THE HOLY BIBLE

NEW REVISED STANDARD VERSION

CATHOLIC EDITION

THE HOLY BIBLE

NEW REVISED STANDARD VERSION

CATHOLIC EDITION

OXFORD UNIVERSITY PRESS

OXFORD · NEW YORK

Oxford University Press

Oxford New York

Athens Auckland Bangkok Bogota Buenos Aires Calcutta
Cape Town Chennai Dar es Salaam Delhi Florence Hong Kong Istanbul
Karachi Kuala Lumpur Madrid Melbourne Mexico City Mumbai
Nairobi Paris Sao Paulo Singapore Taipei Tokyo Toronto Warsaw

and associated companies in

Berlin Ibadan

TABLE OF CONTENTS

The Old Testament

The New Testament

THE BOOKS OF THE BIBLE
IN ALPHABETICAL ORDER

MAPS AND CHARTS

ABBREVIATIONS

The following abbreviations are used for the books of the Bible:

The Old Testament

Gen . . . . Genesis	Prov . . . . Proverbs
Ex . . . . Exodus	Eccl . . . . Ecclesiastes
Lev . . . . Leviticus	Song . . . . Song of Solomon
Num . . . . Numbers	Wis . . . . The Wisdom of Solomon
Deut . . . . Deuteronomy	Sir . . . . Sirach (Ecclesiasticus)
Josh . . . . Joshua	Isa . . . . Isaiah
Judg . . . . Judges	Jer . . . . Jeremiah
Ruth . . . . Ruth	Lam . . . . Lamentations
1 Sam . . . . 1 Samuel	Bar . . . . Baruch
2 Sam . . . . 2 Samuel	Ezek . . . . Ezekiel
1 Kings . . . . 1 Kings	Dan . . . . Daniel
2 Kings . . . . 2 Kings	Hos . . . . Hosea
1 Chr . . . . 1 Chronicles	Joel . . . . Joel
2 Chr . . . . 2 Chronicles	Am . . . . Amos
Ezra . . . . Ezra	Ob . . . . Obadiah
Neh . . . . Nehemiah	Jon . . . . Jonah
Tob . . . . Tobit	Mic . . . . Micah
Jdt . . . . Judith	Nah . . . . Nahum
Esth . . . . Esther	Hab . . . . Habakkuk
1 Macc . . . . 1 Maccabees	Zeph . . . . Zephaniah
2 Macc . . . . 2 Maccabees	Hag . . . . Haggai
Job . . . . Job	Zech . . . . Zechariah
Ps . . . . Psalms	Mal . . . . Malachi

The New Testament

Mt . . . . Matthew	1 Tim . . . . 1 Timothy
Mk . . . . Mark	2 Tim . . . . 2 Timothy
Lk . . . . Luke	Titus . . . . Titus
Jn . . . . John	Philem . . . . Philemon
Acts . . . . Acts of the Apostles	Heb . . . . Hebrews
Rom . . . . Romans	Jas . . . . James
1 Cor . . . . 1 Corinthians	1 Pet . . . . 1 Peter
2 Cor . . . . 2 Corinthians	2 Pet . . . . 2 Peter
Gal . . . . Galatians	1 Jn . . . . 1 John
Eph . . . . Ephesians	2 Jn . . . . 2 John
Phil . . . . Philippians	3 Jn . . . . 3 John
Col . . . . Colossians	Jude . . . . Jude
1 Thess . . . . 1 Thessalonians	Rev . . . . Revelation
2 Thess . . . . 2 Thessalonians	

In the notes to the books of the Old Testament the following abbreviations are used:

Ant.	Josephus, *Antiquities of the Jews*
Aram	Aramaic
Ch, chs	Chapter, chapters
Cn	Correction; made where the text has suffered in transmission and the versions provide no satisfactory restoration but where the Standard Bible Committee agrees with the judgement of competent scholars as to the most probable reconstruction of the original text.
Gk	Septuagint, Greek version of the Old Testament
Heb	Hebrew of the consonantal Masoretic Text of the Old Testament
Josephus	Flavius Josephus (Jewish historian, about A.D. 37 to about 95)
Macc.	The book(s) of the Maccabees
Ms(s)	Manuscript(s)
MT	The Hebrew of the pointed Masoretic Text of the Old Testament
OL	Old Latin
Q Ms(s)	Manuscript(s) found at Qumran by the Dead Sea
Sam	Samaritan Hebrew text of the Old Testament
Syr	Syriac Version of the Old Testament
Syr H	Syriac Version of Origen's Hexapla
Tg	Targum
Vg	Vulgate, Latin Version of the Old Testament

PREFACE

TO THE NEW REVISED STANDARD VERSION

CATHOLIC EDITION

This Catholic edition of the New Revised Standard Version of the Bible has been authorized by the National Conference of Catholic Bishops in the U.S.A. and by the National Council of the Churches of Christ in the U.S.A. It has received the ecclesiastical approval of the Catholic Bishops of both the United States and Canada. The undersigned, who prepared this edition, is a member of the Revised Standard Version Bible Translation Committee as well as an active member and past president of the Catholic Biblical Association of America.

Roman Catholics are already familiar with the accuracy and elegance of the New Revised Standard Version, first published in 1990. It has previously appeared in two major types of edition: an edition of the Old and New Testaments alone, the Bible of most Protestants; and an edition of the Old and New Testaments with the Apocryphal/Deuterocanonical Books placed between the two Testaments. The text of the latter edition received the Imprimatur (official approbation) of the United States and Canadian Catholic Bishops. The New Revised Standard Version is truly an ecumenical translation, for it was produced by Roman Catholic, Eastern Orthodox, Protestant, and Jewish scholars. Because of this Catholic presence no change in the translation was requested for this edition. The only exceptions are the Book of Esther, which exists in two different forms that are explained below, and the Book of Daniel, which includes the deuterocanonical portions that are listed below.

Regarding the number of the books of the Old Testament canon and their arrangement, however, Protestants and Jews on the one hand, and Roman Catholics and Orthodox Christians on the other, hold different beliefs. From the time of the Reformation in the sixteenth century, Protestants have adopted the Jewish canon of the Old Testament, which was established by the rabbis at the end of the first century of the Common Era. This canon includes only those books that were written in Hebrew and Aramaic. In addition to these books, however, Roman Catholics, following the ancient tradition of the Christian church, also hold the Deuterocanonical Books of the Old Testament to be sacred and inspired, and therefore canonical. Protestants and Jews call these books Apocrypha, a word that means "hidden or concealed," an inappropriate title for works that were part of the Greek Old Testament (the Septuagint) from pre-Christian times. The Roman Catholic canon, which was fixed by the time of the Council of Hippo in 393 and reaffirmed by the two Councils of Carthage in 397 and 419, was formally defined by the Council of Trent in 1546. This canon contains seven Deuterocanonical Books: Tobit, Judith, the Wisdom of Solomon, Sirach (the Wisdom of Ben Sira, also known as Ecclesiasticus), Baruch including the Letter of Jeremiah as chapter 6, and 1 and 2 Maccabees; and extra portions of two other books: the Additions to Esther; and the Prayer of Azariah and the Song of the Three Jews inserted between verses 23 and 24 of Daniel 3, Susanna as Daniel 13, and Bel and the Dragon as Daniel 14. Over and above these books and extra portions, the Bible of Greek and Slavonic Orthodox Christians includes 1 Esdras, the Prayer of Manasseh, Psalm 151, and 3 Maccabees. The Slavonic Bible also contains 2 Esdras, and an appendix to the Greek Bible includes 4 Maccabees.

Several of the Deuterocanonical Books were written originally in Hebrew or Aramaic, the rest in Greek. More than two-thirds of the Book of Sirach is now extant in Hebrew, and four fragments of the Book of Tobit in Hebrew and Aramaic were recovered from

Qumran Cave IV. It seems certain that Judith and the additions to Daniel were also written originally in Hebrew. Hebrew is the original language of the prose parts of Baruch; the poetic parts were composed in Greek. The Wisdom of Solomon was written completely in Greek. The original language of 1 Maccabees was Hebrew while 2 Maccabees was composed in Greek.

The Book of Esther has two different forms: the short Hebrew original; and the longer Greek version that contains one hundred and seven additional verses comprising six distinct portions, A through F. It is the translation of the entire Greek version that appears in the Deuterocanonical section of the New Revised Standard Version. In this Catholic edition, however, the translation of the Greek portions has been inserted at the appropriate places of the translation of the Hebrew form of the book. Some of the Greek portions apparently had a Hebrew origin; the others were written in Greek.

What is distinctive about this Catholic edition—as well as every other edition published by Roman Catholics—is that the Deuterocanonical Books and portions are placed in their proper order among the other books of the Old Testament. Thus, Tobit, Judith, the long form of Esther, and 1 and 2 Maccabees are found among the so-called historical books directly after Nehemiah. The Wisdom of Solomon and the Book of Sirach follow after the Song of Solomon among the wisdom books. Because Baruch, the well-known secretary of Jeremiah, is said to be the author of the work that bears his name, the book is placed after Jeremiah and Lamentations. This order of books comes from the Latin Vulgate translated by St. Jerome in the late fourth and early fifth centuries. It is essentially the same order as that found in the fourth-century Codex Vaticanus, one of the oldest extant manuscripts of the Septuagint.

Roman Catholics will welcome this edition of the New Revised Standard Version of the Bible for personal reading and study as well as liturgical usage. Based on the latest manuscript discoveries and critical editions, it offers the fruits of the best biblical scholarship in the idiom of today while being sensitive to the contemporary concern for inclusive language when referring to human beings.

ALEXANDER A. DI LELLA, O.F.M.
Andrews-Kelly-Ryan Distinguished Professor of Biblical Studies
The Catholic University of America

September 30, 1992
Feast of St. Jerome

PREFACE
TO THE NEW REVISED STANDARD VERSION
ANGLICIZED EDITION

T he publication of the New Revised Standard Version of the Bible in 1990 marked the latest stage in the development of an authoritative English language text, a process that started in England with the translation commonly known as the Authorized or King James Version of 1611. The ongoing task of translation had already resulted in the Revised Standard Version of 1952, and a fuller account of this developmental process can be found in the preface To the Reader.

The RSV rapidly found favour throughout the English-speaking world, and in the United Kingdom the translation was quickly adopted by churches, theological colleges, and university faculties as their standard version. In all these places, the RSV was recognized as being authoritative and accurate, impartial in its scholarship, and well-suited to the needs of the Christian community of that period.

The continuance of the Translation Committee's work after the RSV first appeared is a testimony to the fluid nature of the labour with which it is concerned. Bible translators must try to reflect the language of the people for whom they are writing, and the NRSV, recognizing that the English language was evolving rapidly, adopted terms that are familiar to contemporary readers. Yet the English language has developed in different ways in separate countries, and there has been an ongoing divergence between the language as it is used in the United States of America, and the form most commonly used in the British Isles and other countries where British usage is preferred. Therefore, whilst the appearance of the NRSV was warmly welcomed, it soon became apparent that there was a sufficient number of variances between American and British usage to suggest that an edition embodying British usage would be appreciated. The task of producing a text that would meet this need was therefore undertaken, with the convenient (if not strictly accurate) description of an Anglicized Edition.

All those participating in the process of 'anglicization' accepted that no attempt could be made to alter the basic translation in any way; their responsibility was simply to render words that might otherwise be uncertain or awkward into the best generally acceptable equivalent in British usage, whilst at the same time adjusting appropriate points of spelling, grammar, and punctuation.

It is the spelling of various words that will for many present the most obvious examples of change. (Readers may care to note that the verb ending -*ize*, in Britain sometimes regarded as American usage, has been retained where this is etymologically permissable). Other common changes include: the insertion of 'and' into numbers higher than one hundred; the replacement of obsolete (in British usage) past participles such as 'gotten'; the avoidance of subjunctive verbs, still familiar in American but much rarer in British usage; the reinstatement of prepositions such as 'to' and 'for' often elided in US idiom.

The Anglicized Edition's editors also found that words in common use could sometimes have different meanings in various English-speaking cultures, which must affect understanding and interpretation of the text. Thus, references to the (freshwater) Sea of Galilee retain this form, but where the proper name is not given in full, 'sea' is replaced by 'lake', a more unmistakable description for readers to whom sea implies salt water, corresponding to the American 'ocean'. The 'tone' of a particular word may also vary between countries; what is an acceptable 'informal' use in the USA may sometimes be seen as a vulgarism in Britain and other places.

Many smaller alterations have been made, apparently insignificant in themselves, yet which contribute to the overall rendition of the biblical narrative in what may be termed British style.

The intention that lies behind the publication of the New Revised Standard Version Anglicized Edition has been to present an already excellent version of the Scriptures in the form most accessible to its intended readers, so reinforcing their understanding. The editorial work was carried out in Great Britain, but the active support and encouragement of members of the original Translation Committee has ensured that the foundational scholarship which undergirds the NRSV has been retained, and enhanced for those who prefer British usage. It is the earnest hope of all involved in the task that their efforts will enable still more readers to gain fresh insights into the written Word of God.

OXFORD
October 1995

TO THE READER

T his preface is addressed to you by the Committee of translators, who wish to explain, as briefly as possible, the origin and character of our work. The publication of our revision is yet another step in the long, continual process of making the Bible available in the form of the English language that is most widely current in our day. To summarize in a single sentence: the New Revised Standard Version of the Bible is an authorized revision of the Revised Standard Version, published in 1952, which was a revision of the American Standard Version, published in 1901, which, in turn, embodied earlier revisions of the King James Version, published in 1611.

In the course of time, the King James Version came to be regarded as 'the Authorized Version'. With good reason it has been termed 'the noblest monument of English prose', and it has entered, as no other book has, into the making of the personal character and the public institutions of the English-speaking peoples. We owe to it an incalculable debt.

Yet the King James Version has serious defects. By the middle of the nineteenth century, the development of biblical studies and the discovery of many biblical manuscripts more ancient than those on which the King James Version was based made it apparent that these defects were so many as to call for revision. The task was begun, by authority of the Church of England, in 1870. The (British) Revised Version of the Bible was published in 1881–1885; and the American Standard Version, its variant embodying the preferences of the American scholars associated with the work, was published, as was mentioned above, in 1901. In 1928 the copyright of the latter was acquired by the International Council of Religious Education and thus passed into the ownership of the churches of the United States and Canada that were associated in this Council through their boards of education and publication.

The Council appointed a committee of scholars to have charge of the text of the American Standard Version and to undertake inquiry concerning the need for further revision. After studying the questions whether or not revision should be undertaken, and if so, what its nature and extent should be, in 1937 the Council authorized a revision. The scholars who served as members of the Committee worked in two sections, one dealing with the Old Testament and one with the New Testament. In 1946 the Revised Standard Version of the New Testament was published. The publication of the Revised Standard Version of the Bible, containing the Old and New Testaments, took place on September 30, 1952. A translation of the Apocryphal/Deuterocanonical Books of the Old Testament followed in 1957. In 1977 this collection was issued in an expanded edition, containing three additional texts received by Eastern Orthodox communions (3 and 4 Maccabees and Psalm 151). Thereafter the Revised Standard Version gained the distinction of being officially authorized for use by all major Christian churches: Protestant, Anglican, Roman Catholic, and Eastern Orthodox.

The Revised Standard Version Bible Committee is a continuing body, comprising about thirty members, both men and women. Ecumenical in representation, it includes scholars affiliated with various Protestant denominations, as well as several Roman Catholic members, an Eastern Orthodox member, and a Jewish member who serves in the Old Testament section. For a period of time the Committee included several members from Canada and from England.

Because no translation of the Bible is perfect or is acceptable to all groups of readers, and because discoveries of older manuscripts and further investigation of linguistic features of the text continue to become available, renderings of the Bible have proliferated. During the years following the publication of the Revised Standard Version, twenty-six other English translations and revisions of the Bible were produced by committees and by individual scholars—not to mention twenty-five other translations and revisions of the New Testament alone. One of the latter was the second edition of the RSV New Testament, issued in 1971, twenty-five years after its initial publication.

Following the publication of the RSV Old Testament in 1952, significant advances were made in the discovery and interpretation of documents in Semitic languages related to Hebrew. In addition to the information that had become available in the late 1940s from the Dead Sea texts of Isaiah and Habakkuk, subsequent acquisitions from the same area brought to light many other early copies of all the books of the Hebrew Scriptures (except Esther), though most of these copies are fragmentary. During the same period early Greek manuscript copies of books of the New Testament also became available.

In order to take these discoveries into account, along with recent studies of documents in Semitic languages related to Hebrew, in 1974 the Policies Committee of the Revised Standard Version, which is a standing committee of the National Council of the Churches of Christ in the U.S.A., authorized the preparation of a revision of the entire RSV Bible.

For the Old Testament the Committee has made use of the *Biblia Hebraica Stuttgartensia* (1977; ed. sec. emendata, 1983). This is an edition of the Hebrew and Aramaic text as current early in the Christian era and fixed by Jewish scholars (the 'Masoretes') of the sixth to the ninth centuries. The vowel signs, which were added by the Masoretes, are accepted in the main, but where a more probable and convincing reading can be obtained by assuming different vowels, this has been done. No notes are given in such cases, because the vowel points are less ancient and reliable than the consonants. When an alternative reading given by the Masoretes is translated in a footnote, this is identified by the words 'Another reading is'.

Departures from the consonantal text of the best manuscripts have been made only where it seems clear that errors in copying had been made before the text was standardized. Most of the corrections adopted are based on the ancient versions (translations into Greek, Aramaic, Syriac, and Latin), which were made prior to the time of the work of the Masoretes and which therefore may reflect earlier forms of the Hebrew text. In such instances a footnote specifies the version or versions from which the correction has been derived and also gives a translation of the Masoretic Text. Where it was deemed appropriate to do so, information is supplied in footnotes from subsidiary Jewish traditions concerning other textual readings (the *Tiqqune Sopherim*, 'emendations of the scribes'). These are identified in the footnotes as 'Ancient Heb tradition'.

Occasionally it is evident that the text has suffered in transmission and that none of the versions provides a satisfactory restoration. Here we can only follow the best judgement of competent scholars as to the most probable reconstruction of the original text. Such reconstructions are indicated in footnotes by the abbreviation Cn ('Correction'), and a translation of the Masoretic Text is added.

For the Apocryphal/Deuterocanonical Books of the Old Testament the Committee has made use of a number of texts. For most of these books the basic Greek text from which the present translation was made is the edition of the Septuagint prepared by Alfred Rahlfs and published by the Württemberg Bible Society (Stuttgart, 1935). For several of the books the more recently published individual volumes of the Göttingen Septuagint project were utilized. For the book of Tobit it was decided to follow the form of the Greek text found in codex Sinaiticus (supported as it is by evidence from Qumran); where this text is defective, it was supplemented and corrected by other Greek manuscripts. For the three Additions to Daniel (namely, Susanna, the Prayer of Azariah and the Song of the Three Jews, and Bel and the Dragon) the Committee continued to use the Greek version attributed to Theodotion (the so-called 'Theodotion-Daniel'). In translating Ecclesiasticus (Sirach), while constant reference was made to the Hebrew fragments of a large portion of this book (those discovered at Qumran and Masada as well as those recovered from the Cairo Geniza), the Committee generally followed the Greek text (including verse numbers) published by Joseph Ziegler in the Göttingen Septuagint (1965). But in many places the Committee has translated the Hebrew text when this provides a reading that is clearly superior to the Greek; the Syriac and Latin versions were also consulted throughout and occasionally adopted. The basic text adopted in rendering 2 Esdras is the Latin version given in Biblia Sacra, edited by Robert Weber (Stuttgart, 1971). This was supplemented by consulting the Latin text as edited by R. L. Bensly (1895) and by Bruno Violet (1910), as well as by taking into account the several Oriental versions of 2 Esdras, namely, the Syriac, Ethiopic, Arabic (two forms, referred to as Arabic 1 and Arabic 2), Armenian, and Georgian versions. Finally, since the Additions to the Book of Esther are disjointed and quite unintelligible as they stand in most editions of the Apocrypha, we have provided them with their original context by translating the whole of the Greek version of Esther from Robert Hanhart's Göttingen edition (1983).

For the New Testament the Committee has based its work on the most recent edition of The Greek New Testament, prepared by an interconfessional and international committee and published by the United Bible Societies (1966; 3rd ed. corrected, 1983; information concerning changes to be introduced into the critical apparatus of the forthcoming 4th edition was available to the Committee). As in that edition, double brackets are used to enclose a few passages that are generally regarded to be later additions to the text, but which we have retained because of their evident antiquity and their importance in the textual tradition. Only in very rare instances have we replaced the text or the punctuation of the Bible Societies' edition by an alternative that seemed to us to be superior. Here and there in the footnotes the phrase, 'Other ancient authorities read', identifies alternative readings preserved by Greek manuscripts and early versions. In both Testaments, alternative renderings of the text are indicated by the word 'Or'.

As for the style of English adopted for the present revision, among the mandates given to the Committee in 1980 by the Division of Education and Ministry of the National Council of Churches of Christ (which now holds the copyright of the RSV Bible) was the directive to continue in the tradition of the King James Bible, but to introduce such changes as are warranted on the basis of accuracy, clarity, euphony, and current English usage. Within the constraints set by the original texts and by the mandates of the Division, the Committee has followed the maxim, 'As literal as possible, as free as necessary'. As a consequence, the New Revised Standard Version (NRSV) remains essentially a literal translation. Paraphrastic renderings have been adopted only sparingly, and then chiefly to compensate for a deficiency in the English language—the lack of a common gender third person singular pronoun.

During the almost half a century since the publication of the RSV, many in the churches have become sensitive to the danger of linguistic sexism arising from the inherent bias of the English language towards the masculine gender, a bias that in the case of the Bible has often restricted or obscured the meaning of the original text. The mandates from the Division specified that, in references to men and women, masculine-oriented language should be eliminated as far as this can be done without altering passages that reflect the historical situation of ancient patriarchal culture. As can be appreciated, more than once the Committee found that the several mandates stood in tension and even in conflict. The various concerns had to be balanced case by case in order to provide a faithful and acceptable rendering without using contrived English. Only very occasionally has the pronoun 'he' or 'him' been retained in passages where the reference may have been to a woman as well as to a man; for example, in several legal texts in Leviticus and Deuteronomy. In such instances of formal, legal language, the options of either putting the passage in the plural or of introducing additional nouns to avoid masculine pronouns in English seemed to the Committee to obscure the historic structure and literary character of the original. In the vast majority of cases, however, inclusiveness has been attained by simple rephrasing or by introducing plural forms when this does not distort the meaning of the passage. Of course, in narrative and in parable no attempt was made to generalize the sex of individual persons.

Another aspect of style will be detected by readers who compare the more stately English rendering of the Old Testament with the less formal rendering adopted for the New Testament. For example, the traditional distinction between *shall* and *will* in English has been retained in the Old Testament as appropriate in rendering a document that embodies what may be termed the classic form of Hebrew, while in the New Testament the abandonment of such distinctions in the usage of the future tense in English reflects the more colloquial nature of the koine Greek used by most New Testament authors except when they are quoting the Old Testament.

Careful readers will notice that here and there in the Old Testament the word LORD (or in certain cases GOD) is printed in capital letters. This represents the traditional manner in English versions of rendering the Divine Name, the 'Tetragrammaton' (see the notes on Exodus 3.14, 15), following the precedent of the ancient Greek and Latin translators and the long-established practice in the reading of the Hebrew Scriptures in the synagogue. While it is almost if not quite certain that the Name was originally pronounced 'Yahweh', this pronunciation was not indicated when the Masoretes added vowel sounds to the consonantal Hebrew text. To the four consonants YHWH of the Name, which had come to be regarded as too sacred to be pronounced, they attached vowel signs indicating that in its place should be read the Hebrew word *Adonai* meaning 'Lord' (or *Elohim* meaning 'God'). Ancient Greek translators employed the word *Kyrios* ('Lord') for the Name. The Vulgate likewise used the Latin word *Dominus* ('Lord'). The form 'Jehovah' is of late medieval origin; it is a combination of the consonants of the Divine Name and the vowels attached to it by the Masoretes but belonging to an entirely different word. Although the American Standard Version (1901) had used 'Jehovah' to render the Tetragrammaton (the sound of Y being represented by J and the sound of W by V, as in Latin), for two reasons the Committees that produced the RSV and the NRSV returned to the more familiar usage of the King James Version. (1) The word 'Jehovah' does not accurately represent any form of the Name ever used in Hebrew. (2) The use of any proper name for the one and only God, as though there were other gods from whom the true God had to be distinguished, began to be discontinued in Judaism before the Christian era and is inappropriate for the universal faith of the Christian Church.

It will be seen that in the Psalms and in other prayers addressed to God the archaic second person singular pronouns (*thee, thou, thine*) and verb forms (*art, hast, hadst*) are no longer used. Although some readers may regret this change, it should be pointed out that in the original languages neither the Old Testament nor the New makes any linguistic distinction between addressing a human being and addressing the Deity. Furthermore, in the tradition of the King James Version one will not expect to find the use of capital letters for pronouns that refer to the Deity—such capitalization is an unnecessary innovation that has only recently been introduced into a few English translations of the Bible. Finally, we have left to the discretion of the licensed publishers such matters as section headings, cross-references, and clues to the pronunciation of proper names.

This new version seeks to preserve all that is best in the English Bible as it has been known and used through the years. It is intended for use in public reading and congregational worship, as well as in private study, instruction, and meditation. We have resisted the temptation to introduce terms and phrases that merely reflect current moods, and have tried to put the message of the Scriptures in simple, enduring words and expressions that are worthy to stand in the great tradition of the King James Bible and its predecessors.

In traditional Judaism and Christianity, the Bible has been more than a historical document to be preserved or a classic of literature to be cherished and admired; it is recognized as the unique record of God's dealings with people over the ages. The Old Testament sets forth the call of a special people to enter into covenant relation with the God of justice and steadfast love and to bring God's law to the nations. The New Testament records the life and work of Jesus Christ, the one in whom 'the Word became flesh', as well as describes the rise and spread of the early Christian Church. The Bible carries its full message, not to those who regard it simply as a noble literary heritage of the past or who wish to use it to enhance political purposes and advance otherwise desirable goals, but to all persons and communities who read it so that they may discern and understand what God is saying to them. That message must not be disguised in phrases that are no longer clear, or hidden under words that have changed or lost their meaning; it must be presented in language that is direct and plain and meaningful to people today. It is the hope and prayer of the translators that this version of the Bible may continue to hold a large place in congregational life and to speak to all readers, young and old alike, helping them to understand and believe and respond to its message.

For the Committee,
BRUCE M. METZGER

DOGMATIC CONSTITUTION ON
DIVINE REVELATION[a]
DEI VERBUM

18 November 1965

Prologue

1. Hearing the word of God reverently and proclaiming it confidently, this holy synod makes its own the words of St John: "We proclaim to you the eternal life which was with the Father and was made manifest to us—that which we have seen and heard we proclaim also to you, so that you may have fellowship with us; and our fellowship is with the Father and with his Son Jesus Christ" (1 Jn 1:2-3). Following, then, in the steps of the councils of Trent and Vatican I, this synod wishes to set forth the authentic teaching on divine revelation and its transmission. For it wants the whole world to hear the summons to salvation, so that through hearing it may believe, through belief it may hope, through hope it may come to love.[1]

Chapter I
DIVINE REVELATION ITSELF

2. It pleased God, in his goodness and wisdom, to reveal himself and to make known the mystery of his will (see Eph 1:9), which was that people can draw near to the Father, through Christ, the Word made flesh, in the holy Spirit, and thus become sharers in the divine nature (see Eph 2:18; 2 Pet 1:4). By this revelation, then, the invisible God (see Col 1:15; 1 Tim 1:17), from the fullness of his love, addresses men and women as his friends (see Ex 33:11; Jn 15:14-15), and lives among them (see Bar 3:38), in order to invite and receive them into his own company. The pattern of this revelation unfolds through deeds and words which are intrinsically connected: the works performed by God in the history of salvation show forth and confirm the doctrine and realities signified by the words; the words, for their part, proclaim the works, and bring to light the mystery they contain. The most intimate truth thus revealed about God and human salvation shines forth for us in Christ, who is himself both the mediator and the sum total of revelation.[2]

3. God, who creates and conserves all things by his Word (see Jn 1:3), provides constant evidence of himself in created realities (see Rom 1:19-20). Furthermore, wishing to open up the way to heavenly salvation, he manifested himself to our first parents from the very beginning. After the fall, he buoyed them up with the hope of salvation, by promising redemption (see Gen 3:15); and he has never ceased to take care of the human race, in order to give eternal life to all those who seek salvation by persevering in doing good (see Rom 2:6-7). In his own time, God called Abraham and made him into a great nation (see Gen 12:2). After the era of the patriarchs, he taught this nation, through Moses and the prophets, to recognize him as the only living and true God, as a provident Father and just judge. He taught them, too, to look for the promised Saviour. And so, throughout the ages, he prepared the way for the Gospel.

4. After God had spoken many times and in various ways through the prophets, "in these last days he has spoken to us by a Son" (Heb 1:1-2). For he sent his Son, the eternal Word

---

a. Prologue and Chapters 1, 2, 6 translated by Liam Walsh, OP, Chapters 3, 4, 5 by Wilfred Harrington, OP, who have revised their respective chapters for this edition. Further revision was done by AF.

1. St Augustine, *De Catechizandis rudibus*, 4, 8: PL 40, 316.

2. See Mt 11:27; Jn 1:14 and 17; 14:6; 17:1-3; 2 Cor 3:16 and 4:6; Eph 1:3-14.

who enlightens all humankind, to live among them and to tell them about the inner life of God. Hence, Jesus Christ, sent as "a man being men and women",[1] "speaks the words of God" (Jn 3:34), and accomplishes the saving work which the Father gave him to do (see Jn 5:36; 17:4). As a result, he himself—to see whom is to see the Father (see Jn 14:9)—completed and perfected revelation and confirmed it with divine guarantees. Everything to do with his presence and his manifestion of himself was involved in achieving this: his words and works, signs and miracles, but above all his death and glorious resurrection from the dead, and finally his sending of the Spirit of truth. He revealed that God was with us, to deliver us from the darkness of sin and death, and to raise us up to eternal life.

The christian dispensation, therefore, since it is the new and definitive covenant, will never pass away; and no new public revelation is to be expected before the glorious manifestation of our Lord, Jesus Christ (see 1 Tim 6:14 and Tit 2:13).

5. "The obedience of faith" (see Rom 16:26; compare Rom 1:5; 2 Cor 10:5-6) must be our response to God who reveals. By faith one freely commits oneself entirely to God, making "the full submission of intellect and will to God who reveals",[2] and willingly assenting to the revelation given by God. For this faith to be accorded we need the grace of God, anticipating it and assisting it, as well as the interior helps of the holy Spirit, who moves the heart and converts it to God, and opens the eyes of the mind and "makes it easy for all to accept and believe the truth".[3] The same holy Spirit constantly perfects faith by his gifts, so that revelation may be more and more deeply understood.

6. By divine revelation God wished to manifest and communicate both himself and the eternal decrees of his will concerning the salvation of humankind. He wished, in other words, "to share with us divine benefits which entirely surpass the powers of the human mind to understand".[4]

The holy synod professes that "God, the first principle and last end of all things, can be known with certainty from the created world, by the natural light of human reason" (see Rom 1:20). It teaches that it is to his revelation that we must attribute the fact "that those things, which in themselves are not beyond the grasp of human reason, can, in the present condition of the human race, be known by all with ease, with firm certainty, and without the contamination of error".[5]

Chapter II
THE TRANSMISSION OF DIVINE REVELATION

7. God graciously arranged that what he had once revealed for the salvation of all peoples should last forever in its entirety and be transmitted to all generations. Therefore, Christ the Lord, in whom the entire revelation of the most high God is summed up (see 2 Cor 1:20; 3:16-4:6), having fulfilled in his own person and promulgated with his own lips the Gospel promised beforehand by the prophets, commanded the apostles to preach it to everyone as the source of all saving truth and moral law, communicating God's gifts to them.[6] This was faithfully done: it was done by the apostles who handed on, by oral preaching, by their example, by their dispositions, what they themselves had received— whether from the lips of Christ, from his way of life and his works, or by coming to know it through the prompting of the holy Spirit; it was done by those apostles and others as-

---

1. *Letter to Diognetus*, 7,4: Funk, *Patres Apostolici*, I, p. 403.
2. Vatican Council I, Dogmatic Constitution on the Catholic Faith, *Dei Filius*, ch. 3: Denz. 1789 (3008).
3. Council of Orange II, canon 7: Denz. 180 (377). Vatican Council I, loc. cit.: Denz. 1791 (3010).
4. Vatican Council I, Dogmatic Constitution on the Catholic Faith, *Dei Filius*, ch. 2: Denz. 1786 (3005).
5. Ibid.: Denz. 1785 and 1786 (3004 and 3005).
6. See Mt 28:19-20 and Mk 16:15. Council of Trent, Decree *On the Canonical Scriptures*: Denz. 783 (1501).

sociated with them who, under the inspiration of the same holy Spirit, committed the message of salvation to writing.[1]

In order that the full and living Gospel might always be preserved in the church the apostles left bishops as their successors. They gave them "their own position of teaching authority".[2] This sacred tradition, then, and the sacred scripture of both Testaments, are like a mirror, in which the church, during its pilgrim journey here on earth, contemplates God, from whom it receives everything, until such time as it is brought to see him face to face as he really is (see Jn 3:2).

8. Thus, the apostolic preaching, which is expressed in a special way in the inspired books, was to be preserved in a continuous line of succession until the end of time. Hence the apostles, in handing on what they themselves had received, warn the faithful to maintain the traditions which they had learned either by word of mouth or by letter (see 2 Th 2:15), and to fight for the faith that had been handed on to them once and for all (see Jude 3).[3] What was handed on by the apostles comprises everything that serves to make the people of God live their lives in holiness and increase their faith. In this way the church, in its doctrine, life and worship, perpetuates and transmits to every generation all that it itself is, all that it believes.

The tradition that comes from the apostles makes progress in the church, with the help of the holy Spirit.[4] There is a growth in insight into the realities and words that are being passed on. This comes about through the contemplation and study of believers who ponder these things in their hearts (see Lk 2:19 and 51). It comes from the intimate sense of spiritual realities which they experience. And it comes from the preaching of those who, on succeeding to the office of bishop, have received the sure charism of truth. Thus, as the centuries go by, the church is always advancing towards the plenitude of divine truth, until eventually the words of God are fulfilled in it.

The sayings of the church Fathers are a witness to the life-giving presence of this tradition, showing how its riches are poured out in the practice and life of the believing and praying church. By means of the same tradition, the full canon of the sacred books is known to the church and the holy scriptures themselves are more thoroughly understood and constantly made effective in the church. Thus God, who spoke in the past, continues to converse with the spouse of his beloved Son. And the holy Spirit, through whom the living voice of the Gospel rings out in the church—and through it in the world—leads believers to the full truth and makes the word of Christ dwell in them in all its richness (see Col 3:16).

9. Sacred tradition and sacred scripture, then, are bound closely together, and communicate one with the other. Flowing from the same divine well-spring, both of them merge, in a sense, and move towards the same goal. Sacred scripture is the utterance of God put down as it is in writing under the inspiration of the holy Spirit. And tradition transmits in its entirety the word of God which has been entrusted to the apostles by Christ the Lord and the holy Spirit; it transmits it to the successors of the apostles so that, enlightened by the Spirit of truth, they may faithfully preserve, expound and disseminate it by their preaching. Thus it is that the church does not draw its certainty about all revealed truths from the holy scriptures alone. Hence, both scripture and tradition must be accepted and honored with equal devotion and reverence.[5]

10. Tradition and scripture make up a single sacred deposit of the word of God, which is entrusted to the church. By adhering to it the entire holy people, united to its pastors,

---

1. See Council of Trent, loc. cit.; Vatican Council I, Dogmatic Constitution of the Catholic Faith, *Dei Filius*, ch. 2: Denz. 1787 (3006).
2. St Irenaeus, *Adv. Haer.*, III, 3, 1: PG 7, 848; Harvey, 2, p. 9.
3. See Council of Nicea II: Denz. 303 (602). Council of Constantinople IV, Session X, can. 1: Denz. 336 (650-652).
4. See First Vatican Council, Dogmatic Constitution on the Catholic Faith, *Dei Filius*, ch. 4: Denz. 1800 (3020).
5. See Council of Trent, Decree *On the Canonical Scriptures*: Denz. 783 (1501).

remains always faithful to the teaching of the apostles, to the communion of life, to the breaking of bread and the prayers (see Acts 2:42, Greek text). So, in maintaining, practicing and professing the faith that has been handed on there is a unique interplay between the bishops and the faithful.[1]

But the task of giving an authentic interpretation of the word of God, whether in its written form or in the form of tradition,[2] has been entrusted to the living teaching office of the church alone.[3] Its authority in this matter is exercised in the name of Jesus Christ. This magisterium is not superior to the word of God, but is rather its servant. It teaches only what has been handed on to it. At the divine command and with the help of the holy Spirit, it listens to this devoutly, guards it reverently and expounds it faithfully. All that it proposes for belief as being divinely revealed it draws from this sole deposit of faith.

It is clear, therefore, that, in the supremely wise arrangement of God, sacred tradition, sacred scripture and the magisterium of the church are so connected and associated that one of them cannot stand without the others. Working together, each in its own way under the action of the one holy Spirit, they all contribute effectively to the salvation of souls.

Chapter III
SACRED SCRIPTURE: ITS DIVINE INSPIRATION AND ITS INTERPRETATION

11. Those things revealed by God which are contained and presented in the text of sacred scripture have been written under the inspiration of the holy Spirit. For holy mother church, relying on the faith of the apostolic age, accepts as sacred and canonical the books of the Old and the New Testaments, whole and entire, with all their parts, on the grounds that, written under the inspiration of the holy Spirit (see Jn 20:31; 2 Tim 3:16; 2 Pet 1:19-21; 3:15-16), they have God as their author, and have been handed on as such to the church itself.[4] To compose the sacred books, God chose certain men who, all the while he employed them in this task, made full use of their powers and faculties[5] so that, though he acted in them and by them,[6] it was as true authors that they consigned to writing whatever he wanted written, and no more.[7]

Since, therefore, all that the inspired authors, or sacred writers, affirm should be regarded as affirmed by the holy Spirit, we must acknowledge that the books of scripture, firmly, faithfully and without error, teach that truth which God, for the sake of our salvation, wished to see confided to the sacred scriptures.[8] Thus "all scripture is inspired by God, and is useful for teaching, for reproof, for correction and for training in righteousness, so that everyone who belongs to God may be proficient, equipped for every good work" (2 Tim 3:16-17, Greek text).

12. Seeing that, in sacred scripture, God speaks through human beings in human fashion,[9] it follows that the interpreters of sacred scripture, if they are to ascertain what God

---

1. See Pius XII, Apost. Const. *Munificentissimus Deus*, 1 Nov. 1950: AAS 42 (1950), p. 756, taken along with the words of St Cyprian, *Epist.* 66, 8: CSEL, III, 2, 733: "The church is the people united to its priests, the flock adhering to its shepherd."
2. See Vatican Council I, Dogmatic Constitution on the Catholic Faith, *Dei Filius*, ch. 3: Denz. 1972 (3011).
3. See Pius XII, Encyclical *Humani Generis*, 12 Aug. 1950: AAS 42 (1950) 568-569: Denz. 2314 (3886).
4. See Vatican Council I, Dogmatic Constitution on the Catholic Faith, *Dei Filius*, ch. 2: Denz. 1787 (3006). Pontifical Biblical Commission, Decree 18 June 1915: Denz. 2180 (3629); EB 420. Holy Office, *Letter*, 22 Dec. 1923: EB 499.
5. See Pius XII, Encyclical *Divino Afflante Spiritu*, 30 Sept. 1943: AAS 35 (1943), p. 314; EB 556.
6. *In* and *through* human beings: see Heb 1:1 and 4:7 (*in*); 2 Kg. 23:2; Mt 1:22 and passim (*through*); Vatican Council I, Scheme on catholic doctrine, note 9: Collectio Lacensis, VII, 522.
7. Leo XIII, Encyclical *Providentissimus Deus*, 18 Nov. 1893: Denz. 1952 (3293); EB 125.
8. See St Augustine, *De Gen.ad Litt.*, 2, 9, 20: PL 34, 270-271; *Epistola* 82, 3: PL 33, 277; CSEL 34, 2, p. 354. St Thomas Aquinas, *De Veritate*, q. 12, 1 2, C. Council of Trent, Session IV, *On the Canonical Scriptures*: Denz. 783 (1501) Leo XIII, Encyclical *Providentissimus Deus*: EB 121, 124, 126-127. Pius XII, Encyclical *Divino Afflante*: EB 539.
9. St Augustine, *De Civitate Dei*, XVII, 6, 2: PL 41, 537: CSEL 40, 2, 228.

has wished to communicate to us, should carefully search out the meaning which the sacred writers really had in mind, that meaning which God had thought well to manifest through the medium of their words.

In determining the intention of the sacred writers, attention must be paid, among other things, to *literary genres*.

The fact is that truth is differently presented and expressed in the various types of historical writing, in prophetical and poetical texts, and in others forms of literary expression. Hence the exegete must look for that meaning which the sacred writers, in given situations and granted the circumstances of their time and culture, intended to express and did in fact express, through the medium of a contemporary literary form.[1] Rightly to understand what the sacred authors wanted to affirm in their work, due attention must be paid both to the customary and characteristic patterns of perception, speech and narrative which prevailed in their time, and to the conventions which people then observed in their dealings with one another.[2]

But since sacred scripture must be read and interpreted with its divine authorship in mind,[3] no less attention must be devoted to the content and unity of the whole of scripture, taking into account the tradition of the entire church and the analogy of faith, if we are to derive their true meaning from the sacred texts. It is the task of exegetes to work, according to these rules, towards a better understanding and explanation of the meaning of sacred scripture in order that their research may help the church's judgment to mature. For, of course, all that has been said about the manner of interpreting scripture is ultimately subject to the judgment of the church which exercises the divinely conferred commission and ministry of watching over and interpreting the word of God.[4]

13. Hence, in sacred scripture, without prejudice to God's truth and holiness, the marvellous "condescension" of eternal wisdom is plain to be seen, "that we may come to know the ineffable loving-kindness of God and see for ourselves the thought and care he has given to accommodating his language to out nature".[5] Indeed the words of God, expressed in human language, are in every way like human speech, just as the Word of the eternal Father, when he took on himself the weak flesh of human beings, became like them.

Chapter IV
THE OLD TESTAMENT

14. In his great love God intended the salvation of the entire human race. In preparation for this, in a special undertaking, he chose for himself a people to whom he would entrust his promises. By his covenant with Abraham (see Gen 15:18) and, through Moses, with the race of Israel (see Ex 24:8), he acquired a people for himself, and to them he revealed himself in words and deeds as the one, true, living God. It was his strategy that Israel might learn by experience God's ways with humanity and by listening to the voice of God speaking to them through the prophets might gradually understand his ways more fully and more clearly, and make them more widely known among the nations (see Ps 21:28-29; 95:1-3; Is 2:14; Jer 3:17). The plan of salvation, foretold, recounted and explained by the sacred authors, appears as the true word of God in the books of the Old Testament, which is why these books, divinely inspired, retain a lasting value: "For whatever was written in former days was written for our instruction, so that by steadfastness and by the encouragement of the scriptures we might have hope" (Rom 15:4).

1. St Augustine, *De Doctrina Christiana*, III, 18, 26; PL 34, 75-76.
2. Pius XII, loc. cit.: Denz. 2294 (3829-3830); EB 557-562.
3. See Benedict XV, Encyclical *Spiritus Paraclitus*, 15 Sept. 1920: EB 469. St Jerome, *In Gal 5*, 19-21: PL 26, 417A.
4. See Vatican Council I, Dogmatic Constitution on the Catholic Faith, *Dei Filius*, c. 2: Denz. 1788 (3007).
5. St John Chrysostom, *In Gen 3*, 8 (homily 17, 1): PG 53, 134. *Attemperatio* corresponds to the Greek *synkatabasis*.

15. The primary objective of the plan and lay-out of the Old Testament was that it should prepare for and declare in prophecy the coming of Christ, universal redeemer, and of the messianic kingdom (see Lk 24:44; Jn 5:39; 1 Pet 1:10), and should indicate it by means of various foreshadowing signs and symbols (see 1 Cor 10:11). For in the context of the human situation before the era of salvation established by Christ, the books of the Old Testament provide an understanding of God and humanity and make clear to all how a just and merciful God deals with humankind. These books, even though they contain matters which are imperfect and provisional, nevertheless contain authentic divine teaching.[1] Christians should accept with reverence these writings, which express a lively sense of God, which are a storehouse of sublime teaching on God and of sound wisdom on human life, as well as a wonderful treasury of prayers; in them, too, the mystery of our salvation is implicitly present.

16. God, the inspirer and author of the books of both Testaments, in his wisdom has so brought it about that the New should be hidden in the Old and that the Old should be made manifest in the New.[2] For, although Christ founded the New Covenant in his blood (see Lk 22:20; 1 Cor 11:25), nevertheless the books of the Old Testament, all of them given a place in the preaching of the Gospel,[3] attain and display their full meaning in the New Testament (see Mt 5:17; Lk 24-27; Rom 16:25-26; 2 Cor 3:14-16) and, in their turn, shed light on it and explain it.

Chapter V
THE NEW TESTAMENT

17. The word of God, which to everyone who has faith contains God's saving power (see Rom 1:16), is set forth and marvellously displays its power in the writings of the New Testament. For when the time had fully come (see Gal 4:4), the Word became flesh and dwelt among us, full of grace and truth (see Jn 1:14). Christ established on earth the kingdom of God, revealed his Father and himself by deeds and words and by his death, resurrection and glorious ascension, as well as by sending the holy Spirit, completed his work. Lifted up from the earth he draws all people to himself (see Jn 10:32, Greek text), for he alone has the words of eternal life (see Jn 6:68). This mystery was not made known to other generations as it has now been revealed to his holy apostles and prophets by the holy Spirit (see Eph 3:4-6, Greek text), that they might preach the Gospel, foster faith in Jesus Christ and the Lord, and bring together the church. The writings of the New Testament stand as a perpetual and divine witness to these realities.

18. It is common knowledge that among all the inspired writings, including those of the New Testament, the Gospels have a special place, and rightly so, because they are our principal source for the life and teaching of the incarnate Word, our Saviour.

The church has always and everywhere maintained, and continues to maintain, the apostolic origin of the four Gospels. The apostles preached, as Christ had charged them to do, and then, under the inspiration of the holy Spirit, they and others of the apostolic age handed on to us in writing the same message they had preached, the foundation of our faith: the fourfold Gospel, according to Matthew, Mark, Luke and John.[4]

19. Holy mother church has firmly and with absolute constancy maintained and continues to maintain, that these four Gospels, whose historicity it unhesitatingly affirms, faithfully hand on what Jesus, the Son of God, while he lived among men and women, really did and taught for their eternal salvation, until the day when he was taken up (see

---

1. Pius XI, Encyclical *Mit brennender Sorge*, 14 March 1937: AAS 29 (1937), p. 151.
2. St Augustine, *Quaest. in Hept.* 2, 73: PL 34, 623.
3. St Irenaeus, *Adv. Haer.*, III, 21, 3: PG 7, 950 (=25, 1) Harvey 2, p. 115. St Cyril of Jerusalem, *Catech.* 4, 35: PG 33, 497. Theodore of Mopsuestia, *In Soph* 1, 4-6: PG 66, 452D-453A.
4. See St Irenaeus, *Adv. Haer.*, III, 11, 8: PG 7, 885; ed. Sagnard, p. 194.

Acts 1:1-2). For, after the ascension of the Lord, the apostles handed on to their hearers what he had said and done, but with that fuller understanding which they, instructed by the glorious events of Christ and enlightened by the Spirit of truth,[1] now enjoyed.[2] The sacred authors, in writing the four Gospels, selected certain of the many elements which had been handed on, either orally or in written form; others they synthesized or explained with an eye to the situation of the churches. They retained the preaching style, but always in such a fashion that they have told us the authentic truth about Jesus.[3] Whether they relied on their own memory and recollections or on the testimony of those who "from the beginning were eyewitnesses and ministers of the word," their purpose in writing was that we might know the "truth" concerning the things of which we have been informed (see Lk 1:2-4).

20. Besides the four Gospels, the New Testament also contains the letters of St Paul and other apostolic writings composed under the inspiration of the holy Spirit. In accordance with God's wise design these writings firmly establish those matters which concern Christ the Lord, formulate more precisely his authentic teaching, preach the saving power of Christ's divine work and foretell its glorious consummation.

For the Lord Jesus was with his apostles as he had promised (see Mt 28:20) and he had sent to them the Spirit, the Counsellor, who would guide them into all the truth (see Jn 16:13).

Chapter VI
SACRED SCRIPTURE IN THE LIFE OF THE CHURCH

21. The church has always venerated the divine scriptures as it has venerated the Body of the Lord, in that it never ceases, above all in the sacred liturgy, to partake of the bread of life and to offer it to the faithful from the one table of the word of God and the Body of Christ. It has always regarded and continues to regard the scriptures, taken together with sacred tradition, as the supreme rule of its faith. For, since they are inspired by God and committed to writing once and for all time, they present God's own word in an unalterable form, and they make the voice of the holy Spirit sound again and again in the words of the prophets and apostles. It follows that all the preaching of the church, as indeed the entire christian religion, should be nourished and ruled by sacred scripture. In the sacred books the Father who is in heaven comes lovingly to meet his children, and talks with them. And such is the force and power of the word of God that it is the church's support and strength, imparting robustness to the faith of its daughters and sons and providing food for their souls. It is a pure and unfailing fount of spiritual life. It is eminently true of holy scripture that: "The word of God is living and active" (Heb 4:12), and "is able to build you up and to give you the inheritance among all those who are sanctified" (Acts 20:32; see 1 Th 2:13).

22. Access to sacred scripture ought to be widely available to the christian faithful. For this reason the church, from the very beginning, made its own the ancient translation of the Old Testament called the Septuagint; it honors also the other eastern translations, and the Latin translations, especially that known as the Vulgate. But since the word of God must be readily available at all times, the church, with motherly concern, sees to it that suitable and correct translations are made into various languages, especially from the original texts of the sacred books. If, when the opportunity presents itself and the authorities of the church agree, these translations are made jointly with churches separated from us, they can then be used by all Christians.

---

1. See Jn 14:26; 16:13.
2. Jn 2:22; 12-16; see 14:26; 16:12-13; 7:39.
3. See The Instruction *Sacra Mater Ecclesia* of the Pontifical Biblical Commission: AAS 56 (1964), p. 715.

23. Taught by the holy Spirit, the spouse of the incarnate Word, which is the church, strives to reach an increasingly more profound understanding of the sacred scriptures, in order to nourish its children with God's words. For this reason also it duly encourages the study of the Fathers, both eastern and western, and of the sacred liturgies. Catholic exegetes and other workers in the field of sacred theology should work diligently together and under the watchful eye of the sacred magisterium. Using appropriate techniques they should together set about examining and explaining the sacred texts in such a way that as many as possible of those who are ministers of God's word may be able to dispense fruitfully the nourishment of the scriptures to the people of God. This nourishment enlightens the mind, strengthens the will and fires the hearts of men and women with the love of God.[1] The holy synod encourages those members of the church who are engaged in biblical studies constantly to renew their efforts, in order to carry on, with complete dedication and in accordance with the mind of the church,[2] the work they have so happily begun.

24. Sacred theology relies on the written word of God, taken together with sacred tradition, as its permanent foundation. By this word it is powerfully strengthened and constantly rejuvenated, as it searches out, under the light of faith, all the truth stored up in the mystery of Christ. The sacred scriptures contain the word of God, and, because they are inspired, they truly are the word of God; therefore, the study of the sacred page should be the very soul of sacred theology.[3] The ministry of the word, too—pastoral preaching, catechetics and all forms of christian instruction, among which the liturgical homily should hold pride of place—gains healthy nourishment and holy vitality from the word of scripture.

25. Therefore, all clerics, particularly priests of Christ and others who, as deacons or catechists, are officially engaged in the ministry of the word, should immerse themselves in the scriptures by constant spiritual reading and diligent study. For it must not happen that any of them become "empty preachers of the word of God to others, not being hearers of the word in their own hearts",[4] when they ought to be sharing the boundless riches of the divine word with the faithful committed to their care, especially in the sacred liturgy. Likewise, the holy synod forcefully and specifically exhorts all the christian faithful, especially those who live the religious life, to learn "the surpassing knowledge of Jesus Christ" (Phil 3:8) by frequent reading of the divine scriptures. "Ignorance of the scriptures is ignorance of Christ".[5] Therefore, let them go gladly to the sacred text itself, whether in the sacred liturgy, which is full of the divine words, or in devout reading, or in such suitable exercises and various other helps which, with the approval and guidance of the pastors of the church, are happily spreading everywhere in our day. Let them remember, however, that prayer should accompany the reading of sacred scripture, so that it becomes a dialogue between God and the human reader. For, "we speak to him when we pray; we listen to him when we read the divine oracles".[6]

It is the duty of bishops, "with whom the apostolic doctrine resides"[7] suitably to instruct the faithful entrusted to them in the correct use of the divine books, especially the New Testament and in particular the Gospels. This is done by translations of the sacred texts which are equipped with necessary and really adequate explanations. Thus, the chil-

---

1. See Pius XII, Encyclical *Divino Afflante*: EB 551, 553, 567. Pontifical Biblical Commission, *Instructio de S. Scriptura in Clericorum Seminariis et Religiosorum Collegiis recte docenda*, 13 May 1950: AAS 42 (1950), p. 495-505.
2. See Pius XII, ibid.: EB 569.
3. See Leo XIII, Encyclical *Providentissimus Deus*: EB 114; Benedict XV, Encyclical *Spiritus Paraclitus*: EB 483.
4. St Augustine, *Serm.* 179: PL 38, 966.
5. St Jerome, *Comm. in Is*, Prol.: PL 24, 17. See Benedict XV, Encyclical *Spiritus Paraclitus*: B 475-480; Pius XII, Encyclical *Divino Afflante*: EB 544.
6. St Ambrose, *De Officiis. ministrorum* I, 20, 88: PL 16, 50.
7. St Irenaeus, *Adv. Haer.* IV, 32, 1: PG 7, 1071; (= 49, 2) Harvey, 2, p. 255.

dren of the church can familiarize themselves safely and profitably with the sacred scriptures, and become steeped in their spirit.

Moreover, editions of sacred scripture, provided with suitable notes, should be prepared for the use even of non-Christians, and adapted to their circumstances. These should be prudently circulated, either by pastors of souls, or by Christians of any walk of life.

26. So may it come that, by the reading and study of the sacred books "the word of God may speed on and triumph" (2 Th 3:1) and the treasure of revelation entrusted to the church may more and more fill people's hearts. Just as from constant attendance at the eucharistic mystery the life of the church draws increase, so a new impulse of spiritual life may be expected from increased veneration of the word of God, which "stands forever" (Is 40:8; see 1 Pet 1:23-25).

MEASURES AND WEIGHTS IN THE BIBLE

HEBREW MEASURES OF LENGTH

Hebrew	NRSV	Equivalence	U.S. Measures
'ammāh	cubit	2 spans	17.49 inches
zéreth	span	3 handbreadths	8.745 inches
ṭṓphaḥ, ṭéphaḥ	handbreadth	4 fingers	2.915 inches
'esba'	finger		0.728 inch

The cubit described in Ezekiel (40.5; 43.13) is equal to seven (not six) handbreadths, namely 20.405 inches.

MEASURES OF LENGTH IN THE NEW TESTAMENT

Greek	NRSV	U.S. Measures
pēchus	cubit	about 1½ feet
orguia	fathom	about 72.44 inches
stadion	stadia, or the equivalent in miles	about 606 feet
milion	mile	about 4,854 feet

HEBREW MEASURES OF CAPACITY

DRY MEASURES

Hebrew	NRSV	Equivalence	U.S. Measures
hṓmer	homer	2 lethechs	6.524 bushels
kōr	measure, cor		
léthekh	lethech	5 ephahs	3.262 bushels
'êphāh	ephah, measure	3 seahs	20.878 quarts
ṣe'āh	measure	3⅓ omers	6.959 quarts
'ṓmer	omer	1⅘ kabs	2.087 quarts
'issārôn	tenth part (of ephah)		
qabh		kab	1.159 quarts

HEBREW MEASURES OF CAPACITY

LIQUID MEASURES

Hebrew	NRSV	Equivalence	U. S. Measures
kōr	measure, cor	10 baths	60.738 gallons
bath	bath	6 hins	6.073 gallons
hîn	hin	3 kabs	1.012 gallons
qabh	kab	4 logs	1.349 quarts
lōgh	log		0.674 pint

MEASURES OF CAPACITY IN THE NEW TESTAMENT

Greek	NRSV	Equivalence	U.S. Measures
batos	measure	(Hebrew) bath	
koros	measure	(Hebrew) kōr	see Table 3
saton	measure	(Hebrew) ṣe'āh	
metrētēs	measure		10.3 gallons
choinix	quart		0.98 dry quart
modios	bushel	(Latin) modius	7.68 dry quarts
xestēs	pot	(Latin) sextarius	0.96 dry pint, or 1.12 fluid pints

HEBREW WEIGHTS

Hebrew	NRSV	Equivalence	U.S. Avoirdupois
kikkār	talent	60 minas	75.558 pounds
māneh	mina	50 shekels	20.148 ounces
shéqel	shekel	2 bekas	176.29 grains
pîm (or payim)	pim	2/3 shekel	117.52 grains
béqa'	beka, half a shekel	10 gerahs	88.14 grains
gērāh	gerah		8.81 grains

The practice of weighing unmarked ingots of metal used in commercial transactions prior to the invention of money explains that the names of the units of weight were used later as indications of value, and as names for monetary standards. There is, however, no direct relation between the shekel-weight and the weight of a shekel piece.

WEIGHTS IN THE NEW TESTAMENT

Greek	NRSV	Equivalence	U.S. Avoirdupois
talenton	talent	(Hebrew) talent	see Table 5
mna	pound	(Hebrew) mina	see Table 5
litra	pound	(Latin) libra	0.719 pound

THE OLD TESTAMENT

GENESIS

Six Days of Creation and the Sabbath

1 In the beginning when God created*a* the heavens and the earth, ²the earth was a formless void and darkness covered the face of the deep, while a wind from God*b* swept over the face of the waters. ³Then God said, 'Let there be light'; and there was light. ⁴And God saw that the light was good; and God separated the light from the darkness. ⁵God called the light Day, and the darkness he called Night. And there was evening and there was morning, the first day.

6 And God said, 'Let there be a dome in the midst of the waters, and let it separate the waters from the waters.' ⁷So God made the dome and separated the waters that were under the dome from the waters that were above the dome. And it was so. ⁸God called the dome Sky. And there was evening and there was morning, the second day.

9 And God said, 'Let the waters under the sky be gathered together into one place, and let the dry land appear.' And it was so. ¹⁰God called the dry land Earth, and the waters that were gathered together he called Seas. And God saw that it was good. ¹¹Then God said, 'Let the earth put forth vegetation: plants yielding seed, and fruit trees of every kind on earth that bear fruit with the seed in it.' And it was so. ¹²The earth brought forth vegetation: plants yielding seed of every kind, and trees of every kind bearing fruit with the seed in it. And God saw that it was good. ¹³And there was evening and there was morning, the third day.

14 And God said, 'Let there be lights in the dome of the sky to separate the day from the night; and let them be for signs and for seasons and for days and years, ¹⁵and let them be lights in the dome of the sky to give light upon the earth.' And it was so. ¹⁶God made the two great lights—the greater light to rule the day and the lesser light to rule the night—and the stars. ¹⁷God set them in the dome of the sky to give light upon the earth, ¹⁸to rule over the day and over the night, and to separate the light from the darkness. And God saw that it was good. ¹⁹And there was evening and there was morning, the fourth day.

20 And God said, 'Let the waters bring forth swarms of living creatures, and let birds fly above the earth across the dome of the sky.' ²¹So God created the great sea monsters and every living creature that moves, of every kind, with which the waters swarm, and every winged bird of every kind. And God saw that it was good. ²²God blessed them, saying, 'Be fruitful and multiply and fill the waters in the seas, and let birds multiply on the earth.' ²³And there was evening and there was morning, the fifth day.

24 And God said, 'Let the earth bring forth living creatures of every kind: cattle and creeping things and wild animals of the earth of every kind.' And it was so. ²⁵God made the wild animals of the earth of every kind, and the cattle of every kind, and everything that creeps upon the ground of every kind. And God saw that it was good.

26 Then God said, 'Let us make humankind*c* in our image, according to our likeness; and let them have dominion over

---

a Or *when God began to create* or *In the beginning God created*   *b* Or *while the spirit of God* or *while a mighty wind*   *c* Heb *adam* the fish of the sea, and over the birds of the air, and over the cattle, and over all the wild animals of the earth, *a* and over every creeping thing that creeps upon the earth.'

²⁷ So God created humankind *b* in his image,
　　in the image of God he created them; *c*
　　male and female he created them.

²⁸ God blessed them, and God said to them, 'Be fruitful and multiply, and fill the earth and subdue it; and have dominion over the fish of the sea and over the birds of the air and over every living thing that moves upon the earth.' ²⁹ God said, 'See, I have given you every plant yielding seed that is upon the face of all the earth, and every tree with seed in its fruit; you shall have them for food. ³⁰ And to every beast of the earth, and to every bird of the air, and to everything that creeps on the earth, everything that has the breath of life, I have given every green plant for food.' And it was so. ³¹ God saw everything that he had made, and indeed, it was very good. And there was evening and there was morning, the sixth day.

2 Thus the heavens and the earth were finished, and all their multitude. ²And on the seventh day God finished the work that he had done, and he rested on the seventh day from all the work that he had done. ³ So God blessed the seventh day and hallowed it, because on it God rested from all the work that he had done in creation.

4 These are the generations of the heavens and the earth when they were created.

Another Account of the Creation

In the day that the LORD *d* God made the earth and the heavens, ⁵ when no plant of the field was yet in the earth and no herb of the field had yet sprung up—for the LORD God had not caused it to rain upon the earth, and there was no one to till the ground; ⁶ but a stream would rise from the earth, and water the whole face of the ground— ⁷ then the LORD God formed man from the dust of the ground, *e* and breathed into his nostrils the breath of life; and the man became a living being. ⁸ And the LORD God planted a garden in Eden, in the east; and there he put the man whom he had

formed. ⁹ Out of the ground the LORD God made to grow every tree that is pleasant to the sight and good for food, the tree of life also in the midst of the garden, and the tree of the knowledge of good and evil.

10 A river flows out of Eden to water the garden, and from there it divides and becomes four branches. ¹¹ The name of the first is Pishon; it is the one that flows around the whole land of Havilah, where there is gold; ¹² and the gold of that land is good; bdellium and onyx stone are there. ¹³ The name of the second river is Gihon; it is the one that flows around the whole land of Cush. ¹⁴ The name of the third river is Tigris, which flows east of Assyria. And the fourth river is the Euphrates.

15 The LORD God took the man and put him in the garden of Eden to till it and keep it. ¹⁶ And the LORD God commanded the man, 'You may freely eat of every tree of the garden; ¹⁷ but of the tree of the knowledge of good and evil you shall not eat, for in the day that you eat of it you shall die.'

18 Then the LORD God said, 'It is not good that the man should be alone; I will make him a helper as his partner.' ¹⁹ So out of the ground the LORD God formed every animal of the field and every bird of the air, and brought them to the man to see what he would call them; and whatever the man called each living creature, that was its name. ²⁰ The man gave names to all cattle, and to the birds of the air, and to every animal of the field; but for the man *f* there was not found a helper as his partner. ²¹ So the LORD God caused a deep sleep to fall upon the man, and he slept; then he took one of his ribs and closed up its place with flesh. ²² And the rib that the LORD God had taken from the man he made into a woman and brought her to the man. ²³ Then the man said,
　　'This at last is bone of my bones
　　　and flesh of my flesh;
　　this one shall be called Woman, *g*
　　for out of Man *h* this one was taken.'

a Syr: Heb *and over all the earth*　　*b* Heb *adam*
c Heb *him*　　*d* Heb *YHWH*, as in other places where "LORD" is spelled with capital letters (see also Exod 3.14-15 with notes).　　*e* Or *formed a man* (Heb *adam*) *of dust from the ground* (Heb *adamah*)　　*f* Or *for Adam*
g Heb *ishshah*　　*h* Heb *ish*

24 Therefore a man leaves his father and his mother and clings to his wife, and they become one flesh. 25 And the man and his wife were both naked, and were not ashamed.

The First Sin and Its Punishment

3 Now the serpent was more crafty than any other wild animal that the LORD God had made. He said to the woman, 'Did God say, "You shall not eat from any tree in the garden"?' 2 The woman said to the serpent, 'We may eat of the fruit of the trees in the garden; 3 but God said, "You shall not eat of the fruit of the tree that is in the middle of the garden, nor shall you touch it, or you shall die." ' 4 But the serpent said to the woman, 'You will not die; 5 for God knows that when you eat of it your eyes will be opened, and you will be like God, *a* knowing good and evil.' 6 So when the woman saw that the tree was good for food, and that it was a delight to the eyes, and that the tree was to be desired to make one wise, she took of its fruit and ate; and she also gave some to her husband, who was with her, and he ate. 7 Then the eyes of both were opened, and they knew that they were naked; and they sewed fig leaves together and made loincloths for themselves.

8 They heard the sound of the LORD God walking in the garden at the time of the evening breeze, and the man and his wife hid themselves from the presence of the LORD God among the trees of the garden. 9 But the LORD God called to the man, and said to him, 'Where are you?' 10 He said, 'I heard the sound of you in the garden, and I was afraid, because I was naked; and I hid myself.' 11 He said, 'Who told you that you were naked? Have you eaten from the tree of which I commanded you not to eat?' 12 The man said, 'The woman whom you gave to be with me, she gave me fruit from the tree, and I ate.' 13 Then the LORD God said to the woman, 'What is this that you have done?' The woman said, 'The serpent tricked me, and I ate.' 14 The LORD God said to the serpent,

'Because you have done this,
    cursed are you among all animals
    and among all wild creatures;
upon your belly you shall go,
    and dust you shall eat
    all the days of your life.
15 I will put enmity between you and
        the woman,
    and between your offspring and
        hers;
he will strike your head,
    and you will strike his heel.'
16 To the woman he said,
    'I will greatly increase your pangs in
        childbearing;
    in pain you shall bring forth
        children,
yet your desire shall be for your
        husband,
    and he shall rule over you.'
17 And to the man *b* he said,
    'Because you have listened to the
        voice of your wife,
    and have eaten of the tree
about which I commanded you,
    "You shall not eat of it",
cursed is the ground because of you;
    in toil you shall eat of it all the days
        of your life;
18 thorns and thistles it shall bring forth
        for you;
    and you shall eat the plants of the
        field.
19 By the sweat of your face
    you shall eat bread
until you return to the ground,
    for out of it you were taken;
you are dust,
    and to dust you shall return.'

20 The man named his wife Eve, *c* because she was the mother of all who live. 21 And the LORD God made garments of skins for the man *d* and for his wife, and clothed them.

22 Then the LORD God said, 'See, the man has become like one of us, knowing good and evil; and now, he might reach out his hand and take also from the tree of life, and eat, and live for ever'— 23 therefore the LORD God sent him forth from the garden of Eden, to till the ground from which he

a Or *gods*   *b* Or *to Adam*   *c* In Heb *Eve* resembles the word for *living*   *d* Or *for Adam* was taken. 24 He drove out the man; and at the east of the garden of Eden he placed the cherubim, and a sword flaming and turning to guard the way to the tree of life.

Cain Murders Abel

4 Now the man knew his wife Eve, and she conceived and bore Cain, saying, 'I have produced*a* a man with the help of the LORD.' 2 Next she bore his brother Abel. Now Abel was a keeper of sheep, and Cain a tiller of the ground. 3 In the course of time Cain brought to the LORD an offering of the fruit of the ground, 4 and Abel for his part brought of the firstlings of his flock, their fat portions. And the LORD had regard for Abel and his offering, 5 but for Cain and his offering he had no regard. So Cain was very angry, and his countenance fell. 6 The LORD said to Cain, 'Why are you angry, and why has your countenance fallen? 7 If you do well, will you not be accepted? And if you do not do well, sin is lurking at the door; its desire is for you, but you must master it.'

8 Cain said to his brother Abel, 'Let us go out to the field.'*b* And when they were in the field, Cain rose up against his brother Abel and killed him. 9 Then the LORD said to Cain, 'Where is your brother Abel?' He said, 'I do not know; am I my brother's keeper?' 10 And the LORD said, 'What have you done? Listen; your brother's blood is crying out to me from the ground! 11 And now you are cursed from the ground, which has opened its mouth to receive your brother's blood from your hand. 12 When you till the ground, it will no longer yield to you its strength; you will be a fugitive and a wanderer on the earth.' 13 Cain said to the LORD, 'My punishment is greater than I can bear! 14 Today you have driven me away from the soil, and I shall be hidden from your face; I shall be a fugitive and a wanderer on the earth, and anyone who meets me may kill me.' 15 Then the LORD said to him, 'Not so!*c* Whoever kills Cain will suffer a sevenfold vengeance.' And the LORD put a mark on Cain, so that no one who came upon him would kill him. 16 Then Cain went away from the presence of the LORD, and settled in the land of Nod,*d* east of Eden.

Beginnings of Civilization

17 Cain knew his wife, and she conceived and bore Enoch; and he built a city, and named it Enoch after his son Enoch. 18 To Enoch was born Irad; and Irad was the father of Mehujael, and Mehujael the father of Methushael, and Methushael the father of Lamech. 19 Lamech took two wives; the name of one was Adah, and the name of the other Zillah. 20 Adah bore Jabal; he was the ancestor of those who live in tents and have livestock. 21 His brother's name was Jubal; he was the ancestor of all those who play the lyre and pipe. 22 Zillah bore Tubal-cain, who made all kinds of bronze and iron tools. The sister of Tubal-cain was Naamah.

23 Lamech said to his wives:
'Adah and Zillah, hear my voice;
you wives of Lamech, listen to what
I say:
I have killed a man for wounding me,
a young man for striking me.
24 If Cain is avenged sevenfold,
truly Lamech seventy-sevenfold.'

25 Adam knew his wife again, and she bore a son and named him Seth, for she said, 'God has appointed*e* for me another child instead of Abel, because Cain killed him.' 26 To Seth also a son was born, and he named him Enosh. At that time people began to invoke the name of the LORD.

Adam's Descendants to Noah and His Sons

5 This is the list of the descendants of Adam. When God created humankind,*f* he made them*g* in the likeness of God. 2 Male and female he created them, and he blessed them and named them 'Humankind'*f* when they were created.

3 When Adam had lived for one hundred and thirty years, he became the father of a son in his likeness, according to his image, and named him Seth. 4 The days of Adam after he became the father of Seth were eight

---

a The verb in Heb resembles the word for *Cain*
b Sam Gk Syr Compare Vg: MT lacks *Let us go out to the field*   *c* Gk Syr Vg: Heb *Therefore*   *d* That is *Wandering*   *e* The verb in Heb resembles the word for *Seth*   *f* Heb *adam*   *g* Heb *him*

hundred years; and he had other sons and daughters. ⁵Thus all the days that Adam lived were nine hundred and thirty years; and he died.

6 When Seth had lived for one hundred and five years, he became the father of Enosh. ⁷Seth lived after the birth of Enosh for eight hundred and seven years, and had other sons and daughters. ⁸Thus all the days of Seth were nine hundred and twelve years; and he died.

9 When Enosh had lived for ninety years, he became the father of Kenan. ¹⁰Enosh lived after the birth of Kenan for eight hundred and fifteen years, and had other sons and daughters. ¹¹Thus all the days of Enosh were nine hundred and five years; and he died.

12 When Kenan had lived for seventy years, he became the father of Mahalalel. ¹³Kenan lived after the birth of Mahalalel for eight hundred and forty years, and had other sons and daughters. ¹⁴Thus all the days of Kenan were nine hundred and ten years; and he died.

15 When Mahalalel had lived for sixty-five years, he became the father of Jared. ¹⁶Mahalalel lived after the birth of Jared for eight hundred and thirty years, and had other sons and daughters. ¹⁷Thus all the days of Mahalalel were eight hundred and ninety-five years; and he died.

18 When Jared had lived for one hundred and sixty-two years he became the father of Enoch. ¹⁹Jared lived after the birth of Enoch for eight hundred years, and had other sons and daughters. ²⁰Thus all the days of Jared were nine hundred and sixty-two years; and he died.

21 When Enoch had lived for sixty-five years, he became the father of Methuselah. ²²Enoch walked with God after the birth of Methuselah for three hundred years, and had other sons and daughters. ²³Thus all the days of Enoch were three hundred and sixty-five years. ²⁴Enoch walked with God; then he was no more, because God took him.

25 When Methuselah had lived for one hundred and eighty-seven years, he became the father of Lamech. ²⁶Methuselah lived after the birth of Lamech for seven hundred

and eighty-two years, and had other sons and daughters. ²⁷Thus all the days of Methuselah were nine hundred and sixty-nine years; and he died.

28 When Lamech had lived for one hundred and eighty-two years, he became the father of a son; ²⁹he named him Noah, saying, 'Out of the ground that the LORD has cursed this one shall bring us relief from our work and from the toil of our hands.' ³⁰Lamech lived after the birth of Noah for five hundred and ninety-five years, and had other sons and daughters. ³¹Thus all the days of Lamech were seven hundred and seventy-seven years; and he died.

32 After Noah was five hundred years old, Noah became the father of Shem, Ham, and Japheth.

The Wickedness of Humankind

6 When people began to multiply on the face of the ground, and daughters were born to them, ²the sons of God saw that they were fair; and they took wives for themselves of all that they chose. ³Then the LORD said, 'My spirit shall not abide*a* in mortals for ever, for they are flesh; their days shall be one hundred and twenty years.' ⁴The Nephilim were on the earth in those days—and also afterwards—when the sons of God went in to the daughters of humans, who bore children to them. These were the heroes that were of old, warriors of renown.

5 The LORD saw that the wickedness of humankind was great in the earth, and that every inclination of the thoughts of their hearts was only evil continually. ⁶And the LORD was sorry that he had made humankind on the earth, and it grieved him to his heart. ⁷So the LORD said, 'I will blot out from the earth the human beings I have created—people together with animals and creeping things and birds of the air, for I am sorry that I have made them.' ⁸But Noah found favour in the sight of the LORD.

Noah Pleases God

9 These are the descendants of Noah. Noah was a righteous man, blameless in his

a Meaning of Heb uncertain

generation; Noah walked with God. 10 And Noah had three sons, Shem, Ham, and Japheth.

11 Now the earth was corrupt in God's sight, and the earth was filled with violence. 12 And God saw that the earth was corrupt; for all flesh had corrupted its ways upon the earth. 13 And God said to Noah, 'I have determined to make an end of all flesh, for the earth is filled with violence because of them; now I am going to destroy them along with the earth. 14 Make yourself an ark of cypress*ª* wood; make rooms in the ark, and cover it inside and out with pitch. 15 This is how you are to make it: the length of the ark three hundred cubits, its width fifty cubits, and its height thirty cubits. 16 Make a roof*ᵇ* for the ark, and finish it to a cubit above; and put the door of the ark in its side; make it with lower, second, and third decks. 17 For my part, I am going to bring a flood of waters on the earth, to destroy from under heaven all flesh in which is the breath of life; everything that is on the earth shall die. 18 But I will establish my covenant with you; and you shall come into the ark, you, your sons, your wife, and your sons' wives with you. 19 And of every living thing, of all flesh, you shall bring two of every kind into the ark, to keep them alive with you; they shall be male and female. 20 Of the birds according to their kinds, and of the animals according to their kinds, of every creeping thing of the ground according to its kind, two of every kind shall come in to you, to keep them alive. 21 Also take with you every kind of food that is eaten, and store it up; and it shall serve as food for you and for them.' 22 Noah did this; he did all that God commanded him.

The Great Flood

7 Then the LORD said to Noah, 'Go into the ark, you and all your household, for I have seen that you alone are righteous before me in this generation. 2 Take with you seven pairs of all clean animals, the male and its mate; and a pair of the animals that are not clean, the male and its mate; 3 and seven pairs of the birds of the air also, male and female, to keep their kind alive on the face of all the earth. 4 For in seven days I will send rain on the earth for forty days and forty nights; and every living thing that I have made I will blot out from the face of the ground.' 5 And Noah did all that the LORD had commanded him.

6 Noah was six hundred years old when the flood of waters came on the earth. 7 And Noah with his sons and his wife and his sons' wives went into the ark to escape the waters of the flood. 8 Of clean animals, and of animals that are not clean, and of birds, and of everything that creeps on the ground, 9 two and two, male and female, went into the ark with Noah, as God had commanded Noah. 10 And after seven days the waters of the flood came on the earth.

11 In the six-hundredth year of Noah's life, in the second month, on the seventeenth day of the month, on that day all the fountains of the great deep burst forth, and the windows of the heavens were opened. 12 The rain fell on the earth for forty days and forty nights. 13 On the very same day Noah with his sons, Shem and Ham and Japheth, and Noah's wife and the three wives of his sons, entered the ark, 14 they and every wild animal of every kind, and all domestic animals of every kind, and every creeping thing that creeps on the earth, and every bird of every kind—every bird, every winged creature. 15 They went into the ark with Noah, two and two of all flesh in which there was the breath of life. 16 And those that entered, male and female of all flesh, went in as God had commanded him; and the LORD shut him in.

17 The flood continued for forty days on the earth; and the waters increased, and bore up the ark, and it rose high above the earth. 18 The waters swelled and increased greatly on the earth; and the ark floated on the face of the waters. 19 The waters swelled so mightily on the earth that all the high mountains under the whole heaven were covered; 20 the waters swelled above the mountains, covering them fifteen cubits deep. 21 And all flesh died that moved on the earth, birds, domestic animals, wild animals, all swarming creatures that swarm on

a Meaning of Heb uncertain   *b* Or *window*

the earth, and all human beings; 22 everything on dry land in whose nostrils was the breath of life died. 23 He blotted out every living thing that was on the face of the ground, human beings and animals and creeping things and birds of the air; they were blotted out from the earth. Only Noah was left, and those that were with him in the ark. 24 And the waters swelled on the earth for one hundred and fifty days.

The Flood Subsides

8 But God remembered Noah and all the wild animals and all the domestic animals that were with him in the ark. And God made a wind blow over the earth, and the waters subsided; 2 the fountains of the deep and the windows of the heavens were closed, the rain from the heavens was restrained, 3 and the waters gradually receded from the earth. At the end of one hundred and fifty days the waters had abated; 4 and in the seventh month, on the seventeenth day of the month, the ark came to rest on the mountains of Ararat. 5 The waters continued to abate until the tenth month; in the tenth month, on the first day of the month, the tops of the mountains appeared.

6 At the end of forty days Noah opened the window of the ark that he had made 7 and sent out the raven; and it went to and fro until the waters were dried up from the earth. 8 Then he sent out the dove from him, to see if the waters had subsided from the face of the ground; 9 but the dove found no place to set its foot, and it returned to him to the ark, for the waters were still on the face of the whole earth. So he put out his hand and took it and brought it into the ark with him. 10 He waited another seven days, and again he sent out the dove from the ark; 11 and the dove came back to him in the evening, and there in its beak was a freshly plucked olive leaf; so Noah knew that the waters had subsided from the earth. 12 Then he waited another seven days, and sent out the dove; and it did not return to him any more.

13 In the six hundred and first year, in the first month, on the first day of the month, the waters were dried up from the earth; and Noah removed the covering of the ark, and looked, and saw that the face of the ground was drying. 14 In the second month, on the twenty-seventh day of the month, the earth was dry. 15 Then God said to Noah, 16 'Go out of the ark, you and your wife, and your sons and your sons' wives with you. 17 Bring out with you every living thing that is with you of all flesh—birds and animals and every creeping thing that creeps on the earth—so that they may abound on the earth, and be fruitful and multiply on the earth.' 18 So Noah went out with his sons and his wife and his sons' wives. 19 And every animal, every creeping thing, and every bird, everything that moves on the earth, went out of the ark by families.

God's Promise to Noah

20 Then Noah built an altar to the LORD, and took of every clean animal and of every clean bird, and offered burnt-offerings on the altar. 21 And when the LORD smelt the pleasing odour, the LORD said in his heart, 'I will never again curse the ground because of humankind, for the inclination of the human heart is evil from youth; nor will I ever again destroy every living creature as I have done.
22 As long as the earth endures,
seedtime and harvest, cold and
        heat,
summer and winter, day and night,
shall not cease.'

The Covenant with Noah

9 God blessed Noah and his sons, and said to them, 'Be fruitful and multiply, and fill the earth. 2 The fear and dread of you shall rest on every animal of the earth, and on every bird of the air, on everything that creeps on the ground, and on all the fish of the sea; into your hand they are delivered. 3 Every moving thing that lives shall be food for you; and just as I gave you the green plants, I give you everything. 4 Only, you shall not eat flesh with its life, that is, its blood. 5 For your own lifeblood I will surely require a reckoning: from every animal I

will require it and from human beings, each one for the blood of another, I will require a reckoning for human life.

6 Whoever sheds the blood of a
    human,
  by a human shall that person's
    blood be shed;
for in his own image
  God made humankind.

7 And you, be fruitful and multiply, abound on the earth and multiply in it.'

8 Then God said to Noah and to his sons with him, 9 'As for me, I am establishing my covenant with you and your descendants after you, 10 and with every living creature that is with you, the birds, the domestic animals, and every animal of the earth with you, as many as came out of the ark. *a* 11 I establish my covenant with you, that never again shall all flesh be cut off by the waters of a flood, and never again shall there be a flood to destroy the earth.' 12 God said, 'This is the sign of the covenant that I make between me and you and every living creature that is with you, for all future generations: 13 I have set my bow in the clouds, and it shall be a sign of the covenant between me and the earth. 14 When I bring clouds over the earth and the bow is seen in the clouds, 15 I will remember my covenant that is between me and you and every living creature of all flesh; and the waters shall never again become a flood to destroy all flesh. 16 When the bow is in the clouds, I will see it and remember the everlasting covenant between God and every living creature of all flesh that is on the earth.' 17 God said to Noah, 'This is the sign of the covenant that I have established between me and all flesh that is on the earth.'

Noah and His Sons

18 The sons of Noah who went out of the ark were Shem, Ham, and Japheth. Ham was the father of Canaan. 19 These three were the sons of Noah; and from these the whole earth was peopled.

20 Noah, a man of the soil, was the first to plant a vineyard. 21 He drank some of the wine and became drunk, and he lay uncovered in his tent. 22 And Ham, the father of Canaan, saw the nakedness of his father, and told his two brothers outside. 23 Then Shem and Japheth took a garment, laid it on both their shoulders, and walked backwards and covered the nakedness of their father; their faces were turned away, and they did not see their father's nakedness. 24 When Noah awoke from his wine and knew what his youngest son had done to him, 25 he said,
  'Cursed be Canaan;
  lowest of slaves shall he be to his
    brothers.'
26 He also said,
  'Blessed by the LORD my God be
    Shem;
  and let Canaan be his slave.
27 May God make space for *b* Japheth,
  and let him live in the tents of
    Shem;
  and let Canaan be his slave.'

28 After the flood Noah lived for three hundred and fifty years. 29 All the days of Noah were nine hundred and fifty years; and he died.

Nations Descended from Noah

10 These are the descendants of Noah's sons, Shem, Ham, and Japheth; children were born to them after the flood.

2 The descendants of Japheth: Gomer, Magog, Madai, Javan, Tubal, Meshech, and Tiras. 3 The descendants of Gomer: Ashkenaz, Riphath, and Togarmah. 4 The descendants of Javan: Elishah, Tarshish, Kittim, and Rodanim. *c* 5 From these the coastland peoples spread. These are the descendants of Japheth *d* in their lands, with their own language, by their families, in their nations.

6 The descendants of Ham: Cush, Egypt, Put, and Canaan. 7 The descendants of Cush: Seba, Havilah, Sabtah, Raamah, and Sabteca. The descendants of Raamah: Sheba and Dedan. 8 Cush became the father of Nimrod; he was the first on earth to become a mighty warrior. 9 He was a mighty hunter before the LORD; therefore it is said,

---

a Gk: Heb adds *every animal of the earth*   *b* Heb *yapht*, a play on *Japheth*   *c* Heb Mss Sam Gk See 1 Chr 1.7: MT *Dodanim*   *d* Compare verses 20, 31. Heb lacks *These are the descendants of Japheth*

'Like Nimrod a mighty hunter before the LORD.' ¹⁰ The beginning of his kingdom was Babel, Erech, and Accad, all of them in the land of Shinar. ¹¹ From that land he went into Assyria, and built Nineveh, Rehobothir, Calah, and ¹² Resen between Nineveh and Calah; that is the great city. ¹³ Egypt became the father of Ludim, Anamim, Lehabim, Naphtuhim, ¹⁴ Pathrusim, Casluhim, and Caphtorim, from which the Philistines come.ᵃ

15 Canaan became the father of Sidon his firstborn, and Heth, ¹⁶ and the Jebusites, the Amorites, the Girgashites, ¹⁷ the Hivites, the Arkites, the Sinites, ¹⁸ the Arvadites, the Zemarites, and the Hamathites. Afterwards the families of the Canaanites spread abroad. ¹⁹ And the territory of the Canaanites extended from Sidon, in the direction of Gerar, as far as Gaza, and in the direction of Sodom, Gomorrah, Admah, and Zeboiim, as far as Lasha. ²⁰ These are the descendants of Ham, by their families, their languages, their lands, and their nations.

21 To Shem also, the father of all the children of Eber, the elder brother of Japheth, children were born. ²² The descendants of Shem: Elam, Asshur, Arpachshad, Lud, and Aram. ²³ The descendants of Aram: Uz, Hul, Gether, and Mash. ²⁴ Arpachshad became the father of Shelah; and Shelah became the father of Eber. ²⁵ To Eber were born two sons: the name of one was Peleg,ᵇ for in his days the earth was divided, and his brother's name was Joktan. ²⁶ Joktan became the father of Almodad, Sheleph, Hazarmaveth, Jerah, ²⁷ Hadoram, Uzal, Diklah, ²⁸ Obal, Abimael, Sheba, ²⁹ Ophir, Havilah, and Jobab; all these were the descendants of Joktan. ³⁰ The territory in which they lived extended from Mesha in the direction of Sephar, the hill country of the east. ³¹ These are the descendants of Shem, by their families, their languages, their lands, and their nations.

32 These are the families of Noah's sons, according to their genealogies, in their

a Cn: Heb *Casluhim, from which the Philistines come, and Caphtorim*   *b* That is *Division*

The Table of Nations

Gomer

Lud (Lydia)

TURKEY

HITTITES

Ashkenaz (Scythians)

Javan (Greeks)

Mediterranean Sea

Kittim (Cyprus)

LEBANON

Aram (Syria)

Asshur (Assyria)

IRAN

Madai (Medes)

AMORITES

ISRAEL

CANAAN

IRAQ

PHILISTINES

PUT

JORDAN

EGYPT

Joktan (Arabia)

SAUDI ARABIA

Red Sea

Elam (Persia)

Arpachshad

Euphrates River

Tigris River

0   100   200 Mi.
0   100   200   300 Km.

Descendants of Japheth
DESCENDANTS OF HAM
Descendants of Shem

nations; and from these the nations spread abroad on the earth after the flood.

The Tower of Babel

11 Now the whole earth had one language and the same words. 2 And as they migrated from the east,*a* they came upon a plain in the land of Shinar and settled there. 3 And they said to one another, 'Come, let us make bricks, and burn them thoroughly.' And they had brick for stone, and bitumen for mortar. 4 Then they said, 'Come, let us build ourselves a city, and a tower with its top in the heavens, and let us make a name for ourselves; otherwise we shall be scattered abroad upon the face of the whole earth.' 5 The LORD came down to see the city and the tower, which mortals had built. 6 And the LORD said, 'Look, they are one people, and they have all one language; and this is only the beginning of what they will do; nothing that they propose to do will now be impossible for them. 7 Come, let us go down, and confuse their language there, so that they will not understand one another's speech.' 8 So the LORD scattered them abroad from there over the face of all the earth, and they left off building the city. 9 Therefore it was called Babel, because there the LORD confused*b* the language of all the earth; and from there the LORD scattered them abroad over the face of all the earth.

Descendants of Shem

10 These are the descendants of Shem. When Shem was one hundred years old, he became the father of Arpachshad two years after the flood; 11 and Shem lived after the birth of Arpachshad for five hundred years, and had other sons and daughters.

12 When Arpachshad had lived for thirty-five years, he became the father of Shelah; 13 and Arpachshad lived after the birth of Shelah for four hundred and three years, and had other sons and daughters.

14 When Shelah had lived for thirty years, he became the father of Eber; 15 and Shelah lived after the birth of Eber for four hundred and three years, and had other sons and daughters.

16 When Eber had lived for thirty-four years, he became the father of Peleg; 17 and Eber lived after the birth of Peleg for four hundred and thirty years, and had other sons and daughters.

18 When Peleg had lived for thirty years, he became the father of Reu; 19 and Peleg lived after the birth of Reu for two hundred and nine years, and had other sons and daughters.

20 When Reu had lived for thirty-two years, he became the father of Serug; 21 and Reu lived after the birth of Serug for two hundred and seven years, and had other sons and daughters.

22 When Serug had lived for thirty years, he became the father of Nahor; 23 and Serug lived after the birth of Nahor for two hundred years, and had other sons and daughters.

24 When Nahor had lived for twenty-nine years, he became the father of Terah; 25 and Nahor lived after the birth of Terah for one hundred and nineteen years, and had other sons and daughters.

26 When Terah had lived for seventy years, he became the father of Abram, Nahor, and Haran.

Descendants of Terah

27 Now these are the descendants of Terah. Terah was the father of Abram, Nahor, and Haran; and Haran was the father of Lot. 28 Haran died before his father Terah in the land of his birth, in Ur of the Chaldeans. 29 Abram and Nahor took wives; the name of Abram's wife was Sarai, and the name of Nahor's wife was Milcah. She was the daughter of Haran the father of Milcah and Iscah. 30 Now Sarai was barren; she had no child. 31 Terah took his son Abram and his grandson Lot son of Haran, and his daughter-in-law Sarai, his son Abram's wife, and they went out together from Ur of the Chaldeans to go into the land of Canaan; but when they came to Haran, they settled there. 32 The days of Terah were two hun-

a Or *migrated eastward*   *b* Heb *balal*, meaning *to confuse* dred and five years; and Terah died in Haran.

The Call of Abram

12 Now the LORD said to Abram, 'Go from your country and your kindred and your father's house to the land that I will show you. ²I will make of you a great nation, and I will bless you, and make your name great, so that you will be a blessing. ³I will bless those who bless you, and the one who curses you I will curse; and in you all the families of the earth shall be blessed.'ᵃ

4 So Abram went, as the LORD had told him; and Lot went with him. Abram was seventy-five years old when he departed from Haran. ⁵Abram took his wife Sarai and his brother's son Lot, and all the possessions that they had gathered, and the persons whom they had acquired in Haran; and they set forth to go to the land of Canaan. When they had come to the land of Canaan, ⁶Abram passed through the land to the place at Shechem, to the oakᵇ of Moreh.

At that time the Canaanites were in the land. ⁷Then the LORD appeared to Abram, and said, 'To your offspringᶜ I will give this land.' So he built there an altar to the LORD, who had appeared to him. ⁸From there he moved on to the hill country on the east of Bethel, and pitched his tent, with Bethel on the west and Ai on the east; and there he built an altar to the LORD and invoked the name of the LORD. ⁹And Abram journeyed on by stages towards the Negeb.

Abram and Sarai in Egypt

10 Now there was a famine in the land. So Abram went down to Egypt to reside there as an alien, for the famine was severe in the land. ¹¹When he was about to enter Egypt, he said to his wife Sarai, 'I know well that you are a woman beautiful in appearance; ¹²and when the Egyptians see you, they will say, "This is his wife"; then they will kill me, but they will let you live. ¹³Say

a Or *by you all the families of the earth shall bless themselves*   *b* Or *terebinth*   *c* Heb *seed*

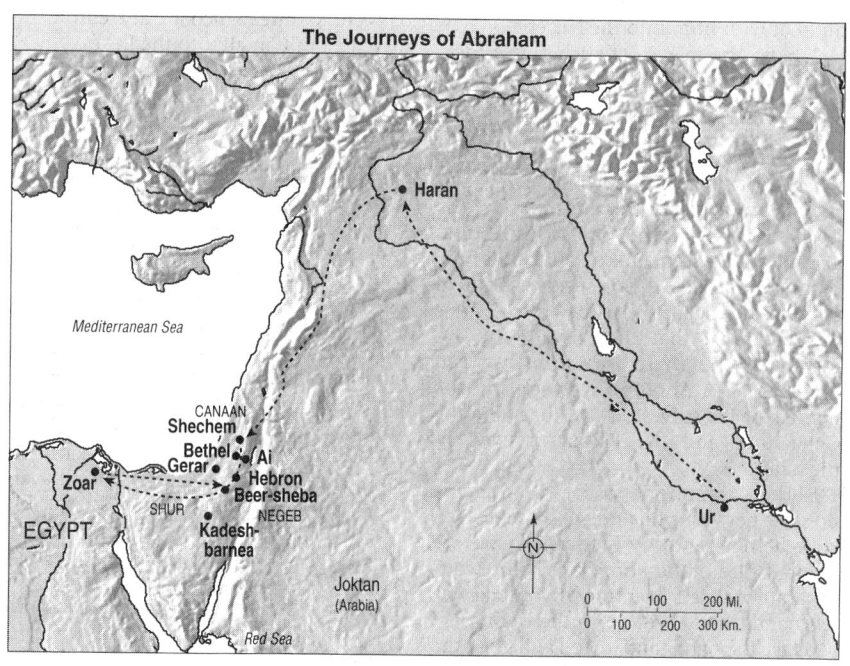

The Journeys of Abraham

you are my sister, so that it may go well with me because of you, and that my life may be spared on your account.' 14 When Abram entered Egypt the Egyptians saw that the woman was very beautiful. 15 When the officials of Pharaoh saw her, they praised her to Pharaoh. And the woman was taken into Pharaoh's house. 16 And for her sake he dealt well with Abram; and he had sheep, oxen, male donkeys, male and female slaves, female donkeys, and camels.

17 But the LORD afflicted Pharaoh and his house with great plagues because of Sarai, Abram's wife. 18 So Pharaoh called Abram, and said, 'What is this you have done to me? Why did you not tell me that she was your wife? 19 Why did you say, "She is my sister", so that I took her for my wife? Now then, here is your wife; take her, and be gone.' 20 And Pharaoh gave his men orders concerning him; and they set him on the way, with his wife and all that he had.

Abram and Lot Separate

13 So Abram went up from Egypt, he and his wife and all that he had, and Lot with him, into the Negeb. 2 Now Abram was very rich in livestock, in silver, and in gold. 3 He journeyed on by stages from the Negeb as far as Bethel, to the place where his tent had been at the beginning, between Bethel and Ai, 4 to the place where he had made an altar at the first; and there Abram called on the name of the LORD. 5 Now Lot, who went with Abram, also had flocks and herds and tents, 6 so that the land could not support both of them living together; for their possessions were so great that they could not live together, 7 and there was strife between the herders of Abram's livestock and the herders of Lot's livestock. At that time the Canaanites and the Perizzites lived in the land.

8 Then Abram said to Lot, 'Let there be no strife between you and me, and between your herders and my herders; for we are kindred. 9 Is not the whole land before you? Separate yourself from me. If you take the left hand, then I will go to the right; or if you take the right hand, then I will go to the

left.' 10 Lot looked about him, and saw that the plain of the Jordan was well watered everywhere like the garden of the LORD, like the land of Egypt, in the direction of Zoar; this was before the LORD had destroyed Sodom and Gomorrah. 11 So Lot chose for himself all the plain of the Jordan, and Lot journeyed eastwards; thus they separated from each other. 12 Abram settled in the land of Canaan, while Lot settled among the cities of the Plain and moved his tent as far as Sodom. 13 Now the people of Sodom were wicked, great sinners against the LORD.

14 The LORD said to Abram, after Lot had separated from him, 'Raise your eyes now, and look from the place where you are, northwards and southwards and eastwards and westwards; 15 for all the land that you see I will give to you and to your offspring*a* for ever. 16 I will make your offspring like the dust of the earth; so that if one can count the dust of the earth, your offspring also can be counted. 17 Rise up, walk through the length and the breadth of the land, for I will give it to you.' 18 So Abram moved his tent, and came and settled by the oaks*b* of Mamre, which are at Hebron; and there he built an altar to the LORD.

Lot's Captivity and Rescue

14 In the days of King Amraphel of Shinar, King Arioch of Ellasar, King Chedorlaomer of Elam, and King Tidal of Goiim, 2 these kings made war with King Bera of Sodom, King Birsha of Gomorrah, King Shinab of Admah, King Shemeber of Zeboiim, and the king of Bela (that is, Zoar). 3 All these joined forces in the Valley of Siddim (that is, the Dead Sea).*c* 4 For twelve years they had served Chedorlaomer, but in the thirteenth year they rebelled. 5 In the fourteenth year Chedorlaomer and the kings who were with him came and subdued the Rephaim in Ashteroth-karnaim, the Zuzim in Ham, the Emim in Shaveh-kiriathaim, 6 and the Horites in the hill country of Seir as far as El-paran on the edge of the wilderness; 7 then they turned back and came to En-mishpat (that is, Kadesh), and subdued all the country of the

a Heb *seed*   *b* Or *terebinths*   *c* Heb *Salt Sea*

Amalekites, and also the Amorites who lived in Hazazon-tamar. ⁸Then the king of Sodom, the king of Gomorrah, the king of Admah, the king of Zeboiim, and the king of Bela (that is, Zoar) went out, and they joined battle in the Valley of Siddim ⁹with King Chedorlaomer of Elam, King Tidal of Goiim, King Amraphel of Shinar, and King Arioch of Ellasar, four kings against five. ¹⁰Now the Valley of Siddim was full of bitumen pits; and as the kings of Sodom and Gomorrah fled, some fell into them, and the rest fled to the hill country. ¹¹So the enemy took all the goods of Sodom and Gomorrah, and all their provisions, and went their way; ¹²they also took Lot, the son of Abram's brother, who lived in Sodom, and his goods, and departed.

13 Then one who had escaped came and told Abram the Hebrew, who was living by the oaks *a* of Mamre the Amorite, brother of Eshcol and of Aner; these were allies of Abram. ¹⁴When Abram heard that his nephew had been taken captive, he led forth his trained men, born in his house, three hundred and eighteen of them, and went in pursuit as far as Dan. ¹⁵He divided his forces against them by night, he and his servants, and routed them and pursued them to Hobah, north of Damascus. ¹⁶Then he brought back all the goods, and also brought back his nephew Lot with his goods, and the women and the people.

Abram Blessed by Melchizedek

17 After his return from the defeat of Chedorlaomer and the kings who were with him, the king of Sodom went out to meet him at the Valley of Shaveh (that is, the King's Valley). ¹⁸And King Melchizedek of Salem brought out bread and wine; he was priest of God Most High. *b* ¹⁹He blessed him and said,

'Blessed be Abram by God Most
     High, *b*
maker of heaven and earth;
²⁰ and blessed be God Most High, *b*
who has delivered your enemies
     into your hand!'
And Abram gave him one-tenth of everything. ²¹Then the king of Sodom said to Abram, 'Give me the people, but take the goods for yourself.' ²²But Abram said to the king of Sodom, 'I have sworn to the LORD, God Most High, *b* maker of heaven and earth, ²³that I would not take a thread or a sandal-thong or anything that is yours, so that you might not say, "I have made Abram rich." ²⁴I will take nothing but what the young men have eaten, and the share of the men who went with me—Aner, Eshcol, and Mamre. Let them take their share.'

God's Covenant with Abram

15 After these things the word of the LORD came to Abram in a vision, 'Do not be afraid, Abram, I am your shield; your reward shall be very great.' ²But Abram said, 'O Lord GOD, what will you give me, for I continue childless, and the heir of my house is Eliezer of Damascus?' *c* ³And Abram said, 'You have given me no offspring, and so a slave born in my house is to be my heir.' ⁴But the word of the LORD came to him, 'This man shall not be your heir; no one but your very own issue shall be your heir.' ⁵He brought him outside and said, 'Look towards heaven and count the stars, if you are able to count them.' Then he said to him, 'So shall your descendants be.' ⁶And he believed the LORD; and the LORD *d* reckoned it to him as righteousness.

7 Then he said to him, 'I am the LORD who brought you from Ur of the Chaldeans, to give you this land to possess.' ⁸But he said, 'O Lord GOD, how am I to know that I shall possess it?' ⁹He said to him, 'Bring me a heifer three years old, a female goat three years old, a ram three years old, a turtle-dove, and a young pigeon.' ¹⁰He brought him all these and cut them in two, laying each half over against the other; but he did not cut the birds in two. ¹¹And when birds of prey came down on the carcasses, Abram drove them away.

12 As the sun was going down, a deep sleep fell upon Abram, and a deep and terrifying darkness descended upon him. ¹³Then the LORD *d* said to Abram, 'Know this for certain, that your offspring shall be

---

a Or *terebinths*   *b* Heb *El Elyon*   *c* Meaning of Heb uncertain   *d* Heb *he* aliens in a land that is not theirs, and shall be slaves there, and they shall be oppressed for four hundred years; [14] but I will bring judgement on the nation that they serve, and afterwards they shall come out with great possessions. [15] As for yourself, you shall go to your ancestors in peace; you shall be buried in a good old age. [16] And they shall come back here in the fourth generation; for the iniquity of the Amorites is not yet complete.'

17 When the sun had gone down and it was dark, a smoking fire-pot and a flaming torch passed between these pieces. [18] On that day the LORD made a covenant with Abram, saying, 'To your descendants I give this land, from the river of Egypt to the great river, the river Euphrates, [19] the land of the Kenites, the Kenizzites, the Kadmonites, [20] the Hittites, the Perizzites, the Rephaim, [21] the Amorites, the Canaanites, the Girgashites, and the Jebusites.'

The Birth of Ishmael

16 Now Sarai, Abram's wife, bore him no children. She had an Egyptian slave-girl whose name was Hagar, [2] and Sarai said to Abram, 'You see that the LORD has prevented me from bearing children; go in to my slave-girl; it may be that I shall obtain children by her.' And Abram listened to the voice of Sarai. [3] So, after Abram had lived for ten years in the land of Canaan, Sarai, Abram's wife, took Hagar the Egyptian, her slave-girl, and gave her to her husband Abram as a wife. [4] He went in to Hagar, and she conceived; and when she saw that she had conceived, she looked with contempt on her mistress. [5] Then Sarai said to Abram, 'May the wrong done to me be on you! I gave my slave-girl to your embrace, and when she saw that she had conceived, she looked on me with contempt. May the LORD judge between you and me!' [6] But Abram said to Sarai, 'Your slave-girl is in your power; do to her as you please.' Then Sarai dealt harshly with her, and she ran away from her.

7 The angel of the LORD found her by a spring of water in the wilderness, the spring on the way to Shur. [8] And he said, 'Hagar, slave-girl of Sarai, where have you come from and where are you going?' She said, 'I am running away from my mistress Sarai.' [9] The angel of the LORD said to her, 'Return to your mistress, and submit to her.' [10] The angel of the LORD also said to her, 'I will so greatly multiply your offspring that they cannot be counted for multitude.' [11] And the angel of the LORD said to her,

'Now you have conceived and shall
  bear a son;
you shall call him Ishmael,[a]
  for the LORD has given heed to your
  affliction.
[12] He shall be a wild ass of a man,
  with his hand against everyone,
  and everyone's hand against him;
  and he shall live at odds with all his
    kin.'

[13] So she named the LORD who spoke to her, 'You are El-roi';[b] for she said, 'Have I really seen God and remained alive after seeing him?'[c] [14] Therefore the well was called Beer-lahai-roi;[d] it lies between Kadesh and Bered.

15 Hagar bore Abram a son; and Abram named his son, whom Hagar bore, Ishmael. [16] Abram was eighty-six years old when Hagar bore him[e] Ishmael.

The Sign of the Covenant

17 When Abram was ninety-nine years old, the LORD appeared to Abram, and said to him, 'I am God Almighty;[f] walk before me, and be blameless. [2] And I will make my covenant between me and you, and will make you exceedingly numerous.' [3] Then Abram fell on his face; and God said to him, [4] 'As for me, this is my covenant with you: You shall be the ancestor of a multitude of nations. [5] No longer shall your name be Abram,[g] but your name shall be Abraham;[h] for I have made you the ancestor of a multitude of nations. [6] I will make you exceedingly fruitful; and I will make nations of you, and kings shall come from you. [7] I will establish my

a That is God hears   b Perhaps God of seeing or God who sees   c Meaning of Heb uncertain   d That is the Well of the Living One who sees me   e Heb Abram f Traditional rendering of Heb El Shaddai   g That is exalted ancestor   h Here taken to mean ancestor of a multitude covenant between me and you, and your offspring after you throughout their generations, for an everlasting covenant, to be God to you and to your offspring *a* after you. [8] And I will give to you, and to your offspring after you, the land where you are now an alien, all the land of Canaan, for a perpetual holding; and I will be their God.'

9 God said to Abraham, 'As for you, you shall keep my covenant, you and your offspring after you throughout their generations. [10] This is my covenant, which you shall keep, between me and you and your offspring after you: Every male among you shall be circumcised. [11] You shall circumcise the flesh of your foreskins, and it shall be a sign of the covenant between me and you. [12] Throughout your generations every male among you shall be circumcised when he is eight days old, including the slave born in your house and the one bought with your money from any foreigner who is not of your offspring. [13] Both the slave born in your house and the one bought with your money must be circumcised. So shall my covenant be in your flesh an everlasting covenant. [14] Any uncircumcised male who is not circumcised in the flesh of his foreskin shall be cut off from his people; he has broken my covenant.'

15 God said to Abraham, 'As for Sarai your wife, you shall not call her Sarai, but Sarah shall be her name. [16] I will bless her, and moreover I will give you a son by her. I will bless her, and she shall give rise to nations; kings of peoples shall come from her.' [17] Then Abraham fell on his face and laughed, and said to himself, 'Can a child be born to a man who is a hundred years old? Can Sarah, who is ninety years old, bear a child?' [18] And Abraham said to God, 'O that Ishmael might live in your sight!' [19] God said, 'No, but your wife Sarah shall bear you a son, and you shall name him Isaac. *b* I will establish my covenant with him as an everlasting covenant for his offspring after him. [20] As for Ishmael, I have heard you; I will bless him and make him fruitful and exceedingly numerous; he shall be the father of twelve princes, and I will make him a great nation. [21] But my cov-

enant I will establish with Isaac, whom Sarah shall bear to you at this season next year.' [22] And when he had finished talking with him, God went up from Abraham.

23 Then Abraham took his son Ishmael and all the slaves born in his house or bought with his money, every male among the men of Abraham's house, and he circumcised the flesh of their foreskins that very day, as God had said to him. [24] Abraham was ninety-nine years old when he was circumcised in the flesh of his foreskin. [25] And his son Ishmael was thirteen years old when he was circumcised in the flesh of his foreskin. [26] That very day Abraham and his son Ishmael were circumcised; [27] and all the men of his house, slaves born in the house and those bought with money from a foreigner, were circumcised with him.

A Son Promised to Abraham and Sarah

18 The LORD appeared to Abraham *c* by the oaks *d* of Mamre, as he sat at the entrance of his tent in the heat of the day. [2] He looked up and saw three men standing near him. When he saw them, he ran from the tent entrance to meet them, and bowed down to the ground. [3] He said, 'My lord, if I find favour with you, do not pass by your servant. [4] Let a little water be brought, and wash your feet, and rest yourselves under the tree. [5] Let me bring a little bread, that you may refresh yourselves, and after that you may pass on—since you have come to your servant.' So they said, 'Do as you have said.' [6] And Abraham hastened into the tent to Sarah, and said, 'Make ready quickly three measures *e* of choice flour, knead it, and make cakes.' [7] Abraham ran to the herd, and took a calf, tender and good, and gave it to the servant, who hastened to prepare it. [8] Then he took curds and milk and the calf that he had prepared, and set it before them; and he stood by them under the tree while they ate.

9 They said to him, 'Where is your wife Sarah?' And he said, 'There, in the tent.' [10] Then one said, 'I will surely return to you in due season, and your wife Sarah shall

a Heb *seed*   *b* That is *he laughs*   *c* Heb *him*
d Or *terebinths*   *e* Heb *seahs*

have a son.' And Sarah was listening at the tent entrance behind him. ¹¹ Now Abraham and Sarah were old, advanced in age; it had ceased to be with Sarah after the manner of women. ¹² So Sarah laughed to herself, saying, 'After I have grown old, and my husband is old, shall I have pleasure?' ¹³ The LORD said to Abraham, 'Why did Sarah laugh, and say, "Shall I indeed bear a child, now that I am old?" ¹⁴ Is anything too wonderful for the LORD? At the set time I will return to you, in due season, and Sarah shall have a son.' ¹⁵ But Sarah denied, saying, 'I did not laugh'; for she was afraid. He said, 'Oh yes, you did laugh.'

Judgement Pronounced on Sodom

16 Then the men set out from there, and they looked towards Sodom; and Abraham went with them to set them on their way. ¹⁷ The LORD said, 'Shall I hide from Abraham what I am about to do, ¹⁸ seeing that Abraham shall become a great and mighty nation, and all the nations of the earth shall be blessed in him?[a] ¹⁹ No, for I have chosen[b] him, that he may charge his children and his household after him to keep the way of the LORD by doing righteousness and justice; so that the LORD may bring about for Abraham what he has promised him.' ²⁰ Then the LORD said, 'How great is the outcry against Sodom and Gomorrah and how very grave their sin! ²¹ I must go down and see whether they have done altogether according to the outcry that has come to me; and if not, I will know.'

22 So the men turned from there, and went towards Sodom, while Abraham remained standing before the LORD.[c] ²³ Then Abraham came near and said, 'Will you indeed sweep away the righteous with the wicked? ²⁴ Suppose there are fifty righteous within the city; will you then sweep away the place and not forgive it for the fifty righteous who are in it? ²⁵ Far be it from you to do such a thing, to slay the righteous with the wicked, so that the righteous fare as the wicked! Far be that from you! Shall not the Judge of all the earth do what is just?' ²⁶ And the LORD said, 'If I find at Sodom fifty righteous in the city, I will forgive the whole place for their sake.' ²⁷ Abraham answered, 'Let me take it upon myself to speak to the Lord, I who am but dust and ashes. ²⁸ Suppose five of the fifty righteous are lacking? Will you destroy the whole city for lack of five?' And he said, 'I will not destroy it if I find forty-five there.' ²⁹ Again he spoke to him, 'Suppose forty are found there.' He answered, 'For the sake of forty I will not do it.' ³⁰ Then he said, 'Oh do not let the Lord be angry if I speak. Suppose thirty are found there.' He answered, 'I will not do it, if I find thirty there.' ³¹ He said, 'Let me take it upon myself to speak to the Lord. Suppose twenty are found there.' He answered, 'For the sake of twenty I will not destroy it.' ³² Then he said, 'Oh do not let the Lord be angry if I speak just once more. Suppose ten are found there.' He answered, 'For the sake of ten I will not destroy it.' ³³ And the LORD went his way, when he had finished speaking to Abraham; and Abraham returned to his place.

The Depravity of Sodom

19 The two angels came to Sodom in the evening, and Lot was sitting in the gateway of Sodom. When Lot saw them, he rose to meet them, and bowed down with his face to the ground. ² He said, 'Please, my lords, turn aside to your servant's house and spend the night, and wash your feet; then you can rise early and go on your way.' They said, 'No; we will spend the night in the square.' ³ But he urged them strongly; so they turned aside to him and entered his house; and he made them a feast, and baked unleavened bread, and they ate. ⁴ But before they lay down, the men of the city, the men of Sodom, both young and old, all the people to the last man, surrounded the house; ⁵ and they called to Lot, 'Where are the men who came to you tonight? Bring them out to us, so that we may know them.' ⁶ Lot went out of the door to the men, shut the door after him, ⁷ and said, 'I beg you, my brothers, do not act so wickedly. ⁸ Look, I have two

a Or *and all the nations of the earth shall bless themselves by him*   *b* Heb *known*   *c* Another ancient tradition reads *while the* LORD *remained standing before Abraham* daughters who have not known a man; let me bring them out to you, and do to them as you please; only do nothing to these men, for they have come under the shelter of my roof.' ⁹ But they replied, 'Stand back!' And they said, 'This fellow came here as an alien, and he would play the judge! Now we will deal worse with you than with them.' Then they pressed hard against the man Lot, and came near the door to break it down. ¹⁰ But the men inside reached out their hands and brought Lot into the house with them, and shut the door. ¹¹ And they struck with blindness the men who were at the door of the house, both small and great, so that they were unable to find the door.

Sodom and Gomorrah Destroyed

12 Then the men said to Lot, 'Have you anyone else here? Sons-in-law, sons, daughters, or anyone you have in the city—bring them out of the place. ¹³ For we are about to destroy this place, because the outcry against its people has become great before the LORD, and the LORD has sent us to destroy it.' ¹⁴ So Lot went out and said to his sons-in-law, who were to marry his daughters, 'Up, get out of this place; for the LORD is about to destroy the city.' But he seemed to his sons-in-law to be jesting.

15 When morning dawned, the angels urged Lot, saying, 'Get up, take your wife and your two daughters who are here, or else you will be consumed in the punishment of the city.' ¹⁶ But he lingered; so the men seized him and his wife and his two daughters by the hand, the LORD being merciful to him, and they brought him out and left him outside the city. ¹⁷ When they had brought them outside, they*a* said, 'Flee for your life; do not look back or stop anywhere in the Plain; flee to the hills, or else you will be consumed.' ¹⁸ And Lot said to them, 'Oh, no, my lords; ¹⁹ your servant has found favour with you, and you have shown me great kindness in saving my life; but I cannot flee to the hills, for fear the disaster will overtake me and I die. ²⁰ Look, that city is near enough to flee to, and it is a little one. Let me escape there—is it not a little one?—and my life will be saved!' ²¹ He

said to him, 'Very well, I grant you this favour too, and will not overthrow the city of which you have spoken. ²² Hurry, escape there, for I can do nothing until you arrive there.' Therefore the city was called Zoar.*b* ²³ The sun had risen on the earth when Lot came to Zoar.

24 Then the LORD rained on Sodom and Gomorrah sulphur and fire from the LORD out of heaven; ²⁵ and he overthrew those cities, and all the Plain, and all the inhabitants of the cities, and what grew on the ground. ²⁶ But Lot's wife, behind him, looked back, and she became a pillar of salt.

27 Abraham went early in the morning to the place where he had stood before the LORD; ²⁸ and he looked down towards Sodom and Gomorrah and towards all the land of the Plain, and saw the smoke of the land going up like the smoke of a furnace.

29 So it was that, when God destroyed the cities of the Plain, God remembered Abraham, and sent Lot out of the midst of the overthrow, when he overthrew the cities in which Lot had settled.

The Shameful Origin of Moab and Ammon

30 Now Lot went up out of Zoar and settled in the hills with his two daughters, for he was afraid to stay in Zoar; so he lived in a cave with his two daughters. ³¹ And the firstborn said to the younger, 'Our father is old, and there is not a man on earth to come in to us after the manner of all the world. ³² Come, let us make our father drink wine, and we will lie with him, so that we may preserve offspring through our father.' ³³ So they made their father drink wine that night; and the firstborn went in, and lay with her father; he did not know when she lay down or when she rose. ³⁴ On the next day, the firstborn said to the younger, 'Look, I lay last night with my father; let us make him drink wine tonight also; then you go in and lie with him, so that we may preserve offspring through our father.' ³⁵ So they made their father drink wine that night also; and the younger rose,

a Gk Syr Vg: Heb *he*   *b* That is *Little*

and lay with him; and he did not know when she lay down or when she rose. ³⁶Thus both the daughters of Lot became pregnant by their father. ³⁷The firstborn bore a son, and named him Moab; he is the ancestor of the Moabites to this day. ³⁸The younger also bore a son and named him Ben-ammi; he is the ancestor of the Ammonites to this day.

Abraham and Sarah at Gerar

20 From there Abraham journeyed towards the region of the Negeb, and settled between Kadesh and Shur. While residing in Gerar as an alien, ²Abraham said of his wife Sarah, 'She is my sister.' And King Abimelech of Gerar sent and took Sarah. ³But God came to Abimelech in a dream by night, and said to him, 'You are about to die because of the woman whom you have taken; for she is a married woman.' ⁴Now Abimelech had not approached her; so he said, 'Lord, will you destroy an innocent people? ⁵Did he not himself say to me, "She is my sister"? And she herself said, "He is my brother." I did this in the integrity of my heart and the innocence of my hands.' ⁶Then God said to him in the dream, 'Yes, I know that you did this in the integrity of your heart; furthermore it was I who kept you from sinning against me. Therefore I did not let you touch her. ⁷Now then, return the man's wife; for he is a prophet, and he will pray for you and you shall live. But if you do not restore her, know that you shall surely die, you and all that are yours.'

8 So Abimelech rose early in the morning, and called all his servants and told them all these things; and the men were very much afraid. ⁹Then Abimelech called Abraham, and said to him, 'What have you done to us? How have I sinned against you, that you have brought such great guilt on me and my kingdom? You have done things to me that ought not to be done.' ¹⁰And Abimelech said to Abraham, 'What were you thinking of, that you did this thing?' ¹¹Abraham said, 'I did it because I thought, There is no fear of God at all in this place, and they will kill me because of my wife. ¹²Besides, she is indeed my sister,

the daughter of my father but not the daughter of my mother; and she became my wife. ¹³And when God caused me to wander from my father's house, I said to her, "This is the kindness you must do me: at every place to which we come, say of me, He is my brother." ' ¹⁴Then Abimelech took sheep and oxen, and male and female slaves, and gave them to Abraham, and restored his wife Sarah to him. ¹⁵Abimelech said, 'My land is before you; settle where it pleases you.' ¹⁶To Sarah he said, 'Look, I have given your brother a thousand pieces of silver; it is your exoneration before all who are with you; you are completely vindicated.' ¹⁷Then Abraham prayed to God; and God healed Abimelech, and also healed his wife and female slaves so that they bore children. ¹⁸For the LORD had closed fast all the wombs of the house of Abimelech because of Sarah, Abraham's wife.

The Birth of Isaac

21 The LORD dealt with Sarah as he had said, and the LORD did for Sarah as he had promised. ²Sarah conceived and bore Abraham a son in his old age, at the time of which God had spoken to him. ³Abraham gave the name Isaac to his son whom Sarah bore him. ⁴And Abraham circumcised his son Isaac when he was eight days old, as God had commanded him. ⁵Abraham was a hundred years old when his son Isaac was born to him. ⁶Now Sarah said, 'God has brought laughter for me; everyone who hears will laugh with me.' ⁷And she said, 'Who would ever have said to Abraham that Sarah would nurse children? Yet I have borne him a son in his old age.'

Hagar and Ishmael Sent Away

8 The child grew, and was weaned; and Abraham made a great feast on the day that Isaac was weaned. ⁹But Sarah saw the son of Hagar the Egyptian, whom she had borne to Abraham, playing with her son Isaac.ᵃ ¹⁰So she said to Abraham, 'Cast out this slave woman with her son; for the son

---

a Gk Vg: Heb lacks *with her son Isaac*

of this slave woman shall not inherit along with my son Isaac.' ¹¹ The matter was very distressing to Abraham on account of his son. ¹² But God said to Abraham, 'Do not be distressed because of the boy and because of your slave woman; whatever Sarah says to you, do as she tells you, for it is through Isaac that offspring shall be named after you. ¹³ As for the son of the slave woman, I will make a nation of him also, because he is your offspring.' ¹⁴ So Abraham rose early in the morning, and took bread and a skin of water, and gave it to Hagar, putting it on her shoulder, along with the child, and sent her away. And she departed, and wandered about in the wilderness of Beer-sheba.

15 When the water in the skin was gone, she cast the child under one of the bushes. ¹⁶ Then she went and sat down opposite him a good way off, about the distance of a bowshot; for she said, 'Do not let me look on the death of the child.' And as she sat opposite him, she lifted up her voice and wept. ¹⁷ And God heard the voice of the boy; and the angel of God called to Hagar from heaven, and said to her, 'What troubles you, Hagar? Do not be afraid; for God has heard the voice of the boy where he is. ¹⁸ Come, lift up the boy and hold him fast with your hand, for I will make a great nation of him.' ¹⁹ Then God opened her eyes, and she saw a well of water. She went, and filled the skin with water, and gave the boy a drink.

20 God was with the boy, and he grew up; he lived in the wilderness, and became an expert with the bow. ²¹ He lived in the wilderness of Paran; and his mother got a wife for him from the land of Egypt.

Abraham and Abimelech Make a Covenant

22 At that time Abimelech, with Phicol the commander of his army, said to Abraham, 'God is with you in all that you do; ²³ now therefore swear to me here by God that you will not deal falsely with me or with my offspring or with my posterity, but as I have dealt loyally with you, you will deal with me and with the land where you

have resided as an alien.' ²⁴ And Abraham said, 'I swear it.'

25 When Abraham complained to Abimelech about a well of water that Abimelech's servants had seized, ²⁶ Abimelech said, 'I do not know who has done this; you did not tell me, and I have not heard of it until today.' ²⁷ So Abraham took sheep and oxen and gave them to Abimelech, and the two men made a covenant. ²⁸ Abraham set apart seven ewe lambs of the flock. ²⁹ And Abimelech said to Abraham, 'What is the meaning of these seven ewe lambs that you have set apart?' ³⁰ He said, 'These seven ewe lambs you shall accept from my hand, in order that you may be a witness for me that I dug this well.' ³¹ Therefore that place was called Beer-sheba;^a because there both of them swore an oath. ³² When they had made a covenant at Beer-sheba, Abimelech, with Phicol the commander of his army, left and returned to the land of the Philistines. ³³ Abraham^b planted a tamarisk tree in Beer-sheba, and called there on the name of the Lord, the Everlasting God.^c ³⁴ And Abraham resided as an alien for many days in the land of the Philistines.

The Command to Sacrifice Isaac

22 After these things God tested Abraham. He said to him, 'Abraham!' And he said, 'Here I am.' ² He said, 'Take your son, your only son Isaac, whom you love, and go to the land of Moriah, and offer him there as a burnt-offering on one of the mountains that I shall show you.' ³ So Abraham rose early in the morning, saddled his donkey, and took two of his young men with him, and his son Isaac; he cut the wood for the burnt-offering, and set out and went to the place in the distance that God had shown him. ⁴ On the third day Abraham looked up and saw the place far away. ⁵ Then Abraham said to his young men, 'Stay here with the donkey; the boy and I will go over there; we will worship, and then we will come back to you.' ⁶ Abraham took the wood of the burnt-offering and laid it on his son Isaac, and he himself

a That is *Well of seven* or *Well of the oath*   *b* Heb *He*
c Or *the* Lord, *El Olam*

carried the fire and the knife. So the two of them walked on together. 7 Isaac said to his father Abraham, 'Father!' And he said, 'Here I am, my son.' He said, 'The fire and the wood are here, but where is the lamb for a burnt-offering?' 8 Abraham said, 'God himself will provide the lamb for a burnt-offering, my son.' So the two of them walked on together.

9 When they came to the place that God had shown him, Abraham built an altar there and laid the wood in order. He bound his son Isaac, and laid him on the altar, on top of the wood. 10 Then Abraham reached out his hand and took the knife to kill *a* his son. 11 But the angel of the LORD called to him from heaven, and said, 'Abraham, Abraham!' And he said, 'Here I am.' 12 He said, 'Do not lay your hand on the boy or do anything to him; for now I know that you fear God, since you have not withheld your son, your only son, from me.' 13 And Abraham looked up and saw a ram, caught in a thicket by its horns. Abraham went and took the ram and offered it up as a burnt-offering instead of his son. 14 So Abraham called that place 'The LORD will provide'; *b* as it is said to this day, 'On the mount of the LORD it shall be provided.' *c*

15 The angel of the LORD called to Abraham a second time from heaven, 16 and said, 'By myself I have sworn, says the LORD: Because you have done this, and have not withheld your son, your only son, 17 I will indeed bless you, and I will make your offspring as numerous as the stars of heaven and as the sand that is on the seashore. And your offspring shall possess the gate of their enemies, 18 and by your offspring shall all the nations of the earth gain blessing for themselves, because you have obeyed my voice.' 19 So Abraham returned to his young men, and they arose and went together to Beersheba; and Abraham lived at Beer-sheba.

The Children of Nahor

20 Now after these things it was told Abraham, 'Milcah also has borne children, to your brother Nahor: 21 Uz the firstborn, Buz his brother, Kemuel the father of Aram, 22 Chesed, Hazo, Pildash, Jidlaph, and Be-

thuel.' 23 Bethuel became the father of Rebekah. These eight Milcah bore to Nahor, Abraham's brother. 24 Moreover, his concubine, whose name was Reumah, bore Tebah, Gaham, Tahash, and Maacah.

Sarah's Death and Burial

23 Sarah lived for one hundred and twenty-seven years; this was the length of Sarah's life. 2 And Sarah died at Kiriath-arba (that is, Hebron) in the land of Canaan; and Abraham went in to mourn for Sarah and to weep for her. 3 Abraham rose up from beside his dead, and said to the Hittites, 4 'I am a stranger and an alien residing among you; give me property among you for a burying-place, so that I may bury my dead out of my sight.' 5 The Hittites answered Abraham, 6 'Hear us, my lord; you are a mighty prince among us. Bury your dead in the choicest of our burial places; none of us will withhold from you any burial ground for burying your dead.' 7 Abraham rose and bowed to the Hittites, the people of the land. 8 He said to them, 'If you are willing that I should bury my dead out of my sight, hear me, and entreat for me Ephron son of Zohar, 9 so that he may give me the cave of Machpelah, which he owns; it is at the end of his field. For the full price let him give it to me in your presence as a possession for a burying-place.' 10 Now Ephron was sitting among the Hittites; and Ephron the Hittite answered Abraham in the hearing of the Hittites, of all who went in at the gate of his city, 11 'No, my lord, hear me; I give you the field, and I give you the cave that is in it; in the presence of my people I give it to you; bury your dead.' 12 Then Abraham bowed down before the people of the land. 13 He said to Ephron in the hearing of the people of the land, 'If you only will listen to me! I will give the price of the field; accept it from me, so that I may bury my dead there.' 14 Ephron answered Abraham, 15 'My lord, listen to me; a piece of land worth four hundred shekels of silver—what is that between you and me? Bury your dead.'

a Or to slaughter   *b* Or will see; Heb traditionally transliterated Jehovah Jireh   *c* Or he shall be seen

16Abraham agreed with Ephron; and Abraham weighed out for Ephron the silver that he had named in the hearing of the Hittites, four hundred shekels of silver, according to the weights current among the merchants.

17 So the field of Ephron in Machpelah, which was to the east of Mamre, the field with the cave that was in it and all the trees that were in the field, throughout its whole area, passed 18to Abraham as a possession in the presence of the Hittites, in the presence of all who went in at the gate of his city. 19After this, Abraham buried Sarah his wife in the cave of the field of Machpelah facing Mamre (that is, Hebron) in the land of Canaan. 20The field and the cave that is in it passed from the Hittites into Abraham's possession as a burying-place.

The Marriage of Isaac and Rebekah

24 Now Abraham was old, well advanced in years; and the LORD had blessed Abraham in all things. 2Abraham said to his servant, the oldest of his house, who had charge of all that he had, 'Put your hand under my thigh 3and I will make you swear by the LORD, the God of heaven and earth, that you will not get a wife for my son from the daughters of the Canaanites, among whom I live, 4but will go to my country and to my kindred and get a wife for my son Isaac.' 5The servant said to him, 'Perhaps the woman may not be willing to follow me to this land; must I then take your son back to the land from which you came?' 6Abraham said to him, 'See to it that you do not take my son back there. 7The LORD, the God of heaven, who took me from my father's house and from the land of my birth, and who spoke to me and swore to me, "To your offspring I will give this land", he will send his angel before you; you shall take a wife for my son from there. 8But if the woman is not willing to follow you, then you will be free from this oath of mine; only you must not take my son back there.' 9So the servant put his hand under the thigh of Abraham his master and swore to him concerning this matter.

10 Then the servant took ten of his master's camels and departed, taking all kinds of choice gifts from his master; and he set out and went to Aram-naharaim, to the city of Nahor. 11He made the camels kneel down outside the city by the well of water; it was towards evening, the time when women go out to draw water. 12And he said, 'O LORD, God of my master Abraham, please grant me success today and show steadfast love to my master Abraham. 13I am standing here by the spring of water, and the daughters of the townspeople are coming out to draw water. 14Let the girl to whom I shall say, "Please offer your jar that I may drink", and who shall say, "Drink, and I will water your camels"—let her be the one whom you have appointed for your servant Isaac. By this I shall know that you have shown steadfast love to my master.'

15 Before he had finished speaking, there was Rebekah, who was born to Bethuel son of Milcah, the wife of Nahor, Abraham's brother, coming out with her water-jar on her shoulder. 16The girl was very fair to look upon, a virgin whom no man had known. She went down to the spring, filled her jar, and came up. 17Then the servant ran to meet her and said, 'Please let me sip a little water from your jar.' 18'Drink, my lord,' she said, and quickly lowered her jar upon her hand and gave him a drink. 19When she had finished giving him a drink, she said, 'I will draw for your camels also, until they have finished drinking.' 20So she quickly emptied her jar into the trough and ran again to the well to draw, and she drew for all his camels. 21The man gazed at her in silence to learn whether or not the LORD had made his journey successful.

22 When the camels had finished drinking, the man took a gold nose-ring weighing a half-shekel, and two bracelets for her arms weighing ten gold shekels, 23and said, 'Tell me whose daughter you are. Is there room in your father's house for us to spend the night?' 24She said to him, 'I am the daughter of Bethuel son of Milcah, whom she bore to Nahor.' 25She added, 'We have plenty of straw and fodder and a place to spend the night.' 26The man bowed his head and worshipped the LORD 27and said,

'Blessed be the LORD, the God of my master Abraham, who has not forsaken his steadfast love and his faithfulness towards my master. As for me, the LORD has led me on the way to the house of my master's kin.'

28 Then the girl ran and told her mother's household about these things. 29 Rebekah had a brother whose name was Laban; and Laban ran out to the man, to the spring. 30 As soon as he had seen the nose-ring, and the bracelets on his sister's arms, and when he heard the words of his sister Rebekah, 'Thus the man spoke to me', he went to the man; and there he was, standing by the camels at the spring. 31 He said, 'Come in, O blessed of the LORD. Why do you stand outside when I have prepared the house and a place for the camels?' 32 So the man came into the house; and Laban unloaded the camels, and gave him straw and fodder for the camels, and water to wash his feet and the feet of the men who were with him. 33 Then food was set before him to eat; but he said, 'I will not eat until I have told my errand.' He said, 'Speak on.'

34 So he said, 'I am Abraham's servant. 35 The LORD has greatly blessed my master, and he has become wealthy; he has given him flocks and herds, silver and gold, male and female slaves, camels and donkeys. 36 And Sarah my master's wife bore a son to my master when she was old; and he has given him all that he has. 37 My master made me swear, saying, "You shall not take a wife for my son from the daughters of the Canaanites, in whose land I live; 38 but you shall go to my father's house, to my kindred, and get a wife for my son." 39 I said to my master, "Perhaps the woman will not follow me." 40 But he said to me, "The LORD, before whom I walk, will send his angel with you and make your way successful. You shall get a wife for my son from my kindred, from my father's house. 41 Then you will be free from my oath, when you come to my kindred; even if they will not give her to you, you will be free from my oath."

42 'I came today to the spring, and said, "O LORD, the God of my master Abraham, if now you will only make successful the way I am going! 43 I am standing here by the spring of water; let the young woman who comes out to draw, to whom I shall say, 'Please give me a little water from your jar to drink,' 44 and who will say to me, 'Drink, and I will draw for your camels also'—let her be the woman whom the LORD has appointed for my master's son."

45 'Before I had finished speaking in my heart, there was Rebekah coming out with her water-jar on her shoulder; and she went down to the spring, and drew. I said to her, "Please let me drink." 46 She quickly let down her jar from her shoulder, and said, "Drink, and I will also water your camels." So I drank, and she also watered the camels. 47 Then I asked her, "Whose daughter are you?" She said, "The daughter of Bethuel, Nahor's son, whom Milcah bore to him." So I put the ring on her nose, and the bracelets on her arms. 48 Then I bowed my head and worshipped the LORD, and blessed the LORD, the God of my master Abraham, who had led me by the right way to obtain the daughter of my master's kinsman for his son. 49 Now then, if you will deal loyally and truly with my master, tell me; and if not, tell me, so that I may turn either to the right hand or to the left.'

50 Then Laban and Bethuel answered, 'The thing comes from the LORD; we cannot speak to you anything bad or good. 51 Look, Rebekah is before you; take her and go, and let her be the wife of your master's son, as the LORD has spoken.'

52 When Abraham's servant heard their words, he bowed himself to the ground before the LORD. 53 And the servant brought out jewellery of silver and of gold, and garments, and gave them to Rebekah; he also gave to her brother and to her mother costly ornaments. 54 Then he and the men who were with him ate and drank, and they spent the night there. When they rose in the morning, he said, 'Send me back to my master.' 55 Her brother and her mother said, 'Let the girl remain with us a while, at least ten days; after that she may go.' 56 But he said to them, 'Do not delay me, since the LORD has made my journey successful; let me go, that I may go to my master.' 57 They

said, 'We will call the girl, and ask her.'
[58] And they called Rebekah, and said to her, 'Will you go with this man?' She said, 'I will.' [59] So they sent away their sister Rebekah and her nurse along with Abraham's servant and his men. [60] And they blessed Rebekah and said to her,

'May you, our sister, become
thousands of myriads;
may your offspring gain possession
of the gates of their foes.'

[61] Then Rebekah and her maids rose up, mounted the camels, and followed the man; thus the servant took Rebekah, and went his way.

62 Now Isaac had come from[a] Beer-lahai-roi, and was settled in the Negeb. [63] Isaac went out in the evening to walk[b] in the field; and looking up, he saw camels coming. [64] And Rebekah looked up, and when she saw Isaac, she slipped quickly from the camel, [65] and said to the servant, 'Who is the man over there, walking in the field to meet us?' The servant said, 'It is my master.' So she took her veil and covered herself. [66] And the servant told Isaac all the things that he had done. [67] Then Isaac brought her into his mother Sarah's tent. He took Rebekah, and she became his wife; and he loved her. So Isaac was comforted after his mother's death.

Abraham Marries Keturah

25 Abraham took another wife, whose name was Keturah. [2] She bore him Zimran, Jokshan, Medan, Midian, Ishbak, and Shuah. [3] Jokshan was the father of Sheba and Dedan. The sons of Dedan were Asshurim, Letushim, and Leummim. [4] The sons of Midian were Ephah, Epher, Hanoch, Abida, and Eldaah. All these were the children of Keturah. [5] Abraham gave all he had to Isaac. [6] But to the sons of his concubines Abraham gave gifts, while he was still living, and he sent them away from his son Isaac, eastwards to the east country.

The Death of Abraham

7 This is the length of Abraham's life, one hundred and seventy-five years. [8] Abraham breathed his last and died in a good old age, an old man and full of years, and was gathered to his people. [9] His sons Isaac and Ishmael buried him in the cave of Machpelah, in the field of Ephron son of Zohar the Hittite, east of Mamre, [10] the field that Abraham purchased from the Hittites. There Abraham was buried, with his wife Sarah. [11] After the death of Abraham God blessed his son Isaac. And Isaac settled at Beer-lahai-roi.

Ishmael's Descendants

12 These are the descendants of Ishmael, Abraham's son, whom Hagar the Egyptian, Sarah's slave-girl, bore to Abraham. [13] These are the names of the sons of Ishmael, named in the order of their birth: Nebaioth, the firstborn of Ishmael; and Kedar, Adbeel, Mibsam, [14] Mishma, Dumah, Massa, [15] Hadad, Tema, Jetur, Naphish, and Kedemah. [16] These are the sons of Ishmael and these are their names, by their villages and by their encampments, twelve princes according to their tribes. [17] (This is the length of the life of Ishmael, one hundred and thirty-seven years; he breathed his last and died, and was gathered to his people.) [18] They settled from Havilah to Shur, which is opposite Egypt in the direction of Assyria; he settled down[c] alongside[d] all his people.

The Birth and Youth of Esau and Jacob

19 These are the descendants of Isaac, Abraham's son: Abraham was the father of Isaac, [20] and Isaac was forty years old when he married Rebekah, daughter of Bethuel the Aramean of Paddan-aram, sister of Laban the Aramean. [21] Isaac prayed to the LORD for his wife, because she was barren; and the LORD granted his prayer, and his wife Rebekah conceived. [22] The children struggled together within her; and she said, 'If it is to be this way, why do I live?'[e] So she went to inquire of the LORD. [23] And the LORD said to her,

'Two nations are in your womb,
and two peoples born of you shall
be divided;

a Syr Tg: Heb *from coming to*   b Meaning of Heb word is uncertain   c Heb *he fell*   d Or *down in opposition to*   e Syr: Meaning of Heb uncertain

one shall be stronger than the other,
the elder shall serve the younger.'
24 When her time to give birth was at hand, there were twins in her womb. 25 The first came out red, all his body like a hairy mantle; so they named him Esau. 26 Afterwards his brother came out, with his hand gripping Esau's heel; so he was named Jacob.ᵈ Isaac was sixty years old when she bore them.

27 When the boys grew up, Esau was a skilful hunter, a man of the field, while Jacob was a quiet man, living in tents. 28 Isaac loved Esau, because he was fond of game; but Rebekah loved Jacob.

Esau Sells His Birthright

29 Once when Jacob was cooking a stew, Esau came in from the field, and he was famished. 30 Esau said to Jacob, 'Let me eat some of that red stuff, for I am famished!' (Therefore he was called Edom.ᵇ) 31 Jacob said, 'First sell me your birthright.' 32 Esau said, 'I am about to die; of what use is a birthright to me?' 33 Jacob said, 'Swear to me first.'ᶜ So he swore to him, and sold his birthright to Jacob. 34 Then Jacob gave Esau bread and lentil stew, and he ate and drank, and rose and went his way. Thus Esau despised his birthright.

Isaac and Abimelech

26 Now there was a famine in the land, besides the former famine that had occurred in the days of Abraham. And Isaac went to Gerar, to King Abimelech of the Philistines. 2 The LORD appeared to Isaacᵈ and said, 'Do not go down to Egypt; settle in the land that I shall show you. 3 Reside in this land as an alien, and I will be with you, and will bless you; for to you and to your descendants I will give all these lands, and I will fulfil the oath that I swore to your father Abraham. 4 I will make your offspring as numerous as the stars of heaven, and will give to your offspring all these lands; and all the nations of the earth shall gain blessing for themselves through your offspring, 5 because Abraham obeyed my voice and kept my charge, my commandments, my statutes, and my laws.'

6 So Isaac settled in Gerar. 7 When the men of the place asked him about his wife, he said, 'She is my sister'; for he was afraid to say, 'My wife,' thinking, 'or else the men of the place might kill me for the sake of Rebekah, because she is attractive in appearance.' 8 When Isaac had been there a long time, King Abimelech of the Philistines looked out of a window and saw him fondling his wife Rebekah. 9 So Abimelech called for Isaac, and said, 'So she is your wife! Why then did you say, "She is my sister"?' Isaac said to him, 'Because I thought I might die because of her.' 10 Abimelech said, 'What is this you have done to us? One of the people might easily have lain with your wife, and you would have brought guilt upon us.' 11 So Abimelech warned all the people, saying, 'Whoever touches this man or his wife shall be put to death.'

12 Isaac sowed seed in that land, and in the same year reaped a hundredfold. The LORD blessed him, 13 and the man became rich; he prospered more and more until he became very wealthy. 14 He had possessions of flocks and herds, and a great household, so that the Philistines envied him. 15 (Now the Philistines had stopped up and filled with earth all the wells that his father's servants had dug in the days of his father Abraham.) 16 And Abimelech said to Isaac, 'Go away from us; you have become too powerful for us.'

17 So Isaac departed from there and camped in the valley of Gerar and settled there. 18 Isaac dug again the wells of water that had been dug in the days of his father Abraham; for the Philistines had stopped them up after the death of Abraham; and he gave them the names that his father had given them. 19 But when Isaac's servants dug in the valley and found there a well of spring water, 20 the herders of Gerar quarrelled with Isaac's herders, saying, 'The water is ours.' So he called the well Esek,ᵉ because they contended with him. 21 Then they dug another well, and they quarrelled over that one also; so he called it Sitnah.ᶠ

a That is *He takes by the heel* or *He supplants*   *b* That is *Red*   *c* Heb *today*   *d* Heb *him*   *e* That is *Contention*   *f* That is *Enmity*

22 He moved from there and dug another well, and they did not quarrel over it; so he called it Rehoboth,ᵃ saying, 'Now the LORD has made room for us, and we shall be fruitful in the land.'

23 From there he went up to Beer-sheba. 24 And that very night the LORD appeared to him and said, 'I am the God of your father Abraham; do not be afraid, for I am with you and will bless you and make your offspring numerous for my servant Abraham's sake.' 25 So he built an altar there, called on the name of the LORD, and pitched his tent there. And there Isaac's servants dug a well.

26 Then Abimelech went to him from Gerar, with Ahuzzath his adviser and Phicol the commander of his army. 27 Isaac said to them, 'Why have you come to me, seeing that you hate me and have sent me away from you?' 28 They said, 'We see plainly that the LORD has been with you; so we say, let there be an oath between you and us, and let us make a covenant with you 29 so that you will do us no harm, just as we have not touched you and have done to you nothing but good and have sent you away in peace. You are now the blessed of the LORD.' 30 So he made them a feast, and they ate and drank. 31 In the morning they rose early and exchanged oaths; and Isaac set them on their way, and they departed from him in peace. 32 That same day Isaac's servants came and told him about the well that they had dug, and said to him, 'We have found water!' 33 He called it Shibah;ᵇ therefore the name of the city is Beer-shebaᶜ to this day.

Esau's Hittite Wives

34 When Esau was forty years old, he married Judith daughter of Beeri the Hittite, and Basemath daughter of Elon the Hittite; 35 and they made life bitter for Isaac and Rebekah.

Isaac Blesses Jacob

27 When Isaac was old and his eyes were dim so that he could not see, he called his elder son Esau and said to him, 'My son'; and he answered, 'Here I am.' 2 He said, 'See, I am old; I do not know the day of my death. 3 Now then, take your weapons, your quiver and your bow, and go out to the field, and hunt game for me. 4 Then prepare for me savoury food, such as I like, and bring it to me to eat, so that I may bless you before I die.'

5 Now Rebekah was listening when Isaac spoke to his son Esau. So when Esau went to the field to hunt for game and bring it, 6 Rebekah said to her son Jacob, 'I heard your father say to your brother Esau, 7 "Bring me game, and prepare for me savoury food to eat, that I may bless you before the LORD before I die." 8 Now therefore, my son, obey my word as I command you. 9 Go to the flock, and get me two choice kids, so that I may prepare from them savoury food for your father, such as he likes; 10 and you shall take it to your father to eat, so that he may bless you before he dies.' 11 But Jacob said to his mother Rebekah, 'Look, my brother Esau is a hairy man, and I am a man of smooth skin. 12 Perhaps my father will feel me, and I shall seem to be mocking him, and bring a curse on myself and not a blessing.' 13 His mother said to him, 'Let your curse be on me, my son; only obey my word, and go, get them for me.' 14 So he went and got them and brought them to his mother; and his mother prepared savoury food, such as his father loved. 15 Then Rebekah took the best garments of her elder son Esau, which were with her in the house, and put them on her younger son Jacob; 16 and she put the skins of the kids on his hands and on the smooth part of his neck. 17 Then she handed the savoury food, and the bread that she had prepared, to her son Jacob.

18 So he went in to his father, and said, 'My father'; and he said, 'Here I am; who are you, my son?' 19 Jacob said to his father, 'I am Esau your firstborn. I have done as you told me; now sit up and eat of my game, so that you may bless me.' 20 But Isaac said to his son, 'How is it that you have found it so quickly, my son?' He answered, 'Because the LORD your God granted me

a That is *Broad places* or *Room*   b A word resembling the word for *oath*   c That is *Well of the oath* or *Well of seven* success.' 21 Then Isaac said to Jacob, 'Come near, that I may feel you, my son, to know whether you are really my son Esau or not.' 22 So Jacob went up to his father Isaac, who felt him and said, 'The voice is Jacob's voice, but the hands are the hands of Esau.' 23 He did not recognize him, because his hands were hairy like his brother Esau's hands; so he blessed him. 24 He said, 'Are you really my son Esau?' He answered, 'I am.' 25 Then he said, 'Bring it to me, that I may eat of my son's game and bless you.' So he brought it to him, and he ate; and he brought him wine, and he drank. 26 Then his father Isaac said to him, 'Come near and kiss me, my son.' 27 So he came near and kissed him; and he smelled the smell of his garments, and blessed him, and said,

'Ah, the smell of my son
　　is like the smell of a field that the
　　LORD has blessed.
28 May God give you of the dew of
　　heaven,
　　and of the fatness of the earth,
　　and plenty of grain and wine.
29 Let peoples serve you,
　　and nations bow down to you.
　Be lord over your brothers,
　　and may your mother's sons bow
　　　down to you.
　Cursed be everyone who curses you,
　　and blessed be everyone who
　　　blesses you!'

Esau's Lost Blessing

30 As soon as Isaac had finished blessing Jacob, when Jacob had scarcely gone out from the presence of his father Isaac, his brother Esau came in from his hunting. 31 He also prepared savoury food, and brought it to his father. And he said to his father, 'Let my father sit up and eat of his son's game, so that you may bless me.' 32 His father Isaac said to him, 'Who are you?' He answered, 'I am your firstborn son, Esau.' 33 Then Isaac trembled violently, and said, 'Who was it then that hunted game and brought it to me, and I ate it all *a* before you came, and I have blessed him?—yes, and blessed he shall be!' 34 When Esau heard his father's words, he cried out with an ex-

ceedingly great and bitter cry, and said to his father, 'Bless me, me also, father!' 35 But he said, 'Your brother came deceitfully, and has taken away your blessing.' 36 Esau said, 'Is he not rightly named Jacob? *b* For he has supplanted me these two times. He took away my birthright; and look, now he has taken away my blessing.' Then he said, 'Have you not reserved a blessing for me?' 37 Isaac answered Esau, 'I have already made him your lord, and I have given him all his brothers as servants, and with grain and wine I have sustained him. What then can I do for you, my son?' 38 Esau said to his father, 'Have you only one blessing, father? Bless me, me also, father!' And Esau lifted up his voice and wept.

39 Then his father Isaac answered him:
　'See, away from *c* the fatness of the
　　earth shall your home be,
　　and away from *d* the dew of heaven
　　　on high.
40 By your sword you shall live,
　　and you shall serve your brother;
　but when you break loose, *e*
　　you shall break his yoke from your
　　　neck.'

Jacob Escapes Esau's Fury

41 Now Esau hated Jacob because of the blessing with which his father had blessed him, and Esau said to himself, 'The days of mourning for my father are approaching; then I will kill my brother Jacob.' 42 But the words of her elder son Esau were told to Rebekah; so she sent and called her younger son Jacob and said to him, 'Your brother Esau is consoling himself by planning to kill you. 43 Now therefore, my son, obey my voice; flee at once to my brother Laban in Haran, 44 and stay with him for a while, until your brother's fury turns away— 45 until your brother's anger against you turns away, and he forgets what you have done to him; then I will send, and bring you back from there. Why should I lose both of you in one day?'

46 Then Rebekah said to Isaac, 'I am

a Cn: Heb *of all*　　*b* That is *He supplants* or *He takes by the heel*　　*c* Or *See, of*　　*d* Or *and of*　　*e* Meaning of Heb uncertain weary of my life because of the Hittite women. If Jacob marries one of the Hittite women such as these, one of the women of the land, what good will my life be to me?'

28 Then Isaac called Jacob and blessed him, and charged him, 'You shall not marry one of the Canaanite women. ² Go at once to Paddan-aram to the house of Bethuel, your mother's father; and take as wife from there one of the daughters of Laban, your mother's brother. ³ May God Almighty[a] bless you and make you fruitful and numerous, that you may become a company of peoples. ⁴ May he give to you the blessing of Abraham, to you and to your offspring with you, so that you may take possession of the land where you now live as an alien—land that God gave to Abraham.' ⁵ Thus Isaac sent Jacob away; and he went to Paddan-aram, to Laban son of Bethuel the Aramean, the brother of Rebekah, Jacob's and Esau's mother.

Esau Marries Ishmael's Daughter

6 Now Esau saw that Isaac had blessed Jacob and sent him away to Paddan-aram to take a wife from there, and that as he blessed him he charged him, 'You shall not marry one of the Canaanite women', ⁷ and that Jacob had obeyed his father and his mother and gone to Paddan-aram. ⁸ So when Esau saw that the Canaanite women did not please his father Isaac, ⁹ Esau went to Ishmael and took Mahalath daughter of Abraham's son Ishmael, and sister of Nebaioth, to be his wife in addition to the wives he had.

Jacob's Dream at Bethel

10 Jacob left Beer-sheba and went towards Haran. ¹¹ He came to a certain place and stayed there for the night, because the sun had set. Taking one of the stones of the place, he put it under his head and lay down in that place. ¹² And he dreamed that there was a ladder[b] set up on the earth, the top of it reaching to heaven; and the angels of God were ascending and descending on it. ¹³ And the LORD stood beside him[c] and said, 'I am the LORD, the God of Abraham your father and the God of Isaac; the land

on which you lie I will give to you and to your offspring; ¹⁴ and your offspring shall be like the dust of the earth, and you shall spread abroad to the west and to the east and to the north and to the south; and all the families of the earth shall be blessed[d] in you and in your offspring. ¹⁵ Know that I am with you and will keep you wherever you go, and will bring you back to this land; for I will not leave you until I have done what I have promised you.' ¹⁶ Then Jacob woke from his sleep and said, 'Surely the LORD is in this place—and I did not know it!' ¹⁷ And he was afraid, and said, 'How awesome is this place! This is none other than the house of God, and this is the gate of heaven.'

18 So Jacob rose early in the morning, and he took the stone that he had put under his head and set it up for a pillar and poured oil on the top of it. ¹⁹ He called that place Bethel;[e] but the name of the city was Luz at the first. ²⁰ Then Jacob made a vow, saying, 'If God will be with me, and will keep me in this way that I go, and will give me bread to eat and clothing to wear, ²¹ so that I come again to my father's house in peace, then the LORD shall be my God, ²² and this stone, which I have set up for a pillar, shall be God's house; and of all that you give me I will surely give one-tenth to you.'

Jacob Meets Rachel

29 Then Jacob went on his journey, and came to the land of the people of the east. ² As he looked, he saw a well in the field and three flocks of sheep lying there beside it; for out of that well the flocks were watered. The stone on the well's mouth was large, ³ and when all the flocks were gathered there, the shepherds would roll the stone from the mouth of the well, and water the sheep, and put the stone back in its place on the mouth of the well.

4 Jacob said to them, 'My brothers, where do you come from?' They said, 'We are from Haran.' ⁵ He said to them, 'Do you

a Traditional rendering of Heb *El Shaddai*
b Or *stairway* or *ramp*   c Or *stood above it*   d Or *shall bless themselves*   e That is *House of God*

know Laban son of Nahor?' They said, 'We do.' ⁶He said to them, 'Is it well with him?' 'Yes,' they replied, 'and here is his daughter Rachel, coming with the sheep.' ⁷He said, 'Look, it is still broad daylight; it is not time for the animals to be gathered together. Water the sheep, and go, pasture them.' ⁸But they said, 'We cannot until all the flocks are gathered together, and the stone is rolled from the mouth of the well; then we water the sheep.'

9 While he was still speaking with them, Rachel came with her father's sheep; for she kept them. ¹⁰Now when Jacob saw Rachel, the daughter of his mother's brother Laban, and the sheep of his mother's brother Laban, Jacob went up and rolled the stone from the well's mouth, and watered the flock of his mother's brother Laban. ¹¹Then Jacob kissed Rachel, and wept aloud. ¹²And Jacob told Rachel that he was her father's kinsman, and that he was Rebekah's son; and she ran and told her father.

13 When Laban heard the news about his sister's son Jacob, he ran to meet him; he embraced him and kissed him, and brought him to his house. Jacob*a* told Laban all these things, ¹⁴and Laban said to him, 'Surely you are my bone and my flesh!' And he stayed with him for a month.

Jacob Marries Laban's Daughters

15 Then Laban said to Jacob, 'Because you are my kinsman, should you therefore serve me for nothing? Tell me, what shall your wages be?' ¹⁶Now Laban had two daughters; the name of the elder was Leah, and the name of the younger was Rachel. ¹⁷Leah's eyes were lovely,*b* and Rachel was graceful and beautiful. ¹⁸Jacob loved Rachel; so he said, 'I will serve you seven years for your younger daughter Rachel.' ¹⁹Laban said, 'It is better that I give her to you than that I should give her to any other man; stay with me.' ²⁰So Jacob served seven years for Rachel, and they seemed to him but a few days because of the love he had for her.

21 Then Jacob said to Laban, 'Give me my wife that I may go in to her, for my time is completed.' ²²So Laban gathered together all the people of the place, and made a

feast. ²³But in the evening he took his daughter Leah and brought her to Jacob; and he went in to her. ²⁴(Laban gave his maid Zilpah to his daughter Leah to be her maid.) ²⁵When morning came, it was Leah! And Jacob said to Laban, 'What is this you have done to me? Did I not serve with you for Rachel? Why then have you deceived me?' ²⁶Laban said, 'This is not done in our country—giving the younger before the firstborn. ²⁷Complete the week of this one, and we will give you the other also in return for serving me for another seven years.' ²⁸Jacob did so, and completed her week; then Laban gave him his daughter Rachel as a wife. ²⁹(Laban gave his maid Bilhah to his daughter Rachel to be her maid.) ³⁰So Jacob went in to Rachel also, and he loved Rachel more than Leah. He served Laban*c* for another seven years.

31 When the LORD saw that Leah was unloved, he opened her womb; but Rachel was barren. ³²Leah conceived and bore a son, and she named him Reuben;*d* for she said, 'Because the LORD has looked on my affliction; surely now my husband will love me.' ³³She conceived again and bore a son, and said, 'Because the LORD has heard*e* that I am hated, he has given me this son also'; and she named him Simeon. ³⁴Again she conceived and bore a son, and said, 'Now this time my husband will be joined*f* to me, because I have borne him three sons'; therefore he was named Levi. ³⁵She conceived again and bore a son, and said, 'This time I will praise*g* the LORD'; therefore she named him Judah; then she ceased bearing.

30 When Rachel saw that she bore Jacob no children, she envied her sister; and she said to Jacob, 'Give me children, or I shall die!' ²Jacob became very angry with Rachel and said, 'Am I in the place of God, who has withheld from you the fruit of the womb?' ³Then she said, 'Here is my maid Bilhah; go in to her, that she may bear upon my knees and that I too may have children through her.' ⁴So she gave him her maid Bilhah as a wife; and Ja-

---

a Heb *He*   *b* Meaning of Heb uncertain   *c* Heb *him*
d That is *See, a son*   *e* Heb *shama*   *f* Heb *lawah*
g Heb *hodah*

cob went in to her. ⁵And Bilhah conceived and bore Jacob a son. ⁶Then Rachel said, 'God has judged me, and has also heard my voice and given me a son'; therefore she named him Dan.ᵃ ⁷Rachel's maid Bilhah conceived again and bore Jacob a second son. ⁸Then Rachel said, 'With mighty wrestlings I have wrestledᵇ with my sister, and have prevailed'; so she named him Naphtali.

9 When Leah saw that she had ceased bearing children, she took her maid Zilpah and gave her to Jacob as a wife. ¹⁰Then Leah's maid Zilpah bore Jacob a son. ¹¹And Leah said, 'Good fortune!' so she named him Gad.ᶜ ¹²Leah's maid Zilpah bore Jacob a second son. ¹³And Leah said, 'Happy am I! For the women will call me happy'; so she named him Asher.ᵈ

14 In the days of wheat harvest Reuben went and found mandrakes in the field, and brought them to his mother Leah. Then Rachel said to Leah, 'Please give me some of your son's mandrakes.' ¹⁵But she said to her, 'Is it a small matter that you have taken away my husband? Would you take away my son's mandrakes also?' Rachel said, 'Then he may lie with you tonight for your son's mandrakes.' ¹⁶When Jacob came from the field in the evening, Leah went out to meet him, and said, 'You must come in to me; for I have hired you with my son's mandrakes.' So he lay with her that night. ¹⁷And God heeded Leah, and she conceived and bore Jacob a fifth son. ¹⁸Leah said, 'God has given me my hireᵉ because I gave my maid to my husband'; so she named him Issachar. ¹⁹And Leah conceived again, and she bore Jacob a sixth son. ²⁰Then Leah said, 'God has endowed me with a good dowry; now my husband will honourᶠ me, because I have borne him six sons'; so she named him Zebulun. ²¹Afterwards she bore a daughter, and named her Dinah.

22 Then God remembered Rachel, and God heeded her and opened her womb. ²³She conceived and bore a son, and said, 'God has taken away my reproach'; ²⁴and she named him Joseph,ᵍ saying, 'May the LORD add to me another son!'

Jacob Prospers at Laban's Expense

25 When Rachel had borne Joseph, Jacob said to Laban, 'Send me away, that I may go to my own home and country. ²⁶Give me my wives and my children for whom I have served you, and let me go; for you know very well the service I have given you.' ²⁷But Laban said to him, 'If you will allow me to say so, I have learned by divination that the LORD has blessed me because of you; ²⁸name your wages, and I will give them.' ²⁹Jacob said to him, 'You yourself know how I have served you, and how your cattle have fared with me. ³⁰For you had little before I came, and it has increased abundantly; and the LORD has blessed you wherever I turned. But now when shall I provide for my own household also?' ³¹He said, 'What shall I give you?' Jacob said, 'You shall not give me anything; if you will do this for me, I will again feed your flock and keep it: ³²let me pass through all your flock

Journeys of Jacob

Mediterranean Sea

Yarmuk R.

Jordan River

Shechem

Penuel   Mahanaim?

Succoth   Jabbok R.

CANAAN

Bethel   Ai

Ephrath

Hebron

Dead Sea

Amon R.

Beer-sheba

0   10   20 Mi.
0   10   20

N

a That is He judged   b Heb niphtal   c That is Fortune
d That is Happy   e Heb sakar   f Heb zabal   g That is He adds

today, removing from it every speckled and spotted sheep and every black lamb, and the spotted and speckled among the goats; and such shall be my wages. [33] So my honesty will answer for me later, when you come to look into my wages with you. Every one that is not speckled and spotted among the goats and black among the lambs, if found with me, shall be counted stolen.' [34] Laban said, 'Good! Let it be as you have said.' [35] But that day Laban removed the male goats that were striped and spotted, and all the female goats that were speckled and spotted, every one that had white on it, and every lamb that was black, and put them in charge of his sons; [36] and he set a distance of three days' journey between himself and Jacob, while Jacob was pasturing the rest of Laban's flock.

37 Then Jacob took fresh rods of poplar and almond and plane, and peeled white streaks in them, exposing the white of the rods. [38] He set the rods that he had peeled in front of the flocks in the troughs, that is, the watering-places, where the flocks came to drink. And since they bred when they came to drink, [39] the flocks bred in front of the rods, and so the flocks produced young that were striped, speckled, and spotted. [40] Jacob separated the lambs, and set the faces of the flocks toward the striped and the completely black animals in the flock of Laban; and he put his own droves apart, and did not put them with Laban's flock. [41] Whenever the stronger of the flock were breeding, Jacob laid the rods in the troughs before the eyes of the flock, that they might breed among the rods, [42] but for the feebler of the flock he did not lay them there; so the feebler were Laban's, and the stronger Jacob's. [43] Thus the man grew exceedingly rich, and had large flocks, and male and female slaves, and camels and donkeys.

Jacob Flees with Family and Flocks

31 Now Jacob heard that the sons of Laban were saying, 'Jacob has taken all that was our father's; he has gained all this wealth from what belonged to our father.' [2] And Jacob saw that Laban did not regard him as favourably as he did before.

[3] Then the LORD said to Jacob, 'Return to the land of your ancestors and to your kindred, and I will be with you.' [4] So Jacob sent and called Rachel and Leah into the field where his flock was, [5] and said to them, 'I see that your father does not regard me as favourably as he did before. But the God of my father has been with me. [6] You know that I have served your father with all my strength; [7] yet your father has cheated me and changed my wages ten times, but God did not permit him to harm me. [8] If he said, "The speckled shall be your wages", then all the flock bore speckled; and if he said, "The striped shall be your wages", then all the flock bore striped. [9] Thus God has taken away the livestock of your father, and given them to me.

10 'During the mating of the flock I once had a dream in which I looked up and saw that the male goats that leaped upon the flock were striped, speckled, and mottled. [11] Then the angel of God said to me in the dream, "Jacob," and I said, "Here I am!" [12] And he said, "Look up and see that all the goats that leap on the flock are striped, speckled, and mottled; for I have seen all that Laban is doing to you. [13] I am the God of Bethel, [a] where you anointed a pillar and made a vow to me. Now leave this land at once and return to the land of your birth." ' [14] Then Rachel and Leah answered him, 'Is there any portion or inheritance left to us in our father's house? [15] Are we not regarded by him as foreigners? For he has sold us, and he has been using up the money given for us. [16] All the property that God has taken away from our father belongs to us and to our children; now then, do whatever God has said to you.'

17 So Jacob arose, and set his children and his wives on camels; [18] and he drove away all his livestock, all the property that he had gained, the livestock in his possession that he had acquired in Paddan-aram, to go to his father Isaac in the land of Canaan.

19 Now Laban had gone to shear his sheep, and Rachel stole her father's household gods. [20] And Jacob deceived Laban the

a Cn: Meaning of Heb uncertain

Aramean, in that he did not tell him that he intended to flee. 21 So he fled with all that he had; starting out he crossed the Euphrates, *a* and set his face towards the hill country of Gilead.

Laban Overtakes Jacob

22 On the third day Laban was told that Jacob had fled. 23 So he took his kinsfolk with him and pursued him for seven days until he caught up with him in the hill country of Gilead. 24 But God came to Laban the Aramean in a dream by night, and said to him, 'Take heed that you say not a word to Jacob, either good or bad.'

25 Laban overtook Jacob. Now Jacob had pitched his tent in the hill country, and Laban with his kinsfolk camped in the hill country of Gilead. 26 Laban said to Jacob, 'What have you done? You have deceived me, and carried away my daughters like captives of the sword. 27 Why did you flee secretly and deceive me and not tell me? I would have sent you away with mirth and songs, with tambourine and lyre. 28 And why did you not permit me to kiss my sons and my daughters farewell? What you have done is foolish. 29 It is in my power to do you harm; but the God of your father spoke to me last night, saying, "Take heed that you speak to Jacob neither good nor bad." 30 Even though you had to go because you longed greatly for your father's house, why did you steal my gods?' 31 Jacob answered Laban, 'Because I was afraid, for I thought that you would take your daughters from me by force. 32 But anyone with whom you find your gods shall not live. In the presence of our kinsfolk, point out what I have that is yours, and take it.' Now Jacob did not know that Rachel had stolen the gods. *b*

33 So Laban went into Jacob's tent, and into Leah's tent, and into the tent of the two maids, but he did not find them. And he went out of Leah's tent, and entered Rachel's. 34 Now Rachel had taken the household gods and put them in the camel's saddle, and sat on them. Laban felt all about in the tent, but did not find them. 35 And she said to her father, 'Let not my lord be angry that I cannot rise before you, for the way of women is upon me.' So he searched, but did not find the household gods.

36 Then Jacob became angry, and upbraided Laban. Jacob said to Laban, 'What is my offence? What is my sin, that you have hotly pursued me? 37 Although you have felt about through all my goods, what have you found of all your household goods? Set it here before my kinsfolk and your kinsfolk, so that they may decide between us two. 38 These twenty years I have been with you; your ewes and your female goats have not miscarried, and I have not eaten the rams of your flocks. 39 That which was torn by wild beasts I did not bring to you; I bore the loss of it myself; of my hand you required it, whether stolen by day or stolen by night. 40 It was like this with me: by day the heat consumed me, and the cold by night, and my sleep fled from my eyes. 41 These twenty years I have been in your house; I served you for fourteen years for your two daughters, and six years for your flock, and you have changed my wages ten times. 42 If the God of my father, the God of Abraham and the Fear *c* of Isaac, had not been on my side, surely now you would have sent me away empty-handed. God saw my affliction and the labour of my hands, and rebuked you last night.'

Laban and Jacob Make a Covenant

43 Then Laban answered and said to Jacob, 'The daughters are my daughters, the children are my children, the flocks are my flocks, and all that you see is mine. But what can I do today about these daughters of mine, or about their children whom they have borne? 44 Come now, let us make a covenant, you and I; and let it be a witness between you and me.' 45 So Jacob took a stone, and set it up as a pillar. 46 And Jacob said to his kinsfolk, 'Gather stones,' and they took stones, and made a heap; and they ate there by the heap. 47 Laban called it Jegar-sahadutha: *d* but Jacob called it Galeed. *e* 48 Laban said, 'This heap is a witness between you and me today.' Therefore he

---

a Heb *the river*　*b* Heb *them*　*c* Meaning of Heb uncertain　*d* In Aramaic *The heap of witness*　*e* In Hebrew *The heap of witness* called it Galeed, ⁴⁹and the pillar*ᵃ* Mizpah,*ᵇ* for he said, 'The LORD watch between you and me, when we are absent one from the other. ⁵⁰If you ill-treat my daughters, or if you take wives in addition to my daughters, though no one else is with us, remember that God is witness between you and me.'

51 Then Laban said to Jacob, 'See this heap and see the pillar, which I have set between you and me. ⁵²This heap is a witness, and the pillar is a witness, that I will not pass beyond this heap to you, and you will not pass beyond this heap and this pillar to me, for harm. ⁵³May the God of Abraham and the God of Nahor'—the God of their father—'judge between us.' So Jacob swore by the Fear*ᶜ* of his father Isaac, ⁵⁴and Jacob offered a sacrifice on the height and called his kinsfolk to eat bread; and they ate bread and tarried all night in the hill country.

55*ᵈ* Early in the morning Laban rose up, and kissed his grandchildren and his daughters and blessed them; then he departed and returned home.

32 Jacob went on his way and the angels of God met him; ²and when Jacob saw them he said, 'This is God's camp!' So he called that place Mahanaim.*ᵉ*

Jacob Sends Presents to Appease Esau

3 Jacob sent messengers before him to his brother Esau in the land of Seir, the country of Edom, ⁴instructing them, 'Thus you shall say to my lord Esau: Thus says your servant Jacob, "I have lived with Laban as an alien, and stayed until now; ⁵and I have oxen, donkeys, flocks, male and female slaves; and I have sent to tell my lord, in order that I may find favour in your sight." '

6 The messengers returned to Jacob, saying, 'We came to your brother Esau, and he is coming to meet you, and four hundred men are with him.' ⁷Then Jacob was greatly afraid and distressed; and he divided the people that were with him, and the flocks and herds and camels, into two companies, ⁸thinking, 'If Esau comes to one company and destroys it, then the company that is left will escape.'

9 And Jacob said, 'O God of my father Abraham and God of my father Isaac, O LORD who said to me, "Return to your country and to your kindred, and I will do you good", ¹⁰I am not worthy of the least of all the steadfast love and all the faithfulness that you have shown to your servant, for with only my staff I crossed this Jordan; and now I have become two companies. ¹¹Deliver me, please, from the hand of my brother, from the hand of Esau, for I am afraid of him; he may come and kill us all, the mothers with the children. ¹²Yet you have said, "I will surely do you good, and make your offspring as the sand of the sea, which cannot be counted because of their number." '

13 So he spent that night there, and from what he had with him he took a present for his brother Esau, ¹⁴two hundred female goats and twenty male goats, two hundred ewes and twenty rams, ¹⁵thirty milch camels and their colts, forty cows and ten bulls, twenty female donkeys and ten male donkeys. ¹⁶These he delivered into the hand of his servants, each drove by itself, and said to his servants, 'Pass on ahead of me, and put a space between drove and drove.' ¹⁷He instructed the foremost, 'When Esau my brother meets you, and asks you, "To whom do you belong? Where are you going? And whose are these ahead of you?" ¹⁸then you shall say, "They belong to your servant Jacob; they are a present sent to my lord Esau; and moreover he is behind us." ' ¹⁹He likewise instructed the second and the third and all who followed the droves, 'You shall say the same thing to Esau when you meet him, ²⁰and you shall say, "Moreover your servant Jacob is behind us." ' For he thought, 'I may appease him with the present that goes ahead of me, and afterwards I shall see his face; perhaps he will accept me.' ²¹So the present passed on ahead of him; and he himself spent that night in the camp.

Jacob Wrestles at Peniel

22 The same night he got up and took his two wives, his two maids, and his eleven

---

a Compare Sam: MT lacks *the pillar*　　*b* That is *Watchpost*　　*c* Meaning of Heb uncertain　　*d* Ch 32.1 in Heb　　*e* Here taken to mean *Two camps* children, and crossed the ford of the Jabbok. 23 He took them and sent them across the stream, and likewise everything that he had. 24 Jacob was left alone; and a man wrestled with him until daybreak. 25 When the man saw that he did not prevail against Jacob, he struck him on the hip socket; and Jacob's hip was put out of joint as he wrestled with him. 26 Then he said, 'Let me go, for the day is breaking.' But Jacob said, 'I will not let you go, unless you bless me.' 27 So he said to him, 'What is your name?' And he said, 'Jacob.' 28 Then the man *a* said, 'You shall no longer be called Jacob, but Israel, *b* for you have striven with God and with humans, *c* and have prevailed.' 29 Then Jacob asked him, 'Please tell me your name.' But he said, 'Why is it that you ask my name?' And there he blessed him. 30 So Jacob called the place Peniel, *d* saying, 'For I have seen God face to face, and yet my life is preserved.' 31 The sun rose upon him as he passed Penuel, limping because of his hip. 32 Therefore to this day the Israelites do not eat the thigh muscle that is on the hip socket, because he struck Jacob on the hip socket at the thigh muscle.

Jacob and Esau Meet

33 Now Jacob looked up and saw Esau coming, and four hundred men with him. So he divided the children among Leah and Rachel and the two maids. 2 He put the maids with their children in front, then Leah with her children, and Rachel and Joseph last of all. 3 He himself went on ahead of them, bowing himself to the ground seven times, until he came near his brother.

4 But Esau ran to meet him, and embraced him, and fell on his neck and kissed him, and they wept. 5 When Esau looked up and saw the women and children, he said, 'Who are these with you?' Jacob said, 'The children whom God has graciously given your servant.' 6 Then the maids drew near, they and their children, and bowed down; 7 Leah likewise and her children drew near and bowed down; and finally Joseph and Rachel drew near, and they bowed down. 8 Esau said, 'What do you mean by all this

company that I met?' Jacob answered, 'To find favour with my lord.' 9 But Esau said, 'I have enough, my brother; keep what you have for yourself.' 10 Jacob said, 'No, please; if I find favour with you, then accept my present from my hand; for truly to see your face is like seeing the face of God—since you have received me with such favour. 11 Please accept my gift that is brought to you, because God has dealt graciously with me, and because I have everything I want.' So he urged him, and he took it.

12 Then Esau said, 'Let us journey on our way, and I will go alongside you.' 13 But Jacob said to him, 'My lord knows that the children are frail and that the flocks and herds, which are nursing, are a care to me; and if they are overdriven for one day, all the flocks will die. 14 Let my lord pass on ahead of his servant, and I will lead on slowly, according to the pace of the cattle that are before me and according to the pace of the children, until I come to my lord in Seir.'

15 So Esau said, 'Let me leave with you some of the people who are with me.' But he said, 'Why should my lord be so kind to me?' 16 So Esau returned that day on his way to Seir. 17 But Jacob journeyed to Succoth, *e* and built himself a house, and made booths for his cattle; therefore the place is called Succoth.

Jacob Reaches Shechem

18 Jacob came safely to the city of Shechem, which is in the land of Canaan, on his way from Paddan-aram; and he camped before the city. 19 And from the sons of Hamor, Shechem's father, he bought for one hundred pieces of money *f* the plot of land on which he had pitched his tent. 20 There he erected an altar and called it El-Elohe-Israel. *g*

The Rape of Dinah

34 Now Dinah the daughter of Leah, whom she had borne to Jacob, went out to visit the women of the region. 2 When Shechem son of Hamor the Hivite,

a Heb *he*   *b* That is *The one who strives with God* or *God strives*   *c* Or *with divine and human beings*
d That is *The face of God*   *e* That is *Booths*   *f* Heb *one hundred qesitah*   *g* That is *God, the God of Israel*

prince of the region, saw her, he seized her and lay with her by force. ³And his soul was drawn to Dinah daughter of Jacob; he loved the girl, and spoke tenderly to her. ⁴So Shechem spoke to his father Hamor, saying, 'Get me this girl to be my wife.'

5 Now Jacob heard that Shechem*ᵃ* had defiled his daughter Dinah; but his sons were with his cattle in the field, so Jacob held his peace until they came. ⁶And Hamor the father of Shechem went out to Jacob to speak with him, ⁷just as the sons of Jacob came in from the field. When they heard of it, the men were indignant and very angry, because he had committed an outrage in Israel by lying with Jacob's daughter, for such a thing ought not to be done.

8 But Hamor spoke with them, saying, 'The heart of my son Shechem longs for your daughter; please give her to him in marriage. ⁹Make marriages with us; give your daughters to us, and take our daughters for yourselves. ¹⁰You shall live with us; and the land shall be open to you; live and trade in it, and get property in it.' ¹¹Shechem also said to her father and to her brothers, 'Let me find favour with you, and whatever you say to me I will give. ¹²Put the marriage present and gift as high as you like, and I will give whatever you ask me; only give me the girl to be my wife.'

13 The sons of Jacob answered Shechem and his father Hamor deceitfully, because he had defiled their sister Dinah. ¹⁴They said to them, 'We cannot do this thing, to give our sister to one who is uncircumcised, for that would be a disgrace to us. ¹⁵Only on this condition will we consent to you: that you will become as we are and every male among you be circumcised. ¹⁶Then we will give our daughters to you, and we will take your daughters for ourselves, and we will live among you and become one people. ¹⁷But if you will not listen to us and be circumcised, then we will take our daughter and be gone.'

18 Their words pleased Hamor and Hamor's son Shechem. ¹⁹And the young man did not delay to do the thing, because he was delighted with Jacob's daughter. Now

he was the most honoured of all his family. ²⁰So Hamor and his son Shechem came to the gate of their city and spoke to the men of their city, saying, ²¹'These people are friendly with us; let them live in the land and trade in it, for the land is large enough for them; let us take their daughters in marriage, and let us give them our daughters. ²²Only on this condition will they agree to live among us, to become one people: that every male among us be circumcised as they are circumcised. ²³Will not their livestock, their property, and all their animals be ours? Only let us agree with them, and they will live among us.' ²⁴And all who went out of the city gate heeded Hamor and his son Shechem; and every male was circumcised, all who went out of the gate of his city.

Dinah's Brothers Avenge Their Sister

25 On the third day, when they were still in pain, two of the sons of Jacob, Simeon and Levi, Dinah's brothers, took their swords and came against the city unawares, and killed all the males. ²⁶They killed Hamor and his son Shechem with the sword, and took Dinah out of Shechem's house, and went away. ²⁷And the other sons of Jacob came upon the slain, and plundered the city, because their sister had been defiled. ²⁸They took their flocks and their herds, their donkeys, and whatever was in the city and in the field. ²⁹All their wealth, all their little ones and their wives, all that was in the houses, they captured and made their prey. ³⁰Then Jacob said to Simeon and Levi, 'You have brought trouble on me by making me odious to the inhabitants of the land, the Canaanites and the Perizzites; my numbers are few, and if they gather themselves against me and attack me, I shall be destroyed, both I and my household.' ³¹But they said, 'Should our sister be treated like a whore?'

Jacob Returns to Bethel

35 God said to Jacob, 'Arise, go up to Bethel, and settle there. Make an altar there to the God who appeared to you

a Heb *he*

when you fled from your brother Esau.' ²So Jacob said to his household and to all who were with him, 'Put away the foreign gods that are among you, and purify yourselves, and change your clothes; ³then come, let us go up to Bethel, that I may make an altar there to the God who answered me in the day of my distress and has been with me wherever I have gone.' ⁴So they gave to Jacob all the foreign gods that they had, and the rings that were in their ears; and Jacob hid them under the oak that was near Shechem.

5 As they journeyed, a terror from God fell upon the cities all around them, so that no one pursued them. ⁶Jacob came to Luz (that is, Bethel), which is in the land of Canaan, he and all the people who were with him, ⁷and there he built an altar and called the place El-bethel,*ᵃ* because it was there that God had revealed himself to him when he fled from his brother. ⁸And Deborah, Rebekah's nurse, died, and she was buried under an oak below Bethel. So it was called Allon-bacuth.*ᵇ*

9 God appeared to Jacob again when he came from Paddan-aram, and he blessed him. ¹⁰God said to him, 'Your name is Jacob; no longer shall you be called Jacob, but Israel shall be your name.' So he was called Israel. ¹¹God said to him, 'I am God Almighty:*ᶜ* be fruitful and multiply; a nation and a company of nations shall come from you, and kings shall spring from you. ¹²The land that I gave to Abraham and Isaac I will give to you, and I will give the land to your offspring after you.' ¹³Then God went up from him at the place where he had spoken with him. ¹⁴Jacob set up a pillar in the place where he had spoken with him, a pillar of stone; and he poured out a drink-offering on it, and poured oil on it. ¹⁵So Jacob called the place where God had spoken with him Bethel.

The Birth of Benjamin and the Death of Rachel

16 Then they journeyed from Bethel; and when they were still some distance from Ephrath, Rachel was in childbirth, and she had a difficult labour. ¹⁷When she was

in her difficult labour, the midwife said to her, 'Do not be afraid; for now you will have another son.' ¹⁸As her soul was departing (for she died), she named him Benoni;*ᵈ* but his father called him Benjamin.*ᵉ* ¹⁹So Rachel died, and she was buried on the way to Ephrath (that is, Bethlehem), ²⁰and Jacob set up a pillar at her grave; it is the pillar of Rachel's tomb, which is there to this day. ²¹Israel journeyed on, and pitched his tent beyond the tower of Eder.

22 While Israel lived in that land, Reuben went and lay with Bilhah his father's concubine; and Israel heard of it.

Now the sons of Jacob were twelve. ²³The sons of Leah: Reuben (Jacob's firstborn), Simeon, Levi, Judah, Issachar, and Zebulun. ²⁴The sons of Rachel: Joseph and Benjamin. ²⁵The sons of Bilhah, Rachel's maid: Dan and Naphtali. ²⁶The sons of Zilpah, Leah's maid: Gad and Asher. These were the sons of Jacob who were born to him in Paddan-aram.

The Death of Isaac

27 Jacob came to his father Isaac at Mamre, or Kiriath-arba (that is, Hebron), where Abraham and Isaac had resided as aliens. ²⁸Now the days of Isaac were one hundred and eighty years. ²⁹And Isaac breathed his last; he died and was gathered to his people, old and full of days; and his sons Esau and Jacob buried him.

Esau's Descendants

36 These are the descendants of Esau (that is, Edom). ²Esau took his wives from the Canaanites: Adah daughter of Elon the Hittite, Oholibamah daughter of Anah son*ᶠ* of Zibeon the Hivite, ³and Basemath, Ishmael's daughter, sister of Nebaioth. ⁴Adah bore Eliphaz to Esau; Basemath bore Reuel; ⁵and Oholibamah bore Jeush, Jalam, and Korah. These are the sons of Esau who were born to him in the land of Canaan.

6 Then Esau took his wives, his sons, his daughters, and all the members of his

---

a That is God of Bethel   *b* That is Oak of weeping
c Traditional rendering of Heb El Shaddai   *d* That is
Son of my sorrow   *e* That is Son of the right hand or Son
of the South   *f* Sam Gk Syr: Heb daughter

household, his cattle, all his livestock, and all the property he had acquired in the land of Canaan; and he moved to a land some distance from his brother Jacob. [7] For their possessions were too great for them to live together; the land where they were living could not support them because of their livestock. [8] So Esau settled in the hill country of Seir; Esau is Edom.

9 These are the descendants of Esau, ancestor of the Edomites, in the hill country of Seir. [10] These are the names of Esau's sons: Eliphaz, son of Adah the wife of Esau; Reuel, the son of Esau's wife Basemath. [11] The sons of Eliphaz were Teman, Omar, Zepho, Gatam, and Kenaz. [12] (Timna was a concubine of Eliphaz, Esau's son; she bore Amalek to Eliphaz.) These were the sons of Adah, Esau's wife. [13] These were the sons of Reuel: Nahath, Zerah, Shammah, and Mizzah. These were the sons of Esau's wife Basemath. [14] These were the sons of Esau's wife Oholibamah, daughter of Anah son[a] of Zibeon: she bore to Esau Jeush, Jalam, and Korah.

Clans and Kings of Edom

15 These are the clans[b] of the sons of Esau. The sons of Eliphaz the firstborn of Esau: the clans[b] Teman, Omar, Zepho, Kenaz, [16] Korah, Gatam, and Amalek; these are the clans[b] of Eliphaz in the land of Edom; they are the sons of Adah. [17] These are the sons of Esau's son Reuel: the clans[b] Nahath, Zerah, Shammah, and Mizzah; these are the clans[b] of Reuel in the land of Edom; they are the sons of Esau's wife Basemath. [18] These are the sons of Esau's wife Oholibamah: the clans[b] Jeush, Jalam, and Korah; these are the clans[b] born of Esau's wife Oholibamah, the daughter of Anah. [19] These are the sons of Esau (that is, Edom), and these are their clans.[b]

20 These are the sons of Seir the Horite, the inhabitants of the land: Lotan, Shobal, Zibeon, Anah, [21] Dishon, Ezer, and Dishan; these are the clans[b] of the Horites, the sons of Seir in the land of Edom. [22] The sons of Lotan were Hori and Heman; and Lotan's sister was Timna. [23] These are the sons of Shobal: Alvan, Manahath, Ebal, Shepho, and Onam. [24] These are the sons of Zibeon:

Aiah and Anah; he is the Anah who found the springs[c] in the wilderness, as he pastured the donkeys of his father Zibeon. [25] These are the children of Anah: Dishon and Oholibamah daughter of Anah. [26] These are the sons of Dishon: Hemdan, Eshban, Ithran, and Cheran. [27] These are the sons of Ezer: Bilhan, Zaavan, and Akan. [28] These are the sons of Dishan: Uz and Aran. [29] These are the clans[b] of the Horites: the clans[b] Lotan, Shobal, Zibeon, Anah, [30] Dishon, Ezer, and Dishan; these are the clans[b] of the Horites, clan by clan[d] in the land of Seir.

31 These are the kings who reigned in the land of Edom, before any king reigned over the Israelites. [32] Bela son of Beor reigned in Edom, the name of his city being Dinhabah. [33] Bela died, and Jobab son of Zerah of Bozrah succeeded him as king. [34] Jobab died, and Husham of the land of the Temanites succeeded him as king. [35] Husham died, and Hadad son of Bedad, who defeated Midian in the country of Moab, succeeded him as king, the name of his city being Avith. [36] Hadad died, and Samlah of Masrekah succeeded him as king. [37] Samlah died, and Shaul of Rehoboth on the Euphrates succeeded him as king. [38] Shaul died, and Baal-hanan son of Achbor succeeded him as king. [39] Baal-hanan son of Achbor died, and Hadar succeeded him as king, the name of his city being Pau; his wife's name was Mehetabel, the daughter of Matred, daughter of Me-zahab.

40 These are the names of the clans[b] of Esau, according to their families and their localities by their names: the clans[b] Timna, Alvah, Jetheth, [41] Oholibamah, Elah, Pinon, [42] Kenaz, Teman, Mibzar, [43] Magdiel, and Iram; these are the clans[b] of Edom (that is, Esau, the father of Edom), according to their settlements in the land that they held.

Joseph Dreams of Greatness

37 Jacob settled in the land where his father had lived as an alien, the land of Canaan. [2] This is the story of the family of Jacob.

a Gk Syr: Heb *daughter*   b Or *chiefs*   c Meaning of Heb uncertain   d Or *chief by chief*

Joseph, being seventeen years old, was shepherding the flock with his brothers; he was a helper to the sons of Bilhah and Zilpah, his father's wives; and Joseph brought a bad report of them to their father. 3 Now Israel loved Joseph more than any other of his children, because he was the son of his old age; and he had made him a long robe with sleeves.*a* 4 But when his brothers saw that their father loved him more than all his brothers, they hated him, and could not speak peaceably to him.

5 Once Joseph had a dream, and when he told it to his brothers, they hated him even more. 6 He said to them, 'Listen to this dream that I dreamed. 7 There we were, binding sheaves in the field. Suddenly my sheaf rose and stood upright; then your sheaves gathered around it, and bowed down to my sheaf.' 8 His brothers said to him, 'Are you indeed to reign over us? Are you indeed to have dominion over us?' So they hated him even more because of his dreams and his words.

9 He had another dream, and told it to his brothers, saying, 'Look, I have had another dream: the sun, the moon, and eleven stars were bowing down to me.' 10 But when he told it to his father and to his brothers, his father rebuked him, and said to him, 'What kind of dream is this that you have had? Shall we indeed come, I and your mother and your brothers, and bow to the ground before you?' 11 So his brothers were jealous of him, but his father kept the matter in mind.

Joseph Is Sold by His Brothers

12 Now his brothers went to pasture their father's flock near Shechem. 13 And Israel said to Joseph, 'Are not your brothers pasturing the flock at Shechem? Come, I will send you to them.' He answered, 'Here I am.' 14 So he said to him, 'Go now, see if it is well with your brothers and with the flock; and bring word back to me.' So he sent him from the valley of Hebron.

He came to Shechem, 15 and a man found him wandering in the fields; the man asked him, 'What are you seeking?' 16 'I am seeking my brothers,' he said; 'tell me,

please, where they are pasturing the flock.' 17 The man said, 'They have gone away, for I heard them say, "Let us go to Dothan."' So Joseph went after his brothers, and found them at Dothan. 18 They saw him from a distance, and before he came near to them, they conspired to kill him. 19 They said to one another, 'Here comes this dreamer. 20 Come now, let us kill him and throw him into one of the pits; then we shall say that a wild animal has devoured him, and we shall see what will become of his dreams.' 21 But when Reuben heard it, he delivered him out of their hands, saying, 'Let us not take his life.' 22 Reuben said to them, 'Shed no blood; throw him into this pit here in the wilderness, but lay no hand on him'— that he might rescue him out of their hand and restore him to his father. 23 So when Joseph came to his brothers, they stripped him of his robe, the long robe with sleeves*b* that he wore; 24 and they took him and threw him into a pit. The pit was empty; there was no water in it.

25 Then they sat down to eat; and looking up they saw a caravan of Ishmaelites coming from Gilead, with their camels carrying gum, balm, and resin, on their way to carry it down to Egypt. 26 Then Judah said to his brothers, 'What profit is there if we kill our brother and conceal his blood? 27 Come, let us sell him to the Ishmaelites, and not lay our hands on him, for he is our brother, our own flesh.' And his brothers agreed. 28 When some Midianite traders passed by, they drew Joseph up, lifting him out of the pit, and sold him to the Ishmaelites for twenty pieces of silver. And they took Joseph to Egypt.

29 When Reuben returned to the pit and saw that Joseph was not in the pit, he tore his clothes. 30 He returned to his brothers, and said, 'The boy is gone; and I, where can I turn?' 31 Then they took Joseph's robe, slaughtered a goat, and dipped the robe in the blood. 32 They had the long robe with sleeves*b* taken to their father, and they said, 'This we have found; see now whether it is your son's robe or not.' 33 He recognized it,

a Traditional rendering (compare Gk): a coat of many colours; meaning of Heb uncertain   b See note on 37.3 and said, 'It is my son's robe! A wild animal has devoured him; Joseph is without doubt torn to pieces.' [34] Then Jacob tore his garments, and put sackcloth on his loins, and mourned for his son for many days. [35] All his sons and all his daughters sought to comfort him; but he refused to be comforted, and said, 'No, I shall go down to Sheol to my son, mourning.' Thus his father bewailed him. [36] Meanwhile the Midianites had sold him in Egypt to Potiphar, one of Pharaoh's officials, the captain of the guard.

Judah and Tamar

38 It happened at that time that Judah went down from his brothers and settled near a certain Adullamite whose name was Hirah. [2] There Judah saw the daughter of a certain Canaanite whose name was Shua; he married her and went in to her. [3] She conceived and bore a son; and he named him Er. [4] Again she conceived and bore a son whom she named Onan. [5] Yet again she bore a son, and she named him Shelah. She [a] was in Chezib when she bore him. [6] Judah took a wife for Er his first-born; her name was Tamar. [7] But Er, Judah's firstborn, was wicked in the sight of the LORD, and the LORD put him to death. [8] Then Judah said to Onan, 'Go in to your brother's wife and perform the duty of a brother-in-law to her; raise up offspring for your brother.' [9] But since Onan knew that the offspring would not be his, he spilled his semen on the ground whenever he went in to his brother's wife, so that he would not give offspring to his brother. [10] What he did was displeasing in the sight of the LORD, and he put him to death also. [11] Then Judah said to his daughter-in-law Tamar, 'Remain a widow in your father's house until my son Shelah grows up'—for he feared that he too would die, like his brothers. So Tamar went to live in her father's house.

12 In course of time the wife of Judah, Shua's daughter, died; when Judah's time of mourning was over, [b] he went up to Timnah to his sheep-shearers, he and his friend Hirah the Adullamite. [13] When Tamar was told, 'Your father-in-law is going up to Timnah to shear his sheep', [14] she put off her widow's garments, put on a veil, wrapped herself up, and sat down at the entrance to Enaim, which is on the road to Timnah. She saw that Shelah was grown up, yet she had not been given to him in marriage. [15] When Judah saw her, he thought her to be a prostitute, for she had covered her face. [16] He went over to her at the roadside, and said, 'Come, let me come in to you', for he did not know that she was his daughter-in-law. She said, 'What will you give me, that you may come in to me?' [17] He answered, 'I will send you a kid from the flock.' And she said, 'Only if you give me a pledge, until you send it.' [18] He said, 'What pledge shall I give you?' She replied, 'Your signet and your cord, and the staff that is in your hand.' So he gave them to her, and went in to her, and she conceived by him. [19] Then she got up and went away, and taking off her veil she put on the garments of her widowhood.

20 When Judah sent the kid by his friend the Adullamite, to recover the pledge from the woman, he could not find her. [21] He asked the townspeople, 'Where is the temple prostitute who was at Enaim by the wayside?' But they said, 'No prostitute has been here.' [22] So he returned to Judah, and said, 'I have not found her; moreover, the townspeople said, "No prostitute has been here." ' [23] Judah replied, 'Let her keep the things as her own, otherwise we will be laughed at; you see, I sent this kid, and you could not find her.'

24 About three months later Judah was told, 'Your daughter-in-law Tamar has played the whore; moreover she is pregnant as a result of whoredom.' And Judah said, 'Bring her out, and let her be burned.' [25] As she was being brought out, she sent word to her father-in-law, 'It was the owner of these who made me pregnant.' And she said, 'Take note, please, whose these are, the signet and the cord and the staff.' [26] Then Judah acknowledged them and said, 'She is more in the right than I, since I did not give her to my son Shelah.' And he did not lie with her again.

27 When the time of her delivery came, there were twins in her womb. [28] While she

was in labour, one put out a hand; and the midwife took and bound on his hand a crimson thread, saying, 'This one came out first.' ²⁹ But just then he drew back his hand, and out came his brother; and she said, 'What a breach you have made for yourself!' Therefore he was named Perez.ᵃ ³⁰ Afterwards his brother came out with the crimson thread on his hand; and he was named Zerah.ᵇ

Joseph and Potiphar's Wife

39 Now Joseph was taken down to Egypt, and Potiphar, an officer of Pharaoh, the captain of the guard, an Egyptian, bought him from the Ishmaelites who had brought him down there. ² The LORD was with Joseph, and he became a successful man; he was in the house of his Egyptian master. ³ His master saw that the LORD was with him, and that the LORD caused all that he did to prosper in his hands. ⁴ So Joseph found favour in his sight and attended him; he made him overseer of his house and put him in charge of all that he had. ⁵ From the time that he made him overseer in his house and over all that he had, the LORD blessed the Egyptian's house for Joseph's sake; the blessing of the LORD was on all that he had, in house and field. ⁶ So he left all that he had in Joseph's charge; and, with him there, he had no concern for anything but the food that he ate.

Now Joseph was handsome and good-looking. ⁷ And after a time his master's wife cast her eyes on Joseph and said, 'Lie with me.' ⁸ But he refused and said to his master's wife, 'Look, with me here, my master has no concern about anything in the house, and he has put everything that he has in my hand. ⁹ He is not greater in this house than I am, nor has he kept back anything from me except yourself, because you are his wife. How then could I do this great wickedness, and sin against God?' ¹⁰ And although she spoke to Joseph day after day, he would not consent to lie beside her or to be with her. ¹¹ One day, however, when he went into the house to do his work, and while no one else was in the house, ¹² she caught hold of his garment, saying, 'Lie with me!' But he left his garment in her hand, and fled and ran outside. ¹³ When she saw that he had left his garment in her hand and had fled outside, ¹⁴ she called out to the members of her household and said to them, 'See, my husbandᶜ has brought among us a Hebrew to insult us! He came in to me to lie with me, and I cried out with a loud voice; ¹⁵ and when he heard me raise my voice and cry out, he left his garment beside me, and fled outside.' ¹⁶ Then she kept his garment by her until his master came home, ¹⁷ and she told him the same story, saying, 'The Hebrew servant, whom you have brought among us, came in to me to insult me; ¹⁸ but as soon as I raised my voice and cried out, he left his garment beside me, and fled outside.'

¹⁹ When his master heard the words that his wife spoke to him, saying, 'This is the way your servant treated me', he became enraged. ²⁰ And Joseph's master took him and put him into the prison, the place

Joseph and His Brothers Go to Egypt

Mediterranean Sea

CANAAN
Dothan
Shechem

Bethel

Gaza
Hebron

To Egypt

NEGEB

Dead Sea

N

0   40 Mi.
0   40 Km.

- ·→ Ishmaelite Caravan Route
→ Joseph and His Brothers

ᵃ That is *A breach*   ᵇ That is *Brightness*; perhaps alluding to the crimson thread   ᶜ Heb *he* where the king's prisoners were confined; he remained there in prison. 21 But the LORD was with Joseph and showed him steadfast love; he gave him favour in the sight of the chief jailer. 22 The chief jailer committed to Joseph's care all the prisoners who were in the prison, and whatever was done there, he was the one who did it. 23 The chief jailer paid no heed to anything that was in Joseph's care, because the LORD was with him; and whatever he did, the LORD made it prosper.

The Dreams of Two Prisoners

40 Some time after this, the cupbearer of the king of Egypt and his baker offended their lord the king of Egypt. 2 Pharaoh was angry with his two officers, the chief cupbearer and the chief baker, 3 and he put them in custody in the house of the captain of the guard, in the prison where Joseph was confined. 4 The captain of the guard charged Joseph with them, and he waited on them; and they continued for some time in custody. 5 One night they both dreamed—the cupbearer and the baker of the king of Egypt, who were confined in the prison—each his own dream, and each dream with its own meaning. 6 When Joseph came to them in the morning, he saw that they were troubled. 7 So he asked Pharaoh's officers, who were with him in custody in his master's house, 'Why are your faces downcast today?' 8 They said to him, 'We have had dreams, and there is no one to interpret them.' And Joseph said to them, 'Do not interpretations belong to God? Please tell them to me.'

9 So the chief cupbearer told his dream to Joseph, and said to him, 'In my dream there was a vine before me, 10 and on the vine there were three branches. As soon as it budded, its blossoms came out and the clusters ripened into grapes. 11 Pharaoh's cup was in my hand; and I took the grapes and pressed them into Pharaoh's cup, and placed the cup in Pharaoh's hand.' 12 Then Joseph said to him, 'This is its interpretation: the three branches are three days; 13 within three days Pharaoh will lift up your head and restore you to your office;

and you shall place Pharaoh's cup in his hand, just as you used to do when you were his cupbearer. 14 But remember me when it is well with you; please do me the kindness to make mention of me to Pharaoh, and so get me out of this place. 15 For in fact I was stolen out of the land of the Hebrews; and here also I have done nothing that they should have put me into the dungeon.'

16 When the chief baker saw that the interpretation was favourable, he said to Joseph, 'I also had a dream: there were three cake baskets on my head, 17 and in the uppermost basket there were all sorts of baked food for Pharaoh, but the birds were eating it out of the basket on my head.' 18 And Joseph answered, 'This is its interpretation: the three baskets are three days; 19 within three days Pharaoh will lift up your head—from you!—and hang you on a pole; and the birds will eat the flesh from you.'

20 On the third day, which was Pharaoh's birthday, he made a feast for all his servants, and lifted up the head of the chief cupbearer and the head of the chief baker among his servants. 21 He restored the chief cupbearer to his cupbearing, and he placed the cup in Pharaoh's hand; 22 but the chief baker he hanged, just as Joseph had interpreted to them. 23 Yet the chief cupbearer did not remember Joseph, but forgot him.

Joseph Interprets Pharaoh's Dream

41 After two whole years, Pharaoh dreamed that he was standing by the Nile, 2 and there came up out of the Nile seven sleek and fat cows, and they grazed in the reed grass. 3 Then seven other cows, ugly and thin, came up out of the Nile after them, and stood by the other cows on the bank of the Nile. 4 The ugly and thin cows ate up the seven sleek and fat cows. And Pharaoh awoke. 5 Then he fell asleep and dreamed a second time; seven ears of grain, plump and good, were growing on one stalk. 6 Then seven ears, thin and blighted by the east wind, sprouted after them. 7 The thin ears swallowed up the seven plump and full ears. Pharaoh awoke, and it was a dream. 8 In the morning his spirit was troubled; so he sent and called for all the ma-

gicians of Egypt and all its wise men. Pharaoh told them his dreams, but there was no one who could interpret them to Pharaoh. 9 Then the chief cupbearer said to Pharaoh, 'I remember my faults today. 10 Once Pharaoh was angry with his servants, and put me and the chief baker in custody in the house of the captain of the guard. 11 We dreamed on the same night, he and I, each having a dream with its own meaning. 12 A young Hebrew was there with us, a servant of the captain of the guard. When we told him, he interpreted our dreams to us, giving an interpretation to each according to his dream. 13 As he interpreted to us, so it turned out; I was restored to my office, and the baker was hanged.'

14 Then Pharaoh sent for Joseph, and he was hurriedly brought out of the dungeon. When he had shaved himself and changed his clothes, he came in before Pharaoh. 15 And Pharaoh said to Joseph, 'I have had a dream, and there is no one who can interpret it. I have heard it said of you that when you hear a dream you can interpret it.' 16 Joseph answered Pharaoh, 'It is not I; God will give Pharaoh a favourable answer.' 17 Then Pharaoh said to Joseph, 'In my dream I was standing on the banks of the Nile; 18 and seven cows, fat and sleek, came up out of the Nile and fed in the reed grass. 19 Then seven other cows came up after them, poor, very ugly, and thin. Never had I seen such ugly ones in all the land of Egypt. 20 The thin and ugly cows ate up the first seven fat cows, 21 but when they had eaten them no one would have known that they had done so, for they were still as ugly as before. Then I awoke. 22 I fell asleep a second time*a* and I saw in my dream seven ears of grain, full and good, growing on one stalk, 23 and seven ears, withered, thin, and blighted by the east wind, sprouting after them; 24 and the thin ears swallowed up the seven good ears. But when I told it to the magicians, there was no one who could explain it to me.'

25 Then Joseph said to Pharaoh, 'Pharaoh's dreams are one and the same; God has revealed to Pharaoh what he is about to do. 26 The seven good cows are seven years, and the seven good ears are seven years; the dreams are one. 27 The seven lean and ugly cows that came up after them are seven years, as are the seven empty ears blighted by the east wind. They are seven years of famine. 28 It is as I told Pharaoh; God has shown to Pharaoh what he is about to do. 29 There will come seven years of great plenty throughout all the land of Egypt. 30 After them there will arise seven years of famine, and all the plenty will be forgotten in the land of Egypt; the famine will consume the land. 31 The plenty will no longer be known in the land because of the famine that will follow, for it will be very grievous. 32 And the doubling of Pharaoh's dream means that the thing is fixed by God, and God will shortly bring it about. 33 Now therefore let Pharaoh select a man who is discerning and wise, and set him over the land of Egypt. 34 Let Pharaoh proceed to appoint overseers over the land, and take one-fifth of the produce of the land of Egypt during the seven plenteous years. 35 Let them gather all the food of these good years that are coming, and lay up grain under the authority of Pharaoh for food in the cities, and let them keep it. 36 That food shall be a reserve for the land against the seven years of famine that are to befall the land of Egypt, so that the land may not perish through the famine.'

Joseph's Rise to Power

37 The proposal pleased Pharaoh and all his servants. 38 Pharaoh said to his servants, 'Can we find anyone else like this—one in whom is the spirit of God?' 39 So Pharaoh said to Joseph, 'Since God has shown you all this, there is no one so discerning and wise as you. 40 You shall be over my house, and all my people shall order themselves as you command; only with regard to the throne will I be greater than you.' 41 And Pharaoh said to Joseph, 'See, I have set you over all the land of Egypt.' 42 Removing his signet ring from his hand, Pharaoh put it on Joseph's hand; he arrayed him in garments of fine linen, and put a gold chain around his neck. 43 He had him ride in the chariot of his

a Gk Syr Vg: Heb lacks I fell asleep a second time

second-in-command; and they cried out in front of him, 'Bow the knee!' *a* Thus he set him over all the land of Egypt. ⁴⁴Moreover, Pharaoh said to Joseph, 'I am Pharaoh, and without your consent no one shall lift up hand or foot in all the land of Egypt.' ⁴⁵Pharaoh gave Joseph the name Zaphenath-paneah; and he gave him Asenath daughter of Potiphera, priest of On, as his wife. Thus Joseph gained authority over the land of Egypt.

46 Joseph was thirty years old when he entered the service of Pharaoh king of Egypt. And Joseph went out from the presence of Pharaoh, and went through all the land of Egypt. ⁴⁷During the seven plenteous years the earth produced abundantly. ⁴⁸He gathered up all the food of the seven years when there was plenty *b* in the land of Egypt, and stored up food in the cities; he stored up in every city the food from the fields around it. ⁴⁹So Joseph stored up grain in such abundance—like the sand of the sea—that he stopped measuring it; it was beyond measure.

50 Before the years of famine came, Joseph had two sons, whom Asenath daughter of Potiphera, priest of On, bore to him. ⁵¹Joseph named the firstborn Manasseh, *c* 'For', he said, 'God has made me forget all my hardship and all my father's house.' ⁵²The second he named Ephraim, *d* 'For God has made me fruitful in the land of my misfortunes.'

53 The seven years of plenty that prevailed in the land of Egypt came to an end; ⁵⁴and the seven years of famine began to come, just as Joseph had said. There was famine in every country, but throughout the land of Egypt there was bread. ⁵⁵When all the land of Egypt was famished, the people cried to Pharaoh for bread. Pharaoh said to all the Egyptians, 'Go to Joseph; what he says to you, do.' ⁵⁶And since the famine had spread over all the land, Joseph opened all the storehouses, *e* and sold to the Egyptians, for the famine was severe in the land of Egypt. ⁵⁷Moreover, all the world came to Joseph in Egypt to buy grain, because the famine became severe throughout the world.

Joseph's Brothers Go to Egypt

42 When Jacob learned that there was grain in Egypt, he said to his sons, 'Why do you keep looking at one another? ²I have heard', he said, 'that there is grain in Egypt; go down and buy grain for us there, that we may live and not die.' ³So ten of Joseph's brothers went down to buy grain in Egypt. ⁴But Jacob did not send Joseph's brother Benjamin with his brothers, for he feared that harm might come to him. ⁵Thus the sons of Israel were among the other people who came to buy grain, for the famine had reached the land of Canaan.

6 Now Joseph was governor over the land; it was he who sold to all the people of the land. And Joseph's brothers came and bowed themselves before him with their faces to the ground. ⁷When Joseph saw his brothers, he recognized them, but he treated them like strangers and spoke harshly to them. 'Where do you come from?' he said. They said, 'From the land of Canaan, to buy food.' ⁸Although Joseph had recognized his brothers, they did not recognize him. ⁹Joseph also remembered the dreams that he had dreamed about them. He said to them, 'You are spies; you have come to see the nakedness of the land!' ¹⁰They said to him, 'No, my lord; your servants have come to buy food. ¹¹We are all sons of one man; we are honest men; your servants have never been spies.' ¹²But he said to them, 'No, you have come to see the nakedness of the land!' ¹³They said, 'We, your servants, are twelve brothers, the sons of a certain man in the land of Canaan; the youngest, however, is now with our father, and one is no more.' ¹⁴But Joseph said to them, 'It is just as I have said to you; you are spies! ¹⁵Here is how you shall be tested: as Pharaoh lives, you shall not leave this place unless your youngest brother comes here! ¹⁶Let one of you go and bring your brother, while the rest of you remain in prison, in order that

a Abrek, apparently an Egyptian word similar in sound to the Hebrew word meaning *to kneel*   *b* Sam Gk: MT *the seven years that were*   *c* That is *Making to forget*   *d* From a Hebrew word meaning *to be fruitful*   *e* Gk Vg Compare Syr: Heb *opened all that was in* (or, among) *them* your words may be tested, whether there is truth in you; or else, as Pharaoh lives, surely you are spies.' 17 And he put them all together in prison for three days.

18 On the third day Joseph said to them, 'Do this and you will live, for I fear God: 19 if you are honest men, let one of your brothers stay here where you are imprisoned. The rest of you shall go and carry grain for the famine of your households, 20 and bring your youngest brother to me. Thus your words will be verified, and you shall not die.' And they agreed to do so. 21 They said to one another, 'Alas, we are paying the penalty for what we did to our brother; we saw his anguish when he pleaded with us, but we would not listen. That is why this anguish has come upon us.' 22 Then Reuben answered them, 'Did I not tell you not to wrong the boy? But you would not listen. So now there comes a reckoning for his blood.' 23 They did not know that Joseph understood them, since he spoke with them through an interpreter. 24 He turned away from them and wept; then he returned and spoke to them. And he picked out Simeon and had him bound before their eyes. 25 Joseph then gave orders to fill their bags with grain, to return every man's money to his sack, and to give them provisions for their journey. This was done for them.

Joseph's Brothers Return to Canaan

26 They loaded their donkeys with their grain, and departed. 27 When one of them opened his sack to give his donkey fodder at the lodging-place, he saw his money at the top of the sack. 28 He said to his brothers, 'My money has been put back; here it is in my sack!' At this they lost heart and turned trembling to one another, saying, 'What is this that God has done to us?'

29 When they came to their father Jacob in the land of Canaan, they told him all that had happened to them, saying, 30 'The man, the lord of the land, spoke harshly to us, and charged us with spying on the land. 31 But we said to him, "We are honest men, we are not spies. 32 We are twelve brothers, sons of our father; one is no more, and the youngest is now with our father in the land of Canaan." 33 Then the man, the lord of the land, said to us, "By this I shall know that you are honest men: leave one of your brothers with me, take grain for the famine of your households, and go your way. 34 Bring your youngest brother to me, and I shall know that you are not spies but honest men. Then I will release your brother to you, and you may trade in the land." '

35 As they were emptying their sacks, there in each one's sack was his bag of money. When they and their father saw their bundles of money, they were dismayed. 36 And their father Jacob said to them, 'I am the one you have bereaved of children: Joseph is no more, and Simeon is no more, and now you would take Benjamin. All this has happened to me!' 37 Then Reuben said to his father, 'You may kill my two sons if I do not bring him back to you. Put him in my hands, and I will bring him back to you.' 38 But he said, 'My son shall not go down with you, for his brother is dead, and he alone is left. If harm should come to him on the journey that you are to make, you would bring down my grey hairs with sorrow to Sheol.'

The Brothers Come Again, Bringing Benjamin

43 Now the famine was severe in the land. 2 And when they had eaten up the grain that they had brought from Egypt, their father said to them, 'Go again, buy us a little more food.' 3 But Judah said to him, 'The man solemnly warned us, saying, "You shall not see my face unless your brother is with you." 4 If you will send our brother with us, we will go down and buy you food; 5 but if you will not send him, we will not go down, for the man said to us, "You shall not see my face, unless your brother is with you." ' 6 Israel said, 'Why did you treat me so badly as to tell the man that you had another brother?' 7 They replied, 'The man questioned us carefully about ourselves and our kindred, saying, "Is your father still alive? Have you another brother?" What we told him was in answer to these questions. Could we in any way know

that he would say, "Bring your brother down"?' ⁸Then Judah said to his father Israel, 'Send the boy with me, and let us be on our way, so that we may live and not die—you and we and also our little ones. ⁹I myself will be surety for him; you can hold me accountable for him. If I do not bring him back to you and set him before you, then let me bear the blame for ever. ¹⁰If we had not delayed, we would now have returned twice.'

11 Then their father Israel said to them, 'If it must be so, then do this: take some of the choice fruits of the land in your bags, and carry them down as a present to the man—a little balm and a little honey, gum, resin, pistachio nuts, and almonds. ¹²Take double the money with you. Carry back with you the money that was returned in the top of your sacks; perhaps it was an oversight. ¹³Take your brother also, and be on your way again to the man; ¹⁴may God Almighty*ᵃ* grant you mercy before the man, so that he may send back your other brother and Benjamin. As for me, if I am bereaved of my children, I am bereaved.' ¹⁵So the men took the present, and they took double the money with them, as well as Benjamin. Then they went on their way down to Egypt, and stood before Joseph.

16 When Joseph saw Benjamin with them, he said to the steward of his house, 'Bring the men into the house, and slaughter an animal and make ready, for the men are to dine with me at noon.' ¹⁷The man did as Joseph said, and brought the men to Joseph's house. ¹⁸Now the men were afraid because they were brought to Joseph's house, and they said, 'It is because of the money, replaced in our sacks the first time, that we have been brought in, so that he may have an opportunity to fall upon us, to make slaves of us and take our donkeys.' ¹⁹So they went up to the steward of Joseph's house and spoke with him at the entrance to the house. ²⁰They said, 'Oh, my lord, we came down the first time to buy food; ²¹and when we came to the lodging-place we opened our sacks, and there was each one's money in the top of his sack, our money in full weight. So we have brought

it back with us. ²²Moreover, we have brought down with us additional money to buy food. We do not know who put our money in our sacks.' ²³He replied, 'Rest assured, do not be afraid; your God and the God of your father must have put treasure in your sacks for you; I received your money.' Then he brought Simeon out to them. ²⁴When the steward*ᵇ* had brought the men into Joseph's house, and given them water, and they had washed their feet, and when he had given their donkeys fodder, ²⁵they made the present ready for Joseph's coming at noon, for they had heard that they would dine there.

26 When Joseph came home, they brought him the present that they had carried into the house, and bowed to the ground before him. ²⁷He inquired about their welfare, and said, 'Is your father well, the old man of whom you spoke? Is he still alive?' ²⁸They said, 'Your servant our father is well; he is still alive.' And they bowed their heads and did obeisance. ²⁹Then he looked up and saw his brother Benjamin, his mother's son, and said, 'Is this your youngest brother, of whom you spoke to me? God be gracious to you, my son!' ³⁰With that, Joseph hurried out, because he was overcome with affection for his brother, and he was about to weep. So he went into a private room and wept there. ³¹Then he washed his face and came out; and controlling himself he said, 'Serve the meal.' ³²They served him by himself, and them by themselves, and the Egyptians who ate with him by themselves, because the Egyptians could not eat with the Hebrews, for that is an abomination to the Egyptians. ³³When they were seated before him, the firstborn according to his birthright and the youngest according to his youth, the men looked at one another in amazement. ³⁴Portions were taken to them from Joseph's table, but Benjamin's portion was five times as much as any of theirs. So they drank and were merry with him.

a Traditional rendering of Heb *El Shaddai*   *b* Heb *the man*

Joseph Detains Benjamin

44 Then he commanded the steward of his house, 'Fill the men's sacks with food, as much as they can carry, and put each man's money in the top of his sack. ²Put my cup, the silver cup, in the top of the sack of the youngest, with his money for the grain.' And he did as Joseph told him. ³As soon as the morning was light, the men were sent away with their donkeys. ⁴When they had gone only a short distance from the city, Joseph said to his steward, 'Go, follow after the men; and when you overtake them, say to them, "Why have you returned evil for good? Why have you stolen my silver cup?ᵃ ⁵Is it not from this that my lord drinks? Does he not indeed use it for divination? You have done wrong in doing this." '

6 When he overtook them, he repeated these words to them. ⁷They said to him, 'Why does my lord speak such words as these? Far be it from your servants that they should do such a thing! ⁸Look, the money that we found at the top of our sacks, we brought back to you from the land of Canaan; why then would we steal silver or gold from your lord's house? ⁹Should it be found with any one of your servants, let him die; moreover, the rest of us will become my lord's slaves.' ¹⁰He said, 'Even so; in accordance with your words, let it be: he with whom it is found shall become my slave, but the rest of you shall go free.' ¹¹Then each one quickly lowered his sack to the ground, and each opened his sack. ¹²He searched, beginning with the eldest and ending with the youngest; and the cup was found in Benjamin's sack. ¹³At this they tore their clothes. Then each one loaded his donkey, and they returned to the city.

14 Judah and his brothers came to Joseph's house while he was still there; and they fell to the ground before him. ¹⁵Joseph said to them, 'What deed is this that you have done? Do you not know that one such as I can practise divination?' ¹⁶And Judah said, 'What can we say to my lord? What can we speak? How can we clear ourselves? God has found out the guilt of your servants; here we are then, my lord's slaves,

both we and also the one in whose possession the cup has been found.' ¹⁷But he said, 'Far be it from me that I should do so! Only the one in whose possession the cup was found shall be my slave; but as for you, go up in peace to your father.'

Judah Pleads for Benjamin's Release

18 Then Judah stepped up to him and said, 'O my lord, let your servant please speak a word in my lord's ears, and do not be angry with your servant; for you are like Pharaoh himself. ¹⁹My lord asked his servants, saying, "Have you a father or a brother?" ²⁰And we said to my lord, "We have a father, an old man, and a young brother, the child of his old age. His brother is dead; he alone is left of his mother's children, and his father loves him." ²¹Then you said to your servants, "Bring him down to me, so that I may set my eyes on him." ²²We said to my lord, "The boy cannot leave his father, for if he should leave his father, his father would die." ²³Then you said to your servants, "Unless your youngest brother comes down with you, you shall see my face no more." ²⁴When we went back to your servant my father we told him the words of my lord. ²⁵And when our father said, "Go again, buy us a little food", ²⁶we said, "We cannot go down. Only if our youngest brother goes with us, will we go down; for we cannot see the man's face unless our youngest brother is with us." ²⁷Then your servant my father said to us, "You know that my wife bore me two sons; ²⁸one left me, and I said, Surely he has been torn to pieces; and I have never seen him since. ²⁹If you take this one also from me, and harm comes to him, you will bring down my grey hairs in sorrow to Sheol." ³⁰Now therefore, when I come to your servant my father and the boy is not with us, then, as his life is bound up in the boy's life, ³¹when he sees that the boy is not with us, he will die; and your servants will bring down the grey hairs of your servant our father with sorrow to Sheol. ³²For your servant became surety for the boy to my father, saying, "If I do not bring him back to you, then

ᵃ Gk Compare Vg: Heb lacks *Why have you stolen my silver cup?*

I will bear the blame in the sight of my father all my life." 33 Now therefore, please let your servant remain as a slave to my lord in place of the boy; and let the boy go back with his brothers. 34 For how can I go back to my father if the boy is not with me? I fear to see the suffering that would come upon my father.'

Joseph Reveals Himself to His Brothers

45 Then Joseph could no longer control himself before all those who stood by him, and he cried out, 'Send everyone away from me.' So no one stayed with him when Joseph made himself known to his brothers. 2 And he wept so loudly that the Egyptians heard it, and the household of Pharaoh heard it. 3 Joseph said to his brothers, 'I am Joseph. Is my father still alive?' But his brothers could not answer him, so dismayed were they at his presence.

4 Then Joseph said to his brothers, 'Come closer to me.' And they came closer. He said, 'I am your brother Joseph, whom you sold into Egypt. 5 And now do not be distressed, or angry with yourselves, because you sold me here; for God sent me before you to preserve life. 6 For the famine has been in the land these two years; and there are five more years in which there will be neither ploughing nor harvest. 7 God sent me before you to preserve for you a remnant on earth, and to keep alive for you many survivors. 8 So it was not you who sent me here, but God; he has made me a father to Pharaoh, and lord of all his house and ruler over all the land of Egypt. 9 Hurry and go up to my father and say to him, "Thus says your son Joseph, God has made me lord of all Egypt; come down to me, do not delay. 10 You shall settle in the land of Goshen, and you shall be near me, you and your children and your children's children, as well as your flocks, your herds, and all that you have. 11 I will provide for you there—since there are five more years of famine to come—so that you and your household, and all that you have, will not come to poverty." 12 And now your eyes and the eyes of my brother Benjamin see that it is my own mouth that speaks to you. 13 You

must tell my father how greatly I am honoured in Egypt, and all that you have seen. Hurry and bring my father down here.' 14 Then he fell upon his brother Benjamin's neck and wept, while Benjamin wept upon his neck. 15 And he kissed all his brothers and wept upon them; and after that his brothers talked with him.

16 When the report was heard in Pharaoh's house, 'Joseph's brothers have come', Pharaoh and his servants were pleased. 17 Pharaoh said to Joseph, 'Say to your brothers, "Do this: load your animals and go back to the land of Canaan. 18 Take your father and your households and come to me, so that I may give you the best of the land of Egypt, and you may enjoy the fat of the land." 19 You are further charged to say, "Do this: take wagons from the land of Egypt for your little ones and for your wives, and bring your father, and come. 20 Give no thought to your possessions, for the best of all the land of Egypt is yours." '

21 The sons of Israel did so. Joseph gave them wagons according to the instruction of Pharaoh, and he gave them provisions for the journey. 22 To each one of them he gave a set of garments; but to Benjamin he gave three hundred pieces of silver and five sets of garments. 23 To his father he sent the following: ten donkeys loaded with the good things of Egypt, and ten female donkeys loaded with grain, bread, and provision for his father on the journey. 24 Then he sent his brothers on their way, and as they were leaving he said to them, 'Do not quarrel[a] along the way.'

25 So they went up out of Egypt and came to their father Jacob in the land of Canaan. 26 And they told him, 'Joseph is still alive! He is even ruler over all the land of Egypt.' He was stunned; he could not believe them. 27 But when they told him all the words of Joseph that he had said to them, and when he saw the wagons that Joseph had sent to carry him, the spirit of their father Jacob revived. 28 Israel said, 'Enough! My son Joseph is still alive. I must go and see him before I die.'

a Or be agitated

Jacob Brings His Whole Family to Egypt

46 When Israel set out on his journey with all that he had and came to Beer-sheba, he offered sacrifices to the God of his father Isaac. ²God spoke to Israel in visions of the night, and said, 'Jacob, Jacob.' And he said, 'Here I am.' ³Then he said, 'I am God,*a* the God of your father; do not be afraid to go down to Egypt, for I will make of you a great nation there. ⁴I myself will go down with you to Egypt, and I will also bring you up again; and Joseph's own hand shall close your eyes.'

5 Then Jacob set out from Beer-sheba; and the sons of Israel carried their father Jacob, their little ones, and their wives, in the wagons that Pharaoh had sent to carry him. ⁶They also took their livestock and the goods that they had acquired in the land of Canaan, and they came into Egypt, Jacob and all his offspring with him, ⁷his sons, and his sons' sons with him, his daughters, and his sons' daughters; all his offspring he brought with him into Egypt.

8 Now these are the names of the Israelites, Jacob and his offspring, who came to Egypt. Reuben, Jacob's firstborn, ⁹and the children of Reuben: Hanoch, Pallu, Hezron, and Carmi. ¹⁰The children of Simeon: Jemuel, Jamin, Ohad, Jachin, Zohar, and Shaul,*b* the son of a Canaanite woman. ¹¹The children of Levi: Gershon, Kohath, and Merari. ¹²The children of Judah: Er, Onan, Shelah, Perez, and Zerah (but Er and Onan died in the land of Canaan); and the children of Perez were Hezron and Hamul. ¹³The children of Issachar: Tola, Puvah, Jashub,*c* and Shimron. ¹⁴The children of Zebulun: Sered, Elon, and Jahleel ¹⁵(these are the sons of Leah, whom she bore to Jacob in Paddan-aram, together with his daughter Dinah; in all his sons and his daughters numbered thirty-three). ¹⁶The children of Gad: Ziphion, Haggi, Shuni, Ezbon, Eri, Arodi, and Areli. ¹⁷The children of Asher: Imnah, Ishvah, Ishvi, Beriah, and their sister Serah. The children of Beriah: Heber and Malchiel ¹⁸(these are the children of Zilpah, whom Laban gave to his daughter Leah; and these she bore to Jacob—sixteen persons). ¹⁹The children of Jacob's wife Rachel: Joseph and Benjamin. ²⁰To Joseph in the land of Egypt were born Manasseh and Ephraim, whom Asenath daughter of Potiphera, priest of On, bore to him. ²¹The children of Benjamin: Bela, Becher, Ashbel, Gera, Naaman, Ehi, Rosh, Muppim, Huppim, and Ard ²²(these are the children of Rachel, who were born to Jacob—fourteen persons in all). ²³The children of Dan: Hashum.*d* ²⁴The children of Naphtali: Jahzeel, Guni, Jezer, and Shillem ²⁵(these are the children of Bilhah, whom Laban gave to his daughter Rachel, and these she bore to Jacob—seven persons in all). ²⁶All the persons belonging to Jacob who came into Egypt, who were his own offspring, not including the wives of his sons, were sixty-six persons in all. ²⁷The children of Joseph, who were born to him in Egypt, were two; all the persons of the house of Jacob who came into Egypt were seventy.

Jacob Settles in Goshen

28 Israel*e* sent Judah ahead to Joseph to lead the way before him into Goshen. When they came to the land of Goshen, ²⁹Joseph made ready his chariot and went up to meet his father Israel in Goshen. He presented himself to him, fell on his neck, and wept on his neck a good while. ³⁰Israel said to Joseph, 'I can die now, having seen for myself that you are still alive.' ³¹Joseph said to his brothers and to his father's household, 'I will go up and tell Pharaoh, and will say to him, "My brothers and my father's household, who were in the land of Canaan, have come to me. ³²The men are shepherds, for they have been keepers of livestock; and they have brought their flocks, and their herds, and all that they have." ³³When Pharaoh calls you, and says, "What is your occupation?" ³⁴you shall say, "Your servants have been keepers of livestock from our youth even until now, both we and our ancestors"—in order that you may settle in the land of Goshen, because all shepherds are abhorrent to the Egyptians.'

a Heb *the God*   *b* Or *Saul*   *c* Compare Sam Gk Num 26.24; 1 Chr 7.1: MT *Iob*   *d* Gk: Heb *Hushim*
e Heb *He*

47 So Joseph went and told Pharaoh, 'My father and my brothers, with their flocks and herds and all that they possess, have come from the land of Canaan; they are now in the land of Goshen.' ²From among his brothers he took five men and presented them to Pharaoh. ³Pharaoh said to his brothers, 'What is your occupation?' And they said to Pharaoh, 'Your servants are shepherds, as our ancestors were.' ⁴They said to Pharaoh, 'We have come to reside as aliens in the land; for there is no pasture for your servants' flocks because the famine is severe in the land of Canaan. Now, we ask you, let your servants settle in the land of Goshen.' ⁵Then Pharaoh said to Joseph, 'Your father and your brothers have come to you. ⁶The land of Egypt is before you; settle your father and your brothers in the best part of the land; let them live in the land of Goshen; and if you know that there are capable men among them, put them in charge of my livestock.'

7 Then Joseph brought in his father Jacob, and presented him before Pharaoh, and Jacob blessed Pharaoh. ⁸Pharaoh said to Jacob, 'How many are the years of your life?' ⁹Jacob said to Pharaoh, 'The years of my earthly sojourn are one hundred and thirty; few and hard have been the years of my life. They do not compare with the years of the life of my ancestors during their long sojourn.' ¹⁰Then Jacob blessed Pharaoh, and went out from the presence of Pharaoh. ¹¹Joseph settled his father and his brothers, and granted them a holding in the land of Egypt, in the best part of the land, in the land of Rameses, as Pharaoh had instructed. ¹²And Joseph provided his father, his brothers, and all his father's household with food, according to the number of their dependants.

The Famine in Egypt

13 Now there was no food in all the land, for the famine was very severe. The land of Egypt and the land of Canaan languished because of the famine. ¹⁴Joseph collected all the money to be found in the land of Egypt and in the land of Canaan, in exchange for the grain that they bought; and Joseph brought the money into Pharaoh's house. ¹⁵When the money from the land of Egypt and from the land of Canaan was spent, all the Egyptians came to Joseph, and said, 'Give us food! Why should we die before your eyes? For our money is gone.' ¹⁶And Joseph answered, 'Give me your livestock, and I will give you food in exchange for your livestock, if your money is gone.' ¹⁷So they brought their livestock to Joseph; and Joseph gave them food in exchange for the horses, the flocks, the herds, and the donkeys. That year he supplied them with food in exchange for all their livestock. ¹⁸When that year was ended, they came to him the following year, and said to him, 'We cannot hide from my lord that our money is all spent; and the herds of cattle are my lord's. There is nothing left in the sight of my lord but our bodies and our lands. ¹⁹Shall we die before your eyes, both we and our land? Buy us and our land in exchange for food. We with our land will become slaves to Pharaoh; just give us seed, so that we may live and not die, and that the land may not become desolate.'

20 So Joseph bought all the land of Egypt for Pharaoh. All the Egyptians sold their fields, because the famine was severe upon them; and the land became Pharaoh's. ²¹As for the people, he made slaves of them*a* from one end of Egypt to the other. ²²Only the land of the priests he did not buy; for the priests had a fixed allowance from Pharaoh, and lived on the allowance that Pharaoh gave them; therefore they did not sell their land. ²³Then Joseph said to the people, 'Now that I have this day bought you and your land for Pharaoh, here is seed for you; sow the land. ²⁴And at the harvests you shall give one-fifth to Pharaoh, and four-fifths shall be your own, as seed for the field and as food for yourselves and your households, and as food for your little ones.' ²⁵They said, 'You have saved our lives; may it please my lord, we will be slaves to Pharaoh.' ²⁶So Joseph made it a statute concerning the land of Egypt, and it stands to this day, that Pharaoh should

a Sam Gk Compare Vg: MT *He removed them to the cities*

have the fifth. The land of the priests alone did not become Pharaoh's.

The Last Days of Jacob

27 Thus Israel settled in the land of Egypt, in the region of Goshen; and they gained possessions in it, and were fruitful and multiplied exceedingly. 28 Jacob lived in the land of Egypt for seventeen years; so the days of Jacob, the years of his life, were one hundred and forty-seven years.

29 When the time of Israel's death drew near, he called his son Joseph and said to him, 'If I have found favour with you, put your hand under my thigh and promise to deal loyally and truly with me. Do not bury me in Egypt. 30 When I lie down with my ancestors, carry me out of Egypt and bury me in their burial place.' He answered, 'I will do as you have said.' 31 And he said, 'Swear to me'; and he swore to him. Then Israel bowed himself on the head of his bed.

Jacob Blesses Joseph's Sons

48 After this Joseph was told, 'Your father is ill.' So he took with him his two sons Manasseh and Ephraim. 2 When Jacob was told, 'Your son Joseph has come to you', he *a* summoned his strength and sat up in bed. 3 And Jacob said to Joseph, 'God Almighty *b* appeared to me at Luz in the land of Canaan, and he blessed me, 4 and said to me, "I am going to make you fruitful and increase your numbers; I will make of you a company of peoples, and will give this land to your offspring after you for a perpetual holding." 5 Therefore your two sons, who were born to you in the land of Egypt before I came to you in Egypt, are now mine; Ephraim and Manasseh shall be mine, just as Reuben and Simeon are. 6 As for the offspring born to you after them, they shall be yours. They shall be recorded under the names of their brothers with regard to their inheritance. 7 For when I came from Paddan, Rachel, alas, died in the land of Canaan on the way, while there was still some distance to go to Ephrath; and I buried her there on the way to Ephrath' (that is, Bethlehem).

8 When Israel saw Joseph's sons, he said,

'Who are these?' 9 Joseph said to his father, 'They are my sons, whom God has given me here.' And he said, 'Bring them to me, please, that I may bless them.' 10 Now the eyes of Israel were dim with age, and he could not see well. So Joseph brought them near him; and he kissed them and embraced them. 11 Israel said to Joseph, 'I did not expect to see your face; and here God has let me see your children also.' 12 Then Joseph removed them from his father's knees, *c* and he bowed himself with his face to the earth. 13 Joseph took them both, Ephraim in his right hand towards Israel's left, and Manasseh in his left hand towards Israel's right, and brought them near him. 14 But Israel stretched out his right hand and laid it on the head of Ephraim, who was the younger, and his left hand on the head of Manasseh, crossing his hands, for Manasseh was the firstborn. 15 He blessed Joseph, and said,

'The God before whom my ancestors
    Abraham and Isaac walked,
the God who has been my shepherd
    all my life to this day,
16 the angel who has redeemed me from
    all harm, bless the boys;
and in them let my name be
    perpetuated, and the name of
    my ancestors Abraham and
    Isaac;
and let them grow into a multitude
    on the earth.'

17 When Joseph saw that his father laid his right hand on the head of Ephraim, it displeased him; so he took his father's hand, to remove it from Ephraim's head to Manasseh's head. 18 Joseph said to his father, 'Not so, my father! Since this one is the firstborn, put your right hand on his head.' 19 But his father refused, and said, 'I know, my son, I know; he also shall become a people, and he also shall be great. Nevertheless, his younger brother shall be greater than he, and his offspring shall become a multitude of nations.' 20 So he blessed them that day, saying,

a Heb *Israel*   *b* Traditional rendering of Heb *El Shaddai*   *c* Heb *from his knees*

'By you[a] Israel will invoke blessings,
  saying,
  "God make you[a] like Ephraim and
    like Manasseh." '
So he put Ephraim ahead of Manasseh.
²¹ Then Israel said to Joseph, 'I am about to
die, but God will be with you and will bring
you again to the land of your ancestors. ²² I
now give to you one portion[b] more than to
your brothers, the portion[b] that I took from
the hand of the Amorites with my sword
and with my bow.'

Jacob's Last Words to His Sons

49 Then Jacob called his sons, and
  said: 'Gather around, that I may
tell you what will happen to you in days to
come.
² Assemble and hear, O sons of Jacob;
    listen to Israel your father.

³ 'Reuben, you are my firstborn,
    my might and the first fruits of my
      vigour,
    excelling in rank and excelling in
      power.
⁴ Unstable as water, you shall no
    longer excel
  because you went up on to your
    father's bed;
  then you defiled it—you[c] went up
    on to my couch!

⁵ 'Simeon and Levi are brothers;
    weapons of violence are their
      swords.
⁶ May I never come into their council;
    may I not be joined to their
      company—
  for in their anger they killed men,
    and at their whim they hamstrung
      oxen.
⁷ Cursed be their anger, for it is fierce,
    and their wrath, for it is cruel!
  I will divide them in Jacob,
    and scatter them in Israel.

⁸ 'Judah, your brothers shall praise
    you;
    your hand shall be on the neck of
      your enemies;

your father's sons shall bow down
      before you.
⁹ Judah is a lion's whelp;
    from the prey, my son, you have
      gone up.
  He crouches down, he stretches out
    like a lion,
    like a lioness—who dares rouse
      him up?
¹⁰ The sceptre shall not depart from
      Judah,
    nor the ruler's staff from between
      his feet,
  until tribute comes to him;[d]
    and the obedience of the peoples is
      his.
¹¹ Binding his foal to the vine
    and his donkey's colt to the choice
      vine,
  he washes his garments in wine
    and his robe in the blood of grapes;
¹² his eyes are darker than wine,
    and his teeth whiter than milk.

¹³ 'Zebulun shall settle at the shore of
      the sea;
    he shall be a haven for ships,
    and his border shall be at Sidon.

¹⁴ 'Issachar is a strong donkey,
    lying down between the
      sheepfolds;
¹⁵ he saw that a resting-place was good,
    and that the land was pleasant;
  so he bowed his shoulder to the
    burden,
    and became a slave at forced
      labour.

¹⁶ 'Dan shall judge his people
    as one of the tribes of Israel.
¹⁷ Dan shall be a snake by the roadside,
    a viper along the path,
  that bites the horse's heels
    so that its rider falls backwards.

¹⁸ 'I wait for your salvation, O LORD.

a *you* here is singular in Heb   b Or *mountain-slope*
(Heb *shekem,* a play on the name of the town and
district of Shechem)   c Gk Syr Tg: Heb *he*
d Or *until Shiloh comes* or *until he comes to Shiloh* or
(with Syr) *until he comes to whom it belongs*

¹⁹ 'Gad shall be raided by raiders,
   but he shall raid at their heels.

²⁰ 'Asher's*ᵃ* food shall be rich,
   and he shall provide royal
      delicacies.

²¹ 'Naphtali is a doe let loose
   that bears lovely fawns.*ᵇ*

²² 'Joseph is a fruitful bough,
   a fruitful bough by a spring;
      his branches run over the wall.*ᶜ*
²³ The archers fiercely attacked him;
   they shot at him and pressed him
      hard.
²⁴ Yet his bow remained taut,
   and his arms*ᵈ* were made agile
by the hands of the Mighty One of
      Jacob,
   by the name of the Shepherd, the
      Rock of Israel,
²⁵ by the God of your father, who will
      help you,
   by the Almighty*ᵉ* who will bless you
with blessings of heaven above,
blessings of the deep that lies
      beneath,
blessings of the breasts and of the
      womb.
²⁶ The blessings of your father
   are stronger than the blessings of
      the eternal mountains,
   the bounties*ᶠ* of the everlasting
      hills;
   may they be on the head of Joseph,
      on the brow of him who was set
      apart from his brothers.

²⁷ 'Benjamin is a ravenous wolf,
   in the morning devouring the prey,
      and at evening dividing the spoil.'

28 All these are the twelve tribes of Israel, and this is what their father said to them
when he blessed them, blessing each one
of them with a suitable blessing.

Jacob's Death and Burial

29 Then he charged them, saying to
them, 'I am about to be gathered to my
people. Bury me with my ancestors—in the
cave in the field of Ephron the Hittite, ³⁰in
the cave in the field at Machpelah, near
Mamre, in the land of Canaan, in the field
that Abraham bought from Ephron the Hittite as a burial site. ³¹There Abraham and his
wife Sarah were buried; there Isaac and his
wife Rebekah were buried; and there I
buried Leah— ³²the field and the cave that
is in it were purchased from the Hittites.'
³³When Jacob ended his charge to his sons,
he drew up his feet into the bed, breathed
his last, and was gathered to his people.

50 Then Joseph threw himself on his
father's face and wept over him and
kissed him. ²Joseph commanded the physicians in his service to embalm his father.
So the physicians embalmed Israel; ³they
spent forty days in doing this, for that is the
time required for embalming. And the
Egyptians wept for him for seventy days.

4 When the days of weeping for him
were past, Joseph addressed the household
of Pharaoh, 'If now I have found favour
with you, please speak to Pharaoh as follows: ⁵My father made me swear an oath; he
said, "I am about to die. In the tomb that I
hewed out for myself in the land of Canaan, there you shall bury me." Now therefore let me go up, so that I may bury my father; then I will return.' ⁶Pharaoh answered,
'Go up, and bury your father, as he made
you swear to do.'

7 So Joseph went up to bury his father.
With him went up all the servants of Pharaoh, the elders of his household, and all
the elders of the land of Egypt, ⁸as well as
all the household of Joseph, his brothers,
and his father's household. Only their children, their flocks, and their herds were left
in the land of Goshen. ⁹Both chariots and
charioteers went up with him. It was a very
great company. ¹⁰When they came to the
threshing-floor of Atad, which is beyond
the Jordan, they held there a very great and
sorrowful lamentation; and he observed a
time of mourning for his father for seven

a Gk Vg Syr: Heb *From Asher*   *b* Or *that gives beautiful
words*   *c* Meaning of Heb uncertain   *d* Heb *the arms
of his hands*   *e* Traditional rendering of Heb *Shaddai*
f Cn Compare Gk: Heb *of my progenitors to the
boundaries*

days. ¹¹When the Canaanite inhabitants of the land saw the mourning on the threshing-floor of Atad, they said, 'This is a grievous mourning on the part of the Egyptians.' Therefore the place was named Abel-mizraim;^a it is beyond the Jordan. ¹²Thus his sons did for him as he had instructed them. ¹³They carried him to the land of Canaan and buried him in the cave of the field at Machpelah, the field near Mamre, which Abraham bought as a burial site from Ephron the Hittite. ¹⁴After he had buried his father, Joseph returned to Egypt with his brothers and all who had gone up with him to bury his father.

Joseph Forgives His Brothers

15 Realizing that their father was dead, Joseph's brothers said, 'What if Joseph still bears a grudge against us and pays us back in full for all the wrong that we did to him?' ¹⁶So they approached^b Joseph, saying, 'Your father gave this instruction before he died, ¹⁷"Say to Joseph: I beg you, forgive the crime of your brothers and the wrong they did in harming you." Now therefore please forgive the crime of the servants of the God of your father.' Joseph wept when they spoke to him. ¹⁸Then his brothers also wept,^c fell down before him, and said, 'We are here as your slaves.' ¹⁹But Joseph said to them, 'Do not be afraid! Am I in the place of God? ²⁰Even though you intended to do harm to me, God intended it for good, in order to preserve a numerous people, as he is doing today. ²¹So have no fear; I myself will provide for you and your little ones.' In this way he reassured them, speaking kindly to them.

Joseph's Last Days and Death

22 So Joseph remained in Egypt, he and his father's household; and Joseph lived for one hundred and ten years. ²³Joseph saw Ephraim's children of the third generation; the children of Machir son of Manasseh were also born on Joseph's knees.

24 Then Joseph said to his brothers, 'I am about to die; but God will surely come to you, and bring you up out of this land to the land that he swore to Abraham, to Isaac, and to Jacob.' ²⁵So Joseph made the Israelites swear, saying, 'When God comes to you, you shall carry up my bones from here.' ²⁶And Joseph died, being one hundred and ten years old; he was embalmed and placed in a coffin in Egypt.

---

a That is *mourning* (or *meadow*) *of Egypt*　*b* Gk Syr: Heb *they commanded*　*c* Cn: Heb *also came*

EXODUS

1 These are the names of the sons of Israel who came to Egypt with Jacob, each with his household: ²Reuben, Simeon, Levi, and Judah, ³Issachar, Zebulun, and Benjamin, ⁴Dan and Naphtali, Gad and Asher. ⁵The total number of people born to Jacob was seventy. Joseph was already in Egypt. ⁶Then Joseph died, and all his brothers, and that whole generation. ⁷But the Israelites were fruitful and prolific; they multiplied and grew exceedingly strong, so that the land was filled with them.

The Israelites Are Oppressed

8 Now a new king arose over Egypt, who did not know Joseph. ⁹He said to his people, 'Look, the Israelite people are more numerous and more powerful than we. ¹⁰Come, let us deal shrewdly with them, or they will increase and, in the event of war, join our enemies and fight against us and escape from the land.' ¹¹Therefore they set taskmasters over them to oppress them with forced labour. They built supply cities, Pithom and Rameses, for Pharaoh. ¹²But the more they were oppressed, the more they multiplied and spread, so that the Egyptians came to dread the Israelites. ¹³The Egyptians became ruthless in imposing tasks on the Israelites, ¹⁴and made their lives bitter with hard service in mortar and brick and in every kind of field labour. They were ruthless in all the tasks that they imposed on them.

15 The king of Egypt said to the Hebrew midwives, one of whom was named Shiphrah and the other Puah, ¹⁶'When you act as midwives to the Hebrew women, and see them on the birthstool, if it is a boy, kill him; but if it is a girl, she shall live.' ¹⁷But the midwives feared God; they did not do as the king of Egypt commanded them, but they let the boys live. ¹⁸So the king of Egypt summoned the midwives and said to them, 'Why have you done this, and allowed the boys to live?' ¹⁹The midwives said to Pharaoh, 'Because the Hebrew women are not like the Egyptian women; for they are vigorous and give birth before the midwife comes to them.' ²⁰So God dealt well with the midwives; and the people multiplied and became very strong. ²¹And because the midwives feared God, he gave them families. ²²Then Pharaoh commanded all his people, 'Every boy that is born to the Hebrews*a* you shall throw into the Nile, but you shall let every girl live.'

Birth and Youth of Moses

2 Now a man from the house of Levi went and married a Levite woman. ²The woman conceived and bore a son; and when she saw that he was a fine baby, she hid him for three months. ³When she could hide him no longer she got a papyrus basket for him, and plastered it with bitumen and pitch; she put the child in it and placed it among the reeds on the bank of the river. ⁴His sister stood at a distance, to see what would happen to him.

5 The daughter of Pharaoh came down to bathe at the river, while her attendants walked beside the river. She saw the basket among the reeds and sent her maid to bring it. ⁶When she opened it, she saw the child. He was crying, and she took pity on him. 'This must be one of the Hebrews' children,'

a Sam Gk Tg: Heb lacks *to the Hebrews*

she said. [7] Then his sister said to Pharaoh's daughter, 'Shall I go and get you a nurse from the Hebrew women to nurse the child for you?' [8] Pharaoh's daughter said to her, 'Yes.' So the girl went and called the child's mother. [9] Pharaoh's daughter said to her, 'Take this child and nurse it for me, and I will give you your wages.' So the woman took the child and nursed it. [10] When the child grew up, she brought him to Pharaoh's daughter, and she took him as her son. She named him Moses,[a] 'because', she said, 'I drew him out[b] of the water.'

Moses Flees to Midian

[11] One day, after Moses had grown up, he went out to his people and saw their forced labour. He saw an Egyptian beating a Hebrew, one of his kinsfolk. [12] He looked this way and that, and seeing no one he killed the Egyptian and hid him in the sand. [13] When he went out the next day, he saw two Hebrews fighting; and he said to the one who was in the wrong, 'Why do you strike your fellow Hebrew?' [14] He answered, 'Who made you a ruler and judge over us? Do you mean to kill me as you killed the Egyptian?' Then Moses was afraid and thought, 'Surely the thing is known.' [15] When Pharaoh heard of it, he sought to kill Moses.

But Moses fled from Pharaoh. He settled in the land of Midian, and sat down by a well. [16] The priest of Midian had seven daughters. They came to draw water, and filled the troughs to water their father's flock. [17] But some shepherds came and drove them away. Moses got up and came to their defence and watered their flock. [18] When they returned to their father Reuel, he said, 'How is it that you have come back so soon today?' [19] They said, 'An Egyptian helped us against the shepherds; he even drew water for us and watered the flock.' [20] He said to his daughters, 'Where is he? Why did you leave the man? Invite him to break bread.' [21] Moses agreed to stay with the man, and he gave Moses his daughter Zipporah in marriage. [22] She bore a son, and he named him Gershom; for he said, 'I

have been an alien[c] residing in a foreign land.'

[23] After a long time the king of Egypt died. The Israelites groaned under their slavery, and cried out. Out of the slavery their cry for help rose up to God. [24] God heard their groaning, and God remembered his covenant with Abraham, Isaac, and Jacob. [25] God looked upon the Israelites, and God took notice of them.

Moses at the Burning Bush

3 Moses was keeping the flock of his father-in-law Jethro, the priest of Midian; he led his flock beyond the wilderness, and came to Horeb, the mountain of God. [2] There the angel of the LORD appeared to him in a flame of fire out of a bush; he looked, and the bush was blazing, yet it was not consumed. [3] Then Moses said, 'I must turn aside and look at this great sight, and see why the bush is not burned up.' [4] When the LORD saw that he had turned aside to see, God called to him out of the bush, 'Moses, Moses!' And he said, 'Here I am.' [5] Then he said, 'Come no closer! Remove the sandals from your feet, for the place on which you are standing is holy ground.' [6] He said further, 'I am the God of your father, the God of Abraham, the God of Isaac, and the God of Jacob.' And Moses hid his face, for he was afraid to look at God.

[7] Then the LORD said, 'I have observed the misery of my people who are in Egypt; I have heard their cry on account of their taskmasters. Indeed, I know their sufferings, [8] and I have come down to deliver them from the Egyptians, and to bring them up out of that land to a good and broad land, a land flowing with milk and honey, to the country of the Canaanites, the Hittites, the Amorites, the Perizzites, the Hivites, and the Jebusites. [9] The cry of the Israelites has now come to me; I have also seen how the Egyptians oppress them. [10] So come, I will send you to Pharaoh to bring my people, the Israelites, out of Egypt.' [11] But Moses said to God, 'Who am I that I should go to Pharaoh, and bring the Israelites out of Egypt?' [12] He said, 'I will be

a Heb *Mosheh*   *b* Heb *mashah*   *c* Heb *ger*

with you; and this shall be the sign for you that it is I who sent you: when you have brought the people out of Egypt, you shall worship God on this mountain.'

The Divine Name Revealed

13 But Moses said to God, 'If I come to the Israelites and say to them, "The God of your ancestors has sent me to you", and they ask me, "What is his name?" what shall I say to them?' 14 God said to Moses, 'I AM WHO I AM.' *a* He said further, 'Thus you shall say to the Israelites, "I AM has sent me to you." ' 15 God also said to Moses, 'Thus you shall say to the Israelites, "The LORD, *b* the God of your ancestors, the God of Abraham, the God of Isaac, and the God of Jacob, has sent me to you":

This is my name for ever,
  and this my title for all generations.

16 Go and assemble the elders of Israel, and say to them, "The LORD, the God of your ancestors, the God of Abraham, of Isaac, and of Jacob, has appeared to me, saying: I have given heed to you and to what has been done to you in Egypt. 17 I declare that I will bring you up out of the misery of Egypt, to the land of the Canaanites, the Hittites, the Amorites, the Perizzites, the Hivites, and the Jebusites, a land flowing with milk and honey." 18 They will listen to your voice; and you and the elders of Israel shall go to the king of Egypt and say to him, "'The LORD, the God of the Hebrews, has met with us; let us now go a three days' journey into the wilderness, so that we may sacrifice to the LORD our God." 19 I know, however, that the king of Egypt will not let you go unless compelled by a mighty hand. *c* 20 So I will stretch out my hand and strike Egypt with all my wonders that I will perform in it; after that he will let you go. 21 I will bring this people into such favour with the Egyptians that, when you go, you will not go empty-handed; 22 each woman shall ask her neighbour and any woman living in the neighbour's house for jewellery of silver and of gold, and clothing, and you shall put them on your sons and on your daughters; and so you shall plunder the Egyptians.'

Moses' Miraculous Power

4 Then Moses answered, 'But suppose they do not believe me or listen to me, but say, "The LORD did not appear to you." ' 2 The LORD said to him, 'What is that in your hand?' He said, 'A staff.' 3 And he said, 'Throw it on the ground.' So he threw the staff on the ground, and it became a snake; and Moses drew back from it. 4 Then the LORD said to Moses, 'Reach out your hand, and seize it by the tail'—so he reached out his hand and grasped it, and it became a staff in his hand— 5 'so that they may believe that the LORD, the God of their ancestors, the God of Abraham, the God of Isaac, and the God of Jacob, has appeared to you.'

6 Again, the LORD said to him, 'Put your hand inside your cloak.' He put his hand into his cloak; and when he took it out, his hand was leprous, *d* as white as snow. 7 Then God said, 'Put your hand back into your cloak'—so he put his hand back into his cloak, and when he took it out, it was restored like the rest of his body— 8 'If they will not believe you or heed the first sign, they may believe the second sign. 9 If they will not believe even these two signs or heed you, you shall take some water from the Nile and pour it on the dry ground; and the water that you shall take from the Nile will become blood on the dry ground.'

10 But Moses said to the LORD, 'O my Lord, I have never been eloquent, neither in the past nor even now that you have spoken to your servant; but I am slow of speech and slow of tongue.' 11 Then the LORD said to him, 'Who gives speech to mortals? Who makes them mute or deaf, seeing or blind? Is it not I, the LORD? 12 Now go, and I will be with your mouth and teach you what you are to speak.' 13 But he said, 'O my Lord, please send someone else.' 14 Then the anger of the LORD was kindled against Moses and he said, 'What of your brother Aaron the Levite? I know that he can speak fluently; even now he is coming out to meet you,

a Or I AM WHAT I AM or I WILL BE WHAT I WILL BE
b The word 'LORD' when spelled with capital letters stands for the divine name, YHWH, which is here connected with the verb hayah, 'to be'   *c* Gk Vg: Heb no, not by a mighty hand   *d* A term for several skin diseases; precise meaning uncertain

and when he sees you his heart will be glad. 15 You shall speak to him and put the words in his mouth; and I will be with your mouth and with his mouth, and will teach you what you shall do. 16 He indeed shall speak for you to the people; he shall serve as a mouth for you, and you shall serve as God for him. 17 Take in your hand this staff, with which you shall perform the signs.'

Moses Returns to Egypt

18 Moses went back to his father-in-law Jethro and said to him, 'Please let me go back to my kindred in Egypt and see whether they are still living.' And Jethro said to Moses, 'Go in peace.' 19 The LORD said to Moses in Midian, 'Go back to Egypt; for all those who were seeking your life are dead.' 20 So Moses took his wife and his sons, put them on a donkey, and went back to the land of Egypt; and Moses carried the staff of God in his hand.

21 And the LORD said to Moses, 'When you go back to Egypt, see that you perform before Pharaoh all the wonders that I have put in your power; but I will harden his heart, so that he will not let the people go. 22 Then you shall say to Pharaoh, "Thus says the LORD: Israel is my firstborn son. 23 I said to you, 'Let my son go that he may worship me.' But you refused to let him go; now I will kill your firstborn son." ' 24 On the way, at a place where they spent the night, the LORD met him and tried to kill him. 25 But Zipporah took a flint and cut off her son's foreskin, and touched Moses'*a* feet with it, and said, 'Truly you are a bridegroom of blood to me!' 26 So he let him alone. It was then she said, 'A bridegroom of blood by circumcision.'

27 The LORD said to Aaron, 'Go into the wilderness to meet Moses.' So he went; and he met him at the mountain of God and kissed him. 28 Moses told Aaron all the words of the LORD with which he had sent him, and all the signs with which he had charged him. 29 Then Moses and Aaron went and assembled all the elders of the Israelites. 30 Aaron spoke all the words that the LORD had spoken to Moses, and performed the signs in the sight of the people.

31 The people believed; and when they heard that the LORD had given heed to the Israelites and that he had seen their misery, they bowed down and worshipped.

Bricks without Straw

5 Afterwards Moses and Aaron went to Pharaoh and said, 'Thus says the LORD, the God of Israel, "Let my people go, so that they may celebrate a festival to me in the wilderness." ' 2 But Pharaoh said, 'Who is the LORD, that I should heed him and let Israel go? I do not know the LORD, and I will not let Israel go.' 3 Then they said, 'The God of the Hebrews has revealed himself to us; let us go a three days' journey into the wilderness to sacrifice to the LORD our God, or he will fall upon us with pestilence or sword.' 4 But the king of Egypt said to them, 'Moses and Aaron, why are you taking the people away from their work? Get to your labours!' 5 Pharaoh continued, 'Now they are more numerous than the people of the land *b* and yet you want them to stop working!' 6 That same day Pharaoh commanded the taskmasters of the people, as well as their supervisors, 7 'You shall no longer give the people straw to make bricks, as before; let them go and gather straw for themselves. 8 But you shall require of them the same quantity of bricks as they have made previously; do not diminish it, for they are lazy; that is why they cry, "Let us go and offer sacrifice to our God." 9 Let heavier work be laid on them; then they will labour at it and pay no attention to deceptive words.'

10 So the taskmasters and the supervisors of the people went out and said to the people, 'Thus says Pharaoh, "I will not give you straw. 11 Go and get straw yourselves, wherever you can find it; but your work will not be lessened in the least." ' 12 So the people scattered throughout the land of Egypt, to gather stubble for straw. 13 The taskmasters were urgent, saying, 'Complete your work, the same daily assignment as when you were given straw.' 14 And the supervisors of the Israelites, whom Pharaoh's taskmasters had set over them, were beaten, and

a Heb *his*   *b* Sam: Heb *The people of the land are now many* were asked, 'Why did you not finish the required quantity of bricks yesterday and today, as you did before?'

15 Then the Israelite supervisors came to Pharaoh and cried, 'Why do you treat your servants like this? [16] No straw is given to your servants, yet they say to us, "Make bricks!" Look how your servants are beaten! You are unjust to your own people.'[a] [17] He said, 'You are lazy, lazy; that is why you say, "Let us go and sacrifice to the LORD." [18] Go now, and work; for no straw shall be given you, but you shall still deliver the same number of bricks.' [19] The Israelite supervisors saw that they were in trouble when they were told, 'You shall not lessen your daily number of bricks.' [20] As they left Pharaoh, they came upon Moses and Aaron who were waiting to meet them. [21] They said to them, 'The LORD look upon you and judge! You have brought us into bad odour with Pharaoh and his officials, and have put a sword in their hand to kill us.'

22 Then Moses turned again to the LORD and said, 'O LORD, why have you mistreated this people? Why did you ever send me? [23] Since I first came to Pharaoh to speak in your name, he has mistreated this people, and you have done nothing at all to deliver your people.'

Israel's Deliverance Assured

6 Then the LORD said to Moses, 'Now you shall see what I will do to Pharaoh: Indeed, by a mighty hand he will let them go; by a mighty hand he will drive them out of his land.'

2 God also spoke to Moses and said to him: 'I am the LORD. [3] I appeared to Abraham, Isaac, and Jacob as God Almighty,[b] but by my name "The LORD"[c] I did not make myself known to them. [4] I also established my covenant with them, to give them the land of Canaan, the land in which they resided as aliens. [5] I have also heard the groaning of the Israelites, whom the Egyptians are holding as slaves, and I have remembered my covenant. [6] Say therefore to the Israelites, "I am the LORD, and I will free you from the burdens of the Egyptians and deliver you from slavery to them. I will redeem you with an outstretched arm and with mighty acts of judgement. [7] I will take you as my people, and I will be your God. You shall know that I am the LORD your God, who has freed you from the burdens of the Egyptians. [8] I will bring you into the land that I swore to give to Abraham, Isaac, and Jacob; I will give it to you for a possession. I am the LORD." ' [9] Moses told this to the Israelites; but they would not listen to Moses, because of their broken spirit and their cruel slavery.

10 Then the LORD spoke to Moses, [11] 'Go and tell Pharaoh king of Egypt to let the Israelites go out of his land.' [12] But Moses spoke to the LORD, 'The Israelites have not listened to me; how then shall Pharaoh listen to me, poor speaker that I am?'[d] [13] Thus the LORD spoke to Moses and Aaron, and gave them orders regarding the Israelites and Pharaoh king of Egypt, charging them to free the Israelites from the land of Egypt.

The Genealogy of Moses and Aaron

14 The following are the heads of their ancestral houses: the sons of Reuben, the firstborn of Israel: Hanoch, Pallu, Hezron, and Carmi; these are the families of Reuben. [15] The sons of Simeon: Jemuel, Jamin, Ohad, Jachin, Zohar, and Shaul,[e] the son of a Canaanite woman; these are the families of Simeon. [16] The following are the names of the sons of Levi according to their genealogies: Gershon,[f] Kohath, and Merari, and the length of Levi's life was one hundred and thirty-seven years. [17] The sons of Gershon:[f] Libni and Shimei, by their families. [18] The sons of Kohath: Amram, Izhar, Hebron, and Uzziel, and the length of Kohath's life was one hundred and thirty-three years. [19] The sons of Merari: Mahli and Mushi. These are the families of the Levites according to their genealogies. [20] Amram married Jochebed his father's sister and she bore him Aaron and Moses, and the length of Amram's life was one hundred and thirty-seven years. [21] The sons of Izhar: Korah,

---

a Gk Compare Syr Vg: Heb *beaten, and the sin of your people*   b Traditional rendering of Heb *El Shaddai*   c Heb YHWH; see note at 3.15   d Heb *me? I am uncircumcised of lips*   e Or Saul   f Also spelled *Gershom*; see 2.22

Nepheg, and Zichri. ²²The sons of Uzziel: Mishael, Elzaphan, and Sithri. ²³Aaron married Elisheba, daughter of Amminadab and sister of Nahshon, and she bore him Nadab, Abihu, Eleazar, and Ithamar. ²⁴The sons of Korah: Assir, Elkanah, and Abiasaph; these are the families of the Korahites. ²⁵Aaron's son Eleazar married one of the daughters of Putiel, and she bore him Phinehas. These are the heads of the ancestral houses of the Levites by their families.

26 It was this same Aaron and Moses to whom the Lord said, 'Bring the Israelites out of the land of Egypt, company by company.' ²⁷It was they who spoke to Pharaoh king of Egypt to bring the Israelites out of Egypt, the same Moses and Aaron.

Moses and Aaron Obey God's Commands

28 On the day when the Lord spoke to Moses in the land of Egypt, ²⁹he said to him, 'I am the Lord; tell Pharaoh king of Egypt all that I am speaking to you.' ³⁰But Moses said in the Lord's presence, 'Since I am a poor speaker,ᵃ why would Pharaoh listen to me?'

7 The Lord said to Moses, 'See, I have made you like God to Pharaoh, and your brother Aaron shall be your prophet. ²You shall speak all that I command you, and your brother Aaron shall tell Pharaoh to let the Israelites go out of his land. ³But I will harden Pharaoh's heart, and I will multiply my signs and wonders in the land of Egypt. ⁴When Pharaoh does not listen to you, I will lay my hand upon Egypt and bring my people the Israelites, company by company, out of the land of Egypt by great acts of judgement. ⁵The Egyptians shall know that I am the Lord, when I stretch out my hand against Egypt and bring the Israelites out from among them.' ⁶Moses and Aaron did so; they did just as the Lord commanded them. ⁷Moses was eighty years old and Aaron eighty-three when they spoke to Pharaoh.

Aaron's Miraculous Rod

8 The Lord said to Moses and Aaron, ⁹'When Pharaoh says to you, "Perform a wonder", then you shall say to Aaron, "Take your staff and throw it down before Pharaoh, and it will become a snake."' ¹⁰So Moses and Aaron went to Pharaoh and did as the Lord had commanded; Aaron threw down his staff before Pharaoh and his officials, and it became a snake. ¹¹Then Pharaoh summoned the wise men and the sorcerers; and they also, the magicians of Egypt, did the same by their secret arts. ¹²Each one threw down his staff, and they became snakes; but Aaron's staff swallowed up theirs. ¹³Still Pharaoh's heart was hardened, and he would not listen to them, as the Lord had said.

The First Plague: Water Turned to Blood

14 Then the Lord said to Moses, 'Pharaoh's heart is hardened; he refuses to let the people go. ¹⁵Go to Pharaoh in the morning, as he is going out to the water; stand by at the river bank to meet him, and take in your hand the staff that was turned into a snake. ¹⁶Say to him, "The Lord, the God of the Hebrews, sent me to you to say, 'Let my people go, so that they may worship me in the wilderness.' But until now you have not listened. ¹⁷Thus says the Lord, 'By this you shall know that I am the Lord.' See, with the staff that is in my hand I will strike the water that is in the Nile, and it shall be turned to blood. ¹⁸The fish in the river shall die, the river itself shall stink, and the Egyptians shall be unable to drink water from the Nile."' ¹⁹The Lord said to Moses, 'Say to Aaron, "Take your staff and stretch out your hand over the waters of Egypt—over its rivers, its canals, and its ponds, and all its pools of water—so that they may become blood; and there shall be blood throughout the whole land of Egypt, even in vessels of wood and in vessels of stone."'

20 Moses and Aaron did just as the Lord commanded. In the sight of Pharaoh and of his officials he lifted up the staff and struck the water in the river, and all the water in the river was turned into blood, ²¹and the fish in the river died. The river stank so that the Egyptians could not drink its water, and there was blood throughout the whole land of Egypt. ²²But the magicians of Egypt did

ᵃ Heb *am uncircumcised of lips*; see 6.12

the same by their secret arts; so Pharaoh's heart remained hardened, and he would not listen to them, as the LORD had said. 23 Pharaoh turned and went into his house, and he did not take even this to heart. 24 And all the Egyptians had to dig along the Nile for water to drink, for they could not drink the water of the river.

25 Seven days passed after the LORD had struck the Nile.

The Second Plague: Frogs

8 *a* Then the LORD said to Moses, 'Go to Pharaoh and say to him, "Thus says the LORD: Let my people go, so that they may worship me. 2 If you refuse to let them go, I will plague your whole country with frogs. 3 The river shall swarm with frogs; they shall come up into your palace, into your bedchamber and your bed, and into the houses of your officials and of your people, *b* and into your ovens and your kneading bowls. 4 The frogs shall come up on you and on your people and on all your officials." ' 5 *c* And the LORD said to Moses, 'Say to Aaron, "Stretch out your hand with your staff over the rivers, the canals, and the pools, and make frogs come up on the land of Egypt." ' 6 So Aaron stretched out his hand over the waters of Egypt; and the frogs came up and covered the land of Egypt. 7 But the magicians did the same by their secret arts, and brought frogs up on the land of Egypt.

8 Then Pharaoh called Moses and Aaron, and said, 'Pray to the LORD to take away the frogs from me and my people, and I will let the people go to sacrifice to the LORD.' 9 Moses said to Pharaoh, 'Kindly tell me when I am to pray for you and for your officials and for your people, that the frogs may be removed from you and your houses and be left only in the Nile.' 10 And he said, 'Tomorrow.' Moses said, 'As you say! So that you may know that there is no one like the LORD our God, 11 the frogs shall leave you and your houses and your officials and your people; they shall be left only in the Nile.' 12 Then Moses and Aaron went out from Pharaoh; and Moses cried out to the LORD concerning the frogs that he had

brought upon Pharaoh. *d* 13 And the LORD did as Moses requested: the frogs died in the houses, the courtyards, and the fields. 14 And they gathered them together in heaps, and the land stank. 15 But when Pharaoh saw that there was a respite, he hardened his heart, and would not listen to them, just as the LORD had said.

The Third Plague: Gnats

16 Then the LORD said to Moses, 'Say to Aaron, "Stretch out your staff and strike the dust of the earth, so that it may become gnats throughout the whole land of Egypt." ' 17 And they did so; Aaron stretched out his hand with his staff and struck the dust of the earth, and gnats came on humans and animals alike; all the dust of the earth turned into gnats throughout the whole land of Egypt. 18 The magicians tried to produce gnats by their secret arts, but they could not. There were gnats on both humans and animals. 19 And the magicians said to Pharaoh, 'This is the finger of God!' But Pharaoh's heart was hardened, and he would not listen to them, just as the LORD had said.

The Fourth Plague: Flies

20 Then the LORD said to Moses, 'Rise early in the morning and present yourself before Pharaoh, as he goes out to the water, and say to him, "Thus says the LORD: Let my people go, so that they may worship me. 21 For if you will not let my people go, I will send swarms of flies on you, your officials, and your people, and into your houses; and the houses of the Egyptians shall be filled with swarms of flies; so also the land where they live. 22 But on that day I will set apart the land of Goshen, where my people live, so that no swarms of flies shall be there, that you may know that I the LORD am in this land. 23 Thus I will make a distinction *e* between my people and your people. This sign shall appear tomorrow." ' 24 The LORD did so, and great swarms of flies came into the house of Pharaoh and into his officials'

a Ch 7.26 in Heb   *b* Gk: Heb *upon your people*
c Ch 8.1 in Heb   *d* Or *frogs, as he had agreed with Pharaoh*   *e* Gk Vg: Heb *will set redemption*

houses; in all of Egypt the land was ruined because of the flies.

25 Then Pharaoh summoned Moses and Aaron, and said, 'Go, sacrifice to your God within the land.' 26 But Moses said, 'It would not be right to do so; for the sacrifices that we offer to the LORD our God are offensive to the Egyptians. If we offer in the sight of the Egyptians sacrifices that are offensive to them, will they not stone us? 27 We must go a three days' journey into the wilderness and sacrifice to the LORD our God as he commands us.' 28 So Pharaoh said, 'I will let you go to sacrifice to the LORD your God in the wilderness, provided you do not go very far away. Pray for me.' 29 Then Moses said, 'As soon as I leave you, I will pray to the LORD that the swarms of flies may depart tomorrow from Pharaoh, from his officials, and from his people; only do not let Pharaoh again deal falsely by not letting the people go to sacrifice to the LORD.'

30 So Moses went out from Pharaoh and prayed to the LORD. 31 And the LORD did as Moses asked: he removed the swarms of flies from Pharaoh, from his officials, and from his people; not one remained. 32 But Pharaoh hardened his heart this time also, and would not let the people go.

The Fifth Plague: Livestock Diseased

9 Then the LORD said to Moses, 'Go to Pharaoh, and say to him, "Thus says the LORD, the God of the Hebrews: Let my people go, so that they may worship me. 2 For if you refuse to let them go and still hold them, 3 the hand of the LORD will strike with a deadly pestilence your livestock in the field: the horses, the donkeys, the camels, the herds, and the flocks. 4 But the LORD will make a distinction between the livestock of Israel and the livestock of Egypt, so that nothing shall die of all that belongs to the Israelites." ' 5 The LORD set a time, saying, 'Tomorrow the LORD will do this thing in the land.' 6 And on the next day the LORD did so; all the livestock of the Egyptians died, but of the livestock of the Israelites not one died. 7 Pharaoh inquired and found that not one of the livestock of the Israelites was dead. But the heart of

Pharaoh was hardened, and he would not let the people go.

The Sixth Plague: Boils

8 Then the LORD said to Moses and Aaron, 'Take handfuls of soot from the kiln, and let Moses throw it in the air in the sight of Pharaoh. 9 It shall become fine dust all over the land of Egypt, and shall cause festering boils on humans and animals throughout the whole land of Egypt.' 10 So they took soot from the kiln, and stood before Pharaoh, and Moses threw it in the air, and it caused festering boils on humans and animals. 11 The magicians could not stand before Moses because of the boils, for the boils afflicted the magicians as well as all the Egyptians. 12 But the LORD hardened the heart of Pharaoh, and he would not listen to them, just as the LORD had spoken to Moses.

The Seventh Plague: Thunder and Hail

13 Then the LORD said to Moses, 'Rise up early in the morning and present yourself before Pharaoh, and say to him, "Thus says the LORD, the God of the Hebrews: Let my people go, so that they may worship me. 14 For this time I will send all my plagues upon you yourself, and upon your officials, and upon your people, so that you may know that there is no one like me in all the earth. 15 For by now I could have stretched out my hand and struck you and your people with pestilence, and you would have been cut off from the earth. 16 But this is why I have let you live: to show you my power, and to make my name resound through all the earth. 17 You are still exalting yourself against my people, and will not let them go. 18 Tomorrow at this time I will cause the heaviest hail to fall that has ever fallen in Egypt from the day it was founded until now. 19 Send, therefore, and have your livestock and everything that you have in the open field brought to a secure place; every human or animal that is in the open field and is not brought under shelter will die when the hail comes down upon them." ' 20 Those officials of Pharaoh who feared the word of the LORD hurried their

slaves and livestock off to a secure place. ²¹Those who did not regard the word of the LORD left their slaves and livestock in the open field.

22 The LORD said to Moses, 'Stretch out your hand towards heaven so that hail may fall on the whole land of Egypt, on humans and animals and all the plants of the field in the land of Egypt.' ²³Then Moses stretched out his staff towards heaven, and the LORD sent thunder and hail, and fire came down on the earth. And the LORD rained hail on the land of Egypt; ²⁴there was hail with fire flashing continually in the midst of it, such heavy hail as had never fallen in all the land of Egypt since it became a nation. ²⁵The hail struck down everything that was in the open field throughout all the land of Egypt, both human and animal; the hail also struck down all the plants of the field, and shattered every tree in the field. ²⁶Only in the land of Goshen, where the Israelites were, there was no hail.

27 Then Pharaoh summoned Moses and Aaron, and said to them, 'This time I have sinned; the LORD is in the right, and I and my people are in the wrong. ²⁸Pray to the LORD! Enough of God's thunder and hail! I will let you go; you need stay no longer.' ²⁹Moses said to him, 'As soon as I have gone out of the city, I will stretch out my hands to the LORD; the thunder will cease, and there will be no more hail, so that you may know that the earth is the LORD's. ³⁰But as for you and your officials, I know that you do not yet fear the LORD God.' ³¹(Now the flax and the barley were ruined, for the barley was in the ear and the flax was in bud. ³²But the wheat and the spelt were not ruined, for they are late in coming up.) ³³So Moses left Pharaoh, went out of the city, and stretched out his hands to the LORD; then the thunder and the hail ceased, and the rain no longer poured down on the earth. ³⁴But when Pharaoh saw that the rain and the hail and the thunder had ceased, he sinned once more and hardened his heart, he and his officials. ³⁵So the heart of Pharaoh was hardened, and he would

not let the Israelites go, just as the LORD had spoken through Moses.

The Eighth Plague: Locusts

10 Then the LORD said to Moses, 'Go to Pharaoh; for I have hardened his heart and the heart of his officials, in order that I may show these signs of mine among them, ²and that you may tell your children and grandchildren how I have made fools of the Egyptians and what signs I have done among them—so that you may know that I am the LORD.'

3 So Moses and Aaron went to Pharaoh, and said to him, 'Thus says the LORD, the God of the Hebrews, "How long will you refuse to humble yourself before me? Let my people go, so that they may worship me. ⁴For if you refuse to let my people go, tomorrow I will bring locusts into your country. ⁵They shall cover the surface of the land, so that no one will be able to see the land. They shall devour the last remnant left you after the hail, and they shall devour every tree of yours that grows in the field. ⁶They shall fill your houses, and the houses of all your officials and of all the Egyptians—something that neither your parents nor your grandparents have seen, from the day they came on earth to this day."' Then he turned and went out from Pharaoh.

7 Pharaoh's officials said to him, 'How long shall this fellow be a snare to us? Let the people go, so that they may worship the LORD their God; do you not yet understand that Egypt is ruined?' ⁸So Moses and Aaron were brought back to Pharaoh, and he said to them, 'Go, worship the LORD your God! But which ones are to go?' ⁹Moses said, 'We will go with our young and our old; we will go with our sons and daughters and with our flocks and herds, because we have the LORD's festival to celebrate.' ¹⁰He said to them, 'The LORD indeed will be with you, if ever I let your little ones go with you! Plainly you have some evil purpose in mind. ¹¹No, never! Your men may go and worship the LORD, for that is what you are asking.' And they were driven out from Pharaoh's presence.

12 Then the LORD said to Moses, 'Stretch out your hand over the land of Egypt, so

that the locusts may come upon it and eat every plant in the land, all that the hail has left.' ¹³ So Moses stretched out his staff over the land of Egypt, and the LORD brought an east wind upon the land all that day and all that night; when morning came, the east wind had brought the locusts. ¹⁴ The locusts came upon all the land of Egypt and settled on the whole country of Egypt, such a dense swarm of locusts as had never been before, nor ever shall be again. ¹⁵ They covered the surface of the whole land, so that the land was black; and they ate all the plants in the land and all the fruit of the trees that the hail had left; nothing green was left, no tree, no plant in the field, in all the land of Egypt. ¹⁶ Pharaoh hurriedly summoned Moses and Aaron and said, 'I have sinned against the LORD your God, and against you. ¹⁷ Do forgive my sin just this once, and pray to the LORD your God that at the least he remove this deadly thing from me.' ¹⁸ So he went out from Pharaoh and prayed to the LORD. ¹⁹ The LORD changed the wind into a very strong west wind, which lifted the locusts and drove them into the Red Sea;ᵃ not a single locust was left in all the country of Egypt. ²⁰ But the LORD hardened Pharaoh's heart, and he would not let the Israelites go.

The Ninth Plague: Darkness

21 Then the LORD said to Moses, 'Stretch out your hand towards heaven so that there may be darkness over the land of Egypt, a darkness that can be felt.' ²² So Moses stretched out his hand towards heaven, and there was dense darkness in all the land of Egypt for three days. ²³ People could not see one another, and for three days they could not move from where they were; but all the Israelites had light where they lived. ²⁴ Then Pharaoh summoned Moses, and said, 'Go, worship the LORD. Only your flocks and your herds shall remain behind. Even your children may go with you.' ²⁵ But Moses said, 'You must also let us have sacrifices and burnt-offerings to sacrifice to the LORD our God. ²⁶ Our livestock also must go with us; not a hoof shall be left behind, for we must choose some of them for the worship

of the LORD our God, and we will not know what to use to worship the LORD until we arrive there.' ²⁷ But the LORD hardened Pharaoh's heart, and he was unwilling to let them go. ²⁸ Then Pharaoh said to him, 'Get away from me! Take care that you do not see my face again, for on the day you see my face you shall die.' ²⁹ Moses said, 'Just as you say! I will never see your face again.'

Warning of the Final Plague

11 The LORD said to Moses, 'I will bring one more plague upon Pharaoh and upon Egypt; afterwards he will let you go from here; indeed, when he lets you go, he will drive you away. ² Tell the people that every man is to ask his neighbour and every woman is to ask her neighbour for objects of silver and gold.' ³ The LORD gave the people favour in the sight of the Egyptians. Moreover, Moses himself was a man of great importance in the land of Egypt, in the sight of Pharaoh's officials, and in the sight of the people.

4 Moses said, 'Thus says the LORD: About midnight I will go out through Egypt. ⁵ Every firstborn in the land of Egypt shall die, from the firstborn of Pharaoh who sits on his throne to the firstborn of the female slave who is behind the handmill, and all the firstborn of the livestock. ⁶ Then there will be a loud cry throughout the whole land of Egypt, such as has never been nor will ever be again. ⁷ But not a dog shall growl at any of the Israelites—not at people, not at animals—so that you may know that the LORD makes a distinction between Egypt and Israel. ⁸ Then all these officials of yours shall come down to me, and bow low to me, saying, "Leave us, you and all the people who follow you." After that I will leave.' And in hot anger he left Pharaoh.

9 The LORD said to Moses, 'Pharaoh will not listen to you, in order that my wonders may be multiplied in the land of Egypt.' ¹⁰ Moses and Aaron performed all these wonders before Pharaoh; but the LORD hardened Pharaoh's heart, and he did not let the people of Israel go out of his land.

ᵃ Or *Sea of Reeds*

The First Passover Instituted

12 The LORD said to Moses and Aaron in the land of Egypt: 2 This month shall mark for you the beginning of months; it shall be the first month of the year for you. 3 Tell the whole congregation of Israel that on the tenth of this month they are to take a lamb for each family, a lamb for each household. 4 If a household is too small for a whole lamb, it shall join its closest neighbour in obtaining one; the lamb shall be divided in proportion to the number of people who eat of it. 5 Your lamb shall be without blemish, a year-old male; you may take it from the sheep or from the goats. 6 You shall keep it until the fourteenth day of this month; then the whole assembled congregation of Israel shall slaughter it at twilight. 7 They shall take some of the blood and put it on the two doorposts and the lintel of the houses in which they eat it. 8 They shall eat the lamb that same night; they shall eat it roasted over the fire with unleavened bread and bitter herbs. 9 Do not eat any of it raw or boiled in water, but roasted over the fire, with its head, legs, and inner organs. 10 You shall let none of it remain until the morning; anything that remains until the morning you shall burn. 11 This is how you shall eat it: your loins girded, your sandals on your feet, and your staff in your hand; and you shall eat it hurriedly. It is the passover of the LORD. 12 For I will pass through the land of Egypt that night, and I will strike down every firstborn in the land of Egypt, both human beings and animals; on all the gods of Egypt I will execute judgements: I am the LORD. 13 The blood shall be a sign for you on the houses where you live: when I see the blood, I will pass over you, and no plague shall destroy you when I strike the land of Egypt.

14 This day shall be a day of remembrance for you. You shall celebrate it as a festival to the LORD; throughout your generations you shall observe it as a perpetual ordinance. 15 Seven days you shall eat unleavened bread; on the first day you shall remove leaven from your houses, for whoever eats leavened bread from the first day until the seventh day shall be cut off from Israel. 16 On the first day you shall hold a solemn assembly, and on the seventh day a solemn assembly; no work shall be done on those days; only what everyone must eat, that alone may be prepared by you. 17 You shall observe the festival of unleavened bread, for on this very day I brought your companies out of the land of Egypt: you shall observe this day throughout your generations as a perpetual ordinance. 18 In the first month, from the evening of the fourteenth day until the evening of the twenty-first day, you shall eat unleavened bread. 19 For seven days no leaven shall be found in your houses; for whoever eats what is leavened shall be cut off from the congregation of Israel, whether an alien or a native of the land. 20 You shall eat nothing leavened; in all your settlements you shall eat unleavened bread.

21 Then Moses called all the elders of Israel and said to them, 'Go, select lambs for your families, and slaughter the passover lamb. 22 Take a bunch of hyssop, dip it in the blood that is in the basin, and touch the lintel and the two doorposts with the blood in the basin. None of you shall go outside the door of your house until morning. 23 For the LORD will pass through to strike down the Egyptians; when he sees the blood on the lintel and on the two doorposts, the LORD will pass over that door and will not allow the destroyer to enter your houses to strike you down. 24 You shall observe this rite as a perpetual ordinance for you and your children. 25 When you come to the land that the LORD will give you, as he has promised, you shall keep this observance. 26 And when your children ask you, "What do you mean by this observance?" 27 you shall say, "It is the passover sacrifice to the LORD, for he passed over the houses of the Israelites in Egypt, when he struck down the Egyptians but spared our houses." ' And the people bowed down and worshipped.

28 The Israelites went and did just as the LORD had commanded Moses and Aaron.

The Tenth Plague: Death of the Firstborn

29 At midnight the LORD struck down all the firstborn in the land of Egypt, from the firstborn of Pharaoh who sat on his throne to the firstborn of the prisoner who was in the dungeon, and all the firstborn of the livestock. 30 Pharaoh arose in the night, he and all his officials and all the Egyptians; and there was a loud cry in Egypt, for there was not a house without someone dead. 31 Then he summoned Moses and Aaron in the night, and said, 'Rise up, go away from my people, both you and the Israelites! Go, worship the LORD, as you said. 32 Take your flocks and your herds, as you said, and be gone. And bring a blessing on me too!'

The Exodus: From Rameses to Succoth

33 The Egyptians urged the people to hasten their departure from the land, for they said, 'We shall all be dead.' 34 So the people took their dough before it was leavened, with their kneading-bowls wrapped up in their cloaks on their shoulders. 35 The Israelites had done as Moses told them; they had asked the Egyptians for jewellery of silver and gold, and for clothing, 36 and the LORD had given the people favour in the sight of the Egyptians, so that they let them have what they asked. And so they plundered the Egyptians.

37 The Israelites journeyed from Rameses to Succoth, about six hundred thousand men on foot, besides children. 38 A mixed crowd also went up with them, and livestock in great numbers, both flocks and herds. 39 They baked unleavened cakes of the dough that they had brought out of Egypt; it was not leavened, because they were driven out of Egypt and could not wait, nor had they prepared any provisions for themselves.

40 The time that the Israelites had lived in Egypt was four hundred and thirty years. 41 At the end of four hundred and thirty years, on that very day, all the companies of the LORD went out from the land of Egypt. 42 That was for the LORD a night of vigil, to bring them out of the land of Egypt. That same night is a vigil to be kept for the LORD by all the Israelites throughout their generations.

Directions for the Passover

43 The LORD said to Moses and Aaron: This is the ordinance for the passover: no foreigner shall eat of it, 44 but any slave who has been purchased may eat of it after he has been circumcised; 45 no bound or hired servant may eat of it. 46 It shall be eaten in one house; you shall not take any of the animal outside the house, and you shall not break any of its bones. 47 The whole congregation of Israel shall celebrate it. 48 If an alien who resides with you wants to celebrate the passover to the LORD, all his males shall be circumcised; then he may draw near to celebrate it; he shall be regarded as a native of the land. But no uncircumcised person shall eat of it; 49 there shall be one law for the native and for the alien who resides among you.

50 All the Israelites did just as the LORD had commanded Moses and Aaron. 51 That very day the LORD brought the Israelites out of the land of Egypt, company by company.

13 The LORD said to Moses: 2 Consecrate to me all the firstborn; whatever is the first to open the womb among the Israelites, of human beings and animals, is mine.

The Festival of Unleavened Bread

3 Moses said to the people, 'Remember this day on which you came out of Egypt, out of the house of slavery, because the LORD brought you out from there by strength of hand; no leavened bread shall be eaten. 4 Today, in the month of Abib, you are going out. 5 When the LORD brings you into the land of the Canaanites, the Hittites, the Amorites, the Hivites, and the Jebusites, which he swore to your ancestors to give you, a land flowing with milk and honey, you shall keep this observance in this month. 6 For seven days you shall eat unleavened bread, and on the seventh day there shall be a festival to the LORD. 7 Unleavened bread shall be eaten for seven days; no leavened bread shall be seen in your possession, and no leaven shall be

seen among you in all your territory. 8 You shall tell your child on that day, "It is because of what the LORD did for me when I came out of Egypt." 9 It shall serve for you as a sign on your hand and as a reminder on your forehead, so that the teaching of the LORD may be on your lips; for with a strong hand the LORD brought you out of Egypt. 10 You shall keep this ordinance at its proper time from year to year.

The Consecration of the Firstborn

11 'When the LORD has brought you into the land of the Canaanites, as he swore to you and your ancestors, and has given it to you, 12 you shall set apart to the LORD all that first opens the womb. All the firstborn of your livestock that are males shall be the LORD's. 13 But every firstborn donkey you shall redeem with a sheep; if you do not redeem it, you must break its neck. Every firstborn male among your children you shall redeem. 14 When in the future your child asks you, "What does this mean?" you shall answer, "By strength of hand the LORD brought us out of Egypt, from the house of slavery. 15 When Pharaoh stubbornly refused to let us go, the LORD killed all the firstborn in the land of Egypt, from human firstborn to the firstborn of animals. Therefore I sacrifice to the LORD every male that first opens the womb, but every firstborn of my sons I redeem." 16 It shall serve as a sign on your hand and as an emblem *a* on your forehead that by strength of hand the LORD brought us out of Egypt.'

The Pillars of Cloud and Fire

17 When Pharaoh let the people go, God did not lead them by way of the land of the Philistines, although that was nearer; for God thought, 'If the people face war, they may change their minds and return to Egypt.' 18 So God led the people by the roundabout way of the wilderness towards the Red Sea. *b* The Israelites went up out of the land of Egypt prepared for battle. 19 And Moses took with him the bones of Joseph, who had required a solemn oath of the Israelites, saying, 'God will surely take notice of you, and then you must carry my bones

with you from here.' 20 They set out from Succoth, and camped at Etham, on the edge of the wilderness. 21 The LORD went in front of them in a pillar of cloud by day, to lead them along the way, and in a pillar of fire by night, to give them light, so that they might travel by day and by night. 22 Neither the pillar of cloud by day nor the pillar of fire by night left its place in front of the people.

Crossing the Red Sea

14 Then the LORD said to Moses: 2 'Tell the Israelites to turn back and camp in front of Pi-hahiroth, between Migdol and the sea, in front of Baal-zephon; you shall camp opposite it, by the sea. 3 Pharaoh will say of the Israelites, 'They are wandering aimlessly in the land; the wilderness has closed in on them.' 4 I will harden Pharaoh's heart, and he will pursue them, so that I will gain glory for myself over Pharaoh and all his army; and the Egyptians shall know that I am the LORD. And they did so.'

5 When the king of Egypt was told that the people had fled, the minds of Pharaoh and his officials were changed towards the people, and they said, 'What have we done, letting Israel leave our service?' 6 So he had his chariot made ready, and took his army with him; 7 he took six hundred picked chariots and all the other chariots of Egypt with officers over all of them. 8 The LORD hardened the heart of Pharaoh king of Egypt and he pursued the Israelites, who were going out boldly. 9 The Egyptians pursued them, all Pharaoh's horses and chariots, his chariot drivers and his army; they overtook them camped by the sea, by Pi-hahiroth, in front of Baal-zephon.

10 As Pharaoh drew near, the Israelites looked back, and there were the Egyptians advancing on them. In great fear the Israelites cried out to the LORD. 11 They said to Moses, 'Was it because there were no graves in Egypt that you have taken us away to die in the wilderness? What have you done to us, bringing us out of Egypt? 12 Is this not

a Or *as a frontlet;* meaning of Heb uncertain   *b* Or *Sea of Reeds* the very thing we told you in Egypt, "Let us alone and let us serve the Egyptians"? For it would have been better for us to serve the Egyptians than to die in the wilderness.' 13 But Moses said to the people, 'Do not be afraid, stand firm, and see the deliverance that the LORD will accomplish for you today; for the Egyptians whom you see today you shall never see again. 14 The LORD will fight for you, and you have only to keep still.'

15 Then the LORD said to Moses, 'Why do you cry out to me? Tell the Israelites to go forward. 16 But you lift up your staff, and stretch out your hand over the sea and divide it, that the Israelites may go into the sea on dry ground. 17 Then I will harden the hearts of the Egyptians so that they will go in after them; and so I will gain glory for myself over Pharaoh and all his army, his chariots, and his chariot drivers. 18 And the Egyptians shall know that I am the LORD, when I have gained glory for myself over Pharaoh, his chariots, and his chariot drivers.'

19 The angel of God who was going be-fore the Israelite army moved and went behind them; and the pillar of cloud moved from in front of them and took its place behind them. 20 It came between the army of Egypt and the army of Israel. And so the cloud was there with the darkness, and it lit up the night; one did not come near the other all night.

21 Then Moses stretched out his hand over the sea. The LORD drove the sea back by a strong east wind all night, and turned the sea into dry land; and the waters were divided. 22 The Israelites went into the sea on dry ground, the waters forming a wall for them on their right and on their left. 23 The Egyptians pursued, and went into the sea after them, all of Pharaoh's horses, chariots, and chariot drivers. 24 At the morning watch the LORD in the pillar of fire and cloud looked down upon the Egyptian army, and threw the Egyptian army into panic. 25 He clogged*a* their chariot wheels so that they turned with difficulty. The

a Sam Gk Syr: MT *removed*

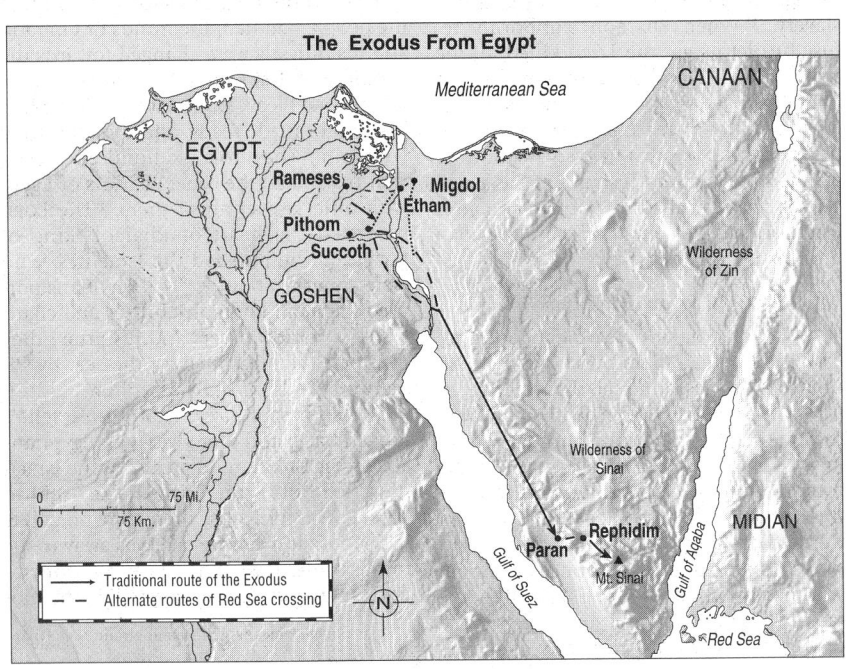

The Exodus From Egypt

Mediterranean Sea

CANAAN

EGYPT

Rameses
Migdol
Etham
Pithom
Succoth

GOSHEN

Wilderness of Zin

Wilderness of Sinai

Rephidim
Paran
Mt. Sinai

MIDIAN

Gulf of Suez

Gulf of Aqaba

Red Sea

0　　　75 Mi.
0　　　75 Km.

→ Traditional route of the Exodus
- - Alternate routes of Red Sea crossing

N

Egyptians said, 'Let us flee from the Israelites, for the LORD is fighting for them against Egypt.'

The Pursuers Drowned

26 Then the LORD said to Moses, 'Stretch out your hand over the sea, so that the water may come back upon the Egyptians, upon their chariots and chariot drivers.' 27 So Moses stretched out his hand over the sea, and at dawn the sea returned to its normal depth. As the Egyptians fled before it, the LORD tossed the Egyptians into the sea. 28 The waters returned and covered the chariots and the chariot drivers, the entire army of Pharaoh that had followed them into the sea; not one of them remained. 29 But the Israelites walked on dry ground through the sea, the waters forming a wall for them on their right and on their left.

30 Thus the LORD saved Israel that day from the Egyptians; and Israel saw the Egyptians dead on the seashore. 31 Israel saw the great work that the LORD did against the Egyptians. So the people feared the LORD and believed in the LORD and in his servant Moses.

The Song of Moses

15 Then Moses and the Israelites sang this song to the LORD:
'I will sing to the LORD, for he has
    triumphed gloriously;
  horse and rider he has thrown into
    the sea.
2 The LORD is my strength and my
    might,[a]
  and he has become my salvation;
  this is my God, and I will praise him,
  my father's God, and I will exalt
    him.
3 The LORD is a warrior;
  the LORD is his name.

4 'Pharaoh's chariots and his army he
    cast into the sea;
  his picked officers were sunk in the
    Red Sea.[b]
5 The floods covered them;
  they went down into the depths
    like a stone.

6 Your right hand, O LORD, glorious in
    power—
  your right hand, O LORD, shattered
    the enemy.
7 In the greatness of your majesty you
    overthrew your adversaries;
  you sent out your fury, it consumed
    them like stubble.
8 At the blast of your nostrils the
    waters piled up,
  the floods stood up in a heap;
  the deeps congealed in the heart of
    the sea.
9 The enemy said, "I will pursue, I will
    overtake,
  I will divide the spoil, my desire
    shall have its fill of them.
  I will draw my sword, my hand
    shall destroy them."
10 You blew with your wind, the sea
    covered them;
  they sank like lead in the mighty
    waters.

11 'Who is like you, O LORD, among the
    gods?
  Who is like you, majestic in
    holiness,
  awesome in splendour, doing
    wonders?
12 You stretched out your right hand,
  the earth swallowed them.

13 'In your steadfast love you led the
    people whom you redeemed;
  you guided them by your strength
    to your holy abode.
14 The peoples heard, they trembled;
  pangs seized the inhabitants of
    Philistia.
15 Then the chiefs of Edom were
    dismayed;
  trembling seized the leaders of
    Moab;
  all the inhabitants of Canaan
    melted away.
16 Terror and dread fell upon them;
  by the might of your arm, they
    became still as a stone
  until your people, O LORD, passed by,

a Or song   b Or Sea of Reeds

until the people whom you
    acquired passed by.
17 You brought them in and planted
    them on the mountain of your
    own possession,
    the place, O LORD, that you made
        your abode,
    the sanctuary, O LORD, that your
    hands have established.
18 The LORD will reign for ever and ever.'
19 When the horses of Pharaoh with his
chariots and his chariot drivers went into
the sea, the LORD brought back the waters of
the sea upon them; but the Israelites
walked through the sea on dry ground.

The Song of Miriam

20 Then the prophet Miriam, Aaron's
sister, took a tambourine in her hand; and
all the women went out after her with tambourines and with dancing. 21 And Miriam
sang to them:
'Sing to the LORD, for he has
    triumphed gloriously;
horse and rider he has thrown into
    the sea.'

Bitter Water Made Sweet

22 Then Moses ordered Israel to set out
from the Red Sea,*a* and they went into the
wilderness of Shur. They went for three days
in the wilderness and found no water.
23 When they came to Marah, they could
not drink the water of Marah because it was
bitter. That is why it was called Marah.*b*
24 And the people complained against Moses, saying, 'What shall we drink?' 25 He
cried out to the LORD; and the LORD showed
him a piece of wood;*c* he threw it into the
water, and the water became sweet.
There the LORD*d* made for them a statute
and an ordinance and there he put them to
the test. 26 He said, 'If you will listen carefully to the voice of the LORD your God, and
do what is right in his sight, and give heed
to his commandments and keep all his statutes, I will not bring upon you any of the
diseases that I brought upon the Egyptians;
for I am the LORD who heals you.'
27 Then they came to Elim, where there
were twelve springs of water and seventy

palm trees; and they camped there by the
water.

Bread from Heaven

16 The whole congregation of the Israelites set out from Elim; and Israel came to the wilderness of Sin, which is
between Elim and Sinai, on the fifteenth
day of the second month after they had departed from the land of Egypt. 2 The whole
congregation of the Israelites complained
against Moses and Aaron in the wilderness.
3 The Israelites said to them, 'If only we had
died by the hand of the LORD in the land of
Egypt, when we sat by the fleshpots and ate
our fill of bread; for you have brought us
out into this wilderness to kill this whole assembly with hunger.'
4 Then the LORD said to Moses, 'I am going to rain bread from heaven for you, and
each day the people shall go out and gather enough for that day. In that way I will
test them, whether they will follow my instruction or not. 5 On the sixth day, when
they prepare what they bring in, it will be
twice as much as they gather on other days.'
6 So Moses and Aaron said to all the Israelites, 'In the evening you shall know that it
was the LORD who brought you out of the
land of Egypt, 7 and in the morning you
shall see the glory of the LORD, because he
has heard your complaining against the
LORD. For what are we, that you complain
against us?' 8 And Moses said, 'When the
LORD gives you meat to eat in the evening
and your fill of bread in the morning, because the LORD has heard the complaining
that you utter against him—what are we?
Your complaining is not against us but
against the LORD.'
9 Then Moses said to Aaron, 'Say to the
whole congregation of the Israelites, "Draw
near to the LORD, for he has heard your complaining." ' 10 And as Aaron spoke to the
whole congregation of the Israelites, they
looked towards the wilderness, and the glory of the LORD appeared in the cloud. 11 The
LORD spoke to Moses and said, 12 'I have
heard the complaining of the Israelites; say

---

a Or *Sea of Reeds*   *b* That is *Bitterness*   *c* Or *a tree*
d Heb *he*

to them, "At twilight you shall eat meat, and in the morning you shall have your fill of bread; then you shall know that I am the LORD your God." ' 13 In the evening quails came up and covered the camp; and in the morning there was a layer of dew around the camp. 14 When the layer of dew lifted, there on the surface of the wilderness was a fine flaky substance, as fine as frost on the ground. 15 When the Israelites saw it, they said to one another, 'What is it?' *a* For they did not know what it was. Moses said to them, 'It is the bread that the LORD has given you to eat. 16 This is what the LORD has commanded: "Gather as much of it as each of you needs, an omer to a person according to the number of persons, all providing for those in their own tents." ' 17 The Israelites did so, some gathering more, some less. 18 But when they measured it with an omer, those who gathered much had nothing over, and those who gathered little had no shortage; they gathered as much as each of them needed. 19 And Moses said to them, 'Let no one leave any of it over until morning.' 20 But they did not listen to Moses; some left part of it until morning, and it bred worms and became foul. And Moses was angry with them. 21 Morning by morning they gathered it, as much as each needed; but when the sun grew hot, it melted.

22 On the sixth day they gathered twice as much food, two omers apiece. When all the leaders of the congregation came and told Moses, 23 he said to them, 'This is what the LORD has commanded: "Tomorrow is a day of solemn rest, a holy sabbath to the LORD; bake what you want to bake and boil what you want to boil, and all that is left over put aside to be kept until morning." ' 24 So they put it aside until morning, as Moses commanded them; and it did not become foul, and there were no worms in it. 25 Moses said, 'Eat it today, for today is a sabbath to the LORD; today you will not find it in the field. 26 For six days you shall gather it; but on the seventh day, which is a sabbath, there will be none.' 27 On the seventh day some of the people went out to gather, and they found

none. 28 The LORD said to Moses, 'How long will you refuse to keep my commandments and instructions? 29 See! The LORD has given you the sabbath, therefore on the sixth day he gives you food for two days; each of you stay where you are; do not leave your place on the seventh day.' 30 So the people rested on the seventh day.

31 The house of Israel called it manna; it was like coriander seed, white, and the taste of it was like wafers made with honey. 32 Moses said, 'This is what the LORD has commanded: "Let an omer of it be kept throughout your generations, in order that they may see the food with which I fed you in the wilderness, when I brought you out of the land of Egypt." ' 33 And Moses said to Aaron, 'Take a jar, and put an omer of manna in it, and place it before the LORD, to be kept throughout your generations.' 34 As the LORD commanded Moses, so Aaron placed it before the covenant, *b* for safekeeping. 35 The Israelites ate manna for forty years, until they came to a habitable land; they ate manna, until they came to the border of the land of Canaan. 36 An omer is a tenth of an ephah.

Water from the Rock

17 From the wilderness of Sin the whole congregation of the Israelites journeyed by stages, as the LORD commanded. They camped at Rephidim, but there was no water for the people to drink. 2 The people quarrelled with Moses, and said, 'Give us water to drink.' Moses said to them, 'Why do you quarrel with me? Why do you test the LORD?' 3 But the people thirsted there for water; and the people complained against Moses and said, 'Why did you bring us out of Egypt, to kill us and our children and livestock with thirst?' 4 So Moses cried out to the LORD, 'What shall I do with this people? They are almost ready to stone me.' 5 The LORD said to Moses, 'Go on ahead of the people, and take some of the elders of Israel with you; take in your hand the staff with which you struck the Nile, and go. 6 I will be standing there in

a Or 'It is manna' (Heb man hu, see verse 31)
b Or treaty or testimony; Heb eduth

front of you on the rock at Horeb. Strike the rock, and water will come out of it, so that the people may drink.' Moses did so, in the sight of the elders of Israel. ⁷ He called the place Massah*a* and Meribah,*b* because the Israelites quarrelled and tested the LORD, saying, 'Is the LORD among us or not?'

Amalek Attacks Israel and Is Defeated

8 Then Amalek came and fought with Israel at Rephidim. ⁹ Moses said to Joshua, 'Choose some men for us and go out; fight with Amalek. Tomorrow I will stand on the top of the hill with the staff of God in my hand.' ¹⁰ So Joshua did as Moses told him, and fought with Amalek, while Moses, Aaron, and Hur went up to the top of the hill. ¹¹ Whenever Moses held up his hand, Israel prevailed; and whenever he lowered his hand, Amalek prevailed. ¹² But Moses' hands grew weary; so they took a stone and put it under him, and he sat on it. Aaron and Hur held up his hands, one on one side, and the other on the other side; so his hands were steady until the sun set. ¹³ And Joshua defeated Amalek and his people with the sword.

14 Then the LORD said to Moses, 'Write this as a reminder in a book and recite it in the hearing of Joshua: I will utterly blot out the remembrance of Amalek from under heaven.' ¹⁵ And Moses built an altar and called it, The LORD is my banner. ¹⁶ He said, 'A hand upon the banner of the LORD!*c* The LORD will have war with Amalek from generation to generation.'

Jethro's Advice

18 Jethro, the priest of Midian, Moses' father-in-law, heard of all that God had done for Moses and for his people Israel, how the LORD had brought Israel out of Egypt. ² After Moses had sent away his wife Zipporah, his father-in-law Jethro took her back, ³ along with her two sons. The name of one was Gershom (for he said, 'I have been an alien*d* in a foreign land'), ⁴ and the name of the other, Eliezer*e* (for he said, 'The God of my father was my help, and delivered me from the sword of Pharaoh'). ⁵ Jethro, Moses' father-in-law, came

into the wilderness where Moses was encamped at the mountain of God, bringing Moses' sons and his wife to him. ⁶ He sent word to Moses, 'I, your father-in-law Jethro, am coming to you, with your wife and her two sons.' ⁷ Moses went out to meet his father-in-law; he bowed down and kissed him; each asked after the other's welfare, and they went into the tent. ⁸ Then Moses told his father-in-law all that the LORD had done to Pharaoh and to the Egyptians for Israel's sake, all the hardship that had beset them on the way, and how the LORD had delivered them. ⁹ Jethro rejoiced for all the good that the LORD had done to Israel, in delivering them from the Egyptians.

10 Jethro said, 'Blessed be the LORD, who has delivered you from the Egyptians and from Pharaoh. ¹¹ Now I know that the LORD is greater than all gods, because he delivered the people from the Egyptians,*f* when they dealt arrogantly with them.' ¹² And Jethro, Moses' father-in-law, brought a burnt-offering and sacrifices to God; and Aaron came with all the elders of Israel to eat bread with Moses' father-in-law in the presence of God.

13 The next day Moses sat as judge for the people, while the people stood around him from morning until evening. ¹⁴ When Moses' father-in-law saw all that he was doing for the people, he said, 'What is this that you are doing for the people? Why do you sit alone, while all the people stand around you from morning until evening?' ¹⁵ Moses said to his father-in-law, 'Because the people come to me to inquire of God. ¹⁶ When they have a dispute, they come to me and I decide between one person and another, and I make known to them the statutes and instructions of God.' ¹⁷ Moses' father-in-law said to him, 'What you are doing is not good. ¹⁸ You will surely wear yourself out, both you and these people with you. For the task is too heavy for you; you cannot do it alone. ¹⁹ Now listen to me. I will give you counsel, and God be with you! You should represent the people before God,

---

a That is *Test*   *b* That is *Quarrel*   *c* Cn: Meaning of Heb uncertain   *d* Heb *ger*   *e* Heb *Eli, my God; ezer,* help   *f* The clause *because . . . Egyptians* has been transposed from verse 10 and you should bring their cases before God; [20] teach them the statutes and instructions and make known to them the way they are to go and the things they are to do. [21] You should also look for able men among all the people, men who fear God, are trustworthy, and hate dishonest gain; set such men over them as officers over thousands, hundreds, fifties, and tens. [22] Let them sit as judges for the people at all times; let them bring every important case to you, but decide every minor case themselves. So it will be easier for you, and they will bear the burden with you. [23] If you do this, and God so commands you, then you will be able to endure, and all these people will go to their home in peace.'

24 So Moses listened to his father-in-law and did all that he had said. [25] Moses chose able men from all Israel and appointed them as heads over the people, as officers over thousands, hundreds, fifties, and tens. [26] And they judged the people at all times; hard cases they brought to Moses, but any minor case they decided themselves. [27] Then Moses let his father-in-law depart, and he went off to his own country.

The Israelites Reach Mount Sinai

19 At the third new moon after the Israelites had gone out of the land of Egypt, on that very day, they came into the wilderness of Sinai. [2] They had journeyed from Rephidim, entered the wilderness of Sinai, and camped in the wilderness; Israel camped there in front of the mountain. [3] Then Moses went up to God; the LORD called to him from the mountain, saying, 'Thus you shall say to the house of Jacob, and tell the Israelites: [4] You have seen what I did to the Egyptians, and how I bore you on eagles' wings and brought you to myself. [5] Now therefore, if you obey my voice and keep my covenant, you shall be my treasured possession out of all the peoples. Indeed, the whole earth is mine, [6] but you shall be for me a priestly kingdom and a holy nation. These are the words that you shall speak to the Israelites.'

7 So Moses came, summoned the elders of the people, and set before them all these words that the LORD had commanded him. [8] The people all answered as one: 'Everything that the LORD has spoken we will do.' Moses reported the words of the people to the LORD. [9] Then the LORD said to Moses, 'I am going to come to you in a dense cloud, in order that the people may hear when I speak with you and so trust you ever after.'

The People Consecrated

When Moses had told the words of the people to the LORD, [10] the LORD said to Moses: 'Go to the people and consecrate them today and tomorrow. Have them wash their clothes [11] and prepare for the third day, because on the third day the LORD will come down upon Mount Sinai in the sight of all the people. [12] You shall set limits for the people all around, saying, "Be careful not to go up the mountain or to touch the edge of it. Any who touch the mountain shall be put to death. [13] No hand shall touch them, but they shall be stoned or shot with arrows; *a* whether animal or human being, they shall not live." When the trumpet sounds a long blast, they may go up on the mountain.' [14] So Moses went down from the mountain to the people. He consecrated the people, and they washed their clothes. [15] And he said to the people, 'Prepare for the third day; do not go near a woman.'

16 On the morning of the third day there was thunder and lightning, as well as a thick cloud on the mountain, and a blast of a trumpet so loud that all the people who were in the camp trembled. [17] Moses brought the people out of the camp to meet God. They took their stand at the foot of the mountain. [18] Now Mount Sinai was wrapped in smoke, because the LORD had descended upon it in fire; the smoke went up like the smoke of a kiln, while the whole mountain shook violently. [19] As the blast of the trumpet grew louder and louder, Moses would speak and God would answer him in thunder. [20] When the LORD descended upon Mount Sinai, to the top of the mountain, the LORD summoned Moses to the top of the mountain, and Moses went up. [21] Then the LORD said to Moses,

a Heb lacks *with arrows*

'Go down and warn the people not to break through to the LORD to look; otherwise many of them will perish. ²²Even the priests who approach the LORD must consecrate themselves or the LORD will break out against them.' ²³Moses said to the LORD, 'The people are not permitted to come up to Mount Sinai; for you yourself warned us, saying, "Set limits around the mountain and keep it holy." ' ²⁴The LORD said to him, 'Go down, and come up bringing Aaron with you; but do not let either the priests or the people break through to come up to the LORD; otherwise he will break out against them.' ²⁵So Moses went down to the people and told them.

The Ten Commandments

20 Then God spoke all these words: 2 I am the LORD your God, who brought you out of the land of Egypt, out of the house of slavery; ³you shall have no other gods before[a] me.

4 You shall not make for yourself an idol, whether in the form of anything that is in heaven above, or that is on the earth beneath, or that is in the water under the earth. ⁵You shall not bow down to them or worship them; for I the LORD your God am a jealous God, punishing children for the iniquity of parents, to the third and the fourth generation of those who reject me, ⁶but showing steadfast love to the thousandth generation[b] of those who love me and keep my commandments.

7 You shall not make wrongful use of the name of the LORD your God, for the LORD will not acquit anyone who misuses his name.

8 Remember the sabbath day, and keep it holy. ⁹For six days you shall labour and do all your work. ¹⁰But the seventh day is a sabbath to the LORD your God; you shall not do any work—you, your son or your daughter, your male or female slave, your livestock, or the alien resident in your towns. ¹¹For in six days the LORD made heaven and earth, the sea, and all that is in them, but rested the seventh day; therefore the LORD blessed the sabbath day and consecrated it.

12 Honour your father and your mother, so that your days may be long in the land that the LORD your God is giving you.

13 You shall not murder.[c]

14 You shall not commit adultery.

15 You shall not steal.

16 You shall not bear false witness against your neighbour.

17 You shall not covet your neighbour's house; you shall not covet your neighbour's wife, or male or female slave, or ox, or donkey, or anything that belongs to your neighbour.

18 When all the people witnessed the thunder and lightning, the sound of the trumpet, and the mountain smoking, they were afraid[d] and trembled and stood at a distance, ¹⁹and said to Moses, 'You speak to us, and we will listen; but do not let God speak to us, or we will die.' ²⁰Moses said to the people, 'Do not be afraid; for God has come only to test you and to put the fear of him upon you so that you do not sin.' ²¹Then the people stood at a distance, while Moses drew near to the thick darkness where God was.

The Law concerning the Altar

22 The LORD said to Moses: Thus you shall say to the Israelites: 'You have seen for yourselves that I spoke with you from heaven. ²³You shall not make gods of silver alongside me, nor shall you make for yourselves gods of gold. ²⁴You need make for me only an altar of earth and sacrifice on it your burnt-offerings and your offerings of well-being, your sheep and your oxen; in every place where I cause my name to be remembered I will come to you and bless you. ²⁵But if you make for me an altar of stone, do not build it of hewn stones; for if you use a chisel upon it you profane it. ²⁶You shall not go up by steps to my altar, so that your nakedness may not be exposed on it.'

The Law concerning Slaves

21 These are the ordinances that you shall set before them:
2 When you buy a male Hebrew slave,

a Or besides   b Or to thousands   c Or kill
d Sam Gk Syr Vg: MT they saw

he shall serve for six years, but in the seventh he shall go out a free person, without debt. ³If he comes in single, he shall go out single; if he comes in married, then his wife shall go out with him. ⁴If his master gives him a wife and she bears him sons or daughters, the wife and her children shall be her master's and he shall go out alone. ⁵But if the slave declares, 'I love my master, my wife, and my children; I will not go out a free person', ⁶then his master shall bring him before God.ᵃ He shall be brought to the door or the doorpost; and his master shall pierce his ear with an awl; and he shall serve him for life.

7 When a man sells his daughter as a slave, she shall not go out as the male slaves do. ⁸If she does not please her master, who designated her for himself, then he shall let her be redeemed; he shall have no right to sell her to a foreign people, since he has dealt unfairly with her. ⁹If he designates her for his son, he shall deal with her as with a daughter. ¹⁰If he takes another wife to himself, he shall not diminish the food, clothing, or marital rights of the first wife.ᵇ ¹¹And if he does not do these three things for her, she shall go out without debt, without payment of money.

The Law concerning Violence

12 Whoever strikes a person mortally shall be put to death. ¹³If it was not premeditated, but came about by an act of God, then I will appoint for you a place to which the killer may flee. ¹⁴But if someone wilfully attacks and kills another by treachery, you shall take the killer from my altar for execution.

15 Whoever strikes father or mother shall be put to death.

16 Whoever kidnaps a person, whether that person has been sold or is still held in possession, shall be put to death.

17 Whoever curses father or mother shall be put to death.

18 When individuals quarrel and one strikes the other with a stone or fist so that the injured party, though not dead, is confined to bed, ¹⁹but recovers and walks around outside with the help of a staff,

then the assailant shall be free of liability, except to pay for the loss of time, and to arrange for full recovery.

20 When a slave-owner strikes a male or female slave with a rod and the slave dies immediately, the owner shall be punished. ²¹But if the slave survives for a day or two, there is no punishment; for the slave is the owner's property.

22 When people who are fighting injure a pregnant woman so that there is a miscarriage, and yet no further harm follows, the one responsible shall be fined what the woman's husband demands, paying as much as the judges determine. ²³If any harm follows, then you shall give life for life, ²⁴eye for eye, tooth for tooth, hand for hand, foot for foot, ²⁵burn for burn, wound for wound, stripe for stripe.

26 When a slave-owner strikes the eye of a male or female slave, destroying it, the owner shall let the slave go, a free person, to compensate for the eye. ²⁷If the owner knocks out a tooth of a male or female slave, the slave shall be let go, a free person, to compensate for the tooth.

Laws concerning Property

28 When an ox gores a man or a woman to death, the ox shall be stoned, and its flesh shall not be eaten; but the owner of the ox shall not be liable. ²⁹If the ox has been accustomed to gore in the past, and its owner has been warned but has not restrained it, and it kills a man or a woman, the ox shall be stoned, and its owner also shall be put to death. ³⁰If a ransom is imposed on the owner, then the owner shall pay whatever is imposed for the redemption of the victim's life. ³¹If it gores a boy or a girl, the owner shall be dealt with according to this same rule. ³²If the ox gores a male or female slave, the owner shall pay to the slave-owner thirty shekels of silver, and the ox shall be stoned.

33 If someone leaves a pit open, or digs a pit and does not cover it, and an ox or a donkey falls into it, ³⁴the owner of the pit shall make restitution, giving money to its owner, but keeping the dead animal.

a Or *to the judges*   *b* Heb *of her*

35 If someone's ox hurts the ox of another, so that it dies, then they shall sell the live ox and divide the price of it; and the dead animal they shall also divide. ³⁶But if it was known that the ox was accustomed to gore in the past, and its owner has not restrained it, the owner shall restore ox for ox, but keep the dead animal.

Laws of Restitution

22 ᵃ When someone steals an ox or a sheep, and slaughters it or sells it, the thief shall pay five oxen for an ox, and four sheep for a sheep.ᵇ The thief shall make restitution, but if unable to do so, shall be sold for the theft. ⁴When the animal, whether ox or donkey or sheep, is found alive in the thief's possession, the thief shall pay double.

2 ᶜ If a thief is found breaking in, and is beaten to death, no blood-guilt is incurred; ³but if it happens after sunrise, blood-guilt is incurred.

5 When someone causes a field or vineyard to be grazed over, or lets livestock loose to graze in someone else's field, restitution shall be made from the best in the owner's field or vineyard.

6 When fire breaks out and catches in thorns so that the stacked grain or the standing grain or the field is consumed, the one who started the fire shall make full restitution.

7 When someone delivers to a neighbour money or goods for safe keeping, and they are stolen from the neighbour's house, then the thief, if caught, shall pay double. ⁸If the thief is not caught, the owner of the house shall be brought before God,ᵈ to determine whether or not the owner had laid hands on the neighbour's goods.

9 In any case of disputed ownership involving ox, donkey, sheep, clothing, or any other loss, of which one party says, 'This is mine', the case of both parties shall come before God;ᵈ the one whom God condemnsᵉ shall pay double to the other.

10 When someone delivers to another a donkey, ox, sheep, or any other animal for safekeeping, and it dies or is injured or is carried off, without anyone seeing it, ¹¹an oath before the LORD shall decide between the two of them that the one has not laid hands on the property of the other; the owner shall accept the oath, and no restitution shall be made. ¹²But if it was stolen, restitution shall be made to its owner. ¹³If it was mangled by beasts, let it be brought as evidence; restitution shall not be made for the mangled remains.

14 When someone borrows an animal from another and it is injured or dies, the owner not being present, full restitution shall be made. ¹⁵If the owner was present, there shall be no restitution; if it was hired, only the hiring fee is due.

Social and Religious Laws

16 When a man seduces a virgin who is not engaged to be married, and lies with her, he shall give the bride-price for her and make her his wife. ¹⁷But if her father refuses to give her to him, he shall pay an amount equal to the bride-price for virgins.

18 You shall not permit a female sorcerer to live.

19 Whoever lies with an animal shall be put to death.

20 Whoever sacrifices to any god, other than the LORD alone, shall be devoted to destruction.

21 You shall not wrong or oppress a resident alien, for you were aliens in the land of Egypt. ²²You shall not abuse any widow or orphan. ²³If you do abuse them, when they cry out to me, I will surely heed their cry; ²⁴my wrath will burn, and I will kill you with the sword, and your wives shall become widows and your children orphans.

25 If you lend money to my people, to the poor among you, you shall not deal with them as a creditor; you shall not exact interest from them. ²⁶If you take your neighbour's cloak in pawn, you shall restore it before the sun goes down; ²⁷for it may be your neighbour's only clothing to use as cover; in what else shall that person

a Ch 21.37 in Heb   b Verses 2, 3, and 4 rearranged thus: 3b, 4, 2, 3a   c Ch 22.1 in Heb   d Or before the judges   e Or the judges condemn sleep? And if your neighbour cries out to me, I will listen, for I am compassionate.

28 You shall not revile God, or curse a leader of your people.

29 You shall not delay to make offerings from the fullness of your harvest and from the outflow of your presses. *a*

The firstborn of your sons you shall give to me. 30 You shall do the same with your oxen and with your sheep: for seven days it shall remain with its mother; on the eighth day you shall give it to me.

31 You shall be people consecrated to me; therefore you shall not eat any meat that is mangled by beasts in the field; you shall throw it to the dogs.

Justice for All

23 You shall not spread a false report. You shall not join hands with the wicked to act as a malicious witness. 2 You shall not follow a majority in wrongdoing; when you bear witness in a lawsuit, you shall not side with the majority so as to pervert justice; 3 nor shall you be partial to the poor in a lawsuit.

4 When you come upon your enemy's ox or donkey going astray, you shall bring it back.

5 When you see the donkey of one who hates you lying under its burden and you would hold back from setting it free, you must help to set it free. *a*

6 You shall not pervert the justice due to your poor in their lawsuits. 7 Keep far from a false charge, and do not kill the innocent or those in the right, for I will not acquit the guilty. 8 You shall take no bribe, for a bribe blinds the officials, and subverts the cause of those who are in the right.

9 You shall not oppress a resident alien; you know the heart of an alien, for you were aliens in the land of Egypt.

Sabbatical Year and Sabbath

10 For six years you shall sow your land and gather in its yield; 11 but the seventh year you shall let it rest and lie fallow, so that the poor of your people may eat; and what they leave the wild animals may eat.

You shall do the same with your vineyard, and with your olive orchard.

12 For six days you shall do your work, but on the seventh day you shall rest, so that your ox and your donkey may have relief, and your home-born slave and the resident alien may be refreshed. 13 Be attentive to all that I have said to you. Do not invoke the names of other gods; do not let them be heard on your lips.

The Annual Festivals

14 Three times in the year you shall hold a festival for me. 15 You shall observe the festival of unleavened bread; as I commanded you, you shall eat unleavened bread for seven days at the appointed time in the month of Abib, for in it you came out of Egypt.

No one shall appear before me empty-handed.

16 You shall observe the festival of harvest, of the first fruits of your labour, of what you sow in the field. You shall observe the festival of ingathering at the end of the year, when you gather in from the field the fruit of your labour. 17 Three times in the year all your males shall appear before the Lord GOD.

18 You shall not offer the blood of my sacrifice with anything leavened, or let the fat of my festival remain until the morning.

19 The choicest of the first fruits of your ground you shall bring into the house of the LORD your God.

You shall not boil a kid in its mother's milk.

The Conquest of Canaan Promised

20 I am going to send an angel in front of you, to guard you on the way and to bring you to the place that I have prepared. 21 Be attentive to him and listen to his voice; do not rebel against him, for he will not pardon your transgression; for my name is in him.

22 But if you listen attentively to his voice and do all that I say, then I will be an enemy to your enemies and a foe to your foes.

a Meaning of Heb uncertain

23 When my angel goes in front of you, and brings you to the Amorites, the Hittites, the Perizzites, the Canaanites, the Hivites, and the Jebusites, and I blot them out, 24 you shall not bow down to their gods, or worship them, or follow their practices, but you shall utterly demolish them and break their pillars in pieces. 25 You shall worship the LORD your God, and I*a* will bless your bread and your water; and I will take sickness away from among you. 26 No one shall miscarry or be barren in your land; I will fulfil the number of your days. 27 I will send my terror in front of you, and will throw into confusion all the people against whom you shall come, and I will make all your enemies turn their backs to you. 28 And I will send the pestilence*b* in front of you, which shall drive out the Hivites, the Canaanites, and the Hittites from before you. 29 I will not drive them out from before you in one year, or the land would become desolate and the wild animals would multiply against you. 30 Little by little I will drive them out from before you, until you have increased and possess the land. 31 I will set your borders from the Red Sea*c* to the sea of the Philistines, and from the wilderness to the Euphrates; for I will hand over to you the inhabitants of the land, and you shall drive them out before you. 32 You shall make no covenant with them and their gods. 33 They shall not live in your land, or they will make you sin against me; for if you worship their gods, it will surely be a snare to you.

The Blood of the Covenant

24 Then he said to Moses, 'Come up to the LORD, you and Aaron, Nadab, and Abihu, and seventy of the elders of Israel, and worship at a distance. 2 Moses alone shall come near the LORD; but the others shall not come near, and the people shall not come up with him.'

3 Moses came and told the people all the words of the LORD and all the ordinances; and all the people answered with one voice, and said, 'All the words that the LORD has spoken we will do.' 4 And Moses wrote down all the words of the LORD. He

rose early in the morning, and built an altar at the foot of the mountain, and set up twelve pillars, corresponding to the twelve tribes of Israel. 5 He sent young men of the people of Israel, who offered burnt-offerings and sacrificed oxen as offerings of well-being to the LORD. 6 Moses took half of the blood and put it in basins, and half of the blood he dashed against the altar. 7 Then he took the book of the covenant, and read it in the hearing of the people; and they said, 'All that the LORD has spoken we will do, and we will be obedient.' 8 Moses took the blood and dashed it on the people, and said, 'See the blood of the covenant that the LORD has made with you in accordance with all these words.'

On the Mountain with God

9 Then Moses and Aaron, Nadab, and Abihu, and seventy of the elders of Israel went up, 10 and they saw the God of Israel. Under his feet there was something like a pavement of sapphire stone, like the very heaven for clearness. 11 God*d* did not lay his hand on the chief men of the people of Israel; also they beheld God, and they ate and drank.

12 The LORD said to Moses, 'Come up to me on the mountain, and wait there; and I will give you the tablets of stone, with the law and the commandment, which I have written for their instruction.' 13 So Moses set out with his assistant Joshua, and Moses went up into the mountain of God. 14 To the elders he had said, 'Wait here for us, until we come to you again; for Aaron and Hur are with you; whoever has a dispute may go to them.'

15 Then Moses went up on the mountain, and the cloud covered the mountain. 16 The glory of the LORD settled on Mount Sinai, and the cloud covered it for six days; on the seventh day he called to Moses out of the cloud. 17 Now the appearance of the glory of the LORD was like a devouring fire on the top of the mountain in the sight of the people of Israel. 18 Moses entered the cloud,

a Gk Vg: Heb *he*   *b* Or *hornets*: Meaning of Heb uncertain   *c* Or *Sea of Reeds*   *d* Heb *He* and went up on the mountain. Moses was on the mountain for forty days and forty nights.

Offerings for the Tabernacle

25 The LORD said to Moses: 2 Tell the Israelites to take for me an offering; from all whose hearts prompt them to give you shall receive the offering for me. 3 This is the offering that you shall receive from them: gold, silver, and bronze, 4 blue, purple, and crimson yarns and fine linen, goats' hair, 5 tanned rams' skins, fine leather,*a* acacia wood, 6 oil for the lamps, spices for the anointing-oil and for the fragrant incense, 7 onyx stones and gems to be set in the ephod and for the breastpiece. 8 And have them make me a sanctuary, so that I may dwell among them. 9 In accordance with all that I show you concerning the pattern of the tabernacle and of all its furniture, so you shall make it.

The Ark of the Covenant

10 They shall make an ark of acacia wood; it shall be two and a half cubits long, a cubit and a half wide, and a cubit and a half high. 11 You shall overlay it with pure gold, inside and outside you shall overlay it, and you shall make a moulding of gold upon it all round. 12 You shall cast four rings of gold for it and put them on its four feet, two rings on one side of it, and two rings on the other side. 13 You shall make poles of acacia wood, and overlay them with gold. 14 And you shall put the poles into the rings on the sides of the ark, by which to carry the ark. 15 The poles shall remain in the rings of the ark; they shall not be taken from it. 16 You shall put into the ark the covenant*b* that I shall give you.

17 Then you shall make a mercy-seat*c* of pure gold; two cubits and a half shall be its length, and a cubit and a half its width. 18 You shall make two cherubim of gold; you shall make them of hammered work, at the two ends of the mercy-seat. *d* 19 Make one cherub at one end, and one cherub at the other; of one piece with the mercy-seat*d* you shall make the cherubim at its two ends. 20 The cherubim shall spread out their wings above, overshadowing the mercy-seat*d* with their wings. They shall face each other; the faces of the cherubim shall be turned towards the mercy-seat. *d* 21 You shall put the mercy-seat*d* on the top of the ark; and in the ark you shall put the covenant*b* that I shall give you. 22 There I will meet you, and from above the mercy-seat, *d* from between the two cherubim that are on the ark of the covenant, *b* I will deliver to you all my commands for the Israelites.

The Table for the Bread of the Presence

23 You shall make a table of acacia wood, two cubits long, one cubit wide, and a cubit and a half high. 24 You shall overlay it with pure gold, and make a moulding of gold round it. 25 You shall make round it a rim a handbreadth wide, and a moulding of gold round the rim. 26 You shall make for it four rings of gold, and fasten the rings to the four corners at its four legs. 27 The rings that hold the poles used for carrying the table shall be close to the rim. 28 You shall make the poles of acacia wood, and overlay them with gold, and the table shall be carried with these. 29 You shall make its plates and dishes for incense, and its flagons and bowls with which to pour drink-offerings; you shall make them of pure gold. 30 And you shall set the bread of the Presence on the table before me always.

The Lampstand

31 You shall make a lampstand of pure gold. The base and the shaft of the lampstand shall be made of hammered work; its cups, its calyxes, and its petals shall be of one piece with it; 32 and there shall be six branches going out of its sides, three branches of the lampstand out of one side of it and three branches of the lampstand out of the other side of it; 33 three cups shaped like almond blossoms, each with calyx and petals, on one branch, and three cups shaped like almond blossoms, each with calyx and petals, on the other branch—so for the six branches going out of the lampstand. 34 On the lampstand itself there shall be four cups shaped like almond

a Meaning of Heb uncertain   *b* Or *treaty*, or *testimony*; Heb *eduth*   *c* Or *a cover*   *d* Or *the cover*

blossoms, each with its calyxes and petals.
35 There shall be a calyx of one piece with it
under the first pair of branches, a calyx of
one piece with it under the next pair of
branches, and a calyx of one piece with it
under the last pair of branches—so for the
six branches that go out of the lampstand.
36 Their calyxes and their branches shall be
of one piece with it, the whole of it one
hammered piece of pure gold. 37 You shall
make the seven lamps for it; and the lamps
shall be set up so as to give light on the
space in front of it. 38 Its snuffers and trays
shall be of pure gold. 39 It, and all these
utensils, shall be made from a talent of
pure gold. 40 And see that you make them
according to the pattern for them, which is
being shown you on the mountain.

The Tabernacle

26 Moreover, you shall make the
tabernacle with ten curtains of fine
twisted linen, and blue, purple, and crimson yarns; you shall make them with cherubim skilfully worked into them. 2 The
length of each curtain shall be twenty-eight
cubits, and the width of each curtain four
cubits; all the curtains shall be of the same
size. 3 Five curtains shall be joined to one
another; and the other five curtains shall be
joined to one another. 4 You shall make
loops of blue on the edge of the outermost
curtain in the first set; and likewise you
shall make loops on the edge of the outermost curtain in the second set. 5 You shall
make fifty loops on the one curtain, and
you shall make fifty loops on the edge of
the curtain that is in the second set; the
loops shall be opposite one another. 6 You
shall make fifty clasps of gold, and join the
curtains to one another with the clasps, so
that the tabernacle may be one whole.

7 You shall also make curtains of goats'
hair for a tent over the tabernacle; you shall
make eleven curtains. 8 The length of each
curtain shall be thirty cubits, and the width
of each curtain four cubits; the eleven curtains shall be of the same size. 9 You shall
join five curtains by themselves, and six curtains by themselves, and the sixth curtain
you shall double over at the front of the

tent. 10 You shall make fifty loops on the
edge of the curtain that is outermost in one
set, and fifty loops on the edge of the curtain that is outermost in the second set.

11 You shall make fifty clasps of bronze,
and put the clasps into the loops, and join
the tent together, so that it may be one
whole. 12 The part that remains of the curtains of the tent, the half-curtain that remains, shall hang over the back of the
tabernacle. 13 The cubit on one side, and the
cubit on the other side, of what remains in
the length of the curtains of the tent, shall
hang over the sides of the tabernacle, on
this side and that side, to cover it. 14 You
shall make for the tent a covering of tanned
rams' skins and an outer covering of fine
leather. *a*

The Framework

15 You shall make upright frames of acacia wood for the tabernacle. 16 Ten cubits
shall be the length of a frame, and a cubit
and a half the width of each frame. 17 There
shall be two pegs in each frame to fit the
frames together; you shall make these for
all the frames of the tabernacle. 18 You shall
make the frames for the tabernacle: twenty
frames for the south side; 19 and you shall
make forty bases of silver under the twenty
frames, two bases under the first frame for
its two pegs, and two bases under the next
frame for its two pegs; 20 and for the second
side of the tabernacle, on the north side
twenty frames, 21 and their forty bases of silver, two bases under the first frame, and
two bases under the next frame; 22 and for
the rear of the tabernacle westward you
shall make six frames. 23 You shall make
two frames for corners of the tabernacle in
the rear; 24 they shall be separate beneath,
but joined at the top, at the first ring; it
shall be the same with both of them; they
shall form the two corners. 25 And so there
shall be eight frames, with their bases of silver, sixteen bases; two bases under the first
frame, and two bases under the next frame.

26 You shall make bars of acacia wood,
five for the frames of one side of the tabernacle, 27 and five bars for the frames of the

a Meaning of Heb uncertain

other side of the tabernacle, and five bars for the frames of the side of the tabernacle at the rear to the west. ²⁸The middle bar, halfway up the frames, shall pass through from end to end. ²⁹You shall overlay the frames with gold, and shall make their rings of gold to hold the bars; and you shall overlay the bars with gold. ³⁰Then you shall erect the tabernacle according to the plan for it that you were shown on the mountain.

The Curtain

31 You shall make a curtain of blue, purple, and crimson yarns, and of fine twisted linen; it shall be made with cherubim skilfully worked into it. ³²You shall hang it on four pillars of acacia overlaid with gold, which have hooks of gold and rest on four bases of silver. ³³You shall hang the curtain under the clasps, and bring the ark of the covenant^a inside, within the curtain; and the curtain shall separate for you the holy place from the most holy. ³⁴You shall put

the mercy-seat^b on the ark of the covenant^a in the most holy place. ³⁵You shall set the table outside the curtain, and the lampstand on the south side of the tabernacle opposite the table; and you shall put the table on the north side.

36 You shall make a screen for the entrance of the tent, of blue, purple, and crimson yarns, and of fine twisted linen, embroidered with needlework. ³⁷You shall make for the screen five pillars of acacia, and overlay them with gold; their hooks shall be of gold, and you shall cast five bases of bronze for them.

The Altar of Burnt-Offering

27 You shall make the altar of acacia wood, five cubits long and five cubits wide; the altar shall be square, and it shall be three cubits high. ²You shall make horns for it on its four corners; its horns shall be of one piece with it, and you shall overlay it with bronze. ³You shall make

a Or *treaty,* or *testimony;* Heb *eduth*   *b* Or *the cover*

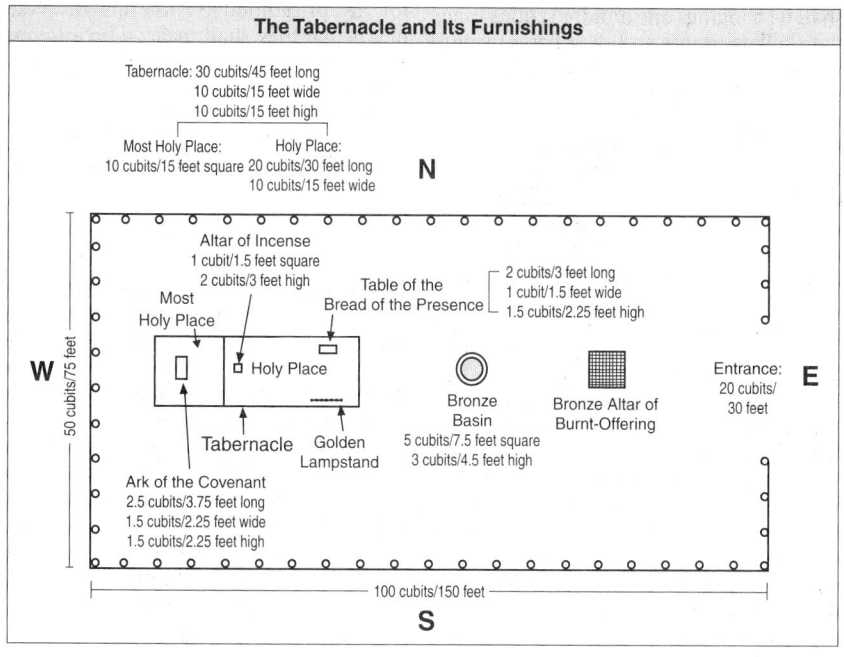

The Tabernacle and Its Furnishings

Tabernacle: 30 cubits/45 feet long
10 cubits/15 feet wide
10 cubits/15 feet high

Most Holy Place: Holy Place:
10 cubits/15 feet square 20 cubits/30 feet long
10 cubits/15 feet wide

N

Altar of Incense
1 cubit/1.5 feet square
2 cubits/3 feet high

Most
Holy Place

Table of the
Bread of the Presence

2 cubits/3 feet long
1 cubit/1.5 feet wide
1.5 cubits/2.25 feet high

Holy Place

W   E

50 cubits/75 feet

Tabernacle   Golden
Lampstand

Bronze
Basin

Bronze Altar of
Burnt-Offering

Entrance:
20 cubits/
30 feet

5 cubits/7.5 feet square
3 cubits/4.5 feet high

Ark of the Covenant
2.5 cubits/3.75 feet long
1.5 cubits/2.25 feet wide
1.5 cubits/2.25 feet high

— 100 cubits/150 feet —

S

pots for it to receive its ashes, and shovels and basins and forks and firepans; you shall make all its utensils of bronze. 4 You shall also make for it a grating, a network of bronze; and on the net you shall make four bronze rings at its four corners. 5 You shall set it under the ledge of the altar so that the net shall extend half-way down the altar. 6 You shall make poles for the altar, poles of acacia wood, and overlay them with bronze; 7 the poles shall be put through the rings, so that the poles shall be on the two sides of the altar when it is carried. 8 You shall make it hollow, with boards. They shall be made just as you were shown on the mountain.

The Court and Its Hangings

9 You shall make the court of the tabernacle. On the south side the court shall have hangings of fine twisted linen one hundred cubits long for that side; 10 its twenty pillars and their twenty bases shall be of bronze, but the hooks of the pillars and their bands shall be of silver. 11 Likewise, for its length on the north side there shall be hangings one hundred cubits long, their pillars twenty and their bases twenty, of bronze, but the hooks of the pillars and their bands shall be of silver. 12 For the width of the court on the west side there shall be fifty cubits of hangings, with ten pillars and ten bases. 13 The width of the court on the front to the east shall be fifty cubits. 14 There shall be fifteen cubits of hangings on one side, with three pillars and three bases. 15 There shall be fifteen cubits of hangings on the other side, with three pillars and three bases. 16 For the gate of the court there shall be a screen twenty cubits long, of blue, purple, and crimson yarns, and of fine twisted linen, embroidered with needlework; it shall have four pillars and with them four bases. 17 All the pillars around the court shall be banded with silver; their hooks shall be of silver, and their bases of bronze. 18 The length of the court shall be one hundred cubits, the width fifty, and the height five cubits, with hangings of fine twisted linen and bases of bronze. 19 All the utensils of the tabernacle for every use,

and all its pegs and all the pegs of the court, shall be of bronze.

The Oil for the Lamp

20 You shall further command the Israelites to bring you pure oil of beaten olives for the light, so that a lamp may be set up to burn regularly. 21 In the tent of meeting, outside the curtain that is before the covenant, *a* Aaron and his sons shall tend it from evening to morning before the LORD. It shall be a perpetual ordinance to be observed throughout their generations by the Israelites.

Vestments for the Priesthood

28 Then bring near to you your brother Aaron, and his sons with him, from among the Israelites, to serve me as priests—Aaron and Aaron's sons, Nadab and Abihu, Eleazar and Ithamar. 2 You shall make sacred vestments for the glorious adornment of your brother Aaron. 3 And you shall speak to all who have ability, whom I have endowed with skill, that they make Aaron's vestments to consecrate him for my priesthood. 4 These are the vestments that they shall make: a breastpiece, an ephod, a robe, a chequered tunic, a turban, and a sash. When they make these sacred vestments for your brother Aaron and his sons to serve me as priests, 5 they shall use gold, blue, purple, and crimson yarns, and fine linen.

The Ephod

6 They shall make the ephod of gold, of blue, purple, and crimson yarns, and of fine twisted linen, skilfully worked. 7 It shall have two shoulder-pieces attached to its two edges, so that it may be joined together. 8 The decorated band on it shall be of the same workmanship and materials, of gold, of blue, purple, and crimson yarns, and of fine twisted linen. 9 You shall take two onyx stones, and engrave on them the names of the sons of Israel, 10 six of their names on one stone, and the names of the remaining six on the other stone, in the order of their birth. 11 As a gem-cutter engraves signets, so

a Or treaty, or testimony; Heb eduth

you shall engrave the two stones with the names of the sons of Israel; you shall mount them in settings of gold filigree. ¹²You shall set the two stones on the shoulder-pieces of the ephod, as stones of remembrance for the sons of Israel; and Aaron shall bear their names before the LORD on his two shoulders for remembrance. ¹³You shall make settings of gold filigree, ¹⁴and two chains of pure gold, twisted like cords; and you shall attach the corded chains to the settings.

The Breastplate

15 You shall make a breastpiece of judgement, in skilled work; you shall make it in the style of the ephod; of gold, of blue and purple and crimson yarns, and of fine twisted linen you shall make it. ¹⁶It shall be square and doubled, a span in length and a span in width. ¹⁷You shall set in it four rows of stones. A row of carnelian, *a* chrysolite, and emerald shall be the first row; ¹⁸and the second row a turquoise, a sapphire, *b* and a moonstone; ¹⁹and the third row a jacinth, an agate, and an amethyst; ²⁰and the fourth row a beryl, an onyx, and a jasper; they shall be set in gold filigree. ²¹There shall be twelve stones with names corresponding to the names of the sons of Israel; they shall be like signets, each engraved with its name, for the twelve tribes. ²²You shall make for the breastpiece chains of pure gold, twisted like cords; ²³and you shall make for the breastpiece two rings of gold, and put the two rings on the two edges of the breastpiece. ²⁴You shall put the two cords of gold in the two rings at the edges of the breastpiece; ²⁵the two ends of the two cords you shall attach to the two settings, and so attach it in front to the shoulder-pieces of the ephod. ²⁶You shall make two rings of gold, and put them at the two ends of the breastpiece, on its inside edge next to the ephod. ²⁷You shall make two rings of gold, and attach them in front to the lower part of the two shoulder-pieces of the ephod, at its joining above the decorated band of the ephod. ²⁸The breast-piece shall be bound by its rings to the rings of the ephod with a blue cord, so that it may lie on the decorated band of the

ephod, and so that the breastpiece shall not come loose from the ephod. ²⁹So Aaron shall bear the names of the sons of Israel in the breastpiece of judgement on his heart when he goes into the holy place, for a continual remembrance before the LORD. ³⁰In the breastpiece of judgement you shall put the Urim and the Thummim, and they shall be on Aaron's heart when he goes in before the LORD; thus Aaron shall bear the judgement of the Israelites on his heart before the LORD continually.

Other Priestly Vestments

31 You shall make the robe of the ephod all of blue. ³²It shall have an opening for the head in the middle of it, with a woven binding round the opening, like the opening in a coat of mail, *c* so that it may not be torn. ³³On its lower hem you shall make pomegranates of blue, purple, and crimson yarns, all round the lower hem, with bells of gold between them all round— ³⁴a golden bell and a pomegranate alternating all round the lower hem of the robe. ³⁵Aaron shall wear it when he ministers, and its sound shall be heard when he goes into the holy place before the LORD, and when he comes out, so that he may not die.

36 You shall make a rosette of pure gold, and engrave on it, like the engraving of a signet, 'Holy to the LORD.' ³⁷You shall fasten it on the turban with a blue cord; it shall be on the front of the turban. ³⁸It shall be on Aaron's forehead, and Aaron shall take on himself any guilt incurred in the holy offering that the Israelites consecrate as their sacred donations; it shall always be on his forehead, in order that they may find favour before the LORD.

39 You shall make the chequered tunic of fine linen, and you shall make a turban of fine linen, and you shall make a sash embroidered with needlework.

40 For Aaron's sons you shall make tunics and sashes and head-dresses; you shall make them for their glorious adornment. ⁴¹You shall put them on your brother Aaron, and on his sons with him, and shall

a The identity of several of these stones is uncertain
b Or *lapis lazuli*   *c* Meaning of Heb uncertain

anoint them and ordain them and consecrate them, so that they may serve me as
priests. 42 You shall make for them linen undergarments to cover their naked flesh; they
shall reach from the hips to the thighs;
43 Aaron and his sons shall wear them when
they go into the tent of meeting, or when
they come near the altar to minister in the
holy place; or they will bring guilt on themselves and die. This shall be a perpetual ordinance for him and for his descendants after him.

The Ordination of the Priests

29 Now this is what you shall do to
them to consecrate them, so that
they may serve me as priests. Take one
young bull and two rams without blemish,
2 and unleavened bread, unleavened cakes
mixed with oil, and unleavened wafers
spread with oil. You shall make them of
choice wheat flour. 3 You shall put them in
one basket and bring them in the basket,
and bring the bull and the two rams. 4 You
shall bring Aaron and his sons to the entrance of the tent of meeting, and wash
them with water. 5 Then you shall take the
vestments, and put on Aaron the tunic and
the robe of the ephod, and the ephod, and
the breastpiece, and gird him with the decorated band of the ephod; 6 and you shall
set the turban on his head, and put the holy
diadem on the turban. 7 You shall take the
anointing-oil, and pour it on his head and
anoint him. 8 Then you shall bring his sons,
and put tunics on them, 9 and you shall gird
them with sashes[a] and tie head-dresses on
them; and the priesthood shall be theirs by
a perpetual ordinance. You shall then ordain Aaron and his sons.

10 You shall bring the bull in front of
the tent of meeting. Aaron and his sons
shall lay their hands on the head of the
bull, 11 and you shall slaughter the bull before the LORD, at the entrance of the tent of
meeting, 12 and shall take some of the
blood of the bull and put it on the horns
of the altar with your finger, and all the
rest of the blood you shall pour out at the
base of the altar. 13 You shall take all the fat
that covers the entrails, and the appendage

of the liver, and the two kidneys with the
fat that is on them, and turn them into
smoke on the altar. 14 But the flesh of the
bull, and its skin, and its dung, you shall
burn with fire outside the camp; it is a sin-
offering.

15 Then you shall take one of the rams,
and Aaron and his sons shall lay their
hands on the head of the ram, 16 and you
shall slaughter the ram, and shall take its
blood and dash it against all sides of the altar. 17 Then you shall cut the ram into its
parts, and wash its entrails and its legs, and
put them with its parts and its head, 18 and
turn the whole ram into smoke on the altar; it is a burnt-offering to the LORD; it is a
pleasing odour, an offering by fire to the
LORD.

19 You shall take the other ram; and
Aaron and his sons shall lay their hands on
the head of the ram, 20 and you shall
slaughter the ram, and take some of its
blood and put it on the lobe of Aaron's
right ear and on the lobes of the right ears
of his sons, and on the thumbs of their
right hands, and on the big toes of their
right feet, and dash the rest of the blood
against all sides of the altar. 21 Then you
shall take some of the blood that is on the
altar, and some of the anointing-oil, and
sprinkle it on Aaron and his vestments and
on his sons and his sons' vestments with
him; then he and his vestments shall be
holy, as well as his sons and his sons' vestments.

22 You shall also take the fat of the ram,
the fat-tail, the fat that covers the entrails,
the appendage of the liver, the two kidneys
with the fat that is on them, and the right
thigh (for it is a ram of ordination), 23 and
one loaf of bread, one cake of bread made
with oil, and one wafer, out of the basket of
unleavened bread that is before the LORD;
24 and you shall place all these on the palms
of Aaron and on the palms of his sons, and
raise them as an elevation-offering before
the LORD. 25 Then you shall take them from
their hands, and turn them into smoke on

a Gk: Heb *sashes, Aaron and his sons*

the altar on top of the burnt-offering of pleasing odour before the LORD; it is an offering by fire to the LORD.

26 You shall take the breast of the ram of Aaron's ordination and raise it as an elevation-offering before the LORD; and it shall be your portion. 27 You shall consecrate the breast that was raised as an elevation-offering and the thigh that was raised as an elevation-offering from the ram of ordination, from that which belonged to Aaron and his sons. 28 These things shall be a perpetual ordinance for Aaron and his sons from the Israelites, for this is an offering; and it shall be an offering by the Israelites from their sacrifice of offerings of well-being, their offering to the LORD.

29 The sacred vestments of Aaron shall be passed on to his sons after him; they shall be anointed in them and ordained in them. 30 The son who is priest in his place shall wear them for seven days, when he comes into the tent of meeting to minister in the holy place.

31 You shall take the ram of ordination, and boil its flesh in a holy place; 32 and Aaron and his sons shall eat the flesh of the ram and the bread that is in the basket, at the entrance of the tent of meeting. 33 They themselves shall eat the food by which atonement is made, to ordain and consecrate them, but no one else shall eat of them, because they are holy. 34 If any of the flesh for the ordination, or of the bread, remains until the morning, then you shall burn the remainder with fire; it shall not be eaten, because it is holy.

35 Thus you shall do to Aaron and to his sons, just as I have commanded you; over seven days you shall ordain them. 36 Also every day you shall offer a bull as a sin-offering for atonement. Also you shall offer a sin-offering for the altar, when you make atonement for it, and shall anoint it, to consecrate it. 37 For seven days you shall make atonement for the altar, and consecrate it, and the altar shall be most holy; whatever touches the altar shall become holy.

The Daily Offerings

38 Now this is what you shall offer on the altar: two lambs a year old regularly each day. 39 One lamb you shall offer in the morning, and the other lamb you shall offer in the evening; 40 and with the first lamb one-tenth of a measure of choice flour mixed with one-fourth of a hin of beaten oil, and one-fourth of a hin of wine for a drink-offering. 41 And the other lamb you shall offer in the evening, and shall offer with it a grain-offering and its drink-offering, as in the morning, for a pleasing odour, an offering by fire to the LORD. 42 It shall be a regular burnt-offering throughout your generations at the entrance of the tent of meeting before the LORD, where I will meet you, to speak to you there. 43 I will meet the Israelites there, and it shall be sanctified by my glory; 44 I will consecrate the tent of meeting and the altar; Aaron also and his sons I will consecrate, to serve me as priests. 45 I will dwell among the Israelites, and I will be their God. 46 And they shall know that I am the LORD their God, who brought them out of the land of Egypt that I might dwell among them; I am the LORD their God.

The Altar of Incense

30 You shall make an altar on which to offer incense; you shall make it of acacia wood. 2 It shall be one cubit long, and one cubit wide; it shall be square, and shall be two cubits high; its horns shall be of one piece with it. 3 You shall overlay it with pure gold, its top, and its sides all round and its horns; and you shall make for it a moulding of gold all round. 4 And you shall make two golden rings for it; under its moulding on two opposite sides of it you shall make them, and they shall hold the poles with which to carry it. 5 You shall make the poles of acacia wood, and overlay them with gold. 6 You shall place it in front of the curtain that is above the ark of the covenant,*a* in front of the mercy-seat*b* that is over the covenant,*a* where I will meet you. 7 Aaron shall offer fragrant

a Or *treaty,* or *testimony;* Heb *eduth*   *b* Or *the cover* incense on it; every morning when he dresses the lamps he shall offer it, 8 and when Aaron sets up the lamps in the evening he shall offer it, a regular incense-offering before the LORD throughout your generations. 9 You shall not offer unholy incense on it, or a burnt-offering, or a grain-offering; and you shall not pour a drink-offering on it. 10 Once a year Aaron shall perform the rite of atonement on its horns. Throughout your generations he shall perform the atonement for it once a year with the blood of the atoning sin-offering. It is most holy to the LORD.

The Half-Shekel for the Sanctuary

11 The LORD spoke to Moses: 12 When you take a census of the Israelites to register them, at registration all of them shall give a ransom for their lives to the LORD, so that no plague may come upon them for being registered. 13 This is what each one who is registered shall give: half a shekel according to the shekel of the sanctuary (the shekel is twenty gerahs), half a shekel as an offering to the LORD. 14 Each one who is registered, from twenty years old and upwards, shall give the LORD's offering. 15 The rich shall not give more, and the poor shall not give less, than the half-shekel, when you bring this offering to the LORD to make atonement for your lives. 16 You shall take the atonement money from the Israelites and shall designate it for the service of the tent of meeting; before the LORD it will be a reminder to the Israelites of the ransom given for your lives.

The Bronze Basin

17 The LORD spoke to Moses: 18 You shall make a bronze basin with a bronze stand for washing. You shall put it between the tent of meeting and the altar, and you shall put water in it; 19 with the water a Aaron and his sons shall wash their hands and their feet. 20 When they go into the tent of meeting, or when they come near the altar to minister, to make an offering by fire to the LORD, they shall wash with water, so that they may not die. 21 They shall wash their hands and their feet, so that they may not die: it shall be a perpetual ordinance for them, for him and for his descendants throughout their generations.

The Anointing-Oil and Incense

22 The LORD spoke to Moses: 23 Take the finest spices: of liquid myrrh five hundred shekels, and of sweet-smelling cinnamon half as much, that is, two hundred and fifty, and two hundred and fifty of aromatic cane, 24 and five hundred of cassia—measured by the sanctuary shekel—and a hin of olive oil; 25 and you shall make of these a sacred anointing-oil blended as by the perfumer; it shall be a holy anointing-oil. 26 With it you shall anoint the tent of meeting and the ark of the covenant, b 27 and the table and all its utensils, and the lampstand and its utensils, and the altar of incense, 28 and the altar of burnt-offering with all its utensils, and the basin with its stand; 29 you shall consecrate them, so that they may be most holy; whatever touches them will become holy. 30 You shall anoint Aaron and his sons, and consecrate them, in order that they may serve me as priests. 31 You shall say to the Israelites, 'This shall be my holy anointing-oil throughout your generations. 32 It shall not be used in any ordinary anointing of the body, and you shall make no other like it in composition; it is holy, and it shall be holy to you. 33 Whoever compounds any like it or whoever puts any of it on an unqualified person shall be cut off from the people.'

34 The LORD said to Moses: Take sweet spices, stacte, and onycha, and galbanum, sweet spices with pure frankincense (an equal part of each), 35 and make an incense blended as by the perfumer, seasoned with salt, pure and holy; 36 and you shall beat some of it into powder, and put part of it before the covenant b in the tent of meeting where I shall meet you; it shall be for you most holy. 37 When you make incense according to this composition, you shall not make it for yourselves; it shall be regarded by you as holy to the LORD. 38 Whoever makes any like it to use as perfume shall be cut off from the people.

a Heb it   b Or treaty, or testimony; Heb eduth

Bezalel and Oholiab

31 The LORD spoke to Moses: ²See, I have called by name Bezalel son of Uri son of Hur, of the tribe of Judah: ³and I have filled him with divine spirit,^a with ability, intelligence, and knowledge in every kind of craft, ⁴to devise artistic designs, to work in gold, silver, and bronze, ⁵in cutting stones for setting, and in carving wood, in every kind of craft. ⁶Moreover, I have appointed with him Oholiab son of Ahisamach, of the tribe of Dan; and I have given skill to all the skilful, so that they may make all that I have commanded you: ⁷the tent of meeting, and the ark of the covenant,^b and the mercy-seat^c that is on it, and all the furnishings of the tent, ⁸the table and its utensils, and the pure lampstand with all its utensils, and the altar of incense, ⁹and the altar of burnt-offering with all its utensils, and the basin with its stand, ¹⁰and the finely worked vestments, the holy vestments for the priest Aaron and the vestments of his sons, for their service as priests, ¹¹and the anointing-oil and the fragrant incense for the holy place. They shall do just as I have commanded you.

The Sabbath Law

12 The LORD said to Moses: ¹³You yourself are to speak to the Israelites: 'You shall keep my sabbaths, for this is a sign between me and you throughout your generations, given in order that you may know that I, the LORD, sanctify you. ¹⁴You shall keep the sabbath, because it is holy for you; everyone who profanes it shall be put to death; whoever does any work on it shall be cut off from among the people. ¹⁵For six days shall work be done, but the seventh day is a sabbath of solemn rest, holy to the LORD; whoever does any work on the sabbath day shall be put to death. ¹⁶Therefore the Israelites shall keep the sabbath, observing the sabbath throughout their generations, as a perpetual covenant. ¹⁷It is a sign for ever between me and the people of Israel that in six days the LORD made heaven and earth, and on the seventh day he rested, and was refreshed.'

The Two Tablets of the Covenant

18 When God^d finished speaking with Moses on Mount Sinai, he gave him the two tablets of the covenant,^b tablets of stone, written with the finger of God.

The Golden Calf

32 When the people saw that Moses delayed to come down from the mountain, the people gathered around Aaron and said to him, 'Come, make gods for us, who shall go before us; as for this Moses, the man who brought us up out of the land of Egypt, we do not know what has become of him.' ²Aaron said to them, 'Take off the gold rings that are on the ears of your wives, your sons, and your daughters, and bring them to me.' ³So all the people took off the gold rings from their ears, and brought them to Aaron. ⁴He took the gold from them, formed it in a mould,^e and cast an image of a calf; and they said, 'These are your gods, O Israel, who brought you up out of the land of Egypt!' ⁵When Aaron saw this, he built an altar before it; and Aaron made proclamation and said, 'Tomorrow shall be a festival to the LORD.' ⁶They rose early the next day, and offered burnt-offerings and brought sacrifices of well-being; and the people sat down to eat and drink, and rose up to revel.

7 The LORD said to Moses, 'Go down at once! Your people, whom you brought up out of the land of Egypt, have acted perversely; ⁸they have been quick to turn aside from the way that I commanded them; they have cast for themselves an image of a calf, and have worshipped it and sacrificed to it, and said, "These are your gods, O Israel, who brought you up out of the land of Egypt!" ' ⁹The LORD said to Moses, 'I have seen this people, how stiff-necked they are. ¹⁰Now let me alone, so that my wrath may burn hot against them and I may consume them; and of you I will make a great nation.'

11 But Moses implored the LORD his

---

a Or *with the spirit of God*   *b* Or *treaty*, or *testimony*; Heb *eduth*   *c* Or *the cover*   *d* Heb *he*
e Or *fashioned it with a graving-tool*; Meaning of Heb uncertain

God, and said, 'O Lord, why does your wrath burn hot against your people, whom you brought out of the land of Egypt with great power and with a mighty hand? 12 Why should the Egyptians say, "It was with evil intent that he brought them out to kill them in the mountains, and to consume them from the face of the earth"? Turn from your fierce wrath; change your mind and do not bring disaster on your people. 13 Remember Abraham, Isaac, and Israel, your servants, how you swore to them by your own self, saying to them, "I will multiply your descendants like the stars of heaven, and all this land that I have promised I will give to your descendants, and they shall inherit it for ever." ' 14 And the Lord changed his mind about the disaster that he planned to bring on his people.

15 Then Moses turned and went down from the mountain, carrying the two tablets of the covenant *a* in his hands, tablets that were written on both sides, written on the front and on the back. 16 The tablets were the work of God, and the writing was the writing of God, engraved upon the tablets. 17 When Joshua heard the noise of the people as they shouted, he said to Moses, 'There is a noise of war in the camp.' 18 But he said,

'It is not the sound made by victors,
or the sound made by losers;
it is the sound of revellers that I hear.'

19 As soon as he came near the camp and saw the calf and the dancing, Moses' anger burned hot, and he threw the tablets from his hands and broke them at the foot of the mountain. 20 He took the calf that they had made, burned it with fire, ground it to powder, scattered it on the water, and made the Israelites drink it.

21 Moses said to Aaron, 'What did this people do to you that you have brought so great a sin upon them?' 22 And Aaron said, 'Do not let the anger of my lord burn hot; you know the people, that they are bent on evil. 23 They said to me, "Make us gods, who shall go before us; as for this Moses, the man who brought us up out of the land of Egypt, we do not know what has become

of him." 24 So I said to them, "Whoever has gold, take it off"; so they gave it to me, and I threw it into the fire, and out came this calf!'

25 When Moses saw that the people were running wild (for Aaron had let them run wild, to the derision of their enemies), 26 then Moses stood in the gate of the camp, and said, 'Who is on the Lord's side? Come to me!' And all the sons of Levi gathered around him. 27 He said to them, 'Thus says the Lord, the God of Israel, "Put your sword on your side, each of you! Go back and forth from gate to gate throughout the camp, and each of you kill your brother, your friend, and your neighbour." ' 28 The sons of Levi did as Moses commanded, and about three thousand of the people fell on that day. 29 Moses said, 'Today you have ordained yourselves *b* for the service of the Lord, each one at the cost of a son or a brother, and so have brought a blessing on yourselves this day.'

30 On the next day Moses said to the people, 'You have sinned a great sin. But now I will go up to the Lord; perhaps I can make atonement for your sin.' 31 So Moses returned to the Lord and said, 'Alas, this people has sinned a great sin; they have made for themselves gods of gold. 32 But now, if you will only forgive their sin—but if not, blot me out of the book that you have written.' 33 But the Lord said to Moses, 'Whoever has sinned against me I will blot out of my book. 34 But now go, lead the people to the place about which I have spoken to you; see, my angel shall go in front of you. Nevertheless, when the day comes for punishment, I will punish them for their sin.'

35 Then the Lord sent a plague on the people, because they made the calf—the one that Aaron made.

The Command to Leave Sinai

33 The Lord said to Moses, 'Go, leave this place, you and the people whom you have brought up out of the land of Egypt, and go to the land of which I

a Or *treaty*, or *testimony*; Heb *eduth*   *b* Gk Vg Compare Tg: Heb *Today ordain yourselves* swore to Abraham, Isaac, and Jacob, saying, "To your descendants I will give it." ²I will send an angel before you, and I will drive out the Canaanites, the Amorites, the Hittites, the Perizzites, the Hivites, and the Jebusites. ³Go up to a land flowing with milk and honey; but I will not go up among you, or I would consume you on the way, for you are a stiff-necked people.'

4 When the people heard these harsh words, they mourned, and no one put on ornaments. ⁵For the LORD had said to Moses, 'Say to the Israelites, "You are a stiff-necked people; if for a single moment I should go up among you, I would consume you. So now take off your ornaments, and I will decide what to do to you." ' ⁶Therefore the Israelites stripped themselves of their ornaments, from Mount Horeb onwards.

The Tent outside the Camp

7 Now Moses used to take the tent and pitch it outside the camp, far off from the camp; he called it the tent of meeting. And everyone who sought the LORD would go out to the tent of meeting, which was outside the camp. ⁸Whenever Moses went out to the tent, all the people would rise and stand, each of them, at the entrance of their tents and watch Moses until he had gone into the tent. ⁹When Moses entered the tent, the pillar of cloud would descend and stand at the entrance of the tent, and the LORD would speak with Moses. ¹⁰When all the people saw the pillar of cloud standing at the entrance of the tent, all the people would rise and bow down, all of them, at the entrance of their tents. ¹¹Thus the LORD used to speak to Moses face to face, as one speaks to a friend. Then he would return to the camp; but his young assistant, Joshua son of Nun, would not leave the tent.

Moses' Intercession

12 Moses said to the LORD, 'See, you have said to me, "Bring up this people"; but you have not let me know whom you will send with me. Yet you have said, "I know you by name, and you have also found favour in my sight." ¹³Now if I have found favour in your sight, show me your ways, so that I may know you and find favour in your sight. Consider too that this nation is your people.' ¹⁴He said, 'My presence will go with you, and I will give you rest.' ¹⁵And he said to him, 'If your presence will not go, do not carry us up from here. ¹⁶For how shall it be known that I have found favour in your sight, I and your people, unless you go with us? In this way, we shall be distinct, I and your people, from every people on the face of the earth.'

17 The LORD said to Moses, 'I will do the very thing that you have asked; for you have found favour in my sight, and I know you by name.' ¹⁸Moses said, 'Show me your glory, I pray.' ¹⁹And he said, 'I will make all my goodness pass before you, and will proclaim before you the name, "The LORD";ᵃ and I will be gracious to whom I will be gracious, and will show mercy on whom I will show mercy. ²⁰But', he said, 'you cannot see my face; for no one shall see me and live.' ²¹And the LORD continued, 'See, there is a place by me where you shall stand on the rock; ²²and while my glory passes by I will put you in a cleft of the rock, and I will cover you with my hand until I have passed by; ²³then I will take away my hand, and you shall see my back; but my face shall not be seen.'

Moses Makes New Tablets

34 The LORD said to Moses, 'Cut two tablets of stone like the former ones, and I will write on the tablets the words that were on the former tablets, which you broke. ²Be ready in the morning, and come up in the morning to Mount Sinai and present yourself there to me, on the top of the mountain. ³No one shall come up with you, and do not let anyone be seen throughout all the mountain; and do not let flocks or herds graze in front of that mountain.' ⁴So Moses cut two tablets of stone like the former ones; and he rose early in the morning and went up on Mount Sinai, as the LORD had commanded him, and took in his hand the two tablets of stone. ⁵The LORD descended in the cloud

a Heb YHWH; see note at 3.15

and stood with him there, and proclaimed the name, 'The LORD.'^a 6 The LORD passed before him, and proclaimed,
'The LORD, the LORD,
a God merciful and gracious,
slow to anger,
and abounding in steadfast love and
faithfulness,
7 keeping steadfast love for the
thousandth generation,^b
forgiving iniquity and transgression
and sin,
yet by no means clearing the guilty,
but visiting the iniquity of the
parents
upon the children
and the children's children,
to the third and the fourth
generation.'
8 And Moses quickly bowed his head towards the earth, and worshipped. 9 He said, 'If now I have found favour in your sight, O Lord, I pray, let the Lord go with us. Although this is a stiff-necked people, pardon our iniquity and our sin, and take us for your inheritance.'

The Covenant Renewed

10 He said: I hereby make a covenant. Before all your people I will perform marvels, such as have not been performed in all the earth or in any nation; and all the people among whom you live shall see the work of the LORD; for it is an awesome thing that I will do with you. 11 Observe what I command you today.
See, I will drive out before you the Amorites, the Canaanites, the Hittites, the Perizzites, the Hivites, and the Jebusites. 12 Take care not to make a covenant with the inhabitants of the land to which you are going, or it will become a snare among you. 13 You shall tear down their altars, break their pillars, and cut down their sacred poles^c 14 (for you shall worship no other god, because the LORD, whose name is Jealous, is a jealous God). 15 You shall not make a covenant with the inhabitants of the land, for when they prostitute themselves to their gods and sacrifice to their gods, someone among them will invite you, and you will eat of the sacrifice. 16 And you will take wives from among their daughters for your sons, and their daughters who prostitute themselves to their gods will make your sons also prostitute themselves to their gods.

17 You shall not make cast idols.

18 You shall keep the festival of unleavened bread. For seven days you shall eat unleavened bread, as I commanded you, at the time appointed in the month of Abib; for in the month of Abib you came out from Egypt.

19 All that first opens the womb is mine, all your male^d livestock, the firstborn of cow and sheep. 20 The firstborn of a donkey you shall redeem with a lamb, or if you will not redeem it you shall break its neck. All the firstborn of your sons you shall redeem.
No one shall appear before me empty-handed.

21 For six days you shall work, but on the seventh day you shall rest; even in ploughing time and in harvest time you shall rest. 22 You shall observe the festival of weeks, the first fruits of wheat harvest, and the festival of ingathering at the turn of the year. 23 Three times in the year all your males shall appear before the LORD God, the God of Israel. 24 For I will cast out nations before you, and enlarge your borders; no one shall covet your land when you go up to appear before the LORD your God three times in the year.

25 You shall not offer the blood of my sacrifice with leaven, and the sacrifice of the festival of the passover shall not be left until the morning.

26 The best of the first fruits of your ground you shall bring to the house of the LORD your God.
You shall not boil a kid in its mother's milk.

27 The LORD said to Moses: Write these words; in accordance with these words I have made a covenant with you and with Israel. 28 He was there with the LORD for forty days and forty nights; he neither ate bread

---

nor drank water. And he wrote on the tablets the words of the covenant, the ten commandments.[a]

The Shining Face of Moses

29 Moses came down from Mount Sinai. As he came down from the mountain with the two tablets of the covenant[b] in his hand, Moses did not know that the skin of his face shone because he had been talking with God. 30 When Aaron and all the Israelites saw Moses, the skin of his face was shining, and they were afraid to come near him. 31 But Moses called to them; and Aaron and all the leaders of the congregation returned to him, and Moses spoke with them. 32 Afterwards all the Israelites came near, and he gave them in commandment all that the LORD had spoken with him on Mount Sinai. 33 When Moses had finished speaking with them, he put a veil on his face; 34 but whenever Moses went in before the LORD to speak with him, he would take the veil off, until he came out; and when he came out, and told the Israelites what he had been commanded, 35 the Israelites would see the face of Moses, that the skin of his face was shining; and Moses would put the veil on his face again, until he went in to speak with him.

Sabbath Regulations

35 Moses assembled all the congregation of the Israelites and said to them: These are the things that the LORD has commanded you to do: 2 For six days shall work be done, but on the seventh day you shall have a holy sabbath of solemn rest to the LORD; whoever does any work on it shall be put to death. 3 You shall kindle no fire in all your dwellings on the sabbath day.

Preparations for Making the Tabernacle

4 Moses said to all the congregation of the Israelites: This is the thing that the LORD has commanded: 5 Take from among you an offering to the LORD; let whoever is of a generous heart bring the LORD's offering: gold, silver, and bronze; 6 blue, purple, and crimson yarns, and fine linen; goats' hair, 7 tanned rams' skins, and fine leather;[c] acacia wood, 8 oil for the light, spices for the anointing-oil and for the fragrant incense, 9 and onyx stones and gems to be set in the ephod and the breastpiece.

10 All who are skilful among you shall come and make all that the LORD has commanded: the tabernacle, 11 its tent and its covering, its clasps and its frames, its bars, its pillars, and its bases; 12 the ark with its poles, the mercy-seat,[d] and the curtain for the screen; 13 the table with its poles and all its utensils, and the bread of the Presence; 14 the lampstand also for the light, with its utensils and its lamps, and the oil for the light; 15 and the altar of incense, with its poles, and the anointing-oil and the fragrant incense, and the screen for the entrance, the entrance of the tabernacle; 16 the altar of burnt-offering, with its grating of bronze, its poles, and all its utensils, the basin with its stand; 17 the hangings of the court, its pillars and its bases, and the screen for the gate of the court; 18 the pegs of the tabernacle and the pegs of the court, and their cords; 19 the finely worked vestments for ministering in the holy place, the holy vestments for the priest Aaron, and the vestments of his sons, for their service as priests.

Offerings for the Tabernacle

20 Then all the congregation of the Israelites withdrew from the presence of Moses. 21 And they came, everyone whose heart was stirred, and everyone whose spirit was willing, and brought the LORD's offering to be used for the tent of meeting, and for all its service, and for the sacred vestments. 22 So they came, both men and women; all who were of a willing heart brought brooches and earings and signet rings and pendants, all sorts of gold objects, everyone bringing an offering of gold to the LORD. 23 And everyone who possessed blue or purple or crimson yarn or fine linen or goats' hair or tanned rams' skins or fine leather,[c] brought them. 24 Everyone who could make an offering of silver or bronze brought it as

a Heb *words*   *b* Or *treaty,* or *testimony;* Heb *eduth*
c Meaning of Heb uncertain   *d* Or *the cover*

the LORD's offering; and everyone who possessed acacia wood of any use in the work, brought it. 25 All the skilful women spun with their hands, and brought what they had spun in blue and purple and crimson yarns and fine linen; 26 all the women whose hearts moved them to use their skill spun the goats' hair. 27 And the leaders brought onyx stones and gems to be set in the ephod and the breastpiece, 28 and spices and oil for the light, and for the anointing-oil, and for the fragrant incense. 29 All the Israelite men and women whose hearts made them willing to bring anything for the work that the LORD had commanded by Moses to be done, brought it as a freewill-offering to the LORD.

Bezalel and Oholiab

30 Then Moses said to the Israelites: See, the LORD has called by name Bezalel son of Uri son of Hur, of the tribe of Judah; 31 he has filled him with divine spirit, *a* with skill, intelligence, and knowledge in every kind of craft, 32 to devise artistic designs, to work in gold, silver, and bronze, 33 in cutting stones for setting, and in carving wood, in every kind of craft. 34 And he has inspired him to teach, both him and Oholiab son of Ahisamach, of the tribe of Dan. 35 He has filled them with skill to do every kind of work done by an artisan or by a designer or by an embroiderer in blue, purple, and crimson yarns, and in fine linen, or by a weaver—by any sort of artisan or skilled designer.

36 Bezalel and Oholiab and everyone skilful to whom the LORD has given skill and understanding to know how to do any work in the construction of the sanctuary shall work in accordance with all that the LORD has commanded.

2 Moses then called Bezalel and Oholiab and everyone skilful to whom the LORD had given skill, everyone whose heart was stirred to come to do the work; 3 and they received from Moses all the freewill-offerings that the Israelites had brought for doing the work on the sanctuary. They still kept bringing him freewill-offerings every morning, 4 so that all the artisans who were doing every sort of task on the sanctuary came, each from the task being performed, 5 and said to Moses, 'The people are bringing much more than enough for doing the work that the LORD has commanded us to do.' 6 So Moses gave command, and word was proclaimed throughout the camp: 'No man or woman is to make anything else as an offering for the sanctuary.' So the people were restrained from bringing; 7 for what they had already brought was more than enough to do all the work.

Construction of the Tabernacle

8 All those with skill among the workers made the tabernacle with ten curtains; they were made of fine twisted linen, and blue, purple, and crimson yarns, with cherubim skilfully worked into them. 9 The length of each curtain was twenty-eight cubits, and the width of each curtain four cubits; all the curtains were of the same size. 10 He joined five curtains to one another, and the other five curtains he joined to one another. 11 He made loops of blue on the edge of the outermost curtain of the first set; likewise he made them on the edge of the outermost curtain of the second set; 12 he made fifty loops on the one curtain, and he made fifty loops on the edge of the curtain that was in the second set; the loops were opposite one another. 13 And he made fifty clasps of gold, and joined the curtains one to the other with clasps; so the tabernacle was one whole.

14 He also made curtains of goats' hair for a tent over the tabernacle; he made eleven curtains. 15 The length of each curtain was thirty cubits, and the width of each curtain four cubits; the eleven curtains were of the same size. 16 He joined five curtains by themselves, and six curtains by themselves. 17 He made fifty loops on the edge of the outermost curtain of one set, and fifty loops on the edge of the other connecting curtain. 18 He made fifty clasps of bronze to join the tent together so that it might be one whole. 19 And he made for the tent a covering of tanned rams' skins and an outer covering of fine leather. *b*

---

a Or *the spirit of God*   *b* Meaning of Heb uncertain

20 Then he made the upright frames for the tabernacle of acacia wood. 21 Ten cubits was the length of a frame, and a cubit and a half the width of each frame. 22 Each frame had two pegs for fitting together; he did this for all the frames of the tabernacle. 23 The frames for the tabernacle he made in this way: twenty frames for the south side; 24 and he made forty bases of silver under the twenty frames, two bases under the first frame for its two pegs, and two bases under the next frame for its two pegs. 25 For the second side of the tabernacle, on the north side, he made twenty frames 26 and their forty bases of silver, two bases under the first frame and two bases under the next frame. 27 For the rear of the tabernacle westward he made six frames. 28 He made two frames for corners of the tabernacle in the rear. 29 They were separate beneath, but joined at the top, at the first ring; he made two of them in this way, for the two corners. 30 There were eight frames with their bases of silver: sixteen bases, under every frame two bases.

31 He made bars of acacia wood, five for the frames of one side of the tabernacle, 32 and five bars for the frames of the other side of the tabernacle, and five bars for the frames of the tabernacle at the rear westward. 33 He made the middle bar to pass through from end to end half-way up the frames. 34 And he overlaid the frames with gold, and made rings of gold for them to hold the bars, and overlaid the bars with gold.

35 He made the curtain of blue, purple, and crimson yarns, and fine twisted linen, with cherubim skilfully worked into it. 36 For it he made four pillars of acacia, and overlaid them with gold; their hooks were of gold, and he cast for them four bases of silver. 37 He also made a screen for the entrance to the tent, of blue, purple, and crimson yarns, and fine twisted linen, embroidered with needlework; 38 and its five pillars with their hooks. He overlaid their capitals and their bases with gold, but their five bases were of bronze.

Making the Ark of the Covenant

37 Bezalel made the ark of acacia wood; it was two and a half cubits long, a cubit and a half wide, and a cubit and a half high. 2 He overlaid it with pure gold inside and outside, and made a moulding of gold round it. 3 He cast for it four rings of gold for its four feet, two rings on one side of it and two rings on its other side. 4 He made poles of acacia wood, and overlaid them with gold, 5 and put the poles into the rings on the sides of the ark, to carry the ark. 6 He made a mercy-seat a of pure gold; two cubits and a half was its length, and a cubit and a half its width. 7 He made two cherubim of hammered gold; at the two ends of the mercy-seat b he made them, 8 one cherub at one end, and one cherub at the other end; of one piece with the mercy-seat b he made the cherubim at its two ends. 9 The cherubim spread out their wings above, overshadowing the mercy-seat b with their wings. They faced one another; the faces of the cherubim were turned towards the mercy-seat. b

Making the Table for the Bread of the Presence

10 He also made the table of acacia wood, two cubits long, one cubit wide, and a cubit and a half high. 11 He overlaid it with pure gold, and made a moulding of gold round it. 12 He made around it a rim a handbreadth wide, and made a moulding of gold round the rim. 13 He cast for it four rings of gold, and fastened the rings to the four corners at its four legs. 14 The rings that held the poles used for carrying the table were close to the rim. 15 He made the poles of acacia wood to carry the table, and overlaid them with gold. 16 And he made the vessels of pure gold that were to be on the table, its plates and dishes for incense, and its bowls and flagons with which to pour drink-offerings.

Making the Lampstand

17 He also made the lampstand of pure gold. The base and the shaft of the lampstand were made of hammered work; its

a Or a cover   b Or the cover

cups, its calyxes, and its petals were of one piece with it. ¹⁸ There were six branches going out of its sides, three branches of the lampstand out of one side of it and three branches of the lampstand out of the other side of it; ¹⁹ three cups shaped like almond blossoms, each with calyx and petals, on one branch, and three cups shaped like almond blossoms, each with calyx and petals, on the other branch—so for the six branches going out of the lampstand. ²⁰ On the lampstand itself there were four cups shaped like almond blossoms, each with its calyxes and petals. ²¹ There was a calyx of one piece with it under the first pair of branches, a calyx of one piece with it under the next pair of branches, and a calyx of one piece with it under the last pair of branches. ²² Their calyxes and their branches were of one piece with it, the whole of it one hammered piece of pure gold. ²³ He made its seven lamps and its snuffers and its trays of pure gold. ²⁴ He made it and all its utensils of a talent of pure gold.

Making the Altar of Incense

25 He made the altar of incense of acacia wood, one cubit long, and one cubit wide; it was square, and was two cubits high; its horns were of one piece with it. ²⁶ He overlaid it with pure gold, its top, and its sides all round, and its horns; and he made for it a moulding of gold all round, ²⁷ and made two golden rings for it under its moulding, on two opposite sides of it, to hold the poles with which to carry it. ²⁸ And he made the poles of acacia wood, and overlaid them with gold.

Making the Anointing-Oil and the Incense

29 He made the holy anointing-oil also, and the pure fragrant incense, blended as by the perfumer.

Making the Altar of Burnt-Offering

38 He made the altar of burnt-offering also of acacia wood; it was five cubits long, and five cubits wide; it was square, and three cubits high. ² He made horns for it on its four corners; its horns were of one piece with it, and he overlaid it with bronze. ³ He made all the utensils of the altar, the pots, the shovels, the basins, the forks, and the firepans: all its utensils he made of bronze. ⁴ He made for the altar a grating, a network of bronze, under its ledge, extending half-way down. ⁵ He cast four rings on the four corners of the bronze grating to hold the poles; ⁶ he made the poles of acacia wood, and overlaid them with bronze. ⁷ And he put the poles through the rings on the sides of the altar, to carry it with them; he made it hollow, with boards.

8 He made the basin of bronze, with its stand of bronze, from the mirrors of the women who served at the entrance to the tent of meeting.

Making the Court of the Tabernacle

9 He made the court; for the south side the hangings of the court were of fine twisted linen, one hundred cubits long; ¹⁰ its twenty pillars and their twenty bases were of bronze, but the hooks of the pillars and their bands were of silver. ¹¹ For the north side there were hangings one hundred cubits long; its twenty pillars and their twenty bases were of bronze, but the hooks of the pillars and their bands were of silver. ¹² For the west side there were hangings fifty cubits long, with ten pillars and ten bases; the hooks of the pillars and their bands were of silver. ¹³ And for the front to the east, fifty cubits. ¹⁴ The hangings for one side of the gate were fifteen cubits, with three pillars and three bases. ¹⁵ And so for the other side; on each side of the gate of the court were hangings of fifteen cubits, with three pillars and three bases. ¹⁶ All the hangings around the court were of fine twisted linen. ¹⁷ The bases for the pillars were of bronze, but the hooks of the pillars and their bands were of silver; the overlaying of their capitals was also of silver, and all the pillars of the court were banded with silver. ¹⁸ The screen for the entrance to the court was embroidered with needlework in blue, purple, and crimson yarns and fine

a Or *treaty*, or *testimony*; Heb *eduth*

twisted linen. It was twenty cubits long and, along the width of it, five cubits high, corresponding to the hangings of the court. ¹⁹There were four pillars; their four bases were of bronze, their hooks of silver, and the overlaying of their capitals and their bands of silver. ²⁰All the pegs for the tabernacle and for the court all around were of bronze.

Materials of the Tabernacle

21 These are the records of the tabernacle, the tabernacle of the covenant, ᵃ which were drawn up at the commandment of Moses, the work of the Levites being under the direction of Ithamar son of the priest Aaron. ²²Bezalel son of Uri son of Hur, of the tribe of Judah, made all that the LORD commanded Moses; ²³and with him was Oholiab son of Ahisamach, of the tribe of Dan, engraver, designer, and embroiderer in blue, purple, and crimson yarns, and in fine linen.

24 All the gold that was used for the work, in all the construction of the sanctuary, the gold from the offering, was twenty-nine talents and seven hundred and thirty shekels, measured by the sanctuary shekel. ²⁵The silver from those of the congregation who were counted was one hundred talents and one thousand seven hundred and seventy-five shekels, measured by the sanctuary shekel; ²⁶a beka a head (that is, half a shekel, measured by the sanctuary shekel), for everyone who was counted in the census, from twenty years old and upwards, for six hundred and three thousand, five hundred and fifty men. ²⁷The hundred talents of silver were for casting the bases of the sanctuary and the bases of the curtain: one hundred bases for the hundred talents, a talent for a base. ²⁸Of the one thousand seven hundred and seventy-five shekels he made hooks for the pillars, and overlaid their capitals and made bands for them. ²⁹The bronze that was contributed was seventy talents and two thousand four hundred shekels; ³⁰with it he made the bases for the entrance of the tent of meeting, the bronze altar and the bronze grating for it and all the utensils of the altar, ³¹the bases

all around the court, and the bases of the gate of the court, all the pegs of the tabernacle, and all the pegs around the court.

Making the Vestments for the Priesthood

39 Of the blue, purple, and crimson yarns they made finely worked vestments, for ministering in the holy place; they made the sacred vestments for Aaron; as the LORD had commanded Moses.

2 He made the ephod of gold, of blue, purple, and crimson yarns, and of fine twisted linen. ³Gold leaf was hammered out and cut into threads to work into the blue, purple, and crimson yarns and into the fine twisted linen, in skilled design. ⁴They made for the ephod shoulder-pieces, joined to it at its two edges. ⁵The decorated band on it was of the same materials and workmanship, of gold, of blue, purple, and crimson yarns, and of fine twisted linen; as the LORD had commanded Moses.

6 The onyx stones were prepared, enclosed in settings of gold filigree and engraved like the engravings of a signet, according to the names of the sons of Israel. ⁷He set them on the shoulder-pieces of the ephod, to be stones of remembrance for the sons of Israel; as the LORD had commanded Moses.

8 He made the breastpiece, in skilled work, like the work of the ephod, of gold, of blue, purple, and crimson yarns, and of fine twisted linen. ⁹It was square; the breastpiece was made double, a span in length and a span in width when doubled. ¹⁰They set in it four rows of stones. A row of carnelian, ᵇ chrysolite, and emerald was the first row; ¹¹and the second row, a turquoise, a sapphire, ᶜ and a moonstone; ¹²and the third row, a jacinth, an agate, and an amethyst; ¹³and the fourth row, a beryl, an onyx, and a jasper; they were enclosed in settings of gold filigree. ¹⁴There were twelve stones with names corresponding to the names of the sons of Israel; they were like signets, each engraved with its name, for the twelve tribes. ¹⁵They made on the

ᵃ Or treaty, or testimony; Heb eduth
ᵇ The identification of several of these stones is uncertain   ᶜ Or lapis lazuli

breastpiece chains of pure gold, twisted like cords; 16 and they made two settings of gold filigree and two gold rings, and put the two rings on the two edges of the breastpiece; 17 and they put the two cords of gold in the two rings at the edges of the breastpiece. 18 Two ends of the two cords they had attached to the two settings of filigree; in this way they attached it in front to the shoulder-pieces of the ephod. 19 Then they made two rings of gold, and put them at the two ends of the breastpiece, on its inside edge next to the ephod. 20 They made two rings of gold, and attached them in front to the lower part of the two shoulder-pieces of the ephod, at its joining above the decorated band of the ephod. 21 They bound the breastpiece by its rings to the rings of the ephod with a blue cord, so that it should lie on the decorated band of the ephod, and that the breastpiece should not come loose from the ephod; as the LORD had commanded Moses.

22 He also made the robe of the ephod woven all of blue yarn; 23 and the opening of the robe in the middle of it was like the opening in a coat of mail, a with a binding round the opening, so that it might not be torn. 24 On the lower hem of the robe they made pomegranates of blue, purple, and crimson yarns, and of fine twisted linen. 25 They also made bells of pure gold, and put the bells between the pomegranates on the lower hem of the robe all round, between the pomegranates; 26 a bell and a pomegranate, a bell and a pomegranate all round on the lower hem of the robe for ministering; as the LORD had commanded Moses.

27 They also made the tunics, woven of fine linen, for Aaron and his sons, 28 and the turban of fine linen, and the headdresses of fine linen, and the linen undergarments of fine twisted linen, 29 and the sash of fine twisted linen, and of blue, purple, and crimson yarns, embroidered with needlework; as the LORD had commanded Moses.

30 They made the rosette of the holy diadem of pure gold, and wrote on it an inscription, like the engraving of a signet,

'Holy to the LORD.' 31 They tied to it a blue cord, to fasten it on the turban above; as the LORD had commanded Moses.

The Work Completed

32 In this way all the work of the tabernacle of the tent of meeting was finished; the Israelites had done everything just as the LORD had commanded Moses. 33 Then they brought the tabernacle to Moses, the tent and all its utensils, its hooks, its frames, its bars, its pillars, and its bases; 34 the covering of tanned rams' skins and the covering of fine leather, a and the curtain for the screen; 35 the ark of the covenant b with its poles and the mercy-seat; c 36 the table with all its utensils, and the bread of the Presence; 37 the pure lampstand with its lamps set on it and all its utensils, and the oil for the light; 38 the golden altar, the anointing-oil and the fragrant incense, and the screen for the entrance of the tent; 39 the bronze altar, and its grating of bronze, its poles, and all its utensils; the basin with its stand; 40 the hangings of the court, its pillars, and its bases, and the screen for the gate of the court, its cords, and its pegs; and all the utensils for the service of the tabernacle, for the tent of meeting; 41 the finely worked vestments for ministering in the holy place, the sacred vestments for the priest Aaron, and the vestments of his sons to serve as priests. 42 The Israelites had done all of the work just as the LORD had commanded Moses. 43 When Moses saw that they had done all the work just as the LORD had commanded, he blessed them.

The Tabernacle Erected and Its Equipment Installed

40 The LORD spoke to Moses: 2 On the first day of the first month you shall set up the tabernacle of the tent of meeting. 3 You shall put in it the ark of the covenant, b and you shall screen the ark with the curtain. 4 You shall bring in the table, and arrange its setting; and you shall bring in the lampstand, and set up its lamps. 5 You shall put the golden altar for

a Meaning of Heb uncertain   b Or treaty, or testimony; Heb eduth   c Or the cover incense before the ark of the covenant, [a] and set up the screen for the entrance of the tabernacle. [6] You shall set the altar of burnt-offering before the entrance of the tabernacle of the tent of meeting, [7] and place the basin between the tent of meeting and the altar, and put water in it. [8] You shall set up the court all around, and hang up the screen for the gate of the court. [9] Then you shall take the anointing-oil, and anoint the tabernacle and all that is in it, and consecrate it and all its furniture, so that it shall become holy. [10] You shall also anoint the altar of burnt-offering and all its utensils, and consecrate the altar, so that the altar shall be most holy. [11] You shall also anoint the basin with its stand, and consecrate it. [12] Then you shall bring Aaron and his sons to the entrance of the tent of meeting, and shall wash them with water, [13] and put on Aaron the sacred vestments, and you shall anoint him and consecrate him, so that he may serve me as priest. [14] You shall bring his sons also and put tunics on them, [15] and anoint them, as you anointed their father, that they may serve me as priests: and their anointing shall admit them to a perpetual priesthood throughout all generations to come.

16 Moses did everything just as the LORD had commanded him. [17] In the first month in the second year, on the first day of the month, the tabernacle was set up. [18] Moses set up the tabernacle; he laid its bases, and set up its frames, and put in its poles, and raised up its pillars; [19] and he spread the tent over the tabernacle, and put the covering of the tent over it; as the LORD had commanded Moses. [20] He took the covenant [a] and put it into the ark, and put the poles on the ark, and set the mercy-seat [b] above the ark; [21] and he brought the ark into the tabernacle, and set up the curtain for screening, and screened the ark of the covenant; [a] as the LORD had commanded Moses. [22] He put the table in the tent of meeting, on the north side of the tabernacle, outside the curtain, [23] and set the bread in order on it before the LORD; as the LORD had commanded Moses. [24] He put the lampstand in the tent of meeting, opposite the table on the south side of the tabernacle, [25] and set up the lamps before the LORD; as the LORD had commanded Moses. [26] He put the golden altar in the tent of meeting before the curtain, [27] and offered fragrant incense on it; as the LORD had commanded Moses. [28] He also put in place the screen for the entrance of the tabernacle. [29] He set the altar of burnt-offering at the entrance of the tabernacle of the tent of meeting, and offered on it the burnt-offering and the grain-offering as the LORD had commanded Moses. [30] He set the basin between the tent of meeting and the altar, and put water in it for washing, [31] with which Moses and Aaron and his sons washed their hands and their feet. [32] When they went into the tent of meeting, and when they approached the altar, they washed; as the LORD had commanded Moses. [33] He set up the court around the tabernacle and the altar, and put up the screen at the gate of the court. So Moses finished the work.

The Cloud and the Glory

34 Then the cloud covered the tent of meeting, and the glory of the LORD filled the tabernacle. [35] Moses was not able to enter the tent of meeting because the cloud settled upon it, and the glory of the LORD filled the tabernacle. [36] Whenever the cloud was taken up from the tabernacle, the Israelites would set out on each stage of their journey; [37] but if the cloud was not taken up, then they did not set out until the day that it was taken up. [38] For the cloud of the LORD was on the tabernacle by day, and fire was in the cloud [c] by night, before the eyes of all the house of Israel at each stage of their journey.

a Or treaty, or testimony; Heb eduth   b Or the cover.
c Heb it

LEVITICUS

The Burnt-Offering

1 The LORD summoned Moses and spoke to him from the tent of meeting, saying: 2 Speak to the people of Israel and say to them: When any of you bring an offering of livestock to the LORD, you shall bring your offering from the herd or from the flock.

3 If the offering is a burnt-offering from the herd, you shall offer a male without blemish; you shall bring it to the entrance of the tent of meeting, for acceptance in your behalf before the LORD. 4 You shall lay your hand on the head of the burnt-offering, and it shall be acceptable in your behalf as atonement for you. 5 The bull shall be slaughtered before the LORD; and Aaron's sons the priests shall offer the blood, dashing the blood against all sides of the altar that is at the entrance of the tent of meeting. 6 The burnt-offering shall be flayed and cut up into its parts. 7 The sons of the priest Aaron shall put fire on the altar and arrange wood on the fire. 8 Aaron's sons the priests shall arrange the parts, with the head and the suet, on the wood that is on the fire on the altar; 9 but its entrails and its legs shall be washed with water. Then the priest shall turn the whole into smoke on the altar as a burnt-offering, an offering by fire of pleasing odour to the LORD.

10 If your gift for a burnt-offering is from the flock, from the sheep or goats, your offering shall be a male without blemish. 11 It shall be slaughtered on the north side of the altar before the LORD, and Aaron's sons the priests shall dash its blood against all sides of the altar. 12 It shall be cut up into its parts, with its head and its suet, and the priest shall arrange them on the wood that is on the fire on the altar; 13 but the entrails and the legs shall be washed with water. Then the priest shall offer the whole and turn it into smoke on the altar; it is a burnt-offering, an offering by fire of pleasing odour to the LORD.

14 If your offering to the LORD is a burnt-offering of birds, you shall choose your offering from turtle-doves or pigeons. 15 The priest shall bring it to the altar and wring off its head, and turn it into smoke on the altar; and its blood shall be drained out against the side of the altar. 16 He shall remove its crop with its contents*a* and throw it at the east side of the altar, in the place for ashes. 17 He shall tear it open by its wings without severing it. Then the priest shall turn it into smoke on the altar, on the wood that is on the fire; it is a burnt-offering, an offering by fire of pleasing odour to the LORD.

Grain-Offerings

2 When anyone presents a grain-offering to the LORD, the offering shall be of choice flour; the worshipper shall pour oil on it, and put frankincense on it, 2 and bring it to Aaron's sons the priests. After taking from it a handful of the choice flour and oil, with all its frankincense, the priest shall turn this token portion into smoke on the altar, an offering by fire of pleasing odour to the LORD. 3 And what is left of the grain-offering shall be for Aaron and his sons, a most holy part of the offerings by fire to the LORD.

4 When you present a grain-offering

a Meaning of Heb uncertain

baked in the oven, it shall be of choice flour: unleavened cakes mixed with oil, or unleavened wafers spread with oil. ⁵If your offering is grain prepared on a griddle, it shall be of choice flour mixed with oil, unleavened; ⁶break it in pieces, and pour oil on it; it is a grain-offering. ⁷If your offering is grain prepared in a pan, it shall be made of choice flour in oil. ⁸You shall bring to the LORD the grain-offering that is prepared in any of these ways; and when it is presented to the priest, he shall take it to the altar. ⁹The priest shall remove from the grain-offering its token portion and turn this into smoke on the altar, an offering by fire of pleasing odour to the LORD. ¹⁰And what is left of the grain-offering shall be for Aaron and his sons; it is a most holy part of the offerings by fire to the LORD.

11 No grain-offering that you bring to the LORD shall be made with leaven, for you must not turn any leaven or honey into smoke as an offering by fire to the LORD. ¹²You may bring them to the LORD as an offering of choice products, but they shall not be offered on the altar for a pleasing odour. ¹³You shall not omit from your grain-offerings the salt of the covenant with your God; with all your offerings you shall offer salt.

14 If you bring a grain-offering of first fruits to the LORD, you shall bring as the grain-offering of your first fruits coarse new grain from fresh ears, parched with fire. ¹⁵You shall add oil to it and lay frankincense on it; it is a grain-offering. ¹⁶And the priest shall turn a token portion of it into smoke—some of the coarse grain and oil with all its frankincense; it is an offering by fire to the LORD.

Offerings of Well-Being

3 If the offering is a sacrifice of well-being, if you offer an animal of the herd, whether male or female, you shall offer one without blemish before the LORD. ²You shall lay your hand on the head of the offering and slaughter it at the entrance of the tent of meeting; and Aaron's sons the priests shall dash the blood against all sides of the altar. ³You shall offer from the sacrifice of well-being, as an offering by fire to the LORD, the fat that covers the entrails and all the fat that is around the entrails; ⁴the two kidneys with the fat that is on them at the loins, and the appendage of the liver, which he shall remove with the kidneys. ⁵Then Aaron's sons shall turn these into smoke on the altar, with the burnt-offering that is on the wood on the fire, as an offering by fire of pleasing odour to the LORD.

6 If your offering for a sacrifice of well-being to the LORD is from the flock, male or female, you shall offer one without blemish. ⁷If you present a sheep as your offering, you shall bring it before the LORD ⁸and lay your hand on the head of the offering. It shall be slaughtered before the tent of meeting, and Aaron's sons shall dash its blood against all sides of the altar. ⁹You shall present its fat from the sacrifice of well-being, as an offering by fire to the LORD: the whole broad tail, which shall be removed close to the backbone, the fat that covers the entrails, and all the fat that is around the entrails; ¹⁰the two kidneys with the fat that is on them at the loins, and the appendage of the liver, which you shall remove with the kidneys. ¹¹Then the priest shall turn these into smoke on the altar as a food-offering by fire to the LORD.

12 If your offering is a goat, you shall bring it before the LORD ¹³and lay your hand on its head; it shall be slaughtered before the tent of meeting; and the sons of Aaron shall dash its blood against all sides of the altar. ¹⁴You shall present as your offering from it, as an offering by fire to the LORD, the fat that covers the entrails, and all the fat that is around the entrails; ¹⁵the two kidneys with the fat that is on them at the loins, and the appendage of the liver, which you shall remove with the kidneys. ¹⁶Then the priest shall turn these into smoke on the altar as a food-offering by fire for a pleasing odour.

All fat is the LORD's. ¹⁷It shall be a perpetual statute throughout your generations, in all your settlements: you must not eat any fat or any blood.

Sin-Offerings

4 The LORD spoke to Moses, saying, 2 Speak to the people of Israel, saying: When anyone sins unintentionally in any of the LORD's commandments about things not to be done, and does any one of them: 3 If it is the anointed priest who sins, thus bringing guilt on the people, he shall offer for the sin that he has committed a bull of the herd without blemish as a sin-offering to the LORD. 4 He shall bring the bull to the entrance of the tent of meeting before the LORD and lay his hand on the head of the bull; the bull shall be slaughtered before the LORD. 5 The anointed priest shall take some of the blood of the bull and bring it into the tent of meeting. 6 The priest shall dip his finger in the blood and sprinkle some of the blood seven times before the LORD in front of the curtain of the sanctuary. 7 The priest shall put some of the blood on the horns of the altar of fragrant incense that is in the tent of meeting before the LORD; and the rest of the blood of the bull he shall pour out at the base of the al-tar of burnt-offering, which is at the entrance of the tent of meeting. 8 He shall remove all the fat from the bull of sin-offering: the fat that covers the entrails and all the fat that is around the entrails; 9 the two kidneys with the fat that is on them at the loins; and the appendage of the liver, which he shall remove with the kidneys, 10 just as these are removed from the ox of the sacrifice of well-being. The priest shall turn them into smoke upon the altar of burnt-offering. 11 But the skin of the bull and all its flesh, as well as its head, its legs, its entrails, and its dung— 12 all the rest of the bull—he shall carry out to a clean place outside the camp, to the ash heap, and shall burn it on a wood fire; at the ash heap it shall be burned.

13 If the whole congregation of Israel errs unintentionally and the matter escapes the notice of the assembly, and they do any one of the things that by the LORD's commandments ought not to be done, and incur guilt; 14 when the sin that they have committed becomes known, the assembly

The Sacrifices of the Old Testament		
Type of Sacrifice		
What (elements)	Why (function)	Where (citation)
Whole burnt-offering		
Male and unblemished cattle, sheep and goats, birds (pigeons for the poor)	Wholly consumed, acknowledging God as Lord of life: atoned for sins; joyful worship	Lev 1.1–17; 6.8–13; 8.18–21; 22.17
Grain-offering		
Grain, flour, frankincense, oil, bread. Only the symbolic portion burned, the rest eaten by priests	Substitute for expensive animal offering; thanksgiving for good crops; joyful worship	Lev 2.1–16; 6.14–23
Sacrifice of well-being		
Any unblemished animal—male or female (cattle or sheep and goats, but not birds since too small for a group to eat)	Not burned up, but eaten by offerers and families. Only fat parts (considered choicest) were burned to God	Lev 3.1–17; 7.11–34
Sin-offering		
If offender were whole people or priest: bull; ordinary person: goat; poor: bird or some fine flour.	To atone for usually unintentional sin (violating something sacred)	Lev 4.1–5,13; 6.24–30
Blood sprinked on altar in outer courtyard if lay offender; in holy interior if priest or whole people offended	To atone for loss of holiness To cleanse from impurity	
Guilt-offering		
A ram sheep (its blood sprinkled on altar). The original wrong must be undone, then additional compensation must be offered to God	Sin-offering cleansed the defiled object or person; guilt-offering was a "pay-back" to God for something that should have been given or done—atonement to remove guilt	Lev 5.14–26; 7.1–6

shall offer a bull of the herd for a sin-offering and bring it before the tent of meeting. ¹⁵ The elders of the congregation shall lay their hands on the head of the bull before the LORD, and the bull shall be slaughtered before the LORD. ¹⁶ The anointed priest shall bring some of the blood of the bull into the tent of meeting, ¹⁷ and the priest shall dip his finger in the blood and sprinkle it seven times before the LORD, in front of the curtain. ¹⁸ He shall put some of the blood on the horns of the altar that is before the LORD in the tent of meeting; and the rest of the blood he shall pour out at the base of the altar of burnt-offering that is at the entrance of the tent of meeting. ¹⁹ He shall remove all its fat and turn it into smoke on the altar. ²⁰ He shall do with the bull just as is done with the bull of sin-offering; he shall do the same with this. The priest shall make atonement for them, and they shall be forgiven. ²¹ He shall carry the bull outside the camp, and burn it as he burned the first bull; it is the sin-offering for the assembly.

22 When a ruler sins, doing unintentionally any one of all the things that by commandments of the LORD his God ought not to be done, and incurs guilt, ²³ once the sin that he has committed is made known to him, he shall bring as his offering a male goat without blemish. ²⁴ He shall lay his hand on the head of the goat; it shall be slaughtered at the spot where the burnt-offering is slaughtered before the LORD; it is a sin-offering. ²⁵ The priest shall take some of the blood of the sin-offering with his finger and put it on the horns of the altar of burnt-offering, and pour out the rest of its blood at the base of the altar of burnt-offering. ²⁶ All its fat he shall turn into smoke on the altar, like the fat of the sacrifice of well-being. Thus the priest shall make atonement on his behalf for his sin, and he shall be forgiven.

27 If anyone of the ordinary people among you sins unintentionally in doing any one of the things that by the LORD's commandments ought not to be done, and incurs guilt, ²⁸ when the sin that you have committed is made known to you, you shall bring a female goat without blemish

as your offering, for the sin that you have committed. ²⁹ You shall lay your hand on the head of the sin-offering; and the sin-offering shall be slaughtered at the place of the burnt-offering. ³⁰ The priest shall take some of its blood with his finger and put it on the horns of the altar of burnt-offering, and he shall pour out the rest of its blood at the base of the altar. ³¹ He shall remove all its fat, as the fat is removed from the offering of well-being, and the priest shall turn it into smoke on the altar for a pleasing odour to the LORD. Thus the priest shall make atonement on your behalf, and you shall be forgiven.

32 If the offering you bring as a sin-offering is a sheep, you shall bring a female without blemish. ³³ You shall lay your hand on the head of the sin-offering; and it shall be slaughtered as a sin-offering at the spot where the burnt-offering is slaughtered. ³⁴ The priest shall take some of the blood of the sin-offering with his finger and put it on the horns of the altar of burnt-offering, and pour out the rest of its blood at the base of the altar. ³⁵ You shall remove all its fat, as the fat of the sheep is removed from the sacrifice of well-being, and the priest shall turn it into smoke on the altar, with the offerings by fire to the LORD. Thus the priest shall make atonement on your behalf for the sin that you have committed, and you shall be forgiven.

5 When any of you sin in that you have heard a public adjuration to testify and—though able to testify as one who has seen or learned of the matter—do not speak up, you are subject to punishment. ² Or when any of you touch any unclean thing—whether the carcass of an unclean beast or the carcass of unclean livestock or the carcass of an unclean swarming thing—and are unaware of it, you have become unclean, and are guilty. ³ Or when you touch human uncleanness—any uncleanness by which one can become unclean—and are unaware of it, when you come to know it, you shall be guilty. ⁴ Or when any of you utter aloud a rash oath for a bad or a good purpose, whatever people utter in an oath, and are unaware of it, when you come to

know it, you shall in any of these be guilty. 5 When you realize your guilt in any of these, you shall confess the sin that you have committed. 6 And you shall bring to the LORD, as your penalty for the sin that you have committed, a female from the flock, a sheep or a goat, as a sin-offering; and the priest shall make atonement on your behalf for your sin.

7 But if you cannot afford a sheep, you shall bring to the LORD, as your penalty for the sin that you have committed, two turtle-doves or two pigeons, one for a sin-offering and the other for a burnt-offering. 8 You shall bring them to the priest, who shall offer first the one for the sin-offering, wringing its head at the nape without severing it. 9 He shall sprinkle some of the blood of the sin-offering on the side of the altar, while the rest of the blood shall be drained out at the base of the altar; it is a sin-offering. 10 And the second he shall offer for a burnt-offering according to the regulation. Thus the priest shall make atonement on your behalf for the sin that you have committed, and you shall be forgiven.

11 But if you cannot afford two turtle-doves or two pigeons, you shall bring as your offering for the sin that you have committed one-tenth of an ephah of choice flour for a sin-offering; you shall not put oil on it or lay frankincense on it, for it is a sin-offering. 12 You shall bring it to the priest, and the priest shall scoop up a handful of it as its memorial portion, and turn this into smoke on the altar, with the offerings by fire to the LORD; it is a sin-offering. 13 Thus the priest shall make atonement on your behalf for whichever of these sins you have committed, and you shall be forgiven. Like the grain-offering, the rest shall be for the priest.

Offerings with Restitution

14 The LORD spoke to Moses, saying: 15 When any of you commit a trespass and sin unintentionally in any of the holy things of the LORD, you shall bring, as your guilt-offering to the LORD, a ram without blemish from the flock, convertible into silver by the sanctuary shekel; it is a guilt-of-

fering. 16 And you shall make restitution for the holy thing in which you were remiss, and shall add one-fifth to it and give it to the priest. The priest shall make atonement on your behalf with the ram of the guilt-offering, and you shall be forgiven.

17 If any of you sin without knowing it, doing any of the things that by the LORD's commandments ought not to be done, you have incurred guilt, and are subject to punishment. 18 You shall bring to the priest a ram without blemish from the flock, or the equivalent, as a guilt-offering; and the priest shall make atonement on your behalf for the error that you committed unintentionally, and you shall be forgiven. 19 It is a guilt-offering; you have incurred guilt before the LORD.

6 *a* The LORD spoke to Moses, saying: 2 When any of you sin and commit a trespass against the LORD by deceiving a neighbour in a matter of a deposit or a pledge, or by robbery, or if you have defrauded a neighbour, 3 or have found something lost and lied about it—if you swear falsely regarding any of the various things that one may do and sin thereby— 4 when you have sinned and realize your guilt, and would restore what you took by robbery or by fraud or the deposit that was committed to you, or the lost thing that you found, 5 or anything else about which you have sworn falsely, you shall repay the principal amount and shall add one-fifth to it. You shall pay it to its owner when you realize your guilt. 6 And you shall bring to the priest, as your guilt-offering to the LORD, a ram without blemish from the flock, or its equivalent, for a guilt-offering. 7 The priest shall make atonement on your behalf before the LORD, and you shall be forgiven for any of the things that one may do and incur guilt thereby.

Instructions concerning Sacrifices

8 *b* The LORD spoke to Moses, saying: 9 Command Aaron and his sons, saying: This is the ritual of the burnt-offering. The burnt-offering itself shall remain on the hearth upon the altar all night until the

a Ch 5.20 in Heb   *b* Ch 6.1 in Heb

morning, while the fire on the altar shall be kept burning. ¹⁰The priest shall put on his linen vestments after putting on his linen undergarments next to his body; and he shall take up the ashes to which the fire has reduced the burnt-offering on the altar, and place them beside the altar. ¹¹Then he shall take off his vestments and put on other garments, and carry the ashes out to a clean place outside the camp. ¹²The fire on the altar shall be kept burning; it shall not go out. Every morning the priest shall add wood to it, lay out the burnt-offering on it, and turn into smoke the fat pieces of the offerings of well-being. ¹³A perpetual fire shall be kept burning on the altar; it shall not go out.

14 This is the ritual of the grain-offering: The sons of Aaron shall offer it before the LORD, in front of the altar. ¹⁵They shall take from it a handful of the choice flour and oil of the grain-offering, with all the frankincense that is on the offering, and they shall turn its memorial portion into smoke on the altar as a pleasing odour to the LORD. ¹⁶Aaron and his sons shall eat what is left of it; it shall be eaten as unleavened cakes in a holy place; in the court of the tent of meeting they shall eat it. ¹⁷It shall not be baked with leaven. I have given it as their portion of my offerings by fire; it is most holy, like the sin-offering and the guilt-offering. ¹⁸Every male among the descendants of Aaron shall eat of it, as their perpetual due throughout your generations, from the LORD's offerings by fire; anything that touches them shall become holy.

19 The LORD spoke to Moses, saying: ²⁰This is the offering that Aaron and his sons shall offer to the LORD on the day when he is anointed: one-tenth of an ephah of choice flour as a regular offering, half of it in the morning and half in the evening. ²¹It shall be made with oil on a griddle; you shall bring it well soaked, as a grain-offering of baked*a* pieces, and you shall present it as a pleasing odour to the LORD. ²²And so the priest, anointed from among Aaron's descendants as a successor, shall prepare it; it is the LORD's—a perpetual due—to be turned entirely into smoke. ²³Every grain-offering of a priest shall be wholly burned; it shall not be eaten.

24 The LORD spoke to Moses, saying: ²⁵Speak to Aaron and his sons, saying: This is the ritual of the sin-offering. The sin-offering shall be slaughtered before the LORD at the spot where the burnt-offering is slaughtered; it is most holy. ²⁶The priest who offers it as a sin-offering shall eat of it; it shall be eaten in a holy place, in the court of the tent of meeting. ²⁷Whatever touches its flesh shall become holy; and when any of its blood is spattered on a garment, you shall wash the bespattered part in a holy place. ²⁸An earthen vessel in which it was boiled shall be broken; but if it is boiled in a bronze vessel, that shall be scoured and rinsed in water. ²⁹Every male among the priests shall eat of it; it is most holy. ³⁰But no sin-offering shall be eaten from which any blood is brought into the tent of meeting for atonement in the holy place; it shall be burned with fire.

7 This is the ritual of the guilt-offering. It is most holy; ²at the spot where the burnt-offering is slaughtered, they shall slaughter the guilt-offering, and its blood shall be dashed against all sides of the altar. ³All its fat shall be offered: the broad tail, the fat that covers the entrails, ⁴the two kidneys with the fat that is on them at the loins, and the appendage of the liver, which shall be removed with the kidneys; ⁵The priest shall turn them into smoke on the altar as an offering by fire to the LORD; it is a guilt-offering. ⁶Every male among the priests shall eat of it; it shall be eaten in a holy place; it is most holy.

7 The guilt-offering is like the sin-offering, there is the same ritual for them; the priest who makes atonement with it shall have it. ⁸So, too, the priest who offers anyone's burnt-offering shall keep the skin of the burnt-offering that he has offered. ⁹And every grain-offering baked in the oven, and all that is prepared in a pan or on a griddle, shall belong to the priest who offers it. ¹⁰But every other grain-offering, mixed with oil or dry, shall belong to all the sons of Aaron equally.

a Meaning of Heb uncertain

Further Instructions

11 This is the ritual of the sacrifice of the offering of well-being that one may offer to the LORD. [12] If you offer it for thanksgiving, you shall offer with the thank-offering unleavened cakes mixed with oil, unleavened wafers spread with oil, and cakes of choice flour well soaked in oil. [13] With your thanksgiving sacrifice of well-being you shall bring your offering with cakes of leavened bread. [14] From this you shall offer one cake from each offering, as a gift to the LORD; it shall belong to the priest who dashes the blood of the offering of well-being. [15] And the flesh of your thanksgiving sacrifice of well-being shall be eaten on the day it is offered; you shall not leave any of it until morning. [16] But if the sacrifice you offer is a votive offering or a freewill-offering, it shall be eaten on the day that you offer your sacrifice, and what is left of it shall be eaten the next day; [17] but what is left of the flesh of the sacrifice shall be burned on the third day. [18] If any of the flesh of your sacrifice of well-being is eaten on the third day, it shall not be acceptable, nor shall it be credited to the one who offers it; it shall be an abomination, and the one who eats of it shall incur guilt.

19 Flesh that touches any unclean thing shall not be eaten; it shall be burned. As for other flesh, all who are clean may eat such flesh. [20] But those who eat flesh from the LORD's sacrifice of well-being while in a state of uncleanness shall be cut off from their kin. [21] When any one of you touches any unclean thing—human uncleanness or an unclean animal or any unclean creature—and then eats flesh from the LORD's sacrifice of well-being, you shall be cut off from your kin.

22 The LORD spoke to Moses, saying: [23] Speak to the people of Israel, saying: You shall eat no fat of ox or sheep or goat. [24] The fat of an animal that died or was torn by wild animals may be put to any other use, except that you must not eat it. [25] If any one of you eats the fat from an animal of which an offering by fire may be made to the LORD, you who eat it shall be cut off from your kin. [26] You must not eat any blood whatever, either of bird or of animal, in any of your settlements. [27] Any one of you who eats any blood shall be cut off from your kin.

28 The LORD spoke to Moses, saying: [29] Speak to the people of Israel, saying: Any one of you who would offer to the LORD your sacrifice of well-being must yourself bring to the LORD your offering from your sacrifice of well-being. [30] Your own hands shall bring the LORD's offering by fire; you shall bring the fat with the breast, so that the breast may be raised as an elevation-offering before the LORD. [31] The priest shall turn the fat into smoke on the altar, but the breast shall belong to Aaron and his sons. [32] And the right thigh from your sacrifices of well-being you shall give to the priest as an offering; [33] the one among the sons of Aaron who offers the blood and fat of the offering of well-being shall have the right thigh for a portion. [34] For I have taken the breast of the elevation-offering, and the thigh that is offered, from the people of Israel, from their sacrifices of well-being, and have given them to Aaron the priest and to his sons, as a perpetual due from the people of Israel. [35] This is the portion allotted to Aaron and to his sons from the offerings made by fire to the LORD, once they have been brought forward to serve the LORD as priests; [36] these the LORD commanded to be given them, when he anointed them, as a perpetual due from the people of Israel throughout their generations.

37 This is the ritual of the burnt-offering, the grain-offering, the sin-offering, the guilt-offering, the offering of ordination, and the sacrifice of well-being, [38] which the LORD commanded Moses on Mount Sinai, when he commanded the people of Israel to bring their offerings to the LORD, in the wilderness of Sinai.

The Rites of Ordination

8 The LORD spoke to Moses, saying: [2] Take Aaron and his sons with him, the vestments, the anointing-oil, the bull of sin-offering, the two rams, and the basket of unleavened bread; [3] and assemble the whole congregation at the entrance of the tent of meeting. [4] And Moses did as the

LORD commanded him. When the congregation was assembled at the entrance of the tent of meeting, [5] Moses said to the congregation, 'This is what the LORD has commanded to be done.'

6 Then Moses brought Aaron and his sons forward, and washed them with water. [7] He put the tunic on him, fastened the sash around him, clothed him with the robe, and put the ephod on him. He then put the decorated band of the ephod around him, tying the ephod to him with it. [8] He placed the breastpiece on him, and in the breastpiece he put the Urim and the Thummim. [9] And he set the turban on his head, and on the turban, in front, he set the golden ornament, the holy crown, as the LORD commanded Moses.

10 Then Moses took the anointing-oil and anointed the tabernacle and all that was in it, and consecrated them. [11] He sprinkled some of it on the altar seven times, and anointed the altar and all its utensils, and the basin and its base, to consecrate them. [12] He poured some of the anointing-oil on Aaron's head and anointed him, to consecrate him. [13] And Moses brought forward Aaron's sons, and clothed them with tunics, and fastened sashes around them, and tied head-dresses on them, as the LORD commanded Moses.

14 He led forward the bull of sin-offering; and Aaron and his sons laid their hands upon the head of the bull of sin-offering, [15] and it was slaughtered. Moses took the blood and with his finger put some on each of the horns of the altar, purifying the altar; then he poured out the blood at the base of the altar. Thus he consecrated it, to make atonement for it. [16] Moses took all the fat that was around the entrails, and the appendage of the liver, and the two kidneys with their fat, and turned them into smoke on the altar. [17] But the bull itself, its skin and flesh and its dung, he burned with fire outside the camp, as the LORD commanded Moses.

18 Then he brought forward the ram of burnt-offering. Aaron and his sons laid their hands on the head of the ram, [19] and it was slaughtered. Moses dashed the blood against all sides of the altar. [20] The ram was cut into its parts, and Moses turned into smoke the head and the parts and the suet. [21] And after the entrails and the legs were washed with water, Moses turned into smoke the whole ram on the altar; it was a burnt-offering for a pleasing odour, an offering by fire to the LORD, as the LORD commanded Moses.

22 Then he brought forward the second ram, the ram of ordination. Aaron and his sons laid their hands on the head of the ram, [23] and it was slaughtered. Moses took some of its blood and put it on the lobe of Aaron's right ear and on the thumb of his right hand and on the big toe of his right foot. [24] After Aaron's sons were brought forward, Moses put some of the blood on the lobes of their right ears and on the thumbs of their right hands and on the big toes of their right feet; and Moses dashed the rest of the blood against all sides of the altar. [25] He took the fat—the broad tail, all the fat that was around the entrails, the appendage of the liver, and the two kidneys with their fat—and the right thigh. [26] From the basket of unleavened bread that was before the LORD, he took one cake of unleavened bread, one cake of bread with oil, and one wafer, and placed them on the fat and on the right thigh. [27] He placed all these on the palms of Aaron and on the palms of his sons, and raised them as an elevation-offering before the LORD. [28] Then Moses took them from their hands and turned them into smoke on the altar with the burnt-offering. This was an ordination-offering for a pleasing odour, an offering by fire to the LORD. [29] Moses took the breast and raised it as an elevation-offering before the LORD; it was Moses' portion of the ram of ordination, as the LORD commanded Moses.

30 Then Moses took some of the anointing-oil and some of the blood that was on the altar and sprinkled them on Aaron and his vestments, and also on his sons and their vestments. Thus he consecrated Aaron and his vestments, and also his sons and their vestments.

31 And Moses said to Aaron and his sons, 'Boil the flesh at the entrance of the tent of

meeting, and eat it there with the bread that is in the basket of ordination-offerings, as I was commanded, "Aaron and his sons shall eat it"; [32] and what remains of the flesh and the bread you shall burn with fire. [33] You shall not go outside the entrance of the tent of meeting for seven days, until the day when your period of ordination is completed. For it will take seven days to ordain you; [34] as has been done today, the LORD has commanded to be done to make atonement for you. [35] You shall remain at the entrance of the tent of meeting day and night for seven days, keeping the LORD's charge so that you do not die; for so I am commanded.' [36] Aaron and his sons did all the things that the LORD commanded through Moses.

Aaron's Priesthood Inaugurated

9 On the eighth day Moses summoned Aaron and his sons and the elders of Israel. [2] He said to Aaron, 'Take a bull calf for a sin-offering and a ram for a burnt-offering, without blemish, and offer them before the LORD. [3] And say to the people of Israel, "Take a male goat for a sin-offering; a calf and a lamb, yearlings without blemish, for a burnt-offering; [4] and an ox and a ram for an offering of well-being to sacrifice before the LORD; and a grain-offering mixed with oil. For today the LORD will appear to you." ' [5] They brought what Moses commanded to the front of the tent of meeting; and the whole congregation drew near and stood before the LORD. [6] And Moses said, 'This is the thing that the LORD commanded you to do, so that the glory of the LORD may appear to you.' [7] Then Moses said to Aaron, 'Draw near to the altar and sacrifice your sin-offering and your burnt-offering, and make atonement for yourself and for the people; and sacrifice the offering of the people, and make atonement for them; as the LORD has commanded.'

8 Aaron drew near to the altar, and slaughtered the calf of the sin-offering, which was for himself. [9] The sons of Aaron presented the blood to him, and he dipped his finger in the blood and put it on the horns of the altar; and the rest of the blood he poured out at the base of the altar. [10] But the fat, the kidneys, and the appendage of the liver from the sin-offering he turned into smoke on the altar, as the LORD commanded Moses; [11] and the flesh and the skin he burned with fire outside the camp.

12 Then he slaughtered the burnt-offering. Aaron's sons brought him the blood, and he dashed it against all sides of the altar. [13] And they brought him the burnt-offering piece by piece, and the head, which he turned into smoke on the altar. [14] He washed the entrails and the legs and, with the burnt-offering, turned them into smoke on the altar.

15 Next he presented the people's offering. He took the goat of the sin-offering that was for the people, and slaughtered it, and presented it as a sin-offering like the first one. [16] He presented the burnt-offering, and sacrificed it according to regulation. [17] He presented the grain-offering, and, taking a handful of it, he turned it into smoke on the altar, in addition to the burnt-offering of the morning.

18 He slaughtered the ox and the ram as a sacrifice of well-being for the people. Aaron's sons brought him the blood, which he dashed against all sides of the altar, [19] and the fat of the ox and of the ram—the broad tail, the fat that covers the entrails, the two kidneys and the fat on them,[a] and the appendage of the liver. [20] They first laid the fat on the breasts, and the fat was turned into smoke on the altar; [21] and the breasts and the right thigh Aaron raised as an elevation-offering before the LORD, as Moses had commanded.

22 Aaron lifted his hands towards the people and blessed them; and he came down after sacrificing the sin-offering, the burnt-offering, and the offering of well-being. [23] Moses and Aaron entered the tent of meeting, and then came out and blessed the people; and the glory of the LORD appeared to all the people. [24] Fire came out from the LORD and consumed the burnt-offering and the fat on the altar; and when all the people saw it, they shouted and fell on their faces.

a Gk: Heb *the broad tail, and that which covers, and the kidneys*

Nadab and Abihu

10 Now Aaron's sons, Nadab and Abihu, each took his censer, put fire in it, and laid incense on it; and they offered unholy fire before the Lord, such as he had not commanded them. ²And fire came out from the presence of the Lord and consumed them, and they died before the Lord. ³Then Moses said to Aaron, 'This is what the Lord meant when he said,

"Through those who are near me
I will show myself holy,
and before all the people
I will be glorified." '

And Aaron was silent.

4 Moses summoned Mishael and Elzaphan, sons of Uzziel the uncle of Aaron, and said to them, 'Come forward, and carry your kinsmen away from the front of the sanctuary to a place outside the camp.' ⁵They came forward and carried them by their tunics out of the camp, as Moses had ordered. ⁶And Moses said to Aaron and to his sons Eleazar and Ithamar, 'Do not dishevel your hair, and do not tear your vestments, or you will die and wrath will strike all the congregation; but your kindred, the whole house of Israel, may mourn the burning that the Lord has sent. ⁷You shall not go outside the entrance of the tent of meeting, or you will die; for the anointing-oil of the Lord is on you.' And they did as Moses had ordered.

8 And the Lord spoke to Aaron: ⁹Drink no wine or strong drink, neither you nor your sons, when you enter the tent of meeting, that you may not die; it is a statute for ever throughout your generations. ¹⁰You are to distinguish between the holy and the common, and between the unclean and the clean; ¹¹and you are to teach the people of Israel all the statutes that the Lord has spoken to them through Moses.

12 Moses spoke to Aaron and to his remaining sons, Eleazar and Ithamar: Take the grain-offering that is left from the Lord's offerings by fire, and eat it unleavened beside the altar, for it is most holy; ¹³you shall eat it in a holy place, because it is your due and your sons' due, from the offerings by fire to the Lord; for so I am

commanded. ¹⁴But the breast that is elevated and the thigh that is raised, you and your sons and daughters as well may eat in any clean place; for they have been assigned to you and your children from the sacrifices of the offerings of well-being of the people of Israel. ¹⁵The thigh that is raised and the breast that is elevated they shall bring, together with the offerings by fire of the fat, to raise for an elevation-offering before the Lord; they are to be your due and that of your children for ever, as the Lord has commanded.

16 Then Moses made inquiry about the goat of the sin-offering, and—it had already been burned! He was angry with Eleazar and Ithamar, Aaron's remaining sons, and said, ¹⁷'Why did you not eat the sin-offering in the sacred area? For it is most holy, and God^a has given it to you that you may remove the guilt of the congregation, to make atonement on their behalf before the Lord. ¹⁸Its blood was not brought into the inner part of the sanctuary. You should certainly have eaten it in the sanctuary, as I commanded.' ¹⁹And Aaron spoke to Moses, 'See, today they offered their sin-offering and their burnt-offering before the Lord; and yet such things as these have befallen me! If I had eaten the sin-offering today, would it have been agreeable to the Lord?' ²⁰And when Moses heard that, he agreed.

Clean and Unclean Foods

11 The Lord spoke to Moses and Aaron, saying to them: ²Speak to the people of Israel, saying:

From among all the land animals, these are the creatures that you may eat. ³Any animal that has divided hoofs and is cloven-footed and chews the cud—such you may eat. ⁴But among those that chew the cud or have divided hoofs, you shall not eat the following: the camel, for even though it chews the cud, it does not have divided hoofs; it is unclean for you. ⁵The rock-badger, for even though it chews the cud, it does not have divided hoofs; it is unclean for you. ⁶The hare, for even though it chews the cud, it does not have divided hoofs; it

_a_ Heb _he_

is unclean for you. 7The pig, for even though it has divided hoofs and is cloven-footed, it does not chew the cud; it is unclean for you. 8Of their flesh you shall not eat, and their carcasses you shall not touch; they are unclean for you.

9 These you may eat, of all that are in the waters. Everything in the waters that has fins and scales, whether in the seas or in the streams—such you may eat. 10But anything in the seas or the streams that does not have fins and scales, of the swarming creatures in the waters and among all the other living creatures that are in the waters—they are detestable to you 11and detestable they shall remain. Of their flesh you shall not eat, and their carcasses you shall regard as detestable. 12Everything in the waters that does not have fins and scales is detestable to you.

13 These you shall regard as detestable among the birds. They shall not be eaten; they are an abomination: the eagle, the vulture, the osprey, 14the buzzard, the kite of any kind; 15every raven of any kind; 16the ostrich, the nighthawk, the seagull, the hawk of any kind; 17the little owl, the cormorant, the great owl, 18the water-hen, the desert-owl,*a* the carrion vulture, 19the stork, the heron of any kind, the hoopoe, and the bat.*b*

20 All winged insects that walk upon all fours are detestable to you. 21But among the winged insects that walk on all fours you may eat those that have jointed legs above their feet, with which to leap on the ground. 22Of them you may eat: the locust according to its kind, the bald locust according to its kind, the cricket according to its kind, and the grasshopper according to its kind. 23But all other winged insects that have four feet are detestable to you.

Unclean Animals

24 By these you shall become unclean; whoever touches the carcass of any of them shall be unclean until the evening, 25and whoever carries any part of the carcass of any of them shall wash his clothes and be unclean until the evening. 26Every animal that has divided hoofs but is not cloven-footed or does not chew the cud is unclean

for you; everyone who touches one of them shall be unclean. 27All that walk on their paws, among the animals that walk on all fours, are unclean for you; whoever touches the carcass of any of them shall be unclean until the evening, 28and the one who carries the carcass shall wash his clothes and be unclean until the evening; they are unclean for you.

29 These are unclean for you among the creatures that swarm upon the earth: the weasel, the mouse, the great lizard according to its kind, 30the gecko, the land-crocodile, the lizard, the sand-lizard, and the chameleon. 31These are unclean for you among all that swarm; whoever touches one of them when they are dead shall be unclean until the evening. 32And anything upon which any of them falls when they are dead shall be unclean, whether an article of wood or cloth or skin or sacking, any article that is used for any purpose; it shall be dipped into water, and it shall be unclean until the evening, and then it shall be clean. 33And if any of them falls into any earthen vessel, all that is in it shall be unclean, and you shall break the vessel. 34Any food that could be eaten shall be unclean if water from any such vessel comes upon it; and any liquid that could be drunk shall be unclean if it was in any such vessel. 35Everything on which any part of the carcass falls shall be unclean; whether an oven or stove, it shall be broken in pieces; they are unclean, and shall remain unclean for you. 36But a spring or a cistern holding water shall be clean, while whatever touches the carcass in it shall be unclean. 37If any part of their carcass falls upon any seed set aside for sowing, it is clean; 38but if water is put on the seed and any part of their carcass falls on it, it is unclean for you.

39 If an animal of which you may eat dies, anyone who touches its carcass shall be unclean until the evening. 40Those who eat of its carcass shall wash their clothes and be unclean until the evening; and those who carry the carcass shall wash their clothes and be unclean until the evening.

a Or *pelican*   *b* Identification of several of the birds in verses 13-19 is uncertain

41 All creatures that swarm upon the earth are detestable; they shall not be eaten. 42 Whatever moves on its belly, and whatever moves on all fours, or whatever has many feet, all the creatures that swarm upon the earth, you shall not eat; for they are detestable. 43 You shall not make yourselves detestable with any creature that swarms; you shall not defile yourselves with them, and so become unclean. 44 For I am the LORD your God; sanctify yourselves therefore, and be holy, for I am holy. You shall not defile yourselves with any swarming creature that moves on the earth. 45 For I am the LORD who brought you up from the land of Egypt, to be your God; you shall be holy, for I am holy.

46 This is the law pertaining to land animal and bird and every living creature that moves through the waters and every creature that swarms upon the earth, 47 to make a distinction between the unclean and the clean, and between the living creature that may be eaten and the living creature that may not be eaten.

Purification of Women after Childbirth

12 The LORD spoke to Moses, saying: 2 Speak to the people of Israel, saying:

If a woman conceives and bears a male child, she shall be ceremonially unclean for seven days; as at the time of her menstruation, she shall be unclean. 3 On the eighth day the flesh of his foreskin shall be circumcised. 4 Her time of blood purification shall be thirty-three days; she shall not touch any holy thing, or come into the sanctuary, until the days of her purification are completed. 5 If she bears a female child, she shall be unclean for two weeks, as in her menstruation; her time of blood purification shall be sixty-six days.

6 When the days of her purification are completed, whether for a son or for a daughter, she shall bring to the priest at the entrance of the tent of meeting a lamb in its first year for a burnt-offering, and a pigeon or a turtle-dove for a sin-offering. 7 He shall offer it before the LORD, and make atonement on her behalf; then she shall be clean from her flow of blood. This is the law for her who bears a child, male or female. 8 If she cannot afford a sheep, she shall take two turtle-doves or two pigeons, one for a burnt-offering and the other for a sin-offering; and the priest shall make atonement on her behalf, and she shall be clean.

Leprosy: Varieties and Symptoms

13 The LORD spoke to Moses and Aaron, saying: 2 When a person has on the skin of his body a swelling or an eruption or a spot, and it turns into a leprous[a] disease on the skin of his body, he shall be brought to Aaron the priest or to one of his sons the priests. 3 The priest shall examine the disease on the skin of his body, and if the hair in the diseased area has turned white and the disease appears to be deeper than the skin of his body, it is a leprous[a] disease; after the priest has examined him he shall pronounce him ceremonially unclean. 4 But if the spot is white in the skin of his body, and appears no deeper than the skin, and the hair in it has not turned white, the priest shall confine the diseased person for seven days. 5 The priest shall examine him on the seventh day, and if he sees that the disease is checked and the disease has not spread in the skin, then the priest shall confine him for seven days more. 6 The priest shall examine him again on the seventh day, and if the disease has abated and the disease has not spread in the skin, the priest shall pronounce him clean; it is only an eruption; and he shall wash his clothes, and be clean. 7 But if the eruption spreads in the skin after he has shown himself to the priest for his cleansing, he shall appear again before the priest. 8 The priest shall make an examination, and if the eruption has spread in the skin, the priest shall pronounce him unclean; it is a leprous[a] disease.

9 When a person contracts a leprous[a] disease, he shall be brought to the priest. 10 The priest shall make an examination, and if there is a white swelling in the skin

a A term for several skin diseases; precise meaning uncertain that has turned the hair white, and there is quick raw flesh in the swelling, ¹¹ it is a chronic leprous *ᵃ* disease in the skin of his body. The priest shall pronounce him unclean; he shall not confine him, for he is unclean. ¹² But if the disease breaks out in the skin, so that it covers all the skin of the diseased person from head to foot, so far as the priest can see, ¹³ then the priest shall make an examination, and if the disease has covered all his body, he shall pronounce him clean of the disease; since it has all turned white, he is clean. ¹⁴ But if raw flesh ever appears on him, he shall be unclean; ¹⁵ the priest shall examine the raw flesh and pronounce him unclean. Raw flesh is unclean, for it is a leprous *ᵃ* disease. ¹⁶ But if the raw flesh again turns white, he shall come to the priest; ¹⁷ the priest shall examine him, and if the disease has turned white, the priest shall pronounce the diseased person clean. He is clean.

18 When there is on the skin of one's body a boil that has healed, ¹⁹ and in the place of the boil there appears a white swelling or a reddish-white spot, it shall be shown to the priest. ²⁰ The priest shall make an examination, and if it appears deeper than the skin and its hair has turned white, the priest shall pronounce him unclean; this is a leprous *ᵃ* disease, broken out in the boil. ²¹ But if the priest examines it and the hair on it is not white, nor is it deeper than the skin but has abated, the priest shall confine him for seven days. ²² If it spreads in the skin, the priest shall pronounce him unclean; it is diseased. ²³ But if the spot remains in one place and does not spread, it is the scar of the boil; the priest shall pronounce him clean.

24 Or, when the body has a burn on the skin and the raw flesh of the burn becomes a spot, reddish-white or white, ²⁵ the priest shall examine it. If the hair in the spot has turned white and it appears deeper than the skin, it is a leprous *ᵃ* disease; it has broken out in the burn, and the priest shall pronounce him unclean. This is a leprous *ᵃ* disease. ²⁶ But if the priest examines it and the hair in the spot is not white, and it is no deeper than the skin but has abated, the

priest shall confine him for seven days. ²⁷ The priest shall examine him on the seventh day; if it is spreading in the skin, the priest shall pronounce him unclean. This is a leprous *ᵃ* disease. ²⁸ But if the spot remains in one place and does not spread in the skin but has abated, it is a swelling from the burn, and the priest shall pronounce him clean; for it is the scar of the burn.

29 When a man or woman has a disease on the head or in the beard, ³⁰ the priest shall examine the disease. If it appears deeper than the skin and the hair in it is yellow and thin, the priest shall pronounce him unclean; it is an itch, a leprous *ᵃ* disease of the head or the beard. ³¹ If the priest examines the itching disease, and it appears no deeper than the skin and there is no black hair in it, the priest shall confine the person with the itching disease for seven days. ³² On the seventh day the priest shall examine the itch; if the itch has not spread, and there is no yellow hair in it, and the itch appears to be no deeper than the skin, ³³ he shall shave, but the itch he shall not shave. The priest shall confine the person with the itch for seven days more. ³⁴ On the seventh day the priest shall examine the itch; if the itch has not spread in the skin and it appears to be no deeper than the skin, the priest shall pronounce him clean. He shall wash his clothes and be clean. ³⁵ But if the itch spreads in the skin after he was pronounced clean, ³⁶ the priest shall examine him. If the itch has spread in the skin, the priest need not seek for the yellow hair; he is unclean. ³⁷ But if in his eyes the itch is checked, and black hair has grown in it, the itch is healed, he is clean; and the priest shall pronounce him clean.

38 When a man or a woman has spots on the skin of the body, white spots, ³⁹ the priest shall make an examination, and if the spots on the skin of the body are of a dull white, it is a rash that has broken out on the skin; he is clean.

40 If anyone loses the hair from his head, he is bald but he is clean. ⁴¹ If he loses the hair from his forehead and temples, he

ᵃ A term for several skin diseases; precise meaning uncertain has baldness of the forehead but he is clean. ⁴²But if there is on the bald head or the bald forehead a reddish-white diseased spot, it is a leprousᵃ disease breaking out on his bald head or his bald forehead. ⁴³The priest shall examine him; if the diseased swelling is reddish-white on his bald head or on his bald forehead, which resembles a leprousᵃ disease in the skin of the body, ⁴⁴he is leprous,ᵃ he is unclean. The priest shall pronounce him unclean; the disease is on his head.

45 The person who has the leprousᵃ disease shall wear torn clothes and let the hair of his head be dishevelled; and he shall cover his upper lip and cry out, 'Unclean, unclean.' ⁴⁶He shall remain unclean as long as he has the disease; he is unclean. He shall live alone; his dwelling shall be outside the camp.

47 Concerning clothing: when a leprousᵃ disease appears in it, in woollen or linen cloth, ⁴⁸in warp or woof of linen or wool, or in a skin or in anything made of skin, ⁴⁹if the disease shows greenish or reddish in the garment, whether in warp or woof or in skin or in anything made of skin, it is a leprousᵃ disease and shall be shown to the priest. ⁵⁰The priest shall examine the disease, and put the diseased article aside for seven days. ⁵¹He shall examine the disease on the seventh day. If the disease has spread in the cloth, in warp or woof, or in the skin, whatever be the use of the skin, this is a spreading leprousᵃ disease; it is unclean. ⁵²He shall burn the clothing, whether diseased in warp or woof, woollen or linen, or anything of skin, for it is a spreading leprousᵃ disease; it shall be burned in fire.

53 If the priest makes an examination, and the disease has not spread in the clothing, in warp or woof or in anything of skin, ⁵⁴the priest shall command them to wash the article in which the disease appears, and he shall put it aside for seven days more. ⁵⁵The priest shall examine the diseased article after it has been washed. If the diseased spot has not changed colour, though the disease has not spread, it is unclean; you shall burn it in fire, whether the leprousᵃ spot is on the inside or on the outside.

56 If the priest makes an examination, and the disease has abated after it is washed, he shall tear the spot out of the cloth, in warp or woof, or out of skin. ⁵⁷If it appears again in the garment, in warp or woof, or in anything of skin, it is spreading; you shall burn with fire that in which the disease appears. ⁵⁸But the cloth, warp or woof, or anything of skin from which the disease disappears when you have washed it, shall then be washed a second time, and it shall be clean.

59 This is the ritual for a leprousᵃ disease in a cloth of wool or linen, either in warp or woof, or in anything of skin, to decide whether it is clean or unclean.

Purification of Lepers and Leprous Houses

14 The LORD spoke to Moses, saying: ²This shall be the ritual for the leprousᵃ person at the time of his cleansing:

He shall be brought to the priest; ³the priest shall go out of the camp, and the priest shall make an examination. If the disease is healed in the leprousᵃ person, ⁴the priest shall command that two living clean birds and cedar wood and crimson yarn and hyssop be brought for the one who is to be cleansed. ⁵The priest shall command that one of the birds be slaughtered over fresh water in an earthen vessel. ⁶He shall take the living bird with the cedar wood and the crimson yarn and the hyssop, and dip them and the living bird in the blood of the bird that was slaughtered over the fresh water. ⁷He shall sprinkle it seven times upon the one who is to be cleansed of the leprousᵃ disease; then he shall pronounce him clean, and he shall let the living bird go into the open field. ⁸The one who is to be cleansed shall wash his clothes, and shave off all his hair, and bathe himself in water, and he shall be clean. After that he shall come into the camp, but shall live outside his tent for seven days. ⁹On the seventh day he shall shave all his hair: of head, beard,

ᵃ A term for several skin diseases; precise meaning uncertain eyebrows; he shall shave all his hair. Then he shall wash his clothes, and bathe his body in water, and he shall be clean.

10 On the eighth day he shall take two male lambs without blemish, and one ewe lamb in its first year without blemish, and a grain-offering of three-tenths of an ephah of choice flour mixed with oil, and one log*a* of oil. [11] The priest who cleanses shall set the person to be cleansed, along with these things, before the LORD, at the entrance of the tent of meeting. [12] The priest shall take one of the lambs, and offer it as a guilt-offering, along with the log*a* of oil, and raise them as an elevation-offering before the LORD. [13] He shall slaughter the lamb in the place where the sin-offering and the burnt-offering are slaughtered in the holy place; for the guilt-offering, like the sin-offering, belongs to the priest: it is most holy. [14] The priest shall take some of the blood of the guilt-offering and put it on the lobe of the right ear of the one to be cleansed, and on the thumb of the right hand, and on the big toe of the right foot. [15] The priest shall take some of the log*a* of oil and pour it into the palm of his own left hand, [16] and dip his right finger in the oil that is in his left hand and sprinkle some oil with his finger seven times before the LORD. [17] Some of the oil that remains in his hand the priest shall put on the lobe of the right ear of the one to be cleansed, and on the thumb of the right hand, and on the big toe of the right foot, on top of the blood of the guilt-offering. [18] The rest of the oil that is in the priest's hand he shall put on the head of the one to be cleansed. Then the priest shall make atonement on his behalf before the LORD: [19] the priest shall offer the sin-offering, to make atonement for the one to be cleansed from his uncleanness. Afterwards he shall slaughter the burnt-offering; [20] and the priest shall offer the burnt-offering and the grain-offering on the altar. Thus the priest shall make atonement on his behalf and he shall be clean.

21 But if he is poor and cannot afford so much, he shall take one male lamb for a guilt-offering to be elevated, to make atonement on his behalf, and one-tenth of an ephah of choice flour mixed with oil for a grain-offering, and a log*a* of oil; [22] also two turtle-doves or two pigeons, such as he can afford, one for a sin-offering and the other for a burnt-offering. [23] On the eighth day he shall bring them for his cleansing to the priest, to the entrance of the tent of meeting, before the LORD; [24] and the priest shall take the lamb of the guilt-offering and the log*a* of oil, and the priest shall raise them as an elevation-offering before the LORD. [25] The priest shall slaughter the lamb of the guilt-offering and shall take some of the blood of the guilt-offering, and put it on the lobe of the right ear of the one to be cleansed, and on the thumb of the right hand, and on the big toe of the right foot. [26] The priest shall pour some of the oil into the palm of his own left hand, [27] and shall sprinkle with his right finger some of the oil that is in his left hand seven times before the LORD. [28] The priest shall put some of the oil that is in his hand on the lobe of the right ear of the one to be cleansed, and on the thumb of the right hand, and the big toe of the right foot, where the blood of the guilt-offering was placed. [29] The rest of the oil that is in the priest's hand he shall put on the head of the one to be cleansed, to make atonement on his behalf before the LORD. [30] And he shall offer, of the turtle-doves or pigeons such as he can afford, [31] one*b* for a sin-offering and the other for a burnt-offering, along with a grain-offering; and the priest shall make atonement before the LORD on behalf of the one being cleansed. [32] This is the ritual for one who has a leprous*c* disease, who cannot afford the offerings for his cleansing.

33 The LORD spoke to Moses and Aaron, saying:

34 When you come into the land of Canaan, which I give you for a possession, and I put a leprous*c* disease in a house in the land of your possession, [35] the owner of the house shall come and tell the priest, saying, 'There seems to me to be some sort of disease in my house.' [36] The priest shall

---

a A liquid measure　*b* Gk Syr: Heb *afford, [31]such as he can afford, one*　*c* A term for several skin diseases; precise meaning uncertain command that they empty the house before the priest goes to examine the disease, or all that is in the house will become unclean; and afterwards the priest shall go in to inspect the house. 37 He shall examine the disease; if the disease is in the walls of the house with greenish or reddish spots, and if it appears to be deeper than the surface, 38 the priest shall go outside to the door of the house and shut up the house for seven days. 39 The priest shall come again on the seventh day and make an inspection; if the disease has spread in the walls of the house, 40 the priest shall command that the stones in which the disease appears be taken out and thrown into an unclean place outside the city. 41 He shall have the inside of the house scraped thoroughly, and the plaster that is scraped off shall be dumped in an unclean place outside the city. 42 They shall take other stones and put them in the place of those stones, and take other plaster and plaster the house.

43 If the disease breaks out again in the house, after he has taken out the stones and scraped the house and plastered it, 44 the priest shall go and make inspection; if the disease has spread in the house, it is a spreading leprous*a* disease in the house; it is unclean. 45 He shall have the house torn down, its stones and timber and all the plaster of the house, and taken outside the city to an unclean place. 46 All who enter the house while it is shut up shall be unclean until the evening; 47 and all who sleep in the house shall wash their clothes; and all who eat in the house shall wash their clothes.

48 If the priest comes and makes an inspection, and the disease has not spread in the house after the house was plastered, the priest shall pronounce the house clean; the disease is healed. 49 For the cleansing of the house he shall take two birds, with cedar wood and crimson yarn and hyssop, 50 and shall slaughter one of the birds over fresh water in an earthen vessel, 51 and shall take the cedar wood and the hyssop and the crimson yarn, along with the living bird, and dip them in the blood of the slaughtered bird and the fresh water, and sprinkle

the house seven times. 52 Thus he shall cleanse the house with the blood of the bird, and with the fresh water, and with the living bird, and with the cedar wood and hyssop and crimson yarn; 53 and he shall let the living bird go out of the city into the open field; so he shall make atonement for the house, and it shall be clean.

54 This is the ritual for any leprous*a* disease: for an itch, 55 for leprous*a* diseases in clothing and houses, 56 and for a swelling or an eruption or a spot, 57 to determine when it is unclean and when it is clean. This is the ritual for leprous*a* diseases.

Concerning Bodily Discharges

15 The LORD spoke to Moses and Aaron, saying: 2 Speak to the people of Israel and say to them:

When any man has a discharge from his member,*b* his discharge makes him ceremonially unclean. 3 The uncleanness of his discharge is this: whether his member*b* flows with his discharge, or his member*b* is stopped from discharging, it is uncleanness for him. 4 Every bed on which the one with the discharge lies shall be unclean; and everything on which he sits shall be unclean. 5 Anyone who touches his bed shall wash his clothes, and bathe in water, and be unclean until the evening. 6 All who sit on anything on which the one with the discharge has sat shall wash their clothes, and bathe in water, and be unclean until the evening. 7 All who touch the body of the one with the discharge shall wash their clothes, and bathe in water, and be unclean until the evening. 8 If the one with the discharge spits on persons who are clean, then they shall wash their clothes, and bathe in water, and be unclean until the evening. 9 Any saddle on which the one with the discharge rides shall be unclean. 10 All who touch anything that was under him shall be unclean until the evening, and all who carry such a thing shall wash their clothes, and bathe in water, and be unclean until the evening. 11 All those whom the one with the discharge touches without his having

a A term for several skin diseases; precise meaning uncertain   *b* Heb *flesh* rinsed his hands in water shall wash their clothes, and bathe in water, and be unclean until the evening. ¹²Any earthen vessel that the one with the discharge touches shall be broken; and every vessel of wood shall be rinsed in water.

13 When the one with a discharge is cleansed of his discharge, he shall count seven days for his cleansing; he shall wash his clothes and bathe his body in fresh water, and he shall be clean. ¹⁴On the eighth day he shall take two turtle-doves or two pigeons and come before the LORD to the entrance of the tent of meeting and give them to the priest. ¹⁵The priest shall offer them, one for a sin-offering and the other for a burnt-offering; and the priest shall make atonement on his behalf before the LORD for his discharge.

16 If a man has an emission of semen, he shall bathe his whole body in water, and be unclean until the evening. ¹⁷Everything made of cloth or of skin on which the semen falls shall be washed with water, and be unclean until the evening. ¹⁸If a man lies with a woman and has an emission of semen, both of them shall bathe in water, and be unclean until the evening.

19 When a woman has a discharge of blood that is her regular discharge from her body, she shall be in her impurity for seven days, and whoever touches her shall be unclean until the evening. ²⁰Everything upon which she lies during her impurity shall be unclean; everything also upon which she sits shall be unclean. ²¹Whoever touches her bed shall wash his clothes, and bathe in water, and be unclean until the evening. ²²Whoever touches anything upon which she sits shall wash his clothes, and bathe in water, and be unclean until the evening; ²³whether it is the bed or anything upon which she sits, when he touches it he shall be unclean until the evening. ²⁴If any man lies with her, and her impurity falls on him, he shall be unclean for seven days; and every bed on which he lies shall be unclean.

25 If a woman has a discharge of blood for many days, not at the time of her impurity, or if she has a discharge beyond the time of her impurity, for all the days of the discharge she shall continue in uncleanness; as in the days of her impurity, she shall be unclean. ²⁶Every bed on which she lies during all the days of her discharge shall be treated as the bed of her impurity; and everything on which she sits shall be unclean, as in the uncleanness of her impurity. ²⁷Whoever touches these things shall be unclean, and shall wash his clothes, and bathe in water, and be unclean until the evening. ²⁸If she is cleansed of her discharge, she shall count seven days, and after that she shall be clean. ²⁹On the eighth day she shall take two turtle-doves or two pigeons and bring them to the priest at the entrance of the tent of meeting. ³⁰The priest shall offer one for a sin-offering and the other for a burnt-offering; and the priest shall make atonement on her behalf before the LORD for her unclean discharge.

31 Thus you shall keep the people of Israel separate from their uncleanness, so that they do not die in their uncleanness by defiling my tabernacle that is in their midst.

32 This is the ritual for those who have a discharge: for him who has an emission of semen, becoming unclean thereby, ³³for her who is in the infirmity of her period, for anyone, male or female, who has a discharge, and for the man who lies with a woman who is unclean.

The Day of Atonement

16 The LORD spoke to Moses after the death of the two sons of Aaron, when they drew near before the LORD and died. ²The LORD said to Moses:

Tell your brother Aaron not to come just at any time into the sanctuary inside the curtain before the mercy-seat*a* that is upon the ark, or he will die; for I appear in the cloud upon the mercy-seat.*a* ³Thus shall Aaron come into the holy place: with a young bull for a sin-offering and a ram for a burnt-offering. ⁴He shall put on the holy linen tunic, and shall have the linen undergarments next to his body, fasten the linen sash, and wear the linen turban; these are the holy vestments. He shall bathe his

a Or *the cover*

body in water, and then put them on. ⁵ He shall take from the congregation of the people of Israel two male goats for a sin-offering, and one ram for a burnt-offering.

6 Aaron shall offer the bull as a sin-offering for himself, and shall make atonement for himself and for his house. ⁷ He shall take the two goats and set them before the LORD at the entrance of the tent of meeting; ⁸ and Aaron shall cast lots on the two goats, one lot for the LORD and the other lot for Azazel.ᵃ ⁹ Aaron shall present the goat on which the lot fell for the LORD, and offer it as a sin-offering; ¹⁰ but the goat on which the lot fell for Azazelᵃ shall be presented alive before the LORD to make atonement over it, so that it may be sent away into the wilderness to Azazel.ᵃ

11 Aaron shall present the bull as a sin-offering for himself, and shall make atonement for himself and for his house; he shall slaughter the bull as a sin-offering for himself. ¹² He shall take a censer full of coals of fire from the altar before the LORD, and two handfuls of crushed sweet incense, and he shall bring it inside the curtain ¹³ and put the incense on the fire before the LORD, so that the cloud of the incense may cover the mercy-seatᵇ that is upon the covenant,ᶜ or he will die. ¹⁴ He shall take some of the blood of the bull, and sprinkle it with his finger on the front of the mercy-seat,ᵇ and before the mercy-seatᵇ he shall sprinkle the blood with his finger seven times.

15 He shall slaughter the goat of the sin-offering that is for the people and bring its blood inside the curtain, and do with its blood as he did with the blood of the bull, sprinkling it upon the mercy-seatᵇ and before the mercy-seat.ᵇ ¹⁶ Thus he shall make atonement for the sanctuary, because of the uncleannesses of the people of Israel, and because of their transgressions, all their sins; and so he shall do for the tent of meeting, which remains with them in the midst of their uncleannesses. ¹⁷ No one shall be in the tent of meeting from the time he enters to make atonement in the sanctuary until he comes out and has made atonement for himself and for his house and for all the assembly of Israel. ¹⁸ Then he shall go

out to the altar that is before the LORD and make atonement on its behalf, and shall take some of the blood of the bull and of the blood of the goat, and put it on each of the horns of the altar. ¹⁹ He shall sprinkle some of the blood on it with his finger seven times, and cleanse it and hallow it from the uncleannesses of the people of Israel.

20 When he has finished atoning for the holy place and the tent of meeting and the altar, he shall present the live goat. ²¹ Then Aaron shall lay both his hands on the head of the live goat, and confess over it all the iniquities of the people of Israel, and all their transgressions, all their sins, putting them on the head of the goat, and sending it away into the wilderness by means of someone designated for the task.ᵈ ²² The goat shall bear on itself all their iniquities to a barren region; and the goat shall be set free in the wilderness.

23 Then Aaron shall enter the tent of meeting, and shall take off the linen vestments that he put on when he went into the holy place, and shall leave them there. ²⁴ He shall bathe his body in water in a holy place, and put on his vestments; then he shall come out and offer his burnt-offering and the burnt-offering of the people, making atonement for himself and for the people. ²⁵ The fat of the sin-offering he shall turn into smoke on the altar. ²⁶ The one who sets the goat free for Azazelᵃ shall wash his clothes and bathe his body in water, and afterwards may come into the camp. ²⁷ The bull of the sin-offering and the goat of the sin-offering, whose blood was brought in to make atonement in the holy place, shall be taken outside the camp; their skin and their flesh and their dung shall be consumed in fire. ²⁸ The one who burns them shall wash his clothes and bathe his body in water, and afterwards may come into the camp.

29 This shall be a statute to you for ever: In the seventh month, on the tenth day of the month, you shall deny yourselves,ᵉ and shall do no work, neither the citizen nor

a Traditionally rendered *a scapegoat*   *b* Or *the cover*
c Or *treaty*, or *testament*; Heb *eduth*   *d* Meaning of
Heb uncertain   *e* Or *shall fast*

the alien who resides among you. ³⁰ For on this day atonement shall be made for you, to cleanse you; from all your sins you shall be clean before the LORD. ³¹ It is a sabbath of complete rest to you, and you shall deny yourselves;ª it is a statute for ever. ³² The priest who is anointed and consecrated as priest in his father's place shall make atonement, wearing the linen vestments, the holy vestments. ³³ He shall make atonement for the sanctuary, and he shall make atonement for the tent of meeting and for the altar, and he shall make atonement for the priests and for all the people of the assembly. ³⁴ This shall be an everlasting statute for you, to make atonement for the people of Israel once in the year for all their sins. And Moses did as the LORD had commanded him.

The Slaughtering of Animals

17 The LORD spoke to Moses: 2 Speak to Aaron and his sons and to all the people of Israel and say to them: This is what the LORD has commanded. ³ If anyone of the house of Israel slaughters an ox or a lamb or a goat in the camp, or slaughters it outside the camp, ⁴ and does not bring it to the entrance of the tent of meeting, to present it as an offering to the LORD before the tabernacle of the LORD, he shall be held guilty of bloodshed; he has shed blood, and he shall be cut off from the people. ⁵ This is in order that the people of Israel may bring their sacrifices that they offer in the open field, that they may bring them to the LORD, to the priest at the entrance of the tent of meeting, and offer them as sacrifices of well-being to the LORD. ⁶ The priest shall dash the blood against the altar of the LORD at the entrance of the tent of meeting, and turn the fat into smoke as a pleasing odour to the LORD, ⁷ so that they may no longer offer their sacrifices for goat-demons, to whom they prostitute themselves. This shall be a statute for ever to them throughout their generations.

8 And say to them further: Anyone of the house of Israel or of the aliens who reside among them who offers a burnt-offering or sacrifice, ⁹ and does not bring it to the entrance of the tent of meeting, to sacrifice it to the LORD, shall be cut off from the people.

Eating Blood Prohibited

10 If anyone of the house of Israel or of the aliens who reside among them eats any blood, I will set my face against that person who eats blood, and will cut that person off from the people. ¹¹ For the life of the flesh is in the blood; and I have given it to you for making atonement for your lives on the altar; for, as life, it is the blood that makes atonement. ¹² Therefore I have said to the people of Israel: No person among you shall eat blood, nor shall any alien who resides among you eat blood. ¹³ And anyone of the people of Israel, or of the aliens who reside among them, who hunts down an animal or bird that may be eaten shall pour out its blood and cover it with earth.

14 For the life of every creature—its blood is its life; therefore I have said to the people of Israel: You shall not eat the blood of any creature, for the life of every creature is its blood; whoever eats it shall be cut off. ¹⁵ All persons, citizens or aliens, who eat what dies of itself or what has been torn by wild animals, shall wash their clothes, and bathe themselves in water, and be unclean until the evening; then they shall be clean. ¹⁶ But if they do not wash themselves or bathe their body, they shall bear their guilt.

Sexual Relations

18 The LORD spoke to Moses, saying: 2 Speak to the people of Israel and say to them: I am the LORD your God. ³ You shall not do as they do in the land of Egypt, where you lived, and you shall not do as they do in the land of Canaan, to which I am bringing you. You shall not follow their statutes. ⁴ My ordinances you shall observe and my statutes you shall keep, following them: I am the LORD your God. ⁵ You shall keep my statutes and my ordinances; by doing so one shall live: I am the LORD.

6 None of you shall approach anyone near of kin to uncover nakedness: I am the LORD. ⁷ You shall not uncover the nakedness

a Or *shall fast*

of your father, which is the nakedness of your mother; she is your mother, you shall not uncover her nakedness. 8 You shall not uncover the nakedness of your father's wife; it is the nakedness of your father. 9 You shall not uncover the nakedness of your sister, your father's daughter or your mother's daughter, whether born at home or born abroad. 10 You shall not uncover the nakedness of your son's daughter or of your daughter's daughter, for their nakedness is your own nakedness. 11 You shall not uncover the nakedness of your father's wife's daughter, begotten by your father, since she is your sister. 12 You shall not uncover the nakedness of your father's sister; she is your father's flesh. 13 You shall not uncover the nakedness of your mother's sister, for she is your mother's flesh. 14 You shall not uncover the nakedness of your father's brother, that is, you shall not approach his wife; she is your aunt. 15 You shall not uncover the nakedness of your daughter-in-law: she is your son's wife; you shall not uncover her nakedness. 16 You shall not uncover the nakedness of your brother's wife; it is your brother's nakedness. 17 You shall not uncover the nakedness of a woman and her daughter, and you shall not take*a* her son's daughter or her daughter's daughter to uncover her nakedness; they are your*b* flesh; it is depravity. 18 And you shall not take*a* a woman as a rival to her sister, uncovering her nakedness while her sister is still alive.

19 You shall not approach a woman to uncover her nakedness while she is in her menstrual uncleanness. 20 You shall not have sexual relations with your kinsman's wife, and defile yourself with her. 21 You shall not give any of your offspring to sacrifice them*c* to Molech, and so profane the name of your God: I am the LORD. 22 You shall not lie with a male as with a woman; it is an abomination. 23 You shall not have sexual relations with any animal and defile yourself with it, nor shall any woman give herself to an animal to have sexual relations with it: it is perversion.

24 Do not defile yourselves in any of these ways, for by all these practices the nations I am casting out before you have de-

filed themselves. 25 Thus the land became defiled; and I punished it for its iniquity, and the land vomited out its inhabitants. 26 But you shall keep my statutes and my ordinances and commit none of these abominations, either the citizen or the alien who resides among you 27 (for the inhabitants of the land, who were before you, committed all of these abominations, and the land became defiled); 28 otherwise the land will vomit you out for defiling it, as it vomited out the nation that was before you. 29 For whoever commits any of these abominations shall be cut off from their people. 30 So keep my charge not to commit any of these abominations that were done before you, and not to defile yourselves by them: I am the LORD your God.

Ritual and Moral Holiness

19 The LORD spoke to Moses, saying: 2 Speak to all the congregation of the people of Israel and say to them: You shall be holy, for I the LORD your God am holy. 3 You shall each revere your mother and father, and you shall keep my sabbaths: I am the LORD your God. 4 Do not turn to idols or make cast images for yourselves: I am the LORD your God.

5 When you offer a sacrifice of well-being to the LORD, offer it in such a way that it is acceptable in your behalf. 6 It shall be eaten on the same day you offer it, or on the next day; and anything left over until the third day shall be consumed in fire. 7 If it is eaten at all on the third day, it is an abomination; it will not be acceptable. 8 All who eat it shall be subject to punishment, because they have profaned what is holy to the LORD; and any such person shall be cut off from the people.

9 When you reap the harvest of your land, you shall not reap to the very edges of your field, or gather the gleanings of your harvest. 10 You shall not strip your vineyard bare, or gather the fallen grapes of your vineyard; you shall leave them for the poor and the alien: I am the LORD your God.

11 You shall not steal; you shall not deal

a Or *marry*   *b* Gk: Heb lacks *your*   *c* Heb *to pass them over* falsely; and you shall not lie to one another. ¹²And you shall not swear falsely by my name, profaning the name of your God: I am the LORD.

13 You shall not defraud your neighbour; you shall not steal; and you shall not keep for yourself the wages of a labourer until morning. ¹⁴You shall not revile the deaf or put a stumbling-block before the blind; you shall fear your God: I am the LORD.

15 You shall not render an unjust judgement; you shall not be partial to the poor or defer to the great: with justice you shall judge your neighbour. ¹⁶You shall not go around as a slanderer*ᵃ* among your people, and you shall not profit by the blood*ᵇ* of your neighbour: I am the LORD.

17 You shall not hate in your heart anyone of your kin; you shall reprove your neighbour, or you will incur guilt yourself. ¹⁸You shall not take vengeance or bear a grudge against any of your people, but you shall love your neighbour as yourself: I am the LORD.

19 You shall keep my statutes. You shall not let your animals breed with a different kind; you shall not sow your field with two kinds of seed; nor shall you put on a garment made of two different materials.

20 If a man has sexual relations with a woman who is a slave, designated for another man but not ransomed or given her freedom, an inquiry shall be held. They shall not be put to death, since she has not been freed; ²¹but he shall bring a guilt-offering for himself to the LORD, at the entrance of the tent of meeting, a ram as guilt-offering. ²²And the priest shall make atonement for him with the ram of guilt-offering before the LORD for his sin that he committed; and the sin he committed shall be forgiven him.

23 When you come into the land and plant all kinds of trees for food, then you shall regard their fruit as forbidden;*ᶜ* for three years it shall be forbidden*ᵈ* to you; it must not be eaten. ²⁴In the fourth year all their fruit shall be set apart for rejoicing in the LORD. ²⁵But in the fifth year you may

eat of their fruit, that their yield may be increased for you: I am the LORD your God.

26 You shall not eat anything with its blood. You shall not practise augury or witchcraft. ²⁷You shall not round off the hair on your temples or mar the edges of your beard. ²⁸You shall not make any gashes in your flesh for the dead or tattoo any marks upon you: I am the LORD.

29 Do not profane your daughter by making her a prostitute, so that the land may not become prostituted and full of depravity. ³⁰You shall keep my sabbaths and reverence my sanctuary: I am the LORD.

31 Do not turn to mediums or wizards; do not seek them out, to be defiled by them: I am the LORD your God.

32 You shall rise before the aged, and defer to the old; and you shall fear your God: I am the LORD.

33 When an alien resides with you in your land, you shall not oppress the alien. ³⁴The alien who resides with you shall be to you as the citizen among you; you shall love the alien as yourself, for you were aliens in the land of Egypt: I am the LORD your God.

35 You shall not cheat in measuring length, weight, or quantity. ³⁶You shall have honest balances, honest weights, an honest ephah, and an honest hin: I am the LORD your God, who brought you out of the land of Egypt. ³⁷You shall keep all my statutes and all my ordinances, and observe them: I am the LORD.

Penalties for Violations of Holiness

20 The LORD spoke to Moses, saying: ²Say further to the people of Israel: Any of the people of Israel, or of the aliens who reside in Israel, who give any of their offspring to Molech shall be put to death; the people of the land shall stone them to death. ³I myself will set my face against them, and will cut them off from the people, because they have given of their offspring to Molech, defiling my sanctuary and profaning my holy name. ⁴And if the

a Meaning of Heb uncertain　　*b* Heb stand against the blood　　*c* Heb as their uncircumcision
d Heb uncircumcision

people of the land should ever close their eyes to them, when they give of their offspring to Molech, and do not put them to death, ⁵I myself will set my face against them and against their family, and will cut them off from among their people, them and all who follow them in prostituting themselves to Molech.

6 If any turn to mediums and wizards, prostituting themselves to them, I will set my face against them, and will cut them off from the people. ⁷Consecrate yourselves therefore, and be holy; for I am the Lord your God. ⁸Keep my statutes, and observe them; I am the Lord; I sanctify you. ⁹All who curse father or mother shall be put to death; having cursed father or mother, their blood is upon them.

10 If a man commits adultery with the wife of*a* his neighbour, both the adulterer and the adulteress shall be put to death. ¹¹The man who lies with his father's wife has uncovered his father's nakedness; both of them shall be put to death; their blood is upon them. ¹²If a man lies with his daughter-in-law, both of them shall be put to death; they have committed perversion; their blood is upon them. ¹³If a man lies with a male as with a woman, both of them have committed an abomination; they shall be put to death; their blood is upon them. ¹⁴If a man takes a wife and her mother also, it is depravity; they shall be burned to death, both he and they, that there may be no depravity among you. ¹⁵If a man has sexual relations with an animal, he shall be put to death; and you shall kill the animal. ¹⁶If a woman approaches any animal and has sexual relations with it, you shall kill the woman and the animal; they shall be put to death, their blood is upon them.

17 If a man takes his sister, a daughter of his father or a daughter of his mother, and sees her nakedness, and she sees his nakedness, it is a disgrace, and they shall be cut off in the sight of their people; he has uncovered his sister's nakedness, he shall be subject to punishment. ¹⁸If a man lies with a woman having her sickness and uncovers her nakedness, he has laid bare her flow and she has laid bare her flow of blood;

both of them shall be cut off from their people. ¹⁹You shall not uncover the nakedness of your mother's sister or of your father's sister, for that is to lay bare one's own flesh; they shall be subject to punishment. ²⁰If a man lies with his uncle's wife, he has uncovered his uncle's nakedness; they shall be subject to punishment; they shall die childless. ²¹If a man takes his brother's wife, it is impurity; he has uncovered his brother's nakedness; they shall be childless.

22 You shall keep all my statutes and all my ordinances, and observe them, so that the land to which I bring you to settle in may not vomit you out. ²³You shall not follow the practices of the nation that I am driving out before you. Because they did all these things, I abhorred them. ²⁴But I have said to you: You shall inherit their land, and I will give it to you to possess, a land flowing with milk and honey. I am the Lord your God; I have separated you from the peoples. ²⁵You shall therefore make a distinction between the clean animal and the unclean, and between the unclean bird and the clean; you shall not bring abomination on yourselves by animal or by bird or by anything with which the ground teems, which I have set apart for you to hold unclean. ²⁶You shall be holy to me; for I the Lord am holy, and I have separated you from the other peoples to be mine.

27 A man or a woman who is a medium or a wizard shall be put to death; they shall be stoned to death, their blood is upon them.

The Holiness of Priests

21 The Lord said to Moses: Speak to the priests, the sons of Aaron, and say to them:

No one shall defile himself for a dead person among his relatives, ²except for his nearest kin: his mother, his father, his son, his daughter, his brother; ³likewise, for a virgin sister, close to him because she has had no husband, he may defile himself for her. ⁴But he shall not defile himself as a husband among his people and so profane himself. ⁵They shall not make bald spots

a Heb repeats *if a man commits adultery with the wife of* upon their heads, or shave off the edges of their beards, or make any gashes in their flesh. 6 They shall be holy to their God, and not profane the name of their God; for they offer the LORD's offerings by fire, the food of their God; therefore they shall be holy. 7 They shall not marry a prostitute or a woman who has been defiled; neither shall they marry a woman divorced from her husband. For they are holy to their God, 8 and you shall treat them as holy, since they offer the food of your God; they shall be holy to you, for I the LORD, I who sanctify you, am holy. 9 When the daughter of a priest profanes herself through prostitution, she profanes her father; she shall be burned to death.

10 The priest who is exalted above his fellows, on whose head the anointing-oil has been poured and who has been consecrated to wear the vestments, shall not dishevel his hair, nor tear his vestments. 11 He shall not go where there is a dead body; he shall not defile himself even for his father or mother. 12 He shall not go outside the sanctuary and thus profane the sanctuary of his God; for the consecration of the anointing-oil of his God is upon him: I am the LORD. 13 He shall marry only a woman who is a virgin. 14 A widow, or a divorced woman, or a woman who has been defiled, a prostitute, these he shall not marry. He shall marry a virgin of his own kin, 15 that he may not profane his offspring among his kin; for I am the LORD; I sanctify him.

16 The LORD spoke to Moses, saying: 17 Speak to Aaron and say: No one of your offspring throughout their generations who has a blemish may approach to offer the food of his God. 18 For no one who has a blemish shall draw near, one who is blind or lame, or one who has a mutilated face or a limb too long, 19 or one who has a broken foot or a broken hand, 20 or a hunchback, or a dwarf, or a man with a blemish in his eyes or an itching disease or scabs or crushed testicles. 21 No descendant of Aaron the priest who has a blemish shall come near to offer the LORD's offerings by fire; since he has a blemish, he shall not come near to offer the food of his God. 22 He may eat the food of his God, of the most holy as well as of the holy. 23 But he shall not come near the curtain or approach the altar, because he has a blemish, that he may not profane my sanctuaries; for I am the LORD; I sanctify them. 24 Thus Moses spoke to Aaron and to his sons and to all the people of Israel.

The Use of Holy Offerings

22 The LORD spoke to Moses, saying: 2 Direct Aaron and his sons to deal carefully with the sacred donations of the people of Israel, which they dedicate to me, so that they may not profane my holy name; I am the LORD. 3 Say to them: If anyone among all your offspring throughout your generations comes near the sacred donations, which the people of Israel dedicate to the LORD, while he is in a state of uncleanness, that person shall be cut off from my presence: I am the LORD. 4 No one of Aaron's offspring who has a leprous a disease or suffers a discharge may eat of the sacred donations until he is clean. Whoever touches anything made unclean by a corpse or a man who has had an emission of semen, 5 and whoever touches any swarming thing by which he may be made unclean or any human being by whom he may be made unclean—whatever his uncleanness may be— 6 the person who touches any such shall be unclean until evening and shall not eat of the sacred donations unless he has washed his body in water. 7 When the sun sets he shall be clean; and afterwards he may eat of the sacred donations, for they are his food. 8 That which died or was torn by wild animals he shall not eat, becoming unclean by it: I am the LORD. 9 They shall keep my charge, so that they may not incur guilt and die in the sanctuary b for having profaned it: I am the LORD; I sanctify them.

10 No lay person shall eat of the sacred donations. No bound or hired servant of the priest shall eat of the sacred donations; 11 but if a priest acquires anyone by purchase, the person may eat of them; and those that are born in his house may eat of

---

a A term for several skin diseases; precise meaning uncertain · b Vg: Heb *incur guilt for it and die in it* his food. [12] If a priest's daughter marries a layman, she shall not eat of the offering of the sacred donations; [13] but if a priest's daughter is widowed or divorced, without offspring, and returns to her father's house, as in her youth, she may eat of her father's food. No lay person shall eat of it. [14] If a man eats of the sacred donation unintentionally, he shall add one-fifth of its value to it, and give the sacred donation to the priest. [15] No one shall profane the sacred donations of the people of Israel, which they offer to the LORD, [16] causing them to bear guilt requiring a guilt-offering, by eating their sacred donations: for I am the LORD; I sanctify them.

Acceptable Offerings

17 The LORD spoke to Moses, saying: [18] Speak to Aaron and his sons and all the people of Israel and say to them: When anyone of the house of Israel or of the aliens residing in Israel presents an offering, whether in payment of a vow or as a freewill-offering that is offered to the LORD as a burnt-offering, [19] to be acceptable in your behalf it shall be a male without blemish, of the cattle or the sheep or the goats. [20] You shall not offer anything that has a blemish, for it will not be acceptable in your behalf.

21 When anyone offers a sacrifice of well-being to the LORD, in fulfilment of a vow or as a freewill-offering, from the herd or from the flock, to be acceptable it must be perfect; there shall be no blemish in it. [22] Anything blind, or injured, or maimed, or having a discharge or an itch or scabs— these you shall not offer to the LORD or put any of them on the altar as offerings by fire to the LORD. [23] An ox or a lamb that has a limb too long or too short you may present for a freewill-offering; but it will not be accepted for a vow. [24] Any animal that has its testicles bruised or crushed or torn or cut, you shall not offer to the LORD; such you shall not do within your land, [25] nor shall you accept any such animals from a foreigner to offer as food to your God; since they are mutilated, with a blemish in them, they shall not be accepted in your behalf.

26 The LORD spoke to Moses, saying:

[27] When an ox or a sheep or a goat is born, it shall remain for seven days with its mother, and from the eighth day onwards it shall be acceptable as the LORD's offering by fire. [28] But you shall not slaughter, from the herd or the flock, an animal with its young on the same day. [29] When you sacrifice a thanksgiving-offering to the LORD, you shall sacrifice it so that it may be acceptable in your behalf. [30] It shall be eaten on the same day; you shall not leave any of it until morning: I am the LORD.

31 Thus you shall keep my commandments and observe them: I am the LORD. [32] You shall not profane my holy name, that I may be sanctified among the people of Israel: I am the LORD; I sanctify you, [33] I who brought you out of the land of Egypt to be your God: I am the LORD.

Appointed Festivals

23 The LORD spoke to Moses, saying: [2] Speak to the people of Israel and say to them: These are the appointed festivals of the LORD that you shall proclaim as holy convocations, my appointed festivals.

The Sabbath, Passover, and Unleavened Bread

3 For six days shall work be done; but the seventh day is a sabbath of complete rest, a holy convocation; you shall do no work: it is a sabbath to the LORD throughout your settlements.

4 These are the appointed festivals of the LORD, the holy convocations, which you shall celebrate at the time appointed for them. [5] In the first month, on the fourteenth day of the month, at twilight, [a] there shall be a passover-offering to the LORD, [6] and on the fifteenth day of the same month is the festival of unleavened bread to the LORD; for seven days you shall eat unleavened bread. [7] On the first day you shall have a holy convocation; you shall not work at your occupations. [8] For seven days you shall present the LORD's offerings by fire; on the seventh day there shall be a holy convocation: you shall not work at your occupations.

a Heb *between the two evenings*

The Offering of First Fruits

9 The LORD spoke to Moses: 10 Speak to the people of Israel and say to them: When you enter the land that I am giving you and you reap its harvest, you shall bring the sheaf of the first fruits of your harvest to the priest. 11 He shall raise the sheaf before the LORD, so that you may find acceptance; on the day after the sabbath the priest shall raise it. 12 On the day when you raise the sheaf, you shall offer a lamb a year old, without blemish, as a burnt-offering to the LORD. 13 And the grain-offering with it shall be two-tenths of an ephah of choice flour mixed with oil, an offering by fire of pleasing odour to the LORD; and the drink-offering with it shall be of wine, one-fourth of a hin. 14 You shall eat no bread or parched grain or fresh ears until that very day, until you have brought the offering of your God: it is a statute for ever throughout your generations in all your settlements.

The Festival of Weeks

15 And from the day after the sabbath, from the day on which you bring the sheaf of the elevation-offering, you shall count off seven weeks; they shall be complete. 16 You shall count until the day after the seventh sabbath, fifty days; then you shall present an offering of new grain to the LORD. 17 You shall bring from your settlements two loaves of bread as an elevation-offering, each made of two-tenths of an ephah; they shall be of choice flour, baked with leaven, as first fruits to the LORD. 18 You shall present with the bread seven lambs a year old without blemish, one young bull, and two rams; they shall be a burnt-offering to the LORD, along with their grain-offering and their drink-offerings, an offering by fire of pleasing odour to the LORD. 19 You shall also offer one male goat for a sin-offering, and two male lambs a year old as a sacrifice of well-being. 20 The priest shall raise them with the bread of the first fruits as an elevation-offering before the LORD, together with the two lambs; they shall be holy to the LORD for the priest. 21 On that same day you shall make proclamation; you shall hold a holy convocation; you shall not

work at your occupations. This is a statute for ever in all your settlements throughout your generations.

22 When you reap the harvest of your land, you shall not reap to the very edges of your field, or gather the gleanings of your harvest; you shall leave them for the poor and for the alien: I am the LORD your God.

The Festival of Trumpets

23 The LORD spoke to Moses, saying: 24 Speak to the people of Israel, saying: In the seventh month, on the first day of the month, you shall observe a day of complete rest, a holy convocation commemorated with trumpet blasts. 25 You shall not work at your occupations; and you shall present the LORD's offering by fire.

The Day of Atonement

26 The LORD spoke to Moses, saying: 27 Now, the tenth day of this seventh month is the day of atonement; it shall be a holy convocation for you: you shall deny yourselves a and present the LORD's offering by fire; 28 and you shall do no work during that entire day; for it is a day of atonement, to make atonement on your behalf before the LORD your God. 29 For anyone who does not practise self-denial b during that entire day shall be cut off from the people. 30 And anyone who does any work during that entire day, such a one I will destroy from the midst of the people. 31 You shall do no work: it is a statute for ever throughout your generations in all your settlements. 32 It shall be to you a sabbath of complete rest, and you shall deny yourselves; a on the ninth day of the month at evening, from evening to evening you shall keep your sabbath.

The Festival of Booths

33 The LORD spoke to Moses, saying: 34 Speak to the people of Israel, saying: On the fifteenth day of this seventh month, and lasting seven days, there shall be the festival of booths c to the LORD. 35 The first day shall be a holy convocation; you shall

a Or shall fast   b Or does not fast   c Or tabernacles: Heb succoth not work at your occupations. ³⁶ For seven days you shall present the LORD's offerings by fire; on the eighth day you shall observe a holy convocation and present the LORD's offerings by fire; it is a solemn assembly; you shall not work at your occupations.

37 These are the appointed festivals of the LORD, which you shall celebrate as times of holy convocation, for presenting to the LORD offerings by fire—burnt-offerings and grain-offerings, sacrifices and drink-offerings, each on its proper day— ³⁸ apart from the sabbaths of the LORD, and apart from your gifts, and apart from all your votive offerings, and apart from all your freewill-offerings, which you give to the LORD.

39 Now, the fifteenth day of the seventh month, when you have gathered in the produce of the land, you shall keep the festival of the LORD, lasting seven days; a complete rest on the first day, and a complete rest on the eighth day. ⁴⁰ On the first day you shall take the fruit of majestic*a* trees, branches of palm trees, boughs of leafy trees, and willows of the brook; and you shall rejoice before the LORD your God for seven days. ⁴¹ You shall keep it as a festival to the LORD seven days in the year; you shall keep it in the seventh month as a statute for ever throughout your generations. ⁴² You shall live in booths for seven days; all that are citizens in Israel shall live in booths, ⁴³ so that your generations may know that I made the people of Israel live in booths when I brought them out of the land of Egypt: I am the LORD your God.

44 Thus Moses declared to the people of Israel the appointed festivals of the LORD.

The Lamp

24 The LORD spoke to Moses, saying: ² Command the people of Israel to bring you pure oil of beaten olives for the lamp, that a light may be kept burning regularly. ³ Aaron shall set it up in the tent of meeting, outside the curtain of the covenant,*b* to burn from evening to morning before the LORD regularly; it shall be a statute for ever throughout your generations. ⁴ He shall set up the lamps on the lampstand of pure gold*c* before the LORD regularly.

The Bread for the Tabernacle

5 You shall take choice flour, and bake twelve loaves of it; two-tenths of an ephah shall be in each loaf. ⁶ You shall place them in two rows, six in a row, on the table of pure gold.*d* ⁷ You shall put pure frankincense with each row, to be a token offering for the bread, as an offering by fire to the LORD. ⁸ Every sabbath day Aaron shall set them in order before the LORD regularly as a commitment of the people of Israel, as a covenant for ever. ⁹ They shall be for Aaron and his descendants, who shall eat them in a holy place, for they are most holy portions for him from the offerings by fire to the LORD, a perpetual due.

Blasphemy and Its Punishment

10 A man whose mother was an Israelite and whose father was an Egyptian came out among the people of Israel; and the Israelite woman's son and a certain Israelite began fighting in the camp. ¹¹ The Israelite woman's son blasphemed the Name in a curse. And they brought him to Moses— now his mother's name was Shelomith, daughter of Dibri, of the tribe of Dan— ¹² and they put him in custody, until the decision of the LORD should be made clear to them.

13 The LORD said to Moses, saying: ¹⁴ Take the blasphemer outside the camp; and let all who were within hearing lay their hands on his head, and let the whole congregation stone him. ¹⁵ And speak to the people of Israel, saying: Anyone who curses God shall bear the sin. ¹⁶ One who blasphemes the name of the LORD shall be put to death; the whole congregation shall stone the blasphemer. Aliens as well as citizens, when they blaspheme the Name, shall be put to death. ¹⁷ Anyone who kills a human being shall be put to death. ¹⁸ Anyone who kills an animal shall make restitution for it, life for life. ¹⁹ Anyone who maims another shall suffer the same injury

a Meaning of Heb uncertain   *b* Or *treaty*, or *testament;* Heb *eduth*   *c* Heb *pure lampstand*   *d* Heb *pure table* in return: 20 fracture for fracture, eye for eye, tooth for tooth; the injury inflicted is the injury to be suffered. 21 One who kills an animal shall make restitution for it; but one who kills a human being shall be put to death. 22 You shall have one law for the alien and for the citizen: for I am the LORD your God. 23 Moses spoke thus to the people of Israel; and they took the blasphemer outside the camp, and stoned him to death. The people of Israel did as the LORD had commanded Moses.

The Sabbatical Year

25 The LORD spoke to Moses on Mount Sinai, saying: 2 Speak to the people of Israel and say to them: When you enter the land that I am giving you, the land shall observe a sabbath for the LORD. 3 For six years you shall sow your field, and for six years you shall prune your vineyard, and gather in their yield; 4 but in the seventh year there shall be a sabbath of complete rest for the land, a sabbath for the LORD: you shall not sow your field or prune your vineyard. 5 You shall not reap the aftergrowth of your harvest or gather the grapes of your unpruned vine: it shall be a year of complete rest for the land. 6 You may eat what the land yields during its sabbath— you, your male and female slaves, your hired and your bound labourers who live with you; 7 for your livestock also, and for the wild animals in your land all its yield shall be for food.

The Year of Jubilee

8 You shall count off seven weeks*a* of years, seven times seven years, so that the period of seven weeks of years gives forty-nine years. 9 Then you shall have the trumpet sounded loud; on the tenth day of the seventh month—on the day of atonement—you shall have the trumpet sounded throughout all your land. 10 And you shall hallow the fiftieth year and you shall proclaim liberty throughout the land to all its inhabitants. It shall be a jubilee for you: you shall return, every one of you, to your property and every one of you to your family. 11 That fiftieth year shall be a jubilee for you:

you shall not sow, or reap the aftergrowth, or harvest the unpruned vines. 12 For it is a jubilee; it shall be holy to you: you shall eat only what the field itself produces.

13 In this year of jubilee you shall return, every one of you, to your property. 14 When you make a sale to your neighbour or buy from your neighbour, you shall not cheat one another. 15 When you buy from your neighbour, you shall pay only for the number of years since the jubilee; the seller shall charge you only for the remaining crop-years. 16 If the years are more, you shall increase the price, and if the years are fewer, you shall diminish the price; for it is a certain number of harvests that are being sold to you. 17 You shall not cheat one another, but you shall fear your God; for I am the LORD your God.

18 You shall observe my statutes and faithfully keep my ordinances, so that you may live on the land securely. 19 The land will yield its fruit, and you will eat your fill and live on it securely. 20 Should you ask, 'What shall we eat in the seventh year, if we may not sow or gather in our crop?' 21 I will order my blessing for you in the sixth year, so that it will yield a crop for three years. 22 When you sow in the eighth year, you will be eating from the old crop; until the ninth year, when its produce comes in, you shall eat the old. 23 The land shall not be sold in perpetuity, for the land is mine; with me you are but aliens and tenants. 24 Throughout the land that you hold, you shall provide for the redemption of the land.

25 If anyone of your kin falls into difficulty and sells a piece of property, then the next-of-kin shall come and redeem what the relative has sold. 26 If the person has no one to redeem it, but then prospers and finds sufficient means to do so, 27 the years since its sale shall be computed and the difference shall be refunded to the person to whom it was sold, and the property shall be returned. 28 But if there are not sufficient means to recover it, what was sold shall remain with the purchaser until the year of jubilee; in the jubilee it shall be released, and the property shall be returned.

a Or *sabbaths*

29 If anyone sells a dwelling-house in a walled city, it may be redeemed until a year has elapsed since its sale; the right of redemption shall be for one year. 30 If it is not redeemed before a full year has elapsed, a house that is in a walled city shall pass in perpetuity to the purchaser, throughout the generations; it shall not be released in the jubilee. 31 But houses in villages that have no walls around them shall be classed as open country; they may be redeemed, and they shall be released in the jubilee. 32 As for the cities of the Levites, the Levites shall for ever have the right of redemption of the houses in the cities belonging to them. 33 Such property as may be redeemed from the Levites—houses sold in a city belonging to them—shall be released in the jubilee; because the houses in the cities of the Levites are their possession among the people of Israel. 34 But the open land around their cities may not be sold; for that is their possession for all time.

35 If any of your kin fall into difficulty and become dependent on you, a you shall support them; they shall live with you as though resident aliens. 36 Do not take interest in advance or otherwise make a profit from them, but fear your God; let them live with you. 37 You shall not lend them your money at interest taken in advance, or provide them food at a profit. 38 I am the LORD your God, who brought you out of the land of Egypt, to give you the land of Canaan, to be your God.

39 If any who are dependent on you become so impoverished that they sell themselves to you, you shall not make them serve as slaves. 40 They shall remain with you as hired or bound labourers. They shall serve with you until the year of the jubilee. 41 Then they and their children with them shall be free from your authority; they shall go back to their own family and return to their ancestral property. 42 For they are my servants, whom I brought out of the land of Egypt; they shall not be sold as slaves are sold. 43 You shall not rule over them with harshness, but shall fear your God. 44 As for the male and female slaves whom you may have, it is from the nations around you that you may acquire male and female slaves. 45 You may also acquire them from among the aliens residing with you, and from their families that are with you, who have been born in your land; and they may be your property. 46 You may keep them as a possession for your children after you, for them to inherit as property. These you may treat as slaves, but as for your fellow Israelites, no one shall rule over the other with harshness.

47 If resident aliens among you prosper, and if any of your kin fall into difficulty with one of them and sell themselves to an alien, or to a branch of the alien's family, 48 after they have sold themselves they shall have the right of redemption; one of their brothers may redeem them, 49 or their uncle or their uncle's son may redeem them, or anyone of their family who is of their own flesh may redeem them; or if they prosper they may redeem themselves. 50 They shall compute with the purchaser the total from the year when they sold themselves to the alien until the jubilee year; the price of the sale shall be applied to the number of years: the time they were with the owner shall be rated as the time of a hired labourer. 51 If many years remain, they shall pay for their redemption in proportion to the purchase price; 52 and if few years remain until the jubilee year, they shall compute thus: according to the years involved they shall make payment for their redemption. 53 As a labourer hired by the year they shall be under the alien's authority, who shall not, however, rule with harshness over them in your sight. 54 And if they have not been redeemed in any of these ways, they and their children with them shall go free in the jubilee year. 55 For to me the people of Israel are servants; they are my servants whom I brought out from the land of Egypt: I am the LORD your God.

Rewards for Obedience

26 You shall make for yourselves no idols and erect no carved images or pillars, and you shall not place figured stones in your land, to worship at them; for

b Meaning of Heb uncertain

I am the LORD your God. ²You shall keep my sabbaths and reverence my sanctuary: I am the LORD.

3 If you follow my statutes and keep my commandments and observe them faithfully, ⁴I will give you your rains in their season, and the land shall yield its produce, and the trees of the field shall yield their fruit. ⁵Your threshing shall overtake the vintage, and the vintage shall overtake the sowing; you shall eat your bread to the full, and live securely in your land. ⁶And I will grant peace in the land, and you shall lie down, and no one shall make you afraid; I will remove dangerous animals from the land, and no sword shall go through your land. ⁷You shall give chase to your enemies, and they shall fall before you by the sword. ⁸Five of you shall give chase to a hundred, and a hundred of you shall give chase to ten thousand; your enemies shall fall before you by the sword. ⁹I will look with favour upon you and make you fruitful and multiply you; and I will maintain my covenant with you. ¹⁰You shall eat old grain long stored, and you shall have to clear out the old to make way for the new. ¹¹I will place my dwelling in your midst, and I shall not abhor you. ¹²And I will walk among you, and will be your God, and you shall be my people. ¹³I am the LORD your God who brought you out of the land of Egypt, to be their slaves no more; I have broken the bars of your yoke and made you walk erect.

Penalties for Disobedience

14 But if you will not obey me, and do not observe all these commandments, ¹⁵if you spurn my statutes, and abhor my ordinances, so that you will not observe all my commandments, and you break my covenant, ¹⁶I in turn will do this to you: I will bring terror on you; consumption and fever that waste the eyes and cause life to pine away. You shall sow your seed in vain, for your enemies shall eat it. ¹⁷I will set my face against you, and you shall be struck down by your enemies; your foes shall rule over you, and you shall flee though no one pursues you. ¹⁸And if in spite of this you will

not obey me, I will continue to punish you sevenfold for your sins. ¹⁹I will break your proud glory, and I will make your sky like iron and your earth like copper. ²⁰Your strength shall be spent to no purpose: your land shall not yield its produce, and the trees of the land shall not yield their fruit. 21 If you continue hostile to me, and will not obey me, I will continue to plague you sevenfold for your sins. ²²I will let loose wild animals against you, and they shall bereave you of your children and destroy your livestock; they shall make you few in number, and your roads shall be deserted.

23 If in spite of these punishments you have not turned back to me, but continue hostile to me, ²⁴then I too will continue hostile to you: I myself will strike you sevenfold for your sins. ²⁵I will bring the sword against you, executing vengeance for the covenant; and if you withdraw within your cities, I will send pestilence among you, and you shall be delivered into enemy hands. ²⁶When I break your staff of bread, ten women shall bake your bread in a single oven, and they shall dole out your bread by weight; and though you eat, you shall not be satisfied.

27 But if, despite this, you disobey me, and continue hostile to me, ²⁸I will continue hostile to you in fury; I in turn will punish you myself sevenfold for your sins. ²⁹You shall eat the flesh of your sons, and you shall eat the flesh of your daughters. ³⁰I will destroy your high places and cut down your incense-altars; I will heap your carcasses on the carcasses of your idols. I will abhor you. ³¹I will lay your cities waste, will make your sanctuaries desolate, and I will not smell your pleasing odours. ³²I will devastate the land, so that your enemies who come to settle in it shall be appalled at it. ³³And you I will scatter among the nations, and I will unsheathe the sword against you; your land shall be a desolation, and your cities a waste.

34 Then the land shall enjoy*a* its sabbath years as long as it lies desolate, while you are in the land of your enemies; then

---

a Or *make up for*

the land shall rest, and enjoy[a] its sabbath years. [35]As long as it lies desolate, it shall have the rest it did not have on your sabbaths when you were living on it. [36]And as for those of you who survive, I will send faintness into their hearts in the lands of their enemies; the sound of a driven leaf shall put them to flight, and they shall flee as one flees from the sword, and they shall fall though no one pursues. [37]They shall stumble over one another, as if to escape a sword, though no one pursues; and you shall have no power to stand against your enemies. [38]You shall perish among the nations, and the land of your enemies shall devour you. [39]And those of you who survive shall languish in the land of your enemies because of their iniquities; also they shall languish because of the iniquities of their ancestors.

40 But if they confess their iniquity and the iniquity of their ancestors, in that they committed treachery against me and, moreover, that they continued hostile to me— [41]so that I, in turn, continued hostile to them and brought them into the land of their enemies; if then their uncircumcised heart is humbled and they make amends for their iniquity, [42]then will I remember my covenant with Jacob; I will remember also my covenant with Isaac and also my covenant with Abraham, and I will remember the land. [43]For the land shall be deserted by them, and enjoy[a] its sabbath years by lying desolate without them, while they shall make amends for their iniquity, because they dared to spurn my ordinances, and they abhorred my statutes. [44]Yet for all that, when they are in the land of their enemies, I will not spurn them, or abhor them so as to destroy them utterly and break my covenant with them; for I am the LORD their God; [45]but I will remember in their favour the covenant with their ancestors whom I brought out of the land of Egypt in the sight of the nations, to be their God: I am the LORD.

46 These are the statutes and ordinances and laws that the LORD established between himself and the people of Israel on Mount Sinai through Moses.

Votive Offerings

27 The LORD spoke to Moses, saying: [2]Speak to the people of Israel and say to them: When a person makes an explicit vow to the LORD concerning the equivalent for a human being, [3]the equivalent for a male shall be: from twenty to sixty years of age the equivalent shall be fifty shekels of silver by the sanctuary shekel. [4]If the person is a female, the equivalent is thirty shekels. [5]If the age is from five to twenty years of age, the equivalent is twenty shekels for a male and ten shekels for a female. [6]If the age is from one month to five years, the equivalent for a male is five shekels of silver, and for a female the equivalent is three shekels of silver. [7]And if the person is sixty years old or over, then the equivalent for a male is fifteen shekels, and for a female ten shekels. [8]If any cannot afford the equivalent, they shall be brought before the priest and the priest shall assess them; the priest shall assess them according to what each one making a vow can afford.

9 If it concerns an animal that may be brought as an offering to the LORD, any such that may be given to the LORD shall be holy. [10]Another shall not be exchanged or substituted for it, either good for bad or bad for good; and if one animal is substituted for another, both that one and its substitute shall be holy. [11]If it concerns any unclean animal that may not be brought as an offering to the LORD, the animal shall be presented before the priest. [12]The priest shall assess it: whether good or bad, according to the assessment of the priest, so it shall be. [13]But if it is to be redeemed, one-fifth must be added to the assessment.

14 If a person consecrates a house to the LORD, the priest shall assess it: whether good or bad, as the priest assesses it, so it shall stand. [15]And if the one who consecrates the house wishes to redeem it, one-fifth shall be added to its assessed value, and it shall revert to the original owner.

16 If a person consecrates to the LORD any inherited land-holding, its assessment

a Or make up for

shall be in accordance with its seed requirements: fifty shekels of silver to a homer of barley seed. ¹⁷ If the person consecrates the field as of the year of jubilee, that assessment shall stand; ¹⁸ but if the field is consecrated after the jubilee, the priest shall compute the price for it according to the years that remain until the year of jubilee, and the assessment shall be reduced. ¹⁹ And if the one who consecrates the field wishes to redeem it, then one-fifth shall be added to its assessed value, and it shall revert to the original owner; ²⁰ but if the field is not redeemed, or if it has been sold to someone else, it shall no longer be redeemable. ²¹ But when the field is released in the jubilee, it shall be holy to the LORD as a devoted field; it becomes the priest's holding. ²² If someone consecrates to the LORD a field that has been purchased, which is not a part of the inherited land-holding, ²³ the priest shall compute for it the proportionate assessment up to the year of jubilee, and the assessment shall be paid as of that day, a sacred donation to the LORD. ²⁴ In the year of jubilee the field shall return to the one from whom it was bought, whose holding the land is. ²⁵ All assessments shall be by the sanctuary shekel: twenty gerahs shall make a shekel.

26 A firstling of animals, however, which as a firstling belongs to the LORD, cannot be consecrated by anyone; whether ox or sheep, it is the LORD's. ²⁷ If it is an unclean animal, it shall be ransomed at its assessment, with one-fifth added; if it is not redeemed, it shall be sold at its assessment.

28 Nothing that a person owns that has been devoted to destruction for the LORD, be it human or animal, or inherited land-holding, may be sold or redeemed; every devoted thing is most holy to the LORD. ²⁹ No human beings who have been devoted to destruction can be ransomed; they shall be put to death.

30 All tithes from the land, whether the seed from the ground or the fruit from the tree, are the LORD's; they are holy to the LORD. ³¹ If persons wish to redeem any of their tithes, they must add one-fifth to them. ³² All tithes of herd and flock, every tenth one that passes under the shepherd's staff, shall be holy to the LORD. ³³ Let no one inquire whether it is good or bad, or make substitution for it; if one makes substitution for it, then both it and the substitute shall be holy and cannot be redeemed.

34 These are the commandments that the LORD gave to Moses for the people of Israel on Mount Sinai.

NUMBERS

The First Census of Israel

1 The LORD spoke to Moses in the wilderness of Sinai, in the tent of meeting, on the first day of the second month, in the second year after they had come out of the land of Egypt, saying: ²Take a census of the whole congregation of Israelites, in their clans, by ancestral houses, according to the number of names, every male individually; ³from twenty years old and upwards, everyone in Israel able to go to war. You and Aaron shall enrol them, company by company. ⁴A man from each tribe shall be with you, each man the head of his ancestral house. ⁵These are the names of the men who shall assist you:

From Reuben, Elizur son of Shedeur.
⁶ From Simeon, Shelumiel son of Zurishaddai.
⁷ From Judah, Nahshon son of Amminadab.
⁸ From Issachar, Nethanel son of Zuar.
⁹ From Zebulun, Eliab son of Helon.
¹⁰ From the sons of Joseph:
from Ephraim, Elishama son of Ammihud;
from Manasseh, Gamaliel son of Pedahzur.
¹¹ From Benjamin, Abidan son of Gideoni.
¹² From Dan, Ahiezer son of Ammishaddai.
¹³ From Asher, Pagiel son of Ochran.
¹⁴ From Gad, Eliasaph son of Deuel.
¹⁵ From Naphtali, Ahira son of Enan.
¹⁶These were the ones chosen from the congregation, the leaders of their ancestral tribes, the heads of the divisions of Israel.

17 Moses and Aaron took these men who had been designated by name, ¹⁸and on the first day of the second month they assembled the whole congregation together. They registered themselves in their clans, by their ancestral houses, according to the number of names from twenty years old and upwards, individually, ¹⁹as the LORD commanded Moses. So he enrolled them in the wilderness of Sinai.

20 The descendants of Reuben, Israel's firstborn, their lineage, in their clans, by their ancestral houses, according to the number of names, individually, every male from twenty years old and upwards, everyone able to go to war: ²¹those enrolled of the tribe of Reuben were forty-six thousand five hundred.

22 The descendants of Simeon, their lineage, in their clans, by their ancestral houses, those of them that were numbered, according to the number of names, individually, every male from twenty years old and upwards, everyone able to go to war: ²³those enrolled of the tribe of Simeon were fifty-nine thousand three hundred.

24 The descendants of Gad, their lineage, in their clans, by their ancestral houses, according to the number of the names, from twenty years old and upwards, everyone able to go to war: ²⁵those enrolled of the tribe of Gad were forty-five thousand six hundred and fifty.

26 The descendants of Judah, their lineage, in their clans, by their ancestral houses, according to the number of names, from twenty years old and upwards, everyone able to go to war: ²⁷those enrolled of the tribe of Judah were seventy-four thousand six hundred.

28 The descendants of Issachar, their lineage, in their clans, by their ancestral

houses, according to the number of names, from twenty years old and upwards, everyone able to go to war: 29 those enrolled of the tribe of Issachar were fifty-four thousand four hundred.

30 The descendants of Zebulun, their lineage, in their clans, by their ancestral houses, according to the number of names, from twenty years old and upwards, everyone able to go to war: 31 those enrolled of the tribe of Zebulun were fifty-seven thousand four hundred.

32 The descendants of Joseph, namely, the descendants of Ephraim, their lineage, in their clans, by their ancestral houses, according to the number of names, from twenty years old and upwards, everyone able to go to war: 33 those enrolled of the tribe of Ephraim were forty thousand five hundred.

34 The descendants of Manasseh, their lineage, in their clans, by their ancestral houses, according to the number of names, from twenty years old and upwards, everyone able to go to war: 35 those enrolled of the tribe of Manasseh were thirty-two thousand two hundred.

36 The descendants of Benjamin, their lineage, in their clans, by their ancestral houses, according to the number of names, from twenty years old and upwards, everyone able to go to war: 37 those enrolled of the tribe of Benjamin were thirty-five thousand four hundred.

38 The descendants of Dan, their lineage, in their clans, by their ancestral houses, according to the number of names, from twenty years old and upwards, everyone able to go to war: 39 those enrolled of the tribe of Dan were sixty-two thousand seven hundred.

40 The descendants of Asher, their lineage, in their clans, by their ancestral houses, according to the number of names, from twenty years old and upwards, everyone able to go to war: 41 those enrolled of the tribe of Asher were forty-one thousand five hundred.

42 The descendants of Naphtali, their lineage, in their clans, by their ancestral houses, according to the number of names,

from twenty years old and upwards, everyone able to go to war: 43 those enrolled of the tribe of Naphtali were fifty-three thousand four hundred.

44 These are those who were enrolled, whom Moses and Aaron enrolled with the help of the leaders of Israel, twelve men, each representing his ancestral house. 45 So the whole number of the Israelites, by their ancestral houses, from twenty years old and upwards, everyone able to go to war in Israel— 46 their whole number was six hundred and three thousand five hundred and fifty. 47 The Levites, however, were not numbered by their ancestral tribe along with them.

48 The Lord had said to Moses: 49 Only the tribe of Levi you shall not enrol, and you shall not take a census of them with the other Israelites. 50 Rather you shall appoint the Levites over the tabernacle of the covenant, a and over all its equipment, and over all that belongs to it; they are to carry the tabernacle and all its equipment, and they shall tend it, and shall camp around the tabernacle. 51 When the tabernacle is to set out, the Levites shall take it down; and when the tabernacle is to be pitched, the Levites shall set it up. And any outsider who comes near shall be put to death. 52 The other Israelites shall camp in their respective regimental camps, by companies; 53 but the Levites shall camp around the tabernacle of the covenant, a so that there may be no wrath on the congregation of the Israelites; and the Levites shall perform the guard duty of the tabernacle of the covenant. a 54 The Israelites did so; they did just as the Lord commanded Moses.

The Order of Encampment and Marching

2 The Lord spoke to Moses and Aaron, saying: 2 The Israelites shall camp each in their respective regiments, under ensigns by their ancestral houses; they shall camp facing the tent of meeting on every side. 3 Those to camp on the east side towards the sunrise shall be of the regimental encampment of Judah by companies. The leader of the people of Judah shall be Nahshon son of

a Or treaty, or testimony; Heb eduth

Amminadab, [4] with a company as enrolled of seventy-four thousand six hundred. [5] Those to camp next to him shall be the tribe of Issachar. The leader of the Issacharites shall be Nethanel son of Zuar, [6] with a company as enrolled of fifty-four thousand four hundred. [7] Then the tribe of Zebulun: The leader of the Zebulunites shall be Eliab son of Helon, [8] with a company as enrolled of fifty-seven thousand four hundred. [9] The total enrolment of the camp of Judah, by companies, is one hundred and eighty-six thousand four hundred. They shall set out first on the march.

10 On the south side shall be the regimental encampment of Reuben by companies. The leader of the Reubenites shall be Elizur son of Shedeur, [11] with a company as enrolled of forty-six thousand five hundred. [12] And those to camp next to him shall be the tribe of Simeon. The leader of the Simeonites shall be Shelumiel son of Zurishaddai, [13] with a company as enrolled of fifty-nine thousand three hundred. [14] Then the tribe of Gad: The leader of the Gadites shall be Eliasaph son of Reuel, [15] with a company as enrolled of forty-five thousand six hundred and fifty. [16] The total enrolment of the camp of Reuben, by companies, is one hundred and fifty-one thousand four hundred and fifty. They shall set out second.

17 The tent of meeting, with the camp of the Levites, shall set out in the centre of the camps; they shall set out just as they camp, each in position, by their regiments.

18 On the west side shall be the regimental encampment of Ephraim by companies. The leader of the people of Ephraim shall be Elishama son of Ammihud, [19] with a company as enrolled of forty thousand five hundred. [20] Next to him shall be the tribe of Manasseh. The leader of the people of Manasseh shall be Gamaliel son of Pedahzur, [21] with a company as enrolled of thirty-two thousand two hundred. [22] Then the tribe of Benjamin: The leader of the Benjaminites shall be Abidan son of Gideoni, [23] with a company as enrolled of thirty-five thousand four hundred. [24] The total enrolment of the camp of Ephraim, by companies, is one hundred and eight thousand one hundred. They shall set out third on the march.

25 On the north side shall be the regimental encampment of Dan by companies. The leader of the Danites shall be Ahiezer son of Ammishaddai, [26] with a company as enrolled of sixty-two thousand seven hundred. [27] Those to camp next to him shall be the tribe of Asher. The leader of the Asherites shall be Pagiel son of Ochran, [28] with a company as enrolled of forty-one thousand five hundred. [29] Then the tribe of Naphtali: The leader of the Naphtalites shall be Ahira son of Enan, [30] with a company as enrolled of fifty-three thousand four hundred. [31] The total enrolment of the camp of Dan is one hundred and fifty-seven thousand six hundred. They shall set out last, by companies. [a]

32 This was the enrolment of the Israelites by their ancestral houses; the total enrolment in the camps by their companies was six hundred and three thousand five hundred and fifty. [33] Just as the LORD had commanded Moses, the Levites were not enrolled among the other Israelites.

34 The Israelites did just as the LORD had commanded Moses: They camped by regiments, and they set out the same way, everyone by clans, according to ancestral houses.

The Sons of Aaron

3 This is the lineage of Aaron and Moses at the time when the LORD spoke with Moses on Mount Sinai. [2] These are the names of the sons of Aaron: Nadab the firstborn, and Abihu, Eleazar, and Ithamar; [3] these are the names of the sons of Aaron, the anointed priests, whom he ordained to minister as priests. [4] Nadab and Abihu died before the LORD when they offered unholy fire before the LORD in the wilderness of Sinai, and they had no children. Eleazar and Ithamar served as priests in the lifetime of their father Aaron.

The Duties of the Levites

5 Then the LORD spoke to Moses, saying: [6] Bring the tribe of Levi near, and set them

a Compare verses 9, 16, 24: Heb *by their regiments*

before Aaron the priest, so that they may assist him. ⁷They shall perform duties for him and for the whole congregation in front of the tent of meeting, doing service at the tabernacle; ⁸they shall be in charge of all the furnishings of the tent of meeting, and attend to the duties for the Israelites as they do service at the tabernacle. ⁹You shall give the Levites to Aaron and his descendants; they are unreservedly given to him from among the Israelites. ¹⁰But you shall make a register of Aaron and his descendants; it is they who shall attend to the priesthood, and any outsider who comes near shall be put to death.

11 Then the LORD spoke to Moses, saying: ¹²I hereby accept the Levites from among the Israelites as substitutes for all the firstborn that open the womb among the Israelites. The Levites shall be mine, ¹³for all the firstborn are mine; when I killed all the firstborn in the land of Egypt, I consecrated for my own all the firstborn in Israel, both human and animal; they shall be mine. I am the LORD.

A Census of the Levites

14 Then the LORD spoke to Moses in the wilderness of Sinai, saying: ¹⁵Enrol the Levites by ancestral houses and by clans. You shall enrol every male from a month old and upwards. ¹⁶So Moses enrolled them according to the word of the LORD, as he was commanded. ¹⁷The following were the sons of Levi, by their names: Gershon, Kohath, and Merari. ¹⁸These are the names of the sons of Gershon by their clans: Libni and Shimei. ¹⁹The sons of Kohath by their clans: Amram, Izhar, Hebron, and Uzziel. ²⁰The sons of Merari by their clans: Mahli and Mushi. These are the clans of the Levites, by their ancestral houses.

21 To Gershon belonged the clan of the Libnites and the clan of the Shimeites; these were the clans of the Gershonites. ²²Their enrolment, counting all the males from a month old and upwards, was seven thousand five hundred. ²³The clans of the Gershonites were to camp behind the tabernacle on the west, ²⁴with Eliasaph son of Lael as head of the ancestral house of the Gershonites. ²⁵The responsibility of the sons of Gershon in the tent of meeting was to be the tabernacle, the tent with its covering, the screen for the entrance of the tent of meeting, ²⁶the hangings of the court, the screen for the entrance of the court that is around the tabernacle and the altar, and its cords—all the service pertaining to these.

27 To Kohath belonged the clan of the Amramites, the clan of the Izharites, the clan of the Hebronites, and the clan of the Uzzielites; these are the clans of the Kohathites. ²⁸Counting all the males, from a month old and upwards, there were eight thousand six hundred, attending to the duties of the sanctuary. ²⁹The clans of the Kohathites were to camp on the south side of the tabernacle, ³⁰with Elizaphan son of Uzziel as head of the ancestral house of the clans of the Kohathites. ³¹Their responsibility was to be the ark, the table, the lampstand, the altars, the vessels of the sanctuary with which the priests minister, and the screen—all the service pertaining to these. ³²Eleazar son of Aaron the priest was to be chief over the leaders of the Levites, and to have oversight of those who had charge of the sanctuary.

33 To Merari belonged the clan of the Mahlites and the clan of the Mushites: these are the clans of Merari. ³⁴Their enrolment, counting all the males from a month old and upwards, was six thousand two hundred. ³⁵The head of the ancestral house of the clans of Merari was Zuriel son of Abihail; they were to camp on the north side of the tabernacle. ³⁶The responsibility assigned to the sons of Merari was to be the frames of the tabernacle, the bars, the pillars, the bases, and all their accessories—all the service pertaining to these; ³⁷also the pillars of the court all around, with their bases and pegs and cords.

38 Those who were to camp in front of the tabernacle on the east—in front of the tent of meeting towards the east—were Moses and Aaron and Aaron's sons, having charge of the rites within the sanctuary, whatever had to be done for the Israelites; and any outsider who came near was to be put to death. ³⁹The total enrolment of the

Levites whom Moses and Aaron enrolled at the commandment of the Lord, by their clans, all the males from a month old and upwards, was twenty-two thousand.

The Redemption of the Firstborn

40 Then the Lord said to Moses: Enrol all the firstborn males of the Israelites, from a month old and upwards, and count their names. 41 But you shall accept the Levites for me—I am the Lord—as substitutes for all the firstborn among the Israelites, and the livestock of the Levites as substitutes for all the firstborn among the livestock of the Israelites. 42 So Moses enrolled all the firstborn among the Israelites, as the Lord commanded him. 43 The total enrolment, all the firstborn males from a month old and upwards, counting the number of names, was twenty-two thousand two hundred and seventy-three.

44 Then the Lord spoke to Moses, saying: 45 Accept the Levites as substitutes for all the firstborn among the Israelites, and the livestock of the Levites as substitutes for their livestock; and the Levites shall be mine. I am the Lord. 46 As the price of redemption of the two hundred and seventy-three of the firstborn of the Israelites, over and above the number of the Levites, 47 you shall accept five shekels apiece, reckoning by the shekel of the sanctuary, a shekel of twenty gerahs. 48 Give to Aaron and his sons the money by which the excess number of them is redeemed. 49 So Moses took the redemption money from those who were over and above those redeemed by the Levites; 50 from the firstborn of the Israelites he took the money, one thousand three hundred and sixty-five shekels, reckoned by the shekel of the sanctuary; 51 and Moses gave the redemption money to Aaron and his sons, according to the word of the Lord, as the Lord had commanded Moses.

The Kohathites

4 The Lord spoke to Moses and Aaron, saying: 2 Take a census of the Kohathites separate from the other Levites, by their clans and their ancestral houses, 3 from thirty years old up to fifty years old, all who qualify to do work relating to the tent of meeting. 4 The service of the Kohathites relating to the tent of meeting concerns the most holy things.

5 When the camp is to set out, Aaron and his sons shall go in and take down the screening curtain, and cover the ark of the covenant[a] with it; 6 then they shall put on it a covering of fine leather,[b] and spread over that a cloth all of blue, and shall put its poles in place. 7 Over the table of the bread of the Presence they shall spread a blue cloth, and put on it the plates, the dishes for incense, the bowls, and the flagons for the drink-offering; the regular bread also shall be on it; 8 then they shall spread over them a crimson cloth, and cover it with a covering of fine leather,[b] and shall put its poles in place. 9 They shall take a blue cloth, and cover the lampstand for the light, with its lamps, its snuffers, its trays, and all the vessels for oil with which it is supplied; 10 and they shall put it with all its utensils in a covering of fine leather,[b] and put it on the carrying-frame. 11 Over the golden altar they shall spread a blue cloth, and cover it with a covering of fine leather,[b] and shall put its poles in place; 12 and they shall take all the utensils of the service that are used in the sanctuary, and put them in a blue cloth, and cover them with a covering of fine leather,[b] and put them on the carrying-frame. 13 They shall take away the ashes from the altar, and spread a purple cloth over it; 14 and they shall put on it all the utensils of the altar, which are used for the service there, the firepans, the forks, the shovels, and the basins, all the utensils of the altar; and they shall spread on it a covering of fine leather,[b] and shall put its poles in place. 15 When Aaron and his sons have finished covering the sanctuary and all the furnishings of the sanctuary, as the camp sets out, after that the Kohathites shall come to carry these, but they must not touch the holy things, or they will die. These are the things of the tent of meeting that the Kohathites are to carry.

a Or treaty, or testimony; Heb eduth   b Meaning of Heb uncertain

16 Eleazar son of Aaron the priest shall have charge of the oil for the light, the fragrant incense, the regular grain-offering, and the anointing-oil, the oversight of all the tabernacle and all that is in it, in the sanctuary and in its utensils.

17 Then the LORD spoke to Moses and Aaron, saying: [18] You must not let the tribe of the clans of the Kohathites be destroyed from among the Levites. [19] This is how you must deal with them in order that they may live and not die when they come near to the most holy things: Aaron and his sons shall go in and assign each to a particular task or burden. [20] But the Kohathites[a] must not go in to look on the holy things even for a moment; otherwise they will die.

The Gershonites and Merarites

21 Then the LORD spoke to Moses, saying: [22] Take a census of the Gershonites also, by their ancestral houses and by their clans; [23] from thirty years old up to fifty years old you shall enrol them, all who qualify to do work in the tent of meeting. [24] This is the service of the clans of the Gershonites, in serving and bearing burdens: [25] They shall carry the curtains of the tabernacle, and the tent of meeting with its covering, and the outer covering of fine leather[b] that is on top of it, and the screen for the entrance of the tent of meeting, [26] and the hangings of the court, and the screen for the entrance of the gate of the court that is around the tabernacle and the altar, and their cords, and all the equipment for their service; and they shall do all that needs to be done with regard to them. [27] All the service of the Gershonites shall be at the command of Aaron and his sons, in all that they are to carry, and in all that they have to do; and you shall assign to their charge all that they are to carry. [28] This is the service of the clans of the Gershonites relating to the tent of meeting, and their responsibilities are to be under the oversight of Ithamar son of Aaron the priest.

29 As for the Merarites, you shall enrol them by their clans and their ancestral houses; [30] from thirty years old up to fifty years old you shall enrol them, everyone who qualifies to do the work of the tent of meeting. [31] This is what they are charged to carry, as the whole of their service in the tent of meeting: the frames of the tabernacle, with its bars, pillars, and bases, [32] and the pillars of the court all around with their bases, pegs, and cords, with all their equipment and all their related service; and you shall assign by name the objects that they are required to carry. [33] This is the service of the clans of the Merarites, the whole of their service relating to the tent of meeting, under the hand of Ithamar son of Aaron the priest.

Census of the Levites

34 So Moses and Aaron and the leaders of the congregation enrolled the Kohathites, by their clans and their ancestral houses, [35] from thirty years old up to fifty years old, everyone who qualified for work relating to the tent of meeting; [36] and their enrolment by clans was two thousand seven hundred and fifty. [37] This was the enrolment of the clans of the Kohathites, all who served at the tent of meeting, whom Moses and Aaron enrolled according to the commandment of the LORD by Moses.

38 The enrolment of the Gershonites, by their clans and their ancestral houses, [39] from thirty years old up to fifty years old, everyone who qualified for work relating to the tent of meeting— [40] their enrolment by their clans and their ancestral houses was two thousand six hundred and thirty. [41] This was the enrolment of the clans of the Gershonites, all who served at the tent of meeting, whom Moses and Aaron enrolled according to the commandment of the LORD.

42 The enrolment of the clans of the Merarites, by their clans and their ancestral houses, [43] from thirty years old up to fifty years old, everyone who qualified for work relating to the tent of meeting— [44] their enrolment by their clans was three thousand two hundred. [45] This is the enrolment of the clans of the Merarites, whom Moses and Aaron enrolled according to the commandment of the LORD by Moses.

a Heb *they*   *b* Meaning of Heb uncertain

46 All those who were enrolled of the Levites, whom Moses and Aaron and the leaders of Israel enrolled, by their clans and their ancestral houses, 47 from thirty years old up to fifty years old, everyone who qualified to do the work of service and the work of bearing burdens relating to the tent of meeting, 48 their enrolment was eight thousand five hundred and eighty. 49 According to the commandment of the LORD through Moses they were appointed to their several tasks of serving or carrying; thus they were enrolled by him, as the LORD commanded Moses.

Unclean Persons

5 The LORD spoke to Moses, saying: 2 Command the Israelites to put out of the camp everyone who is leprous, *a* or has a discharge, and everyone who is unclean through contact with a corpse; 3 you shall put out both male and female, putting them outside the camp; they must not defile their camp, where I dwell among them. 4 The Israelites did so, putting them outside the camp; as the LORD had spoken to Moses, so the Israelites did.

Confession and Restitution

5 The LORD spoke to Moses, saying: 6 Speak to the Israelites: When a man or a woman wrongs another, breaking faith with the LORD, that person incurs guilt 7 and shall confess the sin that has been committed. The person shall make full restitution for the wrong, adding one-fifth to it, and giving it to the one who was wronged. 8 If the injured party has no next-of-kin to whom restitution may be made for the wrong, the restitution for wrong shall go to the LORD for the priest, in addition to the ram of atonement with which atonement is made for the guilty party. 9 Among all the sacred donations of the Israelites, every gift that they bring to the priest shall be his. 10 The sacred donations of all are their own; whatever anyone gives to the priest shall be his.

Concerning an Unfaithful Wife

11 The LORD spoke to Moses, saying: 12 Speak to the Israelites and say to them: If any man's wife goes astray and is unfaithful to him, 13 if a man has had intercourse with her but it is hidden from her husband, so that she is undetected though she has defiled herself, and there is no witness against her since she was not caught in the act; 14 if a spirit of jealousy comes on him, and he is jealous of his wife who has defiled herself; or if a spirit of jealousy comes on him, and he is jealous of his wife, though she has not defiled herself; 15 then the man shall bring his wife to the priest. And he shall bring the offering required for her, one-tenth of an ephah of barley flour. He shall pour no oil on it and put no frankincense on it, for it is a grain-offering of jealousy, a grain-offering of remembrance, bringing iniquity to remembrance.

16 Then the priest shall bring her near, and set her before the LORD; 17 the priest shall take holy water in an earthen vessel, and take some of the dust that is on the floor of the tabernacle and put it into the water. 18 The priest shall set the woman before the LORD, dishevel the woman's hair, and place in her hands the grain-offering of remembrance, which is the grain-offering of jealousy. In his own hand the priest shall have the water of bitterness that brings the curse. 19 Then the priest shall make her take an oath, saying, 'If no man has lain with you, if you have not turned aside to uncleanness while under your husband's authority, be immune to this water of bitterness that brings the curse. 20 But if you have gone astray while under your husband's authority, if you have defiled yourself and some man other than your husband has had intercourse with you'— 21 let the priest make the woman take the oath of the curse and say to the woman—'the LORD make you an execration and an oath among your people, when the LORD makes your uterus drop, your womb discharge; 22 now may this water that brings the curse enter your bowels and make your womb discharge, your uterus drop!' And the woman shall say, 'Amen. Amen.'

a A term for several skin diseases; precise meaning uncertain

23 Then the priest shall put these curses in writing, and wash them off into the water of bitterness. 24 He shall make the woman drink the water of bitterness that brings the curse, and the water that brings the curse shall enter her and cause bitter pain. 25 The priest shall take the grain-offering of jealousy out of the woman's hand, and shall elevate the grain-offering before the LORD and bring it to the altar; 26 and the priest shall take a handful of the grain-offering, as its memorial portion, and turn it into smoke on the altar, and afterwards shall make the woman drink the water. 27 When he has made her drink the water, then, if she has defiled herself and has been unfaithful to her husband, the water that brings the curse shall enter into her and cause bitter pain, and her womb shall discharge, her uterus drop, and the woman shall become an execration among her people. 28 But if the woman has not defiled herself and is clean, then she shall be immune and be able to conceive children.

29 This is the law in cases of jealousy, when a wife, while under her husband's authority, goes astray and defiles herself, 30 or when a spirit of jealousy comes on a man and he is jealous of his wife; then he shall set the woman before the LORD, and the priest shall apply this entire law to her. 31 The man shall be free from iniquity, but the woman shall bear her iniquity.

The Nazirites

6 The LORD spoke to Moses, saying: 2 Speak to the Israelites and say to them: When either men or women make a special vow, the vow of a nazirite, *a* to separate themselves to the LORD, 3 they shall separate themselves from wine and strong drink; they shall drink no wine vinegar or other vinegar, and shall not drink any grape juice or eat grapes, fresh or dried. 4 All their days as nazirites *b* they shall eat nothing that is produced by the grape-vine, not even the seeds or the skins.

5 All the days of their nazirite vow no razor shall come upon the head; until the time is completed for which they separate themselves to the LORD, they shall be holy;

they shall let the locks of the head grow long.

6 All the days that they separate themselves to the LORD they shall not go near a corpse. 7 Even if their father or mother, brother or sister, should die, they may not defile themselves; because their consecration to God is upon the head. 8 All their days as nazirites *b* they are holy to the LORD.

9 If someone dies very suddenly nearby, defiling the consecrated head, then they shall shave the head on the day of their cleansing; on the seventh day they shall shave it. 10 On the eighth day they shall bring two turtle-doves or two young pigeons to the priest at the entrance of the tent of meeting, 11 and the priest shall offer one as a sin-offering and the other as a burnt-offering, and make atonement for them, because they incurred guilt by reason of the corpse. They shall sanctify the head that same day, 12 and separate themselves to the LORD for their days as nazirites, *b* and bring a male lamb a year old as a guilt-offering. The former time shall be void, because the consecrated head was defiled.

13 This is the law for the nazirites *b* when the time of their consecration has been completed: they shall be brought to the entrance of the tent of meeting, 14 and they shall offer their gift to the LORD, one male lamb a year old without blemish as a burnt-offering, one ewe lamb a year old without blemish as a sin-offering, one ram without blemish as an offering of well-being, 15 and a basket of unleavened bread, cakes of choice flour mixed with oil, and unleavened wafers spread with oil, with their grain-offering and their drink-offerings. 16 The priest shall present them before the LORD and offer their sin-offering and burnt-offering, 17 and shall offer the ram as a sacrifice of well-being to the LORD, with the basket of unleavened bread; the priest also shall make the accompanying grain-offering and drink-offering. 18 Then the nazirites *b* shall shave the consecrated head at the entrance of the tent of meeting, and shall take the hair from the consecrated

a That is *one separated* or *one consecrated*   *b* That is *those separated* or *those consecrated* head and put it on the fire under the sacrifice of well-being. [19] The priest shall take the shoulder of the ram, when it is boiled, and one unleavened cake out of the basket, and one unleavened wafer, and shall put them in the palms of the nazirites,[a] after they have shaved the consecrated head. [20] Then the priest shall elevate them as an elevation-offering before the LORD; they are a holy portion for the priest, together with the breast that is elevated and the thigh that is offered. After that the nazirites[a] may drink wine.

21 This is the law for the nazirites[a] who take a vow. Their offering to the LORD must be in accordance with the nazirite[b] vow, apart from what else they can afford. In accordance with whatever vow they take, so they shall do, following the law for their consecration.

The Priestly Benediction

22 The LORD spoke to Moses, saying: [23] Speak to Aaron and his sons, saying, Thus you shall bless the Israelites: You shall say to them,

24 The LORD bless you and keep you;
25 the LORD make his face to shine upon you, and be gracious to you;
26 the LORD lift up his countenance upon you, and give you peace.

27 So they shall put my name on the Israelites, and I will bless them.

Offerings of the Leaders

7 On the day when Moses had finished setting up the tabernacle, and had anointed and consecrated it with all its furnishings, and had anointed and consecrated the altar with all its utensils, [2] the leaders of Israel, heads of their ancestral houses, the leaders of the tribes, who were over those who were enrolled, made offerings. [3] They brought their offerings before the LORD, six covered wagons and twelve oxen, a wagon for every two of the leaders, and for each one an ox; they presented them before the tabernacle. [4] Then the LORD said to Moses: [5] Accept these from them, that they may be used in performing the service of the tent of meeting, and give them to the Le-

vites, to each according to his service. [6] So Moses took the wagons and the oxen, and gave them to the Levites. [7] Two wagons and four oxen he gave to the Gershonites, according to their service; [8] and four wagons and eight oxen he gave to the Merarites, according to their service, under the direction of Ithamar son of Aaron the priest. [9] But to the Kohathites he gave none, because they were charged with the care of the holy things that had to be carried on the shoulders.

10 The leaders also presented offerings for the dedication of the altar at the time when it was anointed; the leaders presented their offering before the altar. [11] The LORD said to Moses: They shall present their offerings, one leader each day, for the dedication of the altar.

12 The one who presented his offering on the first day was Nahshon son of Amminadab, of the tribe of Judah; [13] his offering was one silver plate weighing one hundred and thirty shekels, one silver basin weighing seventy shekels, according to the shekel of the sanctuary, both of them full of choice flour mixed with oil for a grain-offering; [14] one golden dish weighing ten shekels, full of incense; [15] one young bull, one ram, one male lamb a year old, for a burnt-offering; [16] one male goat for a sin-offering; [17] and for the sacrifice of well-being, two oxen, five rams, five male goats, and five male lambs a year old. This was the offering of Nahshon son of Amminadab.

18 On the second day Nethanel son of Zuar, the leader of Issachar, presented an offering; [19] he presented for his offering one silver plate weighing one hundred and thirty shekels, one silver basin weighing seventy shekels, according to the shekel of the sanctuary, both of them full of choice flour mixed with oil for a grain-offering; [20] one golden dish weighing ten shekels, full of incense; [21] one young bull, one ram, one male lamb a year old, as a burnt-offering; [22] one male goat as a sin-offering; [23] and for the sacrifice of well-being, two oxen, five rams,

a That is those separated or those consecrated   b That is one separated or one consecrated five male goats, and five male lambs a year old. This was the offering of Nethanel son of Zuar.

24 On the third day Eliab son of Helon, the leader of the Zebulunites: 25 his offering was one silver plate weighing one hundred and thirty shekels, one silver basin weighing seventy shekels, according to the shekel of the sanctuary, both of them full of choice flour mixed with oil for a grain-offering; 26 one golden dish weighing ten shekels, full of incense; 27 one young bull, one ram, one male lamb a year old, for a burnt-offering; 28 one male goat for a sin-offering; 29 and for the sacrifice of well-being, two oxen, five rams, five male goats, and five male lambs a year old. This was the offering of Eliab son of Helon.

30 On the fourth day Elizur son of Shedeur, the leader of the Reubenites: 31 his offering was one silver plate weighing one hundred and thirty shekels, one silver basin weighing seventy shekels, according to the shekel of the sanctuary, both of them full of choice flour mixed with oil for a grain-offering; 32 one golden dish weighing ten shekels, full of incense; 33 one young bull, one ram, one male lamb a year old, for a burnt-offering; 34 one male goat for a sin-offering; 35 and for the sacrifice of well-being, two oxen, five rams, five male goats, and five male lambs a year old. This was the offering of Elizur son of Shedeur.

36 On the fifth day Shelumiel son of Zurishaddai, the leader of the Simeonites: 37 his offering was one silver plate weighing one hundred and thirty shekels, one silver basin weighing seventy shekels, according to the shekel of the sanctuary, both of them full of choice flour mixed with oil for a grain-offering; 38 one golden dish weighing ten shekels, full of incense; 39 one young bull, one ram, one male lamb a year old, for a burnt-offering; 40 one male goat for a sin-offering; 41 and for the sacrifice of well-being, two oxen, five rams, five male goats, and five male lambs a year old. This was the offering of Shelumiel son of Zurishaddai.

42 On the sixth day Eliasaph son of Deuel, the leader of the Gadites: 43 his of-

fering was one silver plate weighing one hundred and thirty shekels, one silver basin weighing seventy shekels, according to the shekel of the sanctuary, both of them full of choice flour mixed with oil for a grain-offering; 44 one golden dish weighing ten shekels, full of incense; 45 one young bull, one ram, one male lamb a year old, for a burnt-offering; 46 one male goat for a sin-offering; 47 and for the sacrifice of well-being, two oxen, five rams, five male goats, and five male lambs a year old. This was the offering of Eliasaph son of Deuel.

48 On the seventh day Elishama son of Ammihud, the leader of the Ephraimites: 49 his offering was one silver plate weighing one hundred and thirty shekels, one silver basin weighing seventy shekels, according to the shekel of the sanctuary, both of them full of choice flour mixed with oil for a grain-offering; 50 one golden dish weighing ten shekels, full of incense; 51 one young bull, one ram, one male lamb a year old, for a burnt-offering; 52 one male goat for a sin-offering; 53 and for the sacrifice of well-being, two oxen, five rams, five male goats, and five male lambs a year old. This was the offering of Elishama son of Ammihud.

54 On the eighth day Gamaliel son of Pedahzur, the leader of the Manassites: 55 his offering was one silver plate weighing one hundred and thirty shekels, one silver basin weighing seventy shekels, according to the shekel of the sanctuary, both of them full of choice flour mixed with oil for a grain-offering; 56 one golden dish weighing ten shekels, full of incense; 57 one young bull, one ram, one male lamb a year old, for a burnt-offering; 58 one male goat for a sin-offering; 59 and for the sacrifice of well-being, two oxen, five rams, five male goats, and five male lambs a year old. This was the offering of Gamaliel son of Pedahzur.

60 On the ninth day Abidan son of Gideoni, the leader of the Benjaminites: 61 his offering was one silver plate weighing one hundred and thirty shekels, one silver basin weighing seventy shekels, according to the shekel of the sanctuary, both of them full of choice flour mixed with oil for a grain-offering; 62 one golden dish weighing ten

shekels, full of incense; 63 one young bull, one ram, one male lamb a year old, for a burnt-offering; 64 one male goat for a sin-offering; 65 and for the sacrifice of well-being, two oxen, five rams, five male goats, and five male lambs a year old. This was the offering of Abidan son of Gideoni.

66 On the tenth day Ahiezer son of Ammishaddai, the leader of the Danites: 67 his offering was one silver plate weighing one hundred and thirty shekels, one silver basin weighing seventy shekels, according to the shekel of the sanctuary, both of them full of choice flour mixed with oil for a grain-offering; 68 one golden dish weighing ten shekels, full of incense; 69 one young bull, one ram, one male lamb a year old, for a burnt-offering; 70 one male goat for a sin-offering; 71 and for the sacrifice of well-being, two oxen, five rams, five male goats, and five male lambs a year old. This was the offering of Ahiezer son of Ammishaddai.

72 On the eleventh day Pagiel son of Ochran, the leader of the Asherites: 73 his offering was one silver plate weighing one hundred and thirty shekels, one silver basin weighing seventy shekels, according to the shekel of the sanctuary, both of them full of choice flour mixed with oil for a grain-offering; 74 one golden dish weighing ten shekels, full of incense; 75 one young bull, one ram, one male lamb a year old, for a burnt-offering; 76 one male goat for a sin-offering; 77 and for the sacrifice of well-being, two oxen, five rams, five male goats, and five male lambs a year old. This was the offering of Pagiel son of Ochran.

78 On the twelfth day Ahira son of Enan, the leader of the Naphtalites: 79 his offering was one silver plate weighing one hundred and thirty shekels, one silver basin weighing seventy shekels, according to the shekel of the sanctuary, both of them full of choice flour mixed with oil for a grain-offering; 80 one golden dish weighing ten shekels, full of incense; 81 one young bull, one ram, one male lamb a year old, for a burnt-offering; 82 one male goat for a sin-offering; 83 and for the sacrifice of well-being, two oxen, five rams, five male goats,

and five male lambs a year old. This was the offering of Ahira son of Enan.

84 This was the dedication-offering for the altar, at the time when it was anointed, from the leaders of Israel: twelve silver plates, twelve silver basins, twelve golden dishes, 85 each silver plate weighing one hundred and thirty shekels and each basin seventy, all the silver of the vessels two thousand four hundred shekels according to the shekel of the sanctuary, 86 the twelve golden dishes, full of incense, weighing ten shekels apiece according to the shekel of the sanctuary, all the gold of the dishes being one hundred and twenty shekels; 87 all the livestock for the burnt-offering twelve bulls, twelve rams, twelve male lambs a year old, with their grain-offering; and twelve male goats for a sin-offering; 88 and all the livestock for the sacrifice of well-being twenty-four bulls, the rams sixty, the male goats sixty, the male lambs a year old sixty. This was the dedication-offering for the altar, after it was anointed.

89 When Moses went into the tent of meeting to speak with the LORD, *a* he would hear the voice speaking to him from above the mercy-seat *b* that was on the ark of the covenant *c* from between the two cherubim; thus it spoke to him.

The Seven Lamps

8 The LORD spoke to Moses, saying: 2 Speak to Aaron and say to him: When you set up the lamps, the seven lamps shall give light in front of the lampstand. 3 Aaron did so; he set up its lamps to give light in front of the lampstand, as the LORD had commanded Moses. 4 Now this was how the lampstand was made, out of hammered work of gold. From its base to its flowers, it was hammered work; according to the pattern that the LORD had shown Moses, so he made the lampstand.

Consecration and Service of the Levites

5 The LORD spoke to Moses, saying: 6 Take the Levites from among the Israelites and cleanse them. 7 Thus you shall do to

a Heb *him*   *b* Or *the cover*   *c* Or *treaty,* or *testimony;* Heb *eduth* them, to cleanse them: sprinkle the water of purification on them, have them shave their whole body with a razor and wash their clothes, and so cleanse themselves. 8 Then let them take a young bull and its grain-offering of choice flour mixed with oil, and you shall take another young bull for a sin-offering. 9 You shall bring the Levites before the tent of meeting, and assemble the whole congregation of the Israelites. 10 When you bring the Levites before the LORD, the Israelites shall lay their hands on the Levites, 11 and Aaron shall present the Levites before the LORD as an elevation-offering from the Israelites, that they may perform the service of the LORD. 12 The Levites shall lay their hands on the heads of the bulls, and he shall offer one for a sin-offering and the other for a burnt-offering to the LORD, to make atonement for the Levites. 13 Then you shall have the Levites stand before Aaron and his sons, and you shall present them as an elevation-offering to the LORD.

14 Thus you shall separate the Levites from among the other Israelites, and the Levites shall be mine. 15 Thereafter the Levites may go in to perform service at the tent of meeting, once you have cleansed them and presented them as an elevation-offering. 16 For they are unreservedly given to me from among the Israelites; I have taken them for myself, in place of all that open the womb, the firstborn of all the Israelites. 17 For all the firstborn among the Israelites are mine, both human and animal. On the day that I struck down all the firstborn in the land of Egypt I consecrated them for myself, 18 but I have taken the Levites in place of all the firstborn among the Israelites. 19 Moreover, I have given the Levites as a gift to Aaron and his sons from among the Israelites, to do the service for the Israelites at the tent of meeting, and to make atonement for the Israelites, in order that there may be no plague among the Israelites for coming too close to the sanctuary.

20 Moses and Aaron and the whole congregation of the Israelites did with the Levites accordingly; the Israelites did with the Levites just as the LORD had commanded Moses concerning them. 21 The Levites purified themselves from sin and washed their clothes; then Aaron presented them as an elevation-offering before the LORD, and Aaron made atonement for them to cleanse them. 22 Thereafter the Levites went in to perform their service in the tent of meeting in attendance on Aaron and his sons. As the LORD had commanded Moses concerning the Levites, so they dealt with them.

23 The LORD spoke to Moses, saying: 24 This applies to the Levites: from twenty-five years old and upwards they shall begin to do duty in the service of the tent of meeting; 25 and from the age of fifty years they shall retire from the duty of the service and serve no more. 26 They may assist their brothers in the tent of meeting in carrying out their duties, but they shall perform no service. Thus you shall deal with the Levites in assigning their duties.

The Passover at Sinai

9 The LORD spoke to Moses in the wilderness of Sinai, in the first month of the second year after they had come out of the land of Egypt, saying: 2 Let the Israelites keep the passover at its appointed time. 3 On the fourteenth day of this month, at twilight,[a] you shall keep it at its appointed time; according to all its statutes and all its regulations you shall keep it. 4 So Moses told the Israelites that they should keep the passover. 5 They kept the passover in the first month, on the fourteenth day of the month, at twilight,[a] in the wilderness of Sinai. Just as the LORD had commanded Moses, so the Israelites did. 6 Now there were certain people who were unclean through touching a corpse, so that they could not keep the passover on that day. They came before Moses and Aaron on that day, 7 and said to him, 'Although we are unclean through touching a corpse, why must we be kept from presenting the LORD's offering at its appointed time among the Israelites?' 8 Moses spoke to them, 'Wait, so that I may hear what the LORD will command concerning you.'

a Heb *between the two evenings*

9 The LORD spoke to Moses, saying: 10 Speak to the Israelites, saying: Anyone of you or your descendants who is unclean through touching a corpse, or is away on a journey, shall still keep the passover to the LORD. 11 In the second month on the fourteenth day, at twilight, *a* they shall keep it; they shall eat it with unleavened bread and bitter herbs. 12 They shall leave none of it until morning, nor break a bone of it; according to all the statute for the passover they shall keep it. 13 But anyone who is clean and is not on a journey, and yet refrains from keeping the passover, shall be cut off from the people for not presenting the LORD's offering at its appointed time; such a one shall bear the consequences for the sin. 14 Any alien residing among you who wishes to keep the passover to the LORD shall do so according to the statute of the passover and according to its regulation; you shall have one statute for both the resident alien and the native.

The Cloud and the Fire

15 On the day the tabernacle was set up, the cloud covered the tabernacle, the tent of the covenant; *b* and from evening until morning it was over the tabernacle, having the appearance of fire. 16 It was always so: the cloud covered it by day *c* and the appearance of fire by night. 17 Whenever the cloud lifted from over the tent, then the Israelites would set out; and in the place where the cloud settled down, there the Israelites would camp. 18 At the command of the LORD the Israelites would set out, and at the command of the LORD they would camp. As long as the cloud rested over the tabernacle, they would remain in camp. 19 Even when the cloud continued over the tabernacle for many days, the Israelites would keep the charge of the LORD, and would not set out. 20 Sometimes the cloud would remain for a few days over the tabernacle, and according to the command of the LORD they would remain in camp; then according to the command of the LORD they would set out. 21 Sometimes the cloud would remain

from evening until morning; and when the cloud lifted in the morning, they would set out, or if it continued for a day and a night, when the cloud lifted they would set out. 22 Whether it was two days, or a month, or a longer time, that the cloud continued over the tabernacle, resting upon it, the Israelites would remain in camp and would not set out; but when it lifted they would set out. 23 At the command of the LORD they would camp, and at the command of the LORD they would set out. They kept the charge of the LORD, at the command of the LORD by Moses.

The Silver Trumpets

10 The LORD spoke to Moses, saying: 2 Make two silver trumpets; you shall make them of hammered work; and you shall use them for summoning the congregation, and for breaking camp. 3 When both are blown, the whole congregation shall assemble before you at the entrance of the tent of meeting. 4 But if only one is blown, then the leaders, the heads of the tribes of Israel, shall assemble before you. 5 When you blow an alarm, the camps on the east side shall set out; 6 when you blow a second alarm, the camps on the south side shall set out. An alarm is to be blown whenever they are to set out. 7 But when the assembly is to be gathered, you shall blow, but you shall not sound an alarm. 8 The sons of Aaron, the priests, shall blow the trumpets; this shall be a perpetual institution for you throughout your generations. 9 When you go to war in your land against the adversary who oppresses you, you shall sound an alarm with the trumpets, so that you may be remembered before the LORD your God and be saved from your enemies. 10 Also on your days of rejoicing, at your appointed festivals, and at the beginnings of your months, you shall blow the trumpets over your burnt-offerings and over your sacrifices of well-being; they shall serve as a reminder on your behalf before the LORD your God: I am the LORD your God.

a Heb *between the two evenings*   *b* Or *treaty,* or *testimony;* Heb *eduth*   *c* Gk Syr Vg: Heb lacks *by day*

Departure from Sinai

11 In the second year, in the second month, on the twentieth day of the month, the cloud lifted from over the tabernacle of the covenant.[a] 12 Then the Israelites set out by stages from the wilderness of Sinai, and the cloud settled down in the wilderness of Paran. 13 They set out for the first time at the command of the Lord by Moses. 14 The standard of the camp of Judah set out first, company by company, and over the whole company was Nahshon son of Amminadab. 15 Over the company of the tribe of Issachar was Nethanel son of Zuar; 16 and over the company of the tribe of Zebulun was Eliab son of Helon.

17 Then the tabernacle was taken down, and the Gershonites and the Merarites, who carried the tabernacle, set out. 18 Next the standard of the camp of Reuben set out, company by company; and over the whole company was Elizur son of Shedeur. 19 Over the company of the tribe of Simeon was Shelumiel son of Zurishaddai, 20 and over the company of the tribe of Gad was Eliasaph son of Deuel.

21 Then the Kohathites, who carried the holy things, set out; and the tabernacle was set up before their arrival. 22 Next the standard of the Ephraimite camp set out, company by company, and over the whole company was Elishama son of Ammihud. 23 Over the company of the tribe of Manasseh was Gamaliel son of Pedahzur, 24 and over the company of the tribe of Benjamin was Abidan son of Gideoni.

25 Then the standard of the camp of Dan, acting as the rearguard of all the camps, set out, company by company, and over the whole company was Ahiezer son of Ammishaddai. 26 Over the company of the tribe of Asher was Pagiel son of Ochran, 27 and over the company of the tribe of Naphtali was Ahira son of Enan. 28 This was the order of march of the Israelites, company by company, when they set out.

29 Moses said to Hobab son of Reuel the Midianite, Moses' father-in-law, 'We are setting out for the place of which the Lord said, "I will give it to you"; come with us, and we will treat you well; for the Lord has promised good to Israel.' 30 But he said to him, 'I will not go, but I will go back to my own land and to my kindred.' 31 He said, 'Do not leave us, for you know where we should camp in the wilderness, and you will serve as eyes for us. 32 Moreover, if you go with us, whatever good the Lord does for us, the same we will do for you.'

33 So they set out from the mount of the Lord on three days' journey with the ark of the covenant of the Lord going before them for three days' journey, to seek out a resting-place for them, 34 the cloud of the Lord being over them by day when they set out from the camp.

35 Whenever the ark set out, Moses would say,

> 'Arise, O Lord, let your enemies be
>   scattered,
>   and your foes flee before you.'

36 And whenever it came to rest, he would say,

> 'Return, O Lord of the ten thousand
>   thousands of Israel.'[b]

Complaining in the Desert

11 Now when the people complained in the hearing of the Lord about their misfortunes, the Lord heard it and his anger was kindled. Then the fire of the Lord burned against them, and consumed some outlying parts of the camp. 2 But the people cried out to Moses; and Moses prayed to the Lord, and the fire abated. 3 So that place was called Taberah,[c] because the fire of the Lord burned against them.

4 The rabble among them had a strong craving; and the Israelites also wept again, and said, 'If only we had meat to eat! 5 We remember the fish we used to eat in Egypt for nothing, the cucumbers, the melons, the leeks, the onions, and the garlic; 6 but now our strength is dried up, and there is nothing at all but this manna to look at.'

7 Now the manna was like coriander seed, and its colour was like the colour of gum resin. 8 The people went around and gathered it, ground it in mills or beat it in

a Or treaty, or testimony; Heb eduth   b Meaning of Heb uncertain   c That is Burning mortars, then boiled it in pots and made cakes of it; and the taste of it was like the taste of cakes baked with oil. 9 When the dew fell on the camp in the night, the manna would fall with it.

10 Moses heard the people weeping throughout their families, all at the entrances of their tents. Then the LORD became very angry, and Moses was displeased. 11 So Moses said to the LORD, 'Why have you treated your servant so badly? Why have I not found favour in your sight, that you lay the burden of all this people on me? 12 Did I conceive all this people? Did I give birth to them, that you should say to me, "Carry them in your bosom, as a nurse carries a sucking child", to the land that you promised on oath to their ancestors? 13 Where am I to get meat to give to all this people? For they come weeping to me and say, "Give us meat to eat!" 14 I am not able to carry all this people alone, for they are too heavy for me. 15 If this is the way you are going to treat me, put me to death at once—if I have found favour in your sight—and do not let me see my misery.'

The Seventy Elders

16 So the LORD said to Moses, 'Gather for me seventy of the elders of Israel, whom you know to be the elders of the people and officers over them; bring them to the tent of meeting, and have them take their place there with you. 17 I will come down and talk with you there; and I will take some of the spirit that is on you and put it on them; and they shall bear the burden of the people along with you so that you will not bear it all by yourself. 18 And say to the people: Consecrate yourselves for tomorrow, and you shall eat meat; for you have wailed in the hearing of the LORD, saying, "If only we had meat to eat! Surely it was better for us in Egypt." Therefore the LORD will give you meat, and you shall eat. 19 You shall eat not only one day, or two days, or five days, or ten days, or twenty days, 20 but for a whole month—until it comes out of your nostrils and becomes loathsome to you—because you have rejected the LORD who is among you, and have wailed before him, saying,

"Why did we ever leave Egypt?" ' 21 But Moses said, 'The people I am with number six hundred thousand on foot; and you say, "I will give them meat, that they may eat for a whole month"! 22 Are there enough flocks and herds to slaughter for them? Are there enough fish in the sea to catch for them?' 23 The LORD said to Moses, 'Is the LORD's power limited?a Now you shall see whether my word will come true for you or not.'

24 So Moses went out and told the people the words of the LORD; and he gathered seventy elders of the people, and placed them all around the tent. 25 Then the LORD came down in the cloud and spoke to him, and took some of the spirit that was on him and put it on the seventy elders; and when the spirit rested upon them, they prophesied. But they did not do so again.

26 Two men remained in the camp, one named Eldad, and the other named Medad, and the spirit rested on them; they were among those registered, but they had not gone out to the tent, and so they prophesied in the camp. 27 And a young man ran and told Moses, 'Eldad and Medad are prophesying in the camp.' 28 And Joshua son of Nun, the assistant of Moses, one of his chosen men,b said, 'My lord Moses, stop them!' 29 But Moses said to him, 'Are you jealous for my sake? Would that all the LORD's people were prophets, and that the LORD would put his spirit on them!' 30 And Moses and the elders of Israel returned to the camp.

The Quails

31 Then a wind went out from the LORD, and it brought quails from the sea and let them fall beside the camp, about a day's journey on this side and a day's journey on the other side, all around the camp, about two cubits deep on the ground. 32 So the people worked all that day and night and all the next day, gathering the quails; the least anyone gathered was ten homers; and they spread them out for themselves all around the camp. 33 But while the meat was still between their teeth, before it was consumed, the anger of the LORD was kindled against

a Heb LORD's hand too short?   b Or of Moses from his youth the people, and the LORD struck the people with a very great plague. 34 So that place was called Kibroth-hattaavah, *a* because there they buried the people who had the craving. 35 From Kibroth-hattaavah the people journeyed to Hazeroth.

Aaron and Miriam Jealous of Moses

12 While they were at Hazeroth, Miriam and Aaron spoke against Moses because of the Cushite woman whom he had married (for he had indeed married a Cushite woman); 2 and they said, 'Has the LORD spoken only through Moses? Has he not spoken through us also?' And the LORD heard it. 3 Now the man Moses was very humble, *b* more so than anyone else on the face of the earth. 4 Suddenly the LORD said to Moses, Aaron, and Miriam, 'Come out, you three, to the tent of meeting.' So the three of them came out. 5 Then the LORD came down in a pillar of cloud, and stood at the entrance of the tent, and called Aaron and Miriam; and they both came forward. 6 And he said, 'Hear my words:
When there are prophets among you,
 I the LORD make myself known to
  them in visions;
 I speak to them in dreams.
7 Not so with my servant Moses;
 he is entrusted with all my house.
8 With him I speak face to face—
  clearly, not in riddles;
 and he beholds the form of the
  LORD.
Why then were you not afraid to speak against my servant Moses?' 9 And the anger of the LORD was kindled against them, and he departed.

10 When the cloud went away from over the tent, Miriam had become leprous, *c* as white as snow. And Aaron turned towards Miriam and saw that she was leprous. 11 Then Aaron said to Moses, 'Oh, my lord, do not punish us *d* for a sin that we have so foolishly committed. 12 Do not let her be like one stillborn, whose flesh is half consumed when it comes out of its mother's womb.' 13 And Moses cried to the LORD, 'O God, please heal her.' 14 But the LORD said to Moses, 'If her father had but spat in her face, would she not bear her shame for seven days? Let her be shut out of the camp for seven days, and after that she may be brought in again.' 15 So Miriam was shut out of the camp for seven days; and the people did not set out on the march until Miriam had been brought in again. 16 After that the people set out from Hazeroth, and camped in the wilderness of Paran.

Spies Sent into Canaan

13 The LORD said to Moses, 2 'Send men to spy out the land of Canaan, which I am giving to the Israelites; from each of their ancestral tribes you shall send a man, every one a leader among them.' 3 So Moses sent them from the wilderness of Paran, according to the command of the LORD, all of them leading men among the Israelites. 4 These were their names: From the tribe of Reuben, Shammua son of Zaccur; 5 from the tribe of Simeon, Shaphat son of Hori; 6 from the tribe of Judah, Caleb son of Jephunneh; 7 from the tribe of Issachar, Igal son of Joseph; 8 from the tribe of Ephraim, Hoshea son of Nun; 9 from the tribe of Benjamin, Palti son of Raphu; 10 from the tribe of Zebulun, Gaddiel son of Sodi; 11 from the tribe of Joseph (that is, from the tribe of Manasseh), Gaddi son of Susi; 12 from the tribe of Dan, Ammiel son of Gemalli; 13 from the tribe of Asher, Sethur son of Michael; 14 from the tribe of Naphtali, Nahbi son of Vophsi; 15 from the tribe of Gad, Geuel son of Machi. 16 These were the names of the men whom Moses sent to spy out the land. And Moses changed the name of Hoshea son of Nun to Joshua.

17 Moses sent them to spy out the land of Canaan, and said to them, 'Go up there into the Negeb, and go up into the hill country, 18 and see what the land is like, and whether the people who live in it are strong or weak, whether they are few or many, 19 and whether the land they live in is good or bad, and whether the towns that they live in are unwalled or fortified, 20 and whether the land is rich or poor, and

a That is *Graves of craving* *b* Or *devout* *c* A term for several skin diseases; precise meaning uncertain *d* Heb *do not lay sin upon us* whether there are trees in it or not. Be bold, and bring some of the fruit of the land.' Now it was the season of the first ripe grapes.

21 So they went up and spied out the land from the wilderness of Zin to Rehob, near Lebo-hamath. 22 They went up into the Negeb, and came to Hebron; and Ahiman, Sheshai, and Talmai, the Anakites, were there. (Hebron was built seven years before Zoan in Egypt.) 23 And they came to the Wadi Eshcol, and cut down from there a branch with a single cluster of grapes, and they carried it on a pole between two of them. They also brought some pomegranates and figs. 24 That place was called the Wadi Eshcol, *a* because of the cluster that the Israelites cut down from there.

The Report of the Spies

25 At the end of forty days they returned from spying out the land. 26 And they came to Moses and Aaron and to all the congregation of the Israelites in the wilderness of Paran, at Kadesh; they brought back word to them and to all the congregation, and showed them the fruit of the land. 27 And they told him, 'We came to the land to which you sent us; it flows with milk and honey, and this is its fruit. 28 Yet the people who live in the land are strong, and the towns are fortified and very large; and besides, we saw the descendants of Anak there. 29 The Amalekites live in the land of the Negeb; the Hittites, the Jebusites, and the Amorites live in the hill country; and the Canaanites live by the sea, and along the Jordan.'

30 But Caleb quieted the people before Moses, and said, 'Let us go up at once and occupy it, for we are well able to overcome it.' 31 Then the men who had gone up with him said, 'We are not able to go up against this people, for they are stronger than we are.' 32 So they brought to the Israelites an unfavourable report of the land that they had spied out, saying, 'The land that we have gone through as spies is a land that devours its inhabitants; and all the people that we saw in it are of great size. 33 There we saw the Nephilim (the Anakites come from

the Nephilim); and to ourselves we seemed like grasshoppers, and so we seemed to them.'

The People Rebel

14 Then all the congregation raised a loud cry, and the people wept that night. 2 And all the Israelites complained against Moses and Aaron; the whole congregation said to them, 'Would that we had died in the land of Egypt! Or would that we had died in this wilderness! 3 Why is the LORD bringing us into this land to fall by the sword? Our wives and our little ones will become booty; would it not be better for us to go back to Egypt?' 4 So they said to one another, 'Let us choose a captain, and go back to Egypt.'

5 Then Moses and Aaron fell on their faces before all the assembly of the congregation of the Israelites. 6 And Joshua son of Nun and Caleb son of Jephunneh, who were among those who had spied out the land, tore their clothes 7 and said to all the congregation of the Israelites, 'The land that we went through as spies is an exceedingly good land. 8 If the LORD is pleased with us, he will bring us into this land and give it to us, a land that flows with milk and honey. 9 Only, do not rebel against the LORD; and do not fear the people of the land, for they are no more than bread for us; their protection is removed from them, and the LORD is with us; do not fear them.' 10 But the whole congregation threatened to stone them.

Then the glory of the LORD appeared at the tent of meeting to all the Israelites. 11 And the LORD said to Moses, 'How long will this people despise me? And how long will they refuse to believe in me, in spite of all the signs that I have done among them? 12 I will strike them with pestilence and disinherit them, and I will make of you a nation greater and mightier than they.'

Moses Intercedes for the People

13 But Moses said to the LORD, 'Then the Egyptians will hear of it, for in your might you brought up this people from among

a That is *Cluster*

them, ¹⁴and they will tell the inhabitants of this land. They have heard that you, O LORD, are in the midst of this people; for you, O LORD, are seen face to face, and your cloud stands over them and you go in front of them, in a pillar of cloud by day and in a pillar of fire by night. ¹⁵Now if you kill this people all at one time, then the nations who have heard about you will say, ¹⁶"It is because the LORD was not able to bring this people into the land he swore to give them that he has slaughtered them in the wilderness." ¹⁷And now, therefore, let the power of the LORD be great in the way that you promised when you spoke, saying,
¹⁸ "The LORD is slow to anger,
      and abounding in steadfast love,
      forgiving iniquity and transgression,
      but by no means clearing the guilty,
      visiting the iniquity of the parents
      upon the children
      to the third and the fourth
          generation."
¹⁹Forgive the iniquity of this people according to the greatness of your steadfast love, just as you have pardoned this people, from Egypt even until now."

20 Then the LORD said, 'I do forgive, just as you have asked; ²¹nevertheless—as I live, and as all the earth shall be filled with the glory of the LORD— ²²none of the people who have seen my glory and the signs that I did in Egypt and in the wilderness, and yet have tested me these ten times and have not obeyed my voice, ²³shall see the land that I swore to give to their ancestors; none of those who despised me shall see it. ²⁴But my servant Caleb, because he has a different spirit and has followed me wholeheartedly, I will bring into the land into which he went, and his descendants shall possess it. ²⁵Now, since the Amalekites and the Canaanites live in the valleys, turn tomorrow and set out for the wilderness by the way to the Red Sea.'ᵃ

An Attempted Invasion is Repulsed

26 And the LORD spoke to Moses and to Aaron, saying: ²⁷How long shall this wicked congregation complain against me? I have heard the complaints of the Israelites,

which they complain against me. ²⁸Say to them, 'As I live', says the LORD, 'I will do to you the very things I heard you say: ²⁹your dead bodies shall fall in this very wilderness; and of all your number, included in the census, from twenty years old and upwards, who have complained against me, ³⁰not one of you shall come into the land in which I swore to settle you, except Caleb son of Jephunneh and Joshua son of Nun. ³¹But your little ones, who you said would become booty, I will bring in, and they shall know the land that you have despised. ³²But as for you, your dead bodies shall fall in this wilderness. ³³And your children shall be shepherds in the wilderness for forty years, and shall suffer for your faithlessness, until the last of your dead bodies lies in the wilderness. ³⁴According to the number of the days in which you spied out the land, forty days, for every day a year, you shall bear your iniquity, forty years, and you shall know my displeasure.' ³⁵I the LORD have spoken; surely I will do thus to all this wicked congregation gathered together against me: in this wilderness they shall come to a full end, and there they shall die.

36 And the men whom Moses sent to spy out the land, who returned and made all the congregation complain against him by bringing a bad report about the land— ³⁷the men who brought an unfavourable report about the land died by a plague before the LORD. ³⁸But Joshua son of Nun and Caleb son of Jephunneh alone remained alive, of those men who went to spy out the land.

39 When Moses told these words to all the Israelites, the people mourned greatly. ⁴⁰They rose early in the morning and went up to the heights of the hill country, saying, 'Here we are. We will go up to the place that the LORD has promised, for we have sinned.' ⁴¹But Moses said, 'Why do you continue to transgress the command of the LORD? That will not succeed. ⁴²Do not go up, for the LORD is not with you; do not let yourselves be struck down before your enemies. ⁴³For the Amalekites and the

_a_ Or _Sea of Reeds_

Canaanites will confront you there, and you shall fall by the sword; because you have turned back from following the Lord, the Lord will not be with you.' ⁴⁴But they presumed to go up to the heights of the hill country, even though the ark of the covenant of the Lord, and Moses, had not left the camp. ⁴⁵Then the Amalekites and the Canaanites who lived in that hill country came down and defeated them, pursuing them as far as Hormah.

Various Offerings

15 The Lord spoke to Moses, saying: ²Speak to the Israelites and say to them: When you come into the land you are to inhabit, which I am giving you, ³and you make an offering by fire to the Lord from the herd or from the flock—whether a burnt-offering or a sacrifice, to fulfil a vow or as a freewill-offering or at your appointed festivals—to make a pleasing odour for the Lord, ⁴then whoever presents such an offering to the Lord shall present also a grain-offering, one-tenth of an ephah of choice flour, mixed with one-fourth of a hin of oil. ⁵Moreover, you shall offer one-fourth of a hin of wine as a drink-offering with the burnt-offering or the sacrifice, for each lamb. ⁶For a ram, you shall offer a grain-offering, two-tenths of an ephah of choice flour mixed with one-third of a hin of oil; ⁷and as a drink-offering you shall offer one-third of a hin of wine, a pleasing odour to the Lord. ⁸When you offer a bull as a burnt-offering or a sacrifice, to fulfil a vow or as an offering of well-being to the Lord, ⁹then you shall present with the bull a grain-offering, three-tenths of an ephah of choice flour, mixed with half a hin of oil, ¹⁰and you shall present as a drink-offering half a hin of wine, as an offering by fire, a pleasing odour to the Lord.

11 Thus it shall be done for each ox or ram, or for each of the male lambs or the kids. ¹²According to the number that you offer, so you shall do with each and every one. ¹³Every native Israelite shall do these things in this way, in presenting an offering by fire, a pleasing odour to the Lord. ¹⁴An alien who lives with you, or who takes up permanent residence among you, and wishes to offer an offering by fire, a pleasing odour to the Lord, shall do as you do. ¹⁵As for the assembly, there shall be for both you and the resident alien a single statute, a perpetual statute throughout your generations; you and the alien shall be alike before the Lord. ¹⁶You and the alien who resides with you shall have the same law and the same ordinance.

17 The Lord spoke to Moses, saying: ¹⁸Speak to the Israelites and say to them: After you come into the land to which I am bringing you, ¹⁹whenever you eat of the bread of the land, you shall present a donation to the Lord. ²⁰From your first batch of dough you shall present a loaf as a donation; you shall present it just as you present a donation from the threshing-floor. ²¹Throughout your generations you shall give to the Lord a donation from the first of your batch of dough.

22 But if you unintentionally fail to observe all these commandments that the Lord has spoken to Moses— ²³everything that the Lord has commanded you by Moses, from the day the Lord gave commandment and thereafter, throughout your generations— ²⁴then if it was done unintentionally without the knowledge of the congregation, the whole congregation shall offer one young bull for a burnt-offering, a pleasing odour to the Lord, together with its grain-offering and its drink-offering, according to the ordinance, and one male goat for a sin-offering. ²⁵The priest shall make atonement for all the congregation of the Israelites, and they shall be forgiven; it was unintentional, and they have brought their offering, an offering by fire to the Lord, and their sin-offering before the Lord, for their error. ²⁶All the congregation of the Israelites shall be forgiven, as well as the aliens residing among them, because the whole people was involved in the error.

27 An individual who sins unintentionally shall present a female goat a year old for a sin-offering. ²⁸And the priest shall make atonement before the Lord for the one who commits an error, when it is unintentional,

to make atonement for the person, who then shall be forgiven. ²⁹ For both the native among the Israelites and the alien residing among them—you shall have the same law for anyone who acts in error. ³⁰ But whoever acts high-handedly, whether a native or an alien, affronts the LORD, and shall be cut off from among the people. ³¹ Because of having despised the word of the LORD and broken his commandment, such a person shall be utterly cut off and bear the guilt.

Penalty for Violating the Sabbath

32 When the Israelites were in the wilderness, they found a man gathering sticks on the sabbath day. ³³ Those who found him gathering sticks brought him to Moses, Aaron, and to the whole congregation. ³⁴ They put him in custody, because it was not clear what should be done to him. ³⁵ Then the LORD said to Moses, 'The man shall be put to death; all the congregation shall stone him outside the camp.' ³⁶ The whole congregation brought him outside the camp and stoned him to death, just as the LORD had commanded Moses.

Fringes on Garments

37 The LORD said to Moses: ³⁸ Speak to the Israelites, and tell them to make fringes on the corners of their garments throughout their generations and to put a blue cord on the fringe at each corner. ³⁹ You have the fringe so that, when you see it, you will remember all the commandments of the LORD and do them, and not follow the lust of your own heart and your own eyes. ⁴⁰ So you shall remember and do all my commandments, and you shall be holy to your God. ⁴¹ I am the LORD your God, who brought you out of the land of Egypt, to be your God: I am the LORD your God.

Revolt of Korah, Dathan, and Abiram

16 Now Korah son of Izhar son of Kohath son of Levi, along with Dathan and Abiram sons of Eliab, and On son of Peleth—descendants of Reuben—took ² two hundred and fifty Israelite men, leaders of the congregation, chosen from the assembly, well-known men,ᵃ and they con-

fronted Moses. ³ They assembled against Moses and against Aaron, and said to them, 'You have gone too far! All the congregation are holy, every one of them, and the LORD is among them. So why then do you exalt yourselves above the assembly of the LORD?' ⁴ When Moses heard it, he fell on his face. ⁵ Then he said to Korah and all his company, 'In the morning the LORD will make known who is his, and who is holy, and who will be allowed to approach him; the one whom he will choose he will allow to approach him. ⁶ Do this: take censers, Korah and all yourᵇ company, ⁷ and tomorrow put fire in them, and lay incense on them before the LORD; and the man whom the LORD chooses shall be the holy one. You Levites have gone too far!' ⁸ Then Moses said to Korah, 'Hear now, you Levites! ⁹ Is it too little for you that the God of Israel has separated you from the congregation of Israel, to allow you to approach him in order to perform the duties of the LORD's tabernacle, and to stand before the congregation and serve them? ¹⁰ He has allowed you to approach him, and all your brother Levites with you; yet you seek the priesthood as well! ¹¹ Therefore you and all your company have gathered together against the LORD. What is Aaron that you rail against him?'

12 Moses sent for Dathan and Abiram sons of Eliab; but they said, 'We will not come! ¹³ Is it too little that you have brought us up out of a land flowing with milk and honey to kill us in the wilderness, that you must also lord it over us? ¹⁴ It is clear you have not brought us into a land flowing with milk and honey, or given us an inheritance of fields and vineyards. Would you put out the eyes of these men? We will not come!'

15 Moses was very angry and said to the LORD, 'Pay no attention to their offering. I have not taken one donkey from them, and I have not harmed any one of them.' ¹⁶ And Moses said to Korah, 'As for you and all your company, be present tomorrow before the LORD, you and they and Aaron; ¹⁷ and let

ᵃ Cn: Heb *and they confronted Moses, and two hundred and fifty men . . . well-known men*   ᵇ Heb *his* each one of you take his censer, and put incense on it, and each one of you present his censer before the LORD, two hundred and fifty censers; you also, and Aaron, each his censer.' ¹⁸ So each man took his censer, and they put fire in the censers and laid incense on them, and they stood at the entrance of the tent of meeting with Moses and Aaron. ¹⁹ Then Korah assembled the whole congregation against them at the entrance of the tent of meeting. And the glory of the LORD appeared to the whole congregation.

20 Then the LORD spoke to Moses and to Aaron, saying: ²¹ Separate yourselves from this congregation, so that I may consume them in a moment. ²² They fell on their faces, and said, 'O God, the God of the spirits of all flesh, shall one person sin and you become angry with the whole congregation?'

23 And the LORD spoke to Moses, saying: ²⁴ Say to the congregation: Get away from the dwellings of Korah, Dathan, and Abiram. ²⁵ So Moses got up and went to Dathan and Abiram; the elders of Israel followed him. ²⁶ He said to the congregation, 'Turn away from the tents of these wicked men, and touch nothing of theirs, or you will be swept away for all their sins.' ²⁷ So they got away from the dwellings of Korah, Dathan, and Abiram; and Dathan and Abiram came out and stood at the entrance of their tents, together with their wives, their children, and their little ones. ²⁸ And Moses said, 'This is how you shall know that the LORD has sent me to do all these works; it has not been of my own accord: ²⁹ If these people die a natural death, or if a natural fate comes on them, then the LORD has not sent me. ³⁰ But if the LORD creates something new, and the ground opens its mouth and swallows them up, with all that belongs to them, and they go down alive into Sheol, then you shall know that these men have despised the LORD.'

31 As soon as he finished speaking all these words, the ground under them was split apart. ³² The earth opened its mouth and swallowed them up, along with their households—everyone who belonged to

Korah and all their goods. ³³ So they with all that belonged to them went down alive into Sheol; the earth closed over them, and they perished from the midst of the assembly. ³⁴ All Israel around them fled at their outcry, for they said, 'The earth will swallow us too!' ³⁵ And fire came out from the LORD and consumed the two hundred and fifty men offering the incense.

36 ᵃ Then the LORD spoke to Moses, saying: ³⁷ Tell Eleazar son of Aaron the priest to take the censers out of the blaze; then scatter the fire far and wide. ³⁸ For the censers of these sinners have become holy at the cost of their lives. Make them into hammered plates as a covering for the altar, for they presented them before the LORD and they became holy. Thus they shall be a sign to the Israelites. ³⁹ So Eleazar the priest took the bronze censers that had been presented by those who were burned; and they were hammered out as a covering for the altar— ⁴⁰ a reminder to the Israelites that no outsider, who is not of the descendants of Aaron, shall approach to offer incense before the LORD, so as not to become like Korah and his company—just as the LORD had said to him through Moses.

41 On the next day, however, the whole congregation of the Israelites rebelled against Moses and against Aaron, saying, 'You have killed the people of the LORD.' ⁴² And when the congregation had assembled against them, Moses and Aaron turned towards the tent of meeting; the cloud had covered it and the glory of the LORD appeared. ⁴³ Then Moses and Aaron came to the front of the tent of meeting, ⁴⁴ and the LORD spoke to Moses, saying, ⁴⁵ 'Get away from this congregation, so that I may consume them in a moment.' And they fell on their faces. ⁴⁶ Moses said to Aaron, 'Take your censer, put fire on it from the altar and lay incense on it, and carry it quickly to the congregation and make atonement for them. For wrath has gone out from the LORD; the plague has begun.' ⁴⁷ So Aaron took it as Moses had ordered, and ran into the middle of the assembly, where the plague had already

_a_ Ch 17.1 in Heb

begun among the people. He put on the incense, and made atonement for the people. ⁴⁸ He stood between the dead and the living; and the plague was stopped. ⁴⁹ Those who died by the plague were fourteen thousand seven hundred, besides those who died in the affair of Korah. ⁵⁰ When the plague was stopped, Aaron returned to Moses at the entrance of the tent of meeting.

The Budding of Aaron's Rod

17 ᵃ The LORD spoke to Moses, saying: ² Speak to the Israelites, and get twelve staffs from them, one for each ancestral house, from all the leaders of their ancestral houses. Write each man's name on his staff, ³ and write Aaron's name on the staff of Levi. For there shall be one staff for the head of each ancestral house. ⁴ Place them in the tent of meeting before the covenant, ᵇ where I meet with you. ⁵ And the staff of the man whom I choose shall sprout; thus I will put a stop to the complaints of the Israelites that they continually make against you. ⁶ Moses spoke to the Israelites; and all their leaders gave him staffs, one for each leader, according to their ancestral houses, twelve staffs; and the staff of Aaron was among theirs. ⁷ So Moses placed the staffs before the LORD in the tent of the covenant. ᵇ

8 When Moses went into the tent of the covenant ᵇ on the next day, the staff of Aaron for the house of Levi had sprouted. It put forth buds, produced blossoms, and bore ripe almonds. ⁹ Then Moses brought out all the staffs from before the LORD to all the Israelites; and they looked, and each man took his staff. ¹⁰ And the LORD said to Moses, 'Put back the staff of Aaron before the covenant, ᵇ to be kept as a warning to rebels, so that you may make an end of their complaints against me, or else they will die.' ¹¹ Moses did so; just as the LORD commanded him, so he did.

12 The Israelites said to Moses, 'We are perishing; we are lost, all of us are lost! ¹³ Everyone who approaches the tabernacle of the LORD will die. Are we all to perish?'

Responsibility of Priests and Levites

18 The LORD said to Aaron: You and your sons and your ancestral house with you shall bear responsibility for offences connected with the sanctuary, while you and your sons alone shall bear responsibility for offences connected with the priesthood. ² So bring with you also your brothers of the tribe of Levi, your ancestral tribe, in order that they may be joined to you, and serve you while you and your sons with you are in front of the tent of the covenant. ᵇ ³ They shall perform duties for you and for the whole tent. But they must not approach either the utensils of the sanctuary or the altar, otherwise both they and you will die. ⁴ They are attached to you in order to perform the duties of the tent of meeting, for all the service of the tent; no outsider shall approach you. ⁵ You yourselves shall perform the duties of the sanctuary and the duties of the altar, so that wrath may never again come upon the Israelites. ⁶ It is I who now take your brother Levites from among the Israelites; they are now yours as a gift, dedicated to the LORD, to perform the service of the tent of meeting. ⁷ But you and your sons with you shall diligently perform your priestly duties in all that concerns the altar and the area behind the curtain. I give your priesthood as a gift; ᶜ any outsider who approaches shall be put to death.

The Priests' Portion

8 The LORD spoke to Aaron: I have given you charge of the offerings made to me, all the holy gifts of the Israelites; I have given them to you and your sons as a priestly portion due to you in perpetuity. ⁹ This shall be yours from the most holy things, reserved from the fire: every offering of theirs that they render to me as a most holy thing, whether grain-offering, sin-offering, or guilt-offering, shall belong to you and your sons. ¹⁰ As a most holy thing you shall eat it; every male may eat it; it shall be holy to you. ¹¹ This also is yours: I have given to you, together with

---

ᵃ Ch 17.16 in Heb   ᵇ Or *treaty*, or *testimony*; Heb *eduth*   ᶜ Heb *as a service of gift* your sons and daughters, as a perpetual due, whatever is set aside from the gifts of all the elevation-offerings of the Israelites; everyone who is clean in your house may eat them. 12 All the best of the oil and all the best of the wine and of the grain, the choice produce that they give to the LORD, I have given to you. 13 The first fruits of all that is in their land, which they bring to the LORD, shall be yours; everyone who is clean in your house may eat of it. 14 Every devoted thing in Israel shall be yours. 15 The first issue of the womb of all creatures, human and animal, which is offered to the LORD, shall be yours; but the firstborn of human beings you shall redeem, and the firstborn of unclean animals you shall redeem. 16 Their redemption price, reckoned from one month of age, you shall fix at five shekels of silver, according to the shekel of the sanctuary (that is, twenty gerahs). 17 But the firstborn of a cow, or the firstborn of a sheep, or the firstborn of a goat, you shall not redeem; they are holy. You shall dash their blood on the altar, and shall turn their fat into smoke as an offering by fire for a pleasing odour to the LORD; 18 but their flesh shall be yours, just as the breast that is elevated and as the right thigh are yours. 19 All the holy offerings that the Israelites present to the LORD I have given to you, together with your sons and daughters, as a perpetual due; it is a covenant of salt for ever before the LORD for you and your descendants as well. 20 Then the LORD said to Aaron: You shall have no allotment in their land, nor shall you have any share among them; I am your share and your possession among the Israelites.

21 To the Levites I have given every tithe in Israel for a possession in return for the service that they perform, the service in the tent of meeting. 22 From now on the Israelites shall no longer approach the tent of meeting, or else they will incur guilt and die. 23 But the Levites shall perform the service of the tent of meeting, and they shall bear responsibility for their own offences; it shall be a perpetual statute throughout your generations. But among the Israelites

they shall have no allotment, 24 because I have given to the Levites as their portion the tithe of the Israelites, which they set apart as an offering to the LORD. Therefore I have said of them that they shall have no allotment among the Israelites.

25 Then the LORD spoke to Moses, saying: 26 You shall speak to the Levites, saying: When you receive from the Israelites the tithe that I have given you from them for your portion, you shall set apart an offering from it to the LORD, a tithe of the tithe. 27 It shall be reckoned to you as your gift, the same as the grain of the threshing-floor and the fullness of the wine press. 28 Thus you also shall set apart an offering to the LORD from all the tithes that you receive from the Israelites; and from them you shall give the LORD's offering to the priest Aaron. 29 Out of all the gifts to you, you shall set apart every offering due to the LORD; the best of all of them is the part to be consecrated. 30 Say also to them: When you have set apart the best of it, then the rest shall be reckoned to the Levites as produce of the threshing-floor, and as produce of the wine press. 31 You may eat it in any place, you and your households; for it is your payment for your service in the tent of meeting. 32 You shall incur no guilt by reason of it, when you have offered the best of it. But you shall not profane the holy gifts of the Israelites, on pain of death.

Ceremony of the Red Heifer

19 The LORD spoke to Moses and Aaron, saying: 2 This is a statute of the law that the LORD has commanded: Tell the Israelites to bring you a red heifer without defect, in which there is no blemish and on which no yoke has been laid. 3 You shall give it to the priest Eleazar, and it shall be taken outside the camp and slaughtered in his presence. 4 The priest Eleazar shall take some of its blood with his finger and sprinkle it seven times towards the front of the tent of meeting. 5 Then the heifer shall be burned in his sight; its skin, its flesh, and its blood, with its dung, shall be burned. 6 The priest shall take cedar wood, hyssop, and crimson material, and throw them into the

fire in which the heifer is burning. ⁷Then the priest shall wash his clothes and bathe his body in water, and afterwards he may come into the camp; but the priest shall remain unclean until evening. ⁸The one who burns the heifer*ᵃ* shall wash his clothes in water and bathe his body in water; he shall remain unclean until evening. ⁹Then someone who is clean shall gather up the ashes of the heifer, and deposit them outside the camp in a clean place; and they shall be kept for the congregation of the Israelites for the water for cleansing. It is a purification-offering. ¹⁰The one who gathers the ashes of the heifer shall wash his clothes and be unclean until evening.

This shall be a perpetual statute for the Israelites and for the alien residing among them. ¹¹Those who touch the dead body of any human being shall be unclean for seven days. ¹²They shall purify themselves with the water on the third day and on the seventh day, and so be clean; but if they do not purify themselves on the third day and on the seventh day, they will not become clean. ¹³All who touch a corpse, the body of a human being who has died, and do not purify themselves, defile the tabernacle of the LORD; such persons shall be cut off from Israel. Since water for cleansing was not dashed on them, they remain unclean; their uncleanness is still on them.

¹⁴ This is the law when someone dies in a tent: everyone who comes into the tent, and everyone who is in the tent, shall be unclean for seven days. ¹⁵And every open vessel with no cover fastened on it is unclean. ¹⁶Whoever in the open field touches one who has been killed by a sword, or who has died naturally,*ᵇ* or a human bone, or a grave, shall be unclean for seven days. ¹⁷For the unclean they shall take some ashes of the burnt purification-offering, and running water shall be added in a vessel; ¹⁸then a clean person shall take hyssop, dip it in the water, and sprinkle it on the tent, on all the furnishings, on the persons who were there, and on whoever touched the bone, the slain, the corpse, or the grave. ¹⁹The clean person shall sprinkle the unclean ones on the third day and on the sev-

enth day, thus purifying them on the seventh day. Then they shall wash their clothes and bathe themselves in water, and at evening they shall be clean. ²⁰Any who are unclean but do not purify themselves, those persons shall be cut off from the assembly, for they have defiled the sanctuary of the LORD. Since the water for cleansing has not been dashed on them, they are unclean.

21 It shall be a perpetual statute for them. The one who sprinkles the water for cleansing shall wash his clothes, and whoever touches the water for cleansing shall be unclean until evening. ²²Whatever the unclean person touches shall be unclean, and anyone who touches it shall be unclean until evening.

The Waters of Meribah

20 The Israelites, the whole congregation, came into the wilderness of Zin in the first month, and the people stayed in Kadesh. Miriam died there, and was buried there.

2 Now there was no water for the congregation; so they gathered together against Moses and against Aaron. ³The people quarrelled with Moses and said, 'Would that we had died when our kindred died before the LORD! ⁴Why have you brought the assembly of the LORD into this wilderness for us and our livestock to die here? ⁵Why have you brought us up out of Egypt, to bring us to this wretched place? It is no place for grain, or figs, or vines, or pomegranates; and there is no water to drink.' ⁶Then Moses and Aaron went away from the assembly to the entrance of the tent of meeting; they fell on their faces, and the glory of the LORD appeared to them. ⁷The LORD spoke to Moses, saying: ⁸Take the staff, and assemble the congregation, you and your brother Aaron, and command the rock before their eyes to yield its water. Thus you shall bring water out of the rock for them; thus you shall provide drink for the congregation and their livestock.

9 So Moses took the staff from before the LORD, as he had commanded him.

a Heb *it*   *b* Heb lacks *naturally*

10 Moses and Aaron gathered the assembly together before the rock, and he said to them, 'Listen, you rebels, shall we bring water for you out of this rock?' 11 Then Moses lifted up his hand and struck the rock twice with his staff; water came out abundantly, and the congregation and their livestock drank. 12 But the LORD said to Moses and Aaron, 'Because you did not trust in me, to show my holiness before the eyes of the Israelites, therefore you shall not bring this assembly into the land that I have given them.' 13 These are the waters of Meribah, *d* where the people of Israel quarrelled with the LORD, and by which he showed his holiness.

Passage through Edom Refused

14 Moses sent messengers from Kadesh to the king of Edom, 'Thus says your brother Israel: You know all the adversity that has befallen us: 15 how our ancestors went down to Egypt, and we lived in Egypt for a long time; and the Egyptians oppressed us and our ancestors; 16 and when we cried to the LORD, he heard our voice, and sent an angel and brought us out of Egypt; and here we are in Kadesh, a town on the edge of your territory. 17 Now let us pass through your land. We will not pass through field or vineyard, or drink water from any well; we will go along the King's Highway, not turning aside to the right hand or to the left until we have passed through your territory.'

18 But Edom said to him, 'You shall not pass through, or we will come out with the sword against you.' 19 The Israelites said to him, 'We will stay on the highway; and if we drink of your water, we and our livestock, then we will pay for it. It is only a small matter; just let us pass through on foot.' 20 But he said, 'You shall not pass through.' And Edom came out against them with a large force, heavily armed. 21 Thus Edom refused to give Israel passage through their territory; so Israel turned away from them.

The Death of Aaron

22 They set out from Kadesh, and the Israelites, the whole congregation, came to Mount Hor. 23 Then the LORD said to Moses and Aaron at Mount Hor, on the border of the land of Edom, 24 'Let Aaron be gathered to his people. For he shall not enter the land that I have given to the Israelites, because you rebelled against my command at the waters of Meribah. 25 Take Aaron and his son Eleazar, and bring them up Mount Hor; 26 strip Aaron of his vestments, and put them on his son Eleazar. But Aaron shall be gathered to his people, *b* and shall die there.' 27 Moses did as the LORD had commanded; they went up Mount Hor in the sight of the whole congregation. 28 Moses stripped Aaron of his vestments, and put them on his son Eleazar; and Aaron died there on the top of the mountain. Moses and Eleazar came down from the mountain. 29 When all the congregation saw that Aaron had died, all the house of Israel mourned for Aaron for thirty days.

The Bronze Serpent

21 When the Canaanite, the king of Arad, who lived in the Negeb, heard that Israel was coming by the way of Atharim, he fought against Israel and took some of them captive. 2 Then Israel made a vow to the LORD and said, 'If you will indeed give this people into our hands, then we will utterly destroy their towns.' 3 The LORD listened to the voice of Israel, and handed over the Canaanites; and they utterly destroyed them and their towns; so the place was called Hormah. *c*

4 From Mount Hor they set out by the way to the Red Sea, *d* to go around the land of Edom; but the people became impatient on the way. 5 The people spoke against God and against Moses, 'Why have you brought us up out of Egypt to die in the wilderness? For there is no food and no water, and we detest this miserable food.' 6 Then the LORD sent poisonous *e* serpents among the people, and they bit the people, so that many Israelites died. 7 The people came to Moses and said, 'We have sinned by speaking against the LORD and against you; pray to the LORD to take away the serpents from us.'

a That is *Quarrel*   *b* Heb lacks *to his people*
c Heb *Destruction*   *d* Or *Sea of Reeds*   *e* Or *fiery*; Heb *seraphim*

So Moses prayed for the people. 8 And the LORD said to Moses, 'Make a poisonous*a* serpent, and set it on a pole; and everyone who is bitten shall look at it and live.' 9 So Moses made a serpent of bronze, and put it upon a pole; and whenever a serpent bit someone, that person would look at the serpent of bronze and live.

The Journey to Moab

10 The Israelites set out, and camped in Oboth. 11 They set out from Oboth, and camped at Iye-abarim, in the wilderness bordering Moab towards the sunrise. 12 From there they set out, and camped in the Wadi Zered. 13 From there they set out, and camped on the other side of the Arnon, in*b* the wilderness that extends from the boundary of the Amorites; for the Arnon is the boundary of Moab, between Moab and the Amorites. 14 Wherefore it is said in the Book of the Wars of the LORD,

'Waheb in Suphah and the wadis.
The Arnon 15 and the slopes of the
        wadis
that extend to the seat of Ar,
and lie along the border of Moab.'*c*

16 From there they continued to Beer;*d* that is the well of which the LORD said to Moses, 'Gather the people together, and I will give them water.' 17 Then Israel sang this song:

'Spring up, O well!—Sing to it!—
18 the well that the leaders sank,
    that the nobles of the people dug,
    with the sceptre, with the staff.'

From the wilderness to Mattanah, 19 from Mattanah to Nahaliel, from Nahaliel to Bamoth, 20 and from Bamoth to the valley lying in the region of Moab by the top of Pisgah that overlooks the waste-land.*e*

King Sihon Defeated

21 Then Israel sent messengers to King Sihon of the Amorites, saying, 22 'Let me pass through your land; we will not turn aside into field or vineyard; we will not drink the water of any well; we will go by the King's Highway until we have passed through your territory.' 23 But Sihon would not allow Israel to pass through his territory. Sihon gathered all his people together, and went out against Israel to the wilderness; he came to Jahaz, and fought against Israel. 24 Israel put him to the sword, and took possession of his land from the Arnon to the Jabbok, as far as to the Ammonites; for the boundary of the Ammonites was strong. 25 Israel took all these towns, and Israel settled in all the towns of the Amorites, in Heshbon, and in all its villages. 26 For Heshbon was the city of King Sihon of the Amorites, who had fought against the former king of Moab and captured all his land as far as the Arnon. 27 Therefore the ballad-singers say,

'Come to Heshbon, let it be built;
    let the city of Sihon be established.
28 For fire came out from Heshbon,
    flame from the city of Sihon.
It devoured Ar of Moab,
    and swallowed up*f* the heights of
        the Arnon.
29 Woe to you, O Moab!
    You are undone, O people of
        Chemosh!
He has made his sons fugitives,
    and his daughters captives,
    to an Amorite king, Sihon.
30 So their posterity perished
    from Heshbon*g* to Dibon,
    and we laid waste until fire spread
        to Medeba.'*h*

31 Thus Israel settled in the land of the Amorites. 32 Moses sent to spy out Jazer; and they captured its villages, and dispossessed the Amorites who were there.

King Og Defeated

33 Then they turned and went up the road to Bashan; and King Og of Bashan came out against them, he and all his people, to battle at Edrei. 34 But the LORD said to Moses, 'Do not be afraid of him; for I have given him into your hand, with all his people, and all his land. You shall do to him as you did to King Sihon of the Amorites, who ruled in Heshbon.' 35 So they

a Or *fiery*; Heb *seraph*   *b* Gk: Heb *which is in*
c Meaning of Heb uncertain   *d* That is *Well*
e Or *Jeshimon*   *f* Gk: Heb *and the lords of*   *g* Gk: Heb *we have shot at them; Heshbon has perished*   *h* Compare Sam Gk: Meaning of MT uncertain

killed him, his sons, and all his people, until there was no survivor left; and they took possession of his land.

Balak Summons Balaam to Curse Israel

22 The Israelites set out, and camped in the plains of Moab across the Jordan from Jericho. ²Now Balak son of Zippor saw all that Israel had done to the Amorites. ³Moab was in great dread of the people, because they were so numerous; Moab was overcome with fear of the people of Israel. ⁴And Moab said to the elders of Midian, 'This horde will now lick up all that is around us, as an ox licks up the grass of the field.' Now Balak son of Zippor was king of Moab at that time. ⁵He sent messengers to Balaam son of Beor at Pethor, which is on the Euphrates, in the land of Amaw,ᵃ to summon him, saying, 'A people has come out of Egypt; they have spread over the face of the earth, and they have settled next to me. ⁶Come now, curse this people for me, since they are stronger than I; perhaps I shall be able to defeat them and drive them from the land; for I know that whomsoever you bless is blessed, and whomsoever you curse is cursed.'

7 So the elders of Moab and the elders of Midian departed with the fees for divination in their hand; and they came to Balaam, and gave him Balak's message. ⁸He said to them, 'Stay here tonight, and I will bring back word to you, just as the LORD speaks to me'; so the officials of Moab stayed with Balaam. ⁹God came to Balaam and said, 'Who are these men with you?' ¹⁰Balaam said to God, 'King Balak son of Zippor of Moab has sent me this message: ¹¹"A people has come out of Egypt and has spread over the face of the earth; now come, curse them for me; perhaps I shall be able to fight against them and drive them out." ' ¹²God said to Balaam, 'You shall not go with them; you shall not curse the people, for they are blessed.' ¹³So Balaam rose in the morning, and said to the officials of Balak, 'Go to your own land, for the LORD has refused to let me go with you.' ¹⁴So the officials of Moab rose and went to Balak, and said, 'Balaam refuses to come with us.'

15 Once again Balak sent officials, more numerous and more distinguished than these. ¹⁶They came to Balaam and said to him, 'Thus says Balak son of Zippor: "Do not let anything hinder you from coming to me; ¹⁷for I will surely do you great honour, and whatever you say to me I will do; come, curse this people for me." ' ¹⁸But Balaam replied to the servants of Balak, 'Although Balak were to give me his house full of silver and gold, I could not go beyond the command of the LORD my God, to do less or more. ¹⁹You remain here, as the others did, so that I may learn what more the LORD may say to me.' ²⁰That night God came to Balaam and said to him, 'If the men have come to summon you, get up and go with them; but do only what I tell you to do.' ²¹So Balaam got up in the morning, saddled his donkey, and went with the officials of Moab.

Balaam, the Donkey, and the Angel

22 God's anger was kindled because he was going, and the angel of the LORD took his stand in the road as his adversary. Now he was riding on the donkey, and his two servants were with him. ²³The donkey saw the angel of the LORD standing in the road, with a drawn sword in his hand; so the donkey turned off the road, and went into the field; and Balaam struck the donkey, to turn it back on to the road. ²⁴Then the angel of the LORD stood in a narrow path between the vineyards, with a wall on either side. ²⁵When the donkey saw the angel of the LORD, it scraped against the wall, and scraped Balaam's foot against the wall; so he struck it again. ²⁶Then the angel of the LORD went ahead, and stood in a narrow place, where there was no way to turn either to the right or to the left. ²⁷When the donkey saw the angel of the LORD, it lay down under Balaam; and Balaam's anger was kindled, and he struck the donkey with his staff. ²⁸Then the LORD opened the mouth of the donkey, and it said to Balaam, 'What have I done to you, that you have struck me these three times?' ²⁹Balaam said to the donkey, 'Because you have made a fool of

ᵃ Or land of his kinsfolk

me! I wish I had a sword in my hand! I would kill you right now!' ³⁰But the donkey said to Balaam, 'Am I not your donkey, which you have ridden all your life to this day? Have I been in the habit of treating you in this way?' And he said, 'No.'

31 Then the LORD opened the eyes of Balaam, and he saw the angel of the LORD standing in the road, with his drawn sword in his hand; and he bowed down, falling on his face. ³²The angel of the LORD said to him, 'Why have you struck your donkey these three times? I have come out as an adversary, because your way is perverse*ᵃ* before me. ³³The donkey saw me, and turned away from me these three times. If it had not turned away from me, surely I would by now have killed you and let it live.' ³⁴Then Balaam said to the angel of the LORD, 'I have sinned, for I did not know that you were standing in the road to oppose me. Now therefore, if it is displeasing to you, I will return home.' ³⁵The angel of the LORD said to Balaam, 'Go with the men; but speak only what I tell you to speak.' So Balaam went on with the officials of Balak.

36 When Balak heard that Balaam had come, he went out to meet him at Ir-moab, on the boundary formed by the Arnon, at the farthest point of the boundary. ³⁷Balak said to Balaam, 'Did I not send to summon you? Why did you not come to me? Am I not able to honour you?' ³⁸Balaam said to Balak, 'I have come to you now, but do I have power to say just anything? The word God puts in my mouth, that is what I must say.' ³⁹Then Balaam went with Balak, and they came to Kiriath-huzoth. ⁴⁰Balak sacrificed oxen and sheep, and sent them to Balaam and to the officials who were with him.

Balaam's First Oracle

41 On the next day Balak took Balaam and brought him up to Bamoth-baal; and from there he could see part of the people

23 of Israel.*ᵇ* ¹Then Balaam said to Balak, 'Build me seven altars here, and prepare seven bulls and seven rams for me.' ²Balak did as Balaam had said; and Balak and Balaam offered a bull and a ram on each altar. ³Then Balaam said to Balak, 'Stay here beside your burnt-offerings while I go aside. Perhaps the LORD will come to meet me. Whatever he shows me I will tell you.' And he went to a bare height.

4 Then God met Balaam; and Balaam said to him, 'I have arranged the seven altars, and have offered a bull and a ram on each altar.' ⁵The LORD put a word in Balaam's mouth, and said, 'Return to Balak, and this is what you must say.' ⁶So he returned to Balak,*ᶜ* who was standing beside his burnt-offerings with all the officials of Moab. ⁷Then Balaam*ᵈ* uttered his oracle, saying:

'Balak has brought me from Aram,
  the king of Moab from the eastern
    mountains:
"Come, curse Jacob for me;
  Come, denounce Israel!"
8 How can I curse whom God has not
    cursed?
  How can I denounce those whom
    the LORD has not denounced?
9 For from the top of the crags I see
    him,
  from the hills I behold him.
  Here is a people living alone,
    and not reckoning itself among the
      nations!
10 Who can count the dust of Jacob,
    or number the dust-cloud*ᵉ* of
      Israel?
  Let me die the death of the upright,
    and let my end be like his!'

11 Then Balak said to Balaam, 'What have you done to me? I brought you to curse my enemies, but now you have done nothing but bless them.' ¹²He answered, 'Must I not take care to say what the LORD puts into my mouth?'

Balaam's Second Oracle

13 So Balak said to him, 'Come with me to another place from which you may see them; you shall see only part of them, and shall not see them all; then curse them for me from there.' ¹⁴So he took him to the field of Zophim, to the top of Pisgah. He

---

a Meaning of Heb uncertain   *b* Heb lacks *of Israel*
c Heb *him*   *d* Heb *he*   *e* Or *fourth part*

built seven altars, and offered a bull and a ram on each altar. [15] Balaam said to Balak, 'Stand here beside your burnt-offerings, while I meet the LORD over there.' [16] The LORD met Balaam, put a word into his mouth, and said, 'Return to Balak, and this is what you shall say.' [17] When he came to him, he was standing beside his burnt-offerings with the officials of Moab. Balak said to him, 'What has the LORD said?' [18] Then Balaam uttered his oracle, saying:

'Rise, Balak, and hear;
    listen to me, O son of Zippor:
[19] God is not a human being, that he
        should lie,
    or a mortal, that he should change
        his mind.
Has he promised, and will he not do
        it?
Has he spoken, and will he not
        fulfil it?
[20] See, I received a command to bless;
    he has blessed, and I cannot revoke
        it.
[21] He has not beheld misfortune in
        Jacob;
    nor has he seen trouble in Israel.
The LORD their God is with them,
    acclaimed as a king among them.
[22] God, who brings them out of Egypt,
    is like the horns of a wild ox for
        them.
[23] Surely there is no enchantment
        against Jacob,
    no divination against Israel;
now it shall be said of Jacob and
        Israel,
    "See what God has done!"
[24] Look, a people rising up like a
        lioness,
    and rousing itself like a lion!
It does not lie down until it has eaten
        the prey
    and drunk the blood of the slain.'

25 Then Balak said to Balaam, 'Do not curse them at all, and do not bless them at all.' [26] But Balaam answered Balak, 'Did I not tell you, "Whatever the LORD says, that is what I must do"?'

27 So Balak said to Balaam, 'Come now, I will take you to another place; perhaps it will please God that you may curse them for me from there.' [28] So Balak took Balaam to the top of Peor, which overlooks the waste-land. [a] [29] Balaam said to Balak, 'Build me seven altars here, and prepare seven bulls and seven rams for me.' [30] So Balak did as Balaam had said, and offered a bull and a ram on each altar.

Balaam's Third Oracle

24 Now Balaam saw that it pleased the LORD to bless Israel, so he did not go, as at other times, to look for omens, but set his face towards the wilderness. [2] Balaam looked up and saw Israel camping tribe by tribe. Then the spirit of God came upon him, [3] and he uttered his oracle, saying:

'The oracle of Balaam son of Beor,
    the oracle of the man whose eye is
        clear, [b]
[4] the oracle of one who hears the
        words of God,
    who sees the vision of the
        Almighty, [c]
    who falls down, but with eyes
        uncovered:
[5] how fair are your tents, O Jacob,
    your encampments, O Israel!
[6] Like palm groves that stretch far away,
    like gardens beside a river,
like aloes that the LORD has planted,
    like cedar trees beside the waters.
[7] Water shall flow from his buckets,
    and his seed shall have abundant
        water,
his king shall be higher than Agag,
    and his kingdom shall be exalted.
[8] God, who brings him out of Egypt,
    is like the horns of a wild ox for
        him;
he shall devour the nations that are
        his foes
    and break their bones.
He shall strike with his arrows. [d]
[9] He crouched, he lay down like a lion,
    and like a lioness; who will rouse
        him up?

a Or overlooks Jeshimon   b Or closed or open
c Traditional rendering of Heb Shaddai   d Meaning of Heb uncertain

Blessed is everyone who blesses you,
and cursed is everyone who curses
you.'

10 Then Balak's anger was kindled
against Balaam, and he struck his hands together. Balak said to Balaam, 'I summoned
you to curse my enemies, but instead you
have blessed them these three times. 11 Now
be off with you! Go home! I said, "I will
reward you richly", but the LORD has denied
you any reward.' 12 And Balaam said to Balak, 'Did I not tell your messengers whom
you sent to me, 13 "If Balak should give me
his house full of silver and gold, I would
not be able to go beyond the word of the
LORD, to do either good or bad of my own
will; what the LORD says, that is what I will
say"? 14 So now, I am going to my people; let
me advise you what this people will do to
your people in days to come.'

Balaam's Fourth Oracle

15 So he uttered his oracle, saying:
'The oracle of Balaam son of Beor,
    the oracle of the man whose eye is
        clear,ᵃ
16 the oracle of one who hears the
        words of God,
    and knows the knowledge of the
        Most High,ᵇ
who sees the vision of the Almighty,ᶜ
    who falls down, but with his eyes
        uncovered:
17 I see him, but not now;
    I behold him, but not near—
a star shall come out of Jacob,
    and a sceptre shall rise out of Israel;
it shall crush the borderlandsᵈ of
        Moab,
    and the territoryᵉ of all the
        Shethites.
18 Edom will become a possession,
    Seir a possession of its enemies,ᶠ
        while Israel does valiantly.
19 One out of Jacob shall rule,
    and destroy the survivors of Ir.'

20 Then he looked on Amalek, and uttered his oracle, saying:
'First among the nations was Amalek,
    but its end is to perish for ever.'

21 Then he looked on the Kenite, and uttered his oracle, saying:
'Enduring is your dwelling-place,
    and your nest is set in the rock;
22 yet Kain is destined for burning.
    How long shall Asshur take you
        away captive?'
23 Again he uttered his oracle, saying:
'Alas, who shall live when God does
        this?
24   But ships shall come from Kittim
    and shall afflict Asshur and Eber;
    and he also shall perish for ever.'

25 Then Balaam got up and went back to
his place, and Balak also went his way.

Worship of Baal of Peor

25 While Israel was staying at
Shittim, the people began to have
sexual relations with the women of Moab.
2 These invited the people to the sacrifices
of their gods, and the people ate and
bowed down to their gods. 3 Thus Israel
yoked itself to the Baal of Peor, and the
LORD's anger was kindled against Israel.
4 The LORD said to Moses, 'Take all the
chiefs of the people, and impale them in
the sun before the LORD, in order that the
fierce anger of the LORD may turn away
from Israel.' 5 And Moses said to the judges
of Israel, 'Each of you shall kill any of your
people who have yoked themselves to the
Baal of Peor.'

6 Just then one of the Israelites came
and brought a Midianite woman into his
family, in the sight of Moses and in the
sight of the whole congregation of the Israelites, while they were weeping at the entrance of the tent of meeting. 7 When Phinehas son of Eleazar, son of Aaron the priest,
saw it, he got up and left the congregation.
Taking a spear in his hand, 8 he went after
the Israelite man into the tent, and pierced
the two of them, the Israelite and the
woman, through the belly. So the plague
was stopped among the people of Israel.
9 Nevertheless, those that died by the plague
were twenty-four thousand.

ᵃ Or closed or open   ᵇ Or of Elyon   ᶜ Traditional
rendering of Heb Shaddai   ᵈ Or forehead   ᵉ Some
Mss read skull   ᶠ Heb Seir, its enemies, a possession

10 The LORD spoke to Moses, saying: 11 'Phinehas son of Eleazar, son of Aaron the priest, has turned back my wrath from the Israelites by manifesting such zeal among them on my behalf that in my jealousy I did not consume the Israelites. 12 Therefore say, "I hereby grant him my covenant of peace. 13 It shall be for him and for his descendants after him a covenant of perpetual priesthood, because he was zealous for his God, and made atonement for the Israelites." '

14 The name of the slain Israelite man, who was killed with the Midianite woman, was Zimri son of Salu, head of an ancestral house belonging to the Simeonites. 15 The name of the Midianite woman who was killed was Cozbi daughter of Zur, who was the head of a clan, an ancestral house in Midian.

16 The LORD said to Moses, 17 'Harass the Midianites, and defeat them; 18 for they have harassed you by the trickery with which they deceived you in the affair of Peor, and in the affair of Cozbi, the daughter of a leader of Midian, their sister; she was killed on the day of the plague that resulted from Peor.'

A Census of the New Generation

26 After the plague the LORD said to Moses and to Eleazar son of Aaron the priest, 2 'Take a census of the whole congregation of the Israelites, from twenty years old and upwards, by their ancestral houses, everyone in Israel able to go to war.' 3 Moses and Eleazar the priest spoke with them in the plains of Moab by the Jordan opposite Jericho, saying, 4 'Take a census of the people, a from twenty years old and upwards', as the LORD commanded Moses.

The Israelites, who came out of the land of Egypt, were:

5 Reuben, the firstborn of Israel. The descendants of Reuben: of Hanoch, the clan of the Hanochites; of Pallu, the clan of the Palluites; 6 of Hezron, the clan of the Hezronites; of Carmi, the clan of the Carmites. 7 These are the clans of the Reubenites; the number of those enrolled was forty-three thousand seven hundred and thirty. 8 And the descendants of Pallu: Eliab. 9 The descendants of Eliab: Nemuel, Dathan, and Abiram. These are the same Dathan and Abiram, chosen from the congregation, who rebelled against Moses and Aaron in the company of Korah, when they rebelled against the LORD, 10 and the earth opened its mouth and swallowed them up along with Korah, when that company died, when the fire devoured two hundred and fifty men; and they became a warning. 11 Notwithstanding, the sons of Korah did not die.

12 The descendants of Simeon by their clans: of Nemuel, the clan of the Nemuelites; of Jamin, the clan of the Jaminites; of Jachin, the clan of the Jachinites; 13 of Zerah, the clan of the Zerahites; of Shaul, the clan of the Shaulites. b 14 These are the clans of the Simeonites, twenty-two thousand two hundred.

15 The children of Gad by their clans: of Zephon, the clan of the Zephonites; of Haggi, the clan of the Haggites; of Shuni, the clan of the Shunites; 16 of Ozni, the clan of the Oznites; of Eri, the clan of the Erites; 17 of Arod, the clan of the Arodites; of Areli, the clan of the Arelites. 18 These are the clans of the Gadites: the number of those enrolled was forty thousand five hundred.

19 The sons of Judah: Er and Onan; Er and Onan died in the land of Canaan. 20 The descendants of Judah by their clans were: of Shelah, the clan of the Shelanites; of Perez, the clan of the Perezites; of Zerah, the clan of the Zerahites. 21 The descendants of Perez were: of Hezron, the clan of the Hezronites; of Hamul, the clan of the Hamulites. 22 These are the clans of Judah: the number of those enrolled was seventy-six thousand five hundred.

23 The descendants of Issachar by their clans: of Tola, the clan of the Tolaites; of Puvah, the clan of the Punites; 24 of Jashub, the clan of the Jashubites; of Shimron, the clan of the Shimronites. 25 These are the clans of Issachar: sixty-four thousand three hundred enrolled.

a Heb lacks *take a census of the people*: Compare verse 2
b Or *Saul . . . Saulites*

26 The descendants of Zebulun by their clans: of Sered, the clan of the Seredites; of Elon, the clan of the Elonites; of Jahleel, the clan of the Jahleelites. 27 These are the clans of the Zebulunites; the number of those enrolled was sixty thousand five hundred.

28 The sons of Joseph by their clans: Manasseh and Ephraim. 29 The descendants of Manasseh: of Machir, the clan of the Machirites; and Machir was the father of Gilead; of Gilead, the clan of the Gileadites. 30 These are the descendants of Gilead: of Iezer, the clan of the Iezerites; of Helek, the clan of the Helekites; 31 and of Asriel, the clan of the Asrielites; and of Shechem, the clan of the Shechemites; 32 and of Shemida, the clan of the Shemidaites; and of Hepher, the clan of the Hepherites. 33 Now Zelophehad son of Hepher had no sons, but daughters: and the names of the daughters of Zelophehad were Mahlah, Noah, Hoglah, Milcah, and Tirzah. 34 These are the clans of Manasseh; the number of those enrolled was fifty-two thousand seven hundred.

35 These are the descendants of Ephraim according to their clans: of Shuthelah, the clan of the Shuthelahites; of Becher, the clan of the Becherites; of Tahan, the clan of the Tahanites. 36 And these are the descendants of Shuthelah: of Eran, the clan of the Eranites. 37 These are the clans of the Ephraimites: the number of those enrolled was thirty-two thousand five hundred. These are the descendants of Joseph by their clans.

38 The descendants of Benjamin by their clans: of Bela, the clan of the Belaites; of Ashbel, the clan of the Ashbelites; of Ahiram, the clan of the Ahiramites; 39 of Shephupham, the clan of the Shuphamites; of Hupham, the clan of the Huphamites. 40 And the sons of Bela were Ard and Naaman: of Ard, the clan of the Ardites; of Naaman, the clan of the Naamites. 41 These are the descendants of Benjamin by their clans; the number of those enrolled was forty-five thousand six hundred.

42 These are the descendants of Dan by their clans: of Shuham, the clan of the Shuhamites. These are the clans of Dan by their clans. 43 All the clans of the Shuhamites: sixty-four thousand four hundred enrolled.

44 The descendants of Asher by their families: of Imnah, the clan of the Imnites; of Ishvi, the clan of the Ishvites; of Beriah, the clan of the Beriites. 45 Of the descendants of Beriah: of Heber, the clan of the Heberites; of Malchiel, the clan of the Malchielites. 46 And the name of the daughter of Asher was Serah. 47 These are the clans of the Asherites: the number of those enrolled was fifty-three thousand four hundred.

48 The descendants of Naphtali by their clans: of Jahzeel, the clan of the Jahzeelites; of Guni, the clan of the Gunites; 49 of Jezer, the clan of the Jezerites; of Shillem, the clan of the Shillemites. 50 These are the Naphtalites[a] by their clans: the number of those enrolled was forty-five thousand four hundred.

51 This was the number of the Israelites enrolled: six hundred and one thousand seven hundred and thirty.

52 The LORD spoke to Moses, saying: 53 To these the land shall be apportioned for inheritance according to the number of names. 54 To a large tribe you shall give a large inheritance, and to a small tribe you shall give a small inheritance; every tribe shall be given its inheritance according to its enrolment. 55 But the land shall be apportioned by lot; according to the names of their ancestral tribes they shall inherit. 56 Their inheritance shall be apportioned according to lot between the larger and the smaller.

57 This is the enrolment of the Levites by their clans: of Gershon, the clan of the Gershonites; of Kohath, the clan of the Kohathites; of Merari, the clan of the Merarites. 58 These are the clans of Levi: the clan of the Libnites, the clan of the Hebronites, the clan of the Mahlites, the clan of the Mushites, the clan of the Korahites. Now Kohath was the father of Amram. 59 The name of Amram's wife was Jochebed daughter of Levi, who was born to Levi in Egypt; and she bore to Amram: Aaron, Moses, and

a Heb clans of Naphtali

their sister Miriam. 60 To Aaron were born Nadab, Abihu, Eleazar, and Ithamar. 61 But Nadab and Abihu died when they offered unholy fire before the LORD. 62 The number of those enrolled was twenty-three thousand, every male one month old and upwards; for they were not enrolled among the Israelites because there was no allotment given to them among the Israelites.

63 These were those enrolled by Moses and Eleazar the priest, who enrolled the Israelites in the plains of Moab by the Jordan opposite Jericho. 64 Among these there was not one of those enrolled by Moses and Aaron the priest, who had enrolled the Israelites in the wilderness of Sinai. 65 For the LORD had said of them, 'They shall die in the wilderness.' Not one of them was left, except Caleb son of Jephunneh and Joshua son of Nun.

The Daughters of Zelophehad

27 Then the daughters of Zelophehad came forward. Zelophehad was son of Hepher son of Gilead son of Machir son of Manasseh son of Joseph, a member of the Manassite clans. The names of his daughters were: Mahlah, Noah, Hoglah, Milcah, and Tirzah. 2 They stood before Moses, Eleazar the priest, the leaders, and all the congregation, at the entrance of the tent of meeting, and they said, 3 'Our father died in the wilderness; he was not among the company of those who gathered themselves together against the LORD in the company of Korah, but died for his own sin; and he had no sons. 4 Why should the name of our father be taken away from his clan because he had no son? Give to us a possession among our father's brothers.'

5 Moses brought their case before the LORD. 6 And the LORD spoke to Moses, saying: 7 The daughters of Zelophehad are right in what they are saying; you shall indeed let them possess an inheritance among their father's brothers and pass the inheritance of their father on to them. 8 You shall also say to the Israelites, 'If a man dies, and has no son, then you shall pass his inheritance on to his daughter. 9 If

he has no daughter, then you shall give his inheritance to his brothers. 10 If he has no brothers, then you shall give his inheritance to his father's brothers. 11 And if his father has no brothers, then you shall give his inheritance to the nearest kinsman of his clan, and he shall possess it. It shall be for the Israelites a statute and ordinance, as the LORD commanded Moses.'

Joshua Appointed Moses' Successor

12 The LORD said to Moses, 'Go up this mountain of the Abarim range, and see the land that I have given to the Israelites. 13 When you have seen it, you also shall be gathered to your people, as your brother Aaron was, 14 because you rebelled against my word in the wilderness of Zin when the congregation quarrelled with me. a You did not show my holiness before their eyes at the waters.' (These are the waters of Meribath-kadesh in the wilderness of Zin.) 15 Moses spoke to the LORD, saying, 16 'Let the LORD, the God of the spirits of all flesh, appoint someone over the congregation 17 who shall go out before them and come in before them, who shall lead them out and bring them in, so that the congregation of the LORD may not be like sheep without a shepherd.' 18 So the LORD said to Moses, 'Take Joshua son of Nun, a man in whom is the spirit, and lay your hand upon him; 19 have him stand before Eleazar the priest and all the congregation, and commission him in their sight. 20 You shall give him some of your authority, so that all the congregation of the Israelites may obey. 21 But he shall stand before Eleazar the priest, who shall inquire for him by the decision of the Urim before the LORD; at his word they shall go out, and at his word they shall come in, both he and all the Israelites with him, the whole congregation.' 22 So Moses did as the LORD commanded him. He took Joshua and had him stand before Eleazar the priest and the whole congregation; 23 he laid his hands on him and commissioned him—as the LORD had directed through Moses.

a Heb lacks *with me*

Daily Offerings

28 The LORD spoke to Moses, saying: 2 Command the Israelites, and say to them: My offering, the food for my offerings by fire, my pleasing odour, you shall take care to offer to me at its appointed time. 3 And you shall say to them, This is the offering by fire that you shall offer to the LORD: two male lambs a year old without blemish, daily, as a regular offering. 4 One lamb you shall offer in the morning, and the other lamb you shall offer at twilight;*a* 5 also one-tenth of an ephah of choice flour for a grain-offering, mixed with one-fourth of a hin of beaten oil. 6 It is a regular burnt-offering, ordained at Mount Sinai for a pleasing odour, an offering by fire to the LORD. 7 Its drink-offering shall be one-fourth of a hin for each lamb; in the sanctuary you shall pour out a drink-offering of strong drink to the LORD. 8 The other lamb you shall offer at twilight*a* with a grain-offering and a drink-offering like the one in the morning; you shall offer it as an offering by fire, a pleasing odour to the LORD.

Sabbath Offerings

9 On the sabbath day: two male lambs a year old without blemish, and two-tenths of an ephah of choice flour for a grain-offering, mixed with oil, and its drink-offering— 10 this is the burnt-offering for every sabbath, in addition to the regular burnt-offering and its drink-offering.

Monthly Offerings

11 At the beginnings of your months you shall offer a burnt-offering to the LORD: two young bulls, one ram, seven male lambs a year old without blemish; 12 also three-tenths of an ephah of choice flour for a grain-offering, mixed with oil, for each bull; and two-tenths of choice flour for a grain-offering, mixed with oil, for the one ram; 13 and one-tenth of choice flour mixed with oil as a grain-offering for every lamb— a burnt-offering of pleasing odour, an offering by fire to the LORD. 14 Their drink-offerings shall be half a hin of wine for a bull, one-third of a hin for a ram, and one-fourth

of a hin for a lamb. This is the burnt-offering of every month throughout the months of the year. 15 And there shall be one male goat for a sin-offering to the LORD; it shall be offered in addition to the regular burnt-offering and its drink-offering.

Offerings at Passover

16 On the fourteenth day of the first month there shall be a passover-offering to the LORD. 17 And on the fifteenth day of this month is a festival; for seven days shall unleavened bread be eaten. 18 On the first day there shall be a holy convocation. You shall not work at your occupations. 19 You shall offer an offering by fire, a burnt-offering to the LORD: two young bulls, one ram, and seven male lambs a year old; see that they are without blemish. 20 Their grain-offering shall be of choice flour mixed with oil: three-tenths of an ephah shall you offer for a bull, and two-tenths for a ram; 21 one-tenth shall you offer for each of the seven lambs; 22 also one male goat for a sin-offering, to make atonement for you. 23 You shall offer these in addition to the burnt-offering of the morning, which belongs to the regular burnt-offering. 24 In the same way you shall offer daily, for seven days, the food of an offering by fire, a pleasing odour to the LORD; it shall be offered in addition to the regular burnt-offering and its drink-offering. 25 And on the seventh day you shall have a holy convocation; you shall not work at your occupations.

Offerings at the Festival of Weeks

26 On the day of the first fruits, when you offer a grain-offering of new grain to the LORD at your festival of weeks, you shall have a holy convocation; you shall not work at your occupations. 27 You shall offer a burnt-offering, a pleasing odour to the LORD: two young bulls, one ram, seven male lambs a year old. 28 Their grain-offering shall be of choice flour mixed with oil, three-tenths of an ephah for each bull, two-tenths for one ram, 29 one-tenth for each of the seven lambs; 30 with one male goat, to make atonement for you. 31 In addition to

a Heb between the two evenings

the regular burnt-offering with its grain-offering, you shall offer them and their drink-offering. They shall be without blemish.

Offerings at the Festival of Trumpets

29 On the first day of the seventh month you shall have a holy convocation; you shall not work at your occupations. It is a day for you to blow the trumpets, 2 and you shall offer a burnt-offering, a pleasing odour to the LORD: one young bull, one ram, seven male lambs a year old without blemish. 3 Their grain-offering shall be of choice flour mixed with oil, three-tenths of one ephah for the bull, two-tenths for the ram, 4 and one-tenth for each of the seven lambs; 5 with one male goat for a sin-offering, to make atonement for you. 6 These are in addition to the burnt-offering of the new moon and its grain-offering, and the regular burnt-offering and its grain-offering, and their drink-offerings, according to the ordinance for them, a pleasing odour, an offering by fire to the LORD.

Offerings on the Day of Atonement

7 On the tenth day of this seventh month you shall have a holy convocation, and deny yourselves;*a* you shall do no work. 8 You shall offer a burnt-offering to the LORD, a pleasing odour: one young bull, one ram, seven male lambs a year old. They shall be without blemish. 9 Their grain-offering shall be of choice flour mixed with oil, three-tenths of an ephah for the bull, two-tenths for the one ram, 10 one-tenth for each of the seven lambs; 11 with one male goat for a sin-offering, in addition to the sin-offering of atonement, and the regular burnt-offering and its grain-offering, and their drink-offerings.

Offerings at the Festival of Booths

12 On the fifteenth day of the seventh month you shall have a holy convocation; you shall not work at your occupations. You shall celebrate a festival to the LORD for seven days. 13 You shall offer a burnt-offering, an offering by fire, a pleasing odour to the LORD: thirteen young bulls, two rams, fourteen male lambs a year old. They shall

be without blemish. 14 Their grain-offering shall be of choice flour mixed with oil, three-tenths of an ephah for each of the thirteen bulls, two-tenths for each of the two rams, 15 and one-tenth for each of the fourteen lambs; 16 also one male goat for a sin-offering, in addition to the regular burnt-offering, its grain-offering and its drink-offering.

17 On the second day: twelve young bulls, two rams, fourteen male lambs a year old without blemish, 18 with the grain-offering and the drink-offerings for the bulls, for the rams, and for the lambs, as prescribed in accordance with their number; 19 also one male goat for a sin-offering, in addition to the regular burnt-offering and its grain-offering, and their drink-offerings.

20 On the third day: eleven bulls, two rams, fourteen male lambs a year old without blemish, 21 with the grain-offering and the drink-offerings for the bulls, for the rams, and for the lambs, as prescribed in accordance with their number; 22 also one male goat for a sin-offering, in addition to the regular burnt-offering and its grain-offering and its drink-offering.

23 On the fourth day: ten bulls, two rams, fourteen male lambs a year old without blemish, 24 with the grain-offering and the drink-offerings for the bulls, for the rams, and for the lambs, as prescribed in accordance with their number; 25 also one male goat for a sin-offering, in addition to the regular burnt-offering, its grain-offering and its drink-offering.

26 On the fifth day: nine bulls, two rams, fourteen male lambs a year old without blemish, 27 with the grain-offering and the drink-offerings for the bulls, for the rams, and for the lambs, as prescribed in accordance with their number; 28 also one male goat for a sin-offering, in addition to the regular burnt-offering and its grain-offering and its drink-offering.

29 On the sixth day: eight bulls, two rams, fourteen male lambs a year old without blemish, 30 with the grain-offering and the drink-offerings for the bulls, for the rams, and for the lambs, as prescribed in

a Or *and fast*

accordance with their number; 31 also one male goat for a sin-offering, in addition to the regular burnt-offering, its grain-offering, and its drink-offerings.

32 On the seventh day: seven bulls, two rams, fourteen male lambs a year old without blemish, 33 with the grain-offering and the drink-offerings for the bulls, for the rams, and for the lambs, as prescribed in accordance with their number; 34 also one male goat for a sin-offering, besides the regular burnt-offering, its grain-offering, and its drink-offering.

35 On the eighth day you shall have a solemn assembly; you shall not work at your occupations. 36 You shall offer a burnt-offering, an offering by fire, a pleasing odour to the LORD: one bull, one ram, seven male lambs a year old without blemish, 37 and the grain-offering and the drink-offerings for the bull, for the ram, and for the lambs, as prescribed in accordance with their number; 38 also one male goat for a sin-offering, in addition to the regular burnt-offering and its grain-offering and its drink-offering.

39 These you shall offer to the LORD at your appointed festivals, in addition to your votive offerings and your freewill-offerings, as your burnt-offerings, your grain-offerings, your drink-offerings, and your offerings of well-being.

40 a So Moses told the Israelites everything just as the LORD had commanded Moses.

Vows Made by Women

30 Then Moses said to the heads of the tribes of the Israelites: This is what the LORD has commanded. 2 When a man makes a vow to the LORD, or swears an oath to bind himself by a pledge, he shall not break his word; he shall do according to all that proceeds out of his mouth.

3 When a woman makes a vow to the LORD, or binds herself by a pledge, while within her father's house, in her youth, 4 and her father hears of her vow or her pledge by which she has bound herself, and says nothing to her; then all her vows shall stand, and any pledge by which she has

bound herself shall stand. 5 But if her father expresses disapproval to her at the time that he hears of it, no vow of hers, and no pledge by which she has bound herself, shall stand; and the LORD will forgive her, because her father had expressed to her his disapproval.

6 If she marries, while obligated by her vows or any thoughtless utterance of her lips by which she has bound herself, 7 and her husband hears of it and says nothing to her at the time that he hears, then her vows shall stand, and her pledges by which she has bound herself shall stand. 8 But if, at the time that her husband hears of it, he expresses disapproval to her, then he shall nullify the vow by which she was obligated, or the thoughtless utterance of her lips, by which she bound herself; and the LORD will forgive her. 9 (But every vow of a widow or of a divorced woman, by which she has bound herself, shall be binding upon her.) 10 And if she made a vow in her husband's house, or bound herself by a pledge with an oath, 11 and her husband heard it and said nothing to her, and did not express disapproval to her, then all her vows shall stand, and any pledge by which she bound herself shall stand. 12 But if her husband nullifies them at the time that he hears them, then whatever proceeds out of her lips concerning her vows, or concerning her pledge of herself, shall not stand. Her husband has nullified them, and the LORD will forgive her. 13 Any vow or any binding oath to deny herself, b her husband may allow to stand, or her husband may nullify. 14 But if her husband says nothing to her from day to day, c then he validates all her vows, or all her pledges, by which she is obligated; he has validated them, because he said nothing to her at the time that he heard of them. 15 But if he nullifies them some time after he has heard of them, then he shall bear her guilt.

16 These are the statutes that the LORD commanded Moses concerning a husband and his wife, and a father and his daughter

a Ch 30.1 in Heb   b Or to fast   c Or from that day to the next while she is still young and in her father's house.

War against Midian

31 The LORD spoke to Moses, saying, 2'Avenge the Israelites on the Midianites; afterwards you shall be gathered to your people.' 3 So Moses said to the people, 'Arm some of your number for the war, so that they may go against Midian, to execute the LORD's vengeance on Midian. 4 You shall send a thousand from each of the tribes of Israel to the war.' 5 So out of the thousands of Israel, a thousand from each tribe were conscripted, twelve thousand armed for battle. 6 Moses sent them to the war, a thousand from each tribe, along with Phinehas son of Eleazar the priest, *a* with the vessels of the sanctuary and the trumpets for sounding the alarm in his hand. 7 They did battle against Midian, as the LORD had commanded Moses, and killed every male. 8 They killed the kings of Midian: Evi, Rekem, Zur, Hur, and Reba, the five kings of Midian, in addition to others who were slain by them; and they also killed Balaam son of Beor with the sword. 9 The Israelites took the women of Midian and their little ones captive; and they took all their cattle, their flocks, and all their goods as booty. 10 All their towns where they had settled, and all their encampments, they burned, 11 but they took all the spoil and all the booty, both people and animals. 12 Then they brought the captives and the booty and the spoil to Moses, to Eleazar the priest, and to the congregation of the Israelites, at the camp on the plains of Moab by the Jordan at Jericho.

Return from the War

13 Moses, Eleazar the priest, and all the leaders of the congregation went to meet them outside the camp. 14 Moses became angry with the officers of the army, the commanders of thousands and the commanders of hundreds, who had come from service in the war. 15 Moses said to them, 'Have you allowed all the women to live? 16 These women here, on Balaam's advice, made the Israelites act treacherously against the LORD in the affair of Peor, so that the plague came among the congregation of the LORD. 17 Now therefore, kill every male among the little ones, and kill every woman who has known a man by sleeping with him. 18 But all the young girls who have not known a man by sleeping with him, keep alive for yourselves. 19 Camp outside the camp for seven days; whoever of you has killed any person or touched a corpse, purify yourselves and your captives on the third and on the seventh day. 20 You shall purify every garment, every article of skin, everything made of goats' hair, and every article of wood.'

21 Eleazar the priest said to the troops who had gone to battle: 'This is the statute of the law that the LORD has commanded Moses: 22 gold, silver, bronze, iron, tin, and lead— 23 everything that can withstand fire, shall be passed through fire, and it shall be clean. Nevertheless it shall also be purified with the water for purification; and whatever cannot withstand fire, shall be passed through the water. 24 You must wash your clothes on the seventh day, and you shall be clean; afterwards you may come into the camp.'

Disposition of Captives and Booty

25 The LORD spoke to Moses, saying, 26 'You and Eleazar the priest and the heads of the ancestral houses of the congregation make an inventory of the booty captured, both human and animal. 27 Divide the booty into two parts, between the warriors who went out to battle and all the congregation. 28 From the share of the warriors who went out to battle, set aside as tribute for the LORD one item out of every five hundred, whether persons, oxen, donkeys, sheep, or goats. 29 Take it from their half and give it to Eleazar the priest as an offering to the LORD. 30 But from the Israelites' half you shall take one out of every fifty, whether persons, oxen, donkeys, sheep, or goats—all the animals—and give them to the Levites who have charge of the tabernacle of the LORD.'

a Gk: Heb adds *to the war*

31 Then Moses and Eleazar the priest did as the LORD had commanded Moses:

32 The booty remaining from the spoil that the troops had taken totalled six hundred and seventy-five thousand sheep, 33 seventy-two thousand oxen, 34 sixty-one thousand donkeys, 35 and thirty-two thousand persons in all, women who had not known a man by sleeping with him.

36 The half-share, the portion of those who had gone out to war, was in number three hundred and thirty-seven thousand five hundred sheep and goats, 37 and the LORD's tribute of sheep and goats was six hundred and seventy-five. 38 The oxen were thirty-six thousand, of which the LORD's tribute was seventy-two. 39 The donkeys were thirty thousand five hundred, of which the LORD's tribute was sixty-one. 40 The persons were sixteen thousand, of which the LORD's tribute was thirty-two persons. 41 Moses gave the tribute, the offering for the LORD, to Eleazar the priest, as the LORD had commanded Moses.

42 As for the Israelites' half, which Moses separated from that of the troops, 43 the congregation's half was three hundred and thirty-seven thousand five hundred sheep and goats, 44 thirty-six thousand oxen, 45 thirty thousand five hundred donkeys, 46 and sixteen thousand persons. 47 From the Israelites' half Moses took one of every fifty, both of persons and of animals, and gave them to the Levites who had charge of the tabernacle of the LORD; as the LORD had commanded Moses.

48 Then the officers who were over the thousands of the army, the commanders of thousands and the commanders of hundreds, approached Moses, 49 and said to Moses, 'Your servants have counted the warriors who are under our command, and not one of us is missing. 50 And we have brought the LORD's offering, what each of us found, articles of gold, armlets and bracelets, signet rings, ear-rings, and pendants, to make atonement for ourselves before the LORD.' 51 Moses and Eleazar the priest received the gold from them, all in the form of crafted articles. 52 And all the gold of the offering that they offered to the

LORD, from the commanders of thousands and the commanders of hundreds, was sixteen thousand seven hundred and fifty shekels. 53 (The troops had all taken plunder for themselves.) 54 So Moses and Eleazar the priest received the gold from the commanders of thousands and of hundreds, and brought it into the tent of meeting as a memorial for the Israelites before the LORD.

Conquest and Division of Transjordan

32 Now the Reubenites and the Gadites owned a very great number of cattle. When they saw that the land of Jazer and the land of Gilead was a good place for cattle, 2 the Gadites and the Reubenites came and spoke to Moses, to Eleazar the priest, and to the leaders of the congregation, saying, 3 'Ataroth, Dibon, Jazer, Nimrah, Heshbon, Elealeh, Sebam, Nebo, and Beon— 4 the land that the LORD subdued before the congregation of Israel—is a land for cattle; and your servants have cattle.' 5 They continued, 'If we have found favour in your sight, let this land be given to your servants for a possession; do not make us cross the Jordan.'

6 But Moses said to the Gadites and to the Reubenites, 'Shall your brothers go to war while you sit here? 7 Why will you discourage the hearts of the Israelites from going over into the land that the LORD has given them? 8 Your fathers did this, when I sent them from Kadesh-barnea to see the land. 9 When they went up to the Wadi Eshcol and saw the land, they discouraged the hearts of the Israelites from going into the land that the LORD had given them. 10 The LORD's anger was kindled on that day and he swore, saying, 11 "Surely none of the people who came up out of Egypt, from twenty years old and upwards, shall see the land that I swore to give to Abraham, to Isaac, and to Jacob, because they have not unreservedly followed me— 12 none except Caleb son of Jephunneh the Kenizzite and Joshua son of Nun, for they have unreservedly followed the LORD." 13 And the LORD's anger was kindled against Israel, and he made them wander in the wilderness for forty years, until all the generation that had

done evil in the sight of the LORD had disappeared. 14 And now you, a brood of sinners, have risen in place of your fathers, to increase the LORD's fierce anger against Israel! 15 If you turn away from following him, he will again abandon them in the wilderness; and you will destroy all this people.'

16 Then they came up to him and said, 'We will build sheepfolds here for our flocks, and towns for our little ones, 17 but we will take up arms as a vanguard *a* before the Israelites, until we have brought them to their place. Meanwhile our little ones will stay in the fortified towns because of the inhabitants of the land. 18 We will not return to our homes until all the Israelites have obtained their inheritance. 19 We will not inherit with them on the other side of the Jordan and beyond, because our inheritance has come to us on this side of the Jordan to the east.'

20 So Moses said to them, 'If you do this—if you take up arms to go before the LORD for the war, 21 and all those of you who bear arms cross the Jordan before the LORD, until he has driven out his enemies from before him 22 and the land is subdued before the LORD—then after that you may return and be free of obligation to the LORD and to Israel, and this land shall be your possession before the LORD. 23 But if you do not do this, you have sinned against the LORD; and be sure your sin will find you out. 24 Build towns for your little ones, and folds for your flocks; but do what you have promised.'

25 Then the Gadites and the Reubenites said to Moses, 'Your servants will do as my lord commands. 26 Our little ones, our wives, our flocks, and all our livestock shall remain there in the towns of Gilead; 27 but your servants will cross over, everyone armed for war, to do battle for the LORD, just as my lord orders.'

28 So Moses gave command concerning them to Eleazar the priest, to Joshua son of Nun, and to the heads of the ancestral houses of the Israelite tribes. 29 And Moses said to them, 'If the Gadites and the Reubenites, everyone armed for battle before

the LORD, will cross over the Jordan with you and the land shall be subdued before you, then you shall give them the land of Gilead for a possession; 30 but if they will not cross over with you armed, they shall have possessions among you in the land of Canaan.' 31 The Gadites and the Reubenites answered, 'As the LORD has spoken to your servants, so we will do. 32 We will cross over armed before the LORD into the land of Canaan, but the possession of our inheritance shall remain with us on this side of *b* the Jordan.'

33 Moses gave to them—to the Gadites and to the Reubenites and to the half-tribe of Manasseh son of Joseph—the kingdom of King Sihon of the Amorites and the kingdom of King Og of Bashan, the land and its towns, with the territories of the surrounding towns. 34 And the Gadites rebuilt Dibon, Ataroth, Aroer, 35 Atroth-shophan, Jazer, Jogbehah, 36 Beth-nimrah, and Beth-haran, fortified cities, and folds for sheep. 37 And the Reubenites rebuilt Heshbon, Elealeh, Kiriathaim, 38 Nebo, and Baal-meon (some names being changed), and Sibmah; and they gave names to the towns that they rebuilt. 39 The descendants of Machir son of Manasseh went to Gilead, captured it, and dispossessed the Amorites who were there; 40 so Moses gave Gilead to Machir son of Manasseh, and he settled there. 41 Jair son of Manasseh went and captured their villages, and renamed them Havvoth-jair. *c* 42 And Nobah went and captured Kenath and its villages, and renamed it Nobah after himself.

The Stages of Israel's Journey from Egypt

33 These are the stages by which the Israelites went out of the land of Egypt in military formation under the leadership of Moses and Aaron. 2 Moses wrote down their starting points, stage by stage, by command of the LORD; and these are their stages according to their starting places. 3 They set out from Rameses in the first month, on the fifteenth day of the first

a Cn: Heb *hurrying*   *b* Heb *beyond*   *c* That is *the villages of Jair* month; on the day after the passover the Israelites went out boldly in the sight of all the Egyptians, ⁴while the Egyptians were burying all their firstborn, whom the Lᴏʀᴅ had struck down among them. The Lᴏʀᴅ executed judgements even against their gods.

5 So the Israelites set out from Rameses, and camped at Succoth. ⁶They set out from Succoth, and camped at Etham, which is on the edge of the wilderness. ⁷They set out from Etham, and turned back to Pi-hahiroth, which faces Baal-zephon; and they camped before Migdol. ⁸They set out from Pi-hahiroth, passed through the sea into the wilderness, went a three days' journey in the wilderness of Etham, and camped at Marah. ⁹They set out from Marah and came to Elim; at Elim there were twelve springs of water and seventy palm trees, and they camped there. ¹⁰They set out from Elim and camped by the Red Sea.ᵃ ¹¹They set out from the Red Seaᵃ and camped in the wilderness of Sin. ¹²They set out from the wilderness of Sin and camped at Dophkah. ¹³They set out from Dophkah and camped at Alush. ¹⁴They set out from Alush and camped at Rephidim, where there was no water for the people to drink. ¹⁵They set out from Rephidim and camped in the wilderness of Sinai. ¹⁶They set out from the wilderness of Sinai and camped at Kibroth-hattaavah. ¹⁷They set out from Kibroth-hattaavah and camped at Hazeroth. ¹⁸They set out from Hazeroth and camped at Rithmah. ¹⁹They set out from Rithmah and camped at Rimmon-perez. ²⁰They set out from Rimmon-perez and camped at Libnah. ²¹They set out from Libnah and camped at Rissah. ²²They set out from Rissah and camped at Kehelathah. ²³They set out from Kehelathah and camped at Mount Shepher. ²⁴They set out from Mount Shepher and camped at Haradah. ²⁵They set out from Haradah and camped at Makheloth. ²⁶They set out from Makheloth and camped at Tahath. ²⁷They

a Or Sea of Reeds

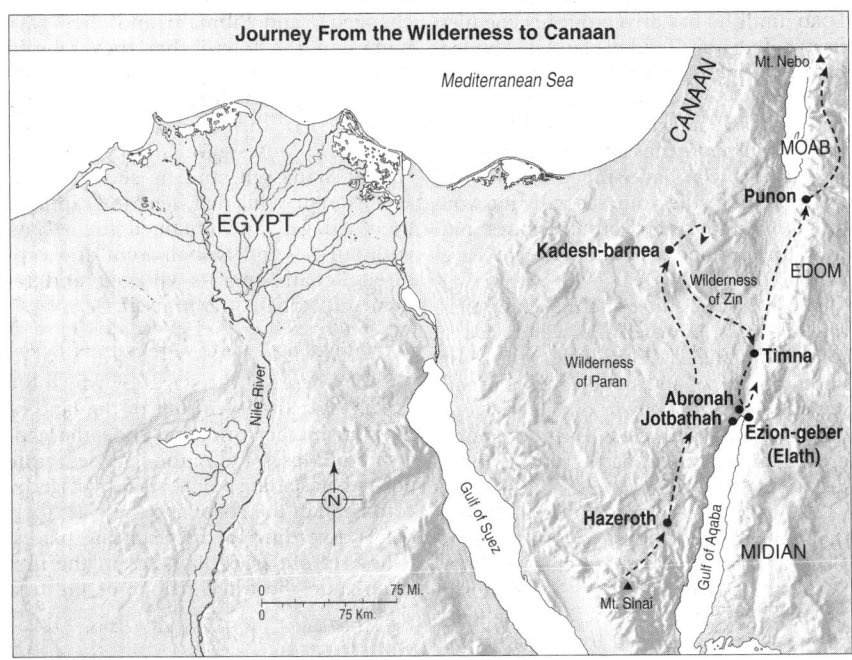

Journey From the Wilderness to Canaan

set out from Tahath and camped at Terah. ²⁸They set out from Terah and camped at Mithkah. ²⁹They set out from Mithkah and camped at Hashmonah. ³⁰They set out from Hashmonah and camped at Moseroth. ³¹They set out from Moseroth and camped at Bene-jaakan. ³²They set out from Bene-jaakan and camped at Hor-haggidgad. ³³They set out from Hor-haggidgad and camped at Jotbathah. ³⁴They set out from Jotbathah and camped at Abronah. ³⁵They set out from Abronah and camped at Ezion-geber. ³⁶They set out from Ezion-geber and camped in the wilderness of Zin (that is, Kadesh). ³⁷They set out from Kadesh and camped at Mount Hor, on the edge of the land of Edom.

38 Aaron the priest went up Mount Hor at the command of the LORD and died there in the fortieth year after the Israelites had come out of the land of Egypt, on the first day of the fifth month. ³⁹Aaron was one hundred and twenty-three years old when he died on Mount Hor.

40 The Canaanite, the king of Arad, who lived in the Negeb in the land of Canaan, heard of the coming of the Israelites.

41 They set out from Mount Hor and camped at Zalmonah. ⁴²They set out from Zalmonah and camped at Punon. ⁴³They set out from Punon and camped at Oboth. ⁴⁴They set out from Oboth and camped at Iye-abarim, in the territory of Moab. ⁴⁵They set out from Iyim and camped at Dibon-gad. ⁴⁶They set out from Dibon-gad and camped at Almon-diblathaim. ⁴⁷They set out from Almon-diblathaim and camped in the mountains of Abarim, before Nebo. ⁴⁸They set out from the mountains of Abarim and camped in the plains of Moab by the Jordan at Jericho; ⁴⁹they camped by the Jordan from Beth-jeshimoth as far as Abel-shittim in the plains of Moab.

Directions for the Conquest of Canaan

50 In the plains of Moab by the Jordan at Jericho, the LORD spoke to Moses, saying: ⁵¹Speak to the Israelites, and say to them: When you cross over the Jordan into the land of Canaan, ⁵²you shall drive out all the inhabitants of the land from before you, destroy all their figured stones, destroy all their cast images, and demolish all their high places. ⁵³You shall take possession of the land and settle in it, for I have given you the land to possess. ⁵⁴You shall apportion the land by lot according to your clans; to a large one you shall give a large inheritance, and to a small one you shall give a small inheritance; the inheritance shall belong to the person on whom the lot falls; according to your ancestral tribes you shall inherit. ⁵⁵But if you do not drive out the inhabitants of the land from before you, then those whom you let remain shall be as barbs in your eyes and thorns in your sides; they shall trouble you in the land where you are settling. ⁵⁶And I will do to you as I thought to do to them.

The Boundaries of the Land

34 The LORD spoke to Moses, saying: ²Command the Israelites, and say to them: When you enter the land of Canaan (this is the land that shall fall to you for an inheritance, the land of Canaan, defined by its boundaries), ³your south sector shall extend from the wilderness of Zin along the side of Edom. Your southern boundary shall begin from the end of the Dead Sea*ᵃ* on the east; ⁴your boundary shall turn south of the ascent of Akrabbim, and cross to Zin, and its outer limit shall be south of Kadesh-barnea; then it shall go on to Hazar-addar, and cross to Azmon; ⁵the boundary shall turn from Azmon to the Wadi of Egypt, and its termination shall be at the Sea.

6 For the western boundary, you shall have the Great Sea and its*ᵇ* coast; this shall be your western boundary.

7 This shall be your northern boundary: from the Great Sea you shall mark out your line to Mount Hor; ⁸from Mount Hor you shall mark it out to Lebo-hamath, and the outer limit of the boundary shall be at Zedad; ⁹then the boundary shall extend to Ziphron, and its end shall be at Hazar-enan; this shall be your northern boundary.

a Heb *Salt Sea*   *b* Syr: Heb lacks *its*

10 You shall mark out your eastern boundary from Hazar-enan to Shepham; [11] and the boundary shall continue down from Shepham to Riblah on the east side of Ain; and the boundary shall go down, and reach the eastern slope of the sea of Chinnereth; [12] and the boundary shall go down to the Jordan, and its end shall be at the Dead Sea.[a] This shall be your land with its boundaries all round.

13 Moses commanded the Israelites, saying: This is the land that you shall inherit by lot, which the LORD has commanded to give to the nine tribes and to the half-tribe; [14] for the tribe of the Reubenites by their ancestral houses and the tribe of the Gadites by their ancestral houses have taken their inheritance, and also the half-tribe of Manasseh; [15] the two tribes and the half-tribe have taken their inheritance beyond the Jordan at Jericho eastwards, towards the sunrise.

Tribal Leaders

16 The LORD spoke to Moses, saying: [17] These are the names of the men who shall apportion the land to you for inheritance: the priest Eleazar and Joshua son of Nun. [18] You shall take one leader of every tribe to apportion the land for inheritance. [19] These are the names of the men: Of the tribe of Judah, Caleb son of Jephunneh. [20] Of the tribe of the Simeonites, Shemuel son of Ammihud. [21] Of the tribe of Benjamin, Elidad son of Chislon. [22] Of the tribe of the Danites a leader, Bukki son of Jogli. [23] Of the Josephites: of the tribe of the Manassites a leader, Hanniel son of Ephod, [24] and of the tribe of the Ephraimites a leader, Kemuel son of Shiphtan. [25] Of the tribe of the Zebulunites a leader, Eli-zaphan son of Parnach. [26] Of the tribe of the Issacharites a leader, Paltiel son of Azzan. [27] And of the tribe of the Asherites a leader, Ahihud son of Shelomi. [28] Of the tribe of the Naphtalites a leader, Pedahel son of Ammihud. [29] These were the ones whom the LORD commanded to apportion the inheritance for the Israelites in the land of Canaan.

Cities for the Levites

35 In the plains of Moab by the Jordan at Jericho, the LORD spoke to Moses, saying: [2] Command the Israelites to give, from the inheritance that they possess, towns for the Levites to live in; you shall also give to the Levites pasture lands surrounding the towns. [3] The towns shall be theirs to live in, and their pasture lands shall be for their cattle, for their livestock, and for all their animals. [4] The pasture lands of the towns, which you shall give to the Levites, shall reach from the wall of the town outwards a thousand cubits all around. [5] You shall measure, outside the town, for the east side two thousand cubits, for the south side two thousand cubits, for the west side two thousand cubits, and for the north side two thousand cubits, with the town in the middle; this shall belong to them as pasture land for their towns.

6 The towns that you give to the Levites shall include the six cities of refuge, where you shall permit a slayer to flee, and in addition to them you shall give forty-two towns. [7] The towns that you give to the Levites shall total forty-eight, with their pasture lands. [8] And as for the towns that you shall give from the possession of the Israelites, from the larger tribes you shall take many, and from the smaller tribes you shall take few; each, in proportion to the inheritance that it obtains, shall give of its towns to the Levites.

Cities of Refuge

9 The LORD spoke to Moses, saying: [10] Speak to the Israelites, and say to them: When you cross the Jordan into the land of Canaan, [11] then you shall select cities to be cities of refuge for you, so that a slayer who kills a person without intent may flee there. [12] The cities shall be for you a refuge from the avenger, so that the slayer may not die until there is a trial before the congregation.

13 The cities that you designate shall be six cities of refuge for you: [14] you shall designate three cities beyond the Jordan, and three cities in the land of Canaan, to be

a Heb Salt Sea

cities of refuge. ¹⁵These six cities shall serve as refuge for the Israelites, for the resident or transient alien among them, so that anyone who kills a person without intent may flee there.

Concerning Murder and Blood-Revenge

16 But anyone who strikes another with an iron object, and death ensues, is a murderer; the murderer shall be put to death. ¹⁷Or anyone who strikes another with a stone in hand that could cause death, and death ensues, is a murderer; the murderer shall be put to death. ¹⁸Or anyone who strikes another with a weapon of wood in hand that could cause death, and death ensues, is a murderer; the murderer shall be put to death. ¹⁹The avenger of blood is the one who shall put the murderer to death; when they meet, the avenger of blood shall execute the sentence. ²⁰Likewise, if someone pushes another from hatred, or hurls something at another, lying in wait, and death ensues, ²¹or in enmity strikes another with the hand, and death ensues, then the one who struck the blow shall be put to death; that person is a murderer; the avenger of blood shall put the murderer to death when they meet.

22 But if someone pushes another suddenly without enmity, or hurls any object without lying in wait, ²³or, while handling any stone that could cause death, unintentionally*a* drops it on another and death ensues, though they were not enemies, and no harm was intended, ²⁴then the congregation shall judge between the slayer and the avenger of blood, in accordance with these ordinances; ²⁵and the congregation shall rescue the slayer from the avenger of blood. Then the congregation shall send the slayer back to the original city of refuge. The slayer shall live in it until the death of the high priest who was anointed with the holy oil. ²⁶But if the slayer shall at any time go outside the bounds of the original city of refuge, ²⁷and is found by the avenger of blood outside the bounds of the city of refuge, and is killed by the avenger, no blood-guilt shall be incurred. ²⁸For the slayer must remain in the city of refuge until the death of the high priest; but after the death of the high priest the slayer may return home.

29 These things shall be a statute and ordinance for you throughout your generations wherever you live.

30 If anyone kills another, the murderer shall be put to death on the evidence of witnesses; but no one shall be put to death on the testimony of a single witness. ³¹Moreover, you shall accept no ransom for the life of a murderer who is subject to the death penalty; a murderer must be put to death. ³²Nor shall you accept ransom for one who has fled to a city of refuge, enabling the fugitive to return to live in the land before the death of the high priest. ³³You shall not pollute the land in which you live; for blood pollutes the land, and no expiation can be made for the land, for the blood that is shed in it, except by the blood of the one who shed it. ³⁴You shall not defile the land in which you live, in which I also dwell; for I the LORD dwell among the Israelites.

Cities of Refuge

Mediterranean Sea

DAN (Northern Settlement)

ASHER

NAPHTALI

MANASSEH

• Kedesh

ZEBULUN

• Golan?

• Ramoth

MANASSEH

Shechem •

EPHRAIM   GAD

DAN   BENJAMIN

• Bezer

JUDAH   REUBEN

Hebron •   Dead Sea

(Kiriath-arba)

SIMEON

0   40 Mi.
0   40 Km.

a Heb *without seeing*

Marriage of Female Heirs

36 The heads of the ancestral houses of the clans of the descendants of Gilead son of Machir son of Manasseh, of the Josephite clans, came forward and spoke in the presence of Moses and the leaders, the heads of the ancestral houses of the Israelites; 2 they said, 'The LORD commanded my lord to give the land for inheritance by lot to the Israelites; and my lord was commanded by the LORD to give the inheritance of our brother Zelophehad to his daughters. 3 But if they are married into another Israelite tribe, then their inheritance will be taken from the inheritance of our ancestors and added to the inheritance of the tribe into which they marry; so it will be taken away from the allotted portion of our inheritance. 4 And when the jubilee of the Israelites comes, then their inheritance will be added to the inheritance of the tribe into which they have married; and their inheritance will be taken from the inheritance of our ancestral tribe.'

5 Then Moses commanded the Israelites according to the word of the LORD, saying, 'The descendants of the tribe of Joseph are right in what they are saying. 6 This is what the LORD commands concerning the daughters of Zelophehad, "Let them marry whom they think best; only it must be into a clan of their father's tribe that they are married, 7 so that no inheritance of the Israelites shall be transferred from one tribe to another; for all Israelites shall retain the inheritance of their ancestral tribes. 8 Every daughter who possesses an inheritance in any tribe of the Israelites shall marry one from the clan of her father's tribe, so that all Israelites may continue to possess their ancestral inheritance. 9 No inheritance shall be transferred from one tribe to another; for each of the tribes of the Israelites shall retain its own inheritance." '

10 The daughters of Zelophehad did as the LORD had commanded Moses. 11 Mahlah, Tirzah, Hoglah, Milcah, and Noah, the daughters of Zelophehad, married sons of their father's brothers. 12 They were married into the clans of the descendants of Manasseh son of Joseph, and their inheritance remained in the tribe of their father's clan.

13 These are the commandments and the ordinances that the LORD commanded through Moses to the Israelites in the plains of Moab by the Jordan at Jericho.

DEUTERONOMY

Events at Horeb Recalled

1 These are the words that Moses spoke to all Israel beyond the Jordan—in the wilderness, on the plain opposite Suph, between Paran and Tophel, Laban, Hazeroth, and Di-zahab. 2 (By the way of Mount Seir it takes eleven days to reach Kadesh-barnea from Horeb.) 3 In the fortieth year, on the first day of the eleventh month, Moses spoke to the Israelites just as the LORD had commanded him to speak to them. 4 This was after he had defeated King Sihon of the Amorites, who reigned in Heshbon, and King Og of Bashan, who reigned in Ashtaroth and*a* in Edrei. 5 Beyond the Jordan in the land of Moab, Moses undertook to expound this law as follows:

6 The LORD our God spoke to us at Horeb, saying, 'You have stayed long enough at this mountain. 7 Resume your journey, and go into the hill country of the Amorites as well as into the neighbouring regions—the Arabah, the hill country, the Shephelah, the Negeb, and the sea coast—the land of the Canaanites and the Lebanon, as far as the great river, the river Euphrates. 8 See, I have set the land before you; go in and take possession of the land that I*b* swore to your ancestors, to Abraham, to Isaac, and to Jacob, to give to them and to their descendants after them.'

Appointment of Tribal Leaders

9 At that time I said to you, 'I am unable by myself to bear you. 10 The LORD your God has multiplied you, so that today you are as numerous as the stars of heaven. 11 May the LORD, the God of your ancestors, increase you a thousand times more and bless you, as he has promised you! 12 But how can I bear the heavy burden of your disputes all by myself? 13 Choose for each of your tribes individuals who are wise, discerning, and reputable to be your leaders.' 14 You answered me, 'The plan you have proposed is a good one.' 15 So I took the leaders of your tribes, wise and reputable individuals, and installed them as leaders over you, commanders of thousands, commanders of hundreds, commanders of fifties, commanders of tens, and officials, throughout your tribes. 16 I charged your judges at that time: 'Give the members of your community a fair hearing, and judge rightly between one person and another, whether citizen or resident alien. 17 You must not be partial in judging: hear out the small and the great alike; you shall not be intimidated by anyone, for the judgement is God's. Any case that is too hard for you, bring to me, and I will hear it.' 18 So I charged you at that time with all the things that you should do.

Israel's Refusal to Enter the Land

19 Then, just as the LORD our God had ordered us, we set out from Horeb and went through all that great and terrible wilderness that you saw, on the way to the hill country of the Amorites, until we reached Kadesh-barnea. 20 I said to you, 'You have reached the hill country of the Amorites, which the LORD our God is giving us. 21 See, the LORD your God has given the land to you; go up, take possession, as the LORD, the God of your ancestors, has promised you; do not fear or be dismayed.'

a Gk Syr Vg Compare Josh 12.4: Heb lacks *and*
b Sam Gk: MT *the* LORD

22 All of you came to me and said, 'Let us send men ahead of us to explore the land for us and bring back a report to us regarding the route by which we should go up and the cities we will come to.' 23 The plan seemed good to me, and I selected twelve of you, one from each tribe. 24 They set out and went up into the hill country, and when they reached the Valley of Eshcol they spied it out 25 and gathered some of the land's produce, which they brought down to us. They brought back a report to us, and said, 'It is a good land that the LORD our God is giving us.'

26 But you were unwilling to go up. You rebelled against the command of the LORD your God; 27 you grumbled in your tents and said, 'It is because the LORD hates us that he has brought us out of the land of Egypt, to hand us over to the Amorites to destroy us. 28 Where are we heading? Our kindred have made our hearts fail by reporting, "The people are stronger and taller than we are; the cities are large and fortified up to heaven! We actually saw there the offspring of the Anakim!" ' 29 I said to you, 'Have no dread or fear of them. 30 The LORD your God, who goes before you, is the one who will fight for you, just as he did for you in Egypt before your very eyes, 31 and in the wilderness, where you saw how the LORD your God carried you, just as one carries a child, all the way that you travelled until you reached this place. 32 But in spite of this, you have no trust in the LORD your God, 33 who goes before you on the way to seek out a place for you to camp, in fire by night, and in the cloud by day, to show you the route you should take.'

The Penalty for Israel's Rebellion

34 When the LORD heard your words, he was wrathful and swore: 35 'Not one of these—not one of this evil generation—shall see the good land that I swore to give to your ancestors, 36 except Caleb son of Jephunneh. He shall see it, and to him and to his descendants I will give the land on which he set foot, because of his complete fidelity to the LORD.' 37 Even with me the LORD was angry on your account, saying,

'You also shall not enter there. 38 Joshua son of Nun, your assistant, shall enter there; encourage him, for he is the one who will secure Israel's possession of it. 39 And as for your little ones, who you thought would become booty, your children, who today do not yet know right from wrong, they shall enter there; to them I will give it, and they shall take possession of it. 40 But as for you, journey back into the wilderness, in the direction of the Red Sea.' a

41 You answered me, 'We have sinned against the LORD! We are ready to go up and fight, just as the LORD our God commanded us.' So all of you strapped on your battle gear, and thought it easy to go up into the hill country. 42 The LORD said to me, 'Say to them, "Do not go up and do not fight, for I am not in the midst of you; otherwise you will be defeated by your enemies." ' 43 Although I told you, you would not listen. You rebelled against the command of the LORD and presumptuously went up into the hill country. 44 The Amorites who lived in that hill country then came out against you and chased you as bees do. They beat you down in Seir as far as Hormah. 45 When you returned and wept before the LORD, the LORD would neither heed your voice nor pay you any attention.

The Desert Years

46 After you had stayed at Kadesh as many days as you did, 1 we journeyed back into the wilderness, in the direction of the Red Sea, a as the LORD had told me, and skirted Mount Seir for many days. 2 Then the LORD said to me: 3 'You have been skirting this hill country long enough. Head north, 4 and charge the people as follows: You are about to pass through the territory of your kindred, the descendants of Esau, who live in Seir. They will be afraid of you, so be very careful 5 not to engage in battle with them, for I will not give you even so much as a foot's length of their land, since I have given Mount Seir to Esau as a possession. 6 You shall purchase food from them for money, so that you may eat; and you shall also buy water from them for

a Or Sea of Reeds

money, so that you may drink. 7 Surely the LORD your God has blessed you in all your undertakings; he knows your going through this great wilderness. These forty years the LORD your God has been with you; you have lacked nothing.' 8 So we passed by our kin, the descendants of Esau who live in Seir, leaving behind the route of the Arabah, and leaving behind Elath and Eziongeber.

When we had headed out along the route of the wilderness of Moab, 9 the LORD said to me: 'Do not harass Moab or engage them in battle, for I will not give you any of its land as a possession, since I have given Ar as a possession to the descendants of Lot.' 10 (The Emim—a large and numerous people, as tall as the Anakim—had formerly inhabited it. 11 Like the Anakim, they are usually reckoned as Rephaim, though the Moabites call them Emim. 12 Moreover, the Horim had formerly inhabited Seir, but the descendants of Esau dispossessed them, destroying them and settling in their place, as Israel has done in the land that the LORD gave them as a possession.) 13 'Now then, proceed to cross over the Wadi Zered.'

So we crossed over the Wadi Zered. 14 And the length of time we had travelled from Kadesh-barnea until we crossed the Wadi Zered was thirty-eight years, until the entire generation of warriors had perished from the camp, as the LORD had sworn concerning them. 15 Indeed, the LORD's own hand was against them, to root them out from the camp, until all had perished.

16 Just as soon as all the warriors had died from among the people, 17 the LORD spoke to me, saying, 18 'Today you are going to cross the boundary of Moab at Ar. 19 When you approach the frontier of the Ammonites, do not harass them or engage them in battle, for I will not give the land of the Ammonites to you as a possession, because I have given it to the descendants of Lot.' 20 (It also is usually reckoned as a land of Rephaim. Rephaim formerly inhabited it, though the Ammonites call them Zamzummim, 21 a strong and numerous people, as tall as the Anakim. But the LORD destroyed them from before the Ammonites

so that they could dispossess them and settle in their place. 22 He did the same for the descendants of Esau, who live in Seir, by destroying the Horim before them so that they could dispossess them and settle in their place even to this day. 23 As for the Avvim, who had lived in settlements in the vicinity of Gaza, the Caphtorim, who came from Caphtor, destroyed them and settled in their place.) 24 'Proceed on your journey and cross the Wadi Arnon. See, I have handed over to you King Sihon the Amorite of Heshbon, and his land. Begin to take possession by engaging him in battle. 25 This day I will begin to put the dread and fear of you upon the peoples everywhere under heaven; when they hear report of you, they will tremble and be in anguish because of you.'

Defeat of King Sihon

26 So I sent messengers from the wilderness of Kedemoth to King Sihon of Heshbon with the following terms of peace: 27 'If you let me pass through your land, I will travel only along the road; I will turn aside neither to the right nor to the left. 28 You shall sell me food for money, so that I may eat, and supply me water for money, so that I may drink. Only allow me to pass through on foot— 29 just as the descendants of Esau who live in Seir have done for me and likewise the Moabites who live in Ar—until I cross the Jordan into the land that the LORD our God is giving us.' 30 But King Sihon of Heshbon was not willing to let us pass through, for the LORD your God had hardened his spirit and made his heart defiant in order to hand him over to you, as he has now done.

31 The LORD said to me, 'See, I have begun to give Sihon and his land over to you. Begin now to take possession of his land.' 32 So when Sihon came out against us, he and all his people for battle at Jahaz, 33 the LORD our God gave him over to us; and we struck him down, along with his offspring and all his people. 34 At that time we captured all his towns, and in each town we utterly destroyed men, women, and children. We left not a single survivor. 35 Only the

livestock we kept as spoil for ourselves, as well as the plunder of the towns that we had captured. ³⁶From Aroer on the edge of the Wadi Arnon (including the town that is in the wadi itself) as far as Gilead, there was no citadel too high for us. The LORD our God gave everything to us. ³⁷You did not encroach, however, on the land of the Ammonites, avoiding the whole upper region of the Wadi Jabbok as well as the towns of the hill country, just as[a] the LORD our God had charged.

Defeat of King Og

3 When we headed up the road to Bashan, King Og of Bashan came out against us, he and all his people, for battle at Edrei. ²The LORD said to me, 'Do not fear him, for I have handed him over to you, along with his people and his land. Do to him as you did to King Sihon of the Amorites, who reigned in Heshbon.' ³So the LORD our God also handed over to us King Og of Bashan and all his people. We struck him down until not a single survivor was left. ⁴At that time we captured all his towns; there was no citadel that we did not take from them—sixty towns, the whole region of Argob, the kingdom of Og in Bashan. ⁵All these were fortress towns with high walls, double gates, and bars, besides a great many villages. ⁶And we utterly destroyed them, as we had done to King Sihon of Heshbon, in each city utterly destroying men, women, and children. ⁷But all the livestock and the plunder of the towns we kept as spoil for ourselves.

8 So at that time we took from the two kings of the Amorites the land beyond the Jordan, from the Wadi Arnon to Mount Hermon ⁹(the Sidonians call Hermon Sirion, while the Amorites call it Senir), ¹⁰all the towns of the tableland, the whole of Gilead, and all of Bashan, as far as Salecah and Edrei, towns of Og's kingdom in Bashan. ¹¹(Now only King Og of Bashan was left of the remnant of the Rephaim. In fact his bed, an iron bed, can still be seen in Rabbah of the Ammonites. By the common cubit it is nine cubits long and four cubits wide.) ¹²As for the land that we took pos-

session of at that time, I gave to the Reubenites and Gadites the territory north of Aroer[b] that is on the edge of the Wadi Arnon, as well as half the hill country of Gilead with its towns, ¹³and I gave to the half-tribe of Manasseh the rest of Gilead and all of Bashan, Og's kingdom. (The whole region of Argob: all that portion of Bashan used to be called a land of Rephaim; ¹⁴Jair the Manassite acquired the whole region of Argob as far as the border of the Geshurites and the Maacathites, and he named them—that is, Bashan—after himself, Havvoth-jair,[c] as it is to this day.) ¹⁵To Machir I gave Gilead. ¹⁶And to the Reubenites and the Gadites I gave the territory from Gilead as far as the Wadi Arnon, with the middle of the wadi as a boundary, and up to the Jabbok, the wadi being the boundary of the Ammonites; ¹⁷the Arabah also, with the Jordan and its banks, from Chinnereth down to the sea of the Arabah, the Dead Sea,[d] with the lower slopes of Pisgah on the east.

18 At that time, I charged you as follows: 'Although the LORD your God has given you this land to occupy, all your troops shall cross over armed as the vanguard of your Israelite kin. ¹⁹Only your wives, your children, and your livestock—I know that you have much livestock—shall stay behind in the towns that I have given to you. ²⁰When the LORD gives rest to your kindred, as to you, and they too have occupied the land that the LORD your God is giving them beyond the Jordan, then each of you may return to the property that I have given to you.' ²¹And I charged Joshua as well at that time, saying: 'Your own eyes have seen everything that the LORD your God has done to these two kings; so the LORD will do to all the kingdoms into which you are about to cross. ²²Do not fear them, for it is the LORD your God who fights for you.'

Moses Views Canaan from Pisgah

23 At that time, too, I entreated the LORD, saying: ²⁴'O Lord GOD, you have only begun to show your servant your greatness

---

a Gk Tg: Heb *and all*   *b* Heb *territory from Aroer*
c That is *Settlement of Jair*   *d* Heb *Salt Sea*

and your might; what god in heaven or on earth can perform deeds and mighty acts like yours! 25 Let me cross over to see the good land beyond the Jordan, that good hill country and the Lebanon.' 26 But the LORD was angry with me on your account and would not heed me. The LORD said to me, 'Enough from you! Never speak to me of this matter again! 27 Go up to the top of Pisgah and look around you to the west, to the north, to the south, and to the east. Look well, for you shall not cross over this Jordan. 28 But charge Joshua, and encourage and strengthen him, because it is he who shall cross over at the head of this people and who shall secure their possession of the land that you will see.' 29 So we remained in the valley opposite Beth-peor.

Moses Commands Obedience

4 So now, Israel, give heed to the statutes and ordinances that I am teaching you to observe, so that you may live to enter and occupy the land that the LORD, the God of your ancestors, is giving you. 2 You must neither add anything to what I command you nor take away anything from it, but keep the commandments of the LORD your God with which I am charging you. 3 You have seen for yourselves what the LORD did with regard to the Baal of Peor—how the LORD your God destroyed from among you everyone who followed the Baal of Peor, 4 while those of you who held fast to the LORD your God are all alive today.

5 See, just as the LORD my God has charged me, I now teach you statutes and ordinances for you to observe in the land that you are about to enter and occupy. 6 You must observe them diligently, for this will show your wisdom and discernment to the peoples, who, when they hear all these statutes, will say, 'Surely this great nation is a wise and discerning people!' 7 For what other great nation has a god so near to it as the LORD our God is whenever we call to him? 8 And what other great nation has statutes and ordinances as just as this entire law that I am setting before you today?

9 But take care and watch yourselves closely, so as neither to forget the things that your eyes have seen nor to let them slip from your mind all the days of your life; make them known to your children and your children's children— 10 how you once stood before the LORD your God at Horeb, when the LORD said to me, 'Assemble the people for me, and I will let them hear my words, so that they may learn to fear me as long as they live on the earth, and may teach their children to do so'; 11 you approached and stood at the foot of the mountain while the mountain was blazing up to the very heavens, shrouded in dark clouds. 12 Then the LORD spoke to you out of the fire. You heard the sound of words but saw no form; there was only a voice. 13 He declared to you his covenant, which he charged you to observe, that is, the ten commandments;*a* and he wrote them on two stone tablets. 14 And the LORD charged me at that time to teach you statutes and ordinances for you to observe in the land that you are about to cross into and occupy.

15 Since you saw no form when the LORD spoke to you at Horeb out of the fire, take care and watch yourselves closely, 16 so that you do not act corruptly by making an idol for yourselves, in the form of any figure—the likeness of male or female, 17 the likeness of any animal that is on the earth, the likeness of any winged bird that flies in the air, 18 the likeness of anything that creeps on the ground, the likeness of any fish that is in the water under the earth. 19 And when you look up to the heavens and see the sun, the moon, and the stars, all the host of heaven, do not be led astray and bow down to them and serve them, things that the LORD your God has allotted to all the peoples everywhere under heaven. 20 But the LORD has taken you and brought you out of the iron-smelter, out of Egypt, to become a people of his very own possession, as you are now.

21 The LORD was angry with me because of you, and he vowed that I should not cross the Jordan and that I should not enter the good land that the LORD your God is

a Heb *the ten words*

giving for your possession. 22 For I am going to die in this land without crossing over the Jordan, but you are going to cross over to take possession of that good land. 23 So be careful not to forget the covenant that the LORD your God made with you, and not to make for yourselves an idol in the form of anything that the LORD your God has forbidden you. 24 For the LORD your God is a devouring fire, a jealous God.

25 When you have had children and children's children, and become complacent in the land, if you act corruptly by making an idol in the form of anything, thus doing what is evil in the sight of the LORD your God, and provoking him to anger, 26 I call heaven and earth to witness against you today that you will soon utterly perish from the land that you are crossing the Jordan to occupy; you will not live long on it, but will be utterly destroyed. 27 The LORD will scatter you among the peoples; only a few of you will be left among the nations where the LORD will lead you. 28 There you will serve other gods made by human hands, objects of wood and stone that neither see, nor hear, nor eat, nor smell. 29 From there you will seek the LORD your God, and you will find him if you search after him with all your heart and soul. 30 In your distress, when all these things have happened to you in time to come, you will return to the LORD your God and heed him. 31 Because the LORD your God is a merciful God, he will neither abandon you nor destroy you; he will not forget the covenant with your ancestors that he swore to them.

32 For ask now about former ages, long before your own, ever since the day that God created human beings on the earth; ask from one end of heaven to the other: has anything so great as this ever happened or has its like ever been heard of? 33 Has any people ever heard the voice of a god speaking out of a fire, as you have heard, and lived? 34 Or has any god ever attempted to go and take a nation for himself from the midst of another nation, by trials, by signs and wonders, by war, by a mighty hand and an outstretched arm, and by terrifying displays of power, as the LORD your God did for you in Egypt before your very eyes? 35 To you it was shown so that you would acknowledge that the LORD is God; there is no other besides him. 36 From heaven he made you hear his voice to discipline you. On earth he showed you his great fire, while you heard his words coming out of the fire. 37 And because he loved your ancestors, he chose their descendants after them. He brought you out of Egypt with his own presence, by his great power, 38 driving out before you nations greater and mightier than yourselves, to bring you in, giving you their land for a possession, as it is still today. 39 So acknowledge today and take to heart that the LORD is God in heaven above and on the earth beneath; there is no other. 40 Keep his statutes and his commandments, which I am commanding you today for your own well-being and that of your descendants after you, so that you may long remain in the land that the LORD your God is giving you for all time.

Cities of Refuge East of the Jordan

41 Then Moses set apart on the east side of the Jordan three cities 42 to which a homicide could flee, someone who unintentionally kills another person, the two not having been at enmity before; the homicide could flee to one of these cities and live: 43 Bezer in the wilderness on the tableland belonging to the Reubenites, Ramoth in Gilead belonging to the Gadites, and Golan in Bashan belonging to the Manassites.

Transition to the Second Address

44 This is the law that Moses set before the Israelites. 45 These are the decrees and the statutes and ordinances that Moses spoke to the Israelites when they had come out of Egypt, 46 beyond the Jordan in the valley opposite Beth-peor, in the land of King Sihon of the Amorites, who reigned at Heshbon, whom Moses and the Israelites defeated when they came out of Egypt. 47 They occupied his land and the land of King Og of Bashan, the two kings of the Amorites on the eastern side of the Jordan:

48 from Aroer, which is on the edge of the Wadi Arnon, as far as Mount Sirion[a] (that is, Hermon), 49 together with all the Arabah on the east side of the Jordan as far as the Sea of the Arabah, under the slopes of Pisgah.

The Ten Commandments

5 Moses convened all Israel, and said to them:

Hear, O Israel, the statutes and ordinances that I am addressing to you today; you shall learn them and observe them diligently. 2 The LORD our God made a covenant with us at Horeb. 3 Not with our ancestors did the LORD make this covenant, but with us, who are all of us here alive today. 4 The LORD spoke with you face to face at the mountain, out of the fire. 5 (At that time I was standing between the LORD and you to declare to you the words[b] of the LORD; for you were afraid because of the fire and did not go up the mountain.) And he said:

6 I am the LORD your God, who brought you out of the land of Egypt, out of the house of slavery; 7 you shall have no other gods before[c] me.

8 You shall not make for yourself an idol, whether in the form of anything that is in heaven above, or that is on the earth beneath, or that is in the water under the earth. 9 You shall not bow down to them or worship them; for I the LORD your God am a jealous God, punishing children for the iniquity of parents, to the third and fourth generation of those who reject me, 10 but showing steadfast love to the thousandth generation[d] of those who love me and keep my commandments.

11 You shall not make wrongful use of the name of the LORD your God, for the LORD will not acquit anyone who misuses his name.

12 Observe the sabbath day and keep it holy, as the LORD your God commanded you. 13 For six days you shall labour and do all your work. 14 But the seventh day is a sabbath to the LORD your God; you shall not do any work—you, or your son or your daughter, or your male or female slave, or your ox or your donkey, or any of your livestock, or the resident alien in your towns, so that your male and female slave may rest as well as you. 15 Remember that you were a slave in the land of Egypt, and the LORD your God brought you out from there with a mighty hand and an outstretched arm; therefore the LORD your God commanded you to keep the sabbath day.

16 Honour your father and your mother, as the LORD your God commanded you, so that your days may be long and that it may go well with you in the land that the LORD your God is giving you.

17 You shall not murder.[e]

18 Neither shall you commit adultery.

19 Neither shall you steal.

20 Neither shall you bear false witness against your neighbour.

21 Neither shall you covet your neighbour's wife.

Neither shall you desire your neighbour's house, or field, or male or female slave, or ox, or donkey, or anything that belongs to your neighbour.

Moses the Mediator of God's Will

22 These words the LORD spoke with a loud voice to your whole assembly at the mountain, out of the fire, the cloud, and the thick darkness, and he added no more. He wrote them on two stone tablets, and gave them to me. 23 When you heard the voice out of the darkness, while the mountain was burning with fire, you approached me, all the heads of your tribes and your elders; 24 and you said, 'Look, the LORD our God has shown us his glory and greatness, and we have heard his voice out of the fire. Today we have seen that God may speak to someone and the person may still live. 25 So now why should we die? For this great fire will consume us; if we hear the voice of the LORD our God any longer, we shall die. 26 For who is there of all flesh that has heard the voice of the living God speaking out of fire, as we have, and remained alive? 27 Go near, you yourself, and hear all that the LORD our God will say. Then tell us every-

a Syr: Heb *Sion*   b Q Mss Sam Gk Syr Vg Tg: MT *word*
c Or *besides*   d Or *to thousands*   e Or *kill*

thing that the LORD our God tells you, and we will listen and do it.'

28 The LORD heard your words when you spoke to me, and the LORD said to me: 'I have heard the words of this people, which they have spoken to you; they are right in all that they have spoken. 29 If only they had such a mind as this, to fear me and to keep all my commandments always, so that it might go well with them and with their children for ever! 30 Go, say to them, "Return to your tents." 31 But you, stand here by me, and I will tell you all the commandments, the statutes and the ordinances, that you shall teach them, so that they may do them in the land that I am giving them to possess.' 32 You must therefore be careful to do as the LORD your God has commanded you; you shall not turn to the right or to the left. 33 You must follow exactly the path that the LORD your God has commanded you, so that you may live, and that it may go well with you, and that you may live long in the land that you are to possess.

The Great Commandment

6 Now this is the commandment—the statutes and the ordinances—that the LORD your God charged me to teach you to observe in the land that you are about to cross into and occupy, 2 so that you and your children and your children's children may fear the LORD your God all the days of your life, and keep all his decrees and his commandments that I am commanding you, so that your days may be long. 3 Hear therefore, O Israel, and observe them diligently, so that it may go well with you, and so that you may multiply greatly in a land flowing with milk and honey, as the LORD, the God of your ancestors, has promised you.

4 Hear, O Israel: The LORD is our God, the LORD alone.*a* 5 You shall love the LORD your God with all your heart, and with all your soul, and with all your might. 6 Keep these words that I am commanding you to-day in your heart. 7 Recite them to your children and talk about them when you are at home and when you are away, when you

lie down and when you rise. 8 Bind them as a sign on your hand, fix them as an emblem*b* on your forehead, 9 and write them on the doorposts of your house and on your gates.

Caution against Disobedience

10 When the LORD your God has brought you into the land that he swore to your ancestors, to Abraham, to Isaac, and to Jacob, to give you—a land with fine, large cities that you did not build, 11 houses filled with all sorts of goods that you did not fill, hewn cisterns that you did not hew, vineyards and olive groves that you did not plant—and when you have eaten your fill, 12 take care that you do not forget the LORD, who brought you out of the land of Egypt, out of the house of slavery. 13 The LORD your God you shall fear; him you shall serve, and by his name alone you shall swear. 14 Do not follow other gods, any of the gods of the peoples who are all around you, 15 because the LORD your God, who is present with you, is a jealous God. The anger of the LORD your God would be kindled against you and he would destroy you from the face of the earth.

16 Do not put the LORD your God to the test, as you tested him at Massah. 17 You must diligently keep the commandments of the LORD your God, and his decrees, and his statutes that he has commanded you. 18 Do what is right and good in the sight of the LORD, so that it may go well with you, and so that you may go in and occupy the good land that the LORD swore to your ancestors to give you, 19 thrusting out all your enemies from before you, as the LORD has promised.

20 When your children ask you in time to come, 'What is the meaning of the decrees and the statutes and the ordinances that the LORD our God has commanded you?' 21 then you shall say to your children, 'We were Pharaoh's slaves in Egypt, but the LORD brought us out of Egypt with a mighty hand. 22 The LORD displayed before our eyes

a Or The LORD our God is one LORD, or The LORD our God, the LORD is one, or The LORD our God, the LORD is one
b Or as a frontlet

great and awesome signs and wonders against Egypt, against Pharaoh and all his household. 23 He brought us out from there in order to bring us in, to give us the land that he promised on oath to our ancestors. 24 Then the LORD commanded us to observe all these statutes, to fear the LORD our God, for our lasting good, so as to keep us alive, as is now the case. 25 If we diligently observe this entire commandment before the LORD our God, as he has commanded us, we will be in the right.'

A Chosen People

7 When the LORD your God brings you into the land that you are about to enter and occupy, and he clears away many nations before you—the Hittites, the Girgashites, the Amorites, the Canaanites, the Perizzites, the Hivites, and the Jebusites, seven nations mightier and more numerous than you— 2 and when the LORD your God gives them over to you and you defeat them, then you must utterly destroy them. Make no covenant with them and show them no mercy. 3 Do not intermarry with them, giving your daughters to their sons or taking their daughters for your sons, 4 for that would turn away your children from following me, to serve other gods. Then the anger of the LORD would be kindled against you, and he would destroy you quickly. 5 But this is how you must deal with them: break down their altars, smash their pillars, hew down their sacred poles,ᵃ and burn their idols with fire. 6 For you are a people holy to the LORD your God; the LORD your God has chosen you out of all the peoples on earth to be his people, his treasured possession.

7 It was not because you were more numerous than any other people that the LORD set his heart on you and chose you— for you were the fewest of all peoples. 8 It was because the LORD loved you and kept the oath that he swore to your ancestors, that the LORD has brought you out with a mighty hand, and redeemed you from the house of slavery, from the hand of Pharaoh king of Egypt. 9 Know therefore that the LORD your God is God, the faithful God

who maintains covenant loyalty with those who love him and keep his commandments, to a thousand generations, 10 and who repays in their own person those who reject him. He does not delay but repays in their own person those who reject him. 11 Therefore, observe diligently the commandment—the statutes and the ordinances—that I am commanding you today.

Blessings for Obedience

12 If you heed these ordinances, by diligently observing them, the LORD your God will maintain with you the covenant loyalty that he swore to your ancestors; 13 he will love you, bless you, and multiply you; he will bless the fruit of your womb and the fruit of your ground, your grain and your wine and your oil, the increase of your cattle and the issue of your flock, in the land that he swore to your ancestors to give you. 14 You shall be the most blessed of peoples, with neither sterility nor barrenness among you or your livestock. 15 The LORD will turn away from you every illness; all the dread diseases of Egypt that you experienced, he will not inflict on you, but he will lay them on all who hate you. 16 You shall devour all the peoples that the LORD your God is giving over to you, showing them no pity; you shall not serve their gods, for that would be a snare to you.

17 If you say to yourself, 'These nations are more numerous than I; how can I dispossess them?' 18 do not be afraid of them. Just remember what the LORD your God did to Pharaoh and to all Egypt, 19 the great trials that your eyes saw, the signs and wonders, the mighty hand and the outstretched arm by which the LORD your God brought you out. The LORD your God will do the same to all the peoples of whom you are afraid. 20 Moreover, the LORD your God will send the pestilenceᵇ against them, until even the survivors and the fugitives are destroyed. 21 Have no dread of them, for the LORD your God, who is present with you, is a great and awesome God. 22 The LORD your God will clear away these nations before

ᵃ Heb *Asherim*   ᵇ Or *hornets*: Meaning of Heb uncertain

you little by little; you will not be able to make a quick end of them, otherwise the wild animals would become too numerous for you. 23 But the LORD your God will give them over to you, and throw them into great panic, until they are destroyed. 24 He will hand their kings over to you and you shall blot out their name from under heaven; no one will be able to stand against you, until you have destroyed them. 25 The images of their gods you shall burn with fire. Do not covet the silver or the gold that is on them and take it for yourself, because you could be ensnared by it; for it is abhorrent to the LORD your God. 26 Do not bring an abhorrent thing into your house, or you will be set apart for destruction like it. You must utterly detest and abhor it, for it is set apart for destruction.

A Warning Not to Forget God in Prosperity

8 This entire commandment that I command you today you must diligently observe, so that you may live and increase, and go in and occupy the land that the LORD promised on oath to your ancestors. 2 Remember the long way that the LORD your God has led you these forty years in the wilderness, in order to humble you, testing you to know what was in your heart, whether or not you would keep his commandments. 3 He humbled you by letting you hunger, then by feeding you with manna, with which neither you nor your ancestors were acquainted, in order to make you understand that one does not live by bread alone, but by every word that comes from the mouth of the LORD.ᵃ 4 The clothes on your back did not wear out and your feet did not swell these forty years. 5 Know then in your heart that as a parent disciplines a child so the LORD your God disciplines you. 6 Therefore keep the commandments of the LORD your God, by walking in his ways and by fearing him. 7 For the LORD your God is bringing you into a good land, a land with flowing streams, with springs and underground waters welling up in valleys and hills, 8 a land of wheat and barley, of vines and fig trees and pomegranates, a land of

olive trees and honey, 9 a land where you may eat bread without scarcity, where you will lack nothing, a land whose stones are iron and from whose hills you may mine copper. 10 You shall eat your fill and bless the LORD your God for the good land that he has given you.

11 Take care that you do not forget the LORD your God, by failing to keep his commandments, his ordinances, and his statutes, which I am commanding you today. 12 When you have eaten your fill and have built fine houses and live in them, 13 and when your herds and flocks have multiplied, and your silver and gold is multiplied, and all that you have is multiplied, 14 then do not exalt yourself, forgetting the LORD your God, who brought you out of the land of Egypt, out of the house of slavery, 15 who led you through the great and terrible wilderness, an arid waste-land with poisonousᵇ snakes and scorpions. He made water flow for you from flint rock, 16 and fed you in the wilderness with manna that your ancestors did not know, to humble you and to test you, and in the end to do you good. 17 Do not say to yourself, 'My power and the might of my own hand have gained me this wealth.' 18 But remember the LORD your God, for it is he who gives you power to get wealth, so that he may confirm his covenant that he swore to your ancestors, as he is doing today. 19 If you do forget the LORD your God and follow other gods to serve and worship them, I solemnly warn you today that you shall surely perish. 20 Like the nations that the LORD is destroying before you, so shall you perish, because you would not obey the voice of the LORD your God.

The Consequences of Rebelling against God

9 Hear, O Israel! You are about to cross the Jordan today, to go in and dispossess nations larger and mightier than you, great cities, fortified to the heavens, 2 a strong and tall people, the offspring of the Anakim, whom you know. You have heard

---

a Or *by anything that the* LORD *decrees*   *b* Or *fiery*; Heb *seraph* it said of them, 'Who can stand up to the Anakim?' [3] Know then today that the LORD your God is the one who crosses over before you as a devouring fire; he will defeat them and subdue them before you, so that you may dispossess and destroy them quickly, as the LORD has promised you.

4 When the LORD your God thrusts them out before you, do not say to yourself, 'It is because of my righteousness that the LORD has brought me in to occupy this land'; it is rather because of the wickedness of these nations that the LORD is dispossessing them before you. [5] It is not because of your righteousness or the uprightness of your heart that you are going in to occupy their land; but because of the wickedness of those nations that the LORD your God is dispossessing them before you, in order to fulfil the promise that the LORD made on oath to your ancestors, to Abraham, to Isaac, and to Jacob.

6 Know, then, that the LORD your God is not giving you this good land to occupy because of your righteousness; for you are a stubborn people. [7] Remember and do not forget how you provoked the LORD your God to wrath in the wilderness; you have been rebellious against the LORD from the day you came out of the land of Egypt until you came to this place.

8 Even at Horeb you provoked the LORD to wrath, and the LORD was so angry with you that he was ready to destroy you. [9] When I went up the mountain to receive the stone tablets, the tablets of the covenant that the LORD made with you, I remained on the mountain for forty days and forty nights; I neither ate bread nor drank water. [10] And the LORD gave me the two stone tablets written with the finger of God; on them were all the words that the LORD had spoken to you at the mountain out of the fire on the day of the assembly. [11] At the end of forty days and forty nights the LORD gave me the two stone tablets, the tablets of the covenant. [12] Then the LORD said to me, 'Get up, go down quickly from here, for your people whom you have brought from Egypt have acted corruptly. They have been quick to turn from the way that I commanded them; they have cast an image for themselves.' [13] Furthermore, the LORD said to me, 'I have seen that this people is indeed a stubborn people. [14] Let me alone that I may destroy them and blot out their name from under heaven; and I will make of you a nation mightier and more numerous than they.'

15 So I turned and went down from the mountain, while the mountain was ablaze; the two tablets of the covenant were in my two hands. [16] Then I saw that you had indeed sinned against the LORD your God, by casting for yourselves an image of a calf; you had been quick to turn from the way that the LORD had commanded you. [17] So I took hold of the two tablets and flung them from my two hands, smashing them before your eyes. [18] Then I lay prostrate before the LORD as before, for forty days and forty nights; I neither ate bread nor drank water, because of all the sin you had committed, provoking the LORD by doing what was evil in his sight. [19] For I was afraid that the anger that the LORD bore against you was so fierce that he would destroy you. But the LORD listened to me that time also. [20] The LORD was so angry with Aaron that he was ready to destroy him, but I interceded also on behalf of Aaron at that same time. [21] Then I took the sinful thing you had made, the calf, and burned it with fire and crushed it, grinding it thoroughly, until it was reduced to dust; and I threw the dust of it into the stream that runs down the mountain.

22 At Taberah also, and at Massah, and at Kibroth-hattaavah, you provoked the LORD to wrath. [23] And when the LORD sent you from Kadesh-barnea, saying, 'Go up and occupy the land that I have given you', you rebelled against the command of the LORD your God, neither trusting him nor obeying him. [24] You have been rebellious against the LORD as long as he has[a] known you.

25 Throughout the forty days and forty nights that I lay prostrate before the LORD when the LORD intended to destroy you, [26] I prayed to the LORD and said, 'Lord GOD, do not destroy the people who are your very

a Sam Gk: MT I have

own possession, whom you redeemed in your greatness, whom you brought out of Egypt with a mighty hand. ²⁷ Remember your servants, Abraham, Isaac, and Jacob; pay no attention to the stubbornness of this people, their wickedness and their sin, ²⁸ otherwise the land from which you have brought us might say, "Because the LORD was not able to bring them into the land that he promised them, and because he hated them, he has brought them out to let them die in the wilderness." ²⁹ For they are the people of your very own possession, whom you brought out by your great power and by your outstretched arm.'

The Second Pair of Tablets

10 At that time the LORD said to me, 'Carve out two tablets of stone like the former ones, and come up to me on the mountain, and make an ark of wood. ² I will write on the tablets the words that were on the former tablets, which you smashed, and you shall put them in the ark.' ³ So I made an ark of acacia wood, cut two tablets of stone like the former ones, and went up the mountain with the two tablets in my hand. ⁴ Then he wrote on the tablets the same words as before, the ten commandments^a that the LORD had spoken to you on the mountain out of the fire on the day of the assembly; and the LORD gave them to me. ⁵ So I turned and came down from the mountain, and put the tablets in the ark that I had made; and there they are, as the LORD commanded me.

6 (The Israelites journeyed from Beeroth-bene-jaakan^b to Moserah. There Aaron died, and there he was buried; his son Eleazar succeeded him as priest. ⁷ From there they journeyed to Gudgodah, and from Gudgodah to Jotbathah, a land with flowing streams. ⁸ At that time the LORD set apart the tribe of Levi to carry the ark of the covenant of the LORD, to stand before the LORD to minister to him, and to bless in his name, to this day. ⁹ Therefore Levi has no allotment or inheritance with his kindred; the LORD is his inheritance, as the LORD your God promised him.)

10 I stayed on the mountain for forty days and forty nights, as I had done the first time. And once again the LORD listened to me. The LORD was unwilling to destroy you. ¹¹ The LORD said to me, 'Get up, go on your journey at the head of the people, that they may go in and occupy the land that I swore to their ancestors to give them.'

The Essence of the Law

12 So now, O Israel, what does the LORD your God require of you? Only to fear the LORD your God, to walk in all his ways, to love him, to serve the LORD your God with all your heart and with all your soul, ¹³ and to keep the commandments of the LORD your God^c and his decrees that I am commanding you today, for your own well-being. ¹⁴ Although heaven and the heaven of heavens belong to the LORD your God, the earth with all that is in it, ¹⁵ yet the LORD set his heart in love on your ancestors alone and chose you, their descendants after them, out of all the peoples, as it is today. ¹⁶ Circumcise, then, the foreskin of your heart, and do not be stubborn any longer. ¹⁷ For the LORD your God is God of gods and Lord of lords, the great God, mighty and awesome, who is not partial and takes no bribe, ¹⁸ who executes justice for the orphan and the widow, and who loves the strangers, providing them with food and clothing. ¹⁹ You shall also love the stranger, for you were strangers in the land of Egypt. ²⁰ You shall fear the LORD your God; him alone you shall worship; to him you shall hold fast, and by his name you shall swear. ²¹ He is your praise; he is your God, who has done for you these great and awesome things that your own eyes have seen. ²² Your ancestors went down to Egypt seventy persons; and now the LORD your God has made you as numerous as the stars in heaven.

Rewards for Obedience

11 You shall love the LORD your God, therefore, and keep his charge, his decrees, his ordinances, and his commandments always. ² Remember today that it was

---

a Heb *the ten words*   *b* Or *the wells of the Bene-jaakan*
c Q Ms Gk Syr: MT lacks *your God*

not your children (who have not known or seen the discipline of the LORD your God), but it is you who must acknowledge his greatness, his mighty hand and his outstretched arm, 3 his signs and his deeds that he did in Egypt to Pharaoh, the king of Egypt, and to all his land; 4 what he did to the Egyptian army, to their horses and chariots, how he made the water of the Red Sea*a* flow over them as they pursued you, so that the LORD has destroyed them to this day; 5 what he did to you in the wilderness, until you came to this place; 6 and what he did to Dathan and Abiram, sons of Eliab son of Reuben, how in the midst of all Israel the earth opened its mouth and swallowed them up, along with their households, their tents, and every living being in their company; 7 for it is your own eyes that have seen every great deed that the LORD did.

8 Keep, then, this entire commandment that I am commanding you today, so that you may have strength to go in and occupy the land that you are crossing over to occupy, 9 and so that you may live long in the land that the LORD swore to your ancestors to give to them and their descendants, a land flowing with milk and honey. 10 For the land that you are about to enter to occupy is not like the land of Egypt, from which you have come, where you sow your seed and irrigate by foot like a vegetable garden. 11 But the land that you are crossing over to occupy is a land of hills and valleys, watered by rain from the sky, 12 a land that the LORD your God looks after. The eyes of the LORD your God are always on it, from the beginning of the year to the end of the year.

13 If you will only heed his every commandment*b* that I am commanding you today—loving the LORD your God, and serving him with all your heart and with all your soul— 14 then he*c* will give the rain for your land in its season, the early rain and the later rain, and you will gather in your grain, your wine, and your oil; 15 and he*c* will give grass in your fields for your livestock, and you will eat your fill. 16 Take care, or you will be seduced into turning away, serving other gods and worshipping them,

17 for then the anger of the LORD will be kindled against you and he will shut up the heavens, so that there will be no rain and the land will yield no fruit; then you will perish quickly from the good land that the LORD is giving you.

18 You shall put these words of mine in your heart and soul, and you shall bind them as a sign on your hand, and fix them as an emblem*d* on your forehead. 19 Teach them to your children, talking about them when you are at home and when you are away, when you lie down and when you rise. 20 Write them on the doorposts of your house and on your gates, 21 so that your days and the days of your children may be multiplied in the land that the LORD swore to your ancestors to give them, as long as the heavens are above the earth.

22 If you will diligently observe this entire commandment that I am commanding you, loving the LORD your God, walking in all his ways, and holding fast to him, 23 then the LORD will drive out all these nations before you, and you will dispossess nations larger and mightier than yourselves. 24 Every place on which you set foot shall be yours; your territory shall extend from the wilderness to the Lebanon and from the River, the river Euphrates, to the Western Sea. 25 No one will be able to stand against you; the LORD your God will put the fear and dread of you on all the land on which you set foot, as he promised you.

26 See, I am setting before you today a blessing and a curse: 27 the blessing, if you obey the commandments of the LORD your God that I am commanding you today; 28 and the curse, if you do not obey the commandments of the LORD your God, but turn from the way that I am commanding you today, to follow other gods that you have not known.

29 When the LORD your God has brought you into the land that you are entering to occupy, you shall set the blessing on Mount Gerizim and the curse on Mount Ebal. 30 As you know, they are beyond the

a Or *Sea of Reeds*   *b* Compare Gk: Heb *my commandments*   *c* Sam Gk Vg: MT *I*   *d* Or *as a frontlet*

Jordan, some distance to the west, in the land of the Canaanites who live in the Arabah, opposite Gilgal, beside the oak*a* of Moreh.

31 When you cross the Jordan to go in to occupy the land that the LORD your God is giving you, and when you occupy it and live in it, 32 you must diligently observe all the statutes and ordinances that I am setting before you today.

Pagan Shrines to Be Destroyed

12 These are the statutes and ordinances that you must diligently observe in the land that the LORD, the God of your ancestors, has given you to occupy all the days that you live on the earth.

2 You must demolish completely all the places where the nations whom you are about to dispossess served their gods, on the mountain heights, on the hills, and under every leafy tree. 3 Break down their altars, smash their pillars, burn their sacred poles*b* with fire, and hew down the idols of their gods, and thus blot out their name from their places. 4 You shall not worship the LORD your God in such ways. 5 But you shall seek the place that the LORD your God will choose out of all your tribes as his habitation to put his name there. You shall go there, 6 bringing there your burnt-offerings and your sacrifices, your tithes and your donations, your votive gifts, your freewill-offerings, and the firstlings of your herds and flocks. 7 And you shall eat there in the presence of the LORD your God, you and your households together, rejoicing in all the undertakings in which the LORD your God has blessed you.

8 You shall not act as we are acting here today, all of us according to our own desires, 9 for you have not yet come into the rest and the possession that the LORD your God is giving you. 10 When you cross over the Jordan and live in the land that the LORD your God is allotting to you, and when he gives you rest from your enemies all around so that you live in safety, 11 then you shall bring everything that I command you to the place that the LORD your God will choose as a dwelling for his name: your

burnt-offerings and your sacrifices, your tithes and your donations, and all your choice votive gifts that you vow to the LORD. 12 And you shall rejoice before the LORD your God, you together with your sons and your daughters, your male and female slaves, and the Levites who reside in your towns (since they have no allotment or inheritance with you).

A Prescribed Place of Worship

13 Take care that you do not offer your burnt-offerings at any place you happen to see. 14 But only at the place that the LORD will choose in one of your tribes—there you shall offer your burnt-offerings and there you shall do everything I command you.

15 Yet whenever you desire you may slaughter and eat meat within any of your towns, according to the blessing that the LORD your God has given you; the unclean and the clean may eat of it, as they would of gazelle or deer. 16 The blood, however, you must not eat; you shall pour it out on the ground like water. 17 Nor may you eat within your towns the tithe of your grain, your wine, or your oil, the firstlings of your herds or your flocks, any of your votive gifts that you vow, your freewill-offerings, or your donations; 18 these you shall eat in the presence of the LORD your God at the place that the LORD your God will choose, you together with your son and your daughter, your male and female slaves, and the Levites resident in your towns, rejoicing in the presence of the LORD your God in all your undertakings. 19 Take care that you do not neglect the Levite as long as you live in your land.

20 When the LORD your God enlarges your territory, as he has promised you, and you say, 'I am going to eat some meat', because you wish to eat meat, you may eat meat whenever you have the desire. 21 If the place where the LORD your God will choose to put his name is too far from you, and you slaughter as I have commanded you any of your herd or flock that the LORD has

a Gk Syr: Compare Gen 12.6; Heb *oaks* or *terebinths*
b Heb *Asherim*

given you, then you may eat within your towns whenever you desire. ²²Indeed, just as gazelle or deer is eaten, so you may eat it; the unclean and the clean alike may eat it. ²³Only be sure that you do not eat the blood; for the blood is the life, and you shall not eat the life with the meat. ²⁴Do not eat it; you shall pour it out on the ground like water. ²⁵Do not eat it, so that all may go well with you and your children after you, because you do what is right in the sight of the LORD. ²⁶But the sacred donations that are due from you, and your votive gifts, you shall bring to the place that the LORD will choose. ²⁷You shall present your burnt-offerings, both the meat and the blood, on the altar of the LORD your God; the blood of your other sacrifices shall be poured out beside*a* the altar of the LORD your God, but the meat you may eat.

28 Be careful to obey all these words that I command you today,*b* so that it may go well with you and with your children after you for ever, because you will be doing what is good and right in the sight of the LORD your God.

Warning against Idolatry

29 When the LORD your God has cut off before you the nations whom you are about to enter to dispossess them, when you have dispossessed them and live in their land, ³⁰take care that you are not ensnared into imitating them, after they have been destroyed before you: do not inquire concerning their gods, saying, 'How did these nations worship their gods? I also want to do the same.' ³¹You must not do the same for the LORD your God, because every abhorrent thing that the LORD hates they have done for their gods. They would even burn their sons and their daughters in the fire to their gods. ³²*c* You must diligently observe everything that I command you; do not add to it or take anything from it.

13 *d* If prophets or those who divine by dreams appear among you and promise you omens or portents, ²and the omens or the portents declared by them take place, and they say, 'Let us follow oth-

er gods' (whom you have not known) 'and let us serve them', ³you must not heed the words of those prophets or those who divine by dreams; for the LORD your God is testing you, to know whether you indeed love the LORD your God with all your heart and soul. ⁴The LORD your God you shall follow, him alone you shall fear, his commandments you shall keep, his voice you shall obey, him you shall serve, and to him you shall hold fast. ⁵But those prophets or those who divine by dreams shall be put to death for having spoken treason against the LORD your God—who brought you out of the land of Egypt and redeemed you from the house of slavery—to turn you from the way in which the LORD your God commanded you to walk. So you shall purge the evil from your midst.

6 If anyone secretly entices you—even if it is your brother, your father's son or*e* your mother's son, or your own son or daughter, or the wife you embrace, or your most intimate friend—saying, 'Let us go and worship other gods', whom neither you nor your ancestors have known, ⁷any of the gods of the peoples that are around you, whether near you or far away from you, from one end of the earth to the other, ⁸you must not yield to or heed any such persons. Show them no pity or compassion and do not shield them. ⁹But you shall surely kill them; your own hand shall be first against them to execute them, and afterwards the hand of all the people. ¹⁰Stone them to death for trying to turn you away from the LORD your God, who brought you out of the land of Egypt, out of the house of slavery. ¹¹Then all Israel shall hear and be afraid, and never again do any such wickedness.

12 If you hear it said about one of the towns that the LORD your God is giving you to live in, ¹³that scoundrels from among you have gone out and led the inhabitants of the town astray, saying, 'Let us go and worship other gods', whom you have not known, ¹⁴then you shall inquire and make

a Or *on*   *b* Gk Sam Syr: MT lacks *today*   *c* Ch 13.1 in Heb   *d* Ch 13.2 in Heb   *e* Sam Gk Compare Tg: MT lacks *your father's son or* a thorough investigation. If the charge is established that such an abhorrent thing has been done among you, 15 you shall put the inhabitants of that town to the sword, utterly destroying it and everything in it—even putting its livestock to the sword. 16 All of its spoil you shall gather into its public square; then burn the town and all its spoil with fire, as a whole burnt-offering to the LORD your God. It shall remain a perpetual ruin, never to be rebuilt. 17 Do not let anything devoted to destruction stick to your hand, so that the LORD may turn from his fierce anger and show you compassion, and in his compassion multiply you, as he swore to your ancestors, 18 if you obey the voice of the LORD your God by keeping all his commandments that I am commanding you today, doing what is right in the sight of the LORD your God.

Pagan Practices Forbidden

14 You are children of the LORD your God. You must not lacerate yourselves or shave your forelocks for the dead. 2 For you are a people holy to the LORD your God; it is you the LORD has chosen out of all the peoples on earth to be his people, his treasured possession.

Clean and Unclean Foods

3 You shall not eat any abhorrent thing. 4 These are the animals you may eat: the ox, the sheep, the goat, 5 the deer, the gazelle, the roebuck, the wild goat, the ibex, the antelope, and the mountain-sheep. 6 Any animal that divides the hoof and has the hoof cloven in two, and chews the cud, among the animals, you may eat. 7 Yet of those that chew the cud or have the hoof cloven you shall not eat these: the camel, the hare, and the rock-badger, because they chew the cud but do not divide the hoof; they are unclean for you. 8 And the pig, because it divides the hoof but does not chew the cud, is unclean for you. You shall not eat their meat, and you shall not touch their carcasses.

9 Of all that live in water you may eat these: whatever has fins and scales you may eat. 10 And whatever does not have fins and scales you shall not eat; it is unclean for you.

11 You may eat any clean birds. 12 But these are the ones that you shall not eat: the eagle, the vulture, the osprey, 13 the buzzard, the kite of any kind; 14 every raven of any kind; 15 the ostrich, the nighthawk, the seagull, the hawk of any kind; 16 the little owl and the great owl, the water-hen 17 and the desert-owl, a the carrion vulture and the cormorant, 18 the stork, the heron of any kind; the hoopoe and the bat. b 19 And all winged insects are unclean for you; they shall not be eaten. 20 You may eat any clean winged creature.

21 You shall not eat anything that dies of itself; you may give it to aliens residing in your towns for them to eat, or you may sell it to a foreigner. For you are a people holy to the LORD your God.

You shall not boil a kid in its mother's milk.

Regulations concerning Tithes

22 Set apart a tithe of all the yield of your seed that is brought in yearly from the field. 23 In the presence of the LORD your God, in the place that he will choose as a dwelling for his name, you shall eat the tithe of your grain, your wine, and your oil, as well as the firstlings of your herd and flock, so that you may learn to fear the LORD your God always. 24 But if, when the LORD your God has blessed you, the distance is so great that you are unable to transport it, because the place where the LORD your God will choose to set his name is too far away from you, 25 then you may turn it into money. With the money secure in hand, go to the place that the LORD your God will choose; 26 spend the money for whatever you wish—oxen, sheep, wine, strong drink, or whatever you desire. And you shall eat there in the presence of the LORD your God, you and your household rejoicing together. 27 As for the Levites resident in your towns, do not neglect them, because they have no allotment or inheritance with you.

a Or pelican   b Identification of several of the birds in verses 12-18 is uncertain

28 Every third year you shall bring out the full tithe of your produce for that year, and store it within your towns; 29 the Levites, because they have no allotment or inheritance with you, as well as the resident aliens, the orphans, and the widows in your towns, may come and eat their fill so that the LORD your God may bless you in all the work that you undertake.

Laws concerning the Sabbatical Year

15 Every seventh year you shall grant a remission of debts. 2 And this is the manner of the remission: every creditor shall remit the claim that is held against a neighbour, not exacting it from a neighbour who is a member of the community, because the LORD's remission has been proclaimed. 3 From a foreigner you may exact it, but you must remit your claim on whatever any member of your community owes you. 4 There will, however, be no one in need among you, because the LORD is sure to bless you in the land that the LORD your God is giving you as a possession to occupy, 5 if only you will obey the LORD your God by diligently observing this entire commandment that I command you today. 6 When the LORD your God has blessed you, as he promised you, you will lend to many nations, but you will not borrow; you will rule over many nations, but they will not rule over you.

7 If there is among you anyone in need, a member of your community in any of your towns within the land that the LORD your God is giving you, do not be hard-hearted or tight-fisted towards your needy neighbour. 8 You should rather open your hand, willingly lending enough to meet the need, whatever it may be. 9 Be careful that you do not entertain a mean thought, thinking, 'The seventh year, the year of remission, is near', and therefore view your needy neighbour with hostility and give nothing; your neighbour might cry to the LORD against you, and you would incur guilt. 10 Give liberally and be ungrudging when you do so, for on this account the LORD your God will bless you in all your

work and in all that you undertake. 11 Since there will never cease to be some in need on the earth, I therefore command you, 'Open your hand to the poor and needy neighbour in your land.'

12 If a member of your community, whether a Hebrew man or a Hebrew woman, is sold*a* to you and works for you for six years, in the seventh year you shall set that person free. 13 And when you send a male slave*b* out from you a free person, you shall not send him out empty-handed. 14 Provide liberally out of your flock, your threshing-floor, and your wine press, thus giving to him some of the bounty with which the LORD your God has blessed you. 15 Remember that you were a slave in the land of Egypt, and the LORD your God redeemed you; for this reason I lay this command upon you today. 16 But if he says to you, 'I will not go out from you', because he loves you and your household, since he is well off with you, 17 then you shall take an awl and thrust it through his earlobe into the door, and he shall be your slave*c* for ever.

You shall do the same with regard to your female slave.*d*

18 Do not consider it a hardship when you send them out from you free persons, because for six years they have given you services worth the wages of hired labourers; and the LORD your God will bless you in all that you do.

The Firstborn of Livestock

19 Every firstling male born of your herd and flock you shall consecrate to the LORD your God; you shall not do work with your firstling ox nor shear the firstling of your flock. 20 You shall eat it, you together with your household, in the presence of the LORD your God year by year at the place that the LORD will choose. 21 But if it has any defect—any serious defect, such as lameness or blindness—you shall not sacrifice it to the LORD your God; 22 within your towns you may eat it, the unclean and the clean alike, as you would a gazelle or deer. 23 Its

a Or *sells himself or herself*   *b* Heb *him*
c Or *bondman*   *d* Or *bondwoman*

blood, however, you must not eat; you shall pour it out on the ground like water.

The Passover Reviewed

16 Observe the month[a] of Abib by keeping the passover to the LORD your God, for in the month of Abib the LORD your God brought you out of Egypt by night. 2 You shall offer the passover sacrifice to the LORD your God, from the flock and the herd, at the place that the LORD will choose as a dwelling for his name. 3 You must not eat with it anything leavened. For seven days you shall eat unleavened bread with it—the bread of affliction—because you came out of the land of Egypt in great haste, so that all the days of your life you may remember the day of your departure from the land of Egypt. 4 No leaven shall be seen with you in all your territory for seven days; and none of the meat of what you slaughter on the evening of the first day shall remain until morning. 5 You are not permitted to offer the passover sacrifice within any of your towns that the LORD your God is giving you. 6 But at the place that the LORD your God will choose as a dwelling for his name, only there shall you offer the passover sacrifice, in the evening at sunset, the time of day when you departed from Egypt. 7 You shall cook it and eat it at the place that the LORD your God will choose; the next morning you may go back to your tents. 8 For six days you shall continue to eat unleavened bread, and on the seventh day there shall be a solemn assembly for the LORD your God, when you shall do no work.

The Festival of Weeks Reviewed

9 You shall count seven weeks; begin to count the seven weeks from the time the sickle is first put to the standing grain. 10 Then you shall keep the festival of weeks to the LORD your God, contributing a freewill-offering in proportion to the blessing that you have received from the LORD your God. 11 Rejoice before the LORD your God—you and your sons and your daughters, your male and female slaves, the Levites resident in your towns, as well as the strangers, the orphans, and the widows who are among you—at the place that the LORD your God will choose as a dwelling for his name. 12 Remember that you were a slave in Egypt, and diligently observe these statutes.

The Festival of Booths Reviewed

13 You shall keep the festival of booths[b] for seven days, when you have gathered in the produce from your threshing-floor and your wine press. 14 Rejoice during your festival, you and your sons and your daughters, your male and female slaves, as well as the Levites, the strangers, the orphans, and the widows resident in your towns. 15 For seven days you shall keep the festival to the LORD your God at the place that the LORD will choose; for the LORD your God will bless you in all your produce and in all your undertakings, and you shall surely celebrate.

16 Three times a year all your males shall appear before the LORD your God at the place that he will choose: at the festival of unleavened bread, at the festival of weeks, and at the festival of booths.[b] They shall not appear before the LORD empty-handed; 17 all shall give as they are able, according to the blessing of the LORD your God that he has given you.

Municipal Judges and Officers

18 You shall appoint judges and officials throughout your tribes, in all your towns that the LORD your God is giving you, and they shall render just decisions for the people. 19 You must not distort justice; you must not show partiality; and you must not accept bribes, for a bribe blinds the eyes of the wise and subverts the cause of those who are in the right. 20 Justice, and only justice, you shall pursue, so that you may live and occupy the land that the LORD your God is giving you.

Forbidden Forms of Worship

21 You shall not plant any tree as a sacred pole[c] beside the altar that you make for the LORD your God; 22 nor shall you set up a

a Or *new moon*   *b* Or *tabernacles*; Heb *succoth*
c Heb *Asherah*

stone pillar—things that the LORD your God hates.

17 You must not sacrifice to the LORD your God an ox or a sheep that has a defect, anything seriously wrong; for that is abhorrent to the LORD your God.

2 If there is found among you, in one of your towns that the LORD your God is giving you, a man or woman who does what is evil in the sight of the LORD your God, and transgresses his covenant 3 by going to serve other gods and worshipping them—whether the sun or the moon or any of the host of heaven, which I have forbidden—4 and if it is reported to you or you hear of it, and you make a thorough inquiry, and the charge is proved true that such an abhorrent thing has occurred in Israel, 5 then you shall bring out to your gates that man or that woman who has committed this crime and you shall stone the man or woman to death. 6 On the evidence of two or three witnesses the death sentence shall be executed; a person must not be put to death on the evidence of only one witness. 7 The hands of the witnesses shall be the first raised against the person to execute the death penalty, and afterwards the hands of all the people. So you shall purge the evil from your midst.

Legal Decisions by Priests and Judges

8 If a judicial decision is too difficult for you to make between one kind of bloodshed and another, one kind of legal right and another, or one kind of assault and another—any such matters of dispute in your towns—then you shall immediately go up to the place that the LORD your God will choose, 9 where you shall consult with the levitical priests and the judge who is in office in those days; they shall announce to you the decision in the case. 10 Carry out exactly the decision that they announce to you from the place that the LORD will choose, diligently observing everything they instruct you. 11 You must carry out fully the law that they interpret for you or the ruling that they announce to you; do not turn aside from the decision that they announce to you, either to the right or to the left. 12 As for anyone who presumes to disobey the priest appointed to minister there to the LORD your God, or the judge, that person shall die. So you shall purge the evil from Israel. 13 All the people will hear and be afraid, and will not act presumptuously again.

Limitations of Royal Authority

14 When you have come into the land that the LORD your God is giving you, and have taken possession of it and settled in it, and you say, 'I will set a king over me, like all the nations that are around me', 15 you may indeed set over you a king whom the LORD your God will choose. One of your own community you may set as king over you; you are not permitted to put a foreigner over you, who is not of your own community. 16 Even so, he must not acquire many horses for himself, or return the people to Egypt in order to acquire more horses, since the LORD has said to you, 'You must never return that way again.' 17 And he must not acquire many wives for himself, or else his heart will turn away; also silver and gold he must not acquire in great quantity for himself. 18 When he has taken the throne of his kingdom, he shall have a copy of this law written for him in the presence of the levitical priests. 19 It shall remain with him and he shall read in it all the days of his life, so that he may learn to fear the LORD his God, diligently observing all the words of this law and these statutes, 20 neither exalting himself above other members of the community nor turning aside from the commandment, either to the right or to the left, so that he and his descendants may reign long over his kingdom in Israel.

Privileges of Priests and Levites

18 The levitical priests, the whole tribe of Levi, shall have no allotment or inheritance within Israel. They may eat the sacrifices that are the LORD's portion[a] 2 but they shall have no inheritance among the other members of the community; the LORD is their inheritance, as he promised them.

a Meaning of Heb uncertain

3 This shall be the priests' due from the people, from those offering a sacrifice, whether an ox or a sheep: they shall give to the priest the shoulder, the two jowls, and the stomach. 4 The first fruits of your grain, your wine, and your oil, as well as the first of the fleece of your sheep, you shall give him. 5 For the LORD your God has chosen Levi[a] out of all your tribes, to stand and minister in the name of the LORD, him and his sons for all time.

6 If a Levite leaves any of your towns, from wherever he has been residing in Israel, and comes to the place that the LORD will choose (and he may come whenever he wishes), 7 then he may minister in the name of the LORD his God, like all his fellow-Levites who stand to minister there before the LORD. 8 They shall have equal portions to eat, even though they have income from the sale of family possessions.[b]

Child-Sacrifice, Divination, and Magic Prohibited

9 When you come into the land that the LORD your God is giving you, you must not learn to imitate the abhorrent practices of those nations. 10 No one shall be found among you who makes a son or daughter pass through fire, or who practises divination, or is a soothsayer, or an augur, or a sorcerer, 11 or one who casts spells, or who consults ghosts or spirits, or who seeks oracles from the dead. 12 For whoever does these things is abhorrent to the LORD; it is because of such abhorrent practices that the LORD your God is driving them out before you. 13 You must remain completely loyal to the LORD your God. 14 Although these nations that you are about to dispossess do give heed to soothsayers and diviners, as for you, the LORD your God does not permit you to do so.

A New Prophet Like Moses

15 The LORD your God will raise up for you a prophet[c] like me from among your own people; you shall heed such a prophet.[d] 16 This is what you requested of the LORD your God at Horeb on the day of the assembly when you said: 'If I hear the voice of the LORD my God any more, or ever again see this great fire, I will die.' 17 Then the LORD replied to me: 'They are right in what they have said. 18 I will raise up for them a prophet[c] like you from among their own people; I will put my words in the mouth of the prophet,[e] who shall speak to them everything that I command. 19 Anyone who does not heed the words that the prophet[f] shall speak in my name, I myself will hold accountable. 20 But any prophet who speaks in the name of other gods, or who presumes to speak in my name a word that I have not commanded the prophet to speak—that prophet shall die.' 21 You may say to yourself, 'How can we recognize a word that the LORD has not spoken?' 22 If a prophet speaks in the name of the LORD but the thing does not take place or prove true, it is a word that the LORD has not spoken. The prophet has spoken it presumptuously; do not be frightened by it.

Laws concerning the Cities of Refuge

19 When the LORD your God has cut off the nations whose land the LORD your God is giving you, and you have dispossessed them and settled in their towns and in their houses, 2 you shall set apart three cities in the land that the LORD your God is giving you to possess. 3 You shall calculate the distances[g] and divide into three regions the land that the LORD your God gives you as a possession, so that any homicide can flee to one of them.

4 Now this is the case of a homicide who might flee there and live, that is, someone who has killed another person unintentionally when the two had not been at enmity before: 5 Suppose someone goes into the forest with another to cut wood, and when one of them swings the axe to cut down a tree, the head slips from the handle and strikes the other person who then dies; the killer may flee to one of these cities and live. 6 But if the distance is too great, the avenger of blood in hot anger might pursue

a Heb him   b Meaning of Heb uncertain
c Or prophets   d Or such prophets   e Or mouths
of the prophets   f Heb he   g Or prepare roads to
them

and overtake and put the killer to death, although a death sentence was not deserved, since the two had not been at enmity before. ⁷Therefore I command you: You shall set apart three cities.

8 If the LORD your God enlarges your territory, as he swore to your ancestors—and he will give you all the land that he promised your ancestors to give you, ⁹provided you diligently observe this entire commandment that I command you today, by loving the LORD your God and walking always in his ways—then you shall add three more cities to these three, ¹⁰so that the blood of an innocent person may not be shed in the land that the LORD your God is giving you as an inheritance, thereby bringing blood-guilt upon you.

11 But if someone at enmity with another lies in wait and attacks and takes the life of that person, and flees into one of these cities, ¹²then the elders of the killer's city shall send to have the culprit taken from there and handed over to the avenger of blood to be put to death. ¹³Show no pity; you shall purge the guilt of innocent blood from Israel, so that it may go well with you.

Property Boundaries

14 You must not move your neighbour's boundary marker, set up by former generations, on the property that will be allotted to you in the land that the LORD your God is giving you to possess.

Law concerning Witnesses

15 A single witness shall not suffice to convict a person of any crime or wrongdoing in connection with any offence that may be committed. Only on the evidence of two or three witnesses shall a charge be sustained. ¹⁶If a malicious witness comes forward to accuse someone of wrongdoing, ¹⁷then both parties to the dispute shall appear before the LORD, before the priests and the judges who are in office in those days, ¹⁸and the judges shall make a thorough inquiry. If the witness is a false witness, having testified falsely against another, ¹⁹then you shall do to the false witness just as the false witness had meant to do to the other. So you shall purge the evil from your midst. ²⁰The rest shall hear and be afraid, and a crime such as this shall never again be committed among you. ²¹Show no pity: life for life, eye for eye, tooth for tooth, hand for hand, foot for foot.

Rules of Warfare

20 When you go out to war against your enemies, and see horses and chariots, an army larger than your own, you shall not be afraid of them; for the LORD your God is with you, who brought you up from the land of Egypt. ²Before you engage in battle, the priest shall come forward and speak to the troops, ³and shall say to them: 'Hear, O Israel! Today you are drawing near to do battle against your enemies. Do not lose heart, or be afraid, or panic, or be in dread of them; ⁴for it is the LORD your God who goes with you, to fight for you against your enemies, to give you victory.' ⁵Then the officials shall address the troops, saying, 'Has anyone built a new house but not dedicated it? He should go back to his house, or he might die in the battle and another dedicate it. ⁶Has anyone planted a vineyard but not yet enjoyed its fruit? He should go back to his house, or he might die in the battle and another be first to enjoy its fruit. ⁷Has anyone become engaged to a woman but not yet married her? He should go back to his house, or he might die in the battle and another marry her.' ⁸The officials shall continue to address the troops, saying, 'Is anyone afraid or disheartened? He should go back to his house, or he might cause the heart of his comrades to fail like his own.' ⁹When the officials have finished addressing the troops, then the commanders shall take charge of them.

10 When you draw near to a town to fight against it, offer it terms of peace. ¹¹If it accepts your terms of peace and surrenders to you, then all the people in it shall serve you in forced labour. ¹²If it does not submit to you peacefully, but makes war against you, then you shall besiege it; ¹³and when the LORD your God gives it into your hand, you shall put all its males to the

sword. 14 You may, however, take as your booty the women, the children, livestock, and everything else in the town, all its spoil. You may enjoy the spoil of your enemies, which the LORD your God has given you. 15 Thus you shall treat all the towns that are very far from you, which are not towns of the nations here. 16 But as for the towns of these peoples that the LORD your God is giving you as an inheritance, you must not let anything that breathes remain alive. 17 You shall annihilate them—the Hittites and the Amorites, the Canaanites and the Perizzites, the Hivites and the Jebusites—just as the LORD your God has commanded, 18 so that they may not teach you to do all the abhorrent things that they do for their gods, and you thus sin against the LORD your God.

19 If you besiege a town for a long time, making war against it in order to take it, you must not destroy its trees by wielding an axe against them. Although you may take food from them, you must not cut them down. Are trees in the field human beings that they should come under siege from you? 20 You may destroy only the trees that you know do not produce food; you may cut them down for use in building siege-works against the town that makes war with you, until it falls.

Law concerning Murder by Persons Unknown

21 If, in the land that the LORD your God is giving you to possess, a body is found lying in open country, and it is not known who struck the person down, 2 then your elders and your judges shall come out to measure the distances to the towns that are near the body. 3 The elders of the town nearest the body shall take a heifer that has never been worked, one that has not pulled in the yoke; 4 the elders of that town shall bring the heifer down to a wadi with running water, which is neither ploughed nor sown, and shall break the heifer's neck there in the wadi. 5 Then the priests, the sons of Levi, shall come forward, for the LORD your God has chosen them to minister to him and to pronounce blessings in the name of the LORD, and by their decision all cases of dispute and assault shall be settled. 6 All the elders of that town nearest the body shall wash their hands over the heifer whose neck was broken in the wadi, 7 and they shall declare: 'Our hands did not shed this blood, nor were we witnesses to it. 8 Absolve, O LORD, your people Israel, whom you redeemed; do not let the guilt of innocent blood remain in the midst of your people Israel.' Then they will be absolved of blood-guilt. 9 So you shall purge the guilt of innocent blood from your midst, because you must do what is right in the sight of the LORD.

Female Captives

10 When you go out to war against your enemies, and the LORD your God hands them over to you and you take them captive, 11 suppose you see among the captives a beautiful woman whom you desire and want to marry, 12 and so you bring her home to your house: she shall shave her head, pare her nails, 13 discard her captive's garb, and shall remain in your house for a full month, mourning for her father and mother; after that you may go in to her and be her husband, and she shall be your wife. 14 But if you are not satisfied with her, you shall let her go free and not sell her for money. You must not treat her as a slave, since you have dishonoured her.

The Right of the Firstborn

15 If a man has two wives, one of them loved and the other disliked, and if both the loved and the disliked have borne him sons, the firstborn being the son of the one who is disliked, 16 then on the day when he wills his possessions to his sons, he is not permitted to treat the son of the loved as the firstborn in preference to the son of the disliked, who is the firstborn. 17 He must acknowledge as firstborn the son of the one who is disliked, giving him a double portion[a] of all that he has; since he is the first issue of his virility, the right of the firstborn is his.

a Heb two-thirds

Rebellious Children

18 If someone has a stubborn and rebellious son who will not obey his father and mother, who does not heed them when they discipline him, 19 then his father and his mother shall take hold of him and bring him out to the elders of his town at the gate of that place. 20 They shall say to the elders of his town, 'This son of ours is stubborn and rebellious. He will not obey us. He is a glutton and a drunkard.' 21 Then all the men of the town shall stone him to death. So you shall purge the evil from your midst; and all Israel will hear, and be afraid.

Miscellaneous Laws

22 When someone is convicted of a crime punishable by death and is executed, and you hang him on a tree, 23 his corpse must not remain all night upon the tree; you shall bury him that same day, for anyone hung on a tree is under God's curse. You must not defile the land that the LORD your God is giving you for possession.

22 You shall not watch your neighbour's ox or sheep straying away and ignore them; you shall take them back to their owner. 2 If the owner does not reside near you or you do not know who the owner is, you shall bring it to your own house, and it shall remain with you until the owner claims it; then you shall return it. 3 You shall do the same with a neighbour's donkey; you shall do the same with a neighbour's garment; and you shall do the same with anything else that your neighbour loses and you find. You may not withhold your help.

4 You shall not see your neighbour's donkey or ox fallen on the road and ignore it; you shall help to lift it up.

5 A woman shall not wear a man's apparel, nor shall a man put on a woman's garment; for whoever does such things is abhorrent to the LORD your God.

6 If you come on a bird's nest, in any tree or on the ground, with fledglings or eggs, with the mother sitting on the fledglings or on the eggs, you shall not take the mother with the young. 7 Let the mother go, taking only the young for yourself, in order that it may go well with you and you may live long.

8 When you build a new house, you shall make a parapet for your roof; otherwise you might have blood-guilt on your house, if anyone should fall from it.

9 You shall not sow your vineyard with a second kind of seed, or the whole yield will have to be forfeited, both the crop that you have sown and the yield of the vineyard itself.

10 You shall not plough with an ox and a donkey yoked together.

11 You shall not wear clothes made of wool and linen woven together.

12 You shall make tassels on the four corners of the cloak with which you cover yourself.

Laws concerning Sexual Relations

13 Suppose a man marries a woman, but after going in to her, he dislikes her 14 and makes up charges against her, slandering her by saying, 'I married this woman; but when I lay with her, I did not find evidence of her virginity.' 15 The father of the young woman and her mother shall then submit the evidence of the young woman's virginity to the elders of the city at the gate. 16 The father of the young woman shall say to the elders: 'I gave my daughter in marriage to this man but he dislikes her; 17 now he has made up charges against her, saying, "I did not find evidence of your daughter's virginity." But here is the evidence of my daughter's virginity.' Then they shall spread out the cloth before the elders of the town. 18 The elders of that town shall take the man and punish him; 19 they shall fine him one hundred shekels of silver (which they shall give to the young woman's father) because he has slandered a virgin of Israel. She shall remain his wife; he shall not be permitted to divorce her as long as he lives.

20 If, however, this charge is true, that evidence of the young woman's virginity was not found, 21 then they shall bring the young woman out to the entrance of her father's house and the men of her town shall stone her to death, because she committed a disgraceful act in Israel by prostituting

herself in her father's house. So you shall purge the evil from your midst.

22 If a man is caught lying with the wife of another man, both of them shall die, the man who lay with the woman as well as the woman. So you shall purge the evil from Israel.

23 If there is a young woman, a virgin already engaged to be married, and a man meets her in the town and lies with her, [24] you shall bring both of them to the gate of that town and stone them to death, the young woman because she did not cry for help in the town and the man because he violated his neighbour's wife. So you shall purge the evil from your midst.

25 But if the man meets the engaged woman in the open country, and the man seizes her and lies with her, then only the man who lay with her shall die. [26] You shall do nothing to the young woman; the young woman has not committed an offence punishable by death, because this case is like that of someone who attacks and murders a neighbour. [27] Since he found her in the open country, the engaged woman may have cried for help, but there was no one to rescue her.

28 If a man meets a virgin who is not engaged, and seizes her and lies with her, and they are caught in the act, [29] the man who lay with her shall give fifty shekels of silver to the young woman's father, and she shall become his wife. Because he violated her he shall not be permitted to divorce her as long as he lives.

30[a] A man shall not marry his father's wife, thereby violating his father's rights.[b]

Those Excluded from the Assembly

23 No one whose testicles are crushed or whose penis is cut off shall be admitted to the assembly of the LORD.

2 Those born of an illicit union shall not be admitted to the assembly of the LORD. Even to the tenth generation, none of their descendants shall be admitted to the assembly of the LORD.

3 No Ammonite or Moabite shall be admitted to the assembly of the LORD. Even to the tenth generation, none of their de-

scendants shall be admitted to the assembly of the LORD, [4] because they did not meet you with food and water on your journey out of Egypt, and because they hired against you Balaam son of Beor, from Pethor of Mesopotamia, to curse you. [5] (Yet the LORD your God refused to heed Balaam; the LORD your God turned the curse into a blessing for you, because the LORD your God loved you.) [6] You shall never promote their welfare or their prosperity as long as you live.

7 You shall not abhor any of the Edomites, for they are your kin. You shall not abhor any of the Egyptians, because you were an alien residing in their land. [8] The children of the third generation that are born to them may be admitted to the assembly of the LORD.

Sanitary, Ritual, and Humanitarian Precepts

9 When you are encamped against your enemies you shall guard against any impropriety.

10 If one of you becomes unclean because of a nocturnal emission, then he shall go outside the camp; he must not come within the camp. [11] When evening comes, he shall wash himself with water, and when the sun has set, he may come back into the camp.

12 You shall have a designated area outside the camp to which you shall go. [13] With your utensils you shall have a trowel; when you relieve yourself outside, you shall dig a hole with it and then cover up your excrement. [14] Because the LORD your God travels along with your camp, to save you and to hand over your enemies to you, therefore your camp must be holy, so that he may not see anything indecent among you and turn away from you.

15 Slaves who have escaped to you from their owners shall not be given back to them. [16] They shall reside with you, in your midst, in any place they choose in any one of your towns, wherever they please; you shall not oppress them.

17 None of the daughters of Israel shall

a Ch 23.1 in Heb　　b Heb uncovering his father's skirt

be a temple prostitute; none of the sons of Israel shall be a temple prostitute. [18] You shall not bring the fee of a prostitute or the wages of a male prostitute[a] into the house of the LORD your God in payment for any vow, for both of these are abhorrent to the LORD your God.

19 You shall not charge interest on loans to another Israelite, interest on money, interest on provisions, interest on anything that is lent. [20] On loans to a foreigner you may charge interest, but on loans to another Israelite you may not charge interest, so that the LORD your God may bless you in all your undertakings in the land that you are about to enter and possess.

21 If you make a vow to the LORD your God, do not postpone fulfilling it; for the LORD your God will surely require it of you, and you would incur guilt. [22] But if you refrain from vowing, you will not incur guilt. [23] Whatever your lips utter you must diligently perform, just as you have freely vowed to the LORD your God with your own mouth.

24 If you go into your neighbour's vineyard, you may eat your fill of grapes, as many as you wish, but you shall not put any in a container.

25 If you go into your neighbour's standing grain, you may pluck the ears with your hand, but you shall not put a sickle to your neighbour's standing grain.

Laws concerning Marriage and Divorce

24 Suppose a man enters into marriage with a woman, but she does not please him because he finds something objectionable about her, and so he writes her a certificate of divorce, puts it in her hand, and sends her out of his house; she then leaves his house [2] and goes off to become another man's wife. [3] Then suppose the second man dislikes her, writes her a bill of divorce, puts it in her hand, and sends her out of his house (or the second man who married her dies); [4] her first husband, who sent her away, is not permitted to take her again to be his wife after she has been defiled; for that would be abhorrent to

the LORD, and you shall not bring guilt on the land that the LORD your God is giving you as a possession.

Miscellaneous Laws

5 When a man is newly married, he shall not go out with the army or be charged with any related duty. He shall be free at home for one year, to be happy with the wife whom he has married.

6 No one shall take a mill or an upper millstone in pledge, for that would be taking a life in pledge.

7 If someone is caught kidnapping another Israelite, enslaving or selling the Israelite, then that kidnapper shall die. So you shall purge the evil from your midst.

8 Guard against an outbreak of a leprous[b] skin disease by being very careful; you shall carefully observe whatever the levitical priests instruct you, just as I have commanded them. [9] Remember what the LORD your God did to Miriam on your journey out of Egypt.

10 When you make your neighbour a loan of any kind, you shall not go into the house to take the pledge. [11] You shall wait outside, while the person to whom you are making the loan brings the pledge out to you. [12] If the person is poor, you shall not sleep in the garment given you as[c] the pledge. [13] You shall give the pledge back by sunset, so that your neighbour may sleep in the cloak and bless you; and it will be to your credit before the LORD your God.

14 You shall not withhold the wages of poor and needy labourers, whether other Israelites or aliens who reside in your land in one of your towns. [15] You shall pay them their wages daily before sunset, because they are poor and their livelihood depends on them; otherwise they might cry to the LORD against you, and you would incur guilt.

16 Parents shall not be put to death for their children, nor shall children be put to death for their parents; only for their own crimes may persons be put to death.

a Heb a dog   b A term for several skin diseases; precise meaning uncertain   c Heb lacks *the garment given you as*

17 You shall not deprive a resident alien or an orphan of justice; you shall not take a widow's garment in pledge. 18 Remember that you were a slave in Egypt and the LORD your God redeemed you from there; therefore I command you to do this.

19 When you reap your harvest in your field and forget a sheaf in the field, you shall not go back to get it; it shall be left for the alien, the orphan, and the widow, so that the LORD your God may bless you in all your undertakings. 20 When you beat your olive trees, do not strip what is left; it shall be for the alien, the orphan, and the widow.

21 When you gather the grapes of your vineyard, do not glean what is left; it shall be for the alien, the orphan, and the widow. 22 Remember that you were a slave in the land of Egypt; therefore I am commanding you to do this.

25 Suppose two persons have a dispute and enter into litigation, and the judges decide between them, declaring one to be in the right and the other to be in the wrong. 2 If the one in the wrong deserves to be flogged, the judge shall make that person lie down and be beaten in his presence with the number of lashes proportionate to the offence. 3 Forty lashes may be given but not more; if more lashes than these are given, your neighbour will be degraded in your sight.

4 You shall not muzzle an ox while it is treading out the grain.

Levirate Marriage

5 When brothers reside together, and one of them dies and has no son, the wife of the deceased shall not be married outside the family to a stranger. Her husband's brother shall go in to her, taking her in marriage, and performing the duty of a husband's brother to her, 6 and the firstborn whom she bears shall succeed to the name of the deceased brother, so that his name may not be blotted out of Israel. 7 But if the man has no desire to marry his brother's widow, then his brother's widow shall go up to the elders at the gate and say, 'My husband's brother refuses to perpetuate his brother's name in Israel; he will not per-

form the duty of a husband's brother to me.' 8 Then the elders of his town shall summon him and speak to him. If he persists, saying, 'I have no desire to marry her', 9 then his brother's wife shall go up to him in the presence of the elders, pull his sandal off his foot, spit in his face, and declare, 'This is what is done to the man who does not build up his brother's house.' 10 Throughout Israel his family shall be known as 'the house of him whose sandal was pulled off.'

Various Commands

11 If men get into a fight with one another, and the wife of one intervenes to rescue her husband from the grip of his opponent by reaching out and seizing his genitals, 12 you shall cut off her hand; show no pity.

13 You shall not have in your bag two kinds of weights, large and small. 14 You shall not have in your house two kinds of measures, large and small. 15 You shall have only a full and honest weight; you shall have only a full and honest measure, so that your days may be long in the land that the LORD your God is giving you. 16 For all who do such things, all who act dishonestly, are abhorrent to the LORD your God.

17 Remember what Amalek did to you on your journey out of Egypt, 18 how he attacked you on the way, when you were faint and weary, and struck down all who lagged behind you; he did not fear God. 19 Therefore when the LORD your God has given you rest from all your enemies on every hand, in the land that the LORD your God is giving you as an inheritance to possess, you shall blot out the remembrance of Amalek from under heaven; do not forget.

First Fruits and Tithes

26 When you have come into the land that the LORD your God is giving you as an inheritance to possess, and you possess it, and settle in it, 2 you shall take some of the first of all the fruit of the ground, which you harvest from the land that the LORD your God is giving you, and you shall put it in a basket and go to the place that the LORD your God will choose as

a dwelling for his name. 3 You shall go to the priest who is in office at that time, and say to him, 'Today I declare to the LORD your God that I have come into the land that the LORD swore to our ancestors to give us.' 4 When the priest takes the basket from your hand and sets it down before the altar of the LORD your God, 5 you shall make this response before the LORD your God: 'A wandering Aramean was my ancestor; he went down into Egypt and lived there as an alien, few in number, and there he became a great nation, mighty and populous. 6 When the Egyptians treated us harshly and afflicted us, by imposing hard labour on us, 7 we cried to the LORD, the God of our ancestors; the LORD heard our voice and saw our affliction, our toil, and our oppression. 8 The LORD brought us out of Egypt with a mighty hand and an outstretched arm, with a terrifying display of power, and with signs and wonders; 9 and he brought us into this place and gave us this land, a land flowing with milk and honey. 10 So now I bring the first of the fruit of the ground that you, O LORD, have given me.' You shall set it down before the LORD your God and bow down before the LORD your God. 11 Then you, together with the Levites and the aliens who reside among you, shall celebrate with all the bounty that the LORD your God has given to you and to your house.

12 When you have finished paying all the tithe of your produce in the third year (which is the year of the tithe), giving it to the Levites, the aliens, the orphans, and the widows, so that they may eat their fill within your towns, 13 then you shall say before the LORD your God: 'I have removed the sacred portion from the house, and I have given it to the Levites, the resident aliens, the orphans, and the widows, in accordance with your entire commandment that you commanded me; I have neither transgressed nor forgotten any of your commandments: 14 I have not eaten of it while in mourning; I have not removed any of it while I was unclean; and I have not offered any of it to the dead. I have obeyed the LORD my God, doing just as you commanded me. 15 Look down from your holy

habitation, from heaven, and bless your people Israel and the ground that you have given us, as you swore to our ancestors—a land flowing with milk and honey.'

Concluding Exhortation

16 This very day the LORD your God is commanding you to observe these statutes and ordinances; so observe them diligently with all your heart and with all your soul. 17 Today you have obtained the LORD's agreement: to be your God; and for you to walk in his ways, to keep his statutes, his commandments, and his ordinances, and to obey him. 18 Today the LORD has obtained your agreement: to be his treasured people, as he promised you, and to keep his commandments; 19 for him to set you high above all nations that he has made, in praise and in fame and in honour; and for you to be a people holy to the LORD your God, as he promised.

The Inscribed Stones and Altar on Mount Ebal

27 Then Moses and the elders of Israel charged all the people as follows: Keep the entire commandment that I am commanding you today. 2 On the day that you cross over the Jordan into the land that the LORD your God is giving you, you shall set up large stones and cover them with plaster. 3 You shall write on them all the words of this law when you have crossed over, to enter the land that the LORD your God is giving you, a land flowing with milk and honey, as the LORD, the God of your ancestors, promised you. 4 So when you have crossed over the Jordan, you shall set up these stones, about which I am commanding you today, on Mount Ebal, and you shall cover them with plaster. 5 And you shall build an altar there to the LORD your God, an altar of stones on which you have not used an iron tool. 6 You must build the altar of the LORD your God of unhewn a stones. Then offer up burnt-offerings on it to the LORD your God, 7 make sacrifices of well-being, and eat them there, rejoicing before the LORD your God. 8 You shall write

a Heb whole

on the stones all the words of this law very clearly.

9 Then Moses and the levitical priests spoke to all Israel, saying: Keep silence and hear, O Israel! This very day you have become the people of the Lord your God. 10Therefore obey the Lord your God, observing his commandments and his statutes that I am commanding you today.

Twelve Curses

11 The same day Moses charged the people as follows: 12When you have crossed over the Jordan, these shall stand on Mount Gerizim for the blessing of the people: Simeon, Levi, Judah, Issachar, Joseph, and Benjamin. 13And these shall stand on Mount Ebal for the curse: Reuben, Gad, Asher, Zebulun, Dan, and Naphtali. 14Then the Levites shall declare in a loud voice to all the Israelites:

15 'Cursed be anyone who makes an idol or casts an image, anything abhorrent to the Lord, the work of an artisan, and sets it up in secret.' All the people shall respond, saying, 'Amen!'

16 'Cursed be anyone who dishonours father or mother.' All the people shall say, 'Amen!'

17 'Cursed be anyone who moves a neighbour's boundary marker.' All the people shall say, 'Amen!'

18 'Cursed be anyone who misleads a blind person on the road.' All the people shall say, 'Amen!'

19 'Cursed be anyone who deprives the alien, the orphan, and the widow of justice.' All the people shall say, 'Amen!'

20 'Cursed be anyone who lies with his father's wife, because he has violated his father's rights.'a All the people shall say, 'Amen!'

21 'Cursed be anyone who lies with any animal.' All the people shall say, 'Amen!'

22 'Cursed be anyone who lies with his sister, whether the daughter of his father or the daughter of his mother.' All the people shall say, 'Amen!'

23 'Cursed be anyone who lies with his mother-in-law.' All the people shall say, 'Amen!'

24 'Cursed be anyone who strikes down a neighbour in secret.' All the people shall say, 'Amen!'

25 'Cursed be anyone who takes a bribe to shed innocent blood.' All the people shall say, 'Amen!'

26 'Cursed be anyone who does not uphold the words of this law by observing them.' All the people shall say, 'Amen!'

Blessings for Obedience

28 If you will only obey the Lord your God, by diligently observing all his commandments that I am commanding you today, the Lord your God will set you high above all the nations of the earth; 2all these blessings shall come upon you and overtake you, if you obey the Lord your God:

3 Blessed shall you be in the city, and blessed shall you be in the field.

4 Blessed shall be the fruit of your womb, the fruit of your ground, and the fruit of your livestock, both the increase of your cattle and the issue of your flock.

5 Blessed shall be your basket and your kneading-bowl.

6 Blessed shall you be when you come in, and blessed shall you be when you go out.

7 The Lord will cause your enemies who rise against you to be defeated before you; they shall come out against you one way, and flee before you seven ways. 8The Lord will command the blessing upon you in your barns, and in all that you undertake; he will bless you in the land that the Lord your God is giving you. 9The Lord will establish you as his holy people, as he has sworn to you, if you keep the commandments of the Lord your God and walk in his ways. 10All the peoples of the earth shall see that you are called by the name of the Lord, and they shall be afraid of you. 11The Lord will make you abound in prosperity, in the fruit of your womb, in the fruit of your livestock, and in the fruit of your ground in the land that the Lord swore to your ancestors to give you. 12The Lord will open for you his rich

a Heb uncovered his father's skirt

storehouse, the heavens, to give the rain of your land in its season and to bless all your undertakings. You will lend to many nations, but you will not borrow. 13 The LORD will make you the head, and not the tail; you shall be only at the top, and not at the bottom—if you obey the commandments of the LORD your God, which I am commanding you today, by diligently observing them, 14 and if you do not turn aside from any of the words that I am commanding you today, either to the right or to the left, following other gods to serve them.

Warnings against Disobedience

15 But if you will not obey the LORD your God by diligently observing all his commandments and decrees, which I am commanding you today, then all these curses shall come upon you and overtake you:

16 Cursed shall you be in the city, and cursed shall you be in the field.

17 Cursed shall be your basket and your kneading-bowl.

18 Cursed shall be the fruit of your womb, the fruit of your ground, the increase of your cattle, and the issue of your flock.

19 Cursed shall you be when you come in, and cursed shall you be when you go out.

20 The LORD will send upon you disaster, panic, and frustration in everything you attempt to do, until you are destroyed and perish quickly, on account of the evil of your deeds, because you have forsaken me. 21 The LORD will make the pestilence cling to you until it has consumed you from the land that you are entering to possess. 22 The LORD will afflict you with consumption, fever, inflammation, with fiery heat and drought, and with blight and mildew; they shall pursue you until you perish. 23 The sky over your head shall be bronze, and the earth under you iron. 24 The LORD will change the rain of your land into powder, and only dust shall come down upon you from the sky until you are destroyed.

25 The LORD will cause you to be defeated before your enemies; you shall go out against them one way and flee before them seven ways. You shall become an object of horror to all the kingdoms of the earth. 26 Your corpses shall be food for every bird of the air and animal of the earth, and there shall be no one to frighten them away. 27 The LORD will afflict you with the boils of Egypt, with ulcers, scurvy, and itch, of which you cannot be healed. 28 The LORD will afflict you with madness, blindness, and confusion of mind; 29 you shall grope about at noon as blind people grope in darkness, but you shall be unable to find your way; and you shall be continually abused and robbed, without anyone to help. 30 You shall become engaged to a woman, but another man shall lie with her. You shall build a house, but not live in it. You shall plant a vineyard, but not enjoy its fruit. 31 Your ox shall be butchered before your eyes, but you shall not eat of it. Your donkey shall be stolen in front of you, and shall not be restored to you. Your sheep shall be given to your enemies, without anyone to help you. 32 Your sons and daughters shall be given to another people, while you look on; you will strain your eyes looking for them all day but be powerless to do anything. 33 A people whom you do not know shall eat up the fruit of your ground and of all your labours; you shall be continually abused and crushed, 34 and driven mad by the sight that your eyes shall see. 35 The LORD will strike you on the knees and on the legs with grievous boils of which you cannot be healed, from the sole of your foot to the crown of your head. 36 The LORD will bring you, and the king whom you set over you, to a nation that neither you nor your ancestors have known, where you shall serve other gods, of wood and stone. 37 You shall become an object of horror, a proverb, and a byword among all the peoples where the LORD will lead you.

38 You shall carry much seed into the field but shall gather little in, for the locust shall consume it. 39 You shall plant vineyards and dress them, but you shall neither drink the wine nor gather the grapes, for the worm shall eat them. 40 You shall have

olive trees throughout all your territory, but you shall not anoint yourself with the oil, for your olives shall drop off. 41 You shall have sons and daughters, but they shall not remain yours, for they shall go into captivity. 42 All your trees and the fruit of your ground the cicada shall take over. 43 Aliens residing among you shall ascend above you higher and higher, while you shall descend lower and lower. 44 They shall lend to you but you shall not lend to them; they shall be the head and you shall be the tail.

45 All these curses shall come upon you, pursuing and overtaking you until you are destroyed, because you did not obey the LORD your God, by observing the commandments and the decrees that he commanded you. 46 They shall be among you and your descendants as a sign and a portent for ever.

47 Because you did not serve the LORD your God joyfully and with gladness of heart for the abundance of everything, 48 therefore you shall serve your enemies whom the LORD will send against you, in hunger and thirst, in nakedness and lack of everything. He will put an iron yoke on your neck until he has destroyed you. 49 The LORD will bring a nation from far away, from the end of the earth, to swoop down on you like an eagle, a nation whose language you do not understand, 50 a grim-faced nation showing no respect to the old or favour to the young. 51 It shall consume the fruit of your livestock and the fruit of your ground until you are destroyed, leaving you neither grain, wine, and oil, nor the increase of your cattle and the issue of your flock, until it has made you perish. 52 It shall besiege you in all your towns until your high and fortified walls, in which you trusted, come down throughout your land; it shall besiege you in all your towns throughout the land that the LORD your God has given you. 53 In the desperate straits to which the enemy siege reduces you, you will eat the fruit of your womb, the flesh of your own sons and daughters whom the LORD your God has given you. 54 Even the most refined and gentle of men among you will begrudge food to his own

brother, to the wife whom he embraces, and to the last of his remaining children, 55 giving to none of them any of the flesh of his children whom he is eating, because nothing else remains to him, in the desperate straits to which the enemy siege will reduce you in all your towns. 56 She who is the most refined and gentle among you, so gentle and refined that she does not venture to set the sole of her foot on the ground, will begrudge food to the husband whom she embraces, to her own son, and to her own daughter, 57 begrudging even the afterbirth that comes out from between her thighs, and the children that she bears, because she is eating them in secret for lack of anything else, in the desperate straits to which the enemy siege will reduce you in your towns.

58 If you do not diligently observe all the words of this law that are written in this book, fearing this glorious and awesome name, the LORD your God, 59 then the LORD will overwhelm both you and your offspring with severe and lasting afflictions and grievous and lasting maladies. 60 He will bring back upon you all the diseases of Egypt, of which you were in dread, and they shall cling to you. 61 Every other malady and affliction, even though not recorded in the book of this law, the LORD will inflict on you until you are destroyed. 62 Although once you were as numerous as the stars in heaven, you shall be left few in number, because you did not obey the LORD your God. 63 And just as the LORD took delight in making you prosperous and numerous, so the LORD will take delight in bringing you to ruin and destruction; you shall be plucked off the land that you are entering to possess. 64 The LORD will scatter you among all peoples, from one end of the earth to the other; and there you shall serve other gods, of wood and stone, which neither you nor your ancestors have known. 65 Among those nations you shall find no ease, no resting-place for the sole of your foot. There the LORD will give you a trembling heart, failing eyes, and a languishing spirit. 66 Your life shall hang in doubt before you; night and day you shall be in dread, with no assur-

ance of your life. ⁶⁷In the morning you shall say, 'If only it were evening!' and at evening you shall say, 'If only it were morning!'—because of the dread that your heart shall feel and the sights that your eyes shall see. ⁶⁸The Lord will bring you back in ships to Egypt, by a route that I promised you would never see again; and there you shall offer yourselves for sale to your enemies as male and female slaves, but there will be no buyer.

29 ᵃ These are the words of the covenant that the Lord commanded Moses to make with the Israelites in the land of Moab, in addition to the covenant that he had made with them at Horeb.

The Covenant Renewed in Moab

2 ᵇ Moses summoned all Israel and said to them: You have seen all that the Lord did before your eyes in the land of Egypt, to Pharaoh and to all his servants and to all his land, ³the great trials that your eyes saw, the signs, and those great wonders. ⁴But to this day the Lord has not given you a mind to understand, or eyes to see, or ears to hear. ⁵I have led you for forty years in the wilderness. The clothes on your back have not worn out, and the sandals on your feet have not worn out; ⁶you have not eaten bread, and you have not drunk wine or strong drink—so that you may know that I am the Lord your God. ⁷When you came to this place, King Sihon of Heshbon and King Og of Bashan came out against us for battle, but we defeated them. ⁸We took their land and gave it as an inheritance to the Reubenites, the Gadites, and the half-tribe of Manasseh. ⁹Therefore diligently observe the words of this covenant, in order that you may succeed ᶜ in everything that you do.

10 You stand assembled today, all of you, before the Lord your God—the leaders of your tribes, ᵈ your elders, and your officials, all the men of Israel, ¹¹your children, your women, and the aliens who are in your camp, both those who cut your wood and those who draw your water— ¹²to enter into the covenant of the Lord your God, sworn by an oath, which the Lord your

God is making with you today; ¹³in order that he may establish you today as his people, and that he may be your God, as he promised you and as he swore to your ancestors, to Abraham, to Isaac, and to Jacob. ¹⁴I am making this covenant, sworn by an oath, not only with you who stand here with us today before the Lord our God, ¹⁵but also with those who are not here with us today. ¹⁶You know how we lived in the land of Egypt, and how we came through the midst of the nations through which you passed. ¹⁷You have seen their detestable things, the filthy idols of wood and stone, of silver and gold, that were among them. ¹⁸It may be that there is among you a man or woman, or a family or tribe, whose heart is already turning away from the Lord our God to serve the gods of those nations. It may be that there is among you a root sprouting poisonous and bitter growth. ¹⁹All who hear the words of this oath and bless themselves, thinking in their hearts, 'We are safe even though we go our own stubborn ways' (thus bringing disaster on moist and dry alike) ᵉ— ²⁰the Lord will be unwilling to pardon them, for the Lord's anger and passion will smoke against them. All the curses written in this book will descend on them, and the Lord will blot out their names from under heaven. ²¹The Lord will single them out from all the tribes of Israel for calamity, in accordance with all the curses of the covenant written in this book of the law. ²²The next generation, your children who rise up after you, as well as the foreigner who comes from a distant country, will see the devastation of that land and the afflictions with which the Lord has afflicted it— ²³all its soil burned out by sulphur and salt, nothing planted, nothing sprouting, unable to support any vegetation, like the destruction of Sodom and Gomorrah, Admah and Zeboiim, which the Lord destroyed in his fierce anger— ²⁴they and indeed all the nations will wonder, 'Why has the Lord done thus to this land? What caused this great display of anger?'

ᵃ Ch 28.69 in Heb   ᵇ Ch 29.1 in Heb   ᶜ Or *deal wisely*   ᵈ Gk Syr: Heb *your leaders, your tribes* ᵉ Meaning of Heb uncertain

25 They will conclude, 'It is because they abandoned the covenant of the Lord, the God of their ancestors, which he made with them when he brought them out of the land of Egypt. 26 They turned and served other gods, worshipping them, gods whom they had not known and whom he had not allotted to them; 27 so the anger of the Lord was kindled against that land, bringing on it every curse written in this book. 28 The Lord uprooted them from their land in anger, fury, and great wrath, and cast them into another land, as is now the case.' 29 The secret things belong to the Lord our God, but the revealed things belong to us and to our children for ever, to observe all the words of this law.

God's Fidelity Assured

30 When all these things have happened to you, the blessings and the curses that I have set before you, if you call them to mind among all the nations where the Lord your God has driven you, 2 and return to the Lord your God, and you and your children obey him with all your heart and with all your soul, just as I am commanding you today, 3 then the Lord your God will restore your fortunes and have compassion on you, gathering you again from all the peoples among whom the Lord your God has scattered you. 4 Even if you are exiled to the ends of the world,[a] from there the Lord your God will gather you, and from there he will bring you back. 5 The Lord your God will bring you into the land that your ancestors possessed, and you will possess it; he will make you more prosperous and numerous than your ancestors.

6 Moreover, the Lord your God will circumcise your heart and the heart of your descendants, so that you will love the Lord your God with all your heart and with all your soul, in order that you may live. 7 The Lord your God will put all these curses on your enemies and on the adversaries who took advantage of you. 8 Then you shall again obey the Lord, observing all his commandments that I am commanding you today, 9 and the Lord your God will make you abundantly prosperous in all your undertakings, in the fruit of your body, in the fruit of your livestock, and in the fruit of your soil. For the Lord will again take delight in prospering you, just as he delighted in prospering your ancestors, 10 when you obey the Lord your God by observing his commandments and decrees that are written in this book of the law, because you turn to the Lord your God with all your heart and with all your soul.

Exhortation to Choose Life

11 Surely, this commandment that I am commanding you today is not too hard for you, nor is it too far away. 12 It is not in heaven, that you should say, 'Who will go up to heaven for us, and get it for us so that we may hear it and observe it?' 13 Neither is it beyond the sea, that you should say, 'Who will cross to the other side of the sea for us, and get it for us so that we may hear it and observe it?' 14 No, the word is very near to you; it is in your mouth and in your heart for you to observe.

15 See, I have set before you today life and prosperity, death and adversity. 16 If you obey the commandments of the Lord your God[b] that I am commanding you today, by loving the Lord your God, walking in his ways, and observing his commandments, decrees, and ordinances, then you shall live and become numerous, and the Lord your God will bless you in the land that you are entering to possess. 17 But if your heart turns away and you do not hear, but are led astray to bow down to other gods and serve them, 18 I declare to you today that you shall perish; you shall not live long in the land that you are crossing the Jordan to enter and possess. 19 I call heaven and earth to witness against you today that I have set before you life and death, blessings and curses. Choose life so that you and your descendants may live, 20 loving the Lord your God, obeying him, and holding fast to him; for that means life to you and length of days, so that you may live in the land that the Lord swore to give to your ancestors, to Abraham, to Isaac, and to Jacob.

a Heb of heaven b Gk: Heb lacks If you obey the commandments of the Lord your God

Joshua Becomes Moses' Successor

31 When Moses had finished speaking all[a] these words to all Israel, [2] he said to them: 'I am now a hundred and twenty years old. I am no longer able to get about, and the LORD has told me, "You shall not cross over this Jordan." [3] The LORD your God himself will cross over before you. He will destroy these nations before you, and you shall dispossess them. Joshua also will cross over before you, as the LORD promised. [4] The LORD will do to them as he did to Sihon and Og, the kings of the Amorites, and to their land, when he destroyed them. [5] The LORD will give them over to you and you shall deal with them in full accord with the command that I have given to you. [6] Be strong and bold; have no fear or dread of them, because it is the LORD your God who goes with you; he will not fail you or forsake you.'

7 Then Moses summoned Joshua and said to him in the sight of all Israel: 'Be strong and bold, for you are the one who will go with this people into the land that the LORD has sworn to their ancestors to give them; and you will put them in possession of it. [8] It is the LORD who goes before you. He will be with you; he will not fail you or forsake you. Do not fear or be dismayed.'

The Law to Be Read Every Seventh Year

9 Then Moses wrote down this law, and gave it to the priests, the sons of Levi, who carried the ark of the covenant of the LORD, and to all the elders of Israel. [10] Moses commanded them: 'Every seventh year, in the scheduled year of remission, during the festival of booths,[b] [11] when all Israel comes to appear before the LORD your God at the place that he will choose, you shall read this law before all Israel in their hearing. [12] Assemble the people—men, women, and children, as well as the aliens residing in your towns—so that they may hear and learn to fear the LORD your God and to observe diligently all the words of this law, [13] and so that their children, who have not known it, may hear and learn to fear the LORD your God, as long as you live in the land that you are crossing over the Jordan to possess.'

Moses and Joshua Receive God's Charge

14 The LORD said to Moses, 'Your time to die is near; call Joshua and present yourselves in the tent of meeting, so that I may commission him.' So Moses and Joshua went and presented themselves in the tent of meeting, [15] and the LORD appeared at the tent in a pillar of cloud; the pillar of cloud stood at the entrance to the tent.

16 The LORD said to Moses, 'Soon you will lie down with your ancestors. Then this people will begin to prostitute themselves to the foreign gods in their midst, the gods of the land into which they are going; they will forsake me, breaking my covenant that I have made with them. [17] My anger will be kindled against them on that day. I will forsake them and hide my face from them; they will become easy prey, and many terrible troubles will come upon them. On that day they will say, "Have not these troubles come upon us because our God is not in our midst?" [18] On that day I will surely hide my face on account of all the evil they have done by turning to other gods. [19] Now therefore write this song, and teach it to the Israelites; put it in their mouths, in order that this song may be a witness for me against the Israelites. [20] For when I have brought them into the land flowing with milk and honey, which I promised on oath to their ancestors, and they have eaten their fill and grown fat, they will turn to other gods and serve them, despising me and breaking my covenant. [21] And when many terrible troubles come upon them, this song will confront them as a witness, because it will not be lost from the mouths of their descendants. For I know what they are inclined to do even now, before I have brought them into the land that I promised them on oath.' [22] That very day Moses wrote this song and taught it to the Israelites.

23 Then the LORD commissioned Joshua son of Nun and said, 'Be strong and bold, for you shall bring the Israelites into the

a Q Ms Gk: MT Moses went and spoke   b Or tabernacles; Heb succoth land that I promised them; I will be with you.'

24 When Moses had finished writing down in a book the words of this law to the very end, 25 Moses commanded the Levites who carried the ark of the covenant of the LORD, saying, 26 'Take this book of the law and put it beside the ark of the covenant of the LORD your God; let it remain there as a witness against you. 27 For I know well how rebellious and stubborn you are. If you already have been so rebellious towards the LORD while I am still alive among you, how much more after my death! 28 Assemble to me all the elders of your tribes and your officials, so that I may recite these words in their hearing and call heaven and earth to witness against them. 29 For I know that after my death you will surely act corruptly, turning aside from the way that I have commanded you. In time to come trouble will befall you, because you will do what is evil in the sight of the LORD, provoking him to anger through the work of your hands.'

The Song of Moses

30 Then Moses recited the words of this song, to the very end, in the hearing of the whole assembly of Israel:

32 Give ear, O heavens, and I will speak;
let the earth hear the words of my mouth.
2 May my teaching drop like the rain,
my speech condense like the dew;
like gentle rain on grass,
like showers on new growth.
3 For I will proclaim the name of the LORD;
ascribe greatness to our God!

4 The Rock, his work is perfect,
and all his ways are just.
A faithful God, without deceit,
just and upright is he;
5 yet his degenerate children have dealt falsely with him, *a*
a perverse and crooked generation.
6 Do you thus repay the LORD,
O foolish and senseless people?

Is not he your father, who created you,
who made you and established you?
7 Remember the days of old,
consider the years long past;
ask your father, and he will inform you;
your elders, and they will tell you.
8 When the Most High *b* apportioned the nations,
when he divided humankind,
he fixed the boundaries of the peoples
according to the number of the gods; *c*
9 the LORD's own portion was his people,
Jacob his allotted share.

10 He sustained *d* him in a desert land,
in a howling wilderness waste;
he shielded him, cared for him,
guarded him as the apple of his eye.
11 As an eagle stirs up its nest,
and hovers over its young;
as it spreads its wings, takes them up,
and bears them aloft on its pinions,
12 the LORD alone guided him;
no foreign god was with him.
13 He set him upon the heights of the land,
and fed him with *e* produce of the field;
he nursed him with honey from the crags,
with oil from flinty rock;
14 curds from the herd, and milk from the flock,
with fat of lambs and rams;
Bashan bulls and goats,
together with the choicest wheat—
you drank fine wine from the blood of grapes.
15 Jacob ate his fill; *f*
Jeshurun grew fat, and kicked.
You grew fat, bloated, and gorged!

a Meaning of Heb uncertain   *b* Traditional rendering of Heb *Elyon*   *c* Q Ms Compare Gk Tg: MT *the Israelites*   *d* Sam Gk Compare Tg: MT *found*   *e* Sam Gk Syr Tg: MT *he ate*   *f* Q Mss Sam Gk: MT lacks *Jacob ate his fill*

He abandoned God who made him,
  and scoffed at the Rock of his
    salvation.
16 They made him jealous with strange
    gods,
  with abhorrent things they
    provoked him.
17 They sacrificed to demons, not God,
  to deities they had never known,
  to new ones recently arrived,
    whom your ancestors had not
     feared.
18 You were unmindful of the Rock that
    bore you;[a]
  you forgot the God who gave you
    birth.

19 The LORD saw it, and was jealous;[b]
  he spurned[c] his sons and
    daughters.
20 He said: I will hide my face from
    them,
  I will see what their end will be;
  for they are a perverse generation,
    children in whom there is no
     faithfulness.
21 They made me jealous with what is
    no god,
  provoked me with their idols.
  So I will make them jealous with
    what is no people,
  provoke them with a foolish
    nation.
22 For a fire is kindled by my anger,
  and burns to the depths of Sheol;
  it devours the earth and its increase,
    and sets on fire the foundations of
    the mountains.
23 I will heap disasters upon them,
  spend my arrows against them:
24 wasting hunger,
    burning consumption,
    bitter pestilence.
  The teeth of beasts I will send against
    them,
    with venom of things crawling in
    the dust.
25 In the street the sword shall bereave,
  and in the chambers terror,
  for young man and woman alike,
    nursing child and old grey head.

26 I thought to scatter them[d]
  and blot out the memory of them
    from humankind;
27 but I feared provocation by the
    enemy,
  for their adversaries might
    misunderstand
  and say, 'Our hand is triumphant;
    it was not the LORD who did all
     this.'

28 They are a nation void of sense;
  there is no understanding in them.
29 If they were wise, they would
    understand this;
  they would discern what the end
    would be.
30 How could one have routed a
    thousand,
  and two put a myriad to flight,
  unless their Rock had sold them,
    the LORD had given them up?
31 Indeed their rock is not like our Rock;
  our enemies are fools.[d]
32 Their vine comes from the vine-stock
    of Sodom,
  from the vineyards of Gomorrah;
  their grapes are grapes of poison,
    their clusters are bitter;
33 their wine is the poison of serpents,
  the cruel venom of asps.

34 Is not this laid up in store with me,
  sealed up in my treasuries?
35 Vengeance is mine, and recompense,
  for the time when their foot shall
    slip;
  because the day of their calamity is at
    hand,
    their doom comes swiftly.

36 Indeed the LORD will vindicate his
    people,
  have compassion on his servants,
  when he sees that their power is
    gone,
    neither bond nor free remaining.

a Or *that begot you* *b* Q Mss Gk: MT lacks *was jealous*
c Cn: Heb *he spurned because of provocation*
d Gk: Meaning of Heb uncertain

37 Then he will say: Where are their
    gods,
    the rock in which they took refuge,
38 who ate the fat of their sacrifices,
    and drank the wine of their
        libations?
Let them rise up and help you,
    let them be your protection!

39 See now that I, even I, am he;
    there is no god besides me.
I kill and I make alive;
    I wound and I heal;
    and no one can deliver from my
        hand.
40 For I lift up my hand to heaven,
    and swear: As I live for ever,
41 when I whet my flashing sword,
    and my hand takes hold on
        judgement;
I will take vengeance on my
        adversaries,
    and will repay those who hate me.
42 I will make my arrows drunk with
        blood,
    and my sword shall devour flesh—
with the blood of the slain and the
        captives,
    from the long-haired enemy.

43 Praise, O heavens, *a* his people,
    worship him, all you gods! *b*
For he will avenge the blood of his
        children, *c*
    and take vengeance on his
        adversaries;
he will repay those who hate him, *b*
    and cleanse the land for his
        people. *d*

44 Moses came and recited all the words
of this song in the hearing of the people,
he and Joshua *e* son of Nun. 45 When Moses
had finished reciting all these words to all
Israel, 46 he said to them: 'Take to heart all
the words that I am giving in witness
against you today; give them as a command
to your children, so that they may diligently observe all the words of this law. 47 This
is no trifling matter for you, but rather your
very life; through it you may live long in

the land that you are crossing over the Jordan to possess.'

Moses' Death Foretold

48 On that very day the LORD addressed
Moses as follows: 49 'Ascend this mountain
of the Abarim, Mount Nebo, which is in
the land of Moab, across from Jericho,
and view the land of Canaan, which I am
giving to the Israelites for a possession;
50 you shall die there on the mountain
that you ascend and shall be gathered to
your kin, as your brother Aaron died on
Mount Hor and was gathered to his kin;
51 because both of you broke faith with me
among the Israelites at the waters of Meribath-kadesh in the wilderness of Zin, by
failing to maintain my holiness among
the Israelites. 52 Although you may view
the land from a distance, you shall not enter it—the land that I am giving to the Israelites.'

Moses' Final Blessing on Israel

33 This is the blessing with which Moses, the man of God, blessed the Israelites before his death. 2 He said:
    The LORD came from Sinai,
    and dawned from Seir upon us; *f*
    he shone forth from Mount Paran.
    With him were myriads of holy
        ones; *g*
    at his right, a host of his own. *h*
3 Indeed, O favourite among *i* peoples,
    all his holy ones were in your
        charge;
they marched at your heels,
    accepted direction from you.
4 Moses charged us with the law,
    as a possession for the assembly of
        Jacob.
5 There arose a king in Jeshurun,
    when the leaders of the people
        assembled—
    the united tribes of Israel.

a Q Ms Gk: MT *nations*   *b* Q Ms Gk: MT lacks this line
c Q Ms Gk: MT *his servants*   *d* Q Ms Sam Gk Vg: MT
his land his people   *e* Sam Gk Syr Vg: MT *Hoshea*
f Gk Syr Vg Compare Tg: Heb *upon them*
g Cn Compare Gk Sam Syr Vg: MT *He came from
Ribeboth-kadesh,*   *h* Cn Compare Gk: meaning of Heb
uncertain   *i* Or *O lover of the*

6 May Reuben live, and not die out,
   even though his numbers are few.

7 And this he said of Judah:
   O LORD, give heed to Judah,
     and bring him to his people;
   strengthen his hands for him,*a*
     and be a help against his
       adversaries.

8 And of Levi he said:
   Give to Levi*b* your Thummim,
     and your Urim to your loyal one,
   whom you tested at Massah,
     with whom you contended at the
       waters of Meribah;
9 who said of his father and mother,
     'I regard them not';
   he ignored his kin,
     and did not acknowledge his
       children.
   For they observed your word,
     and kept your covenant.
10 They teach Jacob your ordinances,
     and Israel your law;
   they place incense before you,
     and whole burnt-offerings on your
       altar.
11 Bless, O LORD, his substance,
     and accept the work of his hands;
   crush the loins of his adversaries,
     of those that hate him, so that they
       do not rise again.

12 Of Benjamin he said:
   The beloved of the LORD rests in
     safety—
   the High God*c* surrounds him all day
     long—
     the beloved*d* rests between his
       shoulders.

13 And of Joseph he said:
   Blessed by the LORD be his land,
     with the choice gifts of heaven
       above,
   and of the deep that lies beneath;
14 with the choice fruits of the sun,
     and the rich yield of the months;
15 with the finest produce of the ancient
     mountains,

and the abundance of the
     everlasting hills;
16 with the choice gifts of the earth and
     its fullness,
   and the favour of the one who
     dwells on Sinai.*e*
   Let these come on the head of
     Joseph,
   on the brow of the prince among
     his brothers.
17 A firstborn*f* bull—majesty is his!
   His horns are the horns of a wild
     ox;
   with them he gores the peoples,
     driving them to*g* the ends of the
       earth;
   such are the myriads of Ephraim,
     such the thousands of Manasseh.

18 And of Zebulun he said:
   Rejoice, Zebulun, in your going out;
     and Issachar, in your tents.
19 They call peoples to the mountain;
     there they offer the right sacrifices;
   for they suck the affluence of the
     seas
   and the hidden treasures of the
     sand.

20 And of Gad he said:
   Blessed be the enlargement of Gad!
     Gad lives like a lion;
   he tears at arm and scalp.
21 He chose the best for himself,
     for there a commander's allotment
       was reserved;
   he came at the head of the people,
     he executed the justice of the LORD,
     and his ordinances for Israel.

22 And of Dan he said:
   Dan is a lion's whelp
     that leaps forth from Bashan.

23 And of Naphtali he said:
   O Naphtali, sated with favour,
     full of the blessing of the LORD,
     possess the west and the south.

a Cn: Heb *with his hands he contended*   *b* Q Ms Gk:
MT lacks *Give to Levi*   *c* Heb *above him*   *d* Heb *he*
e Cn: Heb *in the bush*   *f* Q Ms Gk Syr Vg: MT *His
firstborn*   *g* Cn: Heb *the peoples, together*

24 And of Asher he said:

Most blessed of sons be Asher;
   may he be the favourite of his
      brothers,
   and may he dip his foot in oil.
25 Your bars are iron and bronze;
   and as your days, so is your
      strength.

26 There is none like God, O Jeshurun,
   who rides through the heavens to
      your help,
   majestic through the skies.
27 He subdues the ancient gods,[a]
   shatters[b] the forces of old;[c]
he drove out the enemy before you,
   and said, 'Destroy!'
28 So Israel lives in safety,
   untroubled is Jacob's abode[d]
in a land of grain and wine,
   where the heavens drop down dew.
29 Happy are you, O Israel! Who is like
      you,
   a people saved by the LORD,
the shield of your help,
   and the sword of your triumph!
Your enemies shall come fawning to
      you,
   and you shall tread on their backs.

Moses Dies and Is Buried in the Land of Moab

34 Then Moses went up from the plains of Moab to Mount Nebo, to the top of Pisgah, which is opposite Jericho, and the LORD showed him the whole land: Gilead as far as Dan, 2 all Naphtali, the land of Ephraim and Manasseh, all the land of Judah as far as the Western Sea, 3 the Negeb, and the Plain—that is, the valley of Jericho, the city of palm trees—as far as Zoar. 4 The LORD said to him, 'This is the land of which I swore to Abraham, to Isaac, and to Jacob, saying, "I will give it to your descendants"; I have let you see it with your eyes, but you shall not cross over there.' 5 Then Moses, the servant of the LORD, died there in the land of Moab, at the LORD's command. 6 He was buried in a valley in the land of Moab, opposite Beth-peor, but no one knows his burial place to this day. 7 Moses was one hundred and twenty years old when he died; his sight was unimpaired and his vigour had not abated. 8 The Israelites wept for Moses in the plains of Moab for thirty days; then the period of mourning for Moses was ended.

9 Joshua son of Nun was full of the spirit of wisdom, because Moses had laid his hands on him; and the Israelites obeyed him, doing as the LORD had commanded Moses.

10 Never since has there arisen a prophet in Israel like Moses, whom the LORD knew face to face. 11 He was unequalled for all the signs and wonders that the LORD sent him to perform in the land of Egypt, against Pharaoh and all his servants and his entire land, 12 and for all the mighty deeds and all the terrifying displays of power that Moses performed in the sight of all Israel.

a Or The eternal God is a dwelling-place   b Cn: Heb from underneath   c Or the everlasting arms d Or fountain

JOSHUA

God's Commission to Joshua

1 After the death of Moses the servant of the LORD, the LORD spoke to Joshua son of Nun, Moses' assistant, saying, ²'My servant Moses is dead. Now proceed to cross the Jordan, you and all this people, into the land that I am giving to them, to the Israelites. ³Every place that the sole of your foot will tread upon I have given to you, as I promised to Moses. ⁴From the wilderness and the Lebanon as far as the great river, the river Euphrates, all the land of the Hittites, to the Great Sea in the west shall be your territory. ⁵No one shall be able to stand against you all the days of your life. As I was with Moses, so I will be with you; I will not fail you or forsake you. ⁶Be strong and courageous; for you shall put this people in possession of the land that I swore to their ancestors to give them. ⁷Only be strong and very courageous, being careful to act in accordance with all the law that my servant Moses commanded you; do not turn from it to the right hand or to the left, so that you may be successful wherever you go. ⁸This book of the law shall not depart out of your mouth; you shall meditate on it day and night, so that you may be careful to act in accordance with all that is written in it. For then you shall make your way prosperous, and then you shall be successful. ⁹I hereby command you: Be strong and courageous; do not be frightened or dismayed, for the LORD your God is with you wherever you go.'

Preparations for the Invasion

10 Then Joshua commanded the officers of the people, ¹¹'Pass through the camp, and command the people: "Prepare your provisions; for in three days you are to cross over the Jordan, to go in to take possession of the land that the LORD your God gives you to possess." '

12 To the Reubenites, the Gadites, and the half-tribe of Manasseh Joshua said, ¹³'Remember the word that Moses the servant of the LORD commanded you, saying, "The LORD your God is providing you a place of rest, and will give you this land." ¹⁴Your wives, your little ones, and your livestock shall remain in the land that Moses gave you beyond the Jordan. But all the warriors among you shall cross over armed before your kindred and shall help them, ¹⁵until the LORD gives rest to your kindred as well as to you, and they too take possession of the land that the LORD your God is giving them. Then you shall return to your own land and take possession of it, the land that Moses the servant of the LORD gave you beyond the Jordan to the east.'

16 They answered Joshua: 'All that you have commanded us we will do, and wherever you send us we will go. ¹⁷Just as we obeyed Moses in all things, so we will obey you. Only may the LORD your God be with you, as he was with Moses! ¹⁸Whoever rebels against your orders and disobeys your words, whatever you command, shall be put to death. Only be strong and courageous.'

Spies Sent to Jericho

2 Then Joshua son of Nun sent two men secretly from Shittim as spies, saying, 'Go, view the land, especially Jericho.' So they went, and entered the house of a prostitute whose name was Rahab, and spent the night there. ²The king of Jericho was told, 'Some Israelites have come here tonight to search out the land.' ³Then the king of Jericho sent orders to Rahab, 'Bring out the men who have come to you, who entered your house, for they have come only to search out the whole land.' ⁴But the woman took the two men and hid them. Then she said, 'True, the men came to me, but I did not know where they came from. ⁵And when it was time to close the gate at dark, the men went out. Where the men went I do not know. Pursue them quickly, for you can overtake them.' ⁶She had, however, brought them up to the roof and hidden them with the stalks of flax that she had laid out on the roof. ⁷So the men pursued them on the way to the Jordan as far as the fords. As soon as the pursuers had gone out, the gate was shut.

8 Before they went to sleep, she came up to them on the roof ⁹and said to the men: 'I know that the LORD has given you the land, and that dread of you has fallen on us, and that all the inhabitants of the land melt in fear before you. ¹⁰For we have heard how the LORD dried up the water of the Red Sea*a* before you when you came out of Egypt, and what you did to the two kings of the Amorites that were beyond the Jordan, to Sihon and Og, whom you utterly destroyed. ¹¹As soon as we heard it, our hearts failed, and there was no courage left in any of us because of you. The LORD your God is indeed God in heaven above and on earth below. ¹²Now then, since I have dealt kindly with you, swear to me by the LORD that you in turn will deal kindly with my family. Give me a sign of good faith ¹³that you will spare my father and mother, my brothers and sisters, and all who belong to them, and deliver our lives from death.' ¹⁴The men said to her, 'Our life for yours! If you do not tell this business of ours, then we will deal kindly and faithfully with you when the LORD gives us the land.'

15 Then she let them down by a rope through the window, for her house was on the outer side of the city wall and she resided within the wall itself. ¹⁶She said to them, 'Go towards the hill country, so that the pursuers may not come upon you. Hide yourselves there for three days, until the pursuers have returned; then afterwards you may go on your way.' ¹⁷The men said to her, 'We will be released from this oath that you have made us swear to you ¹⁸if we invade the land and you do not tie this crimson cord in the window through which you let us down, and you do not gather into your house your father and mother, your brothers, and all your family. ¹⁹If any of you go out of the doors of your house into the street, they shall be responsible for their own death, and we shall be innocent; but if a hand is laid upon any who are with you in the house, we shall bear the responsibility for their death. ²⁰But if you tell this business of ours, then we shall be released from this oath that you made us swear to you.' ²¹She said, 'According to your words, so be it.' She sent them away and they departed. Then she tied the crimson cord in the window.

22 They departed and went into the hill country and stayed there for three days, until the pursuers returned. The pursuers had searched all along the way and found nothing. ²³Then the two men came down again from the hill country. They crossed over, came to Joshua son of Nun, and told him all that had happened to them. ²⁴They said to Joshua, 'Truly the LORD has given all the land into our hands; moreover, all the inhabitants of the land melt in fear before us.'

Israel Crosses the Jordan

3 Early in the morning Joshua rose and set out from Shittim with all the Israelites, and they came to the Jordan. They camped there before crossing over. ²At the end of three days the officers went through the camp ³and commanded the people, 'When you see the ark of the covenant of the LORD your God being carried by the levitical priests, then you shall set out from your place. Follow it, ⁴so that you may know the way you should go, for you have not passed this way before. Yet there shall be a space between you and it, a distance of about two thousand cubits; do not come

a Or *Sea of Reeds*

any nearer to it.' ⁵Then Joshua said to the people, 'Sanctify yourselves; for tomorrow the LORD will do wonders among you.' ⁶To the priests Joshua said, 'Take up the ark of the covenant, and pass on in front of the people.' So they took up the ark of the covenant and went in front of the people.

7 The LORD said to Joshua, 'This day I will begin to exalt you in the sight of all Israel, so that they may know that I will be with you as I was with Moses. ⁸You are the one who shall command the priests who bear the ark of the covenant, "When you come to the edge of the waters of the Jordan, you shall stand still in the Jordan." ' ⁹Joshua then said to the Israelites, 'Draw near and hear the words of the LORD your God.' ¹⁰Joshua said, 'By this you shall know that among you is the living God who without fail will drive out from before you the Canaanites, Hittites, Hivites, Perizzites, Girgashites, Amorites, and Jebusites: ¹¹the ark of the covenant of the Lord of all the earth is going to pass before you into the Jordan. ¹²So now select twelve men from the tribes of Israel, one from each tribe. ¹³When the soles of the feet of the priests who bear the ark of the LORD, the Lord of all the earth, rest in the waters of the Jordan, the waters of the Jordan flowing from above shall be cut off; they shall stand in a single heap.'

14 When the people set out from their tents to cross over the Jordan, the priests bearing the ark of the covenant were in front of the people. ¹⁵Now the Jordan overflows all its banks throughout the time of harvest. So when those who bore the ark had come to the Jordan, and the feet of the priests bearing the ark were dipped in the edge of the water, ¹⁶the waters flowing from above stood still, rising up in a single heap far off at Adam, the city that is beside Zarethan, while those flowing towards the sea of the Arabah, the Dead Sea,ᵃ were wholly cut off. Then the people crossed over opposite Jericho. ¹⁷While all Israel were crossing over on dry ground, the priests who bore the ark of the covenant of the LORD stood on dry ground in the middle of the Jordan, until the entire nation finished crossing over the Jordan.

Twelve Stones Set Up at Gilgal

4 When the entire nation had finished crossing over the Jordan, the LORD said to Joshua: ²'Select twelve men from the people, one from each tribe, ³and command them, "Take twelve stones from here out of the middle of the Jordan, from the place where the priests' feet stood, carry them over with you, and lay them down in the place where you camp tonight." ' ⁴Then Joshua summoned the twelve men from the Israelites, whom he had appointed, one from each tribe. ⁵Joshua said to them, 'Pass on before the ark of the LORD your God into the middle of the Jordan, and each of you take up a stone on his shoulder, one for each of the tribes of the Israelites, ⁶so that this may be a sign among you. When your children ask in time to come, "What do those stones mean to you?" ⁷then you shall tell them that the waters of the Jordan were cut off in front of the ark of the covenant of the LORD. When it crossed over the Jordan, the waters of the Jordan were cut off. So these stones shall be to the Israelites a memorial for ever.'

8 The Israelites did as Joshua commanded. They took up twelve stones out of the middle of the Jordan, according to the number of the tribes of the Israelites, as the LORD told Joshua, carried them over with them to the place where they camped, and laid them down there. ⁹(Joshua set up twelve stones in the middle of the Jordan, in the place where the feet of the priests bearing the ark of the covenant had stood; and they are there to this day.)

10 The priests who bore the ark remained standing in the middle of the Jordan, until everything was finished that the LORD commanded Joshua to tell the people, according to all that Moses had commanded Joshua. The people crossed over in haste. ¹¹As soon as all the people had finished crossing over, the ark of the LORD, and the priests, crossed over in front of the people. ¹²The Reubenites, the Gadites, and the half-tribe of Manasseh crossed over armed before the Israelites, as Moses had ordered

ᵃ Heb *Salt Sea*

them. [13] About forty thousand armed for war crossed over before the LORD to the plains of Jericho for battle.

14 On that day the LORD exalted Joshua in the sight of all Israel; and they stood in awe of him, as they had stood in awe of Moses, all the days of his life.

15 The LORD said to Joshua, [16] 'Command the priests who bear the ark of the covenant[a] to come up out of the Jordan.' [17] Joshua therefore commanded the priests, 'Come up out of the Jordan.' [18] When the priests bearing the ark of the covenant of the LORD came up from the middle of the Jordan, and the soles of the priests' feet touched dry ground, the waters of the Jordan returned to their place and overflowed all its banks, as before.

19 The people came up out of the Jordan on the tenth day of the first month, and they camped in Gilgal on the eastern border of Jericho. [20] Those twelve stones, which they had taken out of the Jordan, Joshua set up in Gilgal, [21] saying to the Israelites, 'When your children ask their parents in time to come, "What do these stones mean?" [22] then you shall let your children know, "Israel crossed over the Jordan here on dry ground." [23] For the LORD your God dried up the waters of the Jordan for you until you crossed over, as the LORD your God did to the Red Sea,[b] which he dried up for us until we crossed over, [24] so that all the peoples of the earth may know that the hand of the LORD is mighty, and so that you may fear the LORD your God for ever.'

The New Generation Circumcised

5 When all the kings of the Amorites beyond the Jordan to the west, and all the kings of the Canaanites by the sea, heard that the LORD had dried up the waters of the Jordan for the Israelites until they had crossed over, their hearts failed, and there was no longer any spirit in them, because of the Israelites.

2 At that time the LORD said to Joshua, 'Make flint knives and circumcise the Israelites a second time.' [3] So Joshua made flint knives, and circumcised the Israelites at Gibeath-haaraloth.[c] [4] This is the reason

why Joshua circumcised them: all the males of the people who came out of Egypt, all the warriors, had died during the journey through the wilderness after they had come out of Egypt. [5] Although all the people who came out had been circumcised, yet all the people born on the journey through the wilderness after they had come out of Egypt had not been circumcised. [6] For the Israelites travelled for forty years in the wilderness, until all the nation, the warriors who came out of Egypt, perished, not having listened to the voice of the LORD. To them the LORD swore that he would not let them see the land that he had sworn to their ancestors to give us, a land flowing with milk and honey. [7] So it was their children, whom he raised up in their place, that Joshua circumcised; for they were uncircumcised, because they had not been circumcised on the way.

8 When the circumcising of all the nation was done, they remained in their places in the camp until they were healed. [9] The LORD said to Joshua, 'Today I have rolled away from you the disgrace of Egypt.' And so that place is called Gilgal[d] to this day.

The Passover at Gilgal

10 While the Israelites were encamped in Gilgal they kept the passover in the evening on the fourteenth day of the month in the plains of Jericho. [11] On the day after the passover, on that very day, they ate the produce of the land, unleavened cakes and parched grain. [12] The manna ceased on the day they ate the produce of the land, and the Israelites no longer had manna; they ate the crops of the land of Canaan that year.

Joshua's Vision

13 Once when Joshua was near Jericho, he looked up and saw a man standing before him with a drawn sword in his hand. Joshua went to him and said to him, 'Are you one of us, or one of our adversaries?'

---

a Or *treaty*, or *testimony*; Heb *eduth*   *b* Or *Sea of Reeds*   *c* That is *the Hill of the Foreskins*   *d* Related to Heb *galal* to roll

14 He replied, 'Neither; but as commander of the army of the Lord I have now come.' And Joshua fell on his face to the earth and worshipped, and he said to him, 'What do you command your servant, my lord?' 15 The commander of the army of the Lord said to Joshua, 'Remove the sandals from your feet, for the place where you stand is holy.' And Joshua did so.

Jericho Taken and Destroyed

6 Now Jericho was shut up inside and out because of the Israelites; no one came out and no one went in. 2 The Lord said to Joshua, 'See, I have handed Jericho over to you, along with its king and soldiers. 3 You shall march around the city, all the warriors circling the city once. Thus you shall do for six days, 4 with seven priests bearing seven trumpets of rams' horns before the ark. On the seventh day you shall march around the city seven times, the priests blowing the trumpets. 5 When they make a long blast with the ram's horn, as soon as you hear the sound of the trumpet, then all the people shall shout with a great shout; and the wall of the city will fall down flat, and all the people shall charge straight ahead.' 6 So Joshua son of Nun summoned the priests and said to them, 'Take up the ark of the covenant, and have seven priests carry seven trumpets of rams' horns in front of the ark of the Lord.' 7 To the people he said, 'Go forward and march around the city; have the armed men pass on before the ark of the Lord.'

8 As Joshua had commanded the people, the seven priests carrying the seven trumpets of rams' horns before the Lord went forward, blowing the trumpets, with the ark of the covenant of the Lord following them. 9 And the armed men went before the priests who blew the trumpets; the rearguard came after the ark, while the trumpets blew continually. 10 To the people Joshua gave this command: 'You shall not shout or let your voice be heard, nor shall you utter a word, until the day I tell you to shout. Then you shall shout.' 11 So the ark of the Lord went around the city, circling it once;

and they came into the camp, and spent the night in the camp.

12 Then Joshua rose early in the morning, and the priests took up the ark of the Lord. 13 The seven priests carrying the seven trumpets of rams' horns before the ark of the Lord passed on, blowing the trumpets continually. The armed men went before them, and the rearguard came after the ark of the Lord, while the trumpets blew continually. 14 On the second day they marched around the city once and then returned to the camp. They did this for six days.

15 On the seventh day they rose early, at dawn, and marched around the city in the same manner seven times. It was only on that day that they marched around the city seven times. 16 And at the seventh time, when the priests had blown the trumpets, Joshua said to the people, 'Shout! For the Lord has given you the city. 17 The city and all that is in it shall be devoted to the Lord for destruction. Only Rahab the prostitute and all who are with her in her house shall live, because she hid the messengers we sent. 18 As for you, keep away from the things devoted to destruction, so as not to covet*a* and take any of the devoted things and make the camp of Israel an object for destruction, bringing trouble upon it. 19 But all silver and gold, and vessels of bronze and iron, are sacred to the Lord; they shall go into the treasury of the Lord.' 20 So the people shouted, and the trumpets were blown. As soon as the people heard the sound of the trumpets, they raised a great shout, and the wall fell down flat; so the people charged straight ahead into the city and captured it. 21 Then they devoted to destruction by the edge of the sword all in the city, both men and women, young and old, oxen, sheep, and donkeys.

22 Joshua said to the two men who had spied out the land, 'Go into the prostitute's house, and bring the woman out of it and all who belong to her, as you swore to her.' 23 So the young men who had been spies went in and brought Rahab out, along with her father, her mother, her brothers, and all who belonged to her—they brought all her

---

a Gk: Heb *devote to destruction* Compare 7.21

kindred out—and set them outside the camp of Israel. 24 They burned down the city, and everything in it; only the silver and gold, and the vessels of bronze and iron, they put into the treasury of the house of the LORD. 25 But Rahab the prostitute, with her family and all who belonged to her, Joshua spared. Her family*a* has lived in Israel ever since. For she hid the messengers whom Joshua sent to spy out Jericho.

26 Joshua then pronounced this oath, saying,

'Cursed before the LORD be anyone
    who tries
    to build this city—this Jericho!
At the cost of his firstborn he shall
    lay its foundation,
and at the cost of his youngest he
    shall set up its gates!'

27 So the LORD was with Joshua; and his fame was in all the land.

The Sin of Achan and Its Punishment

7 But the Israelites broke faith in regard to the devoted things: Achan son of Carmi son of Zabdi son of Zerah, of the tribe of Judah, took some of the devoted things; and the anger of the LORD burned against the Israelites.

2 Joshua sent men from Jericho to Ai, which is near Beth-aven, east of Bethel, and said to them, 'Go up and spy out the land.' And the men went up and spied out Ai. 3 Then they returned to Joshua and said to him, 'Not all the people need go up; about two or three thousand men should go up and attack Ai. Since they are so few, do not make the whole people toil up there.' 4 So about three thousand of the people went up there; and they fled before the men of Ai. 5 The men of Ai killed about thirty-six of them, chasing them from outside the gate as far as Shebarim and killing them on the slope. The hearts of the people failed and turned to water.

6 Then Joshua tore his clothes, and fell to the ground on his face before the ark of the LORD until the evening, he and the elders of Israel; and they put dust on their heads. 7 Joshua said, 'Ah, Lord GOD! Why have you brought this people across the Jor-

dan at all, to hand us over to the Amorites so as to destroy us? Would that we had been content to settle beyond the Jordan! 8 O Lord, what can I say, now that Israel has turned their backs to their enemies! 9 The Canaanites and all the inhabitants of the land will hear of it, and surround us, and cut off our name from the earth. Then what will you do for your great name?'

10 The LORD said to Joshua, 'Stand up! Why have you fallen upon your face? 11 Israel has sinned; they have transgressed my covenant that I imposed on them. They have taken some of the devoted things; they have stolen, they have acted deceitfully, and they have put them among their own belongings. 12 Therefore the Israelites are unable to stand before their enemies; they turn their backs to their enemies, because they have become a thing devoted for destruction themselves. I will be with you no more, unless you destroy the devoted things from among you. 13 Proceed to sanctify the people, and say, "Sanctify yourselves for tomorrow; for thus says the LORD, the God of Israel, 'There are devoted things among you, O Israel; you will be unable to stand before your enemies until you take away the devoted things from among you.' 14 In the morning therefore you shall come forward tribe by tribe. The tribe that the LORD takes shall come near by clans, the clan that the LORD takes shall come near by households, and the household that the LORD takes shall come near one by one. 15 And the one who is taken as having the devoted things shall be burned with fire, together with all that he has, for having transgressed the covenant of the LORD, and for having done an outrageous thing in Israel." '

16 So Joshua rose early in the morning, and brought Israel near tribe by tribe, and the tribe of Judah was taken. 17 He brought near the clans of Judah, and the clan of the Zerahites was taken; and he brought near the clan of the Zerahites, family by family,*b* and Zabdi was taken. 18 And he brought near his household one by one, and Achan son of Carmi son of Zabdi son of Zerah, of

a Heb *She*   *b* Mss Syr: MT *man by man*

the tribe of Judah, was taken. [19]Then Joshua said to Achan, 'My son, give glory to the LORD God of Israel and make confession to him. Tell me now what you have done; do not hide it from me.' [20]And Achan answered Joshua, 'It is true; I am the one who sinned against the LORD God of Israel. This is what I did: [21]when I saw among the spoil a beautiful mantle from Shinar, and two hundred shekels of silver, and a bar of gold weighing fifty shekels, then I coveted them and took them. They now lie hidden in the ground inside my tent, with the silver underneath.'

22 So Joshua sent messengers, and they ran to the tent; and there it was, hidden in his tent with the silver underneath. [23]They took them out of the tent and brought them to Joshua and all the Israelites; and they spread them out before the LORD. [24]Then Joshua and all Israel with him took Achan son of Zerah, with the silver, the mantle, and the bar of gold, with his sons and daughters, with his oxen, donkeys, and sheep, and his tent and all that he had; and

they brought them up to the Valley of Achor. [25]Joshua said, 'Why did you bring trouble on us? The LORD is bringing trouble on you today.' And all Israel stoned him to death; they burned them with fire, cast stones on them, [26]and raised over him a great heap of stones that remains to this day. Then the LORD turned from his burning anger. Therefore that place to this day is called the Valley of Achor.[a]

Ai Captured by a Stratagem and Destroyed

8 Then the LORD said to Joshua, 'Do not fear or be dismayed; take all the fighting men with you, and go up now to Ai. See, I have handed over to you the king of Ai with his people, his city, and his land. [2]You shall do to Ai and its king as you did to Jericho and its king; only its spoil and its livestock you may take as booty for yourselves. Set an ambush against the city, behind it.'

3 So Joshua and all the fighting men set out to go up against Ai. Joshua chose thirty thousand warriors and sent them out by night [4]with the command, 'You shall lie in ambush against the city, behind it; do not go very far from the city, but all of you stay alert. [5]I and all the people who are with me will approach the city. When they come out against us, as before, we shall flee from them. [6]They will come out after us until we have drawn them away from the city; for they will say, "They are fleeing from us, as before." While we flee from them, [7]you shall rise up from the ambush and seize the city; for the LORD your God will give it into your hand. [8]And when you have taken the city, you shall set the city on fire, doing as the LORD has ordered; see, I have commanded you.' [9]So Joshua sent them out; and they went to the place of ambush, and lay between Bethel and Ai, to the west of Ai; but Joshua spent that night in the camp.[b]

10 In the morning Joshua rose early and mustered the people, and went up, with the elders of Israel, before the people to Ai. [11]All the fighting men who were with him

The Conquest of Southern Canaan

Mediterranean Sea

Bethel
Upper Beth-horon
Lower Beth-horon
Azekah
Libnah
Lachish
Eglon
Ai
Gilgal
Jericho
Shittim
Gibeon
Hebron
Debir
Dead Sea

N

0   30 Mi.
0   30 Km.

a That is *Trouble*   b Heb *among the people*

went up, and drew near before the city, and camped on the north side of Ai, with a ravine between them and Ai. [12]Taking about five thousand men, he set them in ambush between Bethel and Ai, to the west of the city. [13]So they stationed the forces, the main encampment that was north of the city and its rearguard west of the city. But Joshua spent that night in the valley. [14]When the king of Ai saw this, he and all his people, the inhabitants of the city, hurried out early in the morning to the meeting-place facing the Arabah to meet Israel in battle; but he did not know that there was an ambush against him behind the city. [15]And Joshua and all Israel made a pretence of being beaten before them, and fled in the direction of the wilderness. [16]So all the people who were in the city were called together to pursue them, and as they pursued Joshua they were drawn away from the city. [17]There was not a man left in Ai or Bethel who did not go out after Israel; they left the city open, and pursued Israel.

18 Then the LORD said to Joshua, 'Stretch out the sword that is in your hand towards Ai; for I will give it into your hand.' And Joshua stretched out the sword that was in his hand towards the city. [19]As soon as he stretched out his hand, the troops in ambush rose quickly out of their place and rushed forward. They entered the city, took it, and at once set the city on fire. [20]So when the men of Ai looked back, the smoke of the city was rising to the sky. They had no power to flee this way or that, for the people who fled to the wilderness turned back against the pursuers. [21]When Joshua and all Israel saw that the ambush had taken the city and that the smoke of the city was rising, then they turned back and struck down the men of Ai. [22]And the others came out from the city against them; so they were surrounded by Israelites, some on one side, and some on the other; and Israel struck them down until no one was left who survived or escaped. [23]But the king of Ai was taken alive and brought to Joshua.

24 When Israel had finished slaughtering all the inhabitants of Ai in the open wilderness where they pursued them, and when all of them to the very last had fallen by the edge of the sword, all Israel returned to Ai, and attacked it with the edge of the sword. [25]The total of those who fell that day, both men and women, was twelve thousand—all the people of Ai. [26]For Joshua did not draw back his hand, with which he stretched out the sword, until he had utterly destroyed all the inhabitants of Ai. [27]Only the livestock and the spoil of that city Israel took as their booty, according to the word of the LORD that he had issued to Joshua. [28]So Joshua burned Ai, and made it for ever a heap of ruins, as it is to this day. [29]And he hanged the king of Ai on a tree until evening; and at sunset Joshua commanded, and they took his body down from the tree, threw it down at the entrance of the gate of the city, and raised over it a great heap of stones, which stands there to this day.

Joshua Renews the Covenant

30 Then Joshua built on Mount Ebal an altar to the LORD, the God of Israel, [31]just as Moses the servant of the LORD had commanded the Israelites, as it is written in the book of the law of Moses, 'an altar of unhewn[a] stones, on which no iron tool has been used'; and they offered on it burnt-offerings to the LORD, and sacrificed offerings of well-being. [32]And there, in the presence of the Israelites, Joshua[b] wrote on the stones a copy of the law of Moses, which he had written. [33]All Israel, alien as well as citizen, with their elders and officers and their judges, stood on opposite sides of the ark in front of the levitical priests who carried the ark of the covenant of the LORD, half of them in front of Mount Gerizim and half of them in front of Mount Ebal, as Moses the servant of the LORD had commanded at the first, that they should bless the people of Israel. [34]And afterwards he read all the words of the law, blessings and curses, according to all that is written in the book of the law. [35]There was not a word of all that Moses commanded that Joshua did not read

a Heb *whole*   *b* Heb *he*

before all the assembly of Israel, and the women, and the little ones, and the aliens who resided among them.

The Gibeonites Save Themselves by Trickery

9 Now when all the kings who were beyond the Jordan in the hill country and in the lowland all along the coast of the Great Sea towards Lebanon—the Hittites, the Amorites, the Canaanites, the Perizzites, the Hivites, and the Jebusites—heard of this, 2 they gathered together with one accord to fight Joshua and Israel.

3 But when the inhabitants of Gibeon heard what Joshua had done to Jericho and to Ai, 4 they on their part acted with cunning: they went and prepared provisions, a and took worn-out sacks for their donkeys, and wineskins, worn-out and torn and mended, 5 with worn-out, patched sandals on their feet, and worn-out clothes; and all their provisions were dry and mouldy. 6 They went to Joshua in the camp at Gilgal, and said to him and to the Israelites, 'We have come from a far country; so now make a treaty with us.' 7 But the Israelites said to the Hivites, 'Perhaps you live among us; then how can we make a treaty with you?' 8 They said to Joshua, 'We are your servants.' And Joshua said to them, 'Who are you? And where do you come from?' 9 They said to him, 'Your servants have come from a very far country, because of the name of the LORD your God; for we have heard a report of him, of all that he did in Egypt, 10 and of all that he did to the two kings of the Amorites who were beyond the Jordan, King Sihon of Heshbon, and King Og of Bashan who lived in Ashtaroth. 11 So our elders and all the inhabitants of our country said to us, "Take provisions in your hand for the journey; go to meet them, and say to them, 'We are your servants; come now, make a treaty with us.' " 12 Here is our bread; it was still warm when we took it from our houses as our food for the journey, on the day we set out to come to you, but now, see, it is dry and mouldy; 13 these wineskins were new when we filled them, and see, they are burst; and these garments and sandals of ours are worn out from the very long journey.' 14 So the leaders b partook of their provisions, and did not ask direction from the LORD. 15 And Joshua made peace with them, guaranteeing their lives by a treaty; and the leaders of the congregation swore an oath to them.

16 But when three days had passed after they had made a treaty with them, they heard that they were their neighbours and were living among them. 17 So the Israelites set out and reached their cities on the third day. Now their cities were Gibeon, Chephirah, Beeroth, and Kiriath-jearim. 18 But the Israelites did not attack them, because the leaders of the congregation had sworn to them by the LORD, the God of Israel. Then all the congregation murmured against the leaders. 19 But all the leaders said to all the congregation, 'We have sworn to them by the LORD, the God of Israel, and now we must not touch them. 20 This is what we will do to them: We will let them live, so that wrath may not come upon us, because of the oath that we swore to them.' 21 The leaders said to them, 'Let them live.' So they became hewers of wood and drawers of water for all the congregation, as the leaders had decided concerning them.

22 Joshua summoned them, and said to them, 'Why did you deceive us, saying, "We are very far from you", while in fact you are living among us? 23 Now therefore you are cursed, and some of you shall always be slaves, hewers of wood and drawers of water for the house of my God.' 24 They answered Joshua, 'Because it was told to your servants for a certainty that the LORD your God had commanded his servant Moses to give you all the land, and to destroy all the inhabitants of the land before you; so we were in great fear for our lives because of you, and did this thing. 25 And now we are in your hand: do as it seems good and right in your sight to do to us.' 26 This is what he did for them: he saved them from the Israelites; and they did not kill them. 27 But on that day Joshua made them hewers of

a Cn: Meaning of Heb uncertain   b Gk: Heb men

wood and drawers of water for the congregation and for the altar of the LORD, to continue to this day, in the place that he should choose.

The Sun Stands Still

10 When King Adoni-zedek of Jerusalem heard how Joshua had taken Ai, and had utterly destroyed it, doing to Ai and its king as he had done to Jericho and its king, and how the inhabitants of Gibeon had made peace with Israel and were among them, ²he*a* became greatly frightened, because Gibeon was a large city, like one of the royal cities, and was larger than Ai, and all its men were warriors. ³So King Adoni-zedek of Jerusalem sent a message to King Hoham of Hebron, to King Piram of Jarmuth, to King Japhia of Lachish, and to King Debir of Eglon, saying, ⁴'Come up and help me, and let us attack Gibeon; for it has made peace with Joshua and with the Israelites.' ⁵Then the five kings of the Amorites—the king of Jerusalem, the king of Hebron, the king of Jarmuth, the king of Lachish, and the king of Eglon—gathered their forces, and went up with all their armies and encamped against Gibeon, and made war against it.

6 And the Gibeonites sent to Joshua at the camp in Gilgal, saying, 'Do not abandon your servants; come up to us quickly, and save us, and help us; for all the kings of the Amorites who live in the hill country are gathered against us.' ⁷So Joshua went up from Gilgal, he and all the fighting force with him, all the mighty warriors. ⁸The LORD said to Joshua, 'Do not fear them, for I have handed them over to you; not one of them shall stand before you.' ⁹So Joshua came upon them suddenly, having marched up all night from Gilgal. ¹⁰And the LORD threw them into a panic before Israel, who inflicted a great slaughter on them at Gibeon, chased them by the way of the ascent of Beth-horon, and struck them down as far as Azekah and Makkedah. ¹¹As they fled before Israel, while they were going down the slope of Beth-horon, the LORD threw down huge stones from heaven on them as far as Azekah, and they died; there

were more who died because of the hailstones than the Israelites killed with the sword.

12 On the day when the LORD gave the Amorites over to the Israelites, Joshua spoke to the LORD; and he said in the sight of Israel,
'Sun, stand still at Gibeon,
    and Moon, in the valley of Aijalon.'
¹³ And the sun stood still, and the
        moon stopped,
    until the nation took vengeance on
        their enemies.
Is this not written in the Book of Jashar? The sun stopped in mid-heaven, and did not hurry to set for about a whole day. ¹⁴There has been no day like it before or since, when the LORD heeded a human voice; for the LORD fought for Israel.

15 Then Joshua returned, and all Israel with him, to the camp at Gilgal.

Five Kings Defeated

16 Meanwhile, these five kings fled and hid themselves in the cave at Makkedah. ¹⁷And it was told Joshua, 'The five kings have been found, hidden in the cave at Makkedah.' ¹⁸Joshua said, 'Roll large stones against the mouth of the cave, and set men by it to guard them; ¹⁹but do not stay there yourselves; pursue your enemies, and attack them from the rear. Do not let them enter their towns, for the LORD your God has given them into your hand.' ²⁰When Joshua and the Israelites had finished inflicting a very great slaughter on them, until they were wiped out, and when the survivors had entered into the fortified towns, ²¹all the people returned safe to Joshua in the camp at Makkedah; no one dared to speak*b* against any of the Israelites.

22 Then Joshua said, 'Open the mouth of the cave, and bring those five kings out to me from the cave.' ²³They did so, and brought the five kings out to him from the cave, the king of Jerusalem, the king of Hebron, the king of Jarmuth, the king of Lachish, and the king of Eglon. ²⁴When they brought the kings out to Joshua, Joshua summoned all the Israelites, and said to the

---

a Heb *they*   *b* Heb *moved his tongue*

chiefs of the warriors who had gone with him, 'Come near, put your feet on the necks of these kings.' Then they came near and put their feet on their necks. 25 And Joshua said to them, 'Do not be afraid or dismayed; be strong and courageous; for thus the LORD will do to all the enemies against whom you fight.' 26 Afterwards Joshua struck them down and put them to death, and he hung them on five trees. And they hung on the trees until evening. 27 At sunset Joshua commanded, and they took them down from the trees and threw them into the cave where they had hidden themselves; they set large stones against the mouth of the cave, which remain to this very day.

28 Joshua took Makkedah on that day, and struck it and its king with the edge of the sword; he utterly destroyed every person in it; he left no one remaining. And he did to the king of Makkedah as he had done to the king of Jericho.

29 Then Joshua passed on from Makkedah, and all Israel with him, to Libnah, and fought against Libnah. 30 The LORD gave it also and its king into the hand of Israel; and he struck it with the edge of the sword, and every person in it; he left no one remaining in it; and he did to its king as he had done to the king of Jericho.

31 Next Joshua passed on from Libnah, and all Israel with him, to Lachish, and laid siege to it, and assaulted it. 32 The LORD gave Lachish into the hand of Israel, and he took it on the second day, and struck it with the edge of the sword, and every person in it, as he had done to Libnah.

33 Then King Horam of Gezer came up to help Lachish; and Joshua struck him and his people, leaving him no survivors.

34 From Lachish Joshua passed on with all Israel to Eglon; and they laid siege to it, and assaulted it; 35 and they took it that day, and struck it with the edge of the sword; and every person in it he utterly destroyed that day, as he had done to Lachish.

36 Then Joshua went up with all Israel from Eglon to Hebron; they assaulted it, 37 and took it, and struck it with the edge of the sword, and its king and its towns, and

every person in it; he left no one remaining, just as he had done to Eglon, and utterly destroyed it with every person in it.

38 Then Joshua, with all Israel, turned back to Debir and assaulted it, 39 and he took it with its king and all its towns; they struck them with the edge of the sword, and utterly destroyed every person in it; he left no one remaining, just as he had done to Hebron, and, as he had done to Libnah and its king, so he did to Debir and its king.

40 So Joshua defeated the whole land, the hill country and the Negeb and the lowland and the slopes, and all their kings; he left no one remaining, but utterly destroyed all that breathed, as the LORD God of Israel commanded. 41 And Joshua defeated them from Kadesh-barnea to Gaza, and all the country of Goshen, as far as Gibeon. 42 Joshua took all these kings and their land at one time, because the LORD God of Israel fought for Israel. 43 Then Joshua returned, and all Israel with him, to the camp at Gilgal.

The United Kings of Northern Canaan Defeated

11 When King Jabin of Hazor heard of this, he sent to King Jobab of Madon, to the king of Shimron, to the king of Achshaph, 2 and to the kings who were in the northern hill country, and in the Arabah south of Chinneroth, and in the lowland, and in Naphoth-dor on the west, 3 to the Canaanites in the east and the west, the Amorites, the Hittites, the Perizzites, and the Jebusites in the hill country, and the Hivites under Hermon in the land of Mizpah. 4 They came out, with all their troops, a great army, in number like the sand on the seashore, with very many horses and chariots. 5 All these kings joined their forces, and came and camped together at the waters of Merom, to fight with Israel.

6 And the LORD said to Joshua, 'Do not be afraid of them, for tomorrow at this time I will hand over all of them, slain, to Israel; you shall hamstring their horses, and burn their chariots with fire.' 7 So Joshua came suddenly upon them with all his fighting force, by the waters of Merom, and

fell upon them. 8And the LORD handed them over to Israel, who attacked them and chased them as far as Great Sidon and Misrephoth-maim, and eastwards as far as the valley of Mizpeh. They struck them down, until they had left no one remaining. 9And Joshua did to them as the LORD commanded him; he hamstrung their horses, and burned their chariots with fire.

10 Joshua turned back at that time, and took Hazor, and struck its king down with the sword. Before that time Hazor was the head of all those kingdoms. 11And they put to the sword all who were in it, utterly destroying them; there was no one left who breathed, and he burned Hazor with fire. 12And all the towns of those kings, and all their kings, Joshua took, and struck them with the edge of the sword, utterly destroying them, as Moses the servant of the LORD had commanded. 13But Israel burned none of the towns that stood on mounds except Hazor, which Joshua did burn. 14All the spoil of these towns, and the livestock, the Israelites took for their booty; but all the people they struck down with the edge of the sword, until they had destroyed them, and they did not leave any who breathed. 15As the LORD had commanded his servant Moses, so Moses commanded Joshua, and so Joshua did; he left nothing undone of all that the LORD had commanded Moses.

Summary of Joshua's Conquests

16 So Joshua took all that land: the hill country and all the Negeb and all the land of Goshen and the lowland and the Arabah and the hill country of Israel and its lowland, 17from Mount Halak, which rises towards Seir, as far as Baal-gad in the valley of Lebanon below Mount Hermon. He took all their kings, struck them down, and put them to death. 18Joshua made war a long time with all those kings. 19There was not a town that made peace with the Israelites, except the Hivites, the inhabitants of Gibeon; all were taken in battle. 20For it was the LORD's doing to harden their hearts so that they would come against Israel in battle, in order that they might be utterly destroyed, and might receive no mercy, but be exterminated, just as the LORD had commanded Moses.

21 At that time Joshua came and wiped out the Anakim from the hill country, from Hebron, from Debir, from Anab, and from all the hill country of Judah, and from all the hill country of Israel; Joshua utterly destroyed them with their towns. 22None of the Anakim was left in the land of the Israelites; some remained only in Gaza, in Gath, and in Ashdod. 23So Joshua took the whole land, according to all that the LORD had spoken to Moses; and Joshua gave it for an inheritance to Israel according to their tribal allotments. And the land had rest from war.

The Kings Conquered by Moses

12 Now these are the kings of the land, whom the Israelites defeated, whose land they occupied beyond the Jordan towards the east, from the Wadi Arnon to Mount Hermon, with all the Arabah eastwards: 2King Sihon of the Amorites who lived at Heshbon, and ruled from Aroer,

The Conquest of Northern Canaan

Mediterranean Sea
Sidon
Valley of Mizpah
Tyre
Kedesh
Merom
Hazor
Chinnereth
Sea of Chinnereth
Beth-shan
N
0   20 Mi.
0   30 Km.
From Gilgal

which is on the edge of the Wadi Arnon, and from the middle of the valley as far as the river Jabbok, the boundary of the Ammonites, that is, half of Gilead, 3 and the Arabah to the Sea of Chinneroth eastwards, and in the direction of Beth-jeshimoth, to the sea of the Arabah, the Dead Sea, *a* southwards to the foot of the slopes of Pisgah; 4 and King Og*b* of Bashan, one of the last of the Rephaim, who lived at Ashtaroth and at Edrei 5 and ruled over Mount Hermon and Salecah and all Bashan to the boundary of the Geshurites and the Maacathites, and over half of Gilead to the boundary of King Sihon of Heshbon. 6 Moses, the servant of the LORD, and the Israelites defeated them; and Moses the servant of the LORD gave their land for a possession to the Reubenites and the Gadites and the half-tribe of Manasseh.

The Kings Conquered by Joshua

7 The following are the kings of the land whom Joshua and the Israelites defeated on the west side of the Jordan, from Baal-gad in the valley of Lebanon to Mount Halak, that rises towards Seir (and Joshua gave their land to the tribes of Israel as a possession according to their allotments, 8 in the hill country, in the lowland, in the Arabah, in the slopes, in the wilderness, and in the Negeb, the land of the Hittites, Amorites, Canaanites, Perizzites, Hivites, and Jebusites):

9 the king of Jericho	one
the king of Ai, which is next to Bethel	one
10 the king of Jerusalem	one
the king of Hebron	one
11 the king of Jarmuth	one
the king of Lachish	one
12 the king of Eglon	one
the king of Gezer	one
13 the king of Debir	one
the king of Geder	one
14 the king of Hormah	one
the king of Arad	one
15 the king of Libnah	one
the king of Adullam	one
16 the king of Makkedah	one
the king of Bethel	one
17 the king of Tappuah	one
the king of Hepher	one
18 the king of Aphek	one
the king of Lasharon	one
19 the king of Madon	one
the king of Hazor	one
20 the king of Shimron-meron	one
the king of Achshaph	one
21 the king of Taanach	one
the king of Megiddo	one
22 the king of Kedesh	one
the king of Jokneam in Carmel	one
23 the king of Dor in Naphath-dor	one
the king of Goiim in Galilee, *c*	one
24 the king of Tirzah	one

thirty-one kings in all.

The Parts of Canaan Still Unconquered

13 Now Joshua was old and advanced in years; and the LORD said to him, 'You are old and advanced in years, and very much of the land still remains to be possessed. 2 This is the land that still remains: all the regions of the Philistines, and all those of the Geshurites 3 (from the Shihor, which is east of Egypt, northwards to the boundary of Ekron, it is reckoned as Canaanite; there are five rulers of the Philistines, those of Gaza, Ashdod, Ashkelon, Gath, and Ekron), and those of the Avvim 4 in the south; all the land of the Canaanites, and Mearah that belongs to the Sidonians, to Aphek, to the boundary of the Amorites, 5 and the land of the Gebalites, and all Lebanon, towards the east, from Baal-gad below Mount Hermon to Lebo-hamath, 6 all the inhabitants of the hill country from Lebanon to Misrephoth-maim, even all the Sidonians. I will myself drive them out from before the Israelites; only allot the land to Israel for an inheritance, as I have commanded you. 7 Now therefore divide this land for an inheritance to the nine tribes and the half-tribe of Manasseh.'

The Territory East of the Jordan

8 With the other half-tribe of Manasseh, *d* the Reubenites and the Gadites received their inheritance, which Moses gave

---

a Heb *Salt Sea*   *b* Gk: Heb *the boundary of King Og*
c Gk: Heb *Gilgal*   *d* Cn: Heb *With it*

them, beyond the Jordan eastwards, as Moses the servant of the LORD gave them: [9] from Aroer, which is on the edge of the Wadi Arnon, and the town that is in the middle of the valley, and all the tableland from[a] Medeba as far as Dibon; [10] and all the cities of King Sihon of the Amorites, who reigned in Heshbon, as far as the boundary of the Ammonites; [11] and Gilead, and the region of the Geshurites and Maacathites, and all Mount Hermon, and all Bashan to Salecah; [12] all the kingdom of Og in Bashan, who reigned in Ashtaroth and in Edrei (he alone was left of the survivors of the Rephaim); these Moses had defeated and driven out. [13] Yet the Israelites did not drive out the Geshurites or the Maacathites; but Geshur and Maacath live within Israel to this day.

14 To the tribe of Levi alone Moses gave no inheritance; the offerings by fire to the LORD God of Israel are their inheritance, as he said to them.

The Territory of Reuben

15 Moses gave an inheritance to the tribe of the Reubenites according to their clans. [16] Their territory was from Aroer, which is on the edge of the Wadi Arnon, and the town that is in the middle of the valley, and all the tableland by Medeba; [17] with Heshbon, and all its towns that are in the tableland; Dibon, and Bamoth-baal, and Beth-baal-meon, [18] and Jahaz, and Kedemoth, and Mephaath, [19] and Kiriathaim, and Sibmah, and Zereth-shahar on the hill of the valley, [20] and Beth-peor, and the slopes of Pisgah, and Beth-jeshimoth, [21] that is, all the towns of the tableland, and all the kingdom of King Sihon of the Amorites, who reigned in Heshbon, whom Moses defeated with the leaders of Midian, Evi and Rekem and Zur and Hur and Reba, as princes of Sihon, who lived in the land. [22] Along with the rest of those they put to death, the Israelites also put to the sword Balaam son of Beor, who practised divination. [23] And the border of the Reubenites was the Jordan and its banks. This was the inheritance of the Reubenites according to their families, with their towns and villages.

The Territory of Gad

24 Moses gave an inheritance also to the tribe of the Gadites, according to their families. [25] Their territory was Jazer, and all the towns of Gilead, and half the land of the Ammonites, to Aroer, which is east of Rabbah, [26] and from Heshbon to Ramath-mizpeh and Betonim, and from Mahanaim to the territory of Debir,[b] [27] and in the valley Beth-haram, Beth-nimrah, Succoth, and Zaphon, the rest of the kingdom of King Sihon of Heshbon, the Jordan and its banks, as far as the lower end of the Sea of Chinnereth, eastwards beyond the Jordan. [28] This is the inheritance of the Gadites according to their clans, with their towns and villages.

The Territory of the Half-Tribe of Manasseh (East)

29 Moses gave an inheritance to the half-tribe of Manasseh; it was allotted to the half-tribe of the Manassites according to their families. [30] Their territory extended from Mahanaim, through all Bashan, the whole kingdom of King Og of Bashan, and all the settlements of Jair, which are in Bashan, sixty towns, [31] and half of Gilead, and Ashtaroth, and Edrei, the towns of the kingdom of Og in Bashan; these were allotted to the people of Machir son of Manasseh according to their clans—for half the Machirites.

32 These are the inheritances that Moses distributed in the plains of Moab, beyond the Jordan east of Jericho. [33] But to the tribe of Levi Moses gave no inheritance; the LORD God of Israel is their inheritance, as he said to them.

The Distribution of Territory West of the Jordan

14 These are the inheritances that the Israelites received in the land of Canaan, which the priest Eleazar, and Joshua son of Nun, and the heads of the families of the tribes of the Israelites distributed to them. [2] Their inheritance was by lot, as the LORD had commanded Moses for the

a Compare Gk: Heb lacks *from*   b Gk Syr Vg: Heb *Lidebir* nine and a half tribes. ³For Moses had given an inheritance to the two and a half tribes beyond the Jordan; but to the Levites he gave no inheritance among them. ⁴For the people of Joseph were two tribes, Manasseh and Ephraim; and no portion was given to the Levites in the land, but only towns to live in, with their pasture lands for their flocks and herds. ⁵The Israelites did as the LORD commanded Moses; they allotted the land.

Hebron Allotted to Caleb

6 Then the people of Judah came to Joshua at Gilgal; and Caleb son of Jephunneh the Kenizzite said to him, 'You know what the LORD said to Moses the man of God in Kadesh-barnea concerning you and me. ⁷I was forty years old when Moses the servant of the LORD sent me from Kadesh-barnea to spy out the land; and I brought him an honest report. ⁸But my companions who went up with me made the heart of the people fail; yet I wholeheartedly followed the LORD my God. ⁹And Moses swore on that day, saying, "Surely the land on which your foot has trodden shall be an inheritance for you and your children for ever, because you have wholeheartedly followed the LORD my God." ¹⁰And now, as you see, the LORD has kept me alive, as he said, these forty-five years since the time that the LORD spoke this word to Moses, while Israel was journeying through the wilderness; and here I am today, eighty-five years old. ¹¹I am still as strong today as I was on the day that Moses sent me; my strength now is as my strength was then, for war, and for going and coming. ¹²So now give me this hill country of which the LORD spoke on that day; for you heard on that day how the Anakim were there, with great fortified cities; it may be that the LORD will be with me, and I shall drive them out, as the LORD said.'

13 Then Joshua blessed him, and gave Hebron to Caleb son of Jephunneh for an inheritance. ¹⁴So Hebron became the inheritance of Caleb son of Jephunneh the Kenizzite to this day, because he whole-

heartedly followed the LORD, the God of Israel. ¹⁵Now the name of Hebron formerly was Kiriath-arba;ᵃ this Arba wasᵇ the greatest man among the Anakim. And the land had rest from war.

The Territory of Judah

15 The lot for the tribe of the people of Judah according to their families reached southwards to the boundary of Edom, to the wilderness of Zin at the farthest south. ²And their southern boundary ran from the end of the Dead Sea,ᶜ from the bay that faces southwards; ³it goes out southwards of the ascent of Akrabbim, passes along to Zin, and goes up south of Kadesh-barnea, along by Hezron, up to Addar, makes a turn to Karka, ⁴passes along to Azmon, goes out by the Wadi of Egypt, and comes to its end at the sea. This shall be your southern boundary. ⁵And the eastern boundary is the Dead Sea,ᶜ to the mouth of the Jordan. And the boundary on the north side runs from the bay of the sea at the mouth of the Jordan; ⁶and the boundary goes up to Beth-hoglah, and passes along north of Beth-arabah; and the boundary goes up to the Stone of Bohan, Reuben's son; ⁷and the boundary goes up to Debir from the Valley of Achor, and so northwards, turning towards Gilgal, which is opposite the ascent of Adummim, which is on the south side of the valley; and the boundary passes along to the waters of En-shemesh, and ends at En-rogel; ⁸then the boundary goes up by the valley of the son of Hinnom at the southern slope of the Jebusites (that is, Jerusalem); and the boundary goes up to the top of the mountain that lies over against the valley of Hinnom, on the west, at the northern end of the valley of Rephaim; ⁹then the boundary extends from the top of the mountain to the spring of the Waters of Nephtoah, and from there to the towns of Mount Ephron; then the boundary bends around to Baalah (that is, Kiriath-jearim); ¹⁰and the boundary circles west of Baalah to Mount Seir, passes along

ᵃ That is *the city of Arba*   ᵇ Heb lacks *this Arba was*
ᶜ Heb *Salt Sea*

to the northern slope of Mount Jearim (that is, Chesalon), and goes down to Beth-shemesh, and passes along by Timnah; 11 the boundary goes out to the slope of the hill north of Ekron, then the boundary bends around to Shikkeron, and passes along to Mount Baalah, and goes out to Jabneel; then the boundary comes to an end at the sea. 12 And the western boundary was the Mediterranean with its coast. This is the boundary surrounding the people of Judah according to their families.

Caleb Occupies His Portion

13 According to the commandment of the LORD to Joshua, he gave to Caleb son of Jephunneh a portion among the people of Judah, Kiriath-arba,*a* that is, Hebron (Arba was the father of Anak). 14 And Caleb drove out from there the three sons of Anak: Sheshai, Ahiman, and Talmai, the descendants of Anak. 15 From there he went up against the inhabitants of Debir; now the name of Debir formerly was Kiriath-sepher. 16 And Caleb said, 'Whoever attacks Kiriath-sepher and takes it, to him I will give my daughter Achsah as wife.' 17 Othniel son of Kenaz, the brother of Caleb, took it; and he gave him his daughter Achsah as wife. 18 When she came to him, she urged him to ask her father for a field. As she dismounted from her donkey, Caleb said to her, 'What do you want?' 19 She said to him, 'Give me a present; since you have set me in the land of the Negeb, give me springs of water as well.' So Caleb gave her the upper springs and the lower springs.

The Towns of Judah

20 This is the inheritance of the tribe of the people of Judah according to their families. 21 The towns belonging to the tribe of the people of Judah in the extreme south, towards the boundary of Edom, were Kabzeel, Eder, Jagur, 22 Kinah, Dimonah, Adadah, 23 Kedesh, Hazor, Ithnan, 24 Ziph, Telem, Bealoth, 25 Hazor-hadattah, Kerioth-hezron (that is, Hazor), 26 Amam, Shema, Moladah, 27 Hazar-gaddah, Hesh-

mon, Beth-pelet, 28 Hazar-shual, Beer-sheba, Biziothiah, 29 Baalah, Iim, Ezem, 30 Eltolad, Chesil, Hormah, 31 Ziklag, Madmannah, Sansannah, 32 Lebaoth, Shilhim, Ain, and Rimmon: in all, twenty-nine towns, with their villages.

33 And in the lowlands, Eshtaol, Zorah, Ashnah, 34 Zanoah, En-gannim, Tappuah, Enam, 35 Jarmuth, Adullam, Socoh, Azekah, 36 Shaaraim, Adithaim, Gederah, Gederothaim: fourteen towns with their villages.

37 Zenan, Hadashah, Migdal-gad, 38 Dilan, Mizpeh, Jokthe-el, 39 Lachish, Bozkath, Eglon, 40 Cabbon, Lahmam, Chitlish, 41 Gederoth, Beth-dagon, Naamah, and Makkedah: sixteen towns with their villages.

42 Libnah, Ether, Ashan, 43 Iphtah, Ashnah, Nezib, 44 Keilah, Achzib, and Mareshah: nine towns with their villages.

45 Ekron, with its dependencies and its villages; 46 from Ekron to the sea, all that were near Ashdod, with their villages.

47 Ashdod, its towns and its villages; Gaza, its towns and its villages; to the Wadi of Egypt, and the Great Sea with its coast.

48 And in the hill country, Shamir, Jattir, Socoh, 49 Dannah, Kiriath-sannah (that is, Debir), 50 Anab, Eshtemoh, Anim, 51 Goshen, Holon, and Giloh: eleven towns with their villages.

52 Arab, Dumah, Eshan, 53 Janim, Bethtappuah, Aphekah, 54 Humtah, Kiriath-arba (that is, Hebron), and Zior: nine towns with their villages.

55 Maon, Carmel, Ziph, Juttah, 56 Jezreel, Jokdeam, Zanoah, 57 Kain, Gibeah, and Timnah: ten towns with their villages.

58 Halhul, Beth-zur, Gedor, 59 Maarath, Beth-anoth, and Eltekon: six towns with their villages.

60 Kiriath-baal (that is, Kiriath-jearim) and Rabbah: two towns with their villages.

61 In the wilderness, Beth-arabah, Middin, Secacah, 62 Nibshan, the City of Salt, and En-gedi: six towns with their villages.

63 But the people of Judah could not drive out the Jebusites, the inhabitants of Jerusalem; so the Jebusites live with the people of Judah in Jerusalem to this day.

a That is *the city of Arba*

The Territory of Ephraim

16 The allotment of the Josephites went from the Jordan by Jericho, east of the waters of Jericho, into the wilderness, going up from Jericho into the hill country to Bethel; 2 then going from Bethel to Luz, it passes along to Ataroth, the territory of the Archites; 3 then it goes down westwards to the territory of the Japhletites, as far as the territory of Lower Beth-horon, then to Gezer, and it ends at the sea.

4 The Josephites—Manasseh and Ephraim—received their inheritance.

5 The territory of the Ephraimites by their families was as follows: the boundary of their inheritance on the east was Ataroth-addar as far as Upper Beth-horon, 6 and the boundary goes from there to the sea; on the north is Michmethath; then on the east the boundary makes a turn towards Taanath-shiloh, and passes along beyond it on the east to Janoah, 7 then it goes down from Janoah to Ataroth and to Naarah, and touches Jericho, ending at the Jordan. 8 From Tappuah the boundary goes westwards to the Wadi Kanah, and ends at the sea. Such is the inheritance of the tribe of the Ephraimites by their families, 9 together with the towns that were set apart for the Ephraimites within the inheritance of the Manassites, all those towns with their villages. 10 They did not, however, drive out the Canaanites who lived in Gezer: so the Canaanites have lived within Ephraim to this day but have been made to do forced labour.

The Other Half-Tribe of Manasseh (West)

17 Then allotment was made to the tribe of Manasseh, for he was the firstborn of Joseph. To Machir the firstborn of Manasseh, the father of Gilead, were allotted Gilead and Bashan, because he was a warrior. 2 And allotments were made to the rest of the tribe of Manasseh, by their families, Abiezer, Helek, Asriel, Shechem, Hepher, and Shemida; these were the male descendants of Manasseh son of Joseph, by their families.

3 Now Zelophehad son of Hepher son of Gilead son of Machir son of Manasseh had no sons, but only daughters; and these are the names of his daughters: Mahlah, Noah, Hoglah, Milcah, and Tirzah. 4 They came before the priest Eleazar and Joshua son of Nun and the leaders, and said, 'The LORD commanded Moses to give us an inheritance along with our male kin.' So according to the commandment of the LORD he gave them an inheritance among the kinsmen of their father. 5 Thus there fell to Manasseh ten portions, besides the land of Gilead and Bashan, which is on the other side of the Jordan, 6 because the daughters of Manasseh received an inheritance along with his sons. The land of Gilead was allotted to the rest of the Manassites.

7 The territory of Manasseh reached from Asher to Michmethath, which is east of Shechem; then the boundary goes along southwards to the inhabitants of En-tappuah. 8 The land of Tappuah belonged to Manasseh, but the town of

Division of the Land

Mediterranean Sea

ASHER
NAPHTALI
BASHAN
ZEBULUN
ISSACHAR
MANASSEH
GILEAD
EPHRAIM
GAD
AMMON
DAN
BENJAMIN
PHILISTINES
REUBEN
Dead Sea
JUDAH
SIMEON
MOAB

0   40 Mi.
0   40 Km.

Tappuah on the boundary of Manasseh belonged to the Ephraimites. 9 Then the boundary went down to the Wadi Kanah. The towns here, to the south of the wadi, among the towns of Manasseh, belong to Ephraim. Then the boundary of Manasseh goes along the north side of the wadi and ends at the sea. 10 The land to the south is Ephraim's and that to the north is Manasseh's, with the sea forming its boundary; on the north Asher is reached, and on the east Issachar. 11 Within Issachar and Asher, Manasseh had Beth-shean and its villages, Ibleam and its villages, the inhabitants of Dor and its villages, the inhabitants of En-dor and its villages, the inhabitants of Ta-anach and its villages, and the inhabitants of Megiddo and its villages (the third is Naphath). *a* 12 Yet the Manassites could not take possession of those towns; but the Canaanites continued to live in that land. 13 But when the Israelites grew strong, they put the Canaanites to forced labour, but did not utterly drive them out.

The Tribe of Joseph Protests

14 The tribe of Joseph spoke to Joshua, saying, 'Why have you given me but one lot and one portion as an inheritance, since we are a numerous people, whom all along the LORD has blessed?' 15 And Joshua said to them, 'If you are a numerous people, go up to the forest, and clear ground there for yourselves in the land of the Perizzites and the Rephaim, since the hill country of Ephraim is too narrow for you.' 16 The tribe of Joseph said, 'The hill country is not enough for us; yet all the Canaanites who live in the plain have chariots of iron, both those in Beth-shean and its villages and those in the Valley of Jezreel.' 17 Then Joshua said to the house of Joseph, to Ephraim and Manasseh, 'You are indeed a numerous people, and have great power; you shall not have one lot only, 18 but the hill country shall be yours, for though it is a forest, you shall clear it and possess it to its farthest borders; for you shall drive out the Canaanites, though they have chariots of iron, and though they are strong.'

The Territories of the Remaining Tribes

18 Then the whole congregation of the Israelites assembled at Shiloh, and set up the tent of meeting there. The land lay subdued before them.

2 There remained among the Israelites seven tribes whose inheritance had not yet been apportioned. 3 So Joshua said to the Israelites, 'How long will you be slack about going in and taking possession of the land that the LORD, the God of your ancestors, has given you? 4 Provide three men from each tribe, and I will send them out that they may begin to go throughout the land, writing a description of it with a view to their inheritances. Then come back to me. 5 They shall divide it into seven portions, Judah continuing in its territory on the south, and the house of Joseph in their territory on the north. 6 You shall describe the land in seven divisions and bring the description here to me; and I will cast lots for you here before the LORD our God. 7 The Levites have no portion among you, for the priesthood of the LORD is their heritage; and Gad and Reuben and the half-tribe of Manasseh have received their inheritance beyond the Jordan eastwards, which Moses the servant of the LORD gave them.'

8 So the men started on their way; and Joshua charged those who went to write the description of the land, saying, 'Go throughout the land and write a description of it, and come back to me; and I will cast lots for you here before the LORD in Shiloh.' 9 So the men went and traversed the land and set down in a book a description of it by towns in seven divisions; then they came back to Joshua in the camp at Shiloh, 10 and Joshua cast lots for them in Shiloh before the LORD; and there Joshua apportioned the land to the Israelites, to each a portion.

The Territory of Benjamin

11 The lot of the tribe of Benjamin according to its families came up, and the territory allotted to it fell between the tribe of Judah and the tribe of Joseph. 12 On the

a Meaning of Heb uncertain

north side their boundary began at the Jordan; then the boundary goes up to the slope of Jericho on the north, then up through the hill country westwards; and it ends at the wilderness of Beth-aven. [13] From there the boundary passes along southwards in the direction of Luz, to the slope of Luz (that is, Bethel), then the boundary goes down to Ataroth-addar, on the mountain that lies south of Lower Beth-horon. [14] Then the boundary goes in another direction, turning on the western side southwards from the mountain that lies to the south, opposite Beth-horon, and it ends at Kiriath-baal (that is, Kiriath-jearim), a town belonging to the tribe of Judah. This forms the western side. [15] The southern side begins at the outskirts of Kiriath-jearim; and the boundary goes from there to Ephron,[a] to the spring of the Waters of Nephtoah; [16] then the boundary goes down to the border of the mountain that overlooks the valley of the son of Hinnom, which is at the northern end of the valley of Rephaim; and it then goes down the valley of Hinnom, south of the slope of the Jebusites, and downwards to En-rogel; [17] then it bends in a northerly direction going on to En-shemesh, and from there goes to Geliloth, which is opposite the ascent of Adummim; then it goes down to the Stone of Bohan, Reuben's son; [18] and passing on to the north of the slope of Beth-arabah[b] it goes down to the Arabah; [19] then the boundary passes on to the north of the slope of Beth-hoglah; and the boundary ends at the northern bay of the Dead Sea,[c] at the south end of the Jordan: this is the southern border. [20] The Jordan forms its boundary on the eastern side. This is the inheritance of the tribe of Benjamin, according to its families, boundary by boundary all round.

21 Now the towns of the tribe of Benjamin according to their families were Jericho, Beth-hoglah, Emek-keziz, [22] Beth-arabah, Zemaraim, Bethel, [23] Avvim, Parah, Ophrah, [24] Chephar-ammoni, Ophni, and Geba—twelve towns with their villages: [25] Gibeon, Ramah, Beeroth, [26] Mizpeh, Chephirah, Mozah, [27] Rekem, Irpeel,

Taralah, [28] Zela, Haeleph, Jebus[d] (that is, Jerusalem), Gibeah,[e] and Kiriath-jearim[f]—fourteen towns with their villages. This is the inheritance of the tribe of Benjamin according to its families.

The Territory of Simeon

19 The second lot came out for Simeon, for the tribe of Simeon, according to its families; its inheritance lay within the inheritance of the tribe of Judah. [2] It had for its inheritance Beer-sheba, Sheba, Moladah, [3] Hazar-shual, Balah, Ezem, [4] Eltolad, Bethul, Hormah, [5] Ziklag, Beth-marcaboth, Hazar-susah, [6] Beth-lebaoth, and Sharuhen—thirteen towns with their villages; [7] Ain, Rimmon, Ether, and Ashan—four towns with their villages; [8] together with all the villages all around these towns as far as Baalath-beer, Ramah of the Negeb. This was the inheritance of the tribe of Simeon according to its families. [9] The inheritance of the tribe of Simeon formed part of the territory of Judah; because the portion of the tribe of Judah was too large for them, the tribe of Simeon obtained an inheritance within their inheritance.

The Territory of Zebulun

10 The third lot came up for the tribe of Zebulun, according to its families. The boundary of its inheritance reached as far as Sarid; [11] then its boundary goes up westwards, and on to Maralah, and touches Dabbesheth, then the wadi that is east of Jokneam; [12] from Sarid it goes in the other direction eastwards towards the sunrise to the boundary of Chisloth-tabor; from there it goes to Daberath, then up to Japhia; [13] from there it passes along on the east towards the sunrise to Gath-hepher, to Eth-kazin, and going on to Rimmon it bends towards Neah; [14] then on the north the boundary makes a turn to Hannathon, and it ends at the valley of Iphtah-el; [15] and Kattath, Nahalal, Shimron, Idalah, and Bethlehem—twelve towns with their

a Cn See 15.9. Heb *westwards*   *b* Gk: Heb *to the slope over against the Arabah*   *c* Heb *Salt Sea*   *d* Gk Syr Vg: Heb *the Jebusite*   *e* Heb *Gibeath*   *f* Gk: Heb *Kiriath* villages. [16]This is the inheritance of the tribe of Zebulun, according to its families—these towns with their villages.

The Territory of Issachar

17 The fourth lot came out for Issachar, for the tribe of Issachar, according to its families. [18]Its territory included Jezreel, Chesulloth, Shunem, [19]Hapharaim, Shion, Anaharath, [20]Rabbith, Kishion, Ebez, [21]Remeth, En-gannim, En-haddah, Beth-pazzez; [22]the boundary also touches Tabor, Shahazumah, and Beth-shemesh, and its boundary ends at the Jordan—sixteen towns with their villages. [23]This is the inheritance of the tribe of Issachar, according to its families—the towns with their villages.

The Territory of Asher

24 The fifth lot came out for the tribe of Asher according to its families. [25]Its boundary included Helkath, Hali, Beten, Achshaph, [26]Allammelech, Amad, and Mishal; on the west it touches Carmel and Shihor-libnath, [27]then it turns eastwards, goes to Beth-dagon, and touches Zebulun and the valley of Iphtah-el northwards to Bethemek and Neiel; then it continues in the north to Cabul, [28]Ebron, Rehob, Hammon, Kanah, as far as Great Sidon; [29]then the boundary turns to Ramah, reaching to the fortified city of Tyre; then the boundary turns to Hosah, and it ends at the sea; Mahalab,[a] Achzib, [30]Ummah, Aphek, and Rehob—twenty-two towns with their villages. [31]This is the inheritance of the tribe of Asher according to its families—these towns with their villages.

The Territory of Naphtali

32 The sixth lot came out for the tribe of Naphtali, for the tribe of Naphtali, according to its families. [33]And its boundary ran from Heleph, from the oak in Zaanannim, and Adami-nekeb, and Jabneel, as far as Lakkum; and it ended at the Jordan; [34]then the boundary turns westwards to Aznothtabor, and goes from there to Hukkok, touching Zebulun at the south, and Asher on the west, and Judah on the east at the

Jordan. [35]The fortified towns are Ziddim, Zer, Hammath, Rakkath, Chinnereth, [36]Adamah, Ramah, Hazor, [37]Kedesh, Edrei, Enhazor, [38]Iron, Migdal-el, Horem, Bethanath, and Beth-shemesh—nineteen towns with their villages. [39]This is the inheritance of the tribe of Naphtali according to its families—the towns with their villages.

The Territory of Dan

40 The seventh lot came out for the tribe of Dan, according to its families. [41]The territory of its inheritance included Zorah, Eshtaol, Ir-shemesh, [42]Shaalabbin, Aijalon, Ithlah, [43]Elon, Timnah, Ekron, [44]Eltekeh, Gibbethon, Baalath, [45]Jehud, Bene-berak, Gath-rimmon, [46]Me-jarkon, and Rakkon at the border opposite Joppa. [47]When the territory of the Danites was lost to them, the Danites went up and fought against Leshem, and after capturing it and putting it to the sword, they took possession of it and settled in it, calling Leshem, Dan, after their ancestor Dan. [48]This is the inheritance of the tribe of Dan, according to their families—these towns with their villages.

Joshua's Inheritance

49 When they had finished distributing the several territories of the land as inheritances, the Israelites gave an inheritance among them to Joshua son of Nun. [50]By command of the LORD they gave him the town that he asked for, Timnath-serah in the hill country of Ephraim; he rebuilt the town, and settled in it.

51 These are the inheritances that the priest Eleazar and Joshua son of Nun and the heads of the families of the tribes of the Israelites distributed by lot at Shiloh before the LORD, at the entrance of the tent of meeting. So they finished dividing the land.

The Cities of Refuge

20 Then the LORD spoke to Joshua, saying, [2]'Say to the Israelites, "Appoint the cities of refuge, of which I spoke to you through Moses, [3]so that anyone who kills a person without intent or by mistake may flee there; they shall be for you a refuge

a Cn Compare Gk: Heb *Mehebel*

from the avenger of blood. ⁴The slayer shall flee to one of these cities and shall stand at the entrance of the gate of the city, and explain the case to the elders of that city; then the fugitive shall be taken into the city, and given a place, and shall remain with them. ⁵And if the avenger of blood is in pursuit, they shall not give up the slayer, because the neighbour was killed by mistake, there having been no enmity between them before. ⁶The slayer shall remain in that city until there is a trial before the congregation, until the death of the one who is high priest at the time: then the slayer may return home, to the town in which the deed was done." '

7 So they set apart Kedesh in Galilee in the hill country of Naphtali, and Shechem in the hill country of Ephraim, and Kiriath-arba (that is, Hebron) in the hill country of Judah. ⁸And beyond the Jordan east of Jericho, they appointed Bezer in the wilderness on the tableland, from the tribe of Reuben, and Ramoth in Gilead, from the tribe of Gad, and Golan in Bashan, from the tribe of Manasseh. ⁹These were the cities designated for all the Israelites, and for the aliens residing among them, that anyone who killed a person without intent could flee there, so as not to die by the hand of the avenger of blood, until there was a trial before the congregation.

Cities Allotted to the Levites

21 Then the heads of the families of the Levites came to the priest Eleazar and to Joshua son of Nun and to the heads of the families of the tribes of the Israelites; ²they said to them at Shiloh in the land of Canaan, 'The LORD commanded through Moses that we be given towns to live in, along with their pasture lands for our livestock.' ³So by command of the LORD the Israelites gave to the Levites the following towns and pasture lands out of their inheritance.

4 The lot came out for the families of the Kohathites. So those Levites who were descendants of Aaron the priest received by lot thirteen towns from the tribes of Judah, Simeon, and Benjamin.

5 The rest of the Kohathites received by lot ten towns from the families of the tribe of Ephraim, from the tribe of Dan, and the half-tribe of Manasseh.

6 The Gershonites received by lot thirteen towns from the families of the tribe of Issachar, from the tribe of Asher, from the tribe of Naphtali, and from the half-tribe of Manasseh in Bashan.

7 The Merarites according to their families received twelve towns from the tribe of Reuben, the tribe of Gad, and the tribe of Zebulun.

8 These towns and their pasture lands the Israelites gave by lot to the Levites, as the LORD had commanded through Moses.

9 Out of the tribe of Judah and the tribe of Simeon they gave the following towns mentioned by name, ¹⁰which went to the descendants of Aaron, one of the families of the Kohathites who belonged to the Levites, since the lot fell to them first. ¹¹They gave them Kiriath-arba (Arba being the father of Anak), that is Hebron, in the hill country of Judah, along with the pasture lands around it. ¹²But the fields of the town and its villages had been given to Caleb son of Jephunneh as his holding.

13 To the descendants of Aaron the priest they gave Hebron, the city of refuge for the slayer, with its pasture lands, Libnah with its pasture lands, ¹⁴Jattir with its pasture lands, Eshtemoa with its pasture lands, ¹⁵Holon with its pasture lands, Debir with its pasture lands, ¹⁶Ain with its pasture lands, Juttah with its pasture lands, and Beth-shemesh with its pasture lands—nine towns out of these two tribes. ¹⁷Out of the tribe of Benjamin: Gibeon with its pasture lands, Geba with its pasture lands, ¹⁸Anathoth with its pasture lands, and Almon with its pasture lands—four towns. ¹⁹The towns of the descendants of Aaron—the priests—were thirteen in all, with their pasture lands.

20 As to the rest of the Kohathites belonging to the Kohathite families of the Levites, the towns allotted to them were out of the tribe of Ephraim. ²¹To them were given Shechem, the city of refuge for the slayer, with its pasture lands in the hill country of

Ephraim, Gezer with its pasture lands, 22 Kibzaim with its pasture lands, and Beth-horon with its pasture lands—four towns. 23 Out of the tribe of Dan: Elteke with its pasture lands, Gibbethon with its pasture lands, 24 Aijalon with its pasture lands, Gath-rimmon with its pasture lands—four towns. 25 Out of the half-tribe of Manasseh: Taanach with its pasture lands, and Gath-rimmon with its pasture lands—two towns. 26 The towns of the families of the rest of the Kohathites were ten in all, with their pasture lands.

27 To the Gershonites, one of the families of the Levites, were given out of the half-tribe of Manasseh, Golan in Bashan with its pasture lands, the city of refuge for the slayer, and Beeshterah with its pasture lands—two towns. 28 Out of the tribe of Is-sachar: Kishion with its pasture lands, Dab-erath with its pasture lands, 29 Jarmuth with its pasture lands, En-gannim with its pasture lands—four towns. 30 Out of the tribe of Asher: Mishal with its pasture lands, Ab-don with its pasture lands, 31 Helkath with its pasture lands, and Rehob with its pasture lands—four towns. 32 Out of the tribe of Naphtali: Kedesh in Galilee with its pasture lands, the city of refuge for the slayer, Ham-moth-dor with its pasture lands, and Kartan with its pasture lands—three towns. 33 The towns of the several families of the Ger-shonites were in all thirteen, with their pasture lands.

34 To the rest of the Levites—the Mera-rite families—were given out of the tribe of Zebulun: Jokneam with its pasture lands, Kartah with its pasture lands, 35 Dimnah with its pasture lands, Nahalal with its pasture lands—four towns. 36 Out of the tribe of Reuben: Bezer with its pasture lands, Jah-zah with its pasture lands, 37 Kedemoth with its pasture lands, and Mephaath with its pasture lands—four towns. 38 Out of the tribe of Gad: Ramoth in Gilead with its pasture lands, the city of refuge for the slayer, Mahanaim with its pasture lands, 39 Hesh-bon with its pasture lands, Jazer with its pasture lands—four towns in all. 40 As for the towns of the several Merarite families, that is, the remainder of the families of the Levites, those allotted to them were twelve in all.

41 The towns of the Levites within the holdings of the Israelites were in all forty-eight towns with their pasture lands. 42 Each of these towns had its pasture lands around it; so it was with all these towns.

43 Thus the LORD gave to Israel all the land that he swore to their ancestors that he would give them; and having taken pos-session of it, they settled there. 44 And the LORD gave them rest on every side just as he had sworn to their ancestors; not one of all their enemies had withstood them, for the LORD had given all their enemies into their hands. 45 Not one of all the good promises that the LORD had made to the house of Is-rael had failed; all came to pass.

The Eastern Tribes Return to Their Territory

22 Then Joshua summoned the Reu-benites, the Gadites, and the half-tribe of Manasseh, 2 and said to them, 'You have observed all that Moses the servant of the LORD commanded you, and have obeyed me in all that I have commanded you; 3 you have not forsaken your kindred these many days, down to this day, but have been careful to keep the charge of the LORD your God. 4 And now the LORD your God has given rest to your kindred, as he prom-ised them; therefore turn and go to your tents in the land where your possession lies, which Moses the servant of the LORD gave you on the other side of the Jordan. 5 Take good care to observe the commandment and instruction that Moses the servant of the LORD commanded you, to love the LORD your God, to walk in all his ways, to keep his commandments, and to hold fast to him, and to serve him with all your heart and with all your soul.' 6 So Joshua blessed them and sent them away, and they went to their tents.

7 Now to one half of the tribe of Ma-nasseh Moses had given a possession in Bashan; but to the other half Joshua had given a possession beside their fellow-Is-raelites in the land west of the Jordan. And when Joshua sent them away to their tents

and blessed them, 8 he said to them, 'Go back to your tents with much wealth, and with very much livestock, with silver, gold, bronze, and iron, and with a great quantity of clothing; divide the spoil of your enemies with your kindred.' 9 So the Reubenites and the Gadites and the half-tribe of Manasseh returned home, parting from the Israelites at Shiloh, which is in the land of Canaan, to go to the land of Gilead, their own land of which they had taken possession by command of the LORD through Moses.

A Memorial Altar East of the Jordan

10 When they came to the region*a* near the Jordan that lies in the land of Canaan, the Reubenites and the Gadites and the half-tribe of Manasseh built there an altar by the Jordan, an altar of great size. 11 The Israelites heard that the Reubenites and the Gadites and the half-tribe of Manasseh had built an altar at the frontier of the land of Canaan, in the region*b* near the Jordan, on the side that belongs to the Israelites. 12 And when the people of Israel heard of it, the whole assembly of the Israelites gathered at Shiloh, to make war against them.

13 Then the Israelites sent the priest Phinehas son of Eleazar to the Reubenites and the Gadites and the half-tribe of Manasseh, in the land of Gilead, 14 and with him ten chiefs, one from each of the tribal families of Israel, every one of them the head of a family among the clans of Israel. 15 They came to the Reubenites, the Gadites, and the half-tribe of Manasseh in the land of Gilead, and they said to them, 16 'Thus says the whole congregation of the LORD, "What is this treachery that you have committed against the God of Israel in turning away today from following the LORD, by building yourselves an altar today in rebellion against the LORD? 17 Have we not had enough of the sin at Peor from which even yet we have not cleansed ourselves, and for which a plague came upon the congregation of the LORD, 18 that you must turn away today from following the LORD! If you rebel against the LORD today, he will be angry with the whole congregation of Israel to-

morrow. 19 But now, if your land is unclean, cross over into the LORD's land where the LORD's tabernacle now stands, and take for yourselves a possession among us; only do not rebel against the LORD, or rebel against us*c* by building yourselves an altar other than the altar of the LORD our God. 20 Did not Achan son of Zerah break faith in the matter of the devoted things, and wrath fell upon all the congregation of Israel? And he did not perish alone for his iniquity!" '

21 Then the Reubenites, the Gadites, and the half-tribe of Manasseh said in answer to the heads of the families of Israel, 22 'The LORD, God of gods! The LORD, God of gods! He knows; and let Israel itself know! If it was in rebellion or in breach of faith towards the LORD, do not spare us today 23 for building an altar to turn away from following the LORD; or if we did so to offer burnt-offerings or grain-offerings or offerings of well-being on it, may the LORD himself take vengeance. 24 No! We did it from fear that in time to come your children might say to our children, "What have you to do with the LORD, the God of Israel? 25 For the LORD has made the Jordan a boundary between us and you, you Reubenites and Gadites; you have no portion in the LORD." So your children might make our children cease to worship the LORD. 26 Therefore we said, "Let us now build an altar, not for burnt-offering, nor for sacrifice, 27 but to be a witness between us and you, and between the generations after us, that we do perform the service of the LORD in his presence with our burnt-offerings and sacrifices and offerings of well-being; so that your children may never say to our children in time to come, 'You have no portion in the LORD.' " 28 And we thought, If this should be said to us or to our descendants in time to come, we could say, "Look at this copy of the altar of the LORD, which our ancestors made, not for burnt-offerings, nor for sacrifice, but to be a witness between us and you." 29 Far be it from us that we should rebel against the LORD, and turn away this day from following the LORD by building an altar for burnt-offering, grain-offering, or sacrifice, other

a Or *to Geliloth*   *b* Or *at Geliloth*   *c* Or *make rebels of us* than the altar of the LORD our God that stands before his tabernacle!'

30 When the priest Phinehas and the chiefs of the congregation, the heads of the families of Israel who were with him, heard the words that the Reubenites and the Gadites and the Manassites spoke, they were satisfied. 31 The priest Phinehas son of Eleazar said to the Reubenites and the Gadites and the Manassites, 'Today we know that the LORD is among us, because you have not committed this treachery against the LORD; now you have saved the Israelites from the hand of the LORD.'

32 Then the priest Phinehas son of Eleazar and the chiefs returned from the Reubenites and the Gadites in the land of Gilead to the land of Canaan, to the Israelites, and brought back word to them. 33 The report pleased the Israelites; and the Israelites blessed God and spoke no more of making war against them, to destroy the land where the Reubenites and the Gadites were settled. 34 The Reubenites and the Gadites called the altar Witness;[a] 'For', said they, 'it is a witness between us that the LORD is God.'

Joshua Exhorts the People

23 A long time afterwards, when the LORD had given rest to Israel from all their enemies all around, and Joshua was old and well advanced in years, 2 Joshua summoned all Israel, their elders and heads, their judges and officers, and said to them, 'I am now old and well advanced in years; 3 and you have seen all that the LORD your God has done to all these nations for your sake, for it is the LORD your God who has fought for you. 4 I have allotted to you as an inheritance for your tribes those nations that remain, along with all the nations that I have already cut off, from the Jordan to the Great Sea in the west. 5 The LORD your God will push them back before you, and drive them out of your sight; and you shall possess their land, as the LORD your God promised you. 6 Therefore be very steadfast to observe and do all that is written in the book of the law of Moses, turning aside from it neither to the right nor to

the left, 7 so that you may not be mixed with these nations left here among you, or make mention of the names of their gods, or swear by them, or serve them, or bow yourselves down to them, 8 but hold fast to the LORD your God, as you have done to this day. 9 For the LORD has driven out before you great and strong nations; and as for you, no one has been able to withstand you to this day. 10 One of you puts to flight a thousand, since it is the LORD your God who fights for you, as he promised you. 11 Be very careful, therefore, to love the LORD your God. 12 For if you turn back, and join the survivors of these nations left here among you, and intermarry with them, so that you marry their women and they yours, 13 know assuredly that the LORD your God will not continue to drive out these nations before you; but they shall be a snare and a trap for you, a scourge on your sides, and thorns in your eyes, until you perish from this good land that the LORD your God has given you.

14 'And now I am about to go the way of all the earth, and you know in your hearts and souls, all of you, that not one thing has failed of all the good things that the LORD your God promised concerning you; all have come to pass for you, not one of them has failed. 15 But just as all the good things that the LORD your God promised concerning you have been fulfilled for you, so the LORD will bring upon you all the bad things, until he has destroyed you from this good land that the LORD your God has given you. 16 If you transgress the covenant of the LORD your God, which he enjoined on you, and go and serve other gods and bow down to them, then the anger of the LORD will be kindled against you, and you shall perish quickly from the good land that he has given to you.'

The Tribes Renew the Covenant

24 Then Joshua gathered all the tribes of Israel to Shechem, and summoned the elders, the heads, the judges, and the officers of Israel; and they presented themselves before God. 2 And Joshua

a Cn Compare Syr: Heb lacks *Witness*

said to all the people, 'Thus says the LORD, the God of Israel: Long ago your ancestors—Terah and his sons Abraham and Nahor—lived beyond the Euphrates and served other gods. ³Then I took your father Abraham from beyond the River and led him through all the land of Canaan and made his offspring many. I gave him Isaac; ⁴and to Isaac I gave Jacob and Esau. I gave Esau the hill country of Seir to possess, but Jacob and his children went down to Egypt. ⁵Then I sent Moses and Aaron, and I plagued Egypt with what I did in its midst; and afterwards I brought you out. ⁶When I brought your ancestors out of Egypt, you came to the sea; and the Egyptians pursued your ancestors with chariots and horsemen to the Red Sea.ᵃ ⁷When they cried out to the LORD, he put darkness between you and the Egyptians, and made the sea come upon them and cover them; and your eyes saw what I did to Egypt. Afterwards you lived in the wilderness for a long time. ⁸Then I brought you to the land of the Amorites, who lived on the other side of the Jordan; they fought with you, and I handed them over to you, and you took possession of their land, and I destroyed them before you. ⁹Then King Balak, son of Zippor of Moab, set out to fight against Israel. He sent and invited Balaam son of Beor to curse you, ¹⁰but I would not listen to Balaam; therefore he blessed you; so I rescued you out of his hand. ¹¹When you went over the Jordan and came to Jericho, the citizens of Jericho fought against you, and also the Amorites, the Perizzites, the Canaanites, the Hittites, the Girgashites, the Hivites, and the Jebusites; and I handed them over to you. ¹²I sent the hornetᵇ ahead of you, which drove out before you the two kings of the Amorites; it was not by your sword or by your bow. ¹³I gave you a land on which you had not laboured, and towns that you had not built, and you live in them; you eat the fruit of vineyards and olive groves that you did not plant.

14 'Now therefore revere the LORD, and serve him in sincerity and in faithfulness; put away the gods that your ancestors served beyond the River and in Egypt, and serve the LORD. ¹⁵Now if you are unwilling to serve the LORD, choose this day whom you will serve, whether the gods your ancestors served in the region beyond the River or the gods of the Amorites in whose land you are living; but as for me and my household, we will serve the LORD.'

16 Then the people answered, 'Far be it from us that we should forsake the LORD to serve other gods; ¹⁷for it is the LORD our God who brought us and our ancestors up from the land of Egypt, out of the house of slavery, and who did those great signs in our sight. He protected us along all the way that we went, and among all the peoples through whom we passed; ¹⁸and the LORD drove out before us all the peoples, the Amorites who lived in the land. Therefore we also will serve the LORD, for he is our God.'

19 But Joshua said to the people, 'You cannot serve the LORD, for he is a holy God. He is a jealous God; he will not forgive your transgressions or your sins. ²⁰If you forsake the LORD and serve foreign gods, then he will turn and do you harm, and consume you, after having done you good.' ²¹And the people said to Joshua, 'No, we will serve the LORD!' ²²Then Joshua said to the people, 'You are witnesses against yourselves that you have chosen the LORD, to serve him.' And they said, 'We are witnesses.' ²³He said, 'Then put away the foreign gods that are among you, and incline your hearts to the LORD, the God of Israel.' ²⁴The people said to Joshua, 'The LORD our God we will serve, and him we will obey.' ²⁵So Joshua made a covenant with the people that day, and made statutes and ordinances for them at Shechem. ²⁶Joshua wrote these words in the book of the law of God; and he took a large stone, and set it up there under the oak in the sanctuary of the LORD. ²⁷Joshua said to all the people, 'See, this stone shall be a witness against us; for it has heard all the words of the LORD that he spoke to us; therefore it shall be a witness against you, if you deal falsely with your God.' ²⁸So Joshua sent the people away to their inheritances.

a Or *Sea of Reeds*   *b* Meaning of Heb uncertain

Death of Joshua and Eleazar

29 After these things Joshua son of Nun, the servant of the LORD, died, being one hundred and ten years old. 30They buried him in his own inheritance at Timnath-serah, which is in the hill country of Ephraim, north of Mount Gaash.

31 Israel served the LORD all the days of Joshua, and all the days of the elders who outlived Joshua and had known all the work that the LORD did for Israel.

32 The bones of Joseph, which the Israelites had brought up from Egypt, were buried at Shechem, in the portion of ground that Jacob had bought from the children of Hamor, the father of Shechem, for one hundred pieces of money;*a* it became an inheritance of the descendants of Joseph.

33 Eleazar son of Aaron died; and they buried him at Gibeah, the town of his son Phinehas, which had been given him in the hill country of Ephraim.

a Heb *one hundred qesitah*

JUDGES

Israel's Failure to Complete the Conquest of Canaan

1 After the death of Joshua, the Israelites inquired of the LORD, 'Who shall go up first for us against the Canaanites, to fight against them?' ²The LORD said, 'Judah shall go up. I hereby give the land into his hand.' ³Judah said to his brother Simeon, 'Come up with me into the territory allotted to me, that we may fight against the Canaanites; then I too will go with you into the territory allotted to you.' So Simeon went with him. ⁴Then Judah went up and the LORD gave the Canaanites and the Perizzites into their hand; and they defeated ten thousand of them at Bezek. ⁵They came upon Adoni-bezek at Bezek, and fought against him, and defeated the Canaanites and the Perizzites. ⁶Adoni-bezek fled; but they pursued him, and caught him, and cut off his thumbs and big toes. ⁷Adoni-bezek said, 'Seventy kings with their thumbs and big toes cut off used to pick up scraps under my table; as I have done, so God has paid me back.' They brought him to Jerusalem, and he died there.

8 Then the people of Judah fought against Jerusalem and took it. They put it to the sword and set the city on fire. ⁹Afterwards the people of Judah went down to fight against the Canaanites who lived in the hill country, in the Negeb, and in the lowlands. ¹⁰Judah went against the Canaanites who lived in Hebron (the name of Hebron was formerly Kiriath-arba); and they defeated Sheshai and Ahiman and Talmai.

11 From there they went against the inhabitants of Debir (the name of Debir was formerly Kiriath-sepher). ¹²Then Caleb said, 'Whoever attacks Kiriath-sepher and takes it, I will give him my daughter Achsah as wife.' ¹³And Othniel son of Kenaz, Caleb's younger brother, took it; and he gave him his daughter Achsah as wife. ¹⁴When she came to him, she urged him to ask her father for a field. As she dismounted from her donkey, Caleb said to her, 'What do you want?' ¹⁵She said to him, 'Give me a present; since you have set me in the land of the Negeb, give me also Gulloth-mayim.'ᵃ So Caleb gave her Upper Gulloth and Lower Gulloth.

16 The descendants of Hobabᵇ the Kenite, Moses' father-in-law, went up with the people of Judah from the city of palms into the wilderness of Judah, which lies in the Negeb near Arad. Then they went and settled with the Amalekites.ᶜ ¹⁷Judah went with his brother Simeon, and they defeated the Canaanites who inhabited Zephath, and devoted it to destruction. So the city was called Hormah. ¹⁸Judah took Gaza with its territory, Ashkelon with its territory, and Ekron with its territory. ¹⁹The LORD was with Judah, and he took possession of the hill country, but could not drive out the inhabitants of the plain, because they had chariots of iron. ²⁰Hebron was given to Caleb, as Moses had said; and he drove out from it the three sons of Anak. ²¹But the Benjaminites did not drive out the Jebusites who lived in Jerusalem; so the Jebusites have lived in Jerusalem among the Benjaminites to this day.

22 The house of Joseph also went up against Bethel; and the LORD was with them. ²³The house of Joseph sent out spies

---

a That is *Basins of Water* *b* Gk: Heb lacks *Hobab*
c See 1 Sam 15.6: Heb *people*

to Bethel (the name of the city was formerly Luz). 24 When the spies saw a man coming out of the city, they said to him, 'Show us the way into the city, and we will deal kindly with you.' 25 So he showed them the way into the city; and they put the city to the sword, but they let the man and all his family go. 26 So the man went to the land of the Hittites and built a city, and named it Luz; that is its name to this day.

27 Manasseh did not drive out the inhabitants of Beth-shean and its villages, or Taanach and its villages, or the inhabitants of Dor and its villages, or the inhabitants of Ibleam and its villages, or the inhabitants of Megiddo and its villages; but the Canaanites continued to live in that land. 28 When Israel grew strong, they put the Canaanites to forced labour, but did not in fact drive them out.

29 And Ephraim did not drive out the Canaanites who lived in Gezer; but the Canaanites lived among them in Gezer.

30 Zebulun did not drive out the inhabitants of Kitron, or the inhabitants of Nahalol; but the Canaanites lived among them, and became subject to forced labour.

31 Asher did not drive out the inhabitants of Acco, or the inhabitants of Sidon, or of Ahlab, or of Achzib, or of Helbah, or of Aphik, or of Rehob; 32 but the Asherites lived among the Canaanites, the inhabitants of the land; for they did not drive them out.

33 Naphtali did not drive out the inhabitants of Beth-shemesh, or the inhabitants of Beth-anath, but lived among the Canaanites, the inhabitants of the land; nevertheless the inhabitants of Beth-shemesh and of Beth-anath became subject to forced labour for them.

34 The Amorites pressed the Danites back into the hill country; they did not allow them to come down to the plain. 35 The Amorites continued to live in Har-heres, in Aijalon, and in Shaalbim, but the hand of the house of Joseph rested heavily on them, and they became subject to forced labour. 36 The border of the Amorites ran from the ascent of Akrabbim, from Sela and upwards.

Israel's Disobedience

2 Now the angel of the LORD went up from Gilgal to Bochim, and said, 'I brought you up from Egypt, and brought you into the land that I had promised to your ancestors. I said, "I will never break my covenant with you. 2 For your part, do not make a covenant with the inhabitants of this land; tear down their altars." But you have not obeyed my command. See what you have done! 3 So now I say, I will not drive them out before you; but they shall become adversaries*a* to you, and their gods shall be a snare to you.' 4 When the angel of the LORD spoke these words to all the Israelites, the people lifted up their voices and wept. 5 So they named that place Bochim,*b* and there they sacrificed to the LORD.

Death of Joshua

6 When Joshua dismissed the people, the Israelites all went to their own inheritances to take possession of the land. 7 The people worshipped the LORD all the days of Joshua, and all the days of the elders who outlived Joshua, who had seen all the great work that the LORD had done for Israel. 8 Joshua son of Nun, the servant of the LORD, died at the age of one hundred and ten years. 9 So they buried him within the bounds of his inheritance in Timnath-heres, in the hill country of Ephraim, north of Mount Gaash. 10 Moreover, that whole generation was gathered to their ancestors, and another generation grew up after them, who did not know the LORD or the work that he had done for Israel.

Israel's Unfaithfulness

11 Then the Israelites did what was evil in the sight of the LORD and worshipped the Baals; 12 and they abandoned the LORD, the God of their ancestors, who had brought them out of the land of Egypt; they followed other gods, from among the gods of the peoples who were all around them, and bowed down to them; and they provoked the LORD to anger. 13 They abandoned the LORD, and worshipped Baal and

a OL Vg Compare Gk: Heb *sides*   *b* That is *Weepers*

the Astartes. 14 So the anger of the LORD was kindled against Israel, and he gave them over to plunderers who plundered them, and he sold them into the power of their enemies all around, so that they could no longer withstand their enemies. 15 Whenever they marched out, the hand of the LORD was against them to bring misfortune, as the LORD had warned them and sworn to them; and they were in great distress.

16 Then the LORD raised up judges, who delivered them out of the power of those who plundered them. 17 Yet they did not listen even to their judges; for they lusted after other gods and bowed down to them. They soon turned aside from the way in which their ancestors had walked, who had obeyed the commandments of the LORD; they did not follow their example. 18 Whenever the LORD raised up judges for them, the LORD was with the judge, and he delivered them from the hand of their enemies all the days of the judge; for the LORD would be moved to pity by their groaning because of those who persecuted and oppressed them. 19 But whenever the judge died, they would relapse and behave worse than their ancestors, following other gods, worshipping them and bowing down to them. They would not drop any of their practices or their stubborn ways. 20 So the anger of the LORD was kindled against Israel; and he said, 'Because this people have transgressed my covenant that I commanded their ancestors, and have not obeyed my voice, 21 I will no longer drive out before them any of the nations that Joshua left when he died.' 22 In order to test Israel, whether or not they would take care to walk in the way of the LORD as their ancestors did, 23 the LORD had left those nations, not driving them out at once, and had not handed them over to Joshua.

Nations Remaining in the Land

3 Now these are the nations that the LORD left to test all those in Israel who had no experience of any war in Canaan 2 (it was only that successive generations of Israelites might know war, to teach those who had no experience of it before): 3 the five lords of the Philistines, and all the Canaanites, and the Sidonians, and the Hivites who lived on Mount Lebanon, from Mount Baal-hermon as far as Lebo-hamath. 4 They were for the testing of Israel, to know whether Israel would obey the commandments of the LORD, which he commanded their ancestors by Moses. 5 So the Israelites lived among the Canaanites, the Hittites, the Amorites, the Perizzites, the Hivites, and the Jebusites; 6 and they took their daughters as wives for themselves, and their own daughters they gave to their sons; and they worshipped their gods.

Othniel

7 The Israelites did what was evil in the sight of the LORD, forgetting the LORD their God, and worshipping the Baals and the Asherahs. 8 Therefore the anger of the LORD was kindled against Israel, and he sold them into the hand of King Cushan-rishathaim of Aram-naharaim; and the Israelites served Cushan-rishathaim for eight years. 9 But when the Israelites cried out to the LORD, the LORD raised up a deliverer for the Israelites, who delivered them, Othniel son of Kenaz, Caleb's younger brother. 10 The spirit of the LORD came upon him, and he judged Israel; he went out to war, and the LORD gave King Cushan-rishathaim of Aram into his hand; and his hand prevailed over Cushan-rishathaim. 11 So the land had rest for forty years. Then Othniel son of Kenaz died.

Ehud

12 The Israelites again did what was evil in the sight of the LORD; and the LORD strengthened King Eglon of Moab against Israel, because they had done what was evil in the sight of the LORD. 13 In alliance with the Ammonites and the Amalekites, he went and defeated Israel; and they took possession of the city of palms. 14 So the Israelites served King Eglon of Moab for eighteen years.

15 But when the Israelites cried out to the LORD, the LORD raised up for them a deliverer, Ehud son of Gera, the Benjaminite,

a left-handed man. The Israelites sent tribute by him to King Eglon of Moab. [16] Ehud made for himself a sword with two edges, a cubit in length; and he fastened it on his right thigh under his clothes. [17] Then he presented the tribute to King Eglon of Moab. Now Eglon was a very fat man. [18] When Ehud had finished presenting the tribute, he sent the people who carried the tribute on their way. [19] But he himself turned back at the sculptured stones near Gilgal, and said, 'I have a secret message for you, O king.' So the king said, [a] 'Silence!' and all his attendants went out from his presence. [20] Ehud came to him, while he was sitting alone in his cool roof-chamber, and said, 'I have a message from God for you.' So he rose from his seat. [21] Then Ehud reached with his left hand, took the sword from his right thigh, and thrust it into Eglon's [b] belly; [22] the hilt also went in after the blade, and the fat closed over the blade, for he did not draw the sword out of his belly; and the dirt came out. [c] [23] Then Ehud went out into the vestibule, [d] and closed the doors of the roof-chamber on him, and locked them.

24 After he had gone, the servants came. When they saw that the doors of the roof-chamber were locked, they thought, 'He must be relieving himself [e] in the cool chamber.' [25] So they waited until they were embarrassed. When he still did not open the doors of the roof-chamber, they took the key and opened them. There was their lord lying dead on the floor.

26 Ehud escaped while they delayed, and passed beyond the sculptured stones, and escaped to Seirah. [27] When he arrived, he sounded the trumpet in the hill country of Ephraim; and the Israelites went down with him from the hill country, having him at their head. [28] He said to them, 'Follow after me; for the LORD has given your enemies the Moabites into your hand.' So they went down after him, and seized the fords of the Jordan against the Moabites, and allowed no one to cross over. [29] At that time they killed about ten thousand of the Moabites, all strong, able-bodied men; no one escaped. [30] So Moab was subdued that day under the hand of Israel. And the land had rest for eighty years.

Shamgar

31 After him came Shamgar son of Anath, who killed six hundred of the Philistines with an ox-goad. He too delivered Israel.

Deborah and Barak

4 The Israelites again did what was evil in the sight of the LORD, after Ehud died. [2] So the LORD sold them into the hand of King Jabin of Canaan, who reigned in Hazor; the commander of his army was Sisera, who lived in Harosheth-ha-goiim. [3] Then the Israelites cried out to the LORD for help; for he had nine hundred chariots of iron, and had oppressed the Israelites cruelly for twenty years.

4 At that time Deborah, a prophetess, wife of Lappidoth, was judging Israel. [5] She used to sit under the palm of Deborah between Ramah and Bethel in the hill country of Ephraim; and the Israelites came up to her for judgement. [6] She sent and summoned Barak son of Abinoam from Kedesh in Naphtali, and said to him, 'The LORD, the God of Israel, commands you, "Go, take position at Mount Tabor, bringing ten thousand from the tribe of Naphtali and the tribe of Zebulun. [7] I will draw out Sisera, the general of Jabin's army, to meet you by the Wadi Kishon with his chariots and his troops; and I will give him into your hand." ' [8] Barak said to her, 'If you will go with me, I will go; but if you will not go with me, I will not go.' [9] And she said, 'I will surely go with you; nevertheless, the road on which you are going will not lead to your glory, for the LORD will sell Sisera into the hand of a woman.' Then Deborah got up and went with Barak to Kedesh. [10] Barak summoned Zebulun and Naphtali to Kedesh; and ten thousand warriors went up behind him; and Deborah went up with him.

a Heb he said   b Heb his   c With Tg Vg: Meaning of Heb uncertain   d Meaning of Heb uncertain
e Heb covering his feet

11 Now Heber the Kenite had separated from the other Kenites,*a* that is, the descendants of Hobab the father-in-law of Moses, and had encamped as far away as Elon-bezaanannim, which is near Kedesh.

12 When Sisera was told that Barak son of Abinoam had gone up to Mount Tabor, 13 Sisera called out all his chariots, nine hundred chariots of iron, and all the troops who were with him, from Harosheth-ha-goiim to the Wadi Kishon. 14 Then Deborah said to Barak, 'Up! For this is the day on which the LORD has given Sisera into your hand. The LORD is indeed going out before you.' So Barak went down from Mount Tabor with ten thousand warriors following him. 15 And the LORD threw Sisera and all his chariots and all his army into a panic*b* before Barak; Sisera got down from his chariot and fled away on foot, 16 while Barak pursued the chariots and the army to Harosheth-ha-goiim. All the army of Sisera fell by the sword; no one was left.

17 Now Sisera had fled away on foot to the tent of Jael wife of Heber the Kenite; for there was peace between King Jabin of Hazor and the clan of Heber the Kenite. 18 Jael came out to meet Sisera, and said to him, 'Turn aside, my lord, turn aside to me; have no fear.' So he turned aside to her into the tent, and she covered him with a rug. 19 Then he said to her, 'Please give me a little water to drink; for I am thirsty.' So she opened a skin of milk and gave him a drink and covered him. 20 He said to her, 'Stand at the entrance of the tent, and if anybody comes and asks you, "Is anyone here?" say, "No." ' 21 But Jael wife of Heber took a tent-peg, and took a hammer in her hand, and went softly to him and drove the peg into his temple, until it went down into the ground—he was lying fast asleep from weariness—and he died. 22 Then, as Barak came in pursuit of Sisera, Jael went out to meet him, and said to him, 'Come, and I will show you the man whom you are seeking.' So he went into her tent; and there was Sisera lying dead, with the tent-peg in his temple.

23 So on that day God subdued King Jabin of Canaan before the Israelites. 24 Then the hand of the Israelites bore harder and harder on King Jabin of Canaan, until they destroyed King Jabin of Canaan.

The Song of Deborah

5 Then Deborah and Barak son of Abinoam sang on that day, saying:

2 'When locks are long in Israel,
    when the people offer themselves willingly—
  bless*c* the LORD!

3 'Hear, O kings; give ear, O princes;
    to the LORD I will sing,
  I will make melody to the LORD, the God of Israel.

4 'LORD, when you went out from Seir,
    when you marched from the region of Edom,
  the earth trembled,
    and the heavens poured,
    the clouds indeed poured water.
5 The mountains quaked before the LORD, the One of Sinai,
    before the LORD, the God of Israel.

6 'In the days of Shamgar son of Anath,
    in the days of Jael, caravans ceased
    and travellers kept to the byways.
7 The peasantry prospered in Israel,
    they grew fat on plunder,
  because you arose, Deborah,
    arose as a mother in Israel.
8 When new gods were chosen,
    then war was in the gates.
  Was shield or spear to be seen
    among forty thousand in Israel?
9 My heart goes out to the commanders of Israel
    who offered themselves willingly among the people.
  Bless the LORD.

10 'Tell of it, you who ride on white donkeys,
    you who sit on rich carpets,*d*
    and you who walk by the way.

a Heb *from the Kain*   *b* Heb adds *to the sword; compare verse 16*   *c* Or *You who offer yourselves willingly among the people, bless*   *d* Meaning of Heb uncertain

11 To the sound of musicians[a] at the
    watering-places,
      there they repeat the triumphs of
        the LORD,
      the triumphs of his peasantry in
        Israel.

    Then down to the gates marched the
      people of the LORD.

12 'Awake, awake, Deborah!
    Awake, awake, utter a song!
    Arise, Barak, lead away your captives,
    O son of Abinoam.
13 Then down marched the remnant of
    the noble;
    the people of the LORD marched
      down for him[b] against the
      mighty.
14 From Ephraim they set out[c] into the
    valley,[d]
    following you, Benjamin, with your
      kin;
    from Machir marched down the
      commanders,
    and from Zebulun those who bear
      the marshal's staff;
15 the chiefs of Issachar came with
    Deborah,
    and Issachar faithful to Barak;
    into the valley they rushed out at
      his heels.
    Among the clans of Reuben
      there were great searchings of heart.
16 Why did you tarry among the
    sheepfolds,
    to hear the piping for the flocks?
    Among the clans of Reuben
      there were great searchings of heart.
17 Gilead stayed beyond the Jordan;
    and Dan, why did he abide with
      the ships?
    Asher sat still at the coast of the sea,
    settling down by his landings.
18 Zebulun is a people that scorned
    death;
    Naphtali too, on the heights of the
      field.

19 The kings came, they fought;
    then fought the kings of Canaan,

    at Taanach, by the waters of Megiddo;
    they got no spoils of silver.
20 The stars fought from heaven,
    from their courses they fought
      against Sisera.
21 The torrent Kishon swept them away,
    the onrushing torrent, the torrent
      Kishon.
    March on, my soul, with might!

22 Then loud beat the horses' hoofs
    with the galloping, galloping of his
      steeds.

23 'Curse Meroz, says the angel of the
    LORD,
    curse bitterly its inhabitants,
    because they did not come to the
      help of the LORD,
    to the help of the LORD against the
      mighty.

24 'Most blessed of women be Jael,
    the wife of Heber the Kenite,
    of tent-dwelling women most
      blessed.
25 He asked water and she gave him
    milk,
    she brought him curds in a lordly
      bowl.
26 She put her hand to the tent-peg
    and her right hand to the
      workmen's mallet;
    she struck Sisera a blow,
    she crushed his head,
    she shattered and pierced his
      temple.
27 He sank, he fell,
    he lay still at her feet;
    at her feet he sank, he fell;
    where he sank, there he fell dead.

28 'Out of the window she peered,
    the mother of Sisera gazed[e]
      through the lattice:
    "Why is his chariot so long in
      coming?

---

a Meaning of Heb uncertain   b Gk: Heb me
c Cn: Heb From Ephraim their root   d Gk: Heb in
Amalek   e Gk Compare Tg: Heb exclaimed

Why tarry the hoofbeats of his
    chariots?"
29 Her wisest ladies make answer,
    indeed, she answers the question
      herself:
30 "Are they not finding and dividing
    the spoil?—
  A girl or two for every man;
  spoil of dyed stuffs for Sisera,
    spoil of dyed stuffs embroidered,
  two pieces of dyed work
      embroidered for my neck as
      spoil?"

31 'So perish all your enemies, O Lord!
  But may your friends be like the
    sun as it rises in its might.'

And the land had rest for forty years.

The Midianite Oppression

6 The Israelites did what was evil in the sight of the Lord, and the Lord gave them into the hand of Midian for seven years. 2 The hand of Midian prevailed over Israel; and because of Midian the Israelites provided for themselves hiding-places in the mountains, caves and strongholds. 3 For whenever the Israelites put in seed, the Midianites and the Amalekites and the people of the east would come up against them. 4 They would encamp against them and destroy the produce of the land, as far as the neighbourhood of Gaza, and leave no sustenance in Israel, and no sheep or ox or donkey. 5 For they and their livestock would come up, and they would even bring their tents, as thick as locusts; neither they nor their camels could be counted; so they wasted the land as they came in. 6 Thus Israel was greatly impoverished because of Midian; and the Israelites cried out to the Lord for help.

7 When the Israelites cried to the Lord on account of the Midianites, 8 the Lord sent a prophet to the Israelites; and he said to them, 'Thus says the Lord, the God of Israel: I led you up from Egypt, and brought you out of the house of slavery; 9 and I delivered you from the hand of the Egyptians, and from the hand of all who oppressed you, and drove them out before you, and gave you their land; 10 and I said to you, "I am the Lord your God; you shall not pay reverence to the gods of the Amorites, in whose land you live." But you have not given heed to my voice.'

The Calling of Gideon

11 Now the angel of the Lord came and sat under the oak at Ophrah, which belonged to Joash the Abiezrite, as his son Gideon was beating out wheat in the wine press, to hide it from the Midianites. 12 The angel of the Lord appeared to him and said to him, 'The Lord is with you, you mighty warrior.' 13 Gideon answered him, 'But sir, if the Lord is with us, why then has all this happened to us? And where are all his wonderful deeds that our ancestors recounted to us, saying, "Did not the Lord bring us up from Egypt?" But now the Lord has cast us off, and given us into the hand of Midian.' 14 Then the Lord turned to him and said, 'Go in this might of yours and deliver Israel from the hand of Midian; I hereby commission you.' 15 He responded, 'But sir, how can I deliver Israel? My clan is the weakest in Manasseh, and I am the least in my family.' 16 The Lord said to him, 'But I will be with you, and you shall strike down the Midianites, every one of them.' 17 Then he said to him, 'If now I have found favour with you, then show me a sign that it is you who speak with me. 18 Do not depart from here until I come to you, and bring out my present, and set it before you.' And he said, 'I will stay until you return.'

19 So Gideon went into his house and prepared a kid, and unleavened cakes from an ephah of flour; the meat he put in a basket, and the broth he put in a pot, and brought them to him under the oak and presented them. 20 The angel of God said to him, 'Take the meat and the unleavened cakes, and put them on this rock, and pour out the broth.' And he did so. 21 Then the angel of the Lord reached out the tip of the staff that was in his hand, and touched the meat and the unleavened cakes; and fire sprang up from the rock and consumed the meat and the unleavened cakes; and the

angel of the LORD vanished from his sight. 22 Then Gideon perceived that it was the angel of the LORD; and Gideon said, 'Help me, Lord GOD! For I have seen the angel of the LORD face to face.' 23 But the LORD said to him, 'Peace be to you; do not fear, you shall not die.' 24 Then Gideon built an altar there to the LORD, and called it, The LORD is peace. To this day it still stands at Ophrah, which belongs to the Abiezrites.

25 That night the LORD said to him, 'Take your father's bull, the second bull seven years old, and pull down the altar of Baal that belongs to your father, and cut down the sacred pole[a] that is beside it; 26 and build an altar to the LORD your God on the top of the stronghold here, in proper order; then take the second bull, and offer it as a burnt-offering with the wood of the sacred pole[a] that you shall cut down.' 27 So Gideon took ten of his servants, and did as the LORD had told him; but because he was too afraid of his family and the townspeople to do it by day, he did it by night.

Gideon Destroys the Altar of Baal

28 When the townspeople rose early in the morning, the altar of Baal was broken down, and the sacred pole[a] beside it was cut down, and the second bull was offered on the altar that had been built. 29 So they said to one another, 'Who has done this?' After searching and inquiring, they were told, 'Gideon son of Joash did it.' 30 Then the townspeople said to Joash, 'Bring out your son, so that he may die, for he has pulled down the altar of Baal and cut down the sacred pole[a] beside it.' 31 But Joash said to all who were arrayed against him, 'Will you contend for Baal? Or will you defend his cause? Whoever contends for him shall be put to death by morning. If he is a god, let him contend for himself, because his altar has been pulled down.' 32 Therefore on that day Gideon[b] was called Jerubbaal, that is to say, 'Let Baal contend against him', because he pulled down his altar.

33 Then all the Midianites and the Amalekites and the people of the east came together, and crossing the Jordan they en-

camped in the Valley of Jezreel. 34 But the spirit of the LORD took possession of Gideon; and he sounded the trumpet, and the Abiezrites were called out to follow him. 35 He sent messengers throughout all Manasseh, and they too were called out to follow him. He also sent messengers to Asher, Zebulun, and Naphtali, and they went up to meet them.

The Sign of the Fleece

36 Then Gideon said to God, 'In order to see whether you will deliver Israel by my hand, as you have said, 37 I am going to lay a fleece of wool on the threshing-floor; if there is dew on the fleece alone, and it is dry on all the ground, then I shall know that you will deliver Israel by my hand, as you have said.' 38 And it was so. When he rose early next morning and squeezed the fleece, he wrung enough dew from the fleece to fill a bowl with water. 39 Then Gideon said to God, 'Do not let your anger burn against me, let me speak one more time; let me, please, make trial with the fleece just once more; let it be dry only on the fleece, and on all the ground let there be dew.' 40 And God did so that night. It was dry on the fleece only, and on all the ground there was dew.

Gideon Surprises and Routs the Midianites

7 Then Jerubbaal (that is, Gideon) and all the troops that were with him rose early and encamped beside the spring of Harod; and the camp of Midian was north of them, below[c] the hill of Moreh, in the valley.

2 The LORD said to Gideon, 'The troops with you are too many for me to give the Midianites into their hand. Israel would only take the credit away from me, saying, "My own hand has delivered me." 3 Now therefore proclaim this in the hearing of the troops, "Whoever is fearful and trembling, let him return home." ' Thus Gideon sifted them out;[d] twenty-two thousand returned, and ten thousand remained.

a Heb Asherah   b Heb he   c Heb from   d Cn: Heb home, and depart from Mount Gilead" '

4 Then the LORD said to Gideon, 'The troops are still too many; take them down to the water and I will sift them out for you there. When I say, "This one shall go with you", he shall go with you; and when I say, "This one shall not go with you", he shall not go.' ⁵ So he brought the troops down to the water; and the LORD said to Gideon, 'All those who lap the water with their tongues, as a dog laps, you shall put to one side; all those who kneel down to drink, putting their hands to their mouths, *a* you shall put to the other side.' ⁶ The number of those that lapped was three hundred; but all the rest of the troops knelt down to drink water. ⁷ Then the LORD said to Gideon, 'With the three hundred that lapped I will deliver you, and give the Midianites into your hand. Let all the others go to their homes.' ⁸ So he took the jars of the troops from their hands, *b* and their trumpets; and he sent all the rest of Israel back to their own tents, but retained the three hundred. The camp of Midian was below him in the valley.

9 That same night the LORD said to him,

Battles of Gideon

Mediterranean Sea

Yarmuk R.

Endor
Ophrah
Megiddo
Herod
Beth-shan

Peniel
Succoth
Jogbehah
Rabbah

Bethel

- → Midianites
→ Gideon & his allies

0   10   20 Mi.
0 10   20   30 Km.

Dead Sea

'Get up, attack the camp; for I have given it into your hand.' ¹⁰ But if you fear to attack, go down to the camp with your servant Purah; ¹¹ and you shall hear what they say, and afterwards your hands shall be strengthened to attack the camp.' Then he went down with his servant Purah to the outposts of the armed men that were in the camp. ¹² The Midianites and the Amalekites and all the people of the east lay along the valley as thick as locusts; and their camels were without number, countless as the sand on the seashore. ¹³ When Gideon arrived, there was a man telling a dream to his comrade; and he said, 'I had a dream, and in it a cake of barley bread tumbled into the camp of Midian, and came to the tent, and struck it so that it fell; it turned upside down, and the tent collapsed.' ¹⁴ And his comrade answered, 'This is no other than the sword of Gideon son of Joash, a man of Israel; into his hand God has given Midian and all the army.'

15 When Gideon heard the telling of the dream and its interpretation, he worshipped; and he returned to the camp of Israel, and said, 'Get up; for the LORD has given the army of Midian into your hand.' ¹⁶ After he divided the three hundred men into three companies, and put trumpets into the hands of all of them, and empty jars, with torches inside the jars, ¹⁷ he said to them, 'Look at me, and do the same; when I come to the outskirts of the camp, do as I do. ¹⁸ When I blow the trumpet, I and all who are with me, then you also blow the trumpets around the whole camp, and shout, "For the LORD and for Gideon!" '

19 So Gideon and the hundred who were with him came to the outskirts of the camp at the beginning of the middle watch, when they had just set the watch; and they blew the trumpets and smashed the jars that were in their hands. ²⁰ So the three companies blew the trumpets and broke the jars, holding in their left hands the torches, and in their right hands the trumpets to blow; and they cried, 'A sword for

a Heb places the words *putting their hands to their mouths* after the word *lapped* in verse 6   *b* Cn: Heb *So the people took provisions in their hands* the LORD and for Gideon!' ²¹ Every man stood in his place all around the camp, and all the men in camp ran; they cried out and fled. ²² When they blew the three hundred trumpets, the LORD set every man's sword against his fellow and against all the army; and the army fled as far as Beth-shittah towards Zererah,ᵃ as far as the border of Abel-meholah, by Tabbath. ²³ And the men of Israel were called out from Naphtali and from Asher and from all Manasseh, and they pursued after the Midianites.

24 Then Gideon sent messengers throughout all the hill country of Ephraim, saying, 'Come down against the Midianites and seize the waters against them, as far as Beth-barah, and also the Jordan.' So all the men of Ephraim were called out, and they seized the waters as far as Beth-barah, and also the Jordan. ²⁵ They captured the two captains of Midian, Oreb and Zeeb; they killed Oreb at the rock of Oreb, and Zeeb they killed at the wine press of Zeeb, as they pursued the Midianites. They brought the heads of Oreb and Zeeb to Gideon beyond the Jordan.

Gideon's Triumph and Vengeance

8 Then the Ephraimites said to him, 'What have you done to us, not to call us when you went to fight against the Midianites?' And they upbraided him violently. ² So he said to them, 'What have I done now in comparison with you? Is not the gleaning of the grapes of Ephraim better than the vintage of Abiezer? ³ God has given into your hands the captains of Midian, Oreb and Zeeb; what have I been able to do in comparison with you?' When he said this, their anger against him subsided.

4 Then Gideon came to the Jordan and crossed over, he and the three hundred who were with him, exhausted and famished.ᵇ ⁵ So he said to the people of Succoth, 'Please give some loaves of bread to my followers, for they are exhausted, and I am pursuing Zebah and Zalmunna, the kings of Midian.' ⁶ But the officials of Succoth said, 'Do you already have in your possession the hands of Zebah and Zalmunna, that we should give bread to your army?' ⁷ Gideon

replied, 'Well then, when the LORD has given Zebah and Zalmunna into my hand, I will trample your flesh on the thorns of the wilderness and on briers.' ⁸ From there he went up to Penuel, and made the same request of them; and the people of Penuel answered him as the people of Succoth had answered. ⁹ So he said to the people of Penuel, 'When I come back victorious, I will break down this tower.'

10 Now Zebah and Zalmunna were in Karkor with their army, about fifteen thousand men, all who were left of all the army of the people of the east; for one hundred and twenty thousand men bearing arms had fallen. ¹¹ So Gideon went up by the caravan route east of Nobah and Jogbehah, and attacked the army; for the army was off its guard. ¹² Zebah and Zalmunna fled; and he pursued them and took the two kings of Midian, Zebah and Zalmunna, and threw all the army into a panic.

13 When Gideon son of Joash returned from the battle by the ascent of Heres, ¹⁴ he caught a young man, one of the people of Succoth, and questioned him; and he listed for him the officials and elders of Succoth, seventy-seven people. ¹⁵ Then he came to the people of Succoth, and said, 'Here are Zebah and Zalmunna, about whom you taunted me, saying, "Do you already have in your possession the hands of Zebah and Zalmunna, that we should give bread to your troops who are exhausted?" ' ¹⁶ So he took the elders of the city and he took thorns of the wilderness and briers and with them he trampledᶜ the people of Succoth. ¹⁷ He also broke down the tower of Penuel, and killed the men of the city.

18 Then he said to Zebah and Zalmunna, 'What about the men whom you killed at Tabor?' They answered, 'As you are, so were they, every one of them; they resembled the sons of a king.' ¹⁹ And he replied, 'They were my brothers, the sons of my mother; as the LORD lives, if you had saved them alive, I would not kill you.' ²⁰ So he said to Jether his firstborn, 'Go, kill them!'

---

a Another reading is *Zeredah*　　b Gk: Heb *pursuing*
c With verse 7, Compare Gk: Heb *he taught*

But the boy did not draw his sword, for he was afraid, because he was still a boy. ²¹Then Zebah and Zalmunna said, 'You come and kill us; for as the man is, so is his strength.' So Gideon proceeded to kill Zebah and Zalmunna; and he took the crescents that were on the necks of their camels.

Gideon's Idolatry

22 Then the Israelites said to Gideon, 'Rule over us, you and your son and your grandson also; for you have delivered us out of the hand of Midian.' ²³Gideon said to them, 'I will not rule over you, and my son will not rule over you; the LORD will rule over you.' ²⁴Then Gideon said to them, 'Let me make a request of you; each of you give me an ear-ring he has taken as booty.' (For the enemy*a* had golden earrings, because they were Ishmaelites.) ²⁵'We will willingly give them,' they answered. So they spread a garment, and each threw into it an ear-ring he had taken as booty. ²⁶The weight of the golden ear-rings that he requested was one thousand seven hundred shekels of gold (apart from the crescents and the pendants and the purple garments worn by the kings of Midian, and the collars that were on the necks of their camels). ²⁷Gideon made an ephod of it and put it in his town, in Ophrah; and all Israel prostituted themselves to it there, and it became a snare to Gideon and to his family. ²⁸So Midian was subdued before the Israelites, and they lifted up their heads no more. So the land had rest for forty years in the days of Gideon.

Death of Gideon

29 Jerubbaal son of Joash went to live in his own house. ³⁰Now Gideon had seventy sons, his own offspring, for he had many wives. ³¹His concubine who was in Shechem also bore him a son, and he named him Abimelech. ³²Then Gideon son of Joash died at a good old age, and was buried in the tomb of his father Joash at Ophrah of the Abiezrites.

33 As soon as Gideon died, the Israelites relapsed and prostituted themselves with the Baals, making Baal-berith their god. ³⁴The Israelites did not remember the LORD their God, who had rescued them from the hand of all their enemies on every side; ³⁵and they did not exhibit loyalty to the house of Jerubbaal (that is, Gideon) in return for all the good that he had done to Israel.

Abimelech Attempts to Establish a Monarchy

9 Now Abimelech son of Jerubbaal went to Shechem to his mother's kinsfolk and said to them and to the whole clan of his mother's family, ²'Say in the hearing of all the lords of Shechem, "Which is better for you, that all seventy of the sons of Jerubbaal rule over you, or that one rule over you?" Remember also that I am your bone and your flesh.' ³So his mother's kinsfolk spoke all these words on his behalf in the hearing of all the lords of Shechem; and their hearts inclined to follow Abimelech, for they said, 'He is our brother.' ⁴They gave him seventy pieces of silver out of the temple of Baal-berith with which Abimelech hired worthless and reckless fellows, who followed him. ⁵He went to his father's house at Ophrah, and killed his brothers the sons of Jerubbaal, seventy men, on one stone; but Jotham, the youngest son of Jerubbaal, survived, for he hid himself. ⁶Then all the lords of Shechem and all Beth-millo came together, and they went and made Abimelech king, by the oak of the pillar*b* at Shechem.

The Parable of the Trees

7 When it was told to Jotham, he went and stood on the top of Mount Gerizim, and cried aloud and said to them, 'Listen to me, you lords of Shechem, so that God may listen to you.

⁸ The trees once went out
   to anoint a king over themselves.
So they said to the olive tree,
   "Reign over us."
⁹ The olive tree answered them,
   "Shall I stop producing my rich oil

a Heb *they*   *b* Cn: Meaning of Heb uncertain

by which gods and mortals are
    honoured,
  and go to sway over the trees?"
10 Then the trees said to the fig tree,
  "You come and reign over us."
11 But the fig tree answered them,
  "Shall I stop producing my
    sweetness
  and my delicious fruit,
  and go to sway over the trees?"
12 Then the trees said to the vine,
  "You come and reign over us."
13 But the vine said to them,
  "Shall I stop producing my wine
    that cheers gods and mortals,
  and go to sway over the trees?"
14 So all the trees said to the bramble,
  "You come and reign over us."
15 And the bramble said to the trees,
  "If in good faith you are anointing
    me king over you,
  then come and take refuge in my
    shade;
  but if not, let fire come out of the
    bramble
  and devour the cedars of
    Lebanon."

16 'Now therefore, if you acted in good faith and honour when you made Abimelech king, and if you have dealt well with Jerubbaal and his house, and have done to him as his actions deserved— 17 for my father fought for you, and risked his life, and rescued you from the hand of Midian; 18 but you have risen up against my father's house this day, and have killed his sons, seventy men on one stone, and have made Abimelech, the son of his slave-woman, king over the lords of Shechem, because he is your kinsman— 19 if, I say, you have acted in good faith and honour towards Jerubbaal and towards his house this day, then rejoice in Abimelech, and let him also rejoice in you; 20 but if not, let fire come out from Abimelech, and devour the lords of Shechem, and Beth-millo; and let fire come out from the lords of Shechem, and from Beth-millo, and devour Abimelech.' 21 Then Jotham ran away and fled, going to Beer, where he remained for fear of his brother Abimelech.

The Downfall of Abimelech

22 Abimelech ruled over Israel for three years. 23 But God sent an evil spirit between Abimelech and the lords of Shechem; and the lords of Shechem dealt treacherously with Abimelech. 24 This happened so that the violence done to the seventy sons of Jerubbaal might be avenged[a] and their blood be laid on their brother Abimelech, who killed them, and on the lords of Shechem, who strengthened his hands to kill his brothers. 25 So, out of hostility to him, the lords of Shechem set ambushes on the mountain tops. They robbed all who passed by them along that way; and it was reported to Abimelech.

26 When Gaal son of Ebed moved into Shechem with his kinsfolk, the lords of Shechem put confidence in him. 27 They went out into the field and gathered the grapes from their vineyards, trod them, and celebrated. Then they went into the temple of their god, ate and drank, and ridiculed Abimelech. 28 Gaal son of Ebed said, 'Who is Abimelech, and who are we of Shechem, that we should serve him? Did not the son of Jerubbaal and Zebul his officer serve the men of Hamor father of Shechem? Why then should we serve him? 29 If only this people were under my command! Then I would remove Abimelech; I would say[b] to him, "Increase your army, and come out." '

30 When Zebul the ruler of the city heard the words of Gaal son of Ebed, his anger was kindled. 31 He sent messengers to Abimelech at Arumah,[c] saying, 'Look, Gaal son of Ebed and his kinsfolk have come to Shechem, and they are stirring up[d] the city against you. 32 Now therefore, go by night, you and the troops that are with you, and lie in wait in the fields. 33 Then early in the morning, as soon as the sun rises, get up and rush on the city; and when he and the troops that are with him come out against you, you may deal with them as best you can.'

34 So Abimelech and all the troops with him got up by night and lay in wait against

a Heb *might come*   b Gk: Heb *and he said*   c Cn See
9.41. Heb *Tormah*   d Cn: Heb *are besieging*

Shechem in four companies. ³⁵When Gaal son of Ebed went out and stood in the entrance of the gate of the city, Abimelech and the troops with him rose from the ambush. ³⁶And when Gaal saw them, he said to Zebul, 'Look, people are coming down from the mountain tops!' And Zebul said to him, 'The shadows on the mountains look like people to you.' ³⁷Gaal spoke again and said, 'Look, people are coming down from Tabbur-erez, and one company is coming from the direction of Elon-meonenim.'ᵃ ³⁸Then Zebul said to him, 'Where is your boastᵇ now, you who said, "Who is Abimelech, that we should serve him?" Are not these the troops you made light of? Go out now and fight with them.' ³⁹So Gaal went out at the head of the lords of Shechem, and fought with Abimelech. ⁴⁰Abimelech chased him, and he fled before him. Many fell wounded, up to the entrance of the gate. ⁴¹So Abimelech resided at Arumah; and Zebul drove out Gaal and his kinsfolk, so that they could not live on at Shechem.

42 On the following day the people went out into the fields. When Abimelech was told, ⁴³he took his troops and divided them into three companies, and lay in wait in the fields. When he looked and saw the people coming out of the city, he rose against them and killed them. ⁴⁴Abimelech and the company that wasᶜ with him rushed forward and stood at the entrance of the gate of the city, while the two companies rushed on all who were in the fields and killed them. ⁴⁵Abimelech fought against the city all that day; he took the city, and killed the people that were in it; and he razed the city and sowed it with salt.

46 When all the lords of the Tower of Shechem heard of it, they entered the stronghold of the temple of El-berith. ⁴⁷Abimelech was told that all the lords of the Tower of Shechem were gathered together. ⁴⁸So Abimelech went up to Mount Zalmon, he and all the troops that were with him. Abimelech took an axe in his hand, cut down a bundle of brushwood, and took it up and laid it on his shoulder.

Then he said to the troops with him, 'What you have seen me do, do quickly, as I have done.' ⁴⁹So every one of the troops cut down a bundle and following Abimelech put it against the stronghold, and they set the stronghold on fire over them, so that all the people of the Tower of Shechem also died, about a thousand men and women.

50 Then Abimelech went to Thebez, and encamped against Thebez, and took it. ⁵¹But there was a strong tower within the city, and all the men and women and all the lords of the city fled to it and shut themselves in; and they went to the roof of the tower. ⁵²Abimelech came to the tower, and fought against it, and came near to the entrance of the tower to burn it with fire. ⁵³But a certain woman threw an upper millstone on Abimelech's head, and crushed his skull. ⁵⁴Immediately he called to the young man who carried his armour and said to him, 'Draw your sword and kill me, so people will not say about me, "A woman killed him." ' So the young man thrust him through, and he died. ⁵⁵When the Israelites saw that Abimelech was dead, they all went home. ⁵⁶Thus God repaid Abimelech for the crime he committed against his father in killing his seventy brothers; ⁵⁷and God also made all the wickedness of the people of Shechem fall back on their heads, and on them came the curse of Jotham son of Jerubbaal.

Tola and Jair

10 After Abimelech, Tola son of Puah son of Dodo, a man of Issachar, who lived at Shamir in the hill country of Ephraim, rose to deliver Israel. ²He judged Israel for twenty-three years. Then he died, and was buried at Shamir.

3 After him came Jair the Gileadite, who judged Israel for twenty-two years. ⁴He had thirty sons who rode on thirty donkeys; and they had thirty towns, which are in the land of Gilead, and are called Havvoth-jair to this day. ⁵Jair died, and was buried in Kamon.

ᵃ That is *Diviners' Oak*   ᵇ Heb *mouth*   ᶜ Vg and some Gk Mss: Heb *companies that were*

Oppression by the Ammonites

6 The Israelites again did what was evil in the sight of the LORD, worshipping the Baals and the Astartes, the gods of Aram, the gods of Sidon, the gods of Moab, the gods of the Ammonites, and the gods of the Philistines. Thus they abandoned the LORD, and did not worship him. 7 So the anger of the LORD was kindled against Israel, and he sold them into the hand of the Philistines and into the hand of the Ammonites, 8 and they crushed and oppressed the Israelites that year. For eighteen years they oppressed all the Israelites that were beyond the Jordan in the land of the Amorites, which is in Gilead. 9 The Ammonites also crossed the Jordan to fight against Judah and against Benjamin and against the house of Ephraim; so that Israel was greatly distressed.

10 So the Israelites cried to the LORD, saying, 'We have sinned against you, because we have abandoned our God and have worshipped the Baals.' 11 And the LORD said to the Israelites, 'Did I not deliver you*a* from the Egyptians and from the Amorites, from the Ammonites and from the Philistines? 12 The Sidonians also, and the Amalekites, and the Maonites oppressed you; and you cried to me, and I delivered you out of their hand. 13 Yet you have abandoned me and worshipped other gods; therefore I will deliver you no more. 14 Go and cry to the gods whom you have chosen; let them deliver you in the time of your distress.' 15 And the Israelites said to the LORD, 'We have sinned; do to us whatever seems good to you; but deliver us this day!' 16 So they put away the foreign gods from among them and worshipped the LORD; and he could no longer bear to see Israel suffer.

17 Then the Ammonites were called to arms, and they encamped in Gilead; and the Israelites came together, and they encamped at Mizpah. 18 The commanders of the people of Gilead said to one another, 'Who will begin the fight against the Ammonites? He shall be head over all the inhabitants of Gilead.'

Jephthah

11 Now Jephthah the Gileadite, the son of a prostitute, was a mighty warrior. Gilead was the father of Jephthah. 2 Gilead's wife also bore him sons; and when his wife's sons grew up, they drove Jephthah away, saying to him, 'You shall not inherit anything in our father's house; for you are the son of another woman.' 3 Then Jephthah fled from his brothers and lived in the land of Tob. Outlaws collected around Jephthah and went raiding with him.

4 After a time the Ammonites made war against Israel. 5 And when the Ammonites made war against Israel, the elders of Gilead went to bring Jephthah from the land of Tob. 6 They said to Jephthah, 'Come and be our commander, so that we may fight with the Ammonites.' 7 But Jephthah said to the elders of Gilead, 'Are you not the very ones who rejected me and drove me out of my father's house? So why do you come to me now when you are in trouble?' 8 The elders of Gilead said to Jephthah, 'Nevertheless,

The Twelve Judges

Mediterranean Sea

ASHER
NAPHTALI
Shamgar
ZEBULUN
Elon
ISSACHAR
Ophrah •
Gideon
MANASSEH
• Kamon
Jair
MANASSEH
Tola • Shamir
Jephthah
• *Abdon*
Pirathon •
GAD
EPHRAIM
Deborah
Ehud
Samson BENJAMIN
DAN • Zorah
Ibzan
Bethlehem •
JUDAH
Dead Sea
REUBEN
Othniel • Debir?

Jair Names of Judges

0   20 Mi.
0   20 Km.

a Heb lacks *Did I not deliver you*

we have now turned back to you, so that you may go with us and fight with the Ammonites, and become head over us, over all the inhabitants of Gilead.' 9 Jephthah said to the elders of Gilead, 'If you bring me home again to fight with the Ammonites, and the LORD gives them over to me, I will be your head.' 10 And the elders of Gilead said to Jephthah, 'The LORD will be witness between us; we will surely do as you say.' 11 So Jephthah went with the elders of Gilead, and the people made him head and commander over them; and Jephthah spoke all his words before the LORD at Mizpah.

12 Then Jephthah sent messengers to the king of the Ammonites and said, 'What is there between you and me, that you have come to me to fight against my land?' 13 The king of the Ammonites answered the messengers of Jephthah, 'Because Israel, on coming from Egypt, took away my land from the Arnon to the Jabbok and to the Jordan; now therefore restore it peaceably.' 14 Once again Jephthah sent messengers to the king of the Ammonites 15 and said to him: 'Thus says Jephthah: Israel did not take away the land of Moab or the land of the Ammonites, 16 but when they came up from Egypt, Israel went through the wilderness to the Red Sea *a* and came to Kadesh. 17 Israel then sent messengers to the king of Edom, saying, "Let us pass through your land"; but the king of Edom would not listen. They also sent to the king of Moab, but he would not consent. So Israel remained at Kadesh. 18 Then they journeyed through the wilderness, went around the land of Edom and the land of Moab, arrived on the eastern side of the land of Moab, and camped on the other side of the Arnon. They did not enter the territory of Moab, for the Arnon was the boundary of Moab. 19 Israel then sent messengers to King Sihon of the Amorites, king of Heshbon; and Israel said to him, "Let us pass through your land to our country." 20 But Sihon did not trust Israel to pass through his territory; so Sihon gathered all his people together, and encamped at Jahaz, and fought with Israel. 21 Then the LORD, the God of Israel, gave Si-

hon and all his people into the hand of Israel, and they defeated them; so Israel occupied all the land of the Amorites, who inhabited that country. 22 They occupied all the territory of the Amorites from the Arnon to the Jabbok and from the wilderness to the Jordan. 23 So now the LORD, the God of Israel, has conquered the Amorites for the benefit of his people Israel. Do you intend to take their place? 24 Should you not possess what your god Chemosh gives you to possess? And should we not be the ones to possess everything that the LORD our God has conquered for our benefit? 25 Now are you any better than King Balak son of Zippor of Moab? Did he ever enter into conflict with Israel, or did he ever go to war with them? 26 While Israel lived in Heshbon and its villages, and in Aroer and its villages, and in all the towns that are along the Arnon, for three hundred years, why did you not recover them within that time? 27 It is not I who have sinned against you, but you are the one who does me wrong by making war on me. Let the LORD, who is judge, decide today for the Israelites or for the Ammonites.' 28 But the king of the Ammonites did not heed the message that Jephthah sent him.

Jephthah's Vow

29 Then the spirit of the LORD came upon Jephthah, and he passed through Gilead and Manasseh. He passed on to Mizpah of Gilead, and from Mizpah of Gilead he passed on to the Ammonites. 30 And Jephthah made a vow to the LORD, and said, 'If you will give the Ammonites into my hand, 31 then whoever comes out of the doors of my house to meet me, when I return victorious from the Ammonites, shall be the LORD's, to be offered up by me as a burnt-offering.' 32 So Jephthah crossed over to the Ammonites to fight against them; and the LORD gave them into his hand. 33 He inflicted a massive defeat on them from Aroer to the neighbourhood of Minnith, twenty towns, and as far as Abel-keramim. So the Ammonites were subdued before the people of Israel.

a Or Sea of Reeds

Jephthah's Daughter

34 Then Jephthah came to his home at Mizpah; and there was his daughter coming out to meet him with timbrels and with dancing. She was his only child; he had no son or daughter except her. 35 When he saw her, he tore his clothes, and said, 'Alas, my daughter! You have brought me very low; you have become the cause of great trouble to me. For I have opened my mouth to the LORD, and I cannot take back my vow.' 36 She said to him, 'My father, if you have opened your mouth to the LORD, do to me according to what has gone out of your mouth, now that the LORD has given you vengeance against your enemies, the Ammonites.' 37 And she said to her father, 'Let this thing be done for me: Grant me two months, so that I may go and wander[a] on the mountains, and bewail my virginity, my companions and I.' 38 'Go,' he said and sent her away for two months. So she departed, she and her companions, and bewailed her virginity on the mountains. 39 At the end of two months, she returned to her father, who did with her according to the vow he had made. She had never slept with a man. So there arose an Israelite custom that 40 for four days every year the daughters of Israel would go out to lament the daughter of Jephthah the Gileadite.

Intertribal Dissension

12 The men of Ephraim were called to arms, and they crossed to Zaphon and said to Jephthah, 'Why did you cross over to fight against the Ammonites, and did not call us to go with you? We will burn your house down over you!' 2 Jephthah said to them, 'My people and I were engaged in conflict with the Ammonites who oppressed us[b] severely. But when I called you, you did not deliver me from their hand. 3 When I saw that you would not deliver me, I took my life in my hand, and crossed over against the Ammonites, and the LORD gave them into my hand. Why then have you come up to me this day, to fight against me?' 4 Then Jephthah gathered all the men of Gilead and fought with Ephraim; and the men of Gilead defeated Ephraim, be-cause they said, 'You are fugitives from Ephraim, you Gileadites—in the heart of Ephraim and Manasseh.'[c] 5 Then the Gileadites took the fords of the Jordan against the Ephraimites. Whenever one of the fugitives of Ephraim said, 'Let me go over', the men of Gilead would say to him, 'Are you an Ephraimite?' When he said, 'No', 6 they said to him, 'Then say Shibboleth', and he said, 'Sibboleth', for he could not pronounce it right. Then they seized him and killed him at the fords of the Jordan. Forty-two thousand of the Ephraimites fell at that time.

7 Jephthah judged Israel for six years. Then Jephthah the Gileadite died, and was buried in his town in Gilead.[d]

Ibzan, Elon, and Abdon

8 After him Ibzan of Bethlehem judged Israel. 9 He had thirty sons. He gave his thirty daughters in marriage outside his clan and brought in thirty young women from outside for his sons. He judged Israel for seven years. 10 Then Ibzan died, and was buried at Bethlehem.

11 After him Elon the Zebulunite judged Israel; and he judged Israel for ten years. 12 Then Elon the Zebulunite died, and was buried at Aijalon in the land of Zebulun.

13 After him Abdon son of Hillel the Pirathonite judged Israel. 14 He had forty sons and thirty grandsons, who rode on seventy donkeys; he judged Israel for eight years. 15 Then Abdon son of Hillel the Pirathonite died, and was buried at Pirathon in the land of Ephraim, in the hill country of the Amalekites.

The Birth of Samson

13 The Israelites again did what was evil in the sight of the LORD, and the LORD gave them into the hand of the Philistines for forty years.

2 There was a certain man of Zorah, of the tribe of the Danites, whose name was Manoah. His wife was barren, having borne no children. 3 And the angel of the

a Cn: Heb go down   b Gk OL, Syr H: Heb lacks who oppressed us   c Meaning of Heb uncertain: Gk omits because . . . Manasseh   d Gk: Heb in the towns of Gilead

LORD appeared to the woman and said to her, 'Although you are barren, having borne no children, you shall conceive and bear a son. ⁴Now be careful not to drink wine or strong drink, or to eat anything unclean, ⁵for you shall conceive and bear a son. No razor is to come on his head, for the boy shall be a nazirite*ᵃ* to God from birth. It is he who shall begin to deliver Israel from the hand of the Philistines.' ⁶Then the woman came and told her husband, 'A man of God came to me, and his appearance was like that of an angel*ᵇ* of God, most awe-inspiring; I did not ask him where he came from, and he did not tell me his name; ⁷but he said to me, "You shall conceive and bear a son. So then drink no wine or strong drink, and eat nothing unclean, for the boy shall be a nazirite*ᵃ* to God from birth to the day of his death." '

8 Then Manoah entreated the LORD, and said, 'O LORD, I pray, let the man of God whom you sent come to us again and teach us what we are to do concerning the boy who will be born.' ⁹God listened to Manoah, and the angel of God came again to the woman as she sat in the field; but her husband Manoah was not with her. ¹⁰So the woman ran quickly and told her husband, 'The man who came to me the other day has appeared to me.' ¹¹Manoah got up and followed his wife, and came to the man and said to him, 'Are you the man who spoke to this woman?' And he said, 'I am.' ¹²Then Manoah said, 'Now when your words come true, what is to be the boy's rule of life; what is he to do?' ¹³The angel of the LORD said to Manoah, 'Let the woman give heed to all that I said to her. ¹⁴She may not eat of anything that comes from the vine. She is not to drink wine or strong drink, or eat any unclean thing. She is to observe everything that I commanded her.'

15 Manoah said to the angel of the LORD, 'Allow us to detain you, and prepare a kid for you.' ¹⁶The angel of the LORD said to Manoah, 'If you detain me, I will not eat your food; but if you want to prepare a burnt-offering, then offer it to the LORD.' (For Manoah did not know that he was the angel of the LORD.) ¹⁷Then Manoah said to the angel of the LORD, 'What is your name, so that we may honour you when your words come true?' ¹⁸But the angel of the LORD said to him, 'Why do you ask my name? It is too wonderful.'

19 So Manoah took the kid with the grain-offering, and offered it on the rock to the LORD, to him who works*ᶜ* wonders.*ᵈ* ²⁰When the flame went up towards heaven from the altar, the angel of the LORD ascended in the flame of the altar while Manoah and his wife looked on; and they fell on their faces to the ground. ²¹The angel of the LORD did not appear again to Manoah and his wife. Then Manoah realized that it was the angel of the LORD. ²²And Manoah said to his wife, 'We shall surely die, for we have seen God.' ²³But his wife said to him, 'If the LORD had meant to kill us, he would not have accepted a burnt-offering and a grain-offering at our hands, or shown us all

Five Cities of the Philistines

Mediterranean Sea

PHILISTIA

Ekron •

• Ashdod

• Gath

• Ashkelon

• Gaza

JUDAH

Dead Sea

N

0   40 Mi.
0   40 Km.

a That is *one separated* or *one consecrated*   *b* Or *the angel*   *c* Gk Vg: Heb *and working*   *d* Heb *wonders, while Manoah and his wife looked on* these things, or now announced to us such things as these.'

24 The woman bore a son, and named him Samson. The boy grew, and the LORD blessed him. 25 The spirit of the LORD began to stir him in Mahaneh-dan, between Zorah and Eshtaol.

Samson's Marriage

14 Once Samson went down to Timnah, and at Timnah he saw a Philistine woman. 2 Then he came up, and told his father and mother, 'I saw a Philistine woman at Timnah; now get her for me as my wife.' 3 But his father and mother said to him, 'Is there not a woman among your kin, or among all our*a* people, that you must go to take a wife from the uncircumcised Philistines?' But Samson said to his father, 'Get her for me, because she pleases me.' 4 His father and mother did not know that this was from the LORD; for he was seeking a pretext to act against the Philistines. At that time the Philistines had dominion over Israel.

5 Then Samson went down with his father and mother to Timnah. When he came to the vineyards of Timnah, suddenly a young lion roared at him. 6 The spirit of the LORD rushed on him, and he tore the lion apart with his bare hands as one might tear apart a kid. But he did not tell his father or his mother what he had done. 7 Then he went down and talked with the woman, and she pleased Samson. 8 After a while he returned to marry her, and he turned aside to see the carcass of the lion, and there was a swarm of bees in the body of the lion, and honey. 9 He scraped it out into his hands, and went on, eating as he went. When he came to his father and mother, he gave some to them, and they ate it. But he did not tell them that he had taken the honey from the carcass of the lion.

10 His father went down to the woman, and Samson made a feast there as the young men were accustomed to do. 11 When the people saw him, they brought thirty companions to be with him. 12 Samson said to them, 'Let me now put a riddle to you. If you can explain it to me within the seven

days of the feast, and find it out, then I will give you thirty linen garments and thirty festal garments. 13 But if you cannot explain it to me, then you shall give me thirty linen garments and thirty festal garments.' So they said to him, 'Ask your riddle; let us hear it.' 14 He said to them,

'Out of the eater came something to
    eat.
Out of the strong came something
    sweet.'

But for three days they could not explain the riddle.

15 On the fourth*b* day they said to Samson's wife, 'Coax your husband to explain the riddle to us, or we will burn you and your father's house with fire. Have you invited us here to impoverish us?' 16 So Samson's wife wept before him, saying, 'You hate me; you do not really love me. You have asked a riddle of my people, but you have not explained it to me.' He said to her, 'Look, I have not told my father or my mother. Why should I tell you?' 17 She wept before him for the seven days that their feast lasted; and because she nagged him, on the seventh day he told her. Then she explained the riddle to her people. 18 The men of the town said to him on the seventh day before the sun went down,

'What is sweeter than honey?
What is stronger than a lion?'

And he said to them,

'If you had not ploughed with my
    heifer,
you would not have found out my
    riddle.'

19 Then the spirit of the LORD rushed on him, and he went down to Ashkelon. He killed thirty men of the town, took their spoil, and gave the festal garments to those who had explained the riddle. In hot anger he went back to his father's house. 20 And Samson's wife was given to his companion, who had been his best man.

Samson Defeats the Philistines

15 After a while, at the time of the wheat harvest, Samson went to visit his wife, bringing along a kid. He said, 'I

a Cn: Heb *my*   *b* Gk Syr: Heb *seventh*

want to go into my wife's room.' But her father would not allow him to go in. ²Her father said, 'I was sure that you had rejected her; so I gave her to your companion. Is not her younger sister prettier than she? Why not take her instead?' ³Samson said to them, 'This time, when I do mischief to the Philistines, I will be without blame.' ⁴So Samson went and caught three hundred foxes, and took some torches; and he turned the foxesᵃ tail to tail, and put a torch between each pair of tails. ⁵When he had set fire to the torches, he let the foxes go into the standing grain of the Philistines, and burned up the shocks and the standing grain, as well as the vineyards andᵇ olive groves. ⁶Then the Philistines asked, 'Who has done this?' And they said, 'Samson, the son-in-law of the Timnite, because he has taken Samson's wife and given her to his companion.' So the Philistines came up, and burned her and her father. ⁷Samson said to them, 'If this is what you do, I swear I will not stop until I have taken revenge on you.' ⁸He struck them down hip and thigh with great slaughter; and he went down and lived in the cleft of the rock of Etam.

9 Then the Philistines came up and encamped in Judah, and made a raid on Lehi. ¹⁰The men of Judah said, 'Why have you come up against us?' They said, 'We have come up to bind Samson, to do to him as he did to us.' ¹¹Then three thousand men of Judah went down to the cleft of the rock of Etam, and they said to Samson, 'Do you not know that the Philistines are rulers over us? What then have you done to us?' He replied, 'As they did to me, so I have done to them.' ¹²They said to him, 'We have come down to bind you, so that we may give you into the hands of the Philistines.' Samson answered them, 'Swear to me that you yourselves will not attack me.' ¹³They said to him, 'No, we will only bind you and give you into their hands; we will not kill you.' So they bound him with two new ropes, and brought him up from the rock.

14 When he came to Lehi, the Philistines came shouting to meet him; and the spirit of the LORD rushed on him, and the ropes that were on his arms became like flax that

has caught fire, and his bonds melted off his hands. ¹⁵Then he found a fresh jawbone of a donkey, reached down and took it, and with it he killed a thousand men. ¹⁶And Samson said,

'With the jawbone of a donkey,
    heaps upon heaps,
with the jawbone of a donkey
    I have slain a thousand men.'

¹⁷When he had finished speaking, he threw away the jawbone; and that place was called Ramath-lehi.ᶜ

18 By then he was very thirsty, and he called on the LORD, saying, 'You have granted this great victory by the hand of your servant. Am I now to die of thirst, and fall into the hands of the uncircumcised?' ¹⁹So God split open the hollow place that is at Lehi, and water came from it. When he drank, his spirit returned, and he revived. Therefore it was named En-hakkore,ᵈ which is at Lehi to this day. ²⁰And he judged Israel in the days of the Philistines for twenty years.

Samson and Delilah

16 Once Samson went to Gaza, where he saw a prostitute and went in to her. ²The Gazites were told,ᵉ 'Samson has come here.' So they encircled the place and lay in wait for him all night at the city gate. They kept quiet all night, thinking, 'Let us wait until the light of the morning; then we will kill him.' ³But Samson lay only until midnight. Then at midnight he rose up, took hold of the doors of the city gate and the two posts, pulled them up, bar and all, put them on his shoulders, and carried them to the top of the hill that is in front of Hebron.

4 After this he fell in love with a woman in the valley of Sorek, whose name was Delilah. ⁵The lords of the Philistines came to her and said to her, 'Coax him, and find out what makes his strength so great, and how we may overpower him, so that we may bind him in order to subdue him; and we will each give you eleven hundred pieces of silver.' ⁶So Delilah said to Samson,

ᵃ Heb *them*   ᵇ Gk Tg Vg: Heb lacks *and*   ᶜ That is *The Hill of the Jawbone*   ᵈ That is *The Spring of the One who Called*   ᵉ Gk: Heb lacks *were told*

'Please tell me what makes your strength so great, and how you could be bound, so that one could subdue you.' ⁷ Samson said to her, 'If they bind me with seven fresh bowstrings that are not dried out, then I shall become weak, and be like anyone else.' ⁸ Then the lords of the Philistines brought her seven fresh bowstrings that had not dried out, and she bound him with them. ⁹ While men were lying in wait in an inner chamber, she said to him, 'The Philistines are upon you, Samson!' But he snapped the bowstrings, as a strand of fibre snaps when it touches the fire. So the secret of his strength was not known.

10 Then Delilah said to Samson, 'You have mocked me and told me lies; please tell me how you could be bound.' ¹¹ He said to her, 'If they bind me with new ropes that have not been used, then I shall become weak, and be like anyone else.' ¹² So Delilah took new ropes and bound him with them, and said to him, 'The Philistines are upon you, Samson!' (The men lying in wait were in an inner chamber.) But he snapped the ropes off his arms like a thread.

13 Then Delilah said to Samson, 'Until now you have mocked me and told me lies; tell me how you could be bound.' He said to her, 'If you weave the seven locks of my head with the web and make it tight with the pin, then I shall become weak, and be like anyone else.' ¹⁴ So while he slept, Delilah took the seven locks of his head and wove them into the web,ᵃ and made them tight with the pin. Then she said to him, 'The Philistines are upon you, Samson!' But he awoke from his sleep, and pulled away the pin, the loom, and the web.

15 Then she said to him, 'How can you say, "I love you", when your heart is not with me? You have mocked me three times now and have not told me what makes your strength so great.' ¹⁶ Finally, after she had nagged him with her words day after day, and pestered him, he was tired to death. ¹⁷ So he told her his whole secret, and said to her, 'A razor has never come upon my head; for I have been a naziriteᵇ to God

from my mother's womb. If my head were shaved, then my strength would leave me; I would become weak, and be like anyone else.'

18 When Delilah realized that he had told her his whole secret, she sent and called the lords of the Philistines, saying, 'This time come up, for he has told his whole secret to me.' Then the lords of the Philistines came up to her, and brought the money in their hands. ¹⁹ She let him fall asleep on her lap; and she called a man, and had him shave off the seven locks of his head. He began to weaken,ᶜ and his strength left him. ²⁰ Then she said, 'The Philistines are upon you, Samson!' When he awoke from his sleep, he thought, 'I will go out as at other times, and shake myself free.' But he did not know that the LORD had left him. ²¹ So the Philistines seized him and gouged out his eyes. They brought him down to Gaza and bound him with bronze shackles; and he ground at the mill in the prison. ²² But the hair of his head began to grow again after it had been shaved.

Samson's Death

23 Now the lords of the Philistines gathered to offer a great sacrifice to their god Dagon, and to rejoice; for they said, 'Our god has given Samson our enemy into our hand.' ²⁴ When the people saw him, they praised their god; for they said, 'Our god has given our enemy into our hand, the ravager of our country, who has killed many of us.' ²⁵ And when their hearts were merry, they said, 'Call Samson, and let him entertain us.' So they called Samson out of the prison, and he performed for them. They made him stand between the pillars; ²⁶ and Samson said to the attendant who held him by the hand, 'Let me feel the pillars on which the house rests, so that I may lean against them.' ²⁷ Now the house was full of men and women; all the lords of the Philistines were there; and on the roof there were about three thousand

a Compare Gk: in verses 13–14, Heb lacks *and make it tight . . . into the web*   b That is *one separated* or *one consecrated*   c Gk: Heb *She began to torment him* men and women, who looked on while Samson performed.

28 Then Samson called to the Lord and said, 'Lord God, remember me and strengthen me only this once, O God, so that with this one act of revenge I may pay back the Philistines for my two eyes.'[a] 29 And Samson grasped the two middle pillars on which the house rested, and he leaned his weight against them, his right hand on the one and his left hand on the other. 30 Then Samson said, 'Let me die with the Philistines.' He strained with all his might; and the house fell on the lords and all the people who were in it. So those he killed at his death were more than those he had killed during his life. 31 Then his brothers and all his family came down and took him and brought him up and buried him between Zorah and Eshtaol in the tomb of his father Manoah. He had judged Israel for twenty years.

Micah and the Levite

17 There was a man in the hill country of Ephraim whose name was Micah. 2 He said to his mother, 'The eleven hundred pieces of silver that were taken from you, about which you uttered a curse, and even spoke in my hearing—that silver is in my possession; I took it; but now I will return it to you.'[b] And his mother said, 'May my son be blessed by the Lord!' 3 Then he returned the eleven hundred pieces of silver to his mother; and his mother said, 'I consecrate the silver to the Lord from my hand for my son, to make an idol of cast metal.' 4 So when he returned the money to his mother, his mother took two hundred pieces of silver, and gave it to the silversmith, who made it into an idol of cast metal; and it was in the house of Micah. 5 This man Micah had a shrine, and he made an ephod and teraphim, and installed one of his sons, who became his priest. 6 In those days there was no king in Israel; all the people did what was right in their own eyes.

7 Now there was a young man of Bethlehem in Judah, of the clan of Judah. He was a Levite residing there. 8 This man left the town of Bethlehem in Judah, to live wherever he could find a place. He came to the house of Micah in the hill country of Ephraim to carry on his work.[c] 9 Micah said to him, 'From where do you come?' He replied, 'I am a Levite of Bethlehem in Judah, and I am going to live wherever I can find a place.' 10 Then Micah said to him, 'Stay with me, and be to me a father and a priest, and I will give you ten pieces of silver a year, a set of clothes, and your living.'[d] 11 The Levite agreed to stay with the man; and the young man became to him like one of his sons. 12 So Micah installed the Levite, and the young man became his priest, and was in the house of Micah. 13 Then Micah said, 'Now I know that the Lord will prosper me, because the Levite has become my priest.'

The Migration of Dan

18 In those days there was no king in Israel. And in those days the tribe of the Danites was seeking for itself a territory to live in; for until then no territory among the tribes of Israel had been allotted to them. 2 So the Danites sent five valiant men from the whole number of their clan, from Zorah and from Eshtaol, to spy out the land and to explore it; and they said to them, 'Go, explore the land.' When they came to the hill country of Ephraim, to the house of Micah, they stayed there. 3 While they were at Micah's house, they recognized the voice of the young Levite; so they went over and asked him, 'Who brought you here? What are you doing in this place? What is your business here?' 4 He said to them, 'Micah did such and such for me, and he hired me, and I have become his priest.' 5 Then they said to him, 'Inquire of God that we may know whether the mission we are undertaking will succeed.' 6 The priest replied, 'Go in peace. The mission you are on is under the eye of the Lord.'

7 The five men went on, and when they

---

a Or so that I may be avenged upon the Philistines for one of my two eyes   b The words but now I will return it to you are transposed from the end of verse 3 in Heb   c Or Ephraim, continuing his journey   d Heb living,' and the Levite went came to Laish, they observed the people who were there living securely, after the manner of the Sidonians, quiet and unsuspecting, lacking[a] nothing on earth, and possessing wealth.[b] Furthermore, they were far from the Sidonians and had no dealings with Aram.[c] 8 When they came to their kinsfolk at Zorah and Eshtaol, they said to them, 'What do you report?' 9 They said, 'Come, let us go up against them; for we have seen the land, and it is very good. Will you do nothing? Do not be slow to go, but enter in and possess the land. 10 When you go, you will come to an unsuspecting people. The land is broad—God has indeed given it into your hands—a place where there is no lack of anything on earth.'

11 Six hundred men of the Danite clan, armed with weapons of war, set out from Zorah and Eshtaol, 12 and went up and encamped at Kiriath-jearim in Judah. On this account that place is called Mahaneh-dan[d] to this day; it is west of Kiriath-jearim. 13 From there they passed on to the hill country of Ephraim, and came to the house of Micah.

14 Then the five men who had gone to spy out the land (that is, Laish) said to their comrades, 'Do you know that in these buildings there are an ephod, teraphim, and an idol of cast metal? Now therefore consider what you will do.' 15 So they turned in that direction and came to the house of the young Levite, at the home of Micah, and greeted him. 16 While the six hundred men of the Danites, armed with their weapons of war, stood by the entrance of the gate, 17 the five men who had gone to spy out the land proceeded to enter and take the idol of cast metal, the ephod, and the teraphim.[e] The priest was standing by the entrance of the gate with the six hundred men armed with weapons of war. 18 When the men went into Micah's house and took the idol of cast metal, the ephod, and the teraphim, the priest said to them, 'What are you doing?' 19 They said to him, 'Keep quiet! Put your hand over your mouth, and come with us, and be to us a father and a priest.

Is it better for you to be priest to the house of one person, or to be priest to a tribe and clan in Israel?' 20 Then the priest accepted the offer. He took the ephod, the teraphim, and the idol, and went along with the people.

21 So they resumed their journey, putting the little ones, the livestock, and the goods in front of them. 22 When they were some distance from the home of Micah, the men who were in the houses near Micah's house were called out, and they overtook the Danites. 23 They shouted to the Danites, who turned around and said to Micah, 'What is the matter that you come with such a company?' 24 He replied, 'You take my gods that I made, and the priest, and go away, and what have I left? How then can you ask me, "What is the matter?" ' 25 And the Danites said to him, 'You had better not let your voice be heard among us or else hot-tempered fellows will attack you, and you will lose your life and the lives of your household.' 26 Then the Danites went on their way. When Micah saw that they were too strong for him, he turned and went back to his home.

The Danites Settle in Laish

27 The Danites, having taken what Micah had made, and the priest who belonged to him, came to Laish, to a people quiet and unsuspecting, put them to the sword, and burned down the city. 28 There was no deliverer, because it was far from Sidon and they had no dealings with Aram.[f] It was in the valley that belongs to Beth-rehob. They rebuilt the city, and lived in it. 29 They named the city Dan, after their ancestor Dan, who was born to Israel; but the name of the city was formerly Laish. 30 Then the Danites set up the idol for themselves. Jonathan son of Gershom, son of Moses,[g] and his sons were priests to the tribe of the Danites until the time the land went into captivity. 31 So

a Cn Compare 18.10: Meaning of Heb uncertain
b Meaning of Heb uncertain   c Symmachus: Heb with anyone   d That is Camp of Dan   e Compare 17.4, 5; 18.14: Heb teraphim and the cast metal   f Cn Compare verse 7: Heb with anyone   g Another reading is son of Manasseh

they maintained as their own Micah's idol that he had made, as long as the house of God was at Shiloh.

The Levite's Concubine

19 In those days, when there was no king in Israel, a certain Levite, residing in the remote parts of the hill country of Ephraim, took to himself a concubine from Bethlehem in Judah. 2 But his concubine became angry with[a] him, and she went away from him to her father's house at Bethlehem in Judah, and was there for some four months. 3 Then her husband set out after her, to speak tenderly to her and bring her back. He had with him his servant and a couple of donkeys. When he reached[b] her father's house, the girl's father saw him and came with joy to meet him. 4 His father-in-law, the girl's father, made him stay, and he remained with him for three days; so they ate and drank, and he[c] stayed there. 5 On the fourth day they got up early in the morning, and he prepared to go; but the girl's father said to his son-in-law, 'Fortify yourself with a bit of food, and after that you may go.' 6 So the two men sat and ate and drank together; and the girl's father said to the man, 'Why not spend the night and enjoy yourself?' 7 When the man got up to go, his father-in-law kept urging him until he spent the night there again. 8 On the fifth day he got up early in the morning to leave; and the girl's father said, 'Fortify yourself.' So they lingered[d] until the day declined, and the two of them ate and drank.[e] 9 When the man with his concubine and his servant got up to leave, his father-in-law, the girl's father, said to him, 'Look, the day has worn on until it is almost evening. Spend the night. See, the day has drawn to a close. Spend the night here and enjoy yourself. Tomorrow you can get up early in the morning for your journey, and go home.'

10 But the man would not spend the night; he got up and departed, and arrived opposite Jebus (that is, Jerusalem). He had with him a couple of saddled donkeys, and his concubine was with him.

11 When they were near Jebus, the day was far spent, and the servant said to his master, 'Come now, let us turn aside to this city of the Jebusites, and spend the night in it.' 12 But his master said to him, 'We will not turn aside into a city of foreigners, who do not belong to the people of Israel; but we will continue on to Gibeah.' 13 Then he said to his servant, 'Come, let us try to reach one of these places, and spend the night at Gibeah or at Ramah.' 14 So they passed by and went on their way; and the sun went down on them near Gibeah, which belongs to Benjamin. 15 They turned aside there, to go in and spend the night at Gibeah. He went in and sat down in the open square of the city, but no one took them in to spend the night.

16 Then at evening there was an old man coming from his work in the field. The man was from the hill country of Ephraim, and he was residing in Gibeah. (The people of the place were Benjaminites.) 17 When the old man looked up and saw the wayfarer in the open square of the city, he said, 'Where are you going and where do you come from?' 18 He answered him, 'We are passing from Bethlehem in Judah to the remote parts of the hill country of Ephraim, from which I come. I went to Bethlehem in Judah; and I am going to my home.[f] Nobody has offered to take me in. 19 We your servants have straw and fodder for our donkeys, with bread and wine for me and the woman and the young man along with us. We need nothing more.' 20 The old man said, 'Peace be to you. I will care for all your wants; only do not spend the night in the square.' 21 So he brought him into his house, and fed the donkeys; they washed their feet, and ate and drank.

Gibeah's Crime

22 While they were enjoying themselves, the men of the city, a depraved lot, surrounded the house, and started pounding on the door. They said to the old man,

a Gk OL: Heb *prostituted herself against*   *b* Gk: Heb *she brought him to*   *c* Compare verse 7 and Gk: Heb *they*
d Cn: Heb *Linger*   *e* Gk: Heb lacks *and drank*
f Gk Compare 19.29. Heb *to the house of the* Lord

the master of the house, 'Bring out the man who came into your house, so that we may have intercourse with him.' 23 And the man, the master of the house, went out to them and said to them, 'No, my brothers, do not act so wickedly. Since this man is my guest, do not do this vile thing. 24 Here are my virgin daughter and his concubine; let me bring them out now. Ravish them and do whatever you want to them; but against this man do not do such a vile thing.' 25 But the men would not listen to him. So the man seized his concubine, and put her out to them. They wantonly raped her, and abused her all through the night until the morning. And as the dawn began to break, they let her go. 26 As morning appeared, the woman came and fell down at the door of the man's house where her master was, until it was light.

27 In the morning her master got up, opened the doors of the house, and when he went out to go on his way, there was his concubine lying at the door of the house, with her hands on the threshold. 28 'Get up,' he said to her, 'we are going.' But there was no answer. Then he put her on the donkey; and the man set out for his home. 29 When he had entered his house, he took a knife, and grasping his concubine he cut her into twelve pieces, limb by limb, and sent her throughout all the territory of Israel. 30 Then he commanded the men whom he sent, saying, 'Thus shall you say to all the Israelites, "Has such a thing ever happened[a] since the day that the Israelites came up from the land of Egypt until this day? Consider it, take counsel, and speak out." '

The Other Tribes Attack Benjamin

20 Then all the Israelites came out, from Dan to Beer-sheba, including the land of Gilead, and the congregation assembled in one body before the Lord at Mizpah. 2 The chiefs of all the people, of all the tribes of Israel, presented themselves in the assembly of the people of God, four hundred thousand foot-soldiers bearing arms. 3 (Now the Ben-

jaminites heard that the people of Israel had gone up to Mizpah.) And the Israelites said, 'Tell us, how did this criminal act come about?' 4 The Levite, the husband of the woman who was murdered, answered, 'I came to Gibeah that belongs to Benjamin, I and my concubine, to spend the night. 5 The lords of Gibeah rose up against me, and surrounded the house at night. They intended to kill me, and they raped my concubine until she died. 6 Then I took my concubine and cut her into pieces, and sent her throughout the whole extent of Israel's territory; for they have committed a vile outrage in Israel. 7 So now, you Israelites, all of you, give your advice and counsel here and now.'

8 All the people got up as one, saying, 'We will not any of us go to our tents, nor will any of us return to our houses. 9 But now this is what we will do to Gibeah: we will go up[b] against it by lot. 10 We will take ten men of a hundred throughout all the tribes of Israel, and a hundred of a thousand, and a thousand of ten thousand, to bring provisions for the troops, who are going to repay[c] Gibeah of Benjamin for all the disgrace that they have done in Israel.' 11 So all the men of Israel gathered against the city, united as one.

12 The tribes of Israel sent men through all the tribe of Benjamin, saying, 'What crime is this that has been committed among you? 13 Now then, hand over those scoundrels in Gibeah, so that we may put them to death, and purge the evil from Israel.' But the Benjaminites would not listen to their kinsfolk, the Israelites. 14 The Benjaminites came together out of the towns to Gibeah, to go out to battle against the Israelites. 15 On that day the Benjaminites mustered twenty-six thousand armed men from their towns, besides the inhabitants of Gibeah. 16 Of all this force, there were seven hundred picked men who were left-handed; every one could sling a stone at a hair, and not miss. 17 And the Israelites, apart from Benjamin, mustered

a Compare Gk: Heb 30And all who saw it said, 'Such a thing has not happened or been seen   b Gk: Heb lacks we will go up   c Compare Gk: Meaning of Heb uncertain four hundred thousand armed men, all of them warriors.

18 The Israelites proceeded to go up to Bethel, where they inquired of God, 'Which of us shall go up first to battle against the Benjaminites?' And the LORD answered, 'Judah shall go up first.'

19 Then the Israelites got up in the morning, and encamped against Gibeah. 20The Israelites went out to battle against Benjamin; and the Israelites drew up the battle line against them at Gibeah. 21The Benjaminites came out of Gibeah, and struck down on that day twenty-two thousand of the Israelites. 23ᵃThe Israelites went up and wept before the LORD until the evening; and they inquired of the LORD, 'Shall we again draw near to battle against our kinsfolk the Benjaminites?' And the LORD said, 'Go up against them.' 22The Israelites took courage, and again formed the battle line in the same place where they had formed it on the first day.

24 So the Israelites advanced against the Benjaminites on the second day. 25Benjamin moved out against them from Gibeah the second day, and struck down eighteen thousand of the Israelites, all of them armed men. 26Then all the Israelites, the whole army, went back to Bethel and wept, sitting there before the LORD; they fasted that day until evening. Then they offered burnt-offerings and sacrifices of well-being before the LORD. 27And the Israelites inquired of the LORD (for the ark of the covenant of God was there in those days, 28and Phinehas son of Eleazar, son of Aaron, ministered before it in those days), saying, 'Shall we go out once more to battle against our kinsfolk the Benjaminites, or shall we desist?' The LORD answered, 'Go up, for tomorrow I will give them into your hand.'

29 So Israel stationed men in ambush around Gibeah. 30Then the Israelites went up against the Benjaminites on the third day, and set themselves in array against Gibeah, as before. 31When the Benjaminites went out against the army, they were drawn away from the city. As before they began to inflict casualties on the troops, along the main roads, one of which goes up to Bethel and the other to Gibeah, as well as in the open country, killing about thirty men of Israel. 32The Benjaminites thought, 'They are being routed before us, as previously.' But the Israelites said, 'Let us retreat and draw them away from the city towards the roads.' 33The main body of the Israelites drew back its battle line to Baal-tamar, while those Israelites who were in ambush rushed out of their place westᵇ of Geba. 34There came against Gibeah ten thousand picked men out of all Israel, and the battle was fierce. But the Benjaminites did not realize that disaster was close upon them.

35 The LORD defeated Benjamin before Israel; and the Israelites destroyed twenty-five thousand one hundred men of Benjamin that day, all of them armed.

36 Then the Benjaminites saw that they were defeated.ᶜ

The Israelites gave ground to Benjamin, because they trusted to the troops in ambush that they had stationed against Gibeah. 37The troops in ambush rushed quickly upon Gibeah. Then they put the whole city to the sword. 38Now the agreement between the main body of Israel and the men in ambush was that when they sent up a cloud of smoke out of the city 39the main body of Israel should turn in battle. But Benjamin had begun to inflict casualties on the Israelites, killing about thirty of them; so they thought, 'Surely they are defeated before us, as in the first battle.' 40But when the cloud, a column of smoke, began to rise out of the city, the Benjaminites looked behind them—and there was the whole city going up in smoke towards the sky! 41Then the main body of Israel turned, and the Benjaminites were dismayed, for they saw that disaster was close upon them. 42Therefore they turned away from the Israelites in the direction of the wilderness; but the battle overtook them, and those who came out of the cityᵈ were slaughtering them in between.ᵉ 43Cutting

a Verses 22 and 23 are transposed   b Gk Vg: Heb *in the plain*   c This sentence is continued by verse 45.
d Compare Vg and some Gk Mss: Heb *cities*
e Compare Syr: Meaning of Heb uncertain

down[a] the Benjaminites, they pursued them from Nohah[b] and trod them down as far as a place east of Gibeah. 44 Eighteen thousand Benjaminites fell, all of them courageous fighters. 45 When they turned and fled towards the wilderness to the rock of Rimmon, five thousand of them were cut down on the main roads, and they were pursued as far as Gidom, and two thousand of them were slain. 46 So all who fell that day of Benjamin were twenty-five thousand arms-bearing men, all of them courageous fighters. 47 But six hundred turned and fled towards the wilderness to the rock of Rimmon, and remained at the rock of Rimmon for four months. 48 Meanwhile, the Israelites turned back against the Benjaminites, and put them to the sword—the city, the people, the animals, and all that remained. Also the remaining towns they set on fire.

The Benjaminites Saved from Extinction

21 Now the Israelites had sworn at Mizpah, 'No one of us shall give his daughter in marriage to Benjamin.' 2 And the people came to Bethel, and sat there until evening before God, and they lifted up their voices and wept bitterly. 3 They said, 'O LORD, the God of Israel, why has it come to pass that today there should be one tribe lacking in Israel?' 4 On the next day, the people got up early, and built an altar there, and offered burnt-offerings and sacrifices of well-being. 5 Then the Israelites said, 'Which of all the tribes of Israel did not come up in the assembly to the LORD?' For a solemn oath had been taken concerning whoever did not come up to the LORD to Mizpah, saying, 'That one shall be put to death.' 6 But the Israelites had compassion for Benjamin their kin, and said, 'One tribe is cut off from Israel this day. 7 What shall we do for wives for those who are left, since we have sworn by the LORD that we will not give them any of our daughters as wives?'

8 Then they said, 'Is there anyone from the tribes of Israel who did not come up to the LORD to Mizpah?' It turned out that no one from Jabesh-gilead had come to the

camp, to the assembly. 9 For when the roll was called among the people, not one of the inhabitants of Jabesh-gilead was there. 10 So the congregation sent twelve thousand soldiers there and commanded them, 'Go, put the inhabitants of Jabesh-gilead to the sword, including the women and the little ones. 11 This is what you shall do; every male and every woman that has lain with a male you shall devote to destruction.' 12 And they found among the inhabitants of Jabesh-gilead four hundred young virgins who had never slept with a man and brought them to the camp at Shiloh, which is in the land of Canaan.

13 Then the whole congregation sent word to the Benjaminites who were at the rock of Rimmon, and proclaimed peace to them. 14 Benjamin returned at that time; and they gave them the women whom they had saved alive of the women of Jabesh-gilead; but they did not suffice for them.

15 The people had compassion on Benjamin because the LORD had made a breach in the tribes of Israel. 16 So the elders of the congregation said, 'What shall we do for wives for those who are left, since there are no women left in Benjamin?' 17 And they said, 'There must be heirs for the survivors of Benjamin, in order that a tribe may not be blotted out from Israel. 18 Yet we cannot give any of our daughters to them as wives.' For the Israelites had sworn, 'Cursed be anyone who gives a wife to Benjamin.' 19 So they said, 'Look, the yearly festival of the LORD is taking place at Shiloh, which is north of Bethel, on the east of the highway that goes up from Bethel to Shechem, and south of Lebonah.' 20 And they instructed the Benjaminites, saying, 'Go and lie in wait in the vineyards, 21 and watch; when the young women of Shiloh come out to dance in the dances, then come out of the vineyards and each of you carry off a wife for himself from the young women of Shiloh, and go to the land of Benjamin. 22 Then if their fathers or their brothers come to complain to

---

a Gk: Heb *Surrounding*   b Gk: Heb *pursued them at their resting-place* us, we will say to them, "Be generous and allow us to have them; because we did not capture in battle a wife for each man. But neither did you incur guilt by giving your daughters to them." ' ²³The Benjaminites did so; they took wives for each of them from the dancers whom they abducted. Then they went and returned to their ter-ritory, and rebuilt the towns, and lived in them. ²⁴So the Israelites departed from there at that time by tribes and families, and they went out from there to their own territories.

25 In those days there was no king in Israel; all the people did what was right in their own eyes.

RUTH

Elimelech's Family Goes to Moab

1 In the days when the judges ruled, there was a famine in the land, and a certain man of Bethlehem in Judah went to live in the country of Moab, he and his wife and two sons. 2 The name of the man was Elimelech and the name of his wife Naomi, and the names of his two sons were Mahlon and Chilion; they were Ephrathites from Bethlehem in Judah. They went into the country of Moab and remained there. 3 But Elimelech, the husband of Naomi, died, and she was left with her two sons. 4 These took Moabite wives; the name of one was Orpah and the name of the other Ruth. When they had lived there for about ten years, 5 both Mahlon and Chilion also died, so that the woman was left without her two sons or her husband.

Naomi and Her Moabite Daughters-in-Law

6 Then she started to return with her daughters-in-law from the country of Moab, for she had heard in the country of Moab that the Lord had had consideration for his people and given them food. 7 So she set out from the place where she had been living, she and her two daughters-in-law, and they went on their way to go back to the land of Judah. 8 But Naomi said to her two daughters-in-law, 'Go back each of you to your mother's house. May the Lord deal kindly with you, as you have dealt with the dead and with me. 9 The Lord grant that you may find security, each of you in the house of your husband.' Then she kissed them, and they wept aloud. 10 They said to her, 'No, we will return with you to your people.' 11 But Naomi said, 'Turn back, my daughters, why will you go with me? Do I still have sons in my womb that they may become your husbands? 12 Turn back, my daughters, go your way, for I am too old to have a husband. Even if I thought there was hope for me, even if I should have a husband tonight and bear sons, 13 would you then wait until they were grown? Would you then refrain from marrying? No, my daughters, it has been far more bitter for me than for you, because the hand of the Lord has turned against me.' 14 Then they wept aloud again. Orpah kissed her mother-in-law, but Ruth clung to her.

15 So she said, 'See, your sister-in-law has gone back to her people and to her gods; return after your sister-in-law.' 16 But Ruth said,

'Do not press me to leave you
	or to turn back from following
		you!
Where you go, I will go;
	where you lodge, I will lodge;
your people shall be my people,
	and your God my God.
17 Where you die, I will die—
	there will I be buried.
May the Lord do thus and so to me,
	and more as well,
if even death parts me from you!'

18 When Naomi saw that she was determined to go with her, she said no more to her.

19 So the two of them went on until they came to Bethlehem. When they came to Bethlehem, the whole town was stirred because of them; and the women said, 'Is this Naomi?' 20 She said to them,

'Call me no longer Naomi,*a*
    call me Mara,*b*
    for the Almighty*c* has dealt bitterly
        with me.
21 I went away full,
    but the LORD has brought me back
        empty;
    why call me Naomi
        when the LORD has dealt harshly
        with*d* me,
    and the Almighty*c* has brought
        calamity upon me?'

22 So Naomi returned together with Ruth the Moabite, her daughter-in-law, who came back with her from the country of Moab. They came to Bethlehem at the beginning of the barley harvest.

Ruth Meets Boaz

2 Now Naomi had a kinsman on her husband's side, a prominent rich man, of the family of Elimelech, whose name was Boaz. 2 And Ruth the Moabite said to Naomi, 'Let me go to the field and glean among the ears of grain, behind someone in whose sight I may find favour.' She said to her, 'Go, my daughter.' 3 So she went. She came and gleaned in the field behind the reapers. As it happened, she came to the part of the field belonging to Boaz, who was of the family of Elimelech. 4 Just then Boaz came from Bethlehem. He said to the reapers, 'The LORD be with you.' They answered, 'The LORD bless you.' 5 Then Boaz said to his servant who was in charge of the reapers, 'To whom does this young woman belong?' 6 The servant who was in charge of the reapers answered, 'She is the Moabite who came back with Naomi from the country of Moab. 7 She said, "Please let me glean and gather among the sheaves behind the reapers." So she came, and she has been on her feet from early this morning until now, without resting even for a moment.'*e*

8 Then Boaz said to Ruth, 'Now listen, my daughter, do not go to glean in another field or leave this one, but keep close to my young women. 9 Keep your eyes on the field that is being reaped, and follow behind them. I have ordered the young men not to bother you. If you get thirsty, go to the vessels and drink from what the young men have drawn.' 10 Then she fell prostrate, with her face to the ground, and said to him, 'Why have I found favour in your sight, that you should take notice of me, when I am a foreigner?' 11 But Boaz answered her, 'All that you have done for your mother-in-law since the death of your husband has been fully told me, and how you left your father and mother and your native land and came to a people that you did not know before. 12 May the LORD reward you for your deeds, and may you have a full reward from the LORD, the God of Israel, under whose wings you have come for refuge!' 13 Then she said, 'May I continue to find favour in your sight, my lord, for you have comforted me and spoken kindly to your servant, even though I am not one of your servants.'

14 At mealtime Boaz said to her, 'Come here, and eat some of this bread, and dip

The Book of Ruth

0   30 Mi.
0   30 Km.

N

Jebus   Jericho •
(Jerusalem) •   Heshbon
                        •
Bethlehem•   • Medeba
(Ephrathah)
            Dead   REUBEN
            Sea
JUDAH   Dibon
                    •
                Aroer

        MOAB
            •
        Kir-hareseth

a That is *Pleasant*   *b* That is *Bitter*   *c* Traditional rendering of Heb *Shaddai*   *d* Or *has testified against*   *e* Compare Gk Vg: Meaning of Heb uncertain your morsel in the sour wine.' So she sat beside the reapers, and he heaped up for her some parched grain. She ate until she was satisfied, and she had some left over. [15] When she got up to glean, Boaz instructed his young men, 'Let her glean even among the standing sheaves, and do not reproach her. [16] You must also pull out some handfuls for her from the bundles, and leave them for her to glean, and do not rebuke her.'

17 So she gleaned in the field until evening. Then she beat out what she had gleaned, and it was about an ephah of barley. [18] She picked it up and came into the town, and her mother-in-law saw how much she had gleaned. Then she took out and gave her what was left over after she herself had been satisfied. [19] Her mother-in-law said to her, 'Where did you glean today? And where have you worked? Blessed be the man who took notice of you.' So she told her mother-in-law with whom she had worked, and said, 'The name of the man with whom I worked today is Boaz.' [20] Then Naomi said to her daughter-in-law, 'Blessed be he by the Lord, whose kindness has not forsaken the living or the dead!' Naomi also said to her, 'The man is a relative of ours, one of our nearest kin.'[a] [21] Then Ruth the Moabite said, 'He even said to me, "Stay close by my servants, until they have finished all my harvest." ' [22] Naomi said to Ruth, her daughter-in-law, 'It is better, my daughter, that you go out with his young women, otherwise you might be bothered in another field.' [23] So she stayed close to the young women of Boaz, gleaning until the end of the barley and wheat harvests; and she lived with her mother-in-law.

Ruth and Boaz at the Threshing-Floor

3 Naomi her mother-in-law said to her, 'My daughter, I need to seek some security for you, so that it may be well with you. [2] Now here is our kinsman Boaz, with whose young women you have been working. See, he is winnowing barley tonight at the threshing-floor. [3] Now wash and anoint yourself, and put on your best clothes and go down to the threshing-floor; but do not make yourself known to the man until he has finished eating and drinking. [4] When he lies down, observe the place where he lies; then, go and uncover his feet and lie down; and he will tell you what to do.' [5] She said to her, 'All that you tell me I will do.'

6 So she went down to the threshing-floor and did just as her mother-in-law had instructed her. [7] When Boaz had eaten and drunk, and he was in a contented mood, he went to lie down at the end of the heap of grain. Then she came quietly and uncovered his feet, and lay down. [8] At midnight the man was startled and turned over, and there, lying at his feet, was a woman! [9] He said, 'Who are you?' And she answered, 'I am Ruth, your servant; spread your cloak over your servant, for you are next-of-kin.'[a] [10] He said, 'May you be blessed by the Lord, my daughter; this last instance of your loyalty is better than the first; you have not gone after young men, whether poor or rich. [11] And now, my daughter, do not be afraid; I will do for you all that you ask, for all the assembly of my people know that you are a worthy woman. [12] But now, though it is true that I am a near kinsman, there is another kinsman more closely related than I. [13] Remain this night, and in the morning, if he will act as next-of-kin[a] for you, good; let him do so. If he is not willing to act as next-of-kin[a] for you, then, as the Lord lives, I will act as next-of-kin[a] for you. Lie down until the morning.'

14 So she lay at his feet until morning, but got up before one person could recognize another; for he said, 'It must not be known that the woman came to the threshing-floor.' [15] Then he said, 'Bring the cloak you are wearing and hold it out.' So she held it, and he measured out six measures of barley, and put it on her back; then he went into the city. [16] She came to her mother-in-law, who said, 'How did things go with you,[b] my daughter?' Then she told her all that the man had done for her, [17] saying, 'He gave me these six measures of barley, for he said, "Do not go back to your mother-in-law empty-handed." ' [18] She replied, 'Wait, my daughter, until you learn how the

a Or one with the right to redeem   b Or 'Who are you,

matter turns out, for the man will not rest, but will settle the matter today.'

The Marriage of Boaz and Ruth

4 No sooner had Boaz gone up to the gate and sat down there than the next-of-kin,*a* of whom Boaz had spoken, came passing by. So Boaz said, 'Come over, friend; sit down here.' And he went over and sat down. 2 Then Boaz took ten men of the elders of the city, and said, 'Sit down here'; so they sat down. 3 He then said to the next-of-kin,*a* 'Naomi, who has come back from the country of Moab, is selling the parcel of land that belonged to our kinsman Elimelech. 4 So I thought I would tell you of it, and say: Buy it in the presence of those sitting here, and in the presence of the elders of my people. If you will redeem it, redeem it; but if you will not, tell me, so that I may know; for there is no one prior to you to redeem it, and I come after you.' So he said, 'I will redeem it.' 5 Then Boaz said, 'The day you acquire the field from the hand of Naomi, you are also acquiring Ruth*b* the Moabite, the widow of the dead man, to maintain the dead man's name on his inheritance.' 6 At this, the next-of-kin*a* said, 'I cannot redeem it for myself without damaging my own inheritance. Take my right of redemption yourself, for I cannot redeem it.'

7 Now this was the custom in former times in Israel concerning redeeming and exchanging: to confirm a transaction, one party took off a sandal and gave it to the other; this was the manner of attesting in Israel. 8 So when the next-of-kin*a* said to Boaz, 'Acquire it for yourself', he took off his sandal. 9 Then Boaz said to the elders and all the people, 'Today you are witnesses that I have acquired from the hand of Naomi all that belonged to Elimelech and all that belonged to Chilion and Mahlon. 10 I

have also acquired Ruth the Moabite, the wife of Mahlon, to be my wife, to maintain the dead man's name on his inheritance, in order that the name of the dead may not be cut off from his kindred and from the gate of his native place; today you are witnesses.' 11 Then all the people who were at the gate, along with the elders, said, 'We are witnesses. May the LORD make the woman who is coming into your house like Rachel and Leah, who together built up the house of Israel. May you produce children in Ephrathah and bestow a name in Bethlehem; 12 and, through the children that the LORD will give you by this young woman, may your house be like the house of Perez, whom Tamar bore to Judah.'

The Genealogy of David

13 So Boaz took Ruth and she became his wife. When they came together, the LORD made her conceive, and she bore a son. 14 Then the women said to Naomi, 'Blessed be the LORD, who has not left you this day without next-of-kin;*a* and may his name be renowned in Israel! 15 He shall be to you a restorer of life and a nourisher of your old age; for your daughter-in-law who loves you, who is more to you than seven sons, has borne him.' 16 Then Naomi took the child and laid him in her bosom, and became his nurse. 17 The women of the neighbourhood gave him a name, saying, 'A son has been born to Naomi.' They named him Obed; he became the father of Jesse, the father of David.

18 Now these are the descendants of Perez: Perez became the father of Hezron, 19 Hezron of Ram, Ram of Amminadab, 20 Amminadab of Nahshon, Nahshon of Salmon, 21 Salmon of Boaz, Boaz of Obed, 22 Obed of Jesse, and Jesse of David.

a Or *one with the right to redeem*   *b* OL Vg: Heb *from the hand of Naomi and from Ruth*

1 SAMUEL

Samuel's Birth and Dedication

1 There was a certain man of Ramatha-im, a Zuphite^a from the hill country of Ephraim, whose name was Elkanah son of Jeroham son of Elihu son of Tohu son of Zuph, an Ephraimite. ²He had two wives; the name of one was Hannah, and the name of the other Peninnah. Peninnah had children, but Hannah had no children.

3 Now this man used to go up year by year from his town to worship and to sacrifice to the LORD of hosts at Shiloh, where the two sons of Eli, Hophni and Phinehas, were priests of the LORD. ⁴On the day when Elkanah sacrificed, he would give portions to his wife Peninnah and to all her sons and daughters; ⁵but to Hannah he gave a double portion,^b because he loved her, though the LORD had closed her womb. ⁶Her rival used to provoke her severely, to irritate her, because the LORD had closed her womb. ⁷So it went on year after year; as often as she went up to the house of the LORD, she used to provoke her. Therefore Hannah wept and would not eat. ⁸Her husband Elkanah said to her, 'Hannah, why do you weep? Why do you not eat? Why is your heart sad? Am I not more to you than ten sons?'

9 After they had eaten and drunk at Shiloh, Hannah rose and presented herself before the LORD.^c Now Eli the priest was sitting on the seat beside the doorpost of the temple of the LORD. ¹⁰She was deeply distressed and prayed to the LORD, and wept bitterly. ¹¹She made this vow: 'O LORD of hosts, if only you will look on the misery of your servant, and remember me, and not forget your servant, but will give to your servant a male child, then I will set him before you as a nazirite^d until the day of his death. He shall drink neither wine nor intoxicants,^e and no razor shall touch his head.'

12 As she continued praying before the LORD, Eli observed her mouth. ¹³Hannah was praying silently; only her lips moved, but her voice was not heard; therefore Eli thought she was drunk. ¹⁴So Eli said to her, 'How long will you make a drunken spectacle of yourself? Put away your wine.' ¹⁵But Hannah answered, 'No, my lord, I am a woman deeply troubled; I have drunk neither wine nor strong drink, but I have been pouring out my soul before the LORD. ¹⁶Do not regard your servant as a worthless woman, for I have been speaking out of my great anxiety and vexation all this time.' ¹⁷Then Eli answered, 'Go in peace; the God of Israel grant the petition you have made to him.' ¹⁸And she said, 'Let your servant find favour in your sight.' Then the woman went to her quarters,^f ate and drank with her husband,^g and her countenance was sad no longer.^h

19 They rose early in the morning and worshipped before the LORD; then they went back to their house at Ramah. Elkanah knew his wife Hannah, and the LORD remembered her. ²⁰In due time Hannah conceived and bore a son. She named him Samuel, for she said, 'I have asked him of the LORD.'

a Compare Gk and 1 Chr 6.35-36: Heb *Ramathaim-zophim*   *b* Syr: Meaning of Heb uncertain
c Gk: Heb lacks *and presented herself before the LORD*
d That is *one separated* or *one consecrated*
e Cn Compare Gk Q Ms 1.22: MT *then I will give him to the LORD all the days of his life*   *f* Gk: Heb *went on her way*   *g* Gk: Heb lacks *and drank with her husband*
h Gk: Meaning of Heb uncertain

21 The man Elkanah and all his household went up to offer to the LORD the yearly sacrifice, and to pay his vow. 22 But Hannah did not go up, for she said to her husband, 'As soon as the child is weaned, I will bring him, that he may appear in the presence of the LORD, and remain there for ever; I will offer him as a nazirite*a* for all time.'*b* 23 Her husband Elkanah said to her, 'Do what seems best to you, wait until you have weaned him; only—may the LORD establish his word.'*c* So the woman remained and nursed her son, until she weaned him. 24 When she had weaned him, she took him up with her, along with a three-year-old bull,*d* an ephah of flour, and a skin of wine. She brought him to the house of the LORD at Shiloh; and the child was young. 25 Then they slaughtered the bull, and they brought the child to Eli. 26 And she said, 'Oh, my lord! As you live, my lord, I am the woman who was standing here in your presence, praying to the LORD. 27 For this child I prayed; and the LORD has granted me the petition that I made to him. 28 Therefore I have lent him to the LORD; as long as he lives, he is given to the LORD.'

She left him there for*e* the LORD.

Hannah's Prayer

2 Hannah prayed and said,
'My heart exults in the LORD;
my strength is exalted in my God.*f*
My mouth derides my enemies,
because I rejoice in my*g* victory.

2 'There is no Holy One like the LORD,
no one besides you;
there is no Rock like our God.
3 Talk no more so very proudly,
let not arrogance come from your
mouth;
for the LORD is a God of knowledge,
and by him actions are weighed.
4 The bows of the mighty are broken,
but the feeble gird on strength.
5 Those who were full have hired
themselves out for bread,
but those who were hungry are fat
with spoil.
The barren has borne seven,

but she who has many children is
forlorn.
6 The LORD kills and brings to life;
he brings down to Sheol and raises
up.
7 The LORD makes poor and makes
rich;
he brings low, he also exalts.
8 He raises up the poor from the dust;
he lifts the needy from the ash
heap,
to make them sit with princes
and inherit a seat of honour.*h*
For the pillars of the earth are the
LORD's,
and on them he has set the world.

9 'He will guard the feet of his faithful
ones,
but the wicked shall be cut off in
darkness;
for not by might does one prevail.
10 The LORD! His adversaries shall be
shattered;
the Most High*i* will thunder in
heaven.
The LORD will judge the ends of the
earth;
he will give strength to his king,
and exalt the power of his
anointed.'

Eli's Wicked Sons

11 Then Elkanah went home to Ramah, while the boy remained to minister to the LORD, in the presence of the priest Eli.

12 Now the sons of Eli were scoundrels; they had no regard for the LORD 13 or for the duties of the priests to the people. When anyone offered sacrifice, the priest's servant would come, while the meat was boiling, with a three-pronged fork in his hand, 14 and he would thrust it into the pan, or kettle, or cauldron, or pot; all that the fork

a That is *one separated* or *one consecrated*
b Cn Compare Q Ms: MT lacks *I will offer him as a nazirite for all time*   *c* MT: Q Ms Gk Compare Syr *that which goes out of your mouth*   *d* Q Ms Gk Syr: MT *three bulls*   *e* Gk (Compare Q Ms) and Gk at 2.11: MT *And he* (that is, Elkanah) *worshipped there before*   *f* Gk: Heb *the LORD*   *g* Q Ms: MT *your*   *h* Gk (Compare Q Ms) adds *He grants the vow of the one who vows, and blesses the years of the just*   *i* Cn Heb *against him he*

brought up the priest would take for himself.*a* This is what they did at Shiloh to all the Israelites who came there. [15]Moreover, before the fat was burned, the priest's servant would come and say to the one who was sacrificing, 'Give meat for the priest to roast; for he will not accept boiled meat from you, but only raw.' [16]And if the man said to him, 'Let them burn the fat first, and then take whatever you wish', he would say, 'No, you must give it now; if not, I will take it by force.' [17]Thus the sin of the young men was very great in the sight of the LORD; for they treated the offerings of the LORD with contempt.

The Child Samuel at Shiloh

18 Samuel was ministering before the LORD, a boy wearing a linen ephod. [19]His mother used to make for him a little robe and take it to him each year, when she went up with her husband to offer the yearly sacrifice. [20]Then Eli would bless Elkanah and his wife, and say, 'May the LORD repay*b* you with children by this woman for the gift that she made to*c* the LORD'; and then they would return to their home.

21 And*d* the LORD took note of Hannah; she conceived and bore three sons and two daughters. And the boy Samuel grew up in the presence of the LORD.

Prophecy against Eli's Household

22 Now Eli was very old. He heard all that his sons were doing to all Israel, and how they lay with the women who served at the entrance to the tent of meeting. [23]He said to them, 'Why do you do such things? For I hear of your evil dealings from all these people. [24]No, my sons; it is not a good report that I hear the people of the LORD spreading abroad. [25]If one person sins against another, someone can intercede for the sinner with the LORD;*e* but if someone sins against the LORD, who can make intercession?' But they would not listen to the voice of their father; for it was the will of the LORD to kill them.

26 Now the boy Samuel continued to grow both in stature and in favour with the LORD and with the people.

27 A man of God came to Eli and said to him, 'Thus the LORD has said, "I revealed*f* myself to the family of your ancestor in Egypt when they were slaves*g* to the house of Pharaoh. [28]I chose him out of all the tribes of Israel to be my priest, to go up to my altar, to offer incense, to wear an ephod before me; and I gave to the family of your ancestor all my offerings by fire from the people of Israel. [29]Why then look with greedy eye*h* at my sacrifices and my offerings that I commanded, and honour your sons more than me by fattening yourselves on the choicest parts of every offering of my people Israel?" [30]Therefore the LORD the God of Israel declares: "I promised that your family and the family of your ancestor should go in and out before me for ever"; but now the LORD declares: "Far be it from me; for those who honour me I will honour, and those who despise me shall be treated with contempt. [31]See, a time is coming when I will cut off your strength and the strength of your ancestor's family, so that no one in your family will live to old age. [32]Then in distress you will look with greedy eye*i* on all the prosperity that shall be bestowed upon Israel; and no one in your family shall ever live to old age. [33]The only one of you whom I shall not cut off from my altar shall be spared to weep out his*j* eyes and grieve his*k* heart; all the members of your household shall die by the sword.*l* [34]The fate of your two sons, Hophni and Phinehas, shall be the sign to you— both of them shall die on the same day. [35]I will raise up for myself a faithful priest, who shall do according to what is in my heart and in my mind. I will build him a sure house, and he shall go in and out before my anointed one for ever. [36]Everyone who is left in your family shall come to implore him for a piece of silver or a loaf of bread, and shall say, Please put me in one

a Gk Syr Vg: Heb *with it*   *b* Q Ms Gk: MT *give*
c Q Ms Gk: MT *for the petition that she asked of*
d Q Ms Gk: MT *When*   *e* Gk Compare Q Ms:
another, God will mediate for him   *f* Gk Tg Syr: Heb *Did
I reveal*   *g* Q Ms Gk: MT lacks *slaves*   *h* Q Ms Gk: MT
then kick   *i* Q Ms Gk: MT *will kick*   *j* Q Ms Gk: MT
your   *k* Q Ms Gk: Heb *your*   *l* Q Ms See Gk: MT *die
like mortals*

of the priest's places, that I may eat a morsel of bread." '

Samuel's Calling and Prophetic Activity

3 Now the boy Samuel was ministering to the LORD under Eli. The word of the LORD was rare in those days; visions were not widespread.

2 At that time Eli, whose eyesight had begun to grow dim so that he could not see, was lying down in his room; 3 the lamp of God had not yet gone out, and Samuel was lying down in the temple of the LORD, where the ark of God was. 4 Then the LORD called, 'Samuel! Samuel!'[a] and he said, 'Here I am!' 5 and ran to Eli, and said, 'Here I am, for you called me.' But he said, 'I did not call; lie down again.' So he went and lay down. 6 The LORD called again, 'Samuel!' Samuel got up and went to Eli, and said, 'Here I am, for you called me.' But he said, 'I did not call, my son; lie down again.' 7 Now Samuel did not yet know the LORD, and the word of the LORD had not yet been revealed to him. 8 The LORD called Samuel again, a third time. And he got up and went to Eli, and said, 'Here I am, for you called me.' Then Eli perceived that the LORD was calling the boy. 9 Therefore Eli said to Samuel, 'Go, lie down; and if he calls you, you shall say, "Speak, LORD, for your servant is listening." ' So Samuel went and lay down in his place.

10 Now the LORD came and stood there, calling as before, 'Samuel! Samuel!' And Samuel said, 'Speak, for your servant is listening.' 11 Then the LORD said to Samuel, 'See, I am about to do something in Israel that will make both ears of anyone who hears of it tingle. 12 On that day I will fulfil against Eli all that I have spoken concerning his house, from beginning to end. 13 For I have told him that I am about to punish his house for ever, for the iniquity that he knew, because his sons were blaspheming God,[b] and he did not restrain them. 14 Therefore I swear to the house of Eli that the iniquity of Eli's house shall not be expiated by sacrifice or offering for ever.'

15 Samuel lay there until morning; then he opened the doors of the house of the LORD. Samuel was afraid to tell the vision to Eli. 16 But Eli called Samuel and said, 'Samuel, my son.' He said, 'Here I am.' 17 Eli said, 'What was it that he told you? Do not hide it from me. May God do so to you and more also, if you hide anything from me of all that he told you.' 18 So Samuel told him everything and hid nothing from him. Then he said, 'It is the LORD; let him do what seems good to him.'

19 As Samuel grew up, the LORD was with him and let none of his words fall to the ground. 20 And all Israel from Dan to Beer-sheba knew that Samuel was a trustworthy prophet of the LORD. 21 The LORD continued to appear at Shiloh, for the LORD revealed himself to Samuel at Shiloh by the word of the LORD. 1 And the word of Samuel came to all Israel.

The Ark of God Captured

In those days the Philistines mustered for war against Israel,[c] and Israel went out to battle against them;[d] they encamped at Ebenezer, and the Philistines encamped at Aphek. 2 The Philistines drew up in line against Israel, and when the battle was joined,[e] Israel was defeated by the Philistines, who killed about four thousand men on the field of battle. 3 When the troops came to the camp, the elders of Israel said, 'Why has the LORD put us to rout today before the Philistines? Let us bring the ark of the covenant of the LORD here from Shiloh, so that he may come among us and save us from the power of our enemies.' 4 So the people sent to Shiloh, and brought from there the ark of the covenant of the LORD of hosts, who is enthroned on the cherubim. The two sons of Eli, Hophni and Phinehas, were there with the ark of the covenant of God.

5 When the ark of the covenant of the LORD came into the camp, all Israel gave a mighty shout, so that the earth resounded.

a Q Ms Gk See 3.10: MT *the LORD called Samuel*
b Another reading is *for themselves*   c Gk: Heb lacks *In those days the Philistines mustered for war against Israel*
d Gk: Heb *against the Philistines*   e Meaning of Heb uncertain

6 When the Philistines heard the noise of the shouting, they said, 'What does this great shouting in the camp of the Hebrews mean?' When they learned that the ark of the LORD had come to the camp, 7 the Philistines were afraid; for they said, 'Gods have*a* come into the camp.' They also said, 'Woe to us! For nothing like this has happened before. 8 Woe to us! Who can deliver us from the power of these mighty gods? These are the gods who struck the Egyptians with every sort of plague in the wilderness. 9 Take courage, and be men, O Philistines, in order not to become slaves to the Hebrews as they have been to you; be men and fight.'

10 So the Philistines fought; Israel was defeated, and they fled, everyone to his home. There was a very great slaughter, for there fell of Israel thirty thousand foot-soldiers. 11 The ark of God was captured; and the two sons of Eli, Hophni and Phinehas, died.

Death of Eli

12 A man of Benjamin ran from the battle line, and came to Shiloh the same day, with his clothes torn and with earth upon his head. 13 When he arrived, Eli was sitting upon his seat by the road watching, for his heart trembled for the ark of God. When the man came into the city and told the news, all the city cried out. 14 When Eli heard the sound of the outcry, he said, 'What is this uproar?' Then the man came quickly and told Eli. 15 Now Eli was ninety-eight years old and his eyes were set, so that he could not see. 16 The man said to Eli, 'I have just come from the battle; I fled from the battle today.' He said, 'How did it go, my son?' 17 The messenger replied, 'Israel has fled before the Philistines, and there has also been a great slaughter among the troops; your two sons also, Hophni and Phinehas, are dead, and the ark of God has been captured.' 18 When he mentioned the ark of God, Eli*b* fell over backwards from his seat by the side of the gate; and his neck was broken and he died, for he was an old man, and heavy. He had judged Israel for forty years.

19 Now his daughter-in-law, the wife of Phinehas, was pregnant, about to give birth. When she heard the news that the ark of God was captured, and that her father-in-law and her husband were dead, she bowed and gave birth; for her labour pains overwhelmed her. 20 As she was about to die, the women attending her said to her, 'Do not be afraid, for you have borne a son.' But she did not answer or give heed. 21 She named the child Ichabod, meaning, 'The glory has departed from Israel', because the ark of God had been captured and because of her father-in-law and her husband. 22 She said, 'The glory has departed from Israel, for the ark of God has been captured.'

The Philistines and the Ark

5 When the Philistines captured the ark of God, they brought it from Ebenezer to Ashdod; 2 then the Philistines took the ark of God and brought it into the house of Dagon and placed it beside Dagon. 3 When the people of Ashdod rose early the next day, there was Dagon, fallen on his face to the ground before the ark of the LORD. So they took Dagon and put him back in his place. 4 But when they rose early on the next morning, Dagon had fallen on his face to the ground before the ark of the LORD, and the head of Dagon and both his hands were lying cut off upon the threshold; only the trunk of*c* Dagon was left to him. 5 This is why the priests of Dagon and all who enter the house of Dagon do not step on the threshold of Dagon in Ashdod to this day.

6 The hand of the LORD was heavy upon the people of Ashdod, and he terrified and struck them with tumours, both in Ashdod and in its territory. 7 And when the inhabitants of Ashdod saw how things were, they said, 'The ark of the God of Israel must not remain with us; for his hand is heavy on us and on our god Dagon.' 8 So they sent and gathered together all the lords of the Philistines, and said, 'What shall we do with the ark of the God of Israel?' The inhabitants of Gath replied, 'Let the ark of God be

---

a Or *A god has*　　*b* Heb *he*　　*c* Heb lacks *the trunk of* moved on to us.'[a] So they moved the ark of the God of Israel to Gath.[b] 9 But after they had brought it to Gath,[c] the hand of the LORD was against the city, causing a very great panic; he struck the inhabitants of the city, both young and old, so that tumours broke out on them. 10 So they sent the ark of the God of Israel[d] to Ekron. But when the ark of God came to Ekron, the people of Ekron cried out, 'Why[e] have they brought across to us[f] the ark of the God of Israel to kill us[f] and our[g] people?' 11 They sent therefore and gathered together all the lords of the Philistines, and said, 'Send away the ark of the God of Israel, and let it return to its own place, that it may not kill us and our people.' For there was a deathly panic[h] throughout the whole city. The hand of God was very heavy there; 12 those who did not die were stricken with tumours, and the cry of the city went up to heaven.

The Ark Returned to Israel

6 The ark of the LORD was in the country of the Philistines for seven months. 2 Then the Philistines called for the priests and the diviners and said, 'What shall we do with the ark of the LORD? Tell us what we should send with it to its place.' 3 They said, 'If you send away the ark of the God of Israel, do not send it empty, but by all means return him a guilt-offering. Then you will be healed and will be ransomed;[i] will not his hand then turn from you?' 4 And they said, 'What is the guilt-offering that we should return to him?' They answered, 'Five gold tumours and five gold mice, according to the number of the lords of the Philistines; for the same plague was upon all of you and upon your lords. 5 So you must make images of your tumours and images of your mice that ravage the land, and give glory to the God of Israel; perhaps he will lighten his hand on you and your gods and your land. 6 Why should you harden your hearts as the Egyptians and Pharaoh hardened their hearts? After he had made fools of them, did they not let the people go, and they departed? 7 Now then, get ready a new cart and two milch-cows that have never borne a yoke, and yoke the cows to the cart, but take their calves home, away from them. 8 Take the ark of the LORD and place it on the cart, and put in a box at its side the figures of gold, which you are returning to him as a guilt-offering. Then send it off, and let it go on its way. 9 And watch; if it goes up on the way to its own land, to Beth-shemesh, then it is he who has done us this great harm; but if not, then we shall know that it is not his hand that struck us; it happened to us by chance.'

10 The men did so; they took two milch-cows and yoked them to the cart, and shut up their calves at home. 11 They put the ark of the LORD on the cart, and the box with the gold mice and the images of their tumours. 12 The cows went straight in the direction of Beth-shemesh along one highway, lowing as they went; they turned neither to the right nor to the left, and the lords of the Philistines went after them as far as the border of Beth-shemesh.

13 Now the people of Beth-shemesh were reaping their wheat harvest in the valley. When they looked up and saw the ark, they went with rejoicing to meet it.[j] 14 The cart came into the field of Joshua of Beth-shemesh, and stopped there. A large stone was there; so they split up the wood of the cart and offered the cows as a burnt-offering to the LORD. 15 The Levites took down the ark of the LORD and the box that was beside it, in which were the gold objects, and set them upon the large stone. Then the people of Beth-shemesh offered burnt-offerings and presented sacrifices on that day to the LORD. 16 When the five lords of the Philistines saw it, they returned that day to Ekron.

17 These are the gold tumours, which the Philistines returned as a guilt-offering to the LORD: one for Ashdod, one for Gaza, one for Ashkelon, one for Gath, one for Ekron; 18 also the gold mice, according to the number of all the cities of the Philistines

a Gk Compare Q Ms: MT *They answered, 'Let the ark of the God of Israel be brought across to Gath.'*   b Gk: Heb lacks *to Gath*   c Q Ms: MT lacks *to Gath*   d Q Ms Gk: MT lacks *of Israel*   e Q Ms Gk: MT lacks *Why*   f Heb *me*   g Heb *my*   h Q Ms reads *a panic from the LORD*   i Q Ms Gk: MT *and it will be known to you*   j Gk: Heb *rejoiced to see it* belonging to the five lords, both fortified cities and unwalled villages. The great stone, beside which they set down the ark of the LORD, is a witness to this day in the field of Joshua of Beth-shemesh.

The Ark at Kiriath-jearim

19 The descendants of Jeconiah did not rejoice with the people of Beth-shemesh when they greeted*a* the ark of the LORD; and he killed seventy men of them. *b* The people mourned because the LORD had made a great slaughter among the people. 20 Then the people of Beth-shemesh said, 'Who is able to stand before the LORD, this holy God? To whom shall he go so that we may be rid of him?' 21 So they sent messengers to the inhabitants of Kiriath-jearim, saying, 'The Philistines have returned the ark of the LORD. Come down and take it up to you.'

7 ¹ And the people of Kiriath-jearim came and took up the ark of the LORD, and brought it to the house of Abinadab on the hill. They consecrated his son, Eleazar, to have charge of the ark of the LORD.

2 From the day that the ark was lodged at Kiriath-jearim, a long time passed, some twenty years, and all the house of Israel lamented*c* after the LORD.

Samuel as Judge

3 Then Samuel said to all the house of Israel, 'If you are returning to the LORD with all your heart, then put away the foreign gods and the Astartes from among you. Direct your heart to the LORD, and serve him only, and he will deliver you out of the hand of the Philistines.' 4 So Israel put away the Baals and the Astartes, and they served the LORD only.

5 Then Samuel said, 'Gather all Israel at Mizpah, and I will pray to the LORD for you.' 6 So they gathered at Mizpah, and drew water and poured it out before the LORD. They fasted that day, and said, 'We have sinned against the LORD.' And Samuel judged the people of Israel at Mizpah.

7 When the Philistines heard that the people of Israel had gathered at Mizpah, the lords of the Philistines went up against Israel. And when the people of Israel heard of it they were afraid of the Philistines. 8 The people of Israel said to Samuel, 'Do not cease to cry out to the LORD our God for us, and pray that he may save us from the hand of the Philistines.' 9 So Samuel took a sucking lamb and offered it as a whole burnt-offering to the LORD; Samuel cried out to the LORD for Israel, and the LORD answered him. 10 As Samuel was offering up the burnt-offering, the Philistines drew near to attack Israel; but the LORD thundered with a mighty voice that day against the Philistines and threw them into confusion; and they were routed before Israel. 11 And the men of Israel went out of Mizpah and pursued the Philistines, and struck them down as far as beyond Beth-car.

12 Then Samuel took a stone and set it up between Mizpah and Jeshanah,*d* and named it Ebenezer;*e* for he said, 'Thus far the LORD has helped us.' 13 So the Philistines were subdued and did not again enter the territory of Israel; the hand of the LORD was against the Philistines all the days of Samuel. 14 The towns that the Philistines had taken from Israel were restored to Israel, from Ekron to Gath; and Israel recovered their territory from the hand of the Philistines. There was peace also between Israel and the Amorites.

15 Samuel judged Israel all the days of his life. 16 He went on a circuit year by year to Bethel, Gilgal, and Mizpah; and he judged Israel in all these places. 17 Then he would come back to Ramah, for his home was there; he administered justice there to Israel, and built there an altar to the LORD.

Israel Demands a King

8 When Samuel became old, he made his sons judges over Israel. 2 The name of his firstborn son was Joel, and the name of his second, Abijah; they were judges in Beer-sheba. 3 Yet his sons did not follow in his ways, but turned aside after gain; they took bribes and perverted justice.

a Gk: Heb *And he killed some of the people of Beth-shemesh, because they looked into*   *b* Heb *killed seventy men, fifty thousand men*   *c* Meaning of Heb uncertain   *d* Gk Syr: Heb *Shen*   *e* That is *Stone of Help*

4 Then all the elders of Israel gathered together and came to Samuel at Ramah, ⁵and said to him, 'You are old and your sons do not follow in your ways; appoint for us, then, a king to govern us, like other nations.' ⁶But the thing displeased Samuel when they said, 'Give us a king to govern us.' Samuel prayed to the Lord, ⁷and the Lord said to Samuel, 'Listen to the voice of the people in all that they say to you; for they have not rejected you, but they have rejected me from being king over them. ⁸Just as they have done to me,ᵃ from the day I brought them up out of Egypt to this day, forsaking me and serving other gods, so also they are doing to you. ⁹Now then, listen to their voice; only— you shall solemnly warn them, and show them the ways of the king who shall reign over them.'

10 So Samuel reported all the words of the Lord to the people who were asking him for a king. ¹¹He said, 'These will be the ways of the king who will reign over you: he will take your sons and appoint them to his chariots and to be his horsemen, and to run before his chariots; ¹²and he will appoint for himself commanders of thousands and commanders of fifties, and some to plough his ground and to reap his harvest, and to make his implements of war and the equipment of his chariots. ¹³He will take your daughters to be perfumers and cooks and bakers. ¹⁴He will take the best of your fields and vineyards and olive orchards and give them to his courtiers. ¹⁵He will take one-tenth of your grain and of your vineyards and give it to his officers and his courtiers. ¹⁶He will take your male and female slaves, and the best of your cattleᵇ and donkeys, and put them to his work. ¹⁷He will take one-tenth of your flocks, and you shall be his slaves. ¹⁸And in that day you will cry out because of your king, whom you have chosen for yourselves; but the Lord will not answer you in that day.'

Israel's Request for a King Granted

19 But the people refused to listen to the voice of Samuel; they said, 'No! but we are determined to have a king over us, ²⁰so that we also may be like other nations, and that our king may govern us and go out before us and fight our battles.' ²¹When Samuel had heard all the words of the people, he repeated them in the ears of the Lord. ²²The Lord said to Samuel, 'Listen to their voice and set a king over them.' Samuel then said to the people of Israel, 'Each of you return home.'

Saul Chosen to Be King

9 There was a man of Benjamin whose name was Kish son of Abiel son of Zeror son of Becorath son of Aphiah, a Benjaminite, a man of wealth. ²He had a son whose name was Saul, a handsome young man. There was not a man among the people of Israel more handsome than he; he stood head and shoulders above everyone else.

3 Now the donkeys of Kish, Saul's father, had strayed. So Kish said to his son Saul, 'Take one of the boys with you; go and look

The Cities of Samuel

Mediterranean Sea

Aphek •   • Ebenezer
     • Shiloh
EPHRAIM
   Bethel •
   Mizpah •   Gilgal
   Ramah • • Geba
Kiriath-jearim •   • Jebus
•Ekron   (Jerusalem)
•Ashdod   Beth-shemesh
  •Gath

PHILISTIA

JUDAH

Dead Sea

N

0   30 Mi.
0   30 Km.

ᵃ Gk: Heb lacks *to me*   ᵇ Gk: Heb *young men*

for the donkeys.' [4] He passed through the hill country of Ephraim and passed through the land of Shalishah, but they did not find them. And they passed through the land of Shaalim, but they were not there. Then he passed through the land of Benjamin, but they did not find them.

5 When they came to the land of Zuph, Saul said to the boy who was with him, 'Let us turn back, or my father will stop worrying about the donkeys and worry about us.' [6] But he said to him, 'There is a man of God in this town; he is a man held in honour. Whatever he says always comes true. Let us go there now; perhaps he will tell us about the journey on which we have set out.' [7] Then Saul replied to the boy, 'But if we go, what can we bring the man? For the bread in our sacks is gone, and there is no present to bring to the man of God. What have we?' [8] The boy answered Saul again, 'Here, I have with me a quarter-shekel of silver; I will give it to the man of God, to tell us our way.' [9] (Formerly in Israel, anyone who went to inquire of God would say, 'Come, let us go to the seer'; for the one who is now called a prophet was formerly called a seer.) [10] Saul said to the boy, 'Good; come, let us go.' So they went to the town where the man of God was.

11 As they went up the hill to the town, they met some girls coming out to draw water, and said to them, 'Is the seer here?' [12] They answered, 'Yes, there he is just ahead of you. Hurry; he has come just now to the town, because the people have a sacrifice today at the shrine. [13] As soon as you enter the town, you will find him, before he goes up to the shrine to eat. For the people will not eat until he comes, since he must bless the sacrifice; afterwards those eat who are invited. Now go up, for you will meet him immediately.' [14] So they went up to the town. As they were entering the town, they saw Samuel coming out towards them on his way up to the shrine.

15 Now the day before Saul came, the LORD had revealed to Samuel: [16] 'Tomorrow about this time I will send to you a man from the land of Benjamin, and you

shall anoint him to be ruler over my people Israel. He shall save my people from the hand of the Philistines; for I have seen the suffering of[a] my people, because their outcry has come to me.' [17] When Samuel saw Saul, the LORD told him, 'Here is the man of whom I spoke to you. He it is who shall rule over my people.' [18] Then Saul approached Samuel inside the gate, and said, 'Tell me, please, where is the house of the seer?' [19] Samuel answered Saul, 'I am the seer; go up before me to the shrine, for today you shall eat with me, and in the morning I will let you go and will tell you all that is on your mind. [20] As for your donkeys that were lost three days ago, give no further thought to them, for they have been found. And on whom is all Israel's desire fixed, if not on you and on all your ancestral house?' [21] Saul answered, 'I am only a Benjaminite, from the least of the tribes of Israel, and my family is the humblest of all the families of the tribe of Benjamin. Why then have you spoken to me in this way?'

22 Then Samuel took Saul and his servant-boy and brought them into the hall, and gave them a place at the head of those who had been invited, of whom there were about thirty. [23] And Samuel said to the cook, 'Bring the portion I gave you, the one I asked you to put aside.' [24] The cook took up the thigh and what went with it[b] and set them before Saul. Samuel said, 'See, what was kept is set before you. Eat; for it is set[c] before you at the appointed time, so that you might eat with the guests.'[d]

So Saul ate with Samuel that day. [25] When they came down from the shrine into the town, a bed was spread for Saul[e] on the roof, and he lay down to sleep.[f] [26] Then at the break of dawn[g] Samuel called to Saul upon the roof, 'Get up, so that I may send you on your way.' Saul got up, and both he and Samuel went out into the street.

a Gk: Heb lacks *the suffering of*　b Meaning of Heb uncertain　c Q Ms Gk: MT *it was kept*　d Cn: Heb *it was kept for you, saying, I have invited the people* e Gk: Heb *and he spoke with Saul*　f Gk: Heb lacks *and he lay down to sleep*　g Gk: Heb *and they arose early and at break of dawn*

Samuel Anoints Saul

27 As they were going down to the outskirts of the town, Samuel said to Saul, 'Tell the boy to go on before us, and when he has passed on, stop here yourself for a while, that I may make known to you the word of God.' 1 Samuel took a phial of oil and poured it on his head, and kissed him; he said, 'The LORD has anointed you ruler over his people Israel. You shall reign over the people of the LORD and you will save them from the hand of their enemies all around. Now this shall be the sign to you that the LORD has anointed you ruler*a* over his heritage: 2 When you depart from me today you will meet two men by Rachel's tomb in the territory of Benjamin at Zelzah; they will say to you, "The donkeys that you went to seek are found, and now your father has stopped worrying about them and is worrying about you, saying: What shall I do about my son?" 3 Then you shall go on from there further and come to the oak of Tabor; three men going up to God at Bethel will meet you there, one carrying three kids, another carrying three loaves of bread, and another carrying a skin of wine. 4 They will greet you and give you two loaves of bread, which you shall accept from them. 5 After that you shall come to Gibeath-elohim,*b* at the place where the Philistine garrison is; there, as you come to the town, you will meet a band of prophets coming down from the shrine with harp, tambourine, flute, and lyre playing in front of them; they will be in a prophetic frenzy. 6 Then the spirit of the LORD will possess you, and you will be in a prophetic frenzy along with them and be turned into a different person. 7 Now when these signs meet you, do whatever you see fit to do, for God is with you. 8 And you shall go down to Gilgal ahead of me; then I will come down to you to present burnt-offerings and offer sacrifices of well-being. For seven days you shall wait, until I come to you and show you what you shall do.'

Saul Prophesies

9 As he turned away to leave Samuel, God gave him another heart; and all these signs were fulfilled that day. 10 When they were going from there*c* to Gibeah,*d* a band of prophets met him; and the spirit of God possessed him, and he fell into a prophetic frenzy along with them. 11 When all who knew him before saw how he prophesied with the prophets, the people said to one another, 'What has come over the son of Kish? Is Saul also among the prophets?' 12 A man of the place answered, 'And who is their father?' Therefore it became a proverb, 'Is Saul also among the prophets?' 13 When his prophetic frenzy had ended, he went home.*e*

14 Saul's uncle said to him and to the boy, 'Where did you go?' And he replied, 'To seek the donkeys; and when we saw they were not to be found, we went to Samuel.' 15 Saul's uncle said, 'Tell me what Samuel said to you.' 16 Saul said to his uncle, 'He told us that the donkeys had been found.' But about the matter of the kingship, of which Samuel had spoken, he did not tell him anything.

Saul Proclaimed King

17 Samuel summoned the people to the LORD at Mizpah 18 and said to them,*f* 'Thus says the LORD, the God of Israel, "I brought up Israel out of Egypt, and I rescued you from the hand of the Egyptians and from the hand of all the kingdoms that were oppressing you." 19 But today you have rejected your God, who saves you from all your calamities and your distresses; and you have said, "No! but set a king over us." Now therefore present yourselves before the LORD by your tribes and by your clans.'

20 Then Samuel brought all the tribes of Israel near, and the tribe of Benjamin was taken by lot. 21 He brought the tribe of Benjamin near by its families, and the family of the Matrites was taken by lot. Finally he

a Gk: Heb lacks *over his people Israel. You shall . . . anointed you ruler*   *b* Or *the Hill of God*   *c* Gk: Heb *they came there*   *d* Or *the hill*   *e* Cn: Heb *he came to the shrine*   *f* Heb *to the people of Israel* brought the family of the Matrites near man by man, *a* and Saul the son of Kish was taken by lot. But when they sought him, he could not be found. 22 So they inquired again of the LORD, 'Did the man come here?'*b* and the LORD said, 'See, he has hidden himself among the baggage.' 23 Then they ran and brought him from there. When he took his stand among the people, he was head and shoulders taller than any of them. 24 Samuel said to all the people, 'Do you see the one whom the LORD has chosen? There is no one like him among all the people.' And all the people shouted, 'Long live the king!'

25 Samuel told the people the rights and duties of the kingship; and he wrote them in a book and laid it up before the LORD. Then Samuel sent all the people back to their homes. 26 Saul also went to his home at Gibeah, and with him went warriors whose hearts God had touched. 27 But some worthless fellows said, 'How can this man save us?' They despised him and brought him no present. But he held his peace.

Now Nahash, king of the Ammonites, had been grievously oppressing the Gadites and the Reubenites. He would gouge out the right eye of each of them and would not grant Israel a deliverer. No one was left of the Israelites across the Jordan whose right eye Nahash, king of the Ammonites, had not gouged out. But there were seven thousand men who had escaped from the Ammonites and had entered Jabesh-gilead. *c*

Saul Defeats the Ammonites

11 About a month later, *d* Nahash the Ammonite went up and besieged Jabesh-gilead; and all the men of Jabesh said to Nahash, 'Make a treaty with us, and we will serve you.' 2 But Nahash the Ammonite said to them, 'On this condition I will make a treaty with you, namely that I gouge out everyone's right eye, and thus put disgrace upon all Israel.' 3 The elders of Jabesh said to him, 'Give us seven days' respite that we may send messengers through all the territory of Israel. Then, if there is no one to save us, we will give ourselves up to you.' 4 When the messengers

came to Gibeah of Saul, they reported the matter in the hearing of the people; and all the people wept aloud.

5 Now Saul was coming from the field behind the oxen; and Saul said, 'What is the matter with the people, that they are weeping?' So they told him the message from the inhabitants of Jabesh. 6 And the spirit of God came upon Saul in power when he heard these words, and his anger was greatly kindled. 7 He took a yoke of oxen, and cut them in pieces and sent them throughout all the territory of Israel by messengers, saying, 'Whoever does not come out after Saul and Samuel, so shall it be done to his oxen!' Then the dread of the LORD fell upon the people, and they came out as one. 8 When he mustered them at Bezek, those from Israel were three hundred thousand, and those from Judah seventy *e* thousand. 9 They said to the messengers who had come, 'Thus shall you say to the inhabitants of Jabesh-gilead: "Tomorrow, by the time the sun is hot, you shall have deliverance." ' When the messengers came and told the inhabitants of Jabesh, they rejoiced. 10 So the inhabitants of Jabesh said, 'Tomorrow we will give ourselves up to you, and you may do to us whatever seems good to you.' 11 The next day Saul put the people in three companies. At the morning watch they came into the camp and cut down the Ammonites until the heat of the day; and those who survived were scattered, so that no two of them were left together.

12 The people said to Samuel, 'Who is it that said, "Shall Saul reign over us?" Give them to us so that we may put them to death.' 13 But Saul said, 'No one shall be put to death this day, for today the LORD has brought deliverance to Israel.'

14 Samuel said to the people, 'Come, let us go to Gilgal and there renew the kingship.' 15 So all the people went to Gilgal, and there they made Saul king before the LORD in Gilgal. There they sacrificed offerings of well-being before the LORD, and

a Gk: Heb lacks *Finally . . . man by man*   *b* Gk: Heb *Is there yet a man to come here?*   *c* Q Ms Compare Josephus, *Antiquities* VI.v.1 (68-71): MT lacks *Now Nahash . . . entered Jabesh-gilead.*   *d* Q Ms Gk: MT lacks *About a month later*   *e* Q Ms Gk: MT *thirty* there Saul and all the Israelites rejoiced greatly.

Samuel's Farewell Address

12 Samuel said to all Israel, 'I have listened to you in all that you have said to me, and have set a king over you. [2] See, it is the king who leads you now; I am old and grey, but my sons are with you. I have led you from my youth until this day. [3] Here I am; testify against me before the LORD and before his anointed. Whose ox have I taken? Or whose donkey have I taken? Or whom have I defrauded? Whom have I oppressed? Or from whose hand have I taken a bribe to blind my eyes with it? Testify against me*a* and I will restore it to you.' [4] They said, 'You have not defrauded us or oppressed us or taken anything from the hand of anyone.' [5] He said to them, 'The LORD is witness against you, and his anointed is witness this day, that you have not found anything in my hand.' And they said, 'He is witness.'

6 Samuel said to the people, 'The LORD is witness, who*b* appointed Moses and Aaron and brought your ancestors up out of the land of Egypt. [7] Now therefore take your stand, so that I may enter into judgement with you before the LORD, and I will declare to you*c* all the saving deeds of the LORD that he performed for you and for your ancestors. [8] When Jacob went into Egypt and the Egyptians oppressed them,*d* then your ancestors cried to the LORD and the LORD sent Moses and Aaron, who brought forth your ancestors out of Egypt, and settled them in this place. [9] But they forgot the LORD their God; and he sold them into the hand of Sisera, commander of the army of King Jabin of*e* Hazor, and into the hand of the Philistines, and into the hand of the king of Moab; and they fought against them. [10] Then they cried to the LORD, and said, "We have sinned, because we have forsaken the LORD, and have served the Baals and the Astartes; but now rescue us out of the hand of our enemies, and we will serve you." [11] And the LORD sent Jerubbaal and Barak,*f* and Jephthah, and Samson,*g* and rescued you out of the

hand of your enemies on every side; and you lived in safety. [12] But when you saw that King Nahash of the Ammonites came against you, you said to me, "No, but a king shall reign over us", though the LORD your God was your king. [13] See, here is the king whom you have chosen, for whom you have asked; see, the LORD has set a king over you. [14] If you will fear the LORD and serve him and heed his voice and not rebel against the commandment of the LORD, and if both you and the king who reigns over you will follow the LORD your God, it will be well; [15] but if you will not heed the voice of the LORD, but rebel against the commandment of the LORD, then the hand of the LORD will be against you and your king.*h* [16] Now therefore take your stand and see this great thing that the LORD will do before your eyes. [17] Is it not the wheat harvest today? I will call upon the LORD, that he may send thunder and rain; and you shall know and see that the wickedness that you have done in the sight of the LORD is great in demanding a king for yourselves.' [18] So Samuel called upon the LORD, and the LORD sent thunder and rain that day; and all the people greatly feared the LORD and Samuel.

19 All the people said to Samuel, 'Pray to the LORD your God for your servants, so that we may not die; for we have added to all our sins the evil of demanding a king for ourselves.' [20] And Samuel said to the people, 'Do not be afraid; you have done all this evil, yet do not turn aside from following the LORD, but serve the LORD with all your heart; [21] and do not turn aside after useless things that cannot profit or save, for they are useless. [22] For the LORD will not cast away his people, for his great name's sake, because it has pleased the LORD to make you a people for himself. [23] Moreover as for me, far be it from me that I should sin against the LORD by ceasing to pray for you; and I will instruct you in the good and the right way. [24] Only fear the LORD, and serve

a Gk: Heb lacks *Testify against me*   *b* Gk: Heb lacks *is witness, who*   *c* Gk: Heb lacks *and I will declare to you*
d Gk: Heb lacks *and the Egyptians oppressed them*
e Gk: Heb lacks *King Jabin of*   *f* Gk Syr: Heb *Bedan*
g Gk: Heb *Samuel*   *h* Gk: Heb *and your ancestors*

him faithfully with all your heart; for consider what great things he has done for you. [25] But if you still do wickedly, you shall be swept away, both you and your king.'

Saul's Unlawful Sacrifice

13 Saul was . . . [a] years old when he began to reign; and he reigned for . . . and two [b] years over Israel.

2 Saul chose three thousand out of Israel; two thousand were with Saul in Michmash and the hill country of Bethel, and a thousand were with Jonathan in Gibeah of Benjamin; the rest of the people he sent home to their tents. [3] Jonathan defeated the garrison of the Philistines that was at Geba; and the Philistines heard of it. And Saul blew the trumpet throughout all the land, saying, 'Let the Hebrews hear!' [4] When all Israel heard that Saul had defeated the garrison of the Philistines, and also that Israel had become odious to the Philistines, the people were called out to join Saul at Gilgal.

5 The Philistines mustered to fight with Israel, thirty thousand chariots, and six thousand horsemen, and troops like the sand on the seashore in multitude; they came up and encamped at Michmash, to the east of Beth-aven. [6] When the Israelites saw that they were in distress (for the troops were hard pressed), the people hid themselves in caves and in holes and in rocks and in tombs and in cisterns. [7] Some Hebrews crossed the Jordan to the land of Gad and Gilead. Saul was still at Gilgal, and all the people followed him trembling.

8 He waited for seven days, the time appointed by Samuel; but Samuel did not come to Gilgal, and the people began to slip away from Saul. [c] [9] So Saul said, 'Bring the burnt-offering here to me, and the offerings of well-being.' And he offered the burnt-offering. [10] As soon as he had finished offering the burnt-offering, Samuel arrived; and Saul went out to meet him and salute him. [11] Samuel said, 'What have you done?' Saul replied, 'When I saw that the people were slipping away from me, and that you did not come within the days appointed, and that the Philistines were mus-

tering at Michmash, [12] I said, "Now the Philistines will come down upon me at Gilgal, and I have not entreated the favour of the LORD"; so I forced myself, and offered the burnt-offering.' [13] Samuel said to Saul, 'You have done foolishly; you have not kept the commandment of the LORD your God, which he commanded you. The LORD would have established your kingdom over Israel for ever, [14] but now your kingdom will not continue; the LORD has sought out a man after his own heart; and the LORD has appointed him to be ruler over his people, because you have not kept what the LORD commanded you.' [15] And Samuel left and went on his way from Gilgal. [d] The rest of the people followed Saul to join the army; they went up from Gilgal towards Gibeah of Benjamin. [e]

Preparations for Battle

Saul counted the people who were present with him, about six hundred men. [16] Saul, his son Jonathan, and the people who were present with them stayed in Geba of Benjamin; but the Philistines encamped at Michmash. [17] And raiders came out of the camp of the Philistines in three companies; one company turned towards Ophrah, to the land of Shual, [18] another company turned towards Beth-horon, and another company turned towards the mountain [f] that looks down upon the valley of Zeboim towards the wilderness.

19 Now there was no blacksmith to be found throughout all the land of Israel; for the Philistines said, 'The Hebrews must not make swords or spears for themselves'; [20] so all the Israelites went down to the Philistines to sharpen their ploughshares, mattocks, axes, or sickles; [g] [21] The charge was two-thirds of a shekel [h] for the ploughshares and for the mattocks, and one-third of a shekel for sharpening the axes and for setting the goads. [i] [22] So on the day of the battle neither

a The number is lacking in the Heb text (the verse is lacking in the Septuagint).   b *Two* is not the entire number; something has dropped out.   c Heb *him*
d Gk: Heb *went up from Gilgal to Gibeah of Benjamin*
e Gk: Heb lacks *The rest . . . of Benjamin*
f Cn Compare Gk: Heb *towards the border*   g Gk: Heb *ploughshare*   h Heb *was a pim*   i Cn: Meaning of Heb uncertain

sword nor spear was to be found in the possession of any of the people with Saul and Jonathan; but Saul and his son Jonathan had them.

Jonathan Surprises and Routs the Philistines

23 Now a garrison of the Philistines had gone out to the pass of Michmash.

14 ¹One day Jonathan son of Saul said to the young man who carried his armour, 'Come, let us go over to the Philistine garrison on the other side.' But he did not tell his father. ²Saul was staying in the outskirts of Gibeah under the pomegranate tree that is at Migron; the troops that were with him were about six hundred men, ³along with Ahijah son of Ahitub, Ichabod's brother, son of Phinehas son of Eli, the priest of the LORD in Shiloh, carrying an ephod. Now the people did not know that Jonathan had gone. ⁴In the pass, *a* by which Jonathan tried to go over to the Philistine garrison, there was a rocky crag on one side and a rocky crag on the other; the name of one was Bozez, and the name of the other Seneh. ⁵One crag rose on the north in front of Michmash, and the other on the south in front of Geba.

6 Jonathan said to the young man who carried his armour, 'Come, let us go over to the garrison of these uncircumcised; it may be that the LORD will act for us; for nothing can hinder the LORD from saving by many or by few.' ⁷His armour-bearer said to him, 'Do all that your mind inclines to.*b* I am with you; as your mind is, so is mine.'*c* ⁸Then Jonathan said, 'Now we will cross over to those men and will show ourselves to them. ⁹If they say to us, "Wait until we come to you", then we will stand still in our place, and we will not go up to them. ¹⁰But if they say, "Come up to us", then we will go up; for the LORD has given them into our hand. That will be the sign for us.' ¹¹So both of them showed themselves to the garrison of the Philistines; and the Philistines said, 'Look, Hebrews are coming out of the holes where they have hidden themselves.' ¹²The men of the garrison hailed Jonathan and his armour-bearer, saying, 'Come up to us,

and we will show you something.' Jonathan said to his armour-bearer, 'Come up after me; for the LORD has given them into the hand of Israel.' ¹³Then Jonathan climbed up on his hands and feet, with his armour-bearer following after him. The Philistines*d* fell before Jonathan, and his armour-bearer, coming after him, killed them. ¹⁴In that first slaughter Jonathan and his armour-bearer killed about twenty men within an area about half a furrow long in an acre*e* of land. ¹⁵There was a panic in the camp, in the field, and among all the people; the garrison and even the raiders trembled; the earth quaked; and it became a very great panic.

16 Saul's lookouts in Gibeah of Benjamin were watching as the multitude was surging back and forth.*f* ¹⁷Then Saul said to the troops that were with him, 'Call the roll and see who has gone from us.' When they had called the roll, Jonathan and his armour-bearer were not there. ¹⁸Saul said to Ahijah, 'Bring the ark*g* of God here.' For at that time the ark*g* of God went with the Israelites. ¹⁹While Saul was talking to the priest, the tumult in the camp of the Philistines increased more and more; and Saul said to the priest, 'Withdraw your hand.' ²⁰Then Saul and all the people who were with him rallied and went into the battle; and every sword was against the other, so that there was very great confusion. ²¹Now the Hebrews who previously had been with the Philistines and had gone up with them into the camp turned and joined the Israelites who were with Saul and Jonathan. ²²Likewise, when all the Israelites who had gone into hiding in the hill country of Ephraim heard that the Philistines were fleeing, they too followed closely after them in the battle. ²³So the LORD gave Israel the victory that day.

The battle passed beyond Beth-aven, and the troops with Saul numbered altogether about ten thousand men. The battle spread out over the hill country of Ephraim.

a Heb *Between the passes*   *b* Gk: Heb *Do all that is in your mind. Turn*   *c* Gk: Heb lacks *so is mine*
d Heb *They*   *e* Heb *yoke*   *f* Gk: Heb *they went and there*   *g* Gk *the ephod*

Saul's Rash Oath

24 Now Saul committed a very rash act on that day.[a] He had laid an oath on the troops, saying, 'Cursed be anyone who eats food before it is evening and I have been avenged on my enemies.' So none of the troops tasted food. 25 All the troops[b] came upon a honeycomb; and there was honey on the ground. 26 When the troops came upon the honeycomb, the honey was dripping out; but they did not put their hands to their mouths, for they feared the oath. 27 But Jonathan had not heard his father charge the troops with the oath; so he extended the staff that was in his hand, and dipped the tip of it in the honeycomb, and put his hand to his mouth; and his eyes brightened. 28 Then one of the soldiers said, 'Your father strictly charged the troops with an oath, saying, "Cursed be anyone who eats food this day." And so the troops are faint.' 29 Then Jonathan said, 'My father has troubled the land; see how my eyes have brightened because I tasted a little of this honey. 30 How much better if today the troops had eaten freely of the spoil taken from their enemies; for now the slaughter among the Philistines has not been great.'

31 After they had struck down the Philistines that day from Michmash to Aijalon, the troops were very faint; 32 so the troops flew upon the spoil, and took sheep and oxen and calves, and slaughtered them on the ground; and the troops ate them with the blood. 33 Then it was reported to Saul, 'Look, the troops are sinning against the LORD by eating with the blood.' And he said, 'You have dealt treacherously; roll a large stone before me here.'[c] 34 Saul said, 'Disperse yourselves among the troops, and say to them, "Let all bring their oxen or their sheep, and slaughter them here, and eat; and do not sin against the LORD by eating with the blood."' So all of the troops brought their oxen with them that night, and slaughtered them there. 35 And Saul built an altar to the LORD; it was the first altar that he built to the LORD.

Jonathan in Danger of Death

36 Then Saul said, 'Let us go down after the Philistines by night and despoil them until the morning light; let us not leave one of them.' They said, 'Do whatever seems good to you.' But the priest said, 'Let us draw near to God here.' 37 So Saul inquired of God, 'Shall I go down after the Philistines? Will you give them into the hand of Israel?' But he did not answer him that day. 38 Saul said, 'Come here, all you leaders of the people; and let us find out how this sin has arisen today. 39 For as the LORD lives who saves Israel, even if it is in my son Jonathan, he shall surely die!' But there was no one among all the people who answered him. 40 He said to all Israel, 'You shall be on one side, and I and my son Jonathan will be on the other side.' The people said to Saul, 'Do what seems good to you.' 41 Then Saul said, 'O LORD God of Israel, why have you not answered your servant today? If this guilt is in me or in my son Jonathan, O LORD God of Israel, give Urim; but if this guilt is in your people Israel,[d] give Thummim.' And Jonathan and Saul were indicated by the lot, but the people were cleared. 42 Then Saul said, 'Cast the lot between me and my son Jonathan.' And Jonathan was taken.

43 Then Saul said to Jonathan, 'Tell me what you have done.' Jonathan told him, 'I tasted a little honey with the tip of the staff that was in my hand; here I am, I will die.' 44 Saul said, 'God do so to me and more also; you shall surely die, Jonathan!' 45 Then the people said to Saul, 'Shall Jonathan die, who has accomplished this great victory in Israel? Perish the thought! As the LORD lives, not one hair of his head shall fall to the ground; for he has worked with God today.' So the people ransomed Jonathan, and he did not die. 46 Then Saul withdrew from pursuing the Philistines; and the Philistines went to their own place.

a Gk: Heb *The Israelites were distressed that day*
b Heb *land*   c Gk: Heb *me this day*   d Vg Compare
Gk: Heb 41 *Saul said to the LORD, the God of Israel*

Saul's Continuing Wars

47 When Saul had taken the kingship over Israel, he fought against all his enemies on every side—against Moab, against the Ammonites, against Edom, against the kings of Zobah, and against the Philistines; wherever he turned he routed them. 48 He did valiantly, and struck down the Amalekites, and rescued Israel out of the hands of those who plundered them.

49 Now the sons of Saul were Jonathan, Ishvi, and Malchishua; and the names of his two daughters were these: the name of the firstborn was Merab, and the name of the younger, Michal. 50 The name of Saul's wife was Ahinoam daughter of Ahimaaz. And the name of the commander of his army was Abner son of Ner, Saul's uncle; 51 Kish was the father of Saul, and Ner the father of Abner was the son of Abiel.

52 There was hard fighting against the Philistines all the days of Saul; and when Saul saw any strong or valiant warrior, he took him into his service.

Saul Defeats the Amalekites but Spares Their King

15 Samuel said to Saul, 'The LORD sent me to anoint you king over his people Israel; now therefore listen to the words of the LORD. 2 Thus says the LORD of hosts, "I will punish the Amalekites for what they did in opposing the Israelites when they came up out of Egypt. 3 Now go and attack Amalek, and utterly destroy all that they have; do not spare them, but kill both man and woman, child and infant, ox and sheep, camel and donkey." '

4 So Saul summoned the people, and numbered them in Telaim, two hundred thousand foot-soldiers, and ten thousand soldiers of Judah. 5 Saul came to the city of the Amalekites and lay in wait in the valley. 6 Saul said to the Kenites, 'Go! Leave! Withdraw from among the Amalekites, or I will destroy you with them; for you showed kindness to all the people of Israel when they came up out of Egypt.' So the Kenites withdrew from the Amalekites. 7 Saul defeated the Amalekites, from Havilah as far as Shur, which is east of Egypt. 8 He took

King Agag of the Amalekites alive, but utterly destroyed all the people with the edge of the sword. 9 Saul and the people spared Agag, and the best of the sheep and of the cattle and of the fatlings, and the lambs, and all that was valuable, and would not utterly destroy them; all that was despised and worthless they utterly destroyed.

Saul Rejected as King

10 The word of the LORD came to Samuel: 11 'I regret that I made Saul king, for he has turned back from following me, and has not carried out my commands.' Samuel was angry; and he cried out to the LORD all night. 12 Samuel rose early in the morning to meet Saul, and Samuel was told, 'Saul went to Carmel, where he set up a monument for himself, and on returning he passed on down to Gilgal.' 13 When Samuel came to Saul, Saul said to him, 'May you be blessed by the LORD; I have carried out the command of the LORD.' 14 But Samuel said, 'What then is this bleating of sheep in my ears, and the lowing of cattle that I hear?' 15 Saul said, 'They have brought them from the Amalekites; for the people spared the best of the sheep and the cattle, to sacrifice to the LORD your God; but the rest we have utterly destroyed.' 16 Then Samuel said to Saul, 'Stop! I will tell you what the LORD said to me last night.' He replied, 'Speak.'

17 Samuel said, 'Though you are little in your own eyes, are you not the head of the tribes of Israel? The LORD anointed you king over Israel. 18 And the LORD sent you on a mission, and said, "Go, utterly destroy the sinners, the Amalekites, and fight against them until they are consumed." 19 Why then did you not obey the voice of the LORD? Why did you swoop down on the spoil, and do what was evil in the sight of the LORD?' 20 Saul said to Samuel, 'I have obeyed the voice of the LORD, I have gone on the mission on which the LORD sent me, I have brought Agag the king of Amalek, and I have utterly destroyed the Amalekites. 21 But from the spoil the people took sheep and cattle, the best of the things devoted to destruction, to sacrifice to the LORD your God in Gilgal.' 22 And Samuel said,

'Has the LORD as great delight in
    burnt-offerings and sacrifices,
  as in obedience to the voice of the
    LORD?
Surely, to obey is better than sacrifice,
  and to heed than the fat of rams.'
23 For rebellion is no less a sin than
    divination,
  and stubbornness is like iniquity
    and idolatry.
Because you have rejected the word
    of the LORD,
  he has also rejected you from being
    king.'

24 Saul said to Samuel, 'I have sinned;
for I have transgressed the commandment
of the LORD and your words, because I
feared the people and obeyed their voice.
25 Now therefore, I pray, pardon my sin, and
return with me, so that I may worship the
LORD.' 26 Samuel said to Saul, 'I will not return with you; for you have rejected the
word of the LORD, and the LORD has rejected you from being king over Israel.' 27 As
Samuel turned to go away, Saul caught hold
of the hem of his robe, and it tore. 28 And
Samuel said to him, 'The LORD has torn the
kingdom of Israel from you this very day,
and has given it to a neighbour of yours,
who is better than you. 29 Moreover, the
Glory of Israel will not recant*a* or change
his mind; for he is not a mortal, that he
should change his mind.' 30 Then Saul*b* said,
'I have sinned; yet honour me now before
the elders of my people and before Israel,
and return with me, so that I may worship
the LORD your God.' 31 So Samuel turned
back after Saul; and Saul worshipped the
LORD.

32 Then Samuel said, 'Bring Agag king
of the Amalekites here to me.' And Agag
came to him haltingly.*c* Agag said, 'Surely
this is the bitterness of death.'*d* 33 But Samuel said,

  'As your sword has made women
    childless,
  so your mother shall be childless
    among women.'
And Samuel hewed Agag in pieces before
the LORD in Gilgal.

34 Then Samuel went to Ramah; and

Saul went up to his house in Gibeah of
Saul. 35 Samuel did not see Saul again until
the day of his death, but Samuel grieved
over Saul. And the LORD was sorry that he
had made Saul king over Israel.

David Anointed as King

16 The LORD said to Samuel, 'How
long will you grieve over Saul? I
have rejected him from being king over Israel. Fill your horn with oil and set out; I
will send you to Jesse the Bethlehemite, for
I have provided for myself a king among his
sons.' 2 Samuel said, 'How can I go? If Saul
hears of it, he will kill me.' And the LORD
said, 'Take a heifer with you, and say, "I
have come to sacrifice to the LORD." 3 Invite
Jesse to the sacrifice, and I will show you
what you shall do; and you shall anoint for
me the one whom I name to you.' 4 Samuel
did what the LORD commanded, and came
to Bethlehem. The elders of the city came to
meet him trembling, and said, 'Do you
come peaceably?' 5 He said, 'Peaceably; I
have come to sacrifice to the LORD; sanctify
yourselves and come with me to the sacrifice.' And he sanctified Jesse and his sons
and invited them to the sacrifice.

6 When they came, he looked on Eliab
and thought, 'Surely the LORD's anointed is
now before the LORD.'*e* 7 But the LORD said
to Samuel, 'Do not look on his appearance
or on the height of his stature, because I
have rejected him; for the LORD does not
see as mortals see; they look on the outward appearance, but the LORD looks on the
heart.' 8 Then Jesse called Abinadab, and
made him pass before Samuel. He said,
'Neither has the LORD chosen this one.'
9 Then Jesse made Shammah pass by. And
he said, 'Neither has the LORD chosen this
one.' 10 Jesse made seven of his sons pass before Samuel, and Samuel said to Jesse, 'The
LORD has not chosen any of these.' 11 Samuel
said to Jesse, 'Are all your sons here?' And he
said, 'There remains yet the youngest, but he
is keeping the sheep.' And Samuel said to
Jesse, 'Send and bring him; for we will not

a Q Ms Gk: MT *deceive*   *b* Heb *he*   *c* Cn Compare
Gk: Meaning of Heb uncertain   *d* Q Ms Gk: MT *Surely
the bitterness of death is past*   *e* Heb *him*

sit down until he comes here.' 12 He sent and brought him in. Now he was ruddy, and had beautiful eyes, and was handsome. The LORD said, 'Rise and anoint him; for this is the one.' 13 Then Samuel took the horn of oil, and anointed him in the presence of his brothers; and the spirit of the LORD came mightily upon David from that day forward. Samuel then set out and went to Ramah.

David Plays the Lyre for Saul

14 Now the spirit of the LORD departed from Saul, and an evil spirit from the LORD tormented him. 15 And Saul's servants said to him, 'See now, an evil spirit from God is tormenting you. 16 Let our lord now command the servants who attend you to look for someone who is skilful in playing the lyre; and when the evil spirit from God is upon you, he will play it, and you will feel better.' 17 So Saul said to his servants, 'Provide for me someone who can play well, and bring him to me.' 18 One of the young men answered, 'I have seen a son of Jesse the Bethlehemite who is skilful in playing, a man of valour, a warrior, prudent in speech, and a man of good presence; and the LORD is with him.' 19 So Saul sent messengers to Jesse, and said, 'Send me your son David who is with the sheep.' 20 Jesse took a donkey loaded with bread, a skin of wine, and a kid, and sent them by his son David to Saul. 21 And David came to Saul, and entered his service. Saul loved him greatly, and he became his armour-bearer. 22 Saul sent to Jesse, saying, 'Let David remain in my service, for he has found favour in my sight.' 23 And whenever the evil spirit from God came upon Saul, David took the lyre and played it with his hand, and Saul would be relieved and feel better, and the evil spirit would depart from him.

David and Goliath

17 Now the Philistines gathered their armies for battle; they were gathered at Socoh, which belongs to Judah, and encamped between Socoh and Azekah, in Ephes-dammim. 2 Saul and the Is-raelites gathered and encamped in the valley of Elah, and formed ranks against the Philistines. 3 The Philistines stood on the mountain on one side, and Israel stood on the mountain on the other side, with a valley between them. 4 And there came out from the camp of the Philistines a champion named Goliath, of Gath, whose height was six*a* cubits and a span. 5 He had a helmet of bronze on his head, and he was armoured with a coat of mail; the weight of the coat was five thousand shekels of bronze. 6 He had greaves of bronze on his legs and a javelin of bronze slung between his shoulders. 7 The shaft of his spear was like a weaver's beam, and his spear's head weighed six hundred shekels of iron; and his shield-bearer went before him. 8 He stood and shouted to the ranks of Israel, 'Why have you come out to draw up for battle? Am I not a Philistine, and are you not servants of Saul? Choose a man for yourselves, and let him come down to me. 9 If he is able to fight with me and kill me, then we will be your servants; but if I prevail against him and kill him, then you shall be our servants and serve us.' 10 And the Philistine said, 'Today I defy the ranks of Israel! Give me a man, that we may fight together.' 11 When Saul and all Israel heard these words of the Philistine, they were dismayed and greatly afraid.

12 Now David was the son of an Ephrathite of Bethlehem in Judah, named Jesse, who had eight sons. In the days of Saul the man was already old and advanced in years.*b* 13 The three eldest sons of Jesse had followed Saul to the battle; the names of his three sons who went to the battle were Eliab the firstborn, and next to him Abinadab, and the third Shammah. 14 David was the youngest; the three eldest followed Saul, 15 but David went back and forth from Saul to feed his father's sheep at Bethlehem. 16 For forty days the Philistine came forward and took his stand, morning and evening.

17 Jesse said to his son David, 'Take for your brothers an ephah of this parched

a MT: Q Ms Gk *four*   *b* Gk Syr: Heb *among men*

grain and these ten loaves, and carry them quickly to the camp to your brothers; 18 also take these ten cheeses to the commander of their thousand. See how your brothers fare, and bring some token from them.'

19 Now Saul, and they, and all the men of Israel, were in the valley of Elah, fighting with the Philistines. 20 David rose early in the morning, left someone in charge of the sheep, took the provisions, and went as Jesse had commanded him. He came to the encampment as the army was going forth to the battle line, shouting the war cry. 21 Israel and the Philistines drew up for battle, army against army. 22 David left the things in charge of the keeper of the baggage, ran to the ranks, and went and greeted his brothers. 23 As he talked with them, the champion, the Philistine of Gath, Goliath by name, came up out of the ranks of the Philistines, and spoke the same words as before. And David heard him.

24 All the Israelites, when they saw the man, fled from him and were very much afraid. 25 The Israelites said, 'Have you seen this man who has come up? Surely he has come up to defy Israel. The king will greatly enrich the man who kills him, and will give him his daughter and make his family free in Israel.' 26 David said to the men who stood by him, 'What shall be done for the man who kills this Philistine, and takes away the reproach from Israel? For who is this uncircumcised Philistine that he should defy the armies of the living God?' 27 The people answered him in the same way, 'So shall it be done for the man who kills him.'

28 His eldest brother Eliab heard him talking to the men; and Eliab's anger was kindled against David. He said, 'Why have you come down? With whom have you left those few sheep in the wilderness? I know your presumption and the evil of your heart; for you have come down just to see the battle.' 29 David said, 'What have I done now? It was only a question.' 30 He turned away from him towards another and spoke in the same way; and the people answered him again as before.

31 When the words that David spoke were heard, they repeated them before Saul; and he sent for him. 32 David said to Saul, 'Let no one's heart fail because of him; your servant will go and fight with this Philistine.' 33 Saul said to David, 'You are not able to go against this Philistine to fight with him; for you are just a boy, and he has been a warrior from his youth.' 34 But David said to Saul, 'Your servant used to keep sheep for his father; and whenever a lion or a bear came, and took a lamb from the flock, 35 I went after it and struck it down, rescuing the lamb from its mouth; and if it turned against me, I would catch it by the jaw, strike it down, and kill it. 36 Your servant has killed both lions and bears; and this uncircumcised Philistine shall be like one of them, since he has defied the armies of the living God.' 37 David said, 'The LORD, who saved me from the paw of the lion and from the paw of the bear, will save me from the hand of this Philistine.' So Saul said to David, 'Go, and may the LORD be with you!'

38 Saul clothed David with his armour; he put a bronze helmet on his head and

David's Travels in the Service of Saul

Mediterranean Sea

Ashdod

PHILISTINES

Eglon

Valley of Elah

Ramah
Gibeah of Saul
Nob
Jebus (Jerusalem)
Bethlehem

Salt Sea (Dead Sea)

—N—

0   20 Mi.
0   20 Km.

clothed him with a coat of mail. ³⁹ David strapped Saul's sword over the armour, and he tried in vain to walk, for he was not used to them. Then David said to Saul, 'I cannot walk with these; for I am not used to them.' So David removed them. ⁴⁰ Then he took his staff in his hand, and chose five smooth stones from the wadi, and put them in his shepherd's bag, in the pouch; his sling was in his hand, and he drew near to the Philistine.

41 The Philistine came on and drew near to David, with his shield-bearer in front of him. ⁴² When the Philistine looked and saw David, he disdained him, for he was only a youth, ruddy and handsome in appearance. ⁴³ The Philistine said to David, 'Am I a dog, that you come to me with sticks?' And the Philistine cursed David by his gods. ⁴⁴ The Philistine said to David, 'Come to me, and I will give your flesh to the birds of the air and to the wild animals of the field.' ⁴⁵ But David said to the Philistine, 'You come to me with sword and spear and javelin; but I come to you in the name of the LORD of hosts, the God of the armies of Israel, whom you have defied. ⁴⁶ This very day the LORD will deliver you into my hand, and I will strike you down and cut off your head; and I will give the dead bodies of the Philistine army this very day to the birds of the air and to the wild animals of the earth, so that all the earth may know that there is a God in Israel, ⁴⁷ and that all this assembly may know that the LORD does not save by sword and spear; for the battle is the LORD's and he will give you into our hand.'

48 When the Philistine drew nearer to meet David, David ran quickly towards the battle line to meet the Philistine. ⁴⁹ David put his hand in his bag, took out a stone, slung it, and struck the Philistine on his forehead; the stone sank into his forehead, and he fell face down on the ground.

50 So David prevailed over the Philistine with a sling and a stone, striking down the Philistine and killing him; there was no sword in David's hand. ⁵¹ Then David ran and stood over the Philistine; he grasped his sword, drew it out of its sheath, and killed him; then he cut off his head with it.

When the Philistines saw that their champion was dead, they fled. ⁵² The troops of Israel and Judah rose up with a shout and pursued the Philistines as far as Gath[a] and the gates of Ekron, so that the wounded Philistines fell on the way from Shaaraim as far as Gath and Ekron. ⁵³ The Israelites came back from chasing the Philistines, and they plundered their camp. ⁵⁴ David took the head of the Philistine and brought it to Jerusalem; but he put his armour in his tent.

55 When Saul saw David go out against the Philistine, he said to Abner, the commander of the army, 'Abner, whose son is this young man?' Abner said, 'As your soul lives, O king, I do not know.' ⁵⁶ The king said, 'Inquire whose son the stripling is.' ⁵⁷ On David's return from killing the Philistine, Abner took him and brought him before Saul, with the head of the Philistine in his hand. ⁵⁸ Saul said to him, 'Whose son are you, young man?' And David answered, 'I am the son of your servant Jesse the Bethlehemite.'

Jonathan's Covenant with David

18 When David[b] had finished speaking to Saul, the soul of Jonathan was bound to the soul of David, and Jonathan loved him as his own soul. ² Saul took him that day and would not let him return to his father's house. ³ Then Jonathan made a covenant with David, because he loved him as his own soul. ⁴ Jonathan stripped himself of the robe that he was wearing, and gave it to David, and his armour, and even his sword and his bow and his belt. ⁵ David went out and was successful wherever Saul sent him; as a result, Saul set him over the army. And all the people, even the servants of Saul, approved.

6 As they were coming home, when David returned from killing the Philistine, the women came out of all the towns of Israel, singing and dancing, to meet King Saul, with tambourines, with songs of joy, and with musical instruments.[c] ⁷ And the

a Gk Syr: Heb *Gai*   b Heb *he*   c Or *triangles*, or *three-stringed instruments* women sang to one another as they made merry,

'Saul has killed his thousands,
and David his tens of thousands.'

8 Saul was very angry, for this saying displeased him. He said, 'They have ascribed to David tens of thousands, and to me they have ascribed thousands; what more can he have but the kingdom?' 9 So Saul eyed David from that day on.

Saul Tries to Kill David

10 The next day an evil spirit from God rushed upon Saul, and he raved within his house, while David was playing the lyre, as he did day by day. Saul had his spear in his hand; 11 and Saul threw the spear, for he thought, 'I will pin David to the wall.' But David eluded him twice.

12 Saul was afraid of David, because the LORD was with him but had departed from Saul. 13 So Saul removed him from his presence, and made him a commander of a thousand; and David marched out and came in, leading the army. 14 David had success in all his undertakings; for the LORD was with him. 15 When Saul saw that he had great success, he stood in awe of him. 16 But all Israel and Judah loved David; for it was he who marched out and came in leading them.

David Marries Michal

17 Then Saul said to David, 'Here is my elder daughter Merab; I will give her to you as a wife; only be valiant for me and fight the LORD's battles.' For Saul thought, 'I will not raise a hand against him; let the Philistines deal with him.' 18 David said to Saul, 'Who am I and who are my kinsfolk, my father's family in Israel, that I should be son-in-law to the king?' 19 But at the time when Saul's daughter Merab should have been given to David, she was given to Adriel the Meholathite as a wife.

20 Now Saul's daughter Michal loved David. Saul was told, and the thing pleased him. 21 Saul thought, 'Let me give her to him that she may be a snare for him and that the hand of the Philistines may be against him.' Therefore Saul said to David

a second time, a 'You shall now be my son-in-law.' 22 Saul commanded his servants, 'Speak to David in private and say, "See, the king is delighted with you, and all his servants love you; now then, become the king's son-in-law." ' 23 So Saul's servants reported these words to David in private. And David said, 'Does it seem to you a little thing to become the king's son-in-law, seeing that I am a poor man and of no repute?' 24 The servants of Saul told him, 'This is what David said.' 25 Then Saul said, 'Thus shall you say to David, "The king desires no marriage present except a hundred foreskins of the Philistines, that he may be avenged on the king's enemies." ' Now Saul planned to make David fall by the hand of the Philistines. 26 When his servants told David these words, David was well pleased to be the king's son-in-law. Before the time had expired, 27 David rose and went, along with his men, and killed one hundred b of the Philistines; and David brought their foreskins, which were given in full number to the king, that he might become the king's son-in-law. Saul gave him his daughter Michal as a wife. 28 But when Saul realized that the LORD was with David, and that Saul's daughter Michal loved him, 29 Saul was still more afraid of David. So Saul was David's enemy from that time forward.

30 Then the commanders of the Philistines came out to battle; and as often as they came out, David had more success than all the servants of Saul, so that his fame became very great.

Jonathan Intercedes for David

19 Saul spoke to his son Jonathan and to all his servants about killing David. But Saul's son Jonathan took great delight in David. 2 Jonathan told David, 'My father Saul is trying to kill you; therefore be on guard tomorrow morning; stay in a secret place and hide yourself. 3 I will go out and stand beside my father in the field where you are, and I will speak to my father about you; if I learn anything I will tell

a Heb by two   b Gk Compare 2 Sam 3.14: Heb two hundred

you.' ⁴Jonathan spoke well of David to his father Saul, saying to him, 'The king should not sin against his servant David, because he has not sinned against you, and because his deeds have been of good service to you; ⁵for he took his life in his hand when he attacked the Philistine, and the LORD brought about a great victory for all Israel. You saw it, and rejoiced; why then will you sin against an innocent person by killing David without cause?' ⁶Saul heeded the voice of Jonathan; Saul swore, 'As the LORD lives, he shall not be put to death.' ⁷So Jonathan called David and related all these things to him. Jonathan then brought David to Saul, and he was in his presence as before.

Michal Helps David Escape from Saul

8 Again there was war, and David went out to fight the Philistines. He launched a heavy attack on them, so that they fled before him. ⁹Then an evil spirit from the LORD came upon Saul, as he sat in his house with his spear in his hand, while David was playing music. ¹⁰Saul sought to pin David to the wall with the spear; but he eluded Saul, so that he struck the spear into the wall. David fled and escaped that night.

11 Saul sent messengers to David's house to keep watch over him, planning to kill him in the morning. David's wife Michal told him, 'If you do not save your life tonight, tomorrow you will be killed.' ¹²So Michal let David down through the window; he fled away and escaped. ¹³Michal took an idol[a] and laid it on the bed; she put a net[b] of goats' hair on its head, and covered it with the clothes. ¹⁴When Saul sent messengers to take David, she said, 'He is sick.' ¹⁵Then Saul sent the messengers to see David for themselves. He said, 'Bring him up to me in the bed, that I may kill him.' ¹⁶When the messengers came in, the idol[c] was in the bed, with the covering[b] of goats' hair on its head. ¹⁷Saul said to Michal, 'Why have you deceived me like this, and let my enemy go, so that he has escaped?' Michal answered Saul, 'He said to me, "Let me go; why should I kill you?" '

David Joins Samuel in Ramah

18 Now David fled and escaped; he came to Samuel at Ramah, and told him all that Saul had done to him. He and Samuel went and settled at Naioth. ¹⁹Saul was told, 'David is at Naioth in Ramah.' ²⁰Then Saul sent messengers to take David. When they saw the company of the prophets in a frenzy, with Samuel standing in charge of[b] them, the spirit of God came upon the messengers of Saul, and they also fell into a prophetic frenzy. ²¹When Saul was told, he sent other messengers, and they also fell into a frenzy. Saul sent messengers again the third time, and they also fell into a frenzy. ²²Then he himself went to Ramah. He came to the great well that is in Secu;[d] he asked, 'Where are Samuel and David?' And someone said, 'They are at Naioth in Ramah.' ²³He went there, towards Naioth in Ramah; and the spirit of God came upon him. As he was going, he fell into a prophetic frenzy, until he came to Naioth in Ramah. ²⁴He too stripped off his clothes, and he too fell into a frenzy before Samuel. He lay naked all that day and all that night. Therefore it is said, 'Is Saul also among the prophets?'

The Friendship of David and Jonathan

20 David fled from Naioth in Ramah. He came before Jonathan and said, 'What have I done? What is my guilt? And what is my sin against your father that he is trying to take my life?' ²He said to him, 'Perish the thought! You shall not die. My father does nothing either great or small without disclosing it to me; and why should my father hide this from me? Never!' ³But David also swore, 'Your father knows well that you like me; and he thinks, "Do not let Jonathan know this, or he will be grieved." But truly, as the LORD lives and as you yourself live, there is but a step between me and death.' ⁴Then Jonathan said to David, 'Whatever you say, I will do for you.' ⁵David said to Jonathan,

---

a Heb *took the teraphim*   b Meaning of Heb uncertain
c Heb *the teraphim*   d Gk reads *to the well of the threshing-floor on the bare height*

'Tomorrow is the new moon, and I should not fail to sit with the king at the meal; but let me go, so that I may hide in the field until the third evening. 6 If your father misses me at all, then say, "David earnestly asked leave of me to run to Bethlehem his city; for there is a yearly sacrifice there for all the family." 7 If he says, "Good!" it will be well with your servant; but if he is angry, then know that evil has been determined by him. 8 Therefore deal kindly with your servant, for you have brought your servant into a sacred covenant*a* with you. But if there is guilt in me, kill me yourself; why should you bring me to your father?' 9 Jonathan said, 'Far be it from you! If I knew that it was decided by my father that evil should come upon you, would I not tell you?' 10 Then David said to Jonathan, 'Who will tell me if your father answers you harshly?' 11 Jonathan replied to David, 'Come, let us go out into the field.' So they both went out into the field.

12 Jonathan said to David, 'By the LORD, the God of Israel! When I have sounded out my father, about this time tomorrow, or on the third day, if he is well disposed towards David, shall I not then send and disclose it to you? 13 But if my father intends to do you harm, the LORD do so to Jonathan, and more also, if I do not disclose it to you, and send you away, so that you may go in safety. May the LORD be with you, as he has been with my father. 14 If I am still alive, show me the faithful love of the LORD; but if I die,*b* 15 never cut off your faithful love from my house, even if the LORD were to cut off every one of the enemies of David from the face of the earth.' 16 Thus Jonathan made a covenant with the house of David, saying, 'May the LORD seek out the enemies of David.' 17 Jonathan made David swear again by his love for him; for he loved him as he loved his own life.

18 Jonathan said to him, 'Tomorrow is the new moon; you will be missed, because your place will be empty. 19 On the day after tomorrow, you shall go a long way down; go to the place where you hid yourself earlier, and remain beside the stone there.*b* 20 I will shoot three arrows to the side of it, as though I shot at a mark. 21 Then I will send the boy, saying, "Go, find the arrows." If I say to the boy, "Look, the arrows are on this side of you, collect them", then you are to come, for, as the LORD lives, it is safe for you and there is no danger. 22 But if I say to the young man, "Look, the arrows are beyond you", then go; for the LORD has sent you away. 23 As for the matter about which you and I have spoken, the LORD is witness*c* between you and me for ever.'

24 So David hid himself in the field. When the new moon came, the king sat at the feast to eat. 25 The king sat upon his seat, as at other times, upon the seat by the wall. Jonathan stood, while Abner sat by Saul's side; but David's place was empty. 26 Saul did not say anything that day; for he thought, 'Something has befallen him; he is not clean, surely he is not clean.' 27 But on the second day, the day after the new moon, David's place was empty. And Saul said to his son Jonathan, 'Why has the son of Jesse not come to the feast, either yesterday or today?' 28 Jonathan answered Saul, 'David earnestly asked leave of me to go to Bethlehem; 29 he said, "Let me go; for our family is holding a sacrifice in the city, and my brother has commanded me to be there. So now, if I have found favour in your sight, let me get away, and see my brothers." For this reason he has not come to the king's table.'

30 Then Saul's anger was kindled against Jonathan. He said to him, 'You son of a perverse, rebellious woman! Do I not know that you have chosen the son of Jesse to your own shame, and to the shame of your mother's nakedness? 31 For as long as the son of Jesse lives upon the earth, neither you nor your kingdom shall be established. Now send and bring him to me, for he shall surely die.' 32 Then Jonathan answered his father Saul, 'Why should he be put to death? What has he done?' 33 But Saul threw his spear at him to strike him;

a Heb *a covenant of the* LORD   *b* Meaning of Heb uncertain   *c* Gk: Heb lacks *witness* so Jonathan knew that it was the decision of his father to put David to death. ³⁴ Jonathan rose from the table in fierce anger and ate no food on the second day of the month, for he was grieved for David, and because his father had disgraced him.

35 In the morning Jonathan went out into the field to the appointment with David, and with him was a little boy. ³⁶ He said to the boy, 'Run and find the arrows that I shoot.' As the boy ran, he shot an arrow beyond him. ³⁷ When the boy came to the place where Jonathan's arrow had fallen, Jonathan called after the boy and said, 'Is the arrow not beyond you?' ³⁸ Jonathan called after the boy, 'Hurry, be quick, do not linger.' So Jonathan's boy gathered up the arrows and came to his master. ³⁹ But the boy knew nothing; only Jonathan and David knew the arrangement. ⁴⁰ Jonathan gave his weapons to the boy and said to him, 'Go and carry them to the city.' ⁴¹ As soon as the boy had gone, David rose from beside the stone heap ᵃ and prostrated himself with his face to the ground. He bowed three times, and they kissed each other, and wept with each other; David wept the more. ᵇ ⁴² Then Jonathan said to David, 'Go in peace, since both of us have sworn in the name of the Lord, saying, "The Lord shall be between me and you, and between my descendants and your descendants, for ever." ' He got up and left; and Jonathan went into the city. ᶜ

David and the Holy Bread

21 ᵈ David came to Nob to the priest Ahimelech. Ahimelech came trembling to meet David, and said to him, 'Why are you alone, and no one with you?' ² David said to the priest Ahimelech, 'The king has charged me with a matter, and said to me, "No one must know anything of the matter about which I send you, and with which I have charged you." I have made an appointment ᵉ with the young men for such and such a place. ³ Now then, what have you at hand? Give me five loaves of bread, or whatever is here.' ⁴ The priest answered David, 'I have no ordinary bread at hand, only holy bread—provided that the young

men have kept themselves from women.' ⁵ David answered the priest, 'Indeed, women have been kept from us as always when I go on an expedition; the vessels of the young men are holy even when it is a common journey; how much more today will their vessels be holy?' ⁶ So the priest gave him the holy bread; for there was no bread there except the bread of the Presence, which is removed from before the Lord to be replaced by hot bread on the day it is taken away.

7 Now a certain man of the servants of Saul was there that day, detained before the Lord; his name was Doeg the Edomite, the chief of Saul's shepherds.

8 David said to Ahimelech, 'Is there no spear or sword here with you? I did not bring my sword or my weapons with me, because the king's business required haste.' ⁹ The priest said, 'The sword of Goliath the Philistine, whom you killed in the valley of Elah, is here wrapped in a cloth behind the ephod; if you will take that, take it, for there is none here except that one.' David said, 'There is none like it; give it to me.'

David Flees to Gath

10 David rose and fled that day from Saul; he went to King Achish of Gath. ¹¹ The servants of Achish said to him, 'Is this not David the king of the land? Did they not sing to one another of him in dances,

"Saul has killed his thousands,
    and David his tens of thousands"?'

¹² David took these words to heart and was very much afraid of King Achish of Gath. ¹³ So he changed his behaviour before them; he pretended to be mad when in their presence.ᶠ He scratched marks on the doors of the gate, and let his spittle run down his beard. ¹⁴ Achish said to his servants, 'Look, you see the man is mad; why then have you brought him to me? ¹⁵ Do I lack madmen, that you have brought this fellow to play the madman in my presence? Shall this fellow come into my house?'

---

a Gk: Heb *from beside the south*   *b* Vg: Meaning of Heb uncertain   *c* This sentence is 21.1 in Heb   *d* Ch 21.2 in Heb   *e* Q Ms Vg Compare Gk: Meaning of MT uncertain   *f* Heb *in their hands*

David and His Followers at Adullam

22 David left there and escaped to the cave of Adullam; when his brothers and all his father's house heard of it, they went down there to him. ²Everyone who was in distress, and everyone who was in debt, and everyone who was discontented gathered to him; and he became captain over them. Those who were with him numbered about four hundred.

3 David went from there to Mizpeh of Moab. He said to the king of Moab, 'Please let my father and mother come*ᵃ* to you, until I know what God will do for me.' ⁴He left them with the king of Moab, and they stayed with him all the time that David was in the stronghold. ⁵Then the prophet Gad said to David, 'Do not remain in the stronghold; leave, and go into the land of Judah.' So David left, and went into the forest of Hereth.

Saul Slaughters the Priests at Nob

6 Saul heard that David and those who were with him had been located. Saul was

David the Fugitive From Saul

sitting at Gibeah, under the tamarisk tree on the height, with his spear in his hand, and all his servants were standing around him. ⁷Saul said to his servants who stood around him, 'Hear now, you Benjaminites; will the son of Jesse give every one of you fields and vineyards, will he make you all commanders of thousands and commanders of hundreds? ⁸Is that why all of you have conspired against me? No one discloses to me when my son makes a league with the son of Jesse, none of you is sorry for me or discloses to me that my son has stirred up my servant against me, to lie in wait, as he is doing today.' ⁹Doeg the Edomite, who was in charge of Saul's servants, answered, 'I saw the son of Jesse coming to Nob, to Ahimelech son of Ahitub; ¹⁰he inquired of the LORD for him, gave him provisions, and gave him the sword of Goliath the Philistine.'

11 The king sent for the priest Ahimelech son of Ahitub and for all his father's house, the priests who were at Nob; and all of them came to the king. ¹²Saul said, 'Listen now, son of Ahitub.' He answered, 'Here I am, my lord.' ¹³Saul said to him, 'Why have you conspired against me, you and the son of Jesse, by giving him bread and a sword, and by inquiring of God for him, so that he has risen against me, to lie in wait, as he is doing today?'

14 Then Ahimelech answered the king, 'Who among all your servants is so faithful as David? He is the king's son-in-law, and is quick*ᵇ* to do your bidding, and is honoured in your house. ¹⁵Is today the first time that I have inquired of God for him? By no means! Do not let the king impute anything to his servant or to any member of my father's house; for your servant has known nothing of all this, much or little.' ¹⁶The king said, 'You shall surely die, Ahimelech, you and all your father's house.' ¹⁷The king said to the guard who stood around him, 'Turn and kill the priests of the LORD, because their hand also is with David; they knew that he fled, and did not disclose it to me.' But the servants of the king would not raise their hand to attack the priests of

---

a Syr Vg: Heb *come out*   *b* Heb *and turns aside*

the LORD. ¹⁸Then the king said to Doeg, 'You, Doeg, turn and attack the priests.' Doeg the Edomite turned and attacked the priests; on that day he killed eighty-five who wore the linen ephod. ¹⁹Nob, the city of the priests, he put to the sword; men and women, children and infants, oxen, donkeys, and sheep, he put to the sword.

20 But one of the sons of Ahimelech son of Ahitub, named Abiathar, escaped and fled after David. ²¹Abiathar told David that Saul had killed the priests of the LORD. ²²David said to Abiathar, 'I knew on that day, when Doeg the Edomite was there, that he would surely tell Saul. I am responsible*a* for the lives of all your father's house. ²³Stay with me, and do not be afraid; for the one who seeks my life seeks your life; you will be safe with me.'

David Saves the City of Keilah

23 Now they told David, 'The Philistines are fighting against Keilah, and are robbing the threshing-floors.' ²David inquired of the LORD, 'Shall I go and attack these Philistines?' The LORD said to David, 'Go and attack the Philistines and save Keilah.' ³But David's men said to him, 'Look, we are afraid here in Judah; how much more then if we go to Keilah against the armies of the Philistines?' ⁴Then David inquired of the LORD again. The LORD answered him, 'Yes, go down to Keilah; for I will give the Philistines into your hand.' ⁵So David and his men went to Keilah, fought with the Philistines, brought away their livestock, and dealt them a heavy defeat. Thus David rescued the inhabitants of Keilah.

6 When Abiathar son of Ahimelech fled to David at Keilah, he came down with an ephod in his hand. ⁷Now it was told Saul that David had come to Keilah. And Saul said, 'God has given*b* him into my hand; for he has shut himself in by entering a town that has gates and bars.' ⁸Saul summoned all the people to war, to go down to Keilah, to besiege David and his men. ⁹When David learned that Saul was plotting evil against him, he said to the priest Abiathar, 'Bring the ephod here.' ¹⁰David

said, 'O LORD, the God of Israel, your servant has heard that Saul seeks to come to Keilah, to destroy the city on my account. ¹¹And now, will*c* Saul come down as your servant has heard? O LORD, the God of Israel, I beseech you, tell your servant.' The LORD said, 'He will come down.' ¹²Then David said, 'Will the men of Keilah surrender me and my men into the hand of Saul?' The LORD said, 'They will surrender you.' ¹³Then David and his men, who were about six hundred, set out and left Keilah; they wandered wherever they could go. When Saul was told that David had escaped from Keilah, he gave up the expedition. ¹⁴David remained in the strongholds in the wilderness, in the hill country of the Wilderness of Ziph. Saul sought him every day, but the LORD*d* did not give him into his hand.

David Eludes Saul in the Wilderness

15 David was in the Wilderness of Ziph at Horesh when he learned that*e* Saul had come out to seek his life. ¹⁶Saul's son Jonathan set out and came to David at Horesh; there he strengthened his hand through the LORD.*f* ¹⁷He said to him, 'Do not be afraid; for the hand of my father Saul shall not find you; you shall be king over Israel, and I shall be second to you; my father Saul also knows that this is so.' ¹⁸Then the two of them made a covenant before the LORD; David remained at Horesh, and Jonathan went home.

19 Then some Ziphites went up to Saul at Gibeah and said, 'David is hiding among us in the strongholds of Horesh, on the hill of Hachilah, which is south of Jeshimon. ²⁰Now, O king, whenever you wish to come down, do so; and our part will be to surrender him into the king's hand.' ²¹Saul said, 'May you be blessed by the LORD for showing me compassion! ²²Go and make sure once more; find out exactly where he is, and who has seen him there; for I am told that he is very cunning.

a Gk Vg: Meaning of Heb uncertain   *b* Gk Tg: Heb
made a stranger of   *c* Q Ms Compare Gk: MT *Will the*
men of Keilah surrender me into his hand? Will   *d* Q Ms
Gk: MT *God*   *e* Or *saw that*   *f* Compare Q Ms Gk:
MT *God*

23 Look around and learn all the hiding-places where he lurks, and come back to me with sure information. Then I will go with you; and if he is in the land, I will search him out among all the thousands of Judah.' 24 So they set out and went to Ziph ahead of Saul.

David and his men were in the wilderness of Maon, in the Arabah to the south of Jeshimon. 25 Saul and his men went to search for him. When David was told, he went down to the rock and stayed in the wilderness of Maon. When Saul heard that, he pursued David into the wilderness of Maon. 26 Saul went on one side of the mountain, and David and his men on the other side of the mountain. David was hurrying to get away from Saul, while Saul and his men were closing in on David and his men to capture them. 27 Then a messenger came to Saul, saying, 'Hurry and come; for the Philistines have made a raid on the land.' 28 So Saul stopped pursuing David, and went against the Philistines; therefore that place was called the Rock of Escape.*a* 29 *b* David then went up from there, and lived in the strongholds of En-gedi.

David Spares Saul's Life

24 When Saul returned from following the Philistines, he was told, 'David is in the wilderness of En-gedi.' 2 Then Saul took three thousand chosen men out of all Israel, and went to look for David and his men in the direction of the Rocks of the Wild Goats. 3 He came to the sheepfolds beside the road, where there was a cave; and Saul went in to relieve himself.*c* Now David and his men were sitting in the innermost parts of the cave. 4 The men of David said to him, 'Here is the day of which the LORD said to you, "I will give your enemy into your hand, and you shall do to him as it seems good to you." ' Then David went and stealthily cut off a corner of Saul's cloak. 5 Afterwards David was stricken to the heart because he had cut off a corner of Saul's cloak. 6 He said to his men, 'The LORD forbid that I should do this thing to my lord, the LORD's

anointed, to raise my hand against him; for he is the LORD's anointed.' 7 So David scolded his men severely and did not permit them to attack Saul. Then Saul got up and left the cave, and went on his way.

8 Afterwards David also rose up and went out of the cave and called after Saul, 'My lord the king!' When Saul looked behind him, David bowed with his face to the ground, and did obeisance. 9 David said to Saul, 'Why do you listen to the words of those who say, "David seeks to do you harm"? 10 This very day your eyes have seen how the LORD gave you into my hand in the cave; and some urged me to kill you, but I spared*d* you. I said, "I will not raise my hand against my lord; for he is the LORD's anointed." 11 See, my father, see the corner of your cloak in my hand; for by the fact that I cut off the corner of your cloak, and did not kill you, you may know for certain that there is no wrong or treason in my hands. I have not sinned against you, though you are hunting me to take my life. 12 May the LORD judge between me and you! May the LORD avenge me on you; but my hand shall not be against you. 13 As the ancient proverb says, "Out of the wicked comes forth wickedness"; but my hand shall not be against you. 14 Against whom has the king of Israel come out? Whom do you pursue? A dead dog? A single flea? 15 May the LORD therefore be judge, and give sentence between me and you. May he see to it, and plead my cause, and vindicate me against you.'

16 When David had finished speaking these words to Saul, Saul said, 'Is that your voice, my son David?' Saul lifted up his voice and wept. 17 He said to David, 'You are more righteous than I; for you have repaid me good, whereas I have repaid you evil. 18 Today you have explained how you have dealt well with me, in that you did not kill me when the LORD put me into your hands. 19 For who has ever found an enemy, and sent the enemy safely away?

a Or *Rock of Division*; meaning of Heb uncertain
b Ch 24.1 in Heb   *c* Heb *to cover his feet*   *d* Gk Syr Tg Vg: Heb *it* (my eye) *spared*

So may the LORD reward you with good for what you have done to me this day. 20 Now I know that you shall surely be king, and that the kingdom of Israel shall be established in your hand. 21 Swear to me therefore by the LORD that you will not cut off my descendants after me, and that you will not wipe out my name from my father's house.' 22 So David swore this to Saul. Then Saul went home; but David and his men went up to the stronghold.

Death of Samuel

25 Now Samuel died; and all Israel assembled and mourned for him. They buried him at his home in Ramah.

Then David got up and went down to the wilderness of Paran.

David and the Wife of Nabal

2 There was a man in Maon, whose property was in Carmel. The man was very rich; he had three thousand sheep and a thousand goats. He was shearing his sheep in Carmel. 3 Now the name of the man was Nabal, and the name of his wife Abigail. The woman was clever and beautiful, but the man was surly and mean; he was a Calebite. 4 David heard in the wilderness that Nabal was shearing his sheep. 5 So David sent ten young men; and David said to the young men, 'Go up to Carmel, and go to Nabal, and greet him in my name. 6 Thus you shall salute him: "Peace be to you, and peace be to your house, and peace be to all that you have. 7 I hear that you have shearers; now your shepherds have been with us, and we did them no harm, and they missed nothing, all the time they were in Carmel. 8 Ask your young men, and they will tell you. Therefore let my young men find favour in your sight; for we have come on a feast day. Please give whatever you have at hand to your servants and to your son David." '

9 When David's young men came, they said all this to Nabal in the name of David; and then they waited. 10 But Nabal answered David's servants, 'Who is David? Who is the son of Jesse? There are many servants today who are breaking away from their masters. 11 Shall I take my bread and my water and the meat that I have butchered for my shearers, and give it to men who come from I do not know where?' 12 So David's young men turned away, and came back and told him all this. 13 David said to his men, 'Every man strap on his sword!' And every one of them strapped on his sword; David also strapped on his sword; and about four hundred men went up after David, while two hundred remained with the baggage.

14 But one of the young men told Abigail, Nabal's wife, 'David sent messengers out of the wilderness to salute our master; and he shouted insults at them. 15 Yet the men were very good to us, and we suffered no harm, and we never missed anything when we were in the fields, as long as we were with them; 16 they were a wall to us both by night and by day, all the while we were with them keeping the sheep. 17 Now therefore know this and consider what you should do; for evil has been decided against our master and against all his house; he is so ill-natured that no one can speak to him.'

18 Then Abigail hurried and took two hundred loaves, two skins of wine, five sheep ready dressed, five measures of parched grain, one hundred clusters of raisins, and two hundred cakes of figs. She loaded them on donkeys 19 and said to her young men, 'Go on ahead of me; I am coming after you.' But she did not tell her husband Nabal. 20 As she rode on the donkey and came down under cover of the mountain, David and his men came down towards her; and she met them. 21 Now David had said, 'Surely it was in vain that I protected all that this fellow has in the wilderness, so that nothing was missed of all that belonged to him; but he has returned me evil for good. 22 God do so to David[a] and more also, if by morning I leave as much as one male of all who belong to him.'

23 When Abigail saw David, she hurried and alighted from the donkey, and fell be-

---

a Gk Compare Syr: Heb *the enemies of David*

fore David on her face, bowing to the ground. 24 She fell at his feet and said, 'Upon me alone, my lord, be the guilt; please let your servant speak in your ears, and hear the words of your servant. 25 My lord, do not take seriously this ill-natured fellow Nabal; for as his name is, so is he; Nabal*a* is his name, and folly is with him; but I, your servant, did not see the young men of my lord, whom you sent.

26 'Now then, my lord, as the LORD lives, and as you yourself live, since the LORD has restrained you from blood-guilt and from taking vengeance with your own hand, now let your enemies and those who seek to do evil to my lord be like Nabal. 27 And now let this present that your servant has brought to my lord be given to the young men who follow my lord. 28 Please forgive the trespass of your servant; for the LORD will certainly make my lord a sure house, because my lord is fighting the battles of the LORD; and evil shall not be found in you as long as you live. 29 If anyone should rise up to pursue you and to seek your life, the life of my lord shall be bound in the bundle of the living under the care of the LORD your God; but the lives of your enemies he shall sling out as from the hollow of a sling. 30 When the LORD has done to my lord according to all the good that he has spoken concerning you, and has appointed you prince over Israel, 31 my lord shall have no cause of grief, or pangs of conscience, for having shed blood without cause or for having saved himself. And when the LORD has dealt well with my lord, then remember your servant.'

32 David said to Abigail, 'Blessed be the LORD, the God of Israel, who sent you to meet me today! 33 Blessed be your good sense, and blessed be you, who have kept me today from blood-guilt and from avenging myself by my own hand! 34 For as surely as the LORD the God of Israel lives, who has restrained me from hurting you, unless you had hurried and come to meet me, truly by morning there would not have been left to Nabal as much as one male.' 35 Then David received from her

hand what she had brought him; he said to her, 'Go up to your house in peace; see, I have heeded your voice, and I have granted your petition.'

36 Abigail came to Nabal; he was holding a feast in his house, like the feast of a king. Nabal's heart was merry within him, for he was very drunk; so she told him nothing at all until the morning light. 37 In the morning, when the wine had gone out of Nabal, his wife told him these things, and his heart died within him; he became like a stone. 38 About ten days later the LORD struck Nabal, and he died.

39 When David heard that Nabal was dead, he said, 'Blessed be the LORD who has judged the case of Nabal's insult to me, and has kept back his servant from evil; the LORD has returned the evildoing of Nabal upon his own head.' Then David sent and wooed Abigail, to make her his wife. 40 When David's servants came to Abigail at Carmel, they said to her, 'David has sent us to you to take you to him as his wife.' 41 She rose and bowed down, with her face to the ground, and said, 'Your servant is a slave to wash the feet of the servants of my lord.' 42 Abigail got up hurriedly and rode away on a donkey; her five maids attended her. She went after the messengers of David and became his wife.

43 David also married Ahinoam of Jezreel; both of them became his wives. 44 Saul had given his daughter Michal, David's wife, to Palti son of Laish, who was from Gallim.

David Spares Saul's Life a Second Time

26 Then the Ziphites came to Saul at Gibeah, saying, 'David is in hiding on the hill of Hachilah, which is opposite Jeshimon.'*b* 2 So Saul rose and went down to the Wilderness of Ziph, with three thousand chosen men of Israel, to seek David in the Wilderness of Ziph. 3 Saul encamped on the hill of Hachilah, which is opposite Jeshimon*b* beside the road. But David remained in the wilderness. When he learned that Saul had come after him into the wilderness, 4 David sent out spies, and

a That is *Fool*   *b* Or *opposite the waste-land*

learned that Saul had indeed arrived. 5 Then David set out and came to the place where Saul had encamped; and David saw the place where Saul lay, with Abner son of Ner, the commander of his army. Saul was lying within the encampment, while the army was encamped around him.

6 Then David said to Ahimelech the Hittite, and to Joab's brother Abishai son of Zeruiah, 'Who will go down with me into the camp to Saul?' Abishai said, 'I will go down with you.' 7 So David and Abishai went to the army by night; there Saul lay sleeping within the encampment, with his spear stuck in the ground at his head; and Abner and the army lay around him. 8 Abishai said to David, 'God has given your enemy into your hand today; now therefore let me pin him to the ground with one stroke of the spear; I will not strike him twice.' 9 But David said to Abishai, 'Do not destroy him; for who can raise his hand against the LORD's anointed, and be guiltless?' 10 David said, 'As the LORD lives, the LORD will strike him down; or his day will come to die; or he will go down into battle and perish. 11 The LORD forbid that I should raise my hand against the LORD's anointed; but now take the spear that is at his head, and the water-jar, and let us go.' 12 So David took the spear that was at Saul's head and the water-jar, and they went away. No one saw it, or knew it, nor did anyone awake; for they were all asleep, because a deep sleep from the LORD had fallen upon them.

13 Then David went over to the other side, and stood on top of a hill far away, with a great distance between them. 14 David called to the army and to Abner son of Ner, saying, 'Abner! Will you not answer?' Then Abner replied, 'Who are you that calls to the king?' 15 David said to Abner, 'Are you not a man? Who is like you in Israel? Why then have you not kept watch over your lord the king? For one of the people came in to destroy your lord the king. 16 This thing that you have done is not good. As the LORD lives, you deserve to die, because you have not kept watch over your lord, the LORD's anointed. See

now, where is the king's spear, or the water-jar that was at his head?'

17 Saul recognized David's voice, and said, 'Is that your voice, my son David?' David said, 'It is my voice, my lord, O king.' 18 And he added, 'Why does my lord pursue his servant? For what have I done? What guilt is on my hands? 19 Now therefore let my lord the king hear the words of his servant. If it is the LORD who has stirred you up against me, may he accept an offering; but if it is mortals, may they be cursed before the LORD, for they have driven me out today from my share in the heritage of the LORD, saying, "Go, serve other gods." 20 Now, therefore, do not let my blood fall to the ground, away from the presence of the LORD; for the king of Israel has come out to seek a single flea, like one who hunts a partridge in the mountains.'

21 Then Saul said, 'I have done wrong; come back, my son David, for I will never harm you again, because my life was precious in your sight today; I have been a fool, and have made a great mistake.' 22 David replied, 'Here is the spear, O king! Let one of the young men come over and get it. 23 The LORD rewards everyone for his righteousness and his faithfulness; for the LORD gave you into my hand today, but I would not raise my hand against the LORD's anointed. 24 As your life was precious today in my sight, so may my life be precious in the sight of the LORD, and may he rescue me from all tribulation.' 25 Then Saul said to David, 'Blessed be you, my son David! You will do many things and will succeed in them.' So David went on his way, and Saul returned to his place.

David Serves King Achish of Gath

27 David said in his heart, 'I shall now perish one day by the hand of Saul; there is nothing better for me than to escape to the land of the Philistines; then Saul will despair of seeking me any longer within the borders of Israel, and I shall escape out of his hand.' 2 So David set out and went over, he and the six hundred men who were with him, to King Achish son of Maoch of Gath. 3 David stayed with

Achish at Gath, he and his troops, every man with his household, and David with his two wives, Ahinoam of Jezreel, and Abigail of Carmel, Nabal's widow. 4 When Saul was told that David had fled to Gath, he no longer sought for him.

5 Then David said to Achish, 'If I have found favour in your sight, let a place be given me in one of the country towns, so that I may live there; for why should your servant live in the royal city with you?' 6 So that day Achish gave him Ziklag; therefore Ziklag has belonged to the kings of Judah to this day. 7 The length of time that David lived in the country of the Philistines was one year and four months.

8 Now David and his men went up and made raids on the Geshurites, the Girzites, and the Amalekites; for these were the landed settlements from Telam*a* on the way to Shur and on to the land of Egypt. 9 David struck the land, leaving neither man nor woman alive, but took away the sheep, the oxen, the donkeys, the camels, and the clothing, and came back to Achish. 10 When Achish asked, 'Against whom*b* have you made a raid today?' David would say, 'Against the Negeb of Judah', or 'Against the Negeb of the Jerahmeelites', or 'Against the Negeb of the Kenites.' 11 David left neither man nor woman alive to be brought back to Gath, thinking, 'They might tell about us, and say, "David has done so and so." ' Such was his practice all the time he lived in the country of the Philistines. 12 Achish trusted David, thinking, 'He has made himself utterly abhorrent to his people Israel; therefore he shall always be my servant.'

28 In those days the Philistines gathered their forces for war, to fight against Israel. Achish said to David, 'You know, of course, that you and your men are to go out with me in the army.' 2 David said to Achish, 'Very well, then you shall know what your servant can do.' Achish said to David, 'Very well, I will make you my bodyguard for life.'

Saul Consults a Medium

3 Now Samuel had died, and all Israel had mourned for him and buried him in Ramah, his own city. Saul had expelled the mediums and the wizards from the land. 4 The Philistines assembled, and came and encamped at Shunem. Saul gathered all Israel, and they encamped at Gilboa. 5 When Saul saw the army of the Philistines, he was afraid, and his heart trembled greatly. 6 When Saul inquired of the LORD, the LORD did not answer him, not by dreams, nor by Urim, nor by prophets. 7 Then Saul said to his servants, 'Seek out for me a woman who is a medium, so that I may go to her and inquire of her.' His servants said to him, 'There is a medium at Endor.'

8 So Saul disguised himself and put on other clothes and went there, he and two men with him. They came to the woman by night. And he said, 'Consult a spirit for me, and bring up for me the one whom I name to you.' 9 The woman said to him, 'Surely you know what Saul has done, how he has cut off the mediums and the wizards from the land. Why then are you laying a snare for my life to bring about my death?' 10 But Saul swore to her by the LORD, 'As the LORD lives, no punishment shall come upon you for this thing.' 11 Then the woman said, 'Whom shall I bring up for you?' He answered, 'Bring up Samuel for me.' 12 When the woman saw Samuel, she cried out with a loud voice; and the woman said to Saul, 'Why have you deceived me? You are Saul!' 13 The king said to her, 'Have no fear; what do you see?' The woman said to Saul, 'I see a divine being*c* coming up out of the ground.' 14 He said to her, 'What is his appearance?' She said, 'An old man is coming up; he is wrapped in a robe.' So Saul knew that it was Samuel, and he bowed with his face to the ground, and did obeisance.

15 Then Samuel said to Saul, 'Why have you disturbed me by bringing me up?' Saul answered, 'I am in great distress, for the Philistines are warring against me, and God has turned away from me and answers me no more, either by prophets or by dreams; so I have summoned you to tell me what I should do.' 16 Samuel said, 'Why then do

a Compare Gk 15.4: Heb *from of old*   *b* Q Ms Gk Vg: MT lacks *whom*   *c* Or *a god*; or *gods* you ask me, since the LORD has turned from you and become your enemy? 17 The LORD has done to you just as he spoke by me; for the LORD has torn the kingdom out of your hand, and given it to your neighbour David. 18 Because you did not obey the voice of the LORD, and did not carry out his fierce wrath against Amalek, therefore the LORD has done this thing to you today. 19 Moreover, the LORD will give Israel along with you into the hands of the Philistines; and tomorrow you and your sons shall be with me; the LORD will also give the army of Israel into the hands of the Philistines.'

20 Immediately Saul fell full length on the ground, filled with fear because of the words of Samuel; and there was no strength in him, for he had eaten nothing all day and all night. 21 The woman came to Saul, and when she saw that he was terrified, she said to him, 'Your servant has listened to you; I have taken my life in my hand, and have listened to what you have said to me. 22 Now therefore, you also listen to your servant; let me set a morsel of bread before you. Eat, that you may have strength when you go on your way.' 23 He refused, and said, 'I will not eat.' But his servants, together with the woman, urged him; and he listened to their words. So he got up from the ground and sat on the bed. 24 Now the woman had a fatted calf in the house. She quickly slaughtered it, and she took flour, kneaded it, and baked unleavened cakes. 25 She put them before Saul and his servants, and they ate. Then they rose and went away that night.

The Philistines Reject David

29 Now the Philistines gathered all their forces at Aphek, while the Israelites were encamped by the fountain that is in Jezreel. 2 As the lords of the Philistines were marching on by hundreds and by thousands, and David and his men were marching in the rear with Achish, 3 the commanders of the Philistines said, 'What are these Hebrews doing here?' Achish said to the commanders of the Philistines, 'Is this not David, the servant of King Saul of Israel, who has been with me now for days and years? Since he deserted to me I have found no fault in him to this day.' 4 But the commanders of the Philistines were angry with him; and the commanders of the Philistines said to him, 'Send the man back, so that he may return to the place that you have assigned to him; he shall not go down with us to battle, or else he may become an adversary to us in the battle. For how could this fellow reconcile himself to his lord? Would it not be with the heads of the men here? 5 Is this not David, of whom they sing to one another in dances,

"Saul has killed his thousands,
    and David his tens of thousands"?'

6 Then Achish called David and said to him, 'As the LORD lives, you have been honest, and to me it seems right that you should march out and in with me in the campaign; for I have found nothing wrong in you from the day of your coming to me until today. Nevertheless the lords do not approve of you. 7 So go back now; and go peaceably; do nothing to displease the lords of the Philistines.' 8 David said to Achish, 'But what have I done? What have you found in your servant from the day I entered your service until now, that I should not go and fight against the enemies of my lord the king?' 9 Achish replied to David, 'I know that you are as blameless in my sight as an angel of God; nevertheless, the commanders of the Philistines have said, "He shall not go up with us to the battle." 10 Now then rise early in the morning, you and the servants of your lord who came with you, and go to the place that I appointed for you. As for the evil report, do not take it to heart, for you have done well before me. a Start early in the morning, and leave as soon as you have light.' 11 So David set out with his men early in the morning, to return to the land of the Philistines. But the Philistines went up to Jezreel.

David Avenges the Destruction of Ziklag

30 Now when David and his men came to Ziklag on the third day, the Amalekites had made a raid on the Negeb and on Ziklag. They had attacked Ziklag,

a Gk: Heb lacks *and go to the place . . . done well before me* burned it down, 2 and taken captive the women and all*a* who were in it, both small and great; they killed none of them, but carried them off, and went on their way. 3 When David and his men came to the city, they found it burnt down, and their wives and sons and daughters taken captive. 4 Then David and the people who were with him raised their voices and wept, until they had no more strength to weep. 5 David's two wives also had been taken captive, Ahinoam of Jezreel, and Abigail the widow of Nabal of Carmel. 6 David was in great danger; for the people spoke of stoning him, because all the people were bitter in spirit for their sons and daughters. But David strengthened himself in the LORD his God.

7 David said to the priest Abiathar son of Ahimelech, 'Bring me the ephod.' So Abiathar brought the ephod to David. 8 David inquired of the LORD, 'Shall I pursue this band? Shall I overtake them?' He answered him, 'Pursue; for you shall surely overtake and shall surely rescue.' 9 So David set out, he and the six hundred men who were with him. They came to the Wadi Besor, where those stayed who were left behind. 10 But David went on with the pursuit, he and four hundred men; two hundred stayed behind, too exhausted to cross the Wadi Besor.

11 In the open country they found an Egyptian, and brought him to David. They gave him bread and he ate; they gave him water to drink; 12 they also gave him a piece of fig cake and two clusters of raisins. When he had eaten, his spirit revived; for he had not eaten bread or drunk water for three days and three nights. 13 Then David said to him, 'To whom do you belong? Where are you from?' He said, 'I am a young man of Egypt, servant to an Amalekite. My master left me behind because I fell sick three days ago. 14 We had made a raid on the Negeb of the Cherethites and on that which belongs to Judah and on the Negeb of Caleb; and we burned Ziklag down.' 15 David said to him, 'Will you take me down to this raiding party?' He said, 'Swear to me by God that you will not kill me, or hand me over to my master, and I will take you down to them.'

16 When he had taken him down, they were spread out all over the ground, eating and drinking and dancing, because of the great amount of spoil they had taken from the land of the Philistines and from the land of Judah. 17 David attacked them from twilight until the evening of the next day. Not one of them escaped, except four hundred young men, who mounted camels and fled. 18 David recovered all that the Amalekites had taken; and David rescued his two wives. 19 Nothing was missing, whether small or great, sons or daughters, spoil or anything that had been taken; David brought back everything. 20 David also captured all the flocks and herds, which were driven ahead of the other cattle; people said, 'This is David's spoil.'

21 Then David came to the two hundred men who had been too exhausted to follow David, and who had been left at the Wadi Besor. They went out to meet David and to meet the people who were with him. When David drew near to the people he saluted them. 22 Then all the corrupt and worthless fellows among the men who had gone with David said, 'Because they did not go with us, we will not give them any of the spoil that we have recovered, except that each man may take his wife and children, and leave.' 23 But David said, 'You shall not do so, my brothers, with what the LORD has given us; he has preserved us and handed over to us the raiding party that attacked us. 24 Who would listen to you in this matter? For the share of the one who goes down into the battle shall be the same as the share of the one who stays by the baggage; they shall share alike.' 25 From that day forward he made it a statute and an ordinance for Israel; it continues to the present day.

26 When David came to Ziklag, he sent part of the spoil to his friends, the elders of Judah, saying, 'Here is a present for you from the spoil of the enemies of the LORD'; 27 it was for those in Bethel, in Ramoth of the Negeb, in Jattir, 28 in Aroer, in Siphmoth, in Eshtemoa, 29 in Racal, in the towns of the Jerahmeelites, in the towns of the Kenites, 30 in Hormah, in Bor-ashan, in

a Gk: Heb lacks *and all*

Athach, ³¹in Hebron, all the places where David and his men had roamed.

The Death of Saul and His Sons

31 Now the Philistines fought against Israel; and the men of Israel fled before the Philistines, and many fell*ᵃ* on Mount Gilboa. ²The Philistines overtook Saul and his sons; and the Philistines killed Jonathan and Abinadab and Malchishua, the sons of Saul. ³The battle pressed hard upon Saul; the archers found him, and he was badly wounded by them. ⁴Then Saul said to his armour-bearer, 'Draw your sword and thrust me through with it, so that these uncircumcised may not come and thrust me through, and make sport of me.' But his armour-bearer was unwilling; for he was terrified. So Saul took his own sword and fell upon it. ⁵When his armour-bearer saw that Saul was dead, he also fell upon his sword and died with him. ⁶So Saul and his three sons and his armour-bearer and all his men died together on the same day. ⁷When the men of Israel who were on the other side of the valley and those beyond the Jordan saw that the men of Israel had fled and that Saul and his sons were dead, they forsook their towns and fled; and the Philistines came and occupied them.

8 The next day, when the Philistines came to strip the dead, they found Saul and his three sons fallen on Mount Gilboa. ⁹They cut off his head, stripped off his armour, and sent messengers throughout the land of the Philistines to carry the good news to the houses of their idols and to the people. ¹⁰They put his armour in the temple of Astarte;*ᵇ* and they fastened his body to the wall of Beth-shan. ¹¹But when the inhabitants of Jabesh-gilead heard what the Philistines had done to Saul, ¹²all the valiant men set out, travelled all night long, and took the body of Saul and the bodies of his sons from the wall of Beth-shan. They came to Jabesh and burned them there. ¹³Then they took their bones and buried them under the tamarisk tree in Jabesh, and fasted for seven days.

a Heb *and they fell slain*   *b* Heb plural

2 SAMUEL

David Mourns for Saul and Jonathan

1 After the death of Saul, when David had returned from defeating the Amalekites, David remained two days in Ziklag. ² On the third day, a man came from Saul's camp, with his clothes torn and dirt on his head. When he came to David, he fell to the ground and did obeisance. ³ David said to him, 'Where have you come from?' He said to him, 'I have escaped from the camp of Israel.' ⁴ David said to him, 'How did things go? Tell me!' He answered, 'The army fled from the battle, but also many of the army fell and died; and Saul and his son Jonathan also died.' ⁵ Then David asked the young man who was reporting to him, 'How do you know that Saul and his son Jonathan died?' ⁶ The young man reporting to him said, 'I happened to be on Mount Gilboa; and there was Saul leaning on his spear, while the chariots and the horsemen drew close to him. ⁷ When he looked behind him, he saw me, and called to me. I answered, "Here, sir." ⁸ And he said to me, "Who are you?" I answered him, "I am an Amalekite." ⁹ He said to me, "Come, stand over me and kill me; for convulsions have seized me, and yet my life still lingers." ¹⁰ So I stood over him, and killed him, for I knew that he could not live after he had fallen. I took the crown that was on his head and the armlet that was on his arm, and I have brought them here to my lord.'

11 Then David took hold of his clothes and tore them; and all the men who were with him did the same. ¹² They mourned and wept, and fasted until evening for Saul and for his son Jonathan, and for the army of the LORD and for the house of Israel, because they had fallen by the sword. ¹³ David said to the young man who had reported to him, 'Where do you come from?' He answered, 'I am the son of a resident alien, an Amalekite.' ¹⁴ David said to him, 'Were you not afraid to lift your hand to destroy the LORD's anointed?' ¹⁵ Then David called one of the young men and said, 'Come here and strike him down.' So he struck him down and he died. ¹⁶ David said to him, 'Your blood be on your head; for your own mouth has testified against you, saying, "I have killed the LORD's anointed." '

17 David intoned this lamentation over Saul and his son Jonathan. ¹⁸ (He ordered that The Song of the Bow*a* be taught to the people of Judah; it is written in the Book of Jashar.) He said:

¹⁹ Your glory, O Israel, lies slain upon
      your high places!
   How the mighty have fallen!
²⁰ Tell it not in Gath,
      proclaim it not in the streets of
         Ashkelon;
   or the daughters of the Philistines
         will rejoice,
      the daughters of the uncircumcised
         will exult.

²¹ You mountains of Gilboa,
      let there be no dew or rain upon
         you,
      nor bounteous fields!*b*
   For there the shield of the mighty was
         defiled,
      the shield of Saul, anointed with
         oil no more.

a Heb *that The Bow*   *b* Meaning of Heb uncertain

22 From the blood of the slain,
  from the fat of the mighty,
the bow of Jonathan did not turn
    back,
  nor the sword of Saul return empty.

23 Saul and Jonathan, beloved and
    lovely!
  In life and in death they were not
    divided;
they were swifter than eagles,
  they were stronger than lions.

24 O daughters of Israel, weep over Saul,
  who clothed you with crimson, in
    luxury,
  who put ornaments of gold on your
    apparel.

25 How the mighty have fallen
  in the midst of the battle!

Jonathan lies slain upon your high
    places.
26 I am distressed for you, my brother
    Jonathan;
  greatly beloved were you to me;
  your love to me was wonderful,
    passing the love of women.

27 How the mighty have fallen,
  and the weapons of war perished!

David Anointed King of Judah

2 After this David inquired of the LORD,
'Shall I go up into any of the cities of
Judah?' The LORD said to him, 'Go up.' David said, 'To which shall I go up?' He said,
'To Hebron.' 2 So David went up there,
along with his two wives, Ahinoam of Jezreel, and Abigail the widow of Nabal of
Carmel. 3 David brought up the men who
were with him, every one with his household; and they settled in the towns of Hebron. 4 Then the people of Judah came, and
there they anointed David king over the
house of Judah.

When they told David, 'It was the people
of Jabesh-gilead who buried Saul', 5 David
sent messengers to the people of Jabesh-gilead, and said to them, 'May you be blessed

by the LORD, because you showed this loyalty to Saul your lord, and buried him!
6 Now may the LORD show steadfast love
and faithfulness to you! And I too will reward you because you have done this thing.
7 Therefore let your hands be strong, and be
valiant; for Saul your lord is dead, and the
house of Judah has anointed me king over
them.'

Ishbaal King of Israel

8 But Abner son of Ner, commander of
Saul's army, had taken Ishbaal[a] son of
Saul, and brought him over to Mahanaim.
9 He made him king over Gilead, the Ashurites, Jezreel, Ephraim, Benjamin, and
over all Israel. 10 Ishbaal,[a] Saul's son, was
forty years old when he began to reign
over Israel, and he reigned for two years.
But the house of Judah followed David.
11 The time that David was king in Hebron
over the house of Judah was seven years
and six months.

The Battle of Gibeon

12 Abner son of Ner, and the servants of
Ishbaal[a] son of Saul, went out from Mahanaim to Gibeon. 13 Joab son of Zeruiah,
and the servants of David, went out and
met them at the pool of Gibeon. One
group sat on one side of the pool, while
the other sat on the other side of the pool.
14 Abner said to Joab, 'Let the young men
come forward and have a contest before
us.' Joab said, 'Let them come forward.'
15 So they came forward and were counted
as they passed by, twelve for Benjamin and
Ishbaal[a] son of Saul, and twelve of the servants of David. 16 Each grasped his opponent by the head, and thrust his sword in
his opponent's side; so they fell down together. Therefore that place was called Helkath-hazzurim,[b] which is at Gibeon. 17 The
battle was very fierce that day; and Abner
and the men of Israel were beaten by the
servants of David.

18 The three sons of Zeruiah were there,
Joab, Abishai, and Asahel. Now Asahel was
as swift of foot as a wild gazelle. 19 Asahel

a Gk Compare 1 Chr 8.33; 9.39: Heb Ish-bosheth, 'man
of shame'   b That is Field of Sword-edges

pursued Abner, turning neither to the right nor to the left as he followed him. 20 Then Abner looked back and said, 'Is it you, Asahel?' He answered, 'Yes, it is.' 21 Abner said to him, 'Turn to your right or to your left, and seize one of the young men, and take his spoil.' But Asahel would not turn away from following him. 22 Abner said again to Asahel, 'Turn away from following me; why should I strike you to the ground? How then could I show my face to your brother Joab?' 23 But he refused to turn away. So Abner struck him in the stomach with the butt of his spear, so that the spear came out at his back. He fell there, and died where he lay. And all those who came to the place where Asahel had fallen and died, stood still.

24 But Joab and Abishai pursued Abner. As the sun was going down they came to the hill of Ammah, which lies before Giah on the way to the wilderness of Gibeon. 25 The Benjaminites rallied around Abner and formed a single band; they took their stand on the top of a hill. 26 Then Abner called to Joab, 'Is the sword to keep devouring for ever? Do you not know that the end will be bitter? How long will it be before you order your people to turn from the pursuit of their kinsmen?' 27 Joab said, 'As God lives, if you had not spoken, the people would have continued to pursue their kinsmen, not stopping until morning.' 28 Joab sounded the trumpet and all the people stopped; they no longer pursued Israel or engaged in battle any further.

29 Abner and his men travelled all that night through the Arabah; they crossed the Jordan, and, marching the whole forenoon, *a* they came to Mahanaim. 30 Joab returned from the pursuit of Abner; and when he had gathered all the people together, there were missing of David's servants nineteen men besides Asahel. 31 But the servants of David had killed of Benjamin three hundred and sixty of Abner's men. 32 They took up Asahel and buried him in the tomb of his father, which was at Bethlehem. Joab and his men marched all night, and the day broke upon them at Hebron.

Abner Defects to David

3 There was a long war between the house of Saul and the house of David; David grew stronger and stronger, while the house of Saul became weaker and weaker.

2 Sons were born to David at Hebron: his firstborn was Amnon, of Ahinoam of Jezreel; 3 his second, Chileab, of Abigail the widow of Nabal of Carmel; the third, Absalom son of Maacah, daughter of King Talmai of Geshur; 4 the fourth, Adonijah son of Haggith; the fifth, Shephatiah son of Abital; 5 and the sixth, Ithream, of David's wife Eglah. These were born to David in Hebron.

6 While there was war between the house of Saul and the house of David, Abner was making himself strong in the house of Saul. 7 Now Saul had a concubine whose name was Rizpah daughter of Aiah. And Ishbaal *b* said to Abner, 'Why have you gone in to my father's concubine?' 8 The words of Ishbaal *c* made Abner very angry; he said, 'Am I a dog's head for Judah? Today I keep showing loyalty to the house of your father Saul, to his brothers, and to his friends, and have not given you into the hand of David; and yet you charge me now with a crime concerning this woman. 9 So may God do to Abner and so may he add to it! For just what the LORD has sworn to David, that will I accomplish for him, 10 to transfer the kingdom from the house of Saul, and set up the throne of David over Israel and over Judah, from Dan to Beer-sheba.' 11 And Ishbaal *b* could not answer Abner another word, because he feared him.

12 Abner sent messengers to David at Hebron, *d* saying, 'To whom does the land belong? Make your covenant with me, and I will give you my support to bring all Israel over to you.' 13 He said, 'Good; I will make a covenant with you. But one thing I require of you: you shall never appear in my presence unless you bring Saul's daughter Michal when you come to see me.' 14 Then David sent messengers to Saul's son Ishbaal, *e* saying, 'Give me my wife Michal,

a Meaning of Heb uncertain   *b* Heb *And he*
c Gk Compare 1 Chr 8.33; 9.39: Heb *Ish-bosheth*, 'man of shame'   *d* Gk: Heb *where he was*   *e* Heb *Ish-bosheth*

to whom I became engaged at the price of one hundred foreskins of the Philistines.' [15] Ishbaal[a] sent and took her from her husband Paltiel the son of Laish. [16] But her husband went with her, weeping as he walked behind her all the way to Bahurim. Then Abner said to him, 'Go back home!' So he went back.

17 Abner sent word to the elders of Israel, saying, 'For some time past you have been seeking David as king over you. [18] Now then bring it about; for the LORD has promised David: Through my servant David I will save my people Israel from the hand of the Philistines, and from all their enemies.' [19] Abner also spoke directly to the Benjaminites; then Abner went to tell David at Hebron all that Israel and the whole house of Benjamin were ready to do.

20 When Abner came with twenty men to David at Hebron, David made a feast for Abner and the men who were with him. [21] Abner said to David, 'Let me go and rally all Israel to my lord the king, in order that they may make a covenant with you, and that you may reign over all that your heart desires.' So David dismissed Abner, and he went away in peace.

Abner Is Killed by Joab

22 Just then the servants of David arrived with Joab from a raid, bringing much spoil with them. But Abner was not with David at Hebron, for David[b] had dismissed him, and he had gone away in peace. [23] When Joab and all the army that was with him came, it was told Joab, 'Abner son of Ner came to the king, and he has dismissed him, and he has gone away in peace.' [24] Then Joab went to the king and said, 'What have you done? Abner came to you; why did you dismiss him, so that he got away? [25] You know that Abner son of Ner came to deceive you, and to learn your comings and goings and to learn all that you are doing.'

26 When Joab came out from David's presence, he sent messengers after Abner, and they brought him back from the cistern of Sirah; but David did not know about it. [27] When Abner returned to Hebron, Joab took him aside in the gateway to speak with him privately, and there he stabbed him in the stomach. So he died for shedding[c] the blood of Asahel, Joab's[d] brother. [28] Afterwards, when David heard of it, he said, 'I and my kingdom are for ever guiltless before the LORD for the blood of Abner son of Ner. [29] May the guilt[e] fall on the head of Joab, and on all his father's house; and may the house of Joab never be without one who has a discharge, or who is leprous,[f] or who holds a spindle, or who falls by the sword, or who lacks food!' [30] So Joab and his brother Abishai murdered Abner because he had killed their brother Asahel in the battle at Gibeon.

31 Then David said to Joab and to all the people who were with him, 'Tear your clothes, and put on sackcloth, and mourn over Abner.' And King David followed the bier. [32] They buried Abner at Hebron. The king lifted up his voice and wept at the grave of Abner, and all the people wept. [33] The king lamented for Abner, saying,

'Should Abner die as a fool dies?
[34] Your hands were not bound,
      your feet were not fettered;
    as one falls before the wicked
      you have fallen.'

And all the people wept over him again. [35] Then all the people came to persuade David to eat something while it was still day; but David swore, saying, 'So may God do to me, and more, if I taste bread or anything else before the sun goes down!' [36] All the people took notice of it, and it pleased them; just as everything the king did pleased all the people. [37] So all the people and all Israel understood that day that the king had no part in the killing of Abner son of Ner. [38] And the king said to his servants, 'Do you not know that a prince and a great man has fallen this day in Israel? [39] Today I am powerless, even though anointed king; these men, the sons of Zeruiah, are too violent for me. The LORD pay back the one who does wickedly in accordance with his wickedness!'

a Heb Ish-bosheth   b Heb he   c Heb lacks shedding   d Heb his   e Heb May it   f A term for several skin diseases; precise meaning uncertain

Ishbaal Assassinated

4 When Saul's son Ishbaal[a] heard that Abner had died at Hebron, his courage failed, and all Israel was dismayed. 2 Saul's son had two captains of raiding bands; the name of one was Baanah, and the name of the other Rechab. They were sons of Rimmon, a Benjaminite from Beeroth—for Beeroth is considered to belong to Benjamin. 3 (Now the people of Beeroth had fled to Gittaim and are there as resident aliens to this day).

4 Saul's son Jonathan had a son who was crippled in his feet. He was five years old when the news about Saul and Jonathan came from Jezreel. His nurse picked him up and fled; and, in her haste to flee, it happened that he fell and became lame. His name was Mephibosheth.[b]

5 Now the sons of Rimmon the Beerothite, Rechab and Baanah, set out, and about the heat of the day they came to the house of Ishbaal,[c] while he was taking his noonday rest. 6 They came inside the house as though to take wheat, and they struck him in the stomach; then Rechab and his brother Baanah escaped.[d] 7 Now they had come into the house while he was lying on his couch in his bedchamber; they attacked him, killed him, and beheaded him. Then they took his head and travelled by way of the Arabah all night long. 8 They brought the head of Ishbaal[c] to David at Hebron and said to the king, 'Here is the head of Ishbaal,[c] son of Saul your enemy who sought your life; the LORD has avenged my lord the king this day on Saul and on his offspring.'

9 David answered Rechab and his brother Baanah, the sons of Rimmon the Beerothite, 'As the LORD lives, who has redeemed my life out of every adversity, 10 when the one who told me, "See, Saul is dead", thought he was bringing good news, I seized him and killed him at Ziklag—this was the reward I gave him for his news. 11 How much more then, when wicked men have killed a righteous man on his bed in his own house! And now shall I not require his blood at your hand, and destroy you from the earth?' 12 So David commanded the young men, and they killed them; they cut off their hands and feet, and hung their bodies beside the pool at Hebron. But the head of Ishbaal[c] they took and buried in the tomb of Abner at Hebron.

David Anointed King of All Israel

5 Then all the tribes of Israel came to David at Hebron, and said, 'Look, we are your bone and flesh. 2 For some time, while Saul was king over us, it was you who led out Israel and brought it in. The LORD said to you: It is you who shall be shepherd of my people Israel, you who shall be ruler over Israel.' 3 So all the elders of Israel came to the king at Hebron; and King David made a covenant with them at Hebron before the LORD, and they anointed David king over Israel. 4 David was thirty years old when he began to reign, and he reigned for forty years. 5 At Hebron he reigned over Judah for seven years and six months; and at Jerusalem he reigned over all Israel and Judah for thirty-three years.

Jerusalem Made Capital of the United Kingdom

6 The king and his men marched to Jerusalem against the Jebusites, the inhabitants of the land, who said to David, 'You will not come in here, even the blind and the lame will turn you back'—thinking, 'David cannot come in here.' 7 Nevertheless, David took the stronghold of Zion, which is now the city of David. 8 David had said on that day, 'Whoever wishes to strike down the Jebusites, let him get up the water shaft to attack the lame and the blind, those whom David hates.'[e] Therefore it is said, 'The blind and the lame shall not come into the house.' 9 David occupied the stronghold, and named it the city of David. David built the city all around from the Millo inwards. 10 And David became greater and greater, for the LORD, the God of hosts, was with him.

11 King Hiram of Tyre sent messengers to

a Heb lacks Ishbaal   b In 1 Chr 8.34 and 9.40, Meribbaal   c Heb Ish-bosheth   d Meaning of Heb of verse 6 uncertain   e Another reading is those who hate David

David, along with cedar trees, and carpenters and masons who built David a house. [12] David then perceived that the LORD had established him king over Israel, and that he had exalted his kingdom for the sake of his people Israel.

13 In Jerusalem, after he came from Hebron, David took more concubines and wives; and more sons and daughters were born to David. [14] These are the names of those who were born to him in Jerusalem: Shammua, Shobab, Nathan, Solomon, [15] Ibhar, Elishua, Nepheg, Japhia, [16] Elishama, Eliada, and Eliphelet.

Philistine Attack Repulsed

17 When the Philistines heard that David had been anointed king over Israel, all the Philistines went up in search of David; but David heard about it and went down to the stronghold. [18] Now the Philistines had come and spread out in the valley of Rephaim. [19] David inquired of the LORD, 'Shall I go up against the Philistines? Will you give them into my hand?' The LORD said to David, 'Go up; for I will certainly give the Philistines into your hand.' [20] So David came to Baal-perazim, and David defeated them there. He said, 'The LORD has burst forth against[a] my enemies before me, like a bursting flood.' Therefore that place is called Baal-perazim.[b] [21] The Philistines abandoned their idols there, and David and his men carried them away.

22 Once again the Philistines came up, and were spread out in the valley of Rephaim. [23] When David inquired of the LORD, he said, 'You shall not go up; go round to their rear, and come upon them opposite the balsam trees. [24] When you hear the sound of marching in the tops of the balsam trees, then be on the alert; for then the LORD has gone out before you to strike down the army of the Philistines.' [25] David did just as the LORD had commanded him; and he struck down the Philistines from Geba all the way to Gezer.

a Heb *paraz*   *b* That is *Lord of Bursting Forth*

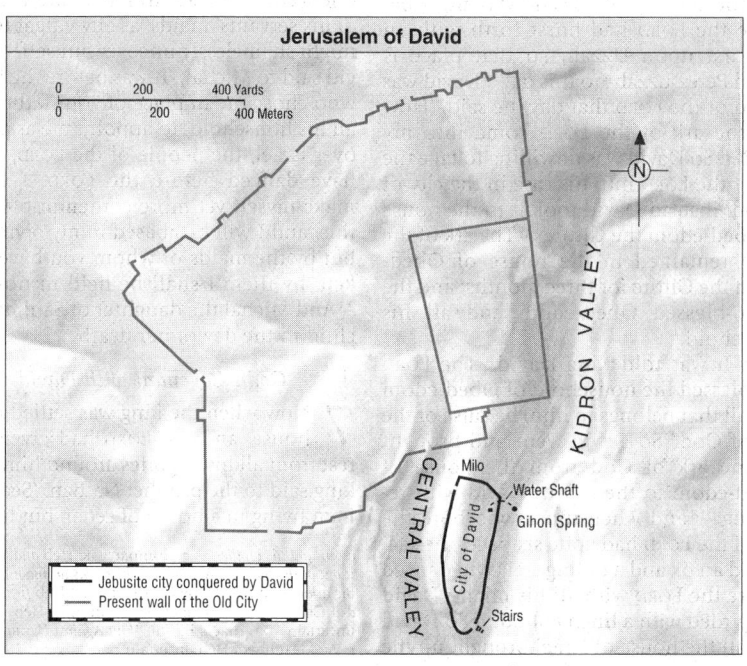

Jerusalem of David

0   200   400 Yards
0   200   400 Meters

KIDRON VALLEY

CENTRAL VALLEY

City of David

Milo
Water Shaft
Gihon Spring

Stairs

N

— Jebusite city conquered by David
-- Present wall of the Old City

David Brings the Ark to Jerusalem

6 David again gathered all the chosen men of Israel, thirty thousand. ²David and all the people with him set out and went from Baale-judah, to bring up from there the ark of God, which is called by the name of the LORD of hosts who is enthroned on the cherubim. ³They carried the ark of God on a new cart, and brought it out of the house of Abinadab, which was on the hill. Uzzah and Ahio, *a* the sons of Abinadab, were driving the new cart ⁴with the ark of God; *b* and Ahio *a* went in front of the ark. ⁵David and all the house of Israel were dancing before the LORD with all their might, with songs *c* and lyres and harps and tambourines and castanets and cymbals.

6 When they came to the threshing-floor of Nacon, Uzzah reached out his hand to the ark of God and took hold of it, for the oxen shook it. ⁷The anger of the LORD was kindled against Uzzah; and God struck him there because he reached out his hand to the ark; *d* and he died there beside the ark of God. ⁸David was angry because the LORD had burst forth with an outburst upon Uzzah; so that place is called Perez-uzzah *e* to this day. ⁹David was afraid of the LORD that day; he said, 'How can the ark of the LORD come into my care?' ¹⁰So David was unwilling to take the ark of the LORD into his care in the city of David; instead David took it to the house of Obed-edom the Gittite. ¹¹The ark of the LORD remained in the house of Obed-edom the Gittite for three months; and the LORD blessed Obed-edom and all his household.

12 It was told King David, 'The LORD has blessed the household of Obed-edom and all that belongs to him, because of the ark of God.' So David went and brought up the ark of God from the house of Obed-edom to the city of David with rejoicing; ¹³and when those who bore the ark of the LORD had gone six paces, he sacrificed an ox and a fatling. ¹⁴David danced before the LORD with all his might; David was girded with a linen ephod. ¹⁵So David and all the house of Israel brought up the ark of the LORD with shouting, and with the sound of the trumpet.

16 As the ark of the LORD came into the city of David, Michal daughter of Saul looked out of the window, and saw King David leaping and dancing before the LORD; and she despised him in her heart.

17 They brought in the ark of the LORD, and set it in its place, inside the tent that David had pitched for it; and David offered burnt-offerings and offerings of well-being before the LORD. ¹⁸When David had finished offering the burnt-offerings and the offerings of well-being, he blessed the people in the name of the LORD of hosts, ¹⁹and distributed food among all the people, the whole multitude of Israel, both men and women, to each a cake of bread, a portion of meat, *f* and a cake of raisins. Then all the people went back to their homes.

20 David returned to bless his household. But Michal the daughter of Saul came out to meet David, and said, 'How the king of Israel honoured himself today, uncovering himself today before the eyes of his servants' maids, as any vulgar fellow might shamelessly uncover himself!' ²¹David said to Michal, 'It was before the LORD, who chose me in place of your father and all his household, to appoint me as prince over Israel, the people of the LORD, that I have danced before the LORD. ²²I will make myself yet more contemptible than this, and I will be abased in my own eyes; but by the maids of whom you have spoken, by them I shall be held in honour.' ²³And Michal the daughter of Saul had no child to the day of her death.

God's Covenant with David

7 Now when the king was settled in his house, and the LORD had given him rest from all his enemies around him, ²the king said to the prophet Nathan, 'See now, I am living in a house of cedar, but the ark

a Or *and his brother*   *b* Compare Gk: Heb *and brought it out of the house of Abinadab, which was on the hill with the ark of God*   *c* Q Ms Gk 1 Chr 13.8: Heb *fir trees*
d 1 Chr 13.10 Compare Q Ms: Meaning of Heb uncertain   *e* That is *Bursting Out Against Uzzah*
f Vg: Meaning of Heb uncertain

of God stays in a tent.' ³Nathan said to the king, 'Go, do all that you have in mind; for the LORD is with you.'

4 But that same night the word of the LORD came to Nathan: ⁵Go and tell my servant David: Thus says the LORD: Are you the one to build me a house to live in? ⁶I have not lived in a house since the day I brought up the people of Israel from Egypt to this day, but I have been moving about in a tent and a tabernacle. ⁷Wherever I have moved about among all the people of Israel, did I ever speak a word with any of the tribal leaders ᵃ of Israel, whom I commanded to shepherd my people Israel, saying, 'Why have you not built me a house of cedar?' ⁸Now therefore thus you shall say to my servant David: Thus says the LORD of hosts: I took you from the pasture, from following the sheep to be prince over my people Israel; ⁹and I have been with you wherever you went, and have cut off all your enemies from before you; and I will make for you a great name, like the name of the great ones of the earth. ¹⁰And I will appoint a place for my people Israel and will plant them, so that they may live in their own place, and be disturbed no more; and evildoers shall afflict them no more, as formerly, ¹¹from the time that I appointed judges over my people Israel; and I will give you rest from all your enemies. Moreover, the LORD declares to you that the LORD will make you a house. ¹²When your days are fulfilled and you lie down with your ancestors, I will raise up your offspring after you, who shall come forth from your body, and I will establish his kingdom. ¹³He shall build a house for my name, and I will establish the throne of his kingdom for ever. ¹⁴I will be a father to him, and he shall be a son to me. When he commits iniquity, I will punish him with a rod such as mortals use, with blows inflicted by human beings. ¹⁵But I will not take ᵇ my steadfast love from him, as I took it from Saul, whom I put away from before you. ¹⁶Your house and your kingdom shall be made sure for ever before me; ᶜ your throne shall be established for ever. ¹⁷In accordance

with all these words and with all this vision, Nathan spoke to David.

David's Prayer

18 Then King David went in and sat before the LORD, and said, 'Who am I, O Lord GOD, and what is my house, that you have brought me thus far? ¹⁹And yet this was a small thing in your eyes, O Lord GOD; you have spoken also of your servant's house for a great while to come. May this be instruction for the people, ᵈ O Lord GOD! ²⁰And what more can David say to you? For you know your servant, O Lord GOD! ²¹Because of your promise, and according to your own heart, you have wrought all this greatness, so that your servant may know it. ²²Therefore you are great, O LORD God; for there is no one like you, and there is no God besides you, according to all that we have heard with our ears. ²³Who is like your people, like Israel? Is there another ᵉ nation on earth whose God went to redeem it as a people, and to make a name for himself, doing great and awesome things for them, ᶠ by driving out ᵍ before his people nations and their gods? ʰ ²⁴And you established your people Israel for yourself to be your people for ever; and you, O LORD, became their God. ²⁵And now, O LORD God, as for the word that you have spoken concerning your servant and concerning his house, confirm it for ever; do as you have promised. ²⁶Thus your name will be magnified for ever in the saying, "The LORD of hosts is God over Israel"; and the house of your servant David will be established before you. ²⁷For you, O LORD of hosts, the God of Israel, have made this revelation to your servant, saying, "I will build you a house"; therefore your servant has found courage to pray this prayer to you. ²⁸And now, O Lord GOD, you are God, and your words are true, and you have promised

a Or *any of the tribes*   b Gk Syr Vg 1 Chr 17.13: Heb *shall not depart*   c Gk Heb Mss: MT *before you*; Compare 2 Sam 7.26, 29   d Meaning of Heb uncertain   e Gk: Heb *one*   f Heb *you* g Gk 1 Chr 17.21: Heb *for your land*   h Cn: Heb *before your people, whom you redeemed for yourself from Egypt, nations and its gods* this good thing to your servant; ²⁹ now therefore may it please you to bless the house of your servant, so that it may continue for ever before you; for you, O Lord GOD, have spoken, and with your blessing shall the house of your servant be blessed for ever.'

David's Wars

8 Some time afterwards, David attacked the Philistines and subdued them; David took Metheg-ammah out of the hand of the Philistines.

2 He also defeated the Moabites and, making them lie down on the ground, measured them off with a cord; he measured two lengths of cord for those who were to be put to death, and one length^a for those who were to be spared. And the Moabites became servants to David and brought tribute.

3 David also struck down King Hadadezer son of Rehob of Zobah, as he went to restore his monument^b at the river Euphrates. ⁴ David took from him one thousand seven hundred horsemen, and twenty thousand foot-soldiers. David hamstrung all the chariot horses, but left enough for a hundred chariots. ⁵ When the Arameans of Damascus came to help King Hadadezer of Zobah, David killed twenty-two thousand men of the Arameans. ⁶ Then David put garrisons among the Arameans of Damascus; and the Arameans became servants to David and brought tribute. The LORD gave victory to David wherever he went. ⁷ David took the gold shields that were carried by the servants of Hadadezer, and brought them to Jerusalem. ⁸ From Betah and from Berothai, towns of Hadadezer, King David took a great amount of bronze.

9 When King Toi of Hamath heard that David had defeated the whole army of Hadadezer, ¹⁰ Toi sent his son Joram to King David, to greet him and to congratulate him because he had fought against Hadadezer and defeated him. Now Hadadezer had often been at war with Toi. Joram brought with him articles of silver, gold, and bronze; ¹¹ these also King David

dedicated to the LORD, together with the silver and gold that he dedicated from all the nations he subdued, ¹² from Edom, Moab, the Ammonites, the Philistines, Amalek, and from the spoil of King Hadadezer son of Rehob of Zobah.

13 David won a name for himself. When he returned, he killed eighteen thousand Edomites^c in the Valley of Salt. ¹⁴ He put garrisons in Edom; throughout all Edom he put garrisons, and all the Edomites became David's servants. And the LORD gave victory to David wherever he went.

David's Officers

15 So David reigned over all Israel; and David administered justice and equity to all his people. ¹⁶ Joab son of Zeruiah was over the army; Jehoshaphat son of Ahilud was recorder; ¹⁷ Zadok son of Ahitub and Ahimelech son of Abiathar were priests; Seraiah was secretary; ¹⁸ Benaiah son of Jehoiada was over^d the Cherethites and the Pelethites; and David's sons were priests.

David's Kindness to Mephibosheth

9 David asked, 'Is there still anyone left of the house of Saul to whom I may show kindness for Jonathan's sake?' ² Now there was a servant of the house of Saul whose name was Ziba, and he was summoned to David. The king said to him, 'Are you Ziba?' And he said, 'At your service!' ³ The king said, 'Is there anyone remaining of the house of Saul to whom I may show the kindness of God?' Ziba said to the king, 'There remains a son of Jonathan; he is crippled in his feet.' ⁴ The king said to him, 'Where is he?' Ziba said to the king, 'He is in the house of Machir son of Ammiel, at Lo-debar.' ⁵ Then King David sent and brought him from the house of Machir son of Ammiel, at Lo-debar. ⁶ Mephibosheth^e son of Jonathan son of Saul came to David, and fell on his face and did obeisance. David said, 'Mephibosheth!'^e He answered, 'I am your servant.' ⁷ David

---

a Heb *one full length*   *b* Compare 1 Sam 15.12 and 2 Sam 18.18   *c* Gk: Heb *returned from striking down eighteen thousand Arameans*   *d* Syr Tg Vg 20.23; 1 Chr 18.17: Heb lacks *was over*   *e* Or *Merib-baal*: See 4.4 note said to him, 'Do not be afraid, for I will show you kindness for the sake of your father Jonathan; I will restore to you all the land of your grandfather Saul, and you yourself shall eat at my table always.' ⁸ He did obeisance and said, 'What is your servant, that you should look upon a dead dog such as I am?'

9 Then the king summoned Saul's servant Ziba, and said to him, 'All that belonged to Saul and to all his house I have given to your master's grandson. ¹⁰ You and your sons and your servants shall till the land for him, and shall bring in the produce, so that your master's grandson may have food to eat; but your master's grandson Mephibosheth ᵃ shall always eat at my table.' Now Ziba had fifteen sons and twenty servants. ¹¹ Then Ziba said to the king, 'According to all that my lord the king commands his servant, so your servant will do.' Mephibosheth ᵃ ate at David's ᵇ table, like one of the king's sons. ¹² Mephibosheth ᵃ had a young son whose name was Mica. And all who lived in Ziba's house became Mephibosheth's ᶜ servants. ¹³ Mephibosheth ᵃ lived in Jerusalem, for he always ate at the king's table. Now he was lame in both his feet.

The Ammonites and Arameans Are Defeated

10 Some time afterwards the king of the Ammonites died, and his son Hanun succeeded him. ² David said, 'I will deal loyally with Hanun son of Nahash, just as his father dealt loyally with me.' So David sent envoys to console him concerning his father. When David's envoys came into the land of the Ammonites, ³ the princes of the Ammonites said to their lord Hanun, 'Do you really think that David is honouring your father just because he has sent messengers with condolences to you? Has not David sent his envoys to you to search the city, to spy it out, and to overthrow it?' ⁴ So Hanun seized David's envoys, shaved off half the beard of each, cut off their garments in the middle at their hips, and sent them away. ⁵ When David was told, he sent to meet them, for the men were greatly ashamed. The king said, 'Remain at Jericho until your beards have grown, and then return.'

6 When the Ammonites saw that they had become odious to David, the Ammonites sent and hired the Arameans of Beth-rehob and the Arameans of Zobah, twenty thousand foot-soldiers, as well as the king of Maacah, one thousand men, and the men of Tob, twelve thousand men. ⁷ When David heard of it, he sent Joab and all the army with the warriors. ⁸ The

David's Conquests

Mediterranean Sea

PHOENICIA

ZOBAH

Damascus

Tyre

ISRAEL

PHILISTIA

Jerusalem

AMMON

Dead Sea

Beer-sheba

Zoar

MOAB

Bozrah

EDOM

N

Elath

| 0 | 60 Mi. |
| 0 | 60 Km. |

a Or *Merib-baal*: See 4.4 note   b Gk: Heb *my*
c Or *Merib-baal's*: See 4.4 note

Ammonites came out and drew up in battle array at the entrance of the gate; but the Arameans of Zobah and of Rehob, and the men of Tob and Maacah, were by themselves in the open country.

9 When Joab saw that the battle was set against him both in front and in the rear, he chose some of the picked men of Israel, and arrayed them against the Arameans; [10] the rest of his men he put in charge of his brother Abishai, and he arrayed them against the Ammonites. [11] He said, 'If the Arameans are too strong for me, then you shall help me; but if the Ammonites are too strong for you, then I will come and help you. [12] Be strong, and let us be courageous for the sake of our people, and for the cities of our God; and may the LORD do what seems good to him.' [13] So Joab and the people who were with him moved forward into battle against the Arameans; and they fled before him. [14] When the Ammonites saw that the Arameans fled, they likewise fled before Abishai, and entered the city. Then Joab returned from fighting against the Ammonites, and came to Jerusalem.

15 But when the Arameans saw that they had been defeated by Israel, they gathered themselves together. [16] Hadadezer sent and brought out the Arameans who were beyond the Euphrates; and they came to Helam, with Shobach the commander of the army of Hadadezer at their head. [17] When it was told to David, he gathered all Israel together, and crossed the Jordan, and came to Helam. The Arameans arrayed themselves against David and fought with him. [18] The Arameans fled before Israel; and David killed of the Arameans seven hundred chariot teams and forty thousand horsemen,[a] and wounded Shobach the commander of their army, so that he died there. [19] When all the kings who were servants of Hadadezer saw that they had been defeated by Israel, they made peace with Israel, and became subject to them. So the Arameans were afraid to help the Ammonites any more.

David Commits Adultery with Bathsheba

11 In the spring of the year, the time when kings go out to battle, David sent Joab with his officers and all Israel with him; they ravaged the Ammonites, and besieged Rabbah. But David remained at Jerusalem.

2 It happened, late one afternoon, when David rose from his couch and was walking about on the roof of the king's house, that he saw from the roof a woman bathing; the woman was very beautiful. [3] David sent someone to inquire about the woman. It was reported, 'This is Bathsheba daughter of Eliam, the wife of Uriah the Hittite.' [4] So David sent messengers to fetch her, and she came to him, and he lay with her. (Now she was purifying herself after her period.) Then she returned to her house. [5] The woman conceived; and she sent and told David, 'I am pregnant.'

6 So David sent word to Joab, 'Send me Uriah the Hittite.' And Joab sent Uriah to David. [7] When Uriah came to him, David asked how Joab and the people fared, and how the war was going. [8] Then David said to Uriah, 'Go down to your house, and wash your feet.' Uriah went out of the king's house, and there followed him a present from the king. [9] But Uriah slept at the entrance of the king's house with all the servants of his lord, and did not go down to his house. [10] When they told David, 'Uriah did not go down to his house', David said to Uriah, 'You have just come from a journey. Why did you not go down to your house?' [11] Uriah said to David, 'The ark and Israel and Judah remain in booths;[b] and my lord Joab and the servants of my lord are camping in the open field; shall I then go to my house, to eat and to drink, and to lie with my wife? As you live, and as your soul lives, I will not do such a thing.' [12] Then David said to Uriah, 'Remain here today also, and tomorrow I will send you back.' So Uriah remained in Jerusalem that day. On the next day, [13] David invited him to eat and drink in his presence and made him drunk; and

a 1 Chr 19.18 and some Gk Mss read *foot-soldiers*
b Or at Succoth

in the evening he went out to lie on his couch with the servants of his lord, but he did not go down to his house.

David Has Uriah Killed

14 In the morning David wrote a letter to Joab, and sent it by the hand of Uriah. [15] In the letter he wrote, 'Set Uriah in the forefront of the hardest fighting, and then draw back from him, so that he may be struck down and die.' [16] As Joab was besieging the city, he assigned Uriah to the place where he knew there were valiant warriors. [17] The men of the city came out and fought with Joab; and some of the servants of David among the people fell. Uriah the Hittite was killed as well. [18] Then Joab sent and told David all the news about the fighting; [19] and he instructed the messenger, 'When you have finished telling the king all the news about the fighting, [20] then, if the king's anger rises, and if he says to you, "Why did you go so near the city to fight? Did you not know that they would shoot from the wall? [21] Who killed Abimelech son of Jerubbaal?[a] Did not a woman throw an upper millstone on him from the wall, so that he died at Thebez? Why did you go so near the wall?" then you shall say, "Your servant Uriah the Hittite is dead too." '

22 So the messenger went, and came and told David all that Joab had sent him to tell. [23] The messenger said to David, 'The men gained an advantage over us, and came out against us in the field; but we drove them back to the entrance of the gate. [24] Then the archers shot at your servants from the wall; some of the king's servants are dead; and your servant Uriah the Hittite is dead also.' [25] David said to the messenger, 'Thus you shall say to Joab, "Do not let this matter trouble you, for the sword devours now one and now another; press your attack on the city, and overthrow it." And encourage him.'

26 When the wife of Uriah heard that her husband was dead, she made lamentation for him. [27] When the mourning was over, David sent and brought her to his house, and she became his wife, and bore him a son.

Nathan Condemns David

But the thing that David had done displeased the LORD, [1] and the LORD sent Nathan to David. He came to him, and said to him, 'There were two men in a certain city, one rich and the other poor. [2] The rich man had very many flocks and herds; [3] but the poor man had nothing but one little ewe lamb, which he had bought. He brought it up, and it grew up with him and with his children; it used to eat of his meagre fare, and drink from his cup, and lie in his bosom, and it was like a daughter to him. [4] Now there came a traveller to the rich man, and he was loath to take one of his own flock or herd to prepare for the wayfarer who had come to him, but he took the poor man's lamb, and prepared that for the guest who had come to him.' [5] Then David's anger was greatly kindled against the man. He said to Nathan, 'As the LORD lives, the man who has done this deserves to die; [6] he shall restore the lamb fourfold, because he did this thing, and because he had no pity.'

7 Nathan said to David, 'You are the man! Thus says the LORD, the God of Israel: I anointed you king over Israel, and I rescued you from the hand of Saul; [8] I gave you your master's house, and your master's wives into your bosom, and gave you the house of Israel and of Judah; and if that had been too little, I would have added as much more. [9] Why have you despised the word of the LORD, to do what is evil in his sight? You have struck down Uriah the Hittite with the sword, and have taken his wife to be your wife, and have killed him with the sword of the Ammonites. [10] Now therefore the sword shall never depart from your house, for you have despised me, and have taken the wife of Uriah the Hittite to be your wife. [11] Thus says the LORD: I will raise up trouble against you from within your own house; and I will take your wives before your eyes, and give them to your neighbour, and he shall lie

---

a Gk Syr Judg 7.1: Heb *Jerubbesheth*

with your wives in the sight of this very sun. 12 For you did it secretly; but I will do this thing before all Israel, and before the sun.' 13 David said to Nathan, 'I have sinned against the LORD.' Nathan said to David, 'Now the LORD has put away your sin; you shall not die. 14 Nevertheless, because by this deed you have utterly scorned the LORD,*a* the child that is born to you shall die.' 15 Then Nathan went to his house.

Bathsheba's Child Dies

The LORD struck the child that Uriah's wife bore to David, and it became very ill. 16 David therefore pleaded with God for the child; David fasted, and went in and lay all night on the ground. 17 The elders of his house stood beside him, urging him to rise from the ground; but he would not, nor did he eat food with them. 18 On the seventh day the child died. And the servants of David were afraid to tell him that the child was dead; for they said, 'While the child was still alive, we spoke to him, and he did not listen to us; how then can we tell him the child is dead? He may do himself some harm.' 19 But when David saw that his servants were whispering together, he perceived that the child was dead; and David said to his servants, 'Is the child dead?' They said, 'He is dead.'

20 Then David rose from the ground, washed, anointed himself, and changed his clothes. He went into the house of the LORD, and worshipped; he then went to his own house; and when he asked, they set food before him and he ate. 21 Then his servants said to him, 'What is this thing that you have done? You fasted and wept for the child while it was alive; but when the child died, you rose and ate food.' 22 He said, 'While the child was still alive, I fasted and wept; for I said, "Who knows? The LORD may be gracious to me, and the child may live." 23 But now he is dead; why should I fast? Can I bring him back again? I shall go to him, but he will not return to me.'

Solomon Is Born

24 Then David consoled his wife Bathsheba, and went to her, and lay with her; and she bore a son, and he named him Solomon. The LORD loved him, 25 and sent a message by the prophet Nathan; so he named him Jedidiah,*b* because of the LORD.

The Ammonites Crushed

26 Now Joab fought against Rabbah of the Ammonites, and took the royal city. 27 Joab sent messengers to David, and said, 'I have fought against Rabbah; moreover, I have taken the water city. 28 Now, then, gather the rest of the people together, and encamp against the city, and take it; or I myself will take the city, and it will be called by my name.' 29 So David gathered all the people together and went to Rabbah, and fought against it and took it. 30 He took the crown of Milcom*c* from his head; the weight of it was a talent of gold, and in it was a precious stone; and it was placed on David's head. He also brought forth the spoil of the city, a very great amount. 31 He brought out the people who were in it, and set them to work with saws and iron picks and iron axes, or sent them to the brickworks. Thus he did to all the cities of the Ammonites. Then David and all the people returned to Jerusalem.

Amnon and Tamar

13 Some time passed. David's son Absalom had a beautiful sister whose name was Tamar; and David's son Amnon fell in love with her. 2 Amnon was so tormented that he made himself ill because of his sister Tamar, for she was a virgin and it seemed impossible to Amnon to do anything to her. 3 But Amnon had a friend whose name was Jonadab, the son of David's brother Shimeah; and Jonadab was a very crafty man. 4 He said to him, 'O son of the king, why are you so haggard morning after morning? Will you not tell me?' Amnon said to him, 'I love Tamar, my

a Ancient scribal tradition: Compare 1 Sam 25.22 note: Heb *scorned the enemies of the LORD*　　*b* That is *Beloved of the LORD*　　*c* Gk See 1 Kings 11.5, 33: Heb *their kings* brother Absalom's sister.' ⁵ Jonadab said to him, 'Lie down on your bed, and pretend to be ill; and when your father comes to see you, say to him, "Let my sister Tamar come and give me something to eat, and prepare the food in my sight, so that I may see it and eat it from her hand." ' ⁶ So Amnon lay down, and pretended to be ill; and when the king came to see him, Amnon said to the king, 'Please let my sister Tamar come and make a couple of cakes in my sight, so that I may eat from her hand.'

7 Then David sent home to Tamar, saying, 'Go to your brother Amnon's house, and prepare food for him.' ⁸ So Tamar went to her brother Amnon's house, where he was lying down. She took dough, kneaded it, made cakes in his sight, and baked the cakes. ⁹ Then she took the pan and set them*a* out before him, but he refused to eat. Amnon said, 'Send out everyone from me.' So everyone went out from him. ¹⁰ Then Amnon said to Tamar, 'Bring the food into the chamber, so that I may eat from your hand.' So Tamar took the cakes she had made, and brought them into the chamber to Amnon her brother. ¹¹ But when she brought them near him to eat, he took hold of her, and said to her, 'Come, lie with me, my sister.' ¹² She answered him, 'No, my brother, do not force me; for such a thing is not done in Israel; do not do anything so vile! ¹³ As for me, where could I carry my shame? And as for you, you would be as one of the scoundrels in Israel. Now therefore, I beg you, speak to the king; for he will not withhold me from you.' ¹⁴ But he would not listen to her; and being stronger than she was, he forced her and lay with her.

15 Then Amnon was seized with a very great loathing for her; indeed, his loathing was even greater than the lust he had felt for her. Amnon said to her, 'Get out!' ¹⁶ But she said to him, 'No, my brother;*b* for this wrong in sending me away is greater than the other that you did to me.' But he would not listen to her. ¹⁷ He called the young man who served him and said, 'Put this woman out of my presence, and bolt the door after her.' ¹⁸ (Now she was

wearing a long robe with sleeves; for this is how the virgin daughters of the king were clothed in earlier times.*c*) So his servant put her out, and bolted the door after her. ¹⁹ But Tamar put ashes on her head, and tore the long robe that she was wearing; she put her hand on her head, and went away, crying aloud as she went.

20 Her brother Absalom said to her, 'Has Amnon your brother been with you? Be quiet for now, my sister; he is your brother; do not take this to heart.' So Tamar remained, a desolate woman, in her brother Absalom's house. ²¹ When King David heard of all these things, he became very angry, but he would not punish his son Amnon, because he loved him, for he was his firstborn.*d* ²² But Absalom spoke to Amnon neither good nor bad; for Absalom hated Amnon, because he had raped his sister Tamar.

Absalom Avenges the Violation of His Sister

23 After two full years Absalom had sheepshearers at Baal-hazor, which is near Ephraim, and Absalom invited all the king's sons. ²⁴ Absalom came to the king, and said, 'Your servant has sheepshearers; will the king and his servants please go with your servant?' ²⁵ But the king said to Absalom, 'No, my son, let us not all go, or else we will be burdensome to you.' He pressed him, but he would not go but gave him his blessing. ²⁶ Then Absalom said, 'If not, please let my brother Amnon go with us.' The king said to him, 'Why should he go with you?' ²⁷ But Absalom pressed him until he let Amnon and all the king's sons go with him. Absalom made a feast like a king's feast.*e* ²⁸ Then Absalom commanded his servants, 'Watch when Amnon's heart is merry with wine, and when I say to you, "Strike Amnon", then kill him. Do not be afraid; have I not myself commanded you? Be courageous and valiant.' ²⁹ So the servants of Absalom

a Heb *and poured*   *b* Cn Compare Gk Vg: Meaning of Heb uncertain   *c* Cn: Heb *were clothed in robes* *d* Q Ms Gk: MT lacks *but he would not punish . . . firstborn*   *e* Gk Compare Q Ms: MT lacks *Absalom made a feast like a king's feast* did to Amnon as Absalom had commanded. Then all the king's sons rose, and each mounted his mule and fled.

30 While they were on the way, the report came to David that Absalom had killed all the king's sons, and not one of them was left. 31 The king rose, tore his garments, and lay on the ground; and all his servants who were standing by tore their garments. 32 But Jonadab, the son of David's brother Shimeah, said, 'Let not my lord suppose that they have killed all the young men the king's sons; Amnon alone is dead. This has been determined by Absalom from the day Amnon*a* raped his sister Tamar. 33 Now therefore, do not let my lord the king take it to heart, as if all the king's sons were dead; for Amnon alone is dead.'

34 But Absalom fled. When the young man who kept watch looked up, he saw many people coming from the Horonaim road*b* by the side of the mountain. 35 Jonadab said to the king, 'See, the king's sons have come; as your servant said, so it has come about.' 36 As soon as he had finished speaking, the king's sons arrived, and raised their voices and wept; and the king and all his servants also wept very bitterly.

37 But Absalom fled, and went to Talmai son of Ammihud, king of Geshur. David mourned for his son day after day. 38 Absalom, having fled to Geshur, stayed there for three years. 39 And the heart of*c* the king went out, yearning for Absalom; for he was now consoled over the death of Amnon.

Absalom Returns to Jerusalem

14 Now Joab son of Zeruiah perceived that the king's mind was on Absalom. 2 Joab sent to Tekoa and brought from there a wise woman. He said to her, 'Pretend to be in mourning; put on mourning garments, do not anoint yourself with oil, but behave like a woman who has been mourning many days for the dead. 3 Go to the king and speak to him as follows.' And Joab put the words into her mouth.

4 When the woman of Tekoa came to the king, she fell on her face to the ground and did obeisance, and said, 'Help, O king!' 5 The king asked her, 'What is your trouble?' She answered, 'Alas, I am a widow; my husband is dead. 6 Your servant had two sons, and they fought with one another in the field; there was no one to part them, and one struck the other and killed him. 7 Now the whole family has risen against your servant. They say, "Give up the man who struck his brother, so that we may kill him for the life of his brother whom he murdered, even if we destroy the heir as well." Thus they would quench my one remaining ember, and leave to my husband neither name nor remnant on the face of the earth.'

8 Then the king said to the woman, 'Go to your house, and I will give orders concerning you.' 9 The woman of Tekoa said to the king, 'On me be the guilt, my lord the king, and on my father's house; let the king and his throne be guiltless.' 10 The king said, 'If anyone says anything to you, bring him to me, and he shall never touch you again.' 11 Then she said, 'Please, may the king keep the LORD your God in mind, so that the avenger of blood may kill no more, and my son not be destroyed.' He said, 'As the LORD lives, not one hair of your son shall fall to the ground.'

12 Then the woman said, 'Please let your servant speak a word to my lord the king.' He said, 'Speak.' 13 The woman said, 'Why then have you planned such a thing against the people of God? For in giving this decision the king convicts himself, inasmuch as the king does not bring his banished one home again. 14 We must all die; we are like water spilled on the ground, which cannot be gathered up. But God will not take away a life; he will devise plans so as not to keep an outcast banished for ever from his presence.*d* 15 Now I have come to say this to my lord the king because the people have made me afraid; your servant thought, "I will speak to the king; it may be that the king will perform

---

a Heb *he*   *b* Cn Compare Gk: Heb *the road behind him*
c Q Ms Gk: MT *And David*   *d* Meaning of Heb uncertain

the request of his servant. 16 For the king will hear, and deliver his servant from the hand of the man who would cut both me and my son off from the heritage of God." 17 Your servant thought, "The word of my lord the king will set me at rest"; for my lord the king is like the angel of God, discerning good and evil. The LORD your God be with you!'

18 Then the king answered the woman, 'Do not withhold from me anything I ask you.' The woman said, 'Let my lord the king speak.' 19 The king said, 'Is the hand of Joab with you in all this?' The woman answered and said, 'As surely as you live, my lord the king, one cannot turn right or left from anything that my lord the king has said. For it was your servant Joab who commanded me; it was he who put all these words into the mouth of your servant. 20 In order to change the course of affairs your servant Joab did this. But my lord has wisdom like the wisdom of the angel of God to know all things that are on the earth.'

21 Then the king said to Joab, 'Very well, I grant this; go, bring back the young man Absalom.' 22 Joab prostrated himself with his face to the ground and did obeisance, and blessed the king; and Joab said, 'Today your servant knows that I have found favour in your sight, my lord the king, in that the king has granted the request of his servant.' 23 So Joab set off, went to Geshur, and brought Absalom to Jerusalem. 24 The king said, 'Let him go to his own house; he is not to come into my presence.' So Absalom went to his own house, and did not come into the king's presence.

David Forgives Absalom

25 Now in all Israel there was no one to be praised so much for his beauty as Absalom; from the sole of his foot to the crown of his head there was no blemish in him. 26 When he cut the hair of his head (for at the end of every year he used to cut it; when it was heavy on him, he cut it), he weighed the hair of his head, two hundred shekels by the king's weight. 27 There were

born to Absalom three sons, and one daughter whose name was Tamar; she was a beautiful woman.

28 So Absalom lived two full years in Jerusalem without coming into the king's presence. 29 Then Absalom sent for Joab to send him to the king; but Joab would not come to him. He sent a second time, but Joab would not come. 30 Then he said to his servants, 'Look, Joab's field is next to mine, and he has barley there; go and set it on fire.' So Absalom's servants set the field on fire. 31 Then Joab rose and went to Absalom at his house, and said to him, 'Why have your servants set my field on fire?' 32 Absalom answered Joab, 'Look, I sent word to you: Come here, that I may send you to the king with the question, "Why have I come from Geshur? It would be better for me to be there still." Now let me go into the king's presence; if there is guilt in me, let him kill me!' 33 Then Joab went to the king and told him; and he summoned Absalom. So he came to the king and prostrated himself with his face to the ground before the king; and the king kissed Absalom.

Absalom Usurps the Throne

15 After this Absalom got himself a chariot and horses, and fifty men to run ahead of him. 2 Absalom used to rise early and stand beside the road into the gate; and when anyone brought a suit before the king for judgement, Absalom would call out and say, 'From what city are you?' When the person said, 'Your servant is of such and such a tribe in Israel', 3 Absalom would say, 'See, your claims are good and right; but there is no one deputed by the king to hear you.' 4 Absalom said moreover, 'If only I were judge in the land! Then all who had a suit or cause might come to me, and I would give them justice.' 5 Whenever people came near to do obeisance to him, he would put out his hand and take hold of them, and kiss them. 6 Thus Absalom did to every Israelite who came to the king for judgement; so Absalom stole the hearts of the people of Israel.

7 At the end of four*a* years Absalom said to the king, 'Please let me go to Hebron and pay the vow that I have made to the LORD. 8 For your servant made a vow while I lived at Geshur in Aram: If the LORD will indeed bring me back to Jerusalem, then I will worship the LORD in Hebron.'*b* 9 The king said to him, 'Go in peace.' So he got up, and went to Hebron. 10 But Absalom sent secret messengers throughout all the tribes of Israel, saying, 'As soon as you hear the sound of the trumpet, then shout: Absalom has become king at Hebron!' 11 Two hundred men from Jerusalem went with Absalom; they were invited guests, and they went in their innocence, knowing nothing of the matter. 12 While Absalom was offering the sacrifices, he sent for*c* Ahithophel the Gilonite, David's counsellor, from his city Giloh. The conspiracy grew in strength, and the people with Absalom kept increasing.

David Flees from Jerusalem

13 A messenger came to David, saying, 'The hearts of the Israelites have gone after Absalom.' 14 Then David said to all his officials who were with him at Jerusalem, 'Get up! Let us flee, or there will be no escape for us from Absalom. Hurry, or he will soon overtake us, and bring disaster down upon us, and attack the city with the edge of the sword.' 15 The king's officials said to the king, 'Your servants are ready to do whatever our lord the king decides.' 16 So the king left, followed by all his household, except ten concubines whom he left behind to look after the house. 17 The king left, followed by all the people; and they stopped at the last house. 18 All his officials passed by him; and all the Cherethites, and all the Pelethites, and all the six hundred Gittites who had followed him from Gath, passed on before the king.

19 Then the king said to Ittai the Gittite, 'Why are you also coming with us? Go back, and stay with the king; for you are a foreigner, and also an exile from your home. 20 You came only yesterday, and shall I today make you wander about with us, while I go wherever I can? Go back, and take your kinsfolk with you; and may the LORD show*d* steadfast love and faithfulness to you.' 21 But Ittai answered the king, 'As the LORD lives, and as my lord the king lives, wherever my lord the king may be, whether for death or for life, there also your servant will be.' 22 David said to Ittai, 'Go then, march on.' So Ittai the Gittite marched on, with all his men and all the little ones who were with him. 23 The whole country wept aloud as all the people passed by; the king crossed the Wadi Kidron, and all the people moved on towards the wilderness.

24 Abiathar came up, and Zadok also, with all the Levites, carrying the ark of the covenant of God. They set down the ark of God, until the people had all passed out of the city. 25 Then the king said to Zadok, 'Carry the ark of God back into the city. If I find favour in the eyes of the LORD, he will bring me back and let me see both it and the place where it remains. 26 But if he says, "I take no pleasure in you", here I am, let him do to me what seems good to him.' 27 The king also said to the priest Zadok, 'Look,*e* go back to the city in peace, you and Abiathar,*f* with your two sons, Ahimaaz your son, and Jonathan son of Abiathar. 28 See, I will wait at the fords of the wilderness until word comes from you to inform me.' 29 So Zadok and Abiathar carried the ark of God back to Jerusalem, and they remained there.

30 But David went up the ascent of the Mount of Olives, weeping as he went, with his head covered and walking barefoot; and all the people who were with him covered their heads and went up, weeping as they went. 31 David was told that Ahithophel was among the conspirators with Absalom. And David said, 'O LORD, I pray you, turn the counsel of Ahithophel into foolishness.'

Hushai Becomes David's Spy

32 When David came to the summit, where God was worshipped, Hushai the

a Gk Syr: Heb *forty*   *b* Gk Mss: Heb lacks *in Hebron*
c Or *he sent*   *d* Gk Compare 2.6: Heb lacks *may the LORD show*   *e* Gk: Heb *Are you a seer* or *Do you see?*
f Cn: Heb lacks *and Abiathar*

Archite came to meet him with his coat torn and earth on his head. 33 David said to him, 'If you go on with me, you will be a burden to me. 34 But if you return to the city and say to Absalom, "I will be your servant, O king; as I have been your father's servant in time past, so now I will be your servant", then you will defeat for me the counsel of Ahithophel. 35 The priests Zadok and Abiathar will be with you there. So whatever you hear from the king's house, tell it to the priests Zadok and Abiathar. 36 Their two sons are with them there, Zadok's son Ahimaaz and Abiathar's son Jonathan; and by them you shall report to me everything you hear.' 37 So Hushai, David's friend, came into the city, just as Absalom was entering Jerusalem.

David's Adversaries

16 When David had passed a little beyond the summit, Ziba the servant of Mephibosheth *a* met him, with a couple of donkeys saddled, carrying two hundred loaves of bread, one hundred bunches of raisins, one hundred of summer fruits, and one skin of wine. 2 The king said to Ziba, 'Why have you brought these?' Ziba answered, 'The donkeys are for the king's household to ride, the bread and summer fruit for the young men to eat, and the wine is for those to drink who faint in the wilderness.' 3 The king said, 'And where is your master's son?' Ziba said to the king, 'He remains in Jerusalem; for he said, "Today the house of Israel will give me back my grandfather's kingdom." ' 4 Then the king said to Ziba, 'All that belonged to Mephibosheth *a* is now yours.' Ziba said, 'I do obeisance; let me find favour in your sight, my lord the king.'

Shimei Curses David

5 When King David came to Bahurim, a man of the family of the house of Saul came out whose name was Shimei son of Gera; he came out cursing. 6 He threw stones at David and at all the servants of King David; now all the people and all the

warriors were on his right and on his left. 7 Shimei shouted while he cursed, 'Out! Out! Murderer! Scoundrel! 8 The LORD has avenged on all of you the blood of the house of Saul, in whose place you have reigned; and the LORD has given the kingdom into the hand of your son Absalom. See, disaster has overtaken you; for you are a man of blood.'

9 Then Abishai son of Zeruiah said to the king, 'Why should this dead dog curse my lord the king? Let me go over and take off his head.' 10 But the king said, 'What have I to do with you, you sons of Zeruiah? If he is cursing because the LORD has said to him, "Curse David", who then shall say, "Why have you done so?" ' 11 David said to Abishai and to all his servants, 'My own son seeks my life; how much more now may this Benjaminite! Let him alone, and let him curse; for the LORD has bidden him. 12 It may be that the LORD will look on my distress, *b* and the LORD will repay me with good for this cursing of me today.' 13 So David and his men went on the road, while Shimei went along on the hillside opposite him and cursed as he went, throwing stones and flinging dust at him. 14 The king and all the people who were with him arrived weary at the Jordan; *c* and there he refreshed himself.

The Counsel of Ahithophel

15 Now Absalom and all the Israelites *d* came to Jerusalem; Ahithophel was with him. 16 When Hushai the Archite, David's friend, came to Absalom, Hushai said to Absalom, 'Long live the king! Long live the king!' 17 Absalom said to Hushai, 'Is this your loyalty to your friend? Why did you not go with your friend?' 18 Hushai said to Absalom, 'No; but the one whom the LORD and this people and all the Israelites have chosen, his I will be, and with him I will remain. 19 Moreover, whom should I serve? Should it not be his son? Just as I have served your father, so I will serve you.'

a Or *Merib-baal*: See 4.4 note   *b* Gk Vg: Heb *iniquity*
c Gk: Heb lacks *at the Jordan*   *d* Gk: Heb *all the people, the men of Israel*

20 Then Absalom said to Ahithophel, 'Give us your counsel; what shall we do?' 21 Ahithophel said to Absalom, 'Go in to your father's concubines, the ones he has left to look after the house; and all Israel will hear that you have made yourself odious to your father, and the hands of all who are with you will be strengthened.' 22 So they pitched a tent for Absalom upon the roof; and Absalom went in to his father's concubines in the sight of all Israel. 23 Now in those days the counsel that Ahithophel gave was as if one consulted the oracle*a* of God; so all the counsel of Ahithophel was esteemed, both by David and by Absalom.

17 Moreover, Ahithophel said to Absalom, 'Let me choose twelve thousand men, and I will set out and pursue David tonight. 2 I will come upon him while he is weary and discouraged, and throw him into a panic; and all the people who are with him will flee. I will strike down only the king, 3 and I will bring all the people back to you as a bride comes home to her husband. You seek the life of only one man,*b* and all the people will be at peace.' 4 The advice pleased Absalom and all the elders of Israel.

The Counsel of Hushai

5 Then Absalom said, 'Call Hushai the Archite also, and let us hear too what he has to say.' 6 When Hushai came to Absalom, Absalom said to him, 'This is what Ahithophel has said; shall we do as he advises? If not, you tell us.' 7 Then Hushai said to Absalom, 'This time the counsel that Ahithophel has given is not good.' 8 Hushai continued, 'You know that your father and his men are warriors, and that they are enraged, like a bear robbed of her cubs in the field. Besides, your father is expert in war; he will not spend the night with the troops. 9 Even now he has hidden himself in one of the pits, or in some other place. And when some of our troops*c* fall at the first attack, whoever hears it will say, "There has been a slaughter among the troops who follow Absalom." 10 Then even the valiant warrior, whose heart is like the heart of a lion, will utterly melt with fear; for all Israel knows that your father is a warrior, and that those who are with him are valiant warriors. 11 But my counsel is that all Israel be gathered to you, from Dan to Beer-sheba, like the sand by the sea for multitude, and that you go to battle in person. 12 So we shall come upon him in whatever place he may be found, and we shall light on him as the dew falls on the ground; and he will not survive, nor will any of those with him. 13 If he withdraws into a city, then all Israel will bring ropes to that city, and we shall drag it into the valley, until not even a pebble is to be found there.' 14 Absalom and all the men of Israel said, 'The counsel of Hushai the Archite is better than the counsel of Ahithophel.' For the LORD had ordained to defeat the good counsel of Ahithophel, so that the LORD might bring ruin on Absalom.

Hushai Warns David to Escape

15 Then Hushai said to the priests Zadok and Abiathar, 'Thus and so did Ahithophel counsel Absalom and the elders of Israel; and thus and so I have counselled. 16 Therefore send quickly and tell David, "Do not lodge tonight at the fords of the wilderness, but by all means cross over; otherwise the king and all the people who are with him will be swallowed up." ' 17 Jonathan and Ahimaaz were waiting at En-rogel; a servant-girl used to go and tell them, and they would go and tell King David; for they could not risk being seen entering the city. 18 But a boy saw them, and told Absalom; so both of them went away quickly, and came to the house of a man at Bahurim, who had a well in his courtyard; and they went down into it. 19 The man's wife took a covering, stretched it over the well's mouth, and spread out grain on it; and nothing was known of it. 20 When Absalom's servants came to the woman at the house, they said, 'Where are Ahimaaz and Jonathan?' The woman said to them, 'They

a Heb *word*   *b* Gk: Heb *like the return of the whole (is) the man whom you seek*   *c* Gk Mss: Heb *some of them* have crossed over the brook*a* of water.' And when they had searched and could not find them, they returned to Jerusalem.

21 After they had gone, the men came up out of the well, and went and told King David. They said to David, 'Go and cross the water quickly; for thus and so has Ahithophel counselled against you.' 22 So David and all the people who were with him set out and crossed the Jordan; by daybreak not one was left who had not crossed the Jordan.

23 When Ahithophel saw that his counsel was not followed, he saddled his donkey and went off home to his own city. He set his house in order, and hanged himself; he died and was buried in the tomb of his father.

24 Then David came to Mahanaim, while Absalom crossed the Jordan with all the men of Israel. 25 Now Absalom had set Amasa over the army in the place of Joab. Amasa was the son of a man named Ithra the Ishmaelite,*b* who had married Abigal daughter of Nahash, sister of Zeruiah, Joab's mother. 26 The Israelites and Absalom encamped in the land of Gilead.

27 When David came to Mahanaim, Shobi son of Nahash from Rabbah of the Ammonites, and Machir son of Ammiel from Lo-debar, and Barzillai the Gileadite from Rogelim 28 brought beds, basins, and earthen vessels, wheat, barley, meal, parched grain, beans and lentils,*c* 29 honey and curds, sheep, and cheese from the herd, for David and the people with him to eat; for they said, 'The troops are hungry and weary and thirsty in the wilderness.'

The Defeat and Death of Absalom

18 Then David mustered the men who were with him, and set over them commanders of thousands and commanders of hundreds. 2 And David divided the army into three groups:*d* one-third under the command of Joab, one-third under the command of Abishai son of Zeruiah, Joab's brother, and one-third under the command of Ittai the Gittite. The king said to the men, 'I myself will

also go out with you.' 3 But the men said, 'You shall not go out. For if we flee, they will not care about us. If half of us die, they will not care about us. But you are worth ten thousand of us;*e* therefore it is better that you send us help from the city.' 4 The king said to them, 'Whatever seems best to you I will do.' So the king stood at the side of the gate, while all the army marched out by hundreds and by thousands. 5 The king gave orders to Joab and Abishai and Ittai, saying, 'Deal gently for my sake with the young man Absalom.' And all the people heard when the king gave orders to all the commanders concerning Absalom.

6 So the army went out into the field against Israel; and the battle was fought in the forest of Ephraim. 7 The men of Israel were defeated there by the servants of David, and the slaughter there was great on that day, twenty thousand men. 8 The battle spread over the face of all the country; and the forest claimed more victims that day than the sword.

9 Absalom happened to meet the servants of David. Absalom was riding on his mule, and the mule went under the thick branches of a great oak. His head caught fast in the oak, and he was left hanging*f* between heaven and earth, while the mule that was under him went on. 10 A man saw it, and told Joab, 'I saw Absalom hanging in an oak.' 11 Joab said to the man who told him, 'What, you saw him! Why then did you not strike him there to the ground? I would have been glad to give you ten pieces of silver and a belt.' 12 But the man said to Joab, 'Even if I felt in my hand the weight of a thousand pieces of silver, I would not raise my hand against the king's son; for in our hearing the king commanded you and Abishai and Ittai, saying: For my sake protect the young man Absalom! 13 On the other hand, if I had dealt treacherously against his life*g* (and there

a Meaning of Heb uncertain   *b* 1 Chr 2.17: Heb *Israelite*   *c* Heb *and lentils and parched grain*
d Gk: Heb *sent forth the army*   *e* Gk Vg Symmachus: Heb *for now there are ten thousand such as we*   *f* Gk Syr Tg: Heb *was put*   *g* Another reading is *at the risk of my life*

is nothing hidden from the king), then you yourself would have stood aloof.' ¹⁴ Joab said, 'I will not waste time like this with you.' He took three spears in his hand, and thrust them into the heart of Absalom, while he was still alive in the oak. ¹⁵ And ten young men, Joab's armour-bearers, surrounded Absalom and struck him, and killed him.

16 Then Joab sounded the trumpet, and the troops came back from pursuing Israel, for Joab restrained the troops. ¹⁷ They took Absalom, threw him into a great pit in the forest, and raised over him a very great heap of stones. Meanwhile all the Israelites fled to their homes. ¹⁸ Now Absalom in his lifetime had taken and set up for himself a pillar that is in the King's Valley, for he said, 'I have no son to keep my name in remembrance'; he called the pillar by his own name. It is called Absalom's Monument to this day.

David Hears of Absalom's Death

19 Then Ahimaaz son of Zadok said, 'Let me run, and carry tidings to the king that the LORD has delivered him from the power of his enemies.' ²⁰ Joab said to him, 'You are not to carry tidings today; you may carry tidings another day, but today you shall not do so, because the king's son is dead.' ²¹ Then Joab said to a Cushite, 'Go, tell the king what you have seen.' The Cushite bowed before Joab, and ran. ²² Then Ahimaaz son of Zadok said again to Joab, 'Come what may, let me also run after the Cushite.' And Joab said, 'Why will you run, my son, seeing that you have no reward ᵃ for the tidings?' ²³ 'Come what may,' he said, 'I will run.' So he said to him, 'Run.' Then Ahimaaz ran by the way of the Plain, and outran the Cushite.

24 Now David was sitting between the two gates. The sentinel went up to the roof of the gate by the wall, and when he looked up, he saw a man running alone. ²⁵ The sentinel shouted and told the king. The king said, 'If he is alone, there are tidings in his mouth.' He kept coming, and drew near. ²⁶ Then the sentinel saw another man running; and the sentinel called to the gate-

keeper and said, 'See, another man running alone!' The king said, 'He also is bringing tidings.' ²⁷ The sentinel said, 'I think the running of the first one is like the running of Ahimaaz son of Zadok.' The king said, 'He is a good man, and comes with good tidings.'

28 Then Ahimaaz cried out to the king, 'All is well!' He prostrated himself before the king with his face to the ground, and said, 'Blessed be the LORD your God, who has delivered up the men who raised their hand against my lord the king.' ²⁹ The king said, 'Is it well with the young man Absalom?' Ahimaaz answered, 'When Joab sent your servant, ᵇ I saw a great tumult, but I do not know what it was.' ³⁰ The king said, 'Turn aside, and stand here.' So he turned aside, and stood still.

31 Then the Cushite came; and the Cushite said, 'Good tidings for my lord the king! For the LORD has vindicated you this day, delivering you from the power of all who rose up against you.' ³² The king said to the Cushite, 'Is it well with the young man Absalom?' The Cushite answered, 'May the enemies of my lord the king, and all who rise up to do you harm, be like that young man.'

David Mourns for Absalom

33 ᶜ The king was deeply moved, and went up to the chamber over the gate, and wept; and as he went, he said, 'O my son Absalom, my son, my son Absalom! Would that I had died instead of you, O Absalom, my son, my son!'

19 It was told Joab, 'The king is weeping and mourning for Absalom.' ² So the victory that day was turned into mourning for all the troops; for the troops heard that day, 'The king is grieving for his son.' ³ The troops stole into the city that day as soldiers steal in who are ashamed when they flee in battle. ⁴ The king covered his face, and the king cried with a loud voice, 'O my son Absalom, O Absalom, my son, my son!' ⁵ Then Joab came into the house to the king, and said, 'Today you

ᵃ Meaning of Heb uncertain   ᵇ Heb the king's servant, your servant   ᶜ Ch 19.1 in Heb have covered with shame the faces of all your officers who have saved your life today, and the lives of your sons and your daughters, and the lives of your wives and your concubines, 6 for love of those who hate you and for hatred of those who love you. You have made it clear today that commanders and officers are nothing to you; for I perceive that if Absalom were alive and all of us were dead today, then you would be pleased. 7 So go out at once and speak kindly to your servants; for I swear by the LORD, if you do not go, not a man will stay with you this night; and this will be worse for you than any disaster that has come upon you from your youth until now.' 8 Then the king got up and took his seat in the gate. The troops were all told, 'See, the king is sitting in the gate'; and all the troops came before the king.

David Recalled to Jerusalem

Meanwhile, all the Israelites had fled to their homes. 9 All the people were disputing throughout all the tribes of Israel, saying, 'The king delivered us from the hand of our enemies, and saved us from the hand of the Philistines; and now he has fled out of the land because of Absalom. 10 But Absalom, whom we anointed over us, is dead in battle. Now therefore why do you say nothing about bringing the king back?'

11 King David sent this message to the priests Zadok and Abiathar, 'Say to the elders of Judah, "Why should you be the last to bring the king back to his house? The talk of all Israel has come to the king. *a* 12 You are my kin, you are my bone and my flesh; why then should you be the last to bring back the king?" 13 And say to Amasa, "Are you not my bone and my flesh? So may God do to me, and more, if you are not the commander of my army from now on, in place of Joab." ' 14 Amasa *b* swayed the hearts of all the people of Judah as one, and they sent word to the king, 'Return, both you and all your servants.' 15 So the king came back to the Jordan; and Judah came to Gilgal to meet the king and to bring him over the Jordan.

16 Shimei son of Gera, the Benjaminite, from Bahurim, hurried to come down with the people of Judah to meet King David; 17 with him were a thousand people from Benjamin. And Ziba, the servant of the house of Saul, with his fifteen sons and his twenty servants, rushed down to the Jordan ahead of the king, 18 while the crossing was taking place, *c* to bring over the king's household, and to do his pleasure.

David's Mercy to Shimei

Shimei son of Gera fell down before the king, as he was about to cross the Jordan, 19 and said to the king, 'May my lord not hold me guilty or remember how your servant did wrong on the day my lord the king left Jerusalem; may the king not bear it in mind. 20 For your servant knows that I have sinned; therefore, see, I have come this day, the first of all the house of Joseph to come down to meet my lord the king.' 21 Abishai son of Zeruiah answered, 'Shall not Shimei be put to death for this, because he cursed the LORD's anointed?' 22 But David said, 'What have I to do with you, you sons of Zeruiah, that you should today become an adversary to me? Shall anyone be put to death in Israel this day? For do I not know that I am this day king over Israel?' 23 The king said to Shimei, 'You shall not die.' And the king gave him his oath.

David and Mephibosheth Meet

24 Mephibosheth *d* grandson of Saul came down to meet the king; he had not taken care of his feet, or trimmed his beard, or washed his clothes, from the day the king left until the day he came back in safety. 25 When he came from Jerusalem to meet the king, the king said to him, 'Why did you not go with me, Mephibosheth?' *d* 26 He answered, 'My lord, O king, my servant deceived me; for your servant said to him, "Saddle a donkey for me, *e* so that I may ride on it and go with the king." For

---

a Gk: Heb *to the king, to his house*   *b* Heb *He*
c Cn: Heb *the ford crossed*   *d* Or *Merib-baal*: See 4.4 note   *e* Gk Syr Vg: Heb *said, "I will saddle a donkey for myself*

your servant is lame. ²⁷He has slandered your servant to my lord the king. But my lord the king is like the angel of God; do therefore what seems good to you. ²⁸For all my father's house were doomed to death before my lord the king; but you set your servant among those who eat at your table. What further right have I, then, to appeal to the king?' ²⁹The king said to him, 'Why speak any more of your affairs? I have decided: you and Ziba shall divide the land.' ³⁰Mephibosheth*a* said to the king, 'Let him take it all, since my lord the king has arrived home safely.'

David's Kindness to Barzillai

31 Now Barzillai the Gileadite had come down from Rogelim; he went on with the king to the Jordan, to escort him over the Jordan. ³²Barzillai was a very aged man, eighty years old. He had provided the king with food while he stayed at Mahanaim, for he was a very wealthy man. ³³The king said to Barzillai, 'Come over with me, and I will provide for you in Jerusalem at my side.' ³⁴But Barzillai said to the king, 'How many years have I still to live, that I should go up with the king to Jerusalem? ³⁵Today I am eighty years old; can I discern what is pleasant and what is not? Can your servant taste what he eats or what he drinks? Can I still listen to the voice of singing men and singing women? Why then should your servant be an added burden to my lord the king? ³⁶Your servant will go a little way over the Jordan with the king. Why should the king recompense me with such a reward? ³⁷Please let your servant return, so that I may die in my own town, near the graves of my father and my mother. But here is your servant Chimham; let him go over with my lord the king; and do for him whatever seems good to you.' ³⁸The king answered, 'Chimham shall go over with me, and I will do for him whatever seems good to you; and all that you desire of me I will do for you.' ³⁹Then all the people crossed over the Jordan, and the king crossed over; the king kissed Barzillai and blessed him, and he returned to his own home. ⁴⁰The king

went on to Gilgal, and Chimham went on with him; all the people of Judah, and also half the people of Israel, brought the king on his way.

41 Then all the people of Israel came to the king, and said to him, 'Why have our kindred the people of Judah stolen you away, and brought the king and his household over the Jordan, and all David's men with him?' ⁴²All the people of Judah answered the people of Israel, 'Because the king is near of kin to us. Why then are you angry over this matter? Have we eaten at all at the king's expense? Or has he given us any gift?' ⁴³But the people of Israel answered the people of Judah, 'We have ten shares in the king, and in David also we have more than you. Why then did you despise us? Were we not the first to speak of bringing back our king?' But the words of the people of Judah were fiercer than the words of the people of Israel.

The Rebellion of Sheba

20 Now a scoundrel named Sheba son of Bichri, a Benjaminite, happened to be there. He sounded the trumpet and cried out,

'We have no portion in David,
no share in the son of Jesse!
Everyone to your tents, O Israel!'

²So all the people of Israel withdrew from David and followed Sheba son of Bichri; but the people of Judah followed their king steadfastly from the Jordan to Jerusalem.

3 David came to his house at Jerusalem; and the king took the ten concubines whom he had left to look after the house, and put them in a house under guard, and provided for them, but did not go in to them. So they were shut up until the day of their death, living as if in widowhood.

4 Then the king said to Amasa, 'Call the men of Judah together to me within three days, and be here yourself.' ⁵So Amasa went to summon Judah; but he delayed beyond the set time that had been appointed him. ⁶David said to Abishai, 'Now Sheba son of Bichri will do us more

a Or Merib-baal: See 4.4 note

harm than Absalom; take your lord's servants and pursue him, or he will find fortified cities for himself, and escape from us.' ⁷Joab's men went out after him, along with the Cherethites, the Pelethites, and all the warriors; they went out from Jerusalem to pursue Sheba son of Bichri. ⁸When they were at the large stone that is in Gibeon, Amasa came to meet them. Now Joab was wearing a soldier's garment and over it was a belt with a sword in its sheath fastened at his waist; as he went forward it fell out. ⁹Joab said to Amasa, 'Is it well with you, my brother?' And Joab took Amasa by the beard with his right hand to kiss him. ¹⁰But Amasa did not notice the sword in Joab's hand; Joab struck him in the belly so that his entrails poured out on the ground, and he died. He did not strike a second blow.

Then Joab and his brother Abishai pursued Sheba son of Bichri. ¹¹And one of Joab's men took his stand by Amasa, and said, 'Whoever favours Joab, and whoever is for David, let him follow Joab.' ¹²Amasa lay wallowing in his blood on the highway, and the man saw that all the people were stopping. Since he saw that all who came by him were stopping, he carried Amasa from the highway into a field, and threw a garment over him. ¹³Once he was removed from the highway, all the people went on after Joab to pursue Sheba son of Bichri.

14 Sheba[a] passed through all the tribes of Israel to Abel of Beth-maacah;[b] and all the Bichrites[c] assembled, and followed him inside. ¹⁵Joab's forces[d] came and besieged him in Abel of Beth-maacah; they threw up a siege-ramp against the city, and it stood against the rampart. Joab's forces were battering the wall to break it down. ¹⁶Then a wise woman called from the city, 'Listen! Listen! Tell Joab, "Come here, I want to speak to you." ' ¹⁷He came near her; and the woman said, 'Are you Joab?' He answered, 'I am.' Then she said to him, 'Listen to the words of your servant.' He answered, 'I am listening.' ¹⁸Then she said, 'They used to say in the old days, "Let them inquire at Abel"; and so they would

settle a matter. ¹⁹I am one of those who are peaceable and faithful in Israel; you seek to destroy a city that is a mother in Israel; why will you swallow up the heritage of the LORD?' ²⁰Joab answered, 'Far be it from me, far be it, that I should swallow up or destroy! ²¹That is not the case! But a man of the hill country of Ephraim, called Sheba son of Bichri, has lifted up his hand against King David; give him up alone, and I will withdraw from the city.' The woman said to Joab, 'His head shall be thrown over the wall to you.' ²²Then the woman went to all the people with her wise plan. And they cut off the head of Sheba son of Bichri, and threw it out to Joab. So he blew the trumpet, and they dispersed from the city, and all went to their homes, while Joab returned to Jerusalem to the king.

23 Now Joab was in command of all the army of Israel;[e] Benaiah son of Jehoiada was in command of the Cherethites and the Pelethites; ²⁴Adoram was in charge of the forced labour; Jehoshaphat son of Ahilud was the recorder; ²⁵Sheva was secretary; Zadok and Abiathar were priests; ²⁶and Ira the Jairite was also David's priest.

David Avenges the Gibeonites

21 Now there was a famine in the days of David for three years, year after year; and David inquired of the LORD. The LORD said, 'There is blood-guilt on Saul and on his house, because he put the Gibeonites to death.' ²So the king called the Gibeonites and spoke to them. (Now the Gibeonites were not of the people of Israel, but of the remnant of the Amorites; although the people of Israel had sworn to spare them, Saul had tried to wipe them out in his zeal for the people of Israel and Judah.) ³David said to the Gibeonites, 'What shall I do for you? How shall I make expiation, that you may bless the heritage of the LORD?' ⁴The Gibeonites said to him, 'It is not a matter of silver or gold between

a Heb *He*   b Compare 20.15: Heb *and Beth-maacah*
c Compare Gk Vg: Heb *Berites*   d Heb *They*
e Cn: Heb *Joab to all the army, Israel*

us and Saul or his house; neither is it for us to put anyone to death in Israel.' He said, 'What do you say that I should do for you?' 5 They said to the king, 'The man who consumed us and planned to destroy us, so that we should have no place in all the territory of Israel— 6 let seven of his sons be handed over to us, and we will impale them before the LORD at Gibeon on the mountain of the LORD.'ᵃ The king said, 'I will hand them over.'

7 But the king spared Mephibosheth,ᵇ the son of Saul's son Jonathan, because of the oath of the LORD that was between them, between David and Jonathan son of Saul. 8 The king took the two sons of Rizpah daughter of Aiah, whom she bore to Saul, Armoni and Mephibosheth;ᵇ and the five sons of Merabᶜ daughter of Saul, whom she bore to Adriel son of Barzillai the Meholathite; 9 he gave them into the hands of the Gibeonites, and they impaled them on the mountain before the LORD. The seven of them perished together. They were put to death in the first days of harvest, at the beginning of the barley harvest.

10 Then Rizpah the daughter of Aiah took sackcloth, and spread it on a rock for herself, from the beginning of harvest until rain fell on them from the heavens; she did not allow the birds of the air to come on the bodiesᵈ by day, or the wild animals by night. 11 When David was told what Rizpah daughter of Aiah, the concubine of Saul, had done, 12 David went and took the bones of Saul and the bones of his son Jonathan from the people of Jabesh-gilead, who had stolen them from the public square of Beth-shan, where the Philistines had hung them up, on the day the Philistines killed Saul on Gilboa. 13 He brought up from there the bones of Saul and the bones of his son Jonathan; and they gathered the bones of those who had been impaled. 14 They buried the bones of Saul and of his son Jonathan in the land of Benjamin in Zela, in the tomb of his father Kish; they did all that the king commanded. After that, God heeded supplications for the land.

Exploits of David's Men

15 The Philistines went to war again with Israel, and David went down together with his servants. They fought against the Philistines, and David grew weary. 16 Ishbi-benob, one of the descendants of the giants, whose spear weighed three hundred shekels of bronze, and who was fitted out with new weapons,ᵉ said he would kill David. 17 But Abishai son of Zeruiah came to his aid, and attacked the Philistine and killed him. Then David's men swore to him, 'You shall not go out with us to battle any longer, so that you do not quench the lamp of Israel.'

18 After this a battle took place with the Philistines, at Gob; then Sibbecai the Hushathite killed Saph, who was one of the descendants of the giants. 19 Then there was another battle with the Philistines at Gob; and Elhanan son of Jaare-oregim, the Bethlehemite, killed Goliath the Gittite, the shaft of whose spear was like a weaver's beam. 20 There was again war at Gath, where there was a man of great size, who had six fingers on each hand, and six toes on each foot, twenty-four in number; he too was descended from the giants. 21 When he taunted Israel, Jonathan son of David's brother Shimei, killed him. 22 These four were descended from the giants in Gath; they fell by the hands of David and his servants.

David's Song of Thanksgiving

22 David spoke to the LORD the words of this song on the day when the LORD delivered him from the hand of all his enemies, and from the hand of Saul. 2 He said:

The LORD is my rock, my fortress, and
    my deliverer,
3   my God, my rock, in whom I take
    refuge,
my shield and the horn of my
    salvation,
my stronghold and my refuge,

a Cn Compare Gk and 21.9: Heb at Gibeah of Saul, the chosen of the LORD   b Or Merib-baal: See 4.4 note
c Two Heb Mss Syr Compare Gk: MT Michal
d Heb them   e Heb was belted anew

my saviour; you save me from
 violence.
4 I call upon the LORD, who is worthy
 to be praised,
 and I am saved from my enemies.

5 For the waves of death encompassed
 me,
 the torrents of perdition assailed
 me;
6 the cords of Sheol entangled me,
 the snares of death confronted me.

7 In my distress I called upon the
 LORD;
 to my God I called.
From his temple he heard my voice,
 and my cry came to his ears.

8 Then the earth reeled and rocked;
 the foundations of the heavens
 trembled
 and quaked, because he was angry.
9 Smoke went up from his nostrils,
 and devouring fire from his mouth;
 glowing coals flamed forth from
 him.
10 He bowed the heavens, and came
 down;
 thick darkness was under his feet.
11 He rode on a cherub, and flew;
 he was seen upon the wings of the
 wind.
12 He made darkness around him a
 canopy,
 thick clouds, a gathering of water.
13 Out of the brightness before him
 coals of fire flamed forth.
14 The LORD thundered from heaven;
 the Most High uttered his voice.
15 He sent out arrows, and scattered
 them
 —lightning, and routed them.
16 Then the channels of the sea were
 seen,
 the foundations of the world were
 laid bare
at the rebuke of the LORD,
 at the blast of the breath of his
 nostrils.

17 He reached from on high, he
 took me,
 he drew me out of mighty waters.
18 He delivered me from my strong
 enemy,
 from those who hated me;
 for they were too mighty for me.
19 They came upon me in the day of my
 calamity,
 but the LORD was my stay.
20 He brought me out into a broad
 place;
 he delivered me, because he
 delighted in me.

21 The LORD rewarded me according to
 my righteousness;
 according to the cleanness of my
 hands he recompensed me.
22 For I have kept the ways of the LORD,
 and have not wickedly departed
 from my God.
23 For all his ordinances were before
 me,
 and from his statutes I did not turn
 aside.
24 I was blameless before him,
 and I kept myself from guilt.
25 Therefore the LORD has recompensed
 me according to my
 righteousness,
 according to my cleanness in his
 sight.

26 With the loyal you show yourself
 loyal;
 with the blameless you show
 yourself blameless;
27 with the pure you show yourself
 pure,
 and with the crooked you show
 yourself perverse.
28 You deliver a humble people,
 but your eyes are upon the haughty
 to bring them down.
29 Indeed, you are my lamp, O LORD,
 the LORD lightens my darkness.
30 By you I can crush a troop,
 and by my God I can leap over a
 wall.
31 This God—his way is perfect;

the promise of the LORD proves
  true;
he is a shield for all who take
  refuge in him.

32 For who is God, but the LORD?
  And who is a rock, except our God?
33 The God who has girded me with
    strength *a*
  has opened wide my path. *b*
34 He made my *c* feet like the feet of
    deer,
  and set me secure on the heights.
35 He trains my hands for war,
  so that my arms can bend a bow of
    bronze.
36 You have given me the shield of your
    salvation,
  and your help *d* has made me
    great.
37 You have made me stride freely,
  and my feet do not slip;
38 I pursued my enemies and destroyed
    them,
  and did not turn back until they
    were consumed.
39 I consumed them; I struck them
    down, so that they did not
    rise;
  they fell under my feet.
40 For you girded me with strength for
    the battle;
  you made my assailants sink under
    me.
41 You made my enemies turn their
    backs to me,
  those who hated me, and I
    destroyed them.
42 They looked, but there was no one to
    save them;
  they cried to the LORD, but he did
    not answer them.
43 I beat them fine like the dust of the
    earth,
  I crushed them and stamped them
    down like the mire of the
    streets.

44 You delivered me from strife with the
    peoples; *e*

you kept me as the head of the
    nations;
  people whom I had not known
    served me.
45 Foreigners came cringing to me;
  as soon as they heard of me, they
    obeyed me.
46 Foreigners lost heart,
  and came trembling out of their
    strongholds.

47 The LORD lives! Blessed be my rock,
  and exalted be my God, the rock of
    my salvation,
48 the God who gave me vengeance
  and brought down peoples under
    me,
49 who brought me out from my
    enemies;
  you exalted me above my
    adversaries,
  you delivered me from the violent.

50 For this I will extol you, O LORD,
    among the nations,
  and sing praises to your name.
51 He is a tower of salvation for his
    king,
  and shows steadfast love to his
    anointed,
  to David and his descendants for
    ever.

The Last Words of David

23 Now these are the last words of
David:
  The oracle of David, son of Jesse,
    the oracle of the man whom God
      exalted, *f*
  the anointed of the God of Jacob,
    the favourite of the Strong One of
      Israel:

2 The spirit of the LORD speaks through
    me,
  his word is upon my tongue.
3 The God of Israel has spoken,

a Q Ms Gk Syr Vg Compare Ps 18.32: MT *God is my
strong refuge*   *b* Meaning of Heb uncertain
c Another reading is *his*   *d* Q Ms: MT *your answering*
e Gk: Heb *from strife with my people*   *f* Q Ms: MT *who
was raised on high*

the Rock of Israel has said to me:
One who rules over people justly,
   ruling in the fear of God,
4 is like the light of morning,
      like the sun rising on a cloudless
         morning,
      gleaming from the rain on the
         grassy land.

5 Is not my house like this with God?
      For he has made with me an
         everlasting covenant,
      ordered in all things and secure.
   Will he not cause to prosper
      all my help and my desire?
6 But the godless are *a* all like thorns
      that are thrown away;
      for they cannot be picked up with
         the hand;
7 to touch them one uses an iron bar
      or the shaft of a spear.
   And they are entirely consumed in
      fire on the spot. *b*

David's Mighty Men

8 These are the names of the warriors
whom David had: Josheb-basshebeth a
Tahchemonite; he was chief of the Three; *c*
he wielded his spear *d* against eight hundred
whom he killed at one time.

9 Next to him among the three warriors
was Eleazar son of Dodo son of Ahohi. He
was with David when they defied the Philistines who were gathered there for battle.
The Israelites withdrew, 10 but he stood his
ground. He struck down the Philistines until his arm grew weary, though his hand
clung to the sword. The LORD brought
about a great victory that day. Then the people came back to him—but only to strip the
dead.

11 Next to him was Shammah son of
Agee, the Hararite. The Philistines gathered
together at Lehi, where there was a plot of
ground full of lentils; and the army fled
from the Philistines. 12 But he took his
stand in the middle of the plot, defended it,
and killed the Philistines; and the LORD
brought about a great victory.

13 Towards the beginning of harvest
three of the thirty *e* chiefs went down to join

David at the cave of Adullam, while a band
of Philistines was encamped in the valley
of Rephaim. 14 David was then in the
stronghold; and the garrison of the Philistines was then at Bethlehem. 15 David said
longingly, 'O that someone would give me
water to drink from the well of Bethlehem
that is by the gate!' 16 Then the three warriors broke through the camp of the Philistines, drew water from the well of Bethlehem that was by the gate, and brought it to
David. But he would not drink of it; he
poured it out to the LORD, 17 for he said,
'The LORD forbid that I should do this. Can
I drink the blood of the men who went at
the risk of their lives?' Therefore he would
not drink it. The three warriors did these
things.

18 Now Abishai son of Zeruiah, the
brother of Joab, was chief of the Thirty. *f*
With his spear he fought against three hundred men and killed them, and won a
name beside the Three. 19 He was the most
renowned of the Thirty, *g* and became their
commander; but he did not attain to the
Three.

20 Benaiah son of Jehoiada was a valiant
warrior *h* from Kabzeel, a doer of great
deeds; he struck down two sons of Ariel *i* of
Moab. He also went down and killed a lion
in a pit on a day when snow had fallen.
21 And he killed an Egyptian, a handsome
man. The Egyptian had a spear in his hand;
but Benaiah went against him with a staff,
snatched the spear out of the Egyptian's
hand, and killed him with his own spear.
22 Such were the things Benaiah son of Jehoiada did, and won a name beside the
three warriors. 23 He was renowned among
the Thirty, but he did not attain to the
Three. And David put him in charge of his
bodyguard.

24 Among the Thirty were Asahel
brother of Joab; Elhanan son of Dodo of
Bethlehem; 25 Shammah of Harod; Elika of

a Heb *But worthlessness*   *b* Heb *in sitting*   *c* Gk Vg
Compare 1 Chr 11.11: Meaning of Heb uncertain
d 1 Chr 11.11: Meaning of Heb uncertain   *e* Heb adds
head   *f* Two Heb Mss Syr: MT *Three*   *g* Syr Compare
1 Chr 11.25: Heb *Was he the most renowned of the Three?*
h Another reading is *the son of Ish-hai*   *i* Gk: Heb
lacks *sons of*

Harod; 26 Helez the Paltite; Ira son of Ikkesh of Tekoa; 27 Abiezer of Anathoth; Me-
bunnai the Hushathite; 28 Zalmon the
Ahohite; Maharai of Netophah; 29 Heleb
son of Baanah of Netophah; Ittai son of
Ribai of Gibeah of the Benjaminites; 30 Be-
naiah of Pirathon; Hiddai of the torrents of
Gaash; 31 Abi-albon the Arbathite; Azmaveth of Bahurim; 32 Eliahba of Shaalbon;
the sons of Jashen: Jonathan 33 son of*a*
Shammah the Hararite; Ahiam son of Sha-
rar the Hararite; 34 Eliphelet son of Ahasbai
of Maacah; Eliam son of Ahithophel the
Gilonite; 35 Hezro*b* of Carmel; Paarai the
Arbite; 36 Igal son of Nathan of Zobah;
Bani the Gadite; 37 Zelek the Ammonite;
Naharai of Beeroth, the armour-bearer of
Joab son of Zeruiah; 38 Ira the Ithrite; Ga-
reb the Ithrite; 39 Uriah the Hittite—thirty-seven in all.

David's Census of Israel and Judah

24 Again the anger of the LORD was
kindled against Israel, and he incited David against them, saying, 'Go,
count the people of Israel and Judah.' 2 So
the king said to Joab and the commanders
of the army,*c* who were with him, 'Go
through all the tribes of Israel, from Dan to
Beer-sheba, and take a census of the people,
so that I may know how many there are.'
3 But Joab said to the king, 'May the LORD
your God increase the number of the people a hundredfold, while the eyes of my
lord the king can still see it! But why does
my lord the king want to do this?' 4 But the
king's word prevailed against Joab and the
commanders of the army. So Joab and
the commanders of the army went out from
the presence of the king to take a census
of the people of Israel. 5 They crossed the
Jordan, and began from*d* Aroer and from
the city that is in the middle of the valley,
towards Gad and on to Jazer. 6 Then they
came to Gilead, and to Kadesh in the land
of the Hittites;*e* and they came to Dan, and
from Dan*f* they went round to Sidon, 7 and
came to the fortress of Tyre and to all the
cities of the Hivites and Canaanites; and
they went out to the Negeb of Judah at
Beer-sheba. 8 So when they had gone

through all the land, they came back to
Jerusalem at the end of nine months and
twenty days. 9 Joab reported to the king the
number of those who had been recorded: in
Israel there were eight hundred thousand
soldiers able to draw the sword, and those
of Judah were five hundred thousand.

Judgement on David's Sin

10 But afterwards, David was stricken to
the heart because he had numbered the
people. David said to the LORD, 'I have
sinned greatly in what I have done. But
now, O LORD, I pray you, take away the guilt
of your servant; for I have done very foolishly.' 11 When David rose in the morning,
the word of the LORD came to the prophet
Gad, David's seer, saying, 12 'Go and say to
David: Thus says the LORD: Three things I offer*g* you; choose one of them, and I will do
it to you.' 13 So Gad came to David and told
him; he asked him, 'Shall three*h* years of
famine come to you on your land? Or will
you flee for three months before your foes
while they pursue you? Or shall there be
three days' pestilence in your land? Now
consider, and decide what answer I shall return to the one who sent me.' 14 Then David
said to Gad, 'I am in great distress; let us
fall into the hand of the LORD, for his mercy is great; but let me not fall into human
hands.'

15 So the LORD sent a pestilence on Israel from that morning until the appointed
time; and seventy thousand of the people
died, from Dan to Beer-sheba. 16 But when
the angel stretched out his hand towards
Jerusalem to destroy it, the LORD relented
concerning the evil, and said to the angel
who was bringing destruction among the
people, 'It is enough; now stay your hand.'
The angel of the LORD was then by the
threshing-floor of Araunah the Jebusite.
17 When David saw the angel who was destroying the people, he said to the LORD, 'I
alone have sinned, and I alone have done

---

a Gk: Heb lacks *son of*   *b* Another reading is *Hezrai*
c 1 Chr 21.2 Gk: Heb *to Joab the commander of the army*
d Gk Mss: Heb *encamped in Aroer south of*   *e* Gk: Heb
to the land of Tahtim-hodshi   *f* Cn Compare Gk: Heb
they came to Dan-jaan and   *g* Or *hold over*
h 1 Chr 21.12 Gk: Heb *seven*

wickedly; but these sheep, what have they done? Let your hand, I pray, be against me and against my father's house.'

David's Altar on the Threshing-Floor

18 That day Gad came to David and said to him, 'Go up and erect an altar to the LORD on the threshing-floor of Araunah the Jebusite.' 19 Following Gad's instructions, David went up, as the LORD had commanded. 20 When Araunah looked down, he saw the king and his servants coming towards him; and Araunah went out and prostrated himself before the king with his face to the ground. 21 Araunah said, 'Why has my lord the king come to his servant?' David said, 'To buy the threshing-floor from you in order to build an altar to the LORD, so that the plague may be averted from the people.'

22 Then Araunah said to David, 'Let my lord the king take and offer up what seems good to him; here are the oxen for the burnt-offering, and the threshing-sledges and the yokes of the oxen for the wood. 23 All this, O king, Araunah gives to the king.' And Araunah said to the king, 'May the LORD your God respond favourably to you.'

24 But the king said to Araunah, 'No, but I will buy them from you for a price; I will not offer burnt-offerings to the LORD my God that cost me nothing.' So David bought the threshing-floor and the oxen for fifty shekels of silver. 25 David built there an altar to the LORD, and offered burnt-offerings and offerings of well-being. So the LORD answered his supplication for the land, and the plague was averted from Israel.

1 KINGS

The Struggle for the Succession

1 King David was old and advanced in years; and although they covered him with clothes, he could not get warm. ² So his servants said to him, 'Let a young virgin be sought for my lord the king, and let her wait on the king, and be his attendant; let her lie in your bosom, so that my lord the king may be warm.' ³ So they searched for a beautiful girl throughout all the territory of Israel, and found Abishag the Shunammite, and brought her to the king. ⁴ The girl was very beautiful. She became the king's attendant and served him, but the king did not know her sexually.

5 Now Adonijah son of Haggith exalted himself, saying, 'I will be king'; he prepared for himself chariots and horsemen, and fifty men to run before him. ⁶ His father had never at any time displeased him by asking, 'Why have you done that?' He was also a very handsome man, and he was born next after Absalom. ⁷ He conferred with Joab son of Zeruiah and with the priest Abiathar, and they supported Adonijah. ⁸ But the priest Zadok, and Benaiah son of Jehoiada, and the prophet Nathan, and Shimei, and Rei, and David's own warriors did not side with Adonijah.

9 Adonijah sacrificed sheep, oxen, and fatted cattle by the stone Zoheleth, which is beside En-rogel, and he invited all his brothers, the king's sons, and all the royal officials of Judah, ¹⁰ but he did not invite the prophet Nathan or Benaiah or the warriors or his brother Solomon.

11 Then Nathan said to Bathsheba, Solomon's mother, 'Have you not heard that Adonijah son of Haggith has become king and our lord David does not know it? ¹² Now therefore come, let me give you advice, so that you may save your own life and the life of your son Solomon. ¹³ Go in at once to King David, and say to him, "Did you not, my lord the king, swear to your servant, saying: Your son Solomon shall succeed me as king, and he shall sit on my throne? Why then is Adonijah king?" ¹⁴ Then while you are still there speaking with the king, I will come in after you and confirm your words.'

15 So Bathsheba went to the king in his room. The king was very old; Abishag the Shunammite was attending the king. ¹⁶ Bathsheba bowed and did obeisance to the king, and the king said, 'What do you wish?' ¹⁷ She said to him, 'My lord, you swore to your servant by the LORD your God, saying: Your son Solomon shall succeed me as king, and he shall sit on my throne. ¹⁸ But now suddenly Adonijah has become king, though you, my lord the king, do not know it. ¹⁹ He has sacrificed oxen, fatted cattle, and sheep in abundance, and has invited all the children of the king, the priest Abiathar, and Joab the commander of the army; but your servant Solomon he has not invited. ²⁰ But you, my lord the king—the eyes of all Israel are on you to tell them who shall sit on the throne of my lord the king after him. ²¹ Otherwise it will come to pass, when my lord the king sleeps with his ancestors, that my son Solomon and I will be counted offenders.'

22 While she was still speaking with the king, the prophet Nathan came in. ²³ The king was told, 'Here is the prophet Nathan.' When he came in before the king,

he did obeisance to the king, with his face to the ground. 24 Nathan said, 'My lord the king, have you said, "Adonijah shall succeed me as king, and he shall sit on my throne"? 25 For today he has gone down and has sacrificed oxen, fatted cattle, and sheep in abundance, and has invited all the king's children, Joab the commander*a* of the army, and the priest Abiathar, who are now eating and drinking before him, and saying, "Long live King Adonijah!" 26 But he did not invite me, your servant, and the priest Zadok, and Benaiah son of Jehoiada, and your servant Solomon. 27 Has this thing been brought about by my lord the king and you have not let your servants know who should sit on the throne of my lord the king after him?'

The Accession of Solomon

28 King David answered, 'Summon Bathsheba to me.' So she came into the king's presence, and stood before the king. 29 The king swore, saying, 'As the LORD lives, who has saved my life from every adversity, 30 as I swore to you by the LORD, the God of Israel, "Your son Solomon shall succeed me as king, and he shall sit on my throne in my place", so will I do this day.' 31 Then Bathsheba bowed with her face to the ground, and did obeisance to the king, and said, 'May my lord King David live for ever!'

32 King David said, 'Summon to me the priest Zadok, the prophet Nathan, and Benaiah son of Jehoiada.' When they came before the king, 33 the king said to them, 'Take with you the servants of your lord, and have my son Solomon ride on my own mule, and bring him down to Gihon. 34 There let the priest Zadok and the prophet Nathan anoint him king over Israel; then blow the trumpet, and say, "Long live King Solomon!" 35 You shall go up following him. Let him enter and sit on my throne; he shall be king in my place; for I have appointed him to be ruler over Israel and over Judah.' 36 Benaiah son of Jehoiada answered the king, 'Amen! May the LORD, the God of my lord the king, so ordain. 37 As the LORD has been

with my lord the king, so may he be with Solomon, and make his throne greater than the throne of my lord King David.'

38 So the priest Zadok, the prophet Nathan, and Benaiah son of Jehoiada, and the Cherethites and the Pelethites, went down and had Solomon ride on King David's mule, and led him to Gihon. 39 There the priest Zadok took the horn of oil from the tent and anointed Solomon. Then they blew the trumpet, and all the people said, 'Long live King Solomon!' 40 And all the people went up following him, playing on pipes and rejoicing with great joy, so that the earth quaked at their noise.

41 Adonijah and all the guests who were with him heard it as they finished feasting. When Joab heard the sound of the trumpet, he said, 'Why is the city in an uproar?' 42 While he was still speaking, Jonathan son of the priest Abiathar arrived. Adonijah said, 'Come in, for you are a worthy man and surely you bring good news.' 43 Jonathan answered Adonijah, 'No, for our lord King David has made Solomon king; 44 the king has sent with him the priest Zadok, the prophet Nathan, and Benaiah son of Jehoiada, and the Cherethites and the Pelethites; and they had him ride on the king's mule; 45 the priest Zadok and the prophet Nathan have anointed him king at Gihon; and they have gone up from there rejoicing, so that the city is in an uproar. This is the noise that you heard. 46 Solomon now sits on the royal throne. 47 Moreover, the king's servants came to congratulate our lord King David, saying, "May God make the name of Solomon more famous than yours, and make his throne greater than your throne." The king bowed in worship on the bed 48 and went on to pray thus, "Blessed be the LORD, the God of Israel, who today has granted one of my offspring*b* to sit on my throne and permitted me to witness it." '

49 Then all the guests of Adonijah got up trembling and went their own ways. 50 Adonijah, fearing Solomon, got up and went to grasp the horns of the altar. 51 Solomon was

a Gk: Heb *the commanders*   *b* Gk: Heb *one*

informed, 'Adonijah is afraid of King Solomon; see, he has laid hold of the horns of the altar, saying, "Let King Solomon swear to me first that he will not kill his servant with the sword." ' 52 So Solomon responded, 'If he proves to be a worthy man, not one of his hairs shall fall to the ground; but if wickedness is found in him, he shall die.' 53 Then King Solomon sent to have him brought down from the altar. He came to do obeisance to King Solomon; and Solomon said to him, 'Go home.'

David's Instruction to Solomon

2 When David's time to die drew near, he charged his son Solomon, saying: 2 'I am about to go the way of all the earth. Be strong, be courageous, 3 and keep the charge of the LORD your God, walking in his ways and keeping his statutes, his commandments, his ordinances, and his testimonies, as it is written in the law of Moses, so that you may prosper in all that you do and wherever you turn. 4 Then the LORD will establish his word that he spoke concerning me: "If your heirs take heed to their way, to walk before me in faithfulness with all their heart and with all their soul, there shall not fail you a successor on the throne of Israel."

5 'Moreover, you know also what Joab son of Zeruiah did to me, how he dealt with the two commanders of the armies of Israel, Abner son of Ner, and Amasa son of Jether, whom he murdered, retaliating in time of peace for blood that had been shed in war, and putting the blood of war on the belt around his waist, and on the sandals on his feet. 6 Act therefore according to your wisdom, but do not let his grey head go down to Sheol in peace. 7 Deal loyally, however, with the sons of Barzillai the Gileadite, and let them be among those who eat at your table; for with such loyalty they met me when I fled from your brother Absalom. 8 There is also with you Shimei son of Gera, the Benjaminite from Bahurim, who cursed me with a terrible curse on the day when I went to Mahanaim; but when he came down to meet me at the Jordan, I swore to him by the LORD, "I

will not put you to death with the sword." 9 Therefore do not hold him guiltless, for you are a wise man; you will know what you ought to do to him, and you must bring his grey head down with blood to Sheol.'

Death of David

10 Then David slept with his ancestors, and was buried in the city of David. 11 The time that David reigned over Israel was forty years; he reigned for seven years in Hebron, and thirty-three years in Jerusalem. 12 So Solomon sat on the throne of his father David; and his kingdom was firmly established.

Solomon Consolidates His Reign

13 Then Adonijah son of Haggith came to Bathsheba, Solomon's mother. She asked, 'Do you come peaceably?' He said, 'Peaceably.' 14 Then he said, 'May I have a word with you?' She said, 'Go on.' 15 He said, 'You know that the kingdom was mine, and that all Israel expected me to reign; however, the kingdom has turned about and become my brother's, for it was his from the LORD. 16 And now I have one request to make of you; do not refuse me.' She said to him, 'Go on.' 17 He said, 'Please ask King Solomon—he will not refuse you—to give me Abishag the Shunammite as my wife.' 18 Bathsheba said, 'Very well; I will speak to the king on your behalf.'

19 So Bathsheba went to King Solomon, to speak to him on behalf of Adonijah. The king rose to meet her, and bowed down to her; then he sat on his throne, and had a throne brought for the king's mother, and she sat on his right. 20 Then she said, 'I have one small request to make of you; do not refuse me.' And the king said to her, 'Make your request, my mother; for I will not refuse you.' 21 She said, 'Let Abishag the Shunammite be given to your brother Adonijah as his wife.' 22 King Solomon answered his mother, 'And why do you ask Abishag the Shunammite for Adonijah? Ask for him the kingdom as well! For he is my elder brother; ask not only for him but also for the priest Abiathar

and for Joab son of Zeruiah!' 23 Then King Solomon swore by the LORD, 'So may God do to me, and more also, for Adonijah has devised this scheme at the risk of his life! 24 Now therefore as the LORD lives, who has established me and placed me on the throne of my father David, and who has made me a house as he promised, today Adonijah shall be put to death.' 25 So King Solomon sent Benaiah son of Jehoiada; he struck him down, and he died.

26 The king said to the priest Abiathar, 'Go to Anathoth, to your estate; for you deserve death. But I will not at this time put you to death, because you carried the ark of the Lord GOD before my father David, and because you shared in all the hardships my father endured.' 27 So Solomon banished Abiathar from being priest to the LORD, thus fulfilling the word of the LORD that he had spoken concerning the house of Eli in Shiloh.

28 When the news came to Joab—for Joab had supported Adonijah though he had not supported Absalom—Joab fled to the tent of the LORD and grasped the horns of the altar. 29 When it was told King Solomon, 'Joab has fled to the tent of the LORD and now is beside the altar', Solomon sent Benaiah son of Jehoiada, saying, 'Go, strike him down.' 30 So Benaiah came to the tent of the LORD and said to him, 'The king commands, "Come out." ' But he said, 'No, I will die here.' Then Benaiah brought the king word again, saying, 'Thus said Joab, and thus he answered me.' 31 The king replied to him, 'Do as he has said, strike him down and bury him; and thus take away from me and from my father's house the guilt for the blood that Joab shed without cause. 32 The LORD will bring back his bloody deeds on his own head, because, without the knowledge of my father David, he attacked and killed with the sword two men more righteous and better than himself, Abner son of Ner, commander of the army of Israel, and Amasa son of Jether, commander of the army of Judah. 33 So shall their blood come back on the head of Joab and on the head of his descendants for ever; but to David, and to

his descendants, and to his house, and to his throne, there shall be peace from the LORD for evermore.' 34 Then Benaiah son of Jehoiada went up and struck him down and killed him; and he was buried at his own house near the wilderness. 35 The king put Benaiah son of Jehoiada over the army in his place, and the king put the priest Zadok in the place of Abiathar.

36 Then the king sent and summoned Shimei, and said to him, 'Build yourself a house in Jerusalem, and live there, and do not go out from there to any place whatever. 37 For on the day you go out, and cross the Wadi Kidron, know for certain that you shall die; your blood shall be on your own head.' 38 And Shimei said to the king, 'The sentence is fair; as my lord the king has said, so will your servant do.' So Shimei lived in Jerusalem for many days.

39 But it happened at the end of three years that two of Shimei's slaves ran away to King Achish son of Maacah of Gath. When it was told Shimei, 'Your slaves are in Gath', 40 Shimei arose and saddled a donkey, and went to Achish in Gath, to search for his slaves; Shimei went and brought his slaves from Gath. 41 When Solomon was told that Shimei had gone from Jerusalem to Gath and returned, 42 the king sent and summoned Shimei, and said to him, 'Did I not make you swear by the LORD, and solemnly adjure you, saying, "Know for certain that on the day you go out and go to any place whatever, you shall die"? And you said to me, "The sentence is fair; I accept." 43 Why then have you not kept your oath to the LORD and the commandment with which I charged you?' 44 The king also said to Shimei, 'You know in your own heart all the evil that you did to my father David; so the LORD will bring back your evil on your own head. 45 But King Solomon shall be blessed, and the throne of David shall be established before the LORD for ever.' 46 Then the king commanded Benaiah son of Jehoiada; and he went out and struck him down, and he died.

So the kingdom was established in the hand of Solomon.

Solomon's Prayer for Wisdom

3 Solomon made a marriage alliance with Pharaoh king of Egypt; he took Pharaoh's daughter and brought her into the city of David, until he had finished building his own house and the house of the LORD and the wall around Jerusalem. ²The people were sacrificing at the high places, however, because no house had yet been built for the name of the LORD.

3 Solomon loved the LORD, walking in the statutes of his father David; only, he sacrificed and offered incense at the high places. ⁴The king went to Gibeon to sacrifice there, for that was the principal high place; Solomon used to offer a thousand burnt-offerings on that altar. ⁵At Gibeon the LORD appeared to Solomon in a dream by night; and God said, 'Ask what I should give you.' ⁶And Solomon said, 'You have shown great and steadfast love to your servant my father David, because he walked before you in faithfulness, in righteousness, and in uprightness of heart towards you;

and you have kept for him this great and steadfast love, and have given him a son to sit on his throne today. ⁷And now, O LORD my God, you have made your servant king in place of my father David, although I am only a little child; I do not know how to go out or come in. ⁸And your servant is in the midst of the people whom you have chosen, a great people, so numerous they cannot be numbered or counted. ⁹Give your servant therefore an understanding mind to govern your people, able to discern between good and evil; for who can govern this your great people?'

10 It pleased the Lord that Solomon had asked this. ¹¹God said to him, 'Because you have asked this, and have not asked for yourself long life or riches, or for the life of your enemies, but have asked for yourself understanding to discern what is right, ¹²I now do according to your word. Indeed I give you a wise and discerning mind; no one like you has been before you and no one like you shall arise after you. ¹³I give you also what you have

Jerusalem of Solomon

not asked, both riches and honour all your life; no other king shall compare with you. 14 If you will walk in my ways, keeping my statutes and my commandments, as your father David walked, then I will lengthen your life.'

15 Then Solomon awoke; it had been a dream. He came to Jerusalem, where he stood before the ark of the covenant of the LORD. He offered up burnt-offerings and of-ferings of well-being, and provided a feast for all his servants.

Solomon's Wisdom in Judgement

16 Later, two women who were prosti-tutes came to the king and stood before him. 17 One woman said, 'Please, my lord, this woman and I live in the same house; and I gave birth while she was in the house. 18 Then on the third day after I gave birth, this woman also gave birth. We were together; there was no one else with us in the house, only the two of us were in the house. 19 Then this woman's son died in the night, because she lay on him. 20 She got up in the middle of the night and took my son from beside me while your servant slept. She laid him at her breast, and laid her dead son at my breast. 21 When I rose in the morning to nurse my son, I saw that he was dead; but when I looked at him closely in the morning, clearly it was not the son I had borne.' 22 But the other woman said, 'No, the living son is mine, and the dead son is yours.' The first said, 'No, the dead son is yours, and the living son is mine.' So they argued before the king. 23 Then the king said, 'One says, "This is my son that is alive, and your son is dead"; while the other says, "Not so! Your son is dead, and my son is the living one." ' 24 So the king said, 'Bring me a sword', and they brought a sword before the king. 25 The king said, 'Divide the liv-ing boy in two; then give half to one, and half to the other.' 26 But the woman whose son was alive said to the king—because compassion for her son burned within her—'Please, my lord, give her the living boy; certainly do not kill him!' The other

said, 'It shall be neither mine nor yours; divide it.' 27 Then the king responded: 'Give the first woman the living boy; do not kill him. She is his mother.' 28 All Israel heard of the judgement that the king had ren-dered; and they stood in awe of the king, because they perceived that the wisdom of God was in him, to execute justice.

Solomon's Administrative Officers

4 King Solomon was king over all Isra-el, 2 and these were his high officials: Azariah son of Zadok was the priest; 3 Eli-horeph and Ahijah sons of Shisha were secretaries; Jehoshaphat son of Ahilud was recorder; 4 Benaiah son of Jehoiada was in command of the army; Zadok and Abia-thar were priests; 5 Azariah son of Nathan was over the officials; Zabud son of Na-than was priest and king's friend; 6 Ahishar was in charge of the palace; and Adoniram son of Abda was in charge of the forced labour.

7 Solomon had twelve officials over all Israel, who provided food for the king and his household; each one had to make pro-vision for one month in the year. 8 These were their names: Ben-hur, in the hill country of Ephraim; 9 Ben-deker, in Makaz, Shaalbim, Beth-shemesh, and Elon-beth-hanan; 10 Ben-hesed, in Arubboth (to him belonged Socoh and all the land of He-pher); 11 Ben-abinadab, in all Naphath-dor (he had Taphath, Solomon's daughter, as his wife); 12 Baana son of Ahilud, in Taa-nach, Megiddo, and all Beth-shean, which is beside Zarethan below Jezreel, and from Beth-shean to Abel-meholah, as far as the other side of Jokmeam; 13 Ben-geber, in Ra-moth-gilead (he had the villages of Jair son of Manasseh, which are in Gilead, and he had the region of Argob, which is in Ba-shan, sixty great cities with walls and bronze bars); 14 Ahinadab son of Iddo, in Mahanaim; 15 Ahimaaz, in Naphtali (he had taken Basemath, Solomon's daughter, as his wife); 16 Baana son of Hushai, in Asher and Bealoth; 17 Jehoshaphat son of Paruah, in Issachar; 18 Shimei son of Ela, in Benjamin; 19 Geber son of Uri, in the land of Gilead, the country of King Sihon of the

Amorites and of King Og of Bashan. And there was one official in the land of Judah.

Magnificence of Solomon's Rule

20 Judah and Israel were as numerous as the sand by the sea; they ate and drank and were happy. 21 ᵃ Solomon was sovereign over all the kingdoms from the Euphrates to the land of the Philistines, even to the border of Egypt; they brought tribute and served Solomon all the days of his life. 22 Solomon's provision for one day was thirty cors of choice flour, and sixty cors of meal, 23 ten fat oxen, and twenty pasture-fed cattle, one hundred sheep, besides deer, gazelles, roebucks, and fatted fowl. 24 For he had dominion over all the region west of the Euphrates from Tiphsah to Gaza, over all the kings west of the Euphrates; and he had peace on all sides. 25 During Solomon's lifetime Judah and Israel lived in safety, from Dan even to Beersheba, all of them under their vines and fig trees. 26 Solomon also had forty thousand stalls of horses for his chariots, and twelve thousand horsemen. 27 Those officials supplied provisions for King Solomon and for all who came to King Solomon's table, each one in his month; they let nothing be lacking. 28 They also brought to the required place barley and straw for the horses and swift steeds, each according to his charge.

Fame of Solomon's Wisdom

29 God gave Solomon very great wisdom, discernment, and breadth of understanding as vast as the sand on the seashore, 30 so that Solomon's wisdom surpassed the wisdom of all the people of the east, and all the wisdom of Egypt. 31 He was wiser than anyone else, wiser than Ethan the Ezrahite, and Heman, Calcol, and Darda, children of Mahol; his fame spread throughout all the surrounding nations. 32 He composed three thousand proverbs, and his songs numbered a thousand and five. 33 He would speak of trees, from the cedar that is in the Lebanon to the hyssop that grows in the wall; he

would speak of animals, and birds, and reptiles, and fish. 34 People came from all the nations to hear the wisdom of Solomon; they came from all the kings of the earth who had heard of his wisdom.

Preparations and Materials for the Temple

5 ᵇ Now King Hiram of Tyre sent his servants to Solomon, when he heard that they had anointed him king in place of his father; for Hiram had always been a friend to David. 2 Solomon sent word to Hiram, saying, 3 'You know that my father David could not build a house for the name of the LORD his God because of the warfare with which his enemies surrounded him, until the LORD put them under the soles of his feet. ᶜ 4 But now the LORD my God has given me rest on every side; there is neither adversary nor misfortune. 5 So I intend to build a house for the name of the LORD my God, as the LORD said to my father David, "Your son, whom I will set on your throne in your place, shall build the house for my name." 6 Therefore command that cedars from the Lebanon be cut for me. My servants will join your servants, and I will give you whatever wages you set for your servants; for you know that there is no one among us who knows how to cut timber like the Sidonians.'

7 When Hiram heard the words of Solomon, he rejoiced greatly, and said, 'Blessed be the LORD today, who has given to David a wise son to be over this great people.' 8 Hiram sent word to Solomon, 'I have heard the message that you have sent to me; I will fulfil all your needs in the matter of cedar and cypress timber. 9 My servants shall bring it down to the sea from the Lebanon; I will make it into rafts to go by sea to the place you indicate. I will have them broken up there for you to take away. And you shall meet my needs by providing food for my household.' 10 So Hiram supplied Solomon's every need for timber of cedar and cypress. 11 Solomon in turn gave Hiram twenty thousand cors

---

ᵃ Ch 5.1 in Heb   ᵇ Ch 5.15 in Heb   ᶜ Gk Tg Vg: Heb *my feet* or *his feet* of wheat as food for his household, and twenty cors of fine oil. Solomon gave this to Hiram year by year. [12] So the LORD gave Solomon wisdom, as he promised him. There was peace between Hiram and Solomon; and the two of them made a treaty.

13 King Solomon conscripted forced labour out of all Israel; the levy numbered thirty thousand men. [14] He sent them to the Lebanon, ten thousand a month in shifts; they would be a month in the Lebanon and two months at home; Adoniram was in charge of the forced labour. [15] Solomon also had seventy thousand labourers and eighty thousand stonecutters in the hill country, [16] besides Solomon's three thousand three hundred supervisors who were over the work, having charge of the people who did the work. [17] At the king's command, they quarried out great, costly stones in order to lay the foundation of the house with dressed stones. [18] So Solomon's builders and Hiram's builders and the Gebalites did the stonecutting and prepared the timber and the stone to build the house.

Solomon Builds the Temple

6 In the four hundred and eightieth year after the Israelites came out of the land of Egypt, in the fourth year of Solomon's reign over Israel, in the month of Ziv, which is the second month, he began to build the house of the LORD. [2] The house that King Solomon built for the LORD was sixty cubits long, twenty cubits wide, and thirty cubits high. [3] The vestibule in front of the nave of the house was twenty cubits wide, across the width of the house. Its depth was ten cubits in front of the house. [4] For the house he made windows with recessed frames.[a] [5] He also built a structure against the wall of the house, running around the walls of the house, both the nave and the inner sanctuary; and he made side chambers all round. [6] The lowest story[b] was five cubits wide, the middle one was six cubits wide, and the third was seven cubits wide; for round the outside of the house he made offsets on the wall in order that the sup-

porting beams should not be inserted into the walls of the house.

7 The house was built with stone finished at the quarry, so that neither hammer nor axe nor any tool of iron was heard in the temple while it was being built.

8 The entrance for the middle story was on the south side of the house: one went up by winding stairs to the middle story, and from the middle story to the third. [9] So he built the house, and finished it; he roofed the house with beams and planks of cedar. [10] He built the structure against the whole house, each story[c] five cubits high, and it was joined to the house with timbers of cedar.

11 Now the word of the LORD came to Solomon, [12] 'Concerning this house that you are building, if you will walk in my statutes, obey my ordinances, and keep all my commandments by walking in them, then I will establish my promise with you, which I made to your father David. [13] I will dwell among the children of Israel, and will not forsake my people Israel.'

14 So Solomon built the house, and finished it. [15] He lined the walls of the house on the inside with boards of cedar; from the floor of the house to the rafters of the ceiling, he covered them on the inside with wood; and he covered the floor of the house with boards of cypress. [16] He built twenty cubits of the rear of the house with boards of cedar from the floor to the rafters, and he built this within as an inner sanctuary, as the most holy place. [17] The house, that is, the nave in front of the inner sanctuary, was forty cubits long. [18] The cedar within the house had carvings of gourds and open flowers; all was cedar, no stone was seen. [19] The inner sanctuary he prepared in the innermost part of the house, to set there the ark of the covenant of the LORD. [20] The interior of the inner sanctuary was twenty cubits long, twenty cubits wide, and twenty cubits high; he overlaid it with pure gold. He also overlaid the altar with cedar.[d] 21 Solomon overlaid

a Gk: Meaning of Heb uncertain   b Gk: Heb *structure*
c Heb lacks *each story*   d Meaning of Heb uncertain

the inside of the house with pure gold, then he drew chains of gold across, in front of the inner sanctuary, and overlaid it with gold. 22 Next he overlaid the whole house with gold, in order that the whole house might be perfect; even the whole altar that belonged to the inner sanctuary he overlaid with gold.

The Furnishings of the Temple

23 In the inner sanctuary he made two cherubim of olive wood, each ten cubits high. 24 Five cubits was the length of one wing of the cherub, and five cubits the length of the other wing of the cherub; it was ten cubits from the tip of one wing to the tip of the other. 25 The other cherub also measured ten cubits; both cherubim had the same measure and the same form. 26 The height of one cherub was ten cubits, and so was that of the other cherub. 27 He put the cherubim in the innermost part of the house; the wings of the cherubim were spread out so that a wing of one was touching one wall, and a wing of the other cherub was touching the other wall; their other wings towards the centre of the house were touching wing to wing. 28 He also overlaid the cherubim with gold.

29 He carved the walls of the house all round about with carved engravings of cherubim, palm trees, and open flowers, in the inner and outer rooms. 30 The floor of the house he overlaid with gold, in the inner and outer rooms.

31 For the entrance to the inner sanctuary he made doors of olive wood; the lintel and the doorposts were five-sided. *a* 32 He covered the two doors of olive wood with carvings of cherubim, palm trees, and open flowers; he overlaid them with gold, and spread gold on the cherubim and on the palm trees.

33 So also he made for the entrance to the nave doorposts of olive wood, each four-sided, 34 and two doors of cypress wood; the two leaves of one door were folding, and the two leaves of the other door were folding. 35 He carved cherubim, palm trees, and open flowers, overlaying them with gold evenly applied upon the carved

work. 36 He built the inner court with three courses of dressed stone to one course of cedar beams.

37 In the fourth year the foundation of the house of the LORD was laid, in the month of Ziv. 38 In the eleventh year, in the month of Bul, which is the eighth month, the house was finished in all its parts, and according to all its specifications. He was seven years in building it.

Solomon's Palace and Other Buildings

7 Solomon was building his own house for thirteen years, and he finished his entire house.

2 He built the House of the Forest of the Lebanon one hundred cubits long, fifty cubits wide, and thirty cubits high, built on four rows of cedar pillars, with cedar beams on the pillars. 3 It was roofed with cedar on the forty-five rafters, fifteen in each row, which were on the pillars. 4 There were window frames in the three rows, facing each other in the three rows. 5 All the doorways and doorposts had four-sided frames, opposite, facing each other in the three rows.

6 He made the Hall of Pillars fifty cubits long and thirty cubits wide. There was a porch in front with pillars, and a canopy in front of them.

7 He made the Hall of the Throne where he was to pronounce judgement, the Hall of Justice, covered with cedar from floor to floor.

8 His own house where he would reside, in the other court behind the hall, was of the same construction. Solomon also made a house like this hall for Pharaoh's daughter, whom he had taken in marriage.

9 All these were made of costly stones, cut according to measure, sawed with saws, back and front, from the foundation to the coping, and from outside to the great court. 10 The foundation was of costly stones, huge stones, stones of eight and ten cubits. 11 There were costly stones above, cut to measure, and cedar wood. 12 The great court had three courses of dressed

a Meaning of Heb uncertain

stone to one layer of cedar beams all round; so had the inner court of the house of the LORD, and the vestibule of the house.

Products of Hiram the Bronzeworker

13 Now King Solomon invited and received Hiram from Tyre. 14 He was the son of a widow of the tribe of Naphtali, whose father, a man of Tyre, had been an artisan in bronze; he was full of skill, intelligence, and knowledge in working bronze. He came to King Solomon, and did all his work.

15 He cast two pillars of bronze. Eighteen cubits was the height of one, and a cord of twelve cubits would encircle it; the second pillar was the same.[a] 16 He also made two capitals of cast bronze, to set on the tops of the pillars; the height of one capital was five cubits, and the height of the other capital was five cubits. 17 There were nets of chequer-work with wreaths of chain-work for the capitals on the tops of the pillars; seven[b] for one capital, and seven[b] for the other capital. 18 He made the columns with two rows round each latticework to cover the capitals that were above the pomegranates; he did the same with the other capital. 19 Now the capitals that were on the tops of the pillars in the vestibule were of lily-work, four cubits high. 20 The capitals were on the two pillars and also above the rounded projection that was beside the lattice-work; there were two hundred pomegranates in rows all round; and so with the other capital. 21 He set up the pillars at the vestibule of the temple; he set up the pillar on the south and called it Jachin; and he set up the pillar on the north and called it Boaz. 22 On the tops of the pillars was lily-work. Thus the work of the pillars was finished.

23 Then he made the cast sea; it was round, ten cubits from brim to brim, and five cubits high. A line of thirty cubits would encircle it completely. 24 Under its brim were panels all round it, each of ten cubits, surrounding the sea; there were two rows of panels, cast when it was cast. 25 It stood on twelve oxen, three facing north, three facing west, three facing south, and

three facing east; the sea was set on them. The hindquarters of each were towards the inside. 26 Its thickness was a handbreadth; its brim was made like the brim of a cup, like the flower of a lily; it held two thousand baths.[c]

27 He also made the ten stands of bronze; each stand was four cubits long, four cubits wide, and three cubits high. 28 This was the construction of the stands: they had borders; the borders were within the frames; 29 on the borders that were set in the frames were lions, oxen, and cherubim. On the frames, both above and below the lions and oxen, there were wreaths of bevelled work. 30 Each stand had four bronze wheels and axles of bronze; at the four corners were supports for a basin. The supports were cast with wreaths at the side of each. 31 Its opening was within the crown whose height was one cubit; its opening was round, as a pedestal is made; it was a cubit and a half wide. At its opening there were carvings; its borders were four-sided, not round. 32 The four wheels were underneath the borders; the axles of the wheels were in the stands; and the height of a wheel was a cubit and a half. 33 The wheels were made like a chariot wheel; their axles, their rims, their spokes, and their hubs were all cast. 34 There were four supports at the four corners of each stand; the supports were of one piece with the stands. 35 On the top of the stand there was a round band half a cubit high; on the top of the stand, its stays and its borders were of one piece with it. 36 On the surfaces of its stays and on its borders he carved cherubim, lions, and palm trees, where each had space, with wreaths all round. 37 In this way he made the ten stands; all of them were cast alike, with the same size and the same form.

38 He made ten basins of bronze; each basin held forty baths,[c] each basin measured four cubits; there was a basin for each of the ten stands. 39 He set five of the stands on the south side of the house, and

a Cn: Heb *and a cord of twelve cubits encircled the second pillar*; Compare Jer 52.21   b Heb: Gk *a net*   c A Heb measure of volume five on the north side of the house; he set the sea on the south-east corner of the house.

40 Hiram also made the pots, the shovels, and the basins. So Hiram finished all the work that he did for King Solomon on the house of the LORD: ⁴¹the two pillars, the two bowls of the capitals that were on the tops of the pillars, the two lattice-works to cover the two bowls of the capitals that were on the tops of the pillars; ⁴²the four hundred pomegranates for the two lattice-works, two rows of pomegranates for each lattice-work, to cover the two bowls of the capitals that were on the pillars; ⁴³the ten stands, the ten basins on the stands; ⁴⁴the one sea, and the twelve oxen underneath the sea.

45 The pots, the shovels, and the basins, all these vessels that Hiram made for King Solomon for the house of the LORD were of burnished bronze. ⁴⁶In the plain of the Jordan the king cast them, in the clay ground between Succoth and Zarethan. ⁴⁷Solomon left all the vessels unweighed, because there were so many of them; the weight of the bronze was not determined.

48 So Solomon made all the vessels that were in the house of the LORD: the golden altar, the golden table for the bread of the Presence, ⁴⁹the lampstands of pure gold, five on the south side and five on the north, in front of the inner sanctuary; the flowers, the lamps, and the tongs, of gold; ⁵⁰the cups, snuffers, basins, dishes for incense, and firepans, of pure gold; the sockets for the doors of the innermost part of the house, the most holy place, and for the doors of the nave of the temple, of gold.

51 Thus all the work that King Solomon did on the house of the LORD was finished. Solomon brought in the things that his father David had dedicated, the silver, the gold, and the vessels, and stored them in the treasuries of the house of the LORD.

Dedication of the Temple

8 Then Solomon assembled the elders of Israel and all the heads of the tribes, the leaders of the ancestral houses of the Israelites, before King Solomon in Jerusalem,

to bring up the ark of the covenant of the LORD out of the city of David, which is Zion. ²All the people of Israel assembled to King Solomon at the festival in the month Ethanim, which is the seventh month. ³And all the elders of Israel came, and the priests carried the ark. ⁴So they brought up the ark of the LORD, the tent of meeting, and all the holy vessels that were in the tent; the priests and the Levites brought them up. ⁵King Solomon and all the congregation of Israel, who had assembled before him, were with him before the ark, sacrificing so many sheep and oxen that they could not be counted or numbered. ⁶Then the priests brought the ark of the covenant of the LORD to its place, in the inner sanctuary of the house, in the most holy place, underneath the wings of the cherubim. ⁷For the cherubim spread out their wings over the place of the ark, so that the cherubim made a covering above the ark and its poles. ⁸The poles were so long that the ends of the poles were seen from the holy place in front of the inner sanctuary; but they could not be seen from outside; they are there to this day. ⁹There was nothing in the ark except the two tablets of stone that Moses had placed there at Horeb, where the LORD made a covenant with the Israelites, when they came out of the land of Egypt. ¹⁰And when the priests came out of the holy place, a cloud filled the house of the LORD, ¹¹so that the priests could not stand to minister because of the cloud; for the glory of the LORD filled the house of the LORD.

12 Then Solomon said,

'The LORD has said that he would
    dwell in thick darkness.
¹³ I have built you an exalted house,
    a place for you to dwell in for ever.'

Solomon's Speech

14 Then the king turned round and blessed all the assembly of Israel, while all the assembly of Israel stood. ¹⁵He said, 'Blessed be the LORD, the God of Israel, who with his hand has fulfilled what he promised with his mouth to my father David, saying, ¹⁶"Since the day that I brought my

people Israel out of Egypt, I have not chosen a city from any of the tribes of Israel in which to build a house, that my name might be there; but I chose David to be over my people Israel." [17] My father David had it in mind to build a house for the name of the LORD, the God of Israel. [18] But the LORD said to my father David, "You did well to consider building a house for my name; [19] nevertheless, you shall not build the house, but your son who shall be born to you shall build the house for my name." [20] Now the LORD has upheld the promise that he made; for I have risen in the place of my father David; I sit on the throne of Israel, as the LORD promised, and have built the house for the name of the LORD, the God of Israel. [21] There I have provided a place for the ark, in which is the covenant of the LORD that he made with our ancestors when he brought them out of the land of Egypt.'

Solomon's Prayer of Dedication

22 Then Solomon stood before the altar of the LORD in the presence of all the assembly of Israel, and spread out his hands to heaven. [23] He said, 'O LORD, God of Israel, there is no God like you in heaven above or on earth beneath, keeping covenant and steadfast love for your servants who walk before you with all their heart, [24] the covenant that you kept for your servant my father David as you declared to him; you promised with your mouth and have this day fulfilled with your hand. [25] Therefore, O LORD, God of Israel, keep for your servant my father David that which you promised him, saying, "There shall never fail you a successor before me to sit on the throne of Israel, if only your children look to their way, to walk before me as you have walked before me." [26] Therefore, O God of Israel, let your word be confirmed, which you promised to your servant my father David.

27 'But will God indeed dwell on the earth? Even heaven and the highest heaven cannot contain you, much less this house that I have built! [28] Have regard to your servant's prayer and his plea, O LORD my God, heeding the cry and the prayer that your servant prays to you today; [29] that your eyes may be open night and day towards this house, the place of which you said, "My name shall be there", that you may heed the prayer that your servant prays towards this place. [30] Hear the plea of your servant and of your people Israel when they pray towards this place; O hear in heaven your dwelling-place; heed and forgive.

31 'If someone sins against a neighbour and is given an oath to swear, and comes and swears before your altar in this house, [32] then hear in heaven, and act, and judge your servants, condemning the guilty by bringing their conduct on their own head, and vindicating the righteous by rewarding them according to their righteousness.

33 'When your people Israel, having sinned against you, are defeated before an enemy but turn again to you, confess your name, pray, and plead with you in this house, [34] then hear in heaven, forgive the sin of your people Israel, and bring them again to the land that you gave to their ancestors.

35 'When heaven is shut up and there is no rain because they have sinned against you, and then they pray towards this place, confess your name, and turn from their sin, because you punish[a] them, [36] then hear in heaven, and forgive the sin of your servants, your people Israel, when you teach them the good way in which they should walk; and grant rain on your land, which you have given to your people as an inheritance.

37 'If there is famine in the land, if there is plague, blight, mildew, locust, or caterpillar; if their enemy besieges them in any[b] of their cities; whatever plague, whatever sickness there is; [38] whatever prayer, whatever plea there is from any individual or from all your people Israel, all knowing the afflictions of their own hearts so that they stretch out their hands towards this house; [39] then hear in heaven your dwelling-place, forgive, act, and render to all whose hearts you know—according to all their ways, for

a Or *when you answer*   *b* Gk Syr: Heb *in the land*

only you know what is in every human heart— [40] so that they may fear you all the days that they live in the land that you gave to our ancestors.

41 'Likewise when a foreigner, who is not of your people Israel, comes from a distant land because of your name [42] —for they shall hear of your great name, your mighty hand, and your outstretched arm— when a foreigner comes and prays towards this house, [43] then hear in heaven your dwelling-place, and do according to all that the foreigner calls to you, so that all the peoples of the earth may know your name and fear you, as do your people Israel, and so that they may know that your name has been invoked on this house that I have built.

44 'If your people go out to battle against their enemy, by whatever way you shall send them, and they pray to the LORD towards the city that you have chosen and the house that I have built for your name, [45] then hear in heaven their prayer and their plea, and maintain their cause.

46 'If they sin against you—for there is no one who does not sin—and you are angry with them and give them to an enemy, so that they are carried away captive to the land of the enemy, far off or near; [47] and if they come to their senses in the land to which they have been taken captive, and repent, and plead with you in the land of their captors, saying, "We have sinned, and have done wrong; we have acted wickedly"; [48] if they repent with all their heart and soul in the land of their enemies, who took them captive, and pray to you towards their land, which you gave to their ancestors, the city that you have chosen, and the house that I have built for your name; [49] then hear in heaven your dwelling-place their prayer and their plea, maintain their cause, [50] and forgive your people who have sinned against you, and all their transgressions that they have committed against you; and grant them compassion in the sight of their captors, so that they may have compassion on them [51] (for they are your people and heritage, which you brought out of Egypt, from the midst of the iron-smelter). [52] Let your eyes be open to the plea of your servant, and to the plea of your people Israel, listening to them whenever they call to you. [53] For you have separated them from among all the peoples of the earth, to be your heritage, just as you promised through Moses, your servant, when you brought our ancestors out of Egypt, O Lord GOD.'

Solomon Blesses the Assembly

54 Now when Solomon finished offering all this prayer and this plea to the LORD, he arose from facing the altar of the LORD, where he had knelt with hands outstretched towards heaven; [55] he stood and blessed all the assembly of Israel with a loud voice:

56 'Blessed be the LORD, who has given rest to his people Israel according to all that he promised; not one word has failed of all his good promise, which he spoke through his servant Moses. [57] The LORD our God be with us, as he was with our ancestors; may he not leave us or abandon us, [58] but incline our hearts to him, to walk in all his ways, and to keep his commandments, his statutes, and his ordinances, which he commanded our ancestors. [59] Let these words of mine, with which I pleaded before the LORD, be near to the LORD our God day and night, and may he maintain the cause of his servant and the cause of his people Israel, as each day requires; [60] so that all the peoples of the earth may know that the LORD is God; there is no other. [61] Therefore devote yourselves completely to the LORD our God, walking in his statutes and keeping his commandments, as at this day.'

Solomon Offers Sacrifices

62 Then the king, and all Israel with him, offered sacrifice before the LORD. [63] Solomon offered as sacrifices of well-being to the LORD twenty-two thousand oxen and one hundred and twenty thousand sheep. So the king and all the people of Israel dedicated the house of the LORD. [64] The same day the king consecrated the middle of the court that was in front of the house of

the LORD; for there he offered the burnt-offerings and the grain-offerings and the fat pieces of the sacrifices of well-being, because the bronze altar that was before the LORD was too small to receive the burnt-offerings and the grain-offerings and the fat pieces of the sacrifices of well-being.

65 So Solomon held the festival at that time, and all Israel with him—a great assembly, people from Lebo-hamath to the Wadi of Egypt—before the LORD our God, for seven days. *a* 66 On the eighth day he sent the people away; and they blessed the king, and went to their tents, joyful and in good spirits because of all the goodness that the LORD had shown to his servant David and to his people Israel.

God Appears Again to Solomon

9 When Solomon had finished building the house of the LORD and the king's house and all that Solomon desired to build, 2 the LORD appeared to Solomon a second time, as he had appeared to him at Gibeon. 3 The LORD said to him, 'I have heard your prayer and your plea, which you made before me; I have consecrated this house that you have built, and put my name there for ever; my eyes and my heart will be there for all time. 4 As for you, if you will walk before me, as David your father walked, with integrity of heart and uprightness, doing according to all that I have commanded you, and keeping my statutes and my ordinances, 5 then I will establish your royal throne over Israel for ever, as I promised your father David, saying, "There shall not fail you a successor on the throne of Israel."

6 'If you turn aside from following me, you or your children, and do not keep my commandments and my statutes that I have set before you, but go and serve other gods and worship them, 7 then I will cut Israel off from the land that I have given them; and the house that I have consecrated for my name I will cast out of my sight; and Israel will become a proverb and a taunt among all peoples. 8 This house will become a heap of ruins; *b* everyone passing by it will be astonished, and will hiss; and they will say, "Why has the LORD done such a thing to this land and to this house?" 9 Then they will say, "Because they have forsaken the LORD their God, who brought their ancestors out of the land of Egypt, and embraced other gods, worshipping them and serving them; therefore the LORD has brought this disaster upon them." '

10 At the end of twenty years, in which Solomon had built the two houses, the house of the LORD and the king's house, 11 King Hiram of Tyre having supplied Solomon with cedar and cypress timber and gold, as much as he desired, King Solomon gave to Hiram twenty cities in the land of Galilee. 12 But when Hiram came from Tyre to see the cities that Solomon had given him, they did not please him. 13 Therefore he said, 'What kind of cities are these that you have given me, my brother?' So they are called the land of Cabul *c* to this day. 14 But Hiram had sent to the king one hundred and twenty talents of gold.

Other Acts of Solomon

15 This is the account of the forced labour that King Solomon conscripted to build the house of the LORD and his own house, the Millo and the wall of Jerusalem, Hazor, Megiddo, Gezer 16 (Pharaoh king of Egypt had gone up and captured Gezer and burned it down, had killed the Canaanites who lived in the city, and had given it as dowry to his daughter, Solomon's wife; 17 so Solomon rebuilt Gezer), Lower Beth-horon, 18 Baalath, Tamar in the wilderness, within the land, 19 as well as all of Solomon's storage cities, the cities for his chariots, the cities for his cavalry, and whatever Solomon desired to build, in Jerusalem, in Lebanon, and in all the land of his dominion. 20 All the people who were left of the Amorites, the Hittites, the Perizzites, the Hivites, and the Jebusites, who were not of the people of Israel— 21 their descendants who were

a Compare Gk: Heb *seven days and seven days, fourteen days* *b* Syr Old Latin: Heb *will become high* *c* Perhaps meaning *a land good for nothing* still left in the land, whom the Israelites were unable to destroy completely—these Solomon conscripted for slave labour, and so they are to this day. 22 But of the Israelites Solomon made no slaves; they were the soldiers, they were his officials, his commanders, his captains, and the commanders of his chariotry and cavalry.

23 These were the chief officers who were over Solomon's work: five hundred and fifty, who had charge of the people who carried on the work.

24 But Pharaoh's daughter went up from the city of David to her own house that Solomon had built for her; then he built the Millo.

25 Three times a year Solomon used to offer up burnt-offerings and sacrifices of well-being on the altar that he built for the LORD, offering incense*a* before the LORD. So he completed the house.

Solomon's Commercial Activity

26 King Solomon built a fleet of ships at Ezion-geber, which is near Eloth on the shore of the Red Sea,*b* in the land of Edom. 27 Hiram sent his servants with the fleet, sailors who were familiar with the sea, together with the servants of Solomon. 28 They went to Ophir, and imported from there four hundred and twenty talents of gold, which they delivered to King Solomon.

Visit of the Queen of Sheba

10 When the queen of Sheba heard of the fame of Solomon, (fame due to*c* the name of the LORD), she came to test him with hard questions. 2 She came to Jerusalem with a very great retinue, with camels bearing spices, and very much gold, and precious stones; and when she came to Solomon, she told him all that was on her mind. 3 Solomon answered all her questions; there was nothing hidden from the king that he could not explain to her. 4 When the queen of Sheba had observed all the wisdom of Solomon, the house that he had built, 5 the food of his table, the seating of his officials, and the attendance of his servants, their clothing, his

valets, and his burnt-offerings that he offered at the house of the LORD, there was no more spirit in her.

6 So she said to the king, 'The report was true that I heard in my own land of your accomplishments and of your wisdom, 7 but I did not believe the reports until I came and my own eyes had seen it. Not even half had been told me; your wisdom and prosperity far surpass the report that I had heard. 8 Happy are your wives!*d* Happy are these your servants, who continually attend you and hear your wisdom! 9 Blessed be the LORD your God, who has delighted in you and set you on the throne of Israel! Because the LORD loved Israel for ever, he has made you king to execute justice and righteousness.' 10 Then she gave the king one hundred and twenty talents of gold, a great quantity of spices, and precious stones; never again did spices come in such quantity as that which the queen of Sheba gave to King Solomon.

11 Moreover, the fleet of Hiram, which carried gold from Ophir, brought from Ophir a great quantity of almug wood and precious stones. 12 From the almug wood the king made supports for the house of the LORD, and for the king's house, lyres also and harps for the singers; no such almug wood has come or been seen to this day.

13 Meanwhile, King Solomon gave to the queen of Sheba every desire that she expressed, as well as what he gave her out of Solomon's royal bounty. Then she returned to her own land, with her servants.

14 The weight of gold that came to Solomon in one year was six hundred and sixty-six talents of gold, 15 besides that which came from the traders and from the business of the merchants, and from all the kings of Arabia and the governors of the land. 16 King Solomon made two hundred large shields of beaten gold; six hundred shekels of gold went into each large shield. 17 He made three hundred shields

a Gk: Heb *offering incense with it that was*　*b* Or *Sea of Reeds*　*c* Meaning of Heb uncertain　*d* Gk Syr: Heb *men* of beaten gold; three minas of gold went into each shield; and the king put them in the House of the Forest of Lebanon. [18] The king also made a great ivory throne, and overlaid it with the finest gold. [19] The throne had six steps. The top of the throne was rounded in the back, and on each side of the seat were arm rests and two lions standing beside the arm rests, [20] while twelve lions were standing, one on each end of a step, on the six steps. Nothing like it was ever made in any kingdom. [21] All King Solomon's drinking vessels were of gold, and all the vessels of the House of the Forest of Lebanon were of pure gold; none were of silver—it was not considered as anything in the days of Solomon. [22] For the king had a fleet of ships of Tarshish at sea with the fleet of Hiram. Once every three years the fleet of ships of Tarshish used to come bringing gold, silver, ivory, apes, and peacocks. [a]

23 Thus King Solomon excelled all the kings of the earth in riches and in wisdom. [24] The whole earth sought the presence of Solomon to hear his wisdom, which God had put into his mind. [25] Every one of them brought a present, objects of silver and gold, garments, weaponry, spices, horses, and mules, so much year by year.

26 Solomon gathered together chariots and horses; he had fourteen hundred chariots and twelve thousand horses, which he stationed in the chariot cities and with the king in Jerusalem. [27] The king made silver as common in Jerusalem as stones, and he made cedars as numerous as the sycamores of the Shephelah. [28] Solomon's import of horses was from Egypt and Kue, and the king's traders received them from Kue at a price. [29] A chariot could be imported from Egypt for six hundred shekels of silver, and a horse for one hundred and fifty; so through the king's traders they were exported to all the kings of the Hittites and the kings of Aram.

Solomon's Errors

11 King Solomon loved many foreign women along with the daughter of Pharaoh: Moabite, Ammonite, Edomite, Sidonian, and Hittite women, [2] from the nations concerning which the Lord had said to the Israelites, 'You shall not enter into marriage with them, neither shall they with you; for they will surely incline your heart to follow their gods;' Solomon clung to these in love. [3] Among his wives were seven hundred princesses and three hundred concubines; and his wives turned away his heart. [4] For when Solomon was old, his wives turned away his heart after other gods; and his heart was not true to the Lord his God, as was the heart of his father David. [5] For Solomon followed Astarte the goddess of the Sidonians, and Milcom the abomination of the Ammonites. [6] So Solomon did what was evil in the sight of the Lord, and did not completely follow the Lord, as his father David had done. [7] Then Solomon built a high place for Chemosh the abomination of Moab, and for Molech the abomination of the Ammonites, on the mountain east of Jerusalem. [8] He did the same for all his foreign wives, who offered incense and sacrificed to their gods.

9 Then the Lord was angry with Solomon, because his heart had turned away from the Lord, the God of Israel, who had appeared to him twice, [10] and had commanded him concerning this matter, that he should not follow other gods; but he did not observe what the Lord commanded. [11] Therefore the Lord said to Solomon, 'Since this has been your mind and you have not kept my covenant and my statutes that I have commanded you, I will surely tear the kingdom from you and give it to your servant. [12] Yet for the sake of your father David I will not do it in your lifetime; I will tear it out of the hand of your son. [13] I will not, however, tear away the entire kingdom; I will give one tribe to your son, for the sake of my servant David and for the sake of Jerusalem, which I have chosen.'

Adversaries of Solomon

14 Then the Lord raised up an adversary against Solomon, Hadad the Edomite; he was of the royal house in Edom. [15] For when David was in Edom, and Joab the

a Or *baboons*

commander of the army went up to bury the dead, he killed every male in Edom [16] (for Joab and all Israel remained there for six months, until he had eliminated every male in Edom); [17] but Hadad fled to Egypt with some Edomites who were servants of his father. He was a young boy at that time. [18] They set out from Midian and came to Paran; they took people with them from Paran and came to Egypt, to Pharaoh king of Egypt, who gave him a house, assigned him an allowance of food, and gave him land. [19] Hadad found great favour in the sight of Pharaoh, so that he gave him his sister-in-law for a wife, the sister of Queen Tahpenes. [20] The sister of Tahpenes gave birth by him to his son Genubath, whom Tahpenes weaned in Pharaoh's house; Genubath was in Pharaoh's house among the children of Pharaoh. [21] When Hadad heard in Egypt that David slept with his ancestors and that Joab the commander of the army was dead, Hadad said to Pharaoh, 'Let me depart, that I may go to my own country.' [22] But Pharaoh said to him, 'What do you lack with me that you now seek to go to your own country?' And he said, 'No, do let me go.'

23 God raised up another adversary against Solomon,[a] Rezon son of Eliada, who had fled from his master, King Hadadezer of Zobah. [24] He gathered followers around him and became leader of a marauding band, after the slaughter by David; they went to Damascus, settled there, and made him king in Damascus. [25] He was an adversary of Israel all the days of Solomon, making trouble as Hadad did; he despised Israel and reigned over Aram.

Jeroboam's Rebellion

26 Jeroboam son of Nebat, an Ephraimite of Zeredah, a servant of Solomon, whose mother's name was Zeruah, a widow, rebelled against the king. [27] The following was the reason he rebelled against the king. Solomon built the Millo, and closed up the gap in the wall[b] of the city of his father David. [28] The man Jeroboam was very able, and when Solomon saw that the young man was industrious he gave him charge over all the forced labour of the house of Joseph. [29] About that time, when Jeroboam was leaving Jerusalem, the prophet Ahijah the Shilonite found him on the road. Ahijah had clothed himself with a new garment. The two of them were alone in the open country [30] when Ahijah laid hold of the new garment he was wearing and tore it into twelve pieces. [31] He then said to Jeroboam: Take for yourself ten pieces; for thus says the LORD, the God of Israel, 'See, I am

The Divided Kingdom

Mediterranean Sea

PHOENICIA

• Damascus

ARAM

Tyre • • Dan

Megiddo •

• Beth-shan

ISRAEL

• Shechem

Joppa •

  Bethel

Ashdod • • Gezer

Ashkelon • Gath • • Jericho

Gaza • Jerusalem

PHILISTIA

Dead
Sea

JUDAH

Beer-sheba •

MOAB

• Bozrah

EDOM

—N—

0   60 Mi.

0   60 Km.

a Heb *him*   *b* Heb lacks *in the wall*

about to tear the kingdom from the hand of Solomon, and will give you ten tribes. ³²One tribe will remain his, for the sake of my servant David and for the sake of Jerusalem, the city that I have chosen out of all the tribes of Israel. ³³This is because he has*ᵃ* forsaken me, worshipped Astarte the goddess of the Sidonians, Chemosh the god of Moab, and Milcom the god of the Ammonites, and has*ᵃ* not walked in my ways, doing what is right in my sight and keeping my statutes and my ordinances, as his father David did. ³⁴Nevertheless, I will not take the whole kingdom away from him but will make him ruler all the days of his life, for the sake of my servant David whom I chose and who did keep my commandments and my statutes; ³⁵but I will take the kingdom away from his son and give it to you—that is, the ten tribes. ³⁶Yet to his son I will give one tribe, so that my servant David may always have a lamp before me in Jerusalem, the city where I have chosen to put my name. ³⁷I will take you, and you shall reign over all that your soul desires; you shall be king over Israel. ³⁸If you will listen to all that I command you, walk in my ways, and do what is right in my sight by keeping my statutes and my commandments, as David my servant did, I will be with you, and will build you an enduring house, as I built for David, and I will give Israel to you. ³⁹For this reason I will punish the descendants of David, but not for ever.' ⁴⁰Solomon sought therefore to kill Jeroboam; but Jeroboam promptly fled to Egypt, to King Shishak of Egypt, and remained in Egypt until the death of Solomon.

Death of Solomon

41 Now the rest of the acts of Solomon, all that he did as well as his wisdom, are they not written in the Book of the Acts of Solomon? ⁴²The time that Solomon reigned in Jerusalem over all Israel was forty years. ⁴³Solomon slept with his ancestors and was buried in the city of his father David; and his son Rehoboam succeeded him.

The Northern Tribes Secede

12 Rehoboam went to Shechem, for all Israel had come to Shechem to make him king. ²When Jeroboam son of Nebat heard of it (for he was still in Egypt, where he had fled from King Solomon), then Jeroboam returned from*ᵇ* Egypt. ³And they sent and called him; and Jeroboam and all the assembly of Israel came and said to Rehoboam, ⁴'Your father made our yoke heavy. Now therefore lighten the hard service of your father and his heavy yoke that he placed on us, and we will serve you.' ⁵He said to them, 'Go away for three days, then come again to me.' So the people went away.

6 Then King Rehoboam took counsel with the older men who had attended his father Solomon while he was still alive, saying, 'How do you advise me to answer this people?' ⁷They answered him, 'If you will be a servant to this people today and serve them, and speak good words to them when you answer them, then they will be your servants for ever.' ⁸But he disregarded the advice that the older men gave him, and consulted the young men who had grown up with him and now attended him. ⁹He said to them, 'What do you advise that we answer this people who have said to me, "Lighten the yoke that your father put on us"?' ¹⁰The young men who had grown up with him said to him, 'Thus you should say to this people who spoke to you, "Your father made our yoke heavy, but you must lighten it for us"; thus you should say to them, "My little finger is thicker than my father's loins. ¹¹Now, whereas my father laid on you a heavy yoke, I will add to your yoke. My father disciplined you with whips, but I will discipline you with scorpions." '

12 So Jeroboam and all the people came to Rehoboam on the third day, as the king had said, 'Come to me again on the third day.' ¹³The king answered the people harshly. He disregarded the advice that the older men had given him ¹⁴and spoke to them according to the advice of the young

a Gk Syr Vg: Heb *they have*   *b* Gk Vg Compare 2 Chr 10.2: Heb *lived in*

The Kings of the Old Testament

The United Monarchy

The length of Saul's reign is not known; David and Solomon are each said to have ruled for forty years, which is often used as a general and somewhat indefinite number. Their reigns must have fallen between about 1020 and 922 (931) B.C., perhaps as follows:

Saul   1020–1000 B.C.
David   1000–961 (or 1000–965) B.C.
Solomon 961–922 (or 965–931) B.C.

The Divided Monarchy: Judah and Israel

Problems of chronology of the kings of Israel and Judah permit no easy solution. The following tables are based on two widely accepted systems of chronology, one developed by W. F. Albright, and the other by E. R. Thiele. The dates of Thiele's system (3rd edition), which are enclosed in parentheses, are presented in simplified form apart from co-regencies and simultaneous claims to the throne. The two columns show the chronological relationships of the kings of the two kingdoms.

JUDAH	ISRAEL
Rehoboam — 922 (931)	922 (931) — Jeroboam I
Abijam — 915 (913)	
Asa — 913 (911)	
	901 (910) — Nadab
	900 (909) — Baasha
	877 (886) — Elah
	876 (885) — Zimri
	876 (885) — Omri, Tibni
	(880) — Omri
Jehoshaphat — 873 (870)	
	869 (874) — Ahab
	850 (853) — Ahaziah
Jehoram — 849 (848)	849 (852) — Jehoram (Joram)
Ahaziah — 842 (841)	842 (841) — Jehu

The Kings of the Old Testament

JUDAH	ISRAEL
Athaliah — 842 (841)	
Joash (Jehoash) — 837 (835)	
	815 (814) — Jehoahaz
	801 (798) — Jehoash (Joash)
Amaziah — 800 (796)	
	786 (782) — Jeroboam II
Azariah (Uzziah) — 783 (767)	
	746 (753) — Zechariah
	745 (752) — Shallum
	745 (752) — Menahem
Jotham — 742 (740)	
	738 (742) — Pekahiah
	737 (740) — Pekah
Ahaz — 735 (732)	
	732 (732) — Hoshea
	721 (723/22) — Fall of Samaria
Hezekiah — 715 (716)	
Manasseh — 687 (687)	
Amon — 642 (643)	
Josiah — 640 (641)	
Jehoahaz — 609 (609)	
Jehoiakim — 609 (609)	
Jehoiachin — 609 (609)	
Zedekiah — 597 (597)	
Fall of Jerusalem — 587 (586)	

men, 'My father made your yoke heavy, but I will add to your yoke; my father disciplined you with whips, but I will discipline you with scorpions.' 15 So the king did not listen to the people, because it was a turn of affairs brought about by the LORD that he might fulfil his word, which the LORD had spoken by Ahijah the Shilonite to Jeroboam son of Nebat.

16 When all Israel saw that the king would not listen to them, the people answered the king,

'What share do we have in David?
We have no inheritance in the son
    of Jesse.
To your tents, O Israel!
Look now to your own house,
    O David.'

So Israel went away to their tents. 17 But Rehoboam reigned over the Israelites who were living in the towns of Judah. 18 When King Rehoboam sent Adoram, who was taskmaster over the forced labour, all Israel stoned him to death. King Rehoboam then hurriedly mounted his chariot to flee to Jerusalem. 19 So Israel has been in rebellion against the house of David to this day.

First Dynasty: Jeroboam Reigns over Israel

20 When all Israel heard that Jeroboam had returned, they sent and called him to the assembly and made him king over all Israel. There was no one who followed the house of David, except the tribe of Judah alone.

21 When Rehoboam came to Jerusalem, he assembled all the house of Judah and the tribe of Benjamin, one hundred and eighty thousand chosen troops to fight against the house of Israel, to restore the kingdom to Rehoboam son of Solomon. 22 But the word of God came to Shemaiah the man of God: 23 Say to King Rehoboam of Judah, son of Solomon, and to all the house of Judah and Benjamin, and to the rest of the people, 24 'Thus says the LORD, You shall not go up or fight against your kindred the people of Israel. Let everyone go home, for this thing is from me.' So they

heeded the word of the LORD and went home again, according to the word of the LORD.

Jeroboam's Golden Calves

25 Then Jeroboam built Shechem in the hill country of Ephraim, and resided there; he went out from there and built Penuel. 26 Then Jeroboam said to himself, 'Now the kingdom may well revert to the house of David. 27 If this people continues to go up to offer sacrifices in the house of the LORD at Jerusalem, the heart of this people will turn again to their master, King Rehoboam of Judah; they will kill me and return to King Rehoboam of Judah.' 28 So the king took counsel, and made two calves of gold. He said to the people, a 'You have gone up to Jerusalem long enough. Here are your gods, O Israel, who brought you up out of the land of Egypt.' 29 He set one in Bethel, and the other he put in Dan. 30 And this thing became a sin, for the people went to worship before the one at Bethel and before the other as far as Dan. b 31 He also made houses c on high places, and appointed priests from among all the people, who were not Levites. 32 Jeroboam appointed a festival on the fifteenth day of the eighth month like the festival that was in Judah, and he offered sacrifices on the altar; so he did in Bethel, sacrificing to the calves that he had made. And he placed in Bethel the priests of the high places that he had made. 33 He went up to the altar that he had made in Bethel on the fifteenth day in the eighth month, in the month that he alone had prescribed; he appointed a festival for the people of Israel, and he went up to the altar to offer incense.

A Man of God from Judah

13 While Jeroboam was standing by the altar to offer incense, a man of God came out of Judah by the word of the LORD to Bethel 2 and proclaimed against the altar by the word of the LORD, and said,

a Gk: Heb to them   b Compare Gk: Heb went to the one as far as Dan   c Gk Vg Compare 13.32: Heb a house

'O altar, altar, thus says the LORD: "A son shall be born to the house of David, Josiah by name; and he shall sacrifice on you the priests of the high places who offer incense on you, and human bones shall be burned on you." ' ³ He gave a sign the same day, saying, 'This is the sign that the LORD has spoken: "The altar shall be torn down, and the ashes that are on it shall be poured out." ' ⁴ When the king heard what the man of God cried out against the altar at Bethel, Jeroboam stretched out his hand from the altar, saying, 'Seize him!' But the hand that he stretched out against him withered so that he could not draw it back to himself. ⁵ The altar also was torn down, and the ashes poured out from the altar, according to the sign that the man of God had given by the word of the LORD. ⁶ The king said to the man of God, 'Entreat now the favour of the LORD your God, and pray for me, so that my hand may be restored to me.' So the man of God entreated the LORD; and the king's hand was restored to him, and became as it was before. ⁷ Then the king said to the man of God, 'Come home with me and dine, and I will give you a gift.' ⁸ But the man of God said to the king, 'If you give me half your kingdom, I will not go in with you; nor will I eat food or drink water in this place. ⁹ For thus I was commanded by the word of the LORD: You shall not eat food, or drink water, or return by the way that you came.' ¹⁰ So he went another way, and did not return by the way that he had come to Bethel.

11 Now there lived an old prophet in Bethel. One of his sons came and told him all that the man of God had done that day in Bethel; the words also that he had spoken to the king, they told to their father. ¹² Their father said to them, 'Which way did he go?' And his sons showed him the way that the man of God who came from Judah had gone. ¹³ Then he said to his sons, 'Saddle a donkey for me.' So they saddled a donkey for him, and he mounted it. ¹⁴ He went after the man of God, and found him sitting under an oak tree. He said to him, 'Are you the man of God who came from Judah?' He answered, 'I am.'

¹⁵ Then he said to him, 'Come home with me and eat some food.' ¹⁶ But he said, 'I cannot return with you, or go in with you; nor will I eat food or drink water with you in this place; ¹⁷ for it was said to me by the word of the LORD: You shall not eat food or drink water there, or return by the way that you came.' ¹⁸ Then the other*a* said to him, 'I also am a prophet as you are, and an angel spoke to me by the word of the LORD: Bring him back with you into your house so that he may eat food and drink water.' But he was deceiving him. ¹⁹ Then the man of God*a* went back with him, and ate food and drank water in his house.

20 As they were sitting at the table, the word of the LORD came to the prophet who had brought him back; ²¹ and he proclaimed to the man of God who came from Judah, 'Thus says the LORD: Because you have disobeyed the word of the LORD, and have not kept the commandment that the LORD your God commanded you, ²² but have come back and have eaten food and drunk water in the place of which he said to you, "Eat no food, and drink no water", your body shall not come to your ancestral tomb.' ²³ After the man of God*a* had eaten food and had drunk, they saddled for him a donkey belonging to the prophet who had brought him back. ²⁴ Then as he went away, a lion met him on the road and killed him. His body was thrown in the road, and the donkey stood beside it; the lion also stood beside the body. ²⁵ People passed by and saw the body thrown in the road, with the lion standing by the body. And they came and told it in the town where the old prophet lived.

26 When the prophet who had brought him back from the way heard of it, he said, 'It is the man of God who disobeyed the word of the LORD; therefore the LORD has given him to the lion, which has torn him and killed him according to the word that the LORD spoke to him.' ²⁷ Then he said to his sons, 'Saddle a donkey for me.' So they saddled one, ²⁸ and he went and found the body thrown in the road, with the donkey

a Heb *he*

and the lion standing beside the body. The lion had not eaten the body or attacked the donkey. 29 The prophet took up the body of the man of God, laid it on the donkey, and brought it back to the city, *a* to mourn and to bury him. 30 He laid the body in his own grave; and they mourned over him, saying, 'Alas, my brother!' 31 After he had buried him, he said to his sons, 'When I die, bury me in the grave in which the man of God is buried; lay my bones beside his bones. 32 For the saying that he proclaimed by the word of the LORD against the altar in Bethel, and against all the houses of the high places that are in the cities of Samaria, shall surely come to pass.'

33 Even after this event Jeroboam did not turn from his evil way, but made priests for the high places again from among all the people; any who wanted to be priests he consecrated for the high places. 34 This matter became sin to the house of Jeroboam, so as to cut it off and to destroy it from the face of the earth.

Judgement on the House of Jeroboam

14 At that time Abijah son of Jeroboam fell sick. 2 Jeroboam said to his wife, 'Go, disguise yourself, so that it will not be known that you are the wife of Jeroboam, and go to Shiloh; for the prophet Ahijah is there, who said of me that I should be king over this people. 3 Take with you ten loaves, some cakes, and a jar of honey, and go to him; he will tell you what shall happen to the child.'

4 Jeroboam's wife did so; she set out and went to Shiloh, and came to the house of Ahijah. Now Ahijah could not see, for his eyes were dim because of his age. 5 But the LORD said to Ahijah, 'The wife of Jeroboam is coming to inquire of you concerning her son; for he is sick. Thus and thus you shall say to her.'

When she came, she pretended to be another woman. 6 But when Ahijah heard the sound of her feet, as she came in at the door, he said, 'Come in, wife of Jeroboam; why do you pretend to be another? For I am charged with heavy tidings for you.

7 Go, tell Jeroboam, "Thus says the LORD, the God of Israel: Because I exalted you from among the people, made you leader over my people Israel, 8 and tore the kingdom away from the house of David to give it to you; yet you have not been like my servant David, who kept my commandments and followed me with all his heart, doing only that which was right in my sight, 9 but you have done evil above all those who were before you and have gone and made for yourself other gods, and cast images, provoking me to anger, and have thrust me behind your back; 10 therefore, I will bring evil upon the house of Jeroboam. I will cut off from Jeroboam every male, both bond and free, in Israel and will consume the house of Jeroboam, just as one burns up dung until it is all gone. 11 Anyone belonging to Jeroboam who dies in the city, the dogs shall eat; and anyone who dies in the open country, the birds of the air shall eat; for the LORD has spoken." 12 Therefore set out, go to your house. When your feet enter the city, the child shall die. 13 All Israel shall mourn for him and bury him; for he alone of Jeroboam's family shall come to the grave, because in him there is found something pleasing to the LORD, the God of Israel, in the house of Jeroboam. 14 Moreover, the LORD will raise up for himself a king over Israel, who shall cut off the house of Jeroboam today, even now! *b*

15 'The LORD will strike Israel, as a reed is shaken in the water; he will root up Israel out of this good land that he gave to their ancestors, and scatter them beyond the Euphrates, because they have made their sacred poles, *c* provoking the LORD to anger. 16 He will give Israel up because of the sins of Jeroboam, which he sinned and which he caused Israel to commit.'

17 Then Jeroboam's wife got up and went away, and she came to Tirzah. As she came to the threshold of the house, the child died. 18 All Israel buried him and mourned for him, according to the word of

a Gk: Heb *he came to the town of the old prophet*
b Meaning of Heb uncertain   *c* Heb *Asherim*

the LORD, which he spoke by his servant the prophet Ahijah.

Death of Jeroboam

19 Now the rest of the acts of Jeroboam, how he warred and how he reigned, are written in the Book of the Annals of the Kings of Israel. 20The time that Jeroboam reigned was twenty-two years; then he slept with his ancestors, and his son Nadab succeeded him.

Rehoboam Reigns over Judah

21 Now Rehoboam son of Solomon reigned in Judah. Rehoboam was forty-one years old when he began to reign, and he reigned for seventeen years in Jerusalem, the city that the LORD had chosen out of all the tribes of Israel, to put his name there. His mother's name was Naamah the Ammonite. 22Judah did what was evil in the sight of the LORD; they provoked him to jealousy with their sins that they committed, more than all that their ancestors had done. 23For they also built for themselves high places, pillars, and sacred poles*a* on every high hill and under every green tree; 24there were also male temple prostitutes in the land. They committed all the abominations of the nations that the LORD drove out before the people of Israel.

25 In the fifth year of King Rehoboam, King Shishak of Egypt came up against Jerusalem; 26he took away the treasures of the house of the LORD and the treasures of the king's house; he took everything. He also took away all the shields of gold that Solomon had made; 27so King Rehoboam made shields of bronze instead, and committed them to the hands of the officers of the guard, who kept the door of the king's house. 28As often as the king went into the house of the LORD, the guard carried them and brought them back to the guardroom.

29 Now the rest of the acts of Rehoboam, and all that he did, are they not written in the Book of the Annals of the Kings of Judah? 30There was war between Rehoboam and Jeroboam continually. 31 Reho-

boam slept with his ancestors and was buried with his ancestors in the city of David. His mother's name was Naamah the Ammonite. His son Abijam succeeded him.

Abijam Reigns over Judah: Idolatry and War

15 Now in the eighteenth year of King Jeroboam son of Nebat, Abijam began to reign over Judah. 2He reigned for three years in Jerusalem. His mother's name was Maacah daughter of Abishalom. 3He committed all the sins that his father did before him; his heart was not true to the LORD his God, like the heart of his father David. 4Nevertheless, for David's sake the LORD his God gave him a lamp in Jerusalem, setting up his son after him, and establishing Jerusalem; 5because David did what was right in the sight of the LORD, and did not turn aside from anything that he commanded him all the days of his life, except in the matter of Uriah the Hittite. 6The war begun between Rehoboam and Jeroboam continued all the days of his life. 7The rest of the acts of Abijam, and all that he did, are they not written in the Book of the Annals of the Kings of Judah? There was war between Abijam and Jeroboam. 8Abijam slept with his ancestors, and they buried him in the city of David. Then his son Asa succeeded him.

Asa Reigns over Judah

9 In the twentieth year of King Jeroboam of Israel, Asa began to reign over Judah; 10he reigned for forty-one years in Jerusalem. His mother's name was Maacah daughter of Abishalom. 11Asa did what was right in the sight of the LORD, as his father David had done. 12He put away the male temple prostitutes out of the land, and removed all the idols that his ancestors had made. 13He also removed his mother Maacah from being queen mother, because she had made an abominable image for Asherah; Asa cut down her image and burned it at the Wadi Kidron.

a Heb *Asherim*

14 But the high places were not taken away. Nevertheless, the heart of Asa was true to the LORD all his days. 15 He brought into the house of the LORD the votive gifts of his father and his own votive gifts—silver, gold, and utensils.

Alliance with Aram against Israel

16 There was war between Asa and King Baasha of Israel all their days. 17 King Baasha of Israel went up against Judah, and built Ramah, to prevent anyone from going out or coming in to King Asa of Judah. 18 Then Asa took all the silver and the gold that were left in the treasures of the house of the LORD and the treasures of the king's house, and gave them into the hands of his servants. King Asa sent them to King Ben-hadad son of Tabrimmon son of Hezion of Aram, who resided in Damascus, saying, 19 'Let there be an alliance between me and you, like that between my father and your father: I am sending you a present of silver and gold; go, break your alliance with King Baasha of Israel, so that he may withdraw from me.' 20 Ben-hadad listened to King Asa, and sent the commanders of his armies against the cities of Israel. He conquered Ijon, Dan, Abel-beth-maacah, and all Chinneroth, with all the land of Naphtali. 21 When Baasha heard of it, he stopped building Ramah and lived in Tirzah. 22 Then King Asa made a proclamation to all Judah; none was exempt: they carried away the stones of Ramah and its timber, with which Baasha had been building; with them King Asa built Geba of Benjamin and Mizpah. 23 Now the rest of all the acts of Asa, all his power, all that he did, and the cities that he built, are they not written in the Book of the Annals of the Kings of Judah? But in his old age he was diseased in his feet. 24 Then Asa slept with his ancestors, and was buried with his ancestors in the city of his father David; his son Jehoshaphat succeeded him.

Nadab Reigns over Israel

25 Nadab son of Jeroboam began to reign over Israel in the second year of King Asa of Judah; he reigned over Israel for two years. 26 He did what was evil in the sight of the LORD, walking in the way of his ancestor and in the sin that he caused Israel to commit.

27 Baasha son of Ahijah, of the house of Issachar, conspired against him; and Baasha struck him down at Gibbethon, which belonged to the Philistines; for Nadab and all Israel were laying siege to Gibbethon. 28 So Baasha killed Nadab[a] in the third year of King Asa of Judah, and succeeded him. 29 As soon as he was king, he killed all the house of Jeroboam; he left to the house of Jeroboam not one that breathed, until he had destroyed it, according to the word of the LORD that he spoke by his servant Ahijah the Shilonite— 30 because of the sins of Jeroboam that he committed and that he caused Israel to commit, and because of the anger to which he provoked the LORD, the God of Israel.

31 Now the rest of the acts of Nadab, and all that he did, are they not written in the Book of the Annals of the Kings of Israel? 32 There was war between Asa and King Baasha of Israel all their days.

Second Dynasty: Baasha Reigns over Israel

33 In the third year of King Asa of Judah, Baasha son of Ahijah began to reign over all Israel at Tirzah; he reigned for twenty-four years. 34 He did what was evil in the sight of the LORD, walking in the way of Jeroboam and in the sin that he caused Israel to commit.

16 The word of the LORD came to Jehu son of Hanani against Baasha, saying, 2 'Since I exalted you out of the dust and made you leader over my people Israel, and you have walked in the way of Jeroboam, and have caused my people Israel to sin, provoking me to anger with their sins, 3 therefore, I will consume Baasha and his house, and I will make your house like the house of Jeroboam son of Nebat. 4 Anyone belonging to Baasha who dies in the city the dogs shall eat; and anyone of his who

a Heb him

dies in the field the birds of the air shall eat.'

5 Now the rest of the acts of Baasha, what he did, and his power, are they not written in the Book of the Annals of the Kings of Israel? 6 Baasha slept with his ancestors, and was buried at Tirzah; and his son Elah succeeded him. 7 Moreover, the word of the LORD came by the prophet Jehu son of Hanani against Baasha and his house, both because of all the evil that he did in the sight of the LORD, provoking him to anger with the work of his hands, in being like the house of Jeroboam, and also because he destroyed it.

Elah Reigns over Israel

8 In the twenty-sixth year of King Asa of Judah, Elah son of Baasha began to reign over Israel in Tirzah; he reigned for two years. 9 But his servant Zimri, commander of half his chariots, conspired against him. When he was at Tirzah, drinking himself drunk in the house of Arza, who was in charge of the palace at Tirzah, 10 Zimri came in and struck him down and killed him, in the twenty-seventh year of King Asa of Judah, and succeeded him.

11 When he began to reign, as soon as he had seated himself on his throne, he killed all the house of Baasha; he did not leave him a single male of his kindred or his friends. 12 Thus Zimri destroyed all the house of Baasha, according to the word of the LORD, which he spoke against Baasha by the prophet Jehu— 13 because of all the sins of Baasha and the sins of his son Elah that they committed, and that they caused Israel to commit, provoking the LORD God of Israel to anger with their idols. 14 Now the rest of the acts of Elah, and all that he did, are they not written in the Book of the Annals of the Kings of Israel?

Third Dynasty: Zimri Reigns over Israel

15 In the twenty-seventh year of King Asa of Judah, Zimri reigned for seven days in Tirzah. Now the troops were encamped against Gibbethon, which belonged to the Philistines, 16 and the troops who were encamped heard it said, 'Zimri has con-

spired, and he has killed the king'; therefore all Israel made Omri, the commander of the army, king over Israel that day in the camp. 17 So Omri went up from Gibbethon, and all Israel with him, and they besieged Tirzah. 18 When Zimri saw that the city was taken, he went into the citadel of the king's house; he burned down the king's house over himself with fire, and died— 19 because of the sins that he committed, doing evil in the sight of the LORD, walking in the way of Jeroboam, and for the sin that he committed, causing Israel to sin. 20 Now the rest of the acts of Zimri, and the conspiracy that he made, are they not written in the Book of the Annals of the Kings of Israel?

Fourth Dynasty: Omri Reigns over Israel

21 Then the people of Israel were divided into two parts; half of the people followed Tibni son of Ginath, to make him king, and half followed Omri. 22 But the people who followed Omri overcame the people who followed Tibni son of Ginath; so Tibni died, and Omri became king. 23 In the thirty-first year of King Asa of Judah, Omri began to reign over Israel; he reigned for twelve years, six of them in Tirzah.

Samaria the New Capital

24 He bought the hill of Samaria from Shemer for two talents of silver; he fortified the hill, and called the city that he built Samaria, after the name of Shemer, the owner of the hill.

25 Omri did what was evil in the sight of the LORD; he did more evil than all who were before him. 26 For he walked in all the way of Jeroboam son of Nebat, and in the sins that he caused Israel to commit, provoking the LORD, the God of Israel, to anger by their idols. 27 Now the rest of the acts of Omri that he did, and the power that he showed, are they not written in the Book of the Annals of the Kings of Israel? 28 Omri slept with his ancestors, and was buried in Samaria; his son Ahab succeeded him.

Ahab Reigns over Israel

29 In the thirty-eighth year of King Asa of Judah, Ahab son of Omri began to reign over Israel; Ahab son of Omri reigned over Israel in Samaria for twenty-two years. 30 Ahab son of Omri did evil in the sight of the LORD more than all who were before him.

Ahab Marries Jezebel and Worships Baal

31 And as if it had been a light thing for him to walk in the sins of Jeroboam son of Nebat, he took as his wife Jezebel daughter of King Ethbaal of the Sidonians, and went and served Baal, and worshipped him. 32 He erected an altar for Baal in the house of Baal, which he built in Samaria. 33 Ahab also made a sacred pole.*a* Ahab did more to provoke the anger of the LORD, the God of Israel, than had all the kings of Israel who were before him. 34 In his days Hiel of Bethel built Jericho; he laid its foundation at the cost of Abiram his first-born, and set up its gates at the cost of his youngest son Segub, according to the word of the LORD, which he spoke by Joshua son of Nun.

Elijah Predicts a Drought

17 Now Elijah the Tishbite, of Tishbe*b* in Gilead, said to Ahab, 'As the LORD the God of Israel lives, before whom I stand, there shall be neither dew nor rain these years, except by my word.' 2 The word of the LORD came to him, saying, 3 'Go from here and turn eastwards, and hide yourself by the Wadi Cherith, which is east of the Jordan. 4 You shall drink from the wadi, and I have commanded the ravens to feed you there.' 5 So he went and did according to the word of the LORD; he went and lived by the Wadi Cherith, which is east of the Jordan. 6 The ravens brought him bread and meat in the morning, and bread and meat in the evening; and he drank from the wadi. 7 But after a while the wadi dried up, because there was no rain in the land.

The Widow of Zarephath

8 Then the word of the LORD came to him, saying, 9 'Go now to Zarephath, which belongs to Sidon, and live there; for I have commanded a widow there to feed you.' 10 So he set out and went to Zarephath. When he came to the gate of the town, a widow was there gathering sticks; he called to her and said, 'Bring me a little water in a vessel, so that I may drink.' 11 As she was going to bring it, he called to her and said, 'Bring me a morsel of bread in your hand.' 12 But she said, 'As the LORD your God lives, I have nothing baked, only a handful of meal in a jar, and a little oil in a jug; I am now gathering a couple of sticks, so that I may go home and prepare it for myself and my son, that we may eat it, and die.' 13 Elijah said to her, 'Do not be afraid; go and do as you have said; but first make me a little cake of it and bring it to me, and afterwards make something for yourself and your son. 14 For thus says the LORD the God of Israel: The jar of meal will not be emptied and the jug of oil will not fail until the day that the LORD sends rain on the earth.' 15 She went and did as Elijah said, so that she as well as he and her household ate for many days. 16 The jar of meal was not emptied, neither did the jug of oil fail, according to the word of the LORD that he spoke by Elijah.

Elijah Revives the Widow's Son

17 After this the son of the woman, the mistress of the house, became ill; his illness was so severe that there was no breath left in him. 18 She then said to Elijah, 'What have you against me, O man of God? You have come to me to bring my sin to remembrance, and to cause the death of my son!' 19 But he said to her, 'Give me your son.' He took him from her bosom, carried him up into the upper chamber where he was lodging, and laid him on his own bed. 20 He cried out to the LORD, 'O LORD my God, have you brought calamity even upon the widow with whom I am staying, by killing her son?' 21 Then he stretched himself upon the child three times, and cried out to the LORD, 'O LORD my God, let this child's life come into him again.' 22 The LORD listened to the voice of Elijah; the life of the child came into him

a Heb *Asherah*   *b* Gk: Heb *of the settlers*

again, and he revived. 23 Elijah took the child, brought him down from the upper chamber into the house, and gave him to his mother; then Elijah said, 'See, your son is alive.' 24 So the woman said to Elijah, 'Now I know that you are a man of God, and that the word of the Lord in your mouth is truth.'

Elijah's Message to Ahab

18 After many days the word of the Lord came to Elijah, in the third year of the drought, *a* saying, 'Go, present yourself to Ahab; I will send rain on the earth.' 2 So Elijah went to present himself to Ahab. The famine was severe in Samaria. 3 Ahab summoned Obadiah, who was in charge of the palace. (Now Obadiah revered the Lord greatly; 4 when Jezebel was killing off the prophets of the Lord, Obadiah took a hundred prophets, hid them fifty to a cave, and provided them with bread and water.) 5 Then Ahab said to Obadiah, 'Go through the land to all the springs of water and to all the

Places in the Ministry of Elijah

Sidon • Damascus •
Zarephath •
Tyre •
Mediterranean Sea
Kishon Valley
Mt. Carmel ▲ • Aphek
Jezreel • • Ramoth-gilead
• Tishbe
Samaria •
Bethel • Gilgal
Jericho •
Kerith Ravine Dead Sea
JUDEA

0   40 Mi.
0   40 Km.

wadis; perhaps we may find grass to keep the horses and mules alive, and not lose some of the animals.' 6 So they divided the land between them to pass through it; Ahab went in one direction by himself, and Obadiah went in another direction by himself.

7 As Obadiah was on the way, Elijah met him; Obadiah recognized him, fell on his face, and said, 'Is it you, my lord Elijah?' 8 He answered him, 'It is I. Go, tell your lord that Elijah is here.' 9 And he said, 'How have I sinned, that you would hand your servant over to Ahab, to kill me? 10 As the Lord your God lives, there is no nation or kingdom to which my lord has not sent to seek you; and when they would say, "He is not here", he would require an oath of the kingdom or nation, that they had not found you. 11 But now you say, "Go, tell your lord that Elijah is here." 12 As soon as I have gone from you, the spirit of the Lord will carry you I know not where; so, when I come and tell Ahab and he cannot find you, he will kill me, although I your servant have revered the Lord from my youth. 13 Has it not been told my lord what I did when Jezebel killed the prophets of the Lord, how I hid a hundred of the Lord's prophets fifty to a cave, and provided them with bread and water? 14 Yet now you say, "Go, tell your lord that Elijah is here"; he will surely kill me.' 15 Elijah said, 'As the Lord of hosts lives, before whom I stand, I will surely show myself to him today.' 16 So Obadiah went to meet Ahab, and told him; and Ahab went to meet Elijah.

17 When Ahab saw Elijah, Ahab said to him, 'Is it you, you troubler of Israel?' 18 He answered, 'I have not troubled Israel; but you have, and your father's house, because you have forsaken the commandments of the Lord and followed the Baals. 19 Now therefore have all Israel assemble for me at Mount Carmel, with the four hundred and fifty prophets of Baal and the four hundred prophets of Asherah, who eat at Jezebel's table.'

a Heb lacks *of the drought*

Elijah's Triumph over the Priests of Baal

20 So Ahab sent to all the Israelites, and assembled the prophets at Mount Carmel. 21 Elijah then came near to all the people, and said, 'How long will you go limping with two different opinions? If the LORD is God, follow him; but if Baal, then follow him.' The people did not answer him a word. 22 Then Elijah said to the people, 'I, even I only, am left a prophet of the LORD; but Baal's prophets number four hundred and fifty. 23 Let two bulls be given to us; let them choose one bull for themselves, cut it in pieces, and lay it on the wood, but put no fire to it; I will prepare the other bull and lay it on the wood, but put no fire to it. 24 Then you call on the name of your god and I will call on the name of the LORD; the god who answers by fire is indeed God.' All the people answered, 'Well spoken!' 25 Then Elijah said to the prophets of Baal, 'Choose for yourselves one bull and prepare it first, for you are many; then call on the name of your god, but put no fire to it.' 26 So they took the bull that was given them, prepared it, and called on the name of Baal from morning until noon, crying, 'O Baal, answer us!' But there was no voice, and no answer. They limped about the altar that they had made. 27 At noon Elijah mocked them, saying, 'Cry aloud! Surely he is a god; either he is meditating, or he has wandered away, or he is on a journey, or perhaps he is asleep and must be awakened.' 28 Then they cried aloud and, as was their custom, they cut themselves with swords and lances until the blood gushed out over them. 29 As midday passed, they raved on until the time of the offering of the oblation, but there was no voice, no answer, and no response.

30 Then Elijah said to all the people, 'Come closer to me'; and all the people came closer to him. First he repaired the altar of the LORD that had been thrown down; 31 Elijah took twelve stones, according to the number of the tribes of the sons of Jacob, to whom the word of the LORD came, saying, 'Israel shall be your name'; 32 with the stones he built an altar in the name of the LORD. Then he made a trench around the altar, large enough to contain two measures of seed. 33 Next he put the wood in order, cut the bull in pieces, and laid it on the wood. He said, 'Fill four jars with water and pour it on the burnt-offering and on the wood.' 34 Then he said, 'Do it a second time'; and they did it a second time. Again he said, 'Do it a third time'; and they did it a third time, 35 so that the water ran all round the altar, and filled the trench also with water.

36 At the time of the offering of the oblation, the prophet Elijah came near and said, 'O LORD, God of Abraham, Isaac, and Israel, let it be known this day that you are God in Israel, that I am your servant, and that I have done all these things at your bidding. 37 Answer me, O LORD, answer me, so that this people may know that you, O LORD, are God, and that you have turned their hearts back.' 38 Then the fire of the LORD fell and consumed the burnt-offering, the wood, the stones, and the dust, and even licked up the water that was in the trench. 39 When all the people saw it, they fell on their faces and said, 'The LORD indeed is God; the LORD indeed is God.' 40 Elijah said to them, 'Seize the prophets of Baal; do not let one of them escape.' Then they seized them; and Elijah brought them down to the Wadi Kishon, and killed them there.

The Drought Ends

41 Elijah said to Ahab, 'Go up, eat and drink; for there is a sound of rushing rain.' 42 So Ahab went up to eat and to drink. Elijah went up to the top of Carmel; there he bowed himself down upon the earth and put his face between his knees. 43 He said to his servant, 'Go up now, look towards the sea.' He went up and looked, and said, 'There is nothing.' Then he said, 'Go again seven times.' 44 At the seventh time he said, 'Look, a little cloud no bigger than a person's hand is rising out of the sea.' Then he said, 'Go and say to Ahab, "Harness your chariot and go down before the rain stops you."' 45 In a little while the heavens grew black with clouds and wind;

there was heavy rain. Ahab rode off and went to Jezreel. 46 But the hand of the LORD was on Elijah; he girded up his loins and ran in front of Ahab to the entrance of Jezreel.

Elijah Flees from Jezebel

19 Ahab told Jezebel all that Elijah had done, and how he had killed all the prophets with the sword. 2 Then Jezebel sent a messenger to Elijah, saying, 'So may the gods do to me, and more also, if I do not make your life like the life of one of them by this time tomorrow.' 3 Then he was afraid; he got up and fled for his life, and came to Beer-sheba, which belongs to Judah; he left his servant there.

4 But he himself went a day's journey into the wilderness, and came and sat down under a solitary broom tree. He asked that he might die: 'It is enough; now, O LORD, take away my life, for I am no better than my ancestors.' 5 Then he lay down under the broom tree and fell asleep. Suddenly an angel touched him and said to him, 'Get up and eat.' 6 He looked, and there at his head was a cake baked on hot stones, and a jar of water. He ate and drank, and lay down again. 7 The angel of the LORD came a second time, touched him, and said, 'Get up and eat, otherwise the journey will be too much for you.' 8 He got up, and ate and drank; then he went in the strength of that food for forty days and forty nights to Horeb the mount of God. 9 At that place he came to a cave, and spent the night there.

Then the word of the LORD came to him, saying, 'What are you doing here, Elijah?' 10 He answered, 'I have been very zealous for the LORD, the God of hosts; for the Israelites have forsaken your covenant, thrown down your altars, and killed your prophets with the sword. I alone am left, and they are seeking my life, to take it away.'

Elijah Meets God at Horeb

11 He said, 'Go out and stand on the mountain before the LORD, for the LORD is about to pass by.' Now there was a great wind, so strong that it was splitting mountains and breaking rocks in pieces before the LORD, but the LORD was not in the wind; and after the wind an earthquake, but the LORD was not in the earthquake; 12 and after the earthquake a fire, but the LORD was not in the fire; and after the fire a sound of sheer silence. 13 When Elijah heard it, he wrapped his face in his mantle and went out and stood at the entrance of the cave. Then there came a voice to him that said, 'What are you doing here, Elijah?' 14 He answered, 'I have been very zealous for the LORD, the God of hosts; for the Israelites have forsaken your covenant, thrown down your altars, and killed your prophets with the sword. I alone am left, and they are seeking my life, to take it away.' 15 Then the LORD said to him, 'Go, return on your way to the wilderness of Damascus; when you arrive, you shall anoint Hazael as king over Aram. 16 Also you shall anoint Jehu son of Nimshi as king over Israel; and you shall anoint Elisha son of Shaphat of Abel-meholah as prophet in your place. 17 Whoever escapes from the sword of Hazael, Jehu shall kill; and whoever escapes from the sword of Jehu, Elisha shall kill. 18 Yet I will leave seven thousand in Israel, all the knees that have not bowed to Baal, and every mouth that has not kissed him.'

Elisha Becomes Elijah's Disciple

19 So he set out from there, and found Elisha son of Shaphat, who was ploughing. There were twelve yoke of oxen ahead of him, and he was with the twelfth. Elijah passed by him and threw his mantle over him. 20 He left the oxen, ran after Elijah, and said, 'Let me kiss my father and my mother, and then I will follow you.' Then Elijah a said to him, 'Go back again; for what have I done to you?' 21 He returned from following him, took the yoke of oxen, and slaughtered them; using the equipment from the oxen, he boiled their flesh, and gave it to the people, and they ate. Then he set out and followed Elijah, and became his servant.

a Heb he

Ahab's Wars with the Arameans

20 King Ben-hadad of Aram gathered all his army together; thirty-two kings were with him, along with horses and chariots. He marched against Samaria, laid siege to it, and attacked it. 2 Then he sent messengers into the city to King Ahab of Israel, and said to him: 'Thus says Ben-hadad: 3 Your silver and gold are mine; your fairest wives and children also are mine.' 4 The king of Israel answered, 'As you say, my lord, O king, I am yours, and all that I have.' 5 The messengers came again and said: 'Thus says Ben-hadad: I sent to you, saying, "Deliver to me your silver and gold, your wives and children"; 6 nevertheless, I will send my servants to you tomorrow about this time, and they shall search your house and the houses of your servants, and lay hands on whatever pleases them, *a* and take it away.'

7 Then the king of Israel called all the elders of the land, and said, 'Look now! See how this man is seeking trouble; for he sent to me for my wives, my children, my silver, and my gold; and I did not refuse him.'

8 Then all the elders and all the people said to him, 'Do not listen or consent.' 9 So he said to the messengers of Ben-hadad, 'Tell my lord the king: All that you first demanded of your servant I will do; but this thing I cannot do.' The messengers left and brought him word again. 10 Ben-hadad sent to him and said, 'The gods do so to me, and more also, if the dust of Samaria will provide a handful for each of the people who follow me.' 11 The king of Israel answered, 'Tell him: One who puts on armour should not brag like one who takes it off.' 12 When Ben-hadad heard this message—now he had been drinking with the kings in the booths—he said to his men, 'Take your positions!' And they took their positions against the city.

Prophetic Opposition to Ahab

13 Then a certain prophet came up to King Ahab of Israel and said, 'Thus says the LORD, Have you seen all this great multitude? Look, I will give it into your hand today; and you shall know that I am the LORD.' 14 Ahab said, 'By whom?' He said, 'Thus says the LORD, By the young men who serve the district governors.' Then he said, 'Who shall begin the battle?' He answered, 'You.' 15 Then he mustered the young men who served the district governors, two hundred and thirty-two; after them he mustered all the people of Israel, seven thousand.

16 They went out at noon, while Ben-hadad was drinking himself drunk in the booths, he and the thirty-two kings allied with him. 17 The young men who served the district governors went out first. Ben-hadad had sent out scouts, *b* and they reported to him, 'Men have come out from Samaria.' 18 He said, 'If they have come out for peace, take them alive; if they have come out for war, take them alive.'

19 But these had already come out of the city: the young men who served the district governors, and the army that followed them. 20 Each killed his man; the Arameans fled and Israel pursued them, but King Ben-hadad of Aram escaped on a horse with the

Places in the Life of Elisha

Sidon
Damascus
Tyre
Mediterranean Sea
N
Shunem
Jezreel
Ramoth-gilead
Dothan · Abel-meholah
Samaria
Bethel · Gilgal
Jericho
Dead Sea
Arad · Kir of Moab
0   40 Mi.
0   40 Km.

a Gk Syr Vg: Heb *you*   *b* Heb lacks *scouts*

cavalry. 21The king of Israel went out, attacked the horses and chariots, and defeated the Arameans with a great slaughter.

22 Then the prophet approached the king of Israel and said to him, 'Come, strengthen yourself, and consider well what you have to do; for in the spring the king of Aram will come up against you.'

The Arameans Are Defeated

23 The servants of the king of Aram said to him, 'Their gods are gods of the hills, and so they were stronger than we; but let us fight against them in the plain, and surely we shall be stronger than they. 24Also do this: remove the kings, each from his post, and put commanders in place of them; 25and muster an army like the army that you have lost, horse for horse, and chariot for chariot; then we will fight against them in the plain, and surely we shall be stronger than they.' He heeded their voice, and did so.

26 In the spring Ben-hadad mustered the Arameans and went up to Aphek to fight against Israel. 27After the Israelites had been mustered and provisioned, they went out to engage them; the people of Israel encamped opposite them like two little flocks of goats, while the Arameans filled the country. 28A man of God approached and said to the king of Israel, 'Thus says the LORD: Because the Arameans have said, "The LORD is a god of the hills but he is not a god of the valleys", therefore I will give all this great multitude into your hand, and you shall know that I am the LORD.' 29They encamped opposite one another for seven days. Then on the seventh day the battle began; the Israelites killed one hundred thousand Aramean foot-soldiers in one day. 30The rest fled into the city of Aphek; and the wall fell on twenty-seven thousand men that were left.

Ben-hadad also fled, and entered the city to hide. 31His servants said to him, 'Look, we have heard that the kings of the house of Israel are merciful kings; let us put sackcloth around our waists and ropes on our heads, and go out to the king of Is-rael; perhaps he will spare your life.' 32So they tied sackcloth around their waists, put ropes on their heads, went to the king of Israel, and said, 'Your servant Ben-hadad says, "Please let me live."' And he said, 'Is he still alive? He is my brother.' 33Now the men were watching for an omen; they quickly took it up from him and said, 'Yes, Ben-hadad is your brother.' Then he said, 'Go and bring him.' So Ben-hadad came out to him; and he had him come up into the chariot. 34Ben-hadad*a* said to him, 'I will restore the towns that my father took from your father; and you may establish bazaars for yourself in Damascus, as my father did in Samaria.' The king of Israel responded,*b* 'I will let you go on those terms.' So he made a treaty with him and let him go.

A Prophet Condemns Ahab

35 At the command of the LORD a certain member of a company of prophets*c* said to another, 'Strike me!' But the man refused to strike him. 36Then he said to him, 'Because you have not obeyed the voice of the LORD, as soon as you have left me, a lion will kill you.' And when he had left him, a lion met him and killed him. 37Then he found another man and said, 'Strike me!' So the man hit him, striking and wounding him. 38Then the prophet departed, and waited for the king along the road, disguising himself with a bandage over his eyes. 39As the king passed by, he cried to the king and said, 'Your servant went out into the thick of the battle; then a soldier turned and brought a man to me, and said, "Guard this man; if he is missing, your life shall be given for his life, or else you shall pay a talent of silver." 40While your servant was busy here and there, he was gone.' The king of Israel said to him, 'So shall your judgement be; you yourself have decided it.' 41Then he quickly took the bandage away from his eyes. The king of Israel recognized him as one of the prophets. 42Then he said to him, 'Thus says the LORD, "Because you have let the

a Heb *He*   *b* Heb lacks *The king of Israel responded*
c Heb *of the sons of the prophets*

man go whom I had devoted to destruction, therefore your life shall be for his life, and your people for his people." ' ⁴³The king of Israel set out towards home, resentful and sullen, and came to Samaria.

Naboth's Vineyard

21 Later the following events took place: Naboth the Jezreelite had a vineyard in Jezreel, beside the palace of King Ahab of Samaria. ²And Ahab said to Naboth, 'Give me your vineyard, so that I may have it for a vegetable garden, because it is near my house; I will give you a better vineyard for it; or, if it seems good to you, I will give you its value in money.' ³But Naboth said to Ahab, 'The LORD forbid that I should give you my ancestral inheritance.' ⁴Ahab went home resentful and sullen because of what Naboth the Jezreelite had said to him; for he had said, 'I will not give you my ancestral inheritance.' He lay down on his bed, turned away his face, and would not eat.

5 His wife Jezebel came to him and said, 'Why are you so depressed that you will not eat?' ⁶He said to her, 'Because I spoke to Naboth the Jezreelite and said to him, "Give me your vineyard for money; or else, if you prefer, I will give you another vineyard for it"; but he answered, "I will not give you my vineyard." ' ⁷His wife Jezebel said to him, 'Do you now govern Israel? Get up, eat some food, and be cheerful; I will give you the vineyard of Naboth the Jezreelite.'

8 So she wrote letters in Ahab's name and sealed them with his seal; she sent the letters to the elders and the nobles who lived with Naboth in his city. ⁹She wrote in the letters, 'Proclaim a fast, and seat Naboth at the head of the assembly; ¹⁰seat two scoundrels opposite him, and have them bring a charge against him, saying, "You have cursed God and the king." Then take him out, and stone him to death.' ¹¹The men of his city, the elders and the nobles who lived in his city, did as Jezebel had sent word to them. Just as it was written in the letters that she had sent to them, ¹²they proclaimed a fast and seated Na-

both at the head of the assembly. ¹³The two scoundrels came in and sat opposite him; and the scoundrels brought a charge against Naboth, in the presence of the people, saying, 'Naboth cursed God and the king.' So they took him outside the city, and stoned him to death. ¹⁴Then they sent to Jezebel, saying, 'Naboth has been stoned; he is dead.'

15 As soon as Jezebel heard that Naboth had been stoned and was dead, Jezebel said to Ahab, 'Go, take possession of the vineyard of Naboth the Jezreelite, which he refused to give you for money; for Naboth is not alive, but dead.' ¹⁶As soon as Ahab heard that Naboth was dead, Ahab set out to go down to the vineyard of Naboth the Jezreelite, to take possession of it.

Elijah Pronounces God's Sentence

17 Then the word of the LORD came to Elijah the Tishbite, saying: ¹⁸Go down to meet King Ahab of Israel, who rules*a* in Samaria; he is now in the vineyard of Naboth, where he has gone to take possession. ¹⁹You shall say to him, 'Thus says the LORD: Have you killed, and also taken possession?' You shall say to him, 'Thus says the LORD: In the place where dogs licked up the blood of Naboth, dogs will also lick up your blood.'

20 Ahab said to Elijah, 'Have you found me, O my enemy?' He answered, 'I have found you. Because you have sold yourself to do what is evil in the sight of the LORD, ²¹I will bring disaster on you; I will consume you, and will cut off from Ahab every male, bond or free, in Israel; ²²and I will make your house like the house of Jeroboam son of Nebat, and like the house of Baasha son of Ahijah, because you have provoked me to anger and have caused Israel to sin. ²³Also concerning Jezebel the LORD said, "The dogs shall eat Jezebel within the bounds of Jezreel." ²⁴Anyone belonging to Ahab who dies in the city the dogs shall eat; and anyone of his who dies in the open country the birds of the air shall eat.'

a Heb *who is*

25 (Indeed, there was no one like Ahab, who sold himself to do what was evil in the sight of the LORD, urged on by his wife Jezebel. 26 He acted most abominably in going after idols, as the Amorites had done, whom the LORD drove out before the Israelites.)

27 When Ahab heard those words, he tore his clothes and put sackcloth over his bare flesh; he fasted, lay in the sackcloth, and went about dejectedly. 28 Then the word of the LORD came to Elijah the Tishbite: 29 'Have you seen how Ahab has humbled himself before me? Because he has humbled himself before me, I will not bring the disaster in his days; but in his son's days I will bring the disaster on his house.'

Joint Campaign with Judah against Aram

22 For three years Aram and Israel continued without war. 2 But in the third year King Jehoshaphat of Judah came down to the king of Israel. 3 The king of Israel said to his servants, 'Do you know that Ramoth-gilead belongs to us, yet we are doing nothing to take it out of the hand of the king of Aram?' 4 He said to Jehoshaphat, 'Will you go with me to battle at Ramoth-gilead?' Jehoshaphat replied to the king of Israel, 'I am as you are; my people are your people, my horses are your horses.'

5 But Jehoshaphat also said to the king of Israel, 'Inquire first for the word of the LORD.' 6 Then the king of Israel gathered the prophets together, about four hundred of them, and said to them, 'Shall I go to battle against Ramoth-gilead, or shall I refrain?' They said, 'Go up; for the LORD will give it into the hand of the king.' 7 But Jehoshaphat said, 'Is there no other prophet of the LORD here of whom we may inquire?' 8 The king of Israel said to Jehoshaphat, 'There is still one other by whom we may inquire of the LORD, Micaiah son of Imlah; but I hate him, for he never prophesies anything favourable about me, but only disaster.' Jehoshaphat said, 'Let the king not say such a thing.' 9 Then the king of Israel summoned an of-

ficer and said, 'Bring quickly Micaiah son of Imlah.' 10 Now the king of Israel and King Jehoshaphat of Judah were sitting on their thrones, arrayed in their robes, at the threshing-floor at the entrance of the gate of Samaria; and all the prophets were prophesying before them. 11 Zedekiah son of Chenaanah made for himself horns of iron, and he said, 'Thus says the LORD: With these you shall gore the Arameans until they are destroyed.' 12 All the prophets were prophesying the same and saying, 'Go up to Ramoth-gilead and triumph; the LORD will give it into the hand of the king.'

Micaiah Predicts Failure

13 The messenger who had gone to summon Micaiah said to him, 'Look, the words of the prophets with one accord are favourable to the king; let your word be like the word of one of them, and speak favourably.' 14 But Micaiah said, 'As the LORD lives, whatever the LORD says to me, that I will speak.'

15 When he had come to the king, the king said to him, 'Micaiah, shall we go to Ramoth-gilead to battle, or shall we refrain?' He answered him, 'Go up and triumph; the LORD will give it into the hand of the king.' 16 But the king said to him, 'How many times must I make you swear to tell me nothing but the truth in the name of the LORD?' 17 Then Micaiah a said, 'I saw all Israel scattered on the mountains, like sheep that have no shepherd; and the LORD said, "These have no master; let each one go home in peace." ' 18 The king of Israel said to Jehoshaphat, 'Did I not tell you that he would not prophesy anything favourable about me, but only disaster?'

19 Then Micaiah a said, 'Therefore hear the word of the LORD: I saw the LORD sitting on his throne, with all the host of heaven standing beside him to the right and to the left of him. 20 And the LORD said, "Who will entice Ahab, so that he may go up and fall at Ramoth-gilead?" Then one said one thing, and another said another, 21 until a spirit came forward and stood before the

a Heb *he*

LORD, saying, "I will entice him." ²²"How?" the LORD asked him. He replied, "I will go out and be a lying spirit in the mouth of all his prophets." Then the LORD*a* said, "You are to entice him, and you shall succeed; go out and do it." ²³So you see, the LORD has put a lying spirit in the mouth of all these your prophets; the LORD has decreed disaster for you.'

24 Then Zedekiah son of Chenaanah came up to Micaiah, slapped him on the cheek, and said, 'Which way did the spirit of the LORD pass from me to speak to you?' ²⁵Micaiah replied, 'You will find out on that day when you go in to hide in an inner chamber.' ²⁶The king of Israel then ordered, 'Take Micaiah, and return him to Amon the governor of the city and to Joash the king's son, ²⁷and say, "Thus says the king: Put this fellow in prison, and feed him on reduced rations of bread and water until I come in peace." ' ²⁸Micaiah said, 'If you return in peace, the LORD has not spoken by me.' And he said, 'Hear, you peoples, all of you!'

Defeat and Death of Ahab

29 So the king of Israel and King Jehoshaphat of Judah went up to Ramoth-gilead. ³⁰The king of Israel said to Jehoshaphat, 'I will disguise myself and go into battle, but you wear your robes.' So the king of Israel disguised himself and went into battle. ³¹Now the king of Aram had commanded the thirty-two captains of his chariots, 'Fight with no one small or great, but only with the king of Israel.' ³²When the captains of the chariots saw Jehoshaphat, they said, 'It is surely the king of Israel.' So they turned to fight against him; and Jehoshaphat cried out. ³³When the captains of the chariots saw that it was not the king of Israel, they turned back from pursuing him. ³⁴But a certain man drew his bow and unknowingly struck the king of Israel between the scale-armour and the breastplate; so he said to the driver of his chariot, 'Turn around, and carry me out of the battle, for I am wounded.' ³⁵The battle grew hot that day, and the king was propped up in his

chariot facing the Arameans, until at evening he died; the blood from the wound had flowed into the bottom of the chariot. ³⁶Then about sunset a shout went through the army, 'Every man to his city, and every man to his country!'

37 So the king died, and was brought to Samaria; they buried the king in Samaria. ³⁸They washed the chariot by the pool of Samaria; the dogs licked up his blood, and the prostitutes washed themselves in it, *b* according to the word of the LORD that he had spoken. ³⁹Now the rest of the acts of Ahab, and all that he did, and the ivory house that he built, and all the cities that he built, are they not written in the Book of the Annals of the Kings of Israel? ⁴⁰So Ahab slept with his ancestors; and his son Ahaziah succeeded him.

Jehoshaphat Reigns over Judah

41 Jehoshaphat son of Asa began to reign over Judah in the fourth year of King Ahab of Israel. ⁴²Jehoshaphat was thirty-five years old when he began to reign, and he reigned for twenty-five years in Jerusalem. His mother's name was Azubah daughter of Shilhi. ⁴³He walked in all the way of his father Asa; he did not turn aside from it, doing what was right in the sight of the LORD; yet the high places were not taken away, and the people still sacrificed and offered incense on the high places. ⁴⁴Jehoshaphat also made peace with the king of Israel.

45 Now the rest of the acts of Jehoshaphat, and his power that he showed, and how he waged war, are they not written in the Book of the Annals of the Kings of Judah? ⁴⁶The remnant of the male temple prostitutes who were still in the land from the days of his father Asa, he exterminated.

47 There was no king in Edom; a deputy was king. ⁴⁸Jehoshaphat made ships of the Tarshish type to go to Ophir for gold; but they did not go, for the ships were wrecked at Ezion-geber. ⁴⁹Then Ahaziah son of Ahab said to Jehoshaphat, 'Let my servants go with your servants in the

a Heb *he*   *b* Heb lacks *in it*

ships', but Jehoshaphat was not willing. [50] Jehoshaphat slept with his ancestors and was buried with his ancestors in the city of his father David; his son Jehoram succeeded him.

Ahaziah Reigns over Israel

51 Ahaziah son of Ahab began to reign over Israel in Samaria in the seventeenth year of King Jehoshaphat of Judah; he reigned for two years over Israel. [52] He did what was evil in the sight of the LORD, and walked in the way of his father and mother, and in the way of Jeroboam son of Nebat, who caused Israel to sin. [53] He served Baal and worshipped him; he provoked the LORD, the God of Israel, to anger, just as his father had done.

2 KINGS

Elijah Denounces Ahaziah

1 After the death of Ahab, Moab rebelled against Israel.

2 Ahaziah had fallen through the lattice in his upper chamber in Samaria, and lay injured; so he sent messengers, telling them, 'Go, inquire of Baal-zebub, the god of Ekron, whether I shall recover from this injury.' ³But the angel of the LORD said to Elijah the Tishbite, 'Get up, go to meet the messengers of the king of Samaria, and say to them, "Is it because there is no God in Israel that you are going to inquire of Baal-zebub, the god of Ekron?" ⁴Now therefore, thus says the LORD, "You shall not leave the bed to which you have gone, but you shall surely die."' So Elijah went.

5 The messengers returned to the king, who said to them, 'Why have you returned?' ⁶They answered him, 'There came a man to meet us, who said to us, "Go back to the king who sent you, and say to him: Thus says the LORD: Is it because there is no God in Israel that you are sending to inquire of Baal-zebub, the god of Ekron? Therefore you shall not leave the bed to which you have gone, but shall surely die."' ⁷He said to them, 'What sort of man was he who came to meet you and told you these things?' ⁸They answered him, 'A hairy man, with a leather belt around his waist.' He said, 'It is Elijah the Tishbite.'

9 Then the king sent to him a captain of fifty with his fifty men. He went up to Elijah, who was sitting on the top of a hill, and said to him, 'O man of God, the king says, "Come down."' ¹⁰But Elijah answered the captain of fifty, 'If I am a man of God, let fire come down from heaven and consume you and your fifty.' Then fire came down from heaven, and consumed him and his fifty.

11 Again the king sent to him another captain of fifty with his fifty. He went up ᵃ and said to him, 'O man of God, this is the king's order: Come down quickly!' ¹²But Elijah answered them, 'If I am a man of God, let fire come down from heaven and consume you and your fifty.' Then the fire of God came down from heaven and consumed him and his fifty.

13 Again the king sent the captain of a third fifty with his fifty. So the third captain of fifty went up, and came and fell on his knees before Elijah, and entreated him, 'O man of God, please let my life, and the life of these fifty servants of yours, be precious in your sight. ¹⁴Look, fire came down from heaven and consumed the two former captains of fifty men with their fifties; but now let my life be precious in your sight.' ¹⁵Then the angel of the LORD said to Elijah, 'Go down with him; do not be afraid of him.' So he set out and went down with him to the king, ¹⁶and said to him, 'Thus says the LORD: Because you have sent messengers to inquire of Baal-zebub, the god of Ekron,—is it because there is no God in Israel to inquire of his word?—therefore you shall not leave the bed to which you have gone, but you shall surely die.'

Death of Ahaziah

17 So he died according to the word of the LORD that Elijah had spoken. His brother ᵇ Jehoram succeeded him as king in the second year of King Jehoram son of

---

a Gk Compare verses 9, 13: Heb *He answered*
b Gk Syr: Heb lacks *His brother*

Jehoshaphat of Judah, because Ahaziah had no son. [18] Now the rest of the acts of Ahaziah that he did, are they not written in the Book of the Annals of the Kings of Israel?

Elijah Ascends to Heaven

2 Now when the LORD was about to take Elijah up to heaven by a whirlwind, Elijah and Elisha were on their way from Gilgal. [2] Elijah said to Elisha, 'Stay here; for the LORD has sent me as far as Bethel.' But Elisha said, 'As the LORD lives, and as you yourself live, I will not leave you.' So they went down to Bethel. [3] The company of prophets[a] who were in Bethel came out to Elisha, and said to him, 'Do you know that today the LORD will take your master away from you?' And he said, 'Yes, I know; keep silent.'

[4] Elijah said to him, 'Elisha, stay here; for the LORD has sent me to Jericho.' But he said, 'As the LORD lives, and as you yourself live, I will not leave you.' So they came to Jericho. [5] The company of prophets[a] who were at Jericho drew near to Elisha, and said to him, 'Do you know that today the LORD will take your master away from you?' And he answered, 'Yes, I know; be silent.'

[6] Then Elijah said to him, 'Stay here; for the LORD has sent me to the Jordan.' But he said, 'As the LORD lives, and as you yourself live, I will not leave you.' So the two of them went on. [7] Fifty men of the company of prophets[a] also went, and stood at some distance from them, as they both were standing by the Jordan. [8] Then Elijah took his mantle and rolled it up, and struck the water; the water was parted to the one side and to the other, until the two of them crossed on dry ground.

[9] When they had crossed, Elijah said to Elisha, 'Tell me what I may do for you, before I am taken from you.' Elisha said, 'Please let me inherit a double share of your spirit.' [10] He responded, 'You have asked a hard thing; yet, if you see me as I am being taken from you, it will be granted you; if not, it will not.' [11] As they continued walking and talking, a chariot of fire and horses of fire separated the two of them, and Elijah ascended in a whirlwind into heaven. [12] Elisha kept watching and crying out, 'Father, father! The chariots of Israel and its horsemen!' But when he could no longer see him, he grasped his own clothes and tore them in two pieces.

Elisha Succeeds Elijah

[13] He picked up the mantle of Elijah that had fallen from him, and went back and stood on the bank of the Jordan. [14] He took the mantle of Elijah that had fallen from him, and struck the water, saying, 'Where is the LORD, the God of Elijah?' When he had struck the water, the water was parted to the one side and to the other, and Elisha went over.

[15] When the company of prophets[a] who were at Jericho saw him at a distance, they declared, 'The spirit of Elijah rests on Elisha.' They came to meet him and bowed to the ground before him. [16] They said to him, 'See now, we have fifty strong men among your servants; please let them go and seek your master; it may be that the spirit of the LORD has caught him up and thrown him down on some mountain or into some valley.' He responded, 'No, do not send them.' [17] But when they urged him until he was ashamed, he said, 'Send them.' So they sent fifty men who searched for three days but did not find him. [18] When they came back to him (he had remained at Jericho), he said to them, 'Did I not say to you, Do not go?'

Elisha Performs Miracles

[19] Now the people of the city said to Elisha, 'The location of this city is good, as my lord sees; but the water is bad, and the land is unfruitful.' [20] He said, 'Bring me a new bowl, and put salt in it.' So they brought it to him. [21] Then he went to the spring of water and threw the salt into it, and said, 'Thus says the LORD, I have made this water wholesome; from now on neither death nor miscarriage shall come from it.' [22] So the water has been wholesome to

---

a Heb sons of the prophets

this day, according to the word that Elisha spoke.

23 He went up from there to Bethel; and while he was going up on the way, some small boys came out of the city and jeered at him, saying, 'Go away, baldhead! Go away, baldhead!' 24 When he turned round and saw them, he cursed them in the name of the LORD. Then two she-bears came out of the woods and mauled forty-two of the boys. 25 From there he went on to Mount Carmel, and then returned to Samaria.

Jehoram Reigns over Israel

3 In the eighteenth year of King Jehoshaphat of Judah, Jehoram son of Ahab became king over Israel in Samaria; he reigned for twelve years. 2 He did what was evil in the sight of the LORD, though not like his father and mother, for he removed the pillar of Baal that his father had made. 3 Nevertheless he clung to the sin of Jeroboam son of Nebat, which he caused Israel to commit; he did not depart from it.

War with Moab

4 Now King Mesha of Moab was a sheep breeder, who used to deliver to the king of Israel one hundred thousand lambs, and the wool of one hundred thousand rams. 5 But when Ahab died, the king of Moab rebelled against the king of Israel. 6 So King Jehoram marched out of Samaria at that time and mustered all Israel. 7 As he went he sent word to King Jehoshaphat of Judah, 'The king of Moab has rebelled against me; will you go with me to battle against Moab?' He answered, 'I will; I am with you, my people are your people, my horses are your horses.' 8 Then he asked, 'By which way shall we march?' Jehoram answered, 'By the way of the wilderness of Edom.'

9 So the king of Israel, the king of Judah, and the king of Edom set out; and when they had made a roundabout march of seven days, there was no water for the army or for the animals that were with them. 10 Then the king of Israel said, 'Alas! The LORD has summoned us, three kings, only to be handed over to Moab.' 11 But Jehoshaphat said, 'Is there no prophet of the LORD here, through whom we may inquire of the LORD?' Then one of the servants of the king of Israel answered, 'Elisha son of Shaphat, who used to pour water on the hands of Elijah, is here.' 12 Jehoshaphat said, 'The word of the LORD is with him.' So the king of Israel and Jehoshaphat and the king of Edom went down to him.

13 Elisha said to the king of Israel, 'What have I to do with you? Go to your father's prophets or to your mother's.' But the king of Israel said to him, 'No; it is the LORD who has summoned us, three kings, only to be handed over to Moab.' 14 Elisha said, 'As the LORD of hosts lives, whom I serve, were it not that I have regard for King Jehoshaphat of Judah, I would give you neither a look nor a glance. 15 But get me a musician.' And then, while the musician was playing, the power of the LORD came on him. 16 And he said, 'Thus says the LORD, "I will make this wadi full of pools." 17 For thus says the LORD, "You shall see neither wind nor rain, but the wadi shall be filled with water, so that you shall drink, you, your cattle, and your animals." 18 This is only a trifle in the sight of the LORD, for he will also hand Moab over to you. 19 You shall conquer every fortified city and every choice city; every good tree you shall fell, all springs of water you shall stop up, and every good piece of land you shall ruin with stones.' 20 The next day, about the time of the morning offering, suddenly water began to flow from the direction of Edom, until the country was filled with water.

21 When all the Moabites heard that the kings had come up to fight against them, all who were able to put on armour, from the youngest to the oldest, were called out and were drawn up at the frontier. 22 When they rose early in the morning, and the sun shone upon the water, the Moabites saw the water opposite them as red as blood. 23 They said, 'This is blood; the kings must have fought together, and killed one another. Now then, Moab, to the spoil!' 24 But

when they came to the camp of Israel, the Israelites rose up and attacked the Moabites, who fled before them; as they entered Moab they continued the attack.*a* 25 The cities they overturned, and on every good piece of land everyone threw a stone, until it was covered; every spring of water they stopped up, and every good tree they felled. Only at Kir-hareseth did the stone walls remain, until the slingers surrounded and attacked it. 26 When the king of Moab saw that the battle was going against him, he took with him seven hundred swordsmen to break through, opposite the king of Edom; but they could not. 27 Then he took his firstborn son who was to succeed him, and offered him as a burnt-offering on the wall. And great wrath came upon Israel, so they withdrew from him and returned to their own land.

Elisha and the Widow's Oil

4 Now the wife of a member of the company of prophets*b* cried to Elisha, 'Your servant my husband is dead; and you know that your servant feared the LORD, but a creditor has come to take my two children as slaves.' 2 Elisha said to her, 'What shall I do for you? Tell me, what do you have in the house?' She answered, 'Your servant has nothing in the house, except a jar of oil.' 3 He said, 'Go outside, borrow vessels from all your neighbours, empty vessels and not just a few. 4 Then go in, and shut the door behind you and your children, and start pouring into all these vessels; when each is full, set it aside.' 5 So she left him and shut the door behind her and her children; they kept bringing vessels to her, and she kept pouring. 6 When the vessels were full, she said to her son, 'Bring me another vessel.' But he said to her, 'There are no more.' Then the oil stopped flowing. 7 She came and told the man of God, and he said, 'Go, sell the oil and pay your debts, and you and your children can live on the rest.'

Elisha Raises the Shunammite's Son

8 One day Elisha was passing through Shunem, where a wealthy woman lived,

who urged him to have a meal. So whenever he passed that way, he would stop there for a meal. 9 She said to her husband, 'Look, I am sure that this man who regularly passes our way is a holy man of God. 10 Let us make a small roof chamber with walls, and put there for him a bed, a table, a chair, and a lamp, so that he can stay there whenever he comes to us.'

11 One day when he came there, he went up to the chamber and lay down there. 12 He said to his servant Gehazi, 'Call the Shunammite woman.' When he had called her, she stood before him. 13 He said to him, 'Say to her, Since you have taken all this trouble for us, what may be done for you? Would you have a word spoken on your behalf to the king or to the commander of the army?' She answered, 'I live among my own people.' 14 He said, 'What then may be done for her?' Gehazi answered, 'Well, she has no son, and her husband is old.' 15 He said, 'Call her.' When he had called her, she stood at the door. 16 He said, 'At this season, in due time, you shall embrace a son.' She replied, 'No, my lord, O man of God; do not deceive your servant.'

17 The woman conceived and bore a son at that season, in due time, as Elisha had declared to her.

18 When the child was older, he went out one day to his father among the reapers. 19 He complained to his father, 'Oh, my head, my head!' The father said to his servant, 'Carry him to his mother.' 20 He carried him and brought him to his mother; the child sat on her lap until noon, and he died. 21 She went up and laid him on the bed of the man of God, closed the door on him, and left. 22 Then she called to her husband, and said, 'Send me one of the servants and one of the donkeys, so that I may quickly go to the man of God and come back again.' 23 He said, 'Why go to him today? It is neither new moon nor sabbath.' She said, 'It will be all right.' 24 Then she saddled the donkey and said to her servant, 'Urge the animal on; do not

a Compare Gk Syr: Meaning of Heb uncertain
b Heb *the sons of the prophets*

hold back for me unless I tell you.' ²⁵So she set out, and came to the man of God at Mount Carmel.

When the man of God saw her coming, he said to Gehazi his servant, 'Look, there is the Shunammite woman; ²⁶run at once to meet her, and say to her, Are you all right? Is your husband all right? Is the child all right?' She answered, 'It is all right.' ²⁷When she came to the man of God at the mountain, she caught hold of his feet. Gehazi approached to push her away. But the man of God said, 'Let her alone, for she is in bitter distress; the LORD has hidden it from me and has not told me.' ²⁸Then she said, 'Did I ask my lord for a son? Did I not say, Do not mislead me?' ²⁹He said to Gehazi, 'Gird up your loins, and take my staff in your hand, and go. If you meet anyone, give no greeting, and if anyone greets you, do not answer; and lay my staff on the face of the child.' ³⁰Then the mother of the child said, 'As the LORD lives, and as you yourself live, I will not leave without you.' So he rose up and followed her. ³¹Gehazi went on ahead and laid the staff on the face of the child, but there was no sound or sign of life. He came back to meet him and told him, 'The child has not awakened.'

³²When Elisha came into the house, he saw the child lying dead on his bed. ³³So he went in and closed the door on the two of them, and prayed to the LORD. ³⁴Then he got up on the bed[a] and lay upon the child, putting his mouth upon his mouth, his eyes upon his eyes, and his hands upon his hands; and while he lay bent over him, the flesh of the child became warm. ³⁵He got down, walked once to and fro in the room, then got up again and bent over him; the child sneezed seven times, and the child opened his eyes. ³⁶Elisha[b] summoned Gehazi and said, 'Call the Shunammite woman.' So he called her. When she came to him, he said, 'Take your son.' ³⁷She came and fell at his feet, bowing to the ground; then she took her son and left.

Elisha Purifies the Pot of Stew

³⁸When Elisha returned to Gilgal, there was a famine in the land. As the company of prophets was[c] sitting before him, he said to his servant, 'Put the large pot on, and make some stew for the company of prophets.'[d] ³⁹One of them went out into the field to gather herbs; he found a wild vine and gathered from it a lapful of wild gourds, and came and cut them up into the pot of stew, not knowing what they were. ⁴⁰They served some for the men to eat. But while they were eating the stew, they cried out, 'O man of God, there is death in the pot!' They could not eat it. ⁴¹He said, 'Then bring some flour.' He threw it into the pot, and said, 'Serve the people and let them eat.' And there was nothing harmful in the pot.

Elisha Feeds One Hundred Men

⁴²A man came from Baal-shalishah, bringing food from the first fruits to the man of God: twenty loaves of barley and fresh ears of grain in his sack. Elisha said, 'Give it to the people and let them eat.' ⁴³But his servant said, 'How can I set this before a hundred people?' So he repeated, 'Give it to the people and let them eat, for thus says the LORD, "They shall eat and have some left." ' ⁴⁴He set it before them, they ate, and had some left, according to the word of the LORD.

The Healing of Naaman

5 Naaman, commander of the army of the king of Aram, was a great man and in high favour with his master, because by him the LORD had given victory to Aram. The man, though a mighty warrior, suffered from leprosy.[e] ²Now the Arameans on one of their raids had taken a young girl captive from the land of Israel, and she served Naaman's wife. ³She said to her mistress, 'If only my lord were with the prophet who is in Samaria! He would cure him of his leprosy.'[e] ⁴So Naaman[b] went in and told his lord just what the girl from the land of Israel had said. ⁵And the king of Aram said, 'Go then, and I will send along a letter to the king of Israel.'

a Heb lacks *on the bed*   *b* Heb *he*   *c* Heb *sons of the prophets were*   *d* Heb *sons of the prophets*   *e* A term for several skin diseases; precise meaning uncertain

He went, taking with him ten talents of silver, six thousand shekels of gold, and ten sets of garments. 6 He brought the letter to the king of Israel, which read, 'When this letter reaches you, know that I have sent to you my servant Naaman, that you may cure him of his leprosy.'*a* 7 When the king of Israel read the letter, he tore his clothes and said, 'Am I God, to give death or life, that this man sends word to me to cure a man of his leprosy?*a* Just look and see how he is trying to pick a quarrel with me.'

8 But when Elisha the man of God heard that the king of Israel had torn his clothes, he sent a message to the king, 'Why have you torn your clothes? Let him come to me, that he may learn that there is a prophet in Israel.' 9 So Naaman came with his horses and chariots, and halted at the entrance of Elisha's house. 10 Elisha sent a messenger to him, saying, 'Go, wash in the Jordan seven times, and your flesh shall be restored and you shall be clean.' 11 But Naaman became angry and went away, saying, 'I thought that for me he would surely come out, and stand and call on the name of the LORD his God, and would wave his hand over the spot, and cure the leprosy!*a* 12 Are not Abana*b* and Pharpar, the rivers of Damascus, better than all the waters of Israel? Could I not wash in them, and be clean?' He turned and went away in a rage. 13 But his servants approached and said to him, 'Father, if the prophet had commanded you to do something difficult, would you not have done it? How much more, when all he said to you was, "Wash, and be clean"?' 14 So he went down and immersed himself seven times in the Jordan, according to the word of the man of God; his flesh was restored like the flesh of a young boy, and he was clean.

15 Then he returned to the man of God, he and all his company; he came and stood before him and said, 'Now I know that there is no God in all the earth except in Israel; please accept a present from your servant.' 16 But he said, 'As the LORD lives, whom I serve, I will accept

nothing!' He urged him to accept, but he refused. 17 Then Naaman said, 'If not, please let two mule-loads of earth be given to your servant; for your servant will no longer offer burnt-offering or sacrifice to any god except the LORD. 18 But may the LORD pardon your servant on one count: when my master goes into the house of Rimmon to worship there, leaning on my arm, and I bow down in the house of Rimmon, when I do bow down in the house of Rimmon, may the LORD pardon your servant on this one count.' 19 He said to him, 'Go in peace.'

Gehazi's Greed

But when Naaman had gone from him a short distance, 20 Gehazi, the servant of Elisha the man of God, thought, 'My master has let that Aramean Naaman off too lightly by not accepting from him what he offered. As the LORD lives, I will run after him and get something out of him.' 21 So Gehazi went after Naaman. When Naaman saw someone running after him, he jumped down from the chariot to meet him and said, 'Is everything all right?' 22 He replied, 'Yes, but my master has sent me to say, "Two members of a company of prophets*c* have just come to me from the hill country of Ephraim; please give them a talent of silver and two changes of clothing." ' 23 Naaman said, 'Please accept two talents.' He urged him, and tied up two talents of silver in two bags, with two changes of clothing, and gave them to two of his servants, who carried them in front of Gehazi.*d* 24 When he came to the citadel, he took the bags*e* from them, and stored them inside; he dismissed the men, and they left.

25 He went in and stood before his master; and Elisha said to him, 'Where have you been, Gehazi?' He answered, 'Your servant has not gone anywhere at all.' 26 But he said to him, 'Did I not go with you in spirit when someone left his chariot to meet you? Is this a time to accept

a A term for several skin diseases; precise meaning uncertain   *b* Another reading is *Amana*   *c* Heb *sons of the prophets*   *d* Heb *him*   *e* Heb lacks *the bags* money and to accept clothing, olive orchards and vineyards, sheep and oxen, and male and female slaves? 27 Therefore the leprosy *a* of Naaman shall cling to you, and to your descendants for ever.' So he left his presence leprous, *a* as white as snow.

The Miracle of the Axehead

6 Now the company of prophets *b* said to Elisha, 'As you see, the place where we live under your charge is too small for us. 2 Let us go to the Jordan, and let us collect logs there, one for each of us, and build a place there for us to live.' He answered, 'Do so.' 3 Then one of them said, 'Please come with your servants.' And he answered, 'I will.' 4 So he went with them. When they came to the Jordan, they cut down trees. 5 But as one was felling a log, his axehead fell into the water; he cried out, 'Alas, master! It was borrowed.' 6 Then the man of God said, 'Where did it fall?' When he showed him the place, he cut off a stick, and threw it in there, and made the iron float. 7 He said, 'Pick it up.' So he reached out his hand and took it.

The Aramean Attack Is Thwarted

8 Once when the king of Aram was at war with Israel, he took counsel with his officers. He said, 'At such and such a place shall be my camp.' 9 But the man of God sent word to the king of Israel, 'Take care not to pass this place, because the Arameans are going down there.' 10 The king of Israel sent word to the place of which the man of God spoke. More than once or twice he warned such a place *c* so that it was on the alert.

11 The mind of the king of Aram was greatly perturbed because of this; he called his officers and said to them, 'Now tell me who among us sides with the king of Israel?' 12 Then one of his officers said, 'No one, my lord king. It is Elisha, the prophet in Israel, who tells the king of Israel the words that you speak in your bedchamber.' 13 He said, 'Go and find where he is; I will send and seize him.' He was told, 'He is in Dothan.' 14 So he sent horses and chariots there

and a great army; they came by night, and surrounded the city.

15 When an attendant of the man of God rose early in the morning and went out, an army with horses and chariots was all around the city. His servant said, 'Alas, master! What shall we do?' 16 He replied, 'Do not be afraid, for there are more with us than there are with them.' 17 Then Elisha prayed: 'O LORD, please open his eyes that he may see.' So the LORD opened the eyes of the servant, and he saw; the mountain was full of horses and chariots of fire all around Elisha. 18 When the Arameans *d* came down against him, Elisha prayed to the LORD, and said, 'Strike this people, please, with blindness.' So he struck them with blindness as Elisha had asked. 19 Elisha said to them, 'This is not the way, and this is not the city; follow me, and I will bring you to the man whom you seek.' And he led them to Samaria.

20 As soon as they entered Samaria, Elisha said, 'O LORD, open the eyes of these men so that they may see.' The LORD opened their eyes, and they saw that they were inside Samaria. 21 When the king of Israel saw them he said to Elisha, 'Father, shall I kill them? Shall I kill them?' 22 He answered, 'No! Did you capture with your sword and your bow those whom you want to kill? Set food and water before them so that they may eat and drink; and let them go to their master.' 23 So he prepared for them a great feast; after they ate and drank, he sent them on their way, and they went to their master. And the Arameans no longer came raiding into the land of Israel.

Ben-hadad's Siege of Samaria

24 Some time later King Ben-hadad of Aram mustered his entire army; he marched against Samaria and laid siege to it. 25 As the siege continued, famine in Samaria became so great that a donkey's head was sold for eighty shekels of silver, and one-fourth of a kab of dove's dung for five shekels of silver. 26 Now as the king of

---

a A term for several skin diseases; precise meaning uncertain   *b* Heb *sons of the prophets*   *c* Heb *warned it*   *d* Heb *they*

Israel was walking on the city wall, a woman cried out to him, 'Help, my lord king!' 27 He said, 'No! Let the LORD help you. How can I help you? From the threshing-floor or from the wine press?' 28 But then the king asked her, 'What is your complaint?' She answered, 'This woman said to me, "Give up your son; we will eat him today, and we will eat my son tomorrow." 29 So we cooked my son and ate him. The next day I said to her, "Give up your son and we will eat him." But she has hidden her son.' 30 When the king heard the words of the woman he tore his clothes—now since he was walking on the city wall, the people could see that he had sackcloth on his body underneath— 31 and he said, 'So may God do to me, and more, if the head of Elisha son of Shaphat stays on his shoulders today.' 32 So he dispatched a man from his presence.

Now Elisha was sitting in his house, and the elders were sitting with him. Before the messenger arrived, Elisha said to the elders, 'Are you aware that this murderer has sent someone to take off my head? When the messenger comes, see that you shut the door and hold it closed against him. Is not the sound of his master's feet behind him?' 33 While he was still speaking with them, the king[a] came down to him and said, 'This trouble is from the LORD! Why should I 7 hope in the LORD any longer?' 1 But Elisha said, 'Hear the word of the LORD: thus says the LORD, Tomorrow about this time a measure of choice meal shall be sold for a shekel, and two measures of barley for a shekel, at the gate of Samaria.' 2 Then the captain on whose hand the king leaned said to the man of God, 'Even if the LORD were to make windows in the sky, could such a thing happen?' But he said, 'You shall see it with your own eyes, but you shall not eat from it.'

The Arameans Flee

3 Now there were four leprous[b] men outside the city gate, who said to one another, 'Why should we sit here until we die? 4 If we say, "Let us enter the city", the famine is in the city, and we shall die there; but if we sit here, we shall also die. Therefore, let us desert to the Aramean camp; if they spare our lives, we shall live; and if they kill us, we shall but die.' 5 So they arose at twilight to go to the Aramean camp; but when they came to the edge of the Aramean camp, there was no one there at all. 6 For the Lord had caused the Aramean army to hear the sound of chariots and of horses, the sound of a great army, so that they said to one another, 'The king of Israel has hired the kings of the Hittites and the kings of Egypt to fight against us.' 7 So they fled away in the twilight and abandoned their tents, their horses, and their donkeys, leaving the camp just as it was, and fled for their lives. 8 When these leprous[b] men had come to the edge of the camp, they went into a tent, ate and drank, carried off silver, gold, and clothing, and went and hid them. Then they came back, entered another tent, carried off things from it, and went and hid them.

9 Then they said to one another, 'What we are doing is wrong. This is a day of good news; if we are silent and wait until the morning light, we will be found guilty; therefore let us go and tell the king's household.' 10 So they came and called to the gatekeepers of the city, and told them, 'We went to the Aramean camp, but there was no one to be seen or heard there, nothing but the horses tied, the donkeys tied, and the tents as they were.' 11 Then the gatekeepers called out and proclaimed it to the king's household. 12 The king got up in the night, and said to his servants, 'I will tell you what the Arameans have prepared against us. They know that we are starving; so they have left the camp to hide themselves in the open country, thinking, "When they come out of the city, we shall take them alive and get into the city." ' 13 One of his servants said, 'Let some men take five of the remaining horses, since those left here will suffer the fate of the whole multitude of Israel that have perished already;[c] let us send and find out.' 14 So they took two mounted men, and

---

a See 7.2: Heb *messenger*   b A term for several skin diseases; precise meaning uncertain   c Compare Gk Syr Vg: Meaning of Heb uncertain the king sent them after the Aramean army, saying, 'Go and find out.' 15 So they went after them as far as the Jordan; the whole way was littered with garments and equipment that the Arameans had thrown away in their haste. So the messengers returned, and told the king.

16 Then the people went out, and plundered the camp of the Arameans. So a measure of choice meal was sold for a shekel, and two measures of barley for a shekel, according to the word of the LORD. 17 Now the king had appointed the captain on whose hand he leaned to have charge of the gate; the people trampled him to death in the gate, just as the man of God had said when the king came down to him. 18 For when the man of God had said to the king, 'Two measures of barley shall be sold for a shekel, and a measure of choice meal for a shekel, about this time tomorrow in the gate of Samaria', 19 the captain had answered the man of God, 'Even if the LORD were to make windows in the sky, could such a thing happen?' And he had answered, 'You shall see it with your own eyes, but you shall not eat from it.' 20 It did indeed happen to him; the people trampled him to death in the gate.

The Shunammite Woman's Land Restored

8 Now Elisha had said to the woman whose son he had restored to life, 'Get up and go with your household, and settle wherever you can; for the LORD has called for a famine, and it will come on the land for seven years.' 2 So the woman got up and did according to the word of the man of God; she went with her household and settled in the land of the Philistines for seven years. 3 At the end of the seven years, when the woman returned from the land of the Philistines, she set out to appeal to the king for her house and her land. 4 Now the king was talking with Gehazi the servant of the man of God, saying, 'Tell me all the great things that Elisha has done.' 5 While he was telling the king how Elisha had restored a dead person to life, the woman whose son he had restored to life appealed to the king for her house and her land. Gehazi said, 'My lord king, here is the woman, and here is her son

whom Elisha restored to life.' 6 When the king questioned the woman, she told him. So the king appointed an official for her, saying, 'Restore all that was hers, together with all the revenue of the fields from the day that she left the land until now.'

Death of Ben-hadad

7 Elisha went to Damascus while King Ben-hadad of Aram was ill. When it was told him, 'The man of God has come here', 8 the king said to Hazael, 'Take a present with you and go to meet the man of God. Inquire of the LORD through him, whether I shall recover from this illness.' 9 So Hazael went to meet him, taking a present with him, all kinds of goods of Damascus, forty camel loads. When he entered and stood before him, he said, 'Your son King Ben-hadad of Aram has sent me to you, saying, "Shall I recover from this illness?" ' 10 Elisha said to him, 'Go, say to him, "You shall certainly recover"; but the LORD has shown me that he shall certainly die.' 11 He fixed his gaze and stared at him, until he was ashamed. Then the man of God wept. 12 Hazael asked, 'Why does my lord weep?' He answered, 'Because I know the evil that you will do to the people of Israel; you will set their fortresses on fire, you will kill their young men with the sword, dash in pieces their little ones, and rip up their pregnant women.' 13 Hazael said, 'What is your servant, who is a mere dog, that he should do this great thing?' Elisha answered, 'The LORD has shown me that you are to be king over Aram.' 14 Then he left Elisha, and went to his master Ben-hadad,[a] who said to him, 'What did Elisha say to you?' And he answered, 'He told me that you would certainly recover.' 15 But the next day he took the bed-cover and dipped it in water and spread it over the king's face, until he died. And Hazael succeeded him.

Jehoram Reigns over Judah

16 In the fifth year of King Joram son of Ahab of Israel,[b] Jehoram son of King Jehoshaphat of Judah began to reign. 17 He was

a Heb lacks *Ben-hadad*　　b Gk Syr: Heb adds *Jehoshaphat being king of Judah,* thirty-two years old when he became king, and he reigned for eight years in Jerusalem. [18] He walked in the way of the kings of Israel, as the house of Ahab had done, for the daughter of Ahab was his wife. He did what was evil in the sight of the LORD. [19] Yet the LORD would not destroy Judah, for the sake of his servant David, since he had promised to give a lamp to him and to his descendants for ever.

20 In his days Edom revolted against the rule of Judah, and set up a king of their own. [21] Then Joram crossed over to Zair with all his chariots. He set out by night and attacked the Edomites and their chariot commanders who had surrounded him;[a] but his army fled home. [22] So Edom has been in revolt against the rule of Judah to this day. Libnah also revolted at the same time. [23] Now the rest of the acts of Joram, and all that he did, are they not written in the Book of the Annals of the Kings of Judah? [24] So Joram slept with his ancestors, and was buried with them in the city of David; his son Ahaziah succeeded him.

Ahaziah Reigns over Judah

25 In the twelfth year of King Joram son of Ahab of Israel, Ahaziah son of King Jehoram of Judah began to reign. [26] Ahaziah was twenty-two years old when he began to reign; he reigned for one year in Jerusalem. His mother's name was Athaliah, a granddaughter of King Omri of Israel. [27] He also walked in the way of the house of Ahab, doing what was evil in the sight of the LORD, as the house of Ahab had done, for he was son-in-law to the house of Ahab.

28 He went with Joram son of Ahab to wage war against King Hazael of Aram at Ramoth-gilead, where the Arameans wounded Joram. [29] King Joram returned to be healed in Jezreel of the wounds that the Arameans had inflicted on him at Ramah, when he fought against King Hazael of Aram. King Ahaziah son of Jehoram of Judah went down to see Joram son of Ahab in Jezreel, because he was wounded.

Anointing of Jehu

9 Then the prophet Elisha called a member of the company of prophets[b] and said to him, 'Gird up your loins; take this flask of oil in your hand, and go to Ramoth-gilead. [2] When you arrive, look there for Jehu son of Jehoshaphat, son of Nimshi; go in and get him to leave his companions, and take him into an inner chamber. [3] Then take the flask of oil, pour it on his head, and say, "Thus says the LORD: I anoint you king over Israel." Then open the door and flee; do not linger.'

4 So the young man, the young prophet, went to Ramoth-gilead. [5] He arrived while the commanders of the army were in council, and he announced, 'I have a message for you, commander.' 'For which one of us?' asked Jehu. 'For you, commander.' [6] So Jehu[c] got up and went inside; the young man poured the oil on his head, saying to him, 'Thus says the LORD the God of Israel: I anoint you king over the people of the LORD, over Israel. [7] You shall strike down the house of your master Ahab, so that I may avenge on Jezebel the blood of my servants the prophets, and the blood of all the servants of the LORD. [8] For the whole house of Ahab shall perish; I will cut off from Ahab every male, bond or free, in Israel. [9] I will make the house of Ahab like the house of Jeroboam son of Nebat, and like the house of Baasha son of Ahijah. [10] The dogs shall eat Jezebel in the territory of Jezreel, and no one shall bury her.' Then he opened the door and fled.

11 When Jehu came back to his master's officers, they said to him, 'Is everything all right? Why did that madman come to you?' He answered them, 'You know the sort and how they babble.' [12] They said, 'Liar! Come on, tell us!' So he said, 'This is just what he said to me: "Thus says the LORD, I anoint you king over Israel." ' [13] Then hurriedly they all took their cloaks and spread them for him on the bare[a] steps; and they blew the trumpet, and proclaimed, 'Jehu is king.'

a Meaning of Heb uncertain   b Heb sons of the prophets   c Heb he

Joram of Israel Killed

14 Thus Jehu son of Jehoshaphat son of Nimshi conspired against Joram. Joram with all Israel had been on guard at Ramoth-gilead against King Hazael of Aram; [15] but King Joram had returned to be healed in Jezreel of the wounds that the Arameans had inflicted on him, when he fought against King Hazael of Aram. So Jehu said, 'If this is your wish, then let no one slip out of the city to go and tell the news in Jezreel.' [16] Then Jehu mounted his chariot and went to Jezreel, where Joram was lying ill. King Ahaziah of Judah had come down to visit Joram.

17 In Jezreel, the sentinel standing on the tower spied the company of Jehu arriving, and said, 'I see a company.' Joram said, 'Take a horseman; send him to meet them, and let him say, "Is it peace?" ' [18] So the horseman went to meet him; he said, 'Thus says the king, "Is it peace?" ' Jehu responded, 'What have you to do with peace? Fall in behind me.' The sentinel reported, saying, 'The messenger reached them, but he is not coming back.' [19] Then he sent out a second horseman, who came to them and said, 'Thus says the king, "Is it peace?" ' Jehu answered, 'What have you to do with peace? Fall in behind me.' [20] Again the sentinel reported, 'He reached them, but he is not coming back. It looks like the driving of Jehu son of Nimshi; for he drives like a maniac.'

21 Joram said, 'Get ready.' And they got his chariot ready. Then King Joram of Israel and King Ahaziah of Judah set out, each in his chariot, and went to meet Jehu; they met him at the property of Naboth the Jezreelite. [22] When Joram saw Jehu, he said, 'Is it peace, Jehu?' He answered, 'What peace can there be, so long as the many whoredoms and sorceries of your mother Jezebel continue?' [23] Then Joram reined about and fled, saying to Ahaziah, 'Treason, Ahaziah!' [24] Jehu drew his bow with all his strength, and shot Joram between the shoulders, so that the arrow pierced his heart; and he sank in his chariot. [25] Jehu said to his aide Bidkar, 'Lift him out, and throw him on the plot of ground belonging to Naboth the Jezreelite; for remember, when you and I rode side by side behind his father Ahab, how the LORD uttered this oracle against him: [26] "For the blood of Naboth and for the blood of his children that I saw yesterday, says the LORD, I swear I will repay you on this very plot of ground." Now therefore lift him out and throw him on the plot of ground, in accordance with the word of the LORD.'

Ahaziah of Judah Killed

27 When King Ahaziah of Judah saw this, he fled in the direction of Beth-haggan. Jehu pursued him, saying, 'Shoot him also!' And they shot him[a] in the chariot at the ascent to Gur, which is by Ibleam. Then he fled to Megiddo, and died there. [28] His officers carried him in a chariot to Jerusalem, and buried him in his tomb with his ancestors in the city of David.

29 In the eleventh year of Joram son of Ahab, Ahaziah began to reign over Judah.

Jezebel's Violent Death

30 When Jehu came to Jezreel, Jezebel heard of it; she painted her eyes, and adorned her head, and looked out of the window. [31] As Jehu entered the gate, she said, 'Is it peace, Zimri, murderer of your master?' [32] He looked up to the window and said, 'Who is on my side? Who?' Two or three eunuchs looked out at him. [33] He said, 'Throw her down.' So they threw her down; some of her blood spattered on the wall and on the horses, which trampled on her. [34] Then he went in and ate and drank; he said, 'See to that cursed woman and bury her; for she is a king's daughter.' [35] But when they went to bury her, they found no more of her than the skull and the feet and the palms of her hands. [36] When they came back and told him, he said, 'This is the word of the LORD, which he spoke by his servant Elijah the Tishbite, "In the territory of Jezreel the dogs shall eat the flesh of Jezebel; [37] the corpse of Jezebel shall be like dung on the field in the territory of Jezreel, so that no one can say, This is Jezebel." '

a Syr Vg Compare Gk: Heb lacks *and they shot him*

Massacre of Ahab's Descendants

10 Now Ahab had seventy sons in Samaria. So Jehu wrote letters and sent them to Samaria, to the rulers of Jezreel,*a* to the elders, and to the guardians of the sons of*b* Ahab, saying, 2 'Since your master's sons are with you and you have at your disposal chariots and horses, a fortified city, and weapons, 3 select the son of your master who is the best qualified, set him on his father's throne, and fight for your master's house.' 4 But they were utterly terrified and said, 'Look, two kings could not withstand him; how then can we stand?' 5 So the steward of the palace, and the governor of the city, along with the elders and the guardians, sent word to Jehu: 'We are your servants; we will do anything you say. We will not make anyone king; do whatever you think right.' 6 Then he wrote them a second letter, saying, 'If you are on my side, and if you are ready to obey me, take the heads of your master's sons and come to me at Jezreel tomorrow at this time.' Now the king's sons, seventy persons, were with the leaders of the city, who were charged with their upbringing. 7 When the letter reached them, they took the king's sons and killed them, seventy persons; they put their heads in baskets and sent them to him at Jezreel. 8 When the messenger came and told him, 'They have brought the heads of the king's sons', he said, 'Lay them in two heaps at the entrance of the gate until the morning.' 9 Then in the morning when he went out, he stood and said to all the people, 'You are innocent. It was I who conspired against my master and killed him; but who struck down all these? 10 Know then that there shall fall to the earth nothing of the word of the LORD, which the LORD spoke concerning the house of Ahab; for the LORD has done what he said through his servant Elijah.' 11 So Jehu killed all who were left of the house of Ahab in Jezreel, all his leaders, close friends, and priests, until he left him no survivor.

12 Then he set out and went to Samaria. On the way, when he was at Beth-eked of the Shepherds, 13 Jehu met relatives of King Ahaziah of Judah and said, 'Who are you?' They answered, 'We are kin of Ahaziah; we have come down to visit the royal princes and the sons of the queen mother.' 14 He said, 'Take them alive.' They took them alive, and slaughtered them at the pit of Beth-eked, forty-two in all; he spared none of them.

15 When he left there, he met Jehonadab son of Rechab coming to meet him; he greeted him, and said to him, 'Is your heart as true to mine as mine is to yours?'*c* Jehonadab answered, 'It is.' Jehu said,*d* 'If it is, give me your hand.' So he gave him his hand. Jehu took him up with him into the chariot. 16 He said, 'Come with me, and see my zeal for the LORD.' So he*e* had him ride in his chariot. 17 When he came to Samaria, he killed all who were left to Ahab in Samaria, until he had wiped them out, according to the word of the LORD that he spoke to Elijah.

Slaughter of Worshippers of Baal

18 Then Jehu assembled all the people and said to them, 'Ahab offered Baal small service; but Jehu will offer much more. 19 Now therefore summon to me all the prophets of Baal, all his worshippers, and all his priests; let none be missing, for I have a great sacrifice to offer to Baal; whoever is missing shall not live.' But Jehu was acting with cunning in order to destroy the worshippers of Baal. 20 Jehu decreed, 'Sanctify a solemn assembly for Baal.' So they proclaimed it. 21 Jehu sent word throughout all Israel; all the worshippers of Baal came, so that there was no one left who did not come. They entered the temple of Baal, until the temple of Baal was filled from wall to wall. 22 He said to the keeper of the wardrobe, 'Bring out the vestments for all the worshippers of Baal.' So he brought out the vestments for them. 23 Then Jehu entered the temple of Baal with Jehonadab son of Rechab; he said to the worshippers of Baal, 'Search and see that there is no worshipper of the LORD

a Or *of the city;* Vg Compare Gk   *b* Gk: Heb lacks *of the sons of*   *c* Gk: Heb *Is it right with your heart, as my heart is with your heart?*   *d* Gk: Heb lacks *Jehu said*   *e* Gk Syr Tg: Heb *they* here among you, but only worshippers of Baal.' 24 Then they proceeded to offer sacrifices and burnt-offerings.

Now Jehu had stationed eighty men outside, saying, 'Whoever allows any of those to escape whom I deliver into your hands shall forfeit his life.' 25 As soon as he had finished presenting the burnt-offering, Jehu said to the guards and to the officers, 'Come in and kill them; let no one escape.' So they put them to the sword. The guards and the officers threw them out, and then went into the citadel of the temple of Baal. 26 They brought out the pillar*a* that was in the temple of Baal, and burned it. 27 Then they demolished the pillar of Baal, and destroyed the temple of Baal, and made it a latrine to this day.

28 Thus Jehu wiped out Baal from Israel. 29 But Jehu did not turn aside from the sins of Jeroboam son of Nebat, which he caused Israel to commit—the golden calves that were in Bethel and in Dan. 30 The LORD said to Jehu, 'Because you have done well in carrying out what I consider right, and in accordance with all that was in my heart have dealt with the house of Ahab, your sons of the fourth generation shall sit on the throne of Israel.' 31 But Jehu was not careful to follow the law of the LORD the God of Israel with all his heart; he did not turn from the sins of Jeroboam, which he caused Israel to commit.

Death of Jehu

32 In those days the LORD began to trim off parts of Israel. Hazael defeated them throughout the territory of Israel: 33 from the Jordan eastwards, all the land of Gilead, the Gadites, the Reubenites, and the Manassites, from Aroer, which is by the Wadi Arnon, that is, Gilead and Bashan. 34 Now the rest of the acts of Jehu, all that he did, and all his power, are they not written in the Book of the Annals of the Kings of Israel? 35 So Jehu slept with his ancestors, and they buried him in Samaria. His son Jehoahaz succeeded him. 36 The time that Jehu reigned over Israel in Samaria was twenty-eight years.

Athaliah Reigns over Judah

11 Now when Athaliah, Ahaziah's mother, saw that her son was dead, she set about to destroy all the royal family. 2 But Jehosheba, King Joram's daughter, Ahaziah's sister, took Joash son of Ahaziah, and stole him away from among the king's children who were about to be killed; she put*b* him and his nurse in a bedroom. Thus she*c* hid him from Athaliah, so that he was not killed; 3 he remained with her for six years, hidden in the house of the LORD, while Athaliah reigned over the land.

Jehoiada Anoints the Child Joash

4 But in the seventh year Jehoiada summoned the captains of the Carites and of the guards and had them come to him in the house of the LORD. He made a covenant with them and put them under oath in the house of the LORD; then he showed them the king's son. 5 He commanded them, 'This is what you are to do: one-third of you, those who go off duty on the sabbath and guard the king's house 6 (another third being at the gate Sur and a third at the gate behind the guards), shall guard the palace; 7 and your two divisions that come on duty in force on the sabbath and guard the house of the LORD*d* 8 shall surround the king, each with weapons in hand; and whoever approaches the ranks is to be killed. Be with the king in his comings and goings.'

9 The captains did according to all that the priest Jehoiada commanded; each brought his men who were to go off duty on the sabbath, with those who were to come on duty on the sabbath, and came to the priest Jehoiada. 10 The priest delivered to the captains the spears and shields that had been King David's, which were in the house of the LORD; 11 the guards stood, every man with his weapons in his hand, from the south side of the house to the north side of the house, around the altar and the house, to guard the king on every

a Gk Vg Syr Tg: Heb *pillars*   *b* With 2 Chr 22.11: Heb lacks *she put*   *c* Gk Syr Vg Compare 2 Chr 22.11: Heb *they*   *d* Heb *the* LORD *to the king* side. [12] Then he brought out the king's son, put the crown on him, and gave him the covenant; [a] they proclaimed him king, and anointed him; they clapped their hands and shouted, 'Long live the king!'

Death of Athaliah

13 When Athaliah heard the noise of the guard and of the people, she went into the house of the LORD to the people; [14] when she looked, there was the king standing by the pillar, according to custom, with the captains and the trumpeters beside the king, and all the people of the land rejoicing and blowing trumpets. Athaliah tore her clothes and cried, 'Treason! Treason!' [15] Then the priest Jehoiada commanded the captains who were set over the army, 'Bring her out between the ranks, and kill with the sword anyone who follows her.' For the priest said, 'Let her not be killed in the house of the LORD.' [16] So they laid hands on her; she went through the horses' entrance to the king's house, and there she was put to death.

17 Jehoiada made a covenant between the LORD and the king and people, that they should be the LORD's people; also between the king and the people. [18] Then all the people of the land went to the house of Baal, and tore it down; his altars and his images they broke in pieces, and they killed Mattan, the priest of Baal, before the altars. The priest posted guards over the house of the LORD. [19] He took the captains, the Carites, the guards, and all the people of the land; then they brought the king down from the house of the LORD, marching through the gate of the guards to the king's house. He took his seat on the throne of the kings. [20] So all the people of the land rejoiced; and the city was quiet after Athaliah had been killed with the sword at the king's house.

21 [b] Jehoash [c] was seven years old when he began to reign.

The Temple Repaired

12 In the seventh year of Jehu, Jehoash began to reign; he reigned for forty years in Jerusalem. His mother's name was Zibiah of Beer-sheba. [2] Jehoash did what was right in the sight of the LORD all his days, because the priest Jehoiada instructed him. [3] Nevertheless, the high places were not taken away; the people continued to sacrifice and make offerings on the high places.

4 Jehoash said to the priests, 'All the money offered as sacred donations that is brought into the house of the LORD, the money for which each person is assessed—the money from the assessment of persons—and the money from the voluntary offerings brought into the house of the LORD, [5] let the priests receive from each of the donors; and let them repair the house wherever any need of repairs is discovered.' [6] But by the twenty-third year of King Jehoash the priests had made no repairs to the house. [7] Therefore King Jehoash summoned the priest Jehoiada with the other priests and said to them, 'Why are you not repairing the house? Now therefore do not accept any more money from your donors but hand it over for the repair of the house.' [8] So the priests agreed that they would neither accept more money from the people nor repair the house.

9 Then the priest Jehoiada took a chest, made a hole in its lid, and set it beside the altar on the right side as one entered the house of the LORD; the priests who guarded the threshold put in it all the money that was brought into the house of the LORD. [10] Whenever they saw that there was a great deal of money in the chest, the king's secretary and the high priest went up, counted the money that was found in the house of the LORD, and tied it up in bags. [11] They would give the money that was weighed out into the hands of the workers who had the oversight of the house of the LORD; then they paid it out to the carpenters and the builders who worked on the house of the LORD, [12] to the masons and the stonecutters, as well as to buy timber and quarried stone for making repairs on the house of the LORD, as well as for any outlay for repairs of the house. [13] But for the house of the LORD no basins of silver, snuffers, bowls, trumpets, or any vessels of

---

a Or *treaty* or *testimony*; Heb *eduth*   b Ch 12.1 in Heb
c Another spelling is *Joash*; see verse 19

gold, or of silver, were made from the money that was brought into the house of the Lord, 14 for that was given to the workers who were repairing the house of the Lord with it. 15 They did not ask for an account from those into whose hand they delivered the money to pay out to the workers, for they dealt honestly. 16 The money from the guilt-offerings and the money from the sin-offerings was not brought into the house of the Lord; it belonged to the priests.

Hazael Threatens Jerusalem

17 At that time King Hazael of Aram went up, fought against Gath, and took it. But when Hazael set his face to go up against Jerusalem, 18 King Jehoash of Judah took all the votive gifts that Jehoshaphat, Jehoram, and Ahaziah, his ancestors, the kings of Judah, had dedicated, as well as his own votive gifts, all the gold that was found in the treasuries of the house of the Lord and of the king's house, and sent these to King Hazael of Aram. Then Hazael withdrew from Jerusalem.

Death of Joash

19 Now the rest of the acts of Joash, and all that he did, are they not written in the Book of the Annals of the Kings of Judah? 20 His servants arose, made a conspiracy, and killed Joash in the house of Millo, on the way that goes down to Silla. 21 It was Jozacar son of Shimeath and Jehozabad son of Shomer, his servants, who struck him down, so that he died. He was buried with his ancestors in the city of David; then his son Amaziah succeeded him.

Jehoahaz Reigns over Israel

13 In the twenty-third year of King Joash son of Ahaziah of Judah, Jehoahaz son of Jehu began to reign over Israel in Samaria; he reigned for seventeen years. 2 He did what was evil in the sight of the Lord, and followed the sins of Jeroboam son of Nebat, which he caused Israel to sin; he did not depart from them. 3 The anger of the Lord was kindled against Israel, so that he gave them repeatedly into

the hand of King Hazael of Aram, then into the hand of Ben-hadad son of Hazael. 4 But Jehoahaz entreated the Lord, and the Lord heeded him; for he saw the oppression of Israel, how the king of Aram oppressed them. 5 Therefore the Lord gave Israel a saviour, so that they escaped from the hand of the Arameans; and the people of Israel lived in their homes as formerly. 6 Nevertheless, they did not depart from the sins of the house of Jeroboam, which he caused Israel to sin, but walked[a] in them; the sacred pole[b] also remained in Samaria. 7 So Jehoahaz was left with an army of not more than fifty horsemen, ten chariots and ten thousand foot-soldiers; for the king of Aram had destroyed them and made them like the dust at threshing. 8 Now the rest of the acts of Jehoahaz and all that he did, including his might, are they not written in the Book of the Annals of the Kings of Israel? 9 So Jehoahaz slept with his ancestors, and they buried him in Samaria; then his son Joash succeeded him.

Jehoash Reigns over Israel

10 In the thirty-seventh year of King Joash of Judah, Jehoash son of Jehoahaz began to reign over Israel in Samaria; he reigned for sixteen years. 11 He also did what was evil in the sight of the Lord; he did not depart from all the sins of Jeroboam son of Nebat, which he caused Israel to sin, but he walked in them. 12 Now the rest of the acts of Joash, and all that he did, as well as the might with which he fought against King Amaziah of Judah, are they not written in the Book of the Annals of the Kings of Israel? 13 So Joash slept with his ancestors, and Jeroboam sat upon his throne; Joash was buried in Samaria with the kings of Israel.

Death of Elisha

14 Now when Elisha had fallen sick with the illness of which he was to die, King Joash of Israel went down to him, and wept before him, crying, 'My father, my father! The chariots of Israel and its horsemen!'

a Gk Syr Tg Vg: Heb *he walked*   *b* Heb *Asherah*

15 Elisha said to him, 'Take a bow and arrows'; so he took a bow and arrows. 16 Then he said to the king of Israel, 'Draw the bow'; and he drew it. Elisha laid his hands on the king's hands. 17 Then he said, 'Open the window to the east'; and he opened it. Elisha said, 'Shoot'; and he shot. Then he said, 'The LORD's arrow of victory, the arrow of victory over Aram! For you shall fight the Arameans in Aphek until you have made an end of them.' 18 He continued, 'Take the arrows'; and he took them. He said to the king of Israel, 'Strike the ground with them'; he struck three times, and stopped. 19 Then the man of God was angry with him, and said, 'You should have struck five or six times; then you would have struck down Aram until you had made an end of it, but now you will strike down Aram only three times.'

20 So Elisha died, and they buried him. Now bands of Moabites used to invade the land in the spring of the year. 21 As a man was being buried, a marauding band was seen and the man was thrown into the grave of Elisha; as soon as the man touched the bones of Elisha, he came to life and stood on his feet.

Israel Recaptures Cities from Aram

22 Now King Hazael of Aram oppressed Israel all the days of Jehoahaz. 23 But the LORD was gracious to them and had compassion on them; he turned towards them, because of his covenant with Abraham, Isaac, and Jacob, and would not destroy them; nor has he banished them from his presence until now.

24 When King Hazael of Aram died, his son Ben-hadad succeeded him. 25 Then Jehoash son of Jehoahaz took again from Ben-hadad son of Hazael the towns that he had taken from his father Jehoahaz in war. Three times Joash defeated him and recovered the towns of Israel.

Amaziah Reigns over Judah

14 In the second year of King Joash son of Joahaz of Israel, King Amaziah son of Joash of Judah, began to reign. 2 He was twenty-five years old when he began to reign, and he reigned for twenty-nine years in Jerusalem. His mother's name was Jehoaddin of Jerusalem. 3 He did what was right in the sight of the LORD, yet not like his ancestor David; in all things he did as his father Joash had done. 4 But the high places were not removed; the people still sacrificed and made offerings on the high places. 5 As soon as the royal power was firmly in his hand he killed his servants who had murdered his father the king. 6 But he did not put to death the children of the murderers; according to what is written in the book of the law of Moses, where the LORD commanded, 'The parents shall not be put to death for the children, or the children be put to death for the parents; but all shall be put to death for their own sins.'

7 He killed ten thousand Edomites in the Valley of Salt and took Sela by storm; he called it Jokthe-el, which is its name to this day.

8 Then Amaziah sent messengers to King Jehoash son of Jehoahaz, son of Jehu, of Israel, saying, 'Come, let us look one another in the face.' 9 King Jehoash of Israel sent word to King Amaziah of Judah, 'A thornbush on Lebanon sent to a' cedar on Lebanon, saying, "Give your daughter to my son for a wife"; but a wild animal of Lebanon passed by and trampled down the thornbush. 10 You have indeed defeated Edom, and your heart has lifted you up. Be content with your glory, and stay at home; for why should you provoke trouble so that you fall, you and Judah with you?'

11 But Amaziah would not listen. So King Jehoash of Israel went up; he and King Amaziah of Judah faced one another in battle at Beth-shemesh, which belongs to Judah. 12 Judah was defeated by Israel; everyone fled home. 13 King Jehoash of Israel captured King Amaziah of Judah son of Jehoash, son of Ahaziah, at Beth-shemesh; he came to Jerusalem, and broke down the wall of Jerusalem from the Ephraim Gate to the Corner Gate, a distance of four hundred cubits. 14 He seized all the gold and silver, and all the vessels that were found in

the house of the LORD and in the treasuries of the king's house, as well as hostages; then he returned to Samaria.

15 Now the rest of the acts that Jehoash did, his might, and how he fought with King Amaziah of Judah, are they not written in the Book of the Annals of the Kings of Israel? 16 Jehoash slept with his ancestors, and was buried in Samaria with the kings of Israel; then his son Jeroboam succeeded him.

17 King Amaziah son of Joash of Judah lived for fifteen years after the death of King Jehoash son of Jehoahaz of Israel. 18 Now the rest of the deeds of Amaziah, are they not written in the Book of the Annals of the Kings of Judah? 19 They made a conspiracy against him in Jerusalem, and he fled to Lachish. But they sent after him to Lachish, and killed him there. 20 They brought him on horses; he was buried in Jerusalem with his ancestors in the city of David. 21 All the people of Judah took Azariah, who was sixteen years old, and made him king to succeed his father Amaziah. 22 He rebuilt Elath and restored it to Judah, after King Amaziah*a* slept with his ancestors.

Jeroboam, Son of Joash, Reigns over Israel

23 In the fifteenth year of King Amaziah son of Joash of Judah, King Jeroboam son of Joash of Israel began to reign in Samaria; he reigned for forty-one years. 24 He did what was evil in the sight of the LORD; he did not depart from all the sins of Jeroboam son of Nebat, which he caused Israel to sin. 25 He restored the border of Israel from Lebo-hamath as far as the Sea of the Arabah, according to the word of the LORD, the God of Israel, which he spoke by his servant Jonah son of Amittai, the prophet, who was from Gath-hepher. 26 For the LORD saw that the distress of Israel was very bitter; there was no one left, bond or free, and no one to help Israel. 27 But the LORD had not said that he would blot out the name of Israel from under heaven, so he saved them by the hand of Jeroboam son of Joash.

28 Now the rest of the acts of Jeroboam, and all that he did, and his might, how he fought, and how he recovered for Israel Damascus and Hamath, which had belonged to Judah, are they not written in the Book of the Annals of the Kings of Israel? 29 Jeroboam slept with his ancestors, the kings of Israel; his son Zechariah succeeded him.

Azariah Reigns over Judah

15 In the twenty-seventh year of King Jeroboam of Israel King Azariah son of Amaziah of Judah began to reign. 2 He was sixteen years old when he began to reign, and he reigned for fifty-two years in Jerusalem. His mother's name was Jecoliah of Jerusalem. 3 He did what was right in the sight of the LORD, just as his father Amaziah had done. 4 Nevertheless, the high places were not taken away; the people still sacrificed and made offerings on the high places. 5 The LORD struck the king, so that he was leprous*b* to the day of his death, and lived in a separate house. Jotham the king's son was in charge of the palace, governing the people of the land. 6 Now the rest of the acts of Azariah, and all that he did, are they not written in the Book of the Annals of the Kings of Judah? 7 Azariah slept with his ancestors; they buried him with his ancestors in the city of David; his son Jotham succeeded him.

Zechariah Reigns over Israel

8 In the thirty-eighth year of King Azariah of Judah, Zechariah son of Jeroboam reigned over Israel in Samaria for six months. 9 He did what was evil in the sight of the LORD, as his ancestors had done. He did not depart from the sins of Jeroboam son of Nebat, which he caused Israel to sin. 10 Shallum son of Jabesh conspired against him, and struck him down in public and killed him, and reigned in place of him. 11 Now the rest of the deeds of Zechariah are written in the Book of the Annals of the Kings of Israel. 12 This was the promise of the LORD that he gave to Jehu: 'Your sons

a Heb *the king*   *b* A term for several skin diseases; precise meaning uncertain shall sit on the throne of Israel to the fourth generation.' And so it happened.

Shallum Reigns over Israel

13 Shallum son of Jabesh began to reign in the thirty-ninth year of King Uzziah of Judah; he reigned for one month in Samaria. 14 Then Menahem son of Gadi came up from Tirzah and came to Samaria; he struck down Shallum son of Jabesh in Samaria and killed him; he reigned in place of him. 15 Now the rest of the deeds of Shallum, including the conspiracy that he made, are written in the Book of the Annals of the Kings of Israel. 16 At that time Menahem sacked Tiphsah, all who were in it and its territory from Tirzah on; because they did not open it to him, he sacked it. He ripped open all the pregnant women in it.

Menahem Reigns over Israel

17 In the thirty-ninth year of King Azariah of Judah, Menahem son of Gadi began to reign over Israel; he reigned for ten years in Samaria. 18 He did what was evil in the sight of the LORD; he did not depart all his days from any of the sins of Jeroboam son of Nebat, which he caused Israel to sin. 19 King Pul of Assyria came against the land; Menahem gave Pul a thousand talents of silver, so that he might help him confirm his hold on the royal power. 20 Menahem exacted the money from Israel, that is, from all the wealthy, fifty shekels of silver from each one, to give to the king of Assyria. So the king of Assyria turned back, and did not stay there in the land. 21 Now the rest of the deeds of Menahem, and all that he did, are they not written in the Book of the Annals of the Kings of Israel? 22 Menahem slept with his ancestors, and his son Pekahiah succeeded him.

Pekahiah Reigns over Israel

23 In the fiftieth year of King Azariah of Judah, Pekahiah son of Menahem began to reign over Israel in Samaria; he reigned for two years. 24 He did what was evil in the sight of the LORD; he did not turn away from the sins of Jeroboam son of Nebat, which he caused Israel to sin. 25 Pekah son of Remaliah, his captain, conspired against him with fifty of the Gileadites, and attacked him in Samaria, in the citadel of the palace along with Argob and Arieh; he killed him, and reigned in place of him. 26 Now the rest of the deeds of Pekahiah, and all that he did, are written in the Book of the Annals of the Kings of Israel.

Pekah Reigns over Israel

27 In the fifty-second year of King Azariah of Judah, Pekah son of Remaliah began to reign over Israel in Samaria; he reigned for twenty years. 28 He did what was evil in the sight of the LORD; he did not depart from the sins of Jeroboam son of Nebat, which he caused Israel to sin.

29 In the days of King Pekah of Israel, King Tiglath-pileser of Assyria came and captured Ijon, Abel-beth-maacah, Janoah, Kedesh, Hazor, Gilead, and Galilee, all the land of Naphtali; and he carried the people captive to Assyria. 30 Then Hoshea son of Elah made a conspiracy against Pekah son of Remaliah, attacked him, and killed him; he reigned in place of him, in the twentieth year of Jotham son of Uzziah. 31 Now the rest of the acts of Pekah, and all that he did, are written in the Book of the Annals of the Kings of Israel.

Jotham Reigns over Judah

32 In the second year of King Pekah son of Remaliah of Israel, King Jotham son of Uzziah of Judah began to reign. 33 He was twenty-five years old when he began to reign and he reigned for sixteen years in Jerusalem. His mother's name was Jerusha daughter of Zadok. 34 He did what was right in the sight of the LORD, just as his father Uzziah had done. 35 Nevertheless, the high places were not removed; the people still sacrificed and made offerings on the high places. He built the upper gate of the house of the LORD. 36 Now the rest of the acts of Jotham, and all that he did, are they not written in the Book of the Annals of the Kings of Judah? 37 In those days the LORD began to send King Rezin of Aram and Pekah son of Remaliah against Judah. 38 Jotham slept

with his ancestors, and was buried with his ancestors in the city of David, his ancestor; his son Ahaz succeeded him.

Ahaz Reigns over Judah

16 In the seventeenth year of Pekah son of Remaliah, King Ahaz son of Jotham of Judah began to reign. ²Ahaz was twenty years old when he began to reign; he reigned for sixteen years in Jerusalem. He did not do what was right in the sight of the LORD his God, as his ancestor David had done, ³but he walked in the way of the kings of Israel. He even made his son pass through fire, according to the abominable practices of the nations whom the LORD drove out before the people of Israel. ⁴He sacrificed and made offerings on the high places, on the hills, and under every green tree.

5 Then King Rezin of Aram and King Pekah son of Remaliah of Israel came up to wage war on Jerusalem; they besieged Ahaz but could not conquer him. ⁶At that time the king of Edom ᵃ recovered Elath for

The Campaign of Tiglath-pileser III

Edom, ᵇ and drove the Judeans from Elath; and the Edomites came to Elath, where they live to this day. ⁷Ahaz sent messengers to King Tiglath-pileser of Assyria, saying, 'I am your servant and your son. Come up, and rescue me from the hand of the king of Aram and from the hand of the king of Israel, who are attacking me.' ⁸Ahaz also took the silver and gold found in the house of the LORD and in the treasures of the king's house, and sent a present to the king of Assyria. ⁹The king of Assyria listened to him; the king of Assyria marched up against Damascus, and took it, carrying its people captive to Kir; then he killed Rezin.

10 When King Ahaz went to Damascus to meet King Tiglath-pileser of Assyria, he saw the altar that was at Damascus. King Ahaz sent to the priest Uriah a model of the altar, and its pattern, exact in all its details. ¹¹The priest Uriah built the altar; in accordance with all that King Ahaz had sent from Damascus, just so did the priest Uriah build it, before King Ahaz arrived from Damascus. ¹²When the king came from Damascus, the king viewed the altar. Then the king drew near to the altar, went up on it, ¹³and offered his burnt-offering and his grain-offering, poured his drink-offering, and dashed the blood of his offerings of well-being against the altar. ¹⁴The bronze altar that was before the LORD he removed from the front of the house, from the place between his altar and the house of the LORD, and put it on the north side of his altar. ¹⁵King Ahaz commanded the priest Uriah, saying, 'Upon the great altar offer the morning burnt-offering, and the evening grain-offering, and the king's burnt-offering, and his grain-offering, with the burnt-offering of all the people of the land, their grain-offering, and their drink-offering; then dash against it all the blood of the burnt-offering, and all the blood of the sacrifice; but the bronze altar shall be for me to inquire by.' ¹⁶The priest Uriah did everything that King Ahaz commanded.

17 Then King Ahaz cut off the frames of the stands, and removed the laver from them; he removed the sea from the bronze

a Cn: Heb King Rezin of Aram   b Cn: Heb Aram

oxen that were under it, and put it on a pediment of stone. [18]The covered portal for use on the sabbath that had been built inside the palace, and the outer entrance for the king, he removed from[a] the house of the LORD. He did this because of the king of Assyria. [19]Now the rest of the acts of Ahaz that he did, are they not written in the Book of the Annals of the Kings of Judah? [20]Ahaz slept with his ancestors, and was buried with his ancestors in the city of David; his son Hezekiah succeeded him.

Hoshea Reigns over Israel

17 In the twelfth year of King Ahaz of Judah, Hoshea son of Elah began to reign in Samaria over Israel; he reigned for nine years. [2]He did what was evil in the sight of the LORD, yet not like the kings of Israel who were before him. [3]King Shalmaneser of Assyria came up against him; Hoshea became his vassal, and paid him tribute. [4]But the king of Assyria found treachery in Hoshea; for he had sent messengers to King So of Egypt, and offered no

tribute to the king of Assyria, as he had done year by year; therefore the king of Assyria confined him and imprisoned him.

Israel Carried Captive to Assyria

5 Then the king of Assyria invaded all the land and came to Samaria; for three years he besieged it. [6]In the ninth year of Hoshea, the king of Assyria captured Samaria; he carried the Israelites away to Assyria. He placed them in Halah, on the Habor, the river of Gozan, and in the cities of the Medes.

7 This occurred because the people of Israel had sinned against the LORD their God, who had brought them up out of the land of Egypt from under the hand of Pharaoh king of Egypt. They had worshipped other gods [8]and walked in the customs of the nations whom the LORD drove out before the people of Israel, and in the customs that the kings of Israel had introduced.[b] [9]The people of Israel secretly did things that were not right against the LORD their God. They built for themselves high places at all their towns, from watch-tower to fortified city; [10]they set up for themselves pillars and sacred poles[c] on every high hill and under every green tree; [11]there they made offerings on all the high places, as the nations did whom the LORD carried away before them. They did wicked things, provoking the LORD to anger; [12]they served idols, of which the LORD had said to them, 'You shall not do this.' [13]Yet the LORD warned Israel and Judah by every prophet and every seer, saying, 'Turn from your evil ways and keep my commandments and my statutes, in accordance with all the law that I commanded your ancestors and that I sent to you by my servants the prophets.' [14]They would not listen but were stubborn, as their ancestors had been, who did not believe in the LORD their God. [15]They despised his statutes, and his covenant that he made with their ancestors, and the warnings that he gave them. They went after false idols and became false; they followed the nations that were around them, concerning

The Campaign of Shalmaneser V

Mediterranean Sea

Damascus

Ijon

Hazor

Acco

Dor

Ashtaroth

Beth-shan

Ramoth-gilead

Samaria

Joppa

Gezer

Jerusalem

Dead Sea

Gaza

N

0   40 Mi.
0   40 Km.

a Cn: Heb lacks *from*   *b* Meaning of Heb uncertain
c Heb *Asherim*

whom the LORD had commanded them that they should not do as they did. [16] They rejected all the commandments of the LORD their God and made for themselves cast images of two calves; they made a sacred pole, [a] worshipped all the host of heaven, and served Baal. [17] They made their sons and their daughters pass through fire; they used divination and augury; and they sold themselves to do evil in the sight of the LORD, provoking him to anger. [18] Therefore the LORD was very angry with Israel and removed them out of his sight; none was left but the tribe of Judah alone.

19 Judah also did not keep the commandments of the LORD their God but walked in the customs that Israel had introduced. [20] The LORD rejected all the descendants of Israel; he punished them and gave them into the hand of plunderers, until he had banished them from his presence.

21 When he had torn Israel from the house of David, they made Jeroboam son of Nebat king. Jeroboam drove Israel from following the LORD and made them commit great sin. [22] The people of Israel continued in all the sins that Jeroboam committed; they did not depart from them [23] until the LORD removed Israel out of his sight, as he had foretold through all his servants the prophets. So Israel was exiled from their own land to Assyria until this day.

Assyria Resettles Samaria

24 The king of Assyria brought people from Babylon, Cuthah, Avva, Hamath, and Sepharvaim, and placed them in the cities of Samaria in place of the people of Israel; they took possession of Samaria, and settled in its cities. [25] When they first settled there, they did not worship the LORD; therefore the LORD sent lions among them, which killed some of them. [26] So the king of Assyria was told, 'The nations that you have carried away and placed in the cities of Samaria do not know the law of the god of the land; therefore he has sent lions among them; they are killing them, because they do not know the law of the god

of the land.' [27] Then the king of Assyria commanded, 'Send there one of the priests whom you carried away from there; let him [b] go and live there, and teach them the law of the god of the land.' [28] So one of the priests whom they had carried away from Samaria came and lived in Bethel; he taught them how they should worship the LORD.

29 But every nation still made gods of its own and put them in the shrines of the high places that the people of Samaria had made, every nation in the cities in which they lived; [30] the people of Babylon made Succoth-benoth, the people of Cuth made Nergal, the people of Hamath made Ashima; [31] the Avvites made Nibhaz and Tartak; the Sepharvites burned their children in the fire to Adrammelech and Anammelech, the gods of Sepharvaim. [32] They also worshipped the LORD and appointed from among themselves all sorts of people as priests of the high places, who sacrificed for them in the shrines of the high places. [33] So they worshipped the LORD, but they also served their own gods, after the manner of the nations from among whom they had been carried away. [34] To this day they continue to practise their former customs.

They do not worship the LORD and they do not follow the statutes or the ordinances or the law or the commandment that the LORD commanded the children of Jacob, whom he named Israel. [35] The LORD had made a covenant with them and commanded them, 'You shall not worship other gods or bow yourselves to them or serve them or sacrifice to them, [36] but you shall worship the LORD, who brought you out of the land of Egypt with great power and with an outstretched arm; you shall bow yourselves to him, and to him you shall sacrifice. [37] The statutes and the ordinances and the law and the commandment that he wrote for you, you shall always be careful to observe. You shall not worship other gods; [38] you shall not forget the covenant that I have made with you. You shall not worship other gods, [39] but you shall

a Heb *Asherah*　　b Syr Vg: Heb *them*

worship the LORD your God; he will deliver you out of the hand of all your enemies.' 40 They would not listen, however, but they continued to practise their former custom.

41 So these nations worshipped the LORD, but also served their carved images; to this day their children and their children's children continue to do as their ancestors did.

Hezekiah's Reign over Judah

18 In the third year of King Hoshea son of Elah of Israel, Hezekiah son of King Ahaz of Judah began to reign. 2 He was twenty-five years old when he began to reign; he reigned for twenty-nine years in Jerusalem. His mother's name was Abi daughter of Zechariah. 3 He did what was right in the sight of the LORD just as his ancestor David had done. 4 He removed the high places, broke down the pillars, and cut down the sacred pole. *a* He broke in pieces the bronze serpent that Moses had made, for until those days the people of Israel had made offerings to it; it was called Nehushtan. 5 He trusted in the LORD the God of Israel; so that there was no one like him among all the kings of Judah after him, or among those who were before him. 6 For he held fast to the LORD; he did not depart from following him but kept the commandments that the LORD commanded Moses. 7 The LORD was with him; wherever he went, he prospered. He rebelled against the king of Assyria and would not serve him. 8 He attacked the Philistines as far as Gaza and its territory, from watch-tower to fortified city.

9 In the fourth year of King Hezekiah, which was the seventh year of King Hoshea son of Elah of Israel, King Shalmaneser of Assyria came up against Samaria, besieged it, 10 and at the end of three years took it. In the sixth year of Hezekiah, which was the ninth year of King Hoshea of Israel, Samaria was taken. 11 The king of Assyria carried the Israelites away to Assyria, settled them in Halah, on the Habor, the river of Gozan, and in the cities of the Medes, 12 because they did not obey the voice of the LORD their God but trans-

gressed his covenant—all that Moses the servant of the LORD had commanded; they neither listened nor obeyed.

Sennacherib Invades Judah

13 In the fourteenth year of King Hezekiah, King Sennacherib of Assyria came up against all the fortified cities of Judah and captured them. 14 King Hezekiah of Judah sent to the king of Assyria at Lachish, saying, 'I have done wrong; withdraw from me; whatever you impose on me I will bear.' The king of Assyria demanded of King Hezekiah of Judah three hundred talents of silver and thirty talents of gold. 15 Hezekiah gave him all the silver that was found in the house of the LORD and in the treasuries of the king's house. 16 At that time Hezekiah stripped the gold from the doors of the temple of the LORD, and from the doorposts that King Hezekiah of Judah had overlaid, and gave it to the king of Assyria. 17 The king of Assyria sent the Tartan, the Rabsaris, and the Rabshakeh with a great army from Lachish to King Hezekiah at Jerusalem. They went up and came to Jerusalem. When they arrived, they came and stood by the conduit of the upper pool, which is on the highway to the Fuller's Field. 18 When they called for the king, there came out to them Eliakim son of Hilkiah, who was in charge of the palace, and Shebnah the secretary, and Joah son of Asaph, the recorder.

19 The Rabshakeh said to them, 'Say to Hezekiah: Thus says the great king, the king of Assyria: On what do you base this confidence of yours? 20 Do you think that mere words are strategy and power for war? On whom do you now rely, that you have rebelled against me? 21 See, you are relying now on Egypt, that broken reed of a staff, which will pierce the hand of anyone who leans on it. Such is Pharaoh king of Egypt to all who rely on him. 22 But if you say to me, "We rely on the LORD our God", is it not he whose high places and altars Hezekiah has removed, saying to Judah and to Jerusalem, "You shall worship before this altar in Jerusalem"? 23 Come

a Heb *Asherah*

now, make a wager with my master the king of Assyria: I will give you two thousand horses, if you are able on your part to set riders on them. 24 How then can you repulse a single captain among the least of my master's servants, when you rely on Egypt for chariots and for horsemen? 25 Moreover, is it without the LORD that I have come up against this place to destroy it? The LORD said to me, Go up against this land, and destroy it.'

26 Then Eliakim son of Hilkiah, and Shebnah, and Joah said to the Rabshakeh, 'Please speak to your servants in the Aramaic language, for we understand it; do not speak to us in the language of Judah within the hearing of the people who are on the wall.' 27 But the Rabshakeh said to them, 'Has my master sent me to speak these words to your master and to you, and not to the people sitting on the wall, who are doomed with you to eat their own dung and to drink their own urine?'

28 Then the Rabshakeh stood and called out in a loud voice in the language of Judah, 'Hear the word of the great king, the king of Assyria! 29 Thus says the king: "Do not let Hezekiah deceive you, for he will not be able to deliver you out of my hand. 30 Do not let Hezekiah make you rely on the LORD by saying, The LORD will surely deliver us, and this city will not be given into the hand of the king of Assyria." 31 Do not listen to Hezekiah; for thus says the king of Assyria: "Make your peace with me and come out to me; then every one of you will eat from your own vine and your own fig tree, and drink water from your own cistern, 32 until I come and take you away to a land like your own land, a land of grain and wine, a land of bread and vineyards, a land of olive oil and honey, that you may live and not die. Do not listen to Hezekiah when he misleads you by saying, The LORD will deliver us. 33 Has any of the gods of the nations ever delivered its land out of the hand of the king of Assyria? 34 Where are the gods of Hamath and Arpad? Where are the gods of Sepharvaim, Hena, and Ivvah? Have they delivered Samaria out of my hand? 35 Who among

all the gods of the countries have delivered their countries out of my hand, that the LORD should deliver Jerusalem out of my hand?" '

36 But the people were silent and answered him not a word, for the king's command was, 'Do not answer him.' 37 Then Eliakim son of Hilkiah, who was in charge of the palace, and Shebna the secretary, and Joah son of Asaph, the recorder, came to Hezekiah with their clothes torn and told him the words of the Rabshakeh.

Hezekiah Consults Isaiah

19 When King Hezekiah heard it, he tore his clothes, covered himself with sackcloth, and went into the house of the LORD. 2 And he sent Eliakim, who was in charge of the palace, and Shebna the secretary, and the senior priests, covered with sackcloth, to the prophet Isaiah son of Amoz. 3 They said to him, 'Thus says Hezekiah, This day is a day of distress, of rebuke, and of disgrace; children have come to birth, and there is no strength to bring them forth. 4 It may be that the LORD your God heard all the words of the Rabshakeh, whom his master the king of Assyria has sent to mock the living God, and will rebuke the words that the LORD your God has heard; therefore lift up your prayer for the remnant that is left.' 5 When the servants of King Hezekiah came to Isaiah, 6 Isaiah said to them, 'Say to your master, "Thus says the LORD: Do not be afraid because of the words that you have heard, with which the servants of the king of Assyria have reviled me. 7 I myself will put a spirit in him, so that he shall hear a rumour and return to his own land; I will cause him to fall by the sword in his own land." '

Sennacherib's Threat

8 The Rabshakeh returned, and found the king of Assyria fighting against Libnah; for he had heard that the king had left Lachish. 9 When the king[a] heard concerning King Tirhakah of Ethiopia,[b] 'See, he has set out to fight against you', he sent messengers again

a Heb *he*   b Or *Nubia*; Heb *Cush*

to Hezekiah, saying, ¹⁰'Thus shall you speak to King Hezekiah of Judah: Do not let your God on whom you rely deceive you by promising that Jerusalem will not be given into the hand of the king of Assyria. ¹¹See, you have heard what the kings of Assyria have done to all lands, destroying them utterly. Shall you be delivered? ¹²Have the gods of the nations delivered them, the nations that my predecessors destroyed, Gozan, Haran, Rezeph, and the people of Eden who were in Telassar? ¹³Where is the king of Hamath, the king of Arpad, the king of the city of Sepharvaim, the king of Hena, or the king of Ivvah?'

Hezekiah's Prayer

14 Hezekiah received the letter from the hand of the messengers and read it; then Hezekiah went up to the house of the LORD and spread it before the LORD. ¹⁵And Hezekiah prayed before the LORD, and said: 'O LORD the God of Israel, who are enthroned above the cherubim, you are God, you alone, of all the kingdoms of the earth; you have made heaven and earth. ¹⁶Incline your ear, O LORD, and hear; open your eyes, O LORD, and see; hear the words of Sennacherib, which he has sent to mock the living God. ¹⁷Truly, O LORD, the kings of Assyria have laid waste the nations and their lands, ¹⁸and have hurled their gods into the fire, though they were no gods but the work of human hands—wood and stone—and so they were destroyed. ¹⁹So now, O LORD our God, save us, I pray you, from his hand, so that all the kingdoms of the earth may know that you, O LORD, are God alone.'

20 Then Isaiah son of Amoz sent to Hezekiah, saying, 'Thus says the LORD, the God of Israel: I have heard your prayer to me about King Sennacherib of Assyria. ²¹This is the word that the LORD has spoken concerning him:

She despises you, she scorns you—
    virgin daughter Zion;
she tosses her head—behind your
        back,
    daughter Jerusalem.

²² 'Whom have you mocked and
        reviled?
    Against whom have you raised your
        voice
and haughtily lifted your eyes?
    Against the Holy One of Israel!
²³ By your messengers you have mocked
        the Lord,
    and you have said, "With my many
        chariots
I have gone up the heights of the
        mountains,
    to the far recesses of Lebanon;
I felled its tallest cedars,
    its choicest cypresses;
I entered its farthest retreat,
    its densest forest.
²⁴ I dug wells
    and drank foreign waters,
I dried up with the sole of my foot
    all the streams of Egypt."

²⁵ 'Have you not heard
    that I determined it long ago?

The Campaign of Sennacherib

Mediterranean
Sea

Damascus

Ijon
Abel-beth-maacah
Hazor
Acco
Ashtaroth
Dor
Megiddo
Ramoth-gilead
Joppa   Aphek
Jerusalem
Lachish   Dead
            Sea
Gaza   Hebron

N

0   40 Mi.
0   40 Km.

I planned from days of old
　　what now I bring to pass,
　that you should make fortified cities
　　crash into heaps of ruins,
26 while their inhabitants, shorn of
　　　strength,
　　are dismayed and confounded;
　they have become like plants of the
　　　field
　　and like tender grass,
　like grass on the housetops,
　　blighted before it is grown.

27 'But I know your rising*a* and your
　　　sitting,
　　your going out and coming in,
　　and your raging against me.
28 Because you have raged against me
　　and your arrogance has come to my
　　　ears,
　I will put my hook in your nose
　　and my bit in your mouth;
　I will turn you back on the way
　　by which you came.

29 'And this shall be the sign for you:
This year you shall eat what grows of itself,
and in the second year what springs from
that; then in the third year sow, reap, plant
vineyards, and eat their fruit. 30 The surviving remnant of the house of Judah shall
again take root downwards, and bear fruit
upwards; 31 for from Jerusalem a remnant
shall go out, and from Mount Zion a band
of survivors. The zeal of the LORD of hosts
will do this.

32 'Therefore thus says the LORD concerning the king of Assyria: He shall not
come into this city, shoot an arrow there,
come before it with a shield, or cast up a
siege-ramp against it. 33 By the way that he
came, by the same he shall return; he shall
not come into this city, says the LORD.
34 For I will defend this city to save it, for
my own sake and for the sake of my servant David.'

Sennacherib's Defeat and Death

35 That very night the angel of the LORD
set out and struck down one hundred and
eighty-five thousand in the camp of the

Assyrians; when morning dawned, they
were all dead bodies. 36 Then King Sennacherib of Assyria left, went home, and
lived at Nineveh. 37 As he was worshipping
in the house of his god Nisroch, his sons
Adrammelech and Sharezer killed him
with the sword, and they escaped into the
land of Ararat. His son Esar-haddon succeeded him.

Hezekiah's Illness

20 In those days Hezekiah became
sick and was at the point of death.
The prophet Isaiah son of Amoz came to
him, and said to him, 'Thus says the LORD:
Set your house in order, for you shall die;
you shall not recover.' 2 Then Hezekiah
turned his face to the wall and prayed to
the LORD: 3 'Remember now, O LORD, I implore you, how I have walked before you
in faithfulness with a whole heart, and
have done what is good in your sight.'
Hezekiah wept bitterly. 4 Before Isaiah had
gone out of the middle court, the word of
the LORD came to him: 5 'Turn back, and
say to Hezekiah prince of my people, Thus
says the LORD, the God of your ancestor
David: I have heard your prayer, I have
seen your tears; indeed, I will heal you; on
the third day you shall go up to the house
of the LORD. 6 I will add fifteen years to
your life. I will deliver you and this city
out of the hand of the king of Assyria; I
will defend this city for my own sake and
for my servant David's sake.' 7 Then Isaiah
said, 'Bring a lump of figs. Let them take
it and apply it to the boil, so that he may
recover.'

8 Hezekiah said to Isaiah, 'What shall be
the sign that the LORD will heal me, and
that I shall go up to the house of the LORD
on the third day?' 9 Isaiah said, 'This is the
sign to you from the LORD, that the LORD
will do the thing that he has promised: the
shadow has now advanced ten intervals;
shall it retreat ten intervals?' 10 Hezekiah answered, 'It is normal for the shadow to
lengthen ten intervals; rather let the shadow retreat ten intervals.' 11 The prophet Isaiah cried to the LORD; and he brought the

a Gk Compare Isa 37.27 Q Ms: MT lacks *rising*

shadow back the ten intervals, by which the sun[a] had declined on the dial of Ahaz.

Envoys from Babylon

12 At that time King Merodach-baladan son of Baladan of Babylon sent envoys with letters and a present to Hezekiah, for he had heard that Hezekiah had been sick. [13] Hezekiah welcomed them;[b] he showed them all his treasure house, the silver, the gold, the spices, the precious oil, his armoury, all that was found in his storehouses; there was nothing in his house or in all his realm that Hezekiah did not show them. [14] Then the prophet Isaiah came to King Hezekiah, and said to him, 'What did these men say? From where did they come to you?' Hezekiah answered, 'They have come from a far country, from Babylon.' [15] He said, 'What have they seen in your house?' Hezekiah answered, 'They have seen all that is in my house; there is nothing in my storehouses that I did not show them.'

16 Then Isaiah said to Hezekiah, 'Hear the word of the LORD: [17] Days are coming when all that is in your house, and that which your ancestors have stored up until this day, shall be carried to Babylon; nothing shall be left, says the LORD. [18] Some of your own sons who are born to you shall be taken away; they shall be eunuchs in the palace of the king of Babylon.' [19] Then Hezekiah said to Isaiah, 'The word of the LORD that you have spoken is good.' For he thought, 'Why not, if there will be peace and security in my days?'

Death of Hezekiah

20 The rest of the deeds of Hezekiah, all his power, how he made the pool and the conduit and brought water into the city, are they not written in the Book of the Annals of the Kings of Judah? [21] Hezekiah slept with his ancestors; and his son Manasseh succeeded him.

Manasseh Reigns over Judah

21 Manasseh was twelve years old when he began to reign; he reigned for fifty-five years in Jerusalem. His mother's name was Hephzibah. [2] He did what was evil in the sight of the LORD, following the abominable practices of the nations that the LORD drove out before the people of Israel. [3] For he rebuilt the high places that his father Hezekiah had destroyed; he erected altars for Baal, made a sacred pole,[c] as King Ahab of Israel had done, worshipped all the host of heaven, and served them. [4] He built altars in the house of the LORD, of which the LORD had said, 'In Jerusalem I will put my name.' [5] He built altars for all the host of heaven in the two courts of the house of the LORD. [6] He made his son pass through fire; he practised soothsaying and augury, and dealt with mediums and with wizards. He did much evil in the sight of the LORD, provoking him to anger. [7] The carved image of Asherah that he had made he set in the house of which the LORD said to David and to his son Solomon, 'In this house, and in Jerusalem, which I have chosen out of all the tribes of Israel, I will put my name for ever; [8] I will not cause the feet of Israel to wander any more out of the land that I gave to their ancestors, if only they will be careful to do according to all that I have commanded them, and according to all the law that my servant Moses commanded them.' [9] But they did not listen; Manasseh misled them to do more evil than the nations had done that the LORD destroyed before the people of Israel.

10 The LORD said by his servants the prophets, [11] 'Because King Manasseh of Judah has committed these abominations, has done things more wicked than all that the Amorites did, who were before him, and has caused Judah also to sin with his idols; [12] therefore thus says the LORD, the God of Israel, I am bringing upon Jerusalem and Judah such evil that the ears of everyone who hears of it will tingle. [13] I will stretch over Jerusalem the measuring line for Samaria, and the plummet for the house of Ahab; I will wipe Jerusalem as one wipes a dish, wiping it and turning it upside down. [14] I will cast off the remnant

a Syr See Isa 38.8 and Tg: Heb *it*   *b* Gk Vg Syr: Heb *When Hezekiah heard about them*   *c* Heb *Asherah* of my heritage, and give them into the hand of their enemies; they shall become a prey and a spoil to all their enemies, [15] because they have done what is evil in my sight and have provoked me to anger, since the day their ancestors came out of Egypt, even to this day.'

16 Moreover, Manasseh shed very much innocent blood, until he had filled Jerusalem from one end to another, besides the sin that he caused Judah to sin so that they did what was evil in the sight of the LORD.

17 Now the rest of the acts of Manasseh, all that he did, and the sin that he committed, are they not written in the Book of the Annals of the Kings of Judah? [18] Manasseh slept with his ancestors, and was buried in the garden of his house, in the garden of Uzza. His son Amon succeeded him.

Amon Reigns over Judah

19 Amon was twenty-two years old when he began to reign; he reigned for two years in Jerusalem. His mother's name was Meshullemeth daughter of Haruz of Jotbah. [20] He did what was evil in the sight of the LORD, as his father Manasseh had done. [21] He walked in all the way in which his father walked, served the idols that his father served, and worshipped them; [22] he abandoned the LORD, the God of his ancestors, and did not walk in the way of the LORD. [23] The servants of Amon conspired against him, and killed the king in his house. [24] But the people of the land killed all those who had conspired against King Amon, and the people of the land made his son Josiah king in place of him. [25] Now the rest of the acts of Amon that he did, are they not written in the Book of the Annals of the Kings of Judah? [26] He was buried in his tomb in the garden of Uzza; then his son Josiah succeeded him.

Josiah Reigns over Judah

22 Josiah was eight years old when he began to reign; he reigned for thirty-one years in Jerusalem. His mother's name was Jedidah daughter of Adaiah of Bozkath. [2] He did what was right in the sight of the LORD, and walked in all the way of his father David; he did not turn aside to the right or to the left.

Hilkiah Finds the Book of the Law

3 In the eighteenth year of King Josiah, the king sent Shaphan son of Azaliah, son of Meshullam, the secretary, to the house of the LORD, saying, [4] 'Go up to the high priest Hilkiah, and have him count the entire sum of the money that has been brought into the house of the LORD, which the keepers of the threshold have collected from the people; [5] let it be given into the hand of the workers who have the oversight of the house of the LORD; let them give it to the workers who are at the house of the LORD, repairing the house, [6] that is, to the carpenters, to the builders, to the masons; and let them use it to buy timber and quarried stone to repair the house. [7] But no account shall be asked from them for the money that is delivered into their hand, for they deal honestly.'

8 The high priest Hilkiah said to Shaphan the secretary, 'I have found the book of the law in the house of the LORD.' When Hilkiah gave the book to Shaphan, he read it. [9] Then Shaphan the secretary came to the king, and reported to the king, 'Your servants have emptied out the money that was found in the house, and have delivered it into the hand of the workers who have oversight of the house of the LORD.' [10] Shaphan the secretary informed the king, 'The priest Hilkiah has given me a book.' Shaphan then read it aloud to the king.

11 When the king heard the words of the book of the law, he tore his clothes. [12] Then the king commanded the priest Hilkiah, Ahikam son of Shaphan, Achbor son of Micaiah, Shaphan the secretary, and the king's servant Asaiah, saying, [13] 'Go, inquire of the LORD for me, for the people, and for all Judah, concerning the words of this book that has been found; for great is the wrath of the LORD that is kindled against us, because our ancestors did not obey the words of this book, to do according to all that is written concerning us.'

14 So the priest Hilkiah, Ahikam, Achbor, Shaphan, and Asaiah went to the prophetess Huldah the wife of Shallum son of Tikvah, son of Harhas, keeper of the wardrobe; she resided in Jerusalem in the Second Quarter, where they consulted her. 15 She declared to them, 'Thus says the LORD, the God of Israel: Tell the man who sent you to me, 16 Thus says the LORD, I will indeed bring disaster on this place and on its inhabitants—all the words of the book that the king of Judah has read. 17 Because they have abandoned me and have made offerings to other gods, so that they have provoked me to anger with all the work of their hands, therefore my wrath will be kindled against this place, and it will not be quenched. 18 But as to the king of Judah, who sent you to inquire of the LORD, thus shall you say to him, Thus says the LORD, the God of Israel: Regarding the words that you have heard, 19 because your heart was penitent, and you humbled yourself before the LORD, when you heard how I spoke against this place, and against its inhabitants, that they should become a desolation and a curse, and because you have torn your clothes and wept before me, I also have heard you, says the LORD. 20 Therefore, I will gather you to your ancestors, and you shall be gathered to your grave in peace; your eyes shall not see all the disaster that I will bring on this place.' They took the message back to the king.

Josiah's Reformation

23 Then the king directed that all the elders of Judah and Jerusalem should be gathered to him. 2 The king went up to the house of the LORD, and with him went all the people of Judah, all the inhabitants of Jerusalem, the priests, the prophets, and all the people, both small and great; he read in their hearing all the words of the book of the covenant that had been found in the house of the LORD. 3 The king stood by the pillar and made a covenant before the LORD, to follow the LORD, keeping his commandments, his decrees, and his statutes, with all his heart and all his soul, to perform the words of this covenant that

were written in this book. All the people joined in the covenant.

4 The king commanded the high priest Hilkiah, the priests of the second order, and the guardians of the threshold, to bring out of the temple of the LORD all the vessels made for Baal, for Asherah, and for all the host of heaven; he burned them outside Jerusalem in the fields of the Kidron, and carried their ashes to Bethel. 5 He deposed the idolatrous priests whom the kings of Judah had ordained to make offerings in the high places at the cities of Judah and around Jerusalem; those also who made offerings to Baal, to the sun, the moon, the constellations, and all the host of the heavens. 6 He brought out the image of *a* Asherah from the house of the LORD, outside Jerusalem, to the Wadi Kidron, burned it at the Wadi Kidron, beat it to dust and threw the dust of it upon the graves of the common people. 7 He broke down the houses of the male temple prostitutes that were in the house of the LORD, where the women did weaving for Asherah. 8 He brought all the priests out of the towns of Judah, and defiled the high places where the priests had made offerings, from Geba to Beer-sheba; he broke down the high places of the gates that were at the entrance of the gate of Joshua the governor of the city, which were on the left at the gate of the city. 9 The priests of the high places, however, did not come up to the altar of the LORD in Jerusalem, but ate unleavened bread among their kindred. 10 He defiled Topheth, which is in the valley of Ben-hinnom, so that no one would make a son or a daughter pass through fire as an offering to Molech. 11 He removed the horses that the kings of Judah had dedicated to the sun, at the entrance to the house of the LORD, by the chamber of the eunuch Nathan-melech, which was in the precincts; *b* then he burned the chariots of the sun with fire. 12 The altars on the roof of the upper chamber of Ahaz, which the kings of Judah had made, and the altars that Manasseh had made in the two courts of the house of the LORD, he pulled down

a Heb lacks *image of*   *b* Meaning of Heb uncertain

from there and broke in pieces, and threw the rubble into the Wadi Kidron. 13 The king defiled the high places that were east of Jerusalem, to the south of the Mount of Destruction, which King Solomon of Israel had built for Astarte the abomination of the Sidonians, for Chemosh the abomination of Moab, and for Milcom the abomination of the Ammonites. 14 He broke the pillars in pieces, cut down the sacred poles, *a* and covered the sites with human bones.

15 Moreover, the altar at Bethel, the high place erected by Jeroboam son of Nebat, who caused Israel to sin—he pulled down that altar along with the high place. He burned the high place, crushing it to dust; he also burned the sacred pole. *b* 16 As Josiah turned, he saw the tombs there on the mount; and he sent and took the bones out of the tombs, and burned them on the altar, and defiled it, according to the word of the LORD that the man of God proclaimed, *c* when Jeroboam stood by the altar at the festival; he turned and looked up at the tomb of the man of God who had predicted these things. 17 Then he said, 'What is that monument that I see?' The people of the city told him, 'It is the tomb of the man of God who came from Judah and predicted these things that you have done against the altar at Bethel.' 18 He said, 'Let him rest; let no one move his bones.' So they let his bones alone, with the bones of the prophet who came out of Samaria. 19 Moreover, Josiah removed all the shrines of the high places that were in the towns of Samaria, which kings of Israel had made, provoking the LORD to anger; he did to them just as he had done at Bethel. 20 He slaughtered on the altars all the priests of the high places who were there, and burned human bones on them. Then he returned to Jerusalem.

The Passover Celebrated

21 The king commanded all the people, 'Keep the passover to the LORD your God as prescribed in this book of the covenant.' 22 No such passover had been kept since the days of the judges who judged Israel, even during all the days of the kings of Israel and of the kings of Judah; 23 but in the eighteenth year of King Josiah this passover was kept to the LORD in Jerusalem.

24 Moreover, Josiah did away with the mediums, wizards, teraphim, *d* idols, and all the abominations that were seen in the land of Judah and in Jerusalem, so that he established the words of the law that were written in the book that the priest Hilkiah had found in the house of the LORD. 25 Before him there was no king like him, who turned to the LORD with all his heart, with all his soul, and with all his might, according to all the law of Moses; nor did any like him arise after him.

26 Still the LORD did not turn from the fierceness of his great wrath, by which his anger was kindled against Judah, because of all the provocations with which Manasseh had provoked him. 27 The LORD said, 'I will remove Judah also out of my sight, as I have removed Israel; and I will reject this city that I have chosen, Jerusalem, and the house of which I said, My name shall be there.'

Josiah Dies in Battle

28 Now the rest of the acts of Josiah, and all that he did, are they not written in the Book of the Annals of the Kings of Judah? 29 In his days Pharaoh Neco king of Egypt went up to the king of Assyria to the river Euphrates. King Josiah went to meet him; but when Pharaoh Neco met him at Megiddo, he killed him. 30 His servants carried him dead in a chariot from Megiddo, brought him to Jerusalem, and buried him in his own tomb. The people of the land took Jehoahaz son of Josiah, anointed him, and made him king in place of his father.

Reign and Captivity of Jehoahaz

31 Jehoahaz was twenty-three years old when he began to reign; he reigned for three months in Jerusalem. His mother's name was Hamutal daughter of Jeremiah

a Heb *Asherim*   *b* Heb *Asherah*   *c* Gk: Heb *proclaimed, who had predicted these things*
d Or *household gods*

of Libnah. 32 He did what was evil in the sight of the LORD, just as his ancestors had done. 33 Pharaoh Neco confined him at Riblah in the land of Hamath, so that he might not reign in Jerusalem, and imposed tribute on the land of one hundred talents of silver and a talent of gold. 34 Pharaoh Neco made Eliakim son of Josiah king in place of his father Josiah, and changed his name to Jehoiakim. But he took Jehoahaz away; he came to Egypt, and died there. 35 Jehoiakim gave the silver and the gold to Pharaoh, but he taxed the land in order to meet Pharaoh's demand for money. He exacted the silver and the gold from the people of the land, from all according to their assessment, to give it to Pharaoh Neco.

Jehoiakim Reigns over Judah

36 Jehoiakim was twenty-five years old when he began to reign; he reigned for eleven years in Jerusalem. His mother's name was Zebidah daughter of Pedaiah of Rumah. 37 He did what was evil in the sight of the LORD, just as all his ancestors had done.

Judah Overrun by Enemies

24 In his days King Nebuchadnezzar of Babylon came up; Jehoiakim became his servant for three years; then he turned and rebelled against him. 2 The LORD sent against him bands of the Chaldeans, bands of the Arameans, bands of the Moabites, and bands of the Ammonites; he sent them against Judah to destroy it, according to the word of the LORD that he spoke by his servants the prophets. 3 Surely this came upon Judah at the command of the LORD, to remove them out of his sight, for the sins of Manasseh, for all that he had committed, 4 and also for the innocent blood that he had shed; for he filled Jerusalem with innocent blood, and the LORD was not willing to pardon. 5 Now the rest of the deeds of Jehoiakim, and all that he did, are they not written in the Book of the Annals of the Kings of Judah? 6 So Jehoiakim slept with his ancestors; then his son Jehoiachin succeeded him. 7 The king of Egypt did not come again out

of his land, for the king of Babylon had taken over all that belonged to the king of Egypt from the Wadi of Egypt to the River Euphrates.

Reign and Captivity of Jehoiachin

8 Jehoiachin was eighteen years old when he began to reign; he reigned for three months in Jerusalem. His mother's name was Nehushta daughter of Elnathan of Jerusalem. 9 He did what was evil in the sight of the LORD, just as his father had done.

10 At that time the servants of King Nebuchadnezzar of Babylon came up to Jerusalem, and the city was besieged. 11 King Nebuchadnezzar of Babylon came to the city, while his servants were besieging it; 12 King Jehoiachin of Judah gave himself up to the king of Babylon, himself, his mother, his servants, his officers, and his palace officials. The king of Babylon took him prisoner in the eighth year of his reign.

Capture of Jerusalem

13 He carried off all the treasures of the house of the LORD, and the treasures of the king's house; he cut in pieces all the vessels of gold in the temple of the LORD, which King Solomon of Israel had made, all this as the LORD had foretold. 14 He carried away all Jerusalem, all the officials, all the warriors, ten thousand captives, all the artisans and the smiths; no one remained, except the poorest people of the land. 15 He carried away Jehoiachin to Babylon; the king's mother, the king's wives, his officials, and the elite of the land, he took into captivity from Jerusalem to Babylon. 16 The king of Babylon brought captive to Babylon all the men of valour, seven thousand, the artisans and the smiths, one thousand, all of them strong and fit for war. 17 The king of Babylon made Mattaniah, Jehoiachin's uncle, king in his place, and changed his name to Zedekiah.

Zedekiah Reigns over Judah

18 Zedekiah was twenty-one years old when he began to reign; he reigned for

eleven years in Jerusalem. His mother's name was Hamutal daughter of Jeremiah of Libnah. [19] He did what was evil in the sight of the LORD, just as Jehoiakim had done. [20] Indeed, Jerusalem and Judah so angered the LORD that he expelled them from his presence.

The Fall and Captivity of Judah

25 Zedekiah rebelled against the king of Babylon. [1] And in the ninth year of his reign, in the tenth month, on the tenth day of the month, King Nebuchadnezzar of Babylon came with all his army against Jerusalem, and laid siege to it; they built siege-works against it all round. [2] So the city was besieged until the eleventh year of King Zedekiah. [3] On the ninth day of the fourth month the famine became so severe in the city that there was no food for the people of the land. [4] Then a breach was made in the city wall;[a] the king with all the soldiers fled[b] by night by the way of the gate between the two walls, by the king's garden, though the Chaldeans were all round the city. They went in the direction of the Arabah. [5] But the army of the Chaldeans pursued the king, and overtook him in the plains of Jericho; all his army was scattered, deserting him. [6] Then they captured the king and brought him up to the king of Babylon at Riblah, who passed sentence on him. [7] They slaughtered the sons of Zedekiah before his eyes, then put out the eyes of Zedekiah; they bound him in fetters and took him to Babylon.

8 In the fifth month, on the seventh day of the month—which was the nineteenth year of King Nebuchadnezzar, king of Babylon—Nebuzaradan, the captain of the bodyguard, a servant of the king of Babylon, came to Jerusalem. [9] He burned the house of the LORD, the king's house, and all the houses of Jerusalem; every great house he burned down. [10] All the army of the Chaldeans who were with the captain of the guard broke down the walls around Jerusalem. [11] Nebuzaradan the captain of the guard carried into exile the rest of the people who were left in the city and the deserters who had defected to the king of Babylon—all the rest of the population. [12] But the captain of the guard left some of the poorest people of the land to be vinedressers and tillers of the soil.

13 The bronze pillars that were in the house of the LORD, as well as the stands and the bronze sea that were in the house of the LORD, the Chaldeans broke in pieces, and carried the bronze to Babylon. [14] They took away the pots, the shovels, the snuffers, the dishes for incense, and all the bronze vessels used in the temple service, [15] as well as the firepans and the basins. What was made of gold the captain of the guard took away for the gold, and what was made of silver, for the silver. [16] As for the two pillars, the one sea, and the stands, which Solomon had made for the house of the LORD, the bronze of all these vessels was beyond weighing. [17] The height of one pillar was eighteen cubits, and on it was a bronze capital; the height of the capital was three cubits; lattice-work and pomegranates, all of

Nebuchadnezzar's Campaigns Against Judah

Damascus

Mediterranean Sea

Hazor

Megiddo

Jerusalem

Azekah   Dead Sea

Lachish   Hebron

0   40 Mi.
0   40 Km.

a Heb lacks *wall*   *b* Gk Compare Jer 39.4; 52.7: Heb lacks *the king* and lacks *fled* bronze, were on the capital all round. The second pillar had the same, with the latticework.

18 The captain of the guard took the chief priest Seraiah, the second priest Zephaniah, and the three guardians of the threshold; 19 from the city he took an officer who had been in command of the soldiers, and five men of the king's council who were found in the city; the secretary who was the commander of the army who mustered the people of the land; and sixty men of the people of the land who were found in the city. 20 Nebuzaradan the captain of the guard took them, and brought them to the king of Babylon at Riblah. 21 The king of Babylon struck them down and put them to death at Riblah in the land of Hamath. So Judah went into exile out of its land.

Gedaliah Made Governor of Judah

22 He appointed Gedaliah son of Ahikam son of Shaphan as governor over the people who remained in the land of Judah, whom King Nebuchadnezzar of Babylon had left. 23 Now when all the captains of the forces and their men heard that the king of Babylon had appointed Gedaliah as governor, they came with their men to Gedaliah at Mizpah, namely, Ishmael son of Nethaniah, Johanan son of Kareah, Seraiah son of Tanhumeth the Netophathite, and Jaazaniah son of the Maacathite. 24 Gedaliah swore to them and their men, saying, 'Do not be afraid because of the Chaldean officials; live in the land, serve the king of Babylon, and it shall be well with you.' 25 But in the seventh month, Ishmael son of Nethaniah son of Elishama, of the royal family, came with ten men; they struck down Gedaliah so that he died, along with the Judeans and Chaldeans who were with him at Mizpah. 26 Then all the people, high and low,*a* and the captains of the forces, set out and went to Egypt; for they were afraid of the Chaldeans.

Jehoiachin Released from Prison

27 In the thirty-seventh year of the exile of King Jehoiachin of Judah, in the twelfth month, on the twenty-seventh day of the month, King Evil-merodach of Babylon, in the year that he began to reign, released King Jehoiachin of Judah from prison; 28 he spoke kindly to him, and gave him a seat above the other seats of the kings who were with him in Babylon. 29 So Jehoiachin put aside his prison clothes. Every day of his life he dined regularly in the king's presence. 30 For his allowance, a regular allowance was given him by the king, a portion every day, as long as he lived.

a Or *young and old*

1 CHRONICLES

From Adam to Abraham

1 Adam, Seth, Enosh; ² Kenan, Maha-lalel, Jared; ³ Enoch, Methuselah, La-mech; ⁴ Noah, Shem, Ham, and Japheth.

5 The descendants of Japheth: Gomer, Magog, Madai, Javan, Tubal, Meshech, and Tiras. ⁶ The descendants of Gomer: Ashke-naz, Diphath,*a* and Togarmah. ⁷ The de-scendants of Javan: Elishah, Tarshish, Kit-tim, and Rodanim.*b*

8 The descendants of Ham: Cush, Egypt, Put, and Canaan. ⁹ The descendants of Cush: Seba, Havilah, Sabta, Raama, and Sabteca. The descendants of Raamah: She-ba and Dedan. ¹⁰ Cush became the father of Nimrod; he was the first to be a mighty one on the earth.

11 Egypt became the father of Ludim, Anamim, Lehabim, Naphtuhim, ¹² Pathru-sim, Casluhim, and Caphtorim, from whom the Philistines come.*c*

13 Canaan became the father of Sidon his firstborn, and Heth, ¹⁴ and the Jebu-sites, the Amorites, the Girgashites, ¹⁵ the Hivites, the Arkites, the Sinites, ¹⁶ the Ar-vadites, the Zemarites, and the Hamath-ites.

17 The descendants of Shem: Elam, As-shur, Arpachshad, Lud, Aram, Uz, Hul, Ge-ther, and Meshech.*d* ¹⁸ Arpachshad became the father of Shelah; and Shelah became the father of Eber. ¹⁹ To Eber were born two sons: the name of one was Peleg (for in his days the earth was divided), and the name of his brother Joktan. ²⁰ Joktan became the father of Almodad, Sheleph, Hazarmaveth, Jerah, ²¹ Hadoram, Uzal, Diklah, ²² Ebal, Abimael, Sheba, ²³ Ophir, Havilah, and Jo-bab; all these were the descendants of Jok-tan.

24 Shem, Arpachshad, Shelah; ²⁵ Eber, Peleg, Reu; ²⁶ Serug, Nahor, Terah; ²⁷ Abram, that is, Abraham.

From Abraham to Jacob

28 The sons of Abraham: Isaac and Ish-mael. ²⁹ These are their genealogies: the firstborn of Ishmael, Nebaioth; and Kedar, Adbeel, Mibsam, ³⁰ Mishma, Dumah, Mas-sa, Hadad, Tema, ³¹ Jetur, Naphish, and Ked-emah. These are the sons of Ishmael. ³² The sons of Keturah, Abraham's concubine: she bore Zimran, Jokshan, Medan, Midian, Ish-bak, and Shuah. The sons of Jokshan: Sheba and Dedan. ³³ The sons of Midian: Ephah, Epher, Hanoch, Abida, and Eldaah. All these were the descendants of Keturah.

34 Abraham became the father of Isaac. The sons of Isaac: Esau and Israel. ³⁵ The sons of Esau: Eliphaz, Reuel, Jeush, Jalam, and Korah. ³⁶ The sons of Eliphaz: Teman, Omar, Zephi, Gatam, Kenaz, Timna, and Amalek. ³⁷ The sons of Reuel: Nahath, Ze-rah, Shammah, and Mizzah.

38 The sons of Seir: Lotan, Shobal, Zib-eon, Anah, Dishon, Ezer, and Dishan. ³⁹ The sons of Lotan: Hori and Homam; and Lotan's sister was Timna. ⁴⁰ The sons of Shobal: Alian, Manahath, Ebal, Shephi, and Onam. The sons of Zibeon: Aiah and Anah. ⁴¹ The sons of Anah: Dishon. The sons of Dishon: Hamran, Eshban, Ithran, and Cheran. ⁴² The sons of Ezer: Bilhan, Zaavan, and Jaakan.*e* The sons of Dishan:*f* Uz and Aran.

a Gen 10.3 *Ripath*; See Gk Vg   *b* Gen 10.4 *Dodanim*; See Syr Vg   *c* Heb *Casluhim, from which the Philistines come, Caphtorim*; See Am 9.7, Jer 47.4   *d* *Mash* in Gen 10.23   *e* Or *and Akan*; See Gen 36.27   *f* See 1.38: Heb *Dishon*

43 These are the kings who reigned in the land of Edom before any king reigned over the Israelites: Bela son of Beor, whose city was called Dinhabah. 44 When Bela died, Jobab son of Zerah of Bozrah succeeded him. 45 When Jobab died, Husham of the land of the Temanites succeeded him. 46 When Husham died, Hadad son of Bedad, who defeated Midian in the country of Moab, succeeded him; and the name of his city was Avith. 47 When Hadad died, Samlah of Masrekah succeeded him. 48 When Samlah died, Shaul*a* of Rehoboth on the Euphrates succeeded him. 49 When Shaul*a* died, Baal-hanan son of Achbor succeeded him. 50 When Baal-hanan died, Hadad succeeded him; the name of his city was Pai, and his wife's name Mehetabel daughter of Matred, daughter of Me-zahab. 51 And Hadad died.

The clans*b* of Edom were: clans*b* Timna, Aliah,*c* Jetheth, 52 Oholibamah, Elah, Pinon, 53 Kenaz, Teman, Mibzar, 54 Magdiel, and Iram; these are the clans*b* of Edom.

The Sons of Israel and the Descendants of Judah

2 These are the sons of Israel: Reuben, Simeon, Levi, Judah, Issachar, Zebulun, 2 Dan, Joseph, Benjamin, Naphtali, Gad, and Asher. 3 The sons of Judah: Er, Onan, and Shelah; these three the Canaanite woman Bath-shua bore to him. Now Er, Judah's firstborn, was wicked in the sight of the LORD, and he put him to death. 4 His daughter-in-law Tamar also bore him Perez and Zerah. Judah had five sons in all.

5 The sons of Perez: Hezron and Hamul. 6 The sons of Zerah: Zimri, Ethan, Heman, Calcol, and Dara,*d* five in all. 7 The sons of Carmi: Achar, the troubler of Israel, who transgressed in the matter of the devoted thing; 8 and Ethan's son was Azariah.

9 The sons of Hezron, who were born to him: Jerahmeel, Ram, and Chelubai. 10 Ram became the father of Amminadab, and Amminadab became the father of Nahshon, prince of the sons of Judah. 11 Nahshon became the father of Salma, Salma of Boaz, 12 Boaz of Obed, Obed of

Jesse. 13 Jesse became the father of Eliab his firstborn, Abinadab the second, Shimea the third, 14 Nethanel the fourth, Raddai the fifth, 15 Ozem the sixth, David the seventh; 16 and their sisters were Zeruiah and Abigail. The sons of Zeruiah: Abishai, Joab, and Asahel, three. 17 Abigail bore Amasa, and the father of Amasa was Jether the Ishmaelite.

18 Caleb son of Hezron had children by his wife Azubah, and by Jerioth; these were her sons: Jesher, Shobab, and Ardon. 19 When Azubah died, Caleb married Ephrath, who bore him Hur. 20 Hur became the father of Uri, and Uri became the father of Bezalel.

21 Afterwards Hezron went in to the daughter of Machir father of Gilead, whom he married when he was sixty years old; and she bore him Segub; 22 and Segub became the father of Jair, who had twenty-three towns in the land of Gilead. 23 But Geshur and Aram took from them Havvoth-jair, Kenath and its villages, sixty towns. All these were descendants of Machir, father of Gilead. 24 After the death of Hezron, in Caleb-ephrathah, Abijah wife of Hezron bore him Ashhur, father of Tekoa.

25 The sons of Jerahmeel, the firstborn of Hezron: Ram his firstborn, Bunah, Oren, Ozem, and Ahijah. 26 Jerahmeel also had another wife, whose name was Atarah; she was the mother of Onam. 27 The sons of Ram, the firstborn of Jerahmeel: Maaz, Jamin, and Eker. 28 The sons of Onam: Shammai and Jada. The sons of Shammai: Nadab and Abishur. 29 The name of Abishur's wife was Abihail, and she bore him Ahban and Molid. 30 The sons of Nadab: Seled and Appaim; and Seled died childless. 31 The son*e* of Appaim: Ishi. The son*e* of Ishi: Sheshan. The son*e* of Sheshan: Ahlai. 32 The sons of Jada, Shammai's brother: Jether and Jonathan; and Jether died childless. 33 The sons of Jonathan: Peleth and Zaza. These were the descendants of Jerahmeel. 34 Now Sheshan had no sons,

---

a Or Saul   *b* Or chiefs   *c* Or Alvah; See Gen 36.40
d Or Darda; Compare Syr Tg some Gk Mss; See
1 Kings 4.31   *e* Heb sons

only daughters; but Sheshan had an Egyptian slave, whose name was Jarha. 35 So Sheshan gave his daughter in marriage to his slave Jarha; and she bore him Attai. 36 Attai became the father of Nathan, and Nathan of Zabad. 37 Zabad became the father of Ephlal, and Ephlal of Obed. 38 Obed became the father of Jehu, and Jehu of Azariah. 39 Azariah became the father of Helez, and Helez of Eleasah. 40 Eleasah became the father of Sismai, and Sismai of Shallum. 41 Shallum became the father of Jekamiah, and Jekamiah of Elishama.

42 The sons of Caleb brother of Jerahmeel: Mesha[a] his firstborn, who was father of Ziph. The sons of Mareshah father of Hebron. 43 The sons of Hebron: Korah, Tappuah, Rekem, and Shema. 44 Shema became father of Raham, father of Jorkeam; and Rekem became the father of Shammai. 45 The son of Shammai: Maon; and Maon was the father of Beth-zur. 46 Ephah also, Caleb's concubine, bore Haran, Moza, and Gazez; and Haran became the father of Gazez. 47 The sons of Jahdai: Regem, Jotham, Geshan, Pelet, Ephah, and Shaaph. 48 Maacah, Caleb's concubine, bore Sheber and Tirhanah. 49 She also bore Shaaph father of Madmannah, Sheva father of Machbenah and father of Gibea; and the daughter of Caleb was Achsah. 50 These were the descendants of Caleb.

The sons[b] of Hur the firstborn of Ephrathah: Shobal father of Kiriath-jearim, 51 Salma father of Bethlehem, and Hareph father of Beth-gader. 52 Shobal father of Kiriath-jearim had other sons: Haroeh, half of the Menuhoth. 53 And the families of Kiriath-jearim: the Ithrites, the Puthites, the Shumathites, and the Mishraites; from these came the Zorathites and the Eshtaolites. 54 The sons of Salma: Bethlehem, the Netophathites, Atroth-beth-joab, and half of the Manahathites, the Zorites. 55 The families also of the scribes that lived at Jabez: the Tirathites, the Shimeathites, and the Sucathites. These are the Kenites who came from Hammath, father of the house of Rechab.

Descendants of David and Solomon

3 These are the sons of David who were born to him in Hebron: the firstborn Amnon, by Ahinoam the Jezreelite; the second Daniel, by Abigail the Carmelite; 2 the third Absalom, son of Maacah, daughter of King Talmai of Geshur; the fourth Adonijah, son of Haggith; 3 the fifth Shephatiah, by Abital; the sixth Ithream, by his wife Eglah; 4 six were born to him in Hebron, where he reigned for seven years and six months. And he reigned for thirty-three years in Jerusalem. 5 These were born to him in Jerusalem: Shimea, Shobab, Nathan, and Solomon, four by Bath-shua, daughter of Ammiel; 6 then Ibhar, Elishama, Eliphelet, 7 Nogah, Nepheg, Japhia, 8 Elishama, Eliada, and Eliphelet, nine. 9 All these were David's sons, besides the sons of the concubines; and Tamar was their sister.

10 The descendants of Solomon: Rehoboam, Abijah his son, Asa his son, Jehoshaphat his son, 11 Joram his son, Ahaziah his son, Joash his son, 12 Amaziah his son, Azariah his son, Jotham his son, 13 Ahaz his son, Hezekiah his son, Manasseh his son, 14 Amon his son, Josiah his son. 15 The sons of Josiah: Johanan the firstborn, the second Jehoiakim, the third Zedekiah, the fourth Shallum. 16 The descendants of Jehoiakim: Jeconiah his son, Zedekiah his son; 17 and the sons of Jeconiah, the captive: Shealtiel his son, 18 Malchiram, Pedaiah, Shenazzar, Jekamiah, Hoshama, and Nedabiah; 19 The sons of Pedaiah: Zerubbabel and Shimei; and the sons of Zerubbabel: Meshullam and Hananiah, and Shelomith was their sister; 20 and Hashubah, Ohel, Berechiah, Hasadiah, and Jushab-hesed, five. 21 The sons of Hananiah: Pelatiah and Jeshaiah, his son[c] Rephaiah, his son[c] Arnan, his son[c] Obadiah, his son[c] Shecaniah. 22 The son[d] of Shecaniah: Shemaiah. And the sons of Shemaiah: Hattush, Igal, Bariah, Neariah, and Shaphat, six. 23 The sons of Neariah: Elioenai, Hizkiah, and Azrikam, three. 24 The sons of Elioenai: Hodaviah, Elia-

a Gk reads Mareshah   b Gk Vg: Heb son
c Gk Compare Syr Vg: Heb sons of   d Heb sons

shib, Pelaiah, Akkub, Johanan, Delaiah, and Anani, seven.

Descendants of Judah

4 The sons of Judah: Perez, Hezron, Carmi, Hur, and Shobal. [2] Reaiah son of Shobal became the father of Jahath, and Jahath became the father of Ahumai and Lahad. These were the families of the Zorathites. [3] These were the sons[a] of Etam: Jezreel, Ishma, and Idbash; and the name of their sister was Hazzelelponi, [4] and Penuel was the father of Gedor, and Ezer the father of Hushah. These were the sons of Hur, the firstborn of Ephrathah, the father of Bethlehem. [5] Ashhur father of Tekoa had two wives, Helah and Naarah; [6] Naarah bore him Ahuzzam, Hepher, Temeni, and Haahashtari.[b] These were the sons of Naarah. [7] The sons of Helah: Zereth, Izhar,[c] and Ethnan. [8] Koz became the father of Anub, Zobebah, and the families of Aharhel son of Harum. [9] Jabez was honoured more than his brothers; and his mother named him Jabez, saying, 'Because I bore him in pain.' [10] Jabez called on the God of Israel, saying, 'Oh that you would bless me and enlarge my border, and that your hand might be with me, and that you would keep me from hurt and harm!' And God granted what he asked. [11] Chelub the brother of Shuhah became the father of Mehir, who was the father of Eshton. [12] Eshton became the father of Beth-rapha, Paseah, and Tehinnah the father of Ir-nahash. These are the men of Recah. [13] The sons of Kenaz: Othniel and Seraiah; and the sons of Othniel: Hathath and Meonothai.[d] [14] Meonothai became the father of Ophrah; and Seraiah became the father of Joab father of Ge-harashim,[e] so-called because they were artisans. [15] The sons of Caleb son of Jephunneh: Iru, Elah, and Naam; and the son[f] of Elah: Kenaz. [16] The sons of Jehallelel: Ziph, Ziphah, Tiria, and Asarel. [17] The sons of Ezrah: Jether, Mered, Epher, and Jalon. These are the sons of Bithiah, daughter of Pharaoh, whom Mered married;[g] and she conceived and bore[h] Miriam, Shammai, and Ishbah father of Eshtemoa. [18] And his Judean wife bore Je-

red father of Gedor, Heber father of Soco, and Jekuthiel father of Zanoah. [19] The sons of the wife of Hodiah, the sister of Naham, were the fathers of Keilah the Garmite and Eshtemoa the Maacathite. [20] The sons of Shimon: Amnon, Rinnah, Ben-hanan, and Tilon. The sons of Ishi: Zoheth and Benzoheth. [21] The sons of Shelah son of Judah: Er father of Lecah, Laadah father of Mareshah, and the families of the guild of linen workers at Beth-ashbea; [22] and Jokim, and the men of Cozeba, and Joash, and Saraph, who married into Moab but returned to Lehem[i] (now the records[j] are ancient). [23] These were the potters and inhabitants of Netaim and Gederah; they lived there with the king in his service.

Descendants of Simeon

24 The sons of Simeon: Nemuel, Jamin, Jarib, Zerah, Shaul;[k] [25] Shallum was his son, Mibsam his son, Mishma his son. [26] The sons of Mishma: Hammuel his son, Zaccur his son, Shimei his son. [27] Shimei had sixteen sons and six daughters; but his brothers did not have many children, nor did all their family multiply like the Judeans. [28] They lived in Beer-sheba, Moladah, Hazar-shual, [29] Bilhah, Ezem, Tolad, [30] Bethuel, Hormah, Ziklag, [31] Beth-marcaboth, Hazar-susim, Beth-biri, and Shaaraim. These were their towns until David became king. [32] And their villages were Etam, Ain, Rimmon, Tochen, and Ashan, five towns, [33] along with all their villages that were around these towns as far as Baal. These were their settlements. And they kept a genealogical record.

34 Meshobab, Jamlech, Joshah son of Amaziah, [35] Joel, Jehu son of Joshibiah son of Seraiah son of Asiel, [36] Elioenai, Jaakobah, Jeshohaiah, Asaiah, Adiel, Jesimiel, Benaiah, [37] Ziza son of Shiphi son of Allon son of Jedaiah son of Shimri son of Shemaiah— [38] these mentioned by name were leaders in their families, and their

---

a Gk Compare Vg: Heb *the father*   b Or *Ahashtari*
c Another reading is *Zohar*   d Gk Vg: Heb lacks *and Meonothai*   e That is *Valley of artisans*   f Heb *sons*
g The clause: *These are . . . married* is transposed from verse 18   h Heb lacks *and bore*   i Vg Compare Gk: Heb *and Jashubi-lehem*   j Or *matters*   k Or *Saul*

clans increased greatly. ³⁹They journeyed to the entrance of Gedor, to the east side of the valley, to seek pasture for their flocks, ⁴⁰where they found rich, good pasture, and the land was very broad, quiet, and peaceful; for the former inhabitants there belonged to Ham. ⁴¹These, registered by name, came in the days of King Hezekiah of Judah, and attacked their tents and the Meunim who were found there, and exterminated them to this day, and settled in their place, because there was pasture there for their flocks. ⁴²And some of them, five hundred men of the Simeonites, went to Mount Seir, having as their leaders Pelatiah, Neariah, Rephaiah, and Uzziel, sons of Ishi; ⁴³they destroyed the remnant of the Amalekites that had escaped, and they have lived there to this day.

Descendants of Reuben

5 The sons of Reuben the firstborn of Israel. (He was the firstborn, but because he defiled his father's bed his birthright was given to the sons of Joseph son of Israel, so that he is not enrolled in the genealogy according to the birthright; ²though Judah became prominent among his brothers and a ruler came from him, yet the birthright belonged to Joseph.) ³The sons of Reuben, the firstborn of Israel: Hanoch, Pallu, Hezron, and Carmi. ⁴The sons of Joel: Shemaiah his son, Gog his son, Shimei his son, ⁵Micah his son, Reaiah his son, Baal his son, ⁶Beerah his son, whom King Tilgath-pilneser of Assyria carried away into exile; he was a chieftain of the Reubenites. ⁷And his kindred by their families, when the genealogy of their generations was reckoned: the chief, Jeiel, and Zechariah, ⁸and Bela son of Azaz, son of Shema, son of Joel, who lived in Aroer, as far as Nebo and Baal-meon. ⁹He also lived to the east as far as the beginning of the desert this side of the Euphrates, because their cattle had multiplied in the land of Gilead. ¹⁰And in the days of Saul they made war on the Hagrites, who fell by their hand; and they lived in their tents throughout all the region east of Gilead.

Descendants of Gad

11 The sons of Gad lived beside them in the land of Bashan as far as Salecah: ¹²Joel the chief, Shapham the second, Janai, and Shaphat in Bashan. ¹³And their kindred according to their clans: Michael, Meshullam, Sheba, Jorai, Jacan, Zia, and Eber, seven. ¹⁴These were the sons of Abihail son of Huri, son of Jaroah, son of Gilead, son of Michael, son of Jeshishai, son of Jahdo, son of Buz; ¹⁵Ahi son of Abdiel, son of Guni, was chief in their clan; ¹⁶and they lived in Gilead, in Bashan and in its towns, and in all the pasture lands of Sharon to their limits. ¹⁷All of these were enrolled by genealogies in the days of King Jotham of Judah, and in the days of King Jeroboam of Israel.

18 The Reubenites, the Gadites, and the half-tribe of Manasseh had valiant warriors, who carried shield and sword, and drew the bow, expert in war, forty-four thousand seven hundred and sixty, ready for service. ¹⁹They made war on the Hagrites, Jetur, Naphish, and Nodab; ²⁰and when they received help against them, the Hagrites and all who were with them were given into their hands, for they cried to God in the battle, and he granted their entreaty because they trusted in him. ²¹They captured their livestock: fifty thousand of their camels, two hundred and fifty thousand sheep, two thousand donkeys, and one hundred thousand captives. ²²Many fell slain, because the war was of God. And they lived in their territory until the exile.

The Half-Tribe of Manasseh

23 The members of the half-tribe of Manasseh lived in the land; they were very numerous from Bashan to Baal-hermon, Senir, and Mount Hermon. ²⁴These were the heads of their clans: Epher,ᵃ Ishi, Eliel, Azriel, Jeremiah, Hodaviah, and Jahdiel, mighty warriors, famous men, heads of their clans. ²⁵But they transgressed against the God of their ancestors, and prostituted themselves to the gods of the peoples of the land, whom God had destroyed before

a Gk Vg: Heb and Epher

them. [26] So the God of Israel stirred up the spirit of King Pul of Assyria, the spirit of King Tilgath-pilneser of Assyria, and he carried them away, namely, the Reubenites, the Gadites, and the half-tribe of Manasseh, and brought them to Halah, Habor, Hara, and the river Gozan, to this day.

Descendants of Levi

6 [a] The sons of Levi: Gershom, [b] Kohath, and Merari. [2] The sons of Kohath: Amram, Izhar, Hebron, and Uzziel. [3] The children of Amram: Aaron, Moses, and Miriam. The sons of Aaron: Nadab, Abihu, Eleazar, and Ithamar. [4] Eleazar became the father of Phinehas, Phinehas of Abishua, [5] Abishua of Bukki, Bukki of Uzzi, [6] Uzzi of Zerahiah, Zerahiah of Meraioth, [7] Meraioth of Amariah, Amariah of Ahitub, [8] Ahitub of Zadok, Zadok of Ahimaaz, [9] Ahimaaz of Azariah, Azariah of Johanan, [10] and Johanan of Azariah (it was he who served as priest in the house that Solomon built in Jerusalem). [11] Azariah became the father of Amariah, Amariah of Ahitub, [12] Ahitub of Zadok, Zadok of Shallum, [13] Shallum of Hilkiah, Hilkiah of Azariah, [14] Azariah of Seraiah, Seraiah of Jehozadak; [15] and Jehozadak went into exile when the LORD sent Judah and Jerusalem into exile by the hand of Nebuchadnezzar.

[16] [c] The sons of Levi: Gershom, Kohath, and Merari. [17] These are the names of the sons of Gershom: Libni and Shimei. [18] The sons of Kohath: Amram, Izhar, Hebron, and Uzziel. [19] The sons of Merari: Mahli and Mushi. These are the clans of the Levites according to their ancestry. [20] Of Gershom: Libni his son, Jahath his son, Zimmah his son, [21] Joah his son, Iddo his son, Zerah his son, Jeatherai his son. [22] The sons of Kohath: Amminadab his son, Korah his son, Assir his son, [23] Elkanah his son, Ebiasaph his son, Assir his son, [24] Tahath his son, Uriel his son, Uzziah his son, and Shaul his son. [25] The sons of Elkanah: Amasai and Ahimoth, [26] Elkanah his son, Zophai his son, Nahath his son, [27] Eliab his son, Jeroham his son, Elkanah his son. [28] The sons of Samuel: Joel [d] his firstborn, the second Abijah. [e] [29] The sons of Merari:

Mahli, Libni his son, Shimei his son, Uzzah his son, [30] Shimea his son, Haggiah his son, and Asaiah his son.

Musicians Appointed by David

[31] These are the men whom David put in charge of the service of song in the house of the LORD, after the ark came to rest there. [32] They ministered with song before the tabernacle of the tent of meeting, until Solomon had built the house of the LORD in Jerusalem; and they performed their service in due order. [33] These are the men who served; and their sons were: Of the Kohathites: Heman, the singer, son of Joel, son of Samuel, [34] son of Elkanah, son of Jeroham, son of Eliel, son of Toah, [35] son of Zuph, son of Elkanah, son of Mahath, son of Amasai, [36] son of Elkanah, son of Joel, son of Azariah, son of Zephaniah, [37] son of Tahath, son of Assir, son of Ebiasaph, son of Korah, [38] son of Izhar, son of Kohath, son of Levi, son of Israel; [39] and his brother Asaph, who stood on his right, namely, Asaph son of Berechiah, son of Shimea, [40] son of Michael, son of Baaseiah, son of Malchijah, [41] son of Ethni, son of Zerah, son of Adaiah, [42] son of Ethan, son of Zimmah, son of Shimei, [43] son of Jahath, son of Gershom, son of Levi. [44] On the left were their kindred the sons of Merari: Ethan son of Kishi, son of Abdi, son of Malluch, [45] son of Hashabiah, son of Amaziah, son of Hilkiah, [46] son of Amzi, son of Bani, son of Shemer, [47] son of Mahli, son of Mushi, son of Merari, son of Levi; [48] and their kindred the Levites were appointed for all the service of the tabernacle of the house of God.

[49] But Aaron and his sons made offerings on the altar of burnt-offering and on the altar of incense, doing all the work of the most holy place, to make atonement for Israel, according to all that Moses the servant of God had commanded. [50] These are the sons of Aaron: Eleazar his son, Phinehas his son, Abishua his son, [51] Bukki

a Ch 5.27 in Heb   b Heb *Gershon*, variant of *Gershom*; See 6.16   c Ch 6.1 in Heb   d Gk Syr Compare verse 33 and 1 Sam 8.2: Heb lacks *Joel*   e Heb reads *Vashni, and Abijah* for *the second Abijah*, taking *the second* as a proper name his son, Uzzi his son, Zerahiah his son, [52] Meraioth his son, Amariah his son, Ahitub his son, [53] Zadok his son, Ahimaaz his son.

Settlements of the Levites

54 These are their dwelling-places according to their settlements within their borders: to the sons of Aaron of the families of Kohathites—for the lot fell to them first— [55] to them they gave Hebron in the land of Judah and its surrounding pasture lands, [56] but the fields of the city and its villages they gave to Caleb son of Jephunneh. [57] To the sons of Aaron they gave the cities of refuge: Hebron, Libnah with its pasture lands, Jattir, Eshtemoa with its pasture lands, [58] Hilen[a] with its pasture lands, Debir with its pasture lands, [59] Ashan with its pasture lands, and Bethshemesh with its pasture lands. [60] From the tribe of Benjamin, Geba with its pasture lands, Alemeth with its pasture lands, and Anathoth with its pasture lands. All their towns throughout their families were thirteen.

61 To the rest of the Kohathites were given by lot out of the family of the tribe, out of the half-tribe, the half of Manasseh, ten towns. [62] To the Gershomites according to their families were allotted thirteen towns out of the tribes of Issachar, Asher, Naphtali, and Manasseh in Bashan. [63] To the Merarites according to their families were allotted twelve towns out of the tribes of Reuben, Gad, and Zebulun. [64] So the people of Israel gave the Levites the towns with their pasture lands. [65] They also gave them by lot out of the tribes of Judah, Simeon, and Benjamin these towns that are mentioned by name.

66 And some of the families of the sons of Kohath had towns of their territory out of the tribe of Ephraim. [67] They were given the cities of refuge: Shechem with its pasture lands in the hill country of Ephraim, Gezer with its pasture lands, [68] Jokmeam with its pasture lands, Beth-horon with its pasture lands, [69] Aijalon with its pasture ~ds, Gath-rimmon with its pasture lands; ¹ out of the half-tribe of Manasseh,

Aner with its pasture lands, and Bileam with its pasture lands, for the rest of the families of the Kohathites.

71 To the Gershomites: out of the half-tribe of Manasseh: Golan in Bashan with its pasture lands and Ashtaroth with its pasture lands; [72] and out of the tribe of Issachar: Kedesh with its pasture lands, Daberath[b] with its pasture lands, [73] Ramoth with its pasture lands, and Anem with its pasture lands; [74] out of the tribe of Asher: Mashal with its pasture lands, Abdon with its pasture lands, [75] Hukok with its pasture lands, and Rehob with its pasture lands; [76] and out of the tribe of Naphtali: Kedesh in Galilee with its pasture lands, Hammon with its pasture lands, and Kiriathaim with its pasture lands. [77] To the rest of the Merarites out of the tribe of Zebulun: Rimmono with its pasture lands, Tabor with its pasture lands, [78] and across the Jordan from Jericho, on the east side of the Jordan, out of the tribe of Reuben: Bezer in the steppe with its pasture lands, Jahzah with its pasture lands, [79] Kedemoth with its pasture lands, and Mephaath with its pasture lands; [80] and out of the tribe of Gad: Ramoth in Gilead with its pasture lands, Mahanaim with its pasture lands, [81] Heshbon with its pasture lands, and Jazer with its pasture lands.

Descendants of Issachar

7 The sons[c] of Issachar: Tola, Puah, Jashub, and Shimron, four. [2] The sons of Tola: Uzzi, Rephaiah, Jeriel, Jahmai, Ibsam, and Shemuel, heads of their ancestral houses, namely of Tola, mighty warriors of their generations, their number in the days of David being twenty-two thousand six hundred. [3] The son[d] of Uzzi: Izrahiah. And the sons of Izrahiah: Michael, Obadiah, Joel, and Isshiah, five, all of them chiefs; [4] and along with them, by their generations, according to their ancestral houses, were units of the fighting force, thirty-six thousand, for they had many wives and

a Other readings Hilez, Holon; See Josh 21.15
b Or Dobrath c Syr Compare Vg: Heb And to the sons
d Heb sons

sons. 5 Their kindred belonging to all the families of Issachar were in all eighty-seven thousand mighty warriors, enrolled by genealogy.

Descendants of Benjamin

6 The sons of Benjamin: Bela, Becher, and Jediael, three. 7 The sons of Bela: Ezbon, Uzzi, Uzziel, Jerimoth, and Iri, five, heads of ancestral houses, mighty warriors; and their enrolment by genealogies was twenty-two thousand and thirty-four. 8 The sons of Becher: Zemirah, Joash, Eliezer, Elioenai, Omri, Jeremoth, Abijah, Anathoth, and Alemeth. All these were the sons of Becher; 9 and their enrolment by genealogies, according to their generations, as heads of their ancestral houses, mighty warriors, was twenty thousand two hundred. 10 The sons of Jediael: Bilhan. And the sons of Bilhan: Jeush, Benjamin, Ehud, Chenaanah, Zethan, Tarshish, and Ahishahar. 11 All these were the sons of Jediael according to the heads of their ancestral houses, mighty warriors, seventeen thousand two hundred, ready for service in war. 12 And Shuppim and Huppim were the sons of Ir, Hushim the son*a* of Aher.

Descendants of Naphtali

13 The descendants of Naphtali: Jahziel, Guni, Jezer, and Shallum, the descendants of Bilhah.

Descendants of Manasseh

14 The sons of Manasseh: Asriel, whom his Aramean concubine bore; she bore Machir the father of Gilead. 15 And Machir took a wife for Huppim and for Shuppim. The name of his sister was Maacah. And the name of the second was Zelophehad; and Zelophehad had daughters. 16 Maacah the wife of Machir bore a son, and she named him Peresh; the name of his brother was Sheresh; and his sons were Ulam and Rekem. 17 The son*a* of Ulam: Bedan. These were the sons of Gilead son of Machir, son of Manasseh. 18 And his sister Hammolecheth bore Ishhod, Abiezer, and Mahlah. 19 The sons of Shemida were Ahian, Shechem, Likhi, and Aniam.

Descendants of Ephraim

20 The sons of Ephraim: Shuthelah, and Bered his son, Tahath his son, Eleadah his son, Tahath his son, 21 Zabad his son, Shuthelah his son, and Ezer and Elead. Now the people of Gath, who were born in the land, killed them, because they came down to raid their cattle. 22 And their father Ephraim mourned for many days, and his brothers came to comfort him. 23 Ephraim*b* went in to his wife, and she conceived and bore a son; and he named him Beriah, because disaster*c* had befallen his house. 24 His daughter was Sheerah, who built both Lower and Upper Beth-horon, and Uzzen-sheerah. 25 Rephah was his son, Resheph his son, Telah his son, Tahan his son, 26 Ladan his son, Ammihud his son, Elishama his son, 27 Nun*d* his son, Joshua his son. 28 Their possessions and settlements were Bethel and its towns, and eastwards Naaran, and westwards Gezer and its towns, Shechem and its towns, as far as Ayyah and its towns; 29 also along the borders of the Manassites, Beth-shean and its towns, Taanach and its towns, Megiddo and its towns, Dor and its towns. In these lived the sons of Joseph son of Israel.

Descendants of Asher

30 The sons of Asher: Imnah, Ishvah, Ishvi, Beriah, and their sister Serah. 31 The sons of Beriah: Heber and Malchiel, who was the father of Birzaith. 32 Heber became the father of Japhlet, Shomer, Hotham, and their sister Shua. 33 The sons of Japhlet: Pasach, Bimhal, and Ashvath. These are the sons of Japhlet. 34 The sons of Shemer: Ahi, Rohgah, Hubbah, and Aram. 35 The sons of Helem*e* his brother: Zophah, Imna, Shelesh, and Amal. 36 The sons of Zophah: Suah, Harnepher, Shual, Beri, Imrah, 37 Bezer, Hod, Shamma, Shilshah, Ithran, and Beera. 38 The sons of Jether: Jephunneh, Pispa, and Ara. 39 The sons of Ulla: Arah, Hanniel, and Rizia. 40 All of these were men of Asher, heads of ancestral houses, select mighty warriors, chief of the princes. Their number enrolled by genealogies, for

a Heb *sons*   *b* Heb *He*   *c* Heb *beraah*   *d* Here spelled *Non*; see Ex 33.11   *e* Or *Hotham*; see 7.32

service in war, was twenty-six thousand men.

Descendants of Benjamin

8 Benjamin became the father of Bela his firstborn, Ashbel the second, Aharah the third, 2 Noah the fourth, and Rapha the fifth. 3 And Bela had sons: Addar, Gera, Abihud, *a* 4 Abishua, Naaman, Ahoah, 5 Gera, Shephuphan, and Huram. 6 These are the sons of Ehud (they were heads of ancestral houses of the inhabitants of Geba, and they were carried into exile to Manahath): 7 Naaman, *b* Ahijah, and Gera, that is, Heglam, *c* who became the father of Uzza and Ahihud. 8 And Shaharaim had sons in the country of Moab after he had sent away his wives Hushim and Baara. 9 He had sons by his wife Hodesh: Jobab, Zibia, Mesha, Malcam, 10 Jeuz, Sachia, and Mirmah. These were his sons, heads of ancestral houses. 11 He also had sons by Hushim: Abitub and Elpaal. 12 The sons of Elpaal: Eber, Misham, and Shemed, who built Ono and Lod with its towns, 13 and Beriah and Shema (they were heads of ancestral houses of the inhabitants of Aijalon, who put to flight the inhabitants of Gath); 14 and Ahio, Shashak, and Jeremoth. 15 Zebadiah, Arad, Eder, 16 Michael, Ishpah, and Joha were sons of Beriah. 17 Zebadiah, Meshullam, Hizki, Heber, 18 Ishmerai, Izliah, and Jobab were the sons of Elpaal. 19 Jakim, Zichri, Zabdi, 20 Elienai, Zillethai, Eliel, 21 Adaiah, Beraiah, and Shimrath were the sons of Shimei. 22 Ishpan, Eber, Eliel, 23 Abdon, Zichri, Hanan, 24 Hananiah, Elam, Anthothijah, 25 Iphdeiah, and Penuel were the sons of Shashak. 26 Shamsherai, Shehariah, Athaliah, 27 Jaareshiah, Elijah, and Zichri were the sons of Jeroham. 28 These were the heads of ancestral houses, according to their generations, chiefs. These lived in Jerusalem.

29 Jeiel *d* the father of Gibeon lived in Gibeon, and the name of his wife was Maacah. 30 His firstborn son: Abdon, then Zur, Kish, Baal, *e* Nadab, 31 Gedor, Ahio, Zecher, 32 and Mikloth, who became the father of Shimeah. Now these also lived opposite their kindred in Jerusalem, with their kin-

dred. 33 Ner became the father of Kish, Kish of Saul, *f* Saul *f* of Jonathan, Malchishua, Abinadab, and Esh-baal; 34 and the son of Jonathan was Merib-baal; and Merib-baal became the father of Micah. 35 The sons of Micah: Pithon, Melech, Tarea, and Ahaz. 36 Ahaz became the father of Jehoaddah; and Jehoaddah became the father of Alemeth, Azmaveth, and Zimri; Zimri became the father of Moza. 37 Moza became the father of Binea; Raphah was his son, Eleasah his son, Azel his son. 38 Azel had six sons, and these are their names: Azrikam, Bocheru, Ishmael, Sheariah, Obadiah, and Hanan; all these were the sons of Azel. 39 The sons of his brother Eshek: Ulam his firstborn, Jeush the second, and Eliphelet the third. 40 The sons of Ulam were mighty warriors, archers, having many children and grandchildren, one hundred and fifty. All these were Benjaminites.

9 So all Israel was enrolled by genealogies; and these are written in the Book of the Kings of Israel. And Judah was taken into exile in Babylon because of their unfaithfulness. 2 Now the first to live again in their possessions in their towns were Israelites, priests, Levites, and temple servants.

Inhabitants of Jerusalem after the Exile

3 And some of the people of Judah, Benjamin, Ephraim, and Manasseh lived in Jerusalem: 4 Uthai son of Ammihud, son of Omri, son of Imri, son of Bani, from the sons of Perez son of Judah. 5 And of the Shilonites: Asaiah the firstborn, and his sons. 6 Of the sons of Zerah: Jeuel and their kin, six hundred and ninety. 7 Of the Benjaminites: Sallu son of Meshullam, son of Hodaviah, son of Hassenuah, 8 Ibneiah son of Jeroham, Elah son of Uzzi, son of Michri, and Meshullam son of Shephatiah, son of Reuel, son of Ibnijah; 9 and their kindred according to their generations, nine hundred and fifty-six. All these were heads of families according to their ancestral houses.

---

a Or *father of Ehud;* see 8.6   *b* Heb *and Naaman*
c Or *he carried them into exile*   *d* Compare 9.35: Heb lacks *Jeiel*   *e* Gk Ms adds *Ner;* Compare 8.33 and 9.36
f Or *Shaul*

Priestly Families

10 Of the priests: Jedaiah, Jehoiarib, Jachin, 11 and Azariah son of Hilkiah, son of Meshullam, son of Zadok, son of Meraioth, son of Ahitub, the chief officer of the house of God; 12 and Adaiah son of Jeroham, son of Pashhur, son of Malchijah, and Maasai son of Adiel, son of Jahzerah, son of Meshullam, son of Meshillemith, son of Immer; 13 besides their kindred, heads of their ancestral houses, one thousand seven hundred and sixty, qualified for the work of the service of the house of God.

Levitical Families

14 Of the Levites: Shemaiah son of Hasshub, son of Azrikam, son of Hashabiah, of the sons of Merari; 15 and Bakbakkar, Heresh, Galal, and Mattaniah son of Mica, son of Zichri, son of Asaph; 16 and Obadiah son of Shemaiah, son of Galal, son of Jeduthun, and Berechiah son of Asa, son of Elkanah, who lived in the villages of the Netophathites.

17 The gatekeepers were: Shallum, Akkub, Talmon, Ahiman; and their kinsman Shallum was the chief, 18 stationed previously in the king's gate on the east side. These were the gatekeepers of the camp of the Levites. 19 Shallum son of Kore, son of Ebiasaph, son of Korah, and his kindred of his ancestral house, the Korahites, were in charge of the work of the service, guardians of the thresholds of the tent, as their ancestors had been in charge of the camp of the LORD, guardians of the entrance. 20 And Phinehas son of Eleazar was chief over them in former times; the LORD was with him. 21 Zechariah son of Meshelemiah was gatekeeper at the entrance of the tent of meeting. 22 All these, who were chosen as gatekeepers at the thresholds, were two hundred and twelve. They were enrolled by genealogies in their villages. David and the seer Samuel established them in their office of trust. 23 So they and their descendants were in charge of the gates of the house of the LORD, that is, the house of the tent, as guards. 24 The gatekeepers were on the four sides, east, west, north, and south;

25 and their kindred who were in their villages were obliged to come in every seven days, in turn, to be with them; 26 for the four chief gatekeepers, who were Levites, were in charge of the chambers and the treasures of the house of God. 27 And they would spend the night near the house of God; for on them lay the duty of watching, and they had charge of opening it every morning.

28 Some of them had charge of the utensils of service, for they were required to count them when they were brought in and taken out. 29 Others of them were appointed over the furniture, and over all the holy utensils, also over the choice flour, the wine, the oil, the incense, and the spices. 30 Others, of the sons of the priests, prepared the mixing of the spices, 31 and Mattithiah, one of the Levites, the firstborn of Shallum the Korahite, was in charge of making the flat cakes. 32 Also some of their kindred of the Kohathites had charge of the rows of bread, to prepare them for each sabbath.

33 Now these are the singers, the heads of ancestral houses of the Levites, living in the chambers of the temple free from other service, for they were on duty day and night. 34 These were heads of ancestral houses of the Levites, according to their generations; these leaders lived in Jerusalem.

The Family of King Saul

35 In Gibeon lived the father of Gibeon, Jeiel, and the name of his wife was Maacah. 36 His firstborn son was Abdon, then Zur, Kish, Baal, Ner, Nadab, 37 Gedor, Ahio, Zechariah, and Mikloth; 38 and Mikloth became the father of Shimeam; and these also lived opposite their kindred in Jerusalem, with their kindred. 39 Ner became the father of Kish, Kish of Saul, Saul of Jonathan, Malchishua, Abinadab, and Esh-baal; 40 and the son of Jonathan was Merib-baal; and Merib-baal became the father of Micah. 41 The sons of Micah: Pithon, Melech, Tahrea, and Ahaz; a 42 and Ahaz became the father of Jarah, and Jarah

a Compare 8.35: Heb lacks *and Ahaz*

of Alemeth, Azmaveth, and Zimri; and Zimri became the father of Moza. ⁴³Moza became the father of Binea; and Rephaiah was his son, Eleasah his son, Azel his son. ⁴⁴Azel had six sons, and these are their names: Azrikam, Bocheru, Ishmael, Sheariah, Obadiah, and Hanan; these were the sons of Azel.

Death of Saul and His Sons

10 Now the Philistines fought against Israel; and the men of Israel fled before the Philistines, and fell slain on Mount Gilboa. ²The Philistines overtook Saul and his sons; and the Philistines killed Jonathan and Abinadab and Malchishua, sons of Saul. ³The battle pressed hard on Saul; and the archers found him, and he was wounded by the archers. ⁴Then Saul said to his armour-bearer, 'Draw your sword, and thrust me through with it, so that these uncircumcised may not come and make sport of me.' But his armour-bearer was unwilling, for he was terrified. So Saul took his own sword and fell on it. ⁵When his armour-bearer saw that Saul was dead, he also fell on his sword and died. ⁶Thus Saul died; he and his three sons and all his house died together. ⁷When all the men of Israel who were in the valley saw that the army*ᵃ* had fled and that Saul and his sons were dead, they abandoned their towns and fled; and the Philistines came and occupied them.

8 The next day when the Philistines came to strip the dead, they found Saul and his sons fallen on Mount Gilboa. ⁹They stripped him and took his head and his armour, and sent messengers throughout the land of the Philistines to carry the good news to their idols and to the people. ¹⁰They put his armour in the temple of their gods, and fastened his head in the temple of Dagon. ¹¹But when all Jabesh-gilead heard everything that the Philistines had done to Saul, ¹²all the valiant warriors got up and took away the body of Saul and the bodies of his sons, and brought them to Jabesh. Then they buried their bones under the oak in Jabesh, and fasted for seven days.

13 So Saul died for his unfaithfulness; he was unfaithful to the Lord in that he did not keep the command of the Lord; moreover, he had consulted a medium, seeking guidance, ¹⁴and did not seek guidance from the Lord. Therefore the Lord*ᵇ* put him to death and turned the kingdom over to David son of Jesse.

David Anointed King of All Israel

11 Then all Israel gathered together to David at Hebron and said, 'See, we are your bone and flesh. ²For some time now, even while Saul was king, it was you who commanded the army of Israel. The Lord your God said to you: It is you who shall be shepherd of my people Israel, you who shall be ruler over my people Israel.' ³So all the elders of Israel came to the king at Hebron, and David made a covenant with them at Hebron before the Lord. And they anointed David king over Israel, according to the word of the Lord by Samuel.

Jerusalem Captured

4 David and all Israel marched to Jerusalem, that is, Jebus where the Jebusites were, the inhabitants of the land. ⁵The inhabitants of Jebus said to David, 'You will not come in here.' Nevertheless, David took the stronghold of Zion, now the city of David. ⁶David had said, 'Whoever attacks the Jebusites first shall be chief and commander.' And Joab son of Zeruiah went up first, so he became chief. ⁷David resided in the stronghold; therefore it was called the city of David. ⁸He built the city all round, from the Millo in a complete circuit; and Joab repaired the rest of the city. ⁹And David became greater and greater, for the Lord of hosts was with him.

David's Mighty Men and Their Exploits

10 Now these are the chiefs of David's warriors, who gave him strong support in his kingdom, together with all Israel, to make him king, according to the word of the Lord concerning Israel. ¹¹This is an account of David's mighty warriors: Jashobeam, son

a Heb *they*   *b* Heb *he*

of Hachmoni,*a* was chief of the Three;*b* he wielded his spear against three hundred whom he killed at one time.

12 And next to him among the three warriors was Eleazar son of Dodo, the Ahohite. 13 He was with David at Pas-dammim when the Philistines were gathered there for battle. There was a plot of ground full of barley. Now the people had fled from the Philistines, 14 but he and David took their stand in the middle of the plot, defended it, and killed the Philistines; and the LORD saved them by a great victory.

15 Three of the thirty chiefs went down to the rock to David at the cave of Adullam, while the army of Philistines was encamped in the valley of Rephaim. 16 David was then in the stronghold; and the garrison of the Philistines was then at Bethlehem. 17 David said longingly, 'O that someone would give me water to drink from the well of Bethlehem that is by the gate!' 18 Then the Three broke through the camp of the Philistines, and drew water from the well of Bethlehem that was by the gate, and

Movements Early in the Life of David

0   30 MI.

0   30 Km.

Aphek

Jebus (Jerusalem)

Bethlehem

Gath

Hebron

Dead Sea

Carmel

Ziklag

Maon

En-gedi

Desert of Maon

→ David's journeys

- - -> After Saul's death

they brought it to David. But David would not drink of it; he poured it out to the LORD, 19 and said, 'My God forbid that I should do this. Can I drink the blood of these men? For at the risk of their lives they brought it.' Therefore he would not drink it. The three warriors did these things.

20 Now Abishai,*c* the brother of Joab, was chief of the Thirty.*d* With his spear he fought against three hundred and killed them, and won a name beside the Three. 21 He was the most renowned*e* of the Thirty,*d* and became their commander; but he did not attain to the Three.

22 Benaiah son of Jehoiada was a valiant man*f* of Kabzeel, a doer of great deeds; he struck down two sons of*g* Ariel of Moab. He also went down and killed a lion in a pit on a day when snow had fallen. 23 And he killed an Egyptian, a man of great stature, five cubits tall. The Egyptian had in his hand a spear like a weaver's beam; but Benaiah went against him with a staff, snatched the spear out of the Egyptian's hand, and killed him with his own spear. 24 Such were the things Benaiah son of Jehoiada did, and he won a name beside the three warriors. 25 He was renowned among the Thirty, but he did not attain to the Three. And David put him in charge of his bodyguard.

26 The warriors of the armies were Asahel brother of Joab, Elhanan son of Dodo of Bethlehem, 27 Shammoth of Harod,*h* Helez the Pelonite, 28 Ira son of Ikkesh of Tekoa, Abiezer of Anathoth, 29 Sibbecai the Hushathite, Ilai the Ahohite, 30 Maharai of Netophah, Heled son of Baanah of Netophah, 31 Ithai son of Ribai of Gibeah of the Benjaminites, Benaiah of Pirathon, 32 Hurai of the wadis of Gaash, Abiel the Arbathite, 33 Azmaveth of Baharum, Eliahba of Shaalbon, 34 Hashem*i* the Gizonite, Jonathan son of Shagee the Hararite, 35 Ahiam son of Sachar the Hararite, Eliphal son of

a Or *a Hachmonite*   *b* Compare 2 Sam 23.8: Heb *Thirty* or *captains*   *c* Gk Vg Tg Compare 2 Sam 23.18: Heb *Abshai*   *d* Syr: Heb *Three*   *e* Compare 2 Sam 23.19: Heb *more renowned among the two*   *f* Syr: Heb *the son of a valiant man*   *g* See 2 Sam 23.20: Heb lacks *sons of*   *h* Compare 2 Sam 23.25: Heb *the Harorite*   *i* Compare Gk and 2 Sam 23.32: Heb *the sons of Hashem*

Ur, [36] Hepher the Mecherathite, Ahijah the Pelonite, [37] Hezro of Carmel, Naarai son of Ezbai, [38] Joel the brother of Nathan, Mibhar son of Hagri, [39] Zelek the Ammonite, Naharai of Beeroth, the armour-bearer of Joab son of Zeruiah, [40] Ira the Ithrite, Gareb the Ithrite, [41] Uriah the Hittite, Zabad son of Ahlai, [42] Adina son of Shiza the Reubenite, a leader of the Reubenites, and thirty with him, [43] Hanan son of Maacah, and Joshaphat the Mithnite, [44] Uzzia the Ashterathite, Shama and Jeiel sons of Hotham the Aroerite, [45] Jediael son of Shimri, and his brother Joha the Tizite, [46] Eliel the Mahavite, and Jeribai and Joshaviah sons of Elnaam, and Ithmah the Moabite, [47] Eliel, and Obed, and Jaasiel the Mezobaite.

David's Followers in the Wilderness

12 The following are those who came to David at Ziklag, while he could not move about freely because of Saul son of Kish; they were among the mighty warriors who helped him in war. [2] They were archers, and could shoot arrows and sling stones with either the right hand or the left; they were Benjaminites, Saul's kindred. [3] The chief was Ahiezer, then Joash, both sons of Shemaah of Gibeah; also Jeziel and Pelet sons of Azmaveth; Beracah, Jehu of Anathoth, [4] Ishmaiah of Gibeon, a warrior among the Thirty and a leader over the Thirty; Jeremiah, [a] Jahaziel, Johanan, Jozabad of Gederah, [5] Eluzai, [b] Jerimoth, Bealiah, Shemariah, Shephatiah the Haruphite; [6] Elkanah, Isshiah, Azarel, Joezer, and Jashobeam, the Korahites; [7] and Joelah and Zebadiah, sons of Jeroham of Gedor.

8 From the Gadites there went over to David at the stronghold in the wilderness mighty and experienced warriors, expert with shield and spear, whose faces were like the faces of lions, and who were swift as gazelles on the mountains: [9] Ezer the chief, Obadiah second, Eliab third, [10] Mishmannah fourth, Jeremiah fifth, [11] Attai sixth, Eliel seventh, [12] Johanan eighth, Elzabad ninth, [13] Jeremiah tenth, Machbannai eleventh. [14] These Gadites were officers of the army, the least equal to a hundred and the greatest to a thousand. [15] These are the men who crossed the Jordan in the first month, when it was overflowing all its banks, and put to flight all those in the valleys, to the east and to the west.

16 Some Benjaminites and Judahites came to the stronghold to David. [17] David went out to meet them and said to them, 'If you have come to me in friendship, to help me, then my heart will be bound to you; but if you have come to betray me to my adversaries, though my hands have done no wrong, then may the God of our ancestors see and give judgement.' [18] Then the spirit came upon Amasai, chief of the Thirty, and he said,

'We are yours, O David;
    and with you, O son of Jesse!
Peace, peace to you,
    and peace to the one who helps
        you!
For your God is the one who helps
        you.'

Then David received them, and made them officers of his troops.

19 Some of the Manassites deserted to David when he came with the Philistines for the battle against Saul. (Yet he did not help them, for the rulers of the Philistines took counsel and sent him away, saying, 'He will desert to his master Saul at the cost of our heads.') [20] As he went to Ziklag these Manassites deserted to him: Adnah, Jozabad, Jediael, Michael, Jozabad, Elihu, and Zillethai, chiefs of the thousands in Manasseh. [21] They helped David against the band of raiders, [c] for they were all warriors and commanders in the army. [22] Indeed from day to day people kept coming to David to help him, until there was a great army, like an army of God.

David's Army at Hebron

23 These are the numbers of the divisions of the armed troops who came to David in Hebron to turn the kingdom of Saul

a Heb verse 5   b Heb verse 6   c Or *as officers of his troops* over to him, according to the word of the LORD. 24 The people of Judah bearing shield and spear numbered six thousand eight hundred armed troops. 25 Of the Simeonites, mighty warriors, seven thousand one hundred. 26 Of the Levites four thousand six hundred. 27 Jehoiada, leader of the house of Aaron, and with him three thousand seven hundred. 28 Zadok, a young warrior, and twenty-two commanders from his own ancestral house. 29 Of the Benjaminites, the kindred of Saul, three thousand, of whom the majority had continued to keep their allegiance to the house of Saul. 30 Of the Ephraimites, twenty thousand eight hundred, mighty warriors, notables in their ancestral houses. 31 Of the half-tribe of Manasseh, eighteen thousand, who were expressly named to come and make David king. 32 Of Issachar, those who had understanding of the times, to know what Israel ought to do, two hundred chiefs, and all their kindred under their command. 33 Of Zebulun, fifty thousand seasoned troops, equipped for battle with all the weapons of war, to help David *a* with singleness of purpose. 34 Of Naphtali, a thousand commanders, with whom there were thirty-seven thousand armed with shield and spear. 35 Of the Danites, twenty-eight thousand six hundred equipped for battle. 36 Of Asher, forty thousand seasoned troops ready for battle. 37 Of the Reubenites and Gadites and the half-tribe of Manasseh from beyond the Jordan, one hundred and twenty thousand armed with all the weapons of war.

38 All these, warriors arrayed in battle order, came to Hebron with full intent to make David king over all Israel; likewise all the rest of Israel were of a single mind to make David king. 39 They were there with David for three days, eating and drinking, for their kindred had provided for them. 40 And also their neighbours, from as far away as Issachar and Zebulun and Naphtali, came bringing food on donkeys, camels, mules, and oxen—abundant provisions of meal, cakes of figs, clusters of raisins, wine, oil, oxen, and sheep, for there was joy in Israel.

The Ark Brought from Kiriath-jearim

13 David consulted with the commanders of the thousands and of the hundreds, with every leader. 2 David said to the whole assembly of Israel, 'If it seems good to you, and if it is the will of the LORD our God, let us send abroad to our kindred who remain in all the land of Israel, including the priests and Levites in the cities that have pasture lands, that they may come together to us; 3 Then let us bring again the ark of our God to us; for we did not turn to it in the days of Saul.' 4 The whole assembly agreed to do so, for the thing pleased all the people.

5 So David assembled all Israel from the Shihor of Egypt to Lebo-hamath, to bring the ark of God from Kiriath-jearim. 6 And David and all Israel went up to Baalah, that is, to Kiriath-jearim, which belongs to Judah, to bring up from there the ark of God, the LORD, who is enthroned on the cherubim, which is called by his *b* name. 7 They carried the ark of God on a new cart, from the house of Abinadab, and Uzzah and Ahio *c* were driving the cart. 8 David and all Israel were dancing before God with all their might, with song and lyres and harps and tambourines and cymbals and trumpets.

9 When they came to the threshing-floor of Chidon, Uzzah put out his hand to hold the ark, for the oxen shook it. 10 The anger of the LORD was kindled against Uzzah; he struck him down because he put out his hand to the ark; and he died there before God. 11 David was angry because the LORD had burst out against Uzzah; so that place is called Perez-uzzah *d* to this day. 12 David was afraid of God that day; he said, 'How can I bring the ark of God into my care?' 13 So David did not take the ark into his care into the city of David; he took it instead to the house of Obed-edom the Gittite. 14 The ark of God remained with the household of Obed-edom in his house for three months, and the LORD blessed the household of Obed-edom and all that he had.

a Gk: Heb lacks *David*   *b* Heb lacks *his*   *c* Or *and his brother*   *d* That is *Bursting Out Against Uzzah*

David Established at Jerusalem

14 King Hiram of Tyre sent messengers to David, along with cedar logs, and masons and carpenters to build a house for him. 2 David then perceived that the LORD had established him as king over Israel, and that his kingdom was highly exalted for the sake of his people Israel.

3 David took more wives in Jerusalem, and David became the father of more sons and daughters. 4 These are the names of the children whom he had in Jerusalem: Shammua, Shobab, and Nathan; Solomon, 5 Ibhar, Elishua, and Elpelet; 6 Nogah, Nepheg, and Japhia; 7 Elishama, Beeliada, and Eliphelet.

Defeat of the Philistines

8 When the Philistines heard that David had been anointed king over all Israel, all the Philistines went up in search of David; and David heard of it and went out against them. 9 Now the Philistines had come and made a raid in the valley of Rephaim. 10 David inquired of God, 'Shall I go up against the Philistines? Will you give them into my hand?' The LORD said to him, 'Go up, and I will give them into your hand.' 11 So he went up to Baal-perazim, and David defeated them there. David said, 'God has burst out[a] against my enemies by my hand, like a bursting flood.' Therefore that place is called Baal-perazim.[b] 12 They abandoned their gods there, and at David's command they were burned.

13 Once again the Philistines made a raid in the valley. 14 When David again inquired of God, God said to him, 'You shall not go up after them; go around and come on them opposite the balsam trees. 15 When you hear the sound of marching in the tops of the balsam trees, then go out to battle; for God has gone out before you to strike down the army of the Philistines.' 16 David did as God had commanded him, and they struck down the Philistine army from Gibeon to Gezer. 17 The fame of David went out into all lands, and the LORD brought the fear of him on all nations.

The Ark Brought to Jerusalem

15 David[c] built houses for himself in the city of David, and he prepared a place for the ark of God and pitched a tent for it. 2 Then David commanded that no one but the Levites were to carry the ark of God, for the LORD had chosen them to carry the ark of the LORD and to minister to him for ever. 3 David assembled all Israel in Jerusalem to bring up the ark of the LORD to its place, which he had prepared for it. 4 Then David gathered together the descendants of Aaron and the Levites: 5 of the sons of Kohath, Uriel the chief, with one hundred and twenty of his kindred; 6 of the sons of Merari, Asaiah the chief, with two hundred and twenty of his kindred; 7 of the sons of Gershom, Joel the chief, with one hundred and thirty of his kindred; 8 of the sons of Elizaphan, Shemaiah the chief, with two hundred of his kindred; 9 of the sons of Hebron, Eliel the chief, with eighty of his kindred; 10 of the sons of Uzziel, Amminadab the chief, with one hundred and twelve of his kindred.

11 David summoned the priests Zadok and Abiathar, and the Levites Uriel, Asaiah, Joel, Shemaiah, Eliel, and Amminadab. 12 He said to them, 'You are the heads of families of the Levites; sanctify yourselves, you and your kindred, so that you may bring up the ark of the LORD, the God of Israel, to the place that I have prepared for it. 13 Because you did not carry it the first time,[d] the LORD our God burst out against us, because we did not give it proper care.' 14 So the priests and the Levites sanctified themselves to bring up the ark of the LORD, the God of Israel. 15 And the Levites carried the ark of God on their shoulders with the poles, as Moses had commanded according to the word of the LORD.

16 David also commanded the chiefs of the Levites to appoint their kindred as the singers to play on musical instruments, on harps and lyres and cymbals, to raise loud sounds of joy. 17 So the Levites appointed Heman son of Joel; and of his kindred Asaph son of Berechiah; and of the sons of

---

a Heb *paraz*　　*b* That is *Lord of Bursting Out*
c Heb *He*　　*d* Meaning of Heb uncertain

Merari, their kindred, Ethan son of Kushaiah; 18 and with them their kindred of the second order, Zechariah, Jaaziel, Shemiramoth, Jehiel, Unni, Eliab, Benaiah, Maaseiah, Mattithiah, Eliphelehu, and Mikneiah, and the gatekeepers Obed-edom and Jeiel. 19 The singers Heman, Asaph, and Ethan were to sound bronze cymbals; 20 Zechariah, Aziel, Shemiramoth, Jehiel, Unni, Eliab, Maaseiah, and Benaiah were to play harps according to Alamoth; 21 but Mattithiah, Eliphelehu, Mikneiah, Obed-edom, Jeiel, and Azaziah were to lead with lyres according to the Sheminith. 22 Chenaniah, leader of the Levites in music, was to direct the music, for he understood it. 23 Berechiah and Elkanah were to be gatekeepers for the ark. 24 Shebaniah, Joshaphat, Nethanel, Amasai, Zechariah, Benaiah, and Eliezer, the priests, were to blow the trumpets before the ark of God. Obed-edom and Jehiah also were to be gatekeepers for the ark.

25 So David and the elders of Israel, and the commanders of the thousands, went to bring up the ark of the covenant of the LORD from the house of Obed-edom with rejoicing. 26 And because God helped the Levites who were carrying the ark of the covenant of the LORD, they sacrificed seven bulls and seven rams. 27 David was clothed with a robe of fine linen, as also were all the Levites who were carrying the ark, and the singers, and Chenaniah the leader of the music of the singers; and David wore a linen ephod. 28 So all Israel brought up the ark of the covenant of the LORD with shouting, to the sound of the horn, trumpets, and cymbals, and made loud music on harps and lyres.

29 As the ark of the covenant of the LORD came to the city of David, Michal daughter of Saul looked out of the window, and saw King David leaping and dancing; and she despised him in her heart.

The Ark Placed in the Tent

16 They brought in the ark of God, and set it inside the tent that David had pitched for it; and they offered burnt-offerings and offerings of well-being before God. 2 When David had finished offering the burnt-offerings and the offerings of well-being, he blessed the people in the name of the LORD; 3 and he distributed to every person in Israel—man and woman alike—to each a loaf of bread, a portion of meat, *a* and a cake of raisins.

4 He appointed certain of the Levites as ministers before the ark of the LORD, to invoke, to thank, and to praise the LORD, the God of Israel. 5 Asaph was the chief, and second to him Zechariah, Jeiel, Shemiramoth, Jehiel, Mattithiah, Eliab, Benaiah, Obed-edom, and Jeiel, with harps and lyres; Asaph was to sound the cymbals, 6 and the priests Benaiah and Jahaziel were to blow trumpets regularly, before the ark of the covenant of God.

David's Psalm of Thanksgiving

7 Then on that day David first appointed the singing of praises to the LORD by Asaph and his kindred.

8 O give thanks to the LORD, call on his
    name,
    make known his deeds among the
    peoples.
9 Sing to him, sing praises to him,
    tell of all his wonderful works.
10 Glory in his holy name;
    let the hearts of those who seek the
    LORD rejoice.
11 Seek the LORD and his strength,
    seek his presence continually.
12 Remember the wonderful works he
    has done,
    his miracles, and the judgements he
    uttered,
13 O offspring of his servant Israel, *b*
    children of Jacob, his chosen ones.

14 He is the LORD our God;
    his judgements are in all the earth.
15 Remember his covenant for ever,
    the word that he commanded for a
    thousand generations,

---

a Compare Gk Syr Vg: Meaning of Heb uncertain
b Another reading is *Abraham* (compare Ps 105.6)

16 the covenant that he made with
Abraham,
his sworn promise to Isaac,
17 which he confirmed to Jacob as a
statute,
to Israel as an everlasting covenant,
18 saying, 'To you I will give the land of
Canaan
as your portion for an inheritance.'

19 When they were few in number,
of little account, and strangers in
the land,[a]
20 wandering from nation to nation,
from one kingdom to another
people,
21 he allowed no one to oppress them;
he rebuked kings on their account,
22 saying, 'Do not touch my anointed
ones;
do my prophets no harm.'

23 Sing to the LORD, all the earth.
Tell of his salvation from day to
day.
24 Declare his glory among the nations,
his marvellous works among all the
peoples.
25 For great is the LORD, and greatly to
be praised;
he is to be revered above all gods.
26 For all the gods of the peoples are
idols,
but the LORD made the heavens.
27 Honour and majesty are before him;
strength and joy are in his place.

28 Ascribe to the LORD, O families of the
peoples,
ascribe to the LORD glory and
strength.
29 Ascribe to the LORD the glory due his
name;
bring an offering, and come before
him.
Worship the LORD in holy splendour;
30 tremble before him, all the earth.
The world is firmly established; it
shall never be moved.
31 Let the heavens be glad, and let the
earth rejoice,

and let them say among the
nations, 'The LORD is king!'
32 Let the sea roar, and all that fills it;
let the field exult, and everything in
it.
33 Then shall the trees of the forest sing
for joy
before the LORD, for he comes to
judge the earth.
34 O give thanks to the LORD, for he is
good;
for his steadfast love endures for
ever.

35 Say also:
'Save us, O God of our salvation,
and gather and rescue us from
among the nations,
that we may give thanks to your holy
name,
and glory in your praise.
36 Blessed be the LORD, the God of
Israel,
from everlasting to everlasting.'
Then all the people said 'Amen!' and
praised the LORD.

Regular Worship Maintained

37 David left Asaph and his kinsfolk
there before the ark of the covenant of the
LORD to minister regularly before the ark as
each day required, 38 and also Obed-edom
and his[b] sixty-eight kinsfolk; while Obed-
edom son of Jeduthun and Hosah were to
be gatekeepers. 39 And he left the priest Zadok and his kindred the priests before the
tabernacle of the LORD in the high place
that was at Gibeon, 40 to offer burnt-offerings to the LORD on the altar of burnt-offering regularly, morning and evening, according to all that is written in the law of
the LORD that he commanded Israel.
41 With them were Heman and Jeduthun,
and the rest of those chosen and expressly
named to render thanks to the LORD, for
his steadfast love endures for ever. 42 Heman and Jeduthun had with them trumpets and cymbals for the music, and instruments for sacred song. The sons of
Jeduthun were appointed to the gate.

a Heb in it   b Gk Syr Vg: Heb their

43 Then all the people departed to their homes, and David went home to bless his household.

God's Covenant with David

17 Now when David settled in his house, David said to the prophet Nathan, 'I am living in a house of cedar, but the ark of the covenant of the LORD is under a tent.' 2 Nathan said to David, 'Do all that you have in mind, for God is with you.'

3 But that same night the word of the LORD came to Nathan, saying: 4 Go and tell my servant David: Thus says the LORD: You shall not build me a house to live in. 5 For I have not lived in a house since the day I brought out Israel to this very day, but I have lived in a tent and a tabernacle.a 6 Wherever I have moved about among all Israel, did I ever speak a word with any of the judges of Israel, whom I commanded to shepherd my people, saying, Why have you not built me a house of cedar? 7 Now therefore, thus you shall say to my servant David: Thus says the LORD of hosts: I took you from the pasture, from following the sheep, to be ruler over my people Israel; 8 and I have been with you wherever you went, and have cut off all your enemies before you; and I will make for you a name, like the name of the great ones of the earth. 9 I will appoint a place for my people Israel, and will plant them, so that they may live in their own place, and be disturbed no more; and evildoers shall wear them down no more, as they did formerly, 10 from the time that I appointed judges over my people Israel; and I will subdue all your enemies.

Moreover, I declare to you that the LORD will build you a house. 11 When your days are fulfilled to go to be with your ancestors, I will raise up your offspring after you, one of your own sons, and I will establish his kingdom. 12 He shall build a house for me, and I will establish his throne for ever. 13 I will be a father to him, and he shall be a son to me. I will not take my steadfast love from him, as I took it from him who was before you, 14 but I

will confirm him in my house and in my kingdom for ever, and his throne shall be established for ever. 15 In accordance with all these words and all this vision, Nathan spoke to David.

David's Prayer

16 Then King David went in and sat before the LORD, and said, 'Who am I, O LORD God, and what is my house, that you have brought me thus far? 17 And even this was a small thing in your sight, O God; you have also spoken of your servant's house for a great while to come. You regard me as someone of high rank,b O LORD God! 18 And what more can David say to you for honouring your servant? You know your servant. 19 For your servant's sake, O LORD, and according to your own heart, you have done all these great deeds, making known all these great things. 20 There is no one like you, O LORD, and there is no God besides you, according to all that we have heard with our ears. 21 Who is like your people Israel, one nation on the earth whom God went to redeem to be his people, making for yourself a name for great and terrible things, in driving out nations before your people whom you redeemed from Egypt? 22 And you made your people Israel to be your people for ever; and you, O LORD, became their God.

23 'And now, O LORD, as for the word that you have spoken concerning your servant and concerning his house, let it be established for ever, and do as you have promised. 24 Thus your name will be established and magnified for ever in the saying, "The LORD of hosts, the God of Israel, is Israel's God"; and the house of your servant David will be established in your presence. 25 For you, my God, have revealed to your servant that you will build a house for him; therefore your servant has found it possible to pray before you. 26 And now, O LORD, you are God, and you have promised this good thing to your servant; 27 therefore may it please you to bless the house of your servant, that it may continue for ever

a Gk 2 Sam 7.6: Heb *but I have been from tent to tent and from tabernacle*   b Meaning of Heb uncertain before you. For you, O LORD, have blessed and are blessed *a* for ever.'

David's Kingdom Established and Extended

18 Some time afterwards, David attacked the Philistines and subdued them; he took Gath and its villages from the Philistines.

2 He defeated Moab, and the Moabites became subject to David and brought tribute.

3 David also struck down King Hadadezer of Zobah, towards Hamath, *b* as he went to set up a monument at the river Euphrates. 4 David took from him one thousand chariots, seven thousand cavalry, and twenty thousand foot-soldiers. David hamstrung all the chariot horses, but left one hundred of them. 5 When the Arameans of Damascus came to help King Hadadezer of Zobah, David killed twenty-two thousand Arameans. 6 Then David put garrisons *c* in Aram of Damascus; and the Arameans became subject to David, and brought tribute. The LORD gave victory to David wherever he went. 7 David took the gold shields that were carried by the servants of Hadadezer, and brought them to Jerusalem. 8 From Tibhath and from Cun, cities of Hadadezer, David took a vast quantity of bronze; with it Solomon made the bronze sea and the pillars and the vessels of bronze.

9 When King Tou of Hamath heard that David had defeated the whole army of King Hadadezer of Zobah, 10 he sent his son Hadoram to King David, to greet him and to congratulate him, because he had fought against Hadadezer and defeated him. Now Hadadezer had often been at war with Tou. He sent all sorts of articles of gold, of silver, and of bronze; 11 these also King David dedicated to the LORD, together with the silver and gold that he had carried off from all the nations, from Edom, Moab, the Ammonites, the Philistines, and Amalek.

12 Abishai son of Zeruiah killed eighteen thousand Edomites in the Valley of Salt. 13 He put garrisons in Edom; and all

the Edomites became subject to David. And the LORD gave victory to David wherever he went.

David's Administration

14 So David reigned over all Israel; and he administered justice and equity to all his people. 15 Joab son of Zeruiah was over the army; Jehoshaphat son of Ahilud was recorder; 16 Zadok son of Ahitub and Ahimelech son of Abiathar were priests; Shavsha was secretary; 17 Benaiah son of Jehoiada was over the Cherethites and the Pelethites; and David's sons were the chief officials in the service of the king.

Defeat of the Ammonites and Arameans

19 Some time afterwards, King Nahash of the Ammonites died, and his son succeeded him. 2 David said, 'I will deal loyally with Hanun son of Nahash, for his father dealt loyally with me.' So David sent messengers to console him concerning his father. When David's servants came to Hanun in the land of the Ammonites, to console him, 3 the officials of the Ammonites said to Hanun, 'Do you think, because David has sent people to console you, that he is honouring your father? Have not his servants come to you to search and to overthrow and to spy out the land?' 4 So Hanun seized David's servants, shaved them, cut off their garments in the middle at their hips, and sent them away; 5 and they departed. When David was told about the men, he sent messengers to them, for they felt greatly humiliated. The king said, 'Remain at Jericho until your beards have grown, and then return.'

6 When the Ammonites saw that they had made themselves odious to David, Hanun and the Ammonites sent a thousand talents of silver to hire chariots and cavalry from Mesopotamia, from Aram-maacah and from Zobah. 7 They hired thirty-two thousand chariots and the king of Maacah with his army, who came and camped before Medeba. And the Ammonites were mustered from their cities

a Or *and it is blessed*   *b* Meaning of Heb uncertain
c Gk Vg 2 Sam 8.6 Compare Syr: Heb lacks *garrisons*

and came to battle. [8]When David heard of it, he sent Joab and all the army of the warriors. [9]The Ammonites came out and drew up in battle array at the entrance of the city, and the kings who had come were by themselves in the open country. 10 When Joab saw that the line of battle was set against him both in front and in the rear, he chose some of the picked men of Israel and arrayed them against the Arameans; [11]the rest of his troops he put in charge of his brother Abishai, and they were arrayed against the Ammonites. [12]He said, 'If the Arameans are too strong for me, then you shall help me; but if the Ammonites are too strong for you, then I will help you. [13]Be strong, and let us be courageous for our people and for the cities of our God; and may the LORD do what seems good to him.' [14]So Joab and the troops who were with him advanced towards the Arameans for battle; and they fled before him. [15]When the Ammonites saw that the Arameans fled, they likewise fled before Abishai, Joab's brother, and entered the city. Then Joab came to Jerusalem.

16 But when the Arameans saw that they had been defeated by Israel, they sent messengers and brought out the Arameans who were beyond the Euphrates, with Shophach the commander of the army of Hadadezer at their head. [17]When David was informed, he gathered all Israel together, crossed the Jordan, came to them, and drew up his forces against them. When David set the battle in array against the Arameans, they fought with him. [18]The Arameans fled before Israel; and David killed seven thousand Aramean charioteers and forty thousand foot-soldiers, and also killed Shophach the commander of their army. [19]When the servants of Hadadezer saw that they had been defeated by Israel, they made peace with David, and became subject to him. So the Arameans were not willing to help the Ammonites any more.

Siege and Capture of Rabbah

20 In the spring of the year, the time when kings go out to battle, Joab led out the army, ravaged the country of the Ammonites, and came and besieged Rabbah. But David remained at Jerusalem. Joab attacked Rabbah, and overthrew it. [2]David took the crown of Milcom[a] from his head; he found that it weighed a talent of gold, and in it was a precious stone; and it was placed on David's head. He also brought out the booty of the city, a very great amount. [3]He brought out the people who were in it, and set them to work[b] with saws and iron picks and axes.[c] Thus David did to all the cities of the Ammonites. Then David and all the people returned to Jerusalem.

Exploits against the Philistines

4 After this, war broke out with the Philistines at Gezer; then Sibbecai the Hushathite killed Sippai, who was one of the descendants of the giants; and the Philistines were subdued. [5]Again there was war with the Philistines; and Elhanan son of Jair killed Lahmi the brother of Goliath the Gittite, the shaft of whose spear was like a weaver's beam. [6]Again there was war at Gath, where there was a man of great size, who had six fingers on each hand, and six toes on each foot, twenty-four in number; he also was descended from the giants. [7]When he taunted Israel, Jonathan son of Shimea, David's brother, killed him. [8]These were descended from the giants in Gath; they fell by the hand of David and his servants.

The Census and Plague

21 Satan stood up against Israel, and incited David to count the people of Israel. [2]So David said to Joab and the commanders of the army, 'Go, number Israel, from Beer-sheba to Dan, and bring me a report, so that I may know their number.' [3]But Joab said, 'May the LORD increase the number of his people a hundredfold! Are they not, my lord the king, all of them my lord's servants? Why then should my lord require this? Why should he bring guilt on Israel?' [4]But the king's

a Gk Vg See 1 Kings 11.5, 33: MT *of their king*
b Compare 2 Sam 12.31: Heb *and he sawed*
c Compare 2 Sam 12.31: Heb *saws*

word prevailed against Joab. So Joab departed and went throughout all Israel, and came back to Jerusalem. [5] Joab gave the total count of the people to David. In all Israel there were one million one hundred thousand men who drew the sword, and in Judah four hundred and seventy thousand who drew the sword. [6] But he did not include Levi and Benjamin in the numbering, for the king's command was abhorrent to Joab.

[7] But God was displeased with this thing, and he struck Israel. [8] David said to God, 'I have sinned greatly in that I have done this thing. But now, I pray you, take away the guilt of your servant; for I have done very foolishly.' [9] The LORD spoke to Gad, David's seer, saying, [10] 'Go and say to David, "Thus says the LORD: Three things I offer you; choose one of them, so that I may do it to you." ' [11] So Gad came to David and said to him, 'Thus says the LORD, "Take your choice: [12] either three years of famine; or three months of devastation by your foes, while the sword of your enemies overtakes you; or three days of the sword of the LORD, pestilence on the land, and the angel of the LORD destroying throughout all the territory of Israel." Now decide what answer I shall return to the one who sent me.' [13] Then David said to Gad, 'I am in great distress; let me fall into the hand of the LORD, for his mercy is very great; but let me not fall into human hands.'

[14] So the LORD sent a pestilence on Israel; and seventy thousand persons fell in Israel. [15] And God sent an angel to Jerusalem to destroy it; but when he was about to destroy it, the LORD took note and relented concerning the calamity; he said to the destroying angel, 'Enough! Stay your hand.' The angel of the LORD was then standing by the threshing-floor of Ornan the Jebusite. [16] David looked up and saw the angel of the LORD standing between earth and heaven, and in his hand a drawn sword stretched out over Jerusalem. Then David and the elders, clothed in sackcloth, fell on their faces. [17] And David said to God, 'Was it not I who gave the command to count the people? It is I who have sinned and done very wickedly. But these sheep, what have they done? Let your hand, I pray, O LORD my God, be against me and against my father's house; but do not let your people be plagued!'

David's Altar and Sacrifice

[18] Then the angel of the LORD commanded Gad to tell David that he should go up and erect an altar to the LORD on the threshing-floor of Ornan the Jebusite. [19] So David went up following Gad's instructions, which he had spoken in the name of the LORD. [20] Ornan turned and saw the angel; and while his four sons who were with him hid themselves, Ornan continued to thresh wheat. [21] As David came to Ornan, Ornan looked and saw David; he went out from the threshing-floor, and did obeisance to David with his face to the ground. [22] David said to Ornan, 'Give me the site of the threshing-floor that I may build on it an altar to the LORD—give it to me at its full price—so that the plague may be averted from the people.' [23] Then Ornan said to David, 'Take it; and let my lord the king do what seems good to him; see, I present the oxen for burnt-offerings, and the threshing-sledges for the wood, and the wheat for a grain-offering. I give it all.' [24] But King David said to Ornan, 'No; I will buy them for the full price. I will not take for the LORD what is yours, nor offer burnt-offerings that cost me nothing.' [25] So David paid Ornan six hundred shekels of gold by weight for the site. [26] David built there an altar to the LORD and presented burnt-offerings and offerings of well-being. He called upon the LORD, and he answered him with fire from heaven on the altar of burnt-offering. [27] Then the LORD commanded the angel, and he put his sword back into its sheath.

The Place Chosen for the Temple

[28] At that time, when David saw that the LORD had answered him at the threshing-floor of Ornan the Jebusite, he made his sacrifices there. [29] For the tabernacle of the LORD, which Moses had made in the wilderness, and the altar of burnt-offering were at

that time in the high place at Gibeon; ³⁰but David could not go before it to inquire of God, for he was afraid of the sword of the angel of the LORD. ¹Then David said, 'Here shall be the house of the LORD God and here the altar of burnt-offering for Israel.'

David Prepares to Build the Temple

2 David gave orders to gather together the aliens who were residing in the land of Israel, and he set stonecutters to prepare dressed stones for building the house of God. ³David also provided great stores of iron for nails for the doors of the gates and for clamps, as well as bronze in quantities beyond weighing, ⁴and cedar logs without number—for the Sidonians and Tyrians brought great quantities of cedar to David. ⁵For David said, 'My son Solomon is young and inexperienced, and the house that is to be built for the LORD must be exceedingly magnificent, famous and glorified throughout all lands; I will therefore make preparation for it.' So David provided materials in great quantity before his death.

David's Charge to Solomon and the Leaders

6 Then he called for his son Solomon and charged him to build a house for the LORD, the God of Israel. ⁷David said to Solomon, 'My son, I had planned to build a house to the name of the LORD my God. ⁸But the word of the LORD came to me, saying, "You have shed much blood and have waged great wars; you shall not build a house to my name, because you have shed so much blood in my sight on the earth. ⁹See, a son shall be born to you; he shall be a man of peace. I will give him peace from all his enemies on every side; for his name shall be Solomon,ᵃ and I will give peaceᵇ and quiet to Israel in his days. ¹⁰He shall build a house for my name. He shall be a son to me, and I will be a father to him, and I will establish his royal throne in Israel for ever." ¹¹Now, my son, the LORD be with you, so that you may succeed in building the house of the LORD your God,

as he has spoken concerning you. ¹²Only, may the LORD grant you discretion and understanding, so that when he gives you charge over Israel you may keep the law of the LORD your God. ¹³Then you will prosper if you are careful to observe the statutes and the ordinances that the LORD commanded Moses for Israel. Be strong and of good courage. Do not be afraid or dismayed. ¹⁴With great pains I have provided for the house of the LORD one hundred thousand talents of gold, one million talents of silver, and bronze and iron beyond weighing, for there is so much of it; timber and stone too I have provided. To these you must add more. ¹⁵You have an abundance of workers: stonecutters, masons, carpenters, and all kinds of artisans without number, skilled in working ¹⁶gold, silver, bronze, and iron. Now begin the work, and the LORD be with you.'

17 David also commanded all the leaders of Israel to help his son Solomon, saying, ¹⁸'Is not the LORD your God with you? Has he not given you peace on every side? For he has delivered the inhabitants of the land into my hand; and the land is subdued before the LORD and his people. ¹⁹Now set your mind and heart to seek the LORD your God. Go and build the sanctuary of the LORD God so that the ark of the covenant of the LORD and the holy vessels of God may be brought into a house built for the name of the LORD.'

Families of the Levites and Their Functions

23 When David was old and full of days, he made his son Solomon king over Israel.

2 David assembled all the leaders of Israel and the priests and the Levites. ³The Levites, thirty years old and upwards, were counted, and the total was thirty-eight thousand. ⁴'Twenty-four thousand of these', David said, 'shall have charge of the work in the house of the LORD, six thousand shall be officers and judges, ⁵four thousand gatekeepers, and four thousand shall offer praises to the LORD with the in-

a Heb *Shelomoh*   *b* Heb *shalom*

struments that I have made for praise.' ⁶And David organized them in divisions corresponding to the sons of Levi: Gershon,ᵃ Kohath, and Merari.

7 The sons of Gershonᵇ were Ladan and Shimei. ⁸The sons of Ladan: Jehiel the chief, Zetham, and Joel, three. ⁹The sons of Shimei: Shelomoth, Haziel, and Haran, three. These were the heads of families of Ladan. ¹⁰And the sons of Shimei: Jahath, Zina, Jeush, and Beriah. These four were the sons of Shimei. ¹¹Jahath was the chief, and Zizah the second; but Jeush and Beriah did not have many sons, so they were enrolled as a single family.

12 The sons of Kohath: Amram, Izhar, Hebron, and Uzziel, four. ¹³The sons of Amram: Aaron and Moses. Aaron was set apart to consecrate the most holy things, so that he and his sons for ever should make offerings before the LORD, and minister to him and pronounce blessings in his name for ever; ¹⁴but as for Moses the man of God, his sons were to be reckoned among the tribe of Levi. ¹⁵The sons of Moses: Gershom and Eliezer. ¹⁶The sons of Gershom: Shebuel the chief. ¹⁷The sons of Eliezer: Rehabiah the chief; Eliezer had no other sons, but the sons of Rehabiah were very numerous. ¹⁸The sons of Izhar: Shelomith the chief. ¹⁹The sons of Hebron: Jeriah the chief, Amariah the second, Jahaziel the third, and Jekameam the fourth. ²⁰The sons of Uzziel: Micah the chief and Isshiah the second.

21 The sons of Merari: Mahli and Mushi. The sons of Mahli: Eleazar and Kish. ²²Eleazar died having no sons, but only daughters; their kindred, the sons of Kish, married them. ²³The sons of Mushi: Mahli, Eder, and Jeremoth, three.

24 These were the sons of Levi by their ancestral houses, the heads of families as they were enrolled according to the number of the names of the individuals from twenty years old and upwards who were to do the work for the service of the house of the LORD. ²⁵For David said, 'The LORD, the God of Israel, has given rest to his people; and he resides in Jerusalem for ever. ²⁶And so the Levites no longer need to carry the

tabernacle or any of the things for its service'— ²⁷for according to the last words of David these were the number of the Levites from twenty years old and upwards— ²⁸'but their duty shall be to assist the descendants of Aaron for the service of the house of the LORD, having the care of the courts and the chambers, the cleansing of all that is holy, and any work for the service of the house of God; ²⁹to assist also with the rows of bread, the choice flour for the grain-offering, the wafers of unleavened bread, the baked-offering, the offering mixed with oil, and all measures of quantity or size. ³⁰And they shall stand every morning, thanking and praising the LORD, and likewise at evening, ³¹and whenever burnt-offerings are offered to the LORD on sabbaths, new moons, and appointed festivals, according to the number required of them, regularly before the LORD. ³²Thus they shall keep charge of the tent of meeting and the sanctuary, and shall attend the descendants of Aaron, their kindred, for the service of the house of the LORD.'

Divisions of the Priests

24 The divisions of the descendants of Aaron were these. The sons of Aaron: Nadab, Abihu, Eleazar, and Ithamar. ²But Nadab and Abihu died before their father, and had no sons; so Eleazar and Ithamar became the priests. ³Along with Zadok of the sons of Eleazar, and Ahimelech of the sons of Ithamar, David organized them according to the appointed duties in their service. ⁴Since more chief men were found among the sons of Eleazar than among the sons of Ithamar, they organized them under sixteen heads of ancestral houses of the sons of Eleazar, and eight of the sons of Ithamar. ⁵They organized them by lot, all alike, for there were officers of the sanctuary and officers of God among both the sons of Eleazar and the sons of Ithamar. ⁶The scribe Shemaiah son of Nethanel, a Levite, recorded them in the presence of the king, and the officers, and Zadok the priest, and Ahimelech son

ᵃ Or Gershom; See 1 Chr 6.1, note, and 23.15
ᵇ Vg Compare Gk Syr: Heb to the Gershonite

of Abiathar, and the heads of ancestral houses of the priests and of the Levites; one ancestral house being chosen for Eleazar and one chosen for Ithamar.

7 The first lot fell to Jehoiarib, the second to Jedaiah, 8 the third to Harim, the fourth to Seorim, 9 the fifth to Malchijah, the sixth to Mijamin, 10 the seventh to Hakkoz, the eighth to Abijah, 11 the ninth to Jeshua, the tenth to Shecaniah, 12 the eleventh to Eliashib, the twelfth to Jakim, 13 the thirteenth to Huppah, the fourteenth to Jeshebeab, 14 the fifteenth to Bilgah, the sixteenth to Immer, 15 the seventeenth to Hezir, the eighteenth to Happizzez, 16 the nineteenth to Pethahiah, the twentieth to Jehezkel, 17 the twenty-first to Jachin, the twenty-second to Gamul, 18 the twenty-third to Delaiah, the twenty-fourth to Maaziah. 19 These had as their appointed duty in their service to enter the house of the LORD according to the procedure established for them by their ancestor Aaron, as the LORD God of Israel had commanded him.

Other Levites

20 And of the rest of the sons of Levi: of the sons of Amram, Shubael; of the sons of Shubael, Jehdeiah. 21 Of Rehabiah: of the sons of Rehabiah, Isshiah the chief. 22 Of the Izharites, Shelomoth; of the sons of Shelomoth, Jahath. 23 The sons of Hebron:*a* Jeriah the chief,*b* Amariah the second, Jahaziel the third, Jekameam the fourth. 24 The sons of Uzziel, Micah; of the sons of Micah, Shamir. 25 The brother of Micah, Isshiah; of the sons of Isshiah, Zechariah. 26 The sons of Merari: Mahli and Mushi. The sons of Jaaziah: Beno.*c* 27 The sons of Merari: of Jaaziah, Beno,*c* Shoham, Zaccur, and Ibri. 28 Of Mahli: Eleazar, who had no sons. 29 Of Kish, the sons of Kish: Jerahmeel. 30 The sons of Mushi: Mahli, Eder, and Jerimoth. These were the sons of the Levites according to their ancestral houses. 31 These also cast lots corresponding to their kindred, the descendants of Aaron, in the presence of King David, Zadok, Ahimelech, and the heads of ancestral houses of the priests and of the Levites, the chief as well as the youngest brother.

The Temple Musicians

25 David and the officers of the army also set apart for the service the sons of Asaph, and of Heman, and of Jeduthun, who were to prophesy with lyres, harps, and cymbals. The list of those who did the work and of their duties was: 2 Of the sons of Asaph: Zaccur, Joseph, Nethaniah, and Asarelah, sons of Asaph, under the direction of Asaph, who prophesied under the direction of the king. 3 Of Jeduthun, the sons of Jeduthun: Gedaliah, Zeri, Jeshaiah, Shimei,*d* Hashabiah, and Mattithiah, six, under the direction of their father Jeduthun, who prophesied with the lyre in thanksgiving and praise to the LORD. 4 Of Heman, the sons of Heman: Bukkiah, Mattaniah, Uzziel, Shebuel, and Jerimoth, Hananiah, Hanani, Eliathah, Giddalti, and Romamti-ezer, Joshbekashah, Mallothi, Hothir, Mahazioth. 5 All these were the sons of Heman the king's seer, according to the promise of God to exalt him; for God had given Heman fourteen sons and three daughters. 6 They were all under the direction of their father for the music in the house of the LORD with cymbals, harps, and lyres for the service of the house of God. Asaph, Jeduthun, and Heman were under the order of the king. 7 They and their kindred, who were trained in singing to the LORD, all of whom were skilful, numbered two hundred and eighty-eight. 8 And they cast lots for their duties, small and great, teacher and pupil alike.

9 The first lot fell for Asaph to Joseph; the second to Gedaliah, to him and his brothers and his sons, twelve; 10 the third to Zaccur, his sons and his brothers, twelve; 11 the fourth to Izri, his sons and his brothers, twelve; 12 the fifth to Nethaniah, his sons and his brothers, twelve; 13 the sixth to Bukkiah, his sons and his brothers, twelve; 14 the seventh to Jesarelah,*e* his sons and his brothers, twelve; 15 the eighth to Jesha-

a See 23.19: Heb lacks Hebron   b See 23.19: Heb lacks the chief   c Or his son: Meaning of Heb uncertain   d One Ms: Gk: MT lacks Shimei   e Or Asarelah; see 25.2 iah, his sons and his brothers, twelve; [16] the ninth to Mattaniah, his sons and his brothers, twelve; [17] the tenth to Shimei, his sons and his brothers, twelve; [18] the eleventh to Azarel, his sons and his brothers, twelve; [19] the twelfth to Hashabiah, his sons and his brothers, twelve; [20] to the thirteenth, Shubael, his sons and his brothers, twelve; [21] to the fourteenth, Mattithiah, his sons and his brothers, twelve; [22] to the fifteenth, to Jeremoth, his sons and his brothers, twelve; [23] to the sixteenth, to Hananiah, his sons and his brothers, twelve; [24] to the seventeenth, to Joshbekashah, his sons and his brothers, twelve; [25] to the eighteenth, to Hanani, his sons and his brothers, twelve; [26] to the nineteenth, to Mallothi, his sons and his brothers, twelve; [27] to the twentieth, to Eliathah, his sons and his brothers, twelve; [28] to the twenty-first, to Hothir, his sons and his brothers, twelve; [29] to the twenty-second, to Giddalti, his sons and his brothers, twelve; [30] to the twenty-third, to Mahazioth, his sons and his brothers, twelve; [31] to the twenty-fourth, to Romamti-ezer, his sons and his brothers, twelve.

The Gatekeepers

26 As for the divisions of the gatekeepers: of the Korahites, Meshelemiah son of Kore, of the sons of Asaph. [2] Meshelemiah had sons: Zechariah the firstborn, Jediael the second, Zebadiah the third, Jathniel the fourth, [3] Elam the fifth, Jehohanan the sixth, Eliehoenai the seventh. [4] Obed-edom had sons: Shemaiah the firstborn, Jehozabad the second, Joah the third, Sachar the fourth, Nethanel the fifth, [5] Ammiel the sixth, Issachar the seventh, Peullethai the eighth; for God blessed him. [6] Also to his son Shemaiah sons were born who exercised authority in their ancestral houses, for they were men of great ability. [7] The sons of Shemaiah: Othni, Rephael, Obed, and Elzabad, whose brothers were able men, Elihu and Semachiah. [8] All these, sons of Obed-edom with their sons and brothers, were able men qualified for the service; sixty-two of Obed-edom. [9] Meshelemiah had sons and brothers, able men, eighteen. [10] Hosah, of

the sons of Merari, had sons: Shimri the chief (for though he was not the firstborn, his father made him chief), [11] Hilkiah the second, Tebaliah the third, Zechariah the fourth: all the sons and brothers of Hosah totalled thirteen.

12 These divisions of the gatekeepers, corresponding to their leaders, had duties, just as their kindred did, ministering in the house of the LORD; [13] and they cast lots by ancestral houses, small and great alike, for their gates. [14] The lot for the east fell to Shelemiah. They cast lots also for his son Zechariah, a prudent counsellor, and his lot came out for the north. [15] Obed-edom's came out for the south, and to his sons was allotted the storehouse. [16] For Shuppim and Hosah it came out for the west, at the gate of Shallecheth on the ascending road. Guard corresponded to guard. [17] On the east there were six Levites each day, [a] on the north four each day, on the south four each day, as well as two and two at the storehouse; [18] and for the colonnade [b] on the west there were four at the road and two at the colonnade. [b] [19] These were the divisions of the gatekeepers among the Korahites and the sons of Merari.

The Treasurers, Officers, and Judges

20 And of the Levites, Ahijah had charge of the treasuries of the house of God and the treasuries of the dedicated gifts. [21] The sons of Ladan, the sons of the Gershonites belonging to Ladan, the heads of families belonging to Ladan the Gershonite: Jehieli. [c] 22 The sons of Jehieli, Zetham and his brother Joel, were in charge of the treasuries of the house of the LORD. [23] Of the Amramites, the Izharites, the Hebronites, and the Uzzielites: [24] Shebuel son of Gershom, son of Moses, was chief officer in charge of the treasuries. [25] His brothers: from Eliezer were his son Rehabiah, his son Jeshaiah, his son Joram, his son Zichri, and his son Shelomoth. [26] This Shelomoth and his brothers were in charge of all the treasuries of the dedicated gifts that King David, and the heads of families, and the officers of

a Gk: Heb lacks *each day*   *b* Heb *parbar*: meaning uncertain   *c* The Hebrew text of verse 21 is confused the thousands and the hundreds, and the commanders of the army, had dedicated. 27 From booty won in battles they dedicated gifts for the maintenance of the house of the LORD. 28 Also all that Samuel the seer, and Saul son of Kish, and Abner son of Ner, and Joab son of Zeruiah had dedicated—all dedicated gifts were in the care of Shelomoth*a* and his brothers.

29 Of the Izharites, Chenaniah and his sons were appointed to outside duties for Israel, as officers and judges. 30 Of the Hebronites, Hashabiah and his brothers, one thousand seven hundred men of ability, had the oversight of Israel west of the Jordan for all the work of the LORD and for the service of the king. 31 Of the Hebronites, Jerijah was chief of the Hebronites. (In the fortieth year of David's reign search was made, of whatever genealogy or family, and men of great ability among them were found at Jazer in Gilead.) 32 King David appointed him and his brothers, two thousand seven hundred men of ability, heads of families, to have the oversight of the Reubenites, the Gadites, and the half-tribe of the Manassites for everything pertaining to God and for the affairs of the king.

The Military Divisions

27 This is the list of the people of Israel, the heads of families, the commanders of the thousands and the hundreds, and their officers who served the king in all matters concerning the divisions that came and went, month after month throughout the year, each division numbering twenty-four thousand:

2 Jashobeam son of Zabdiel was in charge of the first division in the first month; in his division were twenty-four thousand. 3 He was a descendant of Perez, and was chief of all the commanders of the army for the first month. 4 Dodai the Ahohite was in charge of the division of the second month; Mikloth was the chief officer of his division. In his division were twenty-four thousand. 5 The third commander, for the third month, was Benaiah son of the priest Jehoiada, as chief; in his division were twenty-four thousand. 6 This is the Benaiah

who was a mighty man of the Thirty and in command of the Thirty; his son Ammizabad was in charge of his division.*b* 7 Asahel brother of Joab was fourth, for the fourth month, and his son Zebadiah after him; in his division were twenty-four thousand. 8 The fifth commander, for the fifth month, was Shamhuth, the Izrahite; in his division were twenty-four thousand. 9 Sixth, for the sixth month, was Ira son of Ikkesh the Tekoite; in his division were twenty-four thousand. 10 Seventh, for the seventh month, was Helez the Pelonite, of the Ephraimites; in his division were twenty-four thousand. 11 Eighth, for the eighth month, was Sibbecai the Hushathite, of the Zerahites; in his division were twenty-four thousand. 12 Ninth, for the ninth month, was Abiezer of Anathoth, a Benjaminite; in his division were twenty-four thousand. 13 Tenth, for the tenth month, was Maharai of Netophah, of the Zerahites; in his division were twenty-four thousand. 14 Eleventh, for the eleventh month, was Benaiah of Pirathon, of the Ephraimites; in his division were twenty-four thousand. 15 Twelfth, for the twelfth month, was Heldai the Netophathite, of Othniel; in his division were twenty-four thousand.

Leaders of Tribes

16 Over the tribes of Israel, for the Reubenites, Eliezer son of Zichri was chief officer; for the Simeonites, Shephatiah son of Maacah; 17 for Levi, Hashabiah son of Kemuel; for Aaron, Zadok; 18 for Judah, Elihu, one of David's brothers; for Issachar, Omri son of Michael; 19 for Zebulun, Ishmaiah son of Obadiah; for Naphtali, Jerimoth son of Azriel; 20 for the Ephraimites, Hoshea son of Azaziah; for the half-tribe of Manasseh, Joel son of Pedaiah; 21 for the half-tribe of Manasseh in Gilead, Iddo son of Zechariah; for Benjamin, Jaasiel son of Abner; 22 for Dan, Azarel son of Jeroham. These were the leaders of the tribes of Israel. 23 David did not count those below twenty years of age, for the LORD had promised to make Israel as numerous as the stars of heaven. 24 Joab son

a Gk Compare 26.28: Heb *Shelomith*   *b* Gk Vg: Heb *Ammizabad was his division* of Zeruiah began to count them, but did not finish; yet wrath came upon Israel for this, and the number was not entered into the account of the Annals of King David.

Other Civic Officials

25 Over the king's treasuries was Azmaveth son of Adiel. Over the treasuries in the country, in the cities, in the villages, and in the towers, was Jonathan son of Uzziah. 26 Over those who did the work of the field, tilling the soil, was Ezri son of Chelub. 27 Over the vineyards was Shimei the Ramathite. Over the produce of the vineyards for the wine cellars was Zabdi the Shiphmite. 28 Over the olive and sycamore trees in the Shephelah was Baal-hanan the Gederite. Over the stores of oil was Joash. 29 Over the herds that pastured in Sharon was Shitrai the Sharonite. Over the herds in the valleys was Shaphat son of Adlai. 30 Over the camels was Obil the Ishmaelite. Over the donkeys was Jehdeiah the Meronothite. Over the flocks was Jaziz the Hagrite. 31 All these were stewards of King David's property.

32 Jonathan, David's uncle, was a counsellor, being a man of understanding and a scribe; Jehiel son of Hachmoni attended the king's sons. 33 Ahithophel was the king's counsellor, and Hushai the Archite was the king's friend. 34 After Ahithophel came Jehoiada son of Benaiah, and Abiathar. Joab was commander of the king's army.

Solomon Instructed to Build the Temple

28 David assembled at Jerusalem all the officials of Israel, the officials of the tribes, the officers of the divisions that served the king, the commanders of the thousands, the commanders of the hundreds, the stewards of all the property and cattle of the king and his sons, together with the palace officials, the mighty warriors, and all the warriors. 2 Then King David rose to his feet and said: 'Hear me, my brothers and my people. I had planned to build a house of rest for the ark of the covenant of the LORD, for the footstool of our God; and I made preparations for build-

ing. 3 But God said to me, "You shall not build a house for my name, for you are a warrior and have shed blood." 4 Yet the LORD God of Israel chose me from all my ancestral house to be king over Israel for ever; for he chose Judah as leader, and in the house of Judah my father's house, and among my father's sons he took delight in making me king over all Israel. 5 And of all my sons, for the LORD has given me many, he has chosen my son Solomon to sit upon the throne of the kingdom of the LORD over Israel. 6 He said to me, "It is your son Solomon who shall build my house and my courts, for I have chosen him to be a son to me, and I will be a father to him. 7 I will establish his kingdom for ever if he continues resolute in keeping my commandments and my ordinances, as he is today." 8 Now therefore in the sight of all Israel, the assembly of the LORD, and in the hearing of our God, observe and search out all the commandments of the LORD your God; that you may possess this good land, and leave it for an inheritance to your children after you for ever.

9 'And you, my son Solomon, know the God of your father, and serve him with single mind and willing heart; for the LORD searches every mind, and understands every plan and thought. If you seek him, he will be found by you; but if you forsake him, he will abandon you for ever. 10 Take heed now, for the LORD has chosen you to build a house as the sanctuary; be strong, and act.'

11 Then David gave his son Solomon the plan of the vestibule of the temple, and of its houses, its treasuries, its upper rooms, and its inner chambers, and of the room for the mercy-seat;a 12 and the plan of all that he had in mind: for the courts of the house of the LORD, all the surrounding chambers, the treasuries of the house of God, and the treasuries for dedicated gifts; 13 for the divisions of the priests and of the Levites, and all the work of the service in the house of the LORD; for all the vessels for the service in the house of the LORD, 14 the weight of gold for all golden vessels for

a Or the cover

each service, the weight of silver vessels for each service, 15 the weight of the golden lampstands and their lamps, the weight of gold for each lampstand and its lamps, the weight of silver for a lampstand and its lamps, according to the use of each in the service, 16 the weight of gold for each table for the rows of bread, the silver for the silver tables, 17 and pure gold for the forks, the basins, and the cups; for the golden bowls and the weight of each; for the silver bowls and the weight of each; 18 for the altar of incense made of refined gold, and its weight; also his plan for the golden chariot of the cherubim that spread their wings and covered the ark of the covenant of the LORD.

19 'All this, in writing at the LORD's direction, he made clear to me—the plan of all the works.'

20 David said further to his son Solomon, 'Be strong and of good courage, and act. Do not be afraid or dismayed; for the LORD God, my God, is with you. He will not fail you or forsake you, until all the work for the service of the house of the LORD is finished. 21 Here are the divisions of the priests and the Levites for all the service of the house of God; and with you in all the work will be every volunteer who has skill for any kind of service; also the officers and all the people will be wholly at your command.'

Offerings for Building the Temple

29 King David said to the whole assembly, 'My son Solomon, whom alone God has chosen, is young and inexperienced, and the work is great; for the temple*a* will not be for mortals but for the LORD God. 2 So I have provided for the house of my God, so far as I was able, the gold for the things of gold, the silver for the things of silver, and the bronze for the things of bronze, the iron for the things of iron, and wood for the things of wood, besides great quantities of onyx and stones for setting, antimony, coloured stones, all sorts of precious stones, and marble in abundance. 3 Moreover, in addition to all that I have provided for the holy house, I

have a treasure of my own of gold and silver, and because of my devotion to the house of my God I give it to the house of my God: 4 three thousand talents of gold, of the gold of Ophir, and seven thousand talents of refined silver, for overlaying the walls of the house, 5 and for all the work to be done by artisans, gold for the things of gold and silver for the things of silver. Who then will offer willingly, consecrating themselves today to the LORD?'

6 Then the leaders of ancestral houses made their freewill-offerings, as did also the leaders of the tribes, the commanders of the thousands and of the hundreds, and the officers over the king's work. 7 They gave for the service of the house of God five thousand talents and ten thousand darics of gold, ten thousand talents of silver, eighteen thousand talents of bronze, and one hundred thousand talents of iron. 8 Whoever had precious stones gave them to the treasury of the house of the LORD, into the care of Jehiel the Gershonite. 9 Then the people rejoiced because these had given willingly, for with single mind they had offered freely to the LORD; King David also rejoiced greatly.

David's Praise to God

10 Then David blessed the LORD in the presence of all the assembly; David said: 'Blessed are you, O LORD, the God of our ancestor Israel, for ever and ever. 11 Yours, O LORD, are the greatness, the power, the glory, the victory, and the majesty; for all that is in the heavens and on the earth is yours; yours is the kingdom, O LORD, and you are exalted as head above all. 12 Riches and honour come from you, and you rule over all. In your hand are power and might; and it is in your hand to make great and to give strength to all. 13 And now, our God, we give thanks to you and praise your glorious name.

14 'But who am I, and what is my people, that we should be able to make this freewill-offering? For all things come from you, and of your own have we given you. 15 For we are aliens and transients before

a Heb *fortress*

you, as were all our ancestors; our days on the earth are like a shadow, and there is no hope. 16 O LORD our God, all this abundance that we have provided for building you a house for your holy name comes from your hand and is all your own. 17 I know, my God, that you search the heart, and take pleasure in uprightness; in the uprightness of my heart I have freely offered all these things, and now I have seen your people, who are present here, offering freely and joyously to you. 18 O LORD, the God of Abraham, Isaac, and Israel, our ancestors, keep for ever such purposes and thoughts in the hearts of your people, and direct their hearts towards you. 19 Grant to my son Solomon that with single mind he may keep your commandments, your decrees, and your statutes, performing all of them, and that he may build the temple*a* for which I have made provision.'

20 Then David said to the whole assembly, 'Bless the LORD your God.' And all the assembly blessed the LORD, the God of their ancestors, and bowed their heads and prostrated themselves before the LORD and the king. 21 On the next day they offered sacrifices and burnt-offerings to the LORD, a thousand bulls, a thousand rams, and a thousand lambs, with their libations, and sacrifices in abundance for all Israel; 22 and they ate and drank before the LORD on that day with great joy.

Solomon Anointed King

They made David's son Solomon king a second time; they anointed him as the LORD's prince, and Zadok as priest. 23 Then Solomon sat on the throne of the LORD, succeeding his father David as king; he prospered, and all Israel obeyed him. 24 All the leaders and the mighty warriors, and also all the sons of King David, pledged their allegiance to King Solomon. 25 The LORD highly exalted Solomon in the sight of all Israel, and bestowed upon him such royal majesty as had not been on any king before him in Israel.

Summary of David's Reign

26 Thus David son of Jesse reigned over all Israel. 27 The period that he reigned over Israel was forty years; he reigned for seven years in Hebron and thirty-three years in Jerusalem. 28 He died at a good old age, full of days, riches, and honour; and his son Solomon succeeded him. 29 Now the acts of King David, from first to last, are written in the records of the seer Samuel, and in the records of the prophet Nathan, and in the records of the seer Gad, 30 with accounts of all his rule and his might and of the events that befell him and Israel and all the kingdoms of the earth.

a Heb *fortress*

2 CHRONICLES

Solomon Requests Wisdom

1 Solomon son of David established himself in his kingdom; the LORD his God was with him and made him exceedingly great.

2 Solomon summoned all Israel, the commanders of the thousands and of the hundreds, the judges, and all the leaders of all Israel, the heads of families. ³Then Solomon, and the whole assembly with him, went to the high place that was at Gibeon; for God's tent of meeting, which Moses the servant of the LORD had made in the wilderness, was there. ⁴(But David had brought the ark of God up from Kiriath-jearim to the place that David had prepared for it; for he had pitched a tent for it in Jerusalem.) ⁵Moreover, the bronze altar that Bezalel son of Uri, son of Hur, had made was there in front of the tabernacle of the LORD. And Solomon and the assembly inquired at it. ⁶Solomon went up there to the bronze altar before the LORD, which was at the tent of meeting, and offered a thousand burnt-offerings on it.

7 That night God appeared to Solomon, and said to him, 'Ask what I should give you.' ⁸Solomon said to God, 'You have shown great and steadfast love to my father David, and have made me succeed him as king. ⁹O LORD God, let your promise to my father David now be fulfilled, for you have made me king over a people as numerous as the dust of the earth. ¹⁰Give me now wisdom and knowledge to go out and come in before this people, for who can rule this great people of yours?' ¹¹God answered Solomon, 'Because this was in your heart, and you have not asked for possessions, wealth, honour, or the life of those who hate you, and have not even asked for long life, but have asked for wisdom and knowledge for yourself that you may rule my people over whom I have made you king, ¹²wisdom and knowledge are granted to you. I will also give you riches, possessions, and honour, such as none of the kings had who were before you, and none after you shall have the like.' ¹³So Solomon came from*a* the high place at Gibeon, from the tent of meeting, to Jerusalem. And he reigned over Israel.

Solomon's Military and Commercial Activity

14 Solomon gathered together chariots and horses; he had fourteen hundred chariots and twelve thousand horses, which he stationed in the chariot cities and with the king in Jerusalem. ¹⁵The king made silver and gold as common in Jerusalem as stone, and he made cedar as plentiful as the sycomore of the Shephelah. ¹⁶Solomon's horses were imported from Egypt and Kue; the king's traders received them from Kue at the prevailing price. ¹⁷They imported from Egypt, and then exported, a chariot for six hundred shekels of silver, and a horse for one hundred and fifty; so through them these were exported to all the kings of the Hittites and the kings of Aram.

Preparations for Building the Temple

2 *b* Solomon decided to build a temple for the name of the LORD, and a royal palace for himself. ²*c* Solomon conscripted seventy thousand labourers and eighty

a Gk Vg: Heb *to*   b Ch 1.18 in Heb   c Ch 2.1 in Heb

thousand stonecutters in the hill country, with three thousand six hundred to oversee them.

Alliance with Huram of Tyre

3 Solomon sent word to King Huram of Tyre: 'Once you dealt with my father David and sent him cedar to build himself a house to live in. ⁴I am now about to build a house for the name of the LORD my God and dedicate it to him for offering fragrant incense before him, and for the regular offering of the rows of bread, and for burnt-offerings morning and evening, on the sabbaths and the new moons and the appointed festivals of the LORD our God, as ordained for ever for Israel. ⁵The house that I am about to build will be great, for our God is greater than other gods. ⁶But who is able to build him a house, since heaven, even highest heaven, cannot contain him? Who am I to build a house for him, except as a place to make offerings before him? ⁷So now send me an artisan skilled to work in gold, silver, bronze, and iron, and in purple, crimson, and blue fabrics, trained also in engraving, to join the skilled workers who are with me in Judah and Jerusalem, whom my father David provided. ⁸Send me also cedar, cypress, and algum timber from Lebanon, for I know that your servants are skilled in cutting Lebanon timber. My servants will work with your servants ⁹to prepare timber for me in abundance, for the house I am about to build will be great and wonderful. ¹⁰I will provide for your servants, those who cut the timber, twenty thousand cors of crushed wheat, twenty thousand cors of barley, twenty thousand baths*ᵃ* of wine, and twenty thousand baths of oil.'

11 Then King Huram of Tyre answered in a letter that he sent to Solomon, 'Because the LORD loves his people he has made you king over them.' ¹²Huram also said, 'Blessed be the LORD God of Israel, who made heaven and earth, who has given King David a wise son, endowed with discretion and understanding, who will build a temple for the LORD, and a royal palace for himself.

13 'I have dispatched Huram-abi, a skilled artisan, endowed with understanding, ¹⁴the son of one of the Danite women, his father a Tyrian. He is trained to work in gold, silver, bronze, iron, stone, and wood, and in purple, blue, and crimson fabrics and fine linen, and to do all sorts of engraving and execute any design that may be assigned him, with your artisans, the artisans of my lord, your father David. ¹⁵Now, as for the wheat, barley, oil, and wine, of which my lord has spoken, let him send them to his servants. ¹⁶We will cut whatever timber you need from Lebanon, and bring it to you as rafts by sea to Joppa; you will take it up to Jerusalem.'

17 Then Solomon took a census of all the aliens who were residing in the land of Israel, after the census that his father David had taken; and there were found to be one hundred and fifty-three thousand six hundred. ¹⁸Seventy thousand of them he assigned as labourers, eighty thousand as stonecutters in the hill country, and three thousand six hundred as overseers to make the people work.

Solomon Builds the Temple

3 Solomon began to build the house of the LORD in Jerusalem on Mount Moriah, where the LORD had appeared to his father David, at the place that David had designated, on the threshing-floor of Ornan the Jebusite. ²He began to build on the second day of the second month of the fourth year of his reign. ³These are Solomon's measurements*ᵇ* for building the house of God: the length, in cubits of the old standard, was sixty cubits, and the width twenty cubits. ⁴The vestibule in front of the nave of the house was twenty cubits long, across the width of the house;*ᶜ* and its height was one hundred and twenty cubits. He overlaid it on the inside with pure gold. ⁵The nave he lined with cypress,

---

a A Hebrew measure of volume   *b* Syr: Heb *foundations*   *c* Compare 1 Kings 6.3: Meaning of Heb uncertain covered it with fine gold, and made palms and chains on it. 6 He adorned the house with settings of precious stones. The gold was gold from Parvaim. 7 So he lined the house with gold—its beams, its thresholds, its walls, and its doors; and he carved cherubim on the walls.

8 He made the most holy place; its length, corresponding to the width of the house, was twenty cubits, and its width was twenty cubits; he overlaid it with six hundred talents of fine gold. 9 The weight of the nails was fifty shekels of gold. He overlaid the upper chambers with gold.

10 In the most holy place he made two carved cherubim and overlaid*a* them with gold. 11 The wings of the cherubim together extended twenty cubits: one wing of one, five cubits long, touched the wall of the house, and its other wing, five cubits long, touched the wing of the other cherub; 12 and of this cherub, one wing, five cubits long, touched the wall of the house, and the other wing, also five cubits long, was joined to the wing of the first cherub.

13 The wings of these cherubim extended twenty cubits; the cherubim*b* stood on their feet, facing the nave. 14 And Solomon*c* made the curtain of blue and purple and crimson fabrics and fine linen, and worked cherubim into it.

15 In front of the house he made two pillars thirty-five cubits high, with a capital of five cubits on the top of each. 16 He made encircling*d* chains and put them on the tops of the pillars; and he made one hundred pomegranates, and put them on the chains. 17 He set up the pillars in front of the temple, one on the right, the other on the left; the one on the right he called Jachin, and the one on the left, Boaz.

Furnishings of the Temple

4 He made an altar of bronze, twenty cubits long, twenty cubits wide, and ten cubits high. 2 Then he made the cast sea; it was round, ten cubits from rim to rim, and five cubits high. A line of thirty

a Heb *they overlaid*   *b* Heb *they*   *c* Heb *he*
d Cn: Heb *in the inner sanctuary*

Floor Plan of Solomon's Temple

Ten movable stands of bronze:
4 cubits/6 feet square and 3 cubits/4.5 feet high
each holding a bronze basin 4 cubits/6 feet across

N

Two bronze pillars with their capitals:
23 cubits/34.5 feet high
(may have supported the portico roof)

Inner Sanctuary
or the
Most Holy Place

10 lampstands and tables

Boaz

20 cubits/30 feet

†Ark
2.5 cubits/3.75 feet long
1.5 cubits/2.25 feet wide & long

Doors

Altar of
Incense

Main Hall
or the
Holy Place

Doors

Portico

10 cubits/
15 feet

Jachin

Bronze Altar

20 cubits/30 feet

40 cubits/60 feet

3 floors of side rooms:
each floor: 5 cubits/7.5 feet high

7 cubits/
10.5 feet

Walls of the Most Holy Place:
20 cubits/30 feet high

Walls of the Holy Place:
30 cubits/45 feet high

Bronze "Sea"
10 cubits/15 feet across
5 cubits/17.5 feet high

cubits would encircle it completely. ³ Under it were panels all round, each of ten cubits, surrounding the sea; there were two rows of panels, cast when it was cast. ⁴ It stood on twelve oxen, three facing north, three facing west, three facing south, and three facing east; the sea was set on them. The hindquarters of each were towards the inside. ⁵ Its thickness was a handbreadth; its rim was made like the rim of a cup, like the flower of a lily; it held three thousand baths.ᵃ ⁶ He also made ten basins in which to wash, and set five on the right-hand side, and five on the left. In these they were to rinse what was used for the burnt-offering. The sea was for the priests to wash in.

7 He made ten golden lampstands as prescribed, and set them in the temple, five on the south side and five on the north. ⁸ He also made ten tables and placed them in the temple, five on the right-hand side and five on the left. And he made one hundred basins of gold. ⁹ He made the court of the priests, and the great court, and doors for the court; he overlaid their doors with bronze. ¹⁰ He set the sea at the south-east corner of the house.

11 And Huram made the pots, the shovels, and the basins. Thus Huram finished the work that he did for King Solomon on the house of God: ¹² the two pillars, the bowls, and the two capitals on the top of the pillars; and the two lattice-works to cover the two bowls of the capitals that were on the top of the pillars; ¹³ the four hundred pomegranates for the two lattice-works, two rows of pomegranates for each lattice-work, to cover the two bowls of the capitals that were on the pillars. ¹⁴ He made the stands, the basins on the stands, ¹⁵ the one sea, and the twelve oxen underneath it. ¹⁶ The pots, the shovels, the forks, and all the equipment for these Huram-abi made of burnished bronze for King Solomon for the house of the LORD. ¹⁷ In the plain of the Jordan the king cast them, in the clay ground between Succoth and Zeredah. ¹⁸ Solomon made all these things in great quantities, so that the weight of the bronze was not determined.

19 So Solomon made all the things that were in the house of God: the golden altar, the tables for the bread of the Presence, ²⁰ the lampstands and their lamps of pure gold to burn before the inner sanctuary, as prescribed; ²¹ the flowers, the lamps, and the tongs, of purest gold; ²² the snuffers, basins, ladles, and firepans, of pure gold. As for the entrance to the temple: the inner doors to the most holy place and the doors of the nave of the temple were of gold.

5 Thus all the work that Solomon did for the house of the LORD was finished. Solomon brought in the things that his father David had dedicated, and stored the silver, the gold, and all the vessels in the treasuries of the house of God.

The Ark Brought into the Temple

2 Then Solomon assembled the elders of Israel and all the heads of the tribes, the leaders of the ancestral houses of the people of Israel, in Jerusalem, to bring up the ark of the covenant of the LORD out of the city of David, which is Zion. ³ And all the Israelites assembled before the king at the festival that is in the seventh month. ⁴ And all the elders of Israel came, and the Levites carried the ark. ⁵ So they brought up the ark, the tent of meeting, and all the holy vessels that were in the tent; the priests and the Levites brought them up. ⁶ King Solomon and all the congregation of Israel, who had assembled before him, were before the ark, sacrificing so many sheep and oxen that they could not be numbered or counted. ⁷ Then the priests brought the ark of the covenant of the LORD to its place, in the inner sanctuary of the house, in the most holy place, underneath the wings of the cherubim. ⁸ For the cherubim spread out their wings over the place of the ark, so that the cherubim made a covering above the ark and its poles. ⁹ The poles were so long that the ends of the poles were seen from the holy place in front of the inner sanctuary; but they could not be seen from outside; they are there to this day. ¹⁰ There was nothing

---

a A Hebrew measure of volume

in the ark except the two tablets that Moses put there at Horeb, where the LORD made a covenant[a] with the people of Israel after they came out of Egypt.

11 Now when the priests came out of the holy place (for all the priests who were present had sanctified themselves, without regard to their divisions), 12 all the levitical singers, Asaph, Heman, and Jeduthun, their sons and kindred, arrayed in fine linen, with cymbals, harps, and lyres, stood east of the altar with one hundred and twenty priests who were trumpeters, 13 it was the duty of the trumpeters and singers to make themselves heard in unison in praise and thanksgiving to the LORD, and when the song was raised, with trumpets and cymbals and other musical instruments, in praise to the LORD,

'For he is good,
　for his steadfast love endures for
　　ever',

the house, the house of the LORD, was filled with a cloud, 14 so that the priests could not stand to minister because of the cloud; for the glory of the LORD filled the house of God.

Dedication of the Temple

6 Then Solomon said, 'The LORD has said that he would reside in thick darkness. 2 I have built you an exalted house, a place for you to reside in for ever.'

3 Then the king turned round and blessed all the assembly of Israel, while all the assembly of Israel stood. 4 And he said, 'Blessed be the LORD, the God of Israel, who with his hand has fulfilled what he promised with his mouth to my father David, saying, 5 "Since the day that I brought my people out of the land of Egypt, I have not chosen a city from any of the tribes of Israel in which to build a house, so that my name might be there, and I chose no one as ruler over my people Israel; 6 but I have chosen Jerusalem in order that my name may be there, and I have chosen David to be over my people Israel." 7 My father David had it in mind to build a house for the name of the LORD, the God of Israel. 8 But the LORD said to

my father David, "You did well to consider building a house for my name; 9 nevertheless, you shall not build the house, but your son who shall be born to you shall build the house for my name." 10 Now the LORD has fulfilled his promise that he made; for I have succeeded my father David, and sit on the throne of Israel, as the LORD promised, and have built the house for the name of the LORD, the God of Israel. 11 There I have set the ark, in which is the covenant of the LORD that he made with the people of Israel.'

Solomon's Prayer of Dedication

12 Then Solomon[b] stood before the altar of the LORD in the presence of the whole assembly of Israel, and spread out his hands. 13 Solomon had made a bronze platform five cubits long, five cubits wide, and three cubits high, and had set it in the court; and he stood on it. Then he knelt on his knees in the presence of the whole assembly of Israel, and spread out his hands towards heaven. 14 He said, 'O LORD, God of Israel, there is no God like you, in heaven or on earth, keeping covenant in steadfast love with your servants who walk before you with all their heart— 15 you who have kept for your servant, my father David, what you promised to him. Indeed, you promised with your mouth and this day have fulfilled with your hand. 16 Therefore, O LORD, God of Israel, keep for your servant, my father David, that which you promised him, saying, "There shall never fail you a successor before me to sit on the throne of Israel, if only your children keep to their way, to walk in my law as you have walked before me." 17 Therefore, O LORD, God of Israel, let your word be confirmed, which you promised to your servant David.

18 'But will God indeed reside with mortals on earth? Even heaven and the highest heaven cannot contain you, how much less this house that I have built! 19 Have regard to your servant's prayer and his plea, O LORD my God, heeding the cry and the prayer that your servant prays to

a Heb lacks a covenant　　b Heb he

you. 20 May your eyes be open day and night towards this house, the place where you promised to set your name, and may you heed the prayer that your servant prays towards this place. 21 And hear the plea of your servant and of your people Israel, when they pray towards this place; may you hear from heaven your dwelling-place; hear and forgive.

22 'If someone sins against another and is required to take an oath and comes and swears before your altar in this house, 23 may you hear from heaven, and act, and judge your servants, repaying the guilty by bringing their conduct on their own head, and vindicating those who are in the right by rewarding them in accordance with their righteousness.

24 'When your people Israel, having sinned against you, are defeated before an enemy but turn again to you, confess your name, pray and plead with you in this house, 25 may you hear from heaven, and forgive the sin of your people Israel, and bring them again to the land that you gave to them and to their ancestors.

26 'When heaven is shut up and there is no rain because they have sinned against you, and then they pray towards this place, confess your name, and turn from their sin, because you punish them, 27 may you hear in heaven, forgive the sin of your servants, your people Israel, when you teach them the good way in which they should walk; and send down rain upon your land, which you have given to your people as an inheritance.

28 'If there is famine in the land, if there is plague, blight, mildew, locust, or caterpillar; if their enemies besiege them in any of the settlements of the lands; whatever suffering, whatever sickness there is; 29 whatever prayer, whatever plea from any individual or from all your people Israel, all knowing their own suffering and their own sorrows so that they stretch out their hands towards this house; 30 may you hear from heaven your dwelling-place, forgive, and render to all whose heart you know, according to all their ways, for only you know the human heart. 31 Thus may they

fear you and walk in your ways all the days that they live in the land that you gave to our ancestors.

32 'Likewise when foreigners, who are not of your people Israel, come from a distant land because of your great name, and your mighty hand, and your outstretched arm, when they come and pray towards this house, 33 may you hear from heaven your dwelling-place, and do whatever the foreigners ask of you, in order that all the peoples of the earth may know your name and fear you, as do your people Israel, and that they may know that your name has been invoked on this house that I have built.

34 'If your people go out to battle against their enemies, by whatever way you shall send them, and they pray to you towards this city that you have chosen and the house that I have built for your name, 35 then hear from heaven their prayer and their plea, and maintain their cause.

36 'If they sin against you—for there is no one who does not sin—and you are angry with them and give them to an enemy, so that they are carried away captive to a land far or near; 37 then if they come to their senses in the land to which they have been taken captive, and repent, and plead with you in the land of their captivity, saying, "We have sinned, and have done wrong; we have acted wickedly"; 38 if they repent with all their heart and soul in the land of their captivity, to which they were taken captive, and pray towards their land, which you gave to their ancestors, the city that you have chosen, and the house that I have built for your name, 39 then hear from heaven your dwelling-place their prayer and their pleas, maintain their cause and forgive your people who have sinned against you. 40 Now, O my God, let your eyes be open and your ears attentive to prayer from this place.

41 'Now rise up, O LORD God, and go to your resting-place,
　　you and the ark of your might.
Let your priests, O LORD God, be
　　clothed with salvation,

and let your faithful rejoice in your
  goodness.
42 O LORD God, do not reject your
  anointed one.
  Remember your steadfast love for
  your servant David.'

Solomon Dedicates the Temple

7 When Solomon had ended his prayer,
  fire came down from heaven and consumed the burnt-offering and the sacrifices; and the glory of the LORD filled the
temple. 2 The priests could not enter the
house of the LORD, because the glory of
the LORD filled the LORD's house. 3 When all
the people of Israel saw the fire come down
and the glory of the LORD on the temple,
they bowed down on the pavement with
their faces to the ground, and worshipped
and gave thanks to the LORD, saying,

  'For he is good,
    for his steadfast love endures for
      ever.'

4 Then the king and all the people offered sacrifice before the LORD. 5 King Solomon offered as a sacrifice twenty-two thousand oxen and one hundred and twenty
thousand sheep. So the king and all the
people dedicated the house of God. 6 The
priests stood at their posts; the Levites also,
with the instruments for music to the LORD
that King David had made for giving
thanks to the LORD—for his steadfast love
endures for ever—whenever David offered
praises by their ministry. Opposite them
the priests sounded trumpets; and all Israel stood.

7 Solomon consecrated the middle of
the court that was in front of the house of
the LORD; for there he offered the burnt-offerings and the fat of the offerings of well-
being because the bronze altar Solomon
had made could not hold the burnt-offering and the grain-offering and the fat parts.

8 At that time Solomon held the festival
for seven days, and all Israel with him, a
very great congregation, from Lebo-hamath to the Wadi of Egypt. 9 On the eighth
day they held a solemn assembly; for they
had observed the dedication of the altar for
seven days and the festival for seven days.

10 On the twenty-third day of the seventh
month he sent the people away to their
homes, joyful and in good spirits because
of the goodness that the LORD had shown
to David and to Solomon and to his people Israel.

11 Thus Solomon finished the house of
the LORD and the king's house; all that Solomon had planned to do in the house of
the LORD and in his own house he success-
fully accomplished.

God's Second Appearance to Solomon

12 Then the LORD appeared to Solomon
in the night and said to him: 'I have heard
your prayer, and have chosen this place for
myself as a house of sacrifice. 13 When I
shut up the heavens so that there is no
rain, or command the locust to devour the
land, or send pestilence among my people,
14 if my people who are called by my name
humble themselves, pray, seek my face,
and turn from their wicked ways, then I
will hear from heaven, and will forgive
their sin and heal their land. 15 Now my
eyes will be open and my ears attentive to
the prayer that is made in this place. 16 For
now I have chosen and consecrated this
house so that my name may be there for
ever; my eyes and my heart will be there for
all time. 17 As for you, if you walk before
me, as your father David walked, doing according to all that I have commanded you
and keeping my statutes and my ordinances, 18 then I will establish your royal
throne, as I made covenant with your father David saying, "You shall never lack a
successor to rule over Israel."

19 'But if you*a* turn aside and forsake
my statutes and my commandments that I
have set before you, and go and serve other gods and worship them, 20 then I will
pluck you*b* up from the land that I have
given you;*b* and this house, which I have
consecrated for my name, I will cast out of
my sight, and will make it a proverb and a
byword among all peoples. 21 And regarding this house, now exalted, everyone passing by will be astonished, and say, "Why
has the LORD done such a thing to this land

a The word *you* in this verse is plural   *b* Heb *them* and to this house?" 22 Then they will say, "Because they abandoned the LORD the God of their ancestors who brought them out of the land of Egypt, and they adopted other gods, and worshipped them and served them; therefore he has brought all this calamity upon them." '

Various Activities of Solomon

8 At the end of twenty years, during which Solomon had built the house of the LORD and his own house, 2 Solomon rebuilt the cities that Huram had given to him, and settled the people of Israel in them.

3 Solomon went to Hamath-zobah, and captured it. 4 He built Tadmor in the wilderness and all the storage towns that he built in Hamath. 5 He also built Upper Beth-horon and Lower Beth-horon, fortified cities, with walls, gates, and bars, 6 and Baalath, as well as all Solomon's storage towns, and all the towns for his chariots, the towns for his cavalry, and whatever Solomon desired to build, in Jerusalem, in Lebanon, and in all the land of his dominion. 7 All the people who were left of the Hittites, the Amorites, the Perizzites, the Hivites, and the Jebusites, who were not of Israel, 8 from their descendants who were still left in the land, whom the people of Israel had not destroyed—these Solomon conscripted for forced labour, as is still the case today. 9 But of the people of Israel Solomon made no slaves for his work; they were soldiers, and his officers, the commanders of his chariotry and cavalry. 10 These were the chief officers of King Solomon, two hundred and fifty of them, who exercised authority over the people.

11 Solomon brought Pharaoh's daughter from the city of David to the house that he had built for her, for he said, 'My wife shall not live in the house of King David of Israel, for the places to which the ark of the LORD has come are holy.'

12 Then Solomon offered up burnt-offerings to the LORD on the altar of the LORD that he had built in front of the vestibule, 13 as the duty of each day required, offering according to the commandment of Moses for the sabbaths, the new moons, and the three annual festivals—the festival of unleavened bread, the festival of weeks, and the festival of booths. 14 According to the ordinance of his father David, he appointed the divisions of the priests for their service, and the Levites for their offices of praise and ministry alongside the priests as the duty of each day required, and the gatekeepers in their divisions for the several gates; for so David the man of God had commanded. 15 They did not turn away from what the king had commanded the priests and Levites regarding anything at all, or regarding the treasuries.

16 Thus all the work of Solomon was accomplished from *a* the day the foundation of the house of the LORD was laid until the house of the LORD was finished completely.

17 Then Solomon went to Ezion-geber and Eloth on the shore of the sea, in the land of Edom. 18 Huram sent him, in the care of his servants, ships and servants familiar with the sea. They went to Ophir, together with the servants of Solomon, and imported from there four hundred and fifty talents of gold and brought it to King Solomon.

Visit of the Queen of Sheba

9 When the queen of Sheba heard of the fame of Solomon, she came to Jerusalem to test him with hard questions, having a very great retinue and camels bearing spices and very much gold and precious stones. When she came to Solomon, she discussed with him all that was on her mind. 2 Solomon answered all her questions; there was nothing hidden from Solomon that he could not explain to her. 3 When the queen of Sheba had observed the wisdom of Solomon, the house that he had built, 4 the food of his table, the seating of his officials, and the attendance of his servants, and their clothing, his valets and their clothing, and his burnt-offerings *b* that

a Gk Syr Vg: Heb *to*   *b* Gk Syr Vg 1 Kings 10.5: Heb *ascent* he offered at the house of the LORD, there was no more spirit left in her.

5 So she said to the king, 'The report was true that I heard in my own land of your accomplishments and of your wisdom, 6 but I did not believe the*a* reports until I came and my own eyes saw it. Not even half of the greatness of your wisdom had been told to me; you far surpass the report that I had heard. 7 Happy are your people! Happy are these your servants, who continually attend you and hear your wisdom! 8 Blessed be the LORD your God, who has delighted in you and set you on his throne as king for the LORD your God. Because your God loved Israel and wished to establish them for ever, he has made you king over them, so that you may execute justice and righteousness.' 9 Then she gave the king one hundred and twenty talents of gold, a very great quantity of spices, and precious stones: there were no spices such as those that the queen of Sheba gave to King Solomon.

10 Moreover, the servants of Huram and the servants of Solomon who brought gold from Ophir brought algum wood and precious stones. 11 From the algum wood, the king made steps*b* for the house of the LORD and for the king's house, lyres also and harps for the singers; there never was seen the like of them before in the land of Judah.

12 Meanwhile, King Solomon granted the queen of Sheba every desire that she expressed, well beyond what she had brought to the king. Then she returned to her own land, with her servants.

Solomon's Great Wealth

13 The weight of gold that came to Solomon in one year was six hundred and sixty-six talents of gold, 14 besides that which the traders and merchants brought; and all the kings of Arabia and the governors of the land brought gold and silver to Solomon. 15 King Solomon made two hundred large shields of beaten gold; six hundred

a Heb *their*   *b* Gk Vg: Meaning of Heb uncertain

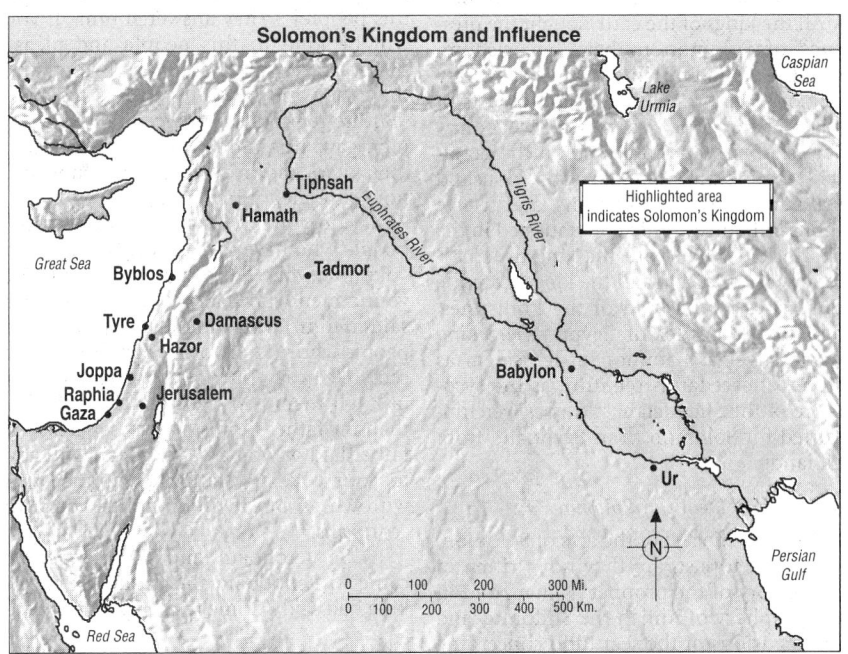

Solomon's Kingdom and Influence

shekels of beaten gold went into each large shield. 16 He made three hundred shields of beaten gold; three hundred shekels of gold went into each shield; and the king put them in the House of the Forest of Lebanon. 17 The king also made a great ivory throne, and overlaid it with pure gold. 18 The throne had six steps and a footstool of gold, which were attached to the throne, and on each side of the seat were arm rests and two lions standing beside the arm rests, 19 while twelve lions were standing, one on each end of a step on the six steps. The like of it was never made in any kingdom. 20 All King Solomon's drinking vessels were of gold, and all the vessels of the House of the Forest of Lebanon were of pure gold; silver was not considered as anything in the days of Solomon. 21 For the king's ships went to Tarshish with the servants of Huram; once every three years the ships of Tarshish used to come bringing gold, silver, ivory, apes, and peacocks.[a]

22 Thus King Solomon excelled all the kings of the earth in riches and in wisdom. 23 All the kings of the earth sought the presence of Solomon to hear his wisdom, which God had put into his mind. 24 Every one of them brought a present, objects of silver and gold, garments, weaponry, spices, horses, and mules, so much year after year. 25 Solomon had four thousand stalls for horses and chariots, and twelve thousand horses, which he stationed in the chariot cities and with the king in Jerusalem. 26 He ruled over all the kings from the Euphrates to the land of the Philistines, and to the border of Egypt. 27 The king made silver as common in Jerusalem as stone, and cedar as plentiful as the sycomore of the Shephelah. 28 Horses were imported for Solomon from Egypt and from all lands.

Death of Solomon

29 Now the rest of the acts of Solomon, from first to last, are they not written in the history of the prophet Nathan, and in the prophecy of Ahijah the Shilonite, and in the visions of the seer Iddo concerning Jeroboam son of Nebat? 30 Solomon reigned in Jerusalem over all Israel for forty years. 31 Solomon slept with his ancestors and was buried in the city of his father David; and his son Rehoboam succeeded him.

The Revolt against Rehoboam

10 Rehoboam went to Shechem, for all Israel had come to Shechem to make him king. 2 When Jeroboam son of Nebat heard of it (for he was in Egypt, where he had fled from King Solomon), then Jeroboam returned from Egypt. 3 They sent and called him; and Jeroboam and all Israel came and said to Rehoboam, 4 'Your father made our yoke heavy. Now therefore lighten the hard service of your father and his heavy yoke that he placed on us, and we will serve you.' 5 He said to them, 'Come to me again in three days.' So the people went away.

6 Then King Rehoboam took counsel with the older men who had attended his father Solomon while he was still alive, saying, 'How do you advise me to answer this people?' 7 They answered him, 'If you will be kind to this people and please them, and speak good words to them, then they will be your servants for ever.' 8 But he rejected the advice that the older men gave him, and consulted the young men who had grown up with him and now attended him. 9 He said to them, 'What do you advise that we answer this people who have said to me, "Lighten the yoke that your father put on us"?' 10 The young men who had grown up with him said to him, 'Thus should you speak to the people who said to you, "Your father made our yoke heavy, but you must lighten it for us"; tell them, "My little finger is thicker than my father's loins. 11 Now, whereas my father laid on you a heavy yoke, I will add to your yoke. My father disciplined you with whips, but I will discipline you with scorpions."'

12 So Jeroboam and all the people came to Rehoboam the third day, as the king had said, 'Come to me again the third

a Or baboons

day.' [13] The king answered them harshly. King Rehoboam rejected the advice of the older men; [14] he spoke to them in accordance with the advice of the young men, 'My father made your yoke heavy, but I will add to it; my father disciplined you with whips, but I will discipline you with scorpions.' [15] So the king did not listen to the people, because it was a turn of affairs brought about by God so that the LORD might fulfil his word, which he had spoken by Ahijah the Shilonite to Jeroboam son of Nebat.

[16] When all Israel saw that the king would not listen to them, the people answered the king,

'What share do we have in David?
We have no inheritance in the son
    of Jesse.
Each of you to your tents, O Israel!
Look now to your own house,
    O David.'

So all Israel departed to their tents. [17] But Rehoboam reigned over the people of Israel who were living in the cities of Judah. [18] When King Rehoboam sent Hadoram, who was taskmaster over the forced labour, the people of Israel stoned him to death. King Rehoboam hurriedly mounted his chariot to flee to Jerusalem. [19] So Israel has been in rebellion against the house of David to this day.

Judah and Benjamin Fortified

11 When Rehoboam came to Jerusalem, he assembled one hundred and eighty thousand chosen troops of the house of Judah and Benjamin to fight against Israel, to restore the kingdom to Rehoboam. [2] But the word of the LORD came to Shemaiah the man of God: [3] Say to King Rehoboam of Judah, son of Solomon, and to all Israel in Judah and Benjamin, [4] 'Thus says the LORD: You shall not go up or fight against your kindred. Let everyone return home, for this thing is from me.' So they heeded the word of the LORD and turned back from the expedition against Jeroboam.

[5] Rehoboam resided in Jerusalem, and he built cities for defence in Judah. [6] He built up Bethlehem, Etam, Tekoa, [7] Bethzur, Soco, Adullam, [8] Gath, Mareshah, Ziph, [9] Adoraim, Lachish, Azekah, [10] Zorah, Aijalon, and Hebron, fortified cities that are in Judah and in Benjamin. [11] He made the fortresses strong, and put commanders in them, and stores of food, oil, and wine. [12] He also put large shields and spears in all the cities, and made them very strong. So he held Judah and Benjamin.

Priests and Levites Support Rehoboam

[13] The priests and the Levites who were in all Israel presented themselves to him from all their territories. [14] The Levites had left their common lands and their holdings and had come to Judah and Jerusalem, because Jeroboam and his sons had prevented them from serving as priests of the LORD, [15] and had appointed his own priests for the high places, and for the goatdemons, and for the calves that he had made. [16] Those who had set their hearts to seek the LORD God of Israel came after them from all the tribes of Israel to Jerusalem to sacrifice to the LORD, the God of their ancestors. [17] They strengthened the kingdom of Judah, and for three years they made Rehoboam son of Solomon secure, for they walked for three years in the way of David and Solomon.

Rehoboam's Marriages

[18] Rehoboam took as his wife Mahalath daughter of Jerimoth son of David, and of Abihail daughter of Eliab son of Jesse. [19] She bore him sons: Jeush, Shemariah, and Zaham. [20] After her he took Maacah daughter of Absalom, who bore him Abijah, Attai, Ziza, and Shelomith. [21] Rehoboam loved Maacah daughter of Absalom more than all his other wives and concubines (he took eighteen wives and sixty concubines, and became the father of twenty-eight sons and sixty daughters). [22] Rehoboam appointed Abijah son of Maacah as chief prince among his brothers, for he intended to make him king. [23] He dealt wisely, and distributed some of his sons through all the districts of Judah and Benjamin, in all the fortified cities; he gave

them abundant provisions, and found many wives for them.

Egypt Attacks Judah

12 When the rule of Rehoboam was established and he grew strong, he abandoned the law of the LORD, he and all Israel with him. ²In the fifth year of King Rehoboam, because they had been unfaithful to the LORD, King Shishak of Egypt came up against Jerusalem ³with twelve hundred chariots and sixty thousand cavalry. A countless army came with him from Egypt—Libyans, Sukkiim, and Ethiopians.ᵃ ⁴He took the fortified cities of Judah and came as far as Jerusalem. ⁵Then the prophet Shemaiah came to Rehoboam and to the officers of Judah, who had gathered at Jerusalem because of Shishak, and said to them, 'Thus says the LORD: You abandoned me, so I have abandoned you to the hand of Shishak.' ⁶Then the officers of Israel and the king humbled themselves and said, 'The LORD is in the right.' ⁷When the LORD saw that they humbled themselves, the word of the LORD came to Shemaiah, saying: 'They have humbled themselves; I will not destroy them, but I will grant them some deliverance, and my wrath shall not be poured out on Jerusalem by the hand of Shishak. ⁸Nevertheless they shall be his servants, so that they may know the difference between serving me and serving the kingdoms of other lands.'

9 So King Shishak of Egypt came up against Jerusalem; he took away the treasures of the house of the LORD and the treasures of the king's house; he took everything. He also took away the shields of gold that Solomon had made; ¹⁰but King Rehoboam made in place of them shields of bronze, and committed them to the hands of the officers of the guard, who kept the door of the king's house. ¹¹Whenever the king went into the house of the LORD, the guard would come along bearing them, and would then bring them back to the guardroom. ¹²Because he humbled himself the wrath of the LORD turned from him, so as not to destroy them completely; moreover, conditions were good in Judah.

Death of Rehoboam

13 So King Rehoboam established himself in Jerusalem and reigned. Rehoboam was forty-one years old when he began to reign; he reigned for seventeen years in Jerusalem, the city that the LORD had chosen out of all the tribes of Israel to put his name there. His mother's name was Naamah the Ammonite. ¹⁴He did evil, for he did not set his heart to seek the LORD.

15 Now the acts of Rehoboam, from first to last, are they not written in the records of the prophet Shemaiah and of the seer Iddo, recorded by genealogy? There were continual wars between Rehoboam and Jeroboam. ¹⁶Rehoboam slept with his ancestors and was buried in the city of David; and his son Abijah succeeded him.

Abijah Reigns over Judah

13 In the eighteenth year of King Jeroboam, Abijah began to reign over Judah. ²He reigned for three years in Jerusalem. His mother's name was Micaiah daughter of Uriel of Gibeah.

Now there was war between Abijah and Jeroboam. ³Abijah engaged in battle, having an army of valiant warriors, four hundred thousand picked men; and Jeroboam drew up his line of battle against him with eight hundred thousand picked mighty warriors. ⁴Then Abijah stood on the slope of Mount Zemaraim that is in the hill country of Ephraim, and said, 'Listen to me, Jeroboam and all Israel! ⁵Do you not know that the LORD God of Israel gave the kingship over Israel for ever to David and his sons by a covenant of salt? ⁶Yet Jeroboam son of Nebat, a servant of Solomon son of David, rose up and rebelled against his lord; ⁷and certain worthless scoundrels gathered round him and defied Rehoboam son of Solomon, when Rehoboam was young and irresolute and could not withstand them.

8 'And now you think that you can withstand the kingdom of the LORD in the hand of the sons of David, because you are a

ᵃ Or *Nubians*; Heb *Cushites*

great multitude and have with you the golden calves that Jeroboam made as gods for you. ⁹Have you not driven out the priests of the LORD, the descendants of Aaron, and the Levites, and made priests for yourselves like the peoples of other lands? Whoever comes to be consecrated with a young bull or seven rams becomes a priest of what are no gods. ¹⁰But as for us, the LORD is our God, and we have not abandoned him. We have priests ministering to the LORD who are descendants of Aaron, and Levites for their service. ¹¹They offer to the LORD every morning and every evening burnt-offerings and fragrant incense, set out the rows of bread on the table of pure gold, and care for the golden lampstand so that its lamps may burn every evening; for we keep the charge of the LORD our God, but you have abandoned him. ¹²See, God is with us at our head, and his priests have their battle trumpets to sound the call to battle against you. O Israelites, do not fight against the LORD, the God of your ancestors; for you cannot succeed.'

13 Jeroboam had sent an ambush around to come on them from behind; thus his troops*a* were in front of Judah, and the ambush was behind them. ¹⁴When Judah turned, the battle was in front of them and behind them. They cried out to the LORD, and the priests blew the trumpets. ¹⁵Then the people of Judah raised the battle shout. And when the people of Judah shouted, God defeated Jeroboam and all Israel before Abijah and Judah. ¹⁶The Israelites fled before Judah, and God gave them into their hands. ¹⁷Abijah and his army defeated them with great slaughter; five hundred thousand picked men of Israel fell slain. ¹⁸Thus the Israelites were subdued at that time, and the people of Judah prevailed, because they relied on the LORD, the God of their ancestors. ¹⁹Abijah pursued Jeroboam, and took cities from him: Bethel with its villages and Jeshanah with its villages and Ephron*b* with its villages. ²⁰Jeroboam did not recover his power in the days of Abijah; the LORD struck him down, and he died. ²¹But Abijah grew strong. He took

fourteen wives, and became the father of twenty-two sons and sixteen daughters. ²²The rest of the acts of Abijah, his behaviour and his deeds, are written in the story of the prophet Iddo.

Asa Reigns

14 *c* So Abijah slept with his ancestors, and they buried him in the city of David. His son Asa succeeded him. In his days the land had rest for ten years. ²*d* Asa did what was good and right in the sight of the LORD his God. ³He took away the foreign altars and the high places, broke down the pillars, hewed down the sacred poles,*e* ⁴and commanded Judah to seek the LORD, the God of their ancestors, and to keep the law and the commandment. ⁵He also removed from all the cities of Judah the high places and the incense altars. And the kingdom had rest under him. ⁶He built fortified cities in Judah while the land had rest. He had no war in those years, for the LORD gave him peace. ⁷He said to Judah, 'Let us build these cities, and surround them with walls and towers, gates and bars; the land is still ours because we have sought the LORD our God; we have sought him, and he has given us peace on every side.' So they built and prospered. ⁸Asa had an army of three hundred thousand from Judah, armed with large shields and spears, and two hundred and eighty thousand troops from Benjamin who carried shields and drew bows; all these were mighty warriors.

Ethiopian Invasion Repulsed

9 Zerah the Ethiopian*f* came out against them with an army of a million men and three hundred chariots, and came as far as Mareshah. ¹⁰Asa went out to meet him, and they drew up their lines of battle in the valley of Zephathah at Mareshah. ¹¹Asa cried to the LORD his God, 'O LORD, there is no difference for you between helping the mighty and the weak. Help us, O LORD our God, for we rely on you, and in your name

a Heb *they*   b Another reading is *Ephrain*
c Ch 13.23 in Heb   d Ch 14.1 in Heb
e Heb *Asherim*   f Or *Nubian*; Heb *Cushite*

we have come against this multitude. O LORD, you are our God; let no mortal prevail against you.' 12 So the LORD defeated the Ethiopians*a* before Asa and before Judah, and the Ethiopians*a* fled. 13 Asa and the army with him pursued them as far as Gerar, and the Ethiopians*a* fell until no one remained alive; for they were broken before the LORD and his army. The people of Judah*b* carried away a great quantity of booty. 14 They defeated all the cities around Gerar, for the fear of the LORD was on them. They plundered all the cities; for there was much plunder in them. 15 They also attacked the tents of those who had livestock,*c* and carried away sheep and goats in abundance, and camels. Then they returned to Jerusalem.

15 The spirit of God came upon Azariah son of Oded. 2 He went out to meet Asa and said to him, 'Hear me, Asa, and all Judah and Benjamin: The LORD is with you, while you are with him. If you seek him, he will be found by you, but if you abandon him, he will abandon you. 3 For a long time Israel was without the true God, and without a teaching priest, and without law; 4 but when in their distress they turned to the LORD, the God of Israel, and sought him, he was found by them. 5 In those times it was not safe for anyone to go or come, for great disturbances afflicted all the inhabitants of the lands. 6 They were broken in pieces, nation against nation and city against city, for God troubled them with every sort of distress. 7 But you, take courage! Do not let your hands be weak, for your work shall be rewarded.'

8 When Asa heard these words, the prophecy of Azariah son of Oded,*d* he took courage, and put away the abominable idols from all the land of Judah and Benjamin and from the towns that he had taken in the hill country of Ephraim. He repaired the altar of the LORD that was in front of the vestibule of the house of the LORD.*e* 9 He gathered all Judah and Benjamin, and those from Ephraim, Manasseh, and Simeon who were residing as aliens with them, for great numbers had deserted

to him from Israel when they saw that the LORD his God was with him. 10 They were gathered at Jerusalem in the third month of the fifteenth year of the reign of Asa. 11 They sacrificed to the LORD on that day, from the booty that they had brought, seven hundred oxen and seven thousand sheep. 12 They entered into a covenant to seek the LORD, the God of their ancestors, with all their heart and with all their soul. 13 Whoever would not seek the LORD, the God of Israel, should be put to death, whether young or old, man or woman. 14 They took an oath to the LORD with a loud voice, and with shouting, and with trumpets, and with horns. 15 All Judah rejoiced over the oath; for they had sworn with all their heart, and had sought him with their whole desire, and he was found by them, and the LORD gave them rest all around.

16 King Asa even removed his mother Maacah from being queen mother because she had made an abominable image for Asherah. Asa cut down her image, crushed it, and burned it at the Wadi Kidron. 17 But the high places were not taken out of Israel. Nevertheless, the heart of Asa was true all his days. 18 He brought into the house of God the votive gifts of his father and his own votive gifts—silver, gold, and utensils. 19 And there was no more war until the thirty-fifth year of the reign of Asa.

Alliance with Aram Condemned

16 In the thirty-sixth year of the reign of Asa, King Baasha of Israel went up against Judah, and built Ramah, to prevent anyone from going out or coming into the territory of*f* King Asa of Judah. 2 Then Asa took silver and gold from the treasures of the house of the LORD and the king's house, and sent them to King Benhadad of Aram, who resided in Damascus, saying, 3 'Let there be an alliance between me and you, like that between my father and your father; I am sending to you silver and gold; go, break your alliance with King

a Or *Nubians*; Heb *Cushites*   *b* Heb *They*   *c* Meaning of Heb uncertain   *d* Compare Syr Vg: Heb *the prophecy, the prophet Obed*   *e* Heb *the vestibule of the* LORD   *f* Heb lacks *the territory of*

Baasha of Israel, so that he may withdraw from me.' [4] Ben-hadad listened to King Asa, and sent the commanders of his armies against the cities of Israel. They conquered Ijon, Dan, Abel-maim, and all the store-cities of Naphtali. [5] When Baasha heard of it, he stopped building Ramah, and let his work cease. [6] Then King Asa brought all Judah, and they carried away the stones of Ramah and its timber, with which Baasha had been building, and with them he built up Geba and Mizpah.

7 At that time the seer Hanani came to King Asa of Judah, and said to him, 'Because you relied on the king of Aram, and did not rely on the LORD your God, the army of the king of Aram has escaped you. [8] Were not the Ethiopians[d] and the Libyans a huge army with exceedingly many chariots and cavalry? Yet because you relied on the LORD, he gave them into your hand. [9] For the eyes of the LORD range throughout the entire earth, to strengthen those whose heart is true to him. You have done foolishly in this; for from now on you will have wars.' [10] Then Asa was angry with the seer, and put him in the stocks, in prison, for he was in a rage with him because of this. And Asa inflicted cruelties on some of the people at the same time.

Asa's Disease and Death

11 The acts of Asa, from first to last, are written in the Book of the Kings of Judah and Israel. [12] In the thirty-ninth year of his reign Asa was diseased in his feet, and his disease became severe; yet even in his disease he did not seek the LORD, but sought help from physicians. [13] Then Asa slept with his ancestors, dying in the forty-first year of his reign. [14] They buried him in the tomb that he had hewn out for himself in the city of David. They laid him on a bier that had been filled with various kinds of spices prepared by the perfumer's art; and they made a very great fire in his honour.

Jehoshaphat's Reign

17 His son Jehoshaphat succeeded him, and strengthened himself against Israel. [2] He placed forces in all the fortified cities of Judah, and set garrisons in the land of Judah, and in the cities of Ephraim that his father Asa had taken. [3] The LORD was with Jehoshaphat, because he walked in the earlier ways of his father;[b] he did not seek the Baals, [4] but sought the God of his father and walked in his commandments, and not according to the ways of Israel. [5] Therefore the LORD established the kingdom in his hand. All Judah brought tribute to Jehoshaphat, and he had great riches and honour. [6] His heart was courageous in the ways of the LORD; and furthermore he removed the high places and the sacred poles[c] from Judah.

7 In the third year of his reign he sent his officials, Ben-hail, Obadiah, Zechariah, Nethanel, and Micaiah, to teach in the cities of Judah. [8] With them were the Levites, Shemaiah, Nethaniah, Zebadiah, Asahel, Shemiramoth, Jehonathan, Adonijah, Tobijah, and Tob-adonijah; and with these Levites, the priests Elishama and Jehoram. [9] They taught in Judah, having the book of the law of the LORD with them; they went around through all the cities of Judah and taught among the people.

10 The fear of the LORD fell on all the kingdoms of the lands around Judah, and they did not make war against Jehoshaphat. [11] Some of the Philistines brought Jehoshaphat presents, and silver for tribute; and the Arabs also brought him seven thousand seven hundred rams and seven thousand seven hundred male goats. [12] Jehoshaphat grew steadily greater. He built fortresses and storage cities in Judah. [13] He carried out great works in the cities of Judah. He had soldiers, mighty warriors, in Jerusalem. [14] This was the muster of them by ancestral houses: Of Judah, the commanders of the thousands: Adnah the commander, with three hundred thousand mighty warriors, [15] and next to him Jehohanan the commander, with two hundred and eighty thousand, [16] and next to him Amasiah son of Zichri, a volunteer for the service of the LORD, with two hundred thousand mighty warriors. [17] Of Benjamin:

a Or *Nubians*; Heb *Cushites* b Another reading is *his father David* c Heb *Asherim*

Eliada, a mighty warrior, with two hundred thousand armed with bow and shield, [18] and next to him Jehozabad with one hundred and eighty thousand armed for war. [19] These were in the service of the king, besides those whom the king had placed in the fortified cities throughout all Judah.

Micaiah Predicts Failure

18 Now Jehoshaphat had great riches and honour; and he made a marriage alliance with Ahab. [2] After some years he went down to Ahab in Samaria. Ahab slaughtered an abundance of sheep and oxen for him and for the people who were with him, and induced him to go up against Ramoth-gilead. [3] King Ahab of Israel said to King Jehoshaphat of Judah, 'Will you go with me to Ramoth-gilead?' He answered him, 'I am with you, my people are your people. We will be with you in the war.'

[4] But Jehoshaphat also said to the king of Israel, 'Inquire first for the word of the LORD.' [5] Then the king of Israel gathered the prophets together, four hundred of them, and said to them, 'Shall we go to battle against Ramoth-gilead, or shall I refrain?' They said, 'Go up; for God will give it into the hand of the king.' [6] But Jehoshaphat said, 'Is there no other prophet of the LORD here of whom we may inquire?' [7] The king of Israel said to Jehoshaphat, 'There is still one other by whom we may inquire of the LORD, Micaiah son of Imlah; but I hate him, for he never prophesies anything favourable about me, but only disaster.' Jehoshaphat said, 'Let the king not say such a thing.' [8] Then the king of Israel summoned an officer and said, 'Bring quickly Micaiah son of Imlah.' [9] Now the king of Israel and King Jehoshaphat of Judah were sitting on their thrones, arrayed in their robes; and they were sitting at the threshing-floor at the entrance of the gate of Samaria; and all the prophets were prophesying before them. [10] Zedekiah son of Chenaanah made for himself horns of iron, and he said, 'Thus says the LORD: With these you shall gore the Arameans until they are destroyed.' [11] All the prophets were prophesying the same and saying, 'Go up to Ramoth-gilead and triumph; the LORD will give it into the hand of the king.'

[12] The messenger who had gone to summon Micaiah said to him, 'Look, the words of the prophets with one accord are favourable to the king; let your word be like the word of one of them, and speak favourably.' [13] But Micaiah said, 'As the LORD lives, whatever my God says, that I will speak.'

[14] When he had come to the king, the king said to him, 'Micaiah, shall we go to Ramoth-gilead to battle, or shall I refrain?' He answered, 'Go up and triumph; they will be given into your hand.' [15] But the king said to him, 'How many times must I make you swear to tell me nothing but the truth in the name of the LORD?' [16] Then Micaiah[a] said, 'I saw all Israel scattered on the mountains, like sheep without a shepherd; and the LORD said, "These have no master; let each one go home in peace." ' [17] The king of Israel said to Jehoshaphat, 'Did I not tell you that he would not prophesy anything favourable about me, but only disaster?'

[18] Then Micaiah[a] said, 'Therefore hear the word of the LORD: I saw the LORD sitting on his throne, with all the host of heaven standing to the right and to the left of him. [19] And the LORD said, "Who will entice King Ahab of Israel, so that he may go up and fall at Ramoth-gilead?" Then one said one thing, and another said another, [20] until a spirit came forward and stood before the LORD, saying, "I will entice him." The LORD asked him, "How?" [21] He replied, "I will go out and be a lying spirit in the mouth of all his prophets." Then the LORD[a] said, "You are to entice him, and you shall succeed; go out and do it." [22] So you see, the LORD has put a lying spirit in the mouth of these your prophets; the LORD has decreed disaster for you.'

[23] Then Zedekiah son of Chenaanah came up to Micaiah, slapped him on the cheek, and said, 'Which way did the spirit of the LORD pass from me to speak to you?' [24] Micaiah replied, 'You will find out on

a Heb *he*

that day when you go in to hide in an inner chamber.' 25 The king of Israel then ordered, 'Take Micaiah, and return him to Amon the governor of the city and to Joash the king's son; 26 and say, "Thus says the king: Put this fellow in prison, and feed him on reduced rations of bread and water until I return in peace." ' 27 Micaiah said, 'If you return in peace, the LORD has not spoken by me.' And he said, 'Hear, you peoples, all of you!'

Defeat and Death of Ahab

28 So the king of Israel and King Jehoshaphat of Judah went up to Ramoth-gilead. 29 The king of Israel said to Jehoshaphat, 'I will disguise myself and go into battle, but you wear your robes.' So the king of Israel disguised himself, and they went into battle. 30 Now the king of Aram had commanded the captains of his chariots, 'Fight with no one small or great, but only with the king of Israel.' 31 When the captains of the chariots saw Jehoshaphat, they said, 'It is the king of Israel.' So they turned to fight against him; and Jehoshaphat cried out, and the LORD helped him. God drew them away from him, 32 for when the captains of the chariots saw that it was not the king of Israel, they turned back from pursuing him. 33 But a certain man drew his bow and unknowingly struck the king of Israel between the scale armour and the breastplate; so he said to the driver of his chariot, 'Turn around, and carry me out of the battle, for I am wounded.' 34 The battle grew hot that day, and the king of Israel propped himself up in his chariot facing the Arameans until evening; then at sunset he died.

19 King Jehoshaphat of Judah returned in safety to his house in Jerusalem. 2 Jehu son of Hanani the seer went out to meet him and said to King Jehoshaphat, 'Should you help the wicked and love those who hate the LORD? Because of this, wrath has gone out against you from the LORD. 3 Nevertheless, some good is found in you, for you destroyed the sacred poles *a* out of the land, and have set your heart to seek God.'

The Reforms of Jehoshaphat

4 Jehoshaphat resided at Jerusalem; then he went out again among the people, from Beer-sheba to the hill country of Ephraim, and brought them back to the LORD, the God of their ancestors. 5 He appointed judges in the land in all the fortified cities of Judah, city by city, 6 and said to the judges, 'Consider what you are doing, for you judge not on behalf of human beings but on the LORD's behalf; he is with you in giving judgement. 7 Now, let the fear of the LORD be upon you; take care what you do, for there is no perversion of justice with the LORD our God, or partiality, or taking of bribes.'

8 Moreover, in Jerusalem Jehoshaphat appointed certain Levites and priests and heads of families of Israel, to give judgement for the LORD and to decide disputed cases. They had their seat at Jerusalem. 9 He charged them: 'This is how you shall act: in the fear of the LORD, in faithfulness, and with your whole heart; 10 whenever a case comes to you from your kindred who live in their cities, concerning bloodshed, law or commandment, statutes or ordinances, then you shall instruct them, so that they may not incur guilt before the LORD and wrath may not come on you and your kindred. Do so, and you will not incur guilt. 11 See, Amariah the chief priest is over you in all matters of the LORD; and Zebadiah son of Ishmael, the governor of the house of Judah, in all the king's matters; and the Levites will serve you as officers. Deal courageously, and may the LORD be with the good!'

Invasion from the East

20 After this the Moabites and Ammonites, and with them some of the Meunites, *b* came against Jehoshaphat for battle. 2 Messengers *c* came and told Jehoshaphat, 'A great multitude is coming against you from Edom, *d* from beyond the sea; already they are at Hazazon-tamar' (that is, En-gedi). 3 Jehoshaphat was afraid; he set himself to seek the LORD,

---

a Heb *Asheroth*   *b* Compare 26.7: Heb *Ammonites*
c Heb *They*   *d* One Ms: MT *Aram*

and proclaimed a fast throughout all Judah. ⁴Judah assembled to seek help from the LORD; from all the towns of Judah they came to seek the LORD.

Jehoshaphat's Prayer and Victory

5 Jehoshaphat stood in the assembly of Judah and Jerusalem, in the house of the LORD, before the new court, ⁶and said, 'O LORD, God of our ancestors, are you not God in heaven? Do you not rule over all the kingdoms of the nations? In your hand are power and might, so that no one is able to withstand you. ⁷Did you not, O our God, drive out the inhabitants of this land before your people Israel, and give it for ever to the descendants of your friend Abraham? ⁸They have lived in it, and in it have built you a sanctuary for your name, saying, ⁹"If disaster comes upon us, the sword, judgement,ᵃ or pestilence, or famine, we will stand before this house, and before you, for your name is in this house, and cry to you in our distress, and you will hear and save." ¹⁰See now, the people of Ammon, Moab, and Mount Seir, whom you would not let Israel invade when they came from the land of Egypt, and whom they avoided and did not destroy— ¹¹they reward us by coming to drive us out of your possession that you have given us to inherit. ¹²O our God, will you not execute judgement upon them? For we are powerless against this great multitude that is coming against us. We do not know what to do, but our eyes are on you.'

13 Meanwhile all Judah stood before the LORD, with their little ones, their wives, and their children. ¹⁴Then the spirit of the LORD came upon Jahaziel son of Zechariah, son of Benaiah, son of Jeiel, son of Mattaniah, a Levite of the sons of Asaph, in the middle of the assembly. ¹⁵He said, 'Listen, all Judah and inhabitants of Jerusalem, and King Jehoshaphat: Thus says the LORD to you: "Do not fear or be dismayed at this great multitude; for the battle is not yours but God's. ¹⁶Tomorrow go down against them; they will come up by the ascent of Ziz; you will find them at the end of the valley, before the wilderness of Jeruel.

¹⁷This battle is not for you to fight; take your position, stand still, and see the victory of the LORD on your behalf, O Judah and Jerusalem." Do not fear or be dismayed; tomorrow go out against them, and the LORD will be with you.'

18 Then Jehoshaphat bowed down with his face to the ground, and all Judah and the inhabitants of Jerusalem fell down before the LORD, worshipping the LORD. ¹⁹And the Levites, of the Kohathites and the Korahites, stood up to praise the LORD, the God of Israel, with a very loud voice.

20 They rose early in the morning and went out into the wilderness of Tekoa; and as they went out, Jehoshaphat stood and said, 'Listen to me, O Judah and inhabitants of Jerusalem! Believe in the LORD your God and you will be established; believe his prophets.' ²¹When he had taken counsel with the people, he appointed those who were to sing to the LORD and praise him in holy splendour, as they went before the army, saying,

'Give thanks to the LORD,
    for his steadfast love endures for
        ever.'

²²As they began to sing and praise, the LORD set an ambush against the Ammonites, Moab, and Mount Seir, who had come against Judah, so that they were routed. ²³For the Ammonites and Moab attacked the inhabitants of Mount Seir, destroying them utterly; and when they had made an end of the inhabitants of Seir, they all helped to destroy one another.

24 When Judah came to the watch-tower of the wilderness, they looked towards the multitude; they were corpses lying on the ground; no one had escaped. ²⁵When Jehoshaphat and his people came to take the booty from them, they found livestockᵇ in great numbers, goods, clothing, and precious things, which they took for themselves until they could carry no more. They spent three days taking the booty, because of its abundance. ²⁶On the fourth day they assembled in the Valley of Beracah, for there they blessed the LORD; therefore that place has been called the Valley of

_a_ Or _the sword of judgement_   _b_ Gk: Heb _among them_

Beracah[a] to this day. 27 Then all the people of Judah and Jerusalem, with Jehoshaphat at their head, returned to Jerusalem with joy, for the LORD had enabled them to rejoice over their enemies. 28 They came to Jerusalem, with harps and lyres and trumpets, to the house of the LORD. 29 The fear of God came on all the kingdoms of the countries when they heard that the LORD had fought against the enemies of Israel. 30 And the realm of Jehoshaphat was quiet, for his God gave him rest all around.

The End of Jehoshaphat's Reign

31 So Jehoshaphat reigned over Judah. He was thirty-five years old when he began to reign; he reigned for twenty-five years in Jerusalem. His mother's name was Azubah daughter of Shilhi. 32 He walked in the way of his father Asa and did not turn aside from it, doing what was right in the sight of the LORD. 33 Yet the high places were not removed; the people had not yet set their hearts upon the God of their ancestors. 34 Now the rest of the acts of Jehoshaphat, from first to last, are written in the Annals of Jehu son of Hanani, which are recorded in the Book of the Kings of Israel. 35 After this King Jehoshaphat of Judah joined with King Ahaziah of Israel, who did wickedly. 36 He joined him in building ships to go to Tarshish; they built the ships in Ezion-geber. 37 Then Eliezer son of Dodavahu of Mareshah prophesied against Jehoshaphat, saying, 'Because you have joined with Ahaziah, the LORD will destroy what you have made.' And the ships were wrecked and were not able to go to Tarshish.

Jehoram's Reign

21 Jehoshaphat slept with his ancestors and was buried with his ancestors in the city of David; his son Jehoram succeeded him. 2 He had brothers, the sons of Jehoshaphat: Azariah, Jehiel, Zechariah, Azariah, Michael, and Shephatiah; all these were the sons of King Jehoshaphat of Judah.[b] 3 Their father gave them many gifts, of silver, gold, and valuable possessions, together with fortified cities in Judah; but he gave the kingdom to Jehoram, because he was the firstborn. 4 When Jehoram had ascended the throne of his father and was established, he put all his brothers to the sword, and also some of the officials of Israel. 5 Jehoram was thirty-two years old when he began to reign; he reigned for eight years in Jerusalem. 6 He walked in the way of the kings of Israel, as the house of Ahab had done; for the daughter of Ahab was his wife. He did what was evil in the sight of the LORD. 7 Yet the LORD would not destroy the house of David because of the covenant that he had made with David, and since he had promised to give a lamp to him and to his descendants for ever.

Revolt of Edom

8 In his days Edom revolted against the rule of Judah and set up a king of their own. 9 Then Jehoram crossed over with his commanders and all his chariots. He set out by night and attacked the Edomites, who had surrounded him and his chariot commanders. 10 So Edom has been in revolt against the rule of Judah to this day. At that time Libnah also revolted against his rule, because he had forsaken the LORD, the God of his ancestors.

Elijah's Letter

11 Moreover, he made high places in the hill country of Judah, and led the inhabitants of Jerusalem into unfaithfulness, and made Judah go astray. 12 A letter came to him from the prophet Elijah, saying: 'Thus says the LORD, the God of your father David: Because you have not walked in the ways of your father Jehoshaphat or in the ways of King Asa of Judah, 13 but have walked in the way of the kings of Israel, and have led Judah and the inhabitants of Jerusalem into unfaithfulness, as the house of Ahab led Israel into unfaithfulness, and because you also have killed your brothers, members of your father's house, who were better than yourself, 14 see, the LORD will bring a great plague on your people, your children, your wives, and all your possessions, 15 and you yourself will have a severe

a That is Blessing   b Gk Syr: Heb Israel

sickness with a disease of your bowels, until your bowels come out, day after day, because of the disease.'

16 The LORD aroused against Jehoram the anger of the Philistines and of the Arabs who are near the Ethiopians. *a* 17 They came up against Judah, invaded it, and carried away all the possessions they found that belonged to the king's house, along with his sons and his wives, so that no son was left to him except Jehoahaz, his youngest son.

Disease and Death of Jehoram

18 After all this the LORD struck him in his bowels with an incurable disease. 19 In course of time, at the end of two years, his bowels came out because of the disease, and he died in great agony. His people made no fire in his honour, like the fires made for his ancestors. 20 He was thirty-two years old when he began to reign; he reigned for eight years in Jerusalem. He departed with no one's regret. They buried him in the city of David, but not in the tombs of the kings.

Ahaziah's Reign

22 The inhabitants of Jerusalem made his youngest son Ahaziah king as his successor; for the troops who came with the Arabs to the camp had killed all the older sons. So Ahaziah son of Jehoram reigned as king of Judah. 2 Ahaziah was forty-two years old when he began to reign; he reigned for one year in Jerusalem. His mother's name was Athaliah, a granddaughter of Omri. 3 He also walked in the ways of the house of Ahab, for his mother was his counsellor in doing wickedly. 4 He did what was evil in the sight of the LORD, as the house of Ahab had done; for after the death of his father they were his counsellors, to his ruin. 5 He even followed their advice, and went with Jehoram son of King Ahab of Israel to make war against King Hazael of Aram at Ramoth-gilead. The Arameans wounded Joram, 6 and he returned to be healed in Jezreel of the wounds that he had received at Ramah, when he fought King Hazael of Aram. And

Ahaziah son of King Jehoram of Judah went down to see Joram son of Ahab in Jezreel, because he was sick.

7 But it was ordained by God that the downfall of Ahaziah should come about through his going to visit Joram. For when he came there he went out with Jehoram to meet Jehu son of Nimshi, whom the LORD had anointed to destroy the house of Ahab. 8 When Jehu was executing judgement on the house of Ahab, he met the officials of Judah and the sons of Ahaziah's brothers, who attended Ahaziah, and he killed them. 9 He searched for Ahaziah, who was captured while hiding in Samaria and was brought to Jehu, and put to death. They buried him, for they said, 'He is the grandson of Jehoshaphat, who sought the LORD with all his heart.' And the house of Ahaziah had no one able to rule the kingdom.

Athaliah Seizes the Throne

10 Now when Athaliah, Ahaziah's mother, saw that her son was dead, she set about to destroy all the royal family of the house of Judah. 11 But Jehoshabeath, the king's daughter, took Joash son of Ahaziah, and stole him away from among the king's children who were about to be killed; she put him and his nurse in a bedroom. Thus Jehoshabeath, daughter of King Jehoram and wife of the priest Jehoiada—because she was a sister of Ahaziah—hid him from Athaliah, so that she did not kill him; 12 he remained with them for six years, hidden in the house of God, while Athaliah reigned over the land.

23 But in the seventh year Jehoiada took courage, and entered into a compact with the commanders of the hundreds, Azariah son of Jeroham, Ishmael son of Jehohanan, Azariah son of Obed, Maaseiah son of Adaiah, and Elishaphat son of Zichri. 2 They went about through Judah and gathered the Levites from all the towns of Judah, and the heads of families of Israel, and they came to Jerusalem. 3 Then the whole assembly made a covenant with the king in the house of God.

a Or *Nubians;* Heb *Cushites*

Jehoiada[a] said to them, 'Here is the king's son! Let him reign, as the LORD promised concerning the sons of David. 4 This is what you are to do: one-third of you, priests and Levites, who come on duty on the sabbath, shall be gatekeepers, 5 one-third shall be at the king's house, and one-third at the Gate of the Foundation; and all the people shall be in the courts of the house of the LORD. 6 Do not let anyone enter the house of the LORD except the priests and ministering Levites; they may enter, for they are holy, but all the other[b] people shall observe the instructions of the LORD. 7 The Levites shall surround the king, each with his weapons in his hand; and whoever enters the house shall be killed. Stay with the king in his comings and goings.'

Joash Crowned King

8 The Levites and all Judah did according to all that the priest Jehoiada commanded; each brought his men, who were to come on duty on the sabbath, with those who were to go off duty on the sabbath; for the priest Jehoiada did not dismiss the divisions. 9 The priest Jehoiada delivered to the captains the spears and the large and small shields that had been King David's, which were in the house of God; 10 and he set all the people as a guard for the king, everyone with weapon in hand, from the south side of the house to the north side of the house, around the altar and the house. 11 Then he brought out the king's son, put the crown on him, and gave him the covenant;[c] they proclaimed him king, and Jehoiada and his sons anointed him; and they shouted, 'Long live the king!'

Athaliah Deposed

12 When Athaliah heard the noise of the people running and praising the king, she went into the house of the LORD to the people; 13 and when she looked, there was the king standing by his pillar at the entrance, and the captains and the trumpeters beside the king, and all the people of the land rejoicing and blowing trumpets, and the singers with their musical in-

struments leading in the celebration. Athaliah tore her clothes, and cried, 'Treason! Treason!' 14 Then the priest Jehoiada brought out the captains who were set over the army, saying to them, 'Bring her out between the ranks; anyone who follows her is to be put to the sword.' For the priest said, 'Do not put her to death in the house of the LORD.' 15 So they laid hands on her; she went into the entrance of the Horse Gate of the king's house, and there they put her to death.

16 Jehoiada made a covenant between himself and all the people and the king that they should be the LORD's people. 17 Then all the people went to the house of Baal, and tore it down; his altars and his images they broke in pieces, and they killed Mattan, the priest of Baal, in front of the altars. 18 Jehoiada assigned the care of the house of the LORD to the levitical priests whom David had organized to be in charge of the house of the LORD, to offer burnt-offerings to the LORD, as it is written in the law of Moses, with rejoicing and with singing, according to the order of David. 19 He stationed the gatekeepers at the gates of the house of the LORD so that no one should enter who was in any way unclean. 20 And he took the captains, the nobles, the governors of the people, and all the people of the land, and they brought the king down from the house of the LORD, marching through the upper gate to the king's house. They set the king on the royal throne. 21 So all the people of the land rejoiced, and the city was quiet after Athaliah had been killed with the sword.

Joash Repairs the Temple

24 Joash was seven years old when he began to reign; he reigned for forty years in Jerusalem; his mother's name was Zibiah of Beer-sheba. 2 Joash did what was right in the sight of the LORD all the days of the priest Jehoiada. 3 Jehoiada got two wives for him, and he became the father of sons and daughters.

---

a Heb *He*   *b* Heb lacks *other*   *c* Or *treaty*, or *testimony*; Heb *eduth*

4 Some time afterwards Joash decided to restore the house of the Lord. 5 He assembled the priests and the Levites and said to them, 'Go out to the cities of Judah and gather money from all Israel to repair the house of your God, year by year; and see that you act quickly.' But the Levites did not act quickly. 6 So the king summoned Jehoiada the chief, and said to him, 'Why have you not required the Levites to bring in from Judah and Jerusalem the tax levied by Moses, the servant of the Lord, on*a* the congregation of Israel for the tent of the covenant?'*b* 7 For the children of Athaliah, that wicked woman, had broken into the house of God, and had even used all the dedicated things of the house of the Lord for the Baals.

8 So the king gave command, and they made a chest, and set it outside the gate of the house of the Lord. 9 A proclamation was made throughout Judah and Jerusalem to bring in for the Lord the tax that Moses the servant of God laid on Israel in the wilderness. 10 All the leaders and all the people rejoiced, and brought their tax and dropped it into the chest until it was full. 11 Whenever the chest was brought to the king's officers by the Levites, when they saw that there was a large amount of money in it, the king's secretary and the officer of the chief priest would come and empty the chest and take it and return it to its place. So they did day after day, and collected money in abundance. 12 The king and Jehoiada gave it to those who had charge of the work of the house of the Lord, and they hired masons and carpenters to restore the house of the Lord, and also workers in iron and bronze to repair the house of the Lord. 13 So those who were engaged in the work laboured, and the repairs went forward at their hands, and they restored the house of God to its proper condition and strengthened it. 14 When they had finished, they brought the rest of the money to the king and Jehoiada, and with it were made utensils for the house of the Lord, utensils for the service and for the burnt-offerings, and ladles, and vessels of gold and silver. They offered burnt-offerings in the house of the Lord regularly all the days of Jehoiada.

Apostasy of Joash

15 But Jehoiada grew old and full of days, and died; he was one hundred and thirty years old at his death. 16 And they buried him in the city of David among the kings, because he had done good in Israel, and for God and his house.

17 Now after the death of Jehoiada the officials of Judah came and did obeisance to the king; then the king listened to them. 18 They abandoned the house of the Lord, the God of their ancestors, and served the sacred poles*c* and the idols. And wrath came upon Judah and Jerusalem for this guilt of theirs. 19 Yet he sent prophets among them to bring them back to the Lord; they testified against them, but they would not listen.

20 Then the spirit of God took possession of*d* Zechariah son of the priest Jehoiada; he stood above the people and said to them, 'Thus says God: Why do you transgress the commandments of the Lord, so that you cannot prosper? Because you have forsaken the Lord, he has also forsaken you.' 21 But they conspired against him, and by command of the king they stoned him to death in the court of the house of the Lord. 22 King Joash did not remember the kindness that Jehoiada, Zechariah's father, had shown him, but killed his son. As he was dying, he said, 'May the Lord see and avenge!'

Death of Joash

23 At the end of the year the army of Aram came up against Joash. They came to Judah and Jerusalem, and destroyed all the officials of the people from among them, and sent all the booty they took to the king of Damascus. 24 Although the army of Aram had come with few men, the Lord delivered into their hand a very great army, because they had abandoned the Lord, the God of their ancestors. Thus they executed judgement on Joash.

a Compare Vg: Heb *and*   *b* Or *treaty*, or *testimony*; Heb *eduth*   *c* Heb *Asherim*   *d* Heb *clothed itself with*

25 When they had withdrawn, leaving him severely wounded, his servants conspired against him because of the blood of the son*a* of the priest Jehoiada, and they killed him on his bed. So he died; and they buried him in the city of David, but they did not bury him in the tombs of the kings. 26 Those who conspired against him were Zabad son of Shimeath the Ammonite, and Jehozabad son of Shimrith the Moabite. 27 Accounts of his sons, and of the many oracles against him, and of the rebuilding*b* of the house of God are written in the Commentary on the Book of the Kings. And his son Amaziah succeeded him.

Reign of Amaziah

25 Amaziah was twenty-five years old when he began to reign, and he reigned for twenty-nine years in Jerusalem. His mother's name was Jehoaddan of Jerusalem. 2 He did what was right in the sight of the LORD, yet not with a true heart. 3 As soon as the royal power was firmly in his hand he killed his servants who had murdered his father the king. 4 But he did not put their children to death, according to what is written in the law, in the book of Moses, where the LORD commanded, 'The parents shall not be put to death for the children, or the children be put to death for the parents; but all shall be put to death for their own sins.'

Slaughter of the Edomites

5 Amaziah assembled the people of Judah, and set them by ancestral houses under commanders of the thousands and of the hundreds for all Judah and Benjamin. He mustered those twenty years old and upwards, and found that they were three hundred thousand picked troops fit for war, able to handle spear and shield. 6 He also hired one hundred thousand mighty warriors from Israel for one hundred talents of silver. 7 But a man of God came to him and said, 'O king, do not let the army of Israel go with you, for the LORD is not with Israel—all these Ephraimites. 8 Rather, go by yourself and act; be strong in battle,

or God will fling you down before the enemy; for God has power to help or to overthrow.' 9 Amaziah said to the man of God, 'But what shall we do about the hundred talents that I have given to the army of Israel?' The man of God answered, 'The LORD is able to give you much more than this.' 10 Then Amaziah discharged the army that had come to him from Ephraim, letting them go home again. But they became very angry with Judah, and returned home in fierce anger.

11 Amaziah took courage, and led out his people; he went to the Valley of Salt, and struck down ten thousand men of Seir. 12 The people of Judah captured another ten thousand alive, took them to the top of Sela, and threw them down from the top of Sela, so that all of them were dashed to pieces. 13 But the men of the army whom Amaziah sent back, not letting them go with him to battle, fell on the cities of Judah from Samaria to Beth-horon; they killed three thousand people in them, and took much booty.

14 Now after Amaziah came from the slaughter of the Edomites, he brought the gods of the people of Seir, set them up as his gods, and worshipped them, making offerings to them. 15 The LORD was angry with Amaziah and sent to him a prophet, who said to him, 'Why have you resorted to a people's gods who could not deliver their own people from your hand?' 16 But as he was speaking the king*c* said to him, 'Have we made you a royal counsellor? Stop! Why should you be put to death?' So the prophet stopped, but said, 'I know that God has determined to destroy you, because you have done this and have not listened to my advice.'

Israel Defeats Judah

17 Then King Amaziah of Judah took counsel and sent to King Joash son of Jehoahaz son of Jehu of Israel, saying, 'Come, let us look one another in the face.' 18 King Joash of Israel sent word to King Amaziah of Judah, 'A thornbush on Lebanon sent to a cedar on Lebanon, saying,

a Gk Vg: Heb *sons*   *b* Heb *founding*   *c* Heb *he*

"Give your daughter to my son for a wife"; but a wild animal of Lebanon passed by and trampled down the thornbush. 19 You say, "See, I have defeated Edom", and your heart has lifted you up in boastfulness. Now stay at home; why should you provoke trouble so that you fall, you and Judah with you?'

20 But Amaziah would not listen—it was God's doing, in order to hand them over, because they had sought the gods of Edom. 21 So King Joash of Israel went up; he and King Amaziah of Judah faced one another in battle at Beth-shemesh, which belongs to Judah. 22 Judah was defeated by Israel; everyone fled home. 23 King Joash of Israel captured King Amaziah of Judah, son of Joash, son of Ahaziah, at Beth-shemesh; he brought him to Jerusalem, and broke down the wall of Jerusalem from the Ephraim Gate to the Corner Gate, a distance of four hundred cubits. 24 He seized all the gold and silver, and all the vessels that were found in the house of God, and Obed-edom with them; he seized also the treasuries of the king's house, also hostages; then he returned to Samaria.

Death of Amaziah

25 King Amaziah son of Joash of Judah, lived fifteen years after the death of King Joash son of Jehoahaz of Israel. 26 Now the rest of the deeds of Amaziah, from first to last, are they not written in the Book of the Kings of Judah and Israel? 27 From the time that Amaziah turned away from the LORD they made a conspiracy against him in Jerusalem, and he fled to Lachish. But they sent after him to Lachish, and killed him there. 28 They brought him back on horses; he was buried with his ancestors in the city of David.

Reign of Uzziah

26 Then all the people of Judah took Uzziah, who was sixteen years old, and made him king to succeed his father Amaziah. 2 He rebuilt Eloth and restored it to Judah, after the king slept with his ancestors. 3 Uzziah was sixteen years old when he began to reign, and he reigned for fifty-two years in Jerusalem. His mother's name was Jecoliah of Jerusalem. 4 He did what was right in the sight of the LORD, just as his father Amaziah had done. 5 He set himself to seek God in the days of Zechariah, who instructed him in the fear of God; and as long as he sought the LORD, God made him prosper.

6 He went out and made war against the Philistines, and broke down the wall of Gath and the wall of Jabneh and the wall of Ashdod; he built cities in the territory of Ashdod and elsewhere among the Philistines. 7 God helped him against the Philistines, against the Arabs who lived in Gurbaal, and against the Meunites. 8 The Ammonites paid tribute to Uzziah, and his fame spread even to the border of Egypt, for he became very strong. 9 Moreover, Uzziah built towers in Jerusalem at the Corner Gate, at the Valley Gate, and at the Angle, and fortified them. 10 He built towers in the wilderness and hewed out many cisterns, for he had large herds, both in the Shephelah and in the plain, and he had farmers and vine-dressers in the hills and in the fertile lands, for he loved the soil. 11 Moreover, Uzziah had an army of soldiers, fit for war, in divisions according to the numbers in the muster made by the secretary Jeiel and the officer Maaseiah, under the direction of Hananiah, one of the king's commanders. 12 The whole number of the heads of ancestral houses of mighty warriors was two thousand six hundred. 13 Under their command was an army of three hundred and seven thousand five hundred, who could make war with mighty power, to help the king against the enemy. 14 Uzziah provided for all the army the shields, spears, helmets, coats of mail, bows, and stones for slinging. 15 In Jerusalem he set up machines, invented by skilled workers, on the towers and the corners for shooting arrows and large stones. And his fame spread far, for he was marvellously helped until he became strong.

Pride and Apostasy

16 But when he had become strong he grew proud, to his destruction. For he was

false to the LORD his God, and entered the temple of the LORD to make offering on the altar of incense. [17] But the priest Azariah went in after him, with eighty priests of the LORD who were men of valour; [18] they withstood King Uzziah, and said to him, 'It is not for you, Uzziah, to make offering to the LORD, but for the priests the descendants of Aaron, who are consecrated to make offering. Go out of the sanctuary; for you have done wrong, and it will bring you no honour from the LORD God.' [19] Then Uzziah was angry. Now he had a censer in his hand to make offering, and when he became angry with the priests a leprous[a] disease broke out on his forehead, in the presence of the priests in the house of the LORD, by the altar of incense. [20] When the chief priest Azariah, and all the priests, looked at him, he was leprous[a] in his forehead. They hurried him out, and he himself hurried to get out, because the LORD had struck him. [21] King Uzziah was leprous[a] to the day of his death, and being leprous[a] lived in a separate house, for he was excluded from the house of the LORD. His son Jotham was in charge of the palace of the king, governing the people of the land.

22 Now the rest of the acts of Uzziah, from first to last, the prophet Isaiah son of Amoz wrote. [23] Uzziah slept with his ancestors; they buried him near his ancestors in the burial field that belonged to the kings, for they said, 'He is leprous.'[a] His son Jotham succeeded him.

Reign of Jotham

27 Jotham was twenty-five years old when he began to reign; he reigned for sixteen years in Jerusalem. His mother's name was Jerushah daughter of Zadok. [2] He did what was right in the sight of the LORD just as his father Uzziah had done—only he did not invade the temple of the LORD. But the people still followed corrupt practices. [3] He built the upper gate of the house of the LORD, and did extensive building on the wall of Ophel. [4] Moreover, he built cities in the hill country of Judah, and forts and towers on the wooded hills.

[5] He fought with the king of the Ammonites and prevailed against them. The Ammonites gave him that year one hundred talents of silver, ten thousand cors of wheat and ten thousand of barley. The Ammonites paid him the same amount in the second and the third years. [6] So Jotham became strong because he ordered his ways before the LORD his God. [7] Now the rest of the acts of Jotham, and all his wars and his ways, are written in the Book of the Kings of Israel and Judah. [8] He was twenty-five years old when he began to reign; he reigned for sixteen years in Jerusalem. [9] Jotham slept with his ancestors, and they buried him in the city of David; and his son Ahaz succeeded him.

Reign of Ahaz

28 Ahaz was twenty years old when he began to reign; he reigned for sixteen years in Jerusalem. He did not do what was right in the sight of the LORD, as his ancestor David had done, [2] but he walked in the ways of the kings of Israel. He even made cast images for the Baals; [3] and he made offerings in the valley of the son of Hinnom, and made his sons pass through fire, according to the abominable practices of the nations whom the LORD drove out before the people of Israel. [4] He sacrificed and made offerings on the high places, on the hills, and under every green tree.

Aram and Israel Defeat Judah

5 Therefore the LORD his God gave him into the hand of the king of Aram, who defeated him and took captive a great number of his people and brought them to Damascus. He was also given into the hand of the king of Israel, who defeated him with great slaughter. [6] Pekah son of Remaliah killed one hundred and twenty thousand in Judah in one day, all of them valiant warriors, because they had abandoned the LORD, the God of their ancestors. [7] And Zichri, a mighty warrior of Ephraim, killed the king's son Maaseiah,

---

a A term for several skin diseases; precise meaning uncertain

Azrikam the commander of the palace, and Elkanah the next in authority to the king.

Intervention of Oded

8 The people of Israel took captive two hundred thousand of their kin, women, sons, and daughters; they also took much booty from them and brought the booty to Samaria. 9 But a prophet of the LORD was there, whose name was Oded; he went out to meet the army that came to Samaria, and said to them, 'Because the LORD, the God of your ancestors, was angry with Judah, he gave them into your hand, but you have killed them in a rage that has reached up to heaven. 10 Now you intend to subjugate the people of Judah and Jerusalem, male and female, as your slaves. But what have you except sins against the LORD your God? 11 Now hear me, and send back the captives whom you have taken from your kindred, for the fierce wrath of the LORD is upon you.' 12 Moreover, certain chiefs of the Ephraimites, Azariah son of Johanan, Berechiah son of Meshillemoth, Jehizkiah son of Shallum, and Amasa son of Hadlai, stood up against those who were coming from the war, 13 and said to them, 'You shall not bring the captives in here, for you propose to bring on us guilt against the LORD in addition to our present sins and guilt. For our guilt is already great, and there is fierce wrath against Israel.' 14 So the warriors left the captives and the booty before the officials and all the assembly. 15 Then those who were mentioned by name got up and took the captives, and with the booty they clothed all that were naked among them; they clothed them, gave them sandals, provided them with food and drink, and anointed them; and carrying all the feeble among them on donkeys, they brought them to their kindred at Jericho, the city of palm trees. Then they returned to Samaria.

Assyria Refuses to Help Judah

16 At that time King Ahaz sent to the king*a* of Assyria for help. 17 For the Edom-ites had again invaded and defeated Judah, and carried away captives. 18 And the Philistines had made raids on the cities in the Shephelah and the Negeb of Judah, and had taken Beth-shemesh, Aijalon, Gederoth, Soco with its villages, Timnah with its villages, and Gimzo with its villages; and they settled there. 19 For the LORD brought Judah low because of King Ahaz of Israel, for he had behaved without restraint in Judah and had been faithless to the LORD. 20 So King Tilgath-pilneser of Assyria came against him, and oppressed him instead of strengthening him. 21 For Ahaz plundered the house of the LORD and the houses of the king and of the officials, and gave tribute to the king of Assyria; but it did not help him.

Apostasy and Death of Ahaz

22 In the time of his distress he became yet more faithless to the LORD—this same King Ahaz. 23 For he sacrificed to the gods of Damascus, which had defeated him, and said, 'Because the gods of the kings of Aram helped them, I will sacrifice to them so that they may help me.' But they were the ruin of him, and of all Israel. 24 Ahaz gathered together the utensils of the house of God, and cut in pieces the utensils of the house of God. He shut up the doors of the house of the LORD and made himself altars in every corner of Jerusalem. 25 In every city of Judah he made high places to make offerings to other gods, provoking to anger the LORD, the God of his ancestors. 26 Now the rest of his acts and all his ways, from first to last, are written in the Book of the Kings of Judah and Israel. 27 Ahaz slept with his ancestors, and they buried him in the city, in Jerusalem; but they did not bring him into the tombs of the kings of Israel. His son Hezekiah succeeded him.

Reign of Hezekiah

29 Hezekiah began to reign when he was twenty-five years old; he reigned for twenty-nine years in Jerusalem. His mother's name was Abijah daughter of

---

a Gk Syr Vg Compare 2 Kings 16.7: Heb *kings*

Zechariah. [2] He did what was right in the sight of the LORD, just as his ancestor David had done.

The Temple Cleansed

[3] In the first year of his reign, in the first month, he opened the doors of the house of the LORD and repaired them. [4] He brought in the priests and the Levites and assembled them in the square on the east. [5] He said to them, 'Listen to me, Levites! Sanctify yourselves, and sanctify the house of the LORD, the God of your ancestors, and carry out the filth from the holy place. [6] For our ancestors have been unfaithful and have done what was evil in the sight of the LORD our God; they have forsaken him, and have turned away their faces from the dwelling of the LORD, and turned their backs. [7] They also shut the doors of the vestibule and put out the lamps, and have not offered incense or made burnt-offerings in the holy place to the God of Israel. [8] Therefore the wrath of the LORD came upon Judah and Jerusalem, and he has made them an object of horror, of astonishment, and of hissing, as you see with your own eyes. [9] Our fathers have fallen by the sword and our sons and our daughters and our wives are in captivity for this. [10] Now it is in my heart to make a covenant with the LORD, the God of Israel, so that his fierce anger may turn away from us. [11] My sons, do not now be negligent, for the LORD has chosen you to stand in his presence to minister to him, and to be his ministers and make offerings to him.'

[12] Then the Levites arose, Mahath son of Amasai, and Joel son of Azariah, of the sons of the Kohathites; and of the sons of Merari, Kish son of Abdi, and Azariah son of Jehallelel; and of the Gershonites, Joah son of Zimmah, and Eden son of Joah; [13] and of the sons of Elizaphan, Shimri and Jeuel; and of the sons of Asaph, Zechariah and Mattaniah; [14] and of the sons of Heman, Jehuel and Shimei; and of the sons of Jeduthun, Shemaiah and Uzziel. [15] They gathered their brothers, sanctified themselves, and went in as the king had commanded, by the words of the LORD, to cleanse the house of the LORD. [16] The priests went into the inner part of the house of the LORD to cleanse it, and they brought out all the unclean things that they found in the temple of the LORD into the court of the house of the LORD; and the Levites took them and carried them out to the Wadi Kidron. [17] They began to sanctify on the first day of the first month, and on the eighth day of the month they came to the vestibule of the LORD; then for eight days they sanctified the house of the LORD, and on the sixteenth day of the first month they finished. [18] Then they went inside to King Hezekiah and said, 'We have cleansed all the house of the LORD, the altar of burnt-offering and all its utensils, and the table for the rows of bread and all its utensils. [19] All the utensils that King Ahaz repudiated during his reign when he was faithless, we have made ready and sanctified; see, they are in front of the altar of the LORD.'

Temple Worship Restored

[20] Then King Hezekiah rose early, assembled the officials of the city, and went up to the house of the LORD. [21] They brought seven bulls, seven rams, seven lambs, and seven male goats for a sin-offering for the kingdom and for the sanctuary and for Judah. He commanded the priests the descendants of Aaron to offer them on the altar of the LORD. [22] So they slaughtered the bulls, and the priests received the blood and dashed it against the altar; they slaughtered the rams and their blood was dashed against the altar; they also slaughtered the lambs and their blood was dashed against the altar. [23] Then the male goats for the sin-offering were brought to the king and the assembly; they laid their hands on them, [24] and the priests slaughtered them and made a sin-offering with their blood at the altar, to make atonement for all Israel. For the king commanded that the burnt-offering and the sin-offering should be made for all Israel.

[25] He stationed the Levites in the house of the LORD with cymbals, harps, and lyres,

according to the commandment of David and of Gad the king's seer and of the prophet Nathan, for the commandment was from the LORD through his prophets. 26 The Levites stood with the instruments of David, and the priests with the trumpets. 27 Then Hezekiah commanded that the burnt-offering be offered on the altar. When the burnt-offering began, the song to the LORD began also, and the trumpets, accompanied by the instruments of King David of Israel. 28 The whole assembly worshipped, the singers sang, and the trumpeters sounded; all this continued until the burnt-offering was finished. 29 When the offering was finished, the king and all who were present with him bowed down and worshipped. 30 King Hezekiah and the officials commanded the Levites to sing praises to the LORD with the words of David and of the seer Asaph. They sang praises with gladness, and they bowed down and worshipped.

31 Then Hezekiah said, 'You have now consecrated yourselves to the LORD; come near, bring sacrifices and thank-offerings to the house of the LORD.' The assembly brought sacrifices and thank-offerings; and all who were of a willing heart brought burnt-offerings. 32 The number of the burnt-offerings that the assembly brought was seventy bulls, one hundred rams, and two hundred lambs; all these were for a burnt-offering to the LORD. 33 The consecrated offerings were six hundred bulls and three thousand sheep. 34 But the priests were too few and could not skin all the burnt-offerings, so, until other priests had sanctified themselves, their kindred, the Levites, helped them until the work was finished—for the Levites were more conscientious[a] than the priests in sanctifying themselves. 35 Besides the great number of burnt-offerings there was the fat of the offerings of well-being, and there were the drink-offerings for the burnt-offerings. Thus the service of the house of the LORD was restored. 36 And Hezekiah and all the people rejoiced because of what God had done for the people; for the thing had come about suddenly.

The Great Passover

30 Hezekiah sent word to all Israel and Judah, and wrote letters also to Ephraim and Manasseh, that they should come to the house of the LORD at Jerusalem, to keep the passover to the LORD the God of Israel. 2 For the king and his officials and all the assembly in Jerusalem had taken counsel to keep the passover in the second month 3 (for they could not keep it at its proper time because the priests had not sanctified themselves in sufficient number, nor had the people assembled in Jerusalem). 4 The plan seemed right to the king and all the assembly. 5 So they decreed the making of a proclamation throughout all Israel, from Beer-sheba to Dan, that the people should come and keep the passover to the LORD the God of Israel, at Jerusalem; for they had not kept it in great numbers as prescribed. 6 So couriers went throughout all Israel and Judah with letters from the king and his officials, as the king had commanded, saying, 'O people of Israel, return to the LORD, the God of Abraham, Isaac, and Israel, so that he may turn again to the remnant of you who have escaped from the hand of the kings of Assyria. 7 Do not be like your ancestors and your kindred, who were faithless to the LORD God of their ancestors, so that he made them a desolation, as you see. 8 Do not now be stiff-necked as your ancestors were, but yield yourselves to the LORD and come to his sanctuary, which he has sanctified for ever, and serve the LORD your God, so that his fierce anger may turn away from you. 9 For as you return to the LORD, your kindred and your children will find compassion with their captors, and return to this land. For the LORD your God is gracious and merciful, and will not turn away his face from you, if you return to him.'

10 So the couriers went from city to city through the country of Ephraim and Manasseh, and as far as Zebulun; but they laughed them to scorn, and mocked them. 11 Only a few from Asher, Manasseh, and

---

a Heb *upright in heart*

Zebulun humbled themselves and came to Jerusalem. 12 The hand of God was also on Judah to give them one heart to do what the king and the officials commanded by the word of the LORD.

13 Many people came together in Jerusalem to keep the festival of unleavened bread in the second month, a very large assembly. 14 They set to work and removed the altars that were in Jerusalem, and all the altars for offering incense they took away and threw into the Wadi Kidron. 15 They slaughtered the passover lamb on the fourteenth day of the second month. The priests and the Levites were ashamed, and they sanctified themselves and brought burnt-offerings into the house of the LORD. 16 They took their accustomed posts according to the law of Moses the man of God; the priests dashed the blood that they received[a] from the hands of the Levites. 17 For there were many in the assembly who had not sanctified themselves; therefore the Levites had to slaughter the passover lamb for everyone who was not clean, to make it holy to the LORD. 18 For a multitude of the people, many of them from Ephraim, Manasseh, Issachar, and Zebulun, had not cleansed themselves, yet they ate the passover otherwise than as prescribed. But Hezekiah prayed for them, saying, 'The good LORD pardon all 19 who set their hearts to seek God, the LORD the God of their ancestors, even though not in accordance with the sanctuary's rules of cleanness.' 20 The LORD heard Hezekiah, and healed the people. 21 The people of Israel who were present at Jerusalem kept the festival of unleavened bread for seven days with great gladness; and the Levites and the priests praised the LORD day by day, accompanied by loud instruments for the LORD. 22 Hezekiah spoke encouragingly to all the Levites who showed good skill in the service of the LORD. So the people ate the food of the festival for seven days, sacrificing offerings of well-being and giving thanks to the LORD the God of their ancestors.

23 Then the whole assembly agreed together to keep the festival for another seven days; so they kept it for another seven days with gladness. 24 For King Hezekiah of Judah gave the assembly a thousand bulls and seven thousand sheep for offerings, and the officials gave the assembly a thousand bulls and ten thousand sheep. The priests sanctified themselves in great numbers. 25 The whole assembly of Judah, the priests and the Levites, and the whole assembly that came out of Israel, and the resident aliens who came out of the land of Israel, and the resident aliens who lived in Judah, rejoiced. 26 There was great joy in Jerusalem, for since the time of Solomon son of King David of Israel there had been nothing like this in Jerusalem. 27 Then the priests and the Levites stood up and blessed the people, and their voice was heard; their prayer came to his holy dwelling in heaven.

Pagan Shrines Destroyed

31 Now when all this was finished, all Israel who were present went out to the cities of Judah and broke down the pillars, hewed down the sacred poles,[b] and pulled down the high places and the altars throughout all Judah and Benjamin, and in Ephraim and Manasseh, until they had destroyed them all. Then all the people of Israel returned to their cities, all to their individual properties.

2 Hezekiah appointed the divisions of the priests and of the Levites, division by division, everyone according to his service, the priests and the Levites, for burnt-offerings and offerings of well-being, to minister in the gates of the camp of the LORD and to give thanks and praise. 3 The contribution of the king from his own possessions was for the burnt-offerings: the burnt-offerings of morning and evening, and the burnt-offerings for the sabbaths, the new moons, and the appointed festivals, as it is written in the law of the LORD. 4 He commanded the people who lived in Jerusalem to give the portion due to the priests and the Levites, so that they might devote themselves to the law of the LORD. 5 As soon as the word spread, the people of Israel gave in abundance the first fruits of

a Heb lacks *that they received*   b Heb *Asherim*

grain, wine, oil, honey, and of all the produce of the field; and they brought in abundantly the tithe of everything. 6 The people of Israel and Judah who lived in the cities of Judah also brought in the tithe of cattle and sheep, and the tithe of the dedicated things that had been consecrated to the LORD their God, and laid them in heaps. 7 In the third month they began to pile up the heaps, and finished them in the seventh month. 8 When Hezekiah and the officials came and saw the heaps, they blessed the LORD and his people Israel. 9 Hezekiah questioned the priests and the Levites about the heaps. 10 The chief priest Azariah, who was of the house of Zadok, answered him, 'Since they began to bring the contributions into the house of the LORD, we have had enough to eat and have plenty to spare; for the LORD has blessed his people, so that we have this great supply left over.'

Reorganization of Priests and Levites

11 Then Hezekiah commanded them to prepare store-chambers in the house of the LORD; and they prepared them. 12 Faithfully they brought in the contributions, the tithes and the dedicated things. The chief officer in charge of them was Conaniah the Levite, with his brother Shimei as second; 13 while Jehiel, Azaziah, Nahath, Asahel, Jerimoth, Jozabad, Eliel, Ismachiah, Mahath, and Benaiah were overseers assisting Conaniah and his brother Shimei, by the appointment of King Hezekiah and of Azariah the chief officer of the house of God. 14 Kore son of Imnah the Levite, keeper of the east gate, was in charge of the freewill-offerings to God, to apportion the contribution reserved for the LORD and the most holy offerings. 15 Eden, Miniamin, Jeshua, Shemaiah, Amariah, and Shecaniah were faithfully assisting him in the cities of the priests, to distribute the portions to their kindred, old and young alike, by divisions, 16 except those enrolled by genealogy, males from three years old and upwards, all who entered the house of the LORD as the duty of each day required, for their service according to their offices, by their divisions.

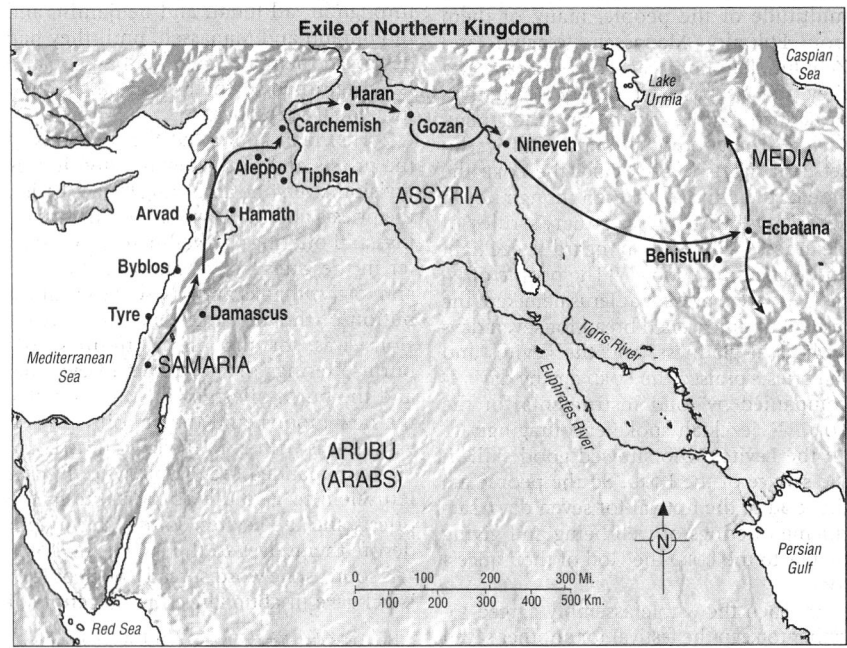

Exile of Northern Kingdom

[17] The enrolment of the priests was according to their ancestral houses; that of the Levites from twenty years old and upwards was according to their offices, by their divisions. [18] The priests were enrolled with all their little children, their wives, their sons, and their daughters, the whole multitude; for they were faithful in keeping themselves holy. [19] And for the descendants of Aaron, the priests, who were in the fields of common land belonging to their towns, town by town, the people designated by name were to distribute portions to every male among the priests and to everyone among the Levites who was enrolled.

[20] Hezekiah did this throughout all Judah; he did what was good and right and faithful before the LORD his God. [21] And every work that he undertook in the service of the house of God, and in accordance with the law and the commandments, to seek his God, he did with all his heart; and he prospered.

Sennacherib's Invasion

32 After these things and these acts of faithfulness, King Sennacherib of Assyria came and invaded Judah and encamped against the fortified cities, thinking to win them for himself. [2] When Hezekiah saw that Sennacherib had come and intended to fight against Jerusalem, [3] he planned with his officers and his warriors to stop the flow of the springs that were outside the city; and they helped him. [4] A great many people were gathered, and they stopped all the springs and the wadi that flowed through the land, saying, 'Why should the Assyrian kings come and find water in abundance?' [5] Hezekiah[a] set to work resolutely and built up the entire wall that was broken down, and raised towers on it,[b] and outside it he built another wall; he also strengthened the Millo in the city of David, and made weapons and shields in abundance. [6] He appointed combat commanders over the people, and gathered them together to him in the square at the gate of the city and spoke encouragingly to them, saying, [7] 'Be strong and of good courage. Do not be afraid or dismayed before the king of Assyria and all the horde that is with him; for there is one greater with us than with him. [8] With him is an arm of flesh; but with us is the LORD our God, to help us and to fight our battles.' The people were encouraged by the words of King Hezekiah of Judah.

[9] After this, while King Sennacherib of Assyria was at Lachish with all his forces, he sent his servants to Jerusalem to King Hezekiah of Judah and to all the people of Judah that were in Jerusalem, saying, [10] 'Thus says King Sennacherib of Assyria: On what are you relying, that you undergo the siege of Jerusalem? [11] Is not Hezekiah misleading you, handing you over to die by famine and by thirst, when he tells you, "The LORD our God will save us from the hand of the king of Assyria"? [12] Was it not this same Hezekiah who took away his high places and his altars and commanded Judah and Jerusalem, saying, "Before one altar you shall worship, and upon it you shall make your offerings"? [13] Do you not know what I and my ancestors have done to all the peoples of other lands? Were the gods of the nations of those lands at all able to save their lands out of my hand? [14] Who among all the gods of those nations that my ancestors utterly destroyed was able to save his people from my hand, that your God should be able to save you from my hand? [15] Now therefore do not let Hezekiah deceive you or mislead you in this fashion, and do not believe him, for no god of any nation or kingdom has been able to save his people from my hand or from the hand of my ancestors. How much less will your God save you out of my hand!'

[16] His servants said still more against the Lord GOD and against his servant Hezekiah. [17] He also wrote letters to throw contempt on the LORD the God of Israel and to speak against him, saying, 'Just as the gods of the nations in other lands did not rescue their people from my hands, so the God of Hezekiah will not rescue his people from my hand.' [18] They shouted it with a loud voice in the language of Judah to

---

a Heb *He*   *b* Vg: Heb *and raised on the towers*

the people of Jerusalem who were on the wall, to frighten and terrify them, in order that they might take the city. 19 They spoke of the God of Jerusalem as if he were like the gods of the peoples of the earth, which are the work of human hands.

Sennacherib's Defeat and Death

20 Then King Hezekiah and the prophet Isaiah son of Amoz prayed because of this and cried to heaven. 21 And the LORD sent an angel who cut off all the mighty warriors and commanders and officers in the camp of the king of Assyria. So he returned in disgrace to his own land. When he came into the house of his god, some of his own sons struck him down there with the sword. 22 So the LORD saved Hezekiah and the inhabitants of Jerusalem from the hand of King Sennacherib of Assyria and from the hand of all his enemies; he gave them rest *a* on every side. 23 Many brought gifts to the LORD in Jerusalem and precious things to King Hezekiah of Judah, so that he was exalted in the sight of all nations from that time onwards.

Hezekiah's Sickness

24 In those days Hezekiah became sick and was at the point of death. He prayed to the LORD, and he answered him and gave him a sign. 25 But Hezekiah did not respond according to the benefit done to him, for his heart was proud. Therefore wrath came upon him and upon Judah and Jerusalem. 26 Then Hezekiah humbled himself for the pride of his heart, both he and the inhabitants of Jerusalem, so that the wrath of the LORD did not come upon them in the days of Hezekiah.

Hezekiah's Prosperity and Achievements

27 Hezekiah had very great riches and honour; and he made for himself treasuries for silver, for gold, for precious stones, for spices, for shields, and for all kinds of costly objects; 28 storehouses also for the yield of grain, wine, and oil; and stalls for all kinds of cattle, and sheepfolds. *b* 29 He likewise provided cities for himself, and flocks and herds in abundance; for God

had given him very great possessions. 30 This same Hezekiah closed the upper outlet of the waters of Gihon and directed them down to the west side of the city of David. Hezekiah prospered in all his works. 31 So also in the matter of the envoys of the officials of Babylon, who had been sent to him to inquire about the sign that had been done in the land, God left him to himself, in order to test him and to know all that was in his heart.

32 Now the rest of the acts of Hezekiah, and his good deeds, are written in the vision of the prophet Isaiah son of Amoz in the Book of the Kings of Judah and Israel. 33 Hezekiah slept with his ancestors, and they buried him on the ascent to the tombs of the descendants of David; and all Judah and the inhabitants of Jerusalem did him honour at his death. His son Manasseh succeeded him.

Reign of Manasseh

33 Manasseh was twelve years old when he began to reign; he reigned for fifty-five years in Jerusalem. 2 He did what was evil in the sight of the LORD, according to the abominable practices of the nations whom the LORD drove out before the people of Israel. 3 For he rebuilt the high places that his father Hezekiah had pulled down, and erected altars to the Baals, made sacred poles, *c* worshipped all the host of heaven, and served them. 4 He built altars in the house of the LORD, of which the LORD had said, 'In Jerusalem shall my name be for ever.' 5 He built altars for all the host of heaven in the two courts of the house of the LORD. 6 He made his son pass through fire in the valley of the son of Hinnom, practised soothsaying and augury and sorcery, and dealt with mediums and with wizards. He did much evil in the sight of the LORD, provoking him to anger. 7 The carved image of the idol that he had made he set in the house of God, of which God said to David and to his son Solomon, 'In this house, and in Jerusalem, which I have chosen out of all the tribes of

a Gk Vg: Heb *guided them*   *b* Gk Vg: Heb *flocks for folds*   *c* Heb *Asheroth*

Israel, I will put my name for ever; ⁸I will never again remove the feet of Israel from the land that I appointed for your ancestors, if only they will be careful to do all that I have commanded them, all the law, the statutes, and the ordinances given through Moses.' ⁹Manasseh misled Judah and the inhabitants of Jerusalem, so that they did more evil than the nations whom the LORD had destroyed before the people of Israel.

Manasseh Restored after Repentance

10 The LORD spoke to Manasseh and to his people, but they gave no heed. ¹¹Therefore the LORD brought against them the commanders of the army of the king of Assyria, who took Manasseh captive in manacles, bound him with fetters, and brought him to Babylon. ¹²While he was in distress he entreated the favour of the LORD his God and humbled himself greatly before the God of his ancestors. ¹³He prayed to him, and God received his entreaty, heard his plea, and restored him again to Jerusalem and to his kingdom. Then Manasseh knew that the LORD indeed was God.

14 Afterwards he built an outer wall for the city of David west of Gihon, in the valley, reaching the entrance at the Fish Gate; he carried it around Ophel, and raised it to a very great height. He also put commanders of the army in all the fortified cities in Judah. ¹⁵He took away the foreign gods and the idol from the house of the LORD, and all the altars that he had built on the mountain of the house of the LORD and in Jerusalem, and he threw them out of the city. ¹⁶He also restored the altar of the LORD and offered on it sacrifices of well-being and of thanksgiving; and he commanded Judah to serve the LORD the God of Israel. ¹⁷The people, however, still sacrificed at the high places, but only to the LORD their God.

Death of Manasseh

18 Now the rest of the acts of Manasseh, his prayer to his God, and the words of the seers who spoke to him in the name of the LORD God of Israel, these are in the Annals

of the Kings of Israel. ¹⁹His prayer, and how God received his entreaty, all his sin and his faithlessness, the sites on which he built high places and set up the sacred poles[a] and the images, before he humbled himself, these are written in the records of the seers.[b] ²⁰So Manasseh slept with his ancestors, and they buried him in his house. His son Amon succeeded him.

Amon's Reign and Death

21 Amon was twenty-two years old when he began to reign; he reigned for two years in Jerusalem. ²²He did what was evil in the sight of the LORD, as his father Manasseh had done. Amon sacrificed to all the images that his father Manasseh had made, and served them. ²³He did not humble himself before the LORD, as his father Manasseh had humbled himself, but this Amon incurred more and more guilt. ²⁴His servants conspired against him and killed him in his house. ²⁵But the people of the land killed all those who had conspired against King Amon; and the people of the land made his son Josiah king to succeed him.

Reign of Josiah

34 Josiah was eight years old when he began to reign; he reigned for thirty-one years in Jerusalem. ²He did what was right in the sight of the LORD, and walked in the ways of his ancestor David; he did not turn aside to the right or to the left. ³For in the eighth year of his reign, while he was still a boy, he began to seek the God of his ancestor David, and in the twelfth year he began to purge Judah and Jerusalem of the high places, the sacred poles,[a] and the carved and the cast images. ⁴In his presence they pulled down the altars of the Baals; he demolished the incense altars that stood above them. He broke down the sacred poles[a] and the carved and the cast images; he made dust of them and scattered it over the graves of those who had sacrificed to them. ⁵He also burned the bones of the priests on their altars, and purged Judah and Jerusalem. ⁶In

a Heb *Asherim*   *b* One Ms Gk: MT *of Hozai*

the towns of Manasseh, Ephraim, and Simeon, and as far as Naphtali, in their ruins*a* all around, 7 he broke down the altars, beat the sacred poles*b* and the images into powder, and demolished all the incense altars throughout all the land of Israel. Then he returned to Jerusalem.

Discovery of the Book of the Law

8 In the eighteenth year of his reign, when he had purged the land and the house, he sent Shaphan son of Azaliah, Maaseiah the governor of the city, and Joah son of Joahaz, the recorder, to repair the house of the LORD his God. 9 They came to the high priest Hilkiah and delivered the money that had been brought into the house of God, which the Levites, the keepers of the threshold, had collected from Manasseh and Ephraim and from all the remnant of Israel and from all Judah and Benjamin and from the inhabitants of Jerusalem. 10 They delivered it to the workers who had the oversight of the house of the LORD, and the workers who were working in the house of the LORD gave it for repairing and restoring the house. 11 They gave it to the carpenters and the builders to buy quarried stone, and timber for tie-beams and joists for the buildings that the kings of Judah had let go to ruin. 12 The people did the work faithfully. Over them were appointed the Levites Jahath and Obadiah, of the sons of Merari, along with Zechariah and Meshullam, of the sons of the Kohathites, to have oversight. Other Levites, all skilful with instruments of music, 13 were over the burden-bearers and directed all who did work in every kind of service; and some of the Levites were scribes, and officials, and gatekeepers.

14 While they were bringing out the money that had been brought into the house of the LORD, the priest Hilkiah found the book of the law of the LORD given through Moses. 15 Hilkiah said to the secretary Shaphan, 'I have found the book of the law in the house of the LORD'; and Hilkiah gave the book to Shaphan. 16 Shaphan brought the book to the king, and further reported to the king, 'All that was

committed to your servants they are doing. 17 They have emptied out the money that was found in the house of the LORD and have delivered it into the hand of the overseers and the workers.' 18 The secretary Shaphan informed the king, 'The priest Hilkiah has given me a book.' Shaphan then read it aloud to the king.

19 When the king heard the words of the law he tore his clothes. 20 Then the king commanded Hilkiah, Ahikam son of Shaphan, Abdon son of Micah, the secretary Shaphan, and the king's servant Asaiah: 21 'Go, inquire of the LORD for me and for those who are left in Israel and in Judah, concerning the words of the book that has been found; for the wrath of the LORD that is poured out on us is great, because our ancestors did not keep the word of the LORD, to act in accordance with all that is written in this book.'

The Prophet Huldah Consulted

22 So Hilkiah and those whom the king had sent went to the prophet Huldah, the wife of Shallum son of Tokhath son of Hasrah, keeper of the wardrobe (who lived in Jerusalem in the Second Quarter) and spoke to her to that effect. 23 She declared to them, 'Thus says the LORD, the God of Israel: Tell the man who sent you to me, 24 Thus says the LORD: I will indeed bring disaster upon this place and upon its inhabitants, all the curses that are written in the book that was read before the king of Judah. 25 Because they have forsaken me and have made offerings to other gods, so that they have provoked me to anger with all the works of their hands, my wrath will be poured out on this place and will not be quenched. 26 But as to the king of Judah, who sent you to inquire of the LORD, thus shall you say to him: Thus says the LORD, the God of Israel: Regarding the words that you have heard, 27 because your heart was penitent and you humbled yourself before God when you heard his words against this place and its inhabitants, and you have humbled yourself before me, and have torn your clothes and wept before me, I

a Meaning of Heb uncertain   *b* Heb *Asherim*

also have heard you, says the LORD. ²⁸ I will gather you to your ancestors and you shall be gathered to your grave in peace; your eyes shall not see all the disaster that I will bring on this place and its inhabitants.' They took the message back to the king.

The Covenant Renewed

29 Then the king sent word and gathered together all the elders of Judah and Jerusalem. ³⁰ The king went up to the house of the LORD, with all the people of Judah, the inhabitants of Jerusalem, the priests and the Levites, all the people both great and small; he read in their hearing all the words of the book of the covenant that had been found in the house of the LORD. ³¹ The king stood in his place and made a covenant before the LORD, to follow the LORD, keeping his commandments, his decrees, and his statutes, with all his heart and all his soul, to perform the words of the covenant that were written in this book. ³² Then he made all who were present in Jerusalem and in Benjamin pledge themselves to it. And the inhabitants of Jerusalem acted according to the covenant of God, the God of their ancestors. ³³ Josiah took away all the abominations from all the territory that belonged to the people of Israel, and made all who were in Israel worship the LORD their God. All his days they did not turn away from following the LORD the God of their ancestors.

Celebration of the Passover

35 Josiah kept a passover to the LORD in Jerusalem; they slaughtered the passover lamb on the fourteenth day of the first month. ² He appointed the priests to their offices and encouraged them in the service of the house of the LORD. ³ He said to the Levites who taught all Israel and who were holy to the LORD, 'Put the holy ark in the house that Solomon son of David, king of Israel, built; you need no longer carry it on your shoulders. Now serve the LORD your God and his people Israel. ⁴ Make preparations by your ancestral houses by your divisions, following the written directions of King David of Israel

and the written directions of his son Solomon. ⁵ Take position in the holy place according to the groupings of the ancestral houses of your kindred the people, and let there be Levites for each division of an ancestral house.ᵃ ⁶ Slaughter the passover lamb, sanctify yourselves, and on behalf of your kindred make preparations, acting according to the word of the LORD by Moses.'

7 Then Josiah contributed to the people, as passover offerings for all that were present, lambs and kids from the flock to the number of thirty thousand, and three thousand bulls; these were from the king's possessions. ⁸ His officials contributed willingly to the people, to the priests, and to the Levites. Hilkiah, Zechariah, and Jehiel, the chief officers of the house of God, gave to the priests for the passover offerings two thousand six hundred lambs and kids and three hundred bulls. ⁹ Conaniah also, and his brothers Shemaiah and Nethanel, and Hashabiah and Jeiel and Jozabad, the chiefs of the Levites, gave to the Levites for the passover offerings five thousand lambs and kids and five hundred bulls.

10 When the service had been prepared for, the priests stood in their place, and the Levites in their divisions according to the king's command. ¹¹ They slaughtered the passover lamb, and the priests dashed the blood that they receivedᵇ from them, while the Levites did the skinning. ¹² They set aside the burnt-offerings so that they might distribute them according to the groupings of the ancestral houses of the people, to offer to the LORD, as it is written in the book of Moses. And they did the same with the bulls. ¹³ They roasted the passover lamb with fire according to the ordinance; and they boiled the holy offerings in pots, in cauldrons, and in pans, and carried them quickly to all the people. ¹⁴ Afterwards they made preparations for themselves and for the priests, because the priests the descendants of Aaron were occupied in offering the burnt-offerings and the fat parts until night; so the Levites

---

a Meaning of Heb uncertain   *b* Heb lacks *that they received* made preparations for themselves and for the priests, the descendants of Aaron. 15The singers, the descendants of Asaph, were in their place according to the command of David, and Asaph, and Heman, and the king's seer Jeduthun. The gatekeepers were at each gate; they did not need to interrupt their service, for their kindred the Levites made preparations for them.

16 So all the service of the LORD was prepared that day, to keep the passover and to offer burnt-offerings on the altar of the LORD, according to the command of King Josiah. 17The people of Israel who were present kept the passover at that time, and the festival of unleavened bread for seven days. 18No passover like it had been kept in Israel since the days of the prophet Samuel; none of the kings of Israel had kept such a passover as was kept by Josiah, by the priests and the Levites, by all Judah and Israel who were present, and by the inhabitants of Jerusalem. 19In the eighteenth year of the reign of Josiah this passover was kept.

Defeat by Pharaoh Neco and Death of Josiah

20 After all this, when Josiah had set the temple in order, King Neco of Egypt went up to fight at Carchemish on the Euphrates, and Josiah went out against him. 21But Neco*a* sent envoys to him, saying, 'What have I to do with you, king of Judah? I am not coming against you today, but against the house with which I am at war; and God has commanded me to hurry. Cease opposing God, who is with me, so that he will not destroy you.' 22But Josiah would not turn away from him, but disguised himself in order to fight with him. He did not listen to the words of Neco from the mouth of God, but joined battle in the plain of Megiddo. 23The archers shot King Josiah; and the king said to his servants, 'Take me away, for I am badly wounded.' 24So his servants took him out of the chariot and carried him in his second chariot*b* and brought him to Jerusalem. There he died, and was buried in the tombs of his

ancestors. All Judah and Jerusalem mourned for Josiah. 25Jeremiah also uttered a lament for Josiah, and all the singing-men and singing-women have spoken of Josiah in their laments to this day. They made these a custom in Israel; they are recorded in the Laments. 26Now the rest of the acts of Josiah and his faithful deeds in accordance with what is written in the law of the LORD, 27and his acts, first and last, are written in the Book of the Kings of Israel and Judah.

Reign of Jehoahaz

36 The people of the land took Jehoahaz son of Josiah and made him king to succeed his father in Jerusalem. 2Jehoahaz was twenty-three years old when he began to reign; he reigned for three months in Jerusalem. 3Then the king of Egypt deposed him in Jerusalem and laid on the land a tribute of one hundred talents of silver and one talent of gold. 4The king of Egypt made his brother Eliakim king over Judah and Jerusalem, and changed his name to Jehoiakim; but Neco took his brother Jehoahaz and carried him to Egypt.

Reign and Captivity of Jehoiakim

5 Jehoiakim was twenty-five years old when he began to reign; he reigned for eleven years in Jerusalem. He did what was evil in the sight of the LORD his God. 6Against him King Nebuchadnezzar of Babylon came up, and bound him with fetters to take him to Babylon. 7Nebuchadnezzar also carried some of the vessels of the house of the LORD to Babylon and put them in his palace in Babylon. 8Now the rest of the acts of Jehoiakim, and the abominations that he did, and what was found against him, are written in the Book of the Kings of Israel and Judah; and his son Jehoiachin succeeded him.

Reign and Captivity of Jehoiachin

9 Jehoiachin was eight years old when he began to reign; he reigned for three months and ten days in Jerusalem. He did

a Heb he   *b* Or the chariot of his deputy

what was evil in the sight of the LORD. ¹⁰In the spring of the year King Nebuchadnezzar sent and brought him to Babylon, along with the precious vessels of the house of the LORD, and made his brother Zedekiah king over Judah and Jerusalem.

Reign of Zedekiah

11 Zedekiah was twenty-one years old when he began to reign; he reigned for eleven years in Jerusalem. ¹²He did what was evil in the sight of the LORD his God. He did not humble himself before the prophet Jeremiah who spoke from the mouth of the LORD. ¹³He also rebelled against King Nebuchadnezzar, who had made him swear by God; he stiffened his neck and hardened his heart against turning to the LORD, the God of Israel. ¹⁴All the leading priests and the people also were exceedingly unfaithful, following all the abominations of the nations; and they polluted the house of the LORD that he had consecrated in Jerusalem.

The Fall of Jerusalem

15 The LORD, the God of their ancestors, sent persistently to them by his messengers, because he had compassion on his people and on his dwelling-place; ¹⁶but they kept mocking the messengers of God, despising his words, and scoffing at his prophets, until the wrath of the LORD against his people became so great that there was no remedy.

17 Therefore he brought up against them the king of the Chaldeans, who killed their youths with the sword in the house of their sanctuary, and had no compassion on young man or young woman, the aged or the feeble; he gave them all into his hand. ¹⁸All the vessels of the house of God, large and small, and the treasures of the house of the LORD, and the treasures of the king and of his officials, all these he brought to Babylon. ¹⁹They burned the house of God, broke down the wall of Jerusalem, burned all its palaces with fire, and destroyed all its precious vessels. ²⁰He took into exile in Babylon those who had escaped from the

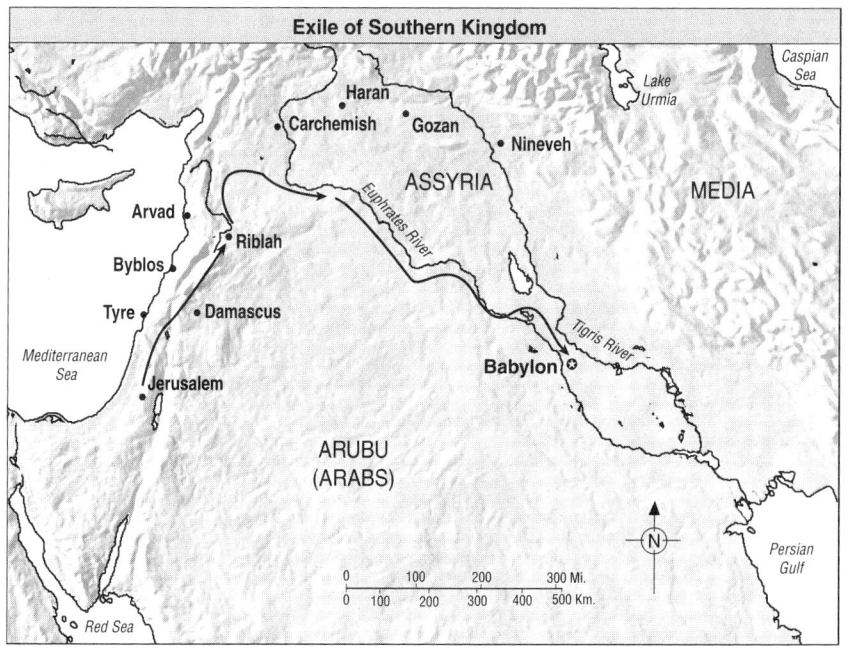

Exile of Southern Kingdom

sword, and they became servants to him and to his sons until the establishment of the kingdom of Persia, 21 to fulfil the word of the LORD by the mouth of Jeremiah, until the land had made up for its sabbaths. All the days that it lay desolate it kept sabbath, to fulfil seventy years.

Cyrus Proclaims Liberty for the Exiles

22 In the first year of King Cyrus of Persia, in fulfilment of the word of the LORD spoken by Jeremiah, the LORD stirred up the spirit of King Cyrus of Persia so that he sent a herald throughout all his kingdom and also declared in a written edict: 23 'Thus says King Cyrus of Persia: The LORD, the God of heaven, has given me all the kingdoms of the earth, and he has charged me to build him a house at Jerusalem, which is in Judah. Whoever is among you of all his people, may the LORD his God be with him! Let him go up.'

EZRA

End of the Babylonian Captivity

1 In the first year of King Cyrus of Persia, in order that the word of the Lord by the mouth of Jeremiah might be accomplished, the Lord stirred up the spirit of King Cyrus of Persia so that he sent a herald throughout all his kingdom, and also in a written edict declared:

2 'Thus says King Cyrus of Persia: The Lord, the God of heaven, has given me all the kingdoms of the earth, and he has charged me to build him a house at Jerusalem in Judah. 3 Any of those among you who are of his people—may their God be with them!—are now permitted to go up to Jerusalem in Judah, and rebuild the house of the Lord, the God of Israel—he is the God who is in Jerusalem; 4 and let all survivors, in whatever place they reside, be assisted by the people of their place with silver and gold, with goods and with animals, besides freewill-offerings for the house of God in Jerusalem.'

5 The heads of the families of Judah and Benjamin, and the priests and the Levites—everyone whose spirit God had stirred—got ready to go up and rebuild the house of the Lord in Jerusalem. 6 All their neighbours aided them with silver vessels, with gold, with goods, with animals, and with valuable gifts, besides all that was freely offered. 7 King Cyrus himself brought out the vessels of the house of the Lord that Nebuchadnezzar had carried away from Jerusalem and placed in the house of his gods. 8 King Cyrus of Persia had them released into the charge of Mithredath the treasurer, who counted them out to Sheshbazzar the prince of Judah. 9 And this was the inventory: gold basins, thirty; silver basins, one thousand; knives, *a* twenty-nine; 10 gold bowls, thirty; other silver bowls, four hundred and ten; other vessels, one thousand; 11 the total of the gold and silver vessels was five thousand four hundred. All these Sheshbazzar brought up, when the exiles were brought up from Babylonia to Jerusalem.

List of the Returned Exiles

2 Now these were the people of the province who came from those captive exiles whom King Nebuchadnezzar of Babylon had carried captive to Babylonia; they returned to Jerusalem and Judah, all to their own towns. 2 They came with Zerubbabel, Jeshua, Nehemiah, Seraiah, Reelaiah, Mordecai, Bilshan, Mispar, Bigvai, Rehum, and Baanah.

The number of the Israelite people: 3 the descendants of Parosh, two thousand one hundred and seventy-two. 4 Of Shephatiah, three hundred and seventy-two. 5 Of Arah, seven hundred and seventy-five. 6 Of Pahath-moab, namely the descendants of Jeshua and Joab, two thousand eight hundred and twelve. 7 Of Elam, one thousand two hundred and fifty-four. 8 Of Zattu, nine hundred and forty-five. 9 Of Zaccai, seven hundred and sixty. 10 Of Bani, six hundred and forty-two. 11 Of Bebai, six hundred and twenty-three. 12 Of Azgad, one thousand two hundred and twenty-two. 13 Of Adonikam, six hundred and sixty-six. 14 Of Bigvai, two thousand and fifty-six. 15 Of Adin, four hundred and fifty-four. 16 Of Ater, namely of Hezekiah, ninety-eight. 17 Of Bezai, three hundred

a Vg: Meaning of Heb uncertain

and twenty-three. ¹⁸Of Jorah, one hundred and twelve. ¹⁹Of Hashum, two hundred and twenty-three. ²⁰Of Gibbar, ninety-five. ²¹Of Bethlehem, one hundred and twenty-three. ²²The people of Netophah, fifty-six. ²³Of Anathoth, one hundred and twenty-eight. ²⁴The descendants of Azmaveth, forty-two. ²⁵Of Kiriatharim, Chephirah, and Beeroth, seven hundred and forty-three. ²⁶Of Ramah and Geba, six hundred and twenty-one. ²⁷The people of Michmas, one hundred and twenty-two. ²⁸Of Bethel and Ai, two hundred and twenty-three. ²⁹The descendants of Nebo, fifty-two. ³⁰Of Magbish, one hundred and fifty-six. ³¹Of the other Elam, one thousand two hundred and fifty-four. ³²Of Harim, three hundred and twenty. ³³Of Lod, Hadid, and Ono, seven hundred and twenty-five. ³⁴Of Jericho, three hundred and forty-five. ³⁵Of Senaah, three thousand six hundred and thirty.

36 The priests: the descendants of Jedaiah, of the house of Jeshua, nine hundred and seventy-three. ³⁷Of Immer, one thousand and fifty-two. ³⁸Of Pashhur, one thousand two hundred and forty-seven. ³⁹Of Harim, one thousand and seventeen.

40 The Levites: the descendants of Jeshua and Kadmiel, of the descendants of Hodaviah, seventy-four. ⁴¹The singers: the descendants of Asaph, one hundred and twenty-eight. ⁴²The descendants of the gatekeepers: of Shallum, of Ater, of Talmon, of Akkub, of Hatita, and of Shobai, in all one hundred and thirty-nine.

43 The temple servants: the descendants of Ziha, Hasupha, Tabbaoth, ⁴⁴Keros, Siaha, Padon, ⁴⁵Lebanah, Hagabah, Akkub, ⁴⁶Hagab, Shamlai, Hanan, ⁴⁷Giddel, Gahar, Reaiah, ⁴⁸Rezin, Nekoda, Gazzam, ⁴⁹Uzza, Paseah, Besai, ⁵⁰Asnah, Meunim, Nephisim, ⁵¹Bakbuk, Hakupha, Harhur, ⁵²Bazluth, Mehida, Harsha, ⁵³Barkos, Sisera, Temah, ⁵⁴Neziah, and Hatipha.

55 The descendants of Solomon's servants: Sotai, Hassophereth, Peruda, ⁵⁶Jaalah, Darkon, Giddel, ⁵⁷Shephatiah, Hattil, Pochereth-hazzebaim, and Ami.

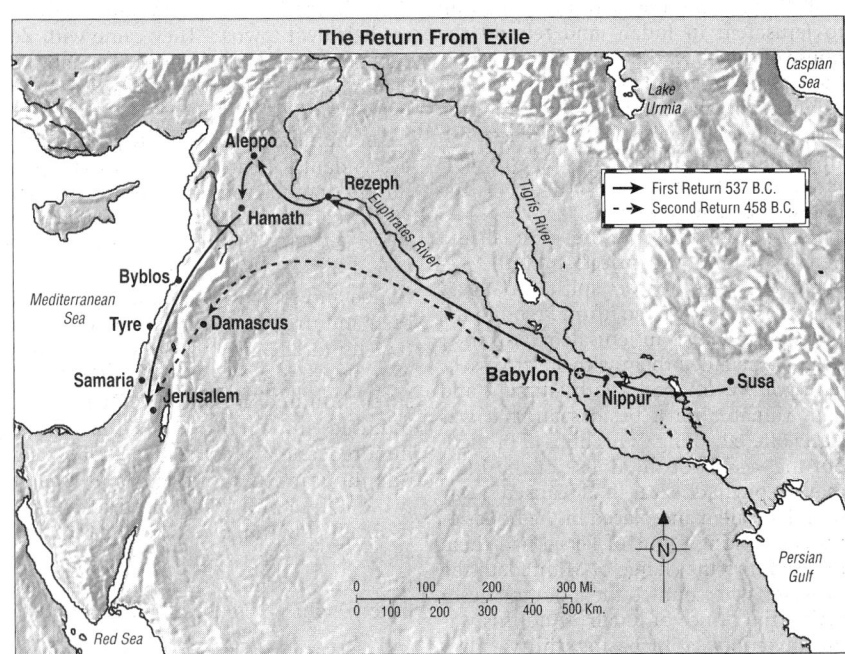

The Return From Exile

58 All the temple servants and the descendants of Solomon's servants were three hundred and ninety-two.

59 The following were those who came up from Tel-melah, Tel-harsha, Cherub, Addan, and Immer, though they could not prove their families or their descent, whether they belonged to Israel: 60 the descendants of Delaiah, Tobiah, and Nekoda, six hundred and fifty-two. 61 Also, of the descendants of the priests: the descendants of Habaiah, Hakkoz, and Barzillai (who had married one of the daughters of Barzillai the Gileadite, and was called by their name). 62 These looked for their entries in the genealogical records, but they were not found there, and so they were excluded from the priesthood as unclean; 63 the governor told them that they were not to partake of the most holy food, until there should be a priest to consult Urim and Thummim.

64 The whole assembly together was forty-two thousand three hundred and sixty, 65 besides their male and female servants, of whom there were seven thousand three hundred and thirty-seven; and they had two hundred male and female singers. 66 They had seven hundred and thirty-six horses, two hundred and forty-five mules, 67 four hundred and thirty-five camels, and six thousand seven hundred and twenty donkeys.

68 As soon as they came to the house of the LORD in Jerusalem, some of the heads of families made freewill-offerings for the house of God, to erect it on its site. 69 According to their resources they gave to the building fund sixty-one thousand darics of gold, five thousand minas of silver, and one hundred priestly robes.

70 The priests, the Levites, and some of the people lived in Jerusalem and its vicinity;[a] and the singers, the gatekeepers, and the temple servants lived in their towns, and all Israel in their towns.

Worship Restored at Jerusalem

3 When the seventh month came, and the Israelites were in the towns, the people gathered together in Jerusalem.

2 Then Jeshua son of Jozadak, with his fellow priests, and Zerubbabel son of Shealtiel with his kin set out to build the altar of the God of Israel, to offer burnt-offerings on it, as prescribed in the law of Moses the man of God. 3 They set up the altar on its foundation, because they were in dread of the neighbouring peoples, and they offered burnt-offerings upon it to the LORD, morning and evening. 4 And they kept the festival of booths,[b] as prescribed, and offered the daily burnt-offerings by number according to the ordinance, as required for each day, 5 and after that the regular burnt-offerings, the offerings at the new moon and at all the sacred festivals of the LORD, and the offerings of everyone who made a freewill-offering to the LORD. 6 From the first day of the seventh month they began to offer burnt-offerings to the LORD. But the foundation of the temple of the LORD was not yet laid. 7 So they gave money to the masons and the carpenters, and food, drink, and oil to the Sidonians and the Tyrians to bring cedar trees from Lebanon to the sea, to Joppa, according to the grant that they had from King Cyrus of Persia.

Foundations Laid for the Temple

8 In the second year after their arrival at the house of God at Jerusalem, in the second month, Zerubbabel son of Shealtiel and Jeshua son of Jozadak made a beginning, together with the rest of their people, the priests and the Levites and all who had come to Jerusalem from the captivity. They appointed the Levites, from twenty years old and upwards, to have the oversight of the work on the house of the LORD. 9 And Jeshua with his sons and his kin, and Kadmiel and his sons, Binnui and Hodaviah[c] along with the sons of Henadad, the Levites, their sons and kin, together took charge of the workers in the house of God.

10 When the builders laid the foundation of the temple of the LORD, the priests in their vestments were stationed to praise

a 1 Esdras 5.46: Heb lacks *lived in Jerusalem and its vicinity*   b Or *tabernacles*; Heb *succoth*
c Compare 2.40; Neh 7.43; 1 Esdras 5.58: Heb *sons of Judah*

Chronology of the Postexilic Era

O.T. Sources	Events in Jerusalem	Persian Rulers

586 B.C. to 500 B.C.

O.T. Sources	Events in Jerusalem	Persian Rulers
	586: Fall of Jerusalem to Babylon; second and final deportation; diaspora Jews in Babylon.	550–530: Cyrus II (the Great) 539: Fall of the Babylonian Empire to Cyrus the Great
Ezra 1–6	538: First wave of the return to Jerusalem begins (groups continue to drift back over the next century). Zerubbabel begins rebuilding the temple in Jerusalem. Samaritans thwart their efforts; rebuilding project halts.	538: Cyrus the Great issues Edict of Toleration, allowing Jews to return home 530–522: Cambyses II 522–486: Darius I
Haggai and Zechariah 1–8	520: The prophets Haggai and Zechariah call for the rebuilding of the temple to continue; works begins.	
	515: In March, the second temple is finished.	

500 B.C. to 400 B.C.

O.T. Sources	Events in Jerusalem	Persian Rulers
Esther Nehemiah's Memiors: Neh 1–7 and 11–13 Malachi	444–432: Nehemiah hears of the plight of Jerusalem while in Persia. He is appointed governor of Judah; the walls around Jerusalem are rebuilt	486–465: Xerxes I ("Ahasuerus" in Esther) 465–423: Artaxerxes I 423: Xerxes II 423–404: Darius II 404–358: Artaxerxes II

400 B.C. to 331 B.C.

O.T. Sources	Events in Jerusalem	Persian Rulers
The "I" narrative— Ezra 7.11–9.15 The "he" narrative— Ezra 10 and Neh 8–19 The king's letter— Ezra 7.12–26 The lists— Ezra 8.1–14; 10.18–44; Neh 10.1–27	398 (?): Ezra, priest and scribe, institutes reforms of worhip. End of O.T. history, c. 400.	331: Alexander the Great conquers the Persian Empire (defeating Darius III); Age of Socrates, Plato, Aristotle; rise of Hellenism

the LORD with trumpets, and the Levites, the sons of Asaph, with cymbals, according to the directions of King David of Israel; 11 and they sang responsively, praising and giving thanks to the LORD,

'For he is good,
   for his steadfast love endures for ever
      towards Israel.'

And all the people responded with a great shout when they praised the LORD, because the foundation of the house of the LORD was laid. 12 But many of the priests and Levites and heads of families, old people who had seen the first house on its foundations, wept with a loud voice when they saw this house, though many shouted aloud for joy, 13 so that the people could not distinguish the sound of the joyful shout from the sound of the people's weeping, for the people shouted so loudly that the sound was heard far away.

Resistance to Rebuilding the Temple

4 When the adversaries of Judah and Benjamin heard that the returned exiles were building a temple to the LORD, the God of Israel, 2 they approached Zerubbabel and the heads of families and said to them, 'Let us build with you, for we worship your God as you do, and we have been sacrificing to him ever since the days of King Esar-haddon of Assyria who brought us here.' 3 But Zerubbabel, Jeshua, and the rest of the heads of families in Israel said to them, 'You shall have no part with us in building a house to our God; but we alone will build to the LORD, the God of Israel, as King Cyrus of Persia has commanded us.'

4 Then the people of the land discouraged the people of Judah, and made them afraid to build, 5 and they bribed officials to frustrate their plan throughout the reign of King Cyrus of Persia and until the reign of King Darius of Persia.

Rebuilding of Jerusalem Opposed

6 In the reign of Ahasuerus, in his accession year, they wrote an accusation against the inhabitants of Judah and Jerusalem.

7 And in the days of Artaxerxes, Bishlam and Mithredath and Tabeel and the rest of their associates wrote to King Artaxerxes of Persia; the letter was written in Aramaic and translated.*a* 8 Rehum the royal deputy and Shimshai the scribe wrote a letter against Jerusalem to King Artaxerxes as follows 9 (then Rehum the royal deputy, Shimshai the scribe, and the rest of their associates, the judges, the envoys, the officials, the Persians, the people of Erech, the Babylonians, the people of Susa, that is, the Elamites, 10 and the rest of the nations whom the great and noble Osnappar deported and settled in the cities of Samaria and in the rest of the province Beyond the River wrote—and now 11 this is a copy of the letter that they sent):

'To King Artaxerxes: Your servants, the people of the province Beyond the River, send greeting. And now 12 may it be known to the king that the Jews who came up from you to us have gone to Jerusalem. They are rebuilding that rebellious and wicked city; they are finishing the walls and repairing the foundations. 13 Now may it be known to the king that, if this city is rebuilt and the walls finished, they will not pay tribute, custom, or toll, and the royal revenue will be reduced. 14 Now because we share the salt of the palace and it is not fitting for us to witness the king's dishonour, therefore we send and inform the king, 15 so that a search may be made in the annals of your ancestors. You will discover in the annals that this is a rebellious city, hurtful to kings and provinces, and that sedition was stirred up in it from long ago. On that account this city was laid waste. 16 We make known to the king that, if this city is rebuilt and its walls finished, you will then have no possession in the province Beyond the River.'

17 The king sent an answer: 'To Rehum the royal deputy and Shimshai the scribe and the rest of their associates who live in Samaria and in the rest of the province Beyond the River, greeting. And now 18 the

---

a Heb adds *in Aramaic,* indicating that 4.8-6.18 is in Aramaic. Another interpretation is *The letter was written in the Aramaic script and set forth in the Aramaic language* letter that you sent to us has been read in translation before me. 19 So I made a decree, and someone searched and discovered that this city has risen against kings from long ago, and that rebellion and sedition have been made in it. 20 Jerusalem has had mighty kings who ruled over the whole province Beyond the River, to whom tribute, custom, and toll were paid. 21 Therefore issue an order that these people be made to cease, and that this city be not rebuilt, until I make a decree. 22 Moreover, take care not to be slack in this matter; why should damage grow to the hurt of the king?'

23 Then when the copy of King Artaxerxes' letter was read before Rehum and the scribe Shimshai and their associates, they hurried to the Jews in Jerusalem and by force and power made them cease. 24 At that time the work on the house of God in Jerusalem stopped and was discontinued until the second year of the reign of King Darius of Persia.

Restoration of the Temple Resumed

5 Now the prophets, Haggai*a* and Zechariah son of Iddo, prophesied to the Jews who were in Judah and Jerusalem, in the name of the God of Israel who was over them. 2 Then Zerubbabel son of Shealtiel and Jeshua son of Jozadak set out to rebuild the house of God in Jerusalem; and with them were the prophets of God, helping them.

3 At the same time Tattenai the governor of the province Beyond the River and Shethar-bozenai and their associates came to them and spoke to them thus, 'Who gave you a decree to build this house and to finish this structure?' 4 They*b* also asked them this: 'What are the names of the men who are building this building?' 5 But the eye of their God was upon the elders of the Jews, and they did not stop them until a report reached Darius and then answer was returned by letter in reply to it.

6 The copy of the letter that Tattenai the governor of the province Beyond the River and Shethar-bozenai and his associates the envoys who were in the province Beyond the River sent to King Darius; 7 they sent him a report, in which was written as follows: 'To Darius the king, all peace! 8 May it be known to the king that we went to the province of Judah, to the house of the great God. It is being built of hewn stone, and timber is laid in the walls; this work is being done diligently and prospers in their hands. 9 Then we spoke to those elders and asked them, "Who gave you a decree to build this house and to finish this structure?" 10 We also asked them their names, for your information, so that we might write down the names of the men at their head. 11 This was their reply to us: "We are the servants of the God of heaven and earth, and we are rebuilding the house that was built many years ago, which a great king of Israel built and finished. 12 But because our ancestors had angered the God of heaven, he gave them into the hand of King Nebuchadnezzar of Babylon, the Chaldean, who destroyed this house and carried away the people to Babylonia. 13 However, King Cyrus of Babylon, in the first year of his reign, made a decree that this house of God should be rebuilt. 14 Moreover, the gold and silver vessels of the house of God, which Nebuchadnezzar had taken out of the temple in Jerusalem and had brought into the temple of Babylon, these King Cyrus took out of the temple of Babylon, and they were delivered to a man named Sheshbazzar, whom he had made governor. 15 He said to him, 'Take these vessels; go and put them in the temple in Jerusalem, and let the house of God be rebuilt on its site.' 16 Then this Sheshbazzar came and laid the foundations of the house of God in Jerusalem; and from that time until now it has been under construction, and it is not yet finished." 17 And now, if it seems good to the king, have a search made in the royal archives there in Babylon, to see whether a decree was issued by King Cyrus for the rebuilding of this house of God in Jerusalem. Let the king send us his pleasure in this matter.'

a Aram adds *the prophet*   *b* Gk Syr: Aram *We*

The Decree of Darius

6 Then King Darius made a decree, and they searched the archives where the documents were stored in Babylon. ² But it was in Ecbatana, the capital in the province of Media, that a scroll was found on which this was written: 'A record. ³ In the first year of his reign, King Cyrus issued a decree: Concerning the house of God at Jerusalem, let the house be rebuilt, the place where sacrifices are offered and burnt-offerings are brought; *a* its height shall be sixty cubits and its width sixty cubits, ⁴ with three courses of hewn stones and one course of timber; let the cost be paid from the royal treasury. ⁵ Moreover, let the gold and silver vessels of the house of God, which Nebuchadnezzar took out of the temple in Jerusalem and brought to Babylon, be restored and brought back to the temple in Jerusalem, each to its place; you shall put them in the house of God.'

6 'Now you, Tattenai, governor of the province Beyond the River, Shethar-bozenai, and you, their associates, the envoys in the province Beyond the River, keep away; ⁷ let the work on this house of God alone; let the governor of the Jews and the elders of the Jews rebuild this house of God on its site. ⁸ Moreover, I make a decree regarding what you shall do for these elders of the Jews for the rebuilding of this house of God: the cost is to be paid to these people, in full and without delay, from the royal revenue, the tribute of the province Beyond the River. ⁹ Whatever is needed—young bulls, rams, or sheep for burnt-offerings to the God of heaven, wheat, salt, wine, or oil, as the priests in Jerusalem require—let that be given to them day by day without fail, ¹⁰ so that they may offer pleasing sacrifices to the God of heaven, and pray for the life of the king and his children. ¹¹ Furthermore, I decree that if anyone alters this edict, a beam shall be pulled out of the house of the perpetrator, who then shall be impaled on it. The house shall be made a dunghill. ¹² May the God who has established his name there overthrow any king or people that shall put forth a hand to al-ter this, or to destroy this house of God in Jerusalem. I, Darius, make a decree; let it be done with all diligence.'

Completion and Dedication of the Temple

13 Then, according to the word sent by King Darius, Tattenai, the governor of the province Beyond the River, Shethar-bozenai, and their associates did with all diligence what King Darius had ordered. ¹⁴ So the elders of the Jews built and prospered, through the prophesying of the prophet Haggai and Zechariah son of Iddo. They finished their building by command of the God of Israel and by decree of Cyrus, Darius, and King Artaxerxes of Persia; ¹⁵ and this house was finished on the third day of the month of Adar, in the sixth year of the reign of King Darius.

16 The people of Israel, the priests and the Levites, and the rest of the returned exiles, celebrated the dedication of this house of God with joy. ¹⁷ They offered at the dedication of this house of God one hundred bulls, two hundred rams, four hundred lambs, and as a sin-offering for all Israel twelve male goats, according to the number of the tribes of Israel. ¹⁸ Then they set the priests in their divisions and the Levites in their courses for the service of God at Jerusalem, as it is written in the book of Moses.

The Passover Celebrated

19 On the fourteenth day of the first month the returned exiles kept the passover. ²⁰ For both the priests and the Levites had purified themselves; all of them were clean. So they killed the passover lamb for all the returned exiles, for their fellow-priests, and for themselves. ²¹ It was eaten by the people of Israel who had returned from exile, and also by all who had joined them and separated themselves from the pollutions of the nations of the land to worship the Lord, the God of Israel. ²² With joy they celebrated the festival of unleavened bread for seven days; for the Lord had made them joyful, and had turned the heart of the king of Assyria to

a Meaning of Aram uncertain

them, so that he aided them in the work on the house of God, the God of Israel.

The Coming and Work of Ezra

7 After this, in the reign of King Artaxerxes of Persia, Ezra son of Seraiah, son of Azariah, son of Hilkiah, ² son of Shallum, son of Zadok, son of Ahitub, ³ son of Amariah, son of Azariah, son of Meraioth, ⁴ son of Zerahiah, son of Uzzi, son of Bukki, ⁵ son of Abishua, son of Phinehas, son of Eleazar, son of the chief priest Aaron— ⁶ this Ezra went up from Babylonia. He was a scribe skilled in the law of Moses that the LORD the God of Israel had given; and the king granted him all that he asked, for the hand of the LORD his God was upon him.

7 Some of the people of Israel, and some of the priests and Levites, the singers and gatekeepers, and the temple servants also went up to Jerusalem, in the seventh year of King Artaxerxes. ⁸ They came to Jerusalem in the fifth month, which was in the seventh year of the king. ⁹ On the first day of the first month the journey up from Babylon was begun, and on the first day of the fifth month he came to Jerusalem, for the gracious hand of his God was upon him. ¹⁰ For Ezra had set his heart to study the law of the LORD, and to do it, and to teach the statutes and ordinances in Israel.

The Letter of Artaxerxes to Ezra

11 This is a copy of the letter that King Artaxerxes gave to the priest Ezra, the scribe, a scholar of the text of the commandments of the LORD and his statutes for Israel: ¹² 'Artaxerxes, king of kings, to the priest Ezra, the scribe of the law of the God of heaven: Peace. ª And now ¹³ I decree that any of the people of Israel or their priests or Levites in my kingdom who freely offers to go to Jerusalem may go with you. ¹⁴ For you are sent by the king and his seven counsellors to make inquiries about Judah and Jerusalem according to the law of your God, which is in your hand, ¹⁵ and also to convey the silver and gold that the king and his counsellors have freely offered to the God of Israel, whose dwelling is in Jerusalem, ¹⁶ with all the silver and gold that you shall find in the whole province of Babylonia, and with the freewill-offerings of the people and the priests, given willingly for the house of their God in Jerusalem. ¹⁷ With this money, then, you shall with all diligence buy bulls, rams, and lambs, and their grain-offerings and their drink-offerings, and you shall offer them on the altar of the house of your God in Jerusalem. ¹⁸ Whatever seems good to you and your colleagues to do with the rest of the silver and gold, you may do, according to the will of your God. ¹⁹ The vessels that have been given you for the service of the house of your God, you shall deliver before the God of Jerusalem. ²⁰ And whatever else is required for the house of your God, which you are responsible for providing, you may provide out of the king's treasury.

21 'I, King Artaxerxes, decree to all the treasurers in the province Beyond the River: Whatever the priest Ezra, the scribe of the law of the God of heaven, requires of you, let it be done with all diligence, ²² up to one hundred talents of silver, one hundred cors of wheat, one hundred baths ᵇ of wine, one hundred baths ᵇ of oil, and unlimited salt. ²³ Whatever is commanded by the God of heaven, let it be done with zeal for the house of the God of heaven, or wrath will come upon the realm of the king and his heirs. ²⁴ We also notify you that it shall not be lawful to impose tribute, custom, or toll on any of the priests, the Levites, the singers, the doorkeepers, the temple servants, or other servants of this house of God.

25 'And you, Ezra, according to the God-given wisdom you possess, appoint magistrates and judges who may judge all the people in the province Beyond the River who know the laws of your God; and you shall teach those who do not know them. ²⁶ All who will not obey the law of your God and the law of the king, let judgement be strictly executed on them,

a Syr Vg 1 Esdras 8.9: Aram *Perfect*　　b A Heb measure of volume whether for death or for banishment or for confiscation of their goods or for imprisonment.'

27 Blessed be the LORD, the God of our ancestors, who put such a thing as this into the heart of the king to glorify the house of the LORD in Jerusalem, 28 and who extended to me steadfast love before the king and his counsellors, and before all the king's mighty officers. I took courage, for the hand of the LORD my God was upon me, and I gathered leaders from Israel to go up with me.

Heads of Families Who Returned with Ezra

8 These are their family heads, and this is the genealogy of those who went up with me from Babylonia, in the reign of King Artaxerxes: 2 Of the descendants of Phinehas, Gershom. Of Ithamar, Daniel. Of David, Hattush, 3 of the descendants of Shecaniah. Of Parosh, Zechariah, with whom were registered one hundred and fifty males. 4 Of the descendants of Pahath-moab, Eliehoenai son of Zerahiah, and with him two hundred males. 5 Of the descendants of Zattu,^{a} Shecaniah son of Jahaziel, and with him three hundred males. 6 Of the descendants of Adin, Ebed son of Jonathan, and with him fifty males. 7 Of the descendants of Elam, Jeshaiah son of Athaliah, and with him seventy males. 8 Of the descendants of Shephatiah, Zebadiah son of Michael, and with him eighty males. 9 Of the descendants of Joab, Obadiah son of Jehiel, and with him two hundred and eighteen males. 10 Of the descendants of Bani,^{b} Shelomith son of Josiphiah, and with him one hundred and sixty males. 11 Of the descendants of Bebai, Zechariah son of Bebai, and with him twenty-eight males. 12 Of the descendants of Azgad, Johanan son of Hakkatan, and with him one hundred and ten males. 13 Of the descendants of Adonikam, those who came later, their names being Eliphelet, Jeuel, and Shemaiah, and with him sixty males. 14 Of the descendants of Bigvai, Uthai and Zaccur, and with them seventy males.

Servants for the Temple

15 I gathered them by the river that runs to Ahava, and there we camped for three days. As I reviewed the people and the priests, I found there none of the descendants of Levi. 16 Then I sent for Eliezer, Ariel, Shemaiah, Elnathan, Jarib, Elnathan, Nathan, Zechariah, and Meshullam, who were leaders, and for Joiarib and Elnathan, who were wise, 17 and sent them to Iddo, the leader at the place called Casiphia, telling them what to say to Iddo and his colleagues the temple servants at Casiphia, namely, to send us ministers for the house of our God. 18 Since the gracious hand of our God was upon us, they brought us a man of discretion, of the descendants of Mahli son of Levi son of Israel, namely Sherebiah, with his sons and kin, eighteen; 19 also Hashabiah and with him Jeshaiah of the descendants of Merari, with his kin and their sons, twenty; 20 besides two hundred and twenty of the temple servants, whom David and his officials had set apart to attend the Levites. These were all mentioned by name.

Fasting and Prayer for Protection

21 Then I proclaimed a fast there, at the river Ahava, that we might deny ourselves^c before our God, to seek from him a safe journey for ourselves, our children, and all our possessions. 22 For I was ashamed to ask the king for a band of soldiers and cavalry to protect us against the enemy on our way, since we had told the king that the hand of our God is gracious to all who seek him, but his power and his wrath are against all who forsake him. 23 So we fasted and petitioned our God for this, and he listened to our entreaty.

Gifts for the Temple

24 Then I set apart twelve of the leading priests: Sherebiah, Hashabiah, and ten of their kin with them. 25 And I weighed out to them the silver and the gold and the vessels, the offering for the house of our God

---

a Gk 1 Esdras 8.32: Heb lacks *of Zattu*
b Gk 1 Esdras 8.36: Heb lacks *Bani* c Or *might fast*

that the king, his counsellors, his lords, and all Israel there present had offered; 26 I weighed out into their hand six hundred and fifty talents of silver, and one hundred silver vessels worth . . . talents,*a* and one hundred talents of gold, 27 twenty gold bowls worth a thousand darics, and two vessels of fine polished bronze as precious as gold. 28 And I said to them, 'You are holy to the LORD, and the vessels are holy; and the silver and the gold are a freewill-offering to the LORD, the God of your ancestors. 29 Guard them and keep them until you weigh them before the chief priests and the Levites and the heads of families in Israel at Jerusalem, within the chambers of the house of the LORD.' 30 So the priests and the Levites took over the silver, the gold, and the vessels as they were weighed out, to bring them to Jerusalem, to the house of our God.

The Return to Jerusalem

31 Then we left the river Ahava on the twelfth day of the first month, to go to Jerusalem; the hand of our God was upon us, and he delivered us from the hand of the enemy and from ambushes along the way. 32 We came to Jerusalem and remained there for three days. 33 On the fourth day, within the house of our God, the silver, the gold, and the vessels were weighed into the hands of the priest Meremoth son of Uriah, and with him was Eleazar son of Phinehas, and with them were the Levites, Jozabad son of Jeshua and Noadiah son of Binnui. 34 The total was counted and weighed, and the weight of everything was recorded.

35 At that time those who had come from captivity, the returned exiles, offered burnt-offerings to the God of Israel, twelve bulls for all Israel, ninety-six rams, seventy-seven lambs, and as a sin-offering twelve male goats; all this was a burnt-offering to the LORD. 36 They also delivered the king's commissions to the king's satraps and to the governors of the province Beyond the River; and they supported the people and the house of God.

Denunciation of Mixed Marriages

9 After these things had been done, the officials approached me and said, 'The people of Israel, the priests, and the Levites have not separated themselves from the peoples of the lands with their abominations, from the Canaanites, the Hittites, the Perizzites, the Jebusites, the Ammonites, the Moabites, the Egyptians, and the Amorites. 2 For they have taken some of their daughters as wives for themselves and for their sons. Thus the holy seed has mixed itself with the peoples of the lands, and in this faithlessness the officials and leaders have led the way.' 3 When I heard this, I tore my garment and my mantle, and pulled hair from my head and beard, and sat appalled. 4 Then all who trembled at the words of the God of Israel, because of the faithlessness of the returned exiles, gathered around me while I sat appalled until the evening sacrifice.

Ezra's Prayer

5 At the evening sacrifice I got up from my fasting, with my garments and my mantle torn, and fell on my knees, spread out my hands to the LORD my God, 6 and said,

'O my God, I am too ashamed and embarrassed to lift my face to you, my God, for our iniquities have risen higher than our heads, and our guilt has mounted up to the heavens. 7 From the days of our ancestors to this day we have been deep in guilt, and for our iniquities we, our kings, and our priests have been handed over to the kings of the lands, to the sword, to captivity, to plundering, and to utter shame, as is now the case. 8 But now for a brief moment favour has been shown by the LORD our God, who has left us a remnant, and given us a stake in his holy place, in order that he*b* may brighten our eyes and grant us a little sustenance in our slavery. 9 For we are slaves; yet our God has not forsaken us in our slavery, but has extended to us his steadfast love before the kings of Persia, to give us new life to set up

a The number of talents is lacking   *b* Heb *our God*

the house of our God, to repair its ruins, and to give us a wall in Judea and Jerusalem.

10 'And now, our God, what shall we say after this? For we have forsaken your commandments, [11] which you commanded by your servants the prophets, saying, "The land that you are entering to possess is a land unclean with the pollutions of the peoples of the lands, with their abominations. They have filled it from end to end with their uncleanness. [12] Therefore do not give your daughters to their sons, neither take their daughters for your sons, and never seek their peace or prosperity, so that you may be strong and eat the good of the land and leave it for an inheritance to your children for ever." [13] After all that has come upon us for our evil deeds and for our great guilt, seeing that you, our God, have punished us less than our iniquities deserved and have given us such a remnant as this, [14] shall we break your commandments again and intermarry with the peoples who practise these abominations? Would you not be angry with us until you destroy us without remnant or survivor? [15] O LORD, God of Israel, you are just, but we have escaped as a remnant, as is now the case. Here we are before you in our guilt, though no one can face you because of this.'

The People's Response

10 While Ezra prayed and made confession, weeping and throwing himself down before the house of God, a very great assembly of men, women, and children gathered to him out of Israel; the people also wept bitterly. [2] Shecaniah son of Jehiel, of the descendants of Elam, addressed Ezra, saying, 'We have broken faith with our God and have married foreign women from the peoples of the land, but even now there is hope for Israel in spite of this. [3] So now let us make a covenant with our God to send away all these wives and their children, according to the counsel of my lord and of those who tremble at the commandment of our God; and let it be done according to the law. [4] Take action, for it is your duty, and we are with you; be strong, and do it.' [5] Then Ezra stood up and made the leading priests, the Levites, and all Israel swear that they would do as had been said. So they swore.

Foreign Wives and Their Children Rejected

6 Then Ezra withdrew from before the house of God, and went to the chamber of Jehohanan son of Eliashib, where he spent the night.[a] He did not eat bread or drink water, for he was mourning over the faithlessness of the exiles. [7] They made a proclamation throughout Judah and Jerusalem to all the returned exiles that they should assemble at Jerusalem, [8] and that if any did not come within three days, by order of the officials and the elders all their property should be forfeited, and they themselves banned from the congregation of the exiles.

9 Then all the people of Judah and Benjamin assembled at Jerusalem within the three days; it was the ninth month, on the twentieth day of the month. All the people sat in the open square before the house of God, trembling because of this matter and because of the heavy rain. [10] Then Ezra the priest stood up and said to them, 'You have trespassed and married foreign women, and so increased the guilt of Israel. [11] Now make confession to the LORD the God of your ancestors, and do his will; separate yourselves from the peoples of the land and from the foreign wives.' [12] Then all the assembly answered with a loud voice, 'It is so; we must do as you have said. [13] But the people are many, and it is a time of heavy rain; we cannot stand in the open. Nor is this a task for one day or for two, for many of us have transgressed in this matter. [14] Let our officials represent the whole assembly, and let all in our towns who have taken foreign wives come at appointed times, and with them the elders and judges of every town, until the fierce wrath of our God on this account is averted from us.' [15] Only Jonathan son of Asahel and Jahzeiah son of Tikvah

a 1 Esdras 9.2: Heb *where he went*

opposed this, and Meshullam and Shabbethai the Levites supported them.

16 Then the returned exiles did so. Ezra the priest selected men,[a] heads of families, according to their families, each of them designated by name. On the first day of the tenth month they sat down to examine the matter. 17 By the first day of the first month they had come to the end of all the men who had married foreign women.

18 There were found of the descendants of the priests who had married foreign women, of the descendants of Jeshua son of Jozadak and his brothers: Maaseiah, Eliezer, Jarib, and Gedaliah. 19 They pledged themselves to send away their wives, and their guilt-offering was a ram of the flock for their guilt. 20 Of the descendants of Immer: Hanani and Zebadiah. 21 Of the descendants of Harim: Maaseiah, Elijah, Shemaiah, Jehiel, and Uzziah. 22 Of the descendants of Pashhur: Elioenai, Maaseiah, Ishmael, Nethanel, Jozabad, and Elasah.

23 Of the Levites: Jozabad, Shimei, Kelaiah (that is, Kelita), Pethahiah, Judah, and Eliezer. 24 Of the singers: Eliashib. Of the gatekeepers: Shallum, Telem, and Uri.

25 And of Israel: of the descendants of Parosh: Ramiah, Izziah, Malchijah, Mijamin, Eleazar, Hashabiah,[b] and Benaiah. 26 Of the descendants of Elam: Mattaniah, Zechariah, Jehiel, Abdi, Jeremoth, and Elijah. 27 Of the descendants of Zattu: Elioenai, Eliashib, Mattaniah, Jeremoth, Zabad, and Aziza. 28 Of the descendants of Bebai: Jehohanan, Hananiah, Zabbai, and Athlai. 29 Of the descendants of Bani: Meshullam, Malluch, Adaiah, Jashub, Sheal, and Jeremoth. 30 Of the descendants of Pahathmoab: Adna, Chelal, Benaiah, Maaseiah, Mattaniah, Bezalel, Binnui, and Manasseh. 31 Of the descendants of Harim: Eliezer, Isshijah, Malchijah, Shemaiah, Shimeon, 32 Benjamin, Malluch, and Shemariah. 33 Of the descendants of Hashum: Mattenai, Mattattah, Zabad, Eliphelet, Jeremai, Manasseh, and Shimei. 34 Of the descendants of Bani: Maadai, Amram, Uel, 35 Benaiah, Bedeiah, Cheluhi, 36 Vaniah, Meremoth, Eliashib, 37 Mattaniah, Mattenai, and Jaasu. 38 Of the descendants of Binnui:[c] Shimei, 39 Shelemiah, Nathan, Adaiah, 40 Machnadebai, Shashai, Sharai, 41 Azarel, Shelemiah, Shemariah, 42 Shallum, Amariah, and Joseph. 43 Of the descendants of Nebo: Jeiel, Mattithiah, Zabad, Zebina, Jaddai, Joel, and Benaiah. 44 All these had married foreign women, and they sent them away with their children.[d]

a 1 Esdras 9.16: Syr: Heb *And there were selected Ezra,*
b 1 Esdras 9.26 Gk: Heb *Malchijah*　　*c* Gk: Heb *Bani, Binnui*　　*d* 1 Esdras 9.36; meaning of Heb uncertain

NEHEMIAH

Nehemiah Prays for His People

1 The words of Nehemiah son of Hacaliah. In the month of Chislev, in the twentieth year, while I was in Susa the capital, 2 one of my brothers, Hanani, came with certain men from Judah; and I asked them about the Jews that survived, those who had escaped the captivity, and about Jerusalem. 3 They replied, 'The survivors there in the province who escaped captivity are in great trouble and shame; the wall of Jerusalem is broken down, and its gates have been destroyed by fire.'

4 When I heard these words I sat down and wept, and mourned for days, fasting and praying before the God of heaven. 5 I said, 'O LORD God of heaven, the great and awesome God who keeps covenant and steadfast love with those who love him and keep his commandments; 6 let your ear be attentive and your eyes open to hear the prayer of your servant that I now pray before you day and night for your servants the people of Israel, confessing the sins of the people of Israel, which we have sinned against you. Both I and my family have sinned. 7 We have offended you deeply, failing to keep the commandments, the statutes, and the ordinances that you commanded your servant Moses. 8 Remember the word that you commanded your servant Moses, "If you are unfaithful, I will scatter you among the peoples; 9 but if you return to me and keep my commandments and do them, though your outcasts are under the farthest skies, I will gather them from there and bring them to the place at which I have chosen to establish my name." 10 They are your servants and your people, whom you redeemed by your great power and your strong hand. 11 O Lord, let your ear be attentive to the prayer of your servant, and to the prayer of your servants who delight in revering your name. Give success to your servant today, and grant him mercy in the sight of this man!'

At the time, I was cupbearer to the king.

Nehemiah Sent to Judah

2 In the month of Nisan, in the twentieth year of King Artaxerxes, when wine was served to him, I carried the wine and gave it to the king. Now, I had never been sad in his presence before. 2 So the king said to me, 'Why is your face sad, since you are not sick? This can only be sadness of the heart.' Then I was very much afraid. 3 I said to the king, 'May the king live for ever! Why should my face not be sad, when the city, the place of my ancestors' graves, lies waste, and its gates have been destroyed by fire?' 4 Then the king said to me, 'What do you request?' So I prayed to the God of heaven. 5 Then I said to the king, 'If it pleases the king, and if your servant has found favour with you, I ask that you send me to Judah, to the city of my ancestors' graves, so that I may rebuild it.' 6 The king said to me (the queen also was sitting beside him), 'How long will you be gone, and when will you return?' So it pleased the king to send me, and I set him a date. 7 Then I said to the king, 'If it pleases the king, let letters be given me to the governors of the province Beyond the River, that they may grant me passage until I arrive in Judah; 8 and a letter to Asaph, the keeper of the king's forest, directing him to give me timber to make beams for the gates of the temple fortress,

and for the wall of the city, and for the house that I shall occupy.' And the king granted me what I asked, for the gracious hand of my God was upon me.

9 Then I came to the governors of the province Beyond the River, and gave them the king's letters. Now the king had sent officers of the army and cavalry with me. 10 When Sanballat the Horonite and Tobiah the Ammonite official heard this, it displeased them greatly that someone had come to seek the welfare of the people of Israel.

Nehemiah's Inspection of the Walls

11 So I came to Jerusalem and was there for three days. 12 Then I got up during the night, I and a few men with me; I told no one what my God had put into my heart to do for Jerusalem. The only animal I took was the animal I rode. 13 I went out by night by the Valley Gate past the Dragon's Spring and to the Dung Gate, and I inspected the walls of Jerusalem that had been broken down and its gates that had been destroyed by fire. 14 Then I went on to the Fountain Gate and to the King's Pool; but there was no place for the animal I was riding to continue. 15 So I went up by way of the valley by night and inspected the wall. Then I turned back and entered by the Valley Gate, and so returned. 16 The officials did not know where I had gone or what I was doing; I had not yet told the Jews, the priests, the nobles, the officials, and the rest that were to do the work.

Decision to Restore the Walls

17 Then I said to them, 'You see the trouble we are in, how Jerusalem lies in ruins with its gates burnt. Come, let us rebuild the wall of Jerusalem, so that we may no longer suffer disgrace.' 18 I told them that the hand of my God had been gracious upon me, and also the words that the king had spoken to me. Then they said, 'Let us start building!' So they committed themselves to the common good. 19 But when Sanballat the Horonite and Tobiah the Ammonite official, and Geshem the Arab heard of it, they mocked and

ridiculed us, saying, 'What is this that you are doing? Are you rebelling against the king?' 20 Then I replied to them, 'The God of heaven is the one who will give us success, and we his servants are going to start building; but you have no share or claim or historic right in Jerusalem.'

Organization of the Work

3 Then the high priest Eliashib set to work with his fellow-priests and rebuilt the Sheep Gate. They consecrated it and set up its doors; they consecrated it as far as the Tower of the Hundred and as far as the Tower of Hananel. 2 And the men of Jericho built next to him. And next to them*a* Zaccur son of Imri built.

3 The sons of Hassenaah built the Fish Gate; they laid its beams and set up its doors, its bolts, and its bars. 4 Next to them Meremoth son of Uriah son of Hakkoz made repairs. Next to them Meshullam son of Berechiah son of Meshezabel made repairs. Next to them Zadok son of Baana made repairs. 5 Next to them the Tekoites made repairs; but their nobles would not put their shoulders to the work of their Lord.*b*

6 Joiada son of Paseah and Meshullam son of Besodeiah repaired the Old Gate; they laid its beams and set up its doors, its bolts, and its bars. 7 Next to them repairs were made by Melatiah the Gibeonite and Jadon the Meronothite—the men of Gibeon and of Mizpah—who were under the jurisdiction of*c* the governor of the province Beyond the River. 8 Next to them Uzziel son of Harhaiah, one of the goldsmiths, made repairs. Next to him Hananiah, one of the perfumers, made repairs; and they restored Jerusalem as far as the Broad Wall. 9 Next to them Rephaiah son of Hur, ruler of half the district of*d* Jerusalem, made repairs. 10 Next to them Jedaiah son of Harumaph made repairs opposite his house; and next to him Hattush son of Hashabneiah made repairs. 11 Malchijah son of Harim and Hasshub son of Pahath-moab repaired another section and the Tower of

a Heb *him*   *b* Or *lords*   *c* Meaning of Heb uncertain   *d* Or *supervisor of half the portion assigned to* the Ovens. [12] Next to him Shallum son of Hallohesh, ruler of half the district of[a] Jerusalem, made repairs, he and his daughters.

[13] Hanun and the inhabitants of Zanoah repaired the Valley Gate; they rebuilt it and set up its doors, its bolts, and its bars, and repaired a thousand cubits of the wall, as far as the Dung Gate.

[14] Malchijah son of Rechab, ruler of the district of[b] Beth-haccherem, repaired the Dung Gate; he rebuilt it and set up its doors, its bolts, and its bars.

[15] And Shallum son of Col-hozeh, ruler of the district of[b] Mizpah, repaired the Fountain Gate; he rebuilt it and covered it and set up its doors, its bolts, and its bars; and he built the wall of the Pool of Shelah of the king's garden, as far as the stairs that go down from the City of David. [16] After him Nehemiah son of Azbuk, ruler of half the district of[a] Beth-zur, repaired from a point opposite the graves of David, as far as the artificial pool and the house of the warriors. [17] After him the Levites made repairs: Rehum son of Bani; next to him Hashabiah, ruler of half the district of[a] Keilah, made repairs for his district. [18] After him their kin made repairs: Binnui,[c] son of Henadad, ruler of half the district of[a] Keilah; [19] next to him Ezer son of Jeshua, ruler[d] of Mizpah, repaired another section opposite the ascent to the armoury at the Angle. [20] After him Baruch son of Zabbai repaired another section from the Angle to the door of the house of the high priest Eliashib. [21] After him Meremoth son of Uriah son of Hakkoz repaired another section from the door of the house of Eliashib to the end of the house of Eliashib. [22] After him the priests, the men of the surrounding area, made repairs. [23] After them Benjamin and Hasshub made repairs opposite their house. After them Azariah son of Maaseiah son of Ananiah made repairs beside his own house. [24] After him Binnui son of Henadad repaired another section, from

a Or *supervisor of half the portion assigned to*
b Or *supervisor of the portion assigned to*   c Gk Syr
Compare verse 24, 10.9: Heb *Bavvai*   d Or *supervisor*

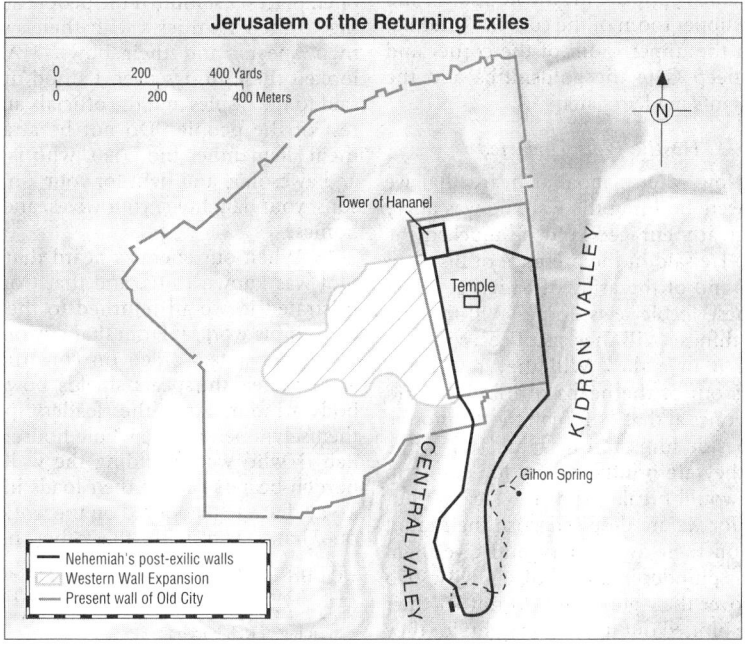

Jerusalem of the Returning Exiles

0   200   400 Yards
0   200   400 Meters

Tower of Hananel

Temple

KIDRON VALLEY

CENTRAL VALLEY

Gihon Spring

—— Nehemiah's post-exilic walls
▨ Western Wall Expansion
— Present wall of Old City

the house of Azariah to the Angle and to the corner. 25 Palal son of Uzai repaired opposite the Angle and the tower projecting from the upper house of the king at the court of the guard. After him Pedaiah son of Parosh 26 and the temple servants living[a] on Ophel made repairs up to a point opposite the Water Gate on the east and the projecting tower. 27 After him the Tekoites repaired another section opposite the great projecting tower as far as the wall of Ophel.

28 Above the Horse Gate the priests made repairs, each one opposite his own house. 29 After them Zadok son of Immer made repairs opposite his own house. After him Shemaiah son of Shecaniah, the keeper of the East Gate, made repairs. 30 After him Hananiah son of Shelemiah and Hanun sixth son of Zalaph repaired another section. After him Meshullam son of Berechiah made repairs opposite his living quarters. 31 After him Malchijah, one of the goldsmiths, made repairs as far as the house of the temple servants and of the merchants, opposite the Muster Gate,[b] and to the upper room of the corner. 32 And between the upper room of the corner and the Sheep Gate the goldsmiths and the merchants made repairs.

Hostile Plots Thwarted

4[c] Now when Sanballat heard that we were building the wall, he was angry and greatly enraged, and he mocked the Jews. 2 He said in the presence of his associates and of the army of Samaria, 'What are these feeble Jews doing? Will they restore things? Will they sacrifice? Will they finish it in a day? Will they revive the stones out of the heaps of rubbish—and burnt ones at that?' 3 Tobiah the Ammonite was beside him, and he said, 'That stone wall they are building—any fox going up on it would break it down!' 4 Hear, O our God, for we are despised; turn their taunt back on their own heads, and give them over as plunder in a land of captivity. 5 Do not cover their guilt, and do not let their sin be blotted out from your sight; for they

have hurled insults in the face of the builders.

6 So we rebuilt the wall, and all the wall was joined together to half its height; for the people had a mind to work.

7[d] But when Sanballat and Tobiah and the Arabs and the Ammonites and the Ashdodites heard that the repairing of the walls of Jerusalem was going forward and the gaps were beginning to be closed, they were very angry, 8 and all plotted together to come and fight against Jerusalem and to cause confusion in it. 9 So we prayed to our God, and set a guard as a protection against them day and night.

10 But Judah said, 'The strength of the burden-bearers is failing, and there is too much rubbish, so that we are unable to work on the wall.' 11 And our enemies said, 'They will not know or see anything before we come upon them and kill them and stop the work.' 12 When the Jews who lived near them came, they said to us ten times, 'From all the places where they live[e] they will come up against us.'[f] 13 So in the lowest parts of the space behind the wall, in open places, I stationed the people according to their families,[g] with their swords, their spears, and their bows. 14 After I looked these things over, I stood up and said to the nobles and the officials and the rest of the people, 'Do not be afraid of them. Remember the LORD, who is great and awesome, and fight for your kin, your sons, your daughters, your wives, and your homes.'

15 When our enemies heard that their plot was known to us, and that God had frustrated it, we all returned to the wall, each to his work. 16 From that day on, half of my servants worked on construction, and half held the spears, shields, bows, and body-armour; and the leaders posted themselves behind the whole house of Judah, 17 who were building the wall. The burden-bearers carried their loads in such a way that each laboured on the work with one hand and with the other held a

---

a Cn: Heb *were living*   b Or *Hammiphkad Gate*
c Ch 3.33 in Heb   d Ch 4.1 in Heb   e Cn: Heb *you return*   f Compare Gk Syr: Meaning of Heb uncertain
g Meaning of Heb uncertain

weapon. 18 And each of the builders had his sword strapped at his side while he built. The man who sounded the trumpet was beside me. 19 And I said to the nobles, the officials, and the rest of the people, 'The work is great and widely spread out, and we are separated far from one another on the wall. 20 Rally to us wherever you hear the sound of the trumpet. Our God will fight for us.'

21 So we laboured at the work, and half of them held the spears from break of dawn until the stars came out. 22 I also said to the people at that time, 'Let every man and his servant pass the night inside Jerusalem, so that they may be a guard for us by night and may labour by day.' 23 So neither I nor my brothers nor my servants nor the men of the guard who followed me ever took off our clothes; each kept his weapon in his right hand.*a*

Nehemiah Deals with Oppression

5 Now there was a great outcry of the people and of their wives against their Jewish kin. 2 For there were those who said, 'With our sons and our daughters, we are many; we must get grain, so that we may eat and stay alive.' 3 There were also those who said, 'We are having to pledge our fields, our vineyards, and our houses in order to get grain during the famine.' 4 And there were those who said, 'We are having to borrow money on our fields and vineyards to pay the king's tax. 5 Now our flesh is the same as that of our kindred; our children are the same as their children; and yet we are forcing our sons and daughters to be slaves, and some of our daughters have been ravished; we are powerless, and our fields and vineyards now belong to others.'

6 I was very angry when I heard their outcry and these complaints. 7 After thinking it over, I brought charges against the nobles and the officials; I said to them, 'You are all taking interest from your own people.' And I called a great assembly to deal with them, 8 and said to them, 'As far as we were able, we have bought back our Jewish kindred who had been sold to other nations; but now you are selling your own kin, who must then be bought back by us!' They were silent, and could not find a word to say. 9 So I said, 'The thing that you are doing is not good. Should you not walk in the fear of our God, to prevent the taunts of the nations our enemies? 10 Moreover, I and my brothers and my servants are lending them money and grain. Let us stop this taking of interest. 11 Restore to them, this very day, their fields, their vineyards, their olive orchards, and their houses, and the interest on money, grain, wine, and oil that you have been exacting from them.' 12 Then they said, 'We will restore everything and demand nothing more from them. We will do as you say.' And I called the priests, and made them take an oath to do as they had promised. 13 I also shook out the fold of my garment and said, 'So may God shake out everyone from house and from property who does not perform this promise. Thus may they be shaken out and emptied.' And all the assembly said, 'Amen', and praised the LORD. And the people did as they had promised.

The Generosity of Nehemiah

14 Moreover, from the time that I was appointed to be their governor in the land of Judah, from the twentieth year to the thirty-second year of King Artaxerxes, twelve years, neither I nor my brothers ate the food allowance of the governor. 15 The former governors who were before me laid heavy burdens on the people, and took food and wine from them, besides forty shekels of silver. Even their servants lorded it over the people. But I did not do so, because of the fear of God. 16 Indeed, I devoted myself to the work on this wall, and acquired no land; and all my servants were gathered there for the work. 17 Moreover, there were at my table one hundred and fifty people, Jews and officials, besides those who came to us from the nations around us. 18 Now that which was prepared for one day was one ox and six choice sheep; also fowls were prepared for me, and every ten days skins of wine in abundance; yet with all this I did not demand

a Cn: Heb *each his weapon the water*

the food allowance of the governor, because of the heavy burden of labour on the people. ¹⁹ Remember for my good, O my God, all that I have done for this people.

Intrigues of Enemies Foiled

6 Now when it was reported to Sanballat and Tobiah and to Geshem the Arab and to the rest of our enemies that I had built the wall and that there was no gap left in it (though up to that time I had not set up the doors in the gates), ² Sanballat and Geshem sent to me, saying, 'Come and let us meet together in one of the villages in the plain of Ono.' But they intended to do me harm. ³ So I sent messengers to them, saying, 'I am doing a great work and I cannot come down. Why should the work stop while I leave it to come down to you?' ⁴ They sent to me four times in this way, and I answered them in the same manner. ⁵ In the same way Sanballat for the fifth time sent his servant to me with an open letter in his hand. ⁶ In it was written, 'It is reported among the nations—and Geshem^a also says it—that you and the Jews intend to rebel; that is why you are building the wall; and according to this report you wish to become their king. ⁷ You have also set up prophets to proclaim in Jerusalem concerning you, "There is a king in Judah!" And now it will be reported to the king according to these words. So come, therefore, and let us confer together.' ⁸ Then I sent to him, saying, 'No such things as you say have been done; you are inventing them out of your own mind' ⁹ —for they all wanted to frighten us, thinking, 'Their hands will drop from the work, and it will not be done.' But now, O God, strengthen my hands.

10 One day when I went into the house of Shemaiah son of Delaiah son of Mehetabel, who was confined to his house, he said, 'Let us meet together in the house of God, within the temple, and let us close the doors of the temple, for they are coming to kill you; indeed, tonight they are coming to kill you.' ¹¹ But I said, 'Should a man like me run away? Would a man like me go into the temple to save his life? I

will not go in!' ¹² Then I perceived and saw that God had not sent him at all, but he had pronounced the prophecy against me because Tobiah and Sanballat had hired him. ¹³ He was hired for this purpose, to intimidate me and make me sin by acting in this way, and so they could give me a bad name, in order to taunt me. ¹⁴ Remember Tobiah and Sanballat, O my God, according to these things that they did, and also the prophetess Noadiah and the rest of the prophets who wanted to make me afraid.

The Wall Completed

15 So the wall was finished on the twenty-fifth day of the month Elul, in fifty-two days. ¹⁶ And when all our enemies heard of it, all the nations around us were afraid^b and fell greatly in their own esteem; for they perceived that this work had been accomplished with the help of our God. ¹⁷ Moreover, in those days the nobles of Judah sent many letters to Tobiah, and Tobiah's letters came to them. ¹⁸ For many in Judah were bound by oath to him, because he was the son-in-law of Shecaniah son of Arah: and his son Jehohanan had married the daughter of Meshullam son of Berechiah. ¹⁹ Also they spoke of his good deeds in my presence, and reported my words to him. And Tobiah sent letters to intimidate me.

7 Now when the wall had been built and I had set up the doors, and the gatekeepers, the singers, and the Levites had been appointed, ² I gave my brother Hanani charge over Jerusalem, along with Hananiah the commander of the citadel— for he was a faithful man and feared God more than many. ³ And I said to them, 'The gates of Jerusalem are not to be opened until the sun is hot; while the gatekeepers^c are still standing guard, let them shut and bar the doors. Appoint guards from among the inhabitants of Jerusalem, some at their watch-posts, and others before their own houses.' ⁴ The city was wide and large, but

<hr>

a Heb *Gashmu*   *b* Another reading is *saw*
c Heb *while they*

the people within it were few and no houses had been built.

Lists of the Returned Exiles

5 Then my God put it into my mind to assemble the nobles and the officials and the people, to be enrolled by genealogy. And I found the book of the genealogy of those who were the first to come back, and I found the following written in it:

6 These are the people of the province who came up out of the captivity of those exiles whom King Nebuchadnezzar of Babylon had carried into exile; they returned to Jerusalem and Judah, each to his town. 7 They came with Zerubbabel, Jeshua, Nehemiah, Azariah, Raamiah, Nahamani, Mordecai, Bilshan, Mispereth, Bigvai, Nehum, Baanah.

The number of the Israelite people: 8 the descendants of Parosh, two thousand one hundred and seventy-two. 9 Of Shephatiah, three hundred and seventy-two. 10 Of Arah, six hundred and fifty-two. 11 Of Pahathmoab, namely the descendants of Jeshua and Joab, two thousand eight hundred and eighteen. 12 Of Elam, one thousand two hundred and fifty-four. 13 Of Zattu, eight hundred and forty-five. 14 Of Zaccai, seven hundred and sixty. 15 Of Binnui, six hundred and forty-eight. 16 Of Bebai, six hundred and twenty-eight. 17 Of Azgad, two thousand three hundred and twenty-two.

18 Of Adonikam, six hundred and sixty-seven. 19 Of Bigvai, two thousand and sixty-seven. 20 Of Adin, six hundred and fifty-five. 21 Of Ater, namely of Hezekiah, ninety-eight. 22 Of Hashum, three hundred and twenty-eight. 23 Of Bezai, three hundred and twenty-four. 24 Of Hariph, one hundred and twelve. 25 Of Gibeon, ninety-five. 26 The people of Bethlehem and Netophah, one hundred and eighty-eight. 27 Of Anathoth, one hundred and twenty-eight. 28 Of Beth-azmaveth, forty-two. 29 Of Kiriath-jearim, Chephirah, and Beeroth, seven hundred and forty-three. 30 Of Ramah and Geba, six hundred and twenty-one. 31 Of Michmas, one hundred and twenty-two. 32 Of Bethel and Ai, one hundred and twenty-three. 33 Of the other Nebo, fifty-two. 34 The descendants of the other Elam, one thousand two hundred and fifty-four. 35 Of Harim, three hundred and twenty. 36 Of Jericho, three hundred and forty-five. 37 Of Lod, Hadid, and Ono, seven hundred and twenty-one. 38 Of Senaah, three thousand nine hundred and thirty.

39 The priests: the descendants of Jedaiah, namely the house of Jeshua, nine hundred and seventy-three. 40 Of Immer, one thousand and fifty-two. 41 Of Pashhur, one thousand two hundred and forty-seven. 42 Of Harim, one thousand and seventeen.

43 The Levites: the descendants of Jeshua, namely of Kadmiel of the descendants

---

The Four Stages of Return from Exile

1. **538 B.C. under Cyrus II**
   Led by Sheshbazzar, who began rebuilding the temple but left it unfinished because of local opposition

2. **521 B.C. under Darius I**
   Led by Zerubbabel and Jeshua, who also encountered opposition but, with the encouragement of the prophets Haggai and Zechariah, completed the temple

3. **458 B.C. under Artaxerxes I or 398 B.C. under Artaxerxes II**
   Led by Ezra, who brought a copy of the Mosaic law

4. **445 B.C. under Artaxerxes I**
   Led by Nehemiah, who rebuilt the walls of Jerusalem and attempted to establish purity of community and worship. (Nehemiah came as governor with his own retinue. He did not, strictly speaking, lead a group of returning exiles.)

of Hodevah, seventy-four. 44 The singers: the descendants of Asaph, one hundred and forty-eight. 45 The gatekeepers: the descendants of Shallum, of Ater, of Talmon, of Akkub, of Hatita, of Shobai, one hundred and thirty-eight.

46 The temple servants: the descendants of Ziha, of Hasupha, of Tabbaoth, 47 of Keros, of Sia, of Padon, 48 of Lebana, of Hagaba, of Shalmai, 49 of Hanan, of Giddel, of Gahar, 50 of Reaiah, of Rezin, of Nekoda, 51 of Gazzam, of Uzza, of Paseah, 52 of Besai, of Meunim, of Nephushesim, 53 of Bakbuk, of Hakupha, of Harhur, 54 of Bazlith, of Mehida, of Harsha, 55 of Barkos, of Sisera, of Temah, 56 of Neziah, of Hatipha.

57 The descendants of Solomon's servants: of Sotai, of Sophereth, of Perida, 58 of Jaala, of Darkon, of Giddel, 59 of Shephatiah, of Hattil, of Pochereth-hazzebaim, of Amon.

60 All the temple servants and the descendants of Solomon's servants were three hundred and ninety-two.

61 The following were those who came up from Tel-melah, Tel-harsha, Cherub, Addon, and Immer, but they could not prove their ancestral houses or their descent, whether they belonged to Israel: 62 the descendants of Delaiah, of Tobiah, of Nekoda, six hundred and forty-two. 63 Also, of the priests: the descendants of Hobaiah, of Hakkoz, of Barzillai (who had married one of the daughters of Barzillai the Gileadite and was called by their name). 64 These sought their registration among those enrolled in the genealogies, but it was not found there, so they were excluded from the priesthood as unclean; 65 the governor told them that they were not to partake of the most holy food, until a priest with Urim and Thummim should come.

66 The whole assembly together was forty-two thousand three hundred and sixty, 67 besides their male and female slaves, of whom there were seven thousand three hundred and thirty-seven; and they had two hundred and forty-five singers, male and female. 68 They had seven hundred and thirty-six horses, two hundred and forty-five mules, *a* 69 four hundred and thirty-five camels, and six thousand seven hundred and twenty donkeys.

70 Now some of the heads of ancestral houses contributed to the work. The governor gave to the treasury one thousand darics of gold, fifty basins, and five hundred and thirty priestly robes. 71 And some of the heads of ancestral houses gave into the building fund twenty thousand darics of gold and two thousand two hundred minas of silver. 72 And what the rest of the people gave was twenty thousand darics of gold, two thousand minas of silver, and sixty-seven priestly robes.

73 So the priests, the Levites, the gatekeepers, the singers, some of the people, the temple servants, and all Israel settled in their towns.

Ezra Summons the People to Obey the Law

When the seventh month came—the people of Israel being settled in their towns— 8 1 all the people gathered together into the square before the Water Gate. They told the scribe Ezra to bring the book of the law of Moses, which the LORD had given to Israel. 2 Accordingly, the priest Ezra brought the law before the assembly, both men and women and all who could hear with understanding. This was on the first day of the seventh month. 3 He read from it facing the square before the Water Gate from early morning until midday, in the presence of the men and the women and those who could understand; and the ears of all the people were attentive to the book of the law. 4 The scribe Ezra stood on a wooden platform that had been made for the purpose; and beside him stood Mattithiah, Shema, Anaiah, Uriah, Hilkiah, and Maaseiah on his right hand; and Pedaiah, Mishael, Malchijah, Hashum, Hash-baddanah, Zechariah, and Meshullam on his left hand. 5 And Ezra opened the book in the sight of all the people, for he was standing above all the people; and when he opened it, all the people stood

---

a Ezra 2.66 and the margins of some Hebrew Mss: MT lacks *They had . . . forty-five mules* up. [6]Then Ezra blessed the LORD, the great God, and all the people answered, 'Amen, Amen', lifting up their hands. Then they bowed their heads and worshipped the LORD with their faces to the ground. [7]Also Jeshua, Bani, Sherebiah, Jamin, Akkub, Shabbethai, Hodiah, Maaseiah, Kelita, Azariah, Jozabad, Hanan, Pelaiah, the Levites,[a] helped the people to understand the law, while the people remained in their places. [8]So they read from the book, from the law of God, with interpretation. They gave the sense, so that the people understood the reading.

9 And Nehemiah, who was the governor, and Ezra the priest and scribe, and the Levites who taught the people said to all the people, 'This day is holy to the LORD your God; do not mourn or weep.' For all the people wept when they heard the words of the law. [10]Then he said to them, 'Go your way, eat the fat and drink sweet wine and send portions of them to those for whom nothing is prepared, for this day is holy to our LORD; and do not be grieved, for the joy of the LORD is your strength.' [11]So the Levites stilled all the people, saying, 'Be quiet, for this day is holy; do not be grieved.' [12]And all the people went their way to eat and drink and to send portions and to make great rejoicing, because they had understood the words that were declared to them.

The Festival of Booths Celebrated

13 On the second day the heads of ancestral houses of all the people, with the priests and the Levites, came together to the scribe Ezra in order to study the words of the law. [14]And they found it written in the law, which the LORD had commanded by Moses, that the people of Israel should live in booths[b] during the festival of the seventh month, [15]and that they should publish and proclaim in all their towns and in Jerusalem as follows, 'Go out to the hills and bring branches of olive, wild olive, myrtle, palm, and other leafy trees to make booths,[b] as it is written.' [16]So the people went out and brought them, and made booths[b] for themselves, each on the

roofs of their houses, and in their courts and in the courts of the house of God, and in the square at the Water Gate and in the square at the Gate of Ephraim. [17]And all the assembly of those who had returned from the captivity made booths[b] and lived in them; for from the days of Jeshua son of Nun to that day the people of Israel had not done so. And there was very great rejoicing. [18]And day by day, from the first day to the last day, he read from the book of the law of God. They kept the festival for seven days; and on the eighth day there was a solemn assembly, according to the ordinance.

National Confession

9 Now on the twenty-fourth day of this month the people of Israel were assembled with fasting and in sackcloth, and with dust on their heads.[c] [2]Then those of Israelite descent separated themselves from all foreigners, and stood and confessed their sins and the iniquities of their ancestors. [3]They stood up in their place and read from the book of the law of the LORD their God for a fourth part of the day, and for another fourth they made confession and worshipped the LORD their God. [4]Then Jeshua, Bani, Kadmiel, Shebaniah, Bunni, Sherebiah, Bani, and Chenani stood on the stairs of the Levites and cried out with a loud voice to the LORD their God. [5]Then the Levites, Jeshua, Kadmiel, Bani, Hashabneiah, Sherebiah, Hodiah, Shebaniah, and Pethahiah, said, 'Stand up and bless the LORD your God from everlasting to everlasting. Blessed be your glorious name, which is exalted above all blessing and praise.'

6 And Ezra said:[d] 'You are the LORD, you alone; you have made heaven, the heaven of heavens, with all their host, the earth and all that is on it, the seas and all that is in them. To all of them you give life, and the host of heaven worships you. [7]You are the LORD, the God who chose Abram and brought him out of Ur of the Chaldeans

---

a 1 Esdras 9.48 Vg: Heb *and the Levites*
b Or *tabernacles*; Heb *succoth*   c Heb *on them*
d Gk: Heb lacks *And Ezra said*

and gave him the name Abraham; 8 and you found his heart faithful before you, and made with him a covenant to give to his descendants the land of the Canaanite, the Hittite, the Amorite, the Perizzite, the Jebusite, and the Girgashite; and you have fulfilled your promise, for you are righteous.

9 'And you saw the distress of our ancestors in Egypt and heard their cry at the Red Sea.ᵃ 10 You performed signs and wonders against Pharaoh and all his servants and all the people of his land, for you knew that they acted insolently against our ancestors. You made a name for yourself, which remains to this day. 11 And you divided the sea before them, so that they passed through the sea on dry land, but you threw their pursuers into the depths, like a stone into mighty waters. 12 Moreover, you led them by day with a pillar of cloud, and by night with a pillar of fire, to give them light on the way in which they should go. 13 You came down also upon Mount Sinai, and spoke with them from heaven, and gave them right ordinances and true laws, good statutes and commandments, 14 and you made known your holy sabbath to them and gave them commandments and statutes and a law through your servant Moses. 15 For their hunger you gave them bread from heaven, and for their thirst you brought water for them out of the rock, and you told them to go in to possess the land that you swore to give them.

16 'But they and our ancestors acted presumptuously and stiffened their necks and did not obey your commandments; 17 they refused to obey, and were not mindful of the wonders that you performed among them; but they stiffened their necks and determined to return to their slavery in Egypt. But you are a God ready to forgive, gracious and merciful, slow to anger and abounding in steadfast love, and you did not forsake them. 18 Even when they had cast an image of a calf for themselves and said, "This is your God who brought you up out of Egypt", and had committed great blasphemies, 19 you in your great mercies did not forsake them in the wilderness; the pillar of cloud that led them in the way did not leave them by day, nor the pillar of fire by night that gave them light on the way by which they should go. 20 You gave your good spirit to instruct them, and did not withhold your manna from their mouths, and gave them water for their thirst. 21 For forty years you sustained them in the wilderness so that they lacked nothing; their clothes did not wear out and their feet did not swell. 22 And you gave them kingdoms and peoples, and allotted to them every corner,ᵇ so they took possession of the land of King Sihon of Heshbon and the land of King Og of Bashan. 23 You multiplied their descendants like the stars of heaven, and brought them into the land that you had told their ancestors to enter and possess. 24 So the descendants went in and possessed the land, and you subdued before them the inhabitants of the land, the Canaanites, and gave them into their hands, with their kings and the peoples of the land, to do with them as they pleased. 25 And they captured fortress cities and a rich land, and took possession of houses filled with all sorts of goods, hewn cisterns, vineyards, olive orchards, and fruit trees in abundance; so they ate, and were filled and became fat, and delighted in your great goodness.

26 'Nevertheless they were disobedient and rebelled against you and cast your law behind their backs and killed your prophets, who had warned them in order to turn them back to you, and they committed great blasphemies. 27 Therefore you gave them into the hands of their enemies, who made them suffer. Then in the time of their suffering they cried out to you and you heard them from heaven, and according to your great mercies you gave them saviours who saved them from the hands of their enemies. 28 But after they had rest, they again did evil before you, and you abandoned them to the hands of their enemies, so that they had dominion over them; yet when they turned and cried to you, you heard from heaven, and many times you rescued

a Or *Sea of Reeds*   b Meaning of Heb uncertain

them according to your mercies. 29 And you warned them in order to turn them back to your law. Yet they acted presumptuously and did not obey your commandments, but sinned against your ordinances, by the observance of which a person shall live. They turned a stubborn shoulder and stiffened their neck and would not obey. 30 For many years you were patient with them, and warned them by your spirit through your prophets; yet they would not listen. Therefore you handed them over to the peoples of the lands. 31 Nevertheless, in your great mercies you did not make an end of them or forsake them, for you are a gracious and merciful God.

32 'Now therefore, our God—the great and mighty and awesome God, keeping covenant and steadfast love—do not treat lightly all the hardship that has come upon us, upon our kings, our officials, our priests, our prophets, our ancestors, and all your people, since the time of the kings of Assyria until today. 33 You have been just in all that has come upon us, for you have dealt faithfully and we have acted wickedly; 34 our kings, our officials, our priests, and our ancestors have not kept your law or heeded the commandments and the warnings that you gave them. 35 Even in their own kingdom, and in the great goodness you bestowed on them, and in the large and rich land that you set before them, they did not serve you and did not turn from their wicked works. 36 Here we are, slaves to this day—slaves in the land that you gave to our ancestors to enjoy its fruit and its good gifts. 37 Its rich yield goes to the kings whom you have set over us because of our sins; they have power also over our bodies and over our livestock at their pleasure, and we are in great distress.'

Those Who Signed the Covenant

38 *a* Because of all this we make a firm agreement in writing, and on that sealed document are inscribed the names of our officials, our Levites, and our priests.

10 *b* Upon the sealed document are the names of Nehemiah the governor, son of Hacaliah, and Zedekiah; 2 Seraiah,

Azariah, Jeremiah, 3 Pashhur, Amariah, Malchijah, 4 Hattush, Shebaniah, Malluch, 5 Harim, Meremoth, Obadiah, 6 Daniel, Ginnethon, Baruch, 7 Meshullam, Abijah, Mijamin, 8 Maaziah, Bilgai, Shemaiah; these are the priests. 9 And the Levites: Jeshua son of Azaniah, Binnui of the sons of Henadad, Kadmiel; 10 and their associates, Shebaniah, Hodiah, Kelita, Pelaiah, Hanan, 11 Mica, Rehob, Hashabiah, 12 Zaccur, Sherebiah, Shebaniah, 13 Hodiah, Bani, Beninu. 14 The leaders of the people: Parosh, Pahath-moab, Elam, Zattu, Bani, 15 Bunni, Azgad, Bebai, 16 Adonijah, Bigvai, Adin, 17 Ater, Hezekiah, Azzur, 18 Hodiah, Hashum, Bezai, 19 Hariph, Anathoth, Nebai, 20 Magpiash, Meshullam, Hezir, 21 Meshezabel, Zadok, Jaddua, 22 Pelatiah, Hanan, Anaiah, 23 Hoshea, Hananiah, Hasshub, 24 Hallohesh, Pilha, Shobek, 25 Rehum, Hashabnah, Maaseiah, 26 Ahiah, Hanan, Anan, 27 Malluch, Harim, and Baanah.

Summary of the Covenant

28 The rest of the people, the priests, the Levites, the gatekeepers, the singers, the temple servants, and all who have separated themselves from the peoples of the lands to adhere to the law of God, their wives, their sons, their daughters, all who have knowledge and understanding, 29 join with their kin, their nobles, and enter into a curse and an oath to walk in God's law, which was given by Moses the servant of God, and to observe and do all the commandments of the LORD our Lord and his ordinances and his statutes. 30 We will not give our daughters to the peoples of the land or take their daughters for our sons; 31 and if the peoples of the land bring in merchandise or any grain on the sabbath day to sell, we will not buy it from them on the sabbath or on a holy day; and we will forego the crops of the seventh year and the exaction of every debt.

32 We also lay on ourselves the obligation to charge ourselves yearly one-third of a shekel for the service of the house of our God: 33 for the rows of bread, the regular grain-offering, the regular burnt-offering,

a Ch 10.1 in Heb   *b Ch 10.2 in Heb*

the sabbaths, the new moons, the appointed festivals, the sacred donations, and the sin-offerings to make atonement for Israel, and for all the work of the house of our God. 34 We have also cast lots among the priests, the Levites, and the people, for the wood-offering, to bring it into the house of our God, by ancestral houses, at appointed times, year by year, to burn on the altar of the LORD our God, as it is written in the law. 35 We obligate ourselves to bring the first fruits of our soil and the first fruits of all fruit of every tree, year by year, to the house of the LORD; 36 also to bring to the house of our God, to the priests who minister in the house of our God, the firstborn of our sons and of our livestock, as it is written in the law, and the firstlings of our herds and of our flocks; 37 and to bring the first of our dough, and our contributions, the fruit of every tree, the wine and the oil, to the priests, to the chambers of the house of our God; and to bring to the Levites the tithes from our soil, for it is the Levites who collect the tithes in all our rural towns. 38 And the priest, the descendant of Aaron, shall be with the Levites when the Levites receive the tithes; and the Levites shall bring up a tithe of the tithes to the house of our God, to the chambers of the storehouse. 39 For the people of Israel and the sons of Levi shall bring the contribution of grain, wine, and oil to the storerooms where the vessels of the sanctuary are, and where the priests that minister, and the gatekeepers and the singers are. We will not neglect the house of our God.

Population of the City Increased

11 Now the leaders of the people lived in Jerusalem; and the rest of the people cast lots to bring one out of ten to live in the holy city Jerusalem, while nine-tenths remained in the other towns. 2 And the people blessed all those who willingly offered to live in Jerusalem.

3 These are the leaders of the province who lived in Jerusalem; but in the towns of Judah all lived on their property in their towns: Israel, the priests, the Levites, the temple servants, and the descendants of Solomon's servants. 4 And in Jerusalem lived some of the Judahites and of the Benjaminites. Of the Judahites: Athaiah son of Uzziah son of Zechariah son of Amariah son of Shephatiah son of Mahalalel, of the descendants of Perez; 5 and Maaseiah son of Baruch son of Col-hozeh son of Hazaiah son of Adaiah son of Joiarib son of Zechariah son of the Shilonite. 6 All the descendants of Perez who lived in Jerusalem were four hundred and sixty-eight valiant warriors.

7 And these are the Benjaminites: Sallu son of Meshullam son of Joed son of Pedaiah son of Kolaiah son of Maaseiah son of Ithiel son of Jeshaiah. 8 And his brothers *a* Gabbai, Sallai: nine hundred and twenty-eight. 9 Joel son of Zichri was their overseer; and Judah son of Hassenuah was second in charge of the city.

10 Of the priests: Jedaiah son of Joiarib, Jachin, 11 Seraiah son of Hilkiah son of Meshullam son of Zadok son of Meraioth son of Ahitub, officer of the house of God, 12 and their associates who did the work of the house, eight hundred and twenty-two; and Adaiah son of Jeroham son of Pelaliah son of Amzi son of Zechariah son of Pashhur son of Malchijah, 13 and his associates, heads of ancestral houses, two hundred and forty-two; and Amashsai son of Azarel son of Ahzai son of Meshillemoth son of Immer, 14 and their associates, valiant warriors, one hundred and twenty-eight; their overseer was Zabdiel son of Haggedolim.

15 And of the Levites: Shemaiah son of Hasshub son of Azrikam son of Hashabiah son of Bunni; 16 and Shabbethai and Jozabad, of the leaders of the Levites, who were over the outside work of the house of God; 17 and Mattaniah son of Mica son of Zabdi son of Asaph, who was the leader to begin the thanksgiving in prayer, and Bakbukiah, the second among his associates; and Abda son of Shammua son of Galal son of Jeduthun. 18 All the Levites in the holy city were two hundred and eighty-four.

19 The gatekeepers, Akkub, Talmon and their associates, who kept watch at the gates, were one hundred and seventy-two.

a Gk Mss: Heb *And after him*

20 And the rest of Israel, and of the priests and the Levites, were in all the towns of Judah, all of them in their inheritance. 21 But the temple servants lived on Ophel; and Ziha and Gishpa were over the temple servants.

22 The overseer of the Levites in Jerusalem was Uzzi son of Bani son of Hashabiah son of Mattaniah son of Mica, of the descendants of Asaph, the singers, in charge of the work of the house of God. 23 For there was a command from the king concerning them, and a settled provision for the singers, as was required every day. 24 And Pethahiah son of Meshezabel, of the descendants of Zerah son of Judah, was at the king's hand in all matters concerning the people.

Villages outside Jerusalem

25 And as for the villages, with their fields, some of the people of Judah lived in Kiriath-arba and its villages, and in Dibon and its villages, and in Jekabzeel and its villages, 26 and in Jeshua and in Moladah and Beth-pelet, 27 in Hazar-shual, in Beersheba and its villages, 28 in Ziklag, in Meconah and its villages, 29 in En-rimmon, in Zorah, in Jarmuth, 30 Zanoah, Adullam, and their villages, Lachish and its fields, and Azekah and its villages. So they camped from Beer-sheba to the valley of Hinnom. 31 The people of Benjamin also lived from Geba onwards, at Michmash, Aija, Bethel and its villages, 32 Anathoth, Nob, Ananiah, 33 Hazor, Ramah, Gittaim, 34 Hadid, Zeboim, Neballat, 35 Lod, and Ono, the valley of artisans. 36 And certain divisions of the Levites in Judah were joined to Benjamin.

A List of Priests and Levites

12 These are the priests and the Levites who came up with Zerubbabel son of Shealtiel, and Jeshua: Seraiah, Jeremiah, Ezra, 2 Amariah, Malluch, Hattush, 3 Shecaniah, Rehum, Meremoth, 4 Iddo, Ginnethoi, Abijah, 5 Mijamin, Maadiah, Bilgah, 6 Shemaiah, Joiarib, Jedaiah, 7 Sallu, Amok, Hilkiah, Jedaiah. These were the leaders of the priests and of their associates in the days of Jeshua.

8 And the Levites: Jeshua, Binnui, Kadmiel, Sherebiah, Judah, and Mattaniah, who with his associates was in charge of the songs of thanksgiving. 9 And Bakbukiah and Unno their associates stood opposite them in the service. 10 Jeshua was the father of Joiakim, Joiakim the father of Eliashib, Eliashib the father of Joiada, 11 Joiada the father of Jonathan, and Jonathan the father of Jaddua.

12 In the days of Joiakim the priests, heads of ancestral houses, were: of Seraiah, Meraiah; of Jeremiah, Hananiah; 13 of Ezra, Meshullam; of Amariah, Jehohanan; 14 of Malluchi, Jonathan; of Shebaniah, Joseph; 15 of Harim, Adna; of Meraioth, Helkai; 16 of Iddo, Zechariah; of Ginnethon, Meshullam; 17 of Abijah, Zichri; of Miniamin, of Moadiah, Piltai; 18 of Bilgah, Shammua; of Shemaiah, Jehonathan; 19 of Joiarib, Mattenai; of Jedaiah, Uzzi; 20 of Sallai, Kallai; of Amok, Eber; 21 of Hilkiah, Hashabiah; of Jedaiah, Nethanel.

22 As for the Levites, in the days of Eliashib, Joiada, Johanan, and Jaddua, there were recorded the heads of ancestral houses; also the priests until the reign of Darius the Persian. 23 The Levites, heads of ancestral houses, were recorded in the Book of the Annals until the days of Johanan son of Eliashib. 24 And the leaders of the Levites: Hashabiah, Sherebiah, and Jeshua son of Kadmiel, with their associates over against them, to praise and to give thanks, according to the commandment of David the man of God, section opposite to section. 25 Mattaniah, Bakbukiah, Obadiah, Meshullam, Talmon, and Akkub were gatekeepers standing guard at the storehouses of the gates. 26 These were in the days of Joiakim son of Jeshua son of Jozadak, and in the days of the governor Nehemiah and of the priest Ezra, the scribe.

Dedication of the City Wall

27 Now at the dedication of the wall of Jerusalem they sought out the Levites in all their places, to bring them to Jerusalem to

celebrate the dedication with rejoicing, with thanksgivings and with singing, with cymbals, harps, and lyres. 28 The companies of the singers gathered together from the circuit around Jerusalem and from the villages of the Netophathites; 29 also from Beth-gilgal and from the region of Geba and Azmaveth; for the singers had built for themselves villages around Jerusalem. 30 And the priests and the Levites purified themselves; and they purified the people and the gates and the wall.

31 Then I brought the leaders of Judah up on to the wall, and appointed two great companies that gave thanks and went in procession. One went to the right on the wall to the Dung Gate; 32 and after them went Hoshaiah and half the officials of Judah, 33 and Azariah, Ezra, Meshullam, 34 Judah, Benjamin, Shemaiah, and Jeremiah, 35 and some of the young priests with trumpets: Zechariah son of Jonathan son of Shemaiah son of Mattaniah son of Micaiah son of Zaccur son of Asaph; 36 and his kindred, Shemaiah, Azarel, Milalai, Gilalai, Maai, Nethanel, Judah, and Hanani, with the musical instruments of David the man of God; and the scribe Ezra went in front of them. 37 At the Fountain Gate, in front of them, they went straight up by the stairs of the city of David, at the ascent of the wall, above the house of David, to the Water Gate on the east.

38 The other company of those who gave thanks went to the left,[a] and I followed them with half of the people on the wall, above the Tower of the Ovens, to the Broad Wall, 39 and above the Gate of Ephraim, and by the Old Gate, and by the Fish Gate and the Tower of Hananel and the Tower of the Hundred, to the Sheep Gate; and they came to a halt at the Gate of the Guard. 40 So both companies of those who gave thanks stood in the house of God, and I and half of the officials with me; 41 and the priests Eliakim, Maaseiah, Miniamin, Micaiah, Elioenai, Zechariah, and Hananiah, with trumpets; 42 and Maaseiah, Shemaiah, Eleazar, Uzzi, Jehohanan, Malchijah, Elam, and Ezer. And the singers sang with Jezrahiah as their leader. 43 They

offered great sacrifices that day and rejoiced, for God had made them rejoice with great joy; the women and children also rejoiced. The joy of Jerusalem was heard far away.

Temple Responsibilities

44 On that day men were appointed over the chambers for the stores, the contributions, the first fruits, and the tithes, to gather into them the portions required by the law for the priests and for the Levites from the fields belonging to the towns; for Judah rejoiced over the priests and the Levites who ministered. 45 They performed the service of their God and the service of purification, as did the singers and the gatekeepers, according to the command of David and his son Solomon. 46 For in the days of David and Asaph long ago there was a leader of the singers, and there were songs of praise and thanksgiving to God. 47 In the days of Zerubbabel and in the days of Nehemiah all Israel gave the daily portions for the singers and the gatekeepers. They set apart that which was for the Levites; and the Levites set apart that which was for the descendants of Aaron.

Foreigners Separated from Israel

13 On that day they read from the book of Moses in the hearing of the people; and in it was found written that no Ammonite or Moabite should ever enter the assembly of God, 2 because they did not meet the Israelites with bread and water, but hired Balaam against them to curse them—yet our God turned the curse into a blessing. 3 When the people heard the law, they separated from Israel all those of foreign descent.

The Reforms of Nehemiah

4 Now before this, the priest Eliashib, who was appointed over the chambers of the house of our God, and who was related to Tobiah, 5 prepared for Tobiah a large room where they had previously put the grain-offering, the frankincense, the vessels, and the tithes of grain, wine, and oil,

a Cn: Heb opposite

which were given by commandment to the Levites, singers, and gatekeepers, and the contributions for the priests. 6 While this was taking place I was not in Jerusalem, for in the thirty-second year of King Artaxerxes of Babylon I went to the king. After some time I asked leave of the king 7 and returned to Jerusalem. I then discovered the wrong that Eliashib had done on behalf of Tobiah, preparing a room for him in the courts of the house of God. 8 And I was very angry, and I threw all the household furniture of Tobiah out of the room. 9 Then I gave orders and they cleansed the chambers, and I brought back the vessels of the house of God, with the grain-offering and the frankincense.

10 I also found out that the portions of the Levites had not been given to them; so that the Levites and the singers, who had conducted the service, had gone back to their fields. 11 So I remonstrated with the officials and said, 'Why is the house of God forsaken?' And I gathered them together and set them in their stations. 12 Then all Judah brought the tithe of the grain, wine, and oil into the storehouses. 13 And I appointed as treasurers over the storehouses the priest Shelemiah, the scribe Zadok, and Pedaiah of the Levites, and as their assistant Hanan son of Zaccur son of Mattaniah, for they were considered faithful; and their duty was to distribute to their associates. 14 Remember me, O my God, concerning this, and do not wipe out my good deeds that I have done for the house of my God and for his service.

Sabbath Reforms Begun

15 In those days I saw in Judah people treading wine presses on the sabbath, and bringing in heaps of grain and loading them on donkeys; and also wine, grapes, figs, and all kinds of burdens, which they brought into Jerusalem on the sabbath day; and I warned them at that time against selling food. 16 Tyrians also, who lived in the city, brought in fish and all kinds of merchandise and sold them on the sabbath to the people of Judah, and in Jerusalem. 17 Then I remonstrated with the nobles of Judah and said to them, 'What is this evil thing that you are doing, profaning the sabbath day? 18 Did not your ancestors act in this way, and did not our God bring all this disaster on us and on this city? Yet you bring more wrath on Israel by profaning the sabbath.'

19 When it began to be dark at the gates of Jerusalem before the sabbath, I commanded that the doors should be shut and gave orders that they should not be opened until after the sabbath. And I set some of my servants over the gates, to prevent any burden from being brought in on the sabbath day. 20 Then the merchants and sellers of all kinds of merchandise spent the night outside Jerusalem once or twice. 21 But I warned them and said to them, 'Why do you spend the night in front of the wall? If you do so again, I will lay hands on you.' From that time on they did not come on the sabbath. 22 And I commanded the Levites that they should purify themselves and come and guard the gates, to keep the sabbath day holy. Remember this also in my favour, O my God, and spare me according to the greatness of your steadfast love.

Mixed Marriages Condemned

23 In those days also I saw Jews who had married women of Ashdod, Ammon, and Moab; 24 and half of their children spoke the language of Ashdod, and they could not speak the language of Judah, but spoke the language of various peoples. 25 And I contended with them and cursed them and beat some of them and pulled out their hair; and I made them take an oath in the name of God, saying, 'You shall not give your daughters to their sons, or take their daughters for your sons or for yourselves. 26 Did not King Solomon of Israel sin on account of such women? Among the many nations there was no king like him, and he was beloved by his God, and God made him king over all Israel; nevertheless, foreign women made even him to sin. 27 Shall we then listen to you and do all this great evil and act treacherously against our God by marrying foreign women?'

28 And one of the sons of Jehoiada, son

of the high priest Eliashib, was the son-in-law of Sanballat the Horonite; I chased him away from me. ²⁹ Remember them, O my God, because they have defiled the priesthood, the covenant of the priests and the Levites.

30 Thus I cleansed them from everything foreign, and I established the duties of the priests and Levites, each in his work; ³¹ and I provided for the wood-offering, at appointed times, and for the first fruits. Remember me, O my God, for good.

TOBIT

1 This book tells the story of Tobit son of Tobiel son of Hananiel son of Aduel son of Gabael son of Raphael of the descendants[a] of Asiel, of the tribe of Naphtali, 2 who in the days of King Shalmaneser[b] of the Assyrians was taken into captivity from Thisbe, which is to the south of Kedesh Naphtali in Upper Galilee, above Asher towards the west, and north of Phogor.

Tobit's Youth and Virtuous Life

3 I, Tobit, walked in the ways of truth and righteousness all the days of my life. I performed many acts of charity for my kindred and my people who had gone with me in exile to Nineveh in the land of the Assyrians. 4 When I was in my own country, in the land of Israel, while I was still a young man, the whole tribe of my ancestor Naphtali deserted the house of David and Jerusalem. This city had been chosen from among all the tribes of Israel, where all the tribes of Israel should offer sacrifice and where the temple, the dwelling of God, had been consecrated and established for all generations for ever.

5 All my kindred and our ancestral house of Naphtali sacrificed to the calf[c] that King Jeroboam of Israel had erected in Dan and on all the mountains of Galilee. 6 But I alone went often to Jerusalem for the festivals, as it is prescribed for all Israel by an everlasting decree. I would hurry off to Jerusalem with the first fruits of the crops and the firstlings of the flock, the tithes of the cattle, and the first shearings of the sheep. 7 I would give these to the priests, the sons of Aaron, at the altar; likewise the tenth of the grain, wine, olive oil, pomegranates, figs, and the rest of the fruits to the sons of Levi who ministered at Jerusalem. Also, for six years I would save up a second tenth in money and go and distribute it in Jerusalem. 8 A third tenth[d] I would give to the orphans and widows and to the converts who had attached themselves to Israel. I would bring it and give it to them in the third year, and we would eat it according to the ordinance decreed concerning it in the law of Moses and according to the instructions of Deborah, the mother of my father Tobiel,[e] for my father had died and left me an orphan. 9 When I became a man I married a woman,[f] a member of our own family, and by her I became the father of a son whom I named Tobias.

Taken Captive to Nineveh

10 After I was carried away captive to Assyria and came as a captive to Nineveh, everyone of my kindred and my people ate the food of the Gentiles, 11 but I kept myself from eating the food of the Gentiles. 12 Because I was mindful of God with all my heart, 13 the Most High gave me favour and good standing with Shalmaneser,[b] and I used to buy everything he needed. 14 Until his death I used to go into Media, and buy for him there. While in the country of Media I left bags of silver worth ten talents in trust with Gabael, the brother of Gabri. 15 But when Shalmaneser[b] died, and his son Sennacherib reigned in his place, the

---

a Other ancient authorities lack *of Raphael son of Raguel of the descendants*   b Gk *Enemessaros*   c Other ancient authorities read *heifer*   d A third tenth added from other ancient authorities   e Lat: Gk *Hananiel*   f Other ancient authorities add *Anna* highways into Media became unsafe and I could no longer go there.

Courage in Burying the Dead

16 In the days of Shalmaneser[a] I performed many acts of charity to my kindred, those of my tribe. 17 I would give my food to the hungry and my clothing to the naked; and if I saw the dead body of any of my people thrown out behind the wall of Nineveh, I would bury it. 18 I also buried any whom King Sennacherib put to death when he came fleeing from Judea in those days of judgement that the king of heaven executed upon him because of his blasphemies. For in his anger he put to death many Israelites; but I would secretly remove the bodies and bury them. So when Sennacherib looked for them he could not find them. 19 Then one of the Ninevites went and informed the king about me, that I was burying them; so I hid myself. But when I realized that the king knew about me and that I was being searched for to be put to death, I was afraid and ran away. 20 Then all my property was confiscated; nothing was left to me that was not taken into the royal treasury, except my wife Anna and my son Tobias.

21 But not forty[b] days passed before two of Sennacherib's[c] sons killed him, and they fled to the mountains of Ararat, and his son Esar-haddon[d] reigned after him. He appointed Ahikar, the son of my brother Hanael[e] over all the accounts of his kingdom, and he had authority over the entire administration. 22 Ahikar interceded for me, and I returned to Nineveh. Now Ahikar was chief cupbearer, keeper of the signet, and in charge of administration of the accounts under King Sennacherib of Assyria; so Esar-haddon[d] reappointed him. He was my nephew and so a close relative.

2 Then during the reign of Esar-haddon[d] I returned home, and my wife Anna and my son Tobias were restored to me. At our festival of Pentecost, which is the sacred festival of weeks, a good dinner was prepared for me and I reclined to eat. 2 When the table was set for me and an abundance of food placed before me, I said to my son Tobias, 'Go, my child, and bring whatever poor person you may find of our people among the exiles in Nineveh, who is wholeheartedly mindful of God,[f] and he shall eat together with me. I will wait for you, until you come back.' 3 So Tobias went to look for some poor person of our people. When he had returned he said, 'Father!' And I replied, 'Here I am, my child.' Then he went on to say, 'Look, father, one of our own people has been murdered and thrown into the market-place, and now he lies there strangled.' 4 Then I sprang up, left the dinner before even tasting it, and removed the body[g] from the square[h] and laid it[g] in one of the rooms until sunset when I might bury it.[g] 5 When I returned, I washed myself and ate my food in sorrow. 6 Then I remembered the prophecy of Amos, how he said against Bethel,[i]

'Your festivals shall be turned into
    mourning,
and all your songs into
    lamentation.'
And I wept.

Tobit Becomes Blind

7 When the sun had set, I went and dug a grave and buried him. 8 And my neighbours laughed and said, 'Is he still not afraid? He has already been hunted down to be put to death for doing this, and he ran away; yet here he is again burying the dead!' 9 That same night I washed myself and went into my courtyard and slept by the wall of the courtyard; and my face was uncovered because of the heat. 10 I did not know that there were sparrows on the wall; their fresh droppings fell into my eyes and produced white films. I went to physicians to be healed, but the more they treated me with ointments the more my vision was obscured by the white films, until I became completely blind. For four years I remained unable to see. All my kindred were

a Gk Enemessaros   b Other ancient authorities read either forty-five or fifty   c Gk his   d Gk Sacherdonos   e Other authorities read Hananael   f Lat: Gk wholeheartedly mindful   g Gk him   h Other ancient authorities lack from the square   i Other ancient authorities read against Bethlehem sorry for me, and Ahikar took care of me for two years before he went to Elymais.

Tobit's Wife Earns Their Livelihood

11 At that time, also, my wife Anna earned money at women's work. 12 She used to send what she made to the owners and they would pay wages to her. One day, the seventh of Dystrus, when she cut off a piece she had woven and sent it to the owners, they paid her full wages and also gave her a kid for a meal. 13 When she returned to me, the kid began to bleat. So I called her and said, 'Where did you get this kid? It is surely not stolen, is it? Return it to the owners; for we have no right to eat anything stolen.' 14 But she said to me, 'It was given to me as a gift in addition to my wages.' But I did not believe her, and told her to return it to the owners. I became flushed with anger against her over this. Then she replied to me, 'Where are your acts of charity? Where are your righteous deeds? These things are known about you!'[a]

Tobit's Prayer

3 Then with much grief and anguish of heart I wept, and with groaning began to pray:
2 'You are righteous, O Lord,
   and all your deeds are just;
   all your ways are mercy and truth;
   you judge the world.[b]
3 And now, O Lord, remember me
   and look favourably upon me.
   Do not punish me for my sins
   and for my unwitting offences
   and those that my ancestors
      committed before you.
   They sinned against you,
4   and disobeyed your
      commandments.
   So you gave us over to plunder, exile,
      and death,
   to become the talk, the byword,
      and an object of reproach,
   among all the nations among
      whom you have dispersed us.
5 And now your many judgements are
   true

in exacting penalty from me for my
   sins.
For we have not kept your
   commandments
and have not walked in accordance
   with truth before you.
6 So now deal with me as you will;
   command my spirit to be taken
      from me,
   so that I may be released from the
      face of the earth and become
      dust.
For it is better for me to die than to
   live,
   because I have had to listen to
      undeserved insults,
   and great is the sorrow within me.
Command, O Lord, that I be released
   from this distress;
   release me to go to the eternal
      home,
   and do not, O Lord, turn your face
      away from me.
For it is better for me to die
   than to see so much distress in my
      life
   and to listen to insults.'

Sarah Falsely Accused

7 On the same day, at Ecbatana in Media, it also happened that Sarah, the daughter of Raguel, was reproached by one of her father's maids. 8 For she had been married to seven husbands, and the wicked demon Asmodeus had killed each of them before they had been with her as is customary for wives. So the maid said to her, 'You are the one who kills[c] your husbands! See, you have already been married to seven husbands and have not borne the name of[d] a single one of them. 9 Why do you beat us? Because your husbands are dead? Go with them! May we never see a son or daughter of yours!'

Sarah's Prayer for Death

10 On that day she was grieved in spirit and wept. When she had gone up to her

a Or to you; Gk with you   b Other ancient authorities
read you render true and righteous judgement for ever
c Other ancient authorities read strangles   d Other
ancient authorities read have had no benefit from

father's upper room, she intended to hang herself. But she thought it over and said, 'Never shall they reproach my father, saying to him, "You had only one beloved daughter but she hanged herself because of her distress." And I shall bring my father in his old age down in sorrow to Hades. It is better for me not to hang myself, but to pray the Lord that I may die and not listen to these reproaches any more.' [11] At that same time, with hands outstretched towards the window, she prayed and said,

'Blessed are you, merciful God!
Blessed is your name for ever;
let all your works praise you for ever.
[12] And now, Lord,[a] I turn my face to you,
and raise my eyes towards you.
[13] Command that I be released from the earth
and not listen to such reproaches any more.
[14] You know, O Master, that I am innocent
of any defilement with a man,
[15] and that I have not disgraced my name
or the name of my father in the land of my exile.
I am my father's only child;
he has no other child to be his heir;
and he has no close relative or other kindred
for whom I should keep myself as wife.
Already seven husbands of mine have died.
Why should I still live?
But if it is not pleasing to you,
O Lord, to take my life,
hear me in my disgrace.'

An Answer to Prayer

16 At that very moment, the prayers of both of them were heard in the glorious presence of God. [17] So Raphael was sent to heal both of them: Tobit, by removing the white films from his eyes, so that he might see God's light with his eyes; and Sarah daughter of Raguel, by giving her in marriage to Tobias son of Tobit, and by setting her free from the wicked demon Asmodeus. For Tobias was entitled to have her before all others who had desired to marry her. At the same time that Tobit returned from the courtyard into his house, Sarah daughter of Raguel came down from her upper room.

Tobit Gives Instructions to His Son

4 That same day Tobit remembered the money that he had left in trust with Gabael at Rages in Media, [2] and he said to himself, 'Now I have asked for death. Why do I not call my son Tobias and explain to him about the money before I die?' [3] Then he called his son Tobias, and when he came to him he said, 'My son, when I die,[b] give me a proper burial. Honour your mother and do not abandon her all the days of her life. Do whatever pleases her, and do not grieve her in anything. [4] Remember her, my son, because she faced many dangers for you while you were in her womb. And when she dies, bury her beside me in the same grave.

5 'Revere the Lord all your days, my son, and refuse to sin or to transgress his commandments. Live uprightly all the days of your life, and do not walk in the ways of wrongdoing; [6] for those who act in accordance with truth will prosper in all their activities. To all those who practise righteousness[c] [7] give alms from your possessions, and do not let your eye begrudge the gift when you make it. Do not turn your face away from anyone who is poor, and the face of God will not be turned away from you. [8] If you have many possessions, make your gift from them in proportion; if few, do not be afraid to give according to the little you have. [9] So you will be laying up a good treasure for yourself against the day of necessity. [10] For almsgiving delivers from death and keeps you from going into the Darkness. [11] Indeed, almsgiving, for all

---

a Other ancient authorities lack *Lord*   b Lat
c The text of codex Sinaiticus goes directly from verse 6 to verse 19, reading *To those who practise righteousness* [19]*the Lord will give good counsel.* In order to fill the lacuna, verses 7 to 18 are derived from other ancient authorities

who practise it, is an excellent offering in the presence of the Most High.

12 'Beware, my son, of every kind of fornication. First of all, marry a woman from among the descendants of your ancestors; do not marry a foreign woman, who is not of your father's tribe; for we are the descendants of the prophets. Remember, my son, that Noah, Abraham, Isaac, and Jacob, our ancestors of old, all took wives from among their kindred. They were blessed in their children, and their posterity will inherit the land. 13 So now, my son, love your kindred, and in your heart do not disdain your kindred, the sons and daughters of your people, by refusing to take a wife for yourself from among them. For in pride there is ruin and great confusion. And in idleness there is loss and dire poverty, because idleness is the mother of famine.

14 'Do not keep over until the next day the wages of those who work for you, but pay them at once. If you serve God you will receive payment. Watch yourself, my son, in everything you do, and discipline yourself in all your conduct. 15 And what you hate, do not do to anyone. Do not drink wine to excess or let drunkenness go with you on your way. 16 Give some of your food to the hungry, and some of your clothing to the naked. Give all your surplus as alms, and do not let your eye begrudge your giving of alms. 17 Place your bread on the grave of the righteous, but give none to sinners. 18 Seek advice from every wise person and do not despise any useful counsel. 19 At all times bless the Lord God, and ask him that your ways may be made straight and that all your paths and plans may prosper. For none of the nations has understanding, but the Lord himself will give them good counsel; but if he chooses otherwise, he casts down to deepest Hades. So now, my child, remember these commandments, and do not let them be erased from your heart.

Money Left in Trust with Gabael

20 'And now, my son, let me explain to you that I left ten talents of silver in trust with Gabael son of Gabrias, at Rages in Media. 21 Do not be afraid, my son, because we have become poor. You have great wealth if you fear God and flee from every sin and do what is good in the sight of the Lord your God.'

The Angel Raphael

5 Then Tobias answered his father Tobit, 'I will do everything that you have commanded me, father; 2 but how can I obtain the money[a] from him, since he does not know me and I do not know him? What evidence[b] am I to give him so that he will recognize and trust me, and give me the money? Also, I do not know the roads to Media, or how to get there.' 3 Then Tobit answered his son Tobias, 'He gave me his bond and I gave him my bond. I[c] divided his in two; we each took one part, and I put one with the money. And now twenty years have passed since I left this money in trust. So now, my son, find yourself a trustworthy man to go with you, and we will pay him wages until you return. But get back the money from Gabael.'[d]

4 So Tobias went out to look for a man to go with him to Media, someone who was acquainted with the way. He went out and found the angel Raphael standing in front of him; but he did not perceive that he was an angel of God. 5 Tobias[e] said to him, 'Where do you come from, young man?' 'From your kindred, the Israelites,' he replied, 'and I have come here to work.' Then Tobias[f] said to him, 'Do you know the way to go to Media?' 6 'Yes,' he replied, 'I have been there many times; I am acquainted with it and know all the roads. I have often travelled to Media, and stayed with our kinsman Gabael who lives in Rages of Media. It is a journey of two days from Ecbatana to Rages; for it lies in a mountainous area, while Ecbatana is in the middle of the plain.' 7 Then Tobias said to him, 'Wait for me, young man, until I go in and tell my father; for I do need you to travel with me, and I will pay you your wages.' 8 He replied, 'All right, I will wait; but do not take too long.'

---

a Gk *it*   *b* Gk *sign*   *c* Other authorities read *He*
d Gk *from him*   *e* Gk *He*   *f* Gk *he*

9 So Tobias[a] went in to tell his father Tobit and said to him, 'I have just found a man who is one of our own Israelite kindred!' He replied, 'Call the man in, my son, so that I may learn about his family and to what tribe he belongs, and whether he is trustworthy enough to go with you.' 10 Then Tobias went out and called him, and said, 'Young man, my father is calling for you.' So he went in to him, and Tobit greeted him first. He replied, 'Joyous greetings to you!' But Tobit retorted, 'What joy is left for me any more? I am a man without eyesight; I cannot see the light of heaven, but I lie in darkness like the dead who no longer see the light. Although still alive, I am among the dead. I hear people but I cannot see them.' But the young man[a] said, 'Take courage; the time is near for God to heal you; take courage.' Then Tobit said to him, 'My son Tobias wishes to go to Media. Can you accompany him and guide him? I will pay your wages, brother.' He answered, 'I can go with him and I know all the roads, for I have often gone to Media and have crossed all its plains, and I am familiar with its mountains and all of its roads.'

11 Then Tobit[a] said to him, 'Brother, of what family are you and from what tribe? Tell me, brother.' 12 He replied, 'Why do you need to know my tribe?' But Tobit[a] said, 'I want to be sure, brother, whose son you are and what your name is.' 13 He replied, 'I am Azariah, the son of the great Hananiah, one of your relatives.' 14 Then Tobit said to him, 'Welcome! God save you, brother. Do not feel bitter towards me, brother, because I wanted to be sure about your ancestry. It turns out that you are a kinsman, and of good and noble lineage. For I knew Hananiah and Nathan,[b] the two sons of Shemeliah,[c] and they used to go with me to Jerusalem and worshipped with me there, and were not led astray. Your kindred are good people; you come of good stock. Hearty welcome!'

15 Then he added, 'I will pay you a drachma a day as wages, as well as expenses for yourself and my son. So go with my son, 16 and[d] I will add something to your wages.' Raphael[e] answered, 'I will go with him; so do not fear. We shall leave in good health and return to you in good health, because the way is safe.' 17 So Tobit[a] said to him, 'Blessings be upon you, brother.'

Then he called his son and said to him, 'Son, prepare supplies for the journey and set out with your brother. May God in heaven bring you safely there and return you in good health to me; and may his angel, my son, accompany you both for your safety.'

Before he went out to start his journey, he kissed his father and mother. Tobit then said to him, 'Have a safe journey.'

18 But his mother[f] began to weep, and said to Tobit, 'Why is it that you have sent my child away? Is he not the staff of our hand as he goes in and out before us? 19 Do not heap money upon money, but let it be a ransom for our child. 20 For the life that is given to us by the Lord is enough for us.' 21 Tobit[e] said to her, 'Do not worry; our child will leave in good health and return to us in good health. Your eyes will see him on the day when he returns to you in good health. Say no more! Do not fear for them, my sister. 22 For a good angel will accompany him; his journey will be successful, and he will come back in good health.'

6 ¹ So she stopped weeping.

Journey to Rages

The young man went out and the angel went with him; ² and the dog came out with him and went along with them. So they both journeyed along, and when the first night overtook them they camped by the Tigris river. ³ Then the young man went down to wash his feet in the Tigris river. Suddenly a large fish leapt up from the water and tried to swallow the young man's foot, and he cried out. ⁴ But the angel said to the young man, 'Catch hold of the fish and hang on to it!' So the young man grasped the fish and drew it up on the

a Gk *he*   b Other ancient authorities read *Jathan* or *Nathaniah*   c Other ancient authorities read *Shemaiah*
d Other ancient authorities add *when you return safely*
e Gk *He*   f Other ancient authorities add *Anna*

land. 5 Then the angel said to him, 'Cut open the fish and take out its gall, heart, and liver. Keep them with you, but throw away the intestines. For its gall, heart, and liver are useful as medicine.' 6 So after cutting open the fish the young man gathered together the gall, heart, and liver; then he roasted and ate some of the fish, and kept some to be salted.

The two continued on their way together until they were near Media.*a* 7 Then the young man questioned the angel and said to him, 'Brother Azariah, what medicinal value is there in the fish's heart and liver, and in the gall?' 8 He replied, 'As for the fish's heart and liver, you must burn them to make a smoke in the presence of a man or woman afflicted by a demon or evil spirit, and every affliction will flee away and never remain with that person any longer. 9 And as for the gall, anoint a person's eyes where white films have appeared on them; blow upon them, upon the white films, and the eyes*b* will be healed.'

Raphael's Instructions

10 When he entered Media and already was approaching Ecbatana,*c* 11 Raphael said to the young man, 'Brother Tobias.' 'Here I am,' he answered. Then Raphael*d* said to him, 'We must stay this night in the home of Raguel. He is your relative, and he has a daughter named Sarah. 12 He has no male heir and no daughter except Sarah only, and you, as next of kin to her, have before all other men a hereditary claim on her. Also it is right for you to inherit her father's possessions. Moreover, the girl is sensible, brave, and very beautiful, and her father is a good man.' 13 He continued, 'You have every right to take her in marriage. So listen to me, brother; tonight I will speak to her father about the girl, so that we may take her to be your bride. When we return from Rages we will celebrate her marriage. For I know that Raguel can by no means keep her from you or promise her to another man without incurring the penalty of death according to the decree of the book of Moses. Indeed he knows that you, rather than any other man, are entitled to marry his daughter. So now listen to me, brother, and tonight we shall speak concerning the girl and arrange her engagement to you. And when we return from Rages we will take her and bring her back with us to your house.'

14 Then Tobias said in answer to Raphael, 'Brother Azariah, I have heard that she already has been married to seven husbands and that they died in the bridal chamber. On the night when they went in to her, they would die. I have heard people saying that it was a demon that killed them. 15 It does not harm her, but it kills anyone who desires to approach her. So now, since I am the only son my father has, I am afraid that I may die and bring my father's and mother's life down to their grave, grieving for me—and they have no other son to bury them.'

16 But Raphael*d* said to him, 'Do you not remember your father's orders when he commanded you to take a wife from your father's house? Now listen to me, brother, and say no more about this demon. Take her. I know that this very night she will be given to you in marriage. 17 When you enter the bridal chamber, take some of the fish's liver and heart, and put them on the embers of the incense. An odour will be given off; 18 the demon will smell it and flee, and will never be seen near her any more. Now when you are about to go to bed with her, both of you must first stand up and pray, imploring the Lord of heaven that mercy and safety may be granted to you. Do not be afraid, for she was set apart for you before the world was made. You will save her, and she will go with you. I presume that you will have children by her, and they will be as brothers to you. Now say no more!' When Tobias heard the words of Raphael and learned that she was his kinswoman,*e* related through his father's lineage, he loved her very much, and his heart was drawn to her.

a Other ancient authorities read *Ecbatana*   *b* Gk *they*
c Other ancient authorities read *Rages*   *d* Gk *he*
e Gk *sister*

Arrival at the Home of Raguel

7 Now when they[a] entered Ecbatana, Tobias[b] said to him, 'Brother Azariah, take me straight to our brother Raguel.' So he took him to Raguel's house, where they found him sitting beside the courtyard door. They greeted him first, and he replied, 'Joyous greetings, brothers; welcome and good health!' Then he brought them into his house. [2] He said to his wife Edna, 'How much the young man resembles my kinsman Tobit!' [3] Then Edna questioned them, saying, 'Where are you from, brothers?' They answered, 'We belong to the descendants of Naphtali who are exiles in Nineveh.' [4] She said to them, 'Do you know our kinsman Tobit?' And they replied, 'Yes, we know him.' Then she asked them, 'Is he[c] in good health?' [5] They replied, 'He is alive and in good health.' And Tobias added, 'He is my father!' [6] At that Raguel jumped up and kissed him and wept. [7] He also spoke to him as follows, 'Blessings on you, my child, son of a good and noble father![d] O most miserable of calamities that such an upright and beneficent man has become blind!' He then embraced his kinsman Tobias and wept. [8] His wife Edna also wept for him, and their daughter Sarah likewise wept. [9] Then Raguel[e] slaughtered a ram from the flock and received them very warmly.

Marriage of Tobias and Sarah

When they had bathed and washed themselves and had reclined to dine, Tobias said to Raphael, 'Brother Azariah, ask Raguel to give me my kinswoman[f] Sarah.' [10] But Raguel overheard it and said to the lad, 'Eat and drink, and be merry tonight. For no one except you, brother, has the right to marry my daughter Sarah. Likewise I am not at liberty to give her to any other man than yourself, because you are my nearest relative. But let me explain to you the true situation more fully, my child. [11] I have given her to seven men of our kinsmen, and all died on the night when they went in to her. But now, my child, eat and drink, and the Lord will act on behalf of you both.' But Tobias said, 'I will neither eat nor drink anything until you settle the things that pertain to me.' So Raguel said, 'I will do so. She is given to you in accordance with the decree in the book of Moses, and it has been decreed from heaven that she should be given to you. Take your kinswoman;[f] from now on you are her brother and she is your sister. She is given to you from today and for ever. May the Lord of heaven, my child, guide and prosper you both this night and grant you mercy and peace.' [12] Then Raguel summoned his daughter Sarah. When she came to him he took her by the hand and gave her to Tobias,[g] saying, 'Take her to be your wife in accordance with the law and decree written in the book of Moses. Take her and bring her safely to your father. And may the God of heaven prosper your journey with his peace.' [13] Then he called her mother and told her to bring writing material; and he wrote out a copy of a marriage contract, to the effect that he gave her to him as wife according to the decree of the law of Moses. [14] Then they began to eat and drink.

[15] Raguel called his wife Edna and said to her, 'Sister, get the other room ready, and take her there.' [16] So she went and made the bed in the room as he had told her, and brought Sarah[h] there. She wept for her daughter.[h] Then, wiping away the tears,[i] she said to her, 'Take courage, my daughter; the Lord of heaven grant you joy[j] in place of your sorrow. Take courage, my daughter.' Then she went out.

Tobias Routs the Demon

8 When they had finished eating and drinking they wanted to retire; so they took the young man and brought him into the bedroom. [2] Then Tobias remembered the words of Raphael, and he took the fish's liver and heart out of the bag where he had them and put them on the embers of the incense. [3] The odour of the

a Other ancient authorities read *he*   b Gk *he*
c Other ancient authorities add *alive and*   d Other ancient authorities add *When he heard that Tobit had lost his sight, he was stricken with grief and wept. Then he said,*
e Gk *he*   f Gk *sister*   g Gk *him*   h Gk *her*
i Other ancient authorities read *the tears of her daughter*
j Other ancient authorities read *favour*

fish so repelled the demon that he fled to the remotest parts[a] of Egypt. But Raphael followed him, and at once bound him there hand and foot.

4 When the parents[b] had gone out and shut the door of the room, Tobias got out of bed and said to Sarah,[c] 'Sister, get up, and let us pray and implore our Lord that he grant us mercy and safety.' 5 So she got up, and they began to pray and implore that they might be kept safe. Tobias[d] began by saying,

'Blessed are you, O God of our
ancestors,
and blessed is your name in all
generations for ever.
Let the heavens and the whole
creation bless you for ever.
6 You made Adam, and for him you
made his wife Eve
as a helper and support.
From the two of them the human
race has sprung.
You said, "It is not good that the man
should be alone;
let us make a helper for him like
himself."
7 I now am taking this kinswoman of
mine,
not because of lust,
but with sincerity.
Grant that she and I may find mercy
and that we may grow old together.'
8 And they both said, 'Amen, Amen.' 9 Then they went to sleep for the night.

But Raguel arose and called his servants to him, and they went and dug a grave, 10 for he said, 'It is possible that he will die and we will become an object of ridicule and derision.' 11 When they had finished digging the grave, Raguel went into his house and called his wife, 12 saying, 'Send one of the maids and have her go in to see if he is alive. But if he is dead, let us bury him without anyone knowing it.' 13 So they sent the maid, lit a lamp, and opened the door; and she went in and found them sound asleep together. 14 Then the maid came out and informed them that he was alive and that nothing was wrong. 15 So

they blessed the God of heaven, and Raguel[b] said,

'Blessed are you, O God, with every
pure blessing;
let all your chosen ones bless you.[e]
Let them bless you for ever.
16 Blessed are you because you have
made me glad.
It has not turned out as I expected,
but you have dealt with us
according to your great mercy.
17 Blessed are you because you had
compassion
on two only children.
Be merciful to them, O Master, and
keep them safe;
bring their lives to fulfilment
in happiness and mercy.'
18 Then he ordered his servants to fill in the grave before daybreak.

Wedding Feast

19 After this he asked his wife to bake many loaves of bread; and he went out to the herd and brought two steers and four rams and ordered them to be slaughtered. So they began to make preparations. 20 Then he called for Tobias and swore on oath to him in these words:[f] 'You shall not leave here for fourteen days, but shall stay here eating and drinking with me; and you shall cheer up my daughter, who has been depressed. 21 Take at once half of what I own and return in safety to your father; the other half will be yours when my wife and I die. Take courage, my child. I am your father and Edna is your mother, and we belong to you as well as to your wife[g] now and for ever. Take courage, my child.'

The Money Recovered

9 Then Tobias called Raphael and said to him, 2 'Brother Azariah, take four servants and two camels with you and travel to Rages. Go to the home of Gabael, give him the bond, get the money, and then bring him with you to the wedding celebration. 4 For you know that my father must be

a Or *fled through the air to the parts*   b Gk *they*
c Gk *her*   d Gk *He*   e Other ancient authorities lack
this line   f Other ancient authorities read *Tobias and
said to him*   g Gk *sister*

counting the days, and if I delay even one day I will upset him very much. 3 You are witness to the oath Raguel has sworn, and I cannot violate his oath.'a 5 So Raphael with the four servants and two camels went to Rages in Media and stayed with Gabael. Raphael b gave him the bond and informed him that Tobit's son Tobias had married and was inviting him to the wedding celebration. So Gabael c got up and counted out to him the money bags, with their seals intact; then they loaded them on the camels. d 6 In the morning they both got up early and went to the wedding celebration. When they came into Raguel's house they found Tobias reclining at table. He sprang up and greeted Gabael, e who wept and blessed him with the words, 'Good and noble son of a father good and noble, upright and generous! May the Lord grant the blessing of heaven to you and your wife, and to your wife's father and mother. Blessed be God, for I see in Tobias the very image of my cousin Tobit.'

Anxiety of the Parents

10 Now, day by day, Tobit kept counting how many days Tobias c would need for going and for returning. And when the days had passed and his son did not appear, 2 he said, 'Is it possible that he has been detained? Or that Gabael has died, and there is no one to give him the money?' 3 And he began to worry. 4 His wife Anna said, 'My child has perished and is no longer among the living.' And she began to weep and mourn for her son, saying, 5 'Woe is me, my child, the light of my eyes, that I let you make the journey.' 6 But Tobit kept saying to her, 'Be quiet and stop worrying, my dear; f he is all right. Probably something unexpected has happened there. The man who went with him is trustworthy and is one of our own kin. Do not grieve for him, my dear; f he will soon be here.' 7 She answered him, 'Be quiet yourself! Stop trying to deceive me! My child has perished.' She would rush out every day and watch the road her son had taken, and would heed no one. g When the sun had set

she would go in and mourn and weep all night long, getting no sleep at all.

Tobias and Sarah Start for Home

Now when the fourteen days of the wedding celebration had ended that Raguel had sworn to observe for his daughter, Tobias came to him and said, 'Send me back, for I know that my father and mother do not believe that they will see me again. So I beg of you, father, to let me go so that I may return to my own father. I have already explained to you how I left him.' 8 But Raguel said to Tobias, 'Stay, my child, stay with me; I will send messengers to your father Tobit and they will inform him about you.' 9 But he said, 'No! I beg you to send me back to my father.' 10 So Raguel promptly gave Tobias his wife Sarah, as well as half of all his property: male and female slaves, oxen and sheep, donkeys and camels, clothing, money, and household goods. 11 Then he saw them safely off; he embraced Tobias e and said, 'Farewell, my child; have a safe journey. The Lord of heaven prosper you and your wife Sarah, and may I see children of yours before I die.' 12 Then he kissed his daughter Sarah and said to her, 'My daughter, honour your father-in-law and your mother-in-law, h since from now on they are as much your parents as those who gave you birth. Go in peace, daughter, and may I hear a good report about you as long as I live.' Then he bade them farewell and let them go. Then Edna said to Tobias, 'My child and dear brother, the Lord of heaven bring you back safely, and may I live long enough to see children of you and of my daughter Sarah before I die. In the sight of the Lord I entrust my daughter to you; do nothing to grieve her all the days of your life. Go in peace, my child. From now on I am your mother and Sarah is your beloved wife. f May we all prosper together all the days of our lives.' Then she kissed them both and

a In other ancient authorities verse 3 precedes verse 4 b Gk He c Gk he d Other ancient authorities lack on the camels e Gk him f Gk sister g Other ancient authorities read and she would eat nothing h Other ancient authorities lack parts of Then . . . mother-in-law saw them safely off. 13 Tobias parted from Raguel with happiness and joy, praising the Lord of heaven and earth, King over all, because he had made his journey a success. Finally, he blessed Raguel and his wife Edna, and said, 'I have been commanded by the Lord to honour you all the days of my life.'*a*

Homeward Journey

11 When they came near to Kaserin, which is opposite Nineveh, Raphael said, 2 'You are aware of how we left your father. 3 Let us run ahead of your wife and prepare the house while they are still on the way.' 4 As they went on together Raphael*b* said to him, 'Have the gall ready.' And the dog*c* went along behind them.

5 Meanwhile, Anna sat looking intently down the road by which her son would come. 6 When she caught sight of him coming, she said to his father, 'Look, your son is coming, and the man who went with him!'

Tobit's Sight Restored

7 Raphael said to Tobias, before he had approached his father, 'I know that his eyes will be opened. 8 Smear the gall of the fish on his eyes; the medicine will make the white films shrink and peel off from his eyes, and your father will regain his sight and see the light.'

9 Then Anna ran up to her son and threw her arms around him, saying, 'Now that I have seen you, my child, I am ready to die.' And she wept. 10 Then Tobit got up and came stumbling out through the courtyard door. Tobias went up to him, 11 with the gall of the fish in his hand, and holding him firmly, he blew into his eyes, saying, 'Take courage, father.' With this he applied the medicine on his eyes, 12 and it made them smart.*d* 13 Next, with both his hands he peeled off the white films from the corners of his eyes. Then Tobit*b* saw his son and*e* threw his arms around him, 14 and he wept and said to him, 'I see you, my son, the light of my eyes!' Then he said,

'Blessed be God,
    and blessed be his great name,

and blessed be all his holy angels.
May his holy name be blessed*f*
    throughout all the ages.
15 Though he afflicted me,
    he has had mercy upon me.*g*
Now I see my son Tobias!'

So Tobit went in rejoicing and praising God at the top of his voice. Tobias reported to his father that his journey had been successful, that he had brought the money, that he had married Raguel's daughter Sarah, and that she was, indeed, on her way there, very near to the gate of Nineveh.

16 Then Tobit, rejoicing and praising God, went out to meet his daughter-in-law at the gate of Nineveh. When the people of Nineveh saw him coming, walking along in full vigour and with no one leading him, they were amazed. 17 Before them all, Tobit acknowledged that God had been merciful to him and had restored his sight. When Tobit met Sarah the wife of his son Tobias, he blessed her saying, 'Come in, my daughter, and welcome. Blessed be your God who has brought you to us, my daughter. Blessed be your father and your mother, blessed be my son Tobias, and blessed be you, my daughter. Come in now to your home, and welcome, with blessing and joy. Come in, my daughter.' So on that day there was rejoicing among all the Jews who were in Nineveh. 18 Ahikar and his nephew Nadab were also present to share Tobit's joy. With merriment they celebrated Tobias's wedding feast for seven days, and many gifts were given to him.*h*

Raphael's Wages

12 When the wedding celebration was ended, Tobit called his son Tobias and said to him, 'My child, see to paying the wages of the man who went with you, and give him a bonus as well.' 2 He replied, 'Father, how much shall I pay him? It would do no harm to give him half of

---

a Lat: Meaning of Gk uncertain   *b* Gk *he*   *c* Codex Sinaiticus reads *And the Lord*   *d* Lat: Meaning of Gk uncertain   *e* Other ancient authorities lack *saw his son and*   *f* Codex Sinaiticus reads *May his great name be upon us and blessed be all the angels*   *g* Lat: Gk lacks this line   *h* Other ancient authorities lack parts of this sentence the possessions brought back with me. ³For he has led me back to you safely, he cured my wife, he brought the money back with me, and he healed you. How much extra shall I give him as a bonus?' ⁴Tobit said, 'He deserves, my child, to receive half of all that he brought back.' ⁵So Tobias*a* called him and said, 'Take for your wages half of all that you brought back, and farewell.'

Raphael's Exhortation

6 Then Raphael*a* called the two of them privately and said to them, 'Bless God and acknowledge him in the presence of all the living for the good things he has done for you. Bless and sing praise to his name. With fitting honour declare to all people the deeds*b* of God. Do not be slow to acknowledge him. ⁷It is good to conceal the secret of a king, but to acknowledge and reveal the works of God, and with fitting honour to acknowledge him. Do good, and evil will not overtake you. ⁸Prayer with fasting*c* is good, but better than both is almsgiving with righteousness. A little with righteousness is better than wealth with wrongdoing.*d* It is better to give alms than to lay up gold. ⁹For almsgiving saves from death and purges away every sin. Those who give alms will enjoy a full life, ¹⁰but those who commit sin and do wrong are their own worst enemies.

Raphael Discloses His Identity

11 'I will now declare the whole truth to you and will conceal nothing from you. Already I have declared it to you when I said, "It is good to conceal the secret of a king, but to reveal with due honour the works of God." ¹²So now, when you and Sarah prayed, it was I who brought and read*e* the record of your prayer before the glory of the Lord, and likewise whenever you buried the dead. ¹³And that time when you did not hesitate to get up and leave your dinner to go and bury the dead, ¹⁴I was sent to you to test you. And at the same time God sent me to heal you and Sarah your daughter-in-law. ¹⁵I am

Raphael, one of the seven angels who stand ready and enter before the glory of the Lord.'

16 The two of them were shaken; they fell face down, for they were afraid. ¹⁷But he said to them, 'Do not be afraid; peace be with you. Bless God for evermore. ¹⁸As for me, when I was with you, I was not acting on my own will, but by the will of God. Bless him each and every day; sing his praises. ¹⁹Although you were watching me, I really did not eat or drink anything—but what you saw was a vision. ²⁰So now get up from the ground,*f* and acknowledge God. See, I am ascending to him who sent me. Write down all these things that have happened to you.' And he ascended. ²¹Then they stood up, and could see him no more. ²²They kept blessing God and singing his praises, and they acknowledged God for these marvellous deeds of his, when an angel of God had appeared to them.

Tobit's Thanksgiving to God

13 Then Tobit*a* said:
'Blessed be God who lives for ever,
　because his kingdom*g* lasts
　　throughout all ages.
² For he afflicts, and he shows mercy;
　he leads down to Hades in the
　　lowest regions of the earth,
　and he brings up from the great
　　abyss,*h*
　and there is nothing that can escape
　　his hand.
³ Acknowledge him before the nations,
　O children of Israel;
　for he has scattered you among
　　them.
⁴ He has shown you his greatness
　even there.
　Exalt him in the presence of every
　　living being,
　because he is our Lord and he is
　　our God;

a Gk *he*　　*b* Gk *words*; other ancient authorities read *words of the deeds*　　*c* Codex Sinaiticus *with sincerity*　　*d* Lat　　*e* Lat: Gk lacks *and read*　　*f* Other ancient authorities read *now bless the Lord on earth*　　*g* Other ancient authorities read *for ever, and his kingdom*　　*h* Gk *from destruction*

he is our Father and he is God for
    ever.

5 He will afflict*a* you for your
    iniquities,
    but he will again show mercy on all
        of you.
He will gather you from all the
    nations
    among whom you have been
        scattered.
6 If you turn to him with all your heart
    and with all your soul,
    to do what is true before him,
then he will turn to you
    and will no longer hide his face
        from you.
So now see what he has done for you;
    acknowledge him at the top of your
        voice.
Bless the Lord of righteousness,
    and exalt the King of the ages.*b*
In the land of my exile I acknowledge
    him,
    and show his power and majesty to
        a nation of sinners:
"Turn back, you sinners, and do what
    is right before him;
    perhaps he may look with favour
        upon you and show you
        mercy."
7 As for me, I exalt my God,
    and my soul rejoices in the King of
        heaven.
8 Let all people speak of his majesty,
    and acknowledge him in Jerusalem.
9 O Jerusalem, the holy city,
    he afflicted*c* you for the deeds of
        your hands,*d*
    but will again have mercy on the
        children of the righteous.
10 Acknowledge the Lord, for he is
    good,*e*
    and bless the King of the ages,
    so that his tent*f* may be rebuilt in
        you in joy.
May he cheer all those within you
    who are captives,
    and love all those within you who
        are distressed,
    to all generations for ever.

11 A bright light will shine to all the
    ends of the earth;
    many nations will come to you
        from far away,
the inhabitants of the remotest parts
        of the earth to your holy name,
    bearing gifts in their hands for the
        King of heaven.
Generation after generation will give
    joyful praise in you;
    the name of the chosen city will
        endure for ever.
12 Cursed are all who speak a harsh
    word against you;
    cursed are all who conquer you
        and pull down your walls,
all who overthrow your towers
    and set your homes on fire.
    But blessed for ever will be all who
        revere you.*g*
13 Go, then, and rejoice over the
    children of the righteous,
    for they will be gathered together
        and will praise the Lord of the ages.
14 Happy are those who love you,
    and happy are those who rejoice in
        your prosperity.
Happy also are all people who grieve
    with you
    because of your afflictions;
for they will rejoice with you
    and witness all your glory for ever.
15 My soul blesses*h* the Lord, the great
    King!
16 For Jerusalem will be built*i* as his
    house for all ages.
How happy I will be if a remnant of
    my descendants should survive
    to see your glory and acknowledge
        the King of heaven.
The gates of Jerusalem will be built
    with sapphire and emerald,
    and all your walls with precious
        stones.

---

a Other ancient authorities read *He afflicted*
b The lacuna in codex Sinaiticus, verses 6b to 10a, is
filled in from other ancient authorities   *c* Other
ancient authorities read *will afflict*   *d* Other ancient
authorities read *your children*   *e* Other ancient
authorities read *Lord worthily*   *f* Or *tabernacle*
g Other ancient authorities read *who build you up*
h Or *O my soul, bless*   *i* Other ancient authorities add
for a city

The towers of Jerusalem will be built
    with gold,
  and their battlements with pure
    gold.
The streets of Jerusalem will be paved
  with ruby and with stones of Ophir.
17 The gates of Jerusalem will sing
    hymns of joy,
  and all her houses will cry,
    "Hallelujah!
  Blessed be the God of Israel!"
  and the blessed will bless the holy
    name for ever and ever.'

Tobit's Final Counsel

14 So ended Tobit's words of praise.
2 Tobit[a] died in peace when he
was one hundred and twelve years old, and
was buried with great honour in Nineveh.
He was sixty-two[b] years old when he lost
his eyesight, and after regaining it he lived
in prosperity, giving alms and continually
blessing God and acknowledging God's
majesty.

3 When he was about to die, he called
his son Tobias and the seven sons of Tobias[c] and gave this command: 'My son,
take your children 4 and hurry off to Media,
for I believe the word of God that Nahum
spoke about Nineveh, that all these things
will take place and overtake Assyria and
Nineveh. Indeed, everything that was spoken by the prophets of Israel, whom God
sent, will occur. None of all their words
will fail, but all will come true at their appointed times. So it will be safer in Media
than in Assyria and Babylon. For I know
and believe that whatever God has said
will be fulfilled and will come true; not a
single word of the prophecies will fail. All
of our kindred, inhabitants of the land of
Israel, will be scattered and taken as captives from the good land; and the whole
land of Israel will be desolate, even
Samaria and Jerusalem will be desolate.
And the temple of God in it will be burned
to the ground, and it will be desolate for a
while.[d]

5 'But God will again have mercy on
them, and God will bring them back into
the land of Israel; and they will rebuild the
temple of God, but not like the first one
until the period when the times of fulfilment shall come. After this they all will return from their exile and will rebuild Jerusalem in splendour; and in it the temple of
God will be rebuilt, just as the prophets of
Israel have said concerning it. 6 Then the
nations in the whole world will all be con-
verted and worship God in truth. They will
all abandon their idols, which deceitfully
have led them into their error; 7 and in
righteousness they will praise the eternal
God. All the Israelites who are saved in
those days and are truly mindful of God
will be gathered together; they will go to
Jerusalem and live in safety for ever in the
land of Abraham, and it will be given over
to them. Those who sincerely love God
will rejoice, but those who commit sin and
injustice will vanish from all the earth.
8,9 So now, my children, I command you,
serve God faithfully and do what is pleasing in his sight. Your children are also to
be commanded to do what is right and to
give alms, and to be mindful of God and to
bless his name at all times with sincerity
and with all their strength. So now, my
son, leave Nineveh; do not remain here.
10 On whatever day you bury your mother
beside me, do not stay overnight within
the confines of the city. For I see that there
is much wickedness within it, and that
much deceit is practised within it, while
the people are without shame. See, my son,
what Nadab did to Ahikar who had reared
him. Was he not, while still alive, brought
down into the earth? For God repaid him
to his face for this shameful treatment.
Ahikar came out into the light, but Nadab
went into the eternal darkness, because he
tried to kill Ahikar. Because he gave alms,
Ahikar[e] escaped the fatal trap that Nadab
had set for him, but Nadab fell into it himself, and was destroyed. 11 So now, my children, see what almsgiving accomplishes,
and what injustice does—it brings death!
But now my breath fails me.'

a Gk He   b Other ancient authorities read *fifty-eight*
c Lat: Gk lacks *and the seven sons of Tobias*   d Lat:
Other ancient authorities read *of God will be in distress
and will be burned for a while*   e Gk *he*; other ancient
authorities read *Manasses*

Death of Tobit and Anna

Then they laid him on his bed, and he died; and he received an honourable funeral. [12] When Tobias's mother died, he buried her beside his father. Then he and his wife and children[a] returned to Media and settled in Ecbatana with Raguel his father-in-law. [13] He treated his parents-in-law[b] with great respect in their old age, and buried them in Ecbatana of Media. He inherited both the property of Raguel and that of his father Tobit. [14] He died highly respected at the age of one hundred and seventeen[c] years. [15] Before he died he heard[d] of the destruction of Nineveh, and he saw its prisoners being led into Media, those whom King Cyaxares[e] of Media had taken captive. Tobias[f] praised God for all he had done to the people of Nineveh and Assyria; before he died he rejoiced over Nineveh, and he blessed the Lord God for ever and ever. Amen.[g]

---

a Codex Sinaiticus lacks *and children*   *b* Gk *them*
c Other authorities read other numbers   *d* Codex
Sinaiticus reads *saw and heard*   *e* Cn: Codex Sinaiticus
Ahikar; other ancient authorities read *Nebuchadnezzar
and Ahasuerus*   *f* Gk *He*   *g* Other ancient authorities
lack *Amen*

JUDITH

Arphaxad Fortifies Ecbatana

1 It was the twelfth year of the reign of Nebuchadnezzar, who ruled over the Assyrians in the great city of Nineveh. In those days Arphaxad ruled over the Medes in Ecbatana. ²He built walls around Ecbatana with hewn stones three cubits thick and six cubits long; he made the walls seventy cubits high and fifty cubits wide. ³At its gates he raised towers one hundred cubits high and sixty cubits wide at the foundations. ⁴He made its gates seventy cubits high and forty cubits wide to allow his armies to march out in force and his infantry to form their ranks. ⁵Then King Nebuchadnezzar made war against King Arphaxad in the great plain that is on the borders of Ragau. ⁶There rallied to him all the people of the hill country and all those who lived along the Euphrates, the Tigris, and the Hydaspes, and, on the plain, Arioch, king of the Elymeans. Thus, many nations joined the forces of the Chaldeans.*ᵃ*

Nebuchadnezzar Issues an Ultimatum

7 Then Nebuchadnezzar, king of the Assyrians, sent messengers to all who lived in Persia and to all who lived in the west, those who lived in Cilicia and Damascus, Lebanon and Antilebanon, and all who lived along the sea coast, ⁸and those among the nations of Carmel and Gilead, and Upper Galilee and the great plain of Esdraelon, ⁹and all who were in Samaria and its towns, and beyond the Jordan as far as Jerusalem and Bethany and Chelous and Kadesh and the river of Egypt, and Tahpanhes and Raamses and the whole land of Goshen, ¹⁰even beyond Tanis and Memphis, and all who lived in Egypt as far as the borders of Ethiopia. ¹¹But all who lived in the whole region disregarded the summons of Nebuchadnezzar, king of the Assyrians, and refused to join him in the war; for they were not afraid of him, but regarded him as only one man.*ᵇ* So they sent back his messengers empty-handed and in disgrace.

12 Then Nebuchadnezzar became very angry with this whole region, and swore by his throne and kingdom that he would take revenge on the whole territory of Cilicia and Damascus and Syria, that he would kill with his sword also all the inhabitants of the land of Moab, and the people of Ammon, and all Judea, and everyone in Egypt, as far as the coasts of the two seas.

Arphaxad Is Defeated

13 In the seventeenth year he led his forces against King Arphaxad and defeated him in battle, overthrowing the whole army of Arphaxad and all his cavalry and all his chariots. ¹⁴Thus he took possession of his towns and came to Ecbatana, captured its towers, plundered its markets, and turned its glory into disgrace. ¹⁵He captured Arphaxad in the mountains of Ragau and struck him down with his spears, thus destroying him once and for all. ¹⁶Then he returned to Nineveh, he and all his combined forces, a vast body of troops; and there he and his forces rested and feasted for one hundred and twenty days.

The Expedition against the West

2 In the eighteenth year, on the twenty-second day of the first month, there was talk in the palace of Nebuchadnezzar,

a Syr: Gk *Cheleoudites*   *b* Or *a man*

king of the Assyrians, about carrying out his revenge on the whole region, just as he had said. [2] He summoned all his ministers and all his nobles and set before them his secret plan and recounted fully, with his own lips, all the wickedness of the region.[a] [3] They decided that everyone who had not obeyed his command should be destroyed.

4 When he had completed his plan, Nebuchadnezzar, king of the Assyrians, called Holofernes, the chief general of his army, second only to himself, and said to him, [5] Thus says the Great King, the lord of the whole earth: Leave my presence and take with you men confident in their strength, one hundred and twenty thousand foot-soldiers and twelve thousand cavalry. [6] March out against all the land to the west, because they disobeyed my orders. [7] Tell them to prepare earth and water, for I am coming against them in my anger, and will cover the whole face of the earth with the feet of my troops, to whom I will hand them over to be plundered. [8] Their wounded shall fill their ravines and gullies, and the swelling river shall be filled with their dead. [9] I will lead them away captive to the ends of the whole earth. [10] You shall go and seize all their territory for me in advance. They must yield themselves to you, and you shall hold them for me until the day of their punishment. [11] But to those who resist show no mercy, but hand them over to slaughter and plunder throughout your whole region. [12] For as I live, and by the power of my kingdom, what I have spoken I will accomplish by my own hand. [13] And you—take care not to transgress any of your lord's commands, but carry them out exactly as I have ordered you; do it without delay.'

Campaign of Holofernes

14 So Holofernes left the presence of his lord, and summoned all the commanders, generals, and officers of the Assyrian army. [15] He mustered the picked troops by divisions as his lord had ordered him to do, one hundred and twenty thousand of them, together with twelve

thousand archers on horseback, [16] and he organized them as a great army is marshalled for a campaign. [17] He took along a vast number of camels and donkeys and mules for transport, and innumerable sheep and oxen and goats for food; [18] also ample rations for everyone, and a huge amount of gold and silver from the royal palace.

19 Then he set out with his whole army, to go ahead of King Nebuchadnezzar and to cover the whole face of the earth to the west with their chariots and cavalry and picked foot-soldiers. [20] Along with them went a mixed crowd like a swarm of locusts, like the dust[b] of the earth—a multitude that could not be counted.

21 They marched for three days from Nineveh to the plain of Bectileth, and camped opposite Bectileth near the mountain that is to the north of Upper Cilicia. [22] From there Holofernes[c] took his whole army, the infantry, cavalry, and chariots, and went up into the hill country. [23] He ravaged Put and Lud, and plundered all the Rassisites and the Ishmaelites on the border of the desert, south of the country of the Chelleans. [24] Then he followed[d] the Euphrates and passed through Mesopotamia and destroyed all the fortified towns along the brook Abron, as far as the sea. [25] He also seized the territory of Cilicia, and killed everyone who resisted him. Then he came to the southern borders of Japheth, facing Arabia. [26] He surrounded all the Midianites, and burned their tents and plundered their sheepfolds. [27] Then he went down into the plain of Damascus during the wheat harvest, and burned all their fields and destroyed their flocks and herds and sacked their towns and ravaged their lands and put all their young men to the sword.

28 So fear and dread of him fell upon all the people who lived along the sea coast, at Sidon and Tyre, and those who lived in Sur and Ocina and all who lived in Jamnia. Those who lived in Azotus and Ascalon feared him greatly.

a Meaning of Gk uncertain   b Gk sand   c Gk he
d Or crossed

Entreaties for Peace

3 They therefore sent messengers to him to sue for peace in these words: 2'We, the servants of Nebuchadnezzar, the Great King, lie prostrate before you. Do with us whatever you will. 3See, our buildings and all our land and all our wheat fields and our flocks and herds and all our encampments*a* lie before you; do with them as you please. 4Our towns and their inhabitants are also your slaves; come and deal with them as you see fit.'

5 The men came to Holofernes and told him all this. 6Then he went down to the sea coast with his army and stationed garrisons in the fortified towns and took picked men from them as auxiliaries. 7These people and all in the countryside welcomed him with garlands and dances and tambourines. 8Yet he demolished all their shrines*b* and cut down their sacred groves; for he had been commissioned to destroy all the gods of the land, so that all nations should worship Nebuchadnezzar alone, and that all their dialects and tribes should call upon him as a god.

9 Then he came towards Esdraelon, near Dothan, facing the great ridge of Judea; 10he camped between Geba and Scythopolis, and remained for a whole month in order to collect all the supplies for his army.

Judea on the Alert

4 When the Israelites living in Judea heard of everything that Holofernes, the general of Nebuchadnezzar, the king of the Assyrians, had done to the nations, and how he had plundered and destroyed all their temples, 2they were therefore greatly terrified at his approach; they were alarmed both for Jerusalem and for the temple of the Lord their God. 3For they had only recently returned from exile, and all the people of Judea had just now gathered together, and the sacred vessels and the altar and the temple had been consecrated after their profanation. 4So they sent word to every district of Samaria, and to Kona, Beth-horon, Belmain, and Jericho, and to Choba and Aesora, and the valley of Salem. 5They immediately seized all the

high hilltops and fortified the villages on them and stored up food in preparation for war—since their fields had recently been harvested.

6 The high priest, Joakim, who was in Jerusalem at the time, wrote to the people of Bethulia and Betomesthaim, which faces Esdraelon opposite the plain near Dothan, 7ordering them to seize the mountain passes, since by them Judea could be invaded; and it would be easy to stop any who tried to enter, for the approach was narrow, wide enough for only two at a time to pass.

Prayer and Penance

8 So the Israelites did as they had been ordered by the high priest Joakim and the senate of the whole people of Israel, in session at Jerusalem. 9And every man of Israel cried out to God with great fervour, and they humbled themselves with much fasting. 10They and their wives and their children and their cattle and every resident alien and hired labourer and purchased slave—they all put sackcloth around their waists. 11And all the Israelite men, women, and children living at Jerusalem prostrated themselves before the temple and put ashes on their heads and spread out their sackcloth before the Lord. 12They even draped the altar with sackcloth and cried out in unison, praying fervently to the God of Israel not to allow their infants to be carried off and their wives to be taken as booty, and the towns they had inherited to be destroyed, and the sanctuary to be profaned and desecrated to the malicious joy of the Gentiles.

13 The Lord heard their prayers and had regard for their distress; for the people fasted for many days throughout Judea and in Jerusalem before the sanctuary of the Lord Almighty. 14The high priest Joakim and all the priests who stood before the Lord and ministered to the Lord, with sackcloth around their loins, offered the daily burnt-offerings, the votive offerings, and freewill-offerings of the people. 15With ashes on their turbans, they cried out to the Lord

a Gk *all the sheepfolds of our tents*   *b* Syr: Gk *borders* with all their might to look with favour on the whole house of Israel.

Council against the Israelites

5 It was reported to Holofernes, the general of the Assyrian army, that the people of Israel had prepared for war and had closed the mountain passes and fortified all the high hilltops and set up barricades in the plains. ² In great anger he called together all the princes of Moab and the commanders of Ammon and all the governors of the coastland, ³ and said to them, 'Tell me, you Canaanites, what people is this that lives in the hill country? What towns do they inhabit? How large is their army, and in what does their power and strength consist? Who rules over them as king and leads their army? ⁴ And why have they alone, of all who live in the west, refused to come out and meet me?'

Achior's Report

5 Then Achior, the leader of all the Ammonites, said to him, 'May my lord please listen to a report from the mouth of your servant, and I will tell you the truth about this people that lives in the mountain district near you. No falsehood shall come from your servant's mouth. ⁶ These people are descended from the Chaldeans. ⁷ At one time they lived in Mesopotamia, because they did not wish to follow the gods of their ancestors who were in Chaldea. ⁸ Since they had abandoned the ways of their ancestors, and worshipped the God of heaven, the God they had come to know, their ancestors*a* drove them out from the presence of their gods. So they fled to Mesopotamia, and lived there for a long time. ⁹ Then their God commanded them to leave the place where they were living and go to the land of Canaan. There they settled, and grew very prosperous in gold and silver and very much livestock. ¹⁰ When a famine spread over the land of Canaan they went down to Egypt and lived there as long as they had food. There they became so great a multitude that their race could not be counted. ¹¹ So the king of Egypt became hostile to them; he exploited them and forced them to make bricks. ¹² They cried out to their God, and he afflicted the whole land of Egypt with incurable plagues. So the Egyptians drove them out of their sight. ¹³ Then God dried up the Red Sea before them, ¹⁴ and he led them by the way of Sinai and Kadesh-barnea. They drove out all the people of the desert, ¹⁵ and took up residence in the land of the Amorites, and by their might destroyed all the inhabitants of Heshbon; and crossing over the Jordan they took possession of all the hill country. ¹⁶ They drove out before them the Canaanites, the Perizzites, the Jebusites, the Shechemites, and all the Gergesites, and lived there a long time.

17 'As long as they did not sin against their God they prospered, for the God who hates iniquity is with them. ¹⁸ But when they departed from the way he had prescribed for them, they were utterly defeated in many battles and were led away captive to a foreign land. The temple of their God was razed to the ground, and their towns were occupied by their enemies. ¹⁹ But now they have returned to their God, and have come back from the places where they were scattered, and have occupied Jerusalem, where their sanctuary is, and have settled in the hill country, because it was uninhabited.

20 'So now, my master and lord, if there is any oversight in this people and they sin against their God and we find out their offence, then we can go up and defeat them. ²¹ But if they are not a guilty nation, then let my lord pass them by; for their Lord and God will defend them, and we shall become the laughing-stock of the whole world.'

22 When Achior had finished saying these things, all the people standing around the tent began to complain; Holofernes' officers and all the inhabitants of the sea coast and Moab insisted that he should be cut to pieces. ²³ They said, 'We are not afraid of the Israelites; they are a people with no strength or power for making war. ²⁴ Therefore let us go ahead, Lord

a Gk they

Holofernes, and your vast army will swallow them up.'

Achior Handed over to the Israelites

6 When the disturbance made by the people outside the council had died down, Holofernes, the commander of the Assyrian army, said to Achior[a] in the presence of all the foreign contingents:

2 'Who are you, Achior and you mercenaries of Ephraim, to prophesy among us as you have done today and tell us not to make war against the people of Israel because their God will defend them? What god is there except Nebuchadnezzar? He will send his forces and destroy them from the face of the earth. Their God will not save them; [3] we the king's[b] servants will destroy them as one man. They cannot resist the might of our cavalry. [4] We will overwhelm them;[c] their mountains will be drunk with their blood, and their fields will be full of their dead. Not even their footprints will survive our attack; they will utterly perish. So says King Nebuchadnezzar, lord of the whole earth. For he has spoken; none of his words shall be in vain.

5 'As for you, Achior, you Ammonite mercenary, you have said these words in a moment of perversity; you shall not see my face again from this day until I take revenge on this race that came out of Egypt. [6] Then at my return the sword of my army and the spear[d] of my servants shall pierce your sides, and you shall fall among their wounded. [7] Now my slaves are going to take you back into the hill country and put you in one of the towns beside the passes. [8] You will not die until you perish along with them. [9] If you really hope in your heart that they will not be taken, then do not look downcast! I have spoken, and none of my words shall fail to come true.'

10 Then Holofernes ordered his slaves, who waited on him in his tent, to seize Achior and take him away to Bethulia and hand him over to the Israelites. [11] So the slaves took him and led him out of the camp into the plain, and from the plain they went up into the hill country and came to the springs below Bethulia.

[12] When the men of the town saw them,[e] they seized their weapons and ran out of the town to the top of the hill, and all the slingers kept them from coming up by throwing stones at them. [13] So having taken shelter below the hill, they bound Achior and left him lying at the foot of the hill, and returned to their master.

14 Then the Israelites came down from their town and found him; they untied him and brought him into Bethulia and placed him before the magistrates of their town, [15] who in those days were Uzziah son of Micah, of the tribe of Simeon, and Chabris son of Gothoniel, and Charmis son of Melchiel. [16] They called together all the elders of the town, and all their young men and women ran to the assembly. They set Achior in the midst of all their people, and Uzziah questioned him about what had happened. [17] He answered and told them what had taken place at the council of Holofernes, and all that he had said in the presence of the Assyrian leaders, and all that Holofernes had boasted he would do against the house of Israel. [18] Then the people fell down and worshipped God, and cried out:

19 'O Lord God of heaven, see their arrogance, and have pity on our people in their humiliation, and look kindly today on the faces of those who are consecrated to you.'

20 Then they reassured Achior, and praised him highly. [21] Uzziah took him from the assembly to his own house and gave a banquet for the elders; and all that night they called on the God of Israel for help.

The Campaign against Bethulia

7 The next day Holofernes ordered his whole army, and all the allies who had joined him, to break camp and move against Bethulia, and to seize the passes up into the hill country and make war on the Israelites. [2] So all their warriors marched off that day; their fighting forces numbered

---

a Other ancient authorities add *and to all the Moabites*
b Gk *his*　　c Other ancient authorities add *with it*
d Lat Syr: Gk *people*　　e Other ancient authorities add *on the top of the hill*

one hundred and seventy thousand infantry and twelve thousand cavalry, not counting the baggage and the foot-soldiers handling it, a very great multitude. ³They encamped in the valley near Bethulia, beside the spring, and they spread out in breadth over Dothan as far as Balbaim and in length from Bethulia to Cyamon, which faces Esdraelon.

4 When the Israelites saw their vast numbers, they were greatly terrified and said to one another, 'They will now strip clean the whole land; neither the high mountains nor the valleys nor the hills will bear their weight.' ⁵Yet they all seized their weapons, and when they had kindled fires on their towers, they remained on guard all that night.

6 On the second day Holofernes led out all his cavalry in full view of the Israelites in Bethulia. ⁷He reconnoitred the approaches to their town, and visited the springs that supplied their water; he seized them and set guards of soldiers over them, and then returned to his army.

8 Then all the chieftains of the Edomites and all the leaders of the Moabites and the commanders of the coastland came to him and said, ⁹'Listen to what we have to say, my lord, and your army will suffer no losses. ¹⁰This people, the Israelites, do not rely on their spears but on the height of the mountains where they live, for it is not easy to reach the tops of their mountains. ¹¹Therefore, my lord, do not fight against them in regular formation, and not a man of your army will fall. ¹²Remain in your camp, and keep all the men in your forces with you; let your servants take possession of the spring of water that flows from the foot of the mountain, ¹³for this is where all the people of Bethulia get their water. So thirst will destroy them, and they will surrender their town. Meanwhile, we and our people will go up to the tops of the nearby mountains and camp there to keep watch to see that no one gets out of the town. ¹⁴They and their wives and children will waste away with famine, and before the sword reaches them they will be strewn about in the streets where they live. ¹⁵Thus

you will pay them back with evil, because they rebelled and did not receive you peaceably.'

16 These words pleased Holofernes and all his attendants, and he gave orders to do as they had said. ¹⁷So the army of the Ammonites moved forward, together with five thousand Assyrians, and they encamped in the valley and seized the water supply and the springs of the Israelites. ¹⁸And the Edomites and Ammonites went up and encamped in the hill country opposite Dothan; and they sent some of their men towards the south and the east, towards Egrebeh, which is near Chusi beside the Wadi Mochmur. The rest of the Assyrian army encamped in the plain, and covered the whole face of the land. Their tents and supply trains spread out in great number, and they formed a vast multitude.

The Distress of the Israelites

19 The Israelites then cried out to the Lord their God, for their courage failed, because all their enemies had surrounded them, and there was no way of escape from them. ²⁰The whole Assyrian army, their infantry, chariots, and cavalry, surrounded them for thirty-four days, until all the water containers of every inhabitant of Bethulia were empty; ²¹their cisterns were going dry, and on no day did they have enough water to drink, for their drinking water was rationed. ²²Their children were listless, and the women and young men fainted from thirst and were collapsing in the streets of the town and in the gateways; they no longer had any strength.

23 Then all the people, the young men, the women, and the children, gathered around Uzziah and the rulers of the town and cried out with a loud voice, and said before all the elders, ²⁴'Let God judge between you and us! You have done us a great injury in not making peace with the Assyrians. ²⁵For now we have no one to help us; God has sold us into their hands, to be strewn before them in thirst and exhaustion. ²⁶Now summon them and surrender the whole town as booty to the

army of Holofernes and to all his forces. [27] For it would be better for us to be captured by them.[a] We shall indeed become slaves, but our lives will be spared, and we shall not witness our little ones dying before our eyes, and our wives and children drawing their last breath. [28] We call to witness against you heaven and earth and our God, the Lord of our ancestors, who punishes us for our sins and the sins of our ancestors; do today the things that we have described!'

[29] Then great and general lamentation arose throughout the assembly, and they cried out to the Lord God with a loud voice. [30] But Uzziah said to them, 'Courage, my brothers and sisters![b] Let us hold out for five days more; by that time the Lord our God will turn his mercy to us again, for he will not forsake us utterly. [31] But if these days pass by, and no help comes for us, I will do as you say.'

[32] Then he dismissed the people to their various posts, and they went up on the walls and towers of their town. The women and children he sent home. In the town they were in great misery.

The Character of Judith

8 Now in those days Judith heard about these things: she was the daughter of Merari son of Ox son of Joseph son of Oziel son of Elkiah son of Ananias son of Gideon son of Raphain son of Ahitub son of Elijah son of Hilkiah son of Eliab son of Nathanael son of Salamiel son of Sarasadai son of Israel. [2] Her husband Manasseh, who belonged to her tribe and family, had died during the barley harvest. [3] For as he stood overseeing those who were binding sheaves in the field, he was overcome by the burning heat, and took to his bed and died in his town Bethulia. So they buried him with his ancestors in the field between Dothan and Balamon. [4] Judith remained as a widow for three years and four months [5] at home where she set up a tent for herself on the roof of her house. She put sackcloth around her waist and dressed in widow's clothing. [6] She fasted all the days of her widowhood, except the day before the sab-

bath and the sabbath itself, the day before the new moon and the day of the new moon, and the festivals and days of rejoicing of the house of Israel. [7] She was beautiful in appearance, and was very lovely to behold. Her husband Manasseh had left her gold and silver, men and women slaves, livestock, and fields; and she maintained this estate. [8] No one spoke ill of her, for she feared God with great devotion.

Judith and the Elders

[9] When Judith heard the harsh words spoken by the people against the ruler, because they were faint for lack of water, and when she heard all that Uzziah said to them, and how he promised them under oath to surrender the town to the Assyrians after five days, [10] she sent her maid, who was in charge of all she possessed, to summon Uzziah and[c] Chabris and Charmis, the elders of her town. [11] They came to her, and she said to them:

'Listen to me, rulers of the people of Bethulia! What you have said to the people today is not right; you have even sworn and pronounced this oath between God and you, promising to surrender the town to our enemies unless the Lord turns and helps us within so many days. [12] Who are you to put God to the test today, and to set yourselves up in the place of[d] God in human affairs? [13] You are putting the Lord Almighty to the test, but you will never learn anything! [14] You cannot plumb the depths of the human heart or understand the workings of the human mind; how do you expect to search out God, who made all these things, and find out his mind or comprehend his thought? No, my brothers, do not anger the Lord our God. [15] For if he does not choose to help us within these five days, he has power to protect us within any time he pleases, or even to destroy us in the presence of our enemies. [16] Do not try to bind the purposes of the Lord our God; for God is not like a human being, to be threatened, or like a mere mor-

---

a Other ancient authorities add *than to die of thirst*
b Gk *Courage, brothers*   c Other ancient authorities lack *Uzziah and* (see verses 28 and 35)   d Or *above*

tal, to be won over by pleading. 17 Therefore, while we wait for his deliverance, let us call upon him to help us, and he will hear our voice if it pleases him.

18 'For never in our generation, nor in these present days, has there been any tribe or family or people or town of ours that worships gods made with hands, as was done in days gone by. 19 That was why our ancestors were handed over to the sword and to pillage, and so they suffered a great catastrophe before our enemies. 20 But we know no other god but him, and so we hope that he will not disdain us or any of our nation. 21 For if we are captured, all Judea will be captured and our sanctuary will be plundered; and he will make us pay for its desecration with our blood. 22 The slaughter of our kindred and the captivity of the land and the desolation of our inheritance—all this he will bring on our heads among the Gentiles, wherever we serve as slaves; and we shall be an offence and a disgrace in the eyes of those who acquire us. 23 For our slavery will not bring us into favour, but the Lord our God will turn it to dishonour.

24 'Therefore, my brothers, let us set an example to our kindred, for their lives depend upon us, and the sanctuary—both the temple and the altar—rests upon us. 25 In spite of everything let us give thanks to the Lord our God, who is putting us to the test as he did our ancestors. 26 Remember what he did with Abraham, and how he tested Isaac, and what happened to Jacob in Syrian Mesopotamia, while he was tending the sheep of Laban, his mother's brother. 27 For he has not tried us with fire, as he did them, to search their hearts, nor has he taken vengeance on us; but the Lord scourges those who are close to him in order to admonish them.'

28 Then Uzziah said to her, 'All that you have said was spoken out of a true heart, and there is no one who can deny your words. 29 Today is not the first time your wisdom has been shown, but from the beginning of your life all the people have recognized your understanding, for your heart's disposition is right. 30 But the people were so thirsty that they compelled us to do for them what we have promised, and made us take an oath that we cannot break. 31 Now since you are a God-fearing woman, pray for us, so that the Lord may send us rain to fill our cisterns. Then we will no longer feel faint from thirst.'

32 Then Judith said to them, 'Listen to me. I am about to do something that will go down through all generations of our descendants. 33 Stand at the town gate tonight so that I may go out with my maid; and within the days after which you have promised to surrender the town to our enemies, the Lord will deliver Israel by my hand. 34 Only, do not try to find out what I am doing; for I will not tell you until I have finished what I am about to do.'

35 Uzziah and the rulers said to her, 'Go in peace, and may the Lord God go before you, to take vengeance on our enemies.' 36 So they returned from the tent and went to their posts.

The Prayer of Judith

9 Then Judith prostrated herself, put ashes on her head, and uncovered the sackcloth she was wearing. At the very time when the evening incense was being offered in the house of God in Jerusalem, Judith cried out to the Lord with a loud voice, and said:

2 'O Lord God of my ancestor Simeon, to whom you gave a sword to take revenge on those strangers who had torn off a virgin's clothing*a* to defile her, and exposed her thighs to put her to shame, and polluted her womb to disgrace her; for you said, "It shall not be done"—yet they did it; 3 so you gave up their rulers to be killed, and their bed, which was ashamed of the deceit they had practised, was stained with blood, and you struck down slaves along with princes, and princes on their thrones. 4 You gave up their wives for booty and their daughters to captivity, and all their booty to be divided among your beloved children who burned with zeal for you and abhorred the pollution

a Cn: Gk *loosed her womb*

of their blood and called on you for help. O God, my God, hear me also, a widow.

5 'For you have done these things and those that went before and those that followed. You have designed the things that are now, and those that are to come. What you had in mind has happened; 6 the things you decided on presented themselves and said, "Here we are!" For all your ways are prepared in advance, and your judgement is with foreknowledge.

7 'Here now are the Assyrians, a greatly increased force, priding themselves on their horses and riders, boasting in the strength of their foot-soldiers, and trusting in shield and spear, in bow and sling. They do not know that you are the Lord who crushes wars; the Lord is your name. 8 Break their strength by your might, and bring down their power in your anger; for they intend to defile your sanctuary, and to pollute the tabernacle where your glorious name resides, and to break off the horns*a* of your altar with the sword. 9 Look at their pride, and send your wrath upon their heads. Give to me, a widow, the strong hand to do what I plan. 10 By the deceit of my lips strike down the slave with the prince and the prince with his servant; crush their arrogance by the hand of a woman.

11 'For your strength does not depend on numbers, nor your might on the powerful. But you are the God of the lowly, helper of the oppressed, upholder of the weak, protector of the forsaken, saviour of those without hope. 12 Please, please, God of my father, God of the heritage of Israel, Lord of heaven and earth, Creator of the waters, King of all your creation, hear my prayer! 13 Make my deceitful words bring wound and bruise on those who have planned cruel things against your covenant, and against your sacred house, and against Mount Zion, and against the house your children possess. 14 Let your whole nation and every tribe know and understand that you are God, the God of all power and might, and that there is no other who protects the people of Israel but you alone!'

Judith Prepares to Go to Holofernes

10 When Judith*b* had stopped crying out to the God of Israel, and had ended all these words, 2 she rose from where she lay prostrate. She called her maid and went down into the house where she lived on sabbaths and on her festal days. 3 She removed the sackcloth she had been wearing, took off her widow's garments, bathed her body with water, and anointed herself with precious ointment. She combed her hair, put on a tiara, and dressed herself in the festive attire that she used to wear while her husband Manasseh was living. 4 She put sandals on her feet, and put on her anklets, bracelets, rings, ear-rings, and all her other jewellery. Thus she made herself very beautiful, to entice the eyes of all the men who might see her. 5 She gave her maid a skin of wine and a flask of oil, and filled a bag with roasted grain, dried fig cakes, and fine bread;*c* then she wrapped up all her dishes and gave them to her to carry.

6 Then they went out to the town gate of Bethulia and found Uzziah standing there with the elders of the town, Chabris and Charmis. 7 When they saw her transformed in appearance and dressed differently, they were very greatly astounded at her beauty and said to her, 8 'May the God of our ancestors grant you favour and fulfil your plans, so that the people of Israel may glory and Jerusalem may be exalted.' She bowed down to God.

9 Then she said to them, 'Order the gate of the town to be opened for me so that I may go out and accomplish the things you have just said to me.' So they ordered the young men to open the gate for her, as she requested. 10 When they had done this, Judith went out, accompanied by her maid. The men of the town watched her until she had gone down the mountain and passed through the valley, where they lost sight of her.

Judith Is Captured

11 As the women*d* were going straight on through the valley, an Assyrian patrol

a Syr: Gk *horn*   *b* Gk *she*   *c* Other ancient authorities add *and cheese*   *d* Gk *they* met her ¹²and took her into custody. They asked her, 'To what people do you belong, and where are you coming from, and where are you going?' She replied, 'I am a daughter of the Hebrews, but I am fleeing from them, for they are about to be handed over to you to be devoured. ¹³I am on my way to see Holofernes the commander of your army, to give him a true report; I will show him a way by which he can go and capture all the hill country without losing one of his men, captured or slain.'

14 When the men heard her words, and observed her face—she was in their eyes marvellously beautiful—they said to her, ¹⁵'You have saved your life by hurrying down to see our lord. Go at once to his tent; some of us will escort you and hand you over to him. ¹⁶When you stand before him, have no fear in your heart, but tell him what you have just said, and he will treat you well.'

17 They chose from their number a hundred men to accompany her and her maid, and they brought them to the tent of Holofernes. ¹⁸There was great excitement in the whole camp, for her arrival was reported from tent to tent. They came and gathered around her as she stood outside the tent of Holofernes, waiting until they told him about her. ¹⁹They marvelled at her beauty and admired the Israelites, judging them by her. They said to one another, 'Who can despise these people, who have women like this among them? It is not wise to leave one of their men alive, for if we let them go they will be able to beguile the whole world!'

Judith Is Brought before Holofernes

20 Then the guards of Holofernes and all his servants came out and led her into the tent. ²¹Holofernes was resting on his bed under a canopy that was woven with purple and gold, emeralds and other precious stones. ²²When they told him of her, he came to the front of the tent, with silver lamps carried before him. ²³When Judith came into the presence of Holofernes*a* and his servants, they all marvelled at the beauty of her face. She prostrated herself and

did obeisance to him, but his slaves raised her up.

11 Then Holofernes said to her, 'Take courage, woman, and do not be afraid in your heart, for I have never hurt anyone who chose to serve Nebuchadnezzar, king of all the earth. ²Even now, if your people who live in the hill country had not slighted me, I would never have lifted my spear against them. They have brought this on themselves. ³But now tell me why you have fled from them and have come over to us. In any event, you have come to safety. Take courage! You will live tonight and ever after. ⁴No one will hurt you. Rather, all will treat you well, as they do the servants of my lord King Nebuchadnezzar.'

Judith Explains Her Presence

5 Judith answered him, 'Accept the words of your slave, and let your servant speak in your presence. I will say nothing false to my lord this night. ⁶If you follow out the words of your servant, God will accomplish something through you, and my lord will not fail to achieve his purposes. ⁷By the life of Nebuchadnezzar, king of the whole earth, and by the power of him who has sent you to direct every living being! Not only do human beings serve him because of you, but also the animals of the field and the cattle and the birds of the air will live, because of your power, under Nebuchadnezzar and all his house. ⁸For we have heard of your wisdom and skill, and it is reported throughout the whole world that you alone are the best in the whole kingdom, the most informed and the most astounding in military strategy.

9 'Now as for Achior's speech in your council, we have heard his words, for the people of Bethulia spared him and he told them all he had said to you. ¹⁰Therefore, lord and master, do not disregard what he said, but keep it in your mind, for it is true. Indeed our nation cannot be punished, nor can the sword prevail against them, unless they sin against their God.

11 'But now, in order that my lord may not be defeated and his purpose frustrated,

a Gk *him*

death will fall upon them, for a sin has overtaken them by which they are about to provoke their God to anger when they do what is wrong. ¹²Since their food supply is exhausted and their water has almost given out, they have planned to kill their livestock and have determined to use all that God by his laws has forbidden them to eat. ¹³They have decided to consume the first fruits of the grain and the tithes of the wine and oil, which they had consecrated and set aside for the priests who minister in the presence of our God in Jerusalem—things it is not lawful for any of the people even to touch with their hands. ¹⁴Since even the people in Jerusalem have been doing this, they have sent messengers there in order to bring back permission from the council of the elders. ¹⁵When the response reaches them and they act upon it, on that very day they will be handed over to you to be destroyed.

16 'So when I, your slave, learned all this, I fled from them. God has sent me to accomplish with you things that will astonish the whole world wherever people shall hear about them. ¹⁷Your servant is indeed God-fearing and serves the God of heaven night and day. So, my lord, I will remain with you; but every night your servant will go out into the valley and pray to God. He will tell me when they have committed their sins. ¹⁸Then I will come and tell you, so that you may go out with your whole army, and not one of them will be able to withstand you. ¹⁹Then I will lead you through Judea, until you come to Jerusalem; there I will set your throne.ᵃ You will drive them like sheep that have no shepherd, and no dog will so much as growl at you. For this was told me to give me foreknowledge; it was announced to me, and I was sent to tell you.'

20 Her words pleased Holofernes and all his servants. They marvelled at her wisdom and said, ²¹'No other woman from one end of the earth to the other looks so beautiful or speaks so wisely!' ²²Then Holofernes said to her, 'God has done well to send you ahead of the people, to strengthen our hands and bring destruc-

tion on those who have despised my lord. ²³You are not only beautiful in appearance, but wise in speech. If you do as you have said, your God shall be my God, and you shall live in the palace of King Nebuchadnezzar and be renowned throughout the whole world.'

Judith as a Guest of Holofernes

12 Then he commanded them to bring her in where his silver dinnerware was kept, and ordered them to set a table for her with some of his own delicacies, and with some of his own wine to drink. ²But Judith said, 'I cannot partake of them, or it will be an offence; but I will have enough with the things I brought with me.' ³Holofernes said to her, 'If your supply runs out, where can we get you more of the same? For none of your people are here with us.' ⁴Judith replied, 'As surely as you live, my lord, your servant will not use up the supplies I have with me before the Lord carries out by my hand what he has determined.'

5 Then the servants of Holofernes brought her into the tent, and she slept until midnight. Towards the morning watch she got up ⁶and sent this message to Holofernes: 'Let my lord now give orders to allow your servant to go out and pray.' ⁷So Holofernes commanded his guards not to hinder her. She remained in the camp for three days. She went out each night to the valley of Bethulia, and bathed at the spring in the camp.ᵇ ⁸After bathing, she prayed the Lord God of Israel to direct her way for the triumph of hisᶜ people. ⁹Then she returned purified and stayed in the tent until she ate her food towards evening.

Judith Attends Holofernes' Banquet

10 On the fourth day Holofernes held a banquet for his personal attendants only, and did not invite any of his officers. ¹¹He said to Bagoas, the eunuch who had charge of his personal affairs, 'Go and persuade the Hebrew woman who is in your care to

a Or chariot   b Other ancient authorities lack in the camp   c Other ancient authorities read her join us and to eat and drink with us. ¹²For it would be a disgrace if we let such a woman go without having intercourse with her. If we do not seduce her, she will laugh at us.'

13 So Bagoas left the presence of Holofernes, and approached her and said, 'Let this pretty girl not hesitate to come to my lord to be honoured in his presence, and to enjoy drinking wine with us, and to become today like one of the Assyrian women who serve in the palace of Nebuchadnezzar.' ¹⁴Judith replied, 'Who am I to refuse my lord? Whatever pleases him I will do at once, and it will be a joy to me until the day of my death.' ¹⁵So she proceeded to dress herself in all her woman's finery. Her maid went ahead and spread for her on the ground before Holofernes the lambskins she had received from Bagoas for her daily use in reclining.

16 Then Judith came in and lay down. Holofernes' heart was ravished with her and his passion was aroused, for he had been waiting for an opportunity to seduce her from the day he first saw her. ¹⁷So Holofernes said to her, 'Have a drink and be merry with us!' ¹⁸Judith said, 'I will gladly drink, my lord, because today is the greatest day in my whole life.' ¹⁹Then she took what her maid had prepared and ate and drank before him. ²⁰Holofernes was greatly pleased with her, and drank a great quantity of wine, much more than he had ever drunk in any one day since he was born.

Judith Beheads Holofernes

13 When evening came, his slaves quickly withdrew. Bagoas closed the tent from outside and shut out the attendants from his master's presence. They went to bed, for they all were weary because the banquet had lasted so long. ²But Judith was left alone in the tent, with Holofernes stretched out on his bed, for he was dead drunk.

3 Now Judith had told her maid to stand outside the bedchamber and to wait for her to come out, as she did on the other days; for she said she would be going out for her prayers. She had said the same

thing to Bagoas. ⁴So everyone went out, and no one, either small or great, was left in the bedchamber. Then Judith, standing beside his bed, said in her heart, 'O Lord God of all might, look in this hour on the work of my hands for the exaltation of Jerusalem. ⁵Now indeed is the time to help your heritage and to carry out my design to destroy the enemies who have risen up against us.'

6 She went up to the bedpost near Holofernes' head, and took down his sword that hung there. ⁷She came close to his bed, took hold of the hair of his head, and said, 'Give me strength today, O Lord God of Israel!' ⁸Then she struck his neck twice with all her might, and cut off his head. ⁹Next she rolled his body off the bed and pulled down the canopy from the posts. Soon afterwards she went out and gave Holofernes' head to her maid, ¹⁰who placed it in her food bag.

Judith Returns to Bethulia

Then the two of them went out together, as they were accustomed to do for prayer. They passed through the camp, circled around the valley, and went up the mountain to Bethulia, and came to its gates. ¹¹From a distance Judith called out to the sentries at the gates, 'Open, open the gate! God, our God, is with us, still showing his power in Israel and his strength against our enemies, as he has done today!'

12 When the people of her town heard her voice, they hurried down to the town gate and summoned the elders of the town. ¹³They all ran together, both small and great, for it seemed unbelievable that she had returned. They opened the gate and welcomed them. Then they lit a fire to give light, and gathered around them. ¹⁴Then she said to them with a loud voice, 'Praise God, O praise him! Praise God, who has not withdrawn his mercy from the house of Israel, but has destroyed our enemies by my hand this very night!'

15 Then she pulled the head out of the bag and showed it to them, and said, 'See here, the head of Holofernes, the commander of the Assyrian army, and here is

the canopy beneath which he lay in his drunken stupor. The Lord has struck him down by the hand of a woman. 16 As the Lord lives, who has protected me on the way I went, I swear that it was my face that seduced him to his destruction, and that he committed no sin with me, to defile and shame me.'

17 All the people were greatly astonished. They bowed down and worshipped God, and said with one accord, 'Blessed are you our God, who have this day humiliated the enemies of your people.'

18 Then Uzziah said to her, 'O daughter, you are blessed by the Most High God above all other women on earth; and blessed be the Lord God, who created the heavens and the earth, who has guided you to cut off the head of the leader of our enemies. 19 Your praise*a* will never depart from the hearts of those who remember the power of God. 20 May God grant this to be a perpetual honour to you, and may he reward you with blessings, because you risked your own life when our nation was brought low, and you averted our ruin, walking in the straight path before our God.' And all the people said, 'Amen. Amen.'

Judith's Counsel

14 Then Judith said to them, 'Listen to me, my friends. Take this head and hang it upon the parapet of your wall. 2 As soon as day breaks and the sun rises on the earth, each of you take up your weapons, and let every able-bodied man go out of the town; set a captain over them, as if you were going down to the plain against the Assyrian outpost; only do not go down. 3 Then they will seize their arms and go into the camp and rouse the officers of the Assyrian army. They will rush into the tent of Holofernes and will not find him. Then panic will come over them, and they will flee before you. 4 Then you and all who live within the borders of Israel will pursue them and cut them down in their tracks. 5 But before you do all this, bring Achior the Ammonite to me so that he may see and recognize the man who de-

spised the house of Israel and sent him to us as if to his death.'

6 So they summoned Achior from the house of Uzziah. When he came and saw the head of Holofernes in the hand of one of the men in the assembly of the people, he fell down on his face in a faint. 7 When they raised him up he threw himself at Judith's feet, and did obeisance to her, and said, 'Blessed are you in every tent of Judah! In every nation those who hear your name will be alarmed. 8 Now tell me what you have done during these days.'

So Judith told him in the presence of the people all that she had done, from the day she left until the moment she began speaking to them. 9 When she had finished, the people raised a great shout and made a joyful noise in their town. 10 When Achior saw all that the God of Israel had done, he believed firmly in God. So he was circumcised, and joined the house of Israel, remaining so to this day.

Holofernes' Death Is Discovered

11 As soon as it was dawn they hung the head of Holofernes on the wall. Then they all took their weapons, and they went out in companies to the mountain passes. 12 When the Assyrians saw them they sent word to their commanders, who then went to the generals and the captains and to all their other officers. 13 They came to Holofernes' tent and said to the steward in charge of all his personal affairs, 'Wake up our lord, for the slaves have been so bold as to come down against us to give battle, to their utter destruction.'

14 So Bagoas went in and knocked at the entry of the tent, for he supposed that he was sleeping with Judith. 15 But when no one answered, he opened it and went into the bedchamber and found him sprawled on the floor dead, with his head missing. 16 He cried out with a loud voice and wept and groaned and shouted, and tore his clothes. 17 Then he went to the tent where Judith had stayed, and when he did not find her, he rushed out to the people and shouted, 18 'The slaves have tricked us!

a Other ancient authorities read *hope*

One Hebrew woman has brought disgrace on the house of King Nebuchadnezzar. Look, Holofernes is lying on the ground, and his head is missing!'

19 When the leaders of the Assyrian army heard this, they tore their tunics and were greatly dismayed, and their loud cries and shouts rose up throughout the camp.

The Assyrians Flee in Panic

15 When the men in the tents heard it, they were amazed at what had happened. ² Overcome with fear and trembling, they did not wait for one another, but with one impulse all rushed out and fled by every path across the plain and through the hill country. ³ Those who had camped in the hills around Bethulia also took to flight. Then the Israelites, everyone that was a soldier, rushed out upon them. ⁴ Uzziah sent men to Betomasthaim*a* and Choba and Kola, and to all the frontiers of Israel, to tell what had taken place and to urge all to rush out upon the enemy to destroy them. ⁵ When the Israelites heard it, with one accord they fell upon the enemy,*b* and cut them down as far as Choba. Those in Jerusalem and all the hill country also came, for they were told what had happened in the camp of the enemy. The men in Gilead and in Galilee outflanked them with great slaughter, even beyond Damascus and its borders. ⁶ The rest of the people of Bethulia fell upon the Assyrian camp and plundered it, acquiring great riches. ⁷ And the Israelites, when they returned from the slaughter, took possession of what remained. Even the villages and towns in the hill country and in the plain got a great amount of booty, since there was a vast quantity of it.

The Israelites Celebrate Their Victory

8 Then the high priest Joakim and the elders of the Israelites who lived in Jerusalem came to witness the good things that the Lord had done for Israel, and to see Judith and to wish her well. ⁹ When they met her, they all blessed her with one accord and said to her, 'You are the glory of Jerusalem, you are the great boast of Israel, you are the great pride of our nation! ¹⁰ You have done all this with your own hand; you have done great good to Israel, and God is well pleased with it. May the Almighty Lord bless you for ever!' And all the people said, 'Amen.'

11 All the people plundered the camp for thirty days. They gave Judith the tent of Holofernes and all his silver dinnerware, his beds, his bowls, and all his furniture. She took them and loaded her mules and hitched up her carts and piled the things on them.

12 All the women of Israel gathered to see her, and blessed her, and some of them performed a dance in her honour. She took ivy-wreathed wands in her hands and distributed them to the women who were with her; ¹³ and she and those who were with her crowned themselves with olive wreaths. She went before all the people in the dance, leading all the women, while all the men of Israel followed, bearing their arms and wearing garlands and singing hymns.

Judith Offers Her Hymn of Praise

14 Judith began this thanksgiving before all Israel, and all the people loudly

16 sang this song of praise. ¹ And Judith said,
Begin a song to my God with
tambourines,
sing to my Lord with cymbals.
Raise to him a new psalm;*c*
exalt him, and call upon his name.
² For the Lord is a God who crushes
wars;
he sets up his camp among his
people;
he delivered me from the hands of
my pursuers.
³ The Assyrian came down from the
mountains of the north;
he came with myriads of his
warriors;
their numbers blocked up the wadis,
and their cavalry covered the hills.

---

a Other ancient authorities add *and Bebai*   *b* Gk *them*
c Other ancient authorities read *a psalm and praise*

4 He boasted that he would burn up
        my territory,
    and kill my young men with the
        sword,
    and dash my infants to the ground,
    and seize my children as booty,
    and take my virgins as spoil.

5 But the Lord Almighty has foiled
        them
    by the hand of a woman. *a*
6 For their mighty one did not fall by
        the hands of the young men,
    nor did the sons of the Titans strike
        him down,
    nor did tall giants set upon him;
    but Judith daughter of Merari
    with the beauty of her countenance
        undid him.

7 For she put away her widow's
        clothing
    to exalt the oppressed in Israel.
    She anointed her face with perfume;
8   she fastened her hair with a tiara
    and put on a linen gown to beguile
        him.
9 Her sandal ravished his eyes,
    her beauty captivated his mind,
    and the sword severed his neck!
10 The Persians trembled at her
        boldness,
    the Medes were daunted at her
        daring.

11 Then my oppressed people shouted;
    my weak people cried out, *b* and the
        enemy *c* trembled;
    they lifted up their voices, and the
        enemy *c* were turned back.
12 Sons of slave-girls pierced them
        through
    and wounded them like the
        children of fugitives;
    they perished before the army of
        my Lord.

13 I will sing to my God a new song:
    O Lord, you are great and glorious,
        wonderful in strength, invincible.
14 Let all your creatures serve you,

for you spoke, and they were made.
    You sent forth your spirit, *d* and it
        formed them; *e*
    there is none that can resist your
        voice.
15 For the mountains shall be shaken to
        their foundations with the
        waters;
    before your glance the rocks shall
        melt like wax.
    But to those who fear you
    you show mercy.
16 For every sacrifice as a fragrant
        offering is a small thing,
    and the fat of all whole burnt-
        offerings to you is a very little
        thing;
    but whoever fears the Lord is great
        for ever.

17 Woe to the nations that rise up
        against my people!
    The Lord Almighty will take
        vengeance on them in the day
        of judgement;
    he will send fire and worms into their
        flesh;
    they shall weep in pain for ever.

18 When they arrived at Jerusalem, they worshipped God. As soon as the people were purified, they offered their burnt-offerings, their freewill-offerings, and their gifts. 19 Judith also dedicated to God all the possessions of Holofernes, which the people had given her; and the canopy that she had taken for herself from his bedchamber she gave as a votive offering. 20 For three months the people continued feasting in Jerusalem before the sanctuary, and Judith remained with them.

The Renown and Death of Judith

21 After this they all returned home to their own inheritances. Judith went to Bethulia, and remained on her estate. For the rest of her life she was honoured throughout the whole country. 22 Many

a Other ancient authorities add *he has confounded them*
b Other ancient authorities read *feared*   *c* Gk *they*
d Or *breath*   *e* Other ancient authorities read *they were created*

desired to marry her, but she gave herself to no man all the days of her life after her husband Manasseh died and was gathered to his people. 23 She became more and more famous, and grew old in her husband's house, reaching the age of one hundred and five. She set her maid free. She died in Bethulia, and they buried her in the cave of her husband Manasseh; 24 and the house of Israel mourned her for seven days. Before she died she distributed her property to all those who were next of kin to her husband Manasseh, and to her own nearest kindred. 25 No one ever again spread terror among the Israelites during the lifetime of Judith, or for a long time after her death.

ESTHER

Note: The deuterocanonical portions of the Book of Esther are translated from the Greek version (Septuagint) and comprise one hundred and seven additional verses that have been inserted at the appropriate places in the translation of the Hebrew form of the book. The disordered chapter numbers come from the displacement of the additions to the end of the Hebrew form of the Book of Esther by St. Jerome in his Latin Vulagte translation and from the subsequent division of the Bible into chapters by Stephen Langton, who numbered the additions consecutively as though they formed a direct continuation of the Hebrew text. The deuterocanonical portions are given in the order found in the Greek text so that they may be read in their proper context, but the chapter and verse numbers conform to those of the King James or Authorized Version. Proper names are given according to their Hebrew rather than their Greek form; for example, Ahasuerus and Mordecai instead of Artaxerxes and Mardocheus. The additions, conveniently indicated by the letters A—F, are located as follows: A, before 1.1; B, after 3.13; C and D, after 4.17; E, after 8.12; F after 10.3.

ADDITION A

Mordecai's Dream

11 *a* 2 In the second year of the reign of Artaxerxes the Great, on the first day of Nisan, Mordecai son of Jair son of Shimei *b* son of Kish, of the tribe of Benjamin, had a dream. 3 He was a Jew living in the city of Susa, a great man, serving in the court of the king. 4 He was one of the captives whom King Nebuchadnezzar of Babylon had brought from Jerusalem with King Jeconiah of Judea. And this was his dream: 5 Noises *c* and confusion, thunders and earthquake, tumult on the earth! 6 Then two great dragons came forward, both ready to fight, and they roared terribly. 7 At their roaring every nation prepared for war, to fight against the righteous nation. 8 It was a day of darkness and gloom, of tribulation and distress, affliction and great tumult on the earth! 9 And the whole righteous nation was troubled; they feared the evils that threatened them, *d* and were ready to perish. 10 Then they cried out to God; and at their outcry, as though from a tiny spring, there came a great river, with abundant water; 11 light came, and the sun rose, and the lowly were exalted and devoured those held in honour.

12 Mordecai saw in this dream what God had determined to do, and after he awoke he had it on his mind, seeking all day to understand it in every detail.

A Plot against the King

12 Now Mordecai took his rest in the courtyard with Gabatha and Thara, the two eunuchs of the king who kept watch in the courtyard. 2 He overheard their conversation and inquired into their purposes, and learned that they were preparing to lay hands on King Artaxerxes; and he informed the king concerning them. 3 Then the king examined the two eunuchs, and after they had confessed it, they were led away to execution. 4 The king made a permanent record of these things, and Mordecai wrote an account of them. 5 And the king ordered Mordecai to serve in the court, and rewarded him for these things. 6 But Haman son of Hammedatha, a Bougean, who was held in great honour by the king, determined to injure Mordecai and his people because of the two eunuchs of the king.

END OF ADDITION A

King Ahasuerus Deposes Queen Vashti

1 This happened in the days of Ahasuerus, the same Ahasuerus who ruled over one hundred and twenty-seven provinces from India to Ethiopia. *e* 2 In those days when King Ahasuerus sat on his royal

a Chapters 11.2—12.6 correspond to chapter A 1-17 in some translations.   *b* Gk *Semeios*   *c* Or *Voices*   *d* Gk *their own evils*   *e* Or *Nubia*; Heb *Cush* throne in the citadel of Susa, ³in the third year of his reign, he gave a banquet for all his officials and ministers. The army of Persia and Media and the nobles and governors of the provinces were present, ⁴while he displayed the great wealth of his kingdom and the splendour and pomp of his majesty for many days, one hundred and eighty days in all.

5 When these days were completed, the king gave for all the people present in the citadel of Susa, both great and small, a banquet lasting for seven days, in the court of the garden of the king's palace. ⁶There were white cotton curtains and blue hangings tied with cords of fine linen and purple to silver rings*a* and marble pillars. There were couches of gold and silver on a mosaic pavement of porphyry, marble, mother-of-pearl, and coloured stones. ⁷Drinks were served in golden goblets, goblets of different kinds, and the royal wine was lavished in accordance with the bounty of the king. ⁸Drinking was by flagons, without restraint; for the king had

given orders to all the officials of his palace to do as each one desired. ⁹Furthermore, Queen Vashti gave a banquet for the women in the palace of King Ahasuerus.

10 On the seventh day, when the king was merry with wine, he commanded Mehuman, Biztha, Harbona, Bigtha and Abagtha, Zethar and Carkas, the seven eunuchs who attended him, ¹¹to bring Queen Vashti before the king, wearing the royal crown, in order to show the peoples and the officials her beauty; for she was fair to behold. ¹²But Queen Vashti refused to come at the king's command conveyed by the eunuchs. At this the king was enraged, and his anger burned within him.

13 Then the king consulted the sages who knew the laws*b* (for this was the king's procedure towards all who were versed in law and custom, ¹⁴and those next to him were Carshena, Shethar, Admatha, Tarshish, Meres, Marsena, and Memucan, the seven officials of Persia and Media, who

a Or *rods*   *b* Cn: Heb *times*

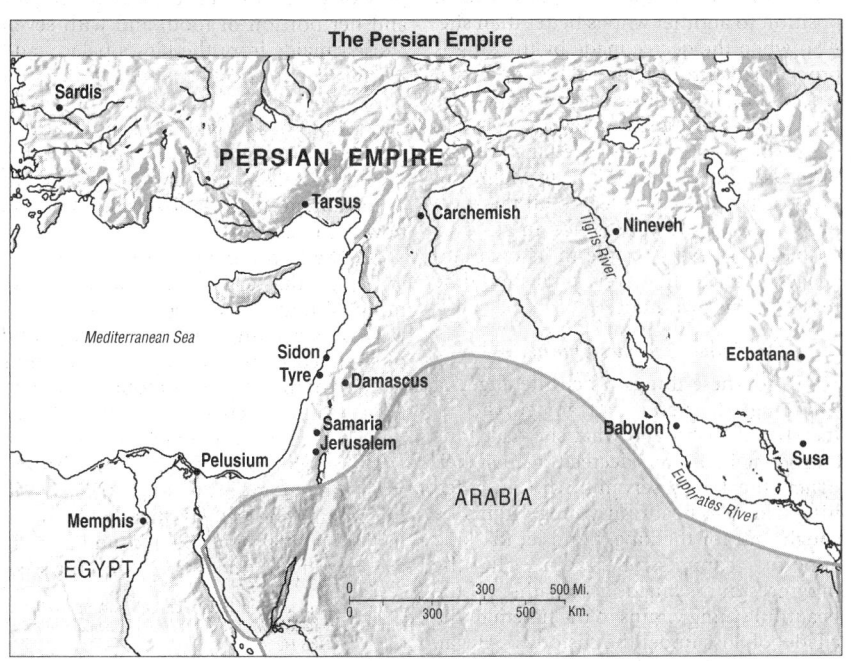

The Persian Empire

had access to the king, and sat first in the kingdom): [15]'According to the law, what is to be done to Queen Vashti because she has not performed the command of King Ahasuerus conveyed by the eunuchs?' [16]Then Memucan said in the presence of the king and the officials, 'Not only has Queen Vashti done wrong to the king, but also to all the officials and all the peoples who are in all the provinces of King Ahasuerus. [17]For this deed of the queen will be made known to all women, causing them to look with contempt on their husbands, since they will say, "King Ahasuerus commanded Queen Vashti to be brought before him, and she did not come." [18]This very day the noble ladies of Persia and Media who have heard of the queen's behaviour will rebel against[a] the king's officials, and there will be no end of contempt and wrath! [19]If it pleases the king, let a royal order go out from him, and let it be written among the laws of the Persians and the Medes so that it may not be altered, that Vashti is never again to come before King Ahasuerus; and let the king give her royal position to another who is better than she. [20]So when the decree made by the king is proclaimed throughout all his kingdom, vast as it is, all women will give honour to their husbands, high and low alike.'

[21] This advice pleased the king and the officials, and the king did as Memucan proposed; [22]he sent letters to all the royal provinces, to every province in its own script and to every people in its own language, declaring that every man should be master in his own house.[b]

Esther Becomes Queen

2 After these things, when the anger of King Ahasuerus had abated, he remembered Vashti and what she had done and what had been decreed against her. [2]Then the king's servants who attended him said, 'Let beautiful young virgins be sought out for the king. [3]And let the king appoint commissioners in all the provinces of his kingdom to gather all the beautiful young virgins to the harem in the citadel of Susa under the custody of Hegai,

the king's eunuch, who is in charge of the women; let their cosmetic treatments be given them. [4]And let the girl who pleases the king be queen instead of Vashti.' This pleased the king, and he did so.

[5] Now there was a Jew in the citadel of Susa whose name was Mordecai son of Jair son of Shimei son of Kish, a Benjaminite. [6]Kish[c] had been carried away from Jerusalem among the captives carried away with King Jeconiah of Judah, whom King Nebuchadnezzar of Babylon had carried away. [7]Mordecai[d] had brought up Hadassah, that is Esther, his cousin, for she had neither father nor mother; the girl was fair and beautiful, and when her father and her mother died, Mordecai adopted her as his own daughter. [8]So when the king's order and his edict were proclaimed, and when many young women were gathered in the citadel of Susa in the custody of Hegai, Esther also was taken into the king's palace and put in the custody of Hegai, who had charge of the women. [9]The girl pleased him and won his favour, and he quickly provided her with her cosmetic treatments and her portion of food, and with seven chosen maids from the king's palace, and advanced her and her maids to the best place in the harem. [10]Esther did not reveal her people or kindred, for Mordecai had charged her not to tell. [11]Every day Mordecai would walk around in front of the court of the harem, to learn how Esther was and how she fared.

[12] The turn came for each girl to go in to King Ahasuerus, after being twelve months under the regulations for the women, since this was the regular period of their cosmetic treatment, six months with oil of myrrh and six months with perfumes and cosmetics for women. [13]When the girl went in to the king she was given whatever she asked for to take with her from the harem to the king's palace. [14]In the evening she went in; then in the morning she came back to the second harem in the custody of Shaashgaz, the king's eu-

---

a Cn: Heb *will tell*   b Heb adds *and speak in accordance with the language of his people*   c Heb *a Benjaminite*
6*who*   d Heb *He*

nuch, who was in charge of the concubines; she did not go in to the king again, unless the king delighted in her and she was summoned by name.

15 When the turn came for Esther daughter of Abihail the uncle of Mordecai, who had adopted her as his own daughter, to go in to the king, she asked for nothing except what Hegai the king's eunuch, who had charge of the women, advised. Now Esther was admired by all who saw her. ¹⁶When Esther was taken to King Ahasuerus in his royal palace in the tenth month, which is the month of Tebeth, in the seventh year of his reign, ¹⁷the king loved Esther more than all the other women; of all the virgins she won his favour and devotion, so that he set the royal crown on her head and made her queen instead of Vashti. ¹⁸Then the king gave a great banquet to all his officials and ministers—'Esther's banquet.' He also granted a holiday*a* to the provinces, and gave gifts with royal liberality.

Mordecai Discovers a Plot

19 When the virgins were being gathered together,*b* Mordecai was sitting at the king's gate. ²⁰Now Esther had not revealed her kindred or her people, as Mordecai had charged her; for Esther obeyed Mordecai just as when she was brought up by him. ²¹In those days, while Mordecai was sitting at the king's gate, Bigthan and Teresh, two of the king's eunuchs, who guarded the threshold, became angry and conspired to assassinate*c* King Ahasuerus. ²²But the matter came to the knowledge of Mordecai, and he told it to Queen Esther, and Esther told the king in the name of Mordecai. ²³When the affair was investigated and found to be so, both the men were hanged on the gallows. It was recorded in the book of the annals in the presence of the king.

Haman Undertakes to Destroy the Jews

3 After these things King Ahasuerus promoted Haman son of Hammedatha the Agagite, and advanced him and set his seat above all the officials who were with him. ²And all the king's servants who were

at the king's gate bowed down and did obeisance to Haman; for the king had so commanded concerning him. But Mordecai did not bow down or do obeisance. ³Then the king's servants who were at the king's gate said to Mordecai, 'Why do you disobey the king's command?' ⁴When they spoke to him day after day and he would not listen to them, they told Haman, in order to see whether Mordecai's words would avail; for he had told them that he was a Jew. ⁵When Haman saw that Mordecai did not bow down or do obeisance to him, Haman was infuriated. ⁶But he thought it beneath him to lay hands on Mordecai alone. So, having been told who Mordecai's people were, Haman plotted to destroy all the Jews, the people of Mordecai, throughout the whole kingdom of Ahasuerus.

7 In the first month, which is the month of Nisan, in the twelfth year of King Ahasuerus, they cast Pur—which means 'the lot'—before Haman for the day and for the month, and the lot fell on the thirteenth day*d* of the twelfth month, which is the month of Adar. ⁸Then Haman said to King Ahasuerus, 'There is a certain people scattered and separated among the peoples in all the provinces of your kingdom; their laws are different from those of every other people, and they do not keep the king's laws, so that it is not appropriate for the king to tolerate them. ⁹If it pleases the king, let a decree be issued for their destruction, and I will pay ten thousand talents of silver into the hands of those who have charge of the king's business, so that they may put it into the king's treasuries.' ¹⁰So the king took his signet ring from his hand and gave it to Haman son of Hammedatha the Agagite, the enemy of the Jews. ¹¹The king said to Haman, 'The money is given to you, and the people as well, to do with them as it seems good to you.'

12 Then the king's secretaries were summoned on the thirteenth day of the first month, and an edict, according to all that

a Or *an amnesty*　　*b* Heb adds *a second time*　　*c* Heb *to lay hands on*　　*d* Cn Compare Gk and verse 13 below: Heb *the twelfth month*

Haman commanded, was written to the king's satraps and to the governors over all the provinces and to the officials of all the peoples, to every province in its own script and every people in its own language; it was written in the name of King Ahasuerus and sealed with the king's ring. ¹³Letters were sent by couriers to all the king's provinces, giving orders to destroy, to kill, and to annihilate all Jews, young and old, women and children, in one day, the thirteenth day of the twelfth month, which is the month of Adar, and to plunder their goods.

Addition B

The King's Letter

13 *a* This is a copy of the letter: 'The Great King, Artaxerxes, writes the following to the governors of the hundred and twenty-seven provinces from India to Ethiopia and to the officials under them:

2 'Having become ruler of many nations and master of the whole world (not elated with presumption of authority but always acting reasonably and with kindness), I have determined to settle the lives of my subjects in lasting tranquillity and, in order to make my kingdom peaceable and open to travel throughout all its extent, to restore the peace desired by all people.

3 'When I asked my counsellors how this might be accomplished, Haman—who excels among us in sound judgement, and is distinguished for his unchanging goodwill and steadfast fidelity, and has attained the second place in the kingdom— ⁴pointed out to us that among all the nations in the world there is scattered a certain hostile people, who have laws contrary to those of every nation and continually disregard the ordinances of kings, so that the unifying of the kingdom that we honourably intend cannot be brought about. ⁵We understand that this people, and it alone, stands constantly in opposition to every nation, perversely following a strange manner of life and laws, and is ill-disposed to our government, doing all the harm

they can so that our kingdom may not attain stability.

6 'Therefore we have decreed that those indicated to you in the letters written by Haman, who is in charge of affairs and is our second father, shall all—wives and children included—be utterly destroyed by the swords of their enemies, without pity or restraint, on the fourteenth day of the twelfth month, Adar, of this present year, ⁷so that those who have long been hostile and remain so may in a single day go down in violence to Hades, and leave our government completely secure and untroubled hereafter.'

End of Addition B

---

3 ¹⁴A copy of the document was to be issued as a decree in every province by proclamation, calling on all the peoples to be ready for that day. ¹⁵The couriers went quickly by order of the king, and the decree was issued in the citadel of Susa. The king and Haman sat down to drink; but the city of Susa was thrown into confusion.

Esther Agrees to Help the Jews

4 When Mordecai learned all that had been done, Mordecai tore his clothes and put on sackcloth and ashes, and went through the city, wailing with a loud and bitter cry; ²he went up to the entrance of the king's gate, for no one might enter the king's gate clothed with sackcloth. ³In every province, wherever the king's command and his decree came, there was great mourning among the Jews, with fasting and weeping and lamenting, and most of them lay in sackcloth and ashes.

4 When Esther's maids and her eunuchs came and told her, the queen was deeply distressed; she sent garments to clothe Mordecai, so that he might take off his sackcloth; but he would not accept them. ⁵Then Esther called for Hathach, one of the king's eunuchs, who had been appointed to attend her, and ordered him to go to Mordecai to learn what was happen-

a Chapter 13.1-7 corresponds to chapter B 1-7 in some translations.

ing and why. 6 Hathach went out to Mordecai in the open square of the city in front of the king's gate, 7 and Mordecai told him all that had happened to him, and the exact sum of money that Haman had promised to pay into the king's treasuries for the destruction of the Jews. 8 Mordecai also gave him a copy of the written decree issued in Susa for their destruction, that he might show it to Esther, explain it to her, and charge her to go to the king to make supplication to him and entreat him for her people.

9 Hathach went and told Esther what Mordecai had said. 10 Then Esther spoke to Hathach and gave him a message for Mordecai, saying, 11 'All the king's servants and the people of the king's provinces know that if any man or woman goes to the king inside the inner court without being called, there is but one law—all alike are to be put to death. Only if the king holds out the golden sceptre to someone, may that person live. I myself have not been called to come in to the king for thirty days.' 12 When they told Mordecai what Esther had said, 13 Mordecai told them to reply to Esther, 'Do not think that in the king's palace you will escape any more than all the other Jews. 14 For if you keep silence at such a time as this, relief and deliverance will rise for the Jews from another quarter, but you and your father's family will perish. Who knows? Perhaps you have come to royal dignity for just such a time as this.' 15 Then Esther said in reply to Mordecai, 16 'Go, gather all the Jews to be found in Susa, and hold a fast on my behalf, and neither eat nor drink for three days, night or day. I and my maids will also fast as you do. After that I will go to the king, though it is against the law; and if I perish, I perish.' 17 Mordecai then went away and did everything as Esther had ordered him.

Mordecai's Prayer

13 8 a Then Mordecai b prayed to the Lord, calling to remembrance all the works of the Lord.

9 He said, 'O Lord, Lord, you rule as King over all things, for the universe is in your power and there is no one who can oppose you when it is your will to save Israel, 10 for you have made heaven and earth and every wonderful thing under heaven. 11 You are Lord of all, and there is no one who can resist you, the Lord. 12 You know all things; you know, O Lord, that it was not in insolence or pride or for any love of glory that I did this, and refused to bow down to this proud Haman; 13 for I would have been willing to kiss the soles of his feet to save Israel! 14 But I did this so that I might not set human glory above the glory of God, and I will not bow down to anyone but you, who are my Lord; and I will not do these things in pride. 15 And now, O Lord God and King, God of Abraham, spare your people; for the eyes of our foes are upon us c to annihilate us, and they desire to destroy the inheritance that has been yours from the beginning. 16 Do not neglect your portion, which you redeemed for yourself out of the land of Egypt. 17 Hear my prayer, and have mercy upon your inheritance; turn our mourning into feasting, that we may live and sing praise to your name, O Lord; do not destroy the lips d of those who praise you.'

18 And all Israel cried out mightily, for their death was before their eyes.

Esther's Prayer

14 Then Queen Esther, seized with deadly anxiety, fled to the Lord. 2 She took off her splendid apparel and put on the garments of distress and mourning, and instead of costly perfumes she covered her head with ashes and dung, and she utterly humbled her body; every part that she loved to adorn she covered with her tangled hair. 3 She prayed to the Lord God of Israel, and said: 'O my Lord, you only are our king; help me, who am alone and have no helper but you, 4 for my danger is in my hand. 5 Ever since I was born I have heard in the tribe of my family that you, O Lord,

---

a Chapters 13.8—15.16 correspond to chapters C 1-30 and D 1-16 in some translations.   b Gk he   c Gk for they are eyeing us   d Gk mouth took Israel out of all the nations, and our ancestors from among all their forebears, for an everlasting inheritance, and that you did for them all that you promised. ⁶And now we have sinned before you, and you have handed us over to our enemies ⁷because we glorified their gods. You are righteous, O Lord! ⁸And now they are not satisfied that we are in bitter slavery, but they have covenanted with their idols ⁹to abolish what your mouth has ordained, and to destroy your inheritance, to stop the mouths of those who praise you and to quench your altar and the glory of your house, ¹⁰to open the mouths of the nations for the praise of vain idols, and to magnify for ever a mortal king.

11 'O Lord, do not surrender your sceptre to what has no being; and do not let them laugh at our downfall; but turn their plan against them, and make an example of him who began this against us. ¹²Remember, O Lord; make yourself known in this time of our affliction, and give me courage, O King of the gods and Master of all dominion! ¹³Put eloquent speech in my mouth before the lion, and turn his heart to hate the man who is fighting against us, so that there may be an end of him and those who agree with him. ¹⁴But save us by your hand, and help me, who am alone and have no helper but you, O Lord. ¹⁵You have knowledge of all things, and you know that I hate the splendour of the wicked and abhor the bed of the uncircumcised and of any alien. ¹⁶You know my necessity—that I abhor the sign of my proud position, which is upon my head on days when I appear in public. I abhor it like a filthy rag, and I do not wear it on the days when I am at leisure. ¹⁷And your servant has not eaten at Haman's table, and I have not honoured the king's feast or drunk the wine of libations. ¹⁸Your servant has had no joy since the day that I was brought here until now, except in you, O Lord God of Abraham. ¹⁹O God, whose might is over all, hear the voice of the despairing, and save us from the hands of evildoers. And save me from my fear!'

END OF ADDITION C

ADDITION D

Esther Is Received by the King

15 On the third day, when she ended her prayer, she took off the garments in which she had worshipped, and arrayed herself in splendid attire. ²Then, majestically adorned, after invoking the aid of the all-seeing God and Saviour, she took two maids with her; ³on one she leaned gently for support, ⁴while the other followed, carrying her train. ⁵She was radiant with perfect beauty, and she looked happy, as if beloved, but her heart was frozen with fear. ⁶When she had gone through all the doors, she stood before the king. He was seated on his royal throne, clothed in the full array of his majesty, all covered with gold and precious stones. He was most terrifying.

7 Lifting his face, flushed with splendour, he looked at her in fierce anger. The queen faltered, and turned pale and faint, and collapsed on the head of the maid who went in front of her. ⁸Then God changed the spirit of the king to gentleness, and in alarm he sprang from his throne and took her in his arms until she came to herself. He comforted her with soothing words, and said to her, ⁹'What is it, Esther? I am your husband.ᵃ Take courage; ¹⁰You shall not die, for our law applies only to our subjects.ᵇ Come near.'

11 Then he raised the golden sceptre and touched her neck with it; ¹²he embraced her, and said, 'Speak to me.' ¹³She said to him, 'I saw you, my lord, like an angel of God, and my heart was shaken with fear at your glory. ¹⁴For you are wonderful, my lord, and your countenance is full of grace.' ¹⁵And while she was speaking, she fainted and fell. ¹⁶Then the king was agitated, and all his servants tried to comfort her.

END OF ADDITION D

---

a Gk *brother*   *b* Meaning of Gk uncertain

Esther's Banquet

5 [a] ³The king said to her, 'What is it, Queen Esther? What is your request? It shall be given you, even to the half of my kingdom.' ⁴Then Esther said, 'If it pleases the king, let the king and Haman come today to a banquet that I have prepared for the king.' ⁵Then the king said, 'Bring Haman quickly, so that we may do as Esther desires.' So the king and Haman came to the banquet that Esther had prepared. ⁶While they were drinking wine, the king said to Esther, 'What is your petition? It shall be granted you. And what is your request? Even to the half of my kingdom, it shall be fulfilled.' ⁷Then Esther said, 'This is my petition and request: ⁸If I have won the king's favour, and if it pleases the king to grant my petition and fulfil my request, let the king and Haman come tomorrow to the banquet that I will prepare for them, and then I will do as the king has said.'

Haman Plans to Have Mordecai Hanged

⁹ Haman went out that day happy and in good spirits. But when Haman saw Mordecai in the king's gate, and observed that he neither rose nor trembled before him, he was infuriated with Mordecai; ¹⁰nevertheless, Haman restrained himself and went home. Then he sent and called for his friends and his wife Zeresh, ¹¹and Haman recounted to them the splendour of his riches, the number of his sons, all the promotions with which the king had honoured him, and how he had advanced him above the officials and the ministers of the king. ¹²Haman added, 'Even Queen Esther let no one but myself come with the king to the banquet that she prepared. Tomorrow also I am invited by her, together with the king. ¹³Yet all this does me no good so long as I see the Jew Mordecai sitting at the king's gate.' ¹⁴Then his wife Zeresh and all his friends said to him, 'Let a gallows fifty cubits high be made, and in the morning tell the king to have Mordecai hanged on it; then go with the king to the banquet in good spirits.' This advice pleased Haman, and he had the gallows made.

The King Honours Mordecai

6 That night the king could not sleep, and he gave orders to bring the book of records, the annals, and they were read to the king. ²It was found written how Mordecai had told about Bigthana and Teresh, two of the king's eunuchs, who guarded the threshold, and who had conspired to assassinate[b] King Ahasuerus. ³Then the king said, 'What honour or distinction has been bestowed on Mordecai for this?' The king's servants who attended him said, 'Nothing has been done for him.' ⁴The king said, 'Who is in the court?' Now Haman had just entered the outer court of the king's palace to speak to the king about having Mordecai hanged on the gallows that he had prepared for him. ⁵So the king's servants told him, 'Haman is there, standing in the court.' The king said, 'Let him come in.' ⁶So Haman came in, and the king said to him, 'What shall be done for the man whom the king wishes to honour?' Haman said to himself, 'Whom would the king wish to honour more than me?' ⁷So Haman said to the king, 'For the man whom the king wishes to honour, ⁸let royal robes be brought, which the king has worn, and a horse that the king has ridden, with a royal crown on its head. ⁹Let the robes and the horse be handed over to one of the king's most noble officials; let him[c] robe the man whom the king wishes to honour, and let him[c] conduct the man on horseback through the open square of the city, proclaiming before him: "Thus shall it be done for the man whom the king wishes to honour." ' ¹⁰Then the king said to Haman, 'Quickly, take the robes and the horse, as you have said, and do so to the Jew Mordecai who sits at the king's gate. Leave out nothing that you have mentioned.' ¹¹So Haman took the robes and the horse and robed Mordecai and led him riding through the open square of the city, proclaiming, 'Thus shall it be done for the man whom the king wishes to honour.'

¹² Then Mordecai returned to the king's gate, but Haman hurried to his house,

---

a In Greek, Chapter D replaces verses 1 and 2 in Hebrew.　*b* Heb *to lay hands on*　*c* Heb *them* mourning and with his head covered. ¹³When Haman told his wife Zeresh and all his friends everything that had happened to him, his advisers and his wife Zeresh said to him, 'If Mordecai, before whom your downfall has begun, is of the Jewish people, you will not prevail against him, but will surely fall before him.'

Haman's Downfall and
Mordecai's Advancement

14 While they were still talking with him, the king's eunuchs arrived and hurried Haman off to the banquet that Esther

7 had prepared. ¹So the king and Haman went in to feast with Queen Esther. ²On the second day, as they were drinking wine, the king again said to Esther, 'What is your petition, Queen Esther? It shall be granted you. And what is your request? Even to the half of my kingdom, it shall be fulfilled.' ³Then Queen Esther answered, 'If I have won your favour, O king, and if it pleases the king, let my life be given me—that is my petition—and the lives of my people—that is my request. ⁴For we have been sold, I and my people, to be destroyed, to be killed, and to be annihilated. If we had been sold merely as slaves, men and women, I would have held my peace; but no enemy can compensate for this damage to the king.'ᵃ ⁵Then King Ahasuerus said to Queen Esther, 'Who is he, and where is he, who has presumed to do this?' ⁶Esther said, 'A foe and enemy, this wicked Haman!' Then Haman was terrified before the king and the queen. ⁷The king rose from the feast in wrath and went into the palace garden, but Haman stayed to beg his life from Queen Esther, for he saw that the king had determined to destroy him. ⁸When the king returned from the palace garden to the banquet hall, Haman had thrown himself on the couch where Esther was reclining; and the king said, 'Will he even assault the queen in my presence, in my own house?' As the words left the mouth of the king, they covered Haman's face. ⁹Then Harbona, one of the eunuchs in attendance on the king, said, 'Look, the very gallows that Haman has

prepared for Mordecai, whose word saved the king, stands at Haman's house, fifty cubits high.' And the king said, 'Hang him on that.' ¹⁰So they hanged Haman on the gallows that he had prepared for Mordecai. Then the anger of the king abated.

8 ¹On that day King Ahasuerus gave to Queen Esther the house of Haman, the enemy of the Jews; and Mordecai came before the king, for Esther had told what he was to her. ²Then the king took off his signet ring, which he had taken from Haman, and gave it to Mordecai. So Esther set Mordecai over the house of Haman.

Esther Saves the Jews

3 Then Esther spoke again to the king; she fell at his feet, weeping and pleading with him to avert the evil design of Haman the Agagite and the plot that he had devised against the Jews. ⁴The king held out the golden sceptre to Esther, ⁵and Esther rose and stood before the king. She said, 'If it pleases the king, and if I have won his favour, and if the thing seems right before the king, and I have his approval, let an order be written to revoke the letters devised by Haman son of Hammedatha the Agagite, which he wrote giving orders to destroy the Jews who are in all the provinces of the king. ⁶For how can I bear to see the calamity that is coming on my people? Or how can I bear to see the destruction of my kindred?' ⁷Then King Ahasuerus said to Queen Esther and to the Jew Mordecai, 'See, I have given Esther the house of Haman, and they have hanged him on the gallows, because he plotted to lay hands on the Jews. ⁸You may write as you please with regard to the Jews, in the name of the king, and seal it with the king's ring; for an edict written in the name of the king and sealed with the king's ring cannot be revoked.'

9 The king's secretaries were summoned at that time, in the third month, which is the month of Sivan, on the twenty-third day; and an edict was written, according to all that Mordecai commanded, to the Jews and to the satraps and the governors and

ᵃ Meaning of Heb uncertain

the officials of the provinces from India to Ethiopia, *a* one hundred and twenty-seven provinces, to every province in its own script and to every people in its own language, and also to the Jews in their script and their language. ¹⁰ He wrote letters in the name of King Ahasuerus, sealed them with the king's ring, and sent them by mounted couriers riding on fast steeds bred from the royal herd. *b* ¹¹ By these letters the king allowed the Jews who were in every city to assemble and defend their lives, to destroy, to kill, and to annihilate any armed force of any people or province that might attack them, with their children and women, and to plunder their goods ¹² on a single day throughout all the provinces of King Ahasuerus, on the thirteenth day of the twelfth month, which is the month of Adar.

ADDITION E

The Decree of Artaxerxes

16 *c* The following is a copy of this letter:

'The Great King, Artaxerxes, to the governors of the provinces from India to Ethiopia, one hundred and twenty-seven provinces, and to those who are loyal to our government, greetings.

2 'Many people, the more they are honoured with the most generous kindness of their benefactors, the more proud do they become, ³ and not only seek to injure our subjects, but in their inability to stand prosperity, they even undertake to scheme against their own benefactors. ⁴ They not only take away thankfulness from others, but, carried away by the boasts of those who know nothing of goodness, they even assume that they will escape the evil-hating justice of God, who always sees everything. ⁵ And often many of those who are set in places of authority have been made in part responsible for the shedding of innocent blood, and have been involved in irremediable calamities, by the persuasion of friends who have been entrusted with the administration of public affairs, ⁶ when these persons by the false trickery of their evil natures beguile the sincere goodwill of their sovereigns.

7 'What has been wickedly accomplished through the pestilent behaviour of those who exercise authority unworthily can be seen, not so much from the more ancient records that we hand on, as from investigation of matters close at hand. *d* ⁸ In the future we will take care to render our kingdom quiet and peaceable for all, ⁹ by changing our methods and always judging what comes before our eyes with more equitable consideration. ¹⁰ For Haman son of Hammedatha, a Macedonian (really an alien to the Persian blood, and quite devoid of our kindliness), having become our guest, ¹¹ enjoyed so fully the goodwill that we have for every nation that he was called our father and was continually bowed down to by all as the person second to the royal throne. ¹² But, unable to restrain his arrogance, he undertook to deprive us of our kingdom and our life, *e* ¹³ and with intricate craft and deceit asked for the destruction of Mordecai, our saviour and perpetual benefactor, and of Esther, the blameless partner of our kingdom, together with their whole nation. ¹⁴ He thought that by these methods he would catch us undefended and would transfer the kingdom of the Persians to the Macedonians.

15 'But we find that the Jews, who were consigned to annihilation by this thrice-accursed man, are not evildoers, but are governed by most righteous laws ¹⁶ and are children of the living God, most high, most mighty, *f* who has directed the kingdom both for us and for our ancestors in the most excellent order.

17 'You will therefore do well not to put in execution the letters sent by Haman son of Hammedatha, ¹⁸ since he, the one who did these things, has been hanged at the gate of Susa with all his household—for God, who rules over all things, has speedily inflicted on him the punishment that he deserved.

a Or *Nubia*; Heb *Cush*   *b* Meaning of Heb uncertain
c Chapter 16.1-24 corresponds to chapter E 1-24 in some translations.   *d* Gk *matters beside* (your) *feet*
e Gk *our spirit*   *f* Gk *greatest*

19 'Therefore post a copy of this letter publicly in every place, and permit the Jews to live under their own laws. 20 And give them reinforcements, so that on the thirteenth day of the twelfth month, Adar, on that very day, they may defend themselves against those who attack them at the time of oppression. 21 For God, who rules over all things, has made this day to be a joy for his chosen people instead of a day of destruction for them.

22 'Therefore you shall observe this with all good cheer as a notable day among your commemorative festivals, 23 so that both now and hereafter it may represent deliverance for you*a* and the loyal Persians, but that it may be a reminder of destruction for those who plot against us.

24 'Every city and country, without exception, that does not act accordingly shall be destroyed in wrath with spear and fire. It shall be made not only impassable for human beings, but also most hateful to wild animals and birds for all time.

END OF ADDITION E

8 13 A copy of the writ was to be issued as a decree in every province and published to all peoples, and the Jews were to be ready on that day to take revenge on their enemies. 14 So the couriers, mounted on their swift royal steeds, hurried out, urged by the king's command. The decree was issued in the citadel of Susa.

15 Then Mordecai went out from the presence of the king, wearing royal robes of blue and white, with a great golden crown and a mantle of fine linen and purple, while the city of Susa shouted and rejoiced. 16 For the Jews there was light and gladness, joy and honour. 17 In every province and in every city, wherever the king's command and his edict came, there was gladness and joy among the Jews, a festival and a holiday. Furthermore, many of the peoples of the country professed to be Jews, because the fear of the Jews had fallen upon them.

Destruction of the Enemies of the Jews

9 Now in the twelfth month, which is the month of Adar, on the thirteenth day, when the king's command and edict were about to be executed, on the very day when the enemies of the Jews hoped to gain power over them, but which had been changed to a day when the Jews would gain power over their foes, 2 the Jews gathered in their cities throughout all the provinces of King Ahasuerus to lay hands on those who had sought their ruin; and no one could withstand them, because the fear of them had fallen upon all peoples. 3 All the officials of the provinces, the satraps and the governors, and the royal officials were supporting the Jews, because the fear of Mordecai had fallen upon them. 4 For Mordecai was powerful in the king's house, and his fame spread throughout all the provinces as the man Mordecai grew more and more powerful. 5 So the Jews struck down all their enemies with the sword, slaughtering, and destroying them, and did as they pleased to those who hated them. 6 In the citadel of Susa the Jews killed and destroyed five hundred people. 7 They killed Parshandatha, Dalphon, Aspatha, 8 Poratha, Adalia, Aridatha, 9 Parmashta, Arisai, Aridai, Vaizatha, 10 the ten sons of Haman son of Hammedatha, the enemy of the Jews; but they did not touch the plunder.

11 That very day the number of those killed in the citadel of Susa was reported to the king. 12 The king said to Queen Esther, 'In the citadel of Susa the Jews have killed five hundred people and also the ten sons of Haman. What have they done in the rest of the king's provinces? Now what is your petition? It shall be granted you. And what further is your request? It shall be fulfilled.' 13 Esther said, 'If it pleases the king, let the Jews who are in Susa be allowed tomorrow also to do according to this day's edict, and let the ten sons of Haman be hanged on the gallows.' 14 So the king commanded this to be done; a decree was issued in Susa, and the ten sons of Haman were

a Other ancient authorities read *for us*

hanged. [15] The Jews who were in Susa gathered also on the fourteenth day of the month of Adar and they killed three hundred people in Susa; but they did not touch the plunder.

16 Now the other Jews who were in the king's provinces also gathered to defend their lives, and gained relief from their enemies, and killed seventy-five thousand of those who hated them; but they laid no hands on the plunder. [17] This was on the thirteenth day of the month of Adar, and on the fourteenth day they rested and made that a day of feasting and gladness.

The Feast of Purim Inaugurated

18 But the Jews who were in Susa gathered on the thirteenth day and on the fourteenth, and rested on the fifteenth day, making that a day of feasting and gladness. [19] Therefore the Jews of the villages, who live in the open towns, hold the fourteenth day of the month of Adar as a day for gladness and feasting, a holiday on which they send gifts of food to one another.

20 Mordecai recorded these things, and sent letters to all the Jews who were in all the provinces of King Ahasuerus, both near and far, [21] enjoining them that they should keep the fourteenth day of the month Adar and also the fifteenth day of the same month, year by year, [22] as the days on which the Jews gained relief from their enemies, and as the month that had been turned for them from sorrow into gladness and from mourning into a holiday; that they should make them days of feasting and gladness, days for sending gifts of food to one another and presents to the poor. [23] So the Jews adopted as a custom what they had begun to do, as Mordecai had written to them.

24 Haman son of Hammedatha the Agagite, the enemy of all the Jews, had plotted against the Jews to destroy them, and had cast Pur—that is, 'the lot'—to crush and destroy them; [25] but when Esther came before the king, he gave orders in writing that the wicked plot that he had devised

against the Jews should come upon his own head, and that he and his sons should be hanged on the gallows. [26] Therefore these days are called Purim, from the word Pur. Thus because of all that was written in this letter, and of what they had faced in this matter, and of what had happened to them, [27] the Jews established and accepted as a custom for themselves and their descendants and all who joined them, that without fail they would continue to observe these two days every year, as it was written and at the time appointed. [28] These days should be remembered and kept throughout every generation, in every family, province, and city; and these days of Purim should never fall into disuse among the Jews, nor should the commemoration of these days cease among their descendants.

29 Queen Esther daughter of Abihail, along with the Jew Mordecai, gave full written authority, confirming this second letter about Purim. [30] Letters were sent wishing peace and security to all the Jews, to the one hundred and twenty-seven provinces of the kingdom of Ahasuerus, [31] and giving orders that these days of Purim should be observed at their appointed seasons, as the Jew Mordecai and Queen Esther enjoined on the Jews, just as they had laid down for themselves and for their descendants regulations concerning their fasts and their lamentations. [32] The command of Queen Esther fixed these practices of Purim, and it was recorded in writing.

10 King Ahasuerus laid tribute on the land and on the islands of the sea. [2] All the acts of his power and might, and the full account of the high honour of Mordecai, to which the king advanced him, are they not written in the annals of the kings of Media and Persia? [3] For Mordecai the Jew was next in rank to King Ahasuerus, and he was powerful among the Jews and popular with his many kindred, for he sought the good of his people and interceded for the welfare of all his descendants.

Mordecai's Dream Fulfilled

4 [a] And Mordecai said, 'These things have come from God; 5 for I remember the dream that I had concerning these matters, and none of them has failed to be fulfilled. 6 There was the little spring that became a river, and there was light and sun and abundant water—the river is Esther, whom the king married and made queen. 7 The two dragons are Haman and myself. 8 The nations are those that gathered to destroy the name of the Jews. 9 And my nation, this is Israel, who cried out to God and was saved. The Lord has saved his people; the Lord has rescued us from all these evils; God has done great signs and wonders, wonders that have never happened among the nations. 10 For this purpose he made two lots, one for the people of God and one for all the nations, 11 and these two lots came to the hour and moment and day of decision before God and among all the nations. 12 And God remembered his people and vindicated his inheritance. 13 So they will observe these days in the month of Adar, on the fourteenth and fifteenth [b] of that month, with an assembly and joy and gladness before God, from generation to generation for ever among his people Israel.'

Postscript

11 1 In the fourth year of the reign of Ptolemy and Cleopatra, Dositheus, who said that he was a priest and a Levite, [c] and his son Ptolemy brought to Egypt [d] the foregoing Letter about Purim, which they said was authentic and had been translated by Lysimachus son of Ptolemy, one of the residents of Jerusalem.

END OF ADDITION F

---

a Chapter 10.4-13 and 11.1 correspond to chapter F 1-11 in some translations.   *b* Other ancient authorities lack *and fifteenth*   *c* Or *priest, and Levitas*   *d* Cn: Gk *brought in*

1 MACCABEES

Alexander the Great

1 After Alexander son of Philip, the Macedonian, who came from the land of Kittim, had defeated[a] King Darius of the Persians and the Medes, he succeeded him as king. (He had previously become king of Greece.) [2] He fought many battles, conquered strongholds, and put to death the kings of the earth. [3] He advanced to the ends of the earth, and plundered many nations. When the earth became quiet before him, he was exalted, and his heart was lifted up. [4] He gathered a very strong army and ruled over countries, nations, and princes, and they became tributary to him.

[5] After this he fell sick and perceived that he was dying. [6] So he summoned his most honoured officers, who had been brought up with him from youth, and divided his kingdom among them while he was still alive. [7] And after Alexander had reigned for twelve years, he died.

[8] Then his officers began to rule, each in his own place. [9] They all put on crowns after his death, and so did their descendants

a Gk adds *and he defeated*

after them for many years; and they caused many evils on the earth.

Antiochus Epiphanes and Renegade Jews

10 From them came forth a sinful root, Antiochus Epiphanes, son of King Antiochus; he had been a hostage in Rome. He began to reign in the one hundred and thirty-seventh year of the kingdom of the Greeks. [a]

11 In those days certain renegades came out from Israel and misled many, saying, 'Let us go and make a covenant with the Gentiles around us, for since we separated from them many disasters have come upon us.' 12 This proposal pleased them, 13 and some of the people eagerly went to the king, who authorized them to observe the ordinances of the Gentiles. 14 So they built a gymnasium in Jerusalem, according to Gentile custom, 15 and removed the marks of circumcision, and abandoned the holy covenant. They joined with the Gentiles and sold themselves to do evil.

Antiochus in Egypt

16 When Antiochus saw that his kingdom was established, he determined to become king of the land of Egypt, in order that he might reign over both kingdoms. 17 So he invaded Egypt with a strong force, with chariots and elephants and cavalry and with a large fleet. 18 He engaged King Ptolemy of Egypt in battle, and Ptolemy turned and fled before him, and many were wounded and fell. 19 They captured the fortified cities in the land of Egypt, and he plundered the land of Egypt.

Persecution of the Jews

20 After subduing Egypt, Antiochus returned in the one hundred and forty-third year. [b] He went up against Israel and came to Jerusalem with a strong force. 21 He arrogantly entered the sanctuary and took the golden altar, the lampstand for the light, and all its utensils. 22 He took also the table for the bread of the Presence, the cups for drink-offerings, the bowls, the golden censers, the curtain, the crowns, and the gold decoration on the front of the temple;

he stripped it all off. 23 He took the silver and the gold, and the costly vessels; he took also the hidden treasures that he found. 24 Taking them all, he went into his own land.

He shed much blood,
  and spoke with great arrogance.
25 Israel mourned deeply in every
    community,
26 rulers and elders groaned,
  young women and young men
    became faint,
  the beauty of the women faded.
27 Every bridegroom took up the
    lament;
  she who sat in the bridal chamber
    was mourning.
28 Even the land trembled for its
    inhabitants,
  and all the house of Jacob was
    clothed with shame.

The Occupation of Jerusalem

29 Two years later the king sent to the cities of Judah a chief collector of tribute, and he came to Jerusalem with a large force. 30 Deceitfully he spoke peaceable words to them, and they believed him; but he suddenly fell upon the city, dealt it a severe blow, and destroyed many people of Israel. 31 He plundered the city, burned it with fire, and tore down its houses and its surrounding walls. 32 They took captive the women and children, and seized the livestock. 33 Then they fortified the city of David with a great strong wall and strong towers, and it became their citadel. 34 They stationed there a sinful people, men who were renegades. These strengthened their position; 35 they stored up arms and food, and collecting the spoils of Jerusalem they stored them there, and became a great menace,

36 for the citadel [c] became an ambush
    against the sanctuary,
  an evil adversary of Israel at all
    times.
37 On every side of the sanctuary they
    shed innocent blood;
  they even defiled the sanctuary.

a 175 BC   b 169 BC   c Gk it

38 Because of them the residents of
   Jerusalem fled;
   she became a dwelling of
      strangers;
   she became strange to her offspring,
   and her children forsook her.
39 Her sanctuary became desolate like a
   desert;
   her feasts were turned into
      mourning,
   her sabbaths into a reproach,
   her honour into contempt.
40 Her dishonour now grew as great as
   her glory;
   her exaltation was turned into
      mourning.

Installation of Gentile Cults

41 Then the king wrote to his whole
kingdom that all should be one people,
42 and that all should give up their particular
customs. 43 All the Gentiles accepted the
command of the king. Many even from Israel
gladly adopted his religion; they sacrificed
to idols and profaned the sabbath.

44 And the king sent letters by messengers
to Jerusalem and the towns of Judah; he directed
them to follow customs strange to
the land, 45 to forbid burnt-offerings and
sacrifices and drink-offerings in the sanctuary,
to profane sabbaths and festivals, 46 to
defile the sanctuary and the priests, 47 to
build altars and sacred precincts and
shrines for idols, to sacrifice swine and
other unclean animals, 48 and to leave their
sons uncircumcised. They were to make
themselves abominable by everything unclean
and profane, 49 so that they would
forget the law and change all the ordinances.
50 He added,*a* 'And whoever does
not obey the command of the king shall
die.'

51 In such words he wrote to his whole
kingdom. He appointed inspectors over all
the people and commanded the towns of
Judah to offer sacrifice, town by town.
52 Many of the people, everyone who forsook
the law, joined them, and they did

a Gk lacks *He added*

The Ptolemaic and Seleucid Kingdoms

Pergamos
Sardis
Tarsus
Carchemish
Antioch
Nineveh
SELEUCID KINGDOM
Tigris River
Mediterranean Sea
Sidon
Tyre
Damascus
Ecbatana
Seleucia
Samaria
Jerusalem
Babylon
Alexandria
Susa
Pelusium
Euphrates River
Memphis
ARABIA
NABATEA
PTOLEMAIC KINGDOM
EGYPT
0   300   500 Mi.
0   300   500   Km.
N

evil in the land; ⁵³they drove Israel into hiding in every place of refuge they had.

54 Now on the fifteenth day of Chislev, in the one hundred and forty-fifth year,ᵃ they erected a desolating sacrilege on the altar of burnt-offering. They also built altars in the surrounding towns of Judah, ⁵⁵and offered incense at the doors of the houses and in the streets. ⁵⁶The books of the law that they found they tore to pieces and burned with fire. ⁵⁷Anyone found possessing the book of the covenant, or anyone who adhered to the law, was condemned to death by decree of the king. ⁵⁸They kept using violence against Israel, against those who were found month after month in the towns. ⁵⁹On the twenty-fifth day of the month they offered sacrifice on the altar that was on top of the altar of burnt-offering. ⁶⁰In accordance with the decree, they put to death the women who had their children circumcised, ⁶¹and their families and those who circumcised them; and they hung the infants from their mothers' necks.

62 But many in Israel stood firm and were resolved in their hearts not to eat unclean food. ⁶³They chose to die rather than to be defiled by food or to profane the holy covenant; and they did die. ⁶⁴Very great wrath came upon Israel.

Mattathias and His Sons

2 In those days Mattathias son of John son of Simeon, a priest of the family of Joarib, moved from Jerusalem and settled in Modein. ²He had five sons, John surnamed Gaddi, ³Simon called Thassi, ⁴Judas called Maccabeus, ⁵Eleazar called Avaran, and Jonathan called Apphus. ⁶He saw the blasphemies being committed in Judah and Jerusalem, ⁷and said,

'Alas! Why was I born to see this,
  the ruin of my people, the ruin of
    the holy city,
  and to live there when it was given
    over to the enemy,
  the sanctuary given over to aliens?
⁸ Her temple has become like a person
    without honour;ᵇ

⁹ her glorious vessels have been
    carried into exile.
  Her infants have been killed in her
    streets,
  her youths by the sword of the foe.
¹⁰ What nation has not inherited her
    palacesᶜ
  and has not seized her spoils?
¹¹ All her adornment has been taken
    away;
  no longer free, she has become a
    slave.
¹² And see, our holy place, our beauty,
  and our glory have been laid waste;
  the Gentiles have profaned them.
¹³   Why should we live any longer?'

14 Then Mattathias and his sons tore their clothes, put on sackcloth, and mourned greatly.

Pagan Worship Refused

15 The king's officers who were enforcing the apostasy came to the town of Modein to make them offer sacrifice. ¹⁶Many from Israel came to them; and Mattathias and his sons were assembled. ¹⁷Then the king's officers spoke to Mattathias as follows: 'You are a leader, honoured and great in this town, and supported by sons and brothers. ¹⁸Now be the first to come and do what the king commands, as all the Gentiles and the people of Judah and those that are left in Jerusalem have done. Then you and your sons will be numbered among the Friends of the king, and you and your sons will be honoured with silver and gold and many gifts.'

19 But Mattathias answered and said in a loud voice: 'Even if all the nations that live under the rule of the king obey him, and have chosen to obey his commandments, everyone of them abandoning the religion of their ancestors, ²⁰I and my sons and my brothers will continue to live by the covenant of our ancestors. ²¹Far be it from us to desert the law and the ordinances. ²²We will not obey the king's words by turning aside from our religion to the right hand or to the left.'

ᵃ 167 BC   ᵇ Meaning of Gk uncertain   ᶜ Other ancient authorities read *has not had a part in her kingdom*

23 When he had finished speaking these words, a Jew came forward in the sight of all to offer sacrifice on the altar in Modein, according to the king's command. 24 When Mattathias saw it, he burned with zeal and his heart was stirred. He gave vent to righteous anger; he ran and killed him on the altar. 25 At the same time he killed the king's officer who was forcing them to sacrifice, and he tore down the altar. 26 Thus he burned with zeal for the law, just as Phinehas did against Zimri son of Salu.

27 Then Mattathias cried out in the town with a loud voice, saying: 'Let everyone who is zealous for the law and supports the covenant come out with me!' 28 Then he and his sons fled to the hills and left all that they had in the town.

29 At that time many who were seeking righteousness and justice went down to the wilderness to live there, 30 they, their sons, their wives, and their livestock, because troubles pressed heavily upon them. 31 And it was reported to the king's officers, and to the troops in Jerusalem the city of David, that those who had rejected the king's command had gone down to the hiding-places in the wilderness. 32 Many pursued them, and overtook them; they encamped opposite them and prepared for battle against them on the sabbath day. 33 They said to them, 'Enough of this! Come out and do what the king commands, and you will live.' 34 But they said, 'We will not come out, nor will we do what the king commands and so profane the sabbath day.' 35 Then the enemy[a] quickly attacked them. 36 But they did not answer them or hurl a stone at them or block up their hiding-places, 37 for they said, 'Let us all die in our innocence; heaven and earth testify for us that you are killing us unjustly.' 38 So they attacked them on the sabbath, and they died, with their wives and children and livestock, to the number of a thousand people.

39 When Mattathias and his friends learned of it, they mourned for them deeply. 40 And all said to their neighbours: 'If we all do as our kindred have done and refuse to fight with the Gentiles for our lives and for our ordinances, they will quickly destroy us from the earth.' 41 So they made this decision that day: 'Let us fight against anyone who comes to attack us on the sabbath day; let us not all die as our kindred died in their hiding-places.'

Counter-Attack

42 Then there united with them a company of Hasideans, mighty warriors of Israel, all who offered themselves willingly for the law. 43 And all who became fugitives to escape their troubles joined them and reinforced them. 44 They organized an army, and struck down sinners in their anger and renegades in their wrath; the survivors fled to the Gentiles for safety. 45 And Mattathias and his friends went around and tore down the altars; 46 they forcibly circumcised all the uncircumcised boys that they found within the borders of Israel. 47 They hunted down the arrogant, and the work prospered in their hands. 48 They rescued the law out of the hands of the Gentiles and kings, and they never let the sinner gain the upper hand.

The Last Words of Mattathias

49 Now the days drew near for Mattathias to die, and he said to his sons: 'Arrogance and scorn have now become strong; it is a time of ruin and furious anger. 50 Now, my children, show zeal for the law, and give your lives for the covenant of our ancestors.

51 'Remember the deeds of the ancestors, which they did in their generations; and you will receive great honour and an everlasting name. 52 Was not Abraham found faithful when tested, and it was reckoned to him as righteousness? 53 Joseph in the time of his distress kept the commandment, and became lord of Egypt. 54 Phinehas our ancestor, because he was deeply zealous, received the covenant of everlasting priesthood. 55 Joshua, because he fulfilled the command, became a judge in Israel. 56 Caleb, because he testified in the assembly, received an inheritance in the land. 57 David, because he was merciful, in-

a Gk they

herited the throne of the kingdom for ever. [58] Elijah, because of great zeal for the law, was taken up into heaven. [59] Hananiah, Azariah, and Mishael believed and were saved from the flame. [60] Daniel, because of his innocence, was delivered from the mouth of the lions.

61 'And so observe, from generation to generation, that none of those who put their trust in him will lack strength. [62] Do not fear the words of sinners, for their splendour will turn into dung and worms. [63] Today they will be exalted, but tomorrow they will not be found, because they will have returned to the dust, and their plans will have perished. [64] My children, be courageous and grow strong in the law, for by it you will gain honour.

65 'Here is your brother Simeon who, I know, is wise in counsel; always listen to him; he shall be your father. [66] Judas Maccabeus has been a mighty warrior from his youth; he shall command the army for you and fight the battle against the peoples.[a] [67] You shall rally around you all who observe the law, and avenge the wrong done to your people. [68] Pay back the Gentiles in full, and obey the commands of the law.'

69 Then he blessed them, and was gathered to his ancestors. [70] He died in the one hundred and forty-sixth year[b] and was buried in the tomb of his ancestors at Modein. And all Israel mourned for him with great lamentation.

The Early Victories of Judas

3 Then his son Judas, who was called Maccabeus, took command in his place. [2] All his brothers and all who had joined his father helped him; they gladly fought for Israel.

3 He extended the glory of his people.
  Like a giant he put on his
      breastplate;
  he bound on his armour of war and
      waged battles,
    protecting the camp by his sword.
4 He was like a lion in his deeds,
    like a lion's cub roaring for prey.
5 He searched out and pursued those
    who broke the law;

  he burned those who troubled his
      people.
6 Lawbreakers shrank back for fear of
      him;
    all the evildoers were confounded;
    and deliverance prospered by his
        hand.
7 He embittered many kings,
    but he made Jacob glad by his
        deeds,
    and his memory is blessed for ever.
8 He went through the cities of Judah;
    he destroyed the ungodly out of the
        land;[c]
    thus he turned away wrath from
        Israel.
9 He was renowned to the ends of the
      earth;
    he gathered in those who were
        perishing.

10 Apollonius now gathered together Gentiles and a large force from Samaria to fight against Israel. [11] When Judas learned of it, he went out to meet him, and he defeated and killed him. Many were wounded and fell, and the rest fled. [12] Then they seized their spoils; and Judas took the sword of Apollonius, and used it in battle for the rest of his life.

13 When Seron, the commander of the Syrian army, heard that Judas had gathered a large company, including a body of faithful soldiers who stayed with him and went out to battle, [14] he said, 'I will make a name for myself and win honour in the kingdom. I will make war on Judas and his companions, who scorn the king's command.' [15] Once again a strong army of godless men went up with him to help him, to take vengeance on the Israelites.

16 When he approached the ascent of Beth-horon, Judas went out to meet him with a small company. [17] But when they saw the army coming to meet them, they said to Judas, 'How can we, few as we are, fight against so great and so strong a multitude? And we are faint, for we have eaten nothing today.' [18] Judas replied, 'It is easy for many to be hemmed in by few, for in the sight of Heaven there is no difference

_a_ Or _of the people_   _b_ 166 BC   _c_ Gk _it_

between saving by many or by few. 19 It is not on the size of the army that victory in battle depends, but strength comes from Heaven. 20 They come against us in great insolence and lawlessness to destroy us and our wives and our children, and to despoil us; 21 but we fight for our lives and our laws. 22 He himself will crush them before us; as for you, do not be afraid of them.'

23 When he finished speaking, he rushed suddenly against Seron and his army, and they were crushed before him. 24 They pursued them*a* down the descent of Beth-horon to the plain; eight hundred of them fell, and the rest fled into the land of the Philistines. 25 Then Judas and his brothers began to be feared, and terror fell on the Gentiles all around them. 26 His fame reached the king, and the Gentiles talked of the battles of Judas.

The Policy of Antiochus

27 When King Antiochus heard these reports, he was greatly angered; and he sent and gathered all the forces of his kingdom, a very strong army. 28 He opened his coffers and gave a year's pay to his forces, and ordered them to be ready for any need. 29 Then he saw that the money in the treasury was exhausted, and that the revenues from the country were small because of the dissension and disaster that he had caused in the land by abolishing the laws that had existed from the earliest days. 30 He feared that he might not have such funds as he had before for his expenses and for the gifts that he used to give more lavishly than preceding kings. 31 He was greatly perplexed in mind; then he determined to go to Persia and collect the revenues from those regions and raise a large fund.

32 He left Lysias, a distinguished man of royal lineage, in charge of the king's affairs from the river Euphrates to the borders of Egypt. 33 Lysias was also to take care of his son Antiochus until he returned. 34 And he turned over to Lysias*b* half of his forces and the elephants, and gave him orders about all that he wanted done. As for the residents of Judea and Jerusalem, 35 Lysias was to send a force against them

to wipe out and destroy the strength of Israel and the remnant of Jerusalem; he was to banish the memory of them from the place, 36 settle aliens in all their territory, and distribute their land by lot. 37 Then the king took the remaining half of his forces and left Antioch his capital in the one hundred and forty-seventh year.*c* He crossed the Euphrates river and went through the upper provinces.

Preparations for Battle

38 Lysias chose Ptolemy son of Dorymenes, and Nicanor and Gorgias, able men among the Friends of the king, 39 and sent with them forty thousand infantry and seven thousand cavalry to go into the land of Judah and destroy it, as the king had commanded. 40 So they set out with their entire force, and when they arrived they encamped near Emmaus in the plain. 41 When the traders of the region heard what was said to them, they took silver and gold in immense amounts, and fetters,*d* and went to the camp to get the Israelites for slaves. And forces from Syria and the land of the Philistines joined with them.

42 Now Judas and his brothers saw that misfortunes had increased and that the forces were encamped in their territory. They also learned what the king had commanded to be done to the people to cause their final destruction. 43 But they said to one another, 'Let us restore the ruins of our people, and fight for our people and the sanctuary.' 44 So the congregation assembled to be ready for battle, and to pray and ask for mercy and compassion.

45 Jerusalem was uninhabited like a
   wilderness;
      not one of her children went in or
      out.
   The sanctuary was trampled down,
      and aliens held the citadel;
      it was a lodging-place for the
      Gentiles.
   Joy was taken from Jacob;
      the flute and the harp ceased to
      play.

---

a Other ancient authorities read *him*   *b* Gk *him*
c 165 BC   *d* Syr: Gk Mss, Vg *slaves*

46 Then they gathered together and went to Mizpah, opposite Jerusalem, because Israel formerly had a place of prayer in Mizpah. 47 They fasted that day, put on sackcloth and sprinkled ashes on their heads, and tore their clothes. 48 And they opened the book of the law to inquire into those matters about which the Gentiles consulted the images of their gods. 49 They also brought the vestments of the priesthood and the first fruits and the tithes, and they stirred up the nazirites[a] who had completed their days; 50 and they cried aloud to Heaven, saying,

'What shall we do with these?
　Where shall we take them?
51 Your sanctuary is trampled down and
　　profaned,
　and your priests mourn in
　　humiliation.
52 Here the Gentiles are assembled
　　against us to destroy us;
　you know what they plot against
　　us.
53 How will we be able to withstand
　　them,
　if you do not help us?'

54 Then they sounded the trumpets and gave a loud shout. 55 After this Judas appointed leaders of the people, in charge of thousands and hundreds and fifties and tens. 56 Those who were building houses, or were about to be married, or were planting a vineyard, or were faint-hearted, he told to go home again, in accordance with the law. 57 Then the army marched out and encamped to the south of Emmaus.

58 And Judas said, 'Arm yourselves and be courageous. Be ready early in the morning to fight with these Gentiles who have assembled against us to destroy us and our sanctuary. 59 It is better for us to die in battle than to see the misfortunes of our nation and of the sanctuary. 60 But as his will in heaven may be, so shall he do.'

The Battle at Emmaus

4 Now Gorgias took five thousand infantry and one thousand picked cavalry, and this division moved out by night 2 to fall upon the camp of the Jews and at-

tack them suddenly. Men from the citadel were their guides. 3 But Judas heard of it, and he and his warriors moved out to attack the king's force in Emmaus 4 while the division was still absent from the camp. 5 When Gorgias entered the camp of Judas by night, he found no one there, so he looked for them in the hills, because he said, 'These men are running away from us.'

6 At daybreak Judas appeared in the plain with three thousand men, but they did not have armour and swords such as they desired. 7 And they saw the camp of the Gentiles, strong and fortified, with cavalry all around it; and these men were trained in war. 8 But Judas said to those who were with him, 'Do not fear their numbers or be afraid when they charge. 9 Remember how our ancestors were saved at the Red Sea, when Pharaoh with his forces pursued them. 10 And now, let us cry to Heaven, to see whether he will favour us and remember his covenant with our ancestors and crush this army before us today. 11 Then all the Gentiles will know that there is one who redeems and saves Israel.'

12 When the foreigners looked up and saw them coming against them, 13 they went out from their camp to battle. Then the men with Judas blew their trumpets 14 and engaged in battle. The Gentiles were crushed, and fled into the plain, 15 and all those in the rear fell by the sword. They pursued them to Gazara, and to the plains of Idumea, and to Azotus and Jamnia; and three thousand of them fell. 16 Then Judas and his force turned back from pursuing them, 17 and he said to the people, 'Do not be greedy for plunder, for there is a battle before us; 18 Gorgias and his force are near us in the hills. But stand now against our enemies and fight them, and afterwards seize the plunder boldly.'

19 Just as Judas was finishing this speech, a detachment appeared, coming out of the hills. 20 They saw that their army[b] had been put to flight, and that the Jews[b] were burning the camp, for the smoke that was seen showed what had

---

a That is *those separated* or *those consecrated*　　*b* Gk *they* happened. [21] When they perceived this, they were greatly frightened, and when they also saw the army of Judas drawn up in the plain for battle, [22] they all fled into the land of the Philistines. [23] Then Judas returned to plunder the camp, and they seized a great amount of gold and silver, and cloth dyed blue and sea purple, and great riches. [24] On their return they sang hymns and praises to Heaven—'For he is good, for his mercy endures for ever.' [25] Thus Israel had a great deliverance that day.

First Campaign of Lysias

26 Those of the foreigners who escaped went and reported to Lysias all that had happened. [27] When he heard it, he was perplexed and discouraged, for things had not happened to Israel as he had intended, nor had they turned out as the king had ordered. [28] But the next year he mustered sixty thousand picked infantry and five thousand cavalry to subdue them. [29] They came into Idumea and encamped at Beth-zur, and Judas met them with ten thousand men.

30 When he saw that their army was strong, he prayed, saying, 'Blessed are you, O Saviour of Israel, who crushed the attack of the mighty warrior by the hand of your servant David, and gave the camp of the Philistines into the hands of Jonathan son of Saul, and of the man who carried his armour. [31] Hem in this army by the hand of your people Israel, and let them be ashamed of their troops and their cavalry. [32] Fill them with cowardice; melt the boldness of their strength; let them tremble in their destruction. [33] Strike them down with the sword of those who love you, and let all who know your name praise you with hymns.'

34 Then both sides attacked, and there fell of the army of Lysias five thousand men; they fell in action.[a] [35] When Lysias saw the rout of his troops and observed the boldness that inspired those of Judas, and how ready they were either to live or to die nobly, he withdrew to Antioch and enlisted mercenaries in order to invade Judea again with an even larger army.

Cleansing and Dedication of the Temple

36 Then Judas and his brothers said, 'See, our enemies are crushed; let us go up to cleanse the sanctuary and dedicate it.' [37] So all the army assembled and went up to Mount Zion. [38] There they saw the sanctuary desolate, the altar profaned, and the gates burned. In the courts they saw bushes sprung up as in a thicket, or as on one of the mountains. They saw also the chambers of the priests in ruins. [39] Then they tore their clothes and mourned with great lamentation; they sprinkled themselves with ashes [40] and fell face down on the ground. And when the signal was given with the trumpets, they cried out to Heaven.

41 Then Judas detailed men to fight against those in the citadel until he had cleansed the sanctuary. [42] He chose blameless priests devoted to the law, [43] and they cleansed the sanctuary and removed the defiled stones to an unclean place. [44] They deliberated what to do about the altar of burnt-offering, which had been profaned. [45] And they thought it best to tear it down, so that it would not be a lasting shame to them that the Gentiles had defiled it. So they tore down the altar, [46] and stored the stones in a convenient place on the temple hill until a prophet should come to tell what to do with them. [47] Then they took unhewn[b] stones, as the law directs, and built a new altar like the former one. [48] They also rebuilt the sanctuary and the interior of the temple, and consecrated the courts. [49] They made new holy vessels, and brought the lampstand, the altar of incense, and the table into the temple. [50] Then they offered incense on the altar and lit the lamps on the lampstand, and these gave light in the temple. [51] They placed the bread on the table and hung up the curtains. Thus they finished all the work they had undertaken.

52 Early in the morning on the twenty-fifth day of the ninth month, which is the

a Or *and some fell on the opposite side*   b Gk *whole*

month of Chislev, in the one hundred and forty-eighth year,[a] 53 they rose and offered sacrifice, as the law directs, on the new altar of burnt-offering that they had built. 54 At the very season and on the very day that the Gentiles had profaned it, it was dedicated with songs and harps and lutes and cymbals. 55 All the people fell on their faces and worshipped and blessed Heaven, who had prospered them. 56 So they celebrated the dedication of the altar for eight days, and joyfully offered burnt-offerings; they offered a sacrifice of well-being and a thanksgiving-offering. 57 They decorated the front of the temple with golden crowns and small shields; they restored the gates and the chambers for the priests, and fitted them with doors. 58 There was very great joy among the people, and the disgrace brought by the Gentiles was removed.

59 Then Judas and his brothers and all the assembly of Israel determined that every year at that season the days of dedication of the altar should be observed with joy and gladness for eight days, beginning with the twenty-fifth day of the month of Chislev.

60 At that time they fortified Mount Zion with high walls and strong towers all round, to keep the Gentiles from coming and trampling them down as they had done before. 61 Judas[b] stationed a garrison there to guard it; he also fortified Beth-zur to guard it, so that the people might have a stronghold that faced Idumea.

Wars with Neighbouring Peoples

5 When the Gentiles all around heard that the altar had been rebuilt and the sanctuary dedicated as it was before, they became very angry, 2 and they determined to destroy the descendants of Jacob who lived among them. So they began to kill and destroy among the people. 3 But Judas made war on the descendants of Esau in Idumea, at Akrabattene, because they kept lying in wait for Israel. He dealt them a heavy blow and humbled them and despoiled them. 4 He also remembered the wickedness of the sons of Baean, who were a trap and a snare to the people and am-

bushed them on the highways. 5 They were shut up by him in their[c] towers; and he encamped against them, vowed their complete destruction, and burned with fire their towers and all who were in them. 6 Then he crossed over to attack the Ammonites, where he found a strong band and many people, with Timothy as their leader. 7 He engaged in many battles with them, and they were crushed before him; he struck them down. 8 He also took Jazer and its villages; then he returned to Judea.

Liberation of Galilean Jews

9 Now the Gentiles in Gilead gathered together against the Israelites who lived in their territory, and planned to destroy them. But they fled to the stronghold of Dathema, 10 and sent to Judas and his brothers a letter that said, 'The Gentiles around us have gathered together to destroy us. 11 They are preparing to come and capture the stronghold to which we have fled, and Timothy is leading their forces. 12 Now then, come and rescue us from their hands, for many of us have fallen, 13 and all our kindred who were in the land of Tob have been killed; the enemy[d] have captured their wives and children and goods, and have destroyed about a thousand people there.'

14 While the letter was still being read, other messengers, with their garments torn, came from Galilee and made a similar report; 15 they said that the people of Ptolemais and Tyre and Sidon, and all Galilee of the Gentiles,[e] had gathered together against them 'to annihilate us.' 16 When Judas and the people heard these messages, a great assembly was called to determine what they should do for their kindred who were in distress and were being attacked by enemies.[f] 17 Then Judas said to his brother Simon, 'Choose your men and go and rescue your kindred in Galilee; Jonathan my brother and I will go to Gilead.' 18 But he left Joseph, son of Zechariah, and Azariah, a leader of the people, with the rest of the forces, in Judea to guard it; 19 and he gave

a 164 BC   b Gk He   c Gk her   d Gk they
e Gk aliens   f Gk them

them this command, 'Take charge of this people, but do not engage in battle with the Gentiles until we return.' 20 Then three thousand men were assigned to Simon to go to Galilee, and eight thousand to Judas for Gilead.

21 So Simon went to Galilee and fought many battles against the Gentiles, and the Gentiles were crushed before him. 22 He pursued them to the gate of Ptolemais; as many as three thousand of the Gentiles fell, and he despoiled them. 23 Then he took the Jews *a* of Galilee and Arbatta, with their wives and children, and all they possessed, and led them to Judea with great rejoicing.

Judas and Jonathan in Gilead

24 Judas Maccabeus and his brother Jonathan crossed the Jordan and made three days' journey into the wilderness. 25 They encountered the Nabateans, who met them peaceably and told them all that had happened to their kindred in Gilead: 26 'Many of them have been shut up in Bozrah and Bosor, in Alema and Chaspho, Maked and Carnaim'—all these towns were strong and large— 27 'and some have been shut up in the other towns of Gilead; the enemy *b* are getting ready to attack the strongholds tomorrow and capture and destroy all these people in a single day.'

28 Then Judas and his army quickly turned back by the wilderness road to Bozrah; and he took the town, and killed every male by the edge of the sword; then he seized all its spoils and burned it with fire. 29 He left the place at night, and they went all the way to the stronghold of Dathema. *c* 30 At dawn they looked out and saw a large company, which could not be counted, carrying ladders and engines of war to capture the stronghold, and attacking the Jews within. *d* 31 So Judas saw that the battle had begun and that the cry of the town went up to Heaven, with trumpets and loud shouts, 32 and he said to the men of his forces, 'Fight today for your kindred!' 33 Then he came up behind them in three companies, who sounded their trumpets and cried aloud in prayer. 34 And when the army of

Timothy realized that it was Maccabeus, they fled before him, and he dealt them a heavy blow. As many as eight thousand of them fell that day.

35 Next he turned aside to Maapha, *e* and fought against it and took it; and he killed every male in it, plundered it, and burned it with fire. 36 From there he marched on and took Chaspho, Maked, and Bosor, and the other towns of Gilead.

37 After these things Timothy gathered another army and encamped opposite Raphon, on the other side of the stream. 38 Judas sent men to spy out the camp, and they reported to him, 'All the Gentiles around us have gathered to him; it is a very large force. 39 They also have hired Arabs to help them, and they are encamped across the stream, ready to come and fight against you.' And Judas went to meet them.

40 Now as Judas and his army drew near to the stream of water, Timothy said to the officers of his forces, 'If he crosses over to us first, we will not be able to resist him, for he will surely defeat us. 41 But if he shows fear and camps on the other side of the river, we will cross over to him and defeat him.' 42 When Judas approached the stream of water, he stationed the officers *f* of the army at the stream and gave them this command, 'Permit no one to encamp, but make them all enter the battle.' 43 Then he crossed over against them first, and the whole army followed him. All the Gentiles were defeated before him, and they threw away their arms and fled into the sacred precincts at Carnaim. 44 But he took the town and burned the sacred precincts with fire, together with all who were in them. Thus Carnaim was conquered; they could stand before Judas no longer.

The Return to Jerusalem

45 Then Judas gathered together all the Israelites in Gilead, the small and the great, with their wives and children and goods, a very large company, to go to the land of Judah. 46 So they came to Ephron. This was a

a Gk *those*   *b* Gk *they*   *c* Gk lacks *of Dathema*. See verse 9   *d* Gk *and they were attacking them*   *e* Other ancient authorities read *Alema*   *f* Or *scribes* large and very strong town on the road, and they could not go around it to the right or to the left; they had to go through it. [47] But the people of the town shut them out and blocked up the gates with stones.

48 Judas sent them this friendly message, 'Let us pass through your land to get to our land. No one will do you harm; we will simply pass by on foot.' But they refused to open to him. [49] Then Judas ordered proclamation to be made to the army that all should encamp where they were. [50] So the men of the forces encamped, and he fought against the town all that day and all the night, and the town was delivered into his hands. [51] He destroyed every male by the edge of the sword, and razed and plundered the town. Then he passed through the town over the bodies of the dead.

52 Then they crossed the Jordan into the large plain before Beth-shan. [53] Judas kept rallying the laggards and encouraging the people all the way until he came to the land of Judah. [54] So they went up to Mount Zion with joy and gladness, and offered burnt-offerings, because they had returned in safety; not one of them had fallen.

Joseph and Azariah Defeated

55 Now while Judas and Jonathan were in Gilead and their[a] brother Simon was in Galilee before Ptolemais, [56] Joseph son of Zechariah, and Azariah, the commanders of the forces, heard of their brave deeds and of the heroic war they had fought. [57] So they said, 'Let us also make a name for ourselves; let us go and make war on the Gentiles around us.' [58] So they issued orders to the men of the forces that were with them and marched against Jamnia. [59] Gorgias and his men came out of the town to meet them in battle. [60] Then Joseph and Azariah were routed, and were pursued to the borders of Judea; as many as two thousand of the people of Israel fell that day. [61] Thus the people suffered a great rout because, thinking to do a brave deed, they did not listen to Judas and his brothers. [62] But they did not belong to the family of those men through whom deliverance was given to Israel.

63 The man Judas and his brothers were greatly honoured in all Israel and among all the Gentiles, wherever their name was heard. [64] People gathered to them and praised them.

Success at Hebron and Philistia

65 Then Judas and his brothers went out and fought the descendants of Esau in the land to the south. He struck Hebron and its villages and tore down its strongholds and burned its towers on all sides. [66] Then he marched off to go into the land of the Philistines, and passed through Marisa.[b] [67] On that day some priests, who wished to do a brave deed, fell in battle, for they went out to battle unwisely. [68] But Judas turned aside to Azotus in the land of the Philistines; he tore down their altars, and the carved images of their gods he burned with fire; he plundered the towns and returned to the land of Judah.

The Last Days of Antiochus Epiphanes

6 King Antiochus was going through the upper provinces when he heard that Elymais in Persia was a city famed for its wealth in silver and gold. [2] Its temple was very rich, containing golden shields, breastplates, and weapons left there by Alexander son of Philip, the Macedonian king who first reigned over the Greeks. [3] So he came and tried to take the city and plunder it, but he could not because his plan had become known to the citizens [4] and they withstood him in battle. So he fled and in great disappointment left there to return to Babylon.

5 Then someone came to him in Persia and reported that the armies that had gone into the land of Judah had been routed; [6] that Lysias had gone first with a strong force, but had turned and fled before the Jews;[c] that the Jews[d] had grown strong from the arms, supplies, and abundant spoils that they had taken from the armies they had cut down; [7] that they had torn

a Gk *his*   b Other ancient authorities read *Samaria*
c Gk *them*   d Gk *they*

down the abomination that he had erected on the altar in Jerusalem; and that they had surrounded the sanctuary with high walls as before, and also Beth-zur, his town.

8 When the king heard this news, he was astounded and badly shaken. He took to his bed and became sick from disappointment, because things had not turned out for him as he had planned. 9 He lay there for many days, because deep disappointment continually gripped him, and he realized that he was dying. 10 So he called all his Friends and said to them, 'Sleep has departed from my eyes and I am downhearted with worry. 11 I said to myself, "To what distress I have come! And into what a great flood I now am plunged! For I was kind and beloved in my power." 12 But now I remember the wrong I did in Jerusalem. I seized all its vessels of silver and gold, and I sent to destroy the inhabitants of Judah without good reason. 13 I know that it is because of this that these misfortunes have come upon me; here I am, perishing of bitter disappointment in a strange land.'

14 Then he called for Philip, one of his Friends, and made him ruler over all his kingdom. 15 He gave him the crown and his robe and the signet, so that he might guide his son Antiochus and bring him up to be king. 16 Thus King Antiochus died there in the one hundred and forty-ninth year.[a] 17 When Lysias learned that the king was dead, he set up Antiochus the king's[b] son to reign. Lysias[c] had brought him up from boyhood; he named him Eupator.

Renewed Attacks from Syria

18 Meanwhile the garrison in the citadel kept hemming Israel in around the sanctuary. They were trying in every way to harm them and strengthen the Gentiles. 19 Judas therefore resolved to destroy them, and assembled all the people to besiege them. 20 They gathered together and besieged the citadel[d] in the one hundred and fiftieth year;[e] and he built siege-towers and other engines of war. 21 But some of the garrison escaped from the siege and some of the ungodly Israelites joined them.

22 They went to the king and said, 'How long will you fail to do justice and to avenge our kindred? 23 We were happy to serve your father, to live by what he said, and to follow his commands. 24 For this reason the sons of our people besieged the citadel[f] and became hostile to us; moreover, they have put to death as many of us as they have caught, and they have seized our inheritances. 25 It is not against us alone that they have stretched out their hands; they have also attacked all the lands on their borders. 26 And see, today they have encamped against the citadel in Jerusalem to take it; they have fortified both the sanctuary and Beth-zur; 27 unless you quickly prevent them, they will do still greater things, and you will not be able to stop them.'

28 The king was enraged when he heard this. He assembled all his Friends, the commanders of his forces and those in authority.[g] 29 Mercenary forces also came to him from other kingdoms and from islands of the seas. 30 The number of his forces was one hundred thousand foot-soldiers, twenty thousand horsemen, and thirty-two elephants accustomed to war. 31 They came through Idumea and encamped against Beth-zur, and for many days they fought and built engines of war; but the Jews[h] sallied out and burned these with fire, and fought courageously.

The Battle at Beth-zechariah

32 Then Judas marched away from the citadel and encamped at Beth-zechariah, opposite the camp of the king. 33 Early in the morning the king set out and took his army by a forced march along the road to Beth-zechariah, and his troops made ready for battle and sounded their trumpets. 34 They offered the elephants the juice of grapes and mulberries, to arouse them for battle. 35 They distributed the animals among the phalanxes; with each elephant they stationed a thousand men armed with coats of mail, and with brass helmets on

a 163 BC   b Gk his   c Gk He   d Gk it   e 162 BC
f Meaning of Gk uncertain   g Gk those over the reins
h Gk they

their heads; and five hundred picked horsemen were assigned to each beast. 36These took their position beforehand wherever the animal was; wherever it went, they went with it, and they never left it. 37On the elephants*a* were wooden towers, strong and covered; they were fastened on each animal by special harness, and on each were four*b* armed men who fought from there, and also its Indian driver. 38The rest of the cavalry were stationed on either side, on the two flanks of the army, to harass the enemy while being themselves protected by the phalanxes. 39When the sun shone on the shields of gold and brass, the hills were ablaze with them and gleamed like flaming torches.

40 Now a part of the king's army was spread out on the high hills, and some troops were on the plain, and they advanced steadily and in good order. 41All who heard the noise made by their multitude, by the marching of the multitude and the clanking of their arms, trembled, for the army was very large and strong. 42But Judas and his army advanced to the battle, and six hundred of the king's army fell. 43Now Eleazar, called Avaran, saw that one of the animals was equipped with royal armour. It was taller than all the others, and he supposed that the king was on it. 44So he gave his life to save his people and to win for himself an everlasting name. 45He courageously ran into the midst of the phalanx to reach it; he killed men right and left, and they parted before him on both sides. 46He got under the elephant, stabbed it from beneath, and killed it; but it fell to the ground upon him and he died. 47When the Jews*c* saw the royal might and the fierce attack of the forces, they turned away in flight.

The Siege of the Temple

48 The soldiers of the king's army went up to Jerusalem against them, and the king encamped in Judea and at Mount Zion. 49He made peace with the people of Bethzur, and they evacuated the town because they had no provisions there to withstand a siege, since it was a sabbatical year for the land. 50So the king took Beth-zur and stationed a guard there to hold it. 51Then he encamped before the sanctuary for many days. He set up siege-towers, engines of war to throw fire and stones, machines to shoot arrows, and catapults. 52The Jews*c* also made engines of war to match theirs, and fought for many days. 53But they had no food in storage,*d* because it was the seventh year; those who had found safety in Judea from the Gentiles had consumed the last of the stores. 54Only a few men were left in the sanctuary; the rest scattered to their own homes, for the famine proved too much for them.

Syria Offers Terms

55 Then Lysias heard that Philip, whom King Antiochus while still living had appointed to bring up his son Antiochus to be king, 56had returned from Persia and Media with the forces that had gone with the king, and that he was trying to seize control of the government. 57So he quickly gave orders to withdraw, and said to the king, to the commanders of the forces, and to the troops, 'Daily we grow weaker, our food supply is scant, the place against which we are fighting is strong, and the affairs of the kingdom press urgently on us. 58Now then, let us come to terms with these people, and make peace with them and with all their nation. 59Let us agree to let them live by their laws as they did before; for it was on account of their laws that we abolished that they became angry and did all these things.'

60 The speech pleased the king and the commanders, and he sent to the Jews*a* an offer of peace, and they accepted it. 61So the king and the commanders gave them their oath. On these conditions the Jews*c* evacuated the stronghold. 62But when the king entered Mount Zion and saw what a strong fortress the place was, he broke the oath he had sworn and gave orders to tear down the wall all round. 63Then he set off in haste and returned to Antioch. He

---

a Gk *them*   *b* Cn: Some authorities read *thirty*; others *thirty-two*   *c* Gk *they*   *d* Other ancient authorities read *in the sanctuary* found Philip in control of the city, but he fought against him, and took the city by force.

Expedition of Bacchides and Alcimus

7 In the one hundred and fifty-first year[a] Demetrius son of Seleucus set out from Rome, sailed with a few men to a town by the sea, and there began to reign. [2] As he was entering the royal palace of his ancestors, the army seized Antiochus and Lysias to bring them to him. [3] But when this act became known to him, he said, 'Do not let me see their faces!' [4] So the army killed them, and Demetrius took his seat on the throne of his kingdom.

[5] Then there came to him all the renegade and godless men of Israel; they were led by Alcimus, who wanted to be high priest. [6] They brought to the king this accusation against the people: 'Judas and his brothers have destroyed all your Friends, and have driven us out of our land. [7] Now then, send a man whom you trust; let him go and see all the ruin that Judas[b] has brought on us and on the land of the king, and let him punish them and all who help them.'

[8] So the king chose Bacchides, one of the king's Friends, governor of the province Beyond the River; he was a great man in the kingdom and was faithful to the king. [9] He sent him, and with him he sent the ungodly Alcimus, whom he made high priest; and he commanded him to take vengeance on the Israelites. [10] So they marched away and came with a large force into the land of Judah; and he sent messengers to Judas and his brothers with peaceable but treacherous words. [11] But they paid no attention to their words, for they saw that they had come with a large force.

[12] Then a group of scribes appeared in a body before Alcimus and Bacchides to ask for just terms. [13] The Hasideans were first among the Israelites to seek peace from them, [14] for they said, 'A priest of the line of Aaron has come with the army, and he will not harm us.' [15] Alcimus[c] spoke peaceable words to them and swore this oath to them, 'We will not seek to injure you or your friends.' [16] So they trusted him; but he seized sixty of them and killed them in one day, in accordance with the word that was written,

[17] 'The flesh of your faithful ones and
their blood
they poured out all around
Jerusalem,
and there was no one to bury them.'

[18] Then the fear and dread of them fell on all the people, for they said, 'There is no truth or justice in them, for they have violated the agreement and the oath that they swore.'

[19] Then Bacchides withdrew from Jerusalem and encamped in Beth-zaith. And he sent and seized many of the men who had deserted to him,[d] and some of the people, and killed them and threw them into a great pit. [20] He placed Alcimus in charge of the country and left with him a force to help him; then Bacchides went back to the king.

[21] Alcimus struggled to maintain his high-priesthood, [22] and all who were troubling their people joined him. They gained control of the land of Judah and did great damage in Israel. [23] And Judas saw all the wrongs that Alcimus and those with him had done among the Israelites; it was more than the Gentiles had done. [24] So Judas[b] went out into all the surrounding parts of Judea, taking vengeance on those who had deserted and preventing those in the city[e] from going out into the country. [25] When Alcimus saw that Judas and those with him had grown strong, and realized that he could not withstand them, he returned to the king and brought malicious charges against them.

Nicanor in Judea

[26] Then the king sent Nicanor, one of his honoured princes, who hated and detested Israel, and he commanded him to destroy the people. [27] So Nicanor came to Jerusalem with a large force, and treacherously sent to Judas and his brothers this

a 161 BC   b Gk he   c Gk He   d Or many of his men who had deserted   e Gk and they were prevented peaceable message, 28 'Let there be no fighting between you and me; I shall come with a few men to see you face to face in peace.' 29 So he came to Judas, and they greeted one another peaceably; but the enemy were preparing to kidnap Judas. 30 It became known to Judas that Nicanor*a* had come to him with treacherous intent, and he was afraid of him and would not meet him again. 31 When Nicanor learned that his plan had been disclosed, he went out to meet Judas in battle near Caphar-salama. 32 About five hundred of the army of Nicanor fell, and the rest*b* fled into the city of David.

Nicanor Threatens the Temple

33 After these events Nicanor went up to Mount Zion. Some of the priests from the sanctuary and some of the elders of the people came out to greet him peaceably and to show him the burnt-offering that was being offered for the king. 34 But he mocked them and derided them and defiled them and spoke arrogantly, 35 and in anger he swore this oath, 'Unless Judas and his army are delivered into my hands this time, then if I return safely I will burn up this house.' And he went out in great anger. 36 At this the priests went in and stood before the altar and the temple; they wept and said,

37 'You chose this house to be called by
        your name,
    and to be for your people a house
        of prayer and supplication.
38 Take vengeance on this man and on
        his army,
    and let them fall by the sword;
    remember their blasphemies,
    and let them live no longer.'

The Death of Nicanor

39 Now Nicanor went out from Jerusalem and encamped in Beth-horon, and the Syrian army joined him. 40 Judas encamped in Adasa with three thousand men. Then Judas prayed and said, 41 'When the messengers from the king spoke blasphemy, your angel went out and struck down one hundred and eighty-five thousand of the Assyrians.*c* 42 So also crush this army before us today; let the rest learn that Nicanor*a* has spoken wickedly against the sanctuary, and judge him according to this wickedness.'

43 So the armies met in battle on the thirteenth day of the month of Adar. The army of Nicanor was crushed, and he himself was the first to fall in the battle. 44 When his army saw that Nicanor had fallen, they threw down their arms and fled. 45 The Jews*b* pursued them a day's journey, from Adasa as far as Gazara, and as they followed they kept sounding the battle-call on the trumpets. 46 People came out of all the surrounding villages of Judea, and they outflanked the enemy*d* and drove them back to their pursuers,*e* so that they all fell by the sword; not even one of them was left. 47 Then the Jews*b* seized the spoils and the plunder; they cut off Nicanor's head and the right hand that he had so arrogantly stretched out, and brought them and displayed them just outside Jerusalem. 48 The people rejoiced greatly and celebrated that day as a day of great gladness. 49 They decreed that this day should be celebrated each year on the thirteenth day of Adar. 50 So the land of Judah had rest for a few days.

A Eulogy of the Romans

8 Now Judas heard of the fame of the Romans, that they were very strong and were well disposed towards all who made an alliance with them, that they pledged friendship to those who came to them, 2 and that they were very strong. He had been told of their wars and of the brave deeds that they were doing among the Gauls, how they had defeated them and forced them to pay tribute, 3 and what they had done in the land of Spain to get control of the silver and gold mines there, 4 and how they had gained control of the whole region by their planning and patience, even though the place was far distant from them. They also subdued the kings who came against them from the

a Gk *he*   *b* Gk *they*   *c* Gk *of them*   *d* Gk *them*
e Gk *these*

ends of the earth, until they crushed them and inflicted great disaster on them; the rest paid them tribute every year. 5 They had crushed in battle and conquered Philip, and King Perseus of the Macedonians,*a* and the others who rose up against them. 6 They also had defeated Antiochus the Great, king of Asia, who went to fight against them with one hundred and twenty elephants and with cavalry and chariots and a very large army. He was crushed by them; 7 they took him alive and decreed that he and those who would reign after him should pay a heavy tribute and give hostages and surrender some of their best provinces, 8 the countries of India, Media, and Lydia. These they took from him and gave to King Eumenes. 9 The Greeks planned to come and destroy them, 10 but this became known to them, and they sent a general against the Greeks*b* and attacked them. Many of them were wounded and fell, and the Romans*c* took captive their wives and children; they plundered them, conquered the land, tore down their strongholds, and enslaved them to this day. 11 The remaining kingdoms and islands, as many as ever opposed them, they destroyed and enslaved; 12 but with their friends and those who rely on them they have kept friendship. They have subdued kings far and near, and as many as have heard of their fame have feared them. 13 Those whom they wish to help and to make kings, they make kings, and those whom they wish they depose; and they have been greatly exalted. 14 Yet for all this not one of them has put on a crown or worn purple as a mark of pride, 15 but they have built for themselves a senate chamber, and every day three hundred and twenty senators constantly deliberate concerning the people, to govern them well. 16 They trust one man each year to rule over them and to control all their land; they all heed the one man, and there is no envy or jealousy among them.

An Alliance with Rome

17 So Judas chose Eupolemus son of John son of Accos, and Jason son of Elea-zar, and sent them to Rome to establish friendship and alliance, 18 and to free themselves from the yoke; for they saw that the kingdom of the Greeks was enslaving Israel completely. 19 They went to Rome, a very long journey; and they entered the senate chamber and spoke as follows: 20 'Judas, who is also called Maccabeus, and his brothers and the people of the Jews have sent us to you to establish alliance and peace with you, so that we may be enrolled as your allies and friends.' 21 The proposal pleased them, 22 and this is a copy of the letter that they wrote in reply, on bronze tablets, and sent to Jerusalem to remain with them there as a memorial of peace and alliance:

23 'May all go well with the Romans and with the nation of the Jews at sea and on land for ever, and may sword and enemy be far from them. 24 If war comes first to Rome or to any of their allies in all their dominion, 25 the nation of the Jews shall act as their allies wholeheartedly, as the occasion may indicate to them. 26 To the enemy that makes war they shall not give or supply grain, arms, money, or ships, just as Rome has decided; and they shall keep their obligations without receiving any return. 27 In the same way, if war comes first to the nation of the Jews, the Romans shall willingly act as their allies, as the occasion may indicate to them. 28 And to their enemies there shall not be given grain, arms, money, or ships, just as Rome has decided; and they shall keep these obligations and do so without deceit. 29 Thus on these terms the Romans make a treaty with the Jewish people. 30 If after these terms are in effect both parties shall determine to add or delete anything, they shall do so at their discretion, and any addition or deletion that they may make shall be valid.

31 'Concerning the wrongs that King Demetrius is doing to them, we have written to him as follows, "Why have you made your yoke heavy on our friends and allies the Jews? 32 If now they appeal again for help against you, we will defend their rights and fight you on sea and on land." '

a Or *Kittim*   *b* Gk *them*   *c* Gk *they*

Bacchides Returns to Judea

9 When Demetrius heard that Nicanor and his army had fallen in battle, he sent Bacchides and Alcimus into the land of Judah a second time, and with them the right wing of the army. 2They went by the road that leads to Gilgal and encamped against Mesaloth in Arbela, and they took it and killed many people. 3In the first month of the one hundred and fifty-second year*a* they encamped against Jerusalem; 4then they marched off and went to Berea with twenty thousand foot-soldiers and two thousand cavalry.

5 Now Judas was encamped in Elasa, and with him were three thousand picked men. 6When they saw the huge number of the enemy forces, they were greatly frightened, and many slipped away from the camp, until no more than eight hundred of them were left.

7 When Judas saw that his army had slipped away and the battle was imminent, he was crushed in spirit, for he had no time to assemble them. 8He became faint, but he said to those who were left, 'Let us get up and go against our enemies. We may have the strength to fight them.' 9But they tried to dissuade him, saying, 'We do not have the strength. Let us rather save our own lives now, and let us come back with our kindred and fight them; we are too few.' 10But Judas said, 'Far be it from us to do such a thing as to flee from them. If our time has come, let us die bravely for our kindred, and leave no cause to question our honour.'

The Last Battle of Judas

11 Then the army of Bacchides*b* marched out from the camp and took its stand for the encounter. The cavalry was divided into two companies, and the slingers and the archers went ahead of the army, as did all the chief warriors. 12Bacchides was on the right wing. Flanked by the two companies, the phalanx advanced to the sound of the trumpets; and the men with Judas also blew their trumpets. 13The earth was shaken by the noise of the armies, and the battle raged from morning until evening.

14 Judas saw that Bacchides and the strength of his army were on the right; then all the stout-hearted men went with him, 15and they crushed the right wing, and he pursued them as far as Mount Azotus. 16When those on the left wing saw that the right wing was crushed, they turned and followed close behind Judas and his men. 17The battle became desperate, and many on both sides were wounded and fell. 18Judas also fell, and the rest fled.

19 Then Jonathan and Simon took their brother Judas and buried him in the tomb of their ancestors at Modein, 20and wept for him. All Israel made great lamentation for him; they mourned for many days and said,

21 'How is the mighty fallen,
      the saviour of Israel!'

22Now the rest of the acts of Judas, and his wars and the brave deeds that he did, and his greatness, have not been recorded, but they were very many.

Jonathan Succeeds Judas

23 After the death of Judas, the renegades emerged in all parts of Israel; all the wrongdoers reappeared. 24In those days a very great famine occurred, and the country went over to their side. 25Bacchides chose the godless and put them in charge of the country. 26They made inquiry and searched for the friends of Judas, and brought them to Bacchides, who took vengeance on them and made sport of them. 27So there was great distress in Israel, such as had not been since the time that prophets ceased to appear among them.

28 Then all the friends of Judas assembled and said to Jonathan, 29'Since the death of your brother Judas there has been no one like him to go against our enemies and Bacchides, and to deal with those of our nation who hate us. 30Now therefore we have chosen you today to take his place as our ruler and leader, to fight our battle.' 31So Jonathan accepted the leadership at that time in place of his brother Judas.

a 160 BC   *b* Gk lacks *of Bacchides*

The Campaigns of Jonathan

32 When Bacchides learned of this, he tried to kill him. 33 But Jonathan and his brother Simon and all who were with him heard of it, and they fled into the wilderness of Tekoa and camped by the water of the pool of Asphar. 34 Bacchides found this out on the sabbath day, and he with all his army crossed the Jordan.

35 So Jonathan[a] sent his brother as leader of the multitude and begged the Nabateans, who were his friends, for permission to store with them the great amount of baggage that they had. 36 But the family of Jambri from Medeba came out and seized John and all that he had, and left with it.

37 After these things it was reported to Jonathan and his brother Simon, 'The family of Jambri are celebrating a great wedding, and are conducting the bride, a daughter of one of the great nobles of Canaan, from Nadabath with a large escort.' 38 Remembering how their brother John had been killed, they went up and hid under cover of the mountain. 39 They looked out and saw a tumultuous procession with a great amount of baggage; and the bridegroom came out with his friends and his brothers to meet them with tambourines and musicians and many weapons. 40 Then they rushed on them from the ambush and began killing them. Many were wounded and fell, and the rest fled to the mountain; and the Jews[b] took all their goods. 41 So the wedding was turned into mourning and the voice of their musicians into a funeral dirge. 42 After they had fully avenged the blood of their brother, they returned to the marshes of the Jordan.

43 When Bacchides heard of this, he came with a large force on the sabbath day to the banks of the Jordan. 44 And Jonathan said to those with him, 'Let us get up now and fight for our lives, for today things are not as they were before. 45 For look! the battle is in front of us and behind us; the water of the Jordan is on this side and on that, with marsh and thicket; there is no place to turn. 46 Cry out now to Heaven that you may be delivered from the hands of our enemies.' 47 So the battle began, and Jonathan stretched out his hand to strike Bacchides, but he eluded him and went to the rear. 48 Then Jonathan and the men with him leapt into the Jordan and swam across to the other side, and the enemy[b] did not cross the Jordan to attack them. 49 And about one thousand of Bacchides' men fell that day.

Bacchides Builds Fortifications

50 Then Bacchides[a] returned to Jerusalem and built strong cities in Judea: the fortress in Jericho, and Emmaus, and Bethhoron, and Bethel, and Timnath, and[c] Pharathon, and Tephon, with high walls and gates and bars. 51 And he placed garrisons in them to harass Israel. 52 He also fortified the town of Beth-zur, and Gazara, and the citadel, and in them he put troops and stores of food. 53 And he took the sons of the leading men of the land as hostages and put them under guard in the citadel at Jerusalem.

54 In the one hundred and fifty-third year,[d] in the second month, Alcimus gave orders to tear down the wall of the inner court of the sanctuary. He tore down the work of the prophets! 55 But he only began to tear it down, for at that time Alcimus was stricken and his work was hindered; his mouth was stopped and he was paralysed, so that he could no longer say a word or give commands concerning his house. 56 And Alcimus died at that time in great agony. 57 When Bacchides saw that Alcimus was dead, he returned to the king, and the land of Judah had rest for two years.

The End of the War

58 Then all the lawless plotted and said, 'See! Jonathan and his men are living in quiet and confidence. So now let us bring Bacchides back, and he will capture them all in one night.' 59 And they went and consulted with him. 60 He started to come with a large force, and secretly sent letters to all his allies in Judea, telling them to seize Jonathan and his men; but they were un-

a Gk he   b Gk they   c Some authorities omit and
d 159 BC

able to do it, because their plan became known. [61] And Jonathan's men[a] seized about fifty of the men of the country who were leaders in this treachery, and killed them.

62 Then Jonathan with his men, and Simon, withdrew to Bethbasi in the wilderness; he rebuilt the parts of it that had been demolished, and they fortified it. [63] When Bacchides learned of this, he assembled all his forces, and sent orders to the men of Judea. [64] Then he came and encamped against Bethbasi; he fought against it for many days and made machines of war.

65 But Jonathan left his brother Simon in the town, while he went out into the country; and he went with only a few men. [66] He struck down Odomera and his kindred and the people of Phasiron in their tents. [67] Then he[b] began to attack and went into battle with his forces; and Simon and his men sallied out from the town and set fire to the machines of war. [68] They fought with Bacchides, and he was crushed by them. They pressed him very hard, for his plan and his expedition had been in vain. [69] So he was very angry at the renegades who had counselled him to come into the country, and he killed many of them. Then he decided to go back to his own land.

70 When Jonathan learned of this, he sent ambassadors to him to make peace with him and obtain release of the captives. [71] He agreed, and did as he said; and he swore to Jonathan[c] that he would not try to harm him as long as he lived. [72] He restored to him the captives whom he had taken previously from the land of Judah; then he turned and went back to his own land, and did not come again into their territory. [73] Thus the sword ceased from Israel. Jonathan settled in Michmash and began to judge the people; and he destroyed the godless out of Israel.

Revolt of Alexander Epiphanes

10 In the one hundred and sixtieth year[d] Alexander Epiphanes, son of Antiochus, landed and occupied Ptolemais. They welcomed him, and there he began to reign. [2] When King Demetrius heard of it, he assembled a very large army and marched out to meet him in battle. [3] Demetrius sent Jonathan a letter in peaceable words to honour him; [4] for he said to himself, 'Let us act first to make peace with him[e] before he makes peace with Alexander against us, [5] for he will remember all the wrongs that we did to him and to his brothers and his nation.' [6] So Demetrius[f] gave him authority to recruit troops, to equip them with arms, and to become his ally; and he commanded that the hostages in the citadel should be released to him.

7 Then Jonathan came to Jerusalem and read the letter in the hearing of all the people and of those in the citadel. [8] They were greatly alarmed when they heard that the king had given him authority to recruit troops. [9] But those in the citadel released the hostages to Jonathan, and he returned them to their parents.

10 And Jonathan took up residence in Jerusalem and began to rebuild and restore

Israel Under the Maccabees

Sidon

Mediterranean Sea

Tyre

Damascus

Panias

Scythopolis

Pella

Ramoth-gilead

Samaria

Joppa

Bethel

Philadelphia

Jericho

Jerusalem

Medeba

Ascalon

Hebron

Dead Sea

Machaerus

Gaza

Masada

Beer-sheba

0   40 Mi.
0   40 Km.

a Gk *they*   b Other ancient authorities read *they*
c Gk *him*   d 152 BC   e Gk *them*   f Gk *he*

the city. ¹¹ He directed those who were doing the work to build the walls and encircle Mount Zion with squared stones, for better fortification; and they did so.

12 Then the foreigners who were in the strongholds that Bacchides had built fled; ¹³ all of them left their places and went back to their own lands. ¹⁴ Only in Bethzur did some remain who had forsaken the law and the commandments, for it served as a place of refuge.

15 Now King Alexander heard of all the promises that Demetrius had sent to Jonathan, and he heard of the battles that Jonathanᵃ and his brothers had fought, of the brave deeds that they had done, and of the troubles that they had endured. ¹⁶ So he said, 'Shall we find another such man? Come now, we will make him our friend and ally.' ¹⁷ And he wrote a letter and sent it to him, in the following words:

Jonathan Becomes High Priest

18 'King Alexander to his brother Jonathan, greetings. ¹⁹ We have heard about you, that you are a mighty warrior and worthy to be our friend. ²⁰ And so we have appointed you today to be the high priest of your nation; you are to be called the king's Friend and you are to take our side and keep friendship with us.' He also sent him a purple robe and a golden crown.

21 So Jonathan put on the sacred vestments in the seventh month of the one hundred and sixtieth year,ᵇ at the festival of booths,ᶜ and he recruited troops and equipped them with arms in abundance. ²² When Demetrius heard of these things he was distressed and said, ²³ 'What is this that we have done? Alexander has overtaken us in forming a friendship with the Jews to strengthen himself. ²⁴ I also will write them words of encouragement and promise them honour and gifts, so that I may have their help.' ²⁵ So he sent a message to them in the following words:

A Letter from Demetrius to Jonathan

'King Demetrius to the nation of the Jews, greetings. ²⁶ Since you have kept your agreement with us and have continued your friendship with us, and have not sided with our enemies, we have heard of it and rejoiced. ²⁷ Now continue still to keep faith with us, and we will repay you with good for what you do for us. ²⁸ We will grant you many immunities and give you gifts.

29 'I now free you and exempt all the Jews from payment of tribute and salt tax and crown levies, ³⁰ and instead of collecting the third of the grain and the half of the fruit of the trees that I should receive, I release them from this day and henceforth. I will not collect them from the land of Judah or from the three districts added to it from Samaria and Galilee, from this day and for all time. ³¹ Jerusalem and its environs, its tithes and its revenues, shall be holy and free from tax. ³² I release also my control of the citadel in Jerusalem and give it to the high priest, so that he may station in it men of his own choice to guard it. ³³ And everyone of the Jews taken as a captive from the land of Judah into any part of my kingdom, I set free without payment; and let all officials cancel also the taxes on their livestock.

34 'All the festivals and sabbaths and new moons and appointed days, and the three days before a festival and the three after a festival—let them all be days of immunity and release for all the Jews who are in my kingdom. ³⁵ No one shall have authority to exact anything from them or annoy any of them about any matter.

36 'Let Jews be enrolled in the king's forces to the number of thirty thousand men, and let the maintenance be given them that is due to all the forces of the king. ³⁷ Let some of them be stationed in the great strongholds of the king, and let some of them be put in positions of trust in the kingdom. Let their officers and leaders be of their own number, and let them live by their own laws, just as the king has commanded in the land of Judah.

38 'As for the three districts that have been added to Judea from the country of Samaria, let them be annexed to Judea so that they may be considered to be under

ᵃ Gk *he*   ᵇ 152 BC   ᶜ Or *tabernacles*

one ruler and obey no other authority than the high priest. 39 Ptolemais and the land adjoining it I have given as a gift to the sanctuary in Jerusalem, to meet the necessary expenses of the sanctuary. 40 I also grant fifteen thousand shekels of silver yearly out of the king's revenues from appropriate places. 41 And all the additional funds that the government officials have not paid as they did in the first years, *a* they shall give from now on for the service of the temple. *b* 42 Moreover, the five thousand shekels of silver that my officials *c* have received every year from the income of the services of the temple, this too is cancelled, because it belongs to the priests who minister there. 43 And all who take refuge at the temple in Jerusalem, or in any of its precincts, because they owe money to the king or are in debt, let them be released and receive back all their property in my kingdom.

44 'Let the cost of rebuilding and restoring the structures of the sanctuary be paid from the revenues of the king. 45 And let the cost of rebuilding the walls of Jerusalem and fortifying it all round, and the cost of rebuilding the walls in Judea, also be paid from the revenues of the king.'

Death of Demetrius

46 When Jonathan and the people heard these words, they did not believe or accept them, because they remembered the great wrongs that Demetrius *d* had done in Israel and how much he had oppressed them. 47 They favoured Alexander, because he had been the first to speak peaceable words to them, and they remained his allies all his days.

48 Now King Alexander assembled large forces and encamped opposite Demetrius. 49 The two kings met in battle, and the army of Demetrius fled, and Alexander *e* pursued him and defeated them. 50 He pressed the battle strongly until the sun set, and on that day Demetrius fell.

Treaty of Ptolemy and Alexander

51 Then Alexander sent ambassadors to Ptolemy king of Egypt with the following

message: 52 'Since I have returned to my kingdom and have taken my seat on the throne of my ancestors, and established my rule—for I crushed Demetrius and gained control of our country; 53 I met him in battle, and he and his army were crushed by us, and we have taken our seat on the throne of his kingdom— 54 now therefore let us establish friendship with one another; give me now your daughter as my wife, and I will become your son-in-law, and will make gifts to you and to her in keeping with your position.'

55 Ptolemy the king replied and said, 'Happy was the day on which you returned to the land of your ancestors and took your seat on the throne of their kingdom. 56 And now I will do for you as you wrote, but meet me at Ptolemais, so that we may see one another, and I will become your father-in-law, as you have said.'

57 So Ptolemy set out from Egypt, he and his daughter Cleopatra, and came to Ptolemais in the one hundred and sixty-second year. *f* 58 King Alexander met him, and Ptolemy *d* gave him his daughter Cleopatra in marriage, and celebrated her wedding at Ptolemais with great pomp, as kings do.

59 Then King Alexander wrote to Jonathan to come and meet him. 60 So he went with pomp to Ptolemais and met the two kings; he gave them and their Friends silver and gold and many gifts, and found favour with them. 61 A group of malcontents from Israel, renegades, gathered together against him to accuse him; but the king paid no attention to them. 62 The king gave orders to take off Jonathan's garments and to clothe him in purple, and they did so. 63 The king also seated him at his side; and he said to his officers, 'Go out with him into the middle of the city and proclaim that no one is to bring charges against him about any matter, and let no one annoy him for any reason.' 64 When his accusers saw the honour that was paid him, in accordance with the proclamation, and saw him clothed in

a Meaning of Gk uncertain   *b* Gk *house*   *c* Gk *they*
d Gk *he*   *e* Other ancient authorities read *Alexander*
fled, and Demetrius   *f* 150 BC

purple, they all fled. 65 Thus the king honoured him and enrolled him among his chief*a* Friends, and made him general and governor of the province. 66 And Jonathan returned to Jerusalem in peace and gladness.

Apollonius Is Defeated by Jonathan

67 In the one hundred and sixty-fifth year*b* Demetrius son of Demetrius came from Crete to the land of his ancestors. 68 When King Alexander heard of it, he was greatly distressed and returned to Antioch. 69 And Demetrius appointed Apollonius the governor of Coelesyria, and he assembled a large force and encamped against Jamnia. Then he sent the following message to the high priest Jonathan:

70 'You are the only one to rise up against us, and I have fallen into ridicule and disgrace because of you. Why do you assume authority against us in the hill country? 71 If you now have confidence in your forces, come down to the plain to meet us, and let us match strength with each other there, for I have with me the power of the cities. 72 Ask and learn who I am and who the others are that are helping us. People will tell you that you cannot stand before us, for your ancestors were twice put to flight in their own land. 73 And now you will not be able to withstand my cavalry and such an army in the plain, where there is no stone or pebble, or place to flee.'

74 When Jonathan heard the words of Apollonius, his spirit was aroused. He chose ten thousand men and set out from Jerusalem, and his brother Simon met him to help him. 75 He encamped before Joppa, but the people of the city closed its gates, for Apollonius had a garrison in Joppa. 76 So they fought against it, and the people of the city became afraid and opened the gates, and Jonathan gained possession of Joppa.

77 When Apollonius heard of it, he mustered three thousand cavalry and a large army, and went to Azotus as though he were going farther. At the same time he advanced into the plain, for he had a large troop of cavalry and put confidence in it. 78 Jonathan*c* pursued him to Azotus, and the armies engaged in battle. 79 Now Apollonius had secretly left a thousand cavalry behind them. 80 Jonathan learned that there was an ambush behind him, for they surrounded his army and shot arrows at his men from early morning until late afternoon. 81 But his men stood fast, as Jonathan had commanded, and the enemy's*d* horses grew tired.

82 Then Simon brought forward his force and engaged the phalanx in battle (for the cavalry was exhausted); they were overwhelmed by him and fled, 83 and the cavalry was dispersed in the plain. They fled to Azotus and entered Beth-dagon, the temple of their idol, for safety. 84 But Jonathan burned Azotus and the surrounding towns and plundered them; and the temple of Dagon, and those who had taken refuge in it, he burned with fire. 85 The number of those who fell by the sword, with those burned alive, came to eight thousand.

86 Then Jonathan left there and encamped against Askalon, and the people of the city came out to meet him with great pomp.

87 He and those with him then returned to Jerusalem with a large amount of booty. 88 When King Alexander heard of these things, he honoured Jonathan still more; 89 and he sent to him a golden buckle, such as it is the custom to give to the King's Kinsmen. He also gave him Ekron and all its environs as his possession.

Ptolemy Invades Syria

11 Then the king of Egypt gathered great forces, like the sand by the seashore, and many ships; and he tried to get possession of Alexander's kingdom by trickery and add it to his own kingdom. 2 He set out for Syria with peaceable words, and the people of the towns opened their gates to him and went to meet him, for King Alexander had commanded them to meet him, since he was Alexander's*e* father-

a Gk *first*   *b* 147 BC   *c* Gk *he*   *d* Gk *their*
e Gk *his*

in-law. ³But when Ptolemy entered the towns he stationed forces as a garrison in each town.

4 When he*ᵃ* approached Azotus, they showed him the burnt-out temple of Dagon, and Azotus and its suburbs destroyed, and the corpses lying about, and the charred bodies of those whom Jonathan*ᵇ* had burned in the war, for they had piled them in heaps along his route. ⁵They also told the king what Jonathan had done, to throw blame on him; but the king kept silent. ⁶Jonathan met the king at Joppa with pomp, and they greeted one another and spent the night there. ⁷And Jonathan went with the king as far as the river called Eleutherus; then he returned to Jerusalem.

8 So King Ptolemy gained control of the coastal cities as far as Seleucia by the sea, and he kept devising wicked designs against Alexander. ⁹He sent envoys to King Demetrius, saying, 'Come, let us make a covenant with each other, and I will give you in marriage my daughter who was Alexander's wife, and you shall reign over your father's kingdom. ¹⁰I now regret that I gave him my daughter, for he has tried to kill me.' ¹¹He threw blame on Alexander*ᶜ* because he coveted his kingdom. ¹²So he took his daughter away from him and gave her to Demetrius. He was estranged from Alexander, and their enmity became manifest.

13 Then Ptolemy entered Antioch and put on the crown of Asia. Thus he put two crowns on his head, the crown of Egypt and that of Asia. ¹⁴Now King Alexander was in Cilicia at that time, because the people of that region were in revolt. ¹⁵When Alexander heard of it, he came against him in battle. Ptolemy marched out and met him with a strong force, and put him to flight. ¹⁶So Alexander fled into Arabia to find protection there, and King Ptolemy was triumphant. ¹⁷Zabdiel the Arab cut off the head of Alexander and sent it to Ptolemy. ¹⁸But King Ptolemy died three days later, and his troops in the strongholds were killed by the inhabitants of the strongholds. ¹⁹So Demetrius became king in the one hundred and sixty-seventh year.*ᵈ*

Jonathan's Diplomacy

20 In those days Jonathan assembled the Judeans to attack the citadel in Jerusalem, and he built many engines of war to use against it. ²¹But certain renegades who hated their nation went to the king and reported to him that Jonathan was besieging the citadel. ²²When he heard this he was angry, and as soon as he heard it he set out and came to Ptolemais; and he wrote to order Jonathan not to continue the siege, but to meet him for a conference at Ptolemais as quickly as possible.

23 When Jonathan heard this, he gave orders to continue the siege. He chose some of the elders of Israel and some of the priests, and put himself in danger, ²⁴for he went to the king at Ptolemais, taking silver and gold and clothing and numerous other gifts. And he won his favour. ²⁵Although certain renegades of his nation kept making complaints against him, ²⁶the king treated him as his predecessors had treated him; he exalted him in the presence of all his Friends. ²⁷He confirmed him in the high-priesthood and in as many other honours as he had formerly had, and caused him to be reckoned among his chief*ᵉ* Friends. ²⁸Then Jonathan asked the king to free Judea and the three districts of Samaria*ᶠ* from tribute, and promised him three hundred talents. ²⁹The king consented, and wrote a letter to Jonathan about all these things; its contents were as follows:

30 'King Demetrius to his brother Jonathan and to the nation of the Jews, greetings. ³¹This copy of the letter that we wrote concerning you to our kinsman Lasthenes we have written to you also, so that you may know what it says. ³²"King Demetrius to his father Lasthenes, greetings. ³³We have determined to do good to the nation of the Jews, who are our friends and fulfil their obligations to us, because of the goodwill they show towards us. ³⁴We have confirmed as their possession both the territory of Judea and the three districts of Aphairema and Lydda and Rathamin; the

latter, with all the region bordering them, were added to Judea from Samaria. To all those who offer sacrifice in Jerusalem we have granted release from[a] the royal taxes that the king formerly received from them each year, from the crops of the land and the fruit of the trees. 35 And the other payments henceforth due to us of the tithes, and the taxes due to us, and the salt pits and the crown taxes due to us—from all these we shall grant them release. 36 And not one of these grants shall be cancelled from this time on for ever. 37 Now therefore take care to make a copy of this, and let it be given to Jonathan and put up in a conspicuous place on the holy mountain." '

The Intrigue of Trypho

38 When King Demetrius saw that the land was quiet before him and that there was no opposition to him, he dismissed all his troops, all of them to their own homes, except the foreign troops that he had recruited from the islands of the nations. So all the troops who had served under his predecessors hated him. 39 A certain Trypho had formerly been one of Alexander's supporters; he saw that all the troops were grumbling against Demetrius. So he went to Imalkue the Arab, who was bringing up Antiochus, the young son of Alexander, 40 and insistently urged him to hand Antiochus[b] over to him, to become king in place of his father. He also reported to Imalkue[b] what Demetrius had done and told of the hatred that the troops of Demetrius[c] had for him; and he stayed there for many days.

41 Now Jonathan sent to King Demetrius the request that he remove the troops of the citadel from Jerusalem, and the troops in the strongholds; for they kept fighting against Israel. 42 And Demetrius sent this message back to Jonathan: 'Not only will I do these things for you and your nation, but I will confer great honour on you and your nation, if I find an opportunity. 43 Now then, you will do well to send me men who will help me, for all my troops have revolted.' 44 So Jonathan sent three thousand stalwart men to him at An-

tioch, and when they came to the king, the king rejoiced at their arrival.

45 Then the people of the city assembled within the city, to the number of a hundred and twenty thousand, and they wanted to kill the king. 46 But the king fled into the palace. Then the people of the city seized the main streets of the city and began to fight. 47 So the king called the Jews to his aid, and they all rallied around him and then spread out through the city; and they killed on that day about one hundred thousand. 48 They set fire to the city and seized a large amount of spoil on that day, and saved the king. 49 When the people of the city saw that the Jews had gained control of the city as they pleased, their courage failed and they cried out to the king with this entreaty: 50 'Grant us peace, and make the Jews stop fighting against us and our city.' 51 And they threw down their arms and made peace. So the Jews gained glory in the sight of the king and of all the people in his kingdom, and they returned to Jerusalem with a large amount of spoil.

52 So King Demetrius sat on the throne of his kingdom, and the land was quiet before him. 53 But he broke his word about all that he had promised; he became estranged from Jonathan and did not repay the favours that Jonathan[d] had done him, but treated him very harshly.

Trypho Seizes Power

54 After this Trypho returned, and with him the young boy Antiochus who began to reign and put on the crown. 55 All the troops that Demetrius had discharged gathered around him; they fought against Demetrius,[b] and he fled and was routed. 56 Trypho captured the elephants[e] and gained control of Antioch. 57 Then the young Antiochus wrote to Jonathan, saying, 'I confirm you in the high-priesthood and set you over the four districts and make you one of the king's Friends.' 58 He also sent him gold plates and a table service, and granted him the right to drink

a Or *Samaria, for all those who offer sacrifice in Jerusalem, in place of*   *b* Gk *him*   *c* Gk *his troops*   *d* Gk *he*   *e* Gk *animals* from gold cups and dress in purple and wear a gold buckle. 59 He appointed Jonathan's*a* brother Simon governor from the Ladder of Tyre to the borders of Egypt.

Campaigns of Jonathan and Simon

60 Then Jonathan set out and travelled beyond the river and among the towns, and all the army of Syria gathered to him as allies. When he came to Askalon, the people of the city met him and paid him honour. 61 From there he went to Gaza, but the people of Gaza shut him out. So he besieged it and burned its suburbs with fire and plundered them. 62 Then the people of Gaza pleaded with Jonathan, and he made peace with them, and took the sons of their rulers as hostages and sent them to Jerusalem. And he passed through the country as far as Damascus.

63 Then Jonathan heard that the officers of Demetrius had come to Kadesh in Galilee with a large army, intending to remove him from office. 64 He went to meet them, but left his brother Simon in the country. 65 Simon encamped before Bethzur and fought against it for many days and hemmed it in. 66 Then they asked him to grant them terms of peace, and he did so. He removed them from there, took possession of the town, and set a garrison over it.

67 Jonathan and his army encamped by the waters of Gennesaret. Early in the morning they marched to the plain of Hazor, 68 and there in the plain the army of the foreigners met him; they had set an ambush against him in the mountains, but they themselves met him face to face. 69 Then the men in ambush emerged from their places and joined battle. 70 All the men with Jonathan fled; not one of them was left except Mattathias son of Absalom and Judas son of Chalphi, commanders of the forces of the army. 71 Jonathan tore his clothes, put dust on his head, and prayed. 72 Then he turned back to the battle against the enemy*b* and routed them, and they fled. 73 When his men who were fleeing saw this, they returned to him and joined him in the pursuit as far as Kadesh, to their camp, and there they encamped. 74 As many as three thousand of the foreigners fell that day. And Jonathan returned to Jerusalem.

Alliances with Rome and Sparta

12 Now when Jonathan saw that the time was favourable for him, he chose men and sent them to Rome to confirm and renew the friendship with them. 2 He also sent letters to the same effect to the Spartans and to other places. 3 So they went to Rome and entered the senate chamber and said, 'The high priest Jonathan and the Jewish nation have sent us to renew the former friendship and alliance with them.' 4 And the Romans*c* gave them letters to the people in every place, asking them to provide for the envoys*b* safe conduct to the land of Judah.

5 This is a copy of the letter that Jonathan wrote to the Spartans: 6 'The high priest Jonathan, the senate of the nation, the priests, and the rest of the Jewish people to their brothers the Spartans, greetings. 7 Already in time past a letter was sent to the high priest Onias from Arius,*d* who was king among you, stating that you are our brothers, as the appended copy shows. 8 Onias welcomed the envoy with honour, and received the letter, which contained a clear declaration of alliance and friendship. 9 Therefore, though we have no need of these things, since we have as encouragement the holy books that are in our hands, 10 we have undertaken to send to renew our family ties and friendship with you, so that we may not become estranged from you, for considerable time has passed since you sent your letter to us. 11 We therefore remember you constantly on every occasion, both at our festivals and on other appropriate days, at the sacrifices that we offer and in our prayers, as it is right and proper to remember brothers. 12 And we rejoice in your glory. 13 But as for ourselves, many trials and many wars have encircled us; the kings around us have waged war against us. 14 We were unwilling to annoy

a Gk his   *b* Gk them   *c* Gk they   *d* Vg Compare verse 20: Gk Darius you and our other allies and friends with these wars, [15] for we have the help that comes from Heaven for our aid, and so we were delivered from our enemies, and our enemies were humbled. [16] We therefore have chosen Numenius son of Antiochus and Antipater son of Jason, and have sent them to Rome to renew our former friendship and alliance with them. [17] We have commanded them to go also to you and greet you and deliver to you this letter from us concerning the renewal of our family ties. [18] And now please send us a reply to this.'

19 This is a copy of the letter that they sent to Onias: [20] 'King Arius of the Spartans, to the high priest Onias, greetings. [21] It has been found in writing concerning the Spartans and the Jews that they are brothers and are of the family of Abraham. [22] And now that we have learned this, please write us concerning your welfare; [23] we on our part write to you that your livestock and your property belong to us, and ours belong to you. We therefore command that our envoys[a] report to you accordingly.'

Further Campaigns of Jonathan and Simon

24 Now Jonathan heard that the commanders of Demetrius had returned, with a larger force than before, to wage war against him. [25] So he marched away from Jerusalem and met them in the region of Hamath, for he gave them no opportunity to invade his own country. [26] He sent spies to their camp, and they returned and reported to him that the enemy[a] were being drawn up in formation to attack the Jews[b] by night. [27] So when the sun had set, Jonathan commanded his troops to be alert and to keep their arms at hand so as to be ready all night for battle, and he stationed outposts around the camp. [28] When the enemy heard that Jonathan and his troops were prepared for battle, they were afraid and were terrified at heart; so they kindled fires in their camp and withdrew.[c] [29] But Jonathan and his troops did not know it until morning, for they saw the fires burning. [30] Then Jonathan pursued them, but he did not overtake them, for they had crossed the Eleutherus river. [31] So Jonathan turned aside against the Arabs who are called Zabadeans, and he crushed them and plundered them. [32] Then he broke camp and went to Damascus, and marched through all that region.

33 Simon also went out and marched through the country as far as Askalon and the neighbouring strongholds. He turned aside to Joppa and took it by surprise, [34] for he had heard that they were ready to hand over the stronghold to those whom Demetrius had sent. And he stationed a garrison there to guard it.

35 When Jonathan returned he convened the elders of the people and planned with them to build strongholds in Judea, [36] to build the walls of Jerusalem still higher, and to erect a high barrier between the citadel and the city to separate it from the city, in order to isolate it so that its garrison[d] could neither buy nor sell. [37] So they gathered together to rebuild the city; part of the wall on the valley to the east had fallen, and he repaired the section called Chaphenatha. [38] Simon also built Adida in the Shephelah; he fortified it and installed gates with bolts.

Trypho Captures Jonathan

39 Then Trypho attempted to become king in Asia and put on the crown, and to raise his hand against King Antiochus. [40] He feared that Jonathan might not permit him to do so, but might make war on him, so he kept seeking to seize and kill him, and he marched out and came to Beth-shan. [41] Jonathan went out to meet him with forty thousand picked warriors, and he came to Beth-shan. [42] When Trypho saw that he had come with a large army, he was afraid to raise his hand against him. [43] So he received him with honour and commended him to all his Friends, and he gave him gifts and commanded his Friends and his troops to obey him as they would himself. [44] Then he said to Jonathan, 'Why

a Gk they   b Gk them   c Other ancient authorities omit and withdrew have you put all these people to so much trouble when we are not at war? 45 Dismiss them now to their homes and choose for yourself a few men to stay with you, and come with me to Ptolemais. I will hand it over to you as well as the other strongholds and the remaining troops and all the officials, and will turn around and go home. For that is why I am here.'

46 Jonathan[a] trusted him and did as he said; he sent away the troops, and they returned to the land of Judah. 47 He kept with himself three thousand men, two thousand of whom he left in Galilee, while one thousand accompanied him. 48 But when Jonathan entered Ptolemais, the people of Ptolemais closed the gates and seized him, and they killed with the sword all who had entered with him.

49 Then Trypho sent troops and cavalry into Galilee and the Great Plain to destroy all Jonathan's soldiers. 50 But they realized that Jonathan had been seized and had perished along with his men, and they encouraged one another and kept marching in close formation, ready for battle. 51 When their pursuers saw that they would fight for their lives, they turned back. 52 So they all reached the land of Judah safely, and they mourned for Jonathan and his companions and were in great fear; and all Israel mourned deeply. 53 All the nations around them tried to destroy them, for they said, 'They have no leader or helper. Now therefore let us make war on them and blot out the memory of them from humankind.'

Simon Takes Command

13 Simon heard that Trypho had assembled a large army to invade the land of Judah and destroy it, 2 and he saw that the people were trembling with fear. So he went up to Jerusalem, and gathering the people together 3 he encouraged them, saying to them, 'You yourselves know what great things my brothers and I and the house of my father have done for the laws and the sanctuary; you know also the wars and the difficulties that my brothers and I have seen. 4 By reason of this all my broth-

ers have perished for the sake of Israel, and I alone am left. 5 And now, far be it from me to spare my life in any time of distress, for I am not better than my brothers. 6 But I will avenge my nation and the sanctuary and your wives and children, for all the nations have gathered together out of hatred to destroy us.'

7 The spirit of the people was rekindled when they heard these words, 8 and they answered in a loud voice, 'You are our leader in place of Judas and your brother Jonathan. 9 Fight our battles, and all that you say to us we will do.' 10 So he assembled all the warriors and hurried to complete the walls of Jerusalem, and he fortified it on every side. 11 He sent Jonathan son of Absalom to Joppa, and with him a considerable army; he drove out its occupants and remained there.

Deceit and Treachery of Trypho

12 Then Trypho left Ptolemais with a large army to invade the land of Judah, and Jonathan was with him under guard. 13 Simon encamped in Adida, facing the plain. 14 Trypho learned that Simon had risen up in place of his brother Jonathan, and that he was about to join battle with him, so he sent envoys to him and said, 15 'It is for the money that your brother Jonathan owed the royal treasury, in connection with the offices he held, that we are detaining him. 16 Send now one hundred talents of silver and two of his sons as hostages, so that when released he will not revolt against us, and we will release him.'

17 Simon knew that they were speaking deceitfully to him, but he sent to get the money and the sons, so that he would not arouse great hostility among the people, who might say, 18 'It was because Simon[b] did not send him the money and the sons, that Jonathan[a] perished.' 19 So he sent the sons and the hundred talents, but Trypho[a] broke his word and did not release Jonathan.

20 After this Trypho came to invade the country and destroy it, and he circled around by the way to Adora. But Simon

a Gk he   b Gk I

and his army kept marching along opposite him to every place he went. 21 Now the men in the citadel kept sending envoys to Trypho urging him to come to them by way of the wilderness and to send them food. 22 So Trypho got all his cavalry ready to go, but that night a very heavy snow fell, and he did not go because of the snow. He marched off and went into the land of Gilead. 23 When he approached Baskama, he killed Jonathan, and he was buried there. 24 Then Trypho turned and went back to his own land.

Jonathan's Tomb

25 Simon sent and took the bones of his brother Jonathan, and buried him in Modein, the city of his ancestors. 26 All Israel bewailed him with great lamentation, and mourned for him for many days. 27 And Simon built a monument over the tomb of his father and his brothers; he made it high so that it might be seen, with polished stone at the front and back. 28 He also erected seven pyramids, opposite one another, for his father and mother and four brothers. 29 For the pyramids*a* he devised an elaborate setting, erecting about them great columns, and on the columns he put suits of armour for a permanent memorial, and beside the suits of armour he carved ships, so that they could be seen by all who sail the sea. 30 This is the tomb that he built in Modein; it remains to this day.

Judea Gains Independence

31 Trypho dealt treacherously with the young King Antiochus; he killed him 32 and became king in his place, putting on the crown of Asia; and he brought great calamity on the land. 33 But Simon built up the strongholds of Judea and walled them all round, with high towers and great walls and gates and bolts, and he stored food in the strongholds. 34 Simon also chose emissaries and sent them to King Demetrius with a request to grant relief to the country, for all that Trypho did was to plunder. 35 King Demetrius sent him a favourable reply to this request, and wrote him a letter as follows, 36 'King Demetrius to Simon,

the high priest and friend of kings, and to the elders and nation of the Jews, greetings. 37 We have received the gold crown and the palm branch that you*b* sent, and we are ready to make a general peace with you and to write to our officials to grant you release from tribute. 38 All the grants that we have made to you remain valid, and let the strongholds that you have built be your possession. 39 We pardon any errors and offences committed to this day, and cancel the crown tax that you owe; and whatever other tax has been collected in Jerusalem shall be collected no longer. 40 And if any of you are qualified to be enrolled in our bodyguard,*c* let them be enrolled, and let there be peace between us.'

41 In the one hundred and seventieth year*d* the yoke of the Gentiles was removed from Israel, 42 and the people began to write in their documents and contracts, 'In the first year of Simon the great high priest and commander and leader of the Jews.'

The Capture of Gazara by Simon

43 In those days Simon*e* encamped against Gazara*f* and surrounded it with troops. He made a siege-engine, brought it up to the city, and battered and captured one tower. 44 The men in the siege-engine leapt out into the city, and a great tumult arose in the city. 45 The men in the city, with their wives and children, went up on the wall with their clothes torn, and they cried out with a loud voice, asking Simon to make peace with them; 46 they said, 'Do not treat us according to our wicked acts but according to your mercy.' 47 So Simon reached an agreement with them and stopped fighting against them. But he expelled them from the city and cleansed the houses in which the idols were located, and then entered it with hymns and praise. 48 He removed all uncleanness from it, and settled in it those who observed the law. He also strengthened its fortifications and built in it a house for himself.

a Gk For these   *b* The word *you* in verses 37-40 is plural   *c* Or *court*   *d* 142 BC   *e* Gk *he*   *f* Cn: Gk *Gaza*

Simon Regains the Citadel at Jerusalem

49 Those who were in the citadel at Jerusalem were prevented from going in and out to buy and sell in the country. So they were very hungry, and many of them perished from famine. 50 Then they cried to Simon to make peace with them, and he did so. But he expelled them from there and cleansed the citadel from its pollutions. 51 On the twenty-third day of the second month, in the one hundred and seventy-first year,*a* the Jews*b* entered it with praise and palm branches, and with harps and cymbals and stringed instruments, and with hymns and songs, because a great enemy had been crushed and removed from Israel. 52 Simon*c* decreed that every year they should celebrate this day with rejoicing. He strengthened the fortifications of the temple hill alongside the citadel, and he and his men lived there. 53 Simon saw that his son John had reached manhood, and so he made him commander of all the forces; and he lived at Gazara.

Capture of Demetrius

14 In the one hundred and seventy-second year*d* King Demetrius assembled his forces and marched into Media to obtain help, so that he could make war against Trypho. 2 When King Arsaces of Persia and Media heard that Demetrius had invaded his territory, he sent one of his generals to take him alive. 3 The general*c* went and defeated the army of Demetrius, and seized him and took him to Arsaces, who put him under guard.

Eulogy of Simon

4 The land*e* had rest all the days of
      Simon.
   He sought the good of his nation;
   his rule was pleasing to them,
      as was the honour shown him, all
         his days.
5 To crown all his honours he took
      Joppa for a harbour,
   and opened a way to the isles of the
         sea.
6 He extended the borders of his
      nation,

and gained full control of the
      country.
7 He gathered a host of captives;
   he ruled over Gazara and Beth-zur
         and the citadel,
   and he removed its uncleanness from
         it;
   and there was none to oppose him.
8 They tilled their land in peace;
   the ground gave its increase,
   and the trees of the plains their
         fruit.
9 Old men sat in the streets;
   they all talked together of good
         things,
   and the youths put on splendid
         military attire.
10 He supplied the towns with food,
   and furnished them with the means
         of defence,
   until his renown spread to the ends
         of the earth.
11 He established peace in the land,
   and Israel rejoiced with great joy.
12 All the people sat under their own
      vines and fig trees,
   and there was none to make them
         afraid.
13 No one was left in the land to fight
      them,
   and the kings were crushed in those
         days.
14 He gave help to all the humble
      among his people;
   he sought out the law,
   and did away with all the renegades
      and outlaws.
15 He made the sanctuary glorious,
   and added to the vessels of the
      sanctuary.

Diplomacy with Rome and Sparta

16 It was heard in Rome, and as far away as Sparta, that Jonathan had died, and they were deeply grieved. 17 When they heard that his brother Simon had become high priest in his stead, and that he was ruling over the country and the towns in it, 18 they wrote to him on bronze tablets to

---

a 141 BC   *b* Gk *they*   *c* Gk *He*   *d* 140 BC
e Other ancient authorities add *of Judah*

renew with him the friendship and alliance that they had established with his brothers Judas and Jonathan. 19 And these were read before the assembly in Jerusalem.

20 This is a copy of the letter that the Spartans sent:

'The rulers and the city of the Spartans to the high priest Simon and to the elders and the priests and the rest of the Jewish people, our brothers, greetings. 21 The envoys who were sent to our people have told us about your glory and honour, and we rejoiced at their coming. 22 We have recorded what they said in our public decrees, as follows, "Numenius son of Antiochus and Antipater son of Jason, envoys of the Jews, have come to us to renew their friendship with us. 23 It has pleased our people to receive these men with honour and to put a copy of their words in the public archives, so that the people of the Spartans may have a record of them. And they have sent a copy of this to the high priest Simon." '

24 After this Simon sent Numenius to Rome with a large gold shield weighing one thousand minas, to confirm the alliance with the Romans. *a*

Official Honours for Simon

25 When the people heard these things they said, 'How shall we thank Simon and his sons? 26 For he and his brothers and the house of his father have stood firm; they have fought and repulsed Israel's enemies and established its freedom.' 27 So they made a record on bronze tablets and put it on pillars on Mount Zion.

This is a copy of what they wrote: 'On the eighteenth day of Elul, in the one hundred and seventy-second year, *b* which is the third year of the great high priest Simon, 28 in Asaramel, *c* in the great assembly of the priests and the people and the rulers of the nation and the elders of the country, the following was proclaimed to us:

29 'Since wars often occurred in the country, Simon son of Mattathias, a priest of the sons *d* of Joarib, and his brothers, exposed themselves to danger and resisted the enemies of their nation, in order that their sanctuary and the law might be preserved; and they brought great glory to their nation. 30 Jonathan rallied the *e* nation, became their high priest, and was gathered to his people. 31 When their enemies decided to invade their country and lay hands on their sanctuary, 32 then Simon rose up and fought for his nation. He spent great sums of his own money; he armed the soldiers of his nation and paid them wages. 33 He fortified the towns of Judea, and Beth-zur on the borders of Judea, where formerly the arms of the enemy had been stored, and he placed there a garrison of Jews. 34 He also fortified Joppa, which is by the sea, and Gazara, which is on the borders of Azotus, where the enemy formerly lived. He settled Jews there, and provided in those towns *d* whatever was necessary for their restoration.

35 'The people saw Simon's faithfulness *f* and the glory that he had resolved to win for his nation, and they made him their leader and high priest, because he had done all these things and because of the justice and loyalty that he had maintained towards his nation. He sought in every way to exalt his people. 36 In his days things prospered in his hands, so that the Gentiles were put out of the *e* country, as were also those in the city of David in Jerusalem, who had built themselves a citadel from which they used to sally forth and defile the environs of the sanctuary, doing great damage to its purity. 37 He settled Jews in it and fortified it for the safety of the country and of the city, and built the walls of Jerusalem higher.

38 'In view of these things King Demetrius confirmed him in the highpriesthood, 39 made him one of his Friends, and paid him high honours. 40 For he had heard that the Jews were addressed by the Romans as friends and allies and brothers, and that the Romans *g* had received the envoys of Simon with honour.

41 'The Jews and their priests have resolved that Simon should be their leader

---

a Gk them   *b* 140 BC   *c* This word resembles the Hebrew words for *the court of the people of God* or *the prince of the people of God*   *d* Meaning of Gk uncertain   *e* Gk *their*   *f* Other ancient authorities read *conduct*   *g* Gk *they* and high priest for ever, until a trustworthy prophet should arise, 42 and that he should be governor over them and that he should take charge of the sanctuary and appoint officials over its tasks and over the country and the weapons and the strongholds, and that he should take charge of the sanctuary, 43 and that he should be obeyed by all, and that all contracts in the country should be written in his name, and that he should be clothed in purple and wear gold.

44 'None of the people or priests shall be permitted to nullify any of these decisions or to oppose what he says, or to convene an assembly in the country without his permission, or to be clothed in purple or put on a gold buckle. 45 Whoever acts contrary to these decisions or rejects any of them shall be liable to punishment.'

46 All the people agreed to grant Simon the right to act in accordance with these decisions. 47 So Simon accepted and agreed to be high priest, to be commander and ethnarch of the Jews and priests, and to be protector of them all.*a* 48 And they gave orders to inscribe this decree on bronze tablets, to put them up in a conspicuous place in the precincts of the sanctuary, 49 and to deposit copies of them in the treasury, so that Simon and his sons might have them.

Letter of Antiochus VII

15 Antiochus, son of King Demetrius, sent a letter from the islands of the sea to Simon, the priest and ethnarch of the Jews, and to all the nation; 2 its contents were as follows: 'King Antiochus to Simon the high priest and ethnarch and to the nation of the Jews, greetings. 3 Whereas certain scoundrels have gained control of the kingdom of our ancestors, and I intend to lay claim to the kingdom so that I may restore it as it formerly was, and have recruited a host of mercenary troops and have equipped warships, 4 and intend to make a landing in the country so that I may proceed against those who have destroyed our country and those who have devastated many cities in my kingdom, 5 now therefore I confirm to you all the tax remissions that the kings before me have granted you, and a release from all the other payments from which they have released you. 6 I permit you to mint your own coinage as money for your country, 7 and I grant freedom to Jerusalem and the sanctuary. All the weapons that you have prepared and the strongholds that you have built and now hold shall remain yours. 8 Every debt you owe to the royal treasury and any such future debts shall be cancelled for you from henceforth and for all time. 9 When we gain control of our kingdom, we will bestow great honour on you and your nation and the temple, so that your glory will become manifest in all the earth.'

10 In the one hundred and seventy-fourth year*b* Antiochus set out and invaded the land of his ancestors. All the troops rallied to him, so that there were only a few with Trypho. 11 Antiochus pursued him, and Trypho*c* came in his flight to Dor, which is by the sea; 12 for he knew that troubles had converged on him, and his troops had deserted him. 13 So Antiochus encamped against Dor, and with him were one hundred and twenty thousand warriors and eight thousand cavalry. 14 He surrounded the town, and the ships joined battle from the sea; he pressed the town hard from land and sea, and permitted no one to leave or enter it.

Rome Supports the Jews

15 Then Numenius and his companions arrived from Rome, with letters to the kings and countries, in which the following was written: 16 'Lucius, consul of the Romans, to King Ptolemy, greetings. 17 The envoys of the Jews have come to us as our friends and allies to renew our ancient friendship and alliance. They had been sent by the high priest Simon and by the Jewish people 18 and have brought a gold shield weighing one thousand minas. 19 We therefore have decided to write to the kings and countries that they should not seek their harm or make war against them and their cities and their country, or make al-

a Or *to preside over them all*   *b* 138 BC   *c* Gk *he* liance with those who war against them. [20]And it has seemed good to us to accept the shield from them. [21]Therefore if any scoundrels have fled to you from their country, hand them over to the high priest Simon, so that he may punish them according to their law.'

22 The consul[a] wrote the same thing to King Demetrius and to Attalus and Ariarathes and Arsaces, [23]and to all the countries, and to Sampsames, [b] and to the Spartans, and to Delos, and to Myndos, and to Sicyon, and to Caria, and to Samos, and to Pamphylia, and to Lycia, and to Halicarnassus, and to Rhodes, and to Phaselis, and to Cos, and to Side, and to Aradus and Gortyna and Cnidus and Cyprus and Cyrene. [24]They also sent a copy of these things to the high priest Simon.

Antiochus VII Threatens Simon

25 King Antiochus besieged Dor for the second time, continually throwing his forces against it and making engines of war; and he shut Trypho up and kept him from going out or in. [26]And Simon sent to Antiochus[c] two thousand picked troops, to fight for him, and silver and gold and a large amount of military equipment. [27]But he refused to receive them, and broke all the agreements he formerly had made with Simon, and became estranged from him. [28]He sent to him Athenobius, one of his Friends, to confer with him, saying, 'You hold control of Joppa and Gazara and the citadel in Jerusalem; they are cities of my kingdom. [29]You have devastated their territory, you have done great damage in the land, and you have taken possession of many places in my kingdom. [30]Now then, hand over the cities that you have seized and the tribute money of the places that you have conquered outside the borders of Judea; [31]or else pay me five hundred talents of silver for the destruction that you have caused and five hundred talents more for the tribute money of the cities. Otherwise we will come and make war on you.'

32 So Athenobius, the king's Friend, came to Jerusalem, and when he saw the splendour of Simon, and the sideboard

with its gold and silver plate, and his great magnificence, he was amazed. When he reported to him the king's message, [33]Simon said to him in reply: 'We have neither taken foreign land nor seized foreign property, but only the inheritance of our ancestors, which at one time had been unjustly taken by our enemies. [34]Now that we have the opportunity, we are firmly holding the inheritance of our ancestors. [35]As for Joppa and Gazara, which you demand, they were causing great damage among the people and to our land; for them we will give you one hundred talents.'

Athenobius[a] did not answer him a word, [36]but returned in wrath to the king and reported to him these words, and also the splendour of Simon and all that he had seen. And the king was very angry.

Victory over Cendebeus

37 Meanwhile Trypho embarked on a ship and escaped to Orthosia. [38]Then the king made Cendebeus commander-in-chief of the coastal country, and gave him troops of infantry and cavalry. [39]He commanded him to encamp against Judea, to build up Kedron and fortify its gates, and to make war on the people; but the king pursued Trypho. [40]So Cendebeus came to Jamnia and began to provoke the people and invade Judea and take the people captive and kill them. [41]He built up Kedron and stationed horsemen and troops there, so that they might go out and make raids along the highways of Judea, as the king had ordered him.

16 John went up from Gazara and reported to his father Simon what Cendebeus had done. [2]And Simon called in his two eldest sons Judas and John, and said to them: 'My brothers and I and my father's house have fought the wars of Israel from our youth until this day, and things have prospered in our hands so that we have delivered Israel many times. [3]But now I have grown old, and you by Heaven's[d] mercy are mature in years. Take my place and my brother's, and go out and fight for

---

a Gk *He*   *b* The name is uncertain   *c* Gk *him*
d Gk *his*

our nation, and may the help that comes from Heaven be with you.'

4 So John*a* chose out of the country twenty thousand warriors and cavalry, and they marched against Cendebeus and camped for the night in Modein. 5 Early in the morning they started out and marched into the plain, where a large force of infantry and cavalry was coming to meet them; and a stream lay between them. 6 Then he and his army lined up against them. He saw that the soldiers were afraid to cross the stream, so he crossed over first; and when his troops saw him, they crossed over after him. 7 Then he divided the army and placed the cavalry in the centre of the infantry, for the cavalry of the enemy were very numerous. 8 They sounded the trumpets, and Cendebeus and his army were put to flight; many of them fell wounded and the rest fled into the stronghold. 9 At that time Judas the brother of John was wounded, but John pursued them until Cendebeus*b* reached Kedron, which he had built. 10 They also fled into the towers that were in the fields of Azotus, and John*b* burned it with fire, and about two thousand of them fell. He then returned to Judea safely.

Murder of Simon and His Sons

11 Now Ptolemy son of Abubus had been appointed governor over the plain of Jericho; he had a large store of silver and gold, 12 for he was son-in-law of the high priest. 13 His heart was lifted up; he determined to get control of the country, and made treacherous plans against Simon and his sons, to do away with them. 14 Now Simon was visiting the towns of the country and attending to their needs, and he went down to Jericho with his sons Mattathias and Judas, in the one hundred and seventy-seventh year, *c* in the eleventh month, which is the month of Shebat. 15 The son of Abubus received them treacherously in the little stronghold called Dok, which he had built; he gave them a great banquet, and hid men there. 16 When Simon and his sons were drunk, Ptolemy and his men rose up, took their weapons, rushed in against Simon in the banqueting-hall and killed him and his two sons, as well as some of his servants. 17 So he committed an act of great treachery and returned evil for good.

John Succeeds Simon

18 Then Ptolemy wrote a report about these things and sent it to the king, asking him to send troops to aid him and to turn over to him the towns and the country. 19 He sent other troops to Gazara to do away with John; he sent letters to the captains asking them to come to him so that he might give them silver and gold and gifts; 20 and he sent other troops to take possession of Jerusalem and the temple hill. 21 But someone ran ahead and reported to John at Gazara that his father and brothers had perished, and that 'he has sent men to kill you also.' 22 When he heard this, he was greatly shocked; he seized the men who came to destroy him and killed them, for he had found out that they were seeking to destroy him.

23 The rest of the acts of John and his wars, and the brave deeds that he did, and the building of the walls that he completed, and his achievements, 24 are written in the annals of his high-priesthood, from the time that he became high priest after his father.

---

a Other ancient authorities read *he*   *b* Gk *he*
c 134 BC

2 MACCABEES

A Letter to the Jews in Egypt

1 The Jews in Jerusalem and those in the land of Judea,

To their Jewish kindred in Egypt,

Greetings and true peace.

2 May God do good to you, and may he remember his covenant with Abraham and Isaac and Jacob, his faithful servants. 3 May he give you all a heart to worship him and to do his will with a strong heart and a willing spirit. 4 May he open your heart to his law and his commandments, and may he bring peace. 5 May he hear your prayers and be reconciled to you, and may he not forsake you in time of evil. 6 We are now praying for you here.

7 In the reign of Demetrius, in the one hundred and sixty-ninth year,[a] we Jews wrote to you, in the critical distress that came upon us in those years after Jason and his company revolted from the holy land and the kingdom 8 and burned the gate and shed innocent blood. We prayed to the Lord and were heard, and we offered sacrifice and grain-offering, and we lit the lamps and set out the loaves. 9 And now see that you keep the festival of booths in the month of Chislev, in the one hundred and eighty-eighth year.[b]

A Letter to Aristobulus

10 The people of Jerusalem and of Judea and the senate and Judas,

To Aristobulus, who is of the family of the anointed priests, teacher of King Ptolemy, and to the Jews in Egypt,

Greetings and good health.

11 Having been saved by God out of grave dangers we thank him greatly for taking our side against the king,[c] 12 for he drove out those who fought against the holy city. 13 When the leader reached Persia with a force that seemed irresistible, they were cut to pieces in the temple of Nanea by a deception employed by the priests of the goddess[d] Nanea. 14 On the pretext of intending to marry her, Antiochus came to the place together with his Friends, to secure most of its treasures as a dowry. 15 When the priests of the temple of Nanea had set out the treasures and Antiochus had come with a few men inside the wall of the sacred precinct, they closed the temple as soon as he entered it. 16 Opening a secret door in the ceiling, they threw stones and struck down the leader and his men; they dismembered them and cut off their heads and threw them to the people outside. 17 Blessed in every way be our God, who has brought judgement on those who have behaved impiously.

Fire Consumes Nehemiah's Sacrifice

18 Since on the twenty-fifth day of Chislev we shall celebrate the purification of the temple, we thought it necessary to notify you, in order that you also may celebrate the festival of booths and the festival of the fire given when Nehemiah, who built the temple and the altar, offered sacrifices.

19 For when our ancestors were being led captive to Persia, the pious priests of that time took some of the fire of the altar and secretly hid it in the hollow of a dry cistern, where they took such precautions that the place was unknown to anyone. 20 But after many years had passed, when it

a 143 BC   b 124 BC   c Cn: Gk as those who array themselves against a king   d Gk lacks the goddess pleased God, Nehemiah, having been commissioned by the king of Persia, sent the descendants of the priests who had hidden the fire to get it. And when they reported to us that they had not found fire but only a thick liquid, he ordered them to dip it out and bring it. 21 When the materials for the sacrifices were presented, Nehemiah ordered the priests to sprinkle the liquid on the wood and on the things laid upon it. 22 When this had been done and some time had passed, and when the sun, which had been clouded over, shone out, a great fire blazed up, so that all marvelled. 23 And while the sacrifice was being consumed, the priests offered prayer—the priests and everyone. Jonathan led, and the rest responded, as did Nehemiah. 24 The prayer was to this effect:

'O Lord, Lord God, Creator of all things, you are awe-inspiring and strong and just and merciful, you alone are king and are kind, 25 you alone are bountiful, you alone are just and almighty and eternal. You rescue Israel from every evil; you chose the ancestors and consecrated them. 26 Accept this sacrifice on behalf of all your people Israel and preserve your portion and make it holy. 27 Gather together our scattered people, set free those who are slaves among the Gentiles, look on those who are rejected and despised, and let the Gentiles know that you are our God. 28 Punish those who oppress and are insolent with pride. 29 Plant your people in your holy place, as Moses promised.'

30 Then the priests sang the hymns. 31 After the materials of the sacrifice had been consumed, Nehemiah ordered that the liquid that was left should be poured on large stones. 32 When this was done, a flame blazed up; but when the light from the altar shone back, it went out. 33 When this matter became known, and it was reported to the king of the Persians that, in the place where the exiled priests had hidden the fire, the liquid had appeared with which Nehemiah and his associates had burned the materials of the sacrifice, 34 the king investigated the matter, and enclosed the place and made it sacred. 35 And with those persons whom the king favoured he exchanged many excellent gifts. 36 Nehemiah and his associates called this 'nephthar', which means purification, but by most people it is called naphtha. [a]

Jeremiah Hides the Tent, Ark, and Altar

2 One finds in the records that the prophet Jeremiah ordered those who were being deported to take some of the fire, as has been mentioned, 2 and that the prophet, after giving them the law, instructed those who were being deported not to forget the commandments of the Lord, or to be led astray in their thoughts on seeing the gold and silver statues and their adornment. 3 And with other similar words he exhorted them that the law should not depart from their hearts.

4 It was also in the same document that the prophet, having received an oracle, ordered that the tent and the ark should follow with him, and that he went out to the mountain where Moses had gone up and had seen the inheritance of God. 5 Jeremiah came and found a cave-dwelling, and he brought there the tent and the ark and the altar of incense; then he sealed up the entrance. 6 Some of those who followed him came up intending to mark the way, but could not find it. 7 When Jeremiah learned of it, he rebuked them and declared: 'The place shall remain unknown until God gathers his people together again and shows his mercy. 8 Then the Lord will disclose these things, and the glory of the Lord and the cloud will appear, as they were shown in the case of Moses, and as Solomon asked that the place should be specially consecrated.'

9 It was also made clear that being possessed of wisdom Solomon [b] offered sacrifice for the dedication and completion of the temple. 10 Just as Moses prayed to the Lord, and fire came down from heaven and consumed the sacrifices, so also Solomon prayed, and the fire came down and consumed the whole burnt-offerings. 11 And Moses said, 'They were consumed because the sin-offering had not been eaten.'

a Gk *nephthai*   *b* Gk *he*

12 Likewise, Solomon also kept the eight days.

13 The same things are reported in the records and in the memoirs of Nehemiah, and also that he founded a library and collected the books about the kings and prophets, and the writings of David, and letters of kings about votive offerings. 14 In the same way Judas also collected all the books that had been lost on account of the war that had come upon us, and they are in our possession. 15 So if you have need of them, send people to get them for you.

16 Since, therefore, we are about to celebrate the purification, we write to you. Will you therefore please keep the days? 17 It is God who has saved all his people, and has returned the inheritance to all, and the kingship and the priesthood and the consecration, 18 as he promised through the law. We have hope in God that he will soon have mercy on us and will gather us from everywhere under heaven into his holy place, for he has rescued us from great evils and has purified the place.

The Compiler's Preface

19 The story of Judas Maccabeus and his brothers, and the purification of the great temple, and the dedication of the altar, 20 and further the wars against Antiochus Epiphanes and his son Eupator, 21 and the appearances that came from heaven to those who fought bravely for Judaism, so that though few in number they seized the whole land and pursued the barbarian hordes, 22 and regained possession of the temple famous throughout the world, and liberated the city, and re-established the laws that were about to be abolished, while the Lord with great kindness became gracious to them— 23 all this, which has been set forth by Jason of Cyrene in five volumes, we shall attempt to condense into a single book. 24 For considering the flood of statistics involved and the difficulty there is for those who wish to enter upon the narratives of history because of the mass of material, 25 we have aimed to please those who wish to read, to make it easy for those who are inclined to

memorize, and to profit all readers. 26 For us who have undertaken the toil of abbreviating, it is no light matter but calls for sweat and loss of sleep, 27 just as it is not easy for one who prepares a banquet and seeks the benefit of others. Nevertheless, to secure the gratitude of many we will gladly endure the uncomfortable toil, 28 leaving the responsibility for exact details to the compiler, while devoting our effort to arriving at the outlines of the condensation. 29 For as the master builder of a new house must be concerned with the whole construction, while the one who undertakes its painting and decoration has to consider only what is suitable for its adornment, such in my judgement is the case with us. 30 It is the duty of the original historian to occupy the ground, to discuss matters from every side, and to take trouble with details, 31 but the one who recasts the narrative should be allowed to strive for brevity of expression and to forego exhaustive treatment. 32 At this point therefore let us begin our narrative, without adding any more to what has already been said; for it would be foolish to lengthen the preface while cutting short the history itself.

Arrival of Heliodorus in Jerusalem

3 While the holy city was inhabited in unbroken peace and the laws were strictly observed because of the piety of the high priest Onias and his hatred of wickedness, 2 it came about that the kings themselves honoured the place and glorified the temple with the finest presents, 3 even to the extent that King Seleucus of Asia defrayed from his own revenues all the expenses connected with the service of the sacrifices.

4 But a man named Simon, of the tribe of Benjamin, who had been made captain of the temple, had a disagreement with the high priest about the administration of the city market. 5 Since he could not prevail over Onias, he went to Apollonius of Tarsus,*a* who at that time was governor of Coelesyria and Phoenicia, 6 and reported to him that the treasury in Jerusalem was full

a Gk *Apollonius son of Tharseas*

of untold sums of money, so that the amount of the funds could not be reckoned, and that they did not belong to the account of the sacrifices, but that it was possible for them to fall under the control of the king. [7] When Apollonius met the king, he told him of the money about which he had been informed. The king[a] chose Heliodorus, who was in charge of his affairs, and sent him with commands to effect the removal of the reported wealth. [8] Heliodorus at once set out on his journey, ostensibly to make a tour of inspection of the cities of Coelesyria and Phoenicia, but in fact to carry out the king's purpose.

9 When he had arrived at Jerusalem and had been kindly welcomed by the high priest of[b] the city, he told about the disclosure that had been made and stated why he had come, and he inquired whether this really was the situation. [10] The high priest explained that there were some deposits belonging to widows and orphans, [11] and also some money of Hyrcanus son of Tobias, a man of very prominent position, and that it totalled in all four hundred talents of silver and two hundred of gold. To such an extent the impious Simon had misrepresented the facts. [12] And he said that it was utterly impossible that wrong should be done to those people who had trusted in the holiness of the place and in the sanctity and inviolability of the temple that is honoured throughout the whole world.

Heliodorus Plans to Rob the Temple

13 But Heliodorus, because of the orders he had from the king, said that this money must in any case be confiscated for the king's treasury. [14] So he set a day and went in to direct the inspection of these funds.

There was no little distress throughout the whole city. [15] The priests prostrated themselves before the altar in their priestly vestments and called towards heaven upon him who had given the law about deposits, that he should keep them safe for those who had deposited them. [16] To see the appearance of the high priest was to be wounded at heart, for his face and the change in his colour disclosed the anguish of his soul. [17] For terror and bodily trembling had come over the man, which plainly showed to those who looked at him the pain lodged in his heart. [18] People also hurried out of their houses in crowds to make a general supplication because the holy place was about to be brought into dishonour. [19] Women, girded with sackcloth under their breasts, thronged the streets. Some of the young women who were kept indoors ran together to the gates, and some to the walls, while others peered out of the windows. [20] And holding up their hands to heaven, they all made supplication. [21] There was something pitiable in the prostration of the whole populace and the anxiety of the high priest in his great anguish.

The Lord Protects His Temple

22 While they were calling upon the Almighty Lord that he would keep what had been entrusted safe and secure for those who had entrusted it, [23] Heliodorus went on with what had been decided. [24] But when he arrived at the treasury with his bodyguard, then and there the Sovereign of spirits and of all authority caused so great a manifestation that all who had been so bold as to accompany him were astounded by the power of God, and became faint with terror. [25] For there appeared to them a magnificently caparisoned horse, with a rider of frightening mien; it rushed furiously at Heliodorus and struck at him with its front hoofs. Its rider was seen to have armour and weapons of gold. [26] Two young men also appeared to him, remarkably strong, gloriously beautiful and splendidly dressed, who stood on either side of him and flogged him continuously, inflicting many blows on him. [27] When he suddenly fell to the ground and deep darkness came over him, his men took him up, put him on a stretcher, [28] and carried him away—this man who had just entered the aforesaid treasury with a great retinue and all his

_a_ Gk He   _b_ Other ancient authorities read _and_

bodyguard but was now unable to help himself. They recognized clearly the sovereign power of God.

Onias Prays for Heliodorus

29 While he lay prostrate, speechless because of the divine intervention and deprived of any hope of recovery, 30 they praised the Lord who had acted marvellously for his own place. And the temple, which a little while before was full of fear and disturbance, was filled with joy and gladness, now that the Almighty Lord had appeared.

31 Some of Heliodorus's friends quickly begged Onias to call upon the Most High to grant life to one who was lying quite at his last breath. 32 So the high priest, fearing that the king might get the notion that some foul play had been perpetrated by the Jews with regard to Heliodorus, offered sacrifice for the man's recovery. 33 While the high priest was making an atonement, the same young men appeared again to Heliodorus dressed in the same clothing, and they stood and said, 'Be very grateful to the high priest Onias, since for his sake the Lord has granted you your life. 34 And see that you, who have been flogged by heaven, report to all people the majestic power of God.' Having said this they vanished.

The Conversion of Heliodorus

35 Then Heliodorus offered sacrifice to the Lord and made very great vows to the Saviour of his life, and having bidden Onias farewell, he marched off with his forces to the king. 36 He bore testimony to all concerning the deeds of the supreme God, which he had seen with his own eyes. 37 When the king asked Heliodorus what sort of person would be suitable to send on another mission to Jerusalem, he replied, 38 'If you have any enemy or plotter against your government, send him there, for you will get him back thoroughly flogged, if he survives at all; for there is certainly some power of God about the place. 39 For he who has his dwelling in heaven watches over that place himself and brings

it aid, and he strikes and destroys those who come to do it injury.' 40 This was the outcome of the episode of Heliodorus and the protection of the treasury.

Simon Accuses Onias

4 The previously mentioned Simon, who had informed about the money against[a] his own country, slandered Onias, saying that it was he who had incited Heliodorus and had been the real cause of the misfortune. 2 He dared to designate as a plotter against the government the man who was the benefactor of the city, the protector of his compatriots, and a zealot for the laws. 3 When his hatred progressed to such a degree that even murders were committed by one of Simon's approved agents, 4 Onias recognized that the rivalry was serious and that Apollonius son of Menestheus,[b] and governor of Coelesyria and Phoenicia, was intensifying the malice of Simon. 5 So he appealed to the king, not accusing his compatriots but having in view the welfare, both public and private, of all the people. 6 For he saw that without the king's attention public affairs could not again reach a peaceful settlement, and that Simon would not stop his folly.

Jason's Reforms

7 When Seleucus died and Antiochus, who was called Epiphanes, succeeded to the kingdom, Jason the brother of Onias obtained the high-priesthood by corruption, 8 promising the king at an interview[c] three hundred and sixty talents of silver, and from another source of revenue eighty talents. 9 In addition to this he promised to pay one hundred and fifty more if permission were given to establish by his authority a gymnasium and a body of youth for it, and to enrol the people of Jerusalem as citizens of Antioch. 10 When the king assented and Jason[d] came to office, he at once shifted his compatriots over to the Greek way of life.

11 He set aside the existing royal concessions to the Jews, secured through John

a Gk *and*   *b* Vg Compare verse 21: Meaning of Gk uncertain   *c* Or *by a petition*   *d* Gk *he* the father of Eupolemus, who went on the mission to establish friendship and alliance with the Romans; and he destroyed the lawful ways of living and introduced new customs contrary to the law. [12] He took delight in establishing a gymnasium right under the citadel, and he induced the noblest of the young men to wear the Greek hat. [13] There was such an extreme of Hellenization and increase in the adoption of foreign ways because of the surpassing wickedness of Jason, who was ungodly and no true[a] high priest, [14] that the priests were no longer intent upon their service at the altar. Despising the sanctuary and neglecting the sacrifices, they hurried to take part in the unlawful proceedings in the wrestling arena after the signal for the discus-throwing, [15] disdaining the honours prized by their ancestors and putting the highest value upon Greek forms of prestige. [16] For this reason heavy disaster overtook them, and those whose ways of living they admired and wished to imitate completely became their enemies and punished them. [17] It is no light thing to show irreverence to the divine laws—a fact that later events will make clear.

Jason Introduces Greek Customs

18 When the quadrennial games were being held at Tyre and the king was present, [19] the vile Jason sent envoys, chosen as being Antiochian citizens from Jerusalem, to carry three hundred silver drachmas for the sacrifice to Hercules. Those who carried the money, however, thought best not to use it for sacrifice, because that was inappropriate, but to expend it for another purpose. [20] So this money was intended by the sender for the sacrifice to Hercules, but by the decision of its carriers it was applied to the construction of triremes.

21 When Apollonius son of Menestheus was sent to Egypt for the coronation[b] of Philometor as king, Antiochus learned that Philometor[c] had become hostile to his government, and he took measures for his own security. Therefore upon arriving at Joppa he proceeded to Jerusalem. [22] He was welcomed magnificently by Jason and the city, and ushered in with a blaze of torches and with shouts. Then he marched his army into Phoenicia.

Menelaus Becomes High Priest

23 After a period of three years Jason sent Menelaus, the brother of the previously mentioned Simon, to carry the money to the king and to complete the records of essential business. [24] But he, when presented to the king, extolled him with an air of authority, and secured the high-priesthood for himself, outbidding Jason by three hundred talents of silver. [25] After receiving the king's orders he returned, possessing no qualification for the high-priesthood, but having the hot temper of a cruel tyrant and the rage of a savage wild beast. [26] So Jason, who after supplanting his own brother was supplanted by another man, was driven as a fugitive into the land of Ammon. [27] Although Menelaus continued to hold the office, he did not pay regularly any of the money promised to the king. [28] When Sostratus the captain of the citadel kept requesting payment—for the collection of the revenue was his responsibility—the two of them were summoned by the king on account of this issue. [29] Menelaus left his own brother Lysimachus as deputy in the high-priesthood, while Sostratus left Crates, the commander of the Cypriot troops.

The Murder of Onias

30 While such was the state of affairs, it happened that the people of Tarsus and of Mallus revolted because their cities had been given as a present to Antiochis, the king's concubine. [31] So the king went hurriedly to settle the trouble, leaving Andronicus, a man of high rank, to act as his deputy. [32] But Menelaus, thinking he had obtained a suitable opportunity, stole some of the gold vessels of the temple and gave them to Andronicus; other vessels, as it happened, he had sold to Tyre and the neighbouring cities. [33] When Onias became

_a_ Gk lacks _true_   _b_ Meaning of Gk uncertain
_c_ Gk _he_

fully aware of these acts, he publicly exposed them, having first withdrawn to a place of sanctuary at Daphne near Antioch. ³⁴Therefore Menelaus, taking Andronicus aside, urged him to kill Onias. Andronicus[a] came to Onias, and resorting to treachery, offered him sworn pledges and gave him his right hand; he persuaded him, though still suspicious, to come out from the place of sanctuary; then, with no regard for justice, he immediately put him out of the way.

Andronicus Is Punished

35 For this reason not only Jews, but many also of other nations, were grieved and displeased at the unjust murder of the man. ³⁶When the king returned from the region of Cilicia, the Jews in the city[b] appealed to him with regard to the unreasonable murder of Onias, and the Greeks shared their hatred of the crime. ³⁷Therefore Antiochus was grieved at heart and filled with pity, and wept because of the moderation and good conduct of the deceased. ³⁸Inflamed with anger, he immediately stripped off the purple robe from Andronicus, tore off his clothes, and led him around the whole city to that very place where he had committed the outrage against Onias, and there he dispatched the bloodthirsty fellow. The Lord thus repaid him with the punishment he deserved.

Unpopularity of Lysimachus and Menelaus

39 When many acts of sacrilege had been committed in the city by Lysimachus with the connivance of Menelaus, and when report of them had spread abroad, the populace gathered against Lysimachus, because many of the gold vessels had already been stolen. ⁴⁰Since the crowds were becoming aroused and filled with anger, Lysimachus armed about three thousand men and launched an unjust attack, under the leadership of a certain Auranus, a man advanced in years and no less advanced in folly. ⁴¹But when the Jews[c] became aware that Lysimachus was attacking them, some picked up stones, some blocks of wood,

and others took handfuls of the ashes that were lying around, and threw them in wild confusion at Lysimachus and his men. ⁴²As a result, they wounded many of them, and killed some, and put all the rest to flight; the temple robber himself they killed close by the treasury.

43 Charges were brought against Menelaus about this incident. ⁴⁴When the king came to Tyre, three men sent by the senate presented the case before him. ⁴⁵But Menelaus, already as good as beaten, promised a substantial bribe to Ptolemy son of Dorymenes to win over the king. ⁴⁶Therefore Ptolemy, taking the king aside into a colonnade as if for refreshment, induced the king to change his mind. ⁴⁷Menelaus, the cause of all the trouble, he acquitted of the charges against him, while he sentenced to death those unfortunate men, who would have been freed uncondemned if they had pleaded even before Scythians. ⁴⁸And so those who had spoken for the city and the villages[d] and the holy vessels quickly suffered the unjust penalty. ⁴⁹Therefore even the Tyrians, showing their hatred of the crime, provided magnificently for their funeral. ⁵⁰But Menelaus, because of the greed of those in power, remained in office, growing in wickedness, having become the chief plotter against his compatriots.

Jason Tries to Regain Control

5 About this time Antiochus made his second invasion of Egypt. ²And it happened that, for almost forty days, there appeared over all the city golden-clad cavalry charging through the air, in companies fully armed with lances and drawn swords— ³troops of cavalry drawn up, attacks and counter-attacks made on this side and on that, brandishing of shields, massing of spears, hurling of missiles, the flash of golden trappings, and armour of all kinds. ⁴Therefore everyone prayed that the apparition might prove to have been a good omen.

5 When a false rumour arose that Anti-

a Gk He   *b* Or *in each city*   *c* Gk *they*   *d* Other ancient authorities read *the people* ochus was dead, Jason took no fewer than a thousand men and suddenly made an assault on the city. When the troops on the wall had been forced back and at last the city was being taken, Menelaus took refuge in the citadel. [6] But Jason kept relentlessly slaughtering his compatriots, not realizing that success at the cost of one's kindred is the greatest misfortune, but imagining that he was setting up trophies of victory over enemies and not over compatriots. [7] He did not, however, gain control of the government; in the end he got only disgrace from his conspiracy, and fled again into the country of the Ammonites. [8] Finally he met a miserable end. Accused[a] before Aretas the ruler of the Arabs, fleeing from city to city, pursued by everyone, hated as a rebel against the laws, and abhorred as the executioner of his country and his compatriots, he was cast ashore in Egypt. [9] There he who had driven many from their own country into exile died in exile, having embarked to go to the Lacedaemonians in hope of finding protection because of their kinship. [10] He who had cast out many to lie unburied had no one to mourn for him; he had no funeral of any sort and no place in the tomb of his ancestors.

[11] When news of what had happened reached the king, he took it to mean that Judea was in revolt. So, raging inwardly, he left Egypt and took the city by storm. [12] He commanded his soldiers to cut down relentlessly everyone they met and to kill those who went into their houses. [13] Then there was massacre of young and old, destruction of boys, women, and children, and slaughter of young girls and infants. [14] Within the total of three days eighty thousand were destroyed, forty thousand in hand-to-hand fighting, and as many were sold into slavery as were killed.

Pillage of the Temple

[15] Not content with this, Antiochus[b] dared to enter the most holy temple in all the world, guided by Menelaus, who had become a traitor both to the laws and to his country. [16] He took the holy vessels with his polluted hands, and swept away with profane hands the votive offerings that other kings had made to enhance the glory and honour of the place. [17] Antiochus was elated in spirit, and did not perceive that the Lord was angered for a little while because of the sins of those who lived in the city, and that this was the reason he was disregarding the holy place. [18] But if it had not happened that they were involved in many sins, this man would have been flogged and turned back from his rash act as soon as he came forward, just as Heliodorus had been, whom King Seleucus sent to inspect the treasury. [19] But the Lord did not choose the nation for the sake of the holy place, but the place for the sake of the nation. [20] Therefore the place itself shared in the misfortunes that befell the nation and afterwards participated in its benefits; and what was forsaken in the wrath of the Almighty was restored again in all its glory when the great Lord became reconciled.

[21] So Antiochus carried off eighteen hundred talents from the temple, and hurried away to Antioch, thinking in his arrogance that he could sail on the land and walk on the sea, because his mind was elated. [22] He left governors to oppress the people: at Jerusalem, Philip, by birth a Phrygian and in character more barbarous than the man who appointed him; [23] and at Gerizim, Andronicus; and besides these Menelaus, who lorded it over his compatriots worse than the others did. In his malice towards the Jewish citizens,[c] [24] Antiochus[b] sent Apollonius, the captain of the Mysians, with an army of twenty-two thousand, and commanded him to kill all the grown men and to sell the women and boys as slaves. [25] When this man arrived in Jerusalem, he pretended to be peaceably disposed and waited until the holy sabbath day; then, finding the Jews not at work, he ordered his troops to parade under arms. [26] He put to the sword all those who came out to see them, then rushed into the city with his armed warriors and killed great numbers of people.

a Cn: Gk *Imprisoned*   b Gk *he*   c Or *worse than the others did in his malice towards the Jewish citizens*

27 But Judas Maccabeus, with about nine others, got away to the wilderness, and kept himself and his companions alive in the mountains as wild animals do; they continued to live on what grew wild, so that they might not share in the defilement.

The Suppression of Judaism

6 Not long after this, the king sent an Athenian[a] senator[b] to compel the Jews to forsake the laws of their ancestors and no longer to live by the laws of God; [2] also to pollute the temple in Jerusalem and to call it the temple of Olympian Zeus, and to call the one in Gerizim the temple of Zeus-the-Friend-of-Strangers, as did the people who lived in that place.

3 Harsh and utterly grievous was the onslaught of evil. [4] For the temple was filled with debauchery and revelling by the Gentiles, who dallied with prostitutes and had intercourse with women within the sacred precincts, and besides brought in things for sacrifice that were unfit. [5] The altar was covered with abominable offerings that were forbidden by the laws. [6] People could neither keep the sabbath, nor observe the festivals of their ancestors, nor so much as confess themselves to be Jews.

7 On the monthly celebration of the king's birthday, the Jews[c] were taken, under bitter constraint, to partake of the sacrifices; and when a festival of Dionysus was celebrated, they were compelled to wear wreaths of ivy and to walk in the procession in honour of Dionysus. [8] At the suggestion of the people of Ptolemais[d] a decree was issued to the neighbouring Greek cities that they should adopt the same policy towards the Jews and make them partake of the sacrifices, [9] and should kill those who did not choose to change over to Greek customs. One could see, therefore, the misery that had come upon them. [10] For example, two women were brought in for having circumcised their children. They publicly paraded them around the city, with their babies hanging at their breasts, and then hurled them down headlong from the wall. [11] Others who had assembled in the caves nearby, in order to observe the seventh day secretly, were betrayed to Philip and were all burned together, because their piety kept them from defending themselves, in view of their regard for that most holy day.

Providential Significance of the Persecution

12 Now I urge those who read this book not to be depressed by such calamities, but to recognize that these punishments were designed not to destroy but to discipline our people. [13] In fact, it is a sign of great kindness not to let the impious alone for long, but to punish them immediately. [14] For in the case of the other nations the Lord waits patiently to punish them until they have reached the full measure of their sins; but he does not deal in this way with us, [15] in order that he should not take vengeance on us afterwards when our sins have reached their height. [16] Therefore he never withdraws his mercy from us. Although he disciplines us with calamities, he does not forsake his own people. [17] Let what we have said serve as a reminder; we must go on briefly with the story.

The Martyrdom of Eleazar

18 Eleazar, one of the scribes in high position, a man now advanced in age and of noble presence, was being forced to open his mouth to eat swine's flesh. [19] But he, welcoming death with honour rather than life with pollution, went up to the rack of his own accord, spitting out the flesh, [20] as all ought to go who have the courage to refuse things that it is not right to taste, even for the natural love of life.

21 Those who were in charge of that unlawful sacrifice took the man aside because of their long acquaintance with him, and privately urged him to bring meat of his own providing, proper for him to use, and to pretend that he was eating the flesh of the sacrificial meal that had been commanded by the king, [22] so that by doing

a Other ancient authorities read *Antiochian*
b Or *Geron an Athenian*   c Gk *they*   d Cn: Gk
suggestion of the Ptolemies (or *of Ptolemy*)

this he might be saved from death, and be treated kindly on account of his old friendship with them. 23 But making a high resolve, worthy of his years and the dignity of his old age and the grey hairs that he had reached with distinction and his excellent life even from childhood, and moreover according to the holy God-given law, he declared himself quickly, telling them to send him to Hades.

24 'Such pretence is not worthy of our time of life,' he said, 'for many of the young might suppose that Eleazar in his ninetieth year had gone over to an alien religion, 25 and through my pretence, for the sake of living a brief moment longer, they would be led astray because of me, while I defile and disgrace my old age. 26 Even if for the present I would avoid the punishment of mortals, yet whether I live or die I will not escape the hands of the Almighty. 27 Therefore, by bravely giving up my life now, I will show myself worthy of my old age 28 and leave to the young a noble example of how to die a good death willingly and nobly for the revered and holy laws.'

When he had said this, he went *a* at once to the rack. 29 Those who a little before had acted towards him with goodwill now changed to ill will, because the words he had uttered were in their opinion sheer madness. *b* 30 When he was about to die under the blows, he groaned aloud and said: 'It is clear to the Lord in his holy knowledge that, though I might have been saved from death, I am enduring terrible sufferings in my body under this beating, but in my soul I am glad to suffer these things because I fear him.'

31 So in this way he died, leaving in his death an example of nobility and a memorial of courage, not only to the young but to the great body of his nation.

The Martyrdom of Seven Brothers

7 It happened also that seven brothers and their mother were arrested and were being compelled by the king, under torture with whips and thongs, to partake of unlawful swine's flesh. 2 One of them, acting as their spokesman, said, 'What do you intend to ask and learn from us? For we are ready to die rather than transgress the laws of our ancestors.'

3 The king fell into a rage, and gave orders to have pans and cauldrons heated. 4 These were heated immediately, and he commanded that the tongue of their spokesman be cut out and that they scalp him and cut off his hands and feet, while the rest of the brothers and the mother looked on. 5 When he was utterly helpless, the king *c* ordered them to take him to the fire, still breathing, and to fry him in a pan. The smoke from the pan spread widely, but the brothers *d* and their mother encouraged one another to die nobly, saying, 6 'The Lord God is watching over us and in truth has compassion on us, as Moses declared in his song that bore witness against the people to their faces, when he said, "And he will have compassion on his servants." *' e*

7 After the first brother had died in this way, they brought forward the second for their sport. They tore off the skin of his head with the hair, and asked him, 'Will you eat rather than have your body punished limb by limb?' 8 He replied in the language of his ancestors and said to them, 'No.' Therefore he in turn underwent tortures as the first brother had done. 9 And when he was at his last breath, he said, 'You accursed wretch, you dismiss us from this present life, but the King of the universe will raise us up to an everlasting renewal of life, because we have died for his laws.'

10 After him, the third was the victim of their sport. When it was demanded, he quickly put out his tongue and courageously stretched forth his hands, 11 and said nobly, 'I got these from Heaven, and because of his laws I disdain them, and from him I hope to get them back again.' 12 As a result the king himself and those with him were astonished at the young man's spirit, for he regarded his sufferings as nothing.

13 After he too had died, they maltreat-

a Other ancient authorities read *was dragged*
b Meaning of Gk uncertain   *c* Gk *he*   *d* Gk *they*
e Gk *slaves*

ed and tortured the fourth in the same way. ¹⁴When he was near death, he said, 'One cannot but choose to die at the hands of mortals and to cherish the hope God gives of being raised again by him. But for you there will be no resurrection to life!'

15 Next they brought forward the fifth and maltreated him. ¹⁶But he looked at the king,ᵃ and said, 'Because you have authority among mortals, though you also are mortal, you do what you please. But do not think that God has forsaken our people. ¹⁷Keep on, and see how his mighty power will torture you and your descendants!'

18 After him they brought forward the sixth. And when he was about to die, he said, 'Do not deceive yourself in vain. For we are suffering these things on our own account, because of our sins against our own God. Thereforeᵇ astounding things have happened. ¹⁹But do not think that you will go unpunished for having tried to fight against God!'

20 The mother was especially admirable and worthy of honourable memory. Although she saw her seven sons perish within a single day, she bore it with good courage because of her hope in the Lord. ²¹She encouraged each of them in the language of their ancestors. Filled with a noble spirit, she reinforced her woman's reasoning with a man's courage, and said to them, ²²'I do not know how you came into being in my womb. It was not I who gave you life and breath, nor I who set in order the elements within each of you. ²³Therefore the Creator of the world, who shaped the beginning of humankind and devised the origin of all things, will in his mercy give life and breath back to you again, since you now forget yourselves for the sake of his laws.'

24 Antiochus felt that he was being treated with contempt, and he was suspicious of her reproachful tone. The youngest brother being still alive, Antiochusᶜ not only appealed to him in words, but promised with oaths that he would make him rich and enviable if he would turn from the ways of his ancestors, and that he would take him for his Friend and

entrust him with public affairs. ²⁵Since the young man would not listen to him at all, the king called the mother to him and urged her to advise the youth to save himself. ²⁶After much urging on his part, she undertook to persuade her son. ²⁷But, leaning close to him, she spoke in their native language as follows, deriding the cruel tyrant: 'My son, have pity on me. I carried you for nine months in my womb, and nursed you for three years, and have reared you and brought you up to this point in your life, and have taken care of you.ᵈ ²⁸I beg you, my child, to look at the heaven and the earth and see everything that is in them, and recognize that God did not make them out of things that existed.ᵉ And in the same way the human race came into being. ²⁹Do not fear this butcher, but prove worthy of your brothers. Accept death, so that in God's mercy I may get you back again along with your brothers.'

30 While she was still speaking, the young man said, 'What are youᶠ waiting for? I will not obey the king's command, but I obey the command of the law that was given to our ancestors through Moses. ³¹But you,ᵍ who have contrived all sorts of evil against the Hebrews, will certainly not escape the hands of God. ³²For we are suffering because of our own sins. ³³And if our living Lord is angry for a little while, to rebuke and discipline us, he will again be reconciled with his own servants.ʰ ³⁴But you, unholy wretch, you most defiled of all mortals, do not be elated in vain and puffed up by uncertain hopes, when you raise your hand against the children of heaven. ³⁵You have not yet escaped the judgement of the almighty, all-seeing God. ³⁶For our brothers after enduring a brief suffering have drunkⁱ of ever-flowing life, under God's covenant; but you, by the judgement of God, will receive just punishment for your arrogance. ³⁷I, like my brothers, give up body and life for the laws of our ancestors, appealing to God to show

---

a Gk at him   b Lat: Other ancient authorities lack Therefore   c Gk he   d Or have borne the burden of your education   e Or God made them out of things that did not exist   f The Gk here for you is plural   g The Gk here for you is singular   h Gk slaves   i Cn: Gk fallen mercy soon to our nation and by trials and plagues to make you confess that he alone is God, 38 and through me and my brothers to bring to an end the wrath of the Almighty that has justly fallen on our whole nation.'

39 The king fell into a rage, and handled him worse than the others, being exasperated at his scorn. 40 So he died in his integrity, putting his whole trust in the Lord.

41 Last of all, the mother died, after her sons.

42 Let this be enough, then, about the eating of sacrifices and the extreme tortures.

The Revolt of Judas Maccabeus

8 Meanwhile Judas, who was also called Maccabeus, and his companions secretly entered the villages and summoned their kindred and enlisted those who had continued in the Jewish faith, and so they gathered about six thousand. 2 They implored the Lord to look upon the people who were oppressed by all; and to have pity on the temple that had been profaned by the godless; 3 to have mercy on the city that was being destroyed and about to be levelled to the ground; to hearken to the blood that cried out to him; 4 to remember also the lawless destruction of the innocent babies and the blasphemies committed against his name; and to show his hatred of evil.

5 As soon as Maccabeus got his army organized, the Gentiles could not withstand him, for the wrath of the Lord had turned to mercy. 6 Coming without warning, he would set fire to towns and villages. He captured strategic positions and put to flight not a few of the enemy. 7 He found the nights most advantageous for such attacks. And talk of his valour spread everywhere.

8 When Philip saw that the man was gaining ground little by little, and that he was pushing ahead with more frequent successes, he wrote to Ptolemy, the governor of Coelesyria and Phoenicia, to come to the aid of the king's government. 9 Then Ptolemy*a* promptly appointed Nicanor son of Patroclus, one of the king's chief*b* Friends, and sent him, in command of no fewer than twenty thousand Gentiles of all nations, to wipe out the whole race of Judea. He associated with him Gorgias, a general and a man of experience in military service. 10 Nicanor determined to make up for the king the tribute due to the Romans, two thousand talents, by selling the captured Jews into slavery. 11 So he immediately sent to the towns on the sea coast, inviting them to buy Jewish slaves and promising to hand over ninety slaves for a talent, not expecting the judgement from the Almighty that was about to overtake him.

Preparation for Battle

12 Word came to Judas concerning Nicanor's invasion; and when he told his companions of the arrival of the army, 13 those who were cowardly and distrustful of God's justice ran off and got away. 14 Others sold all their remaining property, and at the same time implored the Lord to rescue those who had been sold by the ungodly Nicanor before he ever met them, 15 if not for their own sake, then for the sake of the covenants made with their ancestors, and because he had called them by his holy and glorious name. 16 But Maccabeus gathered his forces together, to the number of six thousand, and exhorted them not to be frightened by the enemy and not to fear the great multitude of Gentiles who were wickedly coming against them, but to fight nobly, 17 keeping before their eyes the lawless outrage that the Gentiles*c* had committed against the holy place, and the torture of the derided city, and besides, the overthrow of their ancestral way of life. 18 'For they trust in arms and acts of daring', he said, 'but we trust in the Almighty God, who is able with a single nod to strike down those who are coming against us, and even, if necessary, the whole world.'

19 Moreover, he told them of the occasions when help came to their ancestors;

a Gk he   b Gk one of the first   c Gk they

how, in the time of Sennacherib, when one hundred and eighty-five thousand perished, [20] and the time of the battle against the Galatians that took place in Babylonia, when eight thousand Jews[a] fought along with four thousand Macedonians; yet when the Macedonians were hard pressed, the eight thousand, by the help that came to them from heaven, destroyed one hundred and twenty thousand Galatians[b] and took a great amount of booty.

Judas Defeats Nicanor

21 With these words he filled them with courage and made them ready to die for their laws and their country; then he divided his army into four parts. [22] He appointed his brothers also, Simon and Joseph and Jonathan, each to command a division, putting fifteen hundred men under each. [23] Besides, he appointed Eleazar to read aloud[c] from the holy book, and gave the watchword, 'The help of God'; then, leading the first division himself, he joined battle with Nicanor.

24 With the Almighty as their ally, they killed more than nine thousand of the enemy, and wounded and disabled most of Nicanor's army, and forced them all to flee. [25] They captured the money of those who had come to buy them as slaves. After pursuing them for some distance, they were obliged to return because the hour was late. [26] It was the day before the sabbath, and for that reason they did not continue their pursuit. [27] When they had collected the arms of the enemy and stripped them of their spoils, they kept the sabbath, giving great praise and thanks to the Lord, who had preserved them for that day and allotted it to them as the beginning of mercy. [28] After the sabbath they gave some of the spoils to those who had been tortured and to the widows and orphans, and distributed the rest among themselves and their children. [29] When they had done this, they made common supplication and implored the merciful Lord to be wholly reconciled with his servants.[d]

Judas Defeats Timothy and Bacchides

30 In encounters with the forces of Timothy and Bacchides they killed more than twenty thousand of them and got possession of some exceedingly high strongholds, and they divided a very large amount of plunder, giving to those who had been tortured and to the orphans and widows, and also to the aged, shares equal to their own. [31] They collected the arms of the enemy,[e] and carefully stored all of them in strategic places; the rest of the spoils they carried to Jerusalem. [32] They killed the commander of Timothy's forces, a most wicked man, and one who had greatly troubled the Jews. [33] While they were celebrating the victory in the city of their ancestors, they burned those who had set fire to the sacred gates, Callisthenes and some others, who had fled into one little house; so these received the proper reward for their impiety.[f]

34 The thrice-accursed Nicanor, who had brought the thousand merchants to buy the Jews, [35] having been humbled with the help of the Lord by opponents whom he regarded as of the least account, took off his splendid uniform and made his way alone like a runaway slave across the country until he reached Antioch, having succeeded chiefly in the destruction of his own army! [36] So he who had undertaken to secure tribute for the Romans by the capture of the people of Jerusalem proclaimed that the Jews had a Defender, and that therefore the Jews were invulnerable, because they followed the laws ordained by him.

The Last Campaign of Antiochus Epiphanes

9 About that time, as it happened, Antiochus had retreated in disorder from the region of Persia. [2] He had entered the city called Persepolis and attempted to rob the temples and control the city. Therefore the people rushed to the rescue with arms, and Antiochus and his army were

---

a Gk lacks *Jews*   b Gk lacks *Galatians*   c Meaning of Gk uncertain   d Gk *slaves*   e Gk *their arms*
f Meaning of Gk uncertain

defeated,[a] with the result that Antiochus was put to flight by the inhabitants and beat a shameful retreat. [3] While he was in Ecbatana, news came to him of what had happened to Nicanor and the forces of Timothy. [4] Transported with rage, he conceived the idea of turning upon the Jews the injury done by those who had put him to flight; so he ordered his charioteer to drive without stopping until he completed the journey. But the judgement of heaven rode with him! For in his arrogance he said, 'When I get there I will make Jerusalem a cemetery of Jews.'

[5] But the all-seeing Lord, the God of Israel, struck him with an incurable and invisible blow. As soon as he stopped speaking he was seized with a pain in his bowels, for which there was no relief, and with sharp internal tortures— [6] and that very justly, for he had tortured the bowels of others with many and strange inflictions. [7] Yet he did not in any way stop his insolence, but was even more filled with arrogance, breathing fire in his rage against the Jews, and giving orders to drive even faster. And so it came about that he fell out of his chariot as it was rushing along, and the fall was so hard as to torture every limb of his body. [8] Thus he who only a little while before had thought in his superhuman arrogance that he could command the waves of the sea, and had imagined that he could weigh the high mountains in a balance, was brought down to earth and carried in a litter, making the power of God manifest to all. [9] And so the ungodly man's body swarmed with worms, and while he was still living in anguish and pain, his flesh rotted away, and because of the stench the whole army felt revulsion at his decay. [10] Because of his intolerable stench no one was able to carry the man who a little while before had thought that he could touch the stars of heaven. [11] Then it was that, broken in spirit, he began to lose much of his arrogance and to come to his senses under the scourge of God, for he was tortured with pain at every moment. [12] And when he could not endure his own stench, he uttered these words, 'It is right

to be subject to God; mortals should not think that they are equal to God.'[b]

Antiochus Makes a Promise to God

[13] Then the abominable fellow made a vow to the Lord, who would no longer have mercy on him, stating [14] that the holy city, which he was hurrying to level to the ground and to make a cemetery, he was now declaring to be free; [15] and the Jews, whom he had not considered worth burying but had planned to throw out with their children for the wild animals and for the birds to eat, he would make, all of them, equal to citizens of Athens; [16] and the holy sanctuary, which he had formerly plundered, he would adorn with the finest offerings; and all the holy vessels he would give back, many times over; and the expenses incurred for the sacrifices he would provide from his own revenues; [17] and in addition to all this he also would become a Jew and would visit every inhabited place to proclaim the power of God. [18] But when his sufferings did not in any way abate, for the judgement of God had justly come upon him, he gave up all hope for himself and wrote to the Jews the following letter, in the form of a supplication. This was its content:

Antiochus's Letter and Death

[19] 'To his worthy Jewish citizens, Antiochus their king and general sends hearty greetings and good wishes for their health and prosperity. [20] If you and your children are well and your affairs are as you wish, I am glad. As my hope is in heaven, [21] I remember with affection your esteem and goodwill. On my way back from the region of Persia I suffered an annoying illness, and I have deemed it necessary to take thought for the general security of all. [22] I do not despair of my condition, for I have good hope of recovering from my illness, [23] but I observed that my father, on the occasions when he made expeditions into the upper country, appointed his successor, [24] so that, if anything unexpected hap-

a Gk *they were defeated*   *b* Or *not think thoughts proper only to God* pened or any unwelcome news came, the people throughout the realm would not be troubled, for they would know to whom the government was left. 25 Moreover, I understand how the princes along the borders and the neighbours of my kingdom keep watching for opportunities and waiting to see what will happen. So I have appointed my son Antiochus to be king, whom I have often entrusted and commended to most of you when I hurried off to the upper provinces; and I have written to him what is written here. 26 I therefore urge and beg you to remember the public and private services rendered to you and to maintain your present goodwill, each of you, towards me and my son. 27 For I am sure that he will follow my policy and will treat you with moderation and kindness.'

28 So the murderer and blasphemer, having endured the more intense suffering, such as he had inflicted on others, came to the end of his life by a most pitiable fate, among the mountains in a strange land. 29 And Philip, one of his courtiers, took his body home; then, fearing the son of Antiochus, he withdrew to Ptolemy Philometor in Egypt.

Purification of the Temple

10 Now Maccabeus and his followers, the Lord leading them on, recovered the temple and the city; 2 they tore down the altars that had been built in the public square by the foreigners, and also destroyed the sacred precincts. 3 They purified the sanctuary, and made another altar of sacrifice; then, striking fire out of flint, they offered sacrifices, after a lapse of two years, and they offered incense and lighted lamps and set out the bread of the Presence. 4 When they had done this, they fell prostrate and implored the Lord that they might never again fall into such misfortunes, but that, if they should ever sin, they might be disciplined by him with forbearance and not be handed over to blasphemous and barbarous nations. 5 It happened that on the same day on which the sanctuary had been profaned by the foreigners, the purification of the sanctuary took

place, that is, on the twenty-fifth day of the same month, which was Chislev. 6 They celebrated it for eight days with rejoicing, in the manner of the festival of booths, remembering how not long before, during the festival of booths, they had been wandering in the mountains and caves like wild animals. 7 Therefore, carrying ivy-wreathed wands and beautiful branches and also fronds of palm, they offered hymns of thanksgiving to him who had given success to the purifying of his own holy place. 8 They decreed by public edict, ratified by vote, that the whole nation of the Jews should observe these days every year.

9 Such then was the end of Antiochus, who was called Epiphanes.

Accession of Antiochus Eupator

10 Now we will tell what took place under Antiochus Eupator, who was the son of that ungodly man, and will give a brief summary of the principal calamities of the wars. 11 This man, when he succeeded to the kingdom, appointed one Lysias to have charge of the government and to be chief governor of Coelesyria and Phoenicia. 12 Ptolemy, who was called Macron, took the lead in showing justice to the Jews because of the wrong that had been done to them, and attempted to maintain peaceful relations with them. 13 As a result he was accused before Eupator by the king's Friends. He heard himself called a traitor at every turn, because he had abandoned Cyprus, which Philometor had entrusted to him, and had gone over to Antiochus Epiphanes. Unable to command the respect due to his office,[a] he took poison and ended his life.

Campaign in Idumea

14 When Gorgias became governor of the region, he maintained a force of mercenaries, and at every turn kept attacking the Jews. 15 Besides this, the Idumeans, who had control of important strongholds, were harassing the Jews; they received those who were banished from Jerusalem,

a Cn: Meaning of Gk uncertain

and endeavoured to keep up the war. [16] But Maccabeus and his forces, after making solemn supplication and imploring God to fight on their side, rushed to the strongholds of the Idumeans. [17] Attacking them vigorously, they gained possession of the places, and beat off all who fought upon the wall, and slaughtered those whom they encountered, killing no fewer than twenty thousand.

18 When at least nine thousand took refuge in two very strong towers well equipped to withstand a siege, [19] Maccabeus left Simon and Joseph, and also Zacchaeus and his troops, a force sufficient to besiege them; and he himself set off for places where he was more urgently needed. [20] But those with Simon, who were money-hungry, were bribed by some of those who were in the towers, and on receiving seventy thousand drachmas let some of them slip away. [21] When word of what had happened came to Maccabeus, he gathered the leaders of the people, and accused these men of having sold their kindred for money by setting their enemies free to fight against them. [22] Then he killed these men who had turned traitor, and immediately captured the two towers. [23] Having success at arms in everything he undertook, he destroyed more than twenty thousand in the two strongholds.

Judas Defeats Timothy

24 Now Timothy, who had been defeated by the Jews before, gathered a tremendous force of mercenaries and collected the cavalry from Asia in no small number. He came on, intending to take Judea by storm. [25] As he drew near, Maccabeus and his men sprinkled dust on their heads and girded their loins with sackcloth, in supplication to God. [26] Falling upon the steps before the altar, they implored him to be gracious to them and to be an enemy to their enemies and an adversary to their adversaries, as the law declares. [27] And rising from their prayer they took up their arms and advanced a considerable distance from the city; and when they came near the enemy they halted. [28] Just as dawn was breaking, the two armies joined battle, one having as pledge of success and victory not only their valour but also their reliance on the Lord, while the other made rage their leader in the fight.

29 When the battle became fierce, there appeared to the enemy from heaven five resplendent men on horses with golden bridles, and they were leading the Jews. [30] Two of them took Maccabeus between them, and shielding him with their own armour and weapons, they kept him from being wounded. They showered arrows and thunderbolts on the enemy, so that, confused and blinded, they were thrown into disorder and cut to pieces. [31] Twenty thousand five hundred were slaughtered, besides six hundred cavalry.

32 Timothy himself fled to a stronghold called Gazara, especially well garrisoned, where Chaereas was commander. [33] Then Maccabeus and his men were glad, and they besieged the fort for four days. [34] The men within, relying on the strength of the place, kept blaspheming terribly and uttering wicked words. [35] But at dawn on the fifth day, twenty young men in the army of Maccabeus, fired with anger because of the blasphemies, bravely stormed the wall and with savage fury cut down everyone they met. [36] Others who came up in the same way wheeled around against the defenders and set fire to the towers; they kindled fires and burned the blasphemers alive. Others broke open the gates and let in the rest of the force, and they occupied the city. [37] They killed Timothy, who was hiding in a cistern, and his brother Chaereas, and Apollophanes. [38] When they had accomplished these things, with hymns and thanksgivings they blessed the Lord who shows great kindness to Israel and gives them the victory.

Lysias Besieges Beth-zur

11 Very soon after this, Lysias, the king's guardian and kinsman, who was in charge of the government, being vexed at what had happened, [2] gathered about eighty thousand infantry and all his cavalry and came against the Jews. He in-

tended to make the city a home for Greeks, 3 and to levy tribute on the temple as he did on the sacred places of the other nations, and to put the high-priesthood up for sale every year. 4 He took no account whatever of the power of God, but was elated with his tens of thousands of infantry, and his thousands of cavalry, and his eighty elephants. 5 Invading Judea, he approached Beth-zur, which was a fortified place about five stadia*a* from Jerusalem, and pressed it hard.

6 When Maccabeus and his men got word that Lysias*b* was besieging the strongholds, they and all the people, with lamentations and tears, prayed the Lord to send a good angel to save Israel. 7 Maccabeus himself was the first to take up arms, and he urged the others to risk their lives with him to aid their kindred. Then they eagerly rushed off together. 8 And there, while they were still near Jerusalem, a horseman appeared at their head, clothed in white and brandishing weapons of gold. 9 And together they all praised the merciful God, and were strengthened in heart, ready to assail not only humans but the wildest animals or walls of iron. 10 They advanced in battle order, having their heavenly ally, for the Lord had mercy on them. 11 They hurled themselves like lions against the enemy, and laid low eleven thousand of them and sixteen hundred cavalry, and forced all the rest to flee. 12 Most of them got away stripped and wounded, and Lysias himself escaped by disgraceful flight.

Lysias Makes Peace with the Jews

13 As he was not without intelligence, he pondered over the defeat that had befallen him, and realized that the Hebrews were invincible because the mighty God fought on their side. So he sent to them 14 and persuaded them to settle everything on just terms, promising that he would persuade the king, constraining him to be their friend.*a* 15 Maccabeus, having regard for the common good, agreed to all that Lysias urged. For the king granted every request in behalf of the Jews which Maccabeus delivered to Lysias in writing.

16 The letter written to the Jews by Lysias was to this effect:

'Lysias to the people of the Jews, greetings. 17 John and Absalom, who were sent by you, have delivered your signed communication and have asked about the matters indicated in it. 18 I have informed the king of everything that needed to be brought before him, and he has agreed to what was possible. 19 If you will maintain your goodwill towards the government, I will endeavour in the future to help promote your welfare. 20 And concerning such matters and their details, I have ordered these men and my representatives to confer with you. 21 Farewell. The one hundred and forty-eighth year,*c* the twenty-fourth of Dioscorinthius.'

22 The king's letter ran thus:

'King Antiochus to his brother Lysias, greetings. 23 Now that our father has gone on to the gods, we desire that the subjects of the kingdom be undisturbed in caring for their own affairs. 24 We have heard that the Jews do not consent to our father's change to Greek customs, but prefer their own way of living and ask that their own customs be allowed them. 25 Accordingly, since we choose that this nation also should be free from disturbance, our decision is that their temple be restored to them and that they shall live according to the customs of their ancestors. 26 You will do well, therefore, to send word to them and give them pledges of friendship, so that they may know our policy and be of good cheer and go on happily in the conduct of their own affairs.'

27 To the nation the king's letter was as follows:

'King Antiochus to the senate of the Jews and to the other Jews, greetings. 28 If you are well, it is as we desire. We also are in good health. 29 Menelaus has informed us that you wish to return home and look after your own affairs. 30 Therefore those who go home by the thirtieth of Xanthicus will have our pledge of friendship and full permission 31 for the Jews to enjoy their own food and laws, just as formerly, and none

a Meaning of Gk uncertain   *b* Gk *he*   *c* 164 BC

of them shall be molested in any way for what may have been done in ignorance. [32] And I have also sent Menelaus to encourage you. [33] Farewell. The one hundred and forty-eighth year,[a] the fifteenth of Xanthicus.'

34 The Romans also sent them a letter, which read thus:

'Quintus Memmius and Titus Manius, envoys of the Romans, to the people of the Jews, greetings. [35] With regard to what Lysias the kinsman of the king has granted you, we also give consent. [36] But as to the matters that he decided are to be referred to the king, as soon as you have considered them, send someone promptly so that we may make proposals appropriate for you. For we are on our way to Antioch. [37] Therefore make haste and send messengers so that we may have your judgement. [38] Farewell. The one hundred and forty-eighth year,[a] the fifteenth of Xanthicus.'

Incidents at Joppa and Jamnia

12 When this agreement had been reached, Lysias returned to the king, and the Jews went about their farming.

2 But some of the governors in various places, Timothy and Apollonius son of Gennaeus, as well as Hieronymus and Demophon, and in addition to these Nicanor the governor of Cyprus, would not let them live quietly and in peace. [3] And the people of Joppa did so ungodly a deed as this: they invited the Jews who lived among them to embark, with their wives and children, on boats that they had provided, as though there were no ill will to the Jews;[b] [4] and this was done by public vote of the city. When they accepted, because they wished to live peaceably and suspected nothing, the people of Joppa[c] took them out to sea and drowned them, at least two hundred. [5] When Judas heard of the cruelty visited on his compatriots, he gave orders to his men [6] and, calling upon God, the righteous judge, attacked the murderers of his kindred. He set fire to the harbour by night, burned the boats, and massacred those who had taken refuge

there. [7] Then, because the city's gates were closed, he withdrew, intending to come again and root out the whole community of Joppa. [8] But learning that the people in Jamnia meant in the same way to wipe out the Jews who were living among them, [9] he attacked the Jamnites by night and set fire to the harbour and the fleet, so that the glow of the light was seen in Jerusalem, thirty miles[d] distant.

The Campaign in Gilead

10 When they had gone more than a mile[e] from there, on their march against Timothy, at least five thousand Arabs with five hundred cavalry attacked them. [11] After a hard fight, Judas and his companions, with God's help, were victorious. The defeated nomads begged Judas to grant them pledges of friendship, promising to give him livestock and to help his people[f] in all other ways. [12] Judas, realizing that they might indeed be useful in many ways, agreed to make peace with them; and after receiving his pledges they went back to their tents.

13 He also attacked a certain town that was strongly fortified with earthworks[g] and walls, and inhabited by all sorts of Gentiles. Its name was Caspin. [14] Those who were within, relying on the strength of the walls and on their supply of provisions, behaved most insolently towards Judas and his men, railing at them and even blaspheming and saying unholy things. [15] But Judas and his men, calling upon the great Sovereign of the world, who without battering rams or engines of war overthrew Jericho in the days of Joshua, rushed furiously upon the walls. [16] They took the town by the will of God, and slaughtered untold numbers, so that the adjoining lake, a quarter of a mile[h] wide, appeared to be running over with blood.

Judas Defeats Timothy's Army

17 When they had gone ninety-five miles[i] from there, they came to Charax, to

a 164 BC   b Gk to them   c Gk they   d Gk two hundred and forty stadia   e Gk nine stadia   f Gk them g Meaning of Gk uncertain   h Gk two stadia i Gk seven hundred and fifty stadia the Jews who are called Toubiani. 18 They did not find Timothy in that region, for he had by then left there without accomplishing anything, though in one place he had left a very strong garrison. 19 Dositheus and Sosipater, who were captains under Maccabeus, marched out and destroyed those whom Timothy had left in the stronghold, more than ten thousand men. 20 But Maccabeus arranged his army in divisions, set men[a] in command of the divisions, and hurried after Timothy, who had with him one hundred and twenty thousand infantry and two thousand five hundred cavalry. 21 When Timothy learned of the approach of Judas, he sent off the women and the children and also the baggage to a place called Carnaim; for that place was hard to besiege and difficult of access because of the narrowness of all the approaches. 22 But when Judas's first division appeared, terror and fear came over the enemy at the manifestation to them of him who sees all things. In their flight they rushed headlong in every direction, so that often they were injured by their own men and pierced by the points of their own swords. 23 Judas pressed the pursuit with the utmost vigour, putting the sinners to the sword, and destroyed as many as thirty thousand.

24 Timothy himself fell into the hands of Dositheus and Sosipater and their men. With great guile he begged them to let him go in safety, because he held the parents of most of them, and the brothers of some, to whom no consideration would be shown. 25 And when with many words he had confirmed his solemn promise to restore them unharmed, they let him go, for the sake of saving their kindred.

Judas Wins Other Victories

26 Then Judas[b] marched against Carnaim and the temple of Atargatis, and slaughtered twenty-five thousand people. 27 After the rout and destruction of these, he marched also against Ephron, a fortified town where Lysias lived with multitudes of people of all nationalities.[c] Stalwart young men took their stand before the walls and made a vigorous defence; and great stores of war engines and missiles were there. 28 But the Jews[d] called upon the Sovereign who with power shatters the might of his enemies, and they got the town into their hands, and killed as many as twenty-five thousand of those who were in it.

29 Setting out from there, they hastened to Scythopolis, which is seventy-five miles[e] from Jerusalem. 30 But when the Jews who lived there bore witness to the goodwill that the people of Scythopolis had shown them and their kind treatment of them in times of misfortune, 31 they thanked them and exhorted them to be well disposed to their race in the future also. Then they went up to Jerusalem, as the festival of weeks was close at hand.

Judas Defeats Gorgias

32 After the festival called Pentecost, they hurried against Gorgias, the governor of Idumea, 33 who came out with three thousand infantry and four hundred cavalry. 34 When they joined battle, it happened that a few of the Jews fell. 35 But a certain Dositheus, one of Bacenor's men, who was on horseback and was a strong man, caught hold of Gorgias, and grasping his cloak was dragging him off by main strength, wishing to take the accursed man alive, when one of the Thracian cavalry bore down on him and cut off his arm; so Gorgias escaped and reached Marisa.

36 As Esdris and his men had been fighting for a long time and were weary, Judas called upon the Lord to show himself their ally and leader in the battle. 37 In the language of their ancestors he raised the battle-cry, with hymns; then he charged against Gorgias's troops when they were not expecting it, and put them to flight.

Prayers for Those Killed in Battle

38 Then Judas assembled his army and went to the city of Adullam. As the seventh day was coming on, they purified themselves according to the custom, and kept the sabbath there.

a Gk them   b Gk he   c Meaning of Gk uncertain
d Gk they   e Gk six hundred stadia

39 On the next day, as had now become necessary, Judas and his men went to take up the bodies of the fallen and to bring them back to lie with their kindred in the sepulchres of their ancestors. 40 Then under the tunic of each one of the dead they found sacred tokens of the idols of Jamnia, which the law forbids the Jews to wear. And it became clear to all that this was the reason these men had fallen. 41 So they all blessed the ways of the Lord, the righteous judge, who reveals the things that are hidden; 42 and they turned to supplication, praying that the sin that had been committed might be wholly blotted out. The noble Judas exhorted the people to keep themselves free from sin, for they had seen with their own eyes what had happened as the result of the sin of those who had fallen. 43 He also took up a collection, man by man, to the amount of two thousand drachmas of silver, and sent it to Jerusalem to provide for a sin-offering. In doing this he acted very well and honourably, taking account of the resurrection. 44 For if he were not expecting that those who had fallen would rise again, it would have been superfluous and foolish to pray for the dead. 45 But if he was looking to the splendid reward that is laid up for those who fall asleep in godliness, it was a holy and pious thought. Therefore he made atonement for the dead, so that they might be delivered from their sin.

Menelaus Is Put to Death

13 In the one hundred and forty-ninth year[a] word came to Judas and his men that Antiochus Eupator was coming with a great army against Judea, 2 and with him Lysias, his guardian, who had charge of the government. Each of them had a Greek force of one hundred and ten thousand infantry, five thousand three hundred cavalry, twenty-two elephants, and three hundred chariots armed with scythes.

3 Menelaus also joined them and with utter hypocrisy urged Antiochus on, not for the sake of his country's welfare, but because he thought that he would be estab-

lished in office. 4 But the King of kings aroused the anger of Antiochus against the scoundrel; and when Lysias informed him that this man was to blame for all the trouble, he ordered them to take him to Beroea and to put him to death by the method that is customary in that place. 5 For there is a tower there, fifty cubits high, full of ashes, and it has a rim running round it that on all sides inclines precipitously into the ashes. 6 There they all push to destruction anyone guilty of sacrilege or notorious for other crimes. 7 By such a fate it came about that Menelaus the lawbreaker died, without even burial in the earth. 8 And this was eminently just; because he had committed many sins against the altar whose fire and ashes were holy, he met his death in ashes.

A Battle Near the City of Modein

9 The king with barbarous arrogance was coming to show the Jews things far worse than those that had been done[b] in his father's time. 10 But when Judas heard of this, he ordered the people to call upon the Lord day and night, now more than ever to help those who were on the point of being deprived of the law and their country and the holy temple, 11 and not to let the people who had just begun to revive fall into the hands of the blasphemous Gentiles. 12 When they had all joined in the same petition and had implored the merciful Lord with weeping and fasting and lying prostrate for three days without ceasing, Judas exhorted them and ordered them to stand ready.

13 After consulting privately with the elders, he determined to march out and decide the matter by the help of God before the king's army could enter Judea and get possession of the city. 14 So, committing the decision to the Creator of the world and exhorting his troops to fight bravely to the death for the laws, temple, city, country, and commonwealth, he pitched his camp near Modein. 15 He gave his troops the watchword, 'God's victory', and with a

a 163 BC   *b* Or *the worst of the things that had been done* picked force of the bravest young men, he attacked the king's pavilion at night and killed as many as two thousand men in the camp. He stabbed[a] the leading elephant and its rider. [16]In the end they filled the camp with terror and confusion and withdrew in triumph. [17]This happened, just as day was dawning, because the Lord's help protected him.

Antiochus Makes a Treaty with the Jews

[18] The king, having had a taste of the daring of the Jews, tried strategy in attacking their positions. [19]He advanced against Beth-zur, a strong fortress of the Jews, was turned back, attacked again,[b] and was defeated. [20]Judas sent in to the garrison whatever was necessary. [21]But Rhodocus, a man from the ranks of the Jews, gave secret information to the enemy; he was sought for, caught, and put in prison. [22]The king negotiated a second time with the people in Beth-zur, gave pledges, received theirs, withdrew, attacked Judas and his men, and was defeated; [23]he got word that Philip, who had been left in charge of the government, had revolted in Antioch; he was dismayed, called in the Jews, yielded and swore to observe all their rights, settled with them and offered sacrifice, honoured the sanctuary, and showed generosity to the holy place. [24]He received Maccabeus, left Hegemonides as governor from Ptolemais to Gerar, [25]and went to Ptolemais. The people of Ptolemais were indignant over the treaty; in fact they were so angry that they wanted to annul its terms.[a] [26]Lysias took the public platform, made the best possible defence, convinced them, appeased them, gained their goodwill, and set out for Antioch. This is how the king's attack and withdrawal turned out.

Alcimus Speaks against Judas

14 Three years later, word came to Judas and his men that Demetrius son of Seleucus had sailed into the harbour of Tripolis with a strong army and a fleet, [2]and had taken possession of the country, having made away with Antiochus and his guardian Lysias.

[3] Now a certain Alcimus, who had formerly been high priest but had wilfully defiled himself in the times of separation,[c] realized that there was no way for him to be safe or to have access again to the holy altar, [4]and went to King Demetrius in about the one hundred and fifty-first year,[d] presenting to him a crown of gold and a palm, and besides these some of the customary olive branches from the temple. During that day he kept quiet. [5]But he found an opportunity that furthered his mad purpose when he was invited by Demetrius to a meeting of the council and was asked about the attitude and intentions of the Jews. He answered:

[6] 'Those of the Jews who are called Hasideans, whose leader is Judas Maccabeus, are keeping up war and stirring up sedition, and will not let the kingdom attain tranquillity. [7]Therefore I have laid aside my ancestral glory—I mean the high-priesthood—and have now come here, [8]first because I am genuinely concerned for the interests of the king, and second because I have regard also for my compatriots. For through the folly of those whom I have mentioned our whole nation is now in no small misfortune. [9]Since you are acquainted, O king, with the details of this matter, may it please you to take thought for our country and our hard-pressed nation with the gracious kindness that you show to all. [10]For as long as Judas lives, it is impossible for the government to find peace.' [11]When he had said this, the rest of the king's Friends,[e] who were hostile to Judas, quickly inflamed Demetrius still more. [12]He immediately chose Nicanor, who had been in command of the elephants, appointed him governor of Judea, and sent him off [13]with orders to kill Judas and scatter his troops, and to instal Alcimus as high priest of the great[f] temple. [14]And the Gentiles throughout Judea, who had fled before[a] Judas, flocked to join Nicanor, thinking that the misfortunes and calamities of the Jews would mean prosperity for themselves.

a Meaning of Gk uncertain   b Or faltered   c Other ancient authorities read of mixing   d 161 BC   e Gk of the Friends   f Gk greatest

Nicanor Makes Friends with Judas

15 When the Jews[a] heard of Nicanor's coming and the gathering of the Gentiles, they sprinkled dust on their heads and prayed to him who established his own people for ever and always upholds his own heritage by manifesting himself. 16 At the command of the leader, they[b] set out from there immediately and engaged them in battle at a village called Dessau.[c] 17 Simon, the brother of Judas, had encountered Nicanor, but had been temporarily[d] checked because of the sudden consternation created by the enemy.

18 Nevertheless Nicanor, hearing of the valour of Judas and his troops and their courage in battle for their country, shrank from deciding the issue by bloodshed. 19 Therefore he sent Posidonius, Theodotus, and Mattathias to give and receive pledges of friendship. 20 When the terms had been fully considered, and the leader had informed the people, and it had appeared that they were of one mind, they agreed to the covenant. 21 The leaders[e] set a day on which to meet by themselves. A chariot came forward from each army; seats of honour were set in place; 22 Judas posted armed men in readiness at key places to prevent sudden treachery on the part of the enemy; so they duly held the consultation.

23 Nicanor stayed on in Jerusalem and did nothing out of the way, but dismissed the flocks of people that had gathered. 24 And he kept Judas always in his presence; he was warmly attached to the man. 25 He urged him to marry and have children; so Judas[b] married, settled down, and shared the common life.

Nicanor Turns against Judas

26 But when Alcimus noticed their goodwill for one another, he took the covenant that had been made and went to Demetrius. He told him that Nicanor was disloyal to the government, since he had appointed that conspirator against the kingdom, Judas, to be his successor. 27 The king became excited and, provoked by the false accusations of that depraved man,

wrote to Nicanor, stating that he was displeased with the covenant and commanding him to send Maccabeus to Antioch as a prisoner without delay.

28 When this message came to Nicanor, he was troubled and grieved that he had to annul their agreement when the man had done no wrong. 29 Since it was not possible to oppose the king, he watched for an opportunity to accomplish this by a stratagem. 30 But Maccabeus, noticing that Nicanor was more austere in his dealings with him and was meeting him more rudely than had been his custom, concluded that this austerity did not spring from the best motives. So he gathered not a few of his men, and went into hiding from Nicanor. 31 When the latter became aware that he had been cleverly outwitted by the man, he went to the great[f] and holy temple while the priests were offering the customary sacrifices, and commanded them to hand the man over. 32 When they declared on oath that they did not know where the man was whom he wanted, 33 he stretched out his right hand towards the sanctuary, and swore this oath: 'If you do not hand Judas over to me as a prisoner, I will level this shrine of God to the ground and tear down the altar, and build here a splendid temple to Dionysus.'

34 Having said this, he went away. Then the priests stretched out their hands towards heaven and called upon the constant Defender of our nation, in these words: 35 'O Lord of all, though you have need of nothing, you were pleased that there should be a temple for your habitation among us; 36 so now, O holy One, Lord of all holiness, keep undefiled for ever this house that has been so recently purified.'

Razis Dies for His Country

37 A certain Razis, one of the elders of Jerusalem, was denounced to Nicanor as a man who loved his compatriots and was very well thought of and for his goodwill was called father of the Jews. 38 In former

a Gk they   b Gk he   c Meaning of Gk uncertain
d Other ancient authorities read slowly   e Gk They
f Gk greatest

times, when there was no mingling with the Gentiles, he had been accused of Judaism, and he had most zealously risked body and life for Judaism. 39 Nicanor, wishing to exhibit the enmity that he had for the Jews, sent more than five hundred soldiers to arrest him; 40 for he thought that by arresting[a] him he would do them an injury. 41 When the troops were about to capture the tower and were forcing the door of the courtyard, they ordered that fire be brought and the doors burned. Being surrounded, Razis[b] fell upon his own sword, 42 preferring to die nobly rather than to fall into the hands of sinners and suffer outrages unworthy of his noble birth. 43 But in the heat of the struggle he did not hit exactly, and the crowd was now rushing in through the doors. He courageously ran up on the wall, and bravely threw himself down into the crowd. 44 But as they quickly drew back, a space opened and he fell in the middle of the empty space. 45 Still alive and aflame with anger, he rose, and though his blood gushed forth and his wounds were severe he ran through the crowd; and standing upon a steep rock, 46 with his blood now completely drained from him, he tore out his entrails, took them in both hands, and hurled them at the crowd, calling upon the Lord of life and spirit to give them back to him again. This was the manner of his death.

Nicanor's Arrogance

15 When Nicanor heard that Judas and his troops were in the region of Samaria, he made plans to attack them with complete safety on the day of rest. 2 When the Jews who were compelled to follow him said, 'Do not destroy so savagely and barbarously, but show respect for the day that he who sees all things has honoured and hallowed above other days', 3 the thrice-accursed wretch asked if there were a sovereign in heaven who had commanded the keeping of the sabbath day. 4 When they declared, 'It is the living Lord himself, the Sovereign in heaven, who ordered us to observe the seventh day,' 5 he

replied, 'But I am a sovereign also, on earth, and I command you to take up arms and finish the king's business.' Nevertheless, he did not succeed in carrying out his abominable design.

Judas Prepares the Jews for Battle

6 This Nicanor in his utter boastfulness and arrogance had determined to erect a public monument of victory over Judas and his forces. 7 But Maccabeus did not cease to trust with all confidence that he would get help from the Lord. 8 He exhorted his troops not to fear the attack of the Gentiles, but to keep in mind the former times when help had come to them from heaven, and so to look for the victory that the Almighty would give them. 9 Encouraging them from the law and the prophets, and reminding them also of the struggles they had won, he made them the more eager. 10 When he had aroused their courage, he issued his orders, at the same time pointing out the perfidy of the Gentiles and their violation of oaths. 11 He armed each of them not so much with confidence in shields and spears as with the inspiration of brave words, and he cheered them all by relating a dream, a sort of vision,[a] which was worthy of belief.

12 What he saw was this: Onias, who had been high priest, a noble and good man, of modest bearing and gentle manner, one who spoke fittingly and had been trained from childhood in all that belongs to excellence, was praying with outstretched hands for the whole body of the Jews. 13 Then in the same fashion another appeared, distinguished by his grey hair and dignity, and of marvellous majesty and authority. 14 And Onias spoke, saying, 'This is a man who loves the family of Israel and prays much for the people and the holy city—Jeremiah, the prophet of God.' 15 Jeremiah stretched out his right hand and gave to Judas a golden sword, and as he gave it he addressed him thus: 16 'Take this holy sword, a gift from God, with which you will strike down your adversaries.'

17 Encouraged by the words of Judas, so

---

a Meaning of Gk uncertain   b Gk he

noble and so effective in arousing valour and awaking courage in the souls of the young, they determined not to carry on a campaign*a* but to attack bravely, and to decide the matter by fighting hand to hand with all courage, because the city and the sanctuary and the temple were in danger. 18 Their concern for wives and children, and also for brothers and sisters*b* and relatives, lay upon them less heavily; their greatest and first fear was for the consecrated sanctuary. 19 And those who had to remain in the city were in no little distress, being anxious over the encounter in the open country.

The Defeat and Death of Nicanor

20 When all were now looking forward to the coming issue, and the enemy was already close at hand with their army drawn up for battle, the elephants*c* strategically stationed and the cavalry deployed on the flanks, 21 Maccabeus, observing the masses that were in front of him and the varied supply of arms and the savagery of the elephants, stretched out his hands towards heaven and called upon the Lord who works wonders; for he knew that it is not by arms, but as the Lord*d* decides, that he gains the victory for those who deserve it. 22 He called upon him in these words: 'O Lord, you sent your angel in the time of King Hezekiah of Judea, and he killed fully one hundred and eighty-five thousand in the camp of Sennacherib. 23 So now, O Sovereign of the heavens, send a good angel to spread terror and trembling before us. 24 By the might of your arm may these blasphemers who come against your holy people be struck down.' With these words he ended his prayer.

25 Nicanor and his troops advanced with trumpets and battle-songs, 26 but Judas and his troops met the enemy in battle with invocations to God and prayers. 27 So, fighting with their hands and praying to God in their hearts, they laid low at least thirty-five thousand, and were greatly gladdened by God's manifestation.

28 When the action was over and they were returning with joy, they recognized Nicanor, lying dead, in full armour. 29 Then there was shouting and tumult, and they blessed the Sovereign Lord in the language of their ancestors. 30 Then the man who was ever in body and soul the defender of his people, the man who maintained his youthful goodwill towards his compatriots, ordered them to cut off Nicanor's head and arm and carry them to Jerusalem. 31 When he arrived there and had called his compatriots together and stationed the priests before the altar, he sent for those who were in the citadel. 32 He showed them the vile Nicanor's head and that profane man's arm, which had been boastfully stretched out against the holy house of the Almighty. 33 He cut out the tongue of the ungodly Nicanor and said that he would feed it piecemeal to the birds and would hang up these rewards of his folly opposite the sanctuary. 34 And they all, looking to heaven, blessed the Lord who had manifested himself, saying, 'Blessed is he who has kept his own place undefiled!' 35 Judas*e* hung Nicanor's head from the citadel, a clear and conspicuous sign to everyone of the help of the Lord. 36 And they all decreed by public vote never to let this day go unobserved, but to celebrate the thirteenth day of the twelfth month—which is called Adar in the Aramaic language—the day before Mordecai's day.

37 This, then, is how matters turned out with Nicanor, and from that time the city has been in the possession of the Hebrews. So I will here end my story.

The Compiler's Epilogue

38 If it is well told and to the point, that is what I myself desired; if it is poorly done and mediocre, that was the best I could do. 39 For just as it is harmful to drink wine alone, or, again, to drink water alone, while wine mixed with water is sweet and delicious and enhances one's enjoyment, so also the style of the story delights the ears of those who read the work. And here will be the end.

---

*a Or to remain in camp   b Gk for brothers
c Gk animals   d Gk he   e Gk He*

JOB

Job and His Family

1 There was once a man in the land of Uz whose name was Job. That man was blameless and upright, one who feared God and turned away from evil. ²There were born to him seven sons and three daughters. ³He had seven thousand sheep, three thousand camels, five hundred yoke of oxen, five hundred donkeys, and very many servants; so that this man was the greatest of all the people of the east. ⁴His sons used to go and hold feasts in one another's houses in turn; and they would send and invite their three sisters to eat and drink with them. ⁵And when the feast days had run their course, Job would send and sanctify them, and he would rise early in the morning and offer burnt-offerings according to the number of them all; for Job said, 'It may be that my children have sinned, and cursed God in their hearts.' This is what Job always did.

Attack on Job's Character

6 One day the heavenly beings*a* came to present themselves before the LORD, and Satan*b* also came among them. ⁷The LORD said to Satan,*b* 'Where have you come from?' Satan*b* answered the LORD, 'From going to and fro on the earth, and from walking up and down on it.' ⁸The LORD said to Satan,*b* 'Have you considered my servant Job? There is no one like him on the earth, a blameless and upright man who fears God and turns away from evil.' ⁹Then Satan*b* answered the LORD, 'Does Job fear God for nothing? ¹⁰Have you not put a fence around him and his house and all that he has, on every side? You have blessed the work of his hands, and his possessions have increased in the land. ¹¹But stretch out your hand now, and touch all that he has, and he will curse you to your face.' ¹²The LORD said to Satan,*b* 'Very well, all that he has is in your power; only do not stretch out your hand against him!' So Satan*b* went out from the presence of the LORD.

Job Loses Property and Children

13 One day when his sons and daughters were eating and drinking wine in the eldest brother's house, ¹⁴a messenger came to Job and said, 'The oxen were ploughing and the donkeys were feeding beside them, ¹⁵and the Sabeans fell on them and carried them off, and killed the servants with the edge of the sword; I alone have escaped to tell you.' ¹⁶While he was still speaking, another came and said, 'The fire of God fell from heaven and burned up the sheep and the servants, and consumed them; I alone have escaped to tell you.' ¹⁷While he was still speaking, another came and said, 'The Chaldeans formed three columns, made a raid on the camels and carried them off, and killed the servants with the edge of the sword; I alone have escaped to tell you.' ¹⁸While he was still speaking, another came and said, 'Your sons and daughters were eating and drinking wine in their eldest brother's house, ¹⁹and suddenly a great wind came across the desert, struck the four corners of the house, and it fell on the young people, and they are dead; I alone have escaped to tell you.'

20 Then Job arose, tore his robe, shaved his head, and fell on the ground and worshipped. ²¹He said, 'Naked I came from my

a Heb *sons of God*   *b* Or *the Accuser*; Heb *ha-satan* mother's womb, and naked shall I return there; the LORD gave, and the LORD has taken away; blessed be the name of the LORD.'

22 In all this Job did not sin or charge God with wrongdoing.

Attack on Job's Health

2 One day the heavenly beings[a] came to present themselves before the LORD, and Satan[b] also came among them to present himself before the LORD. [2]The LORD said to Satan,[b] 'Where have you come from?' Satan[c] answered the LORD, 'From going to and fro on the earth, and from walking up and down on it.' [3]The LORD said to Satan,[b] 'Have you considered my servant Job? There is no one like him on the earth, a blameless and upright man who fears God and turns away from evil. He still persists in his integrity, although you incited me against him, to destroy him for no reason.' [4]Then Satan[b] answered the LORD, 'Skin for skin! All that people have they will give to save their lives.[d] [5]But stretch out your hand now and touch his bone and his flesh, and he will curse you to your face.' [6]The LORD said to Satan,[b] 'Very well, he is in your power; only spare his life.'

7 So Satan[b] went out from the presence of the LORD, and inflicted loathsome sores on Job from the sole of his foot to the crown of his head. [8]Job[e] took a potsherd with which to scrape himself, and sat among the ashes.

9 Then his wife said to him, 'Do you still persist in your integrity? Curse[f] God, and die.' [10]But he said to her, 'You speak as any foolish woman would speak. Shall we receive the good at the hand of God, and not receive the bad?' In all this Job did not sin with his lips.

Job's Three Friends

11 Now when Job's three friends heard of all these troubles that had come upon him, each of them set out from his home—Eliphaz the Temanite, Bildad the Shuhite, and Zophar the Naamathite. They met together to go and console and comfort him. [12]When they saw him from a dis-

tance, they did not recognize him, and they raised their voices and wept aloud; they tore their robes and threw dust in the air upon their heads. [13]They sat with him on the ground for seven days and seven nights, and no one spoke a word to him, for they saw that his suffering was very great.

Job Curses the Day He Was Born

3 After this Job opened his mouth and cursed the day of his birth. [2]Job said:

3 'Let the day perish on which I was
    born,
  and the night that said,
    "A man-child is conceived."
4 Let that day be darkness!
  May God above not seek it,
  or light shine on it.
5 Let gloom and deep darkness claim
    it.
  Let clouds settle upon it;
  let the blackness of the day terrify
    it.
6 That night—let thick darkness seize
    it!
  let it not rejoice among the days of
    the year;
  let it not come into the number of
    the months.
7 Yes, let that night be barren;
  let no joyful cry be heard[g] in it.
8 Let those curse it who curse the Sea,[h]
    those who are skilled to rouse up
    Leviathan.
9 Let the stars of its dawn be dark;
  let it hope for light, but have none;
  may it not see the eyelids of the
    morning—
10 because it did not shut the doors of
    my mother's womb,
  and hide trouble from my eyes.

11 'Why did I not die at birth,
  come forth from the womb and
    expire?
12 Why were there knees to receive me,
  or breasts for me to suck?

a Heb sons of God   b Or the Accuser; Heb ha-satan
c Or The Accuser; Heb ha-satan   d Or All that the man
has he will give for his life   e Heb He   f Heb Bless
g Heb come   h Cn: Heb day

13 Now I would be lying down and
      quiet;
    I would be asleep; then I would be
      at rest
14 with kings and counsellors of the
      earth
    who rebuild ruins for themselves,
15 or with princes who have gold,
    who fill their houses with silver.
16 Or why was I not buried like a
      stillborn child,
    like an infant that never sees the
      light?
17 There the wicked cease from
      troubling,
    and there the weary are at rest.
18 There the prisoners are at ease
      together;
    they do not hear the voice of the
      taskmaster.
19 The small and the great are there,
    and the slaves are free from their
      masters.

20 'Why is light given to one in misery,
    and life to the bitter in soul,
21 who long for death, but it does not
      come,
    and dig for it more than for hidden
      treasures;
22 who rejoice exceedingly,
    and are glad when they find the
      grave?
23 Why is light given to one who cannot
      see the way,
    whom God has fenced in?
24 For my sighing comes like*a* my bread,
    and my groanings are poured out
      like water.
25 Truly the thing that I fear comes
      upon me,
    and what I dread befalls me.
26 I am not at ease, nor am I quiet;
    I have no rest; but trouble comes.'

Eliphaz Speaks: Job Has Sinned

4 Then Eliphaz the Temanite answered:
2 'If one ventures a word with you,
      will you be offended?
    But who can keep from speaking?
3 See, you have instructed many;

    you have strengthened the weak
      hands.
4 Your words have supported those
      who were stumbling,
    and you have made firm the feeble
      knees.
5 But now it has come to you, and you
      are impatient;
    it touches you, and you are
      dismayed.
6 Is not your fear of God your
      confidence,
    and the integrity of your ways your
      hope?

7 'Think now, who that was innocent
      ever perished?
    Or where were the upright cut off?
8 As I have seen, those who plough
      iniquity
    and sow trouble reap the same.
9 By the breath of God they perish,
    and by the blast of his anger they
      are consumed.
10 The roar of the lion, the voice of the
      fierce lion,
    and the teeth of the young lions are
      broken.
11 The strong lion perishes for lack of
      prey,
    and the whelps of the lioness are
      scattered.

12 'Now a word came stealing to me,
    my ear received the whisper of it.
13 Amid thoughts from visions of the
      night,
    when deep sleep falls on mortals,
14 dread came upon me, and trembling,
    which made all my bones shake.
15 A spirit glided past my face;
    the hair of my flesh bristled.
16 It stood still,
    but I could not discern its
      appearance.
    A form was before my eyes;
    there was silence, then I heard a
      voice:
17 "Can mortals be righteous before*b*
      God?

a Heb *before*   *b* Or *more than*

Can human beings be pure before[a]
    their Maker?
18 Even in his servants he puts no trust,
    and his angels he charges with
       error;
19 how much more those who live in
    houses of clay,
    whose foundation is in the dust,
    who are crushed like a moth.
20 Between morning and evening they
    are destroyed;
    they perish for ever without any
      regarding it.
21 Their tent-cord is plucked up within
    them,
    and they die devoid of wisdom."

Job Is Corrected by God

5 'Call now; is there anyone who will
    answer you?
    To which of the holy ones will you
    turn?
2 Surely vexation kills the fool,
    and jealousy slays the simple.
3 I have seen fools taking root,
    but suddenly I cursed their
      dwelling.
4 Their children are far from safety,
    they are crushed in the gate,
    and there is no one to deliver them.
5 The hungry eat their harvest,
    and they take it even out of the
      thorns;[b]
    and the thirsty[c] pant after their
      wealth.
6 For misery does not come from the
    earth,
    nor does trouble sprout from the
      ground;
7 but human beings are born to
    trouble
    just as sparks[d] fly upward.

8 'As for me, I would seek God,
    and to God I would commit my
      cause.
9 He does great things and
    unsearchable,
    marvellous things without number.
10 He gives rain on the earth
    and sends waters on the fields;

11 he sets on high those who are lowly,
    and those who mourn are lifted to
      safety.
12 He frustrates the devices of the crafty,
    so that their hands achieve no
      success.
13 He takes the wise in their own
    craftiness;
    and the schemes of the wily are
      brought to a quick end.
14 They meet with darkness in the
    daytime,
    and grope at noonday as in the
      night.
15 But he saves the needy from the
    sword of their mouth,
    from the hand of the mighty.
16 So the poor have hope,
    and injustice shuts its mouth.

17 'How happy is the one whom God
    reproves;
    therefore do not despise the
      discipline of the Almighty.[e]
18 For he wounds, but he binds up;
    he strikes, but his hands heal.
19 He will deliver you from six troubles;
    in seven no harm shall touch you.
20 In famine he will redeem you from
    death,
    and in war from the power of the
      sword.
21 You shall be hidden from the scourge
    of the tongue,
    and shall not fear destruction when
      it comes.
22 At destruction and famine you shall
    laugh,
    and shall not fear the wild animals
      of the earth.
23 For you shall be in league with the
    stones of the field,
    and the wild animals shall be at
      peace with you.
24 You shall know that your tent is safe,
    you shall inspect your fold and
      miss nothing.

a Or *more than*   b Meaning of Heb uncertain
c Aquila Symmachus Syr Vg: Heb *snare*   d Or *birds*;
Heb *sons of Resheph*   e Traditional rendering of Heb
Shaddai

25 You shall know that your descendants
   will be many,
      and your offspring like the grass of
      the earth.
26 You shall come to your grave in ripe
   old age,
      as a shock of grain comes up to the
      threshing-floor in its season.
27 See, we have searched this out; it is
   true.
      Hear, and know it for yourself.'

Job Replies: My Complaint Is Just

6 Then Job answered:
2 'O that my vexation were weighed,
   and all my calamity laid in the
   balances!
3 For then it would be heavier than the
   sand of the sea;
      therefore my words have been rash.
4 For the arrows of the Almighty*a* are in
   me;
      my spirit drinks their poison;
      the terrors of God are arrayed
      against me.
5 Does the wild ass bray over its grass,
   or the ox low over its fodder?
6 Can that which is tasteless be eaten
   without salt,
      or is there any flavour in the juice
      of mallows?*b*
7 My appetite refuses to touch them;
   they are like food that is loathsome
      to me.*b*

8 'O that I might have my request,
   and that God would grant my
   desire;
9 that it would please God to crush me,
   that he would let loose his hand
      and cut me off!
10 This would be my consolation;
   I would even exult*b* in unrelenting
   pain;
      for I have not denied the words of
      the Holy One.
11 What is my strength, that I should
   wait?
      And what is my end, that I should
      be patient?
12 Is my strength the strength of stones,

or is my flesh bronze?
13 In truth I have no help in me,
   and any resource is driven from me.

14 'Those who withhold*c* kindness from
   a friend
      forsake the fear of the Almighty.*a*
15 My companions are treacherous like
   a torrent-bed,
      like freshets that pass away,
16 that run dark with ice,
   turbid with melting snow.
17 In time of heat they disappear;
   when it is hot, they vanish from
   their place.
18 The caravans turn aside from their
   course;
      they go up into the waste, and
      perish.
19 The caravans of Tema look,
   the travellers of Sheba hope.
20 They are disappointed because they
   were confident;
      they come there and are
      confounded.
21 Such you have now become to me;*d*
   you see my calamity, and are afraid.
22 Have I said, "Make me a gift"?
   Or, "From your wealth offer a bribe
      for me"?
23 Or, "Save me from an opponent's
   hand"?
      Or, "Ransom me from the hand of
      oppressors"?

24 'Teach me, and I will be silent;
   make me understand how I have
      gone wrong.
25 How forceful are honest words!
   But your reproof, what does it
      reprove?
26 Do you think that you can reprove
   words,
      as if the speech of the desperate
      were wind?
27 You would even cast lots over the
   orphan,
      and bargain over your friend.

a Traditional rendering of Heb *Shaddai*   *b* Meaning of
Heb uncertain   *c* Syr Vg Compare Tg: Meaning of Heb
uncertain   *d* Cn Compare Gk Syr: Meaning of Heb
uncertain

28 'But now, be pleased to look at me;
     for I will not lie to your face.
29 Turn, I pray, let no wrong be done.
     Turn now, my vindication is at
       stake.
30 Is there any wrong on my tongue?
     Cannot my taste discern calamity?

Job: My Suffering Is without End

7 'Do not human beings have a hard
     service on earth,
     and are not their days like the days
       of a labourer?
2 Like a slave who longs for the
       shadow,
     and like labourers who look for
       their wages,
3 so I am allotted months of
       emptiness,
     and nights of misery are
       apportioned to me.
4 When I lie down I say, "When shall I
     rise?"
     But the night is long,
     and I am full of tossing until dawn.
5 My flesh is clothed with worms and
       dirt;
     my skin hardens, then breaks out
       again.
6 My days are swifter than a weaver's
       shuttle,
     and come to their end without
       hope. *a*

7 'Remember that my life is a breath;
     my eye will never again see good.
8 The eye that beholds me will see me
       no more;
     while your eyes are upon me, I shall
       be gone.
9 As the cloud fades and vanishes,
     so those who go down to Sheol do
       not come up;
10 they return no more to their houses,
     nor do their places know them any
       more.

11 'Therefore I will not restrain my
       mouth;
     I will speak in the anguish of my
       spirit;

I will complain in the bitterness of
       my soul.
12 Am I the Sea, or the Dragon,
     that you set a guard over me?
13 When I say, "My bed will comfort me,
     my couch will ease my complaint",
14 then you scare me with dreams
     and terrify me with visions,
15 so that I would choose strangling
     and death rather than this body.
16 I loathe my life; I would not live for
       ever.
     Let me alone, for my days are a
       breath.
17 What are human beings, that you
       make so much of them,
     that you set your mind on them,
18 visit them every morning,
     test them every moment?
19 Will you not look away from me for a
       while,
     let me alone until I swallow my
       spittle?
20 If I sin, what do I do to you, you
       watcher of humanity?
     Why have you made me your
       target?
     Why have I become a burden to
       you?
21 Why do you not pardon my
       transgression
     and take away my iniquity?
     For now I shall lie in the earth;
     you will seek me, but I shall not be.'

Bildad Speaks: Job Should Repent

8 Then Bildad the Shuhite answered:
2 'How long will you say these things,
     and the words of your mouth be a
       great wind?
3 Does God pervert justice?
     Or does the Almighty *b* pervert the
       right?
4 If your children sinned against him,
     he delivered them into the power of
       their transgression.
5 If you will seek God
     and make supplication to the
       Almighty, *b*

a Or *as the thread runs out*   *b* Traditional rendering of
Heb *Shaddai*

6 if you are pure and upright,
   surely then he will rouse himself
      for you
   and restore to you your rightful
      place.
7 Though your beginning was small,
   your latter days will be very great.

8 'For inquire now of bygone
      generations,
   and consider what their ancestors
      have found;
9 for we are but of yesterday, and we
      know nothing,
   for our days on earth are but a
      shadow.
10 Will they not teach you and tell you
   and utter words out of their
      understanding?

11 'Can papyrus grow where there is no
      marsh?
   Can reeds flourish where there is
      no water?
12 While yet in flower and not cut
      down,
   they wither before any other plant.
13 Such are the paths of all who forget
      God;
   the hope of the godless shall
      perish.
14 Their confidence is gossamer,
   a spider's house their trust.
15 If one leans against its house, it will
      not stand;
   if one lays hold of it, it will not
      endure.
16 The wicked thrive[a] before the sun,
   and their shoots spread over the
      garden.
17 Their roots twine around the
      stoneheap;
   they live among the rocks.[b]
18 If they are destroyed from their
      place,
   then it will deny them, saying, "I
      have never seen you."
19 See, these are their happy ways,[c]
   and out of the earth still others will
      spring.

20 'See, God will not reject a blameless
      person,
   nor take the hand of evildoers.
21 He will yet fill your mouth with
      laughter,
   and your lips with shouts of joy.
22 Those who hate you will be clothed
      with shame,
   and the tent of the wicked will be
      no more.'

Job Replies: There Is No Mediator

9 Then Job answered:
2 'Indeed I know that this is so;
   but how can a mortal be just before
      God?
3 If one wished to contend with him,
   one could not answer him once in
      a thousand.
4 He is wise in heart, and mighty in
      strength
   —who has resisted him, and
      succeeded?—
5 he who removes mountains, and they
      do not know it,
   when he overturns them in his
      anger;
6 who shakes the earth out of its place,
   and its pillars tremble;
7 who commands the sun, and it does
      not rise;
   who seals up the stars;
8 who alone stretched out the heavens
   and trampled the waves of the Sea;[d]
9 who made the Bear and Orion,
   the Pleiades and the chambers of
      the south;
10 who does great things beyond
      understanding,
   and marvellous things without
      number.
11 Look, he passes by me, and I do not
      see him;
   he moves on, but I do not perceive
      him.
12 He snatches away; who can stop him?
   Who will say to him, "What are you
      doing?"

a Heb *He thrives*   b Gk Vg: Meaning of Heb uncertain
c Meaning of Heb uncertain   d Or *trampled the back of
the sea dragon*

13 'God will not turn back his anger;
   the helpers of Rahab bowed
      beneath him.
14 How then can I answer him,
   choosing my words with him?
15 Though I am innocent, I cannot
      answer him;
   I must appeal for mercy to my
      accuser. *a*
16 If I summoned him and he answered
      me,
   I do not believe that he would
      listen to my voice.
17 For he crushes me with a tempest,
   and multiplies my wounds without
      cause;
18 he will not let me get my breath,
   but fills me with bitterness.
19 If it is a contest of strength, he is the
      strong one!
   If it is a matter of justice, who can
      summon him? *b*
20 Though I am innocent, my own
      mouth would condemn me;
   though I am blameless, he would
      prove me perverse.
21 I am blameless; I do not know
      myself;
   I loathe my life.
22 It is all one; therefore I say,
   he destroys both the blameless and
      the wicked.
23 When disaster brings sudden death,
   he mocks at the calamity *c* of the
      innocent.
24 The earth is given into the hand of
      the wicked;
   he covers the eyes of its judges—
   if it is not he, who then is it?

25 'My days are swifter than a runner;
   they flee away, they see no good.
26 They go by like skiffs of reed,
   like an eagle swooping on the
      prey.
27 If I say, "I will forget my complaint;
   I will put off my sad countenance
      and be of good cheer",
28 I become afraid of all my suffering,
   for I know you will not hold me
      innocent.

29 I shall be condemned;
   why then do I labour in vain?
30 If I wash myself with soap
   and cleanse my hands with lye,
31 yet you will plunge me into filth,
   and my own clothes will abhor me.
32 For he is not a mortal, as I am, that I
      might answer him,
   that we should come to trial
      together.
33 There is no umpire *d* between us,
   who might lay his hand on us both.
34 If he would take his rod away from
      me,
   and not let dread of him terrify me,
35 then I would speak without fear of
      him,
   for I know I am not what I am
      thought to be. *e*

Job: I Loathe My Life

10 'I loathe my life;
   I will give free utterance to my
      complaint;
   I will speak in the bitterness of my
      soul.
2 I will say to God, Do not condemn
      me;
   let me know why you contend
      against me.
3 Does it seem good to you to oppress,
   to despise the work of your hands
   and favour the schemes of the
      wicked?
4 Do you have eyes of flesh?
   Do you see as humans see?
5 Are your days like the days of
      mortals,
   or your years like human years,
6 that you seek out my iniquity
   and search for my sin,
7 although you know that I am not
      guilty,
   and there is no one to deliver out
      of your hand?
8 Your hands fashioned and made me;
   and now you turn and destroy me. *f*

a Or *for my right*   *b* Compare Gk: Heb *me*
c Meaning of Heb uncertain   *d* Another reading is
Would that there were an umpire   *e* Cn: Heb *for I am not
so in myself*   *f* Cn Compare Gk Syr: Heb *made me
together all around, and you destroy me*

9 Remember that you fashioned me
   like clay;
   and will you turn me to dust again?
10 Did you not pour me out like milk
   and curdle me like cheese?
11 You clothed me with skin and flesh,
   and knit me together with bones
   and sinews.
12 You have granted me life and
   steadfast love,
   and your care has preserved my
   spirit.
13 Yet these things you hid in your
   heart;
   I know that this was your purpose.
14 If I sin, you watch me,
   and do not acquit me of my
   iniquity.
15 If I am wicked, woe to me!
   If I am righteous, I cannot lift up
   my head,
   for I am filled with disgrace
   and look upon my affliction.
16 Bold as a lion you hunt me;
   you repeat your exploits against me.
17 You renew your witnesses against me,
   and increase your vexation towards
   me;
   you bring fresh troops against me. *a*

18 'Why did you bring me forth from
   the womb?
   Would that I had died before any
   eye had seen me,
19 and were as though I had not been,
   carried from the womb to the grave.
20 Are not the days of my life few? *b*
   Let me alone, that I may find a little
   comfort *c*
21 before I go, never to return,
   to the land of gloom and deep
   darkness,
22 the land of gloom *d* and chaos,
   where light is like darkness.'

*Zophar Speaks: Job's Guilt Deserves
Punishment*

11 Then Zophar the Naamathite answered:
2 'Should a multitude of words go
   unanswered,

and should one full of talk be
   vindicated?
3 Should your babble put others to
   silence,
   and when you mock, shall no one
   shame you?
4 For you say, "My conduct *e* is pure,
   and I am clean in God's *f* sight."
5 But O that God would speak,
   and open his lips to you,
6 and that he would tell you the secrets
   of wisdom!
   For wisdom is many-sided. *g*
Know then that God exacts of you
   less than your guilt deserves.

7 'Can you find out the deep things of
   God?
   Can you find out the limit of the
   Almighty? *h*
8 It is higher than heaven *i*—what can
   you do?
   Deeper than Sheol—what can you
   know?
9 Its measure is longer than the earth,
   and broader than the sea.
10 If he passes through, and imprisons,
   and assembles for judgement, who
   can hinder him?
11 For he knows those who are
   worthless;
   when he sees iniquity, will he not
   consider it?
12 But a stupid person will get
   understanding,
   when a wild ass is born human. *g*

13 'If you direct your heart rightly,
   you will stretch out your hands
   towards him.
14 If iniquity is in your hand, put it far
   away,
   and do not let wickedness reside in
   your tents.

a Cn Compare Gk: Heb *towards me; changes and a troop
are with me*   *b* Cn Compare Gk Syr: Heb *Are not my
days few? Let him cease!*   *c* Heb *that I may brighten up a
little*   *d* Heb *gloom as darkness, deep darkness*
e Gk: Heb *teaching*   *f* Heb *your*   *g* Meaning of Heb
uncertain   *h* Traditional rendering of Heb *Shaddai*
i Heb *The heights of heaven*

15 Surely then you will lift up your face
        without blemish;
    you will be secure, and will not
        fear.
16 You will forget your misery;
    you will remember it as waters that
        have passed away.
17 And your life will be brighter than
        the noonday;
    its darkness will be like the morning.
18 And you will have confidence,
        because there is hope;
    you will be protected*a* and take
        your rest in safety.
19 You will lie down, and no one will
        make you afraid;
    many will entreat your favour.
20 But the eyes of the wicked will fail;
    all way of escape will be lost to
        them,
    and their hope is to breathe their
        last.'

Job Replies: I Am a Laughing-stock

12 Then Job answered:
    2 'No doubt you are the people,
    and wisdom will die with you.
3 But I have understanding as well as
        you;
    I am not inferior to you.
    Who does not know such things as
        these?
4 I am a laughing-stock to my friends;
    I, who called upon God and he
        answered me,
    a just and blameless man, I am a
        laughing-stock.
5 Those at ease have contempt for
        misfortune,*b*
    but it is ready for those whose feet
        are unstable.
6 The tents of robbers are at peace,
    and those who provoke God are
        secure,
    who bring their god in their
        hands.*c*

7 'But ask the animals, and they will
        teach you;
    the birds of the air, and they will
        tell you;

8 ask the plants of the earth,*d* and they
        will teach you;
    and the fish of the sea will declare
        to you.
9 Who among all these does not know
    that the hand of the LORD has done
        this?
10 In his hand is the life of every living
        thing
    and the breath of every human
        being.
11 Does not the ear test words
    as the palate tastes food?
12 Is wisdom with the aged,
    and understanding in length of
        days?

13 'With God*e* are wisdom and strength;
    he has counsel and understanding.
14 If he tears down, no one can rebuild;
    if he shuts someone in, no one can
        open up.
15 If he withholds the waters, they dry
        up;
    if he sends them out, they
        overwhelm the land.
16 With him are strength and wisdom;
    the deceived and the deceiver are
        his.
17 He leads counsellors away stripped,
    and makes fools of judges.
18 He looses the sash of kings,
    and binds a waistcloth on their
        loins.
19 He leads priests away stripped,
    and overthrows the mighty.
20 He deprives of speech those who are
        trusted,
    and takes away the discernment of
        the elders.
21 He pours contempt on princes,
    and looses the belt of the strong.
22 He uncovers the deeps out of
        darkness,
    and brings deep darkness to light.
23 He makes nations great, then
        destroys them;

a Or *you will look around*   b Meaning of Heb uncertain
c Or *whom God brought forth by his hand*; Meaning of
Heb uncertain   d Or *speak to the earth*   e Heb *him*

he enlarges nations, then leads
them away.
24 He strips understanding from the
leaders[a] of the earth,
and makes them wander in a
pathless waste.
25 They grope in the dark without light;
he makes them stagger like a
drunkard.

13 'Look, my eye has seen all this,
my ear has heard and
understood it.
2 What you know, I also know;
I am not inferior to you.
3 But I would speak to the Almighty,[b]
and I desire to argue my case with
God.
4 As for you, you whitewash with lies;
all of you are worthless physicians.
5 If you would only keep silent,
that would be your wisdom!
6 Hear now my reasoning,
and listen to the pleadings of my
lips.
7 Will you speak falsely for God,
and speak deceitfully for him?
8 Will you show partiality towards him,
will you plead the case for God?
9 Will it be well with you when he
searches you out?
Or can you deceive him, as one
person deceives another?
10 He will surely rebuke you
if in secret you show partiality.
11 Will not his majesty terrify you,
and the dread of him fall upon
you?
12 Your maxims are proverbs of ashes,
your defences are defences of clay.

13 'Let me have silence, and I will speak,
and let come on me what may.
14 I will take my flesh in my teeth,
and put my life in my hand.[c]
15 See, he will kill me; I have no hope;[d]
but I will defend my ways to his
face.
16 This will be my salvation,
that the godless shall not come
before him.

17 Listen carefully to my words,
and let my declaration be in your
ears.
18 I have indeed prepared my case;
I know that I shall be vindicated.
19 Who is there that will contend with
me?
For then I would be silent and die.

Job's Despondent Prayer

20 Only grant two things to me,
then I will not hide myself from
your face:
21 withdraw your hand far from me,
and do not let dread of you terrify
me.
22 Then call, and I will answer;
or let me speak, and you reply to
me.
23 How many are my iniquities and my
sins?
Make me know my transgression
and my sin.
24 Why do you hide your face,
and count me as your enemy?
25 Will you frighten a windblown leaf
and pursue dry chaff?
26 For you write bitter things against me,
and make me reap[e] the iniquities of
my youth.
27 You put my feet in the stocks,
and watch all my paths;
you set a bound to the soles of my
feet.
28 One wastes away like a rotten thing,
like a garment that is moth-eaten.

14 'A mortal, born of woman, few
of days and full of trouble,
2 comes up like a flower and withers,
flees like a shadow and does not
last.
3 Do you fix your eyes on such a one?
Do you bring me into judgement
with you?
4 Who can bring a clean thing out of
an unclean?
No one can.

---

a Heb adds *of the people*   b Traditional rendering of
Heb *Shaddai*   c Gk: Heb *Why should I take . . . in my
hand?*   d Or *Though he kill me, yet I will trust in him*
e Heb *inherit*

5 Since their days are determined,
and the number of their months is
known to you,
and you have appointed the
bounds that they cannot pass,
6 look away from them, and desist, [a]
that they may enjoy, like labourers,
their days.

7 'For there is hope for a tree,
if it is cut down, that it will sprout
again,
and that its shoots will not cease.
8 Though its root grows old in the
earth,
and its stump dies in the ground,
9 yet at the scent of water it will bud
and put forth branches like a young
plant.
10 But mortals die, and are laid low;
humans expire, and where are they?
11 As waters fail from a lake,
and a river wastes away and dries
up,
12 so mortals lie down and do not rise
again;
until the heavens are no more, they
will not awake
or be roused out of their sleep.
13 O that you would hide me in Sheol,
that you would conceal me until
your wrath is past,
that you would appoint me a set
time, and remember me!
14 If mortals die, will they live again?
All the days of my service I would
wait
until my release should come.
15 You would call, and I would answer
you;
you would long for the work of
your hands.
16 For then you would not [b] number my
steps,
you would not keep watch over my
sin;
17 my transgression would be sealed up
in a bag,
and you would cover over my
iniquity.

18 'But the mountain falls and crumbles
away,
and the rock is removed from its
place;
19 the waters wear away the stones;
the torrents wash away the soil of
the earth;
so you destroy the hope of mortals.
20 You prevail for ever against them, and
they pass away;
you change their countenance, and
send them away.
21 Their children come to honour, and
they do not know it;
they are brought low, and it goes
unnoticed.
22 They feel only the pain of their own
bodies,
and mourn only for themselves.'

Eliphaz Speaks: Job Undermines Religion

15 Then Eliphaz the Temanite answered:
2 'Should the wise answer with windy
knowledge,
and fill themselves with the east
wind?
3 Should they argue in unprofitable
talk,
or in words with which they can do
no good?
4 But you are doing away with the fear
of God,
and hindering meditation before
God.
5 For your iniquity teaches your mouth,
and you choose the tongue of the
crafty.
6 Your own mouth condemns you, and
not I;
your own lips testify against you.

7 'Are you the firstborn of the human
race?
Were you brought forth before the
hills?
8 Have you listened in the council of
God?
And do you limit wisdom to
yourself?

a Cn: Heb *that they may desist*   b Syr: Heb lacks *not*

9 What do you know that we do not
    know?
    What do you understand that is not
        clear to us?
10 The grey-haired and the aged are on
    our side,
    those older than your father.
11 Are the consolations of God too
    small for you,
    or the word that deals gently with
        you?
12 Why does your heart carry you away,
    and why do your eyes flash, *a*
13 so that you turn your spirit against
    God,
    and let such words go out of your
        mouth?
14 What are mortals, that they can be
    clean?
    Or those born of woman, that they
        can be righteous?
15 God puts no trust even in his holy
    ones,
    and the heavens are not clean in his
        sight;
16 how much less one who is
    abominable and corrupt,
    one who drinks iniquity like water!

17 'I will show you; listen to me;
    what I have seen I will declare—
18 what sages have told,
    and their ancestors have not hidden,
19 to whom alone the land was given,
    and no stranger passed among
        them.
20 The wicked writhe in pain all their
    days,
    through all the years that are laid
        up for the ruthless.
21 Terrifying sounds are in their ears;
    in prosperity the destroyer will
        come upon them.
22 They despair of returning from
    darkness,
    and they are destined for the sword.
23 They wander abroad for bread,
    saying, "Where is it?"
    They know that a day of darkness is
        ready at hand;
24 distress and anguish terrify them;

    they prevail against them, like a
        king prepared for battle.
25 Because they stretched out their
    hands against God,
    and bid defiance to the Almighty, *b*
26 running stubbornly against him
    with a thick-bossed shield;
27 because they have covered their faces
    with their fat,
    and gathered fat upon their loins,
28 they will live in desolate cities,
    in houses that no one should
        inhabit,
    houses destined to become heaps
        of ruins;
29 they will not be rich, and their wealth
    will not endure,
    nor will they strike root in the
        earth; *c*
30 they will not escape from darkness;
    the flame will dry up their shoots,
    and their blossom *d* will be swept
        away *e* by the wind.
31 Let them not trust in emptiness,
    deceiving themselves;
    for emptiness will be their
        recompense.
32 It will be paid in full before their
    time,
    and their branch will not be green.
33 They will shake off their unripe
    grape, like the vine,
    and cast off their blossoms, like the
        olive tree.
34 For the company of the godless is
    barren,
    and fire consumes the tents of
        bribery.
35 They conceive mischief and bring
    forth evil
    and their heart prepares deceit.'

Job Reaffirms His Innocence

16 Then Job answered:
2 'I have heard many such
    things;
    miserable comforters are you all.
3 Have windy words no limit?

---

a Meaning of Heb uncertain   *b* Traditional rendering
of Heb *Shaddai*   *c* Vg: Meaning of Heb uncertain
d Gk: Heb *mouth*   *e* Cn: Heb *will depart*

Or what provokes you that you
    keep on talking?
4 I also could talk as you do,
    if you were in my place;
  I could join words together against
    you,
    and shake my head at you.
5 I could encourage you with my
    mouth,
    and the solace of my lips would
    assuage your pain.

6 'If I speak, my pain is not assuaged,
    and if I forbear, how much of it
    leaves me?
7 Surely now God has worn me out;
    he has*a* made desolate all my
    company.
8 And he has*a* shrivelled me up,
    which is a witness against me;
  my leanness has risen up against me,
    and it testifies to my face.
9 He has torn me in his wrath, and
    hated me;
    he has gnashed his teeth at me;
    my adversary sharpens his eyes
    against me.
10 They have gaped at me with their
    mouths;
    they have struck me insolently on
    the cheek;
    they mass themselves together
    against me.
11 God gives me up to the ungodly,
    and casts me into the hands of the
    wicked.
12 I was at ease, and he broke me in
    two;
    he seized me by the neck and
    dashed me to pieces;
  he set me up as his target;
13   his archers surround me.
  He slashes open my kidneys, and
    shows no mercy;
    he pours out my gall on the
    ground.
14 He bursts upon me again and again;
    he rushes at me like a warrior.
15 I have sewed sackcloth upon my skin,
    and have laid my strength in the
    dust.

16 My face is red with weeping,
    and deep darkness is on my eyelids,
17 though there is no violence in my
    hands,
    and my prayer is pure.

18 'O earth, do not cover my blood;
    let my outcry find no resting-place.
19 Even now, in fact, my witness is in
    heaven,
    and he that vouches for me is on
    high.
20 My friends scorn me;
    my eye pours out tears to God,
21 that he would maintain the right of a
    mortal with God,
    as*b* one does for a neighbour.
22 For when a few years have come,
    I shall go the way from which I
    shall not return.

Job Prays for Relief

17 My spirit is broken, my days are
    extinct,
  the grave is ready for me.
2 Surely there are mockers around me,
    and my eye dwells on their
    provocation.

3 'Lay down a pledge for me with
    yourself;
    who is there that will give surety for
    me?
4 Since you have closed their minds to
    understanding,
    therefore you will not let them
    triumph.
5 Those who denounce friends for
    reward—
    the eyes of their children will fail.

6 'He has made me a byword of the
    peoples,
    and I am one before whom people
    spit.
7 My eye has grown dim from grief,
    and all my members are like a
    shadow.
8 The upright are appalled at this,

a Heb *you have*   *b* Syr Vg Tg: Heb *and*

and the innocent stir themselves up
   against the godless.
9 Yet the righteous hold to their way,
   and they that have clean hands
      grow stronger and stronger.
10 But you, come back now, all of you,
   and I shall not find a sensible
      person among you.
11 My days are past, my plans are
      broken off,
   the desires of my heart.
12 They make night into day;
   "The light", they say, "is near to the
      darkness." *a*
13 If I look for Sheol as my house,
   if I spread my couch in darkness,
14 if I say to the Pit, "You are my father",
   and to the worm, "My mother", or
      "My sister",
15 where then is my hope?
   Who will see my hope?
16 Will it go down to the bars of Sheol?
   Shall we descend together into the
      dust?'

Bildad Speaks: God Punishes the Wicked

18 Then Bildad the Shuhite answered:
   2 'How long will you hunt for
      words?
   Consider, and then we shall speak.
3 Why are we counted as cattle?
   Why are we stupid in your sight?
4 You who tear yourself in your
      anger—
   shall the earth be forsaken because
      of you,
   or the rock be removed out of its
      place?

5 'Surely the light of the wicked is put
      out,
   and the flame of their fire does not
      shine.
6 The light is dark in their tent,
   and the lamp above them is put
      out.
7 Their strong steps are shortened,
   and their own schemes throw them
      down.
8 For they are thrust into a net by their
      own feet,

and they walk into a pitfall.
9 A trap seizes them by the heel;
   a snare lays hold of them.
10 A rope is hid for them in the ground,
   a trap for them in the path.
11 Terrors frighten them on every side,
   and chase them at their heels.
12 Their strength is consumed by
      hunger, *b*
   and calamity is ready for their
      stumbling.
13 By disease their skin is consumed, *c*
   the firstborn of Death consumes
      their limbs.
14 They are torn from the tent in which
      they trusted,
   and are brought to the king of
      terrors.
15 In their tents nothing remains;
   sulphur is scattered upon their
      habitations.
16 Their roots dry up beneath,
   and their branches wither above.
17 Their memory perishes from the
      earth,
   and they have no name in the street.
18 They are thrust from light into
      darkness,
   and driven out of the world.
19 They have no offspring or descendant
      among their people,
   and no survivor where they used to
      live.
20 They of the west are appalled at their
      fate,
   and horror seizes those of the east.
21 Surely such are the dwellings of the
      ungodly,
   such is the place of those who do
      not know God.'

*Job Replies: I Know That My
Redeemer Lives*

19 Then Job answered:
   2 'How long will you torment me,
   and break me in pieces with words?
3 These ten times you have cast
      reproach upon me;
   are you not ashamed to wrong me?

a Meaning of Heb uncertain   *b* Or *Disaster is hungry
for them*   *c* Cn: Heb *It consumes the limbs of his skin*

4 And even if it is true that I have erred,
   my error remains with me.
5 If indeed you magnify yourselves
      against me,
   and make my humiliation an
      argument against me,
6 know then that God has put me in
      the wrong,
   and closed his net around me.
7 Even when I cry out, "Violence!" I am
      not answered;
   I call aloud, but there is no justice.
8 He has walled up my way so that I
      cannot pass,
   and he has set darkness upon my
      paths.
9 He has stripped my glory from me,
   and taken the crown from my head.
10 He breaks me down on every side,
      and I am gone,
   he has uprooted my hope like a
      tree.
11 He has kindled his wrath against me,
   and counts me as his adversary.
12 His troops come on together;
   they have thrown up siege-works[a]
      against me,
   and encamp around my tent.

13 'He has put my family far from me,
   and my acquaintances are wholly
      estranged from me.
14 My relatives and my close friends
      have failed me;
15   the guests in my house have
      forgotten me;
   my serving-girls count me as a
      stranger;
   I have become an alien in their
      eyes.
16 I call to my servant, but he gives me
      no answer;
   I must myself plead with him.
17 My breath is repulsive to my wife;
   I am loathsome to my own family.
18 Even young children despise me;
   when I rise, they talk against me.
19 All my intimate friends abhor me,
   and those whom I loved have
      turned against me.

20 My bones cling to my skin and to my
      flesh,
   and I have escaped by the skin of
      my teeth.
21 Have pity on me, have pity on me,
      O you my friends,
   for the hand of God has touched
      me!
22 Why do you, like God, pursue me,
   never satisfied with my flesh?

23 'O that my words were written down!
   O that they were inscribed in a
      book!
24 O that with an iron pen and with
      lead
   they were engraved on a rock for
      ever!
25 For I know that my Redeemer[b] lives,
   and that at the last he[c] will stand
      upon the earth;[d]
26 and after my skin has been thus
      destroyed,
   then in[e] my flesh I shall see God,[f]
27 whom I shall see on my side,[g]
   and my eyes shall behold, and not
      another.
   My heart faints within me!
28 If you say, "How we will persecute
      him!"
   and, "The root of the matter is
      found in him";
29 be afraid of the sword,
   for wrath brings the punishment of
      the sword,
   so that you may know there is a
      judgement.'

*Zophar Speaks: Wickedness Receives Just
Retribution*

20 Then Zophar the Naamathite answered:
2 'Pay attention! My thoughts urge me
      to answer,
   because of the agitation within me.
3 I hear censure that insults me,
   and a spirit beyond my
      understanding answers me.

a Cn: Heb *their way*   *b* Or *Vindicator*   *c* Or *that he
the Last*   *d* Heb *dust*   *e* Or *without*   *f* Meaning of
Heb of this verse uncertain   *g* Or *for myself*

4 Do you not know this from of old,
  ever since mortals were placed on
  earth,
5 that the exulting of the wicked is
  short,
  and the joy of the godless is but for
  a moment?
6 Even though they mount up high as
  the heavens,
  and their head reaches to the
  clouds,
7 they will perish for ever like their
  own dung;
  those who have seen them will say,
  "Where are they?"
8 They will fly away like a dream, and
  not be found;
  they will be chased away like a
  vision of the night.
9 The eye that saw them will see them
  no more,
  nor will their place behold them
  any longer.
10 Their children will seek the favour of
   the poor,
   and their hands will give back their
   wealth.
11 Their bodies, once full of youth,
   will lie down in the dust with
   them.

12 Though wickedness is sweet in their
   mouth,
   though they hide it under their
   tongues,
13 though they are loath to let it go,
   and hold it in their mouths,
14 yet their food is turned in their
   stomachs;
   it is the venom of asps within
   them.
15 They swallow down riches and vomit
   them up again;
   God casts them out of their bellies.
16 They will suck the poison of asps;
   the tongue of a viper will kill them.
17 They will not look on the rivers,
   the streams flowing with honey and
   curds.
18 They will give back the fruit of their
   toil,

and will not swallow it down;
from the profit of their trading
   they will get no enjoyment.
19 For they have crushed and
      abandoned the poor,
   they have seized a house that they
      did not build.

20 They knew no quiet in their bellies;
   in their greed they let nothing
      escape.
21 There was nothing left after they had
      eaten;
   therefore their prosperity will not
      endure.
22 In full sufficiency they will be in
      distress;
   all the force of misery will come
      upon them.
23 To fill their belly to the full
   God*a* will send his fierce anger into
      them,
   and rain it upon them as their
      food.*b*
24 They will flee from an iron weapon;
   a bronze arrow will strike them
      through.
25 It is drawn forth and comes out of
      their body,
   and the glittering point comes out
      of their gall;
   terrors come upon them.
26 Utter darkness is laid up for their
      treasures;
   a fire fanned by no one will devour
      them;
   what is left in their tent will be
      consumed.
27 The heavens will reveal their iniquity,
   and the earth will rise up against
      them.
28 The possessions of their house will be
      carried away,
   dragged off on the day of God's*c*
      wrath.
29 This is the portion of the wicked
      from God,
   the heritage decreed for them by
      God.'

a Heb *he*   b Cn: Meaning of Heb uncertain
c Heb *his*

*Job Replies: The Wicked Often
Go Unpunished*

21 Then Job answered:
2 'Listen carefully to my words,
and let this be your consolation.
3 Bear with me, and I will speak;
then after I have spoken, mock on.
4 As for me, is my complaint addressed
to mortals?
Why should I not be impatient?
5 Look at me, and be appalled,
and lay your hand upon your
mouth.
6 When I think of it I am dismayed,
and shuddering seizes my flesh.
7 Why do the wicked live on,
reach old age, and grow mighty in
power?
8 Their children are established in their
presence,
and their offspring before their
eyes.
9 Their houses are safe from fear,
and no rod of God is upon them.
10 Their bull breeds without fail;
their cow calves and never
miscarries.
11 They send out their little ones like a
flock,
and their children dance around.
12 They sing to the tambourine and the
lyre,
and rejoice to the sound of the
pipe.
13 They spend their days in prosperity,
and in peace they go down to
Sheol.
14 They say to God, "Leave us alone!
We do not desire to know your
ways.
15 What is the Almighty, *a* that we
should serve him?
And what profit do we get if we
pray to him?"
16 Is not their prosperity indeed their
own achievement?*b*
The plans of the wicked are
repugnant to me.

17 'How often is the lamp of the wicked
put out?

How often does calamity come
upon them?
How often does God*c* distribute
pains in his anger?
18 How often are they like straw before
the wind,
and like chaff that the storm carries
away?
19 You say, "God stores up their iniquity
for their children."
Let it be paid back to them, so that
they may know it.
20 Let their own eyes see their
destruction,
and let them drink of the wrath of
the Almighty.*a*
21 For what do they care for their
household after them,
when the number of their months
is cut off?
22 Will any teach God knowledge,
seeing that he judges those that are
on high?
23 One dies in full prosperity,
being wholly at ease and secure,
24 his loins full of milk
and the marrow of his bones moist.
25 Another dies in bitterness of soul,
never having tasted of good.
26 They lie down alike in the dust,
and the worms cover them.

27 'Oh, I know your thoughts,
and your schemes to wrong me.
28 For you say, "Where is the house of
the prince?
Where is the tent in which the
wicked lived?"
29 Have you not asked those who travel
the roads,
and do you not accept their
testimony,
30 that the wicked are spared on the day
of calamity,
and are rescued on the day of
wrath?
31 Who declares their way to their face,
and who repays them for what they
have done?

a Traditional rendering of Heb *Shaddai*   *b* Heb *in
their hand*   *c* Heb *he*

32 When they are carried to the grave,
    a watch is kept over their tomb.
33 The clods of the valley are sweet to
    them;
    everyone will follow after,
    and those who went before are
    innumerable.
34 How then will you comfort me with
    empty nothings?
    There is nothing left of your
    answers but falsehood.'

Eliphaz Speaks: Job's Wickedness Is Great

22 Then Eliphaz the Temanite an-
    swered:
2 'Can a mortal be of use to God?
    Can even the wisest be of service to
    him?
3 Is it any pleasure to the Almighty*a* if
    you are righteous,
    or is it gain to him if you make
    your ways blameless?
4 Is it for your piety that he reproves
    you,
    and enters into judgement with
    you?
5 Is not your wickedness great?
    There is no end to your iniquities.
6 For you have exacted pledges from
    your family for no reason,
    and stripped the naked of their
    clothing.
7 You have given no water to the weary
    to drink,
    and you have withheld bread from
    the hungry.
8 The powerful possess the land,
    and the favoured live in it.
9 You have sent widows away empty-
    handed,
    and the arms of the orphans you
    have crushed.*b*
10 Therefore snares are around you,
    and sudden terror overwhelms you,
11 or darkness so that you cannot see;
    a flood of water covers you.

12 'Is not God high in the heavens?
    See the highest stars, how lofty they
    are!

13 Therefore you say, "What does God
    know?
    Can he judge through the deep
    darkness?
14 Thick clouds enwrap him, so that he
    does not see,
    and he walks on the dome of
    heaven."
15 Will you keep to the old way
    that the wicked have trod?
16 They were snatched away before their
    time;
    their foundation was washed away
    by a flood.
17 They said to God, "Leave us alone",
    and "What can the Almighty*a* do to
    us?"*c*
18 Yet he filled their houses with good
    things—
    but the plans of the wicked are
    repugnant to me.
19 The righteous see it and are glad;
    the innocent laugh them to scorn,
20 saying, "Surely our adversaries are cut
    off,
    and what they left, the fire has
    consumed."

21 'Agree with God,*d* and be at peace;
    in this way good will come to you.
22 Receive instruction from his mouth,
    and lay up his words in your heart.
23 If you return to the Almighty,*a* you
    will be restored,
    if you remove unrighteousness
    from your tents,
24 if you treat gold like dust,
    and gold of Ophir like the stones of
    the torrent-bed,
25 and if the Almighty*a* is your gold
    and your precious silver,
26 then you will delight in the
    Almighty,*a*
    and lift up your face to God.
27 You will pray to him, and he will
    hear you,
    and you will pay your vows.

a Traditional rendering of Heb *Shaddai*   *b* Gk Syr Tg
Vg: Heb *were crushed*   *c* Gk Syr: Heb *them*
d Heb *him*

28 You will decide on a matter, and it
        will be established for you,
    and light will shine on your ways.
29 When others are humiliated, you say
        it is pride;
    for he saves the humble.
30 He will deliver even those who are
        guilty;
    they will escape because of the
        cleanness of your hands.' *a*

Job Replies: My Complaint Is Bitter

23 Then Job answered:
        2 'Today also my complaint is
        bitter; *b*
    his *c* hand is heavy despite my
        groaning.
3 O that I knew where I might find
        him,
    that I might come even to his
        dwelling!
4 I would lay my case before him,
    and fill my mouth with arguments.
5 I would learn what he would answer
        me,
    and understand what he would say
        to me.
6 Would he contend with me in the
        greatness of his power?
    No; but he would give heed to me.
7 There an upright person could reason
        with him,
    and I should be acquitted for ever
        by my judge.

8 'If I go forward, he is not there;
    or backward, I cannot perceive him;
9 on the left he hides, and I cannot
        behold him;
    I turn *d* to the right, but I cannot see
        him.
10 But he knows the way that I take;
    when he has tested me, I shall
        come out like gold.
11 My foot has held fast to his steps;
    I have kept his way and have not
        turned aside.
12 I have not departed from the
        commandment of his lips;
    I have treasured in *e* my bosom the
        words of his mouth.

13 But he stands alone and who can
        dissuade him?
    What he desires, that he does.
14 For he will complete what he
        appoints for me;
    and many such things are in his
        mind.
15 Therefore I am terrified at his
        presence;
    when I consider, I am in dread of
        him.
16 God has made my heart faint;
    the Almighty *f* has terrified me;
17 If only I could vanish in darkness,
    and thick darkness would cover my
        face! *g*

Job Complains of Violence on the Earth

24 'Why are times not kept by the
        Almighty, *f*
    and why do those who know him
        never see his days?
2 The wicked *h* remove landmarks;
    they seize flocks and pasture
        them.
3 They drive away the donkey of the
        orphan;
    they take the widow's ox for a
        pledge.
4 They thrust the needy off the road;
    the poor of the earth all hide
        themselves.
5 Like wild asses in the desert
        they go out to their toil,
    scavenging in the waste-land
        food for their young.
6 They reap in a field not their own
    and they glean in the vineyard of
        the wicked.
7 They lie all night naked, without
        clothing,
    and have no covering in the cold.
8 They are wet with the rain of the
        mountains,
    and cling to the rock for want of
        shelter.

a Meaning of Heb uncertain   *b* Syr Vg Tg: Heb
rebellious   *c* Gk Syr: Heb *my*   *d* Syr Vg: Heb *he turns*
e Gk Vg: Heb *from*   *f* Traditional rendering of Heb
Shaddai   *g* Or *But I am not destroyed by the darkness; he
has concealed the thick darkness from me*   *h* Gk: Heb
they

9 'There are those who snatch the
   orphan child from the breast,
   and take as a pledge the infant of
   the poor.
10 They go about naked, without
   clothing;
   though hungry, they carry the
   sheaves;
11 between their terraces[a] they press out
   oil;
   they tread the wine presses, but
   suffer thirst.
12 From the city the dying groan,
   and the throat of the wounded cries
   for help;
   yet God pays no attention to their
   prayer.

13 'There are those who rebel against the
   light,
   who are not acquainted with its
   ways,
   and do not stay in its paths.
14 The murderer rises at dusk
   to kill the poor and needy,
   and in the night is like a thief.
15 The eye of the adulterer also waits for
   the twilight,
   saying, "No eye will see me";
   and he disguises his face.
16 In the dark they dig through houses;
   by day they shut themselves up;
   they do not know the light.
17 For deep darkness is morning to all
   of them;
   for they are friends with the terrors
   of deep darkness.

18 'Swift are they on the face of the
   waters;
   their portion in the land is cursed;
   no treader turns towards their
   vineyards.
19 Drought and heat snatch away the
   snow-waters;
   so does Sheol those who have
   sinned.
20 The womb forgets them;
   the worm finds them sweet;
   they are no longer remembered;
   so wickedness is broken like a tree.

21 'They harm[b] the childless woman,
   and do no good to the widow.
22 Yet God[c] prolongs the life of the
   mighty by his power;
   they rise up when they despair of
   life.
23 He gives them security, and they are
   supported;
   his eyes are upon their ways.
24 They are exalted a little while, and
   then are gone;
   they wither and fade like the
   mallow;[d]
   they are cut off like the heads of
   grain.
25 If it is not so, who will prove me a
   liar,
   and show that there is nothing in
   what I say?'

*Bildad Speaks: How Can a Mortal Be
Righteous Before God?*

25 Then Bildad the Shuhite answered:
   2 'Dominion and fear are with
   God;[e]
   he makes peace in his high heaven.
3 Is there any number to his armies?
   Upon whom does his light not
   arise?
4 How then can a mortal be righteous
   before God?
   How can one born of woman be
   pure?
5 If even the moon is not bright
   and the stars are not pure in his
   sight,
6 how much less a mortal, who is a
   maggot,
   and a human being, who is a
   worm!'

*Job Replies: God's Majesty
Is Unsearchable*

26 Then Job answered:
   2 'How you have helped one who
   has no power!
   How you have assisted the arm that
   has no strength!

a Meaning of Heb uncertain   b Gk Tg: Heb *feed on* or
associate with   c Heb *he*   d Gk: Heb *like all others*
e Heb *him*

3 How you have counselled one who
      has no wisdom,
      and given much good advice!
4 With whose help have you uttered
      words,
      and whose spirit has come forth
      from you?
5 The shades below tremble,
      the waters and their inhabitants.
6 Sheol is naked before God,
      and Abaddon has no covering.
7 He stretches out Zaphon[a] over the
      void,
      and hangs the earth upon nothing.
8 He binds up the waters in his thick
      clouds,
      and the cloud is not torn open by
      them.
9 He covers the face of the full moon,
      and spreads over it his cloud.
10 He has described a circle on the face
      of the waters,
      at the boundary between light and
      darkness.
11 The pillars of heaven tremble,
      and are astounded at his rebuke.
12 By his power he stilled the Sea;
      by his understanding he struck
      down Rahab.
13 By his wind the heavens were made
      fair;
      his hand pierced the fleeing
      serpent.
14 These are indeed but the outskirts of
      his ways;
      and how small a whisper do we
      hear of him!
      But the thunder of his power who
      can understand?'

Job Maintains His Integrity

27 Job again took up his discourse
      and said:
2 'As God lives, who has taken away my
      right,
      and the Almighty,[b] who has made
      my soul bitter,
3 as long as my breath is in me
      and the spirit of God is in my
      nostrils,
4 my lips will not speak falsehood,

and my tongue will not utter deceit.
5 Far be it from me to say that you are
      right;
      until I die I will not put away my
      integrity from me.
6 I hold fast my righteousness, and will
      not let it go;
      my heart does not reproach me for
      any of my days.

7 'May my enemy be like the wicked,
      and may my opponent be like the
      unrighteous.
8 For what is the hope of the godless
      when God cuts them off,
      when God takes away their lives?
9 Will God hear their cry
      when trouble comes upon them?
10 Will they take delight in the
      Almighty?[b]
      Will they call upon God at all
      times?
11 I will teach you concerning the hand
      of God;
      that which is with the Almighty[b] I
      will not conceal.
12 All of you have seen it yourselves;
      why then have you become
      altogether vain?

13 'This is the portion of the wicked
      with God,
      and the heritage that oppressors
      receive from the Almighty:[b]
14 If their children are multiplied, it is
      for the sword;
      and their offspring have not
      enough to eat.
15 Those who survive them the
      pestilence buries,
      and their widows make no
      lamentation.
16 Though they heap up silver like
      dust,
      and pile up clothing like clay—
17 they may pile it up, but the just will
      wear it,
      and the innocent will divide the
      silver.

a Or *the north*   b Traditional rendering of Heb
Shaddai

18 They build their houses like nests,
     like booths made by sentinels of
       the vineyard.
19 They go to bed with wealth, but will
     do so no more;
   they open their eyes, and it is gone.
20 Terrors overtake them like a flood;
     in the night a whirlwind carries
       them off.
21 The east wind lifts them up and they
     are gone;
   it sweeps them out of their place.
22 It*a* hurls at them without pity;
     they flee from its*b* power in
       headlong flight.
23 It*a* claps its*b* hands at them,
     and hisses at them from its*b* place.

Interlude: Where Wisdom Is Found

28 'Surely there is a mine for silver,
       and a place for gold to be
       refined.
2 Iron is taken out of the earth,
     and copper is smelted from ore.
3 Miners put*c* an end to darkness,
     and search out to the farthest
       bound
       the ore in gloom and deep
         darkness.
4 They open shafts in a valley away
     from human habitation;
   they are forgotten by travellers,
   they sway suspended, remote from
     people.
5 As for the earth, out of it comes
     bread;
   but underneath it is turned up as by
     fire.
6 Its stones are the place of sapphires,*d*
     and its dust contains gold.

7 'That path no bird of prey knows,
     and the falcon's eye has not seen it.
8 The proud wild animals have not
     trodden it;
   the lion has not passed over it.

9 'They put their hand to the flinty
     rock,
   and overturn mountains by the
     roots.

10 They cut out channels in the rocks,
     and their eyes see every precious
       thing.
11 The sources of the rivers they probe;*e*
     hidden things they bring to light.

12 'But where shall wisdom be found?
     And where is the place of
       understanding?
13 Mortals do not know the way to it,*f*
     and it is not found in the land of
       the living.
14 The deep says, "It is not in me",
     and the sea says, "It is not with
       me."
15 It cannot be bought for gold,
     and silver cannot be weighed out as
       its price.
16 It cannot be valued in the gold of
       Ophir,
     in precious onyx or sapphire.*d*
17 Gold and glass cannot equal it,
     nor can it be exchanged for jewels
       of fine gold.
18 No mention shall be made of coral or
       of crystal;
     the price of wisdom is above pearls.
19 The chrysolite of Ethiopia*g* cannot
       compare with it,
     nor can it be valued in pure gold.

20 'Where then does wisdom come
       from?
     And where is the place of
       understanding?
21 It is hidden from the eyes of all
       living,
     and concealed from the birds of the
       air.
22 Abaddon and Death say,
     "We have heard a rumour of it with
       our ears."

23 'God understands the way to it,
     and he knows its place.
24 For he looks to the ends of the earth,
     and sees everything under the
       heavens.

a Or *He* (that is God)   *b* Or *his*   *c* Heb *He puts*
d Or *lapis lazuli*   *e* Gk Vg: Heb *bind*   *f* Gk: Heb *its
price*   *g* Or *Nubia*; Heb *Cush*

25 When he gave to the wind its weight,
      and apportioned out the waters by
          measure;
26 when he made a decree for the rain,
      and a way for the thunderbolt;
27 then he saw it and declared it;
      he established it, and searched it
          out.
28 And he said to humankind,
      "Truly, the fear of the Lord, that is
          wisdom;
      and to depart from evil is
          understanding." '

Job Finishes His Defence

29 Job again took up his discourse
      and said:
2 'O that I were as in the months of
      old,
      as in the days when God watched
          over me;
3 when his lamp shone over my head,
      and by his light I walked through
          darkness;
4 when I was in my prime,
      when the friendship of God was
          upon my tent;
5 when the Almighty[a] was still with
      me,
      when my children were around me;
6 when my steps were washed with
      milk,
      and the rock poured out for me
          streams of oil!
7 When I went out to the gate of the
      city,
      when I took my seat in the square,
8 the young men saw me and
          withdrew,
      and the aged rose up and stood;
9 the nobles refrained from talking,
      and laid their hands on their
          mouths;
10 the voices of princes were hushed,
      and their tongues stuck to the roof
          of their mouths.
11 When the ear heard, it commended
      me,
      and when the eye saw, it approved;
12 because I delivered the poor who
      cried,

and the orphan who had no helper.
13 The blessing of the wretched came
      upon me,
      and I caused the widow's heart to
          sing for joy.
14 I put on righteousness, and it clothed
      me;
      my justice was like a robe and a
          turban.
15 I was eyes to the blind,
      and feet to the lame.
16 I was a father to the needy,
      and I championed the cause of the
          stranger.
17 I broke the fangs of the unrighteous,
      and made them drop their prey
          from their teeth.
18 Then I thought, "I shall die in my
      nest,
      and I shall multiply my days like
          the phoenix;[b]
19 my roots spread out to the waters,
      with the dew all night on my
          branches;
20 my glory was fresh with me,
      and my bow ever new in my hand."

21 'They listened to me, and waited,
      and kept silence for my counsel.
22 After I spoke they did not speak
          again,
      and my word dropped upon them
          like dew.[c]
23 They waited for me as for the rain;
      they opened their mouths as for the
          spring rain.
24 I smiled on them when they had no
          confidence;
      and the light of my countenance
          they did not extinguish.[d]
25 I chose their way, and sat as chief,
      and I lived like a king among his
          troops,
      like one who comforts mourners.

30 'But now they make sport of me,
      those who are younger than I,
      whose fathers I would have disdained
          to set with the dogs of my flock.

---

a Traditional rendering of Heb *Shaddai*   b Or *like sand*
c Heb lacks *like dew*   d Meaning of Heb uncertain

² What could I gain from the strength
   of their hands?
   All their vigour is gone.
³ Through want and hard hunger
   they gnaw the dry and desolate
   ground,
⁴ they pick mallow and the leaves of
   bushes,
   and to warm themselves the roots
   of broom.
⁵ They are driven out from society;
   people shout after them as after a
   thief.
⁶ In the gullies of wadis they must live,
   in holes in the ground, and in the
   rocks.
⁷ Among the bushes they bray;
   under the nettles they huddle
   together.
⁸ A senseless, disreputable brood,
   they have been whipped out of the
   land.

⁹ 'And now they mock me in song;
   I am a byword to them.
¹⁰ They abhor me, they keep aloof from
   me;
   they do not hesitate to spit at the
   sight of me.
¹¹ Because God has loosed my
   bowstring and humbled me,
   they have cast off restraint in my
   presence.
¹² On my right hand the rabble rise up;
   they send me sprawling,
   and build roads for my ruin.
¹³ They break up my path,
   they promote my calamity;
   no one restrains^a them.
¹⁴ As through a wide breach they come;
   amid the crash they roll on.
¹⁵ Terrors are turned upon me;
   my honour is pursued as by the
   wind,
   and my prosperity has passed away
   like a cloud.

¹⁶ 'And now my soul is poured out
   within me;
   days of affliction have taken hold
   of me.

¹⁷ The night racks my bones,
   and the pain that gnaws me takes
   no rest.
¹⁸ With violence he seizes my garment;^b
   he grasps me by^c the collar of my
   tunic.
¹⁹ He has cast me into the mire,
   and I have become like dust and
   ashes.
²⁰ I cry to you and you do not answer
   me;
   I stand, and you merely look at me.
²¹ You have turned cruel to me;
   with the might of your hand you
   persecute me.
²² You lift me up on the wind, you
   make me ride on it,
   and you toss me about in the roar
   of the storm.
²³ I know that you will bring me to
   death,
   and to the house appointed for all
   living.

²⁴ 'Surely one does not turn against the
   needy,^d
   when in disaster they cry for help.^e
²⁵ Did I not weep for those whose day
   was hard?
   Was not my soul grieved for the
   poor?
²⁶ But when I looked for good, evil came;
   and when I waited for light,
   darkness came.
²⁷ My inward parts are in turmoil, and
   are never still;
   days of affliction come to meet me.
²⁸ I go about in sunless gloom;
   I stand up in the assembly and cry
   for help.
²⁹ I am a brother of jackals,
   and a companion of ostriches.
³⁰ My skin turns black and falls from
   me,
   and my bones burn with heat.
³¹ My lyre is turned to mourning,
   and my pipe to the voice of those
   who weep.

a Cn: Heb *helps*   *b* Gk: Heb *my garment is disfigured*
c Heb *like*   *d* Heb *ruin*   *e* Cn: Meaning of Heb
uncertain

31

'I have made a covenant with my eyes;
how then could I look upon a virgin?

2 What would be my portion from God above,
and my heritage from the Almighty[a] on high?

3 Does not calamity befall the unrighteous,
and disaster the workers of iniquity?

4 Does he not see my ways,
and number all my steps?

5 'If I have walked with falsehood,
and my foot has hurried to deceit—

6 let me be weighed in a just balance,
and let God know my integrity!—

7 if my step has turned aside from the way,
and my heart has followed my eyes,
and if any spot has clung to my hands;

8 then let me sow, and another eat;
and let what grows for me be rooted out.

9 'If my heart has been enticed by a woman,
and I have lain in wait at my neighbour's door;

10 then let my wife grind for another,
and let other men kneel over her.

11 For that would be a heinous crime;
that would be a criminal offence;

12 for that would be a fire consuming down to Abaddon,
and it would burn to the root all my harvest.

13 'If I have rejected the cause of my male or female slaves,
when they brought a complaint against me;

14 what then shall I do when God rises up?
When he makes inquiry, what shall I answer him?

15 Did not he who made me in the womb make them?
And did not one fashion us in the womb?

16 'If I have withheld anything that the poor desired,
or have caused the eyes of the widow to fail,

17 or have eaten my morsel alone,
and the orphan has not eaten from it—

18 for from my youth I reared the orphan[b] like a father,
and from my mother's womb I guided the widow[c]—

19 if I have seen anyone perish for lack of clothing,
or a poor person without covering,

20 whose loins have not blessed me,
and who was not warmed with the fleece of my sheep;

21 if I have raised my hand against the orphan,
because I saw I had supporters at the gate;

22 then let my shoulder blade fall from my shoulder,
and let my arm be broken from its socket.

23 For I was in terror of calamity from God,
and I could not have faced his majesty.

24 'If I have made gold my trust,
or called fine gold my confidence;

25 if I have rejoiced because my wealth was great,
or because my hand had acquired much;

26 if I have looked at the sun[d] when it shone,
or the moon moving in splendour,

27 and my heart has been secretly enticed,
and my mouth has kissed my hand;

28 this also would be an iniquity to be punished by the judges,
for I should have been false to God above.

---

a Traditional rendering of Heb *Shaddai*   b Heb *him*
c Heb *her*   d Heb *the light*

29 'If I have rejoiced at the ruin of those
        who hated me,
        or exulted when evil overtook
            them—
30 I have not let my mouth sin
        by asking for their lives with a
            curse—
31 if those of my tent ever said,
        "O that we might be sated with his
            flesh!" *a*—
32 the stranger has not lodged in the
        street;
        I have opened my doors to the
            traveller—
33 if I have concealed my transgressions
        as others do, *b*
        by hiding my iniquity in my
            bosom,
34 because I stood in great fear of the
        multitude,
        and the contempt of families
            terrified me,
        so that I kept silence, and did not
            go out of doors—
35 O that I had one to hear me!
        (Here is my signature! Let the
            Almighty*c* answer me!)
        O that I had the indictment written
            by my adversary!
36 Surely I would carry it on my
        shoulder;
        I would bind it on me like a crown;
37 I would give him an account of all
        my steps;
        like a prince I would approach him.

38 'If my land has cried out against me,
        and its furrows have wept together;
39 if I have eaten its yield without
        payment,
        and caused the death of its owners;
40 let thorns grow instead of wheat,
        and foul weeds instead of barley.'

The words of Job are ended.

Elihu Rebukes Job's Friends

32 So these three men ceased to answer Job, because he was righteous
in his own eyes. 2 Then Elihu son of
Barachel the Buzite, of the family of Ram,

became angry. He was angry at Job because
he justified himself rather than God; 3 he
was angry also at Job's three friends because they had found no answer, though
they had declared Job to be in the wrong. *d*
4 Now Elihu had waited to speak to Job,
because they were older than he. 5 But when
Elihu saw that there was no answer in the
mouths of these three men, he became angry.
    6 Elihu son of Barachel the Buzite an-
swered:

'I am young in years,
    and you are aged;
therefore I was timid and afraid
    to declare my opinion to you.
7 I said, "Let days speak,
    and many years teach wisdom."
8 But truly it is the spirit in a mortal,
    the breath of the Almighty,*c* that
        makes for understanding.
9 It is not the old*e* that are wise,
    nor the aged that understand what
        is right.
10 Therefore I say, "Listen to me;
    let me also declare my opinion."

11 'See, I waited for your words,
    I listened for your wise sayings,
    while you searched out what to say.
12 I gave you my attention,
    but there was in fact no one that
        confuted Job,
    no one among you that answered
        his words.
13 Yet do not say, "We have found
        wisdom;
    God may vanquish him, not a
        human."
14 He has not directed his words against
        me,
    and I will not answer him with
        your speeches.

15 'They are dismayed, they answer no
        more;
    they have not a word to say.

a Meaning of Heb uncertain   *b* Or *as Adam did*
c Traditional rendering of Heb *Shaddai*   *d* Another
ancient tradition reads *answer, and had put God in the
wrong*   *e* Gk Syr Vg: Heb *many*

¹⁶ And am I to wait, because they do
    not speak,
  because they stand there, and
    answer no more?
¹⁷ I also will give my answer;
  I also will declare my opinion.
¹⁸ For I am full of words;
  the spirit within me constrains me.
¹⁹ My heart is indeed like wine that has
    no vent;
  like new wineskins, it is ready to
    burst.
²⁰ I must speak, so that I may find
    relief;
  I must open my lips and answer.
²¹ I will not show partiality to any
    person
  or use flattery towards anyone.
²² For I do not know how to flatter—
  or my Maker would soon put an
    end to me!

Elihu Rebukes Job

33 ¹ 'But now, hear my speech,
  O Job,
  and listen to all my words.
² See, I open my mouth;
  the tongue in my mouth speaks.
³ My words declare the uprightness of
    my heart,
  and what my lips know they speak
    sincerely.
⁴ The spirit of God has made me,
  and the breath of the Almighty^a
    gives me life.
⁵ Answer me, if you can;
  set your words in order before me;
  take your stand.
⁶ See, before God I am as you are;
  I too was formed from a piece of
    clay.
⁷ No fear of me need terrify you;
  my pressure will not be heavy on
    you.

⁸ 'Surely, you have spoken in my
    hearing,
  and I have heard the sound of your
    words.
⁹ You say, "I am clean, without
    transgression;

I am pure, and there is no iniquity
    in me.
¹⁰ Look, he finds occasions against me,
  he counts me as his enemy;
¹¹ he puts my feet in the stocks,
  and watches all my paths."

¹² 'But in this you are not right. I will
    answer you:
  God is greater than any mortal.
¹³ Why do you contend against him,
  saying, "He will answer none of
    my^b words"?
¹⁴ For God speaks in one way,
  and in two, though people do not
    perceive it.
¹⁵ In a dream, in a vision of the night,
  when deep sleep falls on mortals,
  while they slumber on their beds,
¹⁶ then he opens their ears,
  and terrifies them with warnings,
¹⁷ that he may turn them aside from
    their deeds,
  and keep them from pride,
¹⁸ to spare their souls from the Pit,
  their lives from traversing the
    River.
¹⁹ They are also chastened with pain
    upon their beds,
  and with continual strife in their
    bones,
²⁰ so that their lives loathe bread,
  and their appetites dainty food.
²¹ Their flesh is so wasted away that it
    cannot be seen;
  and their bones, once invisible,
    now stick out.
²² Their souls draw near the Pit,
  and their lives to those who bring
    death.
²³ Then, if there should be for one of
    them an angel,
  a mediator, one of a thousand,
  one who declares a person upright,
²⁴ and he is gracious to that person, and
    says,
  "Deliver him from going down into
    the Pit;
  I have found a ransom;

a Traditional rendering of Heb *Shaddai*   *b* Compare
Gk: Heb *his*

25 let his flesh become fresh with youth;
    let him return to the days of his
      youthful vigour";
26 then he prays to God, and is accepted
      by him,
    he comes into his presence with
      joy,
    and God*a* repays him for his
      righteousness.
27   That person sings to others and
      says,
    "I sinned, and perverted what was
      right,
    and it was not paid back to me.
28 He has redeemed my soul from going
      down to the Pit,
    and my life shall see the light."

29 'God indeed does all these things,
    twice, three times, with mortals,
30 to bring back their souls from the Pit,
    so that they may see the light of
      life.*b*
31 Pay heed, Job, listen to me;
    be silent, and I will speak.
32 If you have anything to say, answer
      me;
    speak, for I desire to justify you.
33 If not, listen to me;
    be silent, and I will teach you
      wisdom.'

Elihu Proclaims God's Justice

34 Then Elihu continued and said:
  2 'Hear my words, you wise men,
    and give ear to me, you who know;
 3 for the ear tests words
    as the palate tastes food.
 4 Let us choose what is right;
    let us determine among ourselves
      what is good.
 5 For Job has said, "I am innocent,
    and God has taken away my right;
 6 in spite of being right I am counted a
      liar;
    my wound is incurable, though I
      am without transgression."
 7 Who is there like Job,
    who drinks up scoffing like water,
 8 who goes in company with evildoers
    and walks with the wicked?

 9 For he has said, "It profits one nothing
    to take delight in God."

10 'Therefore, hear me, you who have
      sense,
    far be it from God that he should
      do wickedness,
    and from the Almighty*c* that he
      should do wrong.
11 For according to their deeds he will
      repay them,
    and according to their ways he will
      make it befall them.
12 Of a truth, God will not do wickedly,
    and the Almighty*c* will not pervert
      justice.
13 Who gave him charge over the earth
    and who laid on him*d* the whole
      world?
14 If he should take back his spirit*e* to
      himself,
    and gather to himself his breath,
15 all flesh would perish together,
    and all mortals return to dust.

16 'If you have understanding, hear this;
    listen to what I say.
17 Shall one who hates justice govern?
    Will you condemn one who is
      righteous and mighty,
18 who says to a king, "You scoundrel!"
    and to princes, "You wicked men!";
19 who shows no partiality to nobles,
    nor regards the rich more than the
      poor,
    for they are all the work of his
      hands?
20 In a moment they die;
    at midnight the people are shaken
      and pass away,
    and the mighty are taken away by
      no human hand.

21 'For his eyes are upon the ways of
      mortals,
    and he sees all their steps.
22 There is no gloom or deep darkness
    where evildoers may hide
      themselves.

a Heb *he*   *b* Syr: Heb *to be lighted with the light of life*
c Traditional rendering of Heb *Shaddai*   *d* Heb lacks
on him   *e* Heb *his heart his spirit*

23 For he has not appointed a time*a* for
    anyone
        to go before God in judgement.
24 He shatters the mighty without
    investigation,
        and sets others in their place.
25 Thus, knowing their works,
        he overturns them in the night, and
        they are crushed.
26 He strikes them for their wickedness
        while others look on,
27 because they turned aside from
    following him,
        and had no regard for any of his
        ways,
28 so that they caused the cry of the
    poor to come to him,
        and he heard the cry of the
        afflicted—
29 When he is quiet, who can condemn?
        When he hides his face, who can
        behold him,
        whether it be a nation or an
        individual?—
30 so that the godless should not reign,
        or those who ensnare the people.

31 'For has anyone said to God,
        "I have endured punishment; I will
        not offend any more;
32 teach me what I do not see;
        if I have done iniquity, I will do it
        no more"?
33 Will he then pay back to suit you,
        because you reject it?
    For you must choose, and not I;
        therefore declare what you know.*b*
34 Those who have sense will say to me,
        and the wise who hear me will say,
35 "Job speaks without knowledge,
        his words are without insight."
36 Would that Job were tried to the
    limit,
        because his answers are those of the
        wicked.
37 For he adds rebellion to his sin;
        he claps his hands among us,
        and multiplies his words against
        God.'

Elihu Condemns Self-Righteousness

35 Elihu continued and said:
    2 'Do you think this to be just?
    You say, "I am in the right before
        God."
3 If you ask, "What advantage have I?
        How am I better off than if I had
        sinned?"
4 I will answer you
        and your friends with you.
5 Look at the heavens and see;
        observe the clouds, which are
        higher than you.
6 If you have sinned, what do you
        accomplish against him?
    And if your transgressions are
        multiplied, what do you do to
        him?
7 If you are righteous, what do you give
        to him;
        or what does he receive from your
        hand?
8 Your wickedness affects others like
    you,
        and your righteousness, other
        human beings.

9 'Because of the multitude of
        oppressions people cry out;
        they call for help because of the
        arm of the mighty.
10 But no one says, "Where is God my
    Maker,
        who gives strength in the night,
11 who teaches us more than the
        animals of the earth,
        and makes us wiser than the birds
        of the air?"
12 There they cry out, but he does not
    answer,
        because of the pride of evildoers.
13 Surely God does not hear an empty
    cry,
        nor does the Almighty*c* regard it.
14 How much less when you say that
        you do not see him,
        that the case is before him, and you
        are waiting for him!

a Cn: Heb *yet*   *b* Meaning of Heb of verses 29-33
uncertain   *c* Traditional rendering of Heb *Shaddai*

15 And now, because his anger does not
  punish,
  and he does not greatly heed
  transgression,[a]
16 Job opens his mouth in empty talk,
  he multiplies words without
  knowledge.'

Elihu Exalts God's Goodness

36 Elihu continued and said:
  2 'Bear with me a little, and I will
  show you,
  for I have yet something to say on
  God's behalf.
3 I will bring my knowledge from far
  away,
  and ascribe righteousness to my
  Maker.
4 For truly my words are not false;
  one who is perfect in knowledge is
  with you.

5 'Surely God is mighty and does not
  despise any;
  he is mighty in strength of
  understanding.
6 He does not keep the wicked alive,
  but gives the afflicted their right.
7 He does not withdraw his eyes from
  the righteous,
  but with kings on the throne
  he sets them for ever, and they are
  exalted.
8 And if they are bound in fetters
  and caught in the cords of
  affliction,
9 then he declares to them their work
  and their transgressions, that they
  are behaving arrogantly.
10 He opens their ears to instruction,
  and commands that they return
  from iniquity.
11 If they listen, and serve him,
  they complete their days in
  prosperity,
  and their years in pleasantness.
12 But if they do not listen, they shall
  perish by the sword,
  and die without knowledge.

13 'The godless in heart cherish anger;
  they do not cry for help when he
  binds them.
14 They die in their youth,
  and their life ends in shame.[b]
15 He delivers the afflicted by their
  affliction,
  and opens their ear by adversity.
16 He also allured you out of distress
  into a broad place where there was
  no constraint,
  and what was set on your table was
  full of fatness.

17 'But you are obsessed with the case of
  the wicked;
  judgement and justice seize you.
18 Beware that wrath does not entice
  you into scoffing,
  and do not let the greatness of the
  ransom turn you aside.
19 Will your cry avail to keep you from
  distress,
  or will all the force of your strength?
20 Do not long for the night,
  when peoples are cut off in their
  place.
21 Beware! Do not turn to iniquity;
  because of that you have been tried
  by affliction.
22 See, God is exalted in his power;
  who is a teacher like him?
23 Who has prescribed for him his way,
  or who can say, "You have done
  wrong"?

Elihu Proclaims God's Majesty

24 'Remember to extol his work,
  of which mortals have sung.
25 All people have looked on it;
  everyone watches it from far away.
26 Surely God is great, and we do not
  know him;
  the number of his years is
  unsearchable.
27 For he draws up the drops of water;
  he distils[c] his mist in rain,
28 which the skies pour down
  and drop upon mortals abundantly.

a Theodotion Symmachus Compare Vg: Meaning of
Heb uncertain   b Heb ends among the temple prostitutes
c Cn: Heb they distil

29 Can anyone understand the
     spreading of the clouds,
   the thunderings of his pavilion?
30 See, he scatters his lightning around
     him
   and covers the roots of the sea.
31 For by these he governs peoples;
   he gives food in abundance.
32 He covers his hands with the
     lightning,
   and commands it to strike the
     mark.
33 Its crashing*a* tells about him;
   he is jealous*a* with anger against
     iniquity.

37 'At this also my heart trembles,
      and leaps out of its place.
2 Listen, listen to the thunder of his
     voice
   and the rumbling that comes from
     his mouth.
3 Under the whole heaven he lets it
     loose,
   and his lightning to the corners of
     the earth.
4 After it his voice roars;
   he thunders with his majestic voice
   and he does not restrain the
     lightnings*b* when his voice is
     heard.
5 God thunders wondrously with his
     voice;
   he does great things that we cannot
     comprehend.
6 For to the snow he says, "Fall on the
     earth";
   and the shower of rain, his heavy
     shower of rain,
7 serves as a sign on everyone's hand,
   so that all whom he has made may
     know it.*c*
8 Then the animals go into their lairs
   and remain in their dens.
9 From its chamber comes the
     whirlwind,
   and cold from the scattering winds.
10 By the breath of God ice is given,
   and the broad waters are frozen
     fast.

11 He loads the thick cloud with
     moisture;
   the clouds scatter his lightning.
12 They turn round and round by his
     guidance,
   to accomplish all that he
     commands them
   on the face of the habitable world.
13 Whether for correction, or for his
     land,
   or for love, he causes it to happen.

14 'Hear this, O Job;
   stop and consider the wondrous
     works of God.
15 Do you know how God lays his
     command upon them,
   and causes the lightning of his
     cloud to shine?
16 Do you know the balancings of the
     clouds,
   the wondrous works of the one
     whose knowledge is perfect,
17 you whose garments are hot
   when the earth is still because of
     the south wind?
18 Can you, like him, spread out the
     skies,
   unyielding as a cast mirror?
19 Teach us what we shall say to him;
   we cannot draw up our case
     because of darkness.
20 Should he be told that I want to
     speak?
   Did anyone ever wish to be
     swallowed up?
21 Now, no one can look on the light
   when it is bright in the skies,
   when the wind has passed and
     cleared them.
22 Out of the north comes golden
     splendour;
   around God is awesome majesty.
23 The Almighty*d*—we cannot find him;
   he is great in power and justice,
   and abundant righteousness he will
     not violate.
24 Therefore mortals fear him;

a Meaning of Heb uncertain   *b* Heb *them*
c Meaning of Heb of verse 7 uncertain   *d* Traditional
rendering of Heb *Shaddai*

and who has given birth to the
  hoar-frost of heaven?
30 The waters become hard like stone,
  and the face of the deep is frozen.

31 'Can you bind the chains of the
      Pleiades,
  or loose the cords of Orion?
32 Can you lead forth the Mazzaroth in
      their season,
    or can you guide the Bear with its
      children?
33 Do you know the ordinances of the
      heavens?
    Can you establish their rule on the
      earth?

34 'Can you lift up your voice to the
      clouds,
    so that a flood of waters may cover
      you?
35 Can you send forth lightnings, so that
      they may go
    and say to you, "Here we are"?
36 Who has put wisdom in the inward
      parts,[a]
    or given understanding to the
      mind?[a]
37 Who has the wisdom to number the
      clouds?
    Or who can tilt the waterskins of
      the heavens,
38 when the dust runs into a mass
    and the clods cling together?

39 'Can you hunt the prey for the lion,
    or satisfy the appetite of the young
      lions,
40 when they crouch in their dens,
    or lie in wait in their covert?
41 Who provides for the raven its prey,
    when its young ones cry to God,
    and wander about for lack of food?

39 'Do you know when the
    mountain goats give birth?
  Do you observe the calving of the
    deer?
2 Can you number the months that
    they fulfil,

and do you know the time when
  they give birth,
3 when they crouch to give birth to
    their offspring,
  and are delivered of their young?
4 Their young ones become strong,
    they grow up in the open;
  they go forth, and do not return to
    them.

5 'Who has let the wild ass go free?
    Who has loosed the bonds of the
      swift ass,
6 to which I have given the steppe for
    its home,
  the salt land for its dwelling-place?
7 It scorns the tumult of the city;
  it does not hear the shouts of the
    driver.
8 It ranges the mountains as its pasture,
  and it searches after every green
    thing.

9 'Is the wild ox willing to serve you?
    Will it spend the night at your crib?
10 Can you tie it in the furrow with
    ropes,
  or will it harrow the valleys after
    you?
11 Will you depend on it because its
      strength is great,
    and will you hand over your labour
      to it?
12 Do you have faith in it that it will
      return,
    and bring your grain to your
      threshing-floor?[b]

13 'The ostrich's wings flap wildly,
    though its pinions lack plumage.[a]
14 For it leaves its eggs to the earth,
    and lets them be warmed on the
      ground,
15 forgetting that a foot may crush
      them,
    and that a wild animal may trample
      them.
16 It deals cruelly with its young, as if
      they were not its own;

a Meaning of Heb uncertain   b Heb your grain and
your threshing-floor

he does not regard any who are
   wise in their own conceit.'

The LORD Answers Job

38 Then the LORD answered Job out
   of the whirlwind:
2 'Who is this that darkens counsel by
      words without knowledge?
3 Gird up your loins like a man,
      I will question you, and you shall
         declare to me.

4 'Where were you when I laid the
      foundation of the earth?
      Tell me, if you have understanding.
5 Who determined its measurements—
      surely you know!
      Or who stretched the line upon it?
6 On what were its bases sunk,
      or who laid its cornerstone
7 when the morning stars sang together
      and all the heavenly beings[a]
         shouted for joy?

8 'Or who shut in the sea with doors
      when it burst out from the
         womb?—
9 when I made the clouds its garment,
      and thick darkness its swaddling
         band,
10 and prescribed bounds for it,
      and set bars and doors,
11 and said, "Thus far shall you come,
         and no farther,
      and here shall your proud waves be
         stopped"?

12 'Have you commanded the morning
         since your days began,
      and caused the dawn to know its
         place,
13 so that it might take hold of the skirts
         of the earth,
      and the wicked be shaken out of it?
14 It is changed like clay under the seal,
      and it is dyed[b] like a garment.
15 Light is withheld from the wicked,
      and their uplifted arm is broken.

16 'Have you entered into the springs of
      the sea,

or walked in the recesses of the
         deep?
17 Have the gates of death been revealed
         to you,
      or have you seen the gates of deep
         darkness?
18 Have you comprehended the expanse
         of the earth?
      Declare, if you know all this.

19 'Where is the way to the dwelling of
         light,
      and where is the place of darkness,
20 that you may take it to its territory
      and that you may discern the paths
         to its home?
21 Surely you know, for you were born
         then,
      and the number of your days is
         great!

22 'Have you entered the storehouses of
         the snow,
      or have you seen the storehouses of
         the hail,
23 which I have reserved for the time of
         trouble,
      for the day of battle and war?
24 What is the way to the place where
         the light is distributed,
      or where the east wind is scattered
         upon the earth?

25 'Who has cut a channel for the
         torrents of rain,
      and a way for the thunderbolt,
26 to bring rain on a land where no one
         lives,
      on the desert, which is empty of
         human life,
27 to satisfy the waste and desolate land,
      and to make the ground put forth
         grass?

28 'Has the rain a father,
      or who has begotten the drops of
         dew?
29 From whose womb did the ice come
         forth,

a Heb sons of God   b Cn: Heb and they stand forth

though its labour should be in
vain, yet it has no fear;
17 because God has made it forget
wisdom,
and given it no share in
understanding.
18 When it spreads its plumes aloft, *a*
it laughs at the horse and its rider.

19 'Do you give the horse its might?
Do you clothe its neck with mane?
20 Do you make it leap like the locust?
Its majestic snorting is terrible.
21 It paws *b* violently, exults mightily;
it goes out to meet the weapons.
22 It laughs at fear, and is not dismayed;
it does not turn back from the
sword.
23 Upon it rattle the quiver,
the flashing spear, and the javelin.
24 With fierceness and rage it swallows
the ground;
it cannot stand still at the sound of
the trumpet.
25 When the trumpet sounds, it says
"Aha!"
From a distance it smells the battle,
the thunder of the captains, and the
shouting.

26 'Is it by your wisdom that the hawk
soars,
and spreads its wings towards the
south?
27 Is it at your command that the eagle
mounts up
and makes its nest on high?
28 It lives on the rock and makes its
home
in the fastness of the rocky crag.
29 From there it spies the prey;
its eyes see it from far away.
30 Its young ones suck up blood;
and where the slain are, there it is.'

40 And the LORD said to Job:
2 'Shall a fault-finder contend
with the Almighty? *c*
Anyone who argues with God must
respond.'

Job's Response to God

3 Then Job answered the LORD:
4 'See, I am of small account; what
shall I answer you?
I lay my hand on my mouth.
5 I have spoken once, and I will not
answer;
twice, but will proceed no further.'

God's Challenge to Job

6 Then the LORD answered Job out of
the whirlwind:
7 'Gird up your loins like a man;
I will question you, and you declare
to me.
8 Will you even put me in the wrong?
Will you condemn me that you
may be justified?
9 Have you an arm like God,
and can you thunder with a voice
like his?

10 'Deck yourself with majesty and
dignity;
clothe yourself with glory and
splendour.
11 Pour out the overflowings of your
anger,
and look on all who are proud, and
abase them.
12 Look on all who are proud, and bring
them low;
tread down the wicked where they
stand.
13 Hide them all in the dust together;
bind their faces in the world
below. *d*
14 Then I will also acknowledge to you
that your own right hand can give
you victory.

15 'Look at Behemoth,
which I made just as I made you;
it eats grass like an ox.
16 Its strength is in its loins,
and its power in the muscles of its
belly.
17 It makes its tail stiff like a cedar;

a Meaning of Heb uncertain   *b* Gk Syr Vg: Heb *they
dig   c* Traditional rendering of Heb *Shaddai
d* Heb *the hidden place*

the sinews of its thighs are knit
together.
18 Its bones are tubes of bronze,
its limbs like bars of iron.

19 'It is the first of the great acts of
God—
only its Maker can approach it with
the sword.
20 For the mountains yield food for it
where all the wild animals play.
21 Under the lotus plants it lies,
in the covert of the reeds and in the
marsh.
22 The lotus trees cover it for shade;
the willows of the wadi surround it.
23 Even if the river is turbulent, it is not
frightened;
it is confident though Jordan rushes
against its mouth.
24 Can one take it with hooks*a*
or pierce its nose with a snare?

41 *b* 'Can you draw out Leviathan*c*
with a fish-hook,
or press down its tongue with a
cord?
2 Can you put a rope in its nose,
or pierce its jaw with a hook?
3 Will it make many supplications to
you?
Will it speak soft words to you?
4 Will it make a covenant with you
to be taken as your servant for ever?
5 Will you play with it as with a bird,
or will you put it on a leash for
your girls?
6 Will traders bargain over it?
Will they divide it up among the
merchants?
7 Can you fill its skin with harpoons,
or its head with fishing-spears?
8 Lay hands on it;
think of the battle; you will not do
it again!
9*d* Any hope of capturing it*e* will be
disappointed;
were not even the gods*f*
overwhelmed at the sight of it?
10 No one is so fierce as to dare to stir it
up.

Who can stand before it?*g*
11 Who can confront it*g* and be safe?*h*
—under the whole heaven, who?*i*

12 'I will not keep silence concerning its
limbs,
or its mighty strength, or its
splendid frame.
13 Who can strip off its outer garment?
Who can penetrate its double coat
of mail?*j*
14 Who can open the doors of its face?
There is terror all around its teeth.
15 Its back*k* is made of shields in rows,
shut up closely as with a seal.
16 One is so near to another
that no air can come between them.
17 They are joined one to another;
they clasp each other and cannot be
separated.
18 Its sneezes flash forth light,
and its eyes are like the eyelids of
the dawn.
19 From its mouth go flaming torches;
sparks of fire leap out.
20 Out of its nostrils comes smoke,
as from a boiling pot and burning
rushes.
21 Its breath kindles coals,
and a flame comes out of its
mouth.
22 In its neck abides strength,
and terror dances before it.
23 The folds of its flesh cling together;
it is firmly cast and immovable.
24 Its heart is as hard as stone,
as hard as the lower millstone.
25 When it raises itself up the gods are
afraid;
at the crashing they are beside
themselves.
26 Though the sword reaches it, it does
not avail,
nor does the spear, the dart, or the
javelin.
27 It counts iron as straw,
and bronze as rotten wood.

a Cn: Heb *in his eyes*   *b* Ch 40.25 in Heb   *c* Or *the crocodile*   *d* Ch 41.1 in Heb   *e* Heb *of it*   *f* Cn Compare Symmachus Syr: Heb *one is*   *g* Heb *me*   *h* Gk: Heb *that I shall repay*   *i* Heb *to me*   *j* Gk: Heb *bridle*   *k* Cn Compare Gk Vg: Heb *pride*

28 The arrow cannot make it flee;
  slingstones, for it, are turned to
    chaff.
29 Clubs are counted as chaff;
  it laughs at the rattle of javelins.
30 Its underparts are like sharp
    potsherds;
  it spreads itself like a threshing-
    sledge on the mire.
31 It makes the deep boil like a pot;
  it makes the sea like a pot of
    ointment.
32 It leaves a shining wake behind it;
  one would think the deep to be
    white-haired.
33 On earth it has no equal,
  a creature without fear.
34 It surveys everything that is lofty;
  it is king over all that are proud.'

Job Is Humbled and Satisfied

42 Then Job answered the LORD:
  2 'I know that you can do all things,
    and that no purpose of yours can
    be thwarted.
3 "Who is this that hides counsel
    without knowledge?"
  Therefore I have uttered what I did
    not understand,
    things too wonderful for me, which
      I did not know.
4 "Hear, and I will speak;
  I will question you, and you declare
    to me."
5 I had heard of you by the hearing of
    the ear,
  but now my eye sees you;
6 therefore I despise myself,
  and repent in dust and ashes.'

Job's Friends Are Humiliated

7 After the LORD had spoken these
words to Job, the LORD said to Eliphaz the
Temanite: 'My wrath is kindled against you
and against your two friends; for you have
not spoken of me what is right, as my servant Job has. 8 Now therefore take seven
bulls and seven rams, and go to my servant
Job, and offer up for yourselves a burnt-offering; and my servant Job shall pray for
you, for I will accept his prayer not to deal
with you according to your folly; for you
have not spoken of me what is right, as my
servant Job has done.' 9 So Eliphaz the Temanite and Bildad the Shuhite and Zophar
the Naamathite went and did what the
LORD had told them; and the LORD accepted Job's prayer.

Job's Fortunes Are Restored Twofold

10 And the LORD restored the fortunes
of Job when he had prayed for his friends;
and the LORD gave Job twice as much as he
had before. 11 Then there came to him all
his brothers and sisters and all who had
known him before, and they ate bread with
him in his house; they showed him sympathy and comforted him for all the evil
that the LORD had brought upon him; and
each of them gave him a piece of money[a]
and a gold ring. 12 The LORD blessed the latter days of Job more than his beginning;
and he had fourteen thousand sheep, six
thousand camels, a thousand yoke of oxen,
and a thousand donkeys. 13 He also had
seven sons and three daughters. 14 He
named the first Jemimah, the second Kezi-
ah, and the third Keren-happuch. 15 In all
the land there were no women so beautiful
as Job's daughters; and their father gave
them an inheritance along with their
brothers. 16 After this Job lived for one hundred and forty years, and saw his children,
and his children's children, four generations. 17 And Job died, old and full of days.

a Heb a qesitah

THE PSALMS

BOOK I

(Psalms 1-41)

Psalm 1

1 Happy are those
  who do not follow the advice of the
    wicked,
  or take the path that sinners tread,
    or sit in the seat of scoffers;
2 but their delight is in the law of the
    LORD,
  and on his law they meditate day
    and night.
3 They are like trees
  planted by streams of water,
  which yield their fruit in its season,
    and their leaves do not wither.
  In all that they do, they prosper.

4 The wicked are not so,
  but are like chaff that the wind
    drives away.
5 Therefore the wicked will not stand
    in the judgement,
  nor sinners in the congregation of
    the righteous;
6 for the LORD watches over the way of
    the righteous,
  but the way of the wicked will
    perish.

Psalm 2

1 Why do the nations conspire,
  and the peoples plot in vain?
2 The kings of the earth set themselves,
  and the rulers take counsel
    together,
against the LORD and his anointed,
    saying,
3 'Let us burst their bonds asunder,
  and cast their cords from us.'

4 He who sits in the heavens laughs;
  the LORD has them in derision.
5 Then he will speak to them in his
    wrath,
  and terrify them in his fury,
    saying,
6 'I have set my king on Zion, my holy
    hill.'

7 I will tell of the decree of the LORD:
  He said to me, 'You are my son;
    today I have begotten you.
8 Ask of me, and I will make the
    nations your heritage,
  and the ends of the earth your
    possession.
9 You shall break them with a rod of
    iron,
  and dash them in pieces like a
    potter's vessel.'

10 Now therefore, O kings, be wise;
  be warned, O rulers of the earth.
11 Serve the LORD with fear,
  with trembling 12 kiss his feet, *a*
  or he will be angry, and you will
    perish in the way;
  for his wrath is quickly kindled.

Happy are all who take refuge
  in him.

a Cn: Meaning of Heb of verses 11b and 12a is
uncertain

Psalm 3

A Psalm of David, when he fled from
his son Absalom.

1 O LORD, how many are my foes!
   Many are rising against me;
2 many are saying to me,
   'There is no help for you*a* in God.'
                                    Selah

3 But you, O LORD, are a shield around
      me,
   my glory, and the one who lifts up
      my head.
4 I cry aloud to the LORD,
   and he answers me from his
      holy hill.   *Selah*

5 I lie down and sleep;
   I wake again, for the LORD sustains
      me.
6 I am not afraid of tens of thousands
      of people
   who have set themselves against me
      all around.

7 Rise up, O LORD!
   Deliver me, O my God!
   For you strike all my enemies on the
      cheek;
   you break the teeth of the wicked.

8 Deliverance belongs to the LORD;
   may your blessing be on your
      people!   *Selah*

Psalm 4

To the leader: with stringed instruments. A
Psalm of David.

1 Answer me when I call, O God of my
      right!
   You gave me room when I was in
      distress.
   Be gracious to me, and hear my
      prayer.

2 How long, you people, shall my
      honour suffer shame?
   How long will you love vain words,
      and seek after lies?   *Selah*

3 But know that the LORD has set apart
      the faithful for himself;
   the LORD hears when I call to him.

4 When you are disturbed,*b* do not sin;
   ponder it on your beds, and be
      silent.   *Selah*
5 Offer right sacrifices,
   and put your trust in the LORD.

6 There are many who say, 'O that we
      might see some good!
   Let the light of your face shine on
      us, O LORD!'
7 You have put gladness in my heart
   more than when their grain and
      wine abound.

8 I will both lie down and sleep in
      peace;
   for you alone, O LORD, make me lie
      down in safety.

Psalm 5

To the leader: for the flutes. A Psalm of David.

1 Give ear to my words, O LORD;
   give heed to my sighing.
2 Listen to the sound of my cry,
   my King and my God,
   for to you I pray.
3 O LORD, in the morning you hear my
      voice;
   in the morning I plead my case to
      you, and watch.

4 For you are not a God who delights
      in wickedness;
   evil will not sojourn with you.
5 The boastful will not stand before
      your eyes;
   you hate all evildoers.
6 You destroy those who speak lies;
   the LORD abhors the bloodthirsty
      and deceitful.

7 But I, through the abundance of your
      steadfast love,
   will enter your house,

a Syr: Heb *him*   *b* Or *are angry*

I will bow down towards your holy
    temple
    in awe of you.
8 Lead me, O LORD, in your
    righteousness
    because of my enemies;
    make your way straight before me.

9 For there is no truth in their mouths;
    their hearts are destruction;
    their throats are open graves;
    they flatter with their tongues.
10 Make them bear their guilt, O God;
    let them fall by their own counsels;
    because of their many transgressions
    cast them out,
    for they have rebelled against you.

11 But let all who take refuge in you
    rejoice;
    let them ever sing for joy.
    Spread your protection over them,
    so that those who love your name
    may exult in you.
12 For you bless the righteous, O LORD;
    you cover them with favour as with
    a shield.

Psalm 6

To the leader: with stringed instruments;
according to The Sheminith.
A Psalm of David.

1 O LORD, do not rebuke me in your
    anger,
    or discipline me in your wrath.
2 Be gracious to me, O LORD, for I am
    languishing;
    O LORD, heal me, for my bones are
    shaking with terror.
3 My soul also is struck with terror,
    while you, O LORD—how long?

4 Turn, O LORD, save my life;
    deliver me for the sake of your
    steadfast love.
5 For in death there is no remembrance
    of you;
    in Sheol who can give you praise?

6 I am weary with my moaning;

every night I flood my bed with
    tears;
    I drench my couch with my
    weeping.
7 My eyes waste away because of grief;
    they grow weak because of all
    my foes.

8 Depart from me, all you workers
    of evil,
    for the LORD has heard the sound of
    my weeping.
9 The LORD has heard my supplication;
    the LORD accepts my prayer.
10 All my enemies shall be ashamed and
    struck with terror;
    they shall turn back, and in a
    moment be put to shame.

Psalm 7

A Shiggaion of David, which he sang to the
LORD concerning Cush, a Benjaminite.

1 O LORD my God, in you I take refuge;
    save me from all my pursuers, and
    deliver me,
2 or like a lion they will tear me apart;
    they will drag me away, with no
    one to rescue.

3 O LORD my God, if I have done this,
    if there is wrong in my hands,
4 if I have repaid my ally with harm
    or plundered my foe without cause,
5 then let the enemy pursue and
    overtake me,
    trample my life to the ground,
    and lay my soul in the dust.   *Selah*

6 Rise up, O LORD, in your anger;
    lift yourself up against the fury of
    my enemies;
    awake, O my God;*a* you have
    appointed a judgement.
7 Let the assembly of the peoples be
    gathered around you,
    and over it take your seat*b* on high.
8 The LORD judges the peoples;
    judge me, O LORD, according to my
    righteousness

a Or *awake for me*   *b* Cn: Heb *return*

and according to the integrity that
is in me.

9 O let the evil of the wicked come to
an end,
but establish the righteous,
you who test the minds and hearts,
O righteous God.
10 God is my shield,
who saves the upright in heart.
11 God is a righteous judge,
and a God who has indignation
every day.

12 If one does not repent, God[a] will
whet his sword;
he has bent and strung his bow;
13 he has prepared his deadly weapons,
making his arrows fiery shafts.
14 See how they conceive evil,
and are pregnant with mischief,
and bring forth lies.
15 They make a pit, digging it out,
and fall into the hole that they have
made.
16 Their mischief returns upon their
own heads,
and on their own heads their
violence descends.

17 I will give to the LORD the thanks due
to his righteousness,
and sing praise to the name of the
LORD, the Most High.

Psalm 8

To the leader: according to The Gittith. A
Psalm of David.

1 O LORD, our Sovereign,
how majestic is your name in all
the earth!

You have set your glory above the
heavens.
2 Out of the mouths of babes and
infants
you have founded a bulwark because
of your foes,
to silence the enemy and the
avenger.

3 When I look at your heavens, the
work of your fingers,
the moon and the stars that you
have established;
4 what are human beings that you are
mindful of them,
mortals[b] that you care for them?

5 Yet you have made them a little lower
than God,[c]
and crowned them with glory and
honour.
6 You have given them dominion over
the works of your hands;
you have put all things under their
feet,
7 all sheep and oxen,
and also the beasts of the field,
8 the birds of the air, and the fish of
the sea,
whatever passes along the paths of
the seas.

9 O LORD, our Sovereign,
how majestic is your name in all
the earth!

Psalm 9

To the leader: according to Muth-labben. A
Psalm of David.

1 I will give thanks to the LORD with
my whole heart;
I will tell of all your wonderful
deeds.
2 I will be glad and exult in you;
I will sing praise to your name,
O Most High.

3 When my enemies turned back,
they stumbled and perished before
you.
4 For you have maintained my just
cause;
you have sat on the throne giving
righteous judgement.

5 You have rebuked the nations, you
have destroyed the wicked;

a Heb he   b Heb ben adam, lit. son of man
c Or than the divine beings or angels: Heb elohim

you have blotted out their name for
    ever and ever.
6 The enemies have vanished in
    everlasting ruins;
    their cities you have rooted out;
    the very memory of them has
    perished.

7 But the LORD sits enthroned for ever,
    he has established his throne for
    judgement.
8 He judges the world with
    righteousness;
    he judges the peoples with equity.

9 The LORD is a stronghold for the
    oppressed,
    a stronghold in times of trouble.
10 And those who know your name put
    their trust in you,
    for you, O LORD, have not forsaken
    those who seek you.

11 Sing praises to the LORD, who dwells
    in Zion.
    Declare his deeds among the
    peoples.
12 For he who avenges blood is mindful
    of them;
    he does not forget the cry of the
    afflicted.

13 Be gracious to me, O LORD.
    See what I suffer from those who
    hate me;
    you are the one who lifts me up
    from the gates of death,
14 so that I may recount all your
    praises,
    and, in the gates of daughter Zion,
    rejoice in your deliverance.

15 The nations have sunk in the pit that
    they made;
    in the net that they hid has their
    own foot been caught.
16 The LORD has made himself known,
    he has executed judgement;
    the wicked are snared in the work
    of their own hands.
                 Higgaion. Selah

17 The wicked shall depart to Sheol,
    all the nations that forget God.

18 For the needy shall not always be
    forgotten,
    nor the hope of the poor perish for
    ever.

19 Rise up, O LORD! Do not let mortals
    prevail;
    let the nations be judged before
    you.
20 Put them in fear, O LORD;
    let the nations know that they are
    only human.   *Selah*

Psalm 10

1 Why, O LORD, do you stand far off?
    Why do you hide yourself in times
    of trouble?
2 In arrogance the wicked persecute the
    poor—
    let them be caught in the schemes
    they have devised.

3 For the wicked boast of the desires of
    their heart,
    those greedy for gain curse and
    renounce the LORD.
4 In the pride of their countenance the
    wicked say, 'God will not seek it
    out';
    all their thoughts are, 'There is no
    God.'

5 Their ways prosper at all times;
    your judgements are on high, out
    of their sight;
    as for their foes, they scoff at them.
6 They think in their heart, 'We shall
    not be moved;
    throughout all generations we shall
    not meet adversity.'

7 Their mouths are filled with cursing
    and deceit and oppression;
    under their tongues are mischief
    and iniquity.
8 They sit in ambush in the villages;
    in hiding-places they murder the
    innocent.

Their eyes stealthily watch for the
  helpless;
9 they lurk in secret like a lion in its
    covert;
  they lurk that they may seize the
    poor;
    they seize the poor and drag them
      off in their net.

10 They stoop, they crouch,
  and the helpless fall by their might.
11 They think in their heart, 'God has
    forgotten,
  he has hidden his face, he will
    never see it.'

12 Rise up, O Lord; O God, lift up your
    hand;
  do not forget the oppressed.
13 Why do the wicked renounce God,
  and say in their hearts, 'You will
    not call us to account'?

14 But you do see! Indeed you note
    trouble and grief,
  that you may take it into your
    hands;
  the helpless commit themselves
    to you;
  you have been the helper of the
    orphan.

15 Break the arm of the wicked and
    evildoers;
  seek out their wickedness until you
    find none.
16 The Lord is king for ever and ever;
  the nations shall perish from his
    land.

17 O Lord, you will hear the desire of
    the meek;
  you will strengthen their heart, you
    will incline your ear
18 to do justice for the orphan and the
    oppressed,
  so that those from earth may strike
    terror no more. *a*

Psalm 11

To the leader. Of David.

1 In the Lord I take refuge; how can
    you say to me,
  'Flee like a bird to the mountains; *b*
2 for look, the wicked bend the bow,
    they have fitted their arrow to the
      string,
    to shoot in the dark at the upright
      in heart.
3 If the foundations are destroyed,
    what can the righteous do?'

4 The Lord is in his holy temple;
    the Lord's throne is in heaven.
    His eyes behold, his gaze examines
      humankind.
5 The Lord tests the righteous and the
      wicked,
    and his soul hates the lover of
      violence.
6 On the wicked he will rain coals of
      fire and sulphur;
    a scorching wind shall be the
      portion of their cup.
7 For the Lord is righteous;
  he loves righteous deeds;
    the upright shall behold his face.

Psalm 12

To the leader: according to The Sheminith.
A Psalm of David.

1 Help, O Lord, for there is no longer
      anyone who is godly;
    the faithful have disappeared from
      humankind.
2 They utter lies to each other;
    with flattering lips and a double
      heart they speak.

3 May the Lord cut off all flattering
      lips,
    the tongue that makes great boasts,
4 those who say, 'With our tongues we
      will prevail;
    our lips are our own—who is our
      master?'

a Meaning of Heb uncertain   *b* Gk Syr Jerome Tg:
Heb *flee to your mountain, O bird*

5 'Because the poor are despoiled,
      because the needy groan,
   I will now rise up,' says the LORD;
   'I will place them in the safety for
      which they long.'
6 The promises of the LORD are
      promises that are pure,
   silver refined in a furnace on the
      ground,
   purified seven times.

7 You, O LORD, will protect us;
   you will guard us from this
      generation for ever.
8 On every side the wicked prowl,
   as vileness is exalted among
      humankind.

Psalm 13

To the leader. A Psalm of David.

1 How long, O LORD? Will you forget
      me for ever?
   How long will you hide your face
      from me?
2 How long must I bear pain[a] in my
      soul,
   and have sorrow in my heart all day
      long?
   How long shall my enemy be exalted
      over me?

3 Consider and answer me, O LORD my
      God!
   Give light to my eyes, or I will sleep
      the sleep of death,
4 and my enemy will say, 'I have
      prevailed';
   my foes will rejoice because I am
      shaken.

5 But I trusted in your steadfast love;
   my heart shall rejoice in your
      salvation.
6 I will sing to the LORD,
   because he has dealt bountifully
      with me.

Psalm 14

To the leader. Of David.

1 Fools say in their hearts, 'There is no
      God.'
   They are corrupt, they do
      abominable deeds;
   there is no one who does good.

2 The LORD looks down from heaven
      on humankind
   to see if there are any who are wise,
   who seek after God.

3 They have all gone astray, they are all
      alike perverse;
   there is no one who does good,
   no, not one.

4 Have they no knowledge, all the
      evildoers
   who eat up my people as they eat
      bread,
   and do not call upon the LORD?

5 There they shall be in great terror,
   for God is with the company of the
      righteous.
6 You would confound the plans of the
      poor,
   but the LORD is their refuge.

7 O that deliverance for Israel would
      come from Zion!
   When the LORD restores the
      fortunes of his people,
   Jacob will rejoice; Israel will be
      glad.

Psalm 15

A Psalm of David.

1 O LORD, who may abide in your tent?
   Who may dwell on your holy hill?

2 Those who walk blamelessly, and do
      what is right,
   and speak the truth from their
      heart;

a Syr: Heb hold counsels

³ who do not slander with their
  tongue,
  and do no evil to their friends,
  nor take up a reproach against their
  neighbours;
⁴ in whose eyes the wicked are
  despised,
  but who honour those who fear the
  LORD;
  who stand by their oath even to their
  hurt;
⁵ who do not lend money at interest,
  and do not take a bribe against the
  innocent.

Those who do these things shall
  never be moved.

Psalm 16

A Miktam of David.

¹ Protect me, O God, for in you I take
  refuge.
² I say to the LORD, 'You are my Lord;
  I have no good apart from you.'ᵃ

³ As for the holy ones in the land, they
  are the noble,
  in whom is all my delight.

⁴ Those who choose another god
  multiply their sorrows;ᵇ
  their drink-offerings of blood I will
  not pour out
  or take their names upon my lips.

⁵ The LORD is my chosen portion and
  my cup;
  you hold my lot.
⁶ The boundary lines have fallen for
  me in pleasant places;
  I have a goodly heritage.

⁷ I bless the LORD who gives me
  counsel;
  in the night also my heart instructs
  me.
⁸ I keep the LORD always before me;
  because he is at my right hand, I
  shall not be moved.

⁹ Therefore my heart is glad, and my
  soul rejoices;
  my body also rests secure.
¹⁰ For you do not give me up to Sheol,
  or let your faithful one see the Pit.

¹¹ You show me the path of life.
  In your presence there is fullness of
  joy;
  in your right hand are pleasures for
  evermore.

Psalm 17

A Prayer of David.

¹ Hear a just cause, O LORD; attend to
  my cry;
  give ear to my prayer from lips free
  of deceit.
² From you let my vindication come;
  let your eyes see the right.

³ If you try my heart, if you visit me by
  night,
  if you test me, you will find no
  wickedness in me;
  my mouth does not transgress.
⁴ As for what others do, by the word of
  your lips
  I have avoided the ways of the
  violent.
⁵ My steps have held fast to your paths;
  my feet have not slipped.

⁶ I call upon you, for you will answer
  me, O God;
  incline your ear to me, hear my
  words.
⁷ Wondrously show your steadfast love,
  O saviour of those who seek refuge
  from their adversaries at your right
  hand.

⁸ Guard me as the apple of the eye;
  hide me in the shadow of your
  wings,
⁹ from the wicked who despoil me,
  my deadly enemies who
  surround me.

a Jerome Tg: Meaning of Heb uncertain
b Cn: Meaning of Heb uncertain

10 They close their hearts to pity;
    with their mouths they speak
        arrogantly.
11 They track me down;[a] now they
    surround me;
    they set their eyes to cast me to the
        ground.
12 They are like a lion eager to tear,
    like a young lion lurking in ambush.

13 Rise up, O LORD, confront them,
    overthrow them!
    By your sword deliver my life from
        the wicked,
14 from mortals—by your hand,
        O LORD—
    from mortals whose portion in life
        is in this world.
    May their bellies be filled with what
        you have stored up for them;
        may their children have more than
            enough;
        may they leave something over to
            their little ones.

15 As for me, I shall behold your face in
    righteousness;
    when I awake I shall be satisfied,
        beholding your likeness.

Psalm 18

To the leader. A Psalm of David the servant of
the LORD, who addressed the words of this
song to the LORD on the day when the LORD
delivered him from the hand of all his
enemies, and from the hand of Saul. He said:

1 I love you, O LORD, my strength.
2 The LORD is my rock, my fortress, and
    my deliverer,
    my God, my rock in whom I take
        refuge,
    my shield, and the horn of my
        salvation, my stronghold.
3 I call upon the LORD, who is worthy
    to be praised;
    so I shall be saved from my
        enemies.

4 The cords of death encompassed me;
    the torrents of perdition
        assailed me;

5 the cords of Sheol entangled me;
    the snares of death confronted me.

6 In my distress I called upon the LORD;
    to my God I cried for help.
    From his temple he heard my voice,
    and my cry to him reached his ears.

7 Then the earth reeled and rocked;
    the foundations also of the
        mountains trembled
    and quaked, because he was angry.
8 Smoke went up from his nostrils,
    and devouring fire from his mouth;
    glowing coals flamed forth from
        him.
9 He bowed the heavens, and came
    down;
    thick darkness was under his feet.
10 He rode on a cherub, and flew;
    he came swiftly upon the wings of
        the wind.
11 He made darkness his covering
    around him,
    his canopy thick clouds dark with
        water.
12 Out of the brightness before him
    there broke through his clouds
    hailstones and coals of fire.
13 The LORD also thundered in the
    heavens,
    and the Most High uttered his
        voice.[b]
14 And he sent out his arrows, and
    scattered them;
    he flashed forth lightnings, and
        routed them.
15 Then the channels of the sea were
    seen,
    and the foundations of the world
        were laid bare
    at your rebuke, O LORD,
    at the blast of the breath of your
        nostrils.

16 He reached down from on high, he
    took me;
    he drew me out of mighty waters.

a One Ms Compare Syr: MT *Our steps*   b Gk See
2 Sam 22.14: Heb adds *hailstones and coals of fire*

17 He delivered me from my strong
    enemy,
    and from those who hated me;
    for they were too mighty for me.
18 They confronted me in the day of my
    calamity;
    but the LORD was my support.
19 He brought me out into a broad
    place;
    he delivered me, because he
    delighted in me.

20 The LORD rewarded me according to
    my righteousness;
    according to the cleanness of my
    hands he recompensed me.
21 For I have kept the ways of the LORD,
    and have not wickedly departed
    from my God.
22 For all his ordinances were before
    me,
    and his statutes I did not put away
    from me.
23 I was blameless before him,
    and I kept myself from guilt.
24 Therefore the LORD has recompensed
    me according to my
    righteousness,
    according to the cleanness of my
    hands in his sight.

25 With the loyal you show yourself
    loyal;
    with the blameless you show
    yourself blameless;
26 with the pure you show yourself
    pure;
    and with the crooked you show
    yourself perverse.
27 For you deliver a humble people,
    but the haughty eyes you bring
    down.
28 It is you who light my lamp;
    the LORD, my God, lights up my
    darkness.
29 By you I can crush a troop,
    and by my God I can leap over a
    wall.
30 This God—his way is perfect;
    the promise of the LORD proves
    true;

    he is a shield for all who take
    refuge in him.

31 For who is God except the LORD?
    And who is a rock besides our
    God?—
32 the God who girded me with
    strength,
    and made my way safe.
33 He made my feet like the feet of a
    deer,
    and set me secure on the heights.
34 He trains my hands for war,
    so that my arms can bend a bow of
    bronze.
35 You have given me the shield of your
    salvation,
    and your right hand has supported
    me;
    your help*a* has made me great.
36 You gave me a wide place for my
    steps under me,
    and my feet did not slip.
37 I pursued my enemies and overtook
    them;
    and did not turn back until they
    were consumed.
38 I struck them down, so that they were
    not able to rise;
    they fell under my feet.
39 For you girded me with strength for
    the battle;
    you made my assailants sink under
    me.
40 You made my enemies turn their
    backs to me,
    and those who hated me I
    destroyed.
41 They cried for help, but there was no
    one to save them;
    they cried to the LORD, but he did
    not answer them.
42 I beat them fine, like dust before the
    wind;
    I cast them out like the mire of the
    streets.

43 You delivered me from strife with the
    peoples;*b*
    you made me head of the nations;

a Or *gentleness*   *b* Gk Tg: Heb *people*

people whom I had not known
    served me.
44 As soon as they heard of me they
    obeyed me;
  foreigners came cringing to me.
45 Foreigners lost heart,
    and came trembling out of their
    strongholds.

46 The LORD lives! Blessed be my rock,
    and exalted be the God of my
    salvation,
47 the God who gave me vengeance
    and subdued peoples under me;
48 who delivered me from my
    enemies;
  indeed, you exalted me above my
    adversaries;
  you delivered me from the
    violent.

49 For this I will extol you, O LORD,
    among the nations,
  and sing praises to your name.
50 Great triumphs he gives to his king,
    and shows steadfast love to his
    anointed,
  to David and his descendants for
    ever.

Psalm 19

To the leader. A Psalm of David.

1 The heavens are telling the glory of
    God;
  and the firmament*a* proclaims his
    handiwork.
2 Day to day pours forth speech,
    and night to night declares
    knowledge.
3 There is no speech, nor are there
    words;
  their voice is not heard;
4 yet their voice*b* goes out through all
    the earth,
  and their words to the end of the
    world.

In the heavens*c* he has set a tent for
    the sun,

5 which comes out like a bridegroom
    from his wedding canopy,
  and like a strong man runs its
    course with joy.
6 Its rising is from the end of the
    heavens,
  and its circuit to the end of them;
  and nothing is hidden from its
    heat.

7 The law of the LORD is perfect,
    reviving the soul;
  the decrees of the LORD are sure,
    making wise the simple;
8 the precepts of the LORD are right,
    rejoicing the heart;
  the commandment of the LORD is
    clear,
    enlightening the eyes;
9 the fear of the LORD is pure,
    enduring for ever;
  the ordinances of the LORD are true
    and righteous altogether.
10 More to be desired are they than
    gold,
    even much fine gold;
  sweeter also than honey,
    and drippings of the honeycomb.

11 Moreover by them is your servant
    warned;
  in keeping them there is great
    reward.
12 But who can detect their errors?
  Clear me from hidden faults.
13 Keep back your servant also from the
    insolent;*d*
  do not let them have dominion
    over me.
Then I shall be blameless,
    and innocent of great
    transgression.

14 Let the words of my mouth and the
    meditation of my heart
  be acceptable to you,
  O LORD, my rock and my redeemer.

a Or *dome*   *b* Gk Jerome Compare Syr: Heb *line*
c Heb *In them*   *d* Or *from proud thoughts*

Psalm 20

To the leader. A Psalm of David.

1 The LORD answer you in the day of
      trouble!
   The name of the God of Jacob
      protect you!
2 May he send you help from the
      sanctuary,
   and give you support from Zion.
3 May he remember all your offerings,
   and regard with favour your burnt
      sacrifices.   *Selah*

4 May he grant you your heart's desire,
   and fulfil all your plans.
5 May we shout for joy over your
      victory,
   and in the name of our God set up
      our banners.
   May the LORD fulfil all your petitions.

6 Now I know that the LORD will help
      his anointed;
   he will answer him from his holy
      heaven
   with mighty victories by his right
      hand.
7 Some take pride in chariots, and
      some in horses,
   but our pride is in the name of the
      LORD our God.
8 They will collapse and fall,
   but we shall rise and stand upright.

9 Give victory to the king, O LORD;
   answer us when we call.*a*

Psalm 21

To the leader. A Psalm of David.

1 In your strength the king rejoices,
      O LORD,
   and in your help how greatly he
      exults!
2 You have given him his heart's desire,
   and have not withheld the request
      of his lips.   *Selah*
3 For you meet him with rich blessings;
   you set a crown of fine gold on his
      head.

4 He asked you for life; you gave it to
      him—
   length of days for ever and ever.
5 His glory is great through your help;
   splendour and majesty you bestow
      on him.
6 You bestow on him blessings for ever;
   you make him glad with the joy of
      your presence.
7 For the king trusts in the LORD,
   and through the steadfast love of
      the Most High he shall not be
      moved.

8 Your hand will find out all your
      enemies;
   your right hand will find out those
      who hate you.
9 You will make them like a fiery
      furnace
   when you appear.
   The LORD will swallow them up in his
      wrath,
   and fire will consume them.
10 You will destroy their offspring from
      the earth,
   and their children from among
      humankind.
11 If they plan evil against you,
   if they devise mischief, they will
      not succeed.
12 For you will put them to flight;
   you will aim at their faces with
      your bows.

13 Be exalted, O LORD, in your strength!
   We will sing and praise your
      power.

Psalm 22

To the leader: according to The Deer of the
Dawn. A Psalm of David.

1 My God, my God, why have you
      forsaken me?
   Why are you so far from helping
      me, from the words of my
      groaning?

a Gk: Heb *give victory, O LORD; let the King answer us
when we call*

2 O my God, I cry by day, but you do
        not answer;
    and by night, but find no rest.

3 Yet you are holy,
        enthroned on the praises of Israel.
4 In you our ancestors trusted;
        they trusted, and you delivered
            them.
5 To you they cried, and were saved;
        in you they trusted, and were not
            put to shame.

6 But I am a worm, and not human;
        scorned by others, and despised by
            the people.
7 All who see me mock at me;
        they make mouths at me, they
            shake their heads;
8 'Commit your cause to the LORD; let
        him deliver—
        let him rescue the one in whom he
            delights!'

9 Yet it was you who took me from the
        womb;
        you kept me safe on my mother's
            breast.
10 On you I was cast from my birth,
        and since my mother bore me you
            have been my God.
11 Do not be far from me,
        for trouble is near
        and there is no one to help.

12 Many bulls encircle me,
        strong bulls of Bashan surround
            me;
13 they open wide their mouths at me,
        like a ravening and roaring lion.

14 I am poured out like water,
        and all my bones are out of joint;
    my heart is like wax;
        it is melted within my breast;
15 my mouth[a] is dried up like a
        potsherd,
        and my tongue sticks to my jaws;
        you lay me in the dust of death.

16 For dogs are all around me;

    a company of evildoers
        encircles me.
    My hands and feet have shrivelled;[b]
17 I can count all my bones.
    They stare and gloat over me;
18 they divide my clothes among
        themselves,
        and for my clothing they cast lots.

19 But you, O LORD, do not be far away!
        O my help, come quickly to my aid!
20 Deliver my soul from the sword,
        my life[c] from the power of the dog!
21   Save me from the mouth of the
            lion!

    From the horns of the wild oxen you
        have rescued[d] me.
22 I will tell of your name to my
        brothers and sisters;[e]
        in the midst of the congregation I
            will praise you:
23 You who fear the LORD, praise him!
        All you offspring of Jacob, glorify
            him;
        stand in awe of him, all you
            offspring of Israel!
24 For he did not despise or abhor
        the affliction of the afflicted;
    he did not hide his face from me,[f]
        but heard when I[g] cried to him.

25 From you comes my praise in the
        great congregation;
        my vows I will pay before those
            who fear him.
26 The poor[h] shall eat and be satisfied;
        those who seek him shall praise the
            LORD.
    May your hearts live for ever!

27 All the ends of the earth shall
        remember
        and turn to the LORD;
    and all the families of the nations
        shall worship before him.[i]
28 For dominion belongs to the LORD,
        and he rules over the nations.

a Cn: Heb *strength*   b Meaning of Heb uncertain
c Heb *my only one*   d Heb *answered*   e Or *kindred*
f Heb *him*   g Heb *he*   h Or *afflicted*   i Gk Syr
Jerome: Heb *you*

²⁹ To him,ᵃ indeed, shall all who sleep
   inᵇ the earth bow down;
   before him shall bow all who go
      down to the dust,
   and I shall live for him.ᶜ
³⁰ Posterity will serve him;
   future generations will be told
      about the Lord,
³¹ andᵈ proclaim his deliverance to a
      people yet unborn,
   saying that he has done it.

Psalm 23

A Psalm of David.

¹ The LORD is my shepherd, I shall not
      want.
²   He makes me lie down in green
         pastures;
   he leads me beside still waters;ᵉ
³   he restores my soul.ᶠ
   He leads me in right pathsᵍ
      for his name's sake.

⁴ Even though I walk through the
      darkest valley,ʰ
   I fear no evil;
   for you are with me;
      your rod and your staff—
      they comfort me.

⁵ You prepare a table before me
      in the presence of my enemies;
   you anoint my head with oil;
      my cup overflows.
⁶ Surelyⁱ goodness and mercyʲ shall
      follow me
      all the days of my life,
   and I shall dwell in the house of the
      LORD
      my whole life long.ᵏ

Psalm 24

Of David. A Psalm.

¹ The earth is the LORD's and all that is
      in it,
      the world, and those who live in it;
² for he has founded it on the seas,
      and established it on the rivers.
³ Who shall ascend the hill of the LORD?

And who shall stand in his holy
      place?
⁴ Those who have clean hands and
      pure hearts,
   who do not lift up their souls to
      what is false,
   and do not swear deceitfully.
⁵ They will receive blessing from the
      LORD,
   and vindication from the God of
      their salvation.
⁶ Such is the company of those who
      seek him,
   who seek the face of the God of
      Jacob.ˡ   *Selah*

⁷ Lift up your heads, O gates!
   and be lifted up, O ancient doors!
   that the King of glory may come in.
⁸ Who is the King of glory?
   The LORD, strong and mighty,
   the LORD, mighty in battle.
⁹ Lift up your heads, O gates!
   and be lifted up, O ancient doors!
   that the King of glory may come in.
¹⁰ Who is this King of glory?
   The LORD of hosts,
   he is the King of glory.   *Selah*

Psalm 25

Of David.

¹ To you, O LORD, I lift up my soul.
² O my God, in you I trust;
      do not let me be put to shame;
      do not let my enemies exult
         over me.
³ Do not let those who wait for you be
      put to shame;
   let them be ashamed who are
      wantonly treacherous.

⁴ Make me to know your ways, O LORD;
   teach me your paths.
⁵ Lead me in your truth, and teach me,

ᵃ Cn: Heb *They have eaten and*   ᵇ Cn: Heb *all the fat
ones*   ᶜ Compare Gk Syr Vg: Heb *and he who cannot
keep himself alive*   ᵈ Compare Gk: Heb *it will be told
about the Lord to the generation,* ³¹*they will come and*
ᵉ Heb *waters of rest*   ᶠ Or *life*   ᵍ Or *paths of
righteousness*   ʰ Or *the valley of the shadow of death*
ⁱ Or *Only*   ʲ Or *kindness*   ᵏ Heb *for length of days*
ˡ Gk Syr: Heb *your face, O Jacob*

for you are the God of my
salvation;
for you I wait all day long.

6 Be mindful of your mercy, O LORD,
and of your steadfast love,
for they have been from of old.
7 Do not remember the sins of my
youth or my transgressions;
according to your steadfast love
remember me,
for your goodness' sake, O LORD!

8 Good and upright is the LORD;
therefore he instructs sinners in the
way.
9 He leads the humble in what is right,
and teaches the humble his way.
10 All the paths of the LORD are steadfast
love and faithfulness,
for those who keep his covenant
and his decrees.

11 For your name's sake, O LORD,
pardon my guilt, for it is great.
12 Who are they that fear the LORD?
He will teach them the way that
they should choose.

13 They will abide in prosperity,
and their children shall possess the
land.
14 The friendship of the LORD is for
those who fear him,
and he makes his covenant known
to them.
15 My eyes are ever towards the LORD,
for he will pluck my feet out of the
net.

16 Turn to me and be gracious to me,
for I am lonely and afflicted.
17 Relieve the troubles of my heart,
and bring me*a* out of my distress.
18 Consider my affliction and my
trouble,
and forgive all my sins.

19 Consider how many are my foes,
and with what violent hatred they
hate me.

20 O guard my life, and deliver me;
do not let me be put to shame, for I
take refuge in you.
21 May integrity and uprightness
preserve me,
for I wait for you.

22 Redeem Israel, O God,
out of all its troubles.

Psalm 26

Of David.

1 Vindicate me, O LORD,
for I have walked in my integrity,
and I have trusted in the LORD
without wavering.
2 Prove me, O LORD, and try me;
test my heart and mind.
3 For your steadfast love is before my
eyes,
and I walk in faithfulness to you.*b*

4 I do not sit with the worthless,
nor do I consort with hypocrites;
5 I hate the company of evildoers,
and will not sit with the wicked.

6 I wash my hands in innocence,
and go around your altar, O LORD,
7 singing aloud a song of thanksgiving,
and telling all your wondrous
deeds.

8 O LORD, I love the house in which
you dwell,
and the place where your glory
abides.
9 Do not sweep me away with sinners,
nor my life with the bloodthirsty,
10 those in whose hands are evil devices,
and whose right hands are full of
bribes.

11 But as for me, I walk in my integrity;
redeem me, and be gracious to me.
12 My foot stands on level ground;
in the great congregation I will
bless the LORD.

a Or *The troubles of my heart are enlarged; bring me*
b Or *in your faithfulness*

Psalm 27

Of David.

1 The Lord is my light and my
     salvation;
   whom shall I fear?
 The Lord is the stronghold[a] of my
     life;
   of whom shall I be afraid?

2 When evildoers assail me
     to devour my flesh—
 my adversaries and foes—
   they shall stumble and fall.

3 Though an army encamp against me,
   my heart shall not fear;
 though war rise up against me,
   yet I will be confident.

4 One thing I asked of the Lord,
   that will I seek after:
 to live in the house of the Lord
   all the days of my life,
 to behold the beauty of the Lord,
   and to inquire in his temple.

5 For he will hide me in his shelter
   in the day of trouble;
 he will conceal me under the cover of
     his tent;
   he will set me high on a rock.

6 Now my head is lifted up
   above my enemies all around me,
 and I will offer in his tent
   sacrifices with shouts of joy;
 I will sing and make melody to the
   Lord.

7 Hear, O Lord, when I cry aloud,
   be gracious to me and answer me!
8 'Come,' my heart says, 'seek his face!'
   Your face, Lord, do I seek.
9   Do not hide your face from me.

 Do not turn your servant away in
     anger,
   you who have been my help.
 Do not cast me off, do not
     forsake me,

 O God of my salvation!
10 If my father and mother forsake me,
   the Lord will take me up.

11 Teach me your way, O Lord,
   and lead me on a level path
   because of my enemies.
12 Do not give me up to the will of
     my adversaries,
   for false witnesses have risen
     against me,
   and they are breathing out violence.

13 I believe that I shall see the goodness
     of the Lord
   in the land of the living.
14 Wait for the Lord;
   be strong, and let your heart take
     courage;
   wait for the Lord!

Psalm 28

Of David.

1 To you, O Lord, I call;
   my rock, do not refuse to hear me,
 for if you are silent to me,
   I shall be like those who go down
     to the Pit.
2 Hear the voice of my supplication,
   as I cry to you for help,
 as I lift up my hands
   towards your most holy sanctuary.[b]

3 Do not drag me away with the
     wicked,
   with those who are workers of evil,
 who speak peace with their
     neighbours,
   while mischief is in their hearts.
4 Repay them according to their work,
   and according to the evil of their
     deeds;
 repay them according to the work of
     their hands;
   render them their due reward.
5 Because they do not regard the works
     of the Lord,
   or the work of his hands,

a Or *refuge*   b Heb *your innermost sanctuary*

he will break them down and build
them up no more.

6 Blessed be the LORD,
for he has heard the sound of my
pleadings.
7 The LORD is my strength and my shield;
in him my heart trusts;
so I am helped, and my heart exults,
and with my song I give thanks to
him.

8 The LORD is the strength of his people;
he is the saving refuge of his
anointed.
9 O save your people, and bless your
heritage;
be their shepherd, and carry them
for ever.

Psalm 29

A Psalm of David.

1 Ascribe to the LORD, O heavenly
beings,[a]
ascribe to the LORD glory and
strength.
2 Ascribe to the LORD the glory of his
name;
worship the LORD in holy
splendour.

3 The voice of the LORD is over the
waters;
the God of glory thunders,
the LORD, over mighty waters.
4 The voice of the LORD is powerful;
the voice of the LORD is full of
majesty.

5 The voice of the LORD breaks the
cedars;
the LORD breaks the cedars of
Lebanon.
6 He makes Lebanon skip like a calf,
and Sirion like a young wild ox.

7 The voice of the LORD flashes forth
flames of fire.
8 The voice of the LORD shakes the
wilderness;

the LORD shakes the wilderness of
Kadesh.

9 The voice of the LORD causes the oaks
to whirl,[b]
and strips the forest bare;
and in his temple all say, 'Glory!'

10 The LORD sits enthroned over the
flood;
the LORD sits enthroned as king for
ever.
11 May the LORD give strength to his
people!
May the LORD bless his people with
peace!

Psalm 30

A Psalm. A Song at the dedication of the
temple. Of David.

1 I will extol you, O LORD, for you have
drawn me up,
and did not let my foes rejoice over
me.
2 O LORD my God, I cried to you for
help,
and you have healed me.
3 O LORD, you brought up my soul
from Sheol,
restored me to life from among
those gone down to the Pit.[c]

4 Sing praises to the LORD, O you his
faithful ones,
and give thanks to his holy name.
5 For his anger is but for a moment;
his favour is for a lifetime.
Weeping may linger for the night,
but joy comes with the morning.

6 As for me, I said in my prosperity,
'I shall never be moved.'
7 By your favour, O LORD,
you had established me as a strong
mountain;
you hid your face;
I was dismayed.

a Heb sons of gods   b Or causes the deer to calve
c Or that I should not go down to the Pit

8 To you, O LORD, I cried,
  and to the LORD I made
    supplication:
9 'What profit is there in my death,
  if I go down to the Pit?
  Will the dust praise you?
  Will it tell of your faithfulness?
10 Hear, O LORD, and be gracious to me!
  O LORD, be my helper!'

11 You have turned my mourning into
    dancing;
  you have taken off my sackcloth
  and clothed me with joy,
12 so that my soul[a] may praise you and
    not be silent.
  O LORD my God, I will give thanks
    to you for ever.

Psalm 31

To the leader. A Psalm of David.

1 In you, O LORD, I seek refuge;
  do not let me ever be put to shame;
  in your righteousness deliver me.
2 Incline your ear to me;
  rescue me speedily.
  Be a rock of refuge for me,
  a strong fortress to save me.

3 You are indeed my rock and my
    fortress;
  for your name's sake lead me and
    guide me,
4 take me out of the net that is hidden
    for me,
  for you are my refuge.
5 Into your hand I commit my spirit;
  you have redeemed me, O LORD,
    faithful God.

6 You hate[b] those who pay regard to
    worthless idols,
  but I trust in the LORD.
7 I will exult and rejoice in your
    steadfast love,
  because you have seen my affliction;
  you have taken heed of my
    adversities,
8 and have not delivered me into the
    hand of the enemy;

  you have set my feet in a broad
    place.

9 Be gracious to me, O LORD, for I am
    in distress;
  my eye wastes away from grief,
  my soul and body also.
10 For my life is spent with sorrow,
  and my years with sighing;
  my strength fails because of my
    misery,[c]
  and my bones waste away.

11 I am the scorn of all my adversaries,
  a horror[d] to my neighbours,
  an object of dread to my
    acquaintances;
  those who see me in the street flee
    from me.
12 I have passed out of mind like one
    who is dead;
  I have become like a broken vessel.
13 For I hear the whispering of many—
  terror all around!—
  as they scheme together against me,
  as they plot to take my life.

14 But I trust in you, O LORD;
  I say, 'You are my God.'
15 My times are in your hand;
  deliver me from the hand of my
    enemies and persecutors.
16 Let your face shine upon your
    servant;
  save me in your steadfast love.
17 Do not let me be put to shame,
    O LORD,
  for I call on you;
  let the wicked be put to shame;
  let them go dumbfounded to Sheol.
18 Let the lying lips be stilled
  that speak insolently against the
    righteous
  with pride and contempt.

19 O how abundant is your goodness
  that you have laid up for those who
    fear you,

a Heb that glory   b One Heb Ms Gk Syr Jerome: MT I
hate   c Gk Syr: Heb my iniquity
d Cn: Heb exceedingly

and accomplished for those who take
	refuge in you,
	in the sight of everyone!
20 In the shelter of your presence you
	hide them
	from human plots;
	you hold them safe under your shelter
	from contentious tongues.

21 Blessed be the LORD,
	for he has wondrously shown his
	steadfast love to me
	when I was beset as a city under
	siege.
22 I had said in my alarm,
	'I am driven far*a* from your sight.'
	But you heard my supplications
	when I cried out to you for help.

23 Love the LORD, all you his saints.
	The LORD preserves the faithful,
	but abundantly repays the one who
	acts haughtily.
24 Be strong, and let your heart take
	courage,
	all you who wait for the LORD.

Psalm 32

Of David. A Maskil.

1 Happy are those whose transgression
	is forgiven,
	whose sin is covered.
2 Happy are those to whom the LORD
	imputes no iniquity,
	and in whose spirit there is no deceit.

3 While I kept silence, my body wasted
	away
	through my groaning all day long.
4 For day and night your hand was
	heavy upon me;
	my strength was dried up*b* as by the
	heat of summer. *Selah*

5 Then I acknowledged my sin to you,
	and I did not hide my iniquity;
	I said, 'I will confess my
	transgressions to the LORD',
	and you forgave the guilt of my sin.
	                                   Selah

6 Therefore let all who are faithful
	offer prayer to you;
	at a time of distress,*c* the rush of
	mighty waters
	shall not reach them.
7 You are a hiding-place for me;
	you preserve me from trouble;
	you surround me with glad cries of
	deliverance. *Selah*

8 I will instruct you and teach you the
	way you should go;
	I will counsel you with my eye
	upon you.
9 Do not be like a horse or a mule,
	without understanding,
	whose temper must be curbed with
	bit and bridle,
	else it will not stay near you.

10 Many are the torments of the wicked,
	but steadfast love surrounds those
	who trust in the LORD.
11 Be glad in the LORD and rejoice,
	O righteous,
	and shout for joy, all you upright in
	heart.

Psalm 33

1 Rejoice in the LORD, O you righteous.
	Praise befits the upright.
2 Praise the LORD with the lyre;
	make melody to him with the harp
	of ten strings.
3 Sing to him a new song;
	play skilfully on the strings, with
	loud shouts.

4 For the word of the LORD is upright,
	and all his work is done in
	faithfulness.
5 He loves righteousness and justice;
	the earth is full of the steadfast love
	of the LORD.

6 By the word of the LORD the heavens
	were made,

a Another reading is *cut off*   *b* Meaning of Heb
uncertain   *c* Cn: Heb *at a time of finding only*

and all their host by the breath of
his mouth.

7 He gathered the waters of the sea as
in a bottle;
he put the deeps in storehouses.

8 Let all the earth fear the LORD;
let all the inhabitants of the world
stand in awe of him.

9 For he spoke, and it came to be;
he commanded, and it stood firm.

10 The LORD brings the counsel of the
nations to nothing;
he frustrates the plans of the
peoples.

11 The counsel of the LORD stands for
ever,
the thoughts of his heart to all
generations.

12 Happy is the nation whose God is the
LORD,
the people whom he has chosen as
his heritage.

13 The LORD looks down from heaven;
he sees all humankind.

14 From where he sits enthroned he
watches
all the inhabitants of the earth—

15 he who fashions the hearts of
them all,
and observes all their deeds.

16 A king is not saved by his great army;
a warrior is not delivered by his
great strength.

17 The war horse is a vain hope for
victory,
and by its great might it cannot
save.

18 Truly the eye of the LORD is on those
who fear him,
on those who hope in his steadfast
love,

19 to deliver their soul from death,
and to keep them alive in famine.

20 Our soul waits for the LORD;
he is our help and shield.

21 Our heart is glad in him,

because we trust in his holy name.

22 Let your steadfast love, O LORD, be
upon us,
even as we hope in you.

Psalm 34

Of David, when he feigned madness before
Abimelech, so that he drove him out, and he
went away.

1 I will bless the LORD at all times;
his praise shall continually be in
my mouth.

2 My soul makes its boast in the LORD;
let the humble hear and be glad.

3 O magnify the LORD with me,
and let us exalt his name together.

4 I sought the LORD, and he answered
me,
and delivered me from all my fears.

5 Look to him, and be radiant;
so your[a] faces shall never be
ashamed.

6 This poor soul cried, and was heard
by the LORD,
and was saved from every trouble.

7 The angel of the LORD encamps
around those who fear him, and
delivers them.

8 O taste and see that the LORD is
good;
happy are those who take refuge in
him.

9 O fear the LORD, you his holy ones,
for those who fear him have no
want.

10 The young lions suffer want and
hunger,
but those who seek the LORD lack
no good thing.

11 Come, O children, listen to me;
I will teach you the fear of the
LORD.

12 Which of you desires life,
and covets many days to enjoy
good?

13 Keep your tongue from evil,
and your lips from speaking deceit.

a Gk Syr Jerome: Heb their

14 Depart from evil, and do good;
     seek peace, and pursue it.

15 The eyes of the LORD are on the
         righteous,
     and his ears are open to their cry.
16 The face of the LORD is against
         evildoers,
     to cut off the remembrance of them
         from the earth.
17 When the righteous cry for help, the
         LORD hears,
     and rescues them from all their
         troubles.
18 The LORD is near to the broken-
         hearted,
     and saves the crushed in spirit.

19 Many are the afflictions of the
         righteous,
     but the LORD rescues them from
         them all.
20 He keeps all their bones;
     not one of them will be broken.
21 Evil brings death to the wicked,
     and those who hate the righteous
         will be condemned.
22 The LORD redeems the life of his
         servants;
     none of those who take refuge in
         him will be condemned.

Psalm 35

Of David.

1 Contend, O LORD, with those who
         contend with me;
     fight against those who fight
         against me!
2 Take hold of shield and buckler,
     and rise up to help me!
3 Draw the spear and javelin
         against my pursuers;
     say to my soul,
         'I am your salvation.'

4 Let them be put to shame and
         dishonour
     who seek after my life.
   Let them be turned back and
         confounded

who devise evil against me.
5 Let them be like chaff before the
         wind,
     with the angel of the LORD driving
         them on.
6 Let their way be dark and slippery,
     with the angel of the LORD pursuing
         them.

7 For without cause they hid their net*a*
         for me;
     without cause they dug a pit*b* for
         my life.
8 Let ruin come on them unawares.
   And let the net that they hid ensnare
         them;
     let them fall in it—to their ruin.

9 Then my soul shall rejoice in the
         LORD,
     exulting in his deliverance.
10 All my bones shall say,
         'O LORD, who is like you?
   You deliver the weak
         from those too strong for them,
         the weak and needy from those
             who despoil them.'

11 Malicious witnesses rise up;
     they ask me about things I do not
         know.
12 They repay me evil for good;
     my soul is forlorn.
13 But as for me, when they were sick,
     I wore sackcloth;
     I afflicted myself with fasting.
   I prayed with head bowed*c* on my
         bosom,
14   as though I grieved for a friend or a
             brother;
   I went about as one who laments for
         a mother,
     bowed down and in mourning.

15 But at my stumbling they gathered in
         glee,
     they gathered together against me;
   ruffians whom I did not know
         tore at me without ceasing;

---

a Heb *a pit, their net*   *b* The word *pit* is transposed
from the preceding line   *c* Or *My prayer turned back*

16 they impiously mocked more and
    more,[a]
    gnashing at me with their teeth.

17 How long, O Lord, will you look on?
    Rescue me from their ravages,
    my life from the lions!
18 Then I will thank you in the great
    congregation;
    in the mighty throng I will
    praise you.

19 Do not let my treacherous enemies
    rejoice over me,
    or those who hate me without
    cause wink the eye.
20 For they do not speak peace,
    but they conceive deceitful words
    against those who are quiet in the
    land.
21 They open wide their mouths against
    me;
    they say, 'Aha, Aha,
    our eyes have seen it.'

22 You have seen, O Lord; do not be
    silent!
    O Lord, do not be far from me!
23 Wake up! Bestir yourself for my
    defence,
    for my cause, my God and my Lord!
24 Vindicate me, O Lord, my God,
    according to your righteousness,
    and do not let them rejoice
    over me.
25 Do not let them say to themselves,
    'Aha, we have our heart's desire.'
    Do not let them say, 'We have
    swallowed you[b] up.'

26 Let all those who rejoice at my
    calamity
    be put to shame and confusion;
    let those who exalt themselves
    against me
    be clothed with shame and
    dishonour.

27 Let those who desire my vindication
    shout for joy and be glad,
    and say evermore,

'Great is the Lord,
    who delights in the welfare of his
    servant.'
28 Then my tongue shall tell of your
    righteousness
    and of your praise all day long.

Psalm 36

To the leader. Of David, the servant
of the Lord.

1 Transgression speaks to the wicked
    deep in their hearts;
    there is no fear of God
    before their eyes.
2 For they flatter themselves in their
    own eyes
    that their iniquity cannot be found
    out and hated.
3 The words of their mouths are
    mischief and deceit;
    they have ceased to act wisely and
    do good.
4 They plot mischief while on their
    beds;
    they are set on a way that is
    not good;
    they do not reject evil.

5 Your steadfast love, O Lord, extends
    to the heavens,
    your faithfulness to the clouds.
6 Your righteousness is like the mighty
    mountains,
    your judgements are like the great
    deep;
    you save humans and animals
    alike, O Lord.

7 How precious is your steadfast love,
    O God!
    All people may take refuge in the
    shadow of your wings.
8 They feast on the abundance of your
    house,
    and you give them drink from the
    river of your delights.
9 For with you is the fountain of life;
    in your light we see light.

a Cn Compare Gk: Heb *like the profanest of mockers of a cake*   b Heb *him*

10 O continue your steadfast love to
        those who know you,
   and your salvation to the upright of
        heart!
11 Do not let the foot of the arrogant
        tread on me,
   or the hand of the wicked drive me
        away.
12 There the evildoers lie prostrate;
   they are thrust down, unable
        to rise.

Psalm 37

Of David.

1 Do not fret because of the wicked;
   do not be envious of wrongdoers,
2 for they will soon fade like the grass,
   and wither like the green herb.

3 Trust in the LORD, and do good;
   so you will live in the land, and
        enjoy security.
4 Take delight in the LORD,
   and he will give you the desires of
        your heart.

5 Commit your way to the LORD;
   trust in him, and he will act.
6 He will make your vindication shine
        like the light,
   and the justice of your cause like
        the noonday.

7 Be still before the LORD, and wait
        patiently for him;
   do not fret over those who prosper
        in their way,
   over those who carry out evil
        devices.

8 Refrain from anger, and forsake
        wrath.
   Do not fret—it leads only to evil.
9 For the wicked shall be cut off,
   but those who wait for the LORD
     shall inherit the land.

10 Yet a little while, and the wicked will
   be no more;

though you look diligently for their
   place, they will not be there.
11 But the meek shall inherit the land,
   and delight in abundant prosperity.

12 The wicked plot against the
        righteous,
   and gnash their teeth at them;
13 but the LORD laughs at the wicked,
   for he sees that their day is
        coming.

14 The wicked draw the sword and bend
        their bows
   to bring down the poor and needy,
   to kill those who walk uprightly;
15 their sword shall enter their own
        heart,
   and their bows shall be broken.

16 Better is a little that the righteous
        person has
   than the abundance of many
        wicked.
17 For the arms of the wicked shall be
        broken,
   but the LORD upholds the righteous.

18 The LORD knows the days of the
        blameless,
   and their heritage will abide for
        ever;
19 they are not put to shame in evil
        times,
   in the days of famine they have
        abundance.

20 But the wicked perish,
   and the enemies of the LORD are
        like the glory of the pastures;
   they vanish—like smoke they
        vanish away.

21 The wicked borrow, and do not pay
        back,
   but the righteous are generous and
        keep giving;
22 for those blessed by the LORD shall
        inherit the land,
   but those cursed by him shall be
        cut off.

23 Our steps[a] are made firm by the
    LORD,
      when he delights in our[b] way;
24 though we stumble,[c] we[d] shall not
        fall headlong,
      for the LORD holds us[e] by the hand.

25 I have been young, and now am old,
      yet I have not seen the righteous
        forsaken
      or their children begging bread.
26 They are ever giving liberally and
        lending,
      and their children become a
        blessing.

27 Depart from evil, and do good;
      so you shall abide for ever.
28 For the LORD loves justice;
      he will not forsake his faithful
        ones.

    The righteous shall be kept safe for
        ever,
      but the children of the wicked shall
        be cut off.
29 The righteous shall inherit the land,
      and live in it for ever.

30 The mouths of the righteous utter
        wisdom,
      and their tongues speak justice.
31 The law of their God is in their
        hearts;
      their steps do not slip.

32 The wicked watch for the righteous,
      and seek to kill them.
33 The LORD will not abandon them to
        their power,
      or let them be condemned when
        they are brought to trial.

34 Wait for the LORD, and keep to his
        way,
      and he will exalt you to inherit the
        land;
      you will look on the destruction of
        the wicked.

35 I have seen the wicked oppressing,

    and towering like a cedar of
      Lebanon.[f]
36 Again I[g] passed by, and they were no
        more;
      though I sought them, they could
        not be found.

37 Mark the blameless, and behold the
        upright,
      for there is posterity for the
        peaceable.
38 But transgressors shall be altogether
        destroyed;
      the posterity of the wicked shall be
        cut off.

39 The salvation of the righteous is from
        the LORD;
      he is their refuge in the time of
        trouble.
40 The LORD helps them and rescues
        them;
      he rescues them from the wicked,
        and saves them,
      because they take refuge in him.

Psalm 38

A Psalm of David, for the memorial offering.

1 O LORD, do not rebuke me in your
        anger,
      or discipline me in your wrath.
2 For your arrows have sunk into me,
      and your hand has come down
        on me.

3 There is no soundness in my flesh
      because of your indignation;
    there is no health in my bones
      because of my sin.
4 For my iniquities have gone over my
        head;
      they weigh like a burden too heavy
        for me.

5 My wounds grow foul and fester
      because of my foolishness;

a Heb *A man's steps*   *b* Heb *his*   *c* Heb *he stumbles*
d Heb *he*   *e* Heb *him*   *f* Gk: Meaning of Heb
uncertain   *g* Gk Syr Jerome: Heb *he*

6 I am utterly bowed down and
        prostrate;
    all day long I go around mourning.
7 For my loins are filled with burning,
        and there is no soundness in my
            flesh.
8 I am utterly spent and crushed;
        I groan because of the tumult of my
            heart.

9 O Lord, all my longing is known
        to you;
    my sighing is not hidden from you.
10 My heart throbs, my strength
        fails me;
    as for the light of my eyes—it also
        has gone from me.
11 My friends and companions stand
        aloof from my affliction,
    and my neighbours stand far off.

12 Those who seek my life lay their
        snares;
    those who seek to hurt me speak of
        ruin,
    and meditate treachery all day long.

13 But I am like the deaf, I do not hear;
    like the mute, who cannot speak.
14 Truly, I am like one who does not
        hear,
    and in whose mouth is no retort.

15 But it is for you, O LORD, that I wait;
    it is you, O Lord my God, who will
        answer.
16 For I pray, 'Only do not let them
        rejoice over me,
    those who boast against me when
        my foot slips.'

17 For I am ready to fall,
    and my pain is ever with me.
18 I confess my iniquity;
    I am sorry for my sin.
19 Those who are my foes without
        cause[a] are mighty,
    and many are those who hate me
        wrongfully.
20 Those who render me evil for good

are my adversaries because I follow
    after good.

21 Do not forsake me, O LORD;
    O my God, do not be far from me;
22 make haste to help me,
    O Lord, my salvation.

Psalm 39

To the leader: to Jeduthun. A Psalm of David.

1 I said, 'I will guard my ways
        that I may not sin with my tongue;
    I will keep a muzzle on my mouth
        as long as the wicked are in my
            presence.'
2 I was silent and still;
        I held my peace to no avail;
    my distress grew worse,
3   my heart became hot within me.
    While I mused, the fire burned;
        then I spoke with my tongue:

4 'LORD, let me know my end,
        and what is the measure of my
            days;
    let me know how fleeting my life is.
5 You have made my days a few
        handbreadths,
    and my lifetime is as nothing in
        your sight.
    Surely everyone stands as a mere
        breath.   *Selah*
6   Surely everyone goes about like a
        shadow.
    Surely for nothing they are in
        turmoil;
    they heap up, and do not know
        who will gather.

7 'And now, O Lord, what do I wait for?
    My hope is in you.
8 Deliver me from all my
        transgressions.
    Do not make me the scorn of the
        fool.
9 I am silent; I do not open my mouth,
    for it is you who have done it.
10 Remove your stroke from me;

a Q Ms: MT *my living foes*

I am worn down by the blows[a] of
    your hand.

11 'You chastise mortals
    in punishment for sin,
    consuming like a moth what is dear
       to them;
    surely everyone is a mere breath.
                        Selah

12 'Hear my prayer, O LORD,
    and give ear to my cry;
    do not hold your peace at my tears.
    For I am your passing guest,
    an alien, like all my forebears.
13 Turn your gaze away from me, that I
    may smile again,
    before I depart and am no more.'

Psalm 40

To the leader. Of David. A Psalm.

1 I waited patiently for the LORD;
    he inclined to me and heard
       my cry.
2 He drew me up from the desolate
       pit,[b]
    out of the miry bog,
    and set my feet upon a rock,
       making my steps secure.
3 He put a new song in my mouth,
    a song of praise to our God.
    Many will see and fear,
       and put their trust in the LORD.

4 Happy are those who make
    the LORD their trust,
    who do not turn to the proud,
       to those who go astray after false
       gods.
5 You have multiplied, O LORD my
       God,
    your wondrous deeds and your
       thoughts towards us;
    none can compare with you.
    Were I to proclaim and tell of them,
       they would be more than can be
       counted.

6 Sacrifice and offering you do not
       desire,

but you have given me an open ear.[c]
Burnt-offering and sin-offering
    you have not required.
7 Then I said, 'Here I am;
    in the scroll of the book it is
       written of me.[d]
8 I delight to do your will, O my God;
    your law is within my heart.'

9 I have told the glad news of
       deliverance
    in the great congregation;
    see, I have not restrained my lips,
       as you know, O LORD.
10 I have not hidden your saving help
       within my heart,
    I have spoken of your faithfulness
       and your salvation;
    I have not concealed your steadfast
       love and your faithfulness
    from the great congregation.

11 Do not, O LORD, withhold
    your mercy from me;
    let your steadfast love and your
       faithfulness
    keep me safe for ever.
12 For evils have encompassed me
       without number;
    my iniquities have overtaken me,
       until I cannot see;
    they are more than the hairs of my
       head,
       and my heart fails me.

13 Be pleased, O LORD, to deliver me;
    O LORD, make haste to help me.
14 Let all those be put to shame and
       confusion
    who seek to snatch away my life;
    let those be turned back and brought
       to dishonour
    who desire my hurt.
15 Let those be appalled because of their
       shame
    who say to me, 'Aha, Aha!'

16 But may all who seek you
    rejoice and be glad in you;

a Heb *hostility*   *b* Cn: Heb *pit of tumult*   *c* Heb *ears you have dug for me*   *d* Meaning of Heb uncertain

may those who love your salvation
  say continually, 'Great is the LORD!'
17 As for me, I am poor and needy,
  but the Lord takes thought for me.
  You are my help and my deliverer;
  do not delay, O my God.

Psalm 41

To the leader. A Psalm of David.

1 Happy are those who consider the
  poor;*a*
  the LORD delivers them in the day
  of trouble.
2 The LORD protects them and keeps
  them alive;
  they are called happy in the land.
  You do not give them up to the will
  of their enemies.
3 The LORD sustains them on their
  sickbed;
  in their illness you heal all their
  infirmities.*b*

4 As for me, I said, 'O LORD, be gracious
  to me;
  heal me, for I have sinned against
  you.'
5 My enemies wonder in malice
  when I will die, and my name
  perish.
6 And when they come to see me, they
  utter empty words,
  while their hearts gather mischief;
  when they go out, they tell it
  abroad.
7 All who hate me whisper together
  about me;
  they imagine the worst for me.

8 They think that a deadly thing has
  fastened on me,
  that I will not rise again from
  where I lie.
9 Even my bosom friend in whom I
  trusted,
  who ate of my bread, has lifted the
  heel against me.
10 But you, O LORD, be gracious to me,
  and raise me up, that I may repay
  them.

11 By this I know that you are pleased
  with me;
  because my enemy has not
  triumphed over me.
12 But you have upheld me because of
  my integrity,
  and set me in your presence for
  ever.

13 Blessed be the LORD, the God of
  Israel,
  from everlasting to everlasting.
  Amen and Amen.

BOOK II

(Psalms 42-72)

Psalm 42

To the leader. A Maskil of the Korahites.

1 As a deer longs for flowing streams,
  so my soul longs for you, O God.
2 My soul thirsts for God,
  for the living God.
  When shall I come and behold
  the face of God?
3 My tears have been my food
  day and night,
  while people say to me continually,
  'Where is your God?'

4 These things I remember,
  as I pour out my soul:
  how I went with the throng,*c*
  and led them in procession to the
  house of God,
  with glad shouts and songs of
  thanksgiving,
  a multitude keeping festival.
5 Why are you cast down, O my soul,
  and why are you disquieted within
  me?
  Hope in God; for I shall again praise
  him,
  my help 6 and my God.

  My soul is cast down within me;
  therefore I remember you

a Or *weak*   *b* Heb *you change all his bed*   *c* Meaning
of Heb uncertain

from the land of Jordan and of
    Hermon,
  from Mount Mizar.
7 Deep calls to deep
    at the thunder of your cataracts;
  all your waves and your billows
    have gone over me.
8 By day the LORD commands his
    steadfast love,
  and at night his song is with me,
    a prayer to the God of my life.

9 I say to God, my rock,
    'Why have you forgotten me?
  Why must I walk about mournfully
    because the enemy oppresses me?'
10 As with a deadly wound in my body,
    my adversaries taunt me,
  while they say to me continually,
    'Where is your God?'

11 Why are you cast down, O my soul,
    and why are you disquieted within
      me?
  Hope in God; for I shall again praise
    him,
    my help and my God.

Psalm 43

1 Vindicate me, O God, and defend my
    cause
  against an ungodly people;
  from those who are deceitful and
    unjust
    deliver me!
2 For you are the God in whom I take
    refuge;
  why have you cast me off?
  Why must I walk about mournfully
    because of the oppression of the
      enemy?

3 O send out your light and your
    truth;
    let them lead me;
  let them bring me to your holy hill
    and to your dwelling.
4 Then I will go to the altar of God,
    to God my exceeding joy;
  and I will praise you with the harp,
    O God, my God.

5 Why are you cast down, O my soul,
    and why are you disquieted within
      me?
  Hope in God; for I shall again praise
    him,
    my help and my God.

Psalm 44

To the leader. Of the Korahites. A Maskil.

1 We have heard with our ears, O God,
    our ancestors have told us,
  what deeds you performed in their
    days,
    in the days of old:
2 you with your own hand drove out
    the nations,
    but them you planted;
  you afflicted the peoples,
    but them you set free;
3 for not by their own sword did they
    win the land,
    nor did their own arm give them
      victory;
  but your right hand, and your arm,
    and the light of your countenance,
    for you delighted in them.

4 You are my King and my God;
    you command *a* victories for Jacob.
5 Through you we push down our foes;
    through your name we tread down
      our assailants.
6 For not in my bow do I trust,
    nor can my sword save me.
7 But you have saved us from our foes,
    and have put to confusion those
      who hate us.
8 In God we have boasted continually,
    and we will give thanks to your
      name for ever.   *Selah*

9 Yet you have rejected us and abased
    us,
    and have not gone out with our
      armies.
10 You made us turn back from the foe,
    and our enemies have taken spoil
      for themselves.

a Gk Syr: Heb *You are my King, O God; command*

11 You have made us like sheep for
        slaughter,
    and have scattered us among
        the nations.
12 You have sold your people for a trifle,
    demanding no high price for them.

13 You have made us the taunt of our
        neighbours,
    the derision and scorn of those
        around us.
14 You have made us a byword among
        the nations,
    a laughing-stock[a] among the
        peoples.
15 All day long my disgrace is before
        me,
    and shame has covered my face
16 at the words of the taunters and
        revilers,
    at the sight of the enemy and the
        avenger.

17 All this has come upon us,
    yet we have not forgotten you,
    or been false to your covenant.
18 Our heart has not turned back,
    nor have our steps departed from
        your way,
19 yet you have broken us in the haunt
        of jackals,
    and covered us with deep darkness.

20 If we had forgotten the name of our
        God,
    or spread out our hands to a
        strange god,
21 would not God discover this?
    For he knows the secrets of the
        heart.
22 Because of you we are being killed all
        day long,
    and accounted as sheep for the
        slaughter.

23 Rouse yourself! Why do you sleep,
        O Lord?
    Awake, do not cast us off for ever!
24 Why do you hide your face?
    Why do you forget our affliction
        and oppression?

25 For we sink down to the dust;
    our bodies cling to the ground.
26 Rise up, come to our help.
    Redeem us for the sake of your
        steadfast love.

Psalm 45

To the leader: according to Lilies. Of the
Korahites. A Maskil. A love song.

1 My heart overflows with a goodly
        theme;
    I address my verses to the king;
    my tongue is like the pen of a ready
        scribe.

2 You are the most handsome of men;
    grace is poured upon your lips;
    therefore God has blessed you for
        ever.
3 Gird your sword on your thigh,
        O mighty one,
    in your glory and majesty.

4 In your majesty ride on victoriously
    for the cause of truth and to
        defend[b] the right;
    let your right hand teach you dread
        deeds.
5 Your arrows are sharp
    in the heart of the king's enemies;
    the peoples fall under you.

6 Your throne, O God,[c] endures for
        ever and ever.
    Your royal sceptre is a sceptre of
        equity;
7 you love righteousness and hate
        wickedness.
    Therefore God, your God, has
        anointed you
    with the oil of gladness beyond
        your companions;
8 your robes are all fragrant with
        myrrh and aloes and cassia.
    From ivory palaces stringed
        instruments make you glad;
9 daughters of kings are among your
        ladies of honour;

a Heb a shaking of the head   b Cn: Heb and the
meekness of   c Or Your throne is a throne of God, it

at your right hand stands the queen
   in gold of Ophir.

10 Hear, O daughter, consider and
   incline your ear;
forget your people and your father's
   house,
11 and the king will desire your
   beauty.
Since he is your lord, bow to him;
12 the people*a* of Tyre will seek your
   favour with gifts,
the richest of the people 13 with all
   kinds of wealth.

The princess is decked in her
   chamber with gold-woven
   robes;*b*
14 in many-coloured robes she is led
   to the king;
behind her the virgins, her
   companions, follow.
15 With joy and gladness they are
   led along
as they enter the palace of the king.

16 In the place of ancestors you,
   O king,*c* shall have sons;
you will make them princes in all
   the earth.
17 I will cause your name to be
   celebrated in all generations;
therefore the peoples will praise
   you for ever and ever.

Psalm 46

To the leader. Of the Korahites. According to
Alamoth. A Song.

1 God is our refuge and strength,
   a very present*d* help in trouble.
2 Therefore we will not fear, though the
   earth should change,
though the mountains shake in the
   heart of the sea;
3 though its waters roar and foam,
though the mountains tremble with
   its tumult.   *Selah*

4 There is a river whose streams make
   glad the city of God,

the holy habitation of the
   Most High.
5 God is in the midst of the city;*e* it
   shall not be moved;
God will help it when the morning
   dawns.
6 The nations are in an uproar, the
   kingdoms totter;
he utters his voice, the earth melts.
7 The Lord of hosts is with us;
   the God of Jacob is our refuge.*f*
             Selah

8 Come, behold the works of the Lord;
   see what desolations he has
   brought on the earth.
9 He makes wars cease to the end of
   the earth;
he breaks the bow, and shatters the
   spear;
he burns the shields with fire.
10 'Be still, and know that I am God!
I am exalted among the nations,
I am exalted in the earth.'
11 The Lord of hosts is with us;
   the God of Jacob is our refuge.*f*
             Selah

Psalm 47

To the leader. Of the Korahites. A Psalm.

1 Clap your hands, all you peoples;
   shout to God with loud songs
   of joy.
2 For the Lord, the Most High, is
   awesome,
a great king over all the earth.
3 He subdued peoples under us,
   and nations under our feet.
4 He chose our heritage for us,
   the pride of Jacob whom he loves.
             Selah

5 God has gone up with a shout,
   the Lord with the sound of a
   trumpet.
6 Sing praises to God, sing praises;

a Heb *daughter*   *b* Or *people.* 13 *All glorious is the
princess within, gold embroidery is her clothing*
c Heb lacks *O king*   *d* Or *well proved*   *e* Heb *of it*
f Or *fortress*

sing praises to our King, sing
   praises.
7 For God is the king of all the earth;
   sing praises with a psalm. *a*

8 God is king over the nations;
   God sits on his holy throne.
9 The princes of the peoples gather
   as the people of the God of
      Abraham.
   For the shields of the earth belong to
      God;
   he is highly exalted.

Psalm 48

A Song. A Psalm of the Korahites.

1 Great is the LORD and greatly to be
      praised
   in the city of our God.
   His holy mountain, 2 beautiful in
      elevation,
   is the joy of all the earth,
   Mount Zion, in the far north,
   the city of the great King.
3 Within its citadels God
   has shown himself a sure defence.

4 Then the kings assembled,
   they came on together.
5 As soon as they saw it, they were
      astounded;
   they were in panic, they took to
      flight;
6 trembling took hold of them there,
   pains as of a woman in labour,
7 as when an east wind shatters
   the ships of Tarshish.
8 As we have heard, so have we seen
   in the city of the LORD of hosts,
   in the city of our God,
   which God establishes for ever.
                                    Selah

9 We ponder your steadfast love,
      O God,
   in the midst of your temple.
10 Your name, O God, like your praise,
   reaches to the ends of the earth.
   Your right hand is filled with victory.
11   Let Mount Zion be glad,

let the towns *b* of Judah rejoice
   because of your judgements.

12 Walk about Zion, go all around it,
   count its towers,
13 consider well its ramparts;
   go through its citadels,
   that you may tell the next generation
14   that this is God,
   our God for ever and ever.
   He will be our guide for ever.

Psalm 49

To the leader. Of the Korahites. A Psalm.

1 Hear this, all you peoples;
   give ear, all inhabitants of the
      world,
2 both low and high,
   rich and poor together.
3 My mouth shall speak wisdom;
   the meditation of my heart shall be
      understanding.
4 I will incline my ear to a proverb;
   I will solve my riddle to the music
      of the harp.

5 Why should I fear in times of trouble,
   when the iniquity of my
      persecutors surrounds me,
6 those who trust in their wealth
   and boast of the abundance of their
      riches?
7 Truly, no ransom avails for one's life, *c*
   there is no price one can give to
      God for it.
8 For the ransom of life is costly,
   and can never suffice,
9 that one should live on for ever
   and never see the grave. *d*

10 When we look at the wise, they die;
   fool and dolt perish together
   and leave their wealth to others.
11 Their graves *e* are their homes for ever,
   their dwelling-places to all
      generations,

a Heb *Maskil*   *b* Heb *daughters*   *c* Another reading
is *no one can ransom a brother*   *d* Heb *the pit*
e Gk Syr Compare Tg: Heb *their inward* (thought)

though they named lands their
    own.

¹² Mortals cannot abide in their pomp;
    they are like the animals that
        perish.

¹³ Such is the fate of the foolhardy,
    the end of those*a* who are pleased
        with their lot.   *Selah*
¹⁴ Like sheep they are appointed for
        Sheol;
    Death shall be their shepherd;
    straight to the grave they descend,*b*
    and their form shall waste away;
    Sheol shall be their home.*c*
¹⁵ But God will ransom my soul from
        the power of Sheol,
    for he will receive me.   *Selah*

¹⁶ Do not be afraid when some become
        rich,
    when the wealth of their houses
        increases.
¹⁷ For when they die they will carry
        nothing away;
    their wealth will not go down after
        them.
¹⁸ Though in their lifetime they count
        themselves happy
    —for you are praised when you do
        well for yourself—
¹⁹ they*d* will go to the company of their
        ancestors,
    who will never again see the light.
²⁰ Mortals cannot abide in their pomp;
    they are like the animals that
        perish.

Psalm 50

A Psalm of Asaph.

¹ The mighty one, God the LORD,
    speaks and summons the earth
    from the rising of the sun to its
        setting.
² Out of Zion, the perfection of beauty,
    God shines forth.

³ Our God comes and does not keep
        silence,
    before him is a devouring fire,

and a mighty tempest all around
    him.
⁴ He calls to the heavens above
    and to the earth, that he may judge
        his people:
⁵ 'Gather to me my faithful ones,
    who made a covenant with me by
        sacrifice!'
⁶ The heavens declare his
        righteousness,
    for God himself is judge.   *Selah*

⁷ 'Hear, O my people, and I will
        speak,
    O Israel, I will testify against you.
    I am God, your God.
⁸ Not for your sacrifices do I rebuke
        you;
    your burnt-offerings are continually
        before me.
⁹ I will not accept a bull from your
        house,
    or goats from your folds.
¹⁰ For every wild animal of the forest is
        mine,
    the cattle on a thousand hills.
¹¹ I know all the birds of the air,*e*
    and all that moves in the field is
        mine.

¹² 'If I were hungry, I would not tell
        you,
    for the world and all that is in it is
        mine.
¹³ Do I eat the flesh of bulls,
    or drink the blood of goats?
¹⁴ Offer to God a sacrifice of
        thanksgiving,*f*
    and pay your vows to the
        Most High.
¹⁵ Call on me in the day of trouble;
    I will deliver you, and you shall
        glorify me.'

¹⁶ But to the wicked God says:
    'What right have you to recite my
        statutes,
    or take my covenant on your lips?

a Tg: Heb *after them*   *b* Cn: Heb *the upright shall have
dominion over them in the morning*   *c* Meaning of Heb
uncertain   *d* Cn: Heb *you*   *e* Gk Syr Tg: Heb
mountains*   *f* Or *make thanksgiving your sacrifice to God*

17 For you hate discipline,
　　and you cast my words behind you.
18 You make friends with a thief when
　　　you see one,
　　and you keep company with
　　　adulterers.

19 'You give your mouth free rein
　　　for evil,
　　and your tongue frames deceit.
20 You sit and speak against your kin;
　　you slander your own mother's
　　　child.
21 These things you have done and I
　　　have been silent;
　　you thought that I was one just like
　　　yourself.
　　But now I rebuke you, and lay the
　　　charge before you.

22 'Mark this, then, you who forget God,
　　or I will tear you apart, and there
　　　will be no one to deliver.
23 Those who bring thanksgiving as
　　　their sacrifice honour me;
　　to those who go the right way*a*
　　I will show the salvation of God.'

Psalm 51

To the leader. A Psalm of David, when the
prophet Nathan came to him, after he had
gone in to Bathsheba.

1 Have mercy on me, O God,
　　according to your steadfast love;
　　according to your abundant mercy
　　blot out my transgressions.
2 Wash me thoroughly from my
　　　iniquity,
　　and cleanse me from my sin.

3 For I know my transgressions,
　　and my sin is ever before me.
4 Against you, you alone, have I sinned,
　　and done what is evil in your sight,
　　so that you are justified in your
　　　sentence
　　and blameless when you pass
　　　judgement.
5 Indeed, I was born guilty,

　　a sinner when my mother
　　　conceived me.

6 You desire truth in the inward being;*b*
　　therefore teach me wisdom in my
　　　secret heart.
7 Purge me with hyssop, and I shall be
　　　clean;
　　wash me, and I shall be whiter than
　　　snow.
8 Let me hear joy and gladness;
　　let the bones that you have crushed
　　　rejoice.
9 Hide your face from my sins,
　　and blot out all my iniquities.

10 Create in me a clean heart, O God,
　　and put a new and right*c* spirit
　　　within me.
11 Do not cast me away from your
　　　presence,
　　and do not take your holy spirit
　　　from me.
12 Restore to me the joy of your
　　　salvation,
　　and sustain in me a willing*d* spirit.

13 Then I will teach transgressors your
　　　ways,
　　and sinners will return to you.
14 Deliver me from bloodshed, O God,
　　O God of my salvation,
　　and my tongue will sing aloud of
　　　your deliverance.

15 O Lord, open my lips,
　　and my mouth will declare your
　　　praise.
16 For you have no delight in sacrifice;
　　if I were to give a burnt-offering,
　　you would not be pleased.
17 The sacrifice acceptable to God*e* is a
　　　broken spirit;
　　a broken and contrite heart, O God,
　　you will not despise.

18 Do good to Zion in your good
　　　pleasure;

a Heb *who set a way*　　*b* Meaning of Heb uncertain
c Or *steadfast*　　*d* Or *generous*　　*e* Or *My sacrifice,
O God,*

rebuild the walls of Jerusalem,
¹⁹ then you will delight in right
sacrifices,
in burnt-offerings and whole burnt-
offerings;
then bulls will be offered on your
altar.

Psalm 52

To the leader. A Maskil of David, when Doeg
the Edomite came to Saul and said to him,
'David has come to the house of Ahimelech.'

¹ Why do you boast, O mighty one,
of mischief done against the
godly?*a*
All day long ²you are plotting
destruction.
Your tongue is like a sharp razor,
you worker of treachery.
³ You love evil more than good,
and lying more than speaking the
truth.   *Selah*
⁴ You love all words that devour,
O deceitful tongue.

⁵ But God will break you down for
ever;
he will snatch and tear you from
your tent;
he will uproot you from the land of
the living.   *Selah*
⁶ The righteous will see, and fear,
and will laugh at the evildoer,*b*
saying,
⁷ 'See the one who would not take
refuge in God,
but trusted in abundant riches,
and sought refuge in wealth!'*c*

⁸ But I am like a green olive tree
in the house of God.
I trust in the steadfast love of God
for ever and ever.
⁹ I will thank you for ever,
because of what you have done.
In the presence of the faithful
I will proclaim*d* your name, for it is
good.

Psalm 53

To the leader: according to Mahalath. A Maskil
of David.

¹ Fools say in their hearts, 'There is no
God.'
They are corrupt, they commit
abominable acts;
there is no one who does good.

² God looks down from heaven on
humankind
to see if there are any who are wise,
who seek after God.

³ They have all fallen away, they are all
alike perverse;
there is no one who does good,
no, not one.

⁴ Have they no knowledge, those
evildoers,
who eat up my people as they eat
bread,
and do not call upon God?

⁵ There they shall be in great terror,
in terror such as has not been.
For God will scatter the bones of the
ungodly;*e*
they will be put to shame,*f* for God
has rejected them.

⁶ O that deliverance for Israel would
come from Zion!
When God restores the fortunes of
his people,
Jacob will rejoice; Israel will be
glad.

Psalm 54

To the leader: with stringed instruments. A
Maskil of David, when the Ziphites went and
told Saul, 'David is in hiding among us.'

¹ Save me, O God, by your name,
and vindicate me by your might.

a Cn Compare Syr: Heb *the kindness of God*
b Heb *him*   *c* Syr Tg: Heb *in his destruction*
d Cn: Heb *wait for*   *e* Cn Compare Gk Syr: Heb *him
who encamps against you*   *f* Gk: Heb *you will put to
shame*

2 Hear my prayer, O God;
  give ear to the words of my mouth.

3 For the insolent have risen
        against me,
     the ruthless seek my life;
     they do not set God before them.
                                    Selah

4 But surely, God is my helper;
     the Lord is the upholder of*a* my
        life.
5 He will repay my enemies for their
     evil.
     In your faithfulness, put an end to
        them.

6 With a freewill-offering I will sacrifice
     to you;
     I will give thanks to your name,
     O LORD, for it is good.
7 For he has delivered me from every
     trouble,
     and my eye has looked in triumph
        on my enemies.

Psalm 55

To the leader: with stringed instruments.
A Maskil of David.

1 Give ear to my prayer, O God;
     do not hide yourself from my
        supplication.
2 Attend to me, and answer me;
     I am troubled in my complaint.
  I am distraught 3 by the noise of the
        enemy,
     because of the clamour of the
        wicked.
  For they bring*b* trouble upon me,
     and in anger they cherish enmity
        against me.

4 My heart is in anguish within me,
     the terrors of death have fallen
        upon me.
5 Fear and trembling come upon me,
     and horror overwhelms me.
6 And I say, 'O that I had wings like a
     dove!
     I would fly away and be at rest;

7 truly, I would flee far away;
     I would lodge in the wilderness;
                                    Selah
8 I would hurry to find a shelter for
     myself
     from the raging wind and tempest.'

9 Confuse, O Lord, confound their
        speech;
     for I see violence and strife in the
        city.
10 Day and night they go around it
     on its walls,
  and iniquity and trouble are
        within it;
11   ruin is in its midst;
  oppression and fraud
     do not depart from its market-
        place.

12 It is not enemies who taunt me—
     I could bear that;
  it is not adversaries who deal
        insolently with me—
     I could hide from them.
13 But it is you, my equal,
     my companion, my familiar friend,
14 with whom I kept pleasant company;
     we walked in the house of God
        with the throng.
15 Let death come upon them;
     let them go down alive to Sheol;
     for evil is in their homes and in
        their hearts.

16 But I call upon God,
     and the LORD will save me.
17 Evening and morning and at noon
     I utter my complaint and moan,
     and he will hear my voice.
18 He will redeem me unharmed
     from the battle that I wage,
     for many are arrayed against me.
19 God, who is enthroned from of old,
                                    Selah

  will hear, and will humble them—
  because they do not change,
     and do not fear God.

a Gk Syr Jerome: Heb *is of those who uphold* or *is with
those who uphold*   *b* Cn Compare Gk: Heb *they cause to
totter*

²⁰ My companion laid hands on a
        friend
     and violated a covenant with me^a
²¹ with speech smoother than butter,
     but with a heart set on war;
     with words that were softer than oil,
     but in fact were drawn swords.

²² Cast your burden^b on the LORD,
     and he will sustain you;
     he will never permit
     the righteous to be moved.

²³ But you, O God, will cast them down
     into the lowest pit;
     the bloodthirsty and treacherous
     shall not live out half their days.
     But I will trust in you.

Psalm 56

To the leader: according to The Dove on Far-
off Terebinths. Of David. A Miktam, when the
Philistines seized him in Gath.

¹ Be gracious to me, O God, for people
        trample on me;
     all day long foes oppress me;
² my enemies trample on me all day
        long,
     for many fight against me.
     O Most High, ³when I am afraid,
     I put my trust in you.
⁴ In God, whose word I praise,
     in God I trust; I am not afraid;
     what can flesh do to me?

⁵ All day long they seek to injure my
        cause;
     all their thoughts are against me for
        evil.
⁶ They stir up strife, they lurk,
     they watch my steps.
     As they hoped to have my life,
⁷   so repay^c them for their crime;
     in wrath cast down the peoples,
        O God!

⁸ You have kept count of my tossings;
     put my tears in your bottle.
     Are they not in your record?
⁹ Then my enemies will retreat

on the day when I call.
     This I know, that^d God is for me.
¹⁰ In God, whose word I praise,
     in the LORD, whose word I praise,
¹¹ in God I trust; I am not afraid.
     What can a mere mortal do to me?

¹² My vows to you I must perform,
        O God;
     I will render thank-offerings to you.
¹³ For you have delivered my soul from
        death,
     and my feet from falling,
     so that I may walk before God
     in the light of life.

Psalm 57

To the leader: Do Not Destroy. Of David. A
Miktam, when he fled from Saul, in the cave.

¹ Be merciful to me, O God, be
        merciful to me,
     for in you my soul takes refuge;
     in the shadow of your wings I will
        take refuge,
     until the destroying storms pass by.
² I cry to God Most High,
     to God who fulfils his purpose for
        me.
³ He will send from heaven and
        save me,
     he will put to shame those who
        trample on me.   *Selah*
     God will send forth his steadfast love
        and his faithfulness.

⁴ I lie down among lions
     that greedily devour^e human prey;
     their teeth are spears and arrows,
     their tongues sharp swords.

⁵ Be exalted, O God, above the
        heavens.
     Let your glory be over all the earth.

⁶ They set a net for my steps;
     my soul was bowed down.
     They dug a pit in my path,

a Heb lacks *with me*   b Or *Cast what he has given you*
c Cn: Heb *rescue*   d Or *because*   e Cn: Heb *are*
aflame for

but they have fallen into it
   themselves.   *Selah*
7 My heart is steadfast, O God,
   my heart is steadfast.
I will sing and make melody.
8   Awake, my soul!
Awake, O harp and lyre!
   I will awake the dawn.
9 I will give thanks to you, O Lord,
   among the peoples;
   I will sing praises to you among the
      nations.
10 For your steadfast love is as high as
   the heavens;
   your faithfulness extends to the
      clouds.

11 Be exalted, O God, above the
   heavens.
   Let your glory be over all the earth.

Psalm 58

To the leader: Do Not Destroy. Of David.
A Miktam.

1 Do you indeed decree what is right,
   you gods?[a]
Do you judge people fairly?
2 No, in your hearts you devise wrongs;
   your hands deal out violence on
      earth.

3 The wicked go astray from the womb;
   they err from their birth, speaking
      lies.
4 They have venom like the venom of a
   serpent,
   like the deaf adder that stops its ear,
5 so that it does not hear the voice of
   charmers
   or of the cunning enchanter.

6 O God, break the teeth in their
   mouths;
   tear out the fangs of the young
      lions, O Lord!
7 Let them vanish like water that runs
   away;
   like grass let them be trodden
      down[b] and wither.

8 Let them be like the snail that
   dissolves into slime;
   like the untimely birth that never
      sees the sun.
9 Sooner than your pots can feel the
   heat of thorns,
   whether green or ablaze, may he
      sweep them away!

10 The righteous will rejoice when they
   see vengeance done;
   they will bathe their feet in the
      blood of the wicked.
11 People will say, 'Surely there is a
   reward for the righteous;
   surely there is a God who judges on
      earth.'

Psalm 59

To the leader: Do Not Destroy. Of David.
A Miktam, when Saul ordered his house to be
watched in order to kill him.

1 Deliver me from my enemies, O my
   God;
   protect me from those who rise up
      against me.
2 Deliver me from those who work evil;
   from the bloodthirsty save me.

3 Even now they lie in wait for my life;
   the mighty stir up strife against me.
For no transgression or sin of mine,
   O Lord,
4   for no fault of mine, they run and
   make ready.

Rouse yourself, come to my help and
   see!
5   You, Lord God of hosts, are God of
   Israel.
Awake to punish all the nations;
   spare none of those who
      treacherously plot evil.   *Selah*

6 Each evening they come back,
   howling like dogs
   and prowling about the city.
7 There they are, bellowing with their
   mouths,

a Or *mighty lords*   *b* Cn: Meaning of Heb uncertain

with sharp words*a* on their lips—
for 'Who', they think,*b* 'will hear
us?'

8 But you laugh at them, O LORD;
    you hold all the nations in
        derision.
9 O my strength, I will watch for you;
    for you, O God, are my fortress.
10 My God in his steadfast love will
        meet me;
    my God will let me look in
        triumph on my enemies.

11 Do not kill them, or my people may
        forget;
    make them totter by your power,
        and bring them down,
    O Lord, our shield.
12 For the sin of their mouths, the
        words of their lips,
    let them be trapped in their pride.
    For the cursing and lies that they
        utter,
13   consume them in wrath;
    consume them until they are no
        more.
    Then it will be known to the ends of
        the earth
    that God rules over Jacob.   *Selah*

14 Each evening they come back,
        howling like dogs
    and prowling about the city.
15 They roam about for food,
    and growl if they do not get
        their fill.

16 But I will sing of your might;
    I will sing aloud of your steadfast
        love in the morning.
    For you have been a fortress for me
    and a refuge on the day of my
        distress.
17 O my strength, I will sing praises to
        you,
    for you, O God, are my fortress,
    the God who shows me steadfast
        love.

Psalm 60

To the leader: according to The Lily of the
Covenant. A Miktam of David; for instruction;
when he struggled with Aram-naharaim and
with Aram-zobah, and when Joab on his
return killed twelve thousand Edomites in the
Valley of Salt.

1 O God, you have rejected us, broken
        our defences;
    you have been angry; now
        restore us!
2 You have caused the land to quake;
        you have torn it open;
    repair the cracks in it, for it is
        tottering.
3 You have made your people suffer
        hard things;
    you have given us wine to drink
        that made us reel.

4 You have set up a banner for those
        who fear you,
    to rally to it out of bowshot.*c*   *Selah*
5 Give victory with your right hand,
        and answer us,*d*
    so that those whom you love may
        be rescued.

6 God has promised in his sanctuary:*e*
    'With exultation I will divide up
        Shechem,
    and portion out the Vale of Succoth.
7 Gilead is mine, and Manasseh is
        mine;
    Ephraim is my helmet;
    Judah is my sceptre.
8 Moab is my wash-basin;
    on Edom I hurl my shoe;
    over Philistia I shout in triumph.'

9 Who will bring me to the fortified
        city?
    Who will lead me to Edom?
10 Have you not rejected us, O God?
    You do not go out, O God, with our
        armies.
11 O grant us help against the foe,
    for human help is worthless.

a Heb *with swords*   *b* Heb lacks *they think*   *c* Gk Syr
Jerome: Heb *because of the truth*   *d* Another reading is
me   *e* Or *by his holiness*

12 With God we shall do valiantly;
    it is he who will tread down our
      foes.

Psalm 61

To the leader: with stringed instruments.
Of David.

1 Hear my cry, O God;
    listen to my prayer.
2 From the end of the earth I call
    to you,
    when my heart is faint.

    Lead me to the rock
    that is higher than I;
3 for you are my refuge,
    a strong tower against the enemy.

4 Let me abide in your tent for ever,
    find refuge under the shelter of
      your wings.   *Selah*
5 For you, O God, have heard my vows;
    you have given me the heritage of
      those who fear your name.

6 Prolong the life of the king;
    may his years endure to all
      generations!
7 May he be enthroned for ever
    before God;
    appoint steadfast love and
      faithfulness to watch over him!

8 So I will always sing praises to your
    name,
    as I pay my vows day after day.

Psalm 62

To the leader: according to Jeduthun. A Psalm
of David.

1 For God alone my soul waits in
    silence;
    from him comes my salvation.
2 He alone is my rock and my
    salvation,
    my fortress; I shall never be shaken.

3 How long will you assail a person,
    will you batter your victim, all
      of you,

    as you would a leaning wall, a
      tottering fence?
4 Their only plan is to bring down a
    person of prominence.
    They take pleasure in falsehood;
    they bless with their mouths,
    but inwardly they curse.   *Selah*

5 For God alone my soul waits in
    silence,
    for my hope is from him.
6 He alone is my rock and my
    salvation,
    my fortress; I shall not be shaken.
7 On God rests my deliverance and my
    honour;
    my mighty rock, my refuge is in
      God.

8 Trust in him at all times, O people;
    pour out your heart before him;
    God is a refuge for us.   *Selah*

9 Those of low estate are but a breath,
    those of high estate are a delusion;
    in the balances they go up;
    they are together lighter than a
      breath.
10 Put no confidence in extortion,
    and set no vain hopes on robbery;
    if riches increase, do not set your
      heart on them.

11 Once God has spoken;
    twice have I heard this:
    that power belongs to God,
12   and steadfast love belongs to you,
      O Lord.
    For you repay to all
    according to their work.

Psalm 63

A Psalm of David, when he was in the
Wilderness of Judah.

1 O God, you are my God, I seek you,
    my soul thirsts for you;
    my flesh faints for you,
    as in a dry and weary land where
      there is no water.

2 So I have looked upon you in the
   sanctuary,
      beholding your power and glory.
3 Because your steadfast love is better
   than life,
      my lips will praise you.
4 So I will bless you as long as I live;
      I will lift up my hands and call on
      your name.

5 My soul is satisfied as with a rich
   feast, [a]
      and my mouth praises you with
      joyful lips
6 when I think of you on my bed,
      and meditate on you in the watches
      of the night;
7 for you have been my help,
      and in the shadow of your wings I
      sing for joy.
8 My soul clings to you;
      your right hand upholds me.

9 But those who seek to destroy my life
      shall go down into the depths of
      the earth;
10 they shall be given over to the power
   of the sword,
      they shall be prey for jackals.
11 But the king shall rejoice in God;
      all who swear by him shall exult,
      for the mouths of liars will be
      stopped.

Psalm 64

To the leader. A Psalm of David.

1 Hear my voice, O God, in my
   complaint;
      preserve my life from the dread
      enemy.
2 Hide me from the secret plots of the
   wicked,
      from the scheming of evildoers,
3 who whet their tongues like swords,
      who aim bitter words like arrows,
4 shooting from ambush at the
   blameless;
      they shoot suddenly and without
      fear.
5 They hold fast to their evil purpose;

they talk of laying snares secretly,
   thinking, 'Who can see us? [b]
6   Who can search out our crimes? [c]
   We have thought out a cunningly
      conceived plot.'
      For the human heart and mind are
      deep.

7 But God will shoot his arrow at them;
      they will be wounded suddenly.
8 Because of their tongue he will bring
   them to ruin; [d]
      all who see them will shake with
      horror.
9 Then everyone will fear;
      they will tell what God has brought
      about,
      and ponder what he has done.

10 Let the righteous rejoice in the LORD
      and take refuge in him.
   Let all the upright in heart glory.

Psalm 65

To the leader. A Psalm of David. A Song.

1 Praise is due to you,
      O God, in Zion;
   and to you shall vows be performed,
2   O you who answer prayer!
   To you all flesh shall come.
3 When deeds of iniquity overwhelm
   us,
      you forgive our transgressions.
4 Happy are those whom you choose
      and bring near
      to live in your courts.
   We shall be satisfied with the
      goodness of your house,
      your holy temple.

5 By awesome deeds you answer us
      with deliverance,
      O God of our salvation;
   you are the hope of all the ends of
      the earth
      and of the farthest seas.

a Heb *with fat and fatness*   b Syr: Heb *them*
c Cn: Heb *They search out crimes*   d Cn: Heb *They will*
bring him to ruin, their tongue being against them

⁶ By your*a* strength you established the
        mountains;
   you are girded with might.
⁷ You silence the roaring of the seas,
        the roaring of their waves,
        the tumult of the peoples.
⁸ Those who live at earth's farthest
            bounds are awed by your signs;
   you make the gateways of the
            morning and the evening shout
            for joy.

⁹ You visit the earth and water it,
        you greatly enrich it;
   the river of God is full of water;
        you provide the people with grain,
        for so you have prepared it.
¹⁰ You water its furrows abundantly,
        settling its ridges,
   softening it with showers,
        and blessing its growth.
¹¹ You crown the year with your bounty;
        your wagon tracks overflow with
            richness.
¹² The pastures of the wilderness
            overflow,
   the hills gird themselves with joy,
¹³ the meadows clothe themselves with
            flocks,
   the valleys deck themselves with
            grain,
   they shout and sing together for joy.

Psalm 66

To the leader. A Song. A Psalm.

¹ Make a joyful noise to God, all the
        earth;
² sing the glory of his name;
        give to him glorious praise.
³ Say to God, 'How awesome are your
        deeds!
   Because of your great power, your
        enemies cringe before you.
⁴ All the earth worships you;
        they sing praises to you,
        sing praises to your name.'   *Selah*

⁵ Come and see what God has done:
   he is awesome in his deeds among
        mortals.

⁶ He turned the sea into dry land;
        they passed through the river
            on foot.
   There we rejoiced in him,
⁷ who rules by his might for ever,
   whose eyes keep watch on the
            nations—
        let the rebellious not exalt
            themselves.   *Selah*

⁸ Bless our God, O peoples,
        let the sound of his praise be
            heard,
⁹ who has kept us among the living,
        and has not let our feet slip.
¹⁰ For you, O God, have tested us;
        you have tried us as silver is tried.
¹¹ You brought us into the net;
        you laid burdens on our backs;
¹² you let people ride over our heads;
        we went through fire and through
            water;
   yet you have brought us out to a
        spacious place.*b*

¹³ I will come into your house with
            burnt-offerings;
   I will pay you my vows,
¹⁴ those that my lips uttered
        and my mouth promised when I
            was in trouble.
¹⁵ I will offer to you burnt-offerings of
            fatlings,
        with the smoke of the sacrifice of
            rams;
   I will make an offering of bulls and
        goats.   *Selah*

¹⁶ Come and hear, all you who fear
            God,
        and I will tell what he has done for
            me.
¹⁷ I cried aloud to him,
        and he was extolled with my
            tongue.
¹⁸ If I had cherished iniquity in my
            heart,
        the Lord would not have listened.
¹⁹ But truly God has listened;

a Gk Jerome: Heb *his*   *b* Cn Compare Gk Syr Jerome
Tg: Heb *to a saturation*

he has given heed to the words of
my prayer.

20 Blessed be God,
because he has not rejected my
prayer
or removed his steadfast love from
me.

Psalm 67

To the leader: with stringed instruments.
A Psalm. A Song.

1 May God be gracious to us and bless
us
and make his face to shine upon us,
Selah
2 that your way may be known upon
earth,
your saving power among all
nations.
3 Let the peoples praise you, O God;
let all the peoples praise you.

4 Let the nations be glad and sing
for joy,
for you judge the peoples with
equity
and guide the nations upon earth.
Selah
5 Let the peoples praise you, O God;
let all the peoples praise you.

6 The earth has yielded its increase;
God, our God, has blessed us.
7 May God continue to bless us;
let all the ends of the earth revere
him.

Psalm 68

To the leader. Of David. A Psalm. A Song.

1 Let God rise up, let his enemies be
scattered;
let those who hate him flee before
him.
2 As smoke is driven away, so drive
them away;
as wax melts before the fire,
let the wicked perish before God.
3 But let the righteous be joyful;

let them exult before God;
let them be jubilant with joy.

4 Sing to God, sing praises to his name;
lift up a song to him who rides
upon the clouds[a]—
his name is the LORD—
be exultant before him.

5 Father of orphans and protector of
widows
is God in his holy habitation.
6 God gives the desolate a home to live
in;
he leads out the prisoners to
prosperity,
but the rebellious live in a parched
land.

7 O God, when you went out before
your people,
when you marched through the
wilderness, *Selah*
8 the earth quaked, the heavens poured
down rain
at the presence of God, the God of
Sinai,
at the presence of God, the God of
Israel.
9 Rain in abundance, O God, you
showered abroad;
you restored your heritage when it
languished;
10 your flock found a dwelling in it;
in your goodness, O God, you
provided for the needy.

11 The Lord gives the command;
great is the company of those[b] who
bore the tidings:
12 'The kings of the armies, they flee,
they flee!'
The women at home divide the spoil,
13 though they stay among the
sheepfolds—
the wings of a dove covered with
silver,
its pinions with green gold.

a Or *cast up a highway for him who rides through the
deserts   b* Or *company of the women*

14 When the Almighty*a* scattered kings
        there,
    snow fell on Zalmon.

15 O mighty mountain, mountain of
        Bashan;
    O many-peaked mountain,
        mountain of Bashan!
16 Why do you look with envy, O many-
        peaked mountain,
    at the mount that God desired for
        his abode,
    where the LORD will reside for ever?

17 With mighty chariotry, twice ten
        thousand,
    thousands upon thousands,
    the Lord came from Sinai into the
        holy place.*b*
18 You ascended the high mount,
    leading captives in your train
    and receiving gifts from people,
    even from those who rebel against
        the LORD God's abiding there.
19 Blessed be the Lord,
    who daily bears us up;
    God is our salvation.   *Selah*
20 Our God is a God of salvation,
    and to GOD, the Lord, belongs
        escape from death.

21 But God will shatter the heads of his
        enemies,
    the hairy crown of those who walk
        in their guilty ways.
22 The Lord said,
    'I will bring them back from
        Bashan,
    I will bring them back from the
        depths of the sea,
23 so that you may bathe*c* your feet in
        blood,
    so that the tongues of your dogs may
        have their share from the foe.'

24 Your solemn processions are seen,*d*
        O God,
    the processions of my God, my
        King, into the sanctuary—
25 the singers in front, the musicians
        last,

between them girls playing
        tambourines:
26 'Bless God in the great congregation,
    the LORD, O you who are of Israel's
        fountain!'
27 There is Benjamin, the least of them,
        in the lead,
    the princes of Judah in a body,
    the princes of Zebulun, the princes
        of Naphtali.

28 Summon your might, O God;
    show your strength, O God, as you
        have done for us before.
29 Because of your temple at Jerusalem
    kings bear gifts to you.
30 Rebuke the wild animals that live
        among the reeds,
    the herd of bulls with the calves of
        the peoples.
    Trample*e* under foot those who lust
        after tribute;
    scatter the peoples who delight in
        war.*f*
31 Let bronze be brought from Egypt;
    let Ethiopia*g* hasten to stretch out
        its hands to God.

32 Sing to God, O kingdoms of the
        earth;
    sing praises to the Lord,   *Selah*
33 O rider in the heavens, the ancient
        heavens;
    listen, he sends out his voice, his
        mighty voice.
34 Ascribe power to God,
    whose majesty is over Israel;
    and whose power is in the skies.
35 Awesome is God in his*h* sanctuary,
    the God of Israel;
    he gives power and strength to his
        people.

    Blessed be God!

a Traditional rendering of Heb *Shaddai*   *b* Cn: Heb
The Lord among them Sinai in the holy (place)   *c* Gk Syr
Tg: Heb *shatter*   *d* Or *have been seen*   *e* Cn: Heb
Trampling   *f* Meaning of Heb of verse 30 is uncertain
g Or *Nubia*; Heb *Cush*   *h* Gk: Heb *from your*

Psalm 69

To the leader: according to Lilies. Of David.

1 Save me, O God,
   for the waters have come up to my
      neck.
2 I sink in deep mire,
   where there is no foothold;
 I have come into deep waters,
   and the flood sweeps over me.
3 I am weary with my crying;
   my throat is parched.
 My eyes grow dim
   with waiting for my God.

4 More in number than the hairs of my
      head
   are those who hate me without
      cause;
 many are those who would destroy
      me,
   my enemies who accuse me falsely.
 What I did not steal
   must I now restore?
5 O God, you know my folly;
   the wrongs I have done are not
      hidden from you.

6 Do not let those who hope in you be
      put to shame because of me,
   O Lord GOD of hosts;
 do not let those who seek you be
      dishonoured because of me,
   O God of Israel.
7 It is for your sake that I have borne
      reproach,
   that shame has covered my face.
8 I have become a stranger to my
      kindred,
   an alien to my mother's children.

9 It is zeal for your house that has
      consumed me;
   the insults of those who insult you
      have fallen on me.
10 When I humbled my soul with
      fasting,[a]
   they insulted me for doing so.
11 When I made sackcloth my clothing,
   I became a byword to them.

12 I am the subject of gossip for those
      who sit in the gate,
   and the drunkards make songs
      about me.

13 But as for me, my prayer is to you,
      O LORD.
   At an acceptable time, O God,
   in the abundance of your steadfast
      love, answer me.
14 With your faithful help [14] rescue me
   from sinking in the mire;
 let me be delivered from my
      enemies
   and from the deep waters.
15 Do not let the flood sweep over me,
   or the deep swallow me up,
   or the Pit close its mouth over me.

16 Answer me, O LORD, for your
      steadfast love is good;
   according to your abundant mercy,
      turn to me.
17 Do not hide your face from your
      servant,
   for I am in distress—make haste to
      answer me.
18 Draw near to me, redeem me,
   set me free because of my enemies.

19 You know the insults I receive,
   and my shame and dishonour;
   my foes are all known to you.
20 Insults have broken my heart,
   so that I am in despair.
 I looked for pity, but there was
      none;
   and for comforters, but I found
      none.
21 They gave me poison for food,
   and for my thirst they gave me
      vinegar to drink.

22 Let their table be a trap for them,
   a snare for their allies.
23 Let their eyes be darkened so that
      they cannot see,
   and make their loins tremble
      continually.

a Gk Syr: Heb I wept, with fasting my soul, or I made my
soul mourn with fasting

24 Pour out your indignation upon them,
 and let your burning anger overtake
  them.
25 May their camp be a desolation;
 let no one live in their tents.
26 For they persecute those whom you
  have struck down,
 and those whom you have
  wounded, they attack still
  more.*a*
27 Add guilt to their guilt;
 may they have no acquittal from
  you.
28 Let them be blotted out of the book
  of the living;
 let them not be enrolled among the
  righteous.
29 But I am lowly and in pain;
 let your salvation, O God, protect
  me.

30 I will praise the name of God with a
  song;
 I will magnify him with
  thanksgiving.
31 This will please the LORD more than
  an ox
 or a bull with horns and hoofs.
32 Let the oppressed see it and be glad;
 you who seek God, let your hearts
  revive.
33 For the LORD hears the needy,
 and does not despise his own that
  are in bonds.

34 Let heaven and earth praise him,
 the seas and everything that moves
  in them.
35 For God will save Zion
 and rebuild the cities of Judah;
 and his servants shall live*b* there and
  possess it;
36 the children of his servants shall
  inherit it,
 and those who love his name shall
  live in it.

Psalm 70

To the leader. Of David, for the
memorial offering.

1 Be pleased, O God, to deliver me.
 O LORD, make haste to help me!
2 Let those be put to shame and
  confusion
 who seek my life.
 Let those be turned back and brought
  to dishonour
 who desire to hurt me.
3 Let those who say, 'Aha, Aha!'
 turn back because of their shame.

4 Let all who seek you
 rejoice and be glad in you.
 Let those who love your salvation
 say evermore, 'God is great!'
5 But I am poor and needy;
 hasten to me, O God!
 You are my help and my deliverer;
 O LORD, do not delay!

Psalm 71

1 In you, O LORD, I take refuge;
 let me never be put to shame.
2 In your righteousness deliver me and
  rescue me;
 incline your ear to me and save me.
3 Be to me a rock of refuge,
 a strong fortress,*c* to save me,
 for you are my rock and my
  fortress.

4 Rescue me, O my God, from the hand
  of the wicked,
 from the grasp of the unjust and
  cruel.
5 For you, O Lord, are my hope,
 my trust, O LORD, from my youth.
6 Upon you I have leaned from my birth;
 it was you who took me from my
  mother's womb.
 My praise is continually of you.

7 I have been like a portent to many,
 but you are my strong refuge.

a Gk Syr: Heb *recount the pain of* *b* Syr: Heb *and they
shall live* *c* Gk Compare 31.3: Heb *to come continually
you have commanded*

8 My mouth is filled with your praise,
  and with your glory all day long.
9 Do not cast me off in the time of old
  age;
    do not forsake me when my
    strength is spent.
10 For my enemies speak concerning
  me,
    and those who watch for my life
    consult together.
11 They say, 'Pursue and seize that
  person
    whom God has forsaken,
    for there is no one to deliver.'

12 O God, do not be far from me;
    O my God, make haste to help me!
13 Let my accusers be put to shame and
  consumed;
    let those who seek to hurt me
    be covered with scorn and disgrace.
14 But I will hope continually,
    and will praise you yet more and
    more.
15 My mouth will tell of your righteous
  acts,
    of your deeds of salvation all day
    long,
    though their number is past my
    knowledge.
16 I will come praising the mighty deeds
    of the Lord GOD,
    I will praise your righteousness,
    yours alone.

17 O God, from my youth you have
    taught me,
    and I still proclaim your wondrous
    deeds.
18 So even to old age and grey hairs,
    O God, do not forsake me,
  until I proclaim your might
    to all the generations to come. *a*
  Your power 19 and your righteousness,
    O God,
    reach the high heavens.

  You who have done great things,
    O God, who is like you?
20 You who have made me see many
    troubles and calamities

will revive me again;
from the depths of the earth
  you will bring me up again.
21 You will increase my honour,
    and comfort me once again.

22 I will also praise you with the harp
    for your faithfulness, O my God;
  I will sing praises to you with the
    lyre,
    O Holy One of Israel.
23 My lips will shout for joy
    when I sing praises to you;
    my soul also, which you have
    rescued.
24 All day long my tongue will talk of
    your righteous help,
  for those who tried to do me harm
    have been put to shame, and
    disgraced.

Psalm 72

Of Solomon.

1 Give the king your justice, O God,
    and your righteousness to a king's
    son.
2 May he judge your people with
    righteousness,
    and your poor with justice.
3 May the mountains yield prosperity
    for the people,
    and the hills, in righteousness.
4 May he defend the cause of the poor
    of the people,
    give deliverance to the needy,
    and crush the oppressor.

5 May he live *b* while the sun endures,
    and as long as the moon,
    throughout all generations.
6 May he be like rain that falls on the
    mown grass,
    like showers that water the earth.
7 In his days may righteousness
    flourish
    and peace abound, until the moon
    is no more.

a Gk Compare Syr: Heb *to a generation, to all that come*
b Gk: Heb *may they fear you*

⁸ May he have dominion from sea to
    sea,
    and from the River to the ends of
    the earth.
⁹ May his foes *a* bow down before him,
    and his enemies lick the dust.
¹⁰ May the kings of Tarshish and of the
    isles
    render him tribute,
    may the kings of Sheba and Seba
    bring gifts.
¹¹ May all kings fall down before him,
    all nations give him service.

¹² For he delivers the needy when they
    call,
    the poor and those who have no
    helper.
¹³ He has pity on the weak and the needy,
    and saves the lives of the needy.
¹⁴ From oppression and violence he
    redeems their life;
    and precious is their blood in his
    sight.

¹⁵ Long may he live!
    May gold of Sheba be given to him.
    May prayer be made for him
    continually,
    and blessings invoked for him all
    day long.
¹⁶ May there be abundance of grain in
    the land;
    may it wave on the tops of the
    mountains;
    may its fruit be like Lebanon;
    and may people blossom in the cities
    like the grass of the field.
¹⁷ May his name endure for ever,
    his fame continue as long as the sun.
    May all nations be blessed in him; *b*
    may they pronounce him happy.

¹⁸ Blessed be the LORD, the God of Israel,
    who alone does wondrous things.
¹⁹ Blessed be his glorious name for ever;
    may his glory fill the whole earth.
          Amen and Amen.

²⁰ The prayers of David son of Jesse are
    ended.

BOOK III

(Psalms 73-89)

Psalm 73

A Psalm of Asaph.

¹ Truly God is good to the upright, *c*
    to those who are pure in heart.
² But as for me, my feet had almost
    stumbled;
    my steps had nearly slipped.
³ For I was envious of the arrogant;
    I saw the prosperity of the wicked.

⁴ For they have no pain;
    their bodies are sound and sleek.
⁵ They are not in trouble as others are;
    they are not plagued like other
    people.
⁶ Therefore pride is their necklace;
    violence covers them like a
    garment.
⁷ Their eyes swell out with fatness;
    their hearts overflow with follies.
⁸ They scoff and speak with malice;
    loftily they threaten oppression.
⁹ They set their mouths against heaven,
    and their tongues range over the
    earth.

¹⁰ Therefore the people turn and praise
    them, *d*
    and find no fault in them. *e*
¹¹ And they say, 'How can God know?
    Is there knowledge in the
    Most High?'
¹² Such are the wicked;
    always at ease, they increase in
    riches.
¹³ All in vain I have kept my heart clean
    and washed my hands in
    innocence.
¹⁴ For all day long I have been plagued,
    and am punished every morning.

¹⁵ If I had said, 'I will talk on in this
    way',

a Cn: Heb *those who live in the wilderness*   *b* Or *bless
themselves by him*   *c* Or *good to Israel*   *d* Cn: Heb *his
people return here*   *e* Cn: Heb *abundant waters are
drained by them*

I would have been untrue to the
circle of your children.
16 But when I thought how to
understand this,
it seemed to me a wearisome task,
17 until I went into the sanctuary
of God;
then I perceived their end.
18 Truly you set them in slippery places;
you make them fall to ruin.
19 How they are destroyed in a moment,
swept away utterly by terrors!
20 They are*a* like a dream when one
awakes;
on awaking you despise their
phantoms.

21 When my soul was embittered,
when I was pricked in heart,
22 I was stupid and ignorant;
I was like a brute beast towards
you.
23 Nevertheless I am continually
with you;
you hold my right hand.
24 You guide me with your counsel,
and afterwards you will receive me
with honour.*b*
25 Whom have I in heaven but you?
And there is nothing on earth that I
desire other than you.
26 My flesh and my heart may fail,
but God is the strength*c* of my
heart and my portion for ever.

27 Indeed, those who are far from you
will perish;
you put an end to those who are
false to you.
28 But for me it is good to be near God;
I have made the Lord GOD my
refuge,
to tell of all your works.

Psalm 74

A Maskil of Asaph.

1 O God, why do you cast us off for
ever?
Why does your anger smoke against
the sheep of your pasture?

2 Remember your congregation, which
you acquired long ago,
which you redeemed to be the tribe
of your heritage.
Remember Mount Zion, where you
came to dwell.
3 Direct your steps to the perpetual
ruins;
the enemy has destroyed everything
in the sanctuary.

4 Your foes have roared within your
holy place;
they set up their emblems there.
5 At the upper entrance they hacked
the wooden trellis with axes.*d*
6 And then, with hatchets and
hammers,
they smashed all its carved work.
7 They set your sanctuary on fire;
they desecrated the dwelling-place
of your name,
bringing it to the ground.
8 They said to themselves, 'We will
utterly subdue them';
they burned all the meeting-places
of God in the land.

9 We do not see our emblems;
there is no longer any prophet,
and there is no one among us who
knows how long.
10 How long, O God, is the foe to scoff?
Is the enemy to revile your name
for ever?
11 Why do you hold back your hand;
why do you keep your hand in*e*
your bosom?

12 Yet God my King is from of old,
working salvation in the earth.
13 You divided the sea by your might;
you broke the heads of the dragons
in the waters.
14 You crushed the heads of Leviathan;
you gave him as food*f* for the
creatures of the wilderness.

a Cn: Heb *Lord*   *b* Or *to glory*   *c* Heb *rock*
d Cn Compare Gk Syr: Meaning of Heb uncertain
e Cn: Heb *do you consume your right hand from*
f Heb *food for the people*

15 You cut openings for springs and
        torrents;
    you dried up ever-flowing streams.
16 Yours is the day, yours also the
        night;
    you established the luminaries*a*
        and the sun.
17 You have fixed all the bounds of the
        earth;
    you made summer and winter.

18 Remember this, O LORD, how the
        enemy scoffs,
    and an impious people reviles your
        name.
19 Do not deliver the soul of your dove
        to the wild animals;
    do not forget the life of your poor
        for ever.

20 Have regard for your*b* covenant,
    for the dark places of the land are
        full of the haunts of violence.
21 Do not let the downtrodden be put
        to shame;
    let the poor and needy praise your
        name.
22 Rise up, O God, plead your cause;
    remember how the impious scoff at
        you all day long.
23 Do not forget the clamour of your
        foes,
    the uproar of your adversaries that
        goes up continually.

Psalm 75

To the leader: Do Not Destroy. A Psalm of
Asaph. A Song.

1 We give thanks to you, O God;
    we give thanks; your name is near.
    People tell of your wondrous deeds.

2 At the set time that I appoint
    I will judge with equity.
3 When the earth totters, with all its
        inhabitants,
    it is I who keep its pillars steady.
                                    Selah

4 I say to the boastful, 'Do not boast',

and to the wicked, 'Do not lift up
        your horn;
5 do not lift up your horn on high,
    or speak with insolent neck.'

6 For not from the east or from the west
    and not from the wilderness comes
        lifting up;
7 but it is God who executes
        judgement,
    putting down one and lifting up
        another.
8 For in the hand of the LORD there is a
        cup
    with foaming wine, well mixed;
    he will pour a draught from it,
    and all the wicked of the earth
    shall drain it down to the dregs.
9 But I will rejoice*c* for ever;
    I will sing praises to the God of
        Jacob.

10 All the horns of the wicked I will cut
        off,
    but the horns of the righteous shall
        be exalted.

Psalm 76

To the leader: with stringed instruments.
A Psalm of Asaph. A Song.

1 In Judah God is known,
    his name is great in Israel.
2 His abode has been established in
        Salem,
    his dwelling-place in Zion.
3 There he broke the flashing arrows,
    the shield, the sword, and the
        weapons of war.   *Selah*

4 Glorious are you, more majestic
    than the everlasting mountains.*d*
5 The stout-hearted were stripped of
        their spoil;
    they sank into sleep;
    none of the troops
    was able to lift a hand.
6 At your rebuke, O God of Jacob,
    both rider and horse lay stunned.

a Or *moon;* Heb *light*   *b* Gk Syr: Heb *the*   *c* Gk: Heb
declare   *d* Gk: Heb *the mountains of prey*

7 But you indeed are awesome!
    Who can stand before you
    when once your anger is roused?
8 From the heavens you uttered
        judgement;
    the earth feared and was still
9 when God rose up to establish
        judgement,
    to save all the oppressed of the
        earth.   *Selah*

10 Human wrath serves only to
        praise you,
    when you bind the last bit of your*a*
        wrath around you.
11 Make vows to the LORD your God,
        and perform them;
    let all who are around him bring
        gifts
    to the one who is awesome,
12 who cuts off the spirit of princes,
    who inspires fear in the kings of the
        earth.

Psalm 77

To the leader: according to Jeduthun.
Of Asaph. A Psalm.

1 I cry aloud to God,
    aloud to God, that he may hear me.
2 In the day of my trouble I seek
        the Lord;
    in the night my hand is stretched
        out without wearying;
    my soul refuses to be comforted.
3 I think of God, and I moan;
    I meditate, and my spirit faints.
                                                    Selah

4 You keep my eyelids from closing;
    I am so troubled that I cannot speak.
5 I consider the days of old,
    and remember the years of long ago.
6 I commune*b* with my heart in the
        night;
    I meditate and search my spirit:*c*
7 'Will the Lord spurn for ever,
    and never again be favourable?
8 Has his steadfast love ceased for ever?
    Are his promises at an end for all
        time?

9 Has God forgotten to be gracious?
    Has he in anger shut up his
        compassion?'   *Selah*
10 And I say, 'It is my grief
    that the right hand of the Most
        High has changed.'

11 I will call to mind the deeds of the
        LORD;
    I will remember your wonders
        of old.
12 I will meditate on all your work,
    and muse on your mighty deeds.
13 Your way, O God, is holy.
    What god is so great as our God?
14 You are the God who works wonders;
    you have displayed your might
        among the peoples.
15 With your strong arm you redeemed
        your people,
    the descendants of Jacob and
        Joseph.   *Selah*

16 When the waters saw you, O God,
    when the waters saw you, they were
        afraid;
    the very deep trembled.
17 The clouds poured out water;
    the skies thundered;
    your arrows flashed on every side.
18 The crash of your thunder was in the
        whirlwind;
    your lightnings lit up the world;
    the earth trembled and shook.
19 Your way was through the sea,
    your path, through the mighty
        waters;
    yet your footprints were unseen.
20 You led your people like a flock
    by the hand of Moses and Aaron.

Psalm 78

A Maskil of Asaph.

1 Give ear, O my people, to my
        teaching;
    incline your ears to the words of
        my mouth.
2 I will open my mouth in a parable;

a Heb lacks *your*   *b* Gk Syr: Heb *My music*
c Syr Jerome: Heb *my spirit searches*

I will utter dark sayings from
   of old,
3 things that we have heard and
      known,
   that our ancestors have told us.
4 We will not hide them from their
      children;
   we will tell to the coming
      generation
   the glorious deeds of the LORD, and
      his might,
   and the wonders that he has done.

5 He established a decree in Jacob,
   and appointed a law in Israel,
   which he commanded our ancestors
      to teach to their children;
6 that the next generation might know
      them,
   the children yet unborn,
   and rise up and tell them to their
      children,
7   so that they should set their hope
      in God,
   and not forget the works of God,
   but keep his commandments;

Places Named in the Psalms

Tyre
Mt. Hermon
BASHAN
Mediterranean
Sea
CANAAN   GILEAD
Shechem
Succoth
Shiloh
Mt. Zion
Jerusalem   AMMON
Dead
Sea
PHILISTIA
MOAB
NEGEB
Zalmon
Kadesh
EDOM
N
0   60 MI.
0   60 Km.

8 and that they should not be like their
      ancestors,
   a stubborn and rebellious
      generation,
   a generation whose heart was not
      steadfast,
   whose spirit was not faithful
      to God.

9 The Ephraimites, armed with[a] the
      bow,
   turned back on the day of battle.
10 They did not keep God's covenant,
   but refused to walk according to his
      law.
11 They forgot what he had done,
   and the miracles that he had shown
      them.
12 In the sight of their ancestors he
      worked marvels
   in the land of Egypt, in the fields of
      Zoan.
13 He divided the sea and let them pass
      through it,
   and made the waters stand like
      a heap.
14 In the daytime he led them with
      a cloud,
   and all night long with a fiery light.
15 He split rocks open in the wilderness,
   and gave them drink abundantly as
      from the deep.
16 He made streams come out of the
      rock,
   and caused waters to flow down
      like rivers.

17 Yet they sinned still more against him,
   rebelling against the Most High in
      the desert.
18 They tested God in their heart
   by demanding the food they craved.
19 They spoke against God, saying,
   'Can God spread a table in the
      wilderness?
20 Even though he struck the rock so
      that water gushed out
   and torrents overflowed,
   can he also give bread,
   or provide meat for his people?'

a Heb *armed with shooting*

21 Therefore, when the LORD heard, he
was full of rage;
a fire was kindled against Jacob,
his anger mounted against Israel,
22 because they had no faith in God,
and did not trust his saving power.
23 Yet he commanded the skies above,
and opened the doors of heaven;
24 he rained down on them manna
to eat,
and gave them the grain of heaven.
25 Mortals ate of the bread of angels;
he sent them food in abundance.
26 He caused the east wind to blow in
the heavens,
and by his power he led out the
south wind;
27 he rained flesh upon them like dust,
winged birds like the sand of the
seas;
28 he let them fall within their camp,
all around their dwellings.
29 And they ate and were well filled,
for he gave them what they craved.
30 But before they had satisfied their
craving,
while the food was still in their
mouths,
31 the anger of God rose against them
and he killed the strongest of them,
and laid low the flower of Israel.

32 In spite of all this they still sinned;
they did not believe in his wonders.
33 So he made their days vanish like a
breath,
and their years in terror.
34 When he killed them, they sought for
him;
they repented and sought God
earnestly.
35 They remembered that God was their
rock,
the Most High God their redeemer.
36 But they flattered him with their
mouths;
they lied to him with their tongues.
37 Their heart was not steadfast towards
him;
they were not true to his covenant.
38 Yet he, being compassionate,

forgave their iniquity,
and did not destroy them;
often he restrained his anger,
and did not stir up all his wrath.
39 He remembered that they were but
flesh,
a wind that passes and does not
come again.
40 How often they rebelled against him
in the wilderness
and grieved him in the desert!
41 They tested God again and again,
and provoked the Holy One of
Israel.
42 They did not keep in mind his power,
or the day when he redeemed them
from the foe;
43 when he displayed his signs in Egypt,
and his miracles in the fields of
Zoan.
44 He turned their rivers to blood,
so that they could not drink of their
streams.
45 He sent among them swarms of flies,
which devoured them,
and frogs, which destroyed them.
46 He gave their crops to the caterpillar,
and the fruit of their labour to the
locust.
47 He destroyed their vines with hail,
and their sycomores with frost.
48 He gave over their cattle to the hail,
and their flocks to thunderbolts.
49 He let loose on them his fierce anger,
wrath, indignation, and distress,
a company of destroying angels.
50 He made a path for his anger;
he did not spare them from death,
but gave their lives over to the
plague.
51 He struck all the firstborn in Egypt,
the first issue of their strength in
the tents of Ham.
52 Then he led out his people like
sheep,
and guided them in the wilderness
like a flock.
53 He led them in safety, so that they
were not afraid;
but the sea overwhelmed their
enemies.

54 And he brought them to his holy hill,
  to the mountain that his right hand
    had won.
55 He drove out nations before them;
  he apportioned them for a
    possession
  and settled the tribes of Israel in
    their tents.

56 Yet they tested the Most High God,
  and rebelled against him.
  They did not observe his decrees,
57 but turned away and were faithless
    like their ancestors;
  they twisted like a treacherous bow.
58 For they provoked him to anger with
    their high places;
  they moved him to jealousy with
    their idols.
59 When God heard, he was full of wrath,
  and he utterly rejected Israel.
60 He abandoned his dwelling at Shiloh,
  the tent where he dwelt among
    mortals,
61 and delivered his power to captivity,
  his glory to the hand of the foe.
62 He gave his people to the sword,
  and vented his wrath on his
    heritage.
63 Fire devoured their young men,
  and their girls had no marriage song.
64 Their priests fell by the sword,
  and their widows made no
    lamentation.
65 Then the Lord awoke as from sleep,
  like a warrior shouting because of
    wine.
66 He put his adversaries to rout;
  he put them to everlasting disgrace.

67 He rejected the tent of Joseph,
  he did not choose the tribe of
    Ephraim;
68 but he chose the tribe of Judah,
  Mount Zion, which he loves.
69 He built his sanctuary like the high
    heavens,
  like the earth, which he has
    founded for ever.
70 He chose his servant David,
  and took him from the sheepfolds;

71 from tending the nursing ewes he
    brought him
  to be the shepherd of his people
    Jacob,
  of Israel, his inheritance.
72 With upright heart he tended them,
  and guided them with skilful hand.

Psalm 79

A Psalm of Asaph.

1 O God, the nations have come into
    your inheritance;
  they have defiled your holy temple;
  they have laid Jerusalem in ruins.
2 They have given the bodies of your
    servants
  to the birds of the air for food,
  the flesh of your faithful to the wild
    animals of the earth.
3 They have poured out their blood
    like water
  all around Jerusalem,
  and there was no one to bury them.
4 We have become a taunt to our
    neighbours,
  mocked and derided by those
    around us.

5 How long, O LORD? Will you be angry
    for ever?
  Will your jealous wrath burn like
    fire?
6 Pour out your anger on the nations
    that do not know you,
  and on the kingdoms
    that do not call on your name.
7 For they have devoured Jacob
  and laid waste his habitation.

8 Do not remember against us the
    iniquities of our ancestors;
  let your compassion come speedily
    to meet us,
  for we are brought very low.
9 Help us, O God of our salvation,
  for the glory of your name;
  deliver us, and forgive our sins,
  for your name's sake.
10 Why should the nations say,
  'Where is their God?'

Let the avenging of the outpoured
    blood of your servants
be known among the nations
    before our eyes.

11 Let the groans of the prisoners come
    before you;
according to your great power
    preserve those doomed to die.
12 Return sevenfold into the bosom of
    our neighbours
    the taunts with which they taunted
        you, O Lord!
13 Then we your people, the flock of
    your pasture,
    will give thanks to you for ever;
    from generation to generation we
        will recount your praise.

Psalm 80

To the leader: on Lilies, a Covenant. Of Asaph.
A Psalm.

1 Give ear, O Shepherd of Israel,
    you who lead Joseph like a flock!
You who are enthroned upon the
    cherubim, shine forth
2   before Ephraim and Benjamin and
        Manasseh.
Stir up your might,
    and come to save us!

3 Restore us, O God;
    let your face shine, that we may be
        saved.

4 O LORD God of hosts,
    how long will you be angry with
        your people's prayers?
5 You have fed them with the bread of
    tears,
    and given them tears to drink in
        full measure.
6 You make us the scorn *a* of our
    neighbours;
    our enemies laugh among
        themselves.

7 Restore us, O God of hosts;
    let your face shine, that we may be
        saved.

8 You brought a vine out of Egypt;
    you drove out the nations and
        planted it.
9 You cleared the ground for it;
    it took deep root and filled the land.
10 The mountains were covered with its
    shade,
    the mighty cedars with its branches;
11 it sent out its branches to the sea,
    and its shoots to the River.
12 Why then have you broken down its
    walls,
    so that all who pass along the way
        pluck its fruit?
13 The boar from the forest ravages it,
    and all that move in the field feed
        on it.

14 Turn again, O God of hosts;
    look down from heaven, and see;
    have regard for this vine,
15   the stock that your right hand
        planted.*b*
16 They have burned it with fire, they
    have cut it down;*c*
    may they perish at the rebuke of
        your countenance.
17 But let your hand be upon the one at
    your right hand,
    the one whom you made strong for
        yourself.
18 Then we will never turn back from
    you;
    give us life, and we will call on your
        name.

19 Restore us, O LORD God of hosts;
    let your face shine, that we may be
        saved.

Psalm 81

To the leader: according to The Gittith.
Of Asaph.

1 Sing aloud to God our strength;
    shout for joy to the God of Jacob.
2 Raise a song, sound the tambourine,
    the sweet lyre with the harp.

a Syr: Heb *strife*   *b* Heb adds *from verse 17 and upon*
the one whom you made strong for yourself   *c* Cn: Heb *it*
is cut down

3 Blow the trumpet at the new moon,
   at the full moon, on our festal day.
4 For it is a statute for Israel,
   an ordinance of the God of Jacob.
5 He made it a decree in Joseph,
   when he went out over[a] the land of
      Egypt.

I hear a voice I had not known:
6 'I relieved your[b] shoulder of the
      burden;
   your[b] hands were freed from the
      basket.
7 In distress you called, and I rescued
      you;
   I answered you in the secret place
      of thunder;
   I tested you at the waters of
      Meribah.   *Selah*
8 Hear, O my people, while I admonish
      you;
   O Israel, if you would but listen to
      me!
9 There shall be no strange god among
      you;
   you shall not bow down to a
      foreign god.
10 I am the LORD your God,
   who brought you up out of the
      land of Egypt.
   Open your mouth wide and I will
      fill it.

11 'But my people did not listen to my
      voice;
   Israel would not submit to me.
12 So I gave them over to their stubborn
      hearts,
   to follow their own counsels.
13 O that my people would listen
      to me,
   that Israel would walk in my ways!
14 Then I would quickly subdue their
      enemies,
   and turn my hand against their
      foes.
15 Those who hate the LORD would
      cringe before him,
   and their doom would last for ever.
16 I would feed you[c] with the finest of
      the wheat,

and with honey from the rock I
   would satisfy you.'

Psalm 82

A Psalm of Asaph.

1 God has taken his place in the divine
      council;
   in the midst of the gods he holds
      judgement:
2 'How long will you judge unjustly
   and show partiality to the wicked?
                                 Selah
3 Give justice to the weak and the
      orphan;
   maintain the right of the lowly and
      the destitute.
4 Rescue the weak and the needy;
   deliver them from the hand of the
      wicked.'

5 They have neither knowledge nor
      understanding,
   they walk around in darkness;
   all the foundations of the earth are
      shaken.

6 I say, 'You are gods,
   children of the Most High, all
      of you;
7 nevertheless, you shall die like
      mortals,
   and fall like any prince.'[d]

8 Rise up, O God, judge the earth;
   for all the nations belong to you!

Psalm 83

A Song. A Psalm of Asaph.

1 O God, do not keep silence;
   do not hold your peace or be still,
      O God!
2 Even now your enemies are in
      tumult;
   those who hate you have raised
      their heads.
3 They lay crafty plans against your
      people;

---

a Or *against*   b Heb *his*   c Cn Compare verse 16b:
Heb *he would feed him*   d Or *fall as one man, O princes*

they consult together against those
    you protect.
4 They say, 'Come, let us wipe them out
    as a nation;
    let the name of Israel be
      remembered no more.'
5 They conspire with one accord;
    against you they make a
      covenant—
6 the tents of Edom and the
    Ishmaelites,
    Moab and the Hagrites,
7 Gebal and Ammon and Amalek,
    Philistia with the inhabitants of
      Tyre;
8 Assyria also has joined them;
    they are the strong arm of the
      children of Lot.   *Selah*

9 Do to them as you did to Midian,
    as to Sisera and Jabin at the Wadi
      Kishon,
10 who were destroyed at En-dor,
    who became dung for the ground.
11 Make their nobles like Oreb and
    Zeeb,
    all their princes like Zebah and
      Zalmunna,
12 who said, 'Let us take the pastures of
    God
    for our own possession.'

13 O my God, make them like whirling
    dust,*a*
    like chaff before the wind.
14 As fire consumes the forest,
    as the flame sets the mountains
      ablaze,
15 so pursue them with your tempest
    and terrify them with your
      hurricane.
16 Fill their faces with shame,
    so that they may seek your name,
      O LORD.
17 Let them be put to shame and
    dismayed for ever;
    let them perish in disgrace.
18 Let them know that you alone,
    whose name is the LORD,
    are the Most High over all the earth.

Psalm 84

*To the leader: according to The Gittith. Of the
Korahites. A Psalm.*

1 How lovely is your dwelling place,
    O LORD of hosts!
2 My soul longs, indeed it faints
    for the courts of the LORD;
    my heart and my flesh sing for joy
    to the living God.

3 Even the sparrow finds a home,
    and the swallow a nest for herself,
    where she may lay her young,
    at your altars, O LORD of hosts,
    my King and my God.
4 Happy are those who live in your
    house,
    ever singing your praise.   *Selah*

5 Happy are those whose strength is in
    you,
    in whose heart are the highways to
      Zion.*b*
6 As they go through the valley of Baca
    they make it a place of springs;
    the early rain also covers it with
      pools.
7 They go from strength to strength;
    the God of gods will be seen
      in Zion.

8 O LORD God of hosts, hear my prayer;
    give ear, O God of Jacob!   *Selah*
9 Behold our shield, O God;
    look on the face of your anointed.

10 For a day in your courts is better
    than a thousand elsewhere.
    I would rather be a doorkeeper in the
      house of my God
    than live in the tents of wickedness.
11 For the LORD God is a sun and shield;
    he bestows favour and honour.
    No good thing does the LORD
      withhold
    from those who walk uprightly.
12 O LORD of hosts,
    happy is everyone who trusts
      in you.

a Or *a tumbleweed*   *b* Heb lacks *to Zion*

Psalm 85

To the leader. Of the Korahites. A Psalm.

1 LORD, you were favourable to your
      land;
    you restored the fortunes of Jacob.
2 You forgave the iniquity of your
      people;
    you pardoned all their sin.   *Selah*
3 You withdrew all your wrath;
    you turned from your hot anger.

4 Restore us again, O God of our
      salvation,
    and put away your indignation
      towards us.
5 Will you be angry with us for ever?
    Will you prolong your anger to all
      generations?
6 Will you not revive us again,
    so that your people may rejoice
      in you?
7 Show us your steadfast love, O LORD,
    and grant us your salvation.

8 Let me hear what God the LORD will
      speak,
    for he will speak peace to his
      people,
    to his faithful, to those who turn to
      him in their hearts.*a*
9 Surely his salvation is at hand for
      those who fear him,
    that his glory may dwell in our
      land.

10 Steadfast love and faithfulness
      will meet;
    righteousness and peace will kiss
      each other.
11 Faithfulness will spring up from the
      ground,
    and righteousness will look down
      from the sky.
12 The LORD will give what is good,
    and our land will yield its increase.
13 Righteousness will go before him,
    and will make a path for his steps.

Psalm 86

A Prayer of David.

1 Incline your ear, O LORD, and answer
      me,
    for I am poor and needy.
2 Preserve my life, for I am devoted to
      you;
    save your servant who trusts in you.
    You are my God; 3 be gracious to me,
      O Lord,
    for to you do I cry all day long.
4 Gladden the soul of your servant,
    for to you, O Lord, I lift up my
      soul.
5 For you, O Lord, are good and
      forgiving,
    abounding in steadfast love to all
      who call on you.
6 Give ear, O LORD, to my prayer;
    listen to my cry of supplication.
7 In the day of my trouble I call
      on you,
    for you will answer me.

8 There is none like you among the
      gods, O Lord,
    nor are there any works like yours.
9 All the nations you have made shall
      come
    and bow down before you, O Lord,
    and shall glorify your name.
10 For you are great and do wondrous
      things;
    you alone are God.
11 Teach me your way, O LORD,
    that I may walk in your truth;
    give me an undivided heart to
      revere your name.
12 I give thanks to you, O Lord my God,
    with my whole heart,
    and I will glorify your name for
      ever.
13 For great is your steadfast love
      towards me;
    you have delivered my soul from
      the depths of Sheol.

14 O God, the insolent rise up against
      me;

a Gk: Heb *but let them not turn back to folly*

a band of ruffians seeks my life,
and they do not set you before them.
15 But you, O Lord, are a God merciful
and gracious,
slow to anger and abounding in
steadfast love and faithfulness.
16 Turn to me and be gracious to me;
give your strength to your servant;
save the child of your serving-maid.
17 Show me a sign of your favour,
so that those who hate me may see
it and be put to shame,
because you, LORD, have helped me
and comforted me.

Psalm 87

Of the Korahites. A Psalm. A Song.

1 On the holy mount stands the city he
founded;
2 the LORD loves the gates of Zion
more than all the dwellings of
Jacob.
3 Glorious things are spoken of you,
O city of God.   *Selah*

4 Among those who know me I
mention Rahab and Babylon;
Philistia too, and Tyre, with
Ethiopia*a*—
'This one was born there,' they say.

5 And of Zion it shall be said,
'This one and that one were born in
it';
for the Most High himself will
establish it.
6 The LORD records, as he registers the
peoples,
'This one was born there.'   *Selah*

7 Singers and dancers alike say,
'All my springs are in you.'

Psalm 88

A Song. A Psalm of the Korahites. To the
leader: according to Mahalath Leannoth.
A Maskil of Heman the Ezrahite.

1 O LORD, God of my salvation,
when, at night, I cry out in your
presence,

2 let my prayer come before you;
incline your ear to my cry.

3 For my soul is full of troubles,
and my life draws near to Sheol.
4 I am counted among those who go
down to the Pit;
I am like those who have no help,
5 like those forsaken among the dead,
like the slain that lie in the grave,
like those whom you remember
no more,
for they are cut off from your hand.
6 You have put me in the depths of the
Pit,
in the regions dark and deep.
7 Your wrath lies heavy upon me,
and you overwhelm me with all
your waves.   *Selah*

8 You have caused my companions to
shun me;
you have made me a thing of
horror to them.
I am shut in so that I cannot escape;
9 my eye grows dim through sorrow.
Every day I call on you, O LORD;
I spread out my hands to you.
10 Do you work wonders for the dead?
Do the shades rise up to praise
you?   *Selah*
11 Is your steadfast love declared in the
grave,
or your faithfulness in Abaddon?
12 Are your wonders known in the
darkness,
or your saving help in the land of
forgetfulness?

13 But I, O LORD, cry out to you;
in the morning my prayer comes
before you.
14 O LORD, why do you cast me off?
Why do you hide your face from
me?
15 Wretched and close to death from my
youth up,
I suffer your terrors; I am desperate.*b*
16 Your wrath has swept over me;
your dread assaults destroy me.

a Or *Nubia*; Heb *Cush*   *b* Meaning of Heb uncertain

17 They surround me like a flood all day
        long;
    from all sides they close in on me.
18 You have caused friend and
        neighbour to shun me;
    my companions are in darkness.

Psalm 89

A Maskil of Ethan the Ezrahite.

1 I will sing of your steadfast love,
        O LORD, *a* for ever;
    with my mouth I will proclaim
        your faithfulness to all
        generations.
2 I declare that your steadfast love is
        established for ever;
    your faithfulness is as firm as the
        heavens.

3 You said, 'I have made a covenant
        with my chosen one,
    I have sworn to my servant David:
4 "I will establish your descendants for
        ever,
    and build your throne for all
        generations." '   *Selah*

5 Let the heavens praise your wonders,
        O LORD,
    your faithfulness in the assembly of
        the holy ones.
6 For who in the skies can be compared
        to the LORD?
    Who among the heavenly beings is
        like the LORD,
7 a God feared in the council of the
        holy ones,
    great and awesome *b* above all that
        are around him?
8 O LORD God of hosts,
    who is as mighty as you, O LORD?
    Your faithfulness surrounds you.
9 You rule the raging of the sea;
    when its waves rise, you still them.
10 You crushed Rahab like a carcass;
    you scattered your enemies with
        your mighty arm.
11 The heavens are yours, the earth also
        is yours;

the world and all that is in it—you
        have founded them.
12 The north and the south *c*—you
        created them;
    Tabor and Hermon joyously praise
        your name.
13 You have a mighty arm;
    strong is your hand, high your right
        hand.
14 Righteousness and justice are the
        foundation of your throne;
    steadfast love and faithfulness go
        before you.
15 Happy are the people who know the
        festal shout,
    who walk, O LORD, in the light of
        your countenance;
16 they exult in your name all day long,
    and extol *d* your righteousness.
17 For you are the glory of their strength;
    by your favour our horn is exalted.
18 For our shield belongs to the LORD,
    our king to the Holy One of Israel.

19 Then you spoke in a vision to your
        faithful one, and said:
    'I have set the crown *e* on one who
        is mighty,
    I have exalted one chosen from the
        people.
20 I have found my servant David;
    with my holy oil I have anointed
        him;
21 my hand shall always remain with
        him;
    my arm also shall strengthen him.
22 The enemy shall not outwit him,
    the wicked shall not humble him.
23 I will crush his foes before him
    and strike down those who hate
        him.
24 My faithfulness and steadfast love
        shall be with him;
    and in my name his horn shall be
        exalted.
25 I will set his hand on the sea
    and his right hand on the rivers.

a Gk: Heb *the steadfast love of the LORD*   *b* Gk Syr: Heb
greatly awesome   *c* Or *Zaphon and Yamin*   *d* Cn: Heb
are exalted in   *e* Cn: Heb *help*

²⁶ He shall cry to me, "You are my
Father,
my God, and the Rock of my
salvation!"
²⁷ I will make him the firstborn,
the highest of the kings of the
earth.
²⁸ For ever I will keep my steadfast love
for him,
and my covenant with him will
stand firm.
²⁹ I will establish his line for ever,
and his throne as long as the
heavens endure.
³⁰ If his children forsake my law
and do not walk according to my
ordinances,
³¹ if they violate my statutes
and do not keep my
commandments,
³² then I will punish their transgression
with the rod
and their iniquity with scourges;
³³ but I will not remove from him my
steadfast love,
or be false to my faithfulness.
³⁴ I will not violate my covenant,
or alter the word that went forth
from my lips.
³⁵ Once and for all I have sworn by my
holiness;
I will not lie to David.
³⁶ His line shall continue for ever,
and his throne endure before me
like the sun.
³⁷ It shall be established for ever like
the moon,
an enduring witness in the skies.'
                                    Selah

³⁸ But now you have spurned and
rejected him;
you are full of wrath against your
anointed.
³⁹ You have renounced the covenant
with your servant;
you have defiled his crown in
the dust.
⁴⁰ You have broken through all
his walls;

you have laid his strongholds
in ruins.
⁴¹ All who pass by plunder him;
he has become the scorn of his
neighbours.
⁴² You have exalted the right hand of his
foes;
you have made all his enemies
rejoice.
⁴³ Moreover, you have turned back the
edge of his sword,
and you have not supported him in
battle.
⁴⁴ You have removed the sceptre from
his hand,ᵃ
and hurled his throne to the
ground.
⁴⁵ You have cut short the days of his
youth;
you have covered him with shame.
                                    Selah

⁴⁶ How long, O LORD? Will you hide
yourself for ever?
How long will your wrath burn like
fire?
⁴⁷ Remember how short my time is—ᵇ
for what vanity you have created all
mortals!
⁴⁸ Who can live and never see death?
Who can escape the power of
Sheol?   *Selah*

⁴⁹ Lord, where is your steadfast love of
old,
which by your faithfulness you
swore to David?
⁵⁰ Remember, O Lord, how your servant
is taunted;
how I bear in my bosom the insults
of the peoples,ᶜ
⁵¹ with which your enemies taunt,
O LORD,
with which they taunted the
footsteps of your anointed.

⁵² Blessed be the LORD for ever.
Amen and Amen.

---

a Cn: Heb *removed his cleanness*   *b* Meaning of Heb
uncertain   *c* Cn: Heb *bosom all of many peoples*

BOOK IV
(Psalms 90-106)

Psalm 90

A Prayer of Moses, the man of God.

1 Lord, you have been our dwelling-
    place[a]
  in all generations.
2 Before the mountains were brought
    forth,
    or ever you had formed the earth
    and the world,
    from everlasting to everlasting you
    are God.

3 You turn us[b] back to dust,
  and say, 'Turn back, you mortals.'
4 For a thousand years in your sight
  are like yesterday when it is past,
  or like a watch in the night.

5 You sweep them away; they are like a
    dream,
    like grass that is renewed in the
    morning;
6 in the morning it flourishes and is
    renewed;
    in the evening it fades and withers.

7 For we are consumed by your anger;
  by your wrath we are overwhelmed.
8 You have set our iniquities
    before you,
    our secret sins in the light of your
    countenance.

9 For all our days pass away under your
    wrath;
    our years come to an end[c] like
    a sigh.
10 The days of our life are seventy years,
    or perhaps eighty, if we are strong;
    even then their span[d] is only toil and
    trouble;
    they are soon gone, and we fly away.

11 Who considers the power of your
    anger?
    Your wrath is as great as the fear
    that is due to you.

12 So teach us to count our days
    that we may gain a wise heart.

13 Turn, O LORD! How long?
    Have compassion on your
    servants!
14 Satisfy us in the morning with your
    steadfast love,
    so that we may rejoice and be glad
    all our days.
15 Make us glad for as many days as you
    have afflicted us,
    and for as many years as we have
    seen evil.
16 Let your work be manifest to your
    servants,
    and your glorious power to their
    children.
17 Let the favour of the Lord our God be
    upon us,
    and prosper for us the work of our
    hands—
    O prosper the work of our hands!

Psalm 91

1 You who live in the shelter of the
    Most High,
    who abide in the shadow of the
    Almighty,[e]
2 will say to the LORD, 'My refuge and
    my fortress;
    my God, in whom I trust.'
3 For he will deliver you from the snare
    of the fowler
    and from the deadly pestilence;
4 he will cover you with his pinions,
    and under his wings you will find
    refuge;
    his faithfulness is a shield and
    buckler.
5 You will not fear the terror of the
    night,
    or the arrow that flies by day,
6 or the pestilence that stalks in
    darkness,
    or the destruction that wastes at
    noonday.

a Another reading is *our refuge*   b Heb *humankind*
c Syr: Heb *we bring our years to an end*   d Cn Compare
Gk Syr Jerome Tg: Heb *pride*   e Traditional rendering
of Heb *Shaddai*

7 A thousand may fall at your side,
  ten thousand at your right hand,
  but it will not come near you.
8 You will only look with your eyes
  and see the punishment of the
    wicked.

9 Because you have made the LORD
    your refuge, *a*
  the Most High your dwelling-place,
10 no evil shall befall you,
  no scourge come near your tent.

11 For he will command his angels
    concerning you
  to guard you in all your ways.
12 On their hands they will bear
    you up,
  so that you will not dash your foot
    against a stone.
13 You will tread on the lion and the
    adder,
  the young lion and the serpent you
    will trample under foot.

14 Those who love me, I will deliver;
  I will protect those who know my
    name.
15 When they call to me, I will answer
    them;
  I will be with them in trouble,
  I will rescue them and honour
    them.
16 With long life I will satisfy them,
  and show them my salvation.

Psalm 92

A Psalm. A Song for the Sabbath Day.

1 It is good to give thanks to the LORD,
  to sing praises to your name,
    O Most High;
2 to declare your steadfast love in the
    morning,
  and your faithfulness by night,
3 to the music of the lute and the harp,
  to the melody of the lyre.
4 For you, O LORD, have made me glad
    by your work;
  at the works of your hands I sing
    for joy.

5 How great are your works, O LORD!
  Your thoughts are very deep!
6 The dullard cannot know,
  the stupid cannot understand this:
7 though the wicked sprout like grass
  and all evildoers flourish,
  they are doomed to destruction for
    ever,
8 but you, O LORD, are on high for
    ever.
9 For your enemies, O LORD,
  for your enemies shall perish;
  all evildoers shall be scattered.

10 But you have exalted my horn like
    that of the wild ox;
  you have poured over me *b*
    fresh oil.
11 My eyes have seen the downfall of my
    enemies;
  my ears have heard the doom of my
    evil assailants.

12 The righteous flourish like the palm
    tree,
  and grow like a cedar in Lebanon.
13 They are planted in the house of the
    LORD;
  they flourish in the courts of our
    God.
14 In old age they still produce fruit;
  they are always green and full
    of sap,
15 showing that the LORD is upright;
  he is my rock, and there is no
    unrighteousness in him.

Psalm 93

1 The LORD is king, he is robed in
    majesty;
  the LORD is robed, he is girded with
    strength.
  He has established the world; it shall
    never be moved;
2 your throne is established from
    of old;
  you are from everlasting.

a Cn: Heb *Because you, LORD, are my refuge; you have
made*   *b* Syr: Meaning of Heb uncertain

3 The floods have lifted up, O LORD,
   the floods have lifted up their
      voice;
   the floods lift up their roaring.
4 More majestic than the thunders of
      mighty waters,
   more majestic than the waves*a* of
      the sea,
   majestic on high is the LORD!

5 Your decrees are very sure;
   holiness befits your house,
   O LORD, for evermore.

Psalm 94

1 O LORD, you God of vengeance,
   you God of vengeance, shine
      forth!
2 Rise up, O judge of the earth;
   give to the proud what they
      deserve!
3 O LORD, how long shall the wicked,
   how long shall the wicked exult?

4 They pour out their arrogant words;
   all the evildoers boast.
5 They crush your people, O LORD,
   and afflict your heritage.
6 They kill the widow and the stranger,
   they murder the orphan,
7 and they say, 'The LORD does not see;
   the God of Jacob does not perceive.'

8 Understand, O dullest of the people;
   fools, when will you be wise?
9 He who planted the ear, does he not
      hear?
   He who formed the eye, does he
      not see?
10 He who disciplines the nations,
   he who teaches knowledge to
      humankind,
   does he not chastise?
11 The LORD knows our thoughts,*b*
   that they are but an empty breath.

12 Happy are those whom you
      discipline, O LORD,
   and whom you teach out of
      your law,

13 giving them respite from days of
      trouble,
   until a pit is dug for the wicked.
14 For the LORD will not forsake his
      people;
   he will not abandon his heritage;
15 for justice will return to the righteous,
   and all the upright in heart will
      follow it.

16 Who rises up for me against the
      wicked?
   Who stands up for me against
      evildoers?
17 If the LORD had not been my help,
   my soul would soon have lived in
      the land of silence.
18 When I thought, 'My foot is slipping',
   your steadfast love, O LORD, held
      me up.
19 When the cares of my heart are many,
   your consolations cheer my soul.
20 Can wicked rulers be allied with you,
   those who contrive mischief by
      statute?
21 They band together against the life of
      the righteous,
   and condemn the innocent to
      death.
22 But the LORD has become my
      stronghold,
   and my God the rock of my refuge.
23 He will repay them for their iniquity
   and wipe them out for their
      wickedness;
   the LORD our God will wipe
      them out.

Psalm 95

1 O come, let us sing to the LORD;
   let us make a joyful noise to the
      rock of our salvation!
2 Let us come into his presence with
      thanksgiving;
   let us make a joyful noise to him
      with songs of praise!
3 For the LORD is a great God,
   and a great King above all gods.

a Cn: Heb *majestic are the waves*   *b* Heb *the thoughts of humankind*

4 In his hand are the depths of the
      earth;
   the heights of the mountains are
      his also.
5 The sea is his, for he made it,
   and the dry land, which his hands
      have formed.

6 O come, let us worship and bow
      down,
   let us kneel before the LORD,
      our Maker!
7 For he is our God,
   and we are the people of his
      pasture,
   and the sheep of his hand.

   O that today you would listen to his
      voice!
8 Do not harden your hearts, as at
      Meribah,
   as on the day at Massah in the
      wilderness,
9 when your ancestors tested me,
   and put me to the proof, though
      they had seen my work.
10 For forty years I loathed that
      generation
   and said, 'They are a people whose
      hearts go astray,
   and they do not regard my ways.'
11 Therefore in my anger I swore,
   'They shall not enter my rest.'

Psalm 96

1 O sing to the LORD a new song;
   sing to the LORD, all the earth.
2 Sing to the LORD, bless his name;
   tell of his salvation from day to day.
3 Declare his glory among the nations,
   his marvellous works among all the
      peoples.
4 For great is the LORD, and greatly to
      be praised;
   he is to be revered above all gods.
5 For all the gods of the peoples are
      idols,
   but the LORD made the heavens.
6 Honour and majesty are before him;
   strength and beauty are in his
      sanctuary.

7 Ascribe to the LORD, O families of the
      peoples,
   ascribe to the LORD glory and
      strength.
8 Ascribe to the LORD the glory due his
      name;
   bring an offering, and come into
      his courts.
9 Worship the LORD in holy splendour;
   tremble before him, all the earth.

10 Say among the nations, 'The LORD is
      king!
   The world is firmly established; it
      shall never be moved.
   He will judge the peoples with
      equity.'
11 Let the heavens be glad, and let the
      earth rejoice;
   let the sea roar, and all that fills it;
12 let the field exult, and everything in
      it.
   Then shall all the trees of the forest
      sing for joy
13 before the LORD; for he is coming,
   for he is coming to judge the earth.
   He will judge the world with
      righteousness,
   and the peoples with his truth.

Psalm 97

1 The LORD is king! Let the earth
      rejoice;
   let the many coastlands be glad!
2 Clouds and thick darkness are all
      around him;
   righteousness and justice are the
      foundation of his throne.
3 Fire goes before him,
   and consumes his adversaries on
      every side.
4 His lightnings light up the world;
   the earth sees and trembles.
5 The mountains melt like wax before
      the LORD,
   before the Lord of all the earth.

6 The heavens proclaim his
      righteousness;
   and all the peoples behold his
      glory.

7 All worshippers of images are put
    to shame,
  those who make their boast in
    worthless idols;
  all gods bow down before him.
8 Zion hears and is glad,
  and the towns[a] of Judah rejoice,
  because of your judgements,
    O God.
9 For you, O LORD, are most high over
    all the earth;
  you are exalted far above all gods.

10 The LORD loves those who hate[b] evil;
  he guards the lives of his faithful;
  he rescues them from the hand of
    the wicked.
11 Light dawns[c] for the righteous,
  and joy for the upright in heart.
12 Rejoice in the LORD, O you righteous,
  and give thanks to his holy name!

Psalm 98

A Psalm.

1 O sing to the LORD a new song,
  for he has done marvellous things.
  His right hand and his holy arm
  have gained him victory.
2 The LORD has made known his
    victory;
  he has revealed his vindication in
    the sight of the nations.
3 He has remembered his steadfast love
    and faithfulness
  to the house of Israel.
  All the ends of the earth have seen
    the victory of our God.

4 Make a joyful noise to the LORD, all
    the earth;
  break forth into joyous song and
    sing praises.
5 Sing praises to the LORD with the
    lyre,
  with the lyre and the sound of
    melody.
6 With trumpets and the sound of the
    horn
  make a joyful noise before the
    King, the LORD.

7 Let the sea roar, and all that fills it;
  the world and those who live in it.
8 Let the floods clap their hands;
  let the hills sing together for joy
9 at the presence of the LORD, for he is
    coming
  to judge the earth.
  He will judge the world with
    righteousness,
  and the peoples with equity.

Psalm 99

1 The LORD is king; let the peoples
    tremble!
  He sits enthroned upon the
    cherubim; let the earth quake!
2 The LORD is great in Zion;
  he is exalted over all the peoples.
3 Let them praise your great and
    awesome name.
  Holy is he!
4 Mighty King,[d] lover of justice,
  you have established equity;
  you have executed justice
  and righteousness in Jacob.
5 Extol the LORD our God;
  worship at his footstool.
  Holy is he!

6 Moses and Aaron were among his
    priests,
  Samuel also was among those who
    called on his name.
  They cried to the LORD, and he
    answered them.
7 He spoke to them in the pillar of
    cloud;
  they kept his decrees,
  and the statutes that he gave them.

8 O LORD our God, you answered them;
  you were a forgiving God to them,
  but an avenger of their
    wrongdoings.
9 Extol the LORD our God,
  and worship at his holy mountain;
  for the LORD our God is holy.

a Heb *daughters*   *b* Cn: Heb *You who love the LORD hate*
c Gk Syr Jerome: Heb *is sown*   *d* Cn: Heb *And a king's
strength*

Psalm 100

A Psalm of thanksgiving.

1 Make a joyful noise to the LORD, all
　　the earth.
2 　Worship the LORD with gladness;
　　come into his presence with
　　　singing.

3 Know that the LORD is God.
　　It is he that made us, and we are
　　　his;[a]
　　we are his people, and the sheep of
　　　his pasture.

4 Enter his gates with thanksgiving,
　　and his courts with praise.
　　Give thanks to him, bless his name.

5 For the LORD is good;
　　his steadfast love endures for ever,
　　and his faithfulness to all
　　　generations.

Psalm 101

Of David. A Psalm.

1 I will sing of loyalty and of justice;
　　to you, O LORD, I will sing.
2 I will study the way that is blameless.
　　When shall I attain it?

　I will walk with integrity of heart
　　within my house;
3 I will not set before my eyes
　　anything that is base.

　I hate the work of those who
　　　fall away;
　　it shall not cling to me.
4 Perverseness of heart shall be far
　　　from me;
　　I will know nothing of evil.

5 One who secretly slanders a neighbour
　　I will destroy.
　A haughty look and an arrogant heart
　　I will not tolerate.

6 I will look with favour on the faithful
　　in the land,

so that they may live with me;
　whoever walks in the way that is
　　blameless
　shall minister to me.

7 No one who practises deceit
　　shall remain in my house;
　no one who utters lies
　　shall continue in my presence.

8 Morning by morning I will destroy
　　all the wicked in the land,
　cutting off all evildoers
　　from the city of the LORD.

Psalm 102

*A prayer of one afflicted, when faint and
pleading before the LORD.*

1 Hear my prayer, O LORD;
　　let my cry come to you.
2 Do not hide your face from me
　　on the day of my distress.
　Incline your ear to me;
　　answer me speedily on the day
　　　when I call.

3 For my days pass away like smoke,
　　and my bones burn like a furnace.
4 My heart is stricken and withered like
　　　grass;
　　I am too wasted to eat my bread.
5 Because of my loud groaning
　　my bones cling to my skin.
6 I am like an owl of the wilderness,
　　like a little owl of the waste places.
7 I lie awake;
　　I am like a lonely bird on the
　　　housetop.
8 All day long my enemies taunt me;
　　those who deride me use my name
　　　for a curse.
9 For I eat ashes like bread,
　　and mingle tears with my drink,
10 because of your indignation and
　　　anger;
　　for you have lifted me up and
　　　thrown me aside.
11 My days are like an evening shadow;
　　I wither away like grass.

a Another reading is and not we ourselves

12 But you, O LORD, are enthroned for
          ever;
     your name endures to all
          generations.
13 You will rise up and have compassion
          on Zion,
     for it is time to favour it;
     the appointed time has come.
14 For your servants hold its stones
          dear,
     and have pity on its dust.
15 The nations will fear the name of the
          LORD,
     and all the kings of the earth your
          glory.
16 For the LORD will build up Zion;
     he will appear in his glory.
17 He will regard the prayer of the
          destitute,
     and will not despise their prayer.

18 Let this be recorded for a generation
          to come,
     so that a people yet unborn may
          praise the LORD:
19 that he looked down from his holy
          height,
     from heaven the LORD looked at the
          earth,
20 to hear the groans of the prisoners,
     to set free those who were doomed
          to die;
21 so that the name of the LORD may be
          declared in Zion,
     and his praise in Jerusalem,
22 when peoples gather together,
     and kingdoms, to worship the
          LORD.

23 He has broken my strength in mid-
          course;
     he has shortened my days.
24 'O my God,' I say, 'do not take
          me away
     at the midpoint of my life,
     you whose years endure
          throughout all generations.'

25 Long ago you laid the foundation of
     the earth,

     and the heavens are the work of
          your hands.
26 They will perish, but you endure;
     they will all wear out like a
          garment.
     You change them like clothing, and
          they pass away;
27 but you are the same, and your
          years have no end.
28 The children of your servants shall
          live secure;
     their offspring shall be established
          in your presence.

Psalm 103

Of David.

1 Bless the LORD, O my soul,
     and all that is within me,
     bless his holy name.
2 Bless the LORD, O my soul,
     and do not forget all his benefits—
3 who forgives all your iniquity,
     who heals all your diseases,
4 who redeems your life from the Pit,
     who crowns you with steadfast love
          and mercy,
5 who satisfies you with good as long
          as you live*a*
     so that your youth is renewed like
          the eagle's.

6 The LORD works vindication
     and justice for all who are
          oppressed.
7 He made known his ways to Moses,
     his acts to the people of Israel.
8 The LORD is merciful and gracious,
     slow to anger and abounding in
          steadfast love.
9 He will not always accuse,
     nor will he keep his anger for ever.
10 He does not deal with us according
          to our sins,
     nor repay us according to our
          iniquities.
11 For as the heavens are high above the
          earth,
     so great is his steadfast love towards
          those who fear him;

a Meaning of Heb uncertain

12 as far as the east is from the west,
so far he removes our
transgressions from us.
13 As a father has compassion for his
children,
so the LORD has compassion for
those who fear him.
14 For he knows how we were made;
he remembers that we are dust.

15 As for mortals, their days are like
grass;
they flourish like a flower of the
field;
16 for the wind passes over it, and it is
gone,
and its place knows it no more.
17 But the steadfast love of the LORD is
from everlasting to everlasting
on those who fear him,
and his righteousness to children's
children,
18 to those who keep his covenant
and remember to do his
commandments.

19 The LORD has established his throne
in the heavens,
and his kingdom rules over all.
20 Bless the LORD, O you his angels,
you mighty ones who do his
bidding,
obedient to his spoken word.
21 Bless the LORD, all his hosts,
his ministers that do his will.
22 Bless the LORD, all his works,
in all places of his dominion.
Bless the LORD, O my soul.

Psalm 104

1 Bless the LORD, O my soul.
O LORD my God, you are very great.
You are clothed with honour and
majesty,
2 wrapped in light as with a garment.
You stretch out the heavens like
a tent,
3 you set the beams of your*a*
chambers on the waters,
you make the clouds your*a* chariot,
you ride on the wings of the wind,

4 you make the winds your*a* messengers,
fire and flame your*a* ministers.

5 You set the earth on its foundations,
so that it shall never be shaken.
6 You cover it with the deep as with a
garment;
the waters stood above the
mountains.
7 At your rebuke they flee;
at the sound of your thunder they
take to flight.
8 They rose up to the mountains, ran
down to the valleys
to the place that you appointed for
them.
9 You set a boundary that they may not
pass,
so that they might not again cover
the earth.

10 You make springs gush forth in the
valleys;
they flow between the hills,
11 giving drink to every wild animal;
the wild asses quench their thirst.
12 By the streams*b* the birds of the air
have their habitation;
they sing among the branches.
13 From your lofty abode you water the
mountains;
the earth is satisfied with the fruit
of your work.

14 You cause the grass to grow for the
cattle,
and plants for people to use,*c*
to bring forth food from the earth,
15 and wine to gladden the human
heart,
oil to make the face shine,
and bread to strengthen the human
heart.
16 The trees of the LORD are watered
abundantly,
the cedars of Lebanon that he
planted.
17 In them the birds build their nests;
the stork has its home in the fir
trees.

a Heb *his*   *b* Heb *By them*   *c* Or *to cultivate*

18 The high mountains are for the wild
     goats;
   the rocks are a refuge for the coneys.
19 You have made the moon to mark the
     seasons;
   the sun knows its time for setting.
20 You make darkness, and it is night,
   when all the animals of the forest
     come creeping out.
21 The young lions roar for their prey,
   seeking their food from God.
22 When the sun rises, they withdraw
   and lie down in their dens.
23 People go out to their work
   and to their labour until the
     evening.

24 O LORD, how manifold are your
     works!
   In wisdom you have made them all;
   the earth is full of your creatures.
25 Yonder is the sea, great and wide,
   creeping things innumerable are
     there,
   living things both small and great.
26 There go the ships,
   and Leviathan that you formed
     to sport in it.

27 These all look to you
   to give them their food in due
     season;
28 when you give to them, they gather it
     up;
   when you open your hand, they are
     filled with good things.
29 When you hide your face, they are
     dismayed;
   when you take away their breath,
     they die
   and return to their dust.
30 When you send forth your spirit,ᵃ
     they are created;
   and you renew the face of the
     ground.

31 May the glory of the LORD endure for
     ever;
   may the LORD rejoice in his works—
32 who looks on the earth and it
     trembles,

who touches the mountains and
     they smoke.
33 I will sing to the LORD as long as I live;
   I will sing praise to my God while I
     have being.
34 May my meditation be pleasing
     to him,
   for I rejoice in the LORD.
35 Let sinners be consumed from the
     earth,
   and let the wicked be no more.
Bless the LORD, O my soul.
Praise the LORD!

Psalm 105

1 O give thanks to the LORD, call on his
     name,
   make known his deeds among the
     peoples.
2 Sing to him, sing praises to him;
   tell of all his wonderful works.
3 Glory in his holy name;
   let the hearts of those who seek the
     LORD rejoice.
4 Seek the LORD and his strength;
   seek his presence continually.
5 Remember the wonderful works he
     has done,
   his miracles, and the judgements he
     has uttered,
6 O offspring of his servant Abraham,ᵇ
   children of Jacob, his chosen ones.

7 He is the LORD our God;
   his judgements are in all the earth.
8 He is mindful of his covenant for
     ever,
   of the word that he commanded,
     for a thousand generations,
9 the covenant that he made with
     Abraham,
   his sworn promise to Isaac,
10 which he confirmed to Jacob as a
     statute,
   to Israel as an everlasting covenant,
11 saying, 'To you I will give the land of
     Canaan
   as your portion for an inheritance.'

a Or *your breath*   *b* Another reading is *Israel* (compare
1 Chr 16.13)

¹² When they were few in number,
of little account, and strangers in it,
¹³ wandering from nation to nation,
from one kingdom to another
people,
¹⁴ he allowed no one to oppress them;
he rebuked kings on their account,
¹⁵ saying, 'Do not touch my anointed
ones;
do my prophets no harm.'

¹⁶ When he summoned famine against
the land,
and broke every staff of bread,
¹⁷ he had sent a man ahead of them,
Joseph, who was sold as a slave.
¹⁸ His feet were hurt with fetters,
his neck was put in a collar of iron;
¹⁹ until what he had said came to pass,
the word of the LORD kept testing
him.
²⁰ The king sent and released him;
the ruler of the peoples set
him free.
²¹ He made him lord of his house,
and ruler of all his possessions,
²² to instruct ᵃ his officials at his
pleasure,
and to teach his elders wisdom.

²³ Then Israel came to Egypt;
Jacob lived as an alien in the land
of Ham.
²⁴ And the LORD made his people very
fruitful,
and made them stronger than their
foes,
²⁵ whose hearts he then turned to hate
his people,
to deal craftily with his servants.

²⁶ He sent his servant Moses,
and Aaron whom he had chosen.
²⁷ They performed his signs among
them,
and miracles in the land of Ham.
²⁸ He sent darkness, and made the land
dark;
they rebelled ᵇ against his words.
²⁹ He turned their waters into blood,
and caused their fish to die.

³⁰ Their land swarmed with frogs,
even in the chambers of their kings.
³¹ He spoke, and there came swarms of
flies,
and gnats throughout their country.
³² He gave them hail for rain,
and lightning that flashed through
their land.
³³ He struck their vines and fig trees,
and shattered the trees of their
country.
³⁴ He spoke, and the locusts came,
and young locusts without number;
³⁵ they devoured all the vegetation in
their land,
and ate up the fruit of their ground.
³⁶ He struck down all the firstborn in
their land,
the first issue of all their strength.

³⁷ Then he brought Israel ᶜ out with
silver and gold,
and there was no one among their
tribes who stumbled.
³⁸ Egypt was glad when they departed,
for dread of them had fallen
upon it.
³⁹ He spread a cloud for a covering,
and fire to give light by night.
⁴⁰ They asked, and he brought quails,
and gave them food from heaven in
abundance.
⁴¹ He opened the rock, and water
gushed out;
it flowed through the desert like a
river.
⁴² For he remembered his holy promise,
and Abraham, his servant.

⁴³ So he brought his people out
with joy,
his chosen ones with singing.
⁴⁴ He gave them the lands of the
nations,
and they took possession of the
wealth of the peoples,
⁴⁵ that they might keep his statutes
and observe his laws.
Praise the LORD!

ᵃ Gk Syr Jerome: Heb *to bind*   ᵇ Cn Compare Gk Syr:
Heb *they did not rebel*   ᶜ Heb *them*

Psalm 106

1 Praise the LORD!
  O give thanks to the LORD, for he is
    good;
  for his steadfast love endures for
    ever.
2 Who can utter the mighty doings of
    the LORD,
  or declare all his praise?
3 Happy are those who observe
    justice,
  who do righteousness at all times.

4 Remember me, O LORD, when you
    show favour to your people;
  help me when you deliver them;
5 that I may see the prosperity of your
    chosen ones,
  that I may rejoice in the gladness of
    your nation,
  that I may glory in your heritage.

6 Both we and our ancestors have
    sinned;
  we have committed iniquity, have
    done wickedly.
7 Our ancestors, when they were in
    Egypt,
  did not consider your wonderful
    works;
  they did not remember the
    abundance of your steadfast
    love,
  but rebelled against the Most High*a*
    at the Red Sea.*b*
8 Yet he saved them for his name's
    sake,
  so that he might make known his
    mighty power.
9 He rebuked the Red Sea,*b* and it
    became dry;
  he led them through the deep as
    through a desert.
10 So he saved them from the hand of
    the foe,
  and delivered them from the hand
    of the enemy.
11 The waters covered their adversaries;
  not one of them was left.
12 Then they believed his words;
  they sang his praise.

13 But they soon forgot his works;
  they did not wait for his counsel.
14 But they had a wanton craving in the
    wilderness,
  and put God to the test in the desert;
15 he gave them what they asked,
  but sent a wasting disease among
    them.

16 They were jealous of Moses in
    the camp,
  and of Aaron, the holy one of
    the LORD.
17 The earth opened and swallowed
    up Dathan,
  and covered the faction of Abiram.
18 Fire also broke out in their company;
  the flame burned up the wicked.

19 They made a calf at Horeb
  and worshipped a cast image.
20 They exchanged the glory of God*c*
  for the image of an ox that eats
    grass.
21 They forgot God, their Saviour,
  who had done great things in Egypt,
22 wondrous works in the land of Ham,
  and awesome deeds by the
    Red Sea.*b*
23 Therefore he said he would destroy
    them—
  had not Moses, his chosen one,
  stood in the breach before him,
  to turn away his wrath from
    destroying them.

24 Then they despised the pleasant land,
  having no faith in his promise.
25 They grumbled in their tents,
  and did not obey the voice of
    the LORD.
26 Therefore he raised his hand and
    swore to them
  that he would make them fall in
    the wilderness,
27 and would disperse*d* their
    descendants among the nations,
  scattering them over the lands.

a Cn Compare 78.17, 56: Heb *rebelled at the sea*
b Or *Sea of Reeds*   *c* Compare Gk Mss: Heb *exchanged
their glory*   *d* Syr Compare Ezek 20.23: Heb *cause to
fall*

28 Then they attached themselves to the
   Baal of Peor,
   and ate sacrifices offered to
      the dead;
29 they provoked the LORD to anger with
   their deeds,
   and a plague broke out among
      them.
30 Then Phinehas stood up and
   interceded,
   and the plague was stopped.
31 And that has been reckoned to him
   as righteousness
   from generation to generation for
      ever.

32 They angered the LORD[a] at the waters
   of Meribah,
   and it went ill with Moses on their
      account;
33 for they made his spirit bitter,
   and he spoke words that were rash.

34 They did not destroy the peoples
   as the LORD commanded them,
35 but they mingled with the nations
   and learned to do as they did.
36 They served their idols,
   which became a snare to them.
37 They sacrificed their sons
   and their daughters to the demons;
38 they poured out innocent blood,
   the blood of their sons and
      daughters,
   whom they sacrificed to the idols of
      Canaan;
   and the land was polluted with
      blood.
39 Thus they became unclean by their
   acts,
   and prostituted themselves in their
      doings.

40 Then the anger of the LORD was
   kindled against his people,
   and he abhorred his heritage;
41 he gave them into the hand of the
   nations,
   so that those who hated them ruled
      over them.
42 Their enemies oppressed them,

and they were brought into
   subjection under their power.
43 Many times he delivered them,
   but they were rebellious in their
      purposes,
   and were brought low through their
      iniquity.
44 Nevertheless, he regarded their distress
   when he heard their cry.
45 For their sake he remembered his
   covenant,
   and showed compassion according
      to the abundance of his
      steadfast love.
46 He caused them to be pitied
   by all who held them captive.

47 Save us, O LORD our God,
   and gather us from among the
      nations,
   that we may give thanks to your holy
      name
   and glory in your praise.

48 Blessed be the LORD, the God of Israel,
   from everlasting to everlasting.
   And let all the people say, 'Amen.'
   Praise the LORD!

BOOK V

(Psalms 107–150)

Psalm 107

1 O give thanks to the LORD, for he is
   good;
   for his steadfast love endures for
      ever.
2 Let the redeemed of the LORD say so,
   those he redeemed from trouble
3 and gathered in from the lands,
   from the east and from the west,
   from the north and from the
      south.[b]

4 Some wandered in desert wastes,
   finding no way to an inhabited
      town;
5 hungry and thirsty,
   their soul fainted within them.

a Heb *him*   *b* Cn: Heb *sea*

6 Then they cried to the LORD in their
   trouble,
   and he delivered them from their
      distress;
7 he led them by a straight way,
   until they reached an inhabited
      town.
8 Let them thank the LORD for his
   steadfast love,
   for his wonderful works to
      humankind.
9 For he satisfies the thirsty,
   and the hungry he fills with good
      things.

10 Some sat in darkness and in gloom,
   prisoners in misery and in irons,
11 for they had rebelled against the
   words of God,
   and spurned the counsel of the
      Most High.
12 Their hearts were bowed down with
   hard labour;
   they fell down, with no one to help.
13 Then they cried to the LORD in their
   trouble,
   and he saved them from their
      distress;
14 he brought them out of darkness and
   gloom,
   and broke their bonds asunder.
15 Let them thank the LORD for his
   steadfast love,
   for his wonderful works to
      humankind.
16 For he shatters the doors of bronze,
   and cuts in two the bars of iron.

17 Some were sick*a* through their sinful
   ways,
   and because of their iniquities
      endured affliction;
18 they loathed any kind of food,
   and they drew near to the gates of
      death.
19 Then they cried to the LORD in their
   trouble,
   and he saved them from their
      distress;
20 he sent out his word and healed them,

and delivered them from
   destruction.
21 Let them thank the LORD for his
   steadfast love,
   for his wonderful works to
      humankind.
22 And let them offer thanksgiving
   sacrifices,
   and tell of his deeds with songs of
      joy.

23 Some went down to the sea in ships,
   doing business on the mighty
      waters;
24 they saw the deeds of the LORD,
   his wondrous works in the deep.
25 For he commanded and raised the
   stormy wind,
   which lifted up the waves of
      the sea.
26 They mounted up to heaven, they
   went down to the depths;
   their courage melted away in their
      calamity;
27 they reeled and staggered like
   drunkards,
   and were at their wits' end.
28 Then they cried to the LORD in their
   trouble,
   and he brought them out from
      their distress;
29 he made the storm be still,
   and the waves of the sea were
      hushed.
30 Then they were glad because they had
   quiet,
   and he brought them to their
      desired haven.
31 Let them thank the LORD for his
   steadfast love,
   for his wonderful works to
      humankind.
32 Let them extol him in the
   congregation of the people,
   and praise him in the assembly of
      the elders.

33 He turns rivers into a desert,
   springs of water into thirsty
      ground,

a Cn: Heb *fools*

34 a fruitful land into a salty waste,
   because of the wickedness of its
     inhabitants.
35 He turns a desert into pools of water,
   a parched land into springs of
     water.
36 And there he lets the hungry live,
   and they establish a town to live in;
37 they sow fields, and plant vineyards,
   and get a fruitful yield.
38 By his blessing they multiply greatly,
   and he does not let their cattle
     decrease.

39 When they are diminished and
     brought low
   through oppression, trouble,
     and sorrow,
40 he pours contempt on princes
   and makes them wander in
     trackless wastes;
41 but he raises up the needy out of
     distress,
   and makes their families like flocks.
42 The upright see it and are glad;
   and all wickedness stops its mouth.
43 Let those who are wise give heed to
     these things,
   and consider the steadfast love of
     the LORD.

Psalm 108

A Song. A Psalm of David.

1 My heart is steadfast, O God, my
     heart is steadfast;[a]
   I will sing and make melody.
   Awake, my soul![b]
2 Awake, O harp and lyre!
   I will awake the dawn.
3 I will give thanks to you, O LORD,
     among the peoples,
   and I will sing praises to you
     among the nations.
4 For your steadfast love is higher than
     the heavens,
   and your faithfulness reaches to the
     clouds.

5 Be exalted, O God, above the
     heavens,

and let your glory be over all the
     earth.
6 Give victory with your right hand,
   and answer me,
   so that those whom you love may
     be rescued.

7 God has promised in his sanctuary:[c]
   'With exultation I will divide up
     Shechem,
   and portion out the Vale of Succoth.
8 Gilead is mine; Manasseh is mine;
   Ephraim is my helmet;
   Judah is my sceptre.
9 Moab is my wash-basin;
   on Edom I hurl my shoe;
   over Philistia I shout in triumph.'

10 Who will bring me to the fortified
     city?
   Who will lead me to Edom?
11 Have you not rejected us, O God?
   You do not go out, O God, with our
     armies.
12 O grant us help against the foe,
   for human help is worthless.
13 With God we shall do valiantly;
   it is he who will tread down
     our foes.

Psalm 109

To the leader. Of David. A Psalm.

1 Do not be silent, O God of my praise.
2 For wicked and deceitful mouths are
     opened against me,
   speaking against me with lying
     tongues.
3 They beset me with words of hate,
   and attack me without cause.
4 In return for my love they accuse me,
   even while I make prayer for them.[d]
5 So they reward me evil for good,
   and hatred for my love.

6 They say,[e] 'Appoint a wicked man
     against him;
   let an accuser stand on his right.

a Heb Mss Gk Syr: MT lacks *my heart is steadfast*
b Compare 57.8: Heb *also my soul*   c Or *by his holiness*
d Syr: Heb *I prayer*   e Heb lacks *They say*

7 When he is tried, let him be found
   guilty;
   let his prayer be counted as sin.
8 May his days be few;
   may another seize his position.
9 May his children be orphans,
   and his wife a widow.
10 May his children wander about
   and beg;
   may they be driven out of*a* the
   ruins they inhabit.
11 May the creditor seize all that he has;
   may strangers plunder the fruits of
   his toil.
12 May there be no one to do him a
   kindness,
   nor anyone to pity his orphaned
   children.
13 May his posterity be cut off;
   may his name be blotted out in the
   second generation.
14 May the iniquity of his father*b* be
   remembered before the LORD,
   and do not let the sin of his mother
   be blotted out.
15 Let them be before the LORD
   continually,
   and may his*c* memory be cut off
   from the earth.
16 For he did not remember to show
   kindness,
   but pursued the poor and needy
   and the broken-hearted to their
   death.
17 He loved to curse; let curses come on
   him.
   He did not like blessing; may it be
   far from him.
18 He clothed himself with cursing as
   his coat,
   may it soak into his body like water,
   like oil into his bones.
19 May it be like a garment that he
   wraps around himself,
   like a belt that he wears every day.'
20 May that be the reward of my
   accusers from the LORD,
   of those who speak evil against my
   life.
21 But you, O LORD my Lord,

act on my behalf for your name's
   sake;
   because your steadfast love is good,
   deliver me.
22 For I am poor and needy,
   and my heart is pierced within me.
23 I am gone like a shadow at evening;
   I am shaken off like a locust.
24 My knees are weak through fasting;
   my body has become gaunt.
25 I am an object of scorn to my
   accusers;
   when they see me, they shake their
   heads.

26 Help me, O LORD my God!
   Save me according to your steadfast
   love.
27 Let them know that this is your hand;
   you, O LORD, have done it.
28 Let them curse, but you will bless.
   Let my assailants be put to shame;*d*
   may your servant be glad.
29 May my accusers be clothed with
   dishonour;
   may they be wrapped in their own
   shame as in a mantle.
30 With my mouth I will give great
   thanks to the LORD;
   I will praise him in the midst of the
   throng.
31 For he stands at the right hand of the
   needy,
   to save them from those who
   would condemn them to death.

Psalm 110

Of David. A Psalm.

1 The LORD says to my lord,
   'Sit at my right hand
   until I make your enemies your
   footstool.'

2 The LORD sends out from Zion
   your mighty sceptre.
   Rule in the midst of your foes.

---

a Gk: Heb *and seek*   *b* Cn: Heb *fathers*   *c* Gk: Heb
their   *d* Gk: Heb *They have risen up and have been put to
shame*

3 Your people will offer themselves
    willingly
    on the day you lead your forces
    on the holy mountains. *a*
  From the womb of the morning,
    like dew, your youth *b* will come to
    you.
4 The LORD has sworn and will not
    change his mind,
    'You are a priest for ever according
    to the order of Melchizedek.' *c*

5 The Lord is at your right hand;
    he will shatter kings on the day of
    his wrath.
6 He will execute judgement among the
    nations,
    filling them with corpses;
  he will shatter heads
    over the wide earth.
7 He will drink from the stream by the
    path;
    therefore he will lift up his head.

Psalm 111

1 Praise the LORD!
  I will give thanks to the LORD with
    my whole heart,
    in the company of the upright, in
    the congregation.
2 Great are the works of the LORD,
    studied by all who delight in them.
3 Full of honour and majesty is
    his work,
    and his righteousness endures for
    ever.
4 He has gained renown by his
    wonderful deeds;
    the LORD is gracious and merciful.
5 He provides food for those who fear
    him;
    he is ever mindful of his covenant.
6 He has shown his people the power
    of his works,
    in giving them the heritage of the
    nations.
7 The works of his hands are faithful
    and just;
    all his precepts are trustworthy.
8 They are established for ever and ever,

to be performed with faithfulness
    and uprightness.
9 He sent redemption to his people;
    he has commanded his covenant
    for ever.
  Holy and awesome is his name.
10 The fear of the LORD is the beginning
    of wisdom;
    all those who practise it *d* have a
    good understanding.
  His praise endures for ever.

Psalm 112

1 Praise the LORD!
  Happy are those who fear the LORD,
    who greatly delight in his
    commandments.
2 Their descendants will be mighty in
    the land;
    the generation of the upright will
    be blessed.
3 Wealth and riches are in their
    houses,
    and their righteousness endures for
    ever.
4 They rise in the darkness as a light for
    the upright;
    they are gracious, merciful, and
    righteous.
5 It is well with those who deal
    generously and lend,
    who conduct their affairs with
    justice.
6 For the righteous will never
    be moved;
    they will be remembered for ever.
7 They are not afraid of evil tidings;
    their hearts are firm, secure in the
    LORD.
8 Their hearts are steady, they will not
    be afraid;
    in the end they will look in
    triumph on their foes.
9 They have distributed freely, they
    have given to the poor;
    their righteousness endures for
    ever;
    their horn is exalted in honour.

a Another reading is *in holy splendour*   *b* Cn: Heb *the
dew of your youth*   *c* Or *for ever, a rightful king by my
edict*   *d* Gk Syr: Heb *them*

10 The wicked see it and are angry;
    they gnash their teeth and melt
       away;
    the desire of the wicked comes
      to nothing.

Psalm 113

1 Praise the LORD!
  Praise, O servants of the LORD;
    praise the name of the LORD.

2 Blessed be the name of the LORD
    from this time on and for
      evermore.
3 From the rising of the sun to its
    setting
    the name of the LORD is to be
      praised.
4 The LORD is high above all nations,
    and his glory above the heavens.

5 Who is like the LORD our God,
    who is seated on high,
6 who looks far down
    on the heavens and the earth?
7 He raises the poor from the dust,
    and lifts the needy from the ash
      heap,
8 to make them sit with princes,
    with the princes of his people.
9 He gives the barren woman a home,
    making her the joyous mother of
      children.
  Praise the LORD!

Psalm 114

1 When Israel went out from Egypt,
    the house of Jacob from a people of
      strange language,
2 Judah became God's*a* sanctuary,
    Israel his dominion.

3 The sea looked and fled;
    Jordan turned back.
4 The mountains skipped like rams,
    the hills like lambs.

5 Why is it, O sea, that you flee?
    O Jordan, that you turn back?

6 O mountains, that you skip like
    rams?
    O hills, like lambs?

7 Tremble, O earth, at the presence of
    the LORD,
    at the presence of the God of
      Jacob,
8 who turns the rock into a pool of
    water,
    the flint into a spring of water.

Psalm 115

1 Not to us, O LORD, not to us, but to
    your name give glory,
    for the sake of your steadfast love
      and your faithfulness.
2 Why should the nations say,
    'Where is their God?'

3 Our God is in the heavens;
    he does whatever he pleases.
4 Their idols are silver and gold,
    the work of human hands.
5 They have mouths, but do not speak;
    eyes, but do not see.
6 They have ears, but do not hear;
    noses, but do not smell.
7 They have hands, but do not feel;
    feet, but do not walk;
    they make no sound in their
      throats.
8 Those who make them are like them;
    so are all who trust in them.

9 O Israel, trust in the LORD!
    He is their help and their shield.
10 O house of Aaron, trust in the LORD!
    He is their help and their shield.
11 You who fear the LORD, trust in
    the LORD!
    He is their help and their shield.

12 The LORD has been mindful of us; he
    will bless us;
    he will bless the house of Israel;
    he will bless the house of Aaron;
13 he will bless those who fear the LORD,
    both small and great.

a Heb *his*

14 May the LORD give you increase,
   both you and your children.
15 May you be blessed by the LORD,
   who made heaven and earth.

16 The heavens are the LORD's heavens,
   but the earth he has given to
      human beings.
17 The dead do not praise the LORD,
   nor do any that go down into
      silence.
18 But we will bless the LORD
   from this time on and for
      evermore.
   Praise the LORD!

Psalm 116

1 I love the LORD, because he has heard
   my voice and my supplications.
2 Because he inclined his ear to me,
   therefore I will call on him as long
      as I live.
3 The snares of death encompassed me;
   the pangs of Sheol laid hold on me;
   I suffered distress and anguish.
4 Then I called on the name of
      the LORD:
   'O LORD, I pray, save my life!'

5 Gracious is the LORD, and righteous;
   our God is merciful.
6 The LORD protects the simple;
   when I was brought low, he saved
      me.
7 Return, O my soul, to your rest,
   for the LORD has dealt bountifully
      with you.

8 For you have delivered my soul from
      death,
   my eyes from tears,
   my feet from stumbling.
9 I walk before the LORD
   in the land of the living.
10 I kept my faith, even when I said,
   'I am greatly afflicted';
11 I said in my consternation,
   'Everyone is a liar.'

12 What shall I return to the LORD
   for all his bounty to me?

13 I will lift up the cup of salvation
   and call on the name of the LORD,
14 I will pay my vows to the LORD
   in the presence of all his people.
15 Precious in the sight of the LORD
   is the death of his faithful ones.
16 O LORD, I am your servant;
   I am your servant, the child of your
      serving-maid.
   You have loosed my bonds.
17 I will offer to you a thanksgiving
      sacrifice
   and call on the name of the LORD.
18 I will pay my vows to the LORD
   in the presence of all his people,
19 in the courts of the house of the LORD,
   in your midst, O Jerusalem.
   Praise the LORD!

Psalm 117

1 Praise the LORD, all you nations!
   Extol him, all you peoples!
2 For great is his steadfast love towards
      us,
   and the faithfulness of the LORD
      endures for ever.
   Praise the LORD!

Psalm 118

1 O give thanks to the LORD, for he is
      good;
   his steadfast love endures for ever!

2 Let Israel say,
   'His steadfast love endures for ever.'
3 Let the house of Aaron say,
   'His steadfast love endures for ever.'
4 Let those who fear the LORD say,
   'His steadfast love endures for ever.'

5 Out of my distress I called on the LORD;
   the LORD answered me and set me
      in a broad place.
6 With the LORD on my side I do not fear.
   What can mortals do to me?
7 The LORD is on my side to help me;
   I shall look in triumph on those
      who hate me.
8 It is better to take refuge in the LORD
   than to put confidence in mortals.

9 It is better to take refuge in the LORD
    than to put confidence in princes.

10 All nations surrounded me;
    in the name of the LORD I cut them
        off!
11 They surrounded me, surrounded me
        on every side;
    in the name of the LORD I cut them
        off!
12 They surrounded me like bees;
    they blazed*a* like a fire of thorns;
    in the name of the LORD I cut them
        off!
13 I was pushed hard,*b* so that I was
        falling,
    but the LORD helped me.
14 The LORD is my strength and my
        might;
    he has become my salvation.

15 There are glad songs of victory in the
        tents of the righteous:
    'The right hand of the LORD does
        valiantly;
16   the right hand of the LORD is
        exalted;
    the right hand of the LORD does
        valiantly.'
17 I shall not die, but I shall live,
    and recount the deeds of the
        LORD.
18 The LORD has punished me severely,
    but he did not give me over to
        death.

19 Open to me the gates of
        righteousness,
    that I may enter through them
    and give thanks to the LORD.
20 This is the gate of the LORD;
    the righteous shall enter through it.

21 I thank you that you have answered
        me
    and have become my salvation.
22 The stone that the builders rejected
    has become the chief cornerstone.
23 This is the LORD's doing;
    it is marvellous in our eyes.

24 This is the day that the LORD has
        made;
    let us rejoice and be glad in it.*c*
25 Save us, we beseech you, O LORD!
    O LORD, we beseech you, give us
        success!

26 Blessed is the one who comes in the
        name of the LORD.*d*
    We bless you from the house of the
        LORD.
27 The LORD is God,
    and he has given us light.
    Bind the festal procession with
        branches,
    up to the horns of the altar.*e*

28 You are my God, and I will give
        thanks to you;
    you are my God, I will extol you.

29 O give thanks to the LORD, for he is
        good,
    for his steadfast love endures for
        ever.

Psalm 119

1 Happy are those whose way is
        blameless,
    who walk in the law of the LORD.
2 Happy are those who keep his
        decrees,
    who seek him with their whole
        heart,
3 who also do no wrong,
    but walk in his ways.
4 You have commanded your precepts
    to be kept diligently.
5 O that my ways may be steadfast
    in keeping your statutes!
6 Then I shall not be put to shame,
    having my eyes fixed on all your
        commandments.
7 I will praise you with an upright
        heart,
    when I learn your righteous
        ordinances.

a Gk: Heb *were extinguished*   *b* Gk Syr Jerome: Heb
You pushed me hard   *c* Or *in him*   *d* Or *Blessed in the
name of the LORD is the one who comes*   *e* Meaning of
Heb uncertain

8 I will observe your statutes;
   do not utterly forsake me.

9 How can young people keep their
      way pure?
   By guarding it according to your
      word.
10 With my whole heart I seek you;
   do not let me stray from your
      commandments.
11 I treasure your word in my heart,
   so that I may not sin against you.
12 Blessed are you, O LORD;
   teach me your statutes.
13 With my lips I declare
   all the ordinances of your mouth.
14 I delight in the way of your decrees
   as much as in all riches.
15 I will meditate on your precepts,
   and fix my eyes on your ways.
16 I will delight in your statutes;
   I will not forget your word.

17 Deal bountifully with your servant,
   so that I may live and observe your
      word.
18 Open my eyes, so that I may behold
   wondrous things out of your law.
19 I live as an alien in the land;
   do not hide your commandments
      from me.
20 My soul is consumed with longing
   for your ordinances at all times.
21 You rebuke the insolent, accursed ones,
   who wander from your
      commandments;
22 take away from me their scorn and
      contempt,
   for I have kept your decrees.
23 Even though princes sit plotting
      against me,
   your servant will meditate on your
      statutes.
24 Your decrees are my delight,
   they are my counsellors.

25 My soul clings to the dust;
   revive me according to your word.
26 When I told of my ways, you
      answered me;
   teach me your statutes.

27 Make me understand the way of your
      precepts,
   and I will meditate on your
      wondrous works.
28 My soul melts away for sorrow;
   strengthen me according to your
      word.
29 Put false ways far from me;
   and graciously teach me your law.
30 I have chosen the way of faithfulness;
   I set your ordinances before me.
31 I cling to your decrees, O LORD;
   let me not be put to shame.
32 I run the way of your
      commandments,
   for you enlarge my understanding.

33 Teach me, O LORD, the way of your
      statutes,
   and I will observe it to the end.
34 Give me understanding, that I may
      keep your law
   and observe it with my whole heart.
35 Lead me in the path of your
      commandments,
   for I delight in it.
36 Turn my heart to your decrees,
   and not to selfish gain.
37 Turn my eyes from looking at
      vanities;
   give me life in your ways.
38 Confirm to your servant your
      promise,
   which is for those who fear you.
39 Turn away the disgrace that I dread,
   for your ordinances are good.
40 See, I have longed for your precepts;
   in your righteousness give me life.

41 Let your steadfast love come to me,
      O LORD,
   your salvation according to your
      promise.
42 Then I shall have an answer for those
      who taunt me,
   for I trust in your word.
43 Do not take the word of truth utterly
      out of my mouth,
   for my hope is in your ordinances.
44 I will keep your law continually,
   for ever and ever.

45 I shall walk at liberty,
     for I have sought your precepts.
46 I will also speak of your decrees
          before kings,
     and shall not be put to shame;
47 I find my delight in your
          commandments,
     because I love them.
48 I revere your commandments, which
          I love,
     and I will meditate on your
          statutes.

49 Remember your word to your servant,
     in which you have made me hope.
50 This is my comfort in my distress,
     that your promise gives me life.
51 The arrogant utterly deride me,
     but I do not turn away from
          your law.
52 When I think of your ordinances
          from of old,
     I take comfort, O LORD.
53 Hot indignation seizes me because of
          the wicked,
     those who forsake your law.
54 Your statutes have been my songs
     wherever I make my home.
55 I remember your name in the night,
          O LORD,
     and keep your law.
56 This blessing has fallen to me,
     for I have kept your precepts.

57 The LORD is my portion;
     I promise to keep your words.
58 I implore your favour with all my
          heart;
     be gracious to me according to your
          promise.
59 When I think of your ways,
     I turn my feet to your decrees;
60 I hurry and do not delay
     to keep your commandments.
61 Though the cords of the wicked
          ensnare me,
     I do not forget your law.
62 At midnight I rise to praise you,
     because of your righteous
          ordinances.

63 I am a companion of all who fear
          you,
     of those who keep your precepts.
64 The earth, O LORD, is full of your
          steadfast love;
     teach me your statutes.

65 You have dealt well with your servant,
     O LORD, according to your word.
66 Teach me good judgement and
          knowledge,
     for I believe in your
          commandments.
67 Before I was humbled I went astray,
     but now I keep your word.
68 You are good and do good;
     teach me your statutes.
69 The arrogant smear me with lies,
     but with my whole heart I keep
          your precepts.
70 Their hearts are fat and gross,
     but I delight in your law.
71 It is good for me that I was humbled,
     so that I might learn your statutes.
72 The law of your mouth is better
          to me
     than thousands of gold and silver
          pieces.

73 Your hands have made and fashioned
          me;
     give me understanding that I may
          learn your commandments.
74 Those who fear you shall see me and
          rejoice,
     because I have hoped in your word.
75 I know, O LORD, that your
          judgements are right,
     and that in faithfulness you have
          humbled me.
76 Let your steadfast love become my
          comfort
     according to your promise to your
          servant.
77 Let your mercy come to me, that I
          may live;
     for your law is my delight.
78 Let the arrogant be put to shame,
     because they have subverted me
          with guile;

as for me, I will meditate on your precepts.

79 Let those who fear you turn to me,
    so that they may know your decrees.
80 May my heart be blameless in your statutes,
    so that I may not be put to shame.

81 My soul languishes for your salvation;
    I hope in your word.
82 My eyes fail with watching for your promise;
    I ask, 'When will you comfort me?'
83 For I have become like a wineskin in the smoke,
    yet I have not forgotten your statutes.
84 How long must your servant endure?
    When will you judge those who persecute me?
85 The arrogant have dug pitfalls for me;
    they flout your law.
86 All your commandments are enduring;
    I am persecuted without cause; help me!
87 They have almost made an end of me on earth;
    but I have not forsaken your precepts.
88 In your steadfast love spare my life,
    so that I may keep the decrees of your mouth.

89 The LORD exists for ever;
    your word is firmly fixed in heaven.
90 Your faithfulness endures to all generations;
    you have established the earth, and it stands fast.
91 By your appointment they stand today,
    for all things are your servants.
92 If your law had not been my delight,
    I would have perished in my misery.
93 I will never forget your precepts,
    for by them you have given me life.
94 I am yours; save me,
    for I have sought your precepts.

95 The wicked lie in wait to destroy me,
    but I consider your decrees.
96 I have seen a limit to all perfection,
    but your commandment is exceedingly broad.

97 Oh, how I love your law!
    It is my meditation all day long.
98 Your commandment makes me wiser than my enemies,
    for it is always with me.
99 I have more understanding than all my teachers,
    for your decrees are my meditation.
100 I understand more than the aged,
    for I keep your precepts.
101 I hold back my feet from every evil way,
    in order to keep your word.
102 I do not turn away from your ordinances,
    for you have taught me.
103 How sweet are your words to my taste,
    sweeter than honey to my mouth!
104 Through your precepts I get understanding;
    therefore I hate every false way.

105 Your word is a lamp to my feet
    and a light to my path.
106 I have sworn an oath and confirmed it,
    to observe your righteous ordinances.
107 I am severely afflicted;
    give me life, O LORD, according to your word.
108 Accept my offerings of praise, O LORD,
    and teach me your ordinances.
109 I hold my life in my hand continually,
    but I do not forget your law.
110 The wicked have laid a snare for me,
    but I do not stray from your precepts.
111 Your decrees are my heritage for ever;
    they are the joy of my heart.
112 I incline my heart to perform your statutes
    for ever, to the end.

113 I hate the double-minded,
　　but I love your law.
114 You are my hiding-place and my
　　　　shield;
　　I hope in your word.
115 Go away from me, you evildoers,
　　that I may keep the
　　　　commandments of my God.
116 Uphold me according to your
　　　　promise, that I may live,
　　and let me not be put to shame in
　　　　my hope.
117 Hold me up, that I may be safe
　　and have regard for your statutes
　　　　continually.
118 You spurn all who go astray from
　　　　your statutes;
　　for their cunning is in vain.
119 All the wicked of the earth you count
　　　　as dross;
　　therefore I love your decrees.
120 My flesh trembles for fear of you,
　　and I am afraid of your judgements.

121 I have done what is just and right;
　　do not leave me to my oppressors.
122 Guarantee your servant's well-being;
　　do not let the godless oppress me.
123 My eyes fail from watching for your
　　　　salvation,
　　and for the fulfilment of your
　　　　righteous promise.
124 Deal with your servant according to
　　　　your steadfast love,
　　and teach me your statutes.
125 I am your servant; give me
　　　　understanding,
　　so that I may know your decrees.
126 It is time for the LORD to act,
　　for your law has been broken.
127 Truly I love your commandments
　　more than gold, more than
　　　　fine gold.
128 Truly I direct my steps by all your
　　　　precepts;[a]
　　I hate every false way.

129 Your decrees are wonderful;
　　therefore my soul keeps them.
130 The unfolding of your words gives
　　　　light;

it imparts understanding to the
　　simple.
131 With open mouth I pant,
　　because I long for your
　　　　commandments.
132 Turn to me and be gracious to me,
　　as is your custom towards those
　　　　who love your name.
133 Keep my steps steady according to
　　　　your promise,
　　and never let iniquity have
　　　　dominion over me.
134 Redeem me from human
　　　　oppression,
　　that I may keep your precepts.
135 Make your face shine upon your
　　　　servant,
　　and teach me your statutes.
136 My eyes shed streams of tears
　　because your law is not kept.

137 You are righteous, O LORD,
　　and your judgements are right.
138 You have appointed your decrees in
　　　　righteousness
　　and in all faithfulness.
139 My zeal consumes me
　　because my foes forget your words.
140 Your promise is well tried,
　　and your servant loves it.
141 I am small and despised,
　　yet I do not forget your precepts.
142 Your righteousness is an everlasting
　　　　righteousness,
　　and your law is the truth.
143 Trouble and anguish have come
　　　　upon me,
　　but your commandments are my
　　　　delight.
144 Your decrees are righteous for ever;
　　give me understanding that I may
　　　　live.

145 With my whole heart I cry; answer
　　　　me, O LORD.
　　I will keep your statutes.
146 I cry to you; save me,
　　that I may observe your decrees.
147 I rise before dawn and cry for help;
　　I put my hope in your words.

a Gk Jerome: Meaning of Heb uncertain

¹⁴⁸ My eyes are awake before each watch
    of the night,
        that I may meditate on your
        promise.
¹⁴⁹ In your steadfast love hear my voice;
        O LORD, in your justice preserve my
        life.
¹⁵⁰ Those who persecute me with evil
        purpose draw near;
        they are far from your law.
¹⁵¹ Yet you are near, O LORD,
        and all your commandments
        are true.
¹⁵² Long ago I learned from your decrees
        that you have established them for
        ever.

¹⁵³ Look on my misery and rescue me,
        for I do not forget your law.
¹⁵⁴ Plead my cause and redeem me;
        give me life according to your
        promise.
¹⁵⁵ Salvation is far from the wicked,
        for they do not seek your statutes.
¹⁵⁶ Great is your mercy, O LORD;
        give me life according to your
        justice.
¹⁵⁷ Many are my persecutors and my
        adversaries,
        yet I do not swerve from your
        decrees.
¹⁵⁸ I look at the faithless with disgust,
        because they do not keep your
        commands.
¹⁵⁹ Consider how I love your precepts;
        preserve my life according to your
        steadfast love.
¹⁶⁰ The sum of your word is truth;
        and every one of your righteous
        ordinances endures for ever.

¹⁶¹ Princes persecute me without cause,
        but my heart stands in awe of your
        words.
¹⁶² I rejoice at your word
        like one who finds great spoil.
¹⁶³ I hate and abhor falsehood,
        but I love your law.
¹⁶⁴ Seven times a day I praise you
        for your righteous ordinances.

¹⁶⁵ Great peace have those who love
        your law;
        nothing can make them stumble.
¹⁶⁶ I hope for your salvation, O LORD,
        and I fulfil your commandments.
¹⁶⁷ My soul keeps your decrees;
        I love them exceedingly.
¹⁶⁸ I keep your precepts and decrees,
        for all my ways are before you.

¹⁶⁹ Let my cry come before you, O LORD;
        give me understanding according to
        your word.
¹⁷⁰ Let my supplication come before
        you;
        deliver me according to your
        promise.
¹⁷¹ My lips will pour forth praise,
        because you teach me your statutes.
¹⁷² My tongue will sing of your promise,
        for all your commandments are
        right.
¹⁷³ Let your hand be ready to help me,
        for I have chosen your precepts.
¹⁷⁴ I long for your salvation, O LORD,
        and your law is my delight.
¹⁷⁵ Let me live that I may praise you,
        and let your ordinances help me.
¹⁷⁶ I have gone astray like a lost sheep;
        seek out your servant,
        for I do not forget your
        commandments.

Psalm 120

A Song of Ascents.

¹ In my distress I cry to the LORD,
        that he may answer me:
² 'Deliver me, O LORD,
        from lying lips,
        from a deceitful tongue.'

³ What shall be given to you?
        And what more shall be done to you,
        you deceitful tongue?
⁴ A warrior's sharp arrows,
        with glowing coals of the broom
        tree!

⁵ Woe is me, that I am an alien in
        Meshech,

that I must live among the tents of
    Kedar.
6 Too long have I had my dwelling
    among those who hate peace.
7 I am for peace;
    but when I speak,
        they are for war.

Psalm 121

A Song of Ascents.

1 I lift up my eyes to the hills—
    from where will my help come?
2 My help comes from the LORD,
    who made heaven and earth.

3 He will not let your foot be moved;
    he who keeps you will not slumber.
4 He who keeps Israel
    will neither slumber nor sleep.

5 The LORD is your keeper;
    the LORD is your shade at your right
        hand.
6 The sun shall not strike you by day,
    nor the moon by night.

7 The LORD will keep you from all evil;
    he will keep your life.
8 The LORD will keep
    your going out and your coming in
    from this time on and for evermore.

Psalm 122

A Song of Ascents. Of David.

1 I was glad when they said to me,
    'Let us go to the house of the LORD!'
2 Our feet are standing
    within your gates, O Jerusalem.

3 Jerusalem—built as a city
    that is bound firmly together.
4 To it the tribes go up,
    the tribes of the LORD,
    as was decreed for Israel,
        to give thanks to the name of
            the LORD.
5 For there the thrones for judgement
        were set up,
    the thrones of the house of David.

6 Pray for the peace of Jerusalem:
    'May they prosper who love you.
7 Peace be within your walls,
    and security within your towers.'
8 For the sake of my relatives and
        friends
    I will say, 'Peace be within you.'
9 For the sake of the house of the LORD
        our God,
    I will seek your good.

Psalm 123

A Song of Ascents.

1 To you I lift up my eyes,
    O you who are enthroned in the
        heavens!
2 As the eyes of servants
    look to the hand of their master,
    as the eyes of a maid
        to the hand of her mistress,
    so our eyes look to the LORD
            our God,
        until he has mercy upon us.

3 Have mercy upon us, O LORD, have
        mercy upon us,
    for we have had more than enough
        of contempt.
4 Our soul has had more than its fill
    of the scorn of those who are
        at ease,
    of the contempt of the proud.

Psalm 124

A Song of Ascents. Of David.

1 If it had not been the LORD who was
        on our side
    —let Israel now say—
2 if it had not been the LORD who was
        on our side,
    when our enemies attacked us,
3 then they would have swallowed us
        up alive,
    when their anger was kindled
        against us;
4 then the flood would have swept us
        away,
    the torrent would have gone
        over us;

5 then over us would have gone
    the raging waters.

6 Blessed be the LORD,
    who has not given us
    as prey to their teeth.
7 We have escaped like a bird
    from the snare of the fowlers;
    the snare is broken,
    and we have escaped.

8 Our help is in the name of the LORD,
    who made heaven and earth.

Psalm 125

A Song of Ascents.

1 Those who trust in the LORD are like
    Mount Zion,
    which cannot be moved, but abides
    for ever.
2 As the mountains surround
    Jerusalem,
    so the LORD surrounds his people,
    from this time on and for
    evermore.
3 For the sceptre of wickedness shall
    not rest
    on the land allotted to the
    righteous,
    so that the righteous may not stretch
    out
    their hands to do wrong.
4 Do good, O LORD, to those who are
    good,
    and to those who are upright in
    their hearts.
5 But those who turn aside to their
    own crooked ways
    the LORD will lead away with
    evildoers.
    Peace be upon Israel!

Psalm 126

A Song of Ascents.

1 When the LORD restored the fortunes
    of Zion,*a*
    we were like those who dream.
2 Then our mouth was filled with
    laughter,

and our tongue with shouts of joy;
    then it was said among the nations,
    'The LORD has done great things for
    them.'
3 The LORD has done great things
    for us,
    and we rejoiced.

4 Restore our fortunes, O LORD,
    like the watercourses in the Negeb.
5 May those who sow in tears
    reap with shouts of joy.
6 Those who go out weeping,
    bearing the seed for sowing,
    shall come home with shouts of joy,
    carrying their sheaves.

Psalm 127

A Song of Ascents. Of Solomon.

1 Unless the LORD builds the house,
    those who build it labour in vain.
    Unless the LORD guards the city,
    the guard keeps watch in vain.
2 It is in vain that you rise up early
    and go late to rest,
    eating the bread of anxious toil;
    for he gives sleep to his beloved.*b*

3 Sons are indeed a heritage from
    the LORD,
    the fruit of the womb a reward.
4 Like arrows in the hand of a warrior
    are the sons of one's youth.
5 Happy is the man who has
    his quiver full of them.
    He shall not be put to shame
    when he speaks with his enemies in
    the gate.

Psalm 128

A Song of Ascents.

1 Happy is everyone who fears the
    LORD,
    who walks in his ways.
2 You shall eat the fruit of the labour of
    your hands;

a Or *brought back those who returned to Zion*   *b* Or *for
he provides for his beloved during sleep*

you shall be happy, and it shall go
   well with you.

3 Your wife will be like a fruitful vine
   within your house;
   your children will be like olive shoots
   around your table.
4 Thus shall the man be blessed
   who fears the LORD.

5 The LORD bless you from Zion.
   May you see the prosperity of
     Jerusalem
   all the days of your life.
6 May you see your children's children.
   Peace be upon Israel!

Psalm 129

A Song of Ascents.

1 'Often have they attacked me from
   my youth'
   —let Israel now say—
2 'often have they attacked me from my
   youth,
   yet they have not prevailed against
   me.
3 Those who plough ploughed on my
   back;
   they made their furrows long.'
4 The LORD is righteous;
   he has cut the cords of the wicked.
5 May all who hate Zion
   be put to shame and turned back.
6 Let them be like the grass on the
   housetops
   that withers before it grows up,
7 with which reapers do not fill their
   hands
   or binders of sheaves their arms,
8 while those who pass by do not say,
   'The blessing of the LORD be upon
   you!
   We bless you in the name of the
   LORD!'

Psalm 130

A Song of Ascents.

1 Out of the depths I cry to you,
   O LORD.

2 Lord, hear my voice!
   Let your ears be attentive
     to the voice of my supplications!

3 If you, O LORD, should mark
     iniquities,
   Lord, who could stand?
4 But there is forgiveness with you,
   so that you may be revered.

5 I wait for the LORD, my soul waits,
   and in his word I hope;
6 my soul waits for the Lord
   more than those who watch for the
     morning,
   more than those who watch for the
     morning.

7 O Israel, hope in the LORD!
   For with the LORD there is steadfast
     love,
   and with him is great power to
     redeem.
8 It is he who will redeem Israel
   from all its iniquities.

Psalm 131

A Song of Ascents. Of David.

1 O LORD, my heart is not lifted up,
   my eyes are not raised too high;
   I do not occupy myself with things
   too great and too marvellous
     for me.
2 But I have calmed and quieted
     my soul,
   like a weaned child with its mother;
   my soul is like the weaned child
     that is with me. *a*

3 O Israel, hope in the LORD
   from this time on and for
     evermore.

Psalm 132

A Song of Ascents.

1 O LORD, remember in David's favour
   all the hardships he endured;
2 how he swore to the LORD

a Or *my soul within me is like a weaned child*

and vowed to the Mighty One of
 Jacob,
3 'I will not enter my house
 or get into my bed;
4 I will not give sleep to my eyes
 or slumber to my eyelids,
5 until I find a place for the LORD,
 a dwelling-place for the Mighty
  One of Jacob.'

6 We heard of it in Ephrathah;
 we found it in the fields of Jaar.
7 'Let us go to his dwelling-place;
 let us worship at his footstool.'

8 Rise up, O LORD, and go to your
 resting-place,
 you and the ark of your might.
9 Let your priests be clothed with
 righteousness,
 and let your faithful shout for joy.
10 For your servant David's sake
 do not turn away the face of your
 anointed one.

11 The LORD swore to David a sure oath
 from which he will not turn back:
 'One of the sons of your body
 I will set on your throne.
12 If your sons keep my covenant
 and my decrees that I shall teach
  them,
 their sons also, for evermore,
 shall sit on your throne.'

13 For the LORD has chosen Zion;
 he has desired it for his habitation:
14 'This is my resting-place for ever;
 here I will reside, for I have desired
  it.
15 I will abundantly bless its provisions;
 I will satisfy its poor with bread.
16 Its priests I will clothe with salvation,
 and its faithful will shout for joy.
17 There I will cause a horn to sprout up
 for David;
 I have prepared a lamp for my
  anointed one.
18 His enemies I will clothe with
 disgrace,
 but on him, his crown will gleam.'

Psalm 133

A Song of Ascents.

1 How very good and pleasant it is
 when kindred live together in
  unity!
2 It is like the precious oil on the head,
 running down upon the beard,
on the beard of Aaron,
 running down over the collar of his
  robes.
3 It is like the dew of Hermon,
 which falls on the mountains of
  Zion.
For there the LORD ordained his
 blessing,
 life for evermore.

Psalm 134

A Song of Ascents.

1 Come, bless the LORD, all you
  servants of the LORD,
 who stand by night in the house of
  the LORD!
2 Lift up your hands to the holy place,
 and bless the LORD.

3 May the LORD, maker of heaven and
 earth,
 bless you from Zion.

Psalm 135

1 Praise the LORD!
 Praise the name of the LORD;
 give praise, O servants of the LORD,
2 you that stand in the house of
  the LORD,
 in the courts of the house of
  our God.
3 Praise the LORD, for the LORD is good;
 sing to his name, for he is gracious.
4 For the LORD has chosen Jacob for
 himself,
 Israel as his own possession.

5 For I know that the LORD is great;
 our Lord is above all gods.
6 Whatever the LORD pleases he does,
 in heaven and on earth,
 in the seas and all deeps.

7 He it is who makes the clouds rise at
   the end of the earth;
   he makes lightnings for the rain
   and brings out the wind from his
      storehouses.

8 He it was who struck down the
   firstborn of Egypt,
   both human beings and animals;
9 he sent signs and wonders
   into your midst, O Egypt,
   against Pharaoh and all his
      servants.
10 He struck down many nations
   and killed mighty kings—
11 Sihon, king of the Amorites,
   and Og, king of Bashan,
   and all the kingdoms of Canaan—
12 and gave their land as a heritage,
   a heritage to his people Israel.

13 Your name, O LORD, endures for ever,
   your renown, O LORD, throughout
      all ages.
14 For the LORD will vindicate his
      people,
   and have compassion on his
      servants.

15 The idols of the nations are silver and
      gold,
   the work of human hands.
16 They have mouths, but they do not
      speak;
   they have eyes, but they do not see;
17 they have ears, but they do not hear,
   and there is no breath in their
      mouths.
18 Those who make them
   and all who trust them
   shall become like them.

19 O house of Israel, bless the LORD!
   O house of Aaron, bless the LORD!
20 O house of Levi, bless the LORD!
   You that fear the LORD, bless
      the LORD!
21 Blessed be the LORD from Zion,
   he who resides in Jerusalem.
   Praise the LORD!

Psalm 136

1 O give thanks to the LORD, for he is
      good,
   for his steadfast love endures for
      ever.
2 O give thanks to the God of gods,
   for his steadfast love endures for
      ever.
3 O give thanks to the Lord of lords,
   for his steadfast love endures for
      ever;

4 who alone does great wonders,
   for his steadfast love endures for
      ever;
5 who by understanding made the
      heavens,
   for his steadfast love endures for
      ever;
6 who spread out the earth on the
      waters,
   for his steadfast love endures for
      ever;
7 who made the great lights,
   for his steadfast love endures for
      ever;
8 the sun to rule over the day,
   for his steadfast love endures for
      ever;
9 the moon and stars to rule over
      the night,
   for his steadfast love endures for
      ever;

10 who struck Egypt through their
      firstborn,
   for his steadfast love endures for
      ever;
11 and brought Israel out from among
      them,
   for his steadfast love endures for
      ever;
12 with a strong hand and an
      outstretched arm,
   for his steadfast love endures for
      ever;
13 who divided the Red Sea[a] in two,
   for his steadfast love endures for
      ever;

a Or Sea of Reeds

14 and made Israel pass through the
      midst of it,
   for his steadfast love endures for
      ever;
15 but overthrew Pharaoh and his army
      in the Red Sea, *a*
   for his steadfast love endures for
      ever;
16 who led his people through the
      wilderness,
   for his steadfast love endures for
      ever;
17 who struck down great kings,
   for his steadfast love endures for
      ever;
18 and killed famous kings,
   for his steadfast love endures for
      ever;
19 Sihon, king of the Amorites,
   for his steadfast love endures for
      ever;
20 and Og, king of Bashan,
   for his steadfast love endures for
      ever;
21 and gave their land as a heritage,
   for his steadfast love endures for
      ever;
22 a heritage to his servant Israel,
   for his steadfast love endures for
      ever.

23 It is he who remembered us in our
      low estate,
   for his steadfast love endures for
      ever;
24 and rescued us from our foes,
   for his steadfast love endures for
      ever;
25 who gives food to all flesh,
   for his steadfast love endures for
      ever.

26 O give thanks to the God of heaven,
   for his steadfast love endures for
      ever.

Psalm 137

1 By the rivers of Babylon—
   there we sat down and there
      we wept
   when we remembered Zion.

2 On the willows *b* there
   we hung up our harps.
3 For there our captors
      asked us for songs,
   and our tormentors asked for mirth,
      saying,
   'Sing us one of the songs of Zion!'

4 How could we sing the LORD's song
   in a foreign land?
5 If I forget you, O Jerusalem,
   let my right hand wither!
6 Let my tongue cling to the roof of my
      mouth,
   if I do not remember you,
   if I do not set Jerusalem
   above my highest joy.

7 Remember, O LORD, against the
      Edomites
   the day of Jerusalem's fall,
   how they said, 'Tear it down! Tear it
      down!
   Down to its foundations!'
8 O daughter Babylon, you devastator! *c*
   Happy shall they be who pay
      you back
   what you have done to us!
9 Happy shall they be who take your
      little ones
   and dash them against the rock!

Psalm 138

Of David.

1 I give you thanks, O LORD, with my
      whole heart;
   before the gods I sing your praise;
2 I bow down towards your holy
      temple
   and give thanks to your name for
      your steadfast love and your
      faithfulness;
   for you have exalted your name and
      your word
   above everything. *d*
3 On the day I called, you answered me,
   you increased my strength of soul. *e*

*a Or Sea of Reeds   b Or poplars   c Or you who are
devastated   d Cn: Heb you have exalted your word above
all your name   e Syr Compare Gk Tg: Heb you made me
arrogant in my soul with strength*

4 All the kings of the earth shall praise
    you, O LORD,
      for they have heard the words of
        your mouth.
5 They shall sing of the ways of the
    LORD,
      for great is the glory of the LORD.
6 For though the LORD is high, he
      regards the lowly;
      but the haughty he perceives from
        far away.

7 Though I walk in the midst of
      trouble,
      you preserve me against the wrath
        of my enemies;
    you stretch out your hand,
      and your right hand delivers me.
8 The LORD will fulfil his purpose
      for me;
      your steadfast love, O LORD,
        endures for ever.
      Do not forsake the work of your
        hands.

Psalm 139

To the leader. Of David. A Psalm.

1 O LORD, you have searched me and
      known me.
2 You know when I sit down and when
      I rise up;
      you discern my thoughts from
        far away.
3 You search out my path and my lying
      down,
      and are acquainted with all
        my ways.
4 Even before a word is on my
      tongue,
      O LORD, you know it completely.
5 You hem me in, behind and before,
      and lay your hand upon me.
6 Such knowledge is too wonderful for
      me;
      it is so high that I cannot attain it.

7 Where can I go from your spirit?
      Or where can I flee from your
        presence?
8 If I ascend to heaven, you are there;

if I make my bed in Sheol, you are
    there.
9 If I take the wings of the morning
      and settle at the farthest limits of
        the sea,
10 even there your hand shall lead me,
      and your right hand shall hold me
        fast.
11 If I say, 'Surely the darkness shall
      cover me,
      and the light around me become
        night',
12 even the darkness is not dark to you;
      the night is as bright as the day,
      for darkness is as light to you.

13 For it was you who formed my
      inward parts;
      you knit me together in my
        mother's womb.
14 I praise you, for I am fearfully and
      wonderfully made.
      Wonderful are your works;
    that I know very well.
15   My frame was not hidden from
      you,
      when I was being made in secret,
        intricately woven in the depths of
          the earth.
16 Your eyes beheld my unformed
      substance.
    In your book were written
      all the days that were formed
        for me,
      when none of them as yet existed.
17 How weighty to me are your
      thoughts, O God!
      How vast is the sum of them!
18 I try to count them—they are more
      than the sand;
      I come to the end[a]—I am still with
        you.

19 O that you would kill the wicked,
      O God,
      and that the bloodthirsty would
        depart from me—
20 those who speak of you maliciously,
      and lift themselves up against you
        for evil![b]

a Or I awake   b Cn: Meaning of Heb uncertain

21 Do I not hate those who hate you,
    O LORD?
    And do I not loathe those who rise
    up against you?
22 I hate them with perfect hatred;
    I count them my enemies.
23 Search me, O God, and know my
    heart;
    test me and know my thoughts.
24 See if there is any wicked*a* way
    in me,
    and lead me in the way everlasting.*b*

Psalm 140

To the leader. A Psalm of David.

1 Deliver me, O LORD, from evildoers;
    protect me from those who are
    violent,
2 who plan evil things in their minds
    and stir up wars continually.
3 They make their tongue sharp as a
    snake's,
    and under their lips is the venom of
    vipers.   *Selah*

4 Guard me, O LORD, from the hands
    of the wicked;
    protect me from the violent
    who have planned my downfall.
5 The arrogant have hidden a trap for
    me,
    and with cords they have spread a
    net;*c*
    along the road they have set snares
    for me.   *Selah*

6 I say to the LORD, 'You are my God;
    give ear, O LORD, to the voice of my
    supplications.'
7 O LORD, my Lord, my strong
    deliverer,
    you have covered my head in
    the day of battle.
8 Do not grant, O LORD, the desires of
    the wicked;
    do not further their evil plot.*d*
                                   Selah

9 Those who surround me lift up their
    heads;*e*

let the mischief of their lips
    overwhelm them!
10 Let burning coals fall on them!
    Let them be flung into pits, no
    more to rise!
11 Do not let the slanderer be
    established in the land;
    let evil speedily hunt down the
    violent!

12 I know that the LORD maintains the
    cause of the needy,
    and executes justice for the poor.
13 Surely the righteous shall give thanks
    to your name;
    the upright shall live in your
    presence.

Psalm 141

A Psalm of David.

1 I call upon you, O LORD; come
    quickly to me;
    give ear to my voice when I call to
    you.
2 Let my prayer be counted as incense
    before you,
    and the lifting up of my hands as
    an evening sacrifice.

3 Set a guard over my mouth, O LORD;
    keep watch over the door of
    my lips.
4 Do not turn my heart to any evil,
    to busy myself with wicked deeds
in company with those who work
    iniquity;
    do not let me eat of their delicacies.

5 Let the righteous strike me;
    let the faithful correct me.
Never let the oil of the wicked anoint
    my head,*f*
    for my prayer is continually*g*
    against their wicked deeds.

a Heb *hurtful*   b Or *the ancient way.* Compare Jer 6.16
c Or *they have spread cords as a net*   d Heb adds *they
are exalted*   e Cn Compare Gk: Heb *those who surround
me are uplifted in head*; Heb divides verses 8 and 9
differently   f Gk: Meaning of Heb uncertain
g Cn: Heb *for continually and my prayer*

6 When they are given over to those
   who shall condemn them,
   then they shall learn that my words
   were pleasant.
7 Like a rock that one breaks apart and
   shatters on the land,
   so shall their bones be strewn at the
   mouth of Sheol. *a*

8 But my eyes are turned towards you,
   O GOD, my Lord;
   in you I seek refuge; do not leave
   me defenceless.
9 Keep me from the trap that they have
   laid for me,
   and from the snares of evildoers.
10 Let the wicked fall into their own nets,
   while I alone escape.

Psalm 142

A Maskil of David. When he was in the cave.
A Prayer.

1 With my voice I cry to the LORD;
   with my voice I make supplication
   to the LORD.
2 I pour out my complaint before him;
   I tell my trouble before him.
3 When my spirit is faint,
   you know my way.

   In the path where I walk
   they have hidden a trap for me.
4 Look on my right hand and see—
   there is no one who takes notice of
   me;
   no refuge remains to me;
   no one cares for me.

5 I cry to you, O LORD;
   I say, 'You are my refuge,
   my portion in the land of the
   living.'
6 Give heed to my cry,
   for I am brought very low.

   Save me from my persecutors,
   for they are too strong for me.
7 Bring me out of prison,
   so that I may give thanks to your
   name.

The righteous will surround me,
   for you will deal bountifully
   with me.

Psalm 143

A Psalm of David.

1 Hear my prayer, O LORD;
   give ear to my supplications in your
   faithfulness;
   answer me in your righteousness.
2 Do not enter into judgement with
   your servant,
   for no one living is righteous before
   you.

3 For the enemy has pursued me,
   crushing my life to the ground,
   making me sit in darkness like
   those long dead.
4 Therefore my spirit faints
   within me;
   my heart within me is appalled.

5 I remember the days of old,
   I think about all your deeds,
   I meditate on the works of your
   hands.
6 I stretch out my hands to you;
   my soul thirsts for you like a
   parched land.   *Selah*

7 Answer me quickly, O LORD;
   my spirit fails.
   Do not hide your face from me,
   or I shall be like those who go
   down to the Pit.
8 Let me hear of your steadfast love in
   the morning,
   for in you I put my trust.
   Teach me the way I should go,
   for to you I lift up my soul.

9 Save me, O LORD, from my enemies;
   I have fled to you for refuge. *b*
10 Teach me to do your will,
   for you are my God.
   Let your good spirit lead me
   on a level path.

a Meaning of Heb of verses 5-7 is uncertain
b One Heb Ms Gk: MT *to you I have hidden*

11 For your name's sake, O LORD,
    preserve my life.
  In your righteousness bring me out
    of trouble.
12 In your steadfast love cut off my
    enemies,
  and destroy all my adversaries,
    for I am your servant.

Psalm 144

Of David.

1 Blessed be the LORD, my rock,
    who trains my hands for war, and
    my fingers for battle;
2 my rock *a* and my fortress,
    my stronghold and my deliverer,
  my shield, in whom I take refuge,
    who subdues the peoples *b*
    under me.

3 O LORD, what are human beings that
    you regard them,
  or mortals that you think of them?
4 They are like a breath;
    their days are like a passing
    shadow.

5 Bow your heavens, O LORD, and come
    down;
  touch the mountains so that they
    smoke.
6 Make the lightning flash and scatter
    them;
  send out your arrows and rout
    them.
7 Stretch out your hand from on high;
    set me free and rescue me from the
    mighty waters,
  from the hand of aliens,
8 whose mouths speak lies,
    and whose right hands are false.

9 I will sing a new song to you, O God;
    upon a ten-stringed harp I will play
    to you,
10 the one who gives victory to kings,
    who rescues his servant David.
11 Rescue me from the cruel sword,
    and deliver me from the hand of
    aliens,

whose mouths speak lies,
    and whose right hands are false.

12 May our sons in their youth
    be like plants full grown,
  our daughters like corner pillars,
    cut for the building of a palace.
13 May our barns be filled
    with produce of every kind;
  may our sheep increase by thousands,
    by tens of thousands in our fields,
14   and may our cattle be heavy with
    young.
  May there be no breach in the walls; *c*
    no exile,
  and no cry of distress in our streets.

15 Happy are the people to whom such
    blessings fall;
  happy are the people whose God is
    the LORD.

Psalm 145

Praise. Of David.

1 I will extol you, my God and King,
    and bless your name for ever
    and ever.
2 Every day I will bless you,
    and praise your name for ever
    and ever.
3 Great is the LORD, and greatly to be
    praised;
  his greatness is unsearchable.

4 One generation shall laud your works
    to another,
  and shall declare your mighty acts.
5 On the glorious splendour of your
    majesty,
  and on your wondrous works, I will
    meditate.
6 The might of your awesome deeds
    shall be proclaimed,
  and I will declare your greatness.
7 They shall celebrate the fame of your
    abundant goodness,

a With 18.2 and 2 Sam 22.2: Heb *my steadfast love*
b Heb Mss Syr Aquila Jerome: MT *my people*
c Heb lacks *in the walls*

and shall sing aloud of your
 righteousness.

8 The LORD is gracious and merciful,
 slow to anger and abounding in
  steadfast love.
9 The LORD is good to all,
 and his compassion is over all that
  he has made.

10 All your works shall give thanks to
  you, O LORD,
 and all your faithful shall bless you.
11 They shall speak of the glory of your
  kingdom,
 and tell of your power,
12 to make known to all people your*a*
  mighty deeds,
 and the glorious splendour of
  your*b* kingdom.
13 Your kingdom is an everlasting
  kingdom,
 and your dominion endures
  throughout all generations.

 The LORD is faithful in all his words,
 and gracious in all his deeds. *c*
14 The LORD upholds all who are falling,
 and raises up all who are bowed
  down.
15 The eyes of all look to you,
 and you give them their food in
  due season.
16 You open your hand,
 satisfying the desire of every living
  thing.
17 The LORD is just in all his ways,
 and kind in all his doings.
18 The LORD is near to all who call
  on him,
 to all who call on him in truth.
19 He fulfils the desire of all who
  fear him;
 he also hears their cry, and saves
  them.
20 The LORD watches over all who
  love him,
 but all the wicked he will destroy.

21 My mouth will speak the praise of
 the LORD,

and all flesh will bless his holy
 name for ever and ever.

Psalm 146

1 Praise the LORD!
 Praise the LORD, O my soul!
2 I will praise the LORD as long as I live;
 I will sing praises to my God all my
  life long.

3 Do not put your trust in princes,
 in mortals, in whom there is no
  help.
4 When their breath departs, they
  return to the earth;
 on that very day their plans perish.

5 Happy are those whose help is the
  God of Jacob,
 whose hope is in the LORD their God,
6 who made heaven and earth,
 the sea, and all that is in them;
who keeps faith for ever;
7 who executes justice for the
  oppressed;
 who gives food to the hungry.

 The LORD sets the prisoners free;
8 the LORD opens the eyes of
  the blind.
 The LORD lifts up those who are
  bowed down;
 the LORD loves the righteous.
9 The LORD watches over the strangers;
 he upholds the orphan and the
  widow,
 but the way of the wicked he brings
  to ruin.

10 The LORD will reign for ever,
 your God, O Zion, for all
  generations.
 Praise the LORD!

Psalm 147

1 Praise the LORD!
 How good it is to sing praises to our
  God;

a Gk Jerome Syr: Heb *his* *b* Heb *his* *c* These two
lines supplied by Q Ms Gk Syr

for he is gracious, and a song of
    praise is fitting.
2 The LORD builds up Jerusalem;
    he gathers the outcasts of Israel.
3 He heals the broken-hearted,
    and binds up their wounds.
4 He determines the number of
    the stars;
    he gives to all of them their names.
5 Great is our Lord, and abundant
    in power;
    his understanding is beyond
    measure.
6 The LORD lifts up the downtrodden;
    he casts the wicked to the ground.

7 Sing to the LORD with thanksgiving;
    make melody to our God on
    the lyre.
8 He covers the heavens with clouds,
    prepares rain for the earth,
    makes grass grow on the hills.
9 He gives to the animals their food,
    and to the young ravens when they
    cry.
10 His delight is not in the strength of
    the horse,
    nor his pleasure in the speed of
    a runner;[a]
11 but the LORD takes pleasure in those
    who fear him,
    in those who hope in his steadfast
    love.

12 Praise the LORD, O Jerusalem!
    Praise your God, O Zion!
13 For he strengthens the bars of
    your gates;
    he blesses your children within
    you.
14 He grants peace[b] within your
    borders;
    he fills you with the finest of wheat.
15 He sends out his command to the
    earth;
    his word runs swiftly.
16 He gives snow like wool;
    he scatters frost like ashes.
17 He hurls down hail like crumbs—
    who can stand before his cold?

18 He sends out his word, and melts
    them;
    he makes his wind blow, and the
    waters flow.
19 He declares his word to Jacob,
    his statutes and ordinances to
    Israel.
20 He has not dealt thus with any other
    nation;
    they do not know his ordinances.
Praise the LORD!

Psalm 148

1 Praise the LORD!
    Praise the LORD from the heavens;
    praise him in the heights!
2 Praise him, all his angels;
    praise him, all his host!

3 Praise him, sun and moon;
    praise him, all you shining stars!
4 Praise him, you highest heavens,
    and you waters above the heavens!

5 Let them praise the name of
    the LORD,
    for he commanded and they
    were created.
6 He established them for ever
    and ever;
    he fixed their bounds, which
    cannot be passed.[c]

7 Praise the LORD from the earth,
    you sea monsters and all deeps,
8 fire and hail, snow and frost,
    stormy wind fulfilling his
    command!

9 Mountains and all hills,
    fruit trees and all cedars!
10 Wild animals and all cattle,
    creeping things and flying birds!

11 Kings of the earth and all peoples,
    princes and all rulers of the earth!
12 Young men and women alike,
    old and young together!

a Heb *legs of a person*   *b* Or *prosperity*   *c* Or *he set a law that cannot pass away*

13 Let them praise the name of the LORD,
    for his name alone is exalted;
    his glory is above earth and heaven.
14 He has raised up a horn for his
       people,
    praise for all his faithful,
    for the people of Israel who are
       close to him.
Praise the LORD!

Psalm 149

1 Praise the LORD!
    Sing to the LORD a new song,
       his praise in the assembly of the
       faithful.
2 Let Israel be glad in its Maker;
    let the children of Zion rejoice in
       their King.
3 Let them praise his name with
       dancing,
    making melody to him with
       tambourine and lyre.
4 For the LORD takes pleasure in
       his people;
    he adorns the humble with
       victory.
5 Let the faithful exult in glory;
    let them sing for joy on their
       couches.
6 Let the high praises of God be in
       their throats
    and two-edged swords in their
       hands,

7 to execute vengeance on the nations
    and punishment on the peoples,
8 to bind their kings with fetters
    and their nobles with chains
       of iron,
9 to execute on them the judgement
       decreed.
    This is glory for all his faithful
       ones.
Praise the LORD!

Psalm 150

1 Praise the LORD!
    Praise God in his sanctuary;
       praise him in his mighty
       firmament! [a]
2 Praise him for his mighty deeds;
       praise him according to his
       surpassing greatness!

3 Praise him with trumpet sound;
       praise him with lute and harp!
4 Praise him with tambourine and
       dance;
    praise him with strings and pipe!
5 Praise him with clanging cymbals;
       praise him with loud clashing
       cymbals!
6 Let everything that breathes praise
       the LORD!
Praise the LORD!

a Or *dome*

PROVERBS

1 The proverbs of Solomon son of David, king of Israel:

Prologue

2 For learning about wisdom and
  instruction,
  for understanding words of insight,
3 for gaining instruction in wise
  dealing,
  righteousness, justice, and equity;
4 to teach shrewdness to the simple,
  knowledge and prudence to the
  young—
5 let the wise also hear and gain in
  learning,
  and the discerning acquire skill,
6 to understand a proverb and a figure,
  the words of the wise and their
  riddles.

7 The fear of the LORD is the beginning
  of knowledge;
  fools despise wisdom and
  instruction.

Warnings against Evil Companions

8 Hear, my child, your father's
  instruction,
  and do not reject your mother's
  teaching;
9 for they are a fair garland for your
  head,
  and pendants for your neck.
10 My child, if sinners entice you,
  do not consent.
11 If they say, 'Come with us, let us lie
  in wait for blood;
  let us wantonly ambush the
  innocent;
12 like Sheol let us swallow them alive

and whole, like those who go down
  to the Pit.
13 We shall find all kinds of costly
  things;
  we shall fill our houses with booty.
14 Throw in your lot among us;
  we will all have one purse'—
15 my child, do not walk in their way,
  keep your foot from their paths;
16 for their feet run to evil,
  and they hurry to shed blood.
17 For in vain is the net baited
  while the bird is looking on;
18 yet they lie in wait—to kill
  themselves!
  and set an ambush—for their own
  lives!
19 Such is the end[a] of all who are greedy
  for gain;
  it takes away the life of its
  possessors.

The Call of Wisdom

20 Wisdom cries out in the street;
  in the squares she raises her voice.
21 At the busiest corner she cries out;
  at the entrance of the city gates she
  speaks:
22 'How long, O simple ones, will you
  love being simple?
  How long will scoffers delight in
  their scoffing
  and fools hate knowledge?
23 Give heed to my reproof;
  I will pour out my thoughts to you;
  I will make my words known
  to you.

---

a Gk: Heb *are the ways*

24 Because I have called and you
        refused,
     have stretched out my hand and no
        one heeded,
25 and because you have ignored all my
        counsel
     and would have none of my
        reproof,
26 I also will laugh at your calamity;
     I will mock when panic strikes you,
27 when panic strikes you like a storm,
     and your calamity comes like a
        whirlwind,
     when distress and anguish come
        upon you.
28 Then they will call upon me, but I
        will not answer;
     they will seek me diligently, but
        will not find me.
29 Because they hated knowledge
     and did not choose the fear of the
        LORD,
30 would have none of my counsel,
     and despised all my reproof,
31 therefore they shall eat the fruit of
        their way
     and be sated with their own devices.
32 For waywardness kills the simple,
     and the complacency of fools
        destroys them;
33 but those who listen to me will be
        secure
     and will live at ease, without dread
        of disaster.'

The Value of Wisdom

2 My child, if you accept my words
     and treasure up my commandments
        within you,
2 making your ear attentive to wisdom
     and inclining your heart to
        understanding;
3 if you indeed cry out for insight,
     and raise your voice for
        understanding;
4 if you seek it like silver,
     and search for it as for hidden
        treasures—
5 then you will understand the fear of
        the LORD
     and find the knowledge of God.

6 For the LORD gives wisdom;
     from his mouth come knowledge
        and understanding;
7 he stores up sound wisdom for the
        upright;
     he is a shield to those who walk
        blamelessly,
8 guarding the paths of justice
     and preserving the way of his
        faithful ones.
9 Then you will understand
        righteousness and justice
     and equity, every good path;
10 for wisdom will come into your
        heart,
     and knowledge will be pleasant to
        your soul;
11 prudence will watch over you;
     and understanding will guard you.
12 It will save you from the way of evil,
     from those who speak perversely,
13 who forsake the paths of uprightness
     to walk in the ways of darkness,
14 who rejoice in doing evil
     and delight in the perverseness
        of evil;
15 those whose paths are crooked,
     and who are devious in their ways.

16 You will be saved from the loose[a]
        woman,
     from the adulteress with her
        smooth words,
17 who forsakes the partner of her youth
     and forgets her sacred covenant;
18 for her way[b] leads down to death,
     and her paths to the shades;
19 those who go to her never come back,
     nor do they regain the paths of life.

20 Therefore walk in the way of the
        good,
     and keep to the paths of the just.
21 For the upright will abide in the land,
     and the innocent will remain in it;
22 but the wicked will be cut off from
        the land,
     and the treacherous will be rooted
        out of it.

a Heb strange   b Cn: Heb house

Admonition to Trust and Honour God

3 My child, do not forget my teaching,
but let your heart keep my
commandments;
2 for length of days and years of life
and abundant welfare they will give
you.

3 Do not let loyalty and faithfulness
forsake you;
bind them round your neck,
write them on the tablet of your
heart.
4 So you will find favour and good
repute
in the sight of God and of people.

5 Trust in the LORD with all your heart,
and do not rely on your own
insight.
6 In all your ways acknowledge him,
and he will make straight your
paths.
7 Do not be wise in your own eyes;
fear the LORD, and turn away from
evil.
8 It will be a healing for your flesh
and a refreshment for your body.

9 Honour the LORD with your
substance
and with the first fruits of all your
produce;
10 then your barns will be filled with
plenty,
and your vats will be bursting with
wine.

11 My child, do not despise the LORD's
discipline
or be weary of his reproof,
12 for the LORD reproves the one he
loves,
as a father the son in whom he
delights.

The True Wealth

13 Happy are those who find wisdom,
and those who get understanding,
14 for her income is better than silver,
and her revenue better than gold.

15 She is more precious than jewels,
and nothing you desire can
compare with her.
16 Long life is in her right hand;
in her left hand are riches and
honour.
17 Her ways are ways of pleasantness,
and all her paths are peace.
18 She is a tree of life to those who lay
hold of her;
those who hold her fast are called
happy.

God's Wisdom in Creation

19 The LORD by wisdom founded the
earth;
by understanding he established
the heavens;
20 by his knowledge the deeps broke
open,
and the clouds drop down the dew.

The True Security

21 My child, do not let these escape
from your sight:
keep sound wisdom and prudence,
22 and they will be life for your soul
and adornment for your neck.
23 Then you will walk on your way
securely
and your foot will not stumble.
24 If you sit down,[a] you will not be
afraid;
when you lie down, your sleep will
be sweet.
25 Do not be afraid of sudden panic,
or of the storm that strikes the
wicked;
26 for the LORD will be your confidence
and will keep your foot from being
caught.

27 Do not withhold good from those to
whom it is due,[b]
when it is in your power to do it.
28 Do not say to your neighbour, 'Go,
and come again;
tomorrow I will give it'—when you
have it with you.

a Gk: Heb *lie down*   *b* Heb *from its owners*

29 Do not plan harm against your
　　neighbour
　　who lives trustingly beside you.
30 Do not quarrel with anyone without
　　cause,
　　when no harm has been done
　　　to you.
31 Do not envy the violent
　　and do not choose any of their
　　　ways;
32 for the perverse are an abomination
　　to the LORD,
　　but the upright are in his
　　　confidence.
33 The LORD's curse is on the house of
　　the wicked,
　　but he blesses the abode of the
　　　righteous.
34 Towards the scorners he is scornful,
　　but to the humble he shows favour.
35 The wise will inherit honour,
　　but stubborn fools, disgrace.

Parental Advice

4 Listen, children, to a father's
　　instruction,
　　and be attentive, that you may
　　　gain[a] insight;
2 for I give you good precepts:
　　do not forsake my teaching.
3 When I was a son with my father,
　　tender, and my mother's favourite,
4 he taught me, and said to me,
　　'Let your heart hold fast my words;
　　keep my commandments, and live.
5 Get wisdom; get insight: do not
　　forget, nor turn away
　　from the words of my mouth.
6 Do not forsake her, and she will keep
　　you;
　　love her, and she will guard you.
7 The beginning of wisdom is this: Get
　　wisdom,
　　and whatever else you get, get
　　　insight.
8 Prize her highly, and she will
　　exalt you;
　　she will honour you if you
　　　embrace her.
9 She will place on your head a fair
　　garland;

she will bestow on you a beautiful
　　crown.'

Admonition to Keep to the Right Path

10 Hear, my child, and accept my
　　words,
　　that the years of your life may
　　　be many.
11 I have taught you the way of
　　wisdom;
　　I have led you in the paths of
　　　uprightness.
12 When you walk, your step will not be
　　hampered;
　　and if you run, you will not
　　　stumble.
13 Keep hold of instruction; do not
　　let go;
　　guard her, for she is your life.
14 Do not enter the path of the wicked,
　　and do not walk in the way of
　　　evildoers.
15 Avoid it; do not go on it;
　　turn away from it and pass on.
16 For they cannot sleep unless they
　　have done wrong;
　　they are robbed of sleep unless they
　　have made someone stumble.
17 For they eat the bread of wickedness
　　and drink the wine of violence.
18 But the path of the righteous is like
　　the light of dawn,
　　which shines brighter and brighter
　　　until full day.
19 The way of the wicked is like deep
　　darkness;
　　they do not know what they
　　　stumble over.
20 My child, be attentive to my words;
　　incline your ear to my sayings.
21 Do not let them escape from
　　your sight;
　　keep them within your heart.
22 For they are life to those who
　　find them,
　　and healing to all their flesh.
23 Keep your heart with all vigilance,
　　for from it flow the springs of life.
24 Put away from you crooked speech,
　　and put devious talk far from you.

a Heb know

25 Let your eyes look directly forwards,
   and your gaze be straight
      before you.
26 Keep straight the path of your feet,
   and all your ways will be sure.
27 Do not swerve to the right or to
      the left;
   turn your foot away from evil.

Warning against Impurity and Infidelity

5 My child, be attentive to my wisdom;
   incline your ear to my
      understanding,
2 so that you may hold on to prudence,
   and your lips may guard
      knowledge.
3 For the lips of a loose*a* woman drip
      honey,
   and her speech is smoother
      than oil;
4 but in the end she is bitter as
      wormwood,
   sharp as a two-edged sword.
5 Her feet go down to death;
   her steps follow the path to Sheol.
6 She does not keep straight to the path
      of life;
   her ways wander, and she does not
      know it.

7 And now, my child,*b* listen to me,
   and do not depart from the words
      of my mouth.
8 Keep your way far from her,
   and do not go near the door of her
      house;
9 or you will give your honour to
      others,
   and your years to the merciless,
10 and strangers will take their fill of
      your wealth,
   and your labours will go to the
      house of an alien;
11 and at the end of your life you will
      groan,
   when your flesh and body are
      consumed,
12 and you say, 'Oh, how I hated
      discipline,
   and my heart despised reproof!

13 I did not listen to the voice of my
      teachers
   or incline my ear to my instructors.
14 Now I am at the point of utter ruin
   in the public assembly.'

15 Drink water from your own cistern,
   flowing water from your own well.
16 Should your springs be scattered
      abroad,
   streams of water in the streets?
17 Let them be for yourself alone,
   and not for sharing with strangers.
18 Let your fountain be blessed,
   and rejoice in the wife of your
      youth,
19   a lovely deer, a graceful doe.
   May her breasts satisfy you at all
      times;
      may you be intoxicated always by
      her love.
20 Why should you be intoxicated, my
      son, by another woman
   and embrace the bosom of an
      adulteress?
21 For human ways are under the eyes of
      the LORD,
   and he examines all their paths.
22 The iniquities of the wicked ensnare
      them,
   and they are caught in the toils of
      their sin.
23 They die for lack of discipline,
   and because of their great folly they
      are lost.

Practical Admonitions

6 My child, if you have given your
   pledge to your neighbour,
   if you have bound yourself to
      another,*c*
2 you are snared by the utterance of
      your lips,*d*
   caught by the words of your mouth.
3 So do this, my child, and save
      yourself,
   for you have come into your
      neighbour's power:

a Heb *strange*   *b* Gk Vg: Heb *children*   *c* Or *a
stranger*   *d* Cn Compare Gk Syr: Heb *the words of your
mouth*

go, hurry,[a] and plead with your
neighbour.
4 Give your eyes no sleep
and your eyelids no slumber;
5 save yourself like a gazelle from the
hunter,[b]
like a bird from the hand of the
fowler.

6 Go to the ant, you lazybones;
consider its ways, and be wise.
7 Without having any chief
or officer or ruler,
8 it prepares its food in summer,
and gathers its sustenance in
harvest.
9 How long will you lie there,
O lazybones?
When will you rise from your
sleep?
10 A little sleep, a little slumber,
a little folding of the hands
to rest,
11 and poverty will come upon you like
a robber,
and want, like an armed warrior.

12 A scoundrel and a villain
goes around with crooked speech,
13 winking the eyes, shuffling the feet,
pointing the fingers,
14 with perverted mind devising evil,
continually sowing discord;
15 on such a one calamity will descend
suddenly;
in a moment, damage beyond
repair.

16 There are six things that the LORD
hates,
seven that are an abomination
to him:
17 haughty eyes, a lying tongue,
and hands that shed innocent
blood,
18 a heart that devises wicked plans,
feet that hurry to run to evil,
19 a lying witness who testifies falsely,
and one who sows discord in a
family.

20 My child, keep your father's
commandment,
and do not forsake your mother's
teaching.
21 Bind them upon your heart always;
tie them around your neck.
22 When you walk, they[c] will lead you;
when you lie down, they[c] will
watch over you;
and when you awake, they[c] will
talk with you.
23 For the commandment is a lamp and
the teaching a light,
and the reproofs of discipline are
the way of life,
24 to preserve you from the wife of
another,[d]
from the smooth tongue of the
adulteress.
25 Do not desire her beauty in your heart,
and do not let her capture you with
her eyelashes;
26 for a prostitute's fee is only a loaf of
bread,[e]
but the wife of another stalks a
man's very life.
27 Can fire be carried in the bosom
without burning one's clothes?
28 Or can one walk on hot coals
without scorching the feet?
29 So is he who sleeps with his
neighbour's wife;
no one who touches her will go
unpunished.
30 Thieves are not despised who
steal only
to satisfy their appetite when they
are hungry.
31 Yet if they are caught, they will pay
sevenfold;
they will forfeit all the goods of
their house.
32 But he who commits adultery has no
sense;
he who does it destroys himself.
33 He will get wounds and dishonour,
and his disgrace will not be wiped
away.

a Or humble yourself   b Cn: Heb from the hand
c Heb it   d Gk: MT the evil woman   e Cn Compare
Gk Syr Vg Tg: Heb for because of a harlot to a piece of
bread

34 For jealousy arouses a husband's fury,
   and he shows no restraint when he
      takes revenge.
35 He will accept no compensation,
   and refuses a bribe no matter how
      great.

The False Attractions of Adultery

7 My child, keep my words
   and store up my commandments
      with you;
2 keep my commandments and live,
   keep my teachings as the apple of
      your eye;
3 bind them on your fingers,
   write them on the tablet of your
      heart.
4 Say to wisdom, 'You are my sister',
   and call insight your intimate
      friend,
5 that they may keep you from the
      loose[a] woman,
   from the adulteress with her
      smooth words.

6 For at the window of my house
   I looked out through my lattice,
7 and I saw among the simple ones,
   I observed among the youths,
   a young man without sense,
8 passing along the street near her
      corner,
   taking the road to her house
9 in the twilight, in the evening,
   at the time of night and darkness.

10 Then a woman comes towards him,
   decked out like a prostitute, wily of
      heart.[b]
11 She is loud and wayward;
   her feet do not stay at home;
12 now in the street, now in the squares,
   and at every corner she lies in wait.
13 She seizes him and kisses him,
   and with impudent face she says to
      him:
14 'I had to offer sacrifices,
   and today I have paid my vows;
15 so now I have come out to meet you,
   to seek you eagerly, and I have
      found you!

16 I have decked my couch with
      coverings,
   coloured spreads of Egyptian linen;
17 I have perfumed my bed with myrrh,
   aloes, and cinnamon.
18 Come, let us take our fill of love until
      morning;
   let us delight ourselves with love.
19 For my husband is not at home;
   he has gone on a long journey.
20 He took a bag of money with him;
   he will not come home until full
      moon.'

21 With much seductive speech she
      persuades him;
   with her smooth talk she
      compels him.
22 Right away he follows her,
   and goes like an ox to the slaughter,
   or bounds like a stag towards
      the trap[c]
23 until an arrow pierces its entrails.
   He is like a bird rushing into a snare,
   not knowing that it will cost him
      his life.

24 And now, my children, listen to me,
   and be attentive to the words of my
      mouth.
25 Do not let your hearts turn aside to
      her ways;
   do not stray into her paths.
26 For many are those she has laid low,
   and numerous are her victims.
27 Her house is the way to Sheol,
   going down to the chambers of
      death.

The Gifts of Wisdom

8 Does not wisdom call,
   and does not understanding raise
      her voice?
2 On the heights, beside the way,
   at the crossroads she takes her
      stand;
3 beside the gates in front of the town,
   at the entrance of the portals she
      cries out:

a Heb *strange*   b Meaning of Heb uncertain
c Cn Compare Gk: Meaning of Heb uncertain

4 'To you, O people, I call,
and my cry is to all that live.
5 O simple ones, learn prudence;
acquire intelligence, you who lack it.
6 Hear, for I will speak noble things,
and from my lips will come what is
right;
7 for my mouth will utter truth;
wickedness is an abomination to
my lips.
8 All the words of my mouth are
righteous;
there is nothing twisted or crooked
in them.
9 They are all straight to one who
understands
and right to those who find
knowledge.
10 Take my instruction instead of silver,
and knowledge rather than choice
gold;
11 for wisdom is better than jewels,
and all that you may desire cannot
compare with her.
12 I, wisdom, live with prudence,[a]
and I attain knowledge and
discretion.
13 The fear of the LORD is hatred of evil.
Pride and arrogance and the way
of evil
and perverted speech I hate.
14 I have good advice and sound
wisdom;
I have insight, I have strength.
15 By me kings reign,
and rulers decree what is just;
16 by me rulers rule,
and nobles, all who govern rightly.
17 I love those who love me,
and those who seek me diligently
find me.
18 Riches and honour are with me,
enduring wealth and prosperity.
19 My fruit is better than gold, even fine
gold,
and my yield than choice silver.
20 I walk in the way of righteousness,
along the paths of justice,
21 endowing with wealth those who
love me,
and filling their treasuries.

Wisdom's Part in Creation

22 The LORD created me at the
beginning[b] of his work,[c]
the first of his acts of long ago.
23 Ages ago I was set up,
at the first, before the beginning of
the earth.
24 When there were no depths I was
brought forth,
when there were no springs
abounding with water.
25 Before the mountains had been
shaped,
before the hills, I was brought
forth—
26 when he had not yet made earth and
fields,[a]
or the world's first bits of soil.
27 When he established the heavens, I
was there,
when he drew a circle on the face of
the deep,
28 when he made firm the skies above,
when he established the fountains
of the deep,
29 when he assigned to the sea its
limit,
so that the waters might not
transgress his command,
when he marked out the foundations
of the earth,
30 then I was beside him, like a master
worker;[d]
and I was daily his[e] delight,
rejoicing before him always,
31 rejoicing in his inhabited world
and delighting in the human race.

32 'And now, my children, listen to me:
happy are those who keep my ways.
33 Hear instruction and be wise,
and do not neglect it.
34 Happy is the one who listens to me,
watching daily at my gates,
waiting beside my doors.
35 For whoever finds me finds life
and obtains favour from the LORD;

a Meaning of Heb uncertain   b Or me as the beginning
c Heb way   d Another reading is little child
e Gk: Heb lacks his

36 but those who miss me injure
        themselves;
   all who hate me love death.'

Wisdom's Feast

9 Wisdom has built her house,
        she has hewn her seven pillars.
2 She has slaughtered her animals, she
        has mixed her wine,
        she has also set her table.
3 She has sent out her servant-girls, she
        calls
        from the highest places in
            the town,
4 'You that are simple, turn in here!'
        To those without sense she says,
5 'Come, eat of my bread
        and drink of the wine I have mixed.
6 Lay aside immaturity, *a* and live,
        and walk in the way of insight.'

General Maxims

7 Whoever corrects a scoffer wins
        abuse;
        whoever rebukes the wicked
            gets hurt.
8 A scoffer who is rebuked will only
        hate you;
        the wise, when rebuked, will
            love you.
9 Give instruction *b* to the wise, and
        they will become wiser still;
        teach the righteous and they will
            gain in learning.
10 The fear of the LORD is the beginning
        of wisdom,
        and the knowledge of the Holy One
            is insight.
11 For by me your days will be
        multiplied,
        and years will be added to your life.
12 If you are wise, you are wise for
        yourself;
        if you scoff, you alone will bear it.

Folly's Invitation and Promise

13 The foolish woman is loud;
        she is ignorant and knows nothing.
14 She sits at the door of her house,
        on a seat at the high places of the
            town,

15 calling to those who pass by,
        who are going straight on their way,
16 'You who are simple, turn in here!'
        And to those without sense she
            says,
17 'Stolen water is sweet,
        and bread eaten in secret is
            pleasant.'
18 But they do not know that the dead *c*
        are there,
        that her guests are in the depths of
            Sheol.

Wise Sayings of Solomon

10 The proverbs of Solomon.

   A wise child makes a glad father,
        but a foolish child is a mother's
            grief.
2 Treasures gained by wickedness do
        not profit,
        but righteousness delivers from
            death.
3 The LORD does not let the righteous
        go hungry,
        but he thwarts the craving of the
            wicked.
4 A slack hand causes poverty,
        but the hand of the diligent makes
            rich.
5 A child who gathers in summer is
        prudent,
        but a child who sleeps in harvest
            brings shame.
6 Blessings are on the head of the
        righteous,
        but the mouth of the wicked
            conceals violence.
7 The memory of the righteous is a
        blessing,
        but the name of the wicked will rot.
8 The wise of heart will heed
        commandments,
        but a babbling fool will come
            to ruin.
9 Whoever walks in integrity walks
        securely,
        but whoever follows perverse ways
            will be found out.

a Or *simpleness*   *b* Heb lacks *instruction*
c Heb *shades*

10 Whoever winks the eye causes
      trouble,
   but the one who rebukes boldly
      makes peace. *a*
11 The mouth of the righteous is a
      fountain of life,
   but the mouth of the wicked
      conceals violence.
12 Hatred stirs up strife,
   but love covers all offences.
13 On the lips of one who has
      understanding wisdom
      is found,
   but a rod is for the back of one who
      lacks sense.
14 The wise lay up knowledge,
   but the babbling of a fool brings
      ruin near.
15 The wealth of the rich is their
      fortress;
   the poverty of the poor is their ruin.
16 The wage of the righteous leads
      to life,
   the gain of the wicked to sin.
17 Whoever heeds instruction is on the
      path to life,
   but one who rejects a rebuke goes
      astray.
18 Lying lips conceal hatred,
   and whoever utters slander is
      a fool.
19 When words are many, transgression
      is not lacking,
   but the prudent are restrained in
      speech.
20 The tongue of the righteous is choice
      silver;
   the mind of the wicked is of
      little worth.
21 The lips of the righteous feed many,
   but fools die for lack of sense.
22 The blessing of the LORD makes rich,
   and he adds no sorrow with it. *b*
23 Doing wrong is like sport to a fool,
   but wise conduct is pleasure to a
      person of understanding.
24 What the wicked dread will come
      upon them,
   but the desire of the righteous will
      be granted.

25 When the tempest passes, the wicked
      are no more,
   but the righteous are established
      for ever.
26 Like vinegar to the teeth, and smoke
      to the eyes,
   so are the lazy to their employers.
27 The fear of the LORD prolongs life,
   but the years of the wicked will be
      short.
28 The hope of the righteous ends in
      gladness,
   but the expectation of the wicked
      comes to nothing.
29 The way of the LORD is a stronghold
      for the upright,
   but destruction for evildoers.
30 The righteous will never be removed,
   but the wicked will not remain in
      the land.
31 The mouth of the righteous brings
      forth wisdom,
   but the perverse tongue will be cut
      off.
32 The lips of the righteous know what
      is acceptable,
   but the mouth of the wicked what
      is perverse.

11 A false balance is an
   abomination to the LORD,
   but an accurate weight is his
      delight.
2 When pride comes, then comes
      disgrace;
   but wisdom is with the humble.
3 The integrity of the upright guides
      them,
   but the crookedness of the
      treacherous destroys them.
4 Riches do not profit in the day
      of wrath,
   but righteousness delivers from
      death.
5 The righteousness of the blameless
      keeps their ways straight,
   but the wicked fall by their own
      wickedness.
6 The righteousness of the upright
      saves them,

a Gk: Heb *but a babbling fool will come to ruin*
b Or *and toil adds nothing to it*

but the treacherous are taken
captive by their schemes.
7 When the wicked die, their hope
perishes,
and the expectation of the godless
comes to nothing.
8 The righteous are delivered from
trouble,
and the wicked get into it instead.
9 With their mouths the godless would
destroy their neighbours,
but by knowledge the righteous are
delivered.
10 When it goes well with the righteous,
the city rejoices;
and when the wicked perish, there
is jubilation.
11 By the blessing of the upright a city is
exalted,
but it is overthrown by the mouth
of the wicked.
12 Whoever belittles another lacks sense,
but an intelligent person remains
silent.
13 A gossip goes about telling secrets,
but one who is trustworthy in spirit
keeps a confidence.
14 Where there is no guidance, a nation*a*
falls,
but in an abundance of counsellors
there is safety.
15 To guarantee loans for a stranger
brings trouble,
but there is safety in refusing
to do so.
16 A gracious woman gets honour,
but she who hates virtue is covered
with shame.*b*
The timid become destitute,*c*
but the aggressive gain riches.
17 Those who are kind reward
themselves,
but the cruel do themselves harm.
18 The wicked earn no real gain,
but those who sow righteousness
get a true reward.
19 Whoever is steadfast in righteousness
will live,
but whoever pursues evil will die.
20 Crooked minds are an abomination
to the LORD,

but those of blameless ways are his
delight.
21 Be assured, the wicked will not go
unpunished,
but those who are righteous will
escape.
22 Like a gold ring in a pig's snout
is a beautiful woman without good
sense.
23 The desire of the righteous ends only
in good;
the expectation of the wicked in
wrath.
24 Some give freely, yet grow all the
richer;
others withhold what is due, and
only suffer want.
25 A generous person will be enriched,
and one who gives water will
get water.
26 The people curse those who hold
back grain,
but a blessing is on the head of
those who sell it.
27 Whoever diligently seeks good seeks
favour,
but evil comes to the one who
searches for it.
28 Those who trust in their riches will
wither,*d*
but the righteous will flourish like
green leaves.
29 Those who trouble their households
will inherit wind,
and the fool will be servant to the
wise.
30 The fruit of the righteous is a tree of
life,
but violence*e* takes lives away.
31 If the righteous are repaid on earth,
how much more the wicked and
the sinner!

12 Whoever loves discipline loves
knowledge,
but those who hate to be rebuked
are stupid.
2 The good obtain favour from the
LORD,

---

a Or *an army*   *b* Compare Gk Syr: Heb lacks *but she
. . . shame*   *c* Gk: Heb lacks *The timid . . . destitute*
d Cn: Heb *fall*   *e* Cn Compare Gk Syr: Heb *a wise man*

but those who devise evil he
condemns.

3 No one finds security by wickedness,
but the root of the righteous will
never be moved.

4 A good wife is the crown of her
husband,
but she who brings shame is like
rottenness in his bones.

5 The thoughts of the righteous
are just;
the advice of the wicked is
treacherous.

6 The words of the wicked are a deadly
ambush,
but the speech of the upright
delivers them.

7 The wicked are overthrown and are
no more,
but the house of the righteous will
stand.

8 One is commended for good sense,
but a perverse mind is despised.

9 Better to be despised and have a
servant,
than to be self-important and lack
food.

10 The righteous know the needs of
their animals,
but the mercy of the wicked is
cruel.

11 Those who till their land will have
plenty of food,
but those who follow worthless
pursuits have no sense.

12 The wicked covet the proceeds of
wickedness, *a*
but the root of the righteous bears
fruit.

13 The evil are ensnared by the
transgression of their lips,
but the righteous escape from
trouble.

14 From the fruit of the mouth one is
filled with good things,
and manual labour has its reward.

15 Fools think their own way is right,
but the wise listen to advice.

16 Fools show their anger at once,
but the prudent ignore an insult.

17 Whoever speaks the truth gives
honest evidence,
but a false witness speaks
deceitfully.

18 Rash words are like sword thrusts,
but the tongue of the wise brings
healing.

19 Truthful lips endure for ever,
but a lying tongue lasts only a
moment.

20 Deceit is in the mind of those who
plan evil,
but those who counsel peace
have joy.

21 No harm happens to the righteous,
but the wicked are filled with
trouble.

22 Lying lips are an abomination to the
LORD,
but those who act faithfully are his
delight.

23 One who is clever conceals
knowledge,
but the mind of a fool *b* broadcasts
folly.

24 The hand of the diligent will rule,
while the lazy will be put to forced
labour.

25 Anxiety weighs down the human
heart,
but a good word cheers it up.

26 The righteous gives good advice
to friends, *c*
but the way of the wicked leads
astray.

27 The lazy do not roast *d* their game,
but the diligent obtain precious
wealth. *d*

28 In the path of righteousness there is
life,
in walking its path there is no
death.

13 A wise child loves discipline, *e*
but a scoffer does not listen to
rebuke.

2 From the fruit of their words good
people eat good things,

a Or *covet the catch of the wicked*   *b* Heb *the heart of
fools*   *c* Syr: Meaning of Heb uncertain   *d* Meaning
of Heb uncertain   *e* Cn: Heb *A wise child the discipline
of his father*

but the desire of the treacherous is
for wrongdoing.

3 Those who guard their mouths
preserve their lives;
those who open wide their lips
come to ruin.

4 The appetite of the lazy craves, and
gets nothing,
while the appetite of the diligent is
richly supplied.

5 The righteous hate falsehood,
but the wicked act shamefully and
disgracefully.

6 Righteousness guards one whose way
is upright,
but sin overthrows the wicked.

7 Some pretend to be rich, yet have
nothing;
others pretend to be poor, yet have
great wealth.

8 Wealth is a ransom for a person's life,
but the poor get no threats.

9 The light of the righteous rejoices,
but the lamp of the wicked
goes out.

10 By insolence the heedless make strife,
but wisdom is with those who take
advice.

11 Wealth hastily gained*a* will dwindle,
but those who gather little by little
will increase it.

12 Hope deferred makes the heart sick,
but a desire fulfilled is a tree of life.

13 Those who despise the word bring
destruction on themselves,
but those who respect the
commandment will be
rewarded.

14 The teaching of the wise is a fountain
of life,
so that one may avoid the snares of
death.

15 Good sense wins favour,
but the way of the faithless is their
ruin.*b*

16 The clever do all things intelligently,
but the fool displays folly.

17 A bad messenger brings trouble,
but a faithful envoy, healing.

18 Poverty and disgrace are for the one
who ignores instruction,

but one who heeds reproof is
honoured.

19 A desire realized is sweet to
the soul,
but to turn away from evil is an
abomination to fools.

20 Whoever walks with the wise
becomes wise,
but the companion of fools suffers
harm.

21 Misfortune pursues sinners,
but prosperity rewards the
righteous.

22 The good leave an inheritance to
their children's children,
but the sinner's wealth is laid up
for the righteous.

23 The field of the poor may yield much
food,
but it is swept away through
injustice.

24 Those who spare the rod hate their
children,
but those who love them are
diligent to discipline them.

25 The righteous have enough to satisfy
their appetite,
but the belly of the wicked is
empty.

14 The wise woman*c* builds her
house,
but the foolish tears it down with
her own hands.

2 Those who walk uprightly fear the
Lord,
but one who is devious in conduct
despises him.

3 The talk of fools is a rod for their
backs,*d*
but the lips of the wise preserve
them.

4 Where there are no oxen, there is no
grain;
abundant crops come by the
strength of the ox.

5 A faithful witness does not lie,
but a false witness breathes
out lies.

a Gk Vg: Heb *from vanity*   *b* Cn Compare Gk Syr Vg
Tg: Heb *is enduring*   *c* Heb *Wisdom of women*
d Cn: Heb *a rod of pride*

6 A scoffer seeks wisdom in vain,
   but knowledge is easy for one who
      understands.
7 Leave the presence of a fool,
   for there you do not find words of
      knowledge.
8 It is the wisdom of the clever to
      understand where they go,
   but the folly of fools misleads.
9 Fools mock at the guilt-offering, *a*
   but the upright enjoy God's favour.
10 The heart knows its own bitterness,
   and no stranger shares its joy.
11 The house of the wicked is
      destroyed,
   but the tent of the upright
      flourishes.
12 There is a way that seems right to a
      person,
   but its end is the way to death. *b*
13 Even in laughter the heart is sad,
   and the end of joy is grief.
14 The perverse get what their ways
      deserve,
   and the good, what their deeds
      deserve. *c*
15 The simple believe everything,
   but the clever consider their steps.
16 The wise are cautious and turn away
      from evil,
   but the fool throws off restraint and
      is careless.
17 One who is quick-tempered acts
      foolishly,
   and the schemer is hated.
18 The simple are adorned with *d* folly,
   but the clever are crowned with
      knowledge.
19 The evil bow down before the good,
   the wicked at the gates of the
      righteous.
20 The poor are disliked even by their
      neighbours,
   but the rich have many friends.
21 Those who despise their neighbours
      are sinners,
   but happy are those who are kind
      to the poor.
22 Do they not err that plan evil?
   Those who plan good find loyalty
      and faithfulness.

23 In all toil there is profit,
   but mere talk leads only to poverty.
24 The crown of the wise is their
      wisdom, *e*
   but folly is the garland *f* of fools.
25 A truthful witness saves lives,
   but one who utters lies is a betrayer.
26 In the fear of the LORD one has strong
      confidence,
   and one's children will have a
      refuge.
27 The fear of the LORD is a fountain of
      life,
   so that one may avoid the snares of
      death.
28 The glory of a king is a multitude of
      people;
   without people a prince is ruined.
29 Whoever is slow to anger has great
      understanding,
   but one who has a hasty temper
      exalts folly.
30 A tranquil mind gives life to the flesh,
   but passion makes the bones rot.
31 Those who oppress the poor insult
      their Maker,
   but those who are kind to the
      needy honour him.
32 The wicked are overthrown by their
      evildoing,
   but the righteous find a refuge in
      their integrity. *g*
33 Wisdom is at home in the mind of
      one who has understanding,
   but it is not *h* known in the heart of
      fools.
34 Righteousness exalts a nation,
   but sin is a reproach to any people.
35 A servant who deals wisely has the
      king's favour,
   but his wrath falls on one who acts
      shamefully.

15 A soft answer turns away wrath,
   but a harsh word stirs up anger.
2 The tongue of the wise dispenses
      knowledge, *i*

---

a Meaning of Heb uncertain   *b* Heb *ways of death*
c Cn: Heb *from upon him*   *d* Or *inherit*
e Cn Compare Gk: Heb *riches*   *f* Cn: Heb *is the folly*
g Gk Syr: Heb *in their death*   *h* Gk Syr: Heb *lacks not*
i Cn: Heb *makes knowledge good*

but the mouths of fools pour
out folly.

3 The eyes of the LORD are in every
place,
keeping watch on the evil and the
good.

4 A gentle tongue is a tree of life,
but perverseness in it breaks the
spirit.

5 A fool despises a parent's instruction,
but the one who heeds admonition
is prudent.

6 In the house of the righteous there is
much treasure,
but trouble befalls the income of
the wicked.

7 The lips of the wise spread
knowledge;
not so the minds of fools.

8 The sacrifice of the wicked is an
abomination to the LORD,
but the prayer of the upright is his
delight.

9 The way of the wicked is an
abomination to the LORD,
but he loves the one who pursues
righteousness.

10 There is severe discipline for one who
forsakes the way,
but one who hates a rebuke
will die.

11 Sheol and Abaddon lie open before
the LORD,
how much more human hearts!

12 Scoffers do not like to be rebuked;
they will not go to the wise.

13 A glad heart makes a cheerful
countenance,
but by sorrow of heart the spirit is
broken.

14 The mind of one who has
understanding seeks
knowledge,
but the mouths of fools feed
on folly.

15 All the days of the poor are hard,
but a cheerful heart has a continual
feast.

16 Better is a little with the fear of the
LORD

than great treasure and trouble with
it.

17 Better is a dinner of vegetables where
love is
than a fatted ox and hatred with it.

18 Those who are hot-tempered stir up
strife,
but those who are slow to anger
calm contention.

19 The way of the lazy is overgrown with
thorns,
but the path of the upright is a level
highway.

20 A wise child makes a glad father,
but the foolish despise their
mothers.

21 Folly is a joy to one who has no
sense,
but a person of understanding
walks straight ahead.

22 Without counsel, plans go wrong,
but with many advisers they
succeed.

23 To make an apt answer is a joy to
anyone,
and a word in season, how good it
is!

24 For the wise the path of life leads
upwards,
in order to avoid Sheol below.

25 The LORD tears down the house of the
proud,
but maintains the widow's
boundaries.

26 Evil plans are an abomination to the
LORD,
but gracious words are pure.

27 Those who are greedy for unjust gain
make trouble for their
households,
but those who hate bribes will live.

28 The mind of the righteous ponders
how to answer,
but the mouth of the wicked pours
out evil.

29 The LORD is far from the wicked,
but he hears the prayer of the
righteous.

30 The light of the eyes rejoices the
heart,
and good news refreshes the body.

31 The ear that heeds wholesome
    admonition
    will lodge among the wise.
32 Those who ignore instruction despise
    themselves,
    but those who heed admonition
    gain understanding.
33 The fear of the LORD is instruction in
    wisdom,
    and humility goes before honour.

16 The plans of the mind belong to mortals,
    but the answer of the tongue is
    from the LORD.
2 All one's ways may be pure in one's
    own eyes,
    but the LORD weighs the spirit.
3 Commit your work to the LORD,
    and your plans will be established.
4 The LORD has made everything for its
    purpose,
    even the wicked for the day of
    trouble.
5 All those who are arrogant are an
    abomination to the LORD;
    be assured, they will not go
    unpunished.
6 By loyalty and faithfulness iniquity is
    atoned for,
    and by the fear of the LORD one
    avoids evil.
7 When the ways of people please
    the LORD,
    he causes even their enemies to be
    at peace with them.
8 Better is a little with righteousness
    than large income with injustice.
9 The human mind plans the way,
    but the LORD directs the steps.
10 Inspired decisions are on the lips of a
    king;
    his mouth does not sin in
    judgement.
11 Honest balances and scales are
    the LORD's;
    all the weights in the bag are
    his work.
12 It is an abomination to kings to
    do evil,

for the throne is established by
    righteousness.
13 Righteous lips are the delight of
    a king,
    and he loves those who speak what
    is right.
14 A king's wrath is a messenger of death,
    and whoever is wise will appease it.
15 In the light of a king's face there
    is life,
    and his favour is like the clouds
    that bring the spring rain.
16 How much better to get wisdom than
    gold!
    To get understanding is to be
    chosen rather than silver.
17 The highway of the upright
    avoids evil;
    those who guard their way preserve
    their lives.
18 Pride goes before destruction,
    and a haughty spirit before a fall.
19 It is better to be of a lowly spirit
    among the poor
    than to divide the spoil with
    the proud.
20 Those who are attentive to a matter
    will prosper,
    and happy are those who trust in
    the LORD.
21 The wise of heart is called perceptive,
    and pleasant speech increases
    persuasiveness.
22 Wisdom is a fountain of life to one
    who has it,
    but folly is the punishment of
    fools.
23 The mind of the wise makes their
    speech judicious,
    and adds persuasiveness to
    their lips.
24 Pleasant words are like a honeycomb,
    sweetness to the soul and health to
    the body.
25 Sometimes there is a way that seems
    to be right,
    but in the end it is the way
    to death.
26 The appetite of workers works for
    them;
    their hunger urges them on.

27 Scoundrels concoct evil,
  and their speech is like a scorching
    fire.
28 A perverse person spreads strife,
  and a whisperer separates close
    friends.
29 The violent entice their neighbours,
  and lead them in a way that is not
    good.
30 One who winks the eyes plans *a*
    perverse things;
  one who compresses the lips brings
    evil to pass.
31 Grey hair is a crown of glory;
  it is gained in a righteous life.
32 One who is slow to anger is better
    than the mighty,
  and one whose temper is controlled
    than one who captures a city.
33 The lot is cast into the lap,
  but the decision is the LORD's alone.

17 Better is a dry morsel with quiet
  than a house full of feasting
    with strife.
2 A slave who deals wisely will rule
    over a child who acts
    shamefully,
  and will share the inheritance as
    one of the family.
3 The crucible is for silver, and the
    furnace is for gold,
  but the LORD tests the heart.
4 An evildoer listens to wicked lips;
  and a liar gives heed to a
    mischievous tongue.
5 Those who mock the poor insult their
    Maker;
  those who are glad at calamity will
    not go unpunished.
6 Grandchildren are the crown of
    the aged,
  and the glory of children is their
    parents.
7 Fine speech is not becoming to
    a fool;
  still less is false speech to a ruler. *b*
8 A bribe is like a magic stone in the
    eyes of those who give it;
  wherever they turn they prosper.
9 One who forgives an affront fosters
    friendship,

but one who dwells on disputes
  will alienate a friend.
10 A rebuke strikes deeper into a
    discerning person
  than a hundred blows into a fool.
11 Evil people seek only rebellion,
  but a cruel messenger will be sent
    against them.
12 Better to meet a she-bear robbed of
    its cubs
  than to confront a fool immersed
    in folly.
13 Evil will not depart from the house
  of one who returns evil for good.
14 The beginning of strife is like letting
    out water;
  so stop before the quarrel
    breaks out.
15 One who justifies the wicked and one
    who condemns the righteous
  are both alike an abomination to
    the LORD.
16 Why should fools have a price
    in hand
  to buy wisdom, when they have no
    mind to learn?
17 A friend loves at all times,
  and kinsfolk are born to share
    adversity.
18 It is senseless to give a pledge,
  to become surety for a neighbour.
19 One who loves transgression
    loves strife;
  one who builds a high threshold
    invites broken bones.
20 The crooked of mind do not prosper,
  and the perverse of tongue fall into
    calamity.
21 The one who begets a fool gets
    trouble;
  the parent of a fool has no joy.
22 A cheerful heart is a good medicine,
  but a downcast spirit dries up
    the bones.
23 The wicked accept a concealed bribe
  to pervert the ways of justice.
24 The discerning person looks to
    wisdom,
  but the eyes of a fool to the ends of
    the earth.

a Gk Syr Vg Tg: Heb *to plan*   *b* Or *a noble person*

25 Foolish children are a grief to their
      father
    and bitterness to her who
      bore them.
26 To impose a fine on the innocent is
      not right,
    or to flog the noble for their
      integrity.
27 One who spares words is
      knowledgeable;
    one who is cool in spirit has
      understanding.
28 Even fools who keep silent are
      considered wise;
    when they close their lips, they are
      deemed intelligent.

18 The one who lives alone is self-
      indulgent,
    showing contempt for all who have
      sound judgement. *a*
2 A fool takes no pleasure in
      understanding,
    but only in expressing personal
      opinion.
3 When wickedness comes, contempt
      comes also;
    and with dishonour comes
      disgrace.
4 The words of the mouth are deep
      waters;
    the fountain of wisdom is a
      gushing stream.
5 It is not right to be partial to
      the guilty,
    or to subvert the innocent in
      judgement.
6 A fool's lips bring strife,
    and a fool's mouth invites a
      flogging.
7 The mouths of fools are their ruin,
    and their lips a snare to themselves.
8 The words of a whisperer are like
      delicious morsels;
    they go down into the inner parts
      of the body.
9 One who is slack in work
    is close kin to a vandal.
10 The name of the LORD is a strong
      tower;
    the righteous run into it and
      are safe.

11 The wealth of the rich is their strong
      city;
    in their imagination it is like a high
      wall.
12 Before destruction one's heart is
      haughty,
    but humility goes before honour.
13 If one gives answer before hearing,
    it is folly and shame.
14 The human spirit will endure sickness;
    but a broken spirit—who can bear?
15 An intelligent mind acquires
      knowledge,
    and the ear of the wise seeks
      knowledge.
16 A gift opens doors;
    it gives access to the great.
17 The one who first states a case seems
      right,
    until the other comes and cross-
      examines.
18 Casting the lot puts an end to disputes
    and decides between powerful
      contenders.
19 An ally offended is stronger than
      a city; *b*
    such quarrelling is like the bars of a
      castle.
20 From the fruit of the mouth one's
      stomach is satisfied;
    the yield of the lips brings
      satisfaction.
21 Death and life are in the power of the
      tongue,
    and those who love it will eat
      its fruits.
22 He who finds a wife finds a
      good thing,
    and obtains favour from the LORD.
23 The poor use entreaties,
    but the rich answer roughly.
24 Some *c* friends play at friendship *d*
    but a true friend sticks closer than
      one's nearest kin.

19 Better the poor walking in
      integrity
    than one perverse of speech who is
      a fool.

a Meaning of Heb uncertain   *b* Gk Syr Vg Tg:
Meaning of Heb uncertain   *c* Syr Tg: Heb A *man of*
d Cn Compare Syr Vg Tg: Meaning of Heb uncertain

2 Desire without knowledge is
      not good,
    and one who moves too hurriedly
      misses the way.
3 One's own folly leads to ruin,
    yet the heart rages against the LORD.
4 Wealth brings many friends,
    but the poor are left friendless.
5 A false witness will not go
      unpunished,
    and a liar will not escape.
6 Many seek the favour of the generous,
    and everyone is a friend to a giver
      of gifts.
7 If the poor are hated even by their
      kin,
    how much more are they shunned
      by their friends!
  When they call after them, they are
      not there. *a*
8 To get wisdom is to love oneself;
    to keep understanding is
      to prosper.
9 A false witness will not go
      unpunished,
    and the liar will perish.
10 It is not fitting for a fool to live
      in luxury,
    much less for a slave to rule over
      princes.
11 Those with good sense are slow
      to anger,
    and it is their glory to overlook an
      offence.
12 A king's anger is like the growling of
      a lion,
    but his favour is like dew on
      the grass.
13 A stupid child is ruin to a father,
    and a wife's quarrelling is a
      continual dripping of rain.
14 House and wealth are inherited from
      parents,
    but a prudent wife is from
      the LORD.
15 Laziness brings on deep sleep;
    an idle person will suffer hunger.
16 Those who keep the commandment
      will live;
    those who are heedless of their
      ways will die.

17 Whoever is kind to the poor lends to
      the LORD,
    and will be repaid in full.
18 Discipline your children while there
      is hope;
    do not set your heart on their
      destruction.
19 A violent-tempered person will pay
      the penalty;
    if you effect a rescue, you will only
      have to do it again. *a*
20 Listen to advice and accept
      instruction,
    that you may gain wisdom for the
      future.
21 The human mind may devise
      many plans,
    but it is the purpose of the LORD
      that will be established.
22 What is desirable in a person
      is loyalty,
    and it is better to be poor than a liar.
23 The fear of the LORD is life indeed;
    filled with it one rests secure
      and suffers no harm.
24 The lazy person buries a hand in the
      dish,
    and will not even bring it back to
      the mouth.
25 Strike a scoffer, and the simple will
      learn prudence;
    reprove the intelligent, and they
      will gain knowledge.
26 Those who do violence to their father
      and chase away their mother
    are children who cause shame and
      bring reproach.
27 Cease straying, my child, from the
      words of knowledge,
    in order that you may hear
      instruction.
28 A worthless witness mocks at justice,
    and the mouth of the wicked
      devours iniquity.
29 Condemnation is ready for scoffers,
    and flogging for the backs of fools.

20 Wine is a mocker, strong drink a
      brawler,
    and whoever is led astray by it is
      not wise.

a Meaning of Heb uncertain

2 The dread anger of a king is like the
   growling of a lion;
   anyone who provokes him to anger
      forfeits life itself.
3 It is honourable to refrain from strife,
   but every fool is quick to quarrel.
4 The lazy person does not plough
      in season;
   harvest comes, and there is nothing
      to be found.
5 The purposes in the human mind are
      like deep water,
   but the intelligent will draw them
      out.
6 Many proclaim themselves loyal,
   but who can find one worthy
      of trust?
7 The righteous walk in integrity—
   happy are the children who follow
      them!
8 A king who sits on the throne of
      judgement
   winnows all evil with his eyes.
9 Who can say, 'I have made my heart
      clean;
   I am pure from my sin'?
10 Diverse weights and diverse measures
   are both alike an abomination to
      the LORD.
11 Even children make themselves
      known by their acts,
   by whether what they do is pure
      and right.
12 The hearing ear and the seeing eye—
   the LORD has made them both.
13 Do not love sleep, or else you will
      come to poverty;
   open your eyes, and you will have
      plenty of bread.
14 'Bad, bad', says the buyer,
   then goes away and boasts.
15 There is gold, and abundance of
      costly stones;
   but the lips informed by knowledge
      are a precious jewel.
16 Take the garment of one who has
      given surety for a stranger;
   seize the pledge given as surety for
      foreigners.
17 Bread gained by deceit is sweet,

but afterwards the mouth will be
   full of gravel.
18 Plans are established by
      taking advice;
   wage war by following wise
      guidance.
19 A gossip reveals secrets;
   therefore do not associate with a
      babbler.
20 If you curse father or mother,
   your lamp will go out in utter
      darkness.
21 An estate quickly acquired in the
      beginning
   will not be blessed in the end.
22 Do not say, 'I will repay evil';
   wait for the LORD, and he will help
      you.
23 Differing weights are an abomination
      to the LORD,
   and false scales are not good.
24 All our steps are ordered by the
      LORD;
   how then can we understand our
      own ways?
25 It is a snare for one to say rashly, 'It is
      holy',
   and begin to reflect only after
      making a vow.
26 A wise king winnows the wicked,
   and drives the wheel over them.
27 The human spirit is the lamp of the
      LORD,
   searching every inmost part.
28 Loyalty and faithfulness preserve the
      king,
   and his throne is upheld by
      righteousness. [a]
29 The glory of youths is their strength,
   but the beauty of the aged is their
      grey hair.
30 Blows that wound cleanse away evil;
   beatings make clean the innermost
      parts.

21 The king's heart is a stream of
   water in the hand of the LORD;
   he turns it wherever he will.
2 All deeds are right in the sight of the
      doer,
   but the LORD weighs the heart.

a Gk: Heb loyalty

3 To do righteousness and justice
    is more acceptable to the Lord than
        sacrifice.
4 Haughty eyes and a proud heart—
    the lamp of the wicked—are sin.
5 The plans of the diligent lead surely
        to abundance,
    but everyone who is hasty comes
        only to want.
6 The getting of treasures by a lying
        tongue
    is a fleeting vapour and a snare[a] of
        death.
7 The violence of the wicked will sweep
        them away,
    because they refuse to do what
        is just.
8 The way of the guilty is crooked,
    but the conduct of the pure is right.
9 It is better to live in a corner of the
        housetop
    than in a house shared with a
        contentious wife.
10 The souls of the wicked desire evil;
    their neighbours find no mercy in
        their eyes.
11 When a scoffer is punished, the
        simple become wiser;
    when the wise are instructed, they
        increase in knowledge.
12 The Righteous One observes the
        house of the wicked;
    he casts the wicked down to ruin.
13 If you close your ear to the cry of the
        poor,
    you will cry out and not be heard.
14 A gift in secret averts anger;
    and a concealed bribe in the
        bosom, strong wrath.
15 When justice is done, it is a joy to the
        righteous,
    but dismay to evildoers.
16 Whoever wanders from the way of
        understanding
    will rest in the assembly of
        the dead.
17 Whoever loves pleasure will suffer
        want;
    whoever loves wine and oil will not
        be rich.

18 The wicked is a ransom for the
        righteous,
    and the faithless for the upright.
19 It is better to live in a desert land
    than with a contentious and fretful
        wife.
20 Precious treasure remains[b] in the
        house of the wise,
    but the fool devours it.
21 Whoever pursues righteousness and
        kindness
    will find life[c] and honour.
22 One wise person went up against a
        city of warriors
    and brought down the stronghold
        in which they trusted.
23 To watch over mouth and tongue
    is to keep out of trouble.
24 The proud, haughty person, named
        'Scoffer',
    acts with arrogant pride.
25 The craving of the lazy person
        is fatal,
    for lazy hands refuse to labour.
26 All day long the wicked covet,[d]
    but the righteous give and do not
        hold back.
27 The sacrifice of the wicked is an
        abomination;
    how much more when brought
        with evil intent.
28 A false witness will perish,
    but a good listener will testify
        successfully.
29 The wicked put on a bold face,
    but the upright give thought to[e]
        their ways.
30 No wisdom, no understanding, no
        counsel,
    can avail against the Lord.
31 The horse is made ready for the day
        of battle,
    but the victory belongs to the Lord.

22 A good name is to be chosen
    rather than great riches,
    and favour is better than silver
        or gold.

a Gk: Heb *seekers*   b Gk: Heb *and oil*   c Gk: Heb *life
and righteousness*   d Gk: Heb *all day long one covets
covetously*   e Another reading is *establish*

2 The rich and the poor have this in
common:
the Lord is the maker of them all.
3 The clever see danger and hide;
but the simple go on, and suffer for
it.
4 The reward for humility and fear of
the Lord
is riches and honour and life.
5 Thorns and snares are in the way of
the perverse;
the cautious will keep far from
them.
6 Train children in the right way,
and when old, they will not stray.
7 The rich rules over the poor,
and the borrower is the slave of the
lender.
8 Whoever sows injustice will reap
calamity,
and the rod of anger will fail.
9 Those who are generous are blessed,
for they share their bread with the
poor.
10 Drive out a scoffer, and strife
goes out;
quarrelling and abuse will cease.
11 Those who love a pure heart and are
gracious in speech
will have the king as a friend.
12 The eyes of the Lord keep watch over
knowledge,
but he overthrows the words of the
faithless.
13 The lazy person says, 'There is a lion
outside!
I shall be killed in the streets!'
14 The mouth of a loose[a] woman is a
deep pit;
he with whom the Lord is angry
falls into it.
15 Folly is bound up in the heart of
a boy,
but the rod of discipline drives it
far away.
16 Oppressing the poor in order to
enrich oneself,
and giving to the rich, will lead
only to loss.

Sayings of the Wise

17 The words of the wise:

Incline your ear and hear my words,[b]
and apply your mind to my
teaching;
18 for it will be pleasant if you keep
them within you,
if all of them are ready on your lips.
19 So that your trust may be in the Lord,
I have made them known to you
today—yes, to you.
20 Have I not written for you thirty
sayings
of admonition and knowledge,
21 to show you what is right and true,
so that you may give a true answer
to those who sent you?

22 Do not rob the poor because they are
poor,
or crush the afflicted at the gate;
23 for the Lord pleads their cause
and despoils of life those who
despoil them.
24 Make no friends with those given to
anger,
and do not associate with
hotheads,
25 or you may learn their ways
and entangle yourself in a snare.
26 Do not be one of those who give
pledges,
who become surety for debts.
27 If you have nothing with which
to pay,
why should your bed be taken from
under you?
28 Do not remove the ancient landmark
that your ancestors set up.
29 Do you see those who are skilful in
their work?
They will serve kings;
they will not serve common people.

23 When you sit down to eat with
a ruler,
observe carefully what[c] is
before you,

---

a Heb *strange*   b Cn Compare Gk: Heb *Incline your
ear, and hear the words of the wise*   c Or *who*

2 and put a knife to your throat
   if you have a big appetite.
3 Do not desire the ruler's*a* delicacies,
   for they are deceptive food.
4 Do not wear yourself out to get rich;
   be wise enough to desist.
5 When your eyes light upon it,
      it is gone;
   for suddenly it takes wings to itself,
   flying like an eagle towards heaven.
6 Do not eat the bread of the stingy;
   do not desire their delicacies;
7 for like a hair in the throat, so
      are they.*b*
   'Eat and drink!' they say to you;
   but they do not mean it.
8 You will vomit up the little you have
      eaten,
   and you will waste your pleasant
      words.
9 Do not speak in the hearing of a fool,
   who will only despise the wisdom
      of your words.
10 Do not remove an ancient landmark
   or encroach on the fields of orphans,
11 for their redeemer is strong;
   he will plead their cause
      against you.
12 Apply your mind to instruction
   and your ear to words of
      knowledge.
13 Do not withhold discipline from
      your children;
   if you beat them with a rod, they
      will not die.
14 If you beat them with the rod,
   you will save their lives from Sheol.
15 My child, if your heart is wise,
   my heart too will be glad.
16 My soul will rejoice
   when your lips speak what is right.
17 Do not let your heart envy sinners,
   but always continue in the fear of
      the LORD.
18 Surely there is a future,
   and your hope will not be cut off.

19 Hear, my child, and be wise,
   and direct your mind in the way.
20 Do not be among winebibbers,
   or among gluttonous eaters of meat;

21 for the drunkard and the glutton will
      come to poverty,
   and drowsiness will clothe them
      with rags.

22 Listen to your father who begot you,
   and do not despise your mother
      when she is old.
23 Buy truth, and do not sell it;
   buy wisdom, instruction, and
      understanding.
24 The father of the righteous will
      greatly rejoice;
   he who begets a wise son will be
      glad in him.
25 Let your father and mother be glad;
   let her who bore you rejoice.

26 My child, give me your heart,
   and let your eyes observe*c* my ways.
27 For a prostitute is a deep pit;
   an adulteress*d* is a narrow well.
28 She lies in wait like a robber
   and increases the number of the
      faithless.

29 Who has woe? Who has sorrow?
   Who has strife? Who has
      complaining?
   Who has wounds without cause?
   Who has redness of eyes?
30 Those who linger late over wine,
   those who keep trying mixed wines.
31 Do not look at wine when it is red,
   when it sparkles in the cup
   and goes down smoothly.
32 At the last it bites like a serpent,
   and stings like an adder.
33 Your eyes will see strange things,
   and your mind utter perverse
      things.
34 You will be like one who lies down in
      the midst of the sea,
   like one who lies on the top of
      a mast.*b*
35 'They struck me', you will say,*e* 'but I
      was not hurt;
   they beat me, but I did not feel it.

a Heb *his*   *b* Meaning of Heb uncertain   *c* Another
reading is *delight in*   *d* Heb *an alien woman*
e Gk Syr Vg Tg: Heb lacks *you will say*

When shall I awake?
I will seek another drink.'

24 Do not envy the wicked,
      nor desire to be with them;
2 for their minds devise violence,
    and their lips talk of mischief.

3 By wisdom a house is built,
    and by understanding it is
      established;
4 by knowledge the rooms are filled
    with all precious and pleasant
      riches.
5 Wise warriors are mightier than
      strong ones,[a]
    and those who have knowledge
      than those who have strength;
6 for by wise guidance you can wage
      your war,
    and in abundance of counsellors
      there is victory.
7 Wisdom is too high for fools;
    in the gate they do not open
      their mouths.

8 Whoever plans to do evil
    will be called a mischief-maker.
9 The devising of folly is sin,
    and the scoffer is an abomination
      to all.

10 If you faint in the day of adversity,
     your strength being small;
11 if you hold back from rescuing those
      taken away to death,
     those who go staggering to the
       slaughter;
12 if you say, 'Look, we did not
      know this'—
     does not he who weighs the heart
       perceive it?
     Does not he who keeps watch over
       your soul know it?
     And will he not repay all according
       to their deeds?

13 My child, eat honey, for it is good,
     and the drippings of the
       honeycomb are sweet to
       your taste.

14 Know that wisdom is such to
       your soul;
     if you find it, you will find a future,
       and your hope will not be cut off.

15 Do not lie in wait like an outlaw
       against the home of the
       righteous;
     do no violence to the place where
       the righteous live;
16 for though they fall seven times, they
       will rise again;
     but the wicked are overthrown by
       calamity.

17 Do not rejoice when your enemies
       fall,
     and do not let your heart be glad
       when they stumble,
18 or else the LORD will see it and be
       displeased,
     and turn away his anger from them.

19 Do not fret because of evildoers.
     Do not envy the wicked;
20 for the evil have no future;
     the lamp of the wicked will go out.

21 My child, fear the LORD and the king,
     and do not disobey either of them;[b]
22 for disaster comes from them
       suddenly,
     and who knows the ruin that both
       can bring?

Further Sayings of the Wise

23   These also are sayings of the wise:

     Partiality in judging is not good.
24 Whoever says to the wicked, 'You are
       innocent',
     will be cursed by peoples, abhorred
       by nations;
25 but those who rebuke the wicked will
       have delight,
     and a good blessing will come
       upon them.
26 One who gives an honest answer
     gives a kiss on the lips.

a Gk Compare Syr Tg: Heb *A wise man is strength*
b Gk: Heb *do not associate with those who change*

27 Prepare your work outside,
    get everything ready for you in the
        field;
    and after that build your house.

28 Do not be a witness against your
        neighbour without cause,
    and do not deceive with your lips.
29 Do not say, 'I will do to others as
        they have done to me;
    I will pay them back for what they
        have done.'

30 I passed by the field of one who was
        lazy,
    by the vineyard of a stupid person;
31 and see, it was all overgrown with
        thorns;
    the ground was covered with
        nettles,
    and its stone wall was broken
        down.
32 Then I saw and considered it;
    I looked and received instruction.
33 A little sleep, a little slumber,
    a little folding of the hands to rest,
34 and poverty will come upon you like
        a robber,
    and want, like an armed warrior.

Further Wise Sayings of Solomon

25 These are other proverbs of Solo-
    mon that the officials of King Hez-
ekiah of Judah copied.

2 It is the glory of God to conceal
        things,
    but the glory of kings is to search
        things out.
3 Like the heavens for height, like the
        earth for depth,
    so the mind of kings is
        unsearchable.
4 Take away the dross from the silver,
    and the smith has material for
        a vessel;
5 take away the wicked from the
        presence of the king,
    and his throne will be established
        in righteousness.

6 Do not put yourself forward in the
        king's presence
    or stand in the place of the great;
7 for it is better to be told, 'Come
        up here',
    than to be put lower in the
        presence of a noble.

What your eyes have seen
8   do not hastily bring into court;
    for*a* what will you do in the end,
        when your neighbour puts you to
            shame?
9 Argue your case with your neighbour
        directly,
    and do not disclose another's
        secret;
10 or else someone who hears you will
        bring shame upon you,
    and your ill repute will have
        no end.

11 A word fitly spoken
    is like apples of gold in a setting of
        silver.
12 Like a gold ring or an ornament
        of gold
    is a wise rebuke to a listening ear.
13 Like the cold of snow in the time
        of harvest
    are faithful messengers to those
        who send them;
    they refresh the spirit of their
        masters.
14 Like clouds and wind without rain
    is one who boasts of a gift never
        given.
15 With patience a ruler may be
        persuaded,
    and a soft tongue can break bones.
16 If you have found honey, eat only
        enough for you,
    or else, having too much, you will
        vomit it.
17 Let your foot be seldom in your
        neighbour's house,
    otherwise the neighbour will
        become weary of you and hate
            you.

a Cn: Heb *or else*

18 Like a war club, a sword, or a sharp
       arrow
   is one who bears false witness
       against a neighbour.
19 Like a bad tooth or a lame foot
   is trust in a faithless person in time
       of trouble.
20 Like vinegar on a wound*a*
   is one who sings songs to a heavy
       heart.
   Like a moth in clothing or a worm in
       wood,
   sorrow gnaws at the human heart.*b*
21 If your enemies are hungry, give them
       bread to eat;
   and if they are thirsty, give them
       water to drink;
22 for you will heap coals of fire on
       their heads,
   and the LORD will reward you.
23 The north wind produces rain,
   and a backbiting tongue, angry
       looks.
24 It is better to live in a corner of the
       housetop
   than in a house shared with a
       contentious wife.
25 Like cold water to a thirsty soul,
   so is good news from a far country.
26 Like a muddied spring or a polluted
       fountain
   are the righteous who give way
       before the wicked.
27 It is not good to eat much honey,
   or to seek honour on top of
       honour.
28 Like a city breached, without walls,
   is one who lacks self-control.

26 Like snow in summer or rain in
       harvest,
   so honour is not fitting for a fool.
2 Like a sparrow in its flitting, like a
       swallow in its flying,
   an undeserved curse goes nowhere.
3 A whip for the horse, a bridle for the
       donkey,
   and a rod for the back of fools.
4 Do not answer fools according to
       their folly,
   or you will be a fool yourself.
5 Answer fools according to their folly,

   or they will be wise in their
       own eyes.
6 It is like cutting off one's foot and
       drinking down violence,
   to send a message by a fool.
7 The legs of a disabled person hang
       limp;
   so does a proverb in the mouth of a
       fool.
8 It is like binding a stone in a sling
   to give honour to a fool.
9 Like a thornbush brandished by the
       hand of a drunkard
   is a proverb in the mouth of a fool.
10 Like an archer who wounds
       everybody
   is one who hires a passing fool or
       drunkard.*c*
11 Like a dog that returns to its vomit
   is a fool who reverts to his folly.
12 Do you see persons wise in their own
       eyes?
   There is more hope for fools than
       for them.
13 The lazy person says, 'There is a lion
       in the road!
   There is a lion in the streets!'
14 As a door turns on its hinges,
   so does a lazy person in bed.
15 The lazy person buries a hand in the
       dish,
   and is too tired to bring it back to
       the mouth.
16 The lazy person is wiser in self-
       esteem
   than seven who can answer
       discreetly.
17 Like somebody who takes a passing
       dog by the ears
   is one who meddles in the quarrel
       of another.
18 Like a maniac who shoots deadly
       firebrands and arrows,
19 so is one who deceives a neighbour
   and says, 'I am only joking!'
20 For lack of wood the fire goes out,
   and where there is no whisperer,
       quarrelling ceases.

a Gk: Heb *Like one who takes off a garment on a cold day,*
like vinegar on lye   *b* Gk Syr Tg: Heb lacks *Like a*
moth . . . human heart   *c* Meaning of Heb uncertain

21 As charcoal is to hot embers and
     wood to fire,
  so is a quarrelsome person for
     kindling strife.
22 The words of a whisperer are like
     delicious morsels;
  they go down into the inner parts
     of the body.
23 Like the glaze[a] covering an earthen
     vessel
  are smooth[b] lips with an evil heart.
24 An enemy dissembles in speaking
  while harbouring deceit within;
25 when an enemy speaks graciously, do
     not believe it,
  for there are seven abominations
     concealed within;
26 though hatred is covered with guile,
  the enemy's wickedness will be
     exposed in the assembly.
27 Whoever digs a pit will fall into it,
  and a stone will come back on the
     one who starts it rolling.
28 A lying tongue hates its victims,
  and a flattering mouth works ruin.

27 Do not boast about tomorrow,
     for you do not know what a day
     may bring.
2 Let another praise you, and not your
     own mouth—
  a stranger, and not your own lips.
3 A stone is heavy, and sand is weighty,
  but a fool's provocation is heavier
     than both.
4 Wrath is cruel, anger is overwhelming,
  but who is able to stand before
     jealousy?
5 Better is open rebuke
  than hidden love.
6 Well meant are the wounds a friend
     inflicts,
  but profuse are the kisses of an
     enemy.
7 The sated appetite spurns honey,
  but to a ravenous appetite even the
     bitter is sweet.
8 Like a bird that strays from its nest
  is one who strays from home.
9 Perfume and incense make the heart
     glad,
  but the soul is torn by trouble.[c]

10 Do not forsake your friend or the
     friend of your parent;
  do not go to the house of your
     kindred on the day of your
     calamity.
  Better is a neighbour who is nearby
     than kindred who are far away.
11 Be wise, my child, and make my heart
     glad,
  so that I may answer whoever
     reproaches me.
12 The clever see danger and hide;
  but the simple go on, and suffer for
     it.
13 Take the garment of one who has
     given surety for a stranger;
  seize the pledge given as surety for
     foreigners.[d]
14 Whoever blesses a neighbour with a
     loud voice,
  rising early in the morning,
  will be counted as cursing.
15 A continual dripping on a rainy day
  and a contentious wife are alike;
16 to restrain her is to restrain the wind
  or to grasp oil in the right hand.[e]
17 Iron sharpens iron,
  and one person sharpens the wits[f]
     of another.
18 Anyone who tends a fig tree will eat
     its fruit,
  and anyone who takes care of a
     master will be honoured.
19 Just as water reflects the face,
  so one human heart reflects
     another.
20 Sheol and Abaddon are never
     satisfied,
  and human eyes are never
     satisfied.
21 The crucible is for silver, and the
     furnace is for gold,
  so a person is tested[g] by being
     praised.
22 Crush a fool in a mortar with a pestle
     along with crushed grain,
  but the folly will not be driven out.

a Cn: Heb *silver of dross*   b Gk: Heb *burning*
c Gk: Heb *the sweetness of a friend is better than one's own*
counsel   d Vg and 20.16: Heb *for a foreign woman*
e Meaning of Heb uncertain   f Heb *face*
g Heb lacks *is tested*

23 Know well the condition of
   your flocks,
   and give attention to your herds;
24 for riches do not last for ever,
   nor a crown for all generations.
25 When the grass is gone, and new
   growth appears,
   and the herbage of the mountains
   is gathered,
26 the lambs will provide your clothing,
   and the goats the price of a field;
27 there will be enough goats' milk for
   your food,
   for the food of your household
   and nourishment for your servant-
   girls.

28 The wicked flee when no one
   pursues,
   but the righteous are as bold as
   a lion.
2 When a land rebels
   it has many rulers;
   but with an intelligent ruler
   there is lasting order. *a*
3 A ruler *b* who oppresses the poor
   is a beating rain that leaves no food.
4 Those who forsake the law praise the
   wicked,
   but those who keep the law struggle
   against them.
5 The evil do not understand justice,
   but those who seek the LORD
   understand it completely.
6 Better to be poor and walk in integrity
   than to be crooked in one's ways
   even though rich.
7 Those who keep the law are wise
   children,
   but companions of gluttons shame
   their parents.
8 One who augments wealth by
   exorbitant interest
   gathers it for another who is kind
   to the poor.
9 When one will not listen to the law,
   even one's prayers are an
   abomination.
10 Those who mislead the upright into
   evil ways
   will fall into pits of their own
   making,

but the blameless will have a
   goodly inheritance.
11 The rich is wise in self-esteem,
   but an intelligent poor person sees
   through the pose.
12 When the righteous triumph, there is
   great glory,
   but when the wicked prevail,
   people go into hiding.
13 No one who conceals transgressions
   will prosper,
   but one who confesses and forsakes
   them will obtain mercy.
14 Happy is the one who is never
   without fear,
   but one who is hard-hearted will
   fall into calamity.
15 Like a roaring lion or a charging bear
   is a wicked ruler over a poor
   people.
16 A ruler who lacks understanding is a
   cruel oppressor;
   but one who hates unjust gain will
   enjoy a long life.
17 If someone is burdened with the
   blood of another,
   let that killer be a fugitive
   until death;
   let no one offer assistance.
18 One who walks in integrity will
   be safe,
   but whoever follows crooked ways
   will fall into the Pit. *c*
19 Anyone who tills the land will have
   plenty of bread,
   but one who follows worthless
   pursuits will have plenty
   of poverty.
20 The faithful will abound with
   blessings,
   but one who is in a hurry to be rich
   will not go unpunished.
21 To show partiality is not good—
   yet for a piece of bread a person
   may do wrong.
22 The miser is in a hurry to get rich
   and does not know that loss is sure
   to come.

a Meaning of Heb uncertain   *b* Cn: Heb *A poor person*
c Syr: Heb *fall all at once*

²³ Whoever rebukes a person will
    afterwards find more favour
  than one who flatters with
    the tongue.
²⁴ Anyone who robs father or mother
    and says, 'That is no crime',
  is partner to a thug.
²⁵ The greedy person stirs up strife,
    but whoever trusts in the LORD will
    be enriched.
²⁶ Those who trust in their own wits are
    fools;
  but those who walk in wisdom
    come through safely.
²⁷ Whoever gives to the poor will lack
    nothing,
  but one who turns a blind eye will
    get many a curse.
²⁸ When the wicked prevail, people go
    into hiding;
  but when they perish, the righteous
    increase.

29 One who is often reproved, yet
    remains stubborn,
  will suddenly be broken beyond
    healing.
² When the righteous are in authority,
    the people rejoice;
  but when the wicked rule, the
    people groan.
³ A child who loves wisdom makes a
    parent glad,
  but to keep company with
    prostitutes is to squander one's
    substance.
⁴ By justice a king gives stability to the
    land,
  but one who makes heavy exactions
    ruins it.
⁵ Whoever flatters a neighbour
    is spreading a net for the
    neighbour's feet.
⁶ In the transgression of the evil there
    is a snare,
  but the righteous sing and rejoice.
⁷ The righteous know the rights of the
    poor;
  the wicked have no such
    understanding.
⁸ Scoffers set a city aflame,
    but the wise turn away wrath.

⁹ If the wise go to law with fools,
    there is ranting and ridicule
    without relief.
¹⁰ The bloodthirsty hate the blameless,
    and they seek the life of the
    upright.
¹¹ A fool gives full vent to anger,
    but the wise quietly holds it back.
¹² If a ruler listens to falsehood,
    all his officials will be wicked.
¹³ The poor and the oppressor have this
    in common:
  the LORD gives light to the eyes of
    both.
¹⁴ If a king judges the poor with equity,
    his throne will be established for
    ever.
¹⁵ The rod and reproof give wisdom,
    but a mother is disgraced by a
    neglected child.
¹⁶ When the wicked are in authority,
    transgression increases,
  but the righteous will look upon
    their downfall.
¹⁷ Discipline your children, and they
    will give you rest;
  they will give delight to your
    heart.
¹⁸ Where there is no prophecy, the
    people cast off restraint,
  but happy are those who keep
    the law.
¹⁹ By mere words servants are not
    disciplined,
  for though they understand, they
    will not give heed.
²⁰ Do you see someone who is hasty
    in speech?
  There is more hope for a fool than
    for anyone like that.
²¹ A slave pampered from childhood
    will come to a bad end. *a*
²² One given to anger stirs up strife,
    and the hothead causes much
    transgression.
²³ A person's pride will bring
    humiliation,
  but one who is lowly in spirit will
    obtain honour.

a Vg: Meaning of Heb uncertain

24 To be a partner of a thief is to hate
   one's own life;
   one hears the victim's curse, but
      discloses nothing. *a*
25 The fear of others*b* lays a snare,
   but one who trusts in the LORD
      is secure.
26 Many seek the favour of a ruler,
   but it is from the LORD that one gets
      justice.
27 The unjust are an abomination to the
      righteous,
   but the upright are an abomination
      to the wicked.

Sayings of Agur

30 The words of Agur son of Jakeh.
   An oracle.

Thus says the man: I am weary, O God,
   I am weary, O God. How can I
      prevail?*c*
2 Surely I am too stupid to be human;
   I do not have human
      understanding.
3 I have not learned wisdom,
   nor have I knowledge of the
      holy ones. *d*
4 Who has ascended to heaven and
      come down?
   Who has gathered the wind in the
      hollow of the hand?
   Who has wrapped up the waters in a
      garment?
   Who has established all the ends of
      the earth?
   What is the person's name?
   And what is the name of the
      person's child?
   Surely you know!

5 Every word of God proves true;
   he is a shield to those who take
      refuge in him.
6 Do not add to his words,
   or else he will rebuke you, and you
      will be found a liar.

7 Two things I ask of you;
   do not deny them to me before
      I die:

8 Remove far from me falsehood and
      lying;
   give me neither poverty nor riches;
   feed me with the food that I need,
9 or I shall be full, and deny you,
   and say, 'Who is the LORD?'
   or I shall be poor, and steal,
   and profane the name of my God.

10 Do not slander a servant to a master,
   or the servant will curse you, and
      you will be held guilty.

11 There are those who curse their
      fathers
   and do not bless their mothers.
12 There are those who are pure in their
      own eyes
   yet are not cleansed of their
      filthiness.
13 There are those—how lofty are their
      eyes,
   how high their eyelids lift!—
14 there are those whose teeth are
      swords,
   whose teeth are knives,
   to devour the poor from off the
      earth,
   the needy from among mortals.

15 The leech*a* has two daughters;
   'Give, give,' they cry.
   Three things are never satisfied;
   four never say, 'Enough':
16 Sheol, the barren womb,
   the earth ever thirsty for water,
   and the fire that never says,
      'Enough.'*a*

17 The eye that mocks a father
   and scorns to obey a mother
   will be pecked out by the ravens of
      the valley
   and eaten by the vultures.

18 Three things are too wonderful
      for me;
   four I do not understand:

a Meaning of Heb uncertain   *b* Or *human fear*
c Or *I am spent.* Meaning of Heb uncertain   *d* Or *Holy One*

¹⁹ the way of an eagle in the sky,
   the way of a snake on a rock,
  the way of a ship on the high seas,
   and the way of a man with a girl.

²⁰ This is the way of an adulteress:
   she eats, and wipes her mouth,
   and says, 'I have done no wrong.'

²¹ Under three things the earth
    trembles;
   under four it cannot bear up:
²² a slave when he becomes king,
   and a fool when glutted with food;
²³ an unloved woman when she gets
    a husband,
   and a maid when she succeeds her
    mistress.

²⁴ Four things on earth are small,
   yet they are exceedingly wise:
²⁵ the ants are a people without strength,
   yet they provide their food in
    the summer;
²⁶ the badgers are a people without
    power,
   yet they make their homes in
    the rocks;
²⁷ the locusts have no king,
   yet all of them march in rank;
²⁸ the lizard^a can be grasped in
    the hand,
   yet it is found in kings' palaces.

²⁹ Three things are stately in their stride;
   four are stately in their gait:
³⁰ the lion, which is mightiest among
    wild animals
   and does not turn back before any;
³¹ the strutting rooster,^b the he-goat,
   and a king striding before^c
    his people.

³² If you have been foolish, exalting
    yourself,
   or if you have been devising evil,
   put your hand on your mouth.
³³ For as pressing milk produces curds,
   and pressing the nose produces
    blood,
   so pressing anger produces strife.

The Teaching of King Lemuel's Mother

31 The words of King Lemuel. An oracle that his mother taught him:

² No, my son! No, son of my womb!
   No, son of my vows!
³ Do not give your strength to women,
   your ways to those who destroy
    kings.
⁴ It is not for kings, O Lemuel,
   it is not for kings to drink wine,
   or for rulers to desire^d strong drink;
⁵ or else they will drink and forget
    what has been decreed,
   and will pervert the rights of all the
    afflicted.
⁶ Give strong drink to one who is
    perishing,
   and wine to those in bitter
    distress;
⁷ let them drink and forget their
    poverty,
   and remember their misery
    no more.
⁸ Speak out for those who cannot
    speak,
   for the rights of all the destitute.^e
⁹ Speak out, judge righteously,
   defend the rights of the poor
    and needy.

Ode to a Capable Wife

¹⁰ A capable wife who can find?
   She is far more precious than
    jewels.
¹¹ The heart of her husband trusts
    in her,
   and he will have no lack of gain.
¹² She does him good, and not harm,
   all the days of her life.
¹³ She seeks wool and flax,
   and works with willing hands.
¹⁴ She is like the ships of the merchant,
   she brings her food from far away.
¹⁵ She rises while it is still night
   and provides food for her
    household
   and tasks for her servant-girls.

a Or *spider*   *b* Gk Syr Tg Compare Vg: Meaning of
Heb uncertain   *c* Meaning of Heb uncertain
d Cn: Heb *where*   *e* Heb *all children of passing away*

16 She considers a field and buys it;
  with the fruit of her hands she
    plants a vineyard.
17 She girds herself with strength,
  and makes her arms strong.
18 She perceives that her merchandise is
    profitable.
  Her lamp does not go out at night.
19 She puts her hands to the distaff,
  and her hands hold the spindle.
20 She opens her hand to the poor,
  and reaches out her hands to
    the needy.
21 She is not afraid for her household
    when it snows,
  for all her household are clothed in
    crimson.
22 She makes herself coverings;
  her clothing is fine linen and purple.
23 Her husband is known in the
    city gates,
  taking his seat among the elders of
    the land.
24 She makes linen garments and sells
    them;

  she supplies the merchant with
    sashes.
25 Strength and dignity are her clothing,
  and she laughs at the time to come.
26 She opens her mouth with wisdom,
  and the teaching of kindness is on
    her tongue.
27 She looks well to the ways of her
    household,
  and does not eat the bread of
    idleness.
28 Her children rise up and call her
    happy;
  her husband too, and he praises her:
29 'Many women have done excellently,
  but you surpass them all.'
30 Charm is deceitful, and beauty
    is vain,
  but a woman who fears the LORD is
    to be praised.
31 Give her a share in the fruit of her
    hands,
  and let her works praise her in the
    city gates.

ECCLESIASTES

Reflections of a Royal Philosopher

1 The words of the Teacher, [a] the son of David, king in Jerusalem.

2 Vanity of vanities, says the Teacher, [a] vanity of vanities! All is vanity.

3 What do people gain from all the toil
at which they toil under the sun?

4 A generation goes, and a generation comes,
but the earth remains for ever.

5 The sun rises and the sun goes down,
and hurries to the place where
it rises.

6 The wind blows to the south,
and goes round to the north;
round and round goes the wind,
and on its circuits the wind returns.

7 All streams run to the sea,
but the sea is not full;
to the place where the streams flow,
there they continue to flow.

8 All things [b] are wearisome;
more than one can express;
the eye is not satisfied with seeing,
or the ear filled with hearing.

9 What has been is what will be,
and what has been done is what
will be done;
there is nothing new under the sun.

10 Is there a thing of which it is said,
'See, this is new'?
It has already been,
in the ages before us.

11 The people of long ago are not
remembered,
nor will there be any remembrance
of people yet to come
by those who come after them.

The Futility of Seeking Wisdom

12 I, the Teacher, [a] when king over Israel in Jerusalem, 13 applied my mind to seek and to search out by wisdom all that is done under heaven; it is an unhappy business that God has given to human beings to be busy with. 14 I saw all the deeds that are done under the sun; and see, all is vanity and a chasing after wind. [c]

15 What is crooked cannot be made
straight,
and what is lacking cannot
be counted.

16 I said to myself, 'I have acquired great wisdom, surpassing all who were over Jerusalem before me; and my mind has had great experience of wisdom and knowledge.' 17 And I applied my mind to know wisdom and to know madness and folly. I perceived that this also is but a chasing after wind. [c]

18 For in much wisdom is much
vexation,
and those who increase knowledge
increase sorrow.

The Futility of Self-Indulgence

2 I said to myself, 'Come now, I will make a test of pleasure; enjoy yourself.' But again, this also was vanity. 2 I said of laughter, 'It is mad', and of pleasure, 'What use is it?' 3 I searched with my mind how to cheer my body with wine—my mind still guiding me with wisdom—and how to lay hold on folly, until I might see what was good for mortals to do under heaven during the few days of their life. 4 I

---

a Heb *Qoheleth*, traditionally rendered *Preacher*
b Or *words*   c Or *a feeding on wind*. See Hos 12.1

made great works; I built houses and planted vineyards for myself; ⁵I made myself gardens and parks, and planted in them all kinds of fruit trees. ⁶I made myself pools from which to water the forest of growing trees. ⁷I bought male and female slaves, and had slaves who were born in my house; I also had great possessions of herds and flocks, more than any who had been before me in Jerusalem. ⁸I also gathered for myself silver and gold and the treasure of kings and of the provinces; I got singers, both men and women, and delights of the flesh, and many concubines.ᵃ

9 So I became great and surpassed all who were before me in Jerusalem; also my wisdom remained with me. ¹⁰Whatever my eyes desired I did not keep from them; I kept my heart from no pleasure, for my heart found pleasure in all my toil, and this was my reward for all my toil. ¹¹Then I considered all that my hands had done and the toil I had spent in doing it, and, again, all was vanity and a chasing after wind,ᵇ and there was nothing to be gained under the sun.

Wisdom and Joy Given to One Who Pleases God

12 So I turned to consider wisdom and madness and folly; for what can the one do who comes after the king? Only what has already been done. ¹³Then I saw that wisdom excels folly as light excels darkness.
¹⁴ The wise have eyes in their head,
    but fools walk in darkness.
Yet I perceived that the same fate befalls all of them. ¹⁵Then I said to myself, 'What happens to the fool will happen to me also; why then have I been so very wise?' And I said to myself that this also is vanity. ¹⁶For there is no enduring remembrance of the wise or of fools, seeing that in the days to come all will have been long forgotten. How can the wise die just like fools? ¹⁷So I hated life, because what is done under the sun was grievous to me; for all is vanity and a chasing after wind.ᵇ

18 I hated all my toil in which I had toiled under the sun, seeing that I must leave it to those who come after me

¹⁹—and who knows whether they will be wise or foolish? Yet they will be master of all for which I toiled and used my wisdom under the sun. This also is vanity. ²⁰So I turned and gave my heart up to despair concerning all the toil of my labours under the sun, ²¹because sometimes one who has toiled with wisdom and knowledge and skill must leave all to be enjoyed by another who did not toil for it. This also is vanity and a great evil. ²²What do mortals get from all the toil and strain with which they toil under the sun? ²³For all their days are full of pain, and their work is a vexation; even at night their minds do not rest. This also is vanity.

24 There is nothing better for mortals than to eat and drink, and find enjoyment in their toil. This also, I saw, is from the hand of God; ²⁵for apart from himᶜ who can eat or who can have enjoyment? ²⁶For to the one who pleases him God gives wisdom and knowledge and joy; but to the sinner he gives the work of gathering and heaping, only to give to one who pleases God. This also is vanity and a chasing after wind.ᵇ

Everything Has Its Time

3 For everything there is a season, and a time for every matter under heaven:
² a time to be born, and a time to die;
    a time to plant, and a time to pluck
        up what is planted;
³ a time to kill, and a time to heal;
    a time to break down, and a time to
        build up;
⁴ a time to weep, and a time to laugh;
    a time to mourn, and a time
        to dance;
⁵ a time to throw away stones, and a
        time to gather stones together;
    a time to embrace, and a time to
        refrain from embracing;
⁶ a time to seek, and a time to lose;
    a time to keep, and a time to
        throw away;
⁷ a time to tear, and a time to sew;

ᵃ Meaning of Heb uncertain   ᵇ Or a feeding on wind.
See Hos 12.1   ᶜ Gk Syr: Heb apart from me

a time to keep silence, and a time to
  speak;
8 a time to love, and a time to hate;
a time for war, and a time for peace.

The God-Given Task

9 What gain have the workers from their
toil? [10] I have seen the business that God
has given to everyone to be busy with. [11] He
has made everything suitable for its time;
moreover, he has put a sense of past and
future into their minds, yet they cannot
find out what God has done from the beginning to the end. [12] I know that there is
nothing better for them than to be happy
and enjoy themselves as long as they live;
[13] moreover, it is God's gift that all should
eat and drink and take pleasure in all their
toil. [14] I know that whatever God does endures for ever; nothing can be added to it,
nor anything taken from it; God has done
this, so that all should stand in awe before
him. [15] That which is, already has been;
that which is to be, already is; and God
seeks out what has gone by. [a]

Judgement and the Future Belong to God

16 Moreover, I saw under the sun that
in the place of justice, wickedness was
there, and in the place of righteousness,
wickedness was there as well. [17] I said in
my heart, God will judge the righteous
and the wicked, for he has appointed a
time for every matter, and for every work.
[18] I said in my heart with regard to human
beings that God is testing them to show
that they are but animals. [19] For the fate of
humans and the fate of animals is the
same; as one dies, so dies the other. They
all have the same breath, and humans
have no advantage over the animals; for
all is vanity. [20] All go to one place; all are
from the dust, and all turn to dust again.
[21] Who knows whether the human spirit
goes upwards and the spirit of animals
goes downwards to the earth? [22] So I saw
that there is nothing better than that all
should enjoy their work, for that is their
lot; who can bring them to see what will
be after them?

4 Again I saw all the oppressions that
are practised under the sun. Look, the
tears of the oppressed—with no one to
comfort them! On the side of their oppressors there was power—with no one to
comfort them. [2] And I thought the dead,
who have already died, more fortunate
than the living, who are still alive; [3] but
better than both is the one who has not yet
been, and has not seen the evil deeds that
are done under the sun.

4 Then I saw that all toil and all skill in
work come from one person's envy of another. This also is vanity and a chasing after wind. [b]
5 Fools fold their hands
    and consume their own flesh.
6 Better is a handful with quiet
    than two handfuls with toil,
    and a chasing after wind. [b]

7 Again, I saw vanity under the sun:
[8] the case of solitary individuals, without
sons or brothers; yet there is no end to all
their toil, and their eyes are never satisfied
with riches. 'For whom am I toiling', they
ask, 'and depriving myself of pleasure?'
This also is vanity and an unhappy business.

The Value of a Friend

9 Two are better than one, because they
have a good reward for their toil. [10] For if
they fall, one will lift up the other; but woe
to one who is alone and falls and does not
have another to help. [11] Again, if two lie together, they keep warm; but how can one
keep warm alone? [12] And though one
might prevail against another, two will
withstand one. A threefold cord is not
quickly broken.

13 Better is a poor but wise youth than
an old but foolish king, who will no longer
take advice. [14] One can indeed come out of
prison to reign, even though born poor in
the kingdom. [15] I saw all the living who,
moving about under the sun, follow that [c]
youth who replaced the king; [d] [16] there was
no end to all those people whom he led.
Yet those who come later will not rejoice

in him. Surely this also is vanity and a chasing after wind.^a

Reverence, Humility, and Contentment

5 ^b Guard your steps when you go to the house of God; to draw near to listen is better than the sacrifice offered by fools; for they do not know how to keep from doing evil.^c ^{2 d} Never be rash with your mouth, nor let your heart be quick to utter a word before God, for God is in heaven, and you upon earth; therefore let your words be few.

3 For dreams come with many cares, and a fool's voice with many words.

4 When you make a vow to God, do not delay fulfilling it; for he has no pleasure in fools. Fulfil what you vow. ⁵ It is better that you should not vow than that you should vow and not fulfil it. ⁶ Do not let your mouth lead you into sin, and do not say before the messenger that it was a mistake; why should God be angry at your words, and destroy the work of your hands?

7 With many dreams come vanities and a multitude of words;^e but fear God.

8 If you see in a province the oppression of the poor and the violation of justice and right, do not be amazed at the matter; for the high official is watched by a higher, and there are yet higher ones over them. ⁹ But all things considered, this is an advantage for a land: a king for a ploughed field.^e

10 The lover of money will not be satisfied with money; nor the lover of wealth, with gain. This also is vanity.

11 When goods increase, those who eat them increase; and what gain has their owner but to see them with his eyes?

12 Sweet is the sleep of labourers, whether they eat little or much; but the surfeit of the rich will not let them sleep.

13 There is a grievous ill that I have seen under the sun: riches were kept by their owners to their hurt, ¹⁴ and those riches were lost in a bad venture; though they are parents of children, they have nothing in their hands. ¹⁵ As they came from their mother's womb, so they shall go again, naked as they came; they shall

take nothing for their toil, which they may carry away with their hands. ¹⁶ This also is a grievous ill: just as they came, so shall they go; and what gain do they have from toiling for the wind? ¹⁷ Besides, all their days they eat in darkness, in much vexation and sickness and resentment.

18 This is what I have seen to be good: it is fitting to eat and drink and find enjoyment in all the toil with which one toils under the sun the few days of the life God gives us; for this is our lot. ¹⁹ Likewise all to whom God gives wealth and possessions and whom he enables to enjoy them, and to accept their lot and find enjoyment in their toil—this is the gift of God. ²⁰ For they will scarcely brood over the days of their lives, because God keeps them occupied with the joy of their hearts.

The Frustration of Desires

6 There is an evil that I have seen under the sun, and it lies heavy upon humankind: ² those to whom God gives wealth, possessions, and honour, so that they lack nothing of all that they desire, yet God does not enable them to enjoy these things, but a stranger enjoys them. This is vanity; it is a grievous ill. ³ A man may beget a hundred children, and live for many years; but however many are the days of his years, if he does not enjoy life's good things, or has no burial, I say that a stillborn child is better off than he. ⁴ For it comes into vanity and goes into darkness, and in darkness its name is covered; ⁵ moreover, it has not seen the sun or known anything; yet it finds rest rather than he. ⁶ Even though he should live a thousand years twice over, yet enjoy no good—do not all go to one place?

7 All human toil is for the mouth, yet the appetite is not satisfied. ⁸ For what advantage have the wise over fools? And what do the poor have who know how to conduct themselves before the living? ⁹ Better is the sight of the eyes than the wandering

of desire; this also is vanity and a chasing after wind.*a*

10 Whatever has come to be has already been named, and it is known what human beings are, and that they are not able to dispute with those who are stronger. 11 The more words, the more vanity, so how is one the better? 12 For who knows what is good for mortals while they live the few days of their vain life, which they pass like a shadow? For who can tell them what will be after them under the sun?

A Disillusioned View of Life

7 A good name is better than
    precious ointment,
and the day of death, than the day
    of birth.
2 It is better to go to the house of
    mourning
    than to go to the house of feasting;
for this is the end of everyone,
    and the living will lay it to heart.
3 Sorrow is better than laughter,
    for by sadness of countenance the
    heart is made glad.
4 The heart of the wise is in the house
    of mourning;
    but the heart of fools is in the
    house of mirth.
5 It is better to hear the rebuke of the
    wise
    than to hear the song of fools.
6 For like the crackling of thorns under
    a pot,
    so is the laughter of fools;
    this also is vanity.
7 Surely oppression makes the wise
    foolish,
    and a bribe corrupts the heart.
8 Better is the end of a thing than its
    beginning;
    the patient in spirit are better than
    the proud in spirit.
9 Do not be quick to anger,
    for anger lodges in the bosom
    of fools.
10 Do not say, 'Why were the former
    days better than these?'
    For it is not from wisdom that you
    ask this.

11 Wisdom is as good as an inheritance,
    an advantage to those who see the
    sun.
12 For the protection of wisdom is like
    the protection of money,
    and the advantage of knowledge is
    that wisdom gives life to the
    one who possesses it.
13 Consider the work of God;
    who can make straight what he has
    made crooked?

14 On the day of prosperity be joyful, and on the day of adversity consider; God has made the one as well as the other, so that mortals may not find out anything that will come after them.

The Riddles of Life

15 In my vain life I have seen everything; there are righteous people who perish in their righteousness, and there are wicked people who prolong their life in their evildoing. 16 Do not be too righteous, and do not act too wise; why should you destroy yourself? 17 Do not be too wicked, and do not be a fool; why should you die before your time? 18 It is good that you should take hold of the one, without letting go of the other; for the one who fears God shall succeed with both.

19 Wisdom gives strength to the wise more than ten rulers that are in a city.

20 Surely there is no one on earth so righteous as to do good without ever sinning.

21 Do not give heed to everything that people say, or you may hear your servant cursing you; 22 your heart knows that many times you have yourself cursed others.

23 All this I have tested by wisdom; I said, 'I will be wise', but it was far from me. 24 That which is, is far off, and deep, very deep; who can find it out? 25 I turned my mind to know and to search out and to seek wisdom and the sum of things, and to know that wickedness is folly and that foolishness is madness. 26 I found more bitter than death the woman who is a trap, whose heart is snares and nets, whose hands are fetters; one who pleases

a Or *a feeding on wind*. See Hos 12.1

God escapes her, but the sinner is taken by her. 27 See, this is what I found, says the Teacher,*a* adding one thing to another to find the sum, 28 which my mind has sought repeatedly, but I have not found. One man among a thousand I found, but a woman among all these I have not found. 29 See, this alone I found, that God made human beings straightforward, but they have devised many schemes.

Obey the King and Enjoy Yourself

8 Who is like the wise man?
And who knows the interpretation of a thing?
Wisdom makes one's face shine,
and the hardness of one's
countenance is changed.

2 Keep*b* the king's command because of your sacred oath. 3 Do not be terrified; go from his presence, do not delay when the matter is unpleasant, for he does whatever he pleases. 4 For the word of the king is powerful, and who can say to him, 'What are you doing?' 5 Whoever obeys a command will meet no harm, and the wise mind will know the time and way. 6 For every matter has its time and way, although the troubles of mortals lie heavy upon them. 7 Indeed, they do not know what is to be, for who can tell them how it will be? 8 No one has power over the wind*c* to restrain the wind,*c* or power over the day of death; there is no discharge from the battle, nor does wickedness deliver those who practise it. 9 All this I observed, applying my mind to all that is done under the sun, while one person exercises authority over another to the other's hurt.

God's Ways Are Inscrutable

10 Then I saw the wicked buried; they used to go in and out of the holy place, and were praised in the city where they had done such things.*d* This also is vanity. 11 Because sentence against an evil deed is not executed speedily, the human heart is fully set to do evil. 12 Though sinners do evil a hundred times and prolong their lives, yet I know that it will be well with those who fear God, because they stand in fear before

him, 13 but it will not be well with the wicked, neither will they prolong their days like a shadow, because they do not stand in fear before God.

14 There is a vanity that takes place on earth, that there are righteous people who are treated according to the conduct of the wicked, and there are wicked people who are treated according to the conduct of the righteous. I said that this also is vanity. 15 So I commend enjoyment, for there is nothing better for people under the sun than to eat, and drink, and enjoy themselves, for this will go with them in their toil through the days of life that God gives them under the sun.

16 When I applied my mind to know wisdom, and to see the business that is done on earth, how one's eyes see sleep neither day nor night, 17 then I saw all the work of God, that no one can find out what is happening under the sun. However much they may toil in seeking, they will not find it out; even though those who are wise claim to know, they cannot find it out.

Take Life as It Comes

9 All this I laid to heart, examining it all, how the righteous and the wise and their deeds are in the hand of God; whether it is love or hate one does not know. Everything that confronts them 2 is vanity,*e* since the same fate comes to all, to the righteous and the wicked, to the good and the evil,*f* to the clean and the unclean, to those who sacrifice and those who do not sacrifice. As are the good, so are the sinners; those who swear are like those who shun an oath. 3 This is an evil in all that happens under the sun, that the same fate comes to everyone. Moreover, the hearts of all are full of evil; madness is in their hearts while they live, and after that they go to the dead. 4 But whoever is joined with all the living has hope, for a living dog is better than a dead lion. 5 The living know that they will die, but the dead know

---

a Qoheleth, traditionally rendered *Preacher*   *b* Heb *I keep*   *c* Or *breath*   *d* Meaning of Heb uncertain
e Syr Compare Gk: Heb *Everything that confronts them* 2 *is everything*   *f* Gk Syr Vg: Heb lacks *and the evil*

nothing; they have no more reward, and even the memory of them is lost. [6]Their love and their hate and their envy have already perished; never again will they have any share in all that happens under the sun.

7 Go, eat your bread with enjoyment, and drink your wine with a merry heart; for God has long ago approved what you do. [8]Let your garments always be white; do not let oil be lacking on your head. [9]Enjoy life with the wife whom you love, all the days of your vain life that are given you under the sun, because that is your portion in life and in your toil at which you toil under the sun. [10]Whatever your hand finds to do, do with your might; for there is no work or thought or knowledge or wisdom in Sheol, to which you are going.

11 Again I saw that under the sun the race is not to the swift, nor the battle to the strong, nor bread to the wise, nor riches to the intelligent, nor favour to the skilful; but time and chance happen to them all. [12]For no one can anticipate the time of disaster. Like fish taken in a cruel net, and like birds caught in a snare, so mortals are snared at a time of calamity, when it suddenly falls upon them.

Wisdom Superior to Folly

13 I have also seen this example of wisdom under the sun, and it seemed important to me. [14]There was a little city with few people in it. A great king came against it and besieged it, building great siegeworks against it. [15]Now there was found in it a poor, wise man, and he by his wisdom delivered the city. Yet no one remembered that poor man. [16]So I said, 'Wisdom is better than might; yet the poor man's wisdom is despised, and his words are not heeded.'

[17] The quiet words of the wise are more
   to be heeded
     than the shouting of a ruler among
     fools.
[18] Wisdom is better than weapons
   of war,
     but one bungler destroys much
     good.

Miscellaneous Observations

10 Dead flies make the perfumer's
   ointment give off a foul odour;
  so a little folly outweighs wisdom
    and honour.
[2] The heart of the wise inclines to the
   right,
   but the heart of a fool to the left.
[3] Even when fools walk on the road,
   they lack sense,
   and show to everyone that they are
    fools.
[4] If the anger of the ruler rises against
    you, do not leave your post,
   for calmness will undo great
    offences.

5 There is an evil that I have seen under the sun, as great an error as if it proceeded from the ruler: [6]folly is set in many high places, and the rich sit in a low place. [7]I have seen slaves on horseback, and princes walking on foot like slaves.

[8] Whoever digs a pit will fall into it;
   and whoever breaks through a wall
    will be bitten by a snake.
[9] Whoever quarries stones will be hurt
   by them;
   and whoever splits logs will be
    endangered by them.
[10] If the iron is blunt, and one does not
   whet the edge,
   then more strength must be
    exerted;
   but wisdom helps one to succeed.
[11] If the snake bites before it is
   charmed,
   there is no advantage in a charmer.

[12] Words spoken by the wise bring them
   favour,
   but the lips of fools consume them.
[13] The words of their mouths begin in
   foolishness,
   and their talk ends in wicked
    madness;
[14] yet fools talk on and on.
   No one knows what is to happen,
   and who can tell anyone what the
    future holds?
[15] The toil of fools wears them out,

for they do not even know the way to town.

16 Alas for you, O land, when your king
    is a servant,[a]
  and your princes feast in the
    morning!
17 Happy are you, O land, when your
    king is a nobleman,
  and your princes feast at the proper
    time—
  for strength, and not for
    drunkenness!
18 Through sloth the roof sinks in,
  and through indolence the house
    leaks.
19 Feasts are made for laughter;
  wine gladdens life,
  and money meets every need.
20 Do not curse the king, even in your
    thoughts,
  or curse the rich, even in your
    bedroom;
  for a bird of the air may carry
    your voice,
  or some winged creature tell
    the matter.

The Value of Diligence

11 Send out your bread upon the
    waters,
  for after many days you will get it
    back.
2 Divide your means seven ways, or
    even eight,
  for you do not know what disaster
    may happen on earth.
3 When clouds are full,
  they empty rain on the earth;
  whether a tree falls to the south or to
    the north,
  in the place where the tree falls,
    there it will lie.
4 Whoever observes the wind will
    not sow;
  and whoever regards the clouds will
    not reap.
5 Just as you do not know how the
breath comes to the bones in the mother's
womb, so you do not know the work of
God, who makes everything.

6 In the morning sow your seed, and at
evening do not let your hands be idle; for
you do not know which will prosper, this
or that, or whether both alike will be good.

Youth and Old Age

7 Light is sweet, and it is pleasant for
the eyes to see the sun.

8 Even those who live for many years
should rejoice in them all; yet let them remember that the days of darkness will be
many. All that comes is vanity.

9 Rejoice, young man, while you are
young, and let your heart cheer you in the
days of your youth. Follow the inclination
of your heart and the desire of your eyes,
but know that for all these things God will
bring you into judgement.

10 Banish anxiety from your mind, and
put away pain from your body; for youth
and the dawn of life are vanity.

12 Remember your creator in the days
of your youth, before the days of
trouble come, and the years draw near when
you will say, 'I have no pleasure in them';
2 before the sun and the light and the moon
and the stars are darkened and the clouds
return with[b] the rain; 3 on the day when the
guards of the house tremble, and the strong
men are bent, and the women who grind
cease working because they are few, and
those who look through the windows see
dimly; 4 when the doors on the street are
shut, and the sound of the grinding is low,
and one rises up at the sound of a bird, and
all the daughters of song are brought low;
5 when one is afraid of heights, and terrors
are in the road; the almond tree blossoms,
the grasshopper drags itself along[c] and desire fails; because all must go to their eternal
home, and the mourners will go about the
streets; 6 before the silver cord is snapped,[d]
and the golden bowl is broken, and the
pitcher is broken at the fountain, and the
wheel broken at the cistern, 7 and the dust
returns to the earth as it was, and the
breath[e] returns to God who gave it. 8 Vanity
of vanities, says the Teacher;[f] all is vanity.

a Or a child   b Or after; Heb 'ahar   c Or is a burden
d Syr Vg Compare Gk: Heb is removed   e Or the spirit
f Qoheleth, traditionally rendered Preacher

Epilogue

9 Besides being wise, the Teacher*a* also taught the people knowledge, weighing and studying and arranging many proverbs. ¹⁰The Teacher*a* sought to find pleasing words, and he wrote words of truth plainly.

11 The sayings of the wise are like goads, and like nails firmly fixed are the collected sayings that are given by one shepherd.*b* ¹²Of anything beyond these, my child, be-ware. Of making many books there is no end, and much study is a weariness of the flesh.

13 The end of the matter; all has been heard. Fear God, and keep his commandments; for that is the whole duty of everyone. ¹⁴For God will bring every deed into judgement, including*c* every secret thing, whether good or evil.

a Qoheleth, traditionally rendered *Preacher*
b Meaning of Heb uncertain   *c* Or *into the judgement on*

THE SONG OF SOLOMON

1 The Song of Songs, which is Solomon's.

Colloquy of Bride and Friends

2 Let him kiss me with the kisses of his
        mouth!
For your love is better than wine,
3   your anointing oils are fragrant,
your name is perfume poured out;
        therefore the maidens love you.
4 Draw me after you, let us make haste.
    The king has brought me into his
        chambers.
We will exult and rejoice in you;
    we will extol your love more
        than wine;
    rightly do they love you.

5 I am black and beautiful,
        O daughters of Jerusalem,
like the tents of Kedar,
        like the curtains of Solomon.
6 Do not gaze at me because I am dark,
        because the sun has gazed on me.
My mother's sons were angry
        with me;
    they made me keeper of the
        vineyards,
    but my own vineyard I have
        not kept!
7 Tell me, you whom my soul loves,
        where you pasture your flock,
        where you make it lie down at noon;
for why should I be like one who
        is veiled
    beside the flocks of your
        companions?

8 If you do not know,
        O fairest among women,
follow the tracks of the flock,
        and pasture your kids
        beside the shepherds' tents.

*Colloquy of Bridegroom, Friends,
        and Bride*

9 I compare you, my love,
        to a mare among Pharaoh's
        chariots.
10 Your cheeks are comely with
        ornaments,
    your neck with strings of jewels.
11 We will make you ornaments
        of gold,
    studded with silver.

12 While the king was on his couch,
        my nard gave forth its fragrance.
13 My beloved is to me a bag of myrrh
        that lies between my breasts.
14 My beloved is to me a cluster of
        henna blossoms
    in the vineyards of En-gedi.

15 Ah, you are beautiful, my love;
        ah, you are beautiful;
        your eyes are doves.
16 Ah, you are beautiful, my beloved,
        truly lovely.
Our couch is green;
17   the beams of our house are cedar,
        our rafters *a* are pine.

2 I am a rose *b* of Sharon,
        a lily of the valleys.

2 As a lily among brambles,
        so is my love among maidens.

a Meaning of Heb uncertain   *b* Heb *crocus*

3 As an apple tree among the trees of
    the wood,
    so is my beloved among young
        men.
  With great delight I sat in his
        shadow,
    and his fruit was sweet to my taste.
4 He brought me to the banqueting
        house,
    and his intention towards me
        was love.
5 Sustain me with raisins,
    refresh me with apples;
    for I am faint with love.
6 O that his left hand were under my
        head,
    and that his right hand embraced
        me!
7 I adjure you, O daughters of
        Jerusalem,
    by the gazelles or the wild does:
    do not stir up or awaken love
        until it is ready!

Springtime Rhapsody

8 The voice of my beloved!
    Look, he comes,
    leaping upon the mountains,
        bounding over the hills.
9 My beloved is like a gazelle
    or a young stag.
  Look, there he stands
        behind our wall,
    gazing in at the windows,
        looking through the lattice.
10 My beloved speaks and says to me:
  'Arise, my love, my fair one,
    and come away;
11 for now the winter is past,
    the rain is over and gone.
12 The flowers appear on the earth;
    the time of singing has come,
  and the voice of the turtle-dove
    is heard in our land.
13 The fig tree puts forth its figs,
    and the vines are in blossom;
        they give forth fragrance.
  Arise, my love, my fair one,
    and come away.
14 O my dove, in the clefts of the rock,
    in the covert of the cliff,

let me see your face,
    let me hear your voice;
  for your voice is sweet,
    and your face is lovely.
15 Catch us the foxes,
    the little foxes,
  that ruin the vineyards—
    for our vineyards are in blossom.'

16 My beloved is mine and I am his;
    he pastures his flock among the
        lilies.
17 Until the day breathes
    and the shadows flee,
  turn, my beloved, be like a gazelle
    or a young stag on the cleft
        mountains. *b*

A Dream of Love

3 Upon my bed at night
    I sought him whom my soul loves;
  I sought him, but found him not;
    I called him, but he gave no
        answer. *b*
2 'I will rise now and go about the city,
    in the streets and in the squares;
  I will seek him whom my soul loves.'
    I sought him, but found him not.
3 The sentinels found me,
    as they went about in the city.
  'Have you seen him whom my soul
        loves?'
4 Scarcely had I passed them,
    when I found him whom my soul
        loves.
  I held him, and would not let him go
    until I brought him into my
        mother's house,
    and into the chamber of her that
        conceived me.
5 I adjure you, O daughters of Jerusalem,
    by the gazelles or the wild does:
  do not stir up or awaken love
    until it is ready!

The Groom and His Party Approach

6 What is that coming up from the
        wilderness,
    like a column of smoke,

a Or *on the mountains of Bether*; meaning of Heb
uncertain   *b* Gk: Heb lacks this line

perfumed with myrrh and
frankincense,
with all the fragrant powders of the
merchant?
7 Look, it is the litter of Solomon!
Around it are sixty mighty men
of the mighty men of Israel,
8 all equipped with swords
and expert in war,
each with his sword at his thigh
because of alarms by night.
9 King Solomon made himself a
palanquin
from the wood of Lebanon.
10 He made its posts of silver,
its back of gold, its seat of purple;
its interior was inlaid with love. *a*
Daughters of Jerusalem,
11 come out.
Look, O daughters of Zion,
at King Solomon,
at the crown with which his mother
crowned him
on the day of his wedding,
on the day of the gladness of
his heart.

The Bride's Beauty Extolled

4 How beautiful you are, my love,
how very beautiful!
Your eyes are doves
behind your veil.
Your hair is like a flock of goats,
moving down the slopes of Gilead.
2 Your teeth are like a flock of
shorn ewes
that have come up from the
washing,
all of which bear twins,
and not one among them is
bereaved.
3 Your lips are like a crimson thread,
and your mouth is lovely.
Your cheeks are like halves of a
pomegranate
behind your veil.
4 Your neck is like the tower of David,
built in courses;
on it hang a thousand bucklers,
all of them shields of warriors.
5 Your two breasts are like two fawns,

twins of a gazelle,
that feed among the lilies.
6 Until the day breathes
and the shadows flee,
I will hasten to the mountain of
myrrh
and the hill of frankincense.
7 You are altogether beautiful,
my love;
there is no flaw in you.
8 Come with me from Lebanon,
my bride;
come with me from Lebanon.
Depart *b* from the peak of Amana,
from the peak of Senir and
Hermon,
from the dens of lions,
from the mountains of leopards.

9 You have ravished my heart, my
sister, my bride,
you have ravished my heart with a
glance of your eyes,
with one jewel of your necklace.
10 How sweet is your love, my sister, my
bride!
how much better is your love than
wine,
and the fragrance of your oils than
any spice!
11 Your lips distil nectar, my bride;
honey and milk are under your
tongue;
the scent of your garments is like
the scent of Lebanon.
12 A garden locked is my sister,
my bride,
a garden locked, a fountain sealed.
13 Your channel *a* is an orchard of
pomegranates
with all choicest fruits,
henna with nard,
14 nard and saffron, calamus and
cinnamon,
with all trees of frankincense,
myrrh and aloes,
with all chief spices—
15 a garden fountain, a well of living
water,
and flowing streams from Lebanon.

a Meaning of Heb uncertain   *b* Or *Look*

16 Awake, O north wind,
    and come, O south wind!
Blow upon my garden
    that its fragrance may be wafted
       abroad.
Let my beloved come to his garden,
    and eat its choicest fruits.

5 I come to my garden, my sister,
    my bride;
I gather my myrrh with my spice,
I eat my honeycomb with my
    honey,
I drink my wine with my milk.

Eat, friends, drink,
    and be drunk with love.

Another Dream

2 I slept, but my heart was awake.
Listen! my beloved is knocking.
'Open to me, my sister, my love,
    my dove, my perfect one;
for my head is wet with dew,
    my locks with the drops of the
       night.'
3 I had put off my garment;
    how could I put it on again?
I had bathed my feet;
    how could I soil them?
4 My beloved thrust his hand into the
    opening,
    and my inmost being yearned
      for him.
5 I arose to open to my beloved,
    and my hands dripped with myrrh,
my fingers with liquid myrrh,
    upon the handles of the bolt.
6 I opened to my beloved,
    but my beloved had turned and was
      gone.
My soul failed me when he spoke.
I sought him, but did not find him;
    I called him, but he gave no answer.
7 Making their rounds in the city
    the sentinels found me;
they beat me, they wounded me,
they took away my mantle,
    those sentinels of the walls.
8 I adjure you, O daughters of
    Jerusalem,

if you find my beloved,
tell him this:
    I am faint with love.

Colloquy of Friends and Bride

9 What is your beloved more than
      another beloved,
    O fairest among women?
What is your beloved more than
      another beloved,
    that you thus adjure us?

10 My beloved is all radiant and ruddy,
    distinguished among ten thousand.
11 His head is the finest gold;
    his locks are wavy,
    black as a raven.
12 His eyes are like doves
    beside springs of water,
bathed in milk,
    fitly set. *a*
13 His cheeks are like beds of spices,
    yielding fragrance.
His lips are lilies,
    distilling liquid myrrh.
14 His arms are rounded gold,
    set with jewels.
His body is ivory work, *a*
    encrusted with sapphires. *b*
15 His legs are alabaster columns,
    set upon bases of gold.
His appearance is like Lebanon,
    choice as the cedars.
16 His speech is most sweet,
    and he is altogether desirable.
This is my beloved and this is
    my friend,
    O daughters of Jerusalem.

6 Where has your beloved gone,
    O fairest among women?
Which way has your beloved turned,
    that we may seek him with you?

2 My beloved has gone down to his
    garden,
    to the beds of spices,
to pasture his flock in the gardens,
    and to gather lilies.

a Meaning of Heb uncertain   *b* Heb *lapis lazuli*

3 I am my beloved's and my beloved is
      mine;
    he pastures his flock among the
      lilies.

The Bride's Matchless Beauty

4 You are beautiful as Tirzah, my love,
    comely as Jerusalem,
    terrible as an army with banners.
5 Turn away your eyes from me,
    for they overwhelm me!
  Your hair is like a flock of goats,
    moving down the slopes of
      Gilead.
6 Your teeth are like a flock of ewes,
    that have come up from the
      washing;
  all of them bear twins,
    and not one among them is
      bereaved.
7 Your cheeks are like halves of a
      pomegranate
  behind your veil.
8 There are sixty queens and eighty
      concubines,
  and maidens without number.
9 My dove, my perfect one, is the only
      one,
    the darling of her mother,
    flawless to her that bore her.
  The maidens saw her and called her
      happy;
    the queens and concubines also,
    and they praised her.
10 'Who is this that looks forth like the
      dawn,
    fair as the moon, bright as the sun,
    terrible as an army with banners?'

11 I went down to the nut orchard,
    to look at the blossoms of the
      valley,
  to see whether the vines had budded,
    whether the pomegranates were in
      bloom.
12 Before I was aware, my fancy set me
    in a chariot beside my prince. *a*

13 *b* Return, return, O Shulammite!
    Return, return, that we may look
      upon you.

Why should you look upon the
    Shulammite,
  as upon a dance before two
    armies? *c*

Expressions of Praise

7 How graceful are your feet in sandals,
  O queenly maiden!
  Your rounded thighs are like jewels,
    the work of a master hand.
2 Your navel is a rounded bowl
    that never lacks mixed wine.
  Your belly is a heap of wheat,
    encircled with lilies.
3 Your two breasts are like two fawns,
    twins of a gazelle.
4 Your neck is like an ivory tower.
  Your eyes are pools in Heshbon,
    by the gate of Bath-rabbim.
  Your nose is like a tower of Lebanon,
    overlooking Damascus.
5 Your head crowns you like Carmel,
    and your flowing locks are like
      purple;
    a king is held captive in the
      tresses. *d*

6 How fair and pleasant you are,
    O loved one, delectable maiden! *e*
7 You are stately *f* as a palm tree,
    and your breasts are like its clusters.
8 I say I will climb the palm tree
    and lay hold of its branches.
  O may your breasts be like clusters of
      the vine,
    and the scent of your breath like
      apples,
9 and your kisses *g* like the best wine
    that goes down *h* smoothly,
    gliding over lips and teeth. *i*

10 I am my beloved's,
    and his desire is for me.
11 Come, my beloved,
    let us go forth into the fields,
    and lodge in the villages;
12 let us go out early to the vineyards,

a Cn: Meaning of Heb uncertain   *b* Ch 7.1 in Heb
c Or *dance of Mahanaim*   *d* Meaning of Heb uncertain
e Syr: Heb *in delights*   *f* Heb *This your stature is*
g Heb *palate*   *h* Heb *down for my lover*   *i* Gk Syr Vg:
Heb *lips of sleepers*

and see whether the vines have
    budded,
whether the grape blossoms have
    opened
    and the pomegranates are
        in bloom.
There I will give you my love.
13 The mandrakes give forth fragrance,
    and over our doors are all choice
        fruits,
    new as well as old,
        which I have laid up for you, O my
        beloved.

8 O that you were like a brother to me,
    who nursed at my mother's breast!
If I met you outside, I would kiss you,
    and no one would despise me.
2 I would lead you and bring you
    into the house of my mother,
    and into the chamber of the one
        who bore me.*a*
I would give you spiced wine
    to drink,
    the juice of my pomegranates.
3 O that his left hand were under
    my head,
    and that his right hand embraced
        me!
4 I adjure you, O daughters of
    Jerusalem,
    do not stir up or awaken love
    until it is ready!

Homecoming

5 Who is that coming up from the
    wilderness,
    leaning upon her beloved?

Under the apple tree I awakened you.
There your mother was in labour
    with you;
    there she who bore you was in
        labour.

6 Set me as a seal upon your heart,
    as a seal upon your arm;
    for love is strong as death,

passion fierce as the grave.
Its flashes are flashes of fire,
    a raging flame.
7 Many waters cannot quench love,
    neither can floods drown it.
If one offered for love
    all the wealth of one's house,
    it would be utterly scorned.

8 We have a little sister,
    and she has no breasts.
What shall we do for our sister,
    on the day when she is spoken for?
9 If she is a wall,
    we will build upon her a
        battlement of silver;
but if she is a door,
    we will enclose her with boards of
        cedar.
10 I was a wall,
    and my breasts were like towers;
then I was in his eyes
    as one who brings*b* peace.
11 Solomon had a vineyard at Baal-
    hamon;
    he entrusted the vineyard to
        keepers;
    each one was to bring for its fruit a
        thousand pieces of silver.
12 My vineyard, my very own, is
    for myself;
    you, O Solomon, may have the
        thousand,
    and the keepers of the fruit two
        hundred!

13 O you who dwell in the gardens,
    my companions are listening for
        your voice;
    let me hear it.

14 Make haste, my beloved,
    and be like a gazelle
or a young stag
    upon the mountains of spices!

a Gk Syr: Heb *my mother; she* (or *you*) *will teach me*
b Or *finds*

THE WISDOM OF SOLOMON

Exhortation to Uprightness

1 Love righteousness, you rulers of
     the earth,
think of the Lord in goodness
and seek him with sincerity of heart;
2 because he is found by those who do
     not put him to the test,
and manifests himself to those who
     do not distrust him.
3 For perverse thoughts separate people
     from God,
and when his power is tested, it
     exposes the foolish;
4 because wisdom will not enter a
     deceitful soul,
or dwell in a body enslaved to sin.
5 For a holy and disciplined spirit will
     flee from deceit,
and will leave foolish thoughts
     behind,
and will be ashamed at the approach
     of unrighteousness.

6 For wisdom is a kindly spirit,
but will not free blasphemers from
     the guilt of their words;
because God is witness of their
     inmost feelings,
and a true observer of their hearts,
     and a hearer of their tongues.
7 Because the spirit of the Lord has
     filled the world,
and that which holds all things
     together knows what is said,
8 therefore those who utter
     unrighteous things will not
     escape notice,
and justice, when it punishes, will
     not pass them by.

9 For inquiry will be made into the
     counsels of the ungodly,
and a report of their words will come
     to the Lord,
to convict them of their lawless
     deeds;
10 because a jealous ear hears all things,
and the sound of grumbling does not
     go unheard.
11 Beware then of useless grumbling,
and keep your tongue from slander;
because no secret word is without
     result,[a]
and a lying mouth destroys the soul.

12 Do not invite death by the error of
     your life,
or bring on destruction by the works
     of your hands;
13 because God did not make death,
and he does not delight in the death
     of the living.
14 For he created all things so that they
     might exist;
the generative forces[b] of the world are
     wholesome,
and there is no destructive poison in
     them,
and the dominion[c] of Hades is not
     on earth.
15 For righteousness is immortal.

Life as the Ungodly See It

16 But the ungodly by their words and
     deeds summoned death;[d]
considering him a friend, they pined
     away
and made a covenant with him,

a Or *will go unpunished*   b Or *the creatures*
c Or *palace*   d Gk *him*

because they are fit to belong to his
company.

2 For they reasoned unsoundly,
saying to themselves,
'Short and sorrowful is our life,
and there is no remedy when a life
comes to its end,
and no one has been known to return
from Hades.
2 For we were born by mere chance,
and hereafter we shall be as though
we had never been,
for the breath in our nostrils is
smoke,
and reason is a spark kindled by the
beating of our hearts;
3 when it is extinguished, the body will
turn to ashes,
and the spirit will dissolve like empty
air.
4 Our name will be forgotten in time,
and no one will remember our
works;
our life will pass away like the traces
of a cloud,
and be scattered like mist
that is chased by the rays of the sun
and overcome by its heat.
5 For our allotted time is the passing of
a shadow,
and there is no return from our
death,
because it is sealed up and no one
turns back.

6 'Come, therefore, let us enjoy the
good things that exist,
and make use of the creation to the
full as in youth.
7 Let us take our fill of costly wine and
perfumes,
and let no flower of spring pass us by.
8 Let us crown ourselves with rosebuds
before they wither.
9 Let none of us fail to share in our
revelry;
everywhere let us leave signs of
enjoyment,
because this is our portion, and this
our lot.

10 Let us oppress the righteous poor
man;
let us not spare the widow
or regard the grey hairs of the aged.
11 But let our might be our law of right,
for what is weak proves itself to be
useless.

12 'Let us lie in wait for the righteous
man,
because he is inconvenient to us and
opposes our actions;
he reproaches us for sins against the
law,
and accuses us of sins against our
training.
13 He professes to have knowledge of
God,
and calls himself a child[a] of the Lord.
14 He became to us a reproof of our
thoughts;
15 the very sight of him is a burden to
us,
because his manner of life is unlike
that of others,
and his ways are strange.
16 We are considered by him as
something base,
and he avoids our ways as unclean;
he calls the last end of the righteous
happy,
and boasts that God is his father.
17 Let us see if his words are true,
and let us test what will happen at
the end of his life;
18 for if the righteous man is God's
child, he will help him,
and will deliver him from the hand
of his adversaries.
19 Let us test him with insult and
torture,
so that we may find out how gentle
he is,
and make trial of his forbearance.
20 Let us condemn him to a shameful
death,
for, according to what he says, he will
be protected.'

a Or servant

Error of the Wicked

21 Thus they reasoned, but they were led astray,
  for their wickedness blinded them,
22 and they did not know the secret purposes of God,
  nor hoped for the wages of holiness,
  nor discerned the prize for blameless souls;
23 for God created us for incorruption,
  and made us in the image of his own eternity,[a]
24 but through the devil's envy death entered the world,
  and those who belong to his company experience it.

The Destiny of the Righteous

3 But the souls of the righteous are in the hand of God,
  and no torment will ever touch them.
2 In the eyes of the foolish they seemed to have died,
  and their departure was thought to be a disaster,
3 and their going from us to be their destruction;
  but they are at peace.
4 For though in the sight of others they were punished,
  their hope is full of immortality.
5 Having been disciplined a little, they will receive great good,
  because God tested them and found them worthy of himself;
6 like gold in the furnace he tried them,
  and like a sacrificial burnt-offering he accepted them.
7 In the time of their visitation they will shine forth,
  and will run like sparks through the stubble.
8 They will govern nations and rule over peoples,
  and the Lord will reign over them for ever.
9 Those who trust in him will understand truth,
  and the faithful will abide with him in love,

because grace and mercy are upon his holy ones,
and he watches over his elect.[b]

The Destiny of the Ungodly

10 But the ungodly will be punished as their reasoning deserves,
  those who disregarded the righteous[c]
  and rebelled against the Lord;
11 for those who despise wisdom and instruction are miserable.
  Their hope is vain, their labours are unprofitable,
  and their works are useless.
12 Their wives are foolish, and their children evil;
13 their offspring are accursed.

On Childlessness

For blessed is the barren woman who is undefiled,
who has not entered into a sinful union;
she will have fruit when God examines souls.
14 Blessed also is the eunuch whose hands have done no lawless deed,
  and who has not devised wicked things against the Lord;
  for special favour will be shown him for his faithfulness,
  and a place of great delight in the temple of the Lord.
15 For the fruit of good labours is renowned,
  and the root of understanding does not fail.
16 But children of adulterers will not come to maturity,
  and the offspring of an unlawful union will perish.
17 Even if they live long they will be held of no account,
  and finally their old age will be without honour.
18 If they die young, they will have no hope

---

a Other ancient authorities read *nature*　b Text of this line uncertain; omitted by some ancient authorities. Compare 4.15　c Or *what is right*

and no consolation on the day of
  judgement.

19 For the end of an unrighteous
  generation is grievous.

4 Better than this is childlessness
    with virtue,
  for in the memory of virtue*a* is
    immortality,
  because it is known both by God and
    by mortals.

2 When it is present, people imitate*b* it,
  and they long for it when it has gone;
  throughout all time it marches,
    crowned in triumph,
  victor in the contest for prizes that
    are undefiled.

3 But the prolific brood of the ungodly
    will be of no use,
  and none of their illegitimate
    seedlings will strike a deep root
  or take a firm hold.

4 For even if they put forth boughs for
    a while,
  standing insecurely they will be
    shaken by the wind,
  and by the violence of the winds they
    will be uprooted.

5 The branches will be broken off
    before they come to maturity,
  and their fruit will be useless,
  not ripe enough to eat, and good for
    nothing.

6 For children born of unlawful unions
  are witnesses of evil against their
    parents when God examines
    them.*c*

7 But the righteous, though they die
    early, will be at rest.

8 For old age is not honoured for
    length of time,
  or measured by number of years;

9 but understanding is grey hair for
    anyone,
  and a blameless life is ripe old age.

10 There were some who pleased God
    and were loved by him,
  and while living among sinners were
    taken up.

11 They were caught up so that evil

might not change their
    understanding
  or guile deceive their souls.

12 For the fascination of wickedness
    obscures what is good,
  and roving desire perverts the
    innocent mind.

13 Being perfected in a short time, they
    fulfilled long years;

14 for their souls were pleasing to the
    Lord,
  therefore he took them quickly from
    the midst of wickedness.

15 Yet the peoples saw and did not
    understand,
  or take such a thing to heart,
  that God's grace and mercy are with
    his elect,
  and that he watches over his holy
    ones.

The Triumph of the Righteous

16 The righteous who have died will
    condemn the ungodly who are
    living,
  and youth that is quickly perfected*d*
    will condemn the prolonged
    old age of the unrighteous.

17 For they will see the end of the wise,
  and will not understand what the
    Lord purposed for them,
  and for what he kept them safe.

18 The unrighteous*e* will see, and will
    have contempt for them,
  but the Lord will laugh them to
    scorn.
  After this they will become
    dishonoured corpses,
  and an outrage among the dead for
    ever;

19 because he will dash them speechless
    to the ground,
  and shake them from the
    foundations;
  they will be left utterly dry and
    barren,
  and they will suffer anguish,
  and the memory of them will perish.

a Gk *it*   *b* Other ancient authorities read *honour*
c Gk *at their examination*   *d* Or *ended*   *e* Gk *They*

The Final Judgement

20 They will come with dread when
   their sins are reckoned up,
and their lawless deeds will convict
   them to their face.

5 Then the righteous will stand with
   great confidence
in the presence of those who have
   oppressed them
and those who make light of their
   labours.

2 When the unrighteous[a] see them,
   they will be shaken with
   dreadful fear,
and they will be amazed at the
   unexpected salvation of the
   righteous.

3 They will speak to one another in
   repentance,
and in anguish of spirit they will
   groan, and say,

4 'These are persons whom we once
   held in derision
and made a byword of reproach—
   fools that we were!
We thought that their lives were
   madness
and that their end was without
   honour.

5 Why have they been numbered
   among the children of God?
And why is their lot among the
   saints?

6 So it was we who strayed from the
   way of truth,
and the light of righteousness did not
   shine on us,
and the sun did not rise upon us.

7 We took our fill of the paths of
   lawlessness and destruction,
and we journeyed through trackless
   deserts,
but the way of the Lord we have not
   known.

8 What has our arrogance profited us?
And what good has our boasted
   wealth brought us?

9 'All those things have vanished like a
   shadow,
and like a rumour that passes by;

10 like a ship that sails through the
   billowy water,
and when it has passed no trace can
   be found,
no track of its keel in the waves;

11 or as, when a bird flies through the
   air,
no evidence of its passage is found;
the light air, lashed by the beat of its
   pinions
and pierced by the force of its rushing
   flight,
is traversed by the movement of its
   wings,
and afterwards no sign of its coming
   is found there;

12 or as, when an arrow is shot at a
   target,
the air, thus divided, comes together
   at once,
so that no one knows its pathway.

13 So we also, as soon as we were born,
   ceased to be,
and we had no sign of virtue to
   show,
but were consumed in our
   wickedness.'

14 Because the hope of the ungodly is
   like thistledown[b] carried by the
   wind,
and like a light frost[c] driven away by
   a storm;
it is dispersed like smoke before the
   wind,
and it passes like the remembrance of
   a guest who stays but a day.

The Reward of the Righteous

15 But the righteous live for ever,
   and their reward is with the Lord;
the Most High takes care of them.

16 Therefore they will receive a glorious
   crown
and a beautiful diadem from the
   hand of the Lord,
because with his right hand he will
   cover them,
and with his arm he will shield them.

a Gk *they*   b Other ancient authorities read *dust*
c Other ancient authorities read *spider's web*

17 The Lord*a* will take his zeal as his
        whole armour,
   and will arm all creation to repel*b* his
        enemies;
18 he will put on righteousness as a
        breastplate,
   and wear impartial justice as a
        helmet;
19 he will take holiness as an invincible
        shield,
20 and sharpen stern wrath for a sword,
   and creation will join with him to
        fight against his frenzied foes.
21 Shafts of lightning will fly with true
        aim,
   and will leap from the clouds to the
        target, as from a well-drawn
        bow,
22 and hailstones full of wrath will be
        hurled as from a catapult;
   the water of the sea will rage against
        them,
   and rivers will relentlessly overwhelm
        them;
23 a mighty wind will rise against them,
   and like a tempest it will winnow
        them away.
   Lawlessness will lay waste the whole
        earth,
   and evildoing will overturn the
        thrones of rulers.

Kings Should Seek Wisdom

6 Listen therefore, O kings, and
    understand;
   learn, O judges of the ends of the
        earth.
2 Give ear, you that rule over
        multitudes,
   and boast of many nations.
3 For your dominion was given you
        from the Lord,
   and your sovereignty from the Most
        High;
   he will search out your works and
        inquire into your plans.
4 Because as servants of his kingdom
        you did not rule rightly,
   or keep the law,
   or walk according to the purpose of
        God,

5 he will come upon you terribly and
        swiftly,
   because severe judgement falls on
        those in high places.
6 For the lowliest may be pardoned in
        mercy,
   but the mighty will be mightily
        tested.
7 For the Lord of all will not stand in
        awe of anyone,
   or show deference to greatness;
   because he himself made both small
        and great,
   and he takes thought for all alike.
8 But a strict inquiry is in store for the
        mighty.
9 To you then, O monarchs, my words
        are directed,
   so that you may learn wisdom and
        not transgress.
10 For they will be made holy who
        observe holy things in holiness,
   and those who have been taught
        them will find a defence.
11 Therefore set your desire on my
        words;
   long for them, and you will be
        instructed.

Description of Wisdom

12 Wisdom is radiant and unfading,
   and she is easily discerned by those
        who love her,
   and is found by those who seek her.
13 She hastens to make herself known to
        those who desire her.
14 One who rises early to seek her will
        have no difficulty,
   for she will be found sitting at the
        gate.
15 To fix one's thought on her is perfect
        understanding,
   and one who is vigilant on her
        account will soon be free from
        care,
16 because she goes about seeking those
        worthy of her,
   and she graciously appears to them
        in their paths,
   and meets them in every thought.

a Gk He   b Or punish

17 The beginning of wisdom*a* is the
    most sincere desire for
    instruction,
  and concern for instruction is love of
    her,
18 and love of her is the keeping of her
    laws,
  and giving heed to her laws is
    assurance of immortality,
19 and immortality brings one near to
    God;
20 so the desire for wisdom leads to a
    kingdom.

21 Therefore if you delight in thrones
    and sceptres, O monarchs over
    the peoples,
  honour wisdom, so that you may
    reign for ever.
22 I will tell you what wisdom is and
    how she came to be,
  and I will hide no secrets from you,
  but I will trace her course from the
    beginning of creation,
  and make knowledge of her clear,
  and I will not pass by the truth;
23 nor will I travel in the company of
    sickly envy,
  for envy*b* does not associate with
    wisdom.
24 The multitude of the wise is the
    salvation of the world,
  and a sensible king is the stability of
    any people.
25 Therefore be instructed by my words,
    and you will profit.

Solomon Like Other Mortals

7 I also am mortal, like everyone else,
    a descendant of the first-formed child
    of earth;
  and in the womb of a mother I was
    moulded into flesh,
2 within the period of ten months,
    compacted with blood,
  from the seed of a man and the
    pleasure of marriage.
3 And when I was born, I began to
    breathe the common air,
  and fell upon the kindred earth;

my first sound was a cry, as is true of
    all.
4 I was nursed with care in swaddling
    cloths.
5 For no king has had a different
    beginning of existence;
6 there is for all one entrance into life,
    and one way out.

Solomon's Respect for Wisdom

7 Therefore I prayed, and
    understanding was given me;
  I called on God, and the spirit of
    wisdom came to me.
8 I preferred her to sceptres and
    thrones,
  and I accounted wealth as nothing in
    comparison with her.
9 Neither did I liken to her any
    priceless gem,
  because all gold is but a little sand in
    her sight,
  and silver will be accounted as clay
    before her.
10 I loved her more than health and
    beauty,
  and I chose to have her rather than
    light,
  because her radiance never ceases.
11 All good things came to me along
    with her,
  and in her hands uncounted wealth.
12 I rejoiced in them all, because
    wisdom leads them;
  but I did not know that she was their
    mother.
13 I learned without guile and I impart
    without grudging;
  I do not hide her wealth,
14 for it is an unfailing treasure for
    mortals;
  those who get it obtain friendship
    with God,
  commended for the gifts that come
    from instruction.

Solomon Prays for Wisdom

15 May God grant me to speak with
    judgement,

a Gk *Her beginning*   *b* Gk *this*

and to have thoughts worthy of what
   I have received;
for he is the guide even of wisdom
   and the corrector of the wise.
16 For both we and our words are in his
      hand,
   as are all understanding and skill in
      crafts.
17 For it is he who gave me unerring
      knowledge of what exists,
   to know the structure of the world
      and the activity of the elements;
18 the beginning and end and middle of
      times,
   the alternations of the solstices and
      the changes of the seasons,
19 the cycles of the year and the
      constellations of the stars,
20 the natures of animals and the
      tempers of wild animals,
   the powers of spirits*a* and the
      thoughts of human beings,
   the varieties of plants and the virtues
      of roots;
21 I learned both what is secret and
      what is manifest,
22 for wisdom, the fashioner of all
      things, taught me.

The Nature of Wisdom

There is in her a spirit that is
      intelligent, holy,
unique, manifold, subtle,
mobile, clear, unpolluted,
distinct, invulnerable, loving the
      good, keen,
irresistible, 23 beneficent, humane,
steadfast, sure, free from anxiety,
all-powerful, overseeing all,
and penetrating through all spirits
that are intelligent, pure, and
      altogether subtle.
24 For wisdom is more mobile than any
      motion;
   because of her pureness she pervades
      and penetrates all things.
25 For she is a breath of the power of
      God,
   and a pure emanation of the glory of
      the Almighty;

therefore nothing defiled gains
      entrance into her.
26 For she is a reflection of eternal light,
   a spotless mirror of the working of
      God,
   and an image of his goodness.
27 Although she is but one, she can do
      all things,
   and while remaining in herself, she
      renews all things;
   in every generation she passes into
      holy souls
   and makes them friends of God, and
      prophets;
28 for God loves nothing so much as the
      person who lives with wisdom.
29 She is more beautiful than the sun,
   and excels every constellation of the
      stars.
   Compared with the light she is found
      to be superior,
30 for it is succeeded by the night,
   but against wisdom evil does not
      prevail.

8 She reaches mightily from one end
      of the earth to the other,
   and she orders all things well.

Solomon's Love for Wisdom

2 I loved her and sought her from my
      youth;
   I desired to take her for my bride,
   and became enamoured of her
      beauty.
3 She glorifies her noble birth by living
      with God,
   and the Lord of all loves her.
4 For she is an initiate in the
      knowledge of God,
   and an associate in his works.
5 If riches are a desirable possession in
      life,
   what is richer than wisdom, the
      active cause of all things?
6 And if understanding is effective,
   who more than she is fashioner of
      what exists?
7 And if anyone loves righteousness,
   her labours are virtues;

a Or *winds*

for she teaches self-control and
    prudence,
justice and courage;
nothing in life is more profitable for
    mortals than these.

8 And if anyone longs for wide
    experience,
she knows the things of old, and
    infers the things to come;
she understands turns of speech and
    the solutions of riddles;
she has foreknowledge of signs and
    wonders
and of the outcome of seasons and
    times.

Wisdom Indispensable to Rulers

9 Therefore I determined to take her to
    live with me,
knowing that she would give me
    good counsel
and encouragement in cares and
    grief.
10 Because of her I shall have glory
    among the multitudes
and honour in the presence of the
    elders, though I am young.
11 I shall be found keen in judgement,
and in the sight of rulers I shall be
    admired.
12 When I am silent they will wait for
    me,
and when I speak they will give heed;
if I speak at greater length,
they will put their hands on their
    mouths.
13 Because of her I shall have
    immortality,
and leave an everlasting
    remembrance to those who
    come after me.
14 I shall govern peoples,
and nations will be subject to me;
15 dread monarchs will be afraid of me
    when they hear of me;
among the people I shall show myself
    capable, and courageous in war.
16 When I enter my house, I shall find
    rest with her;
for companionship with her has no
    bitterness,

and life with her has no pain, but
    gladness and joy.
17 When I considered these things
    inwardly,
and pondered in my heart
that in kinship with wisdom there is
    immortality,
18 and in friendship with her, pure
    delight,
and in the labours of her hands,
    unfailing wealth,
and in the experience of her
    company, understanding,
and renown in sharing her words,
I went about seeking how to get her
    for myself.
19 As a child I was naturally gifted,
and a good soul fell to my lot;
20 or rather, being good, I entered an
    undefiled body.
21 But I perceived that I would not
    possess wisdom unless God
    gave her to me—
and it was a mark of insight to know
    whose gift she was—
so I appealed to the Lord and
    implored him,
and with my whole heart I said:

Solomon's Prayer for Wisdom

9 'O God of my ancestors and Lord of
    mercy,
who have made all things by your
    word,
2 and by your wisdom have formed
    humankind
to have dominion over the creatures
    you have made,
3 and rule the world in holiness and
    righteousness,
and pronounce judgement in
    uprightness of soul,
4 give me the wisdom that sits by your
    throne,
and do not reject me from among
    your servants.
5 For I am your servant,[a] the son of
    your servant-girl,
a man who is weak and short-lived,

a Gk *slave*

with little understanding of
    judgement and laws;
6 for even one who is perfect among
    human beings
will be regarded as nothing without
    the wisdom that comes from
    you.
7 You have chosen me to be king of
    your people
and to be judge over your sons and
    daughters.
8 You have given command to build a
    temple on your holy mountain,
and an altar in the city of your
    habitation,
a copy of the holy tent that you
    prepared from the beginning.
9 With you is wisdom, she who knows
    your works
and was present when you made the
    world;
she understands what is pleasing in
    your sight
and what is right according to your
    commandments.
10 Send her forth from the holy heavens,
and from the throne of your glory
    send her,
that she may labour at my side,
and that I may learn what is pleasing
    to you.
11 For she knows and understands all
    things,
and she will guide me wisely in my
    actions
and guard me with her glory.
12 Then my works will be acceptable,
and I shall judge your people justly,
and shall be worthy of the throne*a* of
    my father.
13 For who can learn the counsel of
    God?
Or who can discern what the Lord
    wills?
14 For the reasoning of mortals is
    worthless,
and our designs are likely to fail;
15 for a perishable body weighs down
    the soul,
and this earthy tent burdens the
    thoughtful*b* mind.

16 We can hardly guess at what is on
    earth,
and what is at hand we find with
    labour;
but who has traced out what is in the
    heavens?
17 Who has learned your counsel,
unless you have given wisdom
and sent your holy spirit from on
    high?
18 And thus the paths of those on earth
    were set right,
and people were taught what pleases
    you,
and were saved by wisdom.'

The Work of Wisdom from Adam to Moses

10 Wisdom*c* protected the first-formed father of the world,
    when he alone had been
    created;
she delivered him from his
    transgression,
2 and gave him strength to rule all
    things.
3 But when an unrighteous man
    departed from her in his anger,
he perished because in rage he killed
    his brother.
4 When the earth was flooded because
    of him, wisdom again saved it,
steering the righteous man by a paltry
    piece of wood.

5 Wisdom*c* also, when the nations in
    wicked agreement had been put
    to confusion,
recognized the righteous man and
    preserved him blameless before
    God,
and kept him strong in the face of his
    compassion for his child.

6 Wisdom*c* rescued a righteous man
    when the ungodly were
    perishing;
he escaped the fire that descended on
    the Five Cities.*d*

a Gk *thrones*   *b* Or *anxious*   *c* Gk *She*   *d* Or *on Pentapolis*

7 Evidence of their wickedness still
remains:
a continually smoking waste-land,
plants bearing fruit that does not
ripen,
and a pillar of salt standing as a
monument to an unbelieving
soul.
8 For because they passed wisdom by,
they not only were hindered from
recognizing the good,
but also left for humankind a
reminder of their folly,
so that their failures could never go
unnoticed.

9 Wisdom rescued from troubles those
who served her.
10 When a righteous man fled from his
brother's wrath,
she guided him on straight paths;
she showed him the kingdom of
God,
and gave him knowledge of holy
things;
she prospered him in his labours,
and increased the fruit of his toil.
11 When his oppressors were covetous,
she stood by him and made him rich.
12 She protected him from his enemies,
and kept him safe from those who
lay in wait for him;
in his arduous contest she gave him
the victory,
so that he might learn that godliness
is more powerful than anything
else.

13 When a righteous man was sold,
wisdom[a] did not desert him,
but delivered him from sin.
She descended with him into the
dungeon,
14 and when he was in prison she did
not leave him,
until she brought him the sceptre of a
kingdom
and authority over his masters.
Those who accused him she showed
to be false,
and she gave him everlasting honour.

Wisdom Led the Israelites out of Egypt

15 A holy people and blameless race
wisdom delivered from a nation of
oppressors.
16 She entered the soul of a servant of
the Lord,
and withstood dread kings with
wonders and signs.
17 She gave to holy people the reward of
their labours;
she guided them along a marvellous
way,
and became a shelter to them by day,
and a starry flame through the night.
18 She brought them over the Red Sea,
and led them through deep waters;
19 but she drowned their enemies,
and cast them up from the depths of
the sea.
20 Therefore the righteous plundered
the ungodly;
they sang hymns, O Lord, to your
holy name,
and praised with one accord your
defending hand;
21 for wisdom opened the mouths of
those who were mute,
and made the tongues of infants
speak clearly.

*Wisdom Led the Israelites through
the Desert*

11 Wisdom[b] prospered their works
by the hand of a holy prophet.
2 They journeyed through an
uninhabited wilderness,
and pitched their tents in untrodden
places.
3 They withstood their enemies and
fought off their foes.
4 When they were thirsty, they called
upon you,
and water was given them out of
flinty rock,
and from hard stone a remedy for
their thirst.
5 For through the very things by which
their enemies were punished,

a Gk *she*   *b* Gk *She*

they themselves received benefit in
their need.

6 Instead of the fountain of an ever-
flowing river,
stirred up and defiled with blood

7 in rebuke for the decree to kill the
infants,
you gave them abundant water
unexpectedly,

8 showing by their thirst at that time
how you punished their enemies.

9 For when they were tried, though
they were being disciplined in
mercy,
they learned how the ungodly were
tormented when judged in
wrath.

10 For you tested them as a parent *a* does
in warning,
but you examined the ungodly *b* as a
stern king does in
condemnation.

11 Whether absent or present, they were
equally distressed,

12 for a twofold grief possessed them,
and a groaning at the memory of
what had occurred.

13 For when they heard that through
their own punishments
the righteous *c* had received benefit,
they perceived it was the Lord's
doing.

14 For though they had mockingly
rejected him who long before
had been cast out and exposed,
at the end of the events they
marvelled at him,
when they felt thirst in a different
way from the righteous.

Punishment of the Wicked

15 In return for their foolish and wicked
thoughts,
which led them astray to worship
irrational serpents and
worthless animals,
you sent upon them a multitude of
irrational creatures to punish
them,

16 so that they might learn that one is

punished by the very things by
which one sins.

17 For your all-powerful hand,
which created the world out of
formless matter,
did not lack the means to send upon
them a multitude of bears, or
bold lions,

18 or newly-created unknown beasts full
of rage,
or such as breathe out fiery breath,
or belch forth a thick pall of smoke,
or flash terrible sparks from their eyes;

19 not only could the harm they did
destroy people, *d*
but the mere sight of them could kill
by fright.

20 Even apart from these, people *c* could
fall at a single breath
when pursued by justice
and scattered by the breath of your
power.
But you have arranged all things by
measure and number and
weight.

God Is Powerful and Merciful

21 For it is always in your power to show
great strength,
and who can withstand the might of
your arm?

22 Because the whole world before you
is like a speck that tips the
scales,
and like a drop of morning dew that
falls on the ground.

23 But you are merciful to all, for you
can do all things,
and you overlook people's sins, so
that they may repent.

24 For you love all things that exist,
and detest none of the things that
you have made,
for you would not have made
anything if you had hated it.

25 How would anything have endured if
you had not willed it?
Or how would anything not called
forth by you have been
preserved?

a Gk *a father*   *b* Gk *those*   *c* Gk *they*   *d* Gk *them*

26 You spare all things, for they are
    yours, O Lord, you who love
    the living.

12 For your immortal spirit is in all
    things.

2 Therefore you correct little by little
    those who trespass,
  and you remind and warn them of
    the things through which they
    sin,
  so that they may be freed from
    wickedness and put their trust
    in you, O Lord.

The Sins of the Canaanites

3 Those who lived long ago in your
    holy land
4 you hated for their detestable
    practices,
  their works of sorcery and unholy
    rites,
5 their merciless slaughter[a] of children,
  and their sacrificial feasting on
    human flesh and blood.
  These initiates from the midst of a
    heathen cult,[b]
6 these parents who murder helpless
    lives,
  you willed to destroy by the hands of
    our ancestors,
7 so that the land most precious of all
    to you
  might receive a worthy colony of the
    servants[c] of God.
8 But even these you spared, since they
    were but mortals,
  and sent wasps[d] as forerunners of
    your army
  to destroy them little by little,
9 though you were not unable to give
    the ungodly into the hands of
    the righteous in battle,
  or to destroy them at one blow by
    dread wild animals or your
    stern word.
10 But judging them little by little you
    gave them an opportunity to
    repent,
  though you were not unaware that
    their origin[e] was evil
  and their wickedness inborn,

and that their way of thinking would
    never change.
11 For they were an accursed race from
    the beginning,
  and it was not through fear of anyone
    that you left them unpunished
    for their sins.

God Is Sovereign

12 For who will say, 'What have you
    done?'
  or will resist your judgement?
  Who will accuse you for the
    destruction of nations that you
    made?
  Or who will come before you to
    plead as an advocate for the
    unrighteous?
13 For neither is there any god besides
    you, whose care is for all
    people,[f]
  to whom you should prove that you
    have not judged unjustly;
14 nor can any king or monarch
    confront you about those
    whom you have punished.
15 You are righteous and you rule all
    things righteously,
  deeming it alien to your power
  to condemn anyone who does not
    deserve to be punished.
16 For your strength is the source of
    righteousness,
  and your sovereignty over all causes
    you to spare all.
17 For you show your strength when
    people doubt the completeness
    of your power,
  and you rebuke any insolence among
    those who know it.[b]
18 Although you are sovereign in
    strength, you judge with
    mildness,
  and with great forbearance you
    govern us;
  for you have power to act whenever
    you choose.

a Gk slaughterers b Meaning of Gk uncertain
c Or children d Or hornets e Or nature f Or all
things

God's Lessons for Israel

19 Through such works you have taught
      your people
   that the righteous must be kind,
   and you have filled your children
      with good hope,
   because you give repentance for sins.
20 For if you punished with such great
      care and indulgence[a]
   the enemies of your servants[b] and
      those deserving of death,
   granting them time and opportunity
      to give up their wickedness,
21 with what strictness you have judged
      your children,
   to whose ancestors you gave oaths
      and covenants full of good
      promises!
22 So while chastening us you scourge
      our enemies ten thousand times
      more,
   so that, when we judge, we may
      meditate upon your goodness,
   and when we are judged, we may
      expect mercy.

The Punishment of the Egyptians

23 Therefore those who lived
      unrighteously, in a life of folly,
   you tormented through their own
      abominations.
24 For they went far astray on the paths
      of error,
   accepting as gods those animals that
      even their enemies[c] despised;
   they were deceived like foolish
      infants.
25 Therefore, as though to children who
      cannot reason,
   you sent your judgement to mock
      them.
26 But those who have not heeded the
      warning of mild rebukes
   will experience the deserved
      judgement of God.
27 For when in their suffering they
      became incensed
   at those creatures that they had
      thought to be gods, being
      punished by means of them,
   they saw and recognized as the true

God the one whom they had
      before refused to know.
   Therefore the utmost condemnation
      came upon them.

The Foolishness of Nature Worship

13 For all people who were
      ignorant of God were foolish by
      nature;
   and they were unable from the good
      things that are seen to know the
      one who exists,
   nor did they recognize the artisan
      while paying heed to his works;
2 but they supposed that either fire or
      wind or swift air,
   or the circle of the stars, or turbulent
      water,
   or the luminaries of heaven were the
      gods that rule the world.
3 If through delight in the beauty of
      these things people assumed
      them to be gods,
   let them know how much better than
      these is their Lord,
   for the author of beauty created
      them.
4 And if people[c] were amazed at their
      power and working,
   let them perceive from them
   how much more powerful is the one
      who formed them.
5 For from the greatness and beauty of
      created things
   comes a corresponding perception of
      their Creator.
6 Yet these people are little to be
      blamed,
   for perhaps they go astray
   while seeking God and desiring to
      find him.
7 For while they live among his works,
      they keep searching,
   and they trust in what they see,
      because the things that are seen
      are beautiful.
8 Yet again, not even they are to be
      excused;

a Other ancient authorities lack and indulgence; others
read and entreaty   b Or children   c Gk they

9 for if they had the power to know so
  much
   that they could investigate the world,
   how did they fail to find sooner the
    Lord of these things?

The Foolishness of Idolatry

10 But miserable, with their hopes set
   on dead things, are those
   who give the name 'gods' to the
    works of human hands,
   gold and silver fashioned with skill,
   and likenesses of animals,
   or a useless stone, the work of an
    ancient hand.
11 A skilled woodcutter may saw down a
   tree easy to handle
   and skilfully strip off all its bark,
   and then with pleasing workmanship
   make a useful vessel that serves life's
    needs,
12 and burn the cast-off pieces of his
   work
   to prepare his food, and eat his fill.
13 But a cast-off piece from among
   them, useful for nothing,
   a stick crooked and full of knots,
   he takes and carves with care in his
    leisure,
   and shapes it with skill gained in
    idleness;[a]
   he forms it in the likeness of a
    human being,
14 or makes it like some worthless
   animal,
   giving it a coat of red paint and
    colouring its surface red
   and covering every blemish in it with
    paint;
15 then he makes a suitable niche for it,
   and sets it in the wall, and fastens it
    there with iron.
16 He takes thought for it, so that it may
   not fall,
   because he knows that it cannot help
    itself,
   for it is only an image and has need
    of help.
17 When he prays about possessions and
   his marriage and children,

he is not ashamed to address a
 lifeless thing.
18 For health he appeals to a thing that
   is weak;
   for life he prays to a thing that is
    dead;
   for aid he entreats a thing that is
    utterly inexperienced;
   for a prosperous journey, a thing that
    cannot take a step;
19 for money-making and work and
   success with his hands
   he asks strength of a thing whose
    hands have no strength.

Folly of a Navigator Praying to an Idol

14 Again, one preparing to sail and
   about to voyage over raging
   waves
   calls upon a piece of wood more
    fragile than the ship that carries
    him.
2 For it was desire for gain that
   planned that vessel,
   and wisdom was the artisan who
    built it;
3 but it is your providence, O Father,
   that steers its course,
   because you have given it a path in
    the sea,
   and a safe way through the waves,
4 showing that you can save from every
   danger,
   so that even a person who lacks skill
    may put to sea.
5 It is your will that works of your
   wisdom should not be without
    effect;
   therefore people trust their lives even
    to the smallest piece of wood,
   and passing through the billows on a
    raft they come safely to land.
6 For even in the beginning, when
   arrogant giants were perishing,
   the hope of the world took refuge on
    a raft,
   and guided by your hand left to the
    world the seed of a new
    generation.

a Other ancient authorities read *with intelligent skill*

7 For blessed is the wood by which
    righteousness comes.

8 But the idol made with hands is
      accursed, and so is the one who
      made it—
  he for having made it, and the
      perishable thing because it was
      named a god.
9 For equally hateful to God are the
      ungodly and their ungodliness;
10 for what was done will be punished
      together with the one who did
      it.
11 Therefore there will be a visitation
      also upon the heathen idols,
  because, though part of what God
      created, they became an
      abomination,
  snares for human souls
  and a trap for the feet of the foolish.

The Origin and Evils of Idolatry

12 For the idea of making idols was the
      beginning of fornication,
  and the invention of them was the
      corruption of life;
13 for they did not exist from the
      beginning,
  nor will they last for ever.
14 For through human vanity they
      entered the world,
  and therefore their speedy end has
      been planned.

15 For a father, consumed with grief at
      an untimely bereavement,
  made an image of his child, who had
      been suddenly taken from him;
  he now honoured as a god what was
      once a dead human being,
  and handed on to his dependants
      secret rites and initiations.
16 Then the ungodly custom, grown
      strong with time, was kept as a
      law,
  and at the command of monarchs
      carved images were worshipped.
17 When people could not honour
      monarchs[a] in their presence,
      since they lived at a distance,

they imagined their appearance far
      away,
  and made a visible image of the king
      whom they honoured,
  so that by their zeal they might flatter
      the absent one as though
      present.

18 Then the ambition of the artisan
      impelled
  even those who did not know the
      king to intensify their worship.
19 For he, perhaps wishing to please his
      ruler,
  skilfully forced the likeness to take
      more beautiful form,
20 and the multitude, attracted by the
      charm of his work,
  now regarded as an object of worship
      the one whom shortly before
      they had honoured as a human
      being.
21 And this became a hidden trap for
      humankind,
  because people, in bondage to
      misfortune or to royal
      authority,
  bestowed on objects of stone or
      wood the name that ought not
      to be shared.

22 Then it was not enough for them to
      err about the knowledge of
      God,
  but though living in great strife due
      to ignorance,
  they call such great evils peace.
23 For whether they kill children in their
      initiations, or celebrate secret
      mysteries,
  or hold frenzied revels with strange
      customs,
24 they no longer keep either their lives
      or their marriages pure,
  but they either treacherously kill one
      another, or grieve one another
      by adultery,
25 and all is a raging riot of blood and
      murder, theft and deceit,

a Gk them

corruption, faithlessness,
tumult, perjury,
26 confusion over what is good,
forgetfulness of favours,
defiling of souls, sexual perversion,
disorder in marriages, adultery, and
debauchery.
27 For the worship of idols not to be
named
is the beginning and cause and end
of every evil.
28 For their worshippers*a* either rave in
exultation,
or prophesy lies, or live
unrighteously, or readily
commit perjury;
29 for because they trust in lifeless idols
they swear wicked oaths and expect
to suffer no harm.
30 But just penalties will overtake them
on two counts:
because they thought wrongly about
God in devoting themselves to
idols,
and because in deceit they swore
unrighteously through
contempt for holiness.
31 For it is not the power of the things
by which people swear,*b*
but the just penalty for those who
sin,
that always pursues the transgression
of the unrighteous.

Benefits of Worshipping the True God

15 But you, our God, are kind and
true,
patient, and ruling all things*c* in
mercy.
2 For even if we sin we are yours,
knowing your power;
but we will not sin, because we know
that you acknowledge us as
yours.
3 For to know you is complete
righteousness,
and to know your power is the root
of immortality.
4 For neither has the evil intent of
human art misled us,
nor the fruitless toil of painters,

a figure stained with varied colours,
5 whose appearance arouses yearning
in fools,
so that they desire*d* the lifeless form
of a dead image.
6 Lovers of evil things and fit for such
objects of hope*e*
are those who either make or desire
or worship them.

The Foolishness of Worshipping
Clay Idols

7 A potter kneads the soft earth
and laboriously moulds each vessel
for our service,
fashioning out of the same clay
both the vessels that serve clean uses
and those for contrary uses, making
all alike;
but which shall be the use of each of
them
the worker in clay decides.
8 With misspent toil, these workers
form a futile god from the same
clay—
these mortals who were made of
earth a short time before
and after a little while go to the earth
from which all mortals are
taken,
when the time comes to return the
souls that were borrowed.
9 But the workers are not concerned
that mortals are destined to die
or that their life is brief,
but they compete with workers in
gold and silver,
and imitate workers in copper;
and they count it a glorious thing to
mould counterfeit gods.
10 Their heart is ashes, their hope is
cheaper than dirt,
and their lives are of less worth than
clay,
11 because they failed to know the one
who formed them
and inspired them with active souls
and breathed a living spirit into
them.

a Gk *they*   *b* Or *of the oaths people swear*   *c* Or *ruling*
the universe   *d* Gk *and he desires*   *e* Gk *such hopes*

12 But they considered our existence an
      idle game,
   and life a festival held for profit,
   for they say one must get money
      however one can, even by base
      means.
13 For these people, more than all
      others, know that they sin
   when they make from earthy matter
      fragile vessels and carved
      images.

14 But most foolish, and more
      miserable than an infant,
   are all the enemies who oppressed
      your people.
15 For they thought that all their
      heathen idols were gods,
   though these have neither the use of
      their eyes to see with,
   nor nostrils with which to draw
      breath,
   nor ears with which to hear,
   nor fingers to feel with,
   and their feet are of no use for
      walking.
16 For a human being made them,
   and one whose spirit is borrowed
      formed them;
   for none can form gods that are like
      themselves.
17 People are mortal, and what they
      make with lawless hands is
      dead;
   for they are better than the objects
      they worship,
   since *a* they have life, but the idols *b*
      never had.

Serpents in the Desert

18 Moreover, they worship even the
      most hateful animals,
   which are worse than all others when
      judged by their lack of
      intelligence;
19 and even as animals they are not so
      beautiful in appearance that
      one would desire them,
   but they have escaped both the praise
      of God and his blessing.

16 Therefore those people *c* were
      deservedly punished through
      such creatures,
   and were tormented by a multitude
      of animals.
2 Instead of this punishment you
      showed kindness to your
      people,
   and you prepared quails to eat,
   a delicacy to satisfy the desire of
      appetite;
3 in order that those people, when they
      desired food,
   might lose the least remnant of
      appetite *d*
   because of the odious creatures sent
      to them,
   while your people, *c* after suffering
      want a short time,
   might partake of delicacies.
4 For it was necessary that upon those
      oppressors inescapable want
      should come,
   while to these others it was merely
      shown how their enemies were
      being tormented.

5 For when the terrible rage of wild
      animals came upon your
      people *e*
   and they were being destroyed by the
      bites of writhing serpents,
   your wrath did not continue to the
      end;
6 they were troubled for a little while
      as a warning,
   and received a symbol of deliverance
      to remind them of your law's
      command.

7 For the one who turned towards it
      was saved, not by the thing that
      was beheld,
   but by you, the Saviour of all.
8 And by this also you convinced our
      enemies
   that it is you who deliver from every
      evil.

*a Other ancient authorities read of which   b Gk but
they   c Gk they   d Gk loathed the necessary appetite
e Gk them*

9 For they were killed by the bites of
         locusts and flies,
   and no healing was found for them,
   because they deserved to be punished
         by such things.
10 But your children were not
         conquered even by the fangs of
         venomous serpents,
   for your mercy came to their help
         and healed them.
11 To remind them of your oracles they
         were bitten,
   and then were quickly delivered,
   so that they would not fall into deep
         forgetfulness
   and become unresponsive*a* to your
         kindness.
12 For neither herb nor poultice cured
         them,
   but it was your word, O Lord, that
         heals all people.
13 For you have power over life and
         death;
   you lead mortals down to the gates of
         Hades and back again.
14 A person in wickedness kills another,
   but cannot bring back the departed
         spirit,
   or set free the imprisoned soul.

Disastrous Storms Strike Egypt

15 To escape from your hand is
         impossible;
16 for the ungodly, refusing to know
         you,
   were flogged by the strength of your
         arm,
   pursued by unusual rains and hail
         and relentless storms,
   and utterly consumed by fire.
17 For—most incredible of all—in water,
         which quenches all things,
   the fire had still greater effect,
   for the universe defends the
         righteous.
18 At one time the flame was restrained,
   so that it might not consume the
         creatures sent against the
         ungodly,
   but that seeing this they might know

that they were being pursued by the
         judgement of God;
19 and at another time even in the midst
         of water it burned more
         intensely than fire,
   to destroy the crops of the
         unrighteous land.

The Israelites Receive Manna

20 Instead of these things you gave your
         people food of angels,
   and without their toil you supplied
         them from heaven with bread
         ready to eat,
   providing every pleasure and suited
         to every taste.
21 For your sustenance manifested your
         sweetness towards your
         children;
   and the bread, ministering*b* to the
         desire of the one who took it,
   was changed to suit everyone's liking.
22 Snow and ice withstood fire without
         melting,
   so that they might know that the
         crops of their enemies
   were being destroyed by the fire that
         blazed in the hail
   and flashed in the showers of rain;
23 whereas the fire,*c* in order that the
         righteous might be fed,
   even forgot its native power.

24 For creation, serving you who made
         it,
   exerts itself to punish the
         unrighteous,
   and in kindness relaxes on behalf of
         those who trust in you.
25 Therefore at that time also, changed
         into all forms,
   it served your all-nourishing bounty,
   according to the desire of those who
         had need,*d*
26 so that your children, whom you
         loved, O Lord, might learn
   that it is not the production of crops
         that feeds humankind

---

a Meaning of Gk uncertain   *b* Gk *and it, ministering*
c Gk *this*   *d* Or *who made supplication*

but that your word sustains those
  who trust in you.

27 For what was not destroyed by fire
  was melted when simply warmed by
    a fleeting ray of the sun,

28 to make it known that one must rise
    before the sun to give you
    thanks,
  and must pray to you at the dawning
    of the light;

29 for the hope of an ungrateful person
    will melt like wintry frost,
  and flow away like waste water.

Terror Strikes the Egyptians at Night

17 Great are your judgements and
  hard to describe;
therefore uninstructed souls have
    gone astray.

2 For when lawless people supposed
    that they held the holy nation
    in their power,
  they themselves lay as captives of
    darkness and prisoners of long
    night,
  shut in under their roofs, exiles from
    eternal providence.

3 For thinking that in their secret sins
    they were unobserved
  behind a dark curtain of
    forgetfulness,
  they were scattered, terribly*a* alarmed,
  and appalled by spectres.

4 For not even the inner chamber that
    held them protected them from
    fear,
  but terrifying sounds rang out around
    them,
  and dismal phantoms with gloomy
    faces appeared.

5 And no power of fire was able to give
    light,
  nor did the brilliant flames of the
    stars
  avail to illumine that hateful night.

6 Nothing was shining through to
    them
  except a dreadful, self-kindled fire,
  and in terror they deemed the things
    that they saw

to be worse than that unseen
    appearance.

7 The delusions of their magic art lay
    humbled,
  and their boasted wisdom was
    scornfully rebuked.

8 For those who promised to drive off
    the fears and disorders of a sick
    soul
  were sick themselves with ridiculous
    fear.

9 For even if nothing disturbing
    frightened them,
  yet, scared by the passing of wild
    animals and the hissing of
    snakes

10 they perished in trembling fear,
  refusing to look even at the air,
    though it nowhere could be
    avoided.

11 For wickedness is a cowardly thing,
    condemned by its own
    testimony;*b*
  distressed by conscience, it has always
    exaggerated*c* the difficulties.

12 For fear is nothing but a giving up of
    the helps that come from
    reason;

13 and hope, defeated by this inward
    weakness,
  prefers ignorance of what causes the
    torment.

14 But throughout the night, which was
    really powerless
  and which came upon them from the
    recesses of powerless Hades,
  they all slept the same sleep,

15 and now were driven by monstrous
    spectres,
  and now were paralysed by their
    souls' surrender;
  for sudden and unexpected fear
    overwhelmed them.

16 And whoever was there fell down,
  and thus was kept shut up in a prison
    not made of iron;

17 for whether they were farmers or
    shepherds

*a Other ancient authorities read unobserved, they were
darkened behind a dark curtain of forgetfulness, terribly
b Meaning of Gk uncertain   c Other ancient
authorities read anticipated*

or workers who toiled in the
wilderness,
they were seized, and endured the
inescapable fate;
for with one chain of darkness they
all were bound.

18 Whether there came a whistling
wind,
or a melodious sound of birds in
wide-spreading branches,
or the rhythm of violently rushing
water,

19 or the harsh crash of rocks hurled
down,
or the unseen running of leaping
animals,
or the sound of the most savage
roaring beasts,
or an echo thrown back from a
hollow of the mountains,
it paralysed them with terror.

20 For the whole world was illumined
with brilliant light,
and went about its work
unhindered,

21 while over those people alone heavy
night was spread,
an image of the darkness that was
destined to receive them;
but still heavier than darkness were
they to themselves.

Light Shines on the Israelites

18 But for your holy ones there was
very great light.
Their enemies[a] heard their voices but
did not see their forms,
and counted them happy for not
having suffered,

2 and were thankful that your holy
ones,[b] though previously
wronged, were doing them no
injury;
and they begged their pardon for
having been at variance with
them.[b]

3 Therefore you provided a flaming
pillar of fire
as a guide for your people's[c]
unknown journey,

and a harmless sun for their glorious
wandering.

4 For their enemies[d] deserved to be
deprived of light and
imprisoned in darkness,
those who had kept your children
imprisoned,
through whom the imperishable light
of the law was to be given to
the world.

The Death of the Egyptian Firstborn

5 When they had resolved to kill the
infants of your holy ones,
and one child had been abandoned
and rescued,
you in punishment took away a
multitude of their children;
and you destroyed them all together
by a mighty flood.

6 That night was made known
beforehand to our ancestors,
so that they might rejoice in sure
knowledge of the oaths in
which they trusted.

7 The deliverance of the righteous and
the destruction of their
enemies
were expected by your people.

8 For by the same means by which you
punished our enemies
you called us to yourself and glorified
us.

9 For in secret the holy children of
good people offered sacrifices,
and with one accord agreed to the
divine law,
so that the saints would share alike
the same things,
both blessings and dangers;
and already they were singing the
praises of the ancestors.[e]

10 But the discordant cry of their
enemies echoed back,
and their piteous lament for their
children was spread abroad.

11 The slave was punished with the
same penalty as the master,

---

a Gk *They*   b Meaning of Gk uncertain   c Gk *their*
d Gk *those persons*   e Other ancient authorities read
dangers, the ancestors already leading the songs of praise

and the commoner suffered the same
loss as the king;

12 and they all together, by one form[a] of
death,
had corpses too many to count.
For the living were not sufficient even
to bury them,
since in one instant their most valued
children had been destroyed.

13 For though they had disbelieved
everything because of their
magic arts,
yet, when their firstborn were
destroyed, they acknowledged
your people to be God's child.

14 For while gentle silence enveloped all
things,
and night in its swift course was now
half gone,

15 your all-powerful word leapt from
heaven, from the royal throne,
into the midst of the land that was
doomed,
a stern warrior

16 carrying the sharp sword of your
authentic command,
and stood and filled all things with
death,
and touched heaven while standing
on the earth.

17 Then at once apparitions in dreadful
dreams greatly troubled them,
and unexpected fears assailed them;

18 and one here and another there,
hurled down half dead,
made known why they were dying;

19 for the dreams that disturbed them
forewarned them of this,
so that they might not perish without
knowing why they suffered.

Threat of Annihilation in the Desert

20 The experience of death touched also
the righteous,
and a plague came upon the
multitude in the desert,
but the wrath did not long
continue.

21 For a blameless man was quick to act
as their champion;

he brought forward the shield of his
ministry,
prayer and propitiation by incense;
he withstood the anger and put an
end to the disaster,
showing that he was your servant.

22 He conquered the wrath[b] not by
strength of body,
not by force of arms,
but by his word he subdued the
avenger,
appealing to the oaths and covenants
given to our ancestors.

23 For when the dead had already fallen
on one another in heaps,
he intervened and held back the
wrath,
and cut off its way to the living.

24 For on his long robe the whole world
was depicted,
and the glories of the ancestors were
engraved on the four rows of
stones,
and your majesty was on the diadem
upon his head.

25 To these the destroyer yielded, these
he[c] feared;
for merely to test the wrath was
enough.

The Red Sea

19 But the ungodly were assailed to
the end by pitiless anger,
for God[d] knew in advance even their
future actions:

2 how, though they themselves had
permitted[e] your people to
depart
and hastily sent them out,
they would change their minds and
pursue them.

3 For while they were still engaged in
mourning,
and were lamenting at the graves of
their dead,
they reached another foolish
decision,

a Gk *name*   *b* Cn: Gk *multitude*   *c* Other ancient
authorities read *they*   *d* Gk *he*   *e* Other ancient
authorities read *had changed their minds to permit*

and pursued as fugitives those whom
they had begged and compelled
to leave.

4 For the fate they deserved drew them
on to this end,
and made them forget what had
happened,
in order that they might fill up the
punishment that their torments
still lacked,

5 and that your people might
experience*a* an incredible
journey,
but they themselves might meet a
strange death.

God Guides and Protects His People

6 For the whole creation in its nature
was fashioned anew,
complying with your commands,
so that your children*b* might be kept
unharmed.

7 The cloud was seen overshadowing
the camp,
and dry land emerging where water
had stood before,
an unhindered way out of the Red
Sea,
and a grassy plain out of the raging
waves,

8 where those protected by your hand
passed through as one nation,
after gazing on marvellous wonders.

9 For they ranged like horses,
and leapt like lambs,
praising you, O Lord, who delivered
them.

10 For they still recalled the events of
their sojourn,
how instead of producing animals
the earth brought forth gnats,
and instead of fish the river spewed
out vast numbers of frogs.

11 Afterwards they saw also a new kind*c*
of birds,
when desire led them to ask for
luxurious food;

12 for, to give them relief, quails came
up from the sea.

The Punishment of the Egyptians

13 The punishments did not come upon
the sinners
without prior signs in the violence of
thunder,
for they justly suffered because of
their wicked acts;
for they practised a more bitter
hatred of strangers.

14 Others had refused to receive
strangers when they came to
them,
but these made slaves of guests who
were their benefactors.

15 And not only so—but, while
punishment of some sort will
come upon the former
for having received strangers with
hostility,

16 the latter, having first received them
with festal celebrations,
afterwards afflicted with terrible
sufferings
those who had already shared the
same rights.

17 They were stricken also with loss of
sight—
just as were those at the door of the
righteous man—
when, surrounded by yawning
darkness,
all of them tried to find the way
through their own doors.

A New Harmony in Nature

18 For the elements changed*d* places
with one another,
as on a harp the notes vary the nature
of the rhythm,
while each note remains the same.*e*
This may be clearly inferred from the
sight of what took place.

19 For land animals were transformed
into water creatures,
and creatures that swim moved over
to the land.

20 Fire even in water retained its normal
power,

a Other ancient authorities read *accomplish*
b Or *servants*   *c* Or *production*   *d* Gk *changing*
e Meaning of Gk uncertain

and water forgot its fire-quenching
nature.
21 Flames, on the contrary, failed to
    consume
the flesh of perishable creatures that
    walked among them,
nor did they melt[h] the crystalline,
    quick-melting kind of heavenly
    food.

Conclusion

22 For in everything, O Lord, you have
    exalted and glorified your
    people,
and you have not neglected to help
    them at all times and in all
    places.

a Cn: Gk *nor could be melted*

ECCLESIASTICUS,
OR THE WISDOM OF JESUS SON OF
SIRACH

THE PROLOGUE

Many great teachings have been given to us through the Law and the Prophets and the others *a* that followed them, and for these we should praise Israel for instruction and wisdom. Now, those who read the scriptures must not only themselves understand them, but must also as lovers of learning be able through the spoken and written word to help the outsiders. So my grandfather Jesus, who had devoted himself especially to the reading of the Law and the Prophets and the other books of our ancestors, and had acquired considerable proficiency in them, was himself also led to write something pertaining to instruction and wisdom, so that by becoming familiar also with his book *b* those who love learning might make even greater progress in living according to the law.

You are invited therefore to read it with goodwill and attention, and to be indulgent in cases where, despite our diligent labour in translating, we may seem to have rendered some phrases imperfectly. For what was originally expressed in Hebrew does not have exactly the same sense when translated into another language. Not only this book, but even the Law itself, the Prophecies, and the rest of the books differ not a little when read in the original.

When I came to Egypt in the thirty-eighth year of the reign of Euergetes and stayed for some time, I found opportunity for no little instruction. *c* It seemed highly necessary that I should myself devote some diligence and labour to the translation of this book. During that time I have applied my skill day and night to complete and publish the book for those living abroad who wished to gain learning and are disposed to live according to the law.

In Praise of Wisdom

1 All wisdom is from the Lord,
  and with him it remains for ever.
2 The sand of the sea, the drops of rain,
  and the days of eternity—who can
    count them?
3 The height of heaven, the breadth of
    the earth,
  the abyss, and wisdom *d*—who can
    search them out?
4 Wisdom was created before all other
    things,
  and prudent understanding from
    eternity. *e*
6 The root of wisdom—to whom has it
    been revealed?
  Her subtleties—who knows them? *f*
8 There is but one who is wise, greatly
    to be feared,
  seated upon his throne—the Lord.
9 It is he who created her;
  he saw her and took her measure;
  he poured her out upon all his
    works,

---

a Or *other books*   *b* Gk *with these things*   *c* Other ancient authorities read *I found a copy affording no little instruction*   *d* Other ancient authorities read *the depth of the abyss*   *e* Other ancient authorities add as verse 5, *The source of wisdom is God's word in the highest heaven, and her ways are the eternal commandments.*   *f* Other ancient authorities add as verse 7, *The knowledge of wisdom—to whom was it manifested? And her abundant experience—who has understood it?*

10 upon all the living according to his
        gift;
    he lavished her upon those who
        love him. *a*

Fear of the Lord Is True Wisdom

11 The fear of the Lord is glory and
        exultation,
    and gladness and a crown of
        rejoicing.
12 The fear of the Lord delights the
        heart,
    and gives gladness and joy and long
        life. *b*
13 Those who fear the Lord will have a
        happy end;
    on the day of their death they will
        be blessed.

14 To fear the Lord is the beginning of
        wisdom;
    she is created with the faithful in
        the womb.
15 She made *c* among human beings an
        eternal foundation,
    and among their descendants she
        will abide faithfully.
16 To fear the Lord is fullness of
        wisdom;
    she inebriates mortals with her
        fruits;
17 she fills their *d* whole house with
        desirable goods,
    and their *d* storehouses with her
        produce.
18 The fear of the Lord is the crown of
        wisdom,
    making peace and perfect health to
        flourish. *e*
19 She rained down knowledge and
        discerning comprehension,
    and she heightened the glory of
        those who held her fast.
20 To fear the Lord is the root of
        wisdom,
    and her branches are long life. *f*

22 Unjust anger cannot be justified,
    for anger tips the scale to one's
        ruin.

23 Those who are patient stay calm until
        the right moment,
    and then cheerfulness comes back
        to them.
24 They hold back their words until the
        right moment;
    then the lips of many tell of their
        good sense.

25 In the treasuries of wisdom are wise
        sayings,
    but godliness is an abomination to
        a sinner.
26 If you desire wisdom, keep the
        commandments,
    and the Lord will lavish her upon
        you.
27 For the fear of the Lord is wisdom
        and discipline,
    fidelity and humility are his
        delight.

28 Do not disobey the fear of the Lord;
    do not approach him with a
        divided mind.
29 Do not be a hypocrite before others,
    and keep watch over your lips.
30 Do not exalt yourself, or you may
        fall
    and bring dishonour upon
        yourself.
    The Lord will reveal your secrets
    and overthrow you before the
        whole congregation,
    because you did not come in the fear
        of the Lord,
    and your heart was full of deceit.

Duties towards God

2 My child, when you come to serve
        the Lord,
    prepare yourself for testing. *g*

---

a Other ancient authorities add *Love of the Lord is
glorious wisdom; to those to whom he appears he apportions
her, that they may see him.   b* Other ancient authorities
add *The fear of the Lord is a gift from the Lord; also for love
he makes firm paths.   c* Gk *made as a nest   d* Other
ancient authorities read *her   e* Other ancient
authorities add *Both are gifts of God for peace; glory opens
out for those who love him. He saw her and took her
measure.   f* Other ancient authorities add as verse 21,
*The fear of the Lord drives away sins; and where it abides, it
will turn away all anger.   g* Or *trials*

2 Set your heart right and be steadfast,
   and do not be impetuous in time of
      calamity.
3 Cling to him and do not depart,
   so that your last days may be
      prosperous.
4 Accept whatever befalls you,
   and in times of humiliation be
      patient.
5 For gold is tested in the fire,
   and those found acceptable, in the
      furnace of humiliation. *a*
6 Trust in him, and he will help you;
   make your ways straight, and hope
      in him.

7 You who fear the Lord, wait for his
      mercy;
   do not stray, or else you may fall.
8 You who fear the Lord, trust in him,
   and your reward will not be lost.
9 You who fear the Lord, hope for good
      things,
   for lasting joy and mercy. *b*
10 Consider the generations of old and
      see:
   has anyone trusted in the Lord and
      been disappointed?
   Or has anyone persevered in the fear
      of the Lord *c* and been forsaken?
   Or has anyone called upon him
      and been neglected?
11 For the Lord is compassionate and
      merciful;
   he forgives sins and saves in time of
      distress.

12 Woe to timid hearts and to slack
      hands,
   and to the sinner who walks a
      double path!
13 Woe to the faint-hearted who have no
      trust!
   Therefore they will have no shelter.
14 Woe to you who have lost your nerve!
   What will you do when the Lord's
      reckoning comes?

15 Those who fear the Lord do not
      disobey his words,

and those who love him keep his
      ways.
16 Those who fear the Lord seek to
      please him,
   and those who love him are filled
      with his law.
17 Those who fear the Lord prepare their
      hearts,
   and humble themselves before
      him.
18 Let us fall into the hands of the Lord,
   but not into the hands of mortals;
   for equal to his majesty is his mercy,
   and equal to his name are his
      works. *d*

Duties towards Parents

3 Listen to me your father,
   O children;
   act accordingly, that you may be
      kept in safety.
2 For the Lord honours a father above
      his children,
   and he confirms a mother's right
      over her children.
3 Those who honour their father atone
      for sins,
4 and those who respect their mother
      are like those who lay up
      treasure.
5 Those who honour their father will
      have joy in their own children,
   and when they pray they will be
      heard.
6 Those who respect their father will
      have long life,
   and those who honour *e* their
      mother obey the Lord;
7 they will serve their parents as their
      masters. *f*
8 Honour your father by word and
      deed,
   that his blessing may come upon
      you.

---

a Other ancient authorities add *in sickness and poverty
put your trust in him*   *b* Other ancient authorities add
For his reward is an everlasting gift with joy.   *c* Gk *of him*
d Syr: Gk lacks this line   *e* Heb: Other ancient
authorities read *comfort*   *f* In other ancient authorities
this line is preceded by *Those who fear the Lord honour
their father,*

9 For a father's blessing strengthens the
  houses of the children,
    but a mother's curse uproots their
    foundations.
10 Do not glorify yourself by
   dishonouring your father,
     for your father's dishonour is no
     glory to you.
11 The glory of one's father is one's own
   glory,
     and it is a disgrace for children not
     to respect their mother.

12 My child, help your father in his old
   age,
     and do not grieve him as long as he
     lives;
13 even if his mind fails, be patient with
   him;
     because you have all your faculties
     do not despise him.
14 For kindness to a father will not be
   forgotten,
     and will be credited to you against
     your sins;
15 in the day of your distress it will be
   remembered in your favour;
     like frost in fair weather, your sins
     will melt away.
16 Whoever forsakes a father is like a
   blasphemer,
     and whoever angers a mother is
     cursed by the Lord.

Humility

17 My child, perform your tasks with
   humility;*a*
     then you will be loved by those
     whom God accepts.
18 The greater you are, the more you
   must humble yourself;
     so you will find favour in the sight
     of the Lord.*b*
20 For great is the might of the Lord;
   but by the humble he is glorified.
21 Neither seek what is too difficult for
   you,
     nor investigate what is beyond your
     power.
22 Reflect upon what you have been
   commanded,

for what is hidden is not your
  concern.
23 Do not meddle in matters that are
   beyond you,
     for more than you can understand
     has been shown to you.
24 For their conceit has led many astray,
   and wrong opinion has impaired
   their judgement.

25 Without eyes there is no light;
   without knowledge there is no
   wisdom.*c*
26 A stubborn mind will fare badly at
   the end,
     and whoever loves danger will
     perish in it.
27 A stubborn mind will be burdened by
   troubles,
     and the sinner adds sin to sins.
28 When calamity befalls the proud,
   there is no healing,
     for an evil plant has taken root in
     him.
29 The mind of the intelligent
   appreciates proverbs,
     and an attentive ear is the desire of
     the wise.

Alms for the Poor

30 As water extinguishes a blazing fire,
   so almsgiving atones for sin.
31 Those who repay favours give
   thought to the future;
     when they fall they will find
     support.

*Duties towards the Poor and the
Oppressed*

4 My child, do not cheat the poor of
  their living,
    and do not keep needy eyes
    waiting.
2 Do not grieve the hungry,
  or anger one in need.
3 Do not add to the troubles of the
  desperate,
    or delay giving to the needy.

---

a Heb: Gk *meekness*   *b* Other ancient authorities add
as verse 19, *Many are lofty and renowned, but to the
humble he reveals his secrets.*   *c* Heb: Other ancient
authorities lack verse 25

4 Do not reject a suppliant in distress,
   or turn your face away from the
      poor.
5 Do not avert your eye from the needy,
   and give no one reason to curse
      you;
6 for if in bitterness of soul some
      should curse you,
   their Creator will hear their prayer.

7 Endear yourself to the congregation;
   bow your head low to the great.
8 Give a hearing to the poor,
   and return their greeting politely.
9 Rescue the oppressed from the
      oppressor;
   and do not be hesitant in giving a
      verdict.
10 Be a father to orphans,
   and be like a husband to their
      mother;
   you will then be like a son of the
      Most High,
   and he will love you more than
      does your mother.

The Rewards of Wisdom

11 Wisdom teaches[a] her children
   and gives help to those who seek
      her.
12 Whoever loves her loves life,
   and those who seek her from early
      morning are filled with joy.
13 Whoever holds her fast inherits glory,
   and the Lord blesses the place she[b]
      enters.
14 Those who serve her minister to the
      Holy One;
   the Lord loves those who love her.
15 Those who obey her will judge the
      nations,
   and all who listen to her will live
      secure.
16 If they remain faithful, they will
      inherit her;
   their descendants will also obtain
      her.
17 For at first she will walk with them
      on tortuous paths;
   she will bring fear and dread upon
      them,

and will torment them by her
      discipline
   until she trusts them,[c]
and she will test them with her
      ordinances.
18 Then she will come straight back to
      them again and gladden them,
   and will reveal her secrets to them.
19 If they go astray she will forsake
      them,
   and hand them over to their ruin.

20 Watch for the opportune time, and
      beware of evil,
   and do not be ashamed to be
      yourself.
21 For there is a shame that leads to sin,
   and there is a shame that is glory
      and favour.
22 Do not show partiality, to your own
      harm,
   or deference, to your downfall.
23 Do not refrain from speaking at the
      proper moment,[d]
   and do not hide your wisdom.[e]
24 For wisdom becomes known through
      speech,
   and education through the words
      of the tongue.
25 Never speak against the truth,
   but be ashamed of your ignorance.
26 Do not be ashamed to confess your
      sins,
   and do not try to stop the current
      of a river.
27 Do not subject yourself to a fool,
   or show partiality to a ruler.
28 Fight to the death for truth,
   and the Lord God will fight for you.

29 Do not be reckless in your speech,
   or sluggish and remiss in your
      deeds.
30 Do not be like a lion in your home,
   or suspicious of your servants.
31 Do not let your hand be stretched out
      to receive
   and closed when it is time to give.

a Heb Syr: Gk exalts   b Or he   c Or until they remain
faithful in their heart   d Heb: Gk at a time of salvation
e So some Gk Mss and Heb Syr Lat: Other Gk Mss lack
and do not hide your wisdom

Precepts for Everyday Living

5 Do not rely on your wealth,
 or say, 'I have enough.'
2 Do not follow your inclination and
   strength
     in pursuing the desires of your
     heart.
3 Do not say, 'Who can have power
   over me?'
     for the Lord will surely punish
     you.

4 Do not say, 'I sinned, yet what has
   happened to me?'
     for the Lord is slow to anger.
5 Do not be so confident of
   forgiveness[a]
     that you add sin to sin.
6 Do not say, 'His mercy is great,
   he will forgive[b] the multitude of
   my sins',
     for both mercy and wrath are with
     him,
     and his anger will rest on sinners.
7 Do not delay to turn back to the
   Lord,
     and do not postpone it from day to
     day;
     for suddenly the wrath of the Lord
     will come upon you,
     and at the time of punishment you
     will perish.
8 Do not depend on dishonest wealth,
   for it will not benefit you on the
   day of calamity.

9 Do not winnow in every wind,
   or follow every path.[c]
10 Stand firm for what you know,
   and let your speech be consistent.
11 Be quick to hear,
   but deliberate in answering.
12 If you know what to say, answer your
   neighbour;
     but if not, put your hand over your
     mouth.

13 Honour and dishonour come from
   speaking,
     and the tongue of mortals may be
     their downfall.

14 Do not be called double-tongued[d]
   and do not lay traps with your
   tongue;
     for shame comes to the thief,
     and severe condemnation to the
     double-tongued.
15 In great and small matters cause no
   harm,[e]

6 1 and do not become an enemy
   instead of a friend;
     for a bad name incurs shame and
     reproach;
     so it is with the double-tongued
     sinner.

2 Do not fall into the grip of passion,[f]
   or you may be torn apart as by a
   bull.[g]
3 Your leaves will be devoured and
   your fruit destroyed,
     and you will be left like a withered
     tree.
4 Evil passion destroys those who have
   it,
     and makes them the laughing-stock
     of their enemies.

Friendship, False and True

5 Pleasant speech multiplies friends,
   and a gracious tongue multiplies
   courtesies.
6 Let those who are friendly with you
   be many,
     but let your advisers be one in a
     thousand.
7 When you gain friends, gain them
   through testing,
     and do not trust them hastily.
8 For there are friends who are such
   when it suits them,
     but they will not stand by you in
     time of trouble.
9 And there are friends who change
   into enemies,
     and tell of the quarrel to your
     disgrace.

a Heb: Gk *atonement*   *b* Heb: Gk *he* (or *it*) *will atone
for*   *c* Gk adds *so it is with the double-tongued sinner*
(see 6.1)   *d* Heb: Gk *a slanderer*   *e* Heb Syr: Gk *be
ignorant*   *f* Heb: Meaning of Gk uncertain
g Meaning of Gk uncertain

10 And there are friends who sit at your
table,
　　but they will not stand by you in
　　time of trouble.
11 When you are prosperous, they
become your second self,
　　and lord it over your servants;
12 but if you are brought low, they turn
against you,
　　and hide themselves from you.
13 Keep away from your enemies,
　　and be on guard with your
　　friends.

14 Faithful friends are a sturdy shelter:
　　whoever finds one has found a
　　treasure.
15 Faithful friends are beyond price;
　　no amount can balance their
　　worth.
16 Faithful friends are life-saving
medicine;
　　and those who fear the Lord will
　　find them.
17 Those who fear the Lord direct their
friendship aright,
　　for as they are, so are their
　　neighbours also.

Blessings of Wisdom

18 My child, from your youth choose
discipline,
　　and when you have grey hair you
　　will still find wisdom.
19 Come to her like one who ploughs
and sows,
　　and wait for her good harvest.
　　For when you cultivate her you will
　　toil but little,
　　and soon you will eat of her
　　produce.
20 She seems very harsh to the
undisciplined;
　　fools cannot remain with her.
21 She will be like a heavy stone to test
them,
　　and they will not delay in casting
　　her aside.
22 For wisdom is like her name;
　　she is not readily perceived by
　　many.

23 Listen, my child, and accept my
judgement;
　　do not reject my counsel.
24 Put your feet into her fetters,
　　and your neck into her collar.
25 Bend your shoulders and carry her,
　　and do not fret under her bonds.
26 Come to her with all your soul,
　　and keep her ways with all your
　　might.
27 Search out and seek, and she will
become known to you;
　　and when you get hold of her, do
　　not let her go.
28 For at last you will find the rest she
gives,
　　and she will be changed into joy for
　　you.
29 Then her fetters will become for you
a strong defence,
　　and her collar a glorious robe.
30 Her yoke*a* is a golden ornament,
　　and her bonds a purple cord.
31 You will wear her like a glorious
robe,
　　and put her on like a splendid
　　crown.*b*

32 If you are willing, my child, you can
be disciplined,
　　and if you apply yourself you will
　　become clever.
33 If you love to listen you will gain
knowledge,
　　and if you pay attention you will
　　become wise.
34 Stand in the company of the elders.
　　Who is wise? Attach yourself to
　　such a one.
35 Be ready to listen to every godly
discourse,
　　and let no wise proverbs escape
　　you.
36 If you see an intelligent person, rise
early to visit him;
　　let your foot wear out his doorstep.
37 Reflect on the statutes of the Lord,
　　and meditate at all times on his
　　commandments.

a Heb: Gk *Upon her*　　*b* Heb: Gk *crown of gladness*

It is he who will give insight to[a] your
mind,
and your desire for wisdom will be
granted.

Miscellaneous Advice

7 Do no evil, and evil will never
overtake you.
2 Stay away from wrong, and it will
turn away from you.
3 Do[b] not sow in the furrows of
injustice,
and you will not reap a sevenfold
crop.

4 Do not seek from the Lord high
office,
or the seat of honour from the
king.
5 Do not assert your righteousness
before the Lord,
or display your wisdom before the
king.
6 Do not seek to become a judge,
or you may be unable to root out
injustice;
you may be partial to the powerful,
and so mar your integrity.
7 Commit no offence against the
public,
and do not disgrace yourself among
the people.

8 Do not commit a sin twice;
not even for one will you go
unpunished.
9 Do not say, 'He will consider the
great number of my gifts,
and when I make an offering to the
Most High God, he will accept
it.'
10 Do not grow weary when you pray;
do not neglect to give alms.
11 Do not ridicule a person who is
embittered in spirit,
for there is One who humbles and
exalts.
12 Do not devise[c] a lie against your
brother,
or do the same to a friend.
13 Refuse to utter any lie,

for it is a habit that results in no
good.
14 Do not babble in the assembly of the
elders,
and do not repeat yourself when
you pray.

15 Do not hate hard labour
or farm work, which was created by
the Most High.
16 Do not enrol in the ranks of sinners;
remember that retribution does not
delay.
17 Humble yourself to the utmost,
for the punishment of the ungodly
is fire and worms.[d]

Relations with Others

18 Do not exchange a friend for money,
or a real brother for the gold of
Ophir.
19 Do not dismiss[e] a wise and good
wife,
for her charm is worth more than
gold.
20 Do not abuse slaves who work
faithfully,
or hired labourers who devote
themselves to their task.
21 Let your soul love intelligent slaves;[f]
do not withhold from them their
freedom.

22 Do you have cattle? Look after them;
if they are profitable to you, keep
them.
23 Do you have children? Discipline
them,
and make them obedient[g] from
their youth.
24 Do you have daughters? Be
concerned for their chastity,[h]
and do not show yourself too
indulgent with them.
25 Give a daughter in marriage, and you
complete a great task;
but give her to a sensible man.

a Heb: Gk will confirm   b Gk My child, do   c Heb:
Gk plough   d Heb for the expectation of mortals is worms
e Heb: Gk deprive yourself of   f Heb Love a wise slave as
yourself   g Gk bend their necks   h Gk body

26 Do you have a wife who pleases
      you?[a] Do not divorce her;
   but do not trust yourself to one
      whom you detest.

27 With all your heart honour your
      father,
   and do not forget the birth pangs of
      your mother.
28 Remember that it was of your
      parents[b] you were born;
   how can you repay what they have
      given to you?

29 With all your soul fear the Lord,
   and revere his priests.
30 With all your might love your Maker,
   and do not neglect his ministers.
31 Fear the Lord and honour the priest,
   and give him his portion, as you
      have been commanded:
   the first fruits, the guilt-offering, the
      gift of the shoulders,
   the sacrifice of sanctification, and
      the first fruits of the holy
      things.

32 Stretch out your hand to the poor,
   so that your blessing may be
      complete.
33 Give graciously to all the living;
   do not withhold kindness even
      from the dead.
34 Do not avoid those who weep,
   but mourn with those who mourn.
35 Do not hesitate to visit the sick,
   because for such deeds you will be
      loved.
36 In all you do, remember the end of
      your life,
   and then you will never sin.

Prudence and Common Sense

8 Do not contend with the powerful,
   or you may fall into their hands.
2 Do not quarrel with the rich,
   in case their resources outweigh
      yours;
   for gold has ruined many,
   and has perverted the minds of
      kings.

3 Do not argue with the loud of
      mouth,
   and do not heap wood on their fire.

4 Do not make fun of one who is ill-
      bred,
   or your ancestors may be insulted.
5 Do not reproach one who is turning
      away from sin;
   remember that we all deserve
      punishment.
6 Do not disdain one who is old,
   for some of us are also growing old.
7 Do not rejoice over anyone's death;
   remember that we must all die.

8 Do not slight the discourse of the
      sages,
   but busy yourself with their maxims;
   because from them you will learn
      discipline
   and how to serve princes.
9 Do not ignore the discourse of the
      aged,
   for they themselves learned from
      their parents;[c]
   from them you learn how to
      understand
   and to give an answer when the
      need arises.

10 Do not kindle the coals of sinners,
   or you may be burned in their
      flaming fire.
11 Do not let the insolent bring you to
      your feet,
   or they may lie in ambush against
      your words.
12 Do not lend to one who is stronger
      than you;
   but if you do lend anything, count
      it as a loss.
13 Do not give surety beyond your means;
   but if you give surety, be prepared
      to pay.

14 Do not go to law against a judge,
   for the decision will favour him
      because of his standing.

a Heb Syr lack *who pleases you*   *b* Gk *them*
c Or *ancestors*

15 Do not go travelling with the reckless,
    or they will be burdensome to you;
  for they will act as they please,
    and through their folly you will
      perish with them.
16 Do not pick a fight with the quick-
      tempered,
    and do not journey with them
      through lonely country,
  because bloodshed means nothing to
      them,
    and where no help is at hand they
      will strike you down.
17 Do not consult with fools,
    for they cannot keep a secret.
18 In the presence of strangers do
      nothing that is to be kept secret,
    for you do not know what they will
      divulge. *a*
19 Do not reveal your thoughts to
      anyone,
    or you may drive away your
      happiness. *b*

Advice Concerning Women

9 Do not be jealous of the wife of
    your bosom,
  or you will teach her an evil lesson
    to your own hurt.
2 Do not give yourself to a woman
    and let her trample down your
      strength.
3 Do not go near a loose woman,
    or you will fall into her snares.
4 Do not dally with a singing-girl,
    or you will be caught by her tricks.
5 Do not look intently at a virgin,
    or you may stumble and incur
      penalties for her.
6 Do not give yourself to prostitutes,
    or you may lose your inheritance.
7 Do not look around in the streets of
      a city,
    or wander about in its deserted
      sections.
8 Turn away your eyes from a shapely
      woman,
    and do not gaze at beauty
      belonging to another;
  many have been seduced by a
      woman's beauty,

and by it passion is kindled like a
    fire.
9 Never dine with another man's wife,
    or revel with her at wine;
  or your heart may turn aside to her,
    and in blood *c* you may be plunged
      into destruction.

Choice of Friends

10 Do not abandon old friends,
    for new ones cannot equal them.
  A new friend is like new wine;
    when it has aged, you can drink it
      with pleasure.

11 Do not envy the success of sinners,
    for you do not know what their end
      will be like.
12 Do not delight in what pleases the
      ungodly;
    remember that they will not be
      held guiltless all their lives.

13 Keep far from those who have power
      to kill,
    and you will not be haunted by the
      fear of death.
  But if you approach them, take no
      false step,
    or they may rob you of your life.
  Know that you are stepping among
      snares,
    and that you are walking on the city
      battlements.

14 As much as you can, aim to know
      your neighbours,
    and consult with the wise.
15 Let your conversation be with
      intelligent people,
    and let all your discussion be about
      the law of the Most High.
16 Let the righteous be your dinner
      companions,
    and let your glory be in the fear of
      the Lord.

a Or *it will bring forth*   *b* Heb: Gk *and let him not*
return a favour to you   *c* Heb: Gk *by your spirit*

Concerning Rulers

17 A work is praised for the skill of the artisan;

so a people's leader is proved wise by his words.

18 The loud of mouth are feared in their city,

and the one who is reckless in speech is hated.

10 A wise magistrate educates his people,

and the rule of an intelligent person is well ordered.

2 As the people's judge is, so are his officials;

as the ruler of the city is, so are all its inhabitants.

3 An undisciplined king ruins his people,

but a city becomes fit to live in through the understanding of its rulers.

4 The government of the earth is in the hand of the Lord,

and over it he will raise up the right leader for the time.

5 Human success is in the hand of the Lord,

and it is he who confers honour upon the lawgiver. *a*

The Sin of Pride

6 Do not get angry with your neighbour for every injury,

and do not resort to acts of insolence.

7 Arrogance is hateful to the Lord and to mortals,

and injustice is outrageous to both.

8 Sovereignty passes from nation to nation

on account of injustice and insolence and wealth. *b*

9 How can dust and ashes be proud? Even in life the human body decays. *c*

10 A long illness baffles the physician; *d*

the king of today will die tomorrow.

11 For when one is dead he inherits maggots and vermin *e* and worms.

12 The beginning of human pride is to forsake the Lord;

the heart has withdrawn from its Maker.

13 For the beginning of pride is sin,

and the one who clings to it pours out abominations.

Therefore the Lord brings upon them unheard-of calamities,

and destroys them completely.

14 The Lord overthrows the thrones of rulers,

and enthrones the lowly in their place.

15 The Lord plucks up the roots of the nations, *f*

and plants the humble in their place.

16 The Lord lays waste the lands of the nations,

and destroys them to the foundations of the earth.

17 He removes some of them and destroys them,

and erases the memory of them from the earth.

18 Pride was not created for human beings,

or violent anger for those born of women.

Persons Deserving Honour

19 Whose offspring are worthy of honour?

Human offspring.

Whose offspring are worthy of honour?

Those who fear the Lord.

Whose offspring are unworthy of honour?

Human offspring.

Whose offspring are unworthy of honour?

Those who break the commandments.

a Heb: Gk *scribe*   *b* Other ancient authorities add here or after verse 9a, *Nothing is more wicked than one who loves money, for such a person puts his own soul up for sale.*   *c* Heb: Meaning of Gk uncertain   *d* Heb Lat: Meaning of Gk uncertain   *e* Heb: Gk *wild animals*   *f* Other ancient authorities read *proud nations*

20 Among family members their leader
    is worthy of honour,
  but those who fear the Lord are
    worthy of honour in his eyes. *a*
22 The rich, and the eminent, and the
    poor—
  their glory is the fear of the Lord.
23 It is not right to despise one who is
    intelligent but poor,
  and it is not proper to honour one
    who is sinful.
24 The prince and the judge and the
    ruler are honoured,
  but none of them is greater than
    one who fears the Lord.
25 Free citizens will serve a wise servant,
  and an intelligent person will not
    complain.

Concerning Humility

26 Do not make a display of your
    wisdom when you do your
    work,
  and do not boast when you are in
    need.
27 Better is the worker who has goods in
    plenty
  than the boaster who lacks bread.

28 My child, honour yourself with
    humility,
  and give yourself the esteem you
    deserve.
29 Who will acquit those who
    condemn *b* themselves?
  And who will honour those who
    dishonour themselves? *c*
30 The poor are honoured for their
    knowledge,
  while the rich are honoured for
    their wealth.
31 One who is honoured in poverty,
    how much more in wealth!
  And one dishonoured in wealth,
    how much more in poverty!

The Deceptiveness of Appearances

11 The wisdom of the humble lifts
    their heads high,
  and seats them among the great.

2 Do not praise individuals for their
    good looks,
  or loathe anyone because of
    appearance alone.
3 The bee is small among flying
    creatures,
  but what it produces is the best of
    sweet things.
4 Do not boast about wearing fine
    clothes,
  and do not exalt yourself when you
    are honoured;
  for the works of the Lord are
    wonderful,
  and his works are concealed from
    humankind.
5 Many kings have had to sit on the
    ground,
  but one who was never thought of
    has worn a crown.
6 Many rulers have been utterly
    disgraced,
  and the honoured have been
    handed over to others.

Deliberation and Caution

7 Do not find fault before you
    investigate;
  examine first, and then criticize.
8 Do not answer before you listen,
  and do not interrupt when another
    is speaking.
9 Do not argue about a matter that
    does not concern you,
  and do not sit with sinners when
    they judge a case.

10 My child, do not busy yourself with
    many matters;
  if you multiply activities, you will
    not be held blameless.
  If you pursue, you will not overtake,
    and by fleeing you will not escape.
11 There are those who work and
    struggle and hurry,
  but are so much the more in want.
12 There are others who are slow and
    need help,

a Other ancient authorities add as verse 21, *The fear of
the Lord is the beginning of acceptance; obduracy and pride
are the beginning of rejection.*   *b* Heb: Gk *sin against*
c Heb Lat: Gk *their own life*

who lack strength and abound in
poverty;
but the eyes of the Lord look kindly
upon them;
he lifts them out of their lowly
condition

13 and raises up their heads
to the amazement of many.

14 Good things and bad, life and death,
poverty and wealth, come from the
Lord. [a]

17 The Lord's gift remains with the
devout,
and his favour brings lasting
success.

18 One becomes rich through diligence
and self-denial,
and the reward allotted to him is
this:

19 when he says, 'I have found rest,
and now I shall feast on my goods!'
he does not know how long it will be
until he leaves them to others and
dies.

20 Stand by your agreement and attend
to it,
and grow old in your work.

21 Do not wonder at the works of a
sinner,
but trust in the Lord and keep at
your job;
for it is easy in the sight of the Lord
to make the poor rich suddenly, in
an instant.

22 The blessing of the Lord is[b] the
reward of the pious,
and quickly God causes his blessing
to flourish.

23 Do not say, 'What do I need,
and what further benefit can be
mine?'

24 Do not say, 'I have enough,
and what harm can come to me
now?'

25 In the day of prosperity, adversity is
forgotten,
and in the day of adversity,
prosperity is not remembered.

26 For it is easy for the Lord on the day
of death
to reward individuals according to
their conduct.

27 An hour's misery makes one forget
past delights,
and at the close of one's life one's
deeds are revealed.

28 Call no one happy before his death;
by how he ends, a person becomes
known. [c]

Care in Choosing Friends

29 Do not invite everyone into your
home,
for many are the tricks of the crafty.

30 Like a decoy partridge in a cage, so is
the mind of the proud,
and like spies they observe your
weakness; [d]

31 for they lie in wait, turning good into
evil,
and to worthy actions they attach
blame.

32 From a spark many coals are kindled,
and a sinner lies in wait to shed
blood.

33 Beware of scoundrels, for they devise
evil,
and they may ruin your reputation
for ever.

34 Receive strangers into your home and
they will stir up trouble for you,
and will make you a stranger to
your own family.

12 If you do good, know to whom
you do it,
and you will be thanked for your
good deeds.

2 Do good to the devout, and you will
be repaid—
if not by them, certainly by the
Most High.

---

a Other ancient authorities add as verses 15 and 16,
[15]*Wisdom, understanding, and knowledge of the law come
from the Lord; affection and the ways of good works come
from him.* [16]*Error and darkness were created with sinners;
evil grows old with those who take pride in malice.*
b Heb: Gk *is in*   *c* Heb: Gk *and through his children a
person becomes known*   *d* Heb: Gk *downfall*

3 No good comes to one who persists
    in evil
  or to one who does not give alms.
4 Give to the devout, but do not help
    the sinner.
5 Do good to the humble, but do not
    give to the ungodly;
  hold back their bread, and do not
    give it to them,
  for by means of it they might
    subdue you;
  then you will receive twice as much
    evil
  for all the good you have done to
    them.
6 For the Most High also hates sinners
  and will inflict punishment on the
    ungodly. *a*
7 Give to one who is good, but do not
    help the sinner.
8 A friend is not known *b* in prosperity,
  nor is an enemy hidden in
    adversity.
9 One's enemies are friendly *c* when
    one prospers,
  but in adversity even one's friend
    disappears.
10 Never trust your enemy,
  for like corrosion in copper, so is
    his wickedness.
11 Even if he humbles himself and
    walks bowed down,
  take care to be on your guard
    against him.
  Be to him like one who polishes a
    mirror,
  to be sure it does not become
    completely tarnished.
12 Do not put him next to you,
  or he may overthrow you and take
    your place.
  Do not let him sit at your right hand,
  or else he may try to take your own
    seat,
  and at last you will realize the truth
    of my words,
  and be stung by what I have said.

13 Who pities a snake-charmer when he
    is bitten,

or all those who go near wild
    animals?
14 So no one pities a person who
    associates with a sinner
  and becomes involved in the
    other's sins.
15 He stands by you for a while,
  but if you falter, he will not be
    there.
16 An enemy speaks sweetly with his
    lips,
  but in his heart he plans to throw
    you into a pit;
  an enemy may have tears in his eyes,
  but if he finds an opportunity he
    will never have enough of your
    blood.
17 If evil comes upon you, you will find
    him there ahead of you;
  pretending to help, he will trip you
    up.
18 Then he will shake his head, and clap
    his hands,
  and whisper much, and show his
    true face.

Caution Regarding Associates

13 Whoever touches pitch gets
    dirty,
  and whoever associates with a
    proud person becomes like
    him.
2 Do not lift a weight too heavy for
    you,
  or associate with one mightier and
    richer than you.
  How can the clay pot associate with
    the iron kettle?
  The pot will strike against it and be
    smashed.
3 A rich person does wrong, and even
    adds insults;
  a poor person suffers wrong, and
    must add apologies.
4 A rich person *d* will exploit you if you
    can be of use to him,
  but if you are in need he will
    abandon you.

a Other ancient authorities add *and he is keeping them
for the day of their punishment*   *b* Other ancient
authorities read *punished*   *c* Heb: Gk *grieved*
d Gk *He*

⁵ If you own something, he will live
    with you;
  he will drain your resources
      without a qualm.
⁶ When he needs you he will deceive
    you,
  and will smile at you and
      encourage you;
  he will speak to you kindly and say,
      'What do you need?'
⁷ He will embarrass you with his
    delicacies,
  until he has drained you two or
      three times,
  and finally he will laugh at you.
  Should he see you afterwards, he will
      pass you by
  and shake his head at you.

⁸ Take care not to be led astray
  and humiliated when you are
      enjoying yourself. ᵃ
⁹ When an influential person invites
    you, be reserved,
  and he will invite you more
      insistently.
¹⁰ Do not be forward, or you may be
    rebuffed;
  do not stand aloof, or you will be
      forgotten.
¹¹ Do not try to treat him as an equal,
  or trust his lengthy conversations;
  for he will test you by prolonged talk,
  and while he smiles he will be
      examining you.
¹² Cruel are those who do not keep your
    secrets;
  they will not spare you harm or
      imprisonment.
¹³ Be on your guard and very careful,
  for you are walking about with your
      own downfall. ᵇ

¹⁵ Every creature loves its like,
  and every person a neighbour.
¹⁶ All living beings associate with their
    own kind,
  and people stick close to those like
      themselves.
¹⁷ What does a wolf have in common
    with a lamb?

No more has a sinner with the
    devout.
¹⁸ What peace is there between a hyena
    and a dog?
  And what peace between the rich
      and the poor?
¹⁹ Wild asses in the wilderness are the
    prey of lions;
  likewise the poor are feeding-
      grounds for the rich.
²⁰ Humility is an abomination to the
    proud;
  likewise the poor are an
      abomination to the rich.

²¹ When the rich person totters, he is
    supported by friends,
  but when the humble ᶜ falls, he is
      pushed away even by friends.
²² If the rich person slips, many come to
    the rescue;
  he speaks unseemly words, but they
      justify him.
  If the humble person slips, they even
      criticize him;
  he talks sense, but is not given a
      hearing.
²³ The rich person speaks and all are
    silent;
  they extol to the clouds what he
      says.
  The poor person speaks and they say,
      'Who is this fellow?'
  And should he stumble, they even
      push him down.
²⁴ Riches are good if they are free from
    sin;
  poverty is evil only in the opinion
      of the ungodly.

²⁵ The heart changes the countenance,
  either for good or for evil. ᵈ
²⁶ The sign of a happy heart is a
    cheerful face,

a Other ancient authorities read *in your folly*   b Other
ancient authorities add as verse 14, *When you hear these
things in your sleep, wake up! During all your life love the
Lord, and call on him for your salvation.*   c Other
ancient authorities read *poor*   d Other ancient
authorities add *and a glad heart makes a cheerful
countenance*

but to devise proverbs requires
painful thinking.

14
Happy are those who do not
blunder with their lips,
and need not suffer remorse for sin.

2 Happy are those whose hearts do not
condemn them,
and who have not given up their
hope.

Responsible Use of Wealth

3 Riches are inappropriate for a small-
minded person;
and of what use is wealth to a
miser?

4 What he denies himself he collects
for others;
and others will live in luxury on his
goods.

5 If one is mean to himself, to whom
will he be generous?
He will not enjoy his own riches.

6 No one is worse than one who is
grudging to himself;
this is the punishment for his
meanness.

7 If ever he does good, it is by mistake;
and in the end he reveals his
meanness.

8 The miser is an evil person;
he turns away and disregards
people.

9 The eye of the greedy person is not
satisfied with his share;
greedy injustice withers the soul.

10 A miser begrudges bread,
and it is lacking at his table.

11 My child, treat yourself well,
according to your means,
and present worthy offerings to the
Lord.

12 Remember that death does not tarry,
and the decree ^{a} of Hades has not
been shown to you.

13 Do good to friends before you die,
and reach out and give to them as
much as you can.

14 Do not deprive yourself of a day's
enjoyment;

do not let your share of desired
good pass by you.

15 Will you not leave the fruit of your
labours to another,
and what you acquired by toil to be
divided by lot?

16 Give, and take, and indulge yourself,
because in Hades one cannot look
for luxury.

17 All living beings become old like a
garment,
for the decree ^{b} from of old is, 'You
must die!'

18 Like abundant leaves on a spreading
tree
that sheds some and puts forth
others,
so are the generations of flesh and
blood:
one dies and another is born.

19 Every work decays and ceases to
exist,
and the one who made it will pass
away with it.

The Happiness of Seeking Wisdom

20 Happy is the person who meditates
on ^{c} wisdom
and reasons intelligently,

21 who ^{d} reflects in his heart on her ways
and ponders her secrets,

22 pursuing her like a hunter,
and lying in wait on her paths;

23 who peers through her windows
and listens at her doors;

24 who camps near her house
and fastens his tent-peg to her
walls;

25 who pitches his tent near her,
and so occupies an excellent
lodging-place;

26 who places his children under her
shelter,
and lodges under her boughs;

27 who is sheltered by her from the
heat,
and dwells in the midst of her
glory.

a Heb Syr: Gk *covenant*   b Heb: Gk *covenant*
c Other ancient authorities read *dies in*
d The structure adopted in verses 21-27 follows the Heb

15 Whoever fears the Lord will do
this,
  and whoever holds to the law will
    obtain wisdom. [a]
2 She will come to meet him like a
    mother,
  and like a young bride she will
    welcome him.
3 She will feed him with the bread of
    learning,
  and give him the water of wisdom
    to drink.
4 He will lean on her and not fall,
  and he will rely on her and not be
    put to shame.
5 She will exalt him above his
    neighbours,
  and will open his mouth in the
    midst of the assembly.
6 He will find gladness and a crown of
    rejoicing,
  and will inherit an everlasting
    name.
7 The foolish will not obtain her,
  and sinners will not see her.
8 She is far from arrogance,
  and liars will never think of her.
9 Praise is unseemly on the lips of a
    sinner,
  for it has not been sent from the
    Lord.
10 For in wisdom must praise be
    uttered,
  and the Lord will make it prosper.

Freedom of Choice

11 Do not say, 'It was the Lord's doing
    that I fell away';
  for he does not do [b] what he hates.
12 Do not say, 'It was he who led me
    astray';
  for he has no need of the sinful.
13 The Lord hates all abominations;
  such things are not loved by those
    who fear him.
14 It was he who created humankind in
    the beginning,
  and he left them in the power of
    their own free choice.
15 If you choose, you can keep the
    commandments,

and to act faithfully is a matter of
    your own choice.
16 He has placed before you fire and
    water;
  stretch out your hand for whichever
    you choose.
17 Before each person are life and death,
  and whichever one chooses will be
    given.
18 For great is the wisdom of the Lord;
  he is mighty in power and sees
    everything;
19 his eyes are on those who fear him,
  and he knows every human action.
20 He has not commanded anyone to be
    wicked,
  and he has not given anyone
    permission to sin.

God's Punishment of Sinners

16 Do not desire a multitude of
worthless [c] children,
  and do not rejoice in ungodly
    offspring.
2 If they multiply, do not rejoice in
    them,
  unless the fear of the Lord is in
    them.
3 Do not trust in their survival,
  or rely on their numbers; [d]
for one can be better than a
    thousand,
  and to die childless is better than to
    have ungodly children.
4 For through one intelligent person a
    city can be filled with people,
  but through a clan of outlaws it
    becomes desolate.

5 Many such things my eye has seen,
  and my ear has heard things more
    striking than these.
6 In an assembly of sinners a fire is
    kindled,
  and in a disobedient nation wrath
    blazes up.
7 He did not forgive the ancient giants
  who revolted in their might.

a Gk her   b Heb: Gk you ought not to do   c Heb: Gk
unprofitable   d Other ancient authorities add For you
will groan in untimely mourning, and will know of their
sudden end.

8 He did not spare the neighbours of
    Lot,
    whom he loathed on account of
        their arrogance.
9 He showed no pity on the doomed
    nation,
    on those dispossessed because of
        their sins;*a*
10 or on the six hundred thousand foot-
    soldiers
    who assembled in their
        stubbornness.*b*
11 Even if there were only one stiff-
    necked person,
    it would be a wonder if he
        remained unpunished.
  For mercy and wrath are with the
    Lord;*c*
    he is mighty to forgive—but he also
        pours out wrath.
12 Great as is his mercy, so also is his
    chastisement;
    he judges a person according to his
        or her deeds.
13 The sinner will not escape with
    plunder,
    and the patience of the godly will
        not be frustrated.
14 He makes room for every act of
    mercy;
    everyone receives in accordance
        with his or her deeds.*d*

17 Do not say, 'I am hidden from the
    Lord,
    and who from on high has me in
        mind?
  Among so many people I am
    unknown,
    for what am I in a boundless
        creation?
18 Lo, heaven and the highest heaven,
    the abyss and the earth, tremble at
        his visitation!*e*
19 The very mountains and the
    foundations of the earth
    quiver and quake when he looks
        upon them.
20 But no human mind can grasp this,
    and who can comprehend his
        ways?

21 Like a tempest that no one can see,
    so most of his works are
        concealed.*f*
22 Who is to announce his acts of
    justice?
    Or who can await them? For his
        decree*g* is far off.'*h*
23 Such are the thoughts of one devoid
    of understanding;
    a senseless and misguided person
        thinks foolishly.

God's Wisdom Seen in Creation

24 Listen to me, my child, and acquire
    knowledge,
    and pay close attention to my
        words.
25 I will impart discipline precisely*i*
    and declare knowledge accurately.

26 When the Lord created*j* his works
    from the beginning,
    and, in making them, determined
        their boundaries,
27 he arranged his works in an eternal
    order,
    and their dominion*k* for all
        generations.
  They neither hunger nor grow weary,
    and they do not abandon their
        tasks.
28 They do not crowd one another,
    and they never disobey his word.
29 Then the Lord looked upon the earth,
    and filled it with his good things.
30 With all kinds of living beings he
    covered its surface,
    and into it they must return.

a Other ancient authorities add *All these things he did to
the hard-hearted nations, and by the multitude of his holy
ones he was not appeased.* *b* Other ancient authorities
add *Chastising, showing mercy, striking, healing, the Lord
persisted in mercy and discipline.* *c* Gk *him* *d* Other
ancient authorities add *¹⁵The Lord hardened Pharaoh so
that he did not recognize him, in order that his works might
be known under heaven. ¹⁶His mercy is manifest to the
whole of creation, and he divided his light and darkness with
a plumb-line.* *e* Other ancient authorities add *The
whole world past and present is in his will.* *f* Meaning of
Gk uncertain: Heb Syr *If I sin, no eye can see me, and if I
am disloyal all in secret, who is to know?* *g* Heb *the
decree:* Gk *the covenant* *h* Other ancient authorities
add *and a scrutiny for all comes at the end* *i* Gk *by
weight* *j* Heb: Gk *judged* *k* Or *elements*

17

The Lord created human beings out of earth,
  and makes them return to it again.

2 He gave them a fixed number of days,
  but granted them authority over everything on the earth. *a*

3 He endowed them with strength like his own, *b*
  and made them in his own image.

4 He put the fear of them *c* in all living beings,
  and gave them dominion over beasts and birds. *d*

6 Discretion and tongue and eyes,
  ears and a mind for thinking he gave them.

7 He filled them with knowledge and understanding,
  and showed them good and evil.

8 He put the fear of him into *e* their hearts
  to show them the majesty of his works. *f*

10 And they will praise his holy name,
9   to proclaim the grandeur of his works.

11 He bestowed knowledge upon them,
  and allotted to them the law of life. *g*

12 He established with them an eternal covenant,
  and revealed to them his decrees.

13 Their eyes saw his glorious majesty,
  and their ears heard the glory of his voice.

14 He said to them, 'Beware of all evil.'
  And he gave commandment to each of them concerning a neighbour.

15 Their ways are always known to him;
  they will not be hid from his eyes. *h*

17 He appointed a ruler for every nation,
  but Israel is the Lord's own portion. *i*

19 All their works are as clear as the sun before him,
  and his eyes are ever upon their ways.

20 Their iniquities are not hidden from him,
  and all their sins are before the Lord. *j*

22 One's almsgiving is like a signet ring with the Lord, *k*
  and he will keep a person's kindness like the apple of his eye. *l*

23 Afterwards he will rise up and repay them,
  and he will bring their recompense on their heads.

24 Yet to those who repent he grants a return,
  and he encourages those who are losing hope.

A Call to Repentance

25 Turn back to the Lord and forsake your sins;
  pray in his presence and lessen your offence.

26 Return to the Most High and turn away from iniquity, *m*
  and hate intensely what he abhors.

27 Who will sing praises to the Most High in Hades
  in place of the living who give thanks?

28 From the dead, as from one who does not exist, thanksgiving has ceased;
  those who are alive and well sing the Lord's praises.

a Lat: Gk *it*   *b* Lat: Gk *proper to them*   *c* Syr: Gk *him*
d Other ancient authorities add as verse 5, *They obtained the use of the five faculties of the Lord; as sixth he distributed to them the gift of mind, and as seventh, reason, the interpreter of one's faculties.*   *e* Other ancient authorities read *He set his eye upon*   *f* Other ancient authorities add *and he gave them to boast of his marvels for ever*   *g* Other ancient authorities add *so that they may know that they who are alive now are mortal*   *h* Other ancient authorities add *16Their ways from youth tend towards evil, and they are unable to make for themselves hearts of flesh in place of their stony hearts. 17For in the division of the nations of the whole earth, he appointed*   *i* Other ancient authorities add as verse 18, *whom, being his firstborn, he brings up with discipline, and allotting to him the light of his love, he does not neglect him.*   *j* Other ancient authorities add as verse 21, *But the Lord, who is gracious and knows how they are formed, has neither left them nor abandoned them, but has spared them.*
k Gk *him*   *l* Other ancient authorities add *apportioning repentance to his sons and daughters*   *m* Other ancient authorities add *for he will lead you out of darkness to the light of health.*

²⁹ How great is the mercy of the Lord,
and his forgiveness for those who
return to him!
³⁰ For not everything is within human
capability,
since human beings are not
immortal.
³¹ What is brighter than the sun? Yet it
can be eclipsed.
So flesh and blood devise evil.
³² He marshals the host of the height of
heaven;
but all human beings are dust and
ashes.

The Majesty of God

18 He who lives for ever created
the whole universe;
² the Lord alone is just. ^a
⁴ To none has he given power to
proclaim his works;
and who can search out his mighty
deeds?
⁵ Who can measure his majestic
power?
And who can fully recount his
mercies?
⁶ It is not possible to diminish or
increase them,
nor is it possible to fathom the
wonders of the Lord.
⁷ When human beings have finished,
they are just beginning,
and when they stop, they are still
perplexed.
⁸ What are human beings, and of what
use are they?
What is good in them, and what is
evil?
⁹ The number of days in their life is
great if they reach one hundred
years. ^b
¹⁰ Like a drop of water from the sea and
a grain of sand,
so are a few years among the days
of eternity.
¹¹ That is why the Lord is patient with
them
and pours out his mercy upon
them.

¹² He sees and recognizes that their end
is miserable;
therefore he grants them
forgiveness all the more.
¹³ The compassion of human beings is
for their neighbours,
but the compassion of the Lord is
for every living thing.
He rebukes and trains and teaches
them,
and turns them back, as a shepherd
his flock.
¹⁴ He has compassion on those who
accept his discipline
and who are eager for his precepts.

The Right Spirit in Giving Alms

¹⁵ My child, do not mix reproach with
your good deeds,
or spoil your gift by harsh words.
¹⁶ Does not the dew give relief from the
scorching heat?
So a word is better than a gift.
¹⁷ Indeed, does not a word surpass a
good gift?
Both are to be found in a gracious
person.
¹⁸ A fool is ungracious and abusive,
and the gift of a grudging giver
makes the eyes dim.

The Need for Reflection and Self-Control

¹⁹ Before you speak, learn;
and before you fall ill, take care of
your health.
²⁰ Before judgement comes, examine
yourself;
and at the time of scrutiny you will
find forgiveness.
²¹ Before falling ill, humble yourself;
and when you have sinned, repent.
²² Let nothing hinder you from paying a
vow promptly,
and do not wait until death to be
released from it.

*a Other ancient authorities add and there is no other
beside him; ³he steers the world with the span of his hand,
and all things obey his will; for he is king of all things by his
power, separating among them the holy things from the
profane.   b Other ancient authorities add but the death
of each one is beyond the calculation of all*

23 Before making a vow, prepare
        yourself;
    do not be like one who puts the
        Lord to the test.
24 Think of his wrath on the day of
        death,
    and of the moment of vengeance
        when he turns away his face.
25 In the time of plenty think of the
        time of hunger;
    in days of wealth think of poverty
        and need.
26 From morning to evening conditions
        change;
    all things move swiftly before the
        Lord.

27 One who is wise is cautious in
        everything;
    when sin is all around, one guards
        against wrongdoing.
28 Every intelligent person knows
        wisdom,
    and praises one who finds her.
29 Those who are skilled in words
        become wise themselves,
    and pour forth apt proverbs. *a*

SELF-CONTROL*b*

30 Do not follow your base desires,
    but restrain your appetites.
31 If you allow your soul to take
        pleasure in base desire,
    it will make you the laughing-stock
        of your enemies.
32 Do not revel in great luxury,
    or you may become impoverished
        by its expense.
33 Do not become a beggar by feasting
        with borrowed money
    when you have nothing in your
        purse. *c*

19 One who does this*d* will not
        become rich;
    one who despises small things will
        fail little by little.
2 Wine and women lead intelligent
        men astray,
    and the man who consorts with
        prostitutes is reckless.

3 Decay and worms will take
        possession of him,
    and the reckless person will be
        snatched away.

Against Loose Talk

4 One who trusts others too quickly
        has a shallow mind,
    and one who sins does wrong to
        himself.
5 One who rejoices in wickedness*e* will
        be condemned,*f*
6   but one who hates gossip has less
        evil.
7 Never repeat a conversation,
    and you will lose nothing at all.
8 With friend or foe do not report it,
    and unless it would be a sin for
        you, do not reveal it;
9 for someone may have heard you and
        watched you,
    and in time will hate you.
10 Have you heard something? Let it die
        with you.
    Be brave, it will not make you
        burst!
11 Having heard something, the fool
        suffers birth-pangs
    like a woman in labour with a
        child.
12 Like an arrow stuck in a person's
        thigh,
    so is gossip inside a fool.

13 Question a friend; perhaps he did not
        do it;
    or if he did, so that he may not do
        it again.
14 Question a neighbour; perhaps he
        did not say it;
    or if he said it, so that he may not
        repeat it.
15 Question a friend, for often it is
        slander;

a Other ancient authorities add *Better is confidence in the
one Lord than clinging with a dead heart to a dead one.*
b This heading is included in the Gk text.   *c* Other
ancient authorities add *for you will be plotting against your
own life*   *d* Heb: Gk *A worker who is a drunkard*
e Other ancient authorities read *heart*   *f* Other
ancient authorities add *but one who withstands pleasures
crowns his life.* *6One who controls the tongue will live
without strife,*

so do not believe everything you hear.

16 A person may make a slip without intending it.
Who has not sinned with his tongue?

17 Question your neighbour before you threaten him;
and let the law of the Most High take its course. *a*

True and False Wisdom

20 The whole of wisdom is fear of the Lord,
and in all wisdom there is the fulfilment of the law. *b*

22 The knowledge of wickedness is not wisdom,
nor is there prudence in the counsel of sinners.

23 There is a cleverness that is detestable,
and there is a fool who merely lacks wisdom.

24 Better are the God-fearing who lack understanding
than the highly intelligent who transgress the law.

25 There is a cleverness that is exact but unjust,
and there are people who abuse favours to gain a verdict.

26 There is the villain bowed down in mourning,
but inwardly he is full of deceit.

27 He hides his face and pretends not to hear,
but when no one notices, he will take advantage of you.

28 Even if lack of strength keeps him from sinning,
he will nevertheless do evil when he finds the opportunity.

29 A person is known by his appearance,
and a sensible person is known when first met face to face.

30 A person's attire and hearty laughter,
and the way he walks, show what he is.

Silence and Speech

20 There is a rebuke that is untimely,
and there is the person who is wise enough to keep silent.

2 How much better it is to rebuke than to fume!

3 And one who admits his fault will be kept from failure.

4 Like a eunuch lusting to violate a girl
is the person who does right under compulsion.

5 Some people keep silent and are thought to be wise,
while others are detested for being talkative.

6 Some people keep silent because they have nothing to say,
while others keep silent because they know when to speak.

7 The wise remain silent until the right moment,
but a boasting fool misses the right moment.

8 Whoever talks too much is detested,
and whoever pretends to authority is hated. *c*

Paradoxes

9 There may be good fortune for a person in adversity,
but a windfall may result in a loss.

10 There is the gift that profits you nothing,
and the gift to be paid back double.

11 There are losses for the sake of glory,
and there are some who have raised their heads from humble circumstances.

12 Some buy much for little,
but pay for it seven times over.

a Other ancient authorities add *and do not be angry.* ¹⁸*The fear of the Lord is the beginning of acceptance, and wisdom obtains his love.* ¹⁹*The knowledge of the Lord's commandments is life-giving discipline; and those who do what is pleasing to him enjoy the fruit of the tree of immortality.*   *b* Other ancient authorities add *and the knowledge of his omnipotence.* ²¹*When a slave says to his master, 'I will not act as you wish', even if later he does it, he angers the one who supports him.*   *c* Other ancient authorities add *How good it is to show repentance when you are reproved, for so you will escape deliberate sin!*

13 The wise make themselves beloved by
    only few words, *a*
    but the courtesies of fools are
        wasted.
14 A fool's gift will profit you nothing, *b*
    for he looks for recompense
        sevenfold. *c*
15 He gives little and upbraids much;
    he opens his mouth like a town
        crier.
    Today he lends and tomorrow he asks
        for it back;
    such a one is hateful to God and
        humans. *d*
16 The fool says, 'I have no friends,
    and I get no thanks for my good
        deeds.
    Those who eat my bread are evil-
        tongued.'
17 How many will ridicule him, and
    how often! *e*

Inappropriate Speech

18 A slip on the pavement is better than
    a slip of the tongue;
    the downfall of the wicked will
        occur just as speedily.
19 A coarse person is like an
    inappropriate story
    continually on the lips of the
        ignorant.
20 A proverb from a fool's lips will be
    rejected,
    for he does not tell it at the proper
        time.

21 One may be prevented from sinning
    by poverty;
    so when he rests he feels no
        remorse.
22 One may lose his life through shame,
    or lose it because of human
        respect. *f*
23 Another out of shame makes
    promises to a friend,
    and so makes an enemy for nothing.

Lying

24 A lie is an ugly blot on a person;
    it is continually on the lips of the
        ignorant.

25 A thief is preferable to a habitual liar,
    but the lot of both is ruin.
26 A liar's way leads to disgrace,
    and his shame is ever with him.

Proverbial Sayings *g*

27 The wise person advances himself by
    his words,
    and one who is sensible pleases the
        great.
28 Those who cultivate the soil heap up
    their harvest,
    and those who please the great
        atone for injustice.
29 Favours and gifts blind the eyes of the
    wise;
    like a muzzle on the mouth they
        stop reproofs.
30 Hidden wisdom and unseen treasure,
    of what value is either?
31 Better are those who hide their folly
    than those who hide their wisdom. *h*

Various Sins

21 Have you sinned, my child? Do
    so no more,
    but ask forgiveness for your past
        sins.
2 Flee from sin as from a snake;
    for if you approach sin, it will bite
        you.
    Its teeth are lion's teeth,
    and can destroy human lives.
3 All lawlessness is like a two-edged
    sword;
    there is no healing for the wound it
        inflicts.

4 Panic and insolence will waste away
    riches;
    thus the house of the proud will be
        laid waste. *i*

a Heb: Gk *by words*   *b* Other ancient authorities add
so it is with the envious who give under compulsion
c Syr: Gk *he has many eyes instead of one*   *d* Other
ancient authorities lack *to God and humans*   *e* Other
ancient authorities add *for he has not honestly received
what he has, and what he does not have is unimportant to
him*   *f* Other ancient authorities read *his foolish look*
g This heading is included in the Gk text.   *h* Other
ancient authorities add *32Unwearied endurance in seeking
the Lord is better than a masterless charioteer of one's own
life.*   *i* Other ancient authorities read *uprooted*

5 The prayer of the poor goes from
        their lips to the ears of God,[a]
    and his judgement comes speedily.
6 Those who hate reproof walk in the
        sinner's steps,
    but those who fear the Lord repent
        in their heart.
7 The mighty in speech are widely
        known;
    when they slip, the sensible person
        knows it.

8 Whoever builds his house with other
        people's money
    ·is like one who gathers stones for
        his burial mound.[b]
9 An assembly of the wicked is like a
        bundle of tow,
    and their end is a blazing fire.
10 The way of sinners is paved with
        smooth stones,
    but at its end is the pit of Hades.

Wisdom and Foolishness

11 Whoever keeps the law controls his
        thoughts,
    and the fulfilment of the fear of the
        Lord is wisdom.
12 One who is not clever cannot be
        taught,
    but there is a cleverness that
        increases bitterness.
13 The knowledge of the wise will
        increase like a flood,
    and their counsel like a life-giving
        spring.
14 The mind[c] of a fool is like a broken
        jar;
    it can hold no knowledge.

15 When an intelligent person hears a
        wise saying,
    he praises it and adds to it;
    when a fool[d] hears it, he laughs at[e] it
        and throws it behind his back.
16 A fool's chatter is like a burden on a
        journey,
    but delight is found in the speech
        of the intelligent.
17 The utterance of a sensible person is
        sought in the assembly,

and they ponder his words in their
    minds.

18 Like a house in ruins is wisdom to a
        fool,
    and to the ignorant, knowledge is
        talk that has no meaning.
19 To a senseless person education is
        fetters on his feet,
    and like manacles on his right
        hand.
20 A fool raises his voice when he
        laughs,
    but the wise[f] smile quietly.
21 To the sensible person education is
        like a golden ornament,
    and like a bracelet on the right
        arm.

22 The foot of a fool rushes into a
        house,
    but an experienced person waits
        respectfully outside.
23 A boor peers into the house from the
        door,
    but a cultivated person remains
        outside.
24 It is ill-mannered for a person to
        listen at a door;
    the discreet would be grieved by the
        disgrace.

25 The lips of babblers speak of what is
        not their concern,[g]
    but the words of the prudent are
        weighed in the balance.
26 The mind of fools is in their mouth,
    but the mouth of the wise is in[h]
        their mind.
27 When an ungodly person curses an
        adversary,[i]
    he curses himself.
28 A whisperer degrades himself
    and is hated in his
        neighbourhood.

a Gk *his ears*   b Other ancient authorities read *for the
winter*   c Syr Lat: Gk *entrails*   d Syr: Gk *reveller*
e Syr: Gk *dislikes*   f Syr Lat: Gk *clever*   g Other
ancient authorities read *of strangers speak of these things*
h Other ancient authorities omit *in*   i Or *curses Satan*

The Idler

22 The idler is like a filthy stone,
and everyone hisses at his
disgrace.
2 The idler is like the filth of dunghills;
anyone that picks it up will shake it
off his hand.

Degenerate Children

3 It is a disgrace to be the father of an
undisciplined son,
and the birth of a daughter is a loss.
4 A sensible daughter obtains a
husband of her own,
but one who acts shamefully is a
grief to her father.
5 An impudent daughter disgraces
father and husband,
and is despised by both.
6 Like music in time of mourning is ill-
timed conversation,
but a thrashing and discipline are
at all times wisdom. *a*

Wisdom and Folly

9 Whoever teaches a fool is like one
who glues potsherds together,
or who rouses a sleeper from deep
slumber.
10 Whoever tells a story to a fool tells it
to a drowsy man;
and at the end he will say, 'What is
it?'
11 Weep for the dead, for he has left the
light behind;
and weep for the fool, for he has
left intelligence behind.
Weep less bitterly for the dead, for he
is at rest;
but the life of the fool is worse than
death.
12 Mourning for the dead lasts seven
days,
but for the foolish or the ungodly it
lasts all the days of their lives.

13 Do not talk much with a senseless
person
or visit an unintelligent person. *b*
Stay clear of him, or you may have
trouble,

and be spattered when he shakes
himself.
Avoid him and you will find rest,
and you will never be wearied by
his lack of sense.
14 What is heavier than lead?
And what is its name except 'Fool'?
15 Sand, salt, and a piece of iron
are easier to bear than a stupid
person.

16 A wooden beam firmly bonded into a
building
is not loosened by an earthquake;
so the mind firmly resolved after due
reflection
will not be afraid in a crisis.
17 A mind settled on an intelligent
thought
is like stucco decoration that makes
a wall smooth.
18 Fences *c* set on a high place
will not stand firm against the
wind;
so a timid mind with a fool's resolve
will not stand firm against any fear.

The Preservation of Friendship

19 One who pricks the eye brings tears,
and one who pricks the heart
makes clear its feelings.
20 One who throws a stone at birds
scares them away,
and one who reviles a friend
destroys a friendship.
21 Even if you draw your sword against a
friend,
do not despair, for there is a way
back.
22 If you open your mouth against your
friend,
do not worry, for reconciliation is
possible.
But as for reviling, arrogance,

a Other ancient authorities add *7Children who are
brought up in a good life conceal the lowly birth of their
parents. 8Children who are disdainfully and boorishly
haughty stain the nobility of their kindred.* *b* Other
ancient authorities add *For being without sense he will
despise everything about you* *c* Other ancient
authorities read *Pebbles*

disclosure of secrets, or a
treacherous blow—
in these cases any friend will take to
flight.

23 Gain the trust of your neighbour in
his poverty,
so that you may rejoice with him in
his prosperity.
Stand by him in time of distress,
so that you may share with him in
his inheritance. *a*

24 The vapour and smoke of the furnace
precede the fire;
so insults precede bloodshed.

25 I am not ashamed to shelter a friend,
and I will not hide from him.

26 But if harm should come to me
because of him,
whoever hears of it will beware of
him.

A Prayer for Help against Sinning

27 Who will set a guard over my mouth,
and an effective seal upon my lips,
so that I may not fall because of
them,
and my tongue may not destroy
me?

23 O Lord, Father and Master of
my life,
do not abandon me to their
designs,
and do not let me fall because of
them!

2 Who will set whips over my thoughts,
and the discipline of wisdom over
my mind,
so as not to spare me in my errors,
and not overlook my *b* sins?

3 Otherwise my mistakes may be
multiplied,
and my sins may abound,
and I may fall before my adversaries,
and my enemy may rejoice over
me. *c*

4 O Lord, Father and God of my life,
do not give me haughty eyes,

5 and remove evil desire from me.

6 Let neither gluttony nor lust
overcome me,

and do not give me over to
shameless passion.

DISCIPLINE OF THE TONGUE d

7 Listen, my children, to instruction
concerning the mouth;
one who observes it will never be
caught.

8 Sinners are overtaken through their
lips;
by them the reviler and the
arrogant are tripped up.

9 Do not accustom your mouth to
oaths,
nor habitually utter the name of
the Holy One;

10 for as a servant who is constantly
under scrutiny
will not lack bruises,
so also the person who always swears
and utters the Name
will never be cleansed *e* from sin.

11 One who swears many oaths is full of
iniquity,
and the scourge will not leave his
house.
If he swears in error, his sin remains
on him,
and if he disregards it, he sins
doubly;
if he swears a false oath, he will not
be justified,
for his house will be filled with
calamities.

Foul Language

12 There is a manner of speaking
comparable to death; *f*
may it never be found in the
inheritance of Jacob!
Such conduct will be far from the
godly,
and they will not wallow in sins.

13 Do not accustom your mouth to
coarse, foul language,
for it involves sinful speech.

a Other ancient authorities add *For one should not always
despise restricted circumstances, or admire a rich person who
is stupid.*   *b* Gk *their*   *c* Other ancient authorities
add *From them the hope of your mercy is remote*   *d* This
heading is included in the Gk text.   *e* Syr *be free*
f Other ancient authorities read *clothed about with death*

14 Remember your father and mother
  when you sit among the great,
 or you may forget yourself in their
    presence,
   and behave like a fool through bad
     habit;
  then you will wish that you had never
     been born,
   and you will curse the day of your
     birth.
15 Those who are accustomed to using
    abusive language
  will never become disciplined as
    long as they live.

Concerning Sexual Sins

16 Two kinds of individuals multiply
    sins,
  and a third incurs wrath.
 Hot passion that blazes like a fire
  will not be quenched until it burns
    itself out;
 one who commits fornication with
    his near of kin
  will never cease until the fire burns
    him up.
17 To a fornicator all bread is sweet;
  he will never weary until he dies.
18 One who sins against his marriage
    bed
  says to himself, 'Who can see me?
 Darkness surrounds me, the walls
    hide me,
  and no one sees me. Why should I
    worry?
 The Most High will not remember
    sins.'
19 His fear is confined to human eyes
  and he does not realize that the
    eyes of the Lord
  are ten thousand times brighter
    than the sun;
 they look upon every aspect of
    human behaviour
  and see into hidden corners.
20 Before the universe was created, it
    was known to him,
  and so it is since its completion.
21 This man will be punished in the
    streets of the city,

and where he least suspects it, he
    will be seized.
22 So it is with a woman who leaves her
    husband
  and presents him with an heir by
    another man.
23 For first of all, she has disobeyed the
    law of the Most High;
  second, she has committed an
    offence against her husband;
 and third, through her fornication
    she has committed adultery
  and brought forth children by
    another man.
24 She herself will be brought before the
    assembly,
  and her punishment will extend to
    her children.
25 Her children will not take root,
  and her branches will not bear
    fruit.
26 She will leave behind an accursed
    memory
  and her disgrace will never be
    blotted out.
27 Those who survive her will recognize
    that nothing is better than the fear
    of the Lord,
  and nothing sweeter than to heed the
    commandments of the Lord. a

THE PRAISE OF WISDOM b

24 Wisdom praises herself,
  and tells of her glory in the
    midst of her people.
2 In the assembly of the Most High she
    opens her mouth,
  and in the presence of his hosts she
    tells of her glory:
3 'I came forth from the mouth of the
    Most High,
  and covered the earth like a mist.
4 I dwelt in the highest heavens,
  and my throne was in a pillar of
    cloud.
5 Alone I compassed the vault of
    heaven

---

a Other ancient authorities add as verse 28, *It is a great
honour to follow God, and to be received by him is long life.*
b This heading is included in the Gk text.

and traversed the depths of the abyss.

6 Over waves of the sea, over all the earth,
    and over every people and nation I have held sway.ᵃ

7 Among all these I sought a resting-place;
    in whose territory should I abide?

8 'Then the Creator of all things gave me a command,
    and my Creator chose the place for my tent.
  He said, "Make your dwelling in Jacob,
    and in Israel receive your inheritance."

9 Before the ages, in the beginning, he created me,
    and for all the ages I shall not cease to be.

10 In the holy tent I ministered before him,
    and so I was established in Zion.

11 Thus in the beloved city he gave me a resting-place,
    and in Jerusalem was my domain.

12 I took root in an honoured people,
    in the portion of the Lord, his heritage.

13 'I grew tall like a cedar in Lebanon,
    and like a cypress on the heights of Hermon.

14 I grew tall like a palm tree in En-gedi,ᵇ
    and like rose-bushes in Jericho;
  like a fair olive tree in the field,
    and like a plane tree beside waterᶜ I grew tall.

15 Like cassia and camel's thorn I gave forth perfume,
    and like choice myrrh I spread my fragrance,
  like galbanum, onycha, and stacte,
    and like the odour of incense in the tent.

16 Like a terebinth I spread out my branches,
    and my branches are glorious and graceful.

17 Like the vine I bud forth delights,
    and my blossoms become glorious and abundant fruit.ᵈ

19 'Come to me, you who desire me,
    and eat your fill of my fruits.

20 For the memory of me is sweeter than honey,
    and the possession of me sweeter than the honeycomb.

21 Those who eat of me will hunger for more,
    and those who drink of me will thirst for more.

22 Whoever obeys me will not be put to shame,
    and those who work with me will not sin.'

Wisdom and the Law

23 All this is the book of the covenant of the Most High God,
    the law that Moses commanded us
    as an inheritance for the congregations of Jacob.ᵉ

25 It overflows, like the Pishon, with wisdom,
    and like the Tigris at the time of the first fruits.

26 It runs over, like the Euphrates, with understanding,
    and like the Jordan at harvest time.

27 It pours forth instruction like the Nile,ᶠ
    like the Gihon at the time of vintage.

28 The first man did not know wisdomᵍ fully,
    nor will the last one fathom her.

---

a Other ancient authorities read *I have acquired a possession*   *b* Other ancient authorities read *on the beaches*   *c* Other ancient authorities omit *beside water*   *d* Other ancient authorities add as verse 18, *I am the mother of beautiful love, of fear, of knowledge, and of holy hope; being eternal, I am given to all my children, to those who are named by him.*   *e* Other ancient authorities add as verse 24, 'Do not cease to be strong in the Lord, cling to him so that he may strengthen you; the Lord Almighty alone is God, and besides him there is no saviour.'*
f Syr: Gk *It makes instruction shine forth like light*
g Gk *her*

29 For her thoughts are more abundant
        than the sea,
    and her counsel deeper than the
        great abyss.

30 As for me, I was like a canal from a
        river,
    like a water channel into a garden.
31 I said, 'I will water my garden
        and drench my flower-beds.'
    And lo, my canal became a river,
        and my river a sea.
32 I will again make instruction shine
        forth like the dawn,
    and I will make it clear from far
        away.
33 I will again pour out teaching like
        prophecy,
    and leave it to all future
        generations.
34 Observe that I have not laboured for
        myself alone,
    but for all who seek wisdom. *a*

Those Who Are Worthy of Praise

25 I take pleasure in three things,
    and they are beautiful in the
    sight of God and of mortals: *b*
    agreement among brothers and
        sisters, friendship among
        neighbours,
    and a wife and husband who live in
        harmony.
2 I hate three kinds of people,
    and I loathe their manner of life:
    a pauper who boasts, a rich person
        who lies,
    and an old fool who commits
        adultery.

3 If you gathered nothing in your
        youth,
    how can you find anything in your
        old age?
4 How attractive is sound judgement in
        the grey-haired,
    and for the aged to possess good
        counsel!
5 How attractive is wisdom in the aged,
    and understanding and counsel in
        the venerable!

6 Rich experience is the crown of the
        aged,
    and their boast is the fear of the
        Lord.

7 I can think of nine whom I would
        call blessed,
    and a tenth my tongue proclaims:
    a man who can rejoice in his
        children;
    a man who lives to see the downfall
        of his foes.
8 Happy the man who lives with a
        sensible wife,
    and one who does not plough with
        ox and ass together. *c*
    Happy is one who does not sin with
        the tongue,
    and one who has not served an
        inferior.
9 Happy is one who finds a friend, *d*
    and one who speaks to attentive
        listeners.
10 How great is one who finds
        wisdom!
    But none is superior to one who
        fears the Lord.
11 Fear of the Lord surpasses
        everything;
    to whom can we compare one who
        has it? *e*

Some Extreme Forms of Evil

13 Any wound, but not a wound of the
        heart!
    Any wickedness, but not the
        wickedness of a woman!
14 Any suffering, but not suffering from
        those who hate!
    And any vengeance, but not the
        vengeance of enemies!
15 There is no venom *f* worse than a
        snake's venom, *f*
    and no anger worse than a
        woman's *g* wrath.

a Gk *her*   *b* Syr Lat: Gk *In three things I was beautiful
and I stood in beauty before the Lord and mortals.*
c Heb Syr: Gk lacks *and one who does not plough with ox
and ass together*   *d* Lat Syr: Gk *good sense*   *e* Other
ancient authorities add as verse 12, *The fear of the Lord is
the beginning of love for him, and faith is the beginning of
clinging to him.*   *f* Syr: Gk *head*   *g* Other ancient
authorities read *an enemy's*

The Evil of a Wicked Woman

16 I would rather live with a lion and a
dragon
than live with an evil woman.
17 A woman's wickedness changes her
appearance,
and darkens her face like that of a
bear.
18 Her husband sits[a] among the
neighbours,
and he cannot help sighing[b]
bitterly.
19 Any iniquity is small compared to a
woman's iniquity;
may a sinner's lot befall her!
20 A sandy ascent for the feet of the
aged—
such is a garrulous wife to a quiet
husband.
21 Do not be ensnared by a woman's
beauty,
and do not desire a woman for her
possessions.[c]
22 There is wrath and impudence and
great disgrace
when a wife supports her husband.
23 Dejected mind, gloomy face,
and wounded heart come from an
evil wife.
Drooping hands and weak knees
come from the wife who does not
make her husband happy.
24 From a woman sin had its
beginning,
and because of her we all die.
25 Allow no outlet to water,
and no boldness of speech to an
evil wife.
26 If she does not go as you direct,
separate her from yourself.

The Joy of a Good Wife

26 Happy is the husband of a good
wife;
the number of his days will be
doubled.
2 A loyal wife brings joy to her
husband,
and he will complete his years in
peace.
3 A good wife is a great blessing;

she will be granted among the
blessings of the man who fears
the Lord.
4 Whether rich or poor, his heart is
content,
and at all times his face is cheerful.

The Worst of Evils: A Wicked Wife

5 Of three things my heart is
frightened,
and of a fourth I am in great fear:[d]
Slander in the city, the gathering of a
mob,
and false accusation—all these are
worse than death.
6 But it is heartache and sorrow when a
wife is jealous of a rival,
and a tongue-lashing makes it
known to all.
7 A bad wife is a chafing yoke;
taking hold of her is like grasping a
scorpion.
8 A drunken wife arouses great anger;
she cannot hide her shame.
9 The haughty stare betrays an unchaste
wife;
her eyelids give her away.

10 Keep strict watch over a headstrong
daughter,
or else, when she finds liberty, she
will make use of it.
11 Be on guard against her impudent
eye,
and do not be surprised if she sins
against you.
12 As a thirsty traveller opens his
mouth
and drinks from any water near
him,
so she will sit in front of every tent-
peg
and open her quiver to the arrow.

The Blessing of a Good Wife

13 A wife's charm delights her husband,
and her skill puts flesh on his
bones.

a Heb Syr: Gk *loses heart*   b Other ancient authorities
read *and listening he sighs*   c Heb Syr: Other Gk
authorities read *for her beauty*   d Syr: Meaning of Gk
uncertain

14 A silent wife is a gift from the Lord,
  and nothing is so precious as her
    self-discipline.
15 A modest wife adds charm to charm,
  and no scales can weigh the value
    of her chastity.
16 Like the sun rising in the heights of
    the Lord,
  so is the beauty of a good wife in
    her well-ordered home.
17 Like the shining lamp on the holy
    lampstand,
  so is a beautiful face on a stately
    figure.
18 Like golden pillars on silver bases,
  so are shapely legs and steadfast
    feet.

Other ancient authorities add verses 19–27:

19 *My child, keep sound the bloom of your*
    youth,
  and do not give your strength to
    strangers.
20 *Seek a fertile field within the whole*
    plain,
  and sow it with your own seed,
    trusting in your fine stock.
21 *So your offspring will prosper,*
  and, having confidence in their good
    descent, will grow great.
22 *A prostitute is regarded as spittle,*
  and a married woman as a tower of
    death to her lovers.
23 *A godless wife is given as a portion to a*
    lawless man,
  but a pious wife is given to the man
    who fears the Lord.
24 *A shameless woman constantly acts*
    disgracefully,
  but a modest daughter will even be
    embarrassed before her husband.
25 *A headstrong wife is regarded as a dog,*
  but one who has a sense of shame will
    fear the Lord.
26 *A wife honouring her husband will seem*
    wise to all,
  but if she dishonours him in her pride
    she will be known to all as
    ungodly.

Happy is the husband of a good wife,
  for the number of his years will be
    doubled.
27 *A loud-voiced and garrulous wife is like*
    a trumpet sounding the charge,
  and every person like this lives in the
    anarchy of war.

Three Depressing Things

28 At two things my heart is grieved,
  and because of a third anger comes
    over me:
  a warrior in want through poverty,
    intelligent men who are treated
      contemptuously,
  and a man who turns back from
      righteousness to sin—
    the Lord will prepare him for the
      sword!

The Temptations of Commerce

29 A merchant can hardly keep from
    wrongdoing,
  nor is a tradesman innocent of
    sin.

27 Many have committed sin for
    gain,[a]
  and those who seek to get rich will
    avert their eyes.
2 As a stake is driven firmly into a
    fissure between stones,
  so sin is wedged in between selling
    and buying.
3 If a person is not steadfast in the fear
    of the Lord,
  his house will be quickly
    overthrown.

Tests in Life

4 When a sieve is shaken, the refuse
    appears;
  so do a person's faults when he
    speaks.
5 The kiln tests the potter's vessels;
  so the test of a person is in his
    conversation.

---

a Other ancient authorities read *a trifle*

6 Its fruit discloses the cultivation of a
tree;
  so a person's speech discloses the
  cultivation of his mind.
7 Do not praise anyone before he
speaks,
  for this is the way people are tested.

Reward and Retribution

8 If you pursue justice, you will attain it
  and wear it like a glorious robe.
9 Birds roost with their own kind,
  so honesty comes home to those
  who practise it.
10 A lion lies in wait for prey;
  so does sin for evildoers.

Varieties of Speech

11 The conversation of the godly is
always wise,
  but the fool changes like the moon.
12 Among stupid people limit your
time,
  but among thoughtful people
  linger on.
13 The talk of fools is offensive,
  and their laughter is wantonly
  sinful.
14 Their cursing and swearing make
one's hair stand on end,
  and their quarrels make others stop
  their ears.
15 The strife of the proud leads to
bloodshed,
  and their abuse is grievous to hear.

Betraying Secrets

16 Whoever betrays secrets destroys
confidence,
  and will never find a congenial
  friend.
17 Love your friend and keep faith with
him;
  but if you betray his secrets, do not
  follow after him.
18 For as a person destroys his enemy,
  so you have destroyed the
    friendship of your neighbour.
19 And as you allow a bird to escape
from your hand,

  so you have let your neighbour go,
  and will not catch him again.
20 Do not go after him, for he is too far
off,
  and has escaped like a gazelle from
  a snare.
21 For a wound may be bandaged,
  and there is reconciliation after
  abuse,
  but whoever has betrayed secrets is
  without hope.

Hypocrisy and Retribution

22 Whoever winks the eye plots
mischief,
  and those who know him will keep
  their distance.
23 In your presence his mouth is all
sweetness,
  and he admires your words;
  but later he will twist his speech
  and with your own words he will
  trip you up.
24 I have hated many things, but him
above all;
  even the Lord hates him.
25 Whoever throws a stone straight up
throws it on his own head,
  and a treacherous blow opens up
  many wounds.
26 Whoever digs a pit will fall into it,
  and whoever sets a snare will be
  caught in it.
27 If a person does evil, it will roll back
upon him,
  and he will not know where it came
  from.
28 Mockery and abuse issue from the
proud,
  but vengeance lies in wait for them
  like a lion.
29 Those who rejoice in the fall of the
godly will be caught in a snare,
  and pain will consume them before
  their death.

Anger and Vengeance

30 Anger and wrath, these also are
abominations,
  yet a sinner holds on to them.

28

The vengeful will face the Lord's vengeance,
  for he keeps a strict account of[a] their sins.

2 Forgive your neighbour the wrong he has done,
  and then your sins will be pardoned when you pray.

3 Does anyone harbour anger against another,
  and expect healing from the Lord?

4 If someone has no mercy towards another like himself,
  can he then seek pardon for his own sins?

5 If a mere mortal harbours wrath,
  who will make an atoning sacrifice for his sins?

6 Remember the end of your life, and set enmity aside;
  remember corruption and death, and be true to the commandments.

7 Remember the commandments, and do not be angry with your neighbour;
  remember the covenant of the Most High, and overlook faults.

8 Refrain from strife, and your sins will be fewer;
  for the hot-tempered kindle strife,

9 and the sinner disrupts friendships
  and sows discord among those who are at peace.

10 In proportion to the fuel, so will the fire burn,
  and in proportion to the obstinacy, so will strife increase;[b]
  in proportion to a person's strength will be his anger,
  and in proportion to his wealth he will increase his wrath.

11 A hasty quarrel kindles a fire,
  and a hasty dispute sheds blood.

The Evil Tongue

12 If you blow on a spark, it will glow;
  if you spit on it, it will be put out;
  yet both come out of your mouth.

13 Curse the gossips and the double-tongued,
  for they destroy the peace of many.

14 Slander[c] has shaken many,
  and scattered them from nation to nation;
  it has destroyed strong cities,
  and overturned the houses of the great.

15 Slander[c] has driven virtuous women from their homes,
  and deprived them of the fruit of their toil.

16 Those who pay heed to slander[d] will not find rest,
  nor will they settle down in peace.

17 The blow of a whip raises a welt,
  but a blow of the tongue crushes the bones.

18 Many have fallen by the edge of the sword,
  but not as many as have fallen because of the tongue.

19 Happy is one who is protected from it,
  who has not been exposed to its anger,
  who has not borne its yoke,
  and has not been bound with its fetters.

20 For its yoke is a yoke of iron,
  and its fetters are fetters of bronze;

21 its death is an evil death,
  and Hades is preferable to it.

22 It has no power over the godly;
  they will not be burned in its flame.

23 Those who forsake the Lord will fall into its power;
  it will burn among them and will not be put out.
  It will be sent out against them like a lion;
  like a leopard it will mangle them.

24a As you fence in your property with thorns,

_____
a Other ancient authorities read *for he firmly establishes*
b Other ancient authorities read *burn*   c Gk A *third tongue*   d Gk *it*

25b so make a door and a bolt for your
        mouth.
24b As you lock up your silver and gold,
25a so make balances and scales for
        your words.
26 Take care not to err with your
        tongue,[a]
        and fall victim to one lying in wait.

On Lending and Borrowing

29 The merciful lend to their
        neighbours;
        by holding out a helping hand they
        keep the commandments.
2 Lend to your neighbour in his time of
        need;
        repay your neighbour when a loan
        falls due.
3 Keep your promise and be honest
        with him,
        and on every occasion you will find
        what you need.
4 Many regard a loan as a windfall,
        and cause trouble to those who
        help them.
5 One kisses another's hands until he
        gets a loan,
        and is deferential in speaking of his
        neighbour's money;
    but at the time for repayment he
        delays,
        and pays back with empty
        promises,
        and finds fault with the time.
6 If he can pay, his creditor[b] will hardly
        get back half,
        and will regard that as a windfall.
    If he cannot pay, the borrower[b] has
        robbed the other of his money,
        and he has needlessly made him an
        enemy;
    he will repay him with curses and
        reproaches,
        and instead of glory will repay him
        with dishonour.
7 Many refuse to lend, not because of
        meanness,
        but from fear[c] of being defrauded
        needlessly.

8 Nevertheless, be patient with

someone in humble
        circumstances,
        and do not keep him waiting for
        your alms.
9 Help the poor for the
        commandment's sake,
        and in their need do not send them
        away empty-handed.
10 Lose your silver for the sake of a
        brother or a friend,
        and do not let it rust under a stone
        and be lost.
11 Lay up your treasure according to the
        commandments of the Most
        High,
        and it will profit you more than
        gold.
12 Store up almsgiving in your treasury,
        and it will rescue you from every
        disaster;
13 better than a stout shield and a
        sturdy spear,
        it will fight for you against the
        enemy.

On Guaranteeing Debts

14 A good person will be surety for his
        neighbour,
        but one who has lost all sense of
        shame will fail him.
15 Do not forget the kindness of your
        guarantor,
        for he has given his life for you.
16 A sinner wastes the property of his
        guarantor,
17   and the ungrateful person
        abandons his rescuer.
18 Being surety has ruined many who
        were prosperous,
        and has tossed them about like
        waves of the sea;
    it has driven the influential into exile,
        and they have wandered among
        foreign nations.
19 The sinner comes to grief through
        surety;
        his pursuit of gain involves him in
        lawsuits.

a Gk *with it*   *b* Gk *he*   *c* Other ancient authorities
read *many refuse to lend, therefore, because of such
meanness; they are afraid*

20 Assist your neighbour to the best of
your ability,
    but be careful not to fall yourself.

Home and Hospitality

21 The necessities of life are water,
bread, and clothing,
    and also a house to assure privacy.
22 Better is the life of the poor under
their own crude roof
    than sumptuous food in the house
of others.
23 Be content with little or much,
    and you will hear no reproach for
being a guest. *a*
24 It is a miserable life to go from house
to house;
    as a guest you should not open
your mouth;
25 you will play the host and provide
drink without being thanked,
    and besides this you will hear rude
words like these:
26 'Come here, stranger, prepare the
table;
    let me eat what you have there.'
27 'Be off, stranger, for an honoured
guest is here;
    my brother has come for a visit,
    and I need the guest-room.'
28 It is hard for a sensitive person to
bear
    scolding about lodging *b* and the
insults of the moneylender.

CONCERNING CHILDREN *c*

30 He who loves his son will whip
him often,
    so that he may rejoice at the way he
turns out.
2 He who disciplines his son will profit
by him,
    and will boast of him among
acquaintances.
3 He who teaches his son will make his
enemies envious,
    and will glory in him among his
friends.
4 When the father dies he will not
seem to be dead,

    for he has left behind him one like
himself,
5 whom in his life he looked upon
with joy
    and at death, without grief.
6 He has left behind him an avenger
against his enemies,
    and one to repay the kindness of
his friends.

7 Whoever spoils his son will bind up
his wounds,
    and will suffer heartache at every
cry.
8 An unbroken horse turns out
stubborn,
    and an unchecked son turns out
headstrong.
9 Pamper a child, and he will terrorize
you;
    play with him, and he will grieve
you.
10 Do not laugh with him, or you will
have sorrow with him,
    and in the end you will gnash your
teeth.
11 Give him no freedom in his youth,
    and do not ignore his errors.
12 Bow down his neck in his youth, *d*
    and beat his sides while he is
young,
    or else he will become stubborn and
disobey you,
    and you will have sorrow of soul
from him. *e*
13 Discipline your son and make his
yoke heavy, *f*
    so that you may not be offended by
his shamelessness.

14 Better off poor, healthy, and fit
    than rich and afflicted in body.
15 Health and fitness are better than any
gold,
    and a robust body than countless
riches.

a Lat: Gk *reproach from your family;* other ancient
authorities lack this line   *b* Or *scolding from the
household*   *c* This heading is included in the Gk text.
d Other ancient authorities lack this line and the
preceding line   *e* Other ancient authorities lack this
line   *f* Heb: Gk *take pains with him*

16 There is no wealth better than health
    of body,
     and no gladness above joy of
     heart.
17 Death is better than a life of misery,
    and eternal sleep*a* than chronic
    sickness.

CONCERNING FOODS*b*

18 Good things poured out upon a
    mouth that is closed
     are like offerings of food placed
     upon a grave.
19 Of what use to an idol is a sacrifice?
     For it can neither eat nor smell.
     So is one punished by the Lord;
20 he sees with his eyes and groans
     as a eunuch groans when
     embracing a girl.*c*

21 Do not give yourself over to sorrow,
    and do not distress yourself
    deliberately.
22 A joyful heart is life itself,
    and rejoicing lengthens one's life
    span.
23 Indulge yourself*d* and take comfort,
    and remove sorrow far from you,
     for sorrow has destroyed many,
     and no advantage ever comes from
     it.
24 Jealousy and anger shorten life,
    and anxiety brings on premature
    old age.
25 Those who are cheerful and merry at
    table
     will benefit from their food.

Right Attitude towards Riches

31 Wakefulness over wealth wastes
    away one's flesh,
     and anxiety about it drives away
     sleep.
2 Wakeful anxiety prevents slumber,
    and a severe illness carries off
    sleep.*e*
3 The rich person toils to amass a
    fortune,
     and when he rests he fills himself
     with his dainties.

4 The poor person toils to make a
    meagre living,
     and if ever he rests he becomes
     needy.
5 One who loves gold will not be
    justified;
     one who pursues money will be led
     astray*f* by it.
6 Many have come to ruin because of
    gold,
     and their destruction has met them
     face to face.
7 It is a stumbling-block to those who
    are avid for it,
     and every fool will be taken captive
     by it.
8 Blessed is the rich person who is
    found blameless,
     and who does not go after gold.
9 Who is he, that we may praise him?
     For he has done wonders among
     his people.
10 Who has been tested by it and been
    found perfect?
     Let it be for him a ground for
     boasting.
    Who has had the power to transgress
     and did not transgress,
     and to do evil and did not do it?
11 His prosperity will be established,*g*
    and the assembly will proclaim his
    acts of charity.

Table Etiquette

12 Are you seated at the table of the
    great?*h*
     Do not be greedy at it,
     and do not say, 'How much food
     there is here!'
13 Remember that a greedy eye is a bad
    thing.
     What has been created more greedy
     than the eye?

a Other ancient authorities lack *eternal sleep*   *b* This
heading is included in the Gk text; other ancient
authorities place the heading before verse 16   *c* Other
ancient authorities add *So is the person who does right
under compulsion*   *d* Other ancient authorities read
Beguile yourself   *e* Other ancient authorities read *sleep
carries off a severe illness*   *f* Heb Syr: Gk *pursues
destruction will be filled*   *g* Other ancient authorities
add *because of this*   *h* Heb Syr: Gk *at a great table*

Therefore it sheds tears for any
    reason.

14 Do not reach out your hand for
    everything you see,
    and do not crowd your neighbour[a]
    at the dish.

15 Judge your neighbour's feelings by
    your own,
    and in every matter be thoughtful.

16 Eat what is set before you like a well-
    bred person,[b]
    and do not chew greedily, or you
    will give offence.

17 Be the first to stop, as befits good
    manners,
    and do not be insatiable, or you
    will give offence.

18 If you are seated among many others,
    do not help yourself[c] before they do.

19 How ample a little is for a well-
    disciplined person!
    He does not breathe heavily when
    in bed.

20 Healthy sleep depends on moderate
    eating;
    he rises early, and feels fit.
    The distress of sleeplessness and of
    nausea
    and colic are with the glutton.

21 If you are overstuffed with food,
    get up to vomit, and you will have
    relief.

22 Listen to me, my child, and do not
    disregard me,
    and in the end you will appreciate
    my words.
    In everything you do be moderate,[d]
    and no sickness will overtake you.

23 People bless someone who is liberal
    with food,
    and their testimony to his
    generosity is trustworthy.

24 The city complains of someone who
    is stingy with food,
    and their testimony to his
    stinginess is accurate.

Temperance in Drinking Wine

25 Do not try to prove your strength by
    wine-drinking,

for wine has destroyed many.

26 As the furnace tests the work of the
    smith,[e]
    so wine tests hearts when the
    insolent quarrel.

27 Wine is very life to human beings
    if taken in moderation.
    What is life to one who is without
    wine?
    It has been created to make people
    happy.

28 Wine drunk at the proper time and in
    moderation
    is rejoicing of heart and gladness of
    soul.

29 Wine drunk to excess leads to
    bitterness of spirit,
    to quarrels and stumbling.

30 Drunkenness increases the anger of a
    fool to his own hurt,
    reducing his strength and adding
    wounds.

31 Do not reprove your neighbour at a
    banquet of wine,
    and do not despise him in his
    merrymaking;
    speak no word of reproach to him,
    and do not distress him by making
    demands of him.

Etiquette at a Banquet

32 If they make you master of the
    feast, do not exalt yourself;
    be among them as one of their
    number.
    Take care of them first and then sit
    down;

2   when you have fulfilled all your
    duties, take your place,
    so that you may be merry along with
    them
    and receive a garland for your
    excellent leadership.

3 Speak, you who are older, for it is
    your right,
    but with accurate knowledge, and
    do not interrupt the music.

---

a Gk him   b Heb: Gk like a human being   c Gk reach
out your hand   d Heb Syr: Gk industrious   e Heb: Gk
tests the hardening of steel by dipping

4 Where there is entertainment, do not
    pour out talk;
  do not display your cleverness at
    the wrong time.
5 A ruby seal in a setting of gold
  is a concert of music at a banquet
    of wine.
6 A seal of emerald in a rich setting of
    gold
  is the melody of music with good
    wine.

7 Speak, you who are young, if you are
    obliged to,
  but no more than twice, and only if
    asked.
8 Be brief; say much in few words;
  be as one who knows and can still
    hold his tongue.
9 Among the great do not act as their
    equal;
  and when another is speaking, do
    not babble.

10 Lightning travels ahead of the
    thunder,
  and approval goes before one who
    is modest.
11 Leave in good time and do not be the
    last;
  go home quickly and do not linger.
12 Amuse yourself there to your heart's
    content,
  but do not sin through proud
    speech.
13 But above all bless your Maker,
  who fills you with his good gifts.

The Providence of God

14 One who seeks God *a* will accept his
    discipline,
  and those who rise early to seek
    him *b* will find favour.
15 One who seeks the law will be filled
    with it,
  but the hypocrite will stumble at it.
16 Those who fear the Lord will form
    true judgements,
  and they will kindle righteous
    deeds like a light.
17 The sinner will shun reproof,

and will find a decision according
    to his liking.

18 A sensible person will not overlook a
    thoughtful suggestion;
  an insolent *c* and proud person will
    not be deterred by fear. *d*
19 Do nothing without deliberation,
  but when you have acted, do not
    regret it.
20 Do not go on a path full of hazards,
  and do not stumble at an obstacle
    twice. *e*
21 Do not be overconfident on a
    smooth *f* road,
22 and give good heed to your paths. *g*
23 Guard *h* yourself in every act,
  for this is the keeping of the
    commandments.

24 One who keeps the law preserves
    himself, *i*
  and one who trusts the Lord will
    not suffer loss.

33

  No evil will befall someone
    who fears the Lord,
  but in trials such a one will be
    rescued again and again.
2 The wise will not hate the law,
  but someone who is hypocritical
    about it is like a boat in a storm.
3 The sensible person will trust in the
    law;
  for such a one the law is as
    dependable as a divine oracle.

4 Prepare what to say, and then you
    will be listened to;
  draw upon your training, and give
    your answer.
5 The heart of a fool is like a cartwheel,
  and his thoughts like a turning axle.
6 A mocking friend is like a stallion
  that neighs no matter who the rider
    is.

a Heb: Gk *who fears the Lord*   *b* Other ancient
authorities lack *to seek him*   *c* Heb: Gk *alien*
d Meaning of Gk uncertain. Other ancient authorities
add *and after acting, with him, without deliberation*
e Heb: Gk *stumble on stony ground*   *f* Or *an unexplored*
g Heb Syr: Gk *and beware of your children*   *h* Heb Syr:
Gk *Trust*   *i* Heb: Gk *who believes the law heeds the
commandments*

Differences in Nature and in Humankind

7 Why is one day more important than
another,
when all the daylight in the year is
from the sun?
8 By the Lord's wisdom they were
distinguished,
and he appointed the different
seasons and festivals.
9 Some days he exalted and hallowed,
and some he made ordinary days.
10 All human beings come from the
ground,
and humankind*a* was created out of
the dust.
11 In the fullness of his knowledge the
Lord distinguished them
and appointed their different
ways.
12 Some he blessed and exalted,
and some he made holy and
brought near to himself;
but some he cursed and brought
low,
and turned them out of their
place.
13 Like clay in the hand of the potter,
to be moulded as he pleases,
so all are in the hand of their Maker,
to be given whatever he decides.

14 Good is the opposite of evil,
and life the opposite of death;
so the sinner is the opposite of the
godly.
15 Look at all the works of the Most
High;
they come in pairs, one the
opposite of the other.

16 Now I was the last to keep vigil;
I was like a gleaner following the
grape-pickers;
17 by the blessing of the Lord I arrived
first,
and like a grape-picker I filled my
wine press.
18 Consider that I have not laboured for
myself alone,
but for all who seek instruction.

19 Hear me, you who are great among
the people,
and you leaders of the
congregation, pay heed!

The Advantage of Independence

20 To son or wife, to brother or friend,
do not give power over yourself, as
long as you live;
and do not give your property to
another,
in case you change your mind and
must ask for it.
21 While you are still alive and have
breath in you,
do not let anyone take your place.
22 For it is better that your children
should ask from you
than that you should look to the
hand of your children.
23 Excel in all that you do;
bring no stain upon your honour.
24 At the time when you end the days of
your life,
in the hour of death, distribute
your inheritance.

The Treatment of Slaves

25 Fodder and a stick and burdens for a
donkey;
bread and discipline and work for a
slave.
26 Set your slave to work, and you will
find rest;
leave his hands idle, and he will
seek liberty.
27 Yoke and thong will bow the neck,
and for a wicked slave there are
racks and tortures.
28 Put him to work, in order that he
may not be idle,
29 for idleness teaches much evil.
30 Set him to work, as is fitting for
him,
and if he does not obey, make his
fetters heavy.
Do not be overbearing towards
anyone,
and do nothing unjust.

a Heb: Gk *Adam*

31 If you have but one slave, treat him
  like yourself,
  because you have bought him with
    blood.
  If you have but one slave, treat him
    like a brother,
  for you will need him as you need
    your life.
32 If you ill-treat him, and he leaves you
    and runs away,
33 which way will you go to seek
    him?

Dreams Mean Nothing

34
The senseless have vain and
false hopes,
  and dreams give wings to fools.
2 As one who catches at a shadow and
    pursues the wind,
  so is anyone who believes in[a]
    dreams.
3 What is seen in dreams is but a
    reflection,
  the likeness of a face looking at
    itself.
4 From an unclean thing what can be
    clean?
  And from something false what can
    be true?
5 Divinations and omens and dreams
    are unreal,
  and like a woman in labour, the
    mind has fantasies.
6 Unless they are sent by intervention
    from the Most High,
  pay no attention to them.
7 For dreams have deceived many,
  and those who put their hope in
    them have perished.
8 Without such deceptions the law will
    be fulfilled,
  and wisdom is complete in the
    mouth of the faithful.

Experience as a Teacher

9 An educated[b] person knows many
    things,
  and one with much experience
    knows what he is talking
    about.

10 An inexperienced person knows few
    things,
11 but he that has travelled acquires
    much cleverness.
12 I have seen many things in my
    travels,
  and I understand more than I can
    express.
13 I have often been in danger of
    death,
  but have escaped because of these
    experiences.

Fear the Lord

14 The spirit of those who fear the Lord
    will live,
15 for their hope is in him who saves
    them.
16 Those who fear the Lord will not be
    timid,
  or play the coward, for he is their
    hope.
17 Happy is the soul that fears the
    Lord!
18 To whom does he look? And who is
    his support?
19 The eyes of the Lord are on those
    who love him,
  a mighty shield and strong
    support,
  a shelter from scorching wind and a
    shade from noonday sun,
  a guard against stumbling and a
    help against falling.
20 He lifts up the soul and makes the
    eyes sparkle;
  he gives health and life and
    blessing.

Offering Sacrifices

21 If one sacrifices ill-gotten goods, the
    offering is blemished;[c]
22 the gifts[d] of the lawless are not
    acceptable.
23 The Most High is not pleased with
    the offerings of the ungodly,
  nor for a multitude of sacrifices
    does he forgive sins.

a Syr: Gk *pays heed to*   b Other ancient authorities
read *A travelled*   c Other ancient authorities read *is
made in mockery*   d Other ancient authorities read
mockeries

24 Like one who kills a son before his
   father's eyes
      is the person who offers a sacrifice
      from the property of the poor.
25 The bread of the needy is the life of
   the poor;
      whoever deprives them of it is a
      murderer.
26 To take away a neighbour's living is
   to commit murder;
27   to deprive an employee of wages is
   to shed blood.

28 When one builds and another tears
   down,
      what do they gain but hard work?
29 When one prays and another curses,
      to whose voice will the Lord listen?
30 If one washes after touching a corpse,
   and touches it again,
      what has been gained by washing?
31 So if someone fasts for his sins,
      and goes again and does the same
      things,
      who will listen to his prayer?
      And what has he gained by
      humbling himself?

The Law and Sacrifices

35 One who keeps the law makes
   many offerings;
2   one who heeds the commandments
   makes an offering of well-being.
3 One who returns a kindness offers
   choice flour,
4   and one who gives alms sacrifices a
   thank-offering.
5 To keep from wickedness is pleasing
   to the Lord,
      and to forsake unrighteousness is
      an atonement.
6 Do not appear before the Lord
   empty-handed,
7   for all that you offer is in fulfilment
   of the commandment.
8 The offering of the righteous enriches
   the altar,
      and its pleasing odour rises before
      the Most High.
9 The sacrifice of the righteous is
   acceptable,

      and it will never be forgotten.
10 Be generous when you worship the
   Lord,
      and do not stint the first fruits of
      your hands.
11 With every gift show a cheerful face,
      and dedicate your tithe with
      gladness.
12 Give to the Most High as he has given
   to you,
      and as generously as you can
      afford.
13 For the Lord is the one who repays,
      and he will repay you sevenfold.

Divine Justice

14 Do not offer him a bribe, for he will
   not accept it;
15   and do not rely on a dishonest
   sacrifice;
   for the Lord is the judge,
      and with him there is no partiality.
16 He will not show partiality to the
   poor;
      but he will listen to the prayer of
      one who is wronged.
17 He will not ignore the supplication of
   the orphan,
      or the widow when she pours out
      her complaint.
18 Do not the tears of the widow run
   down her cheek
19   as she cries out against the one who
   causes them to fall?
20 One whose service is pleasing to the
   Lord will be accepted,
      and his prayer will reach to the
      clouds.
21 The prayer of the humble pierces the
   clouds,
      and it will not rest until it reaches
      its goal;
      it will not desist until the Most High
      responds
22   and does justice to the righteous,
      and executes judgement.
   Indeed, the Lord will not delay,
      and like a warrior[a] will not be
      patient

a Heb: Gk and with them

until he crushes the loins of the
    unmerciful
23 and repays vengeance on the
    nations;
until he destroys the multitude of the
    insolent,
    and breaks the sceptres of the
    unrighteous;
24 until he repays mortals according to
    their deeds,
    and the works of all according to
    their thoughts;
25 until he judges the case of his people
    and makes them rejoice in his
    mercy.
26 His mercy is as welcome in time of
    distress
    as clouds of rain in time of
    drought.

A Prayer for God's People

36 Have mercy upon us, O God*a*
    of all,
2   and put all the nations in fear of
    you.
3   Lift up your hand against foreign
    nations
    and let them see your might.
4   As you have used us to show your
    holiness to them,
    so use them to show your glory to
    us.
5   Then they will know,*b* as we have
    known,
    that there is no God but you,
    O Lord.
6   Give new signs, and work other
    wonders;
7   make your hand and right arm
    glorious.
8   Rouse your anger and pour out your
    wrath;
9   destroy the adversary and wipe out
    the enemy.
10 Hasten the day, and remember the
    appointed time,*c*
    and let people recount your mighty
    deeds.
11 Let survivors be consumed in the
    fiery wrath,

and may those who harm your
    people meet destruction.
12 Crush the heads of hostile rulers
    who say, 'There is no one but
    ourselves.'
13 Gather all the tribes of Jacob,*d*
16 and give them their inheritance, as
    at the beginning.
17 Have mercy, O Lord, on the people
    called by your name,
    on Israel, whom you have named*e*
    your firstborn,
18 Have pity on the city of your
    sanctuary,*f*
    Jerusalem, the place of your
    dwelling.*g*
19 Fill Zion with your majesty,*h*
    and your temple*i* with your glory.
20 Bear witness to those whom you
    created in the beginning,
    and fulfil the prophecies spoken in
    your name.
21 Reward those who wait for you
    and let your prophets be found
    trustworthy.
22 Hear, O Lord, the prayer of your
    servants, according to your
    goodwill towards*j* your people,
    and all who are on the earth will
    know
    that you are the Lord, the God of
    the ages.

Concerning Discrimination

23 The stomach will take any food,
    yet one food is better than another.
24 As the palate tastes the kinds of
    game,
    so an intelligent mind detects false
    words.
25 A perverse mind will cause grief,
    but a person with experience will
    pay him back.

a Heb: Gk *O Master, the God*   *b* Heb: Gk *And let them
know you*   *c* Other ancient authorities read *remember
your oath*   *d* Owing to a dislocation in the Greek Mss
of Sirach, the verse numbers 14 and 15 are not used in
chapter 36, though no text is missing.   *e* Other
ancient authorities read *you have likened to*   *f* Or *on
your holy city*   *g* Heb: Gk *your rest*   *h* Heb Syr: Gk *the
celebration of your wondrous deeds*   *i* Heb Syr: Gk Lat
people*   *j* Heb and two Gk witnesses: Lat and most Gk
witnesses read *according to the blessing of Aaron for*

26 A woman will accept any man as a
   husband,
     but one girl is preferable to
     another.
27 A woman's beauty lights up a man's
   face,
     and there is nothing he desires
     more.
28 If kindness and humility mark her
   speech,
     her husband is more fortunate than
     other men.
29 He who acquires a wife gets his best
   possession,[a]
     a helper fit for him and a pillar of
     support.[b]
30 Where there is no fence, the property
   will be plundered;
     and where there is no wife, a man
     will become a fugitive and a
     wanderer.[c]
31 For who will trust a nimble robber
   that skips from city to city?
   So who will trust a man that has no
   nest,
     but lodges wherever night overtakes
     him?

False Friends

37 Every friend says, 'I too am a
   friend';
     but some friends are friends only in
     name.
2 Is it not a sorrow like that for death
   itself
     when a dear friend turns into an
     enemy?
3 O inclination to evil, why were you
   formed
     to cover the land with deceit?
4 Some companions rejoice in the
   happiness of a friend,
     but in time of trouble they are
     against him.
5 Some companions help a friend for
   their stomachs' sake,
     yet in battle they will carry his
     shield.
6 Do not forget a friend during the
   battle,[d]

and do not be unmindful of him
   when you distribute your spoils.[e]

Caution in Taking Advice

7 All counsellors praise the counsel
   they give,
     but some give counsel in their own
     interest.
8 Be wary of a counsellor,
     and learn first what is his interest,
     for he will take thought for himself.
   He may cast the lot against you
9   and tell you, 'Your way is good',
     and then stand aside to see what
     happens to you.
10 Do not consult one who regards you
   with suspicion;
     hide your intentions from those
     who are jealous of you.
11 Do not consult with a woman about
   her rival
     or with a coward about war,
   with a merchant about business
     or with a buyer about selling,
   with a miser about generosity[f]
     or with the merciless about
     kindness,
   with an idler about any work
     or with a seasonal labourer about
     completing his work,
   with a lazy servant about a big task—
     pay no attention to any advice they
     give.
12 But associate with a godly person
     whom you know to be a keeper of
     the commandments,
   who is like-minded with yourself,
     and who will grieve with you if you
     fail.
13 And heed[g] the counsel of your own
   heart,
     for no one is more faithful to you
     than it is.
14 For our own mind sometimes keeps
   us better informed
     than seven sentinels sitting high on
     a watch-tower.
15 But above all pray to the Most High

a Heb: Gk *enters upon a possession*   b Heb: Gk *rest*
c Heb: Gk *wander about and sigh*   d Heb: Gk *in your
heart*   e Heb: Gk *him in your wealth*   f Heb: Gk
gratitude   g Heb: Gk *establish*

that he may direct your way in
truth.

True and False Wisdom

16 Discussion is the beginning of every
work,
and counsel precedes every
undertaking.
17 The mind is the root of all conduct;
18 it sprouts four branches, *a*
good and evil, life and death;
and it is the tongue that continually
rules them.
19 Some people may be clever enough
to teach many,
and yet be useless to themselves.
20 A skilful speaker may be hated;
he will be destitute of all food,
21 for the Lord has withheld the gift of
charm,
since he is lacking in all wisdom.
22 If a person is wise to his own
advantage,
the fruits of his good sense will be
praiseworthy. *b*
23 A wise person instructs his own
people,
and the fruits of his good sense will
endure.
24 A wise person will have praise heaped
upon him,
and all who see him will call him
happy.
25 The days of a person's life are
numbered,
but the days of Israel are without
number.
26 One who is wise among his people
will inherit honour, *c*
and his name will live for ever.

Concerning Moderation

27 My child, test yourself while you live;
see what is bad for you and do not
give in to it.
28 For not everything is good for
everyone,
and no one enjoys everything.
29 Do not be greedy for every delicacy,
and do not eat without restraint;
30 for overeating brings sickness,

and gluttony leads to nausea.
31 Many have died of gluttony,
but one who guards against it
prolongs his life.

Concerning Physicians and Health

38 Honour physicians for their
services,
for the Lord created them;
2 for their gift of healing comes from
the Most High,
and they are rewarded by the king.
3 The skill of physicians makes them
distinguished,
and in the presence of the great
they are admired.
4 The Lord created medicines out of
the earth,
and the sensible will not despise
them.
5 Was not water made sweet with a tree
in order that its *d* power might be
known?
6 And he gave skill to human beings
that he *e* might be glorified in his
marvellous works.
7 By them the physician *f* heals and
takes away pain;
8 the pharmacist makes a mixture
from them.
God's *g* works will never be finished;
and from him health *h* spreads over
all the earth.

9 My child, when you are ill, do not
delay,
but pray to the Lord, and he will
heal you.
10 Give up your faults and direct your
hands rightly,
and cleanse your heart from all sin.
11 Offer a sweet-smelling sacrifice, and a
memorial portion of choice
flour,
and pour oil on your offering, as
much as you can afford. *i*

a Heb: Gk *As a clue to changes of heart four kinds of
destiny appear*   *b* Other ancient witnesses read
trustworthy   *c* Other ancient authorities read *confidence*
d Or *his*   *e* Or *they*   *f* Heb: Gk *he*   *g* Gk *His*
h Or *peace*   *i* Heb: Lat lacks *as much as you can afford*;
Meaning of Gk uncertain

12 Then give the physician his place, for
   the Lord created him;
   do not let him leave you, for you
   need him.
13 There may come a time when
   recovery lies in the hands of
   physicians, *a*
14 for they too pray to the Lord
   that he will grant them success in
   diagnosis *b*
   and in healing, for the sake of
   preserving life.
15 He who sins against his Maker
   will be defiant towards the
   physician. *c*

On Mourning for the Dead

16 My child, let your tears fall for the
   dead,
   and as one in great pain begin the
   lament.
   Lay out the body with due
   ceremony,
   and do not neglect the burial.
17 Let your weeping be bitter and your
   wailing fervent;
   make your mourning worthy of the
   departed,
   for one day, or two, to avoid
   criticism;
   then be comforted for your grief.
18 For grief may result in death,
   and a sorrowful heart saps one's
   strength.
19 When a person is taken away, sorrow
   is over;
   but the life of the poor weighs
   down the heart.
20 Do not give your heart to grief;
   drive it away, and remember your
   own end.
21 Do not forget, there is no coming
   back;
   you do the dead *d* no good, and you
   injure yourself.
22 Remember his *e* fate, for yours is like
   it;
   yesterday it was his, *f* and today it is
   yours.
23 When the dead is at rest, let his
   remembrance rest too,

and be comforted for him when his
   spirit has departed.

Trades and Crafts

24 The wisdom of the scribe depends on
   the opportunity of leisure;
   only the one who has little business
   can become wise.
25 How can one become wise who
   handles the plough,
   and who glories in the shaft of a
   goad,
   who drives oxen and is occupied with
   their work,
   and whose talk is about bulls?
26 He sets his heart on ploughing
   furrows,
   and he is careful about fodder for
   the heifers.
27 So it is with every artisan and master
   artisan
   who labours by night as well as by
   day;
   those who cut the signets of seals,
   each is diligent in making a great
   variety;
   they set their heart on painting a
   lifelike image,
   and they are careful to finish their
   work.
28 So it is with the smith, sitting by the
   anvil,
   intent on his ironwork;
   the breath of the fire melts his flesh,
   and he struggles with the heat of
   the furnace;
   the sound of the hammer deafens his
   ears, *g*
   and his eyes are on the pattern of
   the object.
   He sets his heart on finishing his
   handiwork,
   and he is careful to complete its
   decoration.
29 So it is with the potter sitting at his
   work
   and turning the wheel with his feet;

a Gk *in their hands*   *b* Heb: Gk *rest*   *c* Heb: Gk *may
he fall into the hands of the physician*   *d* Gk *him*
e Heb: Gk *my*   *f* Heb: Gk *mine*   *g* Cn: Gk *renews
his ear*

he is always deeply concerned over
   his products,
and he produces them in quantity.
30 He moulds the clay with his arm
   and makes it pliable with his feet;
he sets his heart on finishing the
   glazing,
and he takes care in firing*a* the kiln.

31 All these rely on their hands,
   and all are skilful in their own
   work.
32 Without them no city can be
   inhabited,
and wherever they live, they will
   not go hungry.*b*
Yet they are not sought out for the
   council of the people,*c*
33   nor do they attain eminence in the
   public assembly.
They do not sit in the judge's seat,
   nor do they understand the
   decisions of the courts;
they cannot expound discipline or
   judgement,
and they are not found among the
   rulers.*d*
34 But they maintain the fabric of the
   world,
and their concern is for*e* the
   exercise of their trade.

The Activity of the Scribe

How different the one who devotes
   himself
   to the study of the law of the Most
   High!

39 He seeks out the wisdom of all
   the ancients,
and is concerned with prophecies;
2 he preserves the sayings of the
   famous
   and penetrates the subtleties of
   parables;
3 he seeks out the hidden meanings of
   proverbs
   and is at home with the obscurities
   of parables.
4 He serves among the great
   and appears before rulers;
he travels in foreign lands

and learns what is good and evil in
   the human lot.
5 He sets his heart on rising early
   to seek the Lord who made him,
   and to petition the Most High;
he opens his mouth in prayer
   and asks pardon for his sins.

6 If the great Lord is willing,
   he will be filled with the spirit of
   understanding;
he will pour forth words of wisdom
   of his own
   and give thanks to the Lord in
   prayer.
7 The Lord*f* will direct his counsel and
   knowledge,
as he meditates on his mysteries.
8 He will show the wisdom of what he
   has learned,
   and will glory in the law of the
   Lord's covenant.
9 Many will praise his understanding;
   it will never be blotted out.
His memory will not disappear,
   and his name will live through all
   generations.
10 Nations will speak of his wisdom,
   and the congregation will proclaim
   his praise.
11 If he lives long, he will leave a name
   greater than a thousand,
   and if he goes to rest, it is enough*g*
   for him.

A Hymn of Praise to God

12 I have more on my mind to express;
   I am full like the full moon.
13 Listen to me, my faithful children,
   and blossom
   like a rose growing by a stream of
   water.
14 Send out fragrance like incense,
   and put forth blossoms like a lily.
Scatter the fragrance, and sing a
   hymn of praise;
   bless the Lord for all his works.
15 Ascribe majesty to his name

---

a Cn: Gk *cleaning*   *b* Syr: Gk *and people can neither live
nor walk there*   *c* Most ancient authorities lack this line
d Cn: Gk *among parables*   *e* Syr: Gk *prayer is in*
f Gk *He himself*   *g* Cn: Meaning of Gk uncertain

and give thanks to him with praise,
with songs on your lips, and with
  harps;
  this is what you shall say in
    thanksgiving:

16 'All the works of the Lord are very
    good,
  and whatever he commands will be
    done at the appointed time.
17 No one can say, "What is this?" or
    "Why is that?"—
  for at the appointed time all such
    questions will be answered.
  At his word the waters stood in a
    heap,
  and the reservoirs of water at the
    word of his mouth.
18 When he commands, his every
    purpose is fulfilled,
  and none can limit his saving
    power.
19 The works of all are before him,
  and nothing can be hidden from
    his eyes.
20 From the beginning to the end of
    time he can see everything,
  and nothing is too marvellous for
    him.
21 No one can say, "What is this?" or
    "Why is that?"—
  for everything has been created for
    its own purpose.

22 'His blessing covers the dry land like
    a river,
  and drenches it like a flood.
23 But his wrath drives out the nations,
  as when he turned a watered land
    into salt.
24 To the faithful his ways are straight,
  but full of pitfalls for the wicked.
25 From the beginning good things were
    created for the good,
  but for sinners good things and
    bad.*a*
26 The basic necessities of human life
  are water and fire and iron and
    salt
  and wheat flour and milk and
    honey,

the blood of the grape and oil and
  clothing.
27 All these are good for the godly,
  but for sinners they turn into evils.

28 'There are winds created for
    vengeance,
  and in their anger they can dislodge
    mountains;*b*
  on the day of reckoning they will
    pour out their strength
  and calm the anger of their Maker.
29 Fire and hail and famine and
    pestilence,
  all these have been created for
    vengeance;
30 the fangs of wild animals and
    scorpions and vipers,
  and the sword that punishes the
    ungodly with destruction.
31 They take delight in doing his
    bidding,
  always ready for his service on
    earth;
  and when their time comes they
    never disobey his command.'

32 So from the beginning I have been
    convinced of all this
  and have thought it out and left it
    in writing:
33 All the works of the Lord are good,
  and he will supply every need in its
    time.
34 No one can say, 'This is not as good
    as that',
  for everything proves good in its
    appointed time.
35 So now sing praise with all your heart
    and voice,
  and bless the name of the Lord.

Human Wretchedness

40 Hard work was created for
    everyone,
  and a heavy yoke is laid on the
    children of Adam,
  from the day they come forth from
    their mother's womb

a Heb Lat: Gk *sinners bad things*   b Heb Syr: Gk *can
scourge mightily*

until the day they return to[a] the
mother of all the living.[b]

2 Perplexities and fear of heart are
theirs,
and anxious thought of the day of
their death.

3 From the one who sits on a splendid
throne
to the one who grovels in dust and
ashes,

4 from the one who wears purple and a
crown
to the one who is clothed in
sackcloth,

5 there is anger and envy and trouble
and unrest,
and fear of death, and fury and
strife.
And when one rests upon his bed,
his sleep at night confuses his
mind.

6 He gets little or no rest;
he struggles in his sleep as he did
by day.[c]
He is troubled by the visions of his
mind
like one who has escaped from the
battlefield.

7 At the moment he reaches safety he
wakes up,
astonished that his fears were
groundless.

8 To all creatures, human and animal,
but to sinners seven times more,

9 come death and bloodshed and strife
and sword,
calamities and famine and ruin and
plague.

10 All these were created for the
wicked,
and on their account the flood
came.

11 All that is of earth returns to earth,
and what is from above returns
above.[d]

Injustice Will Not Prosper

12 All bribery and injustice will be
blotted out,
but good faith will last for ever.

13 The wealth of the unjust will dry up
like a river,
and crash like a loud clap of
thunder in a storm.

14 As a generous person has cause to
rejoice,
so lawbreakers will utterly fail.

15 The children of the ungodly put out
few branches;
they are unhealthy roots on sheer
rock.

16 The reeds by any water or river bank
are plucked up before any grass;

17 but kindness is like a garden of
blessings,
and almsgiving endures for ever.

The Joys of Life

18 Wealth and wages make life sweet,[e]
but better than either is finding a
treasure.

19 Children and the building of a city
establish one's name,
but better than either is one who
finds wisdom.
Cattle and orchards make one
prosperous;[f]
but a blameless wife is accounted
better than either.

20 Wine and music gladden the heart,
but the love of friends[g] is better
than either.

21 The flute and the harp make sweet
melody,
but a pleasant voice is better than
either.

22 The eye desires grace and beauty,
but the green shoots of grain more
than either.

23 A friend or companion is always
welcome,
but a sensible wife[h] is better than
either.

24 Kindred and helpers are for a time of
trouble,

---

a Other Gk and Lat authorities read *are buried in*
b Heb: Gk *of all*   c Arm: Meaning of Gk uncertain
d Heb Syr: Gk Lat *from the waters returns to the sea*
e Heb: Gk *Life is sweet for the self-reliant worker*
f Heb Syr: Gk lacks *but better . . . prosperous*   g Heb:
Gk *wisdom*   h Heb Compare Syr: Gk *wife with her
husband*

but almsgiving rescues better than
either.
25 Gold and silver make one stand
firm,
but good counsel is esteemed more
than either.
26 Riches and strength build up
confidence,
but the fear of the Lord is better
than either.
There is no want in the fear of the
Lord,
and with it there is no need to seek
for help.
27 The fear of the Lord is like a garden
of blessing,
and covers a person better than any
glory.

The Disgrace of Begging

28 My child, do not lead the life of a
beggar;
it is better to die than to beg.
29 When one looks to the table of
another,
one's way of life cannot be
considered a life.
One loses self-respect with another
person's food,
but one who is intelligent and well
instructed guards against that.
30 In the mouth of the shameless
begging is sweet,
but it kindles a fire inside him.

Concerning Death

41 O death, how bitter is the
thought of you
to one at peace among
possessions,
who has nothing to worry about and
is prosperous in everything,
and still is vigorous enough to
enjoy food!
2 O death, how welcome is your
sentence
to one who is needy and failing in
strength,
worn down by age and anxious about
everything;

to one who is contrary, and has lost
all patience!
3 Do not fear death's decree for you;
remember those who went before
you and those who will come
after.
4 This is the Lord's decree for all flesh;
why then should you reject the will
of the Most High?
Whether life lasts for ten years or a
hundred or a thousand,
there are no questions asked in
Hades.

The Fate of the Wicked

5 The children of sinners are
abominable children,
and they frequent the haunts of the
ungodly.
6 The inheritance of the children of
sinners will perish,
and on their offspring will be a
perpetual disgrace.
7 Children will blame an ungodly
father,
for they suffer disgrace because of
him.
8 Woe to you, the ungodly,
who have forsaken the law of the
Most High God!
9 If you have children, calamity will be
theirs;
you will beget them only for
groaning.
When you stumble, there is lasting
joy; [a]
and when you die, a curse is your
lot.
10 Whatever comes from earth returns to
earth;
so the ungodly go from curse to
destruction.

11 The human body is a fleeting thing,
but a virtuous name will never be
blotted out. [b]
12 Have regard for your name, since it
will outlive you

---

a Heb: Meaning of Gk uncertain   b Heb: Gk *People
grieve over the death of the body, but the bad name of
sinners will be blotted out*

longer than a thousand hoards of
gold.
13 The days of a good life are numbered,
but a good name lasts for ever.

14 My children, be true to your training
and be at peace;
hidden wisdom and unseen
treasure—
of what value is either?

A Series of Contrasts

15 Better are those who hide their folly
than those who hide their
wisdom.
16 Therefore show respect for my
words;
for it is not good to feel shame in
every circumstance,
nor is every kind of abashment to
be approved. [a]

17 Be ashamed of sexual immorality,
before your father or mother;
and of a lie, before a prince or a
ruler;
18 of a crime, before a judge or
magistrate;
and of a breach of the law, before
the congregation and the
people;
of unjust dealing, before your partner
or your friend;
19 and of theft, in the place where you
live.
Be ashamed of breaking an oath or
agreement, [b]
and of leaning on your elbow at
meals;
of surliness in receiving or giving,
20 and of silence, before those who
greet you;
of looking at a prostitute,
21 and of rejecting the appeal of a
relative;
of taking away someone's portion or
gift,
and of gazing at another man's
wife;
22 of meddling with his servant-girl—
and do not approach her bed;

of abusive words, before friends—
and do not be insulting after
making a gift.

42 Be ashamed of repeating what
you hear,
and of betraying secrets.
Then you will show proper shame,
and will find favour with
everyone.

Of the following things do not be
ashamed,
and do not sin to save face:
2 Do not be ashamed of the law of the
Most High and his covenant,
and of rendering judgement to
acquit the ungodly;
3 of keeping accounts with a partner or
with travelling-companions,
and of dividing the inheritance of
friends;
4 of accuracy with scales and weights,
and of acquiring much or little;
5 of profit from dealing with
merchants,
and of frequent disciplining of
children,
and of drawing blood from the
back of a wicked slave.
6 Where there is an untrustworthy wife,
a seal is a good thing;
and where there are many hands,
lock things up.
7 When you make a deposit, be sure it
is counted and weighed,
and when you give or receive, put it
all in writing.
8 Do not be ashamed to correct the
stupid or foolish
or the aged who are guilty of sexual
immorality.
Then you will show your sound
training,
and will be approved by all.

Daughters and Fathers

9 A daughter is a secret anxiety to her
father,

a Heb: Gk and not everything is confidently esteemed by
everyone   b Heb: Gk before the truth of God and the
covenant

and worry over her robs him of
   sleep:
when she is young, for fear she may
   not marry,
   or if married, for fear she may be
      disliked;
10 while a virgin, for fear she may be
   seduced
   and become pregnant in her
      father's house;
   or having a husband, for fear she may
      go astray,
     or, though married, for fear she
      may be barren.
11 Keep strict watch over a headstrong
   daughter,
   or she may make you a laughing-
      stock to your enemies,
  a byword in the city and the assembly
    of *a* the people,
   and put you to shame in public
      gatherings. *b*
See that there is no lattice in her
   room,
   no spot that overlooks the
      approaches to the house. *c*
12 Do not let her parade her beauty
   before any man,
   or spend her time among married
      women; *a*
13 for from garments comes the moth,
   and from a woman comes woman's
      wickedness.
14 Better is the wickedness of a man
   than a woman who does good;
   it is woman who brings shame and
      disgrace.

The Works of God in Nature

15 I will now call to mind the works of
   the Lord,
   and will declare what I have seen.
By the word of the Lord his works are
   made;
   and all his creatures do his will. *d*
16 The sun looks down on everything
   with its light,
   and the work of the Lord is full of
      his glory.
17 The Lord has not empowered even
   his holy ones

to recount all his marvellous works,
which the Lord the Almighty has
   established
   so that the universe may stand firm
      in his glory.
18 He searches out the abyss and the
   human heart;
   he understands their innermost
      secrets.
For the Most High knows all that may
   be known;
   he sees from of old the things that
      are to come. *e*
19 He discloses what has been and what
   is to be,
   and he reveals the traces of hidden
      things.
20 No thought escapes him,
   and nothing is hidden from him.
21 He has set in order the splendours of
   his wisdom;
   he is from all eternity one and the
      same.
Nothing can be added or taken away,
   and he needs no one to be his
      counsellor.
22 How desirable are all his works,
   and how sparkling they are to see! *f*
23 All these things live and remain for
   ever;
   each creature is preserved to meet a
      particular need. *g*
24 All things come in pairs, one
   opposite to the other,
   and he has made nothing
      incomplete.
25 Each supplements the virtues of the
   other.
   Who could ever tire of seeing his
      glory?

The Splendour of the Sun

43 The pride of the higher realms is
     the clear vault of the sky,
   as glorious to behold as the sight of
      the heavens.

---

a Heb: Meaning of Gk uncertain   *b* Heb: Gk *to shame
before the great multitude*   *c* Heb: Gk lacks *See . . . house*
d Syr Compare Heb: most Gk witnesses lack *and all . . .
will*   *e* Heb: Gk *he sees the sign(s) of the age*
f Meaning of Gk uncertain   *g* Heb: Gk *for ever for
every need, and all are obedient*

2 The sun, when it appears, proclaims
     as it rises
   what a marvellous instrument it is,
     the work of the Most High.
3 At noon it parches the land,
   and who can withstand its burning
     heat?
4 A man tending*a* a furnace works in
     burning heat,
   but three times as hot is the sun
     scorching the mountains;
   it breathes out fiery vapours,
   and its bright rays blind the eyes.
5 Great is the Lord who made it;
   at his orders it hurries on its course.

The Splendour of the Moon

6 It is the moon that marks the
     changing seasons,*b*
   governing the times, their
     everlasting sign.
7 From the moon comes the sign for
     festal days,
   a light that wanes when it
     completes its course.
8 The new moon, as its name suggests,
     renews itself;*c*
   how marvellous it is in this change,
   a beacon to the hosts on high,
   shining in the vault of the heavens!

The Glory of the Stars and the Rainbow

9 The glory of the stars is the beauty of
     heaven,
   a glittering array in the heights of
     the Lord.
10 On the orders of the Holy One they
     stand in their appointed places;
   they never relax in their watches.
11 Look at the rainbow, and praise him
     who made it;
   it is exceedingly beautiful in its
     brightness.
12 It encircles the sky with its glorious
     arc;
   the hands of the Most High have
     stretched it out.

The Marvels of Nature

13 By his command he sends the driving
     snow

   and speeds the lightnings of his
     judgement.
14 Therefore the storehouses are
     opened,
   and the clouds fly out like birds.
15 In his majesty he gives the clouds
     their strength,
   and the hailstones are broken in
     pieces.
17a The voice of his thunder rebukes the
     earth;
16   when he appears, the mountains
     shake.
   At his will the south wind blows;
17b so do the storm from the north and
     the whirlwind.
   He scatters the snow like birds flying
     down,
   and its descent is like locusts
     alighting.
18 The eye is dazzled by the beauty of its
     whiteness,
   and the mind is amazed as it falls.
19 He pours frost over the earth like
     salt,
   and icicles form like pointed
     thorns.
20 The cold north wind blows,
   and ice freezes on the water;
   it settles on every pool of water,
   and the water puts it on like a
     breastplate.
21 He consumes the mountains and
     burns up the wilderness,
   and withers the tender grass like
     fire.
22 A mist quickly heals all things;
   the falling dew gives refreshment
     from the heat.

23 By his plan he stilled the deep
   and planted islands in it.
24 Those who sail the sea tell of its
     dangers,
   and we marvel at what we hear.
25 In it are strange and marvellous
     creatures,

a Other ancient authorities read *blowing upon*
b Heb: Meaning of Gk uncertain   *c* Heb: Gk *The
month is named after the moon*

all kinds of living things, and huge
sea-monsters.
26 Because of him each of his
messengers succeeds,
and by his word all things hold
together.

27 We could say more but could never
say enough;
let the final word be: 'He is the all.'
28 Where can we find the strength to
praise him?
For he is greater than all his
works.
29 Awesome is the Lord and very great,
and marvellous is his power.
30 Glorify the Lord and exalt him as
much as you can,
for he surpasses even that.
When you exalt him, summon all
your strength,
and do not grow weary, for you
cannot praise him enough.
31 Who has seen him and can describe
him?
Or who can extol him as he is?
32 Many things greater than these lie
hidden,
for I[a] have seen but few of his
works.
33 For the Lord has made all things,
and to the godly he has given
wisdom.

HYMN IN HONOUR OF OUR ANCESTORS[b]

44 Let us now sing the praises of
famous men,
our ancestors in their generations.
2 The Lord apportioned to them[c] great
glory,
his majesty from the beginning.
3 There were those who ruled in their
kingdoms,
and made a name for themselves by
their valour;
those who gave counsel because they
were intelligent;
those who spoke in prophetic
oracles;
4 those who led the people by their
counsels

and by their knowledge of the
people's lore;
they were wise in their words of
instruction;
5 those who composed musical tunes,
or put verses in writing;
6 rich men endowed with resources,
living peacefully in their homes—
7 all these were honoured in their
generations,
and were the pride of their times.
8 Some of them have left behind a
name,
so that others declare their praise.
9 But of others there is no memory;
they have perished as though they
had never existed;
they have become as though they had
never been born,
they and their children after them.
10 But these also were godly men,
whose righteous deeds have not
been forgotten;
11 their wealth will remain with their
descendants,
and their inheritance with their
children's children.[d]
12 Their descendants stand by the
covenants;
their children also, for their sake.
13 Their offspring will continue for
ever,
and their glory will never be
blotted out.
14 Their bodies are buried in peace,
but their name lives on generation
after generation.
15 The assembly declares[e] their wisdom,
and the congregation proclaims
their praise.

Enoch

16 Enoch pleased the Lord and was
taken up,
an example of repentance to all
generations.

a Heb: Gk *we*   b This title is included in the Gk text.
c Heb: Gk *created*   d Heb Compare Lat Syr: Meaning
of Gk uncertain   e Heb: Gk *Peoples declare*

Noah

17 Noah was found perfect and
        righteous;
    in the time of wrath he kept the
        race alive; *a*
  therefore a remnant was left on the
        earth
    when the flood came.
18 Everlasting covenants were made with
        him
    that all flesh should never again be
        blotted out by a flood.

Abraham

19 Abraham was the great father of a
        multitude of nations,
    and no one has been found like
        him in glory.
20 He kept the law of the Most High,
    and entered into a covenant with
        him;
  he certified the covenant in his flesh,
    and when he was tested he proved
        faithful.
21 Therefore the Lord *b* assured him with
        an oath
    that the nations would be blessed
        through his offspring;
  that he would make him as
        numerous as the dust of the
        earth,
    and exalt his offspring like the
        stars,
  and give them an inheritance from
        sea to sea
    and from the Euphrates *c* to the
        ends of the earth.

Isaac and Jacob

22 To Isaac also he gave the same
        assurance
    for the sake of his father Abraham.
  The blessing of all people and the
        covenant
23   he made to rest on the head of
        Jacob;
  he acknowledged him with his
        blessings,
    and gave him his inheritance;
  he divided his portions,

and distributed them among twelve
        tribes.

Moses

From his descendants the Lord *b*
        brought forth a godly man,
  who found favour in the sight of all

45 1 and was beloved by God and
        people,
  Moses, whose memory is blessed.
2 He made him equal in glory to the
        holy ones,
    and made him great, to the terror
        of his enemies.
3 By his words he performed swift
        miracles; *d*
    the Lord *b* glorified him in the
        presence of kings.
  He gave him commandments for his
        people,
    and revealed to him his glory.
4 For his faithfulness and meekness he
        consecrated him,
    choosing him out of all
        humankind.
5 He allowed him to hear his voice,
    and led him into the dark cloud,
  and gave him the commandments
        face to face,
    the law of life and knowledge,
  so that he might teach Jacob the
        covenant,
    and Israel his decrees.

Aaron

6 He exalted Aaron, a holy man like
        Moses *e*
    who was his brother, of the tribe of
        Levi.
7 He made an everlasting covenant
        with him,
    and gave him the priesthood of the
        people.
  He blessed him with stateliness,
    and put a glorious robe on him.
8 He clothed him in perfect splendour,
    and strengthened him with the
        symbols of authority,

a Heb: Gk *was taken in exchange*   *b* Gk *he*
c Syr: Heb Gk *River*   *d* Heb: Gk *caused signs to cease*
e Gk *him*

the linen undergarments, the long
robe, and the ephod.

9 And he encircled him with
pomegranates,
with many golden bells all round,
to send forth a sound as he walked,
to make their ringing heard in the
temple
as a reminder to his people;

10 with the sacred vestment, of gold and
violet
and purple, the work of an
embroiderer;
with the oracle of judgement, Urim
and Thummim;

11 with twisted crimson, the work of
an artisan;
with precious stones engraved like
seals,
in a setting of gold, the work of a
jeweller,
to commemorate in engraved letters
each of the tribes of Israel;

12 with a gold crown upon his turban,
inscribed like a seal with 'Holiness',
a distinction to be prized, the work of
an expert,
a delight to the eyes, richly
adorned.

13 Before him such beautiful things did
not exist.
No outsider ever put them on,
but only his sons
and his descendants in perpetuity.

14 His sacrifices shall be wholly burned
twice every day continually.

15 Moses ordained him,
and anointed him with holy oil;
it was an everlasting covenant for him
and for his descendants as long as
the heavens endure,
to minister to the Lord[a] and serve as
priest
and bless his people in his name.

16 He chose him out of all the living
to offer sacrifice to the Lord,
incense and a pleasing odour as a
memorial portion,
to make atonement for the[b] people.

17 In his commandments he gave him

authority and statutes and[c]
judgements,
to teach Jacob the testimonies,
and to enlighten Israel with his law.

18 Outsiders conspired against him,
and envied him in the wilderness,
Dathan and Abiram and their
followers
and the company of Korah, in
wrath and anger.

19 The Lord saw it and was not pleased,
and in the heat of his anger they
were destroyed;
he performed wonders against them
to consume them in flaming fire.

20 He added glory to Aaron
and gave him a heritage;
he allotted to him the best of the first
fruits,
and prepared bread of first fruits in
abundance;

21 for they eat the sacrifices of the Lord,
which he gave to him and his
descendants.

22 But in the land of the people he has
no inheritance,
and he has no portion among the
people;
for the Lord[d] himself is his[e]
portion and inheritance.

Phinehas

23 Phinehas son of Eleazar ranks third
in glory
for being zealous in the fear of the
Lord,
and standing firm, when the people
turned away,
in the noble courage of his soul;
and he made atonement for Israel.

24 Therefore a covenant of friendship
was established with him,
that he should be leader of the
sanctuary and of his people,
that he and his descendants should
have
the dignity of the priesthood for
ever.

a Gk him   b Other ancient authorities read his or your
c Heb: Gk authority in covenants of   d Gk he
e Other ancient authorities read your

25 Just as a covenant was established
     with David
          son of Jesse of the tribe of Judah,
     that the king's heritage passes only
          from son to son,
     so the heritage of Aaron is for his
          descendants alone.

26 And now bless the Lord
     who has crowned you with glory.*a*
     May the Lord*b* grant you wisdom of
          mind
     to judge his people with justice,
     so that their prosperity may not
          vanish,
     and that their glory may endure
          through all their generations.

Joshua and Caleb

46 Joshua son of Nun was mighty
     in war,
     and was the successor of Moses in
          the prophetic office.
     He became, as his name implies,
          a great saviour of God's*c* elect,
     to take vengeance on the enemies
          that rose against them,
          so that he might give Israel its
               inheritance.
2 How glorious he was when he lifted
     his hands
          and brandished his sword against
               the cities!
3 Who before him ever stood so firm?
     For he waged the wars of the Lord.
4 Was it not through him that the sun
     stood still
          and one day became as long as
               two?
5 He called upon the Most High, the
     Mighty One,
          when enemies pressed him on
               every side,
     and the great Lord answered him
          with hailstones of mighty power.
6 He overwhelmed that nation in
     battle,
          and on the slope he destroyed his
               opponents,
     so that the nations might know his
          armament,

that he was fighting in the sight of
     the Lord;
     for he was a devoted follower of the
          Mighty One.
7 And in the days of Moses he proved
     his loyalty,
     he and Caleb son of Jephunneh:
     they opposed the congregation,*d*
     restrained the people from sin,
          and stilled their wicked grumbling.
8 And these two alone were spared
     out of six hundred thousand
          infantry,
     to lead the people*e* into their
          inheritance,
     the land flowing with milk and
          honey.
9 The Lord gave Caleb strength,
     which remained with him in his
          old age,
     so that he went up to the hill country,
          and his children obtained it for an
               inheritance,
10 so that all the Israelites might see
     how good it is to follow the Lord.

The Judges

11 The judges also, with their respective
     names,
          whose hearts did not fall into
               idolatry
     and who did not turn away from the
          Lord—
          may their memory be blessed!
12 May their bones send forth new life
     from where they lie,
          and may the names of those who
               have been honoured
     live again in their children!

13 Samuel was beloved by his Lord;
     a prophet of the Lord, he
          established the kingdom
     and anointed rulers over his
          people.
14 By the law of the Lord he judged the
     congregation,
          and the Lord watched over Jacob.

---

a Heb: Gk lacks *And . . . glory*   *b* Gk *he*   *c* Gk *his*
d Other ancient authorities read *the enemy*   *e* Gk *them*

15 By his faithfulness he was proved to
     be a prophet,
   and by his words he became known
     as a trustworthy seer.
16 He called upon the Lord, the Mighty
     One,
   when his enemies pressed him on
     every side,
   and he offered in sacrifice a
     sucking-lamb.
17 Then the Lord thundered from
     heaven,
   and made his voice heard with a
     mighty sound;
18 he subdued the leaders of the
     enemy[a]
   and all the rulers of the
     Philistines.
19 Before the time of his eternal sleep,
   Samuel[b] bore witness before the
     Lord and his anointed:
   'No property, not so much as a pair
     of shoes,
   have I taken from anyone!'
   And no one accused him.
20 Even after he had fallen asleep, he
     prophesied
   and made known to the king his
     death,
   and lifted up his voice from the
     ground
   in prophecy, to blot out the
     wickedness of the people.

Nathan

47 After him Nathan rose up
to prophesy in the days of
David.

David

2 As the fat is set apart from the
     offering of well-being,
   so David was set apart from the
     Israelites.
3 He played with lions as though they
     were young goats,
   and with bears as though they were
     lambs of the flock.
4 In his youth did he not kill a giant,
   and take away the people's disgrace,

when he whirled the stone in the
     sling
   and struck down the boasting
     Goliath?
5 For he called on the Lord, the Most
     High,
   and he gave strength to his right
     arm
   to strike down a mighty warrior,
   and to exalt the power[c] of his
     people.
6 So they glorified him for the tens of
     thousands he conquered,
   and praised him for the blessings
     bestowed by the Lord,
   when the glorious diadem was
     given to him.
7 For he wiped out his enemies on
     every side,
   and annihilated his adversaries the
     Philistines;
   he crushed their power[c] to our own
     day.
8 In all that he did he gave thanks
   to the Holy One, the Most High,
     proclaiming his glory;
   he sang praise with all his heart,
   and he loved his Maker.
9 He placed singers before the altar,
   to make sweet melody with their
     voices.[d]
10 He gave beauty to the festivals,
   and arranged their times
     throughout the year,[e]
   while they praised God's[f] holy
     name,
   and the sanctuary resounded from
     early morning.
11 The Lord took away his sins,
   and exalted his power[c] for ever;
   he gave him a covenant of kingship
   and a glorious throne in Israel.

Solomon

12 After him a wise son rose up
   who because of him lived in
     security:[g]
13 Solomon reigned in an age of peace,

a Heb: Gk *leaders of the people of Tyre*   b Gk *he*
c Gk *horn*   d Other ancient authorities add *and daily
they sing his praises*   e Gk *to completion*   f Gk *his*
g Heb: Gk *in a broad place*

because God made all his borders
   tranquil,
so that he might build a house in his
   name
   and provide a sanctuary to stand
      for ever.

14 How wise you were when you were
      young!
   You overflowed like the Nile*a* with
      understanding.

15 Your influence spread throughout the
      earth,
   and you filled it with proverbs
      having deep meaning.

16 Your fame reached to far-off islands,
   and you were loved for your
      peaceful reign.

17 Your songs, proverbs, and parables,
   and the answers you gave
      astounded the nations.

18 In the name of the Lord God,
   who is called the God of Israel,
   you gathered gold like tin
   and amassed silver like lead.

19 But you brought in women to lie at
      your side,
   and through your body you were
      brought into subjection.

20 You stained your honour
   and defiled your family line,
so that you brought wrath upon your
      children,
   and they were grieved*b* at your folly,

21 because the sovereignty was divided
   and a rebel kingdom arose out of
      Ephraim.

22 But the Lord will never give up his
      mercy,
   or cause any of his works to perish;
he will never blot out the
      descendants of his chosen one,
   or destroy the family line of him
      who loved him.
So he gave a remnant to Jacob,
   and to David a root from his own
      family.

Rehoboam and Jeroboam

23 Solomon rested with his ancestors,
   and left behind him one of his
      sons,

broad in*c* folly and lacking in sense,
   Rehoboam, whose policy drove the
      people to revolt.
Then Jeroboam son of Nebat led
      Israel into sin
   and started Ephraim on its sinful
      ways.

24 Their sins increased more and more,
   until they were exiled from their
      land.

25 For they sought out every kind of
      wickedness,
   until vengeance came upon them.

Elijah

48 Then Elijah arose, a prophet like
     fire,
   and his word burned like a torch.

2 He brought a famine upon them,
   and by his zeal he made them few
      in number.

3 By the word of the Lord he shut up
      the heavens,
   and also three times brought down
      fire.

4 How glorious you were, Elijah, in
      your wondrous deeds!
   Whose glory is equal to yours?

5 You raised a corpse from death
   and from Hades, by the word of the
      Most High.

6 You sent kings down to destruction,
   and famous men, from their
      sickbeds.

7 You heard rebuke at Sinai
   and judgements of vengeance at
      Horeb.

8 You anointed kings to inflict
      retribution,
   and prophets to succeed you.*d*

9 You were taken up by a whirlwind of
      fire,
   in a chariot with horses of fire.

10 At the appointed time, it is written,
      you are destined*e*
   to calm the wrath of God before it
      breaks out in fury,

a Heb: Gk *a river*   *b* Other ancient authorities read *I
was grieved*   *c* Heb (with a play on the name
Rehoboam) Syr: Gk *the people's*   *d* Heb: Gk *him*
e Heb: Gk *are for reproofs*

to turn the hearts of parents to their
children,
   and to restore the tribes of Jacob.
11 Happy are those who saw you
   and were adorned*a* with your love!
For we also shall surely live.*b*

Elisha

12 When Elijah was enveloped in the
whirlwind,
   Elisha was filled with his spirit.
He performed twice as many signs,
   and marvels with every utterance of
   his mouth.*c*
Never in his lifetime did he tremble
before any ruler,
   nor could anyone intimidate him at
   all.
13 Nothing was too hard for him,
   and when he was dead, his body
   prophesied.
14 In his life he did wonders,
   and in death his deeds were
   marvellous.

15 Despite all this the people did not
repent,
   nor did they forsake their sins,
until they were carried off as plunder
from their land,
   and were scattered over all the
   earth.
The people were left very few in
number,
   but with a ruler from the house of
   David.
16 Some of them did what was right,
   but others sinned more and more.

Hezekiah

17 Hezekiah fortified his city,
   and brought water into its midst;
he tunnelled the rock with iron tools,
   and built cisterns for the water.
18 In his days Sennacherib invaded the
country;
   he sent his commander*d* and
   departed;
he shook his fist against Zion,
   and made great boasts in his
   arrogance.

19 Then their hearts were shaken and
their hands trembled,
   and they were in anguish, like
   women in labour.
20 But they called upon the Lord who is
merciful,
   spreading out their hands towards
   him.
The Holy One quickly heard them
from heaven,
   and delivered them through
   Isaiah.
21 The Lord*e* struck down the camp of
the Assyrians,
   and his angel wiped them out.
22 For Hezekiah did what was pleasing
to the Lord,
   and he kept firmly to the ways of
   his ancestor David,
as he was commanded by the
prophet Isaiah,
   who was great and trustworthy in
   his visions.

Isaiah

23 In Isaiah's*f* days the sun went
backwards,
   and he prolonged the life of the
   king.
24 By his dauntless spirit he saw the
future,
   and comforted the mourners in
   Zion.
25 He revealed what was to occur to the
end of time,
   and the hidden things before they
   happened.

Josiah and Other Worthies

49 The name*g* of Josiah is like
blended incense
prepared by the skill of the
perfumer;
his memory*h* is as sweet as honey to
every mouth,
   and like music at a banquet of
   wine.

a Other ancient authorities read *and have died*   *b* Text
and meaning of Gk uncertain   *c* Heb: Gk lacks *He
performed . . . mouth*   *d* Other ancient authorities add
from Lachish   *e* Gk *He*   *f* Gk *his*   *g* Heb: Gk
memory   *h* Heb: Gk *it*

2 He did what was right by reforming
    the people,
  and removing the wicked
    abominations.
3 He kept his heart fixed on the Lord;
  in lawless times he made godliness
    prevail.

4 Except for David and Hezekiah and
    Josiah,
  all of them were great sinners,
  for they abandoned the law of the
    Most High;
  the kings of Judah came to an end.
5 They*a* gave their power to others,
  and their glory to a foreign nation,
6 who set fire to the chosen city of the
    sanctuary,
  and made its streets desolate,
  as Jeremiah had foretold.*b*
7 For they had maltreated him,
  who even in the womb had been
    consecrated a prophet,
  to pluck up and ruin and destroy,
  and likewise to build and to plant.

8 It was Ezekiel who saw the vision of
    glory,
  which God*c* showed him above the
    chariot of the cherubim.
9 For God*d* also mentioned Job
  who held fast to all the ways of
    justice.*e*
10 May the bones of the Twelve
    Prophets
  send forth new life from where they
    lie,
  for they comforted the people of
    Jacob
  and delivered them with confident
    hope.

11 How shall we magnify Zerubbabel?
  He was like a signet ring on the
    right hand,
12 and so was Jeshua son of Jozadak;
  in their days they built the house
  and raised a temple*f* holy to the
    Lord,
  destined for everlasting glory.

13 The memory of Nehemiah also is
    lasting;
  he raised our fallen walls,
  and set up gates and bars,
  and rebuilt our ruined houses.

Retrospect

14 Few have*g* ever been created on earth
    like Enoch,
  for he was taken up from the earth.
15 Nor was anyone ever born like
    Joseph;*h*
  even his bones were cared for.
16 Shem and Seth and Enosh were
    honoured,*i*
  but above every other created living
    being was Adam.

Simon Son of Onias

50 The leader of his brothers and
    the pride of his people*j*
  was the high priest, Simon son of
    Onias,
  who in his life repaired the house,
  and in his time fortified the
    temple.
2 He laid the foundations for the high
    double walls,
  the high retaining walls for the
    temple enclosure.
3 In his days a water cistern was dug,*k*
  a reservoir like the sea in
    circumference.
4 He considered how to save his people
    from ruin,
  and fortified the city against siege.
5 How glorious he was, surrounded by
    the people,
  as he came out of the house of the
    curtain.
6 Like the morning star among the
    clouds,
  like the full moon at the festal
    season;*k*

a Heb *He*   *b* Gk *by the hand of Jeremiah*   *c* Gk *He*
d Gk *he*   *e* Heb Compare Syr: Meaning of Gk
uncertain   *f* Other ancient authorities read *people*
g Heb Syr: Gk *No one has*   *h* Heb Syr: Gk adds *the*
leader of his brothers, the support of the people   *i* Heb: Gk
Shem and Seth were honoured by people   *j* Heb Syr: Gk
lacks this line. Compare 49.15   *k* Heb: Meaning of Gk
uncertain

7 like the sun shining on the temple of
    the Most High,
      like the rainbow gleaming in
        splendid clouds;
8 like roses in the days of first fruits,
      like lilies by a spring of water,
      like a green shoot on Lebanon on a
        summer day;
9 like fire and incense in the censer,
      like a vessel of hammered gold
      studded with all kinds of precious
        stones;
10 like an olive tree laden with fruit,
      and like a cypress towering in the
        clouds.
11 When he put on his glorious robe
      and clothed himself in perfect
        splendour,
      when he went up to the holy altar,
      he made the court of the sanctuary
        glorious.

12 When he received the portions from
    the hands of the priests,
      as he stood by the hearth of the
        altar
      with a garland of brothers around
        him,
      he was like a young cedar on
        Lebanon
      surrounded by the trunks of palm
        trees.
13 All the sons of Aaron in their
    splendour
      held the Lord's offering in their
        hands
      before the whole congregation of
        Israel.
14 Finishing the service at the altars,*a*
      and arranging the offering to the
        Most High, the Almighty,
15 he held out his hand for the cup
      and poured a drink-offering of the
        blood of the grape;
      he poured it out at the foot of the
        altar,
      a pleasing odour to the Most High,
        the king of all.
16 Then the sons of Aaron shouted;
      they blew their trumpets of
        hammered metal;

they sounded a mighty fanfare
      as a reminder before the Most
        High.
17 Then all the people together quickly
    fell to the ground on their faces
    to worship their Lord,
      the Almighty, God Most High.

18 Then the singers praised him with
      their voices
      in sweet and full-toned melody.*b*
19 And the people of the Lord Most
      High offered
      their prayers before the Merciful
        One,
      until the order of worship of the Lord
        was ended,
      and they completed his ritual.
20 Then Simon*c* came down and raised
      his hands
      over the whole congregation of
        Israelites,
      to pronounce the blessing of the Lord
        with his lips,
      and to glory in his name;
21 and they bowed down in worship a
      second time,
      to receive the blessing from the
        Most High.

A Benediction

22 And now bless the God of all,
      who everywhere works great
        wonders,
      who fosters our growth from birth,
      and deals with us according to his
        mercy.
23 May he give us*d* gladness of heart,
      and may there be peace in our*e*
        days
      in Israel, as in the days of old.
24 May he entrust to us his mercy,
      and may he deliver us in our*f* days!

Epilogue

25 Two nations my soul detests,
      and the third is not even a people:

a Other ancient authorities read *altar*   b Other
ancient authorities read *in sweet melody throughout the
house*   c Gk *he*   d Other ancient authorities read *you*
e Other ancient authorities read *your*   f Other ancient
authorities read *his*

26 Those who live in Seir,[a] and the
     Philistines,
   and the foolish people that live in
     Shechem.

27 Instruction in understanding and
     knowledge
   I have written in this book,
   Jesus son of Eleazar son of Sirach[b] of
     Jerusalem,
   whose mind poured forth
     wisdom.
28 Happy are those who concern
     themselves with these things,
   and those who lay them to heart
     will become wise.
29 For if they put them into practice,
     they will be equal to anything,
   for the fear[c] of the Lord is their
     path.

PRAYER OF JESUS SON OF SIRACH[d]

51 I give you thanks, O Lord and
     King,
   and praise you, O God my
     Saviour.
   I give thanks to your name,
2   for you have been my protector and
        helper
   and have delivered me from
     destruction
     and from the trap laid by a
        slanderous tongue,
   from lips that fabricate lies.
   In the face of my adversaries
     you have been my helper 3 and
        delivered me,
     in the greatness of your mercy and
        of your name,
   from grinding teeth about to devour
     me,
     from the hand of those seeking my
        life,
   from the many troubles I endured,
4 from choking fire on every side,
     and from the midst of fire that I
        had not kindled,
5 from the deep belly of Hades,
     from an unclean tongue and lying
        words—

6   the slander of an unrighteous
          tongue to the king.
   My soul drew near to death,
     and my life was on the brink of
        Hades below.
7 They surrounded me on every side,
     and there was no one to help me;
   I looked for human assistance,
     and there was none.
8 Then I remembered your mercy,
     O Lord,
     and your kindness[e] from of old,
   for you rescue those who wait for
     you
     and save them from the hand of
        their enemies.
9 And I sent up my prayer from the
     earth,
     and begged for rescue from death.
10 I cried out, 'Lord, you are my
     Father;[f]
   do not forsake me in the days of
     trouble,
     when there is no help against the
        proud.
11 I will praise your name continually,
     and will sing hymns of
        thanksgiving.'
   My prayer was heard,
12   for you saved me from destruction
     and rescued me in time of trouble.
   For this reason I thank you and praise
     you,
     and I bless the name of the Lord.

Hebrew adds:

Give thanks to the LORD, for he is good,
* for his mercy endures for ever;*

Give thanks to the God of praises,
* for his mercy endures for ever;*

Give thanks to the guardian of Israel,
* for his mercy endures for ever;*

a Heb Compare Lat: Gk *on the mountain of Samaria*
b Heb: Meaning of Gk uncertain   c Heb: Other
ancient authorities read *light*   d This title is included
in the Gk text.   e Other ancient authorities read *work*
f Heb: Gk *the Father of my lord*

Give thanks to him who formed all
    things,
    for his mercy endures for ever;

Give thanks to the redeemer of Israel,
    for his mercy endures for ever;

Give thanks to him who gathers the
    dispersed of Israel,
    for his mercy endures for ever;

Give thanks to him who rebuilt his city
    and his sanctuary,
    for his mercy endures for ever;

Give thanks to him who makes a horn to
    sprout for the house of David,
    for his mercy endures for ever;

Give thanks to him who has chosen the
    sons of Zadok to be priests,
    for his mercy endures for ever;

Give thanks to the shield of Abraham,
    for his mercy endures for ever;

Give thanks to the rock of Isaac,
    for his mercy endures for ever;

Give thanks to the mighty one of Jacob,
    for his mercy endures for ever;

Give thanks to him who has chosen
    Zion,
    for his mercy endures for ever;

Give thanks to the King of the kings of
    kings,
    for his mercy endures for ever;

He has raised up a horn for his people,
    praise for all his loyal ones.

For the children of Israel, the people
    close to him.
    Praise the LORD!

Autobiographical Poem on Wisdom

13 While I was still young, before I went
    on my travels,
    I sought wisdom openly in my
    prayer.
14 Before the temple I asked for her,
    and I will search for her until the
    end.

15 From the first blossom to the
    ripening grape
    my heart delighted in her;
    my foot walked on the straight path;
    from my youth I followed her
    steps.

16 I inclined my ear a little and received
    her,
    and I found for myself much
    instruction.
17 I made progress in her;
    to him who gives wisdom I will
    give glory.

18 For I resolved to live according to
    wisdom,[a]
    and I was zealous for the good,
    and I shall never be disappointed.
19 My soul grappled with wisdom,[a]
    and in my conduct I was strict;[b]

    I spread out my hands to the
    heavens,
    and lamented my ignorance of her.
20 I directed my soul to her,
    and in purity I found her.

    With her I gained understanding
    from the first;
    therefore I will never be forsaken.
21 My heart was stirred to seek her;
    therefore I have gained a prize
    possession.
22 The Lord gave me my tongue as a
    reward,
    and I will praise him with it.

23 Draw near to me, you who are
    uneducated,

a Gk her   b Meaning of Gk uncertain

and lodge in the house of
  instruction.

24 Why do you say you are lacking in
    these things, *a*
  and why do you endure such great
    thirst?

25 I opened my mouth and said,
  Acquire wisdom *b* for yourselves
    without money.

26 Put your neck under her *c* yoke,
  and let your souls receive
    instruction;
  it is to be found close by.

27 See with your own eyes that I have
    laboured but little

and found for myself much
  serenity.

28 Hear but a little of my instruction,
  and through me you will acquire
    silver and gold. *d*

29 May your soul rejoice in God's *e*
    mercy,
  and may you never be ashamed to
    praise him.

30 Do your work in good time,
  and in his own time God *f* will give
    you your reward.

a Cn Compare Heb Syr: Meaning of Gk uncertain
b Heb: Gk lacks *wisdom*   *c* Heb: other ancient
authorities read *the*   *d* Syr Compare Heb: Gk *Get
instruction with a large sum of silver, and you will gain by it
much gold.*   *e* Gk *his*   *f* Gk *he*

ISAIAH

1 The vision of Isaiah son of Amoz,
which he saw concerning Judah and
Jerusalem in the days of Uzziah, Jotham,
Ahaz, and Hezekiah, kings of Judah.

The Wickedness of Judah

2 Hear, O heavens, and listen, O earth;
  for the LORD has spoken:
I reared children and brought
    them up,
  but they have rebelled against me.
3 The ox knows its owner,
  and the donkey its master's crib;
but Israel does not know,
  my people do not understand.

4 Ah, sinful nation,
  people laden with iniquity,
offspring who do evil,
  children who deal corruptly,
who have forsaken the LORD,
  who have despised the Holy One of
    Israel,
  who are utterly estranged!

5 Why do you seek further beatings?
  Why do you continue to rebel?
The whole head is sick,
  and the whole heart faint.
6 From the sole of the foot even to the
    head,
  there is no soundness in it,
but bruises and sores
  and bleeding wounds;
they have not been drained, or
    bound up,
  or softened with oil.

7 Your country lies desolate,
  your cities are burned with fire;
in your very presence
  aliens devour your land;
it is desolate, as overthrown by
  foreigners.
8 And daughter Zion is left
  like a booth in a vineyard,
like a shelter in a cucumber field,
  like a besieged city.
9 If the LORD of hosts
  had not left us a few survivors,
we would have been like Sodom,
  and become like Gomorrah.

10 Hear the word of the LORD,
  you rulers of Sodom!
Listen to the teaching of our God,
  you people of Gomorrah!
11 What to me is the multitude of your
    sacrifices?
  says the LORD;
I have had enough of burnt-offerings
    of rams
  and the fat of fed beasts;
I do not delight in the blood
    of bulls,
  or of lambs, or of goats.

12 When you come to appear
    before me, *a*
  who asked this from your hand?
Trample my courts no more;
13 bringing offerings is futile;
  incense is an abomination to me.
New moon and sabbath and calling
    of convocation—
  I cannot endure solemn assemblies
    with iniquity.

a Or *see my face*

14 Your new moons and your appointed
        festivals
    my soul hates;
  they have become a burden to me,
    I am weary of bearing them.
15 When you stretch out your hands,
    I will hide my eyes from you;
  even though you make many
        prayers,
    I will not listen;
    your hands are full of blood.
16 Wash yourselves; make yourselves
        clean;
    remove the evil of your doings
    from before my eyes;
  cease to do evil,
17   learn to do good;
  seek justice,
    rescue the oppressed,
  defend the orphan,
    plead for the widow.

18 Come now, let us argue it out,
    says the LORD:
  though your sins are like scarlet,
    they shall be like snow;
  though they are red like crimson,
    they shall become like wool.
19 If you are willing and obedient,
    you shall eat the good of the land;
20 but if you refuse and rebel,
    you shall be devoured by the
        sword;
    for the mouth of the LORD has
        spoken.

The Degenerate City

21 How the faithful city
    has become a whore!
    She that was full of justice,
  righteousness lodged in her—
    but now murderers!
22 Your silver has become dross,
    your wine is mixed with water.
23 Your princes are rebels
    and companions of thieves.
  Everyone loves a bribe
    and runs after gifts.
  They do not defend the orphan,
    and the widow's cause does not
        come before them.

24 Therefore says the Sovereign, the
        LORD of hosts, the Mighty One
        of Israel:
  Ah, I will pour out my wrath on my
        enemies,
    and avenge myself on my foes!
25 I will turn my hand against you;
    I will smelt away your dross as with
        lye
    and remove all your alloy.
26 And I will restore your judges as at
        the first,
    and your counsellors as at the
        beginning.
  Afterwards you shall be called the city
        of righteousness,
    the faithful city.

27 Zion shall be redeemed by justice,
    and those in her who repent, by
        righteousness.
28 But rebels and sinners shall be
        destroyed together,
    and those who forsake the LORD
        shall be consumed.
29 For you shall be ashamed of
        the oaks
    in which you delighted;
  and you shall blush for the gardens
    that you have chosen.
30 For you shall be like an oak
    whose leaf withers,
    and like a garden without water.
31 The strong shall become like tinder,
    and their work[b] like a spark;
  they and their work shall burn
        together,
    with no one to quench them.

The Future House of God

2 The word that Isaiah son of Amoz saw
  concerning Judah and Jerusalem.

2 In days to come
    the mountain of the LORD's house
  shall be established as the highest of
        the mountains,
    and shall be raised above
        the hills;
  all the nations shall stream to it.

a Or its makers

3 Many peoples shall come and say,
  'Come, let us go up to the mountain
      of the LORD,
    to the house of the God of Jacob;
  that he may teach us his ways
    and that we may walk in his
      paths.'
  For out of Zion shall go forth
      instruction,
    and the word of the LORD from
      Jerusalem.
4 He shall judge between the nations,
    and shall arbitrate for many
      peoples;
  they shall beat their swords into
      ploughshares,
    and their spears into pruning-
      hooks;
  nation shall not lift up sword against
      nation,
    neither shall they learn war
      any more.

Judgement Pronounced on Arrogance

5 O house of Jacob,
    come, let us walk
    in the light of the LORD!
6 For you have forsaken the ways of*a*
      your people,
    O house of Jacob.
  Indeed they are full of diviners*b* from
      the east
    and of soothsayers like the
      Philistines,
    and they clasp hands with
      foreigners.
7 Their land is filled with silver
      and gold,
    and there is no end to their
      treasures;
  their land is filled with horses,
    and there is no end to their
      chariots.
8 Their land is filled with idols;
    they bow down to the work of their
      hands,
    to what their own fingers
      have made.
9 And so people are humbled,
    and everyone is brought low—
    do not forgive them!

10 Enter into the rock,
    and hide in the dust
  from the terror of the LORD,
    and from the glory of his majesty.
11 The haughty eyes of people shall be
      brought low,
    and the pride of everyone shall be
      humbled;
  and the LORD alone will be exalted on
      that day.
12 For the LORD of hosts has a day
    against all that is proud and lofty,
    against all that is lifted up
      and high;*c*
13 against all the cedars of Lebanon,
    lofty and lifted up;
    and against all the oaks of
      Bashan;
14 against all the high mountains,
    and against all the lofty hills;
15 against every high tower,
    and against every fortified wall;
16 against all the ships of Tarshish,
    and against all the beautiful craft.*d*
17 The haughtiness of people shall be
      humbled,
    and the pride of everyone shall be
      brought low;
  and the LORD alone will be exalted
      on that day.
18 The idols shall utterly pass away.
19 Enter the caves of the rocks
    and the holes of the ground,
  from the terror of the LORD,
    and from the glory of his majesty,
    when he rises to terrify the earth.
20 On that day people will throw away
    to the moles and to the bats
  their idols of silver and their idols of
      gold,
    which they made for themselves to
      worship,
21 to enter the caverns of the rocks
    and the clefts in the crags,
  from the terror of the LORD,
    and from the glory of his majesty,
    when he rises to terrify the earth.
22 Turn away from mortals,

a Heb lacks *the ways of*   *b* Cn: Heb lacks *of diviners*
c Cn Compare Gk: Heb *low*   *d* Compare Gk: Meaning
of Heb uncertain

who have only breath in their
nostrils,
for of what account are they?

3 For now the Sovereign, the LORD
of hosts,
is taking away from Jerusalem and
from Judah
support and staff—
all support of bread,
and all support of water—

2 warrior and soldier,
judge and prophet,
diviner and elder,

3 captain of fifty
and dignitary,
counsellor and skilful magician
and expert enchanter.

4 And I will make boys their princes,
and babes shall rule over them.

5 The people will be oppressed,
everyone by another
and everyone by a neighbour;
the youth will be insolent to
the elder,
and the base to the honourable.

6 Someone will even seize a relative,
a member of the clan, saying,
'You have a cloak;
you shall be our leader,
and this heap of ruins
shall be under your rule.'

7 But the other will cry out on that day,
saying,
'I will not be a healer;
in my house there is neither bread
nor cloak;
you shall not make me
leader of the people.'

8 For Jerusalem has stumbled
and Judah has fallen,
because their speech and their deeds
are against the LORD,
defying his glorious presence.

9 The look on their faces bears witness
against them;
they proclaim their sin like Sodom,
they do not hide it.
Woe to them!

For they have brought evil on
themselves.

10 Tell the innocent how fortunate they
are,
for they shall eat the fruit of their
labours.

11 Woe to the guilty! How unfortunate
they are,
for what their hands have done
shall be done to them.

12 My people—children are their
oppressors,
and women rule over them.
O my people, your leaders mislead
you,
and confuse the course of your
paths.

13 The LORD rises to argue his case;
he stands to judge the peoples.

14 The LORD enters into judgement
with the elders and princes of his
people:
It is you who have devoured the
vineyard;
the spoil of the poor is in your
houses.

15 What do you mean by crushing my
people,
by grinding the face of the poor?
says the Lord GOD of hosts.

16 The LORD said:
Because the daughters of Zion are
haughty
and walk with outstretched necks,
glancing wantonly with their eyes,
mincing along as they go,
tinkling with their feet;

17 the Lord will afflict with scabs
the heads of the daughters of Zion,
and the LORD will lay bare their
secret parts.

18 On that day the Lord will take away
the finery of the anklets, the headbands,
and the crescents; 19 the pendants, the
bracelets, and the scarves; 20 the head-dresses, the armlets, the sashes, the perfume boxes, and the amulets; 21 the signet rings and
nose-rings; 22 the festal robes, the mantles,

the cloaks, and the handbags; 23 the garments of gauze, the linen garments, the turbans, and the veils.

24 Instead of perfume there will be a
    stench;
  and instead of a sash, a rope;
  and instead of well-arranged hair,
    baldness;
  and instead of a rich robe, a
    binding of sackcloth;
  instead of beauty, shame. a
25 Your men shall fall by the sword
  and your warriors in battle.
26 And her gates shall lament and
    mourn;
  ravaged, she shall sit upon the
    ground.

4 Seven women shall take hold of one
man on that day, saying,
'We will eat our own bread and wear
  our own clothes;
just let us be called by your name;
  take away our disgrace.'

The Future Glory of the Survivors in Zion

2 On that day the branch of the LORD shall be beautiful and glorious, and the fruit of the land shall be the pride and glory of the survivors of Israel. 3 Whoever is left in Zion and remains in Jerusalem will be called holy, everyone who has been recorded for life in Jerusalem, 4 once the Lord has washed away the filth of the daughters of Zion and cleansed the bloodstains of Jerusalem from its midst by a spirit of judgement and by a spirit of burning. 5 Then the LORD will create over the whole site of Mount Zion and over its places of assembly a cloud by day and smoke and the shining of a flaming fire by night. Indeed, over all the glory there will be a canopy. 6 It will serve as a pavilion, a shade by day from the heat, and a refuge and a shelter from the storm and rain.

The Song of the Unfruitful Vineyard

5 Let me sing for my beloved
my love-song concerning his
    vineyard:
My beloved had a vineyard
  on a very fertile hill.

2 He dug it and cleared it of stones,
  and planted it with choice vines;
he built a watch-tower in the midst of
    it,
  and hewed out a wine vat in it;
he expected it to yield grapes,
  but it yielded wild grapes.

3 And now, inhabitants of Jerusalem
  and people of Judah,
judge between me
  and my vineyard.
4 What more was there to do for my
    vineyard
  that I have not done in it?
When I expected it to yield grapes,
  why did it yield wild grapes?

5 And now I will tell you
  what I will do to my vineyard.
I will remove its hedge,
  and it shall be devoured;
I will break down its wall,
  and it shall be trampled down.
6 I will make it a waste;
  it shall not be pruned or hoed,
  and it shall be overgrown with
    briers and thorns;
I will also command the clouds
  that they rain no rain upon it.

7 For the vineyard of the LORD
    of hosts
  is the house of Israel,
and the people of Judah
  are his pleasant planting;
he expected justice,
  but saw bloodshed;
righteousness,
  but heard a cry!

Social Injustice Denounced

8 Ah, you who join house to house,
  who add field to field,
until there is room for no one
    but you,
  and you are left to live alone
  in the midst of the land!
9 The LORD of hosts has sworn in my
    hearing:

a Q Ms: MT lacks shame

Surely many houses shall be
    desolate,
    large and beautiful houses, without
    inhabitant.
10 For ten acres of vineyard shall yield
    but one bath,
    and a homer of seed shall yield a
    mere ephah. *a*

11 Ah, you who rise early in the
    morning
    in pursuit of strong drink,
    who linger in the evening
    to be inflamed by wine,
12 whose feasts consist of lyre and
    harp,
    tambourine and flute and wine,
    but who do not regard the deeds of
    the LORD,
    or see the work of his hands!
13 Therefore my people go into exile
    without knowledge;
    their nobles are dying of hunger,
    and their multitude is parched with
    thirst.

14 Therefore Sheol has enlarged its
    appetite
    and opened its mouth beyond
    measure;
    the nobility of Jerusalem *b* and her
    multitude go down,
    her throng and all who exult
    in her.
15 People are bowed down, everyone is
    brought low,
    and the eyes of the haughty are
    humbled.
16 But the LORD of hosts is exalted
    by justice,
    and the Holy God shows himself
    holy by righteousness.
17 Then the lambs shall graze as in their
    pasture,
    fatlings and kids *c* shall feed among
    the ruins.

18 Ah, you who drag iniquity along with
    cords of falsehood,
    who drag sin along as with cart-
    ropes,

19 who say, 'Let him make haste,
    let him speed his work
    that we may see it;
    let the plan of the Holy One of Israel
    hasten to fulfilment,
    that we may know it!'
20 Ah, you who call evil good
    and good evil,
    who put darkness for light
    and light for darkness,
    who put bitter for sweet
    and sweet for bitter!
21 Ah, you who are wise in your
    own eyes,
    and shrewd in your own sight!
22 Ah, you who are heroes in drinking
    wine
    and valiant at mixing drink,
23 who acquit the guilty for a bribe,
    and deprive the innocent of their
    rights!

Foreign Invasion Predicted

24 Therefore, as the tongue of fire
    devours the stubble,
    and as dry grass sinks down in the
    flame,
    so their root will become rotten,
    and their blossom go up like dust;
    for they have rejected the instruction
    of the LORD of hosts,
    and have despised the word of the
    Holy One of Israel.

25 Therefore the anger of the LORD was
    kindled against his people,
    and he stretched out his hand
    against them and struck them;
    the mountains quaked,
    and their corpses were like refuse
    in the streets.
    For all this his anger has not turned
    away,
    and his hand is stretched out still.

26 He will raise a signal for a nation far
    away,

a The Heb *bath, homer,* and *ephah* are measures of
quantity   *b* Heb *her nobility*   *c* Cn Compare Gk:
Heb *aliens*

and whistle for a people at the ends
    of the earth;
Here they come, swiftly, speedily!
27 None of them is weary, none
      stumbles,
    none slumbers or sleeps,
    not a loincloth is loose,
    not a sandal-thong broken;
28 their arrows are sharp,
    all their bows bent,
    their horses' hoofs seem like flint,
    and their wheels like the
      whirlwind.
29 Their roaring is like a lion,
    like young lions they roar;
    they growl and seize their prey,
    they carry it off, and no one
      can rescue.
30 They will roar over it on that day,
    like the roaring of the sea.
And if one looks to the land—
    only darkness and distress;
and the light grows dark with
    clouds.

A Vision of God in the Temple

6 In the year that King Uzziah died, I saw the Lord sitting on a throne, high and lofty; and the hem of his robe filled the temple. 2 Seraphs were in attendance above him; each had six wings: with two they covered their faces, and with two they covered their feet, and with two they flew. 3 And one called to another and said:

  'Holy, holy, holy is the LORD of hosts;
    the whole earth is full of his glory.'

4 The pivots *a* on the thresholds shook at the voices of those who called, and the house filled with smoke. 5 And I said: 'Woe is me! I am lost, for I am a man of unclean lips, and I live among a people of unclean lips; yet my eyes have seen the King, the LORD of hosts!'

6 Then one of the seraphs flew to me, holding a live coal that had been taken from the altar with a pair of tongs. 7 The seraph *b* touched my mouth with it and said: 'Now that this has touched your lips, your guilt has departed and your sin is blotted out.' 8 Then I heard the voice of the Lord saying, 'Whom shall I send, and who

will go for us?' And I said, 'Here am I; send me!' 9 And he said, 'Go and say to this people:

  "Keep listening, but do not
    comprehend;
  keep looking, but do not
    understand."
10 Make the mind of this people dull,
    and stop their ears,
    and shut their eyes,
  so that they may not look with their
    eyes,
    and listen with their ears,
    and comprehend with their minds,
    and turn and be healed.'
11 Then I said, 'How long, O Lord?' And
    he said:
  'Until cities lie waste
    without inhabitant,
  and houses without people,
    and the land is utterly desolate;
12 until the LORD sends everyone
    far away,
    and vast is the emptiness in the
    midst of the land.
13 Even if a tenth part remains in it,
    it will be burned again,
like a terebinth or an oak
    whose stump remains standing
    when it is felled.' *a*
The holy seed is its stump.

Isaiah Reassures King Ahaz

7 In the days of Ahaz son of Jotham son of Uzziah, king of Judah, King Rezin of Aram and King Pekah son of Remaliah of Israel went up to attack Jerusalem, but could not mount an attack against it. 2 When the house of David heard that Aram had allied itself with Ephraim, the heart of Ahaz *c* and the heart of his people shook as the trees of the forest shake before the wind.

3 Then the LORD said to Isaiah, Go out to meet Ahaz, you and your son Shear-jashub, *d* at the end of the conduit of the upper pool on the highway to the Fuller's Field, 4 and say to him, Take heed, be quiet, do not fear, and do not let your heart be

a Meaning of Heb uncertain   *b* Heb *He*   *c* Heb *his heart*   *d* That is *A remnant shall return* faint because of these two smouldering stumps of firebrands, because of the fierce anger of Rezin and Aram and the son of Remaliah. 5 Because Aram—with Ephraim and the son of Remaliah—has plotted evil against you, saying, 6 Let us go up against Judah and cut off Jerusalem *a* and conquer it for ourselves and make the son of Tabeel king in it; 7 therefore thus says the Lord GOD:

It shall not stand,
    and it shall not come to pass.
8 For the head of Aram is Damascus,
    and the head of Damascus is Rezin.
(Within sixty-five years Ephraim will be shattered, no longer a people.)
9 The head of Ephraim is Samaria,
    and the head of Samaria is the son
        of Remaliah.
If you do not stand firm in faith,
    you shall not stand at all.

Isaiah Gives Ahaz the Sign of Immanuel

10 Again the LORD spoke to Ahaz, saying, 11 Ask a sign of the LORD your God; let it be deep as Sheol or high as heaven. 12 But Ahaz said, I will not ask, and I will not put the LORD to the test. 13 Then Isaiah *b* said: 'Hear then, O house of David! Is it too little for you to weary mortals, that you weary my God also? 14 Therefore the Lord himself will give you a sign. Look, the young woman *c* is with child and shall bear a son, and shall name him Immanuel. *d* 15 He shall eat curds and honey by the time he knows how to refuse the evil and choose the good. 16 For before the child knows how to refuse the evil and choose the good, the land before whose two kings you are in dread will be deserted. 17 The LORD will bring on you and on your people and on your ancestral house such days as have not come since the day that Ephraim departed from Judah—the king of Assyria.'

18 On that day the LORD will whistle for the fly that is at the sources of the streams of Egypt, and for the bee that is in the land of Assyria. 19 And they will all come and settle in the steep ravines, and in the clefts of the rocks, and on all the thorn bushes, and on all the pastures.

20 On that day the Lord will shave with a razor hired beyond the River—with the king of Assyria—the head and the hair of the feet, and it will take off the beard as well.

21 On that day one will keep alive a young cow and two sheep, 22 and will eat curds because of the abundance of milk that they give; for everyone that is left in the land shall eat curds and honey.

23 On that day every place where there used to be a thousand vines, worth a thousand shekels of silver, will become briers and thorns. 24 With bow and arrows one will go there, for all the land will be briers and thorns; 25 and as for all the hills that used to be hoed with a hoe, you will not go there for fear of briers and thorns; but they will become a place where cattle are let loose and where sheep tread.

Isaiah's Son a Sign of the Assyrian Invasion

8 Then the LORD said to me, Take a large tablet and write on it in common characters, 'Belonging to Maher-shalal-hash-baz', *e* 2 and have it attested *f* for me by reliable witnesses, the priest Uriah and Zechariah son of Jeberechiah. 3 And I went to the prophetess, and she conceived and bore a son. Then the LORD said to me, Name him Maher-shalal-hash-baz; 4 for before the child knows how to call 'My father' or 'My mother', the wealth of Damascus and the spoil of Samaria will be carried away by the king of Assyria.

5 The LORD spoke to me again: 6 Because this people has refused the waters of Shiloah that flow gently, and melt in fear before *g* Rezin and the son of Remaliah; 7 therefore, the Lord is bringing up against it the mighty flood waters of the River, the king of Assyria and all his glory; it will rise above all its channels and overflow all its banks; 8 it will sweep on into Judah as a flood, and, pouring over, it will reach up to the neck; and its outspread wings will fill the breadth of your land, O Immanuel.

a Heb *cut it off*   *b* Heb *he*   *c* Gk *the virgin*   *d* That is *God is with us*   *e* That is *The spoil speeds, the prey hastens*   *f* Q Ms Gk Syr: MT *and I caused to be attested*   *g* Cn: Meaning of Heb uncertain

⁹ Band together, you peoples, and be
    dismayed;
  listen, all you far countries;
  gird yourselves and be dismayed;
  gird yourselves and be dismayed!
¹⁰ Take counsel together, but it shall be
    brought to naught;
  speak a word, but it will not stand,
  for God is with us. *a*

11 For the LORD spoke thus to me while his hand was strong upon me, and warned me not to walk in the way of this people, saying: ¹²Do not call conspiracy all that this people calls conspiracy, and do not fear what it fears, or be in dread. ¹³But the LORD of hosts, him you shall regard as holy; let him be your fear, and let him be your dread. ¹⁴He will become a sanctuary, a stone one strikes against; for both houses of Israel he will become a rock one stumbles over—a trap and a snare for the inhabitants of Jerusalem. ¹⁵And many among them shall stumble; they shall fall and be broken; they shall be snared and taken.

Disciples of Isaiah

16 Bind up the testimony, seal the teaching among my disciples. ¹⁷I will wait for the LORD, who is hiding his face from the house of Jacob, and I will hope in him. ¹⁸See, I and the children whom the LORD has given me are signs and portents in Israel from the LORD of hosts, who dwells on Mount Zion. ¹⁹Now if people say to you, 'Consult the ghosts and the familiar spirits that chirp and mutter; should not a people consult their gods, the dead on behalf of the living, ²⁰for teaching and for instruction?' surely, those who speak like this will have no dawn! ²¹They will pass through the land, *b* greatly distressed and hungry; when they are hungry, they will be enraged and will curse *c* their king and their gods. They will turn their faces upwards, ²²or they will look to the earth, but will see only distress and darkness, the gloom of anguish; and they will be thrust into thick darkness. *d*

The Righteous Reign of the Coming King

9 *e* But there will be no gloom for those who were in anguish. In the former time he brought into contempt the land of Zebulun and the land of Naphtali, but in the latter time he will make glorious the way of the sea, the land beyond the Jordan, Galilee of the nations.
²*f* The people who walked in
    darkness
  have seen a great light;
  those who lived in a land of deep
    darkness—
  on them light has shined.
3 You have multiplied the nation,
  you have increased its joy;
  they rejoice before you
    as with joy at the harvest,
    as people exult when dividing
      plunder.
4 For the yoke of their burden,
    and the bar across their shoulders,
    the rod of their oppressor,
  you have broken as on the day of
      Midian.
5 For all the boots of the tramping
    warriors
    and all the garments rolled in
      blood
  shall be burned as fuel for the fire.
6 For a child has been born for us,
  a son given to us;
  authority rests upon his shoulders;
    and he is named
  Wonderful Counsellor, Mighty God,
    Everlasting Father, Prince of Peace.
7 His authority shall grow continually,
    and there shall be endless peace
  for the throne of David and his
      kingdom.
  He will establish and uphold it
  with justice and with righteousness
    from this time onwards and for
      evermore.
  The zeal of the LORD of hosts will do
    this.

a Heb *immanu el*   *b* Heb *it*   *c* Or *curse by*
d Meaning of Heb uncertain   *e* Ch 8.23 in Heb
f Ch 9.1 in Heb

Judgement on Arrogance and Oppression

8 The Lord sent a word against Jacob,
  and it fell on Israel;
9 and all the people knew it—
  Ephraim and the inhabitants of
      Samaria—
  but in pride and arrogance of heart
      they said:
10 'The bricks have fallen,
  but we will build with dressed
      stones;
  the sycomores have been cut down,
  but we will put cedars in their
      place.'
11 So the LORD raised adversaries*a*
      against them,
  and stirred up their enemies,
12 the Arameans in the east and the
      Philistines in the west,
  and they devoured Israel with open
      mouth.
  For all this, his anger has not turned
      away;
  his hand is stretched out still.

13 The people did not turn to him who
      struck them,
  or seek the LORD of hosts.
14 So the LORD cut off from Israel head
      and tail,
  palm branch and reed in one day—
15 elders and dignitaries are the head,
  and prophets who teach lies are the
      tail;
16 for those who led this people led
      them astray,
  and those who were led by them
      were left in confusion.
17 That is why the Lord did not have
      pity on*b* their young people,
  or compassion on their orphans
      and widows;
  for everyone was godless and an
      evildoer,
  and every mouth spoke folly.
  For all this, his anger has not turned
      away;
  his hand is stretched out still.

18 For wickedness burned like a fire,
  consuming briers and thorns;
  it kindled the thickets of the forest,
  and they swirled upwards in a
      column of smoke.
19 Through the wrath of the LORD of
      hosts
  the land was burned,
  and the people became like fuel for
      the fire;
  no one spared another.
20 They gorged on the right, but still
      were hungry,
  and they devoured on the left, but
      were not satisfied;
  they devoured the flesh of their own
      kindred;*c*
21 Manasseh devoured Ephraim, and
      Ephraim Manasseh,
  and together they were against
      Judah.
  For all this, his anger has not turned
      away;
  his hand is stretched out still.

10 Ah, you who make iniquitous
      decrees,
  who write oppressive statutes,
2 to turn aside the needy from justice
  and to rob the poor of my people
      of their right,
  that widows may be your spoil,
  and that you may make the
      orphans your prey!
3 What will you do on the day of
      punishment,
  in the calamity that will come from
      far away?
  To whom will you flee for help,
  and where will you leave your
      wealth,
4 so as not to crouch among the
      prisoners
  or fall among the slain?
  For all this, his anger has not turned
      away;
  his hand is stretched out still.

Arrogant Assyria Also Judged

5 Ah, Assyria, the rod of my anger—
  the club in their hands is my fury!

a Cn: Heb *the adversaries of Rezin*   *b* Q Ms: MT *rejoice*
over   *c* Or *arm*

6 Against a godless nation I send him,
   and against the people of my wrath
      I command him,
   to take spoil and seize plunder,
      and to tread them down like the
         mire of the streets.
7 But this is not what he intends,
   nor does he have this in mind;
   but it is in his heart to destroy,
      and to cut off nations not a few.
8 For he says:
   'Are not my commanders all kings?
9 Is not Calno like Carchemish?
   Is not Hamath like Arpad?
   Is not Samaria like Damascus?
10 As my hand has reached to the
         kingdoms of the idols
      whose images were greater than
         those of Jerusalem and Samaria,
11 shall I not do to Jerusalem and
         her idols
      what I have done to Samaria and
         her images?'

12 When the Lord has finished all his
work on Mount Zion and on Jerusalem,
he*a* will punish the arrogant boasting of
the king of Assyria and his haughty pride.
13 For he says:
   'By the strength of my hand I have
         done it,
      and by my wisdom, for I have
         understanding;
   I have removed the boundaries of
         peoples,
      and have plundered their
         treasures;
   like a bull I have brought down
         those who sat on thrones.
14 My hand has found, like a nest,
      the wealth of the peoples;
   and as one gathers eggs that have
         been forsaken,
      so I have gathered all the earth;
   and there was none that moved a
         wing,
      or opened its mouth, or chirped.'

15 Shall the axe vaunt itself over the one
      who wields it,

or the saw magnify itself against the
      one who handles it?
As if a rod should raise the one who
      lifts it up,
   or as if a staff should lift the one
      who is not wood!
16 Therefore the Sovereign, the LORD of
      hosts,
   will send wasting sickness among
         his stout warriors,
   and under his glory a burning will be
         kindled,
      like the burning of fire.
17 The light of Israel will become a fire,
      and his Holy One a flame;
   and it will burn and devour
      his thorns and briers in one day.
18 The glory of his forest and his fruitful
      land
   the LORD will destroy, both soul
         and body,
   and it will be as when an invalid
         wastes away.
19 The remnant of the trees of his forest
      will be so few
   that a child can write them down.

The Repentant Remnant of Israel

20 On that day the remnant of Israel
and the survivors of the house of Jacob will
no more lean on the one who struck them,
but will lean on the LORD, the Holy One of
Israel, in truth. 21 A remnant will return, the
remnant of Jacob, to the mighty God. 22 For
though your people Israel were like the
sand of the sea, only a remnant of them
will return. Destruction is decreed, overflowing with righteousness. 23 For the Lord
GOD of hosts will make a full end, as decreed, in all the earth.*b*

24 Therefore thus says the Lord GOD of
hosts: O my people, who live in Zion, do
not be afraid of the Assyrians when they
beat you with a rod and lift up their staff
against you as the Egyptians did. 25 For in a
very little while my indignation will come
to an end, and my anger will be directed to
their destruction. 26 The LORD of hosts will
wield a whip against them, as when he
struck Midian at the rock of Oreb; his staff

a Heb *I*   *b* Or *land*

will be over the sea, and he will lift it as he did in Egypt. ²⁷ On that day his burden will be removed from your shoulder, and his yoke will be destroyed from your neck.

He has gone up from Rimmon,ᵃ
²⁸   he has come to Aiath;
he has passed through Migron,
   at Michmash he stores his
      baggage;
²⁹ they have crossed over the pass,
   at Geba they lodge for the night;
Ramah trembles,
   Gibeah of Saul has fled.
³⁰ Cry aloud, O daughter Gallim!
   Listen, O Laishah!
   Answer her, O Anathoth!
³¹ Madmenah is in flight,
   the inhabitants of Gebim flee
      for safety.
³² This very day he will halt at Nob,
   he will shake his fist
   at the mount of daughter Zion,
   the hill of Jerusalem.

³³ Look, the Sovereign, the LORD
      of hosts,
   will lop the boughs with terrifying
      power;
   the tallest trees will be cut down,
   and the lofty will be brought low.
³⁴ He will hack down the thickets of the
      forest with an axe,
   and Lebanon with its majestic
      treesᵇ will fall.

The Peaceful Kingdom

11 A shoot shall come out from the
      stock of Jesse,
   and a branch shall grow out of his
      roots.
² The spirit of the LORD shall rest
      on him,
   the spirit of wisdom and
      understanding,
   the spirit of counsel and might,
   the spirit of knowledge and the fear
      of the LORD.
³ His delight shall be in the fear of the
      LORD.

He shall not judge by what his
      eyes see,
   or decide by what his ears hear;
⁴ but with righteousness he shall judge
      the poor,
   and decide with equity for the
      meek of the earth;
he shall strike the earth with the rod
      of his mouth,
   and with the breath of his lips he
      shall kill the wicked.
⁵ Righteousness shall be the belt
      around his waist,
   and faithfulness the belt around his
      loins.

⁶ The wolf shall live with the lamb,
   the leopard shall lie down with the
      kid,
the calf and the lion and the fatling
      together,
   and a little child shall lead them.
⁷ The cow and the bear shall graze,
   their young shall lie down together;
   and the lion shall eat straw like the
      ox.
⁸ The nursing child shall play over the
      hole of the asp,
   and the weaned child shall put its
      hand on the adder's den.
⁹ They will not hurt or destroy
   on all my holy mountain;
for the earth will be full of the
      knowledge of the LORD
   as the waters cover the sea.

Return of the Remnant of Israel and Judah

10 On that day the root of Jesse shall stand as a signal to the peoples; the nations shall inquire of him, and his dwelling shall be glorious.

11 On that day the Lord will extend his hand yet a second time to recover the remnant that is left of his people, from Assyria, from Egypt, from Pathros, from Ethiopia,ᶜ from Elam, from Shinar, from Hamath, and from the coastlands of the sea.

a Cn: Heb *and his yoke from your neck, and a yoke will be destroyed because of fatness*   b Cn Compare Gk Vg: Heb *with a majestic one*   c Or Nubia; Heb *Cush*

12 He will raise a signal for the nations,
    and will assemble the outcasts of
       Israel,
  and gather the dispersed of Judah
  from the four corners of the earth.
13 The jealousy of Ephraim shall
       depart,
    the hostility of Judah shall be
       cut off;
  Ephraim shall not be jealous of
       Judah,
    and Judah shall not be hostile
       towards Ephraim.
14 But they shall swoop down on the
       backs of the Philistines in the
       west;
    together they shall plunder the
       people of the east.
  They shall put forth their hand
       against Edom and Moab,
    and the Ammonites shall
       obey them.
15 And the LORD will utterly destroy
    the tongue of the sea of Egypt;
  and will wave his hand over
       the River
    with his scorching wind;
  and will split it into seven channels,
    and make a way to cross on foot;
16 so there shall be a highway from
       Assyria
    for the remnant that is left of
       his people,
  as there was for Israel
    when they came up from the land
       of Egypt.

Thanksgiving and Praise

12 You will say on that day:
    I will give thanks to you,
       O LORD,
  for though you were angry
       with me,
  your anger turned away,
    and you comforted me.

2 Surely God is my salvation;
  I will trust, and will not be afraid,
  for the LORD GOD[a] is my strength and
       my might;
  he has become my salvation.

3 With joy you will draw water from the
wells of salvation. 4 And you will say on
that day:
  Give thanks to the LORD,
    call on his name;
  make known his deeds among the
       nations;
    proclaim that his name is exalted.

5 Sing praises to the LORD, for he has
       done gloriously;
    let this be known[b] in all the earth.
6 Shout aloud and sing for joy,
    O royal[c] Zion,
  for great in your midst is the Holy
       One of Israel.

Proclamation against Babylon

13 The oracle concerning Babylon
       that Isaiah son of Amoz saw.

2 On a bare hill raise a signal,
    cry aloud to them;
  wave the hand for them to enter
    the gates of the nobles.
3 I myself have commanded my
       consecrated ones,
    have summoned my warriors, my
       proudly exulting ones,
    to execute my anger.

4 Listen, a tumult on the mountains
    as of a great multitude!
  Listen, an uproar of kingdoms,
    of nations gathering together!
  The LORD of hosts is mustering
    an army for battle.
5 They come from a distant land,
    from the end of the heavens,
  the LORD and the weapons of his
       indignation,
    to destroy the whole earth.

6 Wail, for the day of the LORD is near;
    it will come like destruction from
       the Almighty![a]
7 Therefore all hands will be feeble,
    and every human heart will fail,

---

a Heb *for Yah, the* LORD   b Or *this is made known*
c Or *O inhabitant of*   a Traditional rendering of Heb
Shaddai

8 and they will be dismayed.
  Pangs and agony will seize them;
    they will be in anguish like a
      woman in labour.
  They will look aghast at one
      another;
    their faces will be aflame.
9 See, the day of the LORD comes,
    cruel, with wrath and fierce anger,
  to make the earth a desolation,
    and to destroy its sinners from it.
10 For the stars of the heavens and their
      constellations
    will not give their light;
  the sun will be dark at its rising,
    and the moon will not shed
      its light.
11 I will punish the world for its evil,
    and the wicked for their iniquity;
  I will put an end to the pride of
      the arrogant,
    and lay low the insolence of
      tyrants.
12 I will make mortals more rare than
      fine gold,
    and humans than the gold of
      Ophir.
13 Therefore I will make the heavens
      tremble,
    and the earth will be shaken out of
      its place,
  at the wrath of the LORD of hosts
    on the day of his fierce anger.
14 Like a hunted gazelle,
    or like sheep with no one to gather
      them,
  all will turn to their own people,
    and all will flee to their
      own lands.
15 Whoever is found will be thrust
      through,
    and whoever is caught will fall by
      the sword.
16 Their infants will be dashed
      to pieces
    before their eyes;
  their houses will be plundered,
    and their wives ravished.
17 See, I am stirring up the Medes
      against them,
    who have no regard for silver

  and do not delight in gold.
18 Their bows will slaughter the young
      men;
    they will have no mercy on the fruit
      of the womb;
    their eyes will not pity children.
19 And Babylon, the glory of
      kingdoms,
    the splendour and pride of the
      Chaldeans,
  will be like Sodom and Gomorrah
    when God overthrew them.
20 It will never be inhabited
    or lived in for all generations;
  Arabs will not pitch their
      tents there,
    shepherds will not make their
      flocks lie down there.
21 But wild animals will lie
      down there,
    and its houses will be full of
      howling creatures;
  there ostriches will live,
    and there goat-demons will dance.
22 Hyenas will cry in its towers,
    and jackals in the pleasant
      palaces;
  its time is close at hand,
    and its days will not be
      prolonged.

Restoration of Judah

14 But the LORD will have compassion on Jacob and will again choose Israel, and will set them in their own land; and aliens will join them and attach themselves to the house of Jacob. 2 And the nations will take them and bring them to their place, and the house of Israel will possess the nations*a* as male and female slaves in the LORD's land; they will take captive those who were their captors, and rule over those who oppressed them.

Downfall of the King of Babylon

3 When the LORD has given you rest from your pain and turmoil and the hard service with which you were made to serve, 4 you will take up this taunt against the king of Babylon:

a Heb *them*

How the oppressor has ceased!
    How his insolence[a] has ceased!
5 The Lord has broken the staff of the
        wicked,
    the sceptre of rulers,
6 that struck down the peoples
            in wrath
    with unceasing blows,
    that ruled the nations in anger
    with unrelenting persecution.
7 The whole earth is at rest and quiet;
    they break forth into singing.
8 The cypresses exult over you,
    the cedars of Lebanon, saying,
    'Since you were laid low,
    no one comes to cut us down.'
9 Sheol beneath is stirred up
    to meet you when you come;
    it rouses the shades to greet you,
    all who were leaders of the earth;
    it raises from their thrones
    all who were kings of the nations.
10 All of them will speak
    and say to you:
    'You too have become as weak as we
        are!
    You have become like us!'
11 Your pomp is brought down
        to Sheol,
    and the sound of your harps;
    maggots are the bed beneath you,
    and worms are your covering.

12 How you are fallen from heaven,
    O Day Star, son of Dawn!
    How you are cut down to the
        ground,
    you who laid the nations low!
13 You said in your heart,
    'I will ascend to heaven;
    I will raise my throne
    above the stars of God;
    I will sit on the mount of assembly
    on the heights of Zaphon;[b]
14 I will ascend to the tops of the
        clouds,
    I will make myself like the
        Most High.'
15 But you are brought down to Sheol,
    to the depths of the Pit.
16 Those who see you will stare at you,

and ponder over you:
    'Is this the man who made the earth
        tremble,
    who shook kingdoms,
17 who made the world like a desert
    and overthrew its cities,
    who would not let his prisoners go
        home?'
18 All the kings of the nations lie
        in glory,
    each in his own tomb;
19 but you are cast out, away from your
        grave,
    like loathsome carrion,[c]
    clothed with the dead, those pierced
        by the sword,
    who go down to the stones of
        the Pit,
    like a corpse trampled underfoot.
20 You will not be joined with them
        in burial,
    because you have destroyed
        your land,
    you have killed your people.

    May the descendants of evildoers
    nevermore be named!
21 Prepare slaughter for his sons
    because of the guilt of their
        father.[d]
    Let them never rise to possess
        the earth
    or cover the face of the world with
        cities.

22 I will rise up against them, says the
Lord of hosts, and will cut off from Babylon name and remnant, offspring and
posterity, says the Lord. 23 And I will make
it a possession of the hedgehog, and pools
of water, and I will sweep it with the
broom of destruction, says the Lord of
hosts.

An Oracle concerning Assyria

24 The Lord of hosts has sworn:
    As I have designed,
    so shall it be;

a Q Ms Compare Gk Syr Vg: meaning of MT uncertain
b Or assembly in the far north   c Cn Compare Gk: Heb
like a loathed branch   d Syr Compare Gk: Heb fathers

and as I have planned,
so shall it come to pass:

25 I will break the Assyrian in my land,
and on my mountains trample him
under foot;
his yoke shall be removed from them,
and his burden from their
shoulders.

26 This is the plan that is planned
concerning the whole earth;
and this is the hand that is stretched
out
over all the nations.

27 For the LORD of hosts has planned,
and who will annul it?
His hand is stretched out,
and who will turn it back?

An Oracle concerning Philistia

28 In the year that King Ahaz died this oracle came:

29 Do not rejoice, all you Philistines,
that the rod that struck you
is broken,
for from the root of the snake will
come forth an adder,
and its fruit will be a flying
fiery serpent.

30 The firstborn of the poor will graze,
and the needy lie down in safety;
but I will make your root die
of famine,
and your remnant I*a* will kill.

31 Wail, O gate; cry, O city;
melt in fear, O Philistia, all of you!
For smoke comes out of the north,
and there is no straggler in
its ranks.

32 What will one answer the messengers
of the nation?
'The LORD has founded Zion,
and the needy among his people
will find refuge in her.'

An Oracle concerning Moab

15

An oracle concerning Moab.

Because Ar is laid waste in a night,
Moab is undone;

because Kir is laid waste in a night,
Moab is undone.

2 Dibon*b* has gone up to the temple,
to the high places to weep;
over Nebo and over Medeba
Moab wails.
On every head is baldness,
every beard is shorn;

3 in the streets they bind on sackcloth;
on the housetops and in the
squares
everyone wails and melts in tears.

4 Heshbon and Elealeh cry out,
their voices are heard as far
as Jahaz;
therefore the loins of Moab quiver;*c*
his soul trembles.

5 My heart cries out for Moab;
his fugitives flee to Zoar,
to Eglath-shelishiyah.
For at the ascent of Luhith
they go up weeping;
on the road to Horonaim
they raise a cry of destruction;

6 the waters of Nimrim
are a desolation;
the grass is withered, the new growth
fails,
the verdure is no more.

7 Therefore the abundance they
have gained
and what they have laid up
they carry away
over the Wadi of the Willows.

8 For a cry has gone
around the land of Moab;
the wailing reaches to Eglaim,
the wailing reaches to Beer-elim.

9 For the waters of Dibon*d* are full
of blood;
yet I will bring upon Dibon*d* even
more—
a lion for those of Moab who escape,
for the remnant of the land.

16

Send lambs
to the ruler of the land,
from Sela, by way of the desert,
to the mount of daughter Zion.

---

a Q Ms Vg: MT *he*   b Cn: Heb *the house and Dibon*
c Cn Compare Gk Syr: Heb *the armed men of Moab cry
aloud*   d Q Ms Vg Compare Syr: MT *Dimon*

2 Like fluttering birds,
    like scattered nestlings,
  so are the daughters of Moab
    at the fords of the Arnon.
3 'Give counsel,
    grant justice;
  make your shade like night
    at the height of noon;
  hide the outcasts,
    do not betray the fugitive;
4 let the outcasts of Moab
    settle among you;
  be a refuge to them
    from the destroyer.'

When the oppressor is no more,
  and destruction has ceased,
and marauders have vanished from
    the land,
5 then a throne shall be established in
    steadfast love
  in the tent of David,
  and on it shall sit in faithfulness
a ruler who seeks justice
  and is swift to do what is right.

6 We have heard of the pride of Moab
    —how proud he is!—
  of his arrogance, his pride, and his
    insolence;
  his boasts are false.
7 Therefore let Moab wail,
    let everyone wail for Moab.
  Mourn, utterly stricken,
    for the raisin cakes of Kir-hareseth.

8 For the fields of Heshbon languish,
    and the vines of Sibmah,
  whose clusters once made drunk
    the lords of the nations,
  reached to Jazer
    and strayed to the desert;
  their shoots once spread abroad
    and crossed over the sea.
9 Therefore I weep with the weeping of
    Jazer
  for the vines of Sibmah;
  I drench you with my tears,
    O Heshbon and Elealeh;
  for the shout over your fruit harvest
    and your grain harvest has ceased.

10 Joy and gladness are taken away
    from the fruitful field;
  and in the vineyards no songs
      are sung,
    no shouts are raised;
  no treader treads out wine in
      the presses;
    the vintage-shout is hushed. *a*
11 Therefore my heart throbs like a harp
      for Moab,
    and my very soul for Kir-heres.
12 When Moab presents himself, when
he wearies himself upon the high place,
when he comes to his sanctuary to pray, he
will not prevail.
13 This was the word that the LORD
spoke concerning Moab in the past. 14 But
now the LORD says, In three years, like the
years of a hired worker, the glory of Moab
will be brought into contempt, in spite of
all its great multitude; and those who survive will be very few and feeble.

An Oracle concerning Damascus

17 An oracle concerning Damascus.

See, Damascus will cease to be a city,
  and will become a heap of ruins.
2 Her towns will be deserted for ever; *b*
    they will be places for flocks,
    which will lie down, and no one
      will make them afraid.
3 The fortress will disappear from
      Ephraim,
  and the kingdom from Damascus;
and the remnant of Aram will be
  like the glory of the children
      of Israel,
        says the LORD of hosts.

4 On that day
    the glory of Jacob will be
      brought low,
    and the fat of his flesh will
      grow lean.
5 And it shall be as when reapers gather
      standing grain
    and their arms harvest the ears,

a Gk: Heb *I have hushed*   *b* Cn Compare Gk: Heb *the cities of Aroer are deserted*

and as when one gleans the ears
    of grain
  in the Valley of Rephaim.
6 Gleanings will be left in it,
  as when an olive tree is beaten—
two or three berries
  in the top of the highest bough,
four or five
  on the branches of a fruit tree,
    says the LORD God of Israel.

7 On that day people will regard their
Maker, and their eyes will look to the Holy
One of Israel; 8 they will not have regard
for the altars, the work of their hands, and
they will not look to what their own fingers have made, either the sacred poles*a* or
the altars of incense.

9 On that day their strong cities will be
like the deserted places of the Hivites and
the Amorites,*b* which they deserted because of the children of Israel, and there
will be desolation.

10 For you have forgotten the God of
    your salvation,
  and have not remembered the Rock
    of your refuge;
therefore, though you plant pleasant
    plants
  and set out slips of an alien god,
11 though you make them grow on the
    day that you plant them,
  and make them blossom in the
    morning that you sow;
yet the harvest will flee away
  on a day of grief and incurable pain.

12 Ah, the thunder of many peoples,
  they thunder like the thundering of
    the sea!
Ah, the roar of nations,
  they roar like the roaring of mighty
    waters!
13 The nations roar like the roaring of
    many waters,
  but he will rebuke them, and they
    will flee far away,
chased like chaff on the mountains
  before the wind
  and whirling dust before the storm.

14 At evening time, lo, terror!
  Before morning, they are no more.
This is the fate of those who
    despoil us,
  and the lot of those who
    plunder us.

An Oracle concerning Ethiopia

18 Ah, land of whirring wings
  beyond the rivers of Ethiopia,*c*
2 sending ambassadors by the Nile
  in vessels of papyrus on the waters!
Go, you swift messengers,
  to a nation tall and smooth,
to a people feared near and far,
  a nation mighty and conquering,
  whose land the rivers divide.

3 All you inhabitants of the world,
  you who live on the earth,
when a signal is raised on the
    mountains, look!
When a trumpet is blown, listen!
4 For thus the LORD said to me:
I will quietly look from my dwelling
  like clear heat in sunshine,
  like a cloud of dew in the heat
    of harvest.
5 For before the harvest, when the
    blossom is over
  and the flower becomes a ripening
    grape,
he will cut off the shoots with
    pruning-hooks,
  and the spreading branches he will
    hew away.
6 They shall all be left
  to the birds of prey of the
    mountains
  and to the animals of the earth.
And the birds of prey will summer on
    them,
  and all the animals of the earth will
    winter on them.

7 At that time gifts will be brought to
the LORD of hosts from*d* a people tall and
smooth, from a people feared near and far,

a Heb *Asherim*   *b* Cn Compare Gk: Heb *places of the*
wood and the highest bough   *c* Or *Nubia*; Heb *Cush*
d Q Ms Gk Vg: MT *of*

a nation mighty and conquering, whose land the rivers divide, to Mount Zion, the place of the name of the LORD of hosts.

An Oracle concerning Egypt

19 An oracle concerning Egypt.

See, the LORD is riding on a
      swift cloud
   and comes to Egypt;
the idols of Egypt will tremble at his
      presence,
   and the heart of the Egyptians will
      melt within them.
2 I will stir up Egyptians against
      Egyptians,
   and they will fight, one against the
      other,
   neighbour against neighbour,
   city against city, kingdom against
      kingdom;
3 the spirit of the Egyptians within
      them will be emptied out,
   and I will confound their plans;
   they will consult the idols and the
      spirits of the dead
   and the ghosts and the familiar
      spirits;
4 I will deliver the Egyptians
   into the hand of a hard master;
   a fierce king will rule over them,
      says the Sovereign, the LORD
      of hosts.

5 The waters of the Nile will be
      dried up,
   and the river will be parched
      and dry;
6 its canals will become foul,
   and the branches of Egypt's Nile
      will diminish and dry up;
   reeds and rushes will rot away.
7 There will be bare places by
      the Nile,
   on the brink of the Nile;
   and all that is sown by the Nile will
      dry up,
   be driven away, and be no more.
8 Those who fish will mourn;
   all who cast hooks in the Nile will
      lament,

and those who spread nets on the
      water will languish.
9 The workers in flax will be in despair,
   and the carders and those at the
      loom will grow pale.
10 Its weavers will be dismayed,
   and all who work for wages will be
      grieved.

11 The princes of Zoan are utterly
      foolish;
   the wise counsellors of Pharaoh
      give stupid counsel.
How can you say to Pharaoh,
   'I am one of the sages,
   a descendant of ancient kings'?
12 Where now are your sages?
   Let them tell you and make known
   what the LORD of hosts has planned
      against Egypt.
13 The princes of Zoan have become
      fools,
   and the princes of Memphis
      are deluded;
   those who are the cornerstones of its
      tribes
   have led Egypt astray.
14 The LORD has poured into them *a*
   a spirit of confusion;
   and they have made Egypt stagger in
      all its doings
   as a drunkard staggers around
      in vomit.
15 Neither head nor tail, palm branch
      nor reed,
   will be able to do anything for
      Egypt.

16 On that day the Egyptians will be like women, and tremble with fear before the hand that the LORD of hosts raises against them. 17 And the land of Judah will become a terror to the Egyptians; everyone to whom it is mentioned will fear because of the plan that the LORD of hosts is planning against them.

Egypt, Assyria, and Israel Blessed

18 On that day there will be five cities in the land of Egypt that speak the language of

a Gk Compare Tg: Heb *it*

Canaan and swear allegiance to the LORD of hosts. One of these will be called the City of the Sun.

19 On that day there will be an altar to the LORD in the centre of the land of Egypt, and a pillar to the LORD at its border. ²⁰ It will be a sign and a witness to the LORD of hosts in the land of Egypt; when they cry to the LORD because of oppressors, he will send them a saviour, and will defend and deliver them. ²¹ The LORD will make himself known to the Egyptians; and the Egyptians will know the LORD on that day, and will worship with sacrifice and burnt-offering, and they will make vows to the LORD and perform them. ²² The LORD will strike Egypt, striking and healing; they will return to the LORD, and he will listen to their supplications and heal them.

23 On that day there will be a highway from Egypt to Assyria, and the Assyrian will come into Egypt, and the Egyptian into Assyria, and the Egyptians will worship with the Assyrians.

24 On that day Israel will be the third with Egypt and Assyria, a blessing in the midst of the earth, ²⁵ whom the LORD of hosts has blessed, saying, 'Blessed be Egypt my people, and Assyria the work of my hands, and Israel my heritage.'

Isaiah Dramatizes the Conquest of Egypt and Ethiopia

20 In the year that the commander-in-chief, who was sent by King Sargon of Assyria, came to Ashdod and fought against it and took it— ² at that time the LORD had spoken to Isaiah son of Amoz, saying, 'Go, and loose the sackcloth from your loins and take your sandals off your feet', and he had done so, walking naked and barefoot. ³ Then the LORD said, 'Just as my servant Isaiah has walked naked and barefoot for three years as a sign and a portent against Egypt and Ethiopia,ᵃ ⁴ so shall the king of Assyria lead away the Egyptians as captives and the Ethiopiansᵇ as exiles, both the young and the old, naked and barefoot, with buttocks uncovered, to the shame of Egypt. ⁵ And they shall be dismayed and confounded because of

Ethiopiaᵈ their hope and of Egypt their boast. ⁶ On that day the inhabitants of this coastland will say, "See, this is what has happened to those in whom we hoped and to whom we fled for help and deliverance from the king of Assyria! And we, how shall we escape?" '

Oracles concerning Babylon, Edom, and Arabia

21 The oracle concerning the wilderness of the sea.

As whirlwinds in the Negeb
    sweep on,
  it comes from the desert,
  from a terrible land.
² A stern vision is told to me;
  the betrayer betrays,
  and the destroyer destroys.
Go up, O Elam,
  lay siege, O Media;
all the sighing she has caused
  I bring to an end.
³ Therefore my loins are filled
    with anguish;
  pangs have seized me,
  like the pangs of a woman
    in labour;
I am bowed down so that I
    cannot hear,
  I am dismayed so that I
    cannot see.
⁴ My mind reels, horror has
    appalled me;
  the twilight I longed for
  has been turned for me into
    trembling.
⁵ They prepare the table,
  they spread the rugs,
  they eat, they drink.
Rise up, commanders,
  oil the shield!
⁶ For thus the Lord said to me:
'Go, post a lookout,
  let him announce what he sees.
⁷ When he sees riders, horsemen
    in pairs,
  riders on donkeys, riders
    on camels,

a Or *Nubia*; Heb *Cush*   *b* Or *Nubians*; Heb *Cushites*

let him listen diligently,
　very diligently.'
8 Then the watcher*a* called out:
　'Upon a watch-tower I stand,
　　O Lord,
　continually by day,
　and at my post I am stationed
　　throughout the night.
9 Look, there they come, riders,
　　horsemen in pairs!'
Then he responded,
　'Fallen, fallen is Babylon;
　and all the images of her gods
　lie shattered on the ground.'
10 O my threshed and winnowed one,
　what I have heard from the LORD of
　　hosts,
　the God of Israel, I announce
　　to you.

11 The oracle concerning Dumah.

One is calling to me from Seir,
　'Sentinel, what of the night?
　Sentinel, what of the night?'
12 The sentinel says:
　'Morning comes, and also the night.
　If you will inquire, inquire;
　come back again.'

13 The oracle concerning the desert
plain.

In the scrub of the desert plain you
　　will lodge,
　O caravans of Dedanites.
14 Bring water to the thirsty,
　meet the fugitive with bread,
　O inhabitants of the land
　　of Tema.
15 For they have fled from the swords,
　　from the drawn sword,
　from the bent bow,
　　and from the stress of battle.
16 For thus the Lord said to me: Within
a year, according to the years of a hired
worker, all the glory of Kedar will come to
an end; 17 and the remaining bows of Kedar's warriors will be few; for the LORD, the
God of Israel, has spoken.

A Warning of the Destruction of Jerusalem

22 The oracle concerning the valley of
vision.

What do you mean that you have
　　gone up,
　all of you, to the housetops,
2 you that are full of shoutings,
　tumultuous city, exultant town?
Your slain are not slain by the sword,
　nor are they dead in battle.
3 Your rulers have all fled together;
　they were captured without the use
　　of a bow.*b*
All of you who were found were
　　captured,
　though they had fled far away.*c*
4 Therefore I said:
Look away from me,
　let me weep bitter tears;
do not try to comfort me
　for the destruction of my
　　beloved people.

5 For the Lord GOD of hosts has a day
　of tumult and trampling and
　　confusion
　in the valley of vision,
a battering down of walls
　and a cry for help to the
　　mountains.
6 Elam bore the quiver
　with chariots and cavalry,*d*
　and Kir uncovered the shield.
7 Your choicest valleys were full of
　　chariots,
　and the cavalry took their stand at
　　the gates.
8 He has taken away the covering
　of Judah.

On that day you looked to the weapons
of the House of the Forest, 9 and you saw
that there were many breaches in the city
of David, and you collected the waters of
the lower pool. 10 You counted the houses
of Jerusalem, and you broke down the

a Q Ms: MT *a lion*   *b* Or *without their bows*   *c* Gk Syr
Vg: Heb *fled from far away*   *d* Meaning of Heb
uncertain

houses to fortify the wall. ¹¹ You made a reservoir between the two walls for the water of the old pool. But you did not look to him who did it, or have regard for him who planned it long ago.

¹² On that day the Lord GOD of hosts
  called to weeping and mourning,
    to baldness and putting on
      sackcloth;
¹³ but instead there was joy and
    festivity,
  killing oxen and slaughtering
    sheep,
  eating meat and drinking wine.
  'Let us eat and drink,
    for tomorrow we die.'
¹⁴ The LORD of hosts has revealed
    himself in my ears:
  Surely this iniquity will not be
    forgiven you until you die,
  says the Lord GOD of hosts.

Denunciation of Self-Seeking Officials

15 Thus says the Lord GOD of hosts: Come, go to this steward, to Shebna, who is master of the household, and say to him: ¹⁶ What right do you have here? Who are your relatives here, that you have cut out a tomb here for yourself, cutting a tomb on the height, and carving a habitation for yourself in the rock? ¹⁷ The LORD is about to hurl you away violently, my man. He will seize firm hold of you, ¹⁸ whirl you round and round, and throw you like a ball into a wide land; there you shall die, and there your splendid chariots shall lie, O you disgrace to your master's house! ¹⁹ I will thrust you from your office, and you will be pulled down from your post.

20 On that day I will call my servant Eliakim son of Hilkiah, ²¹ and will clothe him with your robe and bind your sash on him. I will commit your authority to his hand, and he shall be a father to the inhabitants of Jerusalem and to the house of Judah. ²² I will place on his shoulder the key of the house of David; he shall open, and no one shall shut; he shall shut, and no one shall open. ²³ I will fasten him like a peg in a secure place, and he will become a throne of

honour to his ancestral house. ²⁴ And they will hang on him the whole weight of his ancestral house, the offspring and issue, every small vessel, from the cups to all the flagons. ²⁵ On that day, says the LORD of hosts, the peg that was fastened in a secure place will give way; it will be cut down and fall, and the load that was on it will perish, for the LORD has spoken.

An Oracle concerning Tyre

23 The oracle concerning Tyre.

  Wail, O ships of Tarshish,
    for your fortress is destroyed. ᵃ
  When they came in from Cyprus
    they learned of it.
² Be still, O inhabitants of the coast,
    O merchants of Sidon;
  your messengers crossed over
    the sea ᵇ
³   and were on the mighty waters;
  your revenue was the grain of Shihor,
    the harvest of the Nile;
  you were the merchant of the
    nations.
⁴ Be ashamed, O Sidon, for the sea has
    spoken,
  the fortress of the sea, saying:
  'I have neither laboured nor given
    birth,
  I have neither reared young men
    nor brought up young women.'
⁵ When the report comes to Egypt,
    they will be in anguish over the
      report about Tyre.
⁶ Cross over to Tarshish—
    wail, O inhabitants of the coast!
⁷ Is this your exultant city
    whose origin is from days of old,
  whose feet carried her
    to settle far away?
⁸ Who has planned this
    against Tyre, the bestower
      of crowns,
  whose merchants were princes,
    whose traders were the honoured
      ones of the earth?

ᵃ Cn Compare verse 14: Heb *for it is destroyed, without houses*   ᵇ Q Ms: MT *crossing over the sea, they replenished you*

9 The LORD of hosts has planned it—
  to defile the pride of all glory,
  to shame all the honoured ones of
    the earth.
10 Cross over to your own land,
  O ships of[a] Tarshish;
  this is a harbour[b] no more.
11 He has stretched out his hand over
    the sea,
  he has shaken the kingdoms;
  the LORD has given command
      concerning Canaan
  to destroy its fortresses.
12 He said:
  You will exult no longer,
  O oppressed virgin daughter Sidon;
  rise, cross over to Cyprus—
  even there you will have no rest.

13 Look at the land of the Chaldeans!
This is the people; it was not Assyria. They
destined Tyre for wild animals. They erected their siege-towers, they tore down her
palaces, they made her a ruin.[c]
14 Wail, O ships of Tarshish,
  for your fortress is destroyed.
15 From that day Tyre will be forgotten for
seventy years, the lifetime of one king. At
the end of seventy years, it will happen to
Tyre as in the song about the prostitute:
16 Take a harp,
  go about the city,
  you forgotten prostitute!
  Make sweet melody,
  sing many songs,
  that you may be remembered.
17 At the end of seventy years, the LORD will
visit Tyre, and she will return to her trade,
and will prostitute herself with all the
kingdoms of the world on the face of the
earth. 18 Her merchandise and her wages
will be dedicated to the LORD; her profits[d]
will not be stored or hoarded, but her merchandise will supply abundant food and
fine clothing for those who live in the presence of the LORD.

Impending Judgement on the Earth

24 Now the Lord is about to lay
waste the earth and make
it desolate,

  and he will twist its surface and
    scatter its inhabitants.
2 And it shall be, as with the people, so
    with the priest;
  as with the slave, so with his
    master;
  as with the maid, so with her
    mistress;
  as with the buyer, so with the seller;
  as with the lender, so with the
    borrower;
  as with the creditor, so with
    the debtor.
3 The earth shall be utterly laid waste
    and utterly despoiled;
  for the LORD has spoken this word.

4 The earth dries up and withers,
  the world languishes and withers;
  the heavens languish together with
    the earth.
5 The earth lies polluted
    under its inhabitants;
  for they have transgressed laws,
    violated the statutes,
    broken the everlasting covenant.
6 Therefore a curse devours the earth,
  and its inhabitants suffer for their
    guilt;
  therefore the inhabitants of the earth
    dwindled,
  and few people are left.
7 The wine dries up,
  the vine languishes,
  all the merry-hearted sigh.
8 The mirth of the timbrels is stilled,
  the noise of the jubilant
    has ceased,
  the mirth of the lyre is stilled.
9 No longer do they drink wine with
    singing;
  strong drink is bitter to those who
    drink it.
10 The city of chaos is broken down,
  every house is shut up so that no
    one can enter.
11 There is an outcry in the streets for
    lack of wine;

a Cn Compare Gk: Heb *like the Nile, daughter*
b Cn: Heb *restraint*   c Meaning of Heb uncertain
d Heb *it*

all joy has reached its eventide;
the gladness of the earth is
banished.
12 Desolation is left in the city,
the gates are battered into ruins.
13 For thus it shall be on the earth
and among the nations,
as when an olive tree is beaten,
as at the gleaning when the grape
harvest is ended.

14 They lift up their voices, they sing for
joy;
they shout from the west over the
majesty of the LORD.
15 Therefore in the east give glory to the
LORD;
in the coastlands of the sea glorify
the name of the LORD, the God
of Israel.
16 From the ends of the earth we hear
songs of praise,
of glory to the Righteous One.
But I say, I pine away,
I pine away. Woe is me!
For the treacherous deal treacherously,
the treacherous deal very
treacherously.

17 Terror, and the pit, and the snare
are upon you, O inhabitant of the
earth!
18 Whoever flees at the sound of
the terror
shall fall into the pit,
and whoever climbs out of the pit
shall be caught in the snare.
For the windows of heaven are
opened,
and the foundations of the earth
tremble.
19 The earth is utterly broken,
the earth is torn asunder,
the earth is violently shaken.
20 The earth staggers like a drunkard,
it sways like a hut;
its transgression lies heavy upon it,
and it falls, and will not rise again.

21 On that day the LORD will punish
the host of heaven in heaven,

and on earth the kings of the earth.
22 They will be gathered together
like prisoners in a pit;
they will be shut up in a prison,
and after many days they will be
punished.
23 Then the moon will be abashed,
and the sun ashamed;
for the LORD of hosts will reign
on Mount Zion and in Jerusalem,
and before his elders he will manifest
his glory.

Praise for Deliverance from Oppression

25 O LORD, you are my God;
I will exalt you, I will praise
your name;
for you have done wonderful things,
plans formed of old, faithful
and sure.
2 For you have made the city a heap,
the fortified city a ruin;
the palace of aliens is a city
no more,
it will never be rebuilt.
3 Therefore strong peoples will glorify
you;
cities of ruthless nations will
fear you.
4 For you have been a refuge to
the poor,
a refuge to the needy in their
distress,
a shelter from the rainstorm and a
shade from the heat.
When the blast of the ruthless was
like a winter rainstorm,
5 the noise of aliens like heat in a dry
place,
you subdued the heat with the shade
of clouds;
the song of the ruthless
was stilled.

6 On this mountain the LORD of hosts
will make for all peoples
a feast of rich food, a feast of well-
matured wines,
of rich food filled with marrow, of
well-matured wines strained
clear.

7 And he will destroy on this mountain
   the shroud that is cast over all
     peoples,
   the sheet that is spread over all
     nations;
8   he will swallow up death for ever.
Then the Lord GOD will wipe away
   the tears from all faces,
  and the disgrace of his people he
     will take away from all
   the earth,
  for the LORD has spoken.
9 It will be said on that day,
  Lo, this is our God; we have waited
    for him, so that he might save
    us.
  This is the LORD for whom we have
    waited;
  let us be glad and rejoice in his
    salvation.
10 For the hand of the LORD will rest on
   this mountain.

  The Moabites shall be trodden down
   in their place
  as straw is trodden down in a dung-
   pit.
11 Though they spread out their hands
   in the midst of it,
  as swimmers spread out their hands
   to swim,
  their pride will be laid low despite
   the struggle[a] of their hands.
12 The high fortifications of his walls
   will be brought down,
  laid low, cast to the ground, even to
   the dust.

Judah's Song of Victory

26 On that day this song will be sung
    in the land of Judah:
We have a strong city;
  he sets up victory
  like walls and bulwarks.
2 Open the gates,
  so that the righteous nation that
   keeps faith
  may enter in.
3 Those of steadfast mind you keep
   in peace—
  in peace because they trust in you.

4 Trust in the LORD for ever,
  for in the LORD GOD[b]
  you have an everlasting rock.
5 For he has brought low
  the inhabitants of the height;
  the lofty city he lays low.
He lays it low to the ground,
  casts it to the dust.
6 The foot tramples it,
  the feet of the poor,
  the steps of the needy.

7 The way of the righteous is level;
  O Just One, you make smooth the
   path of the righteous.
8 In the path of your judgements,
  O LORD, we wait for you;
  your name and your renown
  are the soul's desire.
9 My soul yearns for you in the night,
  my spirit within me earnestly seeks
   you.
For when your judgements are in the
   earth,
  the inhabitants of the world learn
   righteousness.
10 If favour is shown to the wicked,
  they do not learn righteousness;
  in the land of uprightness they deal
   perversely
  and do not see the majesty of
   the LORD.
11 O LORD, your hand is lifted up,
  but they do not see it.
Let them see your zeal for your
   people, and be ashamed.
  Let the fire for your adversaries
   consume them.
12 O LORD, you will ordain peace
   for us,
  for indeed, all that we have done,
   you have done for us.
13 O LORD our God,
  other lords besides you have ruled
   over us,
  but we acknowledge your
   name alone.
14 The dead do not live;
  shades do not rise—

a Meaning of Heb uncertain   *b* Heb *in Yah, the* LORD

because you have punished and
   destroyed them,
   and wiped out all memory of them.
15 But you have increased the nation,
   O LORD,
   you have increased the nation; you
   are glorified;
   you have enlarged all the borders of
   the land.

16 O LORD, in distress they sought you,
   they poured out a prayer *a*
   when your chastening was
   on them.
17 Like a woman with child,
   who writhes and cries out in
   her pangs
   when she is near her time,
   so were we because of you, O LORD;
18 we were with child, we writhed,
   but we gave birth only to wind.
   We have won no victories on earth,
   and no one is born to inhabit
   the world.
19 Your dead shall live, their corpses *b*
   shall rise.
   O dwellers in the dust, awake and
   sing for joy!
   For your dew is a radiant dew,
   and the earth will give birth to
   those long dead. *c*

20 Come, my people, enter your
   chambers,
   and shut your doors behind you;
   hide yourselves for a little while
   until the wrath is past.
21 For the LORD comes out from
   his place
   to punish the inhabitants of the
   earth for their iniquity;
   the earth will disclose the blood shed
   on it,
   and will no longer cover its slain.

Israel's Redemption

27 On that day the LORD with his cruel and great and strong sword will
punish Leviathan the fleeing serpent,
Leviathan the twisting serpent, and he will
kill the dragon that is in the sea.

2 On that day:
   A pleasant vineyard, sing about it!
3 I, the LORD, am its keeper;
   every moment I water it.
   I guard it night and day
   so that no one can harm it;
4 I have no wrath.
   If it gives me thorns and briers,
   I will march to battle against it.
   I will burn it up.
5 Or else let it cling to me for
      protection,
   let it make peace with me,
   let it make peace with me.

6 In days to come *d* Jacob shall
      take root,
   Israel shall blossom and put
      forth shoots,
   and fill the whole world with fruit.

7 Has he struck them down as he struck
      down those who struck them?
   Or have they been killed as their
      killers were killed?
8 By expulsion, *a* by exile you struggled
      against them;
   with his fierce blast he removed
      them on the day of the
      east wind.
9 Therefore by this the guilt of Jacob
      will be expiated,
   and this will be the full fruit of the
      removal of his sin:
   when he makes all the stones of the
      altars
      like chalkstones crushed to pieces,
      no sacred poles *a* or incense altars
      will remain standing.
10 For the fortified city is solitary,
   a habitation deserted and forsaken,
      like the wilderness;
   the calves graze there,
      there they lie down, and strip its
      branches.
11 When its boughs are dry, they
      are broken;

a Meaning of Heb uncertain   *b* Cn Compare Syr Tg:
Heb *my corpse*   *c* Heb *to the shades*   *d* Heb *Those to
come*   *e* Heb *Asherim*

women come and make a fire
   of them.
For this is a people without
      understanding;
   therefore he that made them will
      not have compassion on them,
   he that formed them will show
      them no favour.

12 On that day the LORD will thresh
from the channel of the Euphrates to the
Wadi of Egypt, and you will be gathered
one by one, O people of Israel. 13And on
that day a great trumpet will be blown, and
those who were lost in the land of Assyria
and those who were driven out to the land
of Egypt will come and worship the LORD
on the holy mountain at Jerusalem.

Judgement on Corrupt Rulers, Priests, and Prophets

28 Ah, the proud garland of the
         drunkards of Ephraim,
   and the fading flower of its glorious
      beauty,
   which is on the head of those
      bloated with rich food, of those
      overcome with wine!
2 See, the Lord has one who is mighty
      and strong;
   like a storm of hail, a destroying
      tempest,
   like a storm of mighty, overflowing
      waters;
   with his hand he will hurl them
      down to the earth.
3 Trampled under foot will be
   the proud garland of the drunkards
      of Ephraim.
4 And the fading flower of its glorious
      beauty,
   which is on the head of those
      bloated with rich food,
   will be like a first-ripe fig before the
      summer;
   whoever sees it, eats it up
   as soon as it comes to hand.

5 On that day the LORD of hosts will be
      a garland of glory,

and a diadem of beauty, to the
      remnant of his people;
6 and a spirit of justice to the one who
      sits in judgement,
   and strength to those who turn
      back the battle at the gate.

7 These also reel with wine
   and stagger with strong drink;
the priest and the prophet reel with
      strong drink,
   they are confused with wine,
   they stagger with strong drink;
they err in vision,
   they stumble in giving judgement.
8 All tables are covered with filthy vomit;
   no place is clean.

9 'Whom will he teach knowledge,
   and to whom will he explain
      the message?
Those who are weaned from milk,
   those taken from the breast?
10 For it is precept upon precept,
      precept upon precept,
   line upon line, line upon line,
   here a little, there a little.'a

11 Truly, with stammering lip
   and with alien tongue
he will speak to this people,
12   to whom he has said,
'This is rest;
   give rest to the weary;
and this is repose';
   yet they would not hear.
13 Therefore the word of the LORD will
      be to them,
   'Precept upon precept, precept
      upon precept,
   line upon line, line upon line,
   here a little, there a little';a
in order that they may go, and fall
      backwards,
   and be broken, and snared,
      and taken.

14 Therefore hear the word of the LORD,
      you scoffers
   who rule this people in Jerusalem.

a Meaning of Heb of this verse uncertain

15 Because you have said, 'We have
made a covenant with death,
and with Sheol we have an
agreement;
when the overwhelming scourge
passes through
it will not come to us;
for we have made lies our refuge,
and in falsehood we have taken
shelter';
16 therefore thus says the Lord GOD,
See, I am laying in Zion a foundation
stone,
a tested stone,
a precious cornerstone, a sure
foundation:
'One who trusts will not panic.'
17 And I will make justice the line,
and righteousness the plummet;
hail will sweep away the refuge
of lies,
and waters will overwhelm the
shelter.
18 Then your covenant with death will
be annulled,
and your agreement with Sheol will
not stand;
when the overwhelming scourge
passes through
you will be beaten down by it.
19 As often as it passes through, it will
take you;
for morning by morning it will pass
through,
by day and by night;
and it will be sheer terror to
understand the message.
20 For the bed is too short to stretch
oneself on it,
and the covering too narrow to
wrap oneself in it.
21 For the LORD will rise up as on Mount
Perazim,
he will rage as in the valley of
Gibeon
to do his deed—strange is his
deed!—
and to work his work—alien is his
work!
22 Now therefore do not scoff,

or your bonds will be made
stronger;
for I have heard a decree of
destruction
from the Lord GOD of hosts upon
the whole land.

23 Listen, and hear my voice;
Pay attention, and hear my speech.
24 Do those who plough for sowing
plough continually?
Do they continually open and
harrow their ground?
25 When they have levelled its surface,
do they not scatter dill, sow
cummin,
and plant wheat in rows
and barley in its proper place,
and spelt as the border?
26 For they are well instructed;
their God teaches them.

27 Dill is not threshed with a threshing-
sledge,
nor is a cartwheel rolled over
cummin;
but dill is beaten out with a stick,
and cummin with a rod.
28 Grain is crushed for bread,
but one does not thresh it for ever;
one drives the cartwheel and horses
over it,
but does not pulverize it.
29 This also comes from the LORD
of hosts;
he is wonderful in counsel,
and excellent in wisdom.

The Siege of Jerusalem

29 Ah, Ariel, Ariel,
the city where David
encamped!
Add year to year;
let the festivals run their round.
2 Yet I will distress Ariel,
and there shall be moaning and
lamentation,
and Jerusalem*a* shall be to me like
an Ariel.*b*

a Heb *she*   b Probable meaning, *altar hearth*; compare
Ezek 43.15

3 And like David*a* I will encamp
        against you;
    I will besiege you with towers
    and raise siege-works against you.
4 Then deep from the earth you
        shall speak,
    from low in the dust your words
        shall come;
    your voice shall come from the
        ground like the voice of
        a ghost,
        and your speech shall whisper out
        of the dust.

5 But the multitude of your foes*b* shall
        be like fine dust,
    and the multitude of tyrants like
        flying chaff.
    And in an instant, suddenly,
6   you will be visited by the LORD
        of hosts
    with thunder and earthquake and
        great noise,
        with whirlwind and tempest, and
        the flame of a devouring fire.
7 And the multitude of all the nations
        that fight against Ariel,
    all that fight against her and her
        stronghold, and who
        distress her,
    shall be like a dream, a vision
        of the night.
8 Just as when a hungry person dreams
        of eating
    and wakes up still hungry,
    or a thirsty person dreams of
        drinking
    and wakes up faint, still thirsty,
    so shall the multitude of all the
        nations be
    that fight against Mount Zion.

9 Stupefy yourselves and be in a
        stupor,
    blind yourselves and be blind!
    Be drunk, but not from wine;
        stagger, but not from strong drink!
10 For the LORD has poured out
        upon you
    a spirit of deep sleep;

he has closed your eyes, you
        prophets,
    and covered your heads, you seers.
11 The vision of all this has become for
you like the words of a sealed document. If
it is given to those who can read, with the
command, 'Read this', they say, 'We cannot, for it is sealed.' 12 And if it is given to
those who cannot read, saying, 'Read this',
they say, 'We cannot read.'

13 The Lord said:
    Because these people draw near with
        their mouths
    and honour me with their lips,
        while their hearts are far from me,
    and their worship of me is a human
        commandment learned
        by rote;
14 so I will again do
    amazing things with this people,
        shocking and amazing.
    The wisdom of their wise shall
        perish,
        and the discernment of the
        discerning shall be hidden.

15 Ha! You who hide a plan too deep
        for the LORD,
    whose deeds are in the dark,
    and who say, 'Who sees us? Who
        knows us?'
16 You turn things upside down!
    Shall the potter be regarded as the
        clay?
    Shall the thing made say of its
        maker,
        'He did not make me';
    or the thing formed say of the one
        who formed it,
        'He has no understanding'?

Hope for the Future

17 Shall not Lebanon in a very little
        while
    become a fruitful field,
    and the fruitful field be regarded as
        a forest?
18 On that day the deaf shall hear
    the words of a scroll,

a Gk: Meaning of Heb uncertain   *b* Cn: Heb *strangers*

and out of their gloom and darkness
the eyes of the blind shall see.
19 The meek shall obtain fresh joy in the
LORD,
and the neediest people shall exult
in the Holy One of Israel.
20 For the tyrant shall be no more,
and the scoffer shall cease to be;
all those alert to do evil shall be cut
off—
21 those who cause a person to lose a
lawsuit,
who set a trap for the arbiter in the
gate,
and without grounds deny justice
to the one in the right.

22 Therefore thus says the LORD, who redeemed Abraham, concerning the house of
Jacob:
No longer shall Jacob be ashamed,
no longer shall his face grow pale.
23 For when he sees his children,
the work of my hands, in his midst,
they will sanctify my name;
they will sanctify the Holy One of
Jacob,
and will stand in awe of the God of
Israel.
24 And those who err in spirit will come
to understanding,
and those who grumble will accept
instruction.

The Futility of Reliance on Egypt

30 Oh, rebellious children, says the
LORD,
who carry out a plan, but not mine;
who make an alliance, but against my
will,
adding sin to sin;
2 who set out to go down to Egypt
without asking for my counsel,
to take refuge in the protection of
Pharaoh,
and to seek shelter in the shadow
of Egypt;
3 Therefore the protection of Pharaoh
shall become your shame,
and the shelter in the shadow of
Egypt your humiliation.

4 For though his officials are at Zoan
and his envoys reach Hanes,
5 everyone comes to shame
through a people that cannot profit
them,
that brings neither help nor profit,
but shame and disgrace.

6 An oracle concerning the animals of
the Negeb.
Through a land of trouble and
distress,
of lioness and roaring^a lion,
of viper and flying serpent,
they carry their riches on the backs of
donkeys,
and their treasures on the humps of
camels,
to a people that cannot profit
them.
7 For Egypt's help is worthless and
empty,
therefore I have called her,
'Rahab who sits still.'^{b}

A Rebellious People

8 Go now, write it before them on
a tablet,
and inscribe it in a book,
so that it may be for the time to come
as a witness for ever.
9 For they are a rebellious people,
faithless children,
children who will not hear
the instruction of the LORD;
10 who say to the seers, 'Do not see';
and to the prophets, 'Do not
prophesy to us what is right;
speak to us smooth things,
prophesy illusions;
11 leave the way, turn aside from
the path,
let us hear no more about the Holy
One of Israel.'
12 Therefore thus says the Holy One of
Israel:
Because you reject this word,
and put your trust in oppression
and deceit,
and rely on them;

a Cn: Heb *from them*   *b* Meaning of Heb uncertain

13 therefore this iniquity shall become
          for you
        like a break in a high wall, bulging
            out, and about to collapse,
        whose crash comes suddenly, in an
            instant;
14 its breaking is like that of a potter's
          vessel
        that is smashed so ruthlessly
      that among its fragments not a sherd
          is found
        for taking fire from the hearth,
        or dipping water out of the cistern.

15 For thus said the Lord GOD, the Holy
          One of Israel:
      In returning and rest you shall
              be saved;
        in quietness and in trust shall be
            your strength.
      But you refused 16 and said,
      'No! We will flee upon horses'—
        therefore you shall flee!
      and, 'We will ride upon swift
            steeds'—
        therefore your pursuers shall be
            swift!
17 A thousand shall flee at the threat of
          one,
        at the threat of five you shall flee,
      until you are left
        like a flagstaff on the top of
            a mountain,
        like a signal on a hill.

God's Promise to Zion

18 Therefore the LORD waits to be
          gracious to you;
        therefore he will rise up to show
            mercy to you.
      For the LORD is a God of justice;
        blessed are all those who wait for
            him.

19 Truly, O people in Zion, inhabitants
of Jerusalem, you shall weep no more. He
will surely be gracious to you at the sound
of your cry; when he hears it, he will answer you. 20 Though the Lord may give you
the bread of adversity and the water of affliction, yet your Teacher will not hide
himself any more, but your eyes shall see

your Teacher. 21 And when you turn to the
right or when you turn to the left, your ears
shall hear a word behind you, saying, 'This
is the way; walk in it.' 22 Then you will defile your silver-covered idols and your
gold-plated images. You will scatter them
like filthy rags; you will say to them, 'Away
with you!'

23 He will give rain for the seed with
which you sow the ground, and grain, the
produce of the ground, which will be rich
and plenteous. On that day your cattle will
graze in broad pastures; 24 and the oxen
and donkeys that till the ground will eat
silage, which has been winnowed with
shovel and fork. 25 On every lofty mountain and every high hill there will be
brooks running with water—on a day of
the great slaughter, when the towers fall.
26 Moreover, the light of the moon will be
like the light of the sun, and the light of
the sun will be sevenfold, like the light of
seven days, on the day when the LORD
binds up the injuries of his people, and
heals the wounds inflicted by his blow.

Judgement on Assyria

27 See, the name of the LORD comes
          from far away,
        burning with his anger, and in thick
            rising smoke; [a]
      his lips are full of indignation,
        and his tongue is like a devouring
            fire;
28 his breath is like an overflowing
          stream
        that reaches up to the neck—
      to sift the nations with the sieve of
            destruction,
        and to place on the jaws of the
            peoples a bridle that leads them
            astray.

29 You shall have a song as in the night
when a holy festival is kept; and gladness
of heart, as when one sets out to the sound
of the flute to go to the mountain of the
LORD, to the Rock of Israel. 30 And the LORD
will cause his majestic voice to be heard
and the descending blow of his arm to be

a Meaning of Heb uncertain

seen, in furious anger and a flame of devouring fire, with a cloudburst and tempest and hailstones. 31 The Assyrian will be terror-stricken at the voice of the LORD, when he strikes with his rod. 32 And every stroke of the staff of punishment that the LORD lays upon him will be to the sound of timbrels and lyres; battling with brandished arm he will fight with him. 33 For his burning-place[a] has long been prepared; truly it is made ready for the king,[b] its pyre made deep and wide, with fire and wood in abundance; the breath of the LORD, like a stream of sulphur, kindles it.

Alliance with Egypt Is Futile

31 Alas for those who go down to
Egypt for help
and who rely on horses,
who trust in chariots because they are
many
and in horsemen because they are
very strong,
but do not look to the Holy One
of Israel
or consult the LORD!
2 Yet he too is wise and brings
disaster;
he does not call back his words,
but will rise against the house of the
evildoers,
and against the helpers of those
who work iniquity.
3 The Egyptians are human, and
not God;
their horses are flesh, and
not spirit.
When the LORD stretches out
his hand,
the helper will stumble, and the
one helped will fall,
and they will all perish together.

4 For thus the LORD said to me,
As a lion or a young lion growls over
its prey,
and—when a band of shepherds is
called out against it—
is not terrified by their shouting
or daunted at their noise,

so the LORD of hosts will
come down
to fight upon Mount Zion and
upon its hill.
5 Like birds hovering overhead, so the
LORD of hosts
will protect Jerusalem;
he will protect and deliver it,
he will spare and rescue it.

6 Turn back to him whom you[c] have deeply betrayed, O people of Israel. 7 For on that day all of you shall throw away your idols of silver and idols of gold, which your hands have sinfully made for you.
8 'Then the Assyrian shall fall by a
sword, not of mortals;
and a sword, not of humans, shall
devour him;
he shall flee from the sword,
and his young men shall be put to
forced labour.
9 His rock shall pass away in terror,
and his officers desert the standard
in panic,'
says the LORD, whose fire is in Zion,
and whose furnace is in Jerusalem.

Government with Justice Predicted

32 See, a king will reign in
righteousness,
and princes will rule with justice.
2 Each will be like a hiding-place from
the wind,
a covert from the tempest,
like streams of water in a dry place,
like the shade of a great rock in a
weary land.
3 Then the eyes of those who have sight
will not be closed,
and the ears of those who have
hearing will listen.
4 The minds of the rash will have good
judgement,
and the tongues of stammerers will
speak readily and distinctly.
5 A fool will no longer be called
noble,

a Or *Topheth*   *b* Or *Molech*   *c* Heb *they*

nor a villain be said to be
  honourable.
6 For fools speak folly,
  and their minds plot iniquity:
to practise ungodliness,
  to utter error concerning the LORD,
to leave the craving of the hungry
  unsatisfied,
  and to deprive the thirsty of drink.
7 The villainies of villains are evil;
  they devise wicked devices
to ruin the poor with lying words,
  even when the plea of the needy is
  right.
8 But those who are noble plan noble
  things,
  and by noble things they stand.

Complacent Women Warned of Disaster

9 Rise up, you women who are at ease,
  hear my voice;
  you complacent daughters, listen to
  my speech.
10 In little more than a year
  you will shudder, you complacent
  ones;
  for the vintage will fail,
  the fruit harvest will not come.
11 Tremble, you women who are at ease,
  shudder, you complacent ones;
strip, and make yourselves bare,
  and put sackcloth on your loins.
12 Beat your breasts for the pleasant
  fields,
  for the fruitful vine,
13 for the soil of my people
  growing up in thorns and briers;
yes, for all the joyous houses
  in the jubilant city.
14 For the palace will be forsaken,
  the populous city deserted;
the hill and the watch-tower
  will become dens for ever,
the joy of wild asses,
  a pasture for flocks;
15 until a spirit from on high is poured
  out on us,
  and the wilderness becomes a
  fruitful field,
  and the fruitful field is deemed
  a forest.

The Peace of God's Reign

16 Then justice will dwell in the
  wilderness,
  and righteousness abide in the
  fruitful field.
17 The effect of righteousness will
  be peace,
  and the result of righteousness,
  quietness and trust for ever.
18 My people will abide in a peaceful
  habitation,
  in secure dwellings, and in quiet
  resting-places.
19 The forest will disappear completely, *a*
  and the city will be utterly laid low.
20 Happy will you be who sow beside
  every stream,
  who let the ox and the donkey
  range freely.

A Prophecy of Deliverance from Foes

33 Ah, you destroyer,
  who yourself have not been
  destroyed;
you treacherous one,
  with whom no one has dealt
  treacherously!
When you have ceased to destroy,
  you will be destroyed;
and when you have stopped dealing
  treacherously,
  you will be dealt with
  treacherously.

2 O LORD, be gracious to us; we wait for
  you.
  Be our arm every morning,
  our salvation in the time of
  trouble.
3 At the sound of tumult, peoples fled;
  before your majesty, nations
  scattered.
4 Spoil was gathered as the caterpillar
  gathers;
  as locusts leap, they leapt *b* upon it.
5 The LORD is exalted, he dwells
  on high;
  he filled Zion with justice and
  righteousness;

a Cn: Heb *And it will hail when the forest comes down*
b Meaning of Heb uncertain

6 he will be the stability of your times,
  abundance of salvation, wisdom,
     and knowledge;
  the fear of the LORD is Zion's
     treasure. *a*

7 Listen! the valiant *b* cry in the streets;
  the envoys of peace weep bitterly.
8 The highways are deserted,
  travellers have left the road.
  The treaty is broken,
    its oaths *c* are despised,
    its obligation *d* is disregarded.
9 The land mourns and languishes;
    Lebanon is confounded and
       withers away;
  Sharon is like a desert;
    and Bashan and Carmel shake off
       their leaves.

10 'Now I will arise,' says the LORD,
   'now I will lift myself up;
   now I will be exalted.
11 You conceive chaff, you bring
       forth stubble;
   your breath is a fire that will
       consume you.
12 And the peoples will be as if burned
       to lime,
   like thorns cut down, that are
       burned in the fire.'

13 Hear, you who are far away, what I
       have done;
   and you who are near, acknowledge
       my might.
14 The sinners in Zion are afraid;
   trembling has seized the godless:
   'Who among us can live with the
       devouring fire?
   Who among us can live with
       everlasting flames?'
15 Those who walk righteously and
       speak uprightly,
   who despise the gain of oppression,
   who wave away a bribe instead of
       accepting it,
   who stop their ears from hearing of
       bloodshed
   and shut their eyes from looking on
       evil,

16 they will live on the heights;
   their refuge will be the fortresses of
       rocks;
   their food will be supplied, their
       water assured.

The Land of the Majestic King

17 Your eyes will see the king in his
       beauty;
   they will behold a land that
       stretches far away.
18 Your mind will muse on the terror:
   'Where is the one who counted?
   Where is the one who weighed the
       tribute?
   Where is the one who counted the
       towers?'
19 No longer will you see the insolent
       people,
   the people of an obscure speech
       that you cannot comprehend,
   stammering in a language that you
       cannot understand.
20 Look on Zion, the city of our
       appointed festivals!
   Your eyes will see Jerusalem,
   a quiet habitation, an immovable
       tent,
   whose stakes will never be pulled up,
   and none of whose ropes will
       be broken.
21 But there the LORD in majesty will be
       for us
   a place of broad rivers and streams,
   where no galley with oars can go,
   nor stately ship can pass.
22 For the LORD is our judge, the LORD is
       our ruler,
   the LORD is our king; he will
       save us.

23 Your rigging hangs loose;
   it cannot hold the mast firm in its
       place,
   or keep the sail spread out.

   Then prey and spoil in abundance
       will be divided;

a Heb *his treasure*; meaning of Heb uncertain
b Meaning of Heb uncertain   *c* Q Ms: MT *cities*
d Or *everyone*

even the lame will fall to
plundering.
24 And no inhabitant will say, 'I am
sick';
the people who live there will be
forgiven their iniquity.

Judgement on the Nations

34 Draw near, O nations, to hear;
O peoples, give heed!
Let the earth hear, and all that fills it;
the world, and all that comes from
it.
2 For the LORD is enraged against all
the nations,
and furious against all their
hordes;
he has doomed them, has given
them over for slaughter.
3 Their slain shall be cast out,
and the stench of their corpses shall
rise;
the mountains shall flow with their
blood.
4 All the host of heaven shall rot
away,
and the skies roll up like a scroll.
All their host shall wither
like a leaf withering on a vine,
or fruit withering on a fig tree.

5 When my sword has drunk its fill in
the heavens,
lo, it will descend upon Edom,
upon the people I have doomed to
judgement.
6 The LORD has a sword; it is sated with
blood,
it is gorged with fat,
with the blood of lambs and
goats,
with the fat of the kidneys
of rams.
For the LORD has a sacrifice in
Bozrah,
a great slaughter in the land
of Edom.
7 Wild oxen shall fall with them,
and young steers with the
mighty bulls.

Their land shall be soaked with
blood,
and their soil made rich with fat.

8 For the LORD has a day of vengeance,
a year of vindication by Zion's
cause. *a*
9 And the streams of Edom *b* shall be
turned into pitch,
and her soil into sulphur;
her land shall become burning
pitch.
10 Night and day it shall not be
quenched;
its smoke shall go up for ever.
From generation to generation it
shall lie waste;
no one shall pass through it for
ever and ever.
11 But the hawk *c* and the hedgehog *c*
shall possess it;
the owl *c* and the raven shall live in
it.
He shall stretch the line of confusion
over it,
and the plummet of chaos over *d* its
nobles.
12 They shall name it No Kingdom
There,
and all its princes shall be
nothing.
13 Thorns shall grow over its
strongholds,
nettles and thistles in its
fortresses.
It shall be the haunt of jackals,
an abode for ostriches.
14 Wildcats shall meet with hyenas,
goat-demons shall call to
each other;
there too Lilith shall repose,
and find a place to rest.
15 There shall the owl nest
and lay and hatch and brood in its
shadow;
there too the buzzards shall gather,
each one with its mate.
16 Seek and read from the book of
the LORD:

a Or *of recompense by Zion's defender*   *b* Heb *her*
streams   *c* Identification uncertain   *d* Heb lacks *over*

Not one of these shall be missing;
    none shall be without its mate.
For the mouth of the LORD has
        commanded,
    and his spirit has gathered them.
17 He has cast the lot for them,
    his hand has portioned it out to
        them with the line;
they shall possess it for ever,
    from generation to generation they
        shall live in it.

The Return of the Redeemed to Zion

35 The wilderness and the dry land
        shall be glad,
    the desert shall rejoice and
        blossom;
like the crocus 2 it shall blossom
        abundantly,
    and rejoice with joy and singing.
The glory of Lebanon shall be given
        to it,
    the majesty of Carmel and Sharon.
They shall see the glory of the LORD,
    the majesty of our God.

3 Strengthen the weak hands,
    and make firm the feeble knees.
4 Say to those who are of a fearful
        heart,
    'Be strong, do not fear!
Here is your God.
    He will come with vengeance,
with terrible recompense.
    He will come and save you.'

5 Then the eyes of the blind shall
        be opened,
    and the ears of the deaf unstopped;
6 then the lame shall leap like a deer,
    and the tongue of the speechless
        sing for joy.
For waters shall break forth in the
        wilderness,
    and streams in the desert;
7 the burning sand shall become
        a pool,
    and the thirsty ground springs
        of water;
the haunt of jackals shall become
    a swamp,[a]

the grass shall become reeds and
    rushes.

8 A highway shall be there,
    and it shall be called the Holy Way;
the unclean shall not travel on it,[b]
    but it shall be for God's people;[c]
no traveller, not even fools, shall go
    astray.
9 No lion shall be there,
    nor shall any ravenous beast come
        up on it;
they shall not be found there,
    but the redeemed shall walk there.
10 And the ransomed of the LORD shall
        return,
    and come to Zion with singing;
everlasting joy shall be upon their
        heads;
    they shall obtain joy and gladness,
    and sorrow and sighing shall
        flee away.

Sennacherib Threatens Jerusalem

36 In the fourteenth year of King Hez-
        ekiah, King Sennacherib of Assyria
came up against all the fortified cities of Judah and captured them. 2 The king of Assyria sent the Rabshakeh from Lachish to
King Hezekiah at Jerusalem, with a great
army. He stood by the conduit of the upper
pool on the highway to the Fuller's Field.
3 And there came out to him Eliakim son of
Hilkiah, who was in charge of the palace,
and Shebna the secretary, and Joah son of
Asaph, the recorder.

4 The Rabshakeh said to them, 'Say to
Hezekiah: Thus says the great king, the
king of Assyria: On what do you base this
confidence of yours? 5 Do you think that
mere words are strategy and power for war?
On whom do you now rely, that you have
rebelled against me? 6 See, you are relying
on Egypt, that broken reed of a staff, which
will pierce the hand of anyone who leans
on it. Such is Pharaoh king of Egypt to all
who rely on him. 7 But if you say to me,
"We rely on the LORD our God", is it not he
whose high places and altars Hezekiah has

---

a Cn: Heb *in the haunt of jackals is her resting-place*
b Or *pass it by*   *c* Cn: Heb *for them*

removed, saying to Judah and to Jerusalem, "You shall worship before this altar"? 8 Come now, make a wager with my master the king of Assyria: I will give you two thousand horses, if you are able on your part to set riders on them. 9 How then can you repulse a single captain among the least of my master's servants, when you rely on Egypt for chariots and for horsemen? 10 Moreover, is it without the LORD that I have come up against this land to destroy it? The LORD said to me, Go up against this land, and destroy it.'

11 Then Eliakim, Shebna, and Joah said to the Rabshakeh, 'Please speak to your servants in Aramaic, for we understand it; do not speak to us in the language of Judah within the hearing of the people who are on the wall.' 12 But the Rabshakeh said, 'Has my master sent me to speak these words to your master and to you, and not to the people sitting on the wall, who are doomed with you to eat their own dung and drink their own urine?'

13 Then the Rabshakeh stood and called out in a loud voice in the language of Judah, 'Hear the words of the great king, the king of Assyria! 14 Thus says the king: "Do not let Hezekiah deceive you, for he will not be able to deliver you. 15 Do not let Hezekiah make you rely on the LORD by saying, The LORD will surely deliver us; this city will not be given into the hand of the king of Assyria." 16 Do not listen to Hezekiah; for thus says the king of Assyria: "Make your peace with me and come out to me; then every one of you will eat from your own vine and your own fig tree and drink water from your own cistern, 17 until I come and take you away to a land like your own land, a land of grain and wine, a land of bread and vineyards. 18 Do not let Hezekiah mislead you by saying, The LORD will save us. Has any of the gods of the nations saved their land out of the hand of the king of Assyria? 19 Where are the gods of Hamath and Arpad? Where are the gods of Sepharvaim? Have they delivered Samaria out of my hand? 20 Who among all the gods of these countries have saved their

The Assyrian Empire

Sardis

Tarsus   Carchemish   Nineveh

Tigris River

ASSYRIAN EMPIRE

Mediterranean Sea   Sidon   Ecbatana

Tyre   Damascus

Samaria   Babylon   Susa

Jerusalem

Pelusium   Euphrates River

Memphis

EGYPT

N

0   300   500 Mi.
0   300   500   Km.

countries out of my hand, that the LORD should save Jerusalem out of my hand?" '

21 But they were silent and answered him not a word, for the king's command was, 'Do not answer him.' 22 Then Eliakim son of Hilkiah, who was in charge of the palace, and Shebna the secretary, and Joah son of Asaph, the recorder, came to Hezekiah with their clothes torn, and told him the words of the Rabshakeh.

Hezekiah Consults Isaiah

37 When King Hezekiah heard it, he tore his clothes, covered himself with sackcloth, and went into the house of the LORD. 2 And he sent Eliakim, who was in charge of the palace, and Shebna the secretary, and the senior priests, covered with sackcloth, to the prophet Isaiah son of Amoz. 3 They said to him, 'Thus says Hezekiah, This day is a day of distress, of rebuke, and of disgrace; children have come to birth, and there is no strength to bring them forth. 4 It may be that the LORD your God heard the words of the Rabshakeh, whom his master the king of Assyria has sent to mock the living God, and will rebuke the words that the LORD your God has heard; therefore lift up your prayer for the remnant that is left.'

5 When the servants of King Hezekiah came to Isaiah, 6 Isaiah said to them, 'Say to your master, "Thus says the LORD: Do not be afraid because of the words that you have heard, with which the servants of the king of Assyria have reviled me. 7 I myself will put a spirit in him, so that he shall hear a rumour, and return to his own land; I will cause him to fall by the sword in his own land." '

8 The Rabshakeh returned, and found the king of Assyria fighting against Libnah; for he had heard that the king had left Lachish. 9 Now the king[a] heard concerning King Tirhakah of Ethiopia,[b] 'He has set out to fight against you.' When he heard it, he sent messengers to Hezekiah, saying, 10 'Thus shall you speak to King Hezekiah of Judah: Do not let your God on whom you rely deceive you by promising that Jerusalem will not be given into the hand of the king of Assyria. 11 See, you have heard what the kings of Assyria have done to all lands, destroying them utterly. Shall you be delivered? 12 Have the gods of the nations delivered them, the nations that my predecessors destroyed, Gozan, Haran, Rezeph, and the people of Eden who were in Telassar? 13 Where is the king of Hamath, the king of Arpad, the king of the city of Sepharvaim, the king of Hena, or the king of Ivvah?'

Hezekiah's Prayer

14 Hezekiah received the letter from the hand of the messengers and read it; then Hezekiah went up to the house of the LORD and spread it before the LORD. 15 And Hezekiah prayed to the LORD, saying: 16 'O LORD of hosts, God of Israel, who are enthroned above the cherubim, you are God, you alone, of all the kingdoms of the earth; you have made heaven and earth. 17 Incline your ear, O LORD, and hear; open your eyes, O LORD, and see; hear all the words of Sennacherib, which he has sent to mock the living God. 18 Truly, O LORD, the kings of Assyria have laid waste all the nations and their lands, 19 and have hurled their gods into the fire, though they were no gods, but the work of human hands— wood and stone—and so they were destroyed. 20 So now, O LORD our God, save us from his hand, so that all the kingdoms of the earth may know that you alone are the LORD.'

21 Then Isaiah son of Amoz sent to Hezekiah, saying: 'Thus says the LORD, the God of Israel: Because you have prayed to me concerning King Sennacherib of Assyria, 22 this is the word that the LORD has spoken concerning him:

> She despises you, she scorns you—
>   virgin daughter Zion;
> she tosses her head—behind
>   your back,
>   daughter Jerusalem.

23 'Whom have you mocked and
    reviled?

---

a Heb *he*   *b* Or *Nubia*; Heb *Cush*

Against whom have you raised your
voice
and haughtily lifted your eyes?
Against the Holy One of Israel!
24 By your servants you have mocked
the Lord,
and you have said, "With my many
chariots
I have gone up the heights of the
mountains,
to the far recesses of Lebanon;
I felled its tallest cedars,
its choicest cypresses;
I came to its remotest height,
its densest forest.
25 I dug wells
and drank waters,
I dried up with the sole of my foot
all the streams of Egypt."

26 'Have you not heard
that I determined it long ago?
I planned from days of old
what now I bring to pass,
that you should make fortified cities
crash into heaps of ruins,
27 while their inhabitants, shorn of
strength,
are dismayed and confounded;
they have become like plants of
the field
and like tender grass,
like grass on the housetops,
blighted[a] before it is grown.

28 'I know your rising up[b] and your
sitting down,
your going out and coming in,
and your raging against me.
29 Because you have raged against me
and your arrogance has come to my
ears,
I will put my hook in your nose
and my bit in your mouth;
I will turn you back on the way
by which you came.

30 'And this shall be the sign for you:
This year eat what grows of itself, and in
the second year what springs from that;
then in the third year sow, reap, plant vineyards, and eat their fruit. 31 The surviving
remnant of the house of Judah shall again
take root downwards, and bear fruit upwards; 32 for from Jerusalem a remnant
shall go out, and from Mount Zion a band
of survivors. The zeal of the LORD of hosts
will do this.

33 'Therefore thus says the LORD concerning the king of Assyria: He shall not
come into this city, shoot an arrow there,
come before it with a shield, or cast up a
siege-ramp against it. 34 By the way that he
came, by the same he shall return; he shall
not come into this city, says the LORD.
35 For I will defend this city to save it, for
my own sake and for the sake of my servant David.'

Sennacherib's Defeat and Death

36 Then the angel of the LORD set out
and struck down one hundred and eighty-
five thousand in the camp of the Assyrians;
when morning dawned, they were all dead
bodies. 37 Then King Sennacherib of Assyria left, went home, and lived at Nineveh.
38 As he was worshipping in the house of
his god Nisroch, his sons Adrammelech
and Sharezer killed him with the sword,
and they escaped into the land of Ararat.
His son Esar-haddon succeeded him.

Hezekiah's Illness

38 In those days Hezekiah became
sick and was at the point of death.
The prophet Isaiah son of Amoz came to
him, and said to him, 'Thus says the LORD:
Set your house in order, for you shall die;
you shall not recover.' 2 Then Hezekiah
turned his face to the wall, and prayed to
the LORD: 3 'Remember now, O LORD, I implore you, how I have walked before you in
faithfulness with a whole heart, and have
done what is good in your sight.' And Hezekiah wept bitterly.

4 Then the word of the LORD came to
Isaiah: 5 'Go and say to Hezekiah, Thus says
the LORD, the God of your ancestor David:
I have heard your prayer, I have seen your
tears; I will add fifteen years to your life. 6 I

a With 2 Kings 19.26: Heb field   b Q Ms Gk: MT lacks
your rising up

will deliver you and this city out of the hand of the king of Assyria, and defend this city.

7 'This is the sign to you from the LORD, that the LORD will do this thing that he has promised: ⁸See, I will make the shadow cast by the declining sun on the dial of Ahaz turn back ten steps.' So the sun turned back on the dial the ten steps by which it had declined.ᵃ

9 A writing of King Hezekiah of Judah, after he had been sick and had recovered from his sickness:

¹⁰ I said: In the noontide of my days
    I must depart;
 I am consigned to the gates of Sheol
    for the rest of my years.
¹¹ I said, I shall not see the LORD
    in the land of the living;
 I shall look upon mortals no more
    among the inhabitants of
    the world.
¹² My dwelling is plucked up and
    removed from me
    like a shepherd's tent;
 like a weaver I have rolled up my life;
    he cuts me off from the loom;
 from day to night you bring me to an
    end;ᵃ
¹³   I cry for helpᵇ until morning;
 like a lion he breaks all my bones;
    from day to night you bring me to
    an end.ᵃ

¹⁴ Like a swallow or a craneᵃ I clamour,
    I moan like a dove.
 My eyes are weary with looking
    upwards.
    O Lord, I am oppressed; be my
    security!
¹⁵ But what can I say? For he has spoken
    to me,
    and he himself has done it.
 All my sleep has fledᶜ
    because of the bitterness of
    my soul.

¹⁶ O Lord, by these things people live,
    and in all these is the life of
    my spirit.ᵃ

    O restore me to health and make
    me live!
¹⁷ Surely it was for my welfare
    that I had great bitterness;
 but you have held backᵈ my life
    from the pit of destruction,
 for you have cast all my sins
    behind your back.
¹⁸ For Sheol cannot thank you,
    death cannot praise you;
 those who go down to the Pit cannot
    hope
    for your faithfulness.
¹⁹ The living, the living, they
    thank you,
    as I do this day;
 fathers make known to children
    your faithfulness.

²⁰ The LORD will save me,
    and we will sing to stringed
    instrumentsᵉ
 all the days of our lives,
    at the house of the LORD.

21 Now Isaiah had said, 'Let them take a lump of figs, and apply it to the boil, so that he may recover.' ²²Hezekiah also had said, 'What is the sign that I shall go up to the house of the LORD?'

Envoys from Babylon Welcomed

39 At that time King Merodach-bala-dan son of Baladan of Babylon sent envoys with letters and a present to Hezekiah, for he heard that he had been sick and had recovered. ²Hezekiah wel-comed them; he showed them his treasure-house, the silver, the gold, the spices, the precious oil, his whole armoury, all that was found in his storehouses. There was nothing in his house or in all his realm that Hezekiah did not show them. ³Then the prophet Isaiah came to King Hezekiah and said to him, 'What did these men say? From where did they come to you?' Heze-kiah answered, 'They have come to me from a far country, from Babylon.' ⁴He

ᵃ Meaning of Heb uncertain   ᵇ Cn: Meaning of Heb uncertain   ᶜ Cn Compare Syr: Heb *I will walk slowly all my years*   ᵈ Cn Compare Gk Vg: Heb *loved*   ᵉ Heb *my stringed instruments*

said, 'What have they seen in your house?'
Hezekiah answered, 'They have seen all
that is in my house; there is nothing in my
storehouses that I did not show them.'

5 Then Isaiah said to Hezekiah, 'Hear
the word of the Lord of hosts: 6 Days are
coming when all that is in your house, and
that which your ancestors have stored up
until this day, shall be carried to Babylon;
nothing shall be left, says the Lord. 7 Some
of your own sons who are born to you
shall be taken away; they shall be eunuchs
in the palace of the king of Babylon.' 8 Then
Hezekiah said to Isaiah, 'The word of the
Lord that you have spoken is good.' For he
thought, 'There will be peace and security
in my days.'

God's People Are Comforted

40 Comfort, O comfort my people,
    says your God.
2 Speak tenderly to Jerusalem,
  and cry to her
that she has served her term,
  that her penalty is paid,
that she has received from the Lord's
    hand
    double for all her sins.

3 A voice cries out:
'In the wilderness prepare the way of
    the Lord,
  make straight in the desert a
    highway for our God.
4 Every valley shall be lifted up,
  and every mountain and hill be
    made low;
the uneven ground shall become
    level,
  and the rough places a plain.
5 Then the glory of the Lord shall
    be revealed,
  and all people shall see it together,
for the mouth of the Lord has
    spoken.'

6 A voice says, 'Cry out!'
  And I said, 'What shall I cry?'
All people are grass,
  their constancy is like the flower of
    the field.

7 The grass withers, the flower fades,
  when the breath of the Lord blows
    upon it;
  surely the people are grass.
8 The grass withers, the flower fades;
  but the word of our God will stand
    for ever.
9 Get you up to a high mountain,
  O Zion, herald of good tidings; a
lift up your voice with strength,
  O Jerusalem, herald of good
    tidings, b
  lift it up, do not fear;
say to the cities of Judah,
  'Here is your God!'
10 See, the Lord God comes with
    might,
  and his arm rules for him;
his reward is with him,
  and his recompense before him.
11 He will feed his flock like a
    shepherd;
  he will gather the lambs in
    his arms,
and carry them in his bosom,
  and gently lead the mother sheep.

12 Who has measured the waters in the
    hollow of his hand
  and marked off the heavens with a
    span,
enclosed the dust of the earth in
    a measure,
  and weighed the mountains
    in scales
  and the hills in a balance?
13 Who has directed the spirit of
    the Lord,
  or as his counsellor has instructed
    him?
14 Whom did he consult for his
    enlightenment,
  and who taught him the path of
    justice?
Who taught him knowledge,
  and showed him the way of
    understanding?
15 Even the nations are like a drop from
    a bucket,

a Or O herald of good tidings to Zion   b Or O herald of
good tidings to Jerusalem

and are accounted as dust on
the scales;
see, he takes up the isles like fine
dust.
16 Lebanon would not provide fuel
enough,
nor are its animals enough for a
burnt-offering.
17 All the nations are as nothing before
him;
they are accounted by him as less
than nothing and emptiness.

18 To whom then will you liken God,
or what likeness compare
with him?
19 An idol? —A workman casts it,
and a goldsmith overlays it
with gold,
and casts for it silver chains.
20 As a gift one chooses mulberry
wood[a]
—wood that will not rot—
then seeks out a skilled artisan
to set up an image that will
not topple.

21 Have you not known? Have you
not heard?
Has it not been told you from the
beginning?
Have you not understood from the
foundations of the earth?
22 It is he who sits above the circle of
the earth,
and its inhabitants are like
grasshoppers;
who stretches out the heavens like a
curtain,
and spreads them like a tent to live
in;
23 who brings princes to naught,
and makes the rulers of the earth as
nothing.

24 Scarcely are they planted, scarcely
sown,
scarcely has their stem taken root in
the earth,
when he blows upon them, and they
wither,

and the tempest carries them off
like stubble.

25 To whom then will you compare me,
or who is my equal? says the Holy
One.
26 Lift up your eyes on high and see:
Who created these?
He who brings out their host and
numbers them,
calling them all by name;
because he is great in strength,
mighty in power,
not one is missing.

27 Why do you say, O Jacob,
and speak, O Israel,
'My way is hidden from the LORD,
and my right is disregarded by my
God'?
28 Have you not known? Have you
not heard?
The LORD is the everlasting God,
the Creator of the ends of
the earth.
He does not faint or grow weary;
his understanding is unsearchable.
29 He gives power to the faint,
and strengthens the powerless.
30 Even youths will faint and be weary,
and the young will fall exhausted;
31 but those who wait for the LORD shall
renew their strength,
they shall mount up with wings
like eagles,
they shall run and not be weary,
they shall walk and not faint.

Israel Assured of God's Help

41 Listen to me in silence,
O coastlands;
let the peoples renew their
strength;
let them approach, then let
them speak;
let us together draw near for
judgement.

2 Who has roused a victor from
the east,

a Meaning of Heb uncertain

summoned him to his service?
He delivers up nations to him,
  and tramples kings under foot;
he makes them like dust with
    his sword,
  like driven stubble with his bow.

3 He pursues them and passes
    on safely,
  scarcely touching the path with his
    feet.

4 Who has performed and done this,
  calling the generations from the
    beginning?
  I, the LORD, am first,
  and will be with the last.

5 The coastlands have seen and
    are afraid,
  the ends of the earth tremble;
  they have drawn near and come.

6 Each one helps the other,
  saying to one another, 'Take
    courage!'

7 The artisan encourages the
    goldsmith,
  and the one who smooths with the
    hammer encourages the one
    who strikes the anvil,
  saying of the soldering, 'It is good';
    and they fasten it with nails so that
    it cannot be moved.

8 But you, Israel, my servant,
  Jacob, whom I have chosen,
  the offspring of Abraham,
  my friend;

9 you whom I took from the ends of
    the earth,
  and called from its farthest
    corners,
  saying to you, 'You are my servant,
  I have chosen you and not cast you
    off';

10 do not fear, for I am with you,
  do not be afraid, for I am your
    God;
  I will strengthen you, I will help you,
  I will uphold you with my
    victorious right hand.

11 Yes, all who are incensed
    against you
  shall be ashamed and disgraced;

those who strive against you
  shall be as nothing and
    shall perish.

12 You shall seek those who contend
    with you,
  but you shall not find them;
  those who war against you
  shall be as nothing at all.

13 For I, the LORD your God,
  hold your right hand;
  it is I who say to you, 'Do not fear,
  I will help you.'

14 Do not fear, you worm Jacob,
  you insect*a* Israel!
  I will help you, says the LORD;
  your Redeemer is the Holy One of
    Israel.

15 Now, I will make of you a threshing-
    sledge,
  sharp, new, and having teeth;
  you shall thresh the mountains and
    crush them,
  and you shall make the hills
    like chaff.

16 You shall winnow them and the wind
  shall carry them away,
  and the tempest shall scatter
    them.
  Then you shall rejoice in the LORD;
  in the Holy One of Israel you shall
    glory.

17 When the poor and needy seek
    water,
  and there is none,
  and their tongue is parched
    with thirst,
  I the LORD will answer them,
  I the God of Israel will not forsake
    them.

18 I will open rivers on the bare
    heights,*b*
  and fountains in the midst of
    the valleys;
  I will make the wilderness a pool
    of water,
  and the dry land springs of water.

19 I will put in the wilderness
  the cedar,

a Syr: Heb *men of*   *b* Or *trails*

the acacia, the myrtle, and
the olive;
I will set in the desert the cypress,
the plane and the pine together,
20 so that all may see and know,
all may consider and understand,
that the hand of the LORD has
done this,
the Holy One of Israel has created
it.

The Futility of Idols

21 Set forth your case, says the LORD;
bring your proofs, says the King of
Jacob.
22 Let them bring them, and tell us
what is to happen.
Tell us the former things, what they
are,
so that we may consider them,
and that we may know their
outcome;
or declare to us the things to come.
23 Tell us what is to come hereafter,
that we may know that you
are gods;
do good, or do harm,
that we may be afraid and
terrified.
24 You, indeed, are nothing
and your work is nothing at all;
whoever chooses you is an
abomination.

25 I stirred up one from the north, and
he has come,
from the rising of the sun he was
summoned by name.*a*
He shall trample*b* on rulers as on
mortar,
as the potter treads clay.
26 Who declared it from the beginning,
so that we might know,
and beforehand, so that we might
say, 'He is right'?
There was no one who declared it,
none who proclaimed,
none who heard your words.
27 I first have declared it to Zion,*c*
and I give to Jerusalem a herald of
good tidings.

28 But when I look there is no one;
among these there is no
counsellor
who, when I ask, gives an answer.
29 No, they are all a delusion;
their works are nothing;
their images are empty wind.

The Servant, a Light to the Nations

42 Here is my servant, whom I
uphold,
my chosen, in whom my soul
delights;
I have put my spirit upon him;
he will bring forth justice to the
nations.
2 He will not cry or lift up his voice,
or make it heard in the street;
3 a bruised reed he will not break,
and a dimly burning wick he will
not quench;
he will faithfully bring forth
justice.
4 He will not grow faint or be crushed
until he has established justice in
the earth;
and the coastlands wait for his
teaching.

5 Thus says God, the LORD,
who created the heavens and
stretched them out,
who spread out the earth and what
comes from it,
who gives breath to the people upon
it
and spirit to those who walk in it:
6 I am the LORD, I have called you in
righteousness,
I have taken you by the hand and
kept you;
I have given you as a covenant to the
people,*d*
a light to the nations,
7 to open the eyes that are blind,
to bring out the prisoners from the
dungeon,

---

a Cn Compare Q Ms Gk: MT *and he shall call on my
name*   *b* Cn: Heb *come*   *c* Cn: Heb *First to Zion—
Behold, behold them*   *d* Meaning of Heb uncertain

from the prison those who sit in
darkness.

8 I am the LORD, that is my name;
my glory I give to no other,
nor my praise to idols.

9 See, the former things have come
to pass,
and new things I now declare;
before they spring forth,
I tell you of them.

A Hymn of Praise

10 Sing to the LORD a new song,
his praise from the end of the
earth!
Let the sea roar *a* and all that fills it,
the coastlands and their
inhabitants.

11 Let the desert and its towns lift up
their voice,
the villages that Kedar inhabits;
let the inhabitants of Sela sing
for joy,
let them shout from the tops of the
mountains.

12 Let them give glory to the LORD,
and declare his praise in the
coastlands.

13 The LORD goes forth like a soldier,
like a warrior he stirs up his fury;
he cries out, he shouts aloud,
he shows himself mighty against
his foes.

14 For a long time I have held my
peace,
I have kept still and restrained
myself;
now I will cry out like a woman
in labour,
I will gasp and pant.

15 I will lay waste mountains and hills,
and dry up all their herbage;
I will turn the rivers into islands,
and dry up the pools.

16 I will lead the blind
by a road they do not know,
by paths they have not known
I will guide them.
I will turn the darkness before them
into light,

the rough places into level ground.
These are the things I will do,
and I will not forsake them.

17 They shall be turned back and utterly
put to shame—
those who trust in carved images,
who say to cast images,
'You are our gods.'

18 Listen, you that are deaf;
and you that are blind, look up and
see!

19 Who is blind but my servant,
or deaf like my messenger whom I
send?
Who is blind like my dedicated one,
or blind like the servant of
the LORD?

20 He sees many things, but does *b* not
observe them;
his ears are open, but he does
not hear.

Israel's Disobedience

21 The LORD was pleased, for the sake of
his righteousness,
to magnify his teaching and make it
glorious.

22 But this is a people robbed and
plundered,
all of them are trapped in holes
and hidden in prisons;
they have become a prey with no one
to rescue,
a spoil with no one to say,
'Restore!'

23 Who among you will give heed
to this,
who will attend and listen for the
time to come?

24 Who gave up Jacob to the spoiler,
and Israel to the robbers?
Was it not the LORD, against whom
we have sinned,
in whose ways they would
not walk,
and whose law they would
not obey?

a Cn Compare Ps 96.11; 98.7: Heb *Those who go down to
the sea*   *b* Heb *You see many things but do*

25 So he poured upon him the heat of
his anger
and the fury of war;
it set him on fire all around, but he
did not understand;
it burned him, but he did not take
it to heart.

Restoration and Protection Promised

43 But now thus says the LORD,
he who created you, O Jacob,
he who formed you, O Israel:
Do not fear, for I have redeemed
you;
I have called you by name, you are
mine.
2 When you pass through the waters, I
will be with you;
and through the rivers, they shall
not overwhelm you;
when you walk through fire you shall
not be burned,
and the flame shall not
consume you.
3 For I am the LORD your God,
the Holy One of Israel, your
Saviour.
I give Egypt as your ransom,
Ethiopia*a* and Seba in exchange for
you.
4 Because you are precious in
my sight,
and honoured, and I love you,
I give people in return for you,
nations in exchange for your life.
5 Do not fear, for I am with you;
I will bring your offspring from the
east,
and from the west I will
gather you;
6 I will say to the north, 'Give
them up',
and to the south, 'Do not
withhold;
bring my sons from far away
and my daughters from the end of
the earth—
7 everyone who is called by my name,
whom I created for my glory,
whom I formed and made.'

8 Bring forth the people who are blind,
yet have eyes,
who are deaf, yet have ears!
9 Let all the nations gather together,
and let the peoples assemble.
Who among them declared this,
and foretold to us the former
things?
Let them bring their witnesses to
justify them,
and let them hear and say, 'It
is true.'
10 You are my witnesses, says the LORD,
and my servant whom I have
chosen,
so that you may know and
believe me
and understand that I am he.
Before me no god was formed,
nor shall there be any after me.
11 I, I am the LORD,
and besides me there is no
saviour.
12 I declared and saved and
proclaimed,
when there was no strange god
among you;
and you are my witnesses, says the
LORD.
13 I am God, and also henceforth I
am He;
there is no one who can deliver
from my hand;
I work and who can hinder it?

14 Thus says the LORD,
your Redeemer, the Holy One
of Israel:
For your sake I will send to Babylon
and break down all the bars,
and the shouting of the Chaldeans
will be turned to
lamentation.*b*
15 I am the LORD, your Holy One,
the Creator of Israel, your King.
16 Thus says the LORD,
who makes a way in the sea,
a path in the mighty waters,
17 who brings out chariot and horse,
army and warrior;

a Or *Nubia*; Heb *Cush*   *b* Meaning of Heb uncertain

they lie down, they cannot rise,
 they are extinguished, quenched
  like a wick:

18 Do not remember the former things,
 or consider the things of old.
19 I am about to do a new thing;
 now it springs forth, do you not
  perceive it?
 I will make a way in the wilderness
 and rivers in the desert.
20 The wild animals will honour me,
 the jackals and the ostriches;
 for I give water in the wilderness,
 rivers in the desert,
 to give drink to my chosen people,
21 the people whom I formed
  for myself
 so that they might declare
  my praise.

22 Yet you did not call upon me,
 O Jacob;
 but you have been weary of me,
 O Israel!
23 You have not brought me your sheep
 for burnt-offerings,
 or honoured me with your
  sacrifices.
 I have not burdened you with
  offerings,
 or wearied you with frankincense.
24 You have not bought me sweet cane
 with money,
 or satisfied me with the fat of your
  sacrifices.
 But you have burdened me with your
  sins;
 you have wearied me with your
  iniquities.

25 I, I am He
 who blots out your transgressions
  for my own sake,
 and I will not remember your sins.
26 Accuse me, let us go to trial;
 set forth your case, so that you may
  be proved right.
27 Your first ancestor sinned,
 and your interpreters transgressed
  against me.

28 Therefore I profaned the princes of
 the sanctuary,
 I delivered Jacob to utter
  destruction,
 and Israel to reviling.

God's Blessing on Israel

44 But now hear, O Jacob
 my servant,
 Israel whom I have chosen!
2 Thus says the LORD who made you,
 who formed you in the womb and
  will help you:
 Do not fear, O Jacob my servant,
 Jeshurun whom I have chosen.
3 For I will pour water on the
  thirsty land,
 and streams on the dry ground;
 I will pour my spirit upon your
  descendants,
 and my blessing on your
  offspring.
4 They shall spring up like a green
 tamarisk,
 like willows by flowing streams.
5 This one will say, 'I am the LORD's',
 another will be called by the name
  of Jacob,
 yet another will write on the hand,
 'The LORD's',
 and adopt the name of Israel.

6 Thus says the LORD, the King
 of Israel
 and his Redeemer, the LORD
 of hosts:
 I am the first and I am the last;
 besides me there is no god.
7 Who is like me? Let them
  proclaim it,
 let them declare and set it forth
  before me.
 Who has announced from of old the
  things to come? *a*
 Let them tell us *b* what is yet to be.
8 Do not fear, or be afraid;
 have I not told you from of old and
  declared it?
 You are my witnesses!

a Cn: Heb *from my placing an eternal people and things to come* *b* Tg: Heb *them*

Is there any god besides me?
There is no other rock; I know not
one.

The Absurdity of Idol-Worship

9 All who make idols are nothing, and the things they delight in do not profit; their witnesses neither see nor know. And so they will be put to shame. 10 Who would fashion a god or cast an image that can do no good? 11 Look, all its devotees shall be put to shame; the artisans too are merely human. Let them all assemble, let them stand up; they shall be terrified, they shall all be put to shame.

12 The blacksmith fashions it*a* and works it over the coals, shaping it with hammers, and forging it with his strong arm; he becomes hungry and his strength fails, he drinks no water and is faint. 13 The carpenter stretches a line, marks it out with a stylus, fashions it with planes, and marks it with a compass; he makes it in human form, with human beauty, to be set up in a shrine. 14 He cuts down cedars or chooses a holm tree or an oak and lets it grow strong among the trees of the forest. He plants a cedar and the rain nourishes it. 15 Then it can be used as fuel. Part of it he takes and warms himself; he kindles a fire and bakes bread. Then he makes a god and worships it, makes it a carved image and bows down before it. 16 Half of it he burns in the fire; over this half he roasts meat, eats it, and is satisfied. He also warms himself and says, 'Ah, I am warm, I can feel the fire!' 17 The rest of it he makes into a god, his idol, bows down to it, and worships it; he prays to it and says, 'Save me, for you are my god!'

18 They do not know, nor do they comprehend; for their eyes are shut, so that they cannot see, and their minds as well, so that they cannot understand. 19 No one considers, nor is there knowledge or discernment to say, 'Half of it I burned in the fire; I also baked bread on its coals, I roasted meat and have eaten. Now shall I make the rest of it an abomination? Shall I fall down before a block of wood?' 20 He feeds on ashes; a deluded mind has led him astray, and he cannot save himself or say, 'Is not this thing in my right hand a fraud?'

Israel Is Not Forgotten

21 Remember these things, O Jacob,
and Israel, for you are my servant;
I formed you, you are my servant;
O Israel, you will not be forgotten
by me.
22 I have swept away your transgressions
like a cloud,
and your sins like mist;
return to me, for I have redeemed
you.

23 Sing, O heavens, for the LORD has
done it;
shout, O depths of the earth;
break forth into singing,
O mountains,
O forest, and every tree in it!
For the LORD has redeemed Jacob,
and will be glorified in Israel.

24 Thus says the LORD, your Redeemer,
who formed you in the womb:
I am the LORD, who made all things,
who alone stretched out the
heavens,
who by myself spread out
the earth;
25 who frustrates the omens of liars,
and makes fools of diviners;
who turns back the wise,
and makes their knowledge
foolish;
26 who confirms the word of his
servant,
and fulfils the prediction of his
messengers;
who says of Jerusalem, 'It shall be
inhabited',
and of the cities of Judah, 'They
shall be rebuilt,
and I will raise up their ruins';
27 who says to the deep, 'Be dry—
I will dry up your rivers';
28 who says of Cyrus, 'He is my
shepherd,

a Cn: Heb *an axe*

and he shall carry out all my
   purpose';
and who says of Jerusalem, 'It shall
   be rebuilt',
   and of the temple, 'Your
     foundation shall be laid.'

Cyrus, God's Instrument

45 Thus says the Lord to his
      anointed, to Cyrus,
  whose right hand I have grasped
to subdue nations before him
   and strip kings of their robes,
to open doors before him—
   and the gates shall not be closed:
2 I will go before you
   and level the mountains,*a*
I will break in pieces the doors
     of bronze
   and cut through the bars of iron,
3 I will give you the treasures of
     darkness
   and riches hidden in secret places,
so that you may know that it is I, the
     LORD,
   the God of Israel, who call you by
     your name.
4 For the sake of my servant Jacob,
   and Israel my chosen,
I call you by your name,
   I surname you, though you do not
     know me.
5 I am the LORD, and there is no other;
   besides me there is no god.
   I arm you, though you do not know
     me,
6 so that they may know, from the
     rising of the sun
   and from the west, that there is no
     one besides me;
   I am the LORD, and there is
     no other.
7 I form light and create darkness,
   I make weal and create woe;
   I the LORD do all these things.

8 Shower, O heavens, from above,
   and let the skies rain down
     righteousness;
   let the earth open, that salvation may
     spring up,*b*

   and let it cause righteousness to
     sprout up also;
   I the LORD have created it.

9 Woe to you who strive with your
     Maker,
   earthen vessels with the potter!*c*
Does the clay say to the one who
     fashions it, 'What are you
     making?'
   or 'Your work has no handles'?
10 Woe to anyone who says to a father,
     'What are you begetting?'
   or to a woman, 'With what are you
     in labour?'
11 Thus says the LORD,
   the Holy One of Israel, and its
     Maker:
Will you question me*d* about my
     children,
   or command me concerning the
     work of my hands?
12 I made the earth,
   and created humankind upon it;
it was my hands that stretched out
     the heavens,
   and I commanded all their host.
13 I have aroused Cyrus*e* in
     righteousness,
   and I will make all his paths
     straight;
he shall build my city
   and set my exiles free,
not for price or reward,
   says the LORD of hosts.
14 Thus says the LORD:
The wealth of Egypt and the
     merchandise of Ethiopia,*f*
   and the Sabeans, tall of stature,
shall come over to you and be yours,
   they shall follow you;
   they shall come over in chains and
     bow down to you.
They will make supplication to you,
     saying,
   'God is with you alone, and there is
     no other;
   there is no god besides him.'

a Q Ms Gk: MT *the swellings*   *b* Q Ms: MT *that they
may bring forth salvation*   *c* Cn: Heb *with the potsherds,*
or *with the potters*   *d* Cn: Heb *Ask me of things to come*
e Heb *him*   *f* Or *Nubia*; Heb *Cush*

15 Truly, you are a God who hides
    himself,
    O God of Israel, the Saviour.
16 All of them are put to shame and
    confounded,
    the makers of idols go in confusion
    together.
17 But Israel is saved by the LORD
    with everlasting salvation;
    you shall not be put to shame or
    confounded
    to all eternity.

18 For thus says the LORD,
    who created the heavens
        (he is God!),
    who formed the earth and made it
        (he established it;
    he did not create it a chaos,
        he formed it to be inhabited!):
    I am the LORD, and there is no other.
19 I did not speak in secret,
    in a land of darkness;
    I did not say to the offspring
        of Jacob,
    'Seek me in chaos.'
    I the LORD speak the truth,
    I declare what is right.

Idols Cannot Save Babylon

20 Assemble yourselves and come
    together,
    draw near, you survivors of the
        nations!
    They have no knowledge—
        those who carry about their
        wooden idols,
    and keep on praying to a god
        that cannot save.
21 Declare and present your case;
    let them take counsel together!
    Who told this long ago?
        Who declared it of old?
    Was it not I, the LORD?
        There is no other god besides me,
    a righteous God and a Saviour;
        there is no one besides me.

22 Turn to me and be saved,
    all the ends of the earth!

For I am God, and there is
    no other.
23 By myself I have sworn,
    from my mouth has gone forth in
        righteousness
    a word that shall not return:
    'To me every knee shall bow,
        every tongue shall swear.'

24 Only in the LORD, it shall be said
        of me,
    are righteousness and strength;
    all who were incensed against him
        shall come to him and be
        ashamed.
25 In the LORD all the offspring of Israel
    shall triumph and glory.

46 Bel bows down, Nebo stoops,
    their idols are on beasts
        and cattle;
    these things you carry are loaded
        as burdens on weary animals.
2 They stoop, they bow down
        together;
    they cannot save the burden,
        but themselves go into captivity.

3 Listen to me, O house of Jacob,
    all the remnant of the house of
        Israel,
    who have been borne by me from
        your birth,
    carried from the womb;
4 even to your old age I am he,
    even when you turn grey I will carry
        you.
    I have made, and I will bear;
        I will carry and will save.

5 To whom will you liken me and
        make me equal,
    and compare me, as though we
        were alike?
6 Those who lavish gold from the
        purse,
    and weigh out silver in the
        scales—
    they hire a goldsmith, who makes it
        into a god;
    then they fall down and worship!

7 They lift it to their shoulders, they
        carry it,
    they set it in its place, and it stands
        there;
    it cannot move from its place.
    If one cries out to it, it does
        not answer
    or save anyone from trouble.

8 Remember this and consider, *a*
    recall it to mind, you
        transgressors,
9 remember the former things
        of old;
    for I am God, and there is no other;
    I am God, and there is no one like
        me,
10 declaring the end from the
        beginning
    and from ancient times things not
        yet done,
    saying, 'My purpose shall stand,
    and I will fulfil my intention',
11 calling a bird of prey from the east,
    the man for my purpose from a far
        country.
    I have spoken, and I will bring it
        to pass;
    I have planned, and I will do it.

12 Listen to me, you stubborn of heart,
    you who are far from deliverance:
13 I bring near my deliverance, it is not
        far off,
    and my salvation will not tarry;
    I will put salvation in Zion,
    for Israel my glory.

The Humiliation of Babylon

47 Come down and sit in the dust,
        virgin daughter Babylon!
    Sit on the ground without a throne,
        daughter Chaldea!
    For you shall no more be called
        tender and delicate.
2 Take the millstones and grind meal,
        remove your veil,
    strip off your robe, uncover your legs,
        pass through the rivers.
3 Your nakedness shall be uncovered,
    and your shame shall be seen.

I will take vengeance,
    and I will spare no one.
4 Our Redeemer—the LORD of hosts is
        his name—
    is the Holy One of Israel.

5 Sit in silence, and go into darkness,
        daughter Chaldea!
    For you shall no more be called
        the mistress of kingdoms.
6 I was angry with my people,
    I profaned my heritage;
    I gave them into your hand,
        you showed them no mercy;
    on the aged you made your yoke
        exceedingly heavy.
7 You said, 'I shall be mistress for
        ever',
    so that you did not lay these things
        to heart
    or remember their end.

8 Now therefore hear this, you lover of
        pleasures,
    who sit securely,
    who say in your heart,
        'I am, and there is no one besides
            me;
    I shall not sit as a widow
    or know the loss of children'—
9 both these things shall come
        upon you
    in a moment, in one day:
    the loss of children and widowhood
        shall come upon you in full
            measure,
    in spite of your many sorceries
    and the great power of your
        enchantments.

10 You felt secure in your wickedness;
    you said, 'No one sees me.'
    Your wisdom and your knowledge
        led you astray,
    and you said in your heart,
        'I am, and there is no one besides
            me.'
11 But evil shall come upon you,
    which you cannot charm away;
    disaster shall fall upon you,

a Meaning of Heb uncertain

which you will not be able to ward
off;
and ruin shall come on you suddenly,
of which you know nothing.

12 Stand fast in your enchantments
and your many sorceries,
with which you have laboured from
your youth;
perhaps you may be able to succeed,
perhaps you may inspire terror.
13 You are wearied with your many
consultations;
let those who study[a] the heavens
stand up and save you,
those who gaze at the stars
and at each new moon predict
what[b] shall befall you.

14 See, they are like stubble,
the fire consumes them;
they cannot deliver themselves
from the power of the flame.
No coal for warming oneself is this,
no fire to sit before!
15 Such to you are those with whom
you have laboured,
who have trafficked with you from
your youth;
they all wander about in their
own paths;
there is no one to save you.

God the Creator and Redeemer

48 Hear this, O house of Jacob,
who are called by the name of
Israel,
and who came forth from the
loins[c] of Judah;
who swear by the name of the LORD,
and invoke the God of Israel,
but not in truth or right.
2 For they call themselves after the holy
city,
and lean on the God of Israel;
the LORD of hosts is his name.

3 The former things I declared
long ago,
they went out from my mouth and
I made them known;

then suddenly I did them and they
came to pass.
4 Because I know that you are
obstinate,
and your neck is an iron sinew
and your forehead brass,
5 I declared them to you from
long ago,
before they came to pass I
announced them to you,
so that you would not say, 'My idol
did them,
my carved image and my cast image
commanded them.'

6 You have heard; now see all this;
and will you not declare it?
From this time forward I make you
hear new things,
hidden things that you have not
known.
7 They are created now, not long ago;
before today you have never heard
of them,
so that you could not say, 'I already
knew them.'
8 You have never heard, you have never
known,
from of old your ear has not been
opened.
For I knew that you would deal very
treacherously,
and that from birth you were called
a rebel.

9 For my name's sake I defer my anger,
for the sake of my praise I restrain
it for you,
so that I may not cut you off.
10 See, I have refined you, but not like[d]
silver;
I have tested you in the furnace of
adversity.
11 For my own sake, for my own sake, I
do it,
for why should my name[e] be
profaned?
My glory I will not give to another.

a Meaning of Heb uncertain   b Gk Syr Compare Vg:
Heb *from what*   c Cn: Heb *waters*   d Cn: Heb *with*
e Gk Old Latin: Heb *for why should it*

12 Listen to me, O Jacob,
    and Israel, whom I called:
  I am He; I am the first,
    and I am the last.
13 My hand laid the foundation of
    the earth,
    and my right hand spread out
    the heavens;
  when I summon them,
    they stand at attention.

14 Assemble, all of you, and hear!
    Who among them has declared
    these things?
  The LORD loves him;
    he shall perform his purpose on
    Babylon,
    and his arm shall be against the
    Chaldeans.
15 I, even I, have spoken and
    called him,
    I have brought him, and he will
    prosper in his way.
16 Draw near to me, hear this!
    From the beginning I have not
    spoken in secret,
    from the time it came to be I have
    been there.
  And now the Lord GOD has sent me
    and his spirit.

17 Thus says the LORD,
    your Redeemer, the Holy One
    of Israel:
  I am the LORD your God,
    who teaches you for your
    own good,
    who leads you in the way you
    should go.
18 O that you had paid attention to my
    commandments!
    Then your prosperity would have
    been like a river,
    and your success like the waves of
    the sea;
19 your offspring would have been like
    the sand,
    and your descendants like its
    grains;
  their name would never be cut off
    or destroyed from before me.

20 Go out from Babylon, flee from
    Chaldea,
    declare this with a shout of joy,
    proclaim it,
  send it forth to the end of the earth;
    say, 'The LORD has redeemed his
    servant Jacob!'
21 They did not thirst when he led them
    through the deserts;
    he made water flow for them from
    the rock;
    he split open the rock and the
    water gushed out.

22 'There is no peace', says the LORD, 'for
    the wicked.'

The Servant's Mission

49 Listen to me, O coastlands,
    pay attention, you peoples from
    far away!
  The LORD called me before I
    was born,
    while I was in my mother's womb
    he named me.
2 He made my mouth like a sharp
    sword,
    in the shadow of his hand he
    hid me;
  he made me a polished arrow,
    in his quiver he hid me away.
3 And he said to me, 'You are my
    servant,
    Israel, in whom I will be glorified.'
4 But I said, 'I have laboured in vain,
    I have spent my strength for
    nothing and vanity;
  yet surely my cause is with the LORD,
    and my reward with my God.'

5 And now the LORD says,
    who formed me in the womb to be
    his servant,
  to bring Jacob back to him,
    and that Israel might be gathered to
    him,
  for I am honoured in the sight of
    the LORD,
    and my God has become my
    strength—
6 he says,

'It is too light a thing that you should
    be my servant
  to raise up the tribes of Jacob
  and to restore the survivors of
    Israel;
I will give you as a light to the
    nations,
  that my salvation may reach to the
    end of the earth.'

7 Thus says the LORD,
  the Redeemer of Israel and his Holy
    One,
to one deeply despised, abhorred by
    the nations,
  the slave of rulers,
'Kings shall see and stand up,
  princes, and they shall prostrate
    themselves,
because of the LORD, who is faithful,
  the Holy One of Israel, who has
    chosen you.'

Zion's Children to Be Brought Home

8 Thus says the LORD:
In a time of favour I have answered
    you,
  on a day of salvation I have helped
    you;
I have kept you and given you
  as a covenant to the people, *a*
to establish the land,
  to apportion the desolate heritages;
9 saying to the prisoners, 'Come out',
  to those who are in darkness, 'Show
    yourselves.'
They shall feed along the ways,
  on all the bare heights *b* shall be
    their pasture;
10 they shall not hunger or thirst,
  neither scorching wind nor sun
    shall strike them down,
for he who has pity on them will lead
    them,
  and by springs of water will guide
    them.
11 And I will turn all my mountains into
    a road,
  and my highways shall be
    raised up.
12 Lo, these shall come from far away,

and lo, these from the north and
    from the west,
  and these from the land of Syene. *c*

13 Sing for joy, O heavens, and exult,
    O earth;
  break forth, O mountains, into
    singing!
For the LORD has comforted his
    people,
  and will have compassion on his
    suffering ones.

14 But Zion said, 'The LORD has forsaken
    me,
  my Lord has forgotten me.'
15 Can a woman forget her nursing-
    child,
  or show no compassion for the
    child of her womb?
Even these may forget,
  yet I will not forget you.
16 See, I have inscribed you on the
    palms of my hands;
  your walls are continually
    before me.
17 Your builders outdo your
    destroyers, *d*
  and those who laid you waste go
    away from you.
18 Lift up your eyes all around and see;
  they all gather, they come to you.
As I live, says the LORD,
  you shall put all of them on like an
    ornament,
  and like a bride you shall bind
    them on.

19 Surely your waste and your desolate
    places
  and your devastated land—
surely now you will be too crowded
    for your inhabitants,
  and those who swallowed you up
    will be far away.
20 The children born in the time of your
    bereavement
  will yet say in your hearing:

a Meaning of Heb uncertain   *b* Or *the trails*
c Q Ms: MT *Sinim*   *d* Or *Your children come swiftly;*
your destroyers

'The place is too crowded for me;
make room for me to settle.'
21 Then you will say in your heart,
'Who has borne me these?
I was bereaved and barren,
exiled and put away—
so who has reared these?
I was left all alone—
where then have these come
from?'

22 Thus says the Lord GOD:
I will soon lift up my hand to the
nations,
and raise my signal to the peoples;
and they shall bring your sons in
their bosom,
and your daughters shall be carried
on their shoulders.
23 Kings shall be your foster-fathers,
and their queens your nursing-
mothers.
With their faces to the ground they
shall bow down to you,
and lick the dust of your feet.
Then you will know that I am the
LORD;
those who wait for me shall not be
put to shame.

24 Can the prey be taken from the
mighty,
or the captives of a tyrant[a] be
rescued?
25 But thus says the LORD:
Even the captives of the mighty shall
be taken,
and the prey of the tyrant be
rescued;
for I will contend with those who
contend with you,
and I will save your children.
26 I will make your oppressors eat their
own flesh,
and they shall be drunk with their
own blood as with wine.
Then all flesh shall know
that I am the LORD your Saviour,
and your Redeemer, the Mighty
One of Jacob.

50 Thus says the LORD:
Where is your mother's bill of
divorce
with which I put her away?
Or which of my creditors is it
to whom I have sold you?
No, because of your sins you
were sold,
and for your transgressions your
mother was put away.
2 Why was no one there when I came?
Why did no one answer when I
called?
Is my hand shortened, that it cannot
redeem?
Or have I no power to deliver?
By my rebuke I dry up the sea,
I make the rivers a desert;
their fish stink for lack of water,
and die of thirst.[b]
3 I clothe the heavens with blackness,
and make sackcloth their covering.

The Servant's Humiliation
and Vindication

4 The Lord GOD has given me
the tongue of a teacher,[c]
that I may know how to sustain
the weary with a word.
Morning by morning he wakens—
wakens my ear
to listen as those who are taught.
5 The Lord GOD has opened my ear,
and I was not rebellious,
I did not turn backwards.
6 I gave my back to those who
struck me,
and my cheeks to those who pulled
out the beard;
I did not hide my face
from insult and spitting.

7 The Lord GOD helps me;
therefore I have not been
disgraced;
therefore I have set my face
like flint,
and I know that I shall not be put
to shame;

a Q Ms Syr Vg: MT *of a righteous person*   b Or *die on the thirsty ground*   c Cn: Heb *of those who are taught*

8   he who vindicates me is near.
Who will contend with me?
    Let us stand up together.
Who are my adversaries?
    Let them confront me.
9   It is the Lord GOD who helps me;
    who will declare me guilty?
All of them will wear out like a
        garment;
    the moth will eat them up.

10   Who among you fears the LORD
    and obeys the voice of his servant,
who walks in darkness
    and has no light,
yet trusts in the name of the LORD
    and relies upon his God?
11   But all of you are kindlers of fire,
    lighters of firebrands. *a*
Walk in the flame of your fire,
    and among the brands that you
        have kindled!
This is what you shall have from my
        hand:
    you shall lie down in torment.

Blessings in Store for God's People

51   Listen to me, you that pursue
        righteousness,
    you that seek the LORD.
Look to the rock from which you
        were hewn,
    and to the quarry from which
        you were dug.
2   Look to Abraham your father
    and to Sarah who bore you;
for he was but one when I called
        him,
    but I blessed him and made
        him many.
3   For the LORD will comfort Zion;
    he will comfort all her waste
        places,
and will make her wilderness
        like Eden,
    her desert like the garden of
        the LORD;
joy and gladness will be found
        in her,
    thanksgiving and the voice
        of song.

4   Listen to me, my people,
    and give heed to me, my nation;
for a teaching will go out from me,
    and my justice for a light to
        the peoples.
5   I will bring near my deliverance
        swiftly,
    my salvation has gone out
    and my arms will rule the peoples;
the coastlands wait for me,
    and for my arm they hope.
6   Lift up your eyes to the heavens,
    and look at the earth beneath;
for the heavens will vanish like
        smoke,
    the earth will wear out like a
        garment,
    and those who live on it will die
        like gnats; *b*
but my salvation will be for ever,
    and my deliverance will never
        be ended.

7   Listen to me, you who know
        righteousness,
    you people who have my teaching
        in your hearts;
do not fear the reproach of others,
    and do not be dismayed when they
        revile you.
8   For the moth will eat them up like a
        garment,
    and the worm will eat them
        like wool;
but my deliverance will be for ever,
    and my salvation to all generations.

9   Awake, awake, put on strength,
    O arm of the LORD!
Awake, as in days of old,
    the generations of long ago!
Was it not you who cut Rahab in
        pieces,
    who pierced the dragon?
10   Was it not you who dried up the sea,
    the waters of the great deep;
who made the depths of the sea
        a way
    for the redeemed to cross over?

a Syr: Heb *you gird yourselves with firebrands*   *b* Or *in like manner*

11 So the ransomed of the LORD shall
    return,
  and come to Zion with singing;
  everlasting joy shall be upon their
    heads;
    they shall obtain joy and gladness,
    and sorrow and sighing shall
      flee away.

12 I, I am he who comforts you;
  why then are you afraid of a mere
    mortal who must die,
  a human being who fades like
    grass?
13 You have forgotten the LORD, your
    Maker,
  who stretched out the heavens
  and laid the foundations of
    the earth.
  You fear continually all day long
    because of the fury of the
      oppressor,
  who is bent on destruction.
  But where is the fury of the
    oppressor?
14 The oppressed shall speedily be
    released;
    they shall not die and go down to
      the Pit,
    nor shall they lack bread.
15 For I am the LORD your God,
  who stirs up the sea so that its
    waves roar—
    the LORD of hosts is his name.
16 I have put my words in your mouth,
  and hidden you in the shadow of
    my hand,
  stretching out*a* the heavens
  and laying the foundations of
    the earth,
  and saying to Zion, 'You are my
    people.'

17 Rouse yourself, rouse yourself!
  Stand up, O Jerusalem,
  you who have drunk at the hand of
    the LORD
  the cup of his wrath,
  who have drunk to the dregs
    the bowl of staggering.
18 There is no one to guide her

  among all the children she
    has borne;
  there is no one to take her by
    the hand
  among all the children she has
    brought up.
19 These two things have befallen you
    —who will grieve with you?—
  devastation and destruction, famine
    and sword—
  who will comfort you?*b*
20 Your children have fainted,
    they lie at the head of every street
    like an antelope in a net;
  they are full of the wrath of
    the LORD,
    the rebuke of your God.

21 Therefore hear this, you who are
    wounded,*c*
  who are drunk, but not with wine:
22 Thus says your Sovereign, the LORD,
  your God who pleads the cause of
    his people:
  See, I have taken from your hand the
    cup of staggering;
  you shall drink no more
    from the bowl of my wrath.
23 And I will put it into the hand of
    your tormentors,
  who have said to you,
  'Bow down, that we may walk
    on you';
  and you have made your back like
    the ground
  and like the street for them to walk
    on.

Let Zion Rejoice

52 Awake, awake,
    put on your strength, O Zion!
  Put on your beautiful garments,
    O Jerusalem, the holy city;
  for the uncircumcised and the
    unclean
  shall enter you no more.
2 Shake yourself from the dust,
    rise up,
  O captive*d* Jerusalem;

a Syr: Heb *planting*　*b* Q Ms Gk Syr Vg: MT *how may I comfort you?*　*c* Or *humbled*　*d* Cn: Heb *rise up, sit*

loose the bonds from your neck,
O captive daughter Zion!

3 For thus says the LORD: You were sold
for nothing, and you shall be redeemed
without money. 4 For thus says the Lord
GOD: Long ago, my people went down into
Egypt to reside there as aliens; the Assyrian,
too, has oppressed them without cause.
5 Now therefore, what am I doing here, says
the LORD, seeing that my people are taken
away without cause? Their rulers howl, says
the LORD, and continually, all day long, my
name is despised. 6 Therefore my people
shall know my name; therefore on that day
they shall know that it is I who speak; here
am I.

7 How beautiful upon the mountains
    are the feet of the messenger who
        announces peace,
who brings good news,
    who announces salvation,
    who says to Zion, 'Your God
        reigns.'
8 Listen! Your sentinels lift up
        their voices,
    together they sing for joy;
for in plain sight they see
    the return of the LORD to Zion.
9 Break forth together into singing,
    you ruins of Jerusalem;
for the LORD has comforted his
        people,
    he has redeemed Jerusalem.
10 The LORD has bared his holy arm
    before the eyes of all the nations;
and all the ends of the earth
        shall see
    the salvation of our God.

11 Depart, depart, go out from there!
    Touch no unclean thing;
go out from the midst of it, purify
        yourselves,
    you who carry the vessels of
        the LORD.
12 For you shall not go out in haste,
    and you shall not go in flight;
for the LORD will go before you,

and the God of Israel will be your
    rearguard.

The Suffering Servant

13 See, my servant shall prosper;
    he shall be exalted and lifted up,
    and shall be very high.
14 Just as there were many who were
        astonished at him[a]
    —so marred was his appearance,
        beyond human semblance,
    and his form beyond that of
        mortals—
15 so he shall startle[b] many nations;
    kings shall shut their mouths
        because of him;
for that which had not been told
        them they shall see,
    and that which they had not heard
        they shall contemplate.

53 Who has believed what we have
    heard?
And to whom has the arm of the
    LORD been revealed?
2 For he grew up before him like a
        young plant,
    and like a root out of dry ground;
he had no form or majesty that we
        should look at him,
    nothing in his appearance that we
        should desire him.
3 He was despised and rejected
        by others;
    a man of suffering[c] and acquainted
        with infirmity;
and as one from whom others hide
        their faces[d]
    he was despised, and we held him
        of no account.

4 Surely he has borne our infirmities
    and carried our diseases;
yet we accounted him stricken,
    struck down by God, and afflicted.
5 But he was wounded for our
        transgressions,
    crushed for our iniquities;

a Syr Tg: Heb you   b Meaning of Heb uncertain
c Or a man of sorrows   d Or as one who hides his face
from us

upon him was the punishment that
    made us whole,
    and by his bruises we are healed.
6 All we like sheep have gone astray;
    we have all turned to our
        own way,
    and the LORD has laid on him
        the iniquity of us all.

7 He was oppressed, and he was
    afflicted,
    yet he did not open his mouth;
    like a lamb that is led to the
        slaughter,
        and like a sheep that before its
        shearers is silent,
    so he did not open his mouth.
8 By a perversion of justice he was
    taken away.
        Who could have imagined his
        future?
    For he was cut off from the land of
        the living,
        stricken for the transgression of my
        people.
9 They made his grave with the wicked
    and his tomb*a* with the rich,*b*
    although he had done no violence,
    and there was no deceit in
        his mouth.

10 Yet it was the will of the LORD to
    crush him with pain.*c*
    When you make his life an offering
        for sin,*d*
        he shall see his offspring, and shall
        prolong his days;
    through him the will of the LORD
        shall prosper.
11   Out of his anguish he shall
        see light;*e*
    he shall find satisfaction through his
        knowledge.
    The righteous one,*f* my servant,
        shall make many righteous,
    and he shall bear their iniquities.
12 Therefore I will allot him a portion
    with the great,
    and he shall divide the spoil with
        the strong;

because he poured out himself
    to death,
    and was numbered with the
        transgressors;
    yet he bore the sin of many,
    and made intercession for the
        transgressors.

The Eternal Covenant of Peace

54 Sing, O barren one who did
    not bear;
    burst into song and shout,
    you who have not been in labour!
For the children of the desolate
    woman will be more
    than the children of her that is
        married, says the LORD.
2 Enlarge the site of your tent,
    and let the curtains of your
        habitations be stretched out;
    do not hold back; lengthen
        your cords
    and strengthen your stakes.
3 For you will spread out to the right
    and to the left,
    and your descendants will possess
        the nations
    and will settle the desolate towns.

4 Do not fear, for you will not be
    ashamed;
    do not be discouraged, for you will
        not suffer disgrace;
    for you will forget the shame of your
        youth,
    and the disgrace of your
        widowhood you will remember
        no more.
5 For your Maker is your husband,
    the LORD of hosts is his name;
    the Holy One of Israel is your
        Redeemer,
    the God of the whole earth he
        is called.
6 For the LORD has called you
    like a wife forsaken and grieved in
        spirit,

a Q Ms: MT *and in his death*   *b* Cn: Heb *with a rich
person*   *c* Or *by disease*; meaning of Heb uncertain
d Meaning of Heb uncertain   *e* Q Mss: MT lacks *light*
f Or *and he shall find satisfaction. Through his knowledge,
the righteous one*

like the wife of a man's youth when
    she is cast off,
    says your God.
7 For a brief moment I abandoned
    you,
    but with great compassion I will
      gather you.
8 In overflowing wrath for a moment
    I hid my face from you,
    but with everlasting love I will have
      compassion on you,
    says the LORD, your Redeemer.

9 This is like the days of Noah to me:
    Just as I swore that the waters
      of Noah
    would never again go over
      the earth,
    so I have sworn that I will not be
      angry with you
    and will not rebuke you.
10 For the mountains may depart
    and the hills be removed,
    but my steadfast love shall not depart
      from you,
    and my covenant of peace shall not
      be removed,
    says the LORD, who has compassion
      on you.

11 O afflicted one, storm-tossed, and
    not comforted,
    I am about to set your stones in
      antimony,
    and lay your foundations with
      sapphires.[a]
12 I will make your pinnacles of rubies,
    your gates of jewels,
    and all your wall of precious
      stones.
13 All your children shall be taught by
    the LORD,
    and great shall be the prosperity of
      your children.
14 In righteousness you shall be
    established;
    you shall be far from oppression,
      for you shall not fear;
    and from terror, for it shall not
      come near you.
15 If anyone stirs up strife,

    it is not from me;
    whoever stirs up strife with you
      shall fall because of you.
16 See, it is I who have created
    the smith
    who blows the fire of coals,
    and produces a weapon fit for
      its purpose;
    I have also created the ravager
      to destroy.
17 No weapon that is fashioned
    against you shall prosper,
    and you shall confute every tongue
      that rises against you in
      judgement.
    This is the heritage of the servants of
      the LORD
    and their vindication from me, says
      the LORD.

An Invitation to Abundant Life

55 Ho, everyone who thirsts,
    come to the waters;
and you that have no money,
    come, buy and eat!
Come, buy wine and milk
    without money and without price.
2 Why do you spend your money for
    that which is not bread,
    and your labour for that which
      does not satisfy?
    Listen carefully to me, and eat what is
      good,
    and delight yourselves in rich food.
3 Incline your ear, and come to me;
    listen, so that you may live.
    I will make with you an everlasting
      covenant,
    my steadfast, sure love for David.
4 See, I made him a witness to
    the peoples,
    a leader and commander for
      the peoples.
5 See, you shall call nations that you
    do not know,
    and nations that do not know you
      shall run to you,
    because of the LORD your God, the
      Holy One of Israel,
    for he has glorified you.

a Or *lapis lazuli*

6 Seek the LORD while he may
       be found,
    call upon him while he is near;
7 let the wicked forsake their way,
       and the unrighteous their thoughts;
    let them return to the LORD, that he
       may have mercy on them,
    and to our God, for he will
       abundantly pardon.
8 For my thoughts are not your
       thoughts,
       nor are your ways my ways, says the
           LORD.
9 For as the heavens are higher than the
       earth,
       so are my ways higher than
           your ways
    and my thoughts than your
       thoughts.

10 For as the rain and the snow come
       down from heaven,
       and do not return there until they
           have watered the earth,
    making it bring forth and sprout,
       giving seed to the sower and bread
           to the eater,
11 so shall my word be that goes out
       from my mouth;
       it shall not return to me empty,
    but it shall accomplish that which I
       purpose,
       and succeed in the thing for which
           I sent it.

12 For you shall go out in joy,
       and be led back in peace;
    the mountains and the hills
       before you
       shall burst into song,
       and all the trees of the field shall
           clap their hands.
13 Instead of the thorn shall come up
       the cypress;
       instead of the brier shall come up
           the myrtle;
    and it shall be to the LORD for a
       memorial,
       for an everlasting sign that shall not
           be cut off.

The Covenant Extended to All Who Obey

56 Thus says the LORD:
       Maintain justice, and do what is
           right,
    for soon my salvation will come,
       and my deliverance be revealed.

2 Happy is the mortal who does this,
       the one who holds it fast,
    who keeps the sabbath, not
       profaning it,
       and refrains from doing any evil.

3 Do not let the foreigner joined to the
       LORD say,
       'The LORD will surely separate me
           from his people';
    and do not let the eunuch say,
       'I am just a dry tree.'
4 For thus says the LORD:
    To the eunuchs who keep my
       sabbaths,
       who choose the things that
           please me
       and hold fast my covenant,
5 I will give, in my house and within
       my walls,
       a monument and a name
       better than sons and daughters;
    I will give them an everlasting name
       that shall not be cut off.

6 And the foreigners who join
       themselves to the LORD,
       to minister to him, to love the
           name of the LORD,
       and to be his servants,
    all who keep the sabbath, and do not
       profane it,
       and hold fast my covenant—
7 these I will bring to my holy mountain,
       and make them joyful in my house
           of prayer;
    their burnt-offerings and their
       sacrifices
       will be accepted on my altar;
    for my house shall be called a house
       of prayer
       for all peoples.
8 Thus says the Lord GOD,
       who gathers the outcasts of Israel,

I will gather others to them
   besides those already gathered. *a*

The Corruption of Israel's Rulers

9 All you wild animals,
   all you wild animals in the forest,
     come to devour!
10 Israel's *b* sentinels are blind,
   they are all without knowledge;
they are all silent dogs
   that cannot bark;
dreaming, lying down,
   loving to slumber.
11 The dogs have a mighty appetite;
   they never have enough.
The shepherds also have no
     understanding;
   they have all turned to their
     own way,
   to their own gain, one and all.
12 'Come,' they say, 'let us *c* get wine;
   let us fill ourselves with
     strong drink.
And tomorrow will be like today,
   great beyond measure.'

Israel's Futile Idolatry

57 The righteous perish,
   and no one takes it to heart;
the devout are taken away,
   while no one understands.
For the righteous are taken away from
     calamity,
2   and they enter into peace;
those who walk uprightly
   will rest on their couches.
3 But as for you, come here,
   you children of a sorceress,
   you offspring of an adulterer and a
     whore. *d*
4 Whom are you mocking?
   Against whom do you open your
     mouth wide
   and stick out your tongue?
Are you not children of transgression,
   the offspring of deceit—
5 you that burn with lust among
     the oaks,
   under every green tree;
you that slaughter your children in
     the valleys,

   under the clefts of the rocks?
6 Among the smooth stones of the
     valley is your portion;
   they, they, are your lot;
to them you have poured out a drink-
     offering,
   you have brought a grain-offering.
   Shall I be appeased for these
     things?
7 Upon a high and lofty mountain
   you have set your bed,
   and there you went up to offer
     sacrifice.
8 Behind the door and the doorpost
   you have set up your symbol;
for, in deserting me, *e* you have
     uncovered your bed,
   you have gone up to it,
   you have made it wide;
and you have made a bargain for
     yourself with them,
   you have loved their bed,
   you have gazed on their
     nakedness. *f*
9 You journeyed to Molech *g* with oil,
   and multiplied your perfumes;
you sent your envoys far away,
   and sent down even to Sheol.
10 You grew weary from your many
     wanderings,
   but you did not say, 'It is useless.'
You found your desire rekindled,
   and so you did not weaken.

11 Whom did you dread and fear
   so that you lied,
and did not remember me
   or give me a thought?
Have I not kept silent and closed my
     eyes, *h*
   and so you do not fear me?
12 I will concede your righteousness and
     your works,
   but they will not help you.
13 When you cry out, let your collection
     of idols deliver you!
   The wind will carry them off,

a Heb *besides his gathered ones*   *b* Heb *His*   *c* Q Ms
Syr Vg Tg: MT *me*   *d* Heb *an adulterer and she plays the
whore*   *e* Meaning of Heb uncertain   *f* Or *their
phallus*; Heb *the hand*   *g* Or *the king*   *h* Gk Vg: Heb
silent even for a long time

a breath will take them away.
But whoever takes refuge in me shall
    possess the land
and inherit my holy mountain.

A Promise of Help and Healing

14 It shall be said,
  'Build up, build up, prepare the way,
    remove every obstruction from my
      people's way.'
15 For thus says the high and lofty one
  who inhabits eternity, whose name
    is Holy:
  I dwell in the high and holy place,
    and also with those who are
      contrite and humble in spirit,
  to revive the spirit of the humble,
    and to revive the heart of the
      contrite.
16 For I will not continually accuse,
  nor will I always be angry;
  for then the spirits would grow faint
    before me,
  even the souls that I have made.
17 Because of their wicked covetousness
    I was angry;
  I struck them, I hid and was angry;
  but they kept turning back to their
    own ways.
18 I have seen their ways, but I will heal
    them;
  I will lead them and repay them
    with comfort,
  creating for their mourners the fruit
    of the lips. *a*
19 Peace, peace, to the far and the near,
    says the LORD;
  and I will heal them.
20 But the wicked are like the tossing sea
    that cannot keep still;
  its waters toss up mire and mud.
21 There is no peace, says my God, for
    the wicked.

False and True Worship

58 Shout out, do not hold back!
    Lift up your voice like a
      trumpet!
  Announce to my people their
    rebellion,
  to the house of Jacob their sins.

2 Yet day after day they seek me
  and delight to know my ways,
  as if they were a nation that practised
    righteousness
  and did not forsake the ordinance
    of their God;
  they ask of me righteous
    judgements,
  they delight to draw near to God.
3 'Why do we fast, but you do not see?
  Why humble ourselves, but you do
    not notice?'
  Look, you serve your own interest on
    your fast-day,
  and oppress all your workers.
4 Look, you fast only to quarrel and to
    fight
  and to strike with a wicked fist.
  Such fasting as you do today
    will not make your voice heard on
      high.
5 Is such the fast that I choose,
    a day to humble oneself?
  Is it to bow down the head like a
    bulrush,
  and to lie in sackcloth and ashes?
  Will you call this a fast,
    a day acceptable to the LORD?

6 Is not this the fast that I choose:
    to loose the bonds of injustice,
    to undo the thongs of the yoke,
  to let the oppressed go free,
    and to break every yoke?
7 Is it not to share your bread with the
    hungry,
    and bring the homeless poor into
      your house;
  when you see the naked, to
    cover them,
    and not to hide yourself from your
      own kin?
8 Then your light shall break forth like
    the dawn,
    and your healing shall spring
      up quickly;
  your vindicator *b* shall go before you,
    the glory of the LORD shall be your
      rearguard.

a Meaning of Heb uncertain   *b* Or *vindication*

⁹ Then you shall call, and the LORD will
answer;
    you shall cry for help, and he will
say, Here I am.

If you remove the yoke from
among you,
    the pointing of the finger, the
speaking of evil,
¹⁰ if you offer your food to the hungry
    and satisfy the needs of the
afflicted,
then your light shall rise in
the darkness
    and your gloom be like the
noonday.
¹¹ The LORD will guide you continually,
    and satisfy your needs in parched
places,
    and make your bones strong;
and you shall be like a watered
garden,
    like a spring of water,
    whose waters never fail.
¹² Your ancient ruins shall be rebuilt;
    you shall raise up the foundations
of many generations;
you shall be called the repairer of the
breach,
    the restorer of streets to live in.

¹³ If you refrain from trampling the
sabbath,
    from pursuing your own interests
on my holy day;
if you call the sabbath a delight
    and the holy day of the LORD
honourable;
if you honour it, not going your
own ways,
    serving your own interests, or
pursuing your own affairs; ᵃ
¹⁴ then you shall take delight in
the LORD,
    and I will make you ride upon the
heights of the earth;
I will feed you with the heritage of
your ancestor Jacob,
    for the mouth of the LORD has
spoken.

Injustice and Oppression to Be Punished

59 See, the LORD's hand is not too
short to save,
    nor his ear too dull to hear.
² Rather, your iniquities have been
barriers
    between you and your God,
and your sins have hidden his face
from you
    so that he does not hear.
³ For your hands are defiled
with blood,
    and your fingers with iniquity;
your lips have spoken lies,
    your tongue mutters wickedness.
⁴ No one brings suit justly,
    no one goes to law honestly;
they rely on empty pleas, they speak
lies,
    conceiving mischief and begetting
iniquity.
⁵ They hatch adders' eggs,
    and weave the spider's web;
whoever eats their eggs dies,
    and the crushed egg hatches out a
viper.
⁶ Their webs cannot serve as clothing;
    they cannot cover themselves with
what they make.
Their works are works of iniquity,
    and deeds of violence are in their
hands.
⁷ Their feet run to evil,
    and they rush to shed innocent
blood;
their thoughts are thoughts
of iniquity,
    desolation and destruction are in
their highways.
⁸ The way of peace they do not know,
    and there is no justice in
their paths.
Their roads they have made crooked;
    no one who walks in them knows
peace.

⁹ Therefore justice is far from us,
    and righteousness does not
reach us;

---

a Heb *or speaking words*

we wait for light, and lo! there is
    darkness;
  and for brightness, but we walk in
    gloom.
10 We grope like the blind along a wall,
    groping like those who have
     no eyes;
  we stumble at noon as in the
    twilight,
    among the vigorous*a* as though we
     were dead.
11 We all growl like bears;
    like doves we moan mournfully.
  We wait for justice, but there is none;
    for salvation, but it is far from us.
12 For our transgressions before you are
    many,
    and our sins testify against us.
  Our transgressions indeed are
    with us,
    and we know our iniquities:
13 transgressing, and denying the LORD,
    and turning away from following
     our God,
  talking oppression and revolt,
    conceiving lying words and uttering
    them from the heart.
14 Justice is turned back,
    and righteousness stands at a
     distance;
  for truth stumbles in the public
    square,
    and uprightness cannot enter.
15 Truth is lacking,
    and whoever turns from evil is
     despoiled.

  The LORD saw it, and it displeased
    him
    that there was no justice.
16 He saw that there was no one,
    and was appalled that there was no
     one to intervene;
  so his own arm brought him victory,
    and his righteousness upheld him.
17 He put on righteousness like a
    breastplate,
    and a helmet of salvation on
     his head;
  he put on garments of vengeance for
    clothing,

    and wrapped himself in fury as in a
    mantle.
18 According to their deeds, so will
    he repay;
  wrath to his adversaries, requital to
    his enemies;
  to the coastlands he will render
    requital.
19 So those in the west shall fear the
    name of the LORD,
  and those in the east, his glory;
  for he will come like a pent-up
    stream
    that the wind of the LORD drives on.

20 And he will come to Zion as
    Redeemer,
  to those in Jacob who turn from
    transgression, says the LORD.
21 And as for me, this is my covenant with
them, says the LORD: my spirit that is upon
you, and my words that I have put in your
mouth, shall not depart out of your
mouth, or out of the mouths of your children, or out of the mouths of your children's children, says the LORD, from now
on and for ever.

The Ingathering of the Dispersed

60   Arise, shine; for your light
    has come,
  and the glory of the LORD has risen
    upon you.
2 For darkness shall cover the earth,
    and thick darkness the peoples;
  but the LORD will arise upon you,
    and his glory will appear over you.
3 Nations shall come to your light,
    and kings to the brightness of your
    dawn.

4 Lift up your eyes and look around;
    they all gather together, they come
     to you;
  your sons shall come from far away,
    and your daughters shall be carried
     on their nurses' arms.
5 Then you shall see and be radiant;
    your heart shall thrill and rejoice,*b*

a Meaning of Heb uncertain   *b* Heb *be enlarged*

because the abundance of the sea
>   shall be brought to you,
>   the wealth of the nations shall
>   come to you.
6 A multitude of camels shall
>   cover you,
>   the young camels of Midian and
>   Ephah;
>   all those from Sheba shall come.
> They shall bring gold and
>   frankincense,
>   and shall proclaim the praise of the
>   LORD.
7 All the flocks of Kedar shall be
>   gathered to you,
>   the rams of Nebaioth shall minister
>   to you;
> they shall be acceptable on my altar,
>   and I will glorify my glorious
>   house.

8 Who are these that fly like a cloud,
>   and like doves to their windows?
9 For the coastlands shall wait for me,
>   the ships of Tarshish first,
> to bring your children from far away,
>   their silver and gold with them,
> for the name of the LORD your God,
>   and for the Holy One of Israel,
>   because he has glorified you.
10 Foreigners shall build up your walls,
>   and their kings shall minister
>   to you;
> for in my wrath I struck you down,
>   but in my favour I have had mercy
>   on you.
11 Your gates shall always be open;
>   day and night they shall not
>   be shut,
> so that nations shall bring you their
>   wealth,
>   with their kings led in procession.
12 For the nation and kingdom
>   that will not serve you shall perish;
>   those nations shall be utterly
>   laid waste.
13 The glory of Lebanon shall come
>   to you,
>   the cypress, the plane, and the pine,
> to beautify the place of my sanctuary;

and I will glorify where my
>   feet rest.
14 The descendants of those who
>   oppressed you
>   shall come bending low to you,
> and all who despised you
>   shall bow down at your feet;
> they shall call you the City of
>   the LORD,
>   the Zion of the Holy One of Israel.
15 Whereas you have been forsaken and
>   hated,
>   with no one passing through,
> I will make you majestic for ever,
>   a joy from age to age.
16 You shall suck the milk of nations,
>   you shall suck the breasts of kings;
> and you shall know that I, the LORD,
>   am your Saviour
>   and your Redeemer, the Mighty
>   One of Jacob.

17 Instead of bronze I will bring gold,
>   instead of iron I will bring silver;
> instead of wood, bronze,
>   instead of stones, iron.
> I will appoint Peace as your overseer
>   and Righteousness as your
>   taskmaster.
18 Violence shall no more be heard in
>   your land,
>   devastation or destruction within
>   your borders;
> you shall call your walls Salvation,
>   and your gates Praise.

God the Glory of Zion

19 The sun shall no longer be
>   your light by day,
> nor for brightness shall the moon
>   give light to you by night;*a*
> but the LORD will be your everlasting
>   light,
>   and your God will be your glory.
20 Your sun shall no more go down,
>   or your moon withdraw itself;
> for the LORD will be your everlasting
>   light,
>   and your days of mourning shall be
>   ended.

a Q Ms Gk Old Latin Tg: MT lacks *by night*

21 Your people shall all be righteous;
    they shall possess the land for ever.
  They are the shoot that I planted, the
        work of my hands,
    so that I might be glorified.
22 The least of them shall become
        a clan,
    and the smallest one a mighty
        nation;
  I am the LORD;
    in its time I will accomplish
        it quickly.

The Good News of Deliverance

61 The spirit of the Lord GOD is
    upon me,
  because the LORD has
        anointed me;
  he has sent me to bring good news to
        the oppressed,
    to bind up the broken-hearted,
  to proclaim liberty to the captives,
    and release to the prisoners;
2 to proclaim the year of the
        LORD's favour,
    and the day of vengeance of
        our God;
    to comfort all who mourn;
3 to provide for those who mourn in
        Zion—
    to give them a garland instead
        of ashes,
  the oil of gladness instead of
        mourning,
    the mantle of praise instead of a
        faint spirit.
  They will be called oaks of
        righteousness,
    the planting of the LORD, to display
        his glory.
4 They shall build up the ancient ruins,
    they shall raise up the former
        devastations;
  they shall repair the ruined cities,
    the devastations of many
        generations.

5 Strangers shall stand and feed
        your flocks,
    foreigners shall till your land and
        dress your vines;

6 but you shall be called priests of the
        LORD,
    you shall be named ministers of
        our God;
  you shall enjoy the wealth of
        the nations,
    and in their riches you shall glory.
7 Because their[a] shame was double,
    and dishonour was proclaimed as
        their lot,
  therefore they shall possess a double
        portion;
    everlasting joy shall be theirs.

8 For I the LORD love justice,
    I hate robbery and wrongdoing;[b]
  I will faithfully give them their
        recompense,
    and I will make an everlasting
        covenant with them.
9 Their descendants shall be known
        among the nations,
    and their offspring among the
        peoples;
  all who see them shall acknowledge
    that they are a people whom the
        LORD has blessed.
10 I will greatly rejoice in the LORD,
    my whole being shall exult in
        my God;
  for he has clothed me with the
        garments of salvation,
    he has covered me with the robe of
        righteousness,
  as a bridegroom decks himself with a
        garland,
    and as a bride adorns herself with
        her jewels.
11 For as the earth brings forth its shoots,
    and as a garden causes what is
        sown in it to spring up,
  so the Lord GOD will cause
        righteousness and praise
    to spring up before all the nations.

The Vindication and Salvation of Zion

62 For Zion's sake I will not keep
    silent,
  and for Jerusalem's sake I will not
        rest,

a Heb *your*   b Or *robbery with a burnt-offering*

until her vindication shines out like
    the dawn,
    and her salvation like a burning
        torch.
2 The nations shall see your
        vindication,
    and all the kings your glory;
and you shall be called by a
        new name
    that the mouth of the LORD
        will give.
3 You shall be a crown of beauty in the
        hand of the LORD,
    and a royal diadem in the hand of
        your God.
4 You shall no more be termed
        Forsaken, *a*
    and your land shall no more be
        termed Desolate; *b*
but you shall be called My Delight Is
        in Her, *c*
    and your land shall be Married; *d*
for the LORD delights in you,
    and your land shall be married.
5 For as a young man marries a young
        woman,
    so shall your builder *e* marry you,
and as the bridegroom rejoices over
        the bride,
    so shall your God rejoice over you.
6 Upon your walls, O Jerusalem,
        I have posted sentinels;
all day and all night
        they shall never be silent.
You who remind the LORD,
        take no rest,
7 and give him no rest
        until he establishes Jerusalem
    and makes it renowned throughout
        the earth.
8 The LORD has sworn by his right hand
        and by his mighty arm:
I will not again give your grain
    to be food for your enemies,
and foreigners shall not drink
        the wine
    for which you have laboured;
9 but those who garner it shall eat it
        and praise the LORD,
and those who gather it shall drink it
        in my holy courts.

10 Go through, go through the gates,
        prepare the way for the people;
build up, build up the highway,
        clear it of stones,
lift up an ensign over the peoples.
11 The LORD has proclaimed
        to the end of the earth:
Say to daughter Zion,
    'See, your salvation comes;
his reward is with him,
    and his recompense before him.'
12 They shall be called, 'The
        Holy People,
    The Redeemed of the LORD';
and you shall be called, 'Sought Out,
    A City Not Forsaken.'

Vengeance on Edom

63 'Who is this that comes from
        Edom,
    from Bozrah in garments stained
        crimson?
Who is this so splendidly robed,
    marching in his great might?'

'It is I, announcing vindication,
    mighty to save.'

2 'Why are your robes red,
    and your garments like theirs who
        tread the wine press?'

3 'I have trodden the wine press alone,
    and from the peoples no one was
        with me;
I trod them in my anger
    and trampled them in my wrath;
their juice spattered on my garments,
    and stained all my robes.
4 For the day of vengeance was in my
        heart,
    and the year for my redeeming
        work had come.
5 I looked, but there was no helper;
    I stared, but there was no one to
        sustain me;
so my own arm brought me victory,
    and my wrath sustained me.

a Heb *Azubah*   *b* Heb *Shemamah*   *c* Heb *Hephzibah*
d Heb *Beulah*   *e* Cn: Heb *your sons*

6 I trampled down peoples in my
　　anger,
　　I crushed them in my wrath,
　　and I poured out their lifeblood on
　　　the earth.'

God's Mercy Remembered

7 I will recount the gracious deeds of
　　the LORD,
　　the praiseworthy acts of the LORD,
　　because of all that the LORD has done
　　　for us,
　　and the great favour to the house of
　　　Israel
　　that he has shown them according to
　　　his mercy,
　　according to the abundance of his
　　　steadfast love.
8 For he said, 'Surely they are
　　my people,
　　children who will not deal falsely';
　　and he became their saviour
9 　in all their distress.
　　It was no messenger*a* or angel
　　but his presence that saved them;*b*
　　in his love and in his pity he
　　　redeemed them;
　　he lifted them up and carried them
　　　all the days of old.

10 But they rebelled
　　and grieved his holy spirit;
　　therefore he became their enemy;
　　he himself fought against them.
11 Then they*c* remembered the days of
　　old,
　　of Moses his servant.*d*
　　Where is the one who brought them
　　　up out of the sea
　　with the shepherds of his flock?
　　Where is the one who put within them
　　　his holy spirit,
12 who caused his glorious arm
　　to march at the right hand
　　　of Moses,
　　who divided the waters before them
　　to make for himself an everlasting
　　　name,
13 　who led them through the depths?
　　Like a horse in the desert,
　　　they did not stumble.

14 Like cattle that go down into
　　the valley,
　　the spirit of the LORD gave
　　　them rest.
　　Thus you led your people,
　　to make for yourself a glorious
　　　name.

A Prayer of Penitence

15 Look down from heaven and see,
　　from your holy and glorious
　　　habitation.
　　Where are your zeal and your
　　　might?
　　The yearning of your heart and
　　　your compassion?
　　They are withheld from me.
16 For you are our father,
　　though Abraham does not know us
　　and Israel does not acknowledge
　　　us;
　　you, O LORD, are our father;
　　our Redeemer from of old is
　　　your name.
17 Why, O LORD, do you make us stray
　　from your ways
　　and harden our heart, so that we do
　　　not fear you?
　　Turn back for the sake of your
　　　servants,
　　for the sake of the tribes that are
　　　your heritage.
18 Your holy people took possession for
　　a little while;
　　but now our adversaries have
　　　trampled down your sanctuary.
19 We have long been like those whom
　　you do not rule,
　　like those not called by your name.

64 O that you would tear open the
　　heavens and come down,
　　so that the mountains would quake
　　　at your presence—
2*e* as when fire kindles brushwood
　　and the fire causes water to boil—
　　to make your name known to your
　　　adversaries,

---

a Gk: Heb *anguish*   *b* Or *saviour. 9In all their distress he
was distressed; the angel of his presence saved them;*
c Heb *he*   *d* Cn: Heb *his people*   *e* Ch 64.1 in Heb

so that the nations might tremble
    at your presence!
3 When you did awesome deeds that
        we did not expect,
    you came down, the mountains
        quaked at your presence.
4 From ages past no one has heard,
        no ear has perceived,
    no eye has seen any God besides you,
        who works for those who wait
        for him.
5 You meet those who gladly do right,
        those who remember you in
        your ways.
    But you were angry, and we sinned;
        because you hid yourself we
        transgressed.*a*
6 We have all become like one who is
        unclean,
        and all our righteous deeds are like
        a filthy cloth.
    We all fade like a leaf,
        and our iniquities, like the wind,
        take us away.
7 There is no one who calls on
        your name,
    or attempts to take hold of you;
    for you have hidden your face
        from us,
    and have delivered*b* us into the
        hand of our iniquity.
8 Yet, O Lord, you are our Father;
        we are the clay, and you are
        our potter;
    we are all the work of your hand.
9 Do not be exceedingly angry, O Lord,
    and do not remember iniquity for
        ever.
    Now consider, we are all your
        people.
10 Your holy cities have become a
        wilderness,
    Zion has become a wilderness,
    Jerusalem a desolation.
11 Our holy and beautiful house,
        where our ancestors praised you,
    has been burned by fire,
        and all our pleasant places have
        become ruins.
12 After all this, will you restrain
        yourself, O Lord?

Will you keep silent, and punish us
    so severely?

The Righteousness of God's Judgement

65 I was ready to be sought out by
    those who did not ask,
    to be found by those who did not
        seek me.
    I said, 'Here I am, here I am',
        to a nation that did not call on my
        name.
2 I held out my hands all day long
        to a rebellious people,
    who walk in a way that is not good,
        following their own devices;
3 a people who provoke me
        to my face continually,
    sacrificing in gardens
        and offering incense on bricks;
4 who sit inside tombs,
        and spend the night in secret
        places;
    who eat swine's flesh,
        with broth of abominable things in
        their vessels;
5 who say, 'Keep to yourself,
        do not come near me, for I am too
        holy for you.'
    These are a smoke in my nostrils,
        a fire that burns all day long.
6 See, it is written before me:
        I will not keep silent, but I will
        repay;
    I will indeed repay into their laps
7 their*c* iniquities and their*c*
        ancestors' iniquities together,
                    says the Lord;
    because they offered incense on the
        mountains
        and reviled me on the hills,
    I will measure into their laps
        full payment for their actions.
8 Thus says the Lord:
    As the wine is found in the cluster,
        and they say, 'Do not destroy it,
        for there is a blessing in it',
    so I will do for my servants' sake,
        and not destroy them all.

a Meaning of Heb uncertain   *b* Gk Syr Old Latin Tg:
Heb *melted*   *c* Gk Syr: Heb *your*

9 I will bring forth descendants[a] from
    Jacob,
    and from Judah inheritors[b] of my
      mountains;
  my chosen shall inherit it,
    and my servants shall settle there.
10 Sharon shall become a pasture
    for flocks,
    and the Valley of Achor a place for
      herds to lie down,
  for my people who have sought me.
11 But you who forsake the LORD,
    who forget my holy mountain,
  who set a table for Fortune
    and fill cups of mixed wine for
      Destiny,
12 I will destine you to the sword,
    and all of you shall bow down to
      the slaughter;
  because, when I called, you did
      not answer,
    when I spoke, you did not listen,
  but you did what was evil in
      my sight,
    and chose what I did not delight in.
13 Therefore thus says the Lord GOD:
  My servants shall eat,
    but you shall be hungry;
  my servants shall drink,
    but you shall be thirsty;
  my servants shall rejoice,
    but you shall be put to shame;
14 my servants shall sing for gladness of
    heart,
    but you shall cry out for pain
      of heart,
    and shall wail for anguish of spirit.
15 You shall leave your name to my
      chosen to use as a curse,
    and the Lord GOD will put you
      to death;
    but to his servants he will give a
      different name.
16 Then whoever invokes a blessing in
      the land
    shall bless by the God of
      faithfulness,
  and whoever takes an oath in
      the land
    shall swear by the God of
      faithfulness;

because the former troubles are
    forgotten
  and are hidden from my sight.

The Glorious New Creation

17 For I am about to create new heavens
    and a new earth;
  the former things shall not be
      remembered
    or come to mind.
18 But be glad and rejoice for ever
    in what I am creating;
  for I am about to create Jerusalem as
      a joy,
    and its people as a delight.
19 I will rejoice in Jerusalem,
    and delight in my people;
  no more shall the sound of weeping
      be heard in it,
    or the cry of distress.
20 No more shall there be in it
    an infant that lives but a few days,
    or an old person who does not live
      out a lifetime;
  for one who dies at a hundred years
      will be considered a youth,
    and one who falls short of a
      hundred will be considered
      accursed.
21 They shall build houses and inhabit
      them;
    they shall plant vineyards and eat
      their fruit.
22 They shall not build and another
      inhabit;
    they shall not plant and
      another eat;
  for like the days of a tree shall the
      days of my people be,
    and my chosen shall long enjoy the
      work of their hands.
23 They shall not labour in vain,
    or bear children for calamity;[c]
  for they shall be offspring blessed by
      the LORD—
    and their descendants as well.
24 Before they call I will answer,
    while they are yet speaking I
      will hear.

a Or a descendant   b Or an inheritor   c Or sudden
terror

25 The wolf and the lamb shall feed
together,
the lion shall eat straw like the ox;
but the serpent—its food shall
be dust!
They shall not hurt or destroy
on all my holy mountain,
says the LORD.

The Worship God Demands

66 Thus says the LORD:
Heaven is my throne
and the earth is my footstool;
what is the house that you would
build for me,
and what is my resting-place?
2 All these things my hand has made,
and so all these things are mine,*a*
says the LORD.
But this is the one to whom I will
look,
to the humble and contrite
in spirit,
who trembles at my word.

3 Whoever slaughters an ox is like one
who kills a human being;
whoever sacrifices a lamb, like one
who breaks a dog's neck;
whoever presents a grain-offering,
like one who offers swine's
blood;*b*
whoever makes a memorial offering
of frankincense, like one who
blesses an idol.
These have chosen their own ways,
and in their abominations they take
delight;
4 I also will choose to mock*c* them,
and bring upon them what
they fear;
because, when I called, no one
answered,
when I spoke, they did not listen;
but they did what was evil in
my sight,
and chose what did not please me.

The LORD Vindicates Zion

5 Hear the word of the LORD,
you who tremble at his word:

Your own people who hate you
and reject you for my name's sake
have said, 'Let the LORD be glorified,
so that we may see your joy';
but it is they who shall be put
to shame.

6 Listen, an uproar from the city!
A voice from the temple!
The voice of the LORD,
dealing retribution to his enemies!

7 Before she was in labour
she gave birth;
before her pain came upon her
she delivered a son.
8 Who has heard of such a thing?
Who has seen such things?
Shall a land be born in one day?
Shall a nation be delivered in one
moment?
Yet as soon as Zion was in labour
she delivered her children.
9 Shall I open the womb and not
deliver?
says the LORD;
shall I, the one who delivers, shut the
womb?
says your God.

10 Rejoice with Jerusalem, and be glad
for her,
all you who love her;
rejoice with her in joy,
all you who mourn over her—
11 that you may nurse and be satisfied
from her consoling breast;
that you may drink deeply with
delight
from her glorious bosom.

12 For thus says the LORD:
I will extend prosperity to her like a
river,
and the wealth of the nations like
an overflowing stream;
and you shall nurse and be carried on
her arm,
and dandled on her knees.

a Gk Syr: Heb *these things came to be*   *b* Meaning of
Heb uncertain   *c* Or *to punish*

13 As a mother comforts her child,
  so I will comfort you;
  you shall be comforted in
    Jerusalem.

The Reign and Indignation of God

14 You shall see, and your heart shall
    rejoice;
  your bodies*a* shall flourish like the
    grass;
  and it shall be known that the hand
    of the LORD is with his servants,
  and his indignation is against
    his enemies.
15 For the LORD will come in fire,
  and his chariots like the whirlwind,
  to pay back his anger in fury,
  and his rebuke in flames of fire.
16 For by fire will the LORD execute
    judgement,
  and by his sword, on all flesh;
  and those slain by the LORD shall
    be many.

17 Those who sanctify and purify themselves to go into the gardens, following the
one in the centre, eating the flesh of pigs,
vermin, and rodents, shall come to an end
together, says the LORD.

18 For I know*b* their works and their
thoughts, and I am*c* coming to gather all
nations and tongues; and they shall come
and shall see my glory, 19 and I will set a
sign among them. From them I will send
survivors to the nations, to Tarshish, Put,*d*
and Lud—which draw the bow—to Tubal
and Javan, to the coastlands far away that
have not heard of my fame or seen my glory; and they shall declare my glory among
the nations. 20 They shall bring all your
kindred from all the nations as an offering
to the LORD, on horses, and in chariots,
and in litters, and on mules, and on drom-
edaries, to my holy mountain Jerusalem,
says the LORD, just as the Israelites bring a
grain-offering in a clean vessel to the house
of the LORD. 21 And I will also take some of
them as priests and as Levites, says the
LORD.

22 For as the new heavens and the new
    earth,
  which I will make,
  shall remain before me, says
    the LORD,
  so shall your descendants and your
    name remain.
23 From new moon to new moon,
  and from sabbath to sabbath,
  all flesh shall come to worship before
    me,
  says the LORD.

24 And they shall go out and look at the
dead bodies of the people who have rebelled against me; for their worm shall not
die, their fire shall not be quenched, and
they shall be an abhorrence to all flesh.

a Heb *bones*   *b* Gk Syr: Heb lacks *know*   *c* Gk Syr Vg
Tg: Heb *it is*   *d* Gk: Heb *Pul*

JEREMIAH

1 The words of Jeremiah son of Hilkiah, of the priests who were in Anathoth in the land of Benjamin, ²to whom the word of the LORD came in the days of King Josiah son of Amon of Judah, in the thirteenth year of his reign. ³It came also in the days of King Jehoiakim son of Josiah of Judah, and until the end of the eleventh year of King Zedekiah son of Josiah of Judah, until the captivity of Jerusalem in the fifth month.

Jeremiah's Call and Commission

4 Now the word of the LORD came to me saying,
5 'Before I formed you in the womb I knew you,
    and before you were born I consecrated you;
    I appointed you a prophet to the nations.'
⁶Then I said, 'Ah, Lord GOD! Truly I do not know how to speak, for I am only a boy.' ⁷But the LORD said to me,
    'Do not say, "I am only a boy";
    for you shall go to all to whom I send you,
    and you shall speak whatever I command you.
8 Do not be afraid of them,
    for I am with you to deliver you,
                        says the LORD.'
⁹Then the LORD put out his hand and touched my mouth; and the LORD said to me,
    'Now I have put my words in your mouth.
10 See, today I appoint you over nations and over kingdoms,
    to pluck up and to pull down,
    to destroy and to overthrow,
    to build and to plant.'

11 The word of the LORD came to me, saying, 'Jeremiah, what do you see?' And I said, 'I see a branch of an almond tree.'ᵃ ¹²Then the LORD said to me, 'You have seen well, for I am watchingᵇ over my word to perform it.' ¹³The word of the LORD came to me a second time, saying, 'What do you see?' And I said, 'I see a boiling pot, tilted away from the north.'

14 Then the LORD said to me: Out of the north disaster shall break out on all the inhabitants of the land. ¹⁵For now I am calling all the tribes of the kingdoms of the north, says the LORD; and they shall come and all of them shall set their thrones at the entrance of the gates of Jerusalem, against all its surrounding walls and against all the cities of Judah. ¹⁶And I will utter my judgements against them, for all their wickedness in forsaking me; they have made offerings to other gods, and worshipped the works of their own hands. ¹⁷But you, gird up your loins; stand up and tell them everything that I command you. Do not break down before them, or I will break you before them. ¹⁸And I for my part have made you today a fortified city, an iron pillar, and a bronze wall, against the whole land—against the kings of Judah, its princes, its priests, and the people of the land. ¹⁹They will fight against you; but they shall not prevail against you, for I am with you, says the LORD, to deliver you.

a Heb *shaqed*   *b* Heb *shoqed*

God Pleads with Israel to Repent

2 The word of the LORD came to me, saying: 2 Go and proclaim in the hearing of Jerusalem, Thus says the LORD:
I remember the devotion of your
    youth,
    your love as a bride,
how you followed me in the
    wilderness,
    in a land not sown.
3 Israel was holy to the LORD,
    the first fruits of his harvest.
All who ate of it were held guilty;
    disaster came upon them,
                    says the LORD.

4 Hear the word of the LORD, O house of Jacob, and all the families of the house of Israel. 5 Thus says the LORD:
What wrong did your ancestors find
    in me
    that they went far from me,
and went after worthless things, and
    became worthless themselves?
6 They did not say, 'Where is the LORD
    who brought us up from the land
        of Egypt,
who led us in the wilderness,
    in a land of deserts and pits,
in a land of drought and deep
    darkness,
    in a land that no one passes
        through,
    where no one lives?'
7 I brought you into a plentiful land
    to eat its fruits and its good things.
But when you entered you defiled my
    land,
    and made my heritage an
        abomination.
8 The priests did not say, 'Where is the
    LORD?'
    Those who handle the law did not
        know me;
    the rulers*a* transgressed against me;
    the prophets prophesied by Baal,
    and went after things that do
        not profit.

9 Therefore once more I accuse you,
                    says the LORD,
and I accuse your children's
    children.
10 Cross to the coasts of Cyprus
    and look,
    send to Kedar and examine with
        care;
    see if there has ever been such
        a thing.
11 Has a nation changed its gods,
    even though they are no gods?
But my people have changed
    their glory
    for something that does not profit.
12 Be appalled, O heavens, at this,
    be shocked, be utterly desolate,
                    says the LORD,
13 for my people have committed
    two evils:
    they have forsaken me,
    the fountain of living water,
    and dug out cisterns for
        themselves,
    cracked cisterns
    that can hold no water.

14 Is Israel a slave? Is he a home-born
    servant?
    Why then has he become plunder?
15 The lions have roared against him,
    they have roared loudly.
They have made his land a waste;
    his cities are in ruins, without
        inhabitant.
16 Moreover, the people of Memphis
    and Tahpanhes
    have broken the crown of
        your head.
17 Have you not brought this upon
    yourself
    by forsaking the LORD your God,
    while he led you in the way?
18 What then do you gain by going
    to Egypt,
    to drink the waters of the Nile?
Or what do you gain by going to
    Assyria,
    to drink the waters of the
        Euphrates?
19 Your wickedness will punish you,

a Heb *shepherds*

and your apostasies will
    convict you.
Know and see that it is evil and bitter
    for you to forsake the LORD
        your God;
    the fear of me is not in you,
            says the Lord GOD of hosts.

20 For long ago you broke your yoke
    and burst your bonds,
    and you said, 'I will not serve!'
On every high hill
    and under every green tree
    you sprawled and played
        the whore.
21 Yet I planted you as a choice vine,
    from the purest stock.
How then did you turn degenerate
    and become a wild vine?
22 Though you wash yourself with lye
    and use much soap,
    the stain of your guilt is still before
        me,
            says the Lord GOD.
23 How can you say, 'I am not defiled,
    I have not gone after the Baals'?
Look at your way in the valley;
    know what you have done—
a restive young camel interlacing her
        tracks,
24   a wild ass at home in the
        wilderness,
in her heat sniffing the wind!
    Who can restrain her lust?
None who seek her need weary
        themselves;
    in her month they will find her.
25 Keep your feet from going unshod
    and your throat from thirst.
But you said, 'It is hopeless,
    for I have loved strangers,
    and after them I will go.'

26 As a thief is shamed when caught,
    so the house of Israel shall be
        shamed—
    they, their kings, their officials,
    their priests, and their prophets,
27 who say to a tree, 'You are my father',
    and to a stone, 'You gave me birth.'

For they have turned their backs
    to me,
    and not their faces.
But in the time of their trouble they
        say,
    'Come and save us!'
28 But where are your gods
    that you made for yourself?
Let them come, if they can save you,
    in your time of trouble;
for you have as many gods
    as you have towns, O Judah.

29 Why do you complain against me?
    You have all rebelled against me,
                says the LORD.
30 In vain I have struck down
        your children;
    they accepted no correction.
Your own sword devoured your
        prophets
    like a ravening lion.
31 And you, O generation, behold the
        word of the LORD!*a*
Have I been a wilderness to Israel,
    or a land of thick darkness?
Why then do my people say, 'We are
        free,
    we will come to you no more'?
32 Can a girl forget her ornaments,
    or a bride her attire?
Yet my people have forgotten me,
    days without number.

33 How well you direct your course
    to seek lovers!
So that even to wicked women
    you have taught your ways.
34 Also on your skirts is found
    the lifeblood of the innocent poor,
    though you did not catch them
        breaking in.
    Yet in spite of all these things*a*
35 you say, 'I am innocent;
    surely his anger has turned
        from me.'
Now I am bringing you to judgement
    for saying, 'I have not sinned.'
36 How lightly you gad about,
    changing your ways!

a Meaning of Heb uncertain

You shall be put to shame by Egypt
  as you were put to shame
    by Assyria.
37 From there also you will come away
    with your hands on your head;
  for the LORD has rejected those in
      whom you trust,
    and you will not prosper through
      them.

Unfaithful Israel

3 If[a] a man divorces his wife
    and she goes from him
  and becomes another man's wife,
    will he return to her?
  Would not such a land be greatly
      polluted?
  You have played the whore with
      many lovers;
    and would you return to me?
                          says the LORD.
2 Look up to the bare heights,[b]
    and see!
  Where have you not been
      lain with?
  By the waysides you have sat waiting
      for lovers,
    like a nomad in the wilderness.
  You have polluted the land
    with your whoring and
      wickedness.
3 Therefore the showers have been
      withheld,
    and the spring rain has not come;
  yet you have the forehead of
      a whore,
    you refuse to be ashamed.
4 Have you not just now called to me,
    'My Father, you are the friend of my
      youth—
5 will he be angry for ever,
    will he be indignant to the end?'
  This is how you have spoken,
    but you have done all the evil that
      you could.

A Call to Repentance

6 The LORD said to me in the days of
King Josiah: Have you seen what she did,
that faithless one, Israel, how she went up
on every high hill and under every green

tree, and played the whore there? 7 And I
thought, 'After she has done all this she
will return to me'; but she did not return,
and her false sister Judah saw it. 8 She[c] saw
that for all the adulteries of that faithless
one, Israel, I had sent her away with a decree of divorce; yet her false sister Judah
did not fear, but she too went and played
the whore. 9 Because she took her whoredom so lightly, she polluted the land, committing adultery with stone and tree. 10 Yet
for all this her false sister Judah did not return to me with her whole heart, but only
in pretence, says the LORD.

11 Then the LORD said to me: Faithless
Israel has shown herself less guilty than
false Judah. 12 Go, and proclaim these
words towards the north, and say:
  Return, faithless Israel,
                          says the LORD.
  I will not look on you in anger,
    for I am merciful,
                          says the LORD;
  I will not be angry for ever.
13 Only acknowledge your guilt,
    that you have rebelled against the
      LORD your God,
  and scattered your favours among
      strangers under every
        green tree,
    and have not obeyed my voice,
                          says the LORD.
14 Return, O faithless children,
                          says the LORD,
    for I am your master;
  I will take you, one from a city and
      two from a family,
    and I will bring you to Zion.

15 I will give you shepherds after my
own heart, who will feed you with knowledge and understanding. 16 And when you
have multiplied and increased in the land,
in those days, says the LORD, they shall no
longer say, 'The ark of the covenant of the
LORD.' It shall not come to mind, or be remembered, or missed; nor shall another
one be made. 17 At that time Jerusalem
shall be called the throne of the LORD, and

a Q Ms Gk Syr: MT *Saying, If*   b Or *the trails*
c Q Ms Gk Mss Syr: MT *I*

all nations shall gather to it, to the presence of the Lord in Jerusalem, and they shall no longer stubbornly follow their own evil will. ¹⁸ In those days the house of Judah shall join the house of Israel, and together they shall come from the land of the north to the land that I gave your ancestors for a heritage.

¹⁹ I thought
    how I would set you among
        my children,
and give you a pleasant land,
    the most beautiful heritage of all
        the nations.
And I thought you would call me, My
        Father,
    and would not turn from following
        me.
²⁰ Instead, as a faithless wife leaves her
        husband,
    so you have been faithless to me,
        O house of Israel,
                says the Lord.

²¹ A voice on the bare heights*a*
    is heard,
    the plaintive weeping of Israel's
        children,
because they have perverted
    their way,
    they have forgotten the Lord their
        God:
²² Return, O faithless children,
    I will heal your faithlessness.

'Here we come to you;
    for you are the Lord our God.
²³ Truly the hills are*b* a delusion,
    the orgies on the mountains.
Truly in the Lord our God
    is the salvation of Israel.
²⁴ 'But from our youth the shameful thing has devoured all for which our ancestors had laboured, their flocks and their herds, their sons and their daughters. ²⁵ Let us lie down in our shame, and let our dishonour cover us; for we have sinned against the Lord our God, we and our ancestors, from our youth even to this day;

and we have not obeyed the voice of the Lord our God.'

4 If you return, O Israel,
                says the Lord,
    if you return to me,
if you remove your abominations
        from my presence,
    and do not waver,
² and if you swear, 'As the Lord lives!'
    in truth, in justice, and in
        uprightness,
    then nations shall be blessed*c*
        by him,
    and by him they shall boast.

³ For thus says the Lord to the people of Judah and to the inhabitants of Jerusalem:
    Break up your fallow ground,
        and do not sow among thorns.
⁴ Circumcise yourselves to the Lord,
    remove the foreskin of your
        hearts,
    O people of Judah and inhabitants
        of Jerusalem,
or else my wrath will go forth
        like fire,
    and burn with no one to
        quench it,
    because of the evil of your doings.

*Invasion and Desolation of Judah
Threatened*

⁵ Declare in Judah, and proclaim in Jerusalem, and say:
    Blow the trumpet through the land;
        shout aloud*d* and say,
    'Gather together, and let us go
        into the fortified cities!'
⁶ Raise a standard towards Zion,
    flee for safety, do not delay,
    for I am bringing evil from the
        north,
    and a great destruction.
⁷ A lion has gone up from its thicket,
    a destroyer of nations has set out;
    he has gone out from his place
    to make your land a waste;

---

a Or *the trails*   *b* Gk Syr Vg: Heb *Truly from the hills is*
c Or *shall bless themselves*   *d* Or *shout, take your weapons*: Heb *shout, fill* (your hand)

your cities will be ruins
　　without inhabitant.
8 Because of this put on sackcloth,
　　lament and wail:
　'The fierce anger of the LORD
　　has not turned away from us.'

9 On that day, says the LORD, courage shall
fail the king and the officials; the priests
shall be appalled and the prophets astounded. 10 Then I said, 'Ah, Lord GOD,
how utterly you have deceived this people
and Jerusalem, saying, "It shall be well
with you", even while the sword is at the
throat!'

11 At that time it will be said to this
people and to Jerusalem: A hot wind
comes from me out of the bare heights*a* in
the desert towards my poor people, not to
winnow or cleanse— 12 a wind too strong
for that. Now it is I who speak in judgement against them.
13 Look! He comes up like clouds,
　　his chariots like the whirlwind;
　his horses are swifter than eagles—
　　woe to us, for we are ruined!
14 O Jerusalem, wash your heart clean
　　of wickedness
　　so that you may be saved.
　How long shall your evil schemes
　　lodge within you?
15 For a voice declares from Dan
　　and proclaims disaster from Mount
　　　Ephraim.
16 Tell the nations, 'Here they are!'
　　Proclaim against Jerusalem,
　'Besiegers come from a distant land;
　　they shout against the cities of
　　　Judah.
17 They have closed in around her like
　　watchers of a field,
　　because she has rebelled
　　　against me,
　　　　　　　　　　　　says the LORD.
18 Your ways and your doings
　　have brought this upon you.
　This is your doom; how bitter it is!
　　It has reached your very heart.'

Sorrow for a Doomed Nation

19 My anguish, my anguish! I writhe in
　　pain!
　Oh, the walls of my heart!
　My heart is beating wildly;
　　I cannot keep silent;
　for I *b* hear the sound of the trumpet,
　　the alarm of war.
20 Disaster overtakes disaster,
　　the whole land is laid waste.
　Suddenly my tents are destroyed,
　　my curtains in a moment.
21 How long must I see the standard,
　　and hear the sound of the trumpet?
22 'For my people are foolish,
　　they do not know me;
　they are stupid children,
　　they have no understanding.
　They are skilled in doing evil,
　　but do not know how to do good.'

23 I looked on the earth, and lo, it was
　　waste and void;
　　　and to the heavens, and they had
　　　　no light.
24 I looked on the mountains, and lo,
　　they were quaking,
　　and all the hills moved to and fro.
25 I looked, and lo, there was no one at
　　all,
　　and all the birds of the air had fled.
26 I looked, and lo, the fruitful land was
　　a desert,
　　and all its cities were laid in ruins
　before the LORD, before his fierce
　　anger.
27 For thus says the LORD: The whole
land shall be a desolation; yet I will not
make a full end.
28 Because of this the earth shall mourn,
　　and the heavens above grow black;
　for I have spoken, I have purposed;
　　I have not relented nor will I turn
　　　back.

29 At the noise of horseman and archer
　　every town takes to flight;
　they enter thickets; they climb among
　　rocks;

a Or *the trails*　　*b* Another reading is *for you, O my soul,*

all the towns are forsaken,
  and no one lives in them.
30 And you, O desolate one,
  what do you mean that you dress in
        crimson,
    that you deck yourself with
        ornaments of gold,
    that you enlarge your eyes with
        paint?
  In vain you beautify yourself.
    Your lovers despise you;
    they seek your life.
31 For I heard a cry as of a woman
        in labour,
  anguish as of one bringing forth
        her first child,
  the cry of daughter Zion gasping for
        breath,
    stretching out her hands,
  'Woe is me! I am fainting before
        killers!'

The Utter Corruption of God's People

5 Run to and fro through the streets
      of Jerusalem,
    look around and take note!
  Search its squares and see
    if you can find one person
  who acts justly
    and seeks truth—
  so that I may pardon Jerusalem.*a*
2 Although they say, 'As the LORD
      lives',
    yet they swear falsely.
3 O LORD, do your eyes not look
      for truth?
  You have struck them,
    but they felt no anguish;
  you have consumed them,
    but they refused to take
        correction.
  They have made their faces harder
        than rock;
    they have refused to turn back.

4 Then I said, 'These are only
      the poor,
    they have no sense;
  for they do not know the way of
      the LORD,
    the law of their God.

5 Let me go to the rich*b*
    and speak to them;
  surely they know the way of
      the LORD,
    the law of their God.'
  But they all alike had broken
      the yoke,
    they had burst the bonds.

6 Therefore a lion from the forest shall
      kill them,
    a wolf from the desert shall destroy
        them.
  A leopard is watching against
      their cities;
    everyone who goes out of them
        shall be torn in pieces—
  because their transgressions
      are many,
    their apostasies are great.

7 How can I pardon you?
    Your children have forsaken me,
    and have sworn by those who are
        no gods.
  When I fed them to the full,
    they committed adultery
    and trooped to the houses of
        prostitutes.
8 They were well-fed lusty stallions,
    each neighing for his neighbour's
        wife.
9 Shall I not punish them for these
      things?
                              says the LORD;
    and shall I not bring retribution
    on a nation such as this?

10 Go up through her vine-rows
      and destroy,
    but do not make a full end;
  strip away her branches,
    for they are not the LORD's.
11 For the house of Israel and the house
      of Judah
    have been utterly faithless to me,
                              says the LORD.
12 They have spoken falsely of
      the LORD,
    and have said, 'He will do nothing.

a Heb *it*   *b* Or *the great*

No evil will come upon us,
and we shall not see sword or
famine.'
13 The prophets are nothing but wind,
for the word is not in them.
Thus shall it be done to them!

14 Therefore thus says the LORD, the God
of hosts:
Because they[a] have spoken this word,
I am now making my words in your
mouth a fire,
and this people wood, and the fire
shall devour them.
15 I am going to bring upon you
a nation from far away, O house of
Israel,
says the LORD.
It is an enduring nation,
it is an ancient nation,
a nation whose language you do
not know,
nor can you understand what they
say.
16 Their quiver is like an open tomb;
all of them are mighty warriors.
17 They shall eat up your harvest and
your food;
they shall eat up your sons and
your daughters;
they shall eat up your flocks and your
herds;
they shall eat up your vines and
your fig trees;
they shall destroy with the sword
your fortified cities in which
you trust.

18 But even in those days, says the
LORD, I will not make a full end of you.
19 And when your people say, 'Why has the
LORD our God done all these things to us?'
you shall say to them, 'As you have forsak-
en me and served foreign gods in your
land, so you shall serve strangers in a land
that is not yours.'

20 Declare this in the house of Jacob,
proclaim it in Judah:
21 Hear this, O foolish and senseless
people,

who have eyes, but do not see,
who have ears, but do not hear.
22 Do you not fear me? says the LORD;
Do you not tremble before me?
I placed the sand as a boundary for
the sea,
a perpetual barrier that it cannot
pass;
though the waves toss, they cannot
prevail,
though they roar, they cannot pass
over it.
23 But this people has a stubborn and
rebellious heart;
they have turned aside and
gone away.
24 They do not say in their hearts,
'Let us fear the LORD our God,
who gives the rain in its season,
the autumn rain and the
spring rain,
and keeps for us
the weeks appointed for the
harvest.'
25 Your iniquities have turned
these away,
and your sins have deprived you of
good.
26 For scoundrels are found among
my people;
they take over the goods of others.
Like fowlers they set a trap;[b]
they catch human beings.
27 Like a cage full of birds,
their houses are full of treachery;
therefore they have become great and
rich,
28 they have grown fat and sleek.
They know no limits in deeds of
wickedness;
they do not judge with justice
the cause of the orphan, to make
it prosper,
and they do not defend the rights
of the needy.
29 Shall I not punish them for these
things?
says the LORD,
and shall I not bring retribution
on a nation such as this?

a Heb you   b Meaning of Heb uncertain

30 An appalling and horrible thing
   has happened in the land:
31 the prophets prophesy falsely,
   and the priests rule as the prophets
       direct;[a]
   my people love to have it so,
   but what will you do when the end
       comes?

The Imminence and Horror
of the Invasion

6 Flee for safety, O children of
   Benjamin,
   from the midst of Jerusalem!
Blow the trumpet in Tekoa,
   and raise a signal on Beth-
       haccherem;
   for evil looms out of the north,
   and great destruction.
2 I have likened daughter Zion
   to the loveliest pasture.[b]
3 Shepherds with their flocks shall
       come against her.
   They shall pitch their tents around
       her;
   they shall pasture, all in
       their places.
4 'Prepare war against her;
   up, and let us attack at noon!'
'Woe to us, for the day declines,
   the shadows of evening lengthen!'
5 'Up, and let us attack by night,
   and destroy her palaces!'
6 For thus says the LORD of hosts:
Cut down her trees;
   cast up a siege-ramp against
       Jerusalem.
This is the city that must be
       punished;[c]
   there is nothing but oppression
       within her.
7 As a well keeps its water fresh,
   so she keeps fresh her wickedness;
violence and destruction are heard
       within her;
   sickness and wounds are ever
       before me.
8 Take warning, O Jerusalem,
   or I shall turn from you in disgust,
   and make you a desolation,
   an uninhabited land.

9 Thus says the LORD of hosts:
Glean[d] thoroughly as a vine
   the remnant of Israel;
   like a grape-gatherer, pass your hand
       again
   over its branches.

10 To whom shall I speak and give
       warning,
   that they may hear?
See, their ears are closed,[e]
   they cannot listen.
The word of the LORD is to them an
       object of scorn;
   they take no pleasure in it.
11 But I am full of the wrath of
       the LORD;
   I am weary of holding it in.

Pour it out on the children in
       the street,
   and on the gatherings of young
       men as well;
both husband and wife shall
       be taken,
   the old folk and the very aged.
12 Their houses shall be turned over to
       others,
   their fields and wives together;
for I will stretch out my hand
   against the inhabitants of
       the land,
                           says the LORD.

13 For from the least to the greatest
       of them,
   everyone is greedy for unjust gain;
and from prophet to priest,
   everyone deals falsely.
14 They have treated the wound of my
       people carelessly,
   saying, 'Peace, peace',
   when there is no peace.
15 They acted shamefully, they
       committed abomination;
   yet they were not ashamed,
   they did not know how to blush.

a Or rule by their own authority   b Or I will destroy
daughter Zion, the loveliest pasture   c Or the city of
licence   d Cn: Heb They shall glean   e Heb are
uncircumcised

Therefore they shall fall among those
who fall;
at the time that I punish them, they
shall be overthrown,
says the LORD.

16 Thus says the LORD:
Stand at the crossroads, and look,
and ask for the ancient paths,
where the good way lies; and walk in
it,
and find rest for your souls.
But they said, 'We will not walk
in it.'

17 Also I raised up sentinels for you:
'Give heed to the sound of the
trumpet!'
But they said, 'We will not give
heed.'

18 Therefore hear, O nations,
and know, O congregation, what
will happen to them.

19 Hear, O earth; I am going to bring
disaster on this people,
the fruit of their schemes,
because they have not given heed to
my words;
and as for my teaching, they have
rejected it.

20 Of what use to me is frankincense
that comes from Sheba,
or sweet cane from a distant land?
Your burnt-offerings are not
acceptable,
nor are your sacrifices pleasing
to me.

21 Therefore thus says the LORD:
See, I am laying before this people
stumbling-blocks against which
they shall stumble;
parents and children together,
neighbour and friend shall perish.

22 Thus says the LORD:
See, a people is coming from the land
of the north,
a great nation is stirring from the
farthest parts of the earth.

23 They grasp the bow and the javelin,
they are cruel and have no mercy,
their sound is like the roaring sea;
they ride on horses,

equipped like a warrior for battle,
against you, O daughter Zion!

24 'We have heard news of them,
our hands fall helpless;
anguish has taken hold of us,
pain as of a woman in labour.

25 Do not go out into the field,
or walk on the road;
for the enemy has a sword,
terror is on every side.'

26 O my poor people, put on sackcloth,
and roll in ashes;
make mourning as for an only child,
most bitter lamentation:
for suddenly the destroyer
will come upon us.

27 I have made you a tester and a
refiner*a* among my people
so that you may know and test their
ways.

28 They are all stubbornly rebellious,
going about with slanders;
they are bronze and iron,
all of them act corruptly.

29 The bellows blow fiercely,
the lead is consumed by the fire;
in vain the refining goes on,
for the wicked are not removed.

30 They are called 'rejected silver',
for the LORD has rejected them.

Jeremiah Proclaims God's Judgement on the Nation

7 The word that came to Jeremiah from
the LORD: 2 Stand in the gate of the
LORD's house, and proclaim there this
word, and say, Hear the word of the LORD,
all you people of Judah, you that enter
these gates to worship the LORD. 3 Thus says
the LORD of hosts, the God of Israel:
Amend your ways and your doings, and let
me dwell with you*b* in this place. 4 Do not
trust in these deceptive words: 'This is*c* the
temple of the LORD, the temple of the
LORD, the temple of the LORD.'

5 For if you truly amend your ways and

a Or *a fortress*   b Or *and I will let you dwell*
c Heb *They are*

your doings, if you truly act justly one with another, 6 if you do not oppress the alien, the orphan, and the widow, or shed innocent blood in this place, and if you do not go after other gods to your own hurt, 7 then I will dwell with you in this place, in the land that I gave of old to your ancestors for ever and ever.

8 Here you are, trusting in deceptive words to no avail. 9 Will you steal, murder, commit adultery, swear falsely, make offerings to Baal, and go after other gods that you have not known, 10 and then come and stand before me in this house, which is called by my name, and say, 'We are safe!'—only to go on doing all these abominations? 11 Has this house, which is called by my name, become a den of robbers in your sight? You know, I too am watching, says the LORD. 12 Go now to my place that was in Shiloh, where I made my name dwell at first, and see what I did to it for the wickedness of my people Israel. 13 And now, because you have done all these things, says the LORD, and when I spoke to you persistently, you did not listen, and when I called you, you did not answer, 14 therefore I will do to the house that is called by my name, in which you trust, and to the place that I gave to you and to your ancestors, just what I did to Shiloh. 15 And I will cast you out of my sight, just as I cast out all your kinsfolk, all the offspring of Ephraim.

The People's Disobedience

16 As for you, do not pray for this people, do not raise a cry or prayer on their behalf, and do not intercede with me, for I will not hear you. 17 Do you not see what they are doing in the towns of Judah and in the streets of Jerusalem? 18 The children gather wood, the fathers kindle fire, and the women knead dough, to make cakes for the queen of heaven; and they pour out drink-offerings to other gods, to provoke me to anger. 19 Is it I whom they provoke? says the LORD. Is it not themselves, to their own hurt? 20 Therefore thus says the Lord GOD: My anger and my wrath shall be poured out on this place, on human beings and animals, on the trees of the field and the fruit of the ground; it will burn and not be quenched.

21 Thus says the LORD of hosts, the God of Israel: Add your burnt-offerings to your sacrifices, and eat the flesh. 22 For on the day that I brought your ancestors out of the land of Egypt, I did not speak to them or command them concerning burnt-offerings and sacrifices. 23 But this command I gave them, 'Obey my voice, and I will be your God, and you shall be my people; and walk only in the way that I command you, so that it may be well with you.' 24 Yet they did not obey or incline their ear, but, in the stubbornness of their evil will, they walked in their own counsels, and looked backwards rather than forwards. 25 From the day that your ancestors came out of the land of Egypt until this day, I have persistently sent all my servants the prophets to them, day after day; 26 yet they did not listen to me, or pay attention, but they stiffened their necks. They did worse than their ancestors did.

27 So you shall speak all these words to them, but they will not listen to you. You shall call to them, but they will not answer you. 28 You shall say to them: This is the nation that did not obey the voice of the LORD their God, and did not accept discipline; truth has perished; it is cut off from their lips.

29 Cut off your hair and throw it away;
    raise a lamentation on the bare
        heights,ᵃ
    for the LORD has rejected and
        forsaken
    the generation that provoked
        his wrath.

30 For the people of Judah have done evil in my sight, says the LORD; they have set their abominations in the house that is called by my name, defiling it. 31 And they go on building the high placeᵇ of Topheth, which is in the valley of the son of Hinnom, to burn their sons and their daughters in the fire—which I did not command, nor did it come into my mind. 32 Therefore, the days are surely coming, says the LORD,

a Or the trails   b Gk Tg: Heb high places

when it will no more be called Topheth, or the valley of the son of Hinnom, but the valley of Slaughter: for they will bury in Topheth until there is no more room. 33 The corpses of this people will be food for the birds of the air, and for the animals of the earth; and no one will frighten them away. 34 And I will bring to an end the sound of mirth and gladness, the voice of the bride and bridegroom in the cities of Judah and in the streets of Jerusalem; for the land shall become a waste.

8 At that time, says the LORD, the bones of the kings of Judah, the bones of its officials, the bones of the priests, the bones of the prophets, and the bones of the inhabitants of Jerusalem shall be brought out of their tombs; 2 and they shall be spread before the sun and the moon and all the host of heaven, which they have loved and served, which they have followed, and which they have inquired of and worshipped; and they shall not be gathered or buried; they shall be like dung on the surface of the ground. 3 Death shall be preferred to life by all the remnant that remains of this evil family in all the places where I have driven them, says the LORD of hosts.

The Blind Perversity of the Whole Nation

4 You shall say to them, Thus says the
    LORD:
  When people fall, do they not get up
      again?
    If they go astray, do they not turn
      back?
5 Why then has this people a turned
      away
    in perpetual backsliding?
  They have held fast to deceit,
    they have refused to return.
6 I have given heed and listened,
    but they do not speak honestly;
  no one repents of wickedness,
    saying, 'What have I done!'
  All of them turn to their own
      course,
    like a horse plunging headlong into
      battle.
7 Even the stork in the heavens

knows its times;
  and the turtle-dove, swallow, and
      crane b
  observe the time of their coming;
  but my people do not know
    the ordinance of the LORD.

8 How can you say, 'We are wise,
    and the law of the LORD is with us',
  when, in fact, the false pen of
      the scribes
    has made it into a lie?
9 The wise shall be put to shame,
    they shall be dismayed and taken;
  since they have rejected the word
      of the LORD,
    what wisdom is in them?
10 Therefore I will give their wives
      to others
    and their fields to conquerors,
  because from the least to the greatest
    everyone is greedy for unjust gain;
  from prophet to priest
    everyone deals falsely.
11 They have treated the wound of my
      people carelessly,
    saying, 'Peace, peace',
    when there is no peace.
12 They acted shamefully, they
      committed abomination;
    yet they were not at all ashamed,
    they did not know how to blush.
  Therefore they shall fall among those
      who fall;
    at the time when I punish them,
      they shall be overthrown,
                          says the LORD.
13 When I wanted to gather them, says
      the LORD,
    there are c no grapes on the vine,
      nor figs on the fig tree;
  even the leaves are withered,
    and what I gave them has passed
      away from them. b

14 Why do we sit still?
  Gather together, let us go into the
      fortified cities

a One Ms Gk: MT this people, Jerusalem,   b Meaning of Heb uncertain   c Or I will make an end of them, says the LORD. There are

and perish there;
for the LORD our God has doomed us
    to perish,
  and has given us poisoned water to
    drink,
  because we have sinned against the
    LORD.
15 We look for peace, but find no good,
  for a time of healing, but there is
    terror instead.

16 The snorting of their horses is heard
    from Dan;
  at the sound of the neighing of
    their stallions
  the whole land quakes.
They come and devour the land and
    all that fills it,
  the city and those who live in it.
17 See, I am letting snakes loose among
    you,
  adders that cannot be charmed,
  and they shall bite you,
              says the LORD.

The Prophet Mourns for the People

18 My joy is gone, grief is upon me,
  my heart is sick.
19 Hark, the cry of my poor people
  from far and wide in the land:
'Is the LORD not in Zion?
  Is her King not in her?'
('Why have they provoked me to
    anger with their images,
  with their foreign idols?')
20 'The harvest is past, the summer
    is ended,
  and we are not saved.'
21 For the hurt of my poor people I am
    hurt,
  I mourn, and dismay has taken
    hold of me.

22 Is there no balm in Gilead?
  Is there no physician there?
Why then has the health of my poor
    people
  not been restored?

9 *a* O that my head were a spring of
    water,
  and my eyes a fountain of tears,

so that I might weep day and night
  for the slain of my poor people!
2*b* O that I had in the desert
  a traveller's lodging-place,
that I might leave my people
  and go away from them!
For they are all adulterers,
  a band of traitors.
3 They bend their tongues like bows;
  they have grown strong in the land
    for falsehood, and not for truth;
for they proceed from evil to evil,
  and they do not know me, says the
    LORD.

4 Beware of your neighbours,
  and put no trust in any of
    your kin; *c*
for all your kin *d* are supplanters,
  and every neighbour goes around
    like a slanderer.
5 They all deceive their neighbours,
  and no one speaks the truth;
they have taught their tongues to
    speak lies;
they commit iniquity and are too
    weary to repent. *e*
6 Oppression upon oppression, deceit*f*
    upon deceit!
They refuse to know me, says
    the LORD.

7 Therefore, thus says the LORD of
    hosts:
I will now refine and test them,
  for what else can I do with my
    sinful people?*g*
8 Their tongue is a deadly arrow;
  it speaks deceit through the mouth.
They all speak friendly words to their
    neighbours,
  but inwardly are planning to lay an
    ambush.
9 Shall I not punish them for these
    things? says the LORD;
  and shall I not bring retribution
  on a nation such as this?

a Ch 8.23 in Heb   *b* Ch 9.1 in Heb   *c* Heb *in a
brother*   *d* Heb *for every brother*   *e* Cn Compare Gk:
Heb *they weary themselves with iniquity.* 6*Your dwelling*
f Cn: Heb *Your dwelling in the midst of deceit*   *g* Or *my
poor people*

10 Take up*a* weeping and wailing for the
         mountains,
     and a lamentation for the pastures
         of the wilderness,
   because they are laid waste so that no
         one passes through,
     and the lowing of cattle is not
         heard;
   both the birds of the air and the
         animals
     have fled and are gone.
11 I will make Jerusalem a heap of ruins,
     a lair of jackals;
   and I will make the towns of Judah a
         desolation
     without inhabitant.

12 Who is wise enough to understand
this? To whom has the mouth of the LORD
spoken, so that they may declare it? Why is
the land ruined and laid waste like a
wilderness, so that no one passes through?
13 And the LORD says: Because they have
forsaken my law that I set before them, and
have not obeyed my voice, or walked in accordance with it, 14 but have stubbornly
followed their own hearts and have gone
after the Baals, as their ancestors taught
them. 15 Therefore, thus says the LORD of
hosts, the God of Israel: I am feeding this
people with wormwood, and giving them
poisonous water to drink. 16 I will scatter
them among nations that neither they nor
their ancestors have known; and I will send
the sword after them, until I have consumed them.

The People Mourn in Judgement

17 Thus says the LORD of hosts:
   Consider, and call for the mourning-
         women to come;
     send for the skilled women
         to come;
18 let them quickly raise a dirge over us,
     so that our eyes may run down with
         tears,
   and our eyelids flow with water.
19 For a sound of wailing is heard from
         Zion:
   'How we are ruined!
   We are utterly shamed,

   because we have left the land,
     because they have cast down our
         dwellings.'

20 Hear, O women, the word of
         the LORD,
     and let your ears receive the word
         of his mouth;
   teach to your daughters a dirge,
     and each to her neighbour
         a lament.
21 'Death has come up into our
         windows,
     it has entered our palaces,
   to cut off the children from
         the streets
     and the young men from
         the squares.'
22 Speak! Thus says the LORD:
   'Human corpses shall fall
     like dung upon the open field,
   like sheaves behind the reaper,
     and no one shall gather them.'

23 Thus says the LORD: Do not let the
wise boast in their wisdom, do not let the
mighty boast in their might, do not let
the wealthy boast in their wealth; 24 but let
those who boast boast in this, that they understand and know me, that I am the LORD;
I act with steadfast love, justice, and righteousness in the earth, for in these things I
delight, says the LORD.

25 The days are surely coming, says the
LORD, when I will attend to all those who
are circumcised only in the foreskin:
26 Egypt, Judah, Edom, the Ammonites,
Moab, and all those with shaven temples
who live in the desert. For all these nations
are uncircumcised, and all the house of Israel is uncircumcised in heart.

Idolatry Has Brought Ruin on Israel

10 Hear the word that the LORD speaks
to you, O house of Israel. 2 Thus
says the LORD:
   Do not learn the way of the nations,
     or be dismayed at the signs of the
         heavens;

---

a Gk Syr: Heb *I will take up*

for the nations are dismayed
  at them.
3 For the customs of the peoples
    are false:
  a tree from the forest is cut down,
    and worked with an axe by the
      hands of an artisan;
4 people deck it with silver and gold;
    they fasten it with hammer
      and nails
    so that it cannot move.
5 Their idols[a] are like scarecrows in a
      cucumber field,
    and they cannot speak;
  they have to be carried,
    for they cannot walk.
  Do not be afraid of them,
    for they cannot do evil,
    nor is it in them to do good.

6 There is none like you, O LORD;
    you are great, and your name is
      great in might.
7 Who would not fear you, O King of
      the nations?
    For that is your due;
  among all the wise ones of the
      nations
    and in all their kingdoms
    there is no one like you.
8 They are both stupid and foolish;
    the instruction given by idols
    is no better than wood![b]
9 Beaten silver is brought from
      Tarshish,
    and gold from Uphaz.
  They are the work of the artisan and
      of the hands of the goldsmith;
    their clothing is blue and purple;
    they are all the product of skilled
      workers.
10 But the LORD is the true God;
    he is the living God and the
      everlasting King.
  At his wrath the earth quakes,
    and the nations cannot endure his
      indignation.

11 Thus shall you say to them: The gods
who did not make the heavens and the
earth shall perish from the earth and from
under the heavens.[c]

12 It is he who made the earth by
      his power,
    who established the world by
      his wisdom,
    and by his understanding stretched
      out the heavens.
13 When he utters his voice, there is a
      tumult of waters in the heavens,
    and he makes the mist rise from the
      ends of the earth.
  He makes lightnings for the rain,
    and he brings out the wind from
      his storehouses.
14 Everyone is stupid and without
      knowledge;
    goldsmiths are all put to shame by
      their idols;
  for their images are false,
    and there is no breath in them.
15 They are worthless, a work of delusion;
    at the time of their punishment
      they shall perish.
16 Not like these is the LORD,[d] the
      portion of Jacob,
    for he is the one who formed
      all things,
  and Israel is the tribe of his
      inheritance;
    the LORD of hosts is his name.

The Coming Exile

17 Gather up your bundle from the
      ground,
    O you who live under siege!
18 For thus says the LORD:
  I am going to fling away the
      inhabitants of the land
    at this time,
  and I will bring distress on them,
    so that they shall feel it.

19 Woe is me because of my hurt!
    My wound is severe.
  But I said, 'Truly this is my
      punishment,
    and I must bear it.'

a Heb *They*   b Meaning of Heb uncertain   c This
verse is in Aramaic   d Heb lacks *the LORD*

20 My tent is destroyed,
  and all my cords are broken;
my children have gone from me,
  and they are no more;
there is no one to spread my tent
    again,
  and to set up my curtains.
21 For the shepherds are stupid,
  and do not inquire of the LORD;
therefore they have not prospered,
  and all their flock is scattered.

22 Hear, a noise! Listen, it is coming—
  a great commotion from the land
    of the north
to make the cities of Judah a
    desolation,
  a lair of jackals.

23 I know, O LORD, that the way of
    human beings is not in
    their control,
  that mortals as they walk cannot
    direct their steps.
24 Correct me, O LORD, but in
    just measure;
  not in your anger, or you will bring
    me to nothing.

25 Pour out your wrath on the nations
    that do not know you,
  and on the peoples that do not call
    on your name;
for they have devoured Jacob;
  they have devoured him and
    consumed him,
  and have laid waste his habitation.

Israel and Judah Have Broken the Covenant

11 The word that came to Jeremiah from the LORD: 2 Hear the words of this covenant, and speak to the people of Judah and the inhabitants of Jerusalem. 3 You shall say to them, Thus says the LORD, the God of Israel: Cursed be anyone who does not heed the words of this covenant, 4 which I commanded your ancestors when I brought them out of the land of Egypt, from the iron-smelter, saying, Listen to my voice, and do all that I command you. So shall you be my people, and I will be your God, 5 that I may perform the oath that I swore to your ancestors, to give them a land flowing with milk and honey, as at this day. Then I answered, 'So be it, LORD.'

6 And the LORD said to me: Proclaim all these words in the cities of Judah, and in the streets of Jerusalem: Hear the words of this covenant and do them. 7 For I solemnly warned your ancestors when I brought them up out of the land of Egypt, warning them persistently, even to this day, saying, Obey my voice. 8 Yet they did not obey or incline their ear, but everyone walked in the stubbornness of an evil will. So I brought upon them all the words of this covenant, which I commanded them to do, but they did not.

9 And the LORD said to me: Conspiracy exists among the people of Judah and the inhabitants of Jerusalem. 10 They have turned back to the iniquities of their ancestors of old, who refused to heed my words; they have gone after other gods to serve them; the house of Israel and the house of Judah have broken the covenant that I made with their ancestors. 11 Therefore, thus says the LORD, assuredly I am going to bring disaster upon them that they cannot escape; though they cry out to me, I will not listen to them. 12 Then the cities of Judah and the inhabitants of Jerusalem will go and cry out to the gods to whom they make offerings, but they will never save them in the time of their trouble. 13 For your gods have become as many as your towns, O Judah; and as many as the streets of Jerusalem are the altars to shame that you have set up, altars to make offerings to Baal.

14 As for you, do not pray for this people, or lift up a cry or prayer on their behalf, for I will not listen when they call to me in the time of their trouble. 15 What right has my beloved in my house, when she has done vile deeds? Can vows*a* and sacrificial flesh avert your doom? Can you then exult? 16 The LORD once called you, 'A green olive tree, fair with goodly fruit'; but with the roar of a great tempest he will set

a Gk: Heb *Can many*

fire to it, and its branches will be consumed. ¹⁷The LORD of hosts, who planted you, has pronounced evil against you, because of the evil that the house of Israel and the house of Judah have done, provoking me to anger by making offerings to Baal.

Jeremiah's Life Threatened

¹⁸ It was the LORD who made it known
      to me, and I knew;
  then you showed me their
     evil deeds.
¹⁹ But I was like a gentle lamb
   led to the slaughter.
 And I did not know it was
     against me
   that they devised schemes, saying,
 'Let us destroy the tree with its fruit,
   let us cut him off from the land of
     the living,
   so that his name will no longer be
     remembered!'
²⁰ But you, O LORD of hosts, who judge
     righteously,
  who try the heart and the mind,
 let me see your retribution upon
    them,
   for to you I have committed
     my cause.

21 Therefore thus says the LORD concerning the people of Anathoth, who seek your life, and say, 'You shall not prophesy in the name of the LORD, or you will die by our hand'— ²² therefore thus says the LORD of hosts: I am going to punish them; the young men shall die by the sword; their sons and their daughters shall die by famine; ²³ and not even a remnant shall be left of them. For I will bring disaster upon the people of Anathoth, the year of their punishment.

Jeremiah Complains to God

12 You will be in the right, O LORD,
    when I lay charges against you;
 but let me put my case to you.
Why does the way of the guilty
    prosper?
 Why do all who are treacherous
    thrive?

² You plant them, and they take root;
   they grow and bring forth fruit;
 you are near in their mouths
   yet far from their hearts.
³ But you, O LORD, know me;
   You see me and test me—my heart
     is with you.
 Pull them out like sheep for the
    slaughter,
   and set them apart for the day
     of slaughter.
⁴ How long will the land mourn,
   and the grass of every field wither?
 For the wickedness of those who live
    in it
   the animals and the birds are swept
     away,
   and because people said, 'He is
    blind to our ways.'^a

God Replies to Jeremiah

⁵ If you have raced with foot-runners
    and they have wearied you,
 how will you compete with
    horses?
 And if in a safe land you fall down,
   how will you fare in the thickets of
    the Jordan?
⁶ For even your kinsfolk and your own
    family,
   even they have dealt treacherously
    with you;
   they are in full cry after you;
 do not believe them,
   though they speak friendly words
    to you.

⁷ I have forsaken my house,
   I have abandoned my heritage;
 I have given the beloved of my heart
   into the hands of her enemies.
⁸ My heritage has become to me
   like a lion in the forest;
 she has lifted up her voice against
    me—
   therefore I hate her.
⁹ Is the hyena greedy^b for my heritage
    at my command?
   Are the birds of prey all around her?

a Gk: Heb *to our future*   *b* Cn: Heb *Is the hyena, the bird of prey*

Go, assemble all the wild animals;
bring them to devour her.
10 Many shepherds have destroyed
my vineyard,
they have trampled down
my portion,
they have made my pleasant portion
a desolate wilderness.
11 They have made it a desolation;
desolate, it mourns to me.
The whole land is made desolate,
but no one lays it to heart.
12 Upon all the bare heights[a] in
the desert
spoilers have come;
for the sword of the LORD devours
from one end of the land to
the other;
no one shall be safe.
13 They have sown wheat and have
reaped thorns,
they have tired themselves out but
profit nothing.
They shall be ashamed of their[b]
harvests
because of the fierce anger of
the LORD.

14 Thus says the LORD concerning all my evil neighbours who touch the heritage that I have given my people Israel to inherit: I am about to pluck them up from their land, and I will pluck up the house of Judah from among them. 15 And after I have plucked them up, I will again have compassion on them, and I will bring them again to their heritage and to their land, every one of them. 16 And then, if they will diligently learn the ways of my people, to swear by my name, 'As the LORD lives', as they taught my people to swear by Baal, then they shall be built up in the midst of my people. 17 But if any nation will not listen, then I will completely uproot it and destroy it, says the LORD.

The Linen Loincloth

13 Thus said the LORD to me, 'Go and buy yourself a linen loincloth, and put it on your loins, but do not dip it in water.' 2 So I bought a loincloth according to the word of the LORD, and put it on my loins. 3 And the word of the LORD came to me a second time, saying, 4 'Take the loincloth that you bought and are wearing, and go now to the Euphrates,[c] and hide it there in a cleft of the rock.' 5 So I went, and hid it by the Euphrates,[d] as the LORD commanded me. 6 And after many days the LORD said to me, 'Go now to the Euphrates,[c] and take from there the loincloth that I commanded you to hide there.' 7 Then I went to the Euphrates,[c] and dug, and I took the loincloth from the place where I had hidden it. But now the loincloth was ruined; it was good for nothing.

8 Then the word of the LORD came to me: 9 Thus says the LORD: Just so I will ruin the pride of Judah and the great pride of Jerusalem. 10 This evil people, who refuse to hear my words, who stubbornly follow their own will and have gone after other gods to serve them and worship them, shall be like this loincloth, which is good for nothing. 11 For as the loincloth clings to one's loins, so I made the whole house of Israel and the whole house of Judah cling to me, says the LORD, in order that they might be for me a people, a name, a praise, and a glory. But they would not listen.

Symbol of the Wine-Jars

12 You shall speak to them this word: Thus says the LORD, the God of Israel: Every wine-jar should be filled with wine. And they will say to you, 'Do you think we do not know that every wine-jar should be filled with wine?' 13 Then you shall say to them: Thus says the LORD: I am about to fill all the inhabitants of this land—the kings who sit on David's throne, the priests, the prophets, and all the inhabitants of Jerusalem—with drunkenness. 14 And I will dash them one against another, parents and children together, says the LORD. I will not pity or spare or have compassion when I destroy them.

Exile Threatened

15 Hear and give ear; do not be haughty,
for the LORD has spoken.

a Or *the trails* *b* Heb *your* *c* Or *to Parah*; Heb *perath* *d* Or *by Parah*; Heb *perath*

16 Give glory to the LORD your God
    before he brings darkness,
and before your feet stumble
    on the mountains at twilight;
while you look for light,
    he turns it into gloom
    and makes it deep darkness.
17 But if you will not listen,
    my soul will weep in secret for your
        pride;
my eyes will weep bitterly and run
        down with tears,
    because the LORD's flock has been
        taken captive.

18 Say to the king and the queen
        mother:
    'Take a lowly seat,
for your beautiful crown
    has come down from your head.'ᵃ
19 The towns of the Negeb are shut up
    with no one to open them;
all Judah is taken into exile,
    wholly taken into exile.

20 Lift up your eyes and see
    those who come from the north.
Where is the flock that was
        given you,
    your beautiful flock?
21 What will you say when they set as
        head over you
    those whom you have trained
    to be your allies?
Will not pangs take hold of you,
    like those of a woman in labour?
22 And if you say in your heart,
    'Why have these things come upon
        me?'
it is for the greatness of your
        iniquity
    that your skirts are lifted up,
    and you are violated.
23 Can Ethiopiansᵇ change their skin
    or leopards their spots?
Then also you can do good
    who are accustomed to do evil.
24 I will scatter youᶜ like chaff
    driven by the wind from the desert.
25 This is your lot,

the portion I have measured out to
        you, says the LORD,
because you have forgotten me
    and trusted in lies.
26 I myself will lift up your skirts over
        your face,
    and your shame will be seen.
27 I have seen your abominations,
    your adulteries and neighings, your
        shameless prostitutions
    on the hills of the countryside.
Woe to you, O Jerusalem!
    How long will it be
    before you are made clean?

The Great Drought

14 The word of the LORD that came to
    Jeremiah concerning the drought:
2 Judah mourns
    and her gates languish;
they lie in gloom on the ground,
    and the cry of Jerusalem goes up.
3 Her nobles send their servants
        for water;
    they come to the cisterns,
they find no water,
    they return with their vessels empty.
They are ashamed and dismayed
    and cover their heads,
4 because the ground is cracked.
    Because there has been no rain on
        the land
    the farmers are dismayed;
    they cover their heads.
5 Even the doe in the field forsakes her
        newborn fawn
    because there is no grass.
6 The wild asses stand on the bare
        heights,ᵈ
    they pant for air like jackals;
their eyes fail
    because there is no herbage.

7 Although our iniquities testify against
        us,
    act, O LORD, for your name's sake;
our apostasies indeed are many,
    and we have sinned against you.

a Gk Syr Vg: Meaning of Heb uncertain
b Or Nubians; Heb Cushites   c Heb them   d Or the
trails

8 O hope of Israel,
    its saviour in time of trouble,
  why should you be like a stranger in
    the land,
    like a traveller turning aside for the
      night?
9 Why should you be like someone
    confused,
    like a mighty warrior who cannot
      give help?
  Yet you, O Lord, are in the midst of
    us,
    and we are called by your name;
    do not forsake us!

10 Thus says the Lord concerning
    this people:
  Truly they have loved to wander,
    they have not restrained their feet;
  therefore the Lord does not
      accept them,
    now he will remember their
      iniquity
    and punish their sins.

11 The Lord said to me: Do not pray for the welfare of this people. 12 Although they fast, I do not hear their cry, and although they offer burnt-offering and grain-offering, I do not accept them; but by the sword, by famine, and by pestilence I consume them.

Denunciation of Lying Prophets

13 Then I said: 'Ah, Lord God! Here are the prophets saying to them, "You shall not see the sword, nor shall you have famine, but I will give you true peace in this place." ' 14 And the Lord said to me: The prophets are prophesying lies in my name; I did not send them, nor did I command them or speak to them. They are prophesying to you a lying vision, worthless divination, and the deceit of their own minds. 15 Therefore thus says the Lord concerning the prophets who prophesy in my name though I did not send them, and who say, 'Sword and famine shall not come on this land': By sword and famine those prophets shall be consumed. 16 And the people to whom they prophesy shall be thrown out into the streets of Jerusalem, victims of famine and sword. There shall be no one to bury them—themselves, their wives, their sons, and their daughters. For I will pour out their wickedness upon them.

17 You shall say to them this word:
  Let my eyes run down with tears
    night and day,
    and let them not cease,
  for the virgin daughter—my people—
    is struck down with a crushing
      blow,
    with a very grievous wound.
18 If I go out into the field,
    look—those killed by the sword!
  And if I enter the city,
    look—those sick with[a] famine!
  For both prophet and priest ply their
      trade throughout the land,
    and have no knowledge.

The People Plead for Mercy

19 Have you completely rejected Judah?
    Does your heart loathe Zion?
  Why have you struck us down
    so that there is no healing for us?
  We look for peace, but find no good;
    for a time of healing, but there is
      terror instead.
20 We acknowledge our wickedness,
    O Lord,
    the iniquity of our ancestors,
    for we have sinned against you.
21 Do not spurn us, for your name's sake;
    do not dishonour your glorious
      throne;
    remember and do not break your
      covenant with us.
22 Can any idols of the nations
    bring rain?
    Or can the heavens give showers?
  Is it not you, O Lord our God?
    We set our hope on you,
    for it is you who do all this.

Punishment Is Inevitable

15 Then the Lord said to me: Though Moses and Samuel stood before me, yet my heart would not turn towards

a Heb look—the sicknesses of

this people. Send them out of my sight, and let them go! ²And when they say to you, 'Where shall we go?' you shall say to them: Thus says the LORD:

Those destined for pestilence, to
   pestilence,
and those destined for the sword,
   to the sword;
those destined for famine, to famine,
   and those destined for captivity, to
   captivity.

³And I will appoint over them four kinds of destroyers, says the LORD: the sword to kill, the dogs to drag away, and the birds of the air and the wild animals of the earth to devour and destroy. ⁴I will make them a horror to all the kingdoms of the earth because of what King Manasseh son of Hezekiah of Judah did in Jerusalem.

⁵ Who will have pity on you,
   O Jerusalem,
   or who will bemoan you?
Who will turn aside
   to ask about your welfare?
⁶ You have rejected me, says the LORD,
   you are going backwards;
so I have stretched out my hand
   against you and destroyed
   you—
I am weary of relenting.
⁷ I have winnowed them with a
   winnowing-fork
   in the gates of the land;
I have bereaved them, I have
   destroyed my people;
   they did not turn from their ways.
⁸ Their widows became more
   numerous
   than the sand of the seas;
I have brought against the mothers of
   youths
   a destroyer at noonday;
I have made anguish and terror
   fall upon her suddenly.
⁹ She who bore seven has languished;
   she has swooned away;
her sun went down while it was
   yet day;
   she has been shamed and
   disgraced.

And the rest of them I will give to the
   sword
before their enemies,
                              says the LORD.

Jeremiah Complains Again
and Is Reassured

10 Woe is me, my mother, that you ever bore me, a man of strife and contention to the whole land! I have not lent, nor have I borrowed, yet all of them curse me. ¹¹The LORD said: Surely I have intervened in your life*a* for good; surely I have imposed enemies on you in a time of trouble and in a time of distress.*b* ¹²Can iron and bronze break iron from the north?

13 Your wealth and your treasures I will give as plunder, without price, for all your sins, throughout all your territory. ¹⁴I will make you serve your enemies in a land that you do not know, for in my anger a fire is kindled that shall burn for ever.

¹⁵ O LORD, you know;
   remember me and visit me,
   and bring down retribution for me
   on my persecutors.
In your forbearance do not take
   me away;
   know that on your account I suffer
   insult.
¹⁶ Your words were found, and I
   ate them,
   and your words became to me a joy
   and the delight of my heart;
for I am called by your name,
   O LORD, God of hosts.
¹⁷ I did not sit in the company of
   merrymakers,
   nor did I rejoice;
under the weight of your hand I
   sat alone,
   for you had filled me with
   indignation.
¹⁸ Why is my pain unceasing,
   my wound incurable,
   refusing to be healed?
Truly, you are to me like a deceitful
   brook,
   like waters that fail.

a Heb *intervened with you*   *b* Meaning of Heb
uncertain

19 Therefore, thus says the LORD:
  If you turn back, I will take
      you back,
    and you shall stand before me.
  If you utter what is precious, and not
      what is worthless,
    you shall serve as my mouth.
  It is they who will turn to you,
    not you who will turn to them.
20 And I will make you to this people
    a fortified wall of bronze;
  they will fight against you,
    but they shall not prevail over you,
  for I am with you
    to save you and deliver you,
              says the LORD.
21 I will deliver you out of the hand of
    the wicked,
  and redeem you from the grasp of
    the ruthless.

Jeremiah's Celibacy and Message

16 The word of the LORD came to me: 2 You shall not take a wife, nor shall you have sons or daughters in this place. 3 For thus says the LORD concerning the sons and daughters who are born in this place, and concerning the mothers who bear them and the fathers who beget them in this land: 4 They shall die of deadly diseases. They shall not be lamented, nor shall they be buried; they shall become like dung on the surface of the ground. They shall perish by the sword and by famine, and their dead bodies shall become food for the birds of the air and for the wild animals of the earth.

5 For thus says the LORD: Do not enter the house of mourning, or go to lament, or bemoan them; for I have taken away my peace from this people, says the LORD, my steadfast love and mercy. 6 Both great and small shall die in this land; they shall not be buried, and no one shall lament for them; there shall be no gashing, no shaving of the head for them. 7 No one shall break bread *a* for the mourner, to offer comfort for the dead; nor shall anyone give them the cup of consolation to drink for their fathers or their mothers. 8 You shall not go into the house of feasting to sit with them, to eat and drink. 9 For thus says the LORD of hosts, the God of Israel: I am going to banish from this place, in your days and before your eyes, the voice of mirth and the voice of gladness, the voice of the bridegroom and the voice of the bride.

10 And when you tell this people all these words, and they say to you, 'Why has the LORD pronounced all this great evil against us? What is our iniquity? What is the sin that we have committed against the LORD our God?' 11 then you shall say to them: It is because your ancestors have forsaken me, says the LORD, and have gone after other gods and have served and worshipped them, and have forsaken me and have not kept my law; 12 and because you have behaved worse than your ancestors, for here you are, every one of you, following your stubborn, evil will, refusing to listen to me. 13 Therefore I will hurl you out of this land into a land that neither you nor your ancestors have known, and there you shall serve other gods day and night, for I will show you no favour.

God Will Restore Israel

14 Therefore, the days are surely coming, says the LORD, when it shall no longer be said, 'As the LORD lives who brought the people of Israel up out of the land of Egypt', 15 but 'As the LORD lives who brought the people of Israel up out of the land of the north and out of all the lands where he had driven them.' For I will bring them back to their own land that I gave to their ancestors.

16 I am now sending for many fishermen, says the LORD, and they shall catch them; and afterwards I will send for many hunters, and they shall hunt them from every mountain and every hill, and out of the clefts of the rocks. 17 For my eyes are on all their ways; they are not hidden from my presence, nor is their iniquity concealed from my sight. 18 And *b* I will doubly repay their iniquity and their sin, because they have polluted my land with the carcasses of their detestable idols, and have filled my inheritance with their abominations.

a Two Mss Gk: MT *break for them*   *b* Gk: Heb *And first*

19 O LORD, my strength and my
        stronghold,
    my refuge on the day of trouble,
  to you shall the nations come
      from the ends of the earth and say:
  Our ancestors have inherited nothing
        but lies,
      worthless things in which there is
        no profit.
20 Can mortals make for themselves
        gods?
      Such are no gods!

  21 Therefore I am surely going to teach
them, this time I am going to teach them
my power and my might, and they shall
know that my name is the LORD.'

Judah's Sin and Punishment

17 The sin of Judah is written with an
       iron pen; with a diamond point it
is engraved on the tablet of their hearts,
and on the horns of their altars, 2 while
their children remember their altars and
their sacred poles, a beside every green tree,
and on the high hills, 3 on the mountains
in the open country. Your wealth and all
your treasures I will give for spoil as the
price of your sin b throughout all your territory. 4 By your own act you shall lose the
heritage that I gave you, and I will make
you serve your enemies in a land that you
do not know, for in my anger a fire is kindled c that shall burn for ever.

5 Thus says the LORD:
  Cursed are those who trust in
        mere mortals
      and make mere flesh their strength,
    whose hearts turn away from
        the LORD.
6 They shall be like a shrub in
        the desert,
      and shall not see when relief
        comes.
    They shall live in the parched places
        of the wilderness,
      in an uninhabited salt land.

7 Blessed are those who trust in
        the LORD,

    whose trust is the LORD.
8 They shall be like a tree planted
        by water,
      sending out its roots by the stream.
    It shall not fear when heat comes,
      and its leaves shall stay green;
    in the year of drought it is
        not anxious,
      and it does not cease to bear fruit.

9 The heart is devious above all else;
      it is perverse—
        who can understand it?
10 I the LORD test the mind
      and search the heart,
    to give to all according to their ways,
      according to the fruit of
        their doings.

11 Like the partridge hatching what
        it did not lay,
      so are all who amass wealth
        unjustly;
    in mid-life it will leave them,
      and at their end they will prove to
        be fools.

12 O glorious throne, exalted from the
        beginning,
      shrine of our sanctuary!
13 O hope of Israel! O LORD!
    All who forsake you shall be put to
        shame;
    those who turn away from you d shall
        be recorded in the underworld, e
    for they have forsaken the fountain
        of living water, the LORD.

Jeremiah Prays for Vindication

14 Heal me, O LORD, and I shall
        be healed;
      save me, and I shall be saved;
        for you are my praise.
15 See how they say to me,
      'Where is the word of the LORD?
        Let it come!'
16 But I have not run away from being a
        shepherd f in your service,

a Heb *Asherim*   b Cn: Heb *spoil your high places for sin*
c Two Mss Theodotion: *you kindled*   d Heb *me*
e Or *in the earth*   f Meaning of Heb uncertain

nor have I desired the fatal day.
You know what came from my lips;
   it was before your face.
17 Do not become a terror to me;
   you are my refuge on the day
      of disaster;
18 Let my persecutors be shamed,
   but do not let me be shamed;
let them be dismayed,
   but do not let me be dismayed;
bring on them the day of disaster;
   destroy them with double
      destruction!

Hallow the Sabbath Day

19 Thus said the LORD to me: Go and stand in the People's Gate, by which the kings of Judah enter and by which they go out, and in all the gates of Jerusalem, 20 and say to them: Hear the word of the LORD, you kings of Judah, and all Judah, and all the inhabitants of Jerusalem, who enter by these gates. 21 Thus says the LORD: For the sake of your lives, take care that you do not bear a burden on the sabbath day or bring it in by the gates of Jerusalem. 22 And do not carry a burden out of your houses on the sabbath or do any work, but keep the sabbath day holy, as I commanded your ancestors. 23 Yet they did not listen or incline their ear; they stiffened their necks and would not hear or receive instruction.

24 But if you listen to me, says the LORD, and bring in no burden by the gates of this city on the sabbath day, but keep the sabbath day holy and do no work on it, 25 then there shall enter by the gates of this city kings*a* who sit on the throne of David, riding in chariots and on horses, they and their officials, the people of Judah and the inhabitants of Jerusalem; and this city shall be inhabited for ever. 26 And people shall come from the towns of Judah and the places around Jerusalem, from the land of Benjamin, from the Shephelah, from the hill country, and from the Negeb, bringing burnt-offerings and sacrifices, grain-offerings and frankincense, and bringing thank-offerings to the house of the LORD. 27 But if you do not listen to me, to keep the sab-

bath day holy, and to carry in no burden through the gates of Jerusalem on the sabbath day, then I will kindle a fire in its gates; it shall devour the palaces of Jerusalem and shall not be quenched.

The Potter and the Clay

18 The word that came to Jeremiah from the LORD: 2 'Come, go down to the potter's house, and there I will let you hear my words.' 3 So I went down to the potter's house, and there he was working at his wheel. 4 The vessel he was making of clay was spoiled in the potter's hand, and he reworked it into another vessel, as seemed good to him.

5 Then the word of the LORD came to me: 6 Can I not do with you, O house of Israel, just as this potter has done? says the LORD. Just like the clay in the potter's hand, so are you in my hand, O house of Israel. 7 At one moment I may declare concerning a nation or a kingdom, that I will pluck up and break down and destroy it, 8 but if that nation, concerning which I have spoken, turns from its evil, I will change my mind about the disaster that I intended to bring on it. 9 And at another moment I may declare concerning a nation or a kingdom that I will build and plant it, 10 but if it does evil in my sight, not listening to my voice, then I will change my mind about the good that I had intended to do to it. 11 Now, therefore, say to the people of Judah and the inhabitants of Jerusalem: Thus says the LORD: Look, I am a potter shaping evil against you and devising a plan against you. Turn now, all of you from your evil way, and amend your ways and your doings.

Israel's Stubborn Idolatry

12 But they say, 'It is no use! We will follow our own plans, and each of us will act according to the stubbornness of our evil will.'

13 Therefore, thus says the LORD:
   Ask among the nations:
      Who has heard the like of this?

---

a Cn: Heb *kings and officials*

The virgin Israel has done
   a most horrible thing.
[14] Does the snow of Lebanon leave
   the crags of Sirion?[a]
Do the mountain[b] waters run dry,[c]
   the cold flowing streams?
[15] But my people have forgotten me,
   they burn offerings to a delusion;
they have stumbled[d] in their ways,
   in the ancient roads,
and have gone into bypaths,
   not the highway,
[16] making their land a horror,
   a thing to be hissed at for ever.
All who pass by it are horrified
   and shake their heads.
[17] Like the wind from the east,
   I will scatter them before
      the enemy.
I will show them my back, not
   my face,
on the day of their calamity.

A Plot against Jeremiah

18 Then they said, 'Come, let us make plots against Jeremiah—for instruction shall not perish from the priest, nor counsel from the wise, nor the word from the prophet. Come, let us bring charges against him,[e] and let us not heed any of his words.'

[19] Give heed to me, O LORD,
   and listen to what my adversaries
      say!
[20] Is evil a recompense for good?
   Yet they have dug a pit for my life.
Remember how I stood before you
   to speak good for them,
   to turn away your wrath
      from them.
[21] Therefore give their children over to
   famine;
   hurl them out to the power of
      the sword,
let their wives become childless and
   widowed.
May their men meet death by
   pestilence,
their youths be slain by the sword
   in battle.

[22] May a cry be heard from their
   houses,
when you bring the marauder
   suddenly upon them!
For they have dug a pit to catch me,
   and laid snares for my feet.
[23] Yet you, O LORD, know
   all their plotting to kill me.
Do not forgive their iniquity,
   do not blot out their sin from your
      sight.
Let them be tripped up before you;
   deal with them while you are angry.

The Broken Earthenware Jug

19 Thus said the LORD: Go and buy a potter's earthenware jug. Take with you[f] some of the elders of the people and some of the senior priests, [2] and go out to the valley of the son of Hinnom at the entry of the Potsherd Gate, and proclaim there the words that I tell you. [3] You shall say: Hear the word of the LORD, O kings of Judah and inhabitants of Jerusalem. Thus says the LORD of hosts, the God of Israel: I am going to bring such disaster upon this place that the ears of everyone who hears of it will tingle. [4] Because the people have forsaken me, and have profaned this place by making offerings in it to other gods whom neither they nor their ancestors nor the kings of Judah have known, and because they have filled this place with the blood of the innocent, [5] and gone on building the high places of Baal to burn their children in the fire as burnt-offerings to Baal, which I did not command or decree, nor did it enter my mind; [6] therefore the days are surely coming, says the LORD, when this place shall no more be called Topheth, or the valley of the son of Hinnom, but the valley of Slaughter. [7] And in this place I will make void the plans of Judah and Jerusalem, and will make them fall by the sword before their enemies, and by the hand of those who seek their life. I will give their dead bodies for food to the birds of the air and to the wild animals of the

a Cn: Heb *of the field*   *b* Cn: Heb *foreign*   *c* Cn: Heb *Are . . . plucked up?*   *d* Gk Syr Vg: Heb *they made them stumble*   *e* Heb *strike him with the tongue*   *f* Syr Tg Compare Gk: Heb lacks *take with you* earth. 8 And I will make this city a horror, a thing to be hissed at; everyone who passes by it will be horrified and will hiss because of all its disasters. 9 And I will make them eat the flesh of their sons and the flesh of their daughters, and all shall eat the flesh of their neighbours in the siege, and in the distress with which their enemies and those who seek their life afflict them.

10 Then you shall break the jug in the sight of those who go with you, 11 and shall say to them: Thus says the LORD of hosts: So will I break this people and this city, as one breaks a potter's vessel, so that it can never be mended. In Topheth they shall bury until there is no more room to bury. 12 Thus will I do to this place, says the LORD, and to its inhabitants, making this city like Topheth. 13 And the houses of Jerusalem and the houses of the kings of Judah shall be defiled like the place of Topheth— all the houses upon whose roofs offerings have been made to the whole host of heaven, and libations have been poured out to other gods.

14 When Jeremiah came from Topheth, where the LORD had sent him to prophesy, he stood in the court of the LORD's house and said to all the people: 15 Thus says the LORD of hosts, the God of Israel: I am now bringing upon this city and upon all its towns all the disaster that I have pronounced against it, because they have stiffened their necks, refusing to hear my words.

Jeremiah Persecuted by Pashhur

20 Now the priest Pashhur son of Immer, who was chief officer in the house of the LORD, heard Jeremiah prophesying these things. 2 Then Pashhur struck the prophet Jeremiah, and put him in the stocks that were in the upper Benjamin Gate of the house of the LORD. 3 The next morning when Pashhur released Jeremiah from the stocks, Jeremiah said to him, The LORD has named you not Pashhur but 'Terror-all-around.' 4 For thus says the LORD: I am making you a terror to yourself and to all your friends; and they shall fall by the sword of their enemies while you look on.

And I will give all Judah into the hand of the king of Babylon; he shall carry them captive to Babylon, and shall kill them with the sword. 5 I will give all the wealth of this city, all its gains, all its prized belongings, and all the treasures of the kings of Judah into the hand of their enemies, who shall plunder them, and seize them, and carry them to Babylon. 6 And you, Pashhur, and all who live in your house, shall go into captivity, and to Babylon you shall go; there you shall die, and there you shall be buried, you and all your friends, to whom you have prophesied falsely.

Jeremiah Denounces His Persecutors

7 O LORD, you have enticed me,
    and I was enticed;
you have overpowered me,
    and you have prevailed.
I have become a laughing-stock all
        day long;
    everyone mocks me.
8 For whenever I speak, I must cry out,
    I must shout, 'Violence and
        destruction!'
For the word of the LORD has become
        for me
a reproach and derision all
        day long.
9 If I say, 'I will not mention him,
    or speak any more in his name',
then within me there is something
        like a burning fire
    shut up in my bones;
I am weary with holding it in,
    and I cannot.
10 For I hear many whispering:
    'Terror is all around!
Denounce him! Let us denounce
        him!'
    All my close friends
    are watching for me to stumble.
'Perhaps he can be enticed,
    and we can prevail against him,
    and take our revenge on him.'
11 But the LORD is with me like a dread
        warrior;
    therefore my persecutors will
        stumble,
    and they will not prevail.

They will be greatly shamed,
   for they will not succeed.
Their eternal dishonour
   will never be forgotten.
12 O LORD of hosts, you test the
     righteous,
   you see the heart and the mind;
let me see your retribution
     upon them,
   for to you I have committed
     my cause.

13 Sing to the LORD;
   praise the LORD!
For he has delivered the life of
     the needy
   from the hands of evildoers.

14 Cursed be the day
   on which I was born!
The day when my mother bore me,
   let it not be blessed!
15 Cursed be the man
   who brought the news to my father,
     saying,
'A child is born to you, a son',
   making him very glad.
16 Let that man be like the cities
   that the LORD overthrew
     without pity;
   let him hear a cry in the morning
   and an alarm at noon,
17 because he did not kill me in
     the womb;
   so my mother would have been my
     grave,
   and her womb for ever great.
18 Why did I come forth from the womb
   to see toil and sorrow,
   and spend my days in shame?

Jerusalem Will Fall to Nebuchadrezzar

21 This is the word that came to Jeremiah from the LORD, when King Zedekiah sent to him Pashhur son of Malchiah and the priest Zephaniah son of Maaseiah, saying, 2 'Please inquire of the LORD on our behalf, for King Nebuchadrezzar of Babylon is making war against us; perhaps the LORD will perform a wonderful deed for us, as he has often done, and will make him withdraw from us.'

3 Then Jeremiah said to them: 4 Thus you shall say to Zedekiah: Thus says the LORD, the God of Israel: I am going to turn back the weapons of war that are in your hands and with which you are fighting against the king of Babylon and against the Chaldeans who are besieging you outside the walls; and I will bring them together into the centre of this city. 5 I myself will fight against you with outstretched hand and mighty arm, in anger, in fury, and in great wrath. 6 And I will strike down the inhabitants of this city, both human beings and animals; they shall die of a great pestilence. 7 Afterwards, says the LORD, I will give King Zedekiah of Judah, and his servants, and the people in this city—those who survive the pestilence, sword, and famine—into the hands of King Nebuchadrezzar of Babylon, into the hands of their enemies, into the hands of those who seek their lives. He shall strike them down with the edge of the sword; he shall not pity them, or spare them, or have compassion.

8 And to this people you shall say: Thus says the LORD: See, I am setting before you the way of life and the way of death. 9 Those who stay in this city shall die by the sword, by famine, and by pestilence; but those who go out and surrender to the Chaldeans who are besieging you shall live and shall have their lives as a prize of war. 10 For I have set my face against this city for evil and not for good, says the LORD: it shall be given into the hands of the king of Babylon, and he shall burn it with fire.

Message to the House of David

11 To the house of the king of Judah say: Hear the word of the LORD, 12 O house of David! Thus says the LORD:

Execute justice in the morning,
   and deliver from the hand of the
     oppressor
   anyone who has been robbed,
or else my wrath will go forth
     like fire,

and burn, with no one to
　　quench it,
　because of your evil doings.

13 See, I am against you, O inhabitant of
　　the valley,
　O rock of the plain,
　　　　　　　　　　says the LORD;
　you who say, 'Who can come down
　　　against us,
　or who can enter our places
　　of refuge?'
14 I will punish you according to the
　　fruit of your doings,
　　　　　　　　　　says the LORD;
　I will kindle a fire in its forest,
　and it shall devour all that is
　　around it.

Exhortation to Repent

22 Thus says the LORD: Go down to
the house of the king of Judah,
and speak there this word, 2 and say: Hear
the word of the LORD, O King of Judah sitting on the throne of David—you, and
your servants, and your people who enter
these gates. 3 Thus says the LORD: Act with
justice and righteousness, and deliver from
the hand of the oppressor anyone who has
been robbed. And do no wrong or violence
to the alien, the orphan, and the widow,
nor shed innocent blood in this place. 4 For
if you will indeed obey this word, then
through the gates of this house shall enter
kings who sit on the throne of David, riding in chariots and on horses, they, and
their servants, and their people. 5 But if you
will not heed these words, I swear by myself, says the LORD, that this house shall become a desolation. 6 For thus says the LORD
concerning the house of the king of Judah:

　You are like Gilead to me,
　　like the summit of Lebanon;
　but I swear that I will make you
　　a desert,
　an uninhabited city. a
7 I will prepare destroyers against you,
　all with their weapons;
　they shall cut down your choicest
　　cedars
　and cast them into the fire.

8 And many nations will pass by this
city, and all of them will say one to another, 'Why has the LORD dealt in this way with
that great city?' 9 And they will answer, 'Because they abandoned the covenant of the
LORD their God, and worshipped other
gods and served them.'

10 Do not weep for him who is dead,
　　nor bemoan him;
　weep rather for him who goes away,
　　for he shall return no more
　　to see his native land.

Message to the Sons of Josiah

11 For thus says the LORD concerning
Shallum son of King Josiah of Judah, who
succeeded his father Josiah, and who went
away from this place: He shall return here
no more, 12 but in the place where they
have carried him captive he shall die, and
he shall never see this land again.

13 Woe to him who builds his house by
　　unrighteousness,
　and his upper rooms by injustice;
　who makes his neighbours work for
　　nothing,
　and does not give them their wages;
14 who says, 'I will build myself a
　　spacious house
　with large upper rooms',
　and who cuts out windows for it,
　　panelling it with cedar,
　and painting it with vermilion.
15 Are you a king
　　because you compete in cedar?
　Did not your father eat and drink
　　and do justice and righteousness?
　Then it was well with him.
16 He judged the cause of the poor
　　and needy;
　　then it was well.
　Is not this to know me?
　　says the LORD.
17 But your eyes and heart
　　are only on your dishonest gain,
　for shedding innocent blood,
　　and for practising oppression and
　　violence.

a Cn: Heb uninhabited cities

18 Therefore thus says the LORD concerning King Jehoiakim son of Josiah of Judah:

They shall not lament for him,
saying,
'Alas, my brother!' or 'Alas, sister!'
They shall not lament for him,
saying,
'Alas, lord!' or 'Alas, his majesty!'
19 With the burial of a donkey he shall
be buried—
dragged off and thrown out beyond
the gates of Jerusalem.

20 Go up to Lebanon, and cry out,
and lift up your voice in Bashan;
cry out from Abarim,
for all your lovers are crushed.
21 I spoke to you in your prosperity,
but you said, 'I will not listen.'
This has been your way from
your youth,
for you have not obeyed my voice.
22 The wind shall shepherd all your
shepherds,
and your lovers shall go into
captivity;
then you will be ashamed and
dismayed
because of all your wickedness.
23 O inhabitant of Lebanon,
nested among the cedars,
how you will groan*a* when pangs
come upon you,
pain as of a woman in labour!

Judgement on Coniah (Jehoiachin)

24 As I live, says the LORD, even if King Coniah son of Jehoiakim of Judah were the signet ring on my right hand, even from there I would tear you off 25 and give you into the hands of those who seek your life, into the hands of those of whom you are afraid, even into the hands of King Nebuchadrezzar of Babylon and into the hands of the Chaldeans. 26 I will hurl you and the mother who bore you into another country, where you were not born, and there you shall die. 27 But they shall not return to the land to which they long to return.

28 Is this man Coniah a despised broken
pot,
a vessel no one wants?
Why are he and his offspring hurled
out
and cast away in a land that they do
not know?
29 O land, land, land,
hear the word of the LORD!
30 Thus says the LORD:
Record this man as childless,
a man who shall not succeed in his
days;
for none of his offspring shall
succeed
in sitting on the throne of David,
and ruling again in Judah.

Restoration after Exile

23 Woe to the shepherds who destroy and scatter the sheep of my pasture! says the LORD. 2 Therefore, thus says the LORD, the God of Israel, concerning the shepherds who shepherd my people: It is you who have scattered my flock, and have driven them away, and you have not attended to them. So I will attend to you for your evil doings, says the LORD. 3 Then I myself will gather the remnant of my flock out of all the lands where I have driven them, and I will bring them back to their fold, and they shall be fruitful and multiply. 4 I will raise up shepherds over them who will shepherd them, and they shall not fear any longer, or be dismayed, nor shall any be missing, says the LORD.

The Righteous Branch of David

5 The days are surely coming, says the LORD, when I will raise up for David a righteous Branch, and he shall reign as king and deal wisely, and shall execute justice and righteousness in the land. 6 In his days Judah will be saved and Israel will live in safety. And this is the name by which he will be called: 'The LORD is our righteousness.'

7 Therefore, the days are surely coming, says the LORD, when it shall no longer be said, 'As the LORD lives who brought the

a Gk Vg Syr: Heb *will be pitied*

people of Israel up out of the land of Egypt', [8] but 'As the LORD lives who brought out and led the offspring of the house of Israel out of the land of the north and out of all the lands where he[a] had driven them.' Then they shall live in their own land.

False Prophets of Hope Denounced

9　Concerning the prophets:
My heart is crushed within me,
　all my bones shake;
I have become like a drunkard,
　like one overcome by wine,
because of the LORD
　and because of his holy words.
[10] For the land is full of adulterers;
　because of the curse the land
　　mourns,
　and the pastures of the wilderness
　　are dried up.
Their course has been evil,
　and their might is not right.
[11] Both prophet and priest are ungodly;
　even in my house I have found
　　their wickedness,
　　　　　　　　　says the LORD.
[12] Therefore their way shall be to them
　like slippery paths in the darkness,
　into which they shall be driven and
　　fall;
for I will bring disaster upon them
　in the year of their punishment,
　　　　　　　　　says the LORD.
[13] In the prophets of Samaria
　I saw a disgusting thing:
they prophesied by Baal
　and led my people Israel astray.
[14] But in the prophets of Jerusalem
　I have seen a more shocking thing:
they commit adultery and walk
　　in lies;
　they strengthen the hands of
　　evildoers,
　so that no one turns from
　　wickedness;
all of them have become like Sodom
　　to me,
　and its inhabitants like Gomorrah.
[15] Therefore thus says the LORD of hosts
　concerning the prophets:

'I am going to make them eat
　wormwood,
　and give them poisoned water
　　to drink;
for from the prophets of Jerusalem
　ungodliness has spread throughout
　　the land.'

16　Thus says the LORD of hosts: Do not listen to the words of the prophets who prophesy to you; they are deluding you. They speak visions of their own minds, not from the mouth of the LORD. [17] They keep saying to those who despise the word of the LORD, 'It shall be well with you'; and to all who stubbornly follow their own stubborn hearts, they say, 'No calamity shall come upon you.'

[18] For who has stood in the council of
　　the LORD
　so as to see and to hear his word?
　Who has given heed to his word so
　　as to proclaim it?
[19] Look, the storm of the LORD!
　Wrath has gone forth,
a whirling tempest;
　it will burst upon the head of
　　the wicked.
[20] The anger of the LORD will not
　　turn back
　until he has executed and
　　accomplished
　the intents of his mind.
In the latter days you will understand
　it clearly.

[21] I did not send the prophets,
　yet they ran;
I did not speak to them,
　yet they prophesied.
[22] But if they had stood in my council,
　then they would have proclaimed
　　my words to my people,
and they would have turned them
　　from their evil way,
　and from the evil of their doings.

23　Am I a God near by, says the LORD, and not a God far off? [24] Who can hide in

a　Gk: Heb I

secret places so that I cannot see them? says the LORD. Do I not fill heaven and earth? says the LORD. 25 I have heard what the prophets have said who prophesy lies in my name, saying, 'I have dreamed, I have dreamed!' 26 How long? Will the hearts of the prophets ever turn back— those who prophesy lies, and who prophesy the deceit of their own heart? 27 They plan to make my people forget my name by their dreams that they tell one another, just as their ancestors forgot my name for Baal. 28 Let the prophet who has a dream tell the dream, but let the one who has my word speak my word faithfully. What has straw in common with wheat? says the LORD. 29 Is not my word like fire, says the LORD, and like a hammer that breaks a rock in pieces? 30 See, therefore, I am against the prophets, says the LORD, who steal my words from one another. 31 See, I am against the prophets, says the LORD, who use their own tongues and say, 'Says the LORD.' 32 See, I am against those who prophesy lying dreams, says the LORD, and who tell them, and who lead my people astray by their lies and their recklessness, when I did not send them or appoint them; so they do not profit this people at all, says the LORD.

33 When this people, or a prophet, or a priest asks you, 'What is the burden of the LORD?' you shall say to them, 'You are the burden,[a] and I will cast you off, says the LORD.' 34 And as for the prophet, priest, or the people who say, 'The burden of the LORD', I will punish them and their households. 35 Thus shall you say to one another, among yourselves, 'What has the LORD answered?' or 'What has the LORD spoken?' 36 But 'the burden of the LORD' you shall mention no more, for the burden is everyone's own word, and so you pervert the words of the living God, the LORD of hosts, our God. 37 Thus you shall ask the prophet, 'What has the LORD answered you?' or 'What has the LORD spoken?' 38 But if you say, 'the burden of the LORD', thus says the LORD: Because you have said these words, 'the burden of the LORD', when I sent to you, saying, You shall not say, 'the burden

of the LORD', 39 therefore, I will surely lift you up[b] and cast you away from my presence, you and the city that I gave to you and your ancestors. 40 And I will bring upon you everlasting disgrace and perpetual shame, which shall not be forgotten.

The Good and the Bad Figs

24 The LORD showed me two baskets of figs placed before the temple of the LORD. This was after King Nebuchadrezzar of Babylon had taken into exile from Jerusalem King Jeconiah son of Jehoiakim of Judah, together with the officials of Judah, the artisans, and the smiths, and had brought them to Babylon. 2 One basket had very good figs, like first-ripe figs, but the other basket had very bad figs, so bad that they could not be eaten. 3 And the LORD said to me, 'What do you see, Jeremiah?' I said, 'Figs, the good figs very good, and the bad figs very bad, so bad that they cannot be eaten.'

4 Then the word of the LORD came to me: 5 Thus says the LORD, the God of Israel: Like these good figs, so I will regard as good the exiles from Judah, whom I have sent away from this place to the land of the Chaldeans. 6 I will set my eyes upon them for good, and I will bring them back to this land. I will build them up, and not tear them down; I will plant them, and not pluck them up. 7 I will give them a heart to know that I am the LORD; and they shall be my people and I will be their God, for they shall return to me with their whole heart.

8 But thus says the LORD: Like the bad figs that are so bad they cannot be eaten, so will I treat King Zedekiah of Judah, his officials, the remnant of Jerusalem who remain in this land, and those who live in the land of Egypt. 9 I will make them a horror, an evil thing, to all the kingdoms of the earth—a disgrace, a byword, a taunt, and a curse in all the places where I shall drive them. 10 And I will send sword, famine, and pestilence upon them, until they are utterly destroyed from the land that I gave to them and their ancestors.

---

a Gk Vg: Heb *What burden*   *b* Heb Mss Gk Vg: MT *forget you*

The Babylonian Captivity Foretold

25 The word that came to Jeremiah concerning all the people of Judah, in the fourth year of King Jehoiakim son of Josiah of Judah (that was the first year of King Nebuchadrezzar of Babylon), ²which the prophet Jeremiah spoke to all the people of Judah and all the inhabitants of Jerusalem: ³For twenty-three years, from the thirteenth year of King Josiah son of Amon of Judah to this day, the word of the LORD has come to me, and I have spoken persistently to you, but you have not listened. ⁴And though the LORD persistently sent you all his servants the prophets, you have neither listened nor inclined your ears to hear ⁵when they said, 'Turn now, everyone of you, from your evil way and wicked doings, and you will remain upon the land that the LORD has given to you and your ancestors from of old and for ever; ⁶do not go after other gods to serve and worship them, and do not provoke me to anger with the work of your hands. Then I will do you no harm.' ⁷Yet you did not listen to me, says the LORD, and so you have provoked me to anger with the work of your hands to your own harm.

8 Therefore thus says the LORD of hosts: Because you have not obeyed my words, ⁹I am going to send for all the tribes of the north, says the LORD, even for King Nebuchadrezzar of Babylon, my servant, and I will bring them against this land and its inhabitants, and against all these nations around; I will utterly destroy them, and make them an object of horror and of hissing, and an everlasting disgrace.*ᵃ* ¹⁰And I will banish from them the sound of mirth and the sound of gladness, the voice of the bridegroom and the voice of the bride, the sound of the millstones and the light of the lamp. ¹¹This whole land shall become a ruin and a waste, and these nations shall serve the king of Babylon for seventy years. ¹²Then after seventy years are completed, I will punish the king of Babylon and that nation, the land of the Chaldeans, for their iniquity, says the LORD, making the land an everlasting waste. ¹³I will bring upon that land all the words that I have uttered against it, everything written in this book, which Jeremiah prophesied against all the nations. ¹⁴For many nations and great kings shall make slaves of them also; and I will repay them according to their deeds and the work of their hands.

The Cup of God's Wrath

15 For thus the LORD, the God of Israel, said to me: Take from my hand this cup of the wine of wrath, and make all the nations to whom I send you drink it. ¹⁶They shall drink and stagger and go out of their minds because of the sword that I am sending among them.

17 So I took the cup from the LORD's hand, and made all the nations to whom the LORD sent me drink it: ¹⁸Jerusalem and the towns of Judah, its kings and officials, to make them a desolation and a waste, an object of hissing and of cursing, as they are today; ¹⁹Pharaoh king of Egypt, his servants, his officials, and all his people; ²⁰all the mixed people;*ᵇ* all the kings of the land of Uz; all the kings of the land of the Philistines—Ashkelon, Gaza, Ekron, and the remnant of Ashdod; ²¹Edom, Moab, and the Ammonites; ²²all the kings of Tyre, all the kings of Sidon, and the kings of the coastland across the sea; ²³Dedan, Tema, Buz, and all who have shaven temples; ²⁴all the kings of Arabia and all the kings of the mixed peoples*ᵇ* that live in the desert; ²⁵all the kings of Zimri, all the kings of Elam, and all the kings of Media; ²⁶all the kings of the north, far and near, one after another, and all the kingdoms of the world that are on the face of the earth. And after them the king of Sheshach*ᶜ* shall drink.

27 Then you shall say to them, Thus says the LORD of hosts, the God of Israel: Drink, get drunk and vomit, fall and rise no more, because of the sword that I am sending among you.

28 And if they refuse to accept the cup from your hand to drink, then you shall say to them: Thus says the LORD of hosts:

a Gk Compare Syr: Heb *and everlasting desolations*
b Meaning of Heb uncertain   *c* *Sheshach* is a cryptogram for *Babel*, Babylon

You must drink! 29 See, I am beginning to bring disaster on the city that is called by my name, and how can you possibly avoid punishment? You shall not go unpunished, for I am summoning a sword against all the inhabitants of the earth, says the LORD of hosts.

30 You, therefore, shall prophesy against them all these words, and say to them:

The LORD will roar from on high,
    and from his holy habitation utter
        his voice;
he will roar mightily against his fold,
    and shout, like those who tread
        grapes,
    against all the inhabitants of
        the earth.
31 The clamour will resound to the ends
        of the earth,
    for the LORD has an indictment
        against the nations;
he is entering into judgement with all
        flesh,
    and the guilty he will put to
        the sword,
                                    says the LORD.

32 Thus says the LORD of hosts:
    See, disaster is spreading
        from nation to nation,
    and a great tempest is stirring
        from the farthest parts of the earth!

33 Those slain by the LORD on that day shall extend from one end of the earth to the other. They shall not be lamented, or gathered, or buried; they shall become dung on the surface of the ground.

34 Wail, you shepherds, and cry out;
    roll in ashes, you lords of the flock,
    for the days of your slaughter have
        come—and your dispersions, *a*
    and you shall fall like a
        choice vessel.
35 Flight shall fail the shepherds,
    and there shall be no escape for the
        lords of the flock.
36 Hark! the cry of the shepherds,
    and the wail of the lords of
        the flock!

For the LORD is despoiling their
        pasture,
37   and the peaceful folds are
        devastated,
    because of the fierce anger of
        the LORD.
38 Like a lion he has left his covert;
    for their land has become a waste
because of the cruel sword,
    and because of his fierce anger.

Jeremiah's Prophecies in the Temple

26 At the beginning of the reign of King Jehoiakim son of Josiah of Judah, this word came from the LORD: 2 Thus says the LORD: Stand in the court of the LORD's house, and speak to all the cities of Judah that come to worship in the house of the LORD; speak to them all the words that I command you; do not hold back a word. 3 It may be that they will listen, all of them, and will turn from their evil way, that I may change my mind about the disaster that I intend to bring on them because of their evil doings. 4 You shall say to them: Thus says the LORD: If you will not listen to me, to walk in my law that I have set before you, 5 and to heed the words of my servants the prophets whom I send to you urgently—though you have not heeded— 6 then I will make this house like Shiloh, and I will make this city a curse for all the nations of the earth.

7 The priests and the prophets and all the people heard Jeremiah speaking these words in the house of the LORD. 8 And when Jeremiah had finished speaking all that the LORD had commanded him to speak to all the people, then the priests and the prophets and all the people laid hold of him, saying, 'You shall die! 9 Why have you prophesied in the name of the LORD, saying, "This house shall be like Shiloh, and this city shall be desolate, without inhabitant"?' And all the people gathered around Jeremiah in the house of the LORD.

10 When the officials of Judah heard these things, they came up from the king's house to the house of the LORD and took their seat in the entry of the New Gate of

a Meaning of Heb uncertain

the house of the LORD. [11] Then the priests and the prophets said to the officials and to all the people, 'This man deserves the sentence of death because he has prophesied against this city, as you have heard with your own ears.'

12 Then Jeremiah spoke to all the officials and all the people, saying, 'It is the LORD who sent me to prophesy against this house and this city all the words you have heard. [13] Now therefore amend your ways and your doings, and obey the voice of the LORD your God, and the LORD will change his mind about the disaster that he has pronounced against you. [14] But as for me, here I am in your hands. Do with me as seems good and right to you. [15] Only know for certain that if you put me to death, you will be bringing innocent blood upon yourselves and upon this city and its inhabitants, for in truth the LORD sent me to you to speak all these words in your ears.'

16 Then the officials and all the people said to the priests and the prophets, 'This man does not deserve the sentence of death, for he has spoken to us in the name of the LORD our God.' [17] And some of the elders of the land arose and said to all the assembled people, [18] 'Micah of Moresheth, who prophesied during the days of King Hezekiah of Judah, said to all the people of Judah: "Thus says the LORD of hosts,

Zion shall be ploughed as a field;
    Jerusalem shall become a heap
        of ruins,
    and the mountain of the house a
        wooded height."

[19] Did King Hezekiah of Judah and all Judah actually put him to death? Did he not fear the LORD and entreat the favour of the LORD, and did not the LORD change his mind about the disaster that he had pronounced against them? But we are about to bring great disaster on ourselves!'

20 There was another man prophesying in the name of the LORD, Uriah son of Shemaiah from Kiriath-jearim. He prophesied against this city and against this land in words exactly like those of Jeremiah. [21] And when King Jehoiakim, with all his warriors and all the officials, heard his words, the king sought to put him to death; but when Uriah heard of it, he was afraid and fled and escaped to Egypt. [22] Then King Jehoiakim sent[a] Elnathan son of Achbor and men with him to Egypt, [23] and they took Uriah from Egypt and brought him to King Jehoiakim, who struck him down with the sword and threw his dead body into the burial place of the common people.

24 But the hand of Ahikam son of Shaphan was with Jeremiah so that he was not given over into the hands of the people to be put to death.

The Sign of the Yoke

27 In the beginning of the reign of King Zedekiah[b] son of Josiah of Judah, this word came to Jeremiah from the LORD. [2] Thus the LORD said to me: Make yourself a yoke of straps and bars, and put them on your neck. [3] Send word[c] to the king of Edom, the king of Moab, the king of the Ammonites, the king of Tyre, and the king of Sidon by the hand of the envoys who have come to Jerusalem to King Zedekiah of Judah. [4] Give them this charge for their masters: Thus says the LORD of hosts, the God of Israel: This is what you shall say to your masters: [5] It is I who by my great power and my outstretched arm have made the earth, with the people and animals that are on the earth, and I give it to whomsoever I please. [6] Now I have given all these lands into the hand of King Nebuchadnezzar of Babylon, my servant, and I have given him even the wild animals of the field to serve him. [7] All the nations shall serve him and his son and his grandson, until the time of his own land comes; then many nations and great kings shall make him their slave.

8 But if any nation or kingdom will not serve this king, Nebuchadnezzar of Babylon, and put its neck under the yoke of the king of Babylon, then I will punish that nation with the sword, with famine, and with pestilence, says the LORD, until I have completed its[d] destruction by his hand. [9] You, therefore, must not listen to your

a Heb adds men to Egypt   b Another reading is Jehoiakim   c Cn: Heb send them   d Heb their prophets, your diviners, your dreamers,[a] your soothsayers, or your sorcerers, who are saying to you, 'You shall not serve the king of Babylon.' 10 For they are prophesying a lie to you, with the result that you will be removed far from your land; I will drive you out, and you will perish. 11 But any nation that will bring its neck under the yoke of the king of Babylon and serve him, I will leave on its own land, says the LORD, to till it and live there.

12 I spoke to King Zedekiah of Judah in the same way: Bring your necks under the yoke of the king of Babylon, and serve him and his people, and live. 13 Why should you and your people die by the sword, by famine, and by pestilence, as the LORD has spoken concerning any nation that will not serve the king of Babylon? 14 Do not listen to the words of the prophets who are telling you not to serve the king of Babylon, for they are prophesying a lie to you. 15 I have not sent them, says the LORD, but they are prophesying falsely in my name, with the result that I will drive you out and you will perish, you and the prophets who are prophesying to you.

16 Then I spoke to the priests and to all this people, saying, Thus says the LORD: Do not listen to the words of your prophets who are prophesying to you, saying, 'The vessels of the LORD's house will soon be brought back from Babylon', for they are prophesying a lie to you. 17 Do not listen to them; serve the king of Babylon and live. Why should this city become a desolation? 18 If indeed they are prophets, and if the word of the LORD is with them, then let them intercede with the LORD of hosts, that the vessels left in the house of the LORD, in the house of the king of Judah, and in Jerusalem may not go to Babylon. 19 For thus says the LORD of hosts concerning the pillars, the sea, the stands, and the rest of the vessels that are left in this city, 20 which King Nebuchadnezzar of Babylon did not take away when he took into exile from Jerusalem to Babylon King Jeconiah son of Jehoiakim of Judah, and all the nobles of Judah and Jerusalem— 21 thus says the LORD of hosts, the God of Israel, concern-

ing the vessels left in the house of the LORD, in the house of the king of Judah, and in Jerusalem: 22 They shall be carried to Babylon, and there they shall stay, until the day when I give attention to them, says the LORD. Then I will bring them up and restore them to this place.

Hananiah Opposes Jeremiah and Dies

28 In that same year, at the beginning of the reign of King Zedekiah of Judah, in the fifth month of the fourth year, the prophet Hananiah son of Azzur, from Gibeon, spoke to me in the house of the LORD, in the presence of the priests and all the people, saying, 2 Thus says the LORD of hosts, the God of Israel: I have broken the yoke of the king of Babylon. 3 Within two years I will bring back to this place all the vessels of the LORD's house, which King Nebuchadnezzar of Babylon took away from this place and carried to Babylon. 4 I will also bring back to this place King Jeconiah son of Jehoiakim of Judah, and all the exiles from Judah who went to Babylon, says the LORD, for I will break the yoke of the king of Babylon.'

5 Then the prophet Jeremiah spoke to the prophet Hananiah in the presence of the priests and all the people who were standing in the house of the LORD; 6 and the prophet Jeremiah said, 'Amen! May the LORD do so; may the LORD fulfil the words that you have prophesied, and bring back to this place from Babylon the vessels of the house of the LORD, and all the exiles. 7 But listen now to this word that I speak in your hearing and in the hearing of all the people. 8 The prophets who preceded you and me from ancient times prophesied war, famine, and pestilence against many countries and great kingdoms. 9 As for the prophet who prophesies peace, when the word of that prophet comes true, then it will be known that the LORD has truly sent the prophet.'

10 Then the prophet Hananiah took the yoke from the neck of the prophet Jeremiah, and broke it. 11 And Hananiah spoke in the presence of all the people, saying, 'Thus

a Gk Syr Vg: Heb dreams

says the LORD: This is how I will break the yoke of King Nebuchadnezzar of Babylon from the neck of all the nations within two years.' At this, the prophet Jeremiah went his way.

12 Some time after the prophet Hananiah had broken the yoke from the neck of the prophet Jeremiah, the word of the LORD came to Jeremiah: 13 Go, tell Hananiah, Thus says the LORD: You have broken wooden bars only to forge iron bars in place of them! 14 For thus says the LORD of hosts, the God of Israel: I have put an iron yoke on the neck of all these nations so that they may serve King Nebuchadnezzar of Babylon, and they shall indeed serve him; I have even given him the wild animals. 15 And the prophet Jeremiah said to the prophet Hananiah, 'Listen, Hananiah, the LORD has not sent you, and you made this people trust in a lie. 16 Therefore thus says the LORD: I am going to send you off the face of the earth. Within this year you will be dead, because you have spoken rebellion against the LORD.'

17 In that same year, in the seventh month, the prophet Hananiah died.

Jeremiah's Letter to the Exiles in Babylon

29 These are the words of the letter that the prophet Jeremiah sent from Jerusalem to the remaining elders among the exiles, and to the priests, the prophets, and all the people, whom Nebuchadnezzar had taken into exile from Jerusalem to Babylon. 2 This was after King Jeconiah, and the queen mother, the court officials, the leaders of Judah and Jerusalem, the artisans, and the smiths had departed from Jerusalem. 3 The letter was sent by the hand of Elasah son of Shaphan and Gemariah son of Hilkiah, whom King Zedekiah of Judah sent to Babylon to King Nebuchadnezzar of Babylon. It said: 4 Thus says the LORD of hosts, the God of Israel, to all the exiles whom I have sent into exile from Jerusalem to Babylon: 5 Build houses and live in them; plant gardens and eat what they produce. 6 Take wives and have sons and daughters; take wives for your sons, and give your daughters in marriage,

that they may bear sons and daughters; multiply there, and do not decrease. 7 But seek the welfare of the city where I have sent you into exile, and pray to the LORD on its behalf, for in its welfare you will find your welfare. 8 For thus says the LORD of hosts, the God of Israel: Do not let the prophets and the diviners who are among you deceive you, and do not listen to the dreams that they dream,*a* 9 for it is a lie that they are prophesying to you in my name; I did not send them, says the LORD.

10 For thus says the LORD: Only when Babylon's seventy years are completed will I visit you, and I will fulfil to you my promise and bring you back to this place. 11 For surely I know the plans I have for you, says the LORD, plans for your welfare and not for harm, to give you a future with hope. 12 Then when you call upon me and come and pray to me, I will hear you. 13 When you search for me, you will find me; if you seek me with all your heart, 14 I will let you find me, says the LORD, and I will restore your fortunes and gather you from all the nations and all the places where I have driven you, says the LORD, and I will bring you back to the place from which I sent you into exile.

15 Because you have said, 'The LORD has raised up prophets for us in Babylon'— 16 thus says the LORD concerning the king who sits on the throne of David, and concerning all the people who live in this city, your kinsfolk who did not go out with you into exile: 17 Thus says the LORD of hosts, I am going to let loose on them sword, famine, and pestilence, and I will make them like rotten figs that are so bad they cannot be eaten. 18 I will pursue them with the sword, with famine, and with pestilence, and will make them a horror to all the kingdoms of the earth, to be an object of cursing, and horror, and hissing, and a derision among all the nations where I have driven them, 19 because they did not heed my words, says the LORD, when I persistently sent to you my servants the prophets, but they*b* would not listen, says

a Cn: Heb *your dreams that you cause to dream*
b Syr: Heb *you*

the Lord. 20 But now, all you exiles whom I sent away from Jerusalem to Babylon, hear the word of the Lord: 21 Thus says the Lord of hosts, the God of Israel, concerning Ahab son of Kolaiah and Zedekiah son of Maaseiah, who are prophesying a lie to you in my name: I am going to deliver them into the hand of King Nebuchadrezzar of Babylon, and he shall kill them before your eyes. 22 And on account of them this curse shall be used by all the exiles from Judah in Babylon: 'The Lord make you like Zedekiah and Ahab, whom the king of Babylon roasted in the fire', 23 because they have perpetrated outrage in Israel and have committed adultery with their neighbours' wives, and have spoken in my name lying words that I did not command them; I am the one who knows and bears witness, says the Lord.

The Letter of Shemaiah

24 To Shemaiah of Nehelam you shall say: 25 Thus says the Lord of hosts, the God of Israel: In your own name you sent a letter to all the people who are in Jerusalem, and to the priest Zephaniah son of Maaseiah, and to all the priests, saying, 26 The Lord himself has made you priest instead of the priest Jehoiada, so that there may be officers in the house of the Lord to control any madman who plays the prophet, to put him in the stocks and the collar. 27 So now why have you not rebuked Jeremiah of Anathoth who plays the prophet for you? 28 For he has actually sent to us in Babylon, saying, 'It will be a long time; build houses and live in them, and plant gardens and eat what they produce.' 29 The priest Zephaniah read this letter in the hearing of the prophet Jeremiah. 30 Then the word of the Lord came to Jeremiah: 31 Send to all the exiles, saying, Thus says the Lord concerning Shemaiah of Nehelam: Because Shemaiah has prophesied to you, though I did not send him, and has led you to trust in a lie, 32 therefore thus says the Lord: I am going to punish Shemaiah of Nehelam and his descendants; he shall not have anyone living among this people to see *a* the good that I am going to

do to my people, says the Lord, for he has spoken rebellion against the Lord.

Restoration Promised for Israel and Judah

30 The word that came to Jeremiah from the Lord: 2 Thus says the Lord, the God of Israel: Write in a book all the words that I have spoken to you. 3 For the days are surely coming, says the Lord, when I will restore the fortunes of my people, Israel and Judah, says the Lord, and I will bring them back to the land that I gave to their ancestors and they shall take possession of it.

4 These are the words that the Lord spoke concerning Israel and Judah:

5 Thus says the Lord:
We have heard a cry of panic,
    of terror, and no peace.
6 Ask now, and see,
    can a man bear a child?
Why then do I see every man
    with his hands on his loins like a
        woman in labour?
Why has every face turned pale?
7 Alas! that day is so great
    there is none like it;
it is a time of distress for Jacob;
    yet he shall be rescued from it.

8 On that day, says the Lord of hosts, I will break the yoke from off his *b* neck, and I will burst his *b* bonds, and strangers shall no more make a servant of him. 9 But they shall serve the Lord their God and David their king, whom I will raise up for them.

10 But as for you, have no fear, my
        servant Jacob, says the Lord,
    and do not be dismayed, O Israel;
for I am going to save you from
        far away,
    and your offspring from the land of
        their captivity.
Jacob shall return and have quiet and
        ease,
    and no one shall make him afraid.
11 For I am with you, says the Lord, to
        save you;
    I will make an end of all the nations
        among which I scattered you,

a Gk: Heb *and he shall not see*   *b* Cn: Heb *your*

but of you I will not make an end.
I will chastise you in just measure,
  and I will by no means leave you
    unpunished.

12 For thus says the LORD:
Your hurt is incurable,
  your wound is grievous.
13 There is no one to uphold your cause,
  no medicine for your wound,
  no healing for you.
14 All your lovers have forgotten you;
  they care nothing for you;
for I have dealt you the blow of
    an enemy,
  the punishment of a merciless foe,
because your guilt is great,
  because your sins are so numerous.
15 Why do you cry out over your hurt?
Your pain is incurable.
Because your guilt is great,
  because your sins are so numerous,
  I have done these things to you.
16 Therefore all who devour you shall
    be devoured,
  and all your foes, every one of
    them, shall go into captivity;
those who plunder you shall be
    plundered,
  and all who prey on you I will
    make a prey.
17 For I will restore health to you,
  and your wounds I will heal,
                 says the LORD,
because they have called you
    an outcast:
  'It is Zion; no one cares for her!'

18 Thus says the LORD:
I am going to restore the fortunes of
    the tents of Jacob,
  and have compassion on his
    dwellings;
the city shall be rebuilt upon its
    mound,
  and the citadel set on its
    rightful site.
19 Out of them shall come thanksgiving,
  and the sound of merrymakers.
I will make them many, and they
    shall not be few;

I will make them honoured, and
  they shall not be disdained.
20 Their children shall be as of old,
  their congregation shall be
    established before me;
  and I will punish all who oppress
    them.
21 Their prince shall be one of
    their own,
  their ruler shall come from their
    midst;
I will bring him near, and he shall
    approach me,
  for who would otherwise dare to
    approach me?
                    says the LORD.
22 And you shall be my people,
  and I will be your God.

23 Look, the storm of the LORD!
  Wrath has gone forth,
a whirling[a] tempest;
  it will burst upon the head of
    the wicked.
24 The fierce anger of the LORD will not
    turn back
  until he has executed and
    accomplished
  the intents of his mind.
In the latter days you will understand
    this.

The Joyful Return of the Exiles

31 At that time, says the LORD, I will be
   the God of all the families of Israel,
and they shall be my people.
2 Thus says the LORD:
The people who survived the sword
    found grace in the wilderness;
  when Israel sought for rest,
3   the LORD appeared to him[b] from far
    away.[c]
I have loved you with an everlasting
    love;
  therefore I have continued my
    faithfulness to you.
4 Again I will build you, and you shall
    be built,
  O virgin Israel!

a One Ms: Meaning of MT uncertain   b Gk: Heb me
c Or to him long ago

Again you shall take[a] your
    tambourines,
    and go forth in the dance of the
      merrymakers.
5 Again you shall plant vineyards
    on the mountains of Samaria;
the planters shall plant,
    and shall enjoy the fruit.
6 For there shall be a day when
      sentinels will call
    in the hill country of Ephraim:
'Come, let us go up to Zion,
    to the LORD our God.'

7 For thus says the LORD:
Sing aloud with gladness for Jacob,
    and raise shouts for the chief of the
      nations;
proclaim, give praise, and say,
    'Save, O LORD, your people,
    the remnant of Israel.'
8 See, I am going to bring them from
      the land of the north,
    and gather them from the farthest
      parts of the earth,
among them the blind and the lame,
    those with child and those in
      labour, together;
    a great company, they shall return
      here.
9 With weeping they shall come,
    and with consolations[b] I will lead
      them back,
I will let them walk by brooks of
      water,
    in a straight path in which they
      shall not stumble;
for I have become a father to Israel,
    and Ephraim is my firstborn.

10 Hear the word of the LORD,
      O nations,
    and declare it in the coastlands far
      away;
say, 'He who scattered Israel will
      gather him,
    and will keep him as a shepherd a
      flock.'
11 For the LORD has ransomed Jacob,
    and has redeemed him from hands
      too strong for him.

12 They shall come and sing aloud on
      the height of Zion,
    and they shall be radiant over the
      goodness of the LORD,
over the grain, the wine, and the oil,
    and over the young of the flock and
      the herd;
their life shall become like a watered
      garden,
    and they shall never languish again.
13 Then shall the young women rejoice
      in the dance,
    and the young men and the old
      shall be merry.
I will turn their mourning into joy,
    I will comfort them, and give them
      gladness for sorrow.
14 I will give the priests their fill of
      fatness,
    and my people shall be satisfied
      with my bounty,
                says the LORD.

15 Thus says the LORD:
A voice is heard in Ramah,
    lamentation and bitter weeping.
Rachel is weeping for her children;
    she refuses to be comforted for her
      children,
    because they are no more.
16 Thus says the LORD:
Keep your voice from weeping,
    and your eyes from tears;
for there is a reward for your work,
                says the LORD:
    they shall come back from the land
      of the enemy;
17 there is hope for your future,
                says the LORD:
    your children shall come back to
      their own country.

18 Indeed I heard Ephraim pleading:
'You disciplined me, and I took the
      discipline;
    I was like a calf untrained.
Bring me back, let me come back,
    for you are the LORD my God.

a Or *adorn yourself with*   b Gk Compare Vg Tg: Heb
supplications

¹⁹ For after I had turned away I
    repented;
  and after I was discovered, I struck
    my thigh;
  I was ashamed, and I was dismayed
    because I bore the disgrace of my
    youth.'
²⁰ Is Ephraim my dear son?
  Is he the child I delight in?
  As often as I speak against him,
    I still remember him.
  Therefore I am deeply moved
    for him;
  I will surely have mercy on him,
                says the LORD.

²¹ Set up road markers for yourself,
  make yourself signposts;
  consider well the highway,
    the road by which you went.
  Return, O virgin Israel,
    return to these your cities.
²² How long will you waver,
  O faithless daughter?
  For the LORD has created a new thing
    on the earth:
  a woman encompasses*a man.*

23 Thus says the LORD of hosts, the God
of Israel: Once more they shall use these
words in the land of Judah and in its towns
when I restore their fortunes:
  'The LORD bless you, O abode of
    righteousness,
    O holy hill!'
²⁴ And Judah and all its towns shall live
there together, and the farmers and those
who wander*b* with their flocks.
²⁵ I will satisfy the weary,
    and all who are faint I will
      replenish.
26 Thereupon I awoke and looked, and
my sleep was pleasant to me.

Individual Retribution

27 The days are surely coming, says the
LORD, when I will sow the house of Israel
and the house of Judah with the seed of
humans and the seed of animals. ²⁸ And
just as I have watched over them to pluck
up and break down, to overthrow, destroy,

and bring evil, so I will watch over them to
build and to plant, says the LORD. ²⁹ In
those days they shall no longer say:
  'The parents have eaten sour grapes,
    and the children's teeth are set on
    edge.'
³⁰ But all shall die for their own sins; the
teeth of everyone who eats sour grapes
shall be set on edge.

A New Covenant

31 The days are surely coming, says the
LORD, when I will make a new covenant
with the house of Israel and the house of
Judah. ³² It will not be like the covenant
that I made with their ancestors when I
took them by the hand to bring them out
of the land of Egypt—a covenant that they
broke, though I was their husband,*c* says
the LORD. ³³ But this is the covenant that I
will make with the house of Israel after
those days, says the LORD: I will put my law
within them, and I will write it on their
hearts; and I will be their God, and they
shall be my people. ³⁴ No longer shall they
teach one another, or say to each other,
'Know the LORD', for they shall all know
me, from the least of them to the greatest,
says the LORD; for I will forgive their iniquity, and remember their sin no more.

³⁵ Thus says the LORD,
  who gives the sun for light by day
    and the fixed order of the moon
      and the stars for light by night,
  who stirs up the sea so that its waves
    roar—
  the LORD of hosts is his name:
³⁶ If this fixed order were ever to cease
    from my presence, says the LORD,
  then also the offspring of Israel
    would cease
    to be a nation before me for ever.

³⁷ Thus says the LORD:
  If the heavens above can be
    measured,
    and the foundations of the earth
    below can be explored,

a Meaning of Heb uncertain   *b* Cn Compare Syr Vg
Tg: Heb *and they shall wander*   *c* Or *master*

then I will reject all the offspring
of Israel
because of all they have done,
says the LORD.

Jerusalem to Be Enlarged

38 The days are surely coming, says the LORD, when the city shall be rebuilt for the LORD from the tower of Hananel to the Corner Gate. 39 And the measuring line shall go out farther, straight to the hill Gareb, and shall then turn to Goah. 40 The whole valley of the dead bodies and the ashes, and all the fields as far as the Wadi Kidron, to the corner of the Horse Gate towards the east, shall be sacred to the LORD. It shall never again be uprooted or overthrown.

Jeremiah Buys a Field During the Siege

32 The word that came to Jeremiah from the LORD in the tenth year of King Zedekiah of Judah, which was the eighteenth year of Nebuchadrezzar. 2 At that time the army of the king of Babylon was besieging Jerusalem, and the prophet Jeremiah was confined in the court of the guard that was in the palace of the king of Judah, 3 where King Zedekiah of Judah had confined him. Zedekiah had said, 'Why do you prophesy and say: Thus says the LORD: I am going to give this city into the hand of the king of Babylon, and he shall take it; 4 King Zedekiah of Judah shall not escape out of the hands of the Chaldeans, but shall surely be given into the hands of the king of Babylon, and shall speak with him face to face and see him eye to eye; 5 and he shall take Zedekiah to Babylon, and there he shall remain until I attend to him, says the LORD; though you fight against the Chaldeans, you shall not succeed?'

6 Jeremiah said, The word of the LORD came to me: 7 Hanamel son of your uncle Shallum is going to come to you and say, 'Buy my field that is at Anathoth, for the right of redemption by purchase is yours.' 8 Then my cousin Hanamel came to me in the court of the guard, in accordance with the word of the LORD, and said to me, 'Buy my field that is at Anathoth in the land of Benjamin, for the right of possession and redemption is yours; buy it for yourself.' Then I knew that this was the word of the LORD.

9 And I bought the field at Anathoth from my cousin Hanamel, and weighed out the money to him, seventeen shekels of silver. 10 I signed the deed, sealed it, got witnesses, and weighed the money on scales. 11 Then I took the sealed deed of purchase, containing the terms and conditions, and the open copy; 12 and I gave the deed of purchase to Baruch son of Neriah son of Mahseiah, in the presence of my cousin Hanamel, in the presence of the witnesses who signed the deed of purchase, and in the presence of all the Judeans who were sitting in the court of the guard. 13 In their presence I charged Baruch, saying, 14 Thus says the LORD of hosts, the God of Israel: Take these deeds, both this sealed deed of purchase and this open deed, and put them in an earthenware jar, in order that they may last for a long time. 15 For thus says the LORD of hosts, the God of Israel: Houses and fields and vineyards shall again be bought in this land.

Jeremiah Prays for Understanding

16 After I had given the deed of purchase to Baruch son of Neriah, I prayed to the LORD, saying: 17 Ah Lord GOD! It is you who made the heavens and the earth by your great power and by your outstretched arm! Nothing is too hard for you. 18 You show steadfast love to the thousandth generation,[a] but repay the guilt of parents into the laps of their children after them, O great and mighty God whose name is the LORD of hosts, 19 great in counsel and mighty in deed; whose eyes are open to all the ways of mortals, rewarding all according to their ways and according to the fruit of their doings. 20 You showed signs and wonders in the land of Egypt, and to this day in Israel and among all humankind, and have made yourself a name that continues to this very day. 21 You brought your people Israel out of the land of Egypt with signs and wonders, with a strong hand and

a Or to thousands

outstretched arm, and with great terror; [22] and you gave them this land, which you swore to their ancestors to give them, a land flowing with milk and honey; [23] and they entered and took possession of it. But they did not obey your voice or follow your law; of all you commanded them to do, they did nothing. Therefore you have made all these disasters come upon them. [24] See, the siege-ramps have been cast up against the city to take it, and the city, faced with sword, famine, and pestilence, has been given into the hands of the Chaldeans who are fighting against it. What you spoke has happened, as you yourself can see. [25] Yet you, O Lord GOD, have said to me, 'Buy the field for money and get witnesses'—though the city has been given into the hands of the Chaldeans.

God's Assurance of the People's Return

26 The word of the LORD came to Jeremiah: [27] See, I am the LORD, the God of all flesh; is anything too hard for me? [28] Therefore, thus says the LORD: I am going to give this city into the hands of the Chaldeans and into the hand of King Nebuchadrezzar of Babylon, and he shall take it. [29] The Chaldeans who are fighting against this city shall come, set it on fire, and burn it, with the houses on whose roofs offerings have been made to Baal and libations have been poured out to other gods, to provoke me to anger. [30] For the people of Israel and the people of Judah have done nothing but evil in my sight from their youth; the people of Israel have done nothing but provoke me to anger by the work of their hands, says the LORD. [31] This city has aroused my anger and wrath, from the day it was built until this day, so that I will remove it from my sight [32] because of all the evil of the people of Israel and the people of Judah that they did to provoke me to anger—they, their kings and their officials, their priests and their prophets, the citizens of Judah and the inhabitants of Jerusalem. [33] They have turned their backs to me, not their faces; though I have taught them persistently, they would not listen

and accept correction. [34] They set up their abominations in the house that bears my name, and defiled it. [35] They built the high places of Baal in the valley of the son of Hinnom, to offer up their sons and daughters to Molech, though I did not command them, nor did it enter my mind that they should do this abomination, causing Judah to sin.

36 Now therefore, thus says the LORD, the God of Israel, concerning this city of which you say, 'It is being given into the hand of the king of Babylon by the sword, by famine, and by pestilence': [37] See, I am going to gather them from all the lands to which I drove them in my anger and my wrath and in great indignation; I will bring them back to this place, and I will settle them in safety. [38] They shall be my people, and I will be their God. [39] I will give them one heart and one way, that they may fear me for all time, for their own good and the good of their children after them. [40] I will make an everlasting covenant with them, never to draw back from doing good to them; and I will put the fear of me in their hearts, so that they may not turn from me. [41] I will rejoice in doing good to them, and I will plant them in this land in faithfulness, with all my heart and all my soul.

42 For thus says the LORD: Just as I have brought all this great disaster upon this people, so I will bring upon them all the good fortune that I now promise them. [43] Fields shall be bought in this land of which you are saying, It is a desolation, without human beings or animals; it has been given into the hands of the Chaldeans. [44] Fields shall be bought for money, and deeds shall be signed and sealed and witnessed, in the land of Benjamin, in the places around Jerusalem, and in the cities of Judah, of the hill country, of the Shephelah, and of the Negeb; for I will restore their fortunes, says the LORD.

Healing after Punishment

33 The word of the LORD came to Jeremiah a second time, while he was still confined in the court of the guard: [2] Thus says the LORD who made the

earth,[a] the LORD who formed it to establish it—the LORD is his name: 3 Call to me and I will answer you, and will tell you great and hidden things that you have not known. 4 For thus says the LORD, the God of Israel, concerning the houses of this city and the houses of the kings of Judah that were torn down to make a defence against the siege-ramps and before the sword:[b] 5 The Chaldeans are coming in to fight[c] and to fill them with the dead bodies of those whom I shall strike down in my anger and my wrath, for I have hidden my face from this city because of all their wickedness. 6 I am going to bring it recovery and healing; I will heal them and reveal to them abundance[b] of prosperity and security. 7 I will restore the fortunes of Judah and the fortunes of Israel, and rebuild them as they were at first. 8 I will cleanse them from all the guilt of their sin against me, and I will forgive all the guilt of their sin and rebellion against me. 9 And this city[d] shall be to me a name of joy, a praise and a glory before all the nations of the earth who shall hear of all the good that I do for them; they shall fear and tremble because of all the good and all the prosperity I provide for it.

10 Thus says the LORD: In this place of which you say, 'It is a waste without human beings or animals', in the towns of Judah and the streets of Jerusalem that are desolate, without inhabitants, human or animal, there shall once more be heard 11 the voice of mirth and the voice of gladness, the voice of the bridegroom and the voice of the bride, the voices of those who sing, as they bring thank-offerings to the house of the LORD:

'Give thanks to the LORD of hosts,
    for the LORD is good,
    for his steadfast love endures for
        ever!'

For I will restore the fortunes of the land as at first, says the LORD.

12 Thus says the LORD of hosts: In this place that is waste, without human beings or animals, and in all its towns there shall again be pasture for shepherds resting their flocks. 13 In the towns of the hill country, of the Shephelah, and of the Negeb, in the land of Benjamin, the places around Jerusalem, and in the towns of Judah, flocks shall again pass under the hands of the one who counts them, says the LORD.

The Righteous Branch and the Covenant with David

14 The days are surely coming, says the LORD, when I will fulfil the promise I made to the house of Israel and the house of Judah. 15 In those days and at that time I will cause a righteous Branch to spring up for David; and he shall execute justice and righteousness in the land. 16 In those days Judah will be saved and Jerusalem will live in safety. And this is the name by which it will be called: 'The LORD is our righteousness.'

17 For thus says the LORD: David shall never lack a man to sit on the throne of the house of Israel, 18 and the levitical priests shall never lack a man in my presence to offer burnt-offerings, to make grain-offerings, and to make sacrifices for all time.

19 The word of the LORD came to Jeremiah: 20 Thus says the LORD: If any of you could break my covenant with the day and my covenant with the night, so that day and night would not come at their appointed time, 21 only then could my covenant with my servant David be broken, so that he would not have a son to reign on his throne, and my covenant with my ministers the Levites. 22 Just as the host of heaven cannot be numbered and the sands of the sea cannot be measured, so I will increase the offspring of my servant David, and the Levites who minister to me.

23 The word of the LORD came to Jeremiah: 24 Have you not observed how these people say, 'The two families that the LORD chose have been rejected by him', and how they hold my people in such contempt that they no longer regard them as a nation? 25 Thus says the LORD: Only if I had not established my covenant with day and night and the ordinances of heaven and earth, 26 would I reject the offspring of Jacob and

a Gk: Heb it   b Meaning of Heb uncertain
c Cn: Heb They are coming in to fight against the
Chaldeans   d Heb And it

of my servant David and not choose any of his descendants as rulers over the offspring of Abraham, Isaac, and Jacob. For I will restore their fortunes, and will have mercy upon them.

Death in Captivity Predicted for Zedekiah

34 The word that came to Jeremiah from the LORD, when King Nebuchadrezzar of Babylon and all his army and all the kingdoms of the earth and all the peoples under his dominion were fighting against Jerusalem and all its cities: 2 Thus says the LORD, the God of Israel: Go and speak to King Zedekiah of Judah and say to him: Thus says the LORD: I am going to give this city into the hand of the king of Babylon, and he shall burn it with fire. 3 And you yourself shall not escape from his hand, but shall surely be captured and handed over to him; you shall see the king of Babylon eye to eye and speak with him face to face; and you shall go to Babylon. 4 Yet hear the word of the LORD, O King Zedekiah of Judah! Thus says the LORD concerning you: You shall not die by the sword; 5 you shall die in peace. And as spices were burned[a] for your ancestors, the earlier kings who preceded you, so they shall burn spices[b] for you and lament for you, saying, 'Alas, lord!' For I have spoken the word, says the LORD.

6 Then the prophet Jeremiah spoke all these words to Zedekiah king of Judah, in Jerusalem, 7 when the army of the king of Babylon was fighting against Jerusalem and against all the cities of Judah that were left, Lachish and Azekah; for these were the only fortified cities of Judah that remained.

Treacherous Treatment of Slaves

8 The word that came to Jeremiah from the LORD, after King Zedekiah had made a covenant with all the people in Jerusalem to make a proclamation of liberty to them— 9 that all should set free their Hebrew slaves, male and female, so that no one should hold another Judean in slavery. 10 And they obeyed, all the officials and all the people who had entered into the cov-

enant that all would set free their slaves, male or female, so that they would not be enslaved again; they obeyed and set them free. 11 But afterwards they turned about and took back the male and female slaves they had set free, and brought them again into subjection as slaves. 12 The word of the LORD came to Jeremiah from the LORD: 13 Thus says the LORD, the God of Israel: I myself made a covenant with your ancestors when I brought them out of the land of Egypt, out of the house of slavery, saying, 14 'Every seventh year each of you must set free any Hebrews who have been sold to you and have served you for six years; you must set them free from your service.' But your ancestors did not listen to me or incline their ears to me. 15 You yourselves recently repented and did what was right in my sight by proclaiming liberty to one another, and you made a covenant before me in the house that is called by my name; 16 but then you turned about and profaned my name when each of you took back your male and female slaves, whom you had set free according to their desire, and you brought them again into subjection to be your slaves. 17 Therefore, thus says the LORD: You have not obeyed me by granting a release to your neighbours and friends; I am going to grant a release to you, says the LORD—a release to the sword, to pestilence, and to famine. I will make you a horror to all the kingdoms of the earth. 18 And those who transgressed my covenant and did not keep the terms of the covenant that they made before me, I will make like[c] the calf when they cut it in two and passed between its parts: 19 the officials of Judah, the officials of Jerusalem, the eunuchs, the priests, and all the people of the land who passed between the parts of the calf 20 shall be handed over to their enemies and to those who seek their lives. Their corpses shall become food for the birds of the air and the wild animals of the earth. 21 And as for King Zedekiah of Judah and his officials, I will hand them over to their enemies and to those who seek their lives, to

---

a Heb *as there was burning*   *b* Heb *shall burn*
c Cn: Heb lacks *like*

the army of the king of Babylon, which has withdrawn from you. 22 I am going to command, says the LORD, and will bring them back to this city; and they will fight against it, and take it, and burn it with fire. The towns of Judah I will make a desolation without inhabitant.

The Rechabites Commended

35 The word that came to Jeremiah from the LORD in the days of King Jehoiakim son of Josiah of Judah: 2 Go to the house of the Rechabites, and speak with them, and bring them to the house of the LORD, into one of the chambers; then offer them wine to drink. 3 So I took Jaazaniah son of Jeremiah son of Habazziniah, and his brothers, and all his sons, and the whole house of the Rechabites. 4 I brought them to the house of the LORD into the chamber of the sons of Hanan son of Igdaliah, the man of God, which was near the chamber of the officials, above the chamber of Maaseiah son of Shallum, keeper of the threshold. 5 Then I set before the Rechabites pitchers full of wine, and cups; and I said to them, 'Have some wine.' 6 But they answered, 'We will drink no wine, for our ancestor Jonadab son of Rechab commanded us, "You shall never drink wine, neither you nor your children; 7 nor shall you ever build a house, or sow seed; nor shall you plant a vineyard, or even own one; but you shall live in tents all your days, that you may live many days in the land where you reside." 8 We have obeyed the charge of our ancestor Jonadab son of Rechab in all that he commanded us, to drink no wine all our days, ourselves, our wives, our sons, and our daughters, 9 and not to build houses to live in. We have no vineyard or field or seed; 10 but we have lived in tents, and have obeyed and done all that our ancestor Jonadab commanded us. 11 But when King Nebuchadrezzar of Babylon came up against the land, we said, "Come, and let us go to Jerusalem for fear of the army of the Chaldeans and the army of the Arameans." That is why we are living in Jerusalem.'

12 Then the word of the LORD came to Jeremiah: 13 Thus says the LORD of hosts, the God of Israel: Go and say to the people of Judah and the inhabitants of Jerusalem, Can you not learn a lesson and obey my words? says the LORD. 14 The command has been carried out that Jonadab son of Rechab gave to his descendants to drink no wine; and they drink none to this day, for they have obeyed their ancestor's command. But I myself have spoken to you persistently, and you have not obeyed me. 15 I have sent to you all my servants the prophets, sending them persistently, saying, 'Turn now everyone of you from your evil way, and amend your doings, and do not go after other gods to serve them, and then you shall live in the land that I gave to you and your ancestors.' But you did not incline your ear or obey me. 16 The descendants of Jonadab son of Rechab have carried out the command that their ancestor gave them, but this people has not obeyed me. 17 Therefore, thus says the LORD, the God of hosts, the God of Israel: I am going to bring on Judah and on all the inhabitants of Jerusalem every disaster that I have pronounced against them; because I have spoken to them and they have not listened, I have called to them and they have not answered.

18 But to the house of the Rechabites Jeremiah said: Thus says the LORD of hosts, the God of Israel: Because you have obeyed the command of your ancestor Jonadab, and kept all his precepts, and done all that he commanded you, 19 therefore thus says the LORD of hosts, the God of Israel: Jonadab son of Rechab shall not lack a descendant to stand before me for all time.

The Scroll Read in the Temple

36 In the fourth year of King Jehoiakim son of Josiah of Judah, this word came to Jeremiah from the LORD: 2 Take a scroll and write on it all the words that I have spoken to you against Israel and Judah and all the nations, from the day I spoke to you, from the days of Josiah until today. 3 It may be that when the house of Judah hears of all the disasters that I intend to do to them, all of them may turn from

their evil ways, so that I may forgive their iniquity and their sin.

4 Then Jeremiah called Baruch son of Neriah, and Baruch wrote on a scroll at Jeremiah's dictation all the words of the LORD that he had spoken to him. 5 And Jeremiah ordered Baruch, saying, 'I am prevented from entering the house of the LORD; 6 so you go yourself, and on a fast day in the hearing of the people in the LORD's house you shall read the words of the LORD from the scroll that you have written at my dictation. You shall read them also in the hearing of all the people of Judah who come up from their towns. 7 It may be that their plea will come before the LORD, and that all of them will turn from their evil ways, for great is the anger and wrath that the LORD has pronounced against this people.' 8 And Baruch son of Neriah did all that the prophet Jeremiah ordered him about reading from the scroll the words of the LORD in the LORD's house.

9 In the fifth year of King Jehoiakim son of Josiah of Judah, in the ninth month, all the people in Jerusalem and all the people who came from the towns of Judah to Jerusalem proclaimed a fast before the LORD. 10 Then, in the hearing of all the people, Baruch read the words of Jeremiah from the scroll, in the house of the LORD, in the chamber of Gemariah son of Shaphan the secretary, which was in the upper court, at the entry of the New Gate of the LORD's house.

The Scroll Read in the Palace

11 When Micaiah son of Gemariah son of Shaphan heard all the words of the LORD from the scroll, 12 he went down to the king's house, into the secretary's chamber; and all the officials were sitting there: Elishama the secretary, Delaiah son of Shemaiah, Elnathan son of Achbor, Gemariah son of Shaphan, Zedekiah son of Hananiah, and all the officials. 13 And Micaiah told them all the words that he had heard, when Baruch read the scroll in the hearing of the people. 14 Then all the officials sent Jehudi son of Nethaniah son of Shelemiah son of Cushi to say to Baruch, 'Bring the scroll that you read in the hearing of the people, and come.' So Baruch son of Neriah took the scroll in his hand and came to them. 15 And they said to him, 'Sit down and read it to us.' So Baruch read it to them. 16 When they heard all the words, they turned to one another in alarm, and said to Baruch, 'We certainly must report all these words to the king.' 17 Then they questioned Baruch, 'Tell us now, how did you write all these words? Was it at his dictation?' 18 Baruch answered them, 'He dictated all these words to me, and I wrote them with ink on the scroll.' 19 Then the officials said to Baruch, 'Go and hide, you and Jeremiah, and let no one know where you are.'

Jehoiakim Burns the Scroll

20 Leaving the scroll in the chamber of Elishama the secretary, they went to the court of the king; and they reported all the words to the king. 21 Then the king sent Jehudi to get the scroll, and he took it from the chamber of Elishama the secretary; and Jehudi read it to the king and all the officials who stood beside the king. 22 Now the king was sitting in his winter apartment (it was the ninth month), and there was a fire burning in the brazier before him. 23 As Jehudi read three or four columns, the king^a would cut them off with a penknife and throw them into the fire in the brazier, until the entire scroll was consumed in the fire that was in the brazier. 24 Yet neither the king, nor any of his servants who heard all these words, was alarmed, nor did they tear their garments. 25 Even when Elnathan and Delaiah and Gemariah urged the king not to burn the scroll, he would not listen to them. 26 And the king commanded Jerahmeel the king's son and Seraiah son of Azriel and Shelemiah son of Abdeel to arrest the secretary Baruch and the prophet Jeremiah. But the LORD hid them.

Jeremiah Dictates Another

27 Now, after the king had burned the scroll with the words that Baruch wrote at Jeremiah's dictation, the word of the LORD

a Heb he

came to Jeremiah: 28Take another scroll and write on it all the former words that were in the first scroll, which King Jehoiakim of Judah has burned. 29And concerning King Jehoiakim of Judah you shall say: Thus says the LORD, You have dared to burn this scroll, saying, Why have you written in it that the king of Babylon will certainly come and destroy this land, and will cut off from it human beings and animals? 30Therefore thus says the LORD concerning King Jehoiakim of Judah: He shall have no one to sit upon the throne of David, and his dead body shall be cast out to the heat by day and the frost by night. 31And I will punish him and his offspring and his servants for their iniquity; I will bring on them, and on the inhabitants of Jerusalem, and on the people of Judah, all the disasters with which I have threatened them— but they would not listen.

32 Then Jeremiah took another scroll and gave it to the secretary Baruch son of Neriah, who wrote on it at Jeremiah's dictation all the words of the scroll that King Jehoiakim of Judah had burned in the fire; and many similar words were added to them.

Zedekiah's Vain Hope

37 Zedekiah son of Josiah, whom King Nebuchadrezzar of Babylon made king in the land of Judah, succeeded Coniah son of Jehoiakim. 2But neither he nor his servants nor the people of the land listened to the words of the LORD that he spoke through the prophet Jeremiah.

3 King Zedekiah sent Jehucal son of Shelemiah and the priest Zephaniah son of Maaseiah to the prophet Jeremiah saying, 'Please pray for us to the LORD our God.' 4Now Jeremiah was still going in and out among the people, for he had not yet been put in prison. 5Meanwhile, the army of Pharaoh had come out of Egypt; and when the Chaldeans who were besieging Jerusalem heard news of them, they withdrew from Jerusalem.

6 Then the word of the LORD came to the prophet Jeremiah: 7Thus says the LORD, God of Israel: This is what the two of you shall say to the king of Judah, who sent you to me to inquire of me: Pharaoh's army, which set out to help you, is going to return to its own land, to Egypt. 8And the Chaldeans shall return and fight against this city; they shall take it and burn it with fire. 9Thus says the LORD: Do not deceive yourselves, saying, 'The Chaldeans will surely go away from us', for they will not go away. 10Even if you defeated the whole army of Chaldeans who are fighting against you, and there remained of them only wounded men in their tents, they would rise up and burn this city with fire.

Jeremiah Is Imprisoned

11 Now when the Chaldean army had withdrawn from Jerusalem at the approach of Pharaoh's army, 12Jeremiah set out from Jerusalem to go to the land of Benjamin to receive his share of property*a* among the people there. 13When he reached the Benjamin Gate, a sentinel there named Irijah son of Shelemiah son of Hananiah arrested the prophet Jeremiah, saying, 'You are deserting to the Chaldeans.' 14And Jeremiah said, 'That is a lie; I am not deserting to the Chaldeans.' But Irijah would not listen to him, and arrested Jeremiah and brought him to the officials. 15The officials were enraged at Jeremiah, and they beat him and imprisoned him in the house of the secretary Jonathan, for it had been made a prison. 16Thus Jeremiah was put in the cistern house, in the cells, and remained there for many days.

17 Then King Zedekiah sent for him, and received him. The king questioned him secretly in his house, and said, 'Is there any word from the LORD?' Jeremiah said, 'There is!' Then he said, 'You shall be handed over to the king of Babylon.' 18Jeremiah also said to King Zedekiah, 'What wrong have I done to you or your servants or this people, that you have put me in prison? 19Where are your prophets who prophesied to you, saying, "The king of Babylon will not come against you and against this land"? 20Now please hear me, my lord king: be good enough to listen to

a Meaning of Heb uncertain

my plea, and do not send me back to the house of the secretary Jonathan to die there.' 21 So King Zedekiah gave orders, and they committed Jeremiah to the court of the guard; and a loaf of bread was given him daily from the bakers' street, until all the bread of the city was gone. So Jeremiah remained in the court of the guard.

Jeremiah in the Cistern

38 Now Shephatiah son of Mattan, Gedaliah son of Pashhur, Jucal son of Shelemiah, and Pashhur son of Malchiah heard the words that Jeremiah was saying to all the people, 2 Thus says the LORD, Those who stay in this city shall die by the sword, by famine, and by pestilence; but those who go out to the Chaldeans shall live; they shall have their lives as a prize of war, and live. 3 Thus says the LORD, This city shall surely be handed over to the army of the king of Babylon and be taken. 4 Then the officials said to the king, 'This man ought to be put to death, because he is discouraging the soldiers who are left in this city, and all the people, by speaking such words to them. For this man is not seeking the welfare of this people, but their harm.' 5 King Zedekiah said, 'Here he is; he is in your hands; for the king is powerless against you.' 6 So they took Jeremiah and threw him into the cistern of Malchiah, the king's son, which was in the court of the guard, letting Jeremiah down by ropes. Now there was no water in the cistern, but only mud, and Jeremiah sank in the mud.

Jeremiah Is Rescued by Ebed-melech

7 Ebed-melech the Ethiopian, *a* a eunuch in the king's house, heard that they had put Jeremiah into the cistern. The king happened to be sitting at the Benjamin Gate, 8 So Ebed-melech left the king's house and spoke to the king, 9 'My lord king, these men have acted wickedly in all they did to the prophet Jeremiah by throwing him into the cistern to die there of hunger, for there is no bread left in the city.' 10 Then the king commanded Ebed-melech the Ethiopian, *a* 'Take three men with you from here, and pull the prophet Jeremiah up from the cis-

tern before he dies.' 11 So Ebed-melech took the men with him and went to the house of the king, to a wardrobe of *b* the storehouse, and took from there old rags and worn-out clothes, which he let down to Jeremiah in the cistern by ropes. 12 Then Ebed-melech the Ethiopian *a* said to Jeremiah, 'Just put the rags and clothes between your armpits and the ropes.' Jeremiah did so. 13 Then they drew Jeremiah up by the ropes and pulled him out of the cistern. And Jeremiah remained in the court of the guard.

Zedekiah Consults Jeremiah Again

14 King Zedekiah sent for the prophet Jeremiah and received him at the third entrance of the temple of the LORD. The king said to Jeremiah, 'I have something to ask you; do not hide anything from me.' 15 Jeremiah said to Zedekiah, 'If I tell you, you will put me to death, will you not? And if I give you advice, you will not listen to me.' 16 So King Zedekiah swore an oath in secret to Jeremiah, 'As the LORD lives, who gave us our lives, I will not put you to death or hand you over to these men who seek your life.'

17 Then Jeremiah said to Zedekiah, 'Thus says the LORD, the God of hosts, the God of Israel, If you will only surrender to the officials of the king of Babylon, then your life shall be spared, and this city shall not be burned with fire, and you and your house shall live. 18 But if you do not surrender to the officials of the king of Babylon, then this city shall be handed over to the Chaldeans, and they shall burn it with fire, and you yourself shall not escape from their hand.' 19 King Zedekiah said to Jeremiah, 'I am afraid of the Judeans who have deserted to the Chaldeans, for I might be handed over to them and they would abuse me.' 20 Jeremiah said, 'That will not happen. Just obey the voice of the LORD in what I say to you, and it shall go well with you, and your life shall be spared. 21 But if you are determined not to surrender, this is what the LORD has shown me— 22 a vision of all the women remaining in the house of the king of Judah being led out to

a Or *Nubian*; Heb *Cushite*   *b* Cn: Heb *to under*

the officials of the king of Babylon and saying,

"Your trusted friends have
    seduced you
  and have overcome you;
Now that your feet are stuck in
    the mud,
  they desert you."

23 All your wives and your children shall be led out to the Chaldeans, and you yourself shall not escape from their hand, but shall be seized by the king of Babylon; and this city shall be burned with fire.'

24 Then Zedekiah said to Jeremiah, 'Do not let anyone else know of this conversation, or you will die. 25 If the officials should hear that I have spoken with you, and they should come and say to you, "Just tell us what you said to the king; do not conceal it from us, or we will put you to death. What did the king say to you?" 26 then you shall say to them, "I was presenting my plea to the king not to send me back to the house of Jonathan to die there." ' 27 All the officials did come to Jeremiah and questioned him; and he answered them in the very words the king had commanded. So they stopped questioning him, for the conversation had not been overheard. 28 And Jeremiah remained in the court of the guard until the day that Jerusalem was taken.

The Fall of Jerusalem

39 In the ninth year of King Zedekiah of Judah, in the tenth month, King Nebuchadrezzar of Babylon and all his army came against Jerusalem and besieged it; 2 in the eleventh year of Zedekiah, in the fourth month, on the ninth day of the month, a breach was made in the city. 3 When Jerusalem was taken,[a] all the officials of the king of Babylon came and sat in the middle gate: Nergal-sharezer, Samgar-nebo, Sarsechim the Rabsaris, Nergal-sharezer the Rabmag, with all the rest of the officials of the king of Babylon. 4 When King Zedekiah of Judah and all the soldiers saw them, they fled, going out of the city at night by way of the king's garden through the gate between the two walls; and they

went towards the Arabah. 5 But the army of the Chaldeans pursued them, and overtook Zedekiah in the plains of Jericho; and when they had taken him, they brought him up to King Nebuchadrezzar of Babylon, at Riblah, in the land of Hamath; and he passed sentence on him. 6 The king of Babylon slaughtered the sons of Zedekiah at Riblah before his eyes; also the king of Babylon slaughtered all the nobles of Judah. 7 He put out the eyes of Zedekiah, and bound him in fetters to take him to Babylon. 8 The Chaldeans burned the king's house and the houses of the people, and broke down the walls of Jerusalem. 9 Then Nebuzaradan the captain of the guard exiled to Babylon the rest of the people who were left in the city, those who had deserted to him, and the people who remained. 10 Nebuzaradan the captain of the guard left in the land of Judah some of the poor people who owned nothing, and gave them vineyards and fields at the same time.

Jeremiah, Set Free, Remembers Ebed-melech

11 King Nebuchadrezzar of Babylon gave command concerning Jeremiah through Nebuzaradan, the captain of the guard, saying, 12 'Take him, look after him well and do him no harm, but deal with him as he may ask you.' 13 So Nebuzaradan the captain of the guard, Nebushazban the Rabsaris, Nergal-sharezer the Rabmag, and all the chief officers of the king of Babylon sent 14 and took Jeremiah from the court of the guard. They entrusted him to Gedaliah son of Ahikam son of Shaphan to be brought home. So he stayed with his own people.

15 The word of the Lord came to Jeremiah while he was confined in the court of the guard: 16 Go and say to Ebed-melech the Ethiopian:[b] Thus says the Lord of hosts, the God of Israel: I am going to fulfil my words against this city for evil and not for good, and they shall be accomplished in your presence on that day. 17 But I will save you on that day, says the Lord,

---

a This clause has been transposed from 38.28
b Or Nubian; Heb Cushite

and you shall not be handed over to those whom you dread. [18] For I will surely save you, and you shall not fall by the sword; but you shall have your life as a prize of war, because you have trusted in me, says the LORD.

Jeremiah with Gedaliah the Governor

40 The word that came to Jeremiah from the LORD after Nebuzaradan the captain of the guard had let him go from Ramah, when he took him bound in fetters along with all the captives of Jerusalem and Judah who were being exiled to Babylon. [2] The captain of the guard took Jeremiah and said to him, 'The LORD your God threatened this place with this disaster; [3] and now the LORD has brought it about, and has done as he said, because all of you sinned against the LORD and did not obey his voice. Therefore this thing has come upon you. [4] Now look, I have just released you today from the fetters on your hands. If you wish to come with me to Babylon, come, and I will take good care of you; but if you do not wish to come with me to Babylon, you need not come. See, the whole land is before you; go wherever you think it good and right to go. [5] If you remain, [a] then return to Gedaliah son of Ahikam son of Shaphan, whom the king of Babylon appointed governor of the towns of Judah, and stay with him among the people; or go wherever you think it right to go.' So the captain of the guard gave him an allowance of food and a present, and let him go. [6] Then Jeremiah went to Gedaliah son of Ahikam at Mizpah, and stayed with him among the people who were left in the land.

[7] When all the leaders of the forces in the open country and their troops heard that the king of Babylon had appointed Gedaliah son of Ahikam governor in the land, and had committed to him men, women, and children, those of the poorest of the land who had not been taken into exile to Babylon, [8] they went to Gedaliah at Mizpah—Ishmael son of Nethaniah, Johanan son of Kareah, Seraiah son of Tanhumeth, the sons of Ephai the Netopha-

thite, Jezaniah son of the Maacathite, they and their troops. [9] Gedaliah son of Ahikam son of Shaphan swore to them and their troops, saying, 'Do not be afraid to serve the Chaldeans. Stay in the land and serve the king of Babylon, and it shall go well with you. [10] As for me, I am staying at Mizpah to represent you before the Chaldeans who come to us; but as for you, gather wine and summer fruits and oil, and store them in your vessels, and live in the towns that you have taken over.' [11] Likewise, when all the Judeans who were in Moab and among the Ammonites and in Edom and in other lands heard that the king of Babylon had left a remnant in Judah and had appointed Gedaliah son of Ahikam son of Shaphan as governor over them, [12] then all the Judeans returned from all the places to which they had been scattered and came to the land of Judah, to Gedaliah at Mizpah; and they gathered wine and summer fruits in great abundance.

[13] Now Johanan son of Kareah and all the leaders of the forces in the open country came to Gedaliah at Mizpah [14] and said to him, 'Are you at all aware that Baalis king of the Ammonites has sent Ishmael son of Nethaniah to take your life?' But Gedaliah son of Ahikam would not believe them. [15] Then Johanan son of Kareah spoke secretly to Gedaliah at Mizpah, 'Please let me go and kill Ishmael son of Nethaniah, and no one else will know. Why should he take your life, so that all the Judeans who are gathered around you would be scattered, and the remnant of Judah would perish?' [16] But Gedaliah son of Ahikam said to Johanan son of Kareah, 'Do not do such a thing, for you are telling a lie about Ishmael.'

Insurrection against Gedaliah

41 In the seventh month, Ishmael son of Nethaniah son of Elishama, of the royal family, one of the chief officers of the king, came with ten men to Gedaliah son of Ahikam, at Mizpah. As they ate bread together there at Mizpah, [2] Ishmael son of Nethaniah and the ten men with

a Syr: Meaning of Heb uncertain

him got up and struck down Gedaliah son of Ahikam son of Shaphan with the sword and killed him, because the king of Babylon had appointed him governor in the land. ³ Ishmael also killed all the Judeans who were with Gedaliah at Mizpah, and the Chaldean soldiers who happened to be there.

4 On the day after the murder of Gedaliah, before anyone knew of it, ⁵ eighty men arrived from Shechem and Shiloh and Samaria, with their beards shaved and their clothes torn, and their bodies gashed, bringing grain-offerings and incense to present at the temple of the LORD. ⁶ And Ishmael son of Nethaniah came out from Mizpah to meet them, weeping as he came. As he met them, he said to them, 'Come to Gedaliah son of Ahikam.' ⁷ When they reached the middle of the city, Ishmael son of Nethaniah and the men with him slaughtered them, and threw them*a* into a cistern. ⁸ But there were ten men among them who said to Ishmael, 'Do not kill us, for we have stores of wheat, barley, oil, and honey hidden in the fields.' So he refrained, and did not kill them along with their companions.

9 Now the cistern into which Ishmael had thrown all the bodies of the men whom he had struck down was the large cistern*b* that King Asa had made for defence against King Baasha of Israel; Ishmael son of Nethaniah filled that cistern with those whom he had killed. ¹⁰ Then Ishmael took captive all the rest of the people who were in Mizpah, the king's daughters and all the people who were left at Mizpah, whom Nebuzaradan, the captain of the guard, had committed to Gedaliah son of Ahikam. Ishmael son of Nethaniah took them captive and set out to cross over to the Ammonites.

11 But when Johanan son of Kareah and all the leaders of the forces with him heard of all the crimes that Ishmael son of Nethaniah had done, ¹² they took all their men and went to fight against Ishmael son of Nethaniah. They came upon him at the great pool that is in Gibeon. ¹³ And when all the people who were with Ishmael saw

Johanan son of Kareah and all the leaders of the forces with him, they were glad. ¹⁴ So all the people whom Ishmael had carried away captive from Mizpah turned and came back, and went to Johanan son of Kareah. ¹⁵ But Ishmael son of Nethaniah escaped from Johanan with eight men, and went to the Ammonites. ¹⁶ Then Johanan son of Kareah and all the leaders of the forces with him took all the rest of the people whom Ishmael son of Nethaniah had carried away captive*c* from Mizpah after he had slain Gedaliah son of Ahikam—soldiers, women, children, and eunuchs, whom Johanan brought back from Gibeon.*d* ¹⁷ And they set out, and stopped at Geruth Chimham near Bethlehem, intending to go to Egypt ¹⁸ because of the Chaldeans; for they were afraid of them, because Ishmael son of Nethaniah had killed Gedaliah son of Ahikam, whom the king of Babylon had made governor over the land.

Jeremiah Advises Survivors Not to Migrate

42 Then all the commanders of the forces, and Johanan son of Kareah and Azariah*e* son of Hoshaiah, and all the people from the least to the greatest, approached ² the prophet Jeremiah and said, 'Be good enough to listen to our plea, and pray to the LORD your God for us—for all this remnant. For there are only a few of us left out of many, as your eyes can see. ³ Let the LORD your God show us where we should go and what we should do.' ⁴ The prophet Jeremiah said to them, 'Very well: I am going to pray to the LORD your God as you request, and whatever the LORD answers you I will tell you; I will keep nothing back from you.' ⁵ They in their turn said to Jeremiah, 'May the LORD be a true and faithful witness against us if we do not act according to everything that the LORD your God sends us through you. ⁶ Whether it is good or bad, we will obey the voice of the

---

a Syr: Heb lacks *and threw them*; compare verse 9
b Gk: Heb *whom he had killed by the hand of Gedaliah*
c Cn: Heb *whom he recovered from Ishmael son of Nethaniah*   *d* Meaning of Heb uncertain   *e* Gk: Heb *Jezaniah*

LORD our God to whom we are sending you, in order that it may go well with us when we obey the voice of the LORD our God.'

7 At the end of ten days the word of the LORD came to Jeremiah. 8 Then he summoned Johanan son of Kareah and all the commanders of the forces who were with him, and all the people from the least to the greatest, 9 and said to them, 'Thus says the LORD, the God of Israel, to whom you sent me to present your plea before him: 10 If you will only remain in this land, then I will build you up and not pull you down; I will plant you, and not pluck you up; for I am sorry for the disaster that I have brought upon you. 11 Do not be afraid of the king of Babylon, as you have been; do not be afraid of him, says the LORD, for I am with you, to save you and to rescue you from his hand. 12 I will grant you mercy, and he will have mercy on you and restore you to your native soil. 13 But if you continue to say, "We will not stay in this land", thus disobeying the voice of the LORD your God 14 and saying, "No, we will go to the land of Egypt, where we shall not see war, or hear the sound of the trumpet, or be hungry for bread, and there we will stay", 15 then hear the word of the LORD, O remnant of Judah. Thus says the LORD of hosts, the God of Israel: If you are determined to enter Egypt and go to settle there, 16 then the sword that you fear shall overtake you there, in the land of Egypt; and the famine that you dread shall follow close after you into Egypt; and there you shall die. 17 All the people who have determined to go to Egypt to settle there shall die by the sword, by famine, and by pestilence; they shall have no remnant or survivor from the disaster that I am bringing upon them.

18 'For thus says the LORD of hosts, the God of Israel: Just as my anger and my wrath were poured out on the inhabitants of Jerusalem, so my wrath will be poured out on you when you go to Egypt. You shall become an object of execration and horror, of cursing and ridicule. You shall see this place no more. 19 The LORD has said to you, O remnant of Judah, Do not go to Egypt. Be well aware that I have warned you today 20 that you have made a fatal mistake. For you yourselves sent me to the LORD your God, saying, "Pray for us to the LORD our God, and whatever the LORD our God says, tell us and we will do it." 21 So I have told you today, but you have not obeyed the voice of the LORD your God in anything that he sent me to tell you. 22 Be well aware, then, that you shall die by the sword, by famine, and by pestilence in the place where you desire to go and settle.'

Taken to Egypt, Jeremiah Warns of Judgement

43 When Jeremiah finished speaking to all the people all these words of the LORD their God, with which the LORD their God had sent him to them, 2 Azariah son of Hoshaiah and Johanan son of Kareah and all the other insolent men said to Jeremiah, 'You are telling a lie. The LORD our God did not send you to say, "Do not go to Egypt to settle there"; 3 but Baruch son of Neriah is inciting you against us, to hand us over to the Chaldeans, in order that they may kill us or take us into exile in Babylon.' 4 So Johanan son of Kareah and all the commanders of the forces and all the people did not obey the voice of the LORD, to stay in the land of Judah. 5 But Johanan son of Kareah and all the commanders of the forces took all the remnant of Judah who had returned to settle in the land of Judah from all the nations to which they had been driven— 6 the men, the women, the children, the princesses, and everyone whom Nebuzaradan the captain of the guard had left with Gedaliah son of Ahikam son of Shaphan; also the prophet Jeremiah and Baruch son of Neriah. 7 And they came into the land of Egypt, for they did not obey the voice of the LORD. And they arrived at Tahpanhes.

8 Then the word of the LORD came to Jeremiah in Tahpanhes: 9 Take some large stones in your hands, and bury them in the clay pavement*a* that is at the entrance to Pharaoh's palace in Tahpanhes. Let the Judeans see you do it, 10 and say to them,

a Meaning of Heb uncertain

Thus says the LORD of hosts, the God of Israel: I am going to send and take my servant King Nebuchadrezzar of Babylon, and he*a* will set his throne above these stones that I have buried, and he will spread his royal canopy over them. 11 He shall come and ravage the land of Egypt, giving

those who are destined for pestilence,
to pestilence,
and those who are destined for
captivity, to captivity,
and those who are destined for the
sword, to the sword.

12 He*b* shall kindle a fire in the temples of the gods of Egypt; and he shall burn them and carry them away captive; and he shall pick clean the land of Egypt, as a shepherd picks his cloak clean of vermin; and he shall depart from there safely. 13 He shall break the obelisks of Heliopolis, which is in the land of Egypt; and the temples of the gods of Egypt he shall burn with fire.

Denunciation of Persistent Idolatry

44 The word that came to Jeremiah for all the Judeans living in the land of Egypt, at Migdol, at Tahpanhes, at Memphis, and in the land of Pathros, 2 Thus says the LORD of hosts, the God of Israel: You yourselves have seen all the disaster that I have brought on Jerusalem and on all the towns of Judah. Look at them; today they are a desolation, without an inhabitant in them, 3 because of the wickedness that they committed, provoking me to anger, in that they went to make offerings and serve other gods that they had not known, neither they, nor you, nor your ancestors. 4 Yet I persistently sent to you all my servants the prophets, saying, 'I beg you not to do this abominable thing that I hate!' 5 But they did not listen or incline their ear, to turn from their wickedness and make no offerings to other gods. 6 So my wrath and my anger were poured out and kindled in the towns of Judah and in the streets of Jerusalem; and they became a waste and a desolation, as they still are today. 7 And now, thus says the LORD God of hosts, the God of Israel: Why are you doing such great harm to yourselves, to cut off

man and woman, child and infant, from the midst of Judah, leaving yourselves without a remnant? 8 Why do you provoke me to anger with the works of your hands, making offerings to other gods in the land of Egypt where you have come to settle? Will you be cut off and become an object of cursing and ridicule among all the nations of the earth? 9 Have you forgotten the crimes of your ancestors, of the kings of Judah, of their*c* wives, your own crimes and those of your wives, which they committed in the land of Judah and in the streets of Jerusalem? 10 They have shown no contrition or fear to this day, nor have they walked in my law and my statutes that I set before you and before your ancestors.

11 Therefore, thus says the LORD of hosts, the God of Israel: I am determined to bring disaster on you, to bring all Judah to an end. 12 I will take the remnant of Judah who are determined to come to the land of Egypt to settle, and they shall perish, everyone; in the land of Egypt they shall fall; by the sword and by famine they shall perish; from the least to the greatest, they shall die by the sword and by famine; and they shall become an object of execration and horror, of cursing and ridicule. 13 I will punish those who live in the land of Egypt, as I have punished Jerusalem, with the sword, with famine, and with pestilence, 14 so that none of the remnant of Judah who have come to settle in the land of Egypt shall escape or survive or return to the land of Judah. Although they long to go back to live there, they shall not go back, except some fugitives.

15 Then all the men who were aware that their wives had been making offerings to other gods, and all the women who stood by, a great assembly, all the people who lived in Pathros in the land of Egypt, answered Jeremiah: 16 'As for the word that you have spoken to us in the name of the LORD, we are not going to listen to you. 17 Instead, we will do everything that we have vowed, make offerings to the queen of heaven and pour out libations to her, just as we and our ancestors, our kings and

a Gk Syr: Heb *I*   *b* Gk Syr Vg: Heb *I*   *c* Heb *his* our officials, used to do in the towns of Judah and in the streets of Jerusalem. We used to have plenty of food, and prospered, and saw no misfortune. 18 But from the time we stopped making offerings to the queen of heaven and pouring out libations to her, we have lacked everything and have perished by the sword and by famine.' 19 And the women said, *a* 'Indeed we will go on making offerings to the queen of heaven and pouring out libations to her; do you think that we made cakes for her, marked with her image, and poured out libations to her without our husbands being involved?'

20 Then Jeremiah said to all the people, men and women, all the people who were giving him this answer: 21 'As for the offerings that you made in the towns of Judah and in the streets of Jerusalem, you and your ancestors, your kings and your officials, and the people of the land, did not the LORD remember them? Did it not come into his mind? 22 The LORD could no longer bear the sight of your evil doings, the abominations that you committed; therefore your land became a desolation and a waste and a curse, without inhabitant, as it is to this day. 23 It is because you burned offerings, and because you sinned against the LORD and did not obey the voice of the LORD or walk in his law and in his statutes and in his decrees, that this disaster has befallen you, as is still evident today.'

24 Jeremiah said to all the people and all the women, 'Hear the word of the LORD, all you Judeans who are in the land of Egypt, 25 Thus says the LORD of hosts, the God of Israel: You and your wives have accomplished in deeds what you declared in words, saying, "We are determined to perform the vows that we have made, to make offerings to the queen of heaven and to pour out libations to her." By all means, keep your vows and make your libations! 26 Therefore hear the word of the LORD, all you Judeans who live in the land of Egypt: Lo, I swear by my great name, says the LORD, that my name

a Compare Syr: Heb lacks *And the women said*

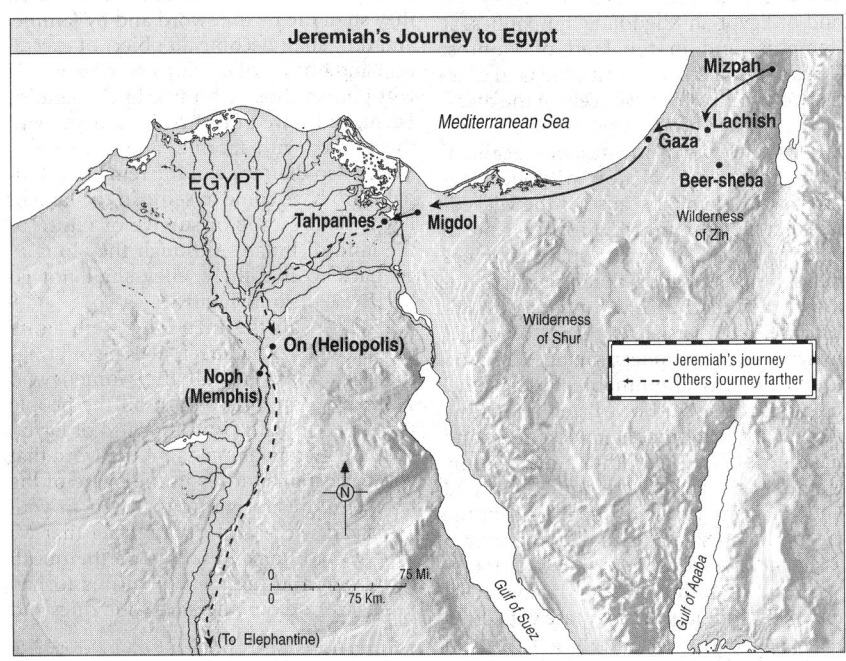

Jeremiah's Journey to Egypt

Mizpah

Lachish

Mediterranean Sea

Gaza

Beer-sheba

EGYPT

Tahpanhes

Migdol

Wilderness of Zin

Wilderness of Shur

On (Heliopolis)

Noph (Memphis)

Jeremiah's journey
Others journey farther

—N—

0   75 Mi.
0   75 Km.

Gulf of Suez

Gulf of Aqaba

(To Elephantine)

shall no longer be pronounced on the lips of any of the people of Judah in all the land of Egypt, saying, "As the Lord GOD lives." 27 I am going to watch over them for harm and not for good; all the people of Judah who are in the land of Egypt shall perish by the sword and by famine, until not one is left. 28 And those who escape the sword shall return from the land of Egypt to the land of Judah, few in number; and all the remnant of Judah, who have come to the land of Egypt to settle, shall know whose words will stand, mine or theirs! 29 This shall be the sign to you, says the LORD, that I am going to punish you in this place, in order that you may know that my words against you will surely be carried out: 30 Thus says the LORD, I am going to give Pharaoh Hophra, king of Egypt, into the hands of his enemies, those who seek his life, just as I gave King Zedekiah of Judah into the hand of King Nebuchadrezzar of Babylon, his enemy who sought his life.'

A Word of Comfort to Baruch

45 The word that the prophet Jeremiah spoke to Baruch son of Neriah, when he wrote these words in a scroll at the dictation of Jeremiah, in the fourth year of King Jehoiakim son of Josiah of Judah: 2 Thus says the LORD, the God of Israel, to you, O Baruch: 3 You said, 'Woe is me! The LORD has added sorrow to my pain; I am weary with my groaning, and I find no rest.' 4 Thus you shall say to him, 'Thus says the LORD: I am going to break down what I have built, and pluck up what I have planted—that is, the whole land. 5 And you, do you seek great things for yourself? Do not seek them; for I am going to bring disaster upon all flesh, says the LORD; but I will give you your life as a prize of war in every place to which you may go.'

Judgement on Egypt

46 The word of the LORD that came to the prophet Jeremiah concerning the nations.

2 Concerning Egypt, about the army of Pharaoh Neco, king of Egypt, which was by the river Euphrates at Carchemish and which King Nebuchadrezzar of Babylon defeated in the fourth year of King Jehoiakim son of Josiah of Judah:

3 Prepare buckler and shield,
    and advance for battle!
4 Harness the horses;
    mount the steeds!
Take your stations with your helmets,
    whet your lances,
    put on your coats of mail!
5 Why do I see them terrified?
    They have fallen back;
their warriors are beaten down,
    and have fled in haste.
They do not look back—
    terror is all around!
                    says the LORD.
6 The swift cannot flee away,
    nor can the warrior escape;
in the north by the river Euphrates
    they have stumbled and fallen.

7 Who is this, rising like the Nile,
    like rivers whose waters surge?
8 Egypt rises like the Nile,
    like rivers whose waters surge.
It said, Let me rise, let me cover the
        earth,
    let me destroy cities and their
        inhabitants.
9 Advance, O horses,
    and dash madly, O chariots!
Let the warriors go forth:
    Ethiopia[a] and Put who carry
        the shield,
    the Ludim, who draw[b] the bow.
10 That day is the day of the Lord GOD
        of hosts,
    a day of retribution,
    to gain vindication from his foes.
The sword shall devour and
        be sated,
    and drink its fill of their blood.
For the Lord GOD of hosts holds
        a sacrifice
    in the land of the north by the river
        Euphrates.
11 Go up to Gilead, and take balm,
    O virgin daughter Egypt!

a Or Nubia; Heb Cush   b Cn: Heb who grasp, who draw

In vain you have used many
      medicines;
  there is no healing for you.
12 The nations have heard of
        your shame,
  and the earth is full of your cry;
  for warrior has stumbled against
        warrior;
    both have fallen together.

Babylonia Will Strike Egypt

13 The word that the LORD spoke to the prophet Jeremiah about the coming of King Nebuchadrezzar of Babylon to attack the land of Egypt:

14 Declare in Egypt, and proclaim
        in Migdol;
    proclaim in Memphis and
        Tahpanhes;
  Say, 'Take your stations and be ready,
    for the sword shall devour those
        around you.'
15 Why has Apis fled?[a]
    Why did your bull not stand?
    —because the LORD thrust
        him down.
16 Your multitude stumbled[b] and fell,
    and one said to another,[c]
  'Come, let us go back to our
        own people
    and to the land of our birth,
  because of the destroying sword.'
17 Give Pharaoh, king of Egypt,
        the name
    'Braggart who missed his chance.'

18 As I live, says the King,
    whose name is the LORD of hosts,
  one is coming
    like Tabor among the mountains,
    and like Carmel by the sea.
19 Pack your bags for exile,
    sheltered daughter Egypt!
  For Memphis shall become a waste,
    a ruin, without inhabitant.

20 A beautiful heifer is Egypt—
    a gadfly from the north lights upon
        her.
21 Even her mercenaries in her midst
    are like fatted calves;

they too have turned and fled
      together,
  they did not stand;
  for the day of their calamity has come
      upon them,
    the time of their punishment.

22 She makes a sound like a snake
        gliding away;
    for her enemies march in force,
  and come against her with axes,
    like those who fell trees.
23 They shall cut down her forest,
                          says the LORD,
    though it is impenetrable,
  because they are more numerous
        than locusts;
    they are without number.
24 Daughter Egypt shall be put
        to shame;
    she shall be handed over to a
        people from the north.

25 The LORD of hosts, the God of Israel, said: See, I am bringing punishment upon Amon of Thebes, and Pharaoh, and Egypt and her gods and her kings, upon Pharaoh and those who trust in him. 26 I will hand them over to those who seek their life, to King Nebuchadrezzar of Babylon and his officers. Afterwards Egypt shall be inhabited as in the days of old, says the LORD.

God Will Save Israel

27 But as for you, have no fear, my
        servant Jacob,
    and do not be dismayed, O Israel;
  for I am going to save you from
        far away,
    and your offspring from the land of
        their captivity.
  Jacob shall return and have quiet and
        ease,
    and no one shall make him afraid.
28 As for you, have no fear, my servant
        Jacob,
                          says the LORD,
  for I am with you.

a Gk: Heb Why was it swept away   b Gk: Meaning of
Heb uncertain   c Gk: Heb and fell one to another and
they said

I will make an end of all the nations
    among which I have banished you,
    but I will not make an end of you!
I will chastise you in just measure,
    and I will by no means leave you
        unpunished.

Judgement on the Philistines

47 The word of the LORD that came to
the prophet Jeremiah concerning
the Philistines, before Pharaoh attacked
Gaza:

2 Thus says the LORD:
See, waters are rising out of the north
    and shall become an overflowing
        torrent;
they shall overflow the land and all
        that fills it,
    the city and those who live in it.
People shall cry out,
    and all the inhabitants of the land
        shall wail.

3 At the noise of the stamping of the
        hoofs of his stallions,
    at the clatter of his chariots, at the
        rumbling of their wheels,
parents do not turn back for children,
    so feeble are their hands,

4 because of the day that is coming
    to destroy all the Philistines,
to cut off from Tyre and Sidon
    every helper that remains.
For the LORD is destroying the
        Philistines,
    the remnant of the coastland
        of Caphtor.

5 Baldness has come upon Gaza,
    Ashkelon is silenced.
O remnant of their power! *a*
    How long will you gash yourselves?

6 Ah, sword of the LORD!
    How long until you are quiet?
Put yourself into your scabbard,
    rest and be still!

7 How can it *b* be quiet,
    when the LORD has given it
        an order?
Against Ashkelon and against the
        seashore—
    there he has appointed it.

Judgement on Moab

48 Concerning Moab.

Thus says the LORD of hosts, the God of Israel:
Alas for Nebo, it is laid waste!
    Kiriathaim is put to shame, it
        is taken;
the fortress is put to shame and
        broken down;

2   the renown of Moab is no more.
In Heshbon they planned evil against
        her:
    'Come, let us cut her off from being
        a nation!'
You also, O Madmen, shall be
    brought to silence; *c*
    the sword shall pursue you.

3 Hark! a cry from Horonaim,
    'Desolation and great destruction!'

4 'Moab is destroyed!'
    her little ones cry out.

5 For at the ascent of Luhith
    they go *d* up weeping bitterly;
for at the descent of Horonaim
    they have heard the distressing cry
        of anguish.

6 Flee! Save yourselves!
    Be like a wild ass *e* in the desert!

7 Surely, because you trusted in your
        strongholds *f* and your treasures,
    you also shall be taken;
Chemosh shall go out into exile,
    with his priests and his attendants.

8 The destroyer shall come upon every
        town,
    and no town shall escape;
the valley shall perish,
    and the plain shall be destroyed,
    as the LORD has spoken.

9 Set aside salt for Moab,
    for she will surely fall;
her towns shall become a desolation,
    with no inhabitant in them.

---

a Gk: Heb *their valley*   *b* Gk Vg: Heb *you*
c The place-name *Madmen* sounds like the Hebrew verb
to be silent   *d* Cn: Heb *he goes*   *e* Gk Aquila: Heb *like
Aroer*   *f* Gk: Heb *works*

10 Accursed is the one who is slack in doing the work of the LORD; and accursed is the one who keeps back the sword from bloodshed.

11 Moab has been at ease from his
    youth,
  settled like wine*a* on its dregs;
 he has not been emptied from vessel
    to vessel,
  nor has he gone into exile;
 therefore his flavour has remained
  and his aroma is unspoiled.
12 Therefore, the time is surely coming, says the LORD, when I shall send to him decanters to decant him, and empty his vessels, and break his*b* jars in pieces. 13 Then Moab shall be ashamed of Chemosh, as the house of Israel was ashamed of Bethel, their confidence.

14 How can you say, 'We are heroes
    and mighty warriors'?
15 The destroyer of Moab and his towns
    has come up,
  and the choicest of his young men
    have gone down to slaughter,
  says the King, whose name is the
    LORD of hosts.
16 The calamity of Moab is near
    at hand
  and his doom approaches swiftly.
17 Mourn over him, all you his
    neighbours,
  and all who know his name;
 say, 'How the mighty sceptre is
    broken,
  the glorious staff!'

18 Come down from glory,
  and sit on the parched ground,
    enthroned daughter Dibon!
 For the destroyer of Moab has come
    up against you;
  he has destroyed your strongholds.
19 Stand by the road and watch,
    you inhabitant of Aroer!
  Ask the man fleeing and the woman
    escaping;
   say, 'What has happened?'

20 Moab is put to shame, for it is broken
    down;
   wail and cry!
 Tell it by the Arnon,
   that Moab is laid waste.

21 Judgement has come upon the tableland, upon Holon, and Jahzah, and Mephaath, 22 and Dibon, and Nebo, and Beth-diblathaim, 23 and Kiriathaim, and Beth-gamul, and Beth-meon, 24 and Kerioth, and Bozrah, and all the towns of the land of Moab, far and near. 25 The horn of Moab is cut off, and his arm is broken, says the LORD.

26 Make him drunk, because he magnified himself against the LORD; let Moab wallow in his vomit; he too shall become a laughing-stock. 27 Israel was a laughing-stock for you, though he was not caught among thieves; but whenever you spoke of him you shook your head!

28 Leave the towns, and live on the rock,
    O inhabitants of Moab!
  Be like the dove that nests
    on the sides of the mouth of
      a gorge.
29 We have heard of the pride of
      Moab—
    he is very proud—
  of his loftiness, his pride, and his
      arrogance,
    and the haughtiness of his heart.
30 I myself know his insolence, says the
      LORD;
    his boasts are false,
    his deeds are false.
31 Therefore I wail for Moab;
    I cry out for all Moab;
   for the people of Kir-heres I mourn.
32 More than for Jazer I weep for you,
    O vine of Sibmah!
  Your branches crossed over the sea,
    reached as far as Jazer;*c*
  upon your summer fruits and
      your vintage
    the destroyer has fallen.

a Heb lacks *like wine*   *b* Gk Aquila: Heb *their*
c Two Mss and Isa 16.8: MT *the sea of Jazer*

33 Gladness and joy have been
        taken away
    from the fruitful land of Moab;
    I have stopped the wine from the
        wine presses;
    no one treads them with shouts of
        joy;
    the shouting is not the shout of joy.

34 Heshbon and Elealeh cry out;*a* as far as Jahaz they utter their voice, from Zoar to Horonaim and Eglath-shelishiyah. For even the waters of Nimrim have become desolate. 35 And I will bring to an end in Moab, says the LORD, those who offer sacrifice at a high place and make offerings to their gods. 36 Therefore my heart moans for Moab like a flute, and my heart moans like a flute for the people of Kir-heres; for the riches they gained have perished.

37 For every head is shaved and every beard cut off; on all the hands there are gashes, and on the loins sackcloth. 38 On all the housetops of Moab and in the squares there is nothing but lamentation; for I have broken Moab like a vessel that no one wants, says the LORD. 39 How it is broken! How they wail! How Moab has turned his back in shame! So Moab has become a derision and a horror to all his neighbours.

40 For thus says the LORD:
    Look, he shall swoop down like
        an eagle,
    and spread his wings against Moab;
41 the towns*b* shall be taken
        and the strongholds seized.
    The hearts of the warriors of Moab,
        on that day,
    shall be like the heart of a woman
        in labour.
42 Moab shall be destroyed as a people,
        because he magnified himself
            against the LORD.
43 Terror, pit, and trap
    are before you, O inhabitants
        of Moab!
                        says the LORD.
44 Everyone who flees from the terror
    shall fall into the pit,

and everyone who climbs out of
        the pit
    shall be caught in the trap.
For I will bring these things*c*
        upon Moab
    in the year of their punishment,
                        says the LORD.

45 In the shadow of Heshbon
        fugitives stop exhausted;
    for a fire has gone out from
        Heshbon,
    a flame from the house of Sihon;
    it has destroyed the forehead
        of Moab,
    the scalp of the people of tumult.*d*
46 Woe to you, O Moab!
    The people of Chemosh have
        perished,
    for your sons have been taken
        captive,
    and your daughters into captivity.
47 Yet I will restore the fortunes of Moab
    in the latter days, says the LORD.
Thus far is the judgement on Moab.

Judgement on the Ammonites

49

Concerning the Ammonites.

Thus says the LORD:
    Has Israel no sons?
        Has he no heir?
    Why then has Milcom dispossessed
        Gad,
    and his people settled in its towns?
2 Therefore, the time is surely coming,
        says the LORD,
    when I will sound the battle alarm
        against Rabbah of the Ammonites;
    it shall become a desolate mound,
        and its villages shall be burned
            with fire;
    then Israel shall dispossess those who
        dispossessed him,
    says the LORD.

3 Wail, O Heshbon, for Ai is laid waste!
    Cry out, O daughters*e* of Rabbah!

a Cn: Heb *From the cry of Heshbon to Elealeh*
b Or *Kerioth*   *c* Gk Syr: Heb *bring upon it*   *d* Or *of Shaon*   *e* Or *villages*

Put on sackcloth,
 lament, and slash yourselves with
  whips!*a*
For Milcom shall go into exile,
 with his priests and his attendants.
4 Why do you boast in your strength?
 Your strength is ebbing,
O faithless daughter.
 You trusted in your treasures,
  saying,
 'Who will attack me?'
5 I am going to bring terror upon you,
 says the Lord GOD of hosts,
 from all your neighbours,
and you will be scattered, each
  headlong,
 with no one to gather the fugitives.
6 But afterwards I will restore the fortunes of the Ammonites, says the LORD.

Judgement on Edom

7 Concerning Edom.

Thus says the LORD of hosts:
 Is there no longer wisdom in
  Teman?
  Has counsel perished from
   the prudent?
  Has their wisdom vanished?
8 Flee, turn back, get down low,
 inhabitants of Dedan!
For I will bring the calamity of Esau
  upon him,
 at the time when I punish him.
9 If grape-gatherers came to you,
 would they not leave gleanings?
If thieves came by night,
 even they would pillage only what
  they wanted.
10 But as for me, I have stripped
  Esau bare,
 I have uncovered his hiding-places,
 and he is not able to conceal
  himself.
His offspring are destroyed,
 his kinsfolk
 and his neighbours; and he is
 no more.
11 Leave your orphans, I will keep them
  alive;
 and let your widows trust in me.

12 For thus says the LORD: If those who
do not deserve to drink the cup still have to
drink it, shall you be the one to go unpunished? You shall not go unpunished; you
must drink it. 13 For by myself I have
sworn, says the LORD, that Bozrah shall become an object of horror and ridicule, a
waste, and an object of cursing; and all her
towns shall be perpetual wastes.
14 I have heard tidings from the LORD,
 and a messenger has been sent
  among the nations:
 'Gather yourselves together and come
  against her,
 and rise up for battle!'
15 For I will make you least among the
  nations,
 despised by humankind.
16 The terror you inspire
 and the pride of your heart have
  deceived you,
you who live in the clefts of
  the rock,*b*
 who hold the height of the hill.
Although you make your nest as high
  as the eagle's,
 from there I will bring you down,
       says the LORD.

17 Edom shall become an object of horror; everyone who passes by it will be horrified and will hiss because of all its disasters. 18 As when Sodom and Gomorrah and
their neighbours were overthrown, says the
LORD, no one shall live there, nor shall anyone settle in it. 19 Like a lion coming up
from the thickets of the Jordan against a
perennial pasture, I will suddenly chase
Edom*c* away from it; and I will appoint
over it whomsoever I choose.*d* For who is
like me? Who can summon me? Who is
the shepherd who can stand before me?
20 Therefore hear the plan that the LORD has
made against Edom and the purposes that
he has formed against the inhabitants of
Teman: Surely the little ones of the flock
shall be dragged away; surely their fold
shall be appalled at their fate. 21 At the
sound of their fall the earth shall tremble;

a Cn: Meaning of Heb uncertain *b* Or *of Sela*
c Heb *him* *d* Or *and I will single out the choicest of his*
rams: Meaning of Heb uncertain

the sound of their cry shall be heard at the Red Sea.[a] [22] Look, he shall mount up and swoop down like an eagle, and spread his wings against Bozrah, and the heart of the warriors of Edom on that day shall be like the heart of a woman in labour.

Judgement on Damascus

23 Concerning Damascus.

Hamath and Arpad are confounded,
for they have heard bad news;
they melt in fear, they are troubled
like the sea[b]
that cannot be quiet.
[24] Damascus has become feeble, she
turned to flee,
and panic seized her;
anguish and sorrows have taken hold
of her,
as of a woman in labour.
[25] How the famous city is forsaken,[c]
the joyful town![d]
[26] Therefore her young men shall fall in
her squares,
and all her soldiers shall be
destroyed on that day,
says the LORD of hosts.
[27] And I will kindle a fire at the wall of
Damascus,
and it shall devour the strongholds
of Ben-hadad.

Judgement on Kedar and Hazor

28 Concerning Kedar and the kingdoms of Hazor that King Nebuchadrezzar of Babylon defeated.

Thus says the LORD:
Rise up, advance against Kedar!
Destroy the people of the east!
[29] Take their tents and their flocks,
their curtains and all their goods;
carry off their camels for yourselves,
and a cry shall go up: 'Terror is all
around!'
[30] Flee, wander far away, hide in
deep places,
O inhabitants of Hazor!
says the LORD.
For King Nebuchadrezzar of Babylon

has made a plan against you
and formed a purpose against you.

[31] Rise up, advance against a nation at
ease,
that lives secure,
says the LORD,
that has no gates or bars,
that lives alone.
[32] Their camels shall become booty,
their herds of cattle a spoil.
I will scatter to every wind
those who have shaven temples,
and I will bring calamity
against them from every side,
says the LORD.
[33] Hazor shall become a lair of jackals,
an everlasting waste;
no one shall live there,
nor shall anyone settle in it.

Judgement on Elam

34 The word of the LORD that came to the prophet Jeremiah concerning Elam, at the beginning of the reign of King Zedekiah of Judah.

35 Thus says the LORD of hosts: I am going to break the bow of Elam, the mainstay of their might; [36] and I will bring upon Elam the four winds from the four quarters of heaven; and I will scatter them to all these winds, and there shall be no nation to which the exiles from Elam shall not come. [37] I will terrify Elam before their enemies, and before those who seek their life; I will bring disaster upon them, my fierce anger, says the LORD. I will send the sword after them, until I have consumed them; [38] and I will set my throne in Elam, and destroy their king and officials, says the LORD.

39 But in the latter days I will restore the fortunes of Elam, says the LORD.

Judgement on Babylon

50 The word that the LORD spoke concerning Babylon, concerning the land of the Chaldeans, by the prophet Jeremiah:

a Or *Sea of Reeds*   b Cn: Heb *there is trouble in the sea*
c Vg: Heb *is not forsaken*   d Syr Vg Tg: Heb *the town of my joy*

2 Declare among the nations
    and proclaim,
  set up a banner and proclaim,
  do not conceal it, say:
Babylon is taken,
  Bel is put to shame,
  Merodach is dismayed.
Her images are put to shame,
  her idols are dismayed.

3 For out of the north a nation has
come up against her; it shall make her land
a desolation, and no one shall live in it;
both human beings and animals shall flee
away.

4 In those days and at that time, says the
LORD, the people of Israel shall come, they
and the people of Judah together; they
shall come weeping as they seek the LORD
their God. 5 They shall ask the way to Zion,
with faces turned towards it, and they shall
come and join*a* themselves to the LORD by
an everlasting covenant that will never be
forgotten.

6 My people have been lost sheep; their
shepherds have led them astray, turning
them away on the mountains; from mountain to hill they have gone, they have forgotten their fold. 7 All who found them
have devoured them, and their enemies
have said, 'We are not guilty, because they
have sinned against the LORD, the true pasture, the LORD, the hope of their ancestors.'

8 Flee from Babylon, and go out of the
land of the Chaldeans, and be like male
goats leading the flock. 9 For I am going to
stir up and bring against Babylon a company of great nations from the land of the
north; and they shall array themselves
against her; from there she shall be taken.
Their arrows are like the arrows of a skilled
warrior who does not return empty-handed. 10 Chaldea shall be plundered; all who
plunder her shall be sated, says the LORD.

11 Though you rejoice, though
    you exult,
  O plunderers of my heritage,

though you frisk about like a heifer
    on the grass,
  and neigh like stallions,
12 your mother shall be utterly shamed,
  and she who bore you shall
    be disgraced.
Lo, she shall be the last of the
    nations,
  a wilderness, dry land, and a desert.
13 Because of the wrath of the LORD she
    shall not be inhabited,
  but shall be an utter desolation;
everyone who passes by Babylon
    shall be appalled
  and hiss because of all her wounds.
14 Take up your positions around
    Babylon,
  all you that bend the bow;
shoot at her, spare no arrows,
  for she has sinned against the LORD.
15 Raise a shout against her from
    all sides,
  'She has surrendered;
her bulwarks have fallen,
  her walls are thrown down.'
For this is the vengeance of the LORD:
  take vengeance on her,
  do to her as she has done.
16 Cut off from Babylon the sower,
  and the wielder of the sickle in
    time of harvest;
because of the destroying sword
  all of them shall return to their
    own people,
  and all of them shall flee to their
    own land.

17 Israel is a hunted sheep driven away
by lions. First the king of Assyria devoured
it, and now at the end King Nebuchadrezzar of Babylon has gnawed its bones.
18 Therefore, thus says the LORD of hosts,
the God of Israel: I am going to punish the
king of Babylon and his land, as I punished the king of Assyria. 19 I will restore Israel to its pasture, and it shall feed on Carmel and in Bashan, and on the hills of
Ephraim and in Gilead its hunger shall be
satisfied. 20 In those days and at that time,
says the LORD, the iniquity of Israel shall be

a Gk: Heb *towards it. Come! They shall join*

sought, and there shall be none; and the sins of Judah, and none shall be found; for I will pardon the remnant that I have spared.

21 Go up to the land of Merathaim;*a*
  go up against her,
and attack the inhabitants of Pekod*b*
  and utterly destroy the last
    of them,*c*
        says the LORD;
  do all that I have commanded you.
22 The noise of battle is in the land,
  and great destruction!
23 How the hammer of the whole earth
  is cut down and broken!
How Babylon has become
  a horror among the nations!
24 You set a snare for yourself and you
    were caught, O Babylon,
  but you did not know it;
you were discovered and seized,
  because you challenged the LORD.
25 The LORD has opened his armoury,
  and brought out the weapons of his
    wrath,
for the Lord GOD of hosts has a task
    to do
  in the land of the Chaldeans.
26 Come against her from every quarter;
  open her granaries;
pile her up like heaps of grain, and
    destroy her utterly;
  let nothing be left of her.
27 Kill all her bulls,
  let them go down to the slaughter.
Alas for them, their day has come,
  the time of their punishment!

28 Listen! Fugitives and refugees from the land of Babylon are coming to declare in Zion the vengeance of the LORD our God, vengeance for his temple.

29 Summon archers against Babylon, all who bend the bow. Encamp all around her; let no one escape. Repay her according to her deeds; just as she has done, do to her—for she has arrogantly defied the LORD, the Holy One of Israel. 30Therefore her young men shall fall in her squares,

and all her soldiers shall be destroyed on that day, says the LORD.

31 I am against you, O arrogant one,
    says the Lord GOD of hosts;
  for your day has come,
    the time when I will punish you.
32 The arrogant one shall stumble
    and fall,
  with no one to raise him up,
  and I will kindle a fire in his cities,
    and it will devour everything
      around him.

33 Thus says the LORD of hosts: The people of Israel are oppressed, and so too are the people of Judah; all their captors have held them fast and refuse to let them go. 34Their Redeemer is strong; the LORD of hosts is his name. He will surely plead their cause, that he may give rest to the earth, but unrest to the inhabitants of Babylon.

35 A sword against the Chaldeans, says
      the LORD,
  and against the inhabitants of
      Babylon,
  and against her officials and
      her sages!
36 A sword against the diviners,
  so that they may become fools!
A sword against her warriors,
  so that they may be destroyed!
37 A sword against her*d* horses and
    against her*d* chariots,
  and against all the foreign troops in
      her midst,
  so that they may become women!
A sword against all her treasures,
  that they may be plundered!
38 A drought*e* against her waters,
  that they may be dried up!
For it is a land of images,
  and they go mad over idols.

39 Therefore wild animals shall live with hyenas in Babylon,*f* and ostriches

a Or *of Double Rebellion*   *b* Or *of Punishment*
c Tg: Heb *destroy after them*   *d* Cn: Heb *his*
e Another reading is *A sword*   *f* Heb lacks *in Babylon*

shall inhabit her; she shall never again be peopled, or inhabited for all generations. ⁴⁰ As when God overthrew Sodom and Gomorrah and their neighbours, says the LORD, so no one shall live there, nor shall anyone settle in her.

41 Look, a people is coming from
        the north;
    a mighty nation and many kings
        are stirring from the farthest parts
            of the earth.
42 They wield bow and spear,
        they are cruel and have no mercy.
    The sound of them is like the roaring
        sea;
    they ride upon horses,
        set in array as a warrior for battle,
        against you, O daughter Babylon!

43 The king of Babylon heard news
        of them,
    and his hands fell helpless;
    anguish seized him,
        pain like that of a woman
            in labour.

44 Like a lion coming up from the thickets of the Jordan against a perennial pasture, I will suddenly chase them away from her; and I will appoint over her whomsoever I choose. *a* For who is like me? Who can summon me? Who is the shepherd who can stand before me? ⁴⁵ Therefore hear the plan that the LORD has made against Babylon, and the purposes that he has formed against the land of the Chaldeans: Surely the little ones of the flock shall be dragged away; surely their *b* fold shall be appalled at their fate. ⁴⁶ At the sound of the capture of Babylon the earth shall tremble, and her cry shall be heard among the nations.

51 Thus says the LORD:
    I am going to stir up a destructive
        wind *c*
    against Babylon
    and against the inhabitants of Leb-
        qamai; *d*

2 and I will send winnowers to Babylon,
        and they shall winnow her.
    They shall empty her land
        when they come against her from
            every side
        on the day of trouble.
3 Let not the archer bend his bow,
        and let him not array himself in his
            coat of mail.
    Do not spare her young men;
        utterly destroy her entire army.
4 They shall fall down slain in the land
        of the Chaldeans,
        and wounded in her streets.
5 Israel and Judah have not been
        forsaken
        by their God, the LORD of hosts,
    though their land is full of guilt
        before the Holy One of Israel.

6 Flee from the midst of Babylon,
        save your lives, each of you!
    Do not perish because of her guilt,
        for this is the time of the LORD's
            vengeance;
        he is repaying her what is due.
7 Babylon was a golden cup in the
        LORD's hand,
        making all the earth drunken;
    the nations drank of her wine,
        and so the nations went mad.
8 Suddenly Babylon has fallen and
        is shattered;
        wail for her!
    Bring balm for her wound;
        perhaps she may be healed.
9 We tried to heal Babylon,
        but she could not be healed.
    Forsake her, and let each of us go
        to our own country;
    for her judgement has reached up
        to heaven
        and has been lifted up even to the
            skies.
10 The LORD has brought forth our
        vindication;
        come, let us declare in Zion
        the work of the LORD our God.

a Or and I will single out the choicest of her rams: Meaning of Heb uncertain   b Syr Gk Tg Compare 49.20: Heb lacks their   c Or stir up the spirit of a destroyer
d Leb-qamai is a cryptogram for Kasdim, Chaldea

[11] Sharpen the arrows!
Fill the quivers!
The LORD has stirred up the spirit of the kings of the Medes, because his purpose concerning Babylon is to destroy it, for that is the vengeance of the LORD, vengeance for his temple.
[12] Raise a standard against the walls of Babylon;
make the watch strong;
post sentinels;
prepare the ambushes;
for the LORD has both planned and done
what he spoke concerning the inhabitants of Babylon.
[13] You who live by mighty waters,
rich in treasures,
your end has come,
the thread of your life is cut.
[14] The LORD of hosts has sworn by himself:
Surely I will fill you with troops like a swarm of locusts,
and they shall raise a shout of victory over you.

[15] It is he who made the earth by his power,
who established the world by his wisdom,
and by his understanding stretched out the heavens.
[16] When he utters his voice there is a tumult of waters in the heavens,
and he makes the mist rise from the ends of the earth.
He makes lightnings for the rain,
and he brings out the wind from his storehouses.
[17] Everyone is stupid and without knowledge;
goldsmiths are all put to shame by their idols;
for their images are false,
and there is no breath in them.
[18] They are worthless, a work of delusion;
at the time of their punishment they shall perish.
[19] Not like these is the LORD,[a] the portion of Jacob,

for he is the one who formed all things,
and Israel is the tribe of his inheritance;
the LORD of hosts is his name.

Israel the Creator's Instrument

[20] You are my war-club, my weapon of battle:
with you I smash nations;
with you I destroy kingdoms;
[21] with you I smash the horse and its rider;
with you I smash the chariot and the charioteer;
[22] with you I smash man and woman;
with you I smash the old man and the boy;
with you I smash the young man and the girl;
[23] with you I smash shepherds and their flocks;
with you I smash farmers and their teams;
with you I smash governors and deputies.

The Doom of Babylon

24 I will repay Babylon and all the inhabitants of Chaldea before your very eyes for all the wrong that they have done in Zion, says the LORD.

[25] I am against you, O destroying mountain,
says the LORD,
that destroys the whole earth;
I will stretch out my hand against you,
and roll you down from the crags,
and make you a burned-out mountain.
[26] No stone shall be taken from you for a corner
and no stone for a foundation,
but you shall be a perpetual waste,
says the LORD.

[27] Raise a standard in the land,
blow the trumpet among the nations;

a Heb lacks the LORD

prepare the nations for war
  against her,
  summon against her the kingdoms,
  Ararat, Minni, and Ashkenaz;
appoint a marshal against her,
  bring up horses like bristling
    locusts.
28 Prepare the nations for war
  against her,
  the kings of the Medes, with their
    governors and deputies,
  and every land under their
    dominion.
29 The land trembles and writhes,
  for the LORD's purposes against
    Babylon stand,
  to make the land of Babylon a
    desolation,
  without inhabitant.
30 The warriors of Babylon have given
    up fighting,
  they remain in their strongholds;
their strength has failed,
  they have become women;
her buildings are set on fire,
  her bars are broken.
31 One runner runs to meet another,
  and one messenger to meet
    another,
  to tell the king of Babylon
    that his city is taken from end
      to end:
32 the fords have been seized,
  the marshes have been burned with
    fire,
  and the soldiers are in panic.
33 For thus says the LORD of hosts, the
    God of Israel:
  Daughter Babylon is like a threshing-
    floor
    at the time when it is trodden;
  yet a little while
    and the time of her harvest
      will come.

34 'King Nebuchadrezzar of Babylon has
    devoured me,
  he has crushed me;
he has made me an empty vessel,
  he has swallowed me like
    a monster;

he has filled his belly with my
    delicacies,
  he has spewed me out.
35 May my torn flesh be avenged on
    Babylon,'
  the inhabitants of Zion shall say.
'May my blood be avenged on the
    inhabitants of Chaldea,'
  Jerusalem shall say.
36 Therefore thus says the LORD:
  I am going to defend your cause
    and take vengeance for you.
  I will dry up her sea
    and make her fountain dry;
37 and Babylon shall become a heap
    of ruins,
  a den of jackals,
  an object of horror and of hissing,
    without inhabitant.

38 Like lions they shall roar together;
  they shall growl like lions' whelps.
39 When they are inflamed, I will set out
    their drink
  and make them drunk, until they
    become merry
  and then sleep a perpetual sleep
    and never wake, says the LORD.
40 I will bring them down like lambs to
    the slaughter,
  like rams and goats.

41 How Sheshach[a] is taken,
  the pride of the whole earth seized!
How Babylon has become
  an object of horror among the
    nations!
42 The sea has risen over Babylon;
  she has been covered by its
    tumultuous waves.
43 Her cities have become an object
    of horror,
  a land of drought and a desert,
  a land in which no one lives,
    and through which no mortal
      passes.
44 I will punish Bel in Babylon,
  and make him disgorge what he
    has swallowed.

a *Sheshach* is a cryptogram for *Babel*, Babylon

The nations shall no longer stream to
   him;
   the wall of Babylon has fallen.

⁴⁵ Come out of her, my people!
   Save your lives, each of you,
   from the fierce anger of the LORD!
⁴⁶ Do not be faint-hearted or fearful
   at the rumours heard in the land—
one year one rumour comes,
   the next year another,
rumours of violence in the land
   and of ruler against ruler.

⁴⁷ Assuredly, the days are coming
   when I will punish the images
      of Babylon;
   her whole land shall be put to shame,
   and all her slain shall fall in
      her midst.
⁴⁸ Then the heavens and the earth,
   and all that is in them,
shall shout for joy over Babylon;
   for the destroyers shall come
      against them out of the north,
                    says the LORD.
⁴⁹ Babylon must fall for the slain of
   Israel,
   as the slain of all the earth have
      fallen because of Babylon.

⁵⁰ You survivors of the sword,
   go, do not linger!
Remember the LORD in a distant land,
   and let Jerusalem come into your
      mind:
⁵¹ We are put to shame, for we have
   heard insults;
   dishonour has covered our face,
for aliens have come
   into the holy places of the
      LORD's house.

⁵² Therefore the time is surely coming,
   says the LORD,
   when I will punish her idols,
and through all her land
   the wounded shall groan.
⁵³ Though Babylon should mount up to
   heaven,

and though she should fortify her
   strong height,
from me destroyers would come
   upon her,
   says the LORD.

⁵⁴ Listen!—a cry from Babylon!
   A great crashing from the land of
      the Chaldeans!
⁵⁵ For the LORD is laying Babylon waste,
   and stilling her loud clamour.
Their waves roar like mighty waters,
   the sound of their clamour
      resounds;
⁵⁶ for a destroyer has come against her,
   against Babylon;
her warriors are taken,
   their bows are broken;
for the LORD is a God of recompense,
   he will repay in full.
⁵⁷ I will make her officials and her sages
   drunk,
   also her governors, her deputies,
      and her warriors;
they shall sleep a perpetual sleep and
   never wake,
   says the King, whose name is the
      LORD of hosts.

⁵⁸ Thus says the LORD of hosts:
The broad wall of Babylon
   shall be levelled to the ground,
and her high gates
   shall be burned with fire.
The peoples exhaust themselves for
   nothing,
   and the nations weary themselves
      only for fire. ᵃ

Jeremiah's Command to Seraiah

59 The word that the prophet Jeremiah
commanded Seraiah son of Neriah son of
Mahseiah, when he went with King Zedekiah of Judah to Babylon, in the fourth
year of his reign. Seraiah was the quarter-
master. ⁶⁰ Jeremiah wrote in a ᵇ scroll all the
disasters that would come on Babylon, all
these words that are written concerning
Babylon. ⁶¹ And Jeremiah said to Seraiah:

ᵃ Gk Syr Compare Hab 2.13: Heb *and the nations for
fire, and they are weary*   ᵇ Or *one*

'When you come to Babylon, see that you read all these words, 62 and say, "O Lord, you yourself threatened to destroy this place so that neither human beings nor animals shall live in it, and it shall be desolate for ever." 63 When you finish reading this scroll, tie a stone to it, and throw it into the middle of the Euphrates, 64 and say, "Thus shall Babylon sink, to rise no more, because of the disasters that I am bringing on her." '[a]

Thus far are the words of Jeremiah.

The Destruction of Jerusalem Recalled

52 Zedekiah was twenty-one years old when he began to reign; he reigned for eleven years in Jerusalem. His mother's name was Hamutal daughter of Jeremiah of Libnah. 2 He did what was evil in the sight of the Lord, just as Jehoiakim had done. 3 Indeed, Jerusalem and Judah so angered the Lord that he expelled them from his presence.

Zedekiah rebelled against the king of Babylon. 4 And in the ninth year of his reign, in the tenth month, on the tenth day of the month, King Nebuchadrezzar of Babylon came with all his army against Jerusalem, and they laid siege to it; they built siege-works against it all round. 5 So the city was besieged until the eleventh year of King Zedekiah. 6 On the ninth day of the fourth month the famine became so severe in the city that there was no food for the people of the land. 7 Then a breach was made in the city wall;[b] and all the soldiers fled and went out from the city by night by the way of the gate between the two walls, by the king's garden, though the Chaldeans were all round the city. They went in the direction of the Arabah. 8 But the army of the Chaldeans pursued the king, and overtook Zedekiah in the plains of Jericho; and all his army was scattered, deserting him. 9 Then they captured the king, and brought him up to the king of Babylon at Riblah in the land of Hamath, and he passed sentence on him. 10 The king of Babylon killed the sons of Zedekiah before his eyes, and also killed all the officers of Judah at Riblah. 11 He put out the eyes of Zedekiah, and

bound him in fetters, and the king of Babylon took him to Babylon, and put him in prison until the day of his death.

12 In the fifth month, on the tenth day of the month—which was the nineteenth year of King Nebuchadrezzar, king of Babylon—Nebuzaradan the captain of the bodyguard who served the king of Babylon, entered Jerusalem. 13 He burned the house of the Lord, the king's house, and all the houses of Jerusalem; every great house he burned down. 14 All the army of the Chaldeans, who were with the captain of the guard, broke down all the walls around Jerusalem. 15 Nebuzaradan the captain of the guard carried into exile some of the poorest of the people and the rest of the people who were left in the city and the deserters who had defected to the king of Babylon, together with the rest of the artisans. 16 But Nebuzaradan the captain of the guard left some of the poorest people of the land to be vine-dressers and tillers of the soil.

17 The pillars of bronze that were in the house of the Lord, and the stands and the bronze sea that were in the house of the Lord, the Chaldeans broke in pieces, and carried all the bronze to Babylon. 18 They took away the pots, the shovels, the snuffers, the basins, the ladles, and all the vessels of bronze used in the temple service. 19 The captain of the guard took away the small bowls also, the firepans, the basins, the pots, the lampstands, the ladles, and the bowls for libation, both those of gold and those of silver. 20 As for the two pillars, the one sea, the twelve bronze bulls that were under the sea, and the stands,[c] which King Solomon had made for the house of the Lord, the bronze of all these vessels was beyond weighing. 21 As for the pillars, the height of one pillar was eighteen cubits, its circumference was twelve cubits; it was hollow and its thickness was four fingers. 22 Upon it was a capital of bronze; the height of the capital was five cubits; lattice-work and pomegranates, all of bronze, encircled the top of the capital.

a   Gk: Heb *on her. And they shall weary themselves*
b   Heb lacks *wall*   c   Cn: Heb *that were under the stands*

And the second pillar had the same, with pomegranates. ²³There were ninety-six pomegranates on the sides; all the pomegranates encircling the lattice-work numbered one hundred.

24 The captain of the guard took the chief priest Seraiah, the second priest Zephaniah, and the three guardians of the threshold; ²⁵and from the city he took an officer who had been in command of the soldiers, and seven men of the king's council who were found in the city; the secretary of the commander of the army who mustered the people of the land; and sixty men of the people of the land who were found inside the city. ²⁶Then Nebuzaradan the captain of the guard took them, and brought them to the king of Babylon at Riblah. ²⁷And the king of Babylon struck them down, and put them to death at Riblah in the land of Hamath. So Judah went into exile out of its land.

28 This is the number of the people whom Nebuchadrezzar took into exile: in the seventh year, three thousand and twenty-three Judeans; ²⁹in the eighteenth year of Nebuchadrezzar he took into exile from Jerusalem eight hundred and thirty-two persons; ³⁰in the twenty-third year of Nebuchadrezzar, Nebuzaradan the captain of the guard took into exile of the Judeans seven hundred and forty-five persons; all the people were four thousand six hundred.

Jehoiachin Favoured in Captivity

31 In the thirty-seventh year of the exile of King Jehoiachin of Judah, in the twelfth month, on the twenty-fifth day of the month, King Evil-merodach of Babylon, in the year he began to reign, showed favour to King Jehoiachin of Judah and brought him out of prison; ³²he spoke kindly to him, and gave him a seat above the seats of the other kings who were with him in Babylon. ³³So Jehoiachin put aside his prison clothes, and every day of his life he dined regularly at the king's table. ³⁴For his allowance, a regular daily allowance was given him by the king of Babylon, as long as he lived, up to the day of his death.

LAMENTATIONS

The Deserted City

1 How lonely sits the city
  that once was full of people!
How like a widow she has become,
  she that was great among the
    nations!
She that was a princess among the
    provinces
  has become a vassal.

2 She weeps bitterly in the night,
  with tears on her cheeks;
among all her lovers
  she has no one to comfort her;
all her friends have dealt
    treacherously with her,
  they have become her enemies.

3 Judah has gone into exile with
    suffering
  and hard servitude;
she lives now among the nations,
  and finds no resting-place;
her pursuers have all overtaken her
  in the midst of her distress.

4 The roads to Zion mourn,
  for no one comes to the festivals;
all her gates are desolate,
  her priests groan;
her young girls grieve, *a*
  and her lot is bitter.

5 Her foes have become the masters,
  her enemies prosper,
because the Lord has made her suffer
  for the multitude of her
    transgressions;
her children have gone away,
  captives before the foe.

6 From daughter Zion has departed
  all her majesty.
Her princes have become like stags
  that find no pasture;
they fled without strength
  before the pursuer.

7 Jerusalem remembers,
  in the days of her affliction and
    wandering,
all the precious things
  that were hers in days of old.
When her people fell into the hand
    of the foe,
  and there was no one to help her,
the foe looked on mocking
  over her downfall.

8 Jerusalem sinned grievously,
  so she has become a mockery;
all who honoured her despise her,
  for they have seen her nakedness;
she herself groans,
  and turns her face away.

9 Her uncleanness was in her skirts;
  she took no thought of her future;
her downfall was appalling,
  with none to comfort her.
'O Lord, look at my affliction,
  for the enemy has triumphed!'

10 Enemies have stretched out their hands
  over all her precious things;
she has even seen the nations
  invade her sanctuary,
those whom you forbade
  to enter your congregation.

a Meaning of Heb uncertain

11 All her people groan
   as they search for bread;
they trade their treasures for food
   to revive their strength.
Look, O Lord, and see
   how worthless I have become.

12 Is it nothing to you,*a* all you who
      pass by?
   Look and see
if there is any sorrow like my sorrow,
   which was brought upon me,
which the Lord inflicted
   on the day of his fierce anger.

13 From on high he sent fire;
   it went deep into my bones;
he spread a net for my feet;
   he turned me back;
he has left me stunned,
   faint all day long.

14 My transgressions were bound*a* into a
      yoke;
   by his hand they were fastened
      together;
they weigh on my neck,
   sapping my strength;
the Lord handed me over
   to those whom I cannot withstand.

15 The Lord has rejected
   all my warriors in the midst of me;
he proclaimed a time against me
   to crush my young men;
the Lord has trodden as in a wine
      press
   the virgin daughter Judah.

16 For these things I weep;
   my eyes flow with tears;
for a comforter is far from me,
   one to revive my courage;
my children are desolate,
   for the enemy has prevailed.

17 Zion stretches out her hands,
   but there is no one to comfort her;
the Lord has commanded against
      Jacob

that his neighbours should become
   his foes;
Jerusalem has become
   a filthy thing among them.

18 The Lord is in the right,
   for I have rebelled against his word;
but hear, all you peoples,
   and behold my suffering;
my young women and young men
   have gone into captivity.

19 I called to my lovers
   but they deceived me;
my priests and elders
   perished in the city
while seeking food
   to revive their strength.

20 See, O Lord, how distressed I am;
   my stomach churns,
my heart is wrung within me,
   because I have been very rebellious.
In the street the sword bereaves;
   in the house it is like death.

21 They heard how I was groaning,
   with no one to comfort me.
All my enemies heard of my trouble;
   they are glad that you have done it.
Bring on the day you have
      announced,
   and let them be as I am.

22 Let all their evildoing come
      before you;
   and deal with them
as you have dealt with me
   because of all my transgressions;
for my groans are many
   and my heart is faint.

God's Warnings Fulfilled

2 How the Lord in his anger
   has humiliated*a* daughter Zion!
He has thrown down from heaven to
      earth
   the splendour of Israel;
he has not remembered his footstool
   on the day of his anger.

a Meaning of Heb uncertain

2 The Lord has destroyed without
     mercy
  all the dwellings of Jacob;
in his wrath he has broken down
    the strongholds of daughter
    Judah;
he has brought down to the ground
    in dishonour
  the kingdom and its rulers.

3 He has cut down in fierce anger
  all the might of Israel;
he has withdrawn his right hand
    from them
  in the face of the enemy;
he has burned like a flaming fire
    in Jacob,
  consuming all around.

4 He has bent his bow like an enemy,
  with his right hand set like a foe;
he has killed all in whom we
    took pride
  in the tent of daughter Zion;
he has poured out his fury like fire.

5 The Lord has become like an
    enemy;
  he has destroyed Israel.
He has destroyed all its palaces,
  laid in ruins its strongholds,
and multiplied in daughter Judah
  mourning and lamentation.

6 He has broken down his booth like a
    garden,
  he has destroyed his tabernacle;
the Lord has abolished in Zion
  festival and sabbath,
and in his fierce indignation has
    spurned
  king and priest.

7 The Lord has scorned his altar,
  disowned his sanctuary;
he has delivered into the hand of the
    enemy
  the walls of her palaces;
a clamour was raised in the house of
    the Lord
  as on a day of festival.

8 The Lord determined to lay in ruins
  the wall of daughter Zion;
he stretched the line;
  he did not withhold his hand from
    destroying;
he caused rampart and wall
  to lament;
  they languish together.

9 Her gates have sunk into the ground;
  he has ruined and broken her bars;
her king and princes are among
    the nations;
  guidance is no more,
and her prophets obtain
  no vision from the Lord.

10 The elders of daughter Zion
  sit on the ground in silence;
they have thrown dust on their heads
  and put on sackcloth;
the young girls of Jerusalem
  have bowed their heads to
    the ground.

11 My eyes are spent with weeping;
  my stomach churns;
my bile is poured out on the ground
  because of the destruction of
    my people,
because infants and babes faint
  in the streets of the city.

12 They cry to their mothers,
  'Where is bread and wine?'
as they faint like the wounded
  in the streets of the city,
as their life is poured out
  on their mothers' bosom.

13 What can I say for you, to what
    compare you,
  O daughter Jerusalem?
To what can I liken you, that I may
    comfort you,
  O virgin daughter Zion?
For vast as the sea is your ruin;
  who can heal you?

14 Your prophets have seen for you
  false and deceptive visions;

they have not exposed your iniquity
    to restore your fortunes,
but have seen oracles for you
    that are false and misleading.

15 All who pass along the way
    clap their hands at you;
they hiss and wag their heads
    at daughter Jerusalem;
'Is this the city that was called
    the perfection of beauty,
    the joy of all the earth?'

16 All your enemies
    open their mouths against you;
they hiss, they gnash their teeth,
    they cry: 'We have devoured her!
Ah, this is the day we longed for;
    at last we have seen it!'

17 The LORD has done what he
      purposed,
    he has carried out his threat;
as he ordained long ago,
    he has demolished without pity;
he has made the enemy rejoice
      over you,
    and exalted the might of your foes.

18 Cry aloud*a* to the Lord!
    O wall of daughter Zion!
Let tears stream down like a torrent
    day and night!
Give yourself no rest,
    your eyes no respite!

19 Arise, cry out in the night,
    at the beginning of the watches!
Pour out your heart like water
    before the presence of the Lord!
Lift your hands to him
    for the lives of your children,
who faint for hunger
    at the head of every street.

20 Look, O LORD, and consider!
    To whom have you done this?
Should women eat their offspring,
    the children they have borne?
Should priest and prophet be killed
    in the sanctuary of the Lord?

21 The young and the old are lying
    on the ground in the streets;
my young women and my
      young men
    have fallen by the sword;
on the day of your anger you have
      killed them,
    slaughtering without mercy.

22 You invited my enemies from
      all around
    as if for a day of festival;
and on the day of the anger of
      the LORD
    no one escaped or survived;
those whom I bore and reared
    my enemy has destroyed.

God's Steadfast Love Endures

3 I am one who has seen affliction
    under the rod of God's*b* wrath;
2 he has driven and brought me
    into darkness without any light;
3 against me alone he turns his hand,
    again and again, all day long.

4 He has made my flesh and my skin
      waste away,
    and broken my bones;
5 he has besieged and enveloped me
    with bitterness and tribulation;
6 he has made me sit in darkness
    like the dead of long ago.

7 He has walled me about so that I
      cannot escape;
    he has put heavy chains on me;
8 though I call and cry for help,
    he shuts out my prayer;
9 he has blocked my ways with hewn
      stones,
    he has made my paths crooked.

10 He is a bear lying in wait for me,
    a lion in hiding;
11 he led me off my way and tore me to
      pieces;
    he has made me desolate;
12 he bent his bow and set me
    as a mark for his arrow.

a Cn: Heb *Their heart cried*   *b* Heb *his*

13 He shot into my vitals
　　the arrows of his quiver;
14 I have become the laughing-stock
　　of all my people,
　　the object of their taunt-songs all
　　　　day long.
15 He has filled me with bitterness,
　　he has glutted me with wormwood.

16 He has made my teeth grind
　　on gravel,
　　and made me cower in ashes;
17 my soul is bereft of peace;
　　I have forgotten what happiness is;
18 so I say, 'Gone is my glory,
　　and all that I had hoped for from
　　　　the LORD.'

19 The thought of my affliction and my
　　　　homelessness
　　is wormwood and gall!
20 My soul continually thinks of it
　　and is bowed down within me.
21 But this I call to mind,
　　and therefore I have hope:

22 The steadfast love of the LORD never
　　　　ceases,[a]
　　his mercies never come to an end;
23 they are new every morning;
　　great is your faithfulness.
24 'The LORD is my portion,' says
　　　　my soul,
　　'therefore I will hope in him.'

25 The LORD is good to those who
　　　　wait for him,
　　to the soul that seeks him.
26 It is good that one should wait quietly
　　for the salvation of the LORD.
27 It is good for one to bear
　　the yoke in youth,
28 to sit alone in silence
　　when the Lord has imposed it,
29 to put one's mouth to the dust
　　(there may yet be hope),
30 to give one's cheek to the smiter,
　　and be filled with insults.

31 For the Lord will not
　　reject for ever.

32 Although he causes grief, he will have
　　　　compassion
　　according to the abundance of his
　　　　steadfast love;
33 for he does not willingly afflict
　　or grieve anyone.

34 When all the prisoners of the land
　　are crushed under foot,
35 when human rights are perverted
　　in the presence of the Most High,
36 when one's case is subverted
　　—does the Lord not see it?

37 Who can command and have
　　it done,
　　if the Lord has not ordained it?
38 Is it not from the mouth of the Most
　　　　High
　　that good and bad come?
39 Why should any who draw breath
　　　　complain
　　about the punishment of
　　　　their sins?

40 Let us test and examine our ways,
　　and return to the LORD.
41 Let us lift up our hearts as well as our
　　　　hands
　　to God in heaven.
42 We have transgressed and rebelled,
　　and you have not forgiven.

43 You have wrapped yourself with
　　　　anger and pursued us,
　　killing without pity;
44 you have wrapped yourself with
　　　　a cloud
　　so that no prayer can pass through.
45 You have made us filth and rubbish
　　among the peoples.

46 All our enemies
　　have opened their mouths against
　　　　us;
47 panic and pitfall have come upon us,
　　devastation and destruction.
48 My eyes flow with rivers of tears
　　because of the destruction of
　　　　my people.

a Syr Tg: Heb LORD, we are not cut off

49 My eyes will flow without ceasing,
    without respite,
50 until the LORD from heaven
    looks down and sees.
51 My eyes cause me grief
    at the fate of all the young women
        in my city.

52 Those who were my enemies without
        cause
    have hunted me like a bird;
53 they flung me alive into a pit
    and hurled stones on me;
54 water closed over my head;
    I said, 'I am lost.'

55 I called on your name, O LORD,
    from the depths of the pit;
56 you heard my plea, 'Do not close
        your ear
    to my cry for help, but give
        me relief!'
57 You came near when I called on you;
    you said, 'Do not fear!'

58 You have taken up my cause, O Lord,
    you have redeemed my life.
59 You have seen the wrong done to me,
        O LORD;
    judge my cause.
60 You have seen all their malice,
    all their plots against me.

61 You have heard their taunts, O LORD,
    all their plots against me.
62 The whispers and murmurs of my
        assailants
    are against me all day long.
63 Whether they sit or rise—see,
    I am the object of their taunt-songs.

64 Pay them back for their deeds,
        O LORD,
    according to the work of their
        hands!
65 Give them anguish of heart;
    your curse be on them!
66 Pursue them in anger and
        destroy them
    from under the LORD's heavens.

The Punishment of Zion

4 How the gold has grown dim,
    how the pure gold is changed!
The sacred stones lie scattered
    at the head of every street.

2 The precious children of Zion,
    worth their weight in fine gold—
how they are reckoned as
        earthen pots,
    the work of a potter's hands!

3 Even the jackals offer the breast
    and nurse their young,
but my people has become cruel,
    like the ostriches in the wilderness.

4 The tongue of the infant sticks
    to the roof of its mouth for thirst;
the children beg for food,
    but no one gives them anything.

5 Those who feasted on delicacies
    perish in the streets;
those who were brought up in purple
    cling to ash heaps.

6 For the chastisement[a] of my people
        has been greater
    than the punishment[b] of Sodom,
which was overthrown in a moment,
    though no hand was laid on it.[c]

7 Her princes were purer than snow,
        whiter than milk;
their bodies were more ruddy
        than coral,
    their hair[c] like sapphire.[d]

8 Now their visage is blacker than soot;
    they are not recognized in
        the streets.
Their skin has shrivelled on
        their bones;
    it has become as dry as wood.

9 Happier were those pierced by
        the sword
    than those pierced by hunger,

a Or iniquity   b Or sin   c Meaning of Heb uncertain
d Or lapis lazuli

whose life drains away, deprived
    of the produce of the field.

10 The hands of compassionate women
        have boiled their own children;
    they became their food
        in the destruction of my people.

11 The LORD gave full vent to his wrath;
        he poured out his hot anger,
    and kindled a fire in Zion
        that consumed its foundations.

12 The kings of the earth did not believe,
        nor did any of the inhabitants
            of the world,
    that foe or enemy could enter
        the gates of Jerusalem.

13 It was for the sins of her prophets
        and the iniquities of her priests,
    who shed the blood of the righteous
        in the midst of her.

14 Blindly they wandered through
        the streets,
        so defiled with blood
    that no one was able
        to touch their garments.

15 'Away! Unclean!' people shouted
        at them;
        'Away! Away! Do not touch!'
    So they became fugitives and
        wanderers;
        it was said among the nations,
        'They shall stay here no longer.'

16 The LORD himself has scattered them,
        he will regard them no more;
    no honour was shown to the priests,
        no favour to the elders.

17 Our eyes failed, ever watching
        vainly for help;
    we were watching eagerly
        for a nation that could not save.

18 They dogged our steps
        so that we could not walk in
            our streets;

our end drew near; our days were
        numbered;
    for our end had come.

19 Our pursuers were swifter
        than the eagles in the heavens;
    they chased us on the mountains,
        they lay in wait for us in the
            wilderness.

20 The LORD's anointed, the breath of
        our life,
        was taken in their pits—
    the one of whom we said, 'Under his
        shadow
        we shall live among the nations.'

21 Rejoice and be glad, O daughter
        Edom,
        you that live in the land of Uz;
    but to you also the cup shall pass;
        you shall become drunk and strip
            yourself bare.

22 The punishment of your iniquity,
        O daughter Zion, is
            accomplished,
    he will keep you in exile no longer;
    but your iniquity, O daughter Edom,
        he will punish,
    he will uncover your sins.

A Plea for Mercy

5 Remember, O LORD, what has
        befallen us;
    look, and see our disgrace!
2 Our inheritance has been turned over
        to strangers,
        our homes to aliens.
3 We have become orphans,
        fatherless;
        our mothers are like widows.
4 We must pay for the water we drink;
        the wood we get must be bought.
5 With a yoke[a] on our necks we are
        hard driven;
    we are weary, we are given no rest.
6 We have made a pact with[b] Egypt and
        Assyria,

a Symmachus: Heb lacks *With a yoke*   b Heb *have given the hand to* to get enough bread.

7 Our ancestors sinned; they are
    no more,
  and we bear their iniquities.
8 Slaves rule over us;
    there is no one to deliver us from
      their hand.
9 We get our bread at the peril of
    our lives,
  because of the sword in the
    wilderness.
10 Our skin is black as an oven
    from the scorching heat of famine.
11 Women are raped in Zion,
    virgins in the towns of Judah.
12 Princes are hung up by their hands;
    no respect is shown to the elders.
13 Young men are compelled to grind,
    and boys stagger under loads
      of wood.
14 The old men have left the city gate,
    the young men their music.
15 The joy of our hearts has ceased;

our dancing has been turned
  to mourning.
16 The crown has fallen from our head;
    woe to us, for we have sinned!
17 Because of this our hearts are sick,
    because of these things our eyes
      have grown dim:
18 because of Mount Zion, which
    lies desolate;
  jackals prowl over it.

19 But you, O Lord, reign for ever;
    your throne endures to all
      generations.
20 Why have you forgotten us
    completely?
  Why have you forsaken us these
    many days?
21 Restore us to yourself, O Lord, that
    we may be restored;
  renew our days as of old—
22 unless you have utterly rejected us,
    and are angry with us beyond
      measure.

BARUCH

1 These are the words of the book that Baruch son of Neriah son of Mahseiah son of Zedekiah son of Hasadiah son of Hilkiah wrote in Babylon, ²in the fifth year, on the seventh day of the month, at the time when the Chaldeans took Jerusalem and burned it with fire.

3 Baruch read the words of this book to Jeconiah son of Jehoiakim, king of Judah, and to all the people who came to hear the book, ⁴and to the nobles and the princes, and to the elders, and to all the people, small and great, all who lived in Babylon by the river Sud.

5 Then they wept, and fasted, and prayed before the Lord; ⁶they collected as much money as each could give, ⁷and sent it to Jerusalem to the high priest*ᵃ* Jehoiakim son of Hilkiah son of Shallum, and to the priests, and to all the people who were present with him in Jerusalem. ⁸At the same time, on the tenth day of Sivan, Baruch*ᵇ* took the vessels of the house of the Lord, which had been carried away from the temple, to return them to the land of Judah—the silver vessels that Zedekiah son of Josiah, king of Judah, had made, ⁹after King Nebuchadnezzar of Babylon had carried away from Jerusalem Jeconiah and the princes and the prisoners and the nobles and the people of the land, and brought them to Babylon.

A Letter to Jerusalem

10 They said: Here we send you money; so buy with the money burnt-offerings and sin-offerings and incense, and prepare a grain-offering, and offer them on the altar of the Lord our God; ¹¹and pray for the life of King Nebuchadnezzar of Babylon, and for the life of his son Belshazzar, so that their days on earth may be like the days of heaven. ¹²The Lord will give us strength, and light to our eyes; we shall live under the protection*ᶜ* of King Nebuchadnezzar of Babylon, and under the protection of his son Belshazzar, and we shall serve them for many days and find favour in their sight. ¹³Pray also for us to the Lord our God, for we have sinned against the Lord our God, and to this day the anger of the Lord and his wrath have not turned away from us. ¹⁴And you shall read aloud this scroll that we are sending you, to make your confession in the house of the Lord on the days of the festivals and at appointed seasons.

Confession of Sins

15 And you shall say: The Lord our God is in the right, but there is open shame on us today, on the people of Judah, on the inhabitants of Jerusalem, ¹⁶and on our kings, our rulers, our priests, our prophets, and our ancestors, ¹⁷because we have sinned before the Lord. ¹⁸We have disobeyed him, and have not heeded the voice of the Lord our God, to walk in the statutes of the Lord that he set before us. ¹⁹From the time when the Lord brought our ancestors out of the land of Egypt until today, we have been disobedient to the Lord our God, and we have been negligent, in not heeding his voice. ²⁰So to this day there have clung to us the calamities and the curse that the Lord declared through his servant Moses at the time when he brought our ancestors out of the land of

a Gk *the priest*   *b* Gk *he*   *c* Gk *in the shadow*

Egypt to give to us a land flowing with milk and honey. 21 We did not listen to the voice of the Lord our God in all the words of the prophets whom he sent to us, 22 but all of us followed the intent of our own wicked hearts by serving other gods and doing what is evil in the sight of the Lord our God.

2 So the Lord carried out the threat he spoke against us: against our judges who ruled Israel, and against our kings and our rulers and the people of Israel and Judah. 2 Under the whole heaven there has not been done the like of what he has done in Jerusalem, in accordance with the threats that were*a* written in the law of Moses. 3 Some of us ate the flesh of their sons and others the flesh of their daughters. 4 He made them subject to all the kingdoms around us, to be an object of scorn and a desolation among all the surrounding peoples, where the Lord has scattered them. 5 They were brought down and not raised up, because our nation*b* sinned against the Lord our God, in not heeding his voice.

6 The Lord our God is in the right, but there is open shame on us and our ancestors this very day. 7 All those calamities with which the Lord threatened us have come upon us. 8 Yet we have not entreated the favour of the Lord by turning away, each of us, from the thoughts of our wicked hearts. 9 And the Lord has kept the calamities ready, and the Lord has brought them upon us, for the Lord is just in all the works that he has commanded us to do. 10 Yet we have not obeyed his voice, to walk in the statutes of the Lord that he set before us.

Prayer for Deliverance

11 And now, O Lord God of Israel, who brought your people out of the land of Egypt with a mighty hand and with signs and wonders and with great power and outstretched arm, and made yourself a name that continues to this day, 12 we have sinned, we have been ungodly, we have done wrong, O Lord our God, against all your ordinances. 13 Let your anger turn away from us, for we are left, few in num-ber, among the nations where you have scattered us. 14 Hear, O Lord, our prayer and our supplication, and for your own sake deliver us, and grant us favour in the sight of those who have carried us into exile; 15 so that all the earth may know that you are the Lord our God, for Israel and his descendants are called by your name.

16 O Lord, look down from your holy dwelling, and consider us. Incline your ear, O Lord, and hear; 17 open your eyes, O Lord, and see, for the dead who are in Hades, whose spirit has been taken from their bodies, will not ascribe glory or justice to the Lord; 18 but the person who is deeply grieved, who walks bowed and feeble, with failing eyes and famished soul, will declare your glory and righteousness, O Lord.

19 For it is not because of any righteous deeds of our ancestors or our kings that we bring before you our prayer for mercy, O Lord our God. 20 For you have sent your anger and your wrath upon us, as you declared by your servants the prophets, saying: 21 Thus says the Lord: Bend your shoulders and serve the king of Babylon, and you will remain in the land that I gave to your ancestors. 22 But if you will not obey the voice of the Lord and will not serve the king of Babylon, 23 I will make to cease from the towns of Judah and from the region around Jerusalem the voice of mirth and the voice of gladness, the voice of the bridegroom and the voice of the bride, and the whole land will be a desolation without inhabitants.

24 But we did not obey your voice, to serve the king of Babylon; and you have carried out your threats, which you spoke by your servants the prophets, that the bones of our kings and the bones of our ancestors would be brought out of their resting-place; 25 and indeed they have been thrown out to the heat of day and the frost of night. They perished in great misery, by famine and sword and pestilence. 26 And the house that is called by your name you have made as it is today, because of the

a Gk in accordance with what is   b Gk because we

wickedness of the house of Israel and the house of Judah.

God's Promise Recalled

27 Yet you have dealt with us, O Lord our God, in all your kindness and in all your great compassion, 28 as you spoke by your servant Moses on the day when you commanded him to write your law in the presence of the people of Israel, saying, 29 'If you will not obey my voice, this very great multitude will surely turn into a small number among the nations, where I will scatter them. 30 For I know that they will not obey me, for they are a stiff-necked people. But in the land of their exile they will come to themselves 31 and know that I am the Lord their God. I will give them a heart that obeys and ears that hear; 32 they will praise me in the land of their exile, and will remember my name 33 and turn from their stubbornness and their wicked deeds; for they will remember the ways of their ancestors, who sinned before the Lord. 34 I will bring them again into the land that I swore to give to their ancestors, to Abraham, Isaac, and Jacob, and they will rule over it; and I will increase them, and they will not be diminished. 35 I will make an everlasting covenant with them to be their God and they shall be my people; and I will never again remove my people Israel from the land that I have given them.'

3 O Lord Almighty, God of Israel, the soul in anguish and the wearied spirit cry out to you. 2 Hear, O Lord, and have mercy, for we have sinned before you. 3 For you are enthroned for ever, and we are perishing for ever. 4 O Lord Almighty, God of Israel, hear now the prayer of the people*a* of Israel, the children of those who sinned before you, who did not heed the voice of the Lord their God, so that calamities have clung to us. 5 Do not remember the iniquities of our ancestors, but in this crisis remember your power and your name. 6 For you are the Lord our God, and it is you, O Lord, whom we will praise. 7 For you have put the fear of you in our hearts so that we call upon your name; and we will praise you in our exile, for we have put

away from our hearts all the iniquity of our ancestors who sinned against you. 8 See, we are today in our exile where you have scattered us, to be reproached and cursed and punished for all the iniquities of our ancestors, who forsook the Lord our God.

In Praise of Wisdom

9 Hear the commandments of life,
      O Israel;
   give ear, and learn wisdom!
10 Why is it, O Israel, why is it that you
         are in the land of your enemies,
      that you are growing old in a
         foreign country,
   that you are defiled with the dead,
11   that you are counted among those
         in Hades?
12 You have forsaken the fountain of
      wisdom.
13 If you had walked in the way of God,
      you would be living in peace for
         ever.
14 Learn where there is wisdom,
      where there is strength,
      where there is understanding,
   so that you may at the same time
         discern
      where there is length of days, and
         life,
      where there is light for the eyes,
         and peace.

15 Who has found her place?
      And who has entered her
         storehouses?
16 Where are the rulers of the nations,
      and those who lorded it over the
         animals on earth;
17 those who made sport of the birds of
      the air,
      and who hoarded up silver and
         gold
   in which people trust,
      and there is no end to their
         getting;
18 those who schemed to get silver, and
      were anxious,
      but there is no trace of their works?

a Gk dead

19 They have vanished and gone down
      to Hades,
    and others have arisen in their
      place.

20 Later generations have seen the light
      of day,
    and have lived upon the earth;
    but they have not learned the way to
      knowledge,
      nor understood her paths,
      nor laid hold of her.
21 Their descendants have strayed far
      from her[a] way.
22 She has not been heard of in Canaan,
    or seen in Teman;
23 the descendants of Hagar, who seek
      for understanding on the earth,
    the merchants of Merran and
      Teman,
    the story-tellers and the seekers for
      understanding,
    have not learned the way to wisdom,
    or given thought to her paths.

24 O Israel, how great is the house of
      God,
    how vast the territory that he
      possesses!
25 It is great and has no bounds;
    it is high and immeasurable.
26 The giants were born there, who were
      famous of old,
    great in stature, expert in war.
27 God did not choose them,
    or give them the way to knowledge;
28 so they perished because they had no
      wisdom,
    they perished through their folly.

29 Who has gone up into heaven, and
      taken her,
    and brought her down from the
      clouds?
30 Who has gone over the sea, and
      found her,
    and will buy her for pure gold?
31 No one knows the way to her,
    or is concerned about the path to
      her.

32 But the one who knows all things
      knows her,
    he found her by his understanding.
    The one who prepared the earth for
      all time
    filled it with four-footed creatures;
33 the one who sends forth the light,
      and it goes;
    he called it, and it obeyed him,
      trembling;
34 the stars shone in their watches, and
      were glad;
    he called them, and they said, 'Here
      we are!'
    They shone with gladness for him
      who made them.
35 This is our God;
    no other can be compared to him.
36 He found the whole way to
      knowledge,
    and gave her to his servant Jacob
    and to Israel, whom he loved.
37 Afterwards she appeared on earth
    and lived with humankind.

4 She is the book of the
      commandments of God,
    the law that endures for ever.
    All who hold her fast will live,
    and those who forsake her will
      die.
2 Turn, O Jacob, and take her;
    walk towards the shining of her
      light.
3 Do not give your glory to another,
    or your advantages to an alien
      people.
4 Happy are we, O Israel,
    for we know what is pleasing to
      God.

Encouragement for Israel

5 Take courage, my people,
    who perpetuate Israel's name!
6 It was not for destruction
    that you were sold to the nations,
    but you were handed over to your
      enemies
    because you angered God.

a Other ancient authorities read *their*

7 For you provoked the one who made
   you
   by sacrificing to demons and not to
   God.
8 You forgot the everlasting God, who
   brought you up,
   and you grieved Jerusalem, who
   reared you.
9 For she saw the wrath that came
   upon you from God,
   and she said:
   Listen, you neighbours of Zion,
   God has brought great sorrow upon
   me;
10 for I have seen the exile of my sons
   and daughters,
   which the Everlasting brought upon
   them.
11 With joy I nurtured them,
   but I sent them away with weeping
   and sorrow.
12 Let no one rejoice over me, a widow
   and bereaved of many;
   I was left desolate because of the sins
   of my children,
   because they turned away from the
   law of God.
13 They had no regard for his statutes;
   they did not walk in the ways of
   God's commandments,
   or tread the paths his righteousness
   showed them.
14 Let the neighbours of Zion come;
   remember the capture of my sons
   and daughters,
   which the Everlasting brought upon
   them.
15 For he brought a distant nation
   against them,
   a nation ruthless and of a strange
   language,
   which had no respect for the aged
   and no pity for a child.
16 They led away the widow's beloved
   sons,
   and bereaved the lonely woman of
   her daughters.

17 But I, how can I help you?
18 For he who brought these calamities
   upon you
   will deliver you from the hand of
   your enemies.
19 Go, my children, go;
   for I have been left desolate.
20 I have taken off the robe of peace
   and put on sackcloth for my
   supplication;
   I will cry to the Everlasting all my
   days.

21 Take courage, my children, cry to
   God,
   and he will deliver you from the
   power and hand of the enemy.
22 For I have put my hope in the
   Everlasting to save you,
   and joy has come to me from the
   Holy One,
   because of the mercy that will soon
   come to you
   from your everlasting saviour. *a*
23 For I sent you out with sorrow and
   weeping,
   but God will give you back to me
   with joy and gladness for ever.
24 For as the neighbours of Zion have
   now seen your capture,
   so they soon will see your salvation
   by God,
   which will come to you with great
   glory
   and with the splendour of the
   Everlasting.
25 My children, endure with patience
   the wrath that has come upon
   you from God.
   Your enemy has overtaken you,
   but you will soon see their
   destruction
   and will tread upon their necks.
26 My pampered children have travelled
   rough roads;
   they were taken away like a flock
   carried off by the enemy.

27 Take courage, my children, and cry to
   God,
   for you will be remembered by the
   one who brought this upon
   you.

a Or *from the Everlasting, your saviour*

28 For just as you were disposed to go
        astray from God,
    return with tenfold zeal to seek
        him.
29 For the one who brought these
        calamities upon you
    will bring you everlasting joy with
        your salvation.

Jerusalem Is Assured of Help

30 Take courage, O Jerusalem,
    for the one who named you will
        comfort you.
31 Wretched will be those who
        mistreated you
    and who rejoiced at your fall.
32 Wretched will be the cities that your
        children served as slaves;
    wretched will be the city that
        received your offspring.
33 For just as she rejoiced at your fall
    and was glad at your ruin,
    so she will be grieved at her own
        desolation.
34 I will take away her pride in her great
        population,
    and her insolence will be turned to
        grief.
35 For fire will come upon her from the
        Everlasting for many days,
    and for a long time she will be
        inhabited by demons.

36 Look towards the east, O Jerusalem,
    and see the joy that is coming to
        you from God.
37 Look, your children are coming,
        whom you sent away;
    they are coming, gathered from east
        and west,
    at the word of the Holy One,
    rejoicing in the glory of God.

5 Take off the garment of your sorrow
        and affliction, O Jerusalem,
    and put on for ever the beauty of
        the glory from God.
2 Put on the robe of the righteousness
        that comes from God;
    put on your head the diadem of the
        glory of the Everlasting;

3 for God will show your splendour
        everywhere under heaven.
4 For God will give you evermore the
        name,
    'Righteous Peace, Godly Glory'.

5 Arise, O Jerusalem, stand upon the
        height;
    look towards the east,
    and see your children gathered from
        west and east
    at the word of the Holy One,
    rejoicing that God has remembered
        them.
6 For they went out from you on foot,
        led away by their enemies;
    but God will bring them back to you,
    carried in glory, as on a royal
        throne.
7 For God has ordered that every high
        mountain and the everlasting
        hills be made low
    and the valleys filled up, to make
        level ground,
    so that Israel may walk safely in the
        glory of God.
8 The woods and every fragrant tree
    have shaded Israel at God's
        command.
9 For God will lead Israel with joy,
    in the light of his glory,
    with the mercy and righteousness
        that come from him.

The Letter of Jeremiah

6 [a] A copy of a letter that Jeremiah sent to
    those who were to be taken to Bab-
ylon as exiles by the king of the Babylonians, to give them the message that God
had commanded him.

The People Face a Long Captivity

2 Because of the sins that you have committed before God, you will be taken to
Babylon as exiles by Nebuchadnezzar, king
of the Babylonians. 3Therefore, when you
have come to Babylon you will remain

a The King James Version (like the Latin Vulgate) prints
The Letter of Jeremiah as Chapter 6 of the Book of
Baruch, and the chapter and verse numbers are here
retained. In the Greek Septuagint, the Letter is separated
from Baruch by the Book of Lamentations.

there for many years, for a long time, up to seven generations; after that I will bring you away from there in peace. ⁴ Now in Babylon you will see gods made of silver and gold and wood, which people carry on their shoulders, and which cause the heathen to fear. ⁵ So beware of becoming at all like the foreigners or of letting fear for these gods*a* possess you ⁶ when you see the multitude before and behind them worshipping them. But say in your heart, 'It is you, O Lord, whom we must worship.' ⁷ For my angel is with you, and he is watching over your lives.

The Helplessness of Idols

8 Their tongues are smoothed by the carpenter, and they themselves are overlaid with gold and silver; but they are false and cannot speak. ⁹ People*b* take gold and make crowns for the heads of their gods, as they might for a girl who loves ornaments. ¹⁰ Sometimes the priests secretly take gold and silver from their gods and spend it on themselves, ¹¹ or even give some of it to the prostitutes on the terrace. They deck their gods*c* out with garments like human beings—these gods of silver and gold and wood ¹² that cannot save themselves from rust and corrosion. When they have been dressed in purple robes, ¹³ their faces are wiped because of the dust from the temple, which is thick upon them. ¹⁴ One of them holds a sceptre, like a district judge, but is unable to destroy anyone who offends it. ¹⁵ Another has a dagger in its right hand, and an axe, but cannot defend itself from war and robbers. ¹⁶ From this it is evident that they are not gods; so do not fear them.

17 For just as someone's dish is useless when it is broken, ¹⁸ so are their gods when they have been set up in the temples. Their eyes are full of the dust raised by the feet of those who enter. And just as the gates are shut on every side against anyone who has offended a king, as though under sentence of death, so the priests make their temples secure with doors and locks and bars, in order that they may not be plundered by robbers. ¹⁹ They light more lamps for them than they light for themselves, though

their gods*d* can see none of them. ²⁰ They are*e* just like a beam of the temple, but their hearts, it is said, are eaten away when crawling creatures from the earth devour them and their robes. They do not notice ²¹ when their faces have been blackened by the smoke of the temple. ²² Bats, swallows, and birds alight on their bodies and heads; and so do cats. ²³ From this you will know that they are not gods; so do not fear them.

24 As for the gold that they wear for beauty—it*f* will not shine unless someone wipes off the tarnish; for even when they were being cast, they did not feel it. ²⁵ They are bought without regard to cost, but there is no breath in them. ²⁶ Having no feet, they are carried on the shoulders of others, revealing to humankind their worthlessness. And those who serve them are put to shame ²⁷ because, if any of these gods falls*g* to the ground, they themselves must pick it up. If anyone sets it upright, it cannot move itself; and if it is tipped over, it cannot straighten itself. Gifts are placed before them just as before the dead. ²⁸ The priests sell the sacrifices that are offered to these gods*h* and use the money themselves. Likewise their wives preserve some of the meat*i* with salt, but give none to the poor or helpless. ²⁹ Sacrifices to them may even be touched by women in their periods or at childbirth. Since you know by these things that they are not gods, do not fear them.

30 For how can they be called gods? Women serve meals for gods of silver and gold and wood; ³¹ and in their temples the priests sit with their clothes torn, their heads and beards shaved, and their heads uncovered. ³² They howl and shout before their gods as some do at a funeral banquet. ³³ The priests take some of the clothing of their gods*j* to clothe their wives and children. ³⁴ Whether one does evil to them or good, they will not be able to repay it. They cannot set up a king or depose one. ³⁵ Likewise they are not able to give either wealth or money; if one makes a vow to them and does not keep it, they will not require it.

a Gk *for them*　　*b* Gk *They*　　*c* Gk *them*　　*d* Gk *they*
e Gk *It is*　　*f* Lat Syr: Gk *they*　　*g* Gk *if they fall*
h Gk *to them*　　*i* Gk *of them*　　*j* Gk *some of their clothing*

[36] They cannot save anyone from death or rescue the weak from the strong. [37] They cannot restore sight to the blind; they cannot rescue one who is in distress. [38] They cannot take pity on a widow or do good to an orphan. [39] These things that are made of wood and overlaid with gold and silver are like stones from the mountain, and those who serve them will be put to shame. [40] Why then must anyone think that they are gods, or call them gods?

The Foolishness of Worshipping Idols

Besides, even the Chaldeans themselves dishonour them; for when they see someone who cannot speak, they bring Bel and pray that the mute may speak, as though Bel[a] were able to understand! [41] Yet they themselves cannot perceive this and abandon them, for they have no sense. [42] And the women, with cords around them, sit along the passageways, burning bran for incense. [43] When one of them is led off by one of the passers-by and is taken to bed by him, she derides the woman next to her, because she was not as attractive as herself and her cord was not broken. [44] Whatever is done for these idols[b] is false. Why then must anyone think that they are gods, or call them gods?

[45] They are made by carpenters and goldsmiths; they can be nothing but what the artisans wish them to be. [46] Those who make them will certainly not live very long themselves; [47] how then can the things that are made by them be gods? They have left only lies and reproach for those who come after. [48] For when war or calamity comes upon them, the priests consult together as to where they can hide themselves and their gods.[b] [49] How then can one fail to see that these are not gods, for they cannot save themselves from war or calamity? [50] Since they are made of wood and overlaid with gold and silver, it will afterwards be known that they are false. [51] It will be manifest to all the nations and kings that they are not gods but the work of human hands, and that there is no work of God in them. [52] Who then can fail to know that they are not gods?[c]

[53] For they cannot set up a king over a country or give rain to people. [54] They cannot judge their own cause or deliver one who is wronged, for they have no power; [55] they are like crows between heaven and earth. When fire breaks out in a temple of wooden gods overlaid with gold or silver, their priests will flee and escape, but the gods[d] will be burned up like timbers. [56] Besides, they can offer no resistance to king or enemy. Why then must anyone admit or think that they are gods?

[57] Gods made of wood and overlaid with silver and gold are unable to save themselves from thieves or robbers. [58] Anyone who can will strip them of their gold and silver and of the robes they wear, and go off with this booty, and they will not be able to help themselves. [59] So it is better to be a king who shows his courage, or a household utensil that serves its owner's need, than to be these false gods; better even the door of a house that protects its contents, than these false gods; better also a wooden pillar in a palace, than these false gods.

[60] For sun and moon and stars are bright, and when sent to do a service, they are obedient. [61] So also the lightning, when it flashes, is widely seen; and the wind likewise blows in every land. [62] When God commands the clouds to go over the whole world, they carry out his command. [63] And the fire sent from above to consume mountains and woods does what it is ordered. But these idols[e] are not to be compared with them in appearance or power. [64] Therefore one must not think that they are gods, nor call them gods, for they are not able either to decide a case or to do good to anyone. [65] Since you know then that they are not gods, do not fear them.

[66] They can neither curse nor bless kings; [67] they cannot show signs in the heavens for the nations, or shine like the sun or give light like the moon. [68] The wild animals are better than they are, for they can flee to shelter and help themselves.

a Gk he   b Gk them   c Meaning of Gk uncertain
d Gk they   e Gk these things

⁶⁹So we have no evidence whatever that they are gods; therefore do not fear them.

70 Like a scarecrow in a cucumber bed, which guards nothing, so are their gods of wood, overlaid with gold and silver. ⁷¹In the same way, their gods of wood, overlaid with gold and silver, are like a thornbush in a garden on which every bird perches; or like a corpse thrown out in the darkness.

⁷²From the purple and linen*a* that rot upon them you will know that they are not gods; and they will finally be consumed themselves, and be a reproach in the land. ⁷³Better, therefore, is someone upright who has no idols; such a person will be far above reproach.

a Cn: Gk *marble,* Syr *silk*

EZEKIEL

The Vision of the Chariot

1 In the thirtieth year, in the fourth month, on the fifth day of the month, as I was among the exiles by the river Chebar, the heavens were opened, and I saw visions of God. 2 On the fifth day of the month (it was the fifth year of the exile of King Jehoiachin), 3 the word of the LORD came to the priest Ezekiel son of Buzi, in the land of the Chaldeans by the river Chebar; and the hand of the LORD was on him there.

4 As I looked, a stormy wind came out of the north: a great cloud with brightness around it and fire flashing forth continually, and in the middle of the fire, something like gleaming amber. 5 In the middle of it was something like four living creatures. This was their appearance: they were of human form. 6 Each had four faces, and each of them had four wings. 7 Their legs were straight, and the soles of their feet were like the sole of a calf's foot; and they sparkled like burnished bronze. 8 Under their wings on their four sides they had human hands. And the four had their faces and their wings thus: 9 their wings touched one another; each of them moved straight ahead, without turning as they moved. 10 As for the appearance of their faces: the four had the face of a human being, the face of a lion on the right side, the face of an ox on the left side, and the face of an eagle; 11 such were their faces. Their wings were spread out above; each creature had two wings, each of which touched the wing of another, while two covered their bodies. 12 Each moved straight ahead; wherever the spirit would go, they went, without turning as they went. 13 In the middle of[a] the living creatures there was something that looked like burning coals of fire, like torches moving to and fro among the living creatures; the fire was bright, and lightning issued from the fire. 14 The living creatures darted to and fro, like a flash of lightning.

15 As I looked at the living creatures, I saw a wheel on the earth beside the living creatures, one for each of the four of them.[b] 16 As for the appearance of the wheels and their construction: their appearance was like the gleaming of beryl; and the four had the same form, their construction being something like a wheel within a wheel. 17 When they moved, they moved in any of the four directions without veering as they moved. 18 Their rims were tall and awesome, for the rims of all four were full of eyes all round. 19 When the living creatures moved, the wheels moved beside them; and when the living creatures rose from the earth, the wheels rose. 20 Wherever the spirit would go, they went, and the wheels rose along with them; for the spirit of the living creatures was in the wheels. 21 When they moved, the others moved; when they stopped, the others stopped; and when they rose from the earth, the wheels rose along with them; for the spirit of the living creatures was in the wheels.

22 Over the heads of the living creatures there was something like a dome, shining like crystal,[c] spread out above their heads. 23 Under the dome their wings were stretched out straight, one towards another; and each of the creatures had two wings covering its body. 24 When they moved, I

---

a Gk OL: Heb *And the appearance of*   b Heb *of their faces*   c Gk: Heb *like the awesome crystal* heard the sound of their wings like the sound of mighty waters, like the thunder of the Almighty,[a] a sound of tumult like the sound of an army; when they stopped, they let down their wings. 25 And there came a voice from above the dome over their heads; when they stopped, they let down their wings.

26 And above the dome over their heads there was something like a throne, in appearance like sapphire;[b] and seated above the likeness of a throne was something that seemed like a human form. 27 Upwards from what appeared like the loins I saw something like gleaming amber, something that looked like fire enclosed all round; and downwards from what looked like the loins I saw something that looked like fire, and there was a splendour all round. 28 Like the bow in a cloud on a rainy day, such was the appearance of the splendour all round. This was the appearance of the likeness of the glory of the LORD.

When I saw it, I fell on my face, and I heard the voice of someone speaking.

The Vision of the Scroll

2 He said to me: O mortal,[c] stand up on your feet, and I will speak with you. 2 And when he spoke to me, a spirit entered into me and set me on my feet; and I heard him speaking to me. 3 He said to me, Mortal, I am sending you to the people of Israel, to a nation[d] of rebels who have rebelled against me; they and their ancestors have transgressed against me to this very day. 4 The descendants are impudent and stubborn. I am sending you to them, and you shall say to them, 'Thus says the Lord GOD.' 5 Whether they hear or refuse to hear (for they are a rebellious house), they shall know that there has been a prophet among them. 6 And you, O mortal, do not be afraid of them, and do not be afraid of their words, though briers and thorns surround you and you live among scorpions; do not be afraid of their words, and do not be dismayed at their looks, for they are a rebellious house. 7 You shall speak my words to them, whether they hear or refuse to hear; for they are a rebellious house.

8 But you, mortal, hear what I say to you; do not be rebellious like that rebellious house; open your mouth and eat what I give you. 9 I looked, and a hand was stretched out to me, and a written scroll was in it. 10 He spread it before me; it had writing on the front and on the back, and written on it were words of lamentation and mourning and woe.

3 He said to me, O mortal, eat what is offered to you; eat this scroll, and go, speak to the house of Israel. 2 So I opened my mouth, and he gave me the scroll to eat. 3 He said to me, Mortal, eat this scroll that I give you and fill your stomach with it. Then I ate it; and in my mouth it was as sweet as honey.

4 He said to me: Mortal, go to the house of Israel and speak my very words to them. 5 For you are not sent to a people of obscure speech and difficult language, but to the house of Israel— 6 not to many peoples of obscure speech and difficult language, whose words you cannot understand. Surely, if I sent you to them, they would listen to you. 7 But the house of Israel will not listen to you, for they are not willing to listen to me; because all the house of Israel have a hard forehead and a stubborn heart. 8 See, I have made your face hard against their faces, and your forehead hard against their foreheads. 9 Like the hardest stone, harder than flint, I have made your forehead; do not fear them or be dismayed at their looks, for they are a rebellious house. 10 He said to me: Mortal, all my words that I shall speak to you receive in your heart and hear with your ears; 11 then go to the exiles, to your people, and speak to them. Say to them, 'Thus says the Lord GOD'; whether they hear or refuse to hear.

Ezekiel at the River Chebar

12 Then the spirit lifted me up, and as the glory of the LORD rose[e] from its place, I

a Traditional rendering of Heb Shaddai　　b Or lapis lazuli　　c Or son of man; Heb ben adam (and so throughout the book when Ezekiel is addressed)　d Syr: Heb to nations　　e Cn: Heb and blessed be the glory of the LORD heard behind me the sound of loud rumbling; [13] it was the sound of the wings of the living creatures brushing against one another, and the sound of the wheels beside them, that sounded like a loud rumbling. [14] The spirit lifted me up and bore me away; I went in bitterness in the heat of my spirit, the hand of the LORD being strong upon me. [15] I came to the exiles at Tel-abib, who lived by the river Chebar.[a] And I sat there among them, stunned, for seven days.

16 At the end of seven days, the word of the LORD came to me: [17] Mortal, I have made you a sentinel for the house of Israel; whenever you hear a word from my mouth, you shall give them warning from me. [18] If I say to the wicked, 'You shall surely die', and you give them no warning, and do not speak to warn the wicked from their wicked way, in order to save their life, those wicked persons shall die for their iniquity; but their blood I will require at your hand. [19] But if you warn the wicked, and they do not turn from their wickedness, or from their wicked way, they shall die for their iniquity; but you will have saved your life. [20] Again, if the righteous turn from their righteousness and commit iniquity, and I lay a stumbling-block before them, they shall die; because you have not warned them, they shall die for their sin, and their righteous deeds that they have done shall not be remembered; but their blood I will require at your hand. [21] If, however, you warn the righteous not to sin, and they do not sin, they shall surely live, because they took warning; and you will have saved your life.

Ezekiel Isolated and Silenced

22 Then the hand of the LORD was upon me there; and he said to me, Rise up, go out into the valley, and there I will speak with you. [23] So I rose up and went out into the valley; and the glory of the LORD stood there, like the glory that I had seen by the river Chebar; and I fell on my face. [24] The spirit entered into me, and set me on my feet; and he spoke with me and said to me: Go, shut yourself inside your house. [25] As

for you, mortal, cords shall be placed on you, and you shall be bound with them, so that you cannot go out among the people; [26] and I will make your tongue cling to the roof of your mouth, so that you shall be speechless and unable to reprove them; for they are a rebellious house. [27] But when I speak with you, I will open your mouth, and you shall say to them, 'Thus says the Lord GOD'; let those who will hear, hear; and let those who refuse to hear, refuse; for they are a rebellious house.

The Siege of Jerusalem Portrayed

4 And you, O mortal, take a brick and set it before you. On it portray a city, Jerusalem; [2] and put siege-works against it, and build a siege-wall against it, and cast up a ramp against it; set camps also against it, and plant battering-rams against it all round. [3] Then take an iron plate and place it as an iron wall between you and the city; set your face towards it, and let it be in a state of siege, and press the siege against it. This is a sign for the house of Israel.

4 Then lie on your left side, and place the punishment of the house of Israel upon it; you shall bear their punishment for the number of the days that you lie there. [5] For I assign to you a number of days, three hundred and ninety days, equal to the number of the years of their punishment; and so you shall bear the punishment of the house of Israel. [6] When you have completed these, you shall lie down a second time, but on your right side, and bear the punishment of the house of Judah; forty days I assign you, one day for each year. [7] You shall set your face towards the siege of Jerusalem, and with your arm bared you shall prophesy against it. [8] See, I am putting cords on you so that you cannot turn from one side to the other until you have completed the days of your siege.

9 And you, take wheat and barley, beans and lentils, millet and spelt; put them into one vessel, and make bread for yourself. During the number of days that you lie on your side, three hundred and ninety days,

a Two Mss Syr: Heb *Chebar, and to where they lived.* Another reading is *Chebar, and I sat where they sat* you shall eat it. ¹⁰The food that you eat shall be twenty shekels a day by weight; at fixed times you shall eat it. ¹¹And you shall drink water by measure, one-sixth of a hin; at fixed times you shall drink. ¹²You shall eat it as a barley-cake, baking it in their sight on human dung. ¹³The LORD said, 'Thus shall the people of Israel eat their bread, unclean, among the nations to which I will drive them.' ¹⁴Then I said, 'Ah Lord GOD! I have never defiled myself; from my youth up until now I have never eaten what died of itself or was torn by animals, nor has carrion flesh come into my mouth.' ¹⁵Then he said to me, 'See, I will let you have cow's dung instead of human dung, on which you may prepare your bread.'

16 Then he said to me, Mortal, I am going to break the staff of bread in Jerusalem; they shall eat bread by weight and with fearfulness; and they shall drink water by measure and in dismay. ¹⁷Lacking bread and water, they will look at one another in dismay, and waste away under their punishment.

A Sword against Jerusalem

5 And you, O mortal, take a sharp sword; use it as a barber's razor and run it over your head and your beard; then take balances for weighing, and divide the hair. ²One-third of the hair you shall burn in the fire inside the city, when the days of the siege are completed; one-third you shall take and strike with the sword all around the city;ᵃ and one-third you shall scatter to the wind, and I will unsheathe the sword after them. ³Then you shall take from these a small number, and bind them in the skirts of your robe. ⁴From these, again, you shall take some, throw them into the fire, and burn them up; from there a fire will come out against all the house of Israel.

5 Thus says the Lord GOD: This is Jerusalem; I have set her in the centre of the nations, with countries all around her. ⁶But she has rebelled against my ordinances and my statutes, becoming more wicked than the nations and the countries all around her, rejecting my ordinances and not following my statutes. ⁷Therefore thus says the Lord GOD: Because you are more turbulent than the nations that are all around you, and have not followed my statutes or kept my ordinances, but have acted according to the ordinances of the nations that are all around you; ⁸therefore thus says the Lord GOD: I, I myself, am coming against you; I will execute judgements among you in the sight of the nations. ⁹And because of all your abominations, I will do to you what I have never yet done, and the like of which I will never do again. ¹⁰Surely, parents shall eat their children in your midst, and children shall eat their parents; I will execute judgements on you, and any of you who survive I will scatter to every wind. ¹¹Therefore, as I live, says the Lord GOD, surely, because you have defiled my sanctuary with all your detestable things and with all your abominations—therefore I will cut you down;ᵇ my eye will not spare, and I will have no pity. ¹²One-third of you shall die of pestilence or be consumed by famine among you; one-third shall fall by the sword around you; and one-third I will scatter to every wind and will unsheathe the sword after them.

13 My anger shall spend itself, and I will vent my fury on them and satisfy myself; and they shall know that I, the LORD, have spoken in my jealousy, when I spend my fury on them. ¹⁴Moreover, I will make you a desolation and an object of mocking among the nations around you, in the sight of all that pass by. ¹⁵You shall beᶜ a mockery and a taunt, a warning and a horror, to the nations around you, when I execute judgements on you in anger and fury, and with furious punishments—I, the LORD, have spoken— ¹⁶when I loose against youᵈ my deadly arrows of famine, arrows for destruction, which I will let loose to destroy you, and when I bring more and more famine upon you, and break your staff of bread. ¹⁷I will send famine and wild animals against you, and they will rob you of your children; pesti-

a Heb *it*   b Another reading is *I will withdraw*
c Gk Syr Vg Tg: Heb *It shall be*   d Heb *them*

lence and bloodshed shall pass through you; and I will bring the sword upon you. I, the LORD, have spoken.

Judgement on Idolatrous Israel

6 The word of the LORD came to me: ² O mortal, set your face towards the mountains of Israel, and prophesy against them, ³ and say, You mountains of Israel, hear the word of the Lord GOD! Thus says the Lord GOD to the mountains and the hills, to the ravines and the valleys: I, I myself will bring a sword upon you, and I will destroy your high places. ⁴ Your altars shall become desolate, and your incense-stands shall be broken; and I will throw down your slain in front of your idols. ⁵ I will lay the corpses of the people of Israel in front of their idols; and I will scatter your bones around your altars. ⁶ Wherever you live, your towns shall be waste and your high places ruined, so that your altars will be waste and ruined, *a* your idols broken and destroyed, your incense-stands cut down, and your works wiped out. ⁷ The slain shall fall in your midst; then you shall know that I am the LORD.

8 But I will spare some. Some of you shall escape the sword among the nations and be scattered through the countries. ⁹ Those of you who escape shall remember me among the nations where they are carried captive, how I was crushed by their wanton heart that turned away from me, and their wanton eyes that turned after their idols. Then they will be loathsome in their own sight for the evils that they have committed, for all their abominations. ¹⁰ And they shall know that I am the LORD; I did not threaten in vain to bring this disaster upon them.

11 Thus says the Lord GOD: Clap your hands and stamp your foot, and say, Alas for all the vile abominations of the house of Israel! For they shall fall by the sword, by famine, and by pestilence. ¹² Those far off shall die of pestilence; those nearby shall fall by the sword; and any who are left and are spared shall die of famine. Thus I will spend my fury upon them. ¹³ And you shall know that I am the LORD,

when their slain lie among their idols around their altars, on every high hill, on all the mountain tops, under every green tree, and under every leafy oak, wherever they offered pleasing odour to all their idols. ¹⁴ I will stretch out my hand against them, and make the land desolate and waste, throughout all their settlements, from the wilderness to Riblah. *b* Then they shall know that I am the LORD.

Impending Disaster

7 The word of the LORD came to me: ² You, O mortal, thus says the Lord GOD to the land of Israel:
An end! The end has come
upon the four corners of the land.
³ Now the end is upon you,
I will let loose my anger
upon you;
I will judge you according to
your ways,
I will punish you for all your
abominations.
⁴ My eye will not spare you, I will have
no pity.
I will punish you for your ways,
while your abominations are
among you.
Then you shall know that I am the LORD.
5 Thus says the Lord GOD:
Disaster after disaster! See, it comes.
⁶ An end has come, the end
has come.
It has awakened against you; see,
it comes!
⁷ Your doom *c* has come to you,
O inhabitant of the land.
The time has come, the day is near—
of tumult, not of revelling on the
mountains.
⁸ Soon now I will pour out my wrath
upon you;
I will spend my anger against you.
I will judge you according to
your ways,
and punish you for all your
abominations.

a Syr Vg Tg: Heb *and be made guilty*   *b* Another reading is *Diblah*   *c* Meaning of Heb uncertain

9 My eye will not spare; I will have no
    pity.
  I will punish you according to your
    ways,
  while your abominations are
    among you.
Then you shall know that it is I the LORD
who strike.
10 See, the day! See, it comes!
  Your doom*a* has gone out.
  The rod has blossomed, pride has
    budded.
11   Violence has grown into a rod
    of wickedness.
  None of them shall remain,
    not their abundance, not their
     wealth;
    no pre-eminence among them.*a*
12 The time has come, the day
    draws near;
    let not the buyer rejoice, nor the
     seller mourn,
    for wrath is upon all their
     multitude.
13 For the sellers shall not return to what
has been sold as long as they remain alive.
For the vision concerns all their multitude;
it shall not be revoked. Because of their iniquity, they cannot maintain their lives.*a*
14 They have blown the horn and made
    everything ready;
    but no one goes to battle,
    for my wrath is upon all their
     multitude.
15 The sword is outside, pestilence and
    famine are inside;
    those in the field die by the sword;
    those in the city—famine and
     pestilence devour them.
16 If any survivors escape,
    they shall be found on the
     mountains
    like doves of the valleys,
  all of them moaning over
    their iniquity.
17 All hands shall grow feeble,
    all knees turn to water.
18 They shall put on sackcloth,
    horror shall cover them.
  Shame shall be on all faces,
    baldness on all their heads.

19 They shall fling their silver into the
    streets,
  their gold shall be treated as
    unclean.
Their silver and gold cannot save them on
the day of the wrath of the LORD. They shall
not satisfy their hunger or fill their stomachs with it. For it was the stumbling-block
of their iniquity. 20 From their*b* beautiful
ornament, in which they took pride, they
made their abominable images, their detestable things; therefore I will make of it
an unclean thing to them.
21 I will hand it over to strangers
    as booty,
    to the wicked of the earth
     as plunder;
    they shall profane it.
22 I will avert my face from them,
    so that they may profane my
     treasured*c* place;
  the violent shall enter it,
    they shall profane it.
23 Make a chain!*a*
  For the land is full of bloody crimes;
    the city is full of violence.
24 I will bring the worst of the nations
    to take possession of their houses.
  I will put an end to the arrogance of
    the strong,
    and their holy places shall be
     profaned.
25 When anguish comes, they will seek
    peace,
    but there shall be none.
26 Disaster comes upon disaster,
    rumour follows rumour;
  they shall keep seeking a vision from
    the prophet;
    instruction shall perish from
     the priest,
    and counsel from the elders.
27 The king shall mourn,
    the prince shall be wrapped
     in despair,
    and the hands of the people of the
     land shall tremble.
  According to their way I will deal
    with them;

a Meaning of Heb uncertain   *b* Syr Symmachus: Heb
its   *c* Or *secret*

according to their own judgements
　　I will judge them.
And they shall know that I am the LORD.

Abominations in the Temple

8 In the sixth year, in the sixth month, on the fifth day of the month, as I sat in my house, with the elders of Judah sitting before me, the hand of the Lord GOD fell upon me there. [2] I looked, and there was a figure that looked like a human being;[a] below what appeared to be its loins it was fire, and above the loins it was like the appearance of brightness, like gleaming amber. [3] It stretched out the form of a hand, and took me by a lock of my head; and the spirit lifted me up between earth and heaven, and brought me in visions of God to Jerusalem, to the entrance of the gateway of the inner court that faces north, to the seat of the image of jealousy, which provokes to jealousy. [4] And the glory of the God of Israel was there, like the vision that I had seen in the valley.

[5] Then God[b] said to me, 'O mortal, lift up your eyes now in the direction of the north.' So I lifted up my eyes towards the north, and there, north of the altar gate, in the entrance, was this image of jealousy. [6] He said to me, 'Mortal, do you see what they are doing, the great abominations that the house of Israel are committing here, to drive me far from my sanctuary? Yet you will see still greater abominations.'

[7] And he brought me to the entrance of the court; I looked, and there was a hole in the wall. [8] Then he said to me, 'Mortal, dig through the wall'; and when I dug through the wall, there was an entrance. [9] He said to me, 'Go in, and see the vile abominations that they are committing here.' [10] So I went in and looked; there, portrayed on the wall all round, were all kinds of creeping things, and loathsome animals, and all the idols of the house of Israel. [11] Before them stood seventy of the elders of the house of Israel, with Jaazaniah son of Shaphan standing among them. Each had his censer in his hand, and the fragrant cloud of incense was ascending. [12] Then he said to me, 'Mortal, have you seen what the elders of the

house of Israel are doing in the dark, each in his room of images? For they say, "The LORD does not see us, the LORD has forsaken the land." ' [13] He said also to me, 'You will see still greater abominations that they are committing.'

[14] Then he brought me to the entrance of the north gate of the house of the LORD; women were sitting there weeping for Tammuz. [15] Then he said to me, 'Have you seen this, O mortal? You will see still greater abominations than these.'

[16] And he brought me into the inner court of the house of the LORD; there, at the entrance of the temple of the LORD, between the porch and the altar, were about twenty-five men, with their backs to the temple of the LORD, and their faces towards the east, prostrating themselves to the sun towards the east. [17] Then he said to me, 'Have you seen this, O mortal? Is it not bad enough that the house of Judah commits the abominations done here? Must they fill the land with violence, and provoke my anger still further? See, they are putting the branch to their nose! [18] Therefore I will act in wrath; my eye will not spare, nor will I have pity; and though they cry in my hearing with a loud voice, I will not listen to them.'

The Slaughter of the Idolaters

9 Then he cried in my hearing with a loud voice, saying, 'Draw near, you executioners of the city, each with his destroying weapon in his hand.' [2] And six men came from the direction of the upper gate, which faces north, each with his weapon for slaughter in his hand; among them was a man clothed in linen, with a writing-case at his side. They went in and stood beside the bronze altar.

[3] Now the glory of the God of Israel had gone up, from the cherub on which it rested, to the threshold of the house. The LORD called to the man clothed in linen, who had the writing-case at his side, [4] and said to him, 'Go through the city, through Jerusalem, and put a mark on the foreheads of those who sigh and groan over all the

_a_ Gk: Heb _like fire_　　_b_ Heb _he_

abominations that are committed in it.' ⁵To the others he said in my hearing, 'Pass through the city after him, and kill; your eye shall not spare, and you shall show no pity. ⁶Cut down old men, young men and young women, little children and women, but touch no one who has the mark. And begin at my sanctuary.' So they began with the elders who were in front of the house. ⁷Then he said to them, 'Defile the house, and fill the courts with the slain. Go!' So they went out and killed in the city. ⁸While they were killing, and I was left alone, I fell prostrate on my face and cried out, 'Ah Lord GOD! will you destroy all who remain of Israel as you pour out your wrath upon Jerusalem?' ⁹He said to me, 'The guilt of the house of Israel and Judah is exceedingly great; the land is full of bloodshed and the city full of perversity; for they say, "The LORD has forsaken the land, and the LORD does not see." ¹⁰As for me, my eye will not spare, nor will I have pity, but I will bring down their deeds upon their heads.'

11 Then the man clothed in linen, with the writing-case at his side, brought back word, saying, 'I have done as you commanded me.'

God's Glory Leaves Jerusalem

10 Then I looked, and above the dome that was over the heads of the cherubim there appeared above them something like a sapphire,ᵃ in form resembling a throne. ²He said to the man clothed in linen, 'Go within the wheel-work underneath the cherubim; fill your hands with burning coals from among the cherubim, and scatter them over the city.' He went in as I looked on. ³Now the cherubim were standing on the south side of the house when the man went in; and a cloud filled the inner court. ⁴Then the glory of the LORD rose up from the cherub to the threshold of the house; the house was filled with the cloud, and the court was full of the brightness of the glory of the LORD. ⁵The sound of the wings of the cherubim was heard as far as the outer court, like the voice of God Almightyᵇ when he speaks.

6 When he commanded the man clothed in linen, 'Take fire from within the wheel-work, from among the cherubim', he went in and stood beside a wheel. ⁷And a cherub stretched out his hand from among the cherubim to the fire that was among the cherubim, took some of it, and put it into the hands of the man clothed in linen, who took it and went out. ⁸The cherubim appeared to have the form of a human hand under their wings.

9 I looked, and there were four wheels beside the cherubim, one beside each cherub; and the appearance of the wheels was like gleaming beryl. ¹⁰And as for their appearance, the four looked alike, something like a wheel within a wheel. ¹¹When they moved, they moved in any of the four directions without veering as they moved; but in whatever direction the front wheel faced, the others followed without veering as they moved. ¹²Their entire body, their rims, their spokes, their wings, and the wheels—the wheels of the four of them—were full of eyes all round. ¹³As for the wheels, they were called in my hearing 'the wheel-work'. ¹⁴Each one had four faces: the first face was that of the cherub, the second face was that of a human being, the third that of a lion, and the fourth that of an eagle.

15 The cherubim rose up. These were the living creatures that I saw by the river Chebar. ¹⁶When the cherubim moved, the wheels moved beside them; and when the cherubim lifted up their wings to rise up from the earth, the wheels at their side did not veer. ¹⁷When they stopped, the others stopped, and when they rose up, the others rose up with them; for the spirit of the living creatures was in them.

18 Then the glory of the LORD went out from the threshold of the house and stopped above the cherubim. ¹⁹The cherubim lifted up their wings and rose up from the earth in my sight as they went out with the wheels beside them. They stopped at the entrance of the east gate of the house of the LORD; and the glory of the God of Israel was above them.

a Or *lapis lazuli*   *b* Traditional rendering of Heb *El Shaddai*

20 These were the living creatures that I saw underneath the God of Israel by the river Chebar; and I knew that they were cherubim. 21 Each had four faces, each four wings, and underneath their wings something like human hands. 22 As for what their faces were like, they were the same faces whose appearance I had seen by the river Chebar. Each one moved straight ahead.

Judgement on Wicked Counsellors

11 The spirit lifted me up and brought me to the east gate of the house of the LORD, which faces east. There, at the entrance of the gateway, were twenty-five men; among them I saw Jaazaniah son of Azzur, and Pelatiah son of Benaiah, officials of the people. 2 He said to me, 'Mortal, these are the men who devise iniquity and who give wicked counsel in this city; 3 they say, "The time is not near to build houses; this city is the pot, and we are the meat." 4 Therefore prophesy against them; prophesy, O mortal.'

5 Then the spirit of the LORD fell upon me, and he said to me, 'Say, Thus says the LORD: This is what you think, O house of Israel; I know the things that come into your mind. 6 You have killed many in this city, and have filled its streets with the slain. 7 Therefore thus says the Lord GOD: The slain whom you have placed within it are the meat, and this city is the pot; but you shall be taken out of it. 8 You have feared the sword; and I will bring the sword upon you, says the Lord GOD. 9 I will take you out of it and give you over to the hands of foreigners, and execute judgements upon you. 10 You shall fall by the sword; I will judge you at the border of Israel. And you shall know that I am the LORD. 11 This city shall not be your pot, and you shall not be the meat inside it; I will judge you at the border of Israel. 12 Then you shall know that I am the LORD, whose statutes you have not followed, and whose ordinances you have not kept, but you have acted according to the ordinances of the nations that are around you.'

13 Now, while I was prophesying, Pela-

tiah son of Benaiah died. Then I fell down on my face, cried with a loud voice, and said, 'Ah Lord GOD! will you make a full end of the remnant of Israel?'

God Will Restore Israel

14 Then the word of the LORD came to me: 15 Mortal, your kinsfolk, your own kin, your fellow exiles,*a* the whole house of Israel, all of them, are those of whom the inhabitants of Jerusalem have said, 'They have gone far from the LORD; to us this land is given for a possession.' 16 Therefore say: Thus says the Lord GOD: Though I removed them far away among the nations, and though I scattered them among the countries, yet I have been a sanctuary to them for a little while*b* in the countries where they have gone. 17 Therefore say: Thus says the Lord GOD: I will gather you from the peoples, and assemble you out of the countries where you have been scattered, and I will give you the land of Israel. 18 When they come there, they will remove from it all its detestable things and all its abominations. 19 I will give them one*c* heart, and put a new spirit within them; I will remove the heart of stone from their flesh and give them a heart of flesh, 20 so that they may follow my statutes and keep my ordinances and obey them. Then they shall be my people, and I will be their God. 21 But as for those whose heart goes after their detestable things and their abominations,*d* I will bring their deeds upon their own heads, says the Lord GOD.

22 Then the cherubim lifted up their wings, with the wheels beside them; and the glory of the God of Israel was above them. 23 And the glory of the LORD ascended from the middle of the city, and stopped on the mountain east of the city. 24 The spirit lifted me up and brought me in a vision by the spirit of God into Chaldea, to the exiles. Then the vision that I had seen left me. 25 And I told the exiles all the things that the LORD had shown me.

a Gk Syr: Heb *people of your kindred*   *b* Or *to some extent*   *c* Another reading is *a new*   *d* Cn: Heb *And to the heart of their detestable things and their abominations their heart goes*

Judah's Captivity Portrayed

12 The word of the LORD came to me: [2]Mortal, you are living in the midst of a rebellious house, who have eyes to see but do not see, who have ears to hear but do not hear; [3]for they are a rebellious house. Therefore, mortal, prepare for yourself an exile's baggage, and go into exile by day in their sight; you shall go like an exile from your place to another place in their sight. Perhaps they will understand, though they are a rebellious house. [4]You shall bring out your baggage by day in their sight, as baggage for exile; and you shall go out yourself at evening in their sight, as those do who go into exile. [5]Dig through the wall in their sight, and carry the baggage through it. [6]In their sight you shall lift the baggage on your shoulder, and carry it out in the dark; you shall cover your face, so that you may not see the land; for I have made you a sign for the house of Israel.

[7]I did just as I was commanded. I brought out my baggage by day, as baggage for exile, and in the evening I dug through the wall with my own hands; I brought it out in the dark, carrying it on my shoulder in their sight.

[8]In the morning the word of the LORD came to me: [9]Mortal, has not the house of Israel, the rebellious house, said to you, 'What are you doing?' [10]Say to them, 'Thus says the Lord GOD: This oracle concerns the prince in Jerusalem and all the house of Israel in it.' [11]Say, 'I am a sign for you: as I have done, so shall it be done to them; they shall go into exile, into captivity.' [12]And the prince who is among them shall lift his baggage on his shoulder in the dark, and shall go out; he[a] shall dig through the wall and carry it through; he shall cover his face, so that he may not see the land with his eyes. [13]I will spread my net over him, and he shall be caught in my snare; and I will bring him to Babylon, the land of the Chaldeans, yet he shall not see it; and he shall die there. [14]I will scatter to every wind all who are around him, his helpers and all his troops; and I will unsheathe the sword behind them. [15]And they shall know that I am the LORD, when I disperse them among the nations and scatter them through the countries. [16]But I will let a few of them escape from the sword, from famine and pestilence, so that they may tell of all their abominations among the nations where they go; then they shall know that I am the LORD.

Judgement Not Postponed

[17]The word of the LORD came to me: [18]Mortal, eat your bread with quaking, and drink your water with trembling and with fearfulness; [19]and say to the people of the land, Thus says the Lord GOD concerning the inhabitants of Jerusalem in the land of Israel: They shall eat their bread with fearfulness, and drink their water in dismay, because their land shall be stripped of all it contains, on account of the violence of all those who live in it. [20]The inhabited cities shall be laid waste, and the land shall become a desolation; and you shall know that I am the LORD.

[21]The word of the LORD came to me: [22]Mortal, what is this proverb of yours about the land of Israel, which says, 'The days are prolonged, and every vision comes to nothing'? [23]Tell them therefore, 'Thus says the Lord GOD: I will put an end to this proverb, and they shall use it no more as a proverb in Israel.' But say to them, The days are near, and the fulfilment of every vision. [24]For there shall no longer be any false vision or flattering divination within the house of Israel. [25]But I the LORD will speak the word that I speak, and it will be fulfilled. It will no longer be delayed; but in your days, O rebellious house, I will speak the word and fulfil it, says the Lord GOD.

[26]The word of the LORD came to me: [27]Mortal, the house of Israel is saying, 'The vision that he sees is for many years ahead; he prophesies for distant times.' [28]Therefore say to them, Thus says the Lord GOD: None of my words will be delayed any longer, but the word that I speak will be fulfilled, says the Lord GOD.

a Gk Syr: Heb *they*

False Prophets Condemned

13 The word of the LORD came to me: ²Mortal, prophesy against the prophets of Israel who are prophesying; say to those who prophesy out of their own imagination: 'Hear the word of the LORD!' ³Thus says the Lord GOD, Alas for the senseless prophets who follow their own spirit, and have seen nothing! ⁴Your prophets have been like jackals among ruins, O Israel. ⁵You have not gone up into the breaches, or repaired a wall for the house of Israel, so that it might stand in battle on the day of the LORD. ⁶They have prophesied falsehood and lying divination; they say, 'Says the LORD', when the LORD has not sent them, and yet they wait for the fulfilment of their word! ⁷Have you not seen a false vision or uttered a lying divination, when you have said, 'Says the LORD', even though I did not speak?

8 Therefore thus says the Lord GOD: Because you have uttered falsehood and prophesied lies, I am against you, says the Lord GOD. ⁹My hand will be against the prophets who see false visions and utter lying divinations; they shall not be in the council of my people, nor be enrolled in the register of the house of Israel, nor shall they enter the land of Israel; and you shall know that I am the Lord GOD. ¹⁰Because, in truth, because they have misled my people, saying, 'Peace', when there is no peace; and because, when the people build a wall, these prophets*ᵃ* smear whitewash on it. ¹¹Say to those who smear whitewash on it that it shall fall. There will be a deluge of rain,*ᵇ* great hailstones will fall, and a stormy wind will break out. ¹²When the wall falls, will it not be said to you, 'Where is the whitewash you smeared on it?' ¹³Therefore thus says the Lord GOD: In my wrath I will make a stormy wind break out, and in my anger there shall be a deluge of rain, and hailstones in wrath to destroy it. ¹⁴I will break down the wall that you have smeared with whitewash, and bring it to the ground, so that its foundation will be laid bare; when it falls, you shall perish within it; and you shall know that I am the LORD. ¹⁵Thus I will spend my wrath upon the wall, and upon those who have smeared it with whitewash; and I will say to you, The wall is no more, nor those who smeared it— ¹⁶the prophets of Israel who prophesied concerning Jerusalem and saw visions of peace for it, when there was no peace, says the Lord GOD.

17 As for you, mortal, set your face against the daughters of your people, who prophesy out of their own imagination; prophesy against them ¹⁸and say, Thus says the Lord GOD: Woe to the women who sew bands on all wrists, and make veils for the heads of people of every height, in the hunt for human lives! Will you hunt down lives among my people, and maintain your own lives? ¹⁹You have profaned me among my people for handfuls of barley and for pieces of bread, putting to death those who should not die and keeping alive those who should not live, by your lies to my people, who listen to lies.

20 Therefore thus says the Lord GOD: I am against your bands with which you hunt lives;*ᶜ* I will tear them from your arms, and let the lives go free, the lives that you hunt down like birds. ²¹I will tear off your veils, and save my people from your hands; they shall no longer be prey in your hands; and you shall know that I am the LORD. ²²Because you have disheartened the righteous falsely, although I have not disheartened them, and you have encouraged the wicked not to turn from their wicked way and save their lives; ²³therefore you shall no longer see false visions nor practise divination; I will save my people from your hand. Then you will know that I am the LORD.

God's Judgements Justified

14 Certain elders of Israel came to me and sat down before me. ²And the word of the LORD came to me: ³Mortal, these men have taken their idols into their hearts, and placed their iniquity as a stumbling-block before them; shall I let myself be consulted by them? ⁴Therefore speak to them, and say to them, Thus says the Lord

a Heb *they*   *b* Heb *rain and you*   *c* Gk Syr: Heb *lives for birds*

GOD: Any of those of the house of Israel who take their idols into their hearts and place their iniquity as a stumbling-block before them, and yet come to the prophet—I the LORD will answer those who come with the multitude of their idols, 5 in order that I may take hold of the hearts of the house of Israel, all of whom are estranged from me through their idols.

6 Therefore say to the house of Israel, Thus says the Lord GOD: Repent and turn away from your idols; and turn away your faces from all your abominations. 7 For any of those of the house of Israel, or of the aliens who reside in Israel, who separate themselves from me, taking their idols into their hearts and placing their iniquity as a stumbling-block before them, and yet come to a prophet to inquire of me by him, I the LORD will answer them myself. 8 I will set my face against them; I will make them a sign and a byword and cut them off from the midst of my people; and you shall know that I am the LORD.

9 If a prophet is deceived and speaks a word, I, the LORD, have deceived that prophet, and I will stretch out my hand against him, and will destroy him from the midst of my people Israel. 10 And they shall bear their punishment—the punishment of the inquirer and the punishment of the prophet shall be the same— 11 so that the house of Israel may no longer go astray from me, nor defile themselves any more with all their transgressions. Then they shall be my people, and I will be their God, says the Lord GOD.

12 The word of the LORD came to me: 13 Mortal, when a land sins against me by acting faithlessly, and I stretch out my hand against it, and break its staff of bread and send famine upon it, and cut off from it human beings and animals, 14 even if Noah, Daniel,*a* and Job, these three, were in it, they would save only their own lives by their righteousness, says the Lord GOD. 15 If I send wild animals through the land to ravage it, so that it is made desolate, and no one may pass through because of the animals; 16 even if these three men were in it, as I live, says the Lord GOD, they would

save neither sons nor daughters; they alone would be saved, but the land would be desolate. 17 Or if I bring a sword upon that land and say, 'Let a sword pass through the land', and I cut off human beings and animals from it; 18 though these three men were in it, as I live, says the Lord GOD, they would save neither sons nor daughters, but they alone would be saved. 19 Or if I send a pestilence into that land, and pour out my wrath upon it with blood, to cut off humans and animals from it; 20 even if Noah, Daniel,*a* and Job were in it, as I live, says the Lord GOD, they would save neither son nor daughter; they would save only their own lives by their righteousness.

21 For thus says the Lord GOD: How much more when I send upon Jerusalem my four deadly acts of judgement, sword, famine, wild animals, and pestilence, to cut off humans and animals from it! 22 Yet, survivors shall be left in it, sons and daughters who will be brought out; they will come out to you. When you see their ways and their deeds, you will be consoled for the evil that I have brought upon Jerusalem, for all that I have brought upon it. 23 They shall console you, when you see their ways and their deeds; and you shall know that it was not without cause that I did all that I have done in it, says the Lord GOD.

The Useless Vine

15 The word of the LORD came to me: 2 O mortal, how does the wood of the vine surpass all other wood— the vine branch that is among the trees of the forest?
3 Is wood taken from it to make anything?
Does one take a peg from it on which to hang any object?
4 It is put in the fire for fuel; when the fire has consumed both ends of it
and the middle of it is charred, is it useful for anything?
5 When it was whole it was used for nothing;

---

a Or, as otherwise read, *Danel*

how much less—when the fire has
    consumed it,
and it is charred—
    can it ever be used for anything!

6 Therefore thus says the Lord GOD: Like
the wood of the vine among the trees of
the forest, which I have given to the fire for
fuel, so I will give up the inhabitants of Jerusalem. 7 I will set my face against them;
although they escape from the fire, the fire
shall still consume them; and you shall
know that I am the LORD, when I set my
face against them. 8 And I will make the
land desolate, because they have acted
faithlessly, says the Lord GOD.

God's Faithless Bride

16 The word of the LORD came to me:
2 Mortal, make known to Jerusa-
lem her abominations, 3 and say, Thus says
the Lord GOD to Jerusalem: Your origin
and your birth were in the land of the
Canaanites; your father was an Amorite,
and your mother a Hittite. 4 As for your
birth, on the day you were born your navel
cord was not cut, nor were you washed
with water to cleanse you, nor rubbed with
salt, nor wrapped in cloths. 5 No eye pitied
you, to do any of these things for you out
of compassion for you; but you were
thrown out in the open field, for you were
abhorred on the day you were born.

6 I passed by you, and saw you flailing
about in your blood. As you lay in your
blood, I said to you, 'Live! 7 and grow up*a*
like a plant of the field.' You grew up and
became tall and arrived at full woman-
hood;*b* your breasts were formed, and your
hair had grown; yet you were naked and
bare.

8 I passed by you again and looked on
you; you were at the age for love. I spread
the edge of my cloak over you, and covered
your nakedness: I pledged myself to you
and entered into a covenant with you, says
the Lord GOD, and you became mine.
9 Then I bathed you with water and washed
off the blood from you, and anointed you
with oil. 10 I clothed you with embroidered
cloth and with sandals of fine leather; I
bound you in fine linen and covered you

with rich fabric.*c* 11 I adorned you with ornaments: I put bracelets on your arms, a
chain on your neck, 12 a ring on your nose,
ear-rings in your ears, and a beautiful
crown upon your head. 13 You were
adorned with gold and silver, while your
clothing was of fine linen, rich fabric,*c* and
embroidered cloth. You had choice flour
and honey and oil for food. You grew exceedingly beautiful, fit to be a queen.
14 Your fame spread among the nations on
account of your beauty, for it was perfect
because of my splendour that I had bestowed on you, says the Lord GOD.

15 But you trusted in your beauty, and
played the whore because of your fame,
and lavished your whorings on any passer-
by.*d* 16 You took some of your garments,
and made for yourself colourful shrines,
and on them played the whore; nothing
like this has ever been or ever shall be.*c*
17 You also took your beautiful jewels of
my gold and my silver that I had given you,
and made for yourself male images, and
with them played the whore; 18 and you
took your embroidered garments to cover
them, and set my oil and my incense before them. 19 Also my bread that I gave
you—I fed you with choice flour and oil
and honey—you set it before them as a
pleasing odour; and so it was, says the Lord
GOD. 20 You took your sons and your
daughters, whom you had borne to me,
and these you sacrificed to them to be devoured. As if your whorings were not
enough! 21 You slaughtered my children
and delivered them up as an offering to
them. 22 And in all your abominations and
your whorings you did not remember the
days of your youth, when you were naked
and bare, flailing about in your blood.

23 After all your wickedness (woe, woe
to you! says the Lord GOD), 24 you built
yourself a platform and made yourself a
lofty place in every square; 25 at the head of
every street you built your lofty place and
prostituted your beauty, offering yourself
to every passer-by, and multiplying your

a Gk Syr: Heb *Live! I made you a myriad*   *b* Cn: Heb
ornament of ornaments   *c* Meaning of Heb uncertain
d Heb adds *let it be his*

whoring. 26 You played the whore with the Egyptians, your lustful neighbours, multiplying your whoring, to provoke me to anger. 27 Therefore I stretched out my hand against you, reduced your rations, and gave you up to the will of your enemies, the daughters of the Philistines, who were ashamed of your lewd behaviour. 28 You played the whore with the Assyrians, because you were insatiable; you played the whore with them, and still you were not satisfied. 29 You multiplied your whoring with Chaldea, the land of merchants; and even with this you were not satisfied.

30 How sick is your heart, says the Lord GOD, that you did all these things, the deeds of a brazen whore; 31 building your platform at the head of every street, and making your lofty place in every square! Yet you were not like a whore, because you scorned payment. 32 Adulterous wife, who receives strangers instead of her husband! 33 Gifts are given to all whores; but you gave your gifts to all your lovers, bribing them to come to you from all around for your whorings. 34 So you were different from other women in your whorings: no one solicited you to play the whore; and you gave payment, while no payment was given to you; you were different.

35 Therefore, O whore, hear the word of the LORD: 36 Thus says the Lord GOD, Because your lust was poured out and your nakedness uncovered in your whoring with your lovers, and because of all your abominable idols, and because of the blood of your children that you gave to them, 37 therefore, I will gather all your lovers, with whom you took pleasure, all those you loved and all those you hated; I will gather them against you from all around, and will uncover your nakedness to them, so that they may see all your nakedness. 38 I will judge you as women who commit adultery and shed blood are judged, and bring blood upon you in wrath and jealousy. 39 I will deliver you into their hands, and they shall throw down your platform and break down your lofty places; they shall strip you of your clothes and take your beautiful objects and leave you naked

and bare. 40 They shall bring up a mob against you, and they shall stone you and cut you to pieces with their swords. 41 They shall burn your houses and execute judgements on you in the sight of many women; I will stop you from playing the whore, and you shall also make no more payments. 42 So I will satisfy my fury on you, and my jealousy shall turn away from you; I will be calm, and will be angry no longer. 43 Because you have not remembered the days of your youth, but have enraged me with all these things; therefore, I have returned your deeds upon your head, says the Lord GOD.

Have you not committed lewdness beyond all your abominations? 44 See, everyone who uses proverbs will use this proverb about you, 'Like mother, like daughter.' 45 You are the daughter of your mother, who loathed her husband and her children; and you are the sister of your sisters, who loathed their husbands and their children. Your mother was a Hittite and your father an Amorite. 46 Your elder sister is Samaria, who lived with her daughters to the north of you; and your younger sister, who lived to the south of you, is Sodom with her daughters. 47 You not only followed their ways, and acted according to their abominations; within a very little time you were more corrupt than they in all your ways. 48 As I live, says the Lord GOD, your sister Sodom and her daughters have not done as you and your daughters have done. 49 This was the guilt of your sister Sodom: she and her daughters had pride, excess of food, and prosperous ease, but did not aid the poor and needy. 50 They were haughty, and did abominable things before me; therefore I removed them when I saw it. 51 Samaria has not committed half your sins; you have committed more abominations than they, and have made your sisters appear righteous by all the abominations that you have committed. 52 Bear your disgrace, you also, for you have brought about for your sisters a more favourable judgement; because of your sins in which you acted more abominably than they, they are more in the right than you.

So be ashamed, you also, and bear your disgrace, for you have made your sisters appear righteous.

53 I will restore their fortunes, the fortunes of Sodom and her daughters and the fortunes of Samaria and her daughters, and I will restore your own fortunes along with theirs, 54 in order that you may bear your disgrace and be ashamed of all that you have done, becoming a consolation to them. 55 As for your sisters, Sodom and her daughters shall return to their former state, Samaria and her daughters shall return to their former state, and you and your daughters shall return to your former state. 56 Was not your sister Sodom a byword in your mouth in the day of your pride, 57 before your wickedness was uncovered? Now you are a mockery to the daughters of Aram*a* and all her neighbours, and to the daughters of the Philistines, those all around who despise you. 58 You must bear the penalty of your lewdness and your abominations, says the LORD.

An Everlasting Covenant

59 Yes, thus says the Lord GOD: I will deal with you as you have done, you who have despised the oath, breaking the covenant; 60 yet I will remember my covenant with you in the days of your youth, and I will establish with you an everlasting covenant. 61 Then you will remember your ways, and be ashamed when I*b* take your sisters, both your elder and your younger, and give them to you as daughters, but not on account of my*c* covenant with you. 62 I will establish my covenant with you, and you shall know that I am the LORD, 63 in order that you may remember and be confounded, and never open your mouth again because of your shame, when I forgive you all that you have done, says the Lord GOD.

The Two Eagles and the Vine

17

The word of the LORD came to me: 2 O mortal, propound a riddle, and speak an allegory to the house of Israel. 3 Say: Thus says the Lord GOD:

A great eagle, with great wings and
    long pinions,
  rich in plumage of many colours,
  came to the Lebanon.
He took the top of the cedar,
4   broke off its topmost shoot;
  he carried it to a land of trade,
    set it in a city of merchants.
5 Then he took a seed from the land,
    placed it in fertile soil;
  a plant*d* by abundant waters,
    he set it like a willow twig.
6 It sprouted and became a vine,
    spreading out, but low;
  its branches turned towards him,
    its roots remained where it stood.
  So it became a vine;
    it brought forth branches,
    put forth foliage.

7 There was another great eagle,
    with great wings and much
      plumage.
  And see! This vine stretched out
    its roots towards him;
  it shot out its branches towards him,
    so that he might water it.
  From the bed where it was planted
8   it was transplanted
  to good soil by abundant waters,
    so that it might produce branches
    and bear fruit
    and become a noble vine.
9 Say: Thus says the Lord GOD:
  Will it prosper?
  Will he not pull up its roots,
    cause its fruit to rot*d* and wither,
    its fresh sprouting leaves to fade?
  No strong arm or mighty army will
      be needed
    to pull it from its roots.
10 When it is transplanted, will
      it thrive?
  When the east wind strikes it,
    will it not utterly wither,
    wither on the bed where it grew?

11 Then the word of the LORD came to me: 12 Say now to the rebellious house: Do you not know what these things mean? Tell

---

a Another reading is *Edom*   *b* Syr: Heb *you*
c Heb lacks *my*   *d* Meaning of Heb uncertain

them: The king of Babylon came to Jerusalem, took its king and its officials, and brought them back with him to Babylon. ¹³He took one of the royal offspring and made a covenant with him, putting him under oath (he had taken away the chief men of the land), ¹⁴so that the kingdom might be humble and not lift itself up, and that by keeping his covenant it might stand. ¹⁵But he rebelled against him by sending ambassadors to Egypt, in order that they might give him horses and a large army. Will he succeed? Can one escape who does such things? Can he break the covenant and yet escape? ¹⁶As I live, says the Lord GOD, surely in the place where the king resides who made him king, whose oath he despised, and whose covenant with him he broke—in Babylon he shall die. ¹⁷Pharaoh with his mighty army and great company will not help him in war, when ramps are cast up and siege-walls built to cut off many lives. ¹⁸Because he despised the oath and broke the covenant, because he gave his hand and yet did all these things, he shall not escape. ¹⁹Therefore, thus says the Lord GOD: As I live, I will surely return upon his head my oath that he despised, and my covenant that he broke. ²⁰I will spread my net over him, and he shall be caught in my snare; I will bring him to Babylon and enter into judgement with him there for the treason he has committed against me. ²¹All the pick*a* of his troops shall fall by the sword, and the survivors shall be scattered to every wind; and you shall know that I, the LORD, have spoken.

Israel Exalted at Last

22 Thus says the Lord GOD:
I myself will take a sprig
  from the lofty top of a cedar;
  I will set it out.
I will break off a tender one
  from the topmost of its
    young twigs;
I myself will plant it
  on a high and lofty mountain.
23 On the mountain height of Israel
  I will plant it,

in order that it may produce boughs
  and bear fruit,
  and become a noble cedar.
Under it every kind of bird will live;
  in the shade of its branches
    will nest
  winged creatures of every kind.
24 All the trees of the field shall know
  that I am the LORD.
I bring low the high tree,
  I make high the low tree;
I dry up the green tree
  and make the dry tree flourish.
I the LORD have spoken;
  I will accomplish it.

Individual Retribution

18 The word of the LORD came to me: ²What do you mean by repeating this proverb concerning the land of Israel, 'The parents have eaten sour grapes, and the children's teeth are set on edge'? ³As I live, says the Lord GOD, this proverb shall no more be used by you in Israel. ⁴Know that all lives are mine; the life of the parent as well as the life of the child is mine: it is only the person who sins that shall die.

5 If a man is righteous and does what is lawful and right— ⁶if he does not eat upon the mountains or lift up his eyes to the idols of the house of Israel, does not defile his neighbour's wife or approach a woman during her menstrual period, ⁷does not oppress anyone, but restores to the debtor his pledge, commits no robbery, gives his bread to the hungry and covers the naked with a garment, ⁸does not take advance or accrued interest, withholds his hand from iniquity, executes true justice between contending parties, ⁹follows my statutes, and is careful to observe my ordinances, acting faithfully—such a one is righteous; he shall surely live, says the Lord GOD.

10 If he has a son who is violent, a shedder of blood, ¹¹who does any of these things (though his father*b* does none of them), who eats upon the mountains, defiles his neighbour's wife, ¹²oppresses the poor and needy, commits robbery, does not restore the pledge, lifts up his eyes to

a Another reading is *fugitives*   *b* Heb *he*

the idols, commits abomination, ¹³ takes advance or accrued interest; shall he then live? He shall not. He has done all these abominable things; he shall surely die; his blood shall be upon himself.

14 But if this man has a son who sees all the sins that his father has done, considers, and does not do likewise, ¹⁵ who does not eat upon the mountains or lift up his eyes to the idols of the house of Israel, does not defile his neighbour's wife, ¹⁶ does not wrong anyone, exacts no pledge, commits no robbery, but gives his bread to the hungry and covers the naked with a garment, ¹⁷ withholds his hand from iniquity,*a* takes no advance or accrued interest, observes my ordinances, and follows my statutes; he shall not die for his father's iniquity; he shall surely live. ¹⁸ As for his father, because he practised extortion, robbed his brother, and did what is not good among his people, he dies for his iniquity.

19 Yet you say, 'Why should not the son suffer for the iniquity of the father?' When the son has done what is lawful and right, and has been careful to observe all my statutes, he shall surely live. ²⁰ The person who sins shall die. A child shall not suffer for the iniquity of a parent, nor a parent suffer for the iniquity of a child; the righteousness of the righteous shall be his own, and the wickedness of the wicked shall be his own.

21 But if the wicked turn away from all their sins that they have committed and keep all my statutes and do what is lawful and right, they shall surely live; they shall not die. ²² None of the transgressions that they have committed shall be remembered against them; for the righteousness that they have done they shall live. ²³ Have I any pleasure in the death of the wicked, says the Lord GOD, and not rather that they should turn from their ways and live? ²⁴ But when the righteous turn away from their righteousness and commit iniquity and do the same abominable things that the wicked do, shall they live? None of the righteous deeds that they have done shall be remembered; for the treachery of which

they are guilty and the sin they have committed, they shall die.

25 Yet you say, 'The way of the Lord is unfair.' Hear now, O house of Israel: Is my way unfair? Is it not your ways that are unfair? ²⁶ When the righteous turn away from their righteousness and commit iniquity, they shall die for it; for the iniquity that they have committed they shall die. ²⁷ Again, when the wicked turn away from the wickedness they have committed and do what is lawful and right, they shall save their life. ²⁸ Because they considered and turned away from all the transgressions that they had committed, they shall surely live; they shall not die. ²⁹ Yet the house of Israel says, 'The way of the Lord is unfair.' O house of Israel, are my ways unfair? Is it not your ways that are unfair?

30 Therefore I will judge you, O house of Israel, all of you according to your ways, says the Lord GOD. Repent and turn from all your transgressions; otherwise iniquity will be your ruin.*b* ³¹ Cast away from you all the transgressions that you have committed against me, and get yourselves a new heart and a new spirit! Why will you die, O house of Israel? ³² For I have no pleasure in the death of anyone, says the Lord GOD. Turn, then, and live.

Israel Degraded

19 As for you, raise up a lamentation for the princes of Israel, ² and say:
What a lioness was your mother
    among lions!
She lay down among young lions,
    rearing her cubs.
³ She raised up one of her cubs;
    he became a young lion,
and he learned to catch prey;
    he devoured humans.
⁴ The nations sounded an alarm
        against him;
    he was caught in their pit;
    and they brought him with hooks
        to the land of Egypt.
⁵ When she saw that she was thwarted,
    that her hope was lost,

she took another of her cubs
and made him a young lion.
6 He prowled among the lions;
he became a young lion,
and he learned to catch prey;
he devoured people.
7 And he ravaged their strongholds,*a*
and laid waste their towns;
the land was appalled, and all in it,
at the sound of his roaring.
8 The nations set upon him
from the provinces all around;
they spread their net over him;
he was caught in their pit.
9 With hooks they put him in a cage,
and brought him to the king
of Babylon;
they brought him into custody,
so that his voice should be heard
no more
on the mountains of Israel.
10 Your mother was like a vine in
a vineyard*b*
transplanted by the water,
fruitful and full of branches
from abundant water.
11 Its strongest stem became
a ruler's sceptre;*c*
it towered aloft
among the thick boughs;
it stood out in its height
with its mass of branches.
12 But it was plucked up in fury,
cast down to the ground;
the east wind dried it up;
its fruit was stripped off,
its strong stem was withered;
the fire consumed it.
13 Now it is transplanted into
the wilderness,
into a dry and thirsty land.
14 And fire has gone out from its stem,
has consumed its branches
and fruit,
so that there remains in it no strong
stem,
no sceptre for ruling.

This is a lamentation, and it is used as a
lamentation.

Israel's Continuing Rebellion

20 In the seventh year, in the fifth month, on the tenth day of the month, certain elders of Israel came to consult the LORD, and sat down before me. 2 And the word of the LORD came to me: 3 Mortal, speak to the elders of Israel, and say to them: Thus says the Lord GOD: Why are you coming? To consult me? As I live, says the Lord GOD, I will not be consulted by you. 4 Will you judge them, mortal, will you judge them? Then let them know the abominations of their ancestors, 5 and say to them: Thus says the Lord GOD: On the day when I chose Israel, I swore to the offspring of the house of Jacob—making myself known to them in the land of Egypt—I swore to them, saying, I am the LORD your God. 6 On that day I swore to them that I would bring them out of the land of Egypt into a land that I had searched out for them, a land flowing with milk and honey, the most glorious of all lands. 7 And I said to them, Cast away the detestable things your eyes feast on, every one of you, and do not defile yourselves with the idols of Egypt; I am the LORD your God. 8 But they rebelled against me and would not listen to me; not one of them cast away the detestable things their eyes feasted on, nor did they forsake the idols of Egypt.

Then I thought I would pour out my wrath upon them and spend my anger against them in the midst of the land of Egypt. 9 But I acted for the sake of my name, that it should not be profaned in the sight of the nations among whom they lived, in whose sight I made myself known to them in bringing them out of the land of Egypt. 10 So I led them out of the land of Egypt and brought them into the wilderness. 11 I gave them my statutes and showed them my ordinances, by whose observance everyone shall live. 12 Moreover, I gave them my sabbaths, as a sign between me and them, so that they might know that I the LORD sanctify them. 13 But the house of Israel rebelled against me in the wilderness; they did not observe my statutes but

---

a Heb *his widows*   *b* Cn: Heb *in your blood*   *c* Heb *Its strongest stems became rulers' sceptres* rejected my ordinances, by whose observance everyone shall live; and my sabbaths they greatly profaned.

Then I thought I would pour out my wrath upon them in the wilderness, to make an end of them. ¹⁴But I acted for the sake of my name, so that it should not be profaned in the sight of the nations, in whose sight I had brought them out. ¹⁵Moreover, I swore to them in the wilderness that I would not bring them into the land that I had given them, a land flowing with milk and honey, the most glorious of all lands, ¹⁶because they rejected my ordinances and did not observe my statutes, and profaned my sabbaths; for their heart went after their idols. ¹⁷Nevertheless, my eye spared them, and I did not destroy them or make an end of them in the wilderness.

18 I said to their children in the wilderness, Do not follow the statutes of your parents, nor observe their ordinances, nor defile yourselves with their idols. ¹⁹I the LORD am your God; follow my statutes, and be careful to observe my ordinances, ²⁰and hallow my sabbaths that they may be a sign between me and you, so that you may know that I the LORD am your God. ²¹But the children rebelled against me; they did not follow my statutes, and were not careful to observe my ordinances, by whose observance everyone shall live; they profaned my sabbaths.

Then I thought I would pour out my wrath upon them and spend my anger against them in the wilderness. ²²But I withheld my hand, and acted for the sake of my name, so that it should not be profaned in the sight of the nations, in whose sight I had brought them out. ²³Moreover, I swore to them in the wilderness that I would scatter them among the nations and disperse them through the countries, ²⁴because they had not executed my ordinances, but had rejected my statutes and profaned my sabbaths, and their eyes were set on their ancestors' idols. ²⁵Moreover, I gave them statutes that were not good and ordinances by which they could not live. ²⁶I defiled them through their very gifts, in

their offering up all their firstborn, in order that I might horrify them, so that they might know that I am the LORD.

27 Therefore, mortal, speak to the house of Israel and say to them, Thus says the Lord GOD: In this again your ancestors blasphemed me, by dealing treacherously with me. ²⁸For when I had brought them into the land that I swore to give them, then wherever they saw any high hill or any leafy tree, there they offered their sacrifices and presented the provocation of their offering; there they sent up their pleasing odours, and there they poured out their drink-offerings. ²⁹(I said to them, What is the high place to which you go? So it is called Bamah*a* to this day.) ³⁰Therefore say to the house of Israel, Thus says the Lord GOD: Will you defile yourselves after the manner of your ancestors and go astray after their detestable things? ³¹When you offer your gifts and make your children pass through the fire, you defile yourselves with all your idols to this day. And shall I be consulted by you, O house of Israel? As I live, says the Lord GOD, I will not be consulted by you.

32 What is in your mind shall never happen—the thought, 'Let us be like the nations, like the tribes of the countries, and worship wood and stone.'

God Will Restore Israel

33 As I live, says the Lord GOD, surely with a mighty hand and an outstretched arm, and with wrath poured out, I will be king over you. ³⁴I will bring you out from the peoples and gather you out of the countries where you are scattered, with a mighty hand and an outstretched arm, and with wrath poured out; ³⁵and I will bring you into the wilderness of the peoples, and there I will enter into judgement with you face to face. ³⁶As I entered into judgement with your ancestors in the wilderness of the land of Egypt, so I will enter into judgement with you, says the Lord GOD. ³⁷I will make you pass under the staff, and will bring you within the bond of the covenant. ³⁸I will purge out the rebels among you,

a That is *High Place*

and those who transgress against me; I will bring them out of the land where they reside as aliens, but they shall not enter the land of Israel. Then you shall know that I am the LORD.

39 As for you, O house of Israel, thus says the Lord GOD: Go, serve your idols, every one of you now and hereafter, if you will not listen to me; but my holy name you shall no more profane with your gifts and your idols.

40 For on my holy mountain, the mountain height of Israel, says the Lord GOD, there all the house of Israel, all of them, shall serve me in the land; there I will accept them, and there I will require your contributions and the choicest of your gifts, with all your sacred things. 41 As a pleasing odour I will accept you, when I bring you out from the peoples, and gather you out of the countries where you have been scattered; and I will manifest my holiness among you in the sight of the nations. 42 You shall know that I am the LORD, when I bring you into the land of Israel, the country that I swore to give to your ancestors. 43 There you shall remember your ways and all the deeds by which you have polluted yourselves; and you shall loathe yourselves for all the evils that you have committed. 44 And you shall know that I am the LORD, when I deal with you for my name's sake, not according to your evil ways or corrupt deeds, O house of Israel, says the Lord GOD.

A Prophecy against the Negeb

45 *a* The word of the LORD came to me: 46 Mortal, set your face towards the south, preach against the south, and prophesy against the forest land in the Negeb; 47 say to the forest of the Negeb, Hear the word of the LORD: Thus says the Lord GOD, I will kindle a fire in you, and it shall devour every green tree in you and every dry tree; the blazing flame shall not be quenched, and all faces from south to north shall be scorched by it. 48 All flesh shall see that I the LORD have kindled it; it shall not be quenched. 49 Then I said, 'Ah Lord GOD!

they are saying of me, "Is he not a maker of allegories?" '

The Drawn Sword of God

21 *b* The word of the LORD came to me: 2 Mortal, set your face towards Jerusalem and preach against the sanctuaries; prophesy against the land of Israel 3 and say to the land of Israel, Thus says the LORD: I am coming against you, and will draw my sword out of its sheath, and will cut off from you both righteous and wicked. 4 Because I will cut off from you both righteous and wicked, therefore my sword shall go out of its sheath against all flesh from south to north; 5 and all flesh shall know that I the LORD have drawn my sword out of its sheath; it shall not be sheathed again. 6 Moan therefore, mortal; moan with breaking heart and bitter grief before their eyes. 7 And when they say to you, 'Why do you moan?' you shall say, 'Because of the news that has come. Every heart will fail and all hands will be feeble, every spirit will faint and all knees will turn to water. See, it comes and it will be fulfilled,' says the Lord GOD.

8 And the word of the LORD came to me: 9 Mortal, prophesy and say: Thus says the Lord; Say:

A sword, a sword is sharpened,
  it is also polished;
10 it is sharpened for slaughter,
  honed to flash like lightning!
How can we make merry?
  You have despised the rod
  and all discipline. *c*
11 The sword *d* is given to be polished,
  to be grasped in the hand;
it is sharpened, the sword is
  polished,
  to be placed in the slayer's hand.
12 Cry and wail, O mortal,
  for it is against my people;
it is against all Israel's princes;
  they are thrown to the sword,
  together with my people.
  Ah! Strike the thigh!
13 For consider: What! If you despise the

a Ch 21.1 in Heb   *b* Ch 21.6 in Heb   *c* Meaning of Heb uncertain   *d* Heb *It*

rod, will it not happen?*a* says the Lord
GOD.

14 And you, mortal, prophesy;
  strike hand to hand.
Let the sword fall twice, thrice;
  it is a sword for killing.
A sword for great slaughter—
  it surrounds them;
15 therefore hearts fail
  and many stumble.
At all their gates I have set
  the point*a* of the sword.
Ah! It is made for flashing,
  it is polished*b* for slaughter.
16 Attack to the right!
  Engage to the left!
  —wherever your edge is directed.
17 I too will strike hand to hand,
  I will satisfy my fury;
  I the LORD have spoken.

18 The word of the LORD came to me:
19 Mortal, mark out two roads for the
sword of the king of Babylon to come;
both of them shall issue from the same
land. And make a signpost, make it for a
fork in the road leading to a city; 20 mark
out the road for the sword to come to Rabbah of the Ammonites or to Judah and to*c*
Jerusalem the fortified. 21 For the king of
Babylon stands at the parting of the way, at
the fork in the two roads, to use divination; he shakes the arrows, he consults the
teraphim,*d* he inspects the liver. 22 Into his
right hand comes the lot for Jerusalem, to
set battering-rams, to call out for slaughter,
for raising the battle cry, to set battering-
rams against the gates, to cast up ramps, to
build siege-towers. 23 But to them it will
seem like a false divination; they have
sworn solemn oaths; but he brings their
guilt to remembrance, bringing about their
capture.

24 Therefore, thus says the Lord GOD:
Because you have brought your guilt to remembrance, in that your transgressions are
uncovered, so that in all your deeds your
sins appear—because you have come to remembrance, you shall be taken in hand.*e*
25 As for you, vile, wicked prince of Israel,
  you whose day has come,
  the time of final punishment,

26 thus says the Lord GOD:
Remove the turban, take off the crown;
  things shall not remain as they are.
Exalt that which is low,
  abase that which is high.
27 A ruin, a ruin, a ruin—
  I will make it!
  (Such has never occurred.)
Until he comes whose right it is;
  to him I will give it.

28 As for you, mortal, prophesy, and
say, Thus says the Lord GOD concerning the
Ammonites, and concerning their reproach; say:
A sword, a sword! Drawn for
    slaughter,
  polished to consume,*f* to flash like
    lightning.
29 Offering false visions for you,
  divining lies for you,
they place you over the necks
  of the vile, wicked ones—
those whose day has come,
  the time of final punishment.
30 Return it to its sheath!
In the place where you were created,
  in the land of your origin,
  I will judge you.
31 I will pour out my indignation upon
    you,
  with the fire of my wrath
  I will blow upon you.
I will deliver you into brutish hands,
  those skilful to destroy.
32 You shall be fuel for the fire,
  your blood shall enter the earth;
you shall be remembered no more,
  for I the LORD have spoken.

The Bloody City

22 The word of the LORD came to me:
2 You, mortal, will you judge, will
you judge the bloody city? Then declare to
it all its abominable deeds. 3 You shall say,
Thus says the Lord GOD: A city! Shedding
blood within itself; its time has come;
making its idols, defiling itself. 4 You have
become guilty by the blood that you have

---

a Meaning of Heb uncertain   *b* Tg: Heb *wrapped up*
c Gk Syr: Heb *Judah in*   *d* Or *the household gods*
e Or *be taken captive*   *f* Cn: Heb *to contain*

shed, and defiled by the idols that you have made; you have brought your day near, the appointed time of your years has come. Therefore I have made you a disgrace before the nations, and a mockery to all the countries. 5 Those who are near and those who are far from you will mock you, you infamous one, full of tumult.

6 The princes of Israel in you, every one according to his power, have been bent on shedding blood. 7 Father and mother are treated with contempt in you; the alien residing within you suffers extortion; the orphan and the widow are wronged in you. 8 You have despised my holy things, and profaned my sabbaths. 9 In you are those who slander to shed blood, those in you who eat upon the mountains, who commit lewdness in your midst. 10 In you they uncover their fathers' nakedness; in you they violate women in their menstrual periods. 11 One commits abomination with his neighbour's wife; another lewdly defiles his daughter-in-law; another in you defiles his sister, his father's daughter. 12 In you, they take bribes to shed blood; you take both advance interest and accrued interest, and make gain of your neighbours by extortion; and you have forgotten me, says the Lord God.

13 See, I strike my hands together at the dishonest gain you have made, and at the blood that has been shed within you. 14 Can your courage endure, or can your hands remain strong in the days when I shall deal with you? I the Lord have spoken, and I will do it. 15 I will scatter you among the nations and disperse you through the countries, and I will purge your filthiness out of you. 16 And I a shall be profaned through you in the sight of the nations; and you shall know that I am the Lord.

17 The word of the Lord came to me: 18 Mortal, the house of Israel has become dross to me; all of them, silver, b bronze, tin, iron, and lead. In the smelter they have become dross. 19 Therefore thus says the Lord God: Because you have all become dross, I will gather you into the midst of Jerusalem. 20 As one gathers silver, bronze, iron, lead, and tin into a smelter, to blow the fire upon them in order to melt them;

so I will gather you in my anger and in my wrath, and I will put you in and melt you. 21 I will gather you and blow upon you with the fire of my wrath, and you shall be melted within it. 22 As silver is melted in a smelter, so you shall be melted in it; and you shall know that I the Lord have poured out my wrath upon you.

23 The word of the Lord came to me: 24 Mortal, say to it: You are a land that is not cleansed, not rained upon in the day of indignation. 25 Its princes c within it are like a roaring lion tearing the prey; they have devoured human lives; they have taken treasure and precious things; they have made many widows within it. 26 Its priests have done violence to my teaching and have profaned my holy things; they have made no distinction between the holy and the common, neither have they taught the difference between the unclean and the clean, and they have disregarded my sabbaths, so that I am profaned among them. 27 Its officials within it are like wolves tearing the prey, shedding blood, destroying lives to get dishonest gain. 28 Its prophets have smeared whitewash on their behalf, seeing false visions and divining lies for them, saying, 'Thus says the Lord God', when the Lord has not spoken. 29 The people of the land have practised extortion and committed robbery; they have oppressed the poor and needy, and have extorted from the alien without redress. 30 And I sought for anyone among them who would repair the wall and stand in the breach before me on behalf of the land, so that I would not destroy it; but I found no one. 31 Therefore I have poured out my indignation upon them; I have consumed them with the fire of my wrath; I have returned their conduct upon their heads, says the Lord God.

Oholah and Oholibah

23 The word of the Lord came to me: 2 Mortal, there were two women, the daughters of one mother; 3 they played

a Gk Syr Vg: Heb you   b Transposed from the end of the verse; compare verse 20   c Gk: Heb indignation. 25 A conspiracy of its prophets the whore in Egypt; they played the whore in their youth; their breasts were caressed there, and their virgin bosoms were fondled. 4 Oholah was the name of the elder and Oholibah the name of her sister. They became mine, and they bore sons and daughters. As for their names, Oholah is Samaria, and Oholibah is Jerusalem.

5 Oholah played the whore while she was mine; she lusted after her lovers the Assyrians, warriors *a* 6 clothed in blue, governors and commanders, all of them handsome young men, mounted horsemen. 7 She bestowed her favours upon them, the choicest men of Assyria all of them; and she defiled herself with all the idols of everyone for whom she lusted. 8 She did not give up her whorings that she had practised since Egypt; for in her youth men had lain with her and fondled her virgin bosom and poured out their lust upon her. 9 Therefore I delivered her into the hands of her lovers, into the hands of the Assyrians, for whom she lusted. 10 These uncovered her nakedness; they seized her sons and her daughters; and they killed her with the sword. Judgement was executed upon her, and she became a byword among women.

11 Her sister Oholibah saw this, yet she was more corrupt than her sister in her lusting and in her whorings, which were worse than those of her sister. 12 She lusted after the Assyrians, governors and commanders, warriors *d* clothed in full armour, mounted horsemen, all of them handsome young men. 13 And I saw that she was defiled; they both took the same way. 14 But she carried her whorings further; she saw male figures carved on the wall, images of the Chaldeans portrayed in vermilion, 15 with belts around their waists, with flowing turbans on their heads, all of them looking like officers—a picture of Babylonians whose native land was Chaldea. 16 When she saw them she lusted after them, and sent messengers to them in Chaldea. 17 And the Babylonians came to her into the bed of love, and they defiled her with their lust; and after she defiled herself with them, she turned from them

in disgust. 18 When she carried on her whorings so openly and flaunted her nakedness, I turned in disgust from her, as I had turned from her sister. 19 Yet she increased her whorings, remembering the days of her youth, when she played the whore in the land of Egypt 20 and lusted after her paramours there, whose members were like those of donkeys, and whose emission was like that of stallions. 21 Thus you longed for the lewdness of your youth, when the Egyptians *b* fondled your bosom and caressed *c* your young breasts.

22 Therefore, O Oholibah, thus says the Lord GOD: I will arouse against you your lovers from whom you turned in disgust, and I will bring them against you from every side: 23 the Babylonians and all the Chaldeans, Pekod and Shoa and Koa, and all the Assyrians with them, handsome young men, governors and commanders all of them, officers and warriors, *d* all of them riding on horses. 24 They shall come against you from the north *e* with chariots and wagons and a host of peoples; they shall set themselves against you on every side with buckler, shield, and helmet, and I will commit the judgement to them, and they shall judge you according to their ordinances. 25 I will direct my indignation against you, in order that they may deal with you in fury. They shall cut off your nose and your ears, and your survivors shall fall by the sword. They shall seize your sons and your daughters, and your survivors shall be devoured by fire. 26 They shall also strip you of your clothes and take away your fine jewels. 27 So I will put an end to your lewdness and your whoring brought from the land of Egypt; you shall not long for them, or remember Egypt any more. 28 For thus says the Lord GOD: I will deliver you into the hands of those whom you hate, into the hands of those from whom you turned in disgust; 29 and they shall deal with you in hatred, and take away all the fruit of your labour, and leave you naked and bare, and the nakedness of

a Meaning of Heb uncertain   *b* Two Mss: MT *from Egypt*   *c* Cn: Heb *for the sake of*   *d* Compare verses 6 and 12: Heb *officers and called ones*   *e* Gk: Meaning of Heb uncertain your whorings shall be exposed. Your lewdness and your whorings ³⁰ have brought this upon you, because you played the whore with the nations, and polluted yourself with their idols. ³¹ You have gone the way of your sister; therefore I will give her cup into your hand. ³² Thus says the Lord GOD:

You shall drink your sister's cup,
    deep and wide;
you shall be scorned and derided,
    it holds so much.
³³ You shall be filled with drunkenness
        and sorrow.
    A cup of horror and desolation
        is the cup of your sister Samaria;
³⁴ you shall drink it and drain it out,
        and gnaw its sherds,
        and tear out your breasts;

for I have spoken, says the Lord GOD. ³⁵ Therefore thus says the Lord GOD: Because you have forgotten me and cast me behind your back, therefore bear the consequences of your lewdness and whorings.

36 The LORD said to me: Mortal, will you judge Oholah and Oholibah? Then declare to them their abominable deeds. ³⁷ For they have committed adultery, and blood is on their hands; with their idols they have committed adultery; and they have even offered up to them for food the children whom they had borne to me. ³⁸ Moreover, this they have done to me: they have defiled my sanctuary on the same day and profaned my sabbaths. ³⁹ For when they had slaughtered their children for their idols, on the same day they came into my sanctuary to profane it. This is what they did in my house.

40 They even sent for men to come from far away, to whom a messenger was sent, and they came. For them you bathed yourself, painted your eyes, and decked yourself with ornaments; ⁴¹ you sat on a stately couch, with a table spread before it on which you had placed my incense and my oil. ⁴² The sound of a raucous multitude was around her, with many of the rabble brought in drunken from the wilderness; and they put bracelets on the arms[a]

of the women, and beautiful crowns upon their heads.

43 Then I said, Ah, she is worn out with adulteries, but they carry on their sexual acts with her. ⁴⁴ For they have gone in to her, as one goes in to a whore. Thus they went in to Oholah and to Oholibah, wanton women. ⁴⁵ But righteous judges shall declare them guilty of adultery and of bloodshed; because they are adulteresses, and blood is on their hands.

46 For thus says the Lord GOD: Bring up an assembly against them, and make them an object of terror and of plunder. ⁴⁷ The assembly shall stone them and with their swords they shall cut them down; they shall kill their sons and their daughters, and burn up their houses. ⁴⁸ Thus will I put an end to lewdness in the land, so that all women may take warning and not commit lewdness as you have done. ⁴⁹ They shall repay you for your lewdness, and you shall bear the penalty for your sinful idolatry; and you shall know that I am the Lord GOD.

The Boiling Pot

24 In the ninth year, in the tenth month, on the tenth day of the month, the word of the LORD came to me: ² Mortal, write down the name of this day, this very day. The king of Babylon has laid siege to Jerusalem this very day. ³ And utter an allegory to the rebellious house and say to them, Thus says the Lord GOD:

Set on the pot, set it on,
    pour in water also;
⁴ put in it the pieces,
    all the good pieces, the thigh and
        the shoulder;
    fill it with choice bones.
⁵ Take the choicest one of the flock,
    pile the logs[b] under it;
    boil its pieces,[c]
    seethe[d] also its bones in it.

6 Therefore, thus says the Lord GOD:
    Woe to the bloody city,
        the pot whose rust is in it,
        whose rust has not gone out of it!

a Heb hands   b Compare verse 10: Heb the bones
c Two Mss: Heb its boilings   d Cn: Heb its bones seethe

Empty it piece by piece,
  making no choice at all. *a*
7 For the blood she shed is inside it;
  she placed it on a bare rock;
  she did not pour it out on the
    ground,
  to cover it with earth.
8 To rouse my wrath, to take
    vengeance,
  I have placed the blood she shed
    on a bare rock,
  so that it may not be covered.
9 Therefore thus says the Lord God:
  Woe to the bloody city!
  I will even make the pile great.
10 Heap up the logs, kindle the fire;
  boil the meat well, mix in
    the spices,
  let the bones be burned.
11 Stand it empty upon the coals,
  so that it may become hot, its
    copper glow,
  its filth melt in it, its rust
    be consumed.
12 In vain I have wearied myself; *b*
  its thick rust does not depart.
  To the fire with its rust! *c*
13 Yet, when I cleansed you in your
    filthy lewdness,
  you did not become clean from
    your filth;
  you shall not again be cleansed
    until I have satisfied my fury upon
    you.
14 I the Lord have spoken; the time is coming, I will act. I will not refrain, I will not
spare, I will not relent. According to your
ways and your doings I will judge you, says
the Lord God.

Ezekiel's Bereavement

15 The word of the Lord came to me:
16 Mortal, with one blow I am about to take
away from you the delight of your eyes; yet
you shall not mourn or weep, nor shall
your tears run down. 17 Sigh, but not aloud;
make no mourning for the dead. Bind on
your turban, and put your sandals on your
feet; do not cover your upper lip or eat the
bread of mourners. *d* 18 So I spoke to the
people in the morning, and at evening my

wife died. And on the next morning I did
as I was commanded.

19 Then the people said to me, 'Will
you not tell us what these things mean for
us, that you are acting in this way?' 20 Then
I said to them: The word of the Lord came
to me: 21 Say to the house of Israel, Thus
says the Lord God: I will profane my sanctuary, the pride of your power, the delight
of your eyes, and your heart's desire; and
your sons and your daughters whom you
left behind shall fall by the sword. 22 And
you shall do as I have done; you shall not
cover your upper lip or eat the bread of
mourners. *d* 23 Your turbans shall be on
your heads and your sandals on your feet;
you shall not mourn or weep, but you shall
pine away in your iniquities and groan to
one another. 24 Thus Ezekiel shall be a sign
to you; you shall do just as he has done.
When this comes, then you shall know that
I am the Lord God.

25 And you, mortal, on the day when I
take from them their stronghold, their joy
and glory, the delight of their eyes and
their heart's affection, and also *e* their sons
and their daughters, 26 on that day, one
who has escaped will come to you to report to you the news. 27 On that day your
mouth shall be opened to the one who has
escaped, and you shall speak and no
longer be silent. So you shall be a sign to
them; and they shall know that I am the
Lord.

Proclamation against Ammon

25 The word of the Lord came to me:
2 Mortal, set your face towards the
Ammonites and prophesy against them.
3 Say to the Ammonites, Hear the word of
the Lord God: Thus says the Lord God, Because you said, 'Aha!' over my sanctuary
when it was profaned, and over the land of
Israel when it was made desolate, and over
the house of Judah when it went into exile;
4 therefore I am handing you over to the
people of the east for a possession. They
shall set their encampments among you

---

a Heb *piece, no lot has fallen on it*   *b* Cn: Meaning of
Heb uncertain   *c* Meaning of Heb uncertain
d Vg Tg: Heb *of men*   *e* Heb lacks *and also*

and pitch their tents in your midst; they shall eat your fruit, and they shall drink your milk. 5 I will make Rabbah a pasture for camels and Ammon a fold for flocks. Then you shall know that I am the LORD. 6 For thus says the Lord GOD: Because you have clapped your hands and stamped your feet and rejoiced with all the malice within you against the land of Israel, 7 therefore I have stretched out my hand against you, and will hand you over as plunder to the nations. I will cut you off from the peoples and will make you perish out of the countries; I will destroy you. Then you shall know that I am the LORD.

Proclamation against Moab

8 Thus says the Lord GOD: Because Moab *a* said, The house of Judah is like all the other nations, 9 therefore I will lay open the flank of Moab from the towns *b* on its frontier, the glory of the country, Beth-jeshimoth, Baal-meon, and Kiriatha-im. 10 I will give it along with Ammon to the people of the east as a possession. Thus Ammon shall be remembered no more among the nations, 11 and I will execute judgements upon Moab. Then they shall know that I am the LORD.

Proclamation against Edom

12 Thus says the Lord GOD: Because Edom acted vengefully against the house of Judah and has grievously offended in taking vengeance upon them, 13 therefore thus says the Lord GOD, I will stretch out my hand against Edom, and cut off from it humans and animals, and I will make it desolate; from Teman even to Dedan they shall fall by the sword. 14 I will lay my vengeance upon Edom by the hand of my people Israel; and they shall act in Edom according to my anger and according to my wrath; and they shall know my vengeance, says the Lord GOD.

Proclamation against Philistia

15 Thus says the Lord GOD: Because with unending hostilities the Philistines acted in vengeance, and with malice of heart took revenge in destruction; 16 there-fore thus says the Lord GOD, I will stretch out my hand against the Philistines, cut off the Cherethites, and destroy the rest of the sea coast. 17 I will execute great vengeance on them with wrathful punishments. Then they shall know that I am the LORD, when I lay my vengeance on them.

Proclamation against Tyre

26 In the eleventh year, on the first day of the month, the word of the LORD came to me: 2 Mortal, because Tyre said concerning Jerusalem,

'Aha, broken is the gateway of
the peoples;
it has swung open to me;
I shall be replenished,
now that it is wasted',

3 therefore, thus says the Lord GOD:
See, I am against you, O Tyre!
I will hurl many nations
against you,
as the sea hurls its waves.
4 They shall destroy the walls of Tyre
and break down its towers.
I will scrape its soil from it
and make it a bare rock.
5 It shall become, in the midst of the
sea,
a place for spreading nets.
I have spoken, says the Lord GOD.
It shall become plunder for
the nations,
6 and its daughter-towns in
the country
shall be killed by the sword.
Then they shall know that I am the LORD.

7 For thus says the Lord GOD: I will bring against Tyre from the north King Nebuchadrezzar of Babylon, king of kings, together with horses, chariots, cavalry, and a great and powerful army. 8 Your daughter-towns in the country he shall put to the sword.
He shall set up a siege-wall
against you,
cast up a ramp against you,
and raise a roof of shields
against you.

a Gk Old Latin: Heb *Moab and Seir*   *b* Heb *towns from its towns*

9 He shall direct the shock of his
 battering-rams against
  your walls
 and break down your towers
  with his axes.
10 His horses shall be so many
 that their dust shall cover you.
 At the noise of cavalry, wheels,
  and chariots
 your very walls shall shake,
 when he enters your gates
 like those entering a breached city.
11 With the hoofs of his horses
 he shall trample all your streets.
 He shall put your people to
  the sword,
  and your strong pillars shall fall to
   the ground.
12 They will plunder your riches
 and loot your merchandise;
 they shall break down your walls
 and destroy your fine houses.
 Your stones and timber and soil
 they shall cast into the water.
13 I will silence the music of
  your songs;
 the sound of your lyres shall be
  heard no more.
14 I will make you a bare rock;
 you shall be a place for
  spreading nets.
 You shall never again be rebuilt,
 for I the LORD have spoken,
 says the Lord GOD.

15 Thus says the Lord GOD to Tyre: Shall not the coastlands shake at the sound of your fall, when the wounded groan, when slaughter goes on within you? 16 Then all the princes of the sea shall step down from their thrones; they shall remove their robes and strip off their embroidered garments. They shall clothe themselves with trembling, and shall sit on the ground; they shall tremble every moment, and be appalled at you. 17 And they shall raise a lamentation over you, and say to you:

How you have vanished[a] from
 the seas,
 O city renowned,
once mighty on the sea,
 you and your inhabitants,[b]

who imposed your[c] terror
 on all the mainland![d]
18 Now the coastlands tremble
 on the day of your fall;
 the coastlands by the sea
 are dismayed at your passing.

19 For thus says the Lord GOD: When I make you a city laid waste, like cities that are not inhabited, when I bring up the deep over you, and the great waters cover you, 20 then I will thrust you down with those who descend into the Pit, to the people of long ago, and I will make you live in the world below, among primeval ruins, with those who go down to the Pit, so that you will not be inhabited or have a place[e] in the land of the living. 21 I will bring you to a dreadful end, and you shall be no more; though sought for, you will never be found again, says the Lord GOD.

Lamentation over Tyre

27 The word of the LORD came to me: 2 Now you, mortal, raise a lamentation over Tyre, 3 and say to Tyre, which sits at the entrance to the sea, merchant of the peoples on many coastlands, Thus says the Lord GOD:

O Tyre, you have said,
 'I am perfect in beauty.'
4 Your borders are in the heart of the
  seas;
 your builders made perfect
  your beauty.
5 They made all your planks
 of fir trees from Senir;
 they took a cedar from Lebanon
  to make a mast for you.
6 From oaks of Bashan
 they made your oars;
 they made your deck of pines[f]
  from the coasts of Cyprus,
  inlaid with ivory.
7 Of fine embroidered linen
  from Egypt
 was your sail,
  serving as your ensign;

a Gk OL Aquila: Heb *have vanished, O inhabited one,*
b Heb *it and its inhabitants* c Heb *their* d Cn: Heb
its inhabitants e Gk: Heb *I will give beauty*
f Or *boxwood*

blue and purple from the coasts
        of Elishah
    was your awning.
8 The inhabitants of Sidon and Arvad
        were your rowers;
    skilled men of Zemer*ᵃ* were
            within you,
        they were your pilots.
9 The elders of Gebal and its artisans
        were within you,
    caulking your seams;
    all the ships of the sea with their
            mariners were within you,
        to barter for your wares.
10 Paras*ᵇ* and Lud and Put
        were in your army,
    your mighty warriors;
    they hung shield and helmet in you;
        they gave you splendour.
11 Men of Arvad and Helech*ᶜ*
        were on your walls all round;
    men of Gamad were at your towers.
    They hung their quivers all round
            your walls;
        they made perfect your beauty.
12 Tarshish did business with you out
of the abundance of your great wealth; silver, iron, tin, and lead they exchanged for
your wares. 13 Javan, Tubal, and Meshech
traded with you; they exchanged human
beings and vessels of bronze for your merchandise. 14 Beth-togarmah exchanged for
your wares horses, war-horses, and mules.
15 The Rhodians*ᵈ* traded with you; many
coastlands were your own special markets;
they brought you in payment ivory tusks
and ebony. 16 Edom*ᵉ* did business with you
because of your abundant goods; they exchanged for your wares turquoise, purple,
embroidered work, fine linen, coral, and
rubies. 17 Judah and the land of Israel traded with you; they exchanged for your merchandise wheat from Minnith, millet,*ᶠ*
honey, oil, and balm. 18 Damascus traded
with you for your abundant goods—because of your great wealth of every kind—
wine of Helbon, and white wool. 19 Vedan
and Javan from Uzal*ᶠ* entered into trade for
your wares; wrought iron, cassia, and sweet
cane were bartered for your merchandise.
20 Dedan traded with you in saddlecloths

for riding. 21 Arabia and all the princes of
Kedar were your favoured dealers in lambs,
rams, and goats; in these they did business
with you. 22 The merchants of Sheba and
Raamah traded with you; they exchanged
for your wares the best of all kinds of
spices, and all precious stones, and gold.
23 Haran, Canneh, Eden, the merchants of
Sheba, Asshur, and Chilmad traded with
you. 24 These traded with you in choice garments, in clothes of blue and embroidered
work, and in carpets of coloured material,
bound with cords and made secure; in
these they traded with you.*ᵍ* 25 The ships of
Tarshish travelled for you in your trade.
    So you were filled and heavily laden
        in the heart of the seas.
26 Your rowers have brought you
        into the high seas.
    The east wind has wrecked you
        in the heart of the seas.
27 Your riches, your wares, your
            merchandise,
        your mariners and your pilots,
    your caulkers, your dealers in
            merchandise,
        and all your warriors within you,
    with all the company
        that is with you,
    sink into the heart of the seas
        on the day of your ruin.
28 At the sound of the cry of your pilots
        the countryside shakes,
29 and down from their ships
        come all that handle the oar.
    The mariners and all the pilots
            of the sea
        stand on the shore
30 and wail aloud over you,
        and cry bitterly.
    They throw dust on their heads
        and wallow in ashes;
31 they make themselves bald for you,
        and put on sackcloth,
    and they weep over you in bitterness
            of soul,
        with bitter mourning.

a Cn Compare Gen 10.18: Heb *your skilled men, O Tyre*
b Or *Persia*   *c* Or *and your army*   *d* Gk: Heb *The
Dedanites*   *e* Another reading is *Aram*   *f* Meaning of
Heb uncertain   *g* Cn: Heb *in your market*

32 In their wailing they raise a
      lamentation for you,
    and lament over you:
    'Who was ever destroyed[a] like Tyre
      in the midst of the sea?
33 When your wares came from the seas,
      you satisfied many peoples;
    with your abundant wealth and
      merchandise
      you enriched the kings of the earth.
34 Now you are wrecked by the seas,
      in the depths of the waters;
    your merchandise and all your crew
      have sunk with you.
35 All the inhabitants of the coastlands
      are appalled at you;
    and their kings are horribly afraid,
      their faces are convulsed.
36 The merchants among the peoples
      hiss at you;
    you have come to a dreadful end
      and shall be no more for ever.'

Proclamation against the King of Tyre

28 The word of the LORD came to me:
      2 Mortal, say to the prince of Tyre,
Thus says the Lord GOD:
    Because your heart is proud
      and you have said, 'I am a god;
    I sit in the seat of the gods,
      in the heart of the seas',
    yet you are but a mortal, and no god,
      though you compare your mind
      with the mind of a god.
3 You are indeed wiser than Daniel;[b]
    no secret is hidden from you;
4 by your wisdom and your
      understanding
    you have amassed wealth
      for yourself,
    and have gathered gold and silver
      into your treasuries.
5 By your great wisdom in trade
      you have increased your wealth,
    and your heart has become proud
      in your wealth.
6 Therefore, thus says the Lord GOD:
    Because you compare your mind
      with the mind of a god,
7 therefore, I will bring strangers
      against you,

    the most terrible of the nations;
    they shall draw their swords against
      the beauty of your wisdom
      and defile your splendour.
8 They shall thrust you down to the Pit,
      and you shall die a violent death
      in the heart of the seas.
9 Will you still say, 'I am a god',
      in the presence of those who
      kill you,
    though you are but a mortal, and no
      god,
    in the hands of those who
      wound you?
10 You shall die the death of the
      uncircumcised
    by the hand of foreigners;
    for I have spoken, says the
      Lord GOD.

Lamentation over the King of Tyre

11 Moreover, the word of the LORD came
to me: 12 Mortal, raise a lamentation over
the king of Tyre, and say to him, Thus says
the Lord GOD:
    You were the signet of perfection,[c]
      full of wisdom and perfect in
      beauty.
13 You were in Eden, the garden of God;
      every precious stone was your
      covering,
    carnelian, chrysolite, and moonstone,
      beryl, onyx, and jasper,
    sapphire,[d] turquoise, and emerald;
      and worked in gold were your
      settings
      and your engravings.[c]
    On the day that you were created
      they were prepared.
14 With an anointed cherub as guardian
      I placed you;[c]
    you were on the holy mountain
      of God;
    you walked among the stones
      of fire.
15 You were blameless in your ways
      from the day that you were created,
    until iniquity was found in you.

---

a Tg Vg: Heb *like silence*   *b* Or, as otherwise read,
Danel   *c* Meaning of Heb uncertain   *d* Or *lapis
lazuli*

16 In the abundance of your trade
　　you were filled with violence, and
　　　you sinned;
　　so I cast you as a profane thing from
　　　　the mountain of God,
　　and the guardian cherub drove you
　　　out
　　from among the stones of fire.
17 Your heart was proud because of your
　　beauty;
　　you corrupted your wisdom for the
　　　sake of your splendour.
I cast you to the ground;
　　I exposed you before kings,
　　to feast their eyes on you.
18 By the multitude of your iniquities,
　　in the unrighteousness of
　　　your trade,
　　you profaned your sanctuaries.
So I brought out fire from
　　　within you;
　　it consumed you,
　　and I turned you to ashes on
　　　the earth
　　in the sight of all who saw you.
19 All who know you among the
　　peoples
　　are appalled at you;
　　you have come to a dreadful end
　　and shall be no more for ever.

Proclamation against Sidon

20 The word of the LORD came to me:
21 Mortal, set your face towards Sidon, and
prophesy against it, 22 and say, Thus says
the Lord GOD:
　　I am against you, O Sidon,
　　　and I will gain glory in your midst.
　　They shall know that I am the LORD
　　　when I execute judgements in it,
　　　and manifest my holiness in it;
23 for I will send pestilence into it,
　　and bloodshed into its streets;
　　and the dead shall fall in its midst,
　　by the sword that is against it on
　　　every side.
　　And they shall know that I am
　　　the LORD.

24 The house of Israel shall no longer
find a pricking brier or a piercing thorn
among all their neighbours who have treat-

ed them with contempt. And they shall
know that I am the Lord GOD.

Future Blessing for Israel

25 Thus says the Lord GOD: When I
gather the house of Israel from the peoples
among whom they are scattered, and manifest my holiness in them in the sight of
the nations, then they shall settle on their
own soil that I gave to my servant Jacob.
26 They shall live in safety in it, and shall
build houses and plant vineyards. They
shall live in safety, when I execute judgements upon all their neighbours who have
treated them with contempt. And they
shall know that I am the LORD their God.

Proclamation against Egypt

29 In the tenth year, in the tenth
month, on the twelfth day of the
month, the word of the LORD came to me:
2 Mortal, set your face against Pharaoh king
of Egypt, and prophesy against him and
against all Egypt; 3 speak, and say, Thus says
the Lord GOD:
　　I am against you,
　　　Pharaoh king of Egypt,
　　the great dragon sprawling
　　　in the midst of its channels,
　　saying, 'My Nile is my own;
　　　I made it for myself.'
4 I will put hooks in your jaws,
　　and make the fish of your channels
　　　stick to your scales.
I will draw you up from your channels,
　　with all the fish of your channels
　　sticking to your scales.
5 I will fling you into the wilderness,
　　you and all the fish of your
　　　channels;
　　you shall fall in the open field,
　　and not be gathered and buried.
To the animals of the earth and to the
　　birds of the air
　　I have given you as food.
6 Then all the inhabitants of Egypt
　　shall know
　　that I am the LORD
because you[a] were a staff of reed
　　to the house of Israel;

---

a Gk Syr Vg: Heb *they*

7 when they grasped you with the
    hand, you broke,
  and tore all their shoulders;
  and when they leaned on you,
      you broke,
  and made all their legs unsteady. *a*

8 Therefore, thus says the Lord GOD: I will bring a sword upon you, and will cut off from you human being and animal; 9 and the land of Egypt shall be a desolation and a waste. Then they shall know that I am the LORD.

Because you*b* said, 'The Nile is mine, and I made it', 10 therefore, I am against you, and against your channels, and I will make the land of Egypt an utter waste and desolation, from Migdol to Syene, as far as the border of Ethiopia.*c* 11 No human foot shall pass through it, and no animal foot shall pass through it; it shall be uninhabited for forty years. 12 I will make the land of Egypt a desolation among desolated countries; and her cities shall be a desolation for forty years among cities that are laid waste. I will scatter the Egyptians among the nations, and disperse them among the countries.

13 Further, thus says the Lord GOD: At the end of forty years I will gather the Egyptians from the peoples among whom they were scattered; 14 and I will restore the fortunes of Egypt, and bring them back to the land of Pathros, the land of their origin; and there they shall be a lowly kingdom. 15 It shall be the most lowly of the kingdoms, and never again exalt itself above the nations; and I will make them so small that they will never again rule over the nations. 16 The Egyptians*d* shall never again be the reliance of the house of Israel; they will recall their iniquity, when they turned to them for aid. Then they shall know that I am the Lord GOD.

Babylonia Will Plunder Egypt

17 In the twenty-seventh year, in the first month, on the first day of the month, the word of the LORD came to me: 18 Mortal, King Nebuchadrezzar of Babylon made his army labour hard against Tyre; every head was made bald and every shoulder was rubbed bare; yet neither he nor his army got anything from Tyre to pay for the labour that he had expended against it. 19 Therefore, thus says the Lord GOD: I will give the land of Egypt to King Nebuchadrezzar of Babylon; and he shall carry off its wealth and despoil it and plunder it; and it shall be the wages for his army. 20 I have given him the land of Egypt as his payment for which he laboured, because they worked for me, says the Lord GOD.

21 On that day I will cause a horn to sprout up for the house of Israel, and I will open your lips among them. Then they shall know that I am the LORD.

Lamentation for Egypt

30 The word of the LORD came to me: 2 Mortal, prophesy, and say, Thus says the Lord GOD:
  Wail, 'Alas for the day!'
3   For a day is near,
    the day of the LORD is near;
  it will be a day of clouds,
    a time of doom*e* for the nations.
4 A sword shall come upon Egypt,
  and anguish shall be in Ethiopia,*c*
  when the slain fall in Egypt,
    and its wealth is carried away,
    and its foundations are torn down.
5 Ethiopia,*c* and Put, and Lud, and all Arabia, and Libya,*f* and the people of the allied land*g* shall fall with them by the sword.

6 Thus says the LORD:
  Those who support Egypt shall fall,
    and its proud might shall
      come down;
  from Migdol to Syene
    they shall fall within it by
      the sword,
  says the Lord GOD.
7 They shall be desolated among other
      desolated countries,
    and their cities shall lie among
      cities laid waste.

a Syr: Heb *stand*   *b* Gk Syr Vg: Heb *he*   *c* Or *Nubia*; Heb *Cush*   *d* Heb *It*   *e* Heb lacks *of doom*
f Compare Gk Syr Vg: Heb *Cub*   *g* Meaning of Heb uncertain

8 Then they shall know that I am
        the LORD,
    when I have set fire to Egypt,
    and all who help it are broken.
    9 On that day, messengers shall go out
from me in ships to terrify the unsuspecting Ethiopians;*a* and anguish shall come
upon them on the day of Egypt's doom;*b*
for it is coming!

10 Thus says the Lord GOD:
    I will put an end to the hordes
        of Egypt,
    by the hand of King
        Nebuchadrezzar of Babylon.
11 ·He and his people with him, the
        most terrible of the nations,
    shall be brought in to destroy
        the land;
    and they shall draw their swords
        against Egypt,
    and fill the land with the slain.
12 I will dry up the channels,
    and will sell the land into the hand
        of evildoers;
    I will bring desolation upon the land
        and everything in it
    by the hand of foreigners;
    I the LORD have spoken.

13 Thus says the Lord GOD:
    I will destroy the idols
        and put an end to the images
        in Memphis;
    there shall no longer be a prince in
        the land of Egypt;
        so I will put fear in the land
        of Egypt.
14 I will make Pathros a desolation,
        and will set fire to Zoan,
    and will execute acts of judgement
        on Thebes.
15 I will pour my wrath upon Pelusium,
    the stronghold of Egypt,
    and cut off the hordes of Thebes.
16 I will set fire to Egypt;
    Pelusium shall be in great agony;
    Thebes shall be breached,
    and Memphis face adversaries
        by day.

17 The young men of On and of Pi-
        beseth shall fall by the sword;
    and the cities themselves*c* shall go
        into captivity.
18 At Tehaphnehes the day shall
        be dark,
    when I break there the dominion of
        Egypt,
    and its proud might shall come to an
        end;
    the city*d* shall be covered by
        a cloud,
    and its daughter-towns shall go
        into captivity.
19 Thus I will execute acts of judgement
        on Egypt.
    Then they shall know that I am the
        LORD.

Proclamation against Pharaoh

20 In the eleventh year, in the first
month, on the seventh day of the month,
the word of the LORD came to me: 21 Mortal, I have broken the arm of Pharaoh king
of Egypt; it has not been bound up for
healing or wrapped with a bandage, so
that it may become strong to wield the
sword. 22 Therefore, thus says the Lord
GOD: I am against Pharaoh king of Egypt,
and will break his arms, both the strong
arm and the one that was broken; and I
will make the sword fall from his hand.
23 I will scatter the Egyptians among the
nations, and disperse them throughout
the lands. 24 I will strengthen the arms of
the king of Babylon, and put my sword in
his hand; but I will break the arms of
Pharaoh, and he will groan before him
with the groans of one mortally wounded.
25 I will strengthen the arms of the king of
Babylon, but the arms of Pharaoh shall
fall. And they shall know that I am the
LORD, when I put my sword into the hand
of the king of Babylon. He shall stretch it
out against the land of Egypt, 26 and I will
scatter the Egyptians among the nations
and disperse them throughout the countries. Then they shall know that I am the
LORD.

a Or *Nubians;* Heb *Cush*   *b* Heb *the day of Egypt*
c Heb *and they*   *d* Heb *she*

The Lofty Cedar

31 In the eleventh year, in the third month, on the first day of the month, the word of the LORD came to me: ²Mortal, say to Pharaoh king of Egypt and to his hordes:

Whom are you like in your greatness?
³   Consider Assyria, a cedar
        of Lebanon,
    with fair branches and forest shade,
        and of great height,
        its top among the clouds.ᵃ
⁴ The waters nourished it,
        the deep made it grow tall,
    making its rivers flowᵇ
        around the place where it was
            planted,
    sending forth its streams
        to all the trees of the field.
⁵ So it towered high
        above all the trees of the field;
    its boughs grew large
        and its branches long,
        from abundant water in its shoots.
⁶ All the birds of the air
        made their nests in its boughs;
    under its branches all the animals of
            the field
        gave birth to their young;
    and in its shade
        all great nations lived.
⁷ It was beautiful in its greatness,
        in the length of its branches;
    for its roots went down
        to abundant water.
⁸ The cedars in the garden of God
        could not rival it,
        nor the fir trees equal its boughs;
    the plane trees were as nothing
        compared with its branches;
    no tree in the garden of God
        was like it in beauty.
⁹ I made it beautiful
        with its mass of branches,
    the envy of all the trees of Eden
        that were in the garden of God.

10 Therefore, thus says the Lord GOD: Because itᶜ towered high and set its top among the clouds,ᵃ and its heart was proud of its height, ¹¹I gave it into the hand of the prince of the nations; he has

dealt with it as its wickedness deserves. I have cast it out. ¹²Foreigners from the most terrible of the nations have cut it down and left it. On the mountains and in all the valleys its branches have fallen, and its boughs lie broken in all the watercourses of the land; and all the peoples of the earth went away from its shade and left it.
¹³ On its fallen trunk settle
        all the birds of the air,
    and among its boughs lodge
        all the wild animals.

¹⁴All this is in order that no trees by the waters may grow to lofty height or set their tops among the clouds,ᵃ and that no trees that drink water may reach up to them in height.

    For all of them are handed over
        to death,
    to the world below;
    along with all mortals,
        with those who go down to the Pit.

15 Thus says the Lord GOD: On the day it went down to Sheol I closed the deep over it and covered it; I restrained its rivers, and its mighty waters were checked. I clothed Lebanon in gloom for it, and all the trees of the field fainted because of it. ¹⁶I made the nations quake at the sound of its fall, when I cast it down to Sheol with those who go down to the Pit; and all the trees of Eden, the choice and best of Lebanon, all that were well watered, were consoled in the world below. ¹⁷They also went down to Sheol with it, to those killed by the sword, along with its allies,ᵈ those who lived in its shade among the nations.

18 Which among the trees of Eden was like you in glory and in greatness? Now you shall be brought down with the trees of Eden to the world below; you shall lie among the uncircumcised, with those who are killed by the sword. This is Pharaoh and all his horde, says the Lord GOD.

Lamentation over Pharaoh and Egypt

32 In the twelfth year, in the twelfth month, on the first day of the month, the word of the LORD came to me:

---

a Gk: Heb *thick boughs*   *b* Gk: Heb *rivers going*
c Syr Vg: Heb *you*   *d* Heb *its arms*

2 Mortal, raise a lamentation over Pharaoh king of Egypt, and say to him:

You consider yourself a lion among
    the nations,
  but you are like a dragon in
    the seas;
  you thrash about in your streams,
    trouble the water with your feet,
    and foul your*a* streams.
3 Thus says the Lord GOD:
  In an assembly of many peoples
    I will throw my net over you;
  and I*b* will haul you up in
    my dragnet.
4 I will throw you on the ground,
  on the open field I will fling you,
  and will cause all the birds of the air
    to settle on you,
  and I will let the wild animals of
    the whole earth gorge
    themselves on you.
5 I will strew your flesh on the
    mountains,
  and fill the valleys with your
    carcass.*c*
6 I will drench the land with your
    flowing blood
    up to the mountains,
    and the watercourses will be filled
    with you.
7 When I blot you out, I will cover the
    heavens,
   and make their stars dark;
  I will cover the sun with a cloud,
    and the moon shall not give
    its light.
8 All the shining lights of the heavens
    I will darken above you,
  and put darkness on your land,
        says the Lord GOD.
9 I will trouble the hearts of many
    peoples,
  as I carry you captive*d* among the
    nations,
  into countries you have not known.
10 I will make many peoples appalled at
    you;
  their kings shall shudder because of
    you.
  When I brandish my sword before
    them,

they shall tremble at every moment
for their lives, each one of them,
  on the day of your downfall.
11 For thus says the Lord GOD:
  The sword of the king of Babylon
    shall come against you.
12 I will cause your hordes to fall
  by the swords of mighty ones,
  all of them most terrible among the
    nations.
They shall bring to ruin the pride of
    Egypt,
  and all its hordes shall perish.
13 I will destroy all its livestock
  from beside abundant waters;
  and no human foot shall trouble
    them any more,
  nor shall the hoofs of cattle trouble
    them.
14 Then I will make their waters clear,
  and cause their streams to run like
    oil, says the Lord GOD.
15 When I make the land of Egypt
    desolate
  and when the land is stripped of all
    that fills it,
  when I strike down all who live in it,
    then they shall know that I am the
    LORD.
16 This is a lamentation; it shall
    be chanted.
  The women of the nations shall
    chant it.
  Over Egypt and all its hordes they
    shall chant it,
    says the Lord GOD.

Dirge over Egypt

17 In the twelfth year, in the first month,*e* on the fifteenth day of the month, the word of the LORD came to me:
18 Mortal, wail over the hordes
    of Egypt,
  and send them down,
  with Egypt*f* and the daughters of
    majestic nations,
    to the world below,
    with those who go down to the Pit.

a Heb *their*   *b* Gk Vg: Heb *they*   *c* Symmachus Syr
Vg: Heb *your height*   *d* Gk: Heb *bring your destruction*
e Gk: Heb lacks *in the first month*   *f* Heb *it*

19 'Whom do you surpass in beauty?
  Go down! Be laid to rest with the
    uncircumcised!'
20 They shall fall among those who are killed by the sword. Egypt[a] has been handed over to the sword; carry away both it and its hordes. 21 The mighty chiefs shall speak of them, with their helpers, out of the midst of Sheol: 'They have come down, they lie still, the uncircumcised, killed by the sword.'

22 Assyria is there, and all its company, their graves all around it, all of them killed, fallen by the sword. 23 Their graves are set in the uttermost parts of the Pit. Its company is all around its grave, all of them killed, fallen by the sword, who spread terror in the land of the living.

24 Elam is there, and all its hordes around its grave; all of them killed, fallen by the sword, who went down uncircumcised into the world below, who spread terror in the land of the living. They bear their shame with those who go down to the Pit. 25 They have made Elam[b] a bed among the slain with all its hordes, their graves all around it, all of them uncircumcised, killed by the sword; for terror of them was spread in the land of the living, and they bear their shame with those who go down to the Pit; they are placed among the slain.

26 Meshech and Tubal are there, and all their multitude, their graves all around them, all of them uncircumcised, killed by the sword; for they spread terror in the land of the living. 27 And they do not lie with the fallen warriors of long ago[c] who went down to Sheol with their weapons of war, whose swords were laid under their heads, and whose shields[d] are upon their bones; for the terror of the warriors was in the land of the living. 28 So you shall be broken and lie among the uncircumcised, with those who are killed by the sword.

29 Edom is there, its kings and all its princes, who for all their might are laid with those who are killed by the sword; they lie with the uncircumcised, with those who go down to the Pit.

30 The princes of the north are there, all of them, and all the Sidonians, who have gone down in shame with the slain, for all the terror that they caused by their might; they lie uncircumcised with those who are killed by the sword, and bear their shame with those who go down to the Pit.

31 When Pharaoh sees them, he will be consoled for all his hordes—Pharaoh and all his army, killed by the sword, says the Lord God. 32 For he[e] spread terror in the land of the living; therefore he shall be laid to rest among the uncircumcised, with those who are slain by the sword—Pharaoh and all his multitude, says the Lord God.

Ezekiel Israel's Sentinel

33 The word of the Lord came to me: 2 O Mortal, speak to your people and say to them, If I bring the sword upon a land, and the people of the land take one of their number as their sentinel; 3 and if the sentinel sees the sword coming upon the land and blows the trumpet and warns the people; 4 then if any who hear the sound of the trumpet do not take warning, and the sword comes and takes them away, their blood shall be upon their own heads. 5 They heard the sound of the trumpet and did not take warning; their blood shall be upon themselves. But if they had taken warning, they would have saved their lives. 6 But if the sentinel sees the sword coming and does not blow the trumpet, so that the people are not warned, and the sword comes and takes any of them, they are taken away in their iniquity, but their blood I will require at the sentinel's hand.

7 So you, mortal, I have made a sentinel for the house of Israel; whenever you hear a word from my mouth, you shall give them warning from me. 8 If I say to the wicked, 'O wicked ones, you shall surely die', and you do not speak to warn the wicked to turn from their ways, the wicked shall die in their iniquity, but their blood I will require at your hand. 9 But if you warn the wicked to turn from their ways, and they do not turn from their ways, the

a Heb *It*   *b* Heb *it*   *c* Gk Old Latin: Heb *of the uncircumcised*   *d* Cn: Heb *iniquities*   *e* Cn: Heb *I* wicked shall die in their iniquity, but you will have saved your life.

God's Justice and Mercy

10 Now you, mortal, say to the house of Israel, Thus you have said: 'Our transgressions and our sins weigh upon us, and we waste away because of them; how then can we live?' ¹¹ Say to them, As I live, says the Lord God, I have no pleasure in the death of the wicked, but that the wicked turn from their ways and live; turn back, turn back from your evil ways; for why will you die, O house of Israel? ¹² And you, mortal, say to your people, The righteousness of the righteous shall not save them when they transgress; and as for the wickedness of the wicked, it shall not make them stumble when they turn from their wickedness; and the righteous shall not be able to live by their righteousness*a* when they sin. ¹³ Though I say to the righteous that they shall surely live, yet if they trust in their righteousness and commit iniquity, none of their righteous deeds shall be remembered; but in the iniquity that they have committed they shall die. ¹⁴ Again, though I say to the wicked, 'You shall surely die', yet if they turn from their sin and do what is lawful and right— ¹⁵ if the wicked restore the pledge, give back what they have taken by robbery, and walk in the statutes of life, committing no iniquity—they shall surely live, they shall not die. ¹⁶ None of the sins that they have committed shall be remembered against them; they have done what is lawful and right, they shall surely live.

17 Yet your people say, 'The way of the Lord is not just', when it is their own way that is not just. ¹⁸ When the righteous turn from their righteousness, and commit iniquity, they shall die for it.*b* ¹⁹ And when the wicked turn from their wickedness, and do what is lawful and right, they shall live by it.*b* ²⁰ Yet you say, 'The way of the Lord is not just.' O house of Israel, I will judge all of you according to your ways!

The Fall of Jerusalem

21 In the twelfth year of our exile, in the tenth month, on the fifth day of the month, someone who had escaped from Jerusalem came to me and said, 'The city has fallen.' ²² Now the hand of the Lord had been upon me the evening before the fugitive came; but he had opened my mouth by the time the fugitive came to me in the morning; so my mouth was opened, and I was no longer unable to speak.

The Survivors in Judah

23 The word of the Lord came to me: ²⁴ Mortal, the inhabitants of these waste places in the land of Israel keep saying, 'Abraham was only one man, yet he got possession of the land; but we are many; the land is surely given to us to possess.' ²⁵ Therefore say to them, Thus says the Lord God: You eat flesh with the blood, and lift up your eyes to your idols, and shed blood; shall you then possess the land? ²⁶ You depend on your swords, you commit abominations, and each of you defiles his neighbour's wife; shall you then possess the land? ²⁷ Say this to them, Thus says the Lord God: As I live, surely those who are in the waste places shall fall by the sword; and those who are in the open field I will give to the wild animals to be devoured; and those who are in strongholds and in caves shall die by pestilence. ²⁸ I will make the land a desolation and a waste, and its proud might shall come to an end; and the mountains of Israel shall be so desolate that no one will pass through. ²⁹ Then they shall know that I am the Lord, when I have made the land a desolation and a waste because of all their abominations that they have committed.

30 As for you, mortal, your people who talk together about you by the walls, and at the doors of the houses, say to one another, each to a neighbour, 'Come and hear what the word is that comes from the Lord.' ³¹ They come to you as people come, and they sit before you as my people, and they hear your words, but they will not obey them. For flattery is on their lips, but their heart is set on their gain. ³² To them you are like a singer of love songs,*c* one who has a beautiful voice and plays well

a Heb *by it*　　*b* Heb *them*　　*c* Cn: Heb *like a love song* on an instrument; they hear what you say, but they will not do it. ³³When this comes—and come it will!—then they shall know that a prophet has been among them.

Israel's False Shepherds

34 The word of the LORD came to me: ²Mortal, prophesy against the shepherds of Israel: prophesy, and say to them—to the shepherds: Thus says the Lord GOD: Ah, you shepherds of Israel who have been feeding yourselves! Should not shepherds feed the sheep? ³You eat the fat, you clothe yourselves with the wool, you slaughter the fatlings; but you do not feed the sheep. ⁴You have not strengthened the weak, you have not healed the sick, you have not bound up the injured, you have not brought back the strayed, you have not sought the lost, but with force and harshness you have ruled them. ⁵So they were scattered, because there was no shepherd; and scattered, they became food for all the wild animals. ⁶My sheep were scattered, they wandered over all the mountains and on every high hill; my sheep were scattered over all the face of the earth, with no one to search or seek for them.

7 Therefore, you shepherds, hear the word of the LORD: ⁸As I live, says the Lord GOD, because my sheep have become a prey, and my sheep have become food for all the wild animals, since there was no shepherd; and because my shepherds have not searched for my sheep, but the shepherds have fed themselves, and have not fed my sheep; ⁹therefore, you shepherds, hear the word of the LORD: ¹⁰Thus says the Lord GOD, I am against the shepherds; and I will demand my sheep at their hand, and put a stop to their feeding the sheep; no longer shall the shepherds feed themselves. I will rescue my sheep from their mouths, so that they may not be food for them.

God the True Shepherd

11 For thus says the Lord GOD: I myself will search for my sheep, and will seek them out. ¹²As shepherds seek out their flocks when they are among their scattered sheep, so I will seek out my sheep. I will rescue them from all the places to which they have been scattered on a day of clouds and thick darkness. ¹³I will bring them out from the peoples and gather them from the countries, and will bring them into their own land; and I will feed them on the mountains of Israel, by the watercourses, and in all the inhabited parts of the land. ¹⁴I will feed them with good pasture, and the mountain heights of Israel shall be their pasture; there they shall lie down in good grazing land, and they shall feed on rich pasture on the mountains of Israel. ¹⁵I myself will be the shepherd of my sheep, and I will make them lie down, says the Lord GOD. ¹⁶I will seek the lost, and I will bring back the strayed, and I will bind up the injured, and I will strengthen the weak, but the fat and the strong I will destroy. I will feed them with justice.

17 As for you, my flock, thus says the Lord GOD: I shall judge between sheep and sheep, between rams and goats: ¹⁸Is it not enough for you to feed on the good pasture, but you must tread down with your feet the rest of your pasture? When you drink of clear water, must you foul the rest with your feet? ¹⁹And must my sheep eat what you have trodden with your feet, and drink what you have fouled with your feet?

20 Therefore, thus says the Lord GOD to them: I myself will judge between the fat sheep and the lean sheep. ²¹Because you pushed with flank and shoulder, and butted at all the weak animals with your horns until you scattered them far and wide, ²²I will save my flock, and they shall no longer be ravaged; and I will judge between sheep and sheep.

23 I will set up over them one shepherd, my servant David, and he shall feed them: he shall feed them and be their shepherd. ²⁴And I, the LORD, will be their God, and my servant David shall be prince among them; I, the LORD, have spoken.

25 I will make with them a covenant of peace and banish wild animals from the land, so that they may live in the wild and sleep in the woods securely. ²⁶I will make them and the region around my hill a

blessing; and I will send down the showers in their season; they shall be showers of blessing. 27 The trees of the field shall yield their fruit, and the earth shall yield its increase. They shall be secure on their soil; and they shall know that I am the LORD, when I break the bars of their yoke, and save them from the hands of those who enslaved them. 28 They shall no more be plunder for the nations, nor shall the animals of the land devour them; they shall live in safety, and no one shall make them afraid. 29 I will provide for them splendid vegetation, so that they shall no more be consumed with hunger in the land, and no longer suffer the insults of the nations. 30 They shall know that I, the LORD their God, am with them, and that they, the house of Israel, are my people, says the Lord GOD. 31 You are my sheep, the sheep of my pasture, *a* and I am your God, says the Lord GOD.

Judgement on Mount Seir

35 The word of the LORD came to me: 2 Mortal, set your face against Mount Seir, and prophesy against it, 3 and say to it, Thus says the Lord GOD:

I am against you, Mount Seir;
  I stretch out my hand against you
  to make you a desolation and
    a waste.
4 I lay your towns in ruins;
  you shall become a desolation,
  and you shall know that I am
    the LORD.

5 Because you cherished an ancient enmity, and gave over the people of Israel to the power of the sword at the time of their calamity, at the time of their final punishment; 6 therefore, as I live, says the Lord GOD, I will prepare you for blood, and blood shall pursue you; since you did not hate bloodshed, bloodshed shall pursue you. 7 I will make Mount Seir a waste and a desolation; and I will cut off from it all who come and go. 8 I will fill its mountains with the slain; on your hills and in your valleys and in all your watercourses those killed with the sword shall fall. 9 I will make you a perpetual desolation, and your

cities shall never be inhabited. Then you shall know that I am the LORD.

10 Because you said, 'These two nations and these two countries shall be mine, and we will take possession of them'—although the LORD was there— 11 therefore, as I live, says the Lord GOD, I will deal with you according to the anger and envy that you showed because of your hatred against them; and I will make myself known among you, *b* when I judge you. 12 You shall know that I, the LORD, have heard all the abusive speech that you uttered against the mountains of Israel, saying, 'They are laid desolate, they are given to us to devour.' 13 And you magnified yourselves against me with your mouth, and multiplied your words against me; I heard it. 14 Thus says the Lord GOD: As the whole earth rejoices, I will make you desolate. 15 As you rejoiced over the inheritance of the house of Israel, because it was desolate, so I will deal with you; you shall be desolate, Mount Seir, and all Edom, all of it. Then they shall know that I am the LORD.

Blessing on Israel

36 And you, mortal, prophesy to the mountains of Israel, and say: O mountains of Israel, hear the word of the LORD. 2 Thus says the Lord GOD: Because the enemy said of you, 'Aha!' and, 'The ancient heights have become our possession', 3 therefore prophesy, and say: Thus says the Lord GOD: Because they made you desolate indeed, and crushed you from all sides, so that you became the possession of the rest of the nations, and you became an object of gossip and slander among the people; 4 therefore, O mountains of Israel, hear the word of the Lord GOD: Thus says the Lord GOD to the mountains and the hills, the watercourses and the valleys, the desolate wastes and the deserted towns, which have become a source of plunder and an object of derision to the rest of the nations all around; 5 therefore thus says the Lord GOD: I am speaking in my hot jealousy against the rest of the nations, and against all

a Gk OL: Heb *pasture, you are people*   *b* Gk: Heb *them*

Edom, who, with wholehearted joy and utter contempt, took my land as their possession, because of its pasture, to plunder it. 6 Therefore prophesy concerning the land of Israel, and say to the mountains and hills, to the watercourses and valleys, Thus says the Lord GOD: I am speaking in my jealous wrath, because you have suffered the insults of the nations; 7 therefore thus says the Lord GOD: I swear that the nations that are all around you shall themselves suffer insults.

8 But you, O mountains of Israel, shall shoot out your branches, and yield your fruit to my people Israel; for they shall soon come home. 9 See now, I am for you; I will turn to you, and you shall be tilled and sown; 10 and I will multiply your population, the whole house of Israel, all of it; the towns shall be inhabited and the waste places rebuilt; 11 and I will multiply human beings and animals upon you. They shall increase and be fruitful; and I will cause you to be inhabited as in your former times, and will do more good to you than ever before. Then you shall know that I am the LORD. 12 I will lead people upon you—my people Israel—and they shall possess you, and you shall be their inheritance. No longer shall you bereave them of children.

13 Thus says the Lord GOD: Because they say to you, 'You devour people, and you bereave your nation of children', 14 therefore you shall no longer devour people and no longer bereave your nation of children, says the Lord GOD; 15 and no longer will I let you hear the insults of the nations, no longer shall you bear the disgrace of the peoples; and no longer shall you cause your nation to stumble, says the Lord GOD.

The Renewal of Israel

16 The word of the LORD came to me: 17 Mortal, when the house of Israel lived on their own soil, they defiled it with their ways and their deeds; their conduct in my sight was like the uncleanness of a woman in her menstrual period. 18 So I poured out my wrath upon them for the blood that they had shed upon the land, and for the idols with which they had defiled it. 19 I scattered them among the nations, and they were dispersed through the countries; in accordance with their conduct and their deeds I judged them. 20 But when they came to the nations, wherever they came, they profaned my holy name, in that it was said of them, 'These are the people of the LORD, and yet they had to go out of his land.' 21 But I had concern for my holy name, which the house of Israel had profaned among the nations to which they came.

22 Therefore say to the house of Israel, Thus says the Lord GOD: It is not for your sake, O house of Israel, that I am about to act, but for the sake of my holy name, which you have profaned among the nations to which you came. 23 I will sanctify my great name, which has been profaned among the nations, and which you have profaned among them; and the nations shall know that I am the LORD, says the Lord GOD, when through you I display my holiness before their eyes. 24 I will take you from the nations, and gather you from all the countries, and bring you into your own land. 25 I will sprinkle clean water upon you, and you shall be clean from all your uncleannesses, and from all your idols I will cleanse you. 26 A new heart I will give you, and a new spirit I will put within you; and I will remove from your body the heart of stone and give you a heart of flesh. 27 I will put my spirit within you, and make you follow my statutes and be careful to observe my ordinances. 28 Then you shall live in the land that I gave to your ancestors; and you shall be my people, and I will be your God. 29 I will save you from all your uncleannesses, and I will summon the grain and make it abundant and lay no famine upon you. 30 I will make the fruit of the tree and the produce of the field abundant, so that you may never again suffer the disgrace of famine among the nations. 31 Then you shall remember your evil ways, and your dealings that were not good; and you shall loathe yourselves for your iniquities and your abominable deeds. 32 It is not for your sake that I will act, says the Lord

GOD; let that be known to you. Be ashamed and dismayed for your ways, O house of Israel.

33 Thus says the Lord GOD: On the day that I cleanse you from all your iniquities, I will cause the towns to be inhabited, and the waste places shall be rebuilt. 34 The land that was desolate shall be tilled, instead of being the desolation that it was in the sight of all who passed by. 35 And they will say, 'This land that was desolate has become like the garden of Eden; and the waste and desolate and ruined towns are now inhabited and fortified.' 36 Then the nations that are left all around you shall know that I, the LORD, have rebuilt the ruined places, and replanted that which was desolate; I, the LORD, have spoken, and I will do it.

37 Thus says the Lord GOD: I will also let the house of Israel ask me to do this for them: to increase their population like a flock. 38 Like the flock for sacrifices,[a] like the flock at Jerusalem during her appointed festivals, so shall the ruined towns be filled with flocks of people. Then they shall know that I am the LORD.

The Valley of Dry Bones

37 The hand of the LORD came upon me, and he brought me out by the spirit of the LORD and set me down in the middle of a valley; it was full of bones. 2 He led me all round them; there were very many lying in the valley, and they were very dry. 3 He said to me, 'Mortal, can these bones live?' I answered, 'O Lord GOD, you know.' 4 Then he said to me, 'Prophesy to these bones, and say to them: O dry bones, hear the word of the LORD. 5 Thus says the Lord GOD to these bones: I will cause breath[b] to enter you, and you shall live. 6 I will lay sinews on you, and will cause flesh to come upon you, and cover you with skin, and put breath[b] in you, and you shall live; and you shall know that I am the LORD.'

7 So I prophesied as I had been commanded; and as I prophesied, suddenly there was a noise, a rattling, and the bones came together, bone to its bone. 8 I looked, and there were sinews on them, and flesh had come upon them, and skin had covered them; but there was no breath in them. 9 Then he said to me, 'Prophesy to the breath, prophesy, mortal, and say to the breath:[c] Thus says the Lord GOD: Come from the four winds, O breath,[c] and breathe upon these slain, that they may live.' 10 I prophesied as he commanded me, and the breath came into them, and they lived, and stood on their feet, a vast multitude.

11 Then he said to me, 'Mortal, these bones are the whole house of Israel. They say, "Our bones are dried up, and our hope is lost; we are cut off completely." 12 Therefore prophesy, and say to them, Thus says the Lord GOD: I am going to open your graves, and bring you up from your graves, O my people; and I will bring you back to the land of Israel. 13 And you shall know that I am the LORD, when I open your graves, and bring you up from your graves, O my people. 14 I will put my spirit within you, and you shall live, and I will place you on your own soil; then you shall know that I, the LORD, have spoken and will act, says the LORD.'

The Two Sticks

15 The word of the LORD came to me: 16 Mortal, take a stick and write on it, 'For Judah, and the Israelites associated with it'; then take another stick and write on it, 'For Joseph (the stick of Ephraim) and all the house of Israel associated with it'; 17 and join them together into one stick, so that they may become one in your hand. 18 And when your people say to you, 'Will you not show us what you mean by these?' 19 say to them, Thus says the Lord GOD: I am about to take the stick of Joseph (which is in the hand of Ephraim) and the tribes of Israel associated with it; and I will put the stick of Judah upon it,[d] and make them one stick, in order that they may be one in my hand. 20 When the sticks on which you write are in your hand before their eyes, 21 then say to them, Thus says the Lord

a Heb *flock of holy things*   b Or *spirit*   c Or *wind* or *spirit*   d Heb *I will put them upon it*

GOD: I will take the people of Israel from the nations among which they have gone, and will gather them from every quarter, and bring them to their own land. 22 I will make them one nation in the land, on the mountains of Israel; and one king shall be king over them all. Never again shall they be two nations, and never again shall they be divided into two kingdoms. 23 They shall never again defile themselves with their idols and their detestable things, or with any of their transgressions. I will save them from all the apostasies into which they have fallen,*a* and will cleanse them. Then they shall be my people, and I will be their God.

24 My servant David shall be king over them; and they shall all have one shepherd. They shall follow my ordinances and be careful to observe my statutes. 25 They shall live in the land that I gave to my servant Jacob, in which your ancestors lived; they and their children and their children's children shall live there for ever; and my servant David shall be their prince for ever. 26 I will make a covenant of peace with them; it shall be an everlasting covenant with them; and I will bless*b* them and multiply them, and will set my sanctuary among them for evermore. 27 My dwelling-place shall be with them; and I will be their God, and they shall be my people. 28 Then the nations shall know that I the LORD sanctify Israel, when my sanctuary is among them for evermore.

Invasion by Gog

38 The word of the LORD came to me: 2 Mortal, set your face towards Gog, of the land of Magog, the chief prince of Meshech and Tubal. Prophesy against him 3 and say: Thus says the Lord GOD: I am against you, O Gog, chief prince of Meshech and Tubal; 4 I will turn you round and put hooks into your jaws, and I will lead you out with all your army, horses and horsemen, all of them clothed in full armour, a great company, all of them with shield and buckler, wielding swords. 5 Persia, Ethiopia,*c* and Put are with them, all of them with buckler and helmet; 6 Gomer

and all its troops; Beth-togarmah from the remotest parts of the north with all its troops—many peoples are with you.

7 Be ready and keep ready, you and all the companies that are assembled around you, and hold yourselves in reserve for them. 8 After many days you shall be mustered; in the latter years you shall go against a land restored from war, a land where people were gathered from many nations on the mountains of Israel, which had long lain waste; its people were brought out from the nations and now are living in safety, all of them. 9 You shall advance, coming on like a storm; you shall be like a cloud covering the land, you and all your troops, and many peoples with you.

10 Thus says the Lord GOD: On that day thoughts will come into your mind, and you will devise an evil scheme. 11 You will say, 'I will go up against the land of unwalled villages; I will fall upon the quiet people who live in safety, all of them living without walls, and having no bars or gates'; 12 to seize spoil and carry off plunder; to assail the waste places that are now inhabited, and the people who were gathered from the nations, who are acquiring cattle and goods, who live at the centre*d* of the earth. 13 Sheba and Dedan and the merchants of Tarshish and all its young warriors*e* will say to you, 'Have you come to seize spoil? Have you assembled your horde to carry off plunder, to carry away silver and gold, to take away cattle and goods, to seize a great amount of booty?'

14 Therefore, mortal, prophesy, and say to Gog: Thus says the Lord GOD: On that day when my people Israel are living securely, you will rouse yourself*f* 15 and come from your place out of the remotest parts of the north, you and many peoples with you, all of them riding on horses, a great horde, a mighty army; 16 you will come up against my people Israel, like a cloud covering the earth. In the latter days I will bring you against my land, so that the nations may know me, when through you,

---

a Another reading is *from all the settlements in which they have sinned*   *b* Tg: Heb *give*   *c* Or *Nubia*; Heb *Cush*   *d* Heb *navel*   *e* Heb *young lions*   *f* Gk: Heb *will you not know?*

O Gog, I display my holiness before their eyes.

Judgement on Gog

17 Thus says the Lord GOD: Are you he of whom I spoke in former days by my servants the prophets of Israel, who in those days prophesied for years that I would bring you against them? 18 On that day, when Gog comes against the land of Israel, says the Lord GOD, my wrath shall be aroused. 19 For in my jealousy and in my blazing wrath I declare: On that day there shall be a great shaking in the land of Israel; 20 the fish of the sea, and the birds of the air, and the animals of the field, and all creeping things that creep on the ground, and all human beings that are on the face of the earth, shall quake at my presence, and the mountains shall be thrown down, and the cliffs shall fall, and every wall shall tumble to the ground. 21 I will summon the sword against Gog*a* in*b* all my mountains, says the Lord GOD; the swords of all will be against their comrades. 22 With pestilence and bloodshed I will enter into judgement with him; and I will pour down torrential rains and hailstones, fire and sulphur, upon him and his troops and the many peoples that are with him. 23 So I will display my greatness and my holiness and make myself known in the eyes of many nations. Then they shall know that I am the LORD.

Gog's Armies Destroyed

39 And you, mortal, prophesy against Gog, and say: Thus says the Lord GOD: I am against you, O Gog, chief prince of Meshech and Tubal! 2 I will turn you round and drive you forwards, and bring you up from the remotest parts of the north, and lead you against the mountains of Israel. 3 I will strike your bow from your left hand, and will make your arrows drop out of your right hand. 4 You shall fall in the mountains of Israel, you and all your troops and the peoples that are with you; I will give you to birds of prey of every kind and to the wild animals to be devoured. 5 You shall fall in the open field; for I have

spoken, says the Lord GOD. 6 I will send fire on Magog and on those who live securely in the coastlands; and they shall know that I am the LORD.

7 My holy name I will make known among my people Israel; and I will not let my holy name be profaned any more; and the nations shall know that I am the LORD, the Holy One in Israel. 8 It has come! It has happened, says the Lord GOD. This is the day of which I have spoken.

9 Then those who live in the towns of Israel will go out and make fires of the weapons and burn them—bucklers and shields, bows and arrows, hand-pikes and spears—and they will make fires of them for seven years. 10 They will not need to take wood out of the field or cut down any trees in the forests, for they will make their fires of the weapons; they will despoil those who despoiled them, and plunder those who plundered them, says the Lord GOD.

The Burial of Gog

11 On that day I will give to Gog a place for burial in Israel, the Valley of the Travellers*c* east of the sea; it shall block the path of the travellers, for there Gog and all his horde will be buried; it shall be called the Valley of Hamon-gog.*d* 12 Seven months the house of Israel shall spend burying them, in order to cleanse the land. 13 All the people of the land shall bury them; and it will bring them honour on the day that I show my glory, says the Lord GOD. 14 They will set apart men to pass through the land regularly and bury any invaders*e* who remain on the face of the land, so as to cleanse it; for seven months they shall make their search. 15 As the searchers*e* pass through the land, anyone who sees a human bone shall set up a sign by it, until the buriers have buried it in the Valley of Hamon-gog.*d* 16 (A city Hamonah*f* is there also.) Thus they shall cleanse the land.

17 As for you, mortal, thus says the Lord GOD: Speak to the birds of every kind and

---

a Heb *him*   *b* Heb *to* or *for*   *c* Or *of the Abarim*
d That is, *the Horde of Gog*   *e* Heb *travellers*   *f* That
is *The Horde*

to all the wild animals: Assemble and come, gather from all around to the sacrificial feast that I am preparing for you, a great sacrificial feast on the mountains of Israel, and you shall eat flesh and drink blood. 18 You shall eat the flesh of the mighty, and drink the blood of the princes of the earth—of rams, of lambs, and of goats, of bulls, all of them fatlings of Bashan. 19 You shall eat fat until you are filled, and drink blood until you are drunk, at the sacrificial feast that I am preparing for you. 20 And you shall be filled at my table with horses and charioteers,*a* with warriors and all kinds of soldiers, says the Lord GOD.

Israel Restored to the Land

21 I will display my glory among the nations; and all the nations shall see my judgement that I have executed, and my hand that I have laid on them. 22 The house of Israel shall know that I am the LORD their God, from that day forward. 23 And the nations shall know that the house of Israel went into captivity for their iniquity, because they dealt treacherously with me. So I hid my face from them and gave them into the hand of their adversaries, and they all fell by the sword. 24 I dealt with them according to their uncleanness and their transgressions, and hid my face from them.

25 Therefore, thus says the Lord GOD: Now I will restore the fortunes of Jacob, and have mercy on the whole house of Israel; and I will be jealous for my holy name. 26 They shall forget*b* their shame, and all the treachery they have practised against me, when they live securely in their land with no one to make them afraid, 27 when I have brought them back from the peoples and gathered them from their enemies' lands, and through them have displayed my holiness in the sight of many nations. 28 Then they shall know that I am the LORD their God because I sent them into exile among the nations, and then gathered them into their own land. I will leave none of them behind; 29 and I will never again hide my face from them, when

I pour out my spirit upon the house of Israel, says the Lord GOD.

The Vision of the New Temple

40 In the twenty-fifth year of our exile, at the beginning of the year, on the tenth day of the month, in the fourteenth year after the city was struck down, on that very day, the hand of the LORD was upon me, and he brought me there. 2 He brought me, in visions of God, to the land of Israel, and set me down upon a very high mountain, on which was a structure like a city to the south. 3 When he brought me there, a man was there, whose appearance shone like bronze, with a linen cord and a measuring reed in his hand; and he was standing in the gateway. 4 The man said to me, 'Mortal, look closely and listen attentively, and set your mind upon all that I shall show you, for you were brought here in order that I might show it to you; declare all that you see to the house of Israel.'

5 Now there was a wall all round the outside of the temple area. The length of the measuring reed in the man's hand was six long cubits, each being a cubit and a handbreadth in length; so he measured the thickness of the wall, one reed; and the height, one reed. 6 Then he went into the gateway facing east, going up its steps, and measured the threshold of the gate, one reed deep.*c* There were 7 recesses, and each recess was one reed wide and one reed deep; and the space between the recesses, five cubits; and the threshold of the gate by the vestibule of the gate at the inner end was one reed deep. 8 Then he measured the inner vestibule of the gateway, one cubit. 9 Then he measured the vestibule of the gateway, eight cubits; and its pilasters, two cubits; and the vestibule of the gate was at the inner end. 10 There were three recesses on either side of the east gate; the three were of the same size; and the pilasters on either side were of the same size. 11 Then he measured the width of the opening of the gateway, ten cubits; and the width of the

a Heb *chariots*   *b* Another reading is *They shall bear*
c Heb *deep, and one threshold, one reed deep*

gateway, thirteen cubits. 12 There was a barrier before the recesses, one cubit on either side; and the recesses were six cubits on either side. 13 Then he measured the gate from the back*a* of one recess to the back*a* of the other, a width of twenty-five cubits, from wall to wall.*b* 14 He measured*c* also the vestibule, twenty cubits; and the gate next to the pilaster on every side of the court.*d* 15 From the front of the gate at the entrance to the end of the inner vestibule of the gate was fifty cubits. 16 The recesses and their pilasters had windows, with shutters*d* on the inside of the gateway all round, and the vestibules also had windows on the inside all round; and on the pilasters were palm trees.

17 Then he brought me into the outer court; there were chambers there, and a pavement, all round the court; thirty chambers fronted on the pavement. 18 The pavement ran along the side of the gates, corresponding to the length of the gates; this was the lower pavement. 19 Then he measured the distance from the inner front of*e* the lower gate to the outer front of the inner court, one hundred cubits.*f*

20 Then he measured the gate of the outer court that faced north—its depth and width. 21 Its recesses, three on either side, and its pilasters and its vestibule were of the same size as those of the first gate; its depth was fifty cubits, and its width twenty-five cubits. 22 Its windows, its vestibule, and its palm trees were of the same size as those of the gate that faced towards the east. Seven steps led up to it; and its vestibule was on the inside.*g* 23 Opposite the gate on the north, as on the east, was a gate to the inner court; he measured from gate to gate, one hundred cubits.

24 Then he led me towards the south, and there was a gate on the south; and he measured its pilasters and its vestibule; they had the same dimensions as the others. 25 There were windows all round in it and in its vestibule, like the windows of the others; its depth was fifty cubits, and its width twenty-five cubits. 26 There were seven steps leading up to it; its vestibule was on the inside.*g* It had palm trees on its pi-lasters, one on either side. 27 There was a gate on the south of the inner court; and he measured from gate to gate towards the south, one hundred cubits.

28 Then he brought me to the inner court by the south gate, and he measured the south gate; it was of the same dimensions as the others. 29 Its recesses, its pilasters, and its vestibule were of the same size as the others; and there were windows all round in it and in its vestibule; its depth was fifty cubits, and its width twenty-five cubits. 30 There were vestibules all round, twenty-five cubits deep and five cubits wide. 31 Its vestibule faced the outer court, and palm trees were on its pilasters, and its stairway had eight steps.

32 Then he brought me to the inner court on the east side, and he measured the gate; it was of the same size as the others. 33 Its recesses, its pilasters, and its vestibule were of the same dimensions as the others; and there were windows all round in it and in its vestibule; its depth was fifty cubits, and its width twenty-five cubits. 34 Its vestibule faced the outer court, and it had palm trees on its pilasters, on either side; and its stairway had eight steps.

35 Then he brought me to the north gate, and he measured it; it had the same dimensions as the others. 36 Its recesses, its pilasters, and its vestibule were of the same size as the others;*h* and it had windows all round. Its depth was fifty cubits, and its width twenty-five cubits. 37 Its vestibule*i* faced the outer court, and it had palm trees on its pilasters, on either side; and its stairway had eight steps.

38 There was a chamber with its door in the vestibule of the gate,*j* where the burnt-offering was to be washed. 39 And in the vestibule of the gate were two tables on either side, on which the burnt-offering and the sin-offering and the guilt-offering were to be slaughtered. 40 On the outside of the

a Gk: Heb *roof*   *b* Heb *opening facing opening*
c Heb *made*   *d* Meaning of Heb uncertain
e Compare Gk: Heb *from before*   *f* Heb adds *the east and the north*   *g* Gk: Heb *before them*   *h* One Ms: Compare verses 29 and 33: MT lacks *were of the same size as the others*   *i* Gk Vg Compare verses 26, 31, 34: Heb *pilasters*   *j* Cn: Heb *at the pilasters of the gates*

vestibule[a] at the entrance of the north gate were two tables; and on the other side of the vestibule of the gate were two tables. [41] Four tables were on the inside, and four tables on the outside of the side of the gate, eight tables, on which the sacrifices were to be slaughtered. [42] There were also four tables of hewn stone for the burnt-offering, a cubit and a half long, and one cubit and a half wide, and one cubit high, on which the instruments were to be laid with which the burnt-offerings and the sacrifices were slaughtered. [43] There were pegs, one handbreadth long, fastened all round the inside. And on the tables the flesh of the offering was to be laid.

[44] On the outside of the inner gateway there were chambers for the singers in the inner court, one[b] at the side of the north gate facing south, the other at the side of the east gate facing north. [45] He said to me, 'This chamber that faces south is for the priests who have charge of the temple, [46] and the chamber that faces north is for the priests who have charge of the altar; these are the descendants of Zadok, who alone among the descendants of Levi may come near to the LORD to minister to him.' [47] He measured the court, one hundred cubits deep, and one hundred cubits wide, a square; and the altar was in front of the temple.

The Temple

[48] Then he brought me to the vestibule of the temple and measured the pilasters of the vestibule, five cubits on either side; and the width of the gate was fourteen cubits; and the side walls of the gate were three cubits[c] on either side. [49] The depth of the vestibule was twenty cubits, and the width twelve[d] cubits; ten steps led up[e] to it; and there were pillars beside the pilasters on either side.

41 Then he brought me to the nave, and measured the pilasters; on each side six cubits was the width of the pilasters.[f] [2] The width of the entrance was ten cubits; and the side walls of the entrance were five cubits on either side. He measured the length of the nave, forty cubits,

and its width, twenty cubits. [3] Then he went into the inner room and measured the pilasters of the entrance, two cubits; and the width of the entrance, six cubits; and the side walls[g] of the entrance, seven cubits. [4] He measured the depth of the room, twenty cubits, and its width, twenty cubits, beyond the nave. And he said to me, This is the most holy place.

[5] Then he measured the wall of the temple, six cubits thick; and the width of the side chambers, four cubits, all round the temple. [6] The side chambers were in three stories, one over another, thirty in each story. There were offsets[h] all round the wall of the temple to serve as supports for the side chambers, so that they should not be supported by the wall of the temple. [7] The passageway[i] of the side chambers widened from story to story; for the structure was supplied with a stairway all round the temple. For this reason the structure became wider from story to story. One ascended from the bottom story to the uppermost story by way of the middle one. [8] I saw also that the temple had a raised platform all around; the foundations of the side chambers measured a full reed of six long cubits. [9] The thickness of the outer wall of the side chambers was five cubits; and the free space between the side chambers of the temple [10] and the chambers of the court was a width of twenty cubits all round the temple on every side. [11] The side chambers opened on to the area left free, one door towards the north, and another door towards the south; and the width of the part that was left free was five cubits all round.

[12] The building that was facing the temple yard on the west side was seventy cubits wide; and the wall of the building was five cubits thick all round, and its depth ninety cubits.

[13] Then he measured the temple, one hundred cubits deep; and the yard and the

a Cn: Heb *to him who goes up*   b Heb lacks *one*
c Gk: Heb *and the width of the gate was three cubits*
d Gk: Heb *eleven*   e Gk: Heb *and by steps that went up*
f Compare Gk: Heb *tent*   g Gk: Heb *width*
h Gk Compare 1 Kings 6.6: Heb *they entered*
i Cn: Heb *it was surrounded*

building with its walls, one hundred cubits deep; [14] also the width of the east front of the temple and the yard, one hundred cubits.

15 Then he measured the depth of the building facing the yard at the west, together with its galleries [a] on either side, one hundred cubits.

The nave of the temple and the inner room and the outer [b] vestibule [16] were panelled, [c] and, all round, all three had windows with recessed [d] frames. Facing the threshold the temple was panelled with wood all round, from the floor up to the windows (now the windows were covered), [17] to the space above the door, even to the inner room, and on the outside. And on all the walls all round in the inner room and the nave there was a pattern. [e] [18] It was formed of cherubim and palm trees, a palm tree between cherub and cherub. Each cherub had two faces: [19] a human face turned towards the palm tree on one side, and the face of a young lion turned towards the palm tree on the other side. They were carved on the whole temple all round; [20] from the floor to the area above the door, cherubim and palm trees were carved on the wall. [f]

21 The doorposts of the nave were square. In front of the holy place was something resembling [22] an altar of wood, three cubits high, two cubits long, and two cubits wide; [g] its corners, its base, [h] and its walls were of wood. He said to me, 'This is the table that stands before the LORD.' [23] The nave and the holy place had each a double door. [24] The doors had two leaves apiece, two swinging leaves for each door. [25] On the doors of the nave were carved cherubim and palm trees, such as were carved on the walls; and there was a canopy of wood in front of the vestibule outside. [26] And there were recessed windows and palm trees on either side, on the side walls of the vestibule. [i]

The Holy Chambers and the Outer Wall

42 Then he led me out into the outer court, towards the north, and he brought me to the chambers that were op-

posite the temple yard and opposite the building on the north. [2] The length of the building that was on the north side [j] was [k] one hundred cubits, and the width fifty cubits. [3] Across the twenty cubits that belonged to the inner court, and facing the pavement that belonged to the outer court, the chambers rose [l] gallery [m] by gallery [m] in three stories. [4] In front of the chambers was a passage on the inner side, ten cubits wide and one hundred cubits deep, [n] and its [o] entrances were on the north. [5] Now the upper chambers were narrower, for the galleries [m] took more away from them than from the lower and middle chambers in the building. [6] For they were in three stories, and they had no pillars like the pillars of the outer [p] court; for this reason the upper chambers were set back from the ground more than the lower and the middle ones. [7] There was a wall outside parallel to the chambers, towards the outer court, opposite the chambers, fifty cubits long. [8] For the chambers on the outer court were fifty cubits long, while those opposite the temple were one hundred cubits long. [9] At the foot of these chambers ran a passage that one entered from the east in order to enter them from the outer court. [10] The width of the passage [q] was fixed by the wall of the court.

On the south [r] also, opposite the vacant area and opposite the building, there were chambers [11] with a passage in front of them; they were similar to the chambers on the north, of the same length and width, with the same exits [s] and arrangements and doors. [12] So the entrances of the chambers to the south were entered through the entrance at the head of the corresponding passage, from the east, along the matching wall. [m]

a Cn: Meaning of Heb uncertain   b Gk: Heb *of the court*   c Gk: Heb *the thresholds*   d Cn Compare Gk 1 Kings 6.4: Meaning of Heb uncertain
e Heb *measures*   f Cn Compare verse 25: Heb *and the wall*   g Gk: Heb lacks *two cubits wide*   h Gk: Heb *length*   i Cn: Heb *vestibule. And the side chambers of the temple and the canopies*   j Gk: Heb *door*   k Gk: Heb *before the length*   l Heb lacks *the chambers rose*
m Meaning of Heb uncertain   n Gk Syr: Heb *a way of one cubit*   o Heb *their*   p Gk: Heb lacks *outer*
q Heb lacks *of the passage*   r Gk: Heb *east*
s Heb *and all their exits*

13 Then he said to me, 'The north chambers and the south chambers opposite the vacant area are the holy chambers, where the priests who approach the LORD shall eat the most holy offerings; there they shall deposit the most holy offerings—the grain-offering, the sin-offering, and the guilt-offering—for the place is holy. 14When the priests enter the holy place, they shall not go out of it into the outer court without laying there the vestments in which they minister, for these are holy; they shall put on other garments before they go near to the area open to the people.'

15 When he had finished measuring the interior of the temple area, he led me out by the gate that faces east, and measured the temple area all round. 16He measured the east side with the measuring reed, five hundred cubits by the measuring reed. 17Then he turned and measured[a] the north side, five hundred cubits by the measuring reed. 18Then he turned and measured[a] the south side, five hundred cubits by the measuring reed. 19Then he turned to the west side and measured, five hundred cubits by the measuring reed. 20He measured it on the four sides. It had a wall around it, five hundred cubits long and five hundred cubits wide, to make a separation between the holy and the common.

The Divine Glory Returns to the Temple

43 Then he brought me to the gate, the gate facing east. 2And there, the glory of the God of Israel was coming from the east; the sound was like the sound of mighty waters; and the earth shone with his glory. 3The[b] vision I saw was like the vision that I had seen when he came to destroy the city, and[c] like the vision that I had seen by the river Chebar; and I fell upon my face. 4As the glory of the LORD entered the temple by the gate facing east, 5the spirit lifted me up, and brought me into the inner court; and the glory of the LORD filled the temple.

6 While the man was standing beside me, I heard someone speaking to me out of the temple. 7He said to me: Mortal, this is the place of my throne and the place for the soles of my feet, where I will reside among the people of Israel for ever. The house of Israel shall no more defile my holy name, neither they nor their kings, by their whoring, and by the corpses of their kings at their death.[d] 8When they placed their threshold by my threshold and their doorposts beside my doorposts, with only a wall between me and them, they were defiling my holy name by their abominations that they committed; therefore I have consumed them in my anger. 9Now let them put away their idolatry and the corpses of their kings far from me, and I will reside among them for ever.

10 As for you, mortal, describe the temple to the house of Israel, and let them measure the pattern; and let them be ashamed of their iniquities. 11When they are ashamed of all that they have done, make known to them the plan of the temple, its arrangement, its exits and its entrances, and its whole form—all its ordinances and its entire plan and all its laws; and write it down in their sight, so that they may observe and follow the entire plan and all its ordinances. 12This is the law of the temple: the whole territory on the top of the mountain all around shall be most holy. This is the law of the temple.

The Altar

13 These are the dimensions of the altar by cubits (the cubit being one cubit and a handbreadth): its base shall be one cubit high,[e] and one cubit wide, with a rim of one span round its edge. This shall be the height of the altar: 14From the base on the ground to the lower ledge, two cubits, with a width of one cubit; and from the smaller ledge to the larger ledge, four cubits, with a width of one cubit; 15and the altar hearth, four cubits; and from the altar hearth projecting upwards, four horns. 16The altar hearth shall be square, twelve cubits long by twelve wide. 17The ledge also shall be square, fourteen cubits long by fourteen

a Gk: Heb *measuring reed all round. He measured*
b Gk: Heb *Like the vision*   c Syr: Heb *and the visions*
d Or *on their high places*   e Gk: Heb lacks *high*

wide, with a rim round it half a cubit wide, and its surrounding base, one cubit. Its steps shall face east.

18 Then he said to me: Mortal, thus says the Lord GOD: These are the ordinances for the altar: On the day when it is erected for offering burnt-offerings upon it and for dashing blood against it, ¹⁹you shall give to the levitical priests of the family of Zadok, who draw near to me to minister to me, says the Lord GOD, a bull for a sin-offering. ²⁰And you shall take some of its blood, and put it on the four horns of the altar, and on the four corners of the ledge, and upon the rim all round; thus you shall purify it and make atonement for it. ²¹You shall also take the bull of the sin-offering, and it shall be burnt in the appointed place belonging to the temple, outside the sacred area.

22 On the second day you shall offer a male goat without blemish for a sin-offering; and the altar shall be purified, as it was purified with the bull. ²³When you have finished purifying it, you shall offer a bull without blemish and a ram from the flock without blemish. ²⁴You shall present them before the LORD, and the priests shall throw salt on them and offer them up as a burnt-offering to the LORD. ²⁵For seven days you shall provide daily a goat for a sin-offering; also a bull and a ram from the flock, without blemish, shall be provided. ²⁶For seven days shall they make atonement for the altar and cleanse it, and so consecrate it. ²⁷When these days are over, then from the eighth day onwards the priests shall offer upon the altar your burnt-offerings and your offerings of well-being; and I will accept you, says the Lord GOD.

The Closed Gate

44 Then he brought me back to the outer gate of the sanctuary, which faces east; and it was shut. ²The LORD said to me: This gate shall remain shut; it shall not be opened, and no one shall enter by it; for the LORD, the God of Israel, has entered by it; therefore it shall remain shut. ³Only the prince, because he is a prince,

may sit in it to eat food before the LORD; he shall enter by way of the vestibule of the gate, and shall go out by the same way.

Admission to the Temple

4 Then he brought me by way of the north gate to the front of the temple; and I looked, and lo! the glory of the LORD filled the temple of the LORD; and I fell upon my face. ⁵The LORD said to me: Mortal, mark well, look closely, and listen attentively to all that I shall tell you concerning all the ordinances of the temple of the LORD and all its laws; and mark well those who may be admitted to ᵃ the temple and all those who are to be excluded from the sanctuary. ⁶Say to the rebellious house, ᵇ to the house of Israel, Thus says the Lord GOD: O house of Israel, let there be an end to all your abominations ⁷in admitting foreigners, uncircumcised in heart and flesh, to be in my sanctuary, profaning my temple when you offer to me my food, the fat and the blood. You ᶜ have broken my covenant with all your abominations. ⁸And you have not kept charge of my sacred offerings; but you have appointed foreigners ᵈ to act for you in keeping my charge in my sanctuary.

9 Thus says the Lord GOD: No foreigner, uncircumcised in heart and flesh, of all the foreigners who are among the people of Israel, shall enter my sanctuary. ¹⁰But the Levites who went far from me, going astray from me after their idols when Israel went astray, shall bear their punishment. ¹¹They shall be ministers in my sanctuary, having oversight at the gates of the temple, and serving in the temple; they shall slaughter the burnt-offering and the sacrifice for the people, and they shall attend on them and serve them. ¹²Because they ministered to them before their idols and made the house of Israel stumble into iniquity, therefore I have sworn concerning them, says the Lord GOD, that they shall bear their punishment. ¹³They shall not come near to me, to serve me as priest, nor come near any of my sacred offerings, the things that are most sacred; but they shall bear

ᵃ Cn: Heb the entrance of   ᵇ Gk: Heb lacks house
ᶜ Gk Syr Vg: Heb They   ᵈ Heb lacks foreigners

their shame, and the consequences of the abominations that they have committed. ¹⁴Yet I will appoint them to keep charge of the temple, to do all its chores, all that is to be done in it.

The Levitical Priests

15 But the levitical priests, the descendants of Zadok, who kept the charge of my sanctuary when the people of Israel went astray from me, shall come near to me to minister to me; and they shall attend me to offer me the fat and the blood, says the Lord God. ¹⁶It is they who shall enter my sanctuary, it is they who shall approach my table, to minister to me, and they shall keep my charge. ¹⁷When they enter the gates of the inner court, they shall wear linen vestments; they shall have nothing of wool on them, while they minister at the gates of the inner court, and within. ¹⁸They shall have linen turbans on their heads, and linen undergarments on their loins; they shall not bind themselves with anything that causes sweat. ¹⁹When they go out into the outer court to the people, they shall remove the vestments in which they have been ministering, and lay them in the holy chambers; and they shall put on other garments, so that they may not communicate holiness to the people with their vestments. ²⁰They shall not shave their heads or let their locks grow long; they shall only trim the hair of their heads. ²¹No priest shall drink wine when he enters the inner court. ²²They shall not marry a widow, or a divorced woman, but only a virgin of the stock of the house of Israel, or a widow who is the widow of a priest. ²³They shall teach my people the difference between the holy and the common, and show them how to distinguish between the unclean and the clean. ²⁴In a controversy they shall act as judges, and they shall decide it according to my judgements. They shall keep my laws and my statutes regarding all my appointed festivals, and they shall keep my sabbaths holy. ²⁵They shall not defile themselves by going near to a dead person; for father or mother, however, and for son or daughter, and

for brother or unmarried sister they may defile themselves. ²⁶After he has become clean, they shall count seven days for him. ²⁷On the day that he goes into the holy place, into the inner court, to minister in the holy place, he shall offer his sin-offering, says the Lord God.

28 This shall be their inheritance: I am their inheritance; and you shall give them no holding in Israel; I am their holding. ²⁹They shall eat the grain-offering, the sin-offering, and the guilt-offering; and every devoted thing in Israel shall be theirs. ³⁰The first of all the first fruits of all kinds, and every offering of all kinds from all your offerings, shall belong to the priests; you shall also give to the priests the first of your dough, in order that a blessing may rest on your house. ³¹The priests shall not eat of anything, whether bird or animal, that died of itself or was torn by animals.

The Holy District

45 When you allot the land as an inheritance, you shall set aside for the Lord a portion of the land as a holy district, twenty-five thousand cubits long and twenty*a* thousand cubits wide; it shall be holy throughout its entire extent. ²Of this, a square plot of five hundred by five hundred cubits shall be for the sanctuary, with fifty cubits for an open space around it. ³In the holy district you shall measure off a section twenty-five thousand cubits long and ten thousand wide, in which shall be the sanctuary, the most holy place. ⁴It shall be a holy portion of the land; it shall be for the priests, who minister in the sanctuary and approach the Lord to minister to him; and it shall be both a place for their houses and a holy place for the sanctuary. ⁵Another section, twenty-five thousand cubits long and ten thousand cubits wide, shall be for the Levites who minister at the temple, as their holding for cities to live in.*b*

6 Alongside the portion set apart as the holy district you shall assign as a holding for the city an area five thousand cubits

---

a Gk: Heb *ten*   *b* Gk: Heb *as their holding, twenty chambers* wide, and twenty-five thousand cubits long; it shall belong to the whole house of Israel.

7 And to the prince shall belong the land on both sides of the holy district and the holding of the city, alongside the holy district and the holding of the city, on the west and on the east, corresponding in length to one of the tribal portions, and extending from the western to the eastern boundary 8 of the land. It is to be his property in Israel. And my princes shall no longer oppress my people; but they shall let the house of Israel have the land according to their tribes.

9 Thus says the Lord GOD: Enough, O princes of Israel! Put away violence and oppression, and do what is just and right. Cease your evictions of my people, says the Lord GOD.

Weights and Measures

10 You shall have honest balances, an honest ephah, and an honest bath.*a* 11 The ephah and the bath shall be of the same measure, the bath containing one-tenth of a homer, and the ephah one-tenth of a homer; the homer shall be the standard measure. 12 The shekel shall be twenty gerahs. Twenty shekels, twenty-five shekels, and fifteen shekels shall make a mina for you.

Offerings

13 This is the offering that you shall make: one-sixth of an ephah from each homer of wheat, and one-sixth of an ephah from each homer of barley, 14 and as the fixed portion of oil,*b* one-tenth of a bath from each cor (the cor,*c* like the homer, contains ten baths); 15 and one sheep from every flock of two hundred, from the pastures of Israel. This is the offering for grain-offerings, burnt-offerings, and offerings of well-being, to make atonement for them, says the Lord GOD. 16 All the people of the land shall join with the prince in Israel in making this offering. 17 But this shall be the obligation of the prince regarding the burnt-offerings, grain-offerings, and drink-offerings at the festivals, the new moons, and the sabbaths, all the appointed festi-

vals of the house of Israel: he shall provide the sin-offerings, grain-offerings, the burnt-offerings, and the offerings of well-being, to make atonement for the house of Israel.

Festivals

18 Thus says the Lord GOD: In the first month, on the first day of the month, you shall take a young bull without blemish, and purify the sanctuary. 19 The priest shall take some of the blood of the sin-offering and put it on the doorposts of the temple, the four corners of the ledge of the altar, and the posts of the gate of the inner court. 20 You shall do the same on the seventh day of the month for anyone who has sinned through error or ignorance; so you shall make atonement for the temple.

21 In the first month, on the fourteenth day of the month, you shall celebrate the festival of the passover, and for seven days unleavened bread shall be eaten. 22 On that day the prince shall provide for himself and all the people of the land a young bull for a sin-offering. 23 And during the seven days of the festival he shall provide as a burnt-offering to the LORD seven young bulls and seven rams without blemish, on each of the seven days; and a male goat daily for a sin-offering. 24 He shall provide as a grain-offering an ephah for each bull, an ephah for each ram, and a hin of oil to each ephah. 25 In the seventh month, on the fifteenth day of the month and for the seven days of the festival, he shall make the same provision for sin-offerings, burnt-offerings, and grain-offerings, and for the oil.

Miscellaneous Regulations

46 Thus says the Lord GOD: The gate of the inner court that faces east shall remain closed on the six working days; but on the sabbath day it shall be opened and on the day of the new moon it shall be opened. 2 The prince shall enter by the vestibule of the gate from outside, and shall take his stand by the post of the gate. The priests shall offer his burnt-offering

a A Heb measure of volume   *b* Cn: Heb *oil, the bath the oil*   *c* Vg: Heb *homer* and his offerings of well-being, and he shall bow down at the threshold of the gate. Then he shall go out, but the gate shall not be closed until evening. ³The people of the land shall bow down at the entrance of that gate before the LORD on the sabbaths and on the new moons. ⁴The burnt-offering that the prince offers to the LORD on the sabbath day shall be six lambs without blemish and a ram without blemish; ⁵and the grain-offering with the ram shall be an ephah, and the grain-offering with the lambs shall be as much as he wishes to give, together with a hin of oil to each ephah. ⁶On the day of the new moon he shall offer a young bull without blemish, and six lambs and a ram, which shall be without blemish; ⁷as a grain-offering he shall provide an ephah with the bull and an ephah with the ram, and with the lambs as much as he wishes, together with a hin of oil to each ephah. ⁸When the prince enters, he shall come in by the vestibule of the gate, and he shall go out by the same way.

9 When the people of the land come before the LORD at the appointed festivals, whoever enters by the north gate to worship shall go out by the south gate; and whoever enters by the south gate shall go out by the north gate: they shall not return by way of the gate by which they entered, but shall go out straight ahead. ¹⁰When they come in, the prince shall come in with them; and when they go out, he shall go out.

11 At the festivals and the appointed seasons the grain-offering with a young bull shall be an ephah, and with a ram an ephah, and with the lambs as much as one wishes to give, together with a hin of oil to an ephah. ¹²When the prince provides a freewill-offering, either a burnt-offering or offerings of well-being as a freewill-offering to the LORD, the gate facing east shall be opened for him; and he shall offer his burnt-offering or his offerings of well-being as he does on the sabbath day. Then he shall go out, and after he has gone out the gate shall be closed.

13 He shall provide a lamb, a yearling without blemish, for a burnt-offering to the LORD daily; morning by morning he shall provide it. ¹⁴And he shall provide a grain-offering with it morning by morning regularly, one-sixth of an ephah, and one-third of a hin of oil to moisten the choice flour, as a grain-offering to the LORD; this is the ordinance for all time. ¹⁵Thus the lamb and the grain-offering and the oil shall be provided, morning by morning, as a regular burnt-offering.

16 Thus says the Lord GOD: If the prince makes a gift to any of his sons out of his inheritance,ᵃ it shall belong to his sons, it is their holding by inheritance. ¹⁷But if he makes a gift out of his inheritance to one of his servants, it shall be his to the year of liberty; then it shall revert to the prince; only his sons may keep a gift from his inheritance. ¹⁸The prince shall not take any of the inheritance of the people, thrusting them out of their holding; he shall give his sons their inheritance out of his own holding, so that none of my people shall be dispossessed of their holding.

19 Then he brought me through the entrance, which was at the side of the gate, to the north row of the holy chambers for the priests; and there I saw a place at the extreme western end of them. ²⁰He said to me, 'This is the place where the priests shall boil the guilt-offering and the sin-offering, and where they shall bake the grain-offering, in order not to bring them out into the outer court and so communicate holiness to the people.'

21 Then he brought me out to the outer court, and led me past the four corners of the court; and in each corner of the court there was a court— ²²in the four corners of the court were smallᵇ courts, forty cubits long and thirty wide; the four were of the same size. ²³On the inside, round each of the four courtsᶜ was a row of masonry, with hearths made at the bottom of the rows all round. ²⁴Then he said to me, 'These are the kitchens where those who serve at the temple shall boil the sacrifices of the people.'

ᵃ Gk: Heb *it is his inheritance*　ᵇ Gk Syr Vg: Meaning of Heb uncertain　ᶜ Heb *the four of them*

Water Flowing from the Temple

47 Then he brought me back to the entrance of the temple; there, water was flowing from below the threshold of the temple towards the east (for the temple faced east); and the water was flowing down from below the south end of the threshold of the temple, south of the altar. ²Then he brought me out by way of the north gate, and led me round on the outside to the outer gate that faces towards the east;ᵃ and the water was coming out on the south side.

3 Going on eastwards with a cord in his hand, the man measured one thousand cubits, and then led me through the water; and it was ankle-deep. ⁴Again he measured one thousand, and led me through the water; and it was knee-deep. Again he measured one thousand, and led me through the water; and it was up to the waist. ⁵Again he measured one thousand, and it was a river that I could not cross, for the water had risen; it was deep enough to swim in, a river that could not be crossed. ⁶He said to me, 'Mortal, have you seen this?'

Then he led me back along the bank of the river. ⁷As I came back, I saw on the bank of the river a great many trees on one side and on the other. ⁸He said to me, 'This water flows towards the eastern region and goes down into the Arabah; and when it enters the sea, the sea of stagnant waters, the water will become fresh. ⁹Wherever the river goes,ᵇ every living creature that swarms will live, and there will be very many fish, once these waters reach there. It will become fresh; and everything will live where the river goes. ¹⁰People will stand fishing beside the seaᶜ from En-gedi to En-eglaim; it will be a place for the spreading of nets; its fish will be of a great many kinds, like the fish of the Great Sea. ¹¹But its swamps and marshes will not become fresh; they are to be left for salt. ¹²On the banks, on both sides of the river, there will grow all kinds of trees for food. Their leaves will not wither nor their fruit fail, but they will bear fresh fruit every month, because the water for them flows from the sanctuary. Their fruit will be for food, and their leaves for healing.'

The New Boundaries of the Land

13 Thus says the Lord GOD: These are the boundaries by which you shall divide the land for inheritance among the twelve tribes of Israel. Joseph shall have two portions. ¹⁴You shall divide it equally; I swore to give it to your ancestors, and this land shall fall to you as your inheritance.

15 This shall be the boundary of the land: On the north side, from the Great Sea by way of Hethlon to Lebo-hamath, and on to Zedad,ᵈ ¹⁶Berothah, Sibraim (which lies between the border of Damascus and the border of Hamath), as far as Hazer-hatticon, which is on the border of Hauran. ¹⁷So the boundary shall run from the sea to Hazar-enon, which is north of the border of Damascus, with the border of Hamath to the north.ᵃ This shall be the north side.

18 On the east side, between Hauran and Damascus; along the Jordan between Gilead and the land of Israel; to the eastern sea and as far as Tamar.ᵉ This shall be the east side.

19 On the south side, it shall run from Tamar as far as the waters of Meribath-kadesh, from there along the Wadi of Egyptᶠ to the Great Sea. This shall be the south side.

20 On the west side, the Great Sea shall be the boundary to a point opposite Lebo-hamath. This shall be the west side.

21 So you shall divide this land among you according to the tribes of Israel. ²²You shall allot it as an inheritance for yourselves and for the aliens who reside among you and have begotten children among you. They shall be to you as citizens of Israel; with you they shall be allotted an inheritance among the tribes of Israel. ²³In whatever tribe aliens reside, there you shall assign them their inheritance, says the Lord GOD.

ᵃ Meaning of Heb uncertain   ᵇ Gk Syr Vg Tg: Heb *the two rivers go*   ᶜ Heb *it*   ᵈ Gk: Heb *Lebo-zedad*, ¹⁶*Hamath*   ᵉ Compare Syr: Heb *you shall measure*   ᶠ Heb lacks *of Egypt*

The Tribal Portions

48 These are the names of the tribes: Beginning at the northern border, on the Hethlon road,[a] from Lebo-hamath, as far as Hazar-enon (which is on the border of Damascus, with Hamath to the north), and[b] extending from the east side to the west,[c] Dan, one portion. [2]Adjoining the territory of Dan, from the east side to the west, Asher, one portion. [3]Adjoining the territory of Asher, from the east side to the west, Naphtali, one portion. [4]Adjoining the territory of Naphtali, from the east side to the west, Manasseh, one portion. [5]Adjoining the territory of Manasseh, from the east side to the west, Ephraim, one portion. [6]Adjoining the territory of Ephraim, from the east side to the west, Reuben, one portion. [7]Adjoining the territory of Reuben, from the east side to the west, Judah, one portion.

8 Adjoining the territory of Judah, from the east side to the west, shall be the portion that you shall set apart, twenty-five thousand cubits in width, and in length equal to one of the tribal portions, from the east side to the west, with the sanctuary in the middle of it. [9]The portion that you shall set apart for the LORD shall be twenty-five thousand cubits in length, and twenty[d] thousand in width. [10]These shall be the allotments of the holy portion: the priests shall have an allotment measuring twenty-five thousand cubits on the northern side, ten thousand cubits in width on the western side, ten thousand in width on the eastern side, and twenty-five thousand in length on the southern side, with the sanctuary of the LORD in the middle of it. [11]This shall be for the consecrated priests, the descendants[e] of Zadok, who kept my charge, who did not go astray when the people of Israel went astray, as the Levites did. [12]It shall belong to them as a special portion from the holy portion of the land, a most holy place, adjoining the territory of the Levites. [13]Alongside the territory of the priests, the Levites shall have an allotment twenty-five thousand cubits in length and ten thousand in width. The whole length shall be twenty-five thousand cubits and the width twenty[f] thousand. [14]They shall not sell or exchange any of it; they shall not transfer this choice portion of the land, for it is holy to the LORD.

15 The remainder, five thousand cubits in width and twenty-five thousand in length, shall be for ordinary use for the city, for dwellings and for open country. In the middle of it shall be the city; [16]and these shall be its dimensions: the north side four thousand five hundred cubits, the south

Ezekiel's Vision of the Land

Mediterranean Sea

Berothah
DAN
ASHER
NAPHTALI
MANASSEH   Damascus
KARNAIM
Tyre
EPHRAIM
HAURAN
REUBEN
GILEAD
JUDAH
Jerusalem   AMMON
BENJAMIN
PHILISTIA
SIMEON   Dead Sea
ISSACHAR   MOAB
ZEBULUN
•Tamar
GAD
EDOM
Meribah of Kadesh

N

0 ___ 60 Mi.
0 ___ 60 Km.

---

a Compare 47.15: Heb *by the side of the way*
b Cn: Heb *and they shall be his*   c Gk Compare verses 2-8: Heb *the east side the west*   d Compare 45.1: Heb *ten*   e One Ms Gk: Heb *of the descendants*
f Gk: Heb *ten*

side four thousand five hundred, the east side four thousand five hundred, and the west side four thousand five hundred. [17] The city shall have open land: on the north two hundred and fifty cubits, on the south two hundred and fifty, on the east two hundred and fifty, on the west two hundred and fifty. [18] The remainder of the length alongside the holy portion shall be ten thousand cubits to the east, and ten thousand to the west, and it shall be alongside the holy portion. Its produce shall be food for the workers of the city. [19] The workers of the city, from all the tribes of Israel, shall cultivate it. [20] The whole portion that you shall set apart shall be twenty-five thousand cubits square, that is, the holy portion together with the property of the city.

21 What remains on both sides of the holy portion and of the property of the city shall belong to the prince. Extending from the twenty-five thousand cubits of the holy portion to the east border, and westwards from the twenty-five thousand cubits to the west border, parallel to the tribal portions, it shall belong to the prince. The holy portion with the sanctuary of the temple in the middle of it, [22] and the property of the Levites and of the city, shall be in the middle of that which belongs to the prince. The portion of the prince shall lie between the territory of Judah and the territory of Benjamin.

23 As for the rest of the tribes: from the east side to the west, Benjamin, one portion. [24] Adjoining the territory of Benjamin, from the east side to the west, Simeon, one portion. [25] Adjoining the territory of Simeon, from the east side to the west, Issachar, one portion. [26] Adjoining the territory of Issachar, from the east side to west, Zebulun, one portion. [27] Adjoining the territory of Zebulun, from the east side to the west, Gad, one portion. [28] And adjoining the territory of Gad to the south, the boundary shall run from Tamar to the waters of Meribath-kadesh, from there along the Wadi of Egypt[a] to the Great Sea. [29] This is the land that you shall allot as an inheritance among the tribes of Israel, and these are their portions, says the Lord GOD.

30 These shall be the exits of the city: On the north side, which is to be four thousand five hundred cubits by measure, [31] three gates, the gate of Reuben, the gate of Judah, and the gate of Levi, the gates of the city being named after the tribes of Israel. [32] On the east side, which is to be four thousand five hundred cubits, three gates, the gate of Joseph, the gate of Benjamin, and the gate of Dan. [33] On the south side, which is to be four thousand five hundred cubits by measure, three gates, the gate of Simeon, the gate of Issachar, and the gate of Zebulun. [34] On the west side, which is to be four thousand five hundred cubits, three gates,[b] the gate of Gad, the gate of Asher, and the gate of Naphtali. [35] The circumference of the city shall be eighteen thousand cubits. And the name of the city from that time on shall be, The LORD is There.

a Heb lacks *of Egypt*   *b* One Ms Gk Syr: MT *their gates three*

DANIEL

Four Young Israelites at the Babylonian Court

1 In the third year of the reign of King Jehoiakim of Judah, King Nebuchadnezzar of Babylon came to Jerusalem and besieged it. ²The Lord let King Jehoiakim of Judah fall into his power, as well as some of the vessels of the house of God. These he brought to the land of Shinar,*ᵃ* and placed the vessels in the treasury of his gods.

3 Then the king commanded his palace master Ashpenaz to bring some of the Israelites of the royal family and of the nobility, ⁴young men without physical defect and handsome, versed in every branch of wisdom, endowed with knowledge and insight, and competent to serve in the king's palace; they were to be taught the literature and language of the Chaldeans. ⁵The king assigned them a daily portion of the royal rations of food and wine. They were to be educated for three years, so that at the end of that time they could be stationed in the king's court. ⁶Among them were Daniel, Hananiah, Mishael, and Azariah, from the

---

a Gk Theodotion: Heb adds *to the house of his own gods*

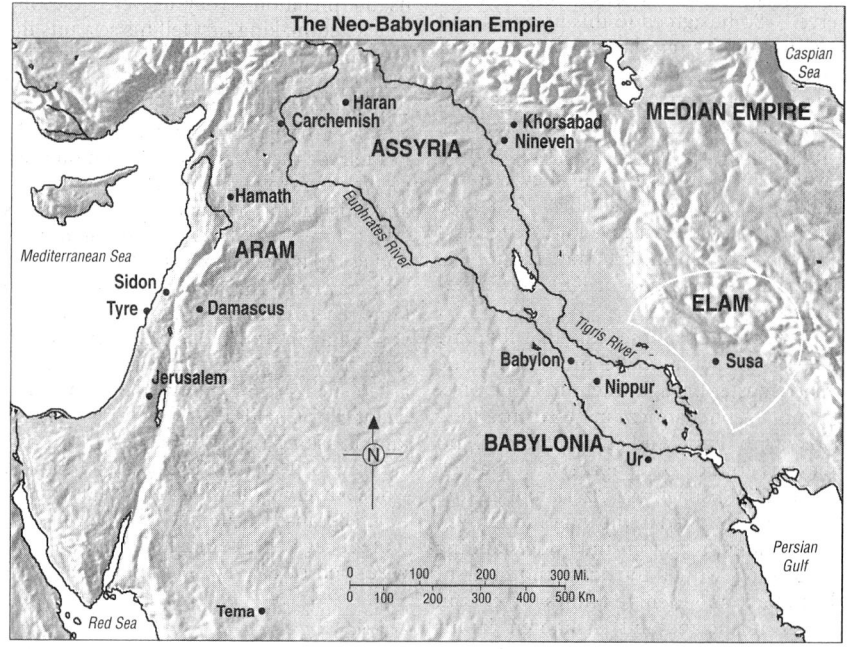

The Neo-Babylonian Empire

tribe of Judah. 7 The palace master gave them other names: Daniel he called Belteshazzar, Hananiah he called Shadrach, Mishael he called Meshach, and Azariah he called Abednego.

8 But Daniel resolved that he would not defile himself with the royal rations of food and wine; so he asked the palace master to allow him not to defile himself. 9 Now God allowed Daniel to receive favour and compassion from the palace master. 10 The palace master said to Daniel, 'I am afraid of my lord the king; he has appointed your food and your drink. If he should see you in poorer condition than the other young men of your own age, you would endanger my head with the king.' 11 Then Daniel asked the guard whom the palace master had appointed over Daniel, Hananiah, Mishael, and Azariah: 12 'Please test your servants for ten days. Let us be given vegetables to eat and water to drink. 13 You can then compare our appearance with the appearance of the young men who eat the royal rations, and deal with your servants according to what you observe.' 14 So he agreed to this proposal and tested them for ten days. 15 At the end of ten days it was observed that they appeared better and fatter than all the young men who had been eating the royal rations. 16 So the guard continued to withdraw their royal rations and the wine they were to drink, and gave them vegetables. 17 To these four young men God gave knowledge and skill in every aspect of literature and wisdom; Daniel also had insight into all visions and dreams.

18 At the end of the time that the king had set for them to be brought in, the palace master brought them into the presence of Nebuchadnezzar, 19 and the king spoke with them. And among them all, no one was found to compare with Daniel, Hananiah, Mishael, and Azariah; therefore they were stationed in the king's court. 20 In every matter of wisdom and understanding concerning which the king inquired of them, he found them ten times better than all the magicians and enchanters in his whole kingdom. 21 And Daniel continued there until the first year of King Cyrus.

Nebuchadnezzar's Dream

2 In the second year of Nebuchadnezzar's reign, Nebuchadnezzar dreamed such dreams that his spirit was troubled and his sleep left him. 2 So the king commanded that the magicians, the enchanters, the sorcerers, and the Chaldeans be summoned to tell the king his dreams. When they came in and stood before the king, 3 he said to them, 'I have had such a dream that my spirit is troubled by the desire to understand it.' 4 The Chaldeans said to the king (in Aramaic),[a] 'O king, live for ever! Tell your servants the dream, and we will reveal the interpretation.' 5 The king answered the Chaldeans, 'This is a public decree: if you do not tell me both the dream and its interpretation, you shall be torn limb from limb, and your houses shall be laid in ruins. 6 But if you do tell me the dream and its interpretation, you shall receive from me gifts and rewards and great honour. Therefore tell me the dream and its interpretation.' 7 They answered a second time, 'Let the king first tell his servants the dream, then we can give its interpretation.' 8 The king answered, 'I know with certainty that you are trying to gain time, because you see I have firmly decreed: 9 if you do not tell me the dream, there is but one verdict for you. You have agreed to speak lying and misleading words to me until things take a turn. Therefore, tell me the dream, and I shall know that you can give me its interpretation.' 10 The Chaldeans answered the king, 'There is no one on earth who can reveal what the king demands! In fact no king, however great and powerful, has ever asked such a thing of any magician or enchanter or Chaldean. 11 The thing that the king is asking is too difficult, and no one can reveal it to the king except the gods, whose dwelling is not with mortals.'

12 Because of this the king flew into a violent rage and commanded that all the wise men of Babylon be destroyed. 13 The

_a_ The text from this point to the end of chapter 7 is in Aramaic decree was issued, and the wise men were about to be executed; and they looked for Daniel and his companions, to execute them. ¹⁴Then Daniel responded with prudence and discretion to Arioch, the king's chief executioner, who had gone out to execute the wise men of Babylon; ¹⁵he asked Arioch, the royal official, 'Why is the decree of the king so urgent?' Arioch then explained the matter to Daniel. ¹⁶So Daniel went in and requested that the king give him time and he would tell the king the interpretation.

God Reveals Nebuchadnezzar's Dream

17 Then Daniel went to his home and informed his companions, Hananiah, Mishael, and Azariah, ¹⁸and told them to seek mercy from the God of heaven concerning this mystery, so that Daniel and his companions with the rest of the wise men of Babylon might not perish. ¹⁹Then the mystery was revealed to Daniel in a vision of the night, and Daniel blessed the God of heaven.

²⁰ Daniel said:
'Blessed be the name of God from
      age to age,
   for wisdom and power are his.
²¹ He changes times and seasons,
      deposes kings and sets up kings;
   he gives wisdom to the wise
      and knowledge to those who have
         understanding.
²² He reveals deep and hidden things;
      he knows what is in the darkness,
      and light dwells with him.
²³ To you, O God of my ancestors,
   I give thanks and praise,
   for you have given me wisdom
      and power,
   and have now revealed to me what
      we asked of you,
   for you have revealed to us what
      the king ordered.'

Daniel Interprets the Dream

24 Therefore Daniel went to Arioch, whom the king had appointed to destroy the wise men of Babylon, and said to him, 'Do not destroy the wise men of Babylon; bring me in before the king, and I will give the king the interpretation.'

25 Then Arioch quickly brought Daniel before the king and said to him: 'I have found among the exiles from Judah a man who can tell the king the interpretation.' ²⁶The king said to Daniel, whose name was Belteshazzar, 'Are you able to tell me the dream that I have seen and its interpretation?' ²⁷Daniel answered the king, 'No wise men, enchanters, magicians, or diviners can show to the king the mystery that the king is asking, ²⁸but there is a God in heaven who reveals mysteries, and he has disclosed to King Nebuchadnezzar what will happen at the end of days. Your dream and the visions of your head as you lay in bed were these: ²⁹To you, O king, as you lay in bed, came thoughts of what would be hereafter, and the revealer of mysteries disclosed to you what is to be. ³⁰But as for me, this mystery has not been revealed to me because of any wisdom that I have more than any other living being, but in order that the interpretation may be known to the king and that you may understand the thoughts of your mind.

31 'You were looking, O king, and lo! there was a great statue. This statue was huge, its brilliance extraordinary; it was standing before you, and its appearance was frightening. ³²The head of that statue was of fine gold, its chest and arms of silver, its middle and thighs of bronze, ³³its legs of iron, its feet partly of iron and partly of clay. ³⁴As you looked on, a stone was cut out, not by human hands, and it struck the statue on its feet of iron and clay and broke them in pieces. ³⁵Then the iron, the clay, the bronze, the silver, and the gold, were all broken in pieces and became like the chaff of the summer threshing-floors; and the wind carried them away, so that not a trace of them could be found. But the stone that struck the statue became a great mountain and filled the whole earth.

36 'This was the dream; now we will tell the king its interpretation. ³⁷You, O king, the king of kings—to whom the God of heaven has given the kingdom, the power, the might, and the glory, ³⁸into whose

hand he has given human beings, wherever they live, the wild animals of the field, and the birds of the air, and whom he has established as ruler over them all—you are the head of gold. 39 After you shall arise another kingdom inferior to yours, and yet a third kingdom of bronze, which shall rule over the whole earth. 40 And there shall be a fourth kingdom, strong as iron; just as iron crushes and smashes everything,ᵃ it shall crush and shatter all these. 41 As you saw the feet and toes partly of potter's clay and partly of iron, it shall be a divided kingdom; but some of the strength of iron shall be in it, as you saw the iron mixed with the clay. 42 As the toes of the feet were part iron and part clay, so the kingdom shall be partly strong and partly brittle. 43 As you saw the iron mixed with clay, so will they mix with one another in marriage,ᵇ but they will not hold together, just as iron does not mix with clay. 44 And in the days of those kings the God of heaven will set up a kingdom that shall never be destroyed, nor shall this kingdom be left to another people. It shall crush all these kingdoms and bring them to an end, and it shall stand for ever; 45 just as you saw that a stone was cut from the mountain not by hands, and that it crushed the iron, the bronze, the clay, the silver, and the gold. The great God has informed the king what shall be hereafter. The dream is certain, and its interpretation trustworthy.'

Daniel and His Friends Promoted

46 Then King Nebuchadnezzar fell on his face, worshipped Daniel, and commanded that a grain-offering and incense be offered to him. 47 The king said to Daniel, 'Truly, your God is God of gods and Lord of kings and a revealer of mysteries, for you have been able to reveal this mystery!' 48 Then the king promoted Daniel, gave him many great gifts, and made him ruler over the whole province of Babylon and chief prefect over all the wise men of Babylon. 49 Daniel made a request of the king, and he appointed Shadrach, Meshach, and Abednego over the affairs of the province of Babylon. But Daniel remained at the king's court.

The Golden Image

3 King Nebuchadnezzar made a golden statue whose height was sixty cubits and whose width was six cubits; he set it up on the plain of Dura in the province of Babylon. 2 Then King Nebuchadnezzar sent for the satraps, the prefects, and the governors, the counsellors, the treasurers, the justices, the magistrates, and all the officials of the provinces, to assemble and come to the dedication of the statue that King Nebuchadnezzar had set up. 3 So the satraps, the prefects, and the governors, the counsellors, the treasurers, the justices, the magistrates, and all the officials of the provinces, assembled for the dedication of the statue that King Nebuchadnezzar had set up. When they were standing before the statue that Nebuchadnezzar had set up, 4 the herald proclaimed aloud, 'You are commanded, O peoples, nations, and languages, 5 that when you hear the sound of the horn, pipe, lyre, trigon, harp, drum, and entire musical ensemble, you are to fall down and worship the golden statue that King Nebuchadnezzar has set up. 6 Whoever does not fall down and worship shall immediately be thrown into a furnace of blazing fire.' 7 Therefore, as soon as all the peoples heard the sound of the horn, pipe, lyre, trigon, harp, drum, and entire musical ensemble, all the peoples, nations, and languages fell down and worshipped the golden statue that King Nebuchadnezzar had set up.

8 Accordingly, at this time certain Chaldeans came forward and denounced the Jews. 9 They said to King Nebuchadnezzar, 'O king, live for ever! 10 You, O king, have made a decree, that everyone who hears the sound of the horn, pipe, lyre, trigon, harp, drum, and entire musical ensemble, shall fall down and worship the golden statue, 11 and whoever does not fall down and worship shall be thrown into a furnace of blazing fire. 12 There are certain Jews whom you have appointed over the af-

---

a Gk Theodotion Syr Vg: Aram adds *and like iron that crushes*   b Aram *by human seed* fairs of the province of Babylon: Shadrach, Meshach, and Abednego. These pay no heed to you, O king. They do not serve your gods and they do not worship the golden statue that you have set up.'

13 Then Nebuchadnezzar in furious rage commanded that Shadrach, Meshach, and Abednego be brought in; so they brought those men before the king. 14 Nebuchadnezzar said to them, 'Is it true, O Shadrach, Meshach, and Abednego, that you do not serve my gods and you do not worship the golden statue that I have set up? 15 Now if you are ready when you hear the sound of the horn, pipe, lyre, trigon, harp, drum, and entire musical ensemble to fall down and worship the statue that I have made, well and good. *a* But if you do not worship, you shall immediately be thrown into a furnace of blazing fire, and who is the god that will deliver you out of my hands?'

16 Shadrach, Meshach, and Abednego answered the king, 'O Nebuchadnezzar, we have no need to present a defence to you in this matter. 17 If our God whom we serve is able to deliver us from the furnace of blazing fire and out of your hand, O king, let him deliver us. *b* 18 But if not, be it known to you, O king, that we will not serve your gods and we will not worship the golden statue that you have set up.'

The Fiery Furnace

19 Then Nebuchadnezzar was so filled with rage against Shadrach, Meshach, and Abednego that his face was distorted. He ordered the furnace to be heated up seven times more than was customary, 20 and ordered some of the strongest guards in his army to bind Shadrach, Meshach, and Abednego and to throw them into the furnace of blazing fire. 21 So the men were bound, still wearing their tunics, *c* their trousers, *c* their hats, and their other garments, and they were thrown into the furnace of blazing fire. 22 Because the king's command was urgent and the furnace was so overheated, the raging flames killed the men who lifted Shadrach, Meshach, and Abednego. 23 But the three men, Shadrach,

Meshach, and Abednego, fell down, bound, into the furnace of blazing fire.

The Prayer of Azariah in the Furnace

24 They walked around in the midst of the flames, singing hymns to God and blessing the Lord. 25 Then Azariah stood still in the fire and prayed aloud:
26 'Blessed are you, O Lord, God of our
    ancestors, and worthy of praise;
    and glorious is your name for ever!
27 For you are just in all you have done;
    all your works are true and your
      ways right,
    and all your judgements are true.
28 You have executed true judgements in
    all you have brought upon us
    and upon Jerusalem, the holy city
      of our ancestors;
    by a true judgement you have
      brought all this upon us
      because of our sins.
29 For we have sinned and broken your
    law in turning away from you;
    in all matters we have sinned
      grievously.
30 We have not obeyed your
    commandments,
    we have not kept them or done
      what you have commanded us
      for our own good.
31 So all that you have brought upon us,
    and all that you have done to us,
    you have done by a true judgement.
32 You have handed us over to our
    enemies, lawless and hateful
      rebels,
    and to an unjust king, the most
      wicked in all the world.
33 And now we cannot open our
    mouths;
    we, your servants who worship you,
      have become a shame and a
      reproach.
34 For your name's sake do not give us
    up for ever,
    and do not annul your covenant.

a Aram lacks *well and good*   *b* Or *If our God whom we serve is able to deliver us, he will deliver us from the furnace of blazing fire and out of your hand, O king.*   *c* Meaning of Aram word uncertain

35 Do not withdraw your mercy from
    us,
  for the sake of Abraham your beloved
    and for the sake of your servant
      Isaac
    and Israel your holy one,
36 to whom you promised
    to multiply their descendants like
      the stars of heaven
    and like the sand on the shore of
      the sea.
37 For we, O Lord, have become fewer
      than any other nation,
    and are brought low this day in all
      the world because of our sins.
38 In our day we have no ruler, or
      prophet, or leader,
    no burnt-offering, or sacrifice, or
      oblation, or incense,
    no place to make an offering before
      you and to find mercy.
39 Yet with a contrite heart and a humble
      spirit may we be accepted,
40 as though it were with burnt-
      offerings of rams and bulls,
    or with tens of thousands of fat
      lambs;
    such may our sacrifice be in your
      sight today,
    and may we unreservedly follow
      you,*a*
    for no shame will come to those
      who trust in you.
41 And now with all our heart we follow
      you;
    we fear you and seek your presence.
42 Do not put us to shame,
    but deal with us in your patience
    and in your abundant mercy.
43 Deliver us in accordance with your
      marvellous works,
    and bring glory to your name,
      O Lord.
44 Let all who do harm to your servants
      be put to shame;
    let them be disgraced and deprived
      of all power,
    and let their strength be broken.
45 Let them know that you alone are the
      Lord God,
    glorious over the whole world.'

The Song of the Three Jews

46 Now the king's servants who threw
them in kept stoking the furnace with
naphtha, pitch, tow, and brushwood.
47 And the flames poured out above the furnace forty-nine cubits, 48 and spread out
and burned those Chaldeans who were
caught near the furnace. 49 But the angel of
the Lord came down into the furnace to be
with Azariah and his companions, and
drove the fiery flame out of the furnace,
50 and made the inside of the furnace as
though a moist wind were whistling
through it. The fire did not touch them at
all and caused them no pain or distress.

51 Then the three with one voice praised
and glorified and blessed God in the furnace:
52 'Blessed are you, O Lord, God of our
      ancestors,
    and to be praised and highly
      exalted for ever;
  And blessed is your glorious, holy
      name,
    and to be highly praised and highly
      exalted for ever.
53 Blessed are you in the temple of your
      holy glory,
    and to be extolled and highly
      glorified for ever.
54 Blessed are you who look into the
      depths from your throne on the
      cherubim,
    and to be praised and highly
      exalted for ever.
55 Blessed are you on the throne of your
      kingdom,
    and to be extolled and highly
      exalted for ever.
56 Blessed are you in the firmament of
      heaven,
    and to be sung and glorified for
      ever.

57 'Bless the Lord, all you works of the
      Lord;
    sing praise to him and highly exalt
      him for ever.
58 Bless the Lord, you heavens;

a Meaning of Gk uncertain

sing praise to him and highly exalt
him for ever.

⁵⁹ Bless the Lord, you angels of the Lord;
sing praise to him and highly exalt
him for ever.

⁶⁰ Bless the Lord, all you waters above
the heavens;
sing praise to him and highly exalt
him for ever.

⁶¹ Bless the Lord, all you powers of the
Lord;
sing praise to him and highly exalt
him for ever.

⁶² Bless the Lord, sun and moon;
sing praise to him and highly exalt
him for ever.

⁶³ Bless the Lord, stars of heaven;
sing praise to him and highly exalt
him for ever.

⁶⁴ 'Bless the Lord, all rain and dew;
sing praise to him and highly exalt
him for ever.

⁶⁵ Bless the Lord, all you winds;
sing praise to him and highly exalt
him for ever.

⁶⁶ Bless the Lord, fire and heat;
sing praise to him and highly exalt
him for ever.

⁶⁷ Bless the Lord, winter cold and
summer heat;
sing praise to him and highly exalt
him for ever.

⁶⁸ Bless the Lord, dews and falling
snow;
sing praise to him and highly exalt
him for ever.

⁶⁹ Bless the Lord, nights and days;
sing praise to him and highly exalt
him for ever.

⁷⁰ Bless the Lord, light and darkness;
sing praise to him and highly exalt
him for ever.

⁷¹ Bless the Lord, ice and cold;
sing praise to him and highly exalt
him for ever.

⁷² Bless the Lord, frosts and snows;
sing praise to him and highly exalt
him for ever.

⁷³ Bless the Lord, lightnings and clouds;

sing praise to him and highly exalt
him for ever.

⁷⁴ 'Let the earth bless the Lord;
let it sing praise to him and highly
exalt him for ever.

⁷⁵ Bless the Lord, mountains and hills;
sing praise to him and highly exalt
him for ever.

⁷⁶ Bless the Lord, all that grows in the
ground;
sing praise to him and highly exalt
him for ever.

⁷⁷ Bless the Lord, seas and rivers;
sing praise to him and highly exalt
him for ever.

⁷⁸ Bless the Lord, you springs;
sing praise to him and highly exalt
him for ever.

⁷⁹ Bless the Lord, you whales and all
that swim in the waters;
sing praise to him and highly exalt
him for ever.

⁸⁰ Bless the Lord, all birds of the air;
sing praise to him and highly exalt
him for ever.

⁸¹ Bless the Lord, all wild animals and
cattle;
sing praise to him and highly exalt
him for ever.

⁸² 'Bless the Lord, all people on earth;
sing praise to him and highly exalt
him for ever.

⁸³ Bless the Lord, O Israel;
sing praise to him and highly exalt
him for ever.

⁸⁴ Bless the Lord, you priests of the
Lord;
sing praise to him and highly exalt
him for ever.

⁸⁵ Bless the Lord, you servants of the
Lord;
sing praise to him and highly exalt
him for ever.

⁸⁶ Bless the Lord, spirits and souls of
the righteous;
sing praise to him and highly exalt
him for ever.

⁸⁷ Bless the Lord, you who are holy and
humble in heart;

sing praise to him and highly exalt
     him for ever.

88 'Bless the Lord, Hananiah, Azariah,
          and Mishael;
     sing praise to him and highly exalt
          him for ever.
     For he has rescued us from Hades
          and saved us from the power[a]
          of death,
          and delivered us from the midst of
               the burning fiery furnace;
          from the midst of the fire he has
               delivered us.
89 Give thanks to the Lord, for he is
          good,
     for his mercy endures for ever.
90 All who worship the Lord, bless the
          God of gods,
     sing praise to him and give thanks
          to him,
     for his mercy endures for ever.'

91 Then King Nebuchadnezzar was astonished and rose up quickly. He said to his
counsellors, 'Was it not three men that we
threw bound into the fire?' They answered
the king, 'True, O king.' 92 He replied, 'But I
see four men unbound, walking in the middle of the fire, and they are not hurt; and the
fourth has the appearance of a god.'[b]
93 Nebuchadnezzar then approached the
door of the furnace of blazing fire and said,
'Shadrach, Meshach, and Abednego, servants of the Most High God, come out!
Come here!' So Shadrach, Meshach, and
Abednego came out from the fire. 94 And
the satraps, the prefects, the governors, and
the king's counsellors gathered together
and saw that the fire had not had any power over the bodies of those men; the hair of
their heads was not singed, their tunics[c]
were not harmed, and not even the smell of
fire came from them. 95 Nebuchadnezzar
said, 'Blessed be the God of Shadrach, Meshach, and Abednego, who has sent his angel and delivered his servants who trusted
in him. They disobeyed the king's command and yielded up their bodies rather
than serve and worship any god except their
own God. 96 Therefore I make a decree: Any
people, nation, or language that utters blas-

phemy against the God of Shadrach, Meshach, and Abednego shall be torn limb
from limb, and their houses laid in ruins;
for there is no other god who is able to deliver in this way.' 97 Then the king promoted Shadrach, Meshach, and Abednego in
the province of Babylon.

Nebuchadnezzar's Second Dream

4[d] King Nebuchadnezzar to all peoples,
nations, and languages that live
throughout the earth: May you have abundant prosperity! 2 The signs and wonders
that the Most High God has worked for me
I am pleased to recount.
3   How great are his signs,
          how mighty his wonders!
     His kingdom is an everlasting
          kingdom,
          and his sovereignty is from
               generation to generation.
4[e] I, Nebuchadnezzar, was living at ease
in my home and prospering in my palace.
5 I saw a dream that frightened me; my fan-
tasies in bed and the visions of my head terrified me. 6 So I made a decree that all the
wise men of Babylon should be brought before me, in order that they might tell me
the interpretation of the dream. 7 Then the
magicians, the enchanters, the Chaldeans,
and the diviners came in, and I told them
the dream, but they could not tell me its interpretation. 8 At last Daniel came in before
me—he who was named Belteshazzar after
the name of my god, and who is endowed
with a spirit of the holy gods[f]—and I told
him the dream: 9 'O Belteshazzar, chief of
the magicians, I know that you are endowed with a spirit of the holy gods[f] and
that no mystery is too difficult for you.
Hear[g] the dream that I saw; tell me its interpretation.
10[h] Upon my bed this is what I saw;
          there was a tree at the centre of the
               earth,
          and its height was great.
11   The tree grew great and strong,

---

a Gk *hand*   *b* Aram *a son of the gods*   *c* Meaning of
Aram word uncertain   *d* Ch 3.31 in Aram   *e* Ch 4.1
in Aram   *f* Or *a holy, divine spirit*   *g* Theodotion:
Aram *The visions of*   *h* Theodotion Syr Compare Gk:
Aram adds *The visions of my head*

its top reached to heaven,
and it was visible to the ends of the
whole earth.
12 Its foliage was beautiful,
its fruit abundant,
and it provided food for all.
The animals of the field found shade
under it,
the birds of the air nested in
its branches,
and from it all living beings
were fed.

13 'I continued looking, in the visions
of my head as I lay in bed, and there was a
holy watcher, coming down from heaven.
14 He cried aloud and said:
"Cut down the tree and chop off
its branches,
strip off its foliage and scatter
its fruit.
Let the animals flee from beneath it
and the birds from its branches.
15 But leave its stump and roots in the
ground,
with a band of iron and bronze,
in the tender grass of the field.
Let him be bathed with the dew
of heaven,
and let his lot be with the animals
of the field
in the grass of the earth.
16 Let his mind be changed from that of
a human,
and let the mind of an animal be
given to him.
And let seven times pass over him.
17 The sentence is rendered by decree of
the watchers,
the decision is given by order of the
holy ones,
in order that all who live may know
that the Most High is sovereign
over the kingdom of mortals;
he gives it to whom he will
and sets over it the lowliest of
human beings."

18 'This is the dream that I, King Nebuchadnezzar, saw. Now you, Belteshazzar,
declare the interpretation, since all the wise
men of my kingdom are unable to tell me
the interpretation. You are able, however,
for you are endowed with a spirit of the
holy gods.'[a]

Daniel Interprets the Second Dream

19 Then Daniel, who was called Belteshazzar, was severely distressed for a while.
His thoughts terrified him. The king said,
'Belteshazzar, do not let the dream or the interpretation terrify you.' Belteshazzar answered, 'My lord, may the dream be for
those who hate you, and its interpretation
for your enemies! 20 The tree that you saw,
which grew great and strong, so that its top
reached to heaven and was visible to the
end of the whole earth, 21 whose foliage was
beautiful and its fruit abundant, and which
provided food for all, under which animals
of the field lived, and in whose branches
the birds of the air had nests— 22 it is you,
O king! You have grown great and strong.
Your greatness has increased and reaches to
heaven, and your sovereignty to the ends of
the earth. 23 And whereas the king saw a
holy watcher coming down from heaven
and saying, "Cut down the tree and destroy
it, but leave its stump and roots in the
ground, with a band of iron and bronze, in
the grass of the field; and let him be bathed
with the dew of heaven, and let his lot be
with the animals of the field, until seven
times pass over him"— 24 this is the interpretation, O king, and it is a decree of the
Most High that has come upon my lord the
king: 25 You shall be driven away from human society, and your dwelling shall be
with the wild animals. You shall be made to
eat grass like oxen, you shall be bathed with
the dew of heaven, and seven times shall
pass over you, until you have learned that
the Most High has sovereignty over the
kingdom of mortals, and gives it to whom
he will. 26 As it was commanded to leave the
stump and roots of the tree, your kingdom
shall be re-established for you from the
time that you learn that Heaven is sovereign. 27 Therefore, O king, may my counsel
be acceptable to you: atone for[b] your sins
with righteousness, and your iniquities

a Or a holy, divine spirit   b Aram break off

with mercy to the oppressed, so that your prosperity may be prolonged.'

Nebuchadnezzar's Humiliation

28 All this came upon King Nebuchadnezzar. 29 At the end of twelve months he was walking on the roof of the royal palace of Babylon, 30 and the king said, 'Is this not magnificent Babylon, which I have built as a royal capital by my mighty power and for my glorious majesty?' 31 While the words were still in the king's mouth, a voice came from heaven: 'O King Nebuchadnezzar, to you it is declared: The kingdom has departed from you! 32 You shall be driven away from human society, and your dwelling shall be with the animals of the field. You shall be made to eat grass like oxen, and seven times shall pass over you, until you have learned that the Most High has sovereignty over the kingdom of mortals and gives it to whom he will.' 33 Immediately the sentence was fulfilled against Nebuchadnezzar. He was driven away from human society, ate grass like oxen, and his body was bathed with the dew of heaven, until his hair grew as long as eagles' feathers and his nails became like birds' claws.

Nebuchadnezzar Praises God

34 When that period was over, I, Nebuchadnezzar, lifted my eyes to heaven, and my reason returned to me.
I blessed the Most High,
    and praised and honoured the one
        who lives for ever.
For his sovereignty is an everlasting
        sovereignty,
    and his kingdom endures from
        generation to generation.
35 All the inhabitants of the earth are
        accounted as nothing,
    and he does what he wills with the
        host of heaven
    and the inhabitants of the earth.
There is no one who can stay
        his hand
    or say to him, 'What are you
        doing?'
36 At that time my reason returned to me; and my majesty and splendour were re-

stored to me for the glory of my kingdom. My counsellors and my lords sought me out, I was re-established over my kingdom, and still more greatness was added to me. 37 Now I, Nebuchadnezzar, praise and extol and honour the King of heaven,
    for all his works are truth,
        and his ways are justice;
    and he is able to bring low
        those who walk in pride.

Belshazzar's Feast

5 King Belshazzar made a great festival for a thousand of his lords, and he was drinking wine in the presence of the thousand.

2 Under the influence of the wine, Belshazzar commanded that they bring in the vessels of gold and silver that his father Nebuchadnezzar had taken out of the temple in Jerusalem, so that the king and his lords, his wives, and his concubines might drink from them. 3 So they brought in the vessels of gold and silver*a* that had been taken out of the temple, the house of God in Jerusalem, and the king and his lords, his wives, and his concubines drank from them. 4 They drank the wine and praised the gods of gold and silver, bronze, iron, wood, and stone.

The Writing on the Wall

5 Immediately the fingers of a human hand appeared and began writing on the plaster of the wall of the royal palace, next to the lampstand. The king was watching the hand as it wrote. 6 Then the king's face turned pale, and his thoughts terrified him. His limbs gave way, and his knees knocked together. 7 The king cried aloud to bring in the enchanters, the Chaldeans, and the diviners; and the king said to the wise men of Babylon, 'Whoever can read this writing and tell me its interpretation shall be clothed in purple, have a chain of gold around his neck, and rank third in the kingdom.' 8 Then all the king's wise men came in, but they could not read the writing or tell the king the interpretation. 9 Then King Belshazzar became greatly ter-

---

a Theodotion Vg: Aram lacks *and silver*

rified and his face turned pale, and his lords were perplexed.

10 The queen, when she heard the discussion of the king and his lords, came into the banqueting-hall. The queen said, 'O king, live for ever! Do not let your thoughts terrify you or your face grow pale. [11] There is a man in your kingdom who is endowed with a spirit of the holy gods. *a* In the days of your father he was found to have enlightenment, understanding, and wisdom like the wisdom of the gods. Your father, King Nebuchadnezzar, made him chief of the magicians, enchanters, Chaldeans, and diviners, *b* [12] because an excellent spirit, knowledge, and understanding to interpret dreams, explain riddles, and solve problems were found in this Daniel, whom the king named Belteshazzar. Now let Daniel be called, and he will give the interpretation.'

The Writing on the Wall Interpreted

13 Then Daniel was brought in before the king. The king said to Daniel, 'So you are Daniel, one of the exiles of Judah, whom my father the king brought from Judah? [14] I have heard of you that a spirit of the gods *c* is in you, and that enlightenment, understanding, and excellent wisdom are found in you. [15] Now the wise men, the enchanters, have been brought in before me to read this writing and tell me its interpretation, but they were not able to give the interpretation of the matter. [16] But I have heard that you can give interpretations and solve problems. Now if you are able to read the writing and tell me its interpretation, you shall be clothed in purple, have a chain of gold around your neck, and rank third in the kingdom.'

17 Then Daniel answered in the presence of the king, 'Let your gifts be for yourself, or give your rewards to someone else! Nevertheless,I will read the writing to the king and let him know the interpretation. [18] O king, the Most High God gave your father Nebuchadnezzar kingship, greatness, glory, and majesty. [19] And because of the greatness that he gave him, all peoples, nations, and languages trembled and feared

before him. He killed those he wanted to kill, kept alive those he wanted to keep alive, honoured those he wanted to honour, and degraded those he wanted to degrade. [20] But when his heart was lifted up and his spirit was hardened so that he acted proudly, he was deposed from his kingly throne, and his glory was stripped from him. [21] He was driven from human society, and his mind was made like that of an animal. His dwelling was with the wild asses, he was fed grass like oxen, and his body was bathed with the dew of heaven, until he learned that the Most High God has sovereignty over the kingdom of mortals, and sets over it whomsoever he will. [22] And you, Belshazzar his son, have not humbled your heart, even though you knew all this! [23] You have exalted yourself against the Lord of heaven! The vessels of his temple have been brought in before you, and you and your lords, your wives and your concubines have been drinking wine from them. You have praised the gods of silver and gold, of bronze, iron, wood, and stone, which do not see or hear or know; but the God in whose power is your very breath, and to whom belong all your ways, you have not honoured.

24 'So from his presence the hand was sent and this writing was inscribed. [25] And this is the writing that was inscribed: MENE, MENE, TEKEL, and PARSIN. [26] This is the interpretation of the matter: MENE, God has numbered the days of *d* your kingdom and brought it to an end; [27] TEKEL, you have been weighed on the scales and found wanting; [28] PERES, *e* your kingdom is divided and given to the Medes and Persians.'

29 Then Belshazzar gave the command, and Daniel was clothed in purple, a chain of gold was put around his neck, and a proclamation was made concerning him that he should rank third in the kingdom.

30 That very night Belshazzar, the Chaldean king, was killed. [31] *f* And Darius the Mede received the kingdom, being about sixty-two years old.

a Or *a holy, divine spirit*   *b* Aram adds *the king your father*   *c* Or *a divine spirit*   *d* Aram lacks *the days of*   *e* The singular of *Parsin*   *f* Ch 6.1 in Aram

The Plot against Daniel

6 It pleased Darius to set over the kingdom one hundred and twenty satraps, stationed throughout the whole kingdom, ²and over them three presidents, including Daniel; to these the satraps gave account, so that the king might suffer no loss. ³Soon Daniel distinguished himself above all the other presidents and satraps because an excellent spirit was in him, and the king planned to appoint him over the whole kingdom. ⁴So the presidents and the satraps tried to find grounds for complaint against Daniel in connection with the kingdom. But they could find no grounds for complaint or any corruption, because he was faithful, and no negligence or corruption could be found in him. ⁵The men said, 'We shall not find any ground for complaint against this Daniel unless we find it in connection with the law of his God.'

6 So the presidents and satraps conspired and came to the king and said to him, 'O King Darius, live for ever! ⁷All the presidents of the kingdom, the prefects and the satraps, the counsellors and the governors, are agreed that the king should establish an ordinance and enforce an interdict, that whoever prays to anyone, divine or human, for thirty days, except to you, O king, shall be thrown into a den of lions. ⁸Now, O king, establish the interdict and sign the document, so that it cannot be changed, according to the law of the Medes and the Persians, which cannot be revoked.' ⁹Therefore King Darius signed the document and interdict.

Daniel in the Lions' Den

10 Although Daniel knew that the document had been signed, he continued to go to his house, which had windows in its upper room open towards Jerusalem, and to get down on his knees three times a day to pray to his God and praise him, just as he had done previously. ¹¹The conspirators came and found Daniel praying and seeking mercy before his God. ¹²Then they approached the king and said concerning the interdict, 'O king! Did you not sign an interdict, that anyone who prays to anyone, divine or human, within thirty days except to you, O king, shall be thrown into a den of lions?' The king answered, 'The thing stands fast, according to the law of the Medes and Persians, which cannot be revoked.' ¹³Then they responded to the king, 'Daniel, one of the exiles from Judah, pays no attention to you, O king, or to the interdict you have signed, but he is saying his prayers three times a day.'

14 When the king heard the charge, he was very much distressed. He was determined to save Daniel, and until the sun went down he made every effort to rescue him. ¹⁵Then the conspirators came to the king and said to him, 'Know, O king, that it is a law of the Medes and Persians that no interdict or ordinance that the king establishes can be changed.'

16 Then the king gave the command, and Daniel was brought and thrown into the den of lions. The king said to Daniel, 'May your God, whom you faithfully serve, deliver you!' ¹⁷A stone was brought and laid on the mouth of the den, and the king sealed it with his own signet and with the signet of his lords, so that nothing might be changed concerning Daniel. ¹⁸Then the king went to his palace and spent the night fasting; no food was brought to him, and sleep fled from him.

Daniel Saved from the Lions

19 Then, at break of day, the king got up and hurried to the den of lions. ²⁰When he came near the den where Daniel was, he cried out anxiously to Daniel, 'O Daniel, servant of the living God, has your God whom you faithfully serve been able to deliver you from the lions?' ²¹Daniel then said to the king, 'O king, live for ever! ²²My God sent his angel and shut the lions' mouths so that they would not hurt me, because I was found blameless before him; and also before you, O king, I have done no wrong.' ²³Then the king was exceedingly glad and commanded that Daniel be taken up out of the den. So Daniel was taken up out of the den, and no kind of harm was found on him, because he had trusted in his God. ²⁴The king gave a command, and those

who had accused Daniel were brought and thrown into the den of lions—they, their children, and their wives. Before they reached the bottom of the den the lions overpowered them and broke all their bones in pieces.

25 Then King Darius wrote to all peoples and nations of every language throughout the whole world: 'May you have abundant prosperity! 26 I make a decree, that in all my royal dominion people should tremble and fear before the God of Daniel:

For he is the living God,
    enduring for ever.
His kingdom shall never be
        destroyed,
    and his dominion has no end.
27 He delivers and rescues,
    he works signs and wonders in
        heaven and on earth;
for he has saved Daniel
    from the power of the lions.'
28 So this Daniel prospered during the reign of Darius and the reign of Cyrus the Persian.

Visions of the Four Beasts

7 In the first year of King Belshazzar of Babylon, Daniel had a dream and visions of his head as he lay in bed. Then he wrote down the dream:[a] 2 I,[b] Daniel, saw in my vision by night the four winds of heaven stirring up the great sea, 3 and four great beasts came up out of the sea, different from one another. 4 The first was like a lion and had eagles' wings. Then, as I watched, its wings were plucked off, and it was lifted up from the ground and made to stand on two feet like a human being; and a human mind was given to it. 5 Another beast appeared, a second one, that looked like a bear. It was raised up on one side, had three tusks[c] in its mouth among its teeth and was told, 'Arise, devour many bodies!' 6 After this, as I watched, another appeared, like a leopard. The beast had four wings of a bird on its back and four heads; and dominion was given to it. 7 After this I saw in the visions by night a fourth beast, terrifying and dreadful and exceedingly strong. It had great iron teeth and was devouring, breaking in pieces, and stamping what was left with its feet. It was different from all the beasts that preceded it, and it had ten horns. 8 I was considering the horns, when another horn appeared, a little one coming up among them; to make room for it, three of the earlier horns were plucked up by the roots. There were eyes like human eyes in this horn, and a mouth speaking arrogantly.

Judgement before the Ancient One

9 As I watched,
    thrones were set in place,
        and an Ancient One[d] took
            his throne;
    his clothing was white as snow,
        and the hair of his head like
            pure wool;
    his throne was fiery flames,
        and its wheels were burning fire.
10 A stream of fire issued
        and flowed out from his presence.
    A thousand thousand served him,
        and ten thousand times ten
            thousand stood attending him.
    The court sat in judgement,
        and the books were opened.
11 I watched then because of the noise of the arrogant words that the horn was speaking. And as I watched, the beast was put to death, and its body destroyed and given over to be burned with fire. 12 As for the rest of the beasts, their dominion was taken away, but their lives were prolonged for a season and a time. 13 As I watched in the night visions,
    I saw one like a human being[e]
        coming with the clouds of heaven.
    And he came to the Ancient One[f]
        and was presented before him.
14 To him was given dominion
        and glory and kingship,
    that all peoples, nations, and
            languages
        should serve him.

a Q Ms Theodotion: MT adds *the beginning of the words; he said*   b Theodotion: Aram *Daniel answered and said, I*   c Or *ribs*   d Aram *an Ancient of Days*
e Aram *one like a son of man*   f Aram *the Ancient of Days*

His dominion is an everlasting
    dominion
    that shall not pass away,
and his kingship is one
    that shall never be destroyed.

Daniel's Visions Interpreted

15 As for me, Daniel, my spirit was troubled within me,[a] and the visions of my head terrified me. 16 I approached one of the attendants to ask him the truth concerning all this. So he said that he would disclose to me the interpretation of the matter: 17 'As for these four great beasts, four kings shall arise out of the earth. 18 But the holy ones of the Most High shall receive the kingdom and possess the kingdom for ever—for ever and ever.'

19 Then I desired to know the truth concerning the fourth beast, which was different from all the rest, exceedingly terrifying, with its teeth of iron and claws of bronze, and which devoured and broke in pieces, and stamped what was left with its feet; 20 and concerning the ten horns that were on its head, and concerning the other horn that came up, and to make room for which three of them fell out—the horn that had eyes and a mouth that spoke arrogantly, and that seemed greater than the others. 21 As I looked, this horn made war with the holy ones and was prevailing over them, 22 until the Ancient One[b] came; then judgement was given for the holy ones of the Most High, and the time arrived when the holy ones gained possession of the kingdom.

23 This is what he said: 'As for the fourth beast,

there shall be a fourth kingdom
    on earth
that shall be different from all the
    other kingdoms;
it shall devour the whole earth,
    and trample it down, and break it
    to pieces.
24 As for the ten horns,
    out of this kingdom ten kings
      shall arise,
    and another shall arise after them.

This one shall be different from the
    former ones,
    and shall put down three kings.
25 He shall speak words against the
    Most High,
    shall wear out the holy ones of the
    Most High,
    and shall attempt to change the
      sacred seasons and the law;
and they shall be given into
    his power
for a time, two times,[c] and half a
    time.
26 Then the court shall sit in judgement,
    and his dominion shall be
      taken away,
to be consumed and totally
    destroyed.
27 The kingship and dominion
    and the greatness of the kingdoms
      under the whole heaven
    shall be given to the people of the
      holy ones of the Most High;
    their kingdom shall be an everlasting
      kingdom,
    and all dominions shall serve and
      obey them.'

28 Here the account ends. As for me, Daniel, my thoughts greatly terrified me, and my face turned pale; but I kept the matter in my mind.

Vision of a Ram and a Goat

8 In the third year of the reign of King Belshazzar a vision appeared to me, Daniel, after the one that had appeared to me at first. 2 In the vision I was looking and saw myself in Susa the capital, in the province of Elam,[d] and I was by the river Ulai.[e] 3 I looked up and saw a ram standing beside the river.[f] It had two horns. Both horns were long, but one was longer than the other, and the longer one came up second. 4 I saw the ram charging westwards and northwards and southwards. All beasts were powerless to withstand it, and no one could rescue from its power; it did as it pleased and became strong.

a Aram troubled in its sheath   b Aram the Ancient of Days   c Aram a time, times   d Gk Theodotion: MT Q Ms repeat in the vision I was looking   e Or the Ulai Gate   f Or gate

5 As I was watching, a male goat appeared from the west, coming across the face of the whole earth without touching the ground. The goat had a horn[a] between its eyes. 6 It came towards the ram with the two horns that I had seen standing beside the river,[b] and it ran at it with savage force. 7 I saw it approaching the ram. It was enraged against it and struck the ram, breaking its two horns. The ram did not have power to withstand it; it threw the ram down to the ground and trampled upon it, and there was no one who could rescue the ram from its power. 8 Then the male goat grew exceedingly great; but at the height of its power, the great horn was broken, and in its place there came up four prominent horns towards the four winds of heaven.

9 Out of one of them came another[c] horn, a little one, which grew exceedingly great towards the south, towards the east, and towards the beautiful land. 10 It grew as high as the host of heaven. It threw down to the earth some of the host and some of the stars, and trampled on them. 11 Even against the prince of the host it acted arrogantly; it took the regular burnt-offering away from him and overthrew the place of his sanctuary. 12 Because of wickedness, the host was given over to it together with the regular burnt-offering;[d] it cast truth to the ground, and kept prospering in what it did. 13 Then I heard a holy one speaking, and another holy one said to the one that spoke, 'For how long is this vision concerning the regular burnt-offering, the transgression that makes desolate, and the giving over of the sanctuary and host to be trampled?'[d] 14 And he answered him,[e] 'For two thousand three hundred evenings and mornings; then the sanctuary shall be restored to its rightful state.'

Gabriel Interprets the Vision

15 When I, Daniel, had seen the vision, I tried to understand it. Then someone appeared standing before me, having the appearance of a man, 16 and I heard a human voice by the Ulai, calling, 'Gabriel, help this man understand the vision.' 17 So he came near where I stood; and when he came, I became frightened and fell prostrate. But he said to me, 'Understand, O mortal,[f] that the vision is for the time of the end.'

18 As he was speaking to me, I fell into a trance, face to the ground; then he touched me and set me on my feet. 19 He said, 'Listen, and I will tell you what will take place later in the period of wrath; for it refers to the appointed time of the end. 20 As for the ram that you saw with the two horns, these are the kings of Media and Persia. 21 The male goat[g] is the king of Greece, and the great horn between its eyes is the first king. 22 As for the horn that was broken, in place of which four others arose, four kingdoms shall arise from his[h] nation, but not with his power.

23 At the end of their rule,
    when the transgressions have
        reached their full measure,
  a king of bold countenance
        shall arise,
        skilled in intrigue.
24 He shall grow strong in power,[i]
    shall cause fearful destruction,
        and shall succeed in what he does.
  He shall destroy the powerful
        and the people of the holy ones.
25 By his cunning
    he shall make deceit prosper under
        his hand,
    and in his own mind he shall
        be great.
  Without warning he shall
        destroy many
    and shall even rise up against the
        Prince of princes.
  But he shall be broken, and not by
        human hands.

26 The vision of the evenings and the mornings that has been told is true. As for you, seal up the vision, for it refers to many days from now.'

27 So I, Daniel, was overcome and lay sick for some days; then I arose and went

---

a Theodotion: Gk *one horn*; Heb *a horn of vision*
b Or *gate*   c Cn Compare 7.8: Heb *one*   d Meaning of Heb uncertain   e Gk Theodotion Syr Vg: Heb *me*
f Heb *son of man*   g Or *shaggy male goat*
h Gk Theodotion Vg: Heb *the*   i Theodotion and one Gk Ms: Heb repeats (from 8.22) *but not with his power*

about the king's business. But I was dismayed by the vision and did not understand it.

Daniel's Prayer for the People

9 In the first year of Darius son of Ahasuerus, by birth a Mede, who became king over the realm of the Chaldeans— 2 in the first year of his reign, I, Daniel, perceived in the books the number of years that, according to the word of the LORD to the prophet Jeremiah, must be fulfilled for the devastation of Jerusalem, namely, seventy years.

3 Then I turned to the Lord God, to seek an answer by prayer and supplication with fasting and sackcloth and ashes. 4 I prayed to the LORD my God and made confession, saying,

'Ah, Lord, great and awesome God, keeping covenant and steadfast love with those who love you and keep your commandments, 5 we have sinned and done wrong, acted wickedly and rebelled, turning aside from your commandments and ordinances. 6 We have not listened to your servants the prophets, who spoke in your name to our kings, our princes, and our ancestors, and to all the people of the land.

7 'Righteousness is on your side, O Lord, but open shame, as at this day, falls on us, the people of Judah, the inhabitants of Jerusalem, and all Israel, those who are near and those who are far away, in all the lands to which you have driven them, because of the treachery that they have committed against you. 8 Open shame, O LORD, falls on us, our kings, our officials, and our ancestors, because we have sinned against you. 9 To the Lord our God belong mercy and forgiveness, for we have rebelled against him, 10 and have not obeyed the voice of the LORD our God by following his laws, which he set before us by his servants the prophets.

11 'All Israel has transgressed your law and turned aside, refusing to obey your voice. So the curse and the oath written in the law of Moses, the servant of God, have been poured out upon us, because we have sinned against you. 12 He has confirmed his words, which he spoke against us and against our rulers, by bringing upon us a calamity so great that what has been done against Jerusalem has never before been done under the whole heaven. 13 Just as it is written in the law of Moses, all this calamity has come upon us. We did not entreat the favour of the LORD our God, turning from our iniquities and reflecting on his a fidelity. 14 So the LORD kept watch over this calamity until he brought it upon us. Indeed, the LORD our God is right in all that he has done; for we have disobeyed his voice.

15 'And now, O Lord our God, who brought your people out of the land of Egypt with a mighty hand and made your name renowned even to this day—we have sinned, we have done wickedly. 16 O Lord, in view of all your righteous acts, let your anger and wrath, we pray, turn away from your city Jerusalem, your holy mountain; because of our sins and the iniquities of our ancestors, Jerusalem and your people have become a disgrace among all our neighbours. 17 Now therefore, O our God, listen to the prayer of your servant and to his supplication, and for your own sake, Lord, b let your face shine upon your desolated sanctuary. 18 Incline your ear, O my God, and hear. Open your eyes and look at our desolation and the city that bears your name. We do not present our supplication before you on the ground of our righteousness, but on the ground of your great mercies. 19 O Lord, hear; O Lord, forgive; O Lord, listen and act and do not delay! For your own sake, O my God, because your city and your people bear your name!'

The Seventy Weeks

20 While I was speaking, and was praying and confessing my sin and the sin of my people Israel, and presenting my supplication before the LORD my God on behalf of the holy mountain of my God— 21 while I was speaking in prayer, the man Gabriel, whom I had seen before in a vision, came to me in swift flight at the time of the evening sacrifice. 22 He came c and said to

a Heb your   b Theodotion Vg Compare Syr: Heb for the Lord's sake   c Gk Syr: Heb He made to understand me, 'Daniel, I have now come out to give you wisdom and understanding. [23] At the beginning of your supplications a word went out, and I have come to declare it, for you are greatly beloved. So consider the word and understand the vision:

24 'Seventy weeks are decreed for your people and your holy city: to finish the transgression, to put an end to sin, and to atone for iniquity, to bring in everlasting righteousness, to seal both vision and prophet, and to anoint a most holy place. [a]
[25] Know therefore and understand: from the time that the word went out to restore and rebuild Jerusalem until the time of an anointed prince, there shall be seven weeks; and for sixty-two weeks it shall be built again with streets and moat, but in a troubled time. [26] After the sixty-two weeks, an anointed one shall be cut off and shall have nothing, and the troops of the prince who is to come shall destroy the city and the sanctuary. Its [b] end shall come with a flood, and to the end there shall be war. Desolations are decreed. [27] He shall make a strong covenant with many for one week, and for half of the week he shall make sacrifice and offering cease; and in their place [c] shall be an abomination that desolates, until the decreed end is poured out upon the desolator.'

Conflict of Nations and Heavenly Powers

10 In the third year of King Cyrus of Persia a word was revealed to Daniel, who was named Belteshazzar. The word was true, and it concerned a great conflict. He understood the word, having received understanding in the vision.

2 At that time I, Daniel, had been mourning for three weeks. [3] I had eaten no rich food, no meat or wine had entered my mouth, and I had not anointed myself at all, for the full three weeks. [4] On the twenty-fourth day of the first month, as I was standing on the bank of the great river (that is, the Tigris), [5] I looked up and saw a man clothed in linen, with a belt of gold from Uphaz around his waist. [6] His body was like beryl, his face like lightning, his eyes like flaming torches, his arms and legs like the gleam of burnished bronze, and the sound of his words like the roar of a multitude. [7] I, Daniel, alone saw the vision; the people who were with me did not see the vision, though a great trembling fell upon them, and they fled and hid themselves. [8] So I was left alone to see this great vision. My strength left me, and my complexion grew deathly pale, and I retained no strength. [9] Then I heard the sound of his words; and when I heard the sound of his words, I fell into a trance, face to the ground.

10 But then a hand touched me and roused me to my hands and knees. [11] He said to me, 'Daniel, greatly beloved, pay attention to the words that I am going to speak to you. Stand on your feet, for I have now been sent to you.' So while he was speaking this word to me, I stood up trembling. [12] He said to me, 'Do not fear, Daniel, for from the first day that you set your mind to gain understanding and to humble yourself before your God, your words have been heard, and I have come because of your words. [13] But the prince of the kingdom of Persia opposed me for twenty-one days. So Michael, one of the chief princes, came to help me, and I left him there with the prince of the kingdom of Persia, [d] [14] and have come to help you understand what is to happen to your people at the end of days. For there is a further vision for those days.'

15 While he was speaking these words to me, I turned my face towards the ground and was speechless. [16] Then one in human form touched my lips, and I opened my mouth to speak, and said to the one who stood before me, 'My lord, because of the vision such pains have come upon me that I retain no strength. [17] How can my lord's servant talk with my lord? For I am shaking, [e] no strength remains in me, and no breath is left in me.'

18 Again one in human form touched me and strengthened me. [19] He said, 'Do not fear, greatly beloved, you are safe. Be strong and courageous!' When he spoke to me, I

a Or thing or one   b Or His   c Cn: Meaning of Heb uncertain   d Gk Theodotion: Heb I was left there with the kings of Persia   e Gk: Heb from now was strengthened and said, 'Let my lord speak, for you have strengthened me.' ²⁰Then he said, 'Do you know why I have come to you? Now I must return to fight against the prince of Persia, and when I am through with him, the prince of Greece will come. ²¹But I am to tell you what is inscribed in the book of truth. There is no one with me who contends against these princes except Michael, your prince. ¹As for me, in the first year of Darius the Mede, I stood up to support and strengthen him.

2 'Now I will announce the truth to you. Three more kings shall arise in Persia. The fourth shall be far richer than all of them, and when he has become strong through his riches, he shall stir up all against the kingdom of Greece. ³Then a warrior king shall arise, who shall rule with great dominion and take action as he pleases. ⁴And while still rising in power, his kingdom shall be broken and divided towards the four winds of heaven, but not to his posterity, nor according to the dominion with which he ruled; for his kingdom shall be uprooted and go to others besides these.

5 'Then the king of the south shall grow strong, but one of his officers shall grow stronger than he and shall rule a realm greater than his own realm. ⁶After some years they shall make an alliance, and the daughter of the king of the south shall come to the king of the north to ratify the agreement. But she shall not retain her power, and his offspring shall not endure. She shall be given up, she and her attendants and her child and the one who supported her.

'In those times ⁷a branch from her roots shall rise up in his place. He shall come against the army and enter the fortress of the king of the north, and he shall take action against them and prevail. ⁸Even their gods, with their idols and with their precious vessels of silver and gold, he shall carry off to Egypt as spoils of war. For some years he shall refrain from attacking the king of the north; ⁹then the latter shall invade the realm of the king of the south, but will return to his own land.

10 'His sons shall wage war and assemble a multitude of great forces, which shall advance like a flood and pass through, and again shall carry the war as far as his fortress. ¹¹Moved with rage, the king of the south shall go out and do battle against the king of the north, who shall muster a great multitude, which shall, however, be defeated by his enemy. ¹²When the multitude has been carried off, his heart shall be exalted, and he shall overthrow tens of thousands, but he shall not prevail. ¹³For the king of the north shall again raise a multitude, larger than the former, and after some years^a he shall advance with a great army and abundant supplies.

14 'In those times many shall rise against the king of the south. The lawless among your own people shall lift themselves up in order to fulfil the vision, but they shall fail. ¹⁵Then the king of the north shall come and throw up siege-works, and take a well-fortified city. And the forces of the south shall not stand, not even his picked troops, for there shall be no strength to resist. ¹⁶But he who comes against him shall take the actions he pleases, and no one shall withstand him. He shall take a position in the beautiful land, and all of it shall be in his power. ¹⁷He shall set his mind to come with the strength of his whole kingdom, and he shall bring terms of peace^b and perform them. In order to destroy the kingdom,^c he shall give him a woman in marriage; but it shall not succeed or be to his advantage. ¹⁸Afterwards he shall turn to the coastlands, and shall capture many. But a commander shall put an end to his insolence; indeed,^d he shall turn his insolence back upon him. ¹⁹Then he shall turn back towards the fortresses of his own land, but he shall stumble and fall, and shall not be found.

20 'Then shall arise in his place one who shall send an official for the glory of the kingdom; but within a few days he shall be broken, though not in anger or in battle. ²¹In his place shall arise a contemptible per-

^a Heb *and at the end of the times years*   ^b Gk: Heb *kingdom, and upright ones with him*   ^c Heb *it*
^d Meaning of Heb uncertain

son on whom royal majesty had not been conferred; he shall come in without warning and obtain the kingdom through intrigue. [22] Armies shall be utterly swept away and broken before him, and the prince of the covenant as well. [23] And after an alliance is made with him, he shall act deceitfully and become strong with a small party. [24] Without warning he shall come into the richest parts[a] of the province and do what none of his predecessors had ever done, lavishing plunder, spoil, and wealth on them. He shall devise plans against strongholds, but only for a time. [25] He shall stir up his power and determination against the king of the south with a great army, and the king of the south shall wage war with a much greater and stronger army. But he shall not succeed, for plots shall be devised against him [26] by those who eat of the royal rations. They shall break him, his army shall be swept away, and many shall fall slain. [27] The two kings, their minds bent on evil, shall sit at one table and exchange lies. But it shall not succeed, for there remains an end at the time appointed. [28] He shall return to his land with great wealth, but his heart shall be set against the holy covenant. He shall work his will, and return to his own land.

29 'At the time appointed he shall return and come into the south, but this time it shall not be as it was before. [30] For ships of Kittim shall come against him, and he shall lose heart and withdraw. He shall be enraged and take action against the holy covenant. He shall turn back and pay heed to those who forsake the holy covenant. [31] Forces sent by him shall occupy and profane the temple and fortress. They shall abolish the regular burnt-offering and set up the abomination that makes desolate. [32] He shall seduce with intrigue those who violate the covenant; but the people who are loyal to their God shall stand firm and take action. [33] The wise among the people shall give understanding to many; for some days, however, they shall fall by sword and flame, and suffer captivity and plunder. [34] When they fall victim, they shall receive a little help, and many shall join them insincerely. [35] Some of the wise shall fall, so

that they may be refined, purified, and cleansed,[b] until the time of the end, for there is still an interval until the time appointed.

36 'The king shall act as he pleases. He shall exalt himself and consider himself greater than any god, and shall speak horrendous things against the God of gods. He shall prosper until the period of wrath is completed, for what is determined shall be done. [37] He shall pay no respect to the gods of his ancestors, or to the one beloved by women; he shall pay no respect to any other god, for he shall consider himself greater than all. [38] He shall honour the god of fortresses instead of these; a god whom his ancestors did not know he shall honour with gold and silver, with precious stones and costly gifts. [39] He shall deal with the strongest fortresses by the help of a foreign god. Those who acknowledge him he shall make more wealthy, and shall appoint them as rulers over many, and shall distribute the land for a price.

The Time of the End

40 'At the time of the end the king of the south shall attack him. But the king of the north shall rush upon him like a whirlwind, with chariots and horsemen, and with many ships. He shall advance against countries and pass through like a flood. [41] He shall come into the beautiful land, and tens of thousands shall fall victim, but Edom and Moab and the main part of the Ammonites shall escape from his power. [42] He shall stretch out his hand against the countries, and the land of Egypt shall not escape. [43] He shall become ruler of the treasures of gold and of silver, and all the riches of Egypt; and the Libyans and the Ethiopians[c] shall follow in his train. [44] But reports from the east and the north shall alarm him, and he shall go out with great fury to bring ruin and complete destruction to many. [45] He shall pitch his palatial tents between the sea and the beautiful holy mountain. Yet he shall come to his end, with no one to help him.

a Or *among the richest men*   *b* Heb *made them white*
c Or *Nubians*; Heb *Cushites*

The Resurrection of the Dead

12 ¹At that time Michael, the great prince, the protector of your people, shall arise. There shall be a time of anguish, such as has never occurred since nations first came into existence. But at that time your people shall be delivered, everyone who is found written in the book. ²Many of those who sleep in the dust of the earth*ᵃ* shall awake, some to everlasting life, and some to shame and everlasting contempt. ³Those who are wise shall shine like the brightness of the sky,*ᵇ* and those who lead many to righteousness, like the stars for ever and ever. ⁴But you, Daniel, keep the words secret and the book sealed until the time of the end. Many shall be running back and forth, and evil*ᶜ* shall increase.'

⁵Then I, Daniel, looked, and two others appeared, one standing on this bank of the stream and one on the other. ⁶One of them said to the man clothed in linen, who was upstream, 'How long shall it be until the end of these wonders?' ⁷The man clothed in linen, who was upstream, raised his right hand and his left hand towards heaven. And I heard him swear by the one who lives for ever that it would be for a time, two times, and half a time,*ᵈ* and that when the shattering of the power of the holy people comes to an end, all these things would be accomplished. ⁸I heard but could not understand; so I said, 'My lord, what shall be the outcome of these things?' ⁹He said, 'Go your way, Daniel, for the words are to remain secret and sealed until the time of the end. ¹⁰Many shall be purified, cleansed, and refined, but the wicked shall continue to act wickedly. None of the wicked shall understand, but those who are wise shall understand. ¹¹From the time that the regular burnt-offering is taken away and the abomination that desolates is set up, there shall be one thousand two hundred and ninety days. ¹²Happy are those who persevere and attain the thousand three hundred and thirty-five days. ¹³But you, go your way,*ᵉ* and rest; you shall rise for your reward at the end of the days.'

Susanna's Beauty Attracts Two Elders

13 There was a man living in Babylon whose name was Joakim. ²He married the daughter of Hilkiah, named Susanna, a very beautiful woman and one who feared the Lord. ³Her parents were righteous, and had trained their daughter according to the law of Moses. ⁴Joakim was very rich, and had a fine garden adjoining his house; the Jews used to come to him because he was the most honoured of them all.

5 That year two elders from the people were appointed as judges. Concerning them the Lord had said: 'Wickedness came forth from Babylon, from elders who were judges, who were supposed to govern the people.' ⁶These men were frequently at Joakim's house, and all who had a case to be tried came to them there.

7 When the people left at noon, Susanna would go into her husband's garden to walk. ⁸Every day the two elders used to see her, going in and walking about, and they began to lust for her. ⁹They suppressed their consciences and turned away their eyes from looking to Heaven or remembering their duty to administer justice. ¹⁰Both were overwhelmed with passion for her, but they did not tell each other of their distress, ¹¹for they were ashamed to disclose their lustful desire to seduce her. ¹²Day after day they watched eagerly to see her.

13 One day they said to each other, 'Let us go home, for it is time for lunch.' So they both left and parted from each other. ¹⁴But turning back, they met again; and when each pressed the other for the reason, they confessed their lust. Then together they arranged for a time when they could find her alone.

The Elders Attempt to Seduce Susanna

15 Once, while they were watching for an opportune day, she went in as before with only two maids, and wished to bathe in the garden, for it was a hot day. ¹⁶No one was there except the two elders, who had

a Or *the land of dust*   . *b* Or *dome*   *c* Cn Compare Gk: Heb *knowledge*   *d* Heb *a time, times, and a half*
e Gk Theodotion: Heb adds *to the end*

hidden themselves and were watching her. [17] She said to her maids, 'Bring me olive oil and ointments, and shut the garden doors so that I can bathe.' [18] They did as she told them: they shut the doors of the garden and went out by the side doors to bring what they had been commanded; they did not see the elders, because they were hiding.

19 When the maids had gone out, the two elders got up and ran to her. [20] They said, 'Look, the garden doors are shut, and no one can see us. We are burning with desire for you; so give your consent, and lie with us. [21] If you refuse, we will testify against you that a young man was with you, and this was why you sent your maids away.'

22 Susanna groaned and said, 'I am completely trapped. For if I do this, it will mean death for me; if I do not, I cannot escape your hands. [23] I choose not to do it; I will fall into your hands, rather than sin in the sight of the Lord.'

24 Then Susanna cried out with a loud voice, and the two elders shouted against her. [25] And one of them ran and opened the garden doors. [26] When the people in the house heard the shouting in the garden, they rushed in at the side door to see what had happened to her. [27] And when the elders told their story, the servants felt very much ashamed, for nothing like this had ever been said about Susanna.

The Elders Testify against Susanna

28 The next day, when the people gathered at the house of her husband Joakim, the two elders came, full of their wicked plot to have Susanna put to death. In the presence of the people they said, [29] 'Send for Susanna daughter of Hilkiah, the wife of Joakim.' [30] So they sent for her. And she came with her parents, her children, and all her relatives.

31 Now Susanna was a woman of great refinement and beautiful in appearance. [32] As she was veiled, the scoundrels ordered her to be unveiled, so that they might feast their eyes on her beauty. [33] Those who were with her and all who saw her were weeping.

34 Then the two elders stood up before the people and laid their hands on her head. [35] Through her tears she looked up towards Heaven, for her heart trusted in the Lord. [36] The elders said, 'While we were walking in the garden alone, this woman came in with two maids, shut the garden doors, and dismissed the maids. [37] Then a young man, who was hiding there, came to her and lay with her. [38] We were in a corner of the garden, and when we saw this wickedness we ran to them. [39] Although we saw them embracing, we could not hold the man, because he was stronger than we are, and he opened the doors and got away. [40] We did, however, seize this woman and asked who the young man was, [41] but she would not tell us. These things we testify.'

Because they were elders of the people and judges, the assembly believed them and condemned her to death.

42 Then Susanna cried out with a loud voice, and said, 'O eternal God, you know what is secret and are aware of all things before they come to be; [43] you know that these men have given false evidence against me. And now I am to die, though I have done none of the wicked things that they have charged against me!'

44 The Lord heard her cry. [45] Just as she was being led off to execution, God stirred up the holy spirit of a young lad named Daniel, [46] and he shouted with a loud voice, 'I want no part in shedding this woman's blood!'

Daniel Rescues Susanna

47 All the people turned to him and asked, 'What is this you are saying?' [48] Taking his stand among them he said, 'Are you such fools, O Israelites, as to condemn a daughter of Israel without examination and without learning the facts? [49] Return to court, for these men have given false evidence against her.'

50 So all the people hurried back. And the rest of the[a] elders said to him, 'Come, sit among us and inform us, for God has given you the standing of an elder.' [51] Daniel said to them, 'Separate them far from each other, and I will examine them.'

a Gk lacks *rest of the*

52 When they were separated from each other, he summoned one of them and said to him, 'You old relic of wicked days, your sins have now come home, which you have committed in the past, 53 pronouncing unjust judgements, condemning the innocent and acquitting the guilty, though the Lord said, "You shall not put an innocent and righteous person to death." 54 Now then, if you really saw this woman, tell me this: Under what tree did you see them being intimate with each other?' He answered, 'Under a mastic tree.' *a* 55 And Daniel said, 'Very well! This lie has cost you your head, for the angel of God has received the sentence from God and will immediately cut *d* you in two.'

56 Then, putting him to one side, he ordered them to bring the other. And he said to him, 'You offspring of Canaan and not of Judah, beauty has beguiled you and lust has perverted your heart. 57 This is how you have been treating the daughters of Israel, and they were intimate with you through fear; but a daughter of Judah would not tolerate your wickedness. 58 Now then, tell me: Under what tree did you catch them being intimate with each other?' He answered, 'Under an evergreen oak.' *b* 59 Daniel said to him, 'Very well! This lie has cost you also your head, for the angel of God is waiting with his sword to split *b* you in two, so as to destroy you both.'

60 Then the whole assembly raised a great shout and blessed God, who saves those who hope in him. 61 And they took action against the two elders, because out of their own mouths Daniel had convicted them of bearing false witness; they did to them as they had wickedly planned to do to their neighbour. 62 Acting in accordance with the law of Moses, they put them to death. Thus innocent blood was spared that day.

63 Hilkiah and his wife praised God for their daughter Susanna, and so did her husband Joakim and all her relatives, because she was found innocent of a shameful deed. 64 And from that day onwards Daniel had a great reputation among the people.

Daniel and the Priests of Bel

14 When King Astyages was laid to rest with his ancestors, Cyrus the Persian succeeded to his kingdom. 2 Daniel was a companion of the king, and was the most honoured of all his Friends.

3 Now the Babylonians had an idol called Bel, and every day they provided for it twelve bushels of choice flour and forty sheep and six measures *c* of wine. 4 The king revered it and went every day to worship it. But Daniel worshipped his own God.

So the king said to him, 'Why do you not worship Bel?' 5 He answered, 'Because I do not revere idols made with hands, but the living God, who created heaven and earth and has dominion over all living creatures.'

6 The king said to him, 'Do you not think that Bel is a living god? Do you not see how much he eats and drinks every day?' 7 And Daniel laughed, and said, 'Do not be deceived, O king, for this thing is only clay inside and bronze outside, and it never ate or drank anything.'

8 Then the king was angry and called the priests of Bel *d* and said to them, 'If you do not tell me who is eating these provisions, you shall die. 9 But if you prove that Bel is eating them, Daniel shall die, because he has spoken blasphemy against Bel.' Daniel said to the king, 'Let it be done as you have said.'

10 Now there were seventy priests of Bel, besides their wives and children. So the king went with Daniel into the temple of Bel. 11 The priests of Bel said, 'See, we are now going outside; you yourself, O king, set out the food and prepare the wine, and shut the door and seal it with your signet. 12 When you return in the morning, if you do not find that Bel has eaten it all, we will die; otherwise Daniel will, who is telling lies about us.' 13 They were unconcerned, for beneath the table they had made a hidden entrance, through which they used to go in regularly and consume the provisions. 14 After they

a The Greek words for *mastic tree* and *cut* are similar, thus forming an ironic wordplay   *b* The Greek words for *evergreen oak* and *split* are similar, thus forming an ironic wordplay   *c* A little more than fifty gallons   *d* Gk *his priests* had gone out, the king set out the food for Bel. Then Daniel ordered his servants to bring ashes, and they scattered them throughout the whole temple in the presence of the king alone. Then they went out, shut the door and sealed it with the king's signet, and departed. 15 During the night the priests came as usual, with their wives and children, and they ate and drank everything.

16 Early in the morning the king rose and came, and Daniel with him. 17 The king said, 'Are the seals unbroken, Daniel?' He answered, 'They are unbroken, O king.' 18 As soon as the doors were opened, the king looked at the table, and shouted in a loud voice, 'You are great, O Bel, and in you there is no deceit at all!'

19 But Daniel laughed and restrained the king from going in. 'Look at the floor', he said, 'and notice whose footprints these are.' 20 The king said, 'I see the footprints of men and women and children.'

21 Then the king was enraged, and he arrested the priests and their wives and children. They showed him the secret doors through which they used to enter to consume what was on the table. 22 Therefore the king put them to death, and gave Bel over to Daniel, who destroyed it and its temple.

Daniel Kills the Dragon

23 Now in that place[a] there was a great dragon, which the Babylonians revered. 24 The king said to Daniel, 'You cannot deny that this is a living god; so worship him.' 25 Daniel said, 'I worship the Lord my God, for he is the living God. 26 But give me permission, O king, and I will kill the dragon without sword or club.' The king said, 'I give you permission.'

27 Then Daniel took pitch, fat, and hair, and boiled them together and made cakes, which he fed to the dragon. The dragon ate them, and burst open. Then Daniel said, 'See what you have been worshipping!'

28 When the Babylonians heard about it, they were very indignant and conspired against the king, saying, 'The king has be-

come a Jew; he has destroyed Bel, and killed the dragon, and slaughtered the priests.' 29 Going to the king, they said, 'Hand Daniel over to us, or else we will kill you and your household.' 30 The king saw that they were pressing him hard, and under compulsion he handed Daniel over to them.

Daniel in the Lions' Den

31 They threw Daniel into the lions' den, and he was there for six days. 32 There were seven lions in the den, and every day they had been given two human bodies and two sheep; but now they were given nothing, so that they would devour Daniel.

33 Now the prophet Habakkuk was in Judea; he had made a stew and had broken bread into a bowl, and was going into the field to take it to the reapers. 34 But the angel of the Lord said to Habakkuk, 'Take the food that you have to Babylon, to Daniel, in the lions' den.' 35 Habakkuk said, 'Sir, I have never seen Babylon, and I know nothing about the den.' 36 Then the angel of the Lord took him by the crown of his head and carried him by his hair; with the speed of the wind[b] he set him down in Babylon, right over the den.

37 Then Habakkuk shouted, 'Daniel, Daniel! Take the food that God has sent you.' 38 Daniel said, 'You have remembered me, O God, and have not forsaken those who love you.' 39 So Daniel got up and ate. And the angel of God immediately returned Habakkuk to his own place.

40 On the seventh day the king came to mourn for Daniel. When he came to the den he looked in, and there sat Daniel! 41 The king shouted with a loud voice, 'You are great, O Lord, the God of Daniel, and there is no other besides you!' 42 Then he pulled Daniel[c] out, and threw into the den those who had attempted his destruction, and they were instantly eaten before his eyes.

---

a Other ancient authorities lack *in that place*   b Or *by the power of his spirit*   c Gk *him*

HOSEA

1 The word of the LORD that came to Hosea son of Beeri, in the days of Kings Uzziah, Jotham, Ahaz, and Hezekiah of Judah, and in the days of King Jeroboam son of Joash of Israel.

The Family of Hosea

2 When the LORD first spoke through Hosea, the LORD said to Hosea, 'Go, take for yourself a wife of whoredom and have children of whoredom, for the land commits great whoredom by forsaking the LORD.' 3 So he went and took Gomer daughter of Diblaim, and she conceived and bore him a son.

4 And the LORD said to him, 'Name him Jezreel;[a] for in a little while I will punish the house of Jehu for the blood of Jezreel, and I will put an end to the kingdom of the house of Israel. 5 On that day I will break the bow of Israel in the valley of Jezreel.'

6 She conceived again and bore a daughter. Then the LORD said to him, 'Name her Lo-ruhamah,[b] for I will no longer have pity on the house of Israel or forgive them. 7 But I will have pity on the house of Judah, and I will save them by the LORD their God; I will not save them by bow, or by sword, or by war, or by horses, or by horsemen.'

8 When she had weaned Lo-ruhamah, she conceived and bore a son. 9 Then the LORD said, 'Name him Lo-ammi,[c] for you are not my people and I am not your God.'[d]

The Restoration of Israel

10[e] Yet the number of the people of Israel shall be like the sand of the sea, which can be neither measured nor numbered; and in the place where it was said to them, 'You are not my people', it shall be said to them, 'Children of the living God.' 11 The people of Judah and the people of Israel shall be gathered together, and they shall appoint for themselves one head; and they shall take possession of[f] the land, for great shall be the day of Jezreel.

2 [g] Say to your brother,[h] Ammi,[i] and to your sister,[j] Ruhamah.[k]

Israel's Infidelity, Punishment, and Redemption

2 Plead with your mother, plead—
   for she is not my wife,
   and I am not her husband—
that she put away her whoring from
      her face,
   and her adultery from between her
      breasts,
3 or I will strip her naked
   and expose her as in the day she
      was born,
and make her like a wilderness,
   and turn her into a parched land,
   and kill her with thirst.
4 Upon her children also I will
      have no pity,
   because they are children of
      whoredom.
5 For their mother has played
      the whore;
   she who conceived them has acted
      shamefully.
   For she said, 'I will go after my lovers;

a That is God sows   b That is Not pitied   c That is Not my people   d Heb I am not yours   e Ch 2.1 in Heb   f Heb rise up from   g Ch 2.3 in Heb   h Gk: Heb brothers   i That is My people   j Gk Vg: Heb sisters   k That is Pitied

they give me my bread and
  my water,
my wool and my flax, my oil and
  my drink.'
6 Therefore I will hedge her*a* way with
    thorns;
  and I will build a wall against her,
  so that she cannot find her paths.
7 She shall pursue her lovers,
    but not overtake them;
  and she shall seek them,
    but shall not find them.
  Then she shall say, 'I will go
    and return to my first husband,
  for it was better with me then than
    now.'
8 She did not know
    that it was I who gave her
    the grain, the wine, and the oil,
  and who lavished upon her silver
    and gold that they used for Baal.
9 Therefore I will take back
    my grain in its time,
    and my wine in its season;
  and I will take away my wool and my
    flax,
  which were to cover her
    nakedness.
10 Now I will uncover her shame
    in the sight of her lovers,
  and no one shall rescue her out of
    my hand.
11 I will put an end to all her mirth,
    her festivals, her new moons, her
      sabbaths,
  and all her appointed festivals.
12 I will lay waste her vines and her fig
    trees,
    of which she said,
  'These are my pay,
    which my lovers have given me.'
  I will make them a forest,
    and the wild animals shall devour
      them.
13 I will punish her for the festival days
    of the Baals,
    when she offered incense to them
  and decked herself with her ring and
    jewellery,
    and went after her lovers,
    and forgot me, says the LORD.

14 Therefore, I will now persuade her,
    and bring her into the wilderness,
    and speak tenderly to her.
15 From there I will give her her
      vineyards,
    and make the Valley of Achor a
      door of hope.
  There she shall respond as in the days
      of her youth,
    as at the time when she came out of
      the land of Egypt.
16 On that day, says the LORD, you will call
me, 'My husband', and no longer will you
call me, 'My Baal'.*b* 17 For I will remove the
names of the Baals from her mouth, and
they shall be mentioned by name no more.
18 I will make for you*c* a covenant on that
day with the wild animals, the birds of the
air, and the creeping things of the ground;
and I will abolish*d* the bow, the sword, and
war from the land; and I will make you lie
down in safety. 19 And I will take you for
my wife for ever; I will take you for my wife
in righteousness and in justice, in steadfast
love, and in mercy. 20 I will take you for my
wife in faithfulness; and you shall know
the LORD.
21 On that day I will answer, says
      the LORD,
    I will answer the heavens
    and they shall answer the earth;
22 and the earth shall answer the grain,
      the wine, and the oil,
    and they shall answer Jezreel;*e*
23   and I will sow him*f* for myself in
      the land.
  And I will have pity on Lo-ruhamah,*g*
    and I will say to Lo-ammi,*h* 'You are
      my people';
    and he shall say, 'You are my God.'

Further Assurances of God's Redeeming Love

3 The LORD said to me again, 'Go, love a
  woman who has a lover and is an
adulteress, just as the LORD loves the people of Israel, though they turn to other
gods and love raisin cakes.' 2 So I bought

a Gk Syr: Heb *your*   *b* That is, *'My master'*
c Heb *them*   *d* Heb *break*   *e* That is *God sows*
f Cn: Heb *her*   *g* That is *Not pitied*   *h* That is
Not my people

her for fifteen shekels of silver and a homer of barley and a measure of wine.*a* 3 And I said to her, 'You must remain as mine for many days; you shall not play the whore, you shall not have intercourse with a man, nor I with you.' 4 For the Israelites shall remain many days without king or prince, without sacrifice or pillar, without ephod or teraphim. 5 Afterwards the Israelites shall return and seek the LORD their God, and David their king; they shall come in awe to the LORD and to his goodness in the latter days.

God Accuses Israel

4 Hear the word of the LORD,
    O people of Israel;
for the LORD has an indictment
    against the inhabitants
    of the land.
There is no faithfulness or loyalty,
    and no knowledge of God in
    the land.
2 Swearing, lying, and murder,
    and stealing and adultery
    break out;
bloodshed follows bloodshed.
3 Therefore the land mourns,
    and all who live in it languish;
together with the wild animals
    and the birds of the air,
    even the fish of the sea are
    perishing.

4 Yet let no one contend,
    and let none accuse,
    for with you is my contention,
    O priest.*b*
5 You shall stumble by day;
    the prophet also shall stumble with
    you by night,
and I will destroy your mother.
6 My people are destroyed for lack of
    knowledge;
because you have rejected
    knowledge,
I reject you from being a priest
    to me.
And since you have forgotten the law
    of your God,
I also will forget your children.

7 The more they increased,
    the more they sinned against me;
they changed*c* their glory
    into shame.
8 They feed on the sin of my people;
    they are greedy for their iniquity.
9 And it shall be like people, like
    priest;
I will punish them for their ways,
    and repay them for their deeds.
10 They shall eat, but not be satisfied;
    they shall play the whore, but not
    multiply;
because they have forsaken the LORD
    to devote themselves to
    11 whoredom.

The Idolatry of Israel

Wine and new wine
    take away the understanding.
12 My people consult a piece of wood,
    and their divining-rod gives
    them oracles.
For a spirit of whoredom has led
    them astray,
    and they have played the whore,
    forsaking their God.
13 They sacrifice on the tops of the
    mountains,
    and make offerings upon the hills,
under oak, poplar, and terebinth,
    because their shade is good.

Therefore your daughters play
    the whore,
    and your daughters-in-law commit
    adultery.
14 I will not punish your daughters
    when they play the whore,
    nor your daughters-in-law when
    they commit adultery;
for the men themselves go aside with
    whores,
    and sacrifice with temple
    prostitutes;
thus a people without understanding
    comes to ruin.

a Gk: Heb *a homer of barley and a lethech of barley*
b Cn: Meaning of Heb uncertain   *c* Ancient Heb tradition: MT *I will change*

15 Though you play the whore, O Israel,
    do not let Judah become guilty.
  Do not enter into Gilgal,
    or go up to Beth-aven,
    and do not swear, 'As the
      LORD lives.'
16 Like a stubborn heifer,
    Israel is stubborn;
  can the LORD now feed them
    like a lamb in a broad pasture?

17 Ephraim is joined to idols—
    let him alone.
18 When their drinking is ended, they
      indulge in sexual orgies;
    they love lewdness more than their
      glory. *a*
19 A wind has wrapped them *b* in
      its wings,
    and they shall be ashamed because
      of their altars. *c*

Impending Judgement on Israel and Judah

5 Hear this, O priests!
  Give heed, O house of Israel!
  Listen, O house of the king!
    For the judgement pertains to you;
    for you have been a snare at Mizpah,
    and a net spread upon Tabor,
2 and a pit dug deep in Shittim; *d*
    but I will punish all of them.

3 I know Ephraim,
    and Israel is not hidden from me;
  for now, O Ephraim, you have played
      the whore;
    Israel is defiled.
4 Their deeds do not permit them
    to return to their God.
  For the spirit of whoredom is within
      them,
    and they do not know the LORD.

5 Israel's pride testifies against him;
    Ephraim *e* stumbles in his guilt;
  Judah also stumbles with them.
6 With their flocks and herds they shall
      go
    to seek the LORD,
  but they will not find him;

he has withdrawn from them.
7 They have dealt faithlessly with the
      LORD;
    for they have borne illegitimate
      children.
  Now the new moon shall devour
    them along with their fields.

8 Blow the horn in Gibeah,
    the trumpet in Ramah.
  Sound the alarm at Beth-aven;
    look behind you, Benjamin!
9 Ephraim shall become a desolation
    on the day of punishment;
  among the tribes of Israel
    I declare what is sure.
10 The princes of Judah have become
    like those who remove the
      landmark;
  on them I will pour out
    my wrath like water.
11 Ephraim is oppressed, crushed in
      judgement,
    because he was determined to go
      after vanity. *f*
12 Therefore I am like maggots to
      Ephraim,
    and like rottenness to the house of
      Judah.
13 When Ephraim saw his sickness,
    and Judah his wound,
  then Ephraim went to Assyria,
    and sent to the great king. *g*
  But he is not able to cure you
    or heal your wound.
14 For I will be like a lion to Ephraim,
    and like a young lion to the house
      of Judah.
  I myself will tear and go away;
    I will carry off, and no one
      shall rescue.
15 I will return again to my place
    until they acknowledge their guilt
      and seek my face.
  In their distress they will beg
    my favour:

a Cn Compare Gk: Meaning of Heb uncertain
b Heb *her*   *c* Gk Syr: Heb *sacrifices*   *d* Cn: Meaning
of Heb uncertain   *e* Heb *Israel and Ephraim*
f Gk: Meaning of Heb uncertain   *g* Cn: Heb *to a king
who will contend*

A Call to Repentance

6 ¹'Come, let us return to the LORD;
　　for it is he who has torn, and he will
　　　heal us;
　　he has struck down, and he will
　　　bind us up.
² After two days he will revive us;
　　on the third day he will raise us up,
　　　that we may live before him.
³ Let us know, let us press on to know
　　　the LORD;
　　his appearing is as sure as
　　　the dawn;
　　he will come to us like the showers,
　　　like the spring rains that water the
　　　　earth.'

Impenitence of Israel and Judah

⁴ What shall I do with you,
　　　O Ephraim?
　　What shall I do with you, O Judah?
　　Your love is like a morning cloud,
　　　like the dew that goes away early.
⁵ Therefore I have hewn them by the
　　　prophets,
　　I have killed them by the words of
　　　my mouth,
　　and my*ᵃ* judgement goes forth as
　　　the light.
⁶ For I desire steadfast love and not
　　　sacrifice,
　　the knowledge of God rather than
　　　burnt-offerings.

⁷ But at*ᵇ* Adam they transgressed the
　　　covenant;
　　there they dealt faithlessly with me.
⁸ Gilead is a city of evildoers,
　　tracked with blood.
⁹ As robbers lie in wait*ᶜ* for someone,
　　so the priests are banded together;*ᵈ*
　　they murder on the road to
　　　Shechem,
　　they commit a monstrous crime.
¹⁰ In the house of Israel I have seen a
　　　horrible thing;
　　Ephraim's whoredom is there, Israel
　　　is defiled.

¹¹ For you also, O Judah, a harvest
　　is appointed.

When I would restore the fortunes of
　　my people,
7 ¹when I would heal Israel,
　　the corruption of Ephraim is revealed,
　　　and the wicked deeds of Samaria;
　　for they deal falsely,
　　　the thief breaks in,
　　　and the bandits raid outside.
² But they do not consider
　　that I remember all their
　　　wickedness.
　　Now their deeds surround them,
　　　they are before my face.
³ By their wickedness they make the
　　　king glad,
　　and the officials by their
　　　treachery.
⁴ They are all adulterers;
　　they are like a heated oven,
　　whose baker does not need to stir the
　　　fire,
　　from the kneading of the dough
　　　until it is leavened.
⁵ On the day of our king the officials
　　became sick with the heat of wine;
　　he stretched out his hand with
　　　mockers.
⁶ For they are kindled*ᵉ* like an oven,
　　　their heart burns within them;
　　all night their anger smoulders;
　　in the morning it blazes like a
　　　flaming fire.
⁷ All of them are hot as an oven,
　　and they devour their rulers.
　　All their kings have fallen;
　　none of them calls upon me.

⁸ Ephraim mixes himself with
　　the peoples;
　　Ephraim is a cake not turned.
⁹ Foreigners devour his strength,
　　but he does not know it;
　　grey hairs are sprinkled upon him,
　　but he does not know it.
¹⁰ Israel's pride testifies against*ᶠ* him;
　　yet they do not return to the LORD
　　　their God,
　　or seek him, for all this.

---

a Gk Syr: Heb *your*　*b* Cn: Heb *like*　*c* Cn: Meaning
of Heb uncertain　*d* Syr: Heb *are a company*
e Gk Syr: Heb *brought near*　*f* Or *humbles*

Futile Reliance on the Nations

11 Ephraim has become like a dove,
    silly and without sense;
    they call upon Egypt, they go
        to Assyria.
12 As they go, I will cast my net
        over them;
    I will bring them down like birds of
        the air;
    I will discipline them according to
        the report made to their
        assembly. *a*
13 Woe to them, for they have strayed
        from me!
    Destruction to them, for they have
        rebelled against me!
    I would redeem them,
        but they speak lies against me.

14 They do not cry to me from the heart,
        but they wail upon their beds;
    they gash themselves for grain
        and wine;
    they rebel against me.
15 It was I who trained and
        strengthened their arms,
    yet they plot evil against me.
16 They turn to that which does not
        profit; *b*
    they have become like a
        defective bow;
    their officials shall fall by the sword
        because of the rage of their tongue.
    So much for their babbling in the
        land of Egypt.

Israel's Apostasy

8 Set the trumpet to your lips!
    One like a vulture *a* is over the house
        of the Lord,
    because they have broken my
        covenant,
    and transgressed my law.
2 Israel cries to me,
    'My God, we—Israel—know you!'
3 Israel has spurned the good;
    the enemy shall pursue him.

4 They made kings, but not
        through me;
    they set up princes, but without my
        knowledge.
    With their silver and gold they made
        idols
    for their own destruction.
5 Your calf is rejected, O Samaria.
    My anger burns against them.
    How long will they be incapable of
        innocence?
6 For it is from Israel,
    an artisan made it;
    it is not God.
    The calf of Samaria
        shall be broken to pieces. *c*

7 For they sow the wind,
    and they shall reap the whirlwind.
    The standing grain has no heads,
        it shall yield no meal;
    if it were to yield,
        foreigners would devour it.
8 Israel is swallowed up;
    now they are among the nations
        as a useless vessel.
9 For they have gone up to Assyria,
    a wild ass wandering alone;
    Ephraim has bargained for lovers.
10 Though they bargain with
        the nations,
    I will now gather them up.
    They shall soon writhe
        under the burden of kings
        and princes.

11 When Ephraim multiplied altars
        to expiate sin,
    they became to him altars for
        sinning.
12 Though I write for him the multitude
        of my instructions,
    they are regarded as a strange thing.
13 Though they offer choice sacrifices, *b*
    though they eat flesh,
    the Lord does not accept them.
    Now he will remember their iniquity,
        and punish their sins;
    they shall return to Egypt.
14 Israel has forgotten his Maker,
    and built palaces;

a Meaning of Heb uncertain   *b* Cn: Meaning of Heb
uncertain   *c* Or *shall go up in flames*

and Judah has multiplied fortified
　　cities;
　　but I will send a fire upon his cities,
　　and it shall devour his strongholds.

Punishment for Israel's Sin

9 Do not rejoice, O Israel!
　　Do not exult[a] as other nations do;
for you have played the whore,
　　departing from your God.
You have loved a prostitute's pay
　　on all threshing-floors.
2 Threshing-floor and wine vat shall
　　not feed them,
　　and the new wine shall fail them.
3 They shall not remain in the land of
　　the LORD;
　　but Ephraim shall return to Egypt,
　　and in Assyria they shall eat
　　unclean food.

4 They shall not pour drink-offerings of
　　wine to the LORD,
　　and their sacrifices shall not please
　　him.
Such sacrifices shall be like mourners'
　　bread;
　　all who eat of it shall be defiled;
for their bread shall be for their
　　hunger only;
　　it shall not come to the house of
　　the LORD.

5 What will you do on the day of
　　appointed festival,
　　and on the day of the festival of the
　　LORD?
6 For even if they escape destruction,
　　Egypt shall gather them,
　　Memphis shall bury them.
Nettles shall possess their precious
　　things of silver;[b]
　　thorns shall be in their tents.

7 The days of punishment have come,
　　the days of recompense have come;
　　Israel cries,[c]
'The prophet is a fool,
　　the man of the spirit is mad!'
Because of your great iniquity,
　　your hostility is great.

8 The prophet is a sentinel for my God
　　over Ephraim,
　　yet a fowler's snare is on all his ways,
　　and hostility in the house of
　　his God.
9 They have deeply corrupted
　　themselves
　　as in the days of Gibeah;
he will remember their iniquity,
　　he will punish their sins.

10 Like grapes in the wilderness,
　　I found Israel.
Like the first fruit on the fig tree,
　　in its first season,
　　I saw your ancestors.
But they came to Baal-peor,
　　and consecrated themselves to a
　　thing of shame,
　　and became detestable like the
　　thing they loved.
11 Ephraim's glory shall fly away like a
　　bird—
　　no birth, no pregnancy, no
　　conception!
12 Even if they bring up children,
　　I will bereave them until no one is
　　left.
Woe to them indeed
　　when I depart from them!
13 Once I saw Ephraim as a young palm
　　planted in a lovely meadow,[b]
　　but now Ephraim must lead out his
　　children for slaughter.
14 Give them, O LORD—
　　what will you give?
Give them a miscarrying womb
　　and dry breasts.

15 Every evil of theirs began at Gilgal;
　　there I came to hate them.
Because of the wickedness of
　　their deeds
　　I will drive them out of my house.
I will love them no more;
　　all their officials are rebels.

16 Ephraim is stricken,
　　their root is dried up,

a Gk: Heb To exultation　　b Meaning of Heb uncertain
c Cn Compare Gk: Heb shall know

they shall bear no fruit.
Even though they give birth,
  I will kill the cherished offspring of
    their womb.
17 Because they have not listened
    to him,
  my God will reject them;
  they shall become wanderers
    among the nations.

Israel's Sin and Captivity

10 Israel is a luxuriant vine
    that yields its fruit.
The more his fruit increased
  the more altars he built;
as his country improved,
  he improved his pillars.
2 Their heart is false;
  now they must bear their guilt.
The LORD*a* will break down
    their altars,
  and destroy their pillars.

3 For now they will say:
  'We have no king,
for we do not fear the LORD,
  and a king—what could he do
    for us?'
4 They utter mere words;
  with empty oaths they make
    covenants;
so litigation springs up like
    poisonous weeds
  in the furrows of the field.
5 The inhabitants of Samaria tremble
  for the calf*b* of Beth-aven.
Its people shall mourn for it,
  and its idolatrous priests shall wail*c*
    over it,
  over its glory that has departed
    from it.
6 The thing itself shall be carried to
    Assyria
  as tribute to the great king.*d*
Ephraim shall be put to shame,
  and Israel shall be ashamed of his
    idol.*e*

7 Samaria's king shall perish
  like a splinter on the face of
    the waters.

8 The high places of Aven, the sin
    of Israel,
  shall be destroyed.
Thorn and thistle shall grow up
  on their altars.
They shall say to the mountains,
    Cover us,
  and to the hills, Fall on us.

9 Since the days of Gibeah you have
    sinned, O Israel;
  there they have continued.
  Shall not war overtake them in
    Gibeah?
10 I will come*f* against the wayward
    people to punish them;
  and nations shall be gathered
    against them
  when they are punished*g* for their
    double iniquity.

11 Ephraim was a trained heifer
  that loved to thresh,
  and I spared her fair neck;
but I will make Ephraim break the
    ground;
  Judah must plough;
  Jacob must harrow for himself.
12 Sow for yourselves righteousness;
  reap steadfast love;
  break up your fallow ground;
for it is time to seek the LORD,
  that he may come and rain
    righteousness upon you.

13 You have ploughed wickedness,
  you have reaped injustice,
  you have eaten the fruit of lies.
Because you have trusted in
    your power
  and in the multitude of your
    warriors,
14 therefore the tumult of war shall rise
    against your people,
  and all your fortresses shall
    be destroyed,
  as Shalman destroyed Beth-arbel on
    the day of battle

a Heb *he*   *b* Gk Syr: Heb *calves*   *c* Cn: Heb *exult*
d Cn: Heb *to a king who will contend*   *e* Cn: Heb
counsel   *f* Cn Compare Gk: Heb *In my desire*
g Gk: Heb *bound*

when mothers were dashed in
  pieces with their children.
15 Thus it shall be done to you,
    O Bethel,
  because of your great wickedness.
  At dawn the king of Israel
    shall be utterly cut off.

God's Compassion Despite Israel's Ingratitude

11 When Israel was a child, I loved
    him,
  and out of Egypt I called my son.
2 The more I[a] called them,
    the more they went from me;[b]
  they kept sacrificing to the Baals,
    and offering incense to idols.

3 Yet it was I who taught Ephraim to
    walk,
    I took them up in my[c] arms;
  but they did not know that I healed
    them.
4 I led them with cords of human
    kindness,
    with bands of love.
  I was to them like those
    who lift infants to their cheeks.[d]
  I bent down to them and fed them.

5 They shall return to the land of
    Egypt,
    and Assyria shall be their king,
  because they have refused to return
    to me.
6 The sword rages in their cities,
    it consumes their oracle-priests,
  and devours because of their
    schemes.
7 My people are bent on turning away
    from me.
  To the Most High they call,
    but he does not raise them up
    at all.[e]

8 How can I give you up, Ephraim?
    How can I hand you over, O Israel?
  How can I make you like Admah?
    How can I treat you like Zeboiim?
  My heart recoils within me;

my compassion grows warm
    and tender.
9 I will not execute my fierce anger;
    I will not again destroy Ephraim;
  for I am God and no mortal,
    the Holy One in your midst,
    and I will not come in wrath.[e]

10 They shall go after the LORD,
    who roars like a lion;
  when he roars,
    his children shall come trembling
    from the west.
11 They shall come trembling like birds
    from Egypt,
    and like doves from the land of
    Assyria;
  and I will return them to their
    homes, says the LORD.

12[f] Ephraim has surrounded me
    with lies,
    and the house of Israel with deceit;
  but Judah still walks[g] with God,
    and is faithful to the Holy One.

12 Ephraim herds the wind,
    and pursues the east wind all
    day long;
  they multiply falsehood and
    violence;
    they make a treaty with Assyria,
    and oil is carried to Egypt.

The Long History of Rebellion

2 The LORD has an indictment against
    Judah,
    and will punish Jacob according to
    his ways,
    and repay him according to
    his deeds.
3 In the womb he tried to supplant his
    brother,
    and in his manhood he strove with
    God.
4 He strove with the angel and
    prevailed,
    he wept and sought his favour;
  he met him at Bethel,

a Gk: Heb *they*   b Gk: Heb *them*   c Gk Syr Vg: Heb
his   d Or *who ease the yoke on their jaws*   e Meaning
of Heb uncertain   f Ch 12.1 in Heb   g Heb *roams*
or *rules*

and there he spoke with him.[a]
5 The LORD the God of hosts,
    the LORD is his name!
6 But as for you, return to your God,
    hold fast to love and justice,
    and wait continually for your God.

7 A trader, in whose hands are false
        balances,
    he loves to oppress.
8 Ephraim has said, 'Ah, I am rich,
    I have gained wealth for myself;
  in all of my gain
    no offence has been found in me
    that would be sin.'[b]
9 I am the LORD your God
    from the land of Egypt;
  I will make you live in tents again,
    as on the days of the appointed
        festival.

10 I spoke to the prophets;
    it was I who multiplied visions,
    and through the prophets I will
        bring destruction.

11 In Gilead[c] there is iniquity,
    they shall surely come to nothing.
   In Gilgal they sacrifice bulls,
    so their altars shall be like
        stone heaps
    on the furrows of the field.
12 Jacob fled to the land of Aram;
    there Israel served for a wife,
    and for a wife he guarded sheep.[d]
13 By a prophet the LORD brought Israel
        up from Egypt,
    and by a prophet he was guarded.
14 Ephraim has given bitter offence,
    so his Lord will bring his crimes
        down on him
    and pay him back for his insults.

Relentless Judgement on Israel

13 When Ephraim spoke, there was
        trembling;
    he was exalted in Israel;
    but he incurred guilt through Baal
        and died.

a Gk Syr: Heb *us*   b Meaning of Heb uncertain
c Compare Syr: Heb *Gilead*   d Heb lacks *sheep*

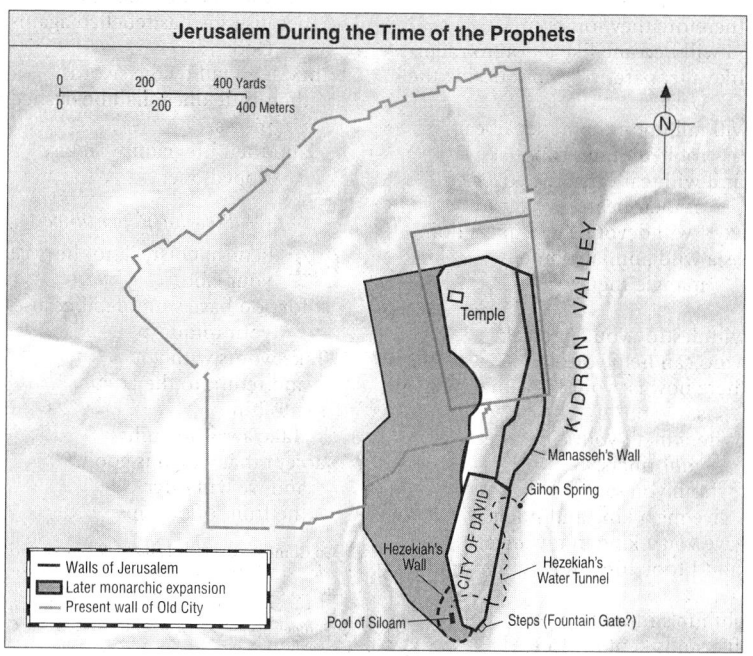

Jerusalem During the Time of the Prophets

0   200   400 Yards
0   200   400 Meters

N

KIDRON VALLEY

Temple

Manasseh's Wall

Gihon Spring

CITY OF DAVID

Hezekiah's
Wall

Hezekiah's
Water Tunnel

Pool of Siloam

Steps (Fountain Gate?)

— Walls of Jerusalem
▓ Later monarchic expansion
— Present wall of Old City

2 And now they keep on sinning
    and make a cast image for
        themselves,
idols of silver made according to
    their understanding,
all of them the work of artisans.
'Sacrifice to these', they say. *a*
    People are kissing calves!
3 Therefore they shall be like the
        morning mist
    or like the dew that goes away early,
like chaff that swirls from the
        threshing-floor
    or like smoke from a window.

4 Yet I have been the LORD your God
    ever since the land of Egypt;
you know no God but me,
    and besides me there is no saviour.
5 It was I who fed *b* you in the
        wilderness,
    in the land of drought.
6 When I fed *c* them, they were
        satisfied;
    they were satisfied, and their heart
        was proud;
    therefore they forgot me.
7 So I will become like a lion to them,
    like a leopard I will lurk beside the
        way.
8 I will fall upon them like a bear
        robbed of her cubs,
    and will tear open the covering
        of their heart;
    there I will devour them like a lion,
        as a wild animal would
            mangle them.

9 I will destroy you, O Israel;
    who can help you? *d*
10 Where now is *e* your king, that he may
        save you?
    Where in all your cities are
        your rulers,
of whom you said,
    'Give me a king and rulers'?
11 I gave you a king in my anger,
    and I took him away in my wrath.

12 Ephraim's iniquity is bound up;
    his sin is kept in store.

13 The pangs of childbirth come
        for him,
    but he is an unwise son;
for at the proper time he does not
        present himself
    at the mouth of the womb.

14 Shall I ransom them from the power
        of Sheol?
    Shall I redeem them from Death?
O Death, where are *f* your plagues?
    O Sheol, where is *f* your
        destruction?
    Compassion is hidden from
        my eyes.

15 Although he may flourish among
        rushes, *g*
    the east wind shall come, a blast
        from the LORD,
    rising from the wilderness;
and his fountain shall dry up,
    his spring shall be parched.
It shall strip his treasury
    of every precious thing.
16 *h* Samaria shall bear her guilt,
    because she has rebelled against her
        God;
they shall fall by the sword,
    their little ones shall be dashed in
        pieces,
    and their pregnant women
        ripped open.

A Plea for Repentance

14 Return, O Israel, to the LORD
    your God,
for you have stumbled because of
    your iniquity.
2 Take words with you
    and return to the LORD;
say to him,
    'Take away all guilt;
accept that which is good,
    and we will offer
    the fruit *i* of our lips.

a Cn Compare Gk: Heb *To these they say sacrifices of
people*   *b* Gk Syr: Heb *knew*   *c* Cn: Heb *according to
their pasture*   *d* Gk Syr: Heb *for in me is your help*
e Gk Syr Vg: Heb *I will be*   *f* Gk Syr: Heb *I will be*
g Or *among brothers*   *h* Ch 14.1 in Heb   *i* Gk Syr:
Heb *bulls*

3 Assyria shall not save us;
  we will not ride upon horses;
we will say no more, "Our God",
  to the work of our hands.
In you the orphan finds mercy.'

Assurance of Forgiveness

4 I will heal their disloyalty;
  I will love them freely,
  for my anger has turned from them.
5 I will be like the dew to Israel;
  he shall blossom like the lily,
  he shall strike root like the forests
    of Lebanon. *a*
6 His shoots shall spread out;
  his beauty shall be like the
    olive tree,
  and his fragrance like that of
    Lebanon.
7 They shall again live beneath
  my *b* shadow,

they shall flourish as a garden; *c*
they shall blossom like the vine,
  their fragrance shall be like the
    wine of Lebanon.

8 O Ephraim, what have I *d* to do with
    idols?
  It is I who answer and look
    after you. *e*
I am like an evergreen cypress;
  your faithfulness *f* comes from me.
9 Those who are wise understand these
    things;
  those who are discerning
    know them.
For the ways of the LORD are right,
  and the upright walk in them,
  but transgressors stumble in them.

a Cn: Heb *like Lebanon*   *b* Heb *his*   *c* Cn: Heb *they shall grow grain*   *d* Or *What more has Ephraim*
e Heb *him*   *f* Heb *your fruit*

JOEL

1 The word of the LORD that came to Joel son of Pethuel:

Lament over the Ruin of the Country

2 Hear this, O elders,
  give ear, all inhabitants of the land!
Has such a thing happened in
    your days,
  or in the days of your ancestors?
3 Tell your children of it,
  and let your children tell their
    children,
  and their children another
    generation.

4 What the cutting locust left,
  the swarming locust has eaten.
What the swarming locust left,
  the hopping locust has eaten,
and what the hopping locust left,
  the destroying locust has eaten.

5 Wake up, you drunkards, and weep;
  and wail, all you wine-drinkers,
over the sweet wine,
  for it is cut off from your mouth.
6 For a nation has invaded my land,
  powerful and innumerable;
its teeth are lions' teeth,
  and it has the fangs of a lioness.
7 It has laid waste my vines,
  and splintered my fig trees;
it has stripped off their bark and
    thrown it down;
  their branches have turned white.

8 Lament like a virgin dressed in
    sackcloth
  for the husband of her youth.

9 The grain-offering and the drink-
    offering are cut off
  from the house of the LORD.
The priests mourn,
  the ministers of the LORD.
10 The fields are devastated,
  the ground mourns;
for the grain is destroyed,
  the wine dries up,
  the oil fails.

11 Be dismayed, you farmers,
  wail, you vine-dressers,
over the wheat and the barley;
  for the crops of the field are
    ruined.
12 The vine withers,
  the fig tree droops.
Pomegranate, palm, and apple—
  all the trees of the field are
    dried up;
surely, joy withers away
  among the people.

A Call to Repentance and Prayer

13 Put on sackcloth and lament,
    you priests;
  wail, you ministers of the altar.
Come, pass the night in sackcloth,
  you ministers of my God!
Grain-offering and drink-offering
  are withheld from the house of
    your God.

14 Sanctify a fast,
  call a solemn assembly.
Gather the elders
  and all the inhabitants of the land
to the house of the LORD your God,
  and cry out to the LORD.

15 Alas for the day!
   For the day of the LORD is near,
      and as destruction from the
         Almighty[a] it comes.
16 Is not the food cut off
      before our eyes,
   joy and gladness
      from the house of our God?

17 The seed shrivels under the clods,[b]
      the storehouses are desolate;
   the granaries are ruined
      because the grain has failed.
18 How the animals groan!
      The herds of cattle wander about
   because there is no pasture for them;
      even the flocks of sheep are dazed.[c]

19 To you, O LORD, I cry.
   For fire has devoured
      the pastures of the wilderness,
   and flames have burned
      all the trees of the field.
20 Even the wild animals cry to you
      because the watercourses are dried
         up,
   and fire has devoured
      the pastures of the wilderness.

2 Blow the trumpet in Zion;
   sound the alarm on my holy
      mountain!
Let all the inhabitants of the land
      tremble,
   for the day of the LORD is coming, it
      is near—
2 a day of darkness and gloom,
      a day of clouds and thick darkness!
   Like blackness spread upon the
      mountains
      a great and powerful army comes;
   their like has never been from of old,
      nor will be again after them
      in ages to come.

3 Fire devours in front of them,
      and behind them a flame burns.
   Before them the land is like the
         garden of Eden,
      but after them a desolate
         wilderness,

   and nothing escapes them.

4 They have the appearance of horses,
      and like warhorses they charge.
5 As with the rumbling of chariots,
      they leap on the tops of the
         mountains,
   like the crackling of a flame of fire
      devouring the stubble,
   like a powerful army
      drawn up for battle.

6 Before them peoples are in anguish,
      all faces grow pale.[b]
7 Like warriors they charge,
      like soldiers they scale the wall.
   Each keeps to its own course,
      they do not swerve from[d]
         their paths.
8 They do not jostle one another,
      each keeps to its own track;
   they burst through the weapons
      and are not halted.
9 They leap upon the city,
      they run upon the walls;
   they climb up into the houses,
      they enter through the windows
         like a thief.

10 The earth quakes before them,
      the heavens tremble.
   The sun and the moon are darkened,
      and the stars withdraw their
         shining.
11 The LORD utters his voice
      at the head of his army;
   how vast is his host!
      Numberless are those who obey his
         command.
   Truly the day of the LORD is great;
      terrible indeed—who can
         endure it?

12 Yet even now, says the LORD,
      return to me with all your heart,
   with fasting, with weeping, and with
         mourning;

a Traditional rendering of Heb *Shaddai*   b Meaning of
Heb uncertain   c Compare Gk Syr Vg: Meaning of
Heb uncertain   d Gk Syr Vg: Heb *they do not take a
pledge along*

13 rend your hearts and not
         your clothing.
    Return to the LORD, your God,
       for he is gracious and merciful,
    slow to anger, and abounding in
         steadfast love,
       and relents from punishing.
14 Who knows whether he will not turn
         and relent,
       and leave a blessing behind him,
    a grain-offering and a drink-offering
       for the LORD, your God?

15 Blow the trumpet in Zion;
       sanctify a fast;
    call a solemn assembly;
16   gather the people.
    Sanctify the congregation;
       assemble the aged;
    gather the children,
       even infants at the breast.
    Let the bridegroom leave his room,
       and the bride her canopy.

17 Between the vestibule and the altar
       let the priests, the ministers of the
         LORD, weep.
    Let them say, 'Spare your people,
         O LORD,
       and do not make your heritage a
         mockery,
       a byword among the nations.
    Why should it be said among the
         peoples,
       "Where is their God?" '

God's Response and Promise

18 Then the LORD became jealous for his
         land,
       and had pity on his people.
19 In response to his people the
         LORD said:
    I am sending you
       grain, wine, and oil,
       and you will be satisfied;
    and I will no more make you
       a mockery among the nations.

20 I will remove the northern army far
       from you,

    and drive it into a parched and
         desolate land,
    its front into the eastern sea,
       and its rear into the western sea;
    its stench and foul smell will rise up.
       Surely he has done great things!

21 Do not fear, O soil;
       be glad and rejoice,
       for the LORD has done great things!
22 Do not fear, you animals of the field,
       for the pastures of the wilderness
         are green;
    the tree bears its fruit,
       the fig tree and vine give their full
         yield.

23 O children of Zion, be glad
       and rejoice in the LORD your God;
    for he has given the early rain[a] for
         your vindication,
       he has poured down for you
         abundant rain,
       the early and the later rain,
       as before.
24 The threshing-floors shall be full
         of grain,
       the vats shall overflow with wine
         and oil.

25 I will repay you for the years
       that the swarming locust has eaten,
    the hopper, the destroyer, and the
         cutter,
       my great army, which I sent against
         you.

26 You shall eat in plenty and be
         satisfied,
       and praise the name of the LORD
         your God,
       who has dealt wondrously with you.
    And my people shall never again be
         put to shame.
27 You shall know that I am in the midst
         of Israel,
       and that I, the LORD, am your God
         and there is no other.
    And my people shall never again
       be put to shame.

a Meaning of Heb uncertain

God's Spirit Poured Out

28 a Then afterwards
> I will pour out my spirit on
> all flesh;
> your sons and your daughters shall
> prophesy,
> your old men shall dream dreams,
> and your young men shall
> see visions.
29 Even on the male and female slaves,
> in those days, I will pour out
> my spirit.

30 I will show portents in the heavens and on the earth, blood and fire and columns of smoke. 31 The sun shall be turned to darkness, and the moon to blood, before the great and terrible day of the LORD comes. 32 Then everyone who calls on the name of the LORD shall be saved; for in Mount Zion and in Jerusalem there shall be those who escape, as the LORD has said, and among the survivors shall be those whom the LORD calls.

3 b For then, in those days and at that time, when I restore the fortunes of Judah and Jerusalem, 2 I will gather all the nations and bring them down to the valley of Jehoshaphat, and I will enter into judgement with them there, on account of my people and my heritage Israel, because they have scattered them among the nations. They have divided my land, 3 and cast lots for my people, and traded boys for prostitutes, and sold girls for wine, and drunk it down.

4 What are you to me, O Tyre and Sidon, and all the regions of Philistia? Are you paying me back for something? If you are paying me back, I will turn your deeds back upon your own heads swiftly and speedily. 5 For you have taken my silver and my gold, and have carried my rich treasures into your temples. c 6 You have sold the people of Judah and Jerusalem to the Greeks, removing them far from their own border. 7 But now I will rouse them to leave the places to which you have sold them, and I will turn your deeds back upon your own heads. 8 I will sell your sons and your daughters into the hand of the people of

Judah, and they will sell them to the Sabeans, to a nation far away; for the LORD has spoken.

Judgement in the Valley of Jehoshaphat

9 Proclaim this among the nations:
> Prepare war, d
> stir up the warriors.
> Let all the soldiers draw near,
> let them come up.
10 Beat your ploughshares into swords,
> and your pruning-hooks into
> spears;
> let the weakling say, 'I am a warrior.'

11 Come quickly, e
> all you nations all around,
> gather yourselves there.
> Bring down your warriors, O LORD.
12 Let the nations rouse themselves,
> and come up to the valley of
> Jehoshaphat;
> for there I will sit to judge
> all the neighbouring nations.

13 Put in the sickle,
> for the harvest is ripe.
> Go in, tread,
> for the wine press is full.
> The vats overflow,
> for their wickedness is great.

14 Multitudes, multitudes,
> in the valley of decision!
> For the day of the LORD is near
> in the valley of decision.
15 The sun and the moon are darkened,
> and the stars withdraw their
> shining.

16 The LORD roars from Zion,
> and utters his voice from
> Jerusalem,
> and the heavens and the earth
> shake.
> But the LORD is a refuge for his
> people,
> a stronghold for the people of
> Israel.

a Ch 3.1 in Heb   b Ch 4.1 in Heb   c Or palaces
d Heb sanctify war   e Meaning of Heb uncertain

The Glorious Future of Judah

17 So you shall know that I, the LORD
        your God,
    dwell in Zion, my holy mountain.
And Jerusalem shall be holy,
    and strangers shall never again pass
        through it.

18 On that day
    the mountains shall drip sweet wine,
    the hills shall flow with milk,
and all the stream beds of Judah
    shall flow with water;
a fountain shall come forth from the
    house of the LORD

and water the Wadi Shittim.

19 Egypt shall become a desolation
    and Edom a desolate wilderness,
because of the violence done to the
        people of Judah,
    in whose land they have shed
        innocent blood.
20 But Judah shall be inhabited for ever,
    and Jerusalem to all generations.
21 I will avenge their blood, and I will
        not clear the guilty, *a*
    for the LORD dwells in Zion.

a Gk Syr: Heb *I will hold innocent their blood that I have*
not held innocent

AMOS

1 The words of Amos, who was among the shepherds of Tekoa, which he saw concerning Israel in the days of King Uzziah of Judah and in the days of King Jeroboam son of Joash of Israel, two years *a* before the earthquake.

Judgement on Israel's Neighbours

2 And he said:
The LORD roars from Zion,
  and utters his voice from Jerusalem;
the pastures of the shepherds wither,
  and the top of Carmel dries up.

3 Thus says the LORD:
For three transgressions of Damascus,
  and for four, I will not revoke the
    punishment; *b*
because they have threshed Gilead
  with threshing-sledges of iron.
4 So I will send a fire on the house
    of Hazael,
  and it shall devour the strongholds
    of Ben-hadad.
5 I will break the gate-bars of
    Damascus,
  and cut off the inhabitants from the
    Valley of Aven,
and the one who holds the sceptre
    from Beth-eden;
  and the people of Aram shall go
    into exile to Kir,
                    says the LORD.

6 Thus says the LORD:
For three transgressions of Gaza,
  and for four, I will not revoke the
    punishment; *b*
because they carried into exile entire
    communities,

to hand them over to Edom.
7 So I will send a fire on the wall
    of Gaza,
  fire that shall devour its
    strongholds.
8 I will cut off the inhabitants from
    Ashdod,
  and the one who holds the sceptre
    from Ashkelon;
I will turn my hand against Ekron,
  and the remnant of the Philistines
    shall perish,
                    says the Lord GOD.

9 Thus says the LORD:
For three transgressions of Tyre,
  and for four, I will not revoke the
    punishment; *b*
because they delivered entire
    communities over to Edom,
  and did not remember the
    covenant of kinship.
10 So I will send a fire on the wall
    of Tyre,
  fire that shall devour its
    strongholds.

11 Thus says the LORD:
For three transgressions of Edom,
  and for four, I will not revoke the
    punishment; *b*
because he pursued his brother with
    the sword
  and cast off all pity;
he maintained his anger perpetually, *c*
  and kept his wrath *d* for ever.
12 So I will send a fire on Teman,

a Or *during two years*   *b* Heb *cause it to return*
c Syr Vg: Heb *and his anger tore perpetually*
d Gk Syr Vg: Heb *and his wrath kept*

and it shall devour the strongholds
   of Bozrah.

13 Thus says the LORD:
For three transgressions of the
   Ammonites,
   and for four, I will not revoke the
      punishment;*a*
because they have ripped open
   pregnant women in Gilead
in order to enlarge their territory.
14 So I will kindle a fire against the wall
   of Rabbah,
   fire that shall devour its strongholds,
with shouting on the day of battle,
   with a storm on the day of the
      whirlwind;
15 then their king shall go into exile,
   he and his officials together,
                says the LORD.

2 Thus says the LORD:
  For three transgressions of Moab,
   and for four, I will not revoke the
      punishment;*a*

God's Judgement in Amos

because he burned to lime
   the bones of the king of Edom.
2 So I will send a fire on Moab,
   and it shall devour the strongholds
      of Kerioth,
and Moab shall die amid uproar,
   amid shouting and the sound of
      the trumpet;
3 I will cut off the ruler from its midst,
   and will kill all its officials
      with him,
                says the LORD.

Judgement on Judah

4 Thus says the LORD:
For three transgressions of Judah,
   and for four, I will not revoke the
      punishment;*a*
because they have rejected the law of
   the LORD,
   and have not kept his statutes,
but they have been led astray by the
   same lies
   after which their ancestors walked.
5 So I will send a fire on Judah,
   and it shall devour the strongholds
      of Jerusalem.

Judgement on Israel

6 Thus says the LORD:
For three transgressions of Israel,
   and for four, I will not revoke the
      punishment;*a*
because they sell the righteous
   for silver,
   and the needy for a pair of
      sandals—
7 they who trample the head of the
      poor into the dust of the earth,
   and push the afflicted out of
      the way;
father and son go in to the same girl,
   so that my holy name is profaned;
8 they lay themselves down beside
      every altar
   on garments taken in pledge;
and in the house of their God
      they drink
   wine bought with fines they
      imposed.

a Heb *cause it to return*

9 Yet I destroyed the Amorite
    before them,
  whose height was like the height of
    cedars,
  and who was as strong as oaks;
  I destroyed his fruit above,
  and his roots beneath.
10 Also I brought you up out of the land
    of Egypt,
  and led you for forty years in
    the wilderness,
  to possess the land of the
    Amorite.
11 And I raised up some of your
    children to be prophets
  and some of your youths to be
    nazirites. *a*
  Is it not indeed so, O people
    of Israel?
               says the LORD.

12 But you made the nazirites *a*
    drink wine,
  and commanded the prophets,
    saying, 'You shall not prophesy.'

13 So, I will press you down in
    your place,
  just as a cart presses down
  when it is full of sheaves. *b*
14 Flight shall perish from the swift,
  and the strong shall not retain their
    strength,
  nor shall the mighty save
    their lives;
15 those who handle the bow shall
    not stand,
  and those who are swift of foot
    shall not save themselves,
  nor shall those who ride horses
    save their lives;
16 and those who are stout of heart
    among the mighty
  shall flee away naked on that day,
            says the LORD.

Israel's Guilt and Punishment

3 Hear this word that the LORD has spoken against you, O people of Israel,
against the whole family that I brought up
out of the land of Egypt:

2 You only have I known
  of all the families of the earth;
  therefore I will punish you
    for all your iniquities.

3 Do two walk together
  unless they have made an
    appointment?
4 Does a lion roar in the forest,
  when it has no prey?
  Does a young lion cry out from
    its den,
  if it has caught nothing?
5 Does a bird fall into a snare on
    the earth,
  when there is no trap for it?
  Does a snare spring up from
    the ground,
  when it has taken nothing?
6 Is a trumpet blown in a city,
  and the people are not afraid?
  Does disaster befall a city,
  unless the LORD has done it?
7 Surely the Lord GOD does nothing,
  without revealing his secret
  to his servants the prophets.
8 The lion has roared;
  who will not fear?
  The Lord GOD has spoken;
  who can but prophesy?

9 Proclaim to the strongholds
    in Ashdod,
  and to the strongholds in the land
    of Egypt,
  and say, 'Assemble yourselves on
    Mount *c* Samaria,
  and see what great tumults are
    within it,
  and what oppressions are in
    its midst.'
10 They do not know how to do right,
    says the LORD,
  those who store up violence and
    robbery in their strongholds.
11 Therefore, thus says the Lord GOD:
  An adversary shall surround the land,
    and strip you of your defence;

a That is, *those separated* or *those consecrated*
b Meaning of Heb uncertain   *c* Gk Syr: Heb *the*
mountains of

and your strongholds shall be
plundered.

12 Thus says the LORD: As the shepherd rescues from the mouth of the lion two legs, or a piece of an ear, so shall the people of Israel who live in Samaria be rescued, with the corner of a couch and part[a] of a bed.

13 Hear, and testify against the house of
Jacob,
    says the Lord GOD, the God
      of hosts:
14 On the day I punish Israel for its
      transgressions,
    I will punish the altars of Bethel,
    and the horns of the altar shall be cut
      off
    and fall to the ground.
15 I will tear down the winter house as
      well as the summer house;
    and the houses of ivory shall
      perish,
    and the great houses[b] shall come to
      an end,
              says the LORD.

4 Hear this word, you cows of Bashan
    who are on Mount Samaria,
  who oppress the poor, who crush the
      needy,
  who say to their husbands, 'Bring
      something to drink!'
2 The Lord GOD has sworn by
      his holiness:
  The time is surely coming
      upon you,
  when they shall take you away with
      hooks,
    even the last of you with fish-
      hooks.
3 Through breaches in the wall you
      shall leave,
    each one straight ahead;
    and you shall be flung out into
      Harmon,[a]
              says the LORD.
4 Come to Bethel—and transgress;
    to Gilgal—and multiply
      transgression;

bring your sacrifices every morning,
    your tithes every three days;
5 bring a thank-offering of leavened
      bread,
    and proclaim freewill-offerings,
      publish them;
  for so you love to do, O people
      of Israel!
           says the Lord GOD.

Israel Rejects Correction

6 I gave you cleanness of teeth in all
      your cities,
    and lack of bread in all your places,
  yet you did not return to me,
             says the LORD.

7 And I also withheld the rain
      from you
    when there were still three months
      to the harvest;
  I would send rain on one city,
    and send no rain on another city;
  one field would be rained upon,
    and the field on which it did not
      rain withered;
8 so two or three towns wandered
      to one town
    to drink water, and were not
      satisfied;
  yet you did not return to me,
             says the LORD.

9 I struck you with blight and mildew;
    I laid waste[c] your gardens and your
      vineyards;
    the locust devoured your fig trees
      and your olive trees;
  yet you did not return to me,
             says the LORD.

10 I sent among you a pestilence after
      the manner of Egypt;
    I killed your young men with
      the sword;
    I carried away your horses;[d]
    and I made the stench of your
      camp go up into your nostrils;

a Meaning of Heb uncertain   b Or *many houses*
c Cn: Heb *the multitude of*   d Heb *with the captivity of
your horses*

yet you did not return to me,
                    says the LORD.

11 I overthrew some of you,
     as when God overthrew Sodom and
         Gomorrah,
     and you were like a brand snatched
         from the fire;
   yet you did not return to me,
                    says the LORD.

12 Therefore, thus I will do to you,
         O Israel;
     because I will do this to you,
     prepare to meet your God, O Israel!

13 For lo, the one who forms the
         mountains, creates the wind,
     reveals his thoughts to mortals,
   makes the morning darkness,
     and treads on the heights of
         the earth—
   the LORD, the God of hosts, is
         his name!

A Lament for Israel's Sin

5 Hear this word that I take up over you
     in lamentation, O house of Israel:
2 Fallen, no more to rise,
     is maiden Israel;
   forsaken on her land,
     with no one to raise her up.

3 For thus says the Lord GOD:
   The city that marched out a thousand
     shall have a hundred left,
   and that which marched out
         a hundred
     shall have ten left. *a*

4 For thus says the LORD to the house
         of Israel:
   Seek me and live;
5   but do not seek Bethel,
   and do not enter into Gilgal
     or cross over to Beer-sheba;
   for Gilgal shall surely go into exile,
     and Bethel shall come to nothing.

6 Seek the LORD and live,

or he will break out against the
         house of Joseph like fire,
     and it will devour Bethel, with no
         one to quench it.
7 Ah, you that turn justice to
         wormwood,
     and bring righteousness to
         the ground!

8 The one who made the Pleiades
         and Orion,
     and turns deep darkness into
         the morning,
     and darkens the day into night,
   who calls for the waters of the sea,
     and pours them out on the surface
         of the earth,
   the LORD is his name,
9 who makes destruction flash out
         against the strong,
     so that destruction comes upon the
         fortress.

10 They hate the one who reproves
         in the gate,
     and they abhor the one who speaks
         the truth.
11 Therefore, because you trample
         on the poor
     and take from them levies of grain,
   you have built houses of hewn stone,
     but you shall not live in them;
   you have planted pleasant vineyards,
     but you shall not drink their wine.
12 For I know how many are your
         transgressions,
     and how great are your sins—
   you who afflict the righteous, who
         take a bribe,
     and push aside the needy in
         the gate.
13 Therefore the prudent will keep silent
         in such a time;
     for it is an evil time.

14 Seek good and not evil,
     that you may live;
   and so the LORD, the God of hosts,
     will be with you,
     just as you have said.

---

a Heb adds *to the house of Israel*

15 Hate evil and love good,
        and establish justice in the gate;
    it may be that the LORD, the God
            of hosts,
        will be gracious to the remnant of
            Joseph.

16 Therefore thus says the LORD, the God
        of hosts, the Lord:
    In all the squares there shall be
            wailing;
        and in all the streets they shall say,
            'Alas! alas!'
    They shall call the farmers to
            mourning,
        and those skilled in lamentation, to
            wailing;
17 in all the vineyards there shall
            be wailing,
        for I will pass through the midst of
            you,

                            says the LORD.

The Day of the LORD a Dark Day

18 Alas for you who desire the day of the
        LORD!
    Why do you want the day of
            the LORD?
    It is darkness, not light;
19   as if someone fled from a lion,
        and was met by a bear;
    or went into the house and rested a
            hand against the wall,
        and was bitten by a snake.
20 Is not the day of the LORD darkness,
            not light,
        and gloom with no brightness in it?

21 I hate, I despise your festivals,
        and I take no delight in your
            solemn assemblies.
22 Even though you offer me your
            burnt-offerings and grain-
            offerings,
        I will not accept them;
    and the offerings of well-being of
            your fatted animals
        I will not look upon.
23 Take away from me the noise of your
            songs;

I will not listen to the melody of
        your harps.
24 But let justice roll down like waters,
        and righteousness like an ever-
            flowing stream.

25 Did you bring to me sacrifices and
offerings the forty years in the wilderness,
O house of Israel? 26 You shall take up
Sakkuth your king, and Kaiwan your star-
god, your images[a] that you made for yourselves; 27 therefore I will take you into exile
beyond Damascus, says the LORD, whose
name is the God of hosts.

Complacent Self-Indulgence Will Be Punished

6 Alas for those who are at ease
        in Zion,
    and for those who feel secure on
            Mount Samaria,
    the notables of the first of the
            nations,
        to whom the house of Israel
            resorts!
2 Cross over to Calneh, and see;
        from there go to Hamath the great;
        then go down to Gath of the
            Philistines.
    Are you better[b] than these kingdoms?
        Or is your[c] territory greater than
            their[d] territory,
3 O you that put far away the evil day,
        and bring near a reign of violence?

4 Alas for those who lie on beds
            of ivory,
        and lounge on their couches,
    and eat lambs from the flock,
        and calves from the stall;
5 who sing idle songs to the sound
            of the harp,
        and like David improvise on
            instruments of music;
6 who drink wine from bowls,
        and anoint themselves with the
            finest oils,
        but are not grieved over the ruin of
            Joseph!

a Heb your images, your star-god   b Or Are they better
c Heb their   d Heb your

7 Therefore they shall now be the first
        to go into exile,
     and the revelry of the loungers shall
        pass away.

8 The Lord GOD has sworn by himself
     (says the LORD, the God of hosts):
   I abhor the pride of Jacob
      and hate his strongholds;
      and I will deliver up the city and all
        that is in it.

9 If ten people remain in one house,
they shall die. 10 And if a relative, one who
burns the dead,[a] shall take up the body to
bring it out of the house, and shall say to
someone in the innermost parts of the
house, 'Is anyone else with you?' the answer will come, 'No.' Then the relative[b]
shall say, 'Hush! We must not mention the
name of the LORD.'

11 See, the LORD commands,
     and the great house shall be
        shattered to bits,
     and the little house to pieces.
12 Do horses run on rocks?
     Does one plough the sea with
        oxen?[c]
   But you have turned justice
        into poison
     and the fruit of righteousness into
        wormwood—
13 you who rejoice in Lo-debar,[d]
     who say, 'Have we not by our own
        strength
     taken Karnaim[e] for ourselves?'
14 Indeed, I am raising up against you a
        nation,
     O house of Israel, says the LORD,
        the God of hosts,
   and they shall oppress you from
        Lebo-hamath
     to the Wadi Arabah.

Locusts, Fire, and a Plumb-Line

7 This is what the Lord GOD showed me:
he was forming locusts at the time the
latter growth began to sprout (it was the
latter growth after the king's mowings).

2 When they had finished eating the grass
of the land, I said,
     'O Lord GOD, forgive, I beg you!
        How can Jacob stand?
        He is so small!'
3 The LORD relented concerning this;
     'It shall not be,' said the LORD.

4 This is what the Lord GOD showed me:
the Lord GOD was calling for a shower of
fire,[f] and it devoured the great deep and
was eating up the land. 5 Then I said,
     'O Lord GOD, cease, I beg you!
        How can Jacob stand?
        He is so small!'
6 The LORD relented concerning this;
     'This also shall not be,' said the
        Lord GOD.

7 This is what he showed me: the Lord
was standing beside a wall built with a
plumb-line, with a plumb-line in his hand.
8 And the LORD said to me, 'Amos, what do
you see?' And I said, 'A plumb-line.' Then
the Lord said,
     'See, I am setting a plumb-line
        in the midst of my people Israel;
        I will never again pass them by;
9 the high places of Isaac shall be made
        desolate,
     and the sanctuaries of Israel shall
        be laid waste,
     and I will rise against the house of
        Jeroboam with the sword.'

Amaziah Complains to the King

10 Then Amaziah, the priest of Bethel,
sent to King Jeroboam of Israel, saying,
'Amos has conspired against you in the
very centre of the house of Israel; the land
is not able to bear all his words. 11 For thus
Amos has said,
     "Jeroboam shall die by the sword,
        and Israel must go into exile
        away from his land." '
12 And Amaziah said to Amos, 'O seer, go,
flee away to the land of Judah, earn your
bread there, and prophesy there; 13 but

a Or who makes a burning for him   b Heb he
c Or Does one plough them with oxen   d Or in a
thing of nothingness   e Or horns   f Or for a
judgement by fire

never again prophesy at Bethel, for it is the king's sanctuary, and it is a temple of the kingdom.'

14 Then Amos answered Amaziah, 'I am *a* no prophet, nor a prophet's son; but I am *a* a herdsman, and a dresser of sycomore trees, 15 and the LORD took me from following the flock, and the LORD said to me, "Go, prophesy to my people Israel."
16 'Now therefore hear the word of the LORD.

You say, "Do not prophesy against Israel,
  and do not preach against the house of Isaac."
17 Therefore, thus says the LORD:
"Your wife shall become a prostitute in the city,
  and your sons and your daughters shall fall by the sword,
  and your land shall be parcelled out by line;
you yourself shall die in an unclean land,
  and Israel shall surely go into exile away from its land." '

The Basket of Fruit

8 This is what the Lord GOD showed me—a basket of summer fruit.*b* 2 He said, 'Amos, what do you see?' And I said, 'A basket of summer fruit.'*b* Then the LORD said to me,

'The end*c* has come upon my people Israel;
  I will never again pass them by.
3 The songs of the temple*d* shall become wailings on that day,'
     says the Lord GOD;
'the dead bodies shall be many,
  cast out in every place. Be silent!'

4 Hear this, you that trample on the needy,
  and bring to ruin the poor of the land,
5 saying, 'When will the new moon be over
  so that we may sell grain;
and the sabbath,
  so that we may offer wheat for sale?

We will make the ephah small and the shekel great,
  and practise deceit with false balances,
6 buying the poor for silver
  and the needy for a pair of sandals,
  and selling the sweepings of the wheat.'

7 The LORD has sworn by the pride of Jacob:
Surely I will never forget any of their deeds.
8 Shall not the land tremble on this account,
  and everyone mourn who lives in it,
and all of it rise like the Nile,
  and be tossed about and sink again, like the Nile of Egypt?

9 On that day, says the Lord GOD,
  I will make the sun go down at noon,
  and darken the earth in broad daylight.
10 I will turn your feasts into mourning,
  and all your songs into lamentation;
I will bring sackcloth on all loins,
  and baldness on every head;
I will make it like the mourning for an only son,
  and the end of it like a bitter day.

11 The time is surely coming, says the Lord GOD,
  when I will send a famine on the land;
not a famine of bread, or a thirst for water,
  but of hearing the words of the LORD.
12 They shall wander from sea to sea,
  and from north to east;
they shall run to and fro, seeking the word of the LORD,
  but they shall not find it.

---

a Or *was* *b* Heb *qayits* *c* Heb *qets* *d* Or *palace*

13 In that day the beautiful young
        women and the young men
    shall faint for thirst.
14 Those who swear by Ashimah
        of Samaria,
    and say, 'As your god lives, O Dan',
    and, 'As the way of Beer-sheba
        lives'—
    they shall fall, and never rise again.

The Destruction of Israel

9 I saw the LORD standing beside[a] the
    altar, and he said:
Strike the capitals until the
        thresholds shake,
    and shatter them on the heads of
        all the people;[b]
and those who are left I will kill with
        the sword;
    not one of them shall flee away,
    not one of them shall escape.

2 Though they dig into Sheol,
    from there shall my hand
        take them;
though they climb up to heaven,
    from there I will bring them
        down.
3 Though they hide themselves on the
        top of Carmel,
    from there I will search out and
        take them;
and though they hide from my sight
        at the bottom of the sea,
    there I will command the
        sea-serpent, and it
        shall bite them.
4 And though they go into captivity in
        front of their enemies,
    there I will command the sword,
        and it shall kill them;
and I will fix my eyes on them
    for harm and not for good.

5 The Lord, GOD of hosts,
he who touches the earth and
        it melts,
    and all who live in it mourn,
and all of it rises like the Nile,
    and sinks again, like the Nile
        of Egypt;

6 who builds his upper chambers in
        the heavens,
    and founds his vault upon
        the earth;
who calls for the waters of the sea,
    and pours them out upon the
        surface of the earth—
the LORD is his name.

7 Are you not like the Ethiopians[c]
        to me,
    O people of Israel? says the LORD.
Did I not bring Israel up from the
        land of Egypt,
    and the Philistines from Caphtor
        and the Arameans from Kir?
8 The eyes of the Lord GOD are upon
        the sinful kingdom,
    and I will destroy it from the face
        of the earth
    —except that I will not utterly
        destroy the house of Jacob,
                        says the LORD.

9 For lo, I will command,
    and shake the house of Israel
        among all the nations
as one shakes with a sieve,
    but no pebble shall fall to
        the ground.
10 All the sinners of my people shall die
        by the sword,
    who say, 'Evil shall not overtake or
        meet us.'

The Restoration of David's Kingdom

11 On that day I will raise up
    the booth of David that is fallen,
and repair its[d] breaches,
    and raise up its[e] ruins,
    and rebuild it as in the days of old;
12 in order that they may possess the
        remnant of Edom
    and all the nations who are called
        by my name,
    says the LORD who does this.

13 The time is surely coming, says
        the LORD,

a Or on   b Heb all of them   c Or Nubians; Heb
Cushites   d Gk: Heb their   e Gk: Heb his

when the one who ploughs shall
  overtake the one who reaps,
and the treader of grapes the one
  who sows the seed;
the mountains shall drip sweet wine,
and all the hills shall flow with it.
14 I will restore the fortunes of my
    people Israel,
  and they shall rebuild the ruined
    cities and inhabit them;

they shall plant vineyards and drink
  their wine,
and they shall make gardens and
  eat their fruit.
15 I will plant them upon their land,
  and they shall never again be
    plucked up
  out of the land that I have
    given them,
            says the Lord your God.

OBADIAH

Proud Edom Will Be Brought Low

1 The vision of Obadiah.

Thus says the Lord GOD concerning
    Edom:
We have heard a report from
    the LORD,
  and a messenger has been sent
    among the nations:
'Rise up! Let us rise against it
    for battle!'
2 I will surely make you least among
    the nations;
  you shall be utterly despised.
3 Your proud heart has deceived you,
  you that live in the clefts of
    the rock, *a*
  whose dwelling is in the heights.
You say in your heart,
  'Who will bring me down to
    the ground?'
4 Though you soar aloft like the eagle,
  though your nest is set among the
    stars,
  from there I will bring you down,
              says the LORD.

Pillage and Slaughter Will Repay Edom's Cruelty

5 If thieves came to you,
  if plunderers by night
  —how you have been destroyed!—
  would they not steal only what they
    wanted?
If grape-gatherers came to you,
  would they not leave gleanings?
6 How Esau has been pillaged,
  his treasures searched out!
7 All your allies have deceived you,
  they have driven you to the border;

your confederates have prevailed
    against you;
  those who ate *b* your bread have set
    a trap for you—
there is no understanding of it.
8 On that day, says the LORD,
  I will destroy the wise out of Edom,
  and understanding out of
    Mount Esau.
9 Your warriors shall be shattered,
  O Teman,
  so that everyone from Mount Esau
    will be cut off.

Edom Wronged His Brother

10 For the slaughter and violence done
    to your brother Jacob,
  shame shall cover you,
  and you shall be cut off for ever.
11 On the day that you stood aside,
  on the day that strangers carried off
    his wealth,
  and foreigners entered his gates
  and cast lots for Jerusalem,
  you too were like one of them.
12 But you should not have gloated *c*
    over *d* your brother
  on the day of his misfortune;
  you should not have rejoiced over the
    people of Judah
  on the day of their ruin;
  you should not have boasted
  on the day of distress.
13 You should not have entered the gate
    of my people
  on the day of their calamity;

---

a Or *clefts of Sela*   *b* Cn: Heb lacks *those who ate*
c Heb *But do not gloat* (and similarly up to and
including verse 14)   *d* Heb *on the day of*

you should not have joined in the
    gloating over Judah's*a* disaster
on the day of his calamity;
you should not have looted his goods
    on the day of his calamity.
14 You should not have stood at
      the crossings
    to cut off his fugitives;
you should not have handed over his
      survivors
    on the day of distress.

15 For the day of the LORD is near
      against all the nations.
    As you have done, it shall be done to
      you;
    your deeds shall return on your
      own head.
16 For as you have drunk on my
      holy mountain,
    all the nations around you
      shall drink;
they shall drink and gulp down,*b*
    and shall be as though they had
      never been.

Israel's Final Triumph

17 But on Mount Zion there shall be
      those that escape,
    and it shall be holy;
and the house of Jacob shall take
      possession of those who
      dispossessed them.

18 The house of Jacob shall be a fire,
    the house of Joseph a flame,
    and the house of Esau stubble;
they shall burn them and
      consume them,
    and there shall be no survivor of
      the house of Esau;
          for the LORD has spoken.
19 Those of the Negeb shall possess
      Mount Esau,
    and those of the Shephelah the
      land of the Philistines;
they shall possess the land of
      Ephraim and the land
      of Samaria,
    and Benjamin shall possess Gilead.
20 The exiles of the Israelites who are in
      Halah*c*
    shall possess*d* Phoenicia as far
      as Zarephath;
and the exiles of Jerusalem who are
      in Sepharad
    shall possess the towns of
      the Negeb.
21 Those who have been saved*e* shall go
      up to Mount Zion
    to rule Mount Esau;
    and the kingdom shall be
      the LORD's.

---

a Heb *his*   *b* Meaning of Heb uncertain
c Cn: Heb *in this army*   *d* Cn: Meaning of Heb
uncertain   *e* Or *Saviours*

JONAH

Jonah Tries to Run Away from God

1 Now the word of the Lord came to Jonah son of Amittai, saying, 2 'Go at once to Nineveh, that great city, and cry out against it; for their wickedness has come up before me.' 3 But Jonah set out to flee to Tarshish from the presence of the Lord. He went down to Joppa and found a ship going to Tarshish; so he paid his fare and went on board, to go with them to Tarshish, away from the presence of the Lord.

4 But the Lord hurled a great wind upon the sea, and such a mighty storm came upon the sea that the ship threatened to break up. 5 Then the mariners were afraid, and each cried to his god. They threw the cargo that was in the ship into the sea, to lighten it for them. Jonah, meanwhile, had gone down into the hold of the ship and had lain down, and was fast asleep. 6 The captain came and said to him, 'What are you doing sound asleep? Get up, call on your god! Perhaps the god will spare us a thought so that we do not perish.'

7 The sailors*a* said to one another, 'Come, let us cast lots, so that we may know on whose account this calamity has come upon us.' So they cast lots, and the lot fell on Jonah. 8 Then they said to him, 'Tell us why this calamity has come upon us. What is your occupation? Where do you come from? What is your country? And of what people are you?' 9 'I am a Hebrew,' he replied. 'I worship the Lord, the God of heaven, who made the sea and the dry land.' 10 Then the men were even more afraid, and said to him, 'What is this that you have done!' For the men knew that he was fleeing from the presence of the Lord, because he had told them so.

11 Then they said to him, 'What shall we do to you, that the sea may quieten down for us?' For the sea was growing more and more tempestuous. 12 He said to them, 'Pick me up and throw me into the sea; then the sea will quieten down for you; for I know it is because of me that this great storm has come upon you.' 13 Nevertheless, the men rowed hard to bring the ship back to land, but they could not, for the sea grew more and more stormy against them. 14 Then they cried out to the Lord, 'Please, O Lord, we pray, do not let us perish on account of this man's life. Do not make us guilty of innocent blood; for you, O Lord, have done as it pleased you.' 15 So they picked Jonah up and threw him into the sea; and the sea ceased from its raging. 16 Then the men feared the Lord even more, and they offered a sacrifice to the Lord and made vows.

17*b* But the Lord provided a large fish to swallow up Jonah; and Jonah was in the belly of the fish for three days and three nights.

A Psalm of Thanksgiving

2 Then Jonah prayed to the Lord his God from the belly of the fish, 2 saying,

'I called to the Lord out of my
distress,
and he answered me;
out of the belly of Sheol I cried,
and you heard my voice.
3 You cast me into the deep,
into the heart of the seas,
and the flood surrounded me;

a Heb *They*   *b* Ch 2.1 in Heb

all your waves and your billows
   passed over me.
4 Then I said, "I am driven away
   from your sight;
how*a* shall I look again
   upon your holy temple?"
5 The waters closed in over me;
   the deep surrounded me;
weeds were wrapped around my head
6   at the roots of the mountains.
I went down to the land
   whose bars closed upon me for
      ever;
yet you brought up my life from the
      Pit,
   O LORD my God.
7 As my life was ebbing away,
   I remembered the LORD;
and my prayer came to you,
   into your holy temple.
8 Those who worship vain idols
   forsake their true loyalty.
9 But I with the voice of thanksgiving
   will sacrifice to you;
what I have vowed I will pay.

Deliverance belongs to the LORD!'
10 Then the LORD spoke to the fish, and it
spewed Jonah out upon the dry land.

Conversion of Nineveh

3 The word of the LORD came to Jonah a
   second time, saying, 2 'Get up, go to
Nineveh, that great city, and proclaim to it
the message that I tell you.' 3 So Jonah set
out and went to Nineveh, according to the
word of the LORD. Now Nineveh was an exceedingly large city, a three days' walk
across. 4 Jonah began to go into the city, going a day's walk. And he cried out, 'Forty
days more, and Nineveh shall be overthrown!' 5 And the people of Nineveh believed God; they proclaimed a fast, and
everyone, great and small, put on sackcloth.

6 When the news reached the king of
Nineveh, he rose from his throne, removed
his robe, covered himself with sackcloth,
and sat in ashes. 7 Then he had a proclama-

a Theodotion: Heb *surely*

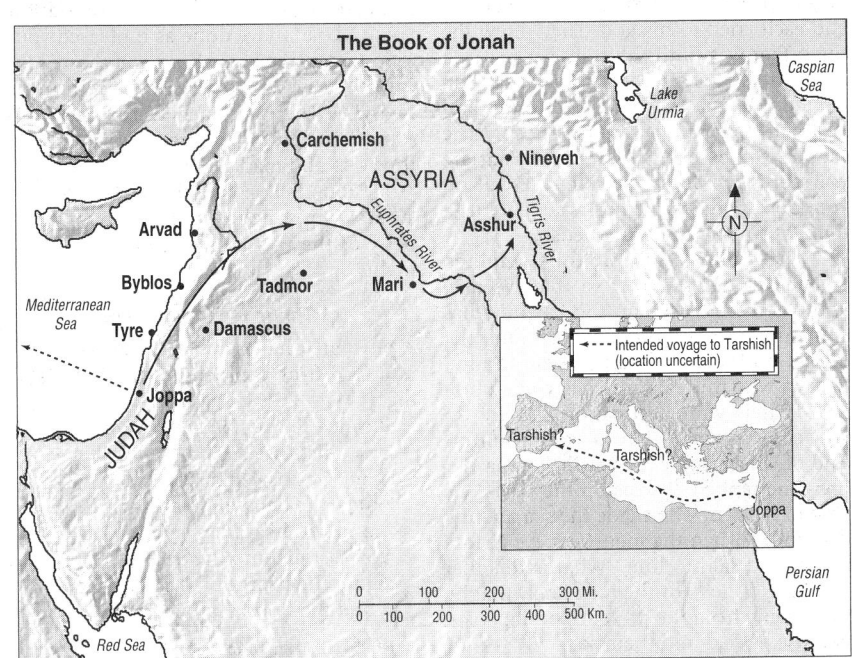

The Book of Jonah

tion made in Nineveh: 'By the decree of the king and his nobles: No human being or animal, no herd or flock, shall taste anything. They shall not feed, nor shall they drink water. 8 Human beings and animals shall be covered with sackcloth, and they shall cry mightily to God. All shall turn from their evil ways and from the violence that is in their hands. 9 Who knows? God may relent and change his mind; he may turn from his fierce anger, so that we do not perish.'

10 When God saw what they did, how they turned from their evil ways, God changed his mind about the calamity that he had said he would bring upon them; and he did not do it.

Jonah's Anger

4 But this was very displeasing to Jonah, and he became angry. 2 He prayed to the LORD and said, 'O LORD! Is not this what I said while I was still in my own country? That is why I fled to Tarshish at the beginning; for I knew that you are a gracious God and merciful, slow to anger, and abounding in steadfast love, and ready to relent from punishing. 3 And now, O LORD, please take my life from me, for it is better for me to die than to live.' 4 And the LORD said, 'Is it right for you to be angry?' 5 Then Jonah went out of the city and sat down east of the city, and made a booth for himself there. He sat under it in the shade, waiting to see what would become of the city.

6 The LORD God appointed a bush,*a* and made it come up over Jonah, to give shade over his head, to save him from his discomfort; so Jonah was very happy about the bush. 7 But when dawn came up the next day, God appointed a worm that attacked the bush, so that it withered. 8 When the sun rose, God prepared a sultry east wind, and the sun beat down on the head of Jonah so that he was faint and asked that he might die. He said, 'It is better for me to die than to live.'

Jonah Is Reproved

9 But God said to Jonah, 'Is it right for you to be angry about the bush?' And he said, 'Yes, angry enough to die.' 10 Then the LORD said, 'You are concerned about the bush, for which you did not labour and which you did not grow; it came into being in a night and perished in a night. 11 And should I not be concerned about Nineveh, that great city, in which there are more than a hundred and twenty thousand people who do not know their right hand from their left, and also many animals?'

a Heb *qiqayon*, possibly *the castor bean plant*

MICAH

1 The word of the Lord that came to Micah of Moresheth in the days of Kings Jotham, Ahaz, and Hezekiah of Judah, which he saw concerning Samaria and Jerusalem.

Judgement Pronounced against Samaria

2 Hear, you peoples, all of you;
    listen, O earth, and all that is in it;
and let the Lord God be a witness
        against you,
    the Lord from his holy temple.
3 For lo, the Lord is coming out of his
        place,
    and will come down and tread
        upon the high places of
        the earth.
4 Then the mountains will melt under
        him
    and the valleys will burst open,
like wax near the fire,
    like waters poured down a
        steep place.
5 All this is for the transgression
        of Jacob
    and for the sins of the house
        of Israel.
What is the transgression of Jacob?
    Is it not Samaria?
And what is the high place *a* of Judah?
    Is it not Jerusalem?
6 Therefore I will make Samaria a heap
        in the open country,
    a place for planting vineyards.
I will pour down her stones into
        the valley,
    and uncover her foundations.
7 All her images shall be beaten
        to pieces,

all her wages shall be burned with
        fire,
    and all her idols I will lay waste;
for as the wages of a prostitute she
        gathered them,
    and as the wages of a prostitute
        they shall again be used.

The Doom of the Cities of Judah

8 For this I will lament and wail;
    I will go barefoot and naked;
I will make lamentation like
        the jackals,
    and mourning like the ostriches.
9 For her wound *b* is incurable.
    It has come to Judah;
it has reached to the gate of
        my people,
    to Jerusalem.

10 Tell it not in Gath,
        weep not at all;
    in Beth-leaphrah
        roll yourselves in the dust.
11 Pass on your way,
        inhabitants of Shaphir,
        in nakedness and shame;
    the inhabitants of Zaanan
        do not come forth;
    Beth-ezel is wailing
        and shall remove its support
            from you.
12 For the inhabitants of Maroth
        wait anxiously for good,
    yet disaster has come down from the
            Lord
        to the gate of Jerusalem.
13 Harness the steeds to the chariots,

a Heb *what are the high places*   *b* Gk Syr Vg: Heb
wounds

inhabitants of Lachish;
it was the beginning of sin
  to daughter Zion,
for in you were found
  the transgressions of Israel.
14 Therefore you shall give parting gifts
    to Moresheth-gath;
the houses of Achzib shall be
    a deception
  to the kings of Israel.
15 I will again bring a conqueror
    upon you,
  inhabitants of Mareshah;
the glory of Israel
  shall come to Adullam.
16 Make yourselves bald and cut off
    your hair
  for your pampered children;
make yourselves as bald as the eagle,
  for they have gone from you
    into exile.

Social Evils Denounced

2 Alas for those who devise
    wickedness

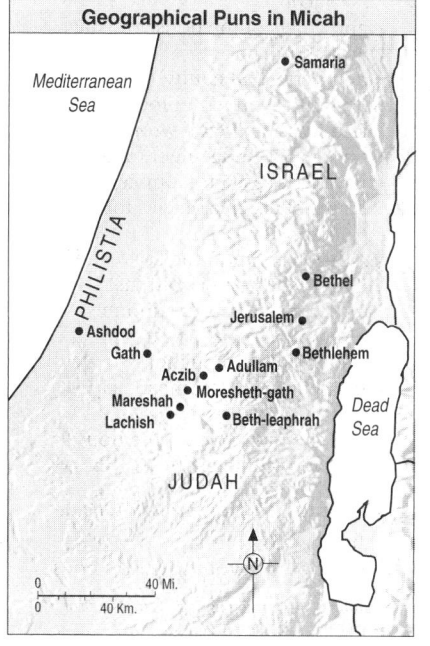

Geographical Puns in Micah

Mediterranean
Sea

ISRAEL

PHILISTIA

• Samaria

• Bethel

Jerusalem •

• Ashdod
Gath •
    Aczib • • Adullam
Mareshah • • Moresheth-gath
Lachish • • Beth-leaphrah

• Bethlehem

Dead
Sea

JUDAH

0   40 Mi.
0   40 Km.

and evil deeds^a on their beds!
When the morning dawns, they
    perform it,
  because it is in their power.
2 They covet fields, and seize them;
    houses, and take them away;
they oppress householder and
    house,
  people and their inheritance.
3 Therefore, thus says the LORD:
Now, I am devising against this
    family an evil
  from which you cannot remove
    your necks;
and you shall not walk haughtily,
  for it will be an evil time.
4 On that day they shall take up a
    taunt-song against you,
  and wail with bitter lamentation,
and say, 'We are utterly ruined;
  the LORD^b alters the inheritance of
    my people;
how he removes it from me!
  Among our captors^c he parcels out
    our fields.'
5 Therefore you will have no one to
    cast the line by lot
  in the assembly of the LORD.

6 'Do not preach'—thus they preach—
  'one should not preach of
    such things;
  disgrace will not overtake us.'
7 Should this be said, O house
    of Jacob?
  Is the LORD's patience exhausted?
  Are these his doings?
Do not my words do good
  to one who walks uprightly?
8 But you rise up against my people^d as
    an enemy;
  you strip the robe from the
    peaceful,^{e}
from those who pass by trustingly
  with no thought of war.
9 The women of my people you
    drive out
  from their pleasant houses;

from their young children you
    take away
  my glory for ever.
¹⁰ Arise and go;
  for this is no place to rest,
  because of uncleanness that destroys
    with a grievous destruction. *a*
¹¹ If someone were to go about uttering
    empty falsehoods,
  saying, 'I will preach to you of wine
    and strong drink',
  such a one would be the preacher
    for this people!

A Promise for the Remnant of Israel

¹² I will surely gather all of you,
    O Jacob,
  I will gather the survivors of Israel;
  I will set them together
    like sheep in a fold,
  like a flock in its pasture;
    it will resound with people.
¹³ The one who breaks out will go up
    before them;
  they will break through and pass
    the gate,
  going out by it.
  Their king will pass on before them,
    the LORD at their head.

Wicked Rulers and Prophets

3 And I said:
  Listen, you heads of Jacob
    and rulers of the house of Israel!
  Should you not know justice?—
² you who hate the good and love
    the evil,
  who tear the skin off my people, *b*
    and the flesh off their bones;
³ who eat the flesh of my people,
    flay their skin off them,
  break their bones in pieces,
    and chop them up like meat *c* in a
      kettle,
    like flesh in a cauldron.

⁴ Then they will cry to the LORD,
    but he will not answer them;
  he will hide his face from them at
    that time,
  because they have acted wickedly.

⁵ Thus says the LORD concerning
    the prophets
  who lead my people astray,
  who cry 'Peace'
    when they have something to eat,
  but declare war against those
    who put nothing into their mouths.
⁶ Therefore it shall be night to you,
    without vision,
  and darkness to you, without
    revelation.
  The sun shall go down upon
    the prophets,
  and the day shall be black
    over them;
⁷ the seers shall be disgraced,
    and the diviners put to shame;
  they shall all cover their lips,
    for there is no answer from God.
⁸ But as for me, I am filled with power,
    with the spirit of the LORD,
  and with justice and might,
  to declare to Jacob his transgression
    and to Israel his sin.

⁹ Hear this, you rulers of the house of
    Jacob
  and chiefs of the house of Israel,
  who abhor justice
    and pervert all equity,
¹⁰ who build Zion with blood
    and Jerusalem with wrong!
¹¹ Its rulers give judgement for a bribe,
    its priests teach for a price,
  its prophets give oracles for
    money;
  yet they lean upon the LORD and say,
    'Surely the LORD is with us!
  No harm shall come upon us.'
¹² Therefore because of you
    Zion shall be ploughed as a field;
  Jerusalem shall become a heap
    of ruins,
  and the mountain of the house a
    wooded height.

Peace and Security through Obedience

4 In days to come
  the mountain of the LORD's house

---

a Meaning of Heb uncertain   *b* Heb *from them*
c Gk: Heb *as*

shall be established as the highest of
the mountains,
and shall be raised up above
the hills.
Peoples shall stream to it,
2   and many nations shall come
and say:
'Come, let us go up to the mountain
of the LORD,
to the house of the God of Jacob;
that he may teach us his ways
and that we may walk in his paths.'
For out of Zion shall go forth
instruction,
and the word of the LORD
from Jerusalem.
3 He shall judge between many
peoples,
and shall arbitrate between strong
nations far away;
they shall beat their swords into
ploughshares,
and their spears into pruning-
hooks;
nation shall not lift up sword against
nation,
neither shall they learn war
any more;
4 but they shall all sit under their own
vines and under their own fig
trees,
and no one shall make them afraid;
for the mouth of the LORD of hosts
has spoken.

5 For all the peoples walk,
each in the name of its god,
but we will walk in the name of the
LORD our God
for ever and ever.

Restoration Promised after Exile

6 On that day, says the LORD,
I will assemble the lame
and gather those who have been
driven away,
and those whom I have afflicted.
7 The lame I will make the remnant,
and those who were cast off, a
strong nation;

and the LORD will reign over them in
Mount Zion
now and for evermore.

8 And you, O tower of the flock,
hill of daughter Zion,
to you it shall come,
the former dominion shall come,
the sovereignty of daughter
Jerusalem.

9 Now why do you cry aloud?
Is there no king in you?
Has your counsellor perished,
that pangs have seized you like a
woman in labour?
10 Writhe and groan,ᵃ O daughter Zion,
like a woman in labour;
for now you shall go forth from
the city
and camp in the open country;
you shall go to Babylon.
There you shall be rescued,
there the LORD will redeem you
from the hands of your enemies.

11 Now many nations
are assembled against you,
saying, 'Let her be profaned,
and let our eyes gaze upon Zion.'
12 But they do not know
the thoughts of the LORD;
they do not understand his plan,
that he has gathered them as
sheaves to the threshing-floor.
13 Arise and thresh,
O daughter Zion,
for I will make your horn iron
and your hoofs bronze;
you shall beat in pieces many peoples,
and shallᵇ devote their gain to the
LORD,
their wealth to the Lord of the
whole earth.

5 ᶜ Now you are walled around with
a wall;ᵈ
siege is laid against us;

a Meaning of Heb uncertain   b Gk Syr Tg: Heb
and I will   c Ch 4.14 in Heb   d Cn Compare Gk:
Meaning of Heb uncertain

with a rod they strike the ruler
    of Israel
upon the cheek.

The Ruler from Bethlehem

2 *a* But you, O Bethlehem of Ephrathah,
    who are one of the little clans
        of Judah,
from you shall come forth for me
    one who is to rule in Israel,
whose origin is from of old,
    from ancient days.
3 Therefore he shall give them up until
        the time
    when she who is in labour has
        brought forth;
then the rest of his kindred shall
        return
    to the people of Israel.
4 And he shall stand and feed his flock
        in the strength of the LORD,
    in the majesty of the name of the
        LORD his God.
And they shall live secure, for now he
        shall be great
    to the ends of the earth;
5 and he shall be the one of peace.

    If the Assyrians come into our land
    and tread upon our soil, *b*
we will raise against them seven
        shepherds
    and eight installed as rulers.
6 They shall rule the land of Assyria
        with the sword,
    and the land of Nimrod with the
        drawn sword; *c*
they *d* shall rescue us from the
        Assyrians
    if they come into our land
    or tread within our border.

The Future Role of the Remnant

7 Then the remnant of Jacob,
    surrounded by many peoples,
shall be like dew from the LORD,
    like showers on the grass,
which do not depend upon people
    or wait for any mortal.
8 And among the nations the remnant
    of Jacob,

surrounded by many peoples,
shall be like a lion among the
        animals of the forest,
    like a young lion among the flocks
        of sheep,
which, when it goes through,
        treads down
    and tears in pieces, with no one to
        deliver.
9 Your hand shall be lifted up over
        your adversaries,
    and all your enemies shall be
        cut off.

10 On that day, says the LORD,
    I will cut off your horses from
        among you
    and will destroy your chariots;
11 and I will cut off the cities of
        your land
    and throw down all your
        strongholds;
12 and I will cut off sorceries from your
        hand,
    and you shall have no more
        soothsayers;
13 and I will cut off your images
    and your pillars from among you,
and you shall bow down no more
    to the work of your hands;
14 and I will uproot your sacred poles *e*
    from among you
    and destroy your towns.
15 And in anger and wrath I will execute
        vengeance
    on the nations that did not obey.

God Challenges Israel

6 Hear what the LORD says:
   Rise, plead your case before
    the mountains,
and let the hills hear your voice.
2 Hear, you mountains, the controversy
    of the LORD,
    and you enduring foundations of
        the earth;
for the LORD has a controversy with
    his people,
    and he will contend with Israel.

a Ch 5.1 in Heb   *b* Gk: Heb *in our palaces*
c Cn: Heb *in its entrances*   *d* Heb *he*   *e* Heb *Asherim*

3 'O my people, what have I done
        to you?
    In what have I wearied you? Answer
        me!
4 For I brought you up from the land
        of Egypt,
    and redeemed you from the house
        of slavery;
    and I sent before you Moses,
        Aaron, and Miriam.
5 O my people, remember now what
        King Balak of Moab devised,
    what Balaam son of Beor answered
        him,
    and what happened from Shittim
        to Gilgal,
    that you may know the saving acts
        of the LORD.'

What God Requires

6 'With what shall I come before
        the LORD,
    and bow myself before God
        on high?
    Shall I come before him with burnt-
        offerings,
    with calves a year old?
7 Will the LORD be pleased with
        thousands of rams,
    with tens of thousands of rivers
        of oil?
    Shall I give my firstborn for my
        transgression,
    the fruit of my body for the sin of
        my soul?'
8 He has told you, O mortal, what
        is good;
    and what does the LORD require of
        you
    but to do justice, and to love
        kindness,
    and to walk humbly with
        your God?

Cheating and Violence to Be Punished

9 The voice of the LORD cries to the
        city
    (it is sound wisdom to fear
        your name):
    Hear, O tribe and assembly of
        the city! [a]

10 Can I forget [b] the treasures of
        wickedness in the house of the
        wicked,
    and the scant measure that is
        accursed?
11 Can I tolerate wicked scales
    and a bag of dishonest weights?
12 Your [c] wealthy are full of violence;
    your [d] inhabitants speak lies,
    with tongues of deceit in
        their mouths.
13 Therefore I have begun [e] to strike you
        down,
    making you desolate because of
        your sins.
14 You shall eat, but not be satisfied,
    and there shall be a gnawing
        hunger within you;
    you shall put away, but not save,
    and what you save, I will hand over
        to the sword.
15 You shall sow, but not reap;
    you shall tread olives, but not
        anoint yourselves with oil;
    you shall tread grapes, but not
        drink wine.
16 For you have kept the statutes
        of Omri [f]
    and all the works of the house
        of Ahab,
    and you have followed their
        counsels.
    Therefore I will make you a
        desolation, and your [g]
        inhabitants an object of hissing;
    so you shall bear the scorn of
        my people.

The Total Corruption of the People

7 Woe is me! For I have become like
        one who,
    after the summer fruit has
        been gathered,
    after the vintage has been gleaned,
    finds no cluster to eat;
        there is no first-ripe fig for which I
            hunger.

a Cn Compare Gk: Heb *tribe, and who has appointed it
yet?*   *b* Cn: Meaning of Heb uncertain   *c* Heb *Whose*
d Heb *whose*   *e* Gk Syr Vg: Heb *have made sick*
f Gk Syr Vg Tg: Heb *the statutes of Omri are kept*
g Heb *its*

2 The faithful have disappeared from
    the land,
  and there is no one left who
    is upright;
they all lie in wait for blood,
  and they hunt each other with nets.
3 Their hands are skilled to do evil;
  the official and the judge ask for a
    bribe,
and the powerful dictate what
    they desire;
  thus they pervert justice. *a*
4 The best of them is like a brier,
  the most upright of them a
    thorn hedge.
The day of their *b* sentinels, of their *b*
    punishment, has come;
  now their confusion is at hand.
5 Put no trust in a friend,
  have no confidence in a loved one;
guard the doors of your mouth
  from her who lies in your embrace;
6 for the son treats the father with
    contempt,
  the daughter rises up against
    her mother,
the daughter-in-law against her
    mother-in-law;
  your enemies are members of your
    own household.
7 But as for me, I will look to the LORD,
  I will wait for the God of my
    salvation;
  my God will hear me.

Penitence and Trust in God

8 Do not rejoice over me, O my enemy;
  when I fall, I shall rise;
when I sit in darkness,
  the LORD will be a light to me.
9 I must bear the indignation of
    the LORD,
  because I have sinned against him,
until he takes my side
  and executes judgement for me.
He will bring me out to the light;
  I shall see his vindication.
10 Then my enemy will see,
  and shame will cover her who said
    to me,
  'Where is the LORD your God?'

My eyes will see her downfall; *c*
  now she will be trodden down
  like the mire of the streets.

A Prophecy of Restoration

11 A day for the building of your walls!
  In that day the boundary shall be
    far extended.
12 In that day they will come to you
    from Assyria to *d* Egypt,
  and from Egypt to the River,
    from sea to sea and from mountain
    to mountain.
13 But the earth will be desolate
    because of its inhabitants,
  for the fruit of their doings.

14 Shepherd your people with your staff,
  the flock that belongs to you,
which lives alone in a forest
  in the midst of a garden land;
let them feed in Bashan and Gilead
  as in the days of old.
15 As in the days when you came out of
    the land of Egypt,
  show us *e* marvellous things.
16 The nations shall see and be ashamed
  of all their might;
they shall lay their hands on
    their mouths;
  their ears shall be deaf;
17 they shall lick dust like a snake,
  like the crawling things of
    the earth;
they shall come trembling out of
    their fortresses;
  they shall turn in dread to the LORD
    our God,
  and they shall stand in fear of you.

God's Compassion and Steadfast Love

18 Who is a God like you, pardoning
    iniquity
  and passing over the transgression
  of the remnant of your *f* possession?
He does not retain his anger for ever,
  because he delights in showing
    clemency.

a Cn: Heb *they weave it*　*b* Heb *your*　*c* Heb
lacks *downfall*　*d* One Ms: MT *Assyria and cities of*
e Cn: Heb *I will show him*　*f* Heb *his*

19 He will again have compassion upon
    us;
    he will tread our iniquities
       under foot.
    You will cast all our[a] sins
    into the depths of the sea.
20 You will show faithfulness to Jacob
    and unswerving loyalty to
       Abraham,
    as you have sworn to our ancestors
       from the days of old.

a Gk Syr Vg Tg: Heb *their*

NAHUM

1 An oracle concerning Nineveh. The book of the vision of Nahum of Elkosh.

The Consuming Wrath of God

2 A jealous and avenging God is
  the LORD,
    the LORD is avenging and wrathful;
  the LORD takes vengeance on his
    adversaries
    and rages against his enemies.
3 The LORD is slow to anger but great in
    power,
    and the LORD will by no means
      clear the guilty.

  His way is in whirlwind and storm,
    and the clouds are the dust of
      his feet.
4 He rebukes the sea and makes it dry,
    and he dries up all the rivers;
  Bashan and Carmel wither,
    and the bloom of Lebanon fades.
5 The mountains quake before him,
    and the hills melt;
  the earth heaves before him,
    the world and all who live in it.

6 Who can stand before his
      indignation?
    Who can endure the heat of
      his anger?
  His wrath is poured out like fire,
    and by him the rocks are broken in
      pieces.
7 The LORD is good,
    a stronghold on a day of trouble;
  he protects those who take refuge in
      him,
8   even in a rushing flood.

He will make a full end of his
    adversaries, *a*
  and will pursue his enemies into
    darkness.
9 Why do you plot against the LORD?
  He will make an end;
    no adversary will rise up twice.
10 Like thorns they are entangled,
    like drunkards they are drunk;
  they are consumed like dry straw.
11 From you one has gone out
    who plots evil against the LORD,
    one who counsels wickedness.

Good News for Judah

12 Thus says the LORD,
  'Though they are at full strength and
      many, *b*
    they will be cut off and pass away.
  Though I have afflicted you,
    I will afflict you no more.
13 And now I will break off his yoke
      from you
    and snap the bonds that bind you.'

14 The LORD has commanded
      concerning you:
    'Your name shall be perpetuated no
      longer;
  from the house of your gods I will cut
      off
    the carved image and the
      cast image.
  I will make your grave, for you
    are worthless.'

15 *c* Look! On the mountains the feet
    of one

---

a Gk: Heb *of her place*   *b* Meaning of Heb uncertain
c Ch 2.1 in Heb

who brings good tidings,
who proclaims peace!
Celebrate your festivals, O Judah,
fulfil your vows,
for never again shall the wicked
invade you;
they are utterly cut off.

The Destruction of the Wicked City

2 A shatterer[a] has come up
against you.
Guard the ramparts;
watch the road;
gird your loins;
collect all your strength.

2 (For the LORD is restoring the majesty
of Jacob,
as well as the majesty of Israel,
though ravagers have ravaged them
and ruined their branches.)

3 The shields of his warriors are red;
his soldiers are clothed in crimson.
The metal on the chariots flashes
on the day when he musters them;
the chargers[b] prance.
4 The chariots race madly through the
streets,
they rush to and fro through
the squares;
their appearance is like torches,
they dart like lightning.
5 He calls his officers;
they stumble as they come forward;
they hasten to the wall,
and the mantelet[c] is set up.
6 The river gates are opened,
the palace trembles.
7 It is decreed[c] that the city[d] be exiled,
its slave women led away,
moaning like doves
and beating their breasts.
8 Nineveh is like a pool
whose waters[e] run away.
'Halt! Halt!'—
but no one turns back.
9 'Plunder the silver,
plunder the gold!
There is no end of treasure!

An abundance of every precious
thing!'

10 Devastation, desolation, and
destruction!
Hearts faint and knees tremble,
all loins quake,
all faces grow pale!
11 What became of the lions' den,
the cave[f] of the young lions,
where the lion goes,
and the lion's cubs, with no one to
disturb them?
12 The lion has torn enough for
his whelps
and strangled prey for his lionesses;
he has filled his caves with prey
and his dens with torn flesh.

13 See, I am against you, says the LORD
of hosts, and I will burn your[g] chariots in
smoke, and the sword shall devour your
young lions; I will cut off your prey from
the earth, and the voice of your messengers
shall be heard no more.

Ruin Imminent and Inevitable

3 Ah! City of bloodshed,
utterly deceitful, full of booty—
no end to the plunder!
2 The crack of whip and rumble
of wheel,
galloping horse and bounding
chariot!
3 Horsemen charging,
flashing sword and glittering spear,
piles of dead,
heaps of corpses,
dead bodies without end—
they stumble over the bodies!
4 Because of the countless debaucheries
of the prostitute,
gracefully alluring, mistress
of sorcery,
who enslaves[h] nations through her
debaucheries,
and peoples through her sorcery,

---

a Cn: Heb *scatterer*   b Cn Compare Gk Syr: Heb
cypresses   c Meaning of Heb uncertain   d Heb *it*
e Cn Compare Gk: Heb *a pool, from the days that she
has become, and they*   f Cn: Heb *pasture*   g Heb *her*
h Heb *sells*

5 I am against you,
　　says the LORD of hosts,
　　and will lift up your skirts over your
　　　face;
　　and I will let nations look on your
　　　nakedness
　　and kingdoms on your shame.
6 I will throw filth at you
　　and treat you with contempt,
　　and make you a spectacle.
7 Then all who see you will shrink
　　　from you and say,
　　'Nineveh is devastated; who will
　　　bemoan her?'
　　Where shall I seek comforters
　　　for you?

8 Are you better than Thebes[a]
　　that sat by the Nile,
　with water around her,
　　her rampart a sea,
　　water her wall?
9 Ethiopia[b] was her strength,
　　Egypt too, and that without limit;
　　Put and the Libyans were her[c]
　　　helpers.

10 Yet she became an exile,
　　she went into captivity;
　even her infants were dashed
　　　in pieces
　　at the head of every street;
　lots were cast for her nobles,
　　all her dignitaries were bound
　　　in fetters.
11 You also will be drunken,
　　you will go into hiding;[d]
　you will seek
　　a refuge from the enemy.
12 All your fortresses are like fig trees
　　with first-ripe figs—
　if shaken they fall
　　into the mouth of the eater.
13 Look at your troops:

they are women in your midst.
The gates of your land
　　are wide open to your foes;
　fire has devoured the bars of
　　your gates.

14 Draw water for the siege,
　　strengthen your forts;
　trample the clay,
　　tread the mortar,
　　take hold of the brick-mould!
15 There the fire will devour you,
　　the sword will cut you off.
　It will devour you like the locust.

Multiply yourselves like the locust,
　　multiply like the grasshopper!
16 You increased your merchants
　　more than the stars of the heavens.
　The locust sheds its skin and
　　　flies away.
17 Your guards are like grasshoppers,
　　your scribes like swarms[d] of locusts
　settling on the fences
　　on a cold day—
　when the sun rises, they fly away;
　　no one knows where they
　　　have gone.

18 Your shepherds are asleep,
　　O king of Assyria;
　　your nobles slumber.
　Your people are scattered on the
　　　mountains
　　with no one to gather them.
19 There is no assuaging your hurt,
　　your wound is mortal.
　All who hear the news about you
　　clap their hands over you.
　For who has ever escaped
　　your endless cruelty?

a Heb *No-amon*　　*b* Or *Nubia*; Heb *Cush*　　*c* Gk: Heb
your　　*d* Meaning of Heb uncertain

HABAKKUK

1 The oracle that the prophet Habakkuk saw.

The Prophet's Complaint

2 O LORD, how long shall I cry for help,
 and you will not listen?
Or cry to you 'Violence!'
 and you will not save?
3 Why do you make me see
 wrongdoing
 and look at trouble?
Destruction and violence are
 before me;
 strife and contention arise.
4 So the law becomes slack
 and justice never prevails.
The wicked surround the righteous—
 therefore judgement comes forth
 perverted.

5 Look at the nations, and see!
 Be astonished! Be astounded!
For a work is being done in your days
 that you would not believe if you
 were told.
6 For I am rousing the Chaldeans,
 that fierce and impetuous nation,
who march through the breadth of
 the earth
 to seize dwellings not their own.
7 Dread and fearsome are they;
 their justice and dignity proceed
 from themselves.
8 Their horses are swifter than
 leopards,
 more menacing than wolves
 at dusk;
 their horses charge.
Their horsemen come from far away;

they fly like an eagle swift
 to devour.
9 They all come for violence,
 with faces pressing *a* forward;
 they gather captives like sand.
10 At kings they scoff,
 and of rulers they make sport.
They laugh at every fortress,
 and heap up earth to take it.
11 Then they sweep by like the wind;
 they transgress and become guilty;
 their own might is their god!

12 Are you not from of old,
 O LORD my God, my Holy One?
 You *b* shall not die.
O LORD, you have marked them for
 judgement;
 and you, O Rock, have established
 them for punishment.
13 Your eyes are too pure to behold evil,
 and you cannot look on
 wrongdoing;
why do you look on the treacherous,
 and are silent when the wicked
 swallow
 those more righteous than they?
14 You have made people like the fish of
 the sea,
 like crawling things that have
 no ruler.

15 The enemy *c* brings all of them up
 with a hook;
he drags them out with his net,
he gathers them in his seine;
 so he rejoices and exults.
16 Therefore he sacrifices to his net

---

a Meaning of Heb uncertain   *b* Ancient Heb
tradition: MT *We*   *c* Heb *He*

and makes offerings to his seine;
for by them his portion is lavish,
    and his food is rich.
17 Is he then to keep on emptying
        his net,
    and destroying nations without
        mercy?

God's Reply to the Prophet's Complaint

2 I will stand at my watch-post,
    and station myself on the rampart;
I will keep watch to see what he will
        say to me,
    and what he*a* will answer
        concerning my complaint.
2 Then the LORD answered me and said:
Write the vision;
    make it plain on tablets,
    so that a runner may read it.
3 For there is still a vision for the
        appointed time;
    it speaks of the end, and does not
        lie.
    If it seems to tarry, wait for it;
    it will surely come, it will not delay.
4 Look at the proud!
    Their spirit is not right in them,
    but the righteous live by
        their faith.*b*
5 Moreover, wealth*c* is treacherous;
    the arrogant do not endure.
They open their throats wide
        as Sheol;
    like Death they never have enough.
They gather all nations for
        themselves,
    and collect all peoples as their own.

The Woes of the Wicked

6 Shall not everyone taunt such people
and, with mocking riddles, say about
them,
    'Alas for you who heap up what is
        not your own!'
    How long will you load yourselves
        with goods taken in pledge?
7 Will not your own creditors suddenly
        rise,
    and those who make you tremble
        wake up?
    Then you will be booty for them.

8 Because you have plundered many
        nations,
    all that survive of the peoples shall
        plunder you—
because of human bloodshed, and
        violence to the earth,
    to cities and all who live in them.

9 'Alas for you who get evil gain for
        your house,
    setting your nest on high
    to be safe from the reach of
        harm!'
10 You have devised shame for
        your house
    by cutting off many peoples;
    you have forfeited your life.
11 The very stones will cry out from the
        wall,
    and the plaster*d* will respond from
        the woodwork.

12 'Alas for you who build a town by
        bloodshed,
    and found a city on iniquity!'
13 Is it not from the LORD of hosts
    that peoples labour only to feed the
        flames,
    and nations weary themselves for
        nothing?
14 But the earth will be filled
    with the knowledge of the glory of
        the LORD,
    as the waters cover the sea.

15 'Alas for you who make your
        neighbours drink,
    pouring out your wrath*e* until they
        are drunk,
    in order to gaze on their
        nakedness!'
16 You will be sated with contempt
        instead of glory.
    Drink, you yourself, and stagger!*f*
The cup in the LORD's right hand
    will come around to you,
    and shame will come upon
        your glory!

a Syr: Heb *I*   *b* Or *faithfulness*   *c* Other Heb Mss
read *wine*   *d* Or *beam*   *e* Or *poison*   *f* Q Ms Gk:
MT *be uncircumcised*

17 For the violence done to Lebanon
     will overwhelm you;
  the destruction of the animals will
     terrify you— *a*
because of human bloodshed and
     violence to the earth,
  to cities and all who live in them.

18 What use is an idol
     once its maker has shaped it—
  a cast image, a teacher of lies?
For its maker trusts in what has been
     made,
  though the product is only an idol
     that cannot speak!
19 Alas for you who say to the wood,
     'Wake up!'
  to silent stone, 'Rouse yourself!'
  Can it teach?
See, it is plated with gold and silver,
  and there is no breath in it at all.

20 But the LORD is in his holy temple;
  let all the earth keep silence before
     him!

3

A prayer of the prophet Habakkuk according to Shigionoth.

The Prophet's Prayer

2 O LORD, I have heard of your renown,
  and I stand in awe, O LORD, of your
     work.
In our own time revive it;
  in our own time make it known;
  in wrath may you remember mercy.
3 God came from Teman,
  the Holy One from Mount Paran.
                                     Selah
His glory covered the heavens,
  and the earth was full of his praise.
4 The brightness was like the sun;
  rays came forth from his hand,
  where his power lay hidden.
5 Before him went pestilence,
  and plague followed close behind.
6 He stopped and shook the earth;
  he looked and made the
     nations tremble.
The eternal mountains were
     shattered;

along his ancient pathways
  the everlasting hills sank low.
7 I saw the tents of Cushan under
     affliction;
  the tent-curtains of the land of
     Midian trembled.
8 Was your wrath against the rivers, *b*
     O LORD?
  Or your anger against the rivers, *b*
  or your rage against the sea, *c*
when you drove your horses,
  your chariots to victory?
9 You brandished your naked bow,
  sated *d* were the arrows at your
     command. *e*   *Selah*
  You split the earth with rivers.
10 The mountains saw you, and
     writhed;
  a torrent of water swept by;
  the deep gave forth its voice.
  The sun *f* raised high its hands;
11 the moon *g* stood still in its exalted
     place,
  at the light of your arrows speeding
     by,
  at the gleam of your flashing
     spear.
12 In fury you trod the earth,
  in anger you trampled nations.
13 You came forth to save your people,
  to save your anointed.
You crushed the head of the
     wicked house,
  laying it bare from foundation
     to roof. *e*   *Selah*
14 You pierced with their *h* own arrows
     the head *i* of his warriors, *j*
  who came like a whirlwind to
     scatter us, *k*
  gloating as if ready to devour the
     poor who were in hiding.
15 You trampled the sea with
     your horses,
  churning the mighty waters.

16 I hear, and I tremble within;
  my lips quiver at the sound.

---

a Gk Syr: Meaning of Heb uncertain   *b* Or *against*
River   *c* Or *against Sea*   *d* Cn: Heb *oaths*
e Meaning of Heb uncertain   *f* Heb *It*   *g* Heb *sun,*
moon   *h* Heb *his*   *i* Or *leader*   *j* Vg Compare Gk
Syr: Meaning of Heb uncertain   *k* Heb *me*

Rottenness enters into my bones,
  and my steps tremble*a* beneath me.
I wait quietly for the day of calamity
  to come upon the people who
    attack us.

Trust and Joy in the Midst of Trouble

17 Though the fig tree does not
    blossom,
  and no fruit is on the vines;
though the produce of the olive fails
  and the fields yield no food;
though the flock is cut off from
    the fold
  and there is no herd in the stalls,

18 yet I will rejoice in the LORD;
  I will exult in the God of my
    salvation.
19 GOD, the Lord, is my strength;
  he makes my feet like the feet of a
    deer,
  and makes me tread upon the
    heights.*b*

To the leader: with stringed*c*
  instruments.

a Cn Compare Gk: Meaning of Heb uncertain
b Heb *my heights*   *c* Heb *my stringed*

ZEPHANIAH

1 The word of the LORD that came to Zephaniah son of Cushi son of Gedaliah son of Amariah son of Hezekiah, in the days of King Josiah son of Amon of Judah.

The Coming Judgement on Judah

2 I will utterly sweep away everything
    from the face of the earth, says the
      LORD.
3 I will sweep away humans and
      animals;
    I will sweep away the birds of the
      air
    and the fish of the sea.
  I will make the wicked stumble. *a*
    I will cut off humanity
    from the face of the earth, says the
      LORD.
4 I will stretch out my hand against
      Judah,
    and against all the inhabitants of
      Jerusalem;
  and I will cut off from this place
      every remnant of Baal
    and the name of the idolatrous
      priests; *b*
5 those who bow down on the roofs
    to the host of the heavens;
  those who bow down and swear to
      the LORD,
    but also swear by Milcom; *c*
6 those who have turned back from
      following the LORD,
    who have not sought the LORD or
      inquired of him.

7 Be silent before the Lord GOD!
    For the day of the LORD is at
      hand;

the LORD has prepared a sacrifice,
    he has consecrated his guests.
8 And on the day of the LORD's sacrifice
  I will punish the officials and the
      king's sons
    and all who dress themselves in
      foreign attire.
9 On that day I will punish
    all who leap over the threshold,
  who fill their master's house
    with violence and fraud.

10 On that day, says the LORD,
    a cry will be heard from the
      Fish Gate,
  a wail from the Second Quarter,
    a loud crash from the hills.
11 The inhabitants of the Mortar wail,
    for all the traders have perished;
    all who weigh out silver are cut off.
12 At that time I will search Jerusalem
      with lamps,
    and I will punish the people
  who rest complacently *d* on
      their dregs,
    those who say in their hearts,
  'The LORD will not do good,
    nor will he do harm.'
13 Their wealth shall be plundered,
    and their houses laid waste.
  Though they build houses,
    they shall not inhabit them;
  though they plant vineyards,
    they shall not drink wine
      from them.

a Cn: Heb *sea, and those who cause the wicked to stumble*
b Compare Gk: Heb *the idolatrous priests with the priests*
c Gk Mss Syr Vg: Heb *Malcam* (or, *their king*)
d Heb *who thicken*

The Great Day of the LORD

14 The great day of the LORD is near,
     near and hastening fast;
   the sound of the day of the LORD
     is bitter,
   the warrior cries aloud there.
15 That day will be a day of wrath,
     a day of distress and anguish,
   a day of ruin and devastation,
     a day of darkness and gloom,
     a day of clouds and thick darkness,
16   a day of trumpet blast and
     battle cry
  against the fortified cities
     and against the lofty battlements.

17 I will bring such distress upon people
     that they shall walk like the blind;
   because they have sinned against
     the LORD,
   their blood shall be poured out
     like dust,
     and their flesh like dung.
18 Neither their silver nor their gold
     will be able to save them
     on the day of the LORD's wrath;
   in the fire of his passion
     the whole earth shall be consumed;
   for a full, a terrible end
     he will make of all the inhabitants
     of the earth.

Judgement on Israel's Enemies

2 Gather together, gather,
    O shameless nation,
2 before you are driven away
     like the drifting chaff, *a*
  before there comes upon you
     the fierce anger of the LORD,
  before there comes upon you
     the day of the LORD's wrath.
3 Seek the LORD, all you humble of the
     land,
    who do his commands;
  seek righteousness, seek humility;
    perhaps you may be hidden
    on the day of the LORD's wrath.
4 For Gaza shall be deserted,
     and Ashkelon shall become a
     desolation;

  Ashdod's people shall be driven out
     at noon,
     and Ekron shall be uprooted.

5 Ah, inhabitants of the sea coast,
     you nation of the Cherethites!
  The word of the LORD is against you,
     O Canaan, land of the Philistines;
     and I will destroy you until no
     inhabitant is left.
6 And you, O sea coast, shall be
     pastures,
    meadows for shepherds
    and folds for flocks.
7 The sea coast shall become the
     possession
    of the remnant of the house
     of Judah,
  on which they shall pasture,
  and in the houses of Ashkelon
    they shall lie down at evening.
  For the LORD their God will be
     mindful of them
    and restore their fortunes.

8 I have heard the taunts of Moab
     and the revilings of the Ammonites,
  how they have taunted my people
    and made boasts against
     their territory.
9 Therefore, as I live, says the LORD of
     hosts,
    the God of Israel,
  Moab shall become like Sodom
    and the Ammonites like Gomorrah,
  a land possessed by nettles and salt-
     pits,
    and a waste for ever.
  The remnant of my people shall
    plunder them,
    and the survivors of my nation
     shall possess them.
10 This shall be their lot in return for
     their pride,
   because they scoffed and boasted
    against the people of the LORD
     of hosts.
11 The LORD will be terrible
     against them;

a Cn Compare Gk Syr: Heb *before a decree is born; like
chaff a day has passed away*

he will shrivel all the gods of
 the earth,
and to him shall bow down,
 each in its place,
 all the coasts and islands of
  the nations.

12 You also, O Ethiopians, *a*
 shall be killed by my sword.

13 And he will stretch out his hand
 against the north,
 and destroy Assyria;
and he will make Nineveh a
 desolation,
 a dry waste like the desert.
14 Herds shall lie down in it,
 every wild animal; *b*
the desert-owl *c* and the screech-owl *c*
 shall lodge on its capitals;
the owl *d* shall hoot at the window,
 the raven *e* croak on the threshold;
 for its cedar-work will be laid bare.
15 Is this the exultant city
 that lived secure,
that said to itself,
 'I am, and there is no one else'?
What a desolation it has become,
 a lair for wild animals!
Everyone who passes by it
 hisses and shakes the fist.

The Wickedness of Jerusalem

3 Ah, soiled, defiled,
 oppressing city!
2 It has listened to no voice;
 it has accepted no correction.
It has not trusted in the LORD;
 it has not drawn near to its God.

3 The officials within it
 are roaring lions;
its judges are evening wolves
 that leave nothing until
  the morning.
4 Its prophets are reckless,
 faithless persons;
its priests have profaned what
 is sacred,
 they have done violence to the law.
5 The LORD within it is righteous;

he does no wrong.
Every morning he renders his
 judgement,
 each dawn without fail;
 but the unjust knows no shame.

6 I have cut off nations;
 their battlements are in ruins;
I have laid waste their streets
 so that no one walks in them;
their cities have been made desolate,
 without people, without
  inhabitants.
7 I said, 'Surely the city *f* will fear me,
 it will accept correction;
it will not lose sight *g*
 of all that I have brought upon it.'
But they were the more eager
 to make all their deeds corrupt.

Punishment and Conversion
of the Nations

8 Therefore wait for me, says the LORD,
 for the day when I arise as
  a witness.
For my decision is to gather nations,
 to assemble kingdoms,
to pour out upon them my
 indignation,
 all the heat of my anger;
for in the fire of my passion
 all the earth shall be consumed.

9 At that time I will change the speech
 of the peoples
 to a pure speech,
that all of them may call on the name
 of the LORD
 and serve him with one accord.
10 From beyond the rivers of Ethiopia *h*
 my suppliants, my scattered ones,
 shall bring my offering.

11 On that day you shall not be put
 to shame
 because of all the deeds by which
  you have rebelled against me;

a Or *Nubians*; Heb *Cushites* *b* Tg Compare Gk: Heb
nation *c* Meaning of Heb uncertain *d* Cn: Heb
a voice *e* Gk Vg: Heb *desolation* *f* Heb *it*
g Gk Syr: Heb *its dwelling will not be cut off*
h Or *Nubia*; Heb *Cush*

for then I will remove from
    your midst
  your proudly exultant ones,
and you shall no longer be haughty
  in my holy mountain.
12 For I will leave in the midst of you
  a people humble and lowly.
They shall seek refuge in the name of
    the LORD—
13   the remnant of Israel;
they shall do no wrong
  and utter no lies,
nor shall a deceitful tongue
  be found in their mouths.
Then they will pasture and lie down,
  and no one shall make them afraid.

A Song of Joy

14 Sing aloud, O daughter Zion;
  shout, O Israel!
Rejoice and exult with all your heart,
  O daughter Jerusalem!
15 The LORD has taken away the
    judgements against you,
  he has turned away your enemies.
The king of Israel, the LORD, is in
    your midst;
  you shall fear disaster no more.
16 On that day it shall be said to
    Jerusalem:

Do not fear, O Zion;
  do not let your hands grow weak.
17 The LORD, your God, is in your midst,
  a warrior who gives victory;
he will rejoice over you with
    gladness,
  he will renew you*a* in his love;
he will exult over you with
    loud singing
18   as on a day of festival.*b*
I will remove disaster from you,*c*
  so that you will not bear reproach
    for it.
19 I will deal with all your oppressors
  at that time.
And I will save the lame
  and gather the outcast,
and I will change their shame
    into praise
  and renown in all the earth.
20 At that time I will bring you home,
  at the time when I gather you;
for I will make you renowned
    and praised
  among all the peoples of the earth,
when I restore your fortunes
  before your eyes, says the LORD.

a Gk Syr: Heb *he will be silent*   *b* Gk Syr: Meaning
of Heb uncertain   *c* Cn: Heb *I will remove from you;*
they were

HAGGAI

The Command to Rebuild the Temple

1 In the second year of King Darius, in the sixth month, on the first day of the month, the word of the Lord came by the prophet Haggai to Zerubbabel son of Shealtiel, governor of Judah, and to Joshua son of Jehozadak, the high priest: ²Thus says the Lord of hosts: These people say the time has not yet come to rebuild the Lord's house. ³Then the word of the Lord came by the prophet Haggai, saying: ⁴Is it a time for you yourselves to live in your panelled houses, while this house lies in ruins? ⁵Now therefore, thus says the Lord of hosts: Consider how you have fared. ⁶You have sown much, and harvested little; you eat, but you never have enough; you drink, but you never have your fill; you clothe yourselves, but no one is warm; and you that earn wages earn wages to put them into a bag with holes.

7 Thus says the Lord of hosts: Consider how you have fared. ⁸Go up to the hills and bring wood and build the house, so that I may take pleasure in it and be honoured, says the Lord. ⁹You have looked for much, and, lo, it came to little; and when you brought it home, I blew it away. Why? says the Lord of hosts. Because my house lies in ruins, while all of you hurry off to your own houses. ¹⁰Therefore the heavens above you have withheld the dew, and the earth has withheld its produce. ¹¹And I have called for a drought on the land and the hills, on the grain, the new wine, the oil, on what the soil produces, on human beings and animals, and on all their labours.

12 Then Zerubbabel son of Shealtiel, and Joshua son of Jehozadak, the high priest, with all the remnant of the people, obeyed the voice of the Lord their God, and the words of the prophet Haggai, as the Lord their God had sent him; and the people feared the Lord. ¹³Then Haggai, the messenger of the Lord, spoke to the people with the Lord's message, saying, I am with you, says the Lord. ¹⁴And the Lord stirred up the spirit of Zerubbabel son of Shealtiel, governor of Judah, and the spirit of Joshua son of Jehozadak, the high priest, and the spirit of all the remnant of the people; and they came and worked on the house of the Lord of hosts, their God, ¹⁵on the twenty-fourth day of the month, in the sixth month.

The Future Glory of the Temple

2 In the second year of King Darius, ¹in the seventh month, on the twenty-first day of the month, the word of the Lord came by the prophet Haggai, saying: ²Speak now to Zerubbabel son of Shealtiel, governor of Judah, and to Joshua son of Jehozadak, the high priest, and to the remnant of the people, and say, ³Who is left among you that saw this house in its former glory? How does it look to you now? Is it not in your sight as nothing? ⁴Yet now take courage, O Zerubbabel, says the Lord; take courage, O Joshua, son of Jehozadak, the high priest; take courage, all you people of the land, says the Lord; work, for I am with you, says the Lord of hosts, ⁵according to the promise that I made you when you came out of Egypt. My spirit abides among you; do not fear. ⁶For thus says the Lord of hosts: Once again, in a little while, I will shake the heavens and the earth and the sea and the dry land; ⁷and I will shake all the nations, so that the treasure of all nations shall come, and I will fill this house with splendour, says the LORD of hosts. ⁸The silver is mine, and the gold is mine, says the LORD of hosts. ⁹The latter splendour of this house shall be greater than the former, says the LORD of hosts; and in this place I will give prosperity, says the LORD of hosts.

A Rebuke and a Promise

10 On the twenty-fourth day of the ninth month, in the second year of Darius, the word of the LORD came by the prophet Haggai, saying: ¹¹Thus says the LORD of hosts: Ask the priests for a ruling: ¹²If one carries consecrated meat in the fold of one's garment, and with the fold touches bread, or stew, or wine, or oil, or any kind of food, does it become holy? The priests answered, 'No.' ¹³Then Haggai said, 'If one who is unclean by contact with a dead body touches any of these, does it become unclean?' The priests answered, 'Yes, it becomes unclean.' ¹⁴Haggai then said, So is it with this people, and with this nation before me, says the LORD; and so with every work of their hands; and what they offer there is unclean. ¹⁵But now, consider what will come to pass from this day on. Before a stone was placed upon a stone in the LORD's temple, ¹⁶how did you fare?ᵃ When one came to a heap of twenty measures, there were but ten; when one came to the wine vat to draw fifty measures, there were but twenty. ¹⁷I struck you and all the products of your toil with blight and mildew and hail; yet you did not return to me, says the LORD. ¹⁸Consider from this day on, from the twenty-fourth day of the ninth month. Since the day that the foundation of the LORD's temple was laid, consider: ¹⁹Is there any seed left in the barn? Do the vine, the fig tree, the pomegranate, and the olive tree still yield nothing? From this day on I will bless you.

God's Promise to Zerubbabel

20 The word of the LORD came a second time to Haggai on the twenty-fourth day of the month: ²¹Speak to Zerubbabel, governor of Judah, saying, I am about to shake the heavens and the earth, ²²and to overthrow the throne of kingdoms; I am about to destroy the strength of the kingdoms of the nations, and overthrow the chariots and their riders; and the horses and their riders shall fall, every one by the sword of a comrade. ²³On that day, says the LORD of hosts, I will take you, O Zerubbabel my servant, son of Shealtiel, says the LORD, and make you like a signet ring; for I have chosen you, says the LORD of hosts.

a Gk: Heb *since they were*

ZECHARIAH

Israel Urged to Repent

1 In the eighth month, in the second year of Darius, the word of the LORD came to the prophet Zechariah son of Berechiah son of Iddo, saying: 2 The LORD was very angry with your ancestors. 3 Therefore say to them, Thus says the LORD of hosts: Return to me, says the LORD of hosts, and I will return to you, says the LORD of hosts. 4 Do not be like your ancestors, to whom the former prophets proclaimed, 'Thus says the LORD of hosts, Return from your evil ways and from your evil deeds.' But they did not hear or heed me, says the LORD. 5 Your ancestors, where are they? And the prophets, do they live for ever? 6 But my words and my statutes, which I commanded my servants the prophets, did they not overtake your ancestors? So they repented and said, 'The LORD of hosts has dealt with us according to our ways and deeds, just as he planned to do.'

First Vision: The Horsemen

7 On the twenty-fourth day of the eleventh month, the month of Shebat, in the second year of Darius, the word of the LORD came to the prophet Zechariah son of Berechiah son of Iddo; and Zechariah[a] said, 8 In the night I saw a man riding on a red horse! He was standing among the myrtle trees in the glen; and behind him were red, sorrel, and white horses. 9 Then I said, 'What are these, my lord?' The angel who talked with me said to me, 'I will show you what they are.' 10 So the man who was standing among the myrtle trees answered, 'They are those whom the LORD has sent to patrol the earth.' 11 Then they spoke to the angel of the LORD who was standing among the myrtle trees, 'We have patrolled the earth, and lo, the whole earth remains at peace.' 12 Then the angel of the LORD said, 'O LORD of hosts, how long will you withhold mercy from Jerusalem and the cities of Judah, with which you have been angry these seventy years?' 13 Then the LORD replied with gracious and comforting words to the angel who talked with me. 14 So the angel who talked with me said to me, Proclaim this message: Thus says the LORD of hosts; I am very jealous for Jerusalem and for Zion. 15 And I am extremely angry with the nations that are at ease; for while I was only a little angry, they made the disaster worse. 16 Therefore, thus says the LORD, I have returned to Jerusalem with compassion; my house shall be built in it, says the LORD of hosts, and the measuring line shall be stretched out over Jerusalem. 17 Proclaim further: Thus says the LORD of hosts: My cities shall again overflow with prosperity; the LORD will again comfort Zion and again choose Jerusalem.

Second Vision: The Horns and the Smiths

18[b] And I looked up and saw four horns. 19 I asked the angel who talked with me, 'What are these?' And he answered me, 'These are the horns that have scattered Judah, Israel, and Jerusalem.' 20 Then the LORD showed me four blacksmiths. 21 And I asked, 'What are they coming to do?' He answered, 'These are the horns that scattered Judah, so that no head could be raised; but these have come to terrify them, to strike down the horns of the nations

a Heb *and he*   *b* Ch 2.1 in Heb

that lifted up their horns against the land of Judah to scatter its people.'[a]

Third Vision: The Man with a Measuring Line

2 [b] I looked up and saw a man with a measuring line in his hand. [2] Then I asked, 'Where are you going?' He answered me, 'To measure Jerusalem, to see what is its width and what is its length.' [3] Then the angel who talked with me came forward, and another angel came forward to meet him, [4] and said to him, 'Run, say to that young man: Jerusalem shall be inhabited like villages without walls, because of the multitude of people and animals in it. [5] For I will be a wall of fire all round it, says the LORD, and I will be the glory within it.'

Interlude: An Appeal to the Exiles

6 Up, up! Flee from the land of the north, says the LORD; for I have spread you abroad like the four winds of heaven, says the LORD. [7] Up! Escape to Zion, you that live with daughter Babylon. [8] For thus said the LORD of hosts (after his glory[c] sent me) regarding the nations that plundered you: Truly, one who touches you touches the apple of my eye.[d] [9] See now, I am going to raise[e] my hand against them, and they shall become plunder for their own slaves. Then you will know that the LORD of hosts has sent me. [10] Sing and rejoice, O daughter Zion! For lo, I will come and dwell in your midst, says the LORD. [11] Many nations shall join themselves to the LORD on that day, and shall be my people; and I will dwell in your midst. And you shall know that the LORD of hosts has sent me to you. [12] The LORD will inherit Judah as his portion in the holy land, and will again choose Jerusalem.

13 Be silent, all people, before the LORD; for he has roused himself from his holy dwelling.

Fourth Vision: Joshua and Satan

3 Then he showed me the high priest Joshua standing before the angel of the LORD, and Satan[f] standing at his right hand to accuse him. [2] And the LORD said to

Satan,[f] 'The LORD rebuke you, O Satan![f] The LORD who has chosen Jerusalem rebuke you! Is not this man a brand plucked from the fire?' [3] Now Joshua was dressed in filthy clothes as he stood before the angel. [4] The angel said to those who were standing before him, 'Take off his filthy clothes.' And to him he said, 'See, I have taken your guilt away from you, and I will clothe you in festal apparel.' [5] And I said, 'Let them put a clean turban on his head.' So they put a clean turban on his head and clothed him in the apparel; and the angel of the LORD was standing by.

6 Then the angel of the LORD assured Joshua, saying [7] 'Thus says the LORD of hosts: If you will walk in my ways and keep my requirements, then you shall rule my house and have charge of my courts, and I will give you the right of access among those who are standing here. [8] Now listen, Joshua, high priest, you and your colleagues who sit before you! For they are an omen of things to come: I am going to bring my servant the Branch. [9] For on the stone that I have set before Joshua, on a single stone with seven facets, I will engrave its inscription, says the LORD of hosts, and I will remove the guilt of this land in a single day. [10] On that day, says the LORD of hosts, you shall invite each other to come under your vine and fig tree.'

Fifth Vision: The Lampstand and Olive Trees

4 The angel who talked with me came again, and wakened me, as one is wakened from sleep. [2] He said to me, 'What do you see?' And I said, 'I see a lampstand all of gold, with a bowl on the top of it; there are seven lamps on it, with seven lips on each of the lamps that are on the top of it. [3] And by it there are two olive trees, one on the right of the bowl and the other on its left.' [4] I said to the angel who talked with me, 'What are these, my lord?' [5] Then the angel who talked with me answered me, 'Do you not know what these are?' I said,

---

a Heb *it*   *b* Ch 2.5 in Heb   *c* Cn: Heb *after glory he*   *d* Heb *his eye*   *e* Or *wave*   *f* Or *the Accuser*; Heb *the Adversary*

'No, my lord.' 6 He said to me, 'This is the word of the LORD to Zerubbabel: Not by might, nor by power, but by my spirit, says the LORD of hosts. 7 What are you, O great mountain? Before Zerubbabel you shall become a plain; and he shall bring out the top stone amid shouts of "Grace, grace to it!" '

8 Moreover, the word of the LORD came to me, saying, 9 'The hands of Zerubbabel have laid the foundation of this house; his hands shall also complete it. Then you will know that the LORD of hosts has sent me to you. 10 For whoever has despised the day of small things shall rejoice, and shall see the plummet in the hand of Zerubbabel.

'These seven are the eyes of the LORD, which range through the whole earth.' 11 Then I said to him, 'What are these two olive trees on the right and the left of the lampstand?' 12 And a second time I said to him, 'What are these two branches of the olive trees, which pour out the oil*a* through the two golden pipes?' 13 He said to me, 'Do you not know what these are?' I said, 'No, my lord.' 14 Then he said, 'These are the two anointed ones who stand by the Lord of the whole earth.'

Sixth Vision: The Flying Scroll

5 Again I looked up and saw a flying scroll. 2 And he said to me, 'What do you see?' I answered, 'I see a flying scroll; its length is twenty cubits, and its width ten cubits.' 3 Then he said to me, 'This is the curse that goes out over the face of the whole land; for everyone who steals shall be cut off according to the writing on one side, and everyone who swears falsely*b* shall be cut off according to the writing on the other side. 4 I have sent it out, says the LORD of hosts, and it shall enter the house of the thief, and the house of anyone who swears falsely by my name; and it shall abide in that house and consume it, both timber and stones.'

Seventh Vision: The Woman in a Basket

5 Then the angel who talked with me came forward and said to me, 'Look up and see what this is that is coming out.' 6 I said,

'What is it?' He said, 'This is a basket*c* coming out.' And he said, 'This is their iniquity*d* in all the land.' 7 Then a leaden cover was lifted, and there was a woman sitting in the basket!*c* 8 And he said, 'This is Wickedness.' So he thrust her back into the basket,*c* and pressed the leaden weight down on its mouth. 9 Then I looked up and saw two women coming forward. The wind was in their wings; they had wings like the wings of a stork, and they lifted up the basket*c* between earth and sky. 10 Then I said to the angel who talked with me, 'Where are they taking the basket?'*c* 11 He said to me, 'To the land of Shinar, to build a house for it; and when this is prepared, they will set the basket*c* down there on its base.'

Eighth Vision: Four Chariots

6 And again I looked up and saw four chariots coming out from between two mountains—mountains of bronze. 2 The first chariot had red horses, the second chariot black horses, 3 the third chariot white horses, and the fourth chariot dappled grey*e* horses. 4 Then I said to the angel who talked with me, 'What are these, my lord?' 5 The angel answered me, 'These are the four winds*f* of heaven going out, after presenting themselves before the LORD of all the earth. 6 The chariot with the black horses goes towards the north country, the white ones go towards the west country,*g* and the dappled ones go towards the south country.' 7 When the steeds came out, they were impatient to get off and patrol the earth. And he said, 'Go, patrol the earth.' So they patrolled the earth. 8 Then he cried out to me, 'Lo, those who go towards the north country have set my spirit at rest in the north country.'

The Coronation of the Branch

9 The word of the LORD came to me: 10 Collect silver and gold*h* from the exiles— from Heldai, Tobijah, and Jedaiah—who have arrived from Babylon; and go the

---

a Cn: Heb *gold*   *b* The word *falsely* added from verse 4
c Heb *ephah*   *d* Gk Compare Syr: Heb *their eye*
e Compare Gk: Meaning of Heb uncertain   *f* Or *spirits*
g Cn: Heb *go after them*   *h* Cn Compare verse 11: Heb lacks *silver and gold*

same day to the house of Josiah son of Zephaniah. [11]Take the silver and gold and make a crown,[a] and set it on the head of the high priest Joshua son of Jehozadak; [12]say to him: Thus says the LORD of hosts: Here is a man whose name is Branch: for he shall branch out in his place, and he shall build the temple of the LORD. [13]It is he that shall build the temple of the LORD; he shall bear royal honour, and shall sit and rule on his throne. There shall be a priest by his throne, with peaceful understanding between the two of them. [14]And the crown[b] shall be in the care of Heldai,[c] Tobijah, Jedaiah, and Josiah[d] son of Zephaniah, as a memorial in the temple of the LORD.

15 Those who are far off shall come and help to build the temple of the LORD; and you shall know that the LORD of hosts has sent me to you. This will happen if you diligently obey the voice of the LORD your God.

Hypocritical Fasting Condemned

7 In the fourth year of King Darius, the word of the LORD came to Zechariah on the fourth day of the ninth month, which is Chislev. [2]Now the people of Bethel had sent Sharezer and Regem-melech and their men, to entreat the favour of the LORD, [3]and to ask the priests of the house of the LORD of hosts and the prophets, 'Should I mourn and practise abstinence in the fifth month, as I have done for so many years?' [4]Then the word of the LORD of hosts came to me: [5]Say to all the people of the land and the priests: When you fasted and lamented in the fifth month and in the seventh, for these seventy years, was it for me that you fasted? [6]And when you eat and when you drink, do you not eat and drink only for yourselves? [7]Were not these the words that the LORD proclaimed by the former prophets, when Jerusalem was inhabited and in prosperity, along with the towns around it, and when the Negeb and the Shephelah were inhabited?

Punishment for Rejecting God's Demands

8 The word of the LORD came to Zecha-

riah, saying: [9]Thus says the LORD of hosts: Render true judgements, show kindness and mercy to one another; [10]do not oppress the widow, the orphan, the alien, or the poor; and do not devise evil in your hearts against one another. [11]But they refused to listen, and turned a stubborn shoulder, and stopped their ears in order not to hear. [12]They made their hearts adamant in order not to hear the law and the words that the LORD of hosts had sent by his spirit through the former prophets. Therefore great wrath came from the LORD of hosts. [13]Just as, when I[e] called, they would not hear, so, when they called, I would not hear, says the LORD of hosts, [14]and I scattered them with a whirlwind among all the nations that they had not known. Thus the land they left was desolate, so that no one went to and fro, and a pleasant land was made desolate.

God's Promises to Zion

8 The word of the LORD of hosts came to me, saying: [2]Thus says the LORD of hosts: I am jealous for Zion with great jealousy, and I am jealous for her with great wrath. [3]Thus says the LORD: I will return to Zion, and will dwell in the midst of Jerusalem; Jerusalem shall be called the faithful city, and the mountain of the LORD of hosts shall be called the holy mountain. [4]Thus says the LORD of hosts: Old men and old women shall again sit in the streets of Jerusalem, each with staff in hand because of their great age. [5]And the streets of the city shall be full of boys and girls playing in its streets. [6]Thus says the LORD of hosts: Even though it seems impossible to the remnant of this people in these days, should it also seem impossible to me, says the LORD of hosts? [7]Thus says the LORD of hosts: I will save my people from the east country and from the west country; [8]and I will bring them to live in Jerusalem. They shall be my people and I will be their God, in faithfulness and in righteousness.

9 Thus says the LORD of hosts: Let your

a Gk Mss Syr Tg: Heb *crowns*   b Gk Syr: Heb *crowns*
c Syr Compare verse 10: Heb *Helem*   d Syr Compare verse 10: Heb *Hen*   e Heb *he*

hands be strong—you that have recently been hearing these words from the mouths of the prophets who were present when the foundation was laid for the rebuilding of the temple, the house of the LORD of hosts. [10] For before those days there were no wages for people or for animals, nor was there any safety from the foe for those who went out or came in, and I set them all against one another. [11] But now I will not deal with the remnant of this people as in the former days, says the LORD of hosts. [12] For there shall be a sowing of peace; the vine shall yield its fruit, the ground shall give its produce, and the skies shall give their dew; and I will cause the remnant of this people to possess all these things. [13] Just as you have been a cursing among the nations, O house of Judah and house of Israel, so I will save you and you shall be a blessing. Do not be afraid, but let your hands be strong.

14 For thus says the LORD of hosts: Just as I purposed to bring disaster upon you, when your ancestors provoked me to wrath, and I did not relent, says the LORD of hosts, [15] so again I have purposed in these days to do good to Jerusalem and to the house of Judah; do not be afraid. [16] These are the things that you shall do: Speak the truth to one another, render in your gates judgements that are true and make for peace, [17] do not devise evil in your hearts against one another, and love no false oath; for all these are things that I hate, says the LORD.

Joyful Fasting

18 The word of the LORD of hosts came to me, saying: [19] Thus says the LORD of hosts: The fast of the fourth month, and the fast of the fifth, and the fast of the seventh, and the fast of the tenth, shall be seasons of joy and gladness, and cheerful festivals for the house of Judah: therefore love truth and peace.

Many Peoples Drawn to Jerusalem

20 Thus says the LORD of hosts: Peoples shall yet come, the inhabitants of many cities; [21] the inhabitants of one city shall go to another, saying, 'Come, let us go to entreat the favour of the LORD, and to seek the LORD of hosts; I myself am going.' [22] Many peoples and strong nations shall come to seek the LORD of hosts in Jerusalem, and to entreat the favour of the LORD. [23] Thus says the LORD of hosts: In those days ten men from nations of every language shall take hold of a Jew, grasping his garment and saying, 'Let us go with you, for we have heard that God is with you.'

Judgement on Israel's Enemies

9 An Oracle.

The word of the LORD is against the
    land of Hadrach
  and will rest upon Damascus.
For to the LORD belongs the capital[a]
    of Aram,[b]
  as do all the tribes of Israel;
2 Hamath also, which borders on it,
    Tyre and Sidon, though they are
      very wise.
3 Tyre has built itself a rampart,
    and heaped up silver like dust,
    and gold like the dirt of the streets.
4 But now, the Lord will strip it of its
      possessions
    and hurl its wealth into the sea,
    and it shall be devoured by fire.

5 Ashkelon shall see it and be afraid;
    Gaza too, and shall writhe in
      anguish;
    Ekron also, because its hopes
      are withered.
The king shall perish from Gaza;
    Ashkelon shall be uninhabited;
6 a mongrel people shall settle
      in Ashdod,
    and I will make an end of the pride
      of Philistia.
7 I will take away its blood from
      its mouth,
    and its abominations from between
      its teeth;
  it too shall be a remnant for our God;
    it shall be like a clan in Judah,

a Heb *eye*   *b* Cn: Heb *of Adam* (or *of humankind*)

and Ekron shall be like the
    Jebusites.
8 Then I will encamp at my house as a
       guard,
    so that no one shall march to
      and fro;
no oppressor shall again overrun
    them,
    for now I have seen with my
      own eyes.

The Coming Ruler of God's People

9 Rejoice greatly, O daughter Zion!
    Shout aloud, O daughter
      Jerusalem!
Lo, your king comes to you;
    triumphant and victorious is he,
humble and riding on a donkey,
    on a colt, the foal of a donkey.
10 He[a] will cut off the chariot
      from Ephraim
    and the warhorse from Jerusalem;
and the battle-bow shall be cut off,
    and he shall command peace to the
      nations;
his dominion shall be from sea
      to sea,
    and from the River to the ends of
      the earth.

11 As for you also, because of the blood
      of my covenant with you,
    I will set your prisoners free from
      the waterless pit.
12 Return to your stronghold,
      O prisoners of hope;
    today I declare that I will restore to
      you double.
13 For I have bent Judah as my bow;
    I have made Ephraim its arrow.
I will arouse your sons, O Zion,
    against your sons, O Greece,
    and wield you like a warrior's
      sword.

14 Then the LORD will appear over them,
    and his arrow go forth like
      lightning;
the Lord GOD will sound the trumpet
    and march forth in the whirlwinds
      of the south.

15 The LORD of hosts will protect them,
    and they shall devour and tread
      down the slingers;[b]
they shall drink their blood[c]
    like wine,
    and be full like a bowl,
    drenched like the corners of
      the altar.

16 On that day the LORD their God will
      save them,
    for they are the flock of his people;
for like the jewels of a crown
    they shall shine on his land.
17 For what goodness and beauty
      are his!
    Grain shall make the young
      men flourish,
    and new wine the young women.

Restoration of Judah and Israel

10 Ask rain from the LORD
    in the season of the spring rain,
from the LORD who makes the storm-
      clouds,
    who gives showers of rain to you,[d]
    the vegetation in the field
      to everyone.
2 For the teraphim[e] utter nonsense,
    and the diviners see lies;
the dreamers tell false dreams,
    and give empty consolation.
Therefore the people wander
    like sheep;
    they suffer for lack of a shepherd.

3 My anger is hot against the
      shepherds,
    and I will punish the leaders;[f]
for the LORD of hosts cares for his
      flock, the house of Judah,
    and will make them like his proud
      warhorse.
4 Out of them shall come the
      cornerstone,
    out of them the tent-peg,
    out of them the battle-bow,
    out of them every commander.

a Gk: Heb I   b Cn: Heb *the slingstones*   c Gk: Heb
shall drink   d Heb *them*   e Or *household gods*
f Or *male goats*

5 Together they shall be like warriors in
        battle,
    trampling the foe in the mud of the
        streets;
    they shall fight, for the LORD is with
        them,
    and they shall put to shame the
        riders on horses.

6 I will strengthen the house of Judah,
    and I will save the house of Joseph.
  I will bring them back because I have
        compassion on them,
    and they shall be as though I had
        not rejected them;
    for I am the LORD their God and I
        will answer them.
7 Then the people of Ephraim shall
        become like warriors,
    and their hearts shall be glad as
        with wine.
  Their children shall see it and rejoice,
    their hearts shall exult in the LORD.

8 I will signal for them and gather
        them in,
    for I have redeemed them,
    and they shall be as numerous as
        they were before.
9 Though I scattered them among
        the nations,
    yet in far countries they shall
        remember me,
    and they shall rear their children
        and return.
10 I will bring them home from the land
        of Egypt,
    and gather them from Assyria;
  I will bring them to the land of
        Gilead and to Lebanon,
    until there is no room for them.
11 They*a* shall pass through the sea of
        distress,
    and the waves of the sea shall be
        struck down,
    and all the depths of the Nile dried
        up.
  The pride of Assyria shall be laid low,
    and the sceptre of Egypt
        shall depart.
12 I will make them strong in the LORD,

and they shall walk in his name,
                            says the LORD.

11 Open your doors, O Lebanon,
        so that fire may devour
        your cedars!
2 Wail, O cypress, for the cedar
        has fallen,
    for the glorious trees are ruined!
  Wail, oaks of Bashan,
    for the thick forest has been felled!
3 Listen, the wail of the shepherds,
    for their glory is despoiled!
  Listen, the roar of the lions,
    for the thickets of the Jordan
        are destroyed!

Two Kinds of Shepherds

4 Thus said the LORD my God: Be a
shepherd of the flock doomed to slaughter.
5 Those who buy them kill them and go unpunished; and those who sell them say,
'Blessed be the LORD, for I have become
rich'; and their own shepherds have no pity
on them. 6 For I will no longer have pity on
the inhabitants of the earth, says the LORD.
I will cause them, every one, to fall each
into the hand of a neighbour, and each
into the hand of the king; and they shall
devastate the earth, and I will deliver no
one from their hand.

7 So, on behalf of the sheep dealers, I
became the shepherd of the flock doomed
to slaughter. I took two staffs; one I named
Favour, the other I named Unity, and I
tended the sheep. 8 In one month I disposed of the three shepherds, for I had become impatient with them, and they also
detested me. 9 So I said, 'I will not be your
shepherd. What is to die, let it die; what is
to be destroyed, let it be destroyed; and let
those that are left devour the flesh of one
another!' 10 I took my staff Favour and
broke it, annulling the covenant that I had
made with all the peoples. 11 So it was annulled on that day, and the sheep dealers,
who were watching me, knew that it was
the word of the LORD. 12 I then said to
them, 'If it seems right to you, give me my
wages; but if not, keep them.' So they

a Gk: Heb *He*

weighed out as my wages thirty shekels of silver. [13] Then the LORD said to me, 'Throw it into the treasury'[a]—this lordly price at which I was valued by them. So I took the thirty shekels of silver and threw them into the treasury[a] in the house of the LORD. [14] Then I broke my second staff Unity, annulling the family ties between Judah and Israel.

15 Then the LORD said to me: Take once more the implements of a worthless shepherd. [16] For I am now raising up in the land a shepherd who does not care for the perishing, or seek the wandering,[b] or heal the maimed, or nourish the healthy,[c] but devours the flesh of the fat ones, tearing off even their hoofs.

[17] Oh, my worthless shepherd,
    who deserts the flock!
May the sword strike his arm
    and his right eye!
Let his arm be completely withered,
    his right eye utterly blinded!

Jerusalem's Victory

12
An Oracle.

The word of the LORD concerning Israel: Thus says the LORD, who stretched out the heavens and founded the earth and formed the human spirit within: [2] See, I am about to make Jerusalem a cup of reeling for all the surrounding peoples; it will be against Judah also in the siege against Jerusalem. [3] On that day I will make Jerusalem a heavy stone for all the peoples; all who lift it shall grievously hurt themselves. And all the nations of the earth shall come together against it. [4] On that day, says the LORD, I will strike every horse with panic, and its rider with madness. But on the house of Judah I will keep a watchful eye, when I strike every horse of the peoples with blindness. [5] Then the clans of Judah shall say to themselves, 'The inhabitants of Jerusalem have strength through the LORD of hosts, their God.'

6 On that day I will make the clans of Judah like a blazing pot on a pile of wood, like a flaming torch among sheaves; and they shall devour to the right and to the left all the surrounding peoples, while Jerusalem shall again be inhabited in its place, in Jerusalem.

7 And the LORD will give victory to the tents of Judah first, so that the glory of the house of David and the glory of the inhabitants of Jerusalem may not be exalted over that of Judah. [8] On that day the LORD will shield the inhabitants of Jerusalem, so that the feeblest among them on that day shall be like David, and the house of David shall be like God, like the angel of the LORD, at their head. [9] And on that day I will seek to destroy all the nations that come against Jerusalem.

Mourning for the Pierced One

10 And I will pour out a spirit of compassion and supplication on the house of David and the inhabitants of Jerusalem, so that, when they look on the one[d] whom they have pierced, they shall mourn for him, as one mourns for an only child, and weep bitterly over him, as one weeps over a firstborn. [11] On that day the mourning in Jerusalem will be as great as the mourning for Hadad-rimmon in the plain of Megiddo. [12] The land shall mourn, each family by itself; the family of the house of David by itself, and their wives by themselves; the family of the house of Nathan by itself, and their wives by themselves; [13] the family of the house of Levi by itself, and their wives by themselves; the family of the Shimeites by itself, and their wives by themselves; [14] and all the families that are left, each by itself, and their wives by themselves.

13
On that day a fountain shall be opened for the house of David and the inhabitants of Jerusalem, to cleanse them from sin and impurity.

Idolatry Cut Off

2 On that day, says the LORD of hosts, I will cut off the names of the idols from the land, so that they shall be remembered no more; and also I will remove from the land

---

a Syr: Heb *it to the potter*   *b* Syr Compare Gk Vg: Heb *the youth*   *c* Meaning of Heb uncertain *d* Heb *on me* the prophets and the unclean spirit. 3 And if any prophets appear again, their fathers and mothers who bore them will say to them, 'You shall not live, for you speak lies in the name of the LORD'; and their fathers and their mothers who bore them shall pierce them through when they prophesy. 4 On that day the prophets will be ashamed, every one, of their visions when they prophesy; they will not put on a hairy mantle in order to deceive, 5 but each of them will say, 'I am no prophet, I am a tiller of the soil; for the land has been my possession *a* since my youth.' 6 And if anyone asks them, 'What are these wounds on your chest?'*b* the answer will be 'The wounds I received in the house of my friends.'

The Shepherd Struck, the Flock Scattered

7 'Awake, O sword, against my
          shepherd,
      against the man who is my
          associate,'
                    says the LORD of hosts.
      Strike the shepherd, that the sheep
          may be scattered;
      I will turn my hand against
          the little ones.
8 In the whole land, says the LORD,
      two-thirds shall be cut off
          and perish,
      and one-third shall be left alive.
9 And I will put this third into the fire,
      refine them as one refines silver,
      and test them as gold is tested.
      They will call on my name,
          and I will answer them.
      I will say, 'They are my people';
          and they will say, 'The LORD is our
                    God.'

Future Warfare and Final Victory

14 See, a day is coming for the LORD, when the plunder taken from you will be divided in your midst. 2 For I will gather all the nations against Jerusalem to battle, and the city shall be taken and the houses looted and the women raped; half the city shall go into exile, but the rest of the people shall not be cut off from the city. 3 Then the LORD will go forth and fight against those nations as when he fights on a day of battle. 4 On that day his feet shall stand on the Mount of Olives, which lies before Jerusalem on the east; and the Mount of Olives shall be split in two from east to west by a very wide valley; so that half of the Mount shall withdraw northwards, and the other half southwards. 5 And you shall flee by the valley of the LORD's mountain,*c* for the valley between the mountains shall reach to Azal;*d* and you shall flee as you fled from the earthquake in the days of King Uzziah of Judah. Then the LORD my God will come, and all the holy ones with him.

6 On that day there shall not be*e* either cold or frost.*f* 7 And there shall be continuous day (it is known to the LORD), not day and not night, for at evening time there shall be light.

8 On that day living waters shall flow out from Jerusalem, half of them to the eastern sea and half of them to the western sea; it shall continue in summer as in winter.

9 And the LORD will become king over all the earth; on that day the LORD will be one and his name one.

10 The whole land shall be turned into a plain from Geba to Rimmon south of Jerusalem. But Jerusalem shall remain aloft on its site from the Gate of Benjamin to the place of the former gate, to the Corner Gate, and from the Tower of Hananel to the king's wine presses. 11 And it shall be inhabited, for never again shall it be doomed to destruction; Jerusalem shall abide in security.

12 This shall be the plague with which the LORD will strike all the peoples that wage war against Jerusalem: their flesh shall rot while they are still on their feet; their eyes shall rot in their sockets, and their tongues shall rot in their mouths. 13 On that day a great panic from the LORD shall fall on them, so that each will seize

a Cn: Heb *for humankind has caused me to possess*
b Heb *wounds between your hands*   *c* Heb *my mountains*
d Meaning of Heb uncertain   *e* Cn: Heb *there shall not be light*   *f* Compare Gk Syr Vg Tg: Meaning of Heb uncertain

the hand of a neighbour, and the hand of one will be raised against the hand of the other; [14] even Judah will fight at Jerusalem. And the wealth of all the surrounding nations shall be collected—gold, silver, and garments in great abundance. [15] And a plague like this plague shall fall on the horses, the mules, the camels, the donkeys, and whatever animals may be in those camps.

16 Then all who survive of the nations that have come against Jerusalem shall go up year by year to worship the King, the LORD of hosts, and to keep the festival of booths. [a] [17] If any of the families of the earth do not go up to Jerusalem to worship the King, the LORD of hosts, there will be no rain upon them. [18] And if the family of Egypt do not go up and present themselves, then on them shall [b] come the plague that the LORD inflicts on the nations that do not go up to keep the festival of booths. [a] [19] Such shall be the punishment of Egypt and the punishment of all the nations that do not go up to keep the festival of booths. [a]

20 On that day there shall be inscribed on the bells of the horses, 'Holy to the LORD.' And the cooking-pots in the house of the LORD shall be as holy as [c] the bowls in front of the altar; [21] and every cooking-pot in Jerusalem and Judah shall be sacred to the LORD of hosts, so that all who sacrifice may come and use them to boil the flesh of the sacrifice. And there shall no longer be traders [d] in the house of the LORD of hosts on that day.

a Or tabernacles; Heb succoth   b Gk Syr: Heb shall not
c Heb shall be like   d Or Canaanites

MALACHI

1 An oracle. The word of the LORD to Israel by Malachi.*a*

Israel Preferred to Edom

2 I have loved you, says the LORD. But you say, 'How have you loved us?' Is not Esau Jacob's brother? says the LORD. Yet I have loved Jacob 3 but I have hated Esau; I have made his hill country a desolation and his heritage a desert for jackals. 4 If Edom says, 'We are shattered but we will rebuild the ruins,' the LORD of hosts says: They may build, but I will tear down, until they are called the wicked country, the people with whom the LORD is angry for ever. 5 Your own eyes shall see this, and you shall say, 'Great is the LORD beyond the borders of Israel!'

Corruption of the Priesthood

6 A son honours his father, and servants their master. If then I am a father, where is the honour due to me? And if I am a master, where is the respect due to me? says the LORD of hosts to you, O priests, who despise my name. You say, 'How have we despised your name?' 7 By offering polluted food on my altar. And you say, 'How have we polluted it?'*b* By thinking that the LORD's table may be despised. 8 When you offer blind animals in sacrifice, is that not wrong? And when you offer those that are lame or sick, is that not wrong? Try presenting that to your governor; will he be pleased with you or show you favour? says the LORD of hosts. 9 And now implore the favour of God, that he may be gracious to us. The fault is yours. Will he show favour to any of you? says the LORD of hosts. 10 O that someone among you would shut the temple*c* doors, so that you would not kindle fire on my altar in vain! I have no pleasure in you, says the LORD of hosts, and I will not accept an offering from your hands. 11 For from the rising of the sun to its setting my name is great among the nations, and in every place incense is offered to my name, and a pure offering; for my name is great among the nations, says the LORD of hosts. 12 But you profane it when you say that the Lord's table is polluted, and the food for it*d* may be despised. 13 'What a weariness this is', you say, and you sniff at me,*e* says the LORD of hosts. You bring what has been taken by violence or is lame or sick, and this you bring as your offering! Shall I accept that from your hand? says the LORD. 14 Cursed be the cheat who has a male in the flock and vows to give it, and yet sacrifices to the Lord what is blemished; for I am a great King, says the LORD of hosts, and my name is reverenced among the nations.

2 And now, O priests, this command is for you. 2 If you will not listen, if you will not lay it to heart to give glory to my name, says the LORD of hosts, then I will send the curse on you and I will curse your blessings; indeed I have already cursed them,*f* because you do not lay it to heart. 3 I will rebuke your offspring, and spread dung on your faces, the dung of your offerings, and I will put you out of my presence.*g*

4 Know, then, that I have sent this command to you, so that my covenant with

---

a Or *by my messenger*   *b* Gk: Heb *you*   *c* Heb lacks *temple*   *d* Compare Syr Tg: Heb *its fruit, its food*   *e* Another reading is *at it*   *f* Heb *it*   *g* Cn Compare Gk Syr: Heb *and he shall bear you to it*

Levi may hold, says the LORD of hosts. [5] My covenant with him was a covenant of life and well-being, which I gave him; this called for reverence, and he revered me and stood in awe of my name. [6] True instruction was in his mouth, and no wrong was found on his lips. He walked with me in integrity and uprightness, and he turned many from iniquity. [7] For the lips of a priest should guard knowledge, and people should seek instruction from his mouth, for he is the messenger of the LORD of hosts. [8] But you have turned aside from the way; you have caused many to stumble by your instruction; you have corrupted the covenant of Levi, says the LORD of hosts, [9] and so I make you despised and abased before all the people, inasmuch as you have not kept my ways but have shown partiality in your instruction.

The Covenant Profaned by Judah

10 Have we not all one father? Has not one God created us? Why then are we faithless to one another, profaning the covenant of our ancestors? [11] Judah has been faithless, and abomination has been committed in Israel and in Jerusalem; for Judah has profaned the sanctuary of the LORD, which he loves, and has married the daughter of a foreign god. [12] May the LORD cut off from the tents of Jacob anyone who does this—any to witness[a] or answer, or to bring an offering to the LORD of hosts.

13 And this you do as well: You cover the LORD's altar with tears, with weeping and groaning because he no longer regards the offering or accepts it with favour at your hand. [14] You ask, 'Why does he not?' Because the LORD was a witness between you and the wife of your youth, to whom you have been faithless, though she is your companion and your wife by covenant. [15] Did not one God make her?[b] Both flesh and spirit are his.[c] And what does the one God[d] desire? Godly offspring. So look to yourselves, and do not let anyone be faithless to the wife of his youth. [16] For I hate[e] divorce, says the LORD, the God of Israel, and covering one's garment with violence,

says the LORD of hosts. So take heed to yourselves and do not be faithless.

17 You have wearied the LORD with your words. Yet you say, 'How have we wearied him?' By saying, 'All who do evil are good in the sight of the LORD, and he delights in them.' Or by asking, 'Where is the God of justice?'

The Coming Messenger

3 See, I am sending my messenger to prepare the way before me, and the Lord whom you seek will suddenly come to his temple. The messenger of the covenant in whom you delight—indeed, he is coming, says the LORD of hosts. [2] But who can endure the day of his coming, and who can stand when he appears?

For he is like a refiner's fire and like fullers' soap; [3] he will sit as a refiner and purifier of silver, and he will purify the descendants of Levi and refine them like gold and silver, until they present offerings to the LORD in righteousness.[f] [4] Then the offering of Judah and Jerusalem will be pleasing to the LORD as in the days of old and as in former years.

5 Then I will draw near to you for judgement; I will be swift to bear witness against the sorcerers, against the adulterers, against those who swear falsely, against those who oppress the hired workers in their wages, the widow, and the orphan, against those who thrust aside the alien, and do not fear me, says the LORD of hosts.

6 For I the LORD do not change; therefore you, O children of Jacob, have not perished. [7] Ever since the days of your ancestors you have turned aside from my statutes and have not kept them. Return to me, and I will return to you, says the LORD of hosts. But you say, 'How shall we return?'

Do Not Rob God

8 Will anyone rob God? Yet you are robbing me! But you say, 'How are we robbing you?' In your tithes and offerings! [9] You are

a Cn Compare Gk: Heb *arouse*   b Or *Has he not made one?*   c Cn: Heb *and a remnant of spirit was his*   d Heb *he*   e Cn: Heb *he hates*   f Or *right offerings to the LORD* cursed with a curse, for you are robbing me—the whole nation of you! [10] Bring the full tithe into the storehouse, so that there may be food in my house, and thus put me to the test, says the LORD of hosts; see if I will not open the windows of heaven for you and pour down for you an overflowing blessing. [11] I will rebuke the locust[a] for you, so that it will not destroy the produce of your soil; and your vine in the field shall not be barren, says the LORD of hosts. [12] Then all nations will count you happy, for you will be a land of delight, says the LORD of hosts.

[13] You have spoken harsh words against me, says the LORD. Yet you say, 'How have we spoken against you?' [14] You have said, 'It is vain to serve God. What do we profit by keeping his command or by going about as mourners before the LORD of hosts? [15] Now we count the arrogant happy; evildoers not only prosper, but when they put God to the test they escape.'

The Reward of the Faithful

[16] Then those who revered the LORD spoke with one another. The LORD took note and listened, and a book of remembrance was written before him of those who revered the LORD and thought on his name. [17] They shall be mine, says the LORD of hosts, my special possession on the day when I act, and I will spare them as parents spare their children who serve them. [18] Then once more you shall see the difference between the righteous and the wicked, between one who serves God and one who does not serve him.

The Great Day of the LORD

4 [b] See, the day is coming, burning like an oven, when all the arrogant and all evildoers will be stubble; the day that comes shall burn them up, says the LORD of hosts, so that it will leave them neither root nor branch. [2] But for you who revere my name the sun of righteousness shall rise, with healing in its wings. You shall go out leaping like calves from the stall. [3] And you shall tread down the wicked, for they will be ashes under the soles of your feet, on the day when I act, says the LORD of hosts.

[4] Remember the teaching of my servant Moses, the statutes and ordinances that I commanded him at Horeb for all Israel.

[5] Lo, I will send you the prophet Elijah before the great and terrible day of the LORD comes. [6] He will turn the hearts of parents to their children and the hearts of children to their parents, so that I will not come and strike the land with a curse.[c]

a Heb *devourer*   b Ch 4.1-6 are Ch 3.19-24 in Heb
c Or *a ban of utter destruction*

THE NEW TESTAMENT

	Matthew	Mark	Luke	John
The Divinity of Jesus				1.1–5
Announcement of the Birth of John the Baptist			1.5–25	
The Betrothal of the Virgin Mary	1.18		1.27	
The Announcement of the Birth of Jesus			1.26–38	
Mary Visits Elizabeth			1.39–56	
Joseph's Dream	1.20–25			
The Birth of John the Baptist			1.57–80	
The Birth of Jesus			2.1–7	
The Visit by the Shepherds			2.8–20	
The Circumcision and Naming of Jesus			2.21	
The Presentation in the Temple			2.22–29	
The Genealogy of Jesus	1.1–17		3.23–38	
The Visit of the Wise Men	2.1–12			
The Flight to Egypt	2.13–15			
The Massacre of the Infants	2.16–18			
The Return from Egypt	2.19–23		2.39	
The Boy Jesus in the Temple			2.41	
With the Teachers in the Temple			2.46–50	
Youth of Jesus			2.51	
The Preaching of John the Baptist	3.1–4	1.1–8	3.1–18	1.6–15
Baptism by John	3.6	1.5	3.21	
The First Testimony of the Baptist to Christ	3.11–12	1.7–8		1.29–34
The Baptism of Jesus	3.13–17	1.9–11	3.21–22	
The Temptation of Jesus	4.1–11	1.12–13	4.1–13	
John the Baptist's Testimony to Himself				1.19–35
The Call of the First Disciples	4.18–22	1.16–20	5.1–11	1.37–51
First Miracle at Cana				2.1–11
Visit to Capernaum				2.12
Cleansing of the Temple	21.12–13	11.15–17	19.45–46	2.13–23
Nicodemus				3.1–21
The Final Witness of the Baptist				3.22–36

	Matthew	Mark	Luke	John
The Samaritan Woman				4.1–42
The Return to Galilee				4.43–45
The Second Sign at Cana				4.46–54
The Cure on a Sabbath				5.1–47
Imprisonment of John the Baptist	4.12; 14.3	1.14–15		3.24
The Beginning of the Galilean Ministry	4.12–17	1.14–15	4.14–15	
The Rejection at Nazareth	13.54–58	6.1–4	4.16–27	
Jesus Preaches at Capernaum	4.13–17			
The Cure of a Man with an Unclean Spirit		1.23–27	4.33–36	
The Cure of Peter's Mother-in-law	8.14–15	1.29–31	4.38–39	
Other Healings	8.16–17	1.32–34	4.40–41	
Circuit through Galilee		1.38–39	4.42–44	
The Cleansing of a Leper	8.1–4	1.40–45	5.12–18	
Retirement for Solitary Prayer		1.45	5.16	
The Healing of a Paralytic	9.1–8	2.1–12	5.18–25	
Call of Matthew	9.9–17	2.13–22	5.27–39	
Ministering to a Great Multitude	4.23–25		6.17–19	
Picking Grain on the Sabbath	12.1–8	2.23–28	6.1–5	
The Man with the Withered Hand	12.9–14	3.1–6	6.6–11	
Retirement for Solitary Prayer			6.12	
The Mission of the Twelve	10.1–4	3.13–19; 6.7–13	6.13–16; 9.1–6	
The Sermon on the Mount	5.1–12		6.20–26	
The Healing of the Centurion's Servant	8.5–13		7.1–10	
The Raising of the Widow's Son			7.11–17	
The Messengers from John the Baptist	11.2–19		7.18–35	
The Pardon of the Sinful Woman			7.36–50	
The Beatitudes	5.2–12		6.20–26	
Galilean Women Follow Jesus			8.1–3	
Jesus and Beelzebul	12.22–28	3.23–30	11.14–23	
Blasphemy against the Holy Spirit	12.31–32			
The Return of the Unclean Spirit	12.43–45	11.24–26		

	Matthew	Mark	Luke	John
The True Family of Jesus	12.46–50	3.31–35	8.19–21	
The Parable of the Sower	13.1–9	4.1–9; 4.14–20	8.6–8; 8.11–15	
The Parable of the Weeds among the Wheat	13.24–30			
The Parable of the Mustard Seed	13.31–32	4.30–32	13.18–19	
The Parable of the Yeast	13.33		13.20–21	
The Parable of the Lamp	5.15	4.21	8.16; 11.33	
The Parable of the Buried Treasure	13.44			
The Parable of the Fine Pearl	13.45–46			
The Parable of the Thrown Net	13.47–48			
The Calming of the Storm at Sea	8.24–27	4.37–41	8.23–25	
The Healing of the Gadarene Demoniacs	8.28–34	5.1–20	8.26–39	
The Parable of the Bridegroom	9.15			
The Parable of the New Cloth	9.16	2.21	5.36	
The Parable of the New Wine in Old Bottles	9.17	2.22	5.37–38	
Miracles: Jairus' Daughter and the Woman with Haemorrhages	9.18–26	5.22–43	8.41–56	
The Healing of Two Blind Men	9.27–31			
The Healing of a Mute Person	9.32–34			
The Mission of the Twelve	10.1–4	6.7–12	9.1–6	
Herod's Opinion of Jesus	14.1–12	6.14–29	9.7–9	
The Return of the Twelve and the Feeding of the Five Thousand	14.13–21	6.31–44	9.10–17	6.1–14
The Walking on the Water	14.22–33	6.47–52		6.16–21
The Bread of Life Discourse				6.22–65
Retirement for Solitary Prayer	14.23	6.46		
The Tradition of the Elders	15.1–20	7.1–23		
The Canaanite Woman's Faith	15.24–29	7.24–30		
The Healing of Many People	15.29–31			
The Feeding of the Four Thousand	15.32–39	8.1–9		
The Demand for a Sign: Weather	16.1–4	8.11–13	12.54–56	
The Yeast of the Pharisees and Sadducees	16.5–12	8.14–21		

	Matthew	Mark	Luke	John
Peter's Confession of Christ	16.13–20	8.27–30	9.18–20	
The First Prediction of the Passion	16.21–23	8.31–38	9.22–27	
The Transfiguration of Jesus	17.1–8	9.2–8	9.28–36	
The Healing of a Boy with a Demon	17.14–21	9.14–25	9.37–43	
The Second Prediction of the Passion	17.22–23	9.30–32	9.43–45	
Payment of the Temple Tax	17.24–27			
The Greatest in the Kingdom	18.1–5	9.33–37	9.46–48	
The Parable of the Lost Sheep	18.10–14		15.1–7	
A Person Who Sins	18.15–20		17.3–4	
A Lesson on Self-denial	18.18			
The Parable of the Unforgiving Servant	18.23–35			
The Departure for Jerusalem			9.51–52	
The Jealousy of the Samaritans			9.53	
The Anger of James and John			9.54–56	
The Festival of Booths				7.1–10
The First Dialogue				7.14–31
Officers Sent to Arrest Jesus				7.32–36
The Woman Caught in Adultery				8.1–11
The Light of the World				8.12–20
Jesus Threatened with Stoning				8.59
The Man Born Blind				9.1–41
The Good Shepherd				10.1–21
The Mission of the Seventy-two			10.1–12	
The Return of the Seventy-two			10.17–20	
The Parable of the Good Samaritan			10.29–37	
The Visit to Martha and Mary			10.38–42	
The Lord's Prayer	6.9–13		11.1–4	
Jesus and Beelzebul	12.22–45	3.23–30	11.14–23	
The Demand for a Sign: Jonah	12.38–42		11.29–32	
God's Providence to Birds and Flowers	10.29–31		12.6–7; 12.24; 12.27–28	
The Parable of the Rich Fool			12.16–20	

	Matthew	Mark	Luke	John
A Call to Repentance			13.1–5	
The Parable of the Barren Fig Tree			13.6–9	
The Cure of the Crippled Woman on the Sabbath			13.10–17	
The Festival of the Dedication				10.22–42
The Attempt to Stone Jesus				10.31
Jesus Retires across the Jordan				10.40
Salvation and Rejection	7.13–14; 7.21–23		13.22–30	
Herod's Desire to Kill Jesus			13.31–33	
The Healing of the Man with Dropsy on the Sabbath			14.1–6	
The Parable of the Great Dinner	22.1–14		14.15–24	
The Parable of the Lost Sheep	18.10–14		15.1–7	
The Parable of the Lost Coin			15.8–10	
The Parable of the Prodigal Son			15.11–32	
The Parable of the Dishonest Manager			16.1–8	
The Parable of the Rich Man and Lazarus			16.19–31	
The Raising of Lazarus				11.38–44
The Return of Jesus from Perea to Bethany				11.11–16
The Resurrection of Lazarus				11.38–44
The Session of the Sanhedrin				11.45–54
The Last Passover				11.55
The Last Journey in Jerusalem	19.1	10.1	17.11	
The Cleansing of the Ten Lepers			17.11–19	
The Parable of the Persistent Widow			18.1–8	
The Parable of the Pharisee and the Tax Collector			18.9–14	
Marriage and Divorce	19.1–12	10.1–12		
Blessing of the Children	19.13–15	10.13–16	18.15–17	
The Rich Young Man	19.16–30	10.17–22	18.18–23	
The Labourers in the Vineyard	20.1–16			
The Third Prediction of the Passion	20.17–19	10.32–34	18.31–34	

	Matthew	Mark	Luke	John
The Request of James and John	20.20–28	10.35–45		
The Healing of Two Blind Men	20.29–34	10.46–52	18.35–43	
Zacchaeus the Tax Collector			19.1–10	
The Parable of the Talents	25.14–30		10.11–27	
The Supper in Simon's House	26.6–13	14.3–9		12.1–9
Mary Anoints Jesus	26.7–13	14.3–9	12.3–8	
The Entry into Jerusalem	21.1–11	11.1–10	19.29–44	12.12–19
The Survey of the Temple		11.11		
The Cursing of the Fig Tree	21.18–19	11.12–14		
The Cleansing of the Temple	21.12–17	11.15–18		
The Lesson of the Fig Tree	21.20–22	11.20–25		
The Authority of Jesus Questioned	21.23–27	11.27–33	20.1–8	
The Parable of the Two Sons	21.28–32			
The Parable of the Tenants	21.33–46	12.1–12	20.9–19	
The Wedding Banquet	22.1–14		14.15–24	
Paying Taxes to the Emperor	22.15–22	12.13–17	20.20–26	
The Question about the Resurrection	22.23–33	12.18–27	20.27–39	
The Greatest Commandment	22.34–40	12.28–34	11.25–28	
The Question about David's Son	22.41–46	12.35–37	20.41–44	
Denunciation of the Scribes and Pharisees	23.1–33	12.38–40	11.37–54	
The Poor Widow's Contribution		12.41–44	21.1–4	
The Coming of Jesus' Hour				12.20–23
The Destruction of the Temple Foretold	24.1–2	13.1–3		
The Parable of the Ten Virgins	25.1–13		19.11–27	
The Judgement of the Nations	25.31–46			
The Conspiracy Against Jesus	26.3–5	14.1–2	22.1–2	
The Betrayal by Judas	26.14–16	14.10–11	22.3–6	18.2–5
Preparation of the Passover	26.17–19	14.12–16	22.7–13	
The Washing of the Disciples' Feet				13.1–17
The Lord's Supper	26.26	14.22	22.14	
The Betrayal Foretold	26.21	14.18	22.21	13.21

	Matthew	Mark	Luke	John
The Giving of the Piece of Bread				13.26–27
The Departure of Judas				13.30
Peter's Denial Predicted	26.31–35	14.27–31	22.21–23	13.36
Blessing the Cup	26.27–28	14.23–24	22.17	
Last Supper Discourses				14.1–14
The Prayer of Jesus				17.1
The Hymn	26.30	14.26		
The Agony in the Garden	26.36; 26.44	14.32–42	22.39–46	18.1
Jesus is Comforted by the Angel			22.43–44	
The Sleep of the Apostles	26.40–45	14.37–41	22.45–46	
The Betrayal and Arrest of Jesus	26.47–50	14.43–45	22.47	18.1–14
Peter Smites Malchus	26.51	14.47	22.50	18.10
Jesus Heals the Ear of Malchus			22.51	
Jesus Forsaken by His Disciples	26.56	14.50		
Jesus Led to Annas				18.12–13
Jesus before the Sanhedrin	26.57	14.53	22.66	
Peter Follows Jesus	26.58	14.54	22.55	18.15
The High Priest's Adjuration	26.63	14.61	22.66	
Jesus Condemned	26.66–67	14.64–65	22.70–71	
Peter's Denial of Jesus	26.69–75	14.66–72	22.54–62	18.17–27
Jesus before Pilate	27.1	15.1	23.1	18.28
The Death of Judas	27.3			
Pilate Comes out to the People				18.29
Pilate Speaks to Jesus Privately				18.33
Mockery by the Soldiers	27.27	15.15	22.63–65	19.1
Jesus Crowned with Thorns	27.29	15.17		19.2
Jesus Exhibited by Pilate				19.5
Jesus Questioned by Pilate	27.11	15.2	23.2	
Jesus Sent by Pilate to Herod			23.6–11	
The Sentence of Death	27.15	15.6	23.17	19.12–16
Pilate Receives a Message from his Wife	27.19			

	Matthew	Mark	Luke	John
Pilate Washes His Hands	27.24			
Pilate Releases Barnabas	27.26	15.15	23.25	
Pilate Delivers Jesus to Be Crucified	27.26	15.15	23.25	19.16
The Way of the Cross	27.32	15.21	23.26	
The Crucifixion	27.33–44	15.22–32	23.33–43	19.17–30
The Death of Jesus	27.45–56	5.33–41	23.44–49	
The Burial of Jesus	27.57–61	15.42–47	23.50–56	19.38–42
The Guard at the Tomb	27.62–66			
The Resurrection of Jesus	28.1–10	16.1–8	24.1–12	20.1–10
The Report of the Guards	28.11–15			
The Appearance to Mary Magdalene		16.9		20.14
The Appearance to the Women Returning Home	28.9			
The Appearance to Two Disciples Going to Emmaus		16.12	24.13	
The Appearance to Peter			24.34	
The Appearance to the Disciples in Jerusalem			24.36	20.19
The Appearance to the Eleven Apostles		16.14		
The Appearance to Thomas				20.27
The Appearance to the Seven Disciples				21.1–22
Jesus and Peter				21.15–19
The Commissioning of the Disciples	28.16–20	16.14		
The Ascension of Jesus		16.19–20	24.50–43	

THE GOSPEL ACCORDING TO
MATTHEW

The Genealogy of Jesus the Messiah

1 An account of the genealogy*a* of Jesus the Messiah,*b* the son of David, the son of Abraham.

2 Abraham was the father of Isaac, and Isaac the father of Jacob, and Jacob the father of Judah and his brothers, ³and Judah the father of Perez and Zerah by Tamar, and Perez the father of Hezron, and Hezron the father of Aram, ⁴and Aram the father of Aminadab, and Aminadab the father of Nahshon, and Nahshon the father of Salmon, ⁵and Salmon the father of Boaz by Rahab, and Boaz the father of Obed by Ruth, and Obed the father of Jesse, ⁶and Jesse the father of King David.

And David was the father of Solomon by the wife of Uriah, ⁷and Solomon the father of Rehoboam, and Rehoboam the father of Abijah, and Abijah the father of Asaph,*c* ⁸and Asaph*c* the father of Jehoshaphat, and Jehoshaphat the father of Joram, and Joram the father of Uzziah, ⁹and Uzziah the father of Jotham, and Jotham the father of Ahaz, and Ahaz the father of Hezekiah, ¹⁰and Hezekiah the father of Manasseh, and Manasseh the father of Amos,*d* and Amos*d* the father of Josiah, ¹¹and Josiah the father of Jechoniah and his brothers, at the time of the deportation to Babylon.

12 And after the deportation to Babylon: Jechoniah was the father of Salathiel, and Salathiel the father of Zerubbabel, ¹³and Zerubbabel the father of Abiud, and Abiud the father of Eliakim, and Eliakim the father of Azor, ¹⁴and Azor the father of Zadok, and Zadok the father of Achim, and Achim the father of Eliud, ¹⁵and Eliud the father of Eleazar, and Eleazar the father of Matthan, and Matthan the father of Jacob, ¹⁶and Jacob the father of Joseph the husband of Mary, of whom Jesus was born, who is called the Messiah.*e*

17 So all the generations from Abraham to David are fourteen generations; and from David to the deportation to Babylon, fourteen generations; and from the deportation to Babylon to the Messiah,*e* fourteen generations.

The Birth of Jesus the Messiah

18 Now the birth of Jesus the Messiah*b* took place in this way. When his mother Mary had been engaged to Joseph, but before they lived together, she was found to be with child from the Holy Spirit. ¹⁹Her husband Joseph, being a righteous man and unwilling to expose her to public disgrace, planned to dismiss her quietly. ²⁰But just when he had resolved to do this, an angel of the Lord appeared to him in a dream and said, 'Joseph, son of David, do not be afraid to take Mary as your wife, for the child conceived in her is from the Holy Spirit. ²¹She will bear a son, and you are to name him Jesus, for he will save his people from their sins.' ²²All this took place to fulfil what had been spoken by the Lord through the prophet:

23 'Look, the virgin shall conceive and
      bear a son,
   and they shall name him
      Emmanuel',

which means, 'God is with us.' ²⁴When Joseph awoke from sleep, he did as the angel

---

a Or *birth* *b* Or *Jesus Christ* *c* Other ancient authorities read *Asa* *d* Other ancient authorities read *Amon* *e* Or *the Christ* of the Lord commanded him; he took her as his wife, 25 but had no marital relations with her until she had borne a son;*a* and he named him Jesus.

The Visit of the Wise Men

2 In the time of King Herod, after Jesus was born in Bethlehem of Judea, wise men*b* from the East came to Jerusalem, 2 asking, 'Where is the child who has been born king of the Jews? For we observed his star at its rising,*c* and have come to pay him homage.' 3 When King Herod heard this, he was frightened, and all Jerusalem with him; 4 and calling together all the chief priests and scribes of the people, he inquired of them where the Messiah*d* was to be born. 5 They told him, 'In Bethlehem of Judea; for so it has been written by the prophet:

6 "And you, Bethlehem, in the land
      of Judah,
    are by no means least among the
      rulers of Judah;
  for from you shall come a ruler
    who is to shepherd*e* my
      people Israel." '

The Journeys of Jesus' Birth

Mediterranean
Sea

GALILEE

Sea of Galilee

Nazareth

SAMARIA

Lebonah

JUDEA

Ashkelon   Jerusalem
Gaza   Hebron   Bethlehem

Dead
Sea

IDUMEA

To Egypt

0   100 Mi.
0   100 Km.

→ To Bethlehem, Egypt
- - - ▶ Return

7 Then Herod secretly called for the wise men*b* and learned from them the exact time when the star had appeared. 8 Then he sent them to Bethlehem, saying, 'Go and search diligently for the child; and when you have found him, bring me word so that I may also go and pay him homage.' 9 When they had heard the king, they set out; and there, ahead of them, went the star that they had seen at its rising,*c* until it stopped over the place where the child was. 10 When they saw that the star had stopped,*f* they were overwhelmed with joy. 11 On entering the house, they saw the child with Mary his mother; and they knelt down and paid him homage. Then, opening their treasure-chests, they offered him gifts of gold, frankincense, and myrrh. 12 And having been warned in a dream not to return to Herod, they left for their own country by another road.

The Escape to Egypt

13 Now after they had left, an angel of the Lord appeared to Joseph in a dream and said, 'Get up, take the child and his mother, and flee to Egypt, and remain there until I tell you; for Herod is about to search for the child, to destroy him.' 14 Then Joseph*g* got up, took the child and his mother by night, and went to Egypt, 15 and remained there until the death of Herod. This was to fulfil what had been spoken by the Lord through the prophet, 'Out of Egypt I have called my son.'

The Massacre of the Infants

16 When Herod saw that he had been tricked by the wise men,*b* he was infuriated, and he sent and killed all the children in and around Bethlehem who were two years old or under, according to the time that he had learned from the wise men.*b* 17 Then was fulfilled what had been spoken through the prophet Jeremiah:

18 'A voice was heard in Ramah,
      wailing and loud lamentation,
    Rachel weeping for her children;

a Other ancient authorities read *her firstborn son*
b Or *astrologers;* Gk *magi* *c* Or *in the East* *d* Or *the
Christ* *e* Or *rule* *f* Gk *saw the star* *g* Gk *he*

she refused to be consoled, because they are no more.'

The Return from Egypt

19 When Herod died, an angel of the Lord suddenly appeared in a dream to Joseph in Egypt and said, 20 'Get up, take the child and his mother, and go to the land of Israel, for those who were seeking the child's life are dead.' 21 Then Joseph[a] got up, took the child and his mother, and went to the land of Israel. 22 But when he heard that Archelaus was ruling over Judea in place of his father Herod, he was afraid to go there. And after being warned in a dream, he went away to the district of Galilee. 23 There he made his home in a town called Nazareth, so that what had been spoken through the prophets might be fulfilled, 'He will be called a Nazorean.'

The Proclamation of John the Baptist

3 In those days John the Baptist appeared in the wilderness of Judea, proclaiming, 2 'Repent, for the kingdom of heaven has come near.'[b] 3 This is the one of whom the prophet Isaiah spoke when he said,

'The voice of one crying out in
the wilderness:
"Prepare the way of the Lord,
make his paths straight." '

4 Now John wore clothing of camel's hair with a leather belt around his waist, and his food was locusts and wild honey. 5 Then the people of Jerusalem and all Judea were going out to him, and all the region along the Jordan, 6 and they were baptized by him in the river Jordan, confessing their sins.

7 But when he saw many Pharisees and Sadducees coming for baptism, he said to them, 'You brood of vipers! Who warned you to flee from the wrath to come? 8 Bear fruit worthy of repentance. 9 Do not presume to say to yourselves, "We have Abraham as our ancestor"; for I tell you, God is able from these stones to raise up children to Abraham. 10 Even now the axe is lying at the root of the trees; every tree therefore that does not bear good fruit is cut down and thrown into the fire.

11 'I baptize you with[c] water for repentance, but one who is more powerful than I is coming after me; I am not worthy to carry his sandals. He will baptize you with[c] the Holy Spirit and fire. 12 His winnowing-fork is in his hand, and he will clear his threshing-floor and will gather his wheat into the granary; but the chaff he will burn with unquenchable fire.'

The Baptism of Jesus

13 Then Jesus came from Galilee to John at the Jordan, to be baptized by him. 14 John would have prevented him, saying, 'I need to be baptized by you, and do you come to me?' 15 But Jesus answered him, 'Let it be so now; for it is proper for us in this way to fulfil all righteousness.' Then he consented. 16 And when Jesus had been baptized, just as he came up from the water, suddenly the heavens were opened to him and he saw the Spirit of God descending like a dove and alighting on him. 17 And a voice from

Jesus' Baptism and Temptation

Mediterranean Sea

GALILEE

Nazareth

Sea of Galilee

Scythopolis

Aenon?
Salim   DECAPOLIS

SAMARIA

PEREA

Jericho
Jerusalem   Bethabara

Wilderness of Judea

Dead Sea

JUDEA

0   40 Mi.
0   40 Km.

N

a Gk he   b Or is at hand   c Or in

heaven said, 'This is my Son, the Beloved,[a] with whom I am well pleased.'

The Temptation of Jesus

4 Then Jesus was led up by the Spirit into the wilderness to be tempted by the devil. 2 He fasted for forty days and forty nights, and afterwards he was famished. 3 The tempter came and said to him, 'If you are the Son of God, command these stones to become loaves of bread.' 4 But he answered, 'It is written,

"One does not live by bread alone,
    but by every word that comes from
        the mouth of God." '

5 Then the devil took him to the holy city and placed him on the pinnacle of the temple, 6 saying to him, 'If you are the Son of God, throw yourself down; for it is written,

"He will command his angels
        concerning you",
    and "On their hands they will bear
        you up,
so that you will not dash your foot
        against a stone." '

7 Jesus said to him, 'Again it is written, "Do not put the Lord your God to the test." '

8 Again, the devil took him to a very high mountain and showed him all the kingdoms of the world and their splendour; 9 and he said to him, 'All these I will give you, if you will fall down and worship me.' 10 Jesus said to him, 'Away with you, Satan! for it is written,

"Worship the Lord your God,
    and serve only him." '

11 Then the devil left him, and suddenly angels came and waited on him.

Jesus Begins His Ministry in Galilee

12 Now when Jesus[b] heard that John had been arrested, he withdrew to Galilee. 13 He left Nazareth and made his home in Capernaum by the lake, in the territory of Zebulun and Naphtali, 14 so that what had been spoken through the prophet Isaiah might be fulfilled:

15 'Land of Zebulun, land of Naphtali,
    on the road by the sea, across the
        Jordan, Galilee of the Gentiles—

16 the people who sat in darkness
        have seen a great light,
    and for those who sat in the region
        and shadow of death
    light has dawned.'

17 From that time Jesus began to proclaim, 'Repent, for the kingdom of heaven has come near.'[c]

Jesus Calls the First Disciples

18 As he walked by the Sea of Galilee, he saw two brothers, Simon, who is called Peter, and Andrew his brother, casting a net into the lake—for they were fishermen. 19 And he said to them, 'Follow me, and I will make you fish for people.' 20 Immediately they left their nets and followed him. 21 As he went from there, he saw two other brothers, James son of Zebedee and his brother John, in the boat with their father Zebedee, mending their nets, and he called them. 22 Immediately they left the boat and their father, and followed him.

Jesus Ministers to Crowds of People

23 Jesus[d] went throughout Galilee, teaching in their synagogues and proclaiming the good news[e] of the kingdom and curing every disease and every sickness among the people. 24 So his fame spread throughout all Syria, and they brought to him all the sick, those who were afflicted with various diseases and pains, demoniacs, epileptics, and paralytics, and he cured them. 25 And great crowds followed him from Galilee, the Decapolis, Jerusalem, Judea, and from beyond the Jordan.

The Beatitudes

5 When Jesus[b] saw the crowds, he went up the mountain; and after he sat down, his disciples came to him. 2 Then he began to speak, and taught them, saying:

3 'Blessed are the poor in spirit, for theirs is the kingdom of heaven.

4 'Blessed are those who mourn, for they will be comforted.

a Or *my beloved Son*   *b* Gk *he*   *c* Or *is at hand*
d Gk *He*   *e* Gk *gospel*

5 'Blessed are the meek, for they will inherit the earth.

6 'Blessed are those who hunger and thirst for righteousness, for they will be filled.

7 'Blessed are the merciful, for they will receive mercy.

8 'Blessed are the pure in heart, for they will see God.

9 'Blessed are the peacemakers, for they will be called children of God.

10 'Blessed are those who are persecuted for righteousness' sake, for theirs is the kingdom of heaven.

11 'Blessed are you when people revile you and persecute you and utter all kinds of evil against you falsely[a] on my account. 12 Rejoice and be glad, for your reward is great in heaven, for in the same way they persecuted the prophets who were before you.

Salt and Light

13 'You are the salt of the earth; but if salt has lost its taste, how can its saltiness be restored? It is no longer good for anything, but is thrown out and trampled under foot.

14 'You are the light of the world. A city built on a hill cannot be hidden. 15 No one after lighting a lamp puts it under the bushel basket, but on the lampstand, and it gives light to all in the house. 16 In the same way, let your light shine before others, so that they may see your good works and give glory to your Father in heaven.

The Law and the Prophets

17 'Do not think that I have come to abolish the law or the prophets; I have come not to abolish but to fulfil. 18 For truly I tell you, until heaven and earth pass away, not one letter,[b] not one stroke of a letter, will pass from the law until all is accomplished. 19 Therefore, whoever breaks[c] one of the least of these commandments, and teaches others to do the same, will be called least in the kingdom of heaven; but whoever does them and teaches them will be called great in the kingdom of heaven. 20 For I tell you, unless your righteousness

exceeds that of the scribes and Pharisees, you will never enter the kingdom of heaven.

Concerning Anger

21 'You have heard that it was said to those of ancient times, "You shall not murder"; and "whoever murders shall be liable to judgement." 22 But I say to you that if you are angry with a brother or sister,[d] you will be liable to judgement; and if you insult[e] a brother or sister,[f] you will be liable to the council; and if you say, "You fool", you will be liable to the hell[g] of fire. 23 So when you are offering your gift at the altar, if you remember that your brother or sister[h] has something against you, 24 leave your gift there before the altar and go; first be reconciled to your brother or sister,[h] and then come and offer your gift. 25 Come to terms quickly with your accuser while you are on the way to court[i] with him, or your accuser may hand you over to the judge, and the judge to the guard, and you will be thrown into prison. 26 Truly I tell you, you will never get out until you have paid the last penny.

Concerning Adultery

27 'You have heard that it was said, "You shall not commit adultery." 28 But I say to you that everyone who looks at a woman with lust has already committed adultery with her in his heart. 29 If your right eye causes you to sin, tear it out and throw it away; it is better for you to lose one of your members than for your whole body to be thrown into hell.[g] 30 And if your right hand causes you to sin, cut it off and throw it away; it is better for you to lose one of your members than for your whole body to go into hell.[g]

Concerning Divorce

31 'It was also said, "Whoever divorces his wife, let him give her a certificate of divorce." 32 But I say to you that anyone who divorces his wife, except on the

a Other ancient authorities lack falsely   b Gk one iota
c Or annuls   d Gk a brother; other ancient authorities
add without cause   e Gk say Raca to (an obscure term
of abuse)   f Gk a brother   g Gk Gehenna
h Gk your brother   i Gk lacks to court

ground of unchastity, causes her to commit adultery; and whoever marries a divorced woman commits adultery.

Concerning Oaths

33 'Again, you have heard that it was said to those of ancient times, "You shall not swear falsely, but carry out the vows you have made to the Lord." 34 But I say to you, Do not swear at all, either by heaven, for it is the throne of God, 35 or by the earth, for it is his footstool, or by Jerusalem, for it is the city of the great King. 36 And do not swear by your head, for you cannot make one hair white or black. 37 Let your word be "Yes, Yes" or "No, No"; anything more than this comes from the evil one. *a*

Concerning Retaliation

38 'You have heard that it was said, "An eye for an eye and a tooth for a tooth." 39 But I say to you, Do not resist an evildoer. But if anyone strikes you on the right cheek, turn the other also; 40 and if anyone wants to sue you and take your coat, give your cloak as well; 41 and if anyone forces you to go one mile, go also the second mile. 42 Give to everyone who begs from you, and do not refuse anyone who wants to borrow from you.

Love for Enemies

43 'You have heard that it was said, "You shall love your neighbour and hate your enemy." 44 But I say to you, Love your enemies and pray for those who persecute you, 45 so that you may be children of your Father in heaven; for he makes his sun rise on the evil and on the good, and sends rain on the righteous and on the unrighteous. 46 For if you love those who love you, what reward do you have? Do not even the tax-collectors do the same? 47 And if you greet only your brothers and sisters, *b* what more are you doing than others? Do not even the Gentiles do the same? 48 Be perfect, therefore, as your heavenly Father is perfect.

Concerning Almsgiving

6 'Beware of practising your piety before others in order to be seen by them; for then you have no reward from your Father in heaven.

2 'So whenever you give alms, do not sound a trumpet before you, as the hypocrites do in the synagogues and in the streets, so that they may be praised by others. Truly I tell you, they have received their reward. 3 But when you give alms, do not let your left hand know what your right hand is doing, 4 so that your alms may be done in secret; and your Father who sees in secret will reward you. *c*

Concerning Prayer

5 'And whenever you pray, do not be like the hypocrites; for they love to stand and pray in the synagogues and at the street corners, so that they may be seen by others. Truly I tell you, they have received their reward. 6 But whenever you pray, go into your room and shut the door and pray to your Father who is in secret; and your Father who sees in secret will reward you. *c*

7 'When you are praying, do not heap up empty phrases as the Gentiles do; for they think that they will be heard because of their many words. 8 Do not be like them, for your Father knows what you need before you ask him.

9 'Pray then in this way:
Our Father in heaven,
   hallowed be your name.
10   Your kingdom come.
    Your will be done,
      on earth as it is in heaven.
11   Give us this day our daily bread. *d*
12   And forgive us our debts,
     as we also have forgiven
      our debtors.
13   And do not bring us to the time of
      trial, *e*
     but rescue us from the evil one. *f*

a Or *evil*   *b* Gk *your brothers*   *c* Other ancient authorities add *openly*   *d* Or *our bread for tomorrow*   *e* Or *us into temptation*   *f* Or *from evil.* Other ancient authorities add, in some form, *For the kingdom and the power and the glory are yours for ever. Amen.*

14 For if you forgive others their trespasses, your heavenly Father will also forgive you; 15 but if you do not forgive others, neither will your Father forgive your trespasses.

Concerning Fasting

16 'And whenever you fast, do not look dismal, like the hypocrites, for they disfigure their faces so as to show others that they are fasting. Truly I tell you, they have received their reward. 17 But when you fast, put oil on your head and wash your face, 18 so that your fasting may be seen not by others but by your Father who is in secret; and your Father who sees in secret will reward you. *a*

Concerning Treasures

19 'Do not store up for yourselves treasures on earth, where moth and rust *b* consume and where thieves break in and steal; 20 but store up for yourselves treasures in heaven, where neither moth nor rust *b* consumes and where thieves do not break in and steal. 21 For where your treasure is, there your heart will be also.

The Sound Eye

22 'The eye is the lamp of the body. So, if your eye is healthy, your whole body will be full of light; 23 but if your eye is unhealthy, your whole body will be full of darkness. If then the light in you is darkness, how great is the darkness!

Serving Two Masters

24 'No one can serve two masters; for a slave will either hate the one and love the other, or be devoted to the one and despise the other. You cannot serve God and wealth. *c*

Do Not Worry

25 'Therefore I tell you, do not worry about your life, what you will eat or what you will drink, *d* or about your body, what you will wear. Is not life more than food, and the body more than clothing? 26 Look at the birds of the air; they neither sow nor reap nor gather into barns, and yet your heavenly Father feeds them. Are you not of more value than they? 27 And can any of you by worrying add a single hour to your span of life? *e* 28 And why do you worry about clothing? Consider the lilies of the field, how they grow; they neither toil nor spin, 29 yet I tell you, even Solomon in all his glory was not clothed like one of these. 30 But if God so clothes the grass of the field, which is alive today and tomorrow is thrown into the oven, will he not much more clothe you—you of little faith? 31 Therefore do not worry, saying, "What will we eat?" or "What will we drink?" or "What will we wear?" 32 For it is the Gentiles who strive for all these things; and indeed your heavenly Father knows that you need all these things. 33 But strive first for the kingdom of God *f* and his *g* righteousness, and all these things will be given to you as well.

34 'So do not worry about tomorrow, for tomorrow will bring worries of its own. Today's trouble is enough for today.

Judging Others

7 'Do not judge, so that you may not be judged. 2 For with the judgement you make you will be judged, and the measure you give will be the measure you get. 3 Why do you see the speck in your neighbour's *h* eye, but do not notice the log in your own eye? 4 Or how can you say to your neighbour, *i* "Let me take the speck out of your eye", while the log is in your own eye? 5 You hypocrite, first take the log out of your own eye, and then you will see clearly to take the speck out of your neighbour's *h* eye.

Profaning the Holy

6 'Do not give what is holy to dogs; and do not throw your pearls before swine, or they will trample them under foot and turn and maul you.

a Other ancient authorities add *openly*   *b* Gk *eating*
c Gk *mammon*   *d* Other ancient authorities lack *or what you will drink*   *e* Or *add one cubit to your height*
f Other ancient authorities lack *of God*   *g* Or *its*
h Gk *brother's*   *i* Gk *brother*

Ask, Search, Knock

7 'Ask, and it will be given to you; search, and you will find; knock, and the door will be opened for you. 8 For everyone who asks receives, and everyone who searches finds, and for everyone who knocks, the door will be opened. 9 Is there anyone among you who, if your child asks for bread, will give a stone? 10 Or if the child asks for a fish, will give a snake? 11 If you then, who are evil, know how to give good gifts to your children, how much more will your Father in heaven give good things to those who ask him!

The Golden Rule

12 'In everything do to others as you would have them do to you; for this is the law and the prophets.

The Narrow Gate

13 'Enter through the narrow gate; for the gate is wide and the road is easy*a* that leads to destruction, and there are many who take it. 14 For the gate is narrow and the road is hard that leads to life, and there are few who find it.

A Tree and Its Fruit

15 'Beware of false prophets, who come to you in sheep's clothing but inwardly are ravenous wolves. 16 You will know them by their fruits. Are grapes gathered from thorns, or figs from thistles? 17 In the same way, every good tree bears good fruit, but the bad tree bears bad fruit. 18 A good tree cannot bear bad fruit, nor can a bad tree bear good fruit. 19 Every tree that does not bear good fruit is cut down and thrown into the fire. 20 Thus you will know them by their fruits.

Concerning Self-Deception

21 'Not everyone who says to me, "Lord, Lord", will enter the kingdom of heaven, but only one who does the will of my Father in heaven. 22 On that day many will say to me, "Lord, Lord, did we not prophesy in your name, and cast out demons in your name, and do many deeds of power in your name?" 23 Then I will declare to them, "I never knew you; go away from me, you evildoers."

Hearers and Doers

24 'Everyone then who hears these words of mine and acts on them will be like a wise man who built his house on rock. 25 The rain fell, the floods came, and the winds blew and beat on that house, but it did not fall, because it had been founded on rock. 26 And everyone who hears these words of mine and does not act on them will be like a foolish man who built his house on sand. 27 The rain fell, and the floods came, and the winds blew and beat against that house, and it fell— and great was its fall!'

28 Now when Jesus had finished saying these things, the crowds were astounded at his teaching, 29 for he taught them as one having authority, and not as their scribes.

Jesus Cleanses a Leper

8 When Jesus*b* had come down from the mountain, great crowds followed him; 2 and there was a leper*c* who came to him and knelt before him, saying, 'Lord, if you choose, you can make me clean.' 3 He stretched out his hand and touched him, saying, 'I do choose. Be made clean!' Immediately his leprosy*c* was cleansed. 4 Then Jesus said to him, 'See that you say nothing to anyone; but go, show yourself to the priest, and offer the gift that Moses commanded, as a testimony to them.'

Jesus Heals a Centurion's Servant

5 When he entered Capernaum, a centurion came to him, appealing to him 6 and saying, 'Lord, my servant is lying at home paralysed, in terrible distress.' 7 And he said to him, 'I will come and cure him.' 8 The centurion answered, 'Lord, I am not worthy to have you come under my roof; but only speak the word, and my servant will be healed. 9 For I also am a man under authority, with soldiers under me; and I

a Other ancient authorities read *for the road is wide and easy*   b Gk *he*   c The terms *leper* and *leprosy* can refer to several diseases say to one, "Go", and he goes, and to another, "Come", and he comes, and to my slave, "Do this", and the slave does it.' [10] When Jesus heard him, he was amazed and said to those who followed him, 'Truly I tell you, in no one[a] in Israel have I found such faith. [11] I tell you, many will come from east and west and will eat with Abraham and Isaac and Jacob in the kingdom of heaven, [12] while the heirs of the kingdom will be thrown into the outer darkness, where there will be weeping and gnashing of teeth.' [13] And to the centurion Jesus said, 'Go; let it be done for you according to your faith.' And the servant was healed in that hour.

Jesus Heals Many at Peter's House

14 When Jesus entered Peter's house, he saw his mother-in-law lying in bed with a fever; [15] he touched her hand, and the fever left her, and she got up and began to serve him. [16] That evening they brought to him many who were possessed by demons; and he cast out the spirits with a word, and cured all who were sick. [17] This was to fulfil what had been spoken through the prophet Isaiah, 'He took our infirmities and bore our diseases.'

Would-Be Followers of Jesus

18 Now when Jesus saw great crowds around him, he gave orders to go over to the other side. [19] A scribe then approached and said, 'Teacher, I will follow you wherever you go.' [20] And Jesus said to him, 'Foxes have holes, and birds of the air have nests; but the Son of Man has nowhere to lay his head.' [21] Another of his disciples said to him, 'Lord, first let me go and bury my father.' [22] But Jesus said to him, 'Follow me, and let the dead bury their own dead.'

Jesus Stills the Storm

23 And when he got into the boat, his disciples followed him. [24] A gale arose on the lake, so great that the boat was being swamped by the waves; but he was asleep. [25] And they went and woke him up, saying, 'Lord, save us! We are perishing!' [26] And he

said to them, 'Why are you afraid, you of little faith?' Then he got up and rebuked the winds and the sea; and there was a dead calm. [27] They were amazed, saying, 'What sort of man is this, that even the winds and the sea obey him?'

Jesus Heals the Gadarene Demoniacs

28 When he came to the other side, to the country of the Gadarenes,[b] two demoniacs coming out of the tombs met him. They were so fierce that no one could pass that way. [29] Suddenly they shouted, 'What have you to do with us, Son of God? Have you come here to torment us before the time?' [30] Now a large herd of swine was feeding at some distance from them. [31] The demons begged him, 'If you cast us out, send us into the herd of swine.' [32] And he said to them, 'Go!' So they came out and entered the swine; and suddenly, the whole herd rushed down the steep bank into the lake and perished in the water. [33] The swineherds ran off, and on going into the town, they told the whole story about what had happened to the demoniacs. [34] Then the whole town came out to meet Jesus; and when they saw him, they begged him to leave their neighbourhood. [9] [1] And after getting into a boat he crossed the water and came to his own town.

Jesus Heals a Paralytic

2 And just then some people were carrying a paralysed man lying on a bed. When Jesus saw their faith, he said to the paralytic, 'Take heart, son; your sins are forgiven.' [3] Then some of the scribes said to themselves, 'This man is blaspheming.' [4] But Jesus, perceiving their thoughts, said, 'Why do you think evil in your hearts? [5] For which is easier, to say, "Your sins are forgiven", or to say, "Stand up and walk"? [6] But so that you may know that the Son of Man has authority on earth to forgive sins'—he then said to the paralytic— 'Stand up, take your bed and go to your

home.' 7 And he stood up and went to his home. 8 When the crowds saw it, they were filled with awe, and they glorified God, who had given such authority to human beings.

The Calling of Matthew

9 As Jesus was walking along, he saw a man called Matthew sitting at the tax booth; and he said to him, 'Follow me.' And he got up and followed him.

10 And as he sat at dinner*a* in the house, many tax-collectors and sinners came and were sitting*b* with him and his disciples. 11 When the Pharisees saw this, they said to his disciples, 'Why does your teacher eat with tax-collectors and sinners?' 12 But when he heard this, he said, 'Those who are well have no need of a physician, but those who are sick. 13 Go and learn what this means, "I desire mercy, not sacrifice." For I have come to call not the righteous but sinners.'

The Question about Fasting

14 Then the disciples of John came to him, saying, 'Why do we and the Pharisees fast often,*c* but your disciples do not fast?' 15 And Jesus said to them, 'The wedding-guests cannot mourn as long as the bridegroom is with them, can they? The days will come when the bridegroom is taken away from them, and then they will fast. 16 No one sews a piece of unshrunk cloth on an old cloak, for the patch pulls away from the cloak, and a worse tear is made. 17 Neither is new wine put into old wineskins; otherwise, the skins burst, and the wine is spilled, and the skins are destroyed; but new wine is put into fresh wineskins, and so both are preserved.'

A Girl Restored to Life and a Woman Healed

18 While he was saying these things to them, suddenly a leader of the synagogue*d* came in and knelt before him, saying, 'My daughter has just died; but come and lay your hand on her, and she will live.' 19 And Jesus got up and followed him, with his disciples. 20 Then suddenly a woman who had been suffering from haemorrhages for twelve years came up behind him and touched the fringe of his cloak, 21 for she said to herself, 'If I only touch his cloak, I will be made well.' 22 Jesus turned, and seeing her he said, 'Take heart, daughter; your faith has made you well.' And instantly the woman was made well. 23 When Jesus came to the leader's house and saw the flute-players and the crowd making a commotion, 24 he said, 'Go away; for the girl is not dead but sleeping.' And they laughed at him. 25 But when the crowd had been put outside, he went in and took her by the hand, and the girl got up. 26 And the report of this spread throughout that district.

Jesus Heals Two Blind Men

27 As Jesus went on from there, two blind men followed him, crying loudly, 'Have mercy on us, Son of David!' 28 When he entered the house, the blind men came to him; and Jesus said to them, 'Do you believe that I am able to do this?' They said to him, 'Yes, Lord.' 29 Then he touched their eyes and said, 'According to your faith let it be done to you.' 30 And their eyes were opened. Then Jesus sternly ordered them, 'See that no one knows of this.' 31 But they went away and spread the news about him throughout that district.

Jesus Heals One Who Was Mute

32 After they had gone away, a demoniac who was mute was brought to him. 33 And when the demon had been cast out, the one who had been mute spoke; and the crowds were amazed and said, 'Never has anything like this been seen in Israel.' 34 But the Pharisees said, 'By the ruler of the demons he casts out the demons.'*e*

The Harvest Is Great, the Labourers Few

35 Then Jesus went about all the cities and villages, teaching in their synagogues, and proclaiming the good news of the kingdom, and curing every disease and

a Gk *reclined*   *b* Gk *were reclining*   *c* Other ancient authorities lack *often*   *d* Gk lacks *of the synagogue*   *e* Other ancient authorities lack this verse every sickness. 36 When he saw the crowds, he had compassion for them, because they were harassed and helpless, like sheep without a shepherd. 37 Then he said to his disciples, 'The harvest is plentiful, but the labourers are few; 38 therefore ask the Lord of the harvest to send out labourers into his harvest.'

The Twelve Apostles

10 Then Jesus *a* summoned his twelve disciples and gave them authority over unclean spirits, to cast them out, and to cure every disease and every sickness. 2 These are the names of the twelve apostles: first, Simon, also known as Peter, and his brother Andrew; James son of Zebedee, and his brother John; 3 Philip and Bartholomew; Thomas and Matthew the tax-collector; James son of Alphaeus, and Thaddaeus; *b* 4 Simon the Cananaean, and Judas Iscariot, the one who betrayed him.

The Mission of the Twelve

5 These twelve Jesus sent out with the following instructions: 'Go nowhere among the Gentiles, and enter no town of the Samaritans, 6 but go rather to the lost sheep of the house of Israel. 7 As you go, proclaim the good news, "The kingdom of heaven has come near." *c* 8 Cure the sick, raise the dead, cleanse the lepers, *d* cast out demons. You received without payment; give without payment. 9 Take no gold, or silver, or copper in your belts, 10 no bag for your journey, or two tunics, or sandals, or a staff; for labourers deserve their food. 11 Whatever town or village you enter, find out who in it is worthy, and stay there until you leave. 12 As you enter the house, greet it. 13 If the house is worthy, let your peace come upon it; but if it is not worthy, let your peace return to you. 14 If anyone will not welcome you or listen to your words, shake off the dust from your feet as you leave that house or town. 15 Truly I tell you, it will be more tolerable for the land of Sodom and Gomorrah on the day of judgement than for that town.

Coming Persecutions

16 'See, I am sending you out like sheep into the midst of wolves; so be wise as serpents and innocent as doves. 17 Beware of them, for they will hand you over to councils and flog you in their synagogues; 18 and you will be dragged before governors and kings because of me, as a testimony to them and the Gentiles. 19 When they hand you over, do not worry about how you are to speak or what you are to say; for what you are to say will be given to you at that time; 20 for it is not you who speak, but the Spirit of your Father speaking through you. 21 Brother will betray brother to death, and a father his child, and children will rise against parents and have them put to death; 22 and you will be hated by all because of my name. But the one who endures to the end will be saved. 23 When they persecute you in one town, flee to the next; for truly I tell you, you will not have gone through all the towns of Israel before the Son of Man comes.

24 'A disciple is not above the teacher, nor a slave above the master; 25 it is enough for the disciple to be like the teacher, and the slave like the master. If they have called the master of the house Beelzebul, how much more will they malign those of his household!

Whom to Fear

26 'So have no fear of them; for nothing is covered up that will not be uncovered, and nothing secret that will not become known. 27 What I say to you in the dark, tell in the light; and what you hear whispered, proclaim from the housetops. 28 Do not fear those who kill the body but cannot kill the soul; rather fear him who can destroy both soul and body in hell. *e* 29 Are not two sparrows sold for a penny? Yet not one of them will fall to the ground unperceived by your Father. 30 And even the hairs of your head are all counted. 31 So do not

---

a Gk *he*   *b* Other ancient authorities read *Lebbaeus,* or *Lebbaeus called Thaddaeus*   *c* Or *is at hand*
d The terms *leper* and *leprosy* can refer to several diseases
e Gk *Gehenna*

be afraid; you are of more value than many sparrows.

32 'Everyone therefore who acknowledges me before others, I also will acknowledge before my Father in heaven; 33 but whoever denies me before others, I also will deny before my Father in heaven.

Not Peace, but a Sword

34 'Do not think that I have come to bring peace to the earth; I have not come to bring peace, but a sword.

35 For I have come to set a man against
   his father,
   and a daughter against her mother,
   and a daughter-in-law against her
      mother-in-law;

36 and one's foes will be members of
   one's own household.

37 Whoever loves father or mother more than me is not worthy of me; and whoever loves son or daughter more than me is not worthy of me; 38 and whoever does not take up the cross and follow me is not worthy of me. 39 Those who find their life will lose it, and those who lose their life for my sake will find it.

Rewards

40 'Whoever welcomes you welcomes me, and whoever welcomes me welcomes the one who sent me. 41 Whoever welcomes a prophet in the name of a prophet will receive a prophet's reward; and whoever welcomes a righteous person in the name of a righteous person will receive the reward of the righteous; 42 and whoever gives even a cup of cold water to one of these little ones in the name of a disciple—truly I tell you, none of these will lose their reward.'

11 Now when Jesus had finished instructing his twelve disciples, he went on from there to teach and proclaim his message in their cities.

Messengers from John the Baptist

2 When John heard in prison what the Messiah[a] was doing, he sent word by his[b] disciples 3 and said to him, 'Are you the one who is to come, or are we to wait for another?' 4 Jesus answered them, 'Go and tell John what you hear and see: 5 the blind receive their sight, the lame walk, the lepers[c] are cleansed, the deaf hear, the dead are raised, and the poor have good news brought to them. 6 And blessed is anyone who takes no offence at me.'

Jesus Praises John the Baptist

7 As they went away, Jesus began to speak to the crowds about John: 'What did you go out into the wilderness to look at? A reed shaken by the wind? 8 What then did you go out to see? Someone[d] dressed in soft robes? Look, those who wear soft robes are in royal palaces. 9 What then did you go out to see? A prophet?[e] Yes, I tell you, and more than a prophet. 10 This is the one about whom it is written,

"See, I am sending my messenger
      ahead of you,
   who will prepare your way
      before you."

11 Truly I tell you, among those born of women no one has arisen greater than John the Baptist; yet the least in the kingdom of heaven is greater than he. 12 From the days of John the Baptist until now the kingdom of heaven has suffered violence,[f] and the violent take it by force. 13 For all the prophets and the law prophesied until John came; 14 and if you are willing to accept it, he is Elijah who is to come. 15 Let anyone with ears[g] listen!

16 'But to what will I compare this generation? It is like children sitting in the market-places and calling to one another,

17   "We played the flute for you, and you
         did not dance;
      we wailed, and you did not
         mourn."

18 For John came neither eating nor drinking, and they say, "He has a demon"; 19 the Son of Man came eating and drinking, and they say, "Look, a glutton and a drunkard,

---

a Or the Christ   b Other ancient authorities read two
of his   c The terms leper and leprosy can refer to several
diseases   d Or Why then did you go out? To see someone
e Other ancient authorities read Why then did you go
out? To see a prophet?   f Or has been coming violently
g Other ancient authorities add to hear

a friend of tax-collectors and sinners!" Yet wisdom is vindicated by her deeds.'*a*

Woes to Unrepentant Cities

20 Then he began to reproach the cities in which most of his deeds of power had been done, because they did not repent. 21 'Woe to you, Chorazin! Woe to you, Bethsaida! For if the deeds of power done in you had been done in Tyre and Sidon, they would have repented long ago in sackcloth and ashes. 22 But I tell you, on the day of judgement it will be more tolerable for Tyre and Sidon than for you. 23 And you, Capernaum,

will you be exalted to heaven?
No, you will be brought down
to Hades.

For if the deeds of power done in you had been done in Sodom, it would have remained until this day. 24 But I tell you that on the day of judgement it will be more tolerable for the land of Sodom than for you.'

Jesus Thanks His Father

25 At that time Jesus said, 'I thank*b* you, Father, Lord of heaven and earth, because you have hidden these things from the wise and the intelligent and have revealed them to infants; 26 yes, Father, for such was your gracious will.*c* 27 All things have been handed over to me by my Father; and no one knows the Son except the Father, and no one knows the Father except the Son and anyone to whom the Son chooses to reveal him.

28 'Come to me, all you that are weary and are carrying heavy burdens, and I will give you rest. 29 Take my yoke upon you, and learn from me; for I am gentle and humble in heart, and you will find rest for your souls. 30 For my yoke is easy, and my burden is light.'

Plucking Grain on the Sabbath

12 At that time Jesus went through the cornfields on the sabbath; his disciples were hungry, and they began to pluck heads of grain and to eat. 2 When the Pharisees saw it, they said to him, 'Look,

your disciples are doing what is not lawful to do on the sabbath.' 3 He said to them, 'Have you not read what David did when he and his companions were hungry? 4 He entered the house of God and ate the bread of the Presence, which it was not lawful for him or his companions to eat, but only for the priests. 5 Or have you not read in the law that on the sabbath the priests in the temple break the sabbath and yet are guiltless? 6 I tell you, something greater than the temple is here. 7 But if you had known what this means, "I desire mercy and not sacrifice", you would not have condemned the guiltless. 8 For the Son of Man is lord of the sabbath.'

The Man with a Withered Hand

9 He left that place and entered their synagogue; 10 a man was there with a withered hand, and they asked him, 'Is it lawful to cure on the sabbath?' so that they might accuse him. 11 He said to them, 'Suppose one of you has only one sheep and it falls into a pit on the sabbath; will you not lay hold of it and lift it out? 12 How much more valuable is a human being than a sheep! So it is lawful to do good on the sabbath.' 13 Then he said to the man, 'Stretch out your hand.' He stretched it out, and it was restored, as sound as the other. 14 But the Pharisees went out and conspired against him, how to destroy him.

God's Chosen Servant

15 When Jesus became aware of this, he departed. Many crowds*d* followed him, and he cured all of them, 16 and he ordered them not to make him known. 17 This was to fulfil what had been spoken through the prophet Isaiah:

18 'Here is my servant, whom I
have chosen,
my beloved, with whom my soul is
well pleased.
I will put my Spirit upon him,

a Other ancient authorities read *children*   *b* Or *praise*
c Or *for so it was well-pleasing in your sight*   *d* Other
ancient authorities lack *crowds*

and he will proclaim justice to the
  Gentiles.
19 He will not wrangle or cry aloud,
  nor will anyone hear his voice
  in the streets.
20 He will not break a bruised reed
  or quench a smouldering wick
  until he brings justice to victory.
21   And in his name the Gentiles will
  hope.'

Jesus and Beelzebul

22 Then they brought to him a demoniac who was blind and mute; and he
cured him, so that the one who had been
mute could speak and see. 23 All the
crowds were amazed and said, 'Can this be
the Son of David?' 24 But when the Pharisees heard it, they said, 'It is only by
Beelzebul, the ruler of the demons, that
this fellow casts out the demons.' 25 He
knew what they were thinking and said to
them, 'Every kingdom divided against itself is laid waste, and no city or house divided against itself will stand. 26 If Satan
casts out Satan, he is divided against himself; how then will his kingdom stand?
27 If I cast out demons by Beelzebul, by
whom do your own exorcists*a* cast them
out? Therefore they will be your judges.
28 But if it is by the Spirit of God that I cast
out demons, then the kingdom of God
has come to you. 29 Or how can one enter
a strong man's house and plunder his
property, without first tying up the strong
man? Then indeed the house can be plundered. 30 Whoever is not with me is against
me, and whoever does not gather with me
scatters. 31 Therefore I tell you, people will
be forgiven for every sin and blasphemy,
but blasphemy against the Spirit will not
be forgiven. 32 Whoever speaks a word
against the Son of Man will be forgiven,
but whoever speaks against the Holy Spirit will not be forgiven, either in this age or
in the age to come.

A Tree and Its Fruit

33 'Either make the tree good, and its
fruit good; or make the tree bad, and its
fruit bad; for the tree is known by its fruit.

34 You brood of vipers! How can you speak
good things, when you are evil? For out of
the abundance of the heart the mouth
speaks. 35 The good person brings good
things out of a good treasure, and the evil
person brings evil things out of an evil
treasure. 36 I tell you, on the day of judgement you will have to give an account for
every careless word you utter; 37 for by your
words you will be justified, and by your
words you will be condemned.'

The Sign of Jonah

38 Then some of the scribes and Pharisees said to him, 'Teacher, we wish to see a
sign from you.' 39 But he answered them,
'An evil and adulterous generation asks for
a sign, but no sign will be given to it except
the sign of the prophet Jonah. 40 For just as
Jonah was for three days and three nights
in the belly of the sea monster, so for three
days and three nights the Son of Man will
be in the heart of the earth. 41 The people
of Nineveh will rise up at the judgement
with this generation and condemn it, because they repented at the proclamation of
Jonah, and see, something greater than Jonah is here! 42 The queen of the South will
rise up at the judgement with this generation and condemn it, because she came
from the ends of the earth to listen to the
wisdom of Solomon, and see, something
greater than Solomon is here!

The Return of the Unclean Spirit

43 'When the unclean spirit has gone
out of a person, it wanders through waterless regions looking for a resting-place, but
it finds none. 44 Then it says, "I will return
to my house from which I came." When it
comes, it finds it empty, swept, and put in
order. 45 Then it goes and brings along sev-
en other spirits more evil than itself, and
they enter and live there; and the last state
of that person is worse than the first. So
will it be also with this evil generation.'

The True Kindred of Jesus

46 While he was still speaking to the
crowds, his mother and his brothers were

a Gk sons

standing outside, wanting to speak to him. [47] Someone told him, 'Look, your mother and your brothers are standing outside, wanting to speak to you.'[a] [48] But to the one who had told him this, Jesus[b] replied, 'Who is my mother, and who are my brothers?' [49] And pointing to his disciples, he said, 'Here are my mother and my brothers! [50] For whoever does the will of my Father in heaven is my brother and sister and mother.'

The Parable of the Sower

13 That same day Jesus went out of the house and sat beside the lake. [2] Such great crowds gathered around him that he got into a boat and sat there, while the whole crowd stood on the beach. [3] And he told them many things in parables, saying: 'Listen! A sower went out to sow. [4] And as he sowed, some seeds fell on the path, and the birds came and ate them up. [5] Other seeds fell on rocky ground, where they did not have much soil, and they sprang up quickly, since they had no depth of soil. [6] But when the sun rose, they were scorched; and since they had no root, they withered away. [7] Other seeds fell among thorns, and the thorns grew up and choked them. [8] Other seeds fell on good soil and brought forth grain, some a hundredfold, some sixty, some thirty. [9] Let anyone with ears[c] listen!'

The Purpose of the Parables

[10] Then the disciples came and asked him, 'Why do you speak to them in parables?' [11] He answered, 'To you it has been given to know the secrets[d] of the kingdom of heaven, but to them it has not been given. [12] For to those who have, more will be given, and they will have an abundance; but from those who have nothing, even what they have will be taken away. [13] The reason I speak to them in parables is that "seeing they do not perceive, and hearing they do not listen, nor do they understand." [14] With them indeed is fulfilled the prophecy of Isaiah that says:

"You will indeed listen, but never understand,

and you will indeed look, but never perceive.

[15] For this people's heart has grown dull,
and their ears are hard of hearing,
and they have shut their eyes;
so that they might not look with their eyes,
and listen with their ears,
and understand with their heart and turn—
and I would heal them."

[16] But blessed are your eyes, for they see, and your ears, for they hear. [17] Truly I tell you, many prophets and righteous people longed to see what you see, but did not see it, and to hear what you hear, but did not hear it.

The Parable of the Sower Explained

[18] 'Hear then the parable of the sower. [19] When anyone hears the word of the kingdom and does not understand it, the evil one comes and snatches away what is sown in the heart; this is what was sown on the path. [20] As for what was sown on rocky ground, this is the one who hears the word and immediately receives it with joy; [21] yet such a person has no root, but endures only for a while, and when trouble or persecution arises on account of the word, that person immediately falls away.[e] [22] As for what was sown among thorns, this is the one who hears the word, but the cares of the world and the lure of wealth choke the word, and it yields nothing. [23] But as for what was sown on good soil, this is the one who hears the word and understands it, who indeed bears fruit and yields, in one case a hundredfold, in another sixty, and in another thirty.'

The Parable of Weeds among the Wheat

[24] He put before them another parable: 'The kingdom of heaven may be compared to someone who sowed good seed in his field; [25] but while everybody was asleep, an enemy came and sowed weeds among the

a Other ancient authorities lack verse 47   b Gk he
c Other ancient authorities add to hear   d Or mysteries
e Gk stumbles

Parables in the Synoptic Gospels

Parable	Matthew	Mark	Luke
The Weeds among the Wheat	13.24–30		
The Buried Treasure	13.44		
The Fine Pearl	13.45–46		
The Thrown Net	13.47–48		
The Unforgiving Servant	18.23–35		
The Labourers in the Vineyard	20.1–16		
The Two Sons	21.28–30		
The Wedding Banquet	22.2–14		
The Talents	25.14–30		
The Judgement of the Nations	25.31–46		
Seed Grows of Itself		4.26–29	
Need for Watchfulness		13.32–37	
The Two Debtors			7.41–42
The Good Samaritan			10.30–35
The Importunate Friend			11.5–8
The Rich Fool			12.16–20
The Vigilant and Faithful Slaves			12.35–40
The Faithful and Prudent Manager			12.42–48
The Barren Fig Tree			13.6–9
The Great Dinner			14.15–24
The Tower			14.28–30
The King Marching into Battle			14.31–33
The Lost Coin			15.8–10
The Prodigal Son			15.11–32
The Dishonest Manager			16.1–8
The Rich Man and Lazarus			16.19–31
Attitude of a Slave			17.7–10
The Persistent Widow			18.2–5
The Pharisee and the Tax Collector			18.9–14
The Ten Pounds			19.11–27
The Two Foundations	7.24–29		6.46–49
The Yeast	13.33		13.20–21
The Lost Sheep	18.10–14		15.1–7
The Lamp	5.15	4.21	8.16; 11.33
The New Cloth	9.16	2.21	5.36
The New Wine in Old Wineskins	9.17	2.22	5.37–38
The Sower	13.1–9	4.1–9	8.4–8
The Mustard Seed	13.31–32	4.30–34	13.18–19
The Tenants	21.33–46	12.1–12	20.9–19
The Lesson of the Fig Tree	24.32–35	13.28–31	21.29

wheat, and then went away. 26 So when the plants came up and bore grain, then the weeds appeared as well. 27 And the slaves of the householder came and said to him, "Master, did you not sow good seed in your field? Where, then, did these weeds come from?" 28 He answered, "An enemy has done this." The slaves said to him, "Then do you want us to go and gather them?" 29 But he replied, "No; for in gathering the weeds you would uproot the wheat along with them. 30 Let both of them grow together until the harvest; and at harvest time I will tell the reapers, Collect the weeds first and bind them in bundles to be burned, but gather the wheat into my barn." '

The Parable of the Mustard Seed

31 He put before them another parable: 'The kingdom of heaven is like a mustard seed that someone took and sowed in his field; 32 it is the smallest of all the seeds, but when it has grown it is the greatest of shrubs and becomes a tree, so that the birds of the air come and make nests in its branches.'

The Parable of the Yeast

33 He told them another parable: 'The kingdom of heaven is like yeast that a woman took and mixed in with*a* three measures of flour until all of it was leavened.'

The Use of Parables

34 Jesus told the crowds all these things in parables; without a parable he told them nothing. 35 This was to fulfil what had been spoken through the prophet:*b*
'I will open my mouth to speak
   in parables;
 I will proclaim what has been
    hidden from the foundation of
    the world.'*c*

Jesus Explains the Parable of the Weeds

36 Then he left the crowds and went into the house. And his disciples approached him, saying, 'Explain to us the parable of the weeds of the field.' 37 He answered, 'The one who sows the good seed is the Son of Man; 38 the field is the world, and the good seed are the children of the kingdom; the weeds are the children of the evil one, 39 and the enemy who sowed them is the devil; the harvest is the end of the age, and the reapers are angels. 40 Just as the weeds are collected and burned up with fire, so will it be at the end of the age. 41 The Son of Man will send his angels, and they will collect out of his kingdom all causes of sin and all evildoers, 42 and they will throw them into the furnace of fire, where there will be weeping and gnashing of teeth. 43 Then the righteous will shine like the sun in the kingdom of their Father. Let anyone with ears*d* listen!

Three Parables

44 'The kingdom of heaven is like treasure hidden in a field, which someone found and hid; then in his joy he goes and sells all that he has and buys that field.

45 'Again, the kingdom of heaven is like a merchant in search of fine pearls; 46 on finding one pearl of great value, he went and sold all that he had and bought it.

47 'Again, the kingdom of heaven is like a net that was thrown into the sea and caught fish of every kind; 48 when it was full, they drew it ashore, sat down, and put the good into baskets but threw out the bad. 49 So it will be at the end of the age. The angels will come out and separate the evil from the righteous 50 and throw them into the furnace of fire, where there will be weeping and gnashing of teeth.

Treasures New and Old

51 'Have you understood all this?' They answered, 'Yes.' 52 And he said to them, 'Therefore every scribe who has been trained for the kingdom of heaven is like the master of a household who brings out of his treasure what is new and what is

a Gk hid in   *b* Other ancient authorities read *the prophet Isaiah*   *c* Other ancient authorities lack *of the world*   *d* Other ancient authorities add *to hear* old! 53 When Jesus had finished these parables, he left that place.

The Rejection of Jesus at Nazareth

54 He came to his home town and began to teach the people[a] in their synagogue, so that they were astounded and said, 'Where did this man get this wisdom and these deeds of power? 55 Is not this the carpenter's son? Is not his mother called Mary? And are not his brothers James and Joseph and Simon and Judas? 56 And are not all his sisters with us? Where then did this man get all this?' 57 And they took offence at him. But Jesus said to them, 'Prophets are not without honour except in their own country and in their own house.' 58 And he did not do many deeds of power there, because of their unbelief.

The Death of John the Baptist

14 At that time Herod the ruler[b] heard reports about Jesus; 2 and he said to his servants, 'This is John the Baptist; he has been raised from the dead, and for this reason these powers are at work in him.' 3 For Herod had arrested John, bound him, and put him in prison on account of Herodias, his brother Philip's wife,[c] 4 because John had been telling him, 'It is not lawful for you to have her.' 5 Though Herod[d] wanted to put him to death, he feared the crowd, because they regarded him as a prophet. 6 But when Herod's birthday came, the daughter of Herodias danced before the company, and she pleased Herod 7 so much that he promised on oath to grant her whatever she might ask. 8 Prompted by her mother, she said, 'Give me the head of John the Baptist here on a platter.' 9 The king was grieved, yet out of regard for his oaths and for the guests, he commanded it to be given; 10 he sent and had John beheaded in the prison. 11 The head was brought on a platter and given to the girl, who brought it to her mother. 12 His disciples came and took the body and buried it; then they went and told Jesus.

Feeding the Five Thousand

13 Now when Jesus heard this, he withdrew from there in a boat to a deserted place by himself. But when the crowds heard it, they followed him on foot from the towns. 14 When he went ashore, he saw a great crowd; and he had compassion for them and cured their sick. 15 When it was evening, the disciples came to him and said, 'This is a deserted place, and the hour is now late; send the crowds away so that they may go into the villages and buy food for themselves.' 16 Jesus said to them, 'They need not go away; you give them something to eat.' 17 They replied, 'We have nothing here but five loaves and two fish.' 18 And he said, 'Bring them here to me.' 19 Then he ordered the crowds to sit down on the grass. Taking the five loaves and the two fish, he looked up to heaven, and blessed and broke the loaves, and gave them to the disciples, and the disciples gave them to the crowds. 20 And all ate and were filled; and they took up what was left over of the broken pieces, twelve baskets full. 21 And those who ate were about five thousand men, besides women and children.

Jesus Walks on the Water

22 Immediately he made the disciples get into the boat and go on ahead to the other side, while he dismissed the crowds. 23 And after he had dismissed the crowds, he went up the mountain by himself to pray. When evening came, he was there alone, 24 but by this time the boat, battered by the waves, was far from the land,[e] for the wind was against them. 25 And early in the morning he came walking towards them on the lake. 26 But when the disciples saw him walking on the lake, they were terrified, saying, 'It is a ghost!' And they cried out in fear. 27 But immediately Jesus spoke to them and said, 'Take heart, it is I; do not be afraid.'

28 Peter answered him, 'Lord, if it is you, command me to come to you on the water.'

a Gk them   b Gk tetrarch   c Other ancient authorities read his brother's wife   d Gk he   e Other ancient authorities read was out on the lake

29 He said, 'Come.' So Peter got out of the boat, started walking on the water, and came towards Jesus. 30 But when he noticed the strong wind,[a] he became frightened, and beginning to sink, he cried out, 'Lord, save me!' 31 Jesus immediately reached out his hand and caught him, saying to him, 'You of little faith, why did you doubt?' 32 When they got into the boat, the wind ceased. 33 And those in the boat worshipped him, saying, 'Truly you are the Son of God.'

Jesus Heals the Sick in Gennesaret

34 When they had crossed over, they came to land at Gennesaret. 35 After the people of that place recognized him, they sent word throughout the region and brought all who were sick to him, 36 and begged him that they might touch even the fringe of his cloak; and all who touched it were healed.

The Tradition of the Elders

15 Then Pharisees and scribes came to Jesus from Jerusalem and said, 2 'Why do your disciples break the tradition of the elders? For they do not wash their hands before they eat.' 3 He answered them, 'And why do you break the commandment of God for the sake of your tradition? 4 For God said,[b] "Honour your father and your mother," and, "Whoever speaks evil of father or mother must surely die." 5 But you say that whoever tells father or mother, "Whatever support you might have had from me is given to God",[c] then that person need not honour the father.[d] 6 So, for the sake of your tradition, you make void the word[e] of God. 7 You hypocrites! Isaiah prophesied rightly about you when he said:

8 "This people honours me with
         their lips,
    but their hearts are far from me;
9 in vain do they worship me,
    teaching human precepts as
         doctrines." '

Things That Defile

10 Then he called the crowd to him and said to them, 'Listen and understand: 11 it is not what goes into the mouth that defiles a person, but it is what comes out of the mouth that defiles.' 12 Then the disciples approached and said to him, 'Do you know that the Pharisees took offence when they heard what you said?' 13 He answered, 'Every plant that my heavenly Father has not planted will be uprooted. 14 Let them alone; they are blind guides of the blind.[f] And if one blind person guides another, both will fall into a pit.' 15 But Peter said to him, 'Explain this parable to us.' 16 Then he said, 'Are you also still without understanding? 17 Do you not see that whatever goes into the mouth enters the stomach, and goes out into the sewer? 18 But what comes out of the mouth proceeds from the heart, and this is what defiles. 19 For out of the heart come evil intentions, murder, adultery, fornication, theft, false witness, slander. 20 These are what defile a person, but to eat with unwashed hands does not defile.'

The Canaanite Woman's Faith

21 Jesus left that place and went away to the district of Tyre and Sidon. 22 Just then a Canaanite woman from that region came out and started shouting, 'Have mercy on me, Lord, Son of David; my daughter is tormented by a demon.' 23 But he did not answer her at all. And his disciples came and urged him, saying, 'Send her away, for she keeps shouting after us.' 24 He answered, 'I was sent only to the lost sheep of the house of Israel.' 25 But she came and knelt before him, saying, 'Lord, help me.' 26 He answered, 'It is not fair to take the children's food and throw it to the dogs.' 27 She said, 'Yes, Lord, yet even the dogs eat the crumbs that fall from their masters' table.' 28 Then Jesus answered her, 'Woman, great is your faith! Let it be done for you as you wish.' And her daughter was healed instantly.

a Other ancient authorities read *the wind*   *b* Other ancient authorities read *commanded, saying*   *c* Or *is an offering*   *d* Other ancient authorities add *or the mother*   *e* Other ancient authorities read *law*; others, *commandment*   *f* Other ancient authorities lack *of the blind*

Jesus Cures Many People

29 After Jesus had left that place, he passed along the Sea of Galilee, and he went up the mountain, where he sat down. 30 Great crowds came to him, bringing with them the lame, the maimed, the blind, the mute, and many others. They put them at his feet, and he cured them, 31 so that the crowd was amazed when they saw the mute speaking, the maimed whole, the lame walking, and the blind seeing. And they praised the God of Israel.

Feeding the Four Thousand

32 Then Jesus called his disciples to him and said, 'I have compassion for the crowd, because they have been with me now for three days and have nothing to eat; and I do not want to send them away hungry, for they might faint on the way.' 33 The disciples said to him, 'Where are we to get enough bread in the desert to feed so great a crowd?' 34 Jesus asked them, 'How many loaves have you?' They said, 'Seven, and a few small fish.' 35 Then ordering the crowd to sit down on the ground, 36 he took the seven loaves and the fish; and after giving thanks he broke them and gave them to the disciples, and the disciples gave them to the crowds. 37 And all of them ate and were filled; and they took up the broken pieces left over, seven baskets full. 38 Those who had eaten were four thousand men, besides women and children. 39 After sending away the crowds, he got into the boat and went to the region of Magadan. [a]

The Demand for a Sign

16 The Pharisees and Sadducees came, and to test Jesus [b] they asked him to show them a sign from heaven. 2 He answered them, 'When it is evening, you say, "It will be fair weather, for the sky is red." 3 And in the morning, "It will be stormy today, for the sky is red and threatening." You know how to interpret the appearance of the sky, but you cannot interpret the signs of the times. [c] 4 An evil and adulterous generation asks for a sign, but no sign will be given to it except the sign of Jonah.' Then he left them and went away.

The Yeast of the Pharisees and Sadducees

5 When the disciples reached the other side, they had forgotten to bring any bread. 6 Jesus said to them, 'Watch out, and beware of the yeast of the Pharisees and Sadducees.' 7 They said to one another, 'It is because we have brought no bread.' 8 And becoming aware of it, Jesus said, 'You of little faith, why are you talking about having no bread? 9 Do you still not perceive? Do you not remember the five loaves for the five thousand, and how many baskets you gathered? 10 Or the seven loaves for the four thousand, and how many baskets you gathered? 11 How could you fail to perceive that I was not speaking about bread? Beware of the yeast of the Pharisees and Sadducees!' 12 Then they understood that he had not told them to beware of the yeast of bread, but of the teaching of the Pharisees and Sadducees.

Peter's Declaration about Jesus

13 Now when Jesus came into the district of Caesarea Philippi, he asked his disciples, 'Who do people say that the Son of Man is?' 14 And they said, 'Some say John the Baptist, but others Elijah, and still others Jeremiah or one of the prophets.' 15 He said to them, 'But who do you say that I am?' 16 Simon Peter answered, 'You are the Messiah, [d] the Son of the living God.' 17 And Jesus answered him, 'Blessed are you, Simon son of Jonah! For flesh and blood has not revealed this to you, but my Father in heaven. 18 And I tell you, you are Peter, [e] and on this rock [f] I will build my church, and the gates of Hades will not prevail against it. 19 I will give you the keys of the kingdom of heaven, and whatever you bind on earth will be bound in heaven, and whatever you loose on earth will be loosed in heaven.' 20 Then he sternly ordered the disciples not to tell anyone that he was [g] the Messiah. [d]

a Other ancient authorities read *Magdala* or *Magdalan*
b Gk *him*   c Other ancient authorities lack 2*When it is . . . of the times*   d Or *the Christ*   e Gk *Petros*
f Gk *petra*   g Other ancient authorities add *Jesus*

Jesus Foretells His Death and Resurrection

21 From that time on, Jesus began to show his disciples that he must go to Jerusalem and undergo great suffering at the hands of the elders and chief priests and scribes, and be killed, and on the third day be raised. 22 And Peter took him aside and began to rebuke him, saying, 'God forbid it, Lord! This must never happen to you.' 23 But he turned and said to Peter, 'Get behind me, Satan! You are a stumbling-block to me; for you are setting your mind not on divine things but on human things.'

The Cross and Self-Denial

24 Then Jesus told his disciples, 'If any want to become my followers, let them deny themselves and take up their cross and follow me. 25 For those who want to save their life will lose it, and those who lose their life for my sake will find it. 26 For what will it profit them if they gain the whole world but forfeit their life? Or what will they give in return for their life?

27 'For the Son of Man is to come with his angels in the glory of his Father, and then he will repay everyone for what has been done. 28 Truly I tell you, there are some standing here who will not taste death before they see the Son of Man coming in his kingdom.'

The Transfiguration

17 Six days later, Jesus took with him Peter and James and his brother John and led them up a high mountain, by themselves. 2 And he was transfigured before them, and his face shone like the sun, and his clothes became dazzling white. 3 Suddenly there appeared to them Moses and Elijah, talking with him. 4 Then Peter said to Jesus, 'Lord, it is good for us to be here; if you wish, I a will make three dwellings b here, one for you, one for Moses, and one for Elijah.' 5 While he was still speaking, suddenly a bright cloud overshadowed them, and from the cloud a voice said, 'This is my Son, the Beloved; c with him I am well pleased; listen to him!' 6 When the disciples heard this, they fell to the ground and were overcome by fear. 7 But Jesus came and touched them, saying, 'Get up and do not be afraid.' 8 And when they looked up, they saw no one except Jesus himself alone.

9 As they were coming down the mountain, Jesus ordered them, 'Tell no one about the vision until after the Son of Man has been raised from the dead.' 10 And the disciples asked him, 'Why, then, do the scribes say that Elijah must come first?' 11 He replied, 'Elijah is indeed coming and will restore all things; 12 but I tell you that Elijah has already come, and they did not recognize him, but they did to him whatever they pleased. So also the Son of Man is about to suffer at their hands.' 13 Then the disciples understood that he was speaking to them about John the Baptist.

Jesus Cures a Boy with a Demon

14 When they came to the crowd, a man came to him, knelt before him, 15 and said, 'Lord, have mercy on my son, for he is an epileptic and he suffers terribly; he often falls into the fire and often into the water. 16 And I brought him to your disciples, but they could not cure him.' 17 Jesus answered, 'You faithless and perverse generation, how much longer must I be with you? How much longer must I put up with you? Bring him here to me.' 18 And Jesus rebuked the demon, d and it e came out of him, and the boy was cured instantly. 19 Then the disciples came to Jesus privately and said, 'Why could we not cast it out?' 20 He said to them, 'Because of your little faith. For truly I tell you, if you have faith the size of a f mustard seed, you will say to this mountain, "Move from here to there", and it will move; and nothing will be impossible for you.' g

Jesus Again Foretells His Death and Resurrection

22 As they were gathering h in Galilee, Jesus said to them, 'The Son of Man is going

a Other ancient authorities read we   b Or tents
c Or my beloved Son   d Gk it or him   e Gk the demon
f Gk faith as a grain of   g Other ancient authorities
add verse 21, But this kind does not come out except by
prayer and fasting   h Other ancient authorities read
living

to be betrayed into human hands, 23 and they will kill him, and on the third day he will be raised.' And they were greatly distressed.

Jesus and the Temple Tax

24 When they reached Capernaum, the collectors of the temple tax*a* came to Peter and said, 'Does your teacher not pay the temple tax?'*a* 25 He said, 'Yes, he does.' And when he came home, Jesus spoke of it first, asking, 'What do you think, Simon? From whom do kings of the earth take toll or tribute? From their children or from others?' 26 When Peter*b* said, 'From others', Jesus said to him, 'Then the children are free. 27 However, so that we do not give offence to them, go to the lake and cast a hook; take the first fish that comes up; and when you open its mouth, you will find a coin;*c* take that and give it to them for you and me.'

True Greatness

18 At that time the disciples came to Jesus and asked, 'Who is the greatest in the kingdom of heaven?' 2 He called a child, whom he put among them, 3 and said, 'Truly I tell you, unless you change and become like children, you will never enter the kingdom of heaven. 4 Whoever becomes humble like this child is the greatest in the kingdom of heaven. 5 Whoever welcomes one such child in my name welcomes me.

Temptations to Sin

6 'If any of you put a stumbling-block before one of these little ones who believe in me, it would be better for you if a great millstone were fastened around your neck and you were drowned in the depth of the sea. 7 Woe to the world because of stumbling-blocks! Occasions for stumbling are bound to come, but woe to the one by whom the stumbling-block comes!

8 'If your hand or your foot causes you to stumble, cut it off and throw it away; it is better for you to enter life maimed or lame than to have two hands or two feet and to be thrown into the eternal fire.

9 And if your eye causes you to stumble, tear it out and throw it away; it is better for you to enter life with one eye than to have two eyes and to be thrown into the hell*d* of fire.

The Parable of the Lost Sheep

10 'Take care that you do not despise one of these little ones; for, I tell you, in heaven their angels continually see the face of my Father in heaven.*e* 12 What do you think? If a shepherd has a hundred sheep, and one of them has gone astray, does he not leave the ninety-nine on the mountains and go in search of the one that went astray? 13 And if he finds it, truly I tell you, he rejoices over it more than over the ninety-nine that never went astray. 14 So it is not the will of your*f* Father in heaven that one of these little ones should be lost.

Reproving Another Who Sins

15 'If another member of the church*g* sins against you,*h* go and point out the fault when the two of you are alone. If the member listens to you, you have regained that one.*i* 16 But if you are not listened to, take one or two others along with you, so that every word may be confirmed by the evidence of two or three witnesses. 17 If the member refuses to listen to them, tell it to the church; and if the offender refuses to listen even to the church, let such a one be to you as a Gentile and a tax-collector. 18 Truly I tell you, whatever you bind on earth will be bound in heaven, and whatever you loose on earth will be loosed in heaven. 19 Again, truly I tell you, if two of you agree on earth about anything you ask, it will be done for you by my Father in heaven. 20 For where two or three are gathered in my name, I am there among them.'

Forgiveness

21 Then Peter came and said to him, 'Lord, if another member of the church*j*

---

a Gk *didrachma*   *b* Gk *he*   *c* Gk *stater*; the stater was worth two didrachmas   *d* Gk *Gehenna*   *e* Other ancient authorities add verse 11, *For the Son of Man came to save the lost*   *f* Other ancient authorities read *my*   *g* Gk *If your brother*   *h* Other ancient authorities lack *against you*   *i* Gk *the brother*   *j* Gk *if my brother* sins against me, how often should I forgive? As many as seven times?' ²²Jesus said to him, 'Not seven times, but, I tell you, seventy-seven*a* times.

The Parable of the Unforgiving Servant

23 'For this reason the kingdom of heaven may be compared to a king who wished to settle accounts with his slaves. ²⁴When he began the reckoning, one who owed him ten thousand talents*b* was brought to him; ²⁵and, as he could not pay, his lord ordered him to be sold, together with his wife and children and all his possessions, and payment to be made. ²⁶So the slave fell on his knees before him, saying, "Have patience with me, and I will pay you everything." ²⁷And out of pity for him, the lord of that slave released him and forgave him the debt. ²⁸But that same slave, as he went out, came upon one of his fellow-slaves who owed him a hundred denarii;*c* and seizing him by the throat, he said, "Pay what you owe." ²⁹Then his fellow-slave fell down and pleaded with him, "Have patience with me, and I will pay you." ³⁰But he refused; then he went and threw him into prison until he should pay the debt. ³¹When his fellow-slaves saw what had happened, they were greatly distressed, and they went and reported to their lord all that had taken place. ³²Then his lord summoned him and said to him, "You wicked slave! I forgave you all that debt because you pleaded with me. ³³Should you not have had mercy on your fellow-slave, as I had mercy on you?" ³⁴And in anger his lord handed him over to be tortured until he should pay his entire debt. ³⁵So my heavenly Father will also do to every one of you, if you do not forgive your brother or sister*d* from your heart.'

Teaching about Divorce

19 When Jesus had finished saying these things, he left Galilee and went to the region of Judea beyond the Jordan. ²Large crowds followed him, and he cured them there.

3 Some Pharisees came to him, and to test him they asked, 'Is it lawful for a man to divorce his wife for any cause?' ⁴He answered, 'Have you not read that the one who made them at the beginning "made them male and female", ⁵and said, "For this reason a man shall leave his father and mother and be joined to his wife, and the two shall become one flesh"? ⁶So they are no longer two, but one flesh. Therefore what God has joined together, let no one separate.' ⁷They said to him, 'Why then did Moses command us to give a certificate of dismissal and to divorce her?' ⁸He said to them, 'It was because you were so hard-hearted that Moses allowed you to divorce your wives, but at the beginning it was not so. ⁹And I say to you, whoever divorces his wife, except for unchastity, and marries another commits adultery.'*e*

10 His disciples said to him, 'If such is the case of a man with his wife, it is better not to marry.' ¹¹But he said to them, 'Not everyone can accept this teaching, but only those to whom it is given. ¹²For there are eunuchs who have been so from birth, and there are eunuchs who have been made eunuchs by others, and there are eunuchs who have made themselves eunuchs for the sake of the kingdom of heaven. Let anyone accept this who can.'

Jesus Blesses Little Children

13 Then little children were being brought to him in order that he might lay his hands on them and pray. The disciples spoke sternly to those who brought them; ¹⁴but Jesus said, 'Let the little children come to me, and do not stop them; for it is to such as these that the kingdom of heaven belongs.' ¹⁵And he laid his hands on them and went on his way.

The Rich Young Man

16 Then someone came to him and said, 'Teacher, what good deed must I do

a Or *seventy times seven*   *b* A talent was worth more than fifteen years' wages of a labourer   *c* The denarius was the usual day's wage for a labourer   *d* Gk *brother*   *e* Other ancient authorities read *except on the ground of unchastity, causes her to commit adultery*; others add at the end of the verse *and he who marries a divorced woman commits adultery* to have eternal life?' ¹⁷And he said to him, 'Why do you ask me about what is good? There is only one who is good. If you wish to enter into life, keep the commandments.' ¹⁸He said to him, 'Which ones?' And Jesus said, 'You shall not murder; You shall not commit adultery; You shall not steal; You shall not bear false witness; ¹⁹Honour your father and mother; also, You shall love your neighbour as yourself.' ²⁰The young man said to him, 'I have kept all these;ᵈ what do I still lack?' ²¹Jesus said to him, 'If you wish to be perfect, go, sell your possessions, and give the moneyᵇ to the poor, and you will have treasure in heaven; then come, follow me.' ²²When the young man heard this word, he went away grieving, for he had many possessions.

23 Then Jesus said to his disciples, 'Truly I tell you, it will be hard for a rich person to enter the kingdom of heaven. ²⁴Again I tell you, it is easier for a camel to go through the eye of a needle than for someone who is rich to enter the kingdom of God.' ²⁵When the disciples heard this, they were greatly astounded and said, 'Then who can be saved?' ²⁶But Jesus looked at them and said, 'For mortals it is impossible, but for God all things are possible.'

27 Then Peter said in reply, 'Look, we have left everything and followed you. What then will we have?' ²⁸Jesus said to them, 'Truly I tell you, at the renewal of all things, when the Son of Man is seated on the throne of his glory, you who have followed me will also sit on twelve thrones, judging the twelve tribes of Israel. ²⁹And everyone who has left houses or brothers or sisters or father or mother or children or fields, for my name's sake, will receive a hundredfold,ᶜ and will inherit eternal life. ³⁰But many who are first will be last, and the last will be first.

The Labourers in the Vineyard

20 'For the kingdom of heaven is like a landowner who went out early in the morning to hire labourers for his vineyard. ²After agreeing with the labour-

ers for the usual daily wage,ᵈ he sent them into his vineyard. ³When he went out about nine o'clock, he saw others standing idle in the market-place; ⁴and he said to them, "You also go into the vineyard, and I will pay you whatever is right." So they went. ⁵When he went out again about noon and about three o'clock, he did the same. ⁶And about five o'clock he went out and found others standing around; and he said to them, "Why are you standing here idle all day?" ⁷They said to him, "Because no one has hired us." He said to them, "You also go into the vineyard." ⁸When evening came, the owner of the vineyard said to his manager, "Call the labourers and give them their pay, beginning with the last and then going to the first." ⁹When those hired about five o'clock came, each of them received the usual daily wage.ᵈ ¹⁰Now when the first came, they thought they would receive more; but each of them also received the usual daily wage.ᵈ ¹¹And when they received it, they grumbled against the landowner, ¹²saying, "These last worked only one hour, and you have made them equal to us who have borne the burden of the day and the scorching heat." ¹³But he replied to one of them, "Friend, I am doing you no wrong; did you not agree with me for the usual daily wage?ᵈ ¹⁴Take what belongs to you and go; I choose to give to this last the same as I give to you. ¹⁵Am I not allowed to do what I choose with what belongs to me? Or are you envious because I am generous?"ᵉ ¹⁶So the last will be first, and the first will be last.'ᶠ

A Third Time Jesus Foretells His Death and Resurrection

17 While Jesus was going up to Jerusalem, he took the twelve disciples aside by themselves, and said to them on the way, ¹⁸'See, we are going up to Jerusalem, and the Son of Man will be handed over to the chief priests and scribes, and they will

ᵃ Other ancient authorities add *from my youth*
ᵇ Gk lacks *the money* ᶜ Other ancient authorities read *manifold* ᵈ Gk *a denarius* ᵉ Gk *is your eye evil because I am good?* ᶠ Other ancient authorities add *for many are called but few are chosen*

condemn him to death; 19then they will hand him over to the Gentiles to be mocked and flogged and crucified; and on the third day he will be raised.'

The Request of the Mother of James and John

20 Then the mother of the sons of Zebedee came to him with her sons, and kneeling before him, she asked a favour of him. 21 And he said to her, 'What do you want?' She said to him, 'Declare that these two sons of mine will sit, one at your right hand and one at your left, in your kingdom.' 22 But Jesus answered, 'You do not know what you are asking. Are you able to drink the cup that I am about to drink?'*a* They said to him, 'We are able.' 23 He said to them, 'You will indeed drink my cup, but to sit at my right hand and at my left, this is not mine to grant, but it is for those for whom it has been prepared by my Father.'

24 When the ten heard it, they were angry with the two brothers. 25 But Jesus called them to him and said, 'You know that the rulers of the Gentiles lord it over them, and their great ones are tyrants over them. 26 It will not be so among you; but whoever wishes to be great among you must be your servant, 27 and whoever wishes to be first among you must be your slave; 28 just as the Son of Man came not to be served but to serve, and to give his life a ransom for many.'

Jesus Heals Two Blind Men

29 As they were leaving Jericho, a large crowd followed him. 30 There were two blind men sitting by the roadside. When they heard that Jesus was passing by, they shouted, 'Lord,*b* have mercy on us, Son of David!' 31 The crowd sternly ordered them to be quiet; but they shouted even more loudly, 'Have mercy on us, Lord, Son of David!' 32 Jesus stood still and called them, saying, 'What do you want me to do for you?' 33 They said to him, 'Lord, let our eyes be opened.' 34 Moved with compassion, Jesus touched their eyes. Immediate-ly they regained their sight and followed him.

Jesus' Triumphal Entry into Jerusalem

21 When they had come near Jerusalem and had reached Bethphage, at the Mount of Olives, Jesus sent two disciples, 2 saying to them, 'Go into the village ahead of you, and immediately you will find a donkey tied, and a colt with her; untie them and bring them to me. 3 If anyone says anything to you, just say this, "The Lord needs them." And he will send them immediately.*c* 4 This took place to fulfil what had been spoken through the prophet, saying,

5 'Tell the daughter of Zion,
  Look, your king is coming to you,
    humble, and mounted on
      a donkey,
      and on a colt, the foal of
      a donkey.'

6 The disciples went and did as Jesus had directed them; 7 they brought the donkey and the colt, and put their cloaks on them, and he sat on them. 8 A very large crowd*d* spread their cloaks on the road, and others cut branches from the trees and spread them on the road. 9 The crowds that went ahead of him and that followed were shouting,

  'Hosanna to the Son of David!
    Blessed is the one who comes in
      the name of the Lord!
  Hosanna in the highest heaven!'

10 When he entered Jerusalem, the whole city was in turmoil, asking, 'Who is this?' 11 The crowds were saying, 'This is the prophet Jesus from Nazareth in Galilee.'

Jesus Cleanses the Temple

12 Then Jesus entered the temple*e* and drove out all who were selling and buying in the temple, and he overturned the tables of the money-changers and the seats of those who sold doves. 13 He said to them, 'It is written,

---

a Other ancient authorities add *or to be baptized with the baptism that I am baptized with?* *b* Other ancient authorities lack *Lord* *c* Or *"The Lord needs them and will send them back immediately."* *d* Or *Most of the crowd* *e* Other ancient authorities add *of God*

"My house shall be called a house
of prayer";
but you are making it a den
of robbers.'

14 The blind and the lame came to him in the temple, and he cured them. 15 But when the chief priests and the scribes saw the amazing things that he did, and heard *a* the children crying out in the temple, 'Hosanna to the Son of David', they became angry 16 and said to him, 'Do you hear what these are saying?' Jesus said to them, 'Yes; have you never read,

"Out of the mouths of infants and
nursing babies
you have prepared praise for
yourself"?'

17 He left them, went out of the city to Bethany, and spent the night there.

Jesus Curses the Fig Tree

18 In the morning, when he returned to the city, he was hungry. 19 And seeing a fig tree by the side of the road, he went to it and found nothing at all on it but leaves. Then he said to it, 'May no fruit ever come from you again!' And the fig tree withered at once. 20 When the disciples saw it, they were amazed, saying, 'How did the fig tree wither at once?' 21 Jesus answered them, 'Truly I tell you, if you have faith and do not doubt, not only will you do what has been done to the fig tree, but even if you say to this mountain, "Be lifted up and thrown into the sea", it will be done. 22 Whatever you ask for in prayer with faith, you will receive.'

The Authority of Jesus Questioned

23 When he entered the temple, the chief priests and the elders of the people came to him as he was teaching, and said, 'By what authority are you doing these things, and who gave you this authority?' 24 Jesus said to them, 'I will also ask you one question; if you tell me the answer, then I will also tell you by what authority I do these things. 25 Did the baptism of John come from heaven, or was it of human origin?' And they argued with one another, 'If we say, "From heaven", he will say to us,

"Why then did you not believe him?" 26 But if we say, "Of human origin", we are afraid of the crowd; for all regard John as a prophet.' 27 So they answered Jesus, 'We do not know.' And he said to them, 'Neither will I tell you by what authority I am doing these things.

The Parable of the Two Sons

28 'What do you think? A man had two sons; he went to the first and said, "Son, go and work in the vineyard today." 29 He answered, "I will not"; but later he changed his mind and went. 30 The father *b* went to the second and said the same; and he answered, "I go, sir"; but he did not go. 31 Which of the two did the will of his father?' They said, 'The first.' Jesus said to them, 'Truly I tell you, the tax-collectors and the prostitutes are going into the kingdom of God ahead of you. 32 For John came to you in the way of righteousness and you did not believe him, but the tax-collectors and the prostitutes believed him; and even after you saw it, you did not change your minds and believe him.

The Parable of the Wicked Tenants

33 'Listen to another parable. There was a landowner who planted a vineyard, put a fence around it, dug a wine press in it, and built a watch-tower. Then he leased it to tenants and went to another country. 34 When the harvest time had come, he sent his slaves to the tenants to collect his produce. 35 But the tenants seized his slaves and beat one, killed another, and stoned another. 36 Again he sent other slaves, more than the first; and they treated them in the same way. 37 Finally he sent his son to them, saying, "They will respect my son." 38 But when the tenants saw the son, they said to themselves, "This is the heir; come, let us kill him and get his inheritance." 39 So they seized him, threw him out of the vineyard, and killed him. 40 Now when the owner of the vineyard comes, what will he do to those tenants?' 41 They said to him, 'He will put those

a Gk lacks *heard*   *b* Gk *He*

wretches to a miserable death, and lease the vineyard to other tenants who will give him the produce at the harvest time.'

42 Jesus said to them, 'Have you never read in the scriptures:

"The stone that the builders rejected
     has become the cornerstone;[a]
this was the Lord's doing,
     and it is amazing in our eyes"?

43 Therefore I tell you, the kingdom of God will be taken away from you and given to a people that produces the fruits of the kingdom.[b] 44 The one who falls on this stone will be broken to pieces; and it will crush anyone on whom it falls.'[c]

45 When the chief priests and the Pharisees heard his parables, they realized that he was speaking about them. 46 They wanted to arrest him, but they feared the crowds, because they regarded him as a prophet.

The Parable of the Wedding Banquet

22 Once more Jesus spoke to them in parables, saying: 2 'The kingdom of heaven may be compared to a king who gave a wedding banquet for his son. 3 He sent his slaves to call those who had been invited to the wedding banquet, but they would not come. 4 Again he sent other slaves, saying, "Tell those who have been invited: Look, I have prepared my dinner, my oxen and my fat calves have been slaughtered, and everything is ready; come to the wedding banquet." 5 But they made light of it and went away, one to his farm, another to his business, 6 while the rest seized his slaves, maltreated them, and killed them. 7 The king was enraged. He sent his troops, destroyed those murderers, and burned their city. 8 Then he said to his slaves, "The wedding is ready, but those invited were not worthy. 9 Go therefore into the main streets, and invite everyone you find to the wedding banquet." 10 Those slaves went out into the streets and gathered all whom they found, both good and bad; so the wedding hall was filled with guests.

11 'But when the king came in to see the guests, he noticed a man there who was not wearing a wedding robe, 12 and he said to him, "Friend, how did you get in here without a wedding robe?" And he was speechless. 13 Then the king said to the attendants, "Bind him hand and foot, and throw him into the outer darkness, where there will be weeping and gnashing of teeth." 14 For many are called, but few are chosen.'

The Question about Paying Taxes

15 Then the Pharisees went and plotted to entrap him in what he said. 16 So they sent their disciples to him, along with the Herodians, saying, 'Teacher, we know that you are sincere, and teach the way of God in accordance with truth, and show deference to no one; for you do not regard people with partiality. 17 Tell us, then, what you think. Is it lawful to pay taxes to the emperor, or not?' 18 But Jesus, aware of their malice, said, 'Why are you putting me to the test, you hypocrites? 19 Show me the coin used for the tax.' And they brought him a denarius. 20 Then he said to them, 'Whose head is this, and whose title?' 21 They answered, 'The emperor's.' Then he said to them, 'Give therefore to the emperor the things that are the emperor's, and to God the things that are God's.' 22 When they heard this, they were amazed; and they left him and went away.

The Question about the Resurrection

23 The same day some Sadducees came to him, saying there is no resurrection;[d] and they asked him a question, saying, 24 'Teacher, Moses said, "If a man dies childless, his brother shall marry the widow, and raise up children for his brother." 25 Now there were seven brothers among us; the first married, and died childless, leaving the widow to his brother. 26 The second did the same, so also the third, down to the seventh. 27 Last of all, the woman herself died. 28 In the resurrection, then, whose wife of the seven will she be? For all of them had married her.'

a Or keystone   b Gk the fruits of it   c Other ancient authorities lack verse 44   d Other ancient authorities read who say that there is no resurrection

29 Jesus answered them, 'You are wrong, because you know neither the scriptures nor the power of God. 30 For in the resurrection they neither marry nor are given in marriage, but are like angels*a* in heaven. 31 And as for the resurrection of the dead, have you not read what was said to you by God, 32 "I am the God of Abraham, the God of Isaac, and the God of Jacob"? He is God not of the dead, but of the living.' 33 And when the crowd heard it, they were astounded at his teaching.

The Greatest Commandment

34 When the Pharisees heard that he had silenced the Sadducees, they gathered together, 35 and one of them, a lawyer, asked him a question to test him. 36 'Teacher, which commandment in the law is the greatest?' 37 He said to him, ' "You shall love the Lord your God with all your heart, and with all your soul, and with all your mind." 38 This is the greatest and first commandment. 39 And a second is like it: "You shall love your neighbour as yourself." 40 On these two commandments hang all the law and the prophets.'

The Question about David's Son

41 Now while the Pharisees were gathered together, Jesus asked them this question: 42 'What do you think of the Messiah?*b* Whose son is he?' They said to him, 'The son of David.' 43 He said to them, 'How is it then that David by the Spirit*c* calls him Lord, saying,

44 "The Lord said to my Lord,
　'Sit at my right hand,
　　until I put your enemies under
　　　your feet' "?

45 If David thus calls him Lord, how can he be his son?' 46 No one was able to give him an answer, nor from that day did anyone dare to ask him any more questions.

Jesus Denounces Scribes and Pharisees

23 Then Jesus said to the crowds and to his disciples, 2 'The scribes and the Pharisees sit on Moses' seat; 3 therefore, do whatever they teach you and follow it; but do not do as they do, for they do not practise what they teach. 4 They tie up heavy burdens, hard to bear,*d* and lay them on the shoulders of others; but they themselves are unwilling to lift a finger to move them. 5 They do all their deeds to be seen by others; for they make their phylacteries broad and their fringes long. 6 They love to have the place of honour at banquets and the best seats in the synagogues, 7 and to be greeted with respect in the marketplaces, and to have people call them rabbi. 8 But you are not to be called rabbi, for you have one teacher, and you are all students.*e* 9 And call no one your father on earth, for you have one Father—the one in heaven. 10 Nor are you to be called instructors, for you have one instructor, the Messiah.*f* 11 The greatest among you will be your servant. 12 All who exalt themselves will be humbled, and all who humble themselves will be exalted.

13 'But woe to you, scribes and Pharisees, hypocrites! For you lock people out of the kingdom of heaven. For you do not go in yourselves, and when others are going in, you stop them.*g* 15 Woe to you, scribes and Pharisees, hypocrites! For you cross sea and land to make a single convert, and you make the new convert twice as much a child of hell*h* as yourselves.

16 'Woe to you, blind guides, who say, "Whoever swears by the sanctuary is bound by nothing, but whoever swears by the gold of the sanctuary is bound by the oath." 17 You blind fools! For which is greater, the gold or the sanctuary that has made the gold sacred? 18 And you say, "Whoever swears by the altar is bound by nothing, but whoever swears by the gift that is on the altar is bound by the oath." 19 How blind you are! For which is greater, the gift or the altar that makes the gift sacred? 20 So whoever swears by the altar, swears by it and by everything on it; 21 and whoever swears by the sanctuary,

a Other ancient authorities add *of God*　*b* Or *Christ*
c Gk *in spirit*　*d* Other ancient authorities lack *hard to bear*　*e* Gk *brothers*　*f* Or *the Christ*　*g* Other authorities add here (or after verse 12) verse 14, *Woe to you, scribes and Pharisees, hypocrites! For you devour widows' houses and for the sake of appearance you make long prayers; therefore you will receive the greater condemnation*　*h* Gk *Gehenna*

swears by it and by the one who dwells in it; 22 and whoever swears by heaven, swears by the throne of God and by the one who is seated upon it.

23 'Woe to you, scribes and Pharisees, hypocrites! For you tithe mint, dill, and cummin, and have neglected the weightier matters of the law: justice and mercy and faith. It is these you ought to have practised without neglecting the others. 24 You blind guides! You strain out a gnat but swallow a camel!

25 'Woe to you, scribes and Pharisees, hypocrites! For you clean the outside of the cup and of the plate, but inside they are full of greed and self-indulgence. 26 You blind Pharisee! First clean the inside of the cup,*a* so that the outside also may become clean.

27 'Woe to you, scribes and Pharisees, hypocrites! For you are like whitewashed tombs, which on the outside look beautiful, but inside they are full of the bones of the dead and of all kinds of filth. 28 So you also on the outside look righteous to others, but inside you are full of hypocrisy and lawlessness.

29 'Woe to you, scribes and Pharisees, hypocrites! For you build the tombs of the prophets and decorate the graves of the righteous, 30 and you say, "If we had lived in the days of our ancestors, we would not have taken part with them in shedding the blood of the prophets." 31 Thus you testify against yourselves that you are descendants of those who murdered the prophets. 32 Fill up, then, the measure of your ancestors. 33 You snakes, you brood of vipers! How can you escape being sentenced to hell?*b* 34 Therefore I send you prophets, sages, and scribes, some of whom you will kill and crucify, and some you will flog in your synagogues and pursue from town to town, 35 so that upon you may come all the righteous blood shed on earth, from the blood of righteous Abel to the blood of Zechariah son of Barachiah, whom you murdered between the sanctuary and the altar. 36 Truly I tell you, all this will come upon this generation.

The Lament over Jerusalem

37 'Jerusalem, Jerusalem, the city that kills the prophets and stones those who are sent to it! How often have I desired to gather your children together as a hen gathers her brood under her wings, and you were not willing! 38 See, your house is left to you, desolate.*c* 39 For I tell you, you will not see me again until you say, "Blessed is the one who comes in the name of the Lord." '

The Destruction of the Temple Foretold

24 As Jesus came out of the temple and was going away, his disciples came to point out to him the buildings of the temple. 2 Then he asked them, 'You see all these, do you not? Truly I tell you, not one stone will be left here upon another; all will be thrown down.'

Signs of the End of the Age

3 When he was sitting on the Mount of Olives, the disciples came to him privately, saying, 'Tell us, when will this be, and what will be the sign of your coming and of the end of the age?' 4 Jesus answered them, 'Beware that no one leads you astray. 5 For many will come in my name, saying, "I am the Messiah!"*d* and they will lead many astray. 6 And you will hear of wars and rumours of wars; see that you are not alarmed; for this must take place, but the end is not yet. 7 For nation will rise against nation, and kingdom against kingdom, and there will be famines*e* and earthquakes in various places: 8 all this is but the beginning of the birth pangs.

Persecutions Foretold

9 'Then they will hand you over to be tortured and will put you to death, and you will be hated by all nations because of my name. 10 Then many will fall away,*f* and they will betray one another and hate one another. 11 And many false prophets will arise and lead many astray. 12 And because of the increase of lawlessness, the love of many

a Other ancient authorities add *and of the plate*
b Gk *Gehenna*   *c* Other ancient authorities lack *desolate*   *d* Or *the Christ*   *e* Other ancient authorities add *and pestilences*   *f* Or *stumble*

will grow cold. ¹³But anyone who endures to the end will be saved. ¹⁴And this good news[a] of the kingdom will be proclaimed throughout the world, as a testimony to all the nations; and then the end will come.

The Desolating Sacrilege

15 'So when you see the desolating sacrilege standing in the holy place, as was spoken of by the prophet Daniel (let the reader understand), ¹⁶then those in Judea must flee to the mountains; ¹⁷someone on the housetop must not go down to take what is in the house; ¹⁸someone in the field must not turn back to get a coat. ¹⁹Woe to those who are pregnant and to those who are nursing infants in those days! ²⁰Pray that your flight may not be in winter or on a sabbath. ²¹For at that time there will be great suffering, such as has not been from the beginning of the world until now, no, and never will be. ²²And if those days had not been cut short, no one would be saved; but for the sake of the elect those days will be cut short. ²³Then if anyone says to you, "Look! Here is the Messiah!"[b] or "There he is!"—do not believe it. ²⁴For false messiahs[c] and false prophets will appear and produce great signs and omens, to lead astray, if possible, even the elect. ²⁵Take note, I have told you beforehand. ²⁶So, if they say to you, "Look! He is in the wilderness", do not go out. If they say, "Look! He is in the inner rooms", do not believe it. ²⁷For as the lightning comes from the east and flashes as far as the west, so will be the coming of the Son of Man. ²⁸Wherever the corpse is, there the vultures will gather.

The Coming of the Son of Man

29 'Immediately after the suffering of those days

the sun will be darkened,
   and the moon will not give
      its light;
the stars will fall from heaven,
   and the powers of heaven will
      be shaken.

³⁰Then the sign of the Son of Man will appear in heaven, and then all the tribes of the earth will mourn, and they will see "the Son of Man coming on the clouds of heaven" with power and great glory. ³¹And he will send out his angels with a loud trumpet call, and they will gather his elect from the four winds, from one end of heaven to the other.

The Lesson of the Fig Tree

32 'From the fig tree learn its lesson: as soon as its branch becomes tender and puts forth its leaves, you know that summer is near. ³³So also, when you see all these things, you know that he[d] is near, at the very gates. ³⁴Truly I tell you, this generation will not pass away until all these things have taken place. ³⁵Heaven and earth will pass away, but my words will not pass away.

The Necessity for Watchfulness

36 'But about that day and hour no one knows, neither the angels of heaven, nor the Son,[e] but only the Father. ³⁷For as the days of Noah were, so will be the coming of the Son of Man. ³⁸For as in those days before the flood they were eating and drinking, marrying and giving in marriage, until the day Noah entered the ark, ³⁹and they knew nothing until the flood came and swept them all away, so too will be the coming of the Son of Man. ⁴⁰Then two will be in the field; one will be taken and one will be left. ⁴¹Two women will be grinding meal together; one will be taken and one will be left. ⁴²Keep awake therefore, for you do not know on what day[f] your Lord is coming. ⁴³But understand this: if the owner of the house had known in what part of the night the thief was coming, he would have stayed awake and would not have let his house be broken into. ⁴⁴Therefore you also must be ready, for the Son of Man is coming at an unexpected hour.

The Faithful or the Unfaithful Slave

45 'Who then is the faithful and wise slave, whom his master has put in charge of his household, to give the other slaves[g]

---

a Or *gospel*   *b* Or *the Christ*   *c* Or *christs*   *d* Or *it*
e Other ancient authorities lack *nor the Son*   *f* Other ancient authorities read *at what hour*   *g* Gk *to give them*

their allowance of food at the proper time? ⁴⁶Blessed is that slave whom his master will find at work when he arrives. ⁴⁷Truly I tell you, he will put that one in charge of all his possessions. ⁴⁸But if that wicked slave says to himself, "My master is delayed", ⁴⁹and he begins to beat his fellow-slaves, and eats and drinks with drunkards, ⁵⁰the master of that slave will come on a day when he does not expect him and at an hour that he does not know. ⁵¹He will cut him in pieces^a and put him with the hypocrites, where there will be weeping and gnashing of teeth.

The Parable of the Ten Bridesmaids

25 'Then the kingdom of heaven will be like this. Ten bridesmaids^b took their lamps and went to meet the bridegroom.^c ²Five of them were foolish, and five were wise. ³When the foolish took their lamps, they took no oil with them; ⁴but the wise took flasks of oil with their lamps. ⁵As the bridegroom was delayed, all of them became drowsy and slept. ⁶But at midnight there was a shout, "Look! Here is the bridegroom! Come out to meet him." ⁷Then all those bridesmaids^b got up and trimmed their lamps. ⁸The foolish said to the wise, "Give us some of your oil, for our lamps are going out." ⁹But the wise replied, "No! there will not be enough for you and for us; you had better go to the dealers and buy some for yourselves." ¹⁰And while they went to buy it, the bridegroom came, and those who were ready went with him into the wedding banquet; and the door was shut. ¹¹Later the other bridesmaids^b came also, saying, "Lord, lord, open to us." ¹²But he replied, "Truly I tell you, I do not know you." ¹³Keep awake therefore, for you know neither the day nor the hour.^d

The Parable of the Talents

14 'For it is as if a man, going on a journey, summoned his slaves and entrusted his property to them; ¹⁵to one he gave five talents,^e to another two, to another one, to each according to his ability. Then he went away. ¹⁶The one who had received the five talents went off at once and traded with them, and made five more talents. ¹⁷In the same way, the one who had the two talents made two more talents. ¹⁸But the one who had received the one talent went off and dug a hole in the ground and hid his master's money. ¹⁹After a long time the master of those slaves came and settled accounts with them. ²⁰Then the one who had received the five talents came forward, bringing five more talents, saying, "Master, you handed over to me five talents; see, I have made five more talents." ²¹His master said to him, "Well done, good and trustworthy slave; you have been trustworthy in a few things, I will put you in charge of many things; enter into the joy of your master." ²²And the one with the two talents also came forward, saying, "Master, you handed over to me two talents; see, I have made two more talents." ²³His master said to him, "Well done, good and trustworthy slave; you have been trustworthy in a few things, I will put you in charge of many things; enter into the joy of your master." ²⁴Then the one who had received the one talent also came forward, saying, "Master, I knew that you were a harsh man, reaping where you did not sow, and gathering where you did not scatter seed; ²⁵so I was afraid, and I went and hid your talent in the ground. Here you have what is yours." ²⁶But his master replied, "You wicked and lazy slave! You knew, did you, that I reap where I did not sow, and gather where I did not scatter? ²⁷Then you ought to have invested my money with the bankers, and on my return I would have received what was my own with interest. ²⁸So take the talent from him, and give it to the one with the ten talents. ²⁹For to all those who have, more will be given, and they will have an abundance; but from those who have nothing, even what they have will be taken away. ³⁰As for this worthless slave, throw him into the outer darkness, where

a Or cut him off   b Gk virgins   c Other ancient authorities add and the bride   d Other ancient authorities add in which the Son of Man is coming   e A talent was worth more than fifteen years' wages of a labourer there will be weeping and gnashing of teeth."

The Judgement of the Nations

31 'When the Son of Man comes in his glory, and all the angels with him, then he will sit on the throne of his glory. 32 All the nations will be gathered before him, and he will separate people one from another as a shepherd separates the sheep from the goats, 33 and he will put the sheep at his right hand and the goats at the left. 34 Then the king will say to those at his right hand, "Come, you that are blessed by my Father, inherit the kingdom prepared for you from the foundation of the world; 35 for I was hungry and you gave me food, I was thirsty and you gave me something to drink, I was a stranger and you welcomed me, 36 I was naked and you gave me clothing, I was sick and you took care of me, I was in prison and you visited me." 37 Then the righteous will answer him, "Lord, when was it that we saw you hungry and gave you food, or thirsty and gave you something to drink? 38 And when was it that we saw you a stranger and welcomed you, or naked and gave you clothing? 39 And when was it that we saw you sick or in prison and visited you?" 40 And the king will answer them, "Truly I tell you, just as you did it to one of the least of these who are members of my family,[a] you did it to me." 41 Then he will say to those at his left hand, "You that are accursed, depart from me into the eternal fire prepared for the devil and his angels; 42 for I was hungry and you gave me no food, I was thirsty and you gave me nothing to drink, 43 I was a stranger and you did not welcome me, naked and you did not give me clothing, sick and in prison and you did not visit me." 44 Then they also will answer, "Lord, when was it that we saw you hungry or thirsty or a stranger or naked or sick or in prison, and did not take care of you?" 45 Then he will answer them, "Truly I tell you, just as you did not do it to one of the least of these, you did not do it to me." 46 And these will go away into eternal punishment, but the righteous into eternal life.'

The Plot to Kill Jesus

26 When Jesus had finished saying all these things, he said to his disciples, 2 'You know that after two days the Passover is coming, and the Son of Man will be handed over to be crucified.'

3 Then the chief priests and the elders of the people gathered in the palace of the high priest, who was called Caiaphas, 4 and they conspired to arrest Jesus by stealth and kill him. 5 But they said, 'Not during the festival, or there may be a riot among the people.'

The Anointing at Bethany

6 Now while Jesus was at Bethany in the house of Simon the leper,[b] 7 a woman came to him with an alabaster jar of very costly ointment, and she poured it on his head as he sat at the table. 8 But when the disciples saw it, they were angry and said, 'Why this waste? 9 For this ointment could have been sold for a large sum, and the money given to the poor.' 10 But Jesus, aware of this, said to them, 'Why do you trouble the woman? She has performed a good service for me. 11 For you always have the poor with you, but you will not always have me. 12 By pouring this ointment on my body she has prepared me for burial. 13 Truly I tell you, wherever this good news[c] is proclaimed in the whole world, what she has done will be told in remembrance of her.'

Judas Agrees to Betray Jesus

14 Then one of the twelve, who was called Judas Iscariot, went to the chief priests 15 and said, 'What will you give me if I betray him to you?' They paid him thirty pieces of silver. 16 And from that moment he began to look for an opportunity to betray him.

The Passover with the Disciples

17 On the first day of Unleavened Bread the disciples came to Jesus, saying, 'Where do you want us to make the preparations for you to eat the Passover?' 18 He said, 'Go

---

a Gk *these my brothers*   *b* The terms *leper* and *leprosy* can refer to several diseases   *c* Or *gospel* into the city to a certain man, and say to him, "The Teacher says, My time is near; I will keep the Passover at your house with my disciples." ' ¹⁹So the disciples did as Jesus had directed them, and they prepared the Passover meal.

20 When it was evening, he took his place with the twelve;ᵃ ²¹and while they were eating, he said, 'Truly I tell you, one of you will betray me.' ²²And they became greatly distressed and began to say to him one after another, 'Surely not I, Lord?' ²³He answered, 'The one who has dipped his hand into the bowl with me will betray me. ²⁴The Son of Man goes as it is written of him, but woe to that one by whom the Son of Man is betrayed! It would have been better for that one not to have been born.' ²⁵Judas, who betrayed him, said, 'Surely not I, Rabbi?' He replied, 'You have said so.'

The Institution of the Lord's Supper

26 While they were eating, Jesus took a loaf of bread, and after blessing it he broke it, gave it to the disciples, and said, 'Take, eat; this is my body.' ²⁷Then he took a cup, and after giving thanks he gave it to them, saying, 'Drink from it, all of you; ²⁸for this is my blood of theᵇ covenant, which is poured out for many for the forgiveness of sins. ²⁹I tell you, I will never again drink of this fruit of the vine until that day when I drink it new with you in my Father's kingdom.'

30 When they had sung the hymn, they went out to the Mount of Olives.

Peter's Denial Foretold

31 Then Jesus said to them, 'You will all become deserters because of me this night; for it is written,

"I will strike the shepherd,
and the sheep of the flock will
be scattered."

³²But after I am raised up, I will go ahead of you to Galilee.' ³³Peter said to him, 'Though all become deserters because of you, I will never desert you.' ³⁴Jesus said to him, 'Truly I tell you, this very night, before the cock crows, you will deny me three

times.' ³⁵Peter said to him, 'Even though I must die with you, I will not deny you.' And so said all the disciples.

Jesus Prays in Gethsemane

36 Then Jesus went with them to a place called Gethsemane; and he said to his disciples, 'Sit here while I go over there and pray.' ³⁷He took with him Peter and the two sons of Zebedee, and began to be grieved and agitated. ³⁸Then he said to them, 'I am deeply grieved, even to death; remain here, and stay awake with me.' ³⁹And going a little farther, he threw himself on the ground and prayed, 'My Father, if it is possible, let this cup pass from me; yet not what I want but what you want.' ⁴⁰Then he came to the disciples and found them sleeping; and he said to Peter, 'So, could you not stay awake with me one hour? ⁴¹Stay awake and pray that you may not come into the time of trial;ᶜ the spirit indeed is willing, but the flesh is weak.' ⁴²Again he went away for the second time and prayed, 'My Father, if this cannot pass unless I drink it, your will be done.' ⁴³Again he came and found them sleeping, for their eyes were heavy. ⁴⁴So leaving them again, he went away and prayed for the third time, saying the same words. ⁴⁵Then he came to the disciples and said to them, 'Are you still sleeping and taking your rest? See, the hour is at hand, and the Son of Man is betrayed into the hands of sinners. ⁴⁶Get up, let us be going. See, my betrayer is at hand.'

The Betrayal and Arrest of Jesus

47 While he was still speaking, Judas, one of the twelve, arrived; with him was a large crowd with swords and clubs, from the chief priests and the elders of the people. ⁴⁸Now the betrayer had given them a sign, saying, 'The one I will kiss is the man; arrest him.' ⁴⁹At once he came up to Jesus and said, 'Greetings, Rabbi!' and kissed him. ⁵⁰Jesus said to him, 'Friend, do what you are here to do.' Then they came and laid hands on Jesus and arrested him.

a Other ancient authorities add *disciples*   *b* Other ancient authorities add *new*   *c* Or *into temptation*

51 Suddenly, one of those with Jesus put his hand on his sword, drew it, and struck the slave of the high priest, cutting off his ear. 52 Then Jesus said to him, 'Put your sword back into its place; for all who take the sword will perish by the sword. 53 Do you think that I cannot appeal to my Father, and he will at once send me more than twelve legions of angels? 54 But how then would the scriptures be fulfilled, which say it must happen in this way?' 55 At that hour Jesus said to the crowds, 'Have you come out with swords and clubs to arrest me as though I were a bandit? Day after day I sat in the temple teaching, and you did not arrest me. 56 But all this has taken place, so that the scriptures of the prophets may be fulfilled.' Then all the disciples deserted him and fled.

Jesus before the High Priest

57 Those who had arrested Jesus took him to Caiaphas the high priest, in whose house the scribes and the elders had gathered. 58 But Peter was following him at a distance, as far as the courtyard of the high priest; and going inside, he sat with the guards in order to see how this would end. 59 Now the chief priests and the whole council were looking for false testimony against Jesus so that they might put him to death, 60 but they found none, though many false witnesses came forward. At last two came forward 61 and said, 'This fellow said, "I am able to destroy the temple of God and to build it in three days." ' 62 The high priest stood up and said, 'Have you no answer? What is it that they testify against you?' 63 But Jesus was silent. Then the high priest said to him, 'I put you under oath before the living God, tell us if you are the Messiah,*a* the Son of God.' 64 Jesus said to him, 'You have said so. But I tell you,

From now on you will see the
    Son of Man
  seated at the right hand of Power
  and coming on the clouds
    of heaven.'

65 Then the high priest tore his clothes and said, 'He has blasphemed! Why do

we still need witnesses? You have now heard his blasphemy. 66 What is your verdict?' They answered, 'He deserves death.' 67 Then they spat in his face and struck him; and some slapped him, 68 saying, 'Prophesy to us, you Messiah!*a* Who is it that struck you?'

Peter's Denial of Jesus

69 Now Peter was sitting outside in the courtyard. A servant-girl came to him and said, 'You also were with Jesus the Galilean.' 70 But he denied it before all of them, saying, 'I do not know what you are talking about.' 71 When he went out to the porch, another servant-girl saw him, and she said to the bystanders, 'This man was with Jesus of Nazareth.'*b* 72 Again he denied it with an oath, 'I do not know the man.' 73 After a little while the bystanders came up and said to Peter, 'Certainly you are also one of them, for your accent betrays you.' 74 Then he began to curse, and he swore an oath, 'I do not know the man!' At that moment the cock crowed. 75 Then Peter remembered what Jesus had said: 'Before the cock crows, you will deny me three times.' And he went out and wept bitterly.

Jesus Brought before Pilate

27 When morning came, all the chief priests and the elders of the people conferred together against Jesus in order to bring about his death. 2 They bound him, led him away, and handed him over to Pilate the governor.

The Suicide of Judas

3 When Judas, his betrayer, saw that Jesus*c* was condemned, he repented and brought back the thirty pieces of silver to the chief priests and the elders. 4 He said, 'I have sinned by betraying innocent*d* blood.' But they said, 'What is that to us? See to it yourself.' 5 Throwing down the pieces of silver in the temple, he departed; and he went and hanged himself. 6 But the chief priests, taking the pieces of silver, said, 'It is not lawful to put them into the treasury,

a Or *Christ*   *b* Gk *the Nazorean*   *c* Gk *he*   *d* Other ancient authorities read *righteous* since they are blood money.' 7 After conferring together, they used them to buy the potter's field as a place to bury foreigners. 8 For this reason that field has been called the Field of Blood to this day. 9 Then was fulfilled what had been spoken through the prophet Jeremiah, *a* 'And they took*b* the thirty pieces of silver, the price of the one on whom a price had been set, *c* on whom some of the people of Israel had set a price, 10 and they gave*d* them for the potter's field, as the Lord commanded me.'

Pilate Questions Jesus

11 Now Jesus stood before the governor; and the governor asked him, 'Are you the King of the Jews?' Jesus said, 'You say so.' 12 But when he was accused by the chief priests and elders, he did not answer. 13 Then Pilate said to him, 'Do you not hear how many accusations they make against you?' 14 But he gave him no answer, not even to a single charge, so that the governor was greatly amazed.

Barabbas or Jesus?

15 Now at the festival the governor was accustomed to release a prisoner for the crowd, anyone whom they wanted. 16 At that time they had a notorious prisoner, called Jesus*e* Barabbas. 17 So after they had gathered, Pilate said to them, 'Whom do you want me to release for you, Jesus*e* Barabbas or Jesus who is called the Messiah?'*f* 18 For he realized that it was out of jealousy that they had handed him over. 19 While he was sitting on the judgement seat, his wife sent word to him, 'Have nothing to do with that innocent man, for today I have suffered a great deal because of a dream about him.' 20 Now the chief priests and the elders persuaded the crowds to ask for Barabbas and to have Jesus killed. 21 The governor again said to them, 'Which of the two do you want me to release for you?' And they said, 'Barabbas.' 22 Pilate said to them, 'Then what should I do with Jesus who is called the Messiah?'*f* All of them said, 'Let him be crucified!' 23 Then he asked, 'Why, what evil has he done?' But

they shouted all the more, 'Let him be crucified!'

Pilate Hands Jesus over to Be Crucified

24 So when Pilate saw that he could do nothing, but rather that a riot was beginning, he took some water and washed his hands before the crowd, saying, 'I am innocent of this man's blood;*g* see to it yourselves.' 25 Then the people as a whole answered, 'His blood be on us and on our children!' 26 So he released Barabbas for them; and after flogging Jesus, he handed him over to be crucified.

The Soldiers Mock Jesus

27 Then the soldiers of the governor took Jesus into the governor's headquarters,*h* and they gathered the whole cohort around him. 28 They stripped him and put a scarlet robe on him, 29 and after twisting some thorns into a crown, they put it on his head. They put a reed in his right hand and knelt before him and mocked him, saying, 'Hail, King of the Jews!' 30 They spat on him, and took the reed and struck him on the head. 31 After mocking him, they stripped him of the robe and put his own clothes on him. Then they led him away to crucify him.

The Crucifixion of Jesus

32 As they went out, they came upon a man from Cyrene named Simon; they compelled this man to carry his cross. 33 And when they came to a place called Golgotha (which means Place of a Skull), 34 they offered him wine to drink, mixed with gall; but when he tasted it, he would not drink it. 35 And when they had crucified him, they divided his clothes among themselves by casting lots;*i* 36 then they sat down there and kept watch over him.

a Other ancient authorities read *Zechariah* or *Isaiah*
b Or *I took*   *c* Or *the price of the precious One*
d Other ancient authorities read *I gave*   *e* Other ancient authorities lack *Jesus*   *f* Or *the Christ*
g Other ancient authorities read *this righteous blood*, or *this righteous man's blood*   *h* Gk *the praetorium*
i Other ancient authorities add *in order that what had been spoken through the prophet might be fulfilled, 'They divided my clothes among themselves, and for my clothing they cast lots.'*

37 Over his head they put the charge against him, which read, 'This is Jesus, the King of the Jews.'

38 Then two bandits were crucified with him, one on his right and one on his left. 39 Those who passed by derided[a] him, shaking their heads 40 and saying, 'You who would destroy the temple and build it in three days, save yourself! If you are the Son of God, come down from the cross.' 41 In the same way the chief priests also, along with the scribes and elders, were mocking him, saying, 42 'He saved others; he cannot save himself.[b] He is the King of Israel; let him come down from the cross now, and we will believe in him. 43 He trusts in God; let God deliver him now, if he wants to; for he said, "I am God's Son." ' 44 The bandits who were crucified with him also taunted him in the same way.

The Death of Jesus

45 From noon on, darkness came over the whole land[c] until three in the afternoon. 46 And about three o'clock Jesus cried with a loud voice, 'Eli, Eli, lema sabachthani?' that is, 'My God, my God, why have you forsaken me?' 47 When some of the bystanders heard it, they said, 'This man is calling for Elijah.' 48 At once one of them ran and got a sponge, filled it with sour wine, put it on a stick, and gave it to him to drink. 49 But the others said, 'Wait, let us see whether Elijah will come to save him.'[d] 50 Then Jesus cried again with a loud voice and breathed his last.[e] 51 At that moment the curtain of the temple was torn in two, from top to bottom. The earth shook, and the rocks were split. 52 The tombs also were opened, and many bodies of the saints who had fallen asleep were raised. 53 After his resurrection they came out of the tombs and entered the holy city and appeared to many. 54 Now when the centurion and those with him, who were keeping watch over Jesus, saw the earthquake and what took place, they were terrified and said, 'Truly this man was God's Son!'[f]

55 Many women were also there, looking on from a distance; they had followed Jesus from Galilee and had provided for him. 56 Among them were Mary Magdalene, and Mary the mother of James and Joseph, and the mother of the sons of Zebedee.

The Burial of Jesus

57 When it was evening, there came a rich man from Arimathea, named Joseph, who was also a disciple of Jesus. 58 He went to Pilate and asked for the body of Jesus; then Pilate ordered it to be given to him. 59 So Joseph took the body and wrapped it in a clean linen cloth 60 and laid it in his own new tomb, which he had hewn in the rock. He then rolled a great stone to the door of the tomb and went away. 61 Mary Magdalene and the other Mary were there, sitting opposite the tomb.

The Guard at the Tomb

62 The next day, that is, after the day of Preparation, the chief priests and the Pharisees gathered before Pilate 63 and said, 'Sir, we remember what that impostor said while he was still alive, "After three days I will rise again." 64 Therefore command that the tomb be made secure until the third day; otherwise his disciples may go and steal him away, and tell the people, "He has been raised from the dead", and the last deception would be worse than the first.' 65 Pilate said to them, 'You have a guard[g] of soldiers; go, make it as secure as you can.'[h] 66 So they went with the guard and made the tomb secure by sealing the stone.

The Resurrection of Jesus

28 After the sabbath, as the first day of the week was dawning, Mary Magdalene and the other Mary went to see the tomb. 2 And suddenly there was a great earthquake; for an angel of the Lord, descending from heaven, came and rolled back the stone and sat on it. 3 His appearance was like lightning, and his clothing

a Or blasphemed   b Or is he unable to save himself?
c Or earth   d Other ancient authorities add And another took a spear and pierced his side, and out came water and blood   e Or gave up his spirit   f Or a son of God   g Or Take a guard   h Gk you know how

Event / Appearance	Matthew	Mark	Luke	John	Acts	1 Cor
The Resurrection and Post-Resurrection Appearances of Jesus						
The empty tomb outside Jerusalem	28.1–8	16.1–8	24.1–12	20.1–9		
To Mary Magdalene at the tomb		16.9–11		20.11–18		
To Mary Magdalene and the other Mary	28.9–10					
To two disciples on the road to Emmaus		16.12–13	24.13–32			
To Peter in Jerusalem			24.34			15.5
To the ten disciples in the upper room			24.36–43	20.19–25		
To the eleven disciples in the upper room		16.14		20.26–31		15.5
To seven disciples fishing on the Sea of Galilee				21.1–3		
To eleven disciples on a mountain in Galilee	28.16–20	16.15–18				
To more than five hundred						15.6
To James						15.7
At the Ascension on the Mt. of Olives		16.19	24.44–49		1.3–8	
To Paul on the road to Damascus					9.1–19 22.3–16 26.9–18	cf. 9.1

white as snow. 4 For fear of him the guards shook and became like dead men. 5 But the angel said to the women, 'Do not be afraid; I know that you are looking for Jesus who was crucified. 6 He is not here; for he has been raised, as he said. Come, see the place where he*a* lay. 7 Then go quickly and tell his disciples, "He has been raised from the dead,*b* and indeed he is going ahead of you to Galilee; there you will see him." This is my message for you.' 8 So they left the tomb quickly with fear and great joy, and ran to tell his disciples. 9 Suddenly Jesus met them and said, 'Greetings!' And they came to him, took hold of his feet, and worshipped him. 10 Then Jesus said to them, 'Do not be afraid; go and tell my brothers to go to Galilee; there they will see me.'

The Report of the Guard

11 While they were going, some of the guard went into the city and told the chief priests everything that had happened. 12 After the priests*c* had assembled with the elders, they devised a plan to give a large sum of money to the soldiers, 13 telling them, 'You must say, "His disciples came by night and stole him away while we were asleep." 14 If this comes to the governor's ears, we will satisfy him and keep you out of trouble.' 15 So they took the money and did as they were directed. And this story is still told among the Jews to this day.

The Commissioning of the Disciples

16 Now the eleven disciples went to Galilee, to the mountain to which Jesus had directed them. 17 When they saw him, they worshipped him; but some doubted. 18 And Jesus came and said to them, 'All authority in heaven and on earth has been given to me. 19 Go therefore and make disciples of all nations, baptizing them in the name of the Father and of the Son and of the Holy Spirit, 20 and teaching them to obey everything that I have commanded you. And remember, I am with you always, to the end of the age.'*d*

a Other ancient authorities read *the Lord*   *b* Other ancient authorities lack *from the dead*   *c* Gk *they*   *d* Other ancient authorities add *Amen*

THE GOSPEL ACCORDING TO
MARK

The Proclamation of John the Baptist

1 The beginning of the good news*a* of Jesus Christ, the Son of God.*b*

2 As it is written in the prophet Isaiah,*c*

'See, I am sending my messenger
    ahead of you,*d*
who will prepare your way;

3 the voice of one crying out in the
        wilderness:
    "Prepare the way of the Lord,
        make his paths straight" ',

4 John the baptizer appeared*e* in the wilderness, proclaiming a baptism of repentance for the forgiveness of sins. 5 And people from the whole Judean countryside and all the people of Jerusalem were going out to him, and were baptized by him in the river Jordan, confessing their sins. 6 Now John was clothed with camel's hair, with a leather belt around his waist, and he ate locusts and wild honey. 7 He proclaimed, 'The one who is more powerful than I is coming after me; I am not worthy to stoop down and untie the thong of his sandals. 8 I have baptized you with*f* water; but he will baptize you with*f* the Holy Spirit.'

The Baptism of Jesus

9 In those days Jesus came from Nazareth of Galilee and was baptized by John in the Jordan. 10 And just as he was coming up out of the water, he saw the heavens torn apart and the Spirit descending like a dove on him. 11 And a voice came from heaven, 'You are my Son, the Beloved;*g* with you I am well pleased.'

The Temptation of Jesus

12 And the Spirit immediately drove him out into the wilderness. 13 He was in the wilderness for forty days, tempted by Satan; and he was with the wild beasts; and the angels waited on him.

The Beginning of the Galilean Ministry

14 Now after John was arrested, Jesus came to Galilee, proclaiming the good news*a* of God,*h* 15 and saying, 'The time is fulfilled, and the kingdom of God has come near;*i* repent, and believe in the good news.'*a*

Jesus Calls the First Disciples

16 As Jesus passed along the Sea of Galilee, he saw Simon and his brother Andrew casting a net into the lake—for they were fishermen. 17 And Jesus said to them, 'Follow me and I will make you fish for people.' 18 And immediately they left their nets and followed him. 19 As he went a little farther, he saw James son of Zebedee and his brother John, who were in their boat mending the nets. 20 Immediately he called them; and they left their father Zebedee in the boat with the hired men, and followed him.

The Man with an Unclean Spirit

21 They went to Capernaum; and when the sabbath came, he entered the synagogue and taught. 22 They were astounded at his teaching, for he taught them as one having authority, and not as the scribes. 23 Just then there was in their synagogue a man with an unclean spirit, 24 and he cried

---

a Or *gospel*   *b* Other ancient authorities lack *the Son of God*   *c* Other ancient authorities read *in the prophets*   *d* Gk *before your face*   *e* Other ancient authorities read *John was baptizing*   *f* Or *in*   *g* Or *my beloved Son*   *h* Other ancient authorities read *of the kingdom*   *i* Or *is at hand* out, 'What have you to do with us, Jesus of Nazareth? Have you come to destroy us? I know who you are, the Holy One of God.' 25 But Jesus rebuked him, saying, 'Be silent, and come out of him!' 26 And the unclean spirit, throwing him into convulsions and crying with a loud voice, came out of him. 27 They were all amazed, and they kept on asking one another, 'What is this? A new teaching—with authority! He*a* commands even the unclean spirits, and they obey him.' 28 At once his fame began to spread throughout the surrounding region of Galilee.

Jesus Heals Many at Simon's House

29 As soon as they*b* left the synagogue, they entered the house of Simon and Andrew, with James and John. 30 Now Simon's mother-in-law was in bed with a fever, and they told him about her at once. 31 He came and took her by the hand and lifted her up. Then the fever left her, and she began to serve them.

32 That evening, at sunset, they brought to him all who were sick or possessed with demons. 33 And the whole city was gathered around the door. 34 And he cured many who were sick with various diseases, and cast out many demons; and he would not permit the demons to speak, because they knew him.

A Preaching Tour in Galilee

35 In the morning, while it was still very dark, he got up and went out to a deserted place, and there he prayed. 36 And Simon and his companions hunted for him. 37 When they found him, they said to him, 'Everyone is searching for you.' 38 He answered, 'Let us go on to the neighbouring towns, so that I may proclaim the message there also; for that is what I came out to do.' 39 And he went throughout Galilee, proclaiming the message in their synagogues and casting out demons.

Jesus Cleanses a Leper

40 A leper*c* came to him begging him, and kneeling*d* he said to him, 'If you choose, you can make me clean.' 41 Moved with pity,*e* Jesus*f* stretched out his hand and touched him, and said to him, 'I do choose. Be made clean!' 42 Immediately the leprosy*c* left him, and he was made clean. 43 After sternly warning him he sent him away at once, 44 saying to him, 'See that you say nothing to anyone; but go, show yourself to the priest, and offer for your cleansing what Moses commanded, as a testimony to them.' 45 But he went out and began to proclaim it freely, and to spread the word, so that Jesus*f* could no longer go into a town openly, but stayed out in the country; and people came to him from every quarter.

Jesus Heals a Paralytic

2 When he returned to Capernaum after some days, it was reported that he was at home. 2 So many gathered around that there was no longer room for them, not even in front of the door; and he was speaking the word to them. 3 Then some people*g* came, bringing to him a paralysed man, carried by four of them. 4 And when they could not bring him to Jesus because of the crowd, they removed the roof above him; and after having dug through it, they let down the mat on which the paralytic lay. 5 When Jesus saw their faith, he said to the paralytic, 'Son, your sins are forgiven.' 6 Now some of the scribes were sitting there, questioning in their hearts, 7 'Why does this fellow speak in this way? It is blasphemy! Who can forgive sins but God alone?' 8 At once Jesus perceived in his spirit that they were discussing these questions among themselves; and he said to them, 'Why do you raise such questions in your hearts? 9 Which is easier, to say to the paralytic, "Your sins are forgiven", or to say, "Stand up and take your mat and walk"? 10 But so that you may know that the Son of Man has authority on earth to forgive sins'—he said to the paralytic— 11 'I say to you, stand up, take your mat and go to your home.' 12 And he stood up,

---

a Or *A new teaching! With authority he*   *b* Other ancient authorities read *he*   *c* The terms *leper* and *leprosy* can refer to several diseases   *d* Other ancient authorities lack *kneeling*   *e* Other ancient authorities read *anger*   *f* Gk *he*   *g* Gk *they* and immediately took the mat and went out before all of them; so that they were all amazed and glorified God, saying, 'We have never seen anything like this!'

Jesus Calls Levi

13 Jesus[a] went out again beside the lake; the whole crowd gathered around him, and he taught them. 14 As he was walking along, he saw Levi son of Alphaeus sitting at the tax booth, and he said to him, 'Follow me.' And he got up and followed him.

15 And as he sat at dinner[b] in Levi's[c] house, many tax-collectors and sinners were also sitting[d] with Jesus and his disciples—for there were many who followed him. 16 When the scribes of[e] the Pharisees saw that he was eating with sinners and tax-collectors, they said to his disciples, 'Why does he eat[f] with tax-collectors and sinners?' 17 When Jesus heard this, he said to them, 'Those who are well have no need of a physician, but those who are sick; I have come to call not the righteous but sinners.'

The Question about Fasting

18 Now John's disciples and the Pharisees were fasting; and people[g] came and said to him, 'Why do John's disciples and the disciples of the Pharisees fast, but your disciples do not fast?' 19 Jesus said to them, 'The wedding-guests cannot fast while the bridegroom is with them, can they? As long as they have the bridegroom with them, they cannot fast. 20 The days will come when the bridegroom is taken away from them, and then they will fast on that day.

21 'No one sews a piece of unshrunk cloth on an old cloak; otherwise, the patch pulls away from it, the new from the old, and a worse tear is made. 22 And no one puts new wine into old wineskins; otherwise, the wine will burst the skins, and the wine is lost, and so are the skins; but one puts new wine into fresh wineskins.'[h]

Pronouncement about the Sabbath

23 One sabbath he was going through the cornfields; and as they made their way

his disciples began to pluck heads of grain. 24 The Pharisees said to him, 'Look, why are they doing what is not lawful on the sabbath?' 25 And he said to them, 'Have you never read what David did when he and his companions were hungry and in need of food? 26 He entered the house of God, when Abiathar was high priest, and ate the bread of the Presence, which it is not lawful for any but the priests to eat, and he gave some to his companions.' 27 Then he said to them, 'The sabbath was made for humankind, and not humankind for the sabbath; 28 so the Son of Man is lord even of the sabbath.'

The Man with a Withered Hand

3 Again he entered the synagogue, and a man was there who had a withered hand. 2 They watched him to see whether he would cure him on the sabbath, so that they might accuse him. 3 And he said to the man who had the withered hand, 'Come forward.' 4 Then he said to them, 'Is it lawful to do good or to do harm on the sabbath, to save life or to kill?' But they were silent. 5 He looked around at them with anger; he was grieved at their hardness of heart and said to the man, 'Stretch out your hand.' He stretched it out, and his hand was restored. 6 The Pharisees went out and immediately conspired with the Herodians against him, how to destroy him.

A Multitude at the Lakeside

7 Jesus departed with his disciples to the lake, and a great multitude from Galilee followed him; 8 hearing all that he was doing, they came to him in great numbers from Judea, Jerusalem, Idumea, beyond the Jordan, and the region around Tyre and Sidon. 9 He told his disciples to have a boat ready for him because of the crowd, so that they would not crush him; 10 for he had cured many, so that all who had diseases pressed upon him to touch him.

a Gk He   b Gk reclined   c Gk his   d Gk reclining
e Other ancient authorities read and   f Other ancient
authorities add and drink   g Gk they   h Other
ancient authorities lack but one puts new wine into fresh
wineskins

[11] Whenever the unclean spirits saw him, they fell down before him and shouted, 'You are the Son of God!' [12] But he sternly ordered them not to make him known.

Jesus Appoints the Twelve

13 He went up the mountain and called to him those whom he wanted, and they came to him. [14] And he appointed twelve, whom he also named apostles,[a] to be with him, and to be sent out to proclaim the message, [15] and to have authority to cast out demons. [16] So he appointed the twelve:[b] Simon (to whom he gave the name Peter); [17] James son of Zebedee and John the brother of James (to whom he gave the name Boanerges, that is, Sons of Thunder); [18] and Andrew, and Philip, and Bartholomew, and Matthew, and Thomas, and James son of Alphaeus, and Thaddaeus, and Simon the Cananaean, [19] and Judas Iscariot, who betrayed him.

Jesus and Beelzebul

Then he went home; [20] and the crowd came together again, so that they could not even eat. [21] When his family heard it, they went out to restrain him, for people were saying, 'He has gone out of his mind.' [22] And the scribes who came down from Jerusalem said, 'He has Beelzebul, and by the ruler of the demons he casts out demons.' [23] And he called them to him, and spoke to them in parables, 'How can Satan cast out Satan? [24] If a kingdom is divided against itself, that kingdom cannot stand. [25] And if a house is divided against itself, that house will not be able to stand. [26] And if Satan has risen up against himself and is divided, he cannot stand, but his end has come. [27] But no one can enter a strong man's house and plunder his property without first tying up the strong man; then indeed the house can be plundered.

28 'Truly I tell you, people will be forgiven for their sins and whatever blasphemies they utter; [29] but whoever blasphemes against the Holy Spirit can never have forgiveness, but is guilty of an eternal sin'— [30] for they had said, 'He has an unclean spirit.'

a Other ancient authorities lack *whom he also named apostles*   b Other ancient authorities lack *So he appointed the twelve*

Lists of the Apostles

Matthew 10.2–4	Mark 3.16–19	Luke 6.14–16	Acts 1.13
Simon . . . Peter	Simon . . . Peter	Simon . . . Peter	Peter
Andrew [Simon's] brother	James son of Zebedee	Andrew [Simon's] brother	John
James son of Zebedee	John the brother of James	James	James
John [son of Zebedee]	Andrew	John	Andrew
Philip	Philip	Philip	Philip
Bartholomew	Bartholomew	Bartholomew	Thomas
Thomas	Matthew	Matthew	Bartholomew
Matthew the tax-collector	Thomas	Thomas	Matthew
James son of Alphaeus	James son of Alphaeus	James son of Alphaeus	James son of Alphaeus
Thaddaeus	Thaddaeus	Simon . . . the Zealot	Simon the Zealot
Simon the Cananaean	Simon the Cananaean	Judas son of James	Judas son of James
Judas Iscariot	Judas Iscariot	Judas Iscariot	

Lists of the apostles appear to be grouped in four groups, with Simon Peter always first in the first group, Philip in the second group, and James son of Alphaeus in the third group. Judas Iscariot is always last in the lists in which he appears.

The True Kindred of Jesus

31 Then his mother and his brothers came; and standing outside, they sent to him and called him. 32 A crowd was sitting around him; and they said to him, 'Your mother and your brothers and sisters*a* are outside, asking for you.' 33 And he replied, 'Who are my mother and my brothers?' 34 And looking at those who sat around him, he said, 'Here are my mother and my brothers! 35 Whoever does the will of God is my brother and sister and mother.'

The Parable of the Sower

4 Again he began to teach beside the lake. Such a very large crowd gathered around him that he got into a boat on the lake and sat there, while the whole crowd was beside the lake on the land. 2 He began to teach them many things in parables, and in his teaching he said to them: 3 'Listen! A sower went out to sow. 4 And as he sowed, some seed fell on the path, and the birds came and ate it up. 5 Other seed fell on rocky ground, where it did not have much soil, and it sprang up quickly, since it had no depth of soil. 6 And when the sun rose, it was scorched; and since it had no root, it withered away. 7 Other seed fell among thorns, and the thorns grew up and choked it, and it yielded no grain. 8 Other seed fell into good soil and brought forth grain, growing up and increasing and yielding thirty and sixty and a hundredfold.' 9 And he said, 'Let anyone with ears to hear listen!'

The Purpose of the Parables

10 When he was alone, those who were around him along with the twelve asked him about the parables. 11 And he said to them, 'To you has been given the secret*b* of the kingdom of God, but for those outside, everything comes in parables; 12 in order that

"they may indeed look, but not
        perceive,
    and may indeed listen, but not
        understand;
so that they may not turn again and
        be forgiven." '

13 And he said to them, 'Do you not understand this parable? Then how will you understand all the parables? 14 The sower sows the word. 15 These are the ones on the path where the word is sown: when they hear, Satan immediately comes and takes away the word that is sown in them. 16 And these are the ones sown on rocky ground: when they hear the word, they immediately receive it with joy. 17 But they have no root, and endure only for a while; then, when trouble or persecution arises on account of the word, immediately they fall away.*c* 18 And others are those sown among the thorns: these are the ones who hear the word, 19 but the cares of the world, and the lure of wealth, and the desire for other things come in and choke the word, and it yields nothing. 20 And these are the ones sown on the good soil: they hear the word and accept it and bear fruit, thirty and sixty and a hundredfold.'

A Lamp under a Bushel Basket

21 He said to them, 'Is a lamp brought in to be put under the bushel basket, or under the bed, and not on the lampstand? 22 For there is nothing hidden, except to be disclosed; nor is anything secret, except to come to light. 23 Let anyone with ears to hear listen!' 24 And he said to them, 'Pay attention to what you hear; the measure you give will be the measure you get, and still more will be given you. 25 For to those who have, more will be given; and from those who have nothing, even what they have will be taken away.'

The Parable of the Growing Seed

26 He also said, 'The kingdom of God is as if someone would scatter seed on the ground, 27 and would sleep and rise night and day, and the seed would sprout and grow, he does not know how. 28 The earth produces of itself, first the stalk, then the head, then the full grain in the head. 29 But when the grain is ripe, at once he goes in with his sickle, because the harvest has come.'

ancient authorities lack *and sisters*
    b ... *c* Or *stumble*

The Parable of the Mustard Seed

30 He also said, 'With what can we compare the kingdom of God, or what parable will we use for it? 31 It is like a mustard seed, which, when sown upon the ground, is the smallest of all the seeds on earth; 32 yet when it is sown it grows up and becomes the greatest of all shrubs, and puts forth large branches, so that the birds of the air can make nests in its shade.'

The Use of Parables

33 With many such parables he spoke the word to them, as they were able to hear it; 34 he did not speak to them except in parables, but he explained everything in private to his disciples.

Jesus Stills a Storm

35 On that day, when evening had come, he said to them, 'Let us go across to the other side.' 36 And leaving the crowd behind, they took him with them in the boat, just as he was. Other boats were with him. 37 A great gale arose, and the waves beat into the boat, so that the boat was already being swamped. 38 But he was in the stern, asleep on the cushion; and they woke him up and said to him, 'Teacher, do you not care that we are perishing?' 39 He woke up and rebuked the wind, and said to the sea, 'Peace! Be still!' Then the wind ceased, and there was a dead calm. 40 He said to them, 'Why are you afraid? Have you still no faith?' 41 And they were filled with great awe and said to one another, 'Who then is this, that even the wind and the sea obey him?'

Jesus Heals the Gerasene Demoniac

5 They came to the other side of the lake, to the country of the Gerasenes.ᵃ 2 And when he had stepped out of the boat, immediately a man out of the tombs with an unclean spirit met him. 3 He lived among the tombs; and no one could restrain him any more, even with a chain; 4 for he had often been restrained with shackles and chains, but the chains he wrenched apart, and the shackles he broke in pieces; and no one had the strength to subdue him. 5 Night and day among the tombs and on the mountains he was always howling and bruising himself with stones. 6 When he saw Jesus from a distance, he ran and bowed down before him; 7 and he shouted at the top of his voice, 'What have you to do with me, Jesus, Son of the Most High God? I adjure you by God, do not torment me.' 8 For he had said to him, 'Come out of the man, you unclean spirit!' 9 Then Jesusᵇ asked him, 'What is your name?' He replied, 'My name is Legion; for we are many.' 10 He begged him earnestly not to send them out of the country. 11 Now there on the hillside a great herd of swine was feeding; 12 and the unclean spiritsᶜ begged him, 'Send us into the swine; let us enter them.' 13 So he gave them permission. And the unclean spirits came out and entered the swine; and the herd, numbering about two thousand, rushed down the steep bank into the lake, and were drowned in the lake.

Jesus' Ministry Beyond Galilee

Mediterranean Sea
Damascus
ITUREA
Caesarea Philippi
Tyre
TRACHONTIS
Raphana
GALILEE
Capernaum
Bethsaida
Nazareth
Hippos
Nain
Abila
Scythopolis
Gadara
Pella
SAMARIA
Dion
Samaria
Gerasa
DECAPOLIS
Philadelphia
Jericho
Bethany
Jerusalem
JUDEA
Dead Sea
0   40 Mi
0   40 Km

ᵃ Other ancient authorities read Gergesenes; others,
ᵇ Gk he   ᶜ Gk they

14 The swineherds ran off and told it in the city and in the country. Then people came to see what it was that had happened. 15 They came to Jesus and saw the demoniac sitting there, clothed and in his right mind, the very man who had had the legion; and they were afraid. 16 Those who had seen what had happened to the demoniac and to the swine reported it. 17 Then they began to beg Jesus*a* to leave their neighbourhood. 18 As he was getting into the boat, the man who had been possessed by demons begged him that he might be with him. 19 But Jesus*b* refused, and said to him, 'Go home to your friends, and tell them how much the Lord has done for you, and what mercy he has shown you.' 20 And he went away and began to proclaim in the Decapolis how much Jesus had done for him; and everyone was amazed.

A Girl Restored to Life and a Woman Healed

21 When Jesus had crossed again in the boat*c* to the other side, a great crowd gathered round him; and he was by the lake. 22 Then one of the leaders of the synagogue named Jairus came and, when he saw him, fell at his feet 23 and begged him repeatedly, 'My little daughter is at the point of death. Come and lay your hands on her, so that she may be made well, and live.' 24 So he went with him.

And a large crowd followed him and pressed in on him. 25 Now there was a woman who had been suffering from haemorrhages for twelve years. 26 She had endured much under many physicians, and had spent all that she had; and she was no better, but rather grew worse. 27 She had heard about Jesus, and came up behind him in the crowd and touched his cloak, 28 for she said, 'If I but touch his clothes, I will be made well.' 29 Immediately her haemorrhage stopped; and she felt in her body that she was healed of her disease. 30 Immediately aware that power had gone forth from him, Jesus turned about in the crowd and said, 'Who touched my clothes?' 31 And his disciples said to him,

'You see the crowd pressing in on you; how can you say, "Who touched me?" ' 32 He looked all round to see who had done it. 33 But the woman, knowing what had happened to her, came in fear and trembling, fell down before him, and told him the whole truth. 34 He said to her, 'Daughter, your faith has made you well; go in peace, and be healed of your disease.'

35 While he was still speaking, some people came from the leader's house to say, 'Your daughter is dead. Why trouble the teacher any further?' 36 But overhearing*d* what they said, Jesus said to the leader of the synagogue, 'Do not fear, only believe.' 37 He allowed no one to follow him except Peter, James, and John, the brother of James. 38 When they came to the house of the leader of the synagogue, he saw a commotion, people weeping and wailing loudly. 39 When he had entered, he said to them, 'Why do you make a commotion and weep? The child is not dead but sleeping.' 40 And they laughed at him. Then he put them all outside, and took the child's father and mother and those who were with him, and went in where the child was. 41 He took her by the hand and said to her, 'Talitha cum', which means, 'Little girl, get up!' 42 And immediately the girl got up and began to walk about (she was twelve years of age). At this they were overcome with amazement. 43 He strictly ordered them that no one should know this, and told them to give her something to eat.

The Rejection of Jesus at Nazareth

6 He left that place and came to his home town, and his disciples followed him. 2 On the sabbath he began to teach in the synagogue, and many who heard him were astounded. They said, 'Where did this man get all this? What is this wisdom that has been given to him? What deeds of power are being done by his hands! 3 Is not this the carpenter, the son of Mary*e* and brother of James and Joses and Judas and Simon, and are not his

---

a Gk him   *b* Gk he   *c* Other ancient authorities lack *in the boat*   *d* Or *ignoring*; other ancient authorities read *hearing*   *e* Other ancient authorities read *son of the carpenter and of Mary* sisters here with us?' And they took offence[a] at him. 4 Then Jesus said to them, 'Prophets are not without honour, except in their home town, and among their own kin, and in their own house.' 5 And he could do no deed of power there, except that he laid his hands on a few sick people and cured them. 6 And he was amazed at their unbelief.

The Mission of the Twelve

Then he went about among the villages teaching. 7 He called the twelve and began to send them out two by two, and gave them authority over the unclean spirits. 8 He ordered them to take nothing for their journey except a staff; no bread, no bag, no money in their belts; 9 but to wear sandals and not to put on two tunics. 10 He said to them, 'Wherever you enter a house, stay there until you leave the place. 11 If any place will not welcome you and they refuse to hear you, as you leave, shake off the dust that is on your feet as a testimony against them.' 12 So they went out and proclaimed that all should repent. 13 They cast out many demons, and anointed with oil many who were sick and cured them.

The Death of John the Baptist

14 King Herod heard of it, for Jesus'[b] name had become known. Some were[c] saying, 'John the baptizer has been raised from the dead; and for this reason these powers are at work in him.' 15 But others said, 'It is Elijah.' And others said, 'It is a prophet, like one of the prophets of old.' 16 But when Herod heard of it, he said, 'John, whom I beheaded, has been raised.'

17 For Herod himself had sent men who arrested John, bound him, and put him in prison on account of Herodias, his brother Philip's wife, because Herod[d] had married her. 18 For John had been telling Herod, 'It is not lawful for you to have your brother's wife.' 19 And Herodias had a grudge against him, and wanted to kill him. But she could not, 20 for Herod feared John, knowing that he was a righteous and holy man, and he protected him. When he heard him, he was greatly perplexed;[e] and

yet he liked to listen to him. 21 But an opportunity came when Herod on his birthday gave a banquet for his courtiers and officers and for the leaders of Galilee. 22 When his daughter Herodias[f] came in and danced, she pleased Herod and his guests; and the king said to the girl, 'Ask me for whatever you wish, and I will give it.' 23 And he solemnly swore to her, 'Whatever you ask me, I will give you, even half of my kingdom.' 24 She went out and said to her mother, 'What should I ask for?' She replied, 'The head of John the baptizer.' 25 Immediately she rushed back to the king and requested, 'I want you to give me at once the head of John the Baptist on a platter.' 26 The king was deeply grieved; yet out of regard for his oaths and for the guests, he did not want to refuse her. 27 Immediately the king sent a soldier of the guard with orders to bring John's[b] head. He went and beheaded him in the prison, 28 brought his head on a platter, and gave it to the girl. Then the girl gave it to her mother. 29 When his disciples heard about it, they came and took his body, and laid it in a tomb.

Feeding the Five Thousand

30 The apostles gathered around Jesus, and told him all that they had done and taught. 31 He said to them, 'Come away to a deserted place all by yourselves and rest a while.' For many were coming and going, and they had no leisure even to eat. 32 And they went away in the boat to a deserted place by themselves. 33 Now many saw them going and recognized them, and they hurried there on foot from all the towns and arrived ahead of them. 34 As he went ashore, he saw a great crowd; and he had compassion for them, because they were like sheep without a shepherd; and he began to teach them many things. 35 When it grew late, his disciples came to him and said, 'This is a deserted place, and the hour is now very late; 36 send them away so that they may go into the surrounding country

a Or stumbled   b Gk his   c Other ancient authorities read He was   d Gk he   e Other ancient authorities read he did many things   f Other ancient authorities read the daughter of Herodias herself and villages and buy something for themselves to eat.' 37 But he answered them, 'You give them something to eat.' They said to him, 'Are we to go and buy two hundred denarii*a* worth of bread, and give it to them to eat?' 38 And he said to them, 'How many loaves have you? Go and see.' When they had found out, they said, 'Five, and two fish.' 39 Then he ordered them to get all the people to sit down in groups on the green grass. 40 So they sat down in groups of hundreds and of fifties. 41 Taking the five loaves and the two fish, he looked up to heaven, and blessed and broke the loaves, and gave them to his disciples to set before the people; and he divided the two fish among them all. 42 And all ate and were filled; 43 and they took up twelve baskets full of broken pieces and of the fish. 44 Those who had eaten the loaves numbered five thousand men.

Jesus Walks on the Water

45 Immediately he made his disciples get into the boat and go on ahead to the other side, to Bethsaida, while he dismissed the crowd. 46 After saying farewell to them, he went up on the mountain to pray.

47 When evening came, the boat was out on the lake, and he was alone on the land. 48 When he saw that they were straining at the oars against an adverse wind, he came towards them early in the morning, walking on the lake. He intended to pass them by. 49 But when they saw him walking on the lake, they thought it was a ghost and cried out; 50 for they all saw him and were terrified. But immediately he spoke to them and said, 'Take heart, it is I; do not be afraid.' 51 Then he got into the boat with them and the wind ceased. And they were utterly astounded, 52 for they did not understand about the loaves, but their hearts were hardened.

Healing the Sick in Gennesaret

53 When they had crossed over, they came to land at Gennesaret and moored the boat. 54 When they got out of the boat, people at once recognized him, 55 and rushed about that whole region and began to bring the sick on mats to wherever they heard he was. 56 And wherever he went, into villages or cities or farms, they laid the sick in the market-places, and begged him that they might touch even the fringe of his cloak; and all who touched it were healed.

The Tradition of the Elders

7 Now when the Pharisees and some of the scribes who had come from Jerusalem gathered around him, 2 they noticed that some of his disciples were eating with defiled hands, that is, without washing them. 3 (For the Pharisees, and all the Jews, do not eat unless they thoroughly wash their hands,*b* thus observing the tradition of the elders; 4 and they do not eat anything from the market unless they wash it;*c* and there are also many other traditions that they observe, the washing of cups, pots, and bronze kettles.*d*) 5 So the Pharisees and the scribes asked him, 'Why do your disciples not live*e* according to the tradition of the elders, but eat with defiled hands?' 6 He said to them, 'Isaiah prophesied rightly about you hypocrites, as it is written,

"This people honours me with
      their lips,
   but their hearts are far from me;
7 in vain do they worship me,
      teaching human precepts as
         doctrines."

8 You abandon the commandment of God and hold to human tradition.'

9 Then he said to them, 'You have a fine way of rejecting the commandment of God in order to keep your tradition! 10 For Moses said, "Honour your father and your mother"; and, "Whoever speaks evil of father or mother must surely die." 11 But you say that if anyone tells father or mother, "Whatever support you might have had from me is Corban" (that is, an offering to God*f*)— 12 then you no longer

a The denarius was the usual day's wage for a labourer
b Meaning of Gk uncertain   *c* Other ancient
authorities read *and when they come from the market-place,
they do not eat unless they purify themselves*   *d* Other
ancient authorities add *and beds*   *e* Gk *walk*
f Gk lacks *to God*

permit doing anything for a father or mother, ¹³thus making void the word of God through your tradition that you have handed on. And you do many things like this.'

14 Then he called the crowd again and said to them, 'Listen to me, all of you, and understand: ¹⁵there is nothing outside a person that by going in can defile, but the things that come out are what defile.'ᵃ

17 When he had left the crowd and entered the house, his disciples asked him about the parable. ¹⁸He said to them, 'Then do you also fail to understand? Do you not see that whatever goes into a person from outside cannot defile, ¹⁹since it enters, not the heart but the stomach, and goes out into the sewer?' (Thus he declared all foods clean.) ²⁰And he said, 'It is what comes out of a person that defiles. ²¹For it is from within, from the human heart, that evil intentions come: fornication, theft, murder, ²²adultery, avarice, wickedness, deceit, licentiousness, envy, slander, pride, folly. ²³All these evil things come from within, and they defile a person.'

The Syrophoenician Woman's Faith

24 From there he set out and went away to the region of Tyre.ᵇ He entered a house and did not want anyone to know he was there. Yet he could not escape notice, ²⁵but a woman whose little daughter had an unclean spirit immediately heard about him, and she came and bowed down at his feet. ²⁶Now the woman was a Gentile, of Syrophoenician origin. She begged him to cast the demon out of her daughter. ²⁷He said to her, 'Let the children be fed first, for it is not fair to take the children's food and throw it to the dogs.' ²⁸But she answered him, 'Sir,ᶜ even the dogs under the table eat the children's crumbs.' ²⁹Then he said to her, 'For saying that, you may go—the demon has left your daughter.' ³⁰So she went home, found the child lying on the bed, and the demon gone.

Jesus Cures a Deaf Man

31 Then he returned from the region of Tyre, and went by way of Sidon towards the Sea of Galilee, in the region of the Decapolis. ³²They brought to him a deaf man who had an impediment in his speech; and they begged him to lay his hand on him. ³³He took him aside in private, away from the crowd, and put his fingers into his ears, and he spat and touched his tongue. ³⁴Then looking up to heaven, he sighed and said to him, 'Ephphatha', that is, 'Be opened.' ³⁵And immediately his ears were opened, his tongue was released, and he spoke plainly. ³⁶Then Jesusᵈ ordered them to tell no one; but the more he ordered them, the more zealously they proclaimed it. ³⁷They were astounded beyond measure, saying, 'He has done everything well; he even makes the deaf to hear and the mute to speak.'

The Territories of Tyre and Sidon

Mediterranean Sea
Sidon
SIDON
▲ Mt. Hermon
Tyre
TYRE
Caesarea Philippi
Gischala
TETRARCHY OF PHILIP
Raphana
Ptolemais
Capernaum
Bethsaida
Jotapata
Sepphoris
Hippos
Dion
Abila
Gadara
GALILEE
Scythopolis
DECAPOLIS
Jordan River
N
0   20 Mi.
0   30 Km.

a Other ancient authorities add verse 16, 'Let anyone with ears to hear listen'   b Other ancient authorities add and Sidon   c Or Lord; other ancient authorities prefix Yes   d Gk he

Feeding the Four Thousand

8 In those days when there was again a great crowd without anything to eat, he called his disciples and said to them, ²'I have compassion for the crowd, because they have been with me now for three days and have nothing to eat. ³If I send them away hungry to their homes, they will faint on the way—and some of them have come from a great distance.' ⁴His disciples replied, 'How can one feed these people with bread here in the desert?' ⁵He asked them, 'How many loaves do you have?' They said, 'Seven.' ⁶Then he ordered the crowd to sit down on the ground; and he took the seven loaves, and after giving thanks he broke them and gave them to his disciples to distribute; and they distributed them to the crowd. ⁷They had also a few small fish; and after blessing them, he ordered that these too should be distributed. ⁸They ate and were filled; and they took up the broken pieces left over, seven baskets full. ⁹Now there were about four thousand people. And he sent them away. ¹⁰And immediately he got into the boat with his disciples and went to the district of Dalmanutha.ᵃ

The Demand for a Sign

11 The Pharisees came and began to argue with him, asking him for a sign from heaven, to test him. ¹²And he sighed deeply in his spirit and said, 'Why does this generation ask for a sign? Truly I tell you, no sign will be given to this generation.' ¹³And he left them, and getting into the boat again, he went across to the other side.

The Yeast of the Pharisees and of Herod

14 Now the disciplesᵇ had forgotten to bring any bread; and they had only one loaf with them in the boat. ¹⁵And he cautioned them, saying, 'Watch out—beware of the yeast of the Pharisees and the yeast of Herod.'ᶜ ¹⁶They said to one another, 'It is because we have no bread.' ¹⁷And becoming aware of it, Jesus said to them, 'Why are you talking about having no bread? Do you still not perceive or understand? Are your hearts hardened? ¹⁸Do you have eyes, and fail to see? Do you have ears, and fail to hear? And do you not remember? ¹⁹When I broke the five loaves for the five thousand, how many baskets full of broken pieces did you collect?' They said to him, 'Twelve.' ²⁰'And the seven for the four thousand, how many baskets full of broken pieces did you collect?' And they said to him, 'Seven.' ²¹Then he said to them, 'Do you not yet understand?'

Jesus Cures a Blind Man at Bethsaida

22 They came to Bethsaida. Some peopleᵈ brought a blind man to him and begged him to touch him. ²³He took the blind man by the hand and led him out of the village; and when he had put saliva on his eyes and laid his hands on him, he asked him, 'Can you see anything?' ²⁴And the manᵉ looked up and said, 'I can see people, but they look like trees, walking.' ²⁵Then Jesusᵉ laid his hands on his eyes again; and he looked intently and his sight was restored, and he saw everything clearly. ²⁶Then he sent him away to his home, saying, 'Do not even go into the village.'ᶠ

Peter's Declaration about Jesus

27 Jesus went on with his disciples to the villages of Caesarea Philippi; and on the way he asked his disciples, 'Who do people say that I am?' ²⁸And they answered him, 'John the Baptist; and others, Elijah; and still others, one of the prophets.' ²⁹He asked them, 'But who do you say that I am?' Peter answered him, 'You are the Messiah.'ᵍ ³⁰And he sternly ordered them not to tell anyone about him.

Jesus Foretells His Death and Resurrection

31 Then he began to teach them that the Son of Man must undergo great suffering, and be rejected by the elders, the chief priests, and the scribes, and be killed, and

---

a Other ancient authorities read *Mageda* or *Magdala*
b Gk *they*   *c* Other ancient authorities read *the Herodians*   *d* Gk *They*   *e* Gk *he*   *f* Other ancient authorities add *or tell anyone in the village*   *g* Or *the Christ*

after three days rise again. ³²He said all this quite openly. And Peter took him aside and began to rebuke him. ³³But turning and looking at his disciples, he rebuked Peter and said, 'Get behind me, Satan! For you are setting your mind not on divine things but on human things.'

34 He called the crowd with his disciples, and said to them, 'If any want to become my followers, let them deny themselves and take up their cross and follow me. ³⁵For those who want to save their life will lose it, and those who lose their life for my sake, and for the sake of the gospel, *a* will save it. ³⁶For what will it profit them to gain the whole world and forfeit their life? ³⁷Indeed, what can they give in return for their life? ³⁸Those who are ashamed of me and of my words *b* in this adulterous and sinful generation, of them the Son of Man will also be ashamed when he comes in the glory of his Father with **9** the holy angels.' ¹And he said to them, 'Truly I tell you, there are some standing here who will not taste death until they see that the kingdom of God has come with *c* power.'

The Transfiguration

2 Six days later, Jesus took with him Peter and James and John, and led them up a high mountain apart, by themselves. And he was transfigured before them, ³and his clothes became dazzling white, such as no one *d* on earth could bleach them. ⁴And there appeared to them Elijah with Moses, who were talking with Jesus. ⁵Then Peter said to Jesus, 'Rabbi, it is good for us to be here; let us make three dwellings, *e* one for you, one for Moses, and one for Elijah.' ⁶He did not know what to say, for they were terrified. ⁷Then a cloud overshadowed them, and from the cloud there came a voice, 'This is my Son, the Beloved; *f* listen to him!' ⁸Suddenly when they looked around, they saw no one with them any more, but only Jesus.

The Coming of Elijah

9 As they were coming down the mountain, he ordered them to tell no one about what they had seen, until after the Son of Man had risen from the dead. ¹⁰So they kept the matter to themselves, questioning what this rising from the dead could mean. ¹¹Then they asked him, 'Why do the scribes say that Elijah must come first?' ¹²He said to them, 'Elijah is indeed coming first to restore all things. How then is it written about the Son of Man, that he is to go through many sufferings and be treated with contempt? ¹³But I tell you that Elijah has come, and they did to him whatever they pleased, as it is written about him.'

The Healing of a Boy with a Spirit

14 When they came to the disciples, they saw a great crowd around them, and some scribes arguing with them. ¹⁵When the whole crowd saw him, they were immediately overcome with awe, and they ran forward to greet him. ¹⁶He asked them, 'What are you arguing about with them?' ¹⁷Someone from the crowd answered him, 'Teacher, I brought you my son; he has a spirit that makes him unable to speak; ¹⁸and whenever it seizes him, it dashes him down; and he foams and grinds his teeth and becomes rigid; and I asked your disciples to cast it out, but they could not do so.' ¹⁹He answered them, 'You faithless generation, how much longer must I be among you? How much longer must I put up with you? Bring him to me.' ²⁰And they brought the boy *g* to him. When the spirit saw him, immediately it threw the boy *g* into convulsions, and he fell on the ground and rolled about, foaming at the mouth. ²¹Jesus *h* asked the father, 'How long has this been happening to him?' And he said, 'From childhood. ²²It has often cast him into the fire and into the water, to destroy him; but if you are able to do anything, have pity on us and help us.' ²³Jesus said to him, 'If you are able!—All things can be done for the one who believes.' ²⁴Immediately the father of the child cried out, *i* 'I believe; help my

a Other ancient authorities read *lose their life for the sake of the gospel*   *b* Other ancient authorities read *and of mine*   *c* Or *in*   *d* Gk *no fuller*   *e* Or *tents*   *f* Or *my beloved Son*   *g* Gk *him*   *h* Gk *He*   *i* Other ancient authorities add *with tears* unbelief!' 25 When Jesus saw that a crowd came running together, he rebuked the unclean spirit, saying to it, 'You spirit that keep this boy from speaking and hearing, I command you, come out of him, and never enter him again!' 26 After crying out and convulsing him terribly, it came out, and the boy was like a corpse, so that most of them said, 'He is dead.' 27 But Jesus took him by the hand and lifted him up, and he was able to stand. 28 When he had entered the house, his disciples asked him privately, 'Why could we not cast it out?' 29 He said to them, 'This kind can come out only through prayer.' *a*

Jesus Again Foretells His Death and Resurrection

30 They went on from there and passed through Galilee. He did not want anyone to know it; 31 for he was teaching his disciples, saying to them, 'The Son of Man is to be betrayed into human hands, and they will kill him, and three days after being killed, he will rise again.' 32 But they did not understand what he was saying and were afraid to ask him.

Who Is the Greatest?

33 Then they came to Capernaum; and when he was in the house he asked them, 'What were you arguing about on the way?' 34 But they were silent, for on the way they had argued with one another about who was the greatest. 35 He sat down, called the twelve, and said to them, 'Whoever wants to be first must be last of all and servant of all.' 36 Then he took a little child and put it among them; and taking it in his arms, he said to them, 37 'Whoever welcomes one such child in my name welcomes me, and whoever welcomes me welcomes not me but the one who sent me.'

Another Exorcist

38 John said to him, 'Teacher, we saw someone *b* casting out demons in your name, and we tried to stop him, because he was not following us.' 39 But Jesus said, 'Do not stop him; for no one who does a deed of power in my name will be able soon af-

terwards to speak evil of me. 40 Whoever is not against us is for us. 41 For truly I tell you, whoever gives you a cup of water to drink because you bear the name of Christ will by no means lose the reward.

Temptations to Sin

42 'If any of you put a stumbling-block before one of these little ones who believe in me, *c* it would be better for you if a great millstone were hung around your neck and you were thrown into the sea. 43 If your hand causes you to stumble, cut it off; it is better for you to enter life maimed than to have two hands and to go to hell, *d* to the unquenchable fire. *e* 45 And if your foot causes you to stumble, cut it off; it is better for you to enter life lame than to have two feet and to be thrown into hell. *d, e* 47 And if your eye causes you to stumble, tear it out; it is better for you to enter the kingdom of God with one eye than to have two eyes and to be thrown into hell, *d* 48 where their worm never dies, and the fire is never quenched.

49 'For everyone will be salted with fire. *f* 50 Salt is good; but if salt has lost its saltiness, how can you season it? *g* Have salt in yourselves, and be at peace with one another.'

Teaching about Divorce

10 He left that place and went to the region of Judea and *h* beyond the Jordan. And crowds again gathered around him; and, as was his custom, he again taught them.

2 Some Pharisees came, and to test him they asked, 'Is it lawful for a man to divorce his wife?' 3 He answered them, 'What did Moses command you?' 4 They said, 'Moses allowed a man to write a certificate of dismissal and to divorce her.' 5 But Jesus said to them, 'Because of your hardness of heart he wrote this commandment for

---

a Other ancient authorities add *and fasting*　　*b* Other ancient authorities add *who does not follow us*　　*c* Other ancient authorities lack *in me*　　*d* Gk *Gehenna*　　*e* Verses 44 and 46 (which are identical with verse 48) are lacking in the best ancient authorities　　*f* Other ancient authorities either add or substitute *and every sacrifice will be salted with salt*　　*g* Or *how can you restore its saltiness?*　　*h* Other ancient authorities lack *and* you. 6 But from the beginning of creation, "God made them male and female." 7 "For this reason a man shall leave his father and mother and be joined to his wife,*a* 8 and the two shall become one flesh." So they are no longer two, but one flesh. 9 Therefore what God has joined together, let no one separate.'

10 Then in the house the disciples asked him again about this matter. 11 He said to them, 'Whoever divorces his wife and marries another commits adultery against her; 12 and if she divorces her husband and marries another, she commits adultery.'

Jesus Blesses Little Children

13 People were bringing little children to him in order that he might touch them; and the disciples spoke sternly to them. 14 But when Jesus saw this, he was indignant and said to them, 'Let the little children come to me; do not stop them; for it is to such as these that the kingdom of God belongs. 15 Truly I tell you, whoever does not receive the kingdom of God as a little child will never enter it.' 16 And he took them up in his arms, laid his hands on them, and blessed them.

The Rich Man

17 As he was setting out on a journey, a man ran up and knelt before him, and asked him, 'Good Teacher, what must I do to inherit eternal life?' 18 Jesus said to him, 'Why do you call me good? No one is good but God alone. 19 You know the commandments: "You shall not murder; You shall not commit adultery; You shall not steal; You shall not bear false witness; You shall not defraud; Honour your father and mother." ' 20 He said to him, 'Teacher, I have kept all these since my youth.' 21 Jesus, looking at him, loved him and said, 'You lack one thing; go, sell what you own, and give the money*b* to the poor, and you will have treasure in heaven; then come, follow me.' 22 When he heard this, he was shocked and went away grieving, for he had many possessions.

23 Then Jesus looked around and said to his disciples, 'How hard it will be for those who have wealth to enter the kingdom of God!' 24 And the disciples were perplexed at these words. But Jesus said to them again, 'Children, how hard it is*c* to enter the kingdom of God! 25 It is easier for a camel to go through the eye of a needle than for someone who is rich to enter the kingdom of God.' 26 They were greatly astounded and said to one another,*d* 'Then who can be saved?' 27 Jesus looked at them and said, 'For mortals it is impossible, but not for God; for God all things are possible.'

28 Peter began to say to him, 'Look, we have left everything and followed you.' 29 Jesus said, 'Truly I tell you, there is no one who has left house or brothers or sisters or mother or father or children or fields, for my sake and for the sake of the good news,*e* 30 who will not receive a hundredfold now in this age—houses, brothers and sisters, mothers and children, and fields, with persecutions—and in the age to come eternal life. 31 But many who are first will be last, and the last will be first.'

A Third Time Jesus Foretells His Death and Resurrection

32 They were on the road, going up to Jerusalem, and Jesus was walking ahead of them; they were amazed, and those who followed were afraid. He took the twelve aside again and began to tell them what was to happen to him, 33 saying, 'See, we are going up to Jerusalem, and the Son of Man will be handed over to the chief priests and the scribes, and they will condemn him to death; then they will hand him over to the Gentiles; 34 they will mock him, and spit upon him, and flog him, and kill him; and after three days he will rise again.'

The Request of James and John

35 James and John, the sons of Zebedee, came forward to him and said to him, 'Teacher, we want you to do for us whatever we ask of you.' 36 And he said to them,

---

a Other ancient authorities lack *and be joined to his wife*
b Gk lacks *the money*   *c* Other ancient authorities add *for those who trust in riches*   *d* Other ancient authorities read *to him*   *e* Or *gospel*

'What is it you want me to do for you?'
37 And they said to him, 'Grant us to sit, one at your right hand and one at your left, in your glory.' 38 But Jesus said to them, 'You do not know what you are asking. Are you able to drink the cup that I drink, or be baptized with the baptism that I am baptized with?' 39 They replied, 'We are able.' Then Jesus said to them, 'The cup that I drink you will drink; and with the baptism with which I am baptized, you will be baptized; 40 but to sit at my right hand or at my left is not mine to grant, but it is for those for whom it has been prepared.'

41 When the ten heard this, they began to be angry with James and John. 42 So Jesus called them and said to them, 'You know that among the Gentiles those whom they recognize as their rulers lord it over them, and their great ones are tyrants over them. 43 But it is not so among you; but whoever wishes to become great among you must be your servant, 44 and whoever wishes to be first among you must be slave of all. 45 For the Son of Man came not to be served but to serve, and to give his life a ransom for many.'

The Healing of Blind Bartimaeus

46 They came to Jericho. As he and his disciples and a large crowd were leaving Jericho, Bartimaeus son of Timaeus, a blind beggar, was sitting by the roadside. 47 When he heard that it was Jesus of Nazareth, he began to shout out and say, 'Jesus, Son of David, have mercy on me!' 48 Many sternly ordered him to be quiet, but he cried out even more loudly, 'Son of David, have mercy on me!' 49 Jesus stood still and said, 'Call him here.' And they called the blind man, saying to him, 'Take heart; get up, he is calling you.' 50 So throwing off his cloak, he sprang up and came to Jesus. 51 Then Jesus said to him, 'What do you want me to do for you?' The blind man said to him, 'My teacher,*a* let me see again.' 52 Jesus said to him, 'Go; your faith has made you well.' Immediately he regained his sight and followed him on the way.

Jesus' Triumphal Entry into Jerusalem

11 When they were approaching Jerusalem, at Bethphage and Bethany, near the Mount of Olives, he sent two of his disciples 2 and said to them, 'Go into the village ahead of you, and immediately as you enter it, you will find tied there a colt that has never been ridden; untie it and bring it. 3 If anyone says to you, "Why are you doing this?" just say this, "The Lord needs it and will send it back here immediately." ' 4 They went away and found a colt tied near a door, outside in the street. As they were untying it, 5 some of the bystanders said to them, 'What are you doing, untying the colt?' 6 They told them what Jesus had said; and they allowed them to take it. 7 Then they brought the colt to Jesus and threw their cloaks on it; and he sat on it. 8 Many people spread their cloaks on the road, and others spread leafy branches that they had cut in the fields. 9 Then those who went ahead and those who followed were shouting,

'Hosanna!
     Blessed is the one who comes in the
          name of the Lord!
10   Blessed is the coming kingdom of
          our ancestor David!
     Hosanna in the highest heaven!'

11 Then he entered Jerusalem and went into the temple; and when he had looked around at everything, as it was already late, he went out to Bethany with the twelve.

Jesus Curses the Fig Tree

12 On the following day, when they came from Bethany, he was hungry. 13 Seeing in the distance a fig tree in leaf, he went to see whether perhaps he would find anything on it. When he came to it, he found nothing but leaves, for it was not the season for figs. 14 He said to it, 'May no one ever eat fruit from you again.' And his disciples heard it.

Jesus Cleanses the Temple

15 Then they came to Jerusalem. And he entered the temple and began to drive

a Aramaic *Rabbouni*

out those who were selling and those who were buying in the temple, and he overturned the tables of the money-changers and the seats of those who sold doves; 16 and he would not allow anyone to carry anything through the temple. 17 He was teaching and saying, 'Is it not written,

"My house shall be called a house of
    prayer for all the nations"?
But you have made it a den
    of robbers.'

18 And when the chief priests and the scribes heard it, they kept looking for a way to kill him; for they were afraid of him, because the whole crowd was spellbound by his teaching. 19 And when evening came, Jesus and his disciples*a* went out of the city.

The Lesson from the Withered Fig Tree

20 In the morning as they passed by, they saw the fig tree withered away to its roots. 21 Then Peter remembered and said to him, 'Rabbi, look! The fig tree that you cursed has withered.' 22 Jesus answered them, 'Have*b* faith in God. 23 Truly I tell you, if you say to this mountain, "Be taken up and thrown into the sea", and if you do not doubt in your heart, but believe that what you say will come to pass, it will be done for you. 24 So I tell you, whatever you ask for in prayer, believe that you have received*c* it, and it will be yours.

25 'Whenever you stand praying, forgive, if you have anything against anyone; so that your Father in heaven may also forgive you your trespasses.'*d*

Jesus' Authority Is Questioned

27 Again they came to Jerusalem. As he was walking in the temple, the chief priests, the scribes, and the elders came to him 28 and said, 'By what authority are you doing these things? Who gave you this authority to do them?' 29 Jesus said to them, 'I will ask you one question; answer me, and I will tell you by what authority I do these things. 30 Did the baptism of John come from heaven, or was it of human origin? Answer me.' 31 They argued with one another, 'If we say, "From heaven", he

will say, "Why then did you not believe him?" 32 But shall we say, "Of human origin"?'—they were afraid of the crowd, for all regarded John as truly a prophet. 33 So they answered Jesus, 'We do not know.' And Jesus said to them, 'Neither will I tell you by what authority I am doing these things.'

The Parable of the Wicked Tenants

12 Then he began to speak to them in parables. 'A man planted a vineyard, put a fence around it, dug a pit for the wine press, and built a watch-tower; then he leased it to tenants and went to another country. 2 When the season came, he sent a slave to the tenants to collect from them his share of the produce of the vineyard. 3 But they seized him, and beat him, and sent him away empty-handed. 4 And again he sent another slave to them; this one they beat over the head and insulted. 5 Then he sent another, and that one they killed. And so it was with many others; some they beat, and others they killed. 6 He had still one other, a beloved son. Finally he sent him to them, saying, "They will respect my son." 7 But those tenants said to one another, "This is the heir; come, let us kill him, and the inheritance will be ours." 8 So they seized him, killed him, and threw him out of the vineyard. 9 What then will the owner of the vineyard do? He will come and destroy the tenants and give the vineyard to others. 10 Have you not read this scripture:

"The stone that the builders rejected
    has become the cornerstone;*e*
11 this was the Lord's doing,
    and it is amazing in our eyes"?'

12 When they realized that he had told this parable against them, they wanted to arrest him, but they feared the crowd. So they left him and went away.

a Gk *they*: other ancient authorities read *he*   *b* Other ancient authorities read *'If you have*   *c* Other ancient authorities read *are receiving*   *d* Other ancient authorities add verse 26, *'But if you do not forgive, neither will your Father in heaven forgive your trespasses.'*   *e* Or *keystone*

The Question about Paying Taxes

13 Then they sent to him some Pharisees and some Herodians to trap him in what he said. 14 And they came and said to him, 'Teacher, we know that you are sincere, and show deference to no one; for you do not regard people with partiality, but teach the way of God in accordance with truth. Is it lawful to pay taxes to the emperor, or not? 15 Should we pay them, or should we not?' But knowing their hypocrisy, he said to them, 'Why are you putting me to the test? Bring me a denarius and let me see it.' 16 And they brought one. Then he said to them, 'Whose head is this, and whose title?' They answered, 'The emperor's.' 17 Jesus said to them, 'Give to the emperor the things that are the emperor's, and to God the things that are God's.' And they were utterly amazed at him.

The Question about the Resurrection

18 Some Sadducees, who say there is no resurrection, came to him and asked him a question, saying, 19 'Teacher, Moses wrote for us that if a man's brother dies, leaving a wife but no child, the man*a* shall marry the widow and raise up children for his brother. 20 There were seven brothers; the first married and, when he died, left no children; 21 and the second married the widow*b* and died, leaving no children; and the third likewise; 22 none of the seven left children. Last of all the woman herself died. 23 In the resurrection*c* whose wife will she be? For the seven had married her.'

24 Jesus said to them, 'Is not this the reason you are wrong, that you know neither the scriptures nor the power of God? 25 For when they rise from the dead, they neither marry nor are given in marriage, but are like angels in heaven. 26 And as for the dead being raised, have you not read in the book of Moses, in the story about the bush, how God said to him, "I am the God of Abraham, the God of Isaac, and the God of Jacob"? 27 He is God not of the dead, but of the living; you are quite wrong.'

The First Commandment

28 One of the scribes came near and heard them disputing with one another, and seeing that he answered them well, he asked him, 'Which commandment is the first of all?' 29 Jesus answered, 'The first is, "Hear, O Israel: the Lord our God, the Lord is one; 30 you shall love the Lord your God with all your heart, and with all your soul, and with all your mind, and with all your strength." 31 The second is this, "You shall love your neighbour as yourself." There is no other commandment greater than these.' 32 Then the scribe said to him, 'You are right, Teacher; you have truly said that "he is one, and besides him there is no other"; 33 and "to love him with all the heart, and with all the understanding, and with all the strength", and "to love one's neighbour as oneself",—this is much more important than all whole burnt-offerings and sacrifices.' 34 When Jesus saw that he answered wisely, he said to him, 'You are not far from the kingdom of God.' After that no one dared to ask him any question.

The Question about David's Son

35 While Jesus was teaching in the temple, he said, 'How can the scribes say that the Messiah*d* is the son of David? 36 David himself, by the Holy Spirit, declared,

"The Lord said to my Lord,
'Sit at my right hand,
    until I put your enemies under your
        feet.' "

37 David himself calls him Lord; so how can he be his son?' And the large crowd was listening to him with delight.

Jesus Denounces the Scribes

38 As he taught, he said, 'Beware of the scribes, who like to walk around in long robes, and to be greeted with respect in the market-places, 39 and to have the best seats in the synagogues and places of honour at banquets! 40 They devour widows' houses and for the sake of appearance say long

a Gk *his brother*   *b* Gk *her*   *c* Other ancient authorities add *when they rise*   *d* Or *the Christ* prayers. They will receive the greater condemnation.'

The Widow's Offering

41 He sat down opposite the treasury, and watched the crowd putting money into the treasury. Many rich people put in large sums. 42 A poor widow came and put in two small copper coins, which are worth a penny. 43 Then he called his disciples and said to them, 'Truly I tell you, this poor widow has put in more than all those who are contributing to the treasury. 44 For all of them have contributed out of their abundance; but she out of her poverty has put in everything she had, all she had to live on.'

The Destruction of the Temple Foretold

13 As he came out of the temple, one of his disciples said to him, 'Look, Teacher, what large stones and what large buildings!' 2 Then Jesus asked him, 'Do you see these great buildings? Not one stone will be left here upon another; all will be thrown down.'

3 When he was sitting on the Mount of Olives opposite the temple, Peter, James, John, and Andrew asked him privately, 4 'Tell us, when will this be, and what will be the sign that all these things are about to be accomplished?' 5 Then Jesus began to say to them, 'Beware that no one leads you astray. 6 Many will come in my name and say, "I am he!"*a* and they will lead many astray. 7 When you hear of wars and rumours of wars, do not be alarmed; this must take place, but the end is still to come. 8 For nation will rise against nation, and kingdom against kingdom; there will be earthquakes in various places; there will be famines. This is but the beginning of the birth pangs.

Persecution Foretold

9 'As for yourselves, beware; for they will hand you over to councils; and you will be beaten in synagogues; and you will stand before governors and kings because of me, as a testimony to them. 10 And the good news*b* must first be proclaimed to all nations. 11 When they bring you to trial and hand you over, do not worry beforehand about what you are to say; but say whatever is given you at that time, for it is not you who speak, but the Holy Spirit. 12 Brother will betray brother to death, and a father his child, and children will rise against parents and have them put to death; 13 and you will be hated by all because of my name. But the one who endures to the end will be saved.

The Desolating Sacrilege

14 'But when you see the desolating sacrilege set up where it ought not to be (let the reader understand), then those in Judea must flee to the mountains; 15 someone on the housetop must not go down or enter the house to take anything away; 16 someone in the field must not turn back to get a coat. 17 Woe to those who are pregnant and to those who are nursing infants in those days! 18 Pray that it may not be in winter. 19 For in those days there will be suffering, such as has not been from the beginning of the creation that God created until now, no, and never will be. 20 And if the Lord had not cut short those days, no one would be saved; but for the sake of the elect, whom he chose, he has cut short those days. 21 And if anyone says to you at that time, "Look! Here is the Messiah!"*c* or "Look! There he is!"—do not believe it. 22 False messiahs*d* and false prophets will appear and produce signs and omens, to lead astray, if possible, the elect. 23 But be alert; I have already told you everything.

The Coming of the Son of Man

24 'But in those days, after that suffering,

the sun will be darkened,
    and the moon will not give
        its light,
25 and the stars will be falling
        from heaven,
    and the powers in the heavens will
        be shaken.

a Gk *I am*   *b* Gk *gospel*   *c* Or *the Christ*
d Or *christs*

26 Then they will see "the Son of Man coming in clouds" with great power and glory. 27 Then he will send out the angels, and gather his elect from the four winds, from the ends of the earth to the ends of heaven.

The Lesson of the Fig Tree

28 'From the fig tree learn its lesson: as soon as its branch becomes tender and puts forth its leaves, you know that summer is near. 29 So also, when you see these things taking place, you know that he[a] is near, at the very gates. 30 Truly I tell you, this generation will not pass away until all these things have taken place. 31 Heaven and earth will pass away, but my words will not pass away.

The Necessity for Watchfulness

32 'But about that day or hour no one knows, neither the angels in heaven, nor the Son, but only the Father. 33 Beware, keep alert;[b] for you do not know when the time will come. 34 It is like a man going on a journey, when he leaves home and puts his slaves in charge, each with his work, and commands the doorkeeper to be on the watch. 35 Therefore, keep awake—for you do not know when the master of the house will come, in the evening, or at midnight, or at cockcrow, or at dawn, 36 or else he may find you asleep when he comes suddenly. 37 And what I say to you I say to all: Keep awake.'

The Plot to Kill Jesus

14 It was two days before the Passover and the festival of Unleavened Bread. The chief priests and the scribes were looking for a way to arrest Jesus[c] by stealth and kill him; 2 for they said, 'Not during the festival, or there may be a riot among the people.'

The Anointing at Bethany

3 While he was at Bethany in the house of Simon the leper,[d] as he sat at the table, a woman came with an alabaster jar of very costly ointment of nard, and she broke open the jar and poured the oint-

ment on his head. 4 But some were there who said to one another in anger, 'Why was the ointment wasted in this way? 5 For this ointment could have been sold for more than three hundred denarii,[e] and the money given to the poor.' And they scolded her. 6 But Jesus said, 'Let her alone; why do you trouble her? She has performed a good service for me. 7 For you always have the poor with you, and you can show kindness to them whenever you wish; but you will not always have me. 8 She has done what she could; she has anointed my body beforehand for its burial. 9 Truly I tell you, wherever the good news[f] is proclaimed in the whole world, what she has done will be told in remembrance of her.'

Judas Agrees to Betray Jesus

10 Then Judas Iscariot, who was one of the twelve, went to the chief priests in order to betray him to them. 11 When they heard it, they were greatly pleased, and promised to give him money. So he began to look for an opportunity to betray him.

The Passover with the Disciples

12 On the first day of Unleavened Bread, when the Passover lamb is sacrificed, his disciples said to him, 'Where do you want us to go and make the preparations for you to eat the Passover?' 13 So he sent two of his disciples, saying to them, 'Go into the city, and a man carrying a jar of water will meet you; follow him, 14 and wherever he enters, say to the owner of the house, "The Teacher asks, Where is my guest room where I may eat the Passover with my disciples?" 15 He will show you a large room upstairs, furnished and ready. Make preparations for us there.' 16 So the disciples set out and went to the city, and found everything as he had told them; and they prepared the Passover meal.

17 When it was evening, he came with

---

a Or it b Other ancient authorities add *and pray*
c Gk *him* d The terms *leper* and *leprosy* can refer to several diseases e The denarius was the usual day's wage for a labourer f Or *gospel*

the twelve. ¹⁸And when they had taken their places and were eating, Jesus said, 'Truly I tell you, one of you will betray me, one who is eating with me.' ¹⁹They began to be distressed and to say to him one after another, 'Surely, not I?' ²⁰He said to them, 'It is one of the twelve, one who is dipping bread*a* into the bowl*b* with me. ²¹For the Son of Man goes as it is written of him, but woe to that one by whom the Son of Man is betrayed! It would have been better for that one not to have been born.'

The Institution of the Lord's Supper

22 While they were eating, he took a loaf of bread, and after blessing it he broke it, gave it to them, and said, 'Take; this is my body.' ²³Then he took a cup, and after giving thanks he gave it to them, and all of them drank from it. ²⁴He said to them, 'This is my blood of the*c* covenant, which is poured out for many. ²⁵Truly I tell you, I will never again drink of the fruit of the vine until that day when I drink it new in the kingdom of God.'

Peter's Denial Foretold

26 When they had sung the hymn, they went out to the Mount of Olives. ²⁷And Jesus said to them, 'You will all become deserters; for it is written,

"I will strike the shepherd,
  and the sheep will be scattered."
²⁸But after I am raised up, I will go before you to Galilee.' ²⁹Peter said to him, 'Even though all become deserters, I will not.' ³⁰Jesus said to him, 'Truly I tell you, this day, this very night, before the cock crows twice, you will deny me three times.' ³¹But he said vehemently, 'Even though I must die with you, I will not deny you.' And all of them said the same.

Jesus Prays in Gethsemane

32 They went to a place called Gethsemane; and he said to his disciples, 'Sit here while I pray.' ³³He took with him Peter and James and John, and began to be distressed and agitated. ³⁴And he said to them, 'I am deeply grieved, even to death;

remain here, and keep awake.' ³⁵And going a little farther, he threw himself on the ground and prayed that, if it were possible, the hour might pass from him. ³⁶He said, 'Abba, *d* Father, for you all things are possible; remove this cup from me; yet, not what I want, but what you want.' ³⁷He came and found them sleeping; and he said to Peter, 'Simon, are you asleep? Could you not keep awake one hour? ³⁸Keep awake and pray that you may not come into the time of trial;*e* the spirit indeed is willing, but the flesh is weak.' ³⁹And again he went away and prayed, saying the same words. ⁴⁰And once more he came and found them sleeping, for their eyes were very heavy; and they did not know what to say to him. ⁴¹He came a third time and said to them, 'Are you still sleeping and taking your rest? Enough! The hour has come; the Son of Man is betrayed into the hands of sinners. ⁴²Get up, let us be going. See, my betrayer is at hand.'

The Betrayal and Arrest of Jesus

43 Immediately, while he was still speaking, Judas, one of the twelve, arrived; and with him there was a crowd with swords and clubs, from the chief priests, the scribes, and the elders. ⁴⁴Now the betrayer had given them a sign, saying, 'The one I will kiss is the man; arrest him and lead him away under guard.' ⁴⁵So when he came, he went up to him at once and said, 'Rabbi!' and kissed him. ⁴⁶Then they laid hands on him and arrested him. ⁴⁷But one of those who stood near drew his sword and struck the slave of the high priest, cutting off his ear. ⁴⁸Then Jesus said to them, 'Have you come out with swords and clubs to arrest me as though I were a bandit? ⁴⁹Day after day I was with you in the temple teaching, and you did not arrest me. But let the scriptures be fulfilled.' ⁵⁰All of them deserted him and fled.

51 A certain young man was following him, wearing nothing but a linen cloth.

---

a Gk lacks *bread*   *b* Other ancient authorities read
same bowl   *c* Other ancient authorities add *new*
d Aramaic for *Father*   *e* Or *into temptation*

They caught hold of him, [52] but he left the linen cloth and ran off naked.

Jesus before the Council

53 They took Jesus to the high priest; and all the chief priests, the elders, and the scribes were assembled. [54] Peter had followed him at a distance, right into the courtyard of the high priest; and he was sitting with the guards, warming himself at the fire. [55] Now the chief priests and the whole council were looking for testimony against Jesus to put him to death; but they found none. [56] For many gave false testimony against him, and their testimony did not agree. [57] Some stood up and gave false testimony against him, saying, [58] 'We heard him say, "I will destroy this temple that is made with hands, and in three days I will build another, not made with hands." ' [59] But even on this point their testimony did not agree. [60] Then the high priest stood up before them and asked Jesus, 'Have you no answer? What is it that they testify against you?' [61] But he was silent and did not answer. Again the high priest asked him, 'Are you the Messiah,[a] the Son of the Blessed One?' [62] Jesus said, 'I am; and

"you will see the Son of Man
   seated at the right hand of
      the Power",
and "coming with the clouds
      of heaven." '

[63] Then the high priest tore his clothes and said, 'Why do we still need witnesses? [64] You have heard his blasphemy! What is your decision?' All of them condemned him as deserving death. [65] Some began to spit on him, to blindfold him, and to strike him, saying to him, 'Prophesy!' The guards also took him over and beat him.

Peter Denies Jesus

66 While Peter was below in the courtyard, one of the servant-girls of the high priest came by. [67] When she saw Peter warming himself, she stared at him and said, 'You also were with Jesus, the man from Nazareth.' [68] But he denied it, saying,

'I do not know or understand what you are talking about.' And he went out into the forecourt.[b] Then the cock crowed.[c] [69] And the servant-girl, on seeing him, began again to say to the bystanders, 'This man is one of them.' [70] But again he denied it. Then after a little while the bystanders again said to Peter, 'Certainly you are one of them; for you are a Galilean.' [71] But he began to curse, and he swore an oath, 'I do not know this man you are talking about.' [72] At that moment the cock crowed for the second time. Then Peter remembered that Jesus had said to him, 'Before the cock crows twice, you will deny me three times.' And he broke down and wept.

Jesus before Pilate

15 As soon as it was morning, the chief priests held a consultation with the elders and scribes and the whole council. They bound Jesus, led him away, and handed him over to Pilate. [2] Pilate asked him, 'Are you the King of the Jews?' He answered him, 'You say so.' [3] Then the chief priests accused him of many things. [4] Pilate asked him again, 'Have you no answer? See how many charges they bring against you.' [5] But Jesus made no further reply, so that Pilate was amazed.

Pilate Hands Jesus over to Be Crucified

6 Now at the festival he used to release a prisoner for them, anyone for whom they asked. [7] Now a man called Barabbas was in prison with the rebels who had committed murder during the insurrection. [8] So the crowd came and began to ask Pilate to do for them according to his custom. [9] Then he answered them, 'Do you want me to release for you the King of the Jews?' [10] For he realized that it was out of jealousy that the chief priests had handed him over. [11] But the chief priests stirred up the crowd to have him release Barabbas for them instead. [12] Pilate spoke to them again, 'Then what do you wish me to do[d]

a Or the Christ   b Or gateway   c Other ancient authorities lack Then the cock crowed   d Other ancient authorities read what should I do with the man you call[a] the King of the Jews?' 13 They shouted back, 'Crucify him!' 14 Pilate asked them, 'Why, what evil has he done?' But they shouted all the more, 'Crucify him!' 15 So Pilate, wishing to satisfy the crowd, released Barabbas for them; and after flogging Jesus, he handed him over to be crucified.

The Soldiers Mock Jesus

16 Then the soldiers led him into the courtyard of the palace (that is, the governor's headquarters[b]); and they called together the whole cohort. 17 And they clothed him in a purple cloak; and after twisting some thorns into a crown, they put it on him. 18 And they began saluting him, 'Hail, King of the Jews!' 19 They struck his head with a reed, spat upon him, and knelt down in homage to him. 20 After mocking him, they stripped him of the purple cloak and put his own clothes on him. Then they led him out to crucify him.

The Crucifixion of Jesus

21 They compelled a passer-by, who was coming in from the country, to carry his cross; it was Simon of Cyrene, the father of Alexander and Rufus. 22 Then they brought Jesus[c] to the place called Golgotha (which means the place of a skull). 23 And they offered him wine mixed with myrrh; but he did not take it. 24 And they crucified him, and divided his clothes among them, casting lots to decide what each should take.

25 It was nine o'clock in the morning when they crucified him. 26 The inscription of the charge against him read, 'The King of the Jews.' 27 And with him they crucified two bandits, one on his right and one on his left.[d] 29 Those who passed by derided[e] him, shaking their heads and saying, 'Aha! You who would destroy the temple and build it in three days, 30 save yourself, and come down from the cross!' 31 In the same way the chief priests, along with the scribes, were also mocking him among themselves and saying, 'He saved others; he cannot save himself. 32 Let the Messiah,[f] the King of Israel, come down from the

cross now, so that we may see and believe.' Those who were crucified with him also taunted him.

The Death of Jesus

33 When it was noon, darkness came over the whole land[g] until three in the afternoon. 34 At three o'clock Jesus cried out with a loud voice, 'Eloi, Eloi, lema sabachthani?' which means, 'My God, my God, why have you forsaken me?'[h] 35 When some of the bystanders heard it, they said, 'Listen, he is calling for Elijah.' 36 And someone ran, filled a sponge with sour wine, put it on a stick, and gave it to him to drink, saying, 'Wait, let us see whether Elijah will come to take him down.' 37 Then Jesus gave a loud cry and breathed his last. 38 And the curtain of the temple was torn in two, from top to bottom. 39 Now when the centurion, who stood facing him, saw that in this way he[i] breathed his last, he said, 'Truly this man was God's Son!'[j]

40 There were also women looking on from a distance; among them were Mary Magdalene, and Mary the mother of James the younger and of Joses, and Salome. 41 These used to follow him and provided for him when he was in Galilee; and there were many other women who had come up with him to Jerusalem.

The Burial of Jesus

42 When evening had come, and since it was the day of Preparation, that is, the day before the sabbath, 43 Joseph of Arimathea, a respected member of the council, who was also himself waiting expectantly for the kingdom of God, went boldly to Pilate and asked for the body of Jesus. 44 Then Pilate wondered if he were already dead; and summoning the centurion, he asked him whether he had been dead for some time. 45 When he learned

a Other ancient authorities lack the man you call
b Gk the praetorium c Gk him d Other ancient authorities add verse 28, And the scripture was fulfilled that says, 'And he was counted among the lawless.'
e Or blasphemed f Or the Christ g Or earth
h Other ancient authorities read made me a reproach
i Other ancient authorities add cried out and j Or a son of God

from the centurion that he was dead, he granted the body to Joseph. ⁴⁶Then Joseph*a* bought a linen cloth, and taking down the body,*b* wrapped it in the linen cloth, and laid it in a tomb that had been hewn out of the rock. He then rolled a stone against the door of the tomb. ⁴⁷Mary Magdalene and Mary the mother of Joses saw where the body*b* was laid.

The Resurrection of Jesus

16 When the sabbath was over, Mary Magdalene, and Mary the mother of James, and Salome bought spices, so that they might go and anoint him. ²And very early on the first day of the week, when the sun had risen, they went to the tomb. ³They had been saying to one another, 'Who will roll away the stone for us from the entrance to the tomb?' ⁴When they looked up, they saw that the stone, which was very large, had already been rolled back. ⁵As they entered the tomb, they saw a young man, dressed in a white robe, sitting on the right side; and they were alarmed. ⁶But he said to them, 'Do not be alarmed; you are looking for Jesus of Nazareth, who was crucified. He has been raised; he is not here. Look, there is the place they laid him. ⁷But go, tell his disciples and Peter that he is going ahead of you to Galilee; there you will see him, just as he told you.' ⁸So they went out and fled from the tomb, for terror and amazement had seized them; and they said nothing to anyone, for they were afraid.*c*

THE SHORTER ENDING OF MARK

⟦And all that had been commanded them they told briefly to those around Peter. And afterwards Jesus himself sent out through them, from east to west, the sacred and imperishable proclamation of eternal salvation.*d*⟧

THE LONGER ENDING OF MARK

Jesus Appears to Mary Magdalene

9 ⟦Now after he rose early on the first day of the week, he appeared first to Mary Magdalene, from whom he had cast out seven demons. ¹⁰She went out and told those who had been with him, while they were mourning and weeping. ¹¹But when they heard that he was alive and had been seen by her, they would not believe it.

Jesus Appears to Two Disciples

12 After this he appeared in another form to two of them, as they were walking into the country. ¹³And they went back and told the rest, but they did not believe them.

Jesus Commissions the Disciples

14 Later he appeared to the eleven themselves as they were sitting at the table; and he upbraided them for their lack of faith and stubbornness, because they had not believed those who saw him after he had risen.*e* ¹⁵And he said to them, 'Go into all the world and proclaim the good news*f* to the whole creation. ¹⁶The one who believes and is baptized will be saved; but the one who does not believe will be condemned. ¹⁷And these signs will accompany those who believe: by using my name they will cast out demons; they will speak in new tongues; ¹⁸they will pick up snakes in their hands,*g* and if they drink any deadly thing, it will not hurt them; they will lay their hands on the sick, and they will recover.'

a Gk *he*   *b* Gk *it*   *c* Some of the most ancient authorities bring the book to a close at the end of verse 8. One authority concludes the book with the shorter ending; others include the shorter ending and then continue with verses 9-20. In most authorities verses 9-20 follow immediately after verse 8, though in some of these authorities the passage is marked as being doubtful.   *d* Other ancient authorities add *Amen*   *e* Other ancient authorities add, in whole or in part, *And they excused themselves, saying, 'This age of lawlessness and unbelief is under Satan, who does not allow the truth and power of God to prevail over the unclean things of the spirits. Therefore reveal your righteousness now'—thus they spoke to Christ. And Christ replied to them, 'The term of years of Satan's power has been fulfilled, but other terrible things draw near. And for those who have sinned I was handed over to death, that they may return to the truth and sin no more, that they may inherit the spiritual and imperishable glory of righteousness that is in heaven.'*   *f* Or *gospel*   *g* Other ancient authorities lack *in their hands*

The Ascension of Jesus

19 So then the Lord Jesus, after he had spoken to them, was taken up into heaven and sat down at the right hand of God. 20 And they went out and proclaimed the good news everywhere, while the Lord worked with them and confirmed the message by the signs that accompanied it. *a*⟧

a Other ancient authorities add *Amen*

THE GOSPEL ACCORDING TO
LUKE

Dedication to Theophilus

1 Since many have undertaken to set down an orderly account of the events that have been fulfilled among us, 2 just as they were handed on to us by those who from the beginning were eyewitnesses and servants of the word, 3 I too decided, after investigating everything carefully from the very first,*a* to write an orderly account for you, most excellent Theophilus, 4 so that you may know the truth concerning the things about which you have been instructed.

The Birth of John the Baptist Foretold

5 In the days of King Herod of Judea, there was a priest named Zechariah, who belonged to the priestly order of Abijah. His wife was a descendant of Aaron, and her name was Elizabeth. 6 Both of them were righteous before God, living blamelessly according to all the commandments and regulations of the Lord. 7 But they had no children, because Elizabeth was barren, and both were getting on in years.

8 Once when he was serving as priest before God and his section was on duty, 9 he was chosen by lot, according to the custom of the priesthood, to enter the sanctuary of the Lord and offer incense. 10 Now at the time of the incense-offering, the whole assembly of the people was praying outside. 11 Then there appeared to him an angel of the Lord, standing at the right side of the altar of incense. 12 When Zechariah saw him, he was terrified; and fear overwhelmed him. 13 But the angel said to him, 'Do not be afraid, Zechariah, for your prayer has been heard. Your wife Elizabeth will bear you a son, and you will name him John. 14 You will have joy and gladness, and many will rejoice at his birth, 15 for he will be great in the sight of the Lord. He must never drink wine or strong drink; even before his birth he will be filled with the Holy Spirit. 16 He will turn many of the people of Israel to the Lord their God. 17 With the spirit and power of Elijah he will go before him, to turn the hearts of parents to their children, and the disobedient to the wisdom of the righteous, to make ready a people prepared for the Lord.' 18 Zechariah said to the angel, 'How will I know that this is so? For I am an old man, and my wife is getting on in years.' 19 The angel replied, 'I am Gabriel. I stand in the presence of God, and I have been sent to speak to you and to bring you this good news. 20 But now, because you did not believe my words, which will be fulfilled in their time, you will become mute, unable to speak, until the day these things occur.'

21 Meanwhile, the people were waiting for Zechariah, and wondered at his delay in the sanctuary. 22 When he did come out, he could not speak to them, and they realized that he had seen a vision in the sanctuary. He kept motioning to them and remained unable to speak. 23 When his time of service was ended, he went to his home.

24 After those days his wife Elizabeth conceived, and for five months she remained in seclusion. She said, 25 'This is what the Lord has done for me when he looked favourably on me and took away

a Or *for a long time*

the disgrace I have endured among my people.'

The Birth of Jesus Foretold

26 In the sixth month the angel Gabriel was sent by God to a town in Galilee called Nazareth, 27 to a virgin engaged to a man whose name was Joseph, of the house of David. The virgin's name was Mary. 28 And he came to her and said, 'Greetings, favoured one! The Lord is with you.'*a* 29 But she was much perplexed by his words and pondered what sort of greeting this might be. 30 The angel said to her, 'Do not be afraid, Mary, for you have found favour with God. 31 And now, you will conceive in your womb and bear a son, and you will name him Jesus. 32 He will be great, and will be called the Son of the Most High, and the Lord God will give to him the throne of his ancestor David. 33 He will reign over the house of Jacob for ever, and of his kingdom there will be no end.' 34 Mary said to the angel, 'How can this be, since I am a virgin?'*b* 35 The angel said to her, 'The Holy Spirit will come upon you, and the power of the Most High will overshadow you; therefore the child to be born*c* will be holy; he will be called Son of God. 36 And now, your relative Elizabeth in her old age has also conceived a son; and this is the sixth month for her who was said to be barren. 37 For nothing will be impossible with God.' 38 Then Mary said, 'Here am I, the servant of the Lord; let it be with me according to your word.' Then the angel departed from her.

Mary Visits Elizabeth

39 In those days Mary set out and went with haste to a Judean town in the hill country, 40 where she entered the house of Zechariah and greeted Elizabeth. 41 When Elizabeth heard Mary's greeting, the child leapt in her womb. And Elizabeth was filled with the Holy Spirit 42 and exclaimed with a loud cry, 'Blessed are you among women, and blessed is the fruit of your womb. 43 And why has this happened to me, that the mother of my Lord comes to me? 44 For as soon as I heard the sound of

your greeting, the child in my womb leapt for joy. 45 And blessed is she who believed that there would be*d* a fulfilment of what was spoken to her by the Lord.'

Mary's Song of Praise

46 And Mary*e* said,
'My soul magnifies the Lord,
47   and my spirit rejoices in God
           my Saviour,
48 for he has looked with favour on the
           lowliness of his servant.
     Surely, from now on all generations
           will call me blessed;
49 for the Mighty One has done great
           things for me,
     and holy is his name.
50 His mercy is for those who fear him
     from generation to generation.
51 He has shown strength with
           his arm;
     he has scattered the proud in the
           thoughts of their hearts.
52 He has brought down the powerful
           from their thrones,
     and lifted up the lowly;
53 he has filled the hungry with
           good things,
     and sent the rich away empty.
54 He has helped his servant Israel,
     in remembrance of his mercy,
55 according to the promise he made to
           our ancestors,
     to Abraham and to his descendants
           for ever.'

56 And Mary remained with her for about three months and then returned to her home.

The Birth of John the Baptist

57 Now the time came for Elizabeth to give birth, and she bore a son. 58 Her neighbours and relatives heard that the Lord had shown his great mercy to her, and they rejoiced with her.

59 On the eighth day they came to circumcise the child, and they were going to name him Zechariah after his father. 60 But

a Other ancient authorities add *Blessed are you among women*   b Gk *I do not know a man*   c Other ancient authorities add *of you*   d Or *believed, for there will be*   e Other ancient authorities read *Elizabeth* his mother said, 'No; he is to be called John.' [61] They said to her, 'None of your relatives has this name.' [62] Then they began motioning to his father to find out what name he wanted to give him. [63] He asked for a writing-tablet and wrote, 'His name is John.' And all of them were amazed. [64] Immediately his mouth was opened and his tongue freed, and he began to speak, praising God. [65] Fear came over all their neighbours, and all these things were talked about throughout the entire hill country of Judea. [66] All who heard them pondered them and said, 'What then will this child become?' For, indeed, the hand of the Lord was with him.

Zechariah's Prophecy

67 Then his father Zechariah was filled with the Holy Spirit and spoke this prophecy:

[68] 'Blessed be the Lord God of Israel,
     for he has looked favourably on his
          people and redeemed them.
[69] He has raised up a mighty saviour[a]
          for us
     in the house of his servant David,
[70] as he spoke through the mouth of his
          holy prophets from of old,
[71]   that we would be saved from our
          enemies and from the hand of
          all who hate us.
[72] Thus he has shown the mercy
          promised to our ancestors,
     and has remembered his
          holy covenant,
[73] the oath that he swore to our
          ancestor Abraham,
     to grant us [74] that we, being rescued
          from the hands of our
          enemies,
     might serve him without fear, [75] in
          holiness and righteousness
     before him all our days.
[76] And you, child, will be called the
          prophet of the Most High;
     for you will go before the Lord to
          prepare his ways,
[77] to give knowledge of salvation to his
          people
     by the forgiveness of their sins.
[78] By the tender mercy of our God,
     the dawn from on high will break
          upon[b] us,
[79] to give light to those who sit in
          darkness and in the shadow of
          death,
     to guide our feet into the way
          of peace.'

80 The child grew and became strong in spirit, and he was in the wilderness until the day he appeared publicly to Israel.

The Birth of Jesus

2 In those days a decree went out from Emperor Augustus that all the world should be registered. [2] This was the first registration and was taken while Quirinius was governor of Syria. [3] All went to their own towns to be registered. [4] Joseph also went from the town of Nazareth in Galilee to Judea, to the city of David called Bethlehem, because he was descended from the

The Holy Land Under Herod the Great

Mediterranean Sea
ITUREA
ABILENE
PHOENICIA
Panias
TRACHONITIS
Raphana
AURANTIS
Nazareth
GALILEE
DECAPOLIS
Samaria
SAMARIA
Joppa
JUDEA
PEREA
ARABIA
Jericho
Jerusalem
Herodium
Machaerus
Gaza
IDUMEA
Masada
Dead Sea
Beersheba
0   40 Mi.
0   40 Km.
N

a Gk *a horn of salvation*   b Other ancient authorities read *has broken upon* house and family of David. 5 He went to be registered with Mary, to whom he was engaged and who was expecting a child. 6 While they were there, the time came for her to deliver her child. 7 And she gave birth to her firstborn son and wrapped him in bands of cloth, and laid him in a manger, because there was no place for them in the inn.

The Shepherds and the Angels

8 In that region there were shepherds living in the fields, keeping watch over their flock by night. 9 Then an angel of the Lord stood before them, and the glory of the Lord shone around them, and they were terrified. 10 But the angel said to them, 'Do not be afraid; for see—I am bringing you good news of great joy for all the people: 11 to you is born this day in the city of David a Saviour, who is the Messiah, *a* the Lord. 12 This will be a sign for you: you will find a child wrapped in bands of cloth and lying in a manger.' 13 And suddenly there was with the angel a multitude of the heavenly host, *b* praising God and saying,

14 'Glory to God in the highest heaven,
　　and on earth peace among those
　　　whom he favours!' *c*

15 When the angels had left them and gone into heaven, the shepherds said to one another, 'Let us go now to Bethlehem and see this thing that has taken place, which the Lord has made known to us.' 16 So they went with haste and found Mary and Joseph, and the child lying in the manger. 17 When they saw this, they made known what had been told them about this child; 18 and all who heard it were amazed at what the shepherds told them. 19 But Mary treasured all these words and pondered them in her heart. 20 The shepherds returned, glorifying and praising God for all they had heard and seen, as it had been told them.

Jesus Is Named

21 After eight days had passed, it was time to circumcise the child; and he was

called Jesus, the name given by the angel before he was conceived in the womb.

Jesus Is Presented in the Temple

22 When the time came for their purification according to the law of Moses, they brought him up to Jerusalem to present him to the Lord 23 (as it is written in the law of the Lord, 'Every firstborn male shall be designated as holy to the Lord'), 24 and they offered a sacrifice according to what is stated in the law of the Lord, 'a pair of turtle-doves or two young pigeons.'

25 Now there was a man in Jerusalem whose name was Simeon; *d* this man was righteous and devout, looking forward to the consolation of Israel, and the Holy Spirit rested on him. 26 It had been revealed to him by the Holy Spirit that he would not see death before he had seen the Lord's Messiah. *e* 27 Guided by the Spirit, Simeon *f* came into the temple; and when the parents brought in the child Jesus, to do for him what was customary under the law, 28 Simeon *g* took him in his arms and praised God, saying,

29 'Master, now you are dismissing your
　　servant *h* in peace,
　　according to your word;
30 for my eyes have seen your
　　salvation,
31 which you have prepared in the
　　presence of all peoples,
32 a light for revelation to the Gentiles
　　and for glory to your people
　　Israel.'

33 And the child's father and mother were amazed at what was being said about him. 34 Then Simeon *d* blessed them and said to his mother Mary, 'This child is destined for the falling and the rising of many in Israel, and to be a sign that will be opposed 35 so that the inner thoughts of many will be revealed—and a sword will pierce your own soul too.'

36 There was also a prophet, Anna *i* the daughter of Phanuel, of the tribe of Asher. She was of a great age, having lived with her

---

a Or *the Christ*   *b* Gk *army*   *c* Other ancient authorities read *peace, goodwill among people*   *d* Gk *Symeon*   *e* Or *the Lord's Christ*   *f* Gk *In the Spirit, he*   *g* Gk *he*   *h* Gk *slave*   *i* Gk *Hanna* husband for seven years after her marriage, [37] then as a widow to the age of eighty-four. She never left the temple but worshipped there with fasting and prayer night and day. [38] At that moment she came, and began to praise God and to speak about the child[a] to all who were looking for the redemption of Jerusalem.

The Return to Nazareth

39 When they had finished everything required by the law of the Lord, they returned to Galilee, to their own town of Nazareth. [40] The child grew and became strong, filled with wisdom; and the favour of God was upon him.

The Boy Jesus in the Temple

41 Now every year his parents went to Jerusalem for the festival of the Passover. [42] And when he was twelve years old, they went up as usual for the festival. [43] When the festival was ended and they started to return, the boy Jesus stayed behind in Jerusalem, but his parents did not know it. [44] Assuming that he was in the group of travellers, they went a day's journey. Then they started to look for him among their relatives and friends. [45] When they did not find him, they returned to Jerusalem to search for him. [46] After three days they found him in the temple, sitting among the teachers, listening to them and asking them questions. [47] And all who heard him were amazed at his understanding and his answers. [48] When his parents[b] saw him they were astonished; and his mother said to him, 'Child, why have you treated us like this? Look, your father and I have been searching for you in great anxiety.' [49] He said to them, 'Why were you searching for me? Did you not know that I must be in my Father's house?'[c] [50] But they did not understand what he said to them. [51] Then he went down with them and came to Nazareth, and was obedient to them. His mother treasured all these things in her heart.

52 And Jesus increased in wisdom and in years,[d] and in divine and human favour.

The Proclamation of John the Baptist

3 In the fifteenth year of the reign of Emperor Tiberius, when Pontius Pilate was governor of Judea, and Herod was ruler[e] of Galilee, and his brother Philip ruler[e] of the region of Ituraea and Trachonitis, and Lysanias ruler[e] of Abilene, [2] during the high-priesthood of Annas and Caiaphas, the word of God came to John son of Zechariah in the wilderness. [3] He went into all the region around the Jordan, proclaiming a baptism of repentance for the forgiveness of sins, [4] as it is written in the book of the words of the prophet Isaiah,

'The voice of one crying out in
    the wilderness:
"Prepare the way of the Lord,
    make his paths straight.
[5] Every valley shall be filled,
    and every mountain and hill shall
        be made low,
and the crooked shall be made
        straight,
    and the rough ways made smooth;
[6] and all flesh shall see the salvation of
        God." '

7 John said to the crowds that came out to be baptized by him, 'You brood of vipers! Who warned you to flee from the wrath to come? [8] Bear fruits worthy of repentance. Do not begin to say to yourselves, "We have Abraham as our ancestor"; for I tell you, God is able from these stones to raise up children to Abraham. [9] Even now the axe is lying at the root of the trees; every tree therefore that does not bear good fruit is cut down and thrown into the fire.'

10 And the crowds asked him, 'What then should we do?' [11] In reply he said to them, 'Whoever has two coats must share with anyone who has none; and whoever has food must do likewise.' [12] Even tax-collectors came to be baptized, and they asked him, 'Teacher, what should we do?' [13] He said to them, 'Collect no more than the amount prescribed for you.' [14] Soldiers also asked him, 'And we, what should we

a Gk him   b Gk they   c Or be about my Father's interests?   d Or in stature   e Gk tetrarch

Rulers During New Testament Times

Roman Emperors

27 B.C.—A.D. 14	Augustus
A.D. 14—37	Tiberius
A.D. 37—41	Caligula
A.D. 41—54	Claudius
A.D. 54—68	Nero
A.D. 68—69	Galba; Otho; Vitellius
A.D. 69—79	Vespasian
A.D. 79—81	Titus
A.D. 81—96	Domitian

Herodian Rulers

37—4 B.C.	Herod the Great, king of the Jews
4 B.C.—A.D. 6	Archelaus, ethnarch of Judea
4 B.C.—A.D. 39	Herod Antipas, tetrarch of Galilee and Perea
4 B.C.—A.D. 34	Philip, tetrarch of Iturea, Trachonitis, etc.
A.D. 37—44	Herod Agrippa I, from 37 to 44 king over the former tetrarchy of Philip, and from 41 to 44 over Judea, Galilee, and Perea
A.D. 53—about 100	Herod Agrippa II, king over the former tetrarchy of Philip and Lysanias, and from 56 (or 61) over parts of Galilee and Perea

Procurators of Judea After the Reign of Archelaus to the Reign of Herod Agrippa I

A.D. 6—8	Coponius
A.D. 9—12	M. Ambivius
A.D. 12—15	Annius Rufus
A.D. 15—26	Valerius Gratus
A.D. 26—36	Pontius Pilate
A.D. 37	Marullus
A.D. 37—41	Herennius Capito

Procurators of Palestine from the Reign of Herod Agrippa I to the Jewish Revolt

A.D. 44—about 46	Cuspius Fadus
A.D. about 46—48	Tiberius Alexander
A.D. 48—52	Ventidius Cumanus
A.D. 52—60	M. Antonius Felix
A.D. 60—62	Porcius Festus
A.D. 62—64	Clodius Albinus
A.D. 64—66	Gessius Florus

do?' He said to them, 'Do not extort money from anyone by threats or false accusation, and be satisfied with your wages.'

15 As the people were filled with expectation, and all were questioning in their hearts concerning John, whether he might be the Messiah,[a] 16 John answered all of them by saying, 'I baptize you with water; but one who is more powerful than I is coming; I am not worthy to untie the thong of his sandals. He will baptize you with[b] the Holy Spirit and fire. 17 His winnowing-fork is in his hand, to clear his threshing-floor and to gather the wheat into his granary; but the chaff he will burn with unquenchable fire.'

18 So, with many other exhortations, he proclaimed the good news to the people. 19 But Herod the ruler,[c] who had been rebuked by him because of Herodias, his brother's wife, and because of all the evil things that Herod had done, 20 added to them all by shutting up John in prison.

The Baptism of Jesus

21 Now when all the people were baptized, and when Jesus also had been baptized and was praying, the heaven was opened, 22 and the Holy Spirit descended upon him in bodily form like a dove. And a voice came from heaven, 'You are my Son, the Beloved;[d] with you I am well pleased.'[e]

The Ancestors of Jesus

23 Jesus was about thirty years old when he began his work. He was the son (as was thought) of Joseph son of Heli, 24 son of Matthat, son of Levi, son of Melchi, son of Jannai, son of Joseph, 25 son of Mattathias, son of Amos, son of Nahum, son of Esli, son of Naggai, 26 son of Maath, son of Mattathias, son of Semein, son of Josech, son of Joda, 27 son of Joanan, son of Rhesa, son of Zerubbabel, son of Shealtiel,[f] son of Neri, 28 son of Melchi, son of Addi, son of Cosam, son of Elmadam, son of Er, 29 son of Joshua, son of Eliezer, son of Jorim, son of Matthat, son of Levi, 30 son of Simeon, son of Judah, son of

Joseph, son of Jonam, son of Eliakim, 31 son of Melea, son of Menna, son of Mattatha, son of Nathan, son of David, 32 son of Jesse, son of Obed, son of Boaz, son of Sala,[g] son of Nahshon, 33 son of Amminadab, son of Admin, son of Arni,[h] son of Hezron, son of Perez, son of Judah, 34 son of Jacob, son of Isaac, son of Abraham, son of Terah, son of Nahor, 35 son of Serug, son of Reu, son of Peleg, son of Eber, son of Shelah, 36 son of Cainan, son of Arphaxad, son of Shem, son of Noah, son of Lamech, 37 son of Methuselah, son of Enoch, son of Jared, son of Mahalaleel, son of Cainan, 38 son of Enos, son of Seth, son of Adam, son of God.

The Temptation of Jesus

4 Jesus, full of the Holy Spirit, returned from the Jordan and was led by the Spirit in the wilderness, 2 where for forty days he was tempted by the devil. He ate nothing at all during those days, and when they were over, he was famished. 3 The devil said to him, 'If you are the Son of God, command this stone to become a loaf of bread.' 4 Jesus answered him, 'It is written, "One does not live by bread alone." '

5 Then the devil[i] led him up and showed him in an instant all the kingdoms of the world. 6 And the devil[i] said to him, 'To you I will give their glory and all this authority; for it has been given over to me, and I give it to anyone I please. 7 If you, then, will worship me, it will be all yours.' 8 Jesus answered him, 'It is written,

"Worship the Lord your God,
    and serve only him." '

9 Then the devil[i] took him to Jerusalem, and placed him on the pinnacle of the temple, saying to him, 'If you are the Son of God, throw yourself down from here, 10 for it is written,

"He will command his angels
    concerning you,
    to protect you",

a Or the Christ   b Or in   c Gk tetrarch   d Or my beloved Son   e Other ancient authorities read You are my Son, today I have begotten you   f Gk Salathiel   g Other ancient authorities read Salmon   h Other ancient authorities read Amminadab, son of Aram; others vary widely   i Gk he

[11] and

> "On their hands they will bear
> > you up,
> so that you will not dash your foot
> > against a stone." '

[12] Jesus answered him, 'It is said, "Do not put the Lord your God to the test." " ' [13] When the devil had finished every test, he departed from him until an opportune time.

The Beginning of the Galilean Ministry

14 Then Jesus, filled with the power of the Spirit, returned to Galilee, and a report about him spread through all the surrounding country. [15] He began to teach in their synagogues and was praised by everyone.

The Rejection of Jesus at Nazareth

16 When he came to Nazareth, where he had been brought up, he went to the synagogue on the sabbath day, as was his custom. He stood up to read, [17] and the scroll of the prophet Isaiah was given to him. He unrolled the scroll and found the place where it was written:

[18] 'The Spirit of the Lord is upon me,
> because he has anointed me
> > to bring good news to the poor.
> He has sent me to proclaim release to
> > the captives
> and recovery of sight to the blind,
> > to let the oppressed go free,
[19] to proclaim the year of the Lord's
> > favour.'

[20] And he rolled up the scroll, gave it back to the attendant, and sat down. The eyes of all in the synagogue were fixed on him. [21] Then he began to say to them, 'Today this scripture has been fulfilled in your hearing.' [22] All spoke well of him and were amazed at the gracious words that came from his mouth. They said, 'Is not this Joseph's son?' [23] He said to them, 'Doubtless you will quote to me this proverb, "Doctor, cure yourself!" And you will say, "Do here also in your home town the things that we have heard you did at Capernaum." ' [24] And he said, 'Truly I tell you, no prophet is accepted in the prophet's home town. [25] But the truth is, there were many widows in Israel in the time of Elijah, when the heaven was shut up for three years and six months, and there was a severe famine over all the land; [26] yet Elijah was sent to none of them except to a widow at Zarephath in Sidon. [27] There were also many lepers[a] in Israel in the time of the prophet Elisha, and none of them was cleansed except Naaman the Syrian.' [28] When they heard this, all in the synagogue were filled with rage. [29] They got up, drove him out of the town, and led him to the brow of the hill on which their town was built, so that they might hurl him off the cliff. [30] But he passed through the midst of them and went on his way.

The Man with an Unclean Spirit

31 He went down to Capernaum, a city in Galilee, and was teaching them on the sabbath. [32] They were astounded at his teaching, because he spoke with authority. [33] In the synagogue there was a man who had the spirit of an unclean demon, and he cried out with a loud voice, [34] 'Let us alone! What have you to do with us, Jesus of Nazareth? Have you come to destroy us? I know who you are, the Holy One of God.' [35] But Jesus rebuked him, saying, 'Be silent, and come out of him!' When the demon had thrown him down before them, he came out of him without having done him any harm. [36] They were all amazed and kept saying to one another, 'What kind of utterance is this? For with authority and power he commands the unclean spirits, and out they come!' [37] And a report about him began to reach every place in the region.

Healings at Simon's House

38 After leaving the synagogue he entered Simon's house. Now Simon's mother-in-law was suffering from a high fever, and they asked him about her. [39] Then he stood over her and rebuked the fever, and it left her. Immediately she got up and began to serve them.

40 As the sun was setting, all those who had any who were sick with various kinds

---

a The terms *leper* and *leprosy* can refer to several diseases of diseases brought them to him; and he laid his hands on each of them and cured them. 41 Demons also came out of many, shouting, 'You are the Son of God!' But he rebuked them and would not allow them to speak, because they knew that he was the Messiah. *a*

Jesus Preaches in the Synagogues

42 At daybreak he departed and went into a deserted place. And the crowds were looking for him; and when they reached him, they wanted to prevent him from leaving them. 43 But he said to them, 'I must proclaim the good news of the kingdom of God to the other cities also; for I was sent for this purpose.' 44 So he continued proclaiming the message in the synagogues of Judea. *b*

Jesus Calls the First Disciples

5 Once while Jesus *c* was standing beside the lake of Gennesaret, and the crowd was pressing in on him to hear the word of God, 2 he saw two boats there at the shore of the lake; the fishermen had gone out of them and were washing their nets. 3 He got into one of the boats, the one belonging to Simon, and asked him to put out a little way from the shore. Then he sat down and taught the crowds from the boat. 4 When he had finished speaking, he said to Simon, 'Put out into the deep water and let down your nets for a catch.' 5 Simon answered, 'Master, we have worked all night long but have caught nothing. Yet if you say so, I will let down the nets.' 6 When they had done this, they caught so many fish that their nets were beginning to break. 7 So they signalled to their partners in the other boat to come and help them. And they came and filled both boats, so that they began to sink. 8 But when Simon Peter saw it, he fell down at Jesus' knees, saying, 'Go away from me, Lord, for I am a sinful man!' 9 For he and all who were with him were amazed at the catch of fish that they had taken; 10 and so also were James and John, sons of Zebedee, who were partners with Simon. Then Jesus said to Simon, 'Do not

be afraid; from now on you will be catching people.' 11 When they had brought their boats to shore, they left everything and followed him.

Jesus Cleanses a Leper

12 Once, when he was in one of the cities, there was a man covered with leprosy. *d* When he saw Jesus, he bowed with his face to the ground and begged him, 'Lord, if you choose, you can make me clean.' 13 Then Jesus *c* stretched out his hand, touched him, and said, 'I do choose. Be made clean.' Immediately the leprosy *d* left him. 14 And he ordered him to tell no one. 'Go', he said, 'and show yourself to the priest, and, as Moses commanded, make an offering for your cleansing, for a testimony to them.' 15 But now more than ever the word about Jesus *e* spread abroad; many crowds would gather to hear him and to be cured of their diseases. 16 But he would withdraw to deserted places and pray.

Jesus Heals a Paralytic

17 One day, while he was teaching, Pharisees and teachers of the law were sitting nearby (they had come from every village of Galilee and Judea and from Jerusalem); and the power of the Lord was with him to heal. *f* 18 Just then some men came, carrying a paralysed man on a bed. They were trying to bring him in and lay him before Jesus; *e* 19 but finding no way to bring him in because of the crowd, they went up on the roof and let him down with his bed through the tiles into the middle of the crowd *g* in front of Jesus. 20 When he saw their faith, he said, 'Friend, *h* your sins are forgiven you.' 21 Then the scribes and the Pharisees began to question, 'Who is this who is speaking blasphemies? Who can forgive sins but God alone?' 22 When Jesus perceived their questionings, he answered them, 'Why do you raise such questions in your hearts?

a Or *the Christ*   *b* Other ancient authorities read *Galilee*   *c* Gk *he*   *d* The terms *leper* and *leprosy* can refer to several diseases   *e* Gk *him*   *f* Other ancient authorities read *was present to heal them*   *g* Gk *into the midst*   *h* Gk *Man*

23 Which is easier, to say, "Your sins are forgiven you", or to say, "Stand up and walk"? 24 But so that you may know that the Son of Man has authority on earth to forgive sins'—he said to the one who was paralysed—'I say to you, stand up and take your bed and go to your home.' 25 Immediately he stood up before them, took what he had been lying on, and went to his home, glorifying God. 26 Amazement seized all of them, and they glorified God and were filled with awe, saying, 'We have seen strange things today.'

Jesus Calls Levi

27 After this he went out and saw a tax-collector named Levi, sitting at the tax booth; and he said to him, 'Follow me.' 28 And he got up, left everything, and followed him.

29 Then Levi gave a great banquet for him in his house; and there was a large crowd of tax-collectors and others sitting at the table[a] with them. 30 The Pharisees and their scribes were complaining to his disciples, saying, 'Why do you eat and drink with tax-collectors and sinners?' 31 Jesus answered, 'Those who are well have no need of a physician, but those who are sick; 32 I have come to call not the righteous but sinners to repentance.'

The Question about Fasting

33 Then they said to him, 'John's disciples, like the disciples of the Pharisees, frequently fast and pray, but your disciples eat and drink.' 34 Jesus said to them, 'You cannot make wedding-guests fast while the bridegroom is with them, can you? 35 The days will come when the bridegroom will be taken away from them, and then they will fast in those days.' 36 He also told them a parable: 'No one tears a piece from a new garment and sews it on an old garment; otherwise the new will be torn, and the piece from the new will not match the old. 37 And no one puts new wine into old wineskins; otherwise the new wine will burst the skins and will be spilled, and the skins will be destroyed. 38 But new wine must be put into fresh wineskins. 39 And no one after drinking old wine desires new wine, but says, "The old is good." '[b]

The Question about the Sabbath

6 One sabbath[c] while Jesus[d] was going through the cornfields, his disciples plucked some heads of grain, rubbed them in their hands, and ate them. 2 But some of the Pharisees said, 'Why are you doing what is not lawful[e] on the sabbath?' 3 Jesus answered, 'Have you not read what David did when he and his companions were hungry? 4 He entered the house of God and took and ate the bread of the Presence, which it is not lawful for any but the priests to eat, and gave some to his companions?' 5 Then he said to them, 'The Son of Man is lord of the sabbath.'

The Man with a Withered Hand

6 On another sabbath he entered the synagogue and taught, and there was a man there whose right hand was withered. 7 The scribes and the Pharisees watched him to see whether he would cure on the sabbath, so that they might find an accusation against him. 8 Even though he knew what they were thinking, he said to the man who had the withered hand, 'Come and stand here.' He got up and stood there. 9 Then Jesus said to them, 'I ask you, is it lawful to do good or to do harm on the sabbath, to save life or to destroy it?' 10 After looking around at all of them, he said to him, 'Stretch out your hand.' He did so, and his hand was restored. 11 But they were filled with fury and discussed with one another what they might do to Jesus.

Jesus Chooses the Twelve Apostles

12 Now during those days he went out to the mountain to pray; and he spent the night in prayer to God. 13 And when day came, he called his disciples and chose twelve of them, whom he also named

---

a Gk *reclining*   b Other ancient authorities read *better*; others lack verse 39   c Other ancient authorities read *On the second first sabbath*   d Gk *he*   e Other ancient authorities add *to do* apostles: 14 Simon, whom he named Peter, and his brother Andrew, and James, and John, and Philip, and Bartholomew, 15 and Matthew, and Thomas, and James son of Alphaeus, and Simon, who was called the Zealot, 16 and Judas son of James, and Judas Iscariot, who became a traitor.

Jesus Teaches and Heals

17 He came down with them and stood on a level place, with a great crowd of his disciples and a great multitude of people from all Judea, Jerusalem, and the coast of Tyre and Sidon. 18 They had come to hear him and to be healed of their diseases; and those who were troubled with unclean spirits were cured. 19 And all in the crowd were trying to touch him, for power came out from him and healed all of them.

Blessings and Woes

20 Then he looked up at his disciples and said:

'Blessed are you who are poor,
for yours is the kingdom of God.
21 'Blessed are you who are hungry now,
for you will be filled.
'Blessed are you who weep now,
for you will laugh.

22 'Blessed are you when people hate you, and when they exclude you, revile you, and defame you*a* on account of the Son of Man. 23 Rejoice on that day and leap for joy, for surely your reward is great in heaven; for that is what their ancestors did to the prophets.

24 'But woe to you who are rich,
for you have received your
consolation.
25 'Woe to you who are full now,
for you will be hungry.
'Woe to you who are laughing now,
for you will mourn and weep.

26 'Woe to you when all speak well of you, for that is what their ancestors did to the false prophets.

Love for Enemies

27 'But I say to you that listen, Love your enemies, do good to those who hate you, 28 bless those who curse you, pray for those who abuse you. 29 If anyone strikes you on the cheek, offer the other also; and from anyone who takes away your coat do not withhold even your shirt. 30 Give to everyone who begs from you; and if anyone takes away your goods, do not ask for them again. 31 Do to others as you would have them do to you.

32 'If you love those who love you, what credit is that to you? For even sinners love those who love them. 33 If you do good to those who do good to you, what credit is that to you? For even sinners do the same. 34 If you lend to those from whom you hope to receive, what credit is that to you? Even sinners lend to sinners, to receive as much again. 35 But love your enemies, do good, and lend, expecting nothing in return.*b* Your reward will be great, and you will be children of the Most High; for he is kind to the ungrateful and the wicked. 36 Be merciful, just as your Father is merciful.

Judging Others

37 'Do not judge, and you will not be judged; do not condemn, and you will not be condemned. Forgive, and you will be forgiven; 38 give, and it will be given to you. A good measure, pressed down, shaken together, running over, will be put into your lap; for the measure you give will be the measure you get back.'

39 He also told them a parable: 'Can a blind person guide a blind person? Will not both fall into a pit? 40 A disciple is not above the teacher, but everyone who is fully qualified will be like the teacher. 41 Why do you see the speck in your neighbour's*c* eye, but do not notice the log in your own eye? 42 Or how can you say to your neighbour,*d* "Friend,*d* let me take out the speck in your eye", when you yourself do not see the log in your own eye? You hypocrite, first take the log out of your own eye, and then you will see clearly to take the speck out of your neighbour's*c* eye.

a Gk cast out your name as evil   *b* Other ancient authorities read despairing of no one   *c* Gk brother's   *d* Gk brother

A Tree and Its Fruit

43 'No good tree bears bad fruit, nor again does a bad tree bear good fruit; 44for each tree is known by its own fruit. Figs are not gathered from thorns, nor are grapes picked from a bramble bush. 45The good person out of the good treasure of the heart produces good, and the evil person out of evil treasure produces evil; for it is out of the abundance of the heart that the mouth speaks.

The Two Foundations

46 'Why do you call me "Lord, Lord", and do not do what I tell you? 47I will show you what someone is like who comes to me, hears my words, and acts on them. 48That one is like a man building a house, who dug deeply and laid the foundation on rock; when a flood arose, the river burst against that house but could not shake it, because it had been well built.ᵃ 49But the one who hears and does not act is like a man who built a house on the ground without a foundation. When the river burst against it, immediately it fell, and great was the ruin of that house.'

Jesus Heals a Centurion's Servant

7 After Jesusᵇ had finished all his sayings in the hearing of the people, he entered Capernaum. 2A centurion there had a slave whom he valued highly, and who was ill and close to death. 3When he heard about Jesus, he sent some Jewish elders to him, asking him to come and heal his slave. 4When they came to Jesus, they appealed to him earnestly, saying, 'He is worthy of having you do this for him, 5for he loves our people, and it is he who built our synagogue for us.' 6And Jesus went with them, but when he was not far from the house, the centurion sent friends to say to him, 'Lord, do not trouble yourself, for I am not worthy to have you come under my roof; 7therefore I did not presume to come to you. But only speak the word, and let my servant be healed. 8For I also am a man set under authority, with soldiers under me; and I say to one, "Go", and he goes, and to another, "Come", and he

comes, and to my slave, "Do this", and the slave does it.' 9When Jesus heard this he was amazed at him, and turning to the crowd that followed him, he said, 'I tell you, not even in Israel have I found such faith.' 10When those who had been sent returned to the house, they found the slave in good health.

Jesus Raises the Widow's Son at Nain

11 Soon afterwardsᶜ he went to a town called Nain, and his disciples and a large crowd went with him. 12As he approached the gate of the town, a man who had died was being carried out. He was his mother's only son, and she was a widow; and with her was a large crowd from the town. 13When the Lord saw her, he had compassion for her and said to her, 'Do not weep.' 14Then he came forward and touched the bier, and the bearers stood still. And he said, 'Young man, I say to you, rise!' 15The dead man sat up and began to speak, and Jesusᵇ gave him to his mother. 16Fear seized all of them; and they glorified God, saying, 'A great prophet has risen among us!' and 'God has looked favourably on his people!' 17This word about him spread throughout Judea and all the surrounding country.

Messengers from John the Baptist

18 The disciples of John reported all these things to him. So John summoned two of his disciples 19and sent them to the Lord to ask, 'Are you the one who is to come, or are we to wait for another?' 20When the men had come to him, they said, 'John the Baptist has sent us to you to ask, "Are you the one who is to come, or are we to wait for another?" ' 21Jesusᵈ had just then cured many people of diseases, plagues, and evil spirits, and had given sight to many who were blind. 22And he answered them, 'Go and tell John what you have seen and heard: the blind receive their sight, the lame walk, the lepersᵉ are cleansed, the deaf hear, the dead are raised,

---

a Other ancient authorities read *founded upon the rock*
b Gk *he*   c Other ancient authorities read *Next day*
d Gk *He*   e The terms *leper* and *leprosy* can refer to several diseases

the poor have good news brought to them. [23] And blessed is anyone who takes no offence at me.'

24 When John's messengers had gone, Jesus[a] began to speak to the crowds about John:[b] 'What did you go out into the wilderness to look at? A reed shaken by the wind? [25] What then did you go out to see? Someone[c] dressed in soft robes? Look, those who put on fine clothing and live in luxury are in royal palaces. [26] What then did you go out to see? A prophet? Yes, I tell you, and more than a prophet. [27] This is the one about whom it is written,

"See, I am sending my messenger
    ahead of you,
who will prepare your way
    before you."

[28] I tell you, among those born of women no one is greater than John; yet the least in the kingdom of God is greater than he.' [29] (And all the people who heard this, including the tax-collectors, acknowledged the justice of God,[d] because they had been baptized with John's baptism. [30] But by refusing to be baptized by him, the Pharisees and the lawyers rejected God's purpose for themselves.)

31 'To what then will I compare the people of this generation, and what are they like? [32] They are like children sitting in the market-place and calling to one another,

"We played the flute for you, and you
    did not dance;
we wailed, and you did not weep."

[33] For John the Baptist has come eating no bread and drinking no wine, and you say, "He has a demon"; [34] the Son of Man has come eating and drinking, and you say, "Look, a glutton and a drunkard, a friend of tax-collectors and sinners!" [35] Nevertheless, wisdom is vindicated by all her children.'

A Sinful Woman Forgiven

36 One of the Pharisees asked Jesus[b] to eat with him, and he went into the Pharisee's house and took his place at the table. [37] And a woman in the city, who was a sinner, having learned that he was eating in the Pharisee's house, brought an alabaster jar of ointment. [38] She stood behind him at his feet, weeping, and began to bathe his feet with her tears and to dry them with her hair. Then she continued kissing his feet and anointing them with the ointment. [39] Now when the Pharisee who had invited him saw it, he said to himself, 'If this man were a prophet, he would have known who and what kind of woman this is who is touching him—that she is a sinner.' [40] Jesus spoke up and said to him, 'Simon, I have something to say to you.' 'Teacher,' he replied, 'speak.' [41] 'A certain creditor had two debtors; one owed five hundred denarii,[e] and the other fifty. [42] When they could not pay, he cancelled the debts for both of them. Now which of them will love him more?' [43] Simon answered, 'I suppose the one for whom he cancelled the greater debt.' And Jesus[a] said to him, 'You have judged rightly.' [44] Then turning towards the woman, he said to Simon, 'Do you see this woman? I entered your house; you gave me no water for my feet, but she has bathed my feet with her tears and dried them with her hair. [45] You gave me no kiss, but from the time I came in she has not stopped kissing my feet. [46] You did not anoint my head with oil, but she has anointed my feet with ointment. [47] Therefore, I tell you, her sins, which were many, have been forgiven; hence she has shown great love. But the one to whom little is forgiven, loves little.' [48] Then he said to her, 'Your sins are forgiven.' [49] But those who were at the table with him began to say among themselves, 'Who is this who even forgives sins?' [50] And he said to the woman, 'Your faith has saved you; go in peace.'

Some Women Accompany Jesus

8 Soon afterwards he went on through cities and villages, proclaiming and bringing the good news of the kingdom of God. The twelve were with him, [2] as well as some women who had been cured of evil

---

a Gk *he*   *b* Gk *him*   *c* Or *Why then did you go out? To see someone*   *d* Or *praised God*   *e* The denarius was the usual day's wage for a labourer spirits and infirmities: Mary, called Magdalene, from whom seven demons had gone out, ³ and Joanna, the wife of Herod's steward Chuza, and Susanna, and many others, who provided for them*a* out of their resources.

The Parable of the Sower

4 When a great crowd gathered and people from town after town came to him, he said in a parable: ⁵ 'A sower went out to sow his seed; and as he sowed, some fell on the path and was trampled on, and the birds of the air ate it up. ⁶ Some fell on the rock; and as it grew up, it withered for lack of moisture. ⁷ Some fell among thorns, and the thorns grew with it and choked it. ⁸ Some fell into good soil, and when it grew, it produced a hundredfold.' As he said this, he called out, 'Let anyone with ears to hear listen!'

The Purpose of the Parables

9 Then his disciples asked him what this parable meant. ¹⁰ He said, 'To you it has been given to know the secrets*b* of the kingdom of God; but to others I speak*c* in parables, so that

"looking they may not perceive,
  and listening they may not
    understand."

The Parable of the Sower Explained

11 'Now the parable is this: The seed is the word of God. ¹² The ones on the path are those who have heard; then the devil comes and takes away the word from their hearts, so that they may not believe and be saved. ¹³ The ones on the rock are those who, when they hear the word, receive it with joy. But these have no root; they believe only for a while and in a time of testing fall away. ¹⁴ As for what fell among the thorns, these are the ones who hear; but as they go on their way, they are choked by the cares and riches and pleasures of life, and their fruit does not mature. ¹⁵ But as for that in the good soil, these are the ones who, when they hear the word, hold it fast in an honest and good heart, and bear fruit with patient endurance.

A Lamp under a Jar

16 'No one after lighting a lamp hides it under a jar, or puts it under a bed, but puts it on a lampstand, so that those who enter may see the light. ¹⁷ For nothing is hidden that will not be disclosed, nor is anything secret that will not become known and come to light. ¹⁸ Then pay attention to how you listen; for to those who have, more will be given; and from those who do not have, even what they seem to have will be taken away.'

The True Kindred of Jesus

19 Then his mother and his brothers came to him, but they could not reach him because of the crowd. ²⁰ And he was told, 'Your mother and your brothers are standing outside, wanting to see you.' ²¹ But he said to them, 'My mother and my brothers are those who hear the word of God and do it.'

Jesus Calms a Storm

22 One day he got into a boat with his disciples, and he said to them, 'Let us go across to the other side of the lake.' So they put out, ²³ and while they were sailing he fell asleep. A gale swept down on the lake, and the boat was filling with water, and they were in danger. ²⁴ They went to him and woke him up, shouting, 'Master, Master, we are perishing!' And he woke up and rebuked the wind and the raging waves; they ceased, and there was a calm. ²⁵ He said to them, 'Where is your faith?' They were afraid and amazed, and said to one another, 'Who then is this, that he commands even the winds and the water, and they obey him?'

Jesus Heals the Gerasene Demoniac

26 Then they arrived at the country of the Gerasenes,*d* which is opposite Galilee. ²⁷ As he stepped out on land, a man of the city who had demons met him. For a long time he had worn*e* no clothes, and he did

not live in a house but in the tombs. 28When he saw Jesus, he fell down before him and shouted at the top of his voice, 'What have you to do with me, Jesus, Son of the Most High God? I beg you, do not torment me'— 29for Jesus*a* had commanded the unclean spirit to come out of the man. (For many times it had seized him; he was kept under guard and bound with chains and shackles, but he would break the bonds and be driven by the demon into the wilds.) 30Jesus then asked him, 'What is your name?' He said, 'Legion'; for many demons had entered him. 31They begged him not to order them to go back into the abyss.

32 Now there on the hillside a large herd of swine was feeding; and the demons*b* begged Jesus*c* to let them enter these. So he gave them permission. 33Then the demons came out of the man and entered the swine, and the herd rushed down the steep bank into the lake and was drowned.

34 When the swineherds saw what had happened, they ran off and told it in the city and in the country. 35Then people came out to see what had happened, and when they came to Jesus, they found the man from whom the demons had gone sitting at the feet of Jesus, clothed and in his right mind. And they were afraid. 36Those who had seen it told them how the one who had been possessed by demons had been healed. 37Then all the people of the surrounding country of the Gerasenes*d* asked Jesus*c* to leave them; for they were seized with great fear. So he got into the boat and returned. 38The man from whom the demons had gone begged that he might be with him; but Jesus*a* sent him away, saying, 39'Return to your home, and declare how much God has done for you.' So he went away, proclaiming throughout the city how much Jesus had done for him.

A Girl Restored to Life and a Woman Healed

40 Now when Jesus returned, the crowd welcomed him, for they were all waiting for him. 41Just then there came a man named Jairus, a leader of the synagogue. He fell at Jesus' feet and begged him to come to his house, 42for he had an only daughter, about twelve years old, who was dying.

As he went, the crowds pressed in on him. 43Now there was a woman who had been suffering from haemorrhages for twelve years; and though she had spent all she had on physicians,*e* no one could cure her. 44She came up behind him and touched the fringe of his clothes, and immediately her haemorrhage stopped. 45Then Jesus asked, 'Who touched me?' When all denied it, Peter*f* said, 'Master, the crowds surround you and press in on you.' 46But Jesus said, 'Someone touched me; for I noticed that power had gone out from me.' 47When the woman saw that she could not remain hidden, she came trembling; and falling down before him, she declared in the presence of all the people why she had touched him, and how she had been immediately healed. 48He said to her, 'Daughter, your faith has made you well; go in peace.'

49 While he was still speaking, someone came from the leader's house to say, 'Your daughter is dead; do not trouble the teacher any longer.' 50When Jesus heard this, he replied, 'Do not fear. Only believe, and she will be saved.' 51When he came to the house, he did not allow anyone to enter with him, except Peter, John, and James, and the child's father and mother. 52They were all weeping and wailing for her; but he said, 'Do not weep; for she is not dead but sleeping.' 53And they laughed at him, knowing that she was dead. 54But he took her by the hand and called out, 'Child, get up!' 55Her spirit returned, and she got up at once. Then he directed them to give her something to eat. 56Her parents were astounded; but he ordered them to tell no one what had happened.

a Gk *he*   *b* Gk *they*   *c* Gk *him*   *d* Other ancient authorities read *Gadarenes*; others, *Gergesenes*   *e* Other ancient authorities lack *and though she had spent all she had on physicians*   *f* Other ancient authorities add *and those who were with him*

The Mission of the Twelve

9 Then Jesus*a* called the twelve together and gave them power and authority over all demons and to cure diseases, 2 and he sent them out to proclaim the kingdom of God and to heal. 3 He said to them, 'Take nothing for your journey, no staff, nor bag, nor bread, nor money—not even an extra tunic. 4 Whatever house you enter, stay there, and leave from there. 5 Wherever they do not welcome you, as you are leaving that town shake the dust off your feet as a testimony against them.' 6 They departed and went through the villages, bringing the good news and curing diseases everywhere.

Herod's Perplexity

7 Now Herod the ruler*b* heard about all that had taken place, and he was perplexed, because it was said by some that John had been raised from the dead, 8 by some that Elijah had appeared, and by others that one of the ancient prophets had arisen. 9 Herod said, 'John I beheaded; but who is this about whom I hear such things?' And he tried to see him.

Feeding the Five Thousand

10 On their return the apostles told Jesus*c* all they had done. He took them with him and withdrew privately to a city called Bethsaida. 11 When the crowds found out about it, they followed him; and he welcomed them, and spoke to them about the kingdom of God, and healed those who needed to be cured.

12 The day was drawing to a close, and the twelve came to him and said, 'Send the crowd away, so that they may go into the surrounding villages and countryside, to lodge and get provisions; for we are here in a deserted place.' 13 But he said to them, 'You give them something to eat.' They said, 'We have no more than five loaves and two fish—unless we are to go and buy food for all these people.' 14 For there were about five thousand men. And he said to his disciples, 'Make them sit down in groups of about fifty each.' 15 They did so and made them all sit down. 16 And taking the five loaves and the two fish, he looked up to heaven, and blessed and broke them, and gave them to the disciples to set before the crowd. 17 And all ate and were filled. What was left over was gathered up, twelve baskets of broken pieces.

Peter's Declaration about Jesus

18 Once when Jesus*a* was praying alone, with only the disciples near him, he asked them, 'Who do the crowds say that I am?' 19 They answered, 'John the Baptist; but others, Elijah; and still others, that one of the ancient prophets has arisen.' 20 He said to them, 'But who do you say that I am?' Peter answered, 'The Messiah*d* of God.'

Jesus Foretells His Death and Resurrection

21 He sternly ordered and commanded them not to tell anyone, 22 saying, 'The Son of Man must undergo great suffering, and be rejected by the elders, chief priests, and scribes, and be killed, and on the third day be raised.'

23 Then he said to them all, 'If any want to become my followers, let them deny themselves and take up their cross daily and follow me. 24 For those who want to save their life will lose it, and those who lose their life for my sake will save it. 25 What does it profit them if they gain the whole world, but lose or forfeit themselves? 26 Those who are ashamed of me and of my words, of them the Son of Man will be ashamed when he comes in his glory and the glory of the Father and of the holy angels. 27 But truly I tell you, there are some standing here who will not taste death before they see the kingdom of God.'

The Transfiguration

28 Now about eight days after these sayings Jesus*a* took with him Peter and John and James, and went up on the mountain to pray. 29 And while he was praying, the appearance of his face changed, and his clothes became dazzling

a Gk *he*   *b* Gk *tetrarch*   *c* Gk *him*   *d* Or *The Christ* white. 30 Suddenly they saw two men, Moses and Elijah, talking to him. 31 They appeared in glory and were speaking of his departure, which he was about to accomplish at Jerusalem. 32 Now Peter and his companions were weighed down with sleep; but since they had stayed awake,*d* they saw his glory and the two men who stood with him. 33 Just as they were leaving him, Peter said to Jesus, 'Master, it is good for us to be here; let us make three dwellings,*b* one for you, one for Moses, and one for Elijah'—not knowing what he said. 34 While he was saying this, a cloud came and overshadowed them; and they were terrified as they entered the cloud. 35 Then from the cloud came a voice that said, 'This is my Son, my Chosen;*c* listen to him!' 36 When the voice had spoken, Jesus was found alone. And they kept silent and in those days told no one any of the things they had seen.

Jesus Heals a Boy with a Demon

37 On the next day, when they had come down from the mountain, a great crowd met him. 38 Just then a man from the crowd shouted, 'Teacher, I beg you to look at my son; he is my only child. 39 Suddenly a spirit seizes him, and all at once he*d* shrieks. It throws him into convulsions until he foams at the mouth; it mauls him and will scarcely leave him. 40 I begged your disciples to cast it out, but they could not.' 41 Jesus answered, 'You faithless and perverse generation, how much longer must I be with you and bear with you? Bring your son here.' 42 While he was coming, the demon dashed him to the ground in convulsions. But Jesus rebuked the unclean spirit, healed the boy, and gave him back to his father. 43 And all were astounded at the greatness of God.

Jesus Again Foretells His Death

While everyone was amazed at all that he was doing, he said to his disciples, 44 'Let these words sink into your ears: The Son of Man is going to be betrayed into human hands.' 45 But they did not understand this saying; its meaning was concealed from them, so that they could not perceive it. And they were afraid to ask him about this saying.

True Greatness

46 An argument arose among them as to which one of them was the greatest. 47 But Jesus, aware of their inner thoughts, took a little child and put it by his side, 48 and said to them, 'Whoever welcomes this child in my name welcomes me, and whoever welcomes me welcomes the one who sent me; for the least among all of you is the greatest.'

Another Exorcist

49 John answered, 'Master, we saw someone casting out demons in your name, and we tried to stop him, because he does not follow with us.' 50 But Jesus said to him, 'Do not stop him; for whoever is not against you is for you.'

A Samaritan Village Refuses to Receive Jesus

51 When the days drew near for him to be taken up, he set his face to go to Jerusalem. 52 And he sent messengers ahead of him. On their way they entered a village of the Samaritans to make ready for him; 53 but they did not receive him, because his face was set towards Jerusalem. 54 When his disciples James and John saw it, they said, 'Lord, do you want us to command fire to come down from heaven and consume them?'*e* 55 But he turned and rebuked them. 56 Then*f* they went on to another village.

Would-Be Followers of Jesus

57 As they were going along the road, someone said to him, 'I will follow you wherever you go.' 58 And Jesus said to him, 'Foxes have holes, and birds of the air have nests; but the Son of Man has nowhere to

---

a Or *but when they were fully awake*   *b* Or *tents*
c Other ancient authorities read *my Beloved*   *d* Or *it*
e Other ancient authorities add *as Elijah did*   *f* Other ancient authorities read *rebuked them, and said, 'You do not know what spirit you are of,* 56 *for the Son of Man has not come to destroy the lives of human beings but to save them.' Then*

lay his head.' ⁵⁹To another he said, 'Follow me.' But he said, 'Lord, first let me go and bury my father.' ⁶⁰But Jesus*a* said to him, 'Let the dead bury their own dead; but as for you, go and proclaim the kingdom of God.' ⁶¹Another said, 'I will follow you, Lord; but let me first say farewell to those at my home.' ⁶²Jesus said to him, 'No one who puts a hand to the plough and looks back is fit for the kingdom of God.'

The Mission of the Seventy

10 After this the Lord appointed seventy*b* others and sent them on ahead of him in pairs to every town and place where he himself intended to go. ²He said to them, 'The harvest is plentiful, but the labourers are few; therefore ask the Lord of the harvest to send out labourers into his harvest. ³Go on your way. See, I am sending you out like lambs into the midst of wolves. ⁴Carry no purse, no bag, no sandals; and greet no one on the road. ⁵Whatever house you enter, first say, "Peace to this house!" ⁶And if anyone is there who shares in peace, your peace will rest on that person; but if not, it will return to you. ⁷Remain in the same house, eating and drinking whatever they provide, for the labourer deserves to be paid. Do not move about from house to house. ⁸Whenever you enter a town and its people welcome you, eat what is set before you; ⁹cure the sick who are there, and say to them, "The kingdom of God has come near to you."*c* ¹⁰But whenever you enter a town and they do not welcome you, go out into its streets and say, ¹¹"Even the dust of your town that clings to our feet, we wipe off in protest against you. Yet know this: the kingdom of God has come near."*d* ¹²I tell you, on that day it will be more tolerable for Sodom than for that town.

Woes to Unrepentant Cities

¹³ 'Woe to you, Chorazin! Woe to you, Bethsaida! For if the deeds of power done in you had been done in Tyre and Sidon, they would have repented long ago, sitting in sackcloth and ashes. ¹⁴But at the judge-

ment it will be more tolerable for Tyre and Sidon than for you. ¹⁵And you, Capernaum,

will you be exalted to heaven?
No, you will be brought down
to Hades.

16 'Whoever listens to you listens to me, and whoever rejects you rejects me, and whoever rejects me rejects the one who sent me.'

The Return of the Seventy

17 The seventy*b* returned with joy, saying, 'Lord, in your name even the demons submit to us!' ¹⁸He said to them, 'I watched Satan fall from heaven like a flash of lightning. ¹⁹See, I have given you authority to tread on snakes and scorpions, and over all the power of the enemy; and nothing will hurt you. ²⁰Nevertheless, do not rejoice at this, that the spirits submit to you, but rejoice that your names are written in heaven.'

Jesus Rejoices

21 At that same hour Jesus*a* rejoiced in the Holy Spirit*e* and said, 'I thank*f* you, Father, Lord of heaven and earth, because you have hidden these things from the wise and the intelligent and have revealed them to infants; yes, Father, for such was your gracious will.*g* ²²All things have been handed over to me by my Father; and no one knows who the Son is except the Father, or who the Father is except the Son and anyone to whom the Son chooses to reveal him.'

23 Then turning to the disciples, Jesus*a* said to them privately, 'Blessed are the eyes that see what you see! ²⁴For I tell you that many prophets and kings desired to see what you see, but did not see it, and to hear what you hear, but did not hear it.'

The Parable of the Good Samaritan

25 Just then a lawyer stood up to test Jesus.*h* 'Teacher,' he said, 'what must I do to

a Gk he   *b* Other ancient authorities read *seventy-two*   *c* Or *is at hand for you*   *d* Or *is at hand*   *e* Other authorities read *in the spirit*   *f* Or *praise*   *g* Or *for so it was well-pleasing in your sight*   *h* Gk *him* inherit eternal life?' ²⁶He said to him, 'What is written in the law? What do you read there?' ²⁷He answered, 'You shall love the Lord your God with all your heart, and with all your soul, and with all your strength, and with all your mind; and your neighbour as yourself.' ²⁸And he said to him, 'You have given the right answer; do this, and you will live.'

29 But wanting to justify himself, he asked Jesus, 'And who is my neighbour?' ³⁰Jesus replied, 'A man was going down from Jerusalem to Jericho, and fell into the hands of robbers, who stripped him, beat him, and went away, leaving him half dead. ³¹Now by chance a priest was going down that road; and when he saw him, he passed by on the other side. ³²So likewise a Levite, when he came to the place and saw him, passed by on the other side. ³³But a Samaritan while travelling came near him; and when he saw him, he was moved with pity. ³⁴He went to him and bandaged his wounds, having poured oil and wine on them. Then he put him on his own animal, brought him to an inn, and took care of him. ³⁵The next day he took out two denarii,ᵃ gave them to the innkeeper, and said, "Take care of him; and when I come back, I will repay you whatever more you spend." ³⁶Which of these three, do you think, was a neighbour to the man who fell into the hands of the robbers?' ³⁷He said, 'The one who showed him mercy.' Jesus said to him, 'Go and do likewise.'

Jesus Visits Martha and Mary

38 Now as they went on their way, he entered a certain village, where a woman named Martha welcomed him into her home. ³⁹She had a sister named Mary, who sat at the Lord's feet and listened to what he was saying. ⁴⁰But Martha was distracted by her many tasks; so she came to him and asked, 'Lord, do you not care that my sister has left me to do all the work by myself? Tell her then to help me.' ⁴¹But the Lord answered her, 'Martha, Martha, you are worried and distracted by many things; ⁴²there is need of only one thing.ᵇ Mary

has chosen the better part, which will not be taken away from her.'

The Lord's Prayer

11 He was praying in a certain place, and after he had finished, one of his disciples said to him, 'Lord, teach us to pray, as John taught his disciples.' ²He said to them, 'When you pray, say:

Father,ᶜ hallowed be your name.
        Your kingdom come.ᵈ
3   Give us each day our daily bread.ᵉ
4   And forgive us our sins,
        for we ourselves forgive everyone
            indebted to us.
        And do not bring us to the time of
            trial.'ᶠ

Perseverance in Prayer

5 And he said to them, 'Suppose one of you has a friend, and you go to him at midnight and say to him, "Friend, lend me three loaves of bread; ⁶for a friend of mine has arrived, and I have nothing to set before him." ⁷And he answers from within, "Do not bother me; the door has already been locked, and my children are with me in bed; I cannot get up and give you anything." ⁸I tell you, even though he will not get up and give him anything because he is his friend, at least because of his persistence he will get up and give him whatever he needs.

9 'So I say to you, Ask, and it will be given to you; search, and you will find; knock, and the door will be opened for you. ¹⁰For everyone who asks receives, and everyone who searches finds, and for everyone who knocks, the door will be opened. ¹¹Is there anyone among you who, if your child asks forᵍ a fish, will give a snake instead of a fish? ¹²Or if the child asks for an egg, will give a scorpion? ¹³If

a The denarius was the usual day's wage for a labourer
b Other ancient authorities read *few things are necessary, or only one*   c Other ancient authorities read *Our Father in heaven*   d A few ancient authorities read *Your Holy Spirit come upon us and cleanse us.* Other ancient authorities add *Your will be done, on earth as in heaven*   e Or *our bread for tomorrow*   f Or *us into temptation.* Other ancient authorities add *but rescue us from the evil one* (or *from evil*)   g Other ancient authorities add *bread, will give a stone; or if your child asks for*

you then, who are evil, know how to give good gifts to your children, how much more will the heavenly Father give the Holy Spirit*a* to those who ask him!'

Jesus and Beelzebul

14 Now he was casting out a demon that was mute; when the demon had gone out, the one who had been mute spoke, and the crowds were amazed. 15 But some of them said, 'He casts out demons by Beelzebul, the ruler of the demons.' 16 Others, to test him, kept demanding from him a sign from heaven. 17 But he knew what they were thinking and said to them, 'Every kingdom divided against itself becomes a desert, and house falls on house. 18 If Satan also is divided against himself, how will his kingdom stand? —for you say that I cast out the demons by Beelzebul. 19 Now if I cast out the demons by Beelzebul, by whom do your exorcists*b* cast them out? Therefore they will be your judges. 20 But if it is by the finger of God that I cast out the demons, then the kingdom of God has come to you. 21 When a strong man, fully armed, guards his castle, his property is safe. 22 But when one stronger than he attacks him and overpowers him, he takes away his armour in which he trusted and divides his plunder. 23 Whoever is not with me is against me, and whoever does not gather with me scatters.

The Return of the Unclean Spirit

24 'When the unclean spirit has gone out of a person, it wanders through waterless regions looking for a resting-place, but not finding any, it says, "I will return to my house from which I came." 25 When it comes, it finds it swept and put in order. 26 Then it goes and brings seven other spirits more evil than itself, and they enter and live there; and the last state of that person is worse than the first.'

True Blessedness

27 While he was saying this, a woman in the crowd raised her voice and said to him, 'Blessed is the womb that bore you

and the breasts that nursed you!' 28 But he said, 'Blessed rather are those who hear the word of God and obey it!'

The Sign of Jonah

29 When the crowds were increasing, he began to say, 'This generation is an evil generation; it asks for a sign, but no sign will be given to it except the sign of Jonah. 30 For just as Jonah became a sign to the people of Nineveh, so the Son of Man will be to this generation. 31 The queen of the South will rise at the judgement with the people of this generation and condemn them, because she came from the ends of the earth to listen to the wisdom of Solomon, and see, something greater than Solomon is here! 32 The people of Nineveh will rise up at the judgement with this generation and condemn it, because they repented at the proclamation of Jonah, and see, something greater than Jonah is here!

The Light of the Body

33 'No one after lighting a lamp puts it in a cellar,*c* but on the lampstand so that those who enter may see the light. 34 Your eye is the lamp of your body. If your eye is healthy, your whole body is full of light; but if it is not healthy, your body is full of darkness. 35 Therefore consider whether the light in you is not darkness. 36 If then your whole body is full of light, with no part of it in darkness, it will be as full of light as when a lamp gives you light with its rays.'

Jesus Denounces Pharisees and Lawyers

37 While he was speaking, a Pharisee invited him to dine with him; so he went in and took his place at the table. 38 The Pharisee was amazed to see that he did not first wash before dinner. 39 Then the Lord said to him, 'Now you Pharisees clean the outside of the cup and of the dish, but inside you are full of greed and wickedness. 40 You fools! Did not the one who made

a Other ancient authorities read *the Father give the Holy Spirit from heaven*   *b* Gk *sons*   *c* Other ancient authorities add *or under the bushel basket* the outside make the inside also? ⁴¹ So give for alms those things that are within; and see, everything will be clean for you.

42 'But woe to you Pharisees! For you tithe mint and rue and herbs of all kinds, and neglect justice and the love of God; it is these you ought to have practised, without neglecting the others. ⁴³ Woe to you Pharisees! For you love to have the seat of honour in the synagogues and to be greeted with respect in the market-places. ⁴⁴ Woe to you! For you are like unmarked graves, and people walk over them without realizing it.'

45 One of the lawyers answered him, 'Teacher, when you say these things, you insult us too.' ⁴⁶ And he said, 'Woe also to you lawyers! For you load people with burdens hard to bear, and you yourselves do not lift a finger to ease them. ⁴⁷ Woe to you! For you build the tombs of the prophets whom your ancestors killed. ⁴⁸ So you are witnesses and approve of the deeds of your ancestors; for they killed them, and you build their tombs. ⁴⁹ Therefore also the Wisdom of God said, "I will send them prophets and apostles, some of whom they will kill and persecute", ⁵⁰ so that this generation may be charged with the blood of all the prophets shed since the foundation of the world, ⁵¹ from the blood of Abel to the blood of Zechariah, who perished between the altar and the sanctuary. Yes, I tell you, it will be charged against this generation. ⁵² Woe to you lawyers! For you have taken away the key of knowledge; you did not enter yourselves, and you hindered those who were entering.'

53 When he went outside, the scribes and the Pharisees began to be very hostile towards him and to cross-examine him about many things, ⁵⁴ lying in wait for him, to catch him in something he might say.

A Warning against Hypocrisy

12 Meanwhile, when the crowd gathered in thousands, so that they trampled on one another, he began to speak first to his disciples, 'Beware of the yeast of the Pharisees, that is, their hypoc-

risy. ² Nothing is covered up that will not be uncovered, and nothing secret that will not become known. ³ Therefore whatever you have said in the dark will be heard in the light, and what you have whispered behind closed doors will be proclaimed from the housetops.

Exhortation to Fearless Confession

4 'I tell you, my friends, do not fear those who kill the body, and after that can do nothing more. ⁵ But I will warn you whom to fear: fear him who, after he has killed, has authority^a to cast into hell.^b Yes, I tell you, fear him! ⁶ Are not five sparrows sold for two pennies? Yet not one of them is forgotten in God's sight. ⁷ But even the hairs of your head are all counted. Do not be afraid; you are of more value than many sparrows.

8 'And I tell you, everyone who acknowledges me before others, the Son of Man also will acknowledge before the angels of God; ⁹ but whoever denies me before others will be denied before the angels of God. ¹⁰ And everyone who speaks a word against the Son of Man will be forgiven; but whoever blasphemes against the Holy Spirit will not be forgiven. ¹¹ When they bring you before the synagogues, the rulers, and the authorities, do not worry about how^c you are to defend yourselves or what you are to say; ¹² for the Holy Spirit will teach you at that very hour what you ought to say.'

The Parable of the Rich Fool

13 Someone in the crowd said to him, 'Teacher, tell my brother to divide the family inheritance with me.' ¹⁴ But he said to him, 'Friend, who set me to be a judge or arbitrator over you?' ¹⁵ And he said to them, 'Take care! Be on your guard against all kinds of greed; for one's life does not consist in the abundance of possessions.' ¹⁶ Then he told them a parable: 'The land of a rich man produced abundantly. ¹⁷ And he thought to himself, "What should I do, for I have no place to store my crops?"

a Or power   b Gk Gehenna   c Other ancient authorities add or what

18 Then he said, "I will do this: I will pull down my barns and build larger ones, and there I will store all my grain and my goods. 19 And I will say to my soul, Soul, you have ample goods laid up for many years; relax, eat, drink, be merry." 20 But God said to him, "You fool! This very night·your life is being demanded of you. And the things you have prepared, whose will they be?" 21 So it is with those who store up treasures for themselves but are not rich towards God.'

Do Not Worry

22 He said to his disciples, 'Therefore I tell you, do not worry about your life, what you will eat, or about your body, what you will wear. 23 For life is more than food, and the body more than clothing. 24 Consider the ravens: they neither sow nor reap, they have neither storehouse nor barn, and yet God feeds them. Of how much more value are you than the birds! 25 And can any of you by worrying add a single hour to your span of life?ᵃ 26 If then you are not able to do so small a thing as that, why do you worry about the rest? 27 Consider the lilies, how they grow: they neither toil nor spin;ᵇ yet I tell you, even Solomon in all his glory was not clothed like one of these. 28 But if God so clothes the grass of the field, which is alive today and tomorrow is thrown into the oven, how much more will he clothe you—you of little faith! 29 And do not keep striving for what you are to eat and what you are to drink, and do not keep worrying. 30 For it is the nations of the world that strive after all these things, and your Father knows that you need them. 31 Instead, strive for hisᶜ kingdom, and these things will be given to you as well.

32 'Do not be afraid, little flock, for it is your Father's good pleasure to give you the kingdom. 33 Sell your possessions, and give alms. Make purses for yourselves that do not wear out, an unfailing treasure in heaven, where no thief comes near and no moth destroys. 34 For where your treasure is, there your heart will be also.

Watchful Slaves

35 'Be dressed for action and have your lamps lit; 36 be like those who are waiting for their master to return from the wedding banquet, so that they may open the door for him as soon as he comes and knocks. 37 Blessed are those slaves whom the master finds alert when he comes; truly I tell you, he will fasten his belt and have them sit down to eat, and he will come and serve them. 38 If he comes during the middle of the night, or near dawn, and finds them so, blessed are those slaves.

39 'But know this: if the owner of the house had known at what hour the thief was coming, heᵈ would not have let his house be broken into. 40 You also must be ready, for the Son of Man is coming at an unexpected hour.'

The Faithful or the Unfaithful Slave

41 Peter said, 'Lord, are you telling this parable for us or for everyone?' 42 And the Lord said, 'Who then is the faithful and prudent manager whom his master will put in charge of his slaves, to give them their allowance of food at the proper time? 43 Blessed is that slave whom his master will find at work when he arrives. 44 Truly I tell you, he will put that one in charge of all his possessions. 45 But if that slave says to himself, "My master is delayed in coming", and if he begins to beat the other slaves, men and women, and to eat and drink and get drunk, 46 the master of that slave will come on a day when he does not expect him and at an hour that he does not know, and will cut him in pieces,ᵉ and put him with the unfaithful. 47 That slave who knew what his master wanted, but did not prepare himself or do what was wanted, will receive a severe beating. 48 But one who did not know and did what deserved a beating will receive a light beating. From everyone to whom much has been given, much will be required; and from one to

---

a Or add a cubit to your stature   b Other ancient authorities read Consider the lilies; they neither spin nor weave   c Other ancient authorities read God's   d Other ancient authorities add would have watched and   e Or cut him off whom much has been entrusted, even more will be demanded.

Jesus the Cause of Division

49 'I came to bring fire to the earth, and how I wish it were already kindled! 50 I have a baptism with which to be baptized, and what stress I am under until it is completed! 51 Do you think that I have come to bring peace to the earth? No, I tell you, but rather division! 52 From now on, five in one household will be divided, three against two and two against three; 53 they will be divided:

father against son
  and son against father,
mother against daughter
  and daughter against mother,
mother-in-law against her daughter-
  in-law
  and daughter-in-law against
    mother-in-law.'

Interpreting the Time

54 He also said to the crowds, 'When you see a cloud rising in the west, you immediately say, "It is going to rain"; and so it happens. 55 And when you see the south wind blowing, you say, "There will be scorching heat"; and it happens. 56 You hypocrites! You know how to interpret the appearance of earth and sky, but why do you not know how to interpret the present time?

Settling with Your Opponent

57 'And why do you not judge for yourselves what is right? 58 Thus, when you go with your accuser before a magistrate, on the way make an effort to settle the case, a or you may be dragged before the judge, and the judge hand you over to the officer, and the officer throw you in prison. 59 I tell you, you will never get out until you have paid the very last penny.'

Repent or Perish

13 At that very time there were some present who told him about the Galileans whose blood Pilate had mingled with their sacrifices. 2 He asked them,

'Do you think that because these Galileans suffered in this way they were worse sinners than all other Galileans? 3 No, I tell you; but unless you repent, you will all perish as they did. 4 Or those eighteen who were killed when the tower of Siloam fell on them—do you think that they were worse offenders than all the others living in Jerusalem? 5 No, I tell you; but unless you repent, you will all perish just as they did.'

The Parable of the Barren Fig Tree

6 Then he told this parable: 'A man had a fig tree planted in his vineyard; and he came looking for fruit on it and found none. 7 So he said to the gardener, "See here! For three years I have come looking for fruit on this fig tree, and still I find none. Cut it down! Why should it be wasting the soil?" 8 He replied, "Sir, let it alone for one more year, until I dig round it and put manure on it. 9 If it bears fruit next year, well and good; but if not, you can cut it down." '

Jesus Heals a Crippled Woman

10 Now he was teaching in one of the synagogues on the sabbath. 11 And just then there appeared a woman with a spirit that had crippled her for eighteen years. She was bent over and was quite unable to stand up straight. 12 When Jesus saw her, he called her over and said, 'Woman, you are set free from your ailment.' 13 When he laid his hands on her, immediately she stood up straight and began praising God. 14 But the leader of the synagogue, indignant because Jesus had cured on the sabbath, kept saying to the crowd, 'There are six days on which work ought to be done; come on those days and be cured, and not on the sabbath day.' 15 But the Lord answered him and said, 'You hypocrites! Does not each of you on the sabbath untie his ox or his donkey from the manger, and lead it away to give it water? 16 And ought not this woman, a daughter of Abraham whom Satan bound for eighteen long years, be set free from this bondage on the

a Gk settle with him

sabbath day?' [17]When he said this, all his opponents were put to shame; and the entire crowd was rejoicing at all the wonderful things that he was doing.

The Parable of the Mustard Seed

18 He said therefore, 'What is the kingdom of God like? And to what should I compare it? [19]It is like a mustard seed that someone took and sowed in the garden; it grew and became a tree, and the birds of the air made nests in its branches.'

The Parable of the Yeast

20 And again he said, 'To what should I compare the kingdom of God? [21]It is like yeast that a woman took and mixed in with[a] three measures of flour until all of it was leavened.'

The Narrow Door

22 Jesus[b] went through one town and village after another, teaching as he made his way to Jerusalem. [23]Someone asked him, 'Lord, will only a few be saved?' He said to them, [24]'Strive to enter through the narrow door; for many, I tell you, will try to enter and will not be able. [25]When once the owner of the house has got up and shut the door, and you begin to stand outside and to knock at the door, saying, "Lord, open to us", then in reply he will say to you, "I do not know where you come from." [26]Then you will begin to say, "We ate and drank with you, and you taught in our streets." [27]But he will say, "I do not know where you come from; go away from me, all you evildoers!" [28]There will be weeping and gnashing of teeth when you see Abraham and Isaac and Jacob and all the prophets in the kingdom of God, and you yourselves thrown out. [29]Then people will come from east and west, from north and south, and will eat in the kingdom of God. [30]Indeed, some are last who will be first, and some are first who will be last.'

The Lament over Jerusalem

31 At that very hour some Pharisees came and said to him, 'Get away from here, for Herod wants to kill you.' [32]He said to them, 'Go and tell that fox for me,[c] "Listen, I am casting out demons and performing cures today and tomorrow, and on the third day I finish my work. [33]Yet today, tomorrow, and the next day I must be on my way, because it is impossible for a prophet to be killed away from Jerusalem." [34]Jerusalem, Jerusalem, the city that kills the prophets and stones those who are sent to it! How often have I desired to gather your children together as a hen gathers her brood under her wings, and you were not willing! [35]See, your house is left to you. And I tell you, you will not see me until the time comes when[d] you say, "Blessed is the one who comes in the name of the Lord." '

Jesus Heals the Man with Dropsy

14 On one occasion when Jesus[e] was going to the house of a leader of the Pharisees to eat a meal on the sabbath, they were watching him closely. [2]Just then, in front of him, there was a man who had dropsy. [3]And Jesus asked the lawyers and Pharisees, 'Is it lawful to cure people on the sabbath, or not?' [4]But they were silent. So Jesus[e] took him and healed him, and sent him away. [5]Then he said to them, 'If one of you has a child[f] or an ox that has fallen into a well, will you not immediately pull it out on a sabbath day?' [6]And they could not reply to this.

Humility and Hospitality

7 When he noticed how the guests chose the places of honour, he told them a parable. [8]'When you are invited by someone to a wedding banquet, do not sit down at the place of honour, in case someone more distinguished than you has been invited by your host; [9]and the host who invited both of you may come and say to you, "Give this person your place", and then in disgrace you would start to take the lowest place. [10]But when you are invited, go and sit down at the lowest place, so that

a Gk *hid in*   *b* Gk *He*   *c* Gk lacks *for me*   *d* Other ancient authorities lack *the time comes when*   *e* Gk *he*   *f* Other ancient authorities read *a donkey* when your host comes, he may say to you, "Friend, move up higher"; then you will be honoured in the presence of all who sit at the table with you. ¹¹ For all who exalt themselves will be humbled, and those who humble themselves will be exalted.'

12 He said also to the one who had invited him, 'When you give a luncheon or a dinner, do not invite your friends or your brothers or your relatives or rich neighbours, in case they may invite you in return, and you would be repaid. ¹³ But when you give a banquet, invite the poor, the crippled, the lame, and the blind. ¹⁴ And you will be blessed, because they cannot repay you, for you will be repaid at the resurrection of the righteous.'

The Parable of the Great Dinner

15 One of the dinner guests, on hearing this, said to him, 'Blessed is anyone who will eat bread in the kingdom of God!' ¹⁶ Then Jesus*a* said to him, 'Someone gave a great dinner and invited many. ¹⁷ At the time for the dinner he sent his slave to say to those who had been invited, "Come; for everything is ready now." ¹⁸ But they all alike began to make excuses. The first said to him, "I have bought a piece of land, and I must go out and see it; please accept my apologies." ¹⁹ Another said, "I have bought five yoke of oxen, and I am going to try them out; please accept my apologies." ²⁰ Another said, "I have just been married, and therefore I cannot come." ²¹ So the slave returned and reported this to his master. Then the owner of the house became angry and said to his slave, "Go out at once into the streets and lanes of the town and bring in the poor, the crippled, the blind, and the lame." ²² And the slave said, "Sir, what you ordered has been done, and there is still room." ²³ Then the master said to the slave, "Go out into the roads and lanes, and compel people to come in, so that my house may be filled. ²⁴ For I tell you,*b* none of those who were invited will taste my dinner." '

The Cost of Discipleship

25 Now large crowds were travelling with him; and he turned and said to them,

²⁶ 'Whoever comes to me and does not hate father and mother, wife and children, brothers and sisters, yes, and even life itself, cannot be my disciple. ²⁷ Whoever does not carry the cross and follow me cannot be my disciple. ²⁸ For which of you, intending to build a tower, does not first sit down and estimate the cost, to see whether he has enough to complete it? ²⁹ Otherwise, when he has laid a foundation and is not able to finish, all who see it will begin to ridicule him, ³⁰ saying, "This fellow began to build and was not able to finish." ³¹ Or what king, going out to wage war against another king, will not sit down first and consider whether he is able with ten thousand to oppose the one who comes against him with twenty thousand? ³² If he cannot, then, while the other is still far away, he sends a delegation and asks for the terms of peace. ³³ So therefore, none of you can become my disciple if you do not give up all your possessions.

About Salt

34 'Salt is good; but if salt has lost its taste, how can its saltiness be restored?*c* ³⁵ It is fit neither for the soil nor for the manure heap; they throw it away. Let anyone with ears to hear listen!'

The Parable of the Lost Sheep

15 Now all the tax-collectors and sinners were coming near to listen to him. ² And the Pharisees and the scribes were grumbling and saying, 'This fellow welcomes sinners and eats with them.'

3 So he told them this parable: ⁴ 'Which one of you, having a hundred sheep and losing one of them, does not leave the ninety-nine in the wilderness and go after the one that is lost until he finds it? ⁵ When he has found it, he lays it on his shoulders and rejoices. ⁶ And when he comes home, he calls together his friends and neighbours, saying to them, "Rejoice with me, for I have found my sheep that was lost." ⁷ Just so, I tell you, there will be more joy in heaven over one sinner who repents

---

a Gk *he*   *b* The Greek word for *you* here is plural
c Or *how can it be used for seasoning?*

than over ninety-nine righteous people who need no repentance.

The Parable of the Lost Coin

8 'Or what woman having ten silver coins,[a] if she loses one of them, does not light a lamp, sweep the house, and search carefully until she finds it? 9 When she has found it, she calls together her friends and neighbours, saying, "Rejoice with me, for I have found the coin that I had lost." 10 Just so, I tell you, there is joy in the presence of the angels of God over one sinner who repents.'

The Parable of the Prodigal and His Brother

11 Then Jesus[b] said, 'There was a man who had two sons. 12 The younger of them said to his father, "Father, give me the share of the property that will belong to me." So he divided his property between them. 13 A few days later the younger son gathered all he had and travelled to a distant country, and there he squandered his property in dissolute living. 14 When he had spent everything, a severe famine took place throughout that country, and he began to be in need. 15 So he went and hired himself out to one of the citizens of that country, who sent him to his fields to feed the pigs. 16 He would gladly have filled himself with[c] the pods that the pigs were eating; and no one gave him anything. 17 But when he came to himself he said, "How many of my father's hired hands have bread enough and to spare, but here I am dying of hunger! 18 I will get up and go to my father, and I will say to him, 'Father, I have sinned against heaven and before you; 19 I am no longer worthy to be called your son; treat me like one of your hired hands.' " 20 So he set off and went to his father. But while he was still far off, his father saw him and was filled with compassion; he ran and put his arms around him and kissed him. 21 Then the son said to him, "Father, I have sinned against heaven and before you; I am no longer worthy to be called your son."[d] 22 But the father said to

his slaves, "Quickly, bring out a robe—the best one—and put it on him; put a ring on his finger and sandals on his feet. 23 And get the fatted calf and kill it, and let us eat and celebrate; 24 for this son of mine was dead and is alive again; he was lost and is found!" And they began to celebrate.

25 'Now his elder son was in the field; and when he came and approached the house, he heard music and dancing. 26 He called one of the slaves and asked what was going on. 27 He replied, "Your brother has come, and your father has killed the fatted calf, because he has got him back safe and sound." 28 Then he became angry and refused to go in. His father came out and began to plead with him. 29 But he answered his father, "Listen! For all these years I have been working like a slave for you, and I have never disobeyed your command; yet you have never given me even a young goat so that I might celebrate with my friends. 30 But when this son of yours came back, who has devoured your property with prostitutes, you killed the fatted calf for him!" 31 Then the father[e] said to him, "Son, you are always with me, and all that is mine is yours. 32 But we had to celebrate and rejoice, because this brother of yours was dead and has come to life; he was lost and has been found." '

The Parable of the Dishonest Manager

16 Then Jesus[e] said to the disciples, 'There was a rich man who had a manager, and charges were brought to him that this man was squandering his property. 2 So he summoned him and said to him, "What is this that I hear about you? Give me an account of your management, because you cannot be my manager any longer." 3 Then the manager said to himself, "What will I do, now that my master is taking the position away from me? I am not strong enough to dig, and I am ashamed to beg. 4 I have decided what to

a Gk drachmas, each worth about a day's wage for a labourer   b Gk he   c Other ancient authorities read filled his stomach with   d Other ancient authorities add Treat me like one of your hired servants   e Gk he do so that, when I am dismissed as manager, people may welcome me into their homes." 5 So, summoning his master's debtors one by one, he asked the first, "How much do you owe my master?" 6 He answered, "A hundred jugs of olive oil." He said to him, "Take your bill, sit down quickly, and make it fifty." 7 Then he asked another, "And how much do you owe?" He replied, "A hundred containers of wheat." He said to him, "Take your bill and make it eighty." 8 And his master commended the dishonest manager because he had acted shrewdly; for the children of this age are more shrewd in dealing with their own generation than are the children of light. 9 And I tell you, make friends for yourselves by means of dishonest wealth[a] so that when it is gone, they may welcome you into the eternal homes.[b]

10 'Whoever is faithful in a very little is faithful also in much; and whoever is dishonest in a very little is dishonest also in much. 11 If then you have not been faithful with the dishonest wealth,[a] who will entrust to you the true riches? 12 And if you have not been faithful with what belongs to another, who will give you what is your own? 13 No slave can serve two masters; for a slave will either hate the one and love the other, or be devoted to the one and despise the other. You cannot serve God and wealth.'[a]

The Law and the Kingdom of God

14 The Pharisees, who were lovers of money, heard all this, and they ridiculed him. 15 So he said to them, 'You are those who justify yourselves in the sight of others; but God knows your hearts; for what is prized by human beings is an abomination in the sight of God.

16 'The law and the prophets were in effect until John came; since then the good news of the kingdom of God is proclaimed, and everyone tries to enter it by force.[c] 17 But it is easier for heaven and earth to pass away, than for one stroke of a letter in the law to be dropped.

18 'Anyone who divorces his wife and marries another commits adultery, and whoever marries a woman divorced from her husband commits adultery.

The Rich Man and Lazarus

19 'There was a rich man who was dressed in purple and fine linen and who feasted sumptuously every day. 20 And at his gate lay a poor man named Lazarus, covered with sores, 21 who longed to satisfy his hunger with what fell from the rich man's table; even the dogs would come and lick his sores. 22 The poor man died and was carried away by the angels to be with Abraham.[d] The rich man also died and was buried. 23 In Hades, where he was being tormented, he looked up and saw Abraham far away with Lazarus by his side.[e] 24 He called out, "Father Abraham, have mercy on me, and send Lazarus to dip the tip of his finger in water and cool my tongue; for I am in agony in these flames." 25 But Abraham said, "Child, remember that during your lifetime you received your good things, and Lazarus in like manner evil things; but now he is comforted here, and you are in agony. 26 Besides all this, between you and us a great chasm has been fixed, so that those who might want to pass from here to you cannot do so, and no one can cross from there to us." 27 He said, "Then, father, I beg you to send him to my father's house— 28 for I have five brothers—that he may warn them, so that they will not also come into this place of torment." 29 Abraham replied, "They have Moses and the prophets; they should listen to them." 30 He said, "No, father Abraham; but if someone goes to them from the dead, they will repent." 31 He said to him, "If they do not listen to Moses and the prophets, neither will they be convinced even if someone rises from the dead." '

Some Sayings of Jesus

17 Jesus[f] said to his disciples, 'Occasions for stumbling are bound to come, but woe to anyone by whom they come! 2 It would be better for you if a mill-

---

a Gk *mammon*   *b* Gk *tents*   *c* Or *everyone is strongly urged to enter it*   *d* Gk *to Abraham's bosom*   *e* Gk *in his bosom*   *f* Gk *He* stone were hung around your neck and you were thrown into the sea than for you to cause one of these little ones to stumble. 3 Be on your guard! If another disciple[a] sins, you must rebuke the offender, and if there is repentance, you must forgive. 4 And if the same person sins against you seven times a day, and turns back to you seven times and says, "I repent", you must forgive.'

5 The apostles said to the Lord, 'Increase our faith!' 6 The Lord replied, 'If you had faith the size of a[b] mustard seed, you could say to this mulberry tree, "Be uprooted and planted in the sea", and it would obey you.

7 'Who among you would say to your slave who has just come in from ploughing or tending sheep in the field, "Come here at once and take your place at the table"? 8 Would you not rather say to him, "Prepare supper for me, put on your apron and serve me while I eat and drink; later you may eat and drink"? 9 Do you thank the slave for doing what was commanded? 10 So you also, when you have done all that you were ordered to do, say, "We are worthless slaves; we have done only what we ought to have done!" '

Jesus Cleanses Ten Lepers

11 On the way to Jerusalem Jesus[c] was going through the region between Samaria and Galilee. 12 As he entered a village, ten lepers[d] approached him. Keeping their distance, 13 they called out, saying, 'Jesus, Master, have mercy on us!' 14 When he saw them, he said to them, 'Go and show yourselves to the priests.' And as they went, they were made clean. 15 Then one of them, when he saw that he was healed, turned back, praising God with a loud voice. 16 He prostrated himself at Jesus'[e] feet and thanked him. And he was a Samaritan. 17 Then Jesus asked, 'Were not ten made clean? But the other nine, where are they? 18 Was none of them found to return and give praise to God except this foreigner?' 19 Then he said to him, 'Get up and go on your way; your faith has made you well.'

The Coming of the Kingdom

20 Once Jesus[c] was asked by the Pharisees when the kingdom of God was coming, and he answered, 'The kingdom of God is not coming with things that can be observed; 21 nor will they say, "Look, here it is!" or "There it is!" For, in fact, the kingdom of God is among[f] you.'

22 Then he said to the disciples, 'The days are coming when you will long to see one of the days of the Son of Man, and you will not see it. 23 They will say to you, "Look there!" or "Look here!" Do not go, do not set off in pursuit. 24 For as the lightning flashes and lights up the sky from one side to the other, so will the Son of Man be in his day.[g] 25 But first he must endure much suffering and be rejected by this generation. 26 Just as it was in the days of Noah, so too it will be in the days of the Son of Man. 27 They were eating and drinking, and marrying and being given in marriage, until the day Noah entered the ark, and the flood came and destroyed all of them. 28 Likewise, just as it was in the days of Lot: they were eating and drinking, buying and selling, planting and building, 29 but on the day that Lot left Sodom, it rained fire and sulphur from heaven and destroyed all of them 30 —it will be like that on the day that the Son of Man is revealed. 31 On that day, anyone on the housetop who has belongings in the house must not come down to take them away; and likewise anyone in the field must not turn back. 32 Remember Lot's wife. 33 Those who try to make their life secure will lose it, but those who lose their life will keep it. 34 I tell you, on that night there will be two in one bed; one will be taken and the other left. 35 There will be two women grinding meal together; one will be taken and the other left.'[h] 37 Then they asked him, 'Where, Lord?' He said to them, 'Where the corpse is, there the vultures will gather.'

a Gk your brother   b Gk faith as a grain of   c Gk he
d The terms leper and leprosy can refer to several diseases
e Gk his   f Or within   g Other ancient authorities
lack in his day   h Other ancient authorities add
verse 36, 'Two will be in the field; one will be taken and the
other left.'

The Parable of the Widow and the Unjust Judge

18 Then Jesus[a] told them a parable about their need to pray always and not to lose heart. 2 He said, 'In a certain city there was a judge who neither feared God nor had respect for people. 3 In that city there was a widow who kept coming to him and saying, "Grant me justice against my opponent." 4 For a while he refused; but later he said to himself, "Though I have no fear of God and no respect for anyone, 5 yet because this widow keeps bothering me, I will grant her justice, so that she may not wear me out by continually coming."'[b] 6 And the Lord said, 'Listen to what the unjust judge says. 7 And will not God grant justice to his chosen ones who cry to him day and night? Will he delay long in helping them? 8 I tell you, he will quickly grant justice to them. And yet, when the Son of Man comes, will he find faith on earth?'

The Parable of the Pharisee and the Tax-Collector

9 He also told this parable to some who trusted in themselves that they were righteous and regarded others with contempt: 10 'Two men went up to the temple to pray, one a Pharisee and the other a tax-collector. 11 The Pharisee, standing by himself, was praying thus, "God, I thank you that I am not like other people: thieves, rogues, adulterers, or even like this tax-collector. 12 I fast twice a week; I give a tenth of all my income." 13 But the tax-collector, standing far off, would not even look up to heaven, but was beating his breast and saying, "God, be merciful to me, a sinner!" 14 I tell you, this man went down to his home justified rather than the other; for all who exalt themselves will be humbled, but all who humble themselves will be exalted.'

Jesus Blesses Little Children

15 People were bringing even infants to him that he might touch them; and when the disciples saw it, they sternly ordered them not to do it. 16 But Jesus called for them and said, 'Let the little children come to me, and do not stop them; for it is to such as these that the kingdom of God belongs. 17 Truly I tell you, whoever does not receive the kingdom of God as a little child will never enter it.'

The Rich Ruler

18 A certain ruler asked him, 'Good Teacher, what must I do to inherit eternal life?' 19 Jesus said to him, 'Why do you call me good? No one is good but God alone. 20 You know the commandments: "You shall not commit adultery; You shall not murder; You shall not steal; You shall not bear false witness; Honour your father and mother."' 21 He replied, 'I have kept all these since my youth.' 22 When Jesus heard this, he said to him, 'There is still one thing lacking. Sell all that you own and distribute the money[c] to the poor, and you will have treasure in heaven; then come, follow me.' 23 But when he heard this, he became sad; for he was very rich. 24 Jesus looked at him and said, 'How hard it is for those who have wealth to enter the kingdom of God! 25 Indeed, it is easier for a camel to go through the eye of a needle than for someone who is rich to enter the kingdom of God.'

26 Those who heard it said, 'Then who can be saved?' 27 He replied, 'What is impossible for mortals is possible for God.'

28 Then Peter said, 'Look, we have left our homes and followed you.' 29 And he said to them, 'Truly I tell you, there is no one who has left house or wife or brothers or parents or children, for the sake of the kingdom of God, 30 who will not get back very much more in this age, and in the age to come eternal life.'

A Third Time Jesus Foretells His Death and Resurrection

31 Then he took the twelve aside and said to them, 'See, we are going up to Jerusalem, and everything that is written about the Son of Man by the prophets will be accomplished. 32 For he will be handed over

a Gk he   b Or so that she may not finally come and slap me in the face   c Gk lacks the money to the Gentiles; and he will be mocked and insulted and spat upon. ³³After they have flogged him, they will kill him, and on the third day he will rise again.' ³⁴But they understood nothing about all these things; in fact, what he said was hidden from them, and they did not grasp what was said.

Jesus Heals a Blind Beggar Near Jericho

35 As he approached Jericho, a blind man was sitting by the roadside begging. ³⁶When he heard a crowd going by, he asked what was happening. ³⁷They told him, 'Jesus of Nazareth*a* is passing by.' ³⁸Then he shouted, 'Jesus, Son of David, have mercy on me!' ³⁹Those who were in front sternly ordered him to be quiet; but he shouted even more loudly, 'Son of David, have mercy on me!' ⁴⁰Jesus stood still and ordered the man to be brought to him; and when he came near, he asked him, ⁴¹'What do you want me to do for you?' He said, 'Lord, let me see again.' ⁴²Jesus said to him, 'Receive your sight; your faith has saved you.' ⁴³Immediately he regained his sight and followed him, glorifying God; and all the people, when they saw it, praised God.

Jesus and Zacchaeus

19 He entered Jericho and was passing through it. ²A man was there named Zacchaeus; he was a chief tax-collector and was rich. ³He was trying to see who Jesus was, but on account of the crowd he could not, because he was short in stature. ⁴So he ran ahead and climbed a sycamore tree to see him, because he was going to pass that way. ⁵When Jesus came to the place, he looked up and said to him, 'Zacchaeus, hurry and come down; for I must stay at your house today.' ⁶So he hurried down and was happy to welcome him. ⁷All who saw it began to grumble and said, 'He has gone to be the guest of one who is a sinner.' ⁸Zacchaeus stood there and said to the Lord, 'Look, half of my possessions, Lord, I will give to the poor; and if I have defrauded anyone of anything, I will pay back four times as much.' ⁹Then Jesus said to him, 'Today salvation has come to this house, because he too is a son of Abraham. ¹⁰For the Son of Man came to seek out and to save the lost.'

The Parable of the Ten Pounds

11 As they were listening to this, he went on to tell a parable, because he was near Jerusalem, and because they supposed that the kingdom of God was to appear immediately. ¹²So he said, 'A nobleman went to a distant country to get royal power for himself and then return. ¹³He summoned ten of his slaves, and gave them ten pounds,*b* and said to them, "Do business with these until I come back." ¹⁴But the citizens of his country hated him and sent a delegation after him, saying, "We do not want this man to rule over us." ¹⁵When he returned, having received royal power, he ordered these slaves, to whom he had given the money, to be summoned so that he might find out what they had gained by trading. ¹⁶The first came forward and said, "Lord, your pound has made ten more pounds." ¹⁷He said to him, "Well done, good slave! Because you have been trustworthy in a very small thing, take charge of ten cities." ¹⁸Then the second came, saying, "Lord, your pound has made five pounds." ¹⁹He said to him, "And you, rule over five cities." ²⁰Then the other came, saying, "Lord, here is your pound. I wrapped it up in a piece of cloth, ²¹for I was afraid of you, because you are a harsh man; you take what you did not deposit, and reap what you did not sow." ²²He said to him, "I will judge you by your own words, you wicked slave! You knew, did you, that I was a harsh man, taking what I did not deposit and reaping what I did not sow? ²³Why then did you not put my money into the bank? Then when I returned, I could have collected it with interest." ²⁴He said to the bystanders, "Take the pound from him and give it to the one who has ten pounds." ²⁵(And they said to him, "Lord, he has ten pounds!") ²⁶"I tell you, to all those who have, more will be given; but from those who have nothing,

a Gk *the Nazorean*   *b* The mina, rendered here by *pound,* was about three months' wages for a labourer even what they have will be taken away. [27] But as for these enemies of mine who did not want me to be king over them— bring them here and slaughter them in my presence." '

Jesus' Triumphal Entry into Jerusalem

28 After he had said this, he went on ahead, going up to Jerusalem.

29 When he had come near Bethphage and Bethany, at the place called the Mount of Olives, he sent two of the disciples, [30] saying, 'Go into the village ahead of you, and as you enter it you will find tied there a colt that has never been ridden. Untie it and bring it here. [31] If anyone asks you, "Why are you untying it?" just say this: "The Lord needs it." ' [32] So those who were sent departed and found it as he had told them. [33] As they were untying the colt, its owners asked them, 'Why are you untying the colt?' [34] They said, 'The Lord needs it.' [35] Then they brought it to Jesus; and after throwing their cloaks on the colt, they set Jesus on it. [36] As he rode along, people kept spreading their cloaks on the road. [37] As he was now approaching the path down from the Mount of Olives, the whole multitude of the disciples began to praise God joyfully with a loud voice for all the deeds of power that they had seen, [38] saying,

'Blessed is the king
    who comes in the name of
        the Lord!
Peace in heaven,
    and glory in the highest heaven!'

[39] Some of the Pharisees in the crowd said to him, 'Teacher, order your disciples to stop.' [40] He answered, 'I tell you, if these were silent, the stones would shout out.'

Jesus Weeps over Jerusalem

41 As he came near and saw the city, he wept over it, [42] saying, 'If you, even you, had only recognized on this day the things that make for peace! But now they are hidden from your eyes. [43] Indeed, the days will come upon you, when your enemies will set up ramparts around you and surround you, and hem you in on every side. [44] They will crush you to the ground, you and your children within you, and they will not leave within you one stone upon another; because you did not recognize the time of your visitation from God.'[a]

Jesus Cleanses the Temple

45 Then he entered the temple and began to drive out those who were selling things there; [46] and he said, 'It is written,

"My house shall be a house
        of prayer";
    but you have made it a den
        of robbers.'

47 Every day he was teaching in the temple. The chief priests, the scribes, and the leaders of the people kept looking for a way to kill him; [48] but they did not find anything they could do, for all the people were spellbound by what they heard.

The Authority of Jesus Questioned

20 One day, as he was teaching the people in the temple and telling the good news, the chief priests and the scribes came with the elders [2] and said to him, 'Tell us, by what authority are you doing these things? Who is it who gave you this authority?' [3] He answered them, 'I will also ask you a question, and you tell me: [4] Did the baptism of John come from heaven, or was it of human origin?' [5] They discussed it with one another, saying, 'If we say, "From heaven", he will say, "Why did you not believe him?" [6] But if we say, "Of human origin", all the people will stone us; for they are convinced that John was a prophet.' [7] So they answered that they did not know where it came from. [8] Then Jesus said to them, 'Neither will I tell you by what authority I am doing these things.'

The Parable of the Wicked Tenants

9 He began to tell the people this parable: 'A man planted a vineyard, and leased it to tenants, and went to another country for a long time. [10] When the season came, he sent a slave to the tenants in order that they might give him his share of the produce of the vineyard; but the tenants beat

a Gk lacks from God

him and sent him away empty-handed. ¹¹ Next he sent another slave; that one also they beat and insulted and sent away empty-handed. ¹² And he sent yet a third; this one also they wounded and threw out. ¹³ Then the owner of the vineyard said, "What shall I do? I will send my beloved son; perhaps they will respect him." ¹⁴ But when the tenants saw him, they discussed it among themselves and said, "This is the heir; let us kill him so that the inheritance may be ours." ¹⁵ So they threw him out of the vineyard and killed him. What then will the owner of the vineyard do to them? ¹⁶ He will come and destroy those tenants and give the vineyard to others.' When they heard this, they said, 'Heaven forbid!' ¹⁷ But he looked at them and said, 'What then does this text mean:

"The stone that the builders rejected
   has become the cornerstone"?ᵃ

¹⁸ Everyone who falls on that stone will be broken to pieces; and it will crush anyone on whom it falls.' ¹⁹ When the scribes and chief priests realized that he had told this parable against them, they wanted to lay hands on him at that very hour, but they feared the people.

The Question about Paying Taxes

20 So they watched him and sent spies who pretended to be honest, in order to trap him by what he said, so as to hand him over to the jurisdiction and authority of the governor. ²¹ So they asked him, 'Teacher, we know that you are right in what you say and teach, and you show deference to no one, but teach the way of God in accordance with truth. ²² Is it lawful for us to pay taxes to the emperor, or not?' ²³ But he perceived their craftiness and said to them, ²⁴ 'Show me a denarius. Whose head and whose title does it bear?' They said, 'The emperor's.' ²⁵ He said to them, 'Then give to the emperor the things that are the emperor's, and to God the things that are God's.' ²⁶ And they were not able in the presence of the people to trap him by what he said; and being amazed by his answer, they became silent.

a Or keystone

Jerusalem During the Ministry of Jesus

0 200 400 Yards	▬▬ Walls of Jerusalem
0 200 400 Meters	▬ ▬ Wall alignment uncertain
	▬▬ Present wall of Old City

Pool of Bethesda

Site of Jesus' trial

MT. OF OLIVES

Golgotha and Tomb of Jesus †

Via Dolorosa

TEMPLE

KIDRON VALLEY

☐ Gethsemane

Bridge

Palace of Herod

Palace of Herod Antipas

Pinnacle of the Temple

UPPER CITY

Gihon Spring

LOWER CITY

N

☐ House of Caiaphas

Upper ☐ Room?

Hezekiah's Water Tunnel

Pool of Siloam

The Question about the Resurrection

27 Some Sadducees, those who say there is no resurrection, came to him 28 and asked him a question, 'Teacher, Moses wrote for us that if a man's brother dies, leaving a wife but no children, the man*a* shall marry the widow and raise up children for his brother. 29 Now there were seven brothers; the first married, and died childless; 30 then the second 31 and the third married her, and so in the same way all seven died childless. 32 Finally the woman also died. 33 In the resurrection, therefore, whose wife will the woman be? For the seven had married her.'

34 Jesus said to them, 'Those who belong to this age marry and are given in marriage; 35 but those who are considered worthy of a place in that age and in the resurrection from the dead neither marry nor are given in marriage. 36 Indeed they cannot die any more, because they are like angels and are children of God, being children of the resurrection. 37 And the fact that the dead are raised Moses himself showed, in the story about the bush, where he speaks of the Lord as the God of Abraham, the God of Isaac, and the God of Jacob. 38 Now he is God not of the dead, but of the living; for to him all of them are alive.' 39 Then some of the scribes answered, 'Teacher, you have spoken well.' 40 For they no longer dared to ask him another question.

The Question about David's Son

41 Then he said to them, 'How can they say that the Messiah*b* is David's son? 42 For David himself says in the book of Psalms,

"The Lord said to my Lord,
'Sit at my right hand,
43   until I make your enemies your
        footstool.' "

44 David thus calls him Lord; so how can he be his son?'

Jesus Denounces the Scribes

45 In the hearing of all the people he said to the*c* disciples, 46 'Beware of the scribes, who like to walk around in long robes, and love to be greeted with respect in the market-places, and to have the best seats in the synagogues and places of honour at banquets. 47 They devour widows' houses and for the sake of appearance say long prayers. They will receive the greater condemnation.'

The Widow's Offering

21 He looked up and saw rich people putting their gifts into the treasury; 2 he also saw a poor widow put in two small copper coins. 3 He said, 'Truly I tell you, this poor widow has put in more than all of them; 4 for all of them have contributed out of their abundance, but she out of her poverty has put in all she had to live on.'

The Destruction of the Temple Foretold

5 When some were speaking about the temple, how it was adorned with beautiful stones and gifts dedicated to God, he said, 6 'As for these things that you see, the days will come when not one stone will be left upon another; all will be thrown down.'

Signs and Persecutions

7 They asked him, 'Teacher, when will this be, and what will be the sign that this is about to take place?' 8 And he said, 'Beware that you are not led astray; for many will come in my name and say, "I am he!"*d* and, "The time is near!"*e* Do not go after them.

9 'When you hear of wars and insurrections, do not be terrified; for these things must take place first, but the end will not follow immediately.' 10 Then he said to them, 'Nation will rise against nation, and kingdom against kingdom; 11 there will be great earthquakes, and in various places famines and plagues; and there will be dreadful portents and great signs from heaven.

12 'But before all this occurs, they will arrest you and persecute you; they will hand you over to synagogues and prisons, and you will be brought before kings and

a Gk his brother   *b* Or the Christ   *c* Other ancient authorities read his   *d* Gk I am   *e* Or at hand governors because of my name. 13 This will give you an opportunity to testify. 14 So make up your minds not to prepare your defence in advance; 15 for I will give you words[a] and a wisdom that none of your opponents will be able to withstand or contradict. 16 You will be betrayed even by parents and brothers, by relatives and friends; and they will put some of you to death. 17 You will be hated by all because of my name. 18 But not a hair of your head will perish. 19 By your endurance you will gain your souls.

The Destruction of Jerusalem Foretold

20 'When you see Jerusalem surrounded by armies, then know that its desolation has come near.[b] 21 Then those in Judea must flee to the mountains, and those inside the city must leave it, and those out in the country must not enter it; 22 for these are days of vengeance, as a fulfilment of all that is written. 23 Woe to those who are pregnant and to those who are nursing infants in those days! For there will be great distress on the earth and wrath against this people; 24 they will fall by the edge of the sword and be taken away as captives among all nations; and Jerusalem will be trampled on by the Gentiles, until the times of the Gentiles are fulfilled.

The Coming of the Son of Man

25 'There will be signs in the sun, the moon, and the stars, and on the earth distress among nations confused by the roaring of the sea and the waves. 26 People will faint from fear and foreboding of what is coming upon the world, for the powers of the heavens will be shaken. 27 Then they will see "the Son of Man coming in a cloud" with power and great glory. 28 Now when these things begin to take place, stand up and raise your heads, because your redemption is drawing near.'

The Lesson of the Fig Tree

29 Then he told them a parable: 'Look at the fig tree and all the trees; 30 as soon as they sprout leaves you can see for your-selves and know that summer is already near. 31 So also, when you see these things taking place, you know that the kingdom of God is near. 32 Truly I tell you, this generation will not pass away until all things have taken place. 33 Heaven and earth will pass away, but my words will not pass away.

Exhortation to Watch

34 'Be on guard so that your hearts are not weighed down with dissipation and drunkenness and the worries of this life, and that day does not catch you unexpectedly, 35 like a trap. For it will come upon all who live on the face of the whole earth. 36 Be alert at all times, praying that you may have the strength to escape all these things that will take place, and to stand before the Son of Man.'

37 Every day he was teaching in the temple, and at night he would go out and spend the night on the Mount of Olives, as it was called. 38 And all the people would get up early in the morning to listen to him in the temple.

The Plot to Kill Jesus

22 Now the festival of Unleavened Bread, which is called the Passover, was near. 2 The chief priests and the scribes were looking for a way to put Jesus[c] to death, for they were afraid of the people.

3 Then Satan entered into Judas called Iscariot, who was one of the twelve; 4 he went away and conferred with the chief priests and officers of the temple police about how he might betray him to them. 5 They were greatly pleased and agreed to give him money. 6 So he consented and began to look for an opportunity to betray him to them when no crowd was present.

The Preparation of the Passover

7 Then came the day of Unleavened Bread, on which the Passover lamb had to be sacrificed. 8 So Jesus[d] sent Peter and John, saying, 'Go and prepare the Passover meal for us that we may eat it.' 9 They asked him, 'Where do you want us to make

a Gk *a mouth*   *b* Or *is at hand*   *c* Gk *him*   *d* Gk *he* preparations for it?' ¹⁰'Listen,' he said to them, 'when you have entered the city, a man carrying a jar of water will meet you; follow him into the house he enters ¹¹and say to the owner of the house, "The teacher asks you, 'Where is the guest room, where I may eat the Passover with my disciples?' " ¹²He will show you a large room upstairs, already furnished. Make preparations for us there.' ¹³So they went and found everything as he had told them; and they prepared the Passover meal.

The Institution of the Lord's Supper

14 When the hour came, he took his place at the table, and the apostles with him. ¹⁵He said to them, 'I have eagerly desired to eat this Passover with you before I suffer; ¹⁶for I tell you, I will not eat it *a* until it is fulfilled in the kingdom of God.' ¹⁷Then he took a cup, and after giving thanks he said, 'Take this and divide it among yourselves; ¹⁸for I tell you that from now on I will not drink of the fruit of the vine until the kingdom of God comes.' ¹⁹Then he took a loaf of bread, and when he had given thanks, he broke it and gave it to them, saying, 'This is my body, which is given for you. Do this in remembrance of me.' ²⁰And he did the same with the cup after supper, saying, 'This cup that is poured out for you is the new covenant in my blood.*b* ²¹But see, the one who betrays me is with me, and his hand is on the table. ²²For the Son of Man is going as it has been determined, but woe to that one by whom he is betrayed!' ²³Then they began to ask one another which one of them it could be who would do this.

The Dispute about Greatness

24 A dispute also arose among them as to which one of them was to be regarded as the greatest. ²⁵But he said to them, 'The kings of the Gentiles lord it over them; and those in authority over them are called benefactors. ²⁶But not so with you; rather the greatest among you must become like the youngest, and the leader like one who serves. ²⁷For who is greater, the one who is at the table or the one who serves? Is it not the one at the table? But I am among you as one who serves.

28 'You are those who have stood by me in my trials; ²⁹and I confer on you, just as my Father has conferred on me, a kingdom, ³⁰so that you may eat and drink at my table in my kingdom, and you will sit on thrones judging the twelve tribes of Israel.

Jesus Predicts Peter's Denial

31 'Simon, Simon, listen! Satan has demanded*c* to sift all of you like wheat, ³²but I have prayed for you that your own faith may not fail; and you, when once you have turned back, strengthen your brothers.' ³³And he said to him, 'Lord, I am ready to go with you to prison and to death!' ³⁴Jesus*d* said, 'I tell you, Peter, the cock will not crow this day, until you have denied three times that you know me.'

Purse, Bag, and Sword

35 He said to them, 'When I sent you out without a purse, bag, or sandals, did you lack anything?' They said, 'No, not a thing.' ³⁶He said to them, 'But now, the one who has a purse must take it, and likewise a bag. And the one who has no sword must sell his cloak and buy one. ³⁷For I tell you, this scripture must be fulfilled in me, "And he was counted among the lawless"; and indeed what is written about me is being fulfilled.' ³⁸They said, 'Lord, look, here are two swords.' He replied, 'It is enough.'

Jesus Prays on the Mount of Olives

39 He came out and went, as was his custom, to the Mount of Olives; and the disciples followed him. ⁴⁰When he reached the place, he said to them, 'Pray that you may not come into the time of trial.'*e* ⁴¹Then he withdrew from them about a stone's throw, knelt down, and prayed, ⁴²'Father, if you are willing, remove this

---

a Other ancient authorities read *never eat it again*
b Other ancient authorities lack, in whole or in part, verses 19b-20 (*which is given . . . in my blood*)
c Or *has obtained permission*   *d* Gk *He*   *e* Or *into temptation*

cup from me; yet, not my will but yours be done.' ⟦ ⁴³Then an angel from heaven appeared to him and gave him strength. ⁴⁴In his anguish he prayed more earnestly, and his sweat became like great drops of blood falling down on the ground.⟧ *a* ⁴⁵When he got up from prayer, he came to the disciples and found them sleeping because of grief, ⁴⁶and he said to them, 'Why are you sleeping? Get up and pray that you may not come into the time of trial.' *b*

The Betrayal and Arrest of Jesus

47 While he was still speaking, suddenly a crowd came, and the one called Judas, one of the twelve, was leading them. He approached Jesus to kiss him; ⁴⁸but Jesus said to him, 'Judas, is it with a kiss that you are betraying the Son of Man?' ⁴⁹When those who were around him saw what was coming, they asked, 'Lord, should we strike with the sword?' ⁵⁰Then one of them struck the slave of the high priest and cut off his right ear. ⁵¹But Jesus said, 'No more of this!' And he touched his ear and healed him. ⁵²Then Jesus said to the chief priests, the officers of the temple police, and the elders who had come for him, 'Have you come out with swords and clubs as if I were a bandit? ⁵³When I was with you day after day in the temple, you did not lay hands on me. But this is your hour, and the power of darkness!'

Peter Denies Jesus

54 Then they seized him and led him away, bringing him into the high priest's house. But Peter was following at a distance. ⁵⁵When they had kindled a fire in the middle of the courtyard and sat down together, Peter sat among them. ⁵⁶Then a servant-girl, seeing him in the firelight, stared at him and said, 'This man also was with him.' ⁵⁷But he denied it, saying, 'Woman, I do not know him.' ⁵⁸A little later someone else, on seeing him, said, 'You also are one of them.' But Peter said, 'Man, I am not!' ⁵⁹Then about an hour later yet another kept insisting, 'Surely this man also was with him; for he is a Galilean.'

⁶⁰But Peter said, 'Man, I do not know what you are talking about!' At that moment, while he was still speaking, the cock crowed. ⁶¹The Lord turned and looked at Peter. Then Peter remembered the word of the Lord, how he had said to him, 'Before the cock crows today, you will deny me three times.' ⁶²And he went out and wept bitterly.

The Mocking and Beating of Jesus

63 Now the men who were holding Jesus began to mock him and beat him; ⁶⁴they also blindfolded him and kept asking him, 'Prophesy! Who is it that struck you?' ⁶⁵They kept heaping many other insults on him.

Jesus before the Council

66 When day came, the assembly of the elders of the people, both chief priests and scribes, gathered together, and they brought him to their council. ⁶⁷They said, 'If you are the Messiah, *c* tell us.' He replied, 'If I tell you, you will not believe; ⁶⁸and if I question you, you will not answer. ⁶⁹But from now on the Son of Man will be seated at the right hand of the power of God.' ⁷⁰All of them asked, 'Are you, then, the Son of God?' He said to them, 'You say that I am.' ⁷¹Then they said, 'What further testimony do we need? We have heard it ourselves from his own lips!'

Jesus before Pilate

23 Then the assembly rose as a body and brought Jesus *d* before Pilate. ²They began to accuse him, saying, 'We found this man perverting our nation, forbidding us to pay taxes to the emperor, and saying that he himself is the Messiah, a king.' *e* ³Then Pilate asked him, 'Are you the king of the Jews?' He answered, 'You say so.' ⁴Then Pilate said to the chief priests and the crowds, 'I find no basis for an accusation against this man.' ⁵But they were insistent and said, 'He stirs up the people by teaching throughout all Judea,

a Other ancient authorities lack verses 43 and 44
b Or *into temptation*　　*c* Or *the Christ*　　*d* Gk *him*
e Or *is an anointed king*

from Galilee where he began even to this place.'

Jesus before Herod

6 When Pilate heard this, he asked whether the man was a Galilean. 7 And when he learned that he was under Herod's jurisdiction, he sent him off to Herod, who was himself in Jerusalem at that time. 8 When Herod saw Jesus, he was very glad, for he had been wanting to see him for a long time, because he had heard about him and was hoping to see him perform some sign. 9 He questioned him at some length, but Jesus*a* gave him no answer. 10 The chief priests and the scribes stood by, vehemently accusing him. 11 Even Herod with his soldiers treated him with contempt and mocked him; then he put an elegant robe on him, and sent him back to Pilate. 12 That same day Herod and Pilate became friends with each other; before this they had been enemies.

Jesus Sentenced to Death

13 Pilate then called together the chief priests, the leaders, and the people, 14 and said to them, 'You brought me this man as one who was perverting the people; and here I have examined him in your presence and have not found this man guilty of any of your charges against him. 15 Neither has Herod, for he sent him back to us. Indeed, he has done nothing to deserve death. 16 I will therefore have him flogged and release him.'*b* 18 Then they all shouted out together, 'Away with this fellow! Release Barabbas for us!' 19 (This was a man who had been put in prison for an insurrection that had taken place in the city, and for murder.) 20 Pilate, wanting to release Jesus, addressed them again; 21 but they kept shouting, 'Crucify, crucify him!' 22 A third time he said to them, 'Why, what evil has he done? I have found in him no ground for the sentence of death; I will therefore have him flogged and then release him.' 23 But they kept urgently demanding with loud shouts that he should be crucified; and

their voices prevailed. 24 So Pilate gave his verdict that their demand should be granted. 25 He released the man they asked for, the one who had been put in prison for insurrection and murder, and he handed Jesus over as they wished.

The Crucifixion of Jesus

26 As they led him away, they seized a man, Simon of Cyrene, who was coming from the country, and they laid the cross on him, and made him carry it behind Jesus. 27 A great number of the people followed him, and among them were women who were beating their breasts and wailing for him. 28 But Jesus turned to them and said, 'Daughters of Jerusalem, do not weep for me, but weep for yourselves and for your children. 29 For the days are surely coming when they will say, "Blessed are the barren, and the wombs that never bore, and the breasts that never nursed." 30 Then they will begin to say to the mountains, "Fall on us"; and to the hills, "Cover us." 31 For if they do this when the wood is green, what will happen when it is dry?'

32 Two others also, who were criminals, were led away to be put to death with him. 33 When they came to the place that is called The Skull, they crucified Jesus*c* there with the criminals, one on his right and one on his left. 〚 34 Then Jesus said, 'Father, forgive them; for they do not know what they are doing.'〛*d* And they cast lots to divide his clothing. 35 And the people stood by, watching; but the leaders scoffed at him, saying, 'He saved others; let him save himself if he is the Messiah*e* of God, his chosen one!' 36 The soldiers also mocked him, coming up and offering him sour wine, 37 and saying, 'If you are the King of the Jews, save yourself!' 38 There was also an inscription over him,*f* 'This is the King of the Jews.'

a Gk *he*   *b* Here, or after verse 19, other ancient authorities add verse 17, *Now he was obliged to release someone for them at the festival*   *c* Gk *him*   *d* Other ancient authorities lack the sentence *Then Jesus . . . what they are doing*   *e* Or *the Christ*   *f* Other ancient authorities add *written in Greek and Latin and Hebrew* (that is, *Aramaic*)

39 One of the criminals who were hanged there kept deriding[a] him and saying, 'Are you not the Messiah?[b] Save yourself and us!' 40But the other rebuked him, saying, 'Do you not fear God, since you are under the same sentence of condemnation? 41And we indeed have been condemned justly, for we are getting what we deserve for our deeds; but this man has done nothing wrong.' 42Then he said, 'Jesus, remember me when you come into[c] your kingdom.' 43He replied, 'Truly I tell you, today you will be with me in Paradise.'

The Death of Jesus

44 It was now about noon, and darkness came over the whole land[d] until three in the afternoon, 45while the sun's light failed;[e] and the curtain of the temple was torn in two. 46Then Jesus, crying with a loud voice, said, 'Father, into your hands I commend my spirit.' Having said this, he breathed his last. 47When the centurion saw what had taken place, he praised God and said, 'Certainly this man was innocent.'[f] 48And when all the crowds who had gathered there for this spectacle saw what had taken place, they returned home, beating their breasts. 49But all his acquaintances, including the women who had followed him from Galilee, stood at a distance, watching these things.

The Burial of Jesus

50 Now there was a good and righteous man named Joseph, who, though a member of the council, 51had not agreed to their plan and action. He came from the Jewish town of Arimathea, and he was waiting expectantly for the kingdom of God. 52This man went to Pilate and asked for the body of Jesus. 53Then he took it down, wrapped it in a linen cloth, and laid it in a rock-hewn tomb where no one had ever been laid. 54It was the day of Preparation, and the sabbath was beginning.[g] 55The women who had come with him from Galilee followed, and they saw the tomb and how his body was laid. 56Then they returned, and prepared spices and ointments.

On the sabbath they rested according to the commandment.

The Resurrection of Jesus

24 But on the first day of the week, at early dawn, they came to the tomb, taking the spices that they had prepared. 2They found the stone rolled away from the tomb, 3but when they went in, they did not find the body.[h] 4While they were perplexed about this, suddenly two men in dazzling clothes stood beside them. 5The women[i] were terrified and bowed their faces to the ground, but the men[j] said to them, 'Why do you look for the living among the dead? He is not here, but has risen.[k] 6Remember how he told you, while he was still in Galilee, 7that the Son of Man must be handed over to sinners, and be crucified, and on the third day rise again.' 8Then they remembered his words, 9and returning from the tomb, they told all this to the eleven and to all the rest. 10Now it was Mary Magdalene, Joanna, Mary the mother of James, and the other women with them who told this to the apostles. 11But these words seemed to them an idle tale, and they did not believe them. 12But Peter got up and ran to the tomb; stooping and looking in, he saw the linen cloths by themselves; then he went home, amazed at what had happened.[l]

The Walk to Emmaus

13 Now on that same day two of them were going to a village called Emmaus, about seven miles[m] from Jerusalem, 14and talking with each other about all these things that had happened. 15While they were talking and discussing, Jesus himself came near and went with them, 16but their

a Or blaspheming   b Or the Christ   c Other ancient authorities read in   d Or earth   e Or the sun was eclipsed. Other ancient authorities read the sun was darkened   f Or righteous   g Gk was dawning   h Other ancient authorities add of the Lord Jesus   i Gk They   j Gk but they   k Other ancient authorities lack He is not here, but has risen   l Other ancient authorities lack verse 12   m Gk sixty stadia; other ancient authorities read a hundred and sixty stadia

eyes were kept from recognizing him.
17 And he said to them, 'What are you discussing with each other while you walk
along?' They stood still, looking sad.*a*
18 Then one of them, whose name was Cle-
opas, answered him, 'Are you the only
stranger in Jerusalem who does not know
the things that have taken place there in
these days?' 19 He asked them, 'What
things?' They replied, 'The things about
Jesus of Nazareth,*b* who was a prophet
mighty in deed and word before God and
all the people, 20 and how our chief priests
and leaders handed him over to be condemned to death and crucified him. 21 But
we had hoped that he was the one to redeem Israel.*c* Yes, and besides all this, it is
now the third day since these things took
place. 22 Moreover, some women of our
group astounded us. They were at the
tomb early this morning, 23 and when they
did not find his body there, they came
back and told us that they had indeed seen
a vision of angels who said that he was
alive. 24 Some of those who were with us
went to the tomb and found it just as the
women had said; but they did not see him.'
25 Then he said to them, 'Oh, how foolish
you are, and how slow of heart to believe
all that the prophets have declared! 26 Was
it not necessary that the Messiah*d* should
suffer these things and then enter into his
glory?' 27 Then beginning with Moses and
all the prophets, he interpreted to them
the things about himself in all the scriptures.

28 As they came near the village to
which they were going, he walked ahead as
if he were going on. 29 But they urged him
strongly, saying, 'Stay with us, because it is
almost evening and the day is now nearly
over.' So he went in to stay with them.
30 When he was at the table with them, he
took bread, blessed and broke it, and gave
it to them. 31 Then their eyes were opened,
and they recognized him; and he vanished
from their sight. 32 They said to each other,
'Were not our hearts burning within us*e*
while he was talking to us on the road,
while he was opening the scriptures to us?'
33 That same hour they got up and returned

to Jerusalem; and they found the eleven
and their companions gathered together.
34 They were saying, 'The Lord has risen indeed, and he has appeared to Simon!'
35 Then they told what had happened on
the road, and how he had been made
known to them in the breaking of the
bread.

Jesus Appears to His Disciples

36 While they were talking about this,
Jesus himself stood among them and said
to them, 'Peace be with you.'*f* 37 They were
startled and terrified, and thought that
they were seeing a ghost. 38 He said to
them, 'Why are you frightened, and why
do doubts arise in your hearts? 39 Look at
my hands and my feet; see that it is I myself. Touch me and see; for a ghost does
not have flesh and bones as you see that I
have.' 40 And when he had said this, he
showed them his hands and his feet.*g*
41 While in their joy they were disbelieving
and still wondering, he said to them, 'Have
you anything here to eat?' 42 They gave him
a piece of broiled fish, 43 and he took it
and ate in their presence.

44 Then he said to them, 'These are my
words that I spoke to you while I was still
with you—that everything written about
me in the law of Moses, the prophets, and
the psalms must be fulfilled.' 45 Then he
opened their minds to understand the
scriptures, 46 and he said to them, 'Thus it
is written, that the Messiah*d* is to suffer
and to rise from the dead on the third day,
47 and that repentance and forgiveness of
sins is to be proclaimed in his name to all
nations, beginning from Jerusalem. 48 You
are witnesses*h* of these things. 49 And see, I
am sending upon you what my Father
promised; so stay here in the city until you
have been clothed with power from on
high.'

a Other ancient authorities read *walk along, looking
sad.'* *b* Other ancient authorities read *Jesus the
Nazorean* *c* Or *to set Israel free* *d* Or *the Christ*
e Other ancient authorities lack *within us* *f* Other
ancient authorities lack *and said to them, 'Peace be with
you.'* *g* Other ancient authorities lack verse 40
h Or *nations. Beginning from Jerusalem* 48*you are
witnesses*

The Ascension of Jesus

50 Then he led them out as far as Bethany, and, lifting up his hands, he blessed them. [51] While he was blessing them, he withdrew from them and was carried up into heaven.[a] [52] And they worshipped him, and[b] returned to Jerusalem with great joy; [53] and they were continually in the temple blessing God.[c]

a Other ancient authorities lack *and was carried up into heaven*   b Other ancient authorities lack *worshipped him, and*   c Other ancient authorities add *Amen*

THE GOSPEL ACCORDING TO
JOHN

The Word Became Flesh

1 In the beginning was the Word, and the Word was with God, and the Word was God. ²He was in the beginning with God. ³All things came into being through him, and without him not one thing came into being. What has come into being ⁴in him was life,ᵃ and the life was the light of all people. ⁵The light shines in the darkness, and the darkness did not overcome it.

6 There was a man sent from God, whose name was John. ⁷He came as a witness to testify to the light, so that all might believe through him. ⁸He himself was not the light, but he came to testify to the light. ⁹The true light, which enlightens everyone, was coming into the world.ᵇ

10 He was in the world, and the world came into being through him; yet the world did not know him. ¹¹He came to what was his own,ᶜ and his own people did not accept him. ¹²But to all who received him, who believed in his name, he gave power to become children of God, ¹³who were born, not of blood or of the will of the flesh or of the will of man, but of God.

14 And the Word became flesh and lived among us, and we have seen his glory, the glory as of a father's only son,ᵈ full of grace and truth. ¹⁵(John testified to him and cried out, 'This was he of whom I said, "He who comes after me ranks ahead of me because he was before me." ') ¹⁶From his fullness we have all received, grace upon grace. ¹⁷The law indeed was given through Moses; grace and truth came through Jesus Christ. ¹⁸No one has ever seen God. It is God the only Son,ᵉ who is close to the Father's heart,ᶠ who has made him known.

The Testimony of John the Baptist

19 This is the testimony given by John when the Jews sent priests and Levites from Jerusalem to ask him, 'Who are you?' ²⁰He confessed and did not deny it, but confessed, 'I am not the Messiah.'ᵍ ²¹And they asked him, 'What then? Are you Elijah?' He said, 'I am not.' 'Are you the prophet?' He answered, 'No.' ²²Then they said to him, 'Who are you? Let us have an answer for those who sent us. What do you say about yourself?' ²³He said,

'I am the voice of one crying out
    in the wilderness,
"Make straight the way of the Lord" ',
as the prophet Isaiah said.

24 Now they had been sent from the Pharisees. ²⁵They asked him, 'Why then are you baptizing if you are neither the Messiah,ᵍ nor Elijah, nor the prophet?' ²⁶John answered them, 'I baptize with water. Among you stands one whom you do not know, ²⁷the one who is coming after me; I am not worthy to untie the thong of his sandal.' ²⁸This took place in Bethany across the Jordan where John was baptizing.

The Lamb of God

29 The next day he saw Jesus coming towards him and declared, 'Here is the

---

a Or ³through him. And without him not one thing came into being that has come into being. ⁴In him was life   *b* Or He was the true light that enlightens everyone coming into the world   *c* Or to his own home   *d* Or the Father's only Son   *e* Other ancient authorities read It is an only Son, God, or It is the only Son   *f* Gk bosom   *g* Or the Christ

Lamb of God who takes away the sin of the world! ³⁰This is he of whom I said, "After me comes a man who ranks ahead of me because he was before me." ³¹I myself did not know him; but I came baptizing with water for this reason, that he might be revealed to Israel.' ³²And John testified, 'I saw the Spirit descending from heaven like a dove, and it remained on him. ³³I myself did not know him, but the one who sent me to baptize with water said to me, "He on whom you see the Spirit descend and remain is the one who baptizes with the Holy Spirit." ³⁴And I myself have seen and have testified that this is the Son of God.'ᵃ

The First Disciples of Jesus

35 The next day John again was standing with two of his disciples, ³⁶and as he watched Jesus walk by, he exclaimed, 'Look, here is the Lamb of God!' ³⁷The two disciples heard him say this, and they followed Jesus. ³⁸When Jesus turned and saw them following, he said to them, 'What are you looking for?' They said to him, 'Rabbi' (which translated means Teacher), 'where are you staying?' ³⁹He said to them, 'Come and see.' They came and saw where he was staying, and they remained with him that day. It was about four o'clock in the afternoon. ⁴⁰One of the two who heard John speak and followed him was Andrew, Simon Peter's brother. ⁴¹He first found his brother Simon and said to him, 'We have found the Messiah' (which is translated Anointedᵇ). ⁴²He brought Simonᶜ to Jesus, who looked at him and said, 'You are Simon son of John. You are to be called Cephas' (which is translated Peterᵈ).

Jesus Calls Philip and Nathanael

43 The next day Jesus decided to go to Galilee. He found Philip and said to him, 'Follow me.' ⁴⁴Now Philip was from Bethsaida, the city of Andrew and Peter. ⁴⁵Philip found Nathanael and said to him, 'We have found him about whom Moses in the law and also the prophets wrote, Jesus son of Joseph from Nazareth.' ⁴⁶Nathanael

said to him, 'Can anything good come out of Nazareth?' Philip said to him, 'Come and see.' ⁴⁷When Jesus saw Nathanael coming towards him, he said of him, 'Here is truly an Israelite in whom there is no deceit!' ⁴⁸Nathanael asked him, 'Where did you come to know me?' Jesus answered, 'I saw you under the fig tree before Philip called you.' ⁴⁹Nathanael replied, 'Rabbi, you are the Son of God! You are the King of Israel!' ⁵⁰Jesus answered, 'Do you believe because I told you that I saw you under the fig tree? You will see greater things than these.' ⁵¹And he said to him, 'Very truly, I tell you,ᵉ you will see heaven opened and the angels of God ascending and descending upon the Son of Man.'

The Wedding at Cana

2 On the third day there was a wedding in Cana of Galilee, and the mother of Jesus was there. ²Jesus and his disciples had also been invited to the wedding. ³When the wine gave out, the mother of Jesus said to him, 'They have no wine.' ⁴And Jesus said to her, 'Woman, what concern is that to you and to me? My hour has not yet come.' ⁵His mother said to the servants, 'Do whatever he tells you.' ⁶Now standing there were six stone water-jars for the Jewish rites of purification, each holding twenty or thirty gallons. ⁷Jesus said to them, 'Fill the jars with water.' And they filled them up to the brim. ⁸He said to them, 'Now draw some out, and take it to the chief steward.' So they took it. ⁹When the steward tasted the water that had become wine, and did not know where it came from (though the servants who had drawn the water knew), the steward called the bridegroom ¹⁰and said to him, 'Everyone serves the good wine first, and then the inferior wine after the guests have become drunk. But you have kept the good wine until now.' ¹¹Jesus did this, the first of his signs, in Cana of Galilee, and revealed

ᵃ Other ancient authorities read *is God's chosen one*
ᵇ Or *Christ*   ᶜ Gk *him*   ᵈ From the word for *rock* in Aramaic (*kepha*) and Greek (*petra*), respectively
ᵉ Both instances of the Greek word for *you* in this verse are plural

Miracles of Jesus

Miracles Showing Power Over Disease and Demons

	Matthew	Mark	Luke	John
A man with leprosy	8.2–4	1.40–42	5.12–13	
A Roman centurion's paralysed servant	8.5–13		7.1–10	
Peter's mother-in-law	8.14–15	1.30–31	4.38–39	
Two demoniacs from Gadara	8.28–34	5.1–15	8.27–35	
A paralysed man	9.2–7	2.3–12	5.18–25	
A woman suffering from haemorrhages	9.20–22	5.25–29	8.43–48	
Two blind men	9.27–31			
A mute demoniac	9.32–33			
A man with a withered hand	12.10–13	3.1–5	6.6–10	
A blind and mute demoniac	12.22		11.14	
A Canaanite woman's demonized daughter	15.21–28	7.24–30		
A young epileptic demoniac	17.14–18	9.17–29	9.38–43	
Two blind men	20.29–34	10.46–52	18.35–43	
A deaf man with a speech impediment		7.31–37		
A man with an unclean spirit		1.23–26	4.33–35	
A blind man at Bethsaida		8.22–26		
A woman crippled by a spirit			13.11–13	
A man with dropsy			14.1–4	
Ten men with leprosy			17.11–19	
The high priest's slave			22.50–51	
A royal official's son at Capernaum				4.46–54
A sick man at the pool of Beth-zatha				5.1–9
A man born blind				9.1–7

Miracles Showing Power Over Nature

	Matthew	Mark	Luke	John
Calming the windstorm on the sea	8.23–27	4.37–41	8.22–25	
Walking on water	14.25	6.48–51		6.19–21
Feeding more than five thousand	14.15–21	6.35–44	9.12–17	6.5–13
Feeding more than four thousand	15.32–38	8.1–9		
A coin in a fish's mouth	17.24–27			
Withering a fig tree	21.18–22	11.12–14, 20–25		
Commanding an amazing catch of fish			5.4–11	
Turning water into wine				2.1–11
Commanding another catch of fish				21.1–11

Miracles Showing Power Over Death

	Matthew	Mark	Luke	John
The daughter of Jairus	9.18–19, 23–25	5.22–24, 38–42	8.41–42, 49–56	
The only son of the widow at Nain			7.11–15	
Lazarus				11.1–44

his glory; and his disciples believed in him.

12 After this he went down to Capernaum with his mother, his brothers, and his disciples; and they remained there for a few days.

Jesus Cleanses the Temple

13 The Passover of the Jews was near, and Jesus went up to Jerusalem. 14 In the temple he found people selling cattle, sheep, and doves, and the money-changers seated at their tables. 15 Making a whip of cords, he drove all of them out of the temple, both the sheep and the cattle. He also poured out the coins of the money-changers and overturned their tables. 16 He told those who were selling the doves, 'Take these things out of here! Stop making my Father's house a market-place!' 17 His disciples remembered that it was written, 'Zeal for your house will consume me.' 18 The Jews then said to him, 'What sign can you show us for doing this?' 19 Jesus answered them, 'Destroy this temple, and in three days I will raise it up.' 20 The Jews then said, 'This temple has been under construction for forty-six years, and will you raise it up in three days?' 21 But he was speaking of the temple of his body. 22 After he was raised from the dead, his disciples remembered that he had said this; and they believed the scripture and the word that Jesus had spoken.

23 When he was in Jerusalem during the Passover festival, many believed in his name because they saw the signs that he was doing. 24 But Jesus on his part would not entrust himself to them, because he knew all people 25 and needed no one to testify about anyone; for he himself knew what was in everyone.

Nicodemus Visits Jesus

3 Now there was a Pharisee named Nicodemus, a leader of the Jews. 2 He came to Jesus[a] by night and said to him, 'Rabbi, we know that you are a teacher who has come from God; for no one can do these signs that you do apart from the presence of God.' 3 Jesus answered him,

'Very truly, I tell you, no one can see the kingdom of God without being born from above.'[b] 4 Nicodemus said to him, 'How can anyone be born after having grown old? Can one enter a second time into the mother's womb and be born?' 5 Jesus answered, 'Very truly, I tell you, no one can enter the kingdom of God without being born of water and Spirit. 6 What is born of the flesh is flesh, and what is born of the Spirit is spirit.[c] 7 Do not be astonished that I said to you, "You[d] must be born from above."[e] 8 The wind[c] blows where it chooses, and you hear the sound of it, but you do not know where it comes from or where it goes. So it is with everyone who is born of the Spirit.' 9 Nicodemus said to him, 'How can these things be?' 10 Jesus answered him, 'Are you a teacher of Israel, and yet you do not understand these things?

11 'Very truly, I tell you, we speak of what we know and testify to what we have seen; yet you[f] do not receive our testimony. 12 If I have told you about earthly things and you do not believe, how can you believe if I tell you about heavenly things? 13 No one has ascended into heaven except the one who descended from heaven, the Son of Man.[g] 14 And just as Moses lifted up the serpent in the wilderness, so must the Son of Man be lifted up, 15 that whoever believes in him may have eternal life.[h]

16 'For God so loved the world that he gave his only Son, so that everyone who believes in him may not perish but may have eternal life.

17 'Indeed, God did not send the Son into the world to condemn the world, but in order that the world might be saved through him. 18 Those who believe in him are not condemned; but those who do not believe are condemned already, because they have not believed in the name of the only Son of God. 19 And this is the judge-

a Gk him   b Or born anew   c The same Greek word means both wind and spirit   d The Greek word for you here is plural   e Or anew   f The Greek word for you here and in verse 12 is plural   g Other ancient authorities add who is in heaven   h Some interpreters hold that the quotation concludes with verse 15 ment, that the light has come into the world, and people loved darkness rather than light because their deeds were evil. [20] For all who do evil hate the light and do not come to the light, so that their deeds may not be exposed. [21] But those who do what is true come to the light, so that it may be clearly seen that their deeds have been done in God.'[a]

Jesus and John the Baptist

22 After this Jesus and his disciples went into the Judean countryside, and he spent some time there with them and baptized. [23] John also was baptizing at Aenon near Salim because water was abundant there; and people kept coming and were being baptized— [24] John, of course, had not yet been thrown into prison.

25 Now a discussion about purification arose between John's disciples and a Jew.[b] [26] They came to John and said to him, 'Rabbi, the one who was with you across the Jordan, to whom you testified, here he is baptizing, and all are going to him.' [27] John answered, 'No one can receive anything except what has been given from heaven. [28] You yourselves are my witnesses that I said, "I am not the Messiah,[c] but I have been sent ahead of him." [29] He who has the bride is the bridegroom. The friend of the bridegroom, who stands and hears him, rejoices greatly at the bridegroom's voice. For this reason my joy has been fulfilled. [30] He must increase, but I must decrease.'[d]

The One Who Comes from Heaven

31 The one who comes from above is above all; the one who is of the earth belongs to the earth and speaks about earthly things. The one who comes from heaven is above all. [32] He testifies to what he has seen and heard, yet no one accepts his testimony. [33] Whoever has accepted his testimony has certified[e] this, that God is true. [34] He whom God has sent speaks the words of God, for he gives the Spirit without measure. [35] The Father loves the Son and has placed all things in his hands. [36] Whoever believes in the Son has eternal life;

whoever disobeys the Son will not see life, but must endure God's wrath.

Jesus and the Woman of Samaria

4 Now when Jesus[f] learned that the Pharisees had heard, 'Jesus is making and baptizing more disciples than John'— [2] although it was not Jesus himself but his disciples who baptized— [3] he left Judea and started back to Galilee. [4] But he had to go through Samaria. [5] So he came to a Samaritan city called Sychar, near the plot of ground that Jacob had given to his son Joseph. [6] Jacob's well was there, and Jesus, tired out by his journey, was sitting by the well. It was about noon.

7 A Samaritan woman came to draw water, and Jesus said to her, 'Give me a drink'. [8] (His disciples had gone to the city to buy food.) [9] The Samaritan woman said to him, 'How is it that you, a Jew, ask a drink of me, a woman of Samaria?' (Jews do not share things in common with Samaritans.)[g] [10] Jesus answered her, 'If you knew the gift of God, and who it is that is saying to you, "Give me a drink", you would have asked him, and he would have given you living water.' [11] The woman said to him, 'Sir, you have no bucket, and the well is deep. Where do you get that living water? [12] Are you greater than our ancestor Jacob, who gave us the well, and with his sons and his flocks drank from it?' [13] Jesus said to her, 'Everyone who drinks of this water will be thirsty again, [14] but those who drink of the water that I will give them will never be thirsty. The water that I will give will become in them a spring of water gushing up to eternal life.' [15] The woman said to him, 'Sir, give me this water, so that I may never be thirsty or have to keep coming here to draw water.'

16 Jesus said to her, 'Go, call your husband, and come back.' [17] The woman answered him, 'I have no husband.' Jesus said to her, 'You are right in saying, "I

---

a Some interpreters hold that the quotation concludes with verse 15   *b* Other ancient authorities read *the Jews*   *c* Or *the Christ*   *d* Some interpreters hold that the quotation continues to the end of verse 36   *e* Gk *set a seal to*   *f* Other ancient authorities read *the Lord*   *g* Other ancient authorities lack this sentence have no husband"; ¹⁸for you have had five husbands, and the one you have now is not your husband. What you have said is true!' ¹⁹The woman said to him, 'Sir, I see that you are a prophet. ²⁰Our ancestors worshipped on this mountain, but you*ᵃ* say that the place where people must worship is in Jerusalem.' ²¹Jesus said to her, 'Woman, believe me, the hour is coming when you will worship the Father neither on this mountain nor in Jerusalem. ²²You worship what you do not know; we worship what we know, for salvation is from the Jews. ²³But the hour is coming, and is now here, when the true worshippers will worship the Father in spirit and truth, for the Father seeks such as these to worship him. ²⁴God is spirit, and those who worship him must worship in spirit and truth.' ²⁵The woman said to him, 'I know that Messiah is coming' (who is called Christ). 'When he comes, he will proclaim all things to us.' ²⁶Jesus said to her, 'I am he,*ᵇ* the one who is speaking to you.'

Jesus in Judea and Samaria

27 Just then his disciples came. They were astonished that he was speaking with a woman, but no one said, 'What do you want?' or, 'Why are you speaking with her?' ²⁸Then the woman left her water-jar and went back to the city. She said to the people, ²⁹'Come and see a man who told me everything I have ever done! He cannot be the Messiah,*ᶜ* can he?' ³⁰They left the city and were on their way to him.

31 Meanwhile the disciples were urging him, 'Rabbi, eat something.' ³²But he said to them, 'I have food to eat that you do not know about.' ³³So the disciples said to one another, 'Surely no one has brought him something to eat?' ³⁴Jesus said to them, 'My food is to do the will of him who sent me and to complete his work. ³⁵Do you not say, "Four months more, then comes the harvest"? But I tell you, look around you, and see how the fields are ripe for harvesting. ³⁶The reaper is already receiving*ᵈ* wages and is gathering fruit for eternal life, so that sower and reaper may rejoice together. ³⁷For here the saying holds true, "One sows and another reaps." ³⁸I sent you to reap that for which you did not labour. Others have laboured, and you have entered into their labour.'

39 Many Samaritans from that city believed in him because of the woman's testimony, 'He told me everything I have ever done.' ⁴⁰So when the Samaritans came to him, they asked him to stay with them; and he stayed there for two days. ⁴¹And many more believed because of his word. ⁴²They said to the woman, 'It is no longer because of what you said that we believe, for we have heard for ourselves, and we know that this is truly the Saviour of the world.'

Jesus Returns to Galilee

43 When the two days were over, he went from that place to Galilee ⁴⁴(for Jesus himself had testified that a prophet has no honour in the prophet's own

a The Greek word for *you* here and in verses 21 and 22 is plural   *b* Gk *I am*   *c* Or *the Christ*   *d* Or ³⁵. . . *the fields are already ripe for harvesting.* ³⁶*The reaper is receiving* country). 45When he came to Galilee, the Galileans welcomed him, since they had seen all that he had done in Jerusalem at the festival; for they too had gone to the festival.

Jesus Heals an Official's Son

46 Then he came again to Cana in Galilee where he had changed the water into wine. Now there was a royal official whose son lay ill in Capernaum. 47When he heard that Jesus had come from Judea to Galilee, he went and begged him to come down and heal his son, for he was at the point of death. 48Then Jesus said to him, 'Unless you*a* see signs and wonders you will not believe.' 49The official said to him, 'Sir, come down before my little boy dies.' 50Jesus said to him, 'Go; your son will live.' The man believed the word that Jesus spoke to him and started on his way. 51As he was going down, his slaves met him and told him that his child was alive. 52So he asked them the hour when he began to recover, and they said to him, 'Yesterday at one in the afternoon the fever left him.' 53The father realized that this was the hour when Jesus had said to him, 'Your son will live.' So he himself believed, along with his whole household. 54Now this was the second sign that Jesus did after coming from Judea to Galilee.

Jesus Heals on the Sabbath

5 After this there was a festival of the Jews, and Jesus went up to Jerusalem. 2 Now in Jerusalem by the Sheep Gate there is a pool, called in Hebrew*b* Bethzatha,*c* which has five porticoes. 3In these lay many invalids—blind, lame, and paralysed.*d* 5One man was there who had been ill for thirty-eight years. 6When Jesus saw him lying there and knew that he had been there a long time, he said to him, 'Do you want to be made well?' 7The sick man answered him, 'Sir, I have no one to put me into the pool when the water is stirred up; and while I am making my way, someone else steps down ahead of me.' 8Jesus said to him, 'Stand up, take your mat and walk.' 9At once the man was

made well, and he took up his mat and began to walk.

Now that day was a sabbath. 10So the Jews said to the man who had been cured, 'It is the sabbath; it is not lawful for you to carry your mat.' 11But he answered them, 'The man who made me well said to me, "Take up your mat and walk." ' 12They asked him, 'Who is the man who said to you, "Take it up and walk"?' 13Now the man who had been healed did not know who it was, for Jesus had disappeared in*e* the crowd that was there. 14Later Jesus found him in the temple and said to him, 'See, you have been made well! Do not sin any more, so that nothing worse happens to you.' 15The man went away and told the Jews that it was Jesus who had made him well. 16Therefore the Jews started persecuting Jesus, because he was doing such things on the sabbath. 17But Jesus answered them, 'My Father is still working, and I also am working.' 18For this reason the Jews were seeking all the more to kill him, because he was not only breaking the sabbath, but was also calling God his own Father, thereby making himself equal to God.

The Authority of the Son

19 Jesus said to them, 'Very truly, I tell you, the Son can do nothing on his own, but only what he sees the Father doing; for whatever the Father*f* does, the Son does likewise. 20The Father loves the Son and shows him all that he himself is doing; and he will show him greater works than these, so that you will be astonished. 21Indeed, just as the Father raises the dead and gives them life, so also the Son gives life to whomsoever he wishes. 22The Father judges no one but has given all judgement to the Son, 23so that all may honour the Son just as they honour the Father. Anyone

---

a Both instances of the Greek word for *you* in this verse are plural   *b* That is, *Aramaic*   *c* Other ancient authorities read *Bethesda*, others *Bethsaida*   *d* Other ancient authorities add, wholly or in part, *waiting for the stirring of the water;* 4*for an angel of the Lord went down at certain seasons into the pool, and stirred up the water; whoever stepped in first after the stirring of the water was made well from whatever disease that person had.*   *e* Or *had left because of*   *f* Gk *that one* who does not honour the Son does not honour the Father who sent him. 24 Very truly, I tell you, anyone who hears my word and believes him who sent me has eternal life, and does not come under judgement, but has passed from death to life.

25 'Very truly, I tell you, the hour is coming, and is now here, when the dead will hear the voice of the Son of God, and those who hear will live. 26 For just as the Father has life in himself, so he has granted the Son also to have life in himself; 27 and he has given him authority to execute judgement, because he is the Son of Man. 28 Do not be astonished at this; for the hour is coming when all who are in their graves will hear his voice 29 and will come out—those who have done good, to the resurrection of life, and those who have done evil, to the resurrection of condemnation.

Witnesses to Jesus

30 'I can do nothing on my own. As I hear, I judge; and my judgement is just, because I seek to do not my own will but the will of him who sent me.

31 'If I testify about myself, my testimony is not true. 32 There is another who testifies on my behalf, and I know that his testimony to me is true. 33 You sent messengers to John, and he testified to the truth. 34 Not that I accept such human testimony, but I say these things so that you may be saved. 35 He was a burning and shining lamp, and you were willing to rejoice for a while in his light. 36 But I have a testimony greater than John's. The works that the Father has given me to complete, the very works that I am doing, testify on my behalf that the Father has sent me. 37 And the Father who sent me has himself testified on my behalf. You have never heard his voice or seen his form, 38 and you do not have his word abiding in you, because you do not believe him whom he has sent.

39 'You search the scriptures because you think that in them you have eternal life; and it is they that testify on my be-

half. 40 Yet you refuse to come to me to have life. 41 I do not accept glory from human beings. 42 But I know that you do not have the love of God in*a* you. 43 I have come in my Father's name, and you do not accept me; if another comes in his own name, you will accept him. 44 How can you believe when you accept glory from one another and do not seek the glory that comes from the one who alone is God? 45 Do not think that I will accuse you before the Father; your accuser is Moses, on whom you have set your hope. 46 If you believed Moses, you would believe me, for he wrote about me. 47 But if you do not believe what he wrote, how will you believe what I say?'

Feeding the Five Thousand

6 After this Jesus went to the other side of the Sea of Galilee, also called the Sea of Tiberias.*b* 2 A large crowd kept following him, because they saw the signs that he was doing for the sick. 3 Jesus went up the mountain and sat down there with his disciples. 4 Now the Passover, the festival of the Jews, was near. 5 When he looked up and saw a large crowd coming towards him, Jesus said to Philip, 'Where are we to buy bread for these people to eat?' 6 He said this to test him, for he himself knew what he was going to do. 7 Philip answered him, 'Six months' wages*c* would not buy enough bread for each of them to get a little.' 8 One of his disciples, Andrew, Simon Peter's brother, said to him, 9 'There is a boy here who has five barley loaves and two fish. But what are they among so many people?' 10 Jesus said, 'Make the people sit down.' Now there was a great deal of grass in the place; so they*d* sat down, about five thousand in all. 11 Then Jesus took the loaves, and when he had given thanks, he distributed them to those who were seated; so also the fish, as much as they wanted. 12 When they were satisfied, he told his disciples, 'Gather up the fragments left over, so that nothing may be lost.' 13 So

a Or *among* *b* Gk *of Galilee of Tiberias* *c* Gk *Two hundred denarii*; the denarius was the usual day's wage for a labourer *d* Gk *the men* they gathered them up, and from the fragments of the five barley loaves, left by those who had eaten, they filled twelve baskets. [14] When the people saw the sign that he had done, they began to say, 'This is indeed the prophet who is to come into the world.'

15 When Jesus realized that they were about to come and take him by force to make him king, he withdrew again to the mountain by himself.

Jesus Walks on the Water

16 When evening came, his disciples went down to the lake, [17] got into a boat, and started across the lake to Capernaum. It was now dark, and Jesus had not yet come to them. [18] The lake became rough because a strong wind was blowing. [19] When they had rowed about three or four miles, [a] they saw Jesus walking on the lake and coming near the boat, and they were terrified. [20] But he said to them, 'It is I; [b] do not be afraid.' [21] Then they wanted to take him into the boat, and immediately the boat reached the land towards which they were going.

The Bread from Heaven

22 The next day the crowd that had stayed on the other side of the lake saw that there had been only one boat there. They also saw that Jesus had not got into the boat with his disciples, but that his disciples had gone away alone. [23] Then some boats from Tiberias came near the place where they had eaten the bread after the Lord had given thanks. [c] [24] So when the crowd saw that neither Jesus nor his disciples were there, they themselves got into the boats and went to Capernaum looking for Jesus.

25 When they found him on the other side of the lake, they said to him, 'Rabbi, when did you come here?' [26] Jesus answered them, 'Very truly, I tell you, you are looking for me, not because you saw signs, but because you ate your fill of the loaves. [27] Do not work for the food that perishes, but for the food that endures for eternal life, which the Son of Man will give you. For it is on him that God the Father has set his seal.' [28] Then they said to him, 'What must we do to perform the works of God?' [29] Jesus answered them, 'This is the work of God, that you believe in him whom he has sent.' [30] So they said to him, 'What sign are you going to give us then, so that we may see it and believe you? What work are you performing? [31] Our ancestors ate the manna in the wilderness; as it is written, "He gave them bread from heaven to eat." ' [32] Then Jesus said to them, 'Very truly, I tell you, it was not Moses who gave you the bread from heaven, but it is my Father who gives you the true bread from heaven. [33] For the bread of God is that which [d] comes down from heaven and gives life to the world.' [34] They said to him, 'Sir, give us this bread always.'

35 Jesus said to them, 'I am the bread of life. Whoever comes to me will never be hungry, and whoever believes in me will

Jesus in Galilee

Mediterranean Sea

Ptolemais

Korazin

Capernaum

Bethsaida

GALILEE

Magdala

Sea of Galilee

Tiberias

Mt. Carmel

Cana

Nazareth

Mt. Tabor

Caesarea

Nain

Scythopolis

Kishon R.

Yarmuk R.

Jordan River

N

0   10 Mi.
0   10 Km.

a Gk *about twenty-five or thirty stadia*   b Gk *I am*
c Other ancient authorities lack *after the Lord had given thanks*   d Or *he who*

never be thirsty. 36 But I said to you that you have seen me and yet do not believe. 37 Everything that the Father gives me will come to me, and anyone who comes to me I will never drive away; 38 for I have come down from heaven, not to do my own will, but the will of him who sent me. 39 And this is the will of him who sent me, that I should lose nothing of all that he has given me, but raise it up on the last day. 40 This is indeed the will of my Father, that all who see the Son and believe in him may have eternal life; and I will raise them up on the last day.'

41 Then the Jews began to complain about him because he said, 'I am the bread that came down from heaven.' 42 They were saying, 'Is not this Jesus, the son of Joseph, whose father and mother we know? How can he now say, "I have come down from heaven"?' 43 Jesus answered them, 'Do not complain among yourselves. 44 No one can come to me unless drawn by the Father who sent me; and I will raise that person up on the last day. 45 It is written in the prophets, "And they shall all be taught by God." Everyone who has heard and learned from the Father comes to me. 46 Not that anyone has seen the Father except the one who is from God; he has seen the Father. 47 Very truly, I tell you, whoever believes has eternal life. 48 I am the bread of life. 49 Your ancestors ate the manna in the wilderness, and they died. 50 This is the bread that comes down from heaven, so that one may eat of it and not die. 51 I am the living bread that came down from heaven. Whoever eats of this bread will live for ever; and the bread that I will give for the life of the world is my flesh.'

52 The Jews then disputed among themselves, saying, 'How can this man give us his flesh to eat?' 53 So Jesus said to them, 'Very truly, I tell you, unless you eat the flesh of the Son of Man and drink his blood, you have no life in you. 54 Those who eat my flesh and drink my blood have eternal life, and I will raise them up on the last day; 55 for my flesh is true food and my blood is true drink. 56 Those who eat my

flesh and drink my blood abide in me, and I in them. 57 Just as the living Father sent me, and I live because of the Father, so whoever eats me will live because of me. 58 This is the bread that came down from heaven, not like that which your ancestors ate, and they died. But the one who eats this bread will live for ever.' 59 He said these things while he was teaching in the synagogue at Capernaum.

The Words of Eternal Life

60 When many of his disciples heard it, they said, 'This teaching is difficult; who can accept it?' 61 But Jesus, being aware that his disciples were complaining about it, said to them, 'Does this offend you? 62 Then what if you were to see the Son of Man ascending to where he was before? 63 It is the spirit that gives life; the flesh is useless. The words that I have spoken to you are spirit and life. 64 But among you there are some who do not believe.' For Jesus knew from the first who were the ones that did not believe, and who was the one that would betray him. 65 And he said, 'For this reason I have told you that no one can come to me unless it is granted by the Father.'

66 Because of this many of his disciples turned back and no longer went about with him. 67 So Jesus asked the twelve, 'Do you also wish to go away?' 68 Simon Peter answered him, 'Lord, to whom can we go? You have the words of eternal life. 69 We have come to believe and know that you are the Holy One of God.'[a] 70 Jesus answered them, 'Did I not choose you, the twelve? Yet one of you is a devil.' 71 He was speaking of Judas son of Simon Iscariot,[b] for he, though one of the twelve, was going to betray him.

The Unbelief of Jesus' Brothers

7 After this Jesus went about in Galilee. He did not wish[c] to go about in Judea because the Jews were looking for an

a Other ancient authorities read the Christ, the Son of the living God   b Other ancient authorities read Judas Iscariot son of Simon; others, Judas son of Simon from Karyot (Kerioth)   c Other ancient authorities read was not at liberty opportunity to kill him. 2 Now the Jewish festival of Booths[a] was near. 3 So his brothers said to him, 'Leave here and go to Judea so that your disciples also may see the works you are doing; 4 for no one who wants[b] to be widely known acts in secret. If you do these things, show yourself to the world.' 5 (For not even his brothers believed in him.) 6 Jesus said to them, 'My time has not yet come, but your time is always here. 7 The world cannot hate you, but it hates me because I testify against it that its works are evil. 8 Go to the festival yourselves. I am not[c] going to this festival, for my time has not yet fully come.' 9 After saying this, he remained in Galilee.

Jesus at the Festival of Booths

10 But after his brothers had gone to the festival, then he also went, not publicly but as it were[d] in secret. 11 The Jews were looking for him at the festival and saying, 'Where is he?' 12 And there was considerable complaining about him among the crowds. While some were saying, 'He is a good man', others were saying, 'No, he is deceiving the crowd.' 13 Yet no one would speak openly about him for fear of the Jews.

14 About the middle of the festival Jesus went up into the temple and began to teach. 15 The Jews were astonished at it, saying, 'How does this man have such learning,[e] when he has never been taught?' 16 Then Jesus answered them, 'My teaching is not mine but his who sent me. 17 Anyone who resolves to do the will of God will know whether the teaching is from God or whether I am speaking on my own. 18 Those who speak on their own seek their own glory; but the one who seeks the glory of him who sent me is true, and there is nothing false in him.

19 'Did not Moses give you the law? Yet none of you keeps the law. Why are you looking for an opportunity to kill me?' 20 The crowd answered, 'You have a demon! Who is trying to kill you?' 21 Jesus answered them, 'I performed one work, and all of you are astonished. 22 Moses gave

you circumcision (it is, of course, not from Moses, but from the patriarchs), and you circumcise a man on the sabbath. 23 If a man receives circumcision on the sabbath in order that the law of Moses may not be broken, are you angry with me because I healed a man's whole body on the sabbath? 24 Do not judge by appearances, but judge with right judgement.'

Is This the Christ?

25 Now some of the people of Jerusalem were saying, 'Is not this the man whom they are trying to kill? 26 And here he is, speaking openly, but they say nothing to him! Can it be that the authorities really know that this is the Messiah?[f] 27 Yet we know where this man is from; but when the Messiah[f] comes, no one will know where he is from.' 28 Then Jesus cried out as he was teaching in the temple, 'You know me, and you know where I am from. I have not come on my own. But the one who sent me is true, and you do not know him. 29 I know him, because I am from him, and he sent me.' 30 Then they tried to arrest him, but no one laid hands on him, because his hour had not yet come. 31 Yet many in the crowd believed in him and were saying, 'When the Messiah[f] comes, will he do more signs than this man has done?'[g]

Officers Are Sent to Arrest Jesus

32 The Pharisees heard the crowd muttering such things about him, and the chief priests and Pharisees sent temple police to arrest him. 33 Jesus then said, 'I will be with you a little while longer, and then I am going to him who sent me. 34 You will search for me, but you will not find me; and where I am, you cannot come.' 35 The Jews said to one another, 'Where does this man intend to go that we will not find him? Does he intend to go to the Dispersion among the Greeks and teach the Greeks? 36 What does he mean by say-

a Or Tabernacles   b Other ancient authorities read
wants it   c Other ancient authorities add yet
d Other ancient authorities lack as it were   e Or this
man know his letters   f Or the Christ   g Other ancient
authorities read is doing

ing, "You will search for me and you will not find me" and, "Where I am, you cannot come"?'

Rivers of Living Water

37 On the last day of the festival, the great day, while Jesus was standing there, he cried out, 'Let anyone who is thirsty come to me, 38 and let the one who believes in me drink. As *a* the scripture has said, "Out of the believer's heart *b* shall flow rivers of living water." ' 39 Now he said this about the Spirit, which believers in him were to receive; for as yet there was no Spirit, *c* because Jesus was not yet glorified.

Division among the People

40 When they heard these words, some in the crowd said, 'This is really the prophet.' 41 Others said, 'This is the Messiah.' *d* But some asked, 'Surely the Messiah *d* does not come from Galilee, does he? 42 Has not the scripture said that the Messiah *d* is descended from David and comes from Bethlehem, the village where David lived?' 43 So there was a division in the crowd because of him. 44 Some of them wanted to arrest him, but no one laid hands on him.

The Unbelief of Those in Authority

45 Then the temple police went back to the chief priests and Pharisees, who asked them, 'Why did you not arrest him?' 46 The police answered, 'Never has anyone spoken like this!' 47 Then the Pharisees replied, 'Surely you have not been deceived too, have you? 48 Has any one of the authorities or of the Pharisees believed in him? 49 But this crowd, which does not know the law—they are accursed.' 50 Nicodemus, who had gone to Jesus *e* before, and who was one of them, asked, 51 'Our law does not judge people without first giving them a hearing to find out what they are doing, does it?' 52 They replied, 'Surely you are not also from Galilee, are you? Search and you will see that no prophet is to arise from Galilee.'

The Woman Caught in Adultery

8 ⟦53 Then each of them went home, 1 while Jesus went to the Mount of Olives. 2 Early in the morning he came again to the temple. All the people came to him and he sat down and began to teach them. 3 The scribes and the Pharisees brought a woman who had been caught in adultery; and making her stand before all of them, 4 they said to him, 'Teacher, this woman was caught in the very act of committing adultery. 5 Now in the law Moses commanded us to stone such women. Now what do you say?' 6 They said this to test him, so that they might have some charge to bring against him. Jesus bent down and wrote with his finger on the ground. 7 When they kept on questioning him, he straightened up and said to them, 'Let anyone among you who is without sin be the first to throw a stone at her.' 8 And once again he bent down and wrote on the ground. *f* 9 When they heard it, they went away, one by one, beginning with the elders; and Jesus was left alone with the woman standing before him. 10 Jesus straightened up and said to her, 'Woman, where are they? Has no one condemned you?' 11 She said, 'No one, sir.' *g* And Jesus said, 'Neither do I condemn you. Go your way, and from now on do not sin again.'⟧ *h*

Jesus the Light of the World

12 Again Jesus spoke to them, saying, 'I am the light of the world. Whoever follows me will never walk in darkness but will have the light of life.' 13 Then the Pharisees said to him, 'You are testifying on your own behalf; your testimony is not valid.' 14 Jesus answered, 'Even if I testify on my own behalf, my testimony is valid because I know where I have come from and where I am going, but you do not know where I come from or where I am going. 15 You

a Or *come to me and drink.* 38 *The one who believes in me, as* *b* Gk *out of his belly* *c* Other ancient authorities read *for as yet the Spirit* (others, *Holy Spirit*) *had not been given* *d* Or *the Christ* *e* Gk *him* *f* Other ancient authorities add *the sins of each of them* *g* Or *Lord* *h* The most ancient authorities lack 7.53—8.11; other authorities add the passage here or after 7.36 or after 21.25 or after Luke 21.38, with variations of text; some mark the passage as doubtful.

judge by human standards;[a] I judge no one. [16]Yet even if I do judge, my judgement is valid; for it is not I alone who judge, but I and the Father[b] who sent me. [17]In your law it is written that the testimony of two witnesses is valid. [18]I testify on my own behalf, and the Father who sent me testifies on my behalf.' [19]Then they said to him, 'Where is your Father?' Jesus answered, 'You know neither me nor my Father. If you knew me, you would know my Father also.' [20]He spoke these words while he was teaching in the treasury of the temple, but no one arrested him, because his hour had not yet come.

Jesus Foretells His Death

[21] Again he said to them, 'I am going away, and you will search for me, but you will die in your sin. Where I am going, you cannot come.' [22]Then the Jews said, 'Is he going to kill himself? Is that what he means by saying, "Where I am going, you cannot come"?' [23]He said to them, 'You are from below, I am from above; you are of this world, I am not of this world. [24]I told you that you would die in your sins, for you will die in your sins unless you believe that I am he.'[c] [25]They said to him, 'Who are you?' Jesus said to them, 'Why do I speak to you at all?[d] [26]I have much to say about you and much to condemn; but the one who sent me is true, and I declare to the world what I have heard from him.' [27]They did not understand that he was speaking to them about the Father. [28]So Jesus said, 'When you have lifted up the Son of Man, then you will realize that I am he,[c] and that I do nothing on my own, but I speak these things as the Father instructed me. [29]And the one who sent me is with me; he has not left me alone, for I always do what is pleasing to him.' [30]As he was saying these things, many believed in him.

True Disciples

[31] Then Jesus said to the Jews who had believed in him, 'If you continue in my word, you are truly my disciples; [32]and you will know the truth, and the truth will make you free.' [33]They answered him, 'We are descendants of Abraham and have never been slaves to anyone. What do you mean by saying, "You will be made free"?'

[34] Jesus answered them, 'Very truly, I tell you, everyone who commits sin is a slave to sin. [35]The slave does not have a permanent place in the household; the son has a place there for ever. [36]So if the Son makes you free, you will be free indeed. [37]I know that you are descendants of Abraham; yet you look for an opportunity to kill me, because there is no place in you for my word. [38]I declare what I have seen in the Father's presence; as for you, you should do what you have heard from the Father.'[e]

Jesus and Abraham

[39] They answered him, 'Abraham is our father.' Jesus said to them, 'If you were Abraham's children, you would be doing[f] what Abraham did, [40]but now you are trying to kill me, a man who has told you the truth that I heard from God. This is not what Abraham did. [41]You are indeed doing what your father does.' They said to him, 'We are not illegitimate children; we have one father, God himself.' [42]Jesus said to them, 'If God were your Father, you would love me, for I came from God and now I am here. I did not come on my own, but he sent me. [43]Why do you not understand what I say? It is because you cannot accept my word. [44]You are from your father the devil, and you choose to do your father's desires. He was a murderer from the beginning and does not stand in the truth, because there is no truth in him. When he lies, he speaks according to his own nature, for he is a liar and the father of lies. [45]But because I tell the truth, you do not believe me. [46]Which of you convicts me of sin? If I tell the truth, why do you not believe me? [47]Whoever is from God hears the words of God. The reason you do not hear them is that you are not from God.'

a Gk *according to the flesh*   b Other ancient authorities read *he*   c Gk *I am*   d Or *What I have told you from the beginning*   e Other ancient authorities read *you do what you have heard from your father*   f Other ancient authorities read *If you are Abraham's children, then do*

48 The Jews answered him, 'Are we not right in saying that you are a Samaritan and have a demon?' 49 Jesus answered, 'I do not have a demon; but I honour my Father, and you dishonour me. 50 Yet I do not seek my own glory; there is one who seeks it and he is the judge. 51 Very truly, I tell you, whoever keeps my word will never see death.' 52 The Jews said to him, 'Now we know that you have a demon. Abraham died, and so did the prophets; yet you say, "Whoever keeps my word will never taste death." 53 Are you greater than our father Abraham, who died? The prophets also died. Who do you claim to be?' 54 Jesus answered, 'If I glorify myself, my glory is nothing. It is my Father who glorifies me, he of whom you say, "He is our God", 55 though you do not know him. But I know him; if I were to say that I do not know him, I would be a liar like you. But I do know him and I keep his word. 56 Your ancestor Abraham rejoiced that he would see my day; he saw it and was glad.' 57 Then the Jews said to him, 'You are not yet fifty years old, and have you seen Abraham?'*a* 58 Jesus said to them, 'Very truly, I tell you, before Abraham was, I am.' 59 So they picked up stones to throw at him, but Jesus hid himself and went out of the temple.

A Man Born Blind Receives Sight

9 As he walked along, he saw a man blind from birth. 2 His disciples asked him, 'Rabbi, who sinned, this man or his parents, that he was born blind?' 3 Jesus answered, 'Neither this man nor his parents sinned; he was born blind so that God's works might be revealed in him. 4 We*b* must work the works of him who sent me*c* while it is day; night is coming when no one can work. 5 As long as I am in the world, I am the light of the world.' 6 When he had said this, he spat on the ground and made mud with the saliva and spread the mud on the man's eyes, 7 saying to him, 'Go, wash in the pool of Siloam' (which means Sent). Then he went and washed and came back able to see. 8 The neighbours and those who had seen him

before as a beggar began to ask, 'Is this not the man who used to sit and beg?' 9 Some were saying, 'It is he.' Others were saying, 'No, but it is someone like him.' He kept saying, 'I am the man.' 10 But they kept asking him, 'Then how were your eyes opened?' 11 He answered, 'The man called Jesus made mud, spread it on my eyes, and said to me, "Go to Siloam and wash." Then I went and washed and received my sight.' 12 They said to him, 'Where is he?' He said, 'I do not know.'

The Pharisees Investigate the Healing

13 They brought to the Pharisees the man who had formerly been blind. 14 Now it was a sabbath day when Jesus made the mud and opened his eyes. 15 Then the Pharisees also began to ask him how he had received his sight. He said to them, 'He put mud on my eyes. Then I washed, and now I see.' 16 Some of the Pharisees said, 'This man is not from God, for he does not observe the sabbath.' But others said, 'How can a man who is a sinner perform such signs?' And they were divided. 17 So they said again to the blind man, 'What do you say about him? It was your eyes he opened.' He said, 'He is a prophet.'

18 The Jews did not believe that he had been blind and had received his sight until they called the parents of the man who had received his sight 19 and asked them, 'Is this your son, who you say was born blind? How then does he now see?' 20 His parents answered, 'We know that this is our son, and that he was born blind; 21 but we do not know how it is that now he sees, nor do we know who opened his eyes. Ask him; he is of age. He will speak for himself.' 22 His parents said this because they were afraid of the Jews; for the Jews had already agreed that anyone who confessed Jesus*d* to be the Messiah*e* would be put out of the synagogue. 23 Therefore his parents said, 'He is of age; ask him.'

24 So for the second time they called the man who had been blind, and they

a Other ancient authorities read *has Abraham seen you?*
b Other ancient authorities read *I*　*c* Other ancient authorities read *us*　*d* Gk *him*　*e* Or *the Christ*

said to him, 'Give glory to God! We know that this man is a sinner.' 25 He answered, 'I do not know whether he is a sinner. One thing I do know, that though I was blind, now I see.' 26 They said to him, 'What did he do to you? How did he open your eyes?' 27 He answered them, 'I have told you already, and you would not listen. Why do you want to hear it again? Do you also want to become his disciples?' 28 Then they reviled him, saying, 'You are his disciple, but we are disciples of Moses. 29 We know that God has spoken to Moses, but as for this man, we do not know where he comes from.' 30 The man answered, 'Here is an astonishing thing! You do not know where he comes from, and yet he opened my eyes. 31 We know that God does not listen to sinners, but he does listen to one who worships him and obeys his will. 32 Never since the world began has it been heard that anyone opened the eyes of a person born blind. 33 If this man were not from God, he could do nothing.' 34 They answered him, 'You were born entirely in sins, and are you trying to teach us?' And they drove him out.

Spiritual Blindness

35 Jesus heard that they had driven him out, and when he found him, he said, 'Do you believe in the Son of Man?'*a* 36 He answered, 'And who is he, sir?*b* Tell me, so that I may believe in him.' 37 Jesus said to him, 'You have seen him, and the one speaking with you is he.' 38 He said, 'Lord,*b* I believe.' And he worshipped him. 39 Jesus said, 'I came into this world for judgement so that those who do not see may see, and those who do see may become blind.' 40 Some of the Pharisees near him heard this and said to him, 'Surely we are not blind, are we?' 41 Jesus said to them, 'If you were blind, you would not have sin. But now that you say, "We see", your sin remains.

Jesus the Good Shepherd

10 'Very truly, I tell you, anyone who does not enter the sheepfold by the gate but climbs in by another way is a thief and a bandit. 2 The one who enters by the gate is the shepherd of the sheep. 3 The gatekeeper opens the gate for him, and the sheep hear his voice. He calls his own sheep by name and leads them out. 4 When he has brought out all his own, he goes ahead of them, and the sheep follow him because they know his voice. 5 They will not follow a stranger, but they will run from him because they do not know the voice of strangers.' 6 Jesus used this figure of speech with them, but they did not understand what he was saying to them.

7 So again Jesus said to them, 'Very truly, I tell you, I am the gate for the sheep. 8 All who came before me are thieves and bandits; but the sheep did not listen to them. 9 I am the gate. Whoever enters by me will be saved, and will come in and go out and find pasture. 10 The thief comes only to steal and kill and destroy. I came that they may have life, and have it abundantly.

11 'I am the good shepherd. The good shepherd lays down his life for the sheep. 12 The hired hand, who is not the shepherd and does not own the sheep, sees the wolf coming and leaves the sheep and runs away—and the wolf snatches them and scatters them. 13 The hired hand runs away because a hired hand does not care for the sheep. 14 I am the good shepherd. I know my own and my own know me, 15 just as the Father knows me and I know the Father. And I lay down my life for the sheep. 16 I have other sheep that do not belong to this fold. I must bring them also, and they will listen to my voice. So there will be one flock, one shepherd. 17 For this reason the Father loves me, because I lay down my life in order to take it up again. 18 No one takes*c* it from me, but I lay it down of my own accord. I have power to lay it down, and I have power to take it up again. I have received this command from my Father.'

19 Again the Jews were divided because of these words. 20 Many of them were say-

a Other ancient authorities read *the Son of God*   *b* Sir and *Lord* translate the same Greek word   *c* Other ancient authorities read *has taken* ing, 'He has a demon and is out of his mind. Why listen to him?' 21 Others were saying, 'These are not the words of one who has a demon. Can a demon open the eyes of the blind?'

Jesus Is Rejected by the Jews

22 At that time the festival of the Dedication took place in Jerusalem. It was winter, 23 and Jesus was walking in the temple, in the portico of Solomon. 24 So the Jews gathered around him and said to him, 'How long will you keep us in suspense? If you are the Messiah,[a] tell us plainly.' 25 Jesus answered, 'I have told you, and you do not believe. The works that I do in my Father's name testify to me; 26 but you do not believe, because you do not belong to my sheep. 27 My sheep hear my voice. I know them, and they follow me. 28 I give them eternal life, and they will never perish. No one will snatch them out of my hand. 29 What my Father has given me is greater than all else, and no one can snatch it out of the Father's hand.[b] 30 The Father and I are one.'

31 The Jews took up stones again to stone him. 32 Jesus replied, 'I have shown you many good works from the Father. For which of these are you going to stone me?' 33 The Jews answered, 'It is not for a good work that we are going to stone you, but for blasphemy, because you, though only a human being, are making yourself God.' 34 Jesus answered, 'Is it not written in your law,[c] "I said, you are gods"? 35 If those to whom the word of God came were called "gods"—and the scripture cannot be annulled— 36 can you say that the one whom the Father has sanctified and sent into the world is blaspheming because I said, "I am God's Son"? 37 If I am not doing the works of my Father, then do not believe me. 38 But if I do them, even though you do not believe me, believe the works, so that you may know and understand[d] that the Father is in me and I am in the Father.' 39 Then they tried to arrest him again, but he escaped from their hands.

40 He went away again across the Jordan to the place where John had been baptizing earlier, and he remained there. 41 Many came to him, and they were saying, 'John performed no sign, but everything that John said about this man was true.' 42 And many believed in him there.

The Death of Lazarus

11 Now a certain man was ill, Lazarus of Bethany, the village of Mary and her sister Martha. 2 Mary was the one who anointed the Lord with perfume and wiped his feet with her hair; her brother Lazarus was ill. 3 So the sisters sent a message to Jesus,[e] 'Lord, he whom you love is ill.' 4 But when Jesus heard it, he said, 'This illness does not lead to death; rather it is for God's glory, so that the Son of God may be glorified through it.' 5 Accordingly, though Jesus loved Martha and her sister and Lazarus, 6 after having heard that Lazarus[f] was ill, he stayed two days longer in the place where he was.

7 Then after this he said to the disciples, 'Let us go to Judea again.' 8 The disciples said to him, 'Rabbi, the Jews were just now trying to stone you, and are you going there again?' 9 Jesus answered, 'Are there not twelve hours of daylight? Those who walk during the day do not stumble, because they see the light of this world. 10 But those who walk at night stumble, because the light is not in them.' 11 After saying this, he told them, 'Our friend Lazarus has fallen asleep, but I am going there to awaken him.' 12 The disciples said to him, 'Lord, if he has fallen asleep, he will be all right.' 13 Jesus, however, had been speaking about his death, but they thought that he was referring merely to sleep. 14 Then Jesus told them plainly, 'Lazarus is dead. 15 For your sake I am glad I was not there, so that you may believe. But let us go to him.' 16 Thomas, who was called the Twin,[g] said to his fellow-disciples, 'Let us also go, that we may die with him.'

a Or the Christ   b Other ancient authorities read My Father who has given them to me is greater than all, and no one can snatch them out of the Father's hand   c Other ancient authorities read in the law   d Other ancient authorities lack and understand; others read and believe   e Gk him   f Gk he   g Gk Didymus

Jesus the Resurrection and the Life

17 When Jesus arrived, he found that Lazarus[a] had already been in the tomb for four days. 18 Now Bethany was near Jerusalem, some two miles[b] away, 19 and many of the Jews had come to Martha and Mary to console them about their brother. 20 When Martha heard that Jesus was coming, she went and met him, while Mary stayed at home. 21 Martha said to Jesus, 'Lord, if you had been here, my brother would not have died. 22 But even now I know that God will give you whatever you ask of him.' 23 Jesus said to her, 'Your brother will rise again.' 24 Martha said to him, 'I know that he will rise again in the resurrection on the last day.' 25 Jesus said to her, 'I am the resurrection and the life.[c] Those who believe in me, even though they die, will live, 26 and everyone who lives and believes in me will never die. Do you believe this?' 27 She said to him, 'Yes, Lord, I believe that you are the Messiah,[d] the Son of God, the one coming into the world.'

Jesus Weeps

28 When she had said this, she went back and called her sister Mary, and told her privately, 'The Teacher is here and is calling for you.' 29 And when she heard it, she got up quickly and went to him. 30 Now Jesus had not yet come to the village, but was still at the place where Martha had met him. 31 The Jews who were with her in the house, consoling her, saw Mary get up quickly and go out. They followed her because they thought that she was going to the tomb to weep there. 32 When Mary came where Jesus was and saw him, she knelt at his feet and said to him, 'Lord, if you had been here, my brother would not have died.' 33 When Jesus saw her weeping, and the Jews who came with her also weeping, he was greatly disturbed in spirit and deeply moved. 34 He said, 'Where have you laid him?' They said to him, 'Lord, come and see.' 35 Jesus began to weep. 36 So the Jews said, 'See how he loved him!' 37 But some of them said, 'Could not he who opened the eyes of the blind man have kept this man from dying?'

Jesus Raises Lazarus to Life

38 Then Jesus, again greatly disturbed, came to the tomb. It was a cave, and a stone was lying against it. 39 Jesus said, 'Take away the stone.' Martha, the sister of the dead man, said to him, 'Lord, already there is a stench because he has been dead for four days.' 40 Jesus said to her, 'Did I not tell you that if you believed, you would see the glory of God?' 41 So they took away the stone. And Jesus looked upwards and said, 'Father, I thank you for having heard me. 42 I knew that you always hear me, but I have said this for the sake of the crowd standing here, so that they may believe that you sent me.' 43 When he had said this, he cried with a loud voice, 'Lazarus, come out!' 44 The dead man came out, his hands and feet bound with strips of cloth, and his face wrapped in a cloth. Jesus said to them, 'Unbind him, and let him go.'

The Plot to Kill Jesus

45 Many of the Jews therefore, who had come with Mary and had seen what Jesus did, believed in him. 46 But some of them went to the Pharisees and told them what he had done. 47 So the chief priests and the Pharisees called a meeting of the council, and said, 'What are we to do? This man is performing many signs. 48 If we let him go on like this, everyone will believe in him, and the Romans will come and destroy both our holy place[e] and our nation.' 49 But one of them, Caiaphas, who was high priest that year, said to them, 'You know nothing at all! 50 You do not understand that it is better for you to have one man die for the people than to have the whole nation destroyed.' 51 He did not say this on his own, but being high priest that year he prophesied that Jesus was about to die for the nation, 52 and not for the nation only, but to gather into one the dispersed chil-

---

a Gk he   *b* Gk *fifteen stadia*   *c* Other ancient authorities lack *and the life*   *d* Or *the Christ*
e Or *our temple*; Greek *our place*

dren of God. [53] So from that day on they planned to put him to death.

54 Jesus therefore no longer walked about openly among the Jews, but went from there to a town called Ephraim in the region near the wilderness; and he remained there with the disciples.

55 Now the Passover of the Jews was near, and many went up from the country to Jerusalem before the Passover to purify themselves. [56] They were looking for Jesus and were asking one another as they stood in the temple, 'What do you think? Surely he will not come to the festival, will he?' [57] Now the chief priests and the Pharisees had given orders that anyone who knew where Jesus[a] was should let them know, so that they might arrest him.

Mary Anoints Jesus

12 Six days before the Passover Jesus came to Bethany, the home of Lazarus, whom he had raised from the dead. [2] There they gave a dinner for him. Martha served, and Lazarus was one of those at the table with him. [3] Mary took a pound of costly perfume made of pure nard, anointed Jesus' feet, and wiped them[b] with her hair. The house was filled with the fragrance of the perfume. [4] But Judas Iscariot, one of his disciples (the one who was about to betray him), said, [5] 'Why was this perfume not sold for three hundred denarii[c] and the money given to the poor?' [6] (He said this not because he cared about the poor, but because he was a thief; he kept the common purse and used to steal what was put into it.) [7] Jesus said, 'Leave her alone. She bought it[d] so that she might keep it for the day of my burial. [8] You always have the poor with you, but you do not always have me.'

The Plot to Kill Lazarus

9 When the great crowd of the Jews learned that he was there, they came not only because of Jesus but also to see Lazarus, whom he had raised from the dead. [10] So the chief priests planned to put Lazarus to death as well, [11] since it was on account of him that many of the Jews were deserting and were believing in Jesus.

Jesus' Triumphal Entry into Jerusalem

12 The next day the great crowd that had come to the festival heard that Jesus was coming to Jerusalem. [13] So they took branches of palm trees and went out to meet him, shouting,
'Hosanna!
Blessed is the one who comes in
the name of the Lord—
the King of Israel!'
[14] Jesus found a young donkey and sat on it; as it is written:
[15] 'Do not be afraid, daughter of Zion.
Look, your king is coming,
sitting on a donkey's colt!'
[16] His disciples did not understand these things at first; but when Jesus was glorified, then they remembered that these things had been written of him and had been done to him. [17] So the crowd that had been with him when he called Lazarus out of the tomb and raised him from the dead continued to testify.[e] [18] It was also because they heard that he had performed this sign that the crowd went to meet him. [19] The Pharisees then said to one another, 'You see, you can do nothing. Look, the world has gone after him!'

Some Greeks Wish to See Jesus

20 Now among those who went up to worship at the festival were some Greeks. [21] They came to Philip, who was from Bethsaida in Galilee, and said to him, 'Sir, we wish to see Jesus.' [22] Philip went and told Andrew; then Andrew and Philip went and told Jesus. [23] Jesus answered them, 'The hour has come for the Son of Man to be glorified. [24] Very truly, I tell you, unless a grain of wheat falls into the earth and dies, it remains just a single grain; but if it dies, it bears much fruit. [25] Those who love their life lose it, and those who hate their life in this world will keep it for eter-

a Gk *he*   b Gk *his feet*   c Three hundred denarii would be nearly a year's wages for a labourer
d Gk lacks *She bought it*   e Other ancient authorities read *with him began to testify that he had called. . .from the dead*

nal life. 26 Whoever serves me must follow me, and where I am, there will my servant be also. Whoever serves me, the Father will honour.

Jesus Speaks about His Death

27 'Now my soul is troubled. And what should I say—"Father, save me from this hour"? No, it is for this reason that I have come to this hour. 28 Father, glorify your name.' Then a voice came from heaven, 'I have glorified it, and I will glorify it again.' 29 The crowd standing there heard it and said that it was thunder. Others said, 'An angel has spoken to him.' 30 Jesus answered, 'This voice has come for your sake, not for mine. 31 Now is the judgement of this world; now the ruler of this world will be driven out. 32 And I, when I am lifted up from the earth, will draw all people*a* to myself.' 33 He said this to indicate the kind of death he was to die. 34 The crowd answered him, 'We have heard from the law that the Messiah*b* remains for ever. How can you say that the Son of Man must be lifted up? Who is this Son of Man?' 35 Jesus said to them, 'The light is with you for a little longer. Walk while you have the light, so that the darkness may not overtake you. If you walk in the darkness, you do not know where you are going. 36 While you have the light, believe in the light, so that you may become children of light.'

The Unbelief of the People

After Jesus had said this, he departed and hid from them. 37 Although he had performed so many signs in their presence, they did not believe in him. 38 This was to fulfil the word spoken by the prophet Isaiah:

'Lord, who has believed our message,
    and to whom has the arm of the
        Lord been revealed?'

39 And so they could not believe, because Isaiah also said,

40 'He has blinded their eyes
    and hardened their heart,
    so that they might not look with their
        eyes,

and understand with their heart
    and turn—
and I would heal them.'

41 Isaiah said this because*c* he saw his glory and spoke about him. 42 Nevertheless many, even of the authorities, believed in him. But because of the Pharisees they did not confess it, for fear that they would be put out of the synagogue; 43 for they loved human glory more than the glory that comes from God.

Summary of Jesus' Teaching

44 Then Jesus cried aloud: 'Whoever believes in me believes not in me but in him who sent me. 45 And whoever sees me sees him who sent me. 46 I have come as light into the world, so that everyone who believes in me should not remain in the darkness. 47 I do not judge anyone who hears my words and does not keep them, for I came not to judge the world, but to save the world. 48 The one who rejects me and does not receive my word has a judge; on the last day the word that I have spoken will serve as judge, 49 for I have not spoken on my own, but the Father who sent me has himself given me a commandment about what to say and what to speak. 50 And I know that his commandment is eternal life. What I speak, therefore, I speak just as the Father has told me.'

Jesus Washes the Disciples' Feet

13 Now before the festival of the Passover, Jesus knew that his hour had come to depart from this world and go to the Father. Having loved his own who were in the world, he loved them to the end. 2 The devil had already put it into the heart of Judas son of Simon Iscariot to betray him. And during supper 3 Jesus, knowing that the Father had given all things into his hands, and that he had come from God and was going to God, 4 got up from the table,*d* took off his outer robe, and tied a towel around himself. 5 Then he poured water into a basin and began to wash the

a Other ancient authorities read *all things*   *b* Or *the Christ*   *c* Other ancient witnesses read *when*
d Gk *from supper*

disciples' feet and to wipe them with the towel that was tied around him. ⁶He came to Simon Peter, who said to him, 'Lord, are you going to wash my feet?' ⁷Jesus answered, 'You do not know now what I am doing, but later you will understand.' ⁸Peter said to him, 'You will never wash my feet.' Jesus answered, 'Unless I wash you, you have no share with me.' ⁹Simon Peter said to him, 'Lord, not my feet only but also my hands and my head!' ¹⁰Jesus said to him, 'One who has bathed does not need to wash, except for the feet,ᵃ but is entirely clean. And youᵇ are clean, though not all of you.' ¹¹For he knew who was to betray him; for this reason he said, 'Not all of you are clean.'

12 After he had washed their feet, had put on his robe, and had returned to the table, he said to them, 'Do you know what I have done to you? ¹³You call me Teacher and Lord—and you are right, for that is what I am. ¹⁴So if I, your Lord and Teacher, have washed your feet, you also ought to wash one another's feet. ¹⁵For I have set you an example, that you also should do as I have done to you. ¹⁶Very truly, I tell you, servantsᶜ are not greater than their master, nor are messengers greater than the one who sent them. ¹⁷If you know these things, you are blessed if you do them. ¹⁸I am not speaking of all of you; I know whom I have chosen. But it is to fulfil the scripture, "The one who ate my breadᵈ has lifted his heel against me." ¹⁹I tell you this now, before it occurs, so that when it does occur, you may believe that I am he.ᵉ ²⁰Very truly, I tell you, whoever receives one whom I send receives me; and whoever receives me receives him who sent me.'

Jesus Foretells His Betrayal

21 After saying this Jesus was troubled in spirit, and declared, 'Very truly, I tell you, one of you will betray me.' ²²The disciples looked at one another, uncertain of whom he was speaking. ²³One of his disciples—the one whom Jesus loved—was reclining next to him; ²⁴Simon Peter therefore motioned to him to ask Jesus of whom he was speaking. ²⁵So while reclin-

ing next to Jesus, he asked him, 'Lord, who is it?' ²⁶Jesus answered, 'It is the one to whom I give this piece of bread when I have dipped it in the dish.'ᶠ So when he had dipped the piece of bread, he gave it to Judas son of Simon Iscariot.ᵍ ²⁷After he received the piece of bread,ʰ Satan entered into him. Jesus said to him, 'Do quickly what you are going to do.' ²⁸Now no one at the table knew why he said this to him. ²⁹Some thought that, because Judas had the common purse, Jesus was telling him, 'Buy what we need for the festival'; or, that he should give something to the poor. ³⁰So, after receiving the piece of bread, he immediately went out. And it was night.

The New Commandment

31 When he had gone out, Jesus said, 'Now the Son of Man has been glorified, and God has been glorified in him. ³²If God has been glorified in him,ⁱ God will also glorify him in himself and will glorify him at once. ³³Little children, I am with you only a little longer. You will look for me; and as I said to the Jews so now I say to you, "Where I am going, you cannot come." ³⁴I give you a new commandment, that you love one another. Just as I have loved you, you also should love one another. ³⁵By this everyone will know that you are my disciples, if you have love for one another.'

Jesus Foretells Peter's Denial

36 Simon Peter said to him, 'Lord, where are you going?' Jesus answered, 'Where I am going, you cannot follow me now; but you will follow afterwards.' ³⁷Peter said to him, 'Lord, why can I not follow you now? I will lay down my life for you.' ³⁸Jesus answered, 'Will you lay down your life for me? Very truly, I tell you, before the cock crows, you will have denied me three times.

a Other ancient authorities lack *except for the feet*
b The Greek word for *you* here is plural   c Gk *slaves*
d Other ancient authorities read *ate bread with me*
e Gk *I am*   f Gk *dipped it*   g Other ancient authorities read *Judas Iscariot son of Simon*; others, *Judas son of Simon from Karyot* (Kerioth)   h Gk *After the piece of bread*   i Other ancient authorities lack *If God has been glorified in him*

Jesus the Way to the Father

14 'Do not let your hearts be troubled. Believe[a] in God, believe also in me. [2] In my Father's house there are many dwelling-places. If it were not so, would I have told you that I go to prepare a place for you?[b] [3] And if I go and prepare a place for you, I will come again and will take you to myself, so that where I am, there you may be also. [4] And you know the way to the place where I am going.'[c] [5] Thomas said to him, 'Lord, we do not know where you are going. How can we know the way?' [6] Jesus said to him, 'I am the way, and the truth, and the life. No one comes to the Father except through me. [7] If you know me, you will know[d] my Father also. From now on you do know him and have seen him.'

[8] Philip said to him, 'Lord, show us the Father, and we will be satisfied.' [9] Jesus said to him, 'Have I been with you all this time, Philip, and you still do not know me? Whoever has seen me has seen the Father. How can you say, "Show us the Father"? [10] Do you not believe that I am in the Father and the Father is in me? The words that I say to you I do not speak on my own; but the Father who dwells in me does his works. [11] Believe me that I am in the Father and the Father is in me; but if you do not, then believe me because of the works themselves. [12] Very truly, I tell you, the one who believes in me will also do the works that I do and, in fact, will do greater works than these, because I am going to the Father. [13] I will do whatever you ask in my name, so that the Father may be glorified in the Son. [14] If in my name you ask me[e] for anything, I will do it.

The Promise of the Holy Spirit

[15] 'If you love me, you will keep[f] my commandments. [16] And I will ask the Father, and he will give you another Advocate,[g] to be with you for ever. [17] This is the Spirit of truth, whom the world cannot receive, because it neither sees him nor knows him. You know him, because he abides with you, and he will be in[h] you. [18] 'I will not leave you orphaned; I am coming to you. [19] In a little while the world will no longer see me, but you will see me; because I live, you also will live. [20] On that day you will know that I am in my Father, and you in me, and I in you. [21] They who have my commandments and keep them are those who love me; and those who love me will be loved by my Father, and I will love them and reveal myself to them.' [22] Judas (not Iscariot) said to him, 'Lord, how is it that you will reveal yourself to us, and not to the world?' [23] Jesus answered him, 'Those who love me will keep my word, and my Father will love them, and we will come to them and make our home with them. [24] Whoever does not love me does not keep my words; and the word that you hear is not mine, but is from the Father who sent me.

[25] 'I have said these things to you while I am still with you. [26] But the Advocate,[g] the Holy Spirit, whom the Father will send in my name, will teach you everything, and remind you of all that I have said to you. [27] Peace I leave with you; my peace I give to you. I do not give to you as the world gives. Do not let your hearts be troubled, and do not let them be afraid. [28] You heard me say to you, "I am going away, and I am coming to you." If you loved me, you would rejoice that I am going to the Father, because the Father is greater than I. [29] And now I have told you this before it occurs, so that when it does occur, you may believe. [30] I will no longer talk much with you, for the ruler of this world is coming. He has no power over me; [31] but I do as the Father has commanded me, so that the world may know that I love the Father. Rise, let us be on our way.

Jesus the True Vine

15 'I am the true vine, and my Father is the vine-grower. [2] He removes every branch in me that bears no fruit.

---

a Or *You believe*   b Or *If it were not so, I would have told you; for I go to prepare a place for you*   c Other ancient authorities read *Where I am going you know, and the way you know*   d Other ancient authorities read *If you had known me, you would have known*   e Other ancient authorities lack *me*   f Other ancient authorities read *me, keep*   g Or *Helper*   h Or *among*

Every branch that bears fruit he prunes*a* to make it bear more fruit. ³You have already been cleansed*a* by the word that I have spoken to you. ⁴Abide in me as I abide in you. Just as the branch cannot bear fruit by itself unless it abides in the vine, neither can you unless you abide in me. ⁵I am the vine, you are the branches. Those who abide in me and I in them bear much fruit, because apart from me you can do nothing. ⁶Whoever does not abide in me is thrown away like a branch and withers; such branches are gathered, thrown into the fire, and burned. ⁷If you abide in me, and my words abide in you, ask for whatever you wish, and it will be done for you. ⁸My Father is glorified by this, that you bear much fruit and become*b* my disciples. ⁹As the Father has loved me, so I have loved you; abide in my love. ¹⁰If you keep my commandments, you will abide in my love, just as I have kept my Father's commandments and abide in his love. ¹¹I have said these things to you so that my joy may be in you, and that your joy may be complete.

12 'This is my commandment, that you love one another as I have loved you. ¹³No one has greater love than this, to lay down one's life for one's friends. ¹⁴You are my friends if you do what I command you. ¹⁵I do not call you servants*c* any longer, because the servant*d* does not know what the master is doing; but I have called you friends, because I have made known to you everything that I have heard from my Father. ¹⁶You did not choose me but I chose you. And I appointed you to go and bear fruit, fruit that will last, so that the Father will give you whatever you ask him in my name. ¹⁷I am giving you these commands so that you may love one another.

The World's Hatred

18 'If the world hates you, be aware that it hated me before it hated you. ¹⁹If you belonged to the world,*e* the world would love you as its own. Because you do not belong to the world, but I have chosen you out of the world—therefore the world

hates you. ²⁰Remember the word that I said to you, "Servants*f* are not greater than their master." If they persecuted me, they will persecute you; if they kept my word, they will keep yours also. ²¹But they will do all these things to you on account of my name, because they do not know him who sent me. ²²If I had not come and spoken to them, they would not have sin; but now they have no excuse for their sin. ²³Whoever hates me hates my Father also. ²⁴If I had not done among them the works that no one else did, they would not have sin. But now they have seen and hated both me and my Father. ²⁵It was to fulfil the word that is written in their law, "They hated me without a cause."

26 'When the Advocate*g* comes, whom I will send to you from the Father, the Spirit of truth who comes from the Father, he will testify on my behalf. ²⁷You also are to testify because you have been with me from the beginning.

16 'I have said these things to you to keep you from stumbling. ²They will put you out of the synagogues. Indeed, an hour is coming when those who kill you will think that by doing so they are offering worship to God. ³And they will do this because they have not known the Father or me. ⁴But I have said these things to you so that when their hour comes you may remember that I told you about them.

The Work of the Spirit

'I did not say these things to you from the beginning, because I was with you. ⁵But now I am going to him who sent me; yet none of you asks me, "Where are you going?" ⁶But because I have said these things to you, sorrow has filled your hearts. ⁷Nevertheless, I tell you the truth: it is to your advantage that I go away, for if I do not go away, the Advocate*g* will not come to you; but if I go, I will send him to you. ⁸And when he comes, he will prove the world wrong about*h* sin and righteous-

a The same Greek root refers to pruning and cleansing
b Or *be*   *c* Gk *slaves*   *d* Gk *slave*   *e* Gk *were of the world*   *f* Gk *Slaves*   *g* Or *Helper*   *h* Or *convict the world of*

ness and judgement: [9] about sin, because they do not believe in me; [10] about righteousness, because I am going to the Father and you will see me no longer; [11] about judgement, because the ruler of this world has been condemned.

12 'I still have many things to say to you, but you cannot bear them now. [13] When the Spirit of truth comes, he will guide you into all the truth; for he will not speak on his own, but will speak whatever he hears, and he will declare to you the things that are to come. [14] He will glorify me, because he will take what is mine and declare it to you. [15] All that the Father has is mine. For this reason I said that he will take what is mine and declare it to you.

Sorrow Will Turn into Joy

16 'A little while, and you will no longer see me, and again a little while, and you will see me.' [17] Then some of his disciples said to one another, 'What does he mean by saying to us, "A little while, and you will no longer see me, and again a little while, and you will see me"; and "Because I am going to the Father"?' [18] They said, 'What does he mean by this "a little while"? We do not know what he is talking about.' [19] Jesus knew that they wanted to ask him, so he said to them, 'Are you discussing among yourselves what I meant when I said, "A little while, and you will no longer see me, and again a little while, and you will see me"? [20] Very truly, I tell you, you will weep and mourn, but the world will rejoice; you will have pain, but your pain will turn into joy. [21] When a woman is in labour, she has pain, because her hour has come. But when her child is born, she no longer remembers the anguish because of the joy of having brought a human being into the world. [22] So you have pain now; but I will see you again, and your hearts will rejoice, and no one will take your joy from you. [23] On that day you will ask nothing of me. [a] Very truly, I tell you, if you ask anything of the Father in my name, he will give it to you. [b] [24] Until now you have not asked for anything in

my name. Ask and you will receive, so that your joy may be complete.

Peace for the Disciples

25 'I have said these things to you in figures of speech. The hour is coming when I will no longer speak to you in figures, but will tell you plainly of the Father. [26] On that day you will ask in my name. I do not say to you that I will ask the Father on your behalf; [27] for the Father himself loves you, because you have loved me and have believed that I came from God. [c] [28] I came from the Father and have come into the world; again, I am leaving the world and am going to the Father.'

29 His disciples said, 'Yes, now you are speaking plainly, not in any figure of speech! [30] Now we know that you know all things, and do not need to have anyone question you; by this we believe that you came from God.' [31] Jesus answered them, 'Do you now believe? [32] The hour is coming, indeed it has come, when you will be scattered, each one to his home, and you will leave me alone. Yet I am not alone because the Father is with me. [33] I have said this to you, so that in me you may have peace. In the world you face persecution. But take courage; I have conquered the world!'

Jesus Prays for His Disciples

17 After Jesus had spoken these words, he looked up to heaven and said, 'Father, the hour has come; glorify your Son so that the Son may glorify you, [2] since you have given him authority over all people, [d] to give eternal life to all whom you have given him. [3] And this is eternal life, that they may know you, the only true God, and Jesus Christ whom you have sent. [4] I glorified you on earth by finishing the work that you gave me to do. [5] So now, Father, glorify me in your own presence with the glory that I had in your presence before the world existed.

6 'I have made your name known to

---

a Or will ask me no question   b Other ancient authorities read Father, he will give it to you in my name   c Other ancient authorities read the Father   d Gk flesh those whom you gave me from the world. They were yours, and you gave them to me, and they have kept your word. 7 Now they know that everything you have given me is from you; 8 for the words that you gave to me I have given to them, and they have received them and know in truth that I came from you; and they have believed that you sent me. 9 I am asking on their behalf; I am not asking on behalf of the world, but on behalf of those whom you gave me, because they are yours. 10 All mine are yours, and yours are mine; and I have been glorified in them. 11 And now I am no longer in the world, but they are in the world, and I am coming to you. Holy Father, protect them in your name that you have given me, so that they may be one, as we are one. 12 While I was with them, I protected them in your name that *a* you have given me. I guarded them, and not one of them was lost except the one destined to be lost, *b* so that the scripture might be fulfilled. 13 But now I am coming to you, and I speak these things in the world so that they may have my joy made complete in themselves. *c* 14 I have given them your word, and the world has hated them because they do not belong to the world, just as I do not belong to the world. 15 I am not asking you to take them out of the world, but I ask you to protect them from the evil one. *d* 16 They do not belong to the world, just as I do not belong to the world. 17 Sanctify them in the truth; your word is truth. 18 As you have sent me into the world, so I have sent them into the world. 19 And for their sakes I sanctify myself, so that they also may be sanctified in truth.

20 'I ask not only on behalf of these, but also on behalf of those who will believe in me through their word, 21 that they may all be one. As you, Father, are in me and I am in you, may they also be in us, *e* so that the world may believe that you have sent me. 22 The glory that you have given me I have given them, so that they may be one, as we are one, 23 I in them and you in me, that they may become completely one, so that the world may know that you have sent me and have loved

them even as you have loved me. 24 Father, I desire that those also, whom you have given me, may be with me where I am, to see my glory, which you have given me because you loved me before the foundation of the world.

25 'Righteous Father, the world does not know you, but I know you; and these know that you have sent me. 26 I made your name known to them, and I will make it known, so that the love with which you have loved me may be in them, and I in them.'

The Betrayal and Arrest of Jesus

18 After Jesus had spoken these words, he went out with his disciples across the Kidron valley to a place where there was a garden, which he and his disciples entered. 2 Now Judas, who betrayed him, also knew the place, because Jesus often met there with his disciples. 3 So Judas brought a detachment of soldiers together with police from the chief priests and the Pharisees, and they came there with lanterns and torches and weapons. 4 Then Jesus, knowing all that was to happen to him, came forward and asked them, 'For whom are you looking?' 5 They answered, 'Jesus of Nazareth.' *f* Jesus replied, 'I am he.' *g* Judas, who betrayed him, was standing with them. 6 When Jesus *h* said to them, 'I am he', *g* they stepped back and fell to the ground. 7 Again he asked them, 'For whom are you looking?' And they said, 'Jesus of Nazareth.' *f* 8 Jesus answered, 'I told you that I am he. *g* So if you are looking for me, let these men go.' 9 This was to fulfil the word that he had spoken, 'I did not lose a single one of those whom you gave me.' 10 Then Simon Peter, who had a sword, drew it, struck the high priest's slave, and cut off his right ear. The slave's name was Malchus. 11 Jesus said to Peter, 'Put your sword back into its sheath. Am I not to drink the cup that the Father has given me?'

a Other ancient authorities read *protected in your name those whom*   *b* Gk *except the son of destruction*   *c* Or *among themselves*   *d* Or *from evil*   *e* Other ancient authorities read *be one in us*   *f* Gk *the Nazorean*   *g* Gk *I am*   *h* Gk *he*

Jesus before the High Priest

12 So the soldiers, their officer, and the Jewish police arrested Jesus and bound him. [13] First they took him to Annas, who was the father-in-law of Caiaphas, the high priest that year. [14] Caiaphas was the one who had advised the Jews that it was better to have one person die for the people.

Peter Denies Jesus

15 Simon Peter and another disciple followed Jesus. Since that disciple was known to the high priest, he went with Jesus into the courtyard of the high priest, [16] but Peter was standing outside at the gate. So the other disciple, who was known to the high priest, went out, spoke to the woman who guarded the gate, and brought Peter in. [17] The woman said to Peter, 'You are not also one of this man's disciples, are you?' He said, 'I am not.' [18] Now the slaves and the police had made a charcoal fire because it was cold, and they were standing round it and warming themselves. Peter also was standing with them and warming himself.

The High Priest Questions Jesus

19 Then the high priest questioned Jesus about his disciples and about his teaching. [20] Jesus answered, 'I have spoken openly to the world; I have always taught in synagogues and in the temple, where all the Jews come together. I have said nothing in secret. [21] Why do you ask me? Ask those who heard what I said to them; they know what I said.' [22] When he had said this, one of the police standing nearby struck Jesus on the face, saying, 'Is that how you answer the high priest?' [23] Jesus answered, 'If I have spoken wrongly, testify to the wrong. But if I have spoken rightly, why do you strike me?' [24] Then Annas sent him bound to Caiaphas the high priest.

Peter Denies Jesus Again

25 Now Simon Peter was standing and warming himself. They asked him, 'You are not also one of his disciples, are you?' He denied it and said, 'I am not.' [26] One of the slaves of the high priest, a relative of the man whose ear Peter had cut off, asked, 'Did I not see you in the garden with him?' [27] Again Peter denied it, and at that moment the cock crowed.

Jesus before Pilate

28 Then they took Jesus from Caiaphas to Pilate's headquarters.[a] It was early in the morning. They themselves did not enter the headquarters,[a] so as to avoid ritual defilement and to be able to eat the Passover. [29] So Pilate went out to them and said, 'What accusation do you bring against this man?' [30] They answered, 'If this man were not a criminal, we would not have handed him over to you.' [31] Pilate said to them, 'Take him yourselves and judge him according to your law.' The Jews replied, 'We are not permitted to put anyone to death.' [32] (This was to fulfil what Jesus had said when he indicated the kind of death he was to die.)

33 Then Pilate entered the headquarters[a] again, summoned Jesus, and asked him, 'Are you the King of the Jews?' [34] Jesus answered, 'Do you ask this on your own, or did others tell you about me?' [35] Pilate replied, 'I am not a Jew, am I? Your own nation and the chief priests have handed you over to me. What have you done?' [36] Jesus answered, 'My kingdom is not from this world. If my kingdom were from this world, my followers would be fighting to keep me from being handed over to the Jews. But as it is, my kingdom is not from here.' [37] Pilate asked him, 'So you are a king?' Jesus answered, 'You say that I am a king. For this I was born, and for this I came into the world, to testify to the truth. Everyone who belongs to the truth listens to my voice.' [38] Pilate asked him, 'What is truth?'

Jesus Sentenced to Death

After he had said this, he went out to the Jews again and told them, 'I find no case against him. [39] But you have a custom that I release someone for you at the Passover. Do you want me to release for you the

a Gk the praetorium

King of the Jews?' ⁴⁰They shouted in reply, 'Not this man, but Barabbas!' Now Barabbas was a bandit.

19 Then Pilate took Jesus and had him flogged. ²And the soldiers wove a crown of thorns and put it on his head, and they dressed him in a purple robe. ³They kept coming up to him, saying, 'Hail, King of the Jews!' and striking him on the face. ⁴Pilate went out again and said to them, 'Look, I am bringing him out to you to let you know that I find no case against him.' ⁵So Jesus came out, wearing the crown of thorns and the purple robe. Pilate said to them, 'Here is the man!' ⁶When the chief priests and the police saw him, they shouted, 'Crucify him! Crucify him!' Pilate said to them, 'Take him yourselves and crucify him; I find no case against him.' ⁷The Jews answered him, 'We have a law, and according to that law he ought to die because he has claimed to be the Son of God.'

8 Now when Pilate heard this, he was more afraid than ever. ⁹He entered his headquarters*a* again and asked Jesus, 'Where are you from?' But Jesus gave him no answer. ¹⁰Pilate therefore said to him, 'Do you refuse to speak to me? Do you not know that I have power to release you, and power to crucify you?' ¹¹Jesus answered him, 'You would have no power over me unless it had been given you from above; therefore the one who handed me over to you is guilty of a greater sin.' ¹²From then on Pilate tried to release him, but the Jews cried out, 'If you release this man, you are no friend of the emperor. Everyone who claims to be a king sets himself against the emperor.'

13 When Pilate heard these words, he brought Jesus outside and sat*b* on the judge's bench at a place called The Stone Pavement, or in Hebrew*c* Gabbatha. ¹⁴Now it was the day of Preparation for the Passover; and it was about noon. He said to the Jews, 'Here is your King!' ¹⁵They cried out, 'Away with him! Away with him! Crucify him!' Pilate asked them, 'Shall I crucify your King?' The chief priests answered, 'We have no king but the emper-

or.' ¹⁶Then he handed him over to them to be crucified.

The Crucifixion of Jesus

So they took Jesus; ¹⁷and carrying the cross by himself, he went out to what is called The Place of the Skull, which in Hebrew*c* is called Golgotha. ¹⁸There they crucified him, and with him two others, one on either side, with Jesus between them. ¹⁹Pilate also had an inscription written and put on the cross. It read, 'Jesus of Nazareth,*d* the King of the Jews.' ²⁰Many of the Jews read this inscription, because the place where Jesus was crucified was near the city; and it was written in Hebrew,*c* in Latin, and in Greek. ²¹Then the chief priests of the Jews said to Pilate, 'Do not write, "The King of the Jews", but, "This man said, I am King of the Jews." ' ²²Pilate answered, 'What I have written I have written.' ²³When the soldiers had crucified Jesus, they took his clothes and divided them into four parts, one for each soldier. They also took his tunic; now the tunic was seamless, woven in one piece from the top. ²⁴So they said to one another, 'Let us not tear it, but cast lots for it to see who will get it.' This was to fulfil what the scripture says,

'They divided my clothes among
   themselves,
   and for my clothing they cast lots.'

²⁵And that is what the soldiers did.

Meanwhile, standing near the cross of Jesus were his mother, and his mother's sister, Mary the wife of Clopas, and Mary Magdalene. ²⁶When Jesus saw his mother and the disciple whom he loved standing beside her, he said to his mother, 'Woman, here is your son.' ²⁷Then he said to the disciple, 'Here is your mother.' And from that hour the disciple took her into his own home.

28 After this, when Jesus knew that all was now finished, he said (in order to fulfil the scripture), 'I am thirsty.' ²⁹A jar full of sour wine was standing there. So they put a sponge full of the wine on a branch of hyssop and held it to his mouth. ³⁰When Jesus had received the wine, he

a Gk *the praetorium*   *b* Or *seated him*   *c* That is, Aramaic   *d* Gk *the Nazorean* said, 'It is finished.' Then he bowed his head and gave up his spirit.

Jesus' Side Is Pierced

31 Since it was the day of Preparation, the Jews did not want the bodies left on the cross during the sabbath, especially because that sabbath was a day of great solemnity. So they asked Pilate to have the legs of the crucified men broken and the bodies removed. 32 Then the soldiers came and broke the legs of the first and of the other who had been crucified with him. 33 But when they came to Jesus and saw that he was already dead, they did not break his legs. 34 Instead, one of the soldiers pierced his side with a spear, and at once blood and water came out. 35 (He who saw this has testified so that you also may believe. His testimony is true, and he knows *a* that he tells the truth.) 36 These things occurred so that the scripture might be fulfilled, 'None of his bones shall be broken.' 37 And again another passage of scripture says, 'They will look on the one whom they have pierced.'

The Burial of Jesus

38 After these things, Joseph of Arimathea, who was a disciple of Jesus, though a secret one because of his fear of the Jews, asked Pilate to let him take away the body of Jesus. Pilate gave him permission; so he came and removed his body. 39 Nicodemus, who had at first come to Jesus by night, also came, bringing a mixture of myrrh and aloes, weighing about a hundred pounds. 40 They took the body of Jesus and wrapped it with the spices in linen cloths, according to the burial custom of the Jews. 41 Now there was a garden in the place where he was crucified, and in the garden there was a new tomb in which no one had ever been laid. 42 And so, because it was the Jewish day of Preparation, and the tomb was nearby, they laid Jesus there.

The Resurrection of Jesus

20 Early on the first day of the week, while it was still dark, Mary Magdalene came to the tomb and saw that the stone had been removed from the tomb. 2 So she ran and went to Simon Peter and the other disciple, the one whom Jesus loved, and said to them, 'They have taken the Lord out of the tomb, and we do not know where they have laid him.' 3 Then Peter and the other disciple set out and went towards the tomb. 4 The two were running together, but the other disciple outran Peter and reached the tomb first. 5 He bent down to look in and saw the linen wrappings lying there, but he did not go in. 6 Then Simon Peter came, following him, and went into the tomb. He saw the linen wrappings lying there, 7 and the cloth that had been on Jesus' head, not lying with the linen wrappings but rolled up in a place by itself. 8 Then the other disciple, who reached the tomb first, also went in, and he saw and believed; 9 for as yet they did not understand the scripture, that he must rise from the dead. 10 Then the disciples returned to their homes.

Jesus Appears to Mary Magdalene

11 But Mary stood weeping outside the tomb. As she wept, she bent over to look *b* into the tomb; 12 and she saw two angels in white, sitting where the body of Jesus had been lying, one at the head and the other at the feet. 13 They said to her, 'Woman, why are you weeping?' She said to them, 'They have taken away my Lord, and I do not know where they have laid him.' 14 When she had said this, she turned round and saw Jesus standing there, but she did not know that it was Jesus. 15 Jesus said to her, 'Woman, why are you weeping? For whom are you looking?' Supposing him to be the gardener, she said to him, 'Sir, if you have carried him away, tell me where you have laid him, and I will take him away.' 16 Jesus said to her, 'Mary!' She turned and said to him in Hebrew, *c* 'Rabbouni!' (which means Teacher). 17 Jesus said to her, 'Do not hold on to me, because I have not yet ascended to the Father. But go to my brothers and say to them, "I am ascending to my Father and your Father, to

my God and your God." ' ¹⁸Mary Magdalene went and announced to the disciples, 'I have seen the Lord'; and she told them that he had said these things to her.

Jesus Appears to the Disciples

19 When it was evening on that day, the first day of the week, and the doors of the house where the disciples had met were locked for fear of the Jews, Jesus came and stood among them and said, 'Peace be with you.' ²⁰After he said this, he showed them his hands and his side. Then the disciples rejoiced when they saw the Lord. ²¹Jesus said to them again, 'Peace be with you. As the Father has sent me, so I send you.' ²²When he had said this, he breathed on them and said to them, 'Receive the Holy Spirit. ²³If you forgive the sins of any, they are forgiven them; if you retain the sins of any, they are retained.'

Jesus and Thomas

24 But Thomas (who was called the Twin[a]), one of the twelve, was not with them when Jesus came. ²⁵So the other disciples told him, 'We have seen the Lord.' But he said to them, 'Unless I see the mark of the nails in his hands, and put my finger in the mark of the nails and my hand in his side, I will not believe.'

26 A week later his disciples were again in the house, and Thomas was with them. Although the doors were shut, Jesus came and stood among them and said, 'Peace be with you.' ²⁷Then he said to Thomas, 'Put your finger here and see my hands. Reach out your hand and put it in my side. Do not doubt but believe.' ²⁸Thomas answered him, 'My Lord and my God!' ²⁹Jesus said to him, 'Have you believed because you have seen me? Blessed are those who have not seen and yet have come to believe.'

The Purpose of This Book

30 Now Jesus did many other signs in the presence of his disciples, which are not written in this book. ³¹But these are written so that you may come to believe[b] that Jesus is the Messiah,[c] the Son of God, and

that through believing you may have life in his name.

Jesus Appears to Seven Disciples

21 After these things Jesus showed himself again to the disciples by the Sea of Tiberias; and he showed himself in this way. ²Gathered there together were Simon Peter, Thomas called the Twin,[a] Nathanael of Cana in Galilee, the sons of Zebedee, and two others of his disciples. ³Simon Peter said to them, 'I am going fishing.' They said to him, 'We will go with you.' They went out and got into the boat, but that night they caught nothing.

4 Just after daybreak, Jesus stood on the beach; but the disciples did not know that it was Jesus. ⁵Jesus said to them, 'Children, you have no fish, have you?' They answered him, 'No.' ⁶He said to them, 'Cast the net to the right side of the boat, and you will find some.' So they cast it, and now they were not able to haul it in because there were so many fish. ⁷That disciple whom Jesus loved said to Peter, 'It is the Lord!' When Simon Peter heard that it was the Lord, he put on some clothes, for he was naked, and jumped into the lake. ⁸But the other disciples came in the boat, dragging the net full of fish, for they were not far from the land, only about a hundred yards[d] off.

9 When they had gone ashore, they saw a charcoal fire there, with fish on it, and bread. ¹⁰Jesus said to them, 'Bring some of the fish that you have just caught.' ¹¹So Simon Peter went aboard and hauled the net ashore, full of large fish, a hundred and fifty-three of them; and though there were so many, the net was not torn. ¹²Jesus said to them, 'Come and have breakfast.' Now none of the disciples dared to ask him, 'Who are you?' because they knew it was the Lord. ¹³Jesus came and took the bread and gave it to them, and did the same with the fish. ¹⁴This was now the third time that Jesus appeared to the disciples after he was raised from the dead.

a Gk Didymus   b Other ancient authorities read may continue to believe   c Or the Christ   d Gk two hundred cubits

Jesus and Peter

15 When they had finished breakfast, Jesus said to Simon Peter, 'Simon son of John, do you love me more than these?' He said to him, 'Yes, Lord; you know that I love you.' Jesus said to him, 'Feed my lambs.' 16 A second time he said to him, 'Simon son of John, do you love me?' He said to him, 'Yes, Lord; you know that I love you.' Jesus said to him, 'Tend my sheep.' 17 He said to him the third time, 'Simon son of John, do you love me?' Peter felt hurt because he said to him the third time, 'Do you love me?' And he said to him, 'Lord, you know everything; you know that I love you.' Jesus said to him, 'Feed my sheep. 18 Very truly, I tell you, when you were younger, you used to fasten your own belt and to go wherever you wished. But when you grow old, you will stretch out your hands, and someone else will fasten a belt around you and take you where you do not wish to go.' 19 (He said this to indicate the kind of death by which he would glorify God.) After this he said to him, 'Follow me.'

Jesus and the Beloved Disciple

20 Peter turned and saw the disciple whom Jesus loved following them; he was the one who had reclined next to Jesus at the supper and had said, 'Lord, who is it that is going to betray you?' 21 When Peter saw him, he said to Jesus, 'Lord, what about him?' 22 Jesus said to him, 'If it is my will that he remain until I come, what is that to you? Follow me!' 23 So the rumour spread in the community*a* that this disciple would not die. Yet Jesus did not say to him that he would not die, but, 'If it is my will that he remain until I come, what is that to you?'*b*

24 This is the disciple who is testifying to these things and has written them, and we know that his testimony is true. 25 But there are also many other things that Jesus did; if every one of them were written down, I suppose that the world itself could not contain the books that would be written.

a Gk *among the brothers*   *b* Other ancient authorities lack *what is that to you*

THE ACTS
OF THE APOSTLES

The Promise of the Holy Spirit

1 In the first book, Theophilus, I wrote about all that Jesus did and taught from the beginning ²until the day when he was taken up to heaven, after giving instructions through the Holy Spirit to the apostles whom he had chosen. ³After his suffering he presented himself alive to them by many convincing proofs, appearing to them over the course of forty days and speaking about the kingdom of God. ⁴While staying*a* with them, he ordered them not to leave Jerusalem, but to wait there for the promise of the Father. 'This', he said, 'is what you have heard from me; ⁵for John baptized with water, but you will be baptized with*b* the Holy Spirit not many days from now.'

The Ascension of Jesus

6 So when they had come together, they asked him, 'Lord, is this the time when you will restore the kingdom to Israel?' ⁷He replied, 'It is not for you to know the times or periods that the Father has set by his own authority. ⁸But you will receive power when the Holy Spirit has come upon you; and you will be my witnesses in Jerusalem, in all Judea and Samaria, and to the ends of the earth.' ⁹When he had said this, as they were watching, he was lifted up, and a cloud took him out of their sight. ¹⁰While he was going and they were gazing up towards heaven, suddenly two men in white robes stood by them. ¹¹They said, 'Men of Galilee, why do you stand looking up towards heaven? This Jesus, who has been taken up from you into heaven, will come in the same way as you saw him go into heaven.'

Matthias Chosen to Replace Judas

12 Then they returned to Jerusalem from the mount called Olivet, which is near Jerusalem, a sabbath day's journey away. ¹³When they had entered the city, they went to the room upstairs where they were staying, Peter, and John, and James, and Andrew, Philip and Thomas, Bartholomew and Matthew, James son of Alphaeus, and Simon the Zealot, and Judas son of*c* James. ¹⁴All these were constantly devoting themselves to prayer, together with certain women, including Mary the mother of Jesus, as well as his brothers.

15 In those days Peter stood up among the believers*d* (together the crowd numbered about one hundred and twenty people) and said, ¹⁶'Friends,*e* the scripture had to be fulfilled, which the Holy Spirit through David foretold concerning Judas, who became a guide for those who arrested Jesus— ¹⁷for he was numbered among us and was allotted his share in this ministry.' ¹⁸(Now this man acquired a field with the reward of his wickedness; and falling headlong,*f* he burst open in the middle and all his bowels gushed out. ¹⁹This became known to all the residents of Jerusalem, so that the field was called in their language Hakeldama, that is, Field of Blood.) ²⁰'For it is written in the book of Psalms,

"Let his homestead become desolate,
   and let there be no one to live
      in it";

and

---

a Or *eating*   *b* Or *by*   *c* Or *the brother of*
d Gk *brothers*   *e* Gk *Men, brothers*   *f* Or *swelling up*

"Let another take his position of
    overseer."

21 So one of the men who have accompanied us throughout the time that the Lord
Jesus went in and out among us, 22 beginning from the baptism of John until the
day when he was taken up from us—one
of these must become a witness with us to
his resurrection.' 23 So they proposed two,
Joseph called Barsabbas, who was also
known as Justus, and Matthias. 24 Then
they prayed and said, 'Lord, you know
everyone's heart. Show us which one of
these two you have chosen 25 to take the
place*a* in this ministry and apostleship
from which Judas turned aside to go to his
own place.' 26 And they cast lots for them,
and the lot fell on Matthias; and he was
added to the eleven apostles.

The Coming of the Holy Spirit

2 When the day of Pentecost had come,
    they were all together in one place.
2 And suddenly from heaven there came a
sound like the rush of a violent wind, and
it filled the entire house where they were
sitting. 3 Divided tongues, as of fire, appeared among them, and a tongue rested
on each of them. 4 All of them were filled
with the Holy Spirit and began to speak in
other languages, as the Spirit gave them
ability.

5 Now there were devout Jews from
every nation under heaven living in Jerusalem. 6 And at this sound the crowd gathered and was bewildered, because each
one heard them speaking in the native
language of each. 7 Amazed and astonished, they asked, 'Are not all these who
are speaking Galileans? 8 And how is it
that we hear, each of us, in our own native
language? 9 Parthians, Medes, Elamites,
and residents of Mesopotamia, Judea and
Cappadocia, Pontus and Asia, 10 Phrygia
and Pamphylia, Egypt and the parts of
Libya belonging to Cyrene, and visitors
from Rome, both Jews and proselytes,
11 Cretans and Arabs—in our own lan-

a Other ancient authorities read *the share*

Countries of the People Mentioned at Pentecost

guages we hear them speaking about God's deeds of power.' 12 All were amazed and perplexed, saying to one another, 'What does this mean?' 13 But others sneered and said, 'They are filled with new wine.'

Peter Addresses the Crowd

14 But Peter, standing with the eleven, raised his voice and addressed them: 'Men of Judea and all who live in Jerusalem, let this be known to you, and listen to what I say. 15 Indeed, these are not drunk, as you suppose, for it is only nine o'clock in the morning. 16 No, this is what was spoken through the prophet Joel:

17 "In the last days it will be, God declares,
    that I will pour out my Spirit upon all flesh,
      and your sons and your daughters shall prophesy,
    and your young men shall see visions,
    and your old men shall dream dreams.
18 Even upon my slaves, both men and women,
    in those days I will pour out my Spirit;
      and they shall prophesy.
19 And I will show portents in the heaven above
    and signs on the earth below,
      blood, and fire, and smoky mist.
20 The sun shall be turned to darkness
    and the moon to blood,
      before the coming of the Lord's great and glorious day.
21 Then everyone who calls on the name of the Lord shall be saved."

22 'You that are Israelites,^{a} listen to what I have to say: Jesus of Nazareth,^{b} a man attested to you by God with deeds of power, wonders, and signs that God did through him among you, as you yourselves know— 23 this man, handed over to you according to the definite plan and foreknowledge of God, you crucified and killed by the hands of those outside the law. 24 But God raised him up, having freed him from death,^{c} because it was impossible for him to be held in its power. 25 For David says concerning him,

"I saw the Lord always before me,
    for he is at my right hand so that I will not be shaken;
26 therefore my heart was glad, and my tongue rejoiced;
    moreover, my flesh will live in hope.
27 For you will not abandon my soul to Hades,
    or let your Holy One experience corruption.
28 You have made known to me the ways of life;
    you will make me full of gladness with your presence."

29 'Fellow Israelites,^{d} I may say to you confidently of our ancestor David that he both died and was buried, and his tomb is with us to this day. 30 Since he was a prophet, he knew that God had sworn with an oath to him that he would put one of his descendants on his throne. 31 Foreseeing this, David^e spoke of the resurrection of the Messiah,^{f} saying,

"He was not abandoned to Hades,
    nor did his flesh experience corruption."

32 This Jesus God raised up, and of that all of us are witnesses. 33 Being therefore exalted at^g the right hand of God, and having received from the Father the promise of the Holy Spirit, he has poured out this that you both see and hear. 34 For David did not ascend into the heavens, but he himself says,

"The Lord said to my Lord,
    'Sit at my right hand,
35   until I make your enemies your footstool.' "

36 Therefore let the entire house of Israel know with certainty that God has made him both Lord and Messiah,^{h} this Jesus whom you crucified.'

a Gk Men, Israelites b Gk the Nazorean c Gk the pains of death d Gk Men, brothers e Gk he f Or the Christ g Or by h Or Christ

The First Converts

37 Now when they heard this, they were cut to the heart and said to Peter and to the other apostles, 'Brothers,[a] what should we do?' 38 Peter said to them, 'Repent, and be baptized every one of you in the name of Jesus Christ so that your sins may be forgiven; and you will receive the gift of the Holy Spirit. 39 For the promise is for you, for your children, and for all who are far away, everyone whom the Lord our God calls to him.' 40 And he testified with many other arguments and exhorted them, saying, 'Save yourselves from this corrupt generation.' 41 So those who welcomed his message were baptized, and that day about three thousand persons were added. 42 They devoted themselves to the apostles' teaching and fellowship, to the breaking of bread and the prayers.

Life among the Believers

43 Awe came upon everyone, because many wonders and signs were being done by the apostles. 44 All who believed were together and had all things in common; 45 they would sell their possessions and goods and distribute the proceeds[b] to all, as any had need. 46 Day by day, as they spent much time together in the temple, they broke bread at home[c] and ate their food with glad and generous[d] hearts, 47 praising God and having the goodwill of all the people. And day by day the Lord added to their number those who were being saved.

Peter Heals a Crippled Beggar

3 One day Peter and John were going up to the temple at the hour of prayer, at three o'clock in the afternoon. 2 And a man lame from birth was being carried in. People would lay him daily at the gate of the temple called the Beautiful Gate so that he could ask for alms from those entering the temple. 3 When he saw Peter and John about to go into the temple, he asked them for alms. 4 Peter looked intently at him, as did John, and said, 'Look at us.' 5 And he fixed his atten-

tion on them, expecting to receive something from them. 6 But Peter said, 'I have no silver or gold, but what I have I give you; in the name of Jesus Christ of Nazareth,[e] stand up and walk.' 7 And he took him by the right hand and raised him up; and immediately his feet and ankles were made strong. 8 Jumping up, he stood and began to walk, and he entered the temple with them, walking and leaping and praising God. 9 All the people saw him walking and praising God, 10 and they recognized him as the one who used to sit and ask for alms at the Beautiful Gate of the temple; and they were filled with wonder and amazement at what had happened to him.

Peter Speaks in Solomon's Portico

11 While he clung to Peter and John, all the people ran together to them in the portico called Solomon's Portico, utterly astonished. 12 When Peter saw it, he addressed the people, 'You Israelites,[f] why do you wonder at this, or why do you stare at us, as though by our own power or piety we had made him walk? 13 The God of Abraham, the God of Isaac, and the God of Jacob, the God of our ancestors has glorified his servant[g] Jesus, whom you handed over and rejected in the presence of Pilate, though he had decided to release him. 14 But you rejected the Holy and Righteous One and asked to have a murderer given to you, 15 and you killed the Author of life, whom God raised from the dead. To this we are witnesses. 16 And by faith in his name, his name itself has made this man strong, whom you see and know; and the faith that is through Jesus[h] has given him this perfect health in the presence of all of you.

17 'And now, friends,[i] I know that you acted in ignorance, as did also your rulers. 18 In this way God fulfilled what he had foretold through all the prophets, that his Messiah[j] would suffer. 19 Repent therefore, and turn to God so that your sins may be

a Gk Men, brothers b Gk them c Or from house to house d Or sincere e Gk the Nazorean f Gk Men, Israelites g Or child h Gk him i Gk brothers j Or his Christ wiped out, [20] so that times of refreshing may come from the presence of the Lord, and that he may send the Messiah[a] appointed for you, that is, Jesus, [21] who must remain in heaven until the time of universal restoration that God announced long ago through his holy prophets. [22] Moses said, "The Lord your God will raise up for you from your own people[b] a prophet like me. You must listen to whatever he tells you. [23] And it will be that everyone who does not listen to that prophet will be utterly rooted out from the people." [24] And all the prophets, as many as have spoken, from Samuel and those after him, also predicted these days. [25] You are the descendants of the prophets and of the covenant that God gave to your ancestors, saying to Abraham, "And in your descendants all the families of the earth shall be blessed." [26] When God raised up his servant,[c] he sent him first to you, to bless you by turning each of you from your wicked ways.'

Peter and John before the Council

4 While Peter and John[d] were speaking to the people, the priests, the captain of the temple, and the Sadducees came to them, [2] much annoyed because they were teaching the people and proclaiming that in Jesus there is the resurrection of the dead. [3] So they arrested them and put them in custody until the next day, for it was already evening. [4] But many of those who heard the word believed; and they numbered about five thousand.

[5] The next day their rulers, elders, and scribes assembled in Jerusalem, [6] with Annas the high priest, Caiaphas, John,[e] and Alexander, and all who were of the high-priestly family. [7] When they had made the prisoners[f] stand in their midst, they inquired, 'By what power or by what name did you do this?' [8] Then Peter, filled with the Holy Spirit, said to them, 'Rulers of the people and elders, [9] if we are questioned today because of a good deed done to someone who was sick and are asked how this man has been healed, [10] let it be known to all of you, and to all the people of Israel, that this man is standing before

you in good health by the name of Jesus Christ of Nazareth,[g] whom you crucified, whom God raised from the dead. [11] This Jesus[h] is

"the stone that was rejected by you,
	the builders;
it has become the cornerstone." [i]

[12] There is salvation in no one else, for there is no other name under heaven given among mortals by which we must be saved.'

[13] Now when they saw the boldness of Peter and John and realized that they were uneducated and ordinary men, they were amazed and recognized them as companions of Jesus. [14] When they saw the man who had been cured standing beside them, they had nothing to say in opposition. [15] So they ordered them to leave the council while they discussed the matter with one another. [16] They said, 'What will we do with them? For it is obvious to all who live in Jerusalem that a notable sign has been done through them; we cannot deny it. [17] But to keep it from spreading further among the people, let us warn them to speak no more to anyone in this name.' [18] So they called them and ordered them not to speak or teach at all in the name of Jesus. [19] But Peter and John answered them, 'Whether it is right in God's sight to listen to you rather than to God, you must judge; [20] for we cannot keep from speaking about what we have seen and heard.' [21] After threatening them again, they let them go, finding no way to punish them because of the people, for all of them praised God for what had happened. [22] For the man on whom this sign of healing had been performed was more than forty years old.

The Believers Pray for Boldness

[23] After they were released, they went to their friends[j] and reported what the chief priests and the elders had said to them. [24] When they heard it, they raised their voices together to God and said,

a Or *the Christ*   *b* Gk *brothers*   *c* Or *child*
d Gk *While they*   *e* Other ancient authorities read
Jonathan   *f* Gk *them*   *g* Gk *the Nazorean*
h Gk *This*   *i* Or *keystone*   *j* Gk *their own*

'Sovereign Lord, who made the heaven and the earth, the sea, and everything in them, 25 it is you who said by the Holy Spirit through our ancestor David, your servant: *a*

"Why did the Gentiles rage,
and the peoples imagine vain
things?
26 The kings of the earth took their
stand,
and the rulers have gathered
together
against the Lord and against his
Messiah." *b*

27 For in this city, in fact, both Herod and Pontius Pilate, with the Gentiles and the peoples of Israel, gathered together against your holy servant *a* Jesus, whom you anointed, 28 to do whatever your hand and your plan had predestined to take place. 29 And now, Lord, look at their threats, and grant to your servants *c* to speak your word with all boldness, 30 while you stretch out your hand to heal, and signs and wonders are performed through the name of your holy servant *a* Jesus.' 31 When they had prayed, the place in which they were gathered together was shaken; and they were all filled with the Holy Spirit and spoke the word of God with boldness.

The Believers Share Their Possessions

32 Now the whole group of those who believed were of one heart and soul, and no one claimed private ownership of any possessions, but everything they owned was held in common. 33 With great power the apostles gave their testimony to the resurrection of the Lord Jesus, and great grace was upon them all. 34 There was not a needy person among them, for as many as owned lands or houses sold them and brought the proceeds of what was sold. 35 They laid it at the apostles' feet, and it was distributed to each as any had need. 36 There was a Levite, a native of Cyprus, Joseph, to whom the apostles gave the name Barnabas (which means 'son of encouragement'). 37 He sold a field that belonged to him, then brought the money, and laid it at the apostles' feet.

Ananias and Sapphira

5 But a man named Ananias, with the consent of his wife Sapphira, sold a piece of property; 2 with his wife's knowledge, he kept back some of the proceeds, and brought only a part and laid it at the apostles' feet. 3 'Ananias,' Peter asked, 'why has Satan filled your heart to lie to the Holy Spirit and to keep back part of the proceeds of the land? 4 While it remained unsold, did it not remain your own? And after it was sold, were not the proceeds at your disposal? How is it that you have contrived this deed in your heart? You did not lie to us *d* but to God!' 5 Now when Ananias heard these words, he fell down and died. And great fear seized all who heard of it. 6 The young men came and wrapped up his body, *e* then carried him out and buried him.

7 After an interval of about three hours his wife came in, not knowing what had happened. 8 Peter said to her, 'Tell me whether you and your husband sold the land for such and such a price.' And she said, 'Yes, that was the price.' 9 Then Peter said to her, 'How is it that you have agreed together to put the Spirit of the Lord to the test? Look, the feet of those who have buried your husband are at the door, and they will carry you out.' 10 Immediately she fell down at his feet and died. When the young men came in they found her dead, so they carried her out and buried her beside her husband. 11 And great fear seized the whole church and all who heard of these things.

The Apostles Heal Many

12 Now many signs and wonders were done among the people through the apostles. And they were all together in Solomon's Portico. 13 None of the rest dared to join them, but the people held them in high esteem. 14 Yet more than ever believers were added to the Lord, great numbers of both men and women, 15 so that they even carried out the sick into the streets, and laid them on cots and mats, in order

a Or *child*   *b* Or *his Christ*   *c* Gk *slaves*   *d* Gk *to men*   *e* Meaning of Gk uncertain that Peter's shadow might fall on some of them as he came by. [16] A great number of people would also gather from the towns around Jerusalem, bringing the sick and those tormented by unclean spirits, and they were all cured.

The Apostles Are Persecuted

17 Then the high priest took action; he and all who were with him (that is, the sect of the Sadducees), being filled with jealousy, [18] arrested the apostles and put them in the public prison. [19] But during the night an angel of the Lord opened the prison doors, brought them out, and said, [20] 'Go, stand in the temple and tell the people the whole message about this life.' [21] When they heard this, they entered the temple at daybreak and went on with their teaching.

When the high priest and those with him arrived, they called together the council and the whole body of the elders of Israel, and sent to the prison to have them brought. [22] But when the temple police went there, they did not find them in the prison; so they returned and reported, [23] 'We found the prison securely locked and the guards standing at the doors, but when we opened them, we found no one inside.' [24] Now when the captain of the temple and the chief priests heard these words, they were perplexed about them, wondering what might be going on. [25] Then someone arrived and announced, 'Look, the men whom you put in prison are standing in the temple and teaching the people!' [26] Then the captain went with the temple police and brought them, but without violence, for they were afraid of being stoned by the people.

27 When they had brought them, they had them stand before the council. The high priest questioned them, [28] saying, 'We gave you strict orders not to teach in this name, [a] yet here you have filled Jerusalem with your teaching and you are determined to bring this man's blood on us.' [29] But Peter and the apostles answered, 'We must obey God rather than any human authority. [b] [30] The God of our ancestors raised up Jesus, whom you had killed by hanging him on a tree. [31] God exalted him at his right hand as Leader and Saviour, so that he might give repentance to Israel and forgiveness of sins. [32] And we are witnesses to these things, and so is the Holy Spirit whom God has given to those who obey him.'

33 When they heard this, they were enraged and wanted to kill them. [34] But a Pharisee in the council named Gamaliel, a teacher of the law, respected by all the people, stood up and ordered the men to be put outside for a short time. [35] Then he said to them, 'Fellow-Israelites, [c] consider carefully what you propose to do to these men. [36] For some time ago Theudas rose up, claiming to be somebody, and a number of men, about four hundred, joined him; but he was killed, and all who followed him were dispersed and disappeared. [37] After him Judas the Galilean rose up at the time of the census and got people to follow him; he also perished, and all who followed him were scattered. [38] So in the present case, I tell you, keep away from these men and let them alone; because if this plan or this undertaking is of human origin, it will fail; [39] but if it is of God, you will not be able to overthrow them—in that case you may even be found fighting against God!'

They were convinced by him, [40] and when they had called in the apostles, they had them flogged. Then they ordered them not to speak in the name of Jesus, and let them go. [41] As they left the council, they rejoiced that they were considered worthy to suffer dishonour for the sake of the name. [42] And every day in the temple and at home [d] they did not cease to teach and proclaim Jesus as the Messiah. [e]

Seven Chosen to Serve

6 Now during those days, when the disciples were increasing in number, the Hellenists complained against the He-

a Other ancient authorities read *Did we not give you strict orders not to teach in this name?*   b Gk *than men*
c Gk *Men, Israelites*   d Or *from house to house*
e Or *the Christ*

brews because their widows were being neglected in the daily distribution of food. 2 And the twelve called together the whole community of the disciples and said, 'It is not right that we should neglect the word of God in order to wait at tables.ᵃ 3 Therefore, friends,ᵇ select from among yourselves seven men of good standing, full of the Spirit and of wisdom, whom we may appoint to this task, 4 while we, for our part, will devote ourselves to prayer and to serving the word.' 5 What they said pleased the whole community, and they chose Stephen, a man full of faith and the Holy Spirit, together with Philip, Prochorus, Nicanor, Timon, Parmenas, and Nicolaus, a proselyte of Antioch. 6 They had these men stand before the apostles, who prayed and laid their hands on them.

7 The word of God continued to spread; the number of the disciples increased greatly in Jerusalem, and a great many of the priests became obedient to the faith.

The Arrest of Stephen

8 Stephen, full of grace and power, did great wonders and signs among the people. 9 Then some of those who belonged to the synagogue of the Freedmen (as it was called), Cyrenians, Alexandrians, and others of those from Cilicia and Asia, stood up and argued with Stephen. 10 But they could not withstand the wisdom and the Spiritᶜ with which he spoke. 11 Then they secretly instigated some men to say, 'We have heard him speak blasphemous words against Moses and God.' 12 They stirred up the people as well as the elders and the scribes; then they suddenly confronted him, seized him, and brought him before the council. 13 They set up false witnesses who said, 'This man never stops saying things against this holy place and the law; 14 for we have heard him say that this Jesus of Nazarethᵈ will destroy this place and will change the customs that Moses handed on to us.' 15 And all who sat in the council looked intently at him, and they saw that his face was like the face of an angel.

Stephen's Speech to the Council

7 Then the high priest asked him, 'Are these things so?' 2 And Stephen replied:

'Brothersᵉ and fathers, listen to me. The God of glory appeared to our ancestor Abraham when he was in Mesopotamia, before he lived in Haran, 3 and said to him, "Leave your country and your relatives and go to the land that I will show you." 4 Then he left the country of the Chaldeans and settled in Haran. After his father died, God had him move from there to this country in which you are now living. 5 He did not give him any of it as a heritage, not even a foot's length, but promised to give it to him as his possession and to his descendants after him, even though he had no child. 6 And God spoke in these terms, that his descendants would be resident aliens in a country belonging to others, who would enslave them and maltreat them for four hundred years. 7 "But I will judge the nation that they serve," said God, "and after that they shall come out and worship me in this place." 8 Then he gave him the covenant of circumcision. And so Abrahamᶠ became the father of Isaac and circumcised him on the eighth day; and Isaac became the father of Jacob, and Jacob of the twelve patriarchs.

9 'The patriarchs, jealous of Joseph, sold him into Egypt; but God was with him, 10 and rescued him from all his afflictions, and enabled him to win favour and to show wisdom when he stood before Pharaoh, king of Egypt, who appointed him ruler over Egypt and over all his household. 11 Now there came a famine throughout Egypt and Canaan, and great suffering, and our ancestors could find no food. 12 But when Jacob heard that there was grain in Egypt, he sent our ancestors there on their first visit. 13 On the second visit Joseph made himself known to his brothers, and Joseph's family became known to Pharaoh. 14 Then Joseph sent and invited his father Jacob and all his relatives to come to him, seventy-five in all;

ᵃ Or keep accounts   ᵇ Gk brothers   ᶜ Or spirit
ᵈ Gk the Nazorean   ᵉ Gk Men, brothers   ᶠ Gk he

[15] so Jacob went down to Egypt. He himself died there as well as our ancestors, [16] and their bodies[a] were brought back to Shechem and laid in the tomb that Abraham had bought for a sum of silver from the sons of Hamor in Shechem.

17 'But as the time drew near for the fulfilment of the promise that God had made to Abraham, our people in Egypt increased and multiplied [18] until another king who had not known Joseph ruled over Egypt. [19] He dealt craftily with our race and forced our ancestors to abandon their infants so that they would die. [20] At this time Moses was born, and he was beautiful before God. For three months he was brought up in his father's house; [21] and when he was abandoned, Pharaoh's daughter adopted him and brought him up as her own son. [22] So Moses was instructed in all the wisdom of the Egyptians and was powerful in his words and deeds.

23 'When he was forty years old, it came into his heart to visit his relatives, the Israelites.[b] [24] When he saw one of them being wronged, he defended the oppressed man and avenged him by striking down the Egyptian. [25] He supposed that his kinsfolk would understand that God through him was rescuing them, but they did not understand. [26] The next day he came to some of them as they were quarrelling and tried to reconcile them, saying, "Men, you are brothers; why do you wrong each other?" [27] But the man who was wronging his neighbour pushed Moses[c] aside, saying, "Who made you a ruler and a judge over us? [28] Do you want to kill me as you killed the Egyptian yesterday?" [29] When he heard this, Moses fled and became a resident alien in the land of Midian. There he became the father of two sons.

30 'Now when forty years had passed, an angel appeared to him in the wilderness of Mount Sinai, in the flame of a burning bush. [31] When Moses saw it, he was amazed at the sight; and as he approached to look, there came the voice of the Lord: [32] "I am the God of your ancestors, the God of Abraham, Isaac, and Ja-

cob." Moses began to tremble and did not dare to look. [33] Then the Lord said to him, "Take off the sandals from your feet, for the place where you are standing is holy ground. [34] I have surely seen the mistreatment of my people who are in Egypt and have heard their groaning, and I have come down to rescue them. Come now, I will send you to Egypt."

35 'It was this Moses whom they rejected when they said, "Who made you a ruler and a judge?" and whom God now sent as both ruler and liberator through the angel who appeared to him in the bush. [36] He led them out, having performed wonders and signs in Egypt, at the Red Sea, and in the wilderness for forty years. [37] This is the Moses who said to the Israelites, "God will raise up a prophet for you from your own people[d] as he raised me up." [38] He is the one who was in the congregation in the wilderness with the angel who spoke to him at Mount Sinai, and with our ancestors; and he received living oracles to give to us. [39] Our ancestors were unwilling to obey him; instead, they pushed him aside, and in their hearts they turned back to Egypt, [40] saying to Aaron, "Make gods for us who will lead the way for us; as for this Moses who led us out from the land of Egypt, we do not know what has happened to him." [41] At that time they made a calf, offered a sacrifice to the idol, and revelled in the works of their hands. [42] But God turned away from them and handed them over to worship the host of heaven, as it is written in the book of the prophets:

"Did you offer to me slain victims
    and sacrifices
  for forty years in the wilderness,
      O house of Israel?
[43] No; you took along the tent
      of Moloch,
    and the star of your god Rephan,
      the images that you made
        to worship;
  so I will remove you beyond
      Babylon."

a Gk they   b Gk his brothers, the sons of Israel
c Gk him   d Gk your brothers

44 'Our ancestors had the tent of testimony in the wilderness, as God[a] directed when he spoke to Moses, ordering him to make it according to the pattern he had seen. 45 Our ancestors in turn brought it in with Joshua when they dispossessed the nations that God drove out before our ancestors. And it was there until the time of David, 46 who found favour with God and asked that he might find a dwelling-place for the house of Jacob.[b] 47 But it was Solomon who built a house for him. 48 Yet the Most High does not dwell in houses made by human hands;[c] as the prophet says,
49 "Heaven is my throne,
    and the earth is my footstool.
What kind of house will you build
        for me, says the Lord,
    or what is the place of my rest?
50 Did not my hand make all these
        things?"

51 'You stiff-necked people, uncircumcised in heart and ears, you are for ever opposing the Holy Spirit, just as your ancestors used to do. 52 Which of the prophets did your ancestors not persecute? They killed those who foretold the coming of the Righteous One, and now you have become his betrayers and murderers. 53 You are the ones that received the law as ordained by angels, and yet you have not kept it.'

The Stoning of Stephen

54 When they heard these things, they became enraged and ground their teeth at Stephen.[d] 55 But filled with the Holy Spirit, he gazed into heaven and saw the glory of God and Jesus standing at the right hand of God. 56 'Look,' he said, 'I see the heavens opened and the Son of Man standing at the right hand of God!' 57 But they covered their ears, and with a loud shout all rushed together against him. 58 Then they dragged him out of the city and began to stone him; and the witnesses laid their coats at the feet of a young man named Saul. 59 While they were stoning Stephen, he prayed, 'Lord Jesus, receive my spirit.' 60 Then he knelt down and cried out in a loud voice, 'Lord, do not hold this sin against them.' When he had said this, he died.[e] 1 And Saul approved of their killing him.

Saul Persecutes the Church

That day a severe persecution began against the church in Jerusalem, and all except the apostles were scattered throughout the countryside of Judea and Samaria. 2 Devout men buried Stephen and made loud lamentation over him. 3 But Saul was ravaging the church by entering house after house; dragging off both men and women, he committed them to prison.

Philip Preaches in Samaria

4 Now those who were scattered went from place to place, proclaiming the word. 5 Philip went down to the city[f] of Samaria and proclaimed the Messiah[g] to them. 6 The crowds with one accord listened eagerly to what was said by Philip, hearing and seeing the signs that he did, 7 for unclean spirits, crying with loud shrieks, came out of many who were possessed; and many others who were paralysed or lame were cured. 8 So there was great joy in that city.

9 Now a certain man named Simon had previously practised magic in the city and amazed the people of Samaria, saying that he was someone great. 10 All of them, from the least to the greatest, listened to him eagerly, saying, 'This man is the power of God that is called Great.' 11 And they listened eagerly to him because for a long time he had amazed them with his magic. 12 But when they believed Philip, who was proclaiming the good news about the kingdom of God and the name of Jesus Christ, they were baptized, both men and women. 13 Even Simon himself believed. After being baptized, he stayed constantly with Philip and was amazed when he saw the signs and great miracles that took place.

14 Now when the apostles at Jerusalem

a Gk he   b Other ancient authorities read for the God of Jacob   c Gk with hands   d Gk him   e Gk fell asleep   f Other ancient authorities read a city
g Or the Christ

heard that Samaria had accepted the word of God, they sent Peter and John to them. ¹⁵The two went down and prayed for them that they might receive the Holy Spirit ¹⁶(for as yet the Spirit had not come*ᵃ* upon any of them; they had only been baptized in the name of the Lord Jesus). ¹⁷Then Peter and John*ᵇ* laid their hands on them, and they received the Holy Spirit. ¹⁸Now when Simon saw that the Spirit was given through the laying on of the apostles' hands, he offered them money, ¹⁹saying, 'Give me also this power so that anyone on whom I lay my hands may receive the Holy Spirit.' ²⁰But Peter said to him, 'May your silver perish with you, because you thought you could obtain God's gift with money! ²¹You have no part or share in this, for your heart is not right before God. ²²Repent therefore of this wickedness of yours, and pray to the Lord that, if possible, the intent of your heart may be forgiven you. ²³For I see that you are in the gall of bitterness and the chains of wickedness.' ²⁴Simon answered, 'Pray for me to the

Lord, that nothing of what you*ᶜ* have said may happen to me.'

25 Now after Peter and John*ᵈ* had testified and spoken the word of the Lord, they returned to Jerusalem, proclaiming the good news to many villages of the Samaritans.

Philip and the Ethiopian Eunuch

26 Then an angel of the Lord said to Philip, 'Get up and go towards the south*ᵉ* to the road that goes down from Jerusalem to Gaza.' (This is a wilderness road.) ²⁷So he got up and went. Now there was an Ethiopian eunuch, a court official of the Candace, queen of the Ethiopians, in charge of her entire treasury. He had come to Jerusalem to worship ²⁸and was returning home; seated in his chariot, he was reading the prophet Isaiah. ²⁹Then the Spirit said to Philip, 'Go over to this chariot and join it.' ³⁰So Philip ran up to it and heard him reading the prophet Isaiah. He asked, 'Do you understand what you are reading?' ³¹He replied, 'How can I, unless someone guides me?' And he invited Philip to get in and sit beside him. ³²Now the passage of the scripture that he was reading was this:

'Like a sheep he was led to the
    slaughter,
  and like a lamb silent before
    its shearer,
    so he does not open his mouth.
³³ In his humiliation justice was denied
    him.
  Who can describe his generation?
    For his life is taken away from the
    earth.'

³⁴The eunuch asked Philip, 'About whom, may I ask you, does the prophet say this, about himself or about someone else?' ³⁵Then Philip began to speak, and starting with this scripture, he proclaimed to him the good news about Jesus. ³⁶As they were going along the road, they came to some water; and the eunuch said, 'Look, here is water! What is to prevent me from being

Philip's and Peter's Missionary Journeys

Mediterranean Sea

Caesarea

SAMARIA

Samaria
Mt. Gerizim

Antipatris

Joppa

Lydda   JUDEA

Jamnia
Azotus   Jerusalem

Betogabris   Bethsura

Dead Sea

Gaza

Jordan River

0   10   20 Mi.
0   10   20   30 Km.

→ Peter's Journeys
⇢ Philip's Journeys

a Gk *fallen*   *b* Gk *they*   *c* The Greek word for *you* and the verb *pray* are plural   *d* Gk *after they* *e* Or *go at noon* baptized?'ᵃ ³⁸He commanded the chariot to stop, and both of them, Philip and the eunuch, went down into the water, and Philipᵇ baptized him. ³⁹When they came up out of the water, the Spirit of the Lord snatched Philip away; the eunuch saw him no more, and went on his way rejoicing. ⁴⁰But Philip found himself at Azotus, and as he was passing through the region, he proclaimed the good news to all the towns until he came to Caesarea.

The Conversion of Saul

9 Meanwhile Saul, still breathing threats and murder against the disciples of the Lord, went to the high priest ²and asked him for letters to the synagogues at Damascus, so that if he found any who belonged to the Way, men or women, he might bring them bound to Jerusalem. ³Now as he was going along and approaching Damascus, suddenly a light from heaven flashed around him. ⁴He fell to the ground and heard a voice saying to him, 'Saul, Saul, why do you persecute me?' ⁵He asked, 'Who are you, Lord?' The reply came, 'I am Jesus, whom you are persecuting. ⁶But get up and enter the city, and you will be told what you are to do.' ⁷The men who were travelling with him stood speechless because they heard the voice but saw no one. ⁸Saul got up from the ground, and though his eyes were open, he could see nothing; so they led him by the hand and brought him into Damascus. ⁹For three days he was without sight, and neither ate nor drank.

10 Now there was a disciple in Damascus named Ananias. The Lord said to him in a vision, 'Ananias.' He answered, 'Here I am, Lord.' ¹¹The Lord said to him, 'Get up and go to the street called Straight, and at the house of Judas look for a man of Tarsus named Saul. At this moment he is praying, ¹²and he has seen in a visionᶜ a man named Ananias come in and lay his hands on him so that he might regain his sight.' ¹³But Ananias answered, 'Lord, I have heard from many about this man, how much evil he has done to your saints in Jerusalem; ¹⁴and here he has authority

from the chief priests to bind all who invoke your name.' ¹⁵But the Lord said to him, 'Go, for he is an instrument whom I have chosen to bring my name before Gentiles and kings and before the people of Israel; ¹⁶I myself will show him how much he must suffer for the sake of my name.' ¹⁷So Ananias went and entered the house. He laid his hands on Saulᵈ and said, 'Brother Saul, the Lord Jesus, who appeared to you on your way here, has sent me so that you may regain your sight and be filled with the Holy Spirit.' ¹⁸And immediately something like scales fell from his eyes, and his sight was restored. Then he got up and was baptized, ¹⁹and after taking some food, he regained his strength.

Saul Preaches in Damascus

For several days he was with the disciples in Damascus, ²⁰and immediately he began to proclaim Jesus in the synagogues, saying, 'He is the Son of God.' ²¹All who heard him were amazed and said, 'Is not this the man who made havoc in Jerusalem among those who invoked this name? And has he not come here for the purpose of bringing them bound before the chief priests?' ²²Saul became increasingly more powerful and confounded the Jews who lived in Damascus by proving that Jesusᵉ was the Messiah.ᶠ

Saul Escapes from the Jews

23 After some time had passed, the Jews plotted to kill him, ²⁴but their plot became known to Saul. They were watching the gates day and night so that they might kill him; ²⁵but his disciples took him by night and let him down through an opening in the wall,ᵍ lowering him in a basket.

Saul in Jerusalem

26 When he had come to Jerusalem, he attempted to join the disciples; and they

---

ᵃ Other ancient authorities add all or most of verse 37,
And Philip said, 'If you believe with all your heart, you may.'
And he replied, 'I believe that Jesus Christ is the Son of God.'
ᵇ Gk he   ᶜ Other ancient authorities lack in a vision
ᵈ Gk him   ᵉ Gk that this   ᶠ Or the Christ
ᵍ Gk through the wall

were all afraid of him, for they did not believe that he was a disciple. 27 But Barnabas took him, brought him to the apostles, and described for them how on the road he had seen the Lord, who had spoken to him, and how in Damascus he had spoken boldly in the name of Jesus. 28 So he went in and out among them in Jerusalem, speaking boldly in the name of the Lord. 29 He spoke and argued with the Hellenists; but they were attempting to kill him. 30 When the believers*a* learned of it, they brought him down to Caesarea and sent him off to Tarsus.

31 Meanwhile the church throughout Judea, Galilee, and Samaria had peace and was built up. Living in the fear of the Lord and in the comfort of the Holy Spirit, it increased in numbers.

The Healing of Aeneas

32 Now as Peter went here and there among all the believers,*b* he came down also to the saints living in Lydda. 33 There he found a man named Aeneas, who had been bedridden for eight years, for he was paralysed. 34 Peter said to him, 'Aeneas, Jesus Christ heals you; get up and make your bed!' And immediately he got up. 35 And all the residents of Lydda and Sharon saw him and turned to the Lord.

Peter in Lydda and Joppa

36 Now in Joppa there was a disciple whose name was Tabitha, which in Greek is Dorcas.*c* She was devoted to good works and acts of charity. 37 At that time she became ill and died. When they had washed her, they laid her in a room upstairs. 38 Since Lydda was near Joppa, the disciples, who heard that Peter was there, sent two men to him with the request, 'Please come to us without delay.' 39 So Peter got up and went with them; and when he arrived, they took him to the room upstairs. All the widows stood beside him, weeping and showing tunics and other clothing that Dorcas had made while she was with them. 40 Peter put all of them outside, and then he knelt down and prayed. He turned to the body and said, 'Tabitha, get up.'

Then she opened her eyes, and seeing Peter, she sat up. 41 He gave her his hand and helped her up. Then calling the saints and widows, he showed her to be alive. 42 This became known throughout Joppa, and many believed in the Lord. 43 Meanwhile he stayed in Joppa for some time with a certain Simon, a tanner.

Peter and Cornelius

10 In Caesarea there was a man named Cornelius, a centurion of the Italian Cohort, as it was called. 2 He was a devout man who feared God with all his household; he gave alms generously to the people and prayed constantly to God. 3 One afternoon at about three o'clock he had a vision in which he clearly saw an angel of God coming in and saying to him, 'Cornelius.' 4 He stared at him in terror and said, 'What is it, Lord?' He answered, 'Your prayers and your alms have ascended as a memorial before God. 5 Now send men to Joppa for a certain Simon who is called Peter; 6 he is lodging with Simon, a tanner, whose house is by the seaside.' 7 When the angel who spoke to him had left, he called two of his slaves and a devout soldier from the ranks of those who served him, 8 and after telling them everything, he sent them to Joppa.

9 About noon the next day, as they were on their journey and approaching the city, Peter went up on the roof to pray. 10 He became hungry and wanted something to eat; and while it was being prepared, he fell into a trance. 11 He saw the heaven opened and something like a large sheet coming down, being lowered to the ground by its four corners. 12 In it were all kinds of four-footed creatures and reptiles and birds of the air. 13 Then he heard a voice saying, 'Get up, Peter; kill and eat.' 14 But Peter said, 'By no means, Lord; for I have never eaten anything that is profane or unclean.' 15 The voice said to him again, a second time, 'What God has made clean, you must not call profane.' 16 This hap-

a Gk *brothers*   *b* Gk *all of them*   *c* The name Tabitha in Aramaic and the name Dorcas in Greek mean *a gazelle* pened three times, and the thing was suddenly taken up to heaven.

17 Now while Peter was greatly puzzled about what to make of the vision that he had seen, suddenly the men sent by Cornelius appeared. They were asking for Simon's house and were standing by the gate. 18 They called out to ask whether Simon, who was called Peter, was staying there. 19 While Peter was still thinking about the vision, the Spirit said to him, 'Look, three*a* men are searching for you. 20 Now get up, go down, and go with them without hesitation; for I have sent them.' 21 So Peter went down to the men and said, 'I am the one you are looking for; what is the reason for your coming?' 22 They answered, 'Cornelius, a centurion, an upright and God-fearing man, who is well spoken of by the whole Jewish nation, was directed by a holy angel to send for you to come to his house and to hear what you have to say.' 23 So Peter*b* invited them in and gave them lodging.

The next day he got up and went with them, and some of the believers*c* from Joppa accompanied him. 24 The following day they came to Caesarea. Cornelius was expecting them and had called together his relatives and close friends. 25 On Peter's arrival Cornelius met him, and falling at his feet, worshipped him. 26 But Peter made him get up, saying, 'Stand up; I am only a mortal.' 27 And as he talked with him, he went in and found that many had assembled; 28 and he said to them, 'You yourselves know that it is unlawful for a Jew to associate with or to visit a Gentile; but God has shown me that I should not call anyone profane or unclean. 29 So when I was sent for, I came without objection. Now may I ask why you sent for me?'

30 Cornelius replied, 'Four days ago at this very hour, at three o'clock, I was praying in my house when suddenly a man in dazzling clothes stood before me. 31 He said, "Cornelius, your prayer has been heard and your alms have been remembered before God. 32 Send therefore to Joppa and ask for Simon, who is called Peter;

he is staying in the home of Simon, a tanner, by the sea." 33 Therefore I sent for you immediately, and you have been kind enough to come. So now all of us are here in the presence of God to listen to all that the Lord has commanded you to say.'

Gentiles Hear the Good News

34 Then Peter began to speak to them: 'I truly understand that God shows no partiality, 35 but in every nation anyone who fears him and does what is right is acceptable to him. 36 You know the message he sent to the people of Israel, preaching peace by Jesus Christ—he is Lord of all. 37 That message spread throughout Judea, beginning in Galilee after the baptism that John announced: 38 how God anointed Jesus of Nazareth with the Holy Spirit and with power; how he went about doing good and healing all who were oppressed by the devil, for God was with him. 39 We are witnesses to all that he did both in Judea and in Jerusalem. They put him to death by hanging him on a tree; 40 but God raised him on the third day and allowed him to appear, 41 not to all the people but to us who were chosen by God as witnesses, and who ate and drank with him after he rose from the dead. 42 He commanded us to preach to the people and to testify that he is the one ordained by God as judge of the living and the dead. 43 All the prophets testify about him that everyone who believes in him receives forgiveness of sins through his name.'

Gentiles Receive the Holy Spirit

44 While Peter was still speaking, the Holy Spirit fell upon all who heard the word. 45 The circumcised believers who had come with Peter were astounded that the gift of the Holy Spirit had been poured out even on the Gentiles, 46 for they heard them speaking in tongues and extolling God. Then Peter said, 47 'Can anyone withhold the water for baptizing these people who have received the Holy Spirit just as

a One ancient authority reads *two*; others lack the word
b Gk *he*   *c* Gk *brothers*

we have?' 48 So he ordered them to be baptized in the name of Jesus Christ. Then they invited him to stay for several days.

Peter's Report to the Church at Jerusalem

11 Now the apostles and the believers[a] who were in Judea heard that the Gentiles had also accepted the word of God. 2 So when Peter went up to Jerusalem, the circumcised believers[b] criticized him, 3 saying, 'Why did you go to uncircumcised men and eat with them?' 4 Then Peter began to explain it to them, step by step, saying, 5 'I was in the city of Joppa praying, and in a trance I saw a vision. There was something like a large sheet coming down from heaven, being lowered by its four corners; and it came close to me. 6 As I looked at it closely I saw four-footed animals, beasts of prey, reptiles, and birds of the air. 7 I also heard a voice saying to me, "Get up, Peter; kill and eat." 8 But I replied, "By no means, Lord; for nothing profane or unclean has ever entered my mouth." 9 But a second time the voice answered from heaven, "What God has made clean, you must not call profane." 10 This happened three times; then everything was pulled up again to heaven. 11 At that very moment three men, sent to me from Caesarea, arrived at the house where we were. 12 The Spirit told me to go with them and not to make a distinction between them and us.[c] These six brothers also accompanied me, and we entered the man's house. 13 He told us how he had seen the angel standing in his house and saying, "Send to Joppa and bring Simon, who is called Peter; 14 he will give you a message by which you and your entire household will be saved." 15 And as I began to speak, the Holy Spirit fell upon them just as it had upon us at the beginning. 16 And I remembered the word of the Lord, how he had said, "John baptized with water, but you will be baptized with the Holy Spirit." 17 If then God gave them the same gift that he gave us when we believed in the Lord Jesus Christ, who was I that I could hinder God?' 18 When they heard this, they were silenced. And they praised God, saying, 'Then God has given even to the Gentiles the repentance that leads to life.'

The Church in Antioch

19 Now those who were scattered because of the persecution that took place over Stephen travelled as far as Phoenicia, Cyprus, and Antioch, and they spoke the word to no one except Jews. 20 But among them were some men of Cyprus and Cyrene who, on coming to Antioch, spoke to the Hellenists[d] also, proclaiming the Lord Jesus. 21 The hand of the Lord was with them, and a great number became believers and turned to the Lord. 22 News of this came to the ears of the church in Jerusalem, and they sent Barnabas to Antioch. 23 When he came and saw the grace of God, he rejoiced, and he exhorted them all to remain faithful to the Lord with steadfast devotion; 24 for he was a good man, full of the Holy Spirit and of faith. And a great many people were brought to the Lord. 25 Then Barnabas went to Tarsus to look for Saul, 26 and when he had found him, he brought him to Antioch. So it was that for an entire year they associated with[e] the church and taught a great many people, and it was in Antioch that the disciples were first called 'Christians'.

27 At that time prophets came down from Jerusalem to Antioch. 28 One of them named Agabus stood up and predicted by the Spirit that there would be a severe famine over all the world; and this took place during the reign of Claudius. 29 The disciples determined that according to their ability, each would send relief to the believers[a] living in Judea; 30 this they did, sending it to the elders by Barnabas and Saul.

James Killed and Peter Imprisoned

12 About that time King Herod laid violent hands upon some who belonged to the church. 2 He had James, the brother of John, killed with the sword.

a Gk *brothers*   *b* Gk lacks *believers*   *c* Or *not to hesitate*   *d* Other ancient authorities read *Greeks*   *e* Or *were guests of*

³After he saw that it pleased the Jews, he proceeded to arrest Peter also. (This was during the festival of Unleavened Bread.) ⁴When he had seized him, he put him in prison and handed him over to four squads of soldiers to guard him, intending to bring him out to the people after the Passover. ⁵While Peter was kept in prison, the church prayed fervently to God for him.

Peter Delivered from Prison

6 The very night before Herod was going to bring him out, Peter, bound with two chains, was sleeping between two soldiers, while guards in front of the door were keeping watch over the prison. ⁷Suddenly an angel of the Lord appeared and a light shone in the cell. He tapped Peter on the side and woke him, saying, 'Get up quickly.' And the chains fell off his wrists. ⁸The angel said to him, 'Fasten your belt and put on your sandals.' He did so. Then he said to him, 'Wrap your cloak around you and follow me.' ⁹Peter*a* went out and followed him; he did not realize that what was happening with the angel's help was real; he thought he was seeing a vision. ¹⁰After they had passed the first and the second guard, they came before the iron gate leading into the city. It opened for them of its own accord, and they went outside and walked along a lane, when suddenly the angel left him. ¹¹Then Peter came to himself and said, 'Now I am sure that the Lord has sent his angel and rescued me from the hands of Herod and from all that the Jewish people were expecting.'

12 As soon as he realized this, he went to the house of Mary, the mother of John whose other name was Mark, where many had gathered and were praying. ¹³When he knocked at the outer gate, a maid named Rhoda came to answer. ¹⁴On recognizing Peter's voice, she was so overjoyed that, instead of opening the gate, she ran in and announced that Peter was standing at the gate. ¹⁵They said to her, 'You are out of your mind!' But she insisted that it was so. They said, 'It is his angel.' ¹⁶Meanwhile, Peter continued knocking; and when they opened the gate, they saw him and were amazed. ¹⁷He motioned to them with his hand to be silent, and described for them how the Lord had brought him out of the prison. And he added, 'Tell this to James and to the believers.'*b* Then he left and went to another place.

18 When morning came, there was no small commotion among the soldiers over what had become of Peter. ¹⁹When Herod had searched for him and could not find him, he examined the guards and ordered them to be put to death. Then he went down from Judea to Caesarea and stayed there.

The Death of Herod

20 Now Herod*c* was angry with the people of Tyre and Sidon. So they came to him in a body; and after winning over Blastus, the king's chamberlain, they asked for a reconciliation, because their country depended on the king's country for food. ²¹On an appointed day Herod put on his royal robes, took his seat on the platform, and delivered a public address to them. ²²The people kept shouting, 'The voice of a god, and not of a mortal!' ²³And immediately, because he had not given the glory to God, an angel of the Lord struck him down, and he was eaten by worms and died.

24 But the word of God continued to advance and gain adherents. ²⁵Then after completing their mission Barnabas and Saul returned to*d* Jerusalem and brought with them John, whose other name was Mark.

Barnabas and Saul Commissioned

13 Now in the church at Antioch there were prophets and teachers: Barnabas, Simeon who was called Niger, Lucius of Cyrene, Manaen a member of the court of Herod the ruler,*e* and Saul. ²While they were worshipping the Lord and fasting, the Holy Spirit said, 'Set apart for me Barnabas and Saul for the work to which I

a Gk He   *b* Gk brothers   *c* Gk he   *d* Other ancient authorities read *from*   *e* Gk *tetrarch* have called them.' ³Then after fasting and praying they laid their hands on them and sent them off.

The Apostles Preach in Cyprus

4 So, being sent out by the Holy Spirit, they went down to Seleucia; and from there they sailed to Cyprus. ⁵When they arrived at Salamis, they proclaimed the word of God in the synagogues of the Jews. And they had John also to assist them. ⁶When they had gone through the whole island as far as Paphos, they met a certain magician, a Jewish false prophet, named Bar-Jesus. ⁷He was with the proconsul, Sergius Paulus, an intelligent man, who summoned Barnabas and Saul and wanted to hear the word of God. ⁸But the magician Elymas (for that is the translation of his name) opposed them and tried to turn the proconsul away from the faith. ⁹But Saul, also known as Paul, filled with the Holy Spirit, looked intently at him ¹⁰and said, 'You son of the devil, you enemy of all righteousness, full of all deceit and villainy, will you

not stop making crooked the straight paths of the Lord? ¹¹And now listen—the hand of the Lord is against you, and you will be blind for a while, unable to see the sun.' Immediately mist and darkness came over him, and he went about groping for someone to lead him by the hand. ¹²When the proconsul saw what had happened, he believed, for he was astonished at the teaching about the Lord.

Paul and Barnabas in Antioch of Pisidia

13 Then Paul and his companions set sail from Paphos and came to Perga in Pamphylia. John, however, left them and returned to Jerusalem; ¹⁴but they went on from Perga and came to Antioch in Pisidia. And on the sabbath day they went into the synagogue and sat down. ¹⁵After the reading of the law and the prophets, the officials of the synagogue sent them a message, saying, 'Brothers, if you have any word of exhortation for the people, give it.' ¹⁶So Paul stood up and with a gesture began to speak:

Paul's First Missionary Journey

'You Israelites,[a] and others who fear God, listen. 17The God of this people Israel chose our ancestors and made the people great during their stay in the land of Egypt, and with uplifted arm he led them out of it. 18For about forty years he put up with[b] them in the wilderness. 19After he had destroyed seven nations in the land of Canaan, he gave them their land as an inheritance 20for about four hundred and fifty years. After that he gave them judges until the time of the prophet Samuel. 21Then they asked for a king; and God gave them Saul son of Kish, a man of the tribe of Benjamin, who reigned for forty years. 22When he had removed him, he made David their king. In his testimony about him he said, "I have found David, son of Jesse, to be a man after my heart, who will carry out all my wishes." 23Of this man's posterity God has brought to Israel a Saviour, Jesus, as he promised; 24before his coming John had already proclaimed a baptism of repentance to all the people of Israel. 25And as John was finishing his work, he said, "What do you suppose that I am? I am not he. No, but one is coming after me; I am not worthy to untie the thong of the sandals[c] on his feet."

26 'My brothers, you descendants of Abraham's family, and others who fear God, to us[d] the message of this salvation has been sent. 27Because the residents of Jerusalem and their leaders did not recognize him or understand the words of the prophets that are read every sabbath, they fulfilled those words by condemning him. 28Even though they found no cause for a sentence of death, they asked Pilate to have him killed. 29When they had carried out everything that was written about him, they took him down from the tree and laid him in a tomb. 30But God raised him from the dead; 31and for many days he appeared to those who came up with him from Galilee to Jerusalem, and they are now his witnesses to the people. 32And we bring you the good news that what God promised to our ancestors 33he has fulfilled for us, their children, by raising Jesus; as also it is written in the second psalm,

"You are my Son;
    today I have begotten you."

34As to his raising him from the dead, no more to return to corruption, he has spoken in this way,

"I will give you the holy promises
    made to David."

35Therefore he has also said in another psalm,

"You will not let your Holy One
    experience corruption."

36For David, after he had served the purpose of God in his own generation, died,[e] was laid beside his ancestors, and experienced corruption; 37but he whom God raised up experienced no corruption. 38Let it be known to you therefore, my brothers, that through this man forgiveness of sins is proclaimed to you; 39by this Jesus[f] everyone who believes is set free from all those sins[g] from which you could not be freed by the law of Moses. 40Beware, therefore, that what the prophets said does not happen to you:
41 "Look, you scoffers!
    Be amazed and perish,
    for in your days I am doing a work,
        a work that you will never believe,
            even if someone tells you." '

42 As Paul and Barnabas[h] were going out, the people urged them to speak about these things again the next sabbath. 43When the meeting of the synagogue broke up, many Jews and devout converts to Judaism followed Paul and Barnabas, who spoke to them and urged them to continue in the grace of God.

44 The next sabbath almost the whole city gathered to hear the word of the Lord.[i] 45But when the Jews saw the crowds, they were filled with jealousy; and blaspheming, they contradicted what was spoken by Paul. 46Then both Paul and Barnabas spoke out boldly, saying, 'It was necessary that the word of God should be spoken first to you. Since you reject it and judge yourselves to be unworthy of eternal life,

we are now turning to the Gentiles. [47] For so the Lord has commanded us, saying,

> "I have set you to be a light for
>   the Gentiles,
>   so that you may bring salvation to
>   the ends of the earth." '

[48] When the Gentiles heard this, they were glad and praised the word of the Lord; and as many as had been destined for eternal life became believers. [49] Thus the word of the Lord spread throughout the region. [50] But the Jews incited the devout women of high standing and the leading men of the city, and stirred up persecution against Paul and Barnabas, and drove them out of their region. [51] So they shook the dust off their feet in protest against them, and went to Iconium. [52] And the disciples were filled with joy and with the Holy Spirit.

Paul and Barnabas in Iconium

14 The same thing occurred in Iconium, where Paul and Barnabas[a] went into the Jewish synagogue and spoke in such a way that a great number of both Jews and Greeks became believers. [2] But the unbelieving Jews stirred up the Gentiles and poisoned their minds against the brothers. [3] So they remained for a long time, speaking boldly for the Lord, who testified to the word of his grace by granting signs and wonders to be done through them. [4] But the residents of the city were divided; some sided with the Jews, and some with the apostles. [5] And when an attempt was made by both Gentiles and Jews, with their rulers, to maltreat them and to stone them, [6] the apostles[a] learned of it and fled to Lystra and Derbe, cities of Lycaonia, and to the surrounding country; [7] and there they continued proclaiming the good news.

Paul and Barnabas in Lystra and Derbe

[8] In Lystra there was a man sitting who could not use his feet and had never walked, for he had been crippled from birth. [9] He listened to Paul as he was speaking. And Paul, looking at him intently and seeing that he had faith to be healed, [10] said in a loud voice, 'Stand upright on your feet.' And the man[b] sprang up and began to walk. [11] When the crowds saw what Paul had done, they shouted in the Lycaonian language, 'The gods have come down to us in human form!' [12] Barnabas they called Zeus, and Paul they called Hermes, because he was the chief speaker. [13] The priest of Zeus, whose temple was just outside the city,[c] brought oxen and garlands to the gates; he and the crowds wanted to offer sacrifice. [14] When the apostles Barnabas and Paul heard of it, they tore their clothes and rushed out into the crowd, shouting, [15] 'Friends,[d] why are you doing this? We are mortals just like you, and we bring you good news, that you should turn from these worthless things to the living God, who made the heaven and the earth and the sea and all that is in them. [16] In past generations he allowed all the nations to follow their own ways; [17] yet he has not left himself without a witness in doing good—giving you rains from heaven and fruitful seasons, and filling you with food and your hearts with joy.' [18] Even with these words, they scarcely restrained the crowds from offering sacrifice to them.

[19] But Jews came there from Antioch and Iconium and won over the crowds. Then they stoned Paul and dragged him out of the city, supposing that he was dead. [20] But when the disciples surrounded him, he got up and went into the city. The next day he went on with Barnabas to Derbe.

The Return to Antioch in Syria

[21] After they had proclaimed the good news to that city and had made many disciples, they returned to Lystra, then on to Iconium and Antioch. [22] There they strengthened the souls of the disciples and encouraged them to continue in the faith, saying, 'It is through many persecutions that we must enter the kingdom of God.' [23] And after they had appointed elders for them in each church, with prayer and fast-

a Gk *they*   *b* Gk *he*   *c* Or *The priest of Zeus-Outside-the-City*   *d* Gk *Men* ing they entrusted them to the Lord in whom they had come to believe.

24 Then they passed through Pisidia and came to Pamphylia. 25 When they had spoken the word in Perga, they went down to Attalia. 26 From there they sailed back to Antioch, where they had been commended to the grace of God for the work*a* that they had completed. 27 When they arrived, they called the church together and related all that God had done with them, and how he had opened a door of faith for the Gentiles. 28 And they stayed there with the disciples for some time.

The Council at Jerusalem

15 Then certain individuals came down from Judea and were teaching the brothers, 'Unless you are circumcised according to the custom of Moses, you cannot be saved.' 2 And after Paul and Barnabas had no small dissension and debate with them, Paul and Barnabas and some of the others were appointed to go up to Jerusalem to discuss this question with the apostles and the elders. 3 So they were sent on their way by the church, and as they passed through both Phoenicia and Samaria, they reported the conversion of the Gentiles, and brought great joy to all the believers.*b* 4 When they came to Jerusalem, they were welcomed by the church and the apostles and the elders, and they reported all that God had done with them. 5 But some believers who belonged to the sect of the Pharisees stood up and said, 'It is necessary for them to be circumcised and ordered to keep the law of Moses.'

6 The apostles and the elders met together to consider this matter. 7 After there had been much debate, Peter stood up and said to them, 'My brothers,*c* you know that in the early days God made a choice among you, that I should be the one through whom the Gentiles would hear the message of the good news and become believers. 8 And God, who knows the human heart, testified to them by giving them the Holy Spirit, just as he did to us; 9 and in cleansing their hearts by faith he

has made no distinction between them and us. 10 Now therefore why are you putting God to the test by placing on the neck of the disciples a yoke that neither our ancestors nor we have been able to bear? 11 On the contrary, we believe that we will be saved through the grace of the Lord Jesus, just as they will.'

12 The whole assembly kept silence, and listened to Barnabas and Paul as they told of all the signs and wonders that God had done through them among the Gentiles. 13 After they finished speaking, James replied, 'My brothers,*c* listen to me. 14 Simeon has related how God first looked favourably on the Gentiles, to take from among them a people for his name. 15 This agrees with the words of the prophets, as it is written,

16 "After this I will return,
    and I will rebuild the dwelling of
        David, which has fallen;
        from its ruins I will rebuild it,
            and I will set it up,
17 so that all other peoples may seek the
        Lord—
    even all the Gentiles over whom my
        name has been called.
    Thus says the Lord, who has been
        making these things 18 known
        from long ago."*d*
19 Therefore I have reached the decision that we should not trouble those Gentiles who are turning to God, 20 but we should write to them to abstain only from things polluted by idols and from fornication and from whatever has been strangled*e* and from blood. 21 For in every city, for generations past, Moses has had those who proclaim him, for he has been read aloud every sabbath in the synagogues.'

The Council's Letter to Gentile Believers

22 Then the apostles and the elders, with the consent of the whole church, decided to choose men from among their

a Or committed in the grace of God to the work
b Gk brothers   *c* Gk Men, brothers   *d* Other ancient authorities read things. *18* Known to God from of old are all his works."   *e* Other ancient authorities lack and from whatever has been strangled

members[a] and to send them to Antioch with Paul and Barnabas. They sent Judas called Barsabbas, and Silas, leaders among the brothers, 23 with the following letter: 'The brothers, both the apostles and the elders, to the believers[b] of Gentile origin in Antioch and Syria and Cilicia, greetings. 24 Since we have heard that certain persons who have gone out from us, though with no instructions from us, have said things to disturb you and have unsettled your minds,[c] 25 we have decided unanimously to choose representatives[d] and send them to you, along with our beloved Barnabas and Paul, 26 who have risked their lives for the sake of our Lord Jesus Christ. 27 We have therefore sent Judas and Silas, who themselves will tell you the same things by word of mouth. 28 For it has seemed good to the Holy Spirit and to us to impose on you no further burden than these essentials: 29 that you abstain from what has been sacrificed to idols and from blood and from what is strangled[e] and from fornication. If you keep yourselves from these, you will do well. Farewell.'

30 So they were sent off and went down to Antioch. When they gathered the congregation together, they delivered the letter. 31 When its members[f] read it, they rejoiced at the exhortation. 32 Judas and Silas, who were themselves prophets, said much to encourage and strengthen the believers.[b] 33 After they had been there for some time, they were sent off in peace by the believers[b] to those who had sent them.[g] 35 But Paul and Barnabas remained in Antioch, and there, with many others, they taught and proclaimed the word of the Lord.

Paul and Barnabas Separate

36 After some days Paul said to Barnabas, 'Come, let us return and visit the believers[b] in every city where we proclaimed the word of the Lord and see how they are doing.' 37 Barnabas wanted to take with them John called Mark. 38 But Paul decided not to take with them one who had deserted them in Pamphylia and had not accompanied them in the work. 39 The disagree-

ment became so sharp that they parted company; Barnabas took Mark with him and sailed away to Cyprus. 40 But Paul chose Silas and set out, the believers[b] commending him to the grace of the Lord. 41 He went through Syria and Cilicia, strengthening the churches.

Timothy Joins Paul and Silas

16 Paul[h] went on also to Derbe and to Lystra, where there was a disciple named Timothy, the son of a Jewish woman who was a believer; but his father was a Greek. 2 He was well spoken of by the believers[b] in Lystra and Iconium. 3 Paul wanted Timothy to accompany him; and he took him and had him circumcised because of the Jews who were in those places, for they all knew that his father was a Greek. 4 As they went from town to town, they delivered to them for observance the decisions that had been reached by the apostles and elders who were in Jerusalem. 5 So the churches were strengthened in the faith and increased in numbers daily.

Paul's Vision of the Man of Macedonia

6 They went through the region of Phrygia and Galatia, having been forbidden by the Holy Spirit to speak the word in Asia. 7 When they had come opposite Mysia, they attempted to go into Bithynia, but the Spirit of Jesus did not allow them; 8 so, passing by Mysia, they went down to Troas. 9 During the night Paul had a vision: there stood a man of Macedonia pleading with him and saying, 'Come over to Macedonia and help us.' 10 When he had seen the vision, we immediately tried to cross over to Macedonia, being convinced that God had called us to proclaim the good news to them.

The Conversion of Lydia

11 We set sail from Troas and took a

---

a Gk *from among them*   *b* Gk *brothers*   *c* Other ancient authorities add *saying, "You must be circumcised and keep the law"*,   *d* Gk *men*   *e* Other ancient authorities lack *and from what is strangled*   *f* Gk *When they*   *g* Other ancient authorities add verse 34, *But it seemed good to Silas to remain there*   *h* Gk *He* straight course to Samothrace, the following day to Neapolis, 12 and from there to Philippi, which is a leading city of the district[a] of Macedonia and a Roman colony. We remained in this city for some days. 13 On the sabbath day we went outside the gate by the river, where we supposed there was a place of prayer; and we sat down and spoke to the women who had gathered there. 14 A certain woman named Lydia, a worshipper of God, was listening to us; she was from the city of Thyatira and a dealer in purple cloth. The Lord opened her heart to listen eagerly to what was said by Paul. 15 When she and her household were baptized, she urged us, saying, 'If you have judged me to be faithful to the Lord, come and stay at my home.' And she prevailed upon us.

Paul and Silas in Prison

16 One day, as we were going to the place of prayer, we met a slave-girl who had a spirit of divination and brought her owners a great deal of money by fortune-telling. 17 While she followed Paul and us, she would cry out, 'These men are slaves of the Most High God, who proclaim to you[b] a way of salvation.' 18 She kept doing this for many days. But Paul, very much annoyed, turned and said to the spirit, 'I order you in the name of Jesus Christ to come out of her.' And it came out that very hour.

19 But when her owners saw that their hope of making money was gone, they seized Paul and Silas and dragged them into the market-place before the authorities. 20 When they had brought them before the magistrates, they said, 'These men are disturbing our city; they are Jews 21 and are advocating customs that are not lawful for us as Romans to adopt or observe.' 22 The crowd joined in attacking them, and the magistrates had them stripped of their clothing and ordered them to be beaten with rods. 23 After they had given them a

a Other authorities read *a city of the first district*
b Other ancient authorities read *to us*

Paul's Second Missionary Journey

severe flogging, they threw them into prison and ordered the jailer to keep them securely. 24 Following these instructions, he put them in the innermost cell and fastened their feet in the stocks.

25 About midnight Paul and Silas were praying and singing hymns to God, and the prisoners were listening to them. 26 Suddenly there was an earthquake, so violent that the foundations of the prison were shaken; and immediately all the doors were opened and everyone's chains were unfastened. 27 When the jailer woke up and saw the prison doors wide open, he drew his sword and was about to kill himself, since he supposed that the prisoners had escaped. 28 But Paul shouted in a loud voice, 'Do not harm yourself, for we are all here.' 29 The jailer*a* called for lights, and rushing in, he fell down trembling before Paul and Silas. 30 Then he brought them outside and said, 'Sirs, what must I do to be saved?' 31 They answered, 'Believe on the Lord Jesus, and you will be saved, you and your household.' 32 They spoke the word of the Lord*b* to him and to all who were in his house. 33 At the same hour of the night he took them and washed their wounds; then he and his entire family were baptized without delay. 34 He brought them up into the house and set food before them; and he and his entire household rejoiced that he had become a believer in God.

35 When morning came, the magistrates sent the police, saying, 'Let those men go.' 36 And the jailer reported the message to Paul, saying, 'The magistrates sent word to let you go; therefore come out now and go in peace.' 37 But Paul replied, 'They have beaten us in public, uncondemned, men who are Roman citizens, and have thrown us into prison; and now are they going to discharge us in secret? Certainly not! Let them come and take us out themselves.' 38 The police reported these words to the magistrates, and they were afraid when they heard that they were Roman citizens; 39 so they came and apologized to them. And they took them out and asked them to leave the city. 40 After

leaving the prison they went to Lydia's home; and when they had seen and encouraged the brothers and sisters*c* there, they departed.

The Uproar in Thessalonica

17 After Paul and Silas*d* had passed through Amphipolis and Apollonia, they came to Thessalonica, where there was a synagogue of the Jews. 2 And Paul went in, as was his custom, and on three sabbath days argued with them from the scriptures, 3 explaining and proving that it was necessary for the Messiah*e* to suffer and to rise from the dead, and saying, 'This is the Messiah,*e* Jesus whom I am proclaiming to you.' 4 Some of them were persuaded and joined Paul and Silas, as did a great many of the devout Greeks and not a few of the leading women. 5 But the Jews became jealous, and with the help of some ruffians in the market-places they formed a mob and set the city in an uproar. While they were searching for Paul and Silas to bring them out to the assembly, they attacked Jason's house. 6 When they could not find them, they dragged Jason and some believers*c* before the city authorities,*f* shouting, 'These people who have been turning the world upside down have come here also, 7 and Jason has entertained them as guests. They are all acting contrary to the decrees of the emperor, saying that there is another king named Jesus.' 8 The people and the city officials were disturbed when they heard this, 9 and after they had taken bail from Jason and the others, they let them go.

Paul and Silas in Beroea

10 That very night the believers*c* sent Paul and Silas off to Beroea; and when they arrived, they went to the Jewish synagogue. 11 These Jews were more receptive than those in Thessalonica, for they welcomed the message very eagerly and examined the scriptures every day to see whether these things were so. 12 Many of

a Gk He　　*b* Other ancient authorities read *word of God*
c Gk *brothers*　　*d* Gk *they*　　*e* Or *the Christ*
f Gk *politarchs*

them therefore believed, including not a few Greek women and men of high standing. 13 But when the Jews of Thessalonica learned that the word of God had been proclaimed by Paul in Beroea as well, they came there too, to stir up and incite the crowds. 14 Then the believers[a] immediately sent Paul away to the coast, but Silas and Timothy remained behind. 15 Those who conducted Paul brought him as far as Athens; and after receiving instructions to have Silas and Timothy join him as soon as possible, they left him.

Paul in Athens

16 While Paul was waiting for them in Athens, he was deeply distressed to see that the city was full of idols. 17 So he argued in the synagogue with the Jews and the devout persons, and also in the market-place[b] every day with those who happened to be there. 18 Also some Epicurean and Stoic philosophers debated with him. Some said, 'What does this babbler want to say?' Others said, 'He seems to be a proclaimer of foreign divinities.' (This was because he was telling the good news about Jesus and the resurrection.) 19 So they took him and brought him to the Areopagus and asked him, 'May we know what this new teaching is that you are presenting? 20 It sounds rather strange to us, so we would like to know what it means.' 21 Now all the Athenians and the foreigners living there would spend their time in nothing but telling or hearing something new.

22 Then Paul stood in front of the Areopagus and said, 'Athenians, I see how extremely religious you are in every way. 23 For as I went through the city and looked carefully at the objects of your worship, I found among them an altar with the inscription, "To an unknown god." What therefore you worship as unknown, this I proclaim to you. 24 The God who made the world and everything in it, he who is Lord of heaven and earth, does not live in shrines made by human hands, 25 nor is he served by human hands, as though he needed anything, since he himself gives to all mortals life and breath and all things. 26 From one ancestor[c] he made all nations to inhabit the whole earth, and he allotted the times of their existence and the boundaries of the places where they would live, 27 so that they would search for God[d] and perhaps grope for him and find him—though indeed he is not far from each one of us. 28 For "In him we live and move and have our being"; as even some of your own poets have said,

"For we too are his offspring."

29 Since we are God's offspring, we ought not to think that the deity is like gold, or silver, or stone, an image formed by the art and imagination of mortals. 30 While God has overlooked the times of human ignorance, now he commands all people everywhere to repent, 31 because he has fixed a day on which he will have the world judged in righteousness by a man whom he has appointed, and of this he has given assurance to all by raising him from the dead.'

32 When they heard of the resurrection of the dead, some scoffed; but others said, 'We will hear you again about this.' 33 At that point Paul left them. 34 But some of them joined him and became believers, including Dionysius the Areopagite and a woman named Damaris, and others with them.

Paul in Corinth

18 After this Paul[e] left Athens and went to Corinth. 2 There he found a Jew named Aquila, a native of Pontus, who had recently come from Italy with his wife Priscilla, because Claudius had ordered all Jews to leave Rome. Paul[f] went to see them, 3 and, because he was of the same trade, he stayed with them, and they worked together—by trade they were tentmakers. 4 Every sabbath he would argue in the synagogue and would try to convince Jews and Greeks.

5 When Silas and Timothy arrived from Macedonia, Paul was occupied with pro-

a Gk brothers   b Or civic centre; Gk agora   c Gk From one; other ancient authorities read From one blood
d Other ancient authorities read the Lord   e Gk he
f Gk He

claiming the word,[a] testifying to the Jews that the Messiah[b] was Jesus. [6]When they opposed and reviled him, in protest he shook the dust from his clothes[c] and said to them, 'Your blood be on your own heads! I am innocent. From now on I will go to the Gentiles.' [7]Then he left the synagogue[d] and went to the house of a man named Titius[e] Justus, a worshipper of God; his house was next door to the synagogue. [8]Crispus, the official of the synagogue, became a believer in the Lord, together with all his household; and many of the Corinthians who heard Paul became believers and were baptized. [9]One night the Lord said to Paul in a vision, 'Do not be afraid, but speak and do not be silent; [10]for I am with you, and no one will lay a hand on you to harm you, for there are many in this city who are my people.' [11]He stayed there for a year and six months, teaching the word of God among them.

[12] But when Gallio was proconsul of Achaia, the Jews made a united attack on Paul and brought him before the tribunal. [13]They said, 'This man is persuading people to worship God in ways that are contrary to the law.' [14]Just as Paul was about to speak, Gallio said to the Jews, 'If it were a matter of crime or serious villainy, I would be justified in accepting the complaint of you Jews; [15]but since it is a matter of questions about words and names and your own law, see to it yourselves; I do not wish to be a judge of these matters.' [16]And he dismissed them from the tribunal. [17]Then all of them[f] seized Sosthenes, the official of the synagogue, and beat him in front of the tribunal. But Gallio paid no attention to any of these things.

Paul's Return to Antioch

[18] After staying there for a considerable time, Paul said farewell to the believers[g] and sailed for Syria, accompanied by Priscilla and Aquila. At Cenchreae he had his hair cut, for he was under a vow. [19]When they reached Ephesus, he left them there, but first he himself went into the synagogue and had a discussion with the Jews. [20]When they asked him to stay longer, he declined; [21]but on taking leave of them, he said, 'I[h] will return to you, if God wills.' Then he set sail from Ephesus.

[22] When he had landed at Caesarea, he went up to Jerusalem[i] and greeted the church, and then went down to Antioch. [23]After spending some time there he departed and went from place to place through the region of Galatia[j] and Phrygia, strengthening all the disciples.

Ministry of Apollos

[24] Now there came to Ephesus a Jew named Apollos, a native of Alexandria. He was an eloquent man, well-versed in the scriptures. [25]He had been instructed in the Way of the Lord; and he spoke with burning enthusiasm and taught accurately the things concerning Jesus, though he knew only the baptism of John. [26]He began to speak boldly in the synagogue; but when Priscilla and Aquila heard him, they took him aside and explained the Way of God to him more accurately. [27]And when he wished to cross over to Achaia, the believers[g] encouraged him and wrote to the disciples to welcome him. On his arrival he greatly helped those who through grace had become believers, [28]for he powerfully refuted the Jews in public, showing by the scriptures that the Messiah[b] is Jesus.

Paul in Ephesus

19 While Apollos was in Corinth, Paul passed through the inland regions and came to Ephesus, where he found some disciples. [2]He said to them, 'Did you receive the Holy Spirit when you became believers?' They replied, 'No, we have not even heard that there is a Holy Spirit.' [3]Then he said, 'Into what then were you baptized?' They answered, 'Into John's baptism.' [4]Paul said, 'John baptized with

---

a Gk *with the word*   *b* Or *the Christ*   *c* Gk *reviled him, he shook out his clothes*   *d* Gk *left there*   *e* Other ancient authorities read *Titus*   *f* Other ancient authorities read *all the Greeks*   *g* Gk *brothers*   *h* Other ancient authorities read *I must at all costs keep the approaching festival in Jerusalem, but I*   *i* Gk *went up*   *j* Gk *the Galatian region* the baptism of repentance, telling the people to believe in the one who was to come after him, that is, in Jesus.' 5 On hearing this, they were baptized in the name of the Lord Jesus. 6 When Paul had laid his hands on them, the Holy Spirit came upon them, and they spoke in tongues and prophesied— 7 altogether there were about twelve of them.

8 He entered the synagogue and for three months spoke out boldly, and argued persuasively about the kingdom of God. 9 When some stubbornly refused to believe and spoke evil of the Way before the congregation, he left them, taking the disciples with him, and argued daily in the lecture hall of Tyrannus.ᵃ 10 This continued for two years, so that all the residents of Asia, both Jews and Greeks, heard the word of the Lord.

The Sons of Sceva

11 God did extraordinary miracles through Paul, 12 so that when the handkerchiefs or aprons that had touched his skin

were brought to the sick, their diseases left them, and the evil spirits came out of them. 13 Then some itinerant Jewish exorcists tried to use the name of the Lord Jesus over those who had evil spirits, saying, 'I adjure you by the Jesus whom Paul proclaims.' 14 Seven sons of a Jewish high priest named Sceva were doing this. 15 But the evil spirit said to them in reply, 'Jesus I know, and Paul I know; but who are you?' 16 Then the man with the evil spirit leapt on them, mastered them all, and so overpowered them that they fled out of the house naked and wounded. 17 When this became known to all residents of Ephesus, both Jews and Greeks, everyone was awestruck; and the name of the Lord Jesus was praised. 18 Also many of those who became believers confessed and disclosed their practices. 19 A number of those who practised magic collected their books and burned them publicly; when the value of

a Other ancient authorities read *of a certain Tyrannus, from eleven o'clock in the morning to four in the afternoon*

Paul's Third Missionary Journey

these books[a] was calculated, it was found to come to fifty thousand silver coins. 20 So the word of the Lord grew mightily and prevailed.

The Riot in Ephesus

21 Now after these things had been accomplished, Paul resolved in the Spirit to go through Macedonia and Achaia, and then to go on to Jerusalem. He said, 'After I have gone there, I must also see Rome.' 22 So he sent two of his helpers, Timothy and Erastus, to Macedonia, while he himself stayed for some time longer in Asia.

23 About that time no little disturbance broke out concerning the Way. 24 A man named Demetrius, a silversmith who made silver shrines of Artemis, brought no little business to the artisans. 25 These he gathered together, with the workers of the same trade, and said, 'Men, you know that we get our wealth from this business. 26 You also see and hear that not only in Ephesus but in almost the whole of Asia this Paul has persuaded and drawn away a considerable number of people by saying that gods made with hands are not gods. 27 And there is danger not only that this trade of ours may come into disrepute but also that the temple of the great goddess Artemis will be scorned, and she will be deprived of her majesty that brought all Asia and the world to worship her.'

28 When they heard this, they were enraged and shouted, 'Great is Artemis of the Ephesians!' 29 The city was filled with the confusion; and people[b] rushed together to the theatre, dragging with them Gaius and Aristarchus, Macedonians who were Paul's travelling-companions. 30 Paul wished to go into the crowd, but the disciples would not let him; 31 even some officials of the province of Asia,[c] who were friendly to him, sent him a message urging him not to venture into the theatre. 32 Meanwhile, some were shouting one thing, some another; for the assembly was in confusion, and most of them did not know why they had come together. 33 Some of the crowd gave instructions to Alexander, whom the Jews had pushed forward. And Alexander motioned for silence and tried to make a defence before the people. 34 But when they recognized that he was a Jew, for about two hours all of them shouted in unison, 'Great is Artemis of the Ephesians!' 35 But when the town clerk had quietened the crowd, he said, 'Citizens of Ephesus, who is there that does not know that the city of the Ephesians is the temple-keeper of the great Artemis and of the statue that fell from heaven?[d] 36 Since these things cannot be denied, you ought to be quiet and do nothing rash. 37 You have brought these men here who are neither temple-robbers nor blasphemers of our[e] goddess. 38 If therefore Demetrius and the artisans with him have a complaint against anyone, the courts are open, and there are proconsuls; let them bring charges there against one another. 39 If there is anything further[f] you want to know, it must be settled in the regular assembly. 40 For we are in danger of being charged with rioting today, since there is no cause that we can give to justify this commotion.' 41 When he had said this, he dismissed the assembly.

Paul Goes to Macedonia and Greece

20 After the uproar had ceased, Paul sent for the disciples; and after encouraging them and saying farewell, he left for Macedonia. 2 When he had gone through those regions and had given the believers[g] much encouragement, he came to Greece, 3 where he stayed for three months. He was about to set sail for Syria when a plot was made against him by the Jews, and so he decided to return through Macedonia. 4 He was accompanied by Sopater son of Pyrrhus from Beroea, by Aristarchus and Secundus from Thessalonica, by Gaius from Derbe, and by Timothy, as well as by Tychicus and Trophimus from Asia. 5 They went ahead and were waiting for us in Troas; 6 but we sailed from Philippi after the days of Unleavened Bread, and in five days we joined

a Gk them   b Gk they   c Gk some of the Asiarchs
d Meaning of Gk uncertain   e Other ancient
authorities read your   f Other ancient authorities read
about other matters   g Gk given them

them in Troas, where we stayed for seven days.

Paul's Farewell Visit to Troas

7 On the first day of the week, when we met to break bread, Paul was holding a discussion with them; since he intended to leave the next day, he continued speaking until midnight. 8 There were many lamps in the room upstairs where we were meeting. 9 A young man named Eutychus, who was sitting in the window, began to sink off into a deep sleep while Paul talked still longer. Overcome by sleep, he fell to the ground three floors below and was picked up dead. 10 But Paul went down, and bending over him took him in his arms, and said, 'Do not be alarmed, for his life is in him.' 11 Then Paul went upstairs, and after he had broken bread and eaten, he continued to converse with them until dawn; then he left. 12 Meanwhile they had taken the boy away alive and were not a little comforted.

The Voyage from Troas to Miletus

13 We went ahead to the ship and set sail for Assos, intending to take Paul on board there; for he had made this arrangement, intending to go by land himself. 14 When he met us in Assos, we took him on board and went to Mitylene. 15 We sailed from there, and on the following day we arrived opposite Chios. The next day we touched at Samos, and *a* the day after that we came to Miletus. 16 For Paul had decided to sail past Ephesus, so that he might not have to spend time in Asia; he was eager to be in Jerusalem, if possible, on the day of Pentecost.

Paul Speaks to the Ephesian Elders

17 From Miletus he sent a message to Ephesus, asking the elders of the church to meet him. 18 When they came to him, he said to them:

'You yourselves know how I lived among you the entire time from the first day that I set foot in Asia, 19 serving the Lord with all humility and with tears, enduring the trials that came to me through the plots of the Jews. 20 I did not shrink from doing anything helpful, proclaiming the message to you and teaching you publicly and from house to house, 21 as I testified to both Jews and Greeks about repentance towards God and faith towards our Lord Jesus. 22 And now, as a captive to the Spirit, *b* I am on my way to Jerusalem, not knowing what will happen to me there, 23 except that the Holy Spirit testifies to me in every city that imprisonment and persecutions are waiting for me. 24 But I do not count my life of any value to myself, if only I may finish my course and the ministry that I received from the Lord Jesus, to testify to the good news of God's grace.

25 'And now I know that none of you, among whom I have gone about proclaiming the kingdom, will ever see my face again. 26 Therefore I declare to you this day that I am not responsible for the blood of any of you, 27 for I did not shrink from declaring to you the whole purpose of God. 28 Keep watch over yourselves and over all the flock, of which the Holy Spirit has made you overseers, to shepherd the church of God *c* that he obtained with the blood of his own Son. *d* 29 I know that after I have gone, savage wolves will come in among you, not sparing the flock. 30 Some even from your own group will come distorting the truth in order to entice the disciples to follow them. 31 Therefore be alert, remembering that for three years I did not cease night or day to warn everyone with tears. 32 And now I commend you to God and to the message of his grace, a message that is able to build you up and to give you the inheritance among all who are sanctified. 33 I coveted no one's silver or gold or clothing. 34 You know for yourselves that I worked with my own hands to support myself and my companions. 35 In all this I have given you an example that by such work we must support the weak, remembering the words of the Lord Jesus, for he himself said, "It is more blessed to give than to receive." '

a Other ancient authorities add *after remaining at Trogyllium*   *b* Or *And now, bound in the spirit*
c Other ancient authorities read *of the Lord*
d Or *with his own blood*; Gk *with the blood of his Own*

36 When he had finished speaking, he knelt down with them all and prayed. 37 There was much weeping among them all; they embraced Paul and kissed him, 38 grieving especially because of what he had said, that they would not see him again. Then they brought him to the ship.

Paul's Journey to Jerusalem

21 When we had parted from them and set sail, we came by a straight course to Cos, and the next day to Rhodes, and from there to Patara.*a* 2 When we found a ship bound for Phoenicia, we went on board and set sail. 3 We came in sight of Cyprus; and leaving it on our left, we sailed to Syria and landed at Tyre, because the ship was to unload its cargo there. 4 We looked up the disciples and stayed there for seven days. Through the Spirit they told Paul not to go on to Jerusalem. 5 When our days there were ended, we left and proceeded on our journey; and all of them, with wives and children, escorted us outside the city. There we knelt down on the beach and prayed 6 and said farewell to one another. Then we went on board the ship, and they returned home.

7 When we had finished*b* the voyage from Tyre, we arrived at Ptolemais; and we greeted the believers*c* and stayed with them for one day. 8 The next day we left and came to Caesarea; and we went into the house of Philip the evangelist, one of the seven, and stayed with him. 9 He had four unmarried daughters*d* who had the gift of prophecy. 10 While we were staying there for several days, a prophet named Agabus came down from Judea. 11 He came to us and took Paul's belt, bound his own feet and hands with it, and said, 'Thus says the Holy Spirit, "This is the way the Jews in Jerusalem will bind the man who owns this belt and will hand him over to the Gentiles." ' 12 When we heard this, we and the people there urged him not to go up to Jerusalem. 13 Then Paul answered, 'What are you doing, weeping and breaking my heart? For I am ready not only to be bound but even to die in Jerusalem for the name of the Lord Jesus.'

14 Since he would not be persuaded, we remained silent except to say, 'The Lord's will be done.'

15 After these days we got ready and started to go up to Jerusalem. 16 Some of the disciples from Caesarea also came along and brought us to the house of Mnason of Cyprus, an early disciple, with whom we were to stay.

Paul Visits James at Jerusalem

17 When we arrived in Jerusalem, the brothers welcomed us warmly. 18 The next day Paul went with us to visit James; and all the elders were present. 19 After greeting them, he related one by one the things that God had done among the Gentiles through his ministry. 20 When they heard it, they praised God. Then they said to him, 'You see, brother, how many thousands of believers there are among the Jews, and they are all zealous for the law. 21 They have been told about you that you teach all the Jews living among the Gentiles to forsake Moses, and that you tell them not to circumcise their children or observe the customs. 22 What then is to be done? They will certainly hear that you have come. 23 So do what we tell you. We have four men who are under a vow. 24 Join these men, go through the rite of purification with them, and pay for the shaving of their heads. Thus all will know that there is nothing in what they have been told about you, but that you yourself observe and guard the law. 25 But as for the Gentiles who have become believers, we have sent a letter with our judgement that they should abstain from what has been sacrificed to idols and from blood and from what is strangled*e* and from fornication.' 26 Then Paul took the men, and the next day, having purified himself, he entered the temple with them, making public the completion of the days of purification when the sacrifice would be made for each of them.

a Other ancient authorities add *and Myra*
b Or *continued*   *c* Gk *brothers*   *d* Gk *four daughters, virgins*,   *e* Other ancient authorities lack *and from what is strangled*

Paul Arrested in the Temple

27 When the seven days were almost completed, the Jews from Asia, who had seen him in the temple, stirred up the whole crowd. They seized him, 28 shouting, 'Fellow-Israelites, help! This is the man who is teaching everyone everywhere against our people, our law, and this place; more than that, he has actually brought Greeks into the temple and has defiled this holy place.' 29 For they had previously seen Trophimus the Ephesian with him in the city, and they supposed that Paul had brought him into the temple. 30 Then all the city was aroused, and the people rushed together. They seized Paul and dragged him out of the temple, and immediately the doors were shut. 31 While they were trying to kill him, word came to the tribune of the cohort that all Jerusalem was in an uproar. 32 Immediately he took soldiers and centurions and ran down to them. When they saw the tribune and the soldiers, they stopped beating Paul. 33 Then the tribune came, arrested him, and ordered him to be bound with two chains; he inquired who he was and what he had done. 34 Some in the crowd shouted one thing, some another; and as he could not learn the facts because of the uproar, he ordered him to be brought into the barracks. 35 When Paul*a* came to the steps, the violence of the mob was so great that he had to be carried by the soldiers. 36 The crowd that followed kept shouting, 'Away with him!'

Paul Defends Himself

37 Just as Paul was about to be brought into the barracks, he said to the tribune, 'May I say something to you?' The tribune*b* replied, 'Do you know Greek? 38 Then you are not the Egyptian who recently stirred up a revolt and led the four thousand assassins out into the wilderness?' 39 Paul replied, 'I am a Jew, from Tarsus in Cilicia, a citizen of an important city; I beg you, let me speak to the people.' 40 When he had given him permission, Paul stood on the steps and motioned to the people for silence; and when there was a great hush, he addressed them in the Hebrew*c* language, saying:

22 'Brothers and fathers, listen to the defence that I now make before you.'

2 When they heard him addressing them in Hebrew,*c* they became even more quiet. Then he said:

3 'I am a Jew, born in Tarsus in Cilicia, but brought up in this city at the feet of Gamaliel, educated strictly according to our ancestral law, being zealous for God, just as all of you are today. 4 I persecuted this Way up to the point of death by binding both men and women and putting them in prison, 5 as the high priest and the whole council of elders can testify about me. From them I also received letters to the brothers in Damascus, and I went there in order to bind those who were there and to bring them back to Jerusalem for punishment.

Paul Tells of His Conversion

6 'While I was on my way and approaching Damascus, about noon a great light from heaven suddenly shone about me. 7 I fell to the ground and heard a voice saying to me, "Saul, Saul, why are you persecuting me?" 8 I answered, "Who are you, Lord?" Then he said to me, "I am Jesus of Nazareth*d* whom you are persecuting." 9 Now those who were with me saw the light but did not hear the voice of the one who was speaking to me. 10 I asked, "What am I to do, Lord?" The Lord said to me, "Get up and go to Damascus; there you will be told everything that has been assigned to you to do." 11 Since I could not see because of the brightness of that light, those who were with me took my hand and led me to Damascus.

12 'A certain Ananias, who was a devout man according to the law and well spoken of by all the Jews living there, 13 came to me; and standing beside me, he said, "Brother Saul, regain your sight!" In that very hour I regained my sight and saw him. 14 Then he said, "The God of our an-

a Gk he   *b* Gk He   *c* That is, *Aramaic*   *d* Gk *the Nazorean* cestors has chosen you to know his will, to see the Righteous One and to hear his own voice; [15] for you will be his witness to all the world of what you have seen and heard. [16] And now why do you delay? Get up, be baptized, and have your sins washed away, calling on his name.'

Paul Sent to the Gentiles

17 'After I had returned to Jerusalem and while I was praying in the temple, I fell into a trance [18] and saw Jesus[a] saying to me, "Hurry and get out of Jerusalem quickly, because they will not accept your testimony about me." [19] And I said, "Lord, they themselves know that in every synagogue I imprisoned and beat those who believed in you. [20] And while the blood of your witness Stephen was shed, I myself was standing by, approving and keeping the coats of those who killed him." [21] Then he said to me, "Go, for I will send you far away to the Gentiles." '

Paul and the Roman Tribune

22 Up to this point they listened to him, but then they shouted, 'Away with such a fellow from the earth! For he should not be allowed to live.' [23] And while they were shouting, throwing off their cloaks, and tossing dust into the air, [24] the tribune directed that he was to be brought into the barracks, and ordered him to be examined by flogging, to find out the reason for this outcry against him. [25] But when they had tied him up with thongs,[b] Paul said to the centurion who was standing by, 'Is it legal for you to flog a Roman citizen who is uncondemned?' [26] When the centurion heard that, he went to the tribune and said to him, 'What are you about to do? This man is a Roman citizen.' [27] The tribune came and asked Paul,[a] 'Tell me, are you a Roman citizen?' And he said, 'Yes.' [28] The tribune answered, 'It cost me a large sum of money to get my citizenship.' Paul said, 'But I was born a citizen.' [29] Immediately those who were about to examine him drew back from him; and the tribune also was afraid, for he realized

that Paul was a Roman citizen and that he had bound him.

Paul before the Council

30 Since he wanted to find out what Paul[c] was being accused of by the Jews, the next day he released him and ordered the chief priests and the entire council to meet. He brought Paul down and had him stand before them.

23 While Paul was looking intently at the council he said, 'Brothers,[d] up to this day I have lived my life with a clear conscience before God.' [2] Then the high priest Ananias ordered those standing near him to strike him on the mouth. [3] At this Paul said to him, 'God will strike you, you whitewashed wall! Are you sitting there to judge me according to the law, and yet in violation of the law you order me to be struck?' [4] Those standing nearby said, 'Do you dare to insult God's high priest?' [5] And Paul said, 'I did not realize, brothers, that he was high priest; for it is written, "You shall not speak evil of a leader of your people." '

6 When Paul noticed that some were Sadducees and others were Pharisees, he called out in the council, 'Brothers, I am a Pharisee, a son of Pharisees. I am on trial concerning the hope of the resurrection[e] of the dead.' [7] When he said this, a dissension began between the Pharisees and the Sadducees, and the assembly was divided. [8] (The Sadducees say that there is no resurrection, or angel, or spirit; but the Pharisees acknowledge all three.) [9] Then a great clamour arose, and certain scribes of the Pharisees' group stood up and contended, 'We find nothing wrong with this man. What if a spirit or an angel has spoken to him?' [10] When the dissension became violent, the tribune, fearing that they would tear Paul to pieces, ordered the soldiers to go down, take him by force, and bring him into the barracks.

11 That night the Lord stood near him and said, 'Keep up your courage! For just

a Gk him   *b* Or *up for the lashes*   *c* Gk *he*
d Gk *Men, brothers*   *e* Gk *concerning hope and resurrection*

as you have testified for me in Jerusalem, so you must bear witness also in Rome.'

The Plot to Kill Paul

12 In the morning the Jews joined in a conspiracy and bound themselves by an oath neither to eat nor drink until they had killed Paul. 13 There were more than forty who joined in this conspiracy. 14 They went to the chief priests and elders and said, 'We have strictly bound ourselves by an oath to taste no food until we have killed Paul. 15 Now then, you and the council must notify the tribune to bring him down to you, on the pretext that you want to make a more thorough examination of his case. And we are ready to do away with him before he arrives.'

16 Now the son of Paul's sister heard about the ambush; so he went and gained entrance to the barracks and told Paul. 17 Paul called one of the centurions and said, 'Take this young man to the tribune, for he has something to report to him.' 18 So he took him, brought him to the tribune, and said, 'The prisoner Paul called me and asked me to bring this young man to you; he has something to tell you.' 19 The tribune took him by the hand, drew him aside privately, and asked, 'What is it that you have to report to me?' 20 He answered, 'The Jews have agreed to ask you to bring Paul down to the council tomorrow, as though they were going to inquire more thoroughly into his case. 21 But do not be persuaded by them, for more than forty of their men are lying in ambush for him. They have bound themselves by an oath neither to eat nor drink until they kill him. They are ready now and are waiting for your consent.' 22 So the tribune dismissed the young man, ordering him, 'Tell no one that you have informed me of this.'

Paul Sent to Felix the Governor

23 Then he summoned two of the centurions and said, 'Get ready to leave by nine o'clock tonight for Caesarea with two hundred soldiers, seventy horsemen, and two hundred spearmen. 24 Also provide mounts for Paul to ride, and take him safe-ly to Felix the governor.' 25 He wrote a letter to this effect:

26 'Claudius Lysias to his Excellency the governor Felix, greetings. 27 This man was seized by the Jews and was about to be killed by them, but when I had learned that he was a Roman citizen, I came with the guard and rescued him. 28 Since I wanted to know the charge for which they accused him, I had him brought to their council. 29 I found that he was accused concerning questions of their law, but was charged with nothing deserving death or imprisonment. 30 When I was informed that there would be a plot against the man, I sent him to you at once, ordering his accusers also to state before you what they have against him. *a* '

31 So the soldiers, according to their instructions, took Paul and brought him during the night to Antipatris. 32 The next day they let the horsemen go on with him, while they returned to the barracks. 33 When they came to Caesarea and delivered the letter to the governor, they presented Paul also before him. 34 On reading the letter, he asked what province he belonged to, and when he learned that he was from Cilicia, 35 he said, 'I will give you a hearing when your accusers arrive.' Then he ordered that he be kept under guard in Herod's headquarters. *b*

Paul before Felix at Caesarea

24 Five days later the high priest Ananias came down with some elders and an attorney, a certain Tertullus, and they reported their case against Paul to the governor. 2 When Paul *c* had been summoned, Tertullus began to accuse him, saying:

'Your Excellency, *d* because of you we have long enjoyed peace, and reforms have been made for this people because of your foresight. 3 We welcome this in every way and everywhere with utmost gratitude. 4 But, to detain you no further, I beg you to hear us briefly with your customary graciousness. 5 We have, in fact, found this

a Other ancient authorities add *Farewell*
b Gk *praetorium*   *c* Gk *he*   *d* Gk lacks *Your Excellency*

man a pestilent fellow, an agitator among all the Jews throughout the world, and a ringleader of the sect of the Nazarenes.[a] [6]He even tried to profane the temple, and so we seized him.[b] [8]By examining him yourself you will be able to learn from him concerning everything of which we accuse him.'

9 The Jews also joined in the charge by asserting that all this was true.

Paul's Defence before Felix

10 When the governor motioned to him to speak, Paul replied:

'I cheerfully make my defence, knowing that for many years you have been a judge over this nation. [11]As you can find out, it is not more than twelve days since I went up to worship in Jerusalem. [12]They did not find me disputing with anyone in the temple or stirring up a crowd either in the synagogues or throughout the city. [13]Neither can they prove to you the charge that they now bring against me. [14]But this I admit to you, that according to the Way, which they call a sect, I worship the God of our ancestors, believing everything laid down according to the law or written in the prophets. [15]I have a hope in God—a hope that they themselves also accept—that there will be a resurrection of both[c] the righteous and the unrighteous. [16]Therefore I do my best always to have a clear conscience towards God and all people. [17]Now after some years I came to bring alms to my nation and to offer sacrifices. [18]While I was doing this, they found me in the temple, completing the rite of purification, without any crowd or disturbance. [19]But there were some Jews from Asia—they ought to be here before you to make an accusation, if they have anything against me. [20]Or let these men here tell what crime they had found when I stood before the council, [21]unless it was this one sentence that I called out while standing before them, "It is about the resurrection of the dead that I am on trial before you today." '

22 But Felix, who was rather well informed about the Way, adjourned the hearing with the comment, 'When Lysias the tribune comes down, I will decide your case.' [23]Then he ordered the centurion to keep him in custody, but to let him have some liberty and not to prevent any of his friends from taking care of his needs.

Paul Held in Custody

24 Some days later when Felix came with his wife Drusilla, who was Jewish, he sent for Paul and heard him speak concerning faith in Christ Jesus. [25]And as he discussed justice, self-control, and the coming judgement, Felix became frightened and said, 'Go away for the present; when I have an opportunity, I will send for you.' [26]At the same time he hoped that money would be given to him by Paul, and for that reason he used to send for him very often and converse with him.

27 After two years had passed, Felix was succeeded by Porcius Festus; and since he wanted to grant the Jews a favour, Felix left Paul in prison.

Paul Appeals to the Emperor

25 Three days after Festus had arrived in the province, he went up from Caesarea to Jerusalem [2]where the chief priests and the leaders of the Jews gave him a report against Paul. They appealed to him [3]and requested, as a favour to them against Paul,[d] to have him transferred to Jerusalem. They were, in fact, planning an ambush to kill him along the way. [4]Festus replied that Paul was being kept at Caesarea, and that he himself intended to go there shortly. [5]'So', he said, 'let those of you who have the authority come down with me, and if there is anything wrong about the man, let them accuse him.'

6 After he had stayed among them for not more than eight or ten days, he went down to Caesarea; the next day he took his seat on the tribunal and ordered Paul to be

---

a Gk *Nazoreans*   *b* Other ancient authorities add *and we would have judged him according to our law.* [7]*But the chief captain Lysias came and with great violence took him out of our hands,* [8]*commanding his accusers to come before you.*   *c* Other ancient authorities read *of the dead, both of*   *d* Gk *him* brought. [7]When he arrived, the Jews who had gone down from Jerusalem surrounded him, bringing many serious charges against him, which they could not prove. [8]Paul said in his defence, 'I have in no way committed an offence against the law of the Jews, or against the temple, or against the emperor.' [9]But Festus, wishing to do the Jews a favour, asked Paul, 'Do you wish to go up to Jerusalem and be tried there before me on these charges?' [10]Paul said, 'I am appealing to the emperor's tribunal; this is where I should be tried. I have done no wrong to the Jews, as you very well know. [11]Now if I am in the wrong and have committed something for which I deserve to die, I am not trying to escape death; but if there is nothing to their charges against me, no one can turn me over to them. I appeal to the emperor.' [12]Then Festus, after he had conferred with his council, replied, 'You have appealed to the emperor; to the emperor you will go.'

Festus Consults King Agrippa

13 After several days had passed, King Agrippa and Bernice arrived at Caesarea to welcome Festus. [14]Since they were staying there for several days, Festus laid Paul's case before the king, saying, 'There is a man here who was left in prison by Felix. [15]When I was in Jerusalem, the chief priests and the elders of the Jews informed me about him and asked for a sentence against him. [16]I told them that it was not the custom of the Romans to hand over anyone before the accused had met the accusers face to face and had been given an opportunity to make a defence against the charge. [17]So when they met here, I lost no time, but on the next day took my seat on the tribunal and ordered the man to be brought. [18]When the accusers stood up, they did not charge him with any of the crimes[a] that I was expecting. [19]Instead they had certain points of disagreement with him about their own religion and about a certain Jesus, who had died, but whom Paul asserted to be alive. [20]Since I was at a loss how to investigate these questions, I asked whether he wished to go to

Jerusalem and be tried there on these charges.[b] [21]But when Paul had appealed to be kept in custody for the decision of his Imperial Majesty, I ordered him to be held until I could send him to the emperor.' [22]Agrippa said to Festus, 'I would like to hear the man myself.' 'Tomorrow', he said, 'you will hear him.'

Paul Brought before Agrippa

23 So on the next day Agrippa and Bernice came with great pomp, and they entered the audience hall with the military tribunes and the prominent men of the city. Then Festus gave the order and Paul was brought in. [24]And Festus said, 'King Agrippa and all here present with us, you see this man about whom the whole Jewish community petitioned me, both in Jerusalem and here, shouting that he ought not to live any longer. [25]But I found that he had done nothing deserving death; and when he appealed to his Imperial Majesty, I decided to send him. [26]But I have nothing definite to write to our sovereign about him. Therefore I have brought him before all of you, and especially before you, King Agrippa, so that, after we have examined him, I may have something to write— [27]for it seems to me unreasonable to send a prisoner without indicating the charges against him.'

Paul Defends Himself before Agrippa

26 Agrippa said to Paul, 'You have permission to speak for yourself.' Then Paul stretched out his hand and began to defend himself:

2 'I consider myself fortunate that it is before you, King Agrippa, I am to make my defence today against all the accusations of the Jews, [3]because you are especially familiar with all the customs and controversies of the Jews; therefore I beg of you to listen to me patiently.

4 'All the Jews know my way of life from my youth, a life spent from the beginning among my own people and in Jerusalem. [5]They have known for a long

a Other ancient authorities read *with anything*
b Gk *on them*

time, if they are willing to testify, that I have belonged to the strictest sect of our religion and lived as a Pharisee. 6 And now I stand here on trial on account of my hope in the promise made by God to our ancestors, 7 a promise that our twelve tribes hope to attain, as they earnestly worship day and night. It is for this hope, your Excellency,*a* that I am accused by Jews! 8 Why is it thought incredible by any of you that God raises the dead?

9 'Indeed, I myself was convinced that I ought to do many things against the name of Jesus of Nazareth.*b* 10 And that is what I did in Jerusalem; with authority received from the chief priests, I not only locked up many of the saints in prison, but I also cast my vote against them when they were being condemned to death. 11 By punishing them often in all the synagogues I tried to force them to blaspheme; and since I was so furiously enraged at them, I pursued them even to foreign cities.

Paul Tells of His Conversion

12 'With this in mind, I was travelling to Damascus with the authority and commission of the chief priests, 13 when at midday along the road, your Excellency,*a* I saw a light from heaven, brighter than the sun, shining around me and my companions. 14 When we had all fallen to the ground, I heard a voice saying to me in the Hebrew*c* language, "Saul, Saul, why are you persecuting me? It hurts you to kick against the goads." 15 I asked, "Who are you, Lord?" The Lord answered, "I am Jesus whom you are persecuting. 16 But get up and stand on your feet; for I have appeared to you for this purpose, to appoint you to serve and testify to the things in which you have seen me*d* and to those in which I will appear to you. 17 I will rescue you from your people and from the Gentiles—to whom I am sending you 18 to open their eyes so that they may turn from darkness to light and from the power of Satan to God, so that they may receive forgiveness of sins and a place among those who are sanctified by faith in me."

Paul Tells of His Preaching

19 'After that, King Agrippa, I was not disobedient to the heavenly vision, 20 but declared first to those in Damascus, then in Jerusalem and throughout the countryside of Judea, and also to the Gentiles, that they should repent and turn to God and do deeds consistent with repentance. 21 For this reason the Jews seized me in the temple and tried to kill me. 22 To this day I have had help from God, and so I stand here, testifying to both small and great, saying nothing but what the prophets and Moses said would take place: 23 that the Messiah*e* must suffer, and that, by being the first to rise from the dead, he would proclaim light both to our people and to the Gentiles.'

Paul Appeals to Agrippa to Believe

24 While he was making this defence, Festus exclaimed, 'You are out of your mind, Paul! Too much learning is driving you insane!' 25 But Paul said, 'I am not out of my mind, most excellent Festus, but I am speaking the sober truth. 26 Indeed the king knows about these things, and to him I speak freely; for I am certain that none of these things has escaped his notice, for this was not done in a corner. 27 King Agrippa, do you believe the prophets? I know that you believe.' 28 Agrippa said to Paul, 'Are you so quickly persuading me to become a Christian?'*f* 29 Paul replied, 'Whether quickly or not, I pray to God that not only you but also all who are listening to me today might become such as I am—except for these chains.'

30 Then the king got up, and with him the governor and Bernice and those who had been seated with them; 31 and as they were leaving, they said to one another, 'This man is doing nothing to deserve death or imprisonment.' 32 Agrippa said to Festus, 'This man could have been set free if he had not appealed to the emperor.'

---

a Gk O *king*   *b* Gk *the Nazorean*   *c* That is, *Aramaic*
d Other ancient authorities read *the things that you have seen*   *e* Or *the Christ*   *f* Or *Quickly you will persuade me to play the Christian*

Paul Sails for Rome

27 When it was decided that we were to sail for Italy, they transferred Paul and some other prisoners to a centurion of the Augustan Cohort, named Julius. ²Embarking on a ship of Adramyttium that was about to set sail to the ports along the coast of Asia, we put to sea, accompanied by Aristarchus, a Macedonian from Thessalonica. ³The next day we put in at Sidon; and Julius treated Paul kindly, and allowed him to go to his friends to be cared for. ⁴Putting out to sea from there, we sailed under the lee of Cyprus, because the winds were against us. ⁵After we had sailed across the sea that is off Cilicia and Pamphylia, we came to Myra in Lycia. ⁶There the centurion found an Alexandrian ship bound for Italy and put us on board. ⁷We sailed slowly for a number of days and arrived with difficulty off Cnidus, and as the wind was against us, we sailed under the lee of Crete off Salmone. ⁸Sailing past it with difficulty, we came to a

place called Fair Havens, near the city of Lasea.

9 Since much time had been lost and sailing was now dangerous, because even the Fast had already gone by, Paul advised them, ¹⁰saying, 'Sirs, I can see that the voyage will be with danger and much heavy loss, not only of the cargo and the ship, but also of our lives.' ¹¹But the centurion paid more attention to the pilot and to the owner of the ship than to what Paul said. ¹²Since the harbour was not suitable for spending the winter, the majority was in favour of putting to sea from there, on the chance that somehow they could reach Phoenix, where they could spend the winter. It was a harbour of Crete, facing southwest and north-west.

The Storm at Sea

13 When a moderate south wind began to blow, they thought they could achieve their purpose; so they weighed anchor and began to sail past Crete, close to the shore. ¹⁴But soon a violent wind, called the

Paul's Journey to Rome

northeaster, rushed down from Crete. [a] [15] Since the ship was caught and could not be turned with its head to the wind, we gave way to it and were driven. [16] By running under the lee of a small island called Cauda [b] we were scarcely able to get the ship's boat under control. [17] After hoisting it up they took measures [c] to undergird the ship; then, fearing that they would run on the Syrtis, they lowered the sea-anchor and so were driven. [18] We were being pounded by the storm so violently that on the next day they began to throw the cargo overboard, [19] and on the third day with their own hands they threw the ship's tackle overboard. [20] When neither sun nor stars appeared for many days, and no small tempest raged, all hope of our being saved was at last abandoned.

[21] Since they had been without food for a long time, Paul then stood up among them and said, 'Men, you should have listened to me and not have set sail from Crete and thereby avoided this damage and loss. [22] I urge you now to keep up your courage, for there will be no loss of life among you, but only of the ship. [23] For last night there stood by me an angel of the God to whom I belong and whom I worship, [24] and he said, "Do not be afraid, Paul; you must stand before the emperor; and indeed, God has granted safety to all those who are sailing with you." [25] So keep up your courage, men, for I have faith in God that it will be exactly as I have been told. [26] But we will have to run aground on some island.'

[27] When the fourteenth night had come, as we were drifting across the sea of Adria, about midnight the sailors suspected that they were nearing land. [28] So they took soundings and found twenty fathoms; a little farther on they took soundings again and found fifteen fathoms. [29] Fearing that we might run on the rocks, they let down four anchors from the stern and prayed for day to come. [30] But when the sailors tried to escape from the ship and had lowered the boat into the sea, on the pretext of putting out anchors from the bow, [31] Paul said to the centurion and the soldiers, 'Unless these men stay in the ship, you cannot be saved.' [32] Then the soldiers cut away the ropes of the boat and set it adrift.

[33] Just before daybreak, Paul urged all of them to take some food, saying, 'Today is the fourteenth day that you have been in suspense and remaining without food, having eaten nothing. [34] Therefore I urge you to take some food, for it will help you survive; for none of you will lose a hair from your heads.' [35] After he had said this, he took bread; and giving thanks to God in the presence of all, he broke it and began to eat. [36] Then all of them were encouraged and took food for themselves. [37] (We were in all two hundred and seventy-six [d] persons in the ship.) [38] After they had satisfied their hunger, they lightened the ship by throwing the wheat into the sea.

The Shipwreck

[39] In the morning they did not recognize the land, but they noticed a bay with a beach, on which they planned to run the ship ashore, if they could. [40] So they cast off the anchors and left them in the sea. At the same time they loosened the ropes that tied the steering-oars; then hoisting the foresail to the wind, they made for the beach. [41] But striking a reef, [e] they ran the ship aground; the bow stuck and remained immovable, but the stern was being broken up by the force of the waves. [42] The soldiers' plan was to kill the prisoners, so that none might swim away and escape; [43] but the centurion, wishing to save Paul, kept them from carrying out their plan. He ordered those who could swim to jump overboard first and make for the land, [44] and the rest to follow, some on planks and others on pieces of the ship. And so it was that all were brought safely to land.

Paul on the Island of Malta

28 After we had reached safety, we then learned that the island was called Malta. [2] The natives showed us un-

a Gk it   b Other ancient authorities read *Clauda*
c Gk *helps*   d Other ancient authorities read
seventy-six; others, *about seventy-six*   e Gk *place of
two seas*

usual kindness. Since it had begun to rain and was cold, they kindled a fire and welcomed all of us round it. ³Paul had gathered a bundle of brushwood and was putting it on the fire, when a viper, driven out by the heat, fastened itself on his hand. ⁴When the natives saw the creature hanging from his hand, they said to one another, 'This man must be a murderer; though he has escaped from the sea, justice has not allowed him to live.' ⁵He, however, shook off the creature into the fire and suffered no harm. ⁶They were expecting him to swell up or drop dead, but after they had waited a long time and saw that nothing unusual had happened to him, they changed their minds and began to say that he was a god.

7 Now in the neighbourhood of that place were lands belonging to the leading man of the island, named Publius, who received us and entertained us hospitably for three days. ⁸It so happened that the father of Publius lay sick in bed with fever and dysentery. Paul visited him and cured him by praying and putting his hands on him. ⁹After this happened, the rest of the people on the island who had diseases also came and were cured. ¹⁰They bestowed many honours on us, and when we were about to sail, they put on board all the provisions we needed.

Paul Arrives at Rome

11 Three months later we set sail on a ship that had wintered at the island, an Alexandrian ship with the Twin Brothers as its figurehead. ¹²We put in at Syracuse and stayed there for three days; ¹³then we weighed anchor and came to Rhegium. After one day there a south wind sprang up, and on the second day we came to Puteoli. ¹⁴There we found believers[a] and were invited to stay with them for seven days. And so we came to Rome. ¹⁵The believers[a] from there, when they heard of us, came as far as the Forum of Appius and Three Taverns to meet us. On seeing them, Paul thanked God and took courage.

16 When we came into Rome, Paul was allowed to live by himself, with the soldier who was guarding him.

Paul and Jewish Leaders in Rome

17 Three days later he called together the local leaders of the Jews. When they had assembled, he said to them, 'Brothers, though I had done nothing against our people or the customs of our ancestors, yet I was arrested in Jerusalem and handed over to the Romans. ¹⁸When they had examined me, the Romans[b] wanted to release me, because there was no reason for the death penalty in my case. ¹⁹But when the Jews objected, I was compelled to appeal to the emperor—even though I had no charge to bring against my nation. ²⁰For this reason therefore I have asked to see you and speak with you,[c] since it is for the sake of the hope of Israel that I am bound with this chain.' ²¹They replied, 'We have received no letters from Judea about you, and none of the brothers coming here has reported or spoken anything evil about you. ²²But we would like to hear from you what you think, for with regard to this sect we know that everywhere it is spoken against.'

Paul Preaches in Rome

23 After they had fixed a day to meet him, they came to him at his lodgings in great numbers. From morning until evening he explained the matter to them, testifying to the kingdom of God and trying to convince them about Jesus both from the law of Moses and from the prophets. ²⁴Some were convinced by what he had said, while others refused to believe. ²⁵So they disagreed with each other; and as they were leaving, Paul made one further statement: 'The Holy Spirit was right in saying to your ancestors through the prophet Isaiah,

²⁶ "Go to this people and say,
  You will indeed listen, but never
      understand,
    and you will indeed look, but never
      perceive.

a Gk brothers   b Gk they   c Or I have asked you to see me and speak with me

27 For this people's heart has
     grown dull,
   and their ears are hard of hearing,
     and they have shut their eyes;
       so that they might not look with
         their eyes,
   and listen with their ears,
 and understand with their heart and
       turn—
     and I would heal them."
28 Let it be known to you then that this

salvation of God has been sent to the Gentiles; they will listen.'[a]

30 He lived there for two whole years at his own expense[b] and welcomed all who came to him, 31 proclaiming the kingdom of God and teaching about the Lord Jesus Christ with all boldness and without hindrance.

_a_ Other ancient authorities add verse 29, _And when he had said these words, the Jews departed, arguing vigorously among themselves_   _b_ Or _in his own rented dwelling_

THE LETTER OF PAUL TO THE
ROMANS

Salutation

1 Paul, a servant^a of Jesus Christ, called to be an apostle, set apart for the gospel of God, ²which he promised beforehand through his prophets in the holy scriptures, ³the gospel concerning his Son, who was descended from David according to the flesh ⁴and was declared to be Son of God with power according to the spirit^b of holiness by resurrection from the dead, Jesus Christ our Lord, ⁵through whom we have received grace and apostleship to bring about the obedience of faith among all the Gentiles for the sake of his name,

⁶including yourselves who are called to belong to Jesus Christ,

7 To all God's beloved in Rome, who are called to be saints:

Grace to you and peace from God our Father and the Lord Jesus Christ.

Prayer of Thanksgiving

8 First, I thank my God through Jesus Christ for all of you, because your faith is proclaimed throughout the world. ⁹For God, whom I serve with my spirit by

a Gk *slave*   b Or *Spirit*

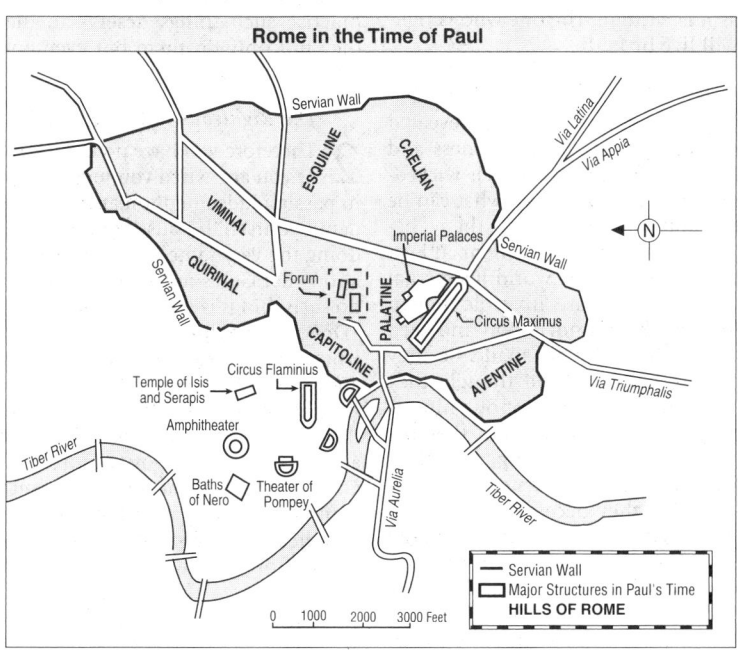

Rome in the Time of Paul

announcing the gospel[a] of his Son, is my witness that without ceasing I remember you always in my prayers, [10] asking that by God's will I may somehow at last succeed in coming to you. [11] For I am longing to see you so that I may share with you some spiritual gift to strengthen you— [12] or rather so that we may be mutually encouraged by each other's faith, both yours and mine. [13] I want you to know, brothers and sisters,[b] that I have often intended to come to you (but thus far have been prevented), in order that I may reap some harvest among you as I have among the rest of the Gentiles. [14] I am a debtor both to Greeks and to barbarians, both to the wise and to the foolish [15]—hence my eagerness to proclaim the gospel to you also who are in Rome.

The Power of the Gospel

[16] For I am not ashamed of the gospel; it is the power of God for salvation to everyone who has faith, to the Jew first and also to the Greek. [17] For in it the righteousness of God is revealed through faith for faith; as it is written, 'The one who is righteous will live by faith.'[c]

The Guilt of Humankind

[18] For the wrath of God is revealed from heaven against all ungodliness and wickedness of those who by their wickedness suppress the truth. [19] For what can be known about God is plain to them, because God has shown it to them. [20] Ever since the creation of the world his eternal power and divine nature, invisible though they are, have been understood and seen through the things he has made. So they are without excuse; [21] for though they knew God, they did not honour him as God or give thanks to him, but they became futile in their thinking, and their senseless minds were darkened. [22] Claiming to be wise, they became fools; [23] and they exchanged the glory of the immortal God for images resembling a mortal human being or birds or four-footed animals or reptiles.

[24] Therefore God gave them up in the lusts of their hearts to impurity, to the degrading of their bodies among themselves, [25] because they exchanged the truth about God for a lie and worshipped and served the creature rather than the Creator, who is blessed for ever! Amen.

[26] For this reason God gave them up to degrading passions. Their women exchanged natural intercourse for unnatural, [27] and in the same way also the men, giving up natural intercourse with women, were consumed with passion for one another. Men committed shameless acts with men and received in their own persons the due penalty for their error.

[28] And since they did not see fit to acknowledge God, God gave them up to a debased mind and to things that should not be done. [29] They were filled with every kind of wickedness, evil, covetousness, malice. Full of envy, murder, strife, deceit, craftiness, they are gossips, [30] slanderers, God-haters,[d] insolent, haughty, boastful, inventors of evil, rebellious towards parents, [31] foolish, faithless, heartless, ruthless. [32] They know God's decree, that those who practise such things deserve to die—yet they not only do them but even applaud others who practise them.

The Righteous Judgement of God

2 Therefore you have no excuse, whoever you are, when you judge others; for in passing judgement on another you condemn yourself, because you, the judge, are doing the very same things. [2] You say,[e] 'We know that God's judgement on those who do such things is in accordance with truth.' [3] Do you imagine, whoever you are, that when you judge those who do such things and yet do them yourself, you will escape the judgement of God? [4] Or do you despise the riches of his kindness and forbearance and patience? Do you not realize that God's kindness is meant to lead you to repentance? [5] But by your hard and impenitent heart you are storing up wrath for yourself on the day of wrath, when God's

---

a Gk my spirit in the gospel   b Gk brothers   c Or The one who is righteous through faith will live   d Or God-hated   e Gk lacks You say righteous judgement will be revealed. 6 For he will repay according to each one's deeds: 7 to those who by patiently doing good seek for glory and honour and immortality, he will give eternal life; 8 while for those who are self-seeking and who obey not the truth but wickedness, there will be wrath and fury. 9 There will be anguish and distress for everyone who does evil, the Jew first and also the Greek, 10 but glory and honour and peace for everyone who does good, the Jew first and also the Greek. 11 For God shows no partiality.

12 All who have sinned apart from the law will also perish apart from the law, and all who have sinned under the law will be judged by the law. 13 For it is not the hearers of the law who are righteous in God's sight, but the doers of the law who will be justified. 14 When Gentiles, who do not possess the law, do instinctively what the law requires, these, though not having the law, are a law to themselves. 15 They show that what the law requires is written on their hearts, to which their own conscience also bears witness; and their conflicting thoughts will accuse or perhaps excuse them 16 on the day when, according to my gospel, God, through Jesus Christ, will judge the secret thoughts of all.

The Jews and the Law

17 But if you call yourself a Jew and rely on the law and boast of your relation to God 18 and know his will and determine what is best because you are instructed in the law, 19 and if you are sure that you are a guide to the blind, a light to those who are in darkness, 20 a corrector of the foolish, a teacher of children, having in the law the embodiment of knowledge and truth, 21 you, then, that teach others, will you not teach yourself? While you preach against stealing, do you steal? 22 You that forbid adultery, do you commit adultery? You that abhor idols, do you rob temples? 23 You that boast in the law, do you dishonour God by breaking the law? 24 For, as it is written, 'The name of God is blasphemed among the Gentiles because of you.'

25 Circumcision indeed is of value if you obey the law; but if you break the law, your circumcision has become uncircumcision. 26 So, if those who are uncircumcised keep the requirements of the law, will not their uncircumcision be regarded as circumcision? 27 Then those who are physically uncircumcised but keep the law will condemn you that have the written code and circumcision but break the law. 28 For a person is not a Jew who is one outwardly, nor is true circumcision something external and physical. 29 Rather, a person is a Jew who is one inwardly, and real circumcision is a matter of the heart— it is spiritual and not literal. Such a person receives praise not from others but from God.

3 Then what advantage has the Jew? Or what is the value of circumcision? 2 Much, in every way. For in the first place the Jews[a] were entrusted with the oracles of God. 3 What if some were unfaithful? Will their faithlessness nullify the faithfulness of God? 4 By no means! Although everyone is a liar, let God be proved true, as it is written,

'So that you may be justified in your
        words,
and prevail in your judging.'[b]

5 But if our injustice serves to confirm the justice of God, what should we say? That God is unjust to inflict wrath on us? (I speak in a human way.) 6 By no means! For then how could God judge the world? 7 But if through my falsehood God's truthfulness abounds to his glory, why am I still being condemned as a sinner? 8 And why not say (as some people slander us by saying that we say), 'Let us do evil so that good may come'? Their condemnation is deserved!

None Is Righteous

9 What then? Are we any better off?[c] No, not at all; for we have already charged that all, both Jews and Greeks, are under the power of sin, 10 as it is written:

---

a Gk they   b Gk when you are being judged   c Or at any disadvantage?

'There is no one who is righteous,
not even one;
11 there is no one who has
understanding,
there is no one who seeks God.
12 All have turned aside, together they
have become worthless;
there is no one who shows
kindness,
there is not even one.'
13 'Their throats are opened graves;
they use their tongues to deceive.'
'The venom of vipers is under
their lips.'
14 'Their mouths are full of cursing
and bitterness.'
15 'Their feet are swift to shed blood;
16 ruin and misery are in their paths,
17 and the way of peace they have
not known.'
18 'There is no fear of God before
their eyes.'

19 Now we know that whatever the law says, it speaks to those who are under the law, so that every mouth may be silenced, and the whole world may be held accountable to God. 20 For 'no human being will be justified in his sight' by deeds prescribed by the law, for through the law comes the knowledge of sin.

Righteousness through Faith

21 But now, irrespective of law, the righteousness of God has been disclosed, and is attested by the law and the prophets, 22 the righteousness of God through faith in Jesus Christ*a* for all who believe. For there is no distinction, 23 since all have sinned and fall short of the glory of God; 24 they are now justified by his grace as a gift, through the redemption that is in Christ Jesus, 25 whom God put forward as a sacrifice of atonement*b* by his blood, effective through faith. He did this to show his righteousness, because in his divine forbearance he had passed over the sins previously committed; 26 it was to prove at the present time that he himself is righteous and that he justifies the one who has faith in Jesus. *c*

27 Then what becomes of boasting? It is

excluded. By what law? By that of works? No, but by the law of faith. 28 For we hold that a person is justified by faith apart from works prescribed by the law. 29 Or is God the God of Jews only? Is he not the God of Gentiles also? Yes, of Gentiles also, 30 since God is one; and he will justify the circumcised on the ground of faith and the uncircumcised through that same faith. 31 Do we then overthrow the law by this faith? By no means! On the contrary, we uphold the law.

The Example of Abraham

4 What then are we to say was gained by*d* Abraham, our ancestor according to the flesh? 2 For if Abraham was justified by works, he has something to boast about, but not before God. 3 For what does the scripture say? 'Abraham believed God, and it was reckoned to him as righteousness.' 4 Now to one who works, wages are not reckoned as a gift but as something due. 5 But to one who without works trusts him who justifies the ungodly, such faith is reckoned as righteousness. 6 So also David speaks of the blessedness of those to whom God reckons righteousness irrespective of works:
7 'Blessed are those whose iniquities
are forgiven,
and whose sins are covered;
8 blessed is the one against whom the
Lord will not reckon sin.'

9 Is this blessedness, then, pronounced only on the circumcised, or also on the uncircumcised? We say, 'Faith was reckoned to Abraham as righteousness.' 10 How then was it reckoned to him? Was it before or after he had been circumcised? It was not after, but before he was circumcised. 11 He received the sign of circumcision as a seal of the righteousness that he had by faith while he was still uncircumcised. The purpose was to make him the ancestor of all who believe without being circumcised and who thus have righteousness reckoned to them, 12 and

a Or *through the faith of Jesus Christ*   *b* Or *a place of atonement*   *c* Or *who has the faith of Jesus*   *d* Other ancient authorities read *say about* likewise the ancestor of the circumcised who are not only circumcised but who also follow the example of the faith that our ancestor Abraham had before he was circumcised.

God's Promise Realized through Faith

13 For the promise that he would inherit the world did not come to Abraham or to his descendants through the law but through the righteousness of faith. 14 If it is the adherents of the law who are to be the heirs, faith is null and the promise is void. 15 For the law brings wrath; but where there is no law, neither is there violation.

16 For this reason it depends on faith, in order that the promise may rest on grace and be guaranteed to all his descendants, not only to the adherents of the law but also to those who share the faith of Abraham (for he is the father of all of us, 17 as it is written, 'I have made you the father of many nations')—in the presence of the God in whom he believed, who gives life to the dead and calls into existence the things that do not exist. 18 Hoping against hope, he believed that he would become 'the father of many nations', according to what was said, 'So numerous shall your descendants be.' 19 He did not weaken in faith when he considered his own body, which was already*a* as good as dead (for he was about a hundred years old), or when he considered the barrenness of Sarah's womb. 20 No distrust made him waver concerning the promise of God, but he grew strong in his faith as he gave glory to God, 21 being fully convinced that God was able to do what he had promised. 22 Therefore his faith*b* 'was reckoned to him as righteousness.' 23 Now the words, 'it was reckoned to him', were written not for his sake alone, 24 but for ours also. It will be reckoned to us who believe in him who raised Jesus our Lord from the dead, 25 who was handed over to death for our trespasses and was raised for our justification.

Results of Justification

5 Therefore, since we are justified by faith, we*c* have peace with God through our Lord Jesus Christ, 2 through whom we have obtained access*d* to this grace in which we stand; and we*e* boast in our hope of sharing the glory of God. 3 And not only that, but we*e* also boast in our sufferings, knowing that suffering produces endurance, 4 and endurance produces character, and character produces hope, 5 and hope does not disappoint us, because God's love has been poured into our hearts through the Holy Spirit that has been given to us.

6 For while we were still weak, at the right time Christ died for the ungodly. 7 Indeed, rarely will anyone die for a righteous person—though perhaps for a good person someone might actually dare to die. 8 But God proves his love for us in that while we still were sinners Christ died for us. 9 Much more surely then, now that we have been justified by his blood, will we be saved through him from the wrath of God.*f* 10 For if while we were enemies, we were reconciled to God through the death of his Son, much more surely, having been reconciled, will we be saved by his life. 11 But more than that, we even boast in God through our Lord Jesus Christ, through whom we have now received reconciliation.

Adam and Christ

12 Therefore, just as sin came into the world through one man, and death came through sin, and so death spread to all because all have sinned— 13 sin was indeed in the world before the law, but sin is not reckoned when there is no law. 14 Yet death exercised dominion from Adam to Moses, even over those whose sins were not like the transgression of Adam, who is a type of the one who was to come.

15 But the free gift is not like the trespass. For if the many died through the one

a Other ancient authorities lack *already*
b Gk *Therefore it*   *c* Other ancient authorities read *let us*   *d* Other ancient authorities add *by faith*
e Or *let us*   *f* Gk *the wrath*

man's trespass, much more surely have the grace of God and the free gift in the grace of the one man, Jesus Christ, abounded for the many. 16 And the free gift is not like the effect of the one man's sin. For the judgement following one trespass brought condemnation, but the free gift following many trespasses brings justification. 17 If, because of the one man's trespass, death exercised dominion through that one, much more surely will those who receive the abundance of grace and the free gift of righteousness exercise dominion in life through the one man, Jesus Christ.

18 Therefore just as one man's trespass led to condemnation for all, so one man's act of righteousness leads to justification and life for all. 19 For just as by the one man's disobedience the many were made sinners, so by the one man's obedience the many will be made righteous. 20 But law came in, with the result that the trespass multiplied; but where sin increased, grace abounded all the more, 21 so that, just as sin exercised dominion in death, so grace might also exercise dominion through justification*a* leading to eternal life through Jesus Christ our Lord.

Dying and Rising with Christ

6 What then are we to say? Should we continue in sin in order that grace may abound? 2 By no means! How can we who died to sin go on living in it? 3 Do you not know that all of us who have been baptized into Christ Jesus were baptized into his death? 4 Therefore we have been buried with him by baptism into death, so that, just as Christ was raised from the dead by the glory of the Father, so we too might walk in newness of life.

5 For if we have been united with him in a death like his, we will certainly be united with him in a resurrection like his. 6 We know that our old self was crucified with him so that the body of sin might be destroyed, and we might no longer be enslaved to sin. 7 For whoever has died is freed from sin. 8 But if we have died with Christ, we believe that we will also live with him. 9 We know that Christ, being

raised from the dead, will never die again; death no longer has dominion over him. 10 The death he died, he died to sin, once for all; but the life he lives, he lives to God. 11 So you also must consider yourselves dead to sin and alive to God in Christ Jesus.

12 Therefore, do not let sin exercise dominion in your mortal bodies, to make you obey their passions. 13 No longer present your members to sin as instruments*b* of wickedness, but present yourselves to God as those who have been brought from death to life, and present your members to God as instruments*b* of righteousness. 14 For sin will have no dominion over you, since you are not under law but under grace.

Slaves of Righteousness

15 What then? Should we sin because we are not under law but under grace? By no means! 16 Do you not know that if you present yourselves to anyone as obedient slaves, you are slaves of the one whom you obey, either of sin, which leads to death, or of obedience, which leads to righteousness? 17 But thanks be to God that you, having once been slaves of sin, have become obedient from the heart to the form of teaching to which you were entrusted, 18 and that you, having been set free from sin, have become slaves of righteousness. 19 I am speaking in human terms because of your natural limitations.*c* For just as you once presented your members as slaves to impurity and to greater and greater iniquity, so now present your members as slaves to righteousness for sanctification.

20 When you were slaves of sin, you were free in regard to righteousness. 21 So what advantage did you then get from the things of which you now are ashamed? The end of those things is death. 22 But now that you have been freed from sin and enslaved to God, the advantage you get is sanctification. The end is eternal life. 23 For the wages of sin is death, but the free gift

a Or *righteousness*   *b* Or *weapons*   *c* Gk *the weakness of your flesh* of God is eternal life in Christ Jesus our Lord.

An Analogy from Marriage

7 Do you not know, brothers and sisters[a]—for I am speaking to those who know the law—that the law is binding on a person only during that person's lifetime? [2]Thus a married woman is bound by the law to her husband as long as he lives; but if her husband dies, she is discharged from the law concerning the husband. [3]Accordingly, she will be called an adulteress if she lives with another man while her husband is alive. But if her husband dies, she is free from that law, and if she marries another man, she is not an adulteress.

4 In the same way, my friends,[a] you have died to the law through the body of Christ, so that you may belong to another, to him who has been raised from the dead in order that we may bear fruit for God. [5]While we were living in the flesh, our sinful passions, aroused by the law, were at work in our members to bear fruit for death. [6]But now we are discharged from the law, dead to that which held us captive, so that we are slaves not under the old written code but in the new life of the Spirit.

The Law and Sin

7 What then should we say? That the law is sin? By no means! Yet, if it had not been for the law, I would not have known sin. I would not have known what it is to covet if the law had not said, 'You shall not covet.' [8]But sin, seizing an opportunity in the commandment, produced in me all kinds of covetousness. Apart from the law sin lies dead. [9]I was once alive apart from the law, but when the commandment came, sin revived [10]and I died, and the very commandment that promised life proved to be death to me. [11]For sin, seizing an opportunity in the commandment, deceived me and through it killed me. [12]So the law is holy, and the commandment is holy and just and good.

13 Did what is good, then, bring death to me? By no means! It was sin, working death in me through what is good, in order that sin might be shown to be sin, and through the commandment might become sinful beyond measure.

The Inner Conflict

14 For we know that the law is spiritual; but I am of the flesh, sold into slavery under sin.[b] [15]I do not understand my own actions. For I do not do what I want, but I do the very thing I hate. [16]Now if I do what I do not want, I agree that the law is good. [17]But in fact it is no longer I that do it, but sin that dwells within me. [18]For I know that nothing good dwells within me, that is, in my flesh. I can will what is right, but I cannot do it. [19]For I do not do the good I want, but the evil I do not want is what I do. [20]Now if I do what I do not want, it is no longer I that do it, but sin that dwells within me.

21 So I find it to be a law that when I want to do what is good, evil lies close at hand. [22]For I delight in the law of God in my inmost self, [23]but I see in my members another law at war with the law of my mind, making me captive to the law of sin that dwells in my members. [24]Wretched man that I am! Who will rescue me from this body of death? [25]Thanks be to God through Jesus Christ our Lord!

So then, with my mind I am a slave to the law of God, but with my flesh I am a slave to the law of sin.

Life in the Spirit

8 There is therefore now no condemnation for those who are in Christ Jesus. [2]For the law of the Spirit[c] of life in Christ Jesus has set you[d] free from the law of sin and of death. [3]For God has done what the law, weakened by the flesh, could not do: by sending his own Son in the likeness of sinful flesh, and to deal with sin,[e] he condemned sin in the flesh, [4]so that the just requirement of the law might be fulfilled in us, who walk not according to the flesh but according to the Spirit.[c] [5]For those

a Gk brothers   b Gk sold under sin   c Or spirit
d Here the Greek word you is singular number; other ancient authorities read me or us   e Or and as a sin-offering

who live according to the flesh set their minds on the things of the flesh, but those who live according to the Spirit*a* set their minds on the things of the Spirit. *a* 6To set the mind on the flesh is death, but to set the mind on the Spirit*a* is life and peace. 7For this reason the mind that is set on the flesh is hostile to God; it does not submit to God's law—indeed it cannot, 8and those who are in the flesh cannot please God.

9 But you are not in the flesh; you are in the Spirit, *a* since the Spirit of God dwells in you. Anyone who does not have the Spirit of Christ does not belong to him. 10But if Christ is in you, though the body is dead because of sin, the Spirit*a* is life because of righteousness. 11If the Spirit of him who raised Jesus from the dead dwells in you, he who raised Christ*b* from the dead will give life to your mortal bodies also through*c* his Spirit that dwells in you.

12 So then, brothers and sisters, *d* we are debtors, not to the flesh, to live according to the flesh— 13for if you live according to the flesh, you will die; but if by the Spirit you put to death the deeds of the body, you will live. 14For all who are led by the Spirit of God are children of God. 15For you did not receive a spirit of slavery to fall back into fear, but you have received a spirit of adoption. When we cry, 'Abba!*e* Father!' 16it is that very Spirit bearing witness*f* with our spirit that we are children of God, 17and if children, then heirs, heirs of God and joint heirs with Christ—if, in fact, we suffer with him so that we may also be glorified with him.

Future Glory

18 I consider that the sufferings of this present time are not worth comparing with the glory about to be revealed to us. 19For the creation waits with eager longing for the revealing of the children of God; 20for the creation was subjected to futility, not of its own will but by the will of the one who subjected it, in hope 21that the creation itself will be set free from its bondage to decay and will obtain the freedom of the glory of the children

of God. 22We know that the whole creation has been groaning in labour pains until now; 23and not only the creation, but we ourselves, who have the first fruits of the Spirit, groan inwardly while we wait for adoption, the redemption of our bodies. 24For in*g* hope we were saved. Now hope that is seen is not hope. For who hopes*h* for what is seen? 25But if we hope for what we do not see, we wait for it with patience.

26 Likewise the Spirit helps us in our weakness; for we do not know how to pray as we ought, but that very Spirit intercedes*i* with sighs too deep for words. 27And God,*j* who searches the heart, knows what is the mind of the Spirit, because the Spirit*k* intercedes for the saints according to the will of God.*l*

28 We know that all things work together for good*m* for those who love God, who are called according to his purpose. 29For those whom he foreknew he also predestined to be conformed to the image of his Son, in order that he might be the firstborn within a large family.*n* 30And those whom he predestined he also called; and those whom he called he also justified; and those whom he justified he also glorified.

God's Love in Christ Jesus

31 What then are we to say about these things? If God is for us, who is against us? 32He who did not withhold his own Son, but gave him up for all of us, will he not with him also give us everything else? 33Who will bring any charge against God's elect? It is God who justifies. 34Who is to condemn? It is Christ Jesus, who died, yes, who was raised, who is at the right hand of God, who indeed intercedes for us.*o*

a Or *spirit*   *b* Other ancient authorities read *the Christ* or *Christ Jesus* or *Jesus Christ*   *c* Other ancient authorities read *on account of*   *d* Gk *brothers* *e* Aramaic for *Father*   *f* Or 15*a spirit of adoption, by which we cry, 'Abba! Father!'* 16*The Spirit itself bears witness* *g* Or *by*   *h* Other ancient authorities read *awaits* *i* Other ancient authorities add *for us*   *j* Gk *the one* *k* Gk *he* or *it*   *l* Gk *according to God*   *m* Other ancient authorities read *God makes all things work together for good*, or *in all things God works for good*   *n* Gk *among many brothers*   *o* Or *Is it Christ Jesus . . . for us?*

35 Who will separate us from the love of Christ? Will hardship, or distress, or persecution, or famine, or nakedness, or peril, or sword? 36 As it is written,

'For your sake we are being killed all
    day long;
we are accounted as sheep to be
    slaughtered.'

37 No, in all these things we are more than conquerors through him who loved us. 38 For I am convinced that neither death, nor life, nor angels, nor rulers, nor things present, nor things to come, nor powers, 39 nor height, nor depth, nor anything else in all creation, will be able to separate us from the love of God in Christ Jesus our Lord.

God's Election of Israel

9 I am speaking the truth in Christ—I am not lying; my conscience confirms it by the Holy Spirit— 2 I have great sorrow and unceasing anguish in my heart. 3 For I could wish that I myself were accursed and cut off from Christ for the sake of my own people,*a* my kindred according to the flesh. 4 They are Israelites, and to them belong the adoption, the glory, the covenants, the giving of the law, the worship, and the promises; 5 to them belong the patriarchs, and from them, according to the flesh, comes the Messiah,*b* who is over all, God blessed for ever.*c* Amen.

6 It is not as though the word of God had failed. For not all Israelites truly belong to Israel, 7 and not all of Abraham's children are his true descendants; but 'It is through Isaac that descendants shall be named after you.' 8 This means that it is not the children of the flesh who are the children of God, but the children of the promise are counted as descendants. 9 For this is what the promise said, 'About this time I will return and Sarah shall have a son.' 10 Nor is that all; something similar happened to Rebecca when she had conceived children by one husband, our ancestor Isaac. 11 Even before they had been born or had done anything good or bad (so that God's purpose of election might continue, 12 not by works but by his call) she was

told, 'The elder shall serve the younger.' 13 As it is written,

'I have loved Jacob,
    but I have hated Esau.'

14 What then are we to say? Is there injustice on God's part? By no means! 15 For he says to Moses,

'I will have mercy on whom I
    have mercy,
and I will have compassion on
    whom I have compassion.'

16 So it depends not on human will or exertion, but on God who shows mercy. 17 For the scripture says to Pharaoh, 'I have raised you up for the very purpose of showing my power in you, so that my name may be proclaimed in all the earth.' 18 So then he has mercy on whomsoever he chooses, and he hardens the heart of whomsoever he chooses.

God's Wrath and Mercy

19 You will say to me then, 'Why then does he still find fault? For who can resist his will?' 20 But who indeed are you, a human being, to argue with God? Will what is moulded say to the one who moulds it, 'Why have you made me like this?' 21 Has the potter no right over the clay, to make out of the same lump one object for special use and another for ordinary use? 22 What if God, desiring to show his wrath and to make known his power, has endured with much patience the objects of wrath that are made for destruction; 23 and what if he has done so in order to make known the riches of his glory for the objects of mercy, which he has prepared beforehand for glory— 24 including us whom he has called, not from the Jews only but also from the Gentiles? 25 As indeed he says in Hosea,

'Those who were not my people I will
    call "my people",
and her who was not beloved I will
    call "beloved". '

26 'And in the very place where it was
    said to them, "You are not my
    people",

a Gk *my brothers*   *b* Or *the Christ*   *c* Or *Messiah, who is God over all, blessed for ever*; or *Messiah. May he who is God over all be blessed for ever*

there they shall be called children
of the living God.'

27 And Isaiah cries out concerning Israel, 'Though the number of the children of Israel were like the sand of the sea, only a remnant of them will be saved; 28 for the Lord will execute his sentence on the earth quickly and decisively.'[a] 29 And as Isaiah predicted,

'If the Lord of hosts had not left
survivors[b] to us,
we would have fared like Sodom
and been made like Gomorrah.'

Israel's Unbelief

30 What then are we to say? Gentiles, who did not strive for righteousness, have attained it, that is, righteousness through faith; 31 but Israel, who did strive for the righteousness that is based on the law, did not succeed in fulfilling that law. 32 Why not? Because they did not strive for it on the basis of faith, but as if it were based on works. They have stumbled over the stumbling-stone, 33 as it is written,

'See, I am laying in Zion a stone that
will make people stumble, a
rock that will make them fall,
and whoever believes in him[c] will
not be put to shame.'

10 Brothers and sisters,[d] my heart's desire and prayer to God for them is that they may be saved. 2 I can testify that they have a zeal for God, but it is not enlightened. 3 For, being ignorant of the righteousness that comes from God, and seeking to establish their own, they have not submitted to God's righteousness. 4 For Christ is the end of the law so that there may be righteousness for everyone who believes.

Salvation Is for All

5 Moses writes concerning the righteousness that comes from the law, that 'the person who does these things will live by them.' 6 But the righteousness that comes from faith says, 'Do not say in your heart, "Who will ascend into heaven?" ' (that is, to bring Christ down) 7 'or "Who will descend into the abyss?" ' (that is, to

bring Christ up from the dead). 8 But what does it say?

'The word is near you,
on your lips and in your heart'
(that is, the word of faith that we proclaim); 9 because[e] if you confess with your lips that Jesus is Lord and believe in your heart that God raised him from the dead, you will be saved. 10 For one believes with the heart and so is justified, and one confesses with the mouth and so is saved. 11 The scripture says, 'No one who believes in him will be put to shame.' 12 For there is no distinction between Jew and Greek; the same Lord is Lord of all and is generous to all who call on him. 13 For, 'Everyone who calls on the name of the Lord shall be saved.'

14 But how are they to call on one in whom they have not believed? And how are they to believe in one of whom they have never heard? And how are they to hear without someone to proclaim him? 15 And how are they to proclaim him unless they are sent? As it is written, 'How beautiful are the feet of those who bring good news!' 16 But not all have obeyed the good news;[f] for Isaiah says, 'Lord, who has believed our message?' 17 So faith comes from what is heard, and what is heard comes through the word of Christ.[g]

18 But I ask, have they not heard? Indeed they have; for

'Their voice has gone out to all
the earth,
and their words to the ends of the
world.'

19 Again I ask, did Israel not understand? First Moses says,

'I will make you jealous of those who
are not a nation;
with a foolish nation I will make
you angry.'

20 Then Isaiah is so bold as to say,

'I have been found by those who did
not seek me;

---

a Other ancient authorities read *for he will finish his work and cut it short in righteousness, because the Lord will make the sentence shortened on the earth*
b Or *descendants*; Gk *seed*   c Or *trusts in it*
d Gk *Brothers*   e Or *namely, that*   f Or *gospel*
g Or *about Christ*; other ancient authorities read *of God*

I have shown myself to those who did not ask for me.'

21 But of Israel he says, 'All day long I have held out my hands to a disobedient and contrary people.'

Israel's Rejection Is Not Final

11 I ask, then, has God rejected his people? By no means! I myself am an Israelite, a descendant of Abraham, a member of the tribe of Benjamin. 2 God has not rejected his people whom he foreknew. Do you not know what the scripture says of Elijah, how he pleads with God against Israel? 3 'Lord, they have killed your prophets, they have demolished your altars; I alone am left, and they are seeking my life.' 4 But what is the divine reply to him? 'I have kept for myself seven thousand who have not bowed the knee to Baal.' 5 So too at the present time there is a remnant, chosen by grace. 6 But if it is by grace, it is no longer on the basis of works, otherwise grace would no longer be grace. *d*

7 What then? Israel failed to obtain what it was seeking. The elect obtained it, but the rest were hardened, 8 as it is written,

'God gave them a sluggish spirit,
    eyes that would not see
    and ears that would not hear,
down to this very day.'

9 And David says,
'Let their table become a snare
        and a trap,
    a stumbling-block and a retribution
        for them;
10 let their eyes be darkened so that
        they cannot see,
    and keep their backs for ever bent.'

The Salvation of the Gentiles

11 So I ask, have they stumbled so as to fall? By no means! But through their stumbling *b* salvation has come to the Gentiles, so as to make Israel *c* jealous. 12 Now if their stumbling *b* means riches for the world, and if their defeat means riches for Gentiles, how much more will their full inclusion mean!

13 Now I am speaking to you Gentiles. Inasmuch then as I am an apostle to the Gentiles, I glorify my ministry 14 in order to make my own people *d* jealous, and thus save some of them. 15 For if their rejection is the reconciliation of the world, what will their acceptance be but life from the dead! 16 If the part of the dough offered as first fruits is holy, then the whole batch is holy; and if the root is holy, then the branches also are holy.

17 But if some of the branches were broken off, and you, a wild olive shoot, were grafted in their place to share the rich root *e* of the olive tree, 18 do not vaunt yourselves over the branches. If you do vaunt yourselves, remember that it is not you that support the root, but the root that supports you. 19 You will say, 'Branches were broken off so that I might be grafted in.' 20 That is true. They were broken off because of their unbelief, but you stand only through faith. So do not become proud, but stand in awe. 21 For if God did not spare the natural branches, perhaps he will not spare you. *f* 22 Note then the kindness and the severity of God: severity towards those who have fallen, but God's kindness towards you, provided you continue in his kindness; otherwise you also will be cut off. 23 And even those of Israel, *g* if they do not persist in unbelief, will be grafted in, for God has the power to graft them in again. 24 For if you have been cut from what is by nature a wild olive tree and grafted, contrary to nature, into a cultivated olive tree, how much more will these natural branches be grafted back into their own olive tree.

All Israel Will Be Saved

25 So that you may not claim to be wiser than you are, brothers and sisters, *h* I want you to understand this mystery: a hardening has come upon part of Israel, until the full number of the Gentiles has

come in. [26] And so all Israel will be saved; as it is written,

> 'Out of Zion will come the Deliverer;
> he will banish ungodliness
> from Jacob.'

[27] 'And this is my covenant with them,
when I take away their sins.'

[28] As regards the gospel they are enemies of God[a] for your sake; but as regards election they are beloved, for the sake of their ancestors; [29] for the gifts and the calling of God are irrevocable. [30] Just as you were once disobedient to God but have now received mercy because of their disobedience, [31] so they have now been disobedient in order that, by the mercy shown to you, they too may now[b] receive mercy. [32] For God has imprisoned all in disobedience so that he may be merciful to all.

[33] O the depth of the riches and wisdom and knowledge of God! How unsearchable are his judgements and how inscrutable his ways!

[34] 'For who has known the mind of the Lord?
Or who has been his counsellor?'

[35] 'Or who has given a gift to him,
to receive a gift in return?'

[36] For from him and through him and to him are all things. To him be the glory for ever. Amen.

The New Life in Christ

12 I appeal to you therefore, brothers and sisters,[c] by the mercies of God, to present your bodies as a living sacrifice, holy and acceptable to God, which is your spiritual[d] worship. [2] Do not be conformed to this world,[e] but be transformed by the renewing of your minds, so that you may discern what is the will of God—what is good and acceptable and perfect.[f]

[3] For by the grace given to me I say to everyone among you not to think of yourself more highly than you ought to think, but to think with sober judgement, each according to the measure of faith that God has assigned. [4] For as in one body we have many members, and not all the members have the same function, [5] so we, who are many, are one body in Christ, and individ-

ually we are members one of another. [6] We have gifts that differ according to the grace given to us: prophecy, in proportion to faith; [7] ministry, in ministering; the teacher, in teaching; [8] the exhorter, in exhortation; the giver, in generosity; the leader, in diligence; the compassionate, in cheerfulness.

Marks of the True Christian

[9] Let love be genuine; hate what is evil, hold fast to what is good; [10] love one another with mutual affection; outdo one another in showing honour. [11] Do not lag in zeal, be ardent in spirit, serve the Lord.[g] [12] Rejoice in hope, be patient in suffering, persevere in prayer. [13] Contribute to the needs of the saints; extend hospitality to strangers.

[14] Bless those who persecute you; bless and do not curse them. [15] Rejoice with those who rejoice, weep with those who weep. [16] Live in harmony with one another; do not be haughty, but associate with the lowly;[h] do not claim to be wiser than you are. [17] Do not repay anyone evil for evil, but take thought for what is noble in the sight of all. [18] If it is possible, so far as it depends on you, live peaceably with all. [19] Beloved, never avenge yourselves, but leave room for the wrath of God;[i] for it is written, 'Vengeance is mine, I will repay, says the Lord.' [20] No, 'if your enemies are hungry, feed them; if they are thirsty, give them something to drink; for by doing this you will heap burning coals on their heads.' [21] Do not be overcome by evil, but overcome evil with good.

Being Subject to Authorities

13 Let every person be subject to the governing authorities; for there is no authority except from God, and those authorities that exist have been instituted by God. [2] Therefore whoever resists authority resists what God has appointed, and those who resist will incur judgement.

---

a Gk lacks *of God*   *b* Other ancient authorities lack *now*   *c* Gk *brothers*   *d* Or *reasonable*   *e* Gk *age*
f Or *what is the good and acceptable and perfect will of God*
g Other ancient authorities read *serve the opportune time*
h Or *give yourselves to humble tasks*   *i* Gk *the wrath*

³For rulers are not a terror to good conduct, but to bad. Do you wish to have no fear of the authority? Then do what is good, and you will receive its approval; ⁴for it is God's servant for your good. But if you do what is wrong, you should be afraid, for the authority *a* does not bear the sword in vain! It is the servant of God to execute wrath on the wrongdoer. ⁵Therefore one must be subject, not only because of wrath but also because of conscience. ⁶For the same reason you also pay taxes, for the authorities are God's servants, busy with this very thing. ⁷Pay to all what is due to them—taxes to whom taxes are due, revenue to whom revenue is due, respect to whom respect is due, honour to whom honour is due.

Love for One Another

8 Owe no one anything, except to love one another; for the one who loves another has fulfilled the law. ⁹The commandments, 'You shall not commit adultery; You shall not murder; You shall not steal; You shall not covet'; and any other commandment, are summed up in this word, 'Love your neighbour as yourself.' ¹⁰Love does no wrong to a neighbour; therefore, love is the fulfilling of the law.

An Urgent Appeal

11 Besides this, you know what time it is, how it is now the moment for you to wake from sleep. For salvation is nearer to us now than when we became believers; ¹²the night is far gone, the day is near. Let us then lay aside the works of darkness and put on the armour of light; ¹³let us live honourably as in the day, not in revelling and drunkenness, not in debauchery and licentiousness, not in quarrelling and jealousy. ¹⁴Instead, put on the Lord Jesus Christ, and make no provision for the flesh, to gratify its desires.

Do Not Judge Another

14 Welcome those who are weak in faith, *b* but not for the purpose of quarrelling over opinions. ²Some believe in eating anything, while the weak eat only vegetables. ³Those who eat must not despise those who abstain, and those who abstain must not pass judgement on those who eat; for God has welcomed them. ⁴Who are you to pass judgement on servants of another? It is before their own lord that they stand or fall. And they will be upheld, for the Lord *c* is able to make them stand.

5 Some judge one day to be better than another, while others judge all days to be alike. Let all be fully convinced in their own minds. ⁶Those who observe the day, observe it in honour of the Lord. Also those who eat, eat in honour of the Lord, since they give thanks to God; while those who abstain, abstain in honour of the Lord and give thanks to God.

7 We do not live to ourselves, and we do not die to ourselves. ⁸If we live, we live to the Lord, and if we die, we die to the Lord; so then, whether we live or whether we die, we are the Lord's. ⁹For to this end Christ died and lived again, so that he might be Lord of both the dead and the living.

10 Why do you pass judgement on your brother or sister? *d* Or you, why do you despise your brother or sister? *d* For we will all stand before the judgement seat of God. *e* ¹¹For it is written,

'As I live, says the Lord, every knee
    shall bow to me,
  and every tongue shall give praise
    to *f* God.'

¹²So then, each of us will be accountable to God. *g*

Do Not Make Another Stumble

13 Let us therefore no longer pass judgement on one another, but resolve instead never to put a stumbling-block or hindrance in the way of another. *h* ¹⁴I know and am persuaded in the Lord Jesus that nothing is unclean in itself; but it is unclean for anyone who thinks it unclean. ¹⁵If your brother or sister *d* is being injured by what you eat, you are no longer

a Gk *it*   *b* Or *conviction*   *c* Other ancient authorities read *for God*   *d* Gk *brother*   *e* Other ancient authorities read *of Christ*   *f* Or *confess*   *g* Other ancient authorities lack *to God*   *h* Gk *of a brother* walking in love. Do not let what you eat cause the ruin of one for whom Christ died. [16] So do not let your good be spoken of as evil. [17] For the kingdom of God is not food and drink but righteousness and peace and joy in the Holy Spirit. [18] The one who thus serves Christ is acceptable to God and has human approval. [19] Let us then pursue what makes for peace and for mutual edification. [20] Do not, for the sake of food, destroy the work of God. Everything is indeed clean, but it is wrong for you to make others fall by what you eat; [21] it is good not to eat meat or drink wine or do anything that makes your brother or sister[a] stumble.[b] [22] The faith that you have, have as your own conviction before God. Blessed are those who have no reason to condemn themselves because of what they approve. [23] But those who have doubts are condemned if they eat, because they do not act from faith;[c] for whatever does not proceed from faith[c] is sin.[d]

Please Others, Not Yourselves

15 We who are strong ought to put up with the failings of the weak, and not to please ourselves. [2] Each of us must please our neighbour for the good purpose of building up the neighbour. [3] For Christ did not please himself; but, as it is written, 'The insults of those who insult you have fallen on me.' [4] For whatever was written in former days was written for our instruction, so that by steadfastness and by the encouragement of the scriptures we might have hope. [5] May the God of steadfastness and encouragement grant you to live in harmony with one another, in accordance with Christ Jesus, [6] so that together you may with one voice glorify the God and Father of our Lord Jesus Christ.

The Gospel for Jews and Gentiles Alike

[7] Welcome one another, therefore, just as Christ has welcomed you, for the glory of God. [8] For I tell you that Christ has become a servant of the circumcised on behalf of the truth of God in order that he

might confirm the promises given to the patriarchs, [9] and in order that the Gentiles might glorify God for his mercy. As it is written,

'Therefore I will confess[e] you among
the Gentiles,
and sing praises to your name';
[10] and again he says,
'Rejoice, O Gentiles, with his people';
[11] and again,
'Praise the Lord, all you Gentiles,
and let all the peoples praise him';
[12] and again Isaiah says,
'The root of Jesse shall come,
the one who rises to rule
the Gentiles;
in him the Gentiles shall hope.'
[13] May the God of hope fill you with all joy and peace in believing, so that you may abound in hope by the power of the Holy Spirit.

Paul's Reason for Writing So Boldly

[14] I myself feel confident about you, my brothers and sisters,[f] that you yourselves are full of goodness, filled with all knowledge, and able to instruct one another. [15] Nevertheless, on some points I have written to you rather boldly by way of reminder, because of the grace given me by God [16] to be a minister of Christ Jesus to the Gentiles in the priestly service of the gospel of God, so that the offering of the Gentiles may be acceptable, sanctified by the Holy Spirit. [17] In Christ Jesus, then, I have reason to boast of my work for God. [18] For I will not venture to speak of anything except what Christ has accomplished[g] through me to win obedience from the Gentiles, by word and deed, [19] by the power of signs and wonders, by the power of the Spirit of God,[h] so that from Jerusalem and as far around as Illyricum I have fully proclaimed the good news[i] of Christ. [20] Thus I make it my ambition to

---

a Gk *brother*   b Other ancient authorities add *or be upset or be weakened*   c Or *conviction*   d Other authorities, some ancient, add here 16.25-27   e Or *thank*   f Gk *brothers*   g Gk *speak of those things that Christ has not accomplished*   h Other ancient authorities read *of the Spirit* or *of the Holy Spirit*   i Or *gospel* proclaim the good news,[a] not where Christ has already been named, so that I do not build on someone else's foundation, 21 but as it is written,

'Those who have never been told of
  him shall see,
and those who have never heard of
  him shall understand.'

Paul's Plan to Visit Rome

22 This is the reason that I have so often been hindered from coming to you. 23 But now, with no further place for me in these regions, I desire, as I have for many years, to come to you 24 when I go to Spain. For I do hope to see you on my journey and to be sent on by you, once I have enjoyed your company for a little while. 25 At present, however, I am going to Jerusalem in a ministry to the saints; 26 for Macedonia and Achaia have been pleased to share their resources with the poor among the saints at Jerusalem. 27 They were pleased to do this, and indeed they owe it to them; for if the Gentiles have come to share in their spiritual blessings, they ought also to be of service to them in material things. 28 So, when I have completed this, and have delivered to them what has been collected,[b] I will set out by way of you to Spain; 29 and I know that when I come to you, I will come in the fullness of the blessing[c] of Christ.

30 I appeal to you, brothers and sisters,[d] by our Lord Jesus Christ and by the love of the Spirit, to join me in earnest prayer to God on my behalf, 31 that I may be rescued from the unbelievers in Judea, and that my ministry[e] to Jerusalem may be acceptable to the saints, 32 so that by God's will I may come to you with joy and be refreshed in your company. 33 The God of peace be with all of you.[f] Amen.

Personal Greetings

16 I commend to you our sister Phoebe, a deacon[g] of the church at Cenchreae, 2 so that you may welcome her in the Lord as is fitting for the saints, and help her in whatever she may require from you, for she has been a benefactor of many and of myself as well.

3 Greet Prisca and Aquila, who work with me in Christ Jesus, 4 and who risked their necks for my life, to whom not only I give thanks, but also all the churches of the Gentiles. 5 Greet the church in their house. Greet my beloved Epaenetus, who was the first convert[g] in Asia for Christ. 6 Greet Mary, who has worked very hard among you. 7 Greet Andronicus and Junia,[i] my relatives[j] who were in prison with me; they are prominent among the apostles, and they were in Christ before I was. 8 Greet Ampliatus, my beloved in the Lord. 9 Greet Urbanus, our co-worker in Christ, and my beloved Stachys. 10 Greet Apelles, who is approved in Christ. Greet those who belong to the family of Aristobulus. 11 Greet my relative[k] Herodion. Greet those in the Lord who belong to the family of Narcissus. 12 Greet those workers in the Lord, Tryphaena and Tryphosa. Greet the beloved Persis, who has worked hard in the Lord. 13 Greet Rufus, chosen in the Lord; and greet his mother—a mother to me also. 14 Greet Asyncritus, Phlegon, Hermes, Patrobas, Hermas, and the brothers and sisters[d] who are with them. 15 Greet Philologus, Julia, Nereus and his sister, and Olympas, and all the saints who are with them. 16 Greet one another with a holy kiss. All the churches of Christ greet you.

Final Instructions

17 I urge you, brothers and sisters,[d] to keep an eye on those who cause dissensions and offences, in opposition to the teaching that you have learned; avoid them. 18 For such people do not serve our Lord Christ, but their own appetites,[l] and by smooth talk and flattery they deceive the hearts of the simple-minded. 19 For while your obedience is known to all, so that I rejoice over you, I want you to be

---

a Or gospel   b Gk have sealed to them this fruit
c Other ancient authorities add of the gospel
d Gk brothers   e Other ancient authorities read my
bringing of a gift   f One ancient authority adds 16.25-
27 here   g Or minister   h Gk first fruits
i Or Junias; other ancient authorities read Julia
j Or compatriots   k Or compatriot   l Gk their own belly

wise in what is good, and guileless in what is evil. ²⁰The God of peace will shortly crush Satan under your feet. The grace of our Lord Jesus Christ be with you. *a*

21 Timothy, my co-worker, greets you; so do Lucius and Jason and Sosipater, my relatives. *b*

22 I Tertius, the writer of this letter, greet you in the Lord. *c*

23 Gaius, who is host to me and to the whole church, greets you. Erastus, the city treasurer, and our brother Quartus, greet you. *d*

Final Doxology

25 Now to God *e* who is able to strengthen you according to my gospel and the proclamation of Jesus Christ, according to the revelation of the mystery that was kept secret for long ages ²⁶but is now disclosed, and through the prophetic writings is made known to all the Gentiles, according to the command of the eternal God, to bring about the obedience of faith— ²⁷to the only wise God, through Jesus Christ, to whom *f* be the glory for ever! Amen. *g*

a Other ancient authorities lack this sentence
b Or *compatriots*   *c* Or *I Tertius, writing this letter in the Lord, greet you*   *d* Other ancient authorities add verse 24, *The grace of our Lord Jesus Christ be with all of you. Amen.*   *e* Gk *the one*   *f* Other ancient authorities lack *to whom.* The verse then reads, *to the only wise God be the glory through Jesus Christ for ever. Amen.*
g Other ancient authorities lack 16.25-27 or include it after 14.23 or 15.33; others put verse 24 after verse 27

THE FIRST LETTER OF PAUL TO THE
CORINTHIANS

Salutation

1 Paul, called to be an apostle of Christ Jesus by the will of God, and our brother Sosthenes,

2 To the church of God that is in Corinth, to those who are sanctified in Christ Jesus, called to be saints, together with all those who in every place call on the name of our Lord Jesus Christ, both their Lord[a] and ours:

3 Grace to you and peace from God our Father and the Lord Jesus Christ.

4 I give thanks to my[b] God always for you because of the grace of God that has been given you in Christ Jesus, 5 for in every way you have been enriched in him, in speech and knowledge of every kind— 6 just as the testimony of[c] Christ has been strengthened among you— 7 so that you are not lacking in any spiritual gift as you wait for the revealing of our Lord Jesus Christ. 8 He will also strengthen you to the end, so that you may be blameless on the day of our Lord Jesus Christ. 9 God is faithful; by him you were called into the

a Gk theirs b Other ancient authorities lack my
c Or to

Corinth in the Time of Paul

To Lechaion

Amphitheater

N

The Forum

Bema

To Philus

Temple of Aphrodite

To Cenchrea

Acrocorinth

Upper Peirene

0
0   500 Meters

fellowship of his Son, Jesus Christ our Lord.

Divisions in the Church

10 Now I appeal to you, brothers and sisters,[a] by the name of our Lord Jesus Christ, that all of you should be in agreement and that there should be no divisions among you, but that you should be united in the same mind and the same purpose. [11] For it has been reported to me by Chloe's people that there are quarrels among you, my brothers and sisters.[b] [12] What I mean is that each of you says, 'I belong to Paul', or 'I belong to Apollos', or 'I belong to Cephas', or 'I belong to Christ.' [13] Has Christ been divided? Was Paul crucified for you? Or were you baptized in the name of Paul? [14] I thank God[c] that I baptized none of you except Crispus and Gaius, [15] so that no one can say that you were baptized in my name. [16] (I did baptize also the household of Stephanas; beyond that, I do not know whether I baptized anyone else.) [17] For Christ did not send me to baptize but to proclaim the gospel, and not with eloquent wisdom, so that the cross of Christ might not be emptied of its power.

Christ the Power and Wisdom of God

18 For the message about the cross is foolishness to those who are perishing, but to us who are being saved it is the power of God. [19] For it is written,

'I will destroy the wisdom of
    the wise,
and the discernment of the
    discerning I will thwart.'

[20] Where is the one who is wise? Where is the scribe? Where is the debater of this age? Has not God made foolish the wisdom of the world? [21] For since, in the wisdom of God, the world did not know God through wisdom, God decided, through the foolishness of our proclamation, to save those who believe. [22] For Jews demand signs and Greeks desire wisdom, [23] but we proclaim Christ crucified, a stumbling-block to Jews and foolishness to Gentiles, [24] but to those who are the called, both Jews and Greeks, Christ the power of God

and the wisdom of God. [25] For God's foolishness is wiser than human wisdom, and God's weakness is stronger than human strength.

26 Consider your own call, brothers and sisters:[a] not many of you were wise by human standards,[d] not many were powerful, not many were of noble birth. [27] But God chose what is foolish in the world to shame the wise; God chose what is weak in the world to shame the strong; [28] God chose what is low and despised in the world, things that are not, to reduce to nothing things that are, [29] so that no one[e] might boast in the presence of God. [30] He is the source of your life in Christ Jesus, who became for us wisdom from God, and righteousness and sanctification and redemption, [31] in order that, as it is written, 'Let the one who boasts, boast in[f] the Lord.'

Proclaiming Christ Crucified

2 When I came to you, brothers and sisters,[a] I did not come proclaiming the mystery[g] of God to you in lofty words or wisdom. [2] For I decided to know nothing among you except Jesus Christ, and him crucified. [3] And I came to you in weakness and in fear and in much trembling. [4] My speech and my proclamation were not with plausible words of wisdom,[h] but with a demonstration of the Spirit and of power, [5] so that your faith might rest not on human wisdom but on the power of God.

The True Wisdom of God

6 Yet among the mature we do speak wisdom, though it is not a wisdom of this age or of the rulers of this age, who are doomed to perish. [7] But we speak God's wisdom, secret and hidden, which God decreed before the ages for our glory. [8] None of the rulers of this age understood this; for if they had, they would not have crucified the Lord of glory. [9] But, as it is written,

a Gk *brothers*   *b* Gk *my brothers*   *c* Other ancient authorities read *I am thankful*   *d* Gk *according to the flesh*   *e* Gk *no flesh*   *f* Or *of*   *g* Other ancient authorities read *testimony*   *h* Other ancient authorities read *the persuasiveness of wisdom*

'What no eye has seen, nor ear heard,
  nor the human heart conceived,
what God has prepared for those
    who love him'—
[10] these things God has revealed to us through the Spirit; for the Spirit searches everything, even the depths of God. [11] For what human being knows what is truly human except the human spirit that is within? So also no one comprehends what is truly God's except the Spirit of God. [12] Now we have received not the spirit of the world, but the Spirit that is from God, so that we may understand the gifts bestowed on us by God. [13] And we speak of these things in words not taught by human wisdom but taught by the Spirit, interpreting spiritual things to those who are spiritual. [a]

14 Those who are unspiritual [b] do not receive the gifts of God's Spirit, for they are foolishness to them, and they are unable to understand them because they are discerned spiritually. [15] Those who are spiritual discern all things, and they are themselves subject to no one else's scrutiny.
[16] 'For who has known the mind
      of the Lord
    so as to instruct him?'
But we have the mind of Christ.

On Divisions in the Corinthian Church

3 And so, brothers and sisters, [c] I could not speak to you as spiritual people, but rather as people of the flesh, as infants in Christ. [2] I fed you with milk, not solid food, for you were not ready for solid food. Even now you are still not ready, [3] for you are still of the flesh. For as long as there is jealousy and quarrelling among you, are you not of the flesh, and behaving according to human inclinations? [4] For when one says, 'I belong to Paul', and another, 'I belong to Apollos', are you not merely human?

5 What then is Apollos? What is Paul? Servants through whom you came to believe, as the Lord assigned to each. [6] I planted, Apollos watered, but God gave the growth. [7] So neither the one who plants nor the one who waters is anything,

but only God who gives the growth. [8] The one who plants and the one who waters have a common purpose, and each will receive wages according to the labour of each. [9] For we are God's servants, working together; you are God's field, God's building.

10 According to the grace of God given to me, like a skilled master builder I laid a foundation, and someone else is building on it. Each builder must choose with care how to build on it. [11] For no one can lay any foundation other than the one that has been laid; that foundation is Jesus Christ. [12] Now if anyone builds on the foundation with gold, silver, precious stones, wood, hay, straw— [13] the work of each builder will become visible, for the Day will disclose it, because it will be revealed with fire, and the fire will test what sort of work each has done. [14] If what has been built on the foundation survives, the builder will receive a reward. [15] If the work is burned, the builder will suffer loss; the builder will be saved, but only as through fire.

16 Do you not know that you are God's temple and that God's Spirit dwells in you? [d] [17] If anyone destroys God's temple, God will destroy that person. For God's temple is holy, and you are that temple.

18 Do not deceive yourselves. If you think that you are wise in this age, you should become fools so that you may become wise. [19] For the wisdom of this world is foolishness with God. For it is written,
    'He catches the wise in their
        craftiness',
[20] and again,
    'The Lord knows the thoughts of the
        wise,
      that they are futile.'
[21] So let no one boast about human leaders. For all things are yours, [22] whether Paul or Apollos or Cephas or the world or life or death or the present or the future—all belong to you, [23] and you belong to Christ, and Christ belongs to God.

---

a Or *interpreting spiritual things in spiritual language,* or *comparing spiritual things with spiritual*   *b* Or *natural*   *c* Gk *brothers*   *d* In verses 16 and 17 the Greek word for *you* is plural

The Ministry of the Apostles

4 Think of us in this way, as servants of Christ and stewards of God's mysteries. ² Moreover, it is required of stewards that they should be found trustworthy. ³ But with me it is a very small thing that I should be judged by you or by any human court. I do not even judge myself. ⁴ I am not aware of anything against myself, but I am not thereby acquitted. It is the Lord who judges me. ⁵ Therefore do not pronounce judgement before the time, before the Lord comes, who will bring to light the things now hidden in darkness and will disclose the purposes of the heart. Then each one will receive commendation from God.

6 I have applied all this to Apollos and myself for your benefit, brothers and sisters, *d* so that you may learn through us the meaning of the saying, 'Nothing beyond what is written', so that none of you will be puffed up in favour of one against another. ⁷ For who sees anything different in you? *b* What do you have that you did not receive? And if you received it, why do you boast as if it were not a gift?

8 Already you have all you want! Already you have become rich! Quite apart from us you have become kings! Indeed, I wish that you had become kings, so that we might be kings with you! ⁹ For I think that God has exhibited us apostles as last of all, as though sentenced to death, because we have become a spectacle to the world, to angels and to mortals. ¹⁰ We are fools for the sake of Christ, but you are wise in Christ. We are weak, but you are strong. You are held in honour, but we in disrepute. ¹¹ To the present hour we are hungry and thirsty, we are poorly clothed and beaten and homeless, ¹² and we grow weary from the work of our own hands. When reviled, we bless; when persecuted, we endure; ¹³ when slandered, we speak kindly. We have become like the rubbish of the world, the dregs of all things, to this very day.

Fatherly Admonition

14 I am not writing this to make you ashamed, but to admonish you as my beloved children. ¹⁵ For though you might have ten thousand guardians in Christ, you do not have many fathers. Indeed, in Christ Jesus I became your father through the gospel. ¹⁶ I appeal to you, then, be imitators of me. ¹⁷ For this reason I sent *c* you Timothy, who is my beloved and faithful child in the Lord, to remind you of my ways in Christ Jesus, as I teach them everywhere in every church. ¹⁸ But some of you, thinking that I am not coming to you, have become arrogant. ¹⁹ But I will come to you soon, if the Lord wills, and I will find out not the talk of these arrogant people but their power. ²⁰ For the kingdom of God depends not on talk but on power. ²¹ What would you prefer? Am I to come to you with a stick, or with love in a spirit of gentleness?

Sexual Immorality Defiles the Church

5 It is actually reported that there is sexual immorality among you, and of a kind that is not found even among pagans; for a man is living with his father's wife. ² And you are arrogant! Should you not rather have mourned, so that he who has done this would have been removed from among you?

3 For though absent in body, I am present in spirit; and as if present I have already pronounced judgement ⁴ in the name of the Lord Jesus on the man who has done such a thing. *d* When you are assembled, and my spirit is present with the power of our Lord Jesus, ⁵ you are to hand this man over to Satan for the destruction of the flesh, so that his spirit may be saved on the day of the Lord. *e*

6 Your boasting is not a good thing. Do you not know that a little yeast leavens the whole batch of dough? ⁷ Clean out the old yeast so that you may be a new batch, as you really are unleavened. For our paschal lamb, Christ, has been sacrificed. ⁸ Therefore, let us celebrate the festival, not with the old yeast, the yeast of malice and evil,

a Gk brothers   *b* Or Who makes you different from another?   *c* Or am sending   *d* Or on the man who has done such a thing in the name of the Lord Jesus   *e* Other ancient authorities add Jesus but with the unleavened bread of sincerity and truth.

Sexual Immorality Must Be Judged

9 I wrote to you in my letter not to associate with sexually immoral persons— [10] not at all meaning the immoral of this world, or the greedy and robbers, or idolaters, since you would then need to go out of the world. [11] But now I am writing to you not to associate with anyone who bears the name of brother or sister[a] who is sexually immoral or greedy, or is an idolater, reviler, drunkard, or robber. Do not even eat with such a one. [12] For what have I to do with judging those outside? Is it not those who are inside that you are to judge? [13] God will judge those outside. 'Drive out the wicked person from among you.'

Lawsuits among Believers

6 When any of you has a grievance against another, do you dare to take it to court before the unrighteous, instead of taking it before the saints? [2] Do you not know that the saints will judge the world? And if the world is to be judged by you, are you incompetent to try trivial cases? [3] Do you not know that we are to judge angels—to say nothing of ordinary matters? [4] If you have ordinary cases, then, do you appoint as judges those who have no standing in the church? [5] I say this to your shame. Can it be that there is no one among you wise enough to decide between one believer[a] and another, [6] but a believer[a] goes to court against a believer[a]—and before unbelievers at that?

7 In fact, to have lawsuits at all with one another is already a defeat for you. Why not rather be wronged? Why not rather be defrauded? [8] But you yourselves wrong and defraud—and believers[b] at that.

9 Do you not know that wrongdoers will not inherit the kingdom of God? Do not be deceived! Fornicators, idolaters, adulterers, male prostitutes, sodomites, [10] thieves, the greedy, drunkards, revilers, robbers—none of these will inherit the kingdom of God. [11] And this is what some of you used to be. But you were washed,

you were sanctified, you were justified in the name of the Lord Jesus Christ and in the Spirit of our God.

Glorify God in Body and Spirit

12 'All things are lawful for me', but not all things are beneficial. 'All things are lawful for me', but I will not be dominated by anything. [13] 'Food is meant for the stomach and the stomach for food',[c] and God will destroy both one and the other. The body is meant not for fornication but for the Lord, and the Lord for the body. [14] And God raised the Lord and will also raise us by his power. [15] Do you not know that your bodies are members of Christ? Should I therefore take the members of Christ and make them members of a prostitute? Never! [16] Do you not know that whoever is united to a prostitute becomes one body with her? For it is said, 'The two shall be one flesh.' [17] But anyone united to the Lord becomes one spirit with him. [18] Shun fornication! Every sin that a person commits is outside the body; but the fornicator sins against the body itself. [19] Or do you not know that your body is a temple[d] of the Holy Spirit within you, which you have from God, and that you are not your own? [20] For you were bought with a price; therefore glorify God in your body.

Directions concerning Marriage

7 Now concerning the matters about which you wrote: 'It is well for a man not to touch a woman.' [2] But because of cases of sexual immorality, each man should have his own wife and each woman her own husband. [3] The husband should give to his wife her conjugal rights, and likewise the wife to her husband. [4] For the wife does not have authority over her own body, but the husband does; likewise the husband does not have authority over his own body, but the wife does. [5] Do not deprive one another except perhaps by agreement for a set time, to devote yourselves to prayer, and then come together again, so that Satan may not tempt you because of

---

a Gk *brother*   *b* Gk *brothers*   *c* The quotation may extend to the word *other*   *d* Or *sanctuary* your lack of self-control. 6This I say by way of concession, not of command. 7I wish that all were as I myself am. But each has a particular gift from God, one having one kind and another a different kind.

8 To the unmarried and the widows I say that it is well for them to remain unmarried as I am. 9But if they are not practising self-control, they should marry. For it is better to marry than to be aflame with passion.

10 To the married I give this command—not I but the Lord—that the wife should not separate from her husband 11(but if she does separate, let her remain unmarried or else be reconciled to her husband), and that the husband should not divorce his wife.

12 To the rest I say—I and not the Lord—that if any believer*a* has a wife who is an unbeliever, and she consents to live with him, he should not divorce her. 13And if any woman has a husband who is an unbeliever, and he consents to live with her, she should not divorce him. 14For the unbelieving husband is made holy through his wife, and the unbelieving wife is made holy through her husband. Otherwise, your children would be unclean, but as it is, they are holy. 15But if the unbelieving partner separates, let it be so; in such a case the brother or sister is not bound. It is to peace that God has called you.*b* 16Wife, for all you know, you might save your husband. Husband, for all you know, you might save your wife.

The Life That the Lord Has Assigned

17 However that may be, let each of you lead the life that the Lord has assigned, to which God called you. This is my rule in all the churches. 18Was anyone at the time of his call already circumcised? Let him not seek to remove the marks of circumcision. Was anyone at the time of his call uncircumcised? Let him not seek circumcision. 19Circumcision is nothing, and uncircumcision is nothing; but obeying the commandments of God is everything. 20Let each of you remain in the condition in which you were called.

21 Were you a slave when called? Do not be concerned about it. Even if you can gain your freedom, make use of your present condition now more than ever.*c* 22For whoever was called in the Lord as a slave is a freed person belonging to the Lord, just as whoever was free when called is a slave of Christ. 23You were bought with a price; do not become slaves of human masters. 24In whatever condition you were called, brothers and sisters,*d* there remain with God.

The Unmarried and the Widows

25 Now concerning virgins, I have no command of the Lord, but I give my opinion as one who by the Lord's mercy is trustworthy. 26I think that, in view of the impending*e* crisis, it is well for you to remain as you are. 27Are you bound to a wife? Do not seek to be free. Are you free from a wife? Do not seek a wife. 28But if you marry, you do not sin, and if a virgin marries, she does not sin. Yet those who marry will experience distress in this life,*f* and I would spare you that. 29I mean, brothers and sisters,*d* the appointed time has grown short; from now on, let even those who have wives be as though they had none, 30and those who mourn as though they were not mourning, and those who rejoice as though they were not rejoicing, and those who buy as though they had no possessions, 31and those who deal with the world as though they had no dealings with it. For the present form of this world is passing away.

32 I want you to be free from anxieties. The unmarried man is anxious about the affairs of the Lord, how to please the Lord; 33but the married man is anxious about the affairs of the world, how to please his wife, 34and his interests are divided. And the unmarried woman and the virgin are anxious about the affairs of the Lord, so that they may be holy in body and spirit; but the married woman is anxious about the affairs of the world, how to please her

a Gk *brother*   *b* Other ancient authorities read *us*
c Or *avail yourself of the opportunity*   *d* Gk *brothers*
e Or *present*   *f* Gk *in the flesh*

husband. [35] I say this for your own benefit, not to put any restraint upon you, but to promote good order and unhindered devotion to the Lord.

36 If anyone thinks that he is not behaving properly towards his fiancée, *a* if his passions are strong, and so it has to be, let him marry as he wishes; it is no sin. Let them marry. [37] But if someone stands firm in his resolve, being under no necessity but having his own desire under control, and has determined in his own mind to keep her as his fiancée, *a* he will do well. [38] So then, he who marries his fiancée *a* does well; and he who refrains from marriage will do better.

39 A wife is bound as long as her husband lives. But if the husband dies, *b* she is free to marry anyone she wishes, only in the Lord. [40] But in my judgement she is more blessed if she remains as she is. And I think that I too have the Spirit of God.

Food Offered to Idols

8 Now concerning food sacrificed to idols: we know that 'all of us possess knowledge.' Knowledge puffs up, but love builds up. [2] Anyone who claims to know something does not yet have the necessary knowledge; [3] but anyone who loves God is known by him.

4 Hence, as to the eating of food offered to idols, we know that 'no idol in the world really exists', and that 'there is no God but one.' [5] Indeed, even though there may be so-called gods in heaven or on earth—as in fact there are many gods and many lords— [6] yet for us there is one God, the Father, from whom are all things and for whom we exist, and one Lord, Jesus Christ, through whom are all things and through whom we exist.

7 It is not everyone, however, who has this knowledge. Since some have become so accustomed to idols until now, they still think of the food they eat as food offered to an idol; and their conscience, being weak, is defiled. [8] 'Food will not bring us close to God.' *c* We are no worse off if we do not eat, and no better off if we do. [9] But take care that this liberty of yours does not somehow become a stumbling-block to the weak. [10] For if others see you, who possess knowledge, eating in the temple of an idol, might they not, since their conscience is weak, be encouraged to the point of eating food sacrificed to idols? [11] So by your knowledge those weak believers for whom Christ died are destroyed. *d* [12] But when you thus sin against members of your family, *e* and wound their conscience when it is weak, you sin against Christ. [13] Therefore, if food is a cause of their falling, *f* I will never eat meat, so that I may not cause one of them *g* to fall.

The Rights of an Apostle

9 Am I not free? Am I not an apostle? Have I not seen Jesus our Lord? Are you not my work in the Lord? [2] If I am not an apostle to others, at least I am to you; for you are the seal of my apostleship in the Lord.

3 This is my defence to those who would examine me. [4] Do we not have the right to our food and drink? [5] Do we not have the right to be accompanied by a believing wife, *h* as do the other apostles and the brothers of the Lord and Cephas? [6] Or is it only Barnabas and I who have no right to refrain from working for a living? [7] Who at any time pays the expenses for doing military service? Who plants a vineyard and does not eat any of its fruit? Or who tends a flock and does not get any of its milk?

8 Do I say this on human authority? Does not the law also say the same? [9] For it is written in the law of Moses, 'You shall not muzzle an ox while it is treading out the grain.' Is it for oxen that God is concerned? [10] Or does he not speak entirely for our sake? It was indeed written for our sake, for whoever ploughs should plough in hope and whoever threshes should thresh in hope of a share in the crop. [11] If we have sown spiritual good among you, is it too much if we reap your material

a Gk *virgin*   *b* Gk *falls asleep*   *c* The quotation may extend to the end of the verse   *d* Gk *the weak brother . . . is destroyed*   *e* Gk *against the brothers*   *f* Gk *my brother's falling*   *g* Gk *cause my brother*   *h* Gk *a sister as wife* benefits? [12] If others share this rightful claim on you, do not we still more?

Nevertheless, we have not made use of this right, but we endure anything rather than put an obstacle in the way of the gospel of Christ. [13] Do you not know that those who are employed in the temple service get their food from the temple, and those who serve at the altar share in what is sacrificed on the altar? [14] In the same way, the Lord commanded that those who proclaim the gospel should get their living by the gospel.

[15] But I have made no use of any of these rights, nor am I writing this so that they may be applied in my case. Indeed, I would rather die than that—no one will deprive me of my ground for boasting! [16] If I proclaim the gospel, this gives me no ground for boasting, for an obligation is laid on me, and woe betide me if I do not proclaim the gospel! [17] For if I do this of my own will, I have a reward; but if not of my own will, I am entrusted with a commission. [18] What then is my reward? Just this: that in my proclamation I may make the gospel free of charge, so as not to make full use of my rights in the gospel.

[19] For though I am free with respect to all, I have made myself a slave to all, so that I might win more of them. [20] To the Jews I became as a Jew, in order to win Jews. To those under the law I became as one under the law (though I myself am not under the law) so that I might win those under the law. [21] To those outside the law I became as one outside the law (though I am not free from God's law but am under Christ's law) so that I might win those outside the law. [22] To the weak I became weak, so that I might win the weak. I have become all things to all people, so that I might by any means save some. [23] I do it all for the sake of the gospel, so that I may share in its blessings.

[24] Do you not know that in a race the runners all compete, but only one receives the prize? Run in such a way that you may win it. [25] Athletes exercise self-control in all things; they do it to receive a perishable garland, but we an imperishable one. [26] So I do not run aimlessly, nor do I box as though beating the air; [27] but I punish my body and enslave it, so that after proclaiming to others I myself should not be disqualified.

Warnings from Israel's History

10 I do not want you to be unaware, brothers and sisters,[a] that our ancestors were all under the cloud, and all passed through the sea, [2] and all were baptized into Moses in the cloud and in the sea, [3] and all ate the same spiritual food, [4] and all drank the same spiritual drink. For they drank from the spiritual rock that followed them, and the rock was Christ. [5] Nevertheless, God was not pleased with most of them, and they were struck down in the wilderness.

[6] Now these things occurred as examples for us, so that we might not desire evil as they did. [7] Do not become idolaters as some of them did; as it is written, 'The people sat down to eat and drink, and they rose up to play.' [8] We must not indulge in sexual immorality as some of them did, and twenty-three thousand fell in a single day. [9] We must not put Christ[b] to the test, as some of them did, and were destroyed by serpents. [10] And do not complain as some of them did, and were destroyed by the destroyer. [11] These things happened to them to serve as an example, and they were written down to instruct us, on whom the ends of the ages have come. [12] So if you think you are standing, watch out that you do not fall. [13] No testing has overtaken you that is not common to everyone. God is faithful, and he will not let you be tested beyond your strength, but with the testing he will also provide the way out so that you may be able to endure it.

[14] Therefore, my dear friends,[c] flee from the worship of idols. [15] I speak as to sensible people; judge for yourselves what I say. [16] The cup of blessing that we bless, is it not a sharing in the blood of Christ? The bread that we break, is it not a sharing in the body of Christ? [17] Because there is one

a Gk *brothers*   b Other ancient authorities read *the Lord*   c Gk *my beloved* bread, we who are many are one body, for we all partake of the one bread. 18 Consider the people of Israel;*a* are not those who eat the sacrifices partners in the altar? 19 What do I imply then? That food sacrificed to idols is anything, or that an idol is anything? 20 No, I imply that what pagans sacrifice, they sacrifice to demons and not to God. I do not want you to be partners with demons. 21 You cannot drink the cup of the Lord and the cup of demons. You cannot partake of the table of the Lord and the table of demons. 22 Or are we provoking the Lord to jealousy? Are we stronger than he?

Do All to the Glory of God

23 'All things are lawful', but not all things are beneficial. 'All things are lawful', but not all things build up. 24 Do not seek your own advantage, but that of others. 25 Eat whatever is sold in the meat market without raising any question on the ground of conscience, 26 for 'the earth and its fullness are the Lord's.' 27 If an unbeliever invites you to a meal and you are disposed to go, eat whatever is set before you without raising any question on the ground of conscience. 28 But if someone says to you, 'This has been offered in sacrifice', then do not eat it, out of consideration for the one who informed you, and for the sake of conscience— 29 I mean the other's conscience, not your own. For why should my liberty be subject to the judgement of someone else's conscience? 30 If I partake with thankfulness, why should I be denounced because of that for which I give thanks?

31 So, whether you eat or drink, or whatever you do, do everything for the glory of God. 32 Give no offence to Jews or to Greeks or to the church of God, 33 just as I try to please everyone in everything I do, not seeking my own advantage, but that of many, so that they may be saved. 11 1 Be imitators of me, as I am of Christ.

Head Coverings

2 I commend you because you remember me in everything and maintain the traditions just as I handed them on to you. 3 But I want you to understand that Christ is the head of every man, and the husband*b* is the head of his wife,*c* and God is the head of Christ. 4 Any man who prays or prophesies with something on his head disgraces his head, 5 but any woman who prays or prophesies with her head unveiled disgraces her head—it is one and the same thing as having her head shaved. 6 For if a woman will not veil herself, then she should cut off her hair; but if it is disgraceful for a woman to have her hair cut off or to be shaved, she should wear a veil. 7 For a man ought not to have his head veiled, since he is the image and reflection*d* of God; but woman is the reflection*d* of man. 8 Indeed, man was not made from woman, but woman from man. 9 Neither was man created for the sake of woman, but woman for the sake of man. 10 For this reason a woman ought to have a symbol of*e* authority on her head,*f* because of the angels. 11 Nevertheless, in the Lord woman is not independent of man or man independent of woman. 12 For just as woman came from man, so man comes through woman; but all things come from God. 13 Judge for yourselves: is it proper for a woman to pray to God with her head unveiled? 14 Does not nature itself teach you that if a man wears long hair, it is degrading to him, 15 but if a woman has long hair, it is her glory? For her hair is given to her for a covering. 16 But if anyone is disposed to be contentious—we have no such custom, nor do the churches of God.

Abuses at the Lord's Supper

17 Now in the following instructions I do not commend you, because when you come together it is not for the better but for the worse. 18 For, to begin with, when you come together as a church, I hear that there are divisions among you; and to some extent I believe it. 19 Indeed, there have to be factions among you, for only so

a Gk *Israel according to the flesh*   *b* The same Greek word means *man* or *husband*   *c* Or *head of the woman*   *d* Or *glory*   *e* Gk lacks *a symbol of*   *f* Or *have freedom of choice regarding her head* will it become clear who among you are genuine. 20 When you come together, it is not really to eat the Lord's supper. 21 For when the time comes to eat, each of you goes ahead with your own supper, and one goes hungry and another becomes drunk. 22 What! Do you not have homes to eat and drink in? Or do you show contempt for the church of God and humiliate those who have nothing? What should I say to you? Should I commend you? In this matter I do not commend you!

The Institution of the Lord's Supper

23 For I received from the Lord what I also handed on to you, that the Lord Jesus on the night when he was betrayed took a loaf of bread, 24 and when he had given thanks, he broke it and said, 'This is my body that is for*a* you. Do this in remembrance of me.' 25 In the same way he took the cup also, after supper, saying, 'This cup is the new covenant in my blood. Do this, as often as you drink it, in remembrance of me.' 26 For as often as you eat this bread and drink the cup, you proclaim the Lord's death until he comes.

Partaking of the Supper Unworthily

27 Whoever, therefore, eats the bread or drinks the cup of the Lord in an unworthy manner will be answerable for the body and blood of the Lord. 28 Examine yourselves, and only then eat of the bread and drink of the cup. 29 For all who eat and drink*b* without discerning the body,*c* eat and drink judgement against themselves. 30 For this reason many of you are weak and ill, and some have died.*d* 31 But if we judged ourselves, we would not be judged. 32 But when we are judged by the Lord, we are disciplined*e* so that we may not be condemned along with the world.

33 So then, my brothers and sisters,*f* when you come together to eat, wait for one another. 34 If you are hungry, eat at home, so that when you come together, it will not be for your condemnation. About the other things I will give instructions when I come.

Spiritual Gifts

12 Now concerning spiritual gifts,*g* brothers and sisters,*f* I do not want you to be uninformed. 2 You know that when you were pagans, you were enticed and led astray to idols that could not speak. 3 Therefore I want you to understand that no one speaking by the Spirit of God ever says 'Let Jesus be cursed!' and no one can say 'Jesus is Lord' except by the Holy Spirit.

4 Now there are varieties of gifts, but the same Spirit; 5 and there are varieties of services, but the same Lord; 6 and there are varieties of activities, but it is the same God who activates all of them in everyone. 7 To each is given the manifestation of the Spirit for the common good. 8 To one is given through the Spirit the utterance of wisdom, and to another the utterance of knowledge according to the same Spirit, 9 to another faith by the same Spirit, to another gifts of healing by the one Spirit, 10 to another the working of miracles, to another prophecy, to another the discernment of spirits, to another various kinds of tongues, to another the interpretation of tongues. 11 All these are activated by one and the same Spirit, who allots to each one individually just as the Spirit chooses.

One Body with Many Members

12 For just as the body is one and has many members, and all the members of the body, though many, are one body, so it is with Christ. 13 For in the one Spirit we were all baptized into one body—Jews or Greeks, slaves or free—and we were all made to drink of one Spirit.

14 Indeed, the body does not consist of one member but of many. 15 If the foot were to say, 'Because I am not a hand, I do not belong to the body', that would not make it any less a part of the body. 16 And if the ear were to say, 'Because I am not an eye, I do not belong to the body', that

a Other ancient authorities read *is broken for*   *b* Other ancient authorities add *in an unworthy manner,*
c Other ancient authorities read *the Lord's body*
d Gk *fallen asleep*   *e* Or *When we are judged, we are being disciplined by the Lord*   *f* Gk *brothers*
g Or *spiritual persons*

would not make it any less a part of the body. 17 If the whole body were an eye, where would the hearing be? If the whole body were hearing, where would the sense of smell be? 18 But as it is, God arranged the members in the body, each one of them, as he chose. 19 If all were a single member, where would the body be? 20 As it is, there are many members, yet one body. 21 The eye cannot say to the hand, 'I have no need of you', nor again the head to the feet, 'I have no need of you.' 22 On the contrary, the members of the body that seem to be weaker are indispensable, 23 and those members of the body that we think less honourable we clothe with greater honour, and our less respectable members are treated with greater respect; 24 whereas our more respectable members do not need this. But God has so arranged the body, giving the greater honour to the inferior member, 25 that there may be no dissension within the body, but the members may have the same care for one another. 26 If one member suffers, all suffer together with it; if one member is honoured, all rejoice together with it.

27 Now you are the body of Christ and individually members of it. 28 And God has appointed in the church first apostles, second prophets, third teachers; then deeds of power, then gifts of healing, forms of assistance, forms of leadership, various kinds of tongues. 29 Are all apostles? Are all prophets? Are all teachers? Do all work miracles? 30 Do all possess gifts of healing? Do all speak in tongues? Do all interpret? 31 But strive for the greater gifts. And I will show you a still more excellent way.

The Gift of Love

13 If I speak in the tongues of mortals and of angels, but do not have love, I am a noisy gong or a clanging cymbal. 2 And if I have prophetic powers, and understand all mysteries and all knowledge, and if I have all faith, so as to remove mountains, but do not have love, I am nothing. 3 If I give away all my possessions, and if I hand over my body so that I may

boast, *a* but do not have love, I gain nothing.

4 Love is patient; love is kind; love is not envious or boastful or arrogant 5 or rude. It does not insist on its own way; it is not irritable or resentful; 6 it does not rejoice in wrongdoing, but rejoices in the truth. 7 It bears all things, believes all things, hopes all things, endures all things.

8 Love never ends. But as for prophecies, they will come to an end; as for tongues, they will cease; as for knowledge, it will come to an end. 9 For we know only in part, and we prophesy only in part; 10 but when the complete comes, the partial will come to an end. 11 When I was a child, I spoke like a child, I thought like a child, I reasoned like a child; when I became an adult, I put an end to childish ways. 12 For now we see in a mirror, dimly, *b* but then we will see face to face. Now I know only in part; then I will know fully, even as I have been fully known. 13 And now faith, hope, and love abide, these three; and the greatest of these is love.

Gifts of Prophecy and Tongues

14 Pursue love and strive for the spiritual gifts, and especially that you may prophesy. 2 For those who speak in a tongue do not speak to other people but to God; for nobody understands them, since they are speaking mysteries in the Spirit. 3 On the other hand, those who prophesy speak to other people for their building up and encouragement and consolation. 4 Those who speak in a tongue build up themselves, but those who prophesy build up the church. 5 Now I would like all of you to speak in tongues, but even more to prophesy. One who prophesies is greater than one who speaks in tongues, unless someone interprets, so that the church may be built up.

6 Now, brothers and sisters, *c* if I come to you speaking in tongues, how will I benefit you unless I speak to you in some revelation or knowledge or prophecy or teaching? 7 It is the same way with lifeless

a Other ancient authorities read *body to be burned*
b Gk *in a riddle*   *c* Gk *brothers*

instruments that produce sound, such as the flute or the harp. If they do not give distinct notes, how will anyone know what is being played? 8 And if the bugle gives an indistinct sound, who will get ready for battle? 9 So with yourselves; if in a tongue you utter speech that is not intelligible, how will anyone know what is being said? For you will be speaking into the air. 10 There are doubtless many different kinds of sounds in the world, and nothing is without sound. 11 If then I do not know the meaning of a sound, I will be a foreigner to the speaker and the speaker a foreigner to me. 12 So with yourselves; since you are eager for spiritual gifts, strive to excel in them for building up the church.

13 Therefore, one who speaks in a tongue should pray for the power to interpret. 14 For if I pray in a tongue, my spirit prays but my mind is unproductive. 15 What should I do then? I will pray with the spirit, but I will pray with the mind also; I will sing praise with the spirit, but I will sing praise with the mind also. 16 Otherwise, if you say a blessing with the spirit, how can anyone in the position of an outsider say the 'Amen' to your thanksgiving, since the outsider does not know what you are saying? 17 For you may give thanks well enough, but the other person is not built up. 18 I thank God that I speak in tongues more than all of you; 19 nevertheless, in church I would rather speak five words with my mind, in order to instruct others also, than ten thousand words in a tongue.

20 Brothers and sisters, *a* do not be children in your thinking; rather, be infants in evil, but in thinking be adults. 21 In the law it is written,

'By people of strange tongues
  and by the lips of foreigners
I will speak to this people;
  yet even then they will not listen to
  me,'

says the Lord. 22 Tongues, then, are a sign not for believers but for unbelievers, while prophecy is not for unbelievers but for believers. 23 If, therefore, the whole church comes together and all speak in tongues, and outsiders or unbelievers enter, will they not say that you are out of your mind? 24 But if all prophesy, an unbeliever or outsider who enters is reproved by all and called to account by all. 25 After the secrets of the unbeliever's heart are disclosed, that person will bow down before God and worship him, declaring, 'God is really among you.'

Orderly Worship

26 What should be done then, my friends? *a* When you come together, each one has a hymn, a lesson, a revelation, a tongue, or an interpretation. Let all things be done for building up. 27 If anyone speaks in a tongue, let there be only two or at most three, and each in turn; and let one interpret. 28 But if there is no one to interpret, let them be silent in church and speak to themselves and to God. 29 Let two or three prophets speak, and let the others weigh what is said. 30 If a revelation is made to someone else sitting nearby, let the first person be silent. 31 For you can all prophesy one by one, so that all may learn and all be encouraged. 32 And the spirits of prophets are subject to the prophets, 33 for God is a God not of disorder but of peace.

(As in all the churches of the saints, 34 women should be silent in the churches. For they are not permitted to speak, but should be subordinate, as the law also says. 35 If there is anything they desire to know, let them ask their husbands at home. For it is shameful for a woman to speak in church. *b* 36 Or did the word of God originate with you? Or are you the only ones it has reached?)

37 Anyone who claims to be a prophet, or to have spiritual powers, must acknowledge that what I am writing to you is a command of the Lord. 38 Anyone who does not recognize this is not to be recognized. 39 So, my friends, *c* be eager to prophesy, and do not forbid speaking in tongues; 40 but all things should be done decently and in order.

a Gk *brothers*   *b* Other ancient authorities put verses 34-35 after verse 40   *c* Gk *my brothers*

The Resurrection of Christ

15 Now I should remind you, brothers and sisters,[a] of the good news[b] that I proclaimed to you, which you in turn received, in which also you stand, 2 through which also you are being saved, if you hold firmly to the message that I proclaimed to you—unless you have come to believe in vain.

3 For I handed on to you as of first importance what I in turn had received: that Christ died for our sins in accordance with the scriptures, 4 and that he was buried, and that he was raised on the third day in accordance with the scriptures, 5 and that he appeared to Cephas, then to the twelve. 6 Then he appeared to more than five hundred brothers and sisters[a] at one time, most of whom are still alive, though some have died.[c] 7 Then he appeared to James, then to all the apostles. 8 Last of all, as to someone untimely born, he appeared also to me. 9 For I am the least of the apostles, unfit to be called an apostle, because I persecuted the church of God. 10 But by the grace of God I am what I am, and his grace towards me has not been in vain. On the contrary, I worked harder than any of them—though it was not I, but the grace of God that is with me. 11 Whether then it was I or they, so we proclaim and so you have come to believe.

The Resurrection of the Dead

12 Now if Christ is proclaimed as raised from the dead, how can some of you say there is no resurrection of the dead? 13 If there is no resurrection of the dead, then Christ has not been raised; 14 and if Christ has not been raised, then our proclamation has been in vain and your faith has been in vain. 15 We are even found to be misrepresenting God, because we testified of God that he raised Christ—whom he did not raise if it is true that the dead are not raised. 16 For if the dead are not raised, then Christ has not been raised. 17 If Christ has not been raised, your faith is futile and you are still in your sins. 18 Then those also who have died[c] in Christ have perished. 19 If for this life only we have hoped in Christ, we are of all people most to be pitied.

20 But in fact Christ has been raised from the dead, the first fruits of those who have died.[c] 21 For since death came through a human being, the resurrection of the dead has also come through a human being; 22 for as all die in Adam, so all will be made alive in Christ. 23 But each in his own order: Christ the first fruits, then at his coming those who belong to Christ. 24 Then comes the end,[d] when he hands over the kingdom to God the Father, after he has destroyed every ruler and every authority and power. 25 For he must reign until he has put all his enemies under his feet. 26 The last enemy to be destroyed is death. 27 For 'God[e] has put all things in subjection under his feet.' But when it says, 'All things are put in subjection', it is plain that this does not include the one who put all things in subjection under him. 28 When all things are subjected to him, then the Son himself will also be subjected to the one who put all things in subjection under him, so that God may be all in all.

29 Otherwise, what will those people do who receive baptism on behalf of the dead? If the dead are not raised at all, why are people baptized on their behalf?

30 And why are we putting ourselves in danger every hour? 31 I die every day! That is as certain, brothers and sisters,[a] as my boasting of you—a boast that I make in Christ Jesus our Lord. 32 If with merely human hopes I fought with wild animals at Ephesus, what would I have gained by it? If the dead are not raised,

'Let us eat and drink,
    for tomorrow we die.'
33 Do not be deceived:
'Bad company ruins good morals.'
34 Come to a sober and right mind, and sin no more; for some people have no knowledge of God. I say this to your shame.

The Resurrection Body

35 But someone will ask, 'How are the dead raised? With what kind of body do

a Gk brothers   b Or gospel   c Gk fallen asleep
d Or Then come the rest   e Gk he

they come?' 36 Fool! What you sow does not come to life unless it dies. 37 And as for what you sow, you do not sow the body that is to be, but a bare seed, perhaps of wheat or of some other grain. 38 But God gives it a body as he has chosen, and to each kind of seed its own body. 39 Not all flesh is alike, but there is one flesh for human beings, another for animals, another for birds, and another for fish. 40 There are both heavenly bodies and earthly bodies, but the glory of the heavenly is one thing, and that of the earthly is another. 41 There is one glory of the sun, and another glory of the moon, and another glory of the stars; indeed, star differs from star in glory.

42 So it is with the resurrection of the dead. What is sown is perishable, what is raised is imperishable. 43 It is sown in dishonour, it is raised in glory. It is sown in weakness, it is raised in power. 44 It is sown a physical body, it is raised a spiritual body. If there is a physical body, there is also a spiritual body. 45 Thus it is written, 'The first man, Adam, became a living being'; the last Adam became a life-giving spirit. 46 But it is not the spiritual that is first, but the physical, and then the spiritual. 47 The first man was from the earth, a man of dust; the second man is *a* from heaven. 48 As was the man of dust, so are those who are of the dust; and as is the man of heaven, so are those who are of heaven. 49 Just as we have borne the image of the man of dust, we will *b* also bear the image of the man of heaven.

50 What I am saying, brothers and sisters, *c* is this: flesh and blood cannot inherit the kingdom of God, nor does the perishable inherit the imperishable. 51 Listen, I will tell you a mystery! We will not all die, *d* but we will all be changed, 52 in a moment, in the twinkling of an eye, at the last trumpet. For the trumpet will sound, and the dead will be raised imperishable, and we will be changed. 53 For this perishable body must put on imperishability, and this mortal body must put on immortality. 54 When this perishable body puts on imperishability, and this mortal body puts on immortality, then the saying that is written will be fulfilled:

'Death has been swallowed up
　in victory.'
55 'Where, O death, is your victory?
　Where, O death, is your sting?'
56 The sting of death is sin, and the power of sin is the law. 57 But thanks be to God, who gives us the victory through our Lord Jesus Christ.

58 Therefore, my beloved, *e* be steadfast, immovable, always excelling in the work of the Lord, because you know that in the Lord your labour is not in vain.

The Collection for the Saints

16 Now concerning the collection for the saints: you should follow the directions I gave to the churches of Galatia. 2 On the first day of every week, each of you is to put aside and save whatever extra you earn, so that collections need not be taken when I come. 3 And when I arrive, I will send any whom you approve with letters to take your gift to Jerusalem. 4 If it seems advisable that I should go also, they will accompany me.

Plans for Travel

5 I will visit you after passing through Macedonia—for I intend to pass through Macedonia— 6 and perhaps I will stay with you or even spend the winter, so that you may send me on my way, wherever I go. 7 I do not want to see you now just in passing, for I hope to spend some time with you, if the Lord permits. 8 But I will stay in Ephesus until Pentecost, 9 for a wide door for effective work has opened to me, and there are many adversaries.

10 If Timothy comes, see that he has nothing to fear among you, for he is doing the work of the Lord just as I am; 11 therefore let no one despise him. Send him on his way in peace, so that he may come to me; for I am expecting him with the brothers.

12 Now concerning our brother Apollos, I strongly urged him to visit you with

a Other ancient authorities add *the Lord*　*b* Other ancient authorities read *let us*　*c* Gk *brothers*
d Gk *fall asleep*　*e* Gk *beloved brothers*

the other brothers, but he was not at all willing[a] to come now. He will come when he has the opportunity.

Final Messages and Greetings

13 Keep alert, stand firm in your faith, be courageous, be strong. [14] Let all that you do be done in love.

15 Now, brothers and sisters,[b] you know that members of the household of Stephanas were the first converts in Achaia, and they have devoted themselves to the service of the saints; [16] I urge you to put yourselves at the service of such people, and of everyone who works and toils with them. [17] I rejoice at the coming of Stephanas and Fortunatus and Achaicus, because they have made up for your absence; [18] for they refreshed my spirit as well as yours. So give recognition to such people.

19 The churches of Asia send greetings. Aquila and Prisca, together with the church in their house, greet you warmly in the Lord. [20] All the brothers and sisters[b] send greetings. Greet one another with a holy kiss.

21 I, Paul, write this greeting with my own hand. [22] Let anyone be accursed who has no love for the Lord. Our Lord, come![c] [23] The grace of the Lord Jesus be with you. [24] My love be with all of you in Christ Jesus.[d]

---

a Or it was not at all God's will for him   b Gk brothers   c Gk Marana tha. These Aramaic words can also be read Maran atha, meaning Our Lord has come   d Other ancient authorities add Amen

THE SECOND LETTER OF PAUL TO THE
CORINTHIANS

Salutation

1 Paul, an apostle of Christ Jesus by the will of God, and Timothy our brother,

To the church of God that is in Corinth, including all the saints throughout Achaia:

2 Grace to you and peace from God our Father and the Lord Jesus Christ.

Paul's Thanksgiving after Affliction

3 Blessed be the God and Father of our Lord Jesus Christ, the Father of mercies and the God of all consolation, 4who consoles us in all our affliction, so that we may be able to console those who are in any affliction with the consolation with which we ourselves are consoled by God. 5For just as the sufferings of Christ are abundant for us, so also our consolation is abundant through Christ. 6If we are being afflicted, it is for your consolation and salvation; if we are being consoled, it is for your consolation, which you experience when you patiently endure the same sufferings that we are also suffering. 7Our hope for you is unshaken; for we know that as you share in our sufferings, so also you share in our consolation.

8 We do not want you to be unaware, brothers and sisters,*a* of the affliction we experienced in Asia; for we were so utterly, unbearably crushed that we despaired of life itself. 9Indeed, we felt that we had received the sentence of death so that we would rely not on ourselves but on God who raises the dead. 10He who rescued us from so deadly a peril will continue to rescue us; on him we have set our hope that he will rescue us again, 11as you also join in helping us by your prayers, so that many will give thanks on our*b* behalf for the blessing granted to us through the prayers of many.

The Postponement of Paul's Visit

12 Indeed, this is our boast, the testimony of our conscience: we have behaved in the world with frankness*c* and godly sincerity, not by earthly wisdom but by the grace of God—and all the more towards you. 13For we write to you nothing other than what you can read and also understand; I hope you will understand until the end— 14as you have already understood us in part—that on the day of the Lord Jesus we are your boast even as you are our boast.

15 Since I was sure of this, I wanted to come to you first, so that you might have a double favour;*d* 16I wanted to visit you on my way to Macedonia, and to come back to you from Macedonia and have you send me on to Judea. 17Was I vacillating when I wanted to do this? Do I make my plans according to ordinary human standards,*e* ready to say 'Yes, yes' and 'No, no' at the same time? 18As surely as God is faithful, our word to you has not been 'Yes and No.' 19For the Son of God, Jesus Christ, whom we proclaimed among you, Silvanus and Timothy and I, was not 'Yes and No'; but in him it is always 'Yes.' 20For in him every one of God's promises is a 'Yes.' For this reason it is through him that we say the 'Amen', to the glory of God. 21But it is God who establishes us with you in Christ and has anointed us, 22by putting his seal on

---

a Gk *brothers*   *b* Other ancient authorities read *your*
c Other ancient authorities read *holiness*   *d* Other ancient authorities read *pleasure*   *e* Gk *according to the flesh*

us and giving us his Spirit in our hearts as a first instalment.

23 But I call on God as witness against me: it was to spare you that I did not come again to Corinth. 24 I do not mean to imply that we lord it over your faith; rather, we are workers with you for your joy, because

2 you stand firm in the faith. 1 So I made up my mind not to make you another painful visit. 2 For if I cause you pain, who is there to make me glad but the one whom I have pained? 3 And I wrote as I did, so that when I came, I might not suffer pain from those who should have made me rejoice; for I am confident about all of you, that my joy would be the joy of all of you. 4 For I wrote to you out of much distress and anguish of heart and with many tears, not to cause you pain, but to let you know the abundant love that I have for you.

Forgiveness for the Offender

5 But if anyone has caused pain, he has caused it not to me, but to some extent— not to exaggerate it—to all of you. 6 This punishment by the majority is enough for such a person; 7 so now instead you should forgive and console him, so that he may not be overwhelmed by excessive sorrow. 8 So I urge you to reaffirm your love for him. 9 I wrote for this reason: to test you and to know whether you are obedient in everything. 10 Anyone whom you forgive, I also forgive. What I have forgiven, if I have forgiven anything, has been for your sake in the presence of Christ. 11 And we do this so that we may not be outwitted by Satan; for we are not ignorant of his designs.

Paul's Anxiety in Troas

12 When I came to Troas to proclaim the good news of Christ, a door was opened for me in the Lord; 13 but my mind could not rest because I did not find my brother Titus there. So I said farewell to them and went on to Macedonia.

14 But thanks be to God, who in Christ always leads us in triumphal procession, and through us spreads in every place the fragrance that comes from knowing him.

15 For we are the aroma of Christ to God among those who are being saved and among those who are perishing; 16 to the one a fragrance from death to death, to the other a fragrance from life to life. Who is sufficient for these things? 17 For we are not peddlers of God's word like so many;*a* but in Christ we speak as persons of sincerity, as persons sent from God and standing in his presence.

Ministers of the New Covenant

3 Are we beginning to commend ourselves again? Surely we do not need, as some do, letters of recommendation to you or from you, do we? 2 You yourselves are our letter, written on our*b* hearts, to be known and read by all; 3 and you show that you are a letter of Christ, prepared by us, written not with ink but with the Spirit of the living God, not on tablets of stone but on tablets of human hearts.

4 Such is the confidence that we have through Christ towards God. 5 Not that we are competent of ourselves to claim anything as coming from us; our competence is from God, 6 who has made us competent to be ministers of a new covenant, not of letter but of spirit; for the letter kills, but the Spirit gives life.

7 Now if the ministry of death, chiselled in letters on stone tablets,*c* came in glory so that the people of Israel could not gaze at Moses' face because of the glory of his face, a glory now set aside, 8 how much more will the ministry of the Spirit come in glory? 9 For if there was glory in the ministry of condemnation, much more does the ministry of justification abound in glory! 10 Indeed, what once had glory has lost its glory because of the greater glory; 11 for if what was set aside came through glory, much more has the permanent come in glory!

12 Since, then, we have such a hope, we act with great boldness, 13 not like Moses, who put a veil over his face to keep the people of Israel from gazing at the end of the glory that*d* was being set aside. 14 But

---

a Other ancient authorities read *like the others*
b Other ancient authorities read *your*   c Gk *on stones*
d Gk *of what*

their minds were hardened. Indeed, to this very day, when they hear the reading of the old covenant, that same veil is still there, since only in Christ is it set aside. 15 Indeed, to this very day whenever Moses is read, a veil lies over their minds; 16 but when one turns to the Lord, the veil is removed. 17 Now the Lord is the Spirit, and where the Spirit of the Lord is, there is freedom. 18 And all of us, with unveiled faces, seeing the glory of the Lord as though reflected in a mirror, are being transformed into the same image from one degree of glory to another; for this comes from the Lord, the Spirit.

Treasure in Clay Jars

4 Therefore, since it is by God's mercy that we are engaged in this ministry, we do not lose heart. 2 We have renounced the shameful things that one hides; we refuse to practise cunning or to falsify God's word; but by the open statement of the truth we commend ourselves to the conscience of everyone in the sight of God. 3 And even if our gospel is veiled, it is veiled to those who are perishing. 4 In their case the god of this world has blinded the minds of the unbelievers, to keep them from seeing the light of the gospel of the glory of Christ, who is the image of God. 5 For we do not proclaim ourselves; we proclaim Jesus Christ as Lord and ourselves as your slaves for Jesus' sake. 6 For it is the God who said, 'Let light shine out of darkness', who has shone in our hearts to give the light of the knowledge of the glory of God in the face of Jesus Christ.

7 But we have this treasure in clay jars, so that it may be made clear that this extraordinary power belongs to God and does not come from us. 8 We are afflicted in every way, but not crushed; perplexed, but not driven to despair; 9 persecuted, but not forsaken; struck down, but not destroyed; 10 always carrying in the body the death of Jesus, so that the life of Jesus may also be made visible in our bodies. 11 For while we live, we are always being given up to death for Jesus' sake, so that the life of Jesus may be made visible in our mortal flesh. 12 So death is at work in us, but life in you.

13 But just as we have the same spirit of faith that is in accordance with scripture— 'I believed, and so I spoke'—we also believe, and so we speak, 14 because we know that the one who raised the Lord Jesus will raise us also with Jesus, and will bring us with you into his presence. 15 Yes, everything is for your sake, so that grace, as it extends to more and more people, may increase thanksgiving, to the glory of God.

Living by Faith

16 So we do not lose heart. Even though our outer nature is wasting away, our inner nature is being renewed day by day. 17 For this slight momentary affliction is preparing us for an eternal weight of glory beyond all measure, 18 because we look not at what can be seen but at what cannot be seen; for what can be seen is temporary, but what cannot be seen is eternal.

5 For we know that if the earthly tent we live in is destroyed, we have a building from God, a house not made with hands, eternal in the heavens. 2 For in this tent we groan, longing to be clothed with our heavenly dwelling— 3 if indeed, when we have taken it off*a* we will not be found naked. 4 For while we are still in this tent, we groan under our burden, because we wish not to be unclothed but to be further clothed, so that what is mortal may be swallowed up by life. 5 He who has prepared us for this very thing is God, who has given us the Spirit as a guarantee.

6 So we are always confident; even though we know that while we are at home in the body we are away from the Lord— 7 for we walk by faith, not by sight. 8 Yes, we do have confidence, and we would rather be away from the body and at home with the Lord. 9 So whether we are at home or away, we make it our aim to please him. 10 For all of us must appear before the judgement seat of Christ, so that each may receive recompense for what has been done in the body, whether good or evil.

a Other ancient authorities read *put it on*

The Ministry of Reconciliation

11 Therefore, knowing the fear of the Lord, we try to persuade others; but we ourselves are well known to God, and I hope that we are also well known to your consciences. 12 We are not commending ourselves to you again, but giving you an opportunity to boast about us, so that you may be able to answer those who boast in outward appearance and not in the heart. 13 For if we are beside ourselves, it is for God; if we are in our right mind, it is for you. 14 For the love of Christ urges us on, because we are convinced that one has died for all; therefore all have died. 15 And he died for all, so that those who live might live no longer for themselves, but for him who died and was raised for them.

16 From now on, therefore, we regard no one from a human point of view;[a] even though we once knew Christ from a human point of view,[a] we know him no longer in that way. 17 So if anyone is in Christ, there is a new creation: everything old has passed away; see, everything has become new! 18 All this is from God, who reconciled us to himself through Christ, and has given us the ministry of reconciliation; 19 that is, in Christ God was reconciling the world to himself,[b] not counting their trespasses against them, and entrusting the message of reconciliation to us. 20 So we are ambassadors for Christ, since God is making his appeal through us; we entreat you on behalf of Christ, be reconciled to God. 21 For our sake he made him to be sin who knew no sin, so that in him we might become the righteousness of God.

6 As we work together with him,[c] we urge you also not to accept the grace of God in vain. 2 For he says,

'At an acceptable time I have listened
    to you,
  and on a day of salvation I have
    helped you.'

See, now is the acceptable time; see, now is the day of salvation! 3 We are putting no obstacle in anyone's way, so that no fault may be found with our ministry, 4 but as servants of God we have commended ourselves in every way: through great endurance, in afflictions, hardships, calamities, 5 beatings, imprisonments, riots, labours, sleepless nights, hunger; 6 by purity, knowledge, patience, kindness, holiness of spirit, genuine love, 7 truthful speech, and the power of God; with the weapons of righteousness for the right hand and for the left; 8 in honour and dishonour, in ill repute and good repute. We are treated as impostors, and yet are true; 9 as unknown, and yet are well known; as dying, and see—we are alive; as punished, and yet not killed; 10 as sorrowful, yet always rejoicing; as poor, yet making many rich; as having nothing, and yet possessing everything.

11 We have spoken frankly to you Corinthians; our heart is wide open to you. 12 There is no restriction in our affections, but only in yours. 13 In return—I speak as to children—open wide your hearts also.

The Temple of the Living God

14 Do not be mismatched with unbelievers. For what partnership is there between righteousness and lawlessness? Or what fellowship is there between light and darkness? 15 What agreement does Christ have with Beliar? Or what does a believer share with an unbeliever? 16 What agreement has the temple of God with idols? For we[d] are the temple of the living God; as God said,

'I will live in them and walk among
    them,
  and I will be their God,
  and they shall be my people.
17 Therefore come out from them,
    and be separate from them, says
    the Lord,
  and touch nothing unclean;
    then I will welcome you,
18 and I will be your father,
    and you shall be my sons and
      daughters,
  says the Lord Almighty.'

7 Since we have these promises, beloved, let us cleanse ourselves from every defilement of body and of spirit, making holiness perfect in the fear of God.

---

a Gk according to the flesh   b Or God was in Christ reconciling the world to himself   c Gk As we work together   d Other ancient authorities read you

Paul's Joy at the Church's Repentance

2 Make room in your hearts*a* for us; we have wronged no one, we have corrupted no one, we have taken advantage of no one. ³I do not say this to condemn you, for I said before that you are in our hearts, to die together and to live together. ⁴I often boast about you; I have great pride in you; I am filled with consolation; I am overjoyed in all our affliction.

5 For even when we came into Macedonia, our bodies had no rest, but we were afflicted in every way—disputes without and fears within. ⁶But God, who consoles the downcast, consoled us by the arrival of Titus, ⁷and not only by his coming, but also by the consolation with which he was consoled about you, as he told us of your longing, your mourning, your zeal for me, so that I rejoiced still more. ⁸For even if I made you sorry with my letter, I do not regret it (though I did regret it, for I see that I grieved you with that letter, though only briefly). ⁹Now I rejoice, not because you were grieved, but because your grief led to repentance; for you felt a godly grief, so that you were not harmed in any way by us. ¹⁰For godly grief produces a repentance that leads to salvation and brings no regret, but worldly grief produces death. ¹¹For see what earnestness this godly grief has produced in you, what eagerness to clear yourselves, what indignation, what alarm, what longing, what zeal, what punishment! At every point you have proved yourselves guiltless in the matter. ¹²So although I wrote to you, it was not on account of the one who did the wrong, nor on account of the one who was wronged, but in order that your zeal for us might be made known to you before God. ¹³In this we find comfort.

In addition to our own consolation, we rejoiced still more at the joy of Titus, because his mind has been set at rest by all of you. ¹⁴For if I have been somewhat boastful about you to him, I was not disgraced; but just as everything we said to you was true, so our boasting to Titus has proved true as well. ¹⁵And his heart goes out all the more to you, as he remembers

the obedience of all of you, and how you welcomed him with fear and trembling. ¹⁶I rejoice, because I have complete confidence in you.

Encouragement to Be Generous

8 We want you to know, brothers and sisters,*b* about the grace of God that has been granted to the churches of Macedonia; ²for during a severe ordeal of affliction, their abundant joy and their extreme poverty have overflowed in a wealth of generosity on their part. ³For, as I can testify, they voluntarily gave according to their means, and even beyond their means, ⁴begging us earnestly for the privilege*c* of sharing in this ministry to the saints— ⁵and this, not merely as we expected; they gave themselves first to the Lord and, by the will of God, to us, ⁶so that we might urge Titus that, as he had already made a beginning, so he should also complete this generous undertaking*d* among you. ⁷Now as you excel in everything—in faith, in speech, in knowledge, in utmost eagerness, and in our love for you*e*—so we want you to excel also in this generous undertaking.*d*

8 I do not say this as a command, but I am testing the genuineness of your love against the earnestness of others. ⁹For you know the generous act*f* of our Lord Jesus Christ, that though he was rich, yet for your sakes he became poor, so that by his poverty you might become rich. ¹⁰And in this matter I am giving my advice: it is appropriate for you who began last year not only to do something but even to desire to do something— ¹¹now finish doing it, so that your eagerness may be matched by completing it according to your means. ¹²For if the eagerness is there, the gift is acceptable according to what one has—not according to what one does not have. ¹³I do not mean that there should be relief for others and pressure on you, but it is a question of a fair balance between ¹⁴your present abundance and their need, so that their abundance may be for your need, in

a Gk lacks *in your hearts*   *b* Gk *brothers*   *c* Gk *grace*
d Gk *this grace*   *e* Other ancient authorities read *your love for us*   *f* Gk *the grace*

order that there may be a fair balance. 15 As it is written,

> 'The one who had much did not have
>   too much,
> and the one who had little did not
>   have too little.'

Commendation of Titus

16 But thanks be to God who put in the heart of Titus the same eagerness for you that I myself have. 17 For he not only accepted our appeal, but since he is more eager than ever, he is going to you of his own accord. 18 With him we are sending the brother who is famous among all the churches for his proclaiming of the good news; [a] 19 and not only that, but he has also been appointed by the churches to travel with us while we are administering this generous undertaking [b] for the glory of the Lord himself [c] and to show our goodwill. 20 We intend that no one should blame us about this generous gift that we are administering, 21 for we intend to do what is right not only in the Lord's sight but also in the sight of others. 22 And with them we are sending our brother whom we have often tested and found eager in many matters, but who is now more eager than ever because of his great confidence in you. 23 As for Titus, he is my partner and co-worker in your service; as for our brothers, they are messengers [d] of the churches, the glory of Christ. 24 Therefore, openly before the churches, show them the proof of your love and of our reason for boasting about you.

The Collection for Christians at Jerusalem

9 Now it is not necessary for me to write to you about the ministry to the saints, 2 for I know your eagerness, which is the subject of my boasting about you to the people of Macedonia, saying that Achaia has been ready since last year; and your zeal has stirred up most of them. 3 But I am sending the brothers in order that our boasting about you may not prove to have been empty in this case, so that you may be ready, as I said you would be; 4 otherwise, if some Macedonians come with me

and find that you are not ready, we would be humiliated—to say nothing of you—in this undertaking. [e] 5 So I thought it necessary to urge the brothers to go on ahead to you, and arrange in advance for this bountiful gift that you have promised, so that it may be ready as a voluntary gift and not as an extortion.

6 The point is this: the one who sows sparingly will also reap sparingly, and the one who sows bountifully will also reap bountifully. 7 Each of you must give as you have made up your mind, not reluctantly or under compulsion, for God loves a cheerful giver. 8 And God is able to provide you with every blessing in abundance, so that by always having enough of everything, you may share abundantly in every good work. 9 As it is written,

> 'He scatters abroad, he gives to
>   the poor;
> his righteousness [f] endures for ever.'

10 He who supplies seed to the sower and bread for food will supply and multiply your seed for sowing and increase the harvest of your righteousness. [f] 11 You will be enriched in every way for your great generosity, which will produce thanksgiving to God through us; 12 for the rendering of this ministry not only supplies the needs of the saints but also overflows with many thanksgivings to God. 13 Through the testing of this ministry you glorify God by your obedience to the confession of the gospel of Christ and by the generosity of your sharing with them and with all others, 14 while they long for you and pray for you because of the surpassing grace of God that he has given you. 15 Thanks be to God for his indescribable gift!

Paul Defends His Ministry

10 I myself, Paul, appeal to you by the meekness and gentleness of Christ—I who am humble when face to face with you, but bold towards you when I am away!— 2 I ask that when I am present I need not show boldness by daring

a Or the gospel   b Gk this grace   c Other ancient authorities lack himself   d Gk apostles   e Other ancient authorities add of boasting   f Or benevolence to oppose those who think we are acting according to human standards. *a* ³Indeed, we live as human beings, *b* but we do not wage war according to human standards; *a* ⁴for the weapons of our warfare are not merely human, *c* but they have divine power to destroy strongholds. We destroy arguments ⁵and every proud obstacle raised up against the knowledge of God, and we take every thought captive to obey Christ. ⁶We are ready to punish every disobedience when your obedience is complete.

7 Look at what is before your eyes. If you are confident that you belong to Christ, remind yourself of this, that just as you belong to Christ, so also do we. ⁸Now, even if I boast a little too much of our authority, which the Lord gave for building you up and not for tearing you down, I will not be ashamed of it. ⁹I do not want to seem as though I am trying to frighten you with my letters. ¹⁰For they say, 'His letters are weighty and strong, but his bodily presence is weak, and his speech contemptible.' ¹¹Let such people understand that what we say by letter when absent, we will also do when present.

12 We do not dare to classify or compare ourselves with some of those who commend themselves. But when they measure themselves by one another, and compare themselves with one another, they do not show good sense. ¹³We, however, will not boast beyond limits, but will keep within the field that God has assigned to us, to reach out even as far as you. ¹⁴For we were not overstepping our limits when we reached you; we were the first to come all the way to you with the good news *d* of Christ. ¹⁵We do not boast beyond limits, that is, in the labours of others; but our hope is that, as your faith increases, our sphere of action among you may be greatly enlarged, ¹⁶so that we may proclaim the good news *d* in lands beyond you, without boasting of work already done in someone else's sphere of action. ¹⁷'Let the one who boasts, boast in the Lord.' ¹⁸For it is not those who commend themselves that are approved, but those whom the Lord commends.

Paul and the False Apostles

11 I wish you would bear with me in a little foolishness. Do bear with me! ²I feel a divine jealousy for you, for I promised you in marriage to one husband, to present you as a chaste virgin to Christ. ³But I am afraid that as the serpent deceived Eve by its cunning, your thoughts will be led astray from a sincere and pure *e* devotion to Christ. ⁴For if someone comes and proclaims another Jesus than the one we proclaimed, or if you receive a different spirit from the one you received, or a different gospel from the one you accepted, you submit to it readily enough. ⁵I think that I am not in the least inferior to these super-apostles. ⁶I may be untrained in speech, but not in knowledge; certainly in every way and in all things we have made this evident to you.

7 Did I commit a sin by humbling myself so that you might be exalted, because I proclaimed God's good news *f* to you free of charge? ⁸I robbed other churches by accepting support from them in order to serve you. ⁹And when I was with you and was in need, I did not burden anyone, for my needs were supplied by the friends *g* who came from Macedonia. So I refrained and will continue to refrain from burdening you in any way. ¹⁰As the truth of Christ is in me, this boast of mine will not be silenced in the regions of Achaia. ¹¹And why? Because I do not love you? God knows I do!

12 And what I do I will also continue to do, in order to deny an opportunity to those who want an opportunity to be recognized as our equals in what they boast about. ¹³For such boasters are false apostles, deceitful workers, disguising themselves as apostles of Christ. ¹⁴And no wonder! Even Satan disguises himself as an angel of light. ¹⁵So it is not strange if his ministers also disguise themselves as ministers of righteousness. Their end will match their deeds.

a Gk *according to the flesh*　*b* Gk *in the flesh*
c Gk *fleshly*　*d* Or *the gospel*　*e* Other ancient authorities lack *and pure*　*f* Gk *the gospel of God*
g Gk *brothers*

Paul's Sufferings as an Apostle

16 I repeat, let no one think that I am a fool; but if you do, then accept me as a fool, so that I too may boast a little. 17 What I am saying in regard to this boastful confidence, I am saying not with the Lord's authority, but as a fool; 18 since many boast according to human standards,[a] I will also boast. 19 For you gladly put up with fools, being wise yourselves! 20 For you put up with it when someone makes slaves of you, or preys upon you, or takes advantage of you, or puts on airs, or gives you a slap in the face. 21 To my shame, I must say, we were too weak for that!

But whatever anyone dares to boast of— I am speaking as a fool—I also dare to boast of that. 22 Are they Hebrews? So am I. Are they Israelites? So am I. Are they descendants of Abraham? So am I. 23 Are they ministers of Christ? I am talking like a madman—I am a better one: with far greater labours, far more imprisonments, with countless floggings, and often near death. 24 Five times I have received from the Jews the forty lashes minus one. 25 Three times I was beaten with rods. Once I received a stoning. Three times I was shipwrecked; for a night and a day I was adrift at sea; 26 on frequent journeys, in danger from rivers, danger from bandits, danger from my own people, danger from Gentiles, danger in the city, danger in the wilderness, danger at sea, danger from false brothers and sisters;[b] 27 in toil and hardship, through many a sleepless night, hungry and thirsty, often without food, cold and naked. 28 And, besides other things, I am under daily pressure because of my anxiety for all the churches. 29 Who is weak, and I am not weak? Who is made to stumble, and I am not indignant?

30 If I must boast, I will boast of the things that show my weakness. 31 The God and Father of the Lord Jesus (blessed be he for ever!) knows that I do not lie. 32 In Damascus, the governor[c] under King Aretas set a guard on the city of Damascus in order to[d] seize me, 33 but I was let down in a basket through a window in the wall,[e] and escaped from his hands.

Paul's Visions and Revelations

12 It is necessary to boast; nothing is to be gained by it, but I will go on to visions and revelations of the Lord. 2 I know a person in Christ who fourteen years ago was caught up to the third heaven—whether in the body or out of the body I do not know; God knows. 3 And I know that such a person—whether in the body or out of the body I do not know; God knows— 4 was caught up into Paradise and heard things that are not to be told, that no mortal is permitted to repeat. 5 On behalf of such a one I will boast, but on my own behalf I will not boast, except of my weaknesses. 6 But if I wish to boast, I will not be a fool, for I will be speaking the truth. But I refrain from it, so that no one may think better of me than what is seen in me or heard from me, 7 even considering the exceptional character of the revelations. Therefore, to keep[f] me from being too elated, a thorn was given to me in the flesh, a messenger of Satan to torment me, to keep me from being too elated.[g] 8 Three times I appealed to the Lord about this, that it would leave me, 9 but he said to me, 'My grace is sufficient for you, for power[h] is made perfect in weakness.' So, I will boast all the more gladly of my weaknesses, so that the power of Christ may dwell in me. 10 Therefore I am content with weaknesses, insults, hardships, persecutions, and calamities for the sake of Christ; for whenever I am weak, then I am strong.

Paul's Concern for the Corinthian Church

11 I have been a fool! You forced me to it. Indeed you should have been the ones commending me, for I am not at all inferior to these super-apostles, even though I am nothing. 12 The signs of a true apostle were performed among you with utmost patience, signs and wonders and mighty works. 13 How have you been worse off

---

a Gk *according to the flesh*   b Gk *brothers*
c Gk *ethnarch*   d Other ancient authorities read *and wanted to*   e Gk *through the wall*   f Other ancient authorities read *To keep*   g Other ancient authorities lack *to keep me from being too elated*   h Other ancient authorities read *my power*

than the other churches, except that I myself did not burden you? Forgive me this wrong!

14 Here I am, ready to come to you this third time. And I will not be a burden, because I do not want what is yours but you; for children ought not to lay up for their parents, but parents for their children. 15 I will most gladly spend and be spent for you. If I love you more, am I to be loved less? 16 Let it be assumed that I did not burden you. Nevertheless (you say) since I was crafty, I took you in by deceit. 17 Did I take advantage of you through any of those whom I sent to you? 18 I urged Titus to go, and sent the brother with him. Titus did not take advantage of you, did he? Did we not conduct ourselves with the same spirit? Did we not take the same steps?

19 Have you been thinking all along that we have been defending ourselves before you? We are speaking in Christ before God. Everything we do, beloved, is for the sake of building you up. 20 For I fear that when I come, I may find you not as I wish, and that you may find me not as you wish; I fear that there may perhaps be quarrelling, jealousy, anger, selfishness, slander, gossip, conceit, and disorder. 21 I fear that when I come again, my God may humble me before you, and that I may have to mourn over many who previously sinned and have not repented of the impurity, sexual immorality, and licentiousness that they have practised.

Further Warning

13 This is the third time I am coming to you. 'Any charge must be sustained by the evidence of two or three witnesses.' 2 I warned those who sinned previously and all the others, and I warn them now while absent, as I did when present on my second visit, that if I come again, I will not be lenient— 3 since you desire proof that Christ is speaking in me. He is not weak in dealing with you, but is powerful in you. 4 For he was crucified in weakness, but lives by the power of God. For we are weak in him,[a] but in dealing with you we will live with him by the power of God.

5 Examine yourselves to see whether you are living in the faith. Test yourselves. Do you not realize that Jesus Christ is in you?—unless, indeed, you fail to pass the test! 6 I hope you will find out that we have not failed. 7 But we pray to God that you may not do anything wrong—not that we may appear to have passed the test, but that you may do what is right, though we may seem to have failed. 8 For we cannot do anything against the truth, but only for the truth. 9 For we rejoice when we are weak and you are strong. This is what we pray for, that you may become perfect. 10 So I write these things while I am away from you, so that when I come, I may not have to be severe in using the authority that the Lord has given me for building up and not for tearing down.

Final Greetings and Benediction

11 Finally, brothers and sisters,[b] farewell.[c] Put things in order, listen to my appeal,[d] agree with one another, live in peace; and the God of love and peace will be with you. 12 Greet one another with a holy kiss. All the saints greet you.

13 The grace of the Lord Jesus Christ, the love of God, and the communion of[e] the Holy Spirit be with all of you.

a Other ancient authorities read *with him*
b Gk *brothers*   c Or *rejoice*   d Or *encourage one another*   e Or *and the sharing in*

THE LETTER OF PAUL TO THE
GALATIANS

Salutation

1 Paul an apostle—sent neither by human commission nor from human authorities, but through Jesus Christ and God the Father, who raised him from the dead— [2] and all the members of God's family[a] who are with me,

To the churches of Galatia:

3 Grace to you and peace from God our Father and the Lord Jesus Christ, [4] who gave himself for our sins to set us free from the present evil age, according to the will of our God and Father, [5] to whom be the glory for ever and ever. Amen.

There Is No Other Gospel

6 I am astonished that you are so quickly deserting the one who called you in the grace of Christ and are turning to a different gospel— [7] not that there is another gospel, but there are some who are confusing you and want to pervert the gospel of Christ. [8] But even if we or an angel[b] from heaven should proclaim to you a gospel contrary to what we proclaimed to you, let that one be accursed! [9] As we have said before, so now I repeat, if anyone proclaims to you a gospel contrary to what you received, let that one be accursed!

10 Am I now seeking human approval, or God's approval? Or am I trying to please people? If I were still pleasing people, I would not be a servant[c] of Christ.

Paul's Vindication of His Apostleship

11 For I want you to know, brothers and sisters,[d] that the gospel that was proclaimed by me is not of human origin; [12] for I did not receive it from a human source, nor was I taught it, but I received it through a revelation of Jesus Christ.

13 You have heard, no doubt, of my earlier life in Judaism. I was violently persecuting the church of God and was trying to destroy it. [14] I advanced in Judaism beyond many among my people of the same age, for I was far more zealous for the traditions of my ancestors. [15] But when God, who had set me apart before I was born and called me through his grace, was pleased [16] to reveal his Son to me,[e] so that I might proclaim him among the Gentiles, I did not confer with any human being, [17] nor did I go up to Jerusalem to those who were already apostles before me, but I went away at once into Arabia, and afterwards I returned to Damascus.

18 Then after three years I did go up to Jerusalem to visit Cephas and stayed with him for fifteen days; [19] but I did not see any other apostle except James the Lord's brother. [20] In what I am writing to you, before God, I do not lie! [21] Then I went into the regions of Syria and Cilicia, [22] and I was still unknown by sight to the churches of Judea that are in Christ; [23] they only heard it said, 'The one who formerly was persecuting us is now proclaiming the faith he once tried to destroy.' [24] And they glorified God because of me.

Paul and the Other Apostles

2 Then after fourteen years I went up again to Jerusalem with Barnabas, taking Titus along with me. [2] I went up in response to a revelation. Then I laid before them (though only in a private meeting

---

a Gk all the brothers   b Or a messenger   c Gk slave
d Gk brothers   e Gk in me

with the acknowledged leaders) the gospel that I proclaim among the Gentiles, in order to make sure that I was not running, or had not run, in vain. 3 But even Titus, who was with me, was not compelled to be circumcised, though he was a Greek. 4 But because of false believers[a] secretly brought in, who slipped in to spy on the freedom we have in Christ Jesus, so that they might enslave us— 5 we did not submit to them even for a moment, so that the truth of the gospel might always remain with you. 6 And from those who were supposed to be acknowledged leaders (what they actually were makes no difference to me; God shows no partiality)—those leaders contributed nothing to me. 7 On the contrary, when they saw that I had been entrusted with the gospel for the uncircumcised, just as Peter had been entrusted with the gospel for the circumcised 8 (for he who worked through Peter making him an apostle to the circumcised also worked through me in sending me to the Gentiles), 9 and when James and Cephas and John, who were acknowledged pillars, recognized the grace that had been given to me, they gave to Barnabas and me the right hand of fellowship, agreeing that we should go to the Gentiles and they to the circumcised. 10 They asked only one thing, that we remember the poor, which was actually what I was[b] eager to do.

Paul Rebukes Peter at Antioch

11 But when Cephas came to Antioch, I opposed him to his face, because he stood self-condemned; 12 for until certain people came from James, he used to eat with the Gentiles. But after they came, he drew back and kept himself separate for fear of the circumcision faction. 13 And the other Jews joined him in this hypocrisy, so that even Barnabas was led astray by their hypocrisy. 14 But when I saw that they were not acting consistently with the truth of the gospel, I said to Cephas before them all, 'If you, though a Jew, live like a Gentile and not like a Jew, how can you compel the Gentiles to live like Jews?'[c]

Jews and Gentiles Are Saved by Faith

15 We ourselves are Jews by birth and not Gentile sinners; 16 yet we know that a person is justified[d] not by the works of the law but through faith in Jesus Christ.[e] And we have come to believe in Christ Jesus, so that we might be justified by faith in Christ,[f] and not by doing the works of the law, because no one will be justified by the works of the law. 17 But if, in our effort to be justified in Christ, we ourselves have been found to be sinners, is Christ then a servant of sin? Certainly not! 18 But if I build up again the very things that I once tore down, then I demonstrate that I am a transgressor. 19 For through the law I died to the law, so that I might live to God. I have been crucified with Christ; 20 and it is no longer I who live, but it is Christ who lives in me. And the life I now live in the flesh I live by faith in the Son of God,[g] who loved me and gave himself for me. 21 I do not nullify the grace of God; for if justification[h] comes through the law, then Christ died for nothing.

Law or Faith

3 You foolish Galatians! Who has bewitched you? It was before your eyes that Jesus Christ was publicly exhibited as crucified! 2 The only thing I want to learn from you is this: Did you receive the Spirit by doing the works of the law or by believing what you heard? 3 Are you so foolish? Having started with the Spirit, are you now ending with the flesh? 4 Did you experience so much for nothing?—if it really was for nothing. 5 Well then, does God[i] supply you with the Spirit and work miracles among you by your doing the works of the law, or by your believing what you heard?

6 Just as Abraham 'believed God, and it was reckoned to him as righteousness', 7 so, you see, those who believe are the descendants of Abraham. 8 And the scripture,

---

a Gk *false brothers*　　*b* Or *had been*　　*c* Some interpreters hold that the quotation extends into the following paragraph　　*d* Or *reckoned as righteous;* and so elsewhere　　*e* Or *the faith of Jesus Christ*　　*f* Or *the faith of Christ*　　*g* Or *by the faith of the Son of God*　　*h* Or *righteousness*　　*i* Gk *he* foreseeing that God would justify the Gentiles by faith, declared the gospel beforehand to Abraham, saying, 'All the Gentiles shall be blessed in you.' 9 For this reason, those who believe are blessed with Abraham who believed.

10 For all who rely on the works of the law are under a curse; for it is written, 'Cursed is everyone who does not observe and obey all the things written in the book of the law.' 11 Now it is evident that no one is justified before God by the law; for 'The one who is righteous will live by faith.' *a* 12 But the law does not rest on faith; on the contrary, 'Whoever does the works of the law *b* will live by them.' 13 Christ redeemed us from the curse of the law by becoming a curse for us—for it is written, 'Cursed is everyone who hangs on a tree'— 14 in order that in Christ Jesus the blessing of Abraham might come to the Gentiles, so that we might receive the promise of the Spirit through faith.

The Promise to Abraham

15 Brothers and sisters, *c* I give an example from daily life: once a person's will *d* has been ratified, no one adds to it or annuls it. 16 Now the promises were made to Abraham and to his offspring; *e* it does not say, 'And to offsprings', *f* as of many; but it says, 'And to your offspring', *e* that is, to one person, who is Christ. 17 My point is this: the law, which came four hundred and thirty years later, does not annul a covenant previously ratified by God, so as to nullify the promise. 18 For if the inheritance comes from the law, it no longer comes from the promise; but God granted it to Abraham through the promise.

The Purpose of the Law

19 Why then the law? It was added because of transgressions, until the offspring *e* would come to whom the promise had been made; and it was ordained through angels by a mediator. 20 Now a mediator involves more than one party; but God is one.

21 Is the law then opposed to the promises of God? Certainly not! For if a law had

been given that could make alive, then righteousness would indeed come through the law. 22 But the scripture has imprisoned all things under the power of sin, so that what was promised through faith in Jesus Christ *g* might be given to those who believe.

23 Now before faith came, we were imprisoned and guarded under the law until faith would be revealed. 24 Therefore the law was our disciplinarian until Christ came, so that we might be justified by faith. 25 But now that faith has come, we are no longer subject to a disciplinarian, 26 for in Christ Jesus you are all children of God through faith. 27 As many of you as were baptized into Christ have clothed yourselves with Christ. 28 There is no longer Jew or Greek, there is no longer slave or free, there is no longer male and female; for all of you are one in Christ Jesus. 29 And if you belong to Christ, then you are Abraham's offspring, *e* heirs according to the promise.

4 My point is this: heirs, as long as they are minors, are no better than slaves, though they are the owners of all the property; 2 but they remain under guardians and trustees until the date set by the father. 3 So with us; while we were minors, we were enslaved to the elemental spirits *h* of the world. 4 But when the fullness of time had come, God sent his Son, born of a woman, born under the law, 5 in order to redeem those who were under the law, so that we might receive adoption as children. 6 And because you are children, God has sent the Spirit of his Son into our *i* hearts, crying, 'Abba! *j* Father!' 7 So you are no longer a slave but a child, and if a child then also an heir, through God. *k*

Paul Reproves the Galatians

8 Formerly, when you did not know God, you were enslaved to beings that by nature are not gods. 9 Now, however, that

a Or The one who is righteous through faith will live
b Gk does them   *c* Gk Brothers   *d* Or covenant (as in verse 17)   *e* Gk seed   *f* Gk seeds   *g* Or through the faith of Jesus Christ   *h* Or the rudiments   *i* Other ancient authorities read your   *j* Aramaic for Father
k Other ancient authorities read an heir of God through Christ

you have come to know God, or rather to be known by God, how can you turn back again to the weak and beggarly elemental spirits?[a] How can you want to be enslaved to them again? [10] You are observing special days, and months, and seasons, and years. [11] I am afraid that my work for you may have been wasted.

12 Friends,[b] I beg you, become as I am, for I also have become as you are. You have done me no wrong. [13] You know that it was because of a physical infirmity that I first announced the gospel to you; [14] though my condition put you to the test, you did not scorn or despise me, but welcomed me as an angel of God, as Christ Jesus. [15] What has become of the goodwill you felt? For I testify that, had it been possible, you would have torn out your eyes and given them to me. [16] Have I now become your enemy by telling you the truth? [17] They make much of you, but for no good purpose; they want to exclude you, so that you may make much of them. [18] It is good to be made much of for a good purpose at all times, and not only when I am present with you. [19] My little children, for whom I am again in the pain of childbirth until Christ is formed in you, [20] I wish I were present with you now and could change my tone, for I am perplexed about you.

The Allegory of Hagar and Sarah

21 Tell me, you who desire to be subject to the law, will you not listen to the law? [22] For it is written that Abraham had two sons, one by a slave woman and the other by a free woman. [23] One, the child of the slave, was born according to the flesh; the other, the child of the free woman, was born through the promise. [24] Now this is an allegory: these women are two covenants. One woman, in fact, is Hagar, from Mount Sinai, bearing children for slavery. [25] Now Hagar is Mount Sinai in Arabia[c] and corresponds to the present Jerusalem, for she is in slavery with her children. [26] But the other woman corresponds to the Jerusalem above; she is free, and she is our mother. [27] For it is written,

'Rejoice, you childless one, you who
    bear no children,
  burst into song and shout, you who
    endure no birth pangs;
for the children of the desolate
    woman are more numerous
  than the children of the one who is
    married.'

[28] Now you,[d] my friends,[e] are children of the promise, like Isaac. [29] But just as at that time the child who was born according to the flesh persecuted the child who was born according to the Spirit, so it is now also. [30] But what does the scripture say? 'Drive out the slave and her child; for the child of the slave will not share the inheritance with the child of the free woman.' [31] So then, friends,[e] we are children, not of the slave but of the free woman. [5] [1] For freedom Christ has set us free. Stand firm, therefore, and do not submit again to a yoke of slavery.

The Nature of Christian Freedom

2 Listen! I, Paul, am telling you that if you let yourselves be circumcised, Christ will be of no benefit to you. [3] Once again I testify to every man who lets himself be circumcised that he is obliged to obey the entire law. [4] You who want to be justified by the law have cut yourselves off from Christ; you have fallen away from grace. [5] For through the Spirit, by faith, we eagerly wait for the hope of righteousness. [6] For in Christ Jesus neither circumcision nor uncircumcision counts for anything; the only thing that counts is faith working[f] through love.

7 You were running well; who prevented you from obeying the truth? [8] Such persuasion does not come from the one who calls you. [9] A little yeast leavens the whole batch of dough. [10] I am confident about you in the Lord that you will not think otherwise. But whoever it is that is confusing you will pay the penalty. [11] But my friends,[e] why am I still being persecuted if I am still preaching circumcision? In that

a Or beggarly rudiments   b Gk Brothers   c Other ancient authorities read For Sinai is a mountain in Arabia   d Other ancient authorities read we   e Gk brothers   f Or made effective case the offence of the cross has been removed. 12 I wish those who unsettle you would castrate themselves!

13 For you were called to freedom, brothers and sisters; *a* only do not use your freedom as an opportunity for self-indulgence, *b* but through love become slaves to one another. 14 For the whole law is summed up in a single commandment, 'You shall love your neighbour as yourself.' 15 If, however, you bite and devour one another, take care that you are not consumed by one another.

The Works of the Flesh

16 Live by the Spirit, I say, and do not gratify the desires of the flesh. 17 For what the flesh desires is opposed to the Spirit, and what the Spirit desires is opposed to the flesh; for these are opposed to each other, to prevent you from doing what you want. 18 But if you are led by the Spirit, you are not subject to the law. 19 Now the works of the flesh are obvious: fornication, impurity, licentiousness, 20 idolatry, sorcery, enmities, strife, jealousy, anger, quarrels, dissensions, factions, 21 envy, *c* drunkenness, carousing, and things like these. I am warning you, as I warned you before: those who do such things will not inherit the kingdom of God.

The Fruit of the Spirit

22 By contrast, the fruit of the Spirit is love, joy, peace, patience, kindness, generosity, faithfulness, 23 gentleness, and self-control. There is no law against such things. 24 And those who belong to Christ Jesus have crucified the flesh with its passions and desires. 25 If we live by the Spirit, let us also be guided by the Spirit. 26 Let us not become conceited, competing against one another, envying one another.

Bear One Another's Burdens

6 My friends, *d* if anyone is detected in a transgression, you who have received the Spirit should restore such a one in a spirit of gentleness. Take care that you yourselves are not tempted. 2 Bear one an-

other's burdens, and in this way you will fulfil *e* the law of Christ. 3 For if those who are nothing think they are something, they deceive themselves. 4 All must test their own work; then that work, rather than their neighbour's work, will become a cause for pride. 5 For all must carry their own loads.

6 Those who are taught the word must share in all good things with their teacher.

7 Do not be deceived; God is not mocked, for you reap whatever you sow. 8 If you sow to your own flesh, you will reap corruption from the flesh; but if you sow to the Spirit, you will reap eternal life from the Spirit. 9 So let us not grow weary in doing what is right, for we will reap at harvest time, if we do not give up. 10 So then, whenever we have an opportunity, let us work for the good of all, and especially for those of the family of faith.

Final Admonitions and Benediction

11 See what large letters I make when I am writing in my own hand! 12 It is those who want to make a good showing in the flesh that try to compel you to be circumcised—only that they may not be persecuted for the cross of Christ. 13 Even the circumcised do not themselves obey the law, but they want you to be circumcised so that they may boast about your flesh. 14 May I never boast of anything except the cross of our Lord Jesus Christ, by which *f* the world has been crucified to me, and I to the world. 15 For *g* neither circumcision nor uncircumcision is anything; but a new creation is everything! 16 As for those who will follow this rule—peace be upon them, and mercy, and upon the Israel of God.

17 From now on, let no one make trouble for me; for I carry the marks of Jesus branded on my body.

18 May the grace of our Lord Jesus Christ be with your spirit, brothers and sisters. *a* Amen.

a Gk *brothers*   *b* Gk *the flesh*   *c* Other ancient authorities add *murder*   *d* Gk *Brothers*   *e* Other ancient authorities read *in this way fulfil*   *f* Or *through whom*   *g* Other ancient authorities add *in Christ Jesus*

THE LETTER OF PAUL TO THE
EPHESIANS

Salutation

1 Paul, an apostle of Christ Jesus by the will of God,

To the saints who are in Ephesus and are faithful*a* in Christ Jesus:

2 Grace to you and peace from God our Father and the Lord Jesus Christ.

Spiritual Blessings in Christ

3 Blessed be the God and Father of our Lord Jesus Christ, who has blessed us in Christ with every spiritual blessing in the heavenly places, 4 just as he chose us in Christ*b* before the foundation of the world to be holy and blameless before him in love. 5 He destined us for adoption as his children through Jesus Christ, according to the good pleasure of his will, 6 to the praise of his glorious grace that he freely bestowed on us in the Beloved. 7 In him we have redemption through his blood, the forgiveness of our trespasses, according to the riches of his grace 8 that he lavished on us. With all wisdom and insight 9 he has made known to us the mystery of his will, according to his good pleasure that he set forth in Christ, 10 as a plan for the fullness of time, to gather up all things in him, things in heaven and things on earth. 11 In Christ we have also obtained

a Other ancient authorities lack *in Ephesus,* reading *saints who are also faithful*   *b* Gk *in him*

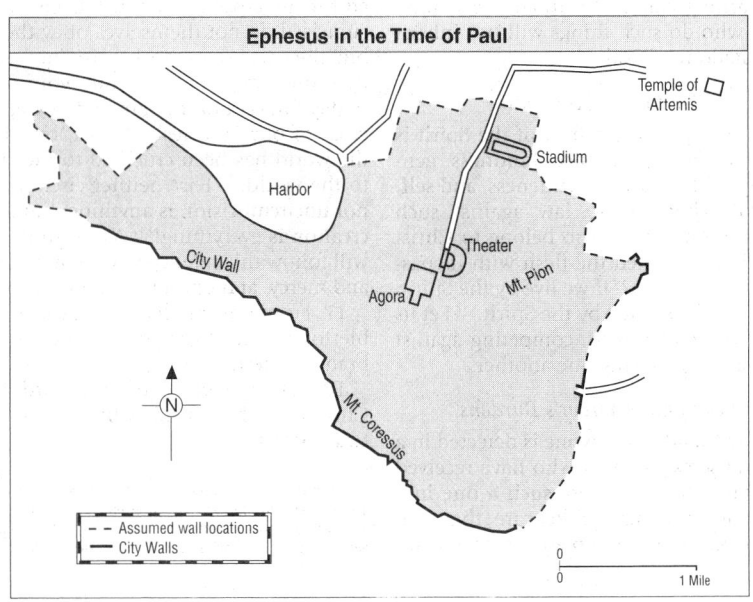

Ephesus in the Time of Paul

Temple of Artemis

Stadium

Harbor

Theater

City Wall

Mt. Pion

Agora

Mt. Coressus

N

- - - Assumed wall locations
—— City Walls

0
0   1 Mile

an inheritance,[a] having been destined according to the purpose of him who accomplishes all things according to his counsel and will, [12] so that we, who were the first to set our hope on Christ, might live for the praise of his glory. [13] In him you also, when you had heard the word of truth, the gospel of your salvation, and had believed in him, were marked with the seal of the promised Holy Spirit; [14] this[b] is the pledge of our inheritance towards redemption as God's own people, to the praise of his glory.

Paul's Prayer

15 I have heard of your faith in the Lord Jesus and your love[c] towards all the saints, and for this reason [16] I do not cease to give thanks for you as I remember you in my prayers. [17] I pray that the God of our Lord Jesus Christ, the Father of glory, may give you a spirit of wisdom and revelation as you come to know him, [18] so that, with the eyes of your heart enlightened, you may know what is the hope to which he has called you, what are the riches of his glorious inheritance among the saints, [19] and what is the immeasurable greatness of his power for us who believe, according to the working of his great power. [20] God[d] put this power to work in Christ when he raised him from the dead and seated him at his right hand in the heavenly places, [21] far above all rule and authority and power and dominion, and above every name that is named, not only in this age but also in the age to come. [22] And he has put all things under his feet and has made him the head over all things for the church, [23] which is his body, the fullness of him who fills all in all.

From Death to Life

2 You were dead through the trespasses and sins [2] in which you once lived, following the course of this world, following the ruler of the power of the air, the spirit that is now at work among those who are disobedient. [3] All of us once lived among them in the passions of our flesh, following the desires of flesh and senses,

and we were by nature children of wrath, like everyone else. [4] But God, who is rich in mercy, out of the great love with which he loved us [5] even when we were dead through our trespasses, made us alive together with Christ[e]—by grace you have been saved— [6] and raised us up with him and seated us with him in the heavenly places in Christ Jesus, [7] so that in the ages to come he might show the immeasurable riches of his grace in kindness towards us in Christ Jesus. [8] For by grace you have been saved through faith, and this is not your own doing; it is the gift of God— [9] not the result of works, so that no one may boast. [10] For we are what he has made us, created in Christ Jesus for good works, which God prepared beforehand to be our way of life.

One in Christ

11 So then, remember that at one time you Gentiles by birth,[f] called 'the uncircumcision' by those who are called 'the circumcision'—a physical circumcision made in the flesh by human hands— [12] remember that you were at that time without Christ, being aliens from the commonwealth of Israel, and strangers to the covenants of promise, having no hope and without God in the world. [13] But now in Christ Jesus you who once were far off have been brought near by the blood of Christ. [14] For he is our peace; in his flesh he has made both groups into one and has broken down the dividing wall, that is, the hostility between us. [15] He has abolished the law with its commandments and ordinances, so that he might create in himself one new humanity in place of the two, thus making peace, [16] and might reconcile both groups to God in one body[g] through the cross, thus putting to death that hostility through it.[h] [17] So he came and proclaimed peace to you who were far off and peace to those who were near; [18] for through him both of us have access in one

a Or been made a heritage   b Other ancient authorities read who   c Other ancient authorities lack and your love   d Gk He   e Other ancient authorities read in Christ   f Gk in the flesh   g Or reconcile both of us in one body for God   h Or in him, or in himself

Spirit to the Father. ¹⁹So then you are no longer strangers and aliens, but you are citizens with the saints and also members of the household of God, ²⁰built upon the foundation of the apostles and prophets, with Christ Jesus himself as the cornerstone.^a ²¹In him the whole structure is joined together and grows into a holy temple in the Lord; ²²in whom you also are built together spiritually^b into a dwelling-place for God.

Paul's Ministry to the Gentiles

3 This is the reason that I Paul am a prisoner for^c Christ Jesus for the sake of you Gentiles— ²for surely you have already heard of the commission of God's grace that was given to me for you, ³and how the mystery was made known to me by revelation, as I wrote above in a few words, ⁴a reading of which will enable you to perceive my understanding of the mystery of Christ. ⁵In former generations this mystery^d was not made known to humankind, as it has now been revealed to his holy apostles and prophets by the Spirit: ⁶that is, the Gentiles have become fellow-heirs, members of the same body, and sharers in the promise in Christ Jesus through the gospel.

7 Of this gospel I have become a servant according to the gift of God's grace that was given to me by the working of his power. ⁸Although I am the very least of all the saints, this grace was given to me to bring to the Gentiles the news of the boundless riches of Christ, ⁹and to make everyone see^e what is the plan of the mystery hidden for ages in^f God who created all things; ¹⁰so that through the church the wisdom of God in its rich variety might now be made known to the rulers and authorities in the heavenly places. ¹¹This was in accordance with the eternal purpose that he has carried out in Christ Jesus our Lord, ¹²in whom we have access to God in boldness and confidence through faith in him.^g ¹³I pray therefore that you^h may not lose heart over my sufferings for you; they are your glory.

Prayer for the Readers

14 For this reason I bow my knees before the Father,ⁱ ¹⁵from whom every family^j in heaven and on earth takes its name. ¹⁶I pray that, according to the riches of his glory, he may grant that you may be strengthened in your inner being with power through his Spirit, ¹⁷and that Christ may dwell in your hearts through faith, as you are being rooted and grounded in love. ¹⁸I pray that you may have the power to comprehend, with all the saints, what is the breadth and length and height and depth, ¹⁹and to know the love of Christ that surpasses knowledge, so that you may be filled with all the fullness of God.

20 Now to him who by the power at work within us is able to accomplish abundantly far more than all we can ask or imagine, ²¹to him be glory in the church and in Christ Jesus to all generations, for ever and ever. Amen.

Unity in the Body of Christ

4 I therefore, the prisoner in the Lord, beg you to lead a life worthy of the calling to which you have been called, ²with all humility and gentleness, with patience, bearing with one another in love, ³making every effort to maintain the unity of the Spirit in the bond of peace. ⁴There is one body and one Spirit, just as you were called to the one hope of your calling, ⁵one Lord, one faith, one baptism, ⁶one God and Father of all, who is above all and through all and in all.

7 But each of us was given grace according to the measure of Christ's gift. ⁸Therefore it is said,

'When he ascended on high he made
captivity itself a captive;
he gave gifts to his people.'

⁹(When it says, 'He ascended', what does it mean but that he had also descended^k into the lower parts of the earth? ¹⁰He who descended is the same one who ascended far

---

^a Or keystone   ^b Gk in the Spirit   ^c Or of   ^d Gk it
^e Other ancient authorities read to bring to light
^f Or by   ^g Or the faith of him   ^h Or I   ⁱ Other
ancient authorities add of our Lord Jesus Christ
^j Gk fatherhood   ^k Other ancient authorities add first

above all the heavens, so that he might fill all things.) [11] The gifts he gave were that some would be apostles, some prophets, some evangelists, some pastors and teachers, [12] to equip the saints for the work of ministry, for building up the body of Christ, [13] until all of us come to the unity of the faith and of the knowledge of the Son of God, to maturity, to the measure of the full stature of Christ. [14] We must no longer be children, tossed to and fro and blown about by every wind of doctrine, by people's trickery, by their craftiness in deceitful scheming. [15] But speaking the truth in love, we must grow up in every way into him who is the head, into Christ, [16] from whom the whole body, joined and knitted together by every ligament with which it is equipped, as each part is working properly, promotes the body's growth in building itself up in love.

The Old Life and the New

17 Now this I affirm and insist on in the Lord: you must no longer live as the Gentiles live, in the futility of their minds. [18] They are darkened in their understanding, alienated from the life of God because of their ignorance and hardness of heart. [19] They have lost all sensitivity and have abandoned themselves to licentiousness, greedy to practise every kind of impurity. [20] That is not the way you learned Christ! [21] For surely you have heard about him and were taught in him, as truth is in Jesus. [22] You were taught to put away your former way of life, your old self, corrupt and deluded by its lusts, [23] and to be renewed in the spirit of your minds, [24] and to clothe yourselves with the new self, created according to the likeness of God in true righteousness and holiness.

Rules for the New Life

25 So then, putting away falsehood, let all of us speak the truth to our neighbours, for we are members of one another. [26] Be angry but do not sin; do not let the sun go down on your anger, [27] and do not make room for the devil. [28] Thieves must give up stealing; rather let them labour and work honestly with their own hands, so as to have something to share with the needy. [29] Let no evil talk come out of your mouths, but only what is useful for building up, [a] as there is need, so that your words may give grace to those who hear. [30] And do not grieve the Holy Spirit of God, with which you were marked with a seal for the day of redemption. [31] Put away from you all bitterness and wrath and anger and wrangling and slander, together with all malice, [32] and be kind to one another, tender-hearted, forgiving one another, as God in Christ has forgiven you. [b]

5 [1] Therefore be imitators of God, as beloved children, [2] and live in love, as Christ loved us [c] and gave himself up for us, a fragrant offering and sacrifice to God.

Renounce Pagan Ways

3 But fornication and impurity of any kind, or greed, must not even be mentioned among you, as is proper among saints. [4] Entirely out of place is obscene, silly, and vulgar talk; but instead, let there be thanksgiving. [5] Be sure of this, that no fornicator or impure person, or one who is greedy (that is, an idolater), has any inheritance in the kingdom of Christ and of God.

6 Let no one deceive you with empty words, for because of these things the wrath of God comes on those who are disobedient. [7] Therefore do not be associated with them. [8] For once you were darkness, but now in the Lord you are light. Live as children of light— [9] for the fruit of the light is found in all that is good and right and true. [10] Try to find out what is pleasing to the Lord. [11] Take no part in the unfruitful works of darkness, but instead expose them. [12] For it is shameful even to mention what such people do secretly; [13] but everything exposed by the light becomes visible, [14] for everything that becomes visible is light. Therefore it says,

'Sleeper, awake!
    Rise from the dead,
    and Christ will shine on you.'

---

a Other ancient authorities read *building up faith*
b Other ancient authorities read *us*   *c* Other ancient authorities read *you*

15 Be careful then how you live, not as unwise people but as wise, ¹⁶ making the most of the time, because the days are evil. ¹⁷ So do not be foolish, but understand what the will of the Lord is. ¹⁸ Do not get drunk with wine, for that is debauchery; but be filled with the Spirit, ¹⁹ as you sing psalms and hymns and spiritual songs among yourselves, singing and making melody to the Lord in your hearts, ²⁰ giving thanks to God the Father at all times and for everything in the name of our Lord Jesus Christ.

The Christian Household

21 Be subject to one another out of reverence for Christ.

22 Wives, be subject to your husbands as you are to the Lord. ²³ For the husband is the head of the wife just as Christ is the head of the church, the body of which he is the Saviour. ²⁴ Just as the church is subject to Christ, so also wives ought to be, in everything, to their husbands.

25 Husbands, love your wives, just as Christ loved the church and gave himself up for her, ²⁶ in order to make her holy by cleansing her with the washing of water by the word, ²⁷ so as to present the church to himself in splendour, without a spot or wrinkle or anything of the kind—yes, so that she may be holy and without blemish. ²⁸ In the same way, husbands should love their wives as they do their own bodies. He who loves his wife loves himself. ²⁹ For no one ever hates his own body, but he nourishes and tenderly cares for it, just as Christ does for the church, ³⁰ because we are members of his body.ᵃ ³¹ 'For this reason a man will leave his father and mother and be joined to his wife, and the two will become one flesh.' ³² This is a great mystery, and I am applying it to Christ and the church. ³³ Each of you, however, should love his wife as himself, and a wife should respect her husband.

Children and Parents

6 Children, obey your parents in the Lord,ᵇ for this is right. ² 'Honour your father and mother'—this is the first commandment with a promise: ³ 'so that it may be well with you and you may live long on the earth.'

4 And, fathers, do not provoke your children to anger, but bring them up in the discipline and instruction of the Lord.

Slaves and Masters

5 Slaves, obey your earthly masters with fear and trembling, in singleness of heart, as you obey Christ; ⁶ not only while being watched, and in order to please them, but as slaves of Christ, doing the will of God from the heart. ⁷ Render service with enthusiasm, as to the Lord and not to men and women, ⁸ knowing that whatever good we do, we will receive the same again from the Lord, whether we are slaves or free.

9 And, masters, do the same to them. Stop threatening them, for you know that both of you have the same Master in heaven, and with him there is no partiality.

The Whole Armour of God

10 Finally, be strong in the Lord and in the strength of his power. ¹¹ Put on the whole armour of God, so that you may be able to stand against the wiles of the devil. ¹² For ourᶜ struggle is not against enemies of blood and flesh, but against the rulers, against the authorities, against the cosmic powers of this present darkness, against the spiritual forces of evil in the heavenly places. ¹³ Therefore take up the whole armour of God, so that you may be able to withstand on that evil day, and having done everything, to stand firm. ¹⁴ Stand therefore, and fasten the belt of truth around your waist, and put on the breastplate of righteousness. ¹⁵ As shoes for your feet put on whatever will make you ready to proclaim the gospel of peace. ¹⁶ With all of these,ᵈ take the shield of faith, with which you will be able to quench all the flaming arrows of the evil one. ¹⁷ Take the helmet of salvation, and the sword of the Spirit, which is the word of God.

---

a Other ancient authorities add *of his flesh and of his bones*   *b* Other ancient authorities lack *in the Lord*   *c* Other ancient authorities read *your*   *d* Or *In all circumstances*

18 Pray in the Spirit at all times in every prayer and supplication. To that end keep alert and always persevere in supplication for all the saints. 19 Pray also for me, so that when I speak, a message may be given to me to make known with boldness the mystery of the gospel, *a* 20 for which I am an ambassador in chains. Pray that I may declare it boldly, as I must speak.

Personal Matters and Benediction

21 So that you also may know how I am and what I am doing, Tychicus will tell you everything. He is a dear brother and a faithful minister in the Lord. 22 I am sending him to you for this very purpose, to let you know how we are, and to encourage your hearts.

23 Peace be to the whole community, *b* and love with faith, from God the Father and the Lord Jesus Christ. 24 Grace be with all who have an undying love for our Lord Jesus Christ. *c*

a Other ancient authorities lack *of the gospel*   *b* Gk *to the brothers*   *c* Other ancient authorities add *Amen*

THE LETTER OF PAUL TO THE
PHILIPPIANS

Salutation

1 Paul and Timothy, servants*a* of Christ Jesus,

To all the saints in Christ Jesus who are in Philippi, with the bishops*b* and deacons:*c*

2 Grace to you and peace from God our Father and the Lord Jesus Christ.

Paul's Prayer for the Philippians

3 I thank my God every time I remember you, 4 constantly praying with joy in every one of my prayers for all of you, 5 because of your sharing in the gospel from the first day until now. 6 I am confident of this, that the one who began a good work among you will bring it to completion by the day of Jesus Christ. 7 It is right for me to think this way about all of you, because you hold me in your heart,*d* for all of you share in God's grace*e* with me, both in my imprisonment and in the defence and confirmation of the gospel. 8 For God is my witness, how I long for all of you with the compassion of Christ Jesus. 9 And this is my prayer, that your love may overflow more and more with knowledge and full insight 10 to help you to determine what is best, so that on the day of Christ you may be pure and blameless, 11 having produced the harvest of righteousness that comes through Jesus Christ for the glory and praise of God.

Paul's Present Circumstances

12 I want you to know, beloved,*f* that what has happened to me has actually helped to spread the gospel, 13 so that it has become known throughout the whole imperial guard*g* and to everyone else that my imprisonment is for Christ; 14 and most of the brothers and sisters,*f* having been made confident in the Lord by my imprisonment, dare to speak the word*h* with greater boldness and without fear.

15 Some proclaim Christ from envy and rivalry, but others from goodwill. 16 These proclaim Christ out of love, knowing that I have been put here for the defence of the gospel; 17 the others proclaim Christ out of selfish ambition, not sincerely but intending to increase my suffering in my imprisonment. 18 What does it matter? Just this, that Christ is proclaimed in every way, whether out of false motives or true; and in that I rejoice.

Yes, and I will continue to rejoice, 19 for I know that through your prayers and the help of the Spirit of Jesus Christ this will result in my deliverance. 20 It is my eager expectation and hope that I will not be put to shame in any way, but that by my speaking with all boldness, Christ will be exalted now as always in my body, whether by life or by death. 21 For to me, living is Christ and dying is gain. 22 If I am to live in the flesh, that means fruitful labour for me; and I do not know which I prefer. 23 I am hard pressed between the two: my desire is to depart and be with Christ, for that is far better; 24 but to remain in the flesh is more necessary for you. 25 Since I am convinced of this, I know that I will remain and continue with all of you for your progress and joy in faith, 26 so that I may

a Gk *slaves*   *b* Or *overseers*   *c* Or *overseers and helpers*
d Or *because I hold you in my heart*   *e* Gk *in grace*
f Gk *brothers*   *g* Gk *whole praetorium*   *h* Other ancient authorities read *word of God*

share abundantly in your boasting in Christ Jesus when I come to you again.

27 Only, live your life in a manner worthy of the gospel of Christ, so that, whether I come and see you or am absent and hear about you, I will know that you are standing firm in one spirit, striving side by side with one mind for the faith of the gospel, 28 and are in no way intimidated by your opponents. For them this is evidence of their destruction, but of your salvation. And this is God's doing. 29 For he has graciously granted you the privilege not only of believing in Christ, but of suffering for him as well— 30 since you are having the same struggle that you saw I had and now hear that I still have.

Imitating Christ's Humility

2 If then there is any encouragement in Christ, any consolation from love, any sharing in the Spirit, any compassion and sympathy, 2 make my joy complete: be of the same mind, having the same love, being in full accord and of one mind. 3 Do nothing from selfish ambition or conceit, but in humility regard others as better than yourselves. 4 Let each of you look not to your own interests, but to the interests of others. 5 Let the same mind be in you that was*a* in Christ Jesus,

6   who, though he was in the form
        of God,
    did not regard equality with God
        as something to be exploited,
7   but emptied himself,
        taking the form of a slave,
        being born in human likeness.
    And being found in human form,
8   he humbled himself
    and became obedient to the point
        of death—
    even death on a cross.

9   Therefore God also highly
        exalted him
    and gave him the name
        that is above every name,
10 so that at the name of Jesus
        every knee should bend,

in heaven and on earth and under
    the earth,
11 and every tongue should confess
        that Jesus Christ is Lord,
    to the glory of God the Father.

Shining as Lights in the World

12 Therefore, my beloved, just as you have always obeyed me, not only in my presence, but much more now in my absence, work out your own salvation with fear and trembling; 13 for it is God who is at work in you, enabling you both to will and to work for his good pleasure.

14 Do all things without murmuring and arguing, 15 so that you may be blameless and innocent, children of God without blemish in the midst of a crooked and perverse generation, in which you shine like stars in the world. 16 It is by your holding fast to the word of life that I can boast on the day of Christ that I did not run in vain or labour in vain. 17 But even if I am being poured out as a libation over the sacrifice and the offering of your faith, I am glad and rejoice with all of you— 18 and in the same way you also must be glad and rejoice with me.

Timothy and Epaphroditus

19 I hope in the Lord Jesus to send Timothy to you soon, so that I may be cheered by news of you. 20 I have no one like him who will be genuinely concerned for your welfare. 21 All of them are seeking their own interests, not those of Jesus Christ. 22 But Timothy's*b* worth you know, how like a son with a father he has served with me in the work of the gospel. 23 I hope therefore to send him as soon as I see how things go with me; 24 and I trust in the Lord that I will also come soon.

25 Still, I think it necessary to send to you Epaphroditus—my brother and co-worker and fellow-soldier, your messenger*c* and minister to my need; 26 for he has been longing for*d* all of you, and has been distressed because you heard that he was ill. 27 He was indeed so ill that he

a Or *that you have*   *b* Gk *his*   *c* Gk *apostle*
d Other ancient authorities read *longing to see*

nearly died. But God had mercy on him, and not only on him but on me also, so that I would not have one sorrow after another. [28] I am the more eager to send him, therefore, in order that you may rejoice at seeing him again, and that I may be less anxious. [29] Welcome him then in the Lord with all joy, and honour such people, [30] because he came close to death for the work of Christ, [a] risking his life to make up for those services that you could not give me.

[3] Finally, my brothers and sisters, [b] rejoice [c] in the Lord.

Breaking with the Past

To write the same things to you is not troublesome to me, and for you it is a safeguard.

[2] Beware of the dogs, beware of the evil workers, beware of those who mutilate the flesh! [d] [3] For it is we who are the circumcision, who worship in the Spirit of God [e] and boast in Christ Jesus and have no confidence in the flesh— [4] even though I, too, have reason for confidence in the flesh.

If anyone else has reason to be confident in the flesh, I have more: [5] circumcised on the eighth day, a member of the people of Israel, of the tribe of Benjamin, a Hebrew born of Hebrews; as to the law, a Pharisee; [6] as to zeal, a persecutor of the church; as to righteousness under the law, blameless.

[7] Yet whatever gains I had, these I have come to regard as loss because of Christ. [8] More than that, I regard everything as loss because of the surpassing value of knowing Christ Jesus my Lord. For his sake I have suffered the loss of all things, and I regard them as rubbish, in order that I may gain Christ [9] and be found in him, not having a righteousness of my own that comes from the law, but one that comes through faith in Christ, [f] the righteousness from God based on faith. [10] I want to know Christ [g] and the power of his resurrection and the sharing of his sufferings by becoming like him in his death, [11] if somehow I may attain the resurrection from the dead.

Pressing towards the Goal

[12] Not that I have already obtained this or have already reached the goal; [h] but I press on to make it my own, because Christ Jesus has made me his own. [13] Beloved, [i] I do not consider that I have made it my own; [j] but this one thing I do: forgetting what lies behind and straining forward to what lies ahead, [14] I press on towards the goal for the prize of the heavenly [k] call of God in Christ Jesus. [15] Let those of us then who are mature be of the same mind; and if you think differently about anything, this too God will reveal to you. [16] Only let us hold fast to what we have attained.

[17] Brothers and sisters, [i] join in imitating me, and observe those who live according to the example you have in us. [18] For many live as enemies of the cross of Christ; I have often told you of them, and now I tell you even with tears. [19] Their end is destruction; their god is the belly; and their glory is in their shame; their minds are set on earthly things. [20] But our citizenship [l] is in heaven, and it is from there that we are expecting a Saviour, the Lord Jesus Christ. [21] He will transform the body of our humiliation [m] so that it may be conformed to the body of his glory, [n] by the power that also enables him to make all things subject

[4] to himself. [1] Therefore, my brothers and sisters, [b] whom I love and long for, my joy and crown, stand firm in the Lord in this way, my beloved.

Exhortations

[2] I urge Euodia and I urge Syntyche to be of the same mind in the Lord. [3] Yes, and I ask you also, my loyal companion, [o] help these women, for they have struggled beside me in the work of the gospel, together with Clement and the rest of my co-workers, whose names are in the book of life.

---

a Other ancient authorities read *of the Lord*   *b* Gk *my brothers*   *c* Or *farewell*   *d* Gk *the mutilation*   *e* Other ancient authorities read *worship God in spirit*   *f* Or *through the faith of Christ*   *g* Gk *him*   *h* Or *have already been made perfect*   *i* Gk *Brothers*   *j* Other ancient authorities read *my own yet*   *k* Gk *upward*   *l* Or *commonwealth*   *m* Or *our humble bodies*   *n* Or *his glorious body*   *o* Or *loyal Syzygus*

4 Rejoice[a] in the Lord always; again I will say, Rejoice.[a] 5 Let your gentleness be known to everyone. The Lord is near. 6 Do not worry about anything, but in everything by prayer and supplication with thanksgiving let your requests be made known to God. 7 And the peace of God, which surpasses all understanding, will guard your hearts and your minds in Christ Jesus.

8 Finally, beloved,[b] whatever is true, whatever is honourable, whatever is just, whatever is pure, whatever is pleasing, whatever is commendable, if there is any excellence and if there is anything worthy of praise, think about[c] these things. 9 Keep on doing the things that you have learned and received and heard and seen in me, and the God of peace will be with you.

Acknowledgment of the Philippians' Gift

10 I rejoice[d] in the Lord greatly that now at last you have revived your concern for me; indeed, you were concerned for me, but had no opportunity to show it.[e] 11 Not that I am referring to being in need; for I have learned to be content with whatever I have. 12 I know what it is to have little, and I know what it is to have plenty. In any and all circumstances I have learned the secret of being well-fed and of going hungry, of having plenty and of being in need. 13 I can do all things through him who strengthens me. 14 In any case, it was kind of you to share my distress.

15 You Philippians indeed know that in the early days of the gospel, when I left Macedonia, no church shared with me in the matter of giving and receiving, except you alone. 16 For even when I was in Thessalonica, you sent me help for my needs more than once. 17 Not that I seek the gift, but I seek the profit that accumulates to your account. 18 I have been paid in full and have more than enough; I am fully satisfied, now that I have received from Epaphroditus the gifts you sent, a fragrant offering, a sacrifice acceptable and pleasing to God. 19 And my God will fully satisfy every need of yours according to his riches in glory in Christ Jesus. 20 To our God and Father be glory for ever and ever. Amen.

Final Greetings and Benediction

21 Greet every saint in Christ Jesus. The friends[b] who are with me greet you. 22 All the saints greet you, especially those of the emperor's household.

23 The grace of the Lord Jesus Christ be with your spirit.[f]

---

a Or *Farewell*   b Gk *brothers*   c Gk *take account of*
d Gk *I rejoiced*   e Gk lacks *to show it*   f Other ancient authorities add *Amen*

THE LETTER OF PAUL TO THE
COLOSSIANS

Salutation

1 Paul, an apostle of Christ Jesus by the will of God, and Timothy our brother,
2 To the saints and faithful brothers and sisters*a* in Christ in Colossae:
Grace to you and peace from God our Father.

Paul Thanks God for the Colossians

3 In our prayers for you we always thank God, the Father of our Lord Jesus Christ, 4 for we have heard of your faith in Christ Jesus and of the love that you have for all the saints, 5 because of the hope laid up for you in heaven. You have heard of this hope before in the word of the truth, the gospel 6 that has come to you. Just as it is bearing fruit and growing in the whole world, so it has been bearing fruit among yourselves from the day you heard it and truly comprehended the grace of God. 7 This you learned from Epaphras, our beloved fellow-servant.*b* He is a faithful minister of Christ on your*c* behalf, 8 and he has made known to us your love in the Spirit.

9 For this reason, since the day we heard it, we have not ceased praying for you and asking that you may be filled with the knowledge of God's*d* will in all spiritual wisdom and understanding, 10 so that you may lead lives worthy of the Lord, fully pleasing to him, as you bear fruit in every good work and as you grow in the knowledge of God. 11 May you be made strong with all the strength that comes from his glorious power, and may you be prepared to endure everything with patience, while joyfully 12 giving thanks to the Father, who has enabled*e* you*f* to share in the inheritance of the saints in the light.

13 He has rescued us from the power of darkness and transferred us into the kingdom of his beloved Son, 14 in whom we have redemption, the forgiveness of sins.*g*

The Supremacy of Christ

15 He is the image of the invisible God, the firstborn of all creation; 16 for in*h* him all things in heaven and on earth were created, things visible and invisible, whether thrones or dominions or rulers or powers—all things have been created through him and for him. 17 He himself is before all things, and in*h* him all things hold together. 18 He is the head of the body, the church; he is the beginning, the firstborn from the dead, so that he might come to have first place in everything. 19 For in him all the fullness of God was pleased to dwell, 20 and through him God was pleased to reconcile to himself all things, whether on earth or in heaven, by making peace through the blood of his cross.

21 And you who were once estranged and hostile in mind, doing evil deeds, 22 he has now reconciled*i* in his fleshly body*j* through death, so as to present you holy and blameless and irreproachable before him— 23 provided that you continue securely established and steadfast in the faith, without shifting from the hope promised by the gospel that you heard, which has been proclaimed to every creature under heaven. I, Paul, became a servant of this gospel.

---

a Gk *brothers*   *b* Gk *slave*   *c* Other ancient authorities read *our*   *d* Gk *his*   *e* Other ancient authorities read *called*   *f* Other ancient authorities read *us*   *g* Other ancient authorities add *through his blood*   *h* Or *by*   *i* Other ancient authorities read *you have now been reconciled*   *j* Gk *in the body of his flesh*

Paul's Interest in the Colossians

24 I am now rejoicing in my sufferings for your sake, and in my flesh I am completing what is lacking in Christ's afflictions for the sake of his body, that is, the church. 25 I became its servant according to God's commission that was given to me for you, to make the word of God fully known, 26 the mystery that has been hidden throughout the ages and generations but has now been revealed to his saints. 27 To them God chose to make known how great among the Gentiles are the riches of the glory of this mystery, which is Christ in you, the hope of glory. 28 It is he whom we proclaim, warning everyone and teaching everyone in all wisdom, so that we may present everyone mature in Christ. 29 For this I toil and struggle with all the energy that he powerfully inspires within me.

2 For I want you to know how much I am struggling for you, and for those in Laodicea, and for all who have not seen me face to face. 2 I want their hearts to be encouraged and united in love, so that they may have all the riches of assured understanding and have the knowledge of God's mystery, that is, Christ himself, *a* 3 in whom are hidden all the treasures of wisdom and knowledge. 4 I am saying this so that no one may deceive you with plausible arguments. 5 For though I am absent in body, yet I am with you in spirit, and I rejoice to see your morale and the firmness of your faith in Christ.

Fullness of Life in Christ

6 As you therefore have received Christ Jesus the Lord, continue to live your lives *b* in him, 7 rooted and built up in him and established in the faith, just as you were taught, abounding in thanksgiving.

8 See to it that no one takes you captive through philosophy and empty deceit, according to human tradition, according to the elemental spirits of the universe, *c* and not according to Christ. 9 For in him the whole fullness of deity dwells bodily, 10 and you have come to fullness in him, who is the head of every ruler and authority. 11 In

him also you were circumcised with a spiritual circumcision, *d* by putting off the body of the flesh in the circumcision of Christ; 12 when you were buried with him in baptism, you were also raised with him through faith in the power of God, who raised him from the dead. 13 And when you were dead in trespasses and the uncircumcision of your flesh, God *e* made you *f* alive together with him, when he forgave us all our trespasses, 14 erasing the record that stood against us with its legal demands. He set this aside, nailing it to the cross. 15 He disarmed *g* the rulers and authorities and made a public example of them, triumphing over them in it.

16 Therefore do not let anyone condemn you in matters of food and drink or of observing festivals, new moons, or sabbaths. 17 These are only a shadow of what is to come, but the substance belongs to Christ. 18 Do not let anyone disqualify you, insisting on self-abasement and worship of angels, dwelling *h* on visions, *i* puffed up without cause by a human way of thinking, *j* 19 and not holding fast to the head, from whom the whole body, nourished and held together by its ligaments and sinews, grows with a growth that is from God.

Warnings against False Teachers

20 If with Christ you died to the elemental spirits of the universe, *c* why do you live as if you still belonged to the world? Why do you submit to regulations, 21 'Do not handle, Do not taste, Do not touch'? 22 All these regulations refer to things that perish with use; they are simply human commands and teachings. 23 These have indeed an appearance of wisdom in promoting self-imposed piety, humility, and severe treatment of the body, but they are of no value in checking self-indulgence. *k*

a Other ancient authorities read *of the mystery of God, both of the Father and of Christ*   *b* Gk *to walk*   *c* Or *the rudiments of the world*   *d* Gk *a circumcision made without hands*   *e* Gk *he*   *f* Other ancient authorities read *made us;* others, *made*   *g* Or *divested himself of*   *h* Other ancient authorities read *not dwelling*   *i* Meaning of Gk uncertain   *j* Gk *by the mind of his flesh*   *k* Or *are of no value, serving only to indulge the flesh*

The New Life in Christ

3 So if you have been raised with Christ, seek the things that are above, where Christ is, seated at the right hand of God. ² Set your minds on things that are above, not on things that are on earth, ³ for you have died, and your life is hidden with Christ in God. ⁴ When Christ who is your*a* life is revealed, then you also will be revealed with him in glory.

5 Put to death, therefore, whatever in you is earthly: fornication, impurity, passion, evil desire, and greed (which is idolatry). ⁶ On account of these the wrath of God is coming on those who are disobedient.*b* ⁷ These are the ways you also once followed, when you were living that life.*c* ⁸ But now you must get rid of all such things—anger, wrath, malice, slander, and abusive*d* language from your mouth. ⁹ Do not lie to one another, seeing that you have stripped off the old self with its practices ¹⁰ and have clothed yourselves with the new self, which is being renewed in knowledge according to the image of its creator. ¹¹ In that renewal*e* there is no longer Greek and Jew, circumcised and uncircumcised, barbarian, Scythian, slave and free; but Christ is all and in all!

12 As God's chosen ones, holy and beloved, clothe yourselves with compassion, kindness, humility, meekness, and patience. ¹³ Bear with one another and, if anyone has a complaint against another, forgive each other; just as the Lord*f* has forgiven you, so you also must forgive. ¹⁴ Above all, clothe yourselves with love, which binds everything together in perfect harmony. ¹⁵ And let the peace of Christ rule in your hearts, to which indeed you were called in the one body. And be thankful. ¹⁶ Let the word of Christ*g* dwell in you richly; teach and admonish one another in all wisdom; and with gratitude in your hearts sing psalms, hymns, and spiritual songs to God.*h* ¹⁷ And whatever you do, in word or deed, do everything in the name of the Lord Jesus, giving thanks to God the Father through him.

Rules for Christian Households

18 Wives, be subject to your husbands, as is fitting in the Lord. ¹⁹ Husbands, love your wives and never treat them harshly.

20 Children, obey your parents in everything, for this is your acceptable duty in the Lord. ²¹ Fathers, do not provoke your children, or they may lose heart. ²² Slaves, obey your earthly masters*i* in everything, not only while being watched and in order to please them, but wholeheartedly, fearing the Lord.*i* ²³ Whatever your task, put yourselves into it, as done for the Lord and not for your masters,*j* ²⁴ since you know that from the Lord you will receive the inheritance as your reward; you serve*k* the Lord Christ. ²⁵ For the wrongdoer will be paid back for whatever wrong has been done, and there is no partiality.

4 ¹ Masters, treat your slaves justly and fairly, for you know that you also have a Master in heaven.

Further Instructions

2 Devote yourselves to prayer, keeping alert in it with thanksgiving. ³ At the same time pray for us as well that God will open to us a door for the word, that we may declare the mystery of Christ, for which I am in prison, ⁴ so that I may reveal it clearly, as I should.

5 Conduct yourselves wisely towards outsiders, making the most of the time.*l* ⁶ Let your speech always be gracious, seasoned with salt, so that you may know how you ought to answer everyone.

Final Greetings and Benediction

7 Tychicus will tell you all the news about me; he is a beloved brother, a faithful minister, and a fellow-servant*m* in the Lord. ⁸ I have sent him to you for this very purpose, so that you may know how we

a Other authorities read *our*   *b* Other ancient authorities lack *on those who are disobedient* (Gk *the children of disobedience*)   *c* Or *living among such people*   *d* Or *filthy*   *e* Gk *its creator,* ¹¹*where*   *f* Other ancient authorities read *just as Christ*   *g* Other ancient authorities read *of God,* or *of the Lord*   *h* Other ancient authorities read *to the Lord*   *i* In Greek the same word is used for *master* and *Lord*   *j* Gk *not for men*   *k* Or *you are slaves of,* or *be slaves of*   *l* Or *opportunity*   *m* Gk *slave* are[a] and that he may encourage your hearts; [9] he is coming with Onesimus, the faithful and beloved brother, who is one of you. They will tell you about everything here.

10 Aristarchus my fellow-prisoner greets you, as does Mark the cousin of Barnabas, concerning whom you have received instructions—if he comes to you, welcome him. [11] And Jesus who is called Justus greets you. These are the only ones of the circumcision among my co-workers for the kingdom of God, and they have been a comfort to me. [12] Epaphras, who is one of you, a servant[b] of Christ Jesus, greets you. He is always wrestling in his prayers on your behalf, so that you may stand mature and fully assured in everything that God wills. [13] For I testify for him that he has worked hard for you and for those in Laodicea and in Hierapolis. [14] Luke, the beloved physician, and Demas greet you. [15] Give my greetings to the brothers and sisters[c] in Laodicea, and to Nympha and the church in her house. [16] And when this letter has been read among you, have it read also in the church of the Laodiceans; and see that you read also the letter from Laodicea. [17] And say to Archippus, 'See that you complete the task that you have received in the Lord.'

18 I, Paul, write this greeting with my own hand. Remember my chains. Grace be with you.[d]

a Other authorities read *that I may know how you are*
b Gk *slave*   c Gk *brothers*   d Other ancient authorities add *Amen*

THE FIRST LETTER OF PAUL TO THE
THESSALONIANS

Salutation

1 Paul, Silvanus, and Timothy,
To the church of the Thessalonians in God the Father and the Lord Jesus Christ:
Grace to you and peace.

The Thessalonians' Faith and Example

2 We always give thanks to God for all of you and mention you in our prayers, constantly ³remembering before our God and Father your work of faith and labour of love and steadfastness of hope in our Lord Jesus Christ. ⁴For we know, brothers and sisters*ᵃ* beloved by God, that he has chosen you, ⁵because our message of the gospel came to you not in word only, but also in power and in the Holy Spirit and with full conviction; just as you know what kind of people we proved to be among you for your sake. ⁶And you became imitators of us and of the Lord, for in spite of persecution you received the word with joy inspired by the Holy Spirit, ⁷so that you became an example to all the believers in Macedonia and in Achaia. ⁸For the word of the Lord has sounded forth from you not only in Macedonia and Achaia, but in every place where your faith in God has become known, so that we have no need to speak about it. ⁹For the people of those regions*ᵇ* report about us what kind of welcome we had among you, and how you turned to God from idols, to serve a living and true God, ¹⁰and to wait for his Son from heaven, whom he raised from the dead—Jesus, who rescues us from the wrath that is coming.

Paul's Ministry in Thessalonica

2 You yourselves know, brothers and sisters,*ᵃ* that our coming to you was not in vain, ²but though we had already suffered and been shamefully maltreated at Philippi, as you know, we had courage in our God to declare to you the gospel of God in spite of great opposition. ³For our appeal does not spring from deceit or impure motives or trickery, ⁴but just as we have been approved by God to be entrusted with the message of the gospel, even so we speak, not to please mortals, but to please God who tests our hearts. ⁵As you know and as God is our witness, we never came with words of flattery or with a pretext for greed; ⁶nor did we seek praise from mortals, whether from you or from others, ⁷though we might have made demands as apostles of Christ. But we were gentle*ᶜ* among you, like a nurse tenderly caring for her own children. ⁸So deeply do we care for you that we are determined to share with you not only the gospel of God but also our own selves, because you have become very dear to us.

9 You remember our labour and toil, brothers and sisters;*ᵈ* we worked night and day, so that we might not burden any of you while we proclaimed to you the gospel of God. ¹⁰You are witnesses, and God also, how pure, upright, and blameless our conduct was towards you believers. ¹¹As you know, we dealt with each one of you like a father with his children, ¹²urging and encouraging you and pleading that you

a Gk *brothers*   *b* Gk *For they*   *c* Other ancient authorities read *infants* should lead a life worthy of God, who calls you into his own kingdom and glory.

13 We also constantly give thanks to God for this, that when you received the word of God that you heard from us, you accepted it not as a human word but as what it really is, God's word, which is also at work in you believers. [14] For you, brothers and sisters,[a] became imitators of the churches of God in Christ Jesus that are in Judea, for you suffered the same things from your own compatriots as they did from the Jews, [15] who killed both the Lord Jesus and the prophets,[b] and drove us out; they displease God and oppose everyone [16] by hindering us from speaking to the Gentiles so that they may be saved. Thus they have constantly been filling up the measure of their sins; but God's wrath has overtaken them at last.[c]

Paul's Desire to Visit the Thessalonians Again

17 As for us, brothers and sisters,[a] when, for a short time, we were made orphans by being separated from you—in person, not in heart—we longed with great eagerness to see you face to face. [18] For we wanted to come to you—certainly I, Paul, wanted to again and again—but Satan blocked our way. [19] For what is our hope or joy or crown of boasting before our Lord Jesus at his coming? Is it not you? [20] Yes, you are our glory and joy!

3 Therefore when we could bear it no longer, we decided to be left alone in Athens; [2] and we sent Timothy, our brother and co-worker for God in proclaiming[d] the gospel of Christ, to strengthen and encourage you for the sake of your faith, [3] so that no one would be shaken by these persecutions. Indeed, you yourselves know that this is what we are destined for. [4] In fact, when we were with you, we told you beforehand that we were to suffer persecution; so it turned out, as you know. [5] For this reason, when I could bear it no longer, I sent to find out about your faith; I was afraid that somehow the tempter had tempted you and that our labour had been in vain.

Timothy's Encouraging Report

6 But Timothy has just now come to us from you, and has brought us the good news of your faith and love. He has told us also that you always remember us kindly and long to see us—just as we long to see you. [7] For this reason, brothers and sisters,[a] during all our distress and persecution we have been encouraged about you through your faith. [8] For we now live, if you continue to stand firm in the Lord. [9] How can we thank God enough for you in return for all the joy that we feel before our God because of you? [10] Night and day we pray most earnestly that we may see you face to face and restore whatever is lacking in your faith.

11 Now may our God and Father himself and our Lord Jesus direct our way to you. [12] And may the Lord make you increase and abound in love for one another and for all, just as we abound in love for you. [13] And may he so strengthen your hearts in holiness that you may be blameless before our God and Father at the coming of our Lord Jesus with all his saints.

A Life Pleasing to God

4 Finally, brothers and sisters,[a] we ask and urge you in the Lord Jesus that, as you learned from us how you ought to live and to please God (as, in fact, you are doing), you should do so more and more. [2] For you know what instructions we gave you through the Lord Jesus. [3] For this is the will of God, your sanctification: that you abstain from fornication; [4] that each one of you knows how to control your own body[e] in holiness and honour, [5] not with lustful passion, like the Gentiles who do not know God; [6] that no one wrongs or exploits a brother or sister[f] in this matter, because the Lord is an avenger in all these things, just as we have already told you beforehand and solemnly warned you. [7] For God did not call us to impurity but in holiness. [8] Therefore whoever rejects this re-

a Gk brothers   b Other ancient authorities read their own prophets   c Or completely or for ever   d Gk lacks proclaiming   e Or how to take a wife for himself   f Gk brother jects not human authority but God, who also gives his Holy Spirit to you.

9 Now concerning love of the brothers and sisters,[a] you do not need to have anyone write to you, for you yourselves have been taught by God to love one another; [10]and indeed you do love all the brothers and sisters[a] throughout Macedonia. But we urge you, beloved,[a] to do so more and more, [11]to aspire to live quietly, to mind your own affairs, and to work with your hands, as we directed you, [12]so that you may behave properly towards outsiders and be dependent on no one.

The Coming of the Lord

13 But we do not want you to be uninformed, brothers and sisters,[a] about those who have died,[b] so that you may not grieve as others do who have no hope. [14]For since we believe that Jesus died and rose again, even so, through Jesus, God will bring with him those who have died.[b] [15]For this we declare to you by the word of the Lord, that we who are alive, who are left until the coming of the Lord, will by no means precede those who have died.[b] [16]For the Lord himself, with a cry of command, with the archangel's call and with the sound of God's trumpet, will descend from heaven, and the dead in Christ will rise first. [17]Then we who are alive, who are left, will be caught up in the clouds together with them to meet the Lord in the air; and so we will be with the Lord for ever. [18]Therefore encourage one another with these words.

5 Now concerning the times and the seasons, brothers and sisters,[a] you do not need to have anything written to you. [2]For you yourselves know very well that the day of the Lord will come like a thief in the night. [3]When they say, 'There is peace and security', then sudden destruction will come upon them, as labour pains come upon a pregnant woman, and there will be no escape! [4]But you, beloved,[a] are not in darkness, for that day to surprise you like a thief; [5]for you are all children of light and children of the day; we are not of the night or of darkness. [6]So then, let us not fall

asleep as others do, but let us keep awake and be sober; [7]for those who sleep sleep at night, and those who are drunk get drunk at night. [8]But since we belong to the day, let us be sober, and put on the breastplate of faith and love, and for a helmet the hope of salvation. [9]For God has destined us not for wrath but for obtaining salvation through our Lord Jesus Christ, [10]who died for us, so that whether we are awake or asleep we may live with him. [11]Therefore encourage one another and build up each other, as indeed you are doing.

Final Exhortations, Greetings, and Benediction

12 But we appeal to you, brothers and sisters,[a] to respect those who labour among you, and have charge of you in the Lord and admonish you; [13]esteem them very highly in love because of their work. Be at peace among yourselves. [14]And we urge you, beloved,[a] to admonish the idlers, encourage the faint-hearted, help the weak, be patient with all of them. [15]See that none of you repays evil for evil, but always seek to do good to one another and to all. [16]Rejoice always, [17]pray without ceasing, [18]give thanks in all circumstances; for this is the will of God in Christ Jesus for you. [19]Do not quench the Spirit. [20]Do not despise the words of prophets,[c] [21]but test everything; hold fast to what is good; [22]abstain from every form of evil.

23 May the God of peace himself sanctify you entirely; and may your spirit and soul and body be kept sound[d] and blameless at the coming of our Lord Jesus Christ. [24]The one who calls you is faithful, and he will do this.

25 Beloved,[e] pray for us.

26 Greet all the brothers and sisters[a] with a holy kiss. [27]I solemnly command you by the Lord that this letter be read to all of them.[f]

28 The grace of our Lord Jesus Christ be with you.[g]

---

a Gk brothers   b Gk fallen asleep   c Gk despise prophecies   d Or complete   e Gk Brothers   f Gk to all the brothers   g Other ancient authorities add Amen

THE SECOND LETTER OF PAUL TO THE
THESSALONIANS

Salutation

1 Paul, Silvanus, and Timothy,
To the church of the Thessalonians in God our Father and the Lord Jesus Christ:

2 Grace to you and peace from God our*a* Father and the Lord Jesus Christ.

Thanksgiving

3 We must always give thanks to God for you, brothers and sisters,*b* as is right, because your faith is growing abundantly, and the love of every one of you for one another is increasing. 4 Therefore we ourselves boast of you among the churches of God for your steadfastness and faith during all your persecutions and the afflictions that you are enduring.

The Judgement at Christ's Coming

5 This is evidence of the righteous judgement of God, and is intended to make you worthy of the kingdom of God, for which you are also suffering. 6 For it is indeed just of God to repay with affliction those who afflict you, 7 and to give relief to the afflicted as well as to us, when the Lord Jesus is revealed from heaven with his mighty angels 8 in flaming fire, inflicting vengeance on those who do not know God and on those who do not obey the gospel of our Lord Jesus. 9 These will suffer the punishment of eternal destruction, separated from the presence of the Lord and from the glory of his might, 10 when he comes to be glorified by his saints and to be marvelled at on that day among all who have believed, because our testimony to you was believed. 11 To this end we always pray for you, asking that our God will make you worthy of his call and will fulfil by his power every good resolve and work of faith, 12 so that the name of our Lord Jesus may be glorified in you, and you in him, according to the grace of our God and the Lord Jesus Christ.

The Man of Lawlessness

2 As to the coming of our Lord Jesus Christ and our being gathered together to him, we beg you, brothers and sisters,*b* 2 not to be quickly shaken in mind or alarmed, either by spirit or by word or by letter, as though from us, to the effect that the day of the Lord is already here. 3 Let no one deceive you in any way; for that day will not come unless the rebellion comes first and the lawless one*c* is revealed, the one destined for destruction.*d* 4 He opposes and exalts himself above every so-called god or object of worship, so that he takes his seat in the temple of God, declaring himself to be God. 5 Do you not remember that I told you these things when I was still with you? 6 And you know what is now restraining him, so that he may be revealed when his time comes. 7 For the mystery of lawlessness is already at work, but only until the one who now restrains it is removed. 8 And then the lawless one will be revealed, whom the Lord Jesus*e* will destroy*f* with the breath of his mouth, annihilating him by the manifestation of his coming. 9 The coming of the lawless one is apparent in the working of Satan, who uses all power, signs, lying wonders, 10 and

a Other ancient authorities read *the*   *b* Gk *brothers*
c Gk *the man of lawlessness*; other ancient authorities read *the man of sin*   *d* Gk *the son of destruction*
e Other ancient authorities lack *Jesus*   *f* Other ancient authorities read *consume*

every kind of wicked deception for those who are perishing, because they refused to love the truth and so be saved. [11] For this reason God sends them a powerful delusion, leading them to believe what is false, [12] so that all who have not believed the truth but took pleasure in unrighteousness will be condemned.

Chosen for Salvation

13 But we must always give thanks to God for you, brothers and sisters[a] beloved by the Lord, because God chose you as the first fruits[b] for salvation through sanctification by the Spirit and through belief in the truth. [14] For this purpose he called you through our proclamation of the good news,[c] so that you may obtain the glory of our Lord Jesus Christ. [15] So then, brothers and sisters,[a] stand firm and hold fast to the traditions that you were taught by us, either by word of mouth or by our letter.

16 Now may our Lord Jesus Christ himself and God our Father, who loved us and through grace gave us eternal comfort and good hope, [17] comfort your hearts and strengthen them in every good work and word.

Request for Prayer

3 Finally, brothers and sisters,[a] pray for us, so that the word of the Lord may spread rapidly and be glorified everywhere, just as it is among you, [2] and that we may be rescued from wicked and evil people; for not all have faith. [3] But the Lord is faithful; he will strengthen you and guard you from the evil one.[d] [4] And we have confidence in the Lord concerning you, that you are doing and will go on doing the things that we command. [5] May the Lord direct your hearts to the love of God and to the steadfastness of Christ.

Warning against Idleness

6 Now we command you, beloved,[a] in the name of our Lord Jesus Christ, to keep away from believers who are[e] living in idleness and not according to the tradition that they[f] received from us. [7] For you yourselves know how you ought to imitate us; we were not idle when we were with you, [8] and we did not eat anyone's bread without paying for it; but with toil and labour we worked night and day, so that we might not burden any of you. [9] This was not because we do not have that right, but in order to give you an example to imitate. [10] For even when we were with you, we gave you this command: Anyone unwilling to work should not eat. [11] For we hear that some of you are living in idleness, mere busybodies, not doing any work. [12] Now such persons we command and exhort in the Lord Jesus Christ to do their work quietly and to earn their own living. [13] Brothers and sisters,[g] do not be weary in doing what is right.

14 Take note of those who do not obey what we say in this letter; have nothing to do with them, so that they may be ashamed. [15] Do not regard them as enemies, but warn them as believers.[h]

Final Greetings and Benediction

16 Now may the Lord of peace himself give you peace at all times in all ways. The Lord be with all of you.

17 I, Paul, write this greeting with my own hand. This is the mark in every letter of mine; it is the way I write. [18] The grace of our Lord Jesus Christ be with all of you.[i]

a Gk brothers   b Other ancient authorities read from the beginning   c Or through our gospel   d Or from evil e Gk from every brother who is   f Other ancient authorities read you   g Gk Brothers   h Gk a brother i Other ancient authorities add Amen

THE FIRST LETTER OF PAUL TO
TIMOTHY

Salutation

1 Paul, an apostle of Christ Jesus by the command of God our Saviour and of Christ Jesus our hope,

2 To Timothy, my loyal child in the faith:

Grace, mercy, and peace from God the Father and Christ Jesus our Lord.

Warning against False Teachers

3 I urge you, as I did when I was on my way to Macedonia, to remain in Ephesus so that you may instruct certain people not to teach any different doctrine, 4 and not to occupy themselves with myths and endless genealogies that promote speculations rather than the divine training*a* that is known by faith. 5 But the aim of such instruction is love that comes from a pure heart, a good conscience, and sincere faith. 6 Some people have deviated from these and turned to meaningless talk, 7 desiring to be teachers of the law, without understanding either what they are saying or the things about which they make assertions.

8 Now we know that the law is good, if one uses it legitimately. 9 This means understanding that the law is laid down not for the innocent but for the lawless and disobedient, for the godless and sinful, for the unholy and profane, for those who kill their father or mother, for murderers, 10 fornicators, sodomites, slave-traders, liars, perjurers, and whatever else is contrary to the sound teaching 11 that conforms to the glorious gospel of the blessed God, which he entrusted to me.

Gratitude for Mercy

12 I am grateful to Christ Jesus our Lord, who has strengthened me, because he judged me faithful and appointed me to his service, 13 even though I was formerly a blasphemer, a persecutor, and a man of violence. But I received mercy because I had acted ignorantly in unbelief, 14 and the grace of our Lord overflowed for me with the faith and love that are in Christ Jesus. 15 The saying is sure and worthy of full acceptance, that Christ Jesus came into the world to save sinners—of whom I am the foremost. 16 But for that very reason I received mercy, so that in me, as the foremost, Jesus Christ might display the utmost patience, making me an example to those who would come to believe in him for eternal life. 17 To the King of the ages, immortal, invisible, the only God, be honour and glory for ever and ever.*b* Amen.

18 I am giving you these instructions, Timothy, my child, in accordance with the prophecies made earlier about you, so that by following them you may fight the good fight, 19 having faith and a good conscience. By rejecting conscience, certain persons have suffered shipwreck in the faith; 20 among them are Hymenaeus and Alexander, whom I have turned over to Satan, so that they may learn not to blaspheme.

Instructions concerning Prayer

2 First of all, then, I urge that supplications, prayers, intercessions, and thanksgivings should be made for everyone, 2 for kings and all who are in high positions, so that we may lead a quiet and peaceable life in all godliness and dignity. 3 This is right and is acceptable in the sight

a Or *plan*   *b* Gk *to the ages of the ages*

of God our Saviour, [4] who desires everyone to be saved and to come to the knowledge of the truth. [5] For

there is one God;
there is also one mediator between
    God and humankind,
Christ Jesus, himself human,
[6]   who gave himself a ransom for all

—this was attested at the right time. [7] For this I was appointed a herald and an apostle (I am telling the truth,[a] I am not lying), a teacher of the Gentiles in faith and truth.

[8] I desire, then, that in every place the men should pray, lifting up holy hands without anger or argument; [9] also that the women should dress themselves modestly and decently in suitable clothing, not with their hair braided, or with gold, pearls, or expensive clothes, [10] but with good works, as is proper for women who profess reverence for God. [11] Let a woman[b] learn in silence with full submission. [12] I permit no woman[b] to teach or to have authority over a man;[c] she is to keep silent. [13] For Adam was formed first, then Eve; [14] and Adam was not deceived, but the woman was deceived and became a transgressor. [15] Yet she will be saved through childbearing, provided they continue in faith and love and holiness, with modesty.

Qualifications of Bishops

3 The saying is sure:[d] whoever aspires to the office of bishop[e] desires a noble task. [2] Now a bishop[f] must be above reproach, married only once,[g] temperate, sensible, respectable, hospitable, an apt teacher, [3] not a drunkard, not violent but gentle, not quarrelsome, and not a lover of money. [4] He must manage his own household well, keeping his children submissive and respectful in every way— [5] for if someone does not know how to manage his own household, how can he take care of God's church? [6] He must not be a recent convert, or he may be puffed up with conceit and fall into the condemnation of the devil. [7] Moreover, he must be well thought of by outsiders, so that he may not fall into disgrace and the snare of the devil.

Qualifications of Deacons

[8] Deacons likewise must be serious, not double-tongued, not indulging in much wine, not greedy for money; [9] they must hold fast to the mystery of the faith with a clear conscience. [10] And let them first be tested; then, if they prove themselves blameless, let them serve as deacons. [11] Women[h] likewise must be serious, not slanderers, but temperate, faithful in all things. [12] Let deacons be married only once,[i] and let them manage their children and their households well; [13] for those who serve well as deacons gain a good standing for themselves and great boldness in the faith that is in Christ Jesus.

The Mystery of Our Religion

[14] I hope to come to you soon, but I am writing these instructions to you so that, [15] if I am delayed, you may know how one ought to behave in the household of God, which is the church of the living God, the pillar and bulwark of the truth. [16] Without any doubt, the mystery of our religion is great:

He[j] was revealed in flesh,
    vindicated[k] in spirit,[l]
    seen by angels,
proclaimed among Gentiles,
    believed in throughout the world,
    taken up in glory.

False Asceticism

4 Now the Spirit expressly says that in later[m] times some will renounce the faith by paying attention to deceitful spirits and teachings of demons, [2] through the hypocrisy of liars whose consciences are seared with a hot iron. [3] They forbid marriage and demand abstinence from foods, which God created to be received with thanksgiving by those who believe and know the truth. [4] For everything created by

a Other ancient authorities add in Christ   b Or wife
c Or her husband   d Some interpreters place these
words at the end of the previous paragraph. Other
ancient authorities read The saying is commonly accepted
e Or overseer   f Or an overseer   g Gk the husband of
one wife   h Or Their wives, or Women deacons
i Gk be husbands of one wife   j Gk Who; other ancient
authorities read God; others, Which   k Or justified
l Or by the Spirit   m Or the last

God is good, and nothing is to be rejected, provided it is received with thanksgiving; [5] for it is sanctified by God's word and by prayer.

A Good Minister of Jesus Christ

6 If you put these instructions before the brothers and sisters,[a] you will be a good servant[b] of Christ Jesus, nourished on the words of the faith and of the sound teaching that you have followed. [7] Have nothing to do with profane myths and old wives' tales. Train yourself in godliness, [8] for, while physical training is of some value, godliness is valuable in every way, holding promise for both the present life and the life to come. [9] The saying is sure and worthy of full acceptance. [10] For to this end we toil and struggle,[c] because we have our hope set on the living God, who is the Saviour of all people, especially of those who believe.

11 These are the things you must insist on and teach. [12] Let no one despise your youth, but set the believers an example in speech and conduct, in love, in faith, in purity. [13] Until I arrive, give attention to the public reading of scripture,[d] to exhorting, to teaching. [14] Do not neglect the gift that is in you, which was given to you through prophecy with the laying on of hands by the council of elders.[e] [15] Put these things into practice, devote yourself to them, so that all may see your progress. [16] Pay close attention to yourself and to your teaching; continue in these things, for in doing this you will save both yourself and your hearers.

Duties towards Believers

5 Do not speak harshly to an older man,[f] but speak to him as to a father, to younger men as brothers, [2] to older women as mothers, to younger women as sisters—with absolute purity.

3 Honour widows who are really widows. [4] If a widow has children or grandchildren, they should first learn their religious duty to their own family and make some repayment to their parents; for this is pleasing in God's sight. [5] The real widow, left alone, has set her hope on God and continues in supplications and prayers night and day; [6] but the widow[g] who lives for pleasure is dead even while she lives. [7] Give these commands as well, so that they may be above reproach. [8] And whoever does not provide for relatives, and especially for family members, has denied the faith and is worse than an unbeliever.

9 Let a widow be put on the list if she is not less than sixty years old and has been married only once;[h] [10] she must be well attested for her good works, as one who has brought up children, shown hospitality, washed the saints' feet, helped the afflicted, and devoted herself to doing good in every way. [11] But refuse to put younger widows on the list; for when their sensual desires alienate them from Christ, they want to marry, [12] and so they incur condemnation for having violated their first pledge. [13] Besides that, they learn to be idle, gadding about from house to house; and they are not merely idle, but also gossips and busybodies, saying what they should not say. [14] So I would have younger widows marry, bear children, and manage their households, so as to give the adversary no occasion to revile us. [15] For some have already turned away to follow Satan. [16] If any believing woman[i] has relatives who are really widows, let her assist them; let the church not be burdened, so that it can assist those who are real widows.

17 Let the elders who rule well be considered worthy of double honour,[j] especially those who labour in preaching and teaching; [18] for the scripture says, 'You shall not muzzle an ox while it is treading out the grain', and, 'The labourer deserves to be paid.' [19] Never accept any accusation against an elder except on the evidence of two or three witnesses. [20] As for those who persist in sin, rebuke them in the presence of all, so that the rest also may stand in

a Gk brothers   b Or deacon   c Other ancient authorities read suffer reproach   d Gk to the reading   e Gk by the presbytery   f Or an elder, or a presbyter   g Gk she   h Gk the wife of one husband   i Other ancient authorities read believing man or woman; others, believing man   j Or compensation fear. 21 In the presence of God and of Christ Jesus and of the elect angels, I warn you to keep these instructions without prejudice, doing nothing on the basis of partiality. 22 Do not ordain*a* anyone hastily, and do not participate in the sins of others; keep yourself pure.

23 No longer drink only water, but take a little wine for the sake of your stomach and your frequent ailments.

24 The sins of some people are conspicuous and precede them to judgement, while the sins of others follow them there. 25 So also good works are conspicuous; and even when they are not, they cannot remain hidden.

6 Let all who are under the yoke of slavery regard their masters as worthy of all honour, so that the name of God and the teaching may not be blasphemed. 2 Those who have believing masters must not be disrespectful to them on the ground that they are members of the church;*b* rather they must serve them all the more, since those who benefit by their service are believers and beloved.*c*

False Teaching and True Riches

Teach and urge these duties. 3 Whoever teaches otherwise and does not agree with the sound words of our Lord Jesus Christ and the teaching that is in accordance with godliness, 4 is conceited, understanding nothing, and has a morbid craving for controversy and for disputes about words. From these come envy, dissension, slander, base suspicions, 5 and wrangling among those who are depraved in mind and bereft of the truth, imagining that godliness is a means of gain.*d* 6 Of course, there is great gain in godliness combined with contentment; 7 for we brought nothing into the world, so that*e* we can take nothing out of it; 8 but if we have food and clothing, we will be content with these. 9 But those who want to be rich fall into temptation and are trapped by many senseless and harmful desires that plunge people into ruin and destruction. 10 For the love of money is a root of all kinds of evil, and in their eagerness to be rich some have wandered away from the faith and pierced themselves with many pains.

The Good Fight of Faith

11 But as for you, man of God, shun all this; pursue righteousness, godliness, faith, love, endurance, gentleness. 12 Fight the good fight of the faith; take hold of the eternal life, to which you were called and for which you made*f* the good confession in the presence of many witnesses. 13 In the presence of God, who gives life to all things, and of Christ Jesus, who in his testimony before Pontius Pilate made the good confession, I charge you 14 to keep the commandment without spot or blame until the manifestation of our Lord Jesus Christ, 15 which he will bring about at the right time—he who is the blessed and only Sovereign, the King of kings and Lord of lords. 16 It is he alone who has immortality and dwells in unapproachable light, whom no one has ever seen or can see; to him be honour and eternal dominion. Amen.

17 As for those who in the present age are rich, command them not to be haughty, or to set their hopes on the uncertainty of riches, but rather on God who richly provides us with everything for our enjoyment. 18 They are to do good, to be rich in good works, generous, and ready to share, 19 thus storing up for themselves the treasure of a good foundation for the future, so that they may take hold of the life that really is life.

Personal Instructions and Benediction

20 Timothy, guard what has been entrusted to you. Avoid the profane chatter and contradictions of what is falsely called knowledge; 21 by professing it some have missed the mark as regards the faith.

Grace be with you.*g*

---

a Gk *Do not lay hands on*   *b* Gk *are brothers*
c Or *since they are believers and beloved, who devote themselves to good deeds*   *d* Other ancient authorities add *Withdraw yourself from such people*   *e* Other ancient authorities read *world—it is certain that*
f Gk *confessed*   *g* The Greek word for *you* here is plural; in other ancient authorities it is singular. Other ancient authorities add *Amen*

THE SECOND LETTER OF PAUL TO
TIMOTHY

Salutation

1 Paul, an apostle of Christ Jesus by the will of God, for the sake of the promise of life that is in Christ Jesus,

2 To Timothy, my beloved child:

Grace, mercy, and peace from God the Father and Christ Jesus our Lord.

Thanksgiving and Encouragement

3 I am grateful to God—whom I worship with a clear conscience, as my ancestors did—when I remember you constantly in my prayers night and day. 4 Recalling your tears, I long to see you so that I may be filled with joy. 5 I am reminded of your sincere faith, a faith that lived first in your grandmother Lois and your mother Eunice and now, I am sure, lives in you. 6 For this reason I remind you to rekindle the gift of God that is within you through the laying on of my hands; 7 for God did not give us a spirit of cowardice, but rather a spirit of power and of love and of self-discipline.

8 Do not be ashamed, then, of the testimony about our Lord or of me his prisoner, but join with me in suffering for the gospel, relying on the power of God, 9 who saved us and called us with a holy calling, not according to our works but according to his own purpose and grace. This grace was given to us in Christ Jesus before the ages began, 10 but it has now been revealed through the appearing of our Saviour Christ Jesus, who abolished death and brought life and immortality to light through the gospel. 11 For this gospel I was appointed a herald and an apostle and a teacher,*a* 12 and for this reason I suffer as I do. But I am not ashamed, for I know the one in whom I have put my trust, and I am

sure that he is able to guard until that day what I have entrusted to him.*b* 13 Hold to the standard of sound teaching that you have heard from me, in the faith and love that are in Christ Jesus. 14 Guard the good treasure entrusted to you, with the help of the Holy Spirit living in us.

15 You are aware that all who are in Asia have turned away from me, including Phygelus and Hermogenes. 16 May the Lord grant mercy to the household of Onesiphorus, because he often refreshed me and was not ashamed of my chain; 17 when he arrived in Rome, he eagerly*c* searched for me and found me 18 —may the Lord grant that he will find mercy from the Lord on that day! And you know very well how much service he rendered in Ephesus.

A Good Soldier of Christ Jesus

2 You then, my child, be strong in the grace that is in Christ Jesus; 2 and what you have heard from me through many witnesses entrust to faithful people who will be able to teach others as well. 3 Share in suffering like a good soldier of Christ Jesus. 4 No one serving in the army gets entangled in everyday affairs; the soldier's aim is to please the enlisting officer. 5 And in the case of an athlete, no one is crowned without competing according to the rules. 6 It is the farmer who does the work who ought to have the first share of the crops. 7 Think over what I say, for the Lord will give you understanding in all things.

8 Remember Jesus Christ, raised from the dead, a descendant of David—that is

---

a Other ancient authorities add *of the Gentiles*
b Or *what has been entrusted to me*   *c* Or *promptly*

my gospel, 9 for which I suffer hardship, even to the point of being chained like a criminal. But the word of God is not chained. 10 Therefore I endure everything for the sake of the elect, so that they may also obtain the salvation that is in Christ Jesus, with eternal glory. 11 The saying is sure:

If we have died with him, we will
    also live with him;
12 if we endure, we will also reign with
    him;
if we deny him, he will also deny us;
13 if we are faithless, he remains
    faithful—
for he cannot deny himself.

A Worker Approved by God

14 Remind them of this, and warn them before God [a] that they are to avoid wrangling over words, which does no good but only ruins those who are listening. 15 Do your best to present yourself to God as one approved by him, a worker who has no need to be ashamed, rightly explaining the word of truth. 16 Avoid profane chatter, for it will lead people into more and more impiety, 17 and their talk will spread like gangrene. Among them are Hymenaeus and Philetus, 18 who have swerved from the truth by claiming that the resurrection has already taken place. They are upsetting the faith of some. 19 But God's firm foundation stands, bearing this inscription: 'The Lord knows those who are his', and, 'Let everyone who calls on the name of the Lord turn away from wickedness.'

20 In a large house there are utensils not only of gold and silver but also of wood and clay, some for special use, some for ordinary. 21 All who cleanse themselves of the things I have mentioned [b] will become special utensils, dedicated and useful to the owner of the house, ready for every good work. 22 Shun youthful passions and pursue righteousness, faith, love, and peace, along with those who call on the Lord from a pure heart. 23 Have nothing to do with stupid and senseless controversies; you know that they breed quarrels. 24 And the Lord's servant [c] must not be quarrel-

some but kindly to everyone, an apt teacher, patient, 25 correcting opponents with gentleness. God may perhaps grant that they will repent and come to know the truth, 26 and that they may escape from the snare of the devil, having been held captive by him to do his will. [d]

Godlessness in the Last Days

3 You must understand this, that in the last days distressing times will come. 2 For people will be lovers of themselves, lovers of money, boasters, arrogant, abusive, disobedient to their parents, ungrateful, unholy, 3 inhuman, implacable, slanderers, profligates, brutes, haters of good, 4 treacherous, reckless, swollen with conceit, lovers of pleasure rather than lovers of God, 5 holding to the outward form of godliness but denying its power. Avoid them! 6 For among them are those who make their way into households and captivate silly women, overwhelmed by their sins and swayed by all kinds of desires, 7 who are always being instructed and can never arrive at a knowledge of the truth. 8 As Jannes and Jambres opposed Moses, so these people, of corrupt mind and counterfeit faith, also oppose the truth. 9 But they will not make much progress, because, as in the case of those two men, [e] their folly will become plain to everyone.

Paul's Charge to Timothy

10 Now you have observed my teaching, my conduct, my aim in life, my faith, my patience, my love, my steadfastness, 11 my persecutions, and my suffering the things that happened to me in Antioch, Iconium, and Lystra. What persecutions I endured! Yet the Lord rescued me from all of them. 12 Indeed, all who want to live a godly life in Christ Jesus will be persecuted. 13 But wicked people and impostors will go from bad to worse, deceiving others and being deceived. 14 But as for you, continue in what you have learned and firmly believed, knowing from whom you learned

a Other ancient authorities read *the Lord*   b Gk *of these things*   c Gk *slave*   d Or *by him, to do his* (that is, God's) *will*   e Gk lacks *two men* it, 15 and how from childhood you have known the sacred writings that are able to instruct you for salvation through faith in Christ Jesus. 16 All scripture is inspired by God and is *a* useful for teaching, for reproof, for correction, and for training in righteousness, 17 so that everyone who belongs to God may be proficient, equipped for every good work.

4 In the presence of God and of Christ Jesus, who is to judge the living and the dead, and in view of his appearing and his kingdom, I solemnly urge you: 2 proclaim the message; be persistent whether the time is favourable or unfavourable; convince, rebuke, and encourage, with the utmost patience in teaching. 3 For the time is coming when people will not put up with sound doctrine, but having itching ears, they will accumulate for themselves teachers to suit their own desires, 4 and will turn away from listening to the truth and wander away to myths. 5 As for you, always be sober, endure suffering, do the work of an evangelist, carry out your ministry fully.

6 As for me, I am already being poured out as a libation, and the time of my departure has come. 7 I have fought the good fight, I have finished the race, I have kept the faith. 8 From now on there is reserved for me the crown of righteousness, which the Lord, the righteous judge, will give to me on that day, and not only to me but also to all who have longed for his appearing.

Personal Instructions

9 Do your best to come to me soon, 10 for Demas, in love with this present world, has deserted me and gone to Thessalonica; Crescens has gone to Galatia, *b* Titus to Dalmatia. 11 Only Luke is with me. Get Mark and bring him with you, for he is useful in my ministry. 12 I have sent Tychicus to Ephesus. 13 When you come, bring the cloak that I left with Carpus at Troas, also the books, and above all the parchments. 14 Alexander the coppersmith did me great harm; the Lord will pay him back for his deeds. 15 You also must beware of him, for he strongly opposed our message.

16 At my first defence no one came to my support, but all deserted me. May it not be counted against them! 17 But the Lord stood by me and gave me strength, so that through me the message might be fully proclaimed and all the Gentiles might hear it. So I was rescued from the lion's mouth. 18 The Lord will rescue me from every evil attack and save me for his heavenly kingdom. To him be the glory for ever and ever. Amen.

Final Greetings and Benediction

19 Greet Prisca and Aquila, and the household of Onesiphorus. 20 Erastus remained in Corinth; Trophimus I left ill in Miletus. 21 Do your best to come before winter. Eubulus sends greetings to you, as do Pudens and Linus and Claudia and all the brothers and sisters. *c*

22 The Lord be with your spirit. Grace be with you. *d*

a Or *Every scripture inspired by God is also*   *b* Other ancient authorities read *Gaul*   *c* Gk *all the brothers*   *d* The Greek word for *you* here is plural. Other ancient authorities add *Amen*

THE LETTER OF PAUL TO
TITUS

Salutation

1 Paul, a servant*a* of God and an apostle of Jesus Christ, for the sake of the faith of God's elect and the knowledge of the truth that is in accordance with godliness, 2 in the hope of eternal life that God, who never lies, promised before the ages began— 3 in due time he revealed his word through the proclamation with which I have been entrusted by the command of God our Saviour,

4 To Titus, my loyal child in the faith we share:

Grace*b* and peace from God the Father and Christ Jesus our Saviour.

Titus in Crete

5 I left you behind in Crete for this reason, that you should put in order what remained to be done, and should appoint elders in every town, as I directed you: 6 someone who is blameless, married only once,*c* whose children are believers, not accused of debauchery and not rebellious. 7 For a bishop,*d* as God's steward, must be blameless; he must not be arrogant or quick-tempered or addicted to wine or violent or greedy for gain; 8 but he must be hospitable, a lover of goodness, prudent, upright, devout, and self-controlled. 9 He must have a firm grasp of the word that is trustworthy in accordance with the teaching, so that he may be able both to preach with sound doctrine and to refute those who contradict it.

10 There are also many rebellious people, idle talkers and deceivers, especially those of the circumcision; 11 they must be silenced, since they are upsetting whole families by teaching for sordid gain what it is not right to teach. 12 It was one of them, their very own prophet, who said,

'Cretans are always liars, vicious
brutes, lazy gluttons.'

13 That testimony is true. For this reason rebuke them sharply, so that they may become sound in the faith, 14 not paying attention to Jewish myths or to commandments of those who reject the truth. 15 To the pure all things are pure, but to the corrupt and unbelieving nothing is pure. Their very minds and consciences are corrupted. 16 They profess to know God, but they deny him by their actions. They are detestable, disobedient, unfit for any good work.

Teach Sound Doctrine

2 But as for you, teach what is consistent with sound doctrine. 2 Tell the older men to be temperate, serious, prudent, and sound in faith, in love, and in endurance.

3 Likewise, tell the older women to be reverent in behaviour, not to be slanderers or slaves to drink; they are to teach what is good, 4 so that they may encourage the young women to love their husbands, to love their children, 5 to be self-controlled, chaste, good managers of the household, kind, being submissive to their husbands, so that the word of God may not be discredited.

6 Likewise, urge the younger men to be self-controlled. 7 Show yourself in all respects a model of good works, and in your teaching show integrity, gravity, 8 and sound speech that cannot be censured;

a Gk *slave*   *b* Other ancient authorities read *Grace, mercy,*   *c* Gk *husband of one wife*   *d* Or *an overseer* then any opponent will be put to shame, having nothing evil to say of us.

9 Tell slaves to be submissive to their masters and to give satisfaction in every respect; they are not to answer back, [10] not to pilfer, but to show complete and perfect fidelity, so that in everything they may be an ornament to the doctrine of God our Saviour.

11 For the grace of God has appeared, bringing salvation to all,[a] [12] training us to renounce impiety and worldly passions, and in the present age to live lives that are self-controlled, upright, and godly, [13] while we wait for the blessed hope and the manifestation of the glory of our great God and Saviour,[b] Jesus Christ. [14] He it is who gave himself for us that he might redeem us from all iniquity and purify for himself a people of his own who are zealous for good deeds.

15 Declare these things; exhort and reprove with all authority.[c] Let no one look down on you.

Maintain Good Deeds

3 Remind them to be subject to rulers and authorities, to be obedient, to be ready for every good work, [2] to speak evil of no one, to avoid quarrelling, to be gentle, and to show every courtesy to everyone. [3] For we ourselves were once foolish, disobedient, led astray, slaves to various passions and pleasures, passing our days in malice and envy, despicable, hating one another. [4] But when the goodness and loving-kindness of God our Saviour appeared, [5] he saved us, not because of any works of righteousness that we had done, but according to his mercy, through the water[d] of rebirth and renewal by the Holy Spirit. [6] This Spirit he poured out on us richly through Jesus Christ our Saviour, [7] so that, having been justified by his grace, we might become heirs according to the hope of eternal life. [8] The saying is sure.

I desire that you insist on these things, so that those who have come to believe in God may be careful to devote themselves to good works; these things are excellent and profitable to everyone. [9] But avoid stupid controversies, genealogies, dissensions, and quarrels about the law, for they are unprofitable and worthless. [10] After a first and second admonition, have nothing more to do with anyone who causes divisions, [11] since you know that such a person is perverted and sinful, being self-condemned.

Final Messages and Benediction

12 When I send Artemas to you, or Tychicus, do your best to come to me at Nicopolis, for I have decided to spend the winter there. [13] Make every effort to send Zenas the lawyer and Apollos on their way, and see that they lack nothing. [14] And let people learn to devote themselves to good works in order to meet urgent needs, so that they may not be unproductive.

15 All who are with me send greetings to you. Greet those who love us in the faith.

Grace be with all of you.[e]

a Or has appeared to all, bringing salvation   b Or of the great God and our Saviour   c Gk commandment   d Gk washing   e Other ancient authorities add Amen

THE LETTER OF PAUL TO
PHILEMON

Salutation

1 Paul, a prisoner of Christ Jesus, and Timothy our brother, *a*

To Philemon our dear friend and co-worker, 2 to Apphia our sister, *b* to Archippus our fellow-soldier, and to the church in your house:

3 Grace to you and peace from God our Father and the Lord Jesus Christ.

Philemon's Love and Faith

4 When I remember you *c* in my prayers, I always thank my God 5 because I hear of your love for all the saints and your faith towards the Lord Jesus. 6 I pray that the sharing of your faith may become effective when you perceive all the good that we *d* may do for Christ. 7 I have indeed received much joy and encouragement from your love, because the hearts of the saints have been refreshed through you, my brother.

Paul's Plea for Onesimus

8 For this reason, though I am bold enough in Christ to command you to do your duty, 9 yet I would rather appeal to you on the basis of love—and I, Paul, do this as an old man, and now also as a prisoner of Christ Jesus. *e* 10 I am appealing to you for my child, Onesimus, whose father I have become during my imprisonment. 11 Formerly he was useless to you, but now he is indeed useful *f* both to you and to me. 12 I am sending him, that is, my own heart, back to you. 13 I wanted to keep him with me, so that he might be of service to me in your place during my imprisonment for the gospel; 14 but I preferred to do nothing without your consent, in order that your good deed might be voluntary and not something forced. 15 Perhaps this is the reason he was separated from you for a while, so that you might have him back for ever, 16 no longer as a slave but as more than a slave, a beloved brother—especially to me but how much more to you, both in the flesh and in the Lord.

17 So if you consider me your partner, welcome him as you would welcome me. 18 If he has wronged you in any way, or owes you anything, charge that to my account. 19 I, Paul, am writing this with my own hand: I will repay it. I say nothing about your owing me even your own self. 20 Yes, brother, let me have this benefit from you in the Lord! Refresh my heart in Christ. 21 Confident of your obedience, I am writing to you, knowing that you will do even more than I say.

22 One thing more—prepare a guest room for me, for I am hoping through your prayers to be restored to you.

Final Greetings and Benediction

23 Epaphras, my fellow-prisoner in Christ Jesus, sends greetings to you, *g* 24 and so do Mark, Aristarchus, Demas, and Luke, my fellow-workers.

25 The grace of the Lord Jesus Christ be with your spirit. *h*

---

a Gk *the brother*   *b* Gk *the sister*   *c* In verses 4 to 21, *you* is singular   *d* Other ancient authorities read *you* (plural)   *e* Or *as an ambassador of Christ Jesus, and now also his prisoner*   *f* The name Onesimus means *useful* or (compare verse 20) *beneficial*   *g* Here *you* is singular   *h* Other ancient authorities add *Amen*

THE LETTER TO THE
HEBREWS

God Has Spoken by His Son

1 Long ago God spoke to our ancestors in many and various ways by the prophets, 2 but in these last days he has spoken to us by a Son, *a* whom he appointed heir of all things, through whom he also created the worlds. 3 He is the reflection of God's glory and the exact imprint of God's very being, and he sustains *b* all things by his powerful word. When he had made purification for sins, he sat down at the right hand of the Majesty on high, 4 having become as much superior to angels as the name he has inherited is more excellent than theirs.

The Son Is Superior to Angels

5 For to which of the angels did God ever say,
'You are my Son;
today I have begotten you'?
Or again,
'I will be his Father,
and he will be my Son'?
6 And again, when he brings the firstborn into the world, he says,
'Let all God's angels worship him.'
7 Of the angels he says,
'He makes his angels winds,
and his servants flames of fire.'
8 But of the Son he says,
'Your throne, O God, is *c* for ever and ever,
and the righteous sceptre is the sceptre of your *d* kingdom.
9 You have loved righteousness and hated wickedness;
therefore God, your God, has anointed you

with the oil of gladness beyond your companions.'
10 And,
'In the beginning, Lord, you founded the earth,
and the heavens are the work of your hands;
11 they will perish, but you remain;
they will all wear out like clothing;
12 like a cloak you will roll them up,
and like clothing *e* they will be changed.
But you are the same,
and your years will never end.'
13 But to which of the angels has he ever said,
'Sit at my right hand
until I make your enemies a footstool for your feet'?
14 Are not all angels *f* spirits in the divine service, sent to serve for the sake of those who are to inherit salvation?

Warning to Pay Attention

2 Therefore we must pay greater attention to what we have heard, so that we do not drift away from it. 2 For if the message declared through angels was valid, and every transgression or disobedience received a just penalty, 3 how can we escape if we neglect so great a salvation? It was declared at first through the Lord, and it was attested to us by those who heard him, 4 while God added his testimony by signs and wonders and various miracles,

a Or *the Son*   *b* Or *bears along*   *c* Or *God is your throne*   *d* Other ancient authorities read *his*
e Other ancient authorities lack *like clothing*
f Gk *all of them*

and by gifts of the Holy Spirit, distributed according to his will.

Exaltation through Abasement

5 Now God[a] did not subject the coming world, about which we are speaking, to angels. [6]But someone has testified somewhere,

'What are human beings that you are
    mindful of them,[b]
  or mortals, that you care for
    them?[c]
[7] You have made them for a little while
    lower[d] than the angels;
  you have crowned them with glory
    and honour,[e]
[8]   subjecting all things under
    their feet.'

Now in subjecting all things to them, God[f] left nothing outside their control. As it is, we do not yet see everything in subjection to them, [9]but we do see Jesus, who for a little while was made lower[g] than the angels, now crowned with glory and honour because of the suffering of death, so that by the grace of God[h] he might taste death for everyone.

10 It was fitting that God,[f] for whom and through whom all things exist, in bringing many children to glory, should make the pioneer of their salvation perfect through sufferings. [11]For the one who sanctifies and those who are sanctified all have one Father.[i] For this reason Jesus[f] is not ashamed to call them brothers and sisters,[j] [12]saying,

'I will proclaim your name to my
    brothers and sisters,[j]
  in the midst of the congregation I
    will praise you.'

[13]And again,

'I will put my trust in him.'

And again,

'Here am I and the children whom
    God has given me.'

14 Since, therefore, the children share flesh and blood, he himself likewise shared the same things, so that through death he might destroy the one who has the power of death, that is, the devil, [15]and free those who all their lives were held in slavery by the fear of death. [16]For it is clear that he did not come to help angels, but the descendants of Abraham. [17]Therefore he had to become like his brothers and sisters[j] in every respect, so that he might be a merciful and faithful high priest in the service of God, to make a sacrifice of atonement for the sins of the people. [18]Because he himself was tested by what he suffered, he is able to help those who are being tested.

Moses a Servant, Christ a Son

3 Therefore, brothers and sisters,[j] holy partners in a heavenly calling, consider that Jesus, the apostle and high priest of our confession, [2]was faithful to the one who appointed him, just as Moses also 'was faithful in all[k] God's[l] house.' [3]Yet Jesus[m] is worthy of more glory than Moses, just as the builder of a house has more honour than the house itself. [4](For every house is built by someone, but the builder of all things is God.) [5]Now Moses was faithful in all God's[l] house as a servant, to testify to the things that would be spoken later. [6]Christ, however, was faithful over God's[l] house as a son, and we are his house if we hold firm[n] the confidence and the pride that belong to hope.

Warning against Unbelief

7 Therefore, as the Holy Spirit says,
'Today, if you hear his voice,
[8] do not harden your hearts as in
    the rebellion,
  as on the day of testing in the
    wilderness,
[9] where your ancestors put me to
    the test,
  though they had seen my works
    [10]for forty years.
Therefore I was angry with that
    generation,

a Gk he   b Gk What is man that you are mindful of him?   c Gk or the son of man that you care for him? In the Hebrew of Psalm 8.4-6 both man and son of man refer to all humankind   d Or them only a little lower   e Other ancient authorities add and set them over the works of your hands   f Gk he   g Or who was made a little lower   h Other ancient authorities read apart from God   i Gk are all of one   j Gk brothers   k Other ancient authorities lack all   l Gk his   m Gk this one   n Other ancient authorities add to the end

and I said, "They always go astray in
    their hearts,
  and they have not known
    my ways."
11 As in my anger I swore,
  "They will not enter my rest." '

12 Take care, brothers and sisters, *a* that
none of you may have an evil, unbelieving
heart that turns away from the living God.
13 But exhort one another every day, as
long as it is called 'today', so that none of
you may be hardened by the deceitfulness
of sin. 14 For we have become partners of
Christ, if only we hold our first confidence
firm to the end. 15 As it is said,

'Today, if you hear his voice,
  do not harden your hearts as in
    the rebellion.'

16 Now who were they who heard and yet
were rebellious? Was it not all those who
left Egypt under the leadership of Moses?
17 But with whom was he angry for forty
years? Was it not those who sinned, whose
bodies fell in the wilderness? 18 And to
whom did he swear that they would not
enter his rest, if not to those who were disobedient? 19 So we see that they were unable to enter because of unbelief.

The Rest That God Promised

4 Therefore, while the promise of entering his rest is still open, let us take
care that none of you should seem to have
failed to reach it. 2 For indeed the good
news came to us just as to them; but the
message they heard did not benefit them,
because they were not united by faith with
those who listened. *b* 3 For we who have believed enter that rest, just as God *c* has said,

'As in my anger I swore,
  "They shall not enter my rest" ',

though his works were finished at the
foundation of the world. 4 For in one place
it speaks about the seventh day as follows:
'And God rested on the seventh day from
all his works.' 5 And again in this place it
says, 'They shall not enter my rest.' 6 Since
therefore it remains open for some to enter
it, and those who formerly received the
good news failed to enter because of disobedience, 7 again he sets a certain day—

'today'—saying through David much later,
in the words already quoted,

'Today, if you hear his voice,
  do not harden your hearts.'

8 For if Joshua had given them rest, God *c*
would not speak later about another day.
9 So then, a sabbath rest still remains for
the people of God; 10 for those who enter
God's rest also cease from their labours as
God did from his. 11 Let us therefore make
every effort to enter that rest, so that no
one may fall through such disobedience as
theirs.

12 Indeed, the word of God is living
and active, sharper than any two-edged
sword, piercing until it divides soul from
spirit, joints from marrow; it is able to
judge the thoughts and intentions of the
heart. 13 And before him no creature is hidden, but all are naked and laid bare to the
eyes of the one to whom we must render
an account.

Jesus the Great High Priest

14 Since, then, we have a great high
priest who has passed through the heavens, Jesus, the Son of God, let us hold fast
to our confession. 15 For we do not have a
high priest who is unable to sympathize
with our weaknesses, but we have one who
in every respect has been tested *d* as we are,
yet without sin. 16 Let us therefore approach the throne of grace with boldness,
so that we may receive mercy and find
grace to help in time of need.

5 Every high priest chosen from among
mortals is put in charge of things pertaining to God on their behalf, to offer
gifts and sacrifices for sins. 2 He is able to
deal gently with the ignorant and wayward, since he himself is subject to weakness; 3 and because of this he must offer
sacrifice for his own sins as well as for
those of the people. 4 And one does not
presume to take this honour, but takes it
only when called by God, just as Aaron
was.

5 So also Christ did not glorify himself

---

a Gk *brothers*   *b* Other ancient authorities read *it did
not meet with faith in those who listened*   *c* Gk *he*
d Or *tempted*

in becoming a high priest, but was appointed by the one who said to him,

'You are my Son,
today I have begotten you';

[6] as he says also in another place,

'You are a priest for ever,
according to the order of
Melchizedek.'

7 In the days of his flesh, Jesus[a] offered up prayers and supplications, with loud cries and tears, to the one who was able to save him from death, and he was heard because of his reverent submission. [8] Although he was a Son, he learned obedience through what he suffered; [9] and having been made perfect, he became the source of eternal salvation for all who obey him, [10] having been designated by God a high priest according to the order of Melchizedek.

Warning against Falling Away

11 About this[b] we have much to say that is hard to explain, since you have become dull in understanding. [12] For though by this time you ought to be teachers, you need someone to teach you again the basic elements of the oracles of God. You need milk, not solid food; [13] for everyone who lives on milk, being still an infant, is unskilled in the word of righteousness. [14] But solid food is for the mature, for those whose faculties have been trained by practice to distinguish good from evil.

The Peril of Falling Away

6 Therefore let us go on towards perfection,[c] leaving behind the basic teaching about Christ, and not laying again the foundation: repentance from dead works and faith towards God, [2] instruction about baptisms, laying on of hands, resurrection of the dead, and eternal judgement. [3] And we will do[d] this, if God permits. [4] For it is impossible to restore again to repentance those who have once been enlightened, and have tasted the heavenly gift, and have shared in the Holy Spirit, [5] and have tasted the goodness of the word of God and the powers of the age to come, [6] and then have fallen away, since on their own they are crucifying again the Son of God and are holding him up to contempt. [7] Ground that drinks up the rain falling on it repeatedly, and that produces a crop useful to those for whom it is cultivated, receives a blessing from God. [8] But if it produces thorns and thistles, it is worthless and on the verge of being cursed; its end is to be burned over.

9 Even though we speak in this way, beloved, we are confident of better things in your case, things that belong to salvation. [10] For God is not unjust; he will not overlook your work and the love that you showed for his sake[e] in serving the saints, as you still do. [11] And we want each one of you to show the same diligence, so as to realize the full assurance of hope to the very end, [12] so that you may not become sluggish, but imitators of those who through faith and patience inherit the promises.

The Certainty of God's Promise

13 When God made a promise to Abraham, because he had no one greater by whom to swear, he swore by himself, [14] saying, 'I will surely bless you and multiply you.' [15] And thus Abraham,[a] having patiently endured, obtained the promise. [16] Human beings, of course, swear by someone greater than themselves, and an oath given as confirmation puts an end to all dispute. [17] In the same way, when God desired to show even more clearly to the heirs of the promise the unchangeable character of his purpose, he guaranteed it by an oath, [18] so that through two unchangeable things, in which it is impossible that God would prove false, we who have taken refuge might be strongly encouraged to seize the hope set before us. [19] We have this hope, a sure and steadfast anchor of the soul, a hope that enters the inner shrine behind the curtain, [20] where Jesus, a forerunner on our behalf, has entered, having become a high priest for ever according to the order of Melchizedek.

a Gk he   b Or him   c Or towards maturity
d Other ancient authorities read let us do   e Gk for his name

The Priestly Order of Melchizedek

7 This 'King Melchizedek of Salem, priest of the Most High God, met Abraham as he was returning from defeating the kings and blessed him'; 2and to him Abraham apportioned 'one-tenth of everything'. His name, in the first place, means 'king of righteousness'; next he is also king of Salem, that is, 'king of peace'. 3Without father, without mother, without genealogy, having neither beginning of days nor end of life, but resembling the Son of God, he remains a priest for ever.

4 See how great he is! Even*a* Abraham the patriarch gave him a tenth of the spoils. 5And those descendants of Levi who receive the priestly office have a commandment in the law to collect tithes*b* from the people, that is, from their kindred,*c* though these also are descended from Abraham. 6But this man, who does not belong to their ancestry, collected tithes*b* from Abraham and blessed him who had received the promises. 7It is beyond dispute that the inferior is blessed by the superior. 8In the one case, tithes are received by those who are mortal; in the other, by one of whom it is testified that he lives. 9One might even say that Levi himself, who receives tithes, paid tithes through Abraham, 10for he was still in the loins of his ancestor when Melchizedek met him.

Another Priest, Like Melchizedek

11 Now if perfection had been attainable through the levitical priesthood—for the people received the law under this priesthood—what further need would there have been to speak of another priest arising according to the order of Melchizedek, rather than one according to the order of Aaron? 12For when there is a change in the priesthood, there is necessarily a change in the law as well. 13Now the one of whom these things are spoken belonged to another tribe, from which no one has ever served at the altar. 14For it is evident that our Lord was descended from Judah, and in connection with that tribe Moses said nothing about priests.

15 It is even more obvious when another priest arises, resembling Melchizedek, 16one who has become a priest, not through a legal requirement concerning physical descent, but through the power of an indestructible life. 17For it is attested of him,

'You are a priest for ever,
　according to the order of
　　Melchizedek.'

18There is, on the one hand, the abrogation of an earlier commandment because it was weak and ineffectual 19(for the law made nothing perfect); there is, on the other hand, the introduction of a better hope, through which we approach God.

20 This was confirmed with an oath; for others who became priests took their office without an oath, 21but this one became a priest with an oath, because of the one who said to him,

'The Lord has sworn
　and will not change his mind,
"You are a priest for ever" '—
22accordingly Jesus has also become the guarantee of a better covenant.

23 Furthermore, the former priests were many in number, because they were prevented by death from continuing in office; 24but he holds his priesthood permanently, because he continues for ever. 25Consequently he is able for all time to save*d* those who approach God through him, since he always lives to make intercession for them.

26 For it was fitting that we should have such a high priest, holy, blameless, undefiled, separated from sinners, and exalted above the heavens. 27Unlike the other*e* high priests, he has no need to offer sacrifices day after day, first for his own sins, and then for those of the people; this he did once for all when he offered himself. 28For the law appoints as high priests those who are subject to weakness, but the word of the oath, which came later than the law, appoints a Son who has been made perfect for ever.

a Other ancient authorities lack *Even*　　*b* Or *a tenth*
c Gk *brothers*　　*d* Or *able to save completely*
e Gk lacks *other*

Mediator of a Better Covenant

8 Now the main point in what we are saying is this: we have such a high priest, one who is seated at the right hand of the throne of the Majesty in the heavens, ²a minister in the sanctuary and the true tent[a] that the Lord, and not any mortal, has set up. ³For every high priest is appointed to offer gifts and sacrifices; hence it is necessary for this priest also to have something to offer. ⁴Now if he were on earth, he would not be a priest at all, since there are priests who offer gifts according to the law. ⁵They offer worship in a sanctuary that is a sketch and shadow of the heavenly one; for Moses, when he was about to erect the tent,[a] was warned, 'See that you make everything according to the pattern that was shown you on the mountain.' ⁶But Jesus[b] has now obtained a more excellent ministry, and to that degree he is the mediator of a better covenant, which has been enacted through better promises. ⁷For if that first covenant had been faultless, there would have been no need to look for a second one.

8 God[c] finds fault with them when he says:

'The days are surely coming, says the Lord,
  when I will establish a new
    covenant with the house
    of Israel
  and with the house of Judah;
⁹ not like the covenant that I made
    with their ancestors,
  on the day when I took them by
    the hand to lead them out
    of the land of Egypt;
for they did not continue in
    my covenant,
  and so I had no concern for them,
    says the Lord.
¹⁰ This is the covenant that I will make
    with the house of Israel
  after those days, says the Lord:
I will put my laws in their minds,
  and write them on their hearts,
and I will be their God,
  and they shall be my people.
¹¹ And they shall not teach one another
or say to each other, "Know
    the Lord",
for they shall all know me,
  from the least of them to
    the greatest.
¹² For I will be merciful towards their
    iniquities,
  and I will remember their sins
    no more.'

¹³In speaking of 'a new covenant', he has made the first one obsolete. And what is obsolete and growing old will soon disappear.

The Earthly and the Heavenly Sanctuaries

9 Now even the first covenant had regulations for worship and an earthly sanctuary. ²For a tent[a] was constructed, the first one, in which were the lampstand, the table, and the bread of the Presence;[d] this is called the Holy Place. ³Behind the second curtain was a tent[a] called the Holy of Holies. ⁴In it stood the golden altar of incense and the ark of the covenant overlaid on all sides with gold, in which there were a golden urn holding the manna, and Aaron's rod that budded, and the tablets of the covenant; ⁵above it were the cherubim of glory overshadowing the mercy-seat.[e] Of these things we cannot speak now in detail.

6 Such preparations having been made, the priests go continually into the first tent[a] to carry out their ritual duties; ⁷but only the high priest goes into the second, and he but once a year, and not without taking the blood that he offers for himself and for the sins committed unintentionally by the people. ⁸By this the Holy Spirit indicates that the way into the sanctuary has not yet been disclosed as long as the first tent[a] is still standing. ⁹This is a symbol[f] of the present time, during which gifts and sacrifices are offered that cannot perfect the conscience of the worshipper, ¹⁰but deal only with food and drink and various baptisms, regulations for the body

a Or tabernacle   b Gk he   c Gk He   d Gk the presentation of the loaves   e Or the place of atonement   f Gk parable imposed until the time comes to set things right.

11 But when Christ came as a high priest of the good things that have come,[a] then through the greater and perfect[b] tent[c] (not made with hands, that is, not of this creation), 12 he entered once for all into the Holy Place, not with the blood of goats and calves, but with his own blood, thus obtaining eternal redemption. 13 For if the blood of goats and bulls, with the sprinkling of the ashes of a heifer, sanctifies those who have been defiled so that their flesh is purified, 14 how much more will the blood of Christ, who through the eternal Spirit[d] offered himself without blemish to God, purify our[e] conscience from dead works to worship the living God!

15 For this reason he is the mediator of a new covenant, so that those who are called may receive the promised eternal inheritance, because a death has occurred that redeems them from the transgressions under the first covenant.[f] 16 Where a will[f] is involved, the death of the one who made it must be established. 17 For a will[f] takes effect only at death, since it is not in force as long as the one who made it is alive. 18 Hence not even the first covenant was inaugurated without blood. 19 For when every commandment had been told to all the people by Moses in accordance with the law, he took the blood of calves and goats,[g] with water and scarlet wool and hyssop, and sprinkled both the scroll itself and all the people, 20 saying, 'This is the blood of the covenant that God has ordained for you.' 21 And in the same way he sprinkled with the blood both the tent[c] and all the vessels used in worship. 22 Indeed, under the law almost everything is purified with blood, and without the shedding of blood there is no forgiveness of sins.

Christ's Sacrifice Takes Away Sin

23 Thus it was necessary for the sketches of the heavenly things to be purified with these rites, but the heavenly things themselves need better sacrifices than these. 24 For Christ did not enter a sanctuary made by human hands, a mere copy of the true one, but he entered into heaven itself, now to appear in the presence of God on our behalf. 25 Nor was it to offer himself again and again, as the high priest enters the Holy Place year after year with blood that is not his own; 26 for then he would have had to suffer again and again since the foundation of the world. But as it is, he has appeared once for all at the end of the age to remove sin by the sacrifice of himself. 27 And just as it is appointed for mortals to die once, and after that the judgement, 28 so Christ, having been offered once to bear the sins of many, will appear a second time, not to deal with sin, but to save those who are eagerly waiting for him.

Christ's Sacrifice Once for All

10 Since the law has only a shadow of the good things to come and not the true form of these realities, it[h] can never, by the same sacrifices that are continually offered year after year, make perfect those who approach. 2 Otherwise, would they not have ceased being offered, since the worshippers, cleansed once for all, would no longer have any consciousness of sin? 3 But in these sacrifices there is a reminder of sin year after year. 4 For it is impossible for the blood of bulls and goats to take away sins. 5 Consequently, when Christ[i] came into the world, he said,

'Sacrifices and offerings you have not
    desired,
  but a body you have prepared
    for me;
6 in burnt-offerings and sin-offerings
    you have taken no pleasure.
7 Then I said, "See, God, I have come
    to do your will, O God"
    (in the scroll of the book[j] it is
    written of me).'

a Other ancient authorities read good things to come
b Gk more perfect   c Or tabernacle   d Other ancient authorities read Holy Spirit   e Other ancient authorities read your   f The Greek word used here means both covenant and will   g Other ancient authorities lack and goats   h Other ancient authorities read they   i Gk he   j Meaning of Gk uncertain

8 When he said above, 'You have neither desired nor taken pleasure in sacrifices and offerings and burnt-offerings and sin-offerings' (these are offered according to the law), 9 then he added, 'See, I have come to do your will.' He abolishes the first in order to establish the second. 10 And it is by God's will[a] that we have been sanctified through the offering of the body of Jesus Christ once for all.

11 And every priest stands day after day at his service, offering again and again the same sacrifices that can never take away sins. 12 But when Christ[b] had offered for all time a single sacrifice for sins, 'he sat down at the right hand of God', 13 and since then has been waiting 'until his enemies would be made a footstool for his feet.' 14 For by a single offering he has perfected for all time those who are sanctified. 15 And the Holy Spirit also testifies to us, for after saying,

16 'This is the covenant that I will make
　　with them
　　after those days, says the Lord:
I will put my laws in their hearts,
　and I will write them on
　　their minds',

17 he also adds,

'I will remember[c] their sins and their
　　lawless deeds no more.'

18 Where there is forgiveness of these, there is no longer any offering for sin.

A Call to Persevere

19 Therefore, my friends,[d] since we have confidence to enter the sanctuary by the blood of Jesus, 20 by the new and living way that he opened for us through the curtain (that is, through his flesh), 21 and since we have a great priest over the house of God, 22 let us approach with a true heart in full assurance of faith, with our hearts sprinkled clean from an evil conscience and our bodies washed with pure water. 23 Let us hold fast to the confession of our hope without wavering, for he who has promised is faithful. 24 And let us consider how to provoke one another to love and good deeds, 25 not neglecting to meet together, as is the habit of some, but encour-

aging one another, and all the more as you see the Day approaching.

26 For if we wilfully persist in sin after having received the knowledge of the truth, there no longer remains a sacrifice for sins, 27 but a fearful prospect of judgement, and a fury of fire that will consume the adversaries. 28 Anyone who has violated the law of Moses dies without mercy 'on the testimony of two or three witnesses.' 29 How much worse punishment do you think will be deserved by those who have spurned the Son of God, profaned the blood of the covenant by which they were sanctified, and outraged the Spirit of grace? 30 For we know the one who said, 'Vengeance is mine, I will repay.' And again, 'The Lord will judge his people.' 31 It is a fearful thing to fall into the hands of the living God.

32 But recall those earlier days when, after you had been enlightened, you endured a hard struggle with sufferings, 33 sometimes being publicly exposed to abuse and persecution, and sometimes being partners with those so treated. 34 For you had compassion for those who were in prison, and you cheerfully accepted the plundering of your possessions, knowing that you yourselves possessed something better and more lasting. 35 Do not, therefore, abandon that confidence of yours; it brings a great reward. 36 For you need endurance, so that when you have done the will of God, you may receive what was promised. 37 For yet

'in a very little while,
　the one who is coming will come
　　and will not delay;
38 but my righteous one will live by faith.
　My soul takes no pleasure in
　　anyone who shrinks back.'

39 But we are not among those who shrink back and so are lost, but among those who have faith and so are saved.

The Meaning of Faith

11 Now faith is the assurance of things hoped for, the conviction of things not seen. 2 Indeed, by faith[e] our

a Gk by that will　　b Gk this one　　c Gk on their minds and I will remember　　d Gk Therefore, brothers　　e Gk by this ancestors received approval. ³ By faith we understand that the worlds were prepared by the word of God, so that what is seen was made from things that are not visible. *a*

The Examples of Abel, Enoch, and Noah

4 By faith Abel offered to God a more acceptable *b* sacrifice than Cain's. Through this he received approval as righteous, God himself giving approval to his gifts; he died, but through his faith *c* he still speaks. ⁵ By faith Enoch was taken so that he did not experience death; and 'he was not found, because God had taken him.' For it was attested before he was taken away that 'he had pleased God.' ⁶ And without faith it is impossible to please God, for whoever would approach him must believe that he exists and that he rewards those who seek him. ⁷ By faith Noah, warned by God about events as yet unseen, respected the warning and built an ark to save his household; by this he condemned the world and became an heir to the righteousness that is in accordance with faith.

The Faith of Abraham

8 By faith Abraham obeyed when he was called to set out for a place that he was to receive as an inheritance; and he set out, not knowing where he was going. ⁹ By faith he stayed for a time in the land he had been promised, as in a foreign land, living in tents, as did Isaac and Jacob, who were heirs with him of the same promise. ¹⁰ For he looked forward to the city that has foundations, whose architect and builder is God. ¹¹ By faith he received power of procreation, even though he was too old—and Sarah herself was barren—because he considered him faithful who had promised. *d* ¹² Therefore from one person, and this one as good as dead, descendants were born, 'as many as the stars of heaven and as the innumerable grains of sand by the seashore.'

13 All of these died in faith without having received the promises, but from a distance they saw and greeted them. They confessed that they were strangers and foreigners on the earth, ¹⁴ for people who speak in this way make it clear that they

are seeking a homeland. ¹⁵ If they had been thinking of the land that they had left behind, they would have had opportunity to return. ¹⁶ But as it is, they desire a better country, that is, a heavenly one. Therefore God is not ashamed to be called their God; indeed, he has prepared a city for them.

17 By faith Abraham, when put to the test, offered up Isaac. He who had received the promises was ready to offer up his only son, ¹⁸ of whom he had been told, 'It is through Isaac that descendants shall be named after you.' ¹⁹ He considered the fact that God is able even to raise someone from the dead—and figuratively speaking, he did receive him back. ²⁰ By faith Isaac invoked blessings for the future on Jacob and Esau. ²¹ By faith Jacob, when dying, blessed each of the sons of Joseph, 'bowing in worship over the top of his staff.' ²² By faith Joseph, at the end of his life, made mention of the exodus of the Israelites and gave instructions about his burial. *e*

The Faith of Moses

23 By faith Moses was hidden by his parents for three months after his birth, because they saw that the child was beautiful; and they were not afraid of the king's edict. *f* ²⁴ By faith Moses, when he was grown up, refused to be called a son of Pharaoh's daughter, ²⁵ choosing rather to share ill-treatment with the people of God than to enjoy the fleeting pleasures of sin. ²⁶ He considered abuse suffered for the Christ *g* to be greater wealth than the treasures of Egypt, for he was looking ahead to the reward. ²⁷ By faith he left Egypt, unafraid of the king's anger; for he persevered as though *h* he saw him who is invisible. ²⁸ By faith he kept the Passover and the sprinkling of blood, so that the destroyer of the firstborn would not touch the firstborn of Israel. *i*

a Or *was not made out of visible things*   *b* Gk *greater* *c* Gk *through it*   *d* Or *By faith Sarah herself, though barren, received power to conceive, even when she was too old, because she considered him faithful who had promised.* *e* Gk *his bones*   *f* Other ancient authorities add *By faith Moses, when he was grown up, killed the Egyptian, because he observed the humiliation of his people* (Gk *brothers*)   *g* Or *the Messiah*   *h* Or *because* *i* Gk *would not touch them*

The Faith of Other Israelite Heroes

29 By faith the people passed through the Red Sea as if it were dry land, but when the Egyptians attempted to do so they were drowned. 30 By faith the walls of Jericho fell after they had been encircled for seven days. 31 By faith Rahab the prostitute did not perish with those who were disobedient, *a* because she had received the spies in peace.

32 And what more should I say? For time would fail me to tell of Gideon, Barak, Samson, Jephthah, of David and Samuel and the prophets— 33 who through faith conquered kingdoms, administered justice, obtained promises, shut the mouths of lions, 34 quenched raging fire, escaped the edge of the sword, won strength out of weakness, became mighty in war, put foreign armies to flight. 35 Women received their dead by resurrection. Others were tortured, refusing to accept release, in order to obtain a better resurrection. 36 Others suffered mocking and flogging, and even chains and imprisonment. 37 They were stoned to death, they were sawn in two, *b* they were killed by the sword; they went about in skins of sheep and goats, destitute, persecuted, tormented— 38 of whom the world was not worthy. They wandered in deserts and mountains, and in caves and holes in the ground.

39 Yet all these, though they were commended for their faith, did not receive what was promised, 40 since God had provided something better so that they would not, without us, be made perfect.

The Example of Jesus

12 Therefore, since we are surrounded by so great a cloud of witnesses, let us also lay aside every weight and the sin that clings so closely, *c* and let us run with perseverance the race that is set before us, 2 looking to Jesus the pioneer and perfecter of our faith, who for the sake of *d* the joy that was set before him endured the cross, disregarding its shame, and has taken his seat at the right hand of the throne of God.

3 Consider him who endured such hostility against himself from sinners, *e* so that you may not grow weary or lose heart. 4 In your struggle against sin you have not yet resisted to the point of shedding your blood. 5 And you have forgotten the exhortation that addresses you as children—

'My child, do not regard lightly the
　discipline of the Lord,
　or lose heart when you are
　　punished by him;
6 for the Lord disciplines those whom
　he loves,
　and chastises every child whom he
　　accepts.'

7 Endure trials for the sake of discipline. God is treating you as children; for what child is there whom a parent does not discipline? 8 If you do not have that discipline in which all children share, then you are illegitimate and not his children. 9 Moreover, we had human parents to discipline us, and we respected them. Should we not be even more willing to be subject to the Father of spirits and live? 10 For they disciplined us for a short time as seemed best to them, but he disciplines us for our good, in order that we may share his holiness. 11 Now, discipline always seems painful rather than pleasant at the time, but later it yields the peaceful fruit of righteousness to those who have been trained by it.

12 Therefore lift your drooping hands and strengthen your weak knees, 13 and make straight paths for your feet, so that what is lame may not be put out of joint, but rather be healed.

Warnings against Rejecting God's Grace

14 Pursue peace with everyone, and the holiness without which no one will see the Lord. 15 See to it that no one fails to obtain the grace of God; that no root of bitterness springs up and causes trouble, and through it many become defiled. 16 See to it that no one becomes like Esau, an immoral and godless person, who sold his

a Or *unbelieving*　　*b* Other ancient authorities add *they were tempted*　　*c* Other ancient authorities read *sin that easily distracts*　　*d* Or *who instead of*　　*e* Other ancient authorities read *such hostility from sinners against themselves* birthright for a single meal. 17 You know that later, when he wanted to inherit the blessing, he was rejected, for he found no chance to repent,[a] even though he sought the blessing[b] with tears.

18 You have not come to something[c] that can be touched, a blazing fire, and darkness, and gloom, and a tempest, 19 and the sound of a trumpet, and a voice whose words made the hearers beg that not another word be spoken to them. 20 (For they could not endure the order that was given, 'If even an animal touches the mountain, it shall be stoned to death.' 21 Indeed, so terrifying was the sight that Moses said, 'I tremble with fear.') 22 But you have come to Mount Zion and to the city of the living God, the heavenly Jerusalem, and to innumerable angels in festal gathering, 23 and to the assembly[d] of the firstborn who are enrolled in heaven, and to God the judge of all, and to the spirits of the righteous made perfect, 24 and to Jesus, the mediator of a new covenant, and to the sprinkled blood that speaks a better word than the blood of Abel.

25 See that you do not refuse the one who is speaking; for if they did not escape when they refused the one who warned them on earth, how much less will we escape if we reject the one who warns from heaven! 26 At that time his voice shook the earth; but now he has promised, 'Yet once more I will shake not only the earth but also the heaven.' 27 This phrase 'Yet once more' indicates the removal of what is shaken—that is, created things—so that what cannot be shaken may remain. 28 Therefore, since we are receiving a kingdom that cannot be shaken, let us give thanks, by which we offer to God an acceptable worship with reverence and awe; 29 for indeed our God is a consuming fire.

Service Well-Pleasing to God

13 Let mutual love continue. 2 Do not neglect to show hospitality to strangers, for by doing that some have entertained angels without knowing it. 3 Remember those who are in prison, as though you were in prison with them; those who

are being tortured, as though you yourselves were being tortured.[e] 4 Let marriage be held in honour by all, and let the marriage bed be kept undefiled; for God will judge fornicators and adulterers. 5 Keep your lives free from the love of money, and be content with what you have; for he has said, 'I will never leave you or forsake you.' 6 So we can say with confidence,

'The Lord is my helper;
    I will not be afraid.
What can anyone do to me?'

7 Remember your leaders, those who spoke the word of God to you; consider the outcome of their way of life, and imitate their faith. 8 Jesus Christ is the same yesterday and today and for ever. 9 Do not be carried away by all kinds of strange teachings; for it is well for the heart to be strengthened by grace, not by regulations about food,[f] which have not benefited those who observe them. 10 We have an altar from which those who officiate in the tent[g] have no right to eat. 11 For the bodies of those animals whose blood is brought into the sanctuary by the high priest as a sacrifice for sin are burned outside the camp. 12 Therefore Jesus also suffered outside the city gate in order to sanctify the people by his own blood. 13 Let us then go to him outside the camp and bear the abuse he endured. 14 For here we have no lasting city, but we are looking for the city that is to come. 15 Through him, then, let us continually offer a sacrifice of praise to God, that is, the fruit of lips that confess his name. 16 Do not neglect to do good and to share what you have, for such sacrifices are pleasing to God.

17 Obey your leaders and submit to them, for they are keeping watch over your souls and will give an account. Let them do this with joy and not with sighing—for that would be harmful to you.

18 Pray for us; we are sure that we have a clear conscience, desiring to act honourably in all things. 19 I urge you all the

a Or no chance to change his father's mind   b Gk it
c Other ancient authorities read a mountain
d Or angels, and to the festal gathering 23 and assembly
e Gk were in the body   f Gk not by foods
g Or tabernacle

more to do this, so that I may be restored to you very soon.

Benediction

20 Now may the God of peace, who brought back from the dead our Lord Jesus, the great shepherd of the sheep, by the blood of the eternal covenant, 21 make you complete in everything good so that you may do his will, working among us[a] that which is pleasing in his sight, through Jesus Christ, to whom be the glory for ever and ever. Amen.

Final Exhortation and Greetings

22 I appeal to you, brothers and sisters,[b] bear with my word of exhortation, for I have written to you briefly. 23 I want you to know that our brother Timothy has been set free; and if he comes in time, he will be with me when I see you. 24 Greet all your leaders and all the saints. Those from Italy send you greetings. 25 Grace be with all of you.[c]

a Other ancient authorities read *you*   b Gk *brothers*
c Other ancient authorities add *Amen*

THE LETTER OF

JAMES

Salutation

1 James, a servant[a] of God and of the Lord Jesus Christ,
To the twelve tribes in the Dispersion:
Greetings.

Faith and Wisdom

2 My brothers and sisters,[b] whenever you face trials of any kind, consider it nothing but joy, 3 because you know that the testing of your faith produces endurance; 4 and let endurance have its full effect, so that you may be mature and complete, lacking in nothing.

5 If any of you is lacking in wisdom, ask God, who gives to all generously and ungrudgingly, and it will be given you. 6 But ask in faith, never doubting, for the one who doubts is like a wave of the sea, driven and tossed by the wind; 7, 8 for the doubter, being double-minded and unstable in every way, must not expect to receive anything from the Lord.

Poverty and Riches

9 Let the believer[c] who is lowly boast in being raised up, 10 and the rich in being brought low, because the rich will disappear like a flower in the field. 11 For the sun rises with its scorching heat and withers the field; its flower falls, and its beauty perishes. It is the same with the rich; in the midst of a busy life, they will wither away.

Trial and Temptation

12 Blessed is anyone who endures temptation. Such a one has stood the test and will receive the crown of life that the Lord[d] has promised to those who love him. 13 No one, when tempted, should say,

'I am being tempted by God'; for God cannot be tempted by evil and he himself tempts no one. 14 But one is tempted by one's own desire, being lured and enticed by it; 15 then, when that desire has conceived, it gives birth to sin, and that sin, when it is fully grown, gives birth to death. 16 Do not be deceived, my beloved.[e]

17 Every generous act of giving, with every perfect gift, is from above, coming down from the Father of lights, with whom there is no variation or shadow due to change.[f] 18 In fulfilment of his own purpose he gave us birth by the word of truth, so that we would become a kind of first fruits of his creatures.

Hearing and Doing the Word

19 You must understand this, my beloved:[e] let everyone be quick to listen, slow to speak, slow to anger; 20 for your anger does not produce God's righteousness. 21 Therefore rid yourselves of all sordidness and rank growth of wickedness, and welcome with meekness the implanted word that has the power to save your souls.

22 But be doers of the word, and not merely hearers who deceive themselves. 23 For if any are hearers of the word and not doers, they are like those who look at themselves[g] in a mirror; 24 for they look at themselves and, on going away, immediately forget what they were like. 25 But those who look into the perfect law, the law of

a Gk slave   b Gk brothers   c Gk brother
d Gk he; other ancient authorities read God
e Gk my beloved brothers   f Other ancient authorities read variation due to a shadow of turning   g Gk at the face of his birth

liberty, and persevere, being not hearers who forget but doers who act—they will be blessed in their doing.

26 If any think they are religious, and do not bridle their tongues but deceive their hearts, their religion is worthless. 27 Religion that is pure and undefiled before God, the Father, is this: to care for orphans and widows in their distress, and to keep oneself unstained by the world.

Warning against Partiality

2 My brothers and sisters, *a* do you with your acts of favouritism really believe in our glorious Lord Jesus Christ? *b* 2 For if a person with gold rings and in fine clothes comes into your assembly, and if a poor person in dirty clothes also comes in, 3 and if you take notice of the one wearing the fine clothes and say, 'Have a seat here, please', while to the one who is poor you say, 'Stand there', or, 'Sit at my feet', *c* 4 have you not made distinctions among yourselves, and become judges with evil thoughts? 5 Listen, my beloved brothers and sisters. *d* Has not God chosen the poor in the world to be rich in faith and to be heirs of the kingdom that he has promised to those who love him? 6 But you have dishonoured the poor. Is it not the rich who oppress you? Is it not they who drag you into court? 7 Is it not they who blaspheme the excellent name that was invoked over you?

8 You do well if you really fulfil the royal law according to the scripture, 'You shall love your neighbour as yourself.' 9 But if you show partiality, you commit sin and are convicted by the law as transgressors. 10 For whoever keeps the whole law but fails in one point has become accountable for all of it. 11 For the one who said, 'You shall not commit adultery', also said, 'You shall not murder.' Now if you do not commit adultery but if you murder, you have become a transgressor of the law. 12 So speak and so act as those who are to be judged by the law of liberty. 13 For judgement will be without mercy to anyone who has shown no mercy; mercy triumphs over judgement.

Faith without Works Is Dead

14 What good is it, my brothers and sisters, *d* if you say you have faith but do not have works? Can faith save you? 15 If a brother or sister is naked and lacks daily food, 16 and one of you says to them, 'Go in peace; keep warm and eat your fill', and yet you do not supply their bodily needs, what is the good of that? 17 So faith by itself, if it has no works, is dead.

18 But someone will say, 'You have faith and I have works.' Show me your faith without works, and I by my works will show you my faith. 19 You believe that God is one; you do well. Even the demons believe—and shudder. 20 Do you want to be shown, you senseless person, that faith without works is barren? 21 Was not our ancestor Abraham justified by works when he offered his son Isaac on the altar? 22 You see that faith was active along with his works, and faith was brought to completion by the works. 23 Thus the scripture was fulfilled that says, 'Abraham believed God, and it was reckoned to him as righteousness', and he was called the friend of God. 24 You see that a person is justified by works and not by faith alone. 25 Likewise, was not Rahab the prostitute also justified by works when she welcomed the messengers and sent them out by another road? 26 For just as the body without the spirit is dead, so faith without works is also dead.

Taming the Tongue

3 Not many of you should become teachers, my brothers and sisters, *d* for you know that we who teach will be judged with greater strictness. 2 For all of us make many mistakes. Anyone who makes no mistakes in speaking is perfect, able to keep the whole body in check with a bridle. 3 If we put bits into the mouths of horses to make them obey us, we guide their whole bodies. 4 Or look at ships: though they are so large that it takes strong winds to drive them, yet they are guided by a very small rudder wherever the will of

a Gk My brothers   *b* Or hold the faith of our glorious Lord Jesus Christ without acts of favouritism   *c* Gk Sit under my footstool   *d* Gk brothers the pilot directs. 5 So also the tongue is a small member, yet it boasts of great exploits.

How great a forest is set ablaze by a small fire! 6 And the tongue is a fire. The tongue is placed among our members as a world of iniquity; it stains the whole body, sets on fire the cycle of nature,*a* and is itself set on fire by hell.*b* 7 For every species of beast and bird, of reptile and sea creature, can be tamed and has been tamed by the human species, 8 but no one can tame the tongue— a restless evil, full of deadly poison. 9 With it we bless the Lord and Father, and with it we curse those who are made in the likeness of God. 10 From the same mouth come blessing and cursing. My brothers and sisters,*c* this ought not to be so. 11 Does a spring pour forth from the same opening both fresh and brackish water? 12 Can a fig tree, my brothers and sisters,*d* yield olives, or a grapevine figs? No more can salt water yield fresh.

Two Kinds of Wisdom

13 Who is wise and understanding among you? Show by your good life that your works are done with gentleness born of wisdom. 14 But if you have bitter envy and selfish ambition in your hearts, do not be boastful and false to the truth. 15 Such wisdom does not come down from above, but is earthly, unspiritual, devilish. 16 For where there is envy and selfish ambition, there will also be disorder and wickedness of every kind. 17 But the wisdom from above is first pure, then peaceable, gentle, willing to yield, full of mercy and good fruits, without a trace of partiality or hypocrisy. 18 And a harvest of righteousness is sown in peace for*e* those who make peace.

Friendship with the World

4 Those conflicts and disputes among you, where do they come from? Do they not come from your cravings that are at war within you? 2 You want something and do not have it; so you commit murder. And you covet*f* something and cannot obtain it; so you engage in disputes and conflicts. You do not have, because you do not

ask. 3 You ask and do not receive, because you ask wrongly, in order to spend what you get on your pleasures. 4 Adulterers! Do you not know that friendship with the world is enmity with God? Therefore whoever wishes to be a friend of the world becomes an enemy of God. 5 Or do you suppose that it is for nothing that the scripture says, 'God*g* yearns jealously for the spirit that he has made to dwell in us'? 6 But he gives all the more grace; therefore it says,

'God opposes the proud,
     but gives grace to the humble.'

7 Submit yourselves therefore to God. Resist the devil, and he will flee from you. 8 Draw near to God, and he will draw near to you. Cleanse your hands, you sinners, and purify your hearts, you double-minded. 9 Lament and mourn and weep. Let your laughter be turned into mourning and your joy into dejection. 10 Humble yourselves before the Lord, and he will exalt you.

Warning against Judging Another

11 Do not speak evil against one another, brothers and sisters.*h* Whoever speaks evil against another or judges another, speaks evil against the law and judges the law; but if you judge the law, you are not a doer of the law but a judge. 12 There is one lawgiver and judge who is able to save and to destroy. So who, then, are you to judge your neighbour?

Boasting about Tomorrow

13 Come now, you who say, 'Today or tomorrow we will go to such and such a town and spend a year there, doing business and making money.' 14 Yet you do not even know what tomorrow will bring. What is your life? For you are a mist that appears for a little while and then vanishes. 15 Instead you ought to say, 'If the Lord wishes, we will live and do this or that.' 16 As it is, you boast in your arrogance; all such boasting is evil. 17 Anyone, then, who knows the

---

a Or *wheel of birth*   *b* Gk *Gehenna*   *c* Gk *My brothers*
d Gk *my brothers*   *e* Or *by*   *f* Or *you murder and you covet*   *g* Gk *He*   *h* Gk *brothers*

right thing to do and fails to do it, commits sin.

Warning to Rich Oppressors

5 Come now, you rich people, weep and wail for the miseries that are coming to you. ²Your riches have rotted, and your clothes are moth-eaten. ³Your gold and silver have rusted, and their rust will be evidence against you, and it will eat your flesh like fire. You have laid up treasure*a* for the last days. ⁴Listen! The wages of the labourers who mowed your fields, which you kept back by fraud, cry out, and the cries of the harvesters have reached the ears of the Lord of hosts. ⁵You have lived on the earth in luxury and in pleasure; you have fattened your hearts on a day of slaughter. ⁶You have condemned and murdered the righteous one, who does not resist you.

Patience in Suffering

7 Be patient, therefore, beloved,*b* until the coming of the Lord. The farmer waits for the precious crop from the earth, being patient with it until it receives the early and the late rains. ⁸You also must be patient. Strengthen your hearts, for the coming of the Lord is near.*c* ⁹Beloved,*d* do not grumble against one another, so that you may not be judged. See, the Judge is standing at the doors! ¹⁰As an example of suffering and patience, beloved,*b* take the prophets who spoke in the name of the Lord. ¹¹Indeed we call blessed those who showed endurance. You have heard of the endurance of Job, and you have seen the

purpose of the Lord, how the Lord is compassionate and merciful.

12 Above all, my beloved,*c* do not swear, either by heaven or by earth or by any other oath, but let your 'Yes' be yes and your 'No' be no, so that you may not fall under condemnation.

The Prayer of Faith

13 Are any among you suffering? They should pray. Are any cheerful? They should sing songs of praise. ¹⁴Are any among you sick? They should call for the elders of the church and have them pray over them, anointing them with oil in the name of the Lord. ¹⁵The prayer of faith will save the sick, and the Lord will raise them up; and anyone who has committed sins will be forgiven. ¹⁶Therefore confess your sins to one another, and pray for one another, so that you may be healed. The prayer of the righteous is powerful and effective. ¹⁷Elijah was a human being like us, and he prayed fervently that it might not rain, and for three years and six months it did not rain on the earth. ¹⁸Then he prayed again, and the heaven gave rain and the earth yielded its harvest.

19 My brothers and sisters,*e* if anyone among you wanders from the truth and is brought back by another, ²⁰you should know that whoever brings back a sinner from wandering will save the sinner's*f* soul from death and will cover a multitude of sins.

a Or *will eat your flesh, since you have stored up fire*
b Gk *brothers* *c* Or *is at hand* *d* Gk *Brothers*
e Gk *My brothers* *f* Gk *his*

THE FIRST LETTER OF
PETER

Salutation

1 Peter, an apostle of Jesus Christ,
To the exiles of the Dispersion in Pontus, Galatia, Cappadocia, Asia, and Bithynia, ²who have been chosen and destined by God the Father and sanctified by the Spirit to be obedient to Jesus Christ and to be sprinkled with his blood:

May grace and peace be yours in abundance.

A Living Hope

3 Blessed be the God and Father of our Lord Jesus Christ! By his great mercy he has given us a new birth into a living hope through the resurrection of Jesus Christ from the dead, ⁴and into an inheritance that is imperishable, undefiled, and unfading, kept in heaven for you, ⁵who are being protected by the power of God through faith for a salvation ready to be revealed in the last time. ⁶In this you rejoice,ᵃ even if now for a little while you have had to suffer various trials, ⁷so that the genuineness of your faith—being more precious than gold that, though perishable, is tested by fire—may be found to result in praise and glory and honour when Jesus Christ is revealed. ⁸Although you have not seenᵇ him, you love him; and even though you do not see him now, you believe in him and rejoice with an indescribable and glorious joy, ⁹for you are receiving the outcome of your faith, the salvation of your souls.

10 Concerning this salvation, the prophets who prophesied of the grace that was to be yours made careful search and inquiry, ¹¹inquiring about the person or time that the Spirit of Christ within them indicated, when it testified in advance to the sufferings destined for Christ and the subsequent glory. ¹²It was revealed to them that they were serving not themselves but you, in regard to the things that have now been announced to you through those who brought you good news by the Holy Spirit sent from heaven—things into which angels long to look!

A Call to Holy Living

13 Therefore prepare your minds for action;ᶜ discipline yourselves; set all your hope on the grace that Jesus Christ will bring you when he is revealed. ¹⁴Like obedient children, do not be conformed to the desires that you formerly had in ignorance. ¹⁵Instead, as he who called you is holy, be holy yourselves in all your conduct; ¹⁶for it is written, 'You shall be holy, for I am holy.'

17 If you invoke as Father the one who judges all people impartially according to their deeds, live in reverent fear during the time of your exile. ¹⁸You know that you were ransomed from the futile ways inherited from your ancestors, not with perishable things like silver or gold, ¹⁹but with the precious blood of Christ, like that of a lamb without defect or blemish. ²⁰He was destined before the foundation of the world, but was revealed at the end of the ages for your sake. ²¹Through him you have come to trust in God, who raised him from the dead and gave him glory, so that your faith and hope are set on God.

22 Now that you have purified your souls by your obedience to the truthᵈ so that you have genuine mutual love, love

---

a Or *Rejoice in this*   *b* Other ancient authorities read *known*   *c* Gk *gird up the loins of your mind*   *d* Other ancient authorities add *through the Spirit* one another deeply[a] from the heart.[b] 23 You have been born anew, not of perishable but of imperishable seed, through the living and enduring word of God.[c] 24 For

'All flesh is like grass
    and all its glory like the flower
        of grass.
The grass withers,
    and the flower falls,
25 but the word of the Lord endures for
        ever.'

That word is the good news that was announced to you.

The Living Stone and a Chosen People

2 Rid yourselves, therefore, of all malice, and all guile, insincerity, envy, and all slander. 2 Like newborn infants, long for the pure, spiritual milk, so that by it you may grow into salvation— 3 if indeed you have tasted that the Lord is good.

4 Come to him, a living stone, though rejected by mortals yet chosen and precious in God's sight, and 5 like living stones, let yourselves be built[d] into a spiritual house, to be a holy priesthood, to offer spiritual sacrifices acceptable to God through Jesus Christ. 6 For it stands in scripture:

'See, I am laying in Zion a stone,
    a cornerstone chosen and precious;
and whoever believes in him[e] will
        not be put to shame.'

7 To you then who believe, he is precious; but for those who do not believe,

'The stone that the builders rejected
    has become the very head of
        the corner',

8 and

'A stone that makes them stumble,
    and a rock that makes them fall.'

They stumble because they disobey the word, as they were destined to do.

9 But you are a chosen race, a royal priesthood, a holy nation, God's own people,[f] in order that you may proclaim the mighty acts of him who called you out of darkness into his marvellous light.

10 Once you were not a people,
    but now you are God's people;
once you had not received mercy,
    but now you have received mercy.

Live as Servants of God

11 Beloved, I urge you as aliens and exiles to abstain from the desires of the flesh that wage war against the soul. 12 Conduct yourselves honourably among the Gentiles, so that, though they malign you as evildoers, they may see your honourable deeds and glorify God when he comes to judge.[g]

13 For the Lord's sake accept the authority of every human institution,[h] whether of the emperor as supreme, 14 or of governors, as sent by him to punish those who do wrong and to praise those who do right. 15 For it is God's will that by doing right you should silence the ignorance of the foolish. 16 As servants[i] of God, live as free people, yet do not use your freedom as a pretext for evil. 17 Honour everyone. Love the family of believers.[j] Fear God. Honour the emperor.

The Example of Christ's Suffering

18 Slaves, accept the authority of your masters with all deference, not only those who are kind and gentle but also those who are harsh. 19 For it is to your credit if, being aware of God, you endure pain while suffering unjustly. 20 If you endure when you are beaten for doing wrong, where is the credit in that? But if you endure when you do right and suffer for it, you have God's approval. 21 For to this you have been called, because Christ also suffered for you, leaving you an example, so that you should follow in his steps.

22 'He committed no sin,
    and no deceit was found in
        his mouth.'

23 When he was abused, he did not return abuse; when he suffered, he did not threaten; but he entrusted himself to the one who judges justly. 24 He himself bore our sins in his body on the cross,[k] so that, free from sins, we might live for righteousness; by his wounds[l] you have been healed. 25 For you were going astray like sheep, but

---

a Or constantly   b Other ancient authorities read a pure heart   c Or through the word of the living and enduring God   d Or you yourselves are being built   e Or it f Gk a people for his possession   g Gk God on the day of visitation   h Or every institution ordained for human beings   i Gk slaves   j Gk Love the brotherhood k Or carried up our sins in his body to the tree   l Gk bruise now you have returned to the shepherd and guardian of your souls.

Wives and Husbands

3 Wives, in the same way, accept the authority of your husbands, so that, even if some of them do not obey the word, they may be won over without a word by their wives' conduct, 2when they see the purity and reverence of your lives. 3Do not adorn yourselves outwardly by braiding your hair, and by wearing gold ornaments or fine clothing; 4rather, let your adornment be the inner self with the lasting beauty of a gentle and quiet spirit, which is very precious in God's sight. 5It was in this way long ago that the holy women who hoped in God used to adorn themselves by accepting the authority of their husbands. 6Thus Sarah obeyed Abraham and called him lord. You have become her daughters as long as you do what is good and never let fears alarm you.

7 Husbands, in the same way, show consideration for your wives in your life together, paying honour to the woman as the weaker sex,ᵃ since they too are also heirs of the gracious gift of life—so that nothing may hinder your prayers.

Suffering for Doing Right

8 Finally, all of you, have unity of spirit, sympathy, love for one another, a tender heart, and a humble mind. 9Do not repay evil for evil or abuse for abuse; but, on the contrary, repay with a blessing. It is for this that you were called—that you might inherit a blessing. 10For

Those who desire life
    and desire to see good days,
let them keep their tongues from evil
    and their lips from speaking deceit;
11 let them turn away from evil and do
        good;
    let them seek peace and pursue it.
12 For the eyes of the Lord are on
        the righteous,
    and his ears are open to their prayer.
But the face of the Lord is against
        those who do evil.'

13 Now who will harm you if you are eager to do what is good? 14But even if you do suffer for doing what is right, you are blessed. Do not fear what they fear,ᵇ and do not be intimidated, 15but in your hearts sanctify Christ as Lord. Always be ready to make your defence to anyone who demands from you an account of the hope that is in you; 16yet do it with gentleness and reverence.ᶜ Keep your conscience clear, so that, when you are maligned, those who abuse you for your good conduct in Christ may be put to shame. 17For it is better to suffer for doing good, if suffering should be God's will, than to suffer for doing evil. 18For Christ also sufferedᵈ for sins once for all, the righteous for the unrighteous, in order to bring youᵉ to God. He was put to death in the flesh, but made alive in the spirit, 19in which also he went and made a proclamation to the spirits in prison, 20who in former times did not obey, when God waited patiently in the days of Noah, during the building of the ark, in which a few, that is, eight people, were saved through water. 21And baptism, which this prefigured, now saves you—not as a removal of dirt from the body, but as an appeal to God forᶠ a good conscience, through the resurrection of Jesus Christ, 22who has gone into heaven and is at the right hand of God, with angels, authorities, and powers made subject to him.

Good Stewards of God's Grace

4 Since therefore Christ suffered in the flesh,ᵍ arm yourselves also with the same intention (for whoever has suffered in the flesh has finished with sin), 2so as to live for the rest of your earthly lifeʰ no longer by human desires but by the will of God. 3You have already spent enough time in doing what the Gentiles like to do, living in licentiousness, passions, drunkenness, revels, carousing, and lawless idolatry. 4They are surprised that you no longer join them in the same excesses of dissipation, and so they blaspheme.ⁱ 5But they will have to give an account to him who stands ready to judge the living and the dead. 6For this is

---

a Gk *vessel*   b Gk *their fear*   c Or *respect*   d Other ancient authorities read *died*   e Other ancient authorities read *us*   f Or *a pledge to God from*   g Other ancient authorities add *for us*; others, *for you*   h Gk *rest of the time in the flesh*   i Or *they malign you* the reason the gospel was proclaimed even to the dead, so that, though they had been judged in the flesh as everyone is judged, they might live in the spirit as God does.

7 The end of all things is near;[a] therefore be serious and discipline yourselves for the sake of your prayers. 8 Above all, maintain constant love for one another, for love covers a multitude of sins. 9 Be hospitable to one another without complaining. 10 Like good stewards of the manifold grace of God, serve one another with whatever gift each of you has received. 11 Whoever speaks must do so as one speaking the very words of God; whoever serves must do so with the strength that God supplies, so that God may be glorified in all things through Jesus Christ. To him belong the glory and the power for ever and ever. Amen.

Suffering as a Christian

12 Beloved, do not be surprised at the fiery ordeal that is taking place among you to test you, as though something strange were happening to you. 13 But rejoice in so far as you are sharing Christ's sufferings, so that you may also be glad and shout for joy when his glory is revealed. 14 If you are reviled for the name of Christ, you are blessed, because the spirit of glory,[b] which is the Spirit of God, is resting on you.[c] 15 But let none of you suffer as a murderer, a thief, a criminal, or even as a mischief-maker. 16 Yet if any of you suffers as a Christian, do not consider it a disgrace, but glorify God because you bear this name. 17 For the time has come for judgement to begin with the household of God; if it begins with us, what will be the end for those who do not obey the gospel of God? 18 And

'If it is hard for the righteous
   to be saved,
  what will become of the ungodly
    and the sinners?'

19 Therefore, let those suffering in accordance with God's will entrust themselves to a faithful Creator, while continuing to do good.

Tending the Flock of God

5 Now as an elder myself and a witness of the sufferings of Christ, as well as one who shares in the glory to be revealed,

I exhort the elders among you 2 to tend the flock of God that is in your charge, exercising the oversight,[d] not under compulsion but willingly, as God would have you do it[e]—not for sordid gain but eagerly. 3 Do not lord it over those in your charge, but be examples to the flock. 4 And when the chief shepherd appears, you will win the crown of glory that never fades away. 5 In the same way, you who are younger must accept the authority of the elders.[f] And all of you must clothe yourselves with humility in your dealings with one another, for

'God opposes the proud,
  but gives grace to the humble.'

6 Humble yourselves therefore under the mighty hand of God, so that he may exalt you in due time. 7 Cast all your anxiety on him, because he cares for you. 8 Discipline yourselves; keep alert.[g] Like a roaring lion your adversary the devil prowls around, looking for someone to devour. 9 Resist him, steadfast in your faith, for you know that your brothers and sisters[h] throughout the world are undergoing the same kinds of suffering. 10 And after you have suffered for a little while, the God of all grace, who has called you to his eternal glory in Christ, will himself restore, support, strengthen, and establish you. 11 To him be the power for ever and ever. Amen.

Final Greetings and Benediction

12 Through Silvanus, whom I consider a faithful brother, I have written this short letter to encourage you, and to testify that this is the true grace of God. Stand fast in it. 13 Your sister church[i] in Babylon, chosen together with you, sends you greetings; and so does my son Mark. 14 Greet one another with a kiss of love.

Peace to all of you who are in Christ.[j]

---

a Or is at hand   b Other ancient authorities add and of power   c Other ancient authorities add On their part he is blasphemed, but on your part he is glorified   d Other ancient authorities lack exercising the oversight   e Other ancient authorities lack as God would have you do it   f Or of those who are older   g Or be vigilant   h Gk your brotherhood   i Gk She who is   j Other ancient authorities add Amen

THE SECOND LETTER OF
PETER

Salutation

1 Simeon*a* Peter, a servant*b* and apostle of Jesus Christ,

To those who have received a faith as precious as ours through the righteousness of our God and Saviour Jesus Christ:*c*

2 May grace and peace be yours in abundance in the knowledge of God and of Jesus our Lord.

The Christian's Call and Election

3 His divine power has given us everything needed for life and godliness, through the knowledge of him who called us by*d* his own glory and goodness. 4 Thus he has given us, through these things, his precious and very great promises, so that through them you may escape from the corruption that is in the world because of lust, and may become participants in the divine nature. 5 For this very reason, you must make every effort to support your faith with goodness, and goodness with knowledge, 6 and knowledge with self-control, and self-control with endurance, and endurance with godliness, 7 and godliness with mutual*e* affection, and mutual*e* affection with love. 8 For if these things are yours and are increasing among you, they keep you from being ineffective and unfruitful in the knowledge of our Lord Jesus Christ. 9 For anyone who lacks these things is short-sighted and blind, and is forgetful of the cleansing of past sins. 10 Therefore, brothers and sisters,*f* be all the more eager to confirm your call and election, for if you do this, you will never stumble. 11 For in this way, entry into the eternal kingdom of our Lord and Saviour Jesus Christ will be richly provided for you.

12 Therefore I intend to keep on reminding you of these things, though you know them already and are established in the truth that has come to you. 13 I think it right, as long as I am in this body,*g* to refresh your memory, 14 since I know that my death*h* will come soon, as indeed our Lord Jesus Christ has made clear to me. 15 And I will make every effort so that after my departure you may be able at any time to recall these things.

Eyewitnesses of Christ's Glory

16 For we did not follow cleverly devised myths when we made known to you the power and coming of our Lord Jesus Christ, but we had been eyewitnesses of his majesty. 17 For he received honour and glory from God the Father when that voice was conveyed to him by the Majestic Glory, saying, 'This is my Son, my Beloved,*i* with whom I am well pleased.' 18 We ourselves heard this voice come from heaven, while we were with him on the holy mountain.

19 So we have the prophetic message more fully confirmed. You will do well to be attentive to this as to a lamp shining in a dark place, until the day dawns and the morning star rises in your hearts. 20 First of all you must understand this, that no prophecy of scripture is a matter of one's own interpretation, 21 because no prophecy

---

a Other ancient authorities read *Simon*   *b* Gk *slave*
c Or *of our God and the Saviour Jesus Christ*   *d* Other ancient authorities read *through*   *e* Gk *brotherly*
f Gk *brothers*   *g* Gk *tent*   *h* Gk *the putting off of my tent*   *i* Other ancient authorities read *my beloved Son*

ever came by human will, but men and women moved by the Holy Spirit spoke from God.[a]

False Prophets and Their Punishment

2 But false prophets also arose among the people, just as there will be false teachers among you, who will secretly bring in destructive opinions. They will even deny the Master who bought them— bringing swift destruction on themselves. [2] Even so, many will follow their licentious ways, and because of these teachers[b] the way of truth will be maligned. [3] And in their greed they will exploit you with deceptive words. Their condemnation, pronounced against them long ago, has not been idle, and their destruction is not asleep.

[4] For if God did not spare the angels when they sinned, but cast them into hell[c] and committed them to chains[d] of deepest darkness to be kept until the judgement; [5] and if he did not spare the ancient world, even though he saved Noah, a herald of righteousness, with seven others, when he brought a flood on a world of the ungodly; [6] and if by turning the cities of Sodom and Gomorrah to ashes he condemned them to extinction[e] and made them an example of what is coming to the ungodly;[f] [7] and if he rescued Lot, a righteous man greatly distressed by the licentiousness of the lawless [8] (for that righteous man, living among them day after day, was tormented in his righteous soul by their lawless deeds that he saw and heard), [9] then the Lord knows how to rescue the godly from trial, and to keep the unrighteous under punishment until the day of judgement [10] —especially those who indulge their flesh in depraved lust, and who despise authority.

Bold and wilful, they are not afraid to slander the glorious ones,[g] [11] whereas angels, though greater in might and power, do not bring against them a slanderous judgement from the Lord.[h] [12] These people, however, are like irrational animals, mere creatures of instinct, born to be caught and killed. They slander what they do not understand, and when those creatures are de-

stroyed,[i] they also will be destroyed, [13] suffering[j] the penalty for doing wrong. They count it a pleasure to revel in the daytime. They are blots and blemishes, revelling in their dissipation[k] while they feast with you. [14] They have eyes full of adultery, insatiable for sin. They entice unsteady souls. They have hearts trained in greed. Accursed children! [15] They have left the straight road and have gone astray, following the road of Balaam son of Bosor,[l] who loved the wages of doing wrong, [16] but was rebuked for his own transgression; a speechless donkey spoke with a human voice and restrained the prophet's madness.

[17] These are waterless springs and mists driven by a storm; for them the deepest darkness has been reserved. [18] For they speak bombastic nonsense, and with licentious desires of the flesh they entice people who have just[m] escaped from those who live in error. [19] They promise them freedom, but they themselves are slaves of corruption; for people are slaves to whatever masters them. [20] For if, after they have escaped the defilements of the world through the knowledge of our Lord and Saviour Jesus Christ, they are again entangled in them and overpowered, the last state has become worse for them than the first. [21] For it would have been better for them never to have known the way of righteousness than, after knowing it, to turn back from the holy commandment that was passed on to them. [22] It has happened to them according to the true proverb,

'The dog turns back to its
        own vomit',

and,

'The sow is washed only to wallow in
        the mud.'

a Other ancient authorities read *but moved by the Holy Spirit saints of God spoke*   b Gk *because of them*   c Gk *Tartaros*   d Other ancient authorities read *pits*   e Other ancient authorities lack *to extinction*   f Other ancient authorities read *an example to those who were to be ungodly*   g Or *angels*; Gk *glories*   h Other ancient authorities read *before the Lord*; others lack the phrase   i Gk *in their destruction*   j Other ancient authorities read *receiving*   k Other ancient authorities read *lovefeasts*   l Other ancient authorities read *Beor*   m Other ancient authorities read *actually*

The Promise of the Lord's Coming

3 This is now, beloved, the second letter I am writing to you; in them I am trying to arouse your sincere intention by reminding you [2] that you should remember the words spoken in the past by the holy prophets, and the commandment of the Lord and Saviour spoken through your apostles. [3] First of all you must understand this, that in the last days scoffers will come, scoffing and indulging their own lusts [4] and saying, 'Where is the promise of his coming? For ever since our ancestors died,[a] all things continue as they were from the beginning of creation!' [5] They deliberately ignore this fact, that by the word of God heavens existed long ago and an earth was formed out of water and by means of water, [6] through which the world of that time was deluged with water and perished. [7] But by the same word the present heavens and earth have been reserved for fire, being kept until the day of judgement and destruction of the godless.

[8] But do not ignore this one fact, beloved, that with the Lord one day is like a thousand years, and a thousand years are like one day. [9] The Lord is not slow about his promise, as some think of slowness, but is patient with you,[b] not wanting any to perish, but all to come to repentance. [10] But the day of the Lord will come like a thief, and then the heavens will pass away with a loud noise, and the elements will be dissolved with fire, and the earth and everything that is done on it will be disclosed.[c]

[11] Since all these things are to be dissolved in this way, what sort of people ought you to be in leading lives of holiness and godliness, [12] waiting for and hastening[d] the coming of the day of God, because of which the heavens will be set ablaze and dissolved, and the elements will melt with fire? [13] But, in accordance with his promise, we wait for new heavens and a new earth, where righteousness is at home.

Final Exhortation and Doxology

[14] Therefore, beloved, while you are waiting for these things, strive to be found by him at peace, without spot or blemish; [15] and regard the patience of our Lord as salvation. So also our beloved brother Paul wrote to you according to the wisdom given to him, [16] speaking of this as he does in all his letters. There are some things in them hard to understand, which the ignorant and unstable twist to their own destruction, as they do the other scriptures. [17] You therefore, beloved, since you are forewarned, beware that you are not carried away with the error of the lawless and lose your own stability. [18] But grow in the grace and knowledge of our Lord and Saviour Jesus Christ. To him be the glory both now and to the day of eternity. Amen.[e]

---

a Gk *our fathers fell asleep*   *b* Other ancient authorities read *on your account*   *c* Other ancient authorities read *will be burned up*   *d* Or *earnestly desiring*   *e* Other ancient authorities lack *Amen*

THE FIRST LETTER OF
JOHN

The Word of Life

1 We declare to you what was from the beginning, what we have heard, what we have seen with our eyes, what we have looked at and touched with our hands, concerning the word of life— ²this life was revealed, and we have seen it and testify to it, and declare to you the eternal life that was with the Father and was revealed to us— ³we declare to you what we have seen and heard so that you also may have fellowship with us; and truly our fellowship is with the Father and with his Son Jesus Christ. ⁴We are writing these things so that our*ᵃ* joy may be complete.

God Is Light

5 This is the message we have heard from him and proclaim to you, that God is light and in him there is no darkness at all. ⁶If we say that we have fellowship with him while we are walking in darkness, we lie and do not do what is true; ⁷but if we walk in the light as he himself is in the light, we have fellowship with one another, and the blood of Jesus his Son cleanses us from all sin. ⁸If we say that we have no sin, we deceive ourselves, and the truth is not in us. ⁹If we confess our sins, he who is faithful and just will forgive us our sins and cleanse us from all unrighteousness. ¹⁰If we say that we have not sinned, we make him a liar, and his word is not in us.

Christ Our Advocate

2 My little children, I am writing these things to you so that you may not sin. But if anyone does sin, we have an advocate with the Father, Jesus Christ the righteous; ²and he is the atoning sacrifice for our sins, and not for ours only but also for the sins of the whole world.

3 Now by this we may be sure that we know him, if we obey his commandments. ⁴Whoever says, 'I have come to know him', but does not obey his commandments, is a liar, and in such a person the truth does not exist; ⁵but whoever obeys his word, truly in this person the love of God has reached perfection. By this we may be sure that we are in him: ⁶whoever says, 'I abide in him', ought to walk just as he walked.

A New Commandment

7 Beloved, I am writing you no new commandment, but an old commandment that you have had from the beginning; the old commandment is the word that you have heard. ⁸Yet I am writing you a new commandment that is true in him and in you, because*ᵇ* the darkness is passing away and the true light is already shining. ⁹Whoever says, 'I am in the light', while hating a brother or sister,*ᶜ* is still in the darkness. ¹⁰Whoever loves a brother or sister*ᵈ* lives in the light, and in such a person*ᵉ* there is no cause for stumbling. ¹¹But whoever hates another believer*ᶠ* is in the darkness, walks in the darkness, and does not know the way to go, because the darkness has brought on blindness.

12 I am writing to you, little children,
  because your sins are forgiven on
    account of his name.
13 I am writing to you, fathers,
  because you know him who is from
    the beginning.

a Other ancient authorities read *your*   *b* Or *that*
c Gk *hating a brother*   *d* Gk *loves a brother*   *e* Or *in it*
f Gk *hates a brother*

I am writing to you, young people,
  because you have conquered
    the evil one.
14 I write to you, children,
  because you know the Father.
I write to you, fathers,
  because you know him who is from
    the beginning.
I write to you, young people,
  because you are strong
  and the word of God abides in you,
    and you have overcome the
      evil one.

15 Do not love the world or the things in the world. The love of the Father is not in those who love the world; 16 for all that is in the world—the desire of the flesh, the desire of the eyes, the pride in riches—comes not from the Father but from the world. 17 And the world and its desire[a] are passing away, but those who do the will of God live for ever.

Warning against Antichrists

18 Children, it is the last hour! As you have heard that antichrist is coming, so now many antichrists have come. From this we know that it is the last hour. 19 They went out from us, but they did not belong to us; for if they had belonged to us, they would have remained with us. But by going out they made it plain that none of them belongs to us. 20 But you have been anointed by the Holy One, and all of you have knowledge.[b] 21 I write to you, not because you do not know the truth, but because you know it, and you know that no lie comes from the truth. 22 Who is the liar but the one who denies that Jesus is the Christ?[c] This is the antichrist, the one who denies the Father and the Son. 23 No one who denies the Son has the Father; everyone who confesses the Son has the Father also. 24 Let what you heard from the beginning abide in you. If what you heard from the beginning abides in you, then you will abide in the Son and in the Father. 25 And this is what he has promised us,[d] eternal life.

26 I write these things to you concerning those who would deceive you. 27 As for you, the anointing that you received from him abides in you, and so you do not need anyone to teach you. But as his anointing teaches you about all things, and is true and is not a lie, and just as it has taught you, abide in him.[e]

28 And now, little children, abide in him, so that when he is revealed we may have confidence and not be put to shame before him at his coming.

Children of God

29 If you know that he is righteous, you may be sure that everyone who does right has been born of him. 3 1 See what love the Father has given us, that we should be called children of God; and that is what we are. The reason the world does not know us is that it did not know him. 2 Beloved, we are God's children now; what we will be has not yet been revealed. What we do know is this: when he[e] is revealed, we will be like him, for we will see him as he is. 3 And all who have this hope in him purify themselves, just as he is pure.

4 Everyone who commits sin is guilty of lawlessness; sin is lawlessness. 5 You know that he was revealed to take away sins, and in him there is no sin. 6 No one who abides in him sins; no one who sins has either seen him or known him. 7 Little children, let no one deceive you. Everyone who does what is right is righteous, just as he is righteous. 8 Everyone who commits sin is a child of the devil; for the devil has been sinning from the beginning. The Son of God was revealed for this purpose, to destroy the works of the devil. 9 Those who have been born of God do not sin, because God's seed abides in them;[f] they cannot sin, because they have been born of God. 10 The children of God and the children of the devil are revealed in this way: all who do not do what is right are not from God, nor are those who do not love their brothers and sisters.[g]

---

a Or *the desire for it*   *b* Other ancient authorities read *you know all things*   *c* Or *the Messiah*   *d* Other ancient authorities read *you*   *e* Or *it*   *f* Or *because the children of God abide in him*   *g* Gk *his brother*

Love One Another

11 For this is the message you have heard from the beginning, that we should love one another. 12 We must not be like Cain who was from the evil one and murdered his brother. And why did he murder him? Because his own deeds were evil and his brother's righteous. 13 Do not be astonished, brothers and sisters, *a* that the world hates you. 14 We know that we have passed from death to life because we love one another. Whoever does not love abides in death. 15 All who hate a brother or sister *b* are murderers, and you know that murderers do not have eternal life abiding in them. 16 We know love by this, that he laid down his life for us—and we ought to lay down our lives for one another. 17 How does God's love abide in anyone who has the world's goods and sees a brother or sister *c* in need and yet refuses help?

18 Little children, let us love, not in word or speech, but in truth and action. 19 And by this we will know that we are from the truth and will reassure our hearts before him 20 whenever our hearts condemn us; for God is greater than our hearts, and he knows everything. 21 Beloved, if our hearts do not condemn us, we have boldness before God; 22 and we receive from him whatever we ask, because we obey his commandments and do what pleases him.

23 And this is his commandment, that we should believe in the name of his Son Jesus Christ and love one another, just as he has commanded us. 24 All who obey his commandments abide in him, and he abides in them. And by this we know that he abides in us, by the Spirit that he has given us.

Testing the Spirits

4 Beloved, do not believe every spirit, but test the spirits to see whether they are from God; for many false prophets have gone out into the world. 2 By this you know the Spirit of God: every spirit that confesses that Jesus Christ has come in the flesh is from God, 3 and every spirit that does not confess Jesus *d* is not from God. And this is the spirit of the antichrist, of which you have heard that it is coming; and now it is already in the world. 4 Little children, you are from God, and have conquered them; for the one who is in you is greater than the one who is in the world. 5 They are from the world; therefore what they say is from the world, and the world listens to them. 6 We are from God. Whoever knows God listens to us, and whoever is not from God does not listen to us. From this we know the spirit of truth and the spirit of error.

God Is Love

7 Beloved, let us love one another, because love is from God; everyone who loves is born of God and knows God. 8 Whoever does not love does not know God, for God is love. 9 God's love was revealed among us in this way: God sent his only Son into the world so that we might live through him. 10 In this is love, not that we loved God but that he loved us and sent his Son to be the atoning sacrifice for our sins. 11 Beloved, since God loved us so much, we also ought to love one another. 12 No one has ever seen God; if we love one another, God lives in us, and his love is perfected in us.

13 By this we know that we abide in him and he in us, because he has given us of his Spirit. 14 And we have seen and do testify that the Father has sent his Son as the Saviour of the world. 15 God abides in those who confess that Jesus is the Son of God, and they abide in God. 16 So we have known and believe the love that God has for us.

God is love, and those who abide in love abide in God, and God abides in them. 17 Love has been perfected among us in this: that we may have boldness on the day of judgement, because as he is, so are we in this world. 18 There is no fear in love, but perfect love casts out fear; for fear has to do with punishment, and whoever fears has not reached perfection in love. 19 We love *e* because he first loved us. 20 Those who say,

a Gk *brothers*   *b* Gk *his brother*   *c* Gk *brother*
d Other ancient authorities read *does away with Jesus*
(Gk *dissolves Jesus*)   *e* Other ancient authorities add
him; others add *God*

'I love God', and hate their brothers or sisters,[a] are liars; for those who do not love a brother or sister[b] whom they have seen, cannot love God whom they have not seen. [21] The commandment we have from him is this: those who love God must love their brothers and sisters[a] also.

Faith Conquers the World

5 Everyone who believes that Jesus is the Christ[c] has been born of God, and everyone who loves the parent loves the child. [2] By this we know that we love the children of God, when we love God and obey his commandments. [3] For the love of God is this, that we obey his commandments. And his commandments are not burdensome, [4] for whatever is born of God conquers the world. And this is the victory that conquers the world, our faith. [5] Who is it that conquers the world but the one who believes that Jesus is the Son of God?

Testimony concerning the Son of God

[6] This is the one who came by water and blood, Jesus Christ, not with the water only but with the water and the blood. And the Spirit is the one that testifies, for the Spirit is the truth. [7] There are three that testify:[d] [8] the Spirit and the water and the blood, and these three agree. [9] If we receive human testimony, the testimony of God is greater; for this is the testimony of God that he has testified to his Son. [10] Those who believe in the Son of God have the testimony in their hearts. Those who do not believe in God[e] have made him a liar by not believing in the testimony that God has given concerning his Son. [11] And this is the testimony: God gave us eternal life, and this life is in his Son. [12] Whoever has the Son has life; whoever does not have the Son of God does not have life.

Epilogue

[13] I write these things to you who believe in the name of the Son of God, so that you may know that you have eternal life.

[14] And this is the boldness we have in him, that if we ask anything according to his will, he hears us. [15] And if we know that he hears us in whatever we ask, we know that we have obtained the requests made of him. [16] If you see your brother or sister[f] committing what is not a mortal sin, you will ask, and God[g] will give life to such a one—to those whose sin is not mortal. There is sin that is mortal; I do not say that you should pray about that. [17] All wrongdoing is sin, but there is sin that is not mortal.

[18] We know that those who are born of God do not sin, but the one who was born of God protects them, and the evil one does not touch them. [19] We know that we are God's children, and that the whole world lies under the power of the evil one. [20] And we know that the Son of God has come and has given us understanding so that we may know him who is true;[h] and we are in him who is true, in his Son Jesus Christ. He is the true God and eternal life.

[21] Little children, keep yourselves from idols.[i]

---

a Gk brothers   b Gk brother   c Or the Messiah   d A few other authorities read (with variations) [7]There are three that testify in heaven, the Father, the Word, and the Holy Spirit, and these three are one. [8]And there are three that testify on earth: e Other ancient authorities read in the Son   f Gk your brother   g Gk he   h Other ancient authorities read know the true God   i Other ancient authorities add Amen

THE SECOND LETTER OF
JOHN

Salutation

1 The elder to the elect lady and her children, whom I love in the truth, and not only I but also all who know the truth, 2 because of the truth that abides in us and will be with us for ever:

3 Grace, mercy, and peace will be with us from God the Father and from*a* Jesus Christ, the Father's Son, in truth and love.

Truth and Love

4 I was overjoyed to find some of your children walking in the truth, just as we have been commanded by the Father. 5 But now, dear lady, I ask you, not as though I were writing you a new commandment, but one we have had from the beginning, let us love one another. 6 And this is love, that we walk according to his commandments; this is the commandment just as you have heard it from the beginning— you must walk in it.

7 Many deceivers have gone out into the world, those who do not confess that Jesus Christ has come in the flesh; any such person is the deceiver and the antichrist! 8 Be on your guard, so that you do not lose what we*b* have worked for, but may receive a full reward. 9 Everyone who does not abide in the teaching of Christ, but goes beyond it, does not have God; whoever abides in the teaching has both the Father and the Son. 10 Do not receive into the house or welcome anyone who comes to you and does not bring this teaching; 11 for to welcome is to participate in the evil deeds of such a person.

Final Greetings

12 Although I have much to write to you, I would rather not use paper and ink; instead I hope to come to you and talk with you face to face, so that our joy may be complete.

13 The children of your elect sister send you their greetings.*c*

a Other ancient authorities add *the Lord*   *b* Other ancient authorities read *you*   *c* Other ancient authorities add *Amen*

THE THIRD LETTER OF
JOHN

Salutation

1 The elder to the beloved Gaius, whom I love in truth.

Gaius Commended for His Hospitality

2 Beloved, I pray that all may go well with you and that you may be in good health, just as it is well with your soul. 3 I was overjoyed when some of the friends*a* arrived and testified to your faithfulness to the truth, namely, how you walk in the truth. 4 I have no greater joy than this, to hear that my children are walking in the truth.

5 Beloved, you do faithfully whatever you do for the friends,*a* even though they are strangers to you; 6 they have testified to your love before the church. You will do well to send them on in a manner worthy of God; 7 for they began their journey for the sake of Christ,*b* accepting no support from non-believers.*c* 8 Therefore we ought to support such people, so that we may become co-workers with the truth.

Diotrephes and Demetrius

9 I have written something to the church; but Diotrephes, who likes to put himself first, does not acknowledge our authority. 10 So if I come, I will call attention to what he is doing in spreading false charges against us. And not content with those charges, he refuses to welcome the friends,*a* and even prevents those who want to do so and expels them from the church.

11 Beloved, do not imitate what is evil but imitate what is good. Whoever does good is from God; whoever does evil has not seen God. 12 Everyone has testified favourably about Demetrius, and so has the truth itself. We also testify for him,*d* and you know that our testimony is true.

Final Greetings

13 I have much to write to you, but I would rather not write with pen and ink; 14 instead I hope to see you soon, and we will talk together face to face.

15 Peace to you. The friends send you their greetings. Greet the friends there, each by name.

---

a Gk *brothers*   *b* Gk *for the sake of the name*   *c* Gk *the Gentiles*   *d* Gk lacks *for him*

THE LETTER OF

JUDE

Salutation

1 Jude,*a* a servant*b* of Jesus Christ and brother of James,

To those who are called, who are beloved*c* in*d* God the Father and kept safe for*d* Jesus Christ:

2 May mercy, peace, and love be yours in abundance.

Occasion of the Letter

3 Beloved, while eagerly preparing to write to you about the salvation we share, I find it necessary to write and appeal to you to contend for the faith that was once for all entrusted to the saints. 4 For certain intruders have stolen in among you, people who long ago were designated for this condemnation as ungodly, who pervert the grace of our God into licentiousness and deny our only Master and Lord, Jesus Christ.*e*

Judgement on False Teachers

5 Now I desire to remind you, though you are fully informed, that the Lord, who once for all saved*f* a people out of the land of Egypt, afterwards destroyed those who did not believe. 6 And the angels who did not keep their own position, but left their proper dwelling, he has kept in eternal chains in deepest darkness for the judgement of the great day. 7 Likewise, Sodom and Gomorrah and the surrounding cities, which, in the same manner as they, indulged in sexual immorality and pursued unnatural lust,*g* serve as an example by undergoing a punishment of eternal fire.

8 Yet in the same way these dreamers also defile the flesh, reject authority, and slander the glorious ones.*h* 9 But when the archangel Michael contended with the devil and disputed about the body of Moses, he did not dare to bring a condemnation of slander*i* against him, but said, 'The Lord rebuke you!' 10 But these people slander whatever they do not understand, and they are destroyed by those things that, like irrational animals, they know by instinct. 11 Woe to them! For they go the way of Cain, and abandon themselves to Balaam's error for the sake of gain, and perish in Korah's rebellion. 12 These are blemishes*j* on your love-feasts, while they feast with you without fear, feeding themselves.*k* They are waterless clouds carried along by the winds; autumn trees without fruit, twice dead, uprooted; 13 wild waves of the sea, casting up the foam of their own shame; wandering stars, for whom the deepest darkness has been reserved for ever.

14 It was also about these that Enoch, in the seventh generation from Adam, prophesied, saying, 'See, the Lord is coming*l* with tens of thousands of his holy ones, 15 to execute judgement on all, and to convict everyone of all the deeds of ungodliness that they have committed in such an ungodly way, and of all the harsh things that ungodly sinners have spoken against him.' 16 These are grumblers and malcontents; they indulge their own lusts; they are bombastic in speech, flattering people to their own advantage.

a Gk *Judas*   *b* Gk *slave*   *c* Other ancient authorities read *sanctified*   *d* Or *by*   *e* Or *the only Master and our Lord Jesus Christ*   *f* Other ancient authorities read *though you were once for all fully informed, that Jesus* (or *Joshua*) *who saved*   *g* Gk *went after other flesh*   *h* Or *angels*; Gk *glories*   *i* Or *condemnation for blasphemy*   *j* Or *reefs*   *k* Or *without fear. They are shepherds who care only for themselves*   *l* Gk *came*

Warnings and Exhortations

17 But you, beloved, must remember the predictions of the apostles of our Lord Jesus Christ; 18 for they said to you, 'In the last time there will be scoffers, indulging their own ungodly lusts.' 19 It is these worldly people, devoid of the Spirit, who are causing divisions. 20 But you, beloved, build yourselves up on your most holy faith; pray in the Holy Spirit; 21 keep yourselves in the love of God; look forward to the mercy of our Lord Jesus Christ that leads to*a* eternal life. 22 And have mercy on some who are wavering; 23 save others by snatching them out of the fire; and have mercy on still others with fear, hating even the tunic defiled by their bodies.*b*

Benediction

24 Now to him who is able to keep you from falling, and to make you stand without blemish in the presence of his glory with rejoicing, 25 to the only God our Saviour, through Jesus Christ our Lord, be glory, majesty, power, and authority, before all time and now and for ever. Amen.

a Gk *Christ to*   *b* Gk *by the flesh*. The Greek text of verses 22-23 is uncertain at several points

THE REVELATION

TO JOHN

Introduction and Salutation

1 The revelation of Jesus Christ, which God gave him to show his servants[a] what must soon take place; he made[b] it known by sending his angel to his servant[c] John, 2 who testified to the word of God and to the testimony of Jesus Christ, even to all that he saw.

3 Blessed is the one who reads aloud the words of the prophecy, and blessed are those who hear and who keep what is written in it; for the time is near.

4 John to the seven churches that are in Asia:

Grace to you and peace from him who is and who was and who is to come, and from the seven spirits who are before his throne, 5 and from Jesus Christ, the faithful witness, the firstborn of the dead, and the ruler of the kings of the earth.

To him who loves us and freed[d] us from our sins by his blood, 6 and made[b] us to be a kingdom, priests serving[e] his God and Father, to him be glory and dominion for ever and ever. Amen.

7 Look! He is coming with the clouds;
  every eye will see him,
  even those who pierced him;
    and on his account all the tribes of
      the earth will wail.
So it is to be. Amen.

8 'I am the Alpha and the Omega', says the Lord God, who is and who was and who is to come, the Almighty.

A Vision of Christ

9 I, John, your brother who share with you in Jesus the persecution and the kingdom and the patient endurance, was on the island called Patmos because of the word of God and the testimony of Jesus.[f] 10 I was in the spirit[g] on the Lord's day, and I heard behind me a loud voice like a trumpet 11 saying, 'Write in a book what you see and send it to the seven churches, to Ephesus, to Smyrna, to Pergamum, to Thyatira, to Sardis, to Philadelphia, and to Laodicea.'

12 Then I turned to see whose voice it was that spoke to me, and on turning I saw seven golden lampstands, 13 and in the midst of the lampstands I saw one like the Son of Man, clothed with a long robe and with a golden sash across his chest. 14 His head and his hair were white as white wool, white as snow; his eyes were like a flame of fire, 15 his feet were like burnished bronze, refined as in a furnace, and his voice was like the sound of many waters. 16 In his right hand he held seven stars, and from his mouth came a sharp, two-edged sword, and his face was like the sun shining with full force.

17 When I saw him, I fell at his feet as though dead. But he placed his right hand on me, saying, 'Do not be afraid; I am the first and the last, 18 and the living one. I was dead, and see, I am alive for ever and ever; and I have the keys of Death and of Hades. 19 Now write what you have seen, what is, and what is to take place after this. 20 As for the mystery of the seven stars that you saw in my right hand, and the seven golden lampstands: the seven stars are the angels of the seven churches, and the seven lampstands are the seven churches.

a Gk *slaves*   b Gk *and he made*   c Gk *slave*
d Other ancient authorities read *washed*
e Gk *priests to*   f Or *testimony to Jesus*
g Or *in the Spirit*

The Message to Ephesus

2 'To the angel of the church in Ephesus write: These are the words of him who holds the seven stars in his right hand, who walks among the seven golden lampstands:

2 'I know your works, your toil and your patient endurance. I know that you cannot tolerate evildoers; you have tested those who claim to be apostles but are not, and have found them to be false. ³I also know that you are enduring patiently and bearing up for the sake of my name, and that you have not grown weary. ⁴But I have this against you, that you have abandoned the love you had at first. ⁵Remember then from what you have fallen; repent, and do the works you did at first. If not, I will come to you and remove your lampstand from its place, unless you repent. ⁶Yet this is to your credit: you hate the works of the Nicolaitans, which I also hate. ⁷Let anyone who has an ear listen to what the Spirit is saying to the churches. To everyone who conquers,

I will give permission to eat from the tree of life that is in the paradise of God.

The Message to Smyrna

8 'And to the angel of the church in Smyrna write: These are the words of the first and the last, who was dead and came to life:

9 'I know your affliction and your poverty, even though you are rich. I know the slander on the part of those who say that they are Jews and are not, but are a synagogue of Satan. ¹⁰Do not fear what you are about to suffer. Beware, the devil is about to throw some of you into prison so that you may be tested, and for ten days you will have affliction. Be faithful until death, and I will give you the crown of life. ¹¹Let anyone who has an ear listen to what the Spirit is saying to the churches. Whoever conquers will not be harmed by the second death.

The Message to Pergamum

12 'And to the angel of the church in

The Seven Churches of the Revelation

MACEDONIA

Black Sea

GALATIA

ASIA

CAPPADOCIA

Aegean Sea

★ Pergamum
★ Thyatira
★ Sardis
Smyrna ★ Philadelphia
Ephesus ★ Laodicea

Patmos⊙

CYPRUS

CRETE

N

Mediterranean Sea

0   300 Mi.
0   300 Km.

Pergamum write: These are the words of him who has the sharp two-edged sword:

13 'I know where you are living, where Satan's throne is. Yet you are holding fast to my name, and you did not deny your faith in me*a* even in the days of Antipas my witness, my faithful one, who was killed among you, where Satan lives. 14 But I have a few things against you: you have some there who hold to the teaching of Balaam, who taught Balak to put a stumbling-block before the people of Israel, so that they would eat food sacrificed to idols and practise fornication. 15 So you also have some who hold to the teaching of the Nicolaitans. 16 Repent then. If not, I will come to you soon and make war against them with the sword of my mouth. 17 Let anyone who has an ear listen to what the Spirit is saying to the churches. To everyone who conquers I will give some of the hidden manna, and I will give a white stone, and on the white stone is written a new name that no one knows except the one who receives it.

The Message to Thyatira

18 'And to the angel of the church in Thyatira write: These are the words of the Son of God, who has eyes like a flame of fire, and whose feet are like burnished bronze:

19 'I know your works—your love, faith, service, and patient endurance. I know that your last works are greater than the first. 20 But I have this against you: you tolerate that woman Jezebel, who calls herself a prophet and is teaching and beguiling my servants*b* to practise fornication and to eat food sacrificed to idols. 21 I gave her time to repent, but she refuses to repent of her fornication. 22 Beware, I am throwing her on a bed, and those who commit adultery with her I am throwing into great distress, unless they repent of her doings; 23 and I will strike her children dead. And all the churches will know that I am the one who searches minds and hearts, and I will give to each of you as your works deserve. 24 But to the rest of you in Thyatira, who do not hold this teaching, who have not learned

what some call "the deep things of Satan", to you I say, I do not lay on you any other burden; 25 only hold fast to what you have until I come. 26 To everyone who conquers and continues to do my works to the end,

I will give authority over the nations;
27 to rule*c* them with an iron rod,

as when clay pots are shattered—
28 even as I also received authority from my Father. To the one who conquers I will also give the morning star. 29 Let anyone who has an ear listen to what the Spirit is saying to the churches.

The Message to Sardis

3 'And to the angel of the church in Sardis write: These are the words of him who has the seven spirits of God and the seven stars:

'I know your works; you have a name for being alive, but you are dead. 2 Wake up, and strengthen what remains and is at the point of death, for I have not found your works perfect in the sight of my God. 3 Remember then what you received and heard; obey it, and repent. If you do not wake up, I will come like a thief, and you will not know at what hour I will come to you. 4 Yet you have still a few people in Sardis who have not soiled their clothes; they will walk with me, dressed in white, for they are worthy. 5 If you conquer, you will be clothed like them in white robes, and I will not blot your name out of the book of life; I will confess your name before my Father and before his angels. 6 Let anyone who has an ear listen to what the Spirit is saying to the churches.

The Message to Philadelphia

7 'And to the angel of the church in Philadelphia write:

These are the words of the holy one,
the true one,
who has the key of David,
who opens and no one will shut,
who shuts and no one opens:
8 'I know your works. Look, I have set before you an open door, which no one is able to shut. I know that you have but little

---

a Or *deny my faith*　　*b* Gk *slaves*　　*c* Or *to shepherd* power, and yet you have kept my word and have not denied my name. ⁹I will make those of the synagogue of Satan who say that they are Jews and are not, but are lying—I will make them come and bow down before your feet, and they will learn that I have loved you. ¹⁰Because you have kept my word of patient endurance, I will keep you from the hour of trial that is coming on the whole world to test the inhabitants of the earth. ¹¹I am coming soon; hold fast to what you have, so that no one may seize your crown. ¹²If you conquer, I will make you a pillar in the temple of my God; you will never go out of it. I will write on you the name of my God, and the name of the city of my God, the new Jerusalem that comes down from my God out of heaven, and my own new name. ¹³Let anyone who has an ear listen to what the Spirit is saying to the churches.

The Message to Laodicea

14 'And to the angel of the church in Laodicea write: The words of the Amen, the faithful and true witness, the origin*a* of God's creation:

15 'I know your works; you are neither cold nor hot. I wish that you were either cold or hot. ¹⁶So, because you are lukewarm, and neither cold nor hot, I am about to spit you out of my mouth. ¹⁷For you say, "I am rich, I have prospered, and I need nothing." You do not realize that you are wretched, pitiable, poor, blind, and naked. ¹⁸Therefore I counsel you to buy from me gold refined by fire so that you may be rich; and white robes to clothe you and to keep the shame of your nakedness from being seen; and salve to anoint your eyes so that you may see. ¹⁹I reprove and discipline those whom I love. Be earnest, therefore, and repent. ²⁰Listen! I am standing at the door, knocking; if you hear my voice and open the door, I will come in to you and eat with you, and you with me. ²¹To the one who conquers I will give a place with me on my throne, just as I myself conquered and sat down with my Father on his throne. ²²Let anyone who has

an ear listen to what the Spirit is saying to the churches.'

The Heavenly Worship

4 After this I looked, and there in heaven a door stood open! And the first voice, which I had heard speaking to me like a trumpet, said, 'Come up here, and I will show you what must take place after this.' ²At once I was in the spirit,*b* and there in heaven stood a throne, with one seated on the throne! ³And the one seated there looks like jasper and cornelian, and around the throne is a rainbow that looks like an emerald. ⁴Around the throne are twenty-four thrones, and seated on the thrones are twenty-four elders, dressed in white robes, with golden crowns on their heads. ⁵Coming from the throne are flashes of lightning, and rumblings and peals of thunder, and in front of the throne burn seven flaming torches, which are the seven spirits of God; ⁶and in front of the throne there is something like a sea of glass, like crystal.

Around the throne, and on each side of the throne, are four living creatures, full of eyes in front and behind: ⁷the first living creature like a lion, the second living creature like an ox, the third living creature with a face like a human face, and the fourth living creature like a flying eagle. ⁸And the four living creatures, each of them with six wings, are full of eyes all around and inside. Day and night without ceasing they sing,

'Holy, holy, holy,
    the Lord God the Almighty,
      who was and is and is to come.'
⁹And whenever the living creatures give glory and honour and thanks to the one who is seated on the throne, who lives for ever and ever, ¹⁰the twenty-four elders fall before the one who is seated on the throne and worship the one who lives for ever and ever; they cast their crowns before the throne, singing,
¹¹ 'You are worthy, our Lord and God,
    to receive glory and honour
      and power,

a Or *beginning*   *b* Or *in the Spirit*

for you created all things,
and by your will they existed and
were created.'

The Scroll and the Lamb

5 Then I saw in the right hand of the
one seated on the throne a scroll written on the inside and on the back, sealed[a]
with seven seals; 2 and I saw a mighty angel
proclaiming with a loud voice, 'Who is
worthy to open the scroll and break its
seals?' 3 And no one in heaven or on earth
or under the earth was able to open the
scroll or to look into it. 4 And I began to
weep bitterly because no one was found
worthy to open the scroll or to look into it.
5 Then one of the elders said to me, 'Do
not weep. See, the Lion of the tribe of Judah, the Root of David, has conquered, so
that he can open the scroll and its seven
seals.'

6 Then I saw between the throne and
the four living creatures and among the elders a Lamb standing as if it had been
slaughtered, having seven horns and seven
eyes, which are the seven spirits of God
sent out into all the earth. 7 He went and
took the scroll from the right hand of the
one who was seated on the throne. 8 When
he had taken the scroll, the four living
creatures and the twenty-four elders fell
before the Lamb, each holding a harp and
golden bowls full of incense, which are the
prayers of the saints. 9 They sing a new
song:

'You are worthy to take the scroll
and to open its seals,
for you were slaughtered and by your
blood you ransomed for God
saints from[b] every tribe and
language and people
and nation;
10 you have made them to be a
kingdom and priests serving[c]
our God,
and they will reign on earth.'

11 Then I looked, and I heard the voice
of many angels surrounding the throne
and the living creatures and the elders;
they numbered myriads of myriads and

thousands of thousands, 12 singing with
full voice,

'Worthy is the Lamb that was
slaughtered
to receive power and wealth and
wisdom and might
and honour and glory and blessing!'
13 Then I heard every creature in heaven
and on earth and under the earth and in
the sea, and all that is in them, singing,

'To the one seated on the throne and
to the Lamb
be blessing and honour and glory
and might
for ever and ever!'
14 And the four living creatures said,
'Amen!' And the elders fell down and worshipped.

The Seven Seals

6 Then I saw the Lamb open one of the
seven seals, and I heard one of the four
living creatures call out, as with a voice of
thunder, 'Come!'[d] 2 I looked, and there was
a white horse! Its rider had a bow; a crown
was given to him, and he came out conquering and to conquer.

3 When he opened the second seal, I
heard the second living creature call out,
'Come!'[d] 4 And out came[e] another horse,
bright red; its rider was permitted to take
peace from the earth, so that people would
slaughter one another; and he was given a
great sword.

5 When he opened the third seal, I
heard the third living creature call out,
'Come!'[d] I looked, and there was a black
horse! Its rider held a pair of scales in his
hand, 6 and I heard what seemed to be a
voice in the midst of the four living creatures saying, 'A quart of wheat for a day's
pay,[f] and three quarts of barley for a day's
pay,[f] but do not damage the olive oil and
the wine!'

7 When he opened the fourth seal, I
heard the voice of the fourth living creature call out, 'Come!'[d] 8 I looked and there
was a pale green horse! Its rider's name

a Or written on the inside, and sealed on the back
b Gk ransomed for God from   c Gk priests to
d Or 'Go!'   e Or went   f Gk a denarius

was Death, and Hades followed with him; they were given authority over a fourth of the earth, to kill with sword, famine, and pestilence, and by the wild animals of the earth.

9 When he opened the fifth seal, I saw under the altar the souls of those who had been slaughtered for the word of God and for the testimony they had given; 10 they cried out with a loud voice, 'Sovereign Lord, holy and true, how long will it be before you judge and avenge our blood on the inhabitants of the earth?' 11 They were each given a white robe and told to rest a little longer, until the number would be complete both of their fellow-servants[a] and of their brothers and sisters,[b] who were soon to be killed as they themselves had been killed.

12 When he opened the sixth seal, I looked, and there came a great earthquake; the sun became black as sackcloth, the full moon became like blood, 13 and the stars of the sky fell to the earth as the fig tree drops its winter fruit when shaken by a gale. 14 The sky vanished like a scroll rolling itself up, and every mountain and island was removed from its place. 15 Then the kings of the earth and the magnates and the generals and the rich and the powerful, and everyone, slave and free, hid in the caves and among the rocks of the mountains, 16 calling to the mountains and rocks, 'Fall on us and hide us from the face of the one seated on the throne and from the wrath of the Lamb; 17 for the great day of their wrath has come, and who is able to stand?'

The 144,000 of Israel Sealed

7 After this I saw four angels standing at the four corners of the earth, holding back the four winds of the earth so that no wind could blow on earth or sea or against any tree. 2 I saw another angel ascending from the rising of the sun, having the seal of the living God, and he called with a loud voice to the four angels who had been given power to damage earth and sea, 3 saying, 'Do not damage the earth or the sea or the trees, until we have marked the servants[a] of our God with a seal on their foreheads.'

4 And I heard the number of those who were sealed, one hundred and forty-four thousand, sealed out of every tribe of the people of Israel:

5 From the tribe of Judah twelve thousand sealed,
from the tribe of Reuben twelve thousand,
from the tribe of Gad twelve thousand,
6 from the tribe of Asher twelve thousand,
from the tribe of Naphtali twelve thousand,
from the tribe of Manasseh twelve thousand,
7 from the tribe of Simeon twelve thousand,
from the tribe of Levi twelve thousand,
from the tribe of Issachar twelve thousand,
8 from the tribe of Zebulun twelve thousand,
from the tribe of Joseph twelve thousand,
from the tribe of Benjamin twelve thousand sealed.

The Multitude from Every Nation

9 After this I looked, and there was a great multitude that no one could count, from every nation, from all tribes and peoples and languages, standing before the throne and before the Lamb, robed in white, with palm branches in their hands. 10 They cried out in a loud voice, saying,

'Salvation belongs to our God who is seated on the throne, and to the Lamb!'

11 And all the angels stood around the throne and around the elders and the four living creatures, and they fell on their faces before the throne and worshipped God, 12 singing,

'Amen! Blessing and glory
and wisdom
and thanksgiving and honour

a Gk slaves   b Gk brothers

and power and might
be to our God for ever and ever!
    Amen.'

13 Then one of the elders addressed me, saying, 'Who are these, robed in white, and where have they come from?' 14 I said to him, 'Sir, you are the one that knows.' Then he said to me, 'These are they who have come out of the great ordeal; they have washed their robes and made them white in the blood of the Lamb.

15 For this reason they are before the
        throne of God,
    and worship him day and night
        within his temple,
    and the one who is seated on the
        throne will shelter them.
16 They will hunger no more, and thirst
        no more;
    the sun will not strike them,
    nor any scorching heat;
17 for the Lamb at the centre of the
        throne will be their shepherd,
    and he will guide them to springs
        of the water of life,
    and God will wipe away every tear
        from their eyes.'

The Seventh Seal and the Golden Censer

8 When the Lamb opened the seventh seal, there was silence in heaven for about half an hour. 2 And I saw the seven angels who stand before God, and seven trumpets were given to them.

3 Another angel with a golden censer came and stood at the altar; he was given a great quantity of incense to offer with the prayers of all the saints on the golden altar that is before the throne. 4 And the smoke of the incense, with the prayers of the saints, rose before God from the hand of the angel. 5 Then the angel took the censer and filled it with fire from the altar and threw it on the earth; and there were peals of thunder, rumblings, flashes of lightning, and an earthquake.

The Seven Trumpets

6 Now the seven angels who had the seven trumpets made ready to blow them.

7 The first angel blew his trumpet, and there came hail and fire, mixed with blood, and they were hurled to the earth; and a third of the earth was burned up, and a third of the trees were burned up, and all green grass was burned up.

8 The second angel blew his trumpet, and something like a great mountain, burning with fire, was thrown into the sea. 9 A third of the sea became blood, a third of the living creatures in the sea died, and a third of the ships were destroyed.

10 The third angel blew his trumpet, and a great star fell from heaven, blazing like a torch, and it fell on a third of the rivers and on the springs of water. 11 The name of the star is Wormwood. A third of the waters became wormwood, and many died from the water, because it was made bitter.

12 The fourth angel blew his trumpet, and a third of the sun was struck, and a third of the moon, and a third of the stars, so that a third of their light was darkened; a third of the day was kept from shining, and likewise the night.

13 Then I looked, and I heard an eagle crying with a loud voice as it flew in midheaven, 'Woe, woe, woe to the inhabitants of the earth, at the blasts of the other trumpets that the three angels are about to blow!'

9 And the fifth angel blew his trumpet, and I saw a star that had fallen from heaven to earth, and he was given the key to the shaft of the bottomless pit; 2 he opened the shaft of the bottomless pit, and from the shaft rose smoke like the smoke of a great furnace, and the sun and the air were darkened with the smoke from the shaft. 3 Then from the smoke came locusts on the earth, and they were given authority like the authority of scorpions of the earth. 4 They were told not to damage the grass of the earth or any green growth or any tree, but only those people who do not have the seal of God on their foreheads. 5 They were allowed to torture them for five months, but not to kill them, and their torture was like the torture of a

scorpion when it stings someone. ⁶And in those days people will seek death but will not find it; they will long to die, but death will flee from them.

7 In appearance the locusts were like horses equipped for battle. On their heads were what looked like crowns of gold; their faces were like human faces, ⁸their hair like women's hair, and their teeth like lions' teeth; ⁹they had scales like iron breastplates, and the noise of their wings was like the noise of many chariots with horses rushing into battle. ¹⁰They have tails like scorpions, with stings, and in their tails is their power to harm people for five months. ¹¹They have as king over them the angel of the bottomless pit; his name in Hebrew is Abaddon,ᵃ and in Greek he is called Apollyon.ᵇ

12 The first woe has passed. There are still two woes to come.

13 Then the sixth angel blew his trumpet, and I heard a voice from the fourᶜ horns of the golden altar before God, ¹⁴saying to the sixth angel who had the trumpet, 'Release the four angels who are bound at the great river Euphrates.' ¹⁵So the four angels were released, who had been held ready for the hour, the day, the month, and the year, to kill a third of humankind. ¹⁶The number of the troops of cavalry was two hundred million; I heard their number. ¹⁷And this was how I saw the horses in my vision: the riders wore breastplates the colour of fire and of sapphireᵈ and of sulphur; the heads of the horses were like lions' heads, and fire and smoke and sulphur came out of their mouths. ¹⁸By these three plagues a third of humankind was killed, by the fire and smoke and sulphur coming out of their mouths. ¹⁹For the power of the horses is in their mouths and in their tails; their tails are like serpents, having heads; and with them they inflict harm.

20 The rest of humankind, who were not killed by these plagues, did not repent of the works of their hands or give up worshipping demons and idols of gold and silver and bronze and stone and wood, which cannot see or hear or walk. ²¹And they did not repent of their murders or their sorceries or their fornication or their thefts.

The Angel with the Little Scroll

10 And I saw another mighty angel coming down from heaven, wrapped in a cloud, with a rainbow over his head; his face was like the sun, and his legs like pillars of fire. ²He held a little scroll open in his hand. Setting his right foot on the sea and his left foot on the land, ³he gave a great shout, like a lion roaring. And when he shouted, the seven thunders sounded. ⁴And when the seven thunders had sounded, I was about to write, but I heard a voice from heaven saying, 'Seal up what the seven thunders have said, and do not write it down.' ⁵Then the angel whom I saw standing on the sea and the land

    raised his right hand to heaven
6   and swore by him who lives for
       ever and ever,

who created heaven and what is in it, the earth and what is in it, and the sea and what is in it: 'There will be no more delay, ⁷but in the days when the seventh angel is to blow his trumpet, the mystery of God will be fulfilled, as he announced to his servantsᵉ the prophets.'

8 Then the voice that I had heard from heaven spoke to me again, saying, 'Go, take the scroll that is open in the hand of the angel who is standing on the sea and on the land.' ⁹So I went to the angel and told him to give me the little scroll; and he said to me, 'Take it, and eat; it will be bitter to your stomach, but sweet as honey in your mouth.' ¹⁰So I took the little scroll from the hand of the angel and ate it; it was sweet as honey in my mouth, but when I had eaten it, my stomach was made bitter.

11 Then they said to me, 'You must prophesy again about many peoples and nations and languages and kings.'

a That is, *Destruction*   *b* That is, *Destroyer*   *c* Other ancient authorities lack *four*   *d* Gk *hyacinth* *e* Gk *slaves*

The Two Witnesses

11 Then I was given a measuring rod like a staff, and I was told, 'Come and measure the temple of God and the altar and those who worship there, ² but do not measure the court outside the temple; leave that out, for it is given over to the nations, and they will trample over the holy city for forty-two months. ³ And I will grant my two witnesses authority to prophesy for one thousand two hundred and sixty days, wearing sackcloth.'

4 These are the two olive trees and the two lampstands that stand before the Lord of the earth. ⁵ And if anyone wants to harm them, fire pours from their mouth and consumes their foes; anyone who wants to harm them must be killed in this manner. ⁶ They have authority to shut the sky, so that no rain may fall during the days of their prophesying, and they have authority over the waters to turn them into blood, and to strike the earth with every kind of plague, as often as they desire.

7 When they have finished their testimony, the beast that comes up from the bottomless pit will make war on them and conquer them and kill them, ⁸ and their dead bodies will lie in the street of the great city that is prophetically*a* called Sodom and Egypt, where also their Lord was crucified. ⁹ For three and a half days members of the peoples and tribes and languages and nations will gaze at their dead bodies and refuse to let them be placed in a tomb; ¹⁰ and the inhabitants of the earth will gloat over them and celebrate and exchange presents, because these two prophets had been a torment to the inhabitants of the earth.

11 But after the three and a half days, the breath*b* of life from God entered them, and they stood on their feet, and those who saw them were terrified. ¹² Then they*c* heard a loud voice from heaven saying to them, 'Come up here!' And they went up to heaven in a cloud while their enemies watched them. ¹³ At that moment there was a great earthquake, and a tenth of the city fell; seven thousand people were killed in the earthquake, and the rest were terrified and gave glory to the God of heaven.

14 The second woe has passed. The third woe is coming very soon.

The Seventh Trumpet

15 Then the seventh angel blew his trumpet, and there were loud voices in heaven, saying,

'The kingdom of the world has
　　become the kingdom of
　　our Lord
　and of his Messiah,*d*
and he will reign for ever and ever.'

16 Then the twenty-four elders who sit on their thrones before God fell on their faces and worshipped God, ¹⁷ singing,

'We give you thanks, Lord
　　God Almighty,
who are and who were,
for you have taken your great power
　and begun to reign.
¹⁸ The nations raged,
　but your wrath has come,
　and the time for judging the dead,
for rewarding your servants,*e*
　　the prophets
and saints and all who fear
　　your name,
　both small and great,
and for destroying those who destroy
　　the earth.'

19 Then God's temple in heaven was opened, and the ark of his covenant was seen within his temple; and there were flashes of lightning, rumblings, peals of thunder, an earthquake, and heavy hail.

The Woman and the Dragon

12 A great portent appeared in heaven: a woman clothed with the sun, with the moon under her feet, and on her head a crown of twelve stars. ² She was pregnant and was crying out in birth pangs, in the agony of giving birth. ³ Then another portent appeared in heaven: a great red dragon, with seven heads and ten horns, and seven diadems on his heads.

a Or *allegorically*; Gk *spiritually*　　*b* Or *the spirit*
c Other ancient authorities read *I*　　*d* Gk *Christ*
e Gk *slaves*

4 His tail swept down a third of the stars of heaven and threw them to the earth. Then the dragon stood before the woman who was about to bear a child, so that he might devour her child as soon as it was born. 5 And she gave birth to a son, a male child, who is to rule[a] all the nations with a rod of iron. But her child was snatched away and taken to God and to his throne; 6 and the woman fled into the wilderness, where she has a place prepared by God, so that there she can be nourished for one thousand two hundred and sixty days.

Michael Defeats the Dragon

7 And war broke out in heaven; Michael and his angels fought against the dragon. The dragon and his angels fought back, 8 but they were defeated, and there was no longer any place for them in heaven. 9 The great dragon was thrown down, that ancient serpent, who is called the Devil and Satan, the deceiver of the whole world—he was thrown down to the earth, and his angels were thrown down with him.

10 Then I heard a loud voice in heaven, proclaiming,

'Now have come the salvation and
        the power
    and the kingdom of our God
    and the authority of his Messiah,[b]
for the accuser of our comrades[c] has
        been thrown down,
    who accuses them day and night
        before our God.
11 But they have conquered him by the
        blood of the Lamb
    and by the word of their testimony,
    for they did not cling to life even in
        the face of death.
12 Rejoice then, you heavens
    and those who dwell in them!
But woe to the earth and the sea,
    for the devil has come down to you
        with great wrath,
    because he knows that his time
        is short!'

The Dragon Fights Again on Earth

13 So when the dragon saw that he had been thrown down to the earth, he pur-

sued[d] the woman who had given birth to the male child. 14 But the woman was given the two wings of the great eagle, so that she could fly from the serpent into the wilderness, to her place where she is nourished for a time, and times, and half a time. 15 Then from his mouth the serpent poured water like a river after the woman, to sweep her away with the flood. 16 But the earth came to the help of the woman; it opened its mouth and swallowed the river that the dragon had poured from his mouth. 17 Then the dragon was angry with the woman, and went off to make war on the rest of her children, those who keep the commandments of God and hold the testimony of Jesus.

The First Beast

18 Then the dragon[e] took his stand on the sand of the seashore. 1 And I saw a beast rising out of the sea, having ten horns and seven heads; and on its horns were ten diadems, and on its heads were blasphemous names. 2 And the beast that I saw was like a leopard, its feet were like a bear's, and its mouth was like a lion's mouth. And the dragon gave it his power and his throne and great authority. 3 One of its heads seemed to have received a death-blow, but its mortal wound[f] had been healed. In amazement the whole earth followed the beast. 4 They worshipped the dragon, for he had given his authority to the beast, and they worshipped the beast, saying, 'Who is like the beast, and who can fight against it?'

5 The beast was given a mouth uttering haughty and blasphemous words, and it was allowed to exercise authority for forty-two months. 6 It opened its mouth to utter blasphemies against God, blaspheming his name and his dwelling, that is, those who dwell in heaven. 7 Also, it was allowed to make war on the saints and to conquer them.[g] It was given authority over every tribe and people and language and nation, 8 and all the inhabitants of the earth will

a Or to shepherd   b Gk Christ   c Gk brothers
d Or persecuted   e Gk Then he; other ancient
authorities read Then I stood   f Gk the plague of its
death   g Other ancient authorities lack this sentence

worship it, everyone whose name has not been written from the foundation of the world in the book of life of the Lamb that was slaughtered. [a]

9 Let anyone who has an ear listen:
10 If you are to be taken captive,

　　into captivity you go;

　if you kill with the sword,

　　with the sword you must be killed.

Here is a call for the endurance and faith of the saints.

The Second Beast

11 Then I saw another beast that rose out of the earth; it had two horns like a lamb and it spoke like a dragon. 12 It exercises all the authority of the first beast on its behalf, and it makes the earth and its inhabitants worship the first beast, whose mortal wound [b] had been healed. 13 It performs great signs, even making fire come down from heaven to earth in the sight of all; 14 and by the signs that it is allowed to perform on behalf of the beast, it deceives the inhabitants of earth, telling them to make an image for the beast that had been wounded by the sword [c] and yet lived; 15 and it was allowed to give breath [d] to the image of the beast, so that the image of the beast could even speak and cause those who would not worship the image of the beast to be killed. 16 Also it causes all, both small and great, both rich and poor, both free and slave, to be marked on the right hand or the forehead, 17 so that no one can buy or sell who does not have the mark, that is, the name of the beast or the number of its name. 18 This calls for wisdom: let anyone with understanding calculate the number of the beast, for it is the number of a person. Its number is six hundred and sixty-six. [e]

The Lamb and the 144,000

14 Then I looked, and there was the Lamb, standing on Mount Zion! And with him were one hundred and forty-four thousand who had his name and his Father's name written on their foreheads. 2 And I heard a voice from heaven like the sound of many waters and like the sound of loud thunder; the voice I heard was like

the sound of harpists playing on their harps, 3 and they sing a new song before the throne and before the four living creatures and before the elders. No one could learn that song except the one hundred forty-four thousand who have been redeemed from the earth. 4 It is these who have not defiled themselves with women, for they are virgins; these follow the Lamb wherever he goes. They have been redeemed from humankind as first fruits for God and the Lamb, 5 and in their mouth no lie was found; they are blameless.

The Messages of the Three Angels

6 Then I saw another angel flying in mid-heaven, with an eternal gospel to proclaim to those who live [f] on the earth—to every nation and tribe and language and people. 7 He said in a loud voice, 'Fear God and give him glory, for the hour of his judgement has come; and worship him who made heaven and earth, the sea and the springs of water.'

8 Then another angel, a second, followed, saying, 'Fallen, fallen is Babylon the great! She has made all nations drink of the wine of the wrath of her fornication.'

9 Then another angel, a third, followed them, crying with a loud voice, 'Those who worship the beast and its image, and receive a mark on their foreheads or on their hands, 10 they will also drink the wine of God's wrath, poured unmixed into the cup of his anger, and they will be tormented with fire and sulphur in the presence of the holy angels and in the presence of the Lamb. 11 And the smoke of their torment goes up for ever and ever. There is no rest day or night for those who worship the beast and its image and for anyone who receives the mark of its name.'

12 Here is a call for the endurance of the saints, those who keep the commandments of God and hold fast to the faith of [g] Jesus.

---

a Or *written in the book of life of the Lamb that was slaughtered from the foundation of the world*　*b* Gk *whose plague of its death*　*c* Or *that had received the plague of the sword*　*d* Or *spirit*　*e* Other ancient authorities read *six hundred and sixteen*　*f* Gk *sit*　*g* Or *to their faith in*

13 And I heard a voice from heaven saying, 'Write this: Blessed are the dead who from now on die in the Lord.' 'Yes,' says the Spirit, 'they will rest from their labours, for their deeds follow them.'

Reaping the Earth's Harvest

14 Then I looked, and there was a white cloud, and seated on the cloud was one like the Son of Man, with a golden crown on his head, and a sharp sickle in his hand! 15 Another angel came out of the temple, calling with a loud voice to the one who sat on the cloud, 'Use your sickle and reap, for the hour to reap has come, because the harvest of the earth is fully ripe.' 16 So the one who sat on the cloud swung his sickle over the earth, and the earth was reaped.

17 Then another angel came out of the temple in heaven, and he too had a sharp sickle. 18 Then another angel came out from the altar, the angel who has authority over fire, and he called with a loud voice to him who had the sharp sickle, 'Use your sharp sickle and gather the clusters of the vine of the earth, for its grapes are ripe.' 19 So the angel swung his sickle over the earth and gathered the vintage of the earth, and he threw it into the great wine press of the wrath of God. 20 And the wine press was trodden outside the city, and blood flowed from the wine press, as high as a horse's bridle, for a distance of about two hundred miles. *a*

The Angels with the Seven Last Plagues

15 Then I saw another portent in heaven, great and amazing: seven angels with seven plagues, which are the last, for with them the wrath of God is ended.

2 And I saw what appeared to be a sea of glass mixed with fire, and those who had conquered the beast and its image and the number of its name standing beside the sea of glass with harps of God in their hands. 3 And they sing the song of Moses, the servant *b* of God, and the song of the Lamb:

'Great and amazing are your deeds,
   Lord God the Almighty!

Just and true are your ways,
   King of the nations! *c*
4 Lord, who will not fear
   and glorify your name?
For you alone are holy.
   All nations will come
   and worship before you,
for your judgements have been
   revealed.'

5 After this I looked, and the temple of the tent *d* of witness in heaven was opened, 6 and out of the temple came the seven angels with the seven plagues, robed in pure bright linen, *e* with golden sashes across their chests. 7 Then one of the four living creatures gave the seven angels seven golden bowls full of the wrath of God, who lives for ever and ever; 8 and the temple was filled with smoke from the glory of God and from his power, and no one could enter the temple until the seven plagues of the seven angels were ended.

The Bowls of God's Wrath

16 Then I heard a loud voice from the temple telling the seven angels, 'Go and pour out on the earth the seven bowls of the wrath of God.'

2 So the first angel went and poured his bowl on the earth, and a foul and painful sore came on those who had the mark of the beast and who worshipped its image.

3 The second angel poured his bowl into the sea, and it became like the blood of a corpse, and every living thing in the sea died.

4 The third angel poured his bowl into the rivers and the springs of water, and they became blood. 5 And I heard the angel of the waters say,

'You are just, O Holy One, who are and were,
   for you have judged these things;
6 because they shed the blood of saints
   and prophets,
   you have given them blood to
   drink.

---

a Gk *one thousand six hundred stadia*   *b* Gk *slave*
c Other ancient authorities read *the ages*
d Or *tabernacle*   *e* Other ancient authorities read *stone*

It is what they deserve!'
7 And I heard the altar respond,

    'Yes, O Lord God, the Almighty,
      your judgements are true and just!'

8 The fourth angel poured his bowl on the sun, and it was allowed to scorch people with fire; 9 they were scorched by the fierce heat, but they cursed the name of God, who had authority over these plagues, and they did not repent and give him glory.

10 The fifth angel poured his bowl on the throne of the beast, and its kingdom was plunged into darkness; people gnawed their tongues in agony, 11 and cursed the God of heaven because of their pains and sores, and they did not repent of their deeds.

12 The sixth angel poured his bowl on the great river Euphrates, and its water was dried up in order to prepare the way for the kings from the east. 13 And I saw three foul spirits like frogs coming from the mouth of the dragon, from the mouth of the beast, and from the mouth of the false prophet. 14 These are demonic spirits, performing signs, who go abroad to the kings of the whole world, to assemble them for battle on the great day of God the Almighty. 15 ('See, I am coming like a thief! Blessed is the one who stays awake and is clothed,*a* not going about naked and exposed to shame.') 16 And they assembled them at the place that in Hebrew is called Harmagedon.

17 The seventh angel poured his bowl into the air, and a loud voice came out of the temple, from the throne, saying, 'It is done!' 18 And there came flashes of lightning, rumblings, peals of thunder, and a violent earthquake, such as had not occurred since people were upon the earth, so violent was that earthquake. 19 The great city was split into three parts, and the cities of the nations fell. God remembered great Babylon and gave her the wine-cup of the fury of his wrath. 20 And every island fled away, and no mountains were to be found; 21 and huge hailstones, each weighing about a hundred pounds,*b* dropped from heaven on people, until they cursed God

for the plague of the hail, so fearful was that plague.

The Great Whore and the Beast

17 Then one of the seven angels who had the seven bowls came and said to me, 'Come, I will show you the judgement of the great whore who is seated on many waters, 2 with whom the kings of the earth have committed fornication, and with the wine of whose fornication the inhabitants of the earth have become drunk.' 3 So he carried me away in the spirit*c* into a wilderness, and I saw a woman sitting on a scarlet beast that was full of blasphemous names, and it had seven heads and ten horns. 4 The woman was clothed in purple and scarlet, and adorned with gold and jewels and pearls, holding in her hand a golden cup full of abominations and the impurities of her fornication; 5 and on her forehead was written a name, a mystery: 'Babylon the great, mother of whores and of earth's abominations.' 6 And I saw that the woman was drunk with the blood of the saints and the blood of the witnesses to Jesus.

When I saw her, I was greatly amazed. 7 But the angel said to me, 'Why are you so amazed? I will tell you the mystery of the woman, and of the beast with seven heads and ten horns that carries her. 8 The beast that you saw was, and is not, and is about to ascend from the bottomless pit and go to destruction. And the inhabitants of the earth, whose names have not been written in the book of life from the foundation of the world, will be amazed when they see the beast, because it was and is not and is to come.

9 'This calls for a mind that has wisdom: the seven heads are seven mountains on which the woman is seated; also, they are seven kings, 10 of whom five have fallen, one is living, and the other has not yet come; and when he comes, he must remain for only a little while. 11 As for the beast that was and is not, it is an eighth but it belongs to the seven, and it goes to

---

a Gk *and keeps his robes*   *b* Gk *weighing about a talent*
c Or *in the Spirit*

destruction. 12And the ten horns that you saw are ten kings who have not yet received a kingdom, but they are to receive authority as kings for one hour, together with the beast. 13These are united in yielding their power and authority to the beast; 14they will make war on the Lamb, and the Lamb will conquer them, for he is Lord of lords and King of kings, and those with him are called and chosen and faithful.'

15 And he said to me, 'The waters that you saw, where the whore is seated, are peoples and multitudes and nations and languages. 16And the ten horns that you saw, they and the beast will hate the whore; they will make her desolate and naked; they will devour her flesh and burn her up with fire. 17For God has put it into their hearts to carry out his purpose by agreeing to give their kingdom to the beast, until the words of God will be fulfilled. 18The woman you saw is the great city that rules over the kings of the earth.'

The Fall of Babylon

18 After this I saw another angel coming down from heaven, having great authority; and the earth was made bright with his splendour. 2He called out with a mighty voice,

'Fallen, fallen is Babylon the great!
    It has become a dwelling-place
        of demons,
a haunt of every foul spirit,
    a haunt of every foul bird,
    a haunt of every foul and
        hateful beast.*a*
3 For all the nations have drunk*b*
    of the wine of the wrath of her
        fornication,
    and the kings of the earth have
        committed fornication
        with her,
    and the merchants of the earth
        have grown rich from the
        power*c* of her luxury.'

4 Then I heard another voice from heaven saying,
'Come out of her, my people,
    so that you do not take part in her
        sins,

and so that you do not share in her
        plagues;
5 for her sins are heaped high
        as heaven,
    and God has remembered
        her iniquities.
6 Render to her as she herself
        has rendered,
    and repay her double for her deeds;
    mix a double draught for her in the
        cup she mixed.
7 As she glorified herself and lived
        luxuriously,
    so give her a like measure of
        torment and grief.
Since in her heart she says,
    "I rule as a queen;
I am no widow,
    and I will never see grief",
8 therefore her plagues will come in a
        single day—
    pestilence and mourning
        and famine—
    and she will be burned with fire;
    for mighty is the Lord God who
        judges her.'

9 And the kings of the earth, who committed fornication and lived in luxury with her, will weep and wail over her when they see the smoke of her burning; 10they will stand far off, in fear of her torment, and say,
'Alas, alas, the great city,
    Babylon, the mighty city!
For in one hour your judgement
        has come.'

11 And the merchants of the earth weep and mourn for her, since no one buys their cargo any more, 12cargo of gold, silver, jewels and pearls, fine linen, purple, silk and scarlet, all kinds of scented wood, all articles of ivory, all articles of costly wood, bronze, iron, and marble, 13cinnamon, spice, incense, myrrh, frankincense, wine, olive oil, choice flour and wheat, cattle

---

a Other ancient authorities lack the words *a haunt of every foul beast* and attach the words *and hateful* to the previous line so as to read *a haunt of every foul and hateful bird*   *b* Other ancient authorities read *She has made all nations drink*   *c* Or *resources* and sheep, horses and chariots, slaves— and human lives.*a*

14 'The fruit for which your soul longed
   has gone from you,
   and all your dainties and
      your splendour
   are lost to you,
   never to be found again!'

15 The merchants of these wares, who gained wealth from her, will stand far off, in fear of her torment, weeping and mourning aloud,

16 'Alas, alas, the great city,
   clothed in fine linen,
      in purple and scarlet,
   adorned with gold,
      with jewels, and with pearls!

17 For in one hour all this wealth has
      been laid waste!'

And all shipmasters and seafarers, sailors and all whose trade is on the sea, stood far off 18 and cried out as they saw the smoke of her burning,

'What city was like the great city?'

19 And they threw dust on their heads, as they wept and mourned, crying out,

'Alas, alas, the great city,
   where all who had ships at sea
   grew rich by her wealth!
For in one hour she has been
   laid waste.'

20 Rejoice over her, O heaven, you saints and apostles and prophets! For God has given judgement for you against her.

21 Then a mighty angel took up a stone like a great millstone and threw it into the sea, saying,

'With such violence Babylon the great
      city
   will be thrown down,
   and will be found no more;

22 and the sound of harpists and
      minstrels and of flautists and
      trumpeters
   will be heard in you no more;
and an artisan of any trade
   will be found in you no more;
and the sound of the millstone
   will be heard in you no more;

23 and the light of a lamp
   will shine in you no more;

and the voice of bridegroom
      and bride
   will be heard in you no more;
for your merchants were the
      magnates of the earth,
   and all nations were deceived by
      your sorcery.

24 And in you*b* was found the blood of
      prophets and of saints,
   and of all who have been
      slaughtered on earth.'

The Rejoicing in Heaven

19 After this I heard what seemed to be the loud voice of a great multitude in heaven, saying,

'Hallelujah!
Salvation and glory and power
   to our God,
2   for his judgements are true
      and just;
   he has judged the great whore
      who corrupted the earth with her
      fornication,
   and he has avenged on her the blood
      of his servants.'*c*

3 Once more they said,
'Hallelujah!
The smoke goes up from her for ever
   and ever.'

4 And the twenty-four elders and the four living creatures fell down and worshipped God who is seated on the throne, saying,

'Amen. Hallelujah!'

5 And from the throne came a voice saying,

'Praise our God,
   all you his servants,*c*
and all who fear him,
   small and great.'

6 Then I heard what seemed to be the voice of a great multitude, like the sound of many waters and like the sound of mighty thunder-peals, crying out,

'Hallelujah!
For the Lord our God
   the Almighty reigns.
7   Let us rejoice and exult
   and give him the glory,

---

a Or *chariots, and human bodies and souls*   *b* Gk *her*
c Gk *slaves*

for the marriage of the Lamb
    has come,
  and his bride has made
    herself ready;
8 to her it has been granted to
    be clothed
  with fine linen, bright and pure'—
for the fine linen is the righteous deeds of
the saints.

9 And the angel said[a] to me, 'Write this:
Blessed are those who are invited to the
marriage supper of the Lamb.' And he said
to me, 'These are true words of God.'
10 Then I fell down at his feet to worship
him, but he said to me, 'You must not do
that! I am a fellow-servant[b] with you and
your comrades[c] who hold the testimony of
Jesus.[d] Worship God! For the testimony of
Jesus[d] is the spirit of prophecy.'

The Rider on the White Horse

11 Then I saw heaven opened, and there
was a white horse! Its rider is called Faithful
and True, and in righteousness he judges
and makes war. 12 His eyes are like a flame
of fire, and on his head are many diadems;
and he has a name inscribed that no one
knows but himself. 13 He is clothed in a
robe dipped in[e] blood, and his name is
called The Word of God. 14 And the armies
of heaven, wearing fine linen, white and
pure, were following him on white horses.
15 From his mouth comes a sharp sword
with which to strike down the nations, and
he will rule[f] them with a rod of iron; he will
tread the wine press of the fury of the wrath
of God the Almighty. 16 On his robe and on
his thigh he has a name inscribed, 'King of
kings and Lord of lords'.

The Beast and Its Armies Defeated

17 Then I saw an angel standing in the
sun, and with a loud voice he called to all
the birds that fly in mid-heaven, 'Come,
gather for the great supper of God, 18 to eat
the flesh of kings, the flesh of captains, the
flesh of the mighty, the flesh of horses and
their riders—flesh of all, both free and
slave, both small and great.' 19 Then I saw
the beast and the kings of the earth with
their armies gathered to make war against

the rider on the horse and against his
army. 20 And the beast was captured, and
with it the false prophet who had performed in its presence the signs by which
he deceived those who had received the
mark of the beast and those who worshipped its image. These two were thrown
alive into the lake of fire that burns with
sulphur. 21 And the rest were killed by the
sword of the rider on the horse, the sword
that came from his mouth; and all the
birds were gorged with their flesh.

The Thousand Years

20 Then I saw an angel coming down
from heaven, holding in his hand
the key to the bottomless pit and a great
chain. 2 He seized the dragon, that ancient
serpent, who is the Devil and Satan, and
bound him for a thousand years, 3 and
threw him into the pit, and locked and
sealed it over him, so that he would deceive the nations no more, until the thousand years were ended. After that he must
be let out for a little while.

4 Then I saw thrones, and those seated
on them were given authority to judge. I
also saw the souls of those who had been
beheaded for their testimony to Jesus[g] and
for the word of God. They had not worshipped the beast or its image and had not
received its mark on their foreheads or
their hands. They came to life and reigned
with Christ for a thousand years. 5 (The rest
of the dead did not come to life until the
thousand years were ended.) This is the
first resurrection. 6 Blessed and holy are
those who share in the first resurrection.
Over these the second death has no power,
but they will be priests of God and of
Christ, and they will reign with him for a
thousand years.

Satan's Doom

7 When the thousand years are ended,
Satan will be released from his prison
8 and will come out to deceive the nations
at the four corners of the earth, Gog and

---

a Gk *he said* *b* Gk *slave* *c* Gk *brothers* *d* Or *to
Jesus* *e* Other ancient authorities read *sprinkled with*
f Or *will shepherd* *g* Or *for the testimony of Jesus*

Magog, in order to gather them for battle; they are as numerous as the sands of the sea. 9 They marched up over the breadth of the earth and surrounded the camp of the saints and the beloved city. And fire came down from heaven*a* and consumed them. 10 And the devil who had deceived them was thrown into the lake of fire and sulphur, where the beast and the false prophet were, and they will be tormented day and night for ever and ever.

The Dead Are Judged

11 Then I saw a great white throne and the one who sat on it; the earth and the heaven fled from his presence, and no place was found for them. 12 And I saw the dead, great and small, standing before the throne, and books were opened. Also another book was opened, the book of life. And the dead were judged according to their works, as recorded in the books. 13 And the sea gave up the dead that were in it, Death and Hades gave up the dead that were in them, and all were judged according to what they had done. 14 Then Death and Hades were thrown into the lake of fire. This is the second death, the lake of fire; 15 and anyone whose name was not found written in the book of life was thrown into the lake of fire.

The New Heaven and the New Earth

21 Then I saw a new heaven and a new earth; for the first heaven and the first earth had passed away, and the sea was no more. 2 And I saw the holy city, the new Jerusalem, coming down out of heaven from God, prepared as a bride adorned for her husband. 3 And I heard a loud voice from the throne saying,

'See, the home*b* of God is
    among mortals.
He will dwell*c* with them;
they will be his peoples,*d*
and God himself will be with them;*e*
4 he will wipe every tear from
        their eyes.
Death will be no more;
mourning and crying and pain
    will be no more,

for the first things have passed away.'

5 And the one who was seated on the throne said, 'See, I am making all things new.' Also he said, 'Write this, for these words are trustworthy and true.' 6 Then he said to me, 'It is done! I am the Alpha and the Omega, the beginning and the end. To the thirsty I will give water as a gift from the spring of the water of life. 7 Those who conquer will inherit these things, and I will be their God and they will be my children. 8 But as for the cowardly, the faithless,*f* the polluted, the murderers, the fornicators, the sorcerers, the idolaters, and all liars, their place will be in the lake that burns with fire and sulphur, which is the second death.'

Vision of the New Jerusalem

9 Then one of the seven angels who had the seven bowls full of the seven last plagues came and said to me, 'Come, I will show you the bride, the wife of the Lamb.' 10 And in the spirit*g* he carried me away to a great, high mountain and showed me the holy city Jerusalem coming down out of heaven from God. 11 It has the glory of God and a radiance like a very rare jewel, like jasper, clear as crystal. 12 It has a great, high wall with twelve gates, and at the gates twelve angels, and on the gates are inscribed the names of the twelve tribes of the Israelites; 13 on the east three gates, on the north three gates, on the south three gates, and on the west three gates. 14 And the wall of the city has twelve foundations, and on them are the twelve names of the twelve apostles of the Lamb.

15 The angel*h* who talked to me had a measuring rod of gold to measure the city and its gates and walls. 16 The city lies foursquare, its length the same as its width; and he measured the city with his rod, fifteen hundred miles;*i* its length and width and height are equal. 17 He also measured its wall, one hundred and forty-four

a Other ancient authorities read *from God, out of heaven,* or *out of heaven from God*   *b* Gk *the tabernacle*
c Gk *will tabernacle*   *d* Other ancient authorities read *people*   *e* Other ancient authorities add *and be their God*   *f* Or *the unbelieving*   *g* Or *in the Spirit*
h Gk *He*   *i* Gk *twelve thousand stadia*

cubits*a* by human measurement, which the angel was using. 18 The wall is built of jasper, while the city is pure gold, clear as glass. 19 The foundations of the wall of the city are adorned with every jewel; the first was jasper, the second sapphire, the third agate, the fourth emerald, 20 the fifth onyx, the sixth cornelian, the seventh chrysolite, the eighth beryl, the ninth topaz, the tenth chrysoprase, the eleventh jacinth, the twelfth amethyst. 21 And the twelve gates are twelve pearls, each of the gates is a single pearl, and the street of the city is pure gold, transparent as glass.

22 I saw no temple in the city, for its temple is the Lord God the Almighty and the Lamb. 23 And the city has no need of sun or moon to shine on it, for the glory of God is its light, and its lamp is the Lamb. 24 The nations will walk by its light, and the kings of the earth will bring their glory into it. 25 Its gates will never be shut by day—and there will be no night there. 26 People will bring into it the glory and the honour of the nations. 27 But nothing unclean will enter it, nor anyone who practises abomination or falsehood, but only those who are written in the Lamb's book of life.

The River of Life

22 Then the angel*b* showed me the river of the water of life, bright as crystal, flowing from the throne of God and of the Lamb 2 through the middle of the street of the city. On either side of the river is the tree of life*c* with its twelve kinds of fruit, producing its fruit each month; and the leaves of the tree are for the healing of the nations. 3 Nothing accursed will be found there any more. But the throne of God and of the Lamb will be in it, and his servants*d* will worship him; 4 they will see his face, and his name will be on their foreheads. 5 And there will be no more night; they need no light of lamp or sun, for the Lord God will be their light, and they will reign for ever and ever.

6 And he said to me, 'These words are trustworthy and true, for the Lord, the God of the spirits of the prophets, has sent his angel to show his servants*d* what must soon take place.'

7 'See, I am coming soon! Blessed is the one who keeps the words of the prophecy of this book.'

Epilogue and Benediction

8 I, John, am the one who heard and saw these things. And when I heard and saw them, I fell down to worship at the feet of the angel who showed them to me; 9 but he said to me, 'You must not do that! I am a fellow-servant*e* with you and your comrades*f* the prophets, and with those who keep the words of this book. Worship God!'

10 And he said to me, 'Do not seal up the words of the prophecy of this book, for the time is near. 11 Let the evildoer still do evil, and the filthy still be filthy, and the righteous still do right, and the holy still be holy.'

12 'See, I am coming soon; my reward is with me, to repay according to everyone's work. 13 I am the Alpha and the Omega, the first and the last, the beginning and the end.'

14 Blessed are those who wash their robes,*g* so that they will have the right to the tree of life and may enter the city by the gates. 15 Outside are the dogs and sorcerers and fornicators and murderers and idolaters, and everyone who loves and practises falsehood.

16 'It is I, Jesus, who sent my angel to you with this testimony for the churches. I am the root and the descendant of David, the bright morning star.'

17 The Spirit and the bride say, 'Come.'
And let everyone who hears say,
'Come.'
And let everyone who is thirsty come.
Let anyone who wishes take the water
of life as a gift.

18 I warn everyone who hears the words of the prophecy of this book: if

a That is, almost seventy-five yards   *b* Gk *he*
c Or *the Lamb.* 2*In the middle of the street of the city, and on either side of the river, is the tree of life*   *d* Gk *slaves*
e Gk *slave*   *f* Gk *brothers*   *g* Other ancient authorities read *do his commandments*

anyone adds to them, God will add to that person the plagues described in this book; ¹⁹ if anyone takes away from the words of the book of this prophecy, God will take away that person's share in the tree of life and in the holy city, which are described in this book.

20 The one who testifies to these things says, 'Surely I am coming soon.'

Amen. Come, Lord Jesus!

21 The grace of the Lord Jesus be with all the saints. Amen. *a*

a Other ancient authorities lack *all*; others lack *the saints*; others lack *Amen*

TABLES OF READINGS
ACCORDING TO THE LECTIONARY
OF THE CATHOLIC CHURCH IN CANADA

TABLE OF READINGS FOR SUNDAYS AND SOLEMNITIES

TABLE OF WEEKDAY READINGS

TABLE OF MOVABLE DATES

PRAYERS AND DEVOTIONS OF
THE CATHOLIC FAITH

CONCORDANCE

TABLES OF READINGS
ACCORDING TO THE LECTIONARY
OF THE CATHOLIC CHURCH IN CANADA

Presently, the Canadian Lectionary is based on the NRSV and includes verses that sometimes go beyond those given in the Roman Missal. The ++ signs in the tables below indicate places marked in the Canadian Lectionary which vary slightly from the passages prescribed in the Roman Missal.

TABLE OF READINGS FOR
SUNDAYS AND SOLEMNITIES

ADVENT SEASON

1st Sunday of Advent—Year A: Isa 2.1–5; Rom 13.11–14; Mt 24.37–44
2nd Sunday of Advent—Year A: Isa 11.1–10; Rom 15.4–9; Mt 3.1–12
3rd Sunday of Advent—Year A: Isa 35.1–6a, 10; Jas 5.7–10; Mt 11.2–11
4th Sunday of Advent—Year A: Isa 7.10–14; Rom 1.1–7; Mt 1.18–24
1st Sunday of Advent—Year B: Isa 63.16b–17; 64.1, 3–8; 1 Cor 1.3–9; Mk 13.31–37++
2nd Sunday of Advent—Year B: Isa 40.1–5, 9–11; 2 Pet 3.8–15; Mk 1.1–8
3rd Sunday of Advent—Year B: Isa 61.1–2a, 10–11; 1 Thess 5.16–24; Jn 1.6–8, 19–28
4th Sunday of Advent—Year B: 2 Sam 7.1–5, 8b-12, 14a, 16; Rom 16.25–27;
    Lk 1.26–38
1st Sunday of Advent—Year C: Jer 33.14–16; 1 Thess 3.12—4.2; Lk 21.25–28, 34–36
2nd Sunday of Advent—Year C: Bar 5.1–9; Phil 1.3–6, 8–11; Lk 3.1–6
3rd Sunday of Advent—Year C: Zeph 3.14–18a; Phil 4.4–7; Lk 3.10–18
4th Sunday of Advent—Year C: Mic 5.2–5a; Heb 10.5–10; Lk 1.39–45

CHRISTMAS SEASON

Vigil of Christmas: Isa 62.1–5; Acts 13.16–17, 22–25; Mt 1.1–25 or 1.18–25
Christmas: During the Night: Isa 9.2–4, 6–7; Titus 2.11–14; Lk 2.1–16++
Christmas: At Dawn: Isa 62.11–12; Titus 3.4–7; Lk 2.15–20
Christmas: During the Day: Isa 52.7–10; Heb 1.1–6; Jn 1.1–18 or 1.1–5, 9–14
Holy Family: Sunday within the Octave of Christmas—Year A: Sir 3.2–6, 12–14;
    Col 3.12–21 or 3.12–17; Mt 2.13–15, 19–23
Holy Family: Sunday within the Octave of Christmas—Year B: Gen 15.1–6; 17.3b-5,
    15–16; 21.1–7++; Heb 11.8, 11–12, 17–19; Lk 2.22–40 or 2.22, 25–27, 34–35, 39–40++
Holy Family: Sunday within the Octave of Christmas—Year C: 1 Sam 1.11, 20–22,
    24–28++; 1 Jn 3.1–2, 21–24; Lk 2.41–52
Mary, Mother of God: Octave of Christmas (Jan. 1)—Years ABC: Num 6.22–27; Gal
    4.4–7; Lk 2.16–21
Second Sunday after Christmas—Years ABC: Sir 24.1–4, 8–12; Eph 1.3–6, 15–19++;
    Jn 1.1–18 or 1.1–5, 9–14
Epiphany of the Lord—Years ABC: Isa 60.1–6; Eph 3.2–3a, 5–6; Mt 2.1–12

Baptism of the Lord: Sunday after Epiphany—Year A: Isa 42.1–4, 6–7; Acts 10.34–38; Mt 3.13–17

Baptism of the Lord: Sunday after Epiphany—Year B: Isa 55.1–11; 1 Jn 5.1–9; Mk 1.7–11

Baptism of the Lord: Sunday after Epiphany—Year C: Isa 40.1–5, 9–11; Titus 2.11–14; 3.4–7; Lk 3.15–16, 21–22

LENTEN SEASON

Ash Wednesday: Joel 2.12–18; 2 Cor 5.20—6.2; Mt 6.1–6, 16–18

1st Sunday of Lent—Year A: Gen 2.7–9, 16–18, 25; 3.1–7++; Rom 5.12–19; Mt 4.1–11

2nd Sunday of Lent—Year A: Gen 12.1–4; 2 Tim 1.8b–10; Mt 17.1–9

3rd Sunday of Lent—Year A: Ex 17.3–7; Rom 5.1–2, 5–8; Jn 4.5–42 or 4.5–15, 19b–26, 39a, 40–42

4th Sunday of Lent—Year A: 1 Sam 16.1b, 6–7, 10–13ab; Eph 5.8–14; Jn 9.1–41 or 9.1, 6–9, 13–17, 34–38

5th Sunday of Lent—Year A: Ezek 37.12–14; Rom 8.8–11; Jn 11.1–45 or 11.3–7, 17, 20–27, 33b–45

Passion (Palm) Sunday—Year A: Isa 50.4–7; Phil 2.6–11; Procession: Mt 21.1–11; Mt 26.14—27.66

1st Sunday of Lent—Year B: Gen 9.8–15; 1 Pet 3.18–22; Mk 1.12–15

2nd Sunday of Lent—Year B: Gen 22.1–2, 9–13, 15–18; Rom 8.31b–35, 37++; Mk 9.2–10

3rd Sunday of Lent—Year B: Ex 20.1–17; 1 Cor 1.18, 22–25++; Jn 2.13–25

4th Sunday of Lent—Year B: 2 Chr 36.14–17a, 19–23++; Eph 2.4–10; Jn 3.14–21

5th Sunday of Lent—Year B: Jer 31.31–34; Heb 5.7–9; Jn 12.20–33

Passion (Palm) Sunday—Year B: Isa 50.4–7; Phil 2.6–11; Procession: Mk 11.1–10 or Jn 12.12–16; Mk 14.1—15.47

1st Sunday of Lent—Year C: Deut 26.4–10; Rom 10.8–13; Lk 4.1–13

2nd Sunday of Lent—Year C: Gen 15.5–12, 17–18; Phil 3.17—4.1; Lk 9.28b–36

3rd Sunday of Lent—Year C: Ex 3.1–8a, 13–15; 1 Cor 10.1–6, 10–12; Lk 13.1–9

4th Sunday of Lent—Year C: Josh 5.9a, 10–12; 2 Cor 5.17–21; Lk 15.1–3, 11–32

5th Sunday of Lent—Year C: Isa 43.16–21; Phil 3.8–14; Jn 8.1–11

Passion (Palm) Sunday—Year C: Isa 50.4–7; Phil 2.6–11; Procession: Lk 19.28–40; Lk 22.14—23.56

Chrism Mass—Years ABC: Isa 61.1–3a, 6a, 8b–9; Rev 1.4–8++; Lk 4.16–21

THE EASTER TRIDUUM

Mass of the Lord's Supper (Holy Thursday)—Years ABC: Ex 12.1–8, 11–14; 1 Cor 11.23–26; Jn 13.1–15

Celebration of the Lord's Passion (Good Friday)—Years ABC: Isa 52.13—53.12; Heb 4.14–16; 5.7–9; Jn 18.1—19.42

Resurrection of the Lord (Easter Vigil)—Years ABC: 1) Gen 1.1–2.2 or 1.1, 26–31a; 2) Gen 22.1–18 or 22.1–2, 9–13, 15–18; 3) Ex 14.15–31; 15.20, 1++; 4) Isa 54.5–14; 5) Isa 55.1–11; 6) Bar 3.9–15, 32–4.4; 7) Ezek 36.16–17a, 18–28; Rom 6.3–11; Year A: Mt 28.1–10; Year B: Mk 16.1–8; Year C: Lk 24.1–12

Resurrection of the Lord (Easter Sunday)—Years ABC: Acts 10.34a, 36–43++; Col 3.1–4 or 1 Cor 5.6b–8; Jn 20.1–18++ or from Vigil. Afternoon Mass: Lk 24.13–35

EASTER SEASON

2nd Sunday of Easter—Year A: Acts 2.42–47; 1 Pet 1.3–9; Jn 20.19–31
3rd Sunday of Easter—Year A: Acts 2.14, 22b-28; 1 Pet 1.17–21; Lk 24.13–35
4th Sunday of Easter—Year A: Acts 2.14a, 36–41; 1 Pet 2.20b-25; Jn 10.1–10
5th Sunday of Easter—Year A: Acts 6.1–7; 1 Pet 2.4–9; Jn 14.1–12
6th Sunday of Easter—Year A: Acts 8.5–8, 14–17; 1 Pet 3.15–18; Jn 14.15–21
Ascension of the Lord—Year A: Acts 1.1–11; Eph 1.17–23; Mt 28.16–20
7th Sunday of Easter—Year A: Acts 1.12–14; 1 Pet 4.13–16; Jn 17.1–11a
Vigil of Pentecost—Years ABC: Gen 11.1–9 or Ex 19.3–8a, 16–20b or Ezek 37.1–14 or
    Joel 2.28–32; Rom 8.22–27; Jn 7.37–39
Extended Vigil of Pentecost—Years ABC: 1) Gen 2.4b-10, 18, 21–25++; 2) Gen 11.1–9;
    3) Ex 19.3–8a, 16–20b; 4) Prov 8.22–31++; 5) Jer 31.31–34++; 6) Ezek 37.1–14;
    7) Joel 2.28–32; Rom 8.22–27; Jn 7.37–39
Pentecost Sunday—Year A: Acts 2.1–11; 1 Cor 12.3b-7, 12–13; Jn 20.19–23
2nd Sunday of Easter—Year B: Acts 4.32–35; 1 Jn 5.1–6; Jn 20.19–31
3rd Sunday of Easter—Year B: Acts 3.13–15, 17–19; 1 Jn 2.1–5; Lk 24.35–48
4th Sunday of Easter—Year B: Acts 4.7–12; 1 Jn 3.1–2; Jn 10.11–18
5th Sunday of Easter—Year B: Acts 9.26–31; 1 Jn 3.18–24; Jn 15.1–8
6th Sunday of Easter—Year B: Acts 10.25–26, 34–35, 44–48; 1 Jn 4.7–10; Jn 15.9–17
Ascension of the Lord—Year B: Acts 1.1–11; Eph 4.1–13 or 4.1–7, 11–13; Mk 16.15–20
7th Sunday of Easter—Year B: Acts 1.15–17, 20ac-26; 1 Jn 4.11–16; Jn 17.11b-19
Vigil of Pentecost—Years ABC: Gen 11.1–9 or Ex 19.3–8a, 16–20b or Ezek 37.1–14 or
    Joel 2.28–32; Rom 8.22–27; Jn 7.37–39
Pentecost Sunday—Year B: Acts 2.1–11; Gal 5.16–25; Jn 15.26–27; 16.12–15
2nd Sunday of Easter—Year C: Acts 5.12–16; Rev 1.9–11a, 12–13, 17–19; Jn 20.19–31
3rd Sunday of Easter—Year C: Acts 5.27b-32, 40b-41; Rev 5.11–14; Jn 21.1–19
4th Sunday of Easter—Year C: Acts 13.14, 43–52; Rev 7.9, 14b-17; Jn 10.27–30
5th Sunday of Easter—Year C: Acts 14.21b-27; Rev 21.1–5a; Jn 13.1, 31–33a, 34–35++
6th Sunday of Easter—Year C: Acts 15.1–2, 22–29; Rev 21.10–14, 22–23; Jn 14.23–29
Ascension of the Lord—Year C: Acts 1.1–11; Heb 9.24–28;10.19–23; Lk 24.46–53
7th Sunday of Easter—Year C: Acts 7.55–60; Rev 22.12–14, 16–17, 20; Jn 17.20–26
Vigil of Pentecost—Years ABC: Gen 11.1–9 or Ex 19.3–8a, 16–20b or Ezek 37.1–14 or
    Joel 2.28–32; Rom 8.22–27; Jn 7.37–39
Pentecost Sunday—Year C: Acts 2.1–11; Rom 8.8–17; Jn 14.15–16, 23b-26

THE SEASON OF THE YEAR: ORDINARY TIME (YEAR A)

1st Sunday: Baptism of the Lord—A: Isa 42.1–4, 6–7; Acts 10.34–38; Mt 3.13–17
2nd Sunday—Year A: Isa 49. 3, 5–6; 1 Cor 1.1–3; Jn 1.29–34
3rd Sunday—Year A: Isa 9.1–4; 1 Cor 1.10–13, 17–18; Mt 4.12–23 or 4.12–17
4th Sunday—Year A: Zeph 2.3, 3.12–13; 1 Cor 1.26–31; Mt 5.1–12a
5th Sunday—Year A: Isa 58.6–10++; 1 Cor 2.1–5; Mt 5.13–16
6th Sunday—Year A: Sir 15.15–20; 1 Cor 2.6–10; Mt 5.17–37 or 5.17, 20–24, 27–28,
    33–34, 37++
7th Sunday—Year A: Lev 19.1–2, 17–18; 1 Cor 3.16–23; Mt 5.38–48
8th Sunday—Year A: Isa 49.13–15++; 1 Cor 4.1–5; Mt 6.24–34
9th Sunday—Year A: Deut 10.12–13a; 11.18, 26–28, 32++; Rom 1.16–17; 3.20–26,
    28++; Mt 7.21–27
10th Sunday—Year A: Hos 6.3–6; Rom 4.18–25; Mt 9.9–13

11th Sunday—Year A: Ex 19.1–6a; Rom 5.6–11; Mt 9.36—10.8
12th Sunday—Year A: Jer 20.7, 10–13++; Rom 5.12–15; Mt 10.26–33
13th Sunday—Year A: 2 Kings 4.8–12a, 14–17++; Rom 6.3–4, 8–11; Mt 10.37–42
14th Sunday—Year A: Zech 9.9–10; Rom 8.9, 11–13; Mt 11.25–30
15th Sunday—Year A: Isa 55.10–11; Rom 8.18–23; Mt 13.1–23 or 13.1–9
16th Sunday—Year A: Wis 12.13, 16–19; Rom 8.26–27; Mt 13.24–43 or 13.24–33
17th Sunday—Year A: 1 Kings 3.5–12++; Rom 8.28–30; Mt 13.44–52 or 13.44–48
18th Sunday—Year A: Isa 55.1–3; Rom 8.35, 37–39; Mt 14.13–21
19th Sunday—Year A: 1 Kings 19.9a, 11–13a; Rom 9.1–5; Mt 14.22–33
20th Sunday—Year A: Isa 56.1, 6–7; Rom 11.13–15, 29–32; Mt 15.21–28
21st Sunday—Year A: Isa 22.15, 19–23; Rom 11.33–36; Mt 16.13–20
22nd Sunday—Year A: Jer 20.7–9; Rom 12.1–2; Mt 16.21–27
23rd Sunday—Year A: Ezek 33.7–9; Rom 13.8–10; Mt 18.15–20
24th Sunday—Year A: Sir 27.30–28.7; Rom 14.7–9; Mt 18.21–35
25th Sunday—Year A: Isa 55.6–9; Phil 1.20c–24, 27; Mt 20.1–16
26th Sunday—Year A: Ezek 18.25–28; Phil 2.1–11 or 2.1–5; Mt 21.28–32
27th Sunday—Year A: Isa 5.1–7; Phil 4.6–9; Mt 21.33–43
28th Sunday—Year A: Isa 25.6–10a; Phil 4.10–14, 19–20++; Mt 22.1–14 or 22.1–10
29th Sunday—Year A: Isa 45.1, 4–6; 1 Thess 1.1–5b; Mt 22.15–21
30th Sunday—Year A: Ex 22.21–27; 1 Thess 1.5c–10; Mt 22.34–40
31st Sunday—Year A: Mal 1.14b—2.2b, 8–10; 1 Thess 2.7b–9, 13; Mt 23.1–12
32nd Sunday—Year A: Wis 6.12–16; 1 Thess 4.13–18 or 4.13–14; Mt 25.1–13
33rd Sunday—Year A: Prov 31.10–13, 16–18, 20, 26, 28–31++; 1 Thess 5.1–6; Mt 24.36; 25.14–30++
34th Sunday: Christ the King—Year A: Ezek 34.11–12, 15–17; 1 Cor 15.20–26, 28; Mt 25.31–46

THE SEASON OF THE YEAR: ORDINARY TIME (YEAR B)

1st Sunday: Baptism of the Lord—B: Isa 55.1–11; 1 Jn 5.1–9; Mk 1.7–11
2nd Sunday—Year B: 1 Sam 3.3b–10, 19; 1 Cor 6.13c–15a, 17–20; Jn 1.35–42
3rd Sunday—Year B: Jon 3.1–5, 10; 1 Cor 7.29–31; Mk 1.14–20
4th Sunday—Year B: Deut 18.15–20; 1 Cor 7.17, 32–35++; Mk 1.21–28
5th Sunday—Year B: Job 7.1–4, 6–7; 1 Cor 9.16–19, 22–23; Mk 1.29–39
6th Sunday—Year B: Lev 13.1–2, 44–46; 1 Cor 10.23—11.1; Mk 1.40–45
7th Sunday—Year B: Isa 43.18–19, 21–22, 24c–25; 2 Cor 1.18–22; Mk 2.1–12
8th Sunday—Year B: Hos 2.14–15, 19–20++; 2 Cor 3.1b–6; Mk 2.18–22
9th Sunday—Year B: Deut 5.12–15; 2 Cor 4.6–11; Mk 2.23—3.6 or 2.23–28
10th Sunday—Year B: Gen 3.8–15++; 2 Cor 4.13—5.1; Mk 3.20–35
11th Sunday—Year B: Ezek 17.22–24; 2 Cor 5.6–10; Mk 4.26–34
12th Sunday—Year B: Job 38.1–4, 8–11++; 2 Cor 5.14–17; Mk 4.35–41
13th Sunday—Year B: Wis 1.13–15; 2.23–24; 2 Cor 8.7, 9, 13–15; Mk 5.21–43 or 5.21–24, 35–43
14th Sunday—Year B: Ezek 2.2–5; 2 Cor 12.7–10; Mk 6.1–6
15th Sunday—Year B: Am 7.12–15; Eph 1.3–14 or 1.3–10; Mk 6.7–13
16th Sunday—Year B: Jer 23.1–6; Eph 2.13–18; Mk 6.30–34
17th Sunday—Year B: 2 Kings 4.42–44; Eph 4.1–6; Jn 6.1–15
18th Sunday—Year B: Ex 16.2–4, 12–15, 31a++; Eph 4.17, 20–24; Jn 6.24–35
19th Sunday—Year B: 1 Kings 19.4–8; Eph 4.30—5.2; Jn 6.41–51
20th Sunday—Year B: Prov 9.1–6; Eph 5.15–20; Jn 6.51–58
21st Sunday—Year B: Jos 24.1–2a, 15–17, 18b; Eph 4.32—5.2; 5.21–32++; Jn 6.53, 60–69

22nd Sunday—Year B: Deut 4.1-2, 6-8; Jas 1.17-18, 21b-22, 27; Mk 7.1-8, 14-15, 21-23
23rd Sunday—Year B: Isa 35.4-7a; Jas 2.1-5; Mk 7.31-37
24th Sunday—Year B: Isa 50.5-9a; Jas 2.14-18; Mk 8.27-35
25th Sunday—Year B: Wis 2.12, 17-20; Jas 3.16—4.3; Mk 9.30-37
26th Sunday—Year B: Num 11.16a, 17c, 25-29; Jas 5.1-6; Mk 9.38-43, 45, 47-48
27th Sunday—Year B: Gen 2.7ab, 8b, 18-24; Heb 2.9-11; Mk 10.2-16 or 10.2-12
28th Sunday—Year B: Wis 7.7-11; Heb 4.12-13; Mk 10.17-30 or 10.17-27
29th Sunday—Year B: Isa 53.4, 10-11++; Heb 4.14-16; Mk 10.35-45 or 10.42-45
30th Sunday—Year B: Jer 31.7-9; Heb 5.1-6; Mk 10.46b-52
31st Sunday—Year B: Deut 6.2-6; Heb 7.23-28; Mk 12.28-34
32nd Sunday—Year B: 1 Kings 17.10-16; Heb 9.24-28; Mk 12.38-44
33rd Sunday—Year B: Dan 12.1-3; Heb 10.11-14, 18; Mk 13.24-32
34th Sunday: Christ the King—Year B: Dan 7.13-14; Rev 1.5-8; Jn 18.33b-37

THE SEASON OF THE YEAR: ORDINARY TIME (YEAR C)

1st Sunday: Baptism of the Lord—C: Isa 40.1-5, 9-11; Titus 2.11-14; 3.4-7; Lk 3.15-16, 21-22
2nd Sunday—Year C: Isa 62.1-5; 1 Cor 12.4-11; Jn 2.1-12
3rd Sunday—Year C: Neh 8.1-4a, 5-6, 8-10++; 1 Cor 12.12-30 or 12.12-14, 27; Lk 1.1-4; 4.14-21
4th Sunday—Year C: Jer 1.4-5, 17-19; 1 Cor 12.31—13.13 or 13.4-13; Lk 4.21-30
5th Sunday—Year C: Isa 6.1-2a, 3-8; 1 Cor 15.1-11 or 15.3-8, 11; Lk 5.1-11
6th Sunday—Year C: Jer 17.5-8; 1 Cor 15.12, 16-20; Lk 6.17, 20-26
7th Sunday—Year C: 1 Sam 26.2, 7-9, 12-13, 22-25++; 1 Cor 15.45-50++; Lk 6.27-38
8th Sunday—Year C: Sir 27.4-7; 1 Cor 15.54-58; Lk 6.39-45
9th Sunday—Year C: 1 Kings 8.41-43; Gal 1.1-2, 6-10; Lk 7.1-10
10th Sunday—Year C: 1 Kings 17.8-9, 17-21a, 22-24++; Gal 1.11-19; Lk 7.11-17
11th Sunday—Year C: 2 Sam 12.7-10, 13; Gal 2.16, 19-21; Lk 7.36—8.3
12th Sunday—Year C: Zech 12.10-11; Gal 3.26-29; Lk 9.18-24
13th Sunday—Year C: 1 Kings 19.16b, 19-21; Gal 5.1, 13-18; Lk 9.51-62
14th Sunday—Year C: Isa 66.10-14c; Gal 6.14-18; Lk 10.1-12, 17-20
15th Sunday—Year C: Deut 30.10-14; Col 1.15-20; Lk 10.25-37
16th Sunday—Year C: Gen 18.1-10a; Col 1.24-28; Lk 10.38-42
17th Sunday—Year C: Gen 18.20-21, 23-32++; Col 2.6-14++; Lk 11.1-13
18th Sunday—Year C: Eccl 1.2, 2.21-23; Col 3.1-5, 9-11; Lk 12.13-21
19th Sunday—Year C: Wis 18.6-9; Heb 11.1-2, 8-19 or 11.1-2, 8-12; Lk 12.32-48 or 12.35-40
20th Sunday—Year C: Jer 38.1-2ab, 4-6, 8-10; Heb 12.1-4; Lk 12.49-53
21st Sunday—Year C: Isa 66.18-21; Heb 12.5-7, 11-13; Lk 13.22-30
22nd Sunday—Year C: Sir 3.17-20, 28-29; Heb 12.18-19, 22-24a; Lk 14.1, 7-14
23rd Sunday—Year C: Wis 9.13-18; Philem 9b-10, 12-17; Lk 14.25-33
24th Sunday—Year C: Ex 32.7-11, 13-14; 1 Tim 1.12-17; Lk 15.1-32 or 15.1-10
25th Sunday—Year C: Am 8.4-7; 1 Tim 2.1-7; Lk 16.1-13 or 16.10-13
26th Sunday—Year C: Am 6.1a, 4-7; 1 Tim 6.11-16; Lk 16.19-31
27th Sunday—Year C: Hab 1.2-3, 2.2-4; 2 Tim 1.6-8, 13-14; Lk 17.5-10
28th Sunday—Year C: 2 Kings 5.14-17; 2 Tim 2.8-13; Lk 17.11-19
29th Sunday—Year C: Ex 17.8-13; 2 Tim 3.14—4.2; Lk 18.1-8
30th Sunday—Year C: Sir 35.15-17, 20-22; 2 Tim 4.6-8, 16-18; Lk 18.9-14
31st Sunday—Year C: Wis 11.22-12.1; 2 Thess 1.11—2.2; Lk 19.1-10

32nd Sunday—Year C: 2 Macc 7.1–2, 9–14++; 2 Thess 2.16—3.5; Lk 20.27–38 or 20.27, 34–38

33rd Sunday—Year C: Mal 4.1–2; 2 Thess 3.7–12; Lk 21.5–19

34th Sunday: Christ the King—Year C: 2 Sam 5.1–3; Col 1.12–20; Lk 23.35–43

SOLEMNITIES OF THE LORD DURING ORDINARY TIME

Trinity Sunday—Year A: Ex 34.4b-6, 8–9; 2 Cor 13.11–13; Jn 3.16–18

Trinity Sunday—Year B: Deut 4.32–34, 39–40; Rom 8.14–17; Mt 28.16–20

Trinity Sunday—Year C: Prov 8.22–31; Rom 5.1–5; Jn 16.12–15

The Body & Blood of Christ—Year A: Deut 8.2–3, 14–16; 1 Cor 10.16–17; Jn 6.51–59

The Body & Blood of Christ—Year B: Ex 24.3–8; Heb 9.11–15; Mk 14.12–16, 22–26

The Body & Blood of Christ—Year C: Gen 14.18–20; 1 Cor 11.23–26; Lk 9.11b-17

The Sacred Heart of Jesus—Year A: Deut 7.6–11; 1 Jn 4.7–16; Mt 11.25–30

The Sacred Heart of Jesus—Year B: Hos 11.1–2a, 3–4, 8ac-9++; Eph 3.8–12, 14–19; Jn 19.31–37

The Sacred Heart of Jesus—Year C: Ezek 34.11–16; Rom 5.5b-11; Lk 15.3–7

FEASTS OF THE LORD AND SOLEMNITIES DURING THE YEAR

Presentation of the Lord (February 2): Mal 3.1–4; Heb 2.10–11, 13b-18++; Lk 2.22–40 or 2.22–32

Joseph, Husband of Mary: Patron of Canada (March 19): 2 Sam 7.4–5a, 12–14a, 16; Rom 4.13, 16–18, 22; Mt 1.16, 18–21, 24a or Lk 2.41–51a

Annunciation of the Lord (March 25): Isa 7.10–14; 8.10d; Heb 10.4–10; Lk 1.26–38

Birth of John the Baptist: Vigil (June 23): Jer 1.4–10; 1 Pet 1.3, 8–12++; Lk 1.5–17

Birth of John the Baptist: During the Day (June 24): Isa 49.1–6; Acts 13.22–26; Lk 1.57–66, 80

Peter and Paul, Apostles: Vigil (June 28): Acts 3.1–10; Gal 1.11–20; Jn 21.15–19

Peter and Paul, Apostles: During the Day (June 29): Acts 12.1–11; 2 Tim 4.6–8, 17–18; Mt 16.13–19

Transfiguration of the Lord (August 6): Dan 7.9–10, 13–14; 2 Pet 1.16–19; Year A: Mt 17.1–9; Year B: Mk 9.2–10; Year C: Lk 9.28b-36

Assumption of Mary: Vigil (August 14): 1 Chr 15.3–4, 15–16; 16.1–2; 1 Cor 15.54–57; Lk 11.27–28

Assumption of Mary: During the Day (August 15): Rev 11.19a; 12.1–6a; 10ab; 1 Cor 15.20–26; Lk 1.39–56

Triumph of the Cross (September 14): Num 21.4b-9; Phil 2.6–11; Jn 3.13–17

All Saints (November 1): Rev 7.2–4, 9–14; 1 Jn 3.1–3; Mt 5.1–12a

All Souls (November 2)—Year A: Lam 3.17–26; 1 Cor 15.51–57; Mt 11.25–30 or Jn 12.23–26

All Souls (November 2)—Year B: Isa 25.6–9; 1 Cor 15.12–26; Mk 8.27–35 or Jn 1.1–5, 9–14

All Souls (November 2)—Year C: Ezek 37.1, 4–6, 12–14; 1 Pet 1.3–9; Lk 7.11–17 or Jn 20.11–18

Dedication of Saint John Lateran (November 9): Ezek 47.1–2, 8–9, 12; 1 Cor 3.9b-11, 16–17; Jn 2.13–22

Immaculate Conception of Mary (December 8): Gen 3.9–15, 20; Eph 1.3–6, 11–12; Lk 1.26–38

TABLE OF WEEKDAY READINGS

ADVENT SEASON

First Week of Advent
Monday: Isa 2.1–5 (Year A Isa 4.2–6); Mt 8.5–11, 13++
Tuesday: Isa 11.1–10; Lk 10.21–24
Wednesday: Isa 25.6–10a; Mt 15.29–37
Thursday: Isa 26.1–6; Mt 7.21, 24–27
Friday: Isa 29.17–24; Mt 9.27–31
Saturday: Isa 30.19–21, 13–26; Mt 9.35; 10.1, 5a, 6–8++

Second Week of Advent
Monday: Isa 35.1–10; Lk 5.17–26
Tuesday: Isa 40.1–11; Mt 18.12–14
Wednesday: Isa 40.25–31; Mt 11.28–30
Thursday: Isa 41.13–20; Mt 11.11–15
Friday: Isa 48.17–19; Mt 11.16–19
Saturday: Sir 48.1–4, 9–11; Mt 17.10–13

Third Week of Advent
Monday: Num 24.2–7, 15–17a; Mt 21.23–27
Tuesday: Zeph 3.1–2, 9–13; Mt 21.28–32
Wednesday: Isa 45.6b–8, 18, 21b–25; Lk 7.18b–23
Thursday: Isa 54.1–10; Lk 7.24–30
Friday: Isa 56.1–3a, 6–8; Jn 5, 16–17, 33–36++

December 17: Gen 49.2, 8–10; Mt 1.1–17
December 18: Jer 23.5–8; Mt 1.18–24
December 19: Judg 13.2–7, 24–25a; Lk 1.5–25
December 20: Isa 7.10–14; 8.10d; Lk 1.26–38
December 21: Song 2.8–14 or Zeph 3.14–18a; Lk 1.39–45
December 22: 1 Sam 1.24–28; Lk 1.46–56
December 23: Mal 3.1–4; 4.5–6; Lk 1.57–66
December 24: 2 Sam 7.1–5, 8–12, 16; Lk 1.67–79

CHRISTMAS SEASON

Octave of Christmas
Second day (St. Stephen): Acts 6.8–10; 7.54–59; Mt 10.17–22
Third day (St. John): 1 Jn 1.1–4; Jn 20.2–8
Fourth day (Holy Innocents): 1 Jn 1.5—2.2; Mt 2.13–18
Fifth day: 1 Jn 2.3–11; Lk 2.22–35
Sixth day: 1 Jn 2.12–17; Lk 2.36–40
Seventh day: 1 Jn 2.18–21; Jn 1.1–18
January 2: 1 Jn 2.22–28; Jn 1.19–28
January 3: 1 Jn 2.29; 3.1–6; Jn 1.29–34
January 4: 1 Jn 3.7–10; Jn 1.35–42

January 5: 1 Jn 3.11–21; Jn 1.43–51
January 6 (if Epiphany not celebrated): 1 Jn 5.5–13; Mk 1.4–5, 7–11++
Readings may vary slightly depending on when Epiphany is celebrated

Week After Epiphany
Monday after Epiphany: 1 Jn 3.22—4.6; Mt 4.12–17, 23–25
Tuesday after Epiphany: 1 Jn 4.7–10; Mk 6.34–44
Wednesday after Epiphany: 1 Jn 4.11–18; Mk 6.45–52
Thursday after Epiphany: 1 Jn 4.19—5.4; Lk 4.14–22a
Friday after Epiphany: 1 Jn 5.5–13; Lk 5.12–16
Saturday after Epiphany: 1 Jn 5.14–21; Jn 3.22–30

LENTEN SEASON

Ash Wednesday: Joel 2.12–18; 2 Cor 5.20—6.2; Mt 6.1–6, 16–18
Thursday after Ash Wednesday: Deut 30.15–20; Lk 9.22–25
Friday after Ash Wednesday: Isa 58.1–9a; Mt 9.14–15
Saturday after Ash Wednesday: Isa 58.9b–14; Lk 5.27–32

First Week of Lent
Monday: Lev 19.1–2, 11–18; Mt 25.31–46
Tuesday: Isa 55.10–11; Mt 6.7–15
Wednesday: Jon 3.1–10; Lk 11.29–32
Thursday: Esth 14.1, 3–5, 12–14; Mt 7.7–12
Friday: Ezek 18.21–28; Mt 5.20–16
Saturday: Deut 26.16–19; Mt 5.43–48

Second Week of Lent
Monday: Dan 9.3, 4b–10++; Lk 6.36–38
Tuesday: Isa 1.10, 16–20, 27–28, 31++; Mt 23.1–12
Wednesday: Jer 18.18–20; Mt 20.17–28
Thursday: Jer 17.5–10; Lk 16.19–31
Friday: Gen 37.3–4, 12–13a, 17b–28; Mt 21.33–43, 45–46
Saturday: Mic 7.14–15, 18–20; Lk 15.1–3, 11–32

Third Week of Lent
Monday: 2 Kings 5.1–15a; Lk 4.24–30
Tuesday: Dan 3.25, 34–43; Mt 18.21–35
Wednesday: Deut 4.1, 5–9; Mt 5.17–19
Thursday: Jer 7.23–28; Lk 11.14–23
Friday: Hos 14.1–9; Mk 12.28b–34
Saturday: Hos 5.15b—6.6++; Lk 18.9–14

Fourth Week of Lent
Monday: Isa 65.17–21; Jn 4.43–54
Tuesday: Ezek 47.1–9, 12; Jn 5.1–16
Wednesday: Isa 49.8–15; Jn 5.16–30
Thursday: Ex 32.7–14; Jn 5.18, 31–47++
Friday: Wis 2.1a, 12–22; Jn 7.1–2, 10, 25–30
Saturday: Jer 11.18–20; Jn 7.40–53

Fifth Week of Lent
Monday: Dan 13. 1–9, 15–17, 19–30, 33–64++; Jn 8.1–11 (Year C: Jn 8.12–20)
Tuesday: Num 21.4–9; Jn 8.21–30
Wednesday: Dan 3.13–20, 24, 49–56, 91–95++; Jn 8.31–42
Thursday: Gen 17.3–9; Jn 8.51–59
Friday: Jer 20.7, 10–13++; Jn 10.31–42
Saturday: Ezek 37.21–28; Jn 11.45–57

Holy Week
Monday: Isa 42.1–7; Jn 12.1–11
Tuesday: Isa 49.1–6; Jn 13.21–33, 36–38
Wednesday: Isa 50.4–9a; Mt 26.14–26

EASTER SEASON

Octave of Easter
Monday: Acts 2.14, 22–33; Mt 28.8–15
Tuesday: Acts 2.36–41; Jn 20.11–18
Wednesday: Acts 3.1–10; Lk 24.13–35
Thursday: Acts 3.11–26; Lk 24.35–48
Friday: Acts 4.1–12; Jn 21.1–14
Saturday: Acts 4.13–21; Mk 16.9–15

Second Week of Easter
Monday: Acts 4.23–31; Jn 3.1–8
Tuesday: Acts 4.32–37; Jn 3.7b–15
Wednesday: Acts 5.17–26; Jn 3.16–21
Thursday: Acts 5.27–33; Jn 3.31–36
Friday: Acts 5.34–42; Jn 6.1–15
Saturday: Acts 6.1–7; Jn 6.16–21

Third Week of Easter
Monday: Acts 6.8–15; Jn 6.22–29
Tuesday: Acts 7.51—8.1a; Jn 6.30–35
Wednesday: Acts 8.1b–8; Jn 6.35–40
Thursday: Acts 8.26–40; Jn 6.44–51
Friday: Acts 9.1–20; Jn 6.52–59
Saturday: Acts 9.31–42; Jn 6.53, 60–69++

Fourth Week of Easter
Monday: Acts 11.1–18; Jn 10.1–10 (Year A: Jn 10.11–18)
Tuesday: Acts 11.19–26; Jn 10.22–30
Wednesday: Acts 12.24—13.5a; Jn 12.44–50
Thursday: Acts 13.13–25; Jn 13.16–20
Friday: Acts 13.26–33; Jn 14.1–6
Saturday: Acts 13.44–52; Jn 14.7–14

Fifth Week of Easter
Monday: Acts 14.5–18; Jn 14.21–26
Tuesday: Acts 14.19–28; Jn 14.27–31a
Wednesday: Acts 15.1–6; Jn 15.1–8

Thursday: Acts 15.7–21; Jn 15.9–11
Friday: Acts 15.22–31; Jn 15.12–17
Saturday: Acts 16.1–10; Jn 15.18–21

Sixth Week of Easter
Monday: Acts 16.11–15; Jn 15.26—16.4a
Tuesday: Acts 16.22–34; Jn 16.5–11
Wednesday: Acts 17.15, 22—18.1; Jn 16.12–15
Thursday: Acts 18.1–8; Jn 16.16–20
Friday: Acts 18.9–18; Jn 16.20–23a
Saturday: Acts 18.23–28; Jn 16.23b–28

Seventh Week of Easter
Monday: Acts 19.1–8; Jn 16.29–33
Tuesday: Acts 20.17–27; Jn 17.1–11a
Wednesday: Acts 20.28–38; Jn 17.11b–19
Thursday: Acts 22.30; 23.6–11; Jn 17.20–26
Friday: Acts 24.27; 25.13b–21++; Jn 21.15–19
Saturday: Acts 28.16–20, 30–31; Jn 21.20–25

SEASON OF THE YEAR
(I is the reading for Year I; II is the reading for Year II; the Gospel is the same each year)

Week One
Monday: I—Heb 1.1–6; II—1 Sam 1.1–8; Mk 1.14–20
Tuesday: I—Heb 2.5–12; II—1 Sam 1.9–20; Mk 1.21–28
Wednesday: I—Heb 2.14–18; II—1 Sam 3.1–10, 19–20; Mk 1.29–39
Thursday: I—Heb 3.7–14; II—1 Sam 4.1c–11; Mk 1.40–45
Friday: I—Heb 4.1–5, 11; II—1 Sam 8.4–7, 10–22a; Mk 2.1–12
Saturday: I—Heb 4.12–16; II—1 Sam 9.1–4, 17–19, 10.1a; Mk 2.13–17

Week Two
Monday: I—Heb 5.1–10; II—1 Sam 15.16–23; Mk 2.18–22
Tuesday: I—Heb 6.10–20; II—1 Sam 16.1–13; Mk 2.23–28
Wednesday: I—Heb 7.1–3, 15–17; II—1 Sam 17.32–33, 37, 40–51; Mk 3.1–6
Thursday: I—Heb 7.25—8.6; II—1 Sam 18.6–9; 19.1–7; Mk 3.7–12
Friday: I—Heb 8.6–13; II—1 Sam 24.2–21; Mk 3.13–19
Saturday: I—Heb 9.2–3, 11–14; II—2 Sam 1.1–4, 11–12, 19, 23–27; Mk 3.20–21

Week Three
Monday: I—Heb 9.15, 24–28; II—2 Sam 5.1–7, 10; Mk 3.22–30
Tuesday: I—Heb 10.1–10; II—2 Sam 6.12b–15, 17–19; Mk 3.31–35
Wednesday: I—Heb 10.11–18; II—2 Sam 7.1–17++; Mk 4.1–20
Thursday: I—Heb 10.19–25; II—2 Sam 7.18–19, 24–29; Mk 4. 21–25
Friday: I—Heb 10.32–39; II—2 Sam 11.1–4a, 5–10a, 13–17; Mk 4.26–34
Saturday: I—Heb 11.1–2, 8–19; II—2 Sam 12.1–7a, 10–17; Mk 4.35–41

Week Four
Monday: I—Heb 11.32–40; II—2 Sam 15.13–14, 30, 16.5–13a; Mk 5.1–20
Tuesday: I—Heb 12.1–4; II—2 Sam 18.9–10, 14b, 24–26a, 30—19.3++; Mk 5.21–43
Wednesday: I—Heb 12.4–7, 11–15; II—2 Sam 24.2, 9–17; Mk 6.1–6

Thursday: I—Heb 12.18–19, 21–24; II—1 Kings 2.1–4, 10–12; Mk 6.7–13
Friday: I—Heb 13.1–8; II—Sir 47.2–11; Mk 6.14–29
Saturday: I—Heb 13.15–17, 20–21; II—1 Kings 3.4–13; Mk 6.30–34

Week Five
Monday: I—Gen 1.1–19; II—1 Kings 8.1–7, 9–13; Mk 6.53–56
Tuesday: I—Gen 1.20–2.4a; II—1 Kings 8.22–23, 27–30; Mk 7.1–13
Wednesday: I—Gen 2.4b–9, 15–17; II—1 Kings 10.1–10; Mk 7.14–23
Thursday: I—Gen 2.18–25; II—1 Kings 11.4–13; Mk 7.24–30
Friday: I—Gen 3.1–8; II—1 Kings 11.29–32, 12.19; Mk 7.31–37
Saturday: I—Gen 3.9–24; II—1 Kings 12.26–32, 13.33–34; Mk 8.1–10

Week Six
Monday: I—Gen 4.1–15, 25; II—Jas 1.1–11; Mk 8.11–13
Tuesday: I—Gen 6.5–8; 7.1–5, 10; II—Jas 1.12–18; Mk 8.14–21
Wednesday: I—Gen 8.6–13, 20–22; II—Jas 1.19–27; Mk 8.22–26
Thursday: I—Gen 9.1–13; II—Jas 2.1–9; Mk 8.27–33
Friday: I—Gen 11.1–9; II—Jas 2.14–24, 26; Mk 8.34—9.1
Saturday: I—Heb 11.1–7; II—Jas 3.1–10; Mk 9.2–13

Week Seven
Monday: I—Sir 1.1–10; II—Jas 3.13–18; Mk 9.14–29
Tuesday: I—Sir 2.1–11; II—Jas 4.1–10; Mk 9.30–37
Wednesday: I—Sir 4.11–19; II—Jas 4.13–17; Mk 9.38–40
Thursday: I—Sir 5.1–8; II—Jas 5.1–6; Mk 9.41–50
Friday: I—Sir 6.5–17; II—Jas 5.9–12; Mk 10.1–12
Saturday: I—Sir 17.1–4, 6–8, 10–15; II—Jas 5.13–20; Mk 10.13–16

Week Eight
Monday: I—Sir 17.24–27, 29; II—1 Pet 1.3–9; Mk 10.17–27
Tuesday: I—Sir 35.1–12; II—1 Pet 1.10–16; Mk 10.28–31
Wednesday: I—Sir 36.1–2, 5–6, 13–22; II—1 Pet 1.18–25; Mk 10.32–45
Thursday: I—Sir 42.15–25; II—1 Pet 2.2–5, 9–12; Mk 10.46–52
Friday: I—Sir 44.1, 9–13; II—1 Pet 4.7–13; Mk 11.11–25
Saturday: I—Sir 51.12b–20; II—Jude 17–25++; Mk 11.27–33

Week Nine
Monday: I—Tob 1.1ad, 2a, 3, 17; 2.1–8++; II—2 Pet 1.1–7; Mk 12.1–12
Tuesday: I—Tob 2.9–14—3.1++; II—2 Pet 3.12–15a, 17–18; Mk 12.13–17
Wednesday: I—Tob 3.1–6a, 7–10a, 11–13, 15b–17a; II—2 Tim 1.1–3, 6–12; Mk 12.18–27
Thursday: I—Tob 7.1, 9–16; 8.1, 4–9++; II—2 Tim 2.8–15; Mk 12.28–34
Friday: I—Tob 11.5–15; II—2 Tim 3.10–17; Mk 12.35–37
Saturday: I—Tob 12.1—20; II—2 Tim 4.1–8; Mk 12.38–44

Week Ten
Monday: I—2 Cor 1.1–7; II—1 Kings 17.1–6; Mt 5.1–12
Tuesday: I—2 Cor 1.18–22; II—1 Kings 17.7–16; Mt 5.13–16
Wednesday: I—2 Cor 3.4–11; II—1 Kings 18.20–39; Mt 5.17–19
Thursday: I—2 Cor 3.15—4.1, 3–6; II—1 Kings 18.41–46; Mt 5.20–26
Friday: I—2 Cor 4.7–15; II—1 Kings 19.9a, 11–16; Mt 5.27–32
Saturday: I—2 Cor 5.14–21; II—1 Kings 19.16b, 19–21; Mt 5.33–37

Week Eleven
Monday: I—2 Cor 6.1–10; II—1 Kings 21.1–16; Mt 5.38–42
Tuesday: I—2 Cor 8.1–9; II—1 Kings 21.17–29; Mt 5.43–48
Wednesday: I—2 Cor 9.6–11; II—2 Kings 2.1, 6–14; Mt 6.1–6, 16–18
Thursday: I—2 Cor 11.1–11; II—Sir 48.1–14; Mt 6.7–15
Friday: I—2 Cor 11.18, 21b–30; II—2 Kings 11.1–4, 9–18, 20; Mt 6.19–23
Saturday: I—2 Cor 12.1–10; II—2 Chr 24.17–25; Mt 6.24–34

Week Twelve
Monday: I—Gen 12.1–9; II—2 Kings 17.5–8, 13–15a, 18; Mt 7.1–5
Tuesday: I—Gen 13.2, 5–18; II—2 Kings 19.9b–11, 14–21, 31–36; Mt 7.6, 12–14
Wednesday: I—Gen 15.1–12, 17–18; II—2 Kings 22.8–13; 23.1–3; Mt 7.15–20
Thursday: I—Gen 16.1–12, 15–16; II—2 Kings 24.8–17; Mt 7.21–29
Friday: I—Gen 17.1, 9–10, 15–22; II—2 Kings 25.1–12; Mt 8.1–4
Saturday: I—Gen 18.1–15; II—Lam 2.2, 10–14, 18–19; Mt 8.5–17

Week Thirteen
Monday: I—Gen 18.16–33; II—Am 2.6–10, 13–16; Mt 8.18–22
Tuesday: I—Gen 19.15–29; II—Am 3.1–8, 4.11–12; Mt 8.23–27
Wednesday: I—Gen 21.5, 8–20; II—Am 5.14–15, 21–24; Mt 8.28–34
Thursday: I—Gen 22.1–19; II—Am 7.10–17; Mt 9.1–8
Friday: I—Gen 23.1–4, 19; 24.1–8, 62–67; II—Am 8.4–6, 9–12; Mt 9.9–13
Saturday: I—Gen 27.1–5, 9–10, 15–29++; II—Am 9.11–15; Mt 9.14–17

Week Fourteen
Monday: I—Gen 28.10–22a; II—Hos 2.14, 15b, 19–20; Mt 9.18–26
Tuesday: I—Gen 32.22–32; II—Hos 8.4–7, 11–13; Mt 9.32–38
Wednesday: I—Gen 41.55–57; 42.5–7a, 17–24; II—Hos 10.1–3, 7–8, 12; Mt 10.1–7
Thursday: I—Gen 44.18–21, 23b–29; 45.1–5; II—Hos 11.1, 3–5b, 8c–9; Mt 10.7–15
Friday: I—Gen 46.1–7, 28–30; II—Hos 14.1–9; Mt 10.16–23
Saturday: I—Gen 49.29–31, 33; 50.15–26++; II—Isa 6.1–8; Mt 10.24–33

Week Fifteen
Monday: I—Ex 1.8–14, 22; II—Isa 1.10–17; Mt 10.34—11.1
Tuesday: I—Ex 2.1–15a; II—Isa 7.1–9; Mt 11.20–24
Wednesday: I—Ex 3.1–6, 9–12; II—Isa 10.5–7, 13–16; Mt 11.25–27
Thursday: I—Ex 3.13–20; II—Isa 26.7–9, 12, 16–19; Mt 11.28–30
Friday: I—Ex 11.10—12.14; II—Isa 38.1–6, 21–22, 7–8; Mt 12.1–8
Saturday: I—Ex 12.37–42; II—Mic 2.1–5; Mt 12.14–21

Week Sixteen
Monday: I Ex 14.5–18; II—Mic 6.1–4, 6–8; Mt 12.38–42
Tuesday: I—Ex 14.21—15.1, 20–21++; II—Mic 7.14–15, 18–20; Mt 12.46–50
Wednesday: I—Ex 16.1–5, 9–15; II—Jer 1.1, 4–10; Mt 13.1–9
Thursday: I—Ex 19.1–2, 9–11, 16–20b; II—Jer 2.1–3, 7–8, 12–13; Mt 13.10–17
Friday: I—Ex 20.1–17; II—Jer 3.14–17; Mt 13.18–23
Saturday: I—Ex 24.3–8; II—Jer 7.1–11; Mt 13.24–30

Week Seventeen
Monday: I—Ex 32.15–24, 30–34; II—Jer 13.1–11; Mt 13.31–35
Tuesday: I—Ex 33.7–11, 34.5b–9, 28; II—Jer 14.17–22; Mt 13.36–43
Wednesday: I—Ex 34.29–35; II—Jer 15.10, 16–21; Mt 13.44–46

Thursday: I—Ex 40.16–21, 34–38; II—Jer 18.1–6; Mt 13.47–52
Friday: I—Lev 23.1, 4–11, 15–16, 27, 34b–37; II—Jer 26.1–9; Mt 13.54–58
Saturday: I—Lev 25.1, 8–17; II—Jer 26.11–16, 24; Mt 14.1–12

Week Eighteen
Monday: I—Num 11.4b–15; II—Jer 28.1–17; Mt 14.13–21 or Mt 14.22–36
Tuesday: I—Num 12.1–13; II—Jer 30.1–2, 12–15, 18–22; Mt 14.22–36 or Mt 15.1–2, 10–14
Wednesday: I—Num 13.1–2, 25–33; 14.1–2b, 26–29, 34–35++; II—Jer 31.1–7; Mt 15.21–28
Thursday: I—Num 20.1–13; II Jer 31.31–34; Mt 16.13–23
Friday: I—Deut 4.32–40; II—Nah 2.1, 3; 3.1–3, 6–7; Mt 16.24–28
Saturday: I—Deut 6.4–13; II—Hab 1.12—2.4; Mt 17.14–20

Week Nineteen
Monday: I—Deut 10.12–22; II—Ezek 1.2–5, 24–28c; Mt 17.22–27
Tuesday: I—Deut 31.1–8; II—Ex 2.8—3.4; Mt 18.1–5, 10, 12–14
Wednesday: I—Deut 34.1–12; II—Ezek 9.1–7; 10.18–22; Mt 18.15–20
Thursday: I—Josh 3.7–10a, 11, 13–17; II—Ezek 12.1–16++; Mt 18.21—19.1
Friday: I—Josh 24.1–13; II—Ezek 16.1–15, 60, 63; Mt 19.3–12
Saturday: I—Josh 24.14–29; II—Ezek 18.1–10, 13b, 30–32; Mt 19.13–15

Week Twenty
Monday: I—Judg 2.11–19; II—Ezek 24.15–24; Mt 19.16–22
Tuesday: I—Judg 6.11–24a; II—Ezek 28.1–10; Mt 19.23–30
Wednesday: I—Judg 9.6–15; II—Ezek 34.1–11; Mt 20.1–16a
Thursday: I—Judg 11.29–39a; II—Ezek 36.23–28; Mt 22.1–14
Friday: I—Ruth 1.1–2ab, 3–6, 14b–16, 22++; II—Ezek 37.1–14; Mt 22.34–40
Saturday: I—Ruth 2.1–3, 8–11; 4.13–17; II—Ezek 43.1–7a; Mt 23.1–12

Week Twenty-one
Monday: I—Thess 1.1–5, 8b–10; II—2 Thess 1.1–5, 11b–12; Mt 23.13–22
Tuesday: I—1 Thess 2.1–8; II—2 Thess 2.1–3a, 14–17; Mt 23.23–26
Wednesday: I—1 Thess 2.9–13; II—2 Thess 3.6–10, 16–18; Mt 23.27–32
Thursday: I—1 Thess 3.7–13; II—1 Cor 1.1–9; Mt 24.42–51
Friday: I—1 Thess 4.1–8; II—1 Cor 1.17–25; Mt 25.1–13
Saturday: I—1 Thess 4.9–11; II—1 Cor 1.26–31; Mt 25.14–30

Week Twenty-two
Monday: I—1 Thess 4.13–18; II—1 Cor 2.1–5; Lk 4.16–30
Tuesday: I—1 Thess 5.1–6, 9–11; II—1 Cor 2.10b–16; Lk 4.31–37
Wednesday: I—Col 1.1–8; II—1 Cor 3.1–9; Lk 4.38–44
Thursday: I—Col 1.9–14; II—1 Cor 3.18–23; Lk 5.1–11
Friday: I—Col 1.15–20; II—1 Cor 4.1–5; Lk 5.33–39
Saturday: I—Col 1.21–23; II—1 Cor 4.6–15; Lk 6.1–5

Week Twenty-three
Monday: I—Col 1.24—2.3; II—1 Cor 5.1–8; Lk 6.6–11
Tuesday: I—Col 2.6–15; II—1 Cor 6.1–11; Lk 6.12–19
Wednesday: I—Col 3.1–11; II—1 Cor 7.1, 17, 25–31++; Lk 6.20–26
Thursday: I—Col 3.12–17; II—1 Cor 8.1b–7, 11–13; Lk 6.27–38
Friday: I—1 Tim 1.1–2, 12–14; II—1 Cor 9.16–19, 22b–27; Lk 6.39–42
Saturday: I—1 Tim 1.15–17; II—1 Cor 10.14–22; Lk 6.43–49

Week Twenty-four
Monday: I—1 Tim 2.1–7++; II—1 Cor 11.17–26, 33; Lk 7.1–10
Tuesday: I—1 Tim 3.1–13; II—1 Cor 12.12–14, 27–31a; Lk 7.11–17
Wednesday: I—1 Tim 3.14–16; II—1 Cor 12.31—13.13; Lk 7.31–35
Thursday: I—1 Tim 4.12–16; II—1 Cor 15.1–11; Lk 7.36–50
Friday: I—1 Tim 6.2c–12; II—1 Cor 15.12–20; Lk 8.1–3
Saturday: I—1 Tim 6.13–16; II—1 Cor 15.36–37, 42–50++; Lk 8.4–15

Week Twenty-five
Monday: I—Ezra 1.1–6; II—Prov 3.27–34; Lk 8.16–18
Tuesday: I—Ezra 4.4–5; 6.1a, 6ad–8, 12b, 14–20++; II—Prov 21.1–6, 10–13; Lk 8.19–21
Wednesday: I—Ezra 9.5–9; II—Prov 30.5–9; Lk 9.1–6
Thursday: I—Hag 1.1–8; II—Eccl 1.2–11; Lk 9.7–9
Friday: I—Hag 2.1–9; II—Eccl 3.1–11; Lk 9.18–22
Saturday: I—Zech 2.5–9, 14–15a; II—Eccl 11.9—12.8; Lk 9.43b–45

Week Twenty-six
Monday: I—Zech 8.1–8; II—Job 1.6–22; Lk 9.46–50
Tuesday: I—Zech 8.20–23; II—Job 3.1–3, 11–17, 20–23; Lk 9.51–56
Wednesday: I—Neh 2.1–8; II—Job 9.1–12, 14–16; Lk 9.57–62
Thursday: I—Neh 8.1–4a, 5–6, 7b–12; II—Job 19.21–27; Lk 10.1–12
Friday: I—Bar 1.15–22; II—Job 38.12–21; 40.3–5; Lk 10.13–16
Saturday: I—Bar 4.5–12, 27–29; II—Job 42.1–3, 5–6, 12–13, 15–17++; Lk 10.17–24

Week Twenty-seven
Monday: I—Jon 1.1—2.1, 10; II—Gal 1.6–12; Lk 10.25–37
Tuesday: I—Jon 3.1–10; II Gal 1.13–24; Lk 10.38–42
Wednesday: I—Jon 4.1–11; II—Gal 2.1–2, 7–14; Lk 11.1–4
Thursday: I—Mal 3.13—4.2; II—Gal 3.1–5; Lk 11.5–13
Friday: I—Joel 1.13–15; 2.1–2; II—Gal 3.6–14++; Lk 11.15–26
Saturday: I—Joel 3.12–21; II—Gal 3.22–29; Lk 11.27–28

Week Twenty-eight
Monday: I—Rom 1.1–7; II—Gal 4.22–24, 26–27, 31—5.1; Lk 11.29–32
Tuesday: I—Rom 1.16–25; II—Gal 5.1–6; Lk 11.37–41
Wednesday: I—Rom 2.1–11; II—Gal 5.18–25; Lk 11.42–46
Thursday: I—Rom 3.21–30; II—Eph 1.1–10; Lk 11.47–54
Friday: I—Rom 4.1–8; II—Eph 1.11–14; Lk 12.1–7
Saturday: I—Rom 4.13, 16–18; II—Eph 1.15–23; Lk 12.8–12

Week Twenty-nine
Monday: I—Rom 4.20–25; II—Eph 2.1–10; Lk 12.13–21
Tuesday: I—Rom 5.12, 15b, 17–21; II Eph 2.12–22; Lk 12.35–38
Wednesday: I—Rom 6.12–18; II—Eph 3.1–12++; Lk 12.39–48
Thursday: I—Rom 6.19–23; II—Eph 3.13–21++; Lk 12.49–53
Friday: I—Rom 7.18–25a; II—Eph 4.1–6; Lk 12.54–59
Saturday: I—Rom 8.1–11; II—Eph 4.7–16; Lk 13.1–9

Week Thirty
Monday: I—Rom 8.11–17++; II—Eph 4.32—5.8; Lk 13.10–17
Tuesday: I—Rom 8.18–25; II—Eph 5.21–33; Lk 13.18–21

Wednesday: I—Rom 8.26–30; II—Eph 6.1–9; Lk 13.22–30
Thursday: I—Rom 3.31b–39; II—Eph 6.10–20; Lk 13.31–35
Friday: I—Rom 9.1–5; II—Phil 1.1–11; Lk 14.1–6
Saturday: I—Rom 11.1–2a, 11–12, 25–29; II—Phil 1.18b–26; Lk 14.1, 7–11

Week Thirty-one
Monday: I—Rom 11.29–36; II—Phil 2.1–4; Lk 14.12–14
Tuesday: I—Rom 12.5–16a; II—Phil 2.5–11; Lk 14.15–24
Wednesday: I—Rom 13.8–10; II—Phil 2.12–18; Lk 14.25–33
Thursday: I—Rom 14.7–12; II—Phil 3.3–8a++; Lk 15.1–10
Friday: I—Rom 15.14–21; II—Phil 3.17–21; 4.1; Lk 16.1–8
Saturday: I—Rom 16.3–9, 16, 22–27; II—Phil 4.10–19; Lk 16.9–15

Week Thirty-two
Monday: I—Wis 1.1–7; II—Titus 1.1–9; Lk 17.1–6
Tuesday: I—Wis 2.23–24—3.9; II—Titus 2.1–8, 11–14; Lk 17.7–10
Wednesday: I—Wis 6.1–11; II—Titus 3.1–7; Lk 17.11–19
Thursday: I—Wis 7.22—8.1; II—Philem 7–20; Lk 17.20–25
Friday: I—Wis 13.1–9; II—2 Jn 4–9; Lk 17.26–37
Saturday: I—Wis 18.14–16; 19.6–9; II—3 Jn 5–8; Lk 18.1–8

Week Thirty-three
Monday: I—1 Macc 1.10–15, 41–43, 54–57, 62–64; II—Rev 1.1–4; 2.1–5a; Lk 18.35–43
Tuesday: I—2 Macc 6.18–31; II—Rev 2.1–6, 14–22; Lk 19.1–10
Wednesday: I—2 Macc 7.1, 20–31; II—Rev 4.1–11; Lk 19.11–28
Thursday: O—1 Macc 2.15–29; II—Rev 5.1–10; Lk 19.41–44
Friday: I—1 Macc 4.36–37, 52–59; II—Rev 10.8–11; Lk 19.45–48
Saturday: I—1 Macc 6.1–13; II—Rev 11.4–12; Lk 20.27–40

Week Thirty-four
Monday: I—Dan 1.1–6, 8–20; II—Rev 14.1–3, 4b–5; Lk 21.1–4
Tuesday: I—Dan 2.3, 9a, 10a, 27a, 31–45++; II—Rev 14.14–19; Lk 21.5–11
Wednesday: I—Dan 5.1–6, 13–14, 16–17, 23–28; II—Rev 15.1–4; Lk 21.12–19
Thursday: I—Dan 6.11–28; II—Rev 18.1–2, 21–23; 19.1–3, 9a; Lk 21.20–28
Friday: I—Dan 7.1–14++; II—Rev 20.1–4, 11–15; 21.1–2; Lk 21.29–33
Saturday: I—Dan 7.15–27; II—Rev 22.1–7; Lk 21.34–36

TABLE OF MOVABLE DATES

Year	Cycle of Readings	Ash Wednesday	Easter	Ascension Sunday	Pentecost	First Sunday of Advent
2000	B II	Mar 8	Apr 23	Jun 4	Jun 11	Dec 3
2001	C I	Feb 28	Apr 15	May 27	Jun 3	Dec 2
2002	A II	Feb 13	Mar 31	May 12	May 19	Dec 1
2003	B I	Mar 5	Apr 20	Jun 1	Jun 8	Nov 30
2004	C II	Feb 25	Apr 11	May 23	May 30	Nov 28
2005	A I	Feb 9	Mar 27	May 8	May 15	Nov 27
2006	B II	Mar 1	Apr 16	May 28	Jun 4	Dec 3
2007	C I	Feb 21	Apr 8	May 20	May 27	Dec 2
2008	A II	Feb 6	Mar 23	May 4	May 11	Nov 30
2009	B I	Feb 25	Apr 12	May 24	May 31	Nov 29
2010	C II	Feb 17	Apr 4	May 16	May 23	Nov 28
2011	A I	Mar 9	Apr 24	Jun 5	Jun 12	Nov 27
2012	B II	Feb 22	Apr 8	May 20	May 27	Dec 2
2013	C I	Feb 13	Mar 31	May 12	May 19	Dec 1
2014	A II	Mar 5	Apr 20	Jun 1	Jun 8	Nov 30
2015	B I	Feb 18	Apr 5	May 17	May 24	Nov 29
2016	C II	Feb 10	Mar 27	May 8	May 15	Nov 27
2017	A I	Mar 1	Apr 16	May 28	Jun 4	Dec 3
2018	B II	Feb 14	Apr 1	May 13	May 20	Dec 2
2019	C I	Mar 6	Apr 21	Jun 2	Jun 9	Dec 1
2020	A II	Feb 26	Apr 12	May 24	May 31	Nov 29
2021	B I	Feb 17	Apr 4	May 16	May 23	Nov 28
2022	C II	Mar 2	Apr 17	May 29	Jun 5	Nov 27
2023	A I	Feb 22	Apr 9	May 21	May 28	Dec 3
2024	B II	Feb 14	Mar 31	May 12	May 19	Dec 1
2025	C I	Mar 5	Apr 20	Jun 1	Jun 8	Nov 30
2026	A II	Feb 18	Apr 5	May 17	May 24	Nov 29
2027	B I	Feb 10	Mar 28	May 9	May 16	Nov 28
2028	C II	Mar 1	Apr 16	May 28	Jun 4	Dec 3
2029	A I	Feb 14	Apr 1	May 13	May 20	Dec 2
2030	B II	Mar 6	Apr 21	Jun 2	Jun 9	Dec 1

PRAYERS AND DEVOTIONS OF
THE CATHOLIC FAITH

Sign of the Cross
In the name of the Father, and of the Son, and of the Holy Spirit. Amen.

The Lord's Prayer
Our Father, who art in heaven, hallowed be Thy name; Thy kingdom come; Thy will be done on earth as it is in heaven. Give us this day our daily bread; and forgive us our trespasses as we forgive those who trespass against us; and lead us not into temptation, but deliver us from evil. Amen.

The Glory Be (Doxology)
Glory be to the Father, and to the Son, and to the Holy Spirit. As it was in the beginning, is now, and ever shall be, world without end. Amen.

The Apostles' Creed
I believe in God, the Father Almighty, Creator of heaven and earth; and in Jesus Christ, His only Son, our Lord; who was conceived by the Holy Spirit, born of the Virgin Mary, suffered under Pontius Pilate, was crucified, died, and was buried. He descended into hell; the third day he arose again from the dead; he ascended into heaven, sitteth at the right hand of God, the Father Almighty; from thence he shall come to judge the living and the dead. I believe in the Holy Spirit, the Holy Catholic Church, the communion of saints, the forgiveness of sins, the resurrection of the body, and life everlasting. Amen.

Prayer to the Holy Spirit
Come, Holy Spirit, fill the hearts of Your faithful, and enkindle in them the fire of Your love. Send forth Your Spirit and they shall be created. And You shall renew the face of the earth.

O God, You instructed the hearts of those who believed in You by the light of the Holy Spirit. Grant us in the same Spirit to be truly wise and ever to rejoice in His consolation: through Christ our Lord. Amen.

Act of Contrition
O my God, I am heartly sorry for having offended You, and I detest all my sins, because of Your just punishments (the loss of heaven and the pains of hell), but most of all because they offend You, my God, who are all-good and deserving of all my love. I firmly resolve, with the help of Your grace, to confess my sins, to do penance, and to amend my life. Amen.

Act of Faith
O my God, I firmly believe that You are one God in three Divine Persons, Father, Son, and Holy Spirit. I believe that Your Divine Son became man, and died for our sins, and that He will come to judge the living and the dead. I believe these and all the truths which the Holy Catholic Church teaches, because You have revealed them, who can neither deceive nor be deceived. Amen.

Act of Hope

O my God, relying on Your almighty power and infinite mercy and promises, I hope to obtain pardon of my sins, the help of Your grace, and life everlasting, through the merits of Jesus Christ, my Lord and Redeemer. Amen.

Act of Love

O my God, I love You above all things, with my whole heart and soul, because You are all-good and worthy of all love. I love my neighbor as myself for the love of You. I forgive all who have injured me, and ask pardon of all whom I have injured. Amen.

The Divine Praises

Blessed be God.
Blessed be His Holy Name.
Blessed be Jesus Christ, true God and true man.
Blessed be the Name of Jesus.
Blessed be His Most Sacred Heart.
Blessed be His Most Precious Blood.
Blessed be Jesus in the Most Holy Sacrament of the Altar.
Blessed be the Holy Spirit, the Paraclete.
Blessed be the great Mother of God, Mary most holy.
Blessed be her holy and Immaculate Conception.
Blessed be her glorious Assumption.
Blessed be the name of Mary, Virgin and Mother.
Blessed be St. Joseph, her most chaste spouse.
Blessed be God, in His angels and in His saints.

The Stations of the Cross

1. Jesus Is Condemned to Death
2. Jesus Takes Up His Cross
3. Jesus Falls the First Time
4. Jesus Meets His Mother
5. Simon of Cyrene Helps to Carry the Cross
6. Veronica Wipes the Face of Jesus
7. Jesus Falls the Second Time
8. Jesus Comforts the Women of Jerusalem
9. Jesus Falls the Third Time
10. Jesus Is Stripped of His Garments
11. Jesus Is Nailed to the Cross
12. Jesus Dies on the Cross
13. Jesus Is Taken Down from the Cross
14. Jesus Is Laid in the Tomb

Prayer Before a Crucifix

Look down upon me, O good and gentle Jesus, while before Your face I humbly kneel, and with burning soul pray and beseech You to fix deep in my heart lively sentiments of faith, hope, and charity, true contrition for my sins, and a firm purpose of amendment; while I contemplate with great love and tender pity Your five wounds, pondering over them within me, calling to mind the words which David Your prophet said of You, my good Jesus: "They have pierced my hands and my feet; they have numbered all my bones."

De Profundis

Out of the depths I have cried unto You, O Lord! Lord, hear my voice. Let Your ears be attentive to the voice of my supplication. If You, O Lord, will mark iniquities: Lord, who shall stand? For with You there is merciful forgiveness; and by reason of Your law I have waited for You, O Lord. My soul has relied on His word; my soul has hoped in the Lord.

From the morning watch even until night; let Israel hope in the Lord. Because with the Lord there is mercy: and with Him plenteous redemption. And He shall redeem Israel from all its iniquities.

Eternal rest grant unto them, O Lord, and let perpetual light shine upon them. May they rest in peace. Amen.

The Jesus Prayer

Lord Jesus Christ, Son of the living God, have mercy on me, a sinner.

The Anima Christi

Soul of Christ, sanctify me.
Body of Christ, save me.
Blood of Christ, inebriate me.
Water from the side of Christ, wash me.
Passion of Christ, strengthen me.
O good Jesus, hear me.
Within Thy wounds hide me.
Permit me not to be separated from Thee.
From the wicked, defend me.
At the hour of death, call me
and bid me come to Thee,
that with all the saints I may praise Thee
forever and ever. Amen.

Morning Offering

O Jesus, through the Immaculate Heart of Mary, I offer You all my prayers, works, joys and sufferings of this day in union with the the Holy Sacrifice of the Mass throughout the world.

I offer them for the intentions of Your Sacred Heart: the salvation of souls, reparation for sin, the reunion of all Christians.

I offer them for the intentions of our bishops, and of all apostles of prayer, and in particular for those recommended by our Holy Father. Amen.

Blessing Before Meals

Bless us, O Lord, and these Your gifts, which we are about to receive from Your bounty. Through Christ our Lord. Amen.

Grace After Meals

We give You thanks for all Your benefits, O Almighty God, who lives and reigns forever; and may the souls of the faithful departed, through the mercy of God, rest in peace. Amen.

Corporal Works of Mercy

Feed the Hungry
Give Drink to the Thirsty
Clothe the Naked
Visit the Imprisoned
Shelter the Homeless
Visit the Sick
Bury the Dead

Spiritual Works of Mercy

Admonish the Sinner
Instruct the Ignorant
Counsel the Doubtful
Comfort the Sorrowful
Bear Wrongs Patiently
Forgive All Injuries
Pray for the Living and the Dead

Guardian Angel

Angel of God, my guardian dear,
to whom God's love commits me here.
Ever this day be at my side,
to light, to guard, to rule and guide. Amen.

St. Michael the Archangel

Saint Michael the Archangel, defend us in battle. Be our protection against the wickedness
and snares of the devil. May God rebuke him, we humbly pray; and do you, O prince of
the heavenly host, by the power of God, thrust into hell Satan and all evil spirits who
wander through the world for the ruin of souls. Amen.

Prayer of St. Ignatius Loyola

Take, O Lord, and receive my entire liberty, my memory, my understanding and my whole
will. All that I am and all that I possess You have given me: I surrender it all to Your love
and Your grace; with these I will be rich enough, and will desire nothing more. Amen.

Prayer of St. Francis of Assisi

Make me, O Lord, an instrument of Your peace.
Where there is hatred, let me sow love;
Where there is injury, pardon;
Where there is doubt, faith;
Where there is despair, hope;
Where there is darkness, light;
Where there is sadness, joy.
O Divine Master, grant that I may not so much seek to be consoled as to console; to be
understood as to understand; to be loved as to love.
For it is in giving that we receive; it is in pardoning that we are pardoned, and it is in dying
that we are born to eternal life. Amen.

Serenity Prayer

God, grant me the serenity to accept the things I cannot change,
the courage to change the things I can,
and the wisdom to know the difference. Amen.

An Irish Blessing Prayer

May the road rise to meet you,
May the wind be at your back,
May the sun shine warm upon your face,
May the rains fall gently upon your field,
May God hold you in the palm of His hand. Amen.

Popular Prayers for the Intercession of the Blessed Virgin Mary

Hail Mary (*Ave Maria*)

Hail Mary, full of grace, the Lord is with thee. Blessed art thou among women, and blessed is the fruit of thy womb, Jesus. Holy Mary, Mother of God, pray for us sinners, now and at the hour of our death. Amen.

The Five Joyful Mysteries of the Rosary

1. The Annunciation (Luke 1.28)
2. The Visitation (Luke 1.42)
3. The Birth of Our Lord (Luke 2.7)
4. The Presentation of Our Lord (Luke 2.28)
5. The Finding of Our Lord in the Temple (Luke 2.46)

The Five Sorrowful Mysteries of the Rosary

1. The Agony in the Garden (Mark 14.35)
2. The Scourging at the Pillar (Mark 15.15)
3. The Crowning with Thorns (Mark 15.17)
4. The Carrying of the Cross (John 19.17)
5. The Crucifixion and Death of Our Lord (Luke 23.33)

The Five Glorious Mysteries of the Rosary

1. The Resurrection (Mark 16.6)
2. The Ascension (Mark 16.19)
3. The Descent of the Holy Spirit (Acts 2.4)
4. The Assumption of Our Blessed Mother into Heaven (Genesis 3.15)
5. The Coronation of Our Blessed Mother (Revelation 12.1)

The Angelus

V. The angel of the Lord declared unto Mary.
R. And she conceived of the Holy Spirit.
Hail Mary, etc.

V. Behold the handmaid of the Lord.
R. Be it done unto me according to Your Word.
Hail Mary, etc.

V. And the Word was made flesh.
R. And dwelt among us.
Hail Mary, etc.

V. Pray for us, O holy Mother of God.
R. That we may be made worthy of the promises of Christ.

Let us pray:
Pour forth, we beseech You, O Lord, Your grace into our hearts: that we, to whom the Incarnation of Christ, Your Son was made known by the message of an Angel, may by His Passion and Cross be brought to the glory of His Resurrection: through the same Christ our Lord. Amen

Queen of Heaven (*Regina Coeli*)
Queen of heaven, rejoice, alleluia:
For He Whom thou didst deserve to bear, alleluia,
Hath risen, as He said, alleluia.
Pray for us to God, alleluia.
V. Rejoice and be glad, O Virgin Mary, alleluia.
R. Because the Lord is truly risen, alleluia.

Let us pray:
O God, who by the resurrection of Your Son, our Lord Jesus Christ, has vouchsafed to make glad the whole world: grant, we beseech You, that through the intercession of the Virgin Mary, His Mother, we may attain the joys of eternal life: through the same Christ our Lord. Amen.

Hail, Holy Queen (*Salve Regina*)
Hail, Holy Queen, Mother of Mercy, our life, our sweetness, and our hope. To you do we cry, poor banished children of Eve. To you do we send up our sighs, mourning and weeping in this valley of tears. Turn, then, most gracious advocate, your eyes of mercy toward us, and after this our exile, show to us the blessed fruit of your womb, Jesus. O clement, O loving, O sweet Virgin Mary.

Pray for us, O Holy Mother of God.
That we may be worthy of the promises of Christ.

The Memorare
Remember, O most gracious Virgin Mary, that never was it known that anyone who fled to your protection, implored your help or sought your intercession, was left unaided. Inspired with this confidence, we fly unto you, O Virgin of virgins, our Mother! To you we come, before you we stand, sinful and sorrowful. O Mother of the Word Incarnate, despise not our petitions, but in your mercy hear and answer us. Amen.

CONCORDANCE TO THE
NEW REVISED STANDARD VERSION

This concordance was prepared for the Catholic Edition of the New Revised Standard Version (NRSV). Special thanks are due to Michael J. McKay, S.T.D. for his editorial assistance.

Entry words are spelled exactly as they appear in the NRSV, North American Edition. Differences in spelling between the North American and Anglicized editions are relatively few (e.g., honor vs. honour) and do not seriously impair the usefulness of the concordance with the Anglicized edition of the NRSV.

Entry words are abbreviated and in bold type in the context lines. Some context lines contain more than one entry word (e.g., at HOLY: Isa 6:3 "**H, h, h** is the LORD of hosts;).

The more important characters in the Bible have concise biographies rather than context lines in order to communicate more information about these significant individuals. When a name is shared by more than one person (e.g., Joseph, Mary), the entry is subdivided into numbered paragraphs.

SPECIAL SYMBOLS

*   Entries marked with an asterisk (e.g., **ABBA***) contain every reference in the NRSV

→   An arrow following an entry heading points to related words for additional study (e.g., **ABIDE** → ABIDES, ABODE)

=   An equals sign marks an alternate proper name for additional study (e.g., **ISRAEL** =JACOB)

⟦⟧   Contexts in double brackets are from passages that are similarly bracketed in the NRSV (e.g., John 7:53–8:11)

Abbreviations for the books of the Bible follow on page 1498.

For further study consult *The Concise Concordance to the New Revised Standard Version* (Oxford University Press, 1993) and *The NRSV Concordance Unabridged* (Zondervan, 1991).

John R. Kohlenberger III

ABBREVIATIONS

The following abbreviations are used for the books of the Bible:

The Old Testament

Gen. . . . . Genesis
Ex . . . . Exodus
Lev . . . . Leviticus
Num. . . . . Numbers
Deut . . . . Deuteronomy
Josh . . . . Joshua
Judg . . . . Judges
Ruth . . . . Ruth
1 Sam. . . . . 1 Samuel
2 Sam. . . . . 2 Samuel
1 Kings . . . . 1 Kings
2 Kings . . . . 2 Kings
1 Chr . . . . 1 Chronicles
2 Chr . . . . 2 Chronicles
Ezra . . . . Ezra
Neh . . . . Nehemiah
Tob . . . . Tobit
Jdt . . . . Judith
Esth. . . . . Esther
1 Macc . . . . 1 Maccabees
2 Macc . . . . 2 Maccabees
Job. . . . . Job
Ps . . . . Psalm

Prov. . . . . Proverbs
Eccl . . . . Ecclesiastes
Song . . . . Song of Solomon
Wis . . . . The Wisdom of Solomon
Sir . . . . Sirach (Ecclesiasticus)
Isa . . . . Isaiah
Jer . . . . Jeremiah
Lam. . . . . Lamentations
Bar. . . . . Baruch
Ezek. . . . . Ezekiel
Dan . . . . Daniel
Hos. . . . . Hosea
Joel . . . . Joel
Am. . . . . Amos
Ob. . . . . Obadiah
Jon . . . . Jonah
Mic . . . . Micah
Nah. . . . . Nahum
Hab . . . . Habakkuk
Zeph . . . . Zephaniah
Hag . . . . Haggai
Zech . . . . Zechariah
Mal. . . . . Malachi

The New Testament

Mt. . . . . Matthew
Mk . . . . Mark
Lk . . . . Luke
Jn. . . . . John
Acts . . . . Acts of the Apostles
Rom . . . . Romans
1 Cor . . . . 1 Corinthians
2 Cor . . . . 2 Corinthians
Gal. . . . . Galatians
Eph . . . . Ephesians
Phil. . . . . Philippians
Col. Colossians
1 Thess . . . . 1 Thessalonians
2 Thess . . . . 2 Thessalonians

1 Tim . . . . 1 Timothy
2 Tim . . . . 2 Timothy
Titus . . . . Titus
Philem . . . . Philemon
Heb. . . . . Hebrews
Jas . . . . James
1 Pet. . . . . 1 Peter
2 Pet. . . . . 2 Peter
1 Jn . . . . 1 John
2 Jn . . . . 2 John
3 Jn . . . . 3 John
Jude. . . . . Jude
Rev. Revelation

A

AARON

Genealogy (Ex 6:16-20; Josh 21:4, 10; 1 Chr 6:3-15). Priesthood of (Ex 28:1; Num 17; Heb 5:1-4; 7), vestments of (Ex 28; 39), consecration of (Ex 29), ordination of (Lev 8).

Spokesman for Moses (Ex 4:14-16, 27-31; 7:1-2). Supported Moses' hands in battle (Ex 17:8-13). Built golden calf (Ex 32; Deut 9:20). Spoke against Moses (Num 12). Priesthood opposed (Num 16); staff budded (Num 17). Forbidden to enter the promised land (Num 20:1-12). Death of (Num 20:22-29; 33:38-39). Praise of (Sir 45:6-22).

ABANDON → ABANDONED

Num	32:15	will again **a** them in the wilderness;
Deut	4:31	will neither **a** you nor destroy you;
2 Chr	15: 2	but if you **a** him, he will **a** you.
Mk	7: 8	You **a** the commandment of God
Acts	2:27	For you will not **a** my soul to Hades
Heb	10:35	Do not, therefore, **a** that confidence

ABANDONED → ABANDON

Deut	29:25	they **a** the covenant of the LORD,
Judg	2:13	**a** the LORD, and worshiped Baal
2 Chr	12: 5	You **a** me, so I have **a** you
Sir	49: 4	for they **a** the law of the Most High;
Isa	54: 7	For a brief moment I **a** you,

ABBA*

Mk	14:36	"**A**, Father, for you all things are possible;
Rom	8:15	When we cry, "**A**! Father!"
Gal	4: 6	into our hearts, crying, "**A**! Father!"

ABEDNEGO* → =AZARIAH

Deported to Babylon with Daniel (Dan 1:1-6). Name changed from Azariah (Dan 1:7). Refused defilement by food (Dan 1:8-20). Refused idol worship (Dan 3:1-12); saved from furnace (Dan 3:13-30).

ABEL

Second son of Adam (Gen 4:2). Offered acceptable sacrifice (Gen 4:4; Heb 11:4; 12:24). Murdered by Cain (Gen 4:8; Mt 23:35; Lk 11:51; 1 Jn 3:12).

ABHOR → ABHORRENT

| Lev | 26:11 | and I shall not **a** you. |

ABHORRENT → ABHOR

| Deut | 14: 3 | You shall not eat any **a** thing. |
| | 18: 9 | not learn to imitate the **a** practices |

ABIATHAR

High priest in days of Saul and David (1 Sam 22; 2 Sam 15; 1 Kings 1-2; Mk 2:26). Escaped Saul's slaughter of priests (1 Sam 22:18-23). Supported David in Absalom's revolt (2 Sam 15:24-29). Supported Adonijah (1 Kings 1:7-42); deposed by Solomon (1 Kings 2:22-35; cf. 1 Sam 2:31-35).

ABIDE → ABIDES, ABODE

Gen	6: 3	My spirit shall not **a** in mortals forever,
Ps	15: 1	O LORD, who may **a** in your tent?
	91: 1	**a** in the shadow of the Almighty,
Wis	3: 9	the faithful will **a** with him in love,
Jn	15: 4	**A** in me as I **a** in you.
1 Cor	13:13	faith, hope, and love, these three;
1 Jn	2:28	And now, little children, **a** in him,

ABIDES → ABIDE

| Hag | 2: 5 | My spirit **a** among you; do not fear. |
| 1 Jn | 3:14 | Whoever does not love **a** in death. |

ABIGAIL

1. Sister of David (1 Chr 2:16-17).
2. Wife of Nabal (1 Sam 25:30); pled for his life with David (1 Sam 25:14-35). Became David's wife after Nabal's death (1 Sam 25:36-42).

ABIHU

Son of Aaron (Ex 6:23; 24:1, 9); killed for offering illicit fire (Lev 10; Num 3:2-4; 1 Chr 24:1-2).

ABIJAH

1. Second son of Samuel (1 Chr 6:28); a corrupt judge (1 Sam 8:1-5).
2. An Aaronic priest (1 Chr 24:10; Lk 1:5).
3. Son of Jeroboam I; died as prophesied by Ahijah (1 Kings 14:1-18).
4. Son of Rehoboam, also called Abijam; king of Judah who

fought Jeroboam I attempting to reunite Israel (1 Kings 14:31-15:8; 2 Chr 12:16-14:1).

ABILITY → ABLE

Ex	31: 3	filled him with divine spirit, with **a**,
Mt	25:15	to each according to his **a**.
Acts	2: 4	as the Spirit gave them **a**.

ABIMELECH

1. King of Gerar who took Abraham's wife Sarah, believing her to be his sister (Gen 20). Covenanted with Abraham (Gen 21:22-33).
2. King of Gerar who took Isaac's wife Rebekah, believing her to be his sister (Gen 26:1-11). Covenanted with Isaac (Gen 26:12-31).
3. Son of Gideon (Judg 8:31). Attempted to become king (Judg 9).

ABIRAM

Sided with Dathan in rebellion against Moses and Aaron (Num 16; 26:9; Deut 11:6; Sir 45:18).

ABISHAI

Son of Zeruiah, David's sister (1 Sam 26:6; 1 Chr 2:16). One of David's chief warriors (1 Chr 11:15-21): against Edom (1 Chr 18:12-13), Ammon (2 Sam 10), Absalom (2 Sam 18), Sheba (2 Sam 20). Wanted to kill Saul (1 Sam 26), killed Abner (2 Sam 2:18-27; 3:22-39).

ABLE → ABILITY

Ex	18:25	Moses chose **a** men from all Israel
Josh	1: 5	No one shall be **a** to stand against
	23: 9	no one has been **a** to withstand you
Jdt	11:18	of them will be **a** to withstand you.
Dan	3:17	God whom we serve is **a** to deliver
Mt	9:28	"Do you believe that I am **a** to do
Mk	10:38	you **a** to drink the cup that I drink,
Rom	14: 4	the Lord is **a** to make them stand.
2 Cor	9: 8	God is **a** to provide you with every
Eph	6:11	**a** to stand against the wiles of the devil.
2 Tim	1:12	he is **a** to guard until that day
Heb	2:18	**a** to help those who are being tested.
	5: 2	is **a** to deal gently with the ignorant
	7:25	he is **a** for all time to save
Rev	5: 3	**a** to open the scroll or to look into it.

ABNER

Cousin of Saul and commander of his army (1 Sam 14:50; 17:55-57; 26). Made Ish-Bosheth king after Saul (2 Sam 2:8-10), but later defected to David (2 Sam 3:6-21). Killed Asahel (2 Sam 2:18-32), for which he was killed by Joab and Abishai (2 Sam 3:22-39).

ABODE → ABIDE

| Ps | 68:16 | mount that God desired for his **a**, |
| Prov | 3:33 | but he blesses the **a** of the righteous. |

ABOLISH → ABOLISHED

| Dan | 11:31 | shall **a** the regular burnt offering |
| Mt | 5:17 | I have come not to **a** but to fulfill. |

ABOLISHED → ABOLISH

| Eph | 2:15 | **a** the law with its commandments |
| 2 Tim | 1:10 | who **a** death and brought life |

ABOMINABLE → ABOMINATION

2 Chr	28: 3	the **a** practices of the nations
1 Macc	1:48	to make themselves **a** by everything
Ezek	7:20	they made their **a** images,

ABOMINATION → ABOMINABLE, ABOMINATIONS

1 Macc	6: 7	that they had torn down the **a** that
Prov	6:16	seven that are an **a** to him:
Sir	1:25	but godliness is an **a** to a sinner.
Dan	9:27	shall be an **a** that desolates,
Rev	21:27	anyone who practices **a** or falsehood

ABOMINATIONS → ABOMINATION

Lev	18:27	committed all of these **a**,
1 Kings	14:24	all the **a** of the nations that the LORD
Ezek	44: 7	broken my covenant with all your **a**.
Rev	17: 5	mother of whores and of earth's **a**."

ABOUND → ABOUNDED, ABOUNDING

| Deut | 28:11 | LORD will make you **a** in prosperity, |
| Rom | 6: 1 | in sin in order that grace may **a**? |

ABOUNDED → ABOUND

| Rom | 5:20 | sin increased, grace **a** all the more, |

ABOUNDING → ABOUND

Ex	34: 6	**a** in steadfast love and faithfulness,
Ps	86: 5	**a** in steadfast love to all who call on
Joel	2:13	to anger, and **a** in steadfast love,
Jon	4: 2	to anger, and **a** in steadfast love,

ABOVE

Deut	4:39	the LORD is God in heaven **a**
Jn	3: 7	'You must be born from **a**.'
Phil	2: 9	the name that is **a** every name,
Col	3: 2	Set your minds on things that are **a**,

ABRAHAM

Abram, son of Terah (Gen 11:26-27), husband of Sarah (Gen 11:29).

Covenant relation with the LORD (Gen 12:1-3; 13:14-17; 15; 17; 22:15-18; Ex 2:24; Neh 9:8; Ps 105; Mic 7:20; Lk 1:68-75; Rom 4; Heb 6:13-15).

Called from Ur, via Haran, to Canaan (Gen 12:1; Acts 7:2-4; Heb 11:8-10). Moved to Egypt, nearly lost Sarah to Pharoah (Gen 12:10-20). Divided the land with Lot; settled in Hebron (Gen 13). Saved Lot from four kings (Gen 14:1-16); blessed by Melchizedek (Gen 14:17-20; Heb 7:1-20). Declared righteous by faith (Gen 15:6; Rom 4:3; Gal 3:6-9; 1 Macc 2:52). Fathered Ishmael by Hagar (Gen 16).

Name changed from Abram (Gen 17:5; Neh 9:7). Circumcised (Gen 17; Rom 4:9-12). Entertained three visitors (Gen 18); promised a son by Sarah (Gen 18:9-15; 17:16). Questioned destruction of Sodom and Gomorrah (Gen 18:16-33). Moved to Gerar; nearly lost Sarah to Abimelech (Gen 20). Fathered Isaac by Sarah (Gen 21:1-7; Acts 7:8; Heb 11:11-12); sent away Hagar and Ishmael (Gen 21:8-21; Gal 4:22-30). Covenant with Abimelech (Gen 21:22-32). Tested by offering Isaac (Gen 22; Heb 11:17-19; Jas 2:21-24). Sarah died; bought field of Ephron for burial (Gen 23). Secured wife for Isaac (Gen 24). Fathered children by Keturah (Gen 25:1-6; 1 Chr 1:32-33). Death (Gen 25:7-11).

Called servant of God (Gen 26:24), friend of God (2 Chr 20:7; Isa 41:8; Jas 2:23), prophet (Gen 20:7), father of Israel (Ex 3:15; Isa 51:2; Mt 3:9; Jn 8:39-58). Praised (Sir 44:19-45:1).

ABSALOM

Son of David by Maacah (2 Sam 3:3; 1 Chr 3:2). Killed Amnon for rape of his sister Tamar; banished by David (2 Sam 13). Returned to Jerusalem; received by David (2 Sam 14). Rebelled against David (2 Sam 15-17). Killed (2 Sam 18).

ABSENT

1 Cor	5: 3	**a** in body, I am present in spirit;
Col	2: 5	For though I am **a** in body,

ABUNDANCE → ABUNDANTLY

Lk	6:45	**a** of the heart that the mouth speaks.
	12:15	one's life does not consist in the **a**
2 Cor	9: 8	provide you with every blessing in **a**

ABUNDANTLY → ABUNDANCE

Jn	10:10	that they may have life, and have it **a**.
Eph	3:20	to accomplish **a** far more than all

ABYSS

Lk	8:31	to order them to go back into the **a**.
Rom	10: 7	'Who will descend into the **a**?'"

ACCEPT → ACCEPTABLE, ACCEPTED

Prov	19:20	Listen to advice and **a** instruction,
Jer	32:33	would not listen and **a** correction.
Mt	19:11	"Not everyone can **a** this teaching,
Jn	1:11	his own people did not **a** him.

ACCEPTABLE → ACCEPT

Ps	19:14	meditation of my heart be **a** to you,
	51:17	sacrifice **a** to God is a broken spirit;
Rom	12: 1	a living sacrifice, holy and **a** to God,

ACCEPTED → ACCEPT

Gen	4: 7	If you do well, will you not be **a**?
Lk	4:24	no prophet is **a** in the prophet's hometown.

ACCESS

Rom	5: 2	we have obtained **a** to this grace
Eph	2:18	have **a** in one Spirit to the Father.

ACCOMPLISH → ACCOMPLISHED

Isa	55:11	but it shall **a** that which I purpose,
Ezek	17:24	I the LORD have spoken; I will **a** it.

ACCOMPLISHED → ACCOMPLISH

Mt	5:18	will pass from the law until all is **a**.

ACCORDING

Ps	28: 4	Repay them **a** to their work,
	119: 9	By guarding it **a** to your word.
Sir	16:12	he judges a person **a** to one's deeds.
Mt	9:29	"**A** to your faith let it be done to you
Rom	8: 4	not **a** to the flesh but **a** to the Spirit.
Heb	2: 4	Holy Spirit, distributed **a** to his will.
1 Jn	5:14	that if we ask anything **a** to his will,
Rev	20:12	dead were judged **a** to their works,

ACCOUNT → ACCOUNTABLE

Mt	12:36	judgment you will have to give an **a**
Heb	4:13	to whom we must render an **a**.

ACCOUNTABLE → ACCOUNT

Rom	14:12	each of us will be **a** to God.

ACCURSED → CURSE

Rom	9: 3	I could wish that I myself were **a**
Rev	22: 3	Nothing **a** will be found there any

ACCUSATION → ACCUSE

Lk	23: 4	no basis for an **a** against this man."

ACCUSE → ACCUSATION, ACCUSER

Ps	103: 9	He will not always **a**,
Zech	3: 1	Satan standing at his right hand to **a**
Mt	12:10	so that they might **a** him.

ACCUSER → ACCUSE

Jn	5:45	your **a** is Moses,
Rev	12:10	the **a** of our comrades has been thrown

ACHAN

Sinned at Jericho; stoned (Josh 7; 22:20; 1 Chr 2:7).

ACHISH

King of Gath before whom David feigned insanity (1 Sam 21:10-15). Later "ally" of David (2 Sam 27-29).

ACKNOWLEDGE

Deut	4:35	you would **a** that the LORD is God;
Prov	3: 6	In all your ways **a** him,
Mt	10:32	I also will **a** before my Father in
Rom	1:28	since they did not see fit to **a** God,

ACT → ACTED, ACTIVE, ACTS

Ps	37: 5	trust in him, and he will **a**.
Rom	14:23	because they do not **a** from faith;
Jas	1:25	hearers who forget but doers who **a**

ACTED → ACT

Ezek	20: 9	But I **a** for the sake of my name,
Acts	3:17	I know that you **a** in ignorance,
1 Tim	1:13	mercy because I had **a** ignorantly

ACTIVE → ACT

Heb	4:12	the word of God is living and **a**,
Jas	2:22	faith was **a** along with his works,

ACTS → ACT

Ex	6: 6	outstretched arm and with mighty **a**
Ps	71:15	mouth will tell of your righteous **a**,
Mt	7:24	hears these words of mine and **a**

ADAM

First man (Tob 8:6; Gen 1:26-2:25; Rom 5:14; 1 Tim 2:13). Sin of (Gen 3; Hos 6:7 [note]; Rom 5:12-21). Children of (Gen 4:1-5:5). Death of (Gen 5:5; Rom 5:12-21; 1 Cor 15:22).

ADD → ADDED

Deut	4: 2	You must neither **a** anything
Prov	30: 6	Do not **a** to his words, or else
Lk	12:25	by worrying **a** a single hour to your

ADDED → ADD

Eccl	3:14	nothing can be **a** to it, nor anything
Sir	42:21	Nothing can be **a** or taken away,

ADDICTED*

Titus	1: 7	or quick-tempered or **a** to wine

ADMONISH → ADMONITION

Col	3:16	and **a** one another in all wisdom;

ADMONITION → ADMONISH

Prov	15: 5	one who heeds **a** is prudent.

ADONIJAH
1. Son of David by Haggith (2 Sam 3:4; 1 Chr 3:2). Attempted to be king after David; killed at Solomon's order (1 Kings 1-2).
2. Levite; teacher of the Law (2 Chr 17:8).

ADOPTION
Rom	8:15	but you have received a spirit of **a.**
	8:23	groan inwardly while we wait for **a,**
Gal	4: 5	that we might receive **a** as children.

ADORNED → ADORNMENT
Lk	21: 5	how it was **a** with beautiful stones
Rev	17: 4	**a** with gold and jewels and pearls,
	21: 2	as a bride **a** for her husband.

ADORNMENT → ADORNED, ADORNS
Prov	3:22	for your soul and **a** for your neck.
1 Pet	3: 4	let your **a** be the inner self with the

ADORNS → ADORNMENT
Isa	61:10	as a bride **a** herself with her jewels.

ADULT* → ADULTS
1 Cor	13:11	an **a,** I put an end to childish ways.

ADULTERERS → ADULTERY
Jer	23:10	For the land is full of **a;**
1 Cor	6: 9	idolaters, **a,** male prostitutes,

ADULTERESS → ADULTERY
Lev	20:10	the **a** shall be put to death.
Prov	2:16	from the **a** with her smooth words,

ADULTERY → ADULTERERS, ADULTERESS
Ex	20:14	You shall not commit **a.**
Jer	3: 9	committing **a** with stone and tree.
Mt	5:28	committed **a** with her in his heart.
Lk	16:18	and marries another commits **a,**
Jn	8: 3	⟦ a woman who had been caught in **a;**⟧

ADULTS* → ADULT
1 Cor	14:20	infants in evil, but in thinking be **a.**

ADVANTAGE
Eccl	7:12	**a** of knowledge is that wisdom gives
Rom	3: 1	Then what **a** has the Jew?
1 Cor	10:24	Do not seek your own **a,** but that of

ADVERSARIES → ADVERSARY
Deut	32:41	I will take vengeance on my **a,**
2 Sam	22:49	you exalted me above my **a,**

ADVERSARY → ADVERSARIES
1 Tim	5:14	give the **a** no occasion to revile us.
1 Pet	5: 8	roaring lion your **a** the devil prowls

ADVERSITY → ADVERSARY
Deut	30:15	life and prosperity, death and **a.**
Isa	48:10	I have tested you in the furnace of **a.**

ADVICE → ADVISERS
2 Chr	10:13	rejected the **a** of the older men;
Tob	4:18	Seek **a** from every wise person
Ps	1: 1	do not follow the **a** of the wicked,
Prov	8:14	I have good **a** and sound wisdom;
Sir	37:11	pay no attention to any **a** they give.

ADVISERS → ADVICE
Prov	15:22	but with many **a** they succeed.

ADVOCATE
Jn	14:26	But the **A,** the Holy Spirit,
	15:26	the **A** comes, whom I will send
1 Jn	2: 1	we have an **a** with the Father,

AFFLICT* → AFFLICTED, AFFLICTION, AFFLICTIONS, AFFLICTS
2 Sam	7:10	evildoers shall **a** them no more,
Lam	3:33	for he does not willingly **a**
2 Thess	1: 6	repay with affliction those who **a**

AFFLICTED → AFFLICT
Deut	26: 6	Egyptians treated us harshly and **a**
Nah	1:12	Though I have **a** you, I will afflict
2 Cor	4: 8	are **a** in every way, but not crushed;

AFFLICTION → AFFLICT
Deut	16: 3	bread with it—the bread of **a—**
Ps	25:18	Consider my **a** and my trouble,
Isa	30:20	of adversity and the water of **a,**

Lam	1: 9	"O LORD, look at my **a,**
2 Cor	4:17	this slight momentary **a** is preparing

AFFLICTIONS → AFFLICT
Ps	34:19	Many are the **a** of the righteous,

AFFLICTS* → AFFLICT
Tob	13: 2	For he **a,** and he shows mercy;

AFRAID → FEAR
Gen	3:10	and I was **a,** because I was naked;
	15: 1	not be **a,** Abram, I am your shield;
Ex	3: 6	his face, for he was **a** to look at God.
Lev	26: 6	and no one shall make you **a;**
Deut	20: 3	Do not lose heart, or be **a,**
Ps	3: 6	I am not **a** of ten thousands
	27: 1	of whom shall I be **a?**
	56:11	in God I trust; I am not **a.**
Isa	12: 2	I will trust, and will not be **a,**
Ezek	2: 6	do not be **a** of their words,
Mt	10:31	So do not be **a;** you are of more
	28:10	Jesus said to them, "Do not be **a;**
Lk	12:32	"Do not be **a,** little flock,
Heb	13: 6	Lord is my helper; I will not be **a.**

AGABUS*
A Christian prophet (Acts 11:28; 21:10).

AGAG
King of Amalekites; not killed by Saul (1 Sam 15).

AGAIN
Job	14:14	If mortals die, will they live **a?**
Eccl	3:20	and all turn to dust **a.**
Mk	8:31	and after three days rise **a.**
Jn	14: 3	I will come **a** and will take you to
Heb	6: 6	they are crucifying a the Son of God
	9:25	Nor was it to offer himself **a** and **a,**

AGE → AGES
Gen	21: 2	bore Abraham a son in his old **a,**
Mt	28:20	with you always, to the end of the **a."**
Gal	1: 4	to set us free from the present evil **a,**

AGES → AGE
Deut	4:32	For ask now about former **a,**
1 Cor	2: 7	decreed before the **a** for our glory.
Col	1:26	has been hidden throughout the **a**
1 Tim	1:17	To the King of the **a,** immortal,

AGREE
Mt	18:19	if two of you **a** on earth about
Mk	14:56	and their testimony did not **a.**
1 Jn	5: 8	and the blood, and these three **a.**

AGRIPPA
Descendant of Herod; king before whom Paul argued his case in Caesarea (Acts 25:13-26:32).

AHAB
1. Son of Omri; king of Israel (1 Kings 16:28-22:40), husband of Jezebel (1 Kings 16:31). Promoted Baal worship (1 Kings 16:31-33); opposed by Elijah (1 Kings 17:1; 18; 21), a prophet (1 Kings 20:35-43), Micaiah (1 Kings 22:1-28). Defeated Ben-Hadad (1 Kings 20). Killed for failing to kill Ben-Hadad and for murder of Naboth (1 Kings 20:35-21:40).
2. A false prophet (Jer 29:21-22).

AHASUERUS → =ARTAXERXES
King of Persia (Ezra 4:6), husband of Esther (called Artaxerxes in Esth 11:1; 12:2; 13:1; 16:1). Deposed Vashti; replaced her with Esther (Esth 1-2). Sealed Haman's edict to annihilate the Jews (Esth 3). Received Esther without having called her (Esth 5:1-8). Honored Mordecai (Esth 6). Hanged Haman (Esth 7). Issued edict allowing Jews to defend themselves (Esth 8). Promoted Mordecai (Esth 8:1-2, 15; 9:4; 10).

AHAZ
Son of Jotham; king of Judah, (2 Kings 16; 2 Chr 28; Mt 1:9). Idolatry of (2 Kings 16:3-4, 10-18; 2 Chr 28:1-4, 22-25). Defeated by Aram and Israel (2 Kings 16:5-6; 2 Chr 28:5-15). Sought help from Assyria rather than the LORD (2 Kings 16:7-9; 2 Chr 28:16-21; Isa 7).

AHAZIAH → =JEHOAHAZ
1. Son of Ahab; king of Israel (1 Kings 22:51-2 Kings 1:18; 2 Chr 20:35-37). Made an unsuccessful alliance with Jehoshaphat (2 Chr 20:35-37). Died for seeking Baal rather than the LORD (2 Kings 1).

2. Son of Jehoram; king of Judah (2 Kings 8:25-29; 9:14-29), also called Jehoahaz (2 Chr 21:17-22:9; 25:23). Killed by Jehu while visiting Joram (2 Kings 9:14-29; 2 Chr 22:1-9).

AHEAD

Mt	11: 10	sending my messenger **a** of you,
Phil	3: 13	straining forward to what lies **a**,
Heb	11: 26	for he was looking **a** to the reward.

AHIJAH

1. Priest during Saul's reign (1 Sam 14:3,18).
2. Prophet of Shiloh (1 Kings 11:29-39; 14:1-18).

AHIKAM

Father of Gedaliah (2 Kings 25:22), protector of Jeremiah (Jer 26:24).

AHIMAAZ

1. Father-in-law of Saul (1 Sam 14:50).
2. Son of Zadok, the high priest, loyal to David (2 Sam 15:27,36; 17:17-20; 18:19-33).

AHIMELECH

1. Priest who helped David in his flight from Saul (1 Sam 21-22).
2. One of David's warriors (1 Sam 26:6).

AHITHOPHEL

One of David's counselors who sided with Absalom (2 Sam 15:12, 31-37; 1 Chr 27:33-34); committed suicide when his advice was ignored (2 Sam 16:15-17:23).

AI

Josh	7: 4	and they fled before the men of **A**.

AIR

Eph	2: 2	the ruler of the power of the **a**,
1 Thess	4: 17	to meet the Lord in the **a**;
Rev	16: 17	angel poured his bowl into the **a**,

ALARMED

Mk	13: 7	and rumors of wars, do not be **a**;
2 Thess	2: 2	to be quickly shaken in mind or **a**,

ALERT

Lk	12: 37	slaves whom the master finds **a**
1 Cor	16: 13	Keep **a**, stand firm in your faith,
Eph	6: 18	keep **a** and always persevere
1 Pet	5: 8	Discipline yourselves, keep **a**.

ALEXANDER

1 Macc	1: 1	**A** son of Philip, the Macedonian,

ALIEN → ALIENS

Ex	2: 22	an **a** residing in a foreign land."
Lev	19: 34	you shall love the **a** as yourself,
Deut	24: 17	You shall not deprive a resident **a**

ALIENS → ALIEN

Gen	15: 13	your offspring shall be **a** in a land
1 Macc	2: 7	the sanctuary given over to **a**?
Eph	2: 19	you are no longer strangers and **a**,
1 Pet	2: 11	I urge you as **a** and exiles to abstain

ALIVE → LIVE

Gen	6: 19	to keep them **a** with you;
Deut	32: 39	I kill and I make **a**; I wound and I heal;
Acts	1: 3	suffering he presented himself **a**
Rom	6: 11	dead to sin and **a** to God
Eph	2: 5	made us **a** together with Christ—
1 Thess	4: 17	Then we who are **a**, who are left,
Rev	1: 18	I am **a** forever and ever;
	19: 20	were thrown **a** into the lake of fire

ALL

Gen	6: 13	to make an end of **a** flesh,
Deut	6: 5	You shall love the LORD your God with **a** your heart, and with **a** your soul, and with **a** your might.
Ps	1: 3	In **a** that they do, they prosper.
Sir	7: 29	With **a** your soul fear the Lord,
Jer	29: 13	if you seek me with **a** your heart,
Lk	10: 27	love the Lord your God with **a** your
Rom	3: 23	**a** have sinned and fall short of the
	6: 10	he died to sin, once for **a**;
1 Cor	6: 12	"**A** things are lawful for me,"
	15: 51	not **a** die, but we will **a** be changed,
2 Cor	5: 15	And he died for **a**,
Eph	1: 23	the fullness of him who fills **a** in **a**.

Phil	4: 13	I can do **a** things through him
Col	3: 11	but Christ is **a** in **a**!
2 Tim	3: 16	**A** scripture is inspired by God
2 Pet	3: 9	but **a** to come to repentance.
Rev	21: 5	"See, I am making **a** things new."

ALMIGHTY → MIGHT

Gen	17: 1	"I am God **A**; walk before me,
Ex	6: 3	Isaac, and Jacob as God **A**,
Ps	91: 1	who abide in the shadow of the **A**,
Bar	3: 1	O Lord **A**, God of Israel,
Rev	1: 8	who was and who is to come, the **A**.
	21: 22	its temple is the Lord God the **A**

ALMS

Tob	12: 8	better to give **a** than to lay up gold.
Sir	7: 10	do not neglect to give **a**.
Mt	6: 2	"So whenever you give **a**,

ALONE → LONELY

Gen	2: 18	not good that the man should be **a**;
Deut	6: 4	The LORD is our God, the LORD **a**.
Isa	2: 11	LORD **a** will be exalted in that day.
Mk	2: 7	Who can forgive sins but God **a**?"
	10: 18	No one is good but God **a**.
Jas	2: 24	justified by works and not by faith **a**

ALPHA

Rev	1: 8	"I am the **A** and the Omega,"
	22: 13	I am the **A** and the Omega,

ALTAR → ALTARS

Gen	22: 9	Isaac, and laid him on the **a**,
Ex	27: 1	shall make the **a** of acacia wood,
	30: 1	an **a** on which to offer incense;
Ezra	3: 2	to build the **a** of the God of Israel,
Jdt	4: 12	even draped the **a** with sackcloth
1 Macc	1: 54	a desolating sacrilege on the **a** of
	4: 47	built a new **a** like the former one.
Mt	5: 24	leave your gift there before the **a**
Heb	13: 10	We have an **a** from which those
Jas	2: 21	he offered his son Isaac on the **a**?
Rev	6: 9	I saw under the **a** the souls of those

ALTARS → ALTAR

Ex	34: 13	You shall tear down their **a**,
Num	3: 31	the table, the lampstand, the **a**,
1 Macc	2: 45	went around and tore down the **a**;

ALWAYS

Mt	28: 20	And remember, I am with you **a**,
Lk	18: 1	to pray **a** and not to lose heart.
Phil	4: 4	Rejoice in the Lord **a**; again I will

AMALEK

Ex	17: 8	Then **A** came and fought with Israel
1 Sam	15: 3	attack **A**, and utterly destroy all

AMASA

Nephew of David (1 Chr 2:17). Commander of Absalom's forces (2 Sam 17:24-27). Returned to David (2 Sam 19:13). Killed by Joab (2 Sam 20:4-13).

AMAZED → AMAZING

Mt	8: 27	**a**, saying, "What sort of man is this,
Mk	6: 6	And he was **a** at their unbelief.
Acts	2: 7	**A** and astonished, they asked,

AMAZIAH

1. Son of Joash; king of Judah (2 Kings 14; 2 Chr 25). Defeated Edom (2 Kings 14:7; 2 Chr 25:5-13); defeated by Israel for worshiping Edom's gods (2 Kings 14:8-14; 2 Chr 25:14-24).
2. Idolatrous priest; opposed Amos (Am 7:10-17).

AMAZING → AMAZED

Mk	12: 11	and it is **a** in our eyes'?"
Rev	15: 3	"Great and **a** are your deeds,

AMBASSADOR* → AMBASSADORS

Eph	6: 20	for which I am an **a** in chains.

AMBASSADORS → AMBASSADOR

2 Cor	5: 20	So we are **a** for Christ,

AMBITION

Phil	2: 3	Do nothing from selfish **a** or conceit
Jas	3: 14	envy and selfish **a** in your hearts,

AMEN

Deut	27: 15	people shall respond, saying, "**A**!"

2 Cor 1:20 through him that we say the "A,"
Rev 3:14 The words of the A, the faithful and

AMMONITE → AMMONITES
Deut 23: 3 No A or Moabite shall be admitted

AMMONITES → AMMONITE
Gen 19:38 the ancestor of the A to this day.
Jer 49: 6 I will restore the fortunes of the A,

AMNON
Firstborn of David (2 Sam 3:2; 1 Chr 3:1). Killed by Absalom for raping his sister Tamar (2 Sam 13).

AMON
1. Son of Manasseh; king of Judah (2 Kings 21:18-26; 1 Chr 3:14; 2 Chr 33:21-25).
2. Ruler of Samaria (1 Kings 22:26; 2 Chr 18:25).

AMORITES
Gen 15:16 iniquity of the A is not yet complete
Num 21:31 Israel settled in the land of the A.

AMOS
Prophet from Tekoa (Am 1:1; 7:10-17; Tob 2:6).

ANANIAS
1. Early disciple; died for lying to God (Acts 5:1-11).
2. Disciple who baptized Saul (Acts 9:10-19).
3. High priest at Paul's arrest (Acts 22:30-24:1).

ANCESTOR → ANCESTORS
Deut 26: 5 "A wandering Aramean was my a;
Mt 3: 9 'We have Abraham as our a';

ANCESTORS → ANCESTOR
Ex 3:13 The God of your a has sent me to
Deut 4:31 not forget the covenant with your a
Lam 5: 7 Our a sinned; they are no more,
Acts 5:30 The God of our a raised up Jesus,
Heb 1: 1 Long ago God spoke to our a in

ANCHOR
Heb 6:19 a sure and steadfast a of the soul,

ANCIENT
Ps 24: 7 and be lifted up, O a doors!
Jer 6:16 ask for the a paths, where the good
Dan 7: 9 and an A One took his throne,
Mic 5: 2 origin is from of old, from a days.
Rev 20: 2 He seized the dragon, that a serpent,

ANDREW*
Apostle; brother of Simon Peter (Mt 4:18; 10:2; Mk 1:16-18, 29; 3:18; 13:3; Lk 6:14; Jn 1:35-44; 6:8-9; 12:22; Acts 1:13).

ANGEL → ANGELS, ARCHANGEL, ARCHANGEL'S
Gen 22:11 the a of the LORD called to him
Ex 3: 2 the a of the LORD appeared to him
23:20 going to send an a in front of you,
Num 22:22 the a of the LORD took his stand in
1 Chr 21:15 sent an a to Jerusalem to destroy it;
Tob 5: 4 the a Raphael standing in front of
1 Macc 7:41 your a went out and struck
Ps 34: 7 The a of the LORD encamps
Sir 48:21 and his a wiped them out.
Isa 37:36 the a of the LORD set out and struck
Bar 6: 7 For my a is with you,
Dan 3:49 But the a of the Lord came down
3:95 who has sent his a and delivered
13:59 a of God is waiting with his sword
14:34 the a of the Lord said to Habakkuk,
6:22 God sent his a and shut the lions'
Mt 1:20 an a of the Lord appeared to him in
Lk 1:26 In the sixth month the a Gabriel
Acts 5:19 during the night an a of the Lord
23: 8 say that there is no resurrection, or a,
2 Cor 11:14 Satan disguises himself as an a of light.
Gal 1: 8 if we or an a from heaven should

ANGELS → ANGEL
Gen 19: 1 The two a came to Sodom in the
28:12 a of God were ascending and
Tob 11:14 and blessed be all his holy a.
Ps 103:20 Bless the LORD, O you his a,
Mk 12:25 but are like a in heaven.
Lk 4:10 command his a concerning you,
Jn 1:51 and the a of God ascending and
Rom 8:38 that neither death, nor life, nor a,

1 Cor 6: 3 not know that we are to judge a—
Col 2:18 on self-abasement and worship of a,
Heb 2: 7 for a little while lower than the a;
1 Pet 1:12 things into which a long to look!
2 Pet 2: 4 not spare the a when they sinned,
Rev 1:20 stars are the a of the seven churches,
7: 1 After this I saw four a standing at
21:12 and at the gates twelve a,

ANGER → ANGRY
Ex 32:19 the dancing, Moses' a burned hot,
34: 6 merciful and gracious, slow to a,
Deut 32:22 For a fire is kindled by my a,
Judg 2:12 and they provoked the LORD to a.
1 Kings 16:13 God of Israel to a with their idols.
Ps 30: 5 For his a is but for a moment;
Prov 12:16 Fools show their a at once,
Eccl 7: 9 Do not be quick to a,
Sir 5: 4 for the Lord is slow to a.
Isa 48: 9 For my name's sake I defer my a,
Joel 2:13 slow to a, and abounding in
Jon 4: 2 slow to a, and abounding in
Mk 3: 5 He looked around at them with a;
Eph 4:26 not let the sun go down on your a,
Jas 1:19 slow to speak, slow to a;
Rev 14:10 unmixed into the cup of his a,

ANGRY → ANGER
Gen 4: 5 So Cain was very a, and his
Jer 3:12 I will not be a forever.
Mt 5:22 that if you are a with a brother or

ANGUISH
Isa 53:11 Out of his a he shall see light;
Dan 12: 1 There shall be a time of a,
Zeph 1:15 a day of distress and a,
Lk 22:44 ⟦ In his a he prayed more earnestly,⟧

ANIMAL → ANIMALS
Gen 2:19 God formed every a of the field
9: 2 dread of you shall rest on every a of
Ps 50:10 every wild a of the forest is mine,

ANIMALS → ANIMAL
Gen 3:14 cursed are you among all a
Lev 26: 6 remove dangerous a from the land,
Ps 36: 6 save humans and a alike, O LORD.

ANNA
1. Prophetess; spoke of the child Jesus (Lk 2:36-38).
2. Wife of Tobit (Tob 1:20; 2:1, 11).

ANNAS*
High priest A.D. 6-15 (Lk 3:2; Jn 18:13, 24; Acts 4:6).

ANNOUNCED → ANNOUNCING
Isa 48: 5 before they came to pass I a them
1 Pet 1:25 the good news that was a to you.

ANNOUNCES → ANNOUNCING
Isa 52: 7 feet of the messenger who a peace,

ANNOUNCING* → ANNOUNCED, ANNOUNCES
Isa 63: 1 I, a vindication, mighty to save."
Rom 1: 9 serve with my spirit by a the gospel

ANNULLED
Jn 10:35 and the scripture cannot be a—

ANOINT → ANOINTED, ANOINTING
Ex 30:30 You shall a Aaron and his sons,
1 Sam 15: 1 "The LORD sent me to a you king
Ps 23: 5 you a my head with oil; my cup
Dan 9:24 and to a a most holy place.

ANOINTED → ANOINT
1 Sam 2:10 and exalt the power of his a."
26: 9 raise his hand against the LORD's a,
1 Chr 16:22 "Do not touch my a ones;
Ps 2: 2 against the LORD and his a, saying,
Isa 61: 1 because the LORD has a me;
Ezek 28:14 With an a cherub as guardian
Dan 9:26 an a one shall be cut off and
Zech 4:14 These are the two a ones who stand
Lk 4:18 he has a me to bring good news to
Jn 1:41 Messiah" (which is translated A).
Jn 12: 3 a Jesus' feet, and wiped them with her hair.

ANOINTING → ANOINT
Ex   30:25 it shall be a holy a oil.
Jas   5:14 a them with oil in the name of the Lord
1 Jn   2:27 as his a teaches you about all things,

ANOTHER
Prov 27: 2 Let a praise you, and not your own
Isa   48:11 My glory I will not give to a.
Jn   14:16 and he will give you a Advocate,
Gal   1: 7 not that there is a gospel,

ANSWER → ANSWERED
1 Kings 18:37 A me, O LORD, a me,
Job   30:20 I cry to you and you do not a me;
Ps   65: 2 O you who a prayer!
Prov 15: 1 A soft a turns away wrath,
Isa   65:24 Before they call I will a,
Lk   23: 9 but Jesus gave him no a.

ANSWERED → ANSWER
1 Chr 21:26 and he a him with fire from heaven
Ps   118:21 I thank you that you have a me

ANT*
Prov   6: 6 Go to the a, you lazybones;

ANTICHRIST*
1 Jn   2:18 As you have heard that a is coming,
       2:22 the a, the one who denies the Father
       4: 3 And this is the spirit of the a,
2 Jn   1: 7 person is the deceiver and the a!

ANTIOCH
Acts 11:26 in A that the disciples were first called
            "Christians."
     13: 1 the church at A there were prophets
Gal   2:11 But when Cephas came to A,

ANTIOCHUS
Antiochus IV Epiphanes, king of the Syrian Greeks B.C. 175-164 (1 Macc 1:10-19). Plundered the temple in Jerusalem (1 Macc 1:20-28). Attempted to force the Hellenization of the Jewish people (1 Macc 1:41-53), including defiling the altar and holy place (1 Macc 1:54-64). His policies sparked the Maccabean revolt.

ANXIETIES → ANXIETY
1 Cor 7:32 I want you to be free from a.

ANXIETY → ANXIETIES
Eccl   11:10 Banish a from your mind,
1 Pet   5: 7 Cast all your a on him, because he

ANYTHING
Gen 18:14 Is a too wonderful for the LORD?
Jer   32:27 is a too hard for me?
Mt   18:19 if two of you agree on earth about a
Jn   16:23 if you ask a of the Father in my name,

APART → PART
Jn   15: 5 a from me you can do nothing.
Rom   3:21 a from law, the righteousness of
Jas   2:20 that faith a from works is barren?

APOLLOS
Christian from Alexandria, learned in the Scriptures; instructed by Aquila and Priscilla (Acts 18:24-28). At Corinth (Acts 19:1; 1 Cor 1:12; 3; Titus 3:13).

APOSTASIES → APOSTASY
Jer   2:19 and your a will convict you.
Ezek 37:23 I will save them from all the a

APOSTASY* → APOSTASIES
1 Macc 2:15 officers who were enforcing the a

APOSTLE → APOSTLES
Rom 11:13 as I am an a to the Gentiles,
1 Cor 9: 1 Am I not an a?
2 Cor 12:12 signs of a true a were performed
Heb   3: 1 a and high priest of our confession,

APOSTLES → APOSTLE
See also Andrew, Bartholomew, Barnabas, James, John, Judas, Matthew, Matthias, Nathanael, Paul, Peter, Philip, Simon, Thaddaeus, Thomas.
Mt   10: 2 the names of the twelve a:
Lk   6:13 of them, whom he also named a:
Acts   2:43 and signs were being done by the a.
1 Cor 12:28 has appointed in the church first a,

APPEAL
Mt   26:53 think that I cannot a to my Father,
Acts 25:11 I a to the emperor."
2 Cor 5:20 God is making his a through us;
Philem 1: 9 rather a to you on the basis of love
1 Pet   3:21 an a to God for a good conscience,

APPEAR → APPEARANCE, APPEARANCES, APPEARED, APPEARING
Mt   24:30 the sign of the Son of Man will a in
Mk   13:22 messiahs and false prophets will a
2 Cor 5:10 a before the judgment seat of Christ,
Heb   9:28 a a second time, not to deal with sin,

APPEARANCE → APPEAR
Ex   24:17 Now the a of the glory of the LORD
1 Sam 16: 7 not look on his a or on the height
Jdt   11:23 You are not only beautiful in a,
Sir   19:29 A person is known by his a,
2 Cor 5:12 those who boast in outward a

APPEARANCES → APPEAR
Jn   7:24 not judge by a, but judge with right

APPEARED → APPEAR
Jn   21:14 that Jesus a to the disciples after he
1 Cor 15: 5 he a to Cephas, then to the twelve.
Heb   9:26 a once for all at the end of the age

APPEARING → APPEAR
Acts   1: 3 a to them during forty days and
2 Tim 4: 8 to all who have longed for his a.

APPETITES
Sir   18:30 base desires, but restrain your a.
Rom 16:18 our Lord Christ, but their own a,

APPLE
Deut 32:10 guarded him as the a of his eye.
Zech   2: 8 touches you touches the a of my eye

APPOINT → APPOINTED
1 Sam 8: 5 a for us, then, a king to govern us,
Isa   60:17 I will a Peace as your overseer

APPOINTED → APPOINT
Lev   23: 2 the a festivals of the LORD
Eccl   3:17 for he has a a time for every matter,
Hab   2: 3 there is still a vision for the a time;
Mk   3:16 So he a the twelve: Simon (to whom
Acts   3:20 that he may send the Messiah a for
Heb   1: 2 whom he a heir of all things,
       9:27 just as it is a for mortals to die once,

APPORTIONED → PORTION
Deut 32: 8 When the Most High a the nations,
Josh 18:10 Joshua a the land to the Israelites,

APPROACH
Sir   1:28 do not a him with a divided mind.
Heb   4:16 a the throne of grace with boldness,
     11: 6 whoever would a him must believe

APPROVAL → APPROVED
Gal   1:10 I now seeking human a, or God's a?
Heb   11: 2 by faith our ancestors received a.
1 Pet   2:20 and suffer for it, you have God's a.

APPROVED → APPROVAL
1 Thess 2: 4 but just as we have been a by God
2 Tim 2:15 to present yourself to God as one a

AQUILA*
Husband of Priscilla; co-worker with Paul, instructor of Apollos (Acts 18; Rom 16:3; 1 Cor 16:19; 2 Tim 4:19).

ARABS
Neh   4: 7 and the A and the Ammonites
1 Macc 5:39 also have hired A to help them,

ARAM → ARAMAIC, ARAMEAN
Judg 10: 6 the gods of A, the gods of Sidon,
2 Chr 16: 7 you relied on the king of A,

ARAMAIC → ARAM
2 Kings 18:26 to your servants in the A language,
Ezra   4: 7 the letter was written in A and

APOSTLE*

Eph   2:20 foundation of the a and prophets,
      4:11 he gave were that some would be a,
Rev   21:14 are the twelve names of the twelve a

Dan   2: 4   Chaldeans said to the king (in **A**),

ARAMEAN → ARAM
Deut   26: 5   "A wandering **A** was my ancestor;

ARARAT
Gen   8: 4   ark came to rest on the mountains of **A**.

ARAUNAH → =ORNAN
2 Sam 24:16   the threshing floor of **A** the Jebusite.

ARCHANGEL* → ANGEL
Jude   1: 9   **a** Michael contended with the devil

ARCHANGEL'S* → ANGEL
1 Thess 4:16   **a** call and with the sound of God's

ARCHITECT*
Heb   11:10   whose **a** and builder is God.

AREOPAGUS
Acts   17:22   Then Paul stood in front of the **A**

ARGUE → ARGUES, ARGUMENT, ARGUMENTS
Job   13: 3   and I desire to **a** my case with God.
Isa   1:18   now, let us **a** it out, says the LORD:
Acts   18: 4   Every sabbath he would **a** in the
Rom   9:20   a human being, to **a** with God?

ARGUES* → ARGUE
Job   40: 2   who **a** with God must respond."

ARGUMENT → ARGUE
Lk   9:46   An **a** arose among them as to which
1 Tim   2: 8   up holy hands without anger or **a**;

ARGUMENTS → ARGUE
2 Cor   10: 4   destroy strongholds. We destroy **a**
Col   2: 4   may deceive you with plausible **a**.

ARIMATHEA
Jn   19:38   After these things, Joseph of **A**,

ARISE → RISE
1 Macc 14:41   until a trustworthy prophet should **a**,
Song   2:10   "**A**, my love, my fair one, and
Isa   60: 1   **A**, shine; for your light has come,
Mt   24:11   false prophets will **a** and lead many

ARK
Gen   6:14   Make yourself an **a** of cypress wood
Ex   25:10   shall make an **a** of acacia wood;
1 Sam   4:11   The **a** of God was captured;
1 Kings 8: 9   There was nothing in the **a** except
2 Macc   2: 4   that the tent and the **a** should follow
1 Pet   3:20   during the building of the **a**,
Rev   11:19   the **a** of his covenant was seen

ARM → ARMIES, ARMOR, ARMS, ARMY
Ex   6: 6   redeem you with an outstretched **a**
Deut   7:19   mighty hand and the outstretched **a**
2 Chr   32: 8   With him is an **a** of flesh;
Job   40: 9   Have you an **a** like God,
Ps   98: 1   his holy **a** have gotten him victory.
Isa   53: 1   the **a** of the LORD been revealed?
Jn   12:38   the **a** of the Lord been revealed?"

ARMIES → ARM
1 Sam 17:36   defied the **a** of the living God."
Lk   21:20   you see Jerusalem surrounded by **a**,
Rev   19:14   the **a** of heaven, wearing fine linen,

ARMOR → ARM
1 Sam 17:38   Saul clothed David with his **a**;
Wis   5:17   will take his zeal as his whole **a**,
Rom   13:12   and put on the **a** of light;
Eph   6:11   Put on the whole **a** of God,

ARMS → ARM
Prov   31:17   and makes her **a** strong.
Hos   11: 3   I took them up in my **a**;
Mk   10:16   And he took them up in his **a**,

ARMY → ARM
Ex   15: 4   and his **a** he cast into the sea;
Josh   5:14   as commander of the **a** of the LORD
Ps   27: 3   Though an **a** encamp against me,
            33:16   A king is not saved by his great **a**;
Rev   19:19   rider on the horse and against his **a**.

AROMA
2 Cor   2:15   For we are the **a** of Christ to God

ARRESTED
Jer   37:14   and a Jeremiah and brought him to
Mt   14: 3   For Herod had a John, bound him,
            26:50   and laid hands on Jesus and a him.
Acts   5:18   **a** the apostles and put them in the
            28:17   yet I was **a** in Jerusalem and handed

ARROGANCE → ARROGANT
Jdt   9:10   their **a** by the hand of a woman.
1 Macc 1:24   much blood, and spoke with great **a**.
Prov   8:13   Pride and **a** and the way of evil
Sir   10: 7   **A** is hateful to the Lord and to
Ezek   7:24   put an end to the **a** of the strong,

ARROGANT → ARROGANCE
Ps   73: 3   For I was envious of the **a**;
Dan   7:11   **a** words that the horn was speaking.
1 Cor   13: 4   love is not envious or boastful or **a**

ARROW → ARROWS
Ps   64: 7   But God will shoot his **a** at them;
Isa   49: 2   he made me a polished **a**,

ARROWS → ARROW
1 Sam 20:20   I will shoot three **a** to the side of it,
Eph   6:16   quench all the flaming **a** of the evil

ARTAXERXES → =AHASUERUS
    1. King of Persia; allowed rebuilding of temple under Ezra (Ezra 4; 7), and of walls of Jerusalem under his cupbearer Nehemiah (Neh 2; 5:14; 13:6).
    2. See Ahasuerus.

ARTEMIS
Acts   19:27   the temple of the great goddess **A**

ASA
    King of Judah (1 Kings 15:8-24; 1 Chr 3:10; 2 Chr 14-16). Godly reformer (2 Chr 15); in later years defeated Israel with help of Aram, not the LORD (1 Kings 15:16-22; 2 Chr 16).

ASAHEL
    Nephew of David, one of his warriors (2 Sam 23:24; 1 Chr 2:16; 11:26; 27:7). Killed by Abner (2 Sam 2); avenged by Joab (2 Sam 3:22-39).

ASAPH
    1. Recorder to Hezekiah (2 Kings 18:18, 37; Isa 36:3, 22).
    2. Levitical musician (1 Chr 6:39; 15:17-19; 16:4-7, 37), seer (2 Chr 29:30). Sons of (1 Chr 25; 2 Chr 5:12; 20:14; 29:13; 35:15; Ezra 2:41; 3:10; Neh 7:44; 11:17; 12:27-47). Psalms of (2 Chr 29:30; Ps 50; 73-83).

ASCEND → ASCENDED, ASCENDING, ASCENTS
Ps   139: 8   If I **a** to heaven, you are there;
Isa   14:13   in your heart, "I will **a** to heaven;
Acts   2:34   David did not **a** into the heavens,
Rom   10: 6   'Who will **a** into heaven?'"

ASCENDED → ASCEND
2 Kings 2:11   Elijah **a** in a whirlwind into heaven.
Jn   3:13   No one has **a** into heaven except

ASCENDING → ASCEND
Gen   28:12   the angels of God were **a** and
Jn   1:51   the angels of God **a** and descending

ASCENTS → ASCEND
    Songs of ascents (Ps 120-134).

ASCRIBE
Deut   32: 3   **a** greatness to our God!
1 Chr   16:29   **A** to the LORD the glory due his
Ps   68:34   **A** power to God,
Sir   39:15   **A** majesty to his name
Bar   2:17   not **a** glory or justice to the Lord;

ASHAMED → SHAME
Gen   2:25   were both naked, and were not **a**.
Ps   10: 1   All my enemies shall be **a** and
Isa   29:22   No longer shall Jacob be **a**,
Mk   8:38   who are **a** of me and of my words
Rom   1:16   For I am not **a** of the gospel;
2 Tim   2:15   a worker who has no need to be **a**,
Heb   2:11   Jesus is not **a** to call them brothers
            11:16   God is not **a** to be called their God;

ASHER
    Son of Jacob by Zilpah (Gen 30:13; 35:26; 46:17; Ex 1:4; 1 Chr 2:2). Tribe of blessed (Gen 49:20; Deut 33:24-25), num-

bered (Num 1:40-41; 26:44-47), allotted land (Josh 10:24-31; Ezek 48:2), failed to fully possess (Judg 1:31-32), failed to support Deborah (Judg 5:17), supported Gideon (Judg 6:35; 7:23) and David (1 Chr 12:36), 12,000 from (Rev 7:6).

ASHERAH → ASHERAHS, ASTARTE
1 Kings 18:19 and the four hundred prophets of **A,**
2 Chr 15:16 made an abominable image for **A.**

ASHERAHS* → ASHERAH
Judg 3: 7 and worshiping the Baals and the **A.**

ASHES
Gen 18:27 I who am but dust and **a.**
Jdt 4:11 the temple and put **a** on their heads
Esth 4: 1 and put on sackcloth and **a,**
Job 42: 6 and repent in dust and **a.**"
Sir 17:32 but all human beings are dust and **a.**
Jon 3: 6 himself with sackcloth, and sat in **a.**
Mt 11:21 long ago in sackcloth and **a.**

ASIA
Acts 16: 6 Holy Spirit to speak the word in **A.**
Rev 1: 4 to the seven churches that are in **A:**

ASIDE → SIDE
Ex 32: 8 quick to turn **a** from the way that I
Deut 28:14 if you do not turn **a** from any of the
Jer 5:23 they have turned **a** and gone away.
Dan 9: 5 turning **a** from your commandments
Rom 3:12 All have turned **a,** together they
Heb 12: 1 also lay **a** every weight and the sin

ASK
Ps 2: 8 **A** of me, and I will make the nations
Isa 65: 1 sought out by those who did not **a,**
Mt 6: 8 knows what you need before you **a**
7: 7 "**A,** and it will be given you;
Jn 16:24 **A** and you will receive,
Jas 4: 3 You **a** and do not receive, because you **a** wrongly,
1 Jn 5:14 we **a** anything according to his will,

ASLEEP → SLEEP
Jon 1: 5 had lain down, and was fast **a.**
Mt 8:24 by the waves; but he was **a.**
1 Thess 5: 6 So then let us not fall **a** as others do,

ASSEMBLE → ASSEMBLY
1 Kings 18:19 all Israel for me at Mount Carmel,
Zeph 3: 8 to gather nations, to **a** kingdoms,
Rev 16:14 to **a** them for battle on the great day

ASSEMBLY → ASSEMBLE
Neh 8: 2 Ezra brought the law before the **a,**
Ps 149: 1 his praise in the **a** of the faithful.
Heb 12:23 the **a** of the firstborn who are

ASSIGNED
Rom 12: 3 the measure of faith that God has **a.**
1 Cor 3: 5 as the Lord **a** to each.
7:17 lead the life that the Lord has **a,**

ASSURANCE
Deut 28:66 in dread, with no **a** of your life.
Heb 6:11 so as to realize the full **a** of hope
11: 1 faith is the **a** of things hoped for,

ASSYRIA
Gen 10:11 From that land he went into **A,**
2 Kings 18:11 of **A** carried the Israelites away to **A,**
Jer 50:18 as I punished the king of **A.**

ASTARTE → ASHERAH, ASTARTES
1 Kings 11: 5 Solomon followed **A** the goddess

ASTARTES → ASTARTE
Judg 2:13 and worshiped Baal and the **A.**

ASTONISHED
Isa 52:14 there were many who were **a** at him
Lk 2:48 his parents saw him they were **a;**
Gal 1: 6 **a** that you are so quickly deserting

ASTRAY → STRAY
Deut 30:17 are led **a** to bow down to other gods
Isa 53: 6 All we like sheep have gone **a;**
Jer 50: 6 their shepherds have led them **a,**
Mt 18:12 go in search of the one that went **a?**
1 Pet 2:25 For you were going **a** like sheep,

ATE → EAT
Gen 3: 6 she took of its fruit and **a;**
Ex 16:35 The Israelites **a** manna forty years,
Ps 78:25 Mortals **a** of the bread of angels;
Ezek 3: 3 I **a** it; and in my mouth it was as
Mt 14:20 And all **a** and were filled;
15:37 And all of them **a** and were filled;
Rev 10:10 from the hand of the angel and **a** it;

ATHALIAH
Granddaughter of Omri; wife of Jehoram and mother of Ahaziah; encouraged their evil ways (2 Kings 8:18, 27; 2 Chr 22:2). At death of Ahaziah she made herself queen, killing all his sons but Joash (2 Kings 11:1-3; 2 Chr 22:10-12); killed six years later when Joash revealed (2 Kings 11:4-16; 2 Chr 23:1-15).

ATHLETE → ATHLETES
2 Tim 2: 5 And in the case of an **a,**

ATHLETES → ATHLETE
1 Cor 9:25 **A** exercise self-control in all things;

ATONE → ATONEMENT
Sir 3: 3 who honor their father **a** for sins,
Dan 9:24 an end to sin, and to **a** for iniquity,

ATONED* → ATONEMENT
Prov 16: 6 and faithfulness iniquity is **a** for,

ATONEMENT → ATONE, ATONED, ATONING
Ex 29:36 a bull as a sin offering for **a.**
30:10 Aaron shall perform the rite of **a**
32:30 perhaps I can make **a** for your sin."
Lev 23:28 for it is a day of **a,**
Rom 3:25 God put forward as a sacrifice of **a**
Heb 2:17 to make a sacrifice of **a** for the sins

ATONING → ATONEMENT
Sir 28: 5 will make an **a** sacrifice for his sins?
1 Jn 2: 2 and he is the **a** sacrifice for our sins,
4:10 sent his Son to be the **a** sacrifice for

ATTAIN → ATTAINED
Ps 139: 6 it is so high that I cannot **a** it.
Prov 8:12 and I **a** knowledge and discretion.
Dan 12:12 those who persevere and **a**
Phil 3:11 **a** the resurrection from the dead.

ATTAINED → ATTAIN
Rom 9:30 not strive for righteousness, have **a**
Phil 3:16 let us hold fast to what we have **a.**

ATTENTION
Num 16:15 "Pay no **a** to their offering.
Job 24:12 yet God pays no **a** to their prayer.
Heb 2: 1 greater **a** to what we have heard,

ATTESTED
Acts 2:22 a man **a** to you by God with deeds
Rom 3:21 and is **a** by the law and the prophets,

AUTHOR*
Wis 13: 3 for the **a** of beauty created them.
Acts 3:15 and you killed the **A** of life,

AUTHORITIES → AUTHORITY
Rom 13: 1 be subject to the governing **a;**
Col 2:15 He disarmed the rulers and **a** and

AUTHORITY → AUTHORITIES
Gen 41:45 Thus Joseph gained **a** over the land
Prov 29: 2 When the righteous are in **a,**
Mk 1:27 A new teaching—with **a!**
Lk 5:24 Son of Man has **a** on earth to forgive
Acts 5:29 obey God rather than any human **a.**
Rom 13: 1 for there is no **a** except from God,
1 Cor 11:10 woman ought to have a symbol of **a**
Col 2:10 who is the head of every ruler and **a.**
1 Tim 2:12 no woman to teach or to have **a** over
Rev 12:10 and the **a** of his Messiah,
20: 4 on them were given **a** to judge.

AVENGE → VENGEANCE
Deut 32:43 he will **a** the blood of his children,
1 Macc 2:67 **a** the wrong done to your people.
Joel 3:21 I will **a** their blood, and I will not
Rom 12:19 Beloved, never **a** yourselves,
Rev 6:10 and **a** our blood on the inhabitants

AVENGER → VENGEANCE
Num 35:12 shall be for you a refuge from the **a**,
Ps   8: 2 to silence the enemy and the **a**.
1 Thess 4: 6 the Lord is an **a** in all these things,

AVENGING → VENGEANCE
Nah   1: 2 A jealous and **a** God is the Lord,

AVOID → AVOIDS
2 Tim 2:16 **A** profane chatter, for it will lead
Titus 3: 9 But **a** stupid controversies,

AVOIDS → AVOID
Prov 16: 6 by the fear of the Lord one **a** evil.

AWAKE
Ps   44:23 **A**, do not cast us off forever!
      57: 8 **A**, my soul! **A**, O harp and lyre!
Isa   51: 9 **A, a**, put on strength, O arm of the Lord!
Dan   12: 2 in the dust of the earth shall **a**,
Mk   14:37 Could you not keep **a** one hour?
Eph   5:14 "Sleeper, **a**! Rise from the dead,
1 Thess 5: 6 but let us keep **a** and be sober;
Rev   16:15 Blessed is the one who stays **a** and

AWE → AWESOME
Ps   119:161 my heart stands in **a** of your words.
Isa   29:23 will stand in **a** of the God of Israel.
Mt   9: 8 saw it, they were filled with **a**,
Acts   2:43 **A** came upon everyone, because
Rom   11:20 do not become proud, but stand in **a**.

AWESOME → AWE
Ex   15:11 majestic in holiness, **a** in splendor,
Deut   6:22 before our eyes great and **a** signs
      10:17 the great God, mighty and **a**,
Neh   1: 5 and **a** God who keeps covenant
Ps   47: 2 For the Lord, the Most High, is **a**,
      65: 5 By **a** deeds you answer us with
      68:35 **A** is God in his sanctuary,
Sir   43:29 **A** is the Lord and very great,
Dan   9: 4 saying, "Ah, Lord, great and **a** God,

AX
2 Kings 6: 5 his **a** head fell into the water;
Mt   3:10 Even now the **a** is lying at the root

AZARIAH → =ABEDNEGO, =UZZIAH
      1. King of Judah; see Uzziah (2 Kings 15:1-7).
      2. Prophet (2 Chr 15:1-8).
      3. Opponent of Jeremiah (Jer 43:2).
      4. Jewish exile; see Abednego (Dan 1:6-19).

AZAZEL
Lev   16: 8 for the Lord and the other lot for **A**.

B

BAAL → BAALS
Num   25: 3 Israel yoked itself to the **B** of Peor,
Judg   2:13 and worshiped **B** and the Astartes.
1 Kings18:25 Elijah said to the prophets of **B**,
      19:18 the knees that have not bowed to **B**,
Jer   2: 8 the prophets prophesied by **B**,
Hos   2:16 no longer will you call me, "My **B**."
Rom   11: 4 not bowed the knee to **B**."

BAALS → BAAL
Judg   3: 7 worshiping the **B** and the Asherahs.
1 Sam 7: 4 So Israel put away the **B** and the

BAASHA
      King of Israel (1 Kings 15:16-16:7; 2 Chr 16:1-6).

BABEL → BABYLON
Gen   11: 9 Therefore it was called **B**,

BABES → BABIES
Ps   8: 2 Out of the mouths of **b** and infants
Isa   3: 4 and **b** shall rule over them.

BABIES → BABES
Mt   21:16 the mouths of infants and nursing **b**

BABYLON → BABEL
2 Kings24:15 into captivity from Jerusalem to **B**.
Ps   137: 1 By the rivers of **B**—there we sat
Isa   14: 4 this taunt against the king of **B**:
      21: 9 he responded, "Fallen, fallen is **B**;

Jer   25:11 serve the king of **B** seventy years.
Dan   14:36 he set him down in **B**,
1 Pet 5:13 Your sister church in **B**, chosen
Rev   14: 8 "Fallen, fallen is **B** the great!

BACK → BACKSLIDING
Gen   19:26 Lot's wife, behind him, looked **b**,
2 Kings20:11 he brought the shadow **b** the ten
Lk   9:62 puts a hand to the plow and looks **b**

BACKSLIDING* → BACK
Jer   8: 5 people turned away in perpetual **b**?

BAD
Prov 20:14 "**B, b**," says the buyer, then goes
Mt   7:17 but the **b** tree bears **b** fruit.
1 Cor 15:33 "**B** company ruins good morals."

BALAAM
      Prophet who attempted to curse Israel (Num 22-24; Deut 23:4-5; 2 Pet 2:15; Jude 11; Rev 2:14). Killed in Israel's vengeance on Midianites (Num 31:8; Josh 13:22).

BALAK
      Moabite king who hired Balaam to curse Israel (Num 22-24; Josh 24:9; Mic 6:5).

BALANCE → BALANCES
Job   31: 6 let me be weighed in a just **b**,
Isa   40:12 in scales and the hills in a **b**?

BALANCES → BALANCE
Lev   19:36 shall have honest **b**, honest weights,
Prov 16:11 Honest **b** and scales are the Lord's;
Sir   28:25 make **b** and scales for your words.

BALM
Jer   8:22 Is there no **b** in Gilead?

BANDIT
Mt   26:55 to arrest me as though I were a **b**?
Jn   10: 1 in by another way is a thief and a **b**.

BANISH
Eccl 11:10 **B** anxiety from your mind,
Rom   11:26 he will **b** ungodliness from Jacob."

BANNER
Ex   17:15 and called it, The Lord is my **b**.

BAPTISM → BAPTIZE
Mk   1: 4 proclaiming a **b** of repentance for
      10:38 be baptized with the **b** that I am
Lk   20: 4 the **b** of John come from heaven,
Acts 18:25 though he knew only the **b** of John.
      19: 3 They answered, "Into John's **b**."
Rom   6: 4 buried with him by **b** into death,
1 Cor 15:29 receive **b** on behalf of the dead?
Eph   4: 5 one Lord, one faith, one **b**,
Col   2:12 when you were buried with him in **b**,
1 Pet 3:21 **b**, which this prefigured, now saves

BAPTISMS* → BAPTIZE
Heb   6: 2 about **b**, laying on of hands,
       9:10 with food and drink and various **b**,

BAPTIST → BAPTIZE
Mt   3: 1 In those days John the **B** appeared
      11:11 has arisen greater than John the **B**;
      14: 8 the head of John the **B** here on a
      16:14 they said, "Some say John the **B**,

BAPTIZE → BAPTISM, BAPTISMS, BAPTIST, BAPTIZED, BAPTIZING
Mt   3:11 "I **b** you with water for repentance,
Lk   3:16 He will **b** you with the Holy Spirit
1 Cor 1:17 For Christ did not send me to **b** but

BAPTIZED → BAPTIZE
Mt   3:13 to John at the Jordan, to be **b**
Acts   1: 5 John **b** with water, but you will be **b** with the Holy Spirit
       2:38 "Repent, and be **b** every one of you
Rom   6: 3 **b** into Christ Jesus were **b** into his
1 Cor 10: 2 all were **b** into Moses in the cloud
      12:13 one Spirit we were all **b** into one

BAPTIZING* → BAPTIZE
Mt   28:19 **b** them in the name of the Father
Jn   4: 1 "Jesus is making and **b** more

BARABBAS*
Prisoner released by Pilate instead of Jesus (Mt 27:16-26; Mk 15:7-15; Lk 23:18-19; Jn 18:40).

BARAK*
Judge who fought with Deborah against Canaanites (Judg 4-5; 1 Sam 12:11; Heb 11:32).

BARBARIAN → BARBARIANS
Col   3: 11   circumcised and uncircumcised, **b**,

BARBARIANS* → BARBARIAN
Rom   1:14   am a debtor both to Greeks and to **b**,

BARBS*
Num   33:55   let remain shall be as **b** in your eyes

BARE → BARED
Ps   18:15   were laid **b** at your rebuke,
Heb   4:13   all are naked and laid **b** to the eyes

BARED* → BARE
Isa   52:10   The LORD has **b** his holy arm

BARN → BARNS
Lk   12:24   they have neither storehouse nor **b**,

BARNABAS* → =JOSEPH
Disciple, originally Joseph (Acts 4:36), prophet (Acts 13:1), apostle (Acts 14:14). Brought Paul to apostles (Acts 9:27), Antioch (Acts 11:22-29; Gal 2:1-13), on the first missionary journey (Acts 13-14). Together at Jerusalem Council, they separated over John Mark (Acts 15). Later co-workers (1 Cor 9:6; Col 4:10).

BARNS* → BARN
Deut   28: 8   the blessing upon you in your **b**,
Ps   144:13   May our **b** be filled, with produce
Lk   12:18   pull down my **b** and build larger

BARREN → BARRENNESS
Gen   11:30   Now Sarai was **b**; she had no child.
Ex   23:26   No one shall miscarry or be **b** in
1 Sam 2: 5   The **b** has borne seven, but she who
Ps   113: 9   He gives the **b** woman a home,
Isa   54: 1   Sing, O **b** one who did not bear;
Lk   1: 7   because Elizabeth was **b**,
Heb   11: 11   too old—and Sarah herself was **b**—

BARRENNESS* → BARREN
Deut   7:14   neither sterility nor **b** among you
Rom   4:19   considered the **b** of Sarah's womb.

BARTHOLOMEW* → =NATHANAEL?
Apostle (Mt 10:3; Mk 3:18; Lk 6:14; Acts 1:13). Possibly also called Nathanael (Jn 1:45-49; 21:2).

BARUCH*
Jeremiah's secretary (Jer 32:12-16; 36; 43:1-6; 45:1-2). Deuterocanonical book ascribed to (Bar 1:1, 3, 8).

BARZILLAI
1. Gileadite who aided David during Absalom's revolt (2 Sam 17:27; 19:31-39).
2. Son-in-law of 1. (Ezra 2:61; Neh 7:63).

BASED*
Rom   9: 31   righteousness that is **b** on the law,
        9:32   but as if it were **b** on works.
Phil   3: 9   righteousness from God **b** on faith.

BASHAN
Num   21:33   King Og of **B** came out against
Ps   22:12   strong bulls of **B** surround me;
Mic   7:14   let them feed in **B** and Gilead as in

BASIN
Ex   30:18   You shall make a bronze **b** with a
1 Kings 7:30   four corners were supports for a **b**.
Jn   13: 5   **b** and began to wash the disciples'

BASIS
Lk   23: 4   "I find no **b** for an accusation
Philem 1: 9   rather appeal to you on the **b** of love

BASKET
Ex   2: 3   she got a papyrus **b** for him,
Mt   5:15   a lamp puts it under the bushel **b**,
Acts   9:25   in the wall, lowering him in a **b**.

BATHING
2 Sam 11: 2   he saw from the roof a woman **b**;

BATHSHEBA*
Wife of Uriah; committed adultery with and married David (2 Sam 11; Ps 51), mother of Solomon (2 Sam 12:24; 1 Kings 1-2; 1 Chr 3:5).

BATTLE
1 Sam 17:47   the **b** is the LORD's and he will give
2 Chr 20:15   for the **b** is not yours but God's.
1 Macc 3:19   the army that victory in **b** depends,
Ps   24: 8   and mighty, the LORD, mighty in **b**.
Eccl   9: 11   nor the **b** to the strong, nor bread to
Rev   16:14   them for **b** on the great day of God
        20: 8   Magog, in order to gather them for **b**;

BEAR → BEARS, BIRTH, BIRTHRIGHT, BORE, BORN, CHILDBEARING, FIRSTBORN
Gen   4:13   punishment is greater than I can **b**!
       17:19   your wife Sarah shall **b** you a son,
Isa   7:14   is with child and shall **b** a son,
Mt   1:23   virgin shall conceive and **b** a son,
       7:18   A good tree cannot **b** bad fruit,
Lk   11:46   load people with burdens hard to **b**,
Jn   15: 2   he prunes to make it **b** more fruit.
Gal   6: 2   **B** one another's burdens,
Col   3:13   **B** with one another and,
Heb   9:28   offered once to **b** the sins of many,
Rev 12: 4   woman who was about to **b** a child,

BEARS → BEAR
Ps   68:19   Blessed be the Lord, who daily **b** us
1 Cor 13: 7   It **b** all things, believes all things,

BEAST → BEASTS
Rev   11: 7   **b** that comes up from the bottomless pit
     13:18   calculate the number of the **b**,
    16: 2   who had the mark of the **b**
   19:20   who had received the mark of the **b**

BEASTS → BEAST
Dan   7: 3   four great **b** came up out of the sea,
Mk   1:13   and he was with the wild **b**;

BEAT → BEATEN, BEATING
Isa   2: 4   shall **b** their swords into plowshares,
Joel   3:10   **B** your plowshares into swords,
Lk   22:63   began to mock him and **b** him;

BEATEN → BEAT
2 Cor 11:25   Three times I was **b** with rods.
1 Pet 2:20   If you endure when you are **b** for

BEATING → BEAT
Ex   2: 11   He saw an Egyptian **b** a Hebrew,
1 Cor 9:26   nor do I box as though **b** the air;

BEAUTIFUL → BEAUTY
Gen   12: 11   you are a woman **b** in appearance,
1 Sam 25: 3   The woman was clever and **b**,
Tob   6:12   girl is sensible, brave, and very **b**,
Jdt   8: 7   She was **b** in appearance,
Esth 2: 7   the girl was fair and **b**,
Job   42:15   no women so **b** as Job's daughters;
Ps   48: 2   **b** in elevation, is the joy of all
Song 1: 5   I am black and **b**, O daughters of
Wis   7:29   She is more **b** than the sun,
Sir   26: 1   and they are **b** in the sight of God
Isa   4: 2   the branch of the LORD shall be **b**
    52: 7   How **b** upon the mountains are the
Dan 13: 2   very **b** woman and one who feared
Acts   3: 2   the temple called the **B** Gate so that
Rom 10:15   **b** are the feet of those who bring

BEAUTY → BEAUTIFUL
2 Sam 14:25   so much for his **b** as Absalom;
Jdt   16: 9   her **b** captivated his mind,
1 Macc 2:12   And see, our holy place, our **b**,
Ps   27: 4   to behold the **b** of the LORD,
Prov 6:25   Do not desire her **b** in your heart,
    31:30   Charm is deceitful, and **b** is vain,
Wis   13: 3   for the author of **b** created them.
Sir   9: 8   not gaze at **b** belonging to another;
Dan 13:56   **b** has beguiled you and lust has
1 Pet 3: 4   with the lasting **b** of a gentle

BED → BEDS
Gen 47:31   bowed himself on the head of his **b**.
Ps   139: 8   if I make my **b** in Sheol, you are

Lk   5:19   let him down with his **b** through the
Heb   13: 4   let the marriage **b** be kept undefiled;

BEDS → BED
Ps   36: 4   They plot mischief while on their **b**;
Mic   2: 1   and evil deeds on their **b**!

BEE* → BEES
Sir   11: 3   The **b** is small among flying
Isa   7:18   the **b** that is in the land of Assyria.

BEER-SHEBA
Gen   21:31   Therefore that place was called **B**;
1 Sam   3:20   And all Israel from Dan to **B** knew

BEES → BEE
Judg   14: 8   a swarm of **b** in the body of the lion,

BEFORE
Ex   20: 3   you shall have no other gods **b** me.
     33: 2   I will send an angel **b** you,
Isa   43:10   **B** me no god was formed,
     65:24   **B** they call I will answer,
Mal   3: 1   my messenger to prepare the way **b**
Mt   6: 8   Father knows what you need **b** you
Lk   22:61   "**B** the cock crows today,
Heb   12: 2   sake of the joy that was set **b** him

BEGGAR → BEGS
Mk   10:46   son of Timaeus, a blind **b**,
Jn   9: 8   who had seen him before as a **b**

BEGINNING
Gen   1: 1   In the **b** when God created the
Ps   111:10   fear of the LORD is the **b** of wisdom;
Prov   1: 7   The fear of the LORD is the **b** of
     8:22   The LORD created me at the **b** of his
Eccl   7: 8   Better is the end of a thing than its **b**
Wis   6:17   The **b** of wisdom is the most sincere
Sir   1:14   To fear the Lord is the **b** of wisdom;
Isa   40:21   Has it not been told you from the **b**?
Mt   24: 8   this is but the **b** of the birth pangs.
Jn   1: 1   In the **b** was the Word,
1 Jn   1: 1   declare to you what was from the **b**,
2 Jn   1: 6   as you have heard it from the **b**—
Rev   21: 6   and the Omega, the **b** and the end.

BEGOTTEN
Ps   2: 7   You are my son; today I have **b** you.
Acts   13:33   are my Son; today I have **b** you.'
Heb   1: 5   are my Son; today I have **b** you"?

BEGS → BEG
Lk   6:30   Give to everyone who **b** from you;

BEHEADED → HEAD
Lk   9: 9   Herod said, "John I **b**;
Rev   20: 4   the souls of those who had been **b**

BEHEMOTH
Job   40:15   "Look at **B**, which I made just as I

BEHIND
Isa   38:17   have cast all my sins **b** your back.
Mt   16:23   said to Peter, "Get **b** me, Satan!
Phil   3:13   forgetting what lies **b** and straining

BEING
Gen   2: 7   and the man became a living **b**.
Num   23:19   God is not a human **b**,
Dan   7:13   one like a human **b** coming with the
Jn   1: 3   All things came into **b** through him,
1 Cor   15:45   Adam, became a living **b**";
Heb   1: 3   the exact imprint of God's very **b**,

BEL*
Babylonian deity (Isa 46:1; Jer 50:2; 51:44; Bar 6:40; Dan 14:3-28).

BELIEF → BELIEVE
2 Thess   2:13   the Spirit and through **b** in the truth.

BELIEVE → BELIEF, BELIEVED, BELIEVER, BELIEVERS, BELIEVES, BELIEVING
Ex   4: 5   that they may **b** that the LORD,
Num   14:11   long will they refuse to **b** in me,
2 Kings   17:14   did not **b** in the LORD their God.
Ps   119:66   for I **b** in your commandments.
Prov   14:15   The simple **b** everything,
Sir   19:15   so do not **b** everything you hear.

Jer   12: 6   do not **b** them, though they speak
Hab   1: 5   you would not **b** if you were told.
Mt   18: 6   one of these little ones who **b** in me,
     24:23   or 'There he is!'—do not **b** it.
Mk   1:15   repent, and **b** in the good news."
     9:24   "I **b**; help my unbelief!"
Lk   24:25   how slow of heart to **b** all that the
Jn   1: 7   so that all might **b** through him.
     3:18   who **b** in him are not condemned;
     5:46   believed Moses, you would **b** me,
     6:29   you **b** in him whom he has sent."
     10:38   you do not **b** me, **b** the works,
     14: 1   **B** in God, **b** also in me.
     17:20   will **b** in me through their word,
     20:29   not seen and yet have come to **b**."
Acts   16:31   answered, "**B** on the Lord Jesus,
     28:24   while others refused to **b**.
Rom   3:22   faith in Jesus Christ for all who **b**.
     10: 9   **b** in your heart that God raised him
1 Cor   15: 2   unless you have come to **b** in vain.
Gal   3: 9   this reason, those who **b** are blessed
1 Thess   4:14   For since we **b** that Jesus died and
Heb   11: 6   would approach him must **b**
Jas   2:19   Even the demons **b**—and shudder.
1 Pet   1: 8   you do not see him now, you **b**
1 Jn   4: 1   Beloved, do not **b** every spirit,
Jude   1: 5   destroyed those who did not **b**.

BELIEVED → BELIEVE
Gen   15: 6   And he **b** the LORD;
Ex   14:31   **b** in the LORD and in his servant
Jdt   14:10   had done, he **b** firmly in God.
1 Macc   2:59   **b** and were saved from the flame.
Isa   53: 1   Who has **b** what we have heard?
Jn   1:12   received him, who **b** in his name,
     12:38   "Lord, who has **b** our message,
     20: 8   also went in, and he saw and **b**;
Acts   2:44   All who **b** were together and had all
Rom   4: 3   "Abraham **b** God, and it was
     10:16   "Lord, who has **b** our message?"
2 Cor   4:13   "I **b**, and so I spoke"—
Gal   3: 6   Just as Abraham "**b** God,
1 Tim   3:16   **b** in throughout the world, taken up
Heb   4: 3   For we who have **b** enter that rest,
Jas   2:23   that says, "Abraham **b** God,

BELIEVER → BELIEVE
1 Cor   6: 6   but a **b** goes to court against a **b**—
     7:12   **b** has a wife who is an unbeliever—
2 Cor   6:15   Or what does a **b** share with an

BELIEVERS → BELIEVE
1 Cor   14:22   a sign not for **b** but for unbelievers,
Gal   2: 4   because of false **b** secretly brought
2 Thess   3: 6   keep away from **b** who are living in
1 Pet   2:17   Love the family of **b**.

BELIEVES → BELIEVE
Jn   3:15   whoever **b** in him may have eternal
     11:26   everyone who lives and **b** in me
Rom   9:33   whoever **b** in him will not be put to
     10:10   **b** with the heart and so is justified,
1 Cor   13: 7   It bears all things, **b** all things,

BELIEVING → BELIEVE
Jn   20:31   through **b** you may have life in his
Gal   3: 5   or by your **b** what you heard?

BELLY
Gen   3:14   upon your **b** you shall go,
Lev   11:42   Whatever moves on its **b**,
Jon   1:17   and Jonah was in the **b** of the fish
Mt   12:40   three days and three nights in the **b**
Phil   3:19   is destruction; their god is the **b**;

BELONG → BELONGS
Deut   29:29   The secret things **b** to the LORD our God, but the revealed things **b** to us
Ps   82: 8   for all the nations **b** to you!
Dan   9: 9   To the Lord our God **b** mercy and
Jn   10:16   sheep that do not **b** to this fold.
     15:19   Because you do not **b** to the world,
Rom   9: 6   not all Israelites truly **b** to Israel,
1 Cor   3:23   you **b** to Christ, and Christ belongs
     12:15   I do not **b** to the body,"

1 Jn 2:19 out from us, but they did not **b** to us;

BELONGS → BELONG
Ps 22:28 For dominion **b** to the LORD,
62:11 I heard this: that power **b** to God,
Jon 2: 9 Deliverance **b** to the LORD!"
Rev 7:10 "Salvation **b** to our God who is

BELOVED → LOVE
Song 2:16 My **b** is mine and I am his;
Mt 3:17 heaven said, "This is my Son, the **B**,
12:18 my **b**, with whom my soul is well
17: 5 "This is my Son, the **B**;
Col 3:12 As God's chosen ones, holy and **b**,
Rev 20: 9 camp of the saints and the **b** city.

BELSHAZZAR*
King of Babylon (Dan 5; Bar 1:11-12).

BELT
1 Sam 18: 4 his sword and his bow and his **b**.
Isa 11: 5 Righteousness shall be the **b** around
Mk 1: 6 with a leather **b** around his waist,
Eph 6:14 the **b** of truth around your waist,

BELTESHAZZAR → See DANIEL

BEN-HADAD*
1. King of Syria in time of Asa (1 Kings 15:18-20; 2 Chr 16:2-4).
2. King of Syria in time of Ahab (1 Kings 20; 2 Kings 6:24; 8:7-15).
3. King of Syria in time of Jehoahaz (2 Kings 13:3, 24-25; Jer 49:27; Am 1:4).

BENAIAH
A commander of David's army (2 Sam 8:18; 20:23; 23:20-30); loyal to Solomon (1 Kings 1:8-2:46; 4:4).

BEND → BENT
Phil 2:10 name of Jesus every knee should **b**,

BENEFICIAL → BENEFIT
1 Cor 6:12 but not all things are **b**.
10:23 lawful," but not all things are **b**.

BENEFIT → BENEFICIAL, BENEFITS
Gal 5: 2 Christ will be of no **b** to you.
Philem 1:20 have this **b** from you in the Lord!
Heb 4: 2 message they heard did not **b** them,

BENEFITS → BENEFIT
Ps 103: 2 and do not forget all his **b**—
1 Cor 9:11 if we reap your material **b**?

BENJAMIN → BENJAMINITE
Twelfth son of Jacob by Rachel (Gen 35:16-24; 46:19-21; 1 Chr 2:2). Jacob refused to send him to Egypt, but relented (Gen 42-45). Tribe of blessed (Gen 49:27; Deut 33:12), numbered (Num 1:37; 26:41), allotted land (Josh 18:11-28; Ezek 48:23), failed to fully possess (Judg 1:21), nearly obliterated (Judg 20-21), sided with Ish-Bosheth (2 Sam 2), but turned to David (1 Chr 12:2, 29). 12,000 from (Rev 7:8).

BENJAMINITE → BENJAMIN
Judg 3:15 the **B**, a left-handed man.
1 Sam 9:21 Saul answered, "I am only a **B**,

BENT → BEND
Hos 11: 4 I **b** down to them and fed them.
Jn 8: 6 ⟦ Jesus **b** down and wrote with his⟧
20: 5 He **b** down to look in and saw

BEREAVE → BEREAVES
Lev 26:22 they shall **b** you of your children
Ezek 36:12 No longer shall you **b** them of

BEREAVES* → BEREAVE
Lam 1:20 In the street the sword **b**;

BESIDES
Deut 32:39 there is no god **b** me.
Ps 18:31 And who is a rock **b** our God?—
Wis 12:13 For neither is there any god **b** you,
Isa 45:21 There is no other god **b** me,
Dan 14:41 there is no other **b** you!"

BEST → GOOD
Deut 33:21 He chose the **b** for himself,
Mk 12:39 the **b** seats in the synagogue and
2 Tim 2:15 your **b** to present yourself to God

BETHANY
Mt 26: 6 Jesus was at **B** in the house of
Jn 11: 1 a certain man was ill, Lazarus of **B**,

BETHEL
Gen 12: 8 the east of **B**, and pitched his tent,
28:19 He called that place **B**;
1 Sam 7:16 a circuit year by year to **B**, Gilgal,

BETHLEHEM
Ruth 4:11 and bestow a name in **B**;
1 Sam 17:12 David was the son of an Ephrathite of **B**
Mic 5: 2 But you, O **B** of Ephrathah,
Mt 2: 1 after Jesus was born in **B** of Judea,
Lk 2:15 "Let us go now to **B** and see this

BETRAY → BETRAYED
Mt 10:21 Brother will **b** brother to death,
Mk 14:11 to look for an opportunity to **b** him.
Jn 13:11 For he knew who was to **b** him;

BETRAYED → BETRAY
Lk 21:16 You will be **b** even by parents and
1 Cor 11:23 Jesus on the night when he was **b**

BETTER → GOOD
1 Sam 15:22 Surely, to obey is **b** than sacrifice,
Tob 12: 8 A little with righteousness is **b** than
Ps 63: 3 your steadfast love is **b** than life,
Prov 15:16 **B** is a little with the fear of
27: 5 **B** is open rebuke than hidden love.
Eccl 2:24 There is nothing **b** for mortals than
9: 4 a living dog is **b** than a dead lion.
Song 1: 2 For your love is **b** than wine,
Sir 40:26 the fear of the Lord is **b** than either.
Dan 1:20 he found them ten times **b** than all
Mt 5:29 it is **b** for you to lose one of your
Mk 14:21 It would have been **b** for that one
Jn 11:50 **b** for you to have one man die for
Rom 14: 5 Some judge one day to be **b** than
Phil 1:23 and be with Christ, for that is far **b**;
2: 3 in humility regard others as **b** than
Heb 7:22 the guarantee of a **b** covenant.
9:23 need **b** sacrifices than these.
1 Pet 3:17 For it is **b** to suffer for doing good,

BETWEEN
Gen 3:15 put enmity **b** you and the woman,
9:13 a sign of the covenant **b** me and
16: 5 the LORD judge **b** you and me!"
Isa 2: 4 He shall judge **b** the nations,
Ezek 34:17 I shall judge **b** sheep and sheep, **b** rams and goats:
Jn 19:18 on either side, with Jesus **b** them.
Rom 10:12 no distinction **b** Jew and Greek;
Eph 2:14 dividing wall, that is, the hostility **b**
1 Tim 2: 5 one mediator **b** God and humankind

BEWARE
Eccl 12:12 anything beyond these, my child, **b**.
Mt 6: 1 "**B** of practicing your piety before
Phil 3: 2 **B** of the dogs, **b** of the evil workers,

BEYOND
Ps 147: 5 his understanding is **b** measure.
Sir 3:23 not meddle in matters that are **b** you
2 Cor 4:17 an eternal weight of glory **b** all
2 Jn 1: 9 but goes **b** it, does not have God;

BEZALEL
Judahite craftsman in charge of building the tabernacle (Ex 31:1-11; 35:30-39:31).

BILDAD*
One of Job's friends (Job 2:11; 8; 18; 25; 42:9).

BILHAH
Servant of Rachel, mother of Jacob's sons Dan and Naphtali (Gen 30:1-7; 35:25; 46:23-25).

BIND → BINDS
Deut 6: 8 **B** them as a sign on your hand,
Prov 6:21 **B** them upon your heart always;
Isa 61: 1 to **b** up the brokenhearted,
Mt 16:19 whatever you **b** on earth will be

BINDS → BIND
Job 5:18 For he wounds, but he **b** up;
Col 3:14 **b** everything together in perfect

BIRD → BIRDS
Gen	1: 21	and every winged **b** of every kind.
Lev	20:25	the unclean **b** and the clean;

BIRDS → BIRD
Gen	1:22	and let **b** multiply on the earth."
	7: 3	and seven pairs of the **b** of the air
Ps	50: 11	I know all the **b** of the air,
Jer	7:33	be food for the **b** of the air, and for
Mt	6:26	Look at the **b** of the air;
Rev	19: 21	the **b** were gorged with their flesh.

BIRTH → BEAR
Deut	32:18	you forgot the God who gave you **b**.
Ps	22:10	On you I was cast from my **b**,
Mt	24: 8	is but the beginning of the **b** pangs.
Jas	1:18	he gave us **b** by the word of truth,
1 Pet	1: 3	given us a new **b** into a living hope

BIRTHRIGHT → BEAR, RIGHT
Gen	25:34	Thus Esau despised his **b**.
Heb	12:16	who sold his **b** for a single meal.

BISHOP
1 Tim	3: 1	whoever aspires to the office of **b**
Titus	1: 7	For a **b**, as God's steward, must be

BIT → BITE, BITS
Num	21: 9	and whenever a serpent **b** someone,
Ps	32: 9	temper must be curbed with **b** and

BITE* → BIT
Sir	21: 2	if you approach sin, it will **b** you.
Gal	5:15	If, however, you **b** and devour one

BITS → BIT
Jas	3: 3	we put **b** into the mouths of horses

BITTER → BITTERNESS
Ex	1:14	made their lives **b** with hard service
	12: 8	with unleavened bread and **b** herbs.
	15:23	water of Marah because it was **b**.
Ruth	1:13	it has been far more **b** for me than
Rev	8: 11	the water, because it was made **b**.

BITTERNESS → BITTER
Num	5:18	the water of **b** that brings the curse.
Prov	14:10	The heart knows its own **b**,
Rom	3:14	mouths are full of cursing and **b**."
Eph	4: 31	Put away from you all **b** and wrath

BLACK
Song	1: 5	I am **b** and beautiful, O daughters
Zech	6: 2	the second chariot **b** horses,
Mt	5:36	cannot make one hair white or **b**.
Rev	6: 5	I looked, and there was a **b** horse!

BLAMELESS
Gen	17: 1	walk before me, and be **b**.
2 Sam	22:26	with the **b** you show yourself **b**;
1 Macc	4:42	chose **b** priests devoted to the law,
Job	1: 1	That man was **b** and upright,
Ps	37:18	The Lord knows the days of the **b**,
Prov	11:20	but those of **b** ways are his delight.
Eph	1: 4	holy and **b** before him in love.
Phil	2:15	so that you may be **b** and innocent,
1 Thess	5:23	and **b** at the coming of our Lord
Titus	1: 7	bishop, as God's steward, must be **b**
Heb	7:26	**b**, undefiled, separated from sinners,
Rev	14: 5	mouth no lie was found; they are **b**.

BLASPHEME → BLASPHEMED, BLASPHEMER,
   BLASPHEMES, BLASPHEMIES, BLASPHEMOUS
Acts	26: 11	I tried to force them to **b**;
1 Tim	1:20	so that they may learn not to **b**.

BLASPHEMED → BLASPHEME
Ezek	20:27	In this again your ancestors **b** me,
Mt	26:65	tore his clothes and said, "He has **b**!

BLASPHEMER → BLASPHEME
Sir	3:16	forsakes a father is like a **b**,
1 Tim	1:13	even though I was formerly a **b**,

BLASPHEMES → BLASPHEME
Lev	24:16	One who **b** the name of the Lord
Lk	12: 10	whoever **b** against the Holy Spirit

BLASPHEMIES → BLASPHEME
1 Macc	2: 6	He saw the **b** being committed in

Mk	3:28	their sins and whatever **b** they utter;
Rev	13: 6	its mouth to utter **b** against God,

BLASPHEMOUS → BLASPHEME
Acts	6: 11	"We have heard him speak **b** words
Rev	13: 1	and on its heads were **b** names.

BLAZING
Ex	3: 2	he looked, and the bush was **b**,
Deut	4: 11	the mountain was **b** up to the very
Heb	12:18	a **b** fire, and darkness, and gloom,

BLEMISH → BLEMISHED
Ex	12: 5	Your lamb shall be without **b**,
Lev	22:20	not offer anything that has a **b**,
Eph	5:27	that she may be holy and without **b**.
Heb	9:14	offered himself without **b** to God,
1 Pet	1: 19	that of a lamb without defect or **b**.
Jude	1:24	to make you stand without **b** in the

BLEMISHED* → BLEMISH
Sir	34:21	ill-gotten goods, the offering is **b**;
Mal	1: 14	yet sacrifices to the Lord what is **b**;

BLESS → BLESSED, BLESSING, BLESSINGS
Gen	12: 2	I will **b** you, and make your name
	17:16	I will **b** her, and moreover I will
	22:17	I will indeed **b** you, and I will make
	26: 3	I will be with you, and will **b** you;
	32:26	not let you go, unless you **b** me."
Ex	20:24	I will come to you and **b** you.
Num	6:24	The Lord **b** you and keep you;
	23:20	See, I received a command to **b**;
Deut	7:13	he will love you, **b** you,
	30:16	the Lord your God will **b** you in
1 Chr	29:20	"B the Lord your God."
Tob	4:19	At all times **b** the Lord God,
Ps	5:12	For you **b** the righteous, O Lord;
	29: 11	the Lord **b** his people with peace!
	34: 1	I will **b** the Lord at all times;
	103: 1	B the Lord, O my soul,
	109:28	Let them curse, but you will **b**.
Sir	32:13	But above all **b** your Maker,
Hag	2:19	From this day on I will **b** you.
Lk	6:28	**b** those who curse you, pray
Rom	12:14	B those who persecute you;
1 Cor	4:12	When reviled, we **b**;
Jas	3: 9	With it we **b** the Lord and Father,

BLESSED → BLESS
Gen	1:22	God **b** them, saying, "Be fruitful
	2: 3	So God **b** the seventh day and
	14:19	He **b** him and said, "B be Abram
Num	24: 9	B is everyone who blesses you,
Tob	3: 11	she prayed and said, "B are you,
Jdt	13:17	one accord, "B are you our God,
Job	1: 21	**b** be the name of the Lord."
	42:12	The Lord **b** the latter days
Ps	118:26	B is the one who comes in the name
Isa	30:18	**b** are all those who wait for him.
Jer	17: 7	B are those who trust in the Lord,
Dan	3:26	"B are you, O Lord, God of our
	13:60	raised a great shout and **b** God,
Mt	5: 3	"B are the poor in spirit,
	16:17	"B are you, Simon son of Jonah!
Mk	10:16	laid his hands on them, and **b** them.
Lk	1:42	"B are you among women,
	6: 20	"B are you who are poor,
Jn	12:13	B is the one who comes in the name
	20:29	B are those who have not seen and
Acts	20:35	It is more **b** to give than to receive.
Gal	3: 8	"All the Gentiles shall be **b** in you."
Eph	1: 3	who has **b** us in Christ
1 Pet	3:14	for doing what is right, you are **b**.
Rev	1: 3	B is the one who reads aloud the
	22: 7	B is the one who keeps the words of

BLESSING → BLESS
Gen	12: 2	so that you will be a **b**.
	22:18	the nations of the earth gain **b** for
	27:36	now he has taken away my **b**."
Deut	11:26	before you today a **b** and a curse:
	23: 5	your God turned the curse into a **b**
Neh	13: 2	our God turned the curse into a **b**.
Tob	8:15	you, O God, with every pure **b**;

Sir	34:20	he gives health and life and **b**.
Ezek	34:26	they shall be showers of **b**.
Mal	3:10	for you an overflowing **b**.
Mk	14:22	of bread, and after **b** it he broke it,
Lk	24:51	While he was **b** them, he withdrew
1 Cor	10:16	The cup of that we bless,
Gal	3:14	in Christ Jesus the **b** of Abraham
Eph	1:3	every spiritual **b** in the heavenly
Rev	5:12	might and honor and glory and **b**!"
	7:12	**B** and glory and wisdom and

BLESSINGS → BLESS

Deut	28:2	all these **b** shall come upon you
Josh	8:34	the words of the law, **b** and curses,
Ps	21:6	You bestow on him **b** forever;
	144:15	Happy are the people to whom such **b**
Prov	10:6	**B** are on the head of the righteous,
Mal	2:2	and I will curse your **b**,
Rom	15:27	come to share in their spiritual **b**,

BLIND → BLINDED, BLINDNESS

Ex	4:11	mute or deaf, seeing or **b**?
Deut	27:18	misleads a **b** person on the road."
Tob	2:10	until I became completely **b**.
Ps	146:8	the LORD opens the eyes of the **b**.
Isa	35:5	the eyes of the **b** shall be opened,
	42:19	Who is **b** but my servant,
Bar	6:37	They cannot restore sight to the **b**;
Mt	11:5	**b** receive their sight, the lame walk,
Lk	6:39	"Can a **b** person guide a **b** person?
Jn	9:25	though I was **b**, now I see."
Rom	2:19	sure that you are a guide to the **b**,
2 Pet	1:9	**b**, and is forgetful of the cleansing

BLINDED → BLIND

Zech	11:17	withered, his right eye utterly **b**!
Jn	12:40	"He has **b** their eyes and hardened
2 Cor	4:4	has **b** the minds of the unbelievers,

BLINDNESS → BLIND

Gen	19:11	And they struck with **b** the men
Deut	28:28	will afflict you with madness, **b**,
1 Jn	2:11	the darkness has brought on **b**.

BLOCK → BLOCKS

Sir	31:7	It is a stumbling **b** to those who are
Isa	44:19	I fall before a **b** of wood?"
Ezek	14:7	their iniquity as a stumbling **b**
Mt	16:23	You are a stumbling **b** to me;
Rom	11:9	a stumbling **b** and a retribution for
1 Cor	1:23	stumbling **b** to Jews and foolishness

BLOCKS → BLOCK

Jer	6:21	before this people stumbling **b**
Mt	18:7	the world because of stumbling **b**!

BLOOD → BLOODSHED

Gen	4:10	your brother's **b** is crying out to me
	9:6	sheds the **b** of a human, by a human shall that person's **b** be shed;
Ex	7:17	and it shall be turned to **b**.
	12:13	when I see the **b**, I will pass over
	24:8	the **b** of the covenant that the LORD
Lev	1:5	the priests shall offer the **b**,
	3:17	you must not eat any fat or any **b**.
	17:11	it is the **b** that makes atonement.
Num	35:33	for **b** pollutes the land,
Ps	72:14	and precious is their **b** in his sight.
Isa	1:11	I do not delight in the **b** of bulls,
Ezek	33:4	**b** shall be upon their own heads.
Joel	2:30	**b** and fire and columns of smoke.
Mt	27:8	field has been called the Field of **B**
Mk	14:24	"This is my **b** of the covenant,
Lk	22:44	⟦ sweat became like great drops of **b**⟧
Jn	1:13	who were born, not of **b**
	6:53	of the Son of Man and drink his **b**,
	19:34	and at once **b** and water came out.
Acts	2:20	to darkness and the moon to **b**,
Rom	5:9	that we have been justified by his **b**,
1 Cor	11:25	cup is the new covenant in my **b**.
Eph	1:7	we have redemption through his **b**,
	6:12	not against enemies of **b** and flesh,
Heb	9:12	the **b** of goats and calves, but with his own **b**,
	9:22	without the shedding of **b** there is no
1 Jn	5:6	the one who came by water and **b**,

Rev	1:5	and freed us from our sins by his **b**,
	5:9	by your **b** you ransomed for God
	6:12	the full moon became like **b**,
	8:9	A third of the sea became **b**,
	12:11	conquered him by the **b** of the Lamb

BLOODSHED → BLOOD, SHED

Isa	5:7	he expected justice, but saw **b**;
Ezek	35:6	you did not hate **b**, **b** shall pursue
Hab	2:8	because of human **b**, and violence

BLOSSOMS

Ex	25:33	three cups shaped like almond **b**,
Num	17:8	It put forth buds, produced **b**,

BLOT

Gen	6:7	"I will **b** out from the earth
Ex	32:32	**b** me out of the book that you have
Ps	51:1	mercy **b** out my transgressions.
Rev	3:5	not **b** your name out of the book of

BLOW → BLOWING

Joel	2:1	**B** the trumpet in Zion; sound the
Rev	8:6	the seven trumpets made ready to **b**

BOAST → BOASTERS, BOASTFUL, BOASTING

Ps	34:2	My soul makes its **b** in the LORD;
Prov	27:1	Do not **b** about tomorrow,
Sir	25:6	and their **b** is the fear of the Lord.
Jer	9:24	but let those who **b** **b** in this,
Rom	2:23	You that **b** in the law,
1 Cor	1:31	the one who boasts, **b** in the Lord."
2 Cor	11:30	If I must **b**, I will **b** of the things that
Gal	6:14	never **b** of anything except the cross
Eph	2:9	of works, so that no one may **b**.

BOASTERS* → BOAST

2 Cor	11:13	For such **b** are false apostles,
2 Tim	3:2	**b**, arrogant, abusive, disobedient to

BOASTFUL → BOAST

Ps	5:5	The **b** will not stand before your
1 Cor	13:4	love is not envious or **b** or arrogant

BOASTING → BOAST

1 Cor	5:6	Your **b** is not a good thing.
1 Thess	2:19	or crown of **b** before our Lord Jesus

BOAZ

Bethlehemite who showed favor to Ruth (Ruth 2), married her (Ruth 4). Ancestor of David (Ruth 4:18-22; 1 Chr 2:12-15), Jesus (Mt 1:5-16; Lk 3:23-32).

BODIES → BODY

Rom	12:1	present your **b** as a living sacrifice,
1 Cor	6:15	that your **b** are members of Christ?
Heb	10:22	and our **b** washed with pure water.

BODILY → BODY

Lk	3:22	upon him in **b** form like a dove.
Col	2:9	the whole fullness of deity dwells **b**,

BODY → BODIES, BODILY

2 Sam	7:12	who shall come forth from your **b**,
Mic	6:7	fruit of my **b** for the sin of my soul?
Mt	6:22	"The eye is the lamp of the **b**.
Mk	14:22	and said, "Take; this is my **b**."
Lk	12:4	do not fear those who kill the **b**,
Jn	2:21	speaking of the temple of his **b**.
Rom	7:24	will rescue me from this **b** of death?
1 Cor	6:13	**b** is meant not for fornication but
	10:17	we who are many are one **b**,
	15:44	It is sown a physical **b**, it is raised a spiritual **b**.
2 Cor	5:8	from the **b** and at home with the Lord.
Eph	4:4	There is one **b** and one Spirit,
Col	2:19	from whom the whole **b**, nourished

BOLD → BOLDNESS

Deut	31:6	Be strong and; have no fear
Prov	28:1	but the righteous are as **b** as a lion.

BOLDNESS → BOLD

Eph	3:12	whom we have access to God in **b**
Heb	4:16	approach the throne of grace with **b**,
1 Jn	4:17	may have **b** on the day of judgment,

BONE → BONES

Gen	2:23	"This at last is **b** of my bones and
Ezek	37:7	the bones came together, **b** to its **b**.

BONES → BONE
Ex	12:46	and you shall not break any of its **b**.
Ps	34:20	He keeps all their **b**; not one of
Jn	19:36	"None of his **b** shall be broken."

BOOK → BOOKS
Ex	17:14	"Write this as a reminder in a **b** and
Deut	31:24	writing down in a **b** the words of
Josh	1: 8	This **b** of the law shall not depart
1 Macc	1:57	possessing the **b** of the covenant,
Ps	69:28	be blotted out of the **b** of the living;
Rev	1:11	"Write in a **b** what you see and
	21:27	who are written in the Lamb's **b**

BOOKS → BOOK
1 Macc	1:56	The **b** of the law that they found
Eccl	12:12	Of making many **b** there is no end,
Dan	7:10	in judgment, and the **b** were opened.
Jn	21:25	world itself could not contain the **b**
Rev	20:12	the throne, and **b** were opened.

BOOTHS
Lev	23:34	the festival of **b** to the LORD.
Ezra	3: 4	kept the festival of **b**, as prescribed,
Zech	14:16	and to keep the festival of **b**.

BORE → BEAR
Isa	53:12	yet he **b** the sin of many,
Mt	8:17	our infirmities and **b** our diseases."
1 Pet	2:24	He himself **b** our sins in his body

BORN → BEAR
Eccl	3: 2	a time to be **b**, and a time to die;
Isa	9: 6	For a child has been **b** for us,
	66: 8	Shall a land be **b** in one day?
Lk	2:11	is **b** this day in the city of David
Jn	3: 7	'You must be **b** from above.'
1 Cor	15: 8	Last of all, as to one untimely **b**,
1 Pet	1:23	You have been **b** anew,
1 Jn	4: 7	everyone who loves is **b** of God

BORROW → BORROWER
Deut	28:12	to many nations, but you will not **b**.
Ps	37:21	The wicked **b**, and do not pay back,
Mt	5:42	anyone who wants to **b** from you.

BORROWER → BORROW
Prov	22: 7	and the **b** is the slave of the lender.

BOUGHT → BUY
1 Cor	6:20	For you were **b** with a price;
2 Pet	2: 1	even deny the Master who **b** them—

BOW → BOWED, RAINBOW
Gen	9:13	I have set my **b** in the clouds,
Ex	20: 5	You shall not **b** down to them or
Ps	95: 6	O come, let us worship and **b** down,
Isa	45:23	"To me every knee shall **b**,
Rom	14:11	every knee shall **b** to me,

BOWED → BOW
Ps	146: 8	The LORD lifts up those who are **b**
Jn	19:30	he **b** his head and gave up his spirit.

BOWLS
Rev	16: 1	the seven **b** of the wrath of God."

BOY → BOYS
Jer	1: 7	to me, "Do not say, 'I am only a **b**';
Lk	2:43	**b** Jesus stayed behind in Jerusalem,

BOYS → BOY
Ex	1:18	and allowed the **b** to live?"
2 Kings	2:24	and mauled forty-two of the **b**.

BRANCH → BRANCHES
Isa	4: 2	On that day the **b** of the LORD shall
	11: 1	and a **b** shall grow out of his roots.
Jer	23: 5	raise up for David a righteous **B**,
Zech	3: 8	going to bring my servant the **B**,
Jn	15: 2	every **b** in me that bears no fruit.

BRANCHES → BRANCH
Jn	15: 5	I am the vine, you are the **b**.
Rom	11:21	if God did not spare the natural **b**,

BREAD
Gen	3:19	sweat of your face you shall eat **b**
Ex	12: 8	with unleavened **b** and bitter herbs.
	25:30	set the **b** of the Presence on the table

Deut	8: 3	that one does not live by **b** alone,
Eccl	11: 1	Send out your **b** upon the waters,
Wis	16:20	from heaven with **b** ready to eat,
Sir	15: 3	will feed him with the **b** of learning,
Mt	6:11	Give us this day our daily **b**.
Lk	4: 4	'One does not live by **b** alone.'"
Jn	6:35	Jesus said to them, "I am the **b** of life.
Acts	2:42	to the breaking of the **b** and the prayers.
1 Cor	10:17	Because there is one **b**,
	11:26	For as often as you eat this **b** and

BREAK → BREAKING, BROKEN, BROKENHEARTED
Ps	2: 9	You shall **b** them with a rod of iron,
Mt	6:19	where thieves **b** in and steal;
Jn	19:33	they did not **b** his legs.

BREASTPIECE → BREASTPLATE
Ex	28:15	You shall make a **b** of judgment,

BREASTPLATE → BREASTPIECE
Wis	5:18	he will put on righteousness as a **b**,
Isa	59:17	He put on righteousness like a **b**,
Eph	6:14	and put on the **b** of righteousness.

BREATH
Gen	2: 7	into his nostrils the **b** of life;
	6:17	all flesh in which is the **b** of life;
Job	7: 7	"Remember that my life is a **b**;
Eccl	12: 7	the **b** returns to God who gave it.
2 Thess	2: 8	will destroy with the **b** of his mouth,

BRIBE
Deut	16:19	for a **b** blinds the eyes of the wise
Prov	6:35	and refuses a **b** no matter how great.

BRIDE → BRIDEGROOM
Isa	62: 5	the bridegroom rejoices over the **b**,
Rev	19: 7	and his **b** has made herself ready;
	21: 9	the **b**, the wife of the Lamb."

BRIDEGROOM → BRIDE
Mt	9:15	as long as the **b** is with them,
Jn	3:29	He who has the bride is the **b**.

BRIDLE
Ps	32: 9	must be curbed with bit and **b**,
Jas	3: 2	the whole body in check with a **b**.

BRIGHT → BRIGHTNESS
Mt	17: 5	suddenly a **b** cloud overshadowed
Rev	15: 6	robed in pure **b** linen,
	22:16	of David, the **b** morning star."

BRIGHTNESS → BRIGHT
Dan	12: 3	wise shall shine like the **b** of the sky
Am	5:20	not light, and gloom with no **b** in it?

BRING → BRINGS, BROUGHT
Gen	6:19	**b** two of every kind into the ark,
Eccl	12:14	will **b** every deed into judgment,
Jer	24: 6	and I will **b** them back to this land.
Mt	10:34	not come to **b** peace, but a sword.
Rom	10:15	the feet of those who **b** good news!"

BRINGS → BRING
1 Sam	2: 6	The LORD kills and **b** to life;
Jas	5:20	that whoever **b** back a sinner

BROKE → BREAK
Ex	32:19	tablets from his hands and **b** them
2 Chr	36:19	**b** down the wall of Jerusalem,
1 Macc	3: 5	and pursued those who **b** the law;
Jer	31:32	a covenant that they **b**,
Mt	14:19	and blessed and **b** the loaves,
1 Cor	11:24	he **b** it and said, "This is my body

BROKEN → BREAK
Neh	1: 3	the wall of Jerusalem is **b** down,
Ps	51:17	acceptable to God is a **b** spirit;
Mt	15:37	they took up the **b** pieces left over,
Lk	20:18	who falls on that stone will be **b**
Rom	11:20	were **b** off because of their unbelief,

BROKENHEARTED → BREAK, HEART
Ps	147: 3	He heals the **b**, and binds up their
Isa	61: 1	the oppressed, to bind up the **b**,

BRONZE
Num	21: 9	look at the serpent of **b** and live.
Deut	28:23	The sky over your head shall be **b**,

Dan 10: 6 legs like the gleam of burnished **b**,
Rev 1:15 his feet were like burnished **b**,

BROOD
Mt 3: 7 he said to them, "You **b** of vipers!
Lk 13:34 a hen gathers her **b** under her wings,

BROTHER → BROTHER'S, BROTHER-IN-LAW,
    BROTHERS
Gen 4: 8 Cain rose up against his **b** Abel,
Mt 5:24 first be reconciled to your **b** or
    10:21 **B** will betray **b** to death,

BROTHER'S → BROTHER
Deut 25: 7 has no desire to marry his **b** widow,
Mk 6:18 lawful for you to have your **b** wife."

BROTHER-IN-LAW* → BROTHER
Gen 38: 8 and perform the duty of a **b** to her;

BROTHERS → BROTHER
Gen 9:25 lowest of slaves shall he be to his **b**.
    37:11 So his **b** were jealous of him,
Mk 3:33 "Who are my mother and my **b?**"
Lk 22:32 turned back, strengthen your **b**."
Heb 2:11 not ashamed to call them **b** and

BROUGHT → BRING
Gen 15: 7 **b** you from Ur of the Chaldeans,
Judg 2: 1 "I **b** you up from Egypt, and **b** you into
2 Chr 36:18 all these he **b** to Babylon.
Ezra 6: 5 **b** back to the temple in Jerusalem,
Rom 6:13 who have been **b** from death to life,
1 Tim 6: 7 for we **b** nothing into the world,

BUILD → BUILDER, BUILDERS, BUILDING, BUILDS,
    BUILT, REBUILD
Gen 11: 4 "Come, let us **b** ourselves a city,
Deut 6:10 fine, large cities that you did not **b**,
Ps 127: 1 those who **b** it labor in vain.
Isa 57:14 said, "**B** up, **b** up, prepare the way,
Mt 16:18 and on this rock I will **b** my church,
    27:40 destroy the temple and **b** it in three
1 Cor 3:10 must choose with care how to **b**
    10:23 are lawful," but not all things **b** up.

BUILDER → BUILD
Heb 3: 4 but the **b** of all things is God.)
    11:10 whose architect and **b** is God.

BUILDERS → BUILD
Ps 118:22 The stone that the **b** rejected has
Mk 12:10 The stone that the **b** rejected has
1 Pet 2: 7 "The stone that the **b** rejected has

BUILDING → BUILD
1 Cor 3: 9 you are God's field, God's **b**.
2 Cor 5: 1 we have a **b** from God,
Eph 4:12 for **b** up the body of Christ,

BUILDS → BUILD
Ps 127: 1 Unless the LORD **b** the house,
Prov 14: 1 The wise woman **b** her house,
1 Cor 8: 1 Knowledge puffs up, but love **b** up.

BUILT → BUILD
1 Kings 6:14 Solomon **b** the house, and finished
Neh 7: 1 the wall had been **b** and I had set up
Tob 13:16 Jerusalem will be **b** as his house for
1 Macc 4:47 **b** a new altar like the former one.
Prov 9: 1 Wisdom has **b** her house,
Dan 9:25 sixty-two weeks it shall be **b** again
Eph 2:20 **b** upon the foundation of the

BULL → BULLS
Ps 50: 9 will not accept a **b** from your house,

BULLS → BULL
1 Chr 29:21 a thousand **b**, a thousand rams,
Ps 22:12 encircle me, strong **b** of Bashan
Isa 1:11 I do not delight in the blood of **b**,
Heb 10: 4 it is impossible for the blood of **b**

BURDEN → BURDENS, BURDENSOME
Ps 55:22 Cast your **b** on the LORD,
Mt 11:30 my yoke is easy, and my **b** is light."
2 Cor 5: 4 in this tent, we groan under our **b**,

BURDENS → BURDEN
Ex 6: 6 free you from the **b** of the Egyptians

Lk 11:46 you load people with **b** hard to bear,
Gal 6: 2 Bear one another's **b**, and

BURDENSOME → BURDEN
1 Jn 5: 3 And his commandments are not **b**,

BURIED → BURY
Rom 6: 4 have been **b** with him by baptism
1 Cor 15: 4 he was **b**, and that he was raised on

BURN → BURNED, BURNING, BURNT
Ex 21:25 **b** for **b**, wound for wound,
Ps 79: 5 Will your jealous wrath **b** like fire?
Jer 7:31 to **b** their sons and their daughters
Mal 4: 1 the day that comes shall **b** them up,
Lk 3:17 but the chaff he will **b** with

BURNED → BURN
Ex 3: 3 and see why the bush is not **b** up."
Jn 15: 6 thrown into the fire, and **b**.
1 Cor 3:15 If the work is **b** up, the builder will

BURNING → BURN
Lk 24:32 "Were not our hearts **b** within us

BURNT → BURN
Ex 40: 6 You shall set the altar of **b** offering
Lev 1: 3 If the offering is a **b** offering from
1 Sam 15:22 LORD as great delight in **b** offerings
1 Macc 1:45 to forbid **b** offerings and sacrifices
    4:56 and joyfully offered **b** offerings;
Ps 51:16 if I were to give a **b** offering,
Dan 8:11 it took the regular **b** offering away
Hos 6: 6 the knowledge of God rather than **b**
Mic 6: 6 Shall I come before him with **b**
Mk 12:33 more important than all whole **b**

BURY → BURIED
Lk 9:60 "Let the dead **b** their own dead;

BUSH
Ex 3: 2 he looked, and the **b** was blazing,
Jon 4: 6 The LORD God appointed a **b**,

BUY → BOUGHT, BUYS
Prov 23:23 **B** truth, and do not sell it;
Isa 55: 1 **b** wine and milk without money
Rev 3:18 to **b** from me gold refined by fire so

BUYS → BUY
Prov 31:16 She considers a field and **b** it;
Mt 13:44 sells all that he has and **b** that field.

BYWORD → WORD
Deut 28:37 and a **b** among all the peoples where
Job 17: 6 He has made me a **b** of the peoples,
Ps 44:14 made us a **b** among the nations,

C

CAESAREA
Mt 16:13 came into the district of **C** Philippi,
Acts 10: 1 **C** there was a man named Cornelius
    25: 4 that Paul was being kept at **C**,

CAIAPHAS*
    High priest at trial of Jesus (Mt 26:3, 57; Lk 3:2; Jn 11:49;
18:13-28); at trial of disciples (Acts 4:6).

CAIN*
    Firstborn of Adam (Gen 4:1), murdered brother Abel (Gen
4:1-25; Heb 11:4; 1 Jn 3:12; Jude 11).

CALAMITIES → CALAMITY
1 Sam 10:19 who saves you from all your **c** and
2 Cor 6: 4 in afflictions, hardships, **c**,
    12:10 and **c** for the sake of Christ;

CALAMITY → CALAMITIES
Prov 1:26 I also will laugh at your **c**;
Dan 9:13 all this **c** has come upon us.
Hab 3:16 wait quietly for the day of **c** to come

CALEB
    Judahite who spied out Canaan (Num 13:6); allowed to enter land (Num 13:30-14:38; Deut 1:36; Sir 46:7-9; 1 Macc 2:56). Given Hebron (Josh 14:6-15:19).

CALF → CALVES
Ex 32: 4 and cast an image of a **c**;

Lk   15:23 And get the fatted c and kill it,

CALL → CALLED, CALLING
Deut   4:26 I c heaven and earth to witness
1 Sam   3: 5 But he said, "I did not c; lie down
1 Kings 18:24 you c on the name of your god and I will c on
            the name of the LORD;
1 Chr 16: 8 thanks to the LORD, c on his name,
Ps   61: 2 From the end of the earth I c to you,
Prov   8: 1 Does not wisdom c, and does
Isa   65:24 Before they c I will answer,
Mt   9:13 to c not the righteous but sinners."
Lk   6:46 "Why do you c me 'Lord, Lord,'
Jn   15:15 I do not c you servants any longer,
Rom 10:12 and is generous to all who c on him.
Phil   3:14 goal for the prize of the heavenly c

CALLED → CALL
2 Sam 22: 7 In my distress I c upon the LORD;
Isa   43: 1 I have c you by name, you are mine.
Mt   23: 8 But you are not to be c rabbi,
1 Cor 7:15 It is to peace that God has c you.
Eph   1:18 the hope to which he has c you,
1 Jn   3: 1 that we should be c children of God;

CALLING → CALL
Rom 11:29 and the c of God are irrevocable.
Eph   4: 1 lead a life worthy of the c to which

CALVES → CALF
1 Kings 12:28 and made two c of gold.
Mal   4: 2 go out leaping like c from the stall.

CAMEL
Mt   23:24 strain out a gnat but swallow a c!
Mk   10:25 c to go through the eye of a needle

CANA
Jn   2: 1 there was a wedding in C

CANAAN → CANAANITE, CANAANITES
Gen   9:25 "Cursed be C; lowest of slaves
Num 13: 2 "Send men to spy out the land of C,
1 Chr 16:18 "To you I will give the land of C

CANAANITE → CANAAN
Gen   28: 1 not marry one of the C women.
Mt   15:22 a C woman from that region came

CANAANITES → CANAAN
Ex   33: 2 I will drive out the C, the Amorites,
Judg 3: 5 So the Israelites lived among the C,

CAPERNAUM
Mt   4:13 and made his home in C by the sea,
Jn   6:59 was teaching in the synagogue at C.

CAPTIVE → CAPTIVITY
2 Kings 15:29 he carried the people c to Assyria.
       24:16 king of Babylon brought c to
Rom   7:23 making me c to the law of sin
Eph   4: 8 he made captivity itself a c;

CAPTIVITY → CAPTIVE
Deut 28:41 for they shall go into c.
Ezra   8:35 those who had come from c,

CARE → CAREFUL, CARELESS, CARES, CARING
Ps   8: 4 mortals that you c for them?
Heb   2: 6 or mortals, that you c for them?
Jas   1:27 to c for orphans and widows in

CAREFUL → CARE
Deut   4:23 So be c not to forget the covenant
Josh 1: 8 you may be c to act in accordance
Eph   5:15 Be c then how you live,

CARELESS* → CARE
Prov 14:16 the fool throws off restraint and is c.
Mt   12:36 to give an account for every c word

CARES → CARE
Lk   8:14 they are choked by the c and riches
1 Pet 5: 7 on him, because he c for you.

CARMEL
1 Kings 18:20 assembled the prophets at Mount C.

CARPENTER'S*
Mt   13:55 Is not this the c son?

CARRY
Ps   28: 9 their shepherd, and c them forever.
Isa   40:11 and c them in his bosom,
Lk   14:27 does not c the cross and follow me

CASE
Job   13: 3 and I desire to argue my c with God.
Isa   41:21 Set forth your c, says the LORD;
Lk   12:58 make an effort to settle the c,
Jn   18:38 "I find no c against him.

CAST
Ex   34:17 You shall not make c idols.
Esth   9:24 Jews to destroy them, and had c Pur
Ps   22:18 and for my clothing they c lots.
      55:22 C your burden on the LORD,
Prov 16:33 The lot is c into the lap,
Mk   3:23 "How can Satan c out Satan?
Jn   19:24 and for my clothing they c lots."
1 Pet 5: 7 C all your anxiety on him,

CATTLE
Gen   1:25 and the c of every kind,
Ps   50:10 the c on a thousand hills.

CAUGHT
2 Cor 12: 2 was c up to the third heaven—
1 Thess 4:17 be c up in the clouds together with

CAUSE
Job   5: 8 and to God I would commit my c.
Ps   9: 4 For you have maintained my just c;
    140:12 LORD maintains the c of the needy,
Jn   15:25 'They hated me without a c.'

CAVE
Gen   23: 9 he may give me the c of Machpelah,
1 Sam 22: 1 and escaped to the c of Adullam;
      24: 3 in the innermost parts of the c.
1 Kings 18: 4 hid them fifty to a c,

CEASE
Gen   8:22 winter, day and night, shall not c."
Jer   31:36 If this fixed order were ever to c
1 Cor 13: 8 as for tongues, they will c;

CEDAR
2 Sam 7: 2 See now, I am living in a house of c,
Ps   92:12 and grow like a c in Lebanon.

CELEBRATE
Lev   23:37 shall c as times of holy convocation,
1 Cor 5: 8 Therefore, let us c the festival,

CENSER
Lev   10: 1 Nadab and Abihu, each took his c,
Ezek 8:11 Each had his c in his hand,
Rev   8: 3 Another angel with a golden c came

CENSUS
Num   1: 2 Take a c of the whole congregation
2 Sam 24: 2 and take a c of the people,

CENTURION
Mt   8: 5 he entered Capernaum, a c came to
Lk   23:47 the c saw what had taken place,
Acts 10: 1 a man named Cornelius, a c

CEPHAS* → =PETER
    Name given to the apostle Peter (Jn 1:42; 1 Cor 1:12; 3:22;
9:5; 15:5; Gal 1:18; 2:9, 11, 14).

CERTIFICATE
Deut 24: 1 and so he writes her a c of divorce,
Mt   5:31 let him give her a c of divorce.'
Mk   10: 4 a man to write a c of dismissal

CHAFF
Ps   1: 4 are like c that the wind drives away.
Lk   3:17 c he will burn with unquenchable

CHAINED* → CHAINS
2 Tim 2: 9 the point of being c like a criminal. But the
           word of God is not c.

CHAINS → CHAINED
Eph   6:20 for which I am an ambassador in c.
Heb 11:36 and even c and imprisonment.
2 Pet 2: 4 them to c of deepest darkness

CHALDEANS
Gen   15: 7 who brought you from Ur of the C,
Dan   1: 4 the literature and language of the C.

CHANGE → CHANGED, CHANGERS
Ex   32:12 c your mind and do not bring
Num   23:19 a mortal, that he should c his mind.
1 Sam 15:29 will not recant or c his mind;
Ps   46: 2 not fear, though the earth should c,
Jer   18: 8 I will c my mind about the disaster
Jas   1:17 is no variation or shadow due to c.

CHANGED → CHANGE
1 Cor 15:51 will not all die, but we will all be c,
Heb   1:12 and like clothing they will be c.

CHANGERS → CHANGE
Mk   11:15 overturned the tables of the money c
Jn   2:15 poured out the coins of the money c

CHARACTER
Rom   5: 4 endurance produces c, and c produces

CHARGE
Mt   25:21 I will put you in c of many things;
Mk   15:26 The inscription of the c against him
Rom   8:33 will bring any c against God's elect?
1 Cor 9:18 I may make the gospel free of c,

CHARIOT → CHARIOTS
2 Kings 2:11 a c of fire and horses of fire
Ps   104: 3 you make the clouds your c,

CHARIOTS → CHARIOT
Ex   14:28 waters returned and covered the c
Zech   6: 1 and saw four c coming out from

CHARM
Prov 31:30 C is deceitful, and beauty is vain,
Sir   7:19 for her c is worth more than gold.
      26:15 A modest wife adds c to c,

CHASTISEMENT → CHASTISES
Sir   16:12 Great as his mercy, so also is his c;
Lam   4: 6 the c of my people has been greater

CHASTISES* → CHASTISEMENT
Heb   12: 6 and c every child whom he accepts.

CHEEK
Ps   3: 7 you strike all my enemies on the c;
Mt   5:39 if anyone strikes you on the right c,

CHEERFUL
Prov 15:13 A glad heart makes a c countenance,
      17:22 A c heart is a good medicine,
2 Cor 9: 7 for God loves a c giver.
Jas   5:13 Are any c? They should sing songs

CHEMOSH
1 Kings 11: 7 Solomon built a high place for C
Jer   48: 7 C shall go out into exile,

CHERUB → CHERUBIM
2 Chr 3:11 touched the wing of the other c;
Ps   18:10 He rode on a c, and flew;
Ezek 10:14 the first face was that of the c,
      28:14 an anointed c as guardian I placed

CHERUBIM → CHERUB
Gen   3:24 the garden of Eden he placed the c,
Ex   25:18 You shall make two c of gold;
Ps   80: 1 You who are enthroned upon the c,
Heb   9: 5 the c of glory overshadowing the

CHIEF
Ps   118:22 has become the c cornerstone.
Mk   15: 3 the c priests accused him of many
1 Pet 5: 4 And when the c shepherd appears,

CHILD → CHILDBEARING, CHILDISH, CHILDREN
Gen   17:17 c be born to a man who is a hundred
1 Kings 3: 7 although I am only a little c;
Isa   11: 6 and a little c shall lead them.
      49:15 Can a woman forget her nursing c,
Hos   11: 1 When Israel was a c, I loved him,
Mt   1:18 with c from the Holy Spirit.
Mk   10:15 the kingdom of God as a little c
Lk   2:12 you will find a c wrapped in bands
1 Cor 13:11 When I was a c, I spoke like a c,

Gal   4: 7 So you are no longer a slave but a c,
Rev   12: 4 that he might devour her c as soon

CHILDBEARING* → CHILD, BEAR
Gen   3:16 greatly increase your pangs in c;
1 Tim 2:15 Yet she will be saved through c,

CHILDISH* → CHILD
1 Cor 13:11 an adult, I put an end to c ways.

CHILDREN → CHILD
Ex   12:26 And when your c ask you,
Deut   6: 7 Recite them to your c and talk about
      11:19 Teach them to your c, talking about
Prov 22: 6 Train c in the right way, and when
Sir   30: 1 CONCERNING C He who loves his son
Mt   3: 9 stones to raise up c to Abraham.
Lk   18:16 "Let the little c come to me,
Jn   1:12 he gave power to become c of God,
Rom   8:14 by the Spirit of God are c of God.
1 Cor 14:20 do not be c in your thinking;
Eph   6: 4 do not provoke your c to anger,
Heb   12: 7 God is treating you as c;
1 Jn   3:10 The c of God and the c of the devil

CHOOSE → CHOOSES, CHOSE, CHOSEN
Deut 12:14 at the place that the LORD will c
      30:19 C life so that you and your
Josh 24:15 c this day whom you will serve,
Jn   15:16 You did not c me but I chose you.

CHOOSES → CHOOSE
Rom   9:18 he has mercy on whomever he c,
1 Cor 12:11 allots to each one individually just as the Spirit c.

CHOSE → CHOOSE
Deut   4:37 he c their descendants after them.
Neh   9: 7 God who c Abram and brought him
Mk   13:20 for the sake of the elect, whom he c,
1 Cor 1:27 God c what is foolish in the world

CHOSEN → CHOOSE
Isa   42: 1 my servant, whom I uphold, my c,
Mt   22:14 For many are called, but few are c."
Rom   11: 5 there is a remnant, c by grace.
1 Pet 2: 6 a cornerstone c and precious;
       2: 9 you are a c race, a royal priesthood,

CHRIST → CHRIST'S, CHRISTIAN, CHRISTIANS,
   MESSIAH
Jn   4:25 Messiah is coming" (who is called C).
Rom   5: 6 right time C died for the ungodly.
       8:35 will separate us from the love of C?
      10: 4 For C is the end of the law so that
1 Cor 1:23 but we proclaim C crucified,
       3:11 that foundation is Jesus C.
      11: 1 Be imitators of me, as I am of C.
      15: 3 C died for our sins in accordance
Gal   5: 1 For freedom C has set us free.
Eph   4:15 into him who is the head, into C,
Phil   1:21 to me, living is C and dying is gain.
       2:11 should confess that Jesus C is Lord,
Col   1:27 C in you, the hope of glory.
Rev   20: 4 reigned with C a thousand years.

CHRIST'S → CHRIST
Col   1:24 what is lacking in C afflictions
1 Pet 4:13 as you are sharing C sufferings,

CHRISTIAN* → CHRIST
Acts 26:28 persuading me to become a C?"
1 Pet 4:16 Yet if any of you suffers as a C,

CHRISTIANS* → CHRIST
Acts 11:26 the disciples were first called "C."

CHURCH
Mt   16:18 and on this rock I will build my c,
Acts   8: 1 persecution began against the c
1 Cor 12:28 has appointed in the c first apostles,
      14: 4 those who prophesy build up the c.
Col   1:18 He is the head of the body, the c;

CIRCUMCISE → CIRCUMCISED, CIRCUMCISION
Gen   17:11 shall c the flesh of your foreskins,
Deut 10:16 C, then, the foreskin of your heart,
Lk   1:59 the eighth day they came to c the
Jn   7:22 and you c a man on the sabbath.

CIRCUMCISED → CIRCUMCISE
Gen   17:10 Every male among you shall be **c**.
1 Macc 1:60 the women who had their children **c**,
Acts   15: 1 **c** according to the custom of Moses,
Gal   6:13 **c** do not themselves obey the law,
Col   2:11 also you were **c** with a spiritual

CIRCUMCISION → CIRCUMCISE
Rom   2:29 and real **c** is a matter of the heart—
Gal   5: 6 For in Christ Jesus neither **c**

CISTERN
Prov   5:15 Drink water from your own **c**,
Jer   38: 6 Jeremiah and threw him into the **c**

CITIES → CITY
Gen   19:25 and he overthrew those **c**,
Josh   20: 2 'Appoint the **c** of refuge,
Rev   16:19 and the **c** of the nations fell.

CITIZENSHIP
Phil   3:20 But our **c** is in heaven,

CITY → CITIES
1 Chr   11: 7 it was called the **c** of David.
Ps   127: 1 Unless the LORD guards the **c**,
Prov   31:31 her works praise her in the **c** gates.
Lam   1: 1 lonely sits the **c** that once was full
Dan   9:24 for your people and your holy **c**:
Mt   5:14 A **c** built on a hill cannot be hid.
Heb   12:22 Zion and to the **c** of the living God,
Rev   21: 2 I saw the holy **c**, the new Jerusalem,

CLAP
Ps   47: 1 **C** your hands, all you peoples;
Isa   55:12 all the trees of the field shall **c** their

CLAY
Isa   45: 9 Does the **c** say to the one who
Jer   18: 6 Just like the **c** in the potter's hand,
Dan   2:33 its feet partly of iron and partly of **c**.
Rom   9:21 Has the potter no right over the **c**,
2 Cor   4: 7 But we have this treasure in **c** jars,
2 Tim   2:20 and silver but also of wood and **c**,

CLEAN → CLEANSE, CLEANSING
Gen   7: 2 seven pairs of all **c** animals,
Lev   10:10 and between the unclean and the **c**;
Ps   51: 7 with hyssop, and I shall be **c**;
Mk   7:19 (Thus he declared all foods **c**.)
Jn   13:10 you are **c**, though not all of you."
Acts   10:15 "What God has made **c**,
Heb   10:22 with our hearts sprinkled **c** from

CLEANSE → CLEAN
Ps   51: 2 and **c** me from my sin.
Sir   38:10 and **c** your heart from all sin.
1 Jn   1: 9 **c** us from all unrighteousness.

CLEANSING → CLEAN
Eph   5:26 by **c** her with the washing of water
2 Pet   1: 9 and is forgetful of the **c** of past sins.

CLEAR → CLEARING
Ps   19: 8 the commandment of the LORD is **c**,
Nah   1: 3 LORD will by no means **c** the guilty.
1 Tim   3: 9 of the faith with a **c** conscience.
Rev   21:18 the city is pure gold, **c** as glass.

CLEARING* → CLEAR
Ex   34: 7 yet by no means **c** the guilty,

CLEFT
Ex   33:22 I will put you in a **c** of the rock,
Deut   14: 6 the hoof and has the hoof **c** in two,

CLINGS
Gen   2:24 and his mother and **c** to his wife,
Ps   119:25 My soul **c** to the dust;
Heb   12: 1 weight and the sin that **c** so closely,

CLOAK
Ex   4: 6 "Put your hand inside your **c**."
        22:26 you take your neighbor's **c** in pawn,
1 Sam   24: 4 cut off a corner of Saul's **c**.
Mk   15:17 And they clothed him in a purple **c**;
Heb   1:12 like a **c** you will roll them up,

CLOTH → SACKCLOTH
Isa   64: 6 righteous deeds are like a filthy **c**.

Lk   2: 7 and wrapped him in bands of **c**,

CLOTHE → CLOTHED, CLOTHES, CLOTHING
Col   3:14 Above all, **c** yourselves with love,
1 Pet   5: 5 you must **c** yourselves with humility

CLOTHED → CLOTHE
2 Cor   5: 2 longing to be **c** with our heavenly
Gal   3:27 have **c** yourselves with Christ.
Rev   12: 1 a woman **c** with the sun,

CLOTHES → CLOTHE
Zech   3: 3 Joshua was dressed with filthy **c** as
Lk   8:44 and touched the fringe of his **c**,

CLOTHING → CLOTHE
Ps   22:18 and for my **c** they cast lots.
Mt   25:36 I was naked and you gave me **c**,
Jn   19:24 and for my **c** they cast lots."

CLOUD → CLOUDS
Ex   13:21 went in front of them in a pillar of **c**
1 Kings 8:10 a **c** filled the house of the LORD,
        18:44 a little **c** no bigger than a person's
Ezek   10: 4 the house was filled with the **c**,
Mk   9: 7 Then a **c** overshadowed them,
Lk   21:27 'the Son of Man coming in a **c**'
Heb   12: 1 by so great a **c** of witnesses,
Rev   14:14 on the **c** was one like the Son of Man,

CLOUDS → CLOUD
Gen   9:13 I have set my bow in the **c**,
Dan   7:13 being coming with the **c** of heaven.
Mt   24:30 'the Son of Man coming on the **c** of
1 Thess 4:17 be caught up in the **c** together with
Rev   1: 7 He is coming with the **c**;

CLUSTER
Num   13:23 from there a branch with a single **c**

COALS
Ps   11: 6 On the wicked he will rain **c** of fire
Prov   25:22 will heap **c** of fire on their heads,
Rom   12:20 will heap burning **c** on their heads."

CODE*
Rom   2:27 condemn you that have the written **c**
        7: 6 slaves not under the old written **c**

COIN*
Mt   17:27 open its mouth, you will find a **c**;
        22:19 Show me the **c** used for the tax."
Lk   15: 9 I have found the **c** that I had lost.'

COLD
Zech   14: 6 that day there shall not be either **c**
Mt   24:12 the love of many will grow **c**.
Rev   3:16 lukewarm, and neither **c** nor hot,

COLLECTOR → COLLECTORS
Mt   10: 3 Thomas and Matthew the tax **c**;
Lk   18:10 one a Pharisee and the other a tax **c**.
        19: 2 he was a chief tax **c** and was rich.

COLLECTORS → COLLECTOR
Mt   5:46 Do even the tax **c** do the same?
        11:19 a friend of tax **c** and sinners!'

COLT
Gen   49:11 his donkey's **c** to the choice vine,
Zech   9: 9 and riding on a donkey, on a **c**,
Jn   12:15 coming, sitting on a donkey's **c**!"

COME → COMES, COMING
Ps   144: 5 your heavens, O LORD, and **c** down;
Isa   59:20 And he will **c** to Zion as Redeemer,
Zech   14: 5 Then the LORD my God will **c**,
Mt   6:10 Your kingdom **c**. Your will be done,
Lk   7:20 'Are you the one who is to **c**,
Jn   6:37 the Father gives me will **c** to me,
1 Cor   16:22 Our Lord, **c**!
Rev   1: 4 who is and who was and who is to **c**,
        22:20 Amen. **C**, Lord Jesus!

COMES → COME
Ps   118:26 one who **c** in the name of the LORD.
Lk   19:38 "Blessed is the king who **c** in the
Jn   14: 6 No one **c** to the Father except through

COMFORT → COMFORTED, COMFORTER, COMFORTERS, COMFORTS
Ps	23: 4	your rod and your staff—they c me.
Isa	40: 1	C, O c my people, says your God.

COMFORTED → COMFORT
Ps	86:17	LORD, have helped me and c me.
Isa	49:13	For the LORD has c his people,
Jer	31:15	she refuses to be c for her children,
Mt	5: 4	those who mourn, for they will be c.

COMFORTER* → COMFORT
Lam	1:16	for a c is far from me,

COMFORTERS → COMFORT
Job	16: 2	miserable c are you all.
Ps	69:20	and for c, but I found none.

COMFORTS → COMFORT
Isa	66:13	As a mother c her child, so I will

COMING → COME
Mal	3: 2	But who can endure the day of his c,
Heb	10:37	is c will come and will not delay;
2 Pet	3: 4	"Where is the promise of his c?
Rev	22:20	"Surely I am c soon."

COMMAND → COMMANDED, COMMANDING, COMMANDMENT, COMMANDMENTS
Ex	34:11	Observe what I c you today.
Deut	1:26	rebelled against the c of the LORD
Judg	2: 2	But you have not obeyed my c.

COMMANDED → COMMAND
Gen	7: 5	Noah did all that the LORD had c
Ex	40:32	as the LORD had c Moses.
Josh	1:16	"All that you have c us we will do,
Mt	28:20	to obey everything that I have c you.
Jn	14:31	but I do as the Father has c me,

COMMANDING → COMMAND
Deut	4:40	c you today for your own well-being
	30:11	c you today is not too hard for you,

COMMANDMENT → COMMAND
Deut	6: 1	Now this is the c—the statutes
Ps	19: 8	c of the LORD is clear,
Mt	22:38	This is the greatest and first c.
Rom	7:12	and the c is holy and just and good.
Gal	5:14	law is summed up in a single c,
1 Jn	3:23	this is his c, that we should believe

COMMANDMENTS → COMMAND
Ex	20: 6	those who love me and keep my c.
Deut	4:13	to observe, that is, the ten c;
1 Macc	2:19	and have chosen to obey his c,
Ps	119:66	for I believe in your c.
Prov	10: 8	The wise of heart will heed c,
Eccl	12:13	Fear God, and keep his c;
Sir	1:26	If you desire wisdom, keep the c,
Mt	19:17	wish to enter into life, keep the c.
	22:40	On these two c hang all the law and
Jn	14:15	If you love me, you will keep my c.
1 Cor	7:19	obeying the c of God is everything.
1 Jn	5: 3	And his c are not burdensome,
Rev	14:12	those who keep the c of God and

COMMENDABLE* → COMMENDATION
Phil	4: 8	whatever is pleasing, whatever is c,

COMMENDATION* → COMMENDABLE, COMMENDED
1 Cor	4: 5	each one will receive c from God.

COMMENDED → COMMENDATION
2 Cor	6: 4	but as servants of God we have c
Heb	11:39	though they were c for their faith,

COMMIT → COMMITS
Deut	5:18	Neither shall you c adultery.
2 Kings	17:21	and made them c great sin.
Ps	31: 5	Into your hand I c my spirit;
Prov	16: 3	C your work to the LORD,
Mt	5:27	'You shall not c adultery.'

COMMITS → COMMIT
Jn	8:34	who c sin is a slave to sin.
Jas	4:17	to do and fails to do it, c sin.

COMMON
Lev	10:10	between the holy and the c,
Ezek	22:26	between the holy and the c,
Acts	2:44	and had all things in c;
1 Cor	10:13	has overtaken you that is not c
	12: 7	of the Spirit for the c good.

COMMUNION*
2 Cor	13:13	the c of the Holy Spirit be with all

COMPANY
1 Cor	15:33	"Bad c ruins good morals."

COMPARE → COMPARING
Prov	8:11	all that you may desire cannot c
Isa	40:18	or what likeness c with him?
Lk	7:31	I c the people of this generation,

COMPARING* → COMPARE
Rom	8:18	of this present time are not worth c

COMPASSION → COMPASSIONATE
Deut	32:36	will vindicate his people, have c
Ps	103:13	As a father has c for his children,
Sir	18:13	the c of the Lord is for every living
Isa	54: 8	with everlasting love I will have c
Jer	12:15	I will again have c on them,
Hos	11: 8	my c grows warm and tender.
Mt	14:14	had c for them and cured their sick.
Rom	9:15	I will have c on whom I have c."
Col	3:12	clothe yourselves with c, kindness,

COMPASSIONATE → COMPASSION
Ex	22:27	I will listen, for I am c.
Sir	2:11	For the Lord is c and merciful;
Jas	5:11	how the Lord is c and merciful.

COMPETE → COMPETING, COMPETITION
Jer	12: 5	how will you c with horses?
1 Cor	9:24	that in a race the runners all c,

COMPETENT
2 Cor	3: 5	Not that we are c of ourselves—

COMPETING* → COMPETE
Gal	5:26	c against one another, envying one
2 Tim	2: 5	is crowned without c according to

COMPLAIN → COMPLAINING, COMPLAINT
Num	14:27	shall this wicked congregation c
Jer	2:29	Why do you c against me?
1 Cor	10:10	And do not c as some of them did,

COMPLAINING → COMPLAIN
Ex	16: 7	has heard your c against the LORD.
1 Pet	4: 9	hospitable to one another without c.

COMPLAINT → COMPLAIN
Job	10: 1	I will give free utterance to my c;
Ps	142: 2	I pour out my c before him;
Hab	2: 1	he will answer concerning my c.
Col	3:13	if anyone has a c against another,

COMPLETE → COMPLETED, COMPLETION
Gen	15:16	iniquity of the Amorites is not yet c.
Lev	23: 3	seventh day is a sabbath of c rest,
Jn	4:34	him who sent me and to c his work.
Rev	6:11	until the number would be c

COMPLETED → COMPLETE
Jer	25:12	Then after seventy years are c,
Dan	11:36	until the period of wrath is c,

COMPLETION → COMPLETE
Phil	1: 6	work among you will bring it to c
Jas	2:22	faith was brought to c by the works.

CONCEALED
Sir	11: 4	his works are c from humankind.
Lk	9:45	its meaning was c from them,

CONCEIT → CONCEITED
Sir	3:24	For their c has led many astray,
Phil	2: 3	nothing from selfish ambition or c,
1 Tim	3: 6	he may be puffed up with c and fall

CONCEITED* → CONCEIT
Gal	5:26	Let us not become c, competing
1 Tim	6: 4	is c, understanding nothing,

CONCEIVE → CONCEIVED

Mt	1:23	the virgin shall c and bear a son,
Lk	1:31	you will c in your womb and bear

CONCEIVED → CONCEIVE

1 Cor	2: 9	ear heard, nor the human heart c,
Jas	1:15	desire has c, it gives birth to sin,

CONDEMN → CONDEMNATION, CONDEMNED

Job	10: 2	I will say to God, Do not c me;
Ps	109:31	save them from those who would c
Lk	11:31	of this generation and c them,
Jn	3:17	not send the Son into the world to c
Rom	8:34	Who is to c?
1 Jn	3:21	Beloved, if our hearts do not c us,

CONDEMNATION → CONDEMN

Mk	12:40	They will receive the greater c."
Rom	5:18	one man's trespass led to c for all,
1 Tim	3: 6	fall into the c of the devil.
Jas	5:12	so that you may not fall under c.

CONDEMNED → CONDEMN

Mt	12:37	and by your words you will be c."
Lk	24:20	handed him over to be c to death
Jn	3:18	Those who believe in him are not c;
	16:11	the ruler of this world has been c.
1 Cor	11:32	disciplined so that we may not be c

CONDUCT

Tob	4:14	and discipline yourself in all your c.
Sir	37:17	The mind is the root of all c;
Ezek	22:31	returned their c upon their heads,
Rom	13: 3	For rulers are not a terror to good c,
1 Pet	1:15	be holy yourselves in all your c;

CONFESS → CONFESSES, CONFESSION

Lev	5: 5	you shall c the sin that you have
	16:21	c over it all the iniquities of the
Ps	38:18	c my iniquity; I am sorry for my sin.
Sir	4:26	Do not be ashamed to c your sins,
Phil	2:11	should c that Jesus Christ is Lord,
1 Jn	1: 9	If we c our sins, he who is faithful
Rev	3: 5	will c your name before my Father

CONFESSES → CONFESS

Rom	10:10	c with the mouth and so is saved.
1 Jn	2:23	who c the Son has the Father also.

CONFESSION → CONFESS

Dan	9: 4	to the LORD my God and made c,
1 Tim	6:12	for which you made the good c in
Heb	4:14	let us hold fast to our c.

CONFIDENCE

Ps	118: 8	in the LORD than to put c in mortals.
Phil	3: 3	and have no c in the flesh—
Heb	10:19	we have c to enter the sanctuary

CONFIRM → CONFIRMED

2 Sam	7:25	c it forever; do as you have
Ps	119:38	to your servant your promise,
Rom	15: 8	that he might c the promises given

CONFIRMED → CONFIRM

Ps	105:10	which he c to Jacob as a statute,
2 Pet	1:19	the prophetic message more fully c.

CONFORMED*

Rom	8:29	predestined to be c to the image of
	12: 2	Do not be c to this world,
Phil	3:21	may be c to the body of his glory,
1 Pet	1:14	do not be c to the desires that you

CONFUSE → CONFUSION

Gen	11: 7	go down, and c their language there,

CONFUSION → CONFUSE

Ex	23:27	and will throw into c all the people
Deut	28:28	blindness, and c of mind;
Ps	44: 7	and have put to c those who hate us.

CONGREGATION

Lev	4:13	c of Israel errs unintentionally
Num	1: 2	a census of the whole c of Israelites,
Ps	1: 5	nor sinners in the c of the righteous;
Heb	2:12	the midst of the c I will praise you."

CONQUER → CONQUERED, CONQUERORS, CONQUERS

Rev	17:14	and the Lamb will c them,
	21: 7	who c will inherit these things,

CONQUERED → CONQUER

Jn	16:33	take courage; I have c the world!"
Heb	11:33	who through faith c kingdoms,
1 Jn	2:13	because you have c the evil one.
Rev	15: 2	who had c the beast and its image

CONQUERORS → CONQUER

Rom	8:37	all these things we are more than c

CONQUERS → CONQUER

1 Jn	5: 4	victory that c the world, our faith.
Rev	2: 7	To everyone who c, I will give

CONSCIENCE

Rom	2:15	their own c also bears witness;
1 Cor	8: 7	and their c, being weak, is defiled.
1 Tim	1: 5	a good c, and sincere faith.
Heb	9:14	purify our c from dead works to
1 Pet	3:21	as an appeal to God for a good c,

CONSECRATE → CONSECRATED

Ex	13: 2	C to me all the firstborn;
	40: 9	and c it and all its furniture,

CONSECRATED → CONSECRATE

Lev	8:30	Thus he c Aaron and his vestments,
2 Chr	7:16	now I have chosen and c this house
Neh	3: 1	They c it and set up its doors;
1 Macc	4:48	of the temple, and c the courts.

CONSIDER → CONSIDERED

Ex	33:13	C too that this nation is your people.
1 Sam	12:24	for c what great things he has done
Ps	107:43	and c the steadfast love of the LORD.
Lk	12:27	C the lilies, how they grow:
Rom	6:11	must c yourselves dead to sin
Jas	1: 2	of any kind, c it nothing but joy,

CONSIDERED → CONSIDER

Prov	17:28	fools who keep silent are c wise;
Heb	11:11	he c him faithful who had promised.

CONSOLATION

Lk	2:25	looking forward to the c of Israel,
2 Cor	1: 3	of mercies and the God of all c,

CONSPIRACY → CONSPIRE

Isa	8:12	not call c all that this people calls c,

CONSPIRE → CONSPIRACY, CONSPIRED

Ps	2: 1	Why do the nations c,
	83: 5	They c with one accord;

CONSPIRED → CONSPIRE

Dan	6: 6	So the presidents and satraps c
Mt	26: 4	and they c to arrest Jesus by stealth

CONSULT → CONSULTED

1 Sam	28: 8	And he said, "C a spirit for me,
Sir	8:17	Do not c with fools, for they cannot
Isa	31: 1	Holy One of Israel or c the LORD!
	40:14	did he c for his enlightenment,

CONSULTED → CONSULT

1 Chr	10:13	had c a medium, seeking guidance,
Ezek	20: 3	Lord GOD, I will not be c by you.

CONSUME → CONSUMED, CONSUMING

Ex	32:12	c them from the face of the earth'?
Num	16:21	so that I may c them in a moment.
Mt	6:19	where moth and rust c and where
Jn	2:17	"Zeal for your house will c me."

CONSUMED → CONSUME

Ex	3: 2	bush was blazing, yet it was not c.
Ps	69: 9	zeal for your house that has c me;
	90: 7	For we are c by your anger;
Zeph	3: 8	all the earth shall be c.
Gal	5:15	that you are not c by one another.

CONSUMING → CONSUME

Heb	12:29	for indeed our God is a c fire.

CONTAIN

2 Chr	2: 6	even highest heaven, cannot c him?
Jn	21:25	world itself could not c the books

CONTEMPT
Dan	12: 2	some to shame and everlasting **c**.
Mk	9:12	sufferings and be treated with **c**?
Heb	6: 6	and are holding them up to **c**.

CONTEND
Isa	49:25	I will **c** with those who **c** with you,
Jude	1: 3	to **c** for the faith that was once for

CONTENT → CONTENTMENT
Sir	29:23	Be **c** with little or much,
2 Cor	12:10	Therefore I am **c** with weaknesses,
Phil	4:11	learned to be **c** with whatever I have
Heb	13: 5	and be **c** with what you have;

CONTENTMENT* → CONTENT
1 Tim	6: 6	gain in godliness combined with **c**;

CONTINUE
1 Chr	17:27	that it may **c** forever before you.
Jn	8:31	"If you **c** in my word,
Acts	13:43	urged them to **c** in the grace of God.
1 Thess	3: 8	if you **c** to stand firm in the Lord.
Heb	8: 9	for they did not **c** in my covenant,

CONTRARY
Gal	1: 8	a gospel **c** to what we proclaimed to
1 Tim	1:10	else is **c** to the sound teaching

CONTRIBUTE* → CONTRIBUTING
Rom	12:13	**C** to the needs of the saints;

CONTRIBUTING* → CONTRIBUTE
Deut	16:10	a freewill offering in proportion to
Mk	12:43	all those who are **c** to the treasury.

CONTRITE
Ps	51:17	broken and **c** heart, O God, you wil
Isa	57:15	who are **c** and humble in spirit,

CONVERT
Mt	23:15	sea and land to make a single **c**,
1 Tim	3: 6	He must not be a recent **c**,

CONVICT → CONVICTION
Deut	19:15	to **c** a person of any crime
Jude	1:15	to **c** everyone of all the deeds of

CONVICTION → CONVICT
Heb	11: 1	the **c** of things not seen.

CONVINCE → CONVINCED, CONVINCING
Acts	28:23	and trying to **c** them about Jesus
2 Tim	4: 2	**c**, rebuke, and encourage,

CONVINCED → CONVINCE
Lk	16:31	neither will they be **c** even if
Rom	8:38	For I am **c** that neither death, nor
2 Cor	5:14	we are **c** that one has died for all;

CONVINCING* → CONVINCE
Acts	1: 3	to them by many **c** proofs,

CONVOCATIONS
Lev	23: 2	that you shall proclaim as holy **c**,

COPPER
Lev	26:19	like iron and your earth like **c**.
Mk	12:42	and put in two small **c** coins,

COPY
Deut	17:18	he shall have a **c** of this law written
Heb	9:24	a mere **c** of the true one,

CORDS
2 Sam	22: 6	the **c** of Sheol entangled me,
Hos	11: 4	led them with **c** of human kindness,

CORNELIUS*
First Gentile Christian (Acts 10).

CORNER → CORNERSTONE
Prov	1:21	At the busiest **c** she cries out;
1 Pet	2: 7	has become the very head of the **c**,"

CORNERSTONE → CORNER, STONE
Ps	118:22	rejected has become the chief **c**.
Isa	28:16	a tested stone, a precious **c**, a sure
Zech	10: 4	Out of them shall come the **c**,
Lk	20:17	builders rejected has become the **c**'?
Eph	2:20	with Christ Jesus himself as the **c**.
1 Pet	2: 6	laying in Zion a stone, a **c** chosen

CORRECT → CORRECTING, CORRECTION
Ps	141: 5	let the faithful **c** me.
Sir	42: 8	Do not be ashamed to **c** the stupid
Jer	10:24	**C** me, O LORD, but in just measure;

CORRECTING* → CORRECT
2 Tim	2:25	**c** opponents with gentleness.

CORRECTION → CORRECT
Jer	5: 3	but they refused to take **c**.
2 Tim	3:16	**c**, and for training in righteousness,

CORRUPT → CORRUPTION
Gen	6:11	Now the earth was **c** in God's sight,
Acts	2:40	yourselves from this **c** generation."
Eph	4:22	your old self, **c** and deluded

CORRUPTION → CORRUPT
Acts	2:31	nor did his flesh experience **c**.'
2 Pet	1: 4	you may escape from the **c**

COST
1 Chr	21:24	burnt offerings that **c** me nothing."
Lk	14:28	not first sit down and estimate the **c**,

COUNCIL → COUNCILS
Jer	23:18	who has stood in the **c** of the LORD
Mt	26:59	the whole **c** were looking for false

COUNCILS* → COUNCIL
Mk	13: 9	for they will hand you over to **c**;

COUNSEL → COUNSELOR, COUNSELORS
Job	38: 2	that darkens **c** by words without
Ps	2: 2	and the rulers take **c** together,
	33:11	The **c** of the LORD stands forever,
Isa	28:29	he is wonderful in **c**, and excellent

COUNSELOR → COUNSEL
Sir	42:21	and he needs no one to be his **c**.
Isa	9: 6	and he is named Wonderful **C**,
Rom	11:34	Or who has been his **c**?"

COUNSELORS → COUNSEL
Prov	11:14	in an abundance of **c** there is safety.
	24: 6	in abundance of **c** there is victory.

COUNT → COUNTED, COUNTS
Gen	13:16	if one can **c** the dust of the earth,
1 Chr	21: 1	incited David to **c** the people of
Ps	90:12	So teach us to **c** our days

COUNTED → COUNT
Eccl	1:15	and what is lacking cannot be **c**.
Mt	10:30	even the hairs of your head are all **c**.

COUNTENANCE
Num	6:26	the LORD lift up his **c** upon you,
Ps	89:15	O LORD, in the light of your **c**;
Prov	15:13	A glad heart makes a cheerful **c**,

COUNTRY
Gen	12: 1	"Go from your **c** and your kindred
Jer	31:17	shall come back to their own **c**.
Jn	4:44	has no honor in the prophet's own **c**).
Heb	11:16	they desire a better **c**, that is,

COURAGE → COURAGEOUS
1 Chr	22:13	Be strong and of good **c**.
Jn	16:33	But take **c**; I have conquered

COURAGEOUS → COURAGE
Josh	1: 6	Be strong and **c**; for you shall put
1 Macc	2:64	be **c** and grow strong in the law,
Dan	10:19	Be strong and **c**!"
1 Cor	16:13	stand firm in your faith, be **c**,

COURT → COURTS
Ex	27: 9	shall make the **c** of the tabernacle.
Prov	25: 8	do not hastily bring into **c**;
Dan	7:10	**c** sat in judgment, and the books
Mt	5:25	while you are on the way to **c**
1 Cor	6: 6	believer goes to **c** against a believer

COURTS → COURT
Ps	84:10	in your **c** is better than a thousand
	96: 8	an offering, and come into his **c**.

COVENANT → COVENANTS
Gen	6:18	But I will establish my **c** with you;
	9: 9	I am establishing my **c** with you

Gen	15:18	the LORD made a **c** with Abram,
Ex	2:24	remembered his **c** with Abraham,
	19: 5	you obey my voice and keep my **c**,
	24: 7	Then he took the book of the **c**,
	40: 3	put in it the ark of the **c**,
Lev	26:42	will I remember my **c** with Jacob;
Judg	2: 1	'I will never break my **c** with you.
1 Kings	8:23	keeping **c** and steadfast love
Ezra	10: 3	now let us make a **c** with our God
Jdt	9:13	planned cruel things against your **c**,
1 Macc	1:15	and abandoned the holy **c**.
Job	31: 1	"I have made a **c** with my eyes;
Ps	105: 8	He is mindful of his **c** forever,
Sir	28: 7	remember the **c** of the Most High,
Isa	61: 8	I will make an everlasting **c** with
Jer	31:31	when I will make a new **c** with
Ezek	16:60	establish with you an everlasting **c**.
Dan	9:27	a strong **c** with many for one week,
Mal	3: 1	The messenger of the **c** in whom
Lk	22:20	is the new **c** in my blood.
1 Cor	11:25	"This cup is the new **c** in my blood.
2 Cor	3: 6	be ministers of a new **c**, not of letter
Heb	7:22	become the guarantee of a better **c**.
	12:24	the mediator of a new **c**,
Rev	11:19	the ark of his **c** was seen within his

COVENANTS → COVENANT

Rom	9: 4	the adoption, the glory, the **c**,
Gal	4:24	an allegory: these women are two **c**.

COVER

Ex	33:22	I will **c** you with my hand
Ps	139:11	"Surely the darkness shall **c** me,
Isa	11: 9	as the waters the **c** the sea.
Jas	5:20	and will **c** a multitude of sins.

COVET

Ex	20:17	shall not **c** your neighbor's house;
Rom	7: 7	had not said, "You shall not **c**."
Jas	4: 2	you **c** something and cannot obtain

CRAFTINESS → CRAFTY

Rom	1:29	of envy, murder, strife, deceit, **c**,
1 Cor	3:19	"He catches the wise in their **c**,"

CRAFTY → CRAFTINESS

Gen	3: 1	serpent was more **c** than any other
2 Cor	12:16	(you say) since I was **c**, I took you

CRAVING*

Num	11: 4	rabble among them had a strong **c**;
Ps	78:30	But before they had satisfied their **c**,

CREATE → CREATED, CREATION, CREATOR

Ps	51:10	**C** in me a clean heart, O God,
Isa	65:17	to **c** new heavens and a new earth;
Eph	2:15	**c** in himself one new humanity

CREATED → CREATE

Gen	1: 1	In the beginning when God **c** the
	1:27	So God **c** humankind in his image,
Deut	32: 6	Is not he your father, who **c** you,
Jdt	13:18	who **c** the heavens and the earth,
Prov	8:22	The LORD **c** me at the beginning of
Wis	2:23	for God **c** us for incorruption,
Sir	1: 4	Wisdom was **c** before all other
Mal	2:10	Has not one God **c** us?
1 Cor	11: 9	Neither was man **c** for the sake of
Eph	2:10	**c** in Christ Jesus for good works,
Col	1:16	all things have been **c** through him
1 Tim	4: 4	For everything **c** by God is good,
Rev	4:11	for you **c** all things, and by your will

CREATION → CREATE

Gen	2: 3	all the work that he had done in **c**.
Mk	10: 6	But from the beginning of **c**,
Rom	8:19	the **c** waits with eager longing for
2 Cor	5:17	anyone is in Christ, there is a new **c**:
Gal	6:15	but a new **c** is everything!
Col	1:15	invisible God, the firstborn of all **c**;
2 Pet	3: 4	they were from the beginning of **c**!"

CREATOR → CREATE

Eccl	12: 1	Remember your **c** in the days of
Rom	1:25	served the creature rather than the C
Col	3:10	according to the image of its **c**.
1 Pet	4:19	to a faithful **C**,

CREATURE → CREATURES

Gen	2:19	the man called every living **c**,
Rom	1:25	worshiped and served the **c** rather

CREATURES → CREATURE

Lev	11: 2	these are the **c** that you may eat.
Ps	104:24	the earth is full of your **c**.
Ezek	1: 5	was something like four living **c**.
Rev	4: 6	are four living **c**, full of eyes
	19: 4	elders and the four living **c** fell

CREDIT → CREDITED

Lk	6:33	what **c** is that to you?
1 Pet	2:20	for doing wrong, what **c** is that?

CREDITED → CREDIT

Lev	7:18	nor shall it be **c** to the one who

CREEPING

Gen	1:24	cattle and **c** things and wild animals
Ps	148:10	**c** things and flying birds!

CRIED → CRY

Ex	2:23	under their slavery, and **c** out.
Num	20:16	when we **c** to the LORD, he heard
Judg	3: 9	the Israelites **c** out to the LORD,
Ps	22: 5	To you they **c**, and were saved;
Mt	27:46	Jesus **c** with a loud voice,

CRIMINAL → CRIMINALS

Jn	18:30	"If this man were not a **c**,
2 Tim	2: 9	the point of being chained like a **c**.
1 Pet	4:15	suffer as a murderer, a thief, a **c**,

CRIMINALS → CRIMINAL

Lk	23:32	Two others also, who were **c**,

CRIMSON

Ex	25: 4	purple, and **c** yarns and fine linen,
Lev	14: 4	cedarwood and **c** yarn and hyssop
Josh	2:21	she tied the **c** cord in the window.

CROOKED

Deut	32: 5	a perverse and **c** generation.
Ps	18:26	the **c** you show yourself perverse.
Eccl	1:15	What is **c** cannot be made straight,
Lk	3: 5	and the **c** shall be made straight,
Phil	2:15	in the midst of a **c** and perverse

CROSS → CROSSROADS

Deut	31: 3	your God himself will **c** over before
Mk	15:30	and come down from the **c**!"
Lk	14:27	the **c** and follow me cannot be my
1 Cor	1:18	the **c** is foolishness to those who are
Gal	6:14	never boast of anything except the **c**
Phil	2: 8	of death—even death on a **c**.
Col	1:20	peace through the blood of his **c**.
Heb	12: 2	was set before him endured the **c**,

CROSSROADS* → CROSS, ROAD

Prov	8: 2	at the **c** she takes her stand;
Jer	6:16	Stand at the **c**, and look, and ask for

CROW*

Lk	22:34	the cock will not **c** this day,

CROWD → CROWDS

Mk	8: 2	"I have compassion for the **c**,
	14:43	a **c** with swords and clubs,

CROWDS → CROWD

Mt	7:28	**c** were astounded at his teaching,

CROWN → CROWNED, CROWNS

Lev	8: 9	the golden ornament, the holy **c**,"
Prov	4: 9	will bestow on you a beautiful **c**."
Sir	1:18	fear of the Lord is the **c** of wisdom,
Lam	5:16	The **c** has fallen from our head;
Jn	19: 2	soldiers wove a **c** of thorns and put
Phil	4: 1	my joy and **c**, stand firm in the Lord
2 Tim	4: 8	there is reserved for me the **c**
1 Pet	5: 4	the **c** of glory that never fades away.
Rev	6: 2	Its rider had a bow; a **c** was given
	14:14	with a golden **c** on his head,

CROWNED → CROWN

Ps	8: 5	and **c** them with glory and honor.
2 Tim	2: 5	no one is **c** without competing
Heb	2: 9	now **c** with glory and honor

CROWNS → CROWN
Rev 4: 10 they cast their **c** before the throne,

CRUCIFIED → CRUCIFY
Mt 27:22 All of them said, "Let him be **c**!"
Lk 24: 7 **c**, and on the third day rise again."
Acts 4: 10 whom you **c**, whom God raised
Rom 6: 6 We know that our old self was **c**
1 Cor 1:23 but we proclaim Christ **c**,
Gal 2:19 I have been **c** with Christ;

CRUCIFY → CRUCIFIED, CRUCIFYING
Lk 23:21 they kept shouting, "**C**, **c** him!"
Jn 19:15 asked them, "Shall I **c** your King?"

CRUCIFYING* → CRUCIFY
Heb 6: 6 they are **c** again the Son of God

CRUSH → CRUSHED
Job 6: 9 that it would please God to **c** me,
Isa 53:10 it was the will of the LORD to **c** him
Dan 2:40 it shall **c** and shatter all these.
Mt 21:44 it will **c** anyone on whom it falls."
Rom 16:20 will shortly **c** Satan under your feet.

CRUSHED → CRUSH
Ps 34:18 and saves the **c** in spirit.
2 Cor 4: 8 afflicted in every way, but not **c**;

CRY → CRIED, CRYING
Ex 2:23 Out of the slavery their **c** for help
Ps 5: 2 Listen to the sound of my **c**,
130: 1 Out of the depths I **c** to you,
Hab 1: 2 how long shall I **c** for help,
Mk 15:37 Then Jesus gave a loud **c**

CRYING → CRY
Gen 4: 10 your brother's blood is **c** out to me
Mk 1: 3 the voice of one **c** out in the
Rev 21: 4 **c** and pain will be no more,

CRYSTAL
Ezek 1:22 shining like **c**, spread out above
Rev 22: 1 river of the water of life, bright as **c**,

CUP
Ps 23: 5 my head with oil; my **c** overflows.
Jer 25:15 my hand this **c** of the wine of wrath,
Mt 10:42 gives even a **c** of cold water to one
26:39 if it is possible, let this **c** pass from
Mk 10:38 you able to drink the **c** that I drink,
Lk 22:17 he took a **c**, and after giving thanks
1 Cor 11:25 **c** is the new covenant in my blood.
Rev 14:10 unmixed into the **c** of his anger,

CURE → CURED
Hos 5:13 But he is not able to **c** you or heal

CURED → CURE
Mt 8:16 and **c** all who were sick.
Acts 5:16 and they were all **c**.

CURSE → ACCURSED, CURSED, CURSES
Gen 8:21 "I will never again **c** the ground
12: 3 and the one who curses you I will **c**;
Num 22:12 not **c** the people, for they are blessed
Deut 21:23 hung on a tree is under God's **c**.
23: 5 God turned the **c** into a blessing
Job 2: 9 **C** God, and die."
Ps 109:28 Let them **c**, but you will bless.
Sir 4: 5 and give no one reason to **c** you;
Mal 4: 6 come and strike the land with a **c**.
Mk 14:71 he began to **c**, and he swore an oath,
Lk 6:28 bless those who **c** you, pray
Rom 12:14 bless and do not **c** them.
Gal 3:13 Christ redeemed us from the **c** of the law by
becoming a **c** for us—

CURSED → CURSE
Gen 3:17 **c** is the ground because of you;
9:25 "**C** be Canaan; lowest of slaves
27:29 **C** be everyone who curses you,
Num 23: 8 can I curse whom God has not **c**?
Job 3: 1 Job opened his mouth and **c** the day
Mk 11:21 fig tree that you **c** has withered."
Gal 3:10 "**C** is everyone who does not
Heb 6: 8 and on the verge of being **c**;
Rev 16: 9 but they **c** the name of God,

CURSES → CURSE
Lev 24:15 who **c** God shall bear the sin.
2 Chr 34:24 all the **c** that are written in the book

CURTAIN
Ex 26:31 You shall make a **c** of blue, purple,
2 Chr 3:14 And Solomon made the **c** of blue
Lk 23:45 the **c** of the temple was torn in two.
Heb 10:20 that he opened for us through the **c**

CUSTOM → CUSTOMS
Esth 9:23 Jews adopted as a **c**
Jn 18:39 But you have a **c** that I release

CUSTOMS → CUSTOM
2 Kings 17: 8 the **c** of the nations whom the LORD
1 Macc 1:42 all should give up their particular **c**.
Acts 16:21 advocating **c** that are not lawful for

CUT
Gen 9:11 never again shall all flesh be **c** off
Ps 37: 9 For the wicked shall be **c** off,
Isa 53: 8 **c** off from the land of the living,
Dan 2:45 a stone was **c** from the mountain
Mt 3:10 does not bear good fruit is **c** down
Mk 9:43 hand causes you to stumble, **c** it off;
Rom 11:22 otherwise you also will be **c** off.

CYMBAL* → CYMBALS
1 Cor 13: 1 I am a noisy gong or a clanging **c**.

CYMBALS → CYMBAL
2 Sam 6: 5 tambourines and castanets and **c**.
Neh 12:27 and with singing, with **c**,
Ps 150: 5 Praise him with clanging **c**;

CYRUS
Persian king who allowed exiles to return (2 Chr 36:22-Ezra 1:8), to rebuild temple (Ezra 5:13-6:14), as appointed by the LORD (Isa 44:28-45:13).

D

DAGON
Judg 16:23 a great sacrifice to their god **D**,
1 Sam 5: 2 and brought it into the house of **D**

DAILY → DAY
Mt 6:11 Give us this day our **d** bread.
Lk 9:23 take up their cross **d** and follow me.

DAMASCUS
Acts 9: 3 was going along and approaching **D**,

DAN
1. Son of Jacob by Bilhah (Gen 30:4-6; 35:25; 46:23). Tribe of blessed (Gen 49:16-17; Deut 33:22), numbered (Num 1:39; 26:43), allotted land (Josh 19:40-48; Ezek 48:1), failed to fully possess (Judg 1:34-35), failed to support Deborah (Judg 5:17), possessed Dan (Judg 18).
2. Northernmost city in Israel (Gen 14:14; Judg 18; 20:1).

DANCE → DANCED
Ps 150: 4 Praise him with tambourine and **d**;
Eccl 3: 4 a time to mourn, and a time to **d**;
Lk 7:32 the flute for you, and you did not **d**;

DANCED → DANCE
2 Sam 6:14 David **d** before the LORD with all
Mt 14: 6 the daughter of Herodias **d** before

DANIEL → =BELTESHAZZAR
1. Hebrew exile to Babylon, name changed to Belteshazzar (Dan 1:6-7). Refused to eat unclean food (Dan 1:8-21). Interpreted Nebuchadnezzar's dreams (Dan 2; 4), writing on the wall (Dan 5). Thrown into lion's den (Dan 6; 14:31-42). Visions of (Dan 7-12). Saves Susanna (Dan 13). Destroys Bel and its priests (Dan 14).
2. Son of David (1 Chr 3:1).

DARE
Mt 22:46 **d** to ask him any more questions.
Rom 5: 7 someone might actually **d** to die.

DARIUS
1. King of Persia (Ezra 4:5), allowed rebuilding of temple (Ezra 5-6).
2. Mede who conquered Babylon (Dan 5:31).

DARK → DARKEST, DARKNESS
Ps	139:12	even the darkness is not **d** to you;
Lk	12: 3	whatever you have said in the **d** will
2 Pet	1:19	as to a lamp shining in a **d** place,

DARKEST* → DARK
| Ps | 23: 4 | though I walk through the **d** valley, |

DARKNESS → DARK
Gen	1: 2	the earth was a formless void and **d**
Ex	10:22	was dense **d** in all the land of Egypt
Deut	5:23	you heard the voice out of the **d**,
Isa	9: 2	walked in **d** have seen a great light;
Joel	2:31	The sun shall be turned to **d**,
Zeph	1:15	a day of **d** and gloom,
Mt	4:16	who sat in **d** have seen a great light,
	6:23	light in you is **d**, how great is the **d!**
Jn	1: 5	light shines in the **d**, and the **d** did not
Eph	5: 8	For once you were **d**, but now in
Col	1:13	from the power of **d** and transferred
1 Jn	1: 5	God is light and in him there is no **d**

DATHAN*
Involved in Korah's rebellion against Moses and Aaron (Num 16:1-27; 26:9; Deut 11:6; Ps 106:17; Sir 45:18).

DAUGHTER → DAUGHTERS
Ex	2: 5	**d** of Pharaoh came down to bathe at
Jdt	10:12	replied, "I am a **d** of the Hebrews,
Esth	2: 7	Mordecai adopted her as his own **d.**
Ps	9:14	and, in the gates of **d** Zion;
Lam	2: 1	in his anger has humiliated **d** Zion!
Mic	7: 6	the **d** rises up against her mother,
Zech	9: 9	Rejoice greatly, O **d** Zion!
Mt	14: 6	the **d** of Herodias danced before the
Lk	12:53	against **d** and **d** against mother,

DAUGHTERS → DAUGHTER
Gen	6: 4	of God went in to the **d** of humans,
	19:36	the **d** of Lot became pregnant by their
Num	27: 1	the **d** of Zelophehad came forward.
Deut	12:31	even burn their sons and their **d** in
Job	42:15	no women so beautiful as Job's **d**;
Joel	2:28	sons and your **d** shall prophesy,
Acts	2:17	sons and your **d** shall prophesy,
2 Cor	6:18	and you shall be my sons and **d**,
1 Pet	3: 6	You have become her **d** as long

DAVID
Son of Jesse (Ruth 4:17-22; 1 Chr 2:13-15), ancestor of Jesus (Mt 1:1-17; Lk 3:31). Wives and children (1 Sam 18; 25:39-44; 2 Sam 3:2-5; 5:13-16; 11:27; 1 Chr 3:1-9).

Anointed king by Samuel (1 Sam 16:1-13). Musician to Saul (1 Sam 16:14-23; 18:10). Killed Goliath (1 Sam 17). Relation with Jonathan (1 Sam 18:1-4; 19:20; 23:16-18; 2 Sam 1). Disfavor of Saul (1 Sam 18:6-23:29). Spared Saul's life (1 Sam 24; 26). Among Philistines (1 Sam 21:10-14; 27:30). Lament for Saul and Jonathan (2 Sam 1).

Anointed king of Judah (2 Sam 2:1-11). Conflict with house of Saul (2 Sam 2-4). Anointed king of Israel (2 Sam 5:1-4; 1 Chr 11:1-3). Conquered Jerusalem (2 Sam 5:6-10; 1 Chr 11;4-9). Brought ark to Jerusalem (2 Sam 6; 1 Chr 13; 15-16). The LORD promised eternal dynasty (2 Sam 7; 1 Chr 17; Ps 132). Showed kindness to Mephibosheth (2 Sam 9). Adultery with Bathsheba, murder of Uriah (2 Sam 11-12). Son Amnon raped daughter Tamar; killed by Absalom (2 Sam 13). Absalom's revolt (2 Sam 14-17); death (2 Sam 18). Sheba's revolt (2 Sam 20). Victories: Philistines (2 Sam 5:17-25; 21:15-22; 1 Chr 14:8-17; 20:4-8), Ammonites (2 Sam 10; 1 Chr 19), various (2 Sam 8; 1 Chr 18). Mighty men (2 Sam 23:8-39; 1 Chr 11-12). Punished for numbering army (2 Sam 24; 1 Chr 21). Appointed Solomon king (1 Kings 1:28-2:9). Prepared for building of temple (1 Chr 22-29). Last words (2 Sam 23:1-7). Death (1 Kings 2:10-12; 1 Chr 29:28).

Psalmist (Mt 22:43-45), musician (Am 6:5), prophet (2 Sam 23:2-7; Acts 1:16; 2:30).

Psalms of: 2 (Acts 4:25), 3-32, 34-41, 51-65, 68-70, 86, 95 (Heb 4:7), 101, 103, 108-110, 122, 124, 131, 133, 138-145.

DAWN → DAWNS
| Isa | 14:12 | from heaven, O Day Star, son of **D!** |
| Hos | 6: 3 | his appearing is as sure as the **d**; |

DAWNS → DAWN
| Ps | 97:11 | Light **d** for the righteous, |

| 2 Pet | 1:19 | until the day **d** and the morning star |

DAY → DAILY, DAYS
Gen	1: 5	God called the light **D**, and
	8:22	**d** and night, shall not cease."
Ex	13:21	of them in a pillar of cloud by **d**,
	20: 8	Remember the sabbath **d**, and keep
Josh	1: 8	you shall meditate on it **d** and night,
Ps	1: 2	his law they meditate **d** and night.
	118:24	is the **d** that the LORD has made;
Isa	66: 8	Shall a land be born in one **d**?
Joel	1:15	For the **d** of the LORD is near,
Zech	14: 1	See, a **d** is coming for the LORD,
Mal	3: 2	who can endure the **d** of his coming,
Mt	25:13	you know neither the **d** nor the hour.
Lk	11: 3	Give us each **d** our daily bread.
	24:46	to rise from the dead on the third **d**,
Jn	6:40	I will raise them up on the last **d**."
Rom	14: 5	Some judge one **d** to be better than
2 Cor	6: 2	see, now is the **d** of salvation!
1 Thess	5: 2	very well that the **d** of the Lord
2 Pet	3: 8	the Lord one **d** is like a thousand years,
	3:10	**d** of the Lord will come like a thief,
1 Jn	4:17	have boldness on the **d** of judgment,
Rev	1:10	I was in the spirit on the Lord's **d**,
	16:14	for battle on the great **d** of God

DAYS → DAY
Gen	1:14	and for seasons and for **d** and years,
	7: 4	rain on the earth for forty **d** and forty
Ex	24:18	on the mountain for forty **d** and
1 Kings	19: 8	that food forty **d** and forty nights
1 Macc	4:56	dedication of the altar for eight **d**,
Ps	90:10	The **d** of our life are seventy years,
Mk	1:13	He was in the wilderness forty **d**,
Eph	5:16	of the time, because the **d** are evil.
2 Tim	3: 1	in the last **d** distressing times will
Heb	1: 2	last **d** he has spoken to us by a Son,

DEACON* → DEACONS
| Rom | 16: 1 | a **d** of the church at Cenchreae, |

DEACONS → DEACON
| 1 Tim | 3: 8 | **D** likewise must be serious, not |

DEAD → DEATH, DIE, DIED, DYING
Num	16:48	stood between the **d** and the living;
Deut	18:11	or who seeks oracles from the **d.**
Ps	115:17	The **d** do not praise the LORD,
Eccl	9: 4	a living dog is better than a **d** lion.
Mt	8:22	and let the **d** bury their own **d.**"
Mk	12:27	God not of the **d**, but of the living;
Lk	24: 5	look for the living among the **d**?
Rom	6:11	must consider yourselves **d** to sin
Eph	2: 1	You were **d** through the trespasses
Col	1:18	the firstborn from the **d**,
1 Pet	4: 5	ready to judge the living and the **d.**
Rev	1: 5	witness, the firstborn of the **d**,
	20:12	And the **d** were judged according to

DEAF
Ex	4:11	Who makes them mute or **d**,
Isa	29:18	On that day the **d** shall hear the
Lk	7:22	the lepers are cleansed, the **d** hear,

DEATH → DEAD
Deut	30:19	that I have set before you life and **d**,
Ruth	1:17	if even **d** parts me from you!"
Ps	22:15	you lay me in the dust of **d**.
Prov	18:21	**D** and life are in the power of the
Song	8: 6	for love is strong as **d**,
Sir	15:17	Before each person are life and **d**,
Isa	25: 7	he will swallow up **d** forever.
Hos	13:14	O **D**, where are your plagues?
Mt	16:28	standing here who will not taste **d**
Lk	1:79	in darkness and in the shadow of **d**,
Jn	5:24	but has passed from **d** to life.
Rom	4:25	handed over to **d** for our trespasses
	6:23	For the wages of sin is **d**,
1 Cor	15:55	"Where, O **d**, is your victory?
2 Cor	2:16	to the one a fragrance from **d** to **d**,
Heb	2:14	through **d** he might destroy the one who has the power of **d**,
1 Jn	3:14	that we have passed from **d** to life
Rev	1:18	I have the keys of **D** and of Hades.

Rev   20:14 D and Hades were thrown into the lake
       21: 4 D will be no more;

DEBAUCHERY
Rom 13:13 not in d and licentiousness,
Eph   5:18 drunk with wine, for that is d;

DEBORAH
Prophetess; led victory over Canaanites (Judg 4-5).

DEBT → DEBTS, INDEBTED
Mt   18:27 released him and forgave him the d.

DEBTS → DEBT
Deut 15: 1 you shall grant a remission of d.
Mt   6:12 And forgive us our d, as we

DECEIT → DECEITFUL, DECEIVE, DECEIVED,
  DECEIVERS
Deut 32: 4 A faithful God, without d,
Isa   53: 9 and there was no d in his mouth.
Rom   1:29 Full of envy, murder, strife, d,
1 Pet 2:22 and no d was found in his mouth."

DECEITFUL → DECEIT
Ps   35:20 but they conceive d words
Zeph 3:13 nor shall a d tongue be found
1 Tim 4: 1 by paying attention to d spirits

DECEIVE → DECEIT
Eph   5: 6 Let no one d you with empty words,
1 Jn   1: 8 that we have no sin, we d ourselves,
Rev   20: 8 to d the nations at the four corners

DECEIVED → DECEIT
Gal   6: 7 Do not be d; God is not mocked,
1 Tim 2:14 was not d, but the woman was d

DECEIVERS* → DECEIT
Titus 1:10 rebellious people, idle talkers and d,
2 Jn   1: 7 Many d have gone out into the

DECISION
Prov 16:33 but the d is the LORD's alone.
Joel   3:14 multitudes, in the valley of d!

DECLARE → DECLARED
Ps   50: 6 The heavens d his righteousness,
Col   4: 3 that we may d the mystery of Christ,

DECLARED → DECLARE
Isa   41:26 Who d it from the beginning,
Mk   7:19 (Thus he d all foods clean.)
Rom   1: 4 and was d to be Son of God

DECREASE
Jn   3:30 He must increase, but I must d."

DECREE → DECREED, DECREES
Ps   2: 7 I will tell of the d of the LORD:
Lk   2: 1 d went out from Emperor Augustus

DECREED → DECREE
Dan   9:24 "Seventy weeks are d for your

DECREES → DECREE
Deut   6: 2 and keep all his d and his
Ps   19: 7 the d of the LORD are sure,
   119: 2 Happy are those who keep his d,

DEDICATED → DEDICATION
1 Kings 8:63 all the people of Israel d the house
Lk   21: 5 beautiful stones and gifts d to God,

DEDICATION → DEDICATED
2 Chr 7: 9 the d of the altar seven days and
Ezra 6:16 the d of this house of God with joy.
1 Macc 4:56 the d of the altar for eight days,

DEED → DEEDS
Eccl 12:14 will bring every d into judgment,
Jer   32:10 I signed the d, sealed it,
Mt   19:16 good d must I do to have eternal life
Col   3:17 And whatever you do, in word or d,

DEEDS → DEED
Deut 3:24 in heaven or on earth can perform d
Ps   9: 1 I will tell of all your wonderful d.
Jer 50:29 Repay her according to her d;
Ob   1:15 your d shall return on your own
Lk   23:41 getting what we deserve for our d,
Rom   2: 6 repay according to each one's d:

Rev   15: 3 "Great and amazing are your d,
    19: 8 the righteous d of the saints.

DEEP → DEPTH, DEPTHS
Gen   1: 2 darkness covered the face of the d,
    7:11 the fountains of the great d burst
Rom   8:26 with sighs too d for words.

DEFECT
1 Pet 1:19 like that of a lamb without d or

DEFEND
Jdt   5:21 for their Lord and God will d them,
Ps   72: 4 May he d the cause of the poor of
Prov 31: 9 d the rights of the poor and needy.

DEFILE → DEFILED
Lev 11:43 you shall not d yourselves
Num 35:34 You shall not d the land
Mk   7:15 things that come out are what d."

DEFILED → DEFILE
1 Macc 1:37 they even d the sanctuary.
Ps   79: 1 they have d your holy temple;

DEFRAUD*
Lev 19:13 You shall not d your neighbor;
Mk 10:19 You shall not d;
1 Cor 6: 8 you yourselves wrong and d—

DEITY
Col   2: 9 whole fullness of d dwells bodily,

DELAY
Deut 7:10 He does not d but repays
Ps 70: 5 my deliverer; O LORD, do not d!
Heb 10:37 will come and will not d;

DELIGHT → DELIGHTS
1 Sam 15:22 "Has the LORD as great d in burnt
Ps   1: 2 but their d is in the law of the LORD,
    40: 8 I d to do your will, O my God;
Prov 8:30 I was daily his d, rejoicing before
Sir   1:27 fidelity and humility are his d.
Rom 7:22 For I d in the law of God in my

DELIGHTS → DELIGHT
Ps   5: 4 not a God who d in wickedness;
Isa 42: 1 chosen, in whom my soul d;

DELILAH*
Philistine who betrayed Samson (Judg 16:4-22).

DELIVER → DELIVERANCE, DELIVERED, DELIVERER,
  DELIVERS
Ex   3: 8 to d them from the Egyptians,
Deut 32:39 and no one can d from my hand.
Dan   3:17 able to d us from the furnace
    6:20 able to d you from the lions?"
Mt   27:43 let God d him now,

DELIVERANCE → DELIVER
Ex   14:13 and see the d that the LORD will
Jdt   8:17 while we wait for his d,
Esth 4:14 d will rise for the Jews from another
Ps   3: 8 D belongs to the LORD;
Phil 1:19 this will turn out for my d.

DELIVERED → DELIVER
Isa 66: 8 Shall a nation be d in one moment?
Dan 12: 1 at that time your people shall be d,

DELIVERER → DELIVER
Ps 140: 7 O LORD, my Lord, my strong d,
Rom 11:26 "Out of Zion will come the D;

DEMON → DEMONIACS, DEMONIC, DEMONS
Tob   3: 8 the wicked d Asmodeus had killed
    6: 8 of a man or woman afflicted by a d
Mt 11:18 and they say, 'He has a d';
   17:18 Jesus rebuked the d, and it came out
Jn   8:48 you are a Samaritan and have a d?"
   10:21 not the words of one who has a d.

DEMONIACS → DEMON
Mt   4:24 d, epileptics, and paralytics, and he
    8:28 two d coming out of the tombs met

DEMONIC* → DEMON
Rev 16:14 These are d spirits, performing signs

DEMONS → DEMON

Deut	32:17	They sacrificed to **d**, not God,
Ps	106:37	and their daughters to the **d**;
Bar	4: 7	by sacrificing to **d** and not
Lk	11:18	that I cast out the **d** by Beelzebul.
1 Cor	10:20	not want you to be partners with **d**.
1 Tim	4: 1	deceitful spirits and teachings of **d**,
Jas	2:19	Even the **d** believe—and shudder.
Rev	9:20	their hands or give up worshiping **d**

DEN

Jer	7:11	a **d** of robbers in your sight?
Dan	6: 7	shall be thrown into a **d** of lions.
Mk	11:17	you have made it a **d** of robbers."

DENARIUS

Mk	12:15	Bring me a **d** and let me see it."

DENIED → DENY

Mt	26:70	But he **d** it before all of them,
1 Tim	5: 8	has **d** the faith and is worse than an
Rev	3: 8	my word and have not **d** my name.

DENIES → DENY

Lk	12: 9	but whoever **d** me before others
1 Jn	2:22	the liar but the one who **d** that Jesus

DENY → DENIED, DENIES

Lev	16:29	you shall **d** yourselves,
	23:27	you shall **d** yourselves
Mt	16:24	let them **d** themselves and take up
2 Tim	2:12	if we **d** him, he will also **d** us;
2 Pet	2: 1	**d** the Master who bought them—

DEPART → DEPARTED

Gen	49:10	The scepter shall not **d** from Judah,
Josh	1: 8	law shall not **d** out of your mouth;
Ps	34:14	**D** from evil, and do good;
Phil	1:23	my desire is to **d** and be with Christ,

DEPARTED → DEPART

1 Sam	4:21	"The glory has **d** from Israel,"

DEPRAVED → DEPRAVITY

1 Tim	6: 5	among those who are **d** in mind
2 Pet	2:10	who indulge their flesh in **d** lust,

DEPRAVITY → DEPRAVED

Lev	20:14	that there may be no **d** among you.

DEPRIVE

Deut	24:17	not **d** a resident alien or an orphan
1 Cor	7: 5	not **d** one another except perhaps

DEPTH → DEEP

Mt	13: 5	since they had no **d** of soil.
Rom	11:33	O the **d** of the riches and wisdom
Eph	3:18	and length and height and **d**,

DEPTHS → DEEP

Ps	130: 1	Out of the **d** I cry to you, O LORD.
1 Cor	2:10	even the **d** of God.

DESCENDANTS

Gen	15:18	saying, "To your **d** I give this land,
Deut	4:37	he chose their **d** after them.
Isa	44: 3	I will pour my spirit upon your **d**,
Rom	9: 7	Abraham's children are his true **d**;
Gal	3: 7	who believe are the **d** of Abraham.

DESCENDED → DESCENDING

Ex	34: 5	LORD **d** in the cloud and stood
Jn	3:13	except the one who **d** from heaven,
Eph	4: 9	does it mean but that he had also **d**

DESCENDING → DESCENDED

Gen	28:12	angels of God were ascending and **d**
Mk	1:10	and the Spirit **d** like a dove
Jn	1:51	the angels of God ascending and **d**

DESERT → DESERTED

Ps	106:14	and put God to the test in the **d**;
Isa	40: 3	make straight in the **d** a highway
Mk	8: 4	with bread here in the **d**?"

DESERTED → DESERT

Mt	26:56	all the disciples **d** him and fled.

DESERVE

Prov	14:14	and the good, what their deeds **d**.
Lk	23:15	he has done nothing to **d** death.

Acts	26:31	man is doing nothing to **d** death
Rev	2:23	give to each of you as your works **d**.

DESIRE → DESIRED, DESIRES

Gen	3:16	your **d** shall be for your husband,
Ps	20: 4	May he grant you your heart's **d**,
Prov	3:15	nothing you **d** can compare with her
Hos	6: 6	I **d** steadfast love and not sacrifice,
Mt	9:13	learn what this means, 'I **d** mercy,
Jas	1:14	But one is tempted by one's own **d**,
1 Jn	2:16	the **d** of the flesh, the **d** of the eyes,

DESIRED → DESIRE

Ps	19:10	More to be **d** are they than gold,
Lk	22:15	I have eagerly **d** to eat this Passover

DESIRES → DESIRE

Ps	37: 4	he will give you the **d** of your heart.
Sir	18:30	Do not follow your base **d**,
Gal	5:16	do not gratify the **d** of the flesh.
1 Tim	2: 4	who **d** everyone to be saved
2 Tim	4: 3	teachers to suit their own **d**,

DESOLATE → DESOLATES, DESOLATING

Ex	23:29	or the land would become **d** and
1 Macc	1:39	sanctuary became **d** like a desert;
Dan	11:31	the abomination that makes **d**.
Mt	23:38	See, your house is left to you, **d**.

DESOLATES → DESOLATE

Dan	9:27	shall be an abomination that **d**,

DESOLATING → DESOLATE

1 Macc	1:54	erected a **d** sacrilege on the altar
Mk	13:14	the **d** sacrilege set up where it ought

DESPAIR → DESPAIRED

2 Cor	4: 8	perplexed, but not driven to **d**;

DESPAIRED* → DESPAIR

2 Cor	1: 8	crushed that we **d** of life itself.

DESPISE → DESPISED

Job	5:17	not **d** the discipline of the Almighty.
Ps	51:17	contrite heart, O God, you will not **d**
Prov	1: 7	fools **d** wisdom and instruction.
Lk	16:13	devoted to the one and **d** the other.

DESPISED → DESPISE

Isa	53: 3	He was **d** and rejected by others;
1 Cor	1:28	God chose what is low and **d** in the

DESTINED

Eph	1: 5	He **d** us for adoption as his children
1 Thess	5: 9	For God has **d** us not for wrath but
1 Pet	1:11	to the sufferings **d** for Christ

DESTROY → DESTROYED, DESTROYER, DESTRUCTION

Gen	6:13	to **d** them along with the earth.
Esth	3: 6	Haman plotted to **d** all the Jews,
Mt	10:28	rather fear him who can **d** both soul
Jn	10:10	comes only to steal and kill and **d**.
Jas	4:12	who is able to save and to **d**.
1 Jn	3: 8	to **d** the works of the devil.

DESTROYED → DESTROY

Dan	6:26	His kingdom shall never be **d**,
1 Cor	15:26	The last enemy to be **d** is death.
2 Cor	5: 1	if the earthly tent we live in is **d**,

DESTROYER → DESTROY

Ex	12:23	not allow the **d** to enter your houses
1 Cor	10:10	and were destroyed by the **d**.

DESTRUCTION → DESTROY

Prov	16:18	Pride goes before **d**, and a haughty
Mt	7:13	and the road is easy that leads to **d**,
Rom	9:22	objects of wrath that are made for **d**;
2 Pet	3:16	and unstable twist to their own **d**,

DEVIL

Mt	4: 1	wilderness to be tempted by the **d**.
Lk	8:12	**d** comes and takes away the word
Jn	8:44	You are from your father the **d**,
Eph	4:27	and do not make room for the **d**.
	6:11	to stand against the wiles of the **d**.
1 Tim	3: 6	fall into the condemnation of the **d**.
Heb	2:14	the power of death, that is, the **d**,
Jas	4: 7	Resist the **d**, and he will flee from

1 Pet   5: 8 lion your adversary the **d** prowls
1 Jn   3: 8 to destroy the works of the **d**.
Jude   1: 9 Michael contended with the **d**
Rev   12: 9 who is called the **D** and Satan,
       20: 2 that ancient serpent, who is the **D**

DEVOTED
Ps   86: 2 Preserve my life, for I am **d** to you;
Mt   6:24 **d** to the one and despise the other.

DEVOUR → DEVOURING
Gal   5:15 you bite and **d** one another,
1 Pet   5: 8 looking for someone to **d**.
Rev   12: 4 that he might **d** her child

DEVOURING → DEVOUR
Ex   24:17 glory of the LORD was like a **d** fire
Deut   9: 3 crosses over before you as a **d** fire;

DEW
Judg   6:37 if there is **d** on the fleece alone,

DICTATED*
Jer   36:18 "He **d** all these words to me,

DIE → DEAD
Gen   2:17 eat of it you shall **d**."
        3: 4 to the woman, "You will not **d**;
Ex   11: 5 firstborn in the land of Egypt shall **d**
Ruth   1:17 Where you **d**, I will **d**—
Job   2: 9 Curse God, and **d**."
Prov   10:21 but fools **d** for lack of sense.
Eccl   3: 2 a time to be born, and a time to **d**;
Isa   22:13 eat and drink, for tomorrow we **d**."
Jer   31:30 But all shall **d** for their own sins;
Mt   26:35 "Even though I must **d** with you,
Jn   11:26 and believes in me will never **d**.
Rom   14: 8 if we **d**, we **d** to the Lord;
1 Cor 15:32 eat and drink, for tomorrow we **d**."
Heb   9:27 it is appointed for mortals to **d** once,

DIED → DEAD
Rom   5: 6 right time Christ **d** for the ungodly.
1 Cor 15: 3 Christ **d** for our sins in accordance
Gal   2:19 the law I **d** to the law,

DIFFERENT
2 Cor 11: 4 or a **d** gospel from the one you
Gal   1: 6 and are turning to a **d** gospel—

DIFFICULT
Dan   4: 9 and that no mystery is too **d**
Jn   6:60 teaching is **d**; who can accept it?"

DILIGENCE → DILIGENTLY
Rom   12: 8 the leader, in **d**;
Heb   6:11 each one of you to show the same **d**

DILIGENTLY → DILIGENCE
Deut   4: 6 You must observe them **d**,
Prov   8:17 and those who seek me **d** find me.

DINAH*
  Only daughter of Jacob, by Leah (Gen 30:21; 46:15). Raped by Shechem; avenged by Simeon and Levi (Gen 34).

DIRECT → DIRECTS
1 Sam   7: 3 **D** your heart to the LORD,
Ps   119:128 I **d** my steps by all your precepts;
2 Thess 3: 5 the Lord **d** your hearts to the love

DIRECTS → DIRECT
Prov   16: 9 but the LORD **d** the steps.
Jas   3: 4 wherever the will of the pilot **d**.

DISAPPOINT*
Rom   5: 5 and hope does not **d** us,

DISASTER
Ex   32:12 your mind and do not bring **d**
Deut   28:20 The LORD will send upon you **d**,
Jer   18: 8 I will change my mind about the **d**
Ezek   7: 5 Thus says the Lord GOD: **D** after **d**!

DISCERNED → DISCERNMENT
1 Cor   2:14 because they are spiritually **d**.

DISCERNING → DISCERNMENT
Deut   4: 6 nation is a wise and **d** people!"
Prov   1: 5 in learning, and the **d** acquire skill,
Sir   1:19 knowledge and **d** comprehension,

1 Cor   1:19 discernment of the **d** I will thwart."

DISCERNMENT → DISCERNED, DISCERNING
1 Kings 4:29 Solomon very great wisdom, **d**,
1 Cor 12:10 prophecy, to another the **d** of spirits,

DISCIPLE → DISCIPLES
Mt   10:24 "A **d** is not above the teacher,
Lk   14:26 even life itself, cannot be my **d**.

DISCIPLES → DISCIPLE
Isa   8:16 seal the teaching among my **d**.
Mt   26:56 all the **d** deserted him and fled.
       28:19 therefore and make **d** of all nations,
Lk   6:13 he called his **d** and chose twelve of
Jn   8:31 in my word, you are truly my **d**;
Acts   11:26 the **d** were first called "Christians."

DISCIPLINE → DISCIPLINED
Job   5:17 not despise the **d** of the Almighty.
Ps   94:12 Happy are those whom you **d**,
Prov   5:23 They die for lack of **d**,
Sir   1:27 fear of the Lord is wisdom and **d**,
Jer   7:28 their God, and did not accept **d**;
Eph   6: 4 in the **d** and instruction of the Lord.
Heb   12: 5 not regard lightly the **d** of the Lord,
1 Pet   5: 8 **D** yourselves, keep alert.

DISCIPLINED → DISCIPLINE
Wis   3: 5 Having been **d** a little, they will
1 Cor 11:32 **d** so that we may not be condemned

DISEASE → DISEASES
Mt   4:23 of the kingdom and curing every **d**
        9:35 curing every **d** and every sickness.

DISEASES → DISEASE
Ex   15:26 **d** that I brought upon the Egyptians;
Ps   103: 3 your iniquity, who heals all your **d**,
Isa   53: 4 our infirmities and carried our **d**;
Mt   8:17 took our infirmities and bore our **d**."

DISGRACE
Josh   5: 9 I have rolled away from you the **d**
1 Macc 4:58 the **d** brought by the Gentiles was
Prov   11: 2 When pride comes, then comes **d**;
Mt   1:19 unwilling to expose her to public **d**,
1 Pet   4:16 do not consider it a **d**,

DISGUISES
2 Cor 11:14 Satan himself as an angel of light.

DISHONEST
Sir   5: 8 Do not depend on **d** wealth,
Jer   22:17 and heart are only on your **d** gain,
Lk   16:10 is **d** in a very little is **d** also in much.

DISHONOR
Jn   8:49 I honor my Father, and you **d** me.
Acts   5:41 considered worthy to suffer **d** for
1 Cor 15:43 It is sown in **d**, it is raised in glory.

DISMAYED
Deut   1:21 do not fear or be **d**."
Josh   1: 9 do not be frightened or **d**,
Jer   17:18 them be **d**, but do not let me be **d**;

DISOBEDIENT → DISOBEY
Neh   9:26 they were **d** and rebelled
Rom   10:21 I have held out my hands to a **d**
       11:30 as you were once **d** to God but have
Titus   3: 3 ourselves were once foolish, **d**, led

DISOBEY → DISOBEDIENT
Lev   26:27 But if, despite this, you **d** me,
Sir   1:28 Do not **d** the fear of the Lord;
1 Pet   2: 8 stumble because they **d** the word,

DISPERSION
Jn   7:35 Does he intend to go to the **D**

DISQUALIFIED* → DISQUALIFY
1 Cor   9:27 to others I myself should not be **d**.

DISQUALIFY* → DISQUALIFIED
Col   2:18 Do not let anyone **d** you,

DISSENSION → DISSENSIONS
1 Cor 12:25 there may be no **d** within the body,
1 Tim   6: 4 From these come envy, **d**, slander,

DISSENSIONS → DISSENSION
Gal 5:20 strife, jealousy, anger, quarrels, **d**,
Titus 3: 9 stupid controversies, genealogies, **d**,

DISTINCTION → DISTINCTIONS
Ex 8:23 I will make a **d** between my people
Lev 11:47 make a **d** between the unclean and
Ezek 22:26 have made no **d** between the holy
Rom 3:22 For there is no **d**,

DISTINCTIONS* → DISTINCTION
Jas 2: 4 you not made **d** among yourselves,

DISTRESS → DISTRESSED
Deut 4:30 In your **d**, when all these things
Judg 2:15 and they were in great **d**.
2 Sam 22: 7 In my **d** I called upon the LORD;
Ps 81: 7 In **d** you called, and I rescued you;
Sir 2:11 and saves in time of **d**.
Jer 30: 7 it is a time of **d** for Jacob;
Lk 21:23 For there will be great **d** on the earth
Rom 8:35 Will hardship, or **d**, or persecution,

DISTRESSED → DISTRESS
Lam 1:20 See, O LORD, how **d** I am;

DISTRIBUTED
Josh 13:32 the inheritances that Moses **d**
Ps 112: 9 They have **d** freely,
Acts 4:35 it was **d** to each as any had need.
Heb 2: 4 gifts of the Holy Spirit, **d** according

DIVIDE → DIVIDED
Ex 14:16 your hand over the sea and **d** it,
Ps 22:18 **d** my clothes among themselves,
Lk 23:34 And they cast lots to **d** his clothing.

DIVIDED → DIVIDE
Lev 11: 3 Any animal that has **d** hoofs
Ps 136:13 who **d** the Red Sea in two,
Lk 11:18 If Satan also is **d** against himself,

DIVINATION → DIVINE
Deut 18:10 who practices **d**, or is a soothsayer,
1 Sam 15:23 For rebellion is no less a sin than **d**,
2 Kings 17:17 they used **d** and augury;

DIVINE → DIVINATION
Rom 1:20 his eternal power and **d** nature,
2 Pet 1: 4 become participants of the **d** nature.

DIVORCE → DIVORCED
Deut 24: 1 so he writes her a certificate of **d**,
Sir 7:26 Do not **d** her;
Isa 50: 1 Where is your mother's bill of **d**
Jer 3: 8 sent her away with a decree of **d**;
Mal 2:16 For I hate **d**, says the LORD,
Mt 5:31 let him give her a certificate of **d**.'
 19: 3 a man to **d** his wife for any cause?"
1 Cor 7:11 the husband should not **d** his wife.

DIVORCED → DIVORCE
Lev 21: 7 neither shall they marry a woman **d**
Mt 5:32 whoever marries a **d** woman

DOCTOR*
Lk 4:23 this proverb, '**D**, cure yourself!'

DOCTRINE → DOCTRINES
Eph 4:14 blown about by every wind of **d**,
1 Tim 1: 3 not to teach any different **d**,
2 Tim 4: 3 people will not put up with sound **d**,
Titus 1: 9 able both to preach with sound **d**

DOCTRINES → DOCTRINE
Mk 7: 7 teaching human precepts as **d**.'

DOEG*
 Edomite; Saul's chief shepherd; murdered 85 priests at Nob
(1 Sam 21:7; 22:6-23; Ps 52).

DOERS → DOES, DONE
Jas 1:22 But be **d** of the word,

DOES → DOERS
Ps 135: 6 Whatever the LORD pleases he **d**,
Eccl 3:14 whatever God **d** endures forever;
Mk 3:35 **d** the will of God is my brother

DOG → DOGS
Judg 7: 5 as a **d** laps, you shall put to one side

Prov 26:11 Like a **d** that returns to its vomit
2 Pet 2:22 "The **d** turns back to its own vomit,"

DOGS → DOG
Mt 7: 6 "Do not give what is holy to **d**;
 15:26 children's food and throw it to the **d**
Phil 3: 2 Beware of the **d**, beware of the evil
Rev 22:15 Outside are the **d** and sorcerers

DOMINION
Gen 1:26 and let them have **d** over
Ps 22:28 For **d** belongs to the LORD,
Dan 7:14 His **d** is an everlasting **d**
Rom 6:14 For sin will have no **d** over you,
Rev 1: 6 to him be glory and **d** forever

DONE → DOERS
Mt 6:10 Your will be **d**, on earth as it is in
 26:42 unless I drink it, your will be **d**."
Rev 16:17 from the throne, saying, "It is **d**!"
 21: 6 Then he said to me, "It is **d**!

DONKEY
Num 22:30 But the **d** said to Balaam,
Judg 15:15 he found a fresh jawbone of a **d**,
Zech 9: 9 humble and riding on a **d**,
Mt 21: 5 humble, and mounted on a **d**,

DOOM → DOOMED
Deut 32:35 their **d** comes swiftly.
Ps 81:15 and their **d** would last forever.

DOOMED → DOOM
Ps 102:20 to set free those who were **d** to die;
1 Cor 2: 6 of this age, who are **d** to perish.

DOOR → DOORPOSTS
Mt 7: 7 knock, and the **d** will be opened for
Lk 13:24 Strive to enter through the narrow **d**
Rev 3:20 I am standing at the **d**, knocking;

DOORPOSTS → DOOR
Ex 12: 7 the blood and put it on the two **d**

DORCAS*
 Disciple; raised from the dead (Acts 9:36-43).

DOUBLE → DOUBLE-TONGUED
Ex 22: 7 then the thief, if caught, shall pay **d**.
Deut 21:17 giving him a **d** portion of all that he
1 Sam 1: 5 but to Hannah he gave a **d** portion,
2 Kings 2: 9 me inherit a **d** share of your spirit.'
Rev 18: 6 and repay her **d** for her deeds;

DOUBLE-TONGUED → DOUBLE, TONGUE
Sir 5:14 Do not be called **d** and do not
1 Tim 3: 8 likewise must be serious, not **d**,

DOUBT → DOUBTED, DOUBTING
Mt 14:31 of little faith, why did you **d**?"
Jn 20:27 Do not **d** but believe."

DOUBTED* → DOUBT
Mt 28:17 they worshiped him; but some **d**.

DOUBTING* → DOUBT
Jas 1: 6 But ask in faith, never **d**,

DOUGH
Ex 12:39 **d** that they had brought out of Egypt
Gal 5: 9 yeast leavens the whole batch of **d**.

DOVE
Gen 8: 8 Then he sent out the **d** from him,
Mk 1:10 Spirit descending like a **d** on him.

DRAGON
Isa 27: 1 and he will kill the **d** that
Dan 14:23 in that place there was a great **d**,
Rev 12: 3 a great red **d**, with seven heads and
 20: 2 seized the **d**, that ancient serpent,

DRANK → DRINK
Ex 24:11 beheld God, and they ate and **d**.
Mk 14:23 and all of them **d** from it.
1 Cor 10: 4 and all **d** the same spiritual drink.

DRAW
Jn 12:32 will **d** all people to myself."
Jas 4: 8 **D** near to God, and he will **d** near

DREAM → DREAMED, DREAMER, DREAMS
1 Kings	3: 5	LORD appeared to Solomon in a **d**
Dan	7: 1	Daniel had a **d** and visions of his
Joel	2:28	your old men shall **d** dreams,
Mt	1:20	of the Lord appeared to him in a **d**
Acts	2:17	and your old men shall **d** dreams.

DREAMED → DREAM
Gen	28:12	he **d** that there was a ladder set up
	41: 1	Pharaoh **d** that he was standing by
Dan	2: 1	Nebuchadnezzar **d** such dreams

DREAMER* → DREAM
Gen	37:19	to one another, "Here comes this **d**.

DREAMS → DREAM
Num	12: 6	I speak to them in **d**.
1 Sam	28: 6	LORD did not answer him, not by **d**,
Sir	34: 7	For **d** have deceived many,

DRIED → DRY
Gen	8:13	the waters were **d** up from the earth;
Josh	5: 1	had **d** up the waters of the Jordan
Isa	51:10	Was it not you who **d** up the sea,

DRINK → DRANK, DRUNK, DRUNKARD, DRUNKENNESS
Gen	19:33	So they made their father **d** wine
Ex	32: 6	the people sat down to eat and **d**,
Eccl	9: 7	and **d** your wine with a merry heart;
Isa	22:13	eat and **d**, for tomorrow we die."
Mt	20:22	to **d** the cup that I am about to **d**?"
Jn	18:11	not to **d** the cup that the Father has
Rom	14:17	kingdom of God is not food and **d**
1 Cor	12:13	we were all made to **d** of one Spirit.
Rev	14:10	also **d** the wine of God's wrath,

DRIVE → DROVE
Ex	23:30	Little by little I will **d** them out
Num	33:52	you shall **d** out all the inhabitants of
Josh	13:13	Yet the Israelites did not **d** out the
Mk	11:15	to **d** out those who were selling
Jn	6:37	comes to me I will never **d** away;

DROSS
Ps	119:119	wicked of the earth you count as **d**;
Isa	1:25	I will smelt away your **d** as with lye
Ezek	22:18	house of Israel has become **d** to me;

DROVE → DRIVE
Josh	24:18	the LORD **d** out before us all the
Mk	1:12	Spirit immediately **d** him out into

DRUNK → DRINK
Gen	9:21	some of the wine and became **d**,
1 Sam	1:13	therefore Eli thought she was **d**.
Jdt	13: 2	on his bed, for he was dead **d**.
Song	5: 1	drink, and be **d** with love.
Jn	2:10	after the guests have become **d**.
Acts	2:15	these are not **d**, as you suppose,
Eph	5:18	Do not get **d** with wine,

DRUNKARD → DRINK
Prov	23:21	for the **d** and the glutton will come
Mt	11:19	they say, 'Look, a glutton and a **d**,
1 Cor	5:11	is an idolater, reviler, **d**, or robber.
1 Tim	3: 3	not a **d**, not violent but gentle,

DRUNKENNESS → DRINK
Tob	4:15	to excess or let **d** go with you
Eccl	10:17	for strength, and not for **d**!
Gal	5:21	**d**, carousing, and things like these.

DRY → DRIED
Gen	1: 9	and let the **d** land appear."
Ex	14:16	may go into the sea on **d** ground.
Josh	3:17	were crossing over on **d** ground,
Judg	6:37	and it is **d** on all the ground,
Ezek	37: 4	**d** bones, hear the word of the LORD.

DUE
1 Chr	16:29	Ascribe to the LORD the glory **d** his
Ps	28: 4	render them their **d** reward.
Mal	1: 6	a father, where is the honor **d** me?
Rom	13: 7	Pay to all what is **d** them—

DULL
Isa	6:10	Make the mind of this people **d**,
	59: 1	nor his ear too **d** to hear.

Mt	13:15	For this people's heart has grown **d**,

DUST
Gen	2: 7	LORD God formed man from the **d**
	3:14	and **d** you shall eat all the days of
	13:16	offspring like the **d** of the earth;
1 Sam	2: 8	He raises up the poor from the **d**;
Ps	103:14	he remembers that we are **d**.
Eccl	3:20	from the **d**, and all turn to **d** again.
Nah	1: 3	and the clouds are the **d** of his feet.
Mt	10:14	shake off the **d** from your feet
1 Cor	15:47	man was from the earth, a man of **d**;

DWELL → DWELLING, DWELLS
Ex	25: 8	so that I may **d** among them.
1 Kings	8:27	But will God indeed **d** on the earth?
Ps	23: 6	and I shall **d** in the house of
Eph	3:17	that Christ may **d** in your hearts
Col	1:19	fullness of God was pleased to **d**,
Rev	21: 3	He will **d** with them as their God;

DWELLING → DWELL
Lev	26:11	I will place my **d** in your midst,
Deut	12:11	will choose as a **d** for his name:
Ps	90: 1	our **d** place in all generations.
Jn	14: 2	my Father's house there are many **d**
2 Cor	5: 2	to be clothed with our heavenly **d**—
Eph	2:22	spiritually into a **d** place for God.

DWELLS → DWELL
Jn	14:10	but the Father who **d** in me
Rom	7:17	but sin that **d** within me.
1 Cor	3:16	and that God's Spirit **d** in you?
Col	2: 9	the whole fullness of deity **d** bodily,

DYING → DEAD
2 Cor	6: 9	as **d**, and see—we are alive;
Phil	1:21	living is Christ and **d** is gain.

E

EAGLE → EAGLES, EAGLES'
Ezek	1:10	the left side, and the face of an **e**;
	17: 3	A great **e**, with great wings and long
Rev	4: 7	fourth living creature like a flying **e**.

EAGLES → EAGLE
Isa	40:31	shall mount up with wings like **e**,

EAGLES' → EAGLE
Ex	19: 4	and how I bore you on **e** wings
Dan	7: 4	like a lion and had **e** wings.

EAR → EARS
Isa	64: 4	has heard, no **e** has perceived,
Lk	22:51	he touched his **e** and healed him.
1 Cor	2: 9	"What no eye has seen, nor **e** heard,
Rev	2: 7	Let anyone who has an **e** listen

EARLY
Deut	11:14	the **e** rain and the later rain,
Lk	24:22	were at the tomb **e** this morning,
Jas	5: 7	receives the **e** and the late rains.

EARS → EAR
Deut	29: 4	or eyes to see, or **e** to hear.
Isa	35: 5	and the **e** of the deaf unstopped;
Mt	11:15	Let anyone with **e** listen!
2 Tim	4: 3	sound doctrine, but having itching **e**,

EARTH → EARTHLY, EARTHQUAKE, EARTHQUAKES
Gen	1: 1	God created the heavens and the **e**,
	6:11	the **e** was corrupt in God's sight,
Ex	19: 5	Indeed, the whole **e** is mine,
Ps	47: 2	a great king over all the **e**.
Sir	40:11	All that is of **e** returns to **e**,
Isa	6: 3	the whole **e** is full of his glory."
	65:17	to create new heavens and a new **e**;
Jer	23:24	Do I not fill heaven and **e**?
Mt	5: 5	the meek, for they will inherit the **e**.
	24:35	Heaven and **e** will pass away,
Lk	5:24	has authority on **e** to forgive sins"—
2 Pet	3:13	wait for new heavens and a new **e**,
Rev	21: 1	I saw a new heaven and a new **e**;

EARTHLY → EARTH
Jn	3:12	If I have told you about **e** things
2 Cor	5: 1	if the **e** tent we live in is destroyed,

EARTHQUAKE → EARTH, QUAKE
1 Kings	19: 11	but the LORD was not in the e;
Mt	28: 2	And suddenly there was a great e;
Acts	16: 26	Suddenly there was an e,
Rev	6: 12	I looked, and there came a great e;

EARTHQUAKES → EARTH, QUAKE
Mt	24: 7	be famines and e in various places:

EASIER → EASY
Mt	9: 5	is e, to say, 'Your sins are forgiven,'
Lk	16: 17	it is e for heaven and earth to pass
	18: 25	e for a camel to go through the eye

EAST
Gen	2: 8	planted a garden in Eden, in the e;
Ps	103: 12	as far as the e is from the west,
Mt	2: 1	wise men from the E came to

EASY → EASIER
Mt	7: 13	road is e that leads to destruction,
	11: 30	For my yoke is e, and my burden is

EAT → ATE, EATING, EATS
Gen	2: 16	freely e of every tree of the garden;
Ex	12: 11	This is how you shall e it:
Lev	3: 17	not e any fat or any blood.
	11: 4	you shall not e the following:
Eccl	2: 24	nothing better for mortals than to e
Mt	26: 26	to the disciples, and said, "Take, e;
Acts	10: 13	"Get up, Peter; kill and e."
1 Cor	10: 31	whether you e or drink, or whatever
Rev	3: 20	I will come in to you and e with you

EATING → EAT
Lk	7: 34	the Son of Man has come e and
Rom	14: 2	Some believe in e anything,
1 Cor	8: 4	as to the e of food offered to idols,

EATS → EAT
Jn	6: 51	e of this bread will live forever;
1 Cor	11: 27	e the bread or drinks the cup of the

EDEN
Gen	2: 8	a garden in E, in the east;
Isa	51: 3	and will make her wilderness like E,
Ezek	28: 13	You were in E, the garden of God;

EDOM → =ESAU
Gen	25: 30	(Therefore he was called E.)
Num	20: 18	But E said to him, "You shall not
Ob	1: 1	says the Lord GOD concerning E:
Mal	1: 4	If E says, "We are shattered but we

EFFORT
Gal	2: 17	in our e to be justified in Christ,
Eph	4: 3	every e to maintain the unity of the
Heb	4: 11	make every e to enter that rest,
2 Pet	1: 5	make every e to support your faith

EGYPT
Gen	12: 10	So Abram went down to E to reside
	37: 28	And they took Joseph to E.
	47: 27	Thus Israel settled in the land of E,
Ex	1: 8	Now a new king arose over E,
	12: 40	in E was four hundred thirty years.
Josh	15: 47	to the Wadi of E, and the Great Sea
Neh	9: 18	God who brought you up out of E,'
Ps	78: 51	He struck all the firstborn in E,
Hos	11: 1	and out of E I called my son.
Mt	2: 15	"Out of E I have called my son."
Rev	11: 8	prophetically called Sodom and E,

EHUD
Judge of Israel (Judg 3:12-30).

ELAH
1. Son of Baasha; king of Israel (1 Kings 16:6-14).
2. Valley in which David fought Goliath (1 Sam 17:2, 19; 21:9).

ELDER → ELDERS
Gen	25: 23	the e shall serve the younger."
Rom	9: 12	"The e shall serve the younger."
1 Tim	5: 19	any accusation against an e except
1 Pet	5: 1	as an e myself and a witness of the

ELDERS → ELDER
Ex	24: 1	and seventy of the e of Israel,

Judg	2: 7	days of the e who outlived Joshua,
Isa	3: 14	enters into judgment with the e
Dan	13: 61	they took action against the two e,
Mt	27: 12	accused by the chief priests and e,
Mk	7: 3	thus observing the tradition of the e;
1 Tim	5: 17	the e who rule well be considered
Jas	5: 14	e of the church and have them pray
1 Pet	5: 5	must accept the authority of the e.
Rev	4: 4	on the thrones are twenty-four e,

ELEAZAR
1. Third son of Aaron (Ex 6:23-25). Succeeded Aaron as high priest (Num 20:26; Deut 10:6). Allotted land to tribes (Josh 14:1). Death (Josh 24:33).
2. Brother of Judas Maccabeus (1 Macc 2:5; 6:43-46).

ELECT → ELECTION
Wis	4: 15	grace and mercy are with his e,
Mt	24: 22	sake of the e those days will be cut
Mk	13: 22	to lead astray, if possible, the e.

ELECTION* → ELECT
Rom	9: 11	God's purpose of e might continue,
	11: 28	but as regards e they are beloved,
2 Pet	1: 10	eager to confirm your call and e,

ELEMENTS
Heb	5: 12	the basic e of the oracles of God.
2 Pet	3: 10	and the e will be dissolved with fire,

ELEVEN
Mt	28: 16	Now the e disciples went to Galilee,
Acts	1: 26	and he was added to the e apostles.

ELI
1. High priest in youth of Samuel (1 Sam 1-4). Blessed Hannah (1 Sam 1:12-18); raised Samuel (1 Sam 2:11-26). Prophesied against because of wicked sons (1 Sam 2:27-36). Death of Eli and sons (1 Sam 4:11-22).
2. "Eli, Eli, lema sabachthani?" (Mt 27:46).

ELIAKIM → =JEHOIAKIM
1. Original name of Jehoiakim (2 Kings 23:34; 2 Chr 36:4).
2. Hezekiah's palace administrator (2 Kings 18:17-37; 19:2; Isa 36:1-22; 37:2).

ELIEZER
1. Servant of Abraham (Gen 15:2).
2. Son of Moses (Ex 18:4; 1 Chr 23:15-17).

ELIHU
A friend of Job (Job 32-37).

ELIJAH
Prophet; predicted famine in Israel (1 Kings 17:1; Jas 5:17). Fed by ravens (1 Kings 17:2-6). Raised Sidonian widow's son (1 Kings 17:7-24). Defeated prophets of Baal at Carmel (1 Kings 18:16-46). Ran from Jezebel (1 Kings 19:1-9). Prophesied death of Azariah (2 Kings 1). Succeeded by Elisha (1 Kings 19:19-21; 2 Kings 2:1-18). Taken to heaven in whirlwind (2 Kings 2:11-12; Sir 48:1-12; 1 Macc 2:58).
Return prophesied (Mal 4:5-6); equated with John the Baptist (Mt 17:9-13; Mk 9:9-13; Lk 1:17). Appeared with Moses in transfiguration of Jesus (Mt 17:1-8; Mk 9:1-8).

ELIMELECH
Ruth	1: 3	But E, the husband of Naomi, died,

ELIPHAZ
A friend of Job (Job 4-5; 15; 22; 42:7, 9).

ELISHA
Prophet; successor of Elijah (1 Kings 19:16-21; Sir 48:12-14); inherited his mantle (2 Kings 2:1-18). Purified bad water (2 Kings 2:19-22). Cursed young men (2 Kings 2:23-25). Aided Israel's defeat of Moab (2 Kings 3). Provided widow with oil (2 Kings 4:1-7). Raised Shunammite woman's son (2 Kings 4:8-37). Purified food (2 Kings 4:38-41). Fed 100 men (2 Kings 4:42-44). Healed Naaman's leprosy (2 Kings 5). Made axhead float (2 Kings 6:1-7). Captured Arameans (2 Kings 6:8-23). Political adviser to Israel (2 Kings 6:24-8:6; 9:1-3; 13:14-19), Aram (2 Kings 8:7-15). Death (2 Kings 13:20).

ELIZABETH*
Mother of John the Baptist (Lk 1:5-58).

ELKANAH
Husband of Hannah, father of Samuel (1 Sam 1-2).

EMMANUEL* → =IMMANUEL
Mt 1:23 and they shall name him **E**,"

EMMAUS
Lk 24:13 were going to a village called **E**,

EMPEROR
Mt 22:17 Is it lawful to pay taxes to the **e**, or
Jn 19:12 you are no friend of the **e**.

EMPTIED → EMPTY
1 Cor 1:17 cross of Christ might not be **e** of its
Phil 2: 7 but **e** himself, taking the form of

EMPTY → EMPTIED, EMPTY-HANDED
Ruth 1:21 the LORD has brought me back **e**;
Isa 55:11 it shall not return to me **e**,
Mt 6: 7 do not heap up **e** phrases
Eph 5: 6 no one deceive you with **e** words,

EMPTY-HANDED → EMPTY, HAND
Ex 23:15 No one shall appear before me **e**.
Ruth 3:17 not go back to your mother-in-law **e**

EN-GEDI
1 Sam 23:29 and lived in the strongholds of **E**.

ENCOURAGE → ENCOURAGEMENT
1 Thess 4:18 **e** one another with these words.
1 Pet 5:12 written this short letter to **e** you

ENCOURAGEMENT → ENCOURAGE
Acts 4:36 Barnabas (which means "son of **e**").
Rom 15: 5 God of steadfastness and **e** grant
Phil 2: 1 If then there is any **e** in Christ,

END → ENDS
Gen 6:13 determined to make an **e** of all flesh,
Prov 14:12 but its **e** is the way to death.
Eccl 12:12 making many books there is no **e**,
Mt 24:13 But the one who endures to the **e**
28:20 always, to the **e** of the age."
Jn 13: 1 he loved them to the **e**.
Rom 10: 4 For Christ is the **e** of the law so that
Rev 22:13 the beginning and the **e**."

ENDOR*
1 Sam 28: 7 "There is a medium at **E**."

ENDS → END
Ps 2: 8 the **e** of the earth your possession.
Isa 40:28 the Creator of the **e** of the earth.
Rom 10:18 their words to the **e** of the world."
1 Cor 13: 8 Love never **e**. But as for prophecies,

ENDURANCE → ENDURE
Lk 8:15 and bear fruit with patient **e**.
Rom 5: 3 knowing that suffering produces **e**,
1 Tim 6:11 godliness, faith, love, **e**,
Heb 10:36 For you need **e**, so that when you
Jas 1: 3 the testing of your faith produces **e**;
2 Pet 1: 6 and self-control with **e**, and **e** with
Rev 1: 9 and the kingdom and the patient **e**,

ENDURE → ENDURANCE, ENDURED, ENDURES
Ps 89:29 his throne as long as the heavens **e**.
Mal 3: 2 who can **e** the day of his coming,
1 Cor 10:13 out so that you may be able to **e** it.
2 Tim 2:12 if we **e**, we will also reign with him;

ENDURED → ENDURE
Heb 12: 2 that was set before him he **e** the cross,

ENDURES → ENDURE
1 Chr 16:41 for his steadfast love **e** forever.
Sir 40:17 and almsgiving **e** forever.
Bar 4: 1 the law that **e** forever.
Mt 10:22 the one who **e** to the end will be saved.
13:21 but **e** only for a while,
Jn 6:27 for the food that **e** for eternal life,
1 Cor 13: 7 hopes all things, **e** all things.
1 Pet 1:25 but the word of the Lord **e** forever."

ENEMIES → ENEMY
Ex 23:22 be an enemy to your **e** and a foe to
Jdt 8:35 to take vengeance on our **e**."
Esth 9: 5 the Jews struck down all their **e**
1 Macc 4:36 said, "See, our **e** are crushed;
Ps 110: 1 until I make your **e** your footstool."
Mt 5:44 But I say to you, Love your **e** and

Lk 20:43 until I make your **e** your footstool."
Rom 5:10 For if while we were **e**,
12:20 "if your **e** are hungry, feed them;

ENEMY → ENEMIES, ENMITY
Mt 13:39 the **e** who sowed them is the devil;
1 Cor 15:26 The last **e** to be destroyed is death.
Jas 4: 4 of the world becomes an **e** of God.

ENGAGED
Mt 1:18 mother Mary had been **e** to Joseph,

ENJOY → ENJOYMENT
Eccl 3:22 that all should **e** their work,
9: 9 **E** life with the wife whom you love,

ENJOYMENT → ENJOY
Eccl 8:15 So I commend **e**, for there is nothing
1 Tim 6:17 with everything for our **e**.

ENLIGHTENED → LIGHT
Rom 10: 2 have a zeal for God, but it is not **e**.
Eph 1:18 with the eyes of your heart **e**,
Heb 6: 4 those who have once been **e**,

ENLIGHTENS* → LIGHT
Jn 1: 9 The true light, which **e** everyone,

ENMITY → ENEMY
Gen 3:15 put **e** between you and the woman,
Jas 4: 4 with the world is **e** with God?

ENOCH
  Walked with God and taken by him (Gen 5:18-24; Heb 11:5; Sir 44:16). Prophet (Jude 14).

ENSLAVE → SLAVE
1 Cor 9:27 but I punish my body and **e** it,
Gal 2: 4 so that they might **e** us—

ENSLAVED → SLAVE
Rom 6: 6 and we might no longer be **e** to sin.
6:22 freed from sin and **e** to God,
Gal 4: 9 want to be **e** to them again?

ENTER → ENTRY
Ex 40:35 Moses was not able to **e** the tent
Num 20:24 not **e** the land that I have given to
Ps 95:11 I swore, "They shall not **e** my rest."
Mt 5:20 will never **e** the kingdom of heaven.
7:13 "**E** through the narrow gate;
Mk 10:15 as a little child will never **e** it."
Jn 3: 5 no one can **e** the kingdom of God
Heb 3:11 'They will not **e** my rest.'"
10:19 have confidence to **e** the sanctuary
Rev 21:27 But nothing unclean will **e** it,

ENTHRONED → THRONE
1 Chr 13: 6 the LORD, who is **e** on the cherubim,
Ps 9: 7 But the LORD sits **e** forever,

ENTRUST → TRUST
Jn 2:24 Jesus on his part would not **e**
1 Pet 4:19 **e** themselves to a faithful Creator,

ENTRUSTED → TRUST
Lk 12:48 the one to whom much has been **e**,
2 Tim 1:12 guard until that day what I have **e** to
Jude 1: 3 the faith that was once for all **e** to

ENVY
Prov 23:17 Do not let your heart **e** sinners,
Mk 7:22 deceit, licentiousness, **e**, slander,
Rom 1:29 Full of **e**, murder, strife, deceit,
Jas 3:16 For where there is **e** and selfish

EPHOD
Ex 28: 6 They shall make the **e** of gold,
Judg 8:27 Gideon made an **e** of it and put it in

EPHRAIM
  1. Second son of Joseph (Gen 41:52; 46:20). Blessed as first-born by Jacob (Gen 48). Tribe of numbered (Num 1:33; 26:37), blessed (Deut 33:17), allotted land (Josh 16:4-9; Ezek 48:5), failed to fully possess (Josh 16:10; Judg 1:29).
  2. Term for the Northern Kingdom (Isa 7:17; Hos 5).

EQUAL → EQUALITY
Isa 40:25 you compare me, or who is my **e**?
46: 5 will you liken me and make me **e**,
Jn 5:18 thereby making himself **e** to God.

EQUALITY* → EQUAL
Phil 2: 6 not regard e with God as something

EQUIPPED
2 Tim 3:17 e for every good work.

ERROR
Lev 5:18 for the e that you committed
Wis 1:12 Do not invite death by the e of your
Rom 1:27 the due penalty for their e.
1 Jn 4: 6 the spirit of truth and the spirit of e.

ESAU → =EDOM
Firstborn of Isaac, twin of Jacob (Gen 25:21-26). Also called Edom (Gen 25:30). Sold Jacob his birthright (Gen 25:29-34); lost blessing (Gen 27). Married Hittites (Gen 26:34), Ishmaelites (Gen 28:6-9). Reconciled to Jacob (Gen 33). Genealogy (Gen 36). The LORD chose Jacob over Esau (Mal 1:2-3), but gave Esau land (Deut 2:2-12). Descendants eventually obliterated (Ob 1-21; Jer 49:7-22).

ESCAPE
Gen 7: 7 went into the ark to e the waters of
Ps 68:20 the LORD, belongs e from death.
Rom 2: 3 you will e the judgment of God?
1 Thess 5: 3 and there will be no e!
Heb 12:25 how much less will we e if we reject
2 Pet 1: 4 you may e from the corruption

ESTABLISH → ESTABLISHED
Gen 6:18 But I will e my covenant with you;
Deut 28: 9 LORD will e you as his holy people,
Ps 89: 4 'I will e your descendants forever,
Ezek 16:60 e with you an everlasting covenant.
Rom 10: 3 and seeking to e their own,
Heb 8: 8 when I will e a new covenant with

ESTABLISHED → ESTABLISH
2 Sam 7:16 your throne shall be e forever.
Ps 89: 2 your steadfast love is e forever;
103:19 The LORD has e his throne in the
Jer 10:12 who e the world by his wisdom,
2 Pet 1:12 you know them already and are e in

ESTHER
Jewess, originally named Hadassah, who lived in Persia; cousin of Mordecai (Esth 2:7). Chosen queen of Xerxes (Esth 2:8-18). Persuaded by Mordecai to foil Haman's plan to exterminate the Jews (Esth 3-4). Revealed Haman's plans to Xerxes, resulting in Haman's death (Esth 7), the Jews' preservation (Esth 8-9), Mordecai's exaltation (Esth 8:15; 9:4; 10). Decreed celebration of Purim (Esth 9:18-32).

ETERNAL → ETERNITY
Mt 25:46 but the righteous into e life."
Mk 10:17 what must I do to inherit e life?"
Jn 3:16 may not perish but may have e life.
4:14 spring of water gushing up to e life.
10:28 I give them e life, and they will
Rom 5: 21 e life through Jesus Christ our Lord.
2 Cor 4:17 an e weight of glory beyond all
Heb 5: 9 the source of e salvation for all who
1 Jn 5:13 may know that you have e life.

ETERNITY → ETERNAL
Wis 2:23 made us in the image of his own e,
Sir 42:21 he is from all e one and the same.
Isa 57:15 high and lofty one who inhabits e,
2 Pet 3:18 glory both now and to the day of e.

ETHIOPIANS
Jer 13:23 Can E change their skin

EUNUCH → EUNUCHS
Jer 38: 7 Ebed-melech the Ethiopian, a e
Acts 8:27 Now there was an Ethiopian e,

EUNUCHS → EUNUCH
Isa 56: 4 To the e who keep my sabbaths,
Mt 19:12 made themselves e for the sake of the

EUPHRATES
Gen 2:14 And the fourth river is the E.
15:18 Egypt to the great river, the river E,
Rev 16:12 poured his bowl on the great river E

EUTYCHUS*
Acts 20: 9 A young man named E,

EVANGELIST* → EVANGELISTS
Acts 21: 8 went into the house of Philip the e,
2 Tim 4: 5 do the work of an e, carry out your

EVANGELISTS* → EVANGELIST
Eph 4:11 some e, some pastors and teachers,

EVE*
Gen 3:20 The man named his wife E,
4: 1 Now the man knew his wife E,
Tob 8: 6 his wife E as a helper and support.
2 Cor 11: 3 afraid that as the serpent deceived E
1 Tim 2:13 For Adam was formed first, then E;

EVENING
Gen 1: 5 there was e and there was morning,
Eccl 11: 6 at e do not let your hands be idle;
Zech 14: 7 for at e time there shall be light.

EVERLASTING → LAST
Gen 9:16 remember the e covenant between
Ps 90: 2 from e to e you are God.
Isa 9: 6 God, E Father, Prince of Peace.
40:28 The LORD is the e God,
Jer 31: 3 I have loved you with an e love;
Dan 4: 3 His kingdom is an e kingdom,

EVERY → EVERYTHING
Gen 7:23 He blotted out e living thing that
Ex 11: 5 E firstborn in the land of Egypt
Deut 8: 3 e word that comes from the mouth
Eccl 12:14 God will bring e deed into judgment
Isa 45:23 "To me e knee shall bow,
Mt 12:25 "E kingdom divided against itself
Rom 14:11 e knee shall bow to me, and e tongue
Phil 2:10 at the name of Jesus e knee should
2 Tim 3:17 equipped for e good work.
1 Jn 4: 1 Beloved, do not believe e spirit,
Rev 21: 4 he will wipe e tear from their eyes.

EVERYTHING → EVERY
Gen 1:31 God saw e that he had made,
Ex 19: 8 "E that the LORD has spoken we will
Eccl 3: 1 For e there is a season,
1 Cor 10:31 do e for the glory of God.
1 Tim 4: 4 For e created by God is good,
2 Pet 1: 3 divine power has given us e needed

EVIDENCE
Deut 17: 6 On the e of two or three witnesses
Dan 13:43 men have given false e against me.
Mt 18:16 by the e of two or three witnesses.

EVIL → EVILDOER, EVILDOERS
Gen 2: 9 tree of the knowledge of good and e.
3: 5 be like God, knowing good and e."
6: 5 their hearts was only e continually.
Ex 32:22 the people, that they are bent on e.
Deut 13: 5 So you shall purge the e from your
Judg 2:11 Then the Israelites did what was e
Tob 12: 7 Do good and e will not overtake
Ps 23: 4 the darkest valley, I fear no e;
Prov 8:13 The fear of the LORD is hatred of e.
Eccl 12:14 secret thing, whether good or e.
Sir 7: 1 Do no e, and e will never overtake
Isa 5:20 you who call e good and good e,
Mt 6:13 but rescue us from the e one.
12:35 e person brings e things out of an e
Lk 6:35 who are e, know how to give good
Jn 17:15 to protect them from the e one.
Rom 12:17 Do not repay anyone e for e,
Eph 5:16 of the time, because the days are e.
1 Tim 6:10 of money is a root of all kinds of e,
1 Pet 2:16 use your freedom as a pretext for e,
1 Jn 5:18 and the e one does not touch them.
2 Jn 1:11 to welcome is to participate in the e
3 Jn 1:11 do not imitate what is e but imitate

EVILDOER → EVIL
Ps 52: 6 and will laugh at the e, saying,
Mt 5:39 But I say to you, Do not resist an e.

EVILDOERS → EVIL
2 Sam 7:10 and e shall afflict them no more,
Ps 34:16 The face of the LORD is against e,
Lk 13:27 go away from me, all you e!'

1 Pet 2:12 though they malign you as **e**,

EXALT → EXALTED, EXALTS
Ex 15: 2 my father's God, and I will **e** him.
Prov 4: 8 Prize her highly, and she will **e** you;
Isa 25: 1 I will **e** you, I will praise your name;
Lk 14:11 who **e** themselves will be humbled,
Jas 4:10 before the Lord, and he will **e** you.

EXALTED → EXALT
Ps 57: 5 Be **e**, O God, above the heavens.
97: 9 you are far above all gods.
Isa 2:11 the LORD alone will be **e** in that day.
Phil 2: 9 highly **e** him and gave him the name

EXALTS → EXALT
Prov 14:34 Righteousness **e** a nation,
Sir 7:11 for there is One who humbles and **e**.

EXAMINE
Sir 18:20 Before judgment comes, **e** yourself;
1 Cor 11:28 **E** yourselves, and only then eat of
2 Cor 13: 5 **E** yourselves to see whether you

EXAMPLE → EXAMPLES
Jn 13:15 For I have set you an **e**,
Phil 3:17 according to the **e** you have in us.

EXAMPLES → EXAMPLE
1 Cor 10: 6 these things occurred as **e** for us,
1 Pet 5: 3 but be **e** to the flock.

EXCEL → EXCELLENCE, EXCELLENT
Sir 33:23 **E** in all that you do;
1 Cor 14:12 strive to **e** in them for building up

EXCELLENCE → EXCEL
Phil 4: 8 if there is any **e** and if there is

EXCELLENT → EXCEL
Isa 28:29 in counsel, and **e** in wisdom.
1 Cor 12:31 I will show you a still more **e** way.
Heb 1: 4 the name he has inherited is more **e**

EXCEPT
2 Sam 22:32 And who is a rock, **e** our God?
Mt 11:27 no one knows the Son **e** the Father,
Lk 11:29 be given to it **e** the sign of Jonah.
Jn 14: 6 No one comes to the Father **e**

EXCHANGED
Ps 106:20 They **e** the glory of God for the
Rom 1:23 **e** the glory of the immortal God

EXCUSE
Jn 15:22 but now they have no **e** for their sin.
Rom 1:20 So they are without **e**;

EXHORT
Titus 2:15 **e** and reprove with all authority.
Heb 3:13 But **e** one another every day,

EXILE → EXILES
2 Kings 25:11 carried into **e** the rest of the people
Ezra 6:21 of Israel who had returned from **e**,

EXILES → EXILE
1 Pet 2:11 I urge you as aliens and **e**

EXIST → EXISTED, EXISTS
1 Cor 8: 6 are all things and for whom we **e**,
Heb 2:10 and through whom all things **e**,

EXISTED → EXIST
2 Pet 3: 5 the word of God heavens **e** long ago
Rev 4:11 by your will they **e** and were created

EXISTS → EXIST
Ps 119:89 The LORD **e** forever;
Heb 11: 6 that he **e** and that he rewards those

EXPECTING
Lk 6:35 and lend, **e** nothing in return.
Phil 3:20 that we are **e** a Savior,

EXPLAIN → EXPLAINED, EXPLAINING
2 Chr 9: 2 Solomon that he could not **e** to her.
Dan 5:12 to interpret dreams, **e** riddles,

EXPLAINED → EXPLAIN
Mk 4:34 but he **e** everything in private to his

EXPLAINING → EXPLAIN
2 Tim 2:15 rightly **e** the word of truth.

EXPOSE → EXPOSED
Mt 1:19 unwilling to **e** her to public disgrace
Eph 5:11 of darkness, but instead **e** them.

EXPOSED → EXPOSE
Jn 3:20 so that their deeds may not be **e**.
Eph 5:13 everything **e** by the light becomes
Heb 10:33 sometimes being publicly **e** to abuse

EYE → EYES, EYEWITNESSES
Ex 21:24 **e** for **e**, tooth for tooth,
Ps 17: 8 Guard me as the apple of the **e**;
Mt 5:29 If your right **e** causes you to sin,
5:38 An **e** for an **e** and a tooth for a tooth.
7: 3 see the speck in your neighbor's **e**,
Mk 10:25 to go through the **e** of a needle
1 Cor 15:52 in the twinkling of an **e**, at the last
Rev 1: 7 the clouds; every **e** will see him,

EYES → EYE
Gen 3: 7 Then the **e** of both were opened,
Deut 29: 4 or **e** to see, or ears to hear.
2 Chr 16: 9 **e** of the LORD range throughout the
Ps 121: 1 I lift up my **e** to the hills—
Prov 3: 7 Do not be wise in your own **e**;
22:12 The **e** of the LORD keep watch over
Isa 11: 3 He shall not judge by what his **e** see,
Jer 9: 1 and my **e** a fountain of tears,
Ezek 1:18 rims of all four were full of **e** all
Dan 10: 6 lightning, his **e** like flaming torches,
Zech 4:10 "These seven are the **e** of the LORD,
Mt 9:30 And their **e** were opened.
13:15 that they might not look with their **e**,
Lk 24:31 their **e** were opened, and they
Eph 1:18 with the **e** of your heart enlightened,
1 Pet 3:12 **e** of the Lord are on the righteous,
1 Jn 2:16 of the flesh, the desire of the **e**,
Rev 1:14 his **e** were like a flame of fire,
4: 6 full of **e** in front and behind:
21: 4 he will wipe every tear from their **e**.

EYEWITNESSES* → EYE, WITNESS
Lk 1: 2 who from the beginning were **e**
2 Pet 1:16 but we had been **e** of his majesty.

EZEKIEL
Priest called to be prophet to the exiles (Ezek 1-3; Sir 49:8). Symbolically acted out destruction of Jerusalem (Ezek 4-5; 12; 24).

EZRA
Priest and teacher of the Law who led a return of exiles to Israel to reestablish temple and worship (Ezra 7-8). Corrected intermarriage of priests (Ezra 9-10). Read Law at celebration of Feast of Tabernacles (Neh 8). Participated in dedication of Jerusalem's walls (Neh 12).

F

FACE → FACES
Gen 1: 2 darkness covered the **f** of the deep,
32:30 saying, "For I have seen God **f** to **f**,
Ex 3: 6 Moses hid his **f**, for he was afraid to
34:30 the skin of his **f** was shining,
Num 6:25 LORD make his **f** to shine upon you,
12: 8 With him I speak **f** to **f**—
Ps 4: 6 Let the light of your **f** shine on us,
Isa 54: 8 wrath for a moment I hid my **f**
Ezek 39:29 I will never again hide my **f** from
Lk 9:29 the appearance of his **f** changed,
2 Cor 3: 7 not gaze at Moses' **f** because of the glory
Rev 1:16 his **f** was like the sun shining with

FACES → FACE
Ezek 1: 6 Each had four **f**, and each
2 Cor 3:18 And all of us, with unveiled **f**,
Rev 9: 7 their **f** were like human **f**,

FACTIONS*
1 Cor 11:19 there have to be **f** among you,
Gal 5:20 anger, quarrels, dissensions, **f**,

FADE → FADES
Ps 37: 2 for they will soon **f** like the grass,

Isa 64: 6 We all f like a leaf,

FADES → FADE
Isa 40: 7 The grass withers, the flower f,
1 Pet 5: 4 crown of glory that never f away.

FAIL → FAILED
Deut 31: 6 he will not f you or forsake you."
Josh 1: 5 I will not f you or forsake you.
Ezek 47:12 will not wither nor their fruit f,
Mk 8:18 Do you have eyes, and f to see?

FAILED → FAIL
Josh 23:14 pass for you, not one of them has f.
1 Kings 8:56 not one word has f of all his good
Rom 9: 6 not as though the word of God had f

FAINT
Ps 142: 3 When my spirit is f, you know my
Isa 40:31 they shall walk and not f.

FAITH → FAITHFUL, FAITHFULNESS, FAITHLESS
Ps 146: 6 in them; who keeps f forever;
Sir 40:12 but good f will last forever.
Isa 7: 9 If you do not stand firm in f,
Hab 2: 4 but the righteous live by their f.
Mt 17:20 have f the size of a mustard seed,
Mk 2: 5 When Jesus saw their f, he said to
Lk 7:50 the woman, "Your f has saved you;
18: 8 comes, will he find f on earth?"
Acts 3:16 and the f that is through Jesus
Rom 1:17 one who is righteous will live by f."
3:28 that a person is justified by f apart
1 Cor 13:13 And now f, hope, and love abide,
Gal 3:11 one who is righteous will live by f."
5: 6 only thing that counts is f working
Eph 4: 5 one Lord, one f, one baptism,
Phil 3: 9 righteousness from God based on f.
1 Tim 6:11 pursue righteousness, godliness, f,
2 Tim 4: 7 finished the race, I have kept the f.
Heb 11: 1 f is the assurance of things hoped
12: 2 the pioneer and perfecter of our f,
Jas 2:17 f by itself, if it has no works, is dead
2:24 by works and not by f alone
2 Pet 1: 1 a f as precious as ours through the
1 Jn 5: 4 that conquers the world, our f.
Jude 1: 3 the f that was once for all entrusted
Rev 2:13 and you did not deny your f in me

FAITHFUL → FAITH
Deut 32: 4 A f God, without deceit, just and
Ps 4: 3 Lord has set apart the f for himself;
116:15 is the death of his f ones.
Wis 3: 9 the f will abide with him in love,
Sir 4:16 If they remain f, they will inherit
Mic 7: 2 The f have disappeared from the
Zech 8: 3 Jerusalem shall be called the f city,
Mt 24:45 "Who then is the f and wise slave,
1 Cor 10:13 God is f, and he will not let you be
1 Thess 5:24 The one who calls you is f,
Heb 10:23 for he who has promised is f.
1 Pet 4:19 to a f Creator,
1 Jn 1: 9 is f and just will forgive us our sins
Rev 1: 5 f witness, the firstborn of the dead,
19:11 Its rider is called F and True,

FAITHFULNESS → FAITH
Ex 34: 6 abounding in steadfast love and f,
Josh 24:14 and serve him in sincerity and in f;
Ps 26: 3 and I walk in f to you.
36: 5 to the heavens, your f to the clouds.
Prov 16: 6 By loyalty and f iniquity is atoned
Isa 11: 5 and f the belt around his loins.
Jer 31: 3 I have continued my f to you.
Lam 3:23 new every morning; great is your f.
Hos 4: 1 There is no f or loyalty, and no
Rom 3: 3 faithlessness nullify the f of God?
Gal 5:22 patience, kindness, generosity, f,

FAITHLESS → FAITH
Jer 3:14 Return, O f children, says the Lord,
Mt 17:17 "You f and perverse generation,
2 Tim 2:13 if we are f, he remains faithful—
Rev 21: 8 But as for the cowardly, the f,

FALL → FALLEN, FALLING, FELL
Ps 91: 7 A thousand may f at your side,
Prov 16:18 and a haughty spirit before a f.
Sir 28:23 Those who forsake the Lord will f
Lk 10:18 "I watched Satan f from heaven like
Rom 9:33 a rock that will make them f,
1 Cor 10:12 watch out that you do not f.
Heb 10:31 a fearful thing to f into the hands of

FALLEN → FALL
2 Sam 1:19 How the mighty have f!
Isa 14:12 f from heaven, O Day Star,
21: 9 he responded, "F, f is Babylon;
Rev 9: 1 I saw a star that had f from heaven
18: 2 "F, f is Babylon the great!

FALLING → FALL
Lk 22:44 ⟦ like great drops of blood f down⟧
Jude 1:24 him who is able to keep you from f,

FALSE
Deut 5:20 Neither shall you bear f witness
2 Kings 17:15 went after f idols and became f;
Bar 6: 8 but they are f and cannot speak.
Dan 13:61 convicted them of bearing f witness;
Mt 7:15 "Beware of f prophets, who come to
Mk 13:22 F messiahs and f prophets will
Heb 6:18 impossible that God would prove f,
2 Pet 2: 1 there will be f teachers among you,
Rev 16:13 and from the mouth of the f prophet.
20:10 where the beast and the f prophet

FAMILIES → FAMILY
Acts 3:25 all the f of the earth shall be blessed.
Titus 1:11 are upsetting whole f by teaching

FAMILY → FAMILIES
Prov 6:19 and one who sows discord in a f.
Gal 6:10 especially for those of the f of faith.
Eph 3:15 from whom every f in heaven and
1 Pet 2:17 Love the f of believers.

FAMINE
Gen 12:10 Now there was a f in the land.
41:27 They are seven years of f.
Ruth 1: 1 there was a f in the land,
Ps 37:19 in the days of f they have abundance
Am 8:11 not a f of bread, or a thirst for water,
Acts 11:28 there would be a severe f over all
Rom 8:35 or distress, or persecution, or f,

FAR
Num 16: 3 "You have gone too f!
1 Sam 7:12 "Thus f the Lord has helped us."
Isa 57:19 Peace, peace, to the f and the near,
Jer 23:23 and not a God f off?
Mk 7: 6 but their hearts are f from me;
12:34 are not f from the kingdom of God."

FAST → FASTED, FASTING
Isa 58: 5 Is such the f that I choose,
Mt 6:16 "And whenever you f,
Lk 18:12 I f twice a week; I give

FASTED → FAST
Mt 4: 2 He f forty days and forty nights,

FASTING → FAST
Mt 6:16 so as to show others that they are f.

FATHER → FATHER'S
Gen 2:24 a man leaves his f and his mother
Ex 20:12 Honor your f and your mother,
21:15 Whoever strikes f or mother shall
2 Sam 7:14 I will be a f to him, and he shall be
Ps 89:26 cry to me, 'You are my F, my God,
Prov 28:24 Anyone who robs f or mother and
Wis 2:16 and boasts that God is his f.
Sir 3: 3 who honor their f atone for sins,
Isa 8: 4 child knows how to call "My f" or
9: 6 Mighty God, Everlasting F, Prince
Jer 3:19 I thought you would call me, My F,
Mal 1: 6 If then I am a f, where is the honor
Mt 6: 9 Our F in heaven, hallowed be your
28:19 the name of the F and of the Son and
Lk 18:20 Honor your f and mother.'"
Jn 5:18 but was also calling God his own F,

Jn	8:44	You are from your f the devil,
	14: 6	comes to the F except through me.
Rom	8:15	When we cry, "Abba! F!"
Gal	4: 6	into your hearts, crying, "Abba! F!"
Eph	6: 2	"Honor your f and mother"—
Heb	1: 5	be his F, and he will be my Son"?
	12: 9	to be subject to the F of spirits
Jas	1:17	coming down from the F of lights,
Rev	3: 5	confess your name before my F

FATHER'S → FATHER

Lk	2:49	that I must be in my F house?"
Jn	1:14	the glory as of a f only son,
	2:16	making my F house a marketplace!"
	10:29	can snatch it out of the F hand.
	14: 2	F house there are many dwelling

FAULT

Sir	11: 7	Do not find f before you investigate;
Rom	9:19	"Why then does he still find f?

FAVOR → FAVORED, FAVORITISM

Gen	6: 8	Noah found f in the sight of the
Ex	33:12	you have also found f in my sight.'
Ps	30: 5	his f is for a lifetime.
Isa	49: 8	In a time of f I have answered you,
Zech	11: 7	I named F, the other I named Unity,
Lk	4:19	proclaim the year of the Lord's f."

FAVORED → FAVOR

Lk	1:28	"Greetings, f one! The Lord is with you."

FAVORITISM* → FAVOR

Jas	2: 1	with your acts of f really believe

FEAR → AFRAID, FEARED, FEARFULLY, FEARS

Gen	22:12	for now I know that you f God,
Deut	6:13	The LORD your God you shall f;
Ps	19: 9	the f of the LORD is pure, enduring
	23: 4	the darkest valley, I f no evil;
	27: 1	and my salvation; whom shall I f?
Prov	1: 7	f of the LORD is the beginning of
Eccl	12:13	F God, and keep his commandments
Sir	1:11	The f of the Lord is glory
Mt	10:28	rather f him who can destroy both
Mk	5:36	"Do not f, only believe."
Phil	2:12	work out your own salvation with f
1 Pet	3:14	Do not f what they f,
1 Jn	4:18	but perfect love casts out f;
Rev	14: 7	"F God and give him glory,

FEARED → FEAR

Ex	14:31	the people f the LORD and believed
Job	1: 1	f God and turned away from evil.
Hag	1:12	and the people f the LORD.

FEARFULLY* → FEAR

Ps	139:14	I am f and wonderfully made.

FEARS → FEAR

Jdt	16:16	whoever f the Lord is great forever.
Ps	34: 4	and delivered me from all my f.
Prov	31:30	a woman who f the LORD is to be
Sir	15: 1	Whoever f the Lord will do this,

FED → FEED

Deut	8:16	f you in the wilderness with manna
Ps	80: 5	have f them with the bread of tears,
Ezek	34: 8	but the shepherds have f themselves,

FEED → FED

Isa	40:11	He will f his flock like a shepherd;
	65:25	wolf and the lamb shall f together,
Jn	21:15	Jesus said to him, "F my lambs."
Rom	12:20	"if your enemies are hungry, f them;

FEET → FOOT

Ps	8: 6	you have put all things under their f,
	119:105	Your word is a lamp to my f
Dan	2:33	its f partly of iron and partly of clay.
Mt	22:44	I put your enemies under your f"?
Lk	24:39	Look at my hands and my f;
Jn	12: 3	anointed Jesus' f, and wiped them with her hair.
	13: 5	and began to wash the disciples' f
Rom	16:20	shortly crush Satan under your f.
1 Cor	15:25	put all his enemies under his f.
Heb	1:13	enemies a footstool for your f"?

Rev	1:15	his f were like burnished bronze,

FELLOWSHIP

Acts	2:42	to the apostles' teaching and f,
2 Cor	6:14	Or what f is there between light and
1 Jn	1: 3	and truly our f is with the Father and

FEMALE

Gen	1:27	male and f he created them.
Mk	10: 6	'God made them male and f.'
Gal	3:28	there is no longer male and f;

FESTIVAL → FESTIVALS

Ex	23:14	in the year you shall hold a f for me.
1 Cor	5: 8	Therefore, let us celebrate the f,

FESTIVALS → FESTIVAL

Lev	23: 2	are the appointed f of the LORD
Neh	10:33	the new moons, the appointed f,
Col	2:16	of food and drink or of observing f,

FEVER

Deut	28:22	will afflict you with consumption, f,
Mk	1:30	mother-in-law was in bed with a f,

FEW

Ps	105:12	When they were f in number,
Eccl	5: 2	therefore let your words be f.
Mt	22:14	many are called, but f are chosen."
Lk	13:23	"Lord, will only a f be saved?"

FIELD → FIELDS

Prov	31:16	She considers a f and buys it;
Mt	6:28	Consider the lilies of the f, how
	13:44	is like treasure hidden in a f,
	24:40	Then two will be in the f;
1 Cor	3: 9	you are God's f, God's building.

FIELDS → FIELD

Lk	2: 8	there were shepherds living in the f,
Jn	4:35	see how the f are ripe for harvesting.

FIG → FIGS

Gen	3: 7	and they sewed f leaves together
Hab	3:17	Though the f tree does not blossom,
Mt	24:32	"From the f tree learn its lesson:
Lk	13: 6	"A man had a f tree planted in his

FIGHT → FOUGHT

Ex	14:14	The LORD will f for you,
Ps	35: 1	f against those who f against me!
1 Tim	1:18	you may f the good f,
2 Tim	4: 7	I have fought the good f,

FIGS → FIG

Jer	24: 1	LORD showed me two baskets of f
Lk	6:44	F are not gathered from thorns,

FILL → FILLED, FULL, FULLNESS

Gen	1:28	and f the earth and subdue it;
	9: 1	fruitful and multiply, and f the earth.
Ps	72:19	may his glory f the whole earth.
Jer	23:24	Do I not f heaven and earth?
Eph	4:10	so that he might f all things.)

FILLED → FILL

Ex	1: 7	so that the land was f with them.
	40:34	glory of the LORD f the tabernacle.
1 Kings	8:11	glory of the LORD f the house of the
Ezek	43: 5	the glory of the LORD f the temple.
Lk	1:15	he will be f with the Holy Spirit.
Acts	2: 4	were f with the Holy Spirit and
Eph	5:18	but be f with the Spirit,

FILTHY

Isa	64: 6	righteous deeds are like a f cloth.
Zech	3: 3	Joshua was dressed with f clothes
Rev	22:11	and the f still be f,

FIND → FINDS, FOUND

Num	32:23	and be sure your sin will f you out.
Deut	4:29	you will f him if you search after
Jer	29:13	you search for me, you will f me;
Mt	11:29	and you will f rest for your souls.
	16:25	lose their life for my sake will f it.
Lk	11: 9	search, and you will f;

FINDS → FIND

Prov	8:35	For whoever f me f life and obtains
	18:22	He who f a wife f a good thing,

FINGER

Ex	8:19	"This is the f of God!"
Deut	9:10	tablets written with the f of God;
Mt	23: 4	themselves are unwilling to lift a f
Lk	11:20	if it is by the f of God that I cast out

FINISHED

Gen	2: 2	on the seventh day God f the work
Ex	40:33	So Moses f the work.
Sir	38: 8	God's works will never be f;
Jn	19:30	received the wine, he said, "It is f."

FIRE → FIERY

Ex	3: 2	appeared to him in a flame of f out
	13:21	and in a pillar of f by night, to give
Lev	9:24	F came out from the LORD and
Num	11: 1	the f of the LORD burned against
Deut	4:24	the LORD your God is a devouring f,
1 Kings	19:12	but the LORD was not in the f;
2 Kings	2:11	a chariot of f and horses of f separated
2 Chr	7: 1	f came down from heaven and
Sir	7:17	punishment of the ungodly is f and
Isa	66:24	their f shall not be quenched,
Dan	3:92	walking in the middle of the f,
Zech	2: 5	For I will be a wall of f all around it,
Mal	3: 2	For he is like a refiner's f and like
Mt	3:11	baptize you with the Holy Spirit and f.
Mk	9:43	to go to hell, to the unquenchable f.
Acts	2: 3	Divided tongues, as of f, appeared
1 Cor	3:13	the f will test what sort of work each
Heb	12:29	indeed our God is a consuming f.
Jas	3: 6	And the tongue is a f.
2 Pet	3:10	elements will be dissolved with f,
Rev	20:14	the second death, the lake of f;

FIRM → FIRMLY

Ex	14:13	"Do not be afraid, stand f,
Isa	7: 9	If you do not stand f in faith,
2 Cor	1:24	because you stand f in the faith.
Eph	6:13	having done everything, to stand f.
Heb	3: 6	if we hold f the confidence

FIRMAMENT

Ps	19: 1	and the f proclaims his handiwork.
	150: 1	praise him in his mighty f!

FIRMLY → FIRM

Ps	119:89	your word is f fixed in heaven.
Eccl	12:11	like nails f fixed are the collected

FIRST → FIRSTBORN

Gen	1: 5	and there was morning, the f day.
Num	18:15	The f issue of the womb of all
Prov	8:22	the f of his acts of long ago.
Isa	41: 4	I, the LORD, am f,
Mt	6:33	But strive f for the kingdom of God
Mk	10:31	But many who are f will be last, and the last will be f."
	16: 2	very early on the f day of the week,
Jn	2:11	Jesus did this, the f of his signs,
Acts	11:26	disciples were f called "Christians."
Rom	1:16	to the Jew f and also to the Greek.
1 Cor	15:45	it is written, "The f man, Adam,
1 Thess	4:16	and the dead in Christ will rise f.
1 Jn	4:19	We love because he f loved us.
Rev	1:17	I am the f and the last,
	20: 5	This is the f resurrection.
	21: 1	the f heaven and the f earth

FIRSTBORN → BEAR, FIRST

Ex	4:22	Thus says the LORD: Israel is my f
	12:29	the LORD struck down all the f
	13: 2	Consecrate to me all the f;
Ps	78:51	He struck all the f in Egypt,
Sir	36:17	whom you have named your f,
Zech	12:10	as one weeps over a f.
Lk	2: 7	And she gave birth to her f son and
Col	1:15	invisible God, the f of all creation;
Heb	1: 6	when he brings the f into the world,
Rev	1: 5	faithful witness, the f of the dead,

FISH

Gen	1:26	have dominion over the f of the sea,
Jon	2: 1	his God from the belly of the f,
Mt	7:10	Or if the child asks for a f, will give

Jn	6: 9	has five barley loaves and two f.

FIVE

1 Sam	17:40	chose f smooth stones from the wadi
Mt	14:19	Taking the f loaves and the two fish,
1 Cor	14:19	church I would rather speak f words

FLAME

Ex	3: 2	in a f of fire out of a bush;
Isa	10:17	and his Holy One a f;
Dan	3:49	drove the fiery f out of the furnace,
Rev	19:12	His eyes are like a f of fire,

FLED → FLEE

Ex	2:15	But Moses f from Pharaoh.
1 Sam	19:18	Now David f and escaped;
Mk	14:50	All of them deserted him and f.
Rev	12: 6	the woman f into the wilderness,
	20:11	and the heaven f from his presence,

FLEE → FLED

Ps	11: 1	"F like a bird to the mountains;
	139: 7	where can I f from your presence?
Isa	30:17	A thousand shall f at the threat of
1 Cor	10:14	f from the worship of idols.
Jas	4: 7	Resist the devil, and he will f from

FLESH

Gen	2:23	is bone of my bones and f of my f;
	2:24	and they become one f.
Job	19:26	then in my f I shall see God,
Ezek	36:26	of stone and give you a heart of f.
Mt	16:17	For f and blood has not revealed this
	26:41	but the f is weak."
Jn	1:14	the Word became f and lived among
	3: 6	What is born of the f is f,
Rom	8: 4	to the f but according to the Spirit.
	8:13	live according to the f, you will die;
2 Cor	12: 7	a thorn was given me in the f,
Gal	5:19	Now the works of the f are obvious:
Eph	6:12	not against enemies of blood and f,
1 Pet	1:24	"All f is like grass and all its glory
1 Jn	4: 2	that Jesus Christ has come in the f

FLOCK

Isa	40:11	He will feed his f like a shepherd;
Ezek	34:22	I will save my f, and they shall no
Mt	26:31	the sheep of the f will be scattered.'
Lk	12:32	"Do not be afraid, little f,
Jn	10:16	So there will be one f, one shepherd.
1 Pet	5: 3	but be examples to the f.

FLOGGED

Jn	19: 1	Pilate took Jesus and had him f.
Acts	5:40	the apostles, they had them f.

FLOOD

Gen	7: 7	the ark to escape the waters of the f.
	9:15	waters shall never again become a f
Ps	29:10	The LORD sits enthroned over the f;
Sir	40:10	and on their account the f came.
2 Pet	2: 5	a f on a world of the ungodly;

FLOW → FLOWING, FLOWS

Zech	14: 8	waters shall f out from Jerusalem,
Jn	7:38	'Out of the believer's heart shall f

FLOWER

Isa	40: 7	The grass withers, the f fades,
1 Pet	1:24	The grass withers, and the f falls,

FLOWING → FLOW

Ex	3: 8	a land f with milk and honey,
Josh	5: 6	a land f with milk and honey.
Ezek	47: 1	water was f from below the
Rev	22: 1	f from the throne of God and

FOE

Ex	23:22	and a f to your foes.
Ps	60:11	O grant us help against the f,

FOLLOW → FOLLOWED

Ex	16: 4	whether they will f my instruction
Deut	6:14	Do not f other gods, any of the gods
1 Kings	18:21	If the LORD is God, f him;
Ps	23: 6	mercy shall f me all the days of my
Lk	9:23	take up their cross daily and f me.
Jn	10:27	I know them, and they f me.

Rev   14: 4 these f the Lamb wherever he goes.

FOLLOWED → FOLLOW
Judg 2:12 they f other gods, from among the
Jer   9:14 have stubbornly f their own hearts
Mk   1:18 they left their nets and f him.
Rev 13: 3 the whole earth f the beast.

FOLLY → FOOL
Prov 13:16 but the fool displays f.
       26: 4 not answer fools according to their f
Eccl   2:13 that wisdom excels f as light excels
Mk   7:22 envy, slander, pride, f.

FOOD → FOODS
Gen   1:30 I have given every green plant for f.
        9: 3 thing that lives shall be f for you;
1 Macc 1:63 to die rather than to be defiled by f
Ps 136:25 who gives f to all flesh,
Mt   6:25 Is not life more than f,
Jn   6:55 for my flesh is true f and my blood
1 Cor 8: 8 "F will not bring us close to God."

FOODS → FOOD
Mk   7:19 (Thus he declared all f clean.)
1 Tim 4: 3 and demand abstinence from f,

FOOL → FOLLY, FOOLISH, FOOLISHNESS, FOOLS
Prov 15: 5 A f despises a parent's instruction,
      20: 3 but every f is quick to quarrel.
Mt   5:22 'You f,' you will be liable to the
2 Cor 11:21 I am speaking as a f—I also dare to

FOOLISH → FOOL
Prov 17:25 F children are a grief to their father
Jer   5:21 O f and senseless people,
Mt   7:26 like a f man who built his house
      25: 2 Five of them were f, and five were
1 Cor 1:20 Has not God made f the wisdom of
Gal   3: 1 f Galatians! Who has bewitched
Titus 3: 3 For we ourselves were once f,

FOOLISHNESS → FOOL
1 Cor 1:18 cross is f to those who are perishing,
      3:19 wisdom of this world is f with God.

FOOLS → FOOL
Ps   14: 1 F say in their hearts, "There is no God."
Prov   1: 7 f despise wisdom and instruction.
    10:21 but f die for lack of sense.
Eccl   5: 4 for he has no pleasure in f.
Rom 1:22 Claiming to be wise, they became f;
1 Cor 4:10 We are f for the sake of Christ,

FOOT → FEET, FOOTSTOOL
Ps   91:12 will not dash your f against a stone.
Mt   18: 8 or your f causes you to stumble,
Lk   4:11 not dash your f against a stone.'"

FOOTSTOOL → FOOT
Ps 110: 1 until I make your enemies your f."
Isa 66: 1 is my throne and the earth is my f;
Heb 10:13 until his enemies would be made a f

FORCES
Mt   5:41 and if anyone f you to go one mile,
Eph   6:12 spiritual f of evil in the heavenly

FOREHEAD → FOREHEADS
Ex   13: 9 and as a reminder on your f,
1 Sam 17:49 and struck the Philistine on his f;
Rev 13:16 marked on the right hand or the f,

FOREHEADS → FOREHEAD
Ezek 9: 4 and put a mark on the f of those
Rev 7: 3 of our God with a seal on their f."
    20: 4 not received its mark on their f

FOREIGN → FOREIGNER, FOREIGNERS
Josh 24:23 "Then put away the f gods that are
Ps   81: 9 you shall not bow down to a f god.

FOREIGNER → FOREIGN
Ex 12:43 no f shall eat of it,
1 Cor 14:11 and the speaker a f to me.

FOREIGNERS → FOREIGN
1 Cor 14:21 by the lips of f I will speak to this
Heb 11:13 were strangers and f on the earth,

FOREKNEW* → KNOW
Rom 8:29 whom he f he also predestined to
    11: 2 not rejected his people whom he f.

FORERUNNER* → RUN
Heb 6:20 a f on our behalf, has entered,

FORESEEING* → SEE
Acts 2:31 F this, David spoke of the
Gal   3: 8 f that God would justify the Gentiles

FORESKIN
Gen 17:14 circumcised in the flesh of his f
Deut 10:16 Circumcise, then, the f of your heart

FORETOLD → TELL
Isa 43: 9 and f to us the former things?
Acts 3:18 this way God fulfilled what he had f

FOREVER
Gen 3:22 the tree of life, and eat, and live f"
     6: 3 spirit shall not abide in mortals f,
Ex   3:15 This is my name f, and this my title
2 Sam 7:13 the throne of his kingdom f.
1 Chr 16:15 Remember his covenant f,
Ps   19: 9 fear of the LORD is pure, enduring f;
   110: 4 "You are a priest f according to the
   117: 2 faithfulness of the LORD endures f.
Eccl 3:14 that whatever God does endures f;
Wis 5:15 But the righteous live f,
Isa 40: 8 the word of our God will stand f.
    51: 6 but my salvation will be f,
Jn   6:51 eats of this bread will live f;
    14:16 another Advocate, to be with you f.
Heb 5: 6 "You are a priest f, according to the
    13: 8 the same yesterday and today and f.
1 Pet 1:25 but the word of the Lord endures f."
Rev 1:18 I am alive f and ever;
    11:15 and he will reign f and ever."
    22: 5 and they will reign f and ever.

FORFEIT
Mk 8:36 the whole world and f their life?

FORGAVE → FORGIVE
Ps   32: 5 and you f the guilt of my sin.
    85: 2 You f the iniquity of your people;
Col 2:13 when he f us all our trespasses,

FORGET → FORGOT, FORGOTTEN
Deut 4:23 So be careful not to f the covenant
    6:12 take care that you do not f the LORD,
Ps 137: 5 If I f you, O Jerusalem, let my right
Prov 4: 5 Get wisdom; get insight: do not f,
Isa 49:15 these may f, yet I will not f you.

FORGIVE → FORGAVE, FORGIVEN, FORGIVENESS, FORGIVING
Gen 18:26 f the whole place for their sake."
Ex 32:32 But now, if you will only f their sin
Num 14:20 the LORD said, "I do f,
1 Kings 8:30 your dwelling place; heed and f.
Neh 9:17 But you are a God ready to f,
Ps   79: 9 and f our sins, for your name's sake.
Sir 5: 6 he will f the multitude of my sins,"
Ezek 16:63 when I f you all that you have done,
Dan 9:19 O Lord, hear; O Lord, f;
Mt   6:12 And f us our debts, as we
Lk   5:24 has authority on earth to f sins"—
1 Jn 1: 9 is faithful and just will f us our sins

FORGIVEN → FORGIVE
Lev 4:20 for them, and they shall be f.
Ps   32: 1 are those whose transgression is f,
Mt   6:12 as we also have f our debtors.
    12:31 against the Spirit will not be f.
Mk 2: 9 to the paralytic, 'Your sins are f,'
Acts 2:38 so that your sins may be f;
Rom 4: 7 are those whose iniquities are f,
Eph 4:32 as God in Christ has f you.

FORGIVENESS → FORGIVE
Mk 1: 4 a baptism of repentance for the f
    3:29 against the Holy Spirit can never have f,
Col 1:14 we have redemption, the f of sins.
Heb 9:22 the shedding of blood there is no f

FORGIVING → FORGIVE
Ex	34: 7	f iniquity and transgression and sin,
Ps	86: 5	For you, O Lord, are good and f,
Eph	4:32	f one another, as God in Christ has

FORGOT → FORGET
Deut	32:18	you f the God who gave you birth.
Jer	23:27	just as their ancestors f my name
Bar	4: 8	You f the everlasting God,
Hos	2:13	and went after her lovers, and f me,

FORGOTTEN → FORGET
Ps	77: 9	Has God f to be gracious?
Isa	49:14	forsaken me, my Lord has f me."
Heb	12: 5	And you have f the exhortation

FORM → FORMED, FORMLESS
Ex	20: 4	in the f of anything that is in heaven
Lk	3:22	descended upon him in bodily f

FORMED → FORM
Gen	2: 7	the Lord God f man from the dust
Ps	139:13	you who f my inward parts;
Gal	4:19	until Christ is f in you,

FORMLESS* → FORM
Gen	1: 2	the earth was a f void and darkness
Wis	11:17	created the world out of f matter,

FORNICATION → FORNICATE, FORNICATORS
Mk	7:21	that evil intentions come: f,
1 Cor	6:13	meant not for f but for the Lord,
Gal	5:19	works of the flesh are obvious: f,
Rev	19: 2	who corrupted the earth with her f,

FORNICATOR* → FORNICATION
Sir	23:17	To a f all bread is sweet;
1 Cor	6:18	but the f sins against the body itself.
Eph	5: 5	that no f or impure person,

FORNICATORS → FORNICATION
1 Tim	1:10	f, sodomites, slave traders, liars,
Rev	22:15	and sorcerers and f and murderers

FORSAKE → FORSAKEN
Deut	31: 6	he will not fail you or f you."
Josh	1: 5	I will not fail you or f you.
Jer	17:13	All who f you shall be put to shame;
Heb	13: 5	"I will never leave you or f you."

FORSAKEN → FORSAKE
Ps	9:10	O Lord, have not f those who seek
	22: 1	my God, why have you f me?
Mt	27:46	my God, why have you f me?"
2 Cor	4: 9	persecuted, but not f;

FORTRESS
2 Sam	22: 2	The Lord is my rock, my f, and my
Ps	71: 3	for you are my rock and my f.

FORTUNES
Deut	30: 3	Lord your God will restore your f
Jer	32:44	I will restore their f, says the Lord.

FORTY
Gen	7: 4	rain on the earth for f days and f
Num	14:34	f days, for every day a year,
1 Kings	19: 8	f days and f nights to Horeb
Jon	3: 4	And he cried out, "F days more,
Mt	4: 2	He fasted f days and f nights,
Heb	3:17	with whom was he angry f years?

FOUGHT → FIGHT
Josh	10:42	the Lord God of Israel f for Israel.
2 Tim	4: 7	I have f the good fight,
Rev	12: 7	and his angels f against the dragon.

FOUND → FIND
Isa	55: 6	Seek the Lord while he may be f,
	65: 1	be f by those who did not seek me.
Lk	15:24	he was lost and is f!'
Rom	10:20	f by those who did not seek me;
Rev	20:15	not f written in the book of life was

FOUNDATION → FOUNDATIONS
1 Kings	6:37	f of the house of the Lord was laid,
Ezra	3: 6	f of the temple of the Lord was not
Isa	28:16	See, I am laying in Zion a f stone,
1 Cor	3:11	that f is Jesus Christ.
Eph	2:20	built upon the f of the apostles and

FOUNDATIONS → FOUNDATION
2 Tim	2:19	But God's firm f stands,
Heb	11:10	looked forward to the city that has f,
Rev	21:14	the wall of the city has twelve f,

FOUNTAIN
Ps	36: 9	For with you is the f of life;
Prov	16:22	Wisdom is a f of life to one who
Jer	9: 1	and my eyes a f of tears,
Joel	3:18	a f shall come forth from the house
Zech	13: 1	a f shall be opened for the house of

FOUR
Ezek	1: 5	something like f living creatures.
	10:14	Each one had f faces:
Rev	4: 6	are f living creatures,

FOXES
Judg	15: 4	went and caught three hundred f,
Lk	9:58	Jesus said to him, "F have holes,

FRAGRANCE → FRAGRANT
2 Cor	2:14	spreads in every place the f

FRAGRANT → FRAGRANCE
Ex	25: 6	anointing oil and for the f incense,
Eph	5: 2	a f offering and sacrifice to God.

FRANKINCENSE → INCENSE
Isa	60: 6	They shall bring gold and f,
Mt	2:11	gifts of gold, f, and myrrh.

FREE → FREED, FREEDOM, FREEWILL
Ex	21: 2	in the seventh he shall go out a f
Ps	146: 7	The Lord sets the prisoners f;
Sir	15:14	he left them in the power of their own f choice
Jn	8:32	and the truth will make you f."
Rom	6:23	but the f gift of God is eternal life
1 Cor	9:21	not f from God's law but am under
Gal	3:28	there is no longer slave or f,
Eph	6: 8	whether we are slaves or f.

FREED → FREE
Acts	2:24	having f him from death,
Rev	1: 5	f us from our sins by his blood,

FREEDOM → FREE
2 Cor	3:17	the Spirit of the Lord is, there is f.
Gal	5: 1	For f Christ has set us free.
1 Pet	2:16	not use your f as a pretext for evil.

FREEWILL → FREE, WILL
Ex	35:29	as a f offering to the Lord.
Ps	54: 6	With a f offering I will sacrifice to

FRIEND → FRIENDS, FRIENDSHIP
Ex	33:11	as one speaks to a f.
Prov	17:17	A f loves at all times,
	18:24	but a true f sticks closer than one's
Sir	7:18	Do not exchange a f for money,
Mt	11:19	a f of tax collectors and sinners!'
Jas	2:23	and he was called the f of God.
	4: 4	a f of the world becomes an enemy

FRIENDS → FRIEND
Job	2:11	when Job's three f heard of all
Sir	6:15	Faithful f are beyond price;
Jn	15:13	to lay down one's life for one's f.
	15:15	but I have called you f,

FRIENDSHIP → FRIEND
Ps	25:14	The f of the Lord is for those who
Jas	4: 4	know that f with the world is enmity

FRINGES*
Num	15:38	to make f on the corners of their
Mt	23: 5	phylacteries broad and their f long.

FRUIT → FRUITFUL, FRUITLESS, FRUITS
Gen	3: 6	she took of its f and ate;
Deut	28: 4	Blessed shall be the f of your womb,
Ps	1: 3	which yield their f in its season,
Prov	8:19	My f is better than gold,
Ezek	47:12	will not wither nor their f fail,
Hos	14: 2	and we will offer the f of our lips.
Mt	3: 8	Bear f worthy of repentance.
Lk	1:42	and blessed is the f of your womb.
	6:44	for each tree is known by its own f.

Jn	15: 2	branch that bears f he prunes to make it bear more f.
Gal	5:22	By contrast, the f of the Spirit is love,
Col	1:10	as you bear f in every good work
Heb	13:15	the f of lips that confess his name.
Rev	22: 2	tree of life with its twelve kinds of f,

FRUITFUL → FRUIT

Gen	1:22	Be f and multiply and fill the waters
	9: 1	said to them, "Be f and multiply,
Ex	1: 7	the Israelites were f and prolific;

FRUITS → FRUIT

Ex	23:16	of the first f of your labor,
Prov	3: 9	with the first f of all your produce;
Mt	7:16	You will know them by their f.
Rom	8:23	who have the first f of the Spirit,
1 Cor	15:23	in his own order: Christ the first f,
Rev	14: 4	as first f for God and the Lamb,

FULFILL → FULFILLED, FULFILLING

Ps	20: 5	May the LORD f all your petitions.
Eccl	5: 4	F what you vow.
Mt	5:17	I have come not to abolish but to f.
Gal	6: 2	way you will f the law of Christ.
Jas	2: 8	really f the royal law according to

FULFILLED → FULFILL

Mk	1:15	"The time is f, and the kingdom
Lk	24:44	prophets, and the psalms must be f."
Rom	8: 4	requirement of the law might be f

FULFILLING → FULFILL

Rom	9:31	did not succeed in f that law.
	13:10	love is the f of the law.

FULL → FILL

Sir	42:16	work of the Lord is f of his glory.
Isa	6: 3	the whole earth is f of his glory."
Ezek	10:12	were f of eyes all around.
	37: 1	it was f of bones.
Mt	6:22	your whole body will be f of light;
Jn	1:14	f of grace and truth.
Rev	4: 6	f of eyes in front and behind:

FULLNESS → FILL

Jn	1:16	From his f we have all received,
1 Cor	10:26	"the earth and its f are the Lord's."
Gal	4: 4	But when the f of time had come,
Eph	1:10	as a plan for the f of time,
	3:19	may be filled with all the f of God.
Col	1:19	in him all the f of God was pleased
	2: 9	in him the whole f of deity dwells

FURNACE

Isa	48:10	have tested you in the f of adversity.
Dan	3: 6	be thrown into a f of blazing fire."
	3:49	of the Lord came down into the f
Mt	13:42	will throw them into the f of fire,

FURNITURE

Ex	25: 9	the tabernacle and of all its f,

FURY

Ps	2: 5	and terrify them in his f,
Lam	2: 4	he has poured out his f like fire.
Rom	2: 8	there will be wrath and f.
Rev	16:19	the wine-cup of the f of his wrath.

FUTILE

Rom	1:21	but they became f in their thinking,
1 Cor	3:20	thoughts of the wise, that they are f.

FUTURE

Prov	24:20	for the evil have no f;
Jer	31:17	hope for your f, says the LORD:
1 Cor	3:22	life or death or the present or the f—
1 Tim	6:19	of a good foundation for the f,

G

GABRIEL*
Angel who interpreted Daniel's visions (Dan 8:16-26; 9:20-27); announced births of John (Lk 1:11-20), Jesus (Lk 1:26-38).

GAD
1. Son of Jacob by Zilpah (Gen 30:9-11; 35:26; 1 Chr 2:2). Tribe of blessed (Gen 49:19; Deut 33:20-21), numbered (Num

1:25; 26:18), allotted land east of the Jordan (Num 32; 34:14; Josh 18:7; 22), west (Ezek 48:27-28), 12,000 from (Rev 7:5).
2. Prophet; seer of David (1 Sam 22:5; 2 Sam 24:11-19; 1 Chr 29:29).

GAIN

Eccl	1: 3	What do people g from all the toil
Lk	9:25	if they g the whole world,
Phil	1:21	living is Christ and dying is g.
	3: 8	in order that I may g Christ
1 Tim	6: 5	that godliness is a means of g.

GALILEAN → GALILEE

Mt	26:69	"You also were with Jesus the G."

GALILEANS → GALILEE

Acts	2: 7	not all these who are speaking G?

GALILEE → GALILEAN, GALILEANS

Isa	9: 1	beyond the Jordan, G of the nations.
Mt	4:15	across the Jordan, G of the Gentiles
Jn	7:41	the Messiah does not come from G,

GAMALIEL
Pharisee (Acts 5:34-39), teacher of Paul (Acts 22:5).

GARDEN

Gen	2: 8	the LORD God planted a g in Eden,
Ezek	28:13	You were in Eden, the g of God;
Jn	19:41	and in the g there was a new tomb

GARMENT → GARMENTS

Gen	39:12	she caught hold of his g,
Deut	22: 5	nor shall a man put on a woman's g;
Ps	102:26	they will all wear out like a g.
Lk	5:36	a new g and sews it on an old g;

GARMENTS → GARMENT

Gen	3:21	the LORD God made g of skins for
Isa	61:10	clothed me with the g of salvation,

GATE → GATES

Mt	7:13	"Enter through the narrow g;
Jn	10: 7	I am the g for the sheep.
Heb	13:12	Jesus also suffered outside the city g

GATES → GATE

Gen	24:60	offspring gain possession of the g
Deut	6: 9	of your house and on your g.
Ps	100: 4	Enter his g with thanksgiving,
Mt	16:18	and the g of Hades will not prevail
Rev	21:21	And the twelve g are twelve pearls,

GATH

1 Sam	17: 4	Goliath, of G, whose height was six
2 Sam	1:20	Tell it not in G, proclaim it not in

GATHER → GATHERED, INGATHERING

Ex	16: 4	and g enough for that day.
Ruth	2: 7	and g among the sheaves behind
Isa	11:12	and g the dispersed of Judah from
Mt	12:30	does not g with me scatters.
Lk	13:34	to g your children together as
Eph	1:10	to g up all things in him,

GATHERED → GATHER

Mt	18:20	two or three are g in my name,
2 Thess	2: 1	Christ and our being g together
Rev	14:19	and g the vintage of the earth,

GAVE → GIVE

Gen	28: 4	land that God g to Abraham."
Ex	31:18	he g him the two tablets of the
1 Kings	4:29	God g Solomon very great wisdom,
Neh	9:15	you g them bread from heaven,
Eccl	12: 7	the breath returns to God who g it.
Mt	25:35	for I was hungry and you g me food,
Jn	1:12	g power to become children of God,
	3:16	loved the world that he g his only Son,
Rom	8:32	but g him up for all of us,
Eph	4:11	The gifts he g were that some would
1 Tim	2: 6	who g himself a ransom

GEDALIAH
Governor of Judah (2 Kings 25:22-26; Jer 39-41).

GEHAZI*
Servant of Elisha (2 Kings 4:12-5:27; 8:4-5).

GENEALOGIES → GENEALOGY
1 Chr 9: 1 So all Israel was enrolled by g;
Neh 7:64 among those enrolled in the g,

GENEALOGY → GENEALOGIES
Mt 1: 1 of the g of Jesus the Messiah,

GENERATION → GENERATIONS
Gen 15:16 come back here in the fourth g;
Ex 20: 6 steadfast love to the thousandth g
34: 7 to the third and the fourth g."
Dan 4:34 his kingdom endures from g to g.
Mt 12:39 evil and adulterous g asks for a sign,
Lk 21:32 this g will not pass away

GENERATIONS → GENERATION
Isa 51: 8 and my salvation to all g.
Lk 1:48 now on all g will call me blessed;

GENEROSITY → GENEROUS
Rom 12: 8 the giver, in g;
Gal 5:22 joy, peace, patience, kindness, g,

GENEROUS → GENEROSITY
Rom 10:12 and is g to all who call on him.
Jas 1:17 Every g act of giving,

GENTILE → GENTILES
1 Macc 1:14 according to G custom,
Mt 18:17 as a G and a tax collector.
Gal 2:14 live like a G and not like a Jew,

GENTILES → GENTILE
Tob 1:11 from eating the food of the G.
1 Macc 1:11 and make a covenant with the G
Lk 21:24 until the times of the G are fulfilled.
Acts 15:19 those G who are turning to God,
Rom 3:29 Is he not the God of G also?
Gal 3: 8 God would justify the G by faith,
Eph 4:17 must no longer live as the G live,

GENTLE → GENTLENESS
Prov 15: 4 A g tongue is a tree of life,
Mt 11:29 for I am g and humble in heart,
1 Pet 3: 4 with the lasting beauty of a g

GENTLENESS → GENTLE
Gal 5:23 g, and self-control. There is no law
Phil 4: 5 Let your g be known to everyone.
1 Tim 6:11 godliness, faith, love, endurance, g.

GETHSEMANE
Mk 14:32 They went to a place called G;

GHOST
Mt 14:26 were terrified, saying, "It is a g!"
Lk 24:39 for a g does not have flesh and

GIANT → GIANTS
Sir 47: 4 In his youth did he not kill a g,

GIANTS → GIANT
1 Chr 20: 4 was one of the descendants of the g;
Sir 16: 7 He did not forgive the ancient g

GIBEON
Josh 10:12 "Sun, stand still at G, and Moon, in
1 Kings 3: 5 G the LORD appeared to Solomon

GIDEON → =JERUBBAAL
Judge, also called Jerubbaal; freed Israel from Midianites (Judg 6-8; Heb 11:32). The fleece (Judg 8:36-40).

GIFT → GIFTS
Num 18: 7 I give your priesthood as a g;
Eccl 5:19 this is the g of God.
Mt 5:23 So when you are offering your g at
Jn 4:10 "If you knew the g of God,
Acts 2:38 will receive the g of the Holy Spirit.
Rom 6:23 but the free g of God is eternal life
1 Cor 7: 7 each has a particular g from God,
Jas 1:17 with every perfect g, is from above,
Rev 21: 6 the thirsty I will give water as a g

GIFTS → GIFT
Deut 12: 6 and your donations, your votive g,
Sir 32:13 who fills you with his good g.
Mt 2:11 offered him g of gold, frankincense,
Lk 11:13 how to give good g to your children,
Rom 11:29 for the g and the calling of God are

1 Cor 12: 1 Now concerning spiritual g,
14: 1 and strive for the spiritual g,
Eph 4: 8 he gave g to his people."
4:11 The g he gave were that some would be apostles,

GILGAL
Josh 5: 9 so that place is called G to this day.
1 Sam 7:16 a circuit year by year to Bethel, G,

GIRL
Ex 1:16 but if it is a g, she shall live."
Mk 5:41 which means, "Little g, get up!"

GIVE → GAVE, GIVEN, GIVER, GIVES
Gen 9: 3 the green plants, I g you everything.
12: 7 your offspring I will g this land."
1 Kings 3: 5 said, "Ask what I should g you."
Tob 12: 9 who g alms enjoy a full life,
Prov 25:21 If your enemies are hungry, g them
30:15 leech has two daughters; "G, g,"
Sir 7:10 do not neglect to g alms.
Ezek 36:26 A new heart I will g you,
Mt 6:11 G us this day our daily bread.
7: 6 "Do not g what is holy to dogs;
Mk 10:45 to g his life a ransom for many."
Jn 10:28 I g them eternal life, and they will
Acts 20:35 more blessed to g than to receive.'"

GIVEN → GIVE
Sir 35:12 Give to the Most High as he has g
Mt 7: 7 "Ask, and it will be g you;
Mk 4:25 to those who have, more will be g;
Lk 22:19 "This is my body, which is g for
Rom 5: 5 the Holy Spirit that has been g to us.

GIVER → GIVE
Rom 12: 8 the g, in generosity;
2 Cor 9: 7 for God loves a cheerful g.

GIVES → GIVE
2 Cor 3: 6 the letter kills, but the Spirit g life.
Jas 4: 6 But he g all the more grace;

GLAD → GLADNESS
Ps 16: 9 Therefore my heart is g, and my
90:15 Make us g as many days as you
Prov 10: 1 A wise child makes a g father,
Mt 5:12 and be g, for your reward is great in
Acts 2:26 heart was g, and my tongue rejoiced

GLADNESS → GLAD
Ps 100: 2 Worship the LORD with g;
Prov 10:28 The hope of the righteous ends in g,
Isa 16:10 Joy and g are taken away from the
Jer 31:13 and give them g for sorrow.
Zeph 3:17 he will rejoice over you with g,
Heb 1: 9 has anointed you with the oil of g

GLASS
Rev 4: 6 there is something like a sea of g,
21:18 the city is pure gold, clear as g.

GLEAN
Deut 24:21 do not g what is left;
Ruth 2: 2 Let me go to the field and g among

GLOOM
Isa 9: 1 there will be no g for those who
Joel 2: 2 a day of darkness and g,
Heb 12:18 and darkness, and g, and a tempest,

GLORIFIED → GLORY
Lev 10: 3 before all the people I will be g.'"
Jn 13:31 "Now the Son of Man has been g,
17: 4 g you on earth by finishing the work
Acts 3:13 has g his servant Jesus,
Rom 8:30 those whom he justified he also g.

GLORIFY → GLORY
Ps 86:12 and I will g your name forever.
Sir 43:30 G the Lord and exalt him as much
Jn 17: 1 g your Son so that the Son may g you,
1 Cor 6:20 therefore g God in your body.
2 Cor 9:13 you g God by your obedience to
Rev 15: 4 who will not fear and g your name?

GLORIOUS → GLORY
Jdt 16:13 O Lord, you are great and g,
Dan 3:26 and g is your name forever!

Jas	2: 1	in our **g** Lord Jesus Christ?

GLORY → GLORIFIED, GLORIFY, GLORIOUS

Ex	24:16	The **g** of the LORD settled on Mount
	33:18	Moses said, "Show me your **g**,
	40:34	**g** of the LORD filled the tabernacle.
1 Sam	4:21	"The **g** has departed from Israel,"
1 Kings	8:11	**g** of the LORD filled the house of the
1 Macc	1:40	dishonor now grew as great as her **g**
Ps	8: 5	crowned them with **g** and honor.
	19: 1	heavens are telling the **g** of God;
	24: 7	that the King of **g** may come in.
Sir	1:11	The fear of the Lord is **g** and
Isa	6: 3	the whole earth is full of his **g**."
	40: 5	the **g** of the LORD shall be revealed,
Bar	5: 4	"Righteous Peace, Godly **G**."
Ezek	11:23	**g** of the LORD ascended from the
	44: 4	**g** of the LORD filled the temple of
Hos	4: 7	they changed their **g** into shame.
Mt	25:31	the Son of Man comes in his **g**,
Lk	2:14	"**G** to God in the highest heaven,
Jn	1:14	and we have seen his **g**,
	12:41	Isaiah said this because he saw his **g**
Rom	3:23	sinned and fall short of the **g** of God;
	8:18	not worth comparing with the **g**
	9: 4	the **g**, the covenants, the giving of
1 Cor	10:31	do everything for the **g** of God.
2 Cor	4:17	for an eternal weight of **g** beyond
Heb	1: 3	reflection of God's **g** and the exact
2 Pet	1:17	conveyed to him by the Majestic **G**,
Rev	4:11	to receive **g** and honor and power,
	21:23	for the **g** of God is its light,

GLUTTON

Prov	23:21	and the **g** will come to poverty,
Mt	11:19	they say, 'Look, a **g** and a drunkard,

GNASHING

Mt	8:12	will be weeping and **g** of teeth."
	25:30	will be weeping and **g** of teeth.'

GNAT*

Mt	23:24	strain out a **g** but swallow a camel!

GO

Ex	5: 1	the God of Israel, 'Let my people **g**,
Josh	1: 9	God is with you wherever you **g**."
Ruth	1:16	Where you **g**, I will **g**;
Mt	28:19	**G** therefore and make disciples of
Jn	14: 3	if I **g** and prepare a place for you,

GOAT → GOATS

Lev	16: 9	Aaron shall present the **g** on which
Dan	8:21	The male **g** is the king of Greece,

GOATS → GOAT

Ps	50:13	or drink the blood of **g**?
Mt	25:32	separates the sheep from the **g**,
Heb	10: 4	for the blood of bulls and **g**

***GOD** → GOD'S, GODDESS, GODLESS, GODLINESS, GODLY, GODS

Gen	1: 1	In the beginning when **G** created
	1:27	So **G** created humankind in his image,
	3: 5	be like **G**, knowing good and evil."
	6: 2	sons of **G** saw that they were fair;
	17: 1	and said to him, "I am **G** Almighty;
Ex	3: 4	**G** called to him out of the bush,
	15: 2	this is my **G**, and I will praise him,
	20: 5	I the LORD your **G** am a jealous **G**,
	34: 6	a **G** merciful and gracious, slow to
Num	23:19	**G** is not a human being,
Deut	4: 7	a **g** so near to it as the LORD our **G**
	6: 5	love the LORD your **G** with all your
Josh	22:34	between us that the LORD is **G**."
1 Sam	2: 2	there is no Rock like our **G**.
1 Kings	8:27	will **G** indeed dwell on the earth?
	18:24	the **g** who answers by fire is indeed **G**.
2 Kings	17: 7	sinned against the LORD their **G**,
2 Chr	2: 5	for our **G** is greater than other gods.
Ezra	6:16	the dedication of this house of **G**
Neh	8:18	read from the book of the law of **G**.
Tob	4:19	At all times bless the Lord **G**,
Ps	19: 1	heavens are telling the glory of **G**;
	22: 1	My **G**, my **G**, why have you forsaken

Ps	46: 1	**G** is our refuge and strength,
	46:10	"Be still, and know that I am **G**!
	47: 7	For **G** is the king of all the earth;
	53: 1	Fools say in their hearts, "There is no **G**."
	68:20	Our **G** is a **G** of salvation,
	90: 2	everlasting to everlasting you are **G**.
	136: 2	O give thanks to the **G** of gods,
	145: 1	I will extol you, my **G** and King,
Eccl	12:13	Fear **G**, and keep his
Sir	32:14	seeks **G** will accept his discipline,
Isa	9: 6	Wonderful Counselor, Mighty **G**,
	12: 2	Surely **G** is my salvation;
	40:28	The LORD is the everlasting **G**,
	44: 6	besides me there is no **g**.
Jer	10:10	But the LORD is the true **G**;
Bar	4: 8	You forgot the everlasting **G**,
Ezek	28: 2	proud and you have said, "I am a **g**;
Dan	14: 4	But Daniel worshiped his own **G**.
Hos	12: 6	But as for you, return to your **G**,
Am	4:12	prepare to meet your **G**,
Mic	6: 8	and to walk humbly with your **G**?
Hab	3:18	I will exult in the **G** of my salvation.
Mal	2:10	Has not one **G** created us?
Mt	1:23	which means, "**G** is with us."
	4: 4	that comes from the mouth of **G**.'"
	4: 7	not put the Lord your **G** to the test.'
	4:10	written, 'Worship the Lord your **G**,
	6:24	You cannot serve **G** and wealth.
	27:40	If you are the Son of **G**,
Mk	1: 1	news of Jesus Christ, the Son of **G**.
	2: 7	Who can forgive sins but **G** alone?"
	10: 9	what **G** has joined together, let no
	12:30	the Lord your **G** with all your heart,
Lk	2:14	"Glory to **G** in the highest heaven,
	18:19	No one is good but **G** alone.
	22:70	"Are you, then, the Son of **G**?"
Jn	1: 1	was with **G**, and the Word was **G**.
	1:18	It is **G** the only Son,
	3:16	**G** so loved the world that he gave his only Son,
	5:18	calling his own Father, thereby making himself equal to **G**.
	20:28	"My Lord and my **G**!"
Acts	5:29	"We must obey **G** rather than any
Rom	4: 3	"Abraham believed **G**, and it was
	6:23	gift of **G** is eternal life in Christ
	8:31	If **G** is for us, who is against us?
1 Cor	10:31	do everything for the glory of **G**.
2 Cor	4: 4	Christ, who is the image of **G**.
	6:16	we are the temple of the living **G**;
Eph	4: 6	one **G** and Father of all,
Phil	2: 6	though he was in the form of **G**,
Col	1:19	fullness of **G** was pleased to dwell,
Titus	2:13	of our great **G** and Savior, Jesus
Heb	4:12	the word of **G** is living and active,
	10:31	to fall into the hands of the living **G**.
	12:29	indeed our **G** is a consuming fire.
Jas	2:23	"Abraham believed **G**,
	4: 8	Draw near to **G**, and he will draw
1 Jn	1: 5	**G** is light and in him there is no
	4:16	**G** is love, and those who abide
	5: 2	love **G** and obey his commandments
Jude	1:21	keep yourselves in the love of **G**;
Rev	4: 8	"Holy, holy, holy, the Lord **G**
	19:13	his name is called The Word of **G**.
	22: 5	for the Lord **G** will be their light,

†GOD [= Yahweh] → †LORD

Gen	15: 2	But Abram said, "O Lord **G**,
2 Sam	7:18	"Who am I, O Lord **G**,
Isa	25: 8	Lord **G** will wipe away the tears
	61: 1	The spirit of the Lord **G** is upon me,

GOD'S → *GOD

Mt	27:43	for he said, 'I am **G** Son.'"
	27:54	"Truly this man was **G** Son!"
Rom	2: 4	that **G** kindness is meant to lead you
1 Cor	3: 9	you are **G** field, **G** building.
	3:16	you are **G** temple and that **G** Spirit
Heb	1: 3	reflection of **G** glory and the exact imprint of **G**
1 Jn	3: 2	Beloved, we are **G** children now;

GODDESS → *GOD

1 Kings	11: 5	Astarte the **g** of the Sidonians,

Acts   19:27   the temple of the great **g** Artemis

GODLESS → *GOD
Job   8:13   the hope of the **g** shall perish.
Ps   119:122 do not let the **g** oppress me.
1 Tim   1: 9   for the **g** and sinful,
2 Pet   3: 7   judgment and destruction of the **g.**

GODLINESS → *GOD
Wis   10:12   **g** is more powerful than anything
1 Tim   4: 7   Train yourself in **g,**
          6: 5   imagining that **g** is a means of gain.
2 Tim   3: 5   outward form of **g** but denying its
Titus   1: 1   truth that is in accordance with **g,**
2 Pet   1: 3   everything needed for life and **g,**

GODLY → *GOD
Sir   37:12   But associate with a **g** person
Bar   5: 4   "Righteous Peace, **G** Glory."
Mal   2:15   the one God desire? **G** offspring.
2 Cor   7:10   For **g** grief produces a repentance
2 Tim   3:12   to live a **g** life in Christ Jesus will
Titus   2:12   are self-controlled, upright, and **g,**
2 Pet   2: 9   how to rescue the **g** from trial,

GODS → *GOD
Gen   31:19   stole her father's household **g.**
Ex   12:12   **g** of Egypt I will execute judgments:
          20: 3   you shall have no other **g** before me.
Judg   2:17   they lusted after other **g** and bowed
2 Kings 17: 7   They had worshiped other **g**
Jn   10:34   in your law, 'I said, you are **g'**?
1 Cor   8: 5   so-called **g** in heaven or on earth—

GOG
Ezek   38:18   **G** comes against the land of Israel,
Rev   20: 8   **G** and Magog, in order to gather

GOLD
Ex   20:23   make for yourselves gods of **g.**
          25:17   shall make a mercy seat of pure **g;**
          25:31   shall make a lampstand of pure **g.**
          28: 6   They shall make the ephod of **g,** of
          32:31   have made for themselves gods of **g.**
1 Kings   6:21   the inside of the house with pure **g,**
Tob   12: 8   better to give alms than to lay up **g.**
Job   28:15   It cannot be gotten for **g,**
         119:127 love your commandments more than **g,**
Sir   31: 5   who loves **g** will not be justified;
Isa   60:17   Instead of bronze I will bring **g,**
Acts   3: 6   Peter said, "I have no silver or **g,**
1 Pet   1: 7   being more precious than **g** that,
Rev   21:21   and the street of the city is pure **g,**

GOLGOTHA
Mt   27:33   **G** (which means Place of a Skull),

GOLIATH
         Giant killed by David (1 Sam 17; 21:9; Sir 47:4).

GOMORRAH
Gen   19:24   LORD rained on Sodom and **G** sulfur
Isa   1: 9   like Sodom, and become like **G.**
Jude   1: 7   Sodom and **G** and the surrounding

GOOD → BEST, BETTER, GOODNESS
Gen   1:31   and indeed, it was very **g.**
          2: 9   tree of the knowledge of **g** and evil.
          3:22   become like one of us, knowing **g**
          50:20 to me, God intended it for **g,**
Deut   6:18   Do what is right and **g** in the sight
2 Chr   7: 3   "For he is **g,** for his steadfast love
Tob   4: 9   laying up a **g** treasure for yourself
Ps   14: 1   there is no one who does **g.**
          34: 8   O taste and see that the LORD is **g;**
          84:11 No **g** thing does the LORD withhold
Prov   18:22   He who finds a wife finds a **g** thing,
Eccl   12:14   every secret thing, whether **g** or evil.
Isa   52: 7   who brings **g** news, who announces
Dan   3:89   to the Lord, for he is **g,**
Mt   5:45   his sun rise on the evil and on the **g,**
          13: 8   Other seeds fell on **g** soil and
          25:21 'Well done, **g** and trustworthy slave;
Mk   10:18   No one is **g** but God alone.
Lk   2:10   I am bringing you **g** news of great
          6:43   "No **g** tree bears bad fruit,
Jn   10:11   "I am the **g** shepherd.

Rom   7:16   I agree that the law is **g.**
          12: 2   is **g** and acceptable and perfect.
          12:21 but overcome evil with **g.**
Eph   2:10   created in Christ Jesus for **g** works,
1 Tim   4: 4   For everything created by God is **g,**
Heb   10: 1   the law has only a shadow of the **g**
1 Pet   3:17   For it is better to suffer for doing **g,**

GOODNESS → GOOD
Ex   33:19   will make all my **g** pass before you,
Ps   23: 6   Surely **g** and mercy shall follow me
Heb   6: 5   tasted the **g** of the word of God and
2 Pet   1: 5   support your faith with **g,** and **g**

GOSHEN
Gen   45:10   You shall settle in the land of **G,**
Ex   8:22   day I will set apart the land of **G,**

GOSPEL
Mk   8:35   and for the sake of the **g,**
Rom   1:16   For I am not ashamed of the **g;**
1 Cor   9:16   woe to me if I do not proclaim the **g**
2 Cor   4: 3   And even if our **g** is veiled,
Gal   1: 6   and are turning to a different **g**—
Phil   1:27   life in a manner worthy of the **g**
Rev   14: 6   an eternal **g** to proclaim to those

GOSSIP
Prov   11:13   A **g** goes about telling secrets,
2 Cor   12:20   selfishness, slander, **g,** conceit,

GRACE → GRACIOUS
Wis   3: 9   **g** and mercy are upon his holy ones,
Jn   1:14   father's only son, full of **g** and truth.
          1:16   we have all received, **g** upon **g.**
Acts   15:11   that we will be saved through the **g**
Rom   3:24   are now justified by his **g** as a gift,
          6: 1   in sin in order that **g** may abound?
          6:14   you are not under law but under **g.**
          11: 6   otherwise **g** would no longer be **g.**
1 Cor   15:10   But by the **g** of God I am what I am,
2 Cor   12: 9   "My **g** is sufficient for you,
Gal   5: 4   you have fallen away from **g.**
Eph   2: 5   by **g** you have been saved—
2 Thess   2:16   through **g** gave us eternal comfort
Titus   2:11   For the **g** of God has appeared,
Heb   4:16   approach the throne of **g** with
Jas   4: 6   But he gives all the more **g;**
1 Pet   5:10   the God of all **g,**
Jude   1: 4   who pervert the **g** of our God into
Rev   22:21   The **g** of the Lord Jesus be with all

GRACIOUS → GRACE
Ex   34: 6   the LORD, a God merciful and **g,**
Num   6:25   to shine upon you, and be **g** to you;
Ezra   8:22   of our God is **g** to all who seek him,
Neh   9:31   for you are a **g** and merciful God.
Ps   77: 9   Has God forgotten to be **g?**
         116: 5   **G** is the LORD, and righteous;
Col   4: 6   Let your speech always be **g,**

GRAFTED
Rom   11:17   were **g** in their place to share the

GRAIN
Lev   2: 1   presents a **g** offering to the LORD,
Deut   25: 4   an ox while it is treading out the **g.**
Mk   2:23   disciples began to pluck heads of **g,**
1 Tim   5:18   an ox while it is treading out the **g,"**

GRAPES
Num   13:23   a branch with a single cluster of **g,**
Isa   5: 2   to yield **g,** but it yielded wild **g.**
Jer   31:29   "The parents have eaten sour **g,**
Mt   7:16   Are **g** gathered from thorns, or figs
Rev   14:18   vine of the earth, for its **g** are ripe."

GRASS
Isa   40: 6   All people are **g,** their constancy is
Mt   6:30   if God so clothes the **g** of the field,
1 Pet   1:24   "All flesh is like **g** and all its glory

GRATIFY*
Rom   13:14   for the flesh, to **g** its desires.
Gal   5:16   do not **g** the desires of the flesh.

GRAVE → GRAVES
Ps   49:14   straight to the **g** they descend,

Isa   53: 9 They made his **g** with the wicked

GRAVES → GRAVE
Ezek   37:12 and bring you up from your **g,**
Lk   11:44 For you are like unmarked **g,**

GRAY
Prov   16:31 **G** hair is a crown of glory;
Sir   6:18 **g** hair you will still find wisdom.

GREAT → GREATER, GREATEST
Gen   1:16 God made the two **g** lights—
       12: 2 I will make of you a **g** nation,
Ex   32:11 **g** power and with a mighty hand?
Deut   10:17 the **g** God, mighty and awesome,
Neh   8: 6 Ezra blessed the LORD, the **g** God,
Jdt   16:13 O Lord, you are **g** and glorious,
Ps   95: 3 the LORD is a **g** God, and a **g** King
Sir   17:29 How **g** is the mercy of the Lord,
Jer   10: 6 you are **g,** and your name is **g**
Lam   3:23 **g** is your faithfulness.
Dan   9: 4 "Ah, Lord, **g** and awesome God,
Joel   2:11 Truly the day of the LORD is **g;**
Mt   4:16 sat in darkness have seen a **g** light,
       13:46 on finding one pearl of **g** value,
       20:26 whoever wishes to be **g** among you
Eph   2: 4 the **g** love with which he loved us
Titus   2:13 of the glory of our **g** God and Savior
Heb   2: 3 if we neglect so **g** a salvation?
       12: 1 by so **g** a cloud of witnesses,
       13:20 the **g** shepherd of the sheep,
Rev   12: 9 The **g** dragon was thrown down,
       14: 8 "Fallen, fallen is Babylon the **g!**
       20:11 I saw a **g** white throne and the one

GREATER → GREAT
Ex   18:11 that the LORD is **g** than all gods,
Mt   12: 6 something **g** than the temple is here.
Mk   12:31 no other commandment **g** than these
Jn   14:12 in fact, will do **g** works than these,
       15:13 No one has **g** love than this,
1 Jn   4: 4 for the one who is in you is **g** than

GREATEST → GREAT
Mt   22:38 the **g** and first commandment.
Lk   9:48 the least among all of you is the **g.**"
1 Cor 13:13 and the **g** of these is love.

GREECE → GREEK, GREEKS
1 Macc 1: 1 had previously become king of **G.)**
Dan   8:21 the male goat is the king of **G,**

GREED → GREEDY
Mt   23:25 but inside they are full of **g**
Lk   12:15 on your guard against all kinds of **g;**
Col   3: 5 evil desire, and **g** (which is idolatry)

GREEDY → GREED
Prov   28:25 The **g** person stirs up strife,
1 Cor   6:10 the **g,** drunkards, revilers, robbers—
Titus   1: 7 to wine or violent or **g** for gain;

GREEK → GREECE
Jn   19:20 in Hebrew, in Latin, and in **G.**
Rom   1:16 to the Jew first and also to the **G.**
Gal   3:28 There is no longer Jew or **G,**

GREEKS → GREECE
1 Cor   1:22 demand signs and **G** desire wisdom,

GREEN
Gen   1:30 I have given every **g** plant for food."
Ps   23: 2 makes me lie down in **g** pastures;

GREW → GROW
1 Sam   2:21 boy Samuel **g** up in the presence of
Isa   53: 2 he **g** up before him like a young
Lk   1:80 child **g** and became strong in spirit,
        2:40 child **g** and became strong, filled

GRIEF → GRIEVE, GRIEVED
Lam   3:32 causes **g,** he will have compassion
2 Cor   7: 9 your **g** led to repentance;

GRIEVE → GRIEF
Eph   4:30 do not **g** the Holy Spirit of God,
1 Thess 4:13 not **g** as others do who have no hope

GRIEVED → GRIEF
Isa   63:10 they rebelled and **g** his holy spirit;
Mt   26:38 "I am deeply **g,** even to death;

GRINDING
Lk   17:35 will be two women **g** meal together;

GROAN → GROANING
Rom   8:23 **g** inwardly while we wait for
2 Cor   5: 2 For in this tent we **g,** longing to be

GROANING → GROAN
Ex   2:24 heard their **g,** and God remembered
Judg   2:18 would be moved to pity by their **g**
Ps   22: 1 from the words of my **g?**

GROUND
Gen   2: 7 formed man from the dust of the **g,**
        3:17 cursed is the **g** because of you;
Ex   3: 5 which you are standing is holy **g.**"
Sir   33:10 All human beings come from the **g,**
Isa   53: 2 and like a root out of dry **g;**
Mt   13: 5 Other seeds fell on rocky **g,**

GROW → GREW, GROWTH
Isa   11: 1 and a branch shall **g** out of his roots.
Ezek   47:12 will **g** all kinds of trees for food.
Col   1:10 as you **g** in the knowledge of God.
2 Pet   3:18 But **g** in the grace and knowledge of

GROWTH → GROW
1 Cor   3: 7 but only God who gives the **g.**
Col   2:19 grows with a **g** that is from God.

GUARANTEE → GUARANTEED
2 Cor   5: 5 who has given us the Spirit as a **g.**
Heb   7:22 Jesus has also become the **g** of a

GUARANTEED* → GUARANTEE
Rom   4:16 promise may rest on grace and be **g**
Heb   6:17 he **g** it by an oath,

GUARD → GUARDIAN, GUARDS
Prov   2:11 and understanding will **g** you.
2 Thess 3: 3 and **g** you from the evil one.
2 Tim   1:12 to **g** until that day what I have

GUARDIAN → GUARD
Sir   51:12 *Give thanks to the* **g** *of Israel,*
1 Pet   2:25 to the shepherd and **g** of your souls.

GUARDS → GUARD
Ps   127: 1 Unless the LORD **g** the city,
Mt   28: 4 the **g** shook and became like dead

GUIDANCE → GUIDE
Prov   11:14 Where there is no **g,** a nation falls,

GUIDE → GUIDANCE
Ps   48:14 He will be our **g** forever.
Isa   58:11 The LORD will **g** you continually,
Lk   6:39 Can a blind person **g** a blind person?
Jn   16:13 he will **g** you into all the truth;

GUILT → GUILTY
Lev   5:15 as your **g** offering to the LORD,
Ps   32: 5 and you forgave the **g** of my sin.
Hos   14: 2 say to him, "Take away all **g;**
Zech   3: 9 I will remove the **g** of this land

GUILTY → GUILT
Ex   23: 7 for I will not acquit the **g.**
Num   14:18 but by no means clearing the **g,**
Dan   13:53 the innocent and acquitting the **g,**
Mk   3:29 but is **g** of an eternal sin"—

H

HABAKKUK
      Prophet to Judah (Hab 1:1; 3:1; Dan 14:33-39).

HADASSAH → See ESTHER

HADES
Sir   21:10 but at its end is the pit of **H.**
Mt   16:18 and the gates of **H** will not prevail
Acts   2:27 not abandon my soul to **H,**
Rev   1:18 I have the keys of Death and of **H.**
       20:14 **H** were thrown into the lake of fire.

HAGAR
Servant of Sarah, wife of Abraham, mother of Ishmael (Gen 16:1-6; 25:12). Driven away by Sarah while pregnant (Gen 16:5-16); after birth of Isaac (Gen 21:9-21; Gal 4:21-31).

HAGGAI*
Post-exilic prophet who encouraged rebuilding of the temple (Ezra 5:1; 6:14; Hag 1-2).

HAIL → HAILSTONES
Ex	9:19	will die when the **h** comes down
Rev	8: 7	came **h** and fire, mixed with blood,

HAILSTONES → HAIL
Josh	10:11	of the **h** the Israelites killed
Rev	16:21	and huge **h**, each weighing about

HAIR → HAIRS
Judg	16:22	**h** of his head began to grow again
Lk	7:44	her tears and dried them with her **h**.
Jn	12: 3	anointed Jesus' feet, and wiped them with her **h**.
1 Cor	11: 6	for a woman to have her **h** cut off
1 Tim	2: 9	not with their **h** braided, or with

HAIRS → HAIR
Ps	40:12	more than the **h** of my head,
Mt	10:30	the **h** of your head are all counted.

HALF
Esth	5: 3	even to the **h** of my kingdom."
Mk	6:23	give you, even **h** of my kingdom."
Lk	19: 8	**h** of my possessions, Lord, I will

HALLELUJAH
Tob	13:17	and all her houses will cry, 'H!
Rev	19: 1	multitude in heaven, saying, "H!

HALLOWED
Gen	2: 3	blessed the seventh day and **h** it,
Mt	6: 9	Father in heaven, **h** be your name.

HAM
Son of Noah (Gen 5:32; 1 Chr 1:4), father of Canaan (Gen 9:18; 10:6-20; 1 Chr 1:8-16). Saw Noah's nakedness (Gen 9:20-27).

HAMAN
Agagite nobleman honored by Xerxes (Esth 3:1-2). Plotted to exterminate the Jews because of Mordecai (Esth 3:3-15). Forced to honor Mordecai (Esth 5-6). Plot exposed by Esther (Esth 5:1-8; 7:1-8). Hanged (Esth 7:9-10).

HANANIAH → =SHADRACH
1. False prophet; adversary of Jeremiah (Jer 28).
2. Original name of Shadrach (Dan 1:6-19; 2:17).

HAND → EMPTY-HANDED, HANDED, HANDS
Ex	3:19	unless compelled by a mighty **h**.
	15: 6	Your right **h**, O LORD, glorious in
Deut	19:21	tooth for tooth, **h** for **h**, foot for foot
1 Kings	18:44	cloud no bigger than a person's **h** is
Jdt	9:10	by the **h** of a woman.
Ps	16: 8	he is at my right **h**, I shall not be
	98: 1	right **h** and his holy arm have gotten
	110: 1	says to my lord, "Sit at my right **h**
Prov	3:16	Long life is in her right **h**;
Isa	5:25	and his **h** is stretched out still.
Dan	5: 5	the fingers of a human **h** appeared
Hab	2:16	The cup in the LORD's right **h** will
Mt	3:12	His winnowing fork is in his **h**,
Mk	9:43	If your **h** causes you to stumble, cut
Lk	20:42	said to my Lord, "Sit at my right **h**,
Jn	10:28	will snatch them out of my **h**.
Rom	8:34	raised, who is at the right **h** of God,
1 Cor	12:15	would say, "Because I am not a **h**,
Heb	10:12	"he sat down at the right **h** of God,"
Rev	1:16	In his right **h** he held seven stars,
	5: 1	saw in the right **h** of the one seated

HANDED → HAND
Mt	27:26	he **h** him over to be crucified.
Rom	4:25	**h** over to death for our trespasses

HANDS → HAND
Ps	24: 4	who have clean **h** and pure hearts,
	115: 7	They have **h**, but do not feel;
Eccl	11: 6	at evening do not let your **h** be idle;
Isa	49:16	inscribed you on the palms of my **h**;

Dan	2:45	was cut from the mountain not by **h**,
Lk	23:46	into your **h** I commend my spirit."
	24:40	he showed them his **h** and his feet.
Jn	3:35	has placed all things in his **h**.
Acts	8:18	the laying on of the apostles' **h**,
Rom	10:21	"All day long I have held out my **h**
Heb	6: 2	laying on of **h**, resurrection of the
	10:31	to fall into the **h** of the living God.

HANNAH*
Wife of Elkanah, mother of Samuel (1 Sam 1). Prayer at dedication of Samuel (1 Sam 2:1-10). Blessed (1 Sam 2:18-21).

HAPPY
Tob	13:14	**H** are those who love you,
Ps	1: 1	**H** are those who do not follow the
	33:12	**H** is the nation whose God is the LORD,
	84:12	**h** is everyone who trusts in you.
Prov	3:13	**H** are those who find wisdom,
Eccl	3:12	nothing better for them than to be **h**
Sir	1:13	who fear the Lord will have a **h** end;

HARD → HARD-HEARTED, HARDEN, HARDENED, HARDENING, HARDSHIP, HARDSHIPS
Ex	1:14	made their lives bitter with **h** service
Jer	32:17	Nothing is too **h** for you.
Mt	7:14	the road is **h** that leads to life,
	19:23	**h** for a rich person to enter the

HARD-HEARTED* → HARD, HEART
Deut	15: 7	do not be **h** or tight-fisted toward
Prov	28:14	one who is **h** will fall into calamity.
Mt	19: 8	you were so **h** that Moses allowed

HARDEN → HARD
Ex	4:21	but I will **h** his heart,
Ps	95: 8	Do not **h** your hearts, as at Meribah,
Heb	3: 8	not **h** your hearts as in the rebellion,

HARDENED → HARD
Ex	10:20	But the LORD **h** Pharaoh's heart,
Mk	8:17	Are your hearts **h**?
Rom	11: 7	elect obtained it, but the rest were **h**,
2 Cor	3:14	But their minds were **h**.

HARDENING* → HARD
Rom	11:25	a **h** has come upon part of Israel,

HARDSHIP → HARD
Rom	8:35	Will **h**, or distress, or persecution,

HARDSHIPS → HARD
2 Cor	12:10	content with weaknesses, insults, **h**,

HARM
Gen	50:20	though you intended to do **h** to me,
Neh	6: 2	But they intended to do me **h**.
Prov	12:21	No **h** happens to the righteous,
Jer	29:11	plans for your welfare and not for **h**,
1 Pet	3:13	who will **h** you if you are eager

HARP → HARPS
Ps	150: 3	praise him with lute and **h**!
Rev	5: 8	each holding a **h** and golden bowls

HARPS → HARP
1 Chr	15:16	on **h** and lyres and cymbals,
Neh	12:27	with cymbals, **h**, and lyres.
Ps	137: 2	the willows there we hung up our **h**.

HARSHLY
Deut	26: 6	When the Egyptians treated us **h**
Col	3:19	your wives and never treat them **h**.
1 Tim	5: 1	Do not speak **h** to an older man,

HARVEST → HARVESTING
Gen	8:22	the earth endures, seedtime and **h**,
Ex	23:16	You shall observe the festival of **h**,
Mt	13:39	**h** is the end of the age, and the
Mk	4:29	with his sickle, because the **h** has come."
Lk	10: 2	He said to them, "The **h** is plentiful,
Rev	14:15	the **h** of the earth is fully ripe."

HARVESTING* → HARVEST
Jn	4:35	and see how the fields are ripe for **h**.

HASTENING*
Zeph	1:14	day of the LORD is near, near and **h**
2 Pet	3:12	and **h** the coming of the day of God,

HATE → HATED, HATING
Ps | 45: 7 | righteousness and **h** wickedness.
| 97:10 | The Lᴏʀᴅ loves those who **h** evil;
Prov | 13: 5 | The righteous **h** falsehood,
Eccl | 3: 8 | a time to love, and a time to **h**;
Am | 5:15 | **H** evil and love good, and establish
Mal | 2:16 | For I **h** divorce, says the Lᴏʀᴅ,
Mt | 5:43 | your neighbor and **h** your enemy.'
Lk | 6:27 | do good to those who **h** you,
Jn | 7: 7 | The world cannot **h** you, but it hates
Rom | 7:15 | but I do the very thing I **h**.

HATED → HATE
Jn | 15:18 | aware that it **h** me before it **h** you.
Rom | 9:13 | loved Jacob, but I have **h** Esau."

HATES → HATE
Deut | 16:22 | things that the Lᴏʀᴅ your God **h**.
Prov | 6:16 | six things that the Lᴏʀᴅ **h**,
Sir | 15:13 | The Lord **h** all abominations;
Jn | 15:23 | Whoever **h** me **h** my Father also.

HAUGHTY
Prov | 6:17 | **h** eyes, a lying tongue, and hands
| 16:18 | and a **h** spirit before a fall.
1 Tim | 6:17 | command them not to be **h**,

HAY*
1 Cor | 3:12 | precious stones, wood, **h**, straw—

HEAD → BEHEADED, HEADS
Isa | 59:17 | and a helmet of salvation on his **h**;
Mt | 8:20 | of Man has nowhere to lay his **h**."
Mk | 6:28 | brought his **h** on a platter,
1 Cor | 11: 3 | Christ is the **h** of every man, and the husband
| | is the **h** of his wife,
Eph | 1:22 | has made him the **h** over all things

HEADS → HEAD
Ezek | 11:21 | bring their deeds upon their own **h**,
Rev | 12: 3 | a great red dragon, with seven **h**

HEAL → HEALED, HEALING, HEALS, HEALTH,
    HEALTHY
Deut | 32:39 | and I make alive; I wound and I **h**;
Eccl | 3: 3 | a time to kill, and a time to **h**;
Isa | 57:19 | says the Lᴏʀᴅ; and I will **h** them.
Jer | 3:22 | I will **h** your faithlessness.
Hos | 14: 4 | I will **h** their disloyalty; I will love
Jn | 12:40 | and turn—and I would **h** them."

HEALED → HEAL
Isa | 6:10 | their minds, and turn and be **h**."
| 53: 5 | and by his bruises we are **h**.
Hos | 11: 3 | but they did not know that I **h** them.
Jas | 5:16 | one another, so that you may be **h**.
1 Pet | 2:24 | by his wounds you have been **h**.

HEALING → HEAL
Prov | 12:18 | but the tongue of the wise brings **h**.
Sir | 38: 2 | gift of **h** comes from the Most High,
Ezek | 47:12 | for food, and their leaves for **h**."
Mal | 4: 2 | shall rise, with **h** in its wings.
1 Cor | 12: 9 | another gifts of **h** by the one Spirit,
Rev | 22: 2 | leaves of the tree are for the **h** of

HEALS → HEAL
Ex | 15:26 | for I am the Lᴏʀᴅ who **h** you."
Ps | 103: 3 | iniquity, who **h** all your diseases,
Wis | 16:12 | your word, O Lord, that **h** all people

HEALTH → HEAL
Sir | 30:15 | **H** and fitness are better than any
3 Jn | 1: 2 | and that you may be in good **h**,

HEALTHY → HEAL
Lk | 11:34 | If your eye is **h**, your whole body

HEAR → HEARD, HEARERS, HEARING, HEARS
Deut | 6: 4 | **H**, O Israel: The Lᴏʀᴅ is our God,
| 31:13 | may **h** and learn to fear the Lᴏʀᴅ
1 Kings | 8:30 | O **h** in heaven your dwelling place;
Sir | 5:11 | Be quick to **h**, but deliberate in
Isa | 59: 1 | nor his ear too dull to **h**.
Jer | 5:21 | who have ears, but do not **h**.
Ezek | 37: 4 | dry bones, **h** the word of the Lᴏʀᴅ.
Mt | 13:17 | to **h** what you **h**, but did not **h** it.
Mk | 12:29 | answered, "The first is, '**H**, O Israel:

Lk | 7:22 | the lepers are cleansed, the deaf **h**,
Heb | 3: 7 | says, "Today, if you **h** his voice,

HEARD → HEAR
Isa | 40:21 | not known? Have you not **h**?
Rom | 10:17 | faith comes from what is **h**,
1 Cor | 2: 9 | "What no eye has seen, nor ear **h**,
1 Jn | 1: 3 | to you what we have seen and **h** so
Rev | 22: 8 | I, John, am the one who **h** and saw

HEARERS → HEAR
Rom | 2:13 | For it is not the **h** of the law who
Jas | 1:22 | merely **h** who deceive themselves.

HEARING → HEAR
Prov | 18:13 | one gives answer before **h**,
Am | 8:11 | but of **h** the words of the Lᴏʀᴅ.
1 Cor | 12:17 | If the whole body were **h**,

HEARS → HEAR
Ps | 69:33 | For the Lᴏʀᴅ **h** the needy,
Prov | 15:29 | but he **h** the prayer of the righteous.
Mt | 7:24 | then who **h** these words of mine
Jn | 5:24 | I tell you, anyone who **h** my word
1 Jn | 5:14 | according to his will, he **h** us.
Rev | 22:18 | I warn everyone who **h** the words

HEART → BROKENHEARTED, HARD-HEARTED,
    HEART'S, HEARTLESS, HEARTS, TENDERHEARTED
Gen | 6: 6 | and it grieved him to his **h**.
Ex | 4:21 | but I will harden his **h**,
| 14: 4 | I will harden Pharaoh's **h**,
Deut | 6: 5 | the Lᴏʀᴅ your God with all your **h**,
| 30:14 | in your mouth and in your **h** for you
Josh | 22: 5 | all your **h** and all your soul.'
1 Sam | 16: 7 | but the Lᴏʀᴅ looks on the **h**."
Ps | 19:14 | meditation of my **h** be acceptable to
| 51:10 | Create in me a clean **h**, O God,
Prov | 3: 5 | Trust in the Lᴏʀᴅ with all your **h**,
| 7: 3 | write them on the tablet of your **h**.
Sir | 1:12 | The fear of the Lord delights the **h**,
Jer | 9:26 | of Israel is uncircumcised in **h**.
Ezek | 36:26 | A new **h** I will give you,
Dan | 3:39 | Yet with a contrite **h** and
Mt | 5: 8 | "Blessed are the pure in **h**, for they
| 5:28 | adultery with her in his **h**.
Mk | 12:30 | the Lord your God with all your **h**,
Lk | 12:34 | treasure is, there your **h** will be also.
Rom | 2:29 | circumcision is a matter of the **h**—
| 10: 9 | believe in your **h** that God raised
Heb | 10:22 | let us approach with a true **h** in full

HEART'S → HEART
Ps | 20: 4 | May he grant you your **h** desire,
Rom | 10: 1 | my **h** desire and prayer to God for

HEARTLESS* → HEART
Rom | 1:31 | foolish, faithless, **h**, ruthless.

HEARTS → HEART
Ps | 95: 8 | not harden your **h**, as at Meribah,
Jer | 31:33 | and I will write it on their **h**;
Mk | 7: 6 | but their **h** are far from me;
Jn | 14: 1 | "Do not let your **h** be troubled.
Rom | 2:15 | law requires is written on their **h**,
| 5: 5 | love has been poured into our **h**
Eph | 3:17 | Christ may dwell in your **h** through
Col | 3:15 | the peace of Christ rule in your **h**,
Heb | 3: 8 | do not harden your **h** as in the
| 10:16 | I will put my laws in their **h**,
2 Pet | 1:19 | and the morning star rises in your **h**.
1 Jn | 3:20 | for God is greater than our **h**,
Rev | 2:23 | the one who searches minds and **h**,

HEAVEN → HEAVENLY, HEAVENS
Gen | 14:19 | by God Most High, maker of **h** and
| 28:12 | the top of it reaching to **h**;
Ex | 16: 4 | "I am going to rain bread from **h**
Deut | 30:12 | "Who will go up to **h** for us,
| 31:28 | and call **h** and earth to witness
1 Kings | 8:27 | **h** and the highest **h** cannot contain
Job | 16:19 | now, in fact, my witness is in **h**,
Eccl | 3: 1 | and a time for every matter under **h**:
Isa | 14:12 | you are fallen from **h**, O Day Star,
Jer | 23:24 | Do I not fill **h** and earth?
Mt | 3: 2 | "Repent, for the kingdom of **h** has

Mt	6: 9	Father in **h**, hallowed be your name.
	24:35	**H** and earth will pass away,
	26:64	and coming on the clouds of **h**."
Mk	10:21	and you will have treasure in **h**;
Lk	10:18	"I watched Satan fall from **h** like a
	19:38	Peace in **h**, and glory in the highest **h**!"
	24:51	and was carried up into **h**.
Jn	3:13	No one has ascended into **h** except the one
		who descended from **h**,
Acts	1:11	same way as you saw him go into **h**.
Rom	10: 6	"Who will ascend into **h**?"
2 Cor	12: 2	was caught up to the third **h**—
Phil	3:20	But our citizenship is in **h**,
1 Thess	1:10	to wait for his Son from **h**,
Heb	9:24	but he entered into **h** itself,
2 Pet	1:18	heard this voice come from **h**,
Rev	4: 1	and there in **h** a door stood open!
	21: 1	I saw a new **h** and a new earth;

HEAVENLY → HEAVEN

Mt	5:48	as your **h** Father is perfect.
2 Cor	5: 2	longing to be clothed with our **h**
Eph	1: 3	spiritual blessing in the **h** places,
Heb	3: 1	holy partners in a **h** calling,

HEAVENS → HEAVEN

Gen	1: 1	when God created the **h** and
	11: 4	and a tower with its top in the **h**,
Deut	10:14	the heaven of **h** belong to the LORD
Ps	57: 5	Be exalted, O God, above the **h**.
	115:16	The **h** are the LORD's **h**,
Isa	65:17	to create new **h** and a new earth;
Jer	10:11	The gods who did not make the **h**
Eph	4:10	who ascended far above all the **h**,
Heb	4:14	priest who has passed through the **h**,
2 Pet	3:10	the **h** will pass away with a loud

HEAVY

Mt	23: 4	They tie up **h** burdens, hard to bear,
Mk	14:40	for their eyes were very **h**;

HEBREW → HEBREWS

Jon	1: 9	"I am a **H**," he replied.
Jn	19:20	and it was written in **H**, in Latin,
Phil	3: 5	of Benjamin, a **H** born of Hebrews;

HEBREWS → HEBREW

Ex	3:18	The LORD, the God of the **H**, has
Jdt	10:12	"I am a daughter of the **H**,
2 Cor	11:22	Are they **H**? So am I.

HEBRON

Gen	13:18	the oaks of Mamre, which are at **H**;
2 Sam	2:11	The time that David was king in **H**

HEEL

Gen	3:15	your head, and you will strike his **h**.
	25:26	with his hand gripping Esau's **h**,
Ps	41: 9	has lifted the **h** against me.
Jn	13:18	has lifted his **h** against me.'

HEIGHT → HIGH

Rom	8:39	nor **h**, nor depth, nor anything else
Eph	3:18	and length and **h** and depth,

HEIGHTS → HIGH

Ps	148: 1	the heavens; praise him in the **h**!
Hab	3:19	and makes me tread upon the **h**.

HEIR → HEIRS

Gen	15: 4	"This man shall not be your **h**;
Gal	4: 7	then also an **h**, through God.
Heb	1: 2	whom he appointed **h** of all things,

HEIRS → HEIR

Rom	8:17	**h**, **h** of God and joint **h** with Christ—
Eph	3: 6	the Gentiles have become fellow **h**,
Titus	3: 7	become **h** according to the hope
1 Pet	3: 7	also **h** of the gracious gift of life—

HELL

Mt	10:28	both soul and body in **h**.
Mk	9:43	to have two hands and to go to **h**,
2 Pet	2: 4	cast them into **h** and committed

HELMET

Isa	59:17	and a **h** of salvation on his head;
Eph	6:17	Take the **h** of salvation, and the

HELP → HELPED, HELPER, HELPS

Ex	18: 4	"The God of my father was my **h**,
Jdt	6:21	called on the God of Israel for **h**.
Ps	33:20	he is our **h** and shield.
	46: 1	a very present **h** in trouble.
Sir	2: 6	Trust in him, and he will **h** you;
Mk	9:24	"I believe; **h** my unbelief!"
Heb	2:18	able to **h** those who are being tested.
	4:16	receive mercy and find grace to **h**

HELPED → HELP

1 Sam	7:12	"Thus far the LORD has **h** us."
Ps	118:13	I was falling, but the LORD **h** me.
Isa	49: 8	on a day of salvation I have **h** you;

HELPER → HELP

Gen	2:18	I will make him a **h** as his partner."
Tob	8: 6	Eve as a **h** and support.
Ps	30:10	O LORD, be my **h**!"
Heb	13: 6	Lord is my **h**; I will not be afraid.

HELPS → HELP

Ps	37:40	The LORD **h** them and rescues them;
Rom	8:26	the Spirit **h** us in our weakness;

HERBS

Ex	12: 8	with unleavened bread and bitter **h**.

HERMON

Deut	3: 8	from the Wadi Arnon to Mount **H**
Ps	133: 3	It is like the dew of **H**,

HEROD → HERODIANS

1. King of Judea; tried to kill Jesus (Mt 2; Lk 1:5).
2. Son of 1. Tetrarch of Galilee who arrested and beheaded John the Baptist (Mt 14:1-12; Mk 6:14-29; Lk 3:1, 19-20; 9:7-9); tried Jesus (Lk 23:6-15).
3. Grandson of 1. King of Judea who killed James (Acts 12:2); arrested Peter (Acts 12:3-19). Death (Acts 12:19-23).

HERODIANS → HEROD

Mk	3: 6	immediately conspired with the **H**
	12:13	some **H** to trap him in what he said.

HERODIAS*

Wife of Herod the Tetrarch who persuaded her daughter to ask for John the Baptist's head (Mt 14:1-12; Mk 6:14-29; Lk 3:19).

HEWN

Ex	20:25	do not build it of **h** stones;
Mk	15:46	laid it in a tomb that had been **h**

HEZEKIAH

King of Judah (Sir 48:17-25). Restored the temple and worship (2 Chr 29-31). Sought the LORD for help against Assyria (2 Kings 18-19; 2 Chr 32:1-23; Isa 36-37). Illness healed (2 Kings 20:1-11; 2 Chr 32:24-26; Isa 38). Judged for showing Babylonians his treasures (2 Kings 20:12-21; 2 Chr 32:31; Isa 39).

HID → HIDE

Gen	3: 8	and his wife **h** themselves from the
Ex	2: 2	a fine baby, she **h** him three months.
	3: 6	Moses **h** his face, for he was afraid
Josh	6:17	live because she **h** the messengers
1 Kings	18:13	**h** a hundred of the LORD's prophets
Isa	49: 2	in the shadow of his hand he **h** me;
	54: 8	wrath for a moment I **h** my face
Mt	25:25	and **h** your talent in the ground.

HIDDEN → HIDE

Ps	19:12	Clear me from **h** faults.
Prov	2: 4	and search for it as for **h** treasures—
Sir	42:20	and nothing is **h** from him.
Isa	40:27	"My way is **h** from the LORD,
Mt	13:44	is like treasure **h** in a field,
Mk	4:22	nothing **h**, except to be disclosed;
Col	3: 3	your life is **h** with Christ in God.
Rev	2:17	the **h** manna, and I will give a white

HIDE → HID, HIDDEN

Deut	31:17	I will forsake them and **h** my face
Ps	13: 1	How long will you **h** your face
	17: 8	**h** me in the shadow of your wings,

HIGH → HEIGHT, HEIGHTS, HIGHER, HIGHEST, HIGHLY

Gen	14:18	he was priest of God Most **H**.

1 Kings	3: 2	were sacrificing at the **h** places,
Ps	91: 1	live in the shelter of the Most H,
Mt	4: 8	a very **h** mountain and showed him
	17: 1	and led them up a **h** mountain,
Mk	5: 7	Jesus, Son of the Most H God?
Eph	4: 8	"When he ascended on **h** he made
Heb	2:17	a merciful and faithful **h** priest
	7:26	that we should have such a **h** priest,

HIGHER → HIGH

Ps	61: 2	Lead me to the rock that is **h** than I;
Isa	55: 9	so are my ways **h** than your ways

HIGHEST → HIGH

1 Kings	8:27	the **h** heaven cannot contain you,
Mt	21: 9	Hosanna in the **h** heaven!"
Lk	2:14	"Glory to God in the **h** heaven,

HIGHLY → HIGH

Ps	47: 9	to God; he is **h** exalted.
Rom	12: 3	not to think of yourself more **h** than

HILL → HILLS

Ps	15: 1	Who may dwell on your holy **h**?
Isa	40: 4	every mountain and **h** be made low;
Mt	5:14	A city built on a **h** cannot be hid.
Lk	3: 5	mountain and **h** shall be made low,

HILLS → HILL

1 Kings	20:23	"Their gods are gods of the **h**,
Ps	50:10	the cattle on a thousand **h**.

HINDER

1 Sam	14: 6	nothing can **h** the LORD from saving
Isa	43:13	I work and who can **h** it?
1 Pet	3: 7	so that nothing may **h** your prayers.

HIP

Gen	32:25	Jacob's **h** was put out of joint

HIRAM

King of Tyre; helped David build his palace (2 Sam 5:11-12; 1 Chr 14:1); helped Solomon build the temple (1 Kings 5; 2 Chr 2) and his navy (1 Kings 9:10-27; 2 Chr 8).

HITTITE → HITTITES

Gen	23:10	Ephron the H answered Abraham
2 Sam	11: 3	the wife of Uriah the **H**."

HITTITES → HITTITE

Deut	20:17	H and the Amorites, the Canaanites
Ezra	9: 1	Canaanites, the **H**, the Perizzites,

HOLD → HOLDS

Ps	73:23	you **h** my right hand.
Isa	41:13	I, the LORD your God, **h** your right
Jn	20:17	Jesus said to her, "Do not **h** on to
Col	1:17	and in him all things **h** together.

HOLDS → HOLD

Ps	37:24	for the LORD **h** us by the hand.
Wis	1: 7	which **h** all things together
Rev	2: 1	who **h** the seven stars in his right

HOLES

Hag	1: 6	to put them into a bag with **h**.
Mt	8:20	Jesus said to him, "Foxes have **h**,

HOLINESS → HOLY

Ex	15:11	Who is like you, majestic in **h**,
Deut	32:51	by failing to maintain my **h** among
Ps	89:35	and for all I have sworn by my **h**;
Rom	1: 4	according to the spirit of **h** by
2 Cor	6: 6	kindness, **h** of spirit, genuine love,
1 Tim	2:15	continue in faith and love and **h**,
Heb	12:14	**h** without which no one will see the

HOLOFERNES

Assyrian general (Jdt 2:4). Beguiled and beheaded by Judith (Jdt 10-13).

HOLY → HOLINESS

Ex	3: 5	which you are standing is **h** ground.
	20: 8	the sabbath day, and keep it **h**.
	26:33	the **h** place from the most **h**.
	29:37	the altar shall be most **h**;
Lev	11:44	and be **h**, for I am **h**.
Josh	5:15	for the place where you stand is **h**."
1 Sam	2: 2	"There is no H One like the LORD,
1 Macc	1:15	and abandoned the **h** covenant.

Ps	2: 6	set my king on Zion, my **h** hill."
	11: 4	The LORD is in his **h** temple;
Wis	4:15	he watches over his **h** ones.
Isa	6: 3	"H, **h**, **h** is the LORD of hosts;
	40:25	who is my equal? says the H One.
Dan	9:24	and to anoint a most **h** place.
Mt	1:18	to be with child from the H Spirit.
	3:11	baptize you with the H Spirit and
	24:15	sacrilege standing in the **h** place,
Mk	1:24	who you are, the H One of God."
	3:29	against the H Spirit can never have
Lk	3:22	the H Spirit descended upon him in
	11:13	heavenly Father give the H Spirit
Jn	14:26	But the Advocate, the H Spirit,
Acts	2: 4	were filled with the H Spirit and
	2:27	your H One experience corruption.
	5: 3	your heart to lie to the H Spirit
Rom	12: 1	living sacrifice, **h** and acceptable to
Eph	1: 4	to be **h** and blameless
	4:30	do not grieve the H Spirit of God,
Heb	6: 4	and have shared in the H Spirit,
1 Pet	1:16	"You shall be **h**, for I am **h**."
1 Jn	2:20	have been anointed by the H One,
Jude	1:14	with ten thousands of his **h** ones,
Rev	4: 8	H, **h**, **h**, the Lord God the Almighty
	21: 2	I saw the **h** city, the new Jerusalem,
	22:11	and the **h** still be **h**."

HOME → HOMELESS, HOMETOWN

Deut	6: 7	when you are at **h** and when you
Ps	68: 6	God gives the desolate a **h**
Jn	14:23	to them and make our **h** with them.
2 Cor	5: 8	the body and at **h** with the Lord.
Rev	21: 3	"See, the **h** of God is among mortals

HOMELESS* → HOME

Isa	58: 7	the **h** poor into your house;
1 Cor	4:11	poorly clothed and beaten and **h**,

HOMETOWN → HOME, TOWN

Mk	6: 4	not without honor, except in their **h**,

HONEST

Lev	19:36	have **h** balances, **h** weights,
Prov	16:11	H balances and scales are the

HONEY

Ex	3: 8	a land flowing with milk and **h**,
Judg	14: 8	bees in the body of the lion, and **h**.
1 Sam	14:26	honeycomb, the **h** was dripping out;
Ps	19:10	sweeter also than **h**, and drippings
Mt	3: 4	and his food was locusts and wild **h**.

HONOR → HONORABLE, HONORED, HONORS

Deut	5:16	H your father and your mother,
1 Chr	29:12	Riches and **h** come from you,
Tob	4: 3	H your mother and do not
Ps	8: 5	and crowned them with glory and **h**.
Eccl	10: 1	little folly outweighs wisdom and **h**.
Isa	29:13	and **h** me with their lips,
Mal	1: 6	a father, where is the **h** due me?
Mt	13:57	not without **h** except in their own
	15: 4	For God said, 'H your father and
Jn	12:26	serves me, the Father will **h**.
Rom	13: 7	**h** to whom **h** is due.
Eph	6: 2	"H your father and mother"—
1 Tim	5:17	considered worthy of double **h**,
Heb	2: 7	crowned them with glory and **h**,
Rev	4:11	to receive glory and **h** and power,

HONORABLE → HONOR

Phil	4: 8	whatever is true, whatever is **h**,

HONORED → HONOR

Hag	1: 8	I may take pleasure in it and be **h**,
1 Cor	12:26	if one member is **h**, all rejoice

HONORS → HONOR

Mal	1: 6	A son **h** his father, and servants
Mt	15: 8	'This people **h** me with their lips,

HOOFS

Lev	11: 3	Any animal that has divided **h**

HOOK → HOOKS

Mt	17:27	go to the sea and cast a **h**;

HOOKS → HOOK

Isa	2: 4	and their spears into pruning h;
Joel	3:10	and your pruning h into spears;

HOPE → HOPED, HOPES

Job	17:15	where then is my h?
Ps	62: 5	for my h is from him.
	146: 5	whose h is in the LORD their God,
Prov	23:18	and your h will not be cut off.
Sir	34:15	their h is in him who saves them.
Isa	8:17	and I will h in him.
Jer	14: 8	O h of Israel, its savior in time of
Dan	13:60	who saves those who h in him.
Lam	3:21	and therefore I have h:
Mt	12:21	in his name the Gentiles will h."
Rom	5: 5	and h does not disappoint us,
	12:12	Rejoice in h, be patient in suffering,
1 Cor	13:13	And now faith, h, and love abide,
Col	1:27	Christ in you, the h of glory.
1 Thess	5: 8	and for a helmet the h of salvation.
Heb	6:19	this h, a sure and steadfast anchor
	7:19	the introduction of a better h,
1 Pet	1: 3	a living h through the resurrection
1 Jn	3: 3	all who have this h in him purify

HOPED → HOPE

Heb	11: 1	faith is the assurance of things h for,
1 Pet	3: 5	the holy women who h in God

HOPES → HOPE

1 Cor	13: 7	believes all things, h all things,

HOREB → =SINAI

Ex	3: 1	came to H, the mountain of God.
Deut	5: 2	God made a covenant with us at H.
1 Kings	19: 8	forty days and forty nights to H

HORN → HORNS

Ps	18: 2	and the h of my salvation,
Dan	7: 8	when another h appeared,
	8: 5	The goat had a h between its eyes.

HORNS → HORN

Gen	22:13	caught in a thicket by its h.
Ex	27: 2	make h for it on its four corners;
Dan	7: 7	that preceded it, and it had ten h.
	8: 3	Both h were long, but one
Zech	1:18	And I looked up and saw four h.
Rev	5: 6	having seven h and seven eyes,
	9:13	from the four h of the golden altar
	17: 3	and it had seven heads and ten h.

HORSE → HORSES

Ex	15: 1	h and rider he has thrown into the
Ps	33:17	The war h is a vain hope for victory,
Zech	1: 8	I saw a man riding on a red h!
Rev	6: 2	I looked, and there was a white h!
	19:11	and there was a white h!

HORSES → HORSE

2 Kings	2:11	a chariot of fire and h of fire
Ps	20: 7	pride in chariots, and some in h,
Joel	2: 4	They have the appearance of h,
Rev	9: 7	appearance the locusts were like h
	19:14	following him on white h.

HOSANNA

Mk	11:10	H in the highest heaven!"
Jn	12:13	went out to meet him, shouting, "H!

HOSEA

Prophet whose wife and family pictured the unfaithfulness of Israel (Hos 1-3).

HOSHEA → =JOSHUA

1. Original name of Joshua (Num 13:8, 16).
2. Last king of Israel (2 Kings 15:30; 17:1-6).

HOSPITABLE* → HOSPITALITY

1 Tim	3: 2	temperate, sensible, respectable, h,
Titus	1: 8	but he must be h, a lover
1 Pet	4: 9	Be h to one another without

HOSPITALITY* → HOSPITABLE

Rom	12:13	of the saints; extend h to strangers.
1 Tim	5:10	has brought up children, shown h,
Heb	13: 2	not neglect to show h to strangers,

HOST → HOSTS

Deut	4:19	all the h of heaven,
2 Kings	17:16	worshiped all the h of heaven
Lk	2:13	angel a multitude of the heavenly h,

HOSTILE → HOSTILITY

Rom	8: 7	that is set on the flesh is h to God;
Col	1:21	once estranged and h in mind,

HOSTILITY → HOSTILE

Eph	2:14	the dividing wall, that is, the h
Heb	12: 3	Consider him who endured such h

HOSTS → HOST

1 Sam	1: 3	and to sacrifice to the LORD of h
Ps	46: 7	The LORD of h is with us;
Isa	48: 2	the LORD of h is his name.

HOT

Rev	3:15	you are neither cold nor h.

HOUR

Mt	6:27	by worrying add a single h to your
	24:36	about that day and h no one knows,
Jn	2: 4	My h has not yet come."
	17: 1	"Father, the h has come;
Rev	3:10	I will keep you from the h of trial
	14: 7	for the h of his judgment has come;

HOUSE → HOUSEHOLD, HOUSES, HOUSETOP, HOUSETOPS, STOREHOUSE

Ex	20:17	shall not covet your neighbor's h;
2 Sam	7:11	that the LORD will make you a h.
1 Chr	22: 1	"Here shall be the h of the LORD
Ezra	1: 5	rebuild the h of the LORD in
Ps	69: 9	zeal for your h that has consumed
	127: 1	Unless the LORD builds the h,
Prov	9: 1	Wisdom has built her h, she has
Isa	56: 7	my h shall be called a h of prayer
Mt	7:24	like a wise man who built his h
	21:13	'My h shall be called a h of prayer';
Mk	3:25	And if a h is divided against itself,
Jn	2:17	"Zeal for your h will consume me."
	14: 2	In my Father's h there are many
1 Pet	2: 5	be built into a spiritual h,

HOUSEHOLD → HOUSE

Josh	24:15	and my h, we will serve the LORD."
Mic	7: 6	enemies are members of your own h
Mt	10:36	will be members of one's own h.
Eph	2:19	and also members of the h of God,
1 Tim	3: 4	He must manage his own h well,
	3:15	how one ought to behave in the h of God
Titus	2: 5	good managers of the h, kind,
1 Pet	4:17	judgment to begin with the h of God

HOUSES → HOUSE

Ex	12:27	passed over the h of the Israelites in
Mt	19:29	everyone who has left h or brothers

HOUSETOP → HOUSE

Mt	24:17	the one on the h must not go down

HOUSETOPS → HOUSE

Mt	10:27	whispered, proclaim from the h.

HULDAH*

Prophetess inquired by Hilkiah for Josiah (2 Kings 22; 2 Chr 34:14-28).

HUMAN → HUMANKIND

Gen	6: 7	blot out from the earth the h beings
Jdt	8:16	for God is not like a h being,
Ps	8: 4	are h beings that you are mindful
Dan	2:34	a stone was cut out, not by h hands,
	5: 5	the fingers of a h hand appeared
Hos	11: 4	I led them with cords of h kindness,
Mt	15: 9	teaching h precepts as doctrines.'"
Acts	5:29	obey God rather than any h
1 Cor	2:13	in words not taught by h wisdom
Phil	2: 7	being born in h likeness.
Rev	4: 7	with a face like a h face,

HUMANKIND → HUMAN

Gen	1:26	"Let us make h in our image,
Mk	2:27	"The sabbath was made for h,
1 Tim	2: 5	one mediator between God and h,

HUMBLE → HUMBLED, HUMBLY, HUMILITY
Num 12: 3 Now the man Moses was very **h**,
Deut 8:16 to **h** you and to test you,
Ps 25: 9 He leads the **h** in what is right,
149: 4 he adorns the **h** with victory.
Sir 3:20 but by the **h** he is glorified.
Isa 57:15 to revive the spirit of the **h**,
Zeph 2: 3 Seek the LORD, all you **h** of the land
Mt 11:29 for I am gentle and **h** in heart,
21: 5 **h**, and mounted on a donkey,
Jas 4:10 **H** yourselves before the Lord,
1 Pet 5: 5 but gives grace to the **h**."

HUMBLED → HUMBLE
Ps 119:71 It is good for me that I was **h**,
Lk 14:11 all who exalt themselves will be **h**,
Phil 2: 8 he **h** himself and became obedient

HUMBLY* → HUMBLE
Mic 6: 8 and to walk **h** with your God?

HUMILITY → HUMBLE
Prov 15:33 and **h** goes before honor.
Sir 1:27 fidelity and **h** are his delight.
Zeph 2: 3 seek righteousness, seek **h**;
Phil 2: 3 but in **h** regard others as better than
Col 3:12 with compassion, kindness, **h**,
1 Pet 5: 5 must clothe yourselves with **h**

HUNDRED
Gen 17:17 born to a man who is a **h** years old?
Isa 65:20 one who dies at a **h** years will be
Rom 4:19 (for he was about a **h** years old),

HUNG
Deut 21:23 **h** on a tree is under God's curse.
Ps 137: 2 the willows there we **h** up our harps.
Mk 9:42 if a great millstone were **h** around

HUNGER → HUNGRY
Deut 8: 3 He humbled you by letting you **h**,
Mt 5: 6 "Blessed are those who **h** and thirst
Rev 7:16 will **h** no more, and thirst no more;

HUNGRY → HUNGER
Ps 50:12 "If I were **h**, I would not tell you,
146: 7 who gives food to the **h**.
Prov 25:21 If your enemies are **h**, give them
Mt 12: 1 his disciples were **h**, and they began
Jn 6:35 comes to me will never be **h**,
Rom 12:20 "if your enemies are **h**, feed them;

HUSBAND → HUSBANDS
Gen 3: 6 and she also gave some to her **h**,
3:16 yet your desire shall be for your **h**,
Prov 31:28 her **h** too, and he praises her:
Sir 26: 1 Happy is the **h** of a good wife;
Isa 54: 5 For your Maker is your **h**,
Jer 31:32 they broke, though I was their **h**,
Hos 2:16 the LORD, you will call me, "My **h**,"
1 Cor 7:10 wife should not separate from her **h**
Eph 5:23 **h** is the head of the wife just as
Rev 21: 2 as a bride adorned for her **h**.

HUSBANDS → HUSBAND
Jn 4:18 for you have had five **h**,
Eph 5:25 **H**, love your wives, just as Christ
Col 3:18 Wives, be subject to your **h**,
Titus 2: 4 the young women to love their **h**,
1 Pet 3: 7 **H**, in the same way, show

HUSHAI
Wise man of David; foiled Absalom's revolt (2 Sam 15:32-37; 16:15-17:16).

HYMN → HYMNS
Sir 44: 1 **H** IN HONOR OF OUR ANCESTORS
Mt 26:30 When they had sung the **h**,

HYMNS → HYMN
Dan 3:24 singing **h** to God and blessing the
Eph 5:19 psalms and **h** and spiritual songs
Col 3:16 in your hearts sing psalms, **h**,

HYPOCRISY → HYPOCRITE, HYPOCRITES
Mt 23:28 but inside you are full of **h** and
Mk 12:15 knowing their **h**, he said to them,
Lk 12: 1 of the Pharisees, that is, their **h**.

Jas 3:17 without a trace of partiality or **h**.

HYPOCRITE → HYPOCRISY
Sir 1:29 Do not be a **h** before others,
Lk 6:42 You **h**, first take the log out of your

HYPOCRITES → HYPOCRISY
Mt 6: 5 you pray, do not be like the **h**;
23:13 to you, scribes and Pharisees, **h**!
Mk 7: 6 prophesied rightly about you **h**,

HYSSOP
Ex 12:22 a bunch of **h**, dip it in the blood that
Num 19: 6 The priest shall take cedarwood, **h**,
Ps 51: 7 Purge me with **h**, and I shall be
Jn 19:29 full of the wine on a branch of **h**

I

I AM
Ex 3:14 God said to Moses, "I AM WHO **I AM**."
Isa 44: 6 I am the first and **I am** the last;
Mt 28:20 **I am** with you always, to the end of
Mk 8:29 "But who do you say that **I am**?"
Jn 6:35 to them, "**I am** the bread of life.
8:12 "**I am** the light of the world.
8:58 before Abraham was, **I am**."
9: 5 **I am** the light of the world."
10: 7 **I am** the gate for the sheep.
10:11 "**I am** the good shepherd.
11:25 "**I am** the resurrection and the life.
14: 6 "**I am** the way, and the truth, and
15: 1 "**I am** the true vine, and my Father
Rev 1: 8 "**I am** the Alpha and the Omega,"
22:20 "Surely **I am** coming soon."

IDLE
Eccl 11: 6 evening do not let your hands be **i**;
2 Thess 3: 7 were not **i** when we were with you,

IDOL → IDOLS
Ex 20: 4 shall not make for yourself an **i**,
Isa 40:19 An **i**?—A workman casts it,
1 Cor 10:19 or that an **i** is anything?

IDOLS → IDOL
Ex 34:17 You shall not make cast **i**.
2 Kings 17:15 went after false **i** and became false;
1 Macc 1:43 they sacrificed to **i** and profaned the
Ps 115: 4 Their **i** are silver and gold,
1 Cor 8: 1 concerning food sacrificed to **i**:

IGNORANCE → IGNORANT
Acts 17:30 overlooked the times of human **i**,
1 Pet 2:15 silence the **i** of the foolish.

IGNORANT → IGNORANCE
Heb 5: 2 He is able to deal gently with the **i**
2 Pet 3:16 the **i** and unstable twist to their own

ILL → ILLNESS
1 Cor 11:30 many of you are weak and **i**,

ILLEGITIMATE
Jn 8:41 said to him, "We are not **i** children;
Heb 12: 8 then you are **i** and not his children.

ILLNESS → ILL
Deut 7:15 will turn away from you every **i**;
Ps 41: 3 their **i** you heal all their infirmities.

IMAGE → IMAGES
Gen 1:26 "Let us make humankind in our **i**,
Deut 27:15 who makes an idol or casts an **i**,
Sir 17: 3 and made them in his own **i**.
1 Cor 15:49 the **i** of the man of heaven.
Col 1:15 He is the **i** of the invisible God,
Rev 20: 4 not worshiped the beast or its **i** and

IMAGES → IMAGE
Num 33:52 destroy all their cast **i**,
Ps 97: 7 All worshipers of **i** are put to shame,

IMITATE → IMITATORS
Heb 13: 7 their way of life, and **i** their faith.
3 Jn 1:11 not what is evil but **i** what is good.

IMITATORS → IMITATE
1 Cor 11: 1 Be **i** of me, as I am of Christ.

Eph 5: 1 be i of God, as beloved children,

IMMANUEL* → =EMMANUEL
Isa 7:14 bear a son, and shall name him I.
8: 8 fill the breadth of your land, O I.

IMMORAL → IMMORALITY
1 Cor 5: 9 not to associate with sexually i
Heb 12:16 an i and godless person,

IMMORALITY → IMMORAL
Sir 41:17 Be ashamed of sexual i,
2 Cor 12:21 sexual i, and licentiousness
Jude 1: 7 indulged in sexual i and pursued

IMMORTAL → IMMORTALITY
Rom 1:23 the glory of the i God for images
1 Tim 1:17 To the King of the ages, i, invisible,

IMMORTALITY → IMMORTAL
1 Cor 15:53 and this mortal body must put on i.
1 Tim 6:16 It is he alone who has i and dwells

IMPERISHABLE
1 Cor 9:25 a perishable wreath, but we an i one.
15:52 and the dead will be raised i,
1 Pet 1: 4 and into an inheritance that is i,

IMPORTANCE* → IMPORTANT
1 Cor 15: 3 of first i what I in turn had received:

IMPORTANT → IMPORTANCE
Mk 12:33 much more i than all whole burnt

IMPOSSIBLE
Zech 8: 6 should it also seem i to me,
Mt 17:20 and nothing will be i for you."
Mk 10:27 "For mortals it is i, but not for God;
Heb 11: 6 without faith it is i to please God,

IMPURE* → IMPURITY
Eph 5: 5 that no fornicator or i person,
1 Thess 2: 3 not spring from deceit or i motives

IMPURITY → IMPURE
Zech 13: 1 to cleanse them from sin and i.
Gal 5:19 fornication, i, licentiousness,
1 Thess 4: 7 did not call us to i but in holiness.

INCENSE → FRANKINCENSE
Ex 25: 6 anointing oil and for the fragrant i,

INCLINATION
Gen 6: 5 and that every i of the thoughts
Eccl 11: 9 Follow the i of your heart and

INCREASE → INCREASED
Gen 3:16 greatly i your pangs in childbearing;
Lk 17: 5 said to the Lord, "I our faith!"
Jn 3:30 He must i, but I must decrease."

INCREASED → INCREASE
Rom 5:20 but where sin i, grace abounded all

INDEBTED* → DEBT
Lk 11: 4 forgive everyone i to us.

INDEPENDENT*
1 Cor 11:11 not i of man or man i of woman.

INFANTS
Ps 8: 2 Out of the mouths of babes and i
Mt 21:16 'Out of the mouths of i and nursing
1 Cor 14:20 i in evil, but in thinking be adults.

INFIRMITIES
Isa 53: 4 borne our i and carried our diseases;
Mt 8:17 took our i and bore our diseases."

INGATHERING → GATHER
Ex 23:16 You shall observe the festival of i

INHERIT → INHERITANCE
Lev 20:24 You shall i their land,
Ps 37:11 But the meek shall i the land,
Zech 2:12 The Lord will i Judah as his portion
Lk 10:25 "what must I do to i eternal life?"
1 Cor 6: 9 wrongdoers will not i the kingdom
Heb 1:14 sake of those who are to i salvation?

INHERITANCE → INHERIT
Ex 34: 9 and take us for your i."
Eph 1:11 In Christ we have also obtained an i,

Col 1:12 share in the i of the saints in the light.
Heb 9:15 the promised eternal i,

INIQUITIES → INIQUITY
Lev 16:22 goat shall bear on itself all their i
Ps 103:10 nor repay us according to our i.
Isa 53:11 and he shall bear their i.
Rom 4: 7 are those whose i are forgiven,
Rev 18: 5 and God has remembered her i.

INIQUITY → INIQUITIES
Ex 34: 7 forgiving i and transgression and sin
Ps 103: 3 who forgives all your i,
Isa 53: 6 Lord has laid on him the i of us all.
Titus 2:14 that he might redeem us from all i

INJURY
Lev 24:20 the i inflicted is the i to be suffered.

INJUSTICE
Hos 10:13 wickedness, you have reaped i,
Rom 9:14 Is there i on God's part?

INN*
Lk 2: 7 there was no place for them in the i.
10:34 brought him to an i, and took care

INNER → INWARDLY
Mt 24:26 He is in the i rooms,' do not believe
2 Cor 4:16 our i nature is being renewed day
1 Pet 3: 4 let your adornment be the i self

INNOCENCE → INNOCENT
Ps 26: 6 I wash my hands in i,
Hos 8: 5 long will they be incapable of i?

INNOCENT → INNOCENCE
Prov 6:17 tongue, and hands that shed i blood,
Mt 10:16 be wise as serpents and i as doves.
27:24 "I am i of this man's blood;

INQUIRE → INQUIRED
Deut 12:30 do not i concerning their gods,

INQUIRED → INQUIRE
Zeph 1: 6 not sought the Lord or i of him.

INSCRIBED → INSCRIPTION
Dan 10:21 what is i in the book of truth.
Rev 19:12 he has a name i that no one

INSCRIPTION → INSCRIBED
Mk 15:26 The i of the charge against him read,
2 Tim 2:19 foundation stands, bearing this i:

INSIGHT
Prov 3: 5 and do not rely on your own i.
Sir 6:37 It is he who will give i to your mind,
Eph 1: 8 With all wisdom and i

INSPIRED
Ex 35:34 And he has i him to teach,
2 Tim 3:16 All scripture is i by God and is

INSTITUTED → INSTITUTION
Rom 13: 1 that exist have been i by God.

INSTITUTION* → INSTITUTED
Num 10: 8 this shall be a perpetual i for you
1 Pet 2:13 the authority of every human i,

INSTRUCT → INSTRUCTED, INSTRUCTION, INSTRUCTOR
Deut 17:10 observing everything they i you.
Neh 9:20 You gave your good spirit to i them,
Rom 15:14 and able to i one another.
1 Cor 14:19 in order to i others also,

INSTRUCTED → INSTRUCT
Isa 40:13 or as his counselor has i him?
Jn 8:28 these things as the Father i me.

INSTRUCTION → INSTRUCT
Prov 8:10 Take my i instead of silver,
Sir 51:26 and let your souls receive i;
Mic 4: 2 For out of Zion shall go forth i,
Rom 15: 4 in former days was written for our i,
1 Tim 1: 5 But the aim of such i is love

INSTRUCTOR → INSTRUCT
Mt 23:10 for you have one i, the Messiah.

INSULTS
Ps	69: 9	the i of those who insult you have
Lk	22:65	heaping many other i on him.
2 Cor	12:10	I am content with weaknesses, i,

INTEGRITY
Job	27: 5	until I die I will not put away my i
Prov	14:32	the righteous find a refuge in their i.
Titus	2: 7	and in your teaching show i, gravity,

INTELLIGENCE → INTELLIGENT
Prov	8: 5	acquire i, you who lack it.
Sir	22:11	fool, for he has left i behind.

INTELLIGENT → INTELLIGENCE
Prov	11:12	but an i person remains silent.
Eccl	9:11	nor riches to the i,

INTENDED → INTENTIONS
Gen	50:20	i to do harm to me, God i it for good,
Jer	18:10	the good that I had i to do to it.

INTENTIONS → INTENDED
Mk	7:21	the human heart, that evil i come:
Heb	4:12	judge the thoughts and i of the heart.

INTERCEDES → INTERCESSION
Rom	8:26	Spirit i with sighs too deep for

INTERCESSION* → INTERCEDES
1 Sam	2:25	against the LORD, who can make i?"
Isa	53:12	and made i for the transgressors.
Heb	7:25	he always lives to make i for them.

INTERMARRY → MARRIAGE
Deut	7: 3	Do not i with them, giving your

INTERPRET → INTERPRETATION, INTERPRETATIONS
Gen	41:15	no one who can i it.
Mt	16: 3	cannot i the signs of the times.
1 Cor	12:30	Do all speak in tongues? Do all i?

INTERPRETATION → INTERPRET
Dan	2: 4	and we will reveal the i."
1 Cor	12:10	to another the i of tongues.
2 Pet	1:20	scripture is a matter of one's own i,

INTERPRETATIONS → INTERPRET
Gen	40: 8	to them, "Do not i belong to God?

INVADE → INVADED
Lam	1:10	the nations i her sanctuary,
Nah	1:15	never again shall the wicked i you;

INVADED → INVADE
2 Kings	17: 5	the king of Assyria i all the land

INVISIBLE
Col	1:15	He is the image of the i God,
1 Tim	1:17	To the King of the ages, immortal, i,

INVITE → INVITED, INVITES
Lk	14:13	when you give a banquet, i the poor,

INVITED → INVITE
Rev	19: 9	Blessed are those who are i to

INVITES → INVITE
Sir	13: 9	When an influential person i you,
1 Cor	10:27	If an unbeliever i you to a meal

INVOKE
Ex	23:13	Do not i the names of other gods;
1 Pet	1:17	If you i as Father the one who

INWARDLY → INNER
Rom	2:29	a person is a Jew who is one i,
	8:23	groan i while we wait for adoption,

IRON
Ps	2: 9	shall break them with a rod of i,
Prov	27:17	I sharpens i, and one person
Dan	2:33	its legs of i, its feet partly of i
Rev	19:15	he will rule them with a rod of i.

IRREVOCABLE
Rom	11:29	gifts and the calling of God are i.

ISAAC
Son of Abraham by Sarah (Gen 17:19; 21:1-7; 1 Chr 1:28). Abrahamic covenant perpetuated with (Gen 17:21; 26:2-5). Offered up by Abraham (Gen 22; Heb 11:17-19). Rebekah taken as wife (Gen 24). Inherited Abraham's estate (Gen 25:5). Father of

Esau and Jacob (Gen 25:19-26; 1 Chr 1:34). Nearly lost Rebekah to Abimelech (Gen 26:1-11). Covenant with Abimelech (Gen 26:12-31). Tricked into blessing Jacob (Gen 27). Death (Gen 35:27-29). Father of Israel (Ex 3:6; Deut 29:13; Rom 9:10).

ISAIAH
Prophet to Judah (Isa 1:1). Called by the LORD (Isa 6). Announced judgment to Ahaz (Isa 7), deliverance from Assyria to Hezekiah (2 Kings 19; Isa 36-37), deliverance from death to Hezekiah (2 Kings 20:1-11; Isa 38). Chronicler of Judah's history (2 Chr 26:22; 32:32).

ISCARIOT
Mt	10: 4	Judas I, the one who betrayed him.
Lk	22: 3	Satan entered into Judas called I,

ISHBAAL*
Son of Saul; would-be king (2 Sam 2:8-4:12).

ISHMAEL
Son of Abraham by Hagar (Gen 16; 1 Chr 1:28). Blessed, but not son of covenant (Gen 17:18-21; Gal 4:21-31). Sent away by Sarah (Gen 21:8-21). Children (Gen 25:12-18; 1 Chr 1:29-31). Death (Gen 25:17).

ISRAEL → ISRAELITE, ISRAELITES, =JACOB
1. Name given to Jacob (Gen 32:28; 35:10).
2. Corporate name of Jacob's descendants; often specifically Northern Kingdom.
Gen	49:28	All these are the twelve tribes of I,
Ex	28:11	with the names of the sons of I;
Num	24:17	and a scepter shall rise out of I;
Deut	6: 4	Hear, O I: The LORD is our God,
Ps	125: 5	Peace be upon I!
Sir	17:17	but I is the Lord's own portion.
Jer	31:31	a new covenant with the house of I
Hos	11: 1	When I was a child, I loved him,
Mt	2: 6	who is to shepherd my people I.'"
Mk	12:29	answered, "The first is, 'Hear, O I,
Lk	22:30	judging the twelve tribes of I.
Acts	1: 6	you will restore the kingdom to I?"
Rom	9: 6	not all Israelites truly belong to I,
Heb	8: 8	a new covenant with the house of I
Rev	7: 4	out of every tribe of the people of I:

ISRAELITE → ISRAEL
Jn	1:47	an I in whom there is no deceit!"
Rom	11: 1	I myself am an I, a descendant of

ISRAELITES → ISRAEL
Ex	2:23	The I groaned under their slavery,
	29:45	I will dwell among the I, and I will

ISSACHAR
Son of Jacob by Leah (Gen 30:18; 35:23; 1 Chr 2:1). Tribe of blessed (Gen 49:14-15; Deut 33:18-19), numbered (Num 1:29; 26:25), allotted land (Josh 19:17-23; Ezek 48:25), assisted Deborah (Judg 5:15), 12,000 from (Rev 7:7).

ITCHING
2 Tim	4: 3	sound doctrine, but having i ears,

J

JACOB → =ISRAEL
1. Son of Isaac, younger twin of Esau (Gen 26:21-26; 1 Chr 1:34). Bought Esau's birthright (Gen 26:29-34); tricked Isaac into blessing him (Gen 27:1-37). Fled to Haran (Gen 28:1-5). Abrahamic covenant perpetuated through (Gen 28:13-15; Mal 1:2). Vision at Bethel (Gen 28:10-22). Served Laban for Rachel and Leah (Gen 29:1-30). Children (Gen 29:31-30:24; 35:16-26; 1 Chr 2-9). Flocks increased (Gen 30:25-43). Returned to Canaan (Gen 31). Wrestled with God; name changed to Israel (Gen 32:22-32). Reconciled to Esau (Gen 33). Returned to Bethel (Gen 35:1-15). Favored Joseph (Gen 37:3). Sent sons to Egypt during famine (Gen 42-43). Settled in Egypt (Gen 46). Blessed Ephraim and Manasseh (Gen 48). Blessed sons (Gen 49:1-28; Heb 11:21). Death (Gen 49:29-33). Burial (Gen 50:1-14).
2. Corporate name of Jacob's descendants; often specifically Northern Kingdom.
1 Macc	1:28	house of J was clothed with shame.
Ps	135: 4	the LORD has chosen J for himself,
Mic	7:20	You will show faithfulness to J
Rom	9:13	"I have loved J,

JAEL*

Woman who killed the Canaanite general, Sisera (Judg 4:17-22; 5:6, 24-27).

JAIRUS

Synagogue ruler whose daughter Jesus raised (Mk 5:22-43; Lk 8:41-56).

JAMES

1. Apostle; brother of John (Mt 4:21-22; 10:2; Mk 3:17; Lk 5:1-10). At transfiguration (Mt 17:1-13; Mk 9:1-13; Lk 9:28-36). Killed by Herod (Acts 12:2).

2. Apostle (Mt 10:3; Mk 3:18; Lk 6:15).

3. Brother of Jesus (Mt 13:55; Mk 6:3; Lk 24:10; Gal 1:19) and Judas (Jude 1). With believers before Pentecost (Acts 1:13). Leader of church at Jerusalem (Acts 12:17; 15; 21:18; Gal 2:9, 12). Author of epistle (Jas 1:1).

JAPHETH

Son of Noah (Gen 5:32; 1 Chr 1:4-5). Blessed (Gen 9:18-28). Sons of (Gen 10:2-5).

JAR → JARS

1 Kings	17:14	The j of meal will not be emptied
Mk	14: 3	alabaster j of very costly ointment
Lk	22:10	man carrying a j of water will meet

JARS → JAR

Jn	2: 6	there were six stone water j for
2 Cor	4: 7	But we have this treasure in clay j,

JEALOUS

Ex	34:14	whose name is J, is a j God).
Deut	4:24	God is a devouring fire, a j God.
	32:16	They made him j with strange gods,
Ezek	39:25	and I will be j for my holy name.
Rom	10:19	"I will make you j of those

JEBUSITES

Ex	3: 8	the Perizzites, the Hivites, and the J.
Josh	15:63	Judah could not drive out the J,

JECONIAH → See JEHOIACHIN

JEHOAHAZ

1. Son of Jehu; king of Israel (2 Kings 13:1-9).

2. Son of Josiah; king of Judah (2 Kings 23:31-34; 2 Chr 36:1-4).

JEHOASH → =JOASH

1. Son of Ahaziah, king of Judah (2 Kings 12). See Joash, 1.

2. Son of Jehoahaz; king of Israel. Defeat of Aram prophesied by Elisha (2 Kings 13:10-25). Defeated Amaziah in Jerusalem (2 Kings 14:1-16). See Joash, 2.

JEHOIACHIN → =CONIAH, =JECONIAH

Son of Jehoiakim; king of Judah exiled by Nebuchadnezzar (2 Kings 24:8-17; 2 Chr 36:8-10; Ezek 1:2). Status improved (2 Kings 25:27-30; Jer 52:31-34).

JEHOIADA

Priest who sheltered Joash from Athaliah (2 Kings 11-12; 2 Chr 22:11-24:16).

JEHOIAKIM → =ELIAKIM

Son of Josiah; made king of Judah by Nebuchadnezzar (2 Kings 23:34-24:6; 2 Chr 36:4-8; Jer 22:18-23). Burned scroll of Jeremiah's prophecies (Jer 36).

JEHORAM → =JORAM

1. Son of Jehoshaphat; king of Judah. Prophesied against by Elijah; killed by the LORD (2 Chr 21). See Joram, 1.

2. Son of Ahab; king of Israel (2 Chr 22:5). Joined Jehoshaphat against Moab (2 Kings 3). See Joram, 2.

JEHOSHAPHAT

1. Son of Asa; king of Judah. Strengthened his kingdom (2 Chr 17). Joined with Ahab against Aram (2 Kings 22; 2 Chr 18). Established judges (2 Chr 19). Joined Joram against Moab (2 Kings 3; 2 Chr 20).

2. Valley of judgment (Joel 3:2, 12).

JEHU

1. Prophet against Baasha (2 Kings 16:1-7).

2. King of Israel. Anointed by Elijah to obliterate house of Ahab (1 Kings 19:16-17); anointed by servant of Elisha (2 Kings 9:1-13). Killed Joram and Ahaziah (2 Kings 9:14-29; 2 Chr 22:7-9), Jezebel (2 Kings 9:30-37), relatives of Ahab (2 Kings 10:1-17; Hos 1:4), ministers of Baal (2 Kings 10:18-29). Death (2 Kings 10:30-36).

JEPHTHAH

Judge from Gilead who delivered Israel from Ammon (Judg 10:6-12:7). Made rash vow concerning his daughter (Judg 11:30-40).

JEREMIAH

Prophet to Judah (Jer 1:1-3). Called by the LORD (Jer 1). Put in stocks (Jer 20:1-3). Threatened for prophesying (Jer 11:18-23; 26). Opposed by Hananiah (Jer 28). Scroll burned (Jer 36). Imprisoned (Jer 37). Thrown into cistern (Jer 38). Forced to Egypt with those fleeing Babylonians (Jer 43).

JERICHO

Josh	6: 2	"See, I have handed J over to you,
1 Kings	16:34	In his days Hiel of Bethel built J;
Lk	18:35	As he approached J, a blind man

JEROBOAM

1. Official of Solomon; rebelled to become first king of Israel (1 Kings 11:26-40; 12:1-20; 2 Chr 10). Idolatry (1 Kings 12:25-33; Tob 1:5; Sir 47:23); judgment for (1 Kings 13-14; 2 Chr 13).

2. Son of Jehoash; king of Israel (1 Kings 14:23-29).

JERUSALEM

2 Sam	5:5	and at J he reigned over all Israel
	15:29	carried the ark of God back to J,
2 Kings	25:10	broke down the walls around J.
Ezra	2: 1	they returned to J and Judah,
Neh	2:17	Come, let us rebuild the wall of J,
1 Macc	1:29	and he came to J with a large force.
Isa	40: 2	Speak tenderly to J,
Lam	1: 8	J sinned grievously, so she has
Dan	9:25	went out to restore and rebuild J
Joel	3: 1	I restore the fortunes of Judah and J,
Mic	4: 2	and the word of the LORD from J.
Zech	1:14	I am very jealous for J and for Zion.
	14: 8	living waters shall flow out from J,
Mt	23:37	"J, J, the city that kills the prophets
Lk	4: 9	Then the devil took him to J,
Gal	4:25	corresponds to the present J,
Heb	12:22	of the living God, the heavenly J,
Rev	21: 2	And I saw the holy city, the new J,

JESSE

Father of David (Ruth 4:17-22; 1 Sam 16; 1 Chr 2:12-17).

JESUS

1. Jesus the Messiah.

LIFE: Genealogy (Mt 1:1-17; Lk 3:21-37). Birth announced (Mt 1:18-25; Lk 1:26-45). Birth (Mt 2:1-12; Lk 2:1-40). Escape to Egypt (Mt 2:13-23). As a boy in the temple (Lk 2:41-52). Baptism (Mt 3:13-17; Mk 1:9-11; Lk 3:21-22; Jn 1:32-34). Temptation (Mt 4:1-11; Mk 1:12-13; Lk 4:1-13). Ministry in Galilee (Mt 4:12-18:35; Mk 1:14-9:50; Lk 4:14-13:9; Jn 1:35-2:11; 4; 6), Transfiguration (Mt 17:1-8; Mk 9:2-8; Lk 9:28-36), on the way to Jerusalem (Mt 19-20; Mk 10; Lk 13:10-19:27), in Jerusalem (Mt 21-25; Mk 11-13; Lk 19:28-21:38; Jn 2:12-3:36; 5; 7-12). Last supper (Mt 26:17-35; Mk 14:12-31; Lk 22:1-38; Jn 13-17). Arrest and trial (Mt 26:36-27:31; Mk 14:43-15:20; Lk 22:39-23:25; Jn 18:1-19:16). Crucifixion (Mt 27:32-66; Mk 15:21-47; Lk 23:26-55; Jn 19:28-42). Resurrection and appearances (Mt 28; Mk 16; Lk 24; Jn 20-21; Acts 1:1-11; 7:56; 9:3-6; 1 Cor 15:1-8; Rev 1:1-20).

MIRACLES. *Healings:* official's son (Jn 4:43-54), demoniac in Capernaum (Mk 1:23-26; Lk 4:33-35), Peter's mother-in-law (Mt 8:14-17; Mk 1:29-31; Lk 4:38-39), leper (Mt 8:2-4; Mk 1:40-45; Lk 5:12-16), paralytic (Mt 9:1-8; Mk 2:1-12; Lk 5:17-26), cripple (Jn 5:1-9), shriveled hand (Mt 12:10-13; Mk 3:1-5; Lk 6:6-11), centurion's servant (Mt 8:5-13; Lk 7:1-10), widow's son raised (Lk 7:11-17), demoniac (Mt 12:22-23; Lk 11:14), Gadarene demoniacs (Mt 8:28-34; Mk 5:1-20; Lk 8:26-39), woman's bleeding and Jairus' daughter (Mt 9:18-26; Mk 5:21-43; Lk 8:40-56), blind man (Mt 9:27-31), mute man (Mt 9:32-33), Canaanite woman's daughter (Mt 15:21-28; Mk 7:24-30), deaf man (Mk 7:31-37), blind man (Mk 8:22-26), demoniac boy (Mt 17:14-18; Mk 9:14-29; Lk 9:37-43), ten lepers (Lk 17:11-19), man born blind (Jn 9:1-7), Lazarus raised (Jn 11), crippled woman (Lk 13:11-17), man with dropsy (Lk 14:1-6), two blind men (Mt 20:29-34; Mk 10:46-52; Lk 18:35-43), Malchus' ear (Lk 22:50-51). *Other Miracles:* water to wine (Jn 2:1-11), catch of fish (Lk 5:1-11), storm stilled (Mt 8:23-27; Mk 4:37-41; Lk 8:22-25), 5,000 fed (Mt 14:15-21; Mk 6:35-44; Lk 9:10-17; Jn 6:1-14), walking on water (Mt 14:25-33; Mk 6:48-

52; Jn 6:15-21), 4,000 fed (Mt 15:32-39; Mk 8:1-9), money from fish (Mt 17:24-27), fig tree cursed (Mt 21:18-22; Mk 11:12-14), catch of fish (Jn 21:1-14).

MAJOR TEACHING: Sermon on the Mount (Mt 5-7; Lk 6:17-49), to Nicodemus (Jn 3), to Samaritan woman (Jn 4), Bread of Life (Jn 6:22-59), at Feast of Tabernacles (Jn 7-8), woes to Pharisees (Mt 23; Lk 11:37-54), Good Shepherd (Jn 10:1-18), Olivet Discourse (Mt 24-25; Mk 13; Lk 21:5-36), Upper Room Discourse (Jn 13-16).

PARABLES: Sower (Mt 13:3-23; Mk 4:3-25; Lk 8:5-18), seed's growth (Mk 4:26-29), wheat and weeds (Mt 13:24-30, 36-43), mustard seed (Mt 13:31-32; Mk 4:30-32), yeast (Mt 13:33; Lk 13:20-21), hidden treasure (Mt 13:44), valuable pearl (Mt 13:45-46), net (Mt 13:47-51), house owner (Mt 13:52), good Samaritan (Lk 10:25-37), unmerciful servant (Mt 18:15-35), lost sheep (Mt 18:10-14; Lk 15:4-7), lost coin (Lk 15:8-10), prodigal son (Lk 15:11-32), dishonest manager (Lk 16:1-13), rich man and Lazarus (Lk 16:19-31), persistent widow (Lk 18:1-8), Pharisee and tax collector (Lk 18:9-14), payment of workers (Mt 20:1-16), tenants and the vineyard (Mt 21:28-46; Mt 12:1-12; Lk 20:9-19), wedding banquet (Mt 22:1-14), faithful servant (Mt 24:45-51), ten virgins (Mt 25:1-13), talents (Mt 25:1-30; Lk 19:12-27).

DISCIPLES see APOSTLES. Call (Jn 1:35-51; Mt 4:18-22; 9:9; Mk 1:16-20; 2:13-14; Lk 5:1-11, 27-28). Named Apostles (Mk 3:13-19; Lk 6:12-16). Twelve sent out (Mt 10; Mk 6:7-11; Lk 9:1-5). Seventy sent out (Lk 10:1-24). Defection of (Jn 6:60-71; Mt 26:56; Mk 14:50-52). Final commission (Mt 28:16-20; Jn 21:15-23; Acts 1:3-8).

Acts	9: 5	"I am J, whom you are persecuting.
1 Cor	8: 6	and one Lord, J Christ,
Phil	2:10	name of J every knee should bend,
2 Thess	2: 1	the coming of our Lord J Christ
1 Tim	1:15	J came into the world to save
Heb	12: 2	to J the pioneer and perfecter of our
	13: 8	J Christ is the same yesterday and
1 Jn	1: 7	the blood of J his Son cleanses us
Rev	1: 1	The revelation of J Christ,
	22:20	Amen. Come, Lord J!

2. Disciple, also called Justus (Col 4:11).
3. Writer of Sirach (Sir Pr:1; 50:27; 51:1).

JETHRO
Father-in-law and adviser of Moses (Ex 3:1; 4:18; 18). Also known as Reuel (Ex 2:18).

JEW → JEWS, JUDAISM

Esth	10: 3	Mordecai the J was next in rank to
Zech	8:23	shall take hold of a J,
Rom	1:16	to the J first and also to the Greek.
	2:29	a person is a J who is one inwardly,
1 Cor	9:20	To the Jews I became as a J,
Col	3:11	there is no longer Greek and J,

JEWEL → JEWELS

| Prov | 20:15 | by knowledge are a precious j. |
| Rev | 21:19 | of the city are adorned with every j; |

JEWELS → JEWEL

Prov	3:15	She is more precious than j,
Isa	54:12	your gates of j, and all your wall
Rev	17: 4	adorned with gold and j and pearls,

JEWS → JEW

Neh	4: 1	enraged, and he mocked the J.
Esth	3:13	to kill, and to annihilate all J,
Mt	2: 2	who has been born king of the J?
	27:11	"Are you the King of the J?"
Jn	4:22	for salvation is from the J.
Rom	3:29	Or is God the God of J only?

JEZEBEL*
Sidonian wife of Ahab (1 Kings 16:31). Promoted Baal worship (1 Kings 16:32-33). Killed prophets of the LORD (1 Kings 18:4, 13). Opposed Elijah (1 Kings 19:1-2). Had Naboth killed (1 Kings 21). Death (1 Kings 21:17-24; 2 Kings 9:30-37). Metaphor of immorality (Rev 2:20).

JEZREEL

| 2 Kings 10: 7 | in baskets and sent them to him at J. |
| Hos 1: 4 | the LORD said to him, "Name him J; |

JOAB
Nephew of David (1 Chr 2:16). Commander of his army (2 Sam 8:16). Victorious over Ammon (2 Sam 10; 1 Chr 19), Rabbah (2 Sam 11; 1 Chr 20), Jerusalem (1 Chr 11:6), Absalom

(2 Sam 18), Sheba (2 Sam 20). Killed Abner (2 Sam 3:22-39), Amasa (2 Sam 20:1-13). Numbered David's army (2 Sam 24; 1 Chr 21). Sided with Adonijah (1 Kings 1:17, 19). Killed by Benaiah (1 Kings 2:5-6, 28-35).

JOASH → =JEHOASH
1. Son of Ahaziah; king of Judah. Sheltered from Athaliah by Jehoiada (2 Kings 11; 2 Chr 22:10-23:21). Repaired temple (2 Chr 24). See Jehoash, 1.
2. Son of Jehoahaz, king of Israel (2 Kings 13; 2 Chr 25:17-25). See Jehoash, 2.

JOB
Wealthy man from Uz; feared God (Job 1:1-5). Integrity tested by disaster (Job 1:6-22), personal affliction (Job 2). Maintained innocence in debate with three friends (Job 3-31), Elihu (Job 32-37). Rebuked by the LORD (Job 38-41). Vindicated and restored to greater stature by the LORD (Job 42). Example of righteousness (Ezek 14:14, 20; Sir 49:9).

JOEL
1. Son of Samuel (1 Sam 8:2; 1 Chr 6:28).
2. Prophet (Joel 1:1; Acts 2:16).

JOHANAN
1. First high priest in the temple (1 Chr 6:9-10).
2. Jewish leader who tried to save Gedaliah from assassination (Jer 40:13-14); took Jews, including Jeremiah, to Egypt (Jer 40-43).

JOHN
1. Son of Zechariah and Elizabeth (Lk 1). Called the Baptist (Mt 3:1-12; Mk 1:2-8). Witness to Jesus (Mt 3:11-12; Mk 1:7-8; Lk 3:15-18; Jn 1:6-35; 3:27-30; 5:33-36). Doubts about Jesus (Mt 11:2-6; Lk 7:18-23). Arrest (Mt 4:12; Mk 1:14). Execution (Mt 14:1-12; Mk 6:14-29; Lk 9:7-9). Ministry compared to Elijah (Mt 11:7-19; Mk 9:11-13; Lk 7:24-35).
2. Apostle; brother of James (Mt 4:21-22; 10:2; Mk 3:17; Lk 5:1-10). At transfiguration (Mt 17:1-13; Mk 9:1-13; Lk 9:28-36). Desire to be greatest (Mk 10:35-45). Leader of church at Jerusalem (Acts 4:1-3; Gal 2:9). Elder who wrote epistles (2 Jn 1; 3 Jn 1). Prophet who wrote Revelation (Rev 1:1; 22:8).
3. Cousin of Barnabas, co-worker with Paul, (Acts 12:12-13:13; 15:37; see Mark).
4. Son of Simon Maccabeus (1 Macc 13:53; 16).

JOIN → JOINED

| Ezek | 37:17 | and j them together into one stick, |
| 2 Tim | 1: 8 | j with me in suffering for the gospel |

JOINED → JOIN

| Mt | 19: 6 | what God has j together, let no one |
| Eph | 2:21 | the whole structure is j together and |

JOINT → JOINTS

Gen	32:25	and Jacob's hip was put out of j
Ps	22:14	and all my bones are out of j;
Rom	8:17	heirs of God and j heirs with Christ

JOINTS → JOINT

| Heb | 4:12 | soul from spirit, j from marrow; |

JONAH
Prophet in days of Jeroboam II (2 Kings 14:25). Called to Nineveh; fled to Tarshish (Jon 1:1-3). Cause of storm; thrown into sea (Jon 1:4-16). Swallowed by fish (Jon 1:17). Prayer (Jon 2). Preached to Nineveh (Jon 3). Attitude reproved by the LORD (Jon 4). Sign of (Mt 12:39-41; Lk 11:29-32).

JONATHAN
1. Son of Saul (1 Sam 13:16; 1 Chr 8:33). Valiant warrior (1 Sam 13-14). Relation to David (1 Sam 18:1-4; 19-20; 23:16-18). Killed at Gilboa (1 Sam 31). Mourned by David (2 Sam 1).
2. Brother and successor of Judas Maccabeus (1 Macc 2:5; 9:28-31).

JOPPA

| Jon | 1: 3 | down to J and found a ship going |
| Acts | 9:43 | he stayed in J for some time with |

JORAM → =JEHORAM
1. Son of Jehoshaphat; king of Judah (2 Kings 8:16-24). See Jehoram, 1.
2. Son of Ahab; king of Israel. Killed with Ahaziah by Jehu (2 Kings 8:25-29; 9:14-26; 2 Chr 22:5-9). See Jehoram, 2.

JORDAN

| Gen | 13:10 | the plain of the J was well watered |
| Num | 34:12 | the boundary shall go down to the J, |

Josh 3:17 dry ground in the middle of the **J**,
Mt 3: 6 were baptized by him in the river **J**,

JOSEPH → =BARNABAS, =BARSABBAS
1. Son of Jacob by Rachel (Gen 30:24; 1 Chr 2:2). Favored by Jacob, hated by brothers (Gen 37:3-4). Dreams (Gen 37:5-11). Sold by brothers (Gen 37:12-36). Served Potiphar; imprisoned by false accusation (Gen 39). Interpreted dreams of Pharaoh's servants (Gen 40), of Pharaoh (Gen 41:4-40). Made greatest in Egypt (Gen 41:41-57). Sold grain to brothers (Gen 42-45). Brought Jacob and sons to Egypt (Gen 46-47). Sons Ephraim and Manasseh blessed (Gen 48). Blessed (Gen 49:22-26; Deut 33:13-17). Death (Gen 50:22-26; Ex 13:19; Heb 11:22). 12,000 from (Rev 7:8).
2. Husband of Mary mother of Jesus (Mt 1:16-24; 2:13-19; Lk 1:27; 2; Jn 1:45).
3. Disciple from Arimathea; buried Jesus in his tomb (Mt 27:57-61; Mk 15:43-47; Lk 24:50-52).
4. Original name of Barnabas (Acts 4:36).

JOSHUA → =HOSHEA, =JESHUA
1. Son of Nun; name changed from Hoshea (Num 13:8, 16; 1 Chr 7:27). Fought Amalekites under Moses (Ex 17:9-14). Servant of Moses on Sinai (Ex 24:13; 32:17). Spied Canaan (Num 13). With Caleb, allowed to enter land (Num 14:6, 30). Succeeded Moses (Deut 1:38; 31:1-8; 34:9).
Charged Israel to conquer Canaan (Josh 1). Crossed Jordan (Josh 3-4). Circumcised sons of wilderness wanderings (Josh 5). Conquered Jericho (Josh 6), Ai (Josh 7-8), five kings at Gibeon (Josh 10:1-28), southern Canaan (Josh 10:29-43), northern Canaan (Josh 11-12). Defeated at Ai (Josh 7). Deceived by Gibeonites (Josh 9). Renewed covenant (Josh 8:30-35; 24:1-27). Divided land among tribes (Josh 13-22). Last words (Josh 23). Death (Josh 24:28-31).
2. High priest during rebuilding of temple (Hag 1-2; Zech 3:1-9; 6:11). See Jeshua.

JOSIAH
Son of Amon; king of Judah (2 Kings 21:26; 1 Chr 3:14). Prophesied (1 Kings 13:2). Book of the Law discovered during his reign (2 Kings 22; 2 Chr 34:14-31). Reforms (2 Kings 23:1-25; 2 Chr 34:1-13; 35:1-19; Sir 49:1-4). Killed in battle (2 Kings 23:29-30; 2 Chr 35:20-27).

JOTHAM
1. Son of Gideon (Judg 9).
2. Son of Azariah (Uzziah); king of Judah (2 Kings 15:32-38; 2 Chr 26:21-27:9).

JOY → JOYFUL
Neh 8:10 the **j** of the LORD is your strength."
Tob 13:17 Jerusalem will sing hymns of **j**,
Job 20: 5 **j** of the godless is but for a moment?
Ps 51:12 Restore to me the **j** of your salvation
Prov 21:15 When justice is done, it is a **j** to the
Isa 12: 3 With **j** you will draw water from
35:10 everlasting **j** shall be upon their
Lam 2:15 of beauty, the **j** of all the earth?"
Bar 5: 9 For God will lead Israel with **j**,
Mt 28: 8 tomb quickly with fear and great **j**,
Mk 4:16 they immediately receive it with **j**.
Lk 1:44 the child in my womb leaped for **j**.
2:10 bringing you good news of great **j**
Jn 16:22 no one will take your **j** from you.
Rom 14:17 but righteousness and peace and **j** in
Gal 5:22 the fruit of the Spirit is love, **j**,
Phil 4: 1 I love and long for, my **j** and crown,
Heb 12: 2 **j** that was set before him endured
Jas 1: 2 consider it nothing but **j**,

JOYFUL → JOY
Jdt 14: 9 and made a **j** noise in their town.
Ps 98: 4 Make a **j** noise to the LORD,

JUBILEE
Lev 25:10 It shall be a **j** for you:
Num 36: 4 when the **j** of the Israelites comes,

JUDAH → JUDEA
1. Son of Jacob by Leah (Gen 29:35; 35:23; 1 Chr 2:1). Did not want to kill Joseph (Gen 37:26-27). Among Canaanites, fathered Perez by Tamar (Gen 38). Tribe of blessed as ruling tribe (Gen 49:8-12; Deut 33:7), numbered (Num 1:27; 26:22), allotted land (Josh 15; Ezek 48:7), failed to fully possess (Josh 15:63; Judg 1:1-20).
2. Name used for Southern Kingdom.

2 Sam 2: 4 David king over the house of **J**.
Lam 1: 3 **J** has gone into exile with suffering
Joel 3: 1 when I restore the fortunes of **J** and
Mic 5: 2 who are one of the little clans of **J**,
Mt 2: 6 least among the rulers of **J**,
Heb 7:14 our Lord was descended from **J**,
Rev 5: 5 See, the Lion of the tribe of **J**,

JUDAISM → JEW
Acts 13:43 devout converts to **J** followed Paul
Gal 1:13 no doubt, of my earlier life in **J**.

JUDAS → =BARSABBAS, =JUDE, =THADDAEUS, MACCABEUS
1. Apostle; son of James (Lk 6:16; Jn 14:22; Acts 1:13). Probably also called Thaddaeus (Mt 10:3; Mk 3:18).
2. Brother of James and Jesus (Mt 13:55; Mk 6:3), also called Jude (Jude 1).
3. Christian prophet (Acts 15:22-32).
4. Apostle, also called Iscariot, who betrayed Jesus (Mt 10:4; 26:14-56; Mk 3:19; 14:10-50; Lk 6:16; 22:3-53; Jn 6:71; 12:4; 13:2-30; 18:2-11). Suicide of (Mt 27:3-5; Acts 1:16-25).
5. Leader of the Maccabean revolt (1 Macc 2:4, 66). Recaptured Jerusalem and rededicated the temple and altar (1 Macc 4:36-61). Death of (1 Macc 9).

JUDE → See JUDAS, 2

JUDEA → JUDAH
Mt 2: 1 Jesus was born in Bethlehem of **J**,
Lk 3: 1 Pontius Pilate was governor of **J**,
Acts 1: 8 my witnesses in Jerusalem, in all **J**

JUDGE → JUDGED, JUDGES, JUDGMENT, JUDGMENTS
Gen 16: 5 the LORD **j** between you and me!"
Ex 2:14 made you a ruler and **j** over us?
1 Sam 2:10 LORD will **j** the ends of the earth;
Ps 96:13 for he is coming to **j** the earth.
Sir 35:15 for the Lord is the **j**,
Isa 11: 3 He shall not **j** by what his eyes see,
Jer 11:20 O LORD of hosts, who **j** righteously,
Ezek 34:17 I shall **j** between sheep and sheep,
Lk 6:37 not **j**, and you will not be judged;
Jn 7:24 Do not **j** by appearances;
18:31 "Take him yourselves and **j** him
Acts 4:19 rather than to God, you must **j**;
Rom 3: 6 then how could God **j** the world?
1 Cor 6: 2 that the saints will **j** the world?
2 Tim 4: 1 who is to **j** the living and the dead,
Heb 12:23 and to God the **j** of all,
Jas 5: 9 See, the **J** is standing at the doors!
Rev 20: 4 on them were given authority to **j**.

JUDGED → JUDGE
Mt 7: 1 not judge, so that you may not be **j**.
1 Cor 11:31 if we **j** ourselves, we would not be **j**.
Jas 3: 1 know that we who teach will be **j**
Rev 20:12 dead were **j** according to their works

JUDGES → JUDGE
Judg 2:16 Then the LORD raised up **j**,
Sir 16:12 **j** a person according to one's deeds.
Lk 11:19 Therefore they will be your **j**.
Jas 4:11 evil against the law and **j** the law;
Rev 19:11 righteousness he **j** and makes war.

JUDGMENT → JUDGE
Ex 6: 6 arm and with mighty acts of **j**.
Ps 1: 5 wicked will not stand in the **j**,
119:66 Teach me good **j** and knowledge,
Eccl 12:14 God will bring every deed into **j**,
Wis 12:12 Or will resist your **j**?
Sir 18:20 Before **j** comes, examine yourself;
Jer 25:31 he is entering into **j** with all flesh,
Dan 7:22 **j** was given for the holy ones of the
Mal 3: 5 Then I will draw near to you for **j**;
Mt 11:24 day of **j** it will be more tolerable for
Jn 16:11 about **j**, because the ruler
Rom 14:10 we will all stand before the **j** seat of
2 Cor 5:10 all of us must appear before the **j**
Heb 9:27 to die once, and after that the **j**,
10:27 but a fearful prospect of **j**,
Jas 2:13 mercy triumphs over **j**.
1 Pet 4:17 for **j** to begin with the household of

1 Jn	4:17	may have boldness on the day of **j**,
Rev	18:10	For in one hour your **j** has come."

JUDGMENTS → JUDGE

Ps	119:75	LORD, that your **j** are right,
Rom	11:33	How unsearchable are his **j** and
Rev	19:2	for his **j** are true and just;

JUDITH

Virtuous widow and heroine of the deuterocanonical book of Judith (Jdt 8-16).

JUST → JUSTICE, JUSTIFICATION, JUSTIFIED, JUSTIFY

Gen	18:25	Judge of all the earth do what is **j**?"
Deut	32:4	without deceit, **j** and upright is he;
Tob	3:2	O Lord, and all your deeds are **j**;
Ps	111:7	works of his hands are faithful and **j**
Sir	18:2	the Lord alone is **j**.
Ezek	33:17	"The way of the Lord is not **j**,"
Rom	7:12	the commandment is holy and **j** and
1 Jn	1:9	he who is faithful and **j** will forgive
Rev	15:3	**J** and true are your ways, King of

JUSTICE → JUST

Ex	23:6	not pervert the **j** due to your poor
1 Kings	7:7	pronounce judgment, the Hall of **J**,
Job	19:7	I call aloud, but there is no **j**.
	37:23	he is great in power and **j**,
Ps	33:5	He loves righteousness and **j**;
	106:3	Happy are those who observe **j**,
Prov	21:15	**j** is done, it is a joy to the righteous,
Isa	30:18	For the LORD is a God of **j**;
	42:4	until he has established **j** in the earth
Jer	9:24	I act with steadfast love, **j**,
Hos	12:6	to your God, hold fast to love and **j**,
Am	5:24	But let **j** roll down like waters,
Mal	2:17	by asking, "Where is the God of **j**?"
Lk	11:42	and neglect **j** and the love of God;

JUSTIFICATION → JUST

Rom	4:25	trespasses and was raised for our **j**.
2 Cor	3:9	more does the ministry of **j** abound
Gal	2:21	for if **j** comes through the law,

JUSTIFIED → JUST

Job	32:2	he **j** himself rather than God;
Mt	12:37	for by your words you will be **j**,
Rom	3:24	they are now **j** by his grace as a gift,
	5:1	Therefore, since we are **j** by faith,
	10:10	believes with the heart and so is **j**,
1 Cor	6:11	were **j** in the name of the Lord Jesus
Gal	2:16	that we might be **j** by faith in Christ,
Jas	2:24	is **j** by works and not by faith alone.

JUSTIFY → JUST

Rom	3:30	and he will **j** the circumcised on the
Gal	3:8	that God would **j** the Gentiles

K

KADESH → KADESH-BARNEA

Num	20:1	and the people stayed in **K**.
Deut	1:46	you had stayed at **K** as many days

KADESH-BARNEA → KADESH

Num	32:8	sent them from **K** to see the land.

KEEP → KEEPER, KEEPS, KEPT

Gen	17:9	for you, you shall **k** my covenant,
Ex	19:5	obey my voice and **k** my covenant,
Num	6:24	The LORD bless you and **k** you;
Deut	5:10	love me and **k** my commandments.
Neh	1:5	love him and **k** his commandments;
Prov	7:2	**k** my commandments and live,
Eccl	3:6	time to **k**, and a time to throw away;
	12:13	Fear God, and **k** his commandments
Sir	1:26	wisdom, **k** the commandments,
Lk	17:33	those who lose their life will **k** it.
Jude	1:24	Now to him who is able to **k** you
Rev	22:9	those who **k** the words of this book.

KEEPER → KEEP

Gen	4:9	am I my brother's **k**?"
Ps	121:5	The LORD is your **k**;

KEEPS → KEEP

Ps	121:3	he who **k** you will not slumber.

Jas	2:10	whoever **k** the whole law but fails

KEPT → KEEP

Mt	19:20	said to him, "I have **k** all these;
Jn	17:6	and they have **k** your word.
2 Tim	4:7	finished the race, I have **k** the faith.

KEY → KEYS

Isa	22:22	on his shoulder the **k** of the house
Lk	11:52	taken away the **k** of knowledge;
Rev	3:7	true one, who has the **k** of David,

KEYS* → KEY

Mt	16:19	you the **k** of the kingdom of heaven,
Rev	1:18	I have the **k** of Death and of Hades.

KIDNAPS*

Ex	21:16	Whoever **k** a person, whether

KIDRON

2 Sam	15:23	the king crossed the Wadi **K**,
Jn	18:1	his disciples across the **K** valley

KILL → KILLED, KILLS

Ex	4:23	now I will **k** your firstborn son.'"
Eccl	3:3	a time to **k**, and a time to heal;
Mt	10:28	not fear those who **k** the body but cannot **k** the soul;
Mk	14:1	to arrest Jesus by stealth and **k** him;

KILLED → KILL

Mk	9:31	after being **k**, he will rise again."
Acts	3:15	and you **k** the Author of life,
Rom	7:11	deceived me and through it **k** me.
2 Cor	6:9	as punished, and yet not **k**;

KILLS → KILL

1 Sam	2:6	The LORD **k** and brings to life;
2 Cor	3:6	the letter **k**, but the Spirit gives life.

KIND → KINDNESS, KINDS

Gen	6:20	two of every **k** shall come in to you,
Ps	145:17	and **k** in all his doings.
1 Cor	13:4	Love is patient; love is **k**;
Eph	4:32	and be **k** to one another,

KINDNESS → KIND

Prov	31:26	teaching of **k** is on her tongue.
Hos	11:4	I led them with cords of human **k**,
Rom	2:4	**k** is meant to lead you to repentance
Gal	5:22	joy, peace, patience, **k**, generosity,

KINDS → KIND

Lev	19:19	not sow your field with two **k** of
1 Cor	12:10	to another various **k** of tongues,
1 Tim	6:10	of money is a root of all **k** of evil,

KING → KINGDOM, KINGS

Ex	1:8	Now a new **k** arose over Egypt,
Deut	17:14	and you say, "I will set a **k** over me,
1 Sam	8:7	rejected me from being **k** over them.
2 Sam	2:4	there they anointed David **k** over
Tob	10:13	Lord of heaven and earth, **K** over all
Jdt	9:12	**K** of all your creation,
Ps	2:6	set my **k** on Zion, my holy hill."
	10:16	The LORD is **k** forever and ever;
Isa	6:5	have seen the **K**, the LORD of hosts!
Jer	10:10	living God and the everlasting **K**.
Mt	2:2	who has been born **k** of the Jews?
	27:37	"This is Jesus, the **K** of the Jews."
Lk	19:38	"Blessed is the **k** who comes in the
Jn	1:49	You are the **K** of Israel!"
1 Tim	1:17	To the **K** of the ages, immortal,
Rev	19:16	"**K** of kings and Lord of lords."

KINGDOM → KING

Ex	19:6	you shall be for me a priestly **k** and
2 Sam	7:12	and I will establish his **k**.
1 Kings	11:31	"See, I am about to tear the **k**
Ps	145:13	Your **k** is an everlasting **k**,
Wis	10:10	she showed him the **k** of God,
Dan	4:3	His **k** is an everlasting **k**,
Mt	4:17	"Repent, for the **k** of heaven has
	5:3	for theirs is the **k** of heaven.
	6:10	Your **k** come. Your will be done,
	13:24	"The **k** of heaven may be compared
Mk	1:15	and the **k** of God has come near;
	6:23	I will give you, even half of my **k**."

Mk	10:24	how hard it is to enter the **k** of God!
	12:34	You are not far from the **k** of God."
	13: 8	and **k** against **k**;
Lk	17:21	in fact, the **k** of God is among you."
	22:16	not eat it until it is fulfilled in the **k**
Jn	3: 5	no one can enter the **k** of God
	18:36	"My **k** is not from this world.
Acts	1: 6	you will restore the **k** to Israel?"
Rom	14:17	the **k** of God is not food and drink
1 Cor	6: 9	wrongdoers will not inherit the **k**
Eph	5: 5	any inheritance in the **k** of Christ
Col	1:13	transferred us into the **k** of his
1 Thess	2:12	calls you into his own **k** and glory.
Heb	12:28	receiving a **k** that cannot be shaken,
2 Pet	1:11	entry into the eternal **k** of our Lord
Rev	11:15	world has become the **k** of our Lord

KINGS → KING

Gen	17: 6	and **k** shall come from you.
Ps	2: 2	The **k** of the earth set themselves,
	138: 4	All the **k** of the earth shall praise
Prov	8:15	By me **k** reign, and rulers decree
Sir	51:12	*Give thanks to the King of the k of k,*
Isa	52:15	**k** shall shut their mouths because of
Dan	7:24	of this kingdom ten **k** shall arise,
Acts	4:26	The **k** of the earth took their stand,
1 Tim	6:15	the King of **k** and Lord of lords.
Rev	19:16	"King of **k** and Lord of lords."

KISS

Ps	2:12	**k** his feet, or he will be angry,
Song	1: 2	Let him **k** me with the kisses of his
Mt	26:48	"The one I will **k** is the man; arrest
2 Cor	13:12	Greet one another with a holy **k**.

KNEE → KNEES

Isa	45:23	"To me every **k** shall bow,
Rom	14:11	says the Lord, every **k** shall bow to
Phil	2:10	at the name of Jesus every **k** should

KNEEL → KNELT

Ps	95: 6	let us **k** before the LORD, our Maker

KNEES → KNEE

1 Kings	19:18	the **k** that have not bowed to Baal,
Eph	3:14	I bow my **k** before the Father,

KNELT → KNEEL

2 Chr	6:13	he **k** on his knees in the presence of
Lk	22:41	about a stone's throw, **k** down,

KNEW → KNOW

Deut	34:10	whom the LORD **k** face to face.
Jer	1: 5	I formed you in the womb I **k** you,
Mt	7:23	will declare to them, 'I never **k** you;
Rom	1:21	they **k** God, they did not honor him

KNOCK → KNOCKING

Lk	11: 9	**k**, and the door will be opened for

KNOCKING → KNOCK

Rev	3:20	I am standing at the door, **k**;

KNOW → FOREKNEW, KNEW, KNOWING,
        KNOWLEDGE, KNOWN, KNOWS

Gen	22:12	for now I **k** that you fear God,
Ex	6: 7	**k** that I am the LORD your God,
1 Kings	8:39	only you **k** what is in every human
Job	19:25	For I **k** that my Redeemer lives,
Ps	46:10	"Be still, and **k** that I am God!
Eccl	8:16	I applied my mind to **k** wisdom,
Isa	1: 3	Israel does not **k**, my people do not
Jer	31:34	"**K** the LORD," for they shall all **k**
Mt	6: 3	left hand **k** what your right hand is
	24:42	do not **k** on what day your Lord is
Lk	11:13	**k** how to give good gifts to your
	22:34	denied three times that you **k** me."
Jn	10:14	I **k** my own and my own **k** me,
	13:35	will **k** that you are my disciples,
	21:24	and we **k** that his testimony is true.
Acts	1: 7	**k** the times or periods that the
Rom	8:28	We **k** that all things work together
1 Cor	8: 2	Anyone who claims to **k** something
	13:12	I **k** only in part; then I will **k** fully,
Eph	3:19	**k** the love of Christ that surpasses
Phil	3:10	to **k** Christ and the power of his
Titus	1:16	profess to **k** God, but they deny him

Heb	8:11	'**K** the Lord,' for they shall all **k** me,
1 Jn	2: 4	Whoever says, "I have come to **k**
	3:16	**k** love by this, that he laid down his
Rev	3: 3	not **k** at what hour I will come to

KNOWING → KNOW

Gen	3:22	like one of us, **k** good and evil;
Jn	18: 4	Jesus, **k** all that was to happen to
Phil	3: 8	surpassing value of **k** Christ Jesus
Heb	13: 2	have entertained angels without **k** it.

KNOWLEDGE → KNOW

Gen	2: 9	the tree of the **k** of good and evil.
Job	21:22	Will any teach God **k**,
Ps	94:10	he who teaches **k** to humankind,
Prov	1: 7	of the LORD is the beginning of **k**;
	8:10	and **k** rather than choice gold;
Eccl	1:18	who increase **k** increase sorrow.
Sir	3:25	without **k** there is no wisdom.
Isa	11: 2	spirit of **k** and the fear of the LORD.
Hos	4: 6	people are destroyed for lack of **k**;
Lk	11:52	you have taken away the key of **k**;
Rom	11:33	riches and wisdom and **k** of God!
1 Cor	8: 1	**K** puffs up, but love builds up.
Eph	3:19	the love of Christ that surpasses **k**,
Col	2: 3	the treasures of wisdom and **k**.
1 Tim	6:20	of what is falsely called **k**;
2 Pet	1: 5	goodness, and goodness with **k**,
1 Jn	2:20	and all of you have **k**.

KNOWN → KNOW

Ps	139: 1	you have searched me and **k** me.
Lk	6:44	for each tree is **k** by its own fruit.
Jn	1:18	Father's heart, who has made him **k**.
Rom	7: 7	I would not have **k** sin.
1 Cor	2:16	For who has **k** the mind of the Lord
Eph	1: 9	made **k** to us the mystery of his will,

KNOWS → KNOW

Ps	94:11	The LORD **k** our thoughts,
	103:14	For he **k** how we were made;
Sir	42:18	Most High **k** all that may be known;
Mt	6: 8	your Father **k** what you need before
	24:36	about that day and hour no one **k**,
Rom	8:27	**k** what is the mind of the Spirit,
2 Tim	2:19	"The Lord **k** those who are his,"
1 Jn	4: 7	loves is born of God and **k** God.

KORAH → KORAHITES
        Levite; led rebels against Moses (Num 16; Jude 11).

KORAHITES → KORAH
        Psalms of: Pss 42; 44-49; 84; 85; 87; 88.

L

LABAN
        Brother of Rebekah (Gen 24:29), father of Rachel and Leah (Gen 29:16). Received Abraham's servant (Gen 24:29-51). Provided daughters as wives for Jacob in exchange for Jacob's service (Gen 29:1-30). Provided flocks for Jacob's service (Gen 30:25-43). Pursued and covenanted with Jacob (Gen 31).

LABOR → LABORER

Ex	1:11	to oppress them with forced **l**.
	20: 9	Six days you shall **l** and do all your
Mic	5: 3	when she who is in **l** has brought forth
Jn	4:38	reap that for which you did not **l**.
1 Cor	15:58	in the Lord your **l** is not in vain

LABORER → LABOR

Lev	19:13	the wages of a **l** until morning.
Lk	10: 7	for the **l** deserves to be paid.
1 Tim	5:18	and, "The **l** deserves to be paid."

LACKED → LACKING

Deut	2: 7	with you; you have **l** nothing."

LACKING → LACKED

Eccl	1:15	and what is **l** cannot be counted.
Lk	18:22	"There is still one thing **l**.
Col	1:24	completing what is **l** in Christ's

LADDER

Gen	28:12	that there was a **l** set up on the earth,

LAID → LAY

Isa	53: 6	the LORD has **l** on him the iniquity

Mk   16: 6   Look, there is the place they l him.
1 Jn   3:16   that he l down his life for us—

LAKE
Rev   19:20   were thrown alive into the l of fire
        20:14   This is the second death, the l of fire

LAMB → LAMBS
Gen   22: 8   "God himself will provide the l for
Ex   12:21   and slaughter the passover l.
Isa   53: 7   like a l that is led to the slaughter,
Mk   14:12   when the Passover l is sacrificed,
Jn   1:29   L of God who takes away the sin of
1 Cor   5: 7   For our paschal l, Christ, has been
1 Pet   1:19   like that of a l without defect or
Rev   5:12   the L that was slaughtered to
        19: 7   for the marriage of the L has come,
        21:23   and its lamp is the L.

LAMBS → LAMB
Isa   40:11   he will gather the l in his arms,
Jn   21:15   Jesus said to him, "Feed my l."

LAME
Isa   35: 6   then the l shall leap like a deer,
Zeph   3:19   And I will save the l and gather the
Mt   11: 5   the l walk, the lepers are cleansed,

LAMENTATION
Lam   2: 5   in daughter Judah mourning and l.

LAMP → LAMPS, LAMPSTAND, LAMPSTANDS
1 Kings 11:36   servant David may always have a l
Ps   18:28   It is you who light my l;
       119:105 Your word is a l to my feet and a
Mt   5:15   lighting a l puts it under the bushel
         6:22   "The eye is the l of the body.
Rev   22: 5   they need no light of l or sun,

LAMPS → LAMP
Ex   25:37   You shall make the seven l for it;
Mt   25: 1   Ten bridesmaids took their l and

LAMPSTAND → LAMP
Ex   25:31   You shall make a l of pure gold.
1 Macc   4:50   and lit the lamps on the l,
Zech   4: 2   And I said, "I see a l all of gold,

LAMPSTANDS → LAMP
Rev   1:20   the seven l are the seven churches.
        11: 4   the two l that stand before the Lord

LAND
Gen   1:10   God called the dry l Earth,
        12: 7   your offspring I will give this l."
Ex   3: 8   a l flowing with milk and honey,
        20: 2   brought you out of the l of Egypt,
Num   13: 2   to spy out the l of Canaan,
Josh   11:23   So Joshua took the whole l,
Judg   1:27   Canaanites continued to live in that l
2 Kings 17: 5   the king of Assyria invaded all the l
        25:21   So Judah went into exile out of its l.
2 Chr   7:14   will forgive their sin and heal their l.
Ps   37:11   But the meek shall inherit the l,
Jer   22:29   O l, l, l, hear the word of the LORD!
Dan   11:41   He shall come into the beautiful l,
Mal   4: 6   come and strike the l with a curse.

LANGUAGE
Gen   11: 9   LORD confused the l of all the earth;
Acts   2: 6   speaking in the native l of each.

LAP
Judg   7: 5   who l the water with their tongues,
Prov   16:33   The lot is cast into the l,

LASHES
Deut   25: 3   Forty l may be given but not more;
2 Cor   11:24   from the Jews the forty l minus one.

LAST → EVERLASTING
2 Sam   23: 1   Now these are the l words of David:
Isa   44: 6   I am the first and I am the l;
Mt   19:30   first will be l, and the l will be first.
Mk   9:35   first must be l of all and servant of
1 Cor   15:26   l enemy to be destroyed is death.
        15:52   twinkling of an eye, at the l trumpet.
2 Tim   3: 1   that in the l days distressing times
Heb   1: 2   l days he has spoken to us by a Son,

1 Jn   2:18   Children, it is the l hour!
Rev   1:17   I am the first and the l,

LAUGH → LAUGHINGSTOCK, LAUGHTER
Gen   18:13   said to Abraham, "Why did Sarah l,
Eccl   3: 4   a time to weep, and a time to l;
Lk   6:21   you who weep now, for you will l.

LAUGHINGSTOCK → LAUGH
Ps   44:14   the nations, a l among the peoples.
Lam   3:14   have become the l of all my people,

LAUGHTER → LAUGH
Ps   126: 2   Then our mouth was filled with l,
Jas   4: 9   Let your l be turned into mourning

LAW → LAWFUL, LAWLESSNESS
Deut   1: 5   Moses undertook to expound this l
        31: 9   Then Moses wrote down this l,
Josh   1: 8   book of the l shall not depart out of
1 Macc   2:48   They rescued the l out of the hands
Ps   1: 2   their delight is in the l of the LORD,
       119:97 Oh, how I love your l!
Jer   31:33   I will put my l within them,
Mt   5:17   come to abolish the l or the prophets
        23:23   the weightier matters of the l:
Lk   24:44   written about me in the l of Moses,
Jn   1:17   l indeed was given through Moses;
Rom   2:15   that what the l requires is written
         6:14   you are not under l but under grace.
        10: 4   For Christ is the end of the l so that
Gal   2:19   through the l I died to the l,
Heb   10: 1   Since the l has only a shadow of the
Jas   2:10   For whoever keeps the whole l but

LAWFUL → LAW
Mt   12:12   So it is l to do good on the sabbath."
1 Cor   6:12   "All things are l for me,"
        10:23   "All things are l," but

LAWLESSNESS → LAW
Sir   21: 3   All l is like a two-edged sword;
2 Thess 2: 7   the mystery of l is already at work,
1 Jn   3: 4   commits sin is guilty of l; sin is l.

LAY → LAID
Mt   8:20   of Man has nowhere to l his head."
        28: 6   Come, see the place where he l.
Jn   10:15   And I l down my life for the sheep.
1 Cor   3:11   no one can l any foundation other

LAZARUS*
    1. Poor man in Jesus' parable (Lk 16:19-31).
    2. Brother of Mary and Martha whom Jesus raised from the dead (Jn 11:1-12:19).

LAZY
Ex   5:17   He said, "You are l, l;
Prov   13: 4   The appetite of the l craves,

LEAD → LEADER, LEADERS, LEADS, LED
Ex   32:34   l the people to the place
Ps   61: 2   L me to the rock that is higher than
Isa   11: 6   and a little child shall l them.
Mk   13:22   to l astray, if possible, the elect.
Rom   2: 4   meant to l you to repentance?

LEADER → LEAD
1 Chr   28: 4   for he chose Judah as l,
Rom   12: 8   the l, in diligence;

LEADERS → LEAD
Isa   3:12   O my people, your l mislead you,
Lk   19:47   the l of the people kept looking for
Heb   13: 7   Remember your l, those who spoke

LEADS → LEAD
Ps   23: 2   he l me beside still waters;
Mk   13: 5   "Beware that no one l you astray.
Rom   6:16   obedience, which l to righteousness

LEAH
    Wife of Jacob (Gen 29:16-30); bore six sons and one daughter (Gen 29:31-30:21; 34:1; 35:23; Ruth 4:11).

LEAPED → LEAPING
Lk   1:41   the child l in her womb.

LEAPING → LEAPED
1 Chr   15:29   and saw King David l and dancing;

Acts 3: 8 walking and l and praising God.

LEARN → LEARNED, LEARNING
Deut 4:10 that they may l to fear me as long as
Isa 1:17 l to do good; seek justice,
1 Tim 2:11 Let a woman l in silence with full

LEARNED → LEARN
Jn 6:45 l from the Father comes to me.
Phil 4:11 I have l to be content with whatever

LEARNING → LEARN
Jn 7:15 "How does this man have such l,
Acts 26:24 Too much l is driving you insane!"

LEAST → LESS
Mt 2: 6 are by no means l among the rulers
5:19 called l in the kingdom of heaven;
Lk 9:48 l among all of you is the greatest."

LEAVE → LEFT
Num 11:20 'Why did we ever l Egypt?'"
Mk 10: 7 this reason a man shall l his father
Jn 14:18 not l you orphaned; I am coming to
Heb 13: 5 said, "I will never l you or forsake

LEAVEN → LEAVENS
Ex 12:15 on the first day you shall remove l

LEAVENS → LEAVEN
Gal 5: 9 A little yeast l the whole batch of

LEAVES
Gen 3: 7 and they sewed fig l together
Ezek 47:12 and their l for healing."
Rev 22: 2 l of the tree are for the healing of

LEBANON
Deut 11:24 from the wilderness to the L and
Isa 40:16 L would not provide fuel enough,

LED → LEAD
Isa 53: 7 like a lamb that is l to the slaughter,
Jer 50: 6 their shepherds have l them astray,
Hos 11: 4 I l them with cords of human
Mt 4: 1 Then Jesus was l up by the Spirit
27:31 they l him away to crucify him.
Lk 21: 8 "Beware that you are not l astray;
Rom 8:14 For all who are l by the Spirit

LEFT → LEAVE
Deut 28:14 either to the right or to the l,
Mt 6: 3 your l hand know what your right
25:33 his right hand and the goats at the l.
Lk 17:34 one will be taken and the other l.

LEGION
Lk 8:30 He said, "L"; for many demons

LEGS
Dan 10: 6 l like the gleam of burnished bronze
Jn 19:33 they did not break his l.
Rev 10: 1 and his l like pillars of fire.

LENDER
Prov 22: 7 the borrower is the slave of the l.

LEPER → LEPROUS
Mt 8: 2 and there was a l who came to him
26: 6 in the house of Simon the l,

LEPERS → LEPROUS
Lk 7:22 the lame walk, the l are cleansed,

LEPROUS → LEPER, LEPERS
Ex 4: 6 he took it out, his hand was l,
Num 12:10 Miriam had become l,

LESS → LEAST
Ex 30:15 and the poor shall not give l,
Ezra 9:13 punished us l than our iniquities

LETTER
Mt 5:18 not one l, not one stroke of a l,
2 Cor 3: 6 the l kills, but the Spirit gives life.

LEVI → LEVITES, LEVITICAL, =MATTHEW
1. Son of Jacob by Leah (Gen 29:34; 46:11; 1 Chr 2:1). With
Simeon avenged rape of Dinah (Gen 34). Tribe of blessed (Gen
49:5-7; Deut 33:8-11), chosen as priests (Num 3-4), numbered
(Num 3:39; 26:62), given cities, but not land (Num 18; 35;

Deut 10:9; Josh 13:14; 21), land (Ezek 48:8-22), 12,000 from
(Rev 7:7).
2. See Matthew.

LEVIATHAN
Job 41: 1 you draw out L with a fishhook,
Ps 74:14 You crushed the heads of L;

LEVITES → LEVI
Num 1:53 L shall camp around the tabernacle
Josh 14: 4 no portion was given to the L in the
Neh 8: 9 L who taught the people said to all

LEVITICAL → LEVI
Heb 7:11 attainable through the l priesthood

LIAR → LIE
Prov 19:22 and it is better to be poor than a l.
Jn 8:44 for he is a l and the father of lies.
Rom 3: 4 Although everyone is a l,
1 Jn 2:22 l but the one who denies that Jesus

LIARS → LIE
1 Tim 1:10 sodomites, slave traders, l, perjurers,
Rev 21: 8 the sorcerers, the idolaters, and all l,

LIBERTY
Lev 25:10 shall proclaim l throughout the land
Isa 61: 1 to proclaim l to the captives,
1 Cor 8: 9 this l of yours does not somehow

LICENTIOUSNESS
Mk 7:22 avarice, wickedness, deceit, l, envy,
Gal 5:19 fornication, impurity, l,
Jude 1: 4 pervert the grace of our God into l

LIE → LIAR, LIARS, LIES, LYING
Num 23:19 that he should l, or a mortal,
Ps 23: 2 makes me l down in green pastures;
Isa 11: 6 leopard shall l down with the kid,
Acts 5: 3 your heart to l to the Holy Spirit
1 Jn 2:21 know that no l comes from the truth.

LIES → LIE
Ps 5: 6 You destroy those who speak l;
Phil 3:13 forgetting what l behind and straining forward
to what l ahead,

LIFE → LIVE
Gen 2: 7 into his nostrils the breath of l;
2: 9 the tree of l also in the midst of the
9: 5 require a reckoning for human l.
Ex 21:23 then you shall give l for l,
Deut 12:23 for the blood is the l,
30:19 Choose l so that you and your
Ps 34:12 Which of you desires l, and covets
Prov 18:21 Death and l are in the power of the tongue,
Eccl 7:12 that wisdom gives l to the one who
Sir 4:12 Whoever loves her loves l,
Isa 53:10 you make his l an offering for sin,
Dan 12: 2 shall awake, some to everlasting l,
Mt 7:14 and the road is hard that leads to l,
10:39 Those who find their l will lose it,
20:28 to give his l a ransom for many."
Mk 10:30 and in the age to come eternal l.
Lk 12:25 a single hour to your span of l?
Jn 1: 4 in him was l, and the l was the light
3:15 believes in him may have eternal l.
6:35 said to them, "I am the bread of l.
11:25 "I am the resurrection and the l.
14: 6 "I am the way, and the truth, and the l.
Acts 3:15 and you killed the Author of l,
Rom 5:21 eternal l through Jesus Christ our
8:11 who raised Christ from the dead will give l
8:38 convinced that neither death, nor l,
2 Cor 3: 6 the letter kills, but the Spirit gives l.
Eph 4: 1 to lead a l worthy of the calling
Phil 4: 3 whose names are in the book of l.
1 Jn 3:14 that we have passed from death to l
5:20 He is the true God and eternal l.
Rev 2: 8 who was dead and came to l:
20: 4 came to l and reigned with Christ
20:12 book was opened, the book of l.
22: 2 the tree of l with its twelve kinds

LIFTED
Isa 52:13 he shall be exalted and l up,

Jn 3:14 so must the Son of Man be l up,

LIGHT → ENLIGHTENED, ENLIGHTENS, LIGHTS
Gen 1: 3 "Let there be l"; and there was l.
Ex 13:21 pillar of fire by night, to give them l,
Ps 27: 1 The LORD is my l and my salvation;
Prov 4:18 the path of the righteous is like the l
Eccl 2:13 that wisdom excels folly as l excels
Isa 9: 2 in darkness have seen a great l;
42: 6 as a covenant to the people, a l
60: 1 Arise, shine; for your l has come,
Mt 4:16 in darkness have seen a great l,
5:14 "You are the l of the world.
11:30 my yoke is easy, and my burden is l.
Jn 1: 9 true l, which enlightens everyone,
8:12 saying, "I am the l of the world.
Rom 13:12 and put on the armor of l;
2 Cor 11:14 Satan disguises himself as an angel of l.
1 Pet 2: 9 of darkness into his marvelous l.
1 Jn 1: 7 walk in the l as he himself is in the l
Rev 22: 5 for the Lord God will be their l,

LIGHTNING
Ex 19:16 third day there was thunder and l,
Dan 10: 6 body was like beryl, his face like l,
Lk 10:18 from heaven like a flash of l.
Rev 4: 5 from the throne are flashes of l,

LIGHTS → LIGHT
Gen 1:16 God made the two great l—
Jas 1:17 coming down from the Father of l,

LIKE → LIKENESS
Gen 3: 5 be l God, knowing good and evil."
Ex 15:11 "Who is l you, O LORD, among the
2 Sam 7:22 for there is no one l you,
Ps 113: 5 Who is l the LORD our God,
Isa 46: 9 I am God, and there is no one l me,
Jer 10: 6 There is none l you, O LORD;
Lk 13:18 "What is the kingdom of God l?
1 Cor 13:11 When I was a child, I spoke l a child
Rev 1:13 I saw one l the Son of Man,
10: 1 his face was l the sun,
16:15 ("See, I am coming l a thief!

LIKENESS → LIKE
Gen 1:26 in our image, according to our l;
Rom 8: 3 his own Son in the l of sinful flesh,
Phil 2: 7 of a slave, being born in human l.

LILIES
Lk 12:27 Consider the l, how they grow:

LINE
Isa 28:10 l upon l, l upon l, here a little,
Am 7: 7 with a plumb l in his hand.

LINEN
Ex 26: 1 with ten curtains of fine twisted l,
Dan 10: 5 and saw a man clothed in l,
Rev 19: 8 for the fine l is the righteous deeds

LION → LION'S, LIONS
1 Sam 17:34 and whenever a l or a bear came,
Eccl 9: 4 a living dog is better than a dead l.
Isa 11: 7 and the l shall eat straw like the ox.
Dan 7: 4 first was like a l and had eagles'
Rev 4: 7 the first living creature like a l,
5: 5 See, the L of the tribe of Judah,

LION'S → LION
2 Tim 4:17 So l was rescued from the l mouth.

LIONS → LION
Dan 6:20 able to deliver you from the l?"

LIPS
Deut 23:23 Whatever your l utter you must
Job 2:10 Job did not sin with his l.
Isa 6: 5 am lost, for I am a man of unclean l,
Mt 15: 8 with their l, but their hearts are far
Heb 13:15 the fruit of l that confess his name.

LISTEN → LISTENS
Ex 23:22 But if you l attentively to his voice
2 Kings 17:40 They would not l, however,
Ps 5: 2 L to the sound of my cry, my King
Prov 4: 1 L, children, to a father's instruction,

Eccl 5: 1 l is better than the sacrifice offered
Sir 11: 8 Do not answer before you l,
Mk 9: 7 my Son, the Beloved; l to him!"
Lk 16:31 'If they do not l to Moses and the
Acts 3:22 You must l to whatever he tells you.
Jas 1:19 be quick to l, slow to speak,

LISTENS → LISTEN
Jn 18:37 Everyone who belongs to the truth l
1 Jn 4: 6 Whoever knows God l to us,

LITTLE
Ex 16:18 who gathered l had no shortage;
Ps 8: 5 have made them a l lower than God,
Prov 15:16 Better is a l with the fear of
Sir 29:23 Be content with l or much,
Mt 8:26 "Why are you afraid, you of l faith?
14:14 "Let the children come to me,
2 Cor 8:15 one who had l did not have too l."
Gal 5: 9 A l yeast leavens the whole batch of
Rev 10: 2 He held a l scroll open in his hand.

LIVE → ALIVE, LIFE, LIVED, LIVES, LIVING
Gen 3:22 and eat, and l forever"—
Ex 1:16 but if it is a girl, she shall l."
33:20 for no one shall see me and l."
Lev 18: 5 by doing so one shall l:
Deut 8: 3 one does not l by bread alone,
Ps 91: 1 l in the shelter of the Most High,
Wis 5:15 But the righteous l forever,
Sir 34:14 those who fear the Lord will l,
Hab 2: 4 but the righteous l by their faith.
Mt 4: 4 'One does not l by bread alone,
Jn 11:25 even though they die, will l,
Rom 1:17 one who is righteous will l by faith."
14: 8 If we l, we l to the Lord,
2 Cor 5:15 those who l might l no longer for
Gal 3:12 does works of the law will l

LIVED → LIVE
Rom 14: 9 to this end Christ died and l again,

LIVES → LIVE
Tob 13: 1 "Blessed be God who l forever,
Job 19:25 For I know that my Redeemer l,
Ps 18:46 The LORD l! Blessed be my rock,
Jn 11:26 and everyone who l and believes
Rom 6:10 but the life he l, he l to God.
1 Jn 3:16 to lay down our l for one another.
Rev 15: 7 of God, who l forever and ever;

LIVING → LIVE
Gen 2: 7 and the man became a l being.
3:20 because she was the mother of all l.
6:19 And of every l thing, of all flesh,
Deut 5:26 the voice of the l God speaking out
Jer 2:13 forsaken me, the fountain of l water,
Zech 14: 8 that day l waters shall flow out from
Mt 16:16 the Messiah, the Son of the l God."
Jn 4:10 he would have given you l water."
6:51 I am the l bread that came down
Rom 12: 1 present your bodies as a l sacrifice,
2 Cor 6:16 For we are the temple of the l God;
Heb 4:12 the word of God is l and active,
1 Pet 2: 4 l stone, though rejected by mortals

LOAVES
Mk 6:41 Taking the five l and the two fish,
8: 6 and he took the seven l,

LOCK
Mt 23:13 you l people out of the kingdom of

LOCUST → LOCUSTS
2 Chr 6:28 if there is plague, blight, mildew, l,
Joel 2:25 years that the swarming l has eaten,

LOCUSTS → LOCUST
Ex 10: 4 I will bring l into your country.
Mt 3: 4 and his food was l and wild honey.
Rev 9: 3 from the smoke came l on the earth,

LOG
Mt 7: 3 do not notice the l in your own eye?

LONELY → ALONE
Ps 25:16 for I am l and afflicted.
Lam 1: 1 How l sits the city that once was full

LONG → LONGING

Ex	20:12	that your days may be l in the land
Ps	13: 1	How l, O LORD?
Prov	3:16	L life is in her right hand;
1 Cor	11:14	that if a man wears l hair,
1 Pet	1:12	things into which angels l to look!
	2: 2	Like newborn infants, l for the pure,
Rev	6:10	how l will it be before you judge

LONGING → LONG

Rom	8:19	the creation waits with eager l for
2 Cor	5: 2	l to be clothed with our heavenly

LOOK → LOOKED, LOOKS

Ex	3: 6	for he was afraid to l at God.
Ps	8: 3	When I l at your heavens,
	80:14	l down from heaven, and see;
Lk	24:39	L at my hands and my feet;

LOOKED → LOOK

Gen	19:26	But Lot's wife, behind him, l back,
Ex	2:25	God l upon the Israelites,
Sir	16:29	Then the Lord l upon the earth,

LOOKS → LOOK

1 Sam	16: 7	but the LORD l on the heart."
Ps	14: 2	The LORD l down from heaven
Mt	5:28	who l at a woman with lust

*LORD → *LORD'S, LORDS

Gen	18:27	take it upon myself to speak to the L
Ex	4:10	Moses said to the LORD, "O my L,
Deut	10:17	God is God of gods and L of lords,
Jdt	6:19	L God of heaven, see their
Ps	16: 2	I say to the LORD, "You are my L;
	110: 1	The LORD says to my l,
Wis	8: 3	and the L of all loves her.
Sir	1: 1	All wisdom is from the L,
Isa	6: 1	I saw the L sitting on a throne, high
Dan	2:47	God is God of gods and L of kings
	3:57	Bless the L, all you works of the L;
	13: 2	and one who feared the L.
Mic	1: 2	the L from his holy temple.
Mt	7:22	many will say to me, 'L, L,
	9:38	the L of the harvest to send out
	12: 8	the Son of Man is l of the sabbath."
Mk	1: 3	'Prepare the way of the L,
	12:29	the L our God, the L is one;
Lk	2:11	who is the Messiah, the L.
	10:27	"You shall love the L your God
	19:38	who comes in the name of the L!
Jn	13:13	You call me Teacher and L—
	20:28	"My L and my God!"
Acts	2:34	'The L said to my L, "Sit at my
Rom	4:24	in him who raised Jesus our L
	10:12	the same L is L of all and
1 Cor	2:16	who has known the mind of the L
	8: 6	and one L, Jesus Christ,
	12: 3	no one can say "Jesus is L" except
2 Cor	3:17	Now the L is the Spirit,
Eph	4: 5	one L, one faith, one baptism,
Phil	2:11	that Jesus Christ is L, to the glory
	4: 5	The L is near.
Col	3:13	just as the L has forgiven you,
1 Thess	4:15	are left until the coming of the L,
1 Tim	6:15	the King of kings and L of lords.
Heb	12:14	without which no one will see the L.
Jas	4:10	Humble yourselves before the L,
1 Pet	3:15	in your hearts sanctify Christ as L.
2 Pet	3: 9	The L is not slow about his promise,
Jude	1: 4	and deny our only Master and L,
Rev	4: 8	"Holy, holy, holy, the L God
	19:16	"King of kings and L of lords."
	22:20	Amen. Come, L Jesus!

†LORD [= Yahweh] → †GOD, †LORD'S

Gen	2: 7	L God formed man from the dust of
	6: 6	the L was sorry that he had made
	13: 4	Abram called on the name of the L.
	18:14	Is anything too wonderful for the L?
	22:14	that place "The L will provide";
Ex	3:15	shall say to the Israelites, 'The L,
	5: 2	But Pharaoh said, "Who is the L,
	6: 7	know that I am the L your God,

Ex	15: 3	The L is a warrior; the L is his name.
	34: 6	and proclaimed, "The L, the L,
Lev	19: 2	for I the L your God am holy.
Num	6:24	The L bless you and keep you;
	14:18	'The L is slow to anger,
Deut	6: 4	The L is our God, the L alone.
Josh	24:15	my household, we will serve the L."
1 Sam	2: 2	"There is no Holy One like the L,
1 Kings	8:11	of the L filled the house of the L.
	18:21	If the L is God, follow him;
1 Chr	16:11	Seek the L and his strength,
Ezra	7:10	his heart to study the law of the L,
Neh	8:10	the joy of the L is your strength."
Job	1:21	the L gave, and the L has taken
	42:12	The L blessed the latter days
Ps	1: 2	their delight is in the law of the L,
	10:16	The L is king forever and ever;
	18: 1	I love you, O L, my strength.
	23: 1	The L is my shepherd, I shall not
	33:12	Happy is the nation whose God is the L
	84:11	For the L God is a sun and shield;
	110: 1	The L says to my lord,
	113: 5	Who is like the L our God,
	125: 2	so the L surrounds his people,
	128: 1	Happy is everyone who fears the L,
	145:18	The L is near to all who call on him,
	150: 6	that breathes praise the L!
Prov	1: 7	fear of the L is the beginning of
	3: 5	Trust in the L with all your heart,
	19:23	The fear of the L is life indeed;
	21: 2	but the L weighs the heart.
Isa	2:11	L alone will be exalted in that day.
	6: 3	"Holy, holy, holy is the L of hosts;
	33:22	the L is our judge, the L is our ruler,
	53: 6	the L has laid on him the iniquity
	64: 8	Yet, O L, you are our Father;
Jer	4: 4	Circumcise yourselves to the L,
	31:34	"Know the L," for they shall all
	32:27	I am the L, the God of all flesh;
Lam	3:25	The L is good to those who wait for
Ezek	3:23	and the glory of the L stood there,
	10:18	the glory of the L went out from
	37: 4	O dry bones, hear the word of the L.
	44: 4	glory of the L filled the temple
	48:35	time on shall be, The L is There.
Hos	14: 1	Return, O Israel, to the L your God,
Joel	1:15	For the day of the L is near,
Am	5: 6	Seek the L and live,
Ob	1:15	the day of the L is near against all
Nah	1: 3	The L is slow to anger but great in
Zeph	1:14	The great day of the L is near,
Zech	14: 9	the L will be one and his name one.
Mal	3: 6	For I the L do not change;
	4: 5	and terrible day of the L comes.

*LORD'S → *LORD

Sir	17:17	but Israel is the L own portion.
Mk	12:11	was the L doing, and it is amazing
Lk	4:19	to proclaim the year of the L favor."
Rom	14: 8	or whether we die, we are the L.
1 Cor	10:26	the earth and its fullness are the L."

†LORD'S [= Yahweh's] → †LORD

Num	11:23	"Is the L power limited?
Deut	32: 9	the L own portion was his people,
Ps	24: 1	The earth is the L and all that is in it
Isa	59: 1	the L hand is not too short to save,
Ob	1:21	and the kingdom shall be the L.

LORDS → *LORD

Deut	10:17	God is God of gods and Lord of l,
Ps	136: 3	O give thanks to the Lord of l,
1 Cor	8: 5	there are many gods and many l—
Rev	19:16	"King of kings and Lord of l."

LOSE → LOSS, LOST

Mk	8:35	who l their life for my sake,
Jn	12:25	Those who love their life l it,
2 Cor	4: 1	in this ministry, we do not l heart.
Heb	12: 3	you may not grow weary or l heart.
2 Jn	1: 8	do not l what we have worked for,

LOSS → LOSE

Sir	32:24	who trusts the Lord will not suffer l.

| 1 Cor | 3:15 | burned up, the builder will suffer l; |
| Phil | 3: 8 | I regard everything as l because of |

LOST → LOSE

Ps	119:176	I have gone astray like a l sheep;
Jer	50: 6	My people have been l sheep;
Ezek	34:16	I will seek the l, and I will bring
Mt	10: 6	to the l sheep of the house of Israel.
Lk	15: 6	I have found my sheep that was l.'
	19:10	came to seek out and to save the l."

LOT → LOT'S, LOTS

1. Nephew of Abraham (Gen 11:27; 12:5). Chose to live in Sodom (Gen 13). Rescued from four kings (Gen 14). Rescued from Sodom (Gen 19:1-29; 2 Pet 2:7). Fathered Moab and Ammon (Gen 19:30-38).

2. Object cast to make decisions.

Num	33:54	You shall apportion the land by l
Esth	3: 7	they cast Pur—which means "the l"
Prov	16:33	The l is cast into the lap,
Jon	1: 7	cast lots, and the l fell on Jonah.
Acts	1:26	and the l fell on Matthias;

LOT'S → LOT, 1

| Gen | 19:26 | L wife, behind him, looked back, |
| Lk | 17:32 | Remember L wife. |

LOTS → LOT, 2

| Ps | 22:18 | and for my clothing they cast l. |
| Mt | 27:35 | among themselves by casting l; |

LOVE → BELOVED, LOVED, LOVER, LOVERS, LOVES

Ex	20: 6	but showing steadfast l to the
	34: 6	and abounding in steadfast l and
Lev	19:18	shall l your neighbor as yourself:
Num	14:18	and abounding in steadfast l,
Deut	6: 5	You shall l the LORD your God
2 Sam	7:15	not take my steadfast l from him,
1 Kings	11: 2	Solomon clung to these in l.
2 Chr	6:42	Remember your steadfast l
Ezra	3:11	his steadfast l endures forever
Neh	1: 5	steadfast l with those who l him
1 Macc	4:33	with the sword of those who l you,
Ps	18: 1	I l you, O LORD, my strength.
	86: 5	abounding in steadfast l to all who
	116: 1	I l the LORD, because he has heard
	119:97	Oh, how I l your law!
	136: 1	for his steadfast l endures forever.
Prov	5:19	you be intoxicated always by her l.
	8:17	I l those who l me,
	19: 8	To get wisdom is to l oneself;
Eccl	3: 8	a time to l, and a time to hate;
Song	1: 2	For your l is better than wine,
	8: 6	for l is strong as death,
Sir	2:15	and those who l him keep his ways.
	7:30	With all your might l your Maker,
Isa	54: 8	but with everlasting l I will have
Lam	3:22	steadfast l of the LORD never ceases,
Dan	9: 4	steadfast l with those who l you
	14:38	have not forsaken those who l you."
Hos	6: 4	Your l is like a morning cloud,
	11: 4	of human kindness, with bands of l.
	14: 4	heal their disloyalty; I will l them
Joel	2:13	and abounding in steadfast l,
Jon	4: 2	and abounding in steadfast l,
Mt	5:44	L your enemies and pray
	6:24	either hate the one and l the other,
Mk	12:31	shall l your neighbor as yourself.'
Lk	6:32	For even sinners l those who l them.
	10:27	"You shall l the Lord your God
Jn	12:25	Those who l their life lose it,
	13:34	new commandment, that you l one
	14:15	"If you l me, you will keep my
	15:13	No one has greater l than this,
	21:16	"Simon son of John, do you l me?"
Rom	5: 5	God's l has been poured into our
	5: 8	But God proves his l for us in that
	12: 9	Let l be genuine; hate what is evil,
	13: 8	anything, except to l one another;
1 Cor	8: 1	Knowledge puffs up, but l builds up.
	13: 4	L is patient; l is kind;
	13:13	and the greatest of these is l.
Gal	5: 6	is faith working through l.
	5:22	the fruit of the Spirit is l, joy,

Eph	2: 4	out of the great l with which he
	3:19	l of Christ that surpasses knowledge
	5:25	Husbands, l your wives,
Col	3:14	Above all, clothe yourselves with l,
1 Thess	5: 8	put on the breastplate of faith and l,
1 Tim	6:10	For the l of money is a root of all
Titus	2: 2	in faith, in l, and in endurance.
Heb	10:24	provoke one another to l and good
	13: 5	your lives free from the l of money,
Jas	2: 8	shall l your neighbor as yourself."
1 Pet	1: 8	you have not seen him, you l him;
2 Pet	1: 7	and mutual affection with l.
1 Jn	2:15	not l the world or the things in the
	3: 1	See what l the Father has given us,
	3:16	We know l by this, that he laid
	4: 7	because l is from God;
	4: 8	does not l does not know God, for God is l.
	5: 3	For the l of God is this,
2 Jn	1: 6	And this is l, that we walk according
Jude	1:21	keep yourselves in the l of God;
Rev	2: 4	abandoned the l you had at first.

LOVED → LOVE

Deut	4:37	And because he l your ancestors,
Jer	31: 3	have l you with an everlasting love;
Hos	11: 1	When Israel was a child, I l him,
Mal	1: 2	I have l you, says the LORD.
Jn	3:16	God so l the world that he gave his
	13: 1	he l them to the end.
	15: 9	the Father has l me, so I have l you;
	15:12	love one another as I have l you.
Gal	2:20	who l me and gave himself for me.
Eph	2: 4	the great love with which he l us
	5: 2	Christ l us and gave himself up for
1 Jn	4:19	We love because he first l us.

LOVER → LOVE

Ps	99: 4	Mighty King, l of justice,
Eccl	5:10	l of money will not be satisfied with
1 Tim	3: 3	quarrelsome, and not a l of money.

LOVERS → LOVE

Jer	3: 1	have played the whore with many l;
Lam	1: 2	all her l she has no one to comfort
Hos	2: 5	For she said, "I will go after my l;
Lk	16:14	Pharisees, who were l of money,
2 Tim	3: 2	For people will be l of themselves,

LOVES → LOVE

Ps	33: 5	He l righteousness and justice;
Prov	3:12	for the LORD reproves the one he l,
	17:17	A friend l at all times,
Wis	8: 3	and the Lord of all l her.
Sir	4:12	Whoever l her l life,
Mt	10:37	Whoever l father or mother more
Lk	7:47	to whom little is forgiven, l little."
Rom	13: 8	who l another has fulfilled the law.
Eph	5:28	He who l his wife l himself.
Heb	12: 6	Lord disciplines those whom he l,
1 Jn	4: 7	who l is born of God and knows
Rev	1: 5	who l us and freed us from our sins

LOW → LOWER, LOWLY

Ps	136:23	who remembered us in our l estate,
Isa	40: 4	every mountain and hill be made l;
Lk	3: 5	mountain and hill shall be made l,

LOWER → LOW

| Ps | 8: 5 | have made them a little l than God, |
| Heb | 2: 7 | made them for a little while l than |

LOWLY → LOW

Jdt	9:11	But you are the God of the l,
Prov	16:19	It is better to be of a l spirit
Lk	1:52	their thrones, and lifted up the l;
Rom	12:16	but associate with the l;

LOYAL → LOYALTY

| 2 Sam | 22:26 | With the l you show yourself l; |
| Dan | 11:32 | who are l to their God |

LOYALTY → LOYAL

Deut	7: 9	God who maintains covenant l
Ruth	3:10	this last instance of your l
Ps	101: 1	I will sing of l and of justice;
Hos	4: 1	There is no faithfulness or l,

LUKE*

Associate of Paul (Col 4:14; 2 Tim 4:11; Philem 24).

LUKEWARM*

| Rev | 3:16 | because you are l, and neither cold |

LUST → LUSTS

| Mt | 5:28 | looks at a woman with l has already |
| 2 Pet | 1: 4 | that is in the world because of l, |

LUSTS → LUST

Rom	1:24	gave them up in the l of their hearts
Eph	4:22	old self, corrupt and deluded by its l
2 Pet	3: 3	scoffing and indulging their own l

LYDIA

| Acts | 16:14 | named L, a worshiper of God, |

LYING → LIE

1 Kings	22:23	a l spirit in the mouth of all these
Prov	6:17	a l tongue, and hands that shed
Wis	1:11	and a l mouth destroys the soul.
Hos	4: 2	Swearing, l, and murder,

LYRE

1 Sam	18:10	while David was playing the l,
Ps	33: 2	Praise the LORD with the l;
Dan	3: 5	pipe, l, trigon, harp, drum,

M

MACCABEUS → JUDAS

| 1 Macc | 2:66 | Judas M has been a mighty warrior |

MACEDONIA

| Acts | 16: 9 | a man of M pleading with him and |

MADE → MAKE

Gen	1:31	God saw everything that he had m,
	2:22	he m into a woman and brought her
	3:21	the LORD God m garments of skins
	6: 6	was sorry that he had m humankind
	15:18	the LORD m a covenant with Abram,
Ex	20:11	For in six days the LORD m heaven
	36: 8	the workers m the tabernacle with
Ps	8: 5	have m them a little lower than God
	118:24	This is the day that the LORD has m;
	139:14	I am fearfully and wonderfully m.
Sir	43:33	For the Lord has m all things,
Jer	27: 5	outstretched arm have m the earth,
Mk	2:27	"The sabbath was m for humankind,
Acts	2:36	that God has m him both Lord and
Eph	2: 5	m us alive together with Christ—
Rev	14: 7	and worship him who m heaven

MADNESS

| Deut | 28:28 | The LORD will afflict you with m, |
| Eccl | 9: 3 | m is in their hearts while they live, |

MAGDALENE

| Mt | 27:56 | Among them were Mary M, |

MAGICIANS

| Ex | 7:11 | and they also, the m of Egypt, |
| Dan | 2: 2 | So the king commanded that the m, |

MAGNIFIES* → MAGNIFY

| Lk | 1:46 | Mary said, "My soul m the Lord, |

MAGNIFY → MAGNIFIES

| Ps | 34: 3 | O m the LORD with me, |

MAJESTIC → MAJESTY

Ex	15:11	Who is like you, m in holiness,
Ps	8: 1	how m is your name in all the earth!
2 Pet	1:17	conveyed to him by the M Glory,

MAJESTY → MAJESTIC

1 Chr	29:11	the glory, the victory, and the m;
Ps	93: 1	The LORD is king, he is robed in m;
Isa	53: 2	or m that we should look at him,
Heb	1: 3	sat down at the right hand of the M
2 Pet	1:16	we had been eyewitnesses of his m.

MAKE → MADE, MAKER

Gen	1:26	"Let us m humankind in our image,
	2:18	will m him a helper as his partner."
	12: 2	I will m of you a great nation,
Ex	20: 4	You shall not m for yourself an idol,
	32: 1	"Come, m gods for us, who shall go

Num	6:25	LORD m his face to shine upon you,
Isa	61: 8	I will m an everlasting covenant
	66:22	and the new earth, which I will m,
Jer	31:31	when I will m a new covenant with
Mt	28:19	and m disciples of all nations,
Mk	1:17	and I will m you fish for people."

MAKER → MAKE

Gen	14:19	God Most High, m of heaven and
Job	4:17	beings be pure before their M?
Ps	95: 6	kneel before the LORD, our M!
Sir	7:30	With all your might love your M,
Isa	54: 5	For your M is your husband,

MALACHI*

Post-exilic prophet (Mal 1:1).

MALE

Gen	1:27	m and female he created them.
	17:10	among you shall be circumcised.
Lev	20:13	If a man lies with a m as with a
Mt	19: 4	'made them m and female,'
Rev	12: 5	she gave birth to a son, a m child,

MALICE

| Rom | 1:29 | wickedness, evil, covetousness, m. |
| 1 Cor | 5: 8 | the old yeast, the yeast of m and |

MAN → MEN

Gen	2: 7	LORD God formed m from the dust
	2:18	not good that the m should be alone;
	32:24	m wrestled with him until daybreak.
1 Sam	13:14	sought out a m after his own heart;
Mt	9: 6	Son of M has authority on earth to
Lk	6: 5	The Son of M is lord of the sabbath.
Jn	9:35	"Do you believe in the Son of M?"
1 Cor	11: 3	that Christ is the head of every m,
Rev	1:13	I saw one like the Son of M,
	14:14	cloud was one like the Son of M,

MANAGE → MANAGERS

| 1 Tim | 3: 4 | He must m his own household well, |
| | 5:14 | children, and m their households, |

MANAGERS* → MANAGE

| Titus | 1: 7 | chaste, good m of the household, |

MANASSEH

1. Firstborn of Joseph (Gen 41:51; 46:20). Blessed by Jacob but not as firstborn (Gen 48). Tribe of blessed (Deut 33:17), numbered (Num 1:35; 26:34), half allotted land east of Jordan (Num 32; Josh 13:8-33), half west (Josh 16; Ezek 48:4), failed to fully possess (Josh 17:12-13; Judg 1:27), 12,000 from (Rev 7:6).

2. Son of Hezekiah; king of Judah (2 Kings 21:1-18; 2 Chr 33:1-20). Judah exiled for his detestable sins (2 Kings 21:10-15). Repented (2 Chr 33:12-19).

MANGER

| Lk | 2:12 | in bands of cloth and lying in a m." |

MANNA

Ex	16:31	The house of Israel called it m;
Josh	5:12	The m ceased on the day they ate
Jn	6:49	ate the m in the wilderness,
Rev	2:17	I will give some of the hidden m,

MANNER

| 1 Cor | 11:27 | cup of the Lord in an unworthy m |
| Phil | 1:27 | life in a m worthy of the gospel |

MANTLE

| 1 Kings | 19:19 | and threw his m over him. |
| 2 Kings | 2: 8 | Elijah took his m and rolled it up, |

MANY

Isa	53:12	yet he bore the sin of m,
Mt	22:14	m are called, but few are chosen."
Mk	10:45	and to give his life a ransom for m."
Jn	20:30	Now Jesus did m other signs in the
Rom	12: 5	who are m, are one body in Christ,

MARAH

| Ex | 15:23 | That is why it was called M. |

MARK → MARKED, MARKS

1. Cousin of Barnabas (Acts 12:12; 15:37-39; Col 4:10; 2 Tim 4:11; Philem 24; 1 Pet 5:13), see John.

2. Brand or symbol:

Gen	4:15	And the LORD put a **m** on Cain,
Ezek	9: 6	but touch no one who has the **m**.
Rev	14: 9	receive a **m** on their foreheads or
	19:20	who had received the **m** of the beast

MARKED → MARK

| Hab | 1:12 | you have **m** them for judgment; |
| Eph | 1:13 | **m** with the seal of the promised |

MARKET → MARKETPLACE

| Mk | 7: 4 | not eat anything from the **m** unless |
| 1 Cor | 10:25 | Eat whatever is sold in the meat **m** |

MARKETPLACE → MARKET

| Jn | 2:16 | Stop making my Father's house a **m** |

MARKS → MARK

1 Macc	1:15	and removed the **m** of circumcision,
1 Cor	7:18	to remove the **m** of circumcision.
Gal	6:17	I carry the **m** of Jesus branded on

MARRIAGE → INTERMARRY, MARRIED, MARRIES

Mt	22:30	are given in **m**, but are like angels
Heb	13: 4	Let **m** be held in honor by all,
Rev	19: 7	for the **m** of the Lamb has come,

MARRIED → MARRIAGE

Mal	2:11	has **m** the daughter of a foreign god.
Mk	12:23	For the seven had **m** her."
1 Tim	3: 2	be above reproach, **m** only once,
Titus	1: 6	**m** only once, whose children are

MARRIES → MARRIAGE

Mk	10:11	and **m** another commits adultery
Rom	7: 3	if she **m** another man, she is not an
1 Cor	7:28	and if a virgin **m**, she does not sin.

MARTHA*

Sister of Mary and Lazarus (Lk 10:38-42; Jn 11; 12:2).

MARVELOUS

Ps	98: 1	for he has done **m** things.
	131: 1	things too great and too **m** for me.
Sir	39:20	and nothing is too **m** for him.

MARY

1. Mother of Jesus (Mt 1:16-25; Lk 1:27-56; 2:1-40). With Jesus at temple (Lk 2:41-52), at the wedding in Cana (Jn 2:1-5), questioning his sanity (Mk 3:21), at the cross (Jn 19:25-27). Among disciples (Acts 1:14).

2. Magdalene; former demoniac (Lk 8:2). Helped support Jesus' ministry (Lk 8:1-3). At the cross (Mt 27:56; Mk 15:40; Jn 19:25), burial (Mt 27:61; Mk 15:47). Saw angel after resurrection (Mt 28:1-10; Mk 16:1-9; Lk 24:1-12); also Jesus (Jn 20:1-18).

3. Sister of Martha and Lazarus (Jn 11). Washed Jesus' feet (Jn 12:1-8).

4. Mother of James and Joses; witnessed crucifixion (Mt 27:56; Mk 15:40) and empty tomb (Mk 16:1; Lk 24:10).

MASTER → MASTERS, TASKMASTERS

Gen	4: 7	desire is for you, but you must **m** it.
Mal	1: 6	if I am a **m**, where is the respect due
Mt	25:21	enter into the joy of your **m**.'
Jn	15:20	Servants are not greater than their **m**
2 Pet	2: 1	deny the **M** who bought them—

MASTERS → MASTER

| Mt | 6:24 | "No one can serve two **m**; |

MATTANIAH → See ZEDEKIAH

MATTATHIAS

Priest who started the Maccabean revolt (1 Macc 2).

MATTER

| Eccl | 3: 1 | a time for every **m** under heaven: |
| | 12:13 | end of the **m**; all has been heard. |

MATTHEW* → =LEVI

Apostle; former tax collector (Mt 9:9-13; 10:3; Mk 3:18; Lk 6:15; Acts 1:13). Also called Levi (Mk 2:14-17; Lk 5:27-32).

MATTHIAS

Disciple chosen to replace Judas (Acts 1:23-26).

MATURE → MATURITY

1 Cor	2: 6	among the **m** we do speak wisdom,
Phil	3:15	who are **m** be of the same mind;
Col	4:12	you may stand **m** and fully assured
Heb	5:14	But solid food is for the **m**,

MATURITY → MATURE

| Eph | 4:13 | to **m**, to the measure of the full |

MEAN → MEANING, MEANS

| Ex | 12:26 | What do you **m** by this observance? |
| Josh | 4: 6 | 'What do those stones **m** to you?' |

MEANING → MEAN

| Gen | 40: 5 | and each dream with its own **m**. |
| Deut | 6:20 | "What is the **m** of the decrees |

MEANS → MEAN

| Mt | 9:13 | learn what this **m**, 'I desire mercy, |
| 1 Cor | 9:22 | that I might by all **m** save some. |

MEASURE

Deut	25:15	have only a full and honest **m**,
Mk	4:24	**m** you give will be the **m** you get,
Lk	6:38	A good **m**, pressed down, shaken
Jn	3:34	for he gives the Spirit without **m**.

MEAT

| Ex | 16:12 | 'At twilight you shall eat **m**, |
| Rom | 14:21 | not to eat **m** or drink wine or do |

MEDIA

| Dan | 8:20 | these are the kings of **M** and Persia. |

MEDIATOR

Gal	3:19	ordained through angels by a **m**.
1 Tim	2: 5	**m** between God and humankind,
Heb	8: 6	he is the **m** of a better covenant,

MEDICINE

| Prov | 17:22 | A cheerful heart is a good **m**, |
| Sir | 6:16 | Faithful friends are life-saving **m**; |

MEDITATE → MEDITATION

Josh	1: 8	you shall **m** on it day and night,
Ps	1: 2	on his law they **m** day and night.
	119:15	I will **m** on your precepts,
Wis	12:22	we may **m** upon your goodness,
Sir	6:37	and **m** at all times on his

MEDITATION → MEDITATE

| Ps | 19:14 | of my mouth and the **m** of my heart |
| | 119:97 | It is my **m** all day long. |

MEDIUM

| Lev | 20:27 | A man or a woman who is a **m** |
| 1 Chr | 10:13 | moreover, he had consulted a **m**, |

MEEK → MEEKNESS

| Ps | 37:11 | But the **m** shall inherit the land, |
| Mt | 5: 5 | "Blessed are the **m**, for they will |

MEEKNESS → MEEK

| Col | 3:12 | kindness, humility, **m**, and patience. |
| Jas | 1:21 | with **m** the implanted word |

MEET → MEETING

Ex	30:36	tent of meeting where I shall **m** with
Am	4:12	prepare to **m** your God,
1 Thess	4:17	together with them to **m** the Lord

MEETING → MEET

| Ex | 27:21 | In the tent of **m**, outside the curtain |
| | 40:34 | the cloud covered the tent of **m**, |

MELCHIZEDEK

Gen	14:18	King **M** of Salem brought out bread
Ps	110: 4	forever according to the order of **M**."
Heb	7: 1	This "King **M** of Salem, priest of

MELT

Deut	1:28	made our hearts **m** by reporting,
Ps	97: 5	The mountains **m** like wax before
2 Pet	3:12	and the elements will **m** with fire?

MEMBERS

Rom	7:23	I see in my **m** another law at war
	12: 5	individually we are **m** one of another.
1 Cor	6:15	that your bodies are **m** of Christ?
	12:18	God arranged the **m** in the body,

MEMORIAL

| Lev | 5:12 | a handful of it as its **m** portion, |
| Josh | 4: 7 | stones shall be to the Israelites a **m** |

MEN → MAN

| Gen | 18: 2 | and saw three **m** standing near him. |
| Sir | 44: 1 | now sing the praises of famous **m**, |

Dan 3:92 "But I see four **m** unbound,
Mt 2: 1 wise **m** from the East came to
Lk 9:30 they saw two **m**, Moses and Elijah,

MENAHEM*
King of Israel (2 Kings 15:14-23).

MENE
Dan 5:25 inscribed: M, M, TEKEL, and PARSIN.

MEPHIBOSHETH
Son of Jonathan shown kindness by David (2 Sam 4:4; 9; 21:7). Accused of siding with Absalom (2 Sam 16:1-4; 19:24-30).

MERCIES → MERCY
Lam 3:22 his **m** never come to an end;
2 Cor 1: 3 the Father of **m** and the God of all

MERCIFUL → MERCY
Deut 4:31 the LORD your God is a **m** God,
Ps 111: 4 the LORD is gracious and **m**.
Sir 2:11 the Lord is compassionate and **m**;
Jer 3:12 not look on you in anger, for I am **m**
Mt 5: 7 "Blessed are the **m**, for they will
Lk 6:36 Be **m**, just as your Father is **m**.
Heb 2:17 be a **m** and faithful high priest

MERCY → MERCIES, MERCIFUL
Ex 25:17 make a **m** seat of pure gold;
1 Chr 21:13 of the LORD, for his **m** is very great;
Ps 40:11 Do not, O LORD, withhold your **m**
Sir 2:17 for equal to his majesty is his **m**,
Dan 9: 9 To the Lord our God belong **m**
Hab 3: 2 in wrath may you remember **m**.
Zech 1:12 will you withhold **m** from Jerusalem
Mt 9:13 learn what this means, 'I desire **m**,
23:23 of the law: justice and **m** and faith.
Rom 9:15 "I will have **m** on whom I have **m**,
Eph 2: 4 But God, who is rich in **m**,
1 Tim 1:13 **m** because I had acted ignorantly
Titus 3: 5 had done, but according to his **m**,
Heb 4:16 so that we may receive **m** and find
Jas 2:13 **m** triumphs over judgment.

MERIBAH
Ex 17: 7 He called the place Massah and M,
Ps 95: 8 Do not harden your hearts, as at M,

MESHACH → =MISHAEL
Hebrew exiled to Babylon; name changed from Mishael (Dan 1:6-7). Refused defilement by food (Dan 1:8-20). Refused to worship idol (Dan 3:1-18); saved from furnace (Dan 3:19-30).

MESSAGE → MESSENGER
Jn 12:38 "Lord, who has believed our **m**,
1 Cor 1:18 the **m** about the cross is foolishness
2 Cor 5:19 entrusting the **m** of reconciliation to

MESSENGER → MESSAGE
Isa 42:19 or deaf like my **m** whom I send?
Mt 11:10 I am sending my **m** ahead of you,
2 Cor 12: 7 a **m** of Satan to torment me,

MESSIAH → CHRIST, MESSIAHS
Mt 16:16 Peter answered, "You are the M,
Lk 2:11 a Savior, who is the M, the Lord.
Acts 2:36 God has made him both Lord and M
Rom 9: 5 according to the flesh, comes the M,
Rev 11:15 kingdom of our Lord and of his M,

MESSIAHS → MESSIAH
Mk 13:22 False **m** and false prophets will

MICAH
1. Idolater from Ephraim (Judg 17-18).
2. Prophet from Moresheth (Jer 26:18-19; Mic 1:1).

MICAIAH
Prophet of the LORD who spoke against Ahab (1 Kings 22:1-28; 2 Chr 18:1-27).

MICHAEL
Archangel (Jude 9); warrior in angelic realm, protector of Israel (Dan 10:13, 21; 12:1; Rev 12:7).

MICHAL*
Daughter of Saul, wife of David (1 Sam 14:49; 18:20-28). Warned David of Saul's plot (1 Sam 19). Saul gave her to Palti-

el (1 Sam 25:44); David retrieved her (2 Sam 3:13-16). Criticized David for dancing before the ark (2 Sam 6:16-23; 1 Chr 15:29).

MIDDLE
Gen 3: 3 tree that is in the **m** of the garden,
Rev 22: 2 the **m** of the street of the city.

MIDIAN → MIDIANITES
Ex 18: 1 Jethro, the priest of M, Moses'

MIDIANITES → MIDIAN
Gen 37:36 the M had sold him in Egypt to
Num 31: 2 "Avenge the Israelites on the M;

MIDWIVES
Ex 1:17 But the **m** feared God; they did not

MIGHT → ALMIGHTY, MIGHTY
2 Chr 6:41 you and the ark of your **m**.
20: 6 In your hand are power and **m**,
Ps 54: 1 and vindicate me by your **m**.
Eccl 9:10 hands find to do, do with your **m**;
Sir 7:30 With all your **m** love your Maker,
Zech 4: 6 **m**, nor by power, but by my spirit,

MIGHTY → MIGHT
Gen 49:24 by the hands of the M One of Jacob,
Ex 6: 1 by a **m** hand he will let them go;
Deut 5:15 a **m** hand and an outstretched arm;
2 Sam 1:19 How the **m** have fallen!
Ps 99: 4 M King, lover of justice, you have
Isa 9: 6 Wonderful Counselor, M God,
Lk 1:49 the M One has done great things
Rev 18: 8 for **m** is the Lord God who judges

MILE
Mt 5:41 one **m**, go also the second **m**.

MILK
Ex 3: 8 a land flowing with **m** and honey,
Heb 5:12 You need **m**, not solid food;
1 Pet 2: 2 long for the pure, spiritual **m**,

MILLSTONE → STONE
Lk 17: 2 better for you if a **m** were hung

MIND → MINDFUL, MINDS
Num 23:19 mortal, that he should change his **m**.
1 Chr 28: 9 for the LORD searches every **m**,
Ps 110: 4 sworn and will not change his **m**,
Sir 37:17 The **m** is the root of all conduct;
Jon 3: 9 God may relent and change his **m**;
Mt 22:37 all your soul, and with all your **m**.'
Rom 1:28 God gave them up to a debased **m**
8: 6 but to set the **m** on the Spirit is life
1 Cor 2:16 who has known the **m** of the Lord
Phil 2: 5 same **m** be in you that was in Christ
Heb 7:21 sworn and will not change his **m**,

MINDFUL → MIND
Ps 8: 4 beings that you are **m** of them,
111: 5 he is ever **m** of his covenant.
Heb 2: 6 beings that you are **m** of them,

MINDS → MIND
2 Cor 4: 4 blinded the **m** of the unbelievers,
Eph 4:23 be renewed in the spirit of your **m**,
Phil 4: 7 guard your hearts and your **m**

MINISTER → MINISTERS, MINISTRY
Ex 28:43 to **m** in the holy place;
Ps. 101: 6 that is blameless shall **m** to me.

MINISTERS → MINISTER
2 Cor 3: 6 to be **m** of a new covenant,
11:15 if his **m** also disguise themselves as **m**

MINISTRY → MINISTER
2 Cor 5:18 has given us the **m** of reconciliation;
Eph 4:12 equip the saints for the work of **m**,
Heb 8: 6 now obtained a more excellent **m**,

MIRACLES → See also JESUS: MIRACLES
Ps 78:11 and the **m** that he had shown them.
Acts 19:11 did extraordinary **m** through Paul,
1 Cor 12:29 Are all teachers? Do all work **m**?
Heb 2: 4 signs and wonders and various **m**,

MIRIAM
Sister of Moses and Aaron (Num 26:59). Led dancing at Red Sea (Ex 15:20-21). Struck with leprosy for criticizing Moses (Num 12). Death (Num 20:1).

MIRROR
1 Cor	13:12	For now we see in a **m**, dimly,
2 Cor	3:18	as though reflected in a **m**,
Jas	1:23	who look at themselves in a **m**;

MISHAEL → See MESHACH

MISUSES
Ex	20: 7	not acquit anyone who **m** his name.

MOAB → MOABITE
Gen	19:37	bore a son, and named him **M**;
Ruth	1: 1	went to live in the country of **M**,
Isa	15: 1	An oracle concerning **M**.

MOABITE → MOAB
Deut	23: 3	**M** shall be admitted to the assembly

MOCK → MOCKED
Ps	22: 7	All who see me **m** at me;
Mk	10:34	they will **m** him, and spit upon him,

MOCKED → MOCK
1 Kings	18:27	At noon Elijah **m** them, saying,
Gal	6: 7	God is not **m**, for you reap

MOLECH
Lev	18:21	to sacrifice them to **M**,

MOMENT → MOMENTARY
Ex	33: 5	single **m** I should go up among you,
Ps	30: 5	For his anger is but for a **m**;
Isa	54: 7	For a brief **m** I abandoned you,
	66: 8	a nation be delivered in one **m**?
1 Cor	15:52	in a **m**, in the twinkling of an eye,

MOMENTARY* → MOMENT
2 Cor	4:17	this slight **m** affliction is preparing

MONEY
Eccl	10:19	and **m** meets every need.
Mk	11:15	the tables of the **m** changers
1 Tim	3: 3	quarrelsome, and not a lover of **m**.
	6:10	love of **m** is a root of all kinds
Heb	13: 5	your lives free from the love of **m**,

MONTH
Ex	12: 2	be the first **m** of the year for you.
Ezek	47:12	they will bear fresh fruit every **m**,
Rev	22: 2	producing its fruit each **m**;

MOON → MOONS
Gen	37: 9	the sun, the **m**, and eleven stars
Deut	17: 3	the sun or the **m** or any of the host
Josh	10:13	sun stood still, and the **m** stopped,
Joel	2:31	to darkness, and the **m** to blood,
Acts	2:20	to darkness and the **m** to blood,
Rev	6:12	the full **m** became like blood,
	21:23	no need of sun or **m** to shine on it,

MOONS → MOON
2 Chr	8:13	the new **m**, and the three annual
Col	2:16	or of observing festivals, new **m**,

MORALS*
1 Cor	15:33	"Bad company ruins good **m**."

MORDECAI
Benjamite exile who raised Esther (Esth 2:5-15). Mordecai's dream (Esth 11; 10:4-13). Exposed plot to kill Xerxes (Esth 2:19-23; 12:1-6). Refused to honor Haman (Esth 3:1-6; 5:9-14). Mordecai's prayer (Esth 13). Charged Esther to foil Haman's plot against the Jews (Esth 4). Xerxes forced Haman to honor Mordecai (Esth 6). Mordecai exalted (Esth 8-10). Established Purim (Esth 9:18-32).

MORE → MOST
Ps	19:10	**M** to be desired are they than gold,
	69:31	will please the LORD **m** than an ox
Eccl	6:11	The **m** words, the **m** vanity,
Mk	4:25	to those who have, **m** will be given;
Lk	12:23	For life is **m** than food,
Rom	8:37	things we are **m** than conquerors
1 Cor	12:31	a still **m** excellent way.
Jas	4: 6	But he gives all the **m** grace;

Rev	7:16	will hunger no **m**, and thirst no **m**;
	21: 4	Death will be no **m**;

MORIAH*
Gen	22: 2	you love, and go to the land of **M**,
2 Chr	3: 1	the LORD in Jerusalem on Mount **M**,

MORNING
Gen	1: 5	and there was **m**, the first day.
Ps	30: 5	but joy comes with the **m**.
Lam	3:23	every **m**; great is your faithfulness.
Lk	24:22	They were at the tomb early this **m**,
2 Pet	1:19	the day dawns and the **m** star rises
Rev	22:16	of David, the bright **m** star."

MORTAL
Num	23:19	**m**, that he should change his mind.
1 Sam	15:29	**m**, that he should change his mind."
1 Cor	15:53	**m** body must put on immortality.
2 Cor	5: 4	is **m** may be swallowed up by life.

MOSES
Levite; brother of Aaron (Ex 6:20; 1 Chr 6:3). Put in basket into Nile; discovered and raised by Pharaoh's daughter (Ex 2:1-10). Fled to Midian after killing Egyptian (Ex 2:11-15). Married to Zipporah, fathered Gershom (Ex 2:16-22).
Called by the LORD to deliver Israel (Ex 3-4). Pharaoh's resistance (Ex 5). Ten plagues (Ex 7-11). Passover and Exodus (Ex 12-13). Led Israel through Red Sea (Ex 14). Song of deliverance (Ex 15:1-21). Brought water from rock (Ex 17:1-7). Raised hands to defeat Amalekites (Ex 17:8-16). Delegated judges (Ex 18; Deut 1:9-18).
Received Law at Sinai (Ex 19-23; 25-31; Jn 1:17). Announced Law to Israel (Ex 19:7-8; 24; 35). Broke tablets because of golden calf (Ex 32; Deut 9). Saw glory of the LORD (Ex 33-34). Supervised building of tabernacle (Ex 36-40). Set apart Aaron and priests (Lev 8-9). Numbered tribes (Num 1-4; 26). Opposed by Aaron and Miriam (Num 12). Sent spies into Canaan (Num 13). Announced forty years of wandering for failure to enter land (Num 14). Opposed by Korah (Num 16). Forbidden to enter land for striking rock (Num 20:1-13; Deut 1:37). Lifted bronze snake for healing (Num 21:4-9; Jn 3:14). Final address to Israel (Deut 1-33). Succeeded by Joshua (Num 27:12-23; Deut 34). Death and burial by God (Deut 34:5-12). Praise of (Sir 45).
Law of (1 Kings 2:3; Ezra 3:2; Mk 12:26; Lk 24:44). Book of (2 Chr 25:12; Neh 13:1). Song of (Ex 15:1-21; Rev 15:3). Prayer of (Ps 90).

MOST → MORE
Gen	14:18	he was priest of God **M** High.
Ex	26:33	the holy place from the **m** holy.
Ps	91: 1	live in the shelter of the **M** High,
Mk	5: 7	Jesus, Son of the **M** High God?
Col	4: 5	making the **m** of the time.
Jude	1:20	yourselves up on your **m** holy faith;

MOTH
Ps	39:11	consuming like a **m** what is dear to
Mt	6:19	where **m** and rust consume and

MOTHER → MOTHER'S, MOTHERS
Gen	2:24	a man leaves his father and his **m**
	3:20	because she was the **m** of all living.
Ex	20:12	Honor your father and your **m**,
Judg	5: 7	Deborah, arose as a **m** in Israel.
Tob	4: 3	Honor your **m** and do not abandon
Prov	31: 1	An oracle that his **m** taught him:
Sir	3: 6	who honor their **m** obey the Lord;
Isa	66:13	As a **m** comforts her child, so I will
Mt	10:37	loves father or **m** more than me is
Lk	14:26	and does not hate father and **m**,
Jn	2: 3	When the wine gave out, the **m** of Jesus said
	19:27	to the disciple, "Here is your **m**."
Gal	4:26	she is free, and she is our **m**.
Eph	5:31	a man will leave his father and **m**
Rev	17: 5	**m** of whores and of earth's

MOTHER'S → MOTHER
Job	1:21	"Naked I came from my **m** womb,
Prov	1: 8	and do not reject your **m** teaching;
Jn	3: 4	a second time into the **m** womb and

MOTHERS → MOTHER
Prov	15:20	but the foolish despise their **m**.
Mk	10:30	brothers and sisters, **m** and children,

MOUNT → MOUNTAIN, MOUNTAINS

Gen	22:14	"On the **m** of the LORD it shall be
Ex	19:20	the LORD descended upon **M** Sinai,
Deut	11:29	blessing on **M** Gerizim and the curse
Ps	78:68	**M** Zion, which he loves.
Mic	4: 7	will reign over them in **M** Zion
Zech	14: 4	the **M** of Olives shall be split in two
Mk	13: 3	he was sitting on the **M** of Olives
Heb	12:22	But you have come to **M** Zion and
Rev	14: 1	the Lamb, standing on **M** Zion!

MOUNTAIN → MOUNT

Ex	3: 1	and came to Horeb, the **m** of God.
	24:18	on the **m** for forty days and forty
Isa	2: 2	the **m** of the LORD's house shall be
Dan	2:45	saw that a stone was cut from the **m**
Mt	4: 8	a very high **m** and showed him all
	17:20	you will say to this **m**, 'Move from
2 Pet	1:18	we were with him on the holy **m**.

MOUNTAINS → MOUNT

Gen	7:20	the waters swelled above the **m**,
Ps	125: 2	As the **m** surround Jerusalem,
Isa	52: 7	beautiful upon the **m** are the feet of
1 Cor	13: 2	have all faith, so as to remove **m**,
Rev	16:20	and no **m** were to be found;

MOURN → MOURNFUL, MOURNING

Eccl	3: 4	a time to **m**, and a time to dance;
Sir	7:34	but **m** with those who **m**.
Zech	12:10	they shall **m** for him,
Mt	5: 4	"Blessed are those who **m**,

MOURNING → MOURN

Ps	30:11	You have turned my **m** into dancing
Isa	61: 3	the oil of gladness instead of **m**,
Rev	21: 4	**m** and crying and pain will be no

MOUTH → MOUTHS

Ex	4:12	Now go, and I will be with your **m**
Deut	8: 3	that comes from the **m** of the LORD.
Ps	19:14	Let the words of my **m**,
Eccl	5: 2	Never be rash with your **m**,
Sir	28:25	and a bolt for your **m**.
Isa	49: 2	He made my **m** like a sharp sword,
Mt	4: 4	every word that comes from the **m**
	15:11	it is not what goes into the **m**
Jas	3:10	From the same **m** come blessing and
Rev	19:15	From his **m** comes a sharp sword

MOUTHS → MOUTH

Ps	115: 5	They have **m**, but do not speak;
Dan	6:22	sent his angel and shut the lions' **m**

MUCH

Ps	19:10	they than gold, even **m** fine gold;
Eccl	12:12	**m** study is a weariness of the flesh.
Lk	12:48	to whom **m** has been given, **m** will be required;
Jn	12:24	but if it dies, it bears **m** fruit.
1 Jn	4:11	since God loved us so **m**,

MUD

Jn	9: 6	and spread the **m** on the man's eyes,
2 Pet	2:22	washed only to wallow in the **m**."

MULTIPLY

Gen	1:28	to them, "Be fruitful and **m**,
	9: 7	And you, be fruitful and **m**,
Deut	6: 3	that you may **m** greatly in a land

MULTITUDE → MULTITUDES

Jas	5:20	and will cover a **m** of sins.
1 Pet	4: 8	for love covers a **m** of sins.

MULTITUDES → MULTITUDE

Joel	3:14	**M**, **m**, in the valley of decision!
Rev	17:15	are peoples and **m** and nations

MURDER → MURDERER, MURDERERS

Ex	20:13	You shall not **m**.
Hos	4: 2	lying, and **m**, and stealing and
Mt	5:21	of ancient times, 'You shall not **m**';

MURDERER → MURDER

Num	35:16	the **m** shall be put to death.
Jn	8:44	He was a **m** from the beginning

MURDERERS → MURDER

1 Jn	3:15	who hate a brother or sister are **m**,

Rev	21: 8	the faithless, the polluted, the **m**,

MUSIC

1 Sam	19: 9	while David was playing **m**.
Ps	92: 3	to the **m** of the lute and the harp,

MUSTARD

Mt	17:20	have faith the size of a **m** seed,
Mk	4:31	It is like a **m** seed, which,

MUTUAL

Rom	12:10	love one another with **m** affection;
Heb	13: 1	Let **m** love continue.

MYRRH

Mt	2:11	gifts of gold, frankincense, and **m**.
Mk	15:23	offered him wine mixed with **m**;

MYSTERY

Dan	2:19	**m** was revealed to Daniel in a vision
Rom	11:25	I want you to understand this **m**:
1 Cor	15:51	Listen, I will tell you a **m**!
Eph	3: 4	my understanding of the **m** of Christ
1 Tim	3: 9	must hold fast to the **m** of the faith
Rev	17: 5	a name, a **m**: "Babylon the great,

MYTHS

2 Pet	1:16	did not follow cleverly devised **m**

N

NAAMAN

Aramean general whose leprosy was cleansed by Elisha (2 Kings 5; Lk 4:27).

NABAL

Wealthy Carmelite the LORD killed for refusing to help David (1 Sam 25). David married Abigail, his widow (1 Sam 25:39-42).

NABOTH

Jezreelite killed for his vineyard (1 Kings 21). Ahab's family punished (1 Kings 21:17-24; 2 Kings 9:21-37).

NADAB

1. Firstborn of Aaron (Ex 6:23); killed with Abihu for offering unauthorized fire (Lev 10; Num 3:4).

2. Son of Jeroboam I; king of Israel (1 Kings 15:25-32).

NAHUM

Prophet against Nineveh (Nah 1:1; Tob 14:4).

NAILING* → NAILS

Col	2:14	He set this aside, **n** it to the cross.

NAILS → NAILING

Eccl	12:11	like **n** firmly fixed are the collected
Jn	20:25	put my finger in the mark of the **n**

NAKED → NAKEDNESS

Gen	2:25	the man and his wife were both **n**,
Job	1:21	"**N** I came from my mother's womb, and **n** shall
2 Cor	5: 3	taken it off we will not be found **n**.

NAKEDNESS → NAKED

Rom	8:35	or persecution, or famine, or **n**,

NAME → NAME'S, NAMES

Gen	2:19	every living creature, that was its **n**.
	4:26	people began to invoke the **n** of
	12: 2	bless you, and make your **n** great,
Ex	3:15	my **n** forever, and this my title
	20: 7	wrongful use of the **n** of the LORD
	34: 5	and proclaimed the **n**, "The LORD."
Num	17: 2	Write each man's **n** on his staff,
Deut	12:11	as a dwelling for his **n**:
Ps	9:10	know your **n** put their trust in you,
Prov	18:10	The **n** of the LORD is a strong tower;
Sir	2:17	and equal to his **n** are his works.
Isa	42: 8	I am the LORD, that is my **n**;
Ezek	20: 9	But I acted for the sake of my **n**,
Joel	2:32	on the **n** of the LORD shall be saved;
Zech	14: 9	the LORD will be one and his **n** one.
Mt	1:21	a son, and you are to **n** him Jesus,
	6: 9	Father in heaven, hallowed be your **n**.
	28:19	baptizing them in the **n** of the Father
Jn	1:12	received him, who believed in his **n**,
	20:31	believing you may have life in his **n**.

Acts 4:12 for there is no other **n** under heaven
Phil 2: 9 gave him the **n** that is above every **n**
Rev 13:17 **n** of the beast or the number of its **n**.
19:13 his **n** is called The Word of God.
22: 4 and his **n** will be on their foreheads.

NAME'S → NAME
Ps 23: 3 in right paths for his **n** sake.

NAMES → NAME
Gen 2:20 The man gave **n** to all cattle,
Ex 28: 9 engrave on them the **n** of the sons
Mt 10: 2 are the **n** of the twelve apostles:
Rev 21:14 the twelve **n** of the twelve apostles

NAOMI*
Wife of Elimelech, mother-in-law of Ruth (Ruth 1:2, 4). Left Bethlehem for Moab during famine (Ruth 1:1). Returned a widow, with Ruth (Ruth 1:6-22). Advised Ruth to seek marriage with Boaz (Ruth 2:17-3:4). Cared for Ruth's son Obed (Ruth 4:13-17).

NAPHTALI
Son of Jacob by Bilhah (Gen 30:8; 35:25; 1 Chr 2:2). Tribe of blessed (Gen 49:21; Deut 33:23), numbered (Num 1:43; 26:50), allotted land (Josh 19:32-39; Ezek 48:3), failed to fully possess (Judg 1:33), supported Deborah (Judg 4:10; 5:18), David (1 Chr 12:34), 12,000 from (Rev 7:6).

NARROW
Lk 13:24 "Strive to enter through the **n** door;

NATHAN
Prophet and chronicler of Israel's history (1 Chr 29:29; 2 Chr 9:29). Announced the Davidic covenant (2 Sam 7; 1 Chr 17). Denounced David's sin with Bathsheba (2 Sam 12). Supported Solomon (1 Kings 1).

NATHANAEL → =BARTHOLOMEW?
Apostle (Jn 1:45-49; 21:2). Probably also called Bartholomew (Mt 10:3).

NATION → NATIONS
Gen 12: 2 I will make of you a great **n**, and
Ex 32:10 and of you I will make a great **n**."
Ps 33:12 Happy is the **n** whose God is the LORD
Prov 14:34 Righteousness exalts a **n**,
Isa 2: 4 **n** shall not lift up sword against **n**,
66: 8 a **n** be delivered in one moment?
Mt 24: 7 For **n** will rise against **n**,
1 Pet 2: 9 a holy **n**, God's own people,

NATIONS → NATION
Gen 18:18 the **n** of the earth shall be blessed in
2 Kings 17:15 followed the **n** that were around
Ps 47: 8 God is king over the **n**;
Isa 2: 2 all the **n** shall stream to it.
42: 1 he will bring forth justice to the **n**.
Am 9:12 and all the **n** who are called
Mt 28:19 and make disciples of all **n**,
Mk 11:17 a house of prayer for all the **n**'?
Rom 4:18 become "the father of many **n**,"
Rev 22: 2 the tree are for the healing of the **n**.

NATURAL → NATURE
Num 16:29 If these people die a **n** death,
Rom 11:21 if God did not spare the **n** branches,

NATURE → NATURAL
Rom 1:20 his eternal power and divine **n**,
2 Pet 1: 4 become participants of the divine **n**.

NAZARETH
Mt 2:23 made his home in a town called **N**,
Jn 1:46 Can anything good come out of **N**?
19:19 "Jesus of **N**, the King of the Jews."

NAZIRITE
Num 6: 2 make a special vow, the vow of a **n**,
Judg 13: 5 boy shall be a **n** to God from birth.

NEAR → NEARSIGHTED
Deut 4: 7 has a god so **n** to it as the LORD
30:14 No, the word is very **n** to you;
Isa 55: 6 call upon him while he is **n**;
Zeph 1:14 The great day of the LORD is **n**,
Lk 10: 9 'The kingdom of God has come **n**
Jas 4: 8 Draw **n** to God, and he will draw **n** to
Rev 22:10 of this book, for the time is **n**.

NEARSIGHTED* → NEAR, SEE
2 Pet 1: 9 lacks these things is **n** and blind,

NEBUCHADNEZZAR
Babylonian king, also spelled Nebuchadrezzar. Subdued and exiled Judah (2 Kings 24-25; 2 Chr 36; Jer 39). Dreams interpreted by Daniel (Dan 2; 4). Worshiped God (Dan 3:28-29; 4:34-37).

NECK → STIFF-NECKED
Prov 3:22 your soul and adornment for your **n**.
Mt 18: 6 were fastened around your **n**

NECO
Pharaoh who killed Josiah (2 Kings 23:29-30; 2 Chr 35:20-22), deposed Jehoahaz (2 Kings 23:33-35; 2 Chr 36:3-4).

NEED → NEEDY
Mt 6: 8 for your Father knows what you **n**
1 Cor 12:21 to the hand, "I have no **n** of you,"
Heb 4:16 and find grace to help in time of **n**.
1 Jn 2:27 you do not **n** anyone to teach you.

NEEDLE
Lk 18:25 a camel to go through the eye of a **n**

NEEDY → NEED
1 Sam 2: 8 he lifts the **n** from the ash heap,
Job 29:16 I was a father to the **n**,
Ps 113: 7 and lifts the **n** from the ash heap,

NEGLECT
Lk 11:42 and **n** justice and the love of God;
1 Tim 4:14 Do not **n** the gift that is in you,
Heb 2: 3 escape if we **n** so great a salvation?

NEHEMIAH
Cupbearer of Artaxerxes (Neh 2:1); governor of Israel (Neh 8:9). Returned to Jerusalem to rebuild walls (Neh 2-6). With Ezra, reestablished worship (Neh 8). Prayer confessing nation's sin (Neh 9). Dedicated wall (Neh 12). Story of the miraculous fire (2 Macc 1).

NEIGHBOR
Lev 19:18 shall love your **n** as yourself:
Deut 5:20 bear false witness against your **n**.
Mt 19:19 You shall love your **n** as yourself."
Jas 2: 8 "You shall love your **n** as yourself."

NESTS
Mt 8:20 and birds of the air have **n**;
Lk 13:19 made **n** in its branches."

NEVER
Ps 15: 5 do these things shall **n** be moved.
Lam 3:22 steadfast love of the LORD **n** ceases,
Dan 2:44 will set up a kingdom that shall **n**
Mt 7:23 will declare to them, 'I **n** knew you;
Jn 10:28 eternal life, and they will **n** perish.
1 Cor 13: 8 Love **n** ends. But as for prophecies,
Heb 13: 5 he has said, "I will **n** leave you or

NEW
Ex 1: 8 Now a **n** king arose over Egypt,
Ps 33: 3 Sing to him a **n** song;
Eccl 1: 9 there is nothing **n** under the sun.
Isa 43:19 I am about to do a **n** thing;
65:17 create **n** heavens and a **n** earth;
Jer 31:31 I will make a **n** covenant with the
Lam 3:23 they are **n** every morning;
Ezek 36:26 A **n** heart I will give you,
Mt 9:17 is **n** wine put into old wineskins;
Mk 1:27 A **n** teaching—with authority!
Lk 22:20 is the **n** covenant in my blood.
Jn 13:34 I give you a **n** commandment,
2 Cor 3: 6 to be ministers of a **n** covenant,
Col 3:10 clothed yourselves with the **n** self,
Heb 8: 8 when I will establish a **n** covenant
1 Pet 1: 3 mercy he has given us a **n** birth into
2 Pet 3:13 we wait for **n** heavens and a **n** earth,
1 Jn 2: 7 writing you no **n** commandment,
Rev 21: 1 I saw a **n** heaven and a **n** earth;
21: 2 I saw the holy city, the **n** Jerusalem,
21: 5 "See, I am making all things **n**."

NEWS
Isa 52: 7 who brings good **n**, who announces
Mt 11: 5 the poor have good **n** brought to

Mk   1:15 repent, and believe in the good **n**."

NICODEMUS
Pharisee who visted Jesus at night (Jn 3). Argued for fair treatment of Jesus (Jn 7:50-52). With Joseph, prepared Jesus for burial (Jn 19:38-42).

NIGHT → NIGHTS
Gen   1: 5 and the darkness he called **N**.
Ex   13:21 a pillar of fire by **n**, to give them
Josh   1: 8 you shall meditate on it day and **n**,
Mt   24:43 part of the **n** the thief was coming,
1 Thess 5: 2 Lord will come like a thief in the **n**.
Rev   22: 5 And there will be no more **n**;

NIGHTS → NIGHT
Gen   7:12 on the earth forty days and forty **n**.
Ex   24:18 mountain for forty days and forty **n**.
1 Kings 19: 8 of that food forty days and forty **n**
Jon   1:17 of the fish three days and three **n**.
Mt   4: 2 He fasted forty days and forty **n**,
         12:40 for three days and three **n** the Son

NILE
Ex   7:17 will strike the water that is in the **N**,

NINEVEH
Jon   1: 2 "Go at once to **N**, that great city,
Nah   1: 1 An oracle concerning **N**.
Mt   12:41 The people of **N** will rise up at the

NOAH
Righteous man (Ezek 14:14, 20) called to build ark (Gen 6-8; Heb 11:7; 1 Pet 3:20; 2 Pet 2:5). God's covenant with (Gen 9:1-17). Drunkenness of (Gen 9:18-23). Blessed sons, cursed Canaan (Gen 9:24-27). Praised (Sir 44:17-18).

NOISE
Ex   32:17 "There is a **n** of war in the camp."
Ps   66: 1 Make a joyful **n** to God, all the earth
2 Pet   3:10 will pass away with a loud **n**,

NOON
Am   8: 9 I will make the sun go down at **n**,
Mk   15:33 When it was **n**, darkness came over

NORTH
Jer   4: 6 I am bringing evil from the **n**,
Dan   11: 6 come to the king of the **n** to ratify

NOTHING
Eccl   1: 9 there is **n** new under the sun.
Sir   39:20 and **n** is too marvelous for him.
Jer   32:17 **N** is too hard for you.
Mt   17:20 and **n** will be impossible for you."
Jn   15: 5 apart from me you can do **n**.
1 Cor   13: 2 but do not have love, I am **n**.

NULLIFY
Rom   3: 3 **n** the faithfulness of God?
Gal   2:21 I do not **n** the grace of God;

NUMBER → NUMBERED, NUMEROUS
Num   1:45 So the whole **n** of the Israelites,
         26:51 the **n** of the Israelites enrolled:
Rom   11:25 until the full **n** of the Gentiles has
Rev   13:18 Its **n** is six hundred sixty-six.

NUMBERED → NUMBER
2 Sam   24:10 because he had **n** the people.

NUMEROUS → NUMBER
Gen   17: 2 and will make you exceedingly **n**."
Ex   1: 9 the Israelite people are more **n**
Zech   10: 8 shall be as **n** as they were before.

NURSING
Isa   49:15 Can a woman forget her **n** child,

O

OATH
Deut   7: 8 and kept the **o** that he swore to your
Neh   13:25 them take an **o** in the name of God,
Ps   132:11 a sure **o** from which he will not turn
Heb   7:20 This was confirmed with an **o**;

OBADIAH
1. Believer who sheltered 100 prophets from Jezebel (1 Kings 18:1-16).

2. Prophet against Edom (Ob 1).

OBEDIENCE → OBEY
Rom   5:19 so by the one man's **o** the many will
Heb   5: 8 learned **o** through what he suffered;

OBEDIENT → OBEY
Ex   24: 7 spoken we will do, and we will be **o**.
Phil   2: 8 and became **o** to the point of death

OBEY → OBEDIENCE, OBEDIENT, OBEYED
Ex   19: 5 if you **o** my voice and keep my
Deut   12:28 Be careful to **o** all these words that
Josh   24:24 we will serve, and him we will **o**."
Mt   28:20 **o** everything that I have commanded
Acts   5:29 "We must **o** God rather than any
Eph   6: 1 Children, **o** your parents in the Lord,
1 Jn   5: 3 love of God is this, that we **o** his

OBEYED → OBEY
Jer   3:13 have not **o** my voice, says the LORD:
Heb   11: 8 By faith Abraham **o** when he was

OBSERVE
Lev   20: 8 Keep my statutes, and **o** them;
Ps   119: 8 I will **o** your statutes;

OBSTACLE
1 Cor   9:12 **o** in the way of the gospel of Christ.
2 Cor   6: 3 are putting no **o** in anyone's way,

OBTAIN → OBTAINED
Rom   11: 7 Israel failed to **o** what it was seeking
2 Tim   2:10 that they may also **o** the salvation

OBTAINED → OBTAIN
Phil   3:12 Not that I have already **o** this
Heb   8: 6 Jesus has now **o** a more excellent

ODOR
Gen   8:21 the LORD smelled the pleasing **o**,
Ex   29:18 it is a pleasing **o**, an offering

OFFENSE
Mk   6: 3 And they took **o** at him.
Gal   5:11 **o** of the cross has been removed.

OFFER → OFFERING, OFFERINGS
Ps   4: 5 **O** right sacrifices, and put your trust
Hos   14: 2 and we will **o** the fruit of our lips.
Heb   9:25 Nor was it to **o** himself again and

OFFERING → OFFER
Gen   4: 4 LORD had regard for Abel and his **o**,
         22: 8 will provide the lamb for a burnt **o**,
2 Chr   7: 1 heaven and consumed the burnt **o**
1 Macc   4:44 what to do about the altar of burnt **o**,
Ps   40: 6 Sacrifice and **o** you do not desire,
Dan   11:31 shall abolish the regular burnt **o**
Eph   5: 2 a fragrant **o** and sacrifice to God.
Heb   10:14 For by a single **o** he has perfected

OFFERINGS → OFFER
1 Sam   15:22 the LORD as great delight in burnt **o**
1 Macc   1:45 to forbid burnt **o** and sacrifices
Hos   6: 6 of God rather than burnt **o**.
Mk   12:33 important than all whole burnt **o**

OFFSPRING
Gen   3:15 and between your **o** and hers;
         12: 7 "To your **o** I will give this land."
2 Sam   7:12 I will raise up your **o** after you,

OHOLIAB
Craftsman who worked on the tabernacle (Ex 31:6; 35:34; 36:1-2; 38:23).

OIL
Ex   25: 6 **o** for the lamps, spices for the anointing **o**
Deut   14:23 your wine, and your **o**, as well
Ps   23: 5 you anoint my head with **o**;
Heb   1: 9 with the **o** of gladness beyond your
Jas   5:14 anointing them with **o** in the name

OLD
Gen   21: 7 I have borne him a son in his **o** age."
Ps   74:12 Yet God my King is from of **o**,
Mk   2:22 puts new wine into **o** wineskins;
Rom   4:19 he was about a hundred years **o**),
Eph   4:22 your **o** self, corrupt and deluded by

OLIVE → OLIVES
Zech	4: 3	And by it there are two o trees,
Rom	11:17	and you, a wild o shoot,
Rev	11: 4	two o trees and the two lampstands

OLIVES → OLIVE
Zech	14: 4	Mount of O shall be split in two
Mt	24: 3	he was sitting on the Mount of O,

OMEGA
Rev	1: 8	"I am the Alpha and the O,"

OMRI
King of Israel (1 Kings 16:21-26).

ONCE → ONE
Ex	30:10	O a year Aaron shall perform the
Rom	6:10	he died, he died to sin, o for all;
Heb	7:27	this he did o for all when he offered
	9:27	it is appointed for mortals to die o,

ONE → FIRST, ONCE
Gen	2:24	and they become o flesh.
Zech	14: 9	the LORD will be o and his name o.
Mk	12:29	the Lord our God, the Lord is o;
Jn	10:30	The Father and I are o."
1 Cor	12:13	For in the o Spirit we were all baptized
Gal	3:28	for all of you are o in Christ Jesus.
Eph	4: 5	o Lord, o faith, o baptism,

ONLY
Gen	22: 2	"Take your son, your o son Isaac,
1 Kings	18:22	"I, even I o, am left a prophet
Jn	1:14	the glory as of a father's o son,
	3:16	that he gave his o Son,
1 Tim	1:17	the o God, be honor and glory
1 Jn	4: 9	God sent his o Son into the world so

OPEN → OPENED, OPENS
Isa	53: 7	so he did not o his mouth.
Rev	5: 2	"Who is worthy to o the scroll

OPENED → OPEN
Gen	3: 7	Then the eyes of both were o,
Dan	7:10	in judgment, and the books were o.
Zech	13: 1	a fountain shall be o for the house
Lk	11: 9	knock, and the door will be o for
Heb	10:20	new and living way that he o for us
Rev	20:12	book was o, the book of life.

OPENS → OPEN
Rev	3: 7	who o and no one will shut,

OPPORTUNITY
Mt	26:16	began to look for an o to betray him.
Gal	5:13	not use your freedom as an o for

OPPRESSED → OPPRESSION
Gen	15:13	shall be o for four hundred years;
Ex	1:12	But the more they were o,
Jdt	9:11	God of the lowly, helper of the o,
Ps	146: 7	who executes justice for the o;
Isa	53: 7	He was o, and he was afflicted,

OPPRESSION → OPPRESSED
Jer	9: 6	O upon o, deceit upon deceit!
Ezek	45: 9	Put away violence and o,

ORACLES
Rom	3: 2	entrusted with the o of God.

ORDAIN → ORDINANCE, ORDINANCES
Ex	29: 9	shall then o Aaron and his sons.
1 Tim	5:22	Do not o anyone hastily,

ORDER
Ps	110: 4	according to the o of Melchizedek."
Heb	5:10	according to the o of Melchizedek.

ORDINANCE → ORDAIN
Ex	12:17	your generations as a perpetual o.
	29: 9	shall be theirs by a perpetual o.

ORDINANCES → ORDAIN
Ps	19: 9	o of the LORD are true and righteous

ORIGIN
Mt	21:26	But if we say, 'Of human o,'
Acts	5:38	or this undertaking is of human o,

ORNAMENTS
Ex	33: 6	stripped themselves of their o,
1 Pet	3: 3	by wearing gold o or fine clothing;

ORPHAN → ORPHANED, ORPHANS
Ex	22:22	You shall not abuse any widow or o.
Hos	14: 3	In you the o finds mercy."

ORPHANED → ORPHAN
Jn	14:18	will not leave you o; I am coming

ORPHANS → ORPHAN
Sir	4:10	Be a father to o, and be like a
Jas	1:27	to care for o and widows in their

OTHER → OTHERS
Ex	20: 3	you shall have no o gods before me.
Judg	2:19	following o gods,
2 Kings	17: 7	They had worshiped o gods
Isa	45: 5	I am the LORD, and there is no o;
Mt	6:24	to the one and despise the o.

OTHERS → OTHER
Lk	6:31	Do to o as you would have them do
Phil	2: 3	but in humility regard o as better

OTHNIEL
Nephew of Caleb (Josh 15:15-19; Judg 1:12-15). Judge who freed Israel from Aram (Judg 3:7-11).

OUTSIDE
Lk	11:39	Pharisees clean the o of the cup and
Heb	13:12	Jesus also suffered o the city gate in
Rev	22:15	O are the dogs and sorcerers and

OUTSTRETCHED → STRETCH
Ex	6: 6	I will redeem you with an o arm
Ps	136:12	an o arm, for his steadfast love
Jer	27: 5	by my great power and my o arm

OUTWARD
1 Sam	16: 7	they look on the o appearance,
2 Cor	5:12	those who boast in o appearance
2 Tim	3: 5	the o form of godliness but denying

OVERCOME
Jn	1: 5	and the darkness did not o it.
Rom	12:21	Do not be o by evil, but o evil with
1 Jn	2:14	and you have o the evil one.

OVERSEERS
Acts	20:28	made you o, to shepherd the church of God

OVERSHADOW* → OVERSHADOWED
Lk	1:35	power of the Most High will o you;

OVERSHADOWED → OVERSHADOW
Lk	9:34	a cloud came and o them;

OWE → OWES
Mt	18:28	he said, 'Pay what you o.'
Rom	13: 8	O no one anything, except to love

OWN
Isa	53: 6	we have all turned to our o way,
Jer	31:30	But all shall die for their o sins;
Jn	1:11	He came to what was his o, and his o people did not accept him.
	10:18	but I lay it down of my o accord.
1 Cor	6:19	and that you are not your o?

OX → OXEN
Deut	25: 4	not muzzle an o while it is treading
Isa	65:25	the lion shall eat straw like the o;
Ezek	1:10	the face of an o on the left side,
1 Tim	5:18	not muzzle an o while it is treading
Rev	4: 7	the second living creature like an o,

P

PAGANS
1 Cor	5: 1	that is not found even among p;
	12: 2	You know that when you were p,

PAIN → PAINS
Gen	3:16	in p you shall bring forth children,
1 Pet	2:19	endure p while suffering unjustly.
Rev	21: 4	and crying and p will be no more,

PAINS → PAIN
Rom	8:22	creation has been groaning in labor p

1 Thess 5: 3 as labor **p** come upon a pregnant

PALM → PALMS
Jn   12:13 So they took branches of **p** trees
Rev   7: 9 robed in white, with **p** branches in

PALMS → PALM
Isa   49:16 I have inscribed you on the **p** of my

PANGS
Gen   3:16 increase your **p** in childbearing;
Mk   13: 8 but the beginning of the birth **p.**
Rev   12: 2 and was crying out in birth **p,**

PARABLE → PARABLES
Ps   78: 2 I will open my mouth in a **p;**
Mt   13:18 "Hear then the **p** of the sower.

PARABLES → PARABLE; See also JESUS: PARABLES
Sir   39: 2 penetrates the subtleties of **p;**
Mt   13:35 I will open my mouth to speak in **p;**

PARADISE
Lk   23:43 today you will be with me in **P."**
2 Cor   12: 4 was caught up into **P** and heard
Rev   2: 7 tree of life that is in the **p** of God.

PARALYTIC → PARALYZED
Mt   9: 2 saw their faith, he said to the **p,**

PARALYZED → PARALYTIC
Jn   5: 3 many invalids—blind, lame, and **p.**
Acts   8: 7 who were **p** or lame were cured.

PARCHMENTS*
2 Tim   4:13 also the books, and above all the **p.**

PARDON
Ex   34: 9 **p** our iniquity and our sin,
Isa   55: 7 our God, for he will abundantly **p.**

PARENT → PARENTS
Deut   8: 5 that as a **p** disciplines a child
Ezek   18:20 nor a **p** suffer for the iniquity of a

PARENTS → PARENT
Sir   48:10 turn the hearts of **p** to their children,
Mal   4: 6 turn the hearts of **p** to their children
Lk   1:17 turn the hearts of **p** to their children,
Eph   6: 1 Children, obey your **p** in the Lord,

PART → APART
1 Cor   13: 9 For we know only in **p,** and we prophesy only
                    in **p;**

PARTAKE
1 Cor   10:17 for we all **p** of the one bread.

PARTIALITY
Deut   16:19 distort justice; you must not show **p;**
Prov   24:23 **P** in judging is not good.
Sir   35:15 and with him there is no **p.**
Rom   2:11 For God shows no **p.**
Jas   3:17 without a trace of **p** or hypocrisy.

PARTICIPANTS → PARTICIPATE
2 Pet   1: 4 may become **p** of the divine nature.

PARTICIPATE* → PARTICIPANTS
1 Tim   5:22 and do not **p** in the sins of others;
2 Jn   1:11 for to welcome is to **p** in the evil

PARTNER → PARTNERS, PARTNERSHIP
Prov   2:17 who forsakes the **p** of her youth
1 Cor   7:15 But if the unbelieving **p** separates,

PARTNERS → PARTNER
1 Cor   10:20 not want you to be **p** with demons.
Heb   3: 1 holy **p** in a heavenly calling,

PARTNERSHIP* → PARTNER
2 Cor   6:14 **p** is there between righteousness

PASHHUR
Priest; opponent of Jeremiah (Jer 20:1-6).

PASS → PASSED, PASSING
Ex   12:13 when I see the blood, I will **p** over
        33:19 make all my goodness **p** before you,
Am   5:17 I will **p** through the midst of you,
Mt   24:35 Heaven and earth will **p** away, but my words
                    will not **p**
2 Pet   3:10 then the heavens will **p** away

PASSED → PASS
Gen   15:17 torch **p** between these pieces.
Ex   12:27 he **p** over the houses of the Israelites
        33:22 with my hand until I have **p** by;
2 Cor   5:17 everything old has **p** away;
1 Jn   3:14 that we have **p** from death to life
Rev   21: 4 for the first things have **p** away."

PASSING → PASS
1 Cor   7:31 present form of this world is **p** away
1 Jn   2:17 the world and its desire are **p** away,

PASSIONS
Gal   5:24 have crucified the flesh with its **p**
2 Tim   2:22 Shun youthful **p** and pursue

PASSOVER
Ex   12:11 It is the **p** of the LORD.
Deut   16: 1 the month of Abib by keeping the **p**
Mk   14:12 when the **P** lamb is sacrificed,

PASTORS*
Eph   4:11 evangelists, some **p** and teachers,

PASTURE → PASTURES
Ps   100: 3 his people, and the sheep of his **p.**
Jer   50: 7 the LORD, the true **p,** the LORD,

PASTURES → PASTURE
Ps   23: 2 He makes me lie down in green **p;**

PATH → PATHS
Ps   16:11 You show me the **p** of life.
       119:105 lamp to my feet and a light to my **p.**
Mt   13: 4 he sowed, some seeds fell on the **p,**

PATHS → PATH
Ps   23: 3 in right **p** for his name's sake.
Prov   3: 6 and he will make straight your **p.**
Mt   3: 3 of the Lord, make his **p** straight.'"
Heb   12:13 and make straight **p** for your feet,

PATIENCE → PATIENT
Mic   2: 7 Is the LORD's **p** exhausted?
Rom   2: 4 his kindness and forbearance and **p?**
Gal   5:22 fruit of the Spirit is love, joy, peace, **p,**
2 Pet   3:15 regard the **p** of our Lord as salvation

PATIENT → PATIENCE
Lk   8:15 and bear fruit with **p** endurance.
Rom   12:12 Rejoice in hope, be **p** in suffering,
1 Cor   13: 4 Love is **p;** love is kind;
2 Pet   3: 9 as some think of slowness, but is **p**

PATTERN
Ex   25:40 make them according to the **p** for
Heb   8: 5 make everything according to the **p**

PAUL → =SAUL
Also called Saul (Acts 13:9). Pharisee from Tarsus (Acts 9:11; Phil 3:5). Apostle (Gal 1). At stoning of Stephen (Acts 8:1). Persecuted Church (Acts 9:1-2; Gal 1:13). Vision of Jesus on road to Damascus (Acts 9:4-9; 26:12-18). In Arabia (Gal 1:17). Preached in Damascus; escaped death through the wall in a basket (Acts 9:19-25). In Jerusalem; back to Tarsus (Acts 9:26-30). Brought to Antioch by Barnabas (Acts 11:22-26). First missionary journey to Cyprus and Galatia (Acts 13-14). Stoned at Lystra (Acts 14:19-20). At Jerusalem council (Acts 15). Split with Barnabas over Mark (Acts 15:36-41).
Second missionary journey with Silas (Acts 16-20). Called to Macedonia (Acts 16:6-10). Freed from prison in Philippi (Acts 16:16-40). In Thessalonica (Acts 17:1-9). Speech in Athens (Acts 17:16-33). In Corinth (Acts 18). In Ephesus (Acts 19). Return to Jerusalem (Acts 20). Farewell to Ephesian elders (Acts 20:13-38). Arrival in Jerusalem (Acts 21:1-26). Arrested (Acts 21:27-36). Addressed crowds (Acts 22), Sanhedrin (Acts 23:1-11). Sent to Caesarea (Acts 23:12-35). Trial before Felix (Acts 24), Festus (Acts 25:1-12). Before Agrippa (Acts 25:13-26:32). Voyage to Rome; shipwreck (Acts 27). Arrival in Rome (Acts 28).

PAVEMENT
Ex   24:10 his feet there was something like a **p**
Jn   19:13 bench at a place called The Stone **P,**

PAY → REPAY
Ex   22: 4 the thief shall **p** double.
Deut   24:15 You shall **p** them their wages daily
Mt   22:17 lawful to **p** taxes to the emperor, or
Rom   13: 7 **P** to all what is due them—

PEACE → PEACEMAKERS
Lev	26: 6	And I will grant **p** in the land,
Ps	122: 6	Pray for the **p** of Jerusalem:
Isa	26: 3	in **p** because they trust in you.
	57:19	P, **p**, to the far and the near,
	57:21	no **p**, says my God, for the wicked.
Jer	6:14	saying, "P, **p**," when there is no **p**.
Mic	5: 5	and he shall be the one of **p**.
Lk	2:14	on earth **p** among those whom he
Jn	14:27	P I leave with you; my **p** I give
Rom	16:20	God of **p** will shortly crush Satan
1 Cor	14:33	is a God not of disorder but of **p**.
Gal	5:22	the fruit of the Spirit is love, joy, **p**,
Eph	4: 3	unity of the Spirit in the bond of **p**.
Phil	4: 7	the **p** of God, which surpasses all
2 Tim	2:22	righteousness, faith, love, and **p**,

PEACEMAKERS* → PEACE
Mt	5: 9	"Blessed are the **p**, for they will be

PEARL* → PEARLS
Mt	13:46	on finding one **p** of great value,
Rev	21:21	each of the gates is a single **p**,

PEARLS → PEARL
Mt	7: 6	do not throw your **p** before swine,

PEKAH*
King of Israel (2 Kings 15:25-31; 2 Chr 28:6; Isa 7:1).

PEKAHIAH*
Son of Menahem; king of Israel (2 Kings 15:22-26).

PENALTY
Rom	1:27	in their own persons the due **p**
2 Pet	2:13	suffering the **p** for doing wrong.

PENTECOST
Acts	2: 1	When the day of P had come,

PEOPLE → PEOPLES
Ex	5: 1	the God of Israel, 'Let my **p** go,
	33:13	that this nation is your **p**."
Deut	4:20	a **p** of his very own possession,
	32: 9	the LORD's own portion was his **p**,
Ruth	1:16	your **p** shall be my **p**,
2 Sam	5: 2	shall be shepherd of my **p** Israel,
Ps	29:11	the LORD bless his **p** with peace!
	125: 2	so the LORD surrounds his **p**,
Isa	40: 1	Comfort, O comfort my **p**, says
	42: 6	given you as a covenant to the **p**,
	53: 8	for the transgression of my **p**.
Jer	50: 6	My **p** have been lost sheep;
Lam	1: 1	sits the city that once was full of **p**!
Dan	9:24	"Seventy weeks are decreed for your **p**
Zech	13: 9	I will say, "They are my **p**,"
Mt	1:21	he will save his **p** from their sins."
Jn	11:50	the **p** than to have the whole nation
	18:14	to have one person die for the **p**.
Rom	9:25	not my **p** I will call 'my **p**,'
Heb	8:10	their God, and they shall be my **p**.
1 Pet	2: 9	a holy nation, God's own **p**,

PEOPLES → PEOPLE
Gen	17:16	kings of **p** shall come from her."
Deut	7: 7	for you were the fewest of all **p**.
Ps	117: 1	Extol him, all you **p**!
Rev	21: 3	they will be his **p**, and God himself

PERFECT → PERFECTED, PERFECTER, PERFECTION
Lev	22:21	to be acceptable it must be **p**;
2 Sam	22:31	This God—his way is **p**;
Ps	19: 7	The law of the LORD is **p**, reviving
Mt	5:48	Be **p**, therefore, as your heavenly Father is **p**.
Rom	12: 2	what is good and acceptable and **p**.
2 Cor	12: 9	for power is made **p** in weakness."
Heb	5: 9	and having been made **p**,
	7:19	(for the law made nothing **p**);
1 Jn	4:18	in love, but **p** love casts out fear;

PERFECTED → PERFECT
Heb	10:14	For by a single offering he has **p**
1 Jn	4:12	God lives in us, and his love is **p** in

PERFECTER* → PERFECT
Heb	12: 2	Jesus the pioneer and **p** of our faith,

PERFECTION → PERFECT
Heb	6: 1	Therefore let us go on toward **p**,
1 Jn	2: 5	the love of God has reached **p**.

PERISH → PERISHABLE
Lev	26:38	You shall **p** among the nations,
Josh	23:13	until you **p** from this good land that
Esth	4:16	and if I **p**, I **p**."
Ps	1: 6	but the way of the wicked will **p**.
Lk	21:18	But not a hair of your head will **p**.
Jn	3:16	who believes in him may not **p**
2 Pet	3: 9	with you, not wanting any to **p**,

PERISHABLE → PERISH
1 Cor	9:25	they do it to receive a **p** wreath,
	15:42	What is sown is **p**, what is raised is
1 Pet	1:23	not of **p** but of imperishable seed,

PERMANENT → PERMANENTLY
2 Cor	3:11	much more has the **p** come in glory!

PERMANENTLY* → PERMANENT
Heb	7:24	but he holds his priesthood **p**,

PERSECUTE → PERSECUTED, PERSECUTION
Mt	5:44	and pray for those who **p** you,
Acts	9: 4	"Saul, Saul, why do you **p** me?"
Rom	12:14	Bless those who **p** you; bless

PERSECUTED → PERSECUTE
Ps	119:86	I am **p** without cause; help me!
Jn	15:20	they **p** me, they will persecute you;
2 Cor	4: 9	**p**, but not forsaken; struck down,
2 Tim	3:12	godly life in Christ Jesus will be **p**.

PERSECUTION → PERSECUTE
Mt	13:21	or **p** arises on account of the word,
Rom	8:35	Will hardship, or distress, or **p**, or
Heb	10:33	publicly exposed to abuse and **p**,

PERSEVERANCE* → PERSEVERE
Heb	12: 1	let us run with **p** the race that is set

PERSEVERE → PERSEVERANCE
Dan	12:12	Happy are those who **p**
Rom	12:12	be patient in suffering, **p** in prayer.

PERSIA → PERSIANS
Ezra	1: 1	the spirit of King Cyrus of P
Dan	8:20	these are the kings of Media and P.

PERSIANS → PERSIA
Dan	6:15	a law of the Medes and P that

PESTILENCE
Deut	32:24	burning consumption, bitter **p**.
Ps	91: 6	or the **p** that stalks in darkness,

PETER → =CEPHAS, =SIMON
Apostle, brother of Andrew, also called Simon (Mt 10:2; Mk 3:16; Lk 6:14; Acts 1:13), and Cephas (Jn 1:42). Confession of Christ (Mt 16:13-20; Mk 8:27-30; Lk 9:18-27). At transfiguration (Mt 17:1-8; Mk 9:2-8; Lk 9:28-36; 2 Pet 1:16-18). Caught fish with coin (Mt 17:24-27). Denial of Jesus predicted (Mt 26:31-35; Mk 14:27-31; Lk 22:31-34; Jn 13:31-38). Denied Jesus (Mt 26:69-75; Mk 14:66-72; Lk 22:54-62; Jn 18:15-27). Commissioned by Jesus to shepherd his flock (Jn 21:15-23).
Speech at Pentecost (Acts 2). Healed beggar (Acts 3:1-10). Speech at temple (Acts 3:11-26), before Sanhedrin (Acts 4:1-22). In Samaria (Acts 8:14-25). Sent by vision to Cornelius (Acts 10). Announced salvation of Gentiles in Jerusalem (Acts 11; 15). Freed from prison (Acts 12). Inconsistency at Antioch (Gal 2:11-21). At Jerusalem Council (Acts 15).

PHARAOH → PHARAOH'S
Gen	41:14	Then P sent for Joseph,
Ex	3:11	"Who am I that I should go to P,
	14:17	I will gain glory for myself over P
Rom	9:17	For the scripture says to P,

PHARAOH'S → PHARAOH
Ex	7: 3	But I will harden P heart,
Heb	11:24	refused to be called a son of P

PHARISEE → PHARISEES
Lk	11:37	a P invited him to dine with him;
Jn	3: 1	a P named Nicodemus,
Acts	5:34	a P in the council named Gamaliel,
Phil	3: 5	as to the law, a P;

PHARISEES → PHARISEE
Mt 5:20 that of the scribes and P,
16: 6 beware of the yeast of the P and
23:13 "But woe to you, scribes and P,

PHILEMON*
Philem 1: 1 To P our dear friend and co-worker,

PHILIP
1. Apostle (Mt 10:3; Mk 3:18; Lk 6:14; Jn 1:43-48; 14:8; Acts 1:13).
2. Deacon (Acts 6:1-7); evangelist in Samaria (Acts 8:4-25), to Ethiopian (Acts 8:26-40).

PHILISTINE → PHILISTINES
1 Sam 17:37 save me from the hand of this P."

PHILISTINES → PHILISTINE
Gen 26: 1 Gerar, to King Abimelech of the P.
1 Sam 5: 1 the P captured the ark of God,
17: 1 the P gathered their armies for battle
2 Sam 8: 1 David attacked the P and subdued
Am 1: 8 the remnant of the P shall perish,

PHILOSOPHERS* → PHILOSOPHY
Acts 17:18 Epicurean and Stoic p debated with

PHILOSOPHY → PHILOSOPHERS
Col 2: 8 no one takes you captive through p

PHINEHAS
1. Grandson of Aaron (Ex 6:25; Josh 22:30-32). Zeal for the LORD (Num 25:7-13; Ps 106:30).
2. A wicked priest (1 Sam 1:3; 2:12-17; 4:1-19).

PHOEBE*
Rom 16: 1 I commend to you our sister P,

PHYSICAL
1 Cor 15:44 It is sown a p body, it is raised a
1 Tim 4: 8 while p training is of some value,

PHYSICIAN → PHYSICIANS
Mt 9:12 who are well have no need of a p,
Col 4:14 Luke, the beloved p, and Demas

PHYSICIANS → PHYSICIAN
Job 13: 4 all of you are worthless p.
Mk 5:26 had endured much under many p,

PIECES
Gen 15:17 torch passed between these p.
Mt 14:20 what was left over of the broken p,
15:37 they took up the broken p left over,
Lk 20:18 on that stone will be broken to p;

PIERCED
Zech 12:10 look on the one whom they have p,
Jn 19:37 look on the one whom they have p."
Rev 1: 7 even those who p him;

PIG
Deut 14: 8 the p, because it divides the hoof

PILATE
Governor of Judea. Questioned Jesus (Mt 27:1-26; Mk 15:15; Lk 22:66-23:25; Jn 18:28-19:16); sent him to Herod (Lk 23:6-12); consented to his crucifixion when crowds chose Barabbas (Mt 27:15-26; Mk 15:6-15; Lk 23:13-25; Jn 19:1-10).

PILLAR → PILLARS
Gen 19:26 back, and she became a p of salt.
Ex 13:21 and in a p of fire by night,

PILLARS → PILLAR
Judg 16:29 Samson grasped the two middle p
1 Kings 7:15 He cast two p of bronze.
Prov 9: 1 she has hewn her seven p.

PIONEER*
Heb 2:10 make the p of their salvation perfect
12: 2 Jesus the p and perfecter of our faith

PIT
Ps 103: 4 who redeems your life from the P,
Sir 21:10 but at its end is the p of Hades.
Rev 20: 3 into the p, and locked and sealed it

PITY
Deut 7:16 showing them no p;
Hos 1: 6 for I will no longer have p
2:23 And I will have p on Lo-ruhamah,

PLACE → PLACES
Gen 28:16 "Surely the LORD is in this p—
Ex 26:33 shall separate for you the holy p
Ps 24: 3 And who shall stand in his holy p?
32: 7 You are a hiding p for me;
Jn 14: 3 And if I go and prepare a p for you,

PLACES → PLACE
Lev 26:30 I will destroy your high p
Ps 78:58 him to anger with their high p;

PLAGUE → PLAGUES
Ex 32:35 the LORD sent a p on the people,
Num 25: 8 So the p was stopped among the
Zech 14:12 the p with which the LORD will
Rev 11: 6 strike the earth with every kind of p,

PLAGUES → PLAGUE
Hos 13:14 O Death, where are your p?
Rev 15: 1 seven angels with seven p, which
22:18 God will add to that person the p

PLAIN
Gen 13:12 among the cities of the P and
Isa 40: 4 and the rough places a p.

PLANNED
Ex 32:14 his mind about the disaster that he p
Isa 46:11 I have p, and I will do it.

PLANT → PLANTED
Gen 1:29 I have given you every p yielding
Eccl 3: 2 time to p, and a time to pluck up

PLANTED → PLANT
Gen 2: 8 the LORD God p a garden in Eden,
Ps 1: 3 like trees p by streams of water,
1 Cor 3: 6 I p, Apollos watered, but God gave

PLEA
1 Kings 8:28 your servant's prayer and his p,
Lam 3:56 heard my p, "Do not close your ear

PLEASE → PLEASED, PLEASES, PLEASING, PLEASURE
Ps 69:31 will p the LORD more than an ox
Sir 2:16 Those who fear the Lord seek to p
Rom 8: 8 who are in the flesh cannot p God.
15: 3 For Christ did not p himself;
1 Cor 10:33 as I try to p everyone in everything
1 Thess 4: 1 how you ought to live and to p God
Heb 11: 6 without faith it is impossible to p God,

PLEASED → PLEASE
Ps 40:13 Be p, O LORD, to deliver me;
Mic 6: 7 Will the LORD be p with thousands
Mt 3:17 Beloved, with whom I am well p."
Col 1:19 the fullness of God was p to dwell,
2 Pet 1:17 Beloved, with whom I am well p."

PLEASES → PLEASE
Ps 115: 3 the heavens; he does whatever he p.
1 Jn 3:22 commandments and do what p him.

PLEASING → PLEASE
Ps 104:34 May my meditation be p to him,
Eph 5:10 to find out what is p to the Lord.
Phil 4:18 a sacrifice acceptable and p to God.

PLEASURE → PLEASE
Prov 21:17 Whoever loves p will suffer want;
Ezek 18:32 I have no p in the death of anyone,
Eph 1: 5 according to the good p of his will,
2 Tim 3: 4 lovers of p rather than lovers of God

PLENTIFUL → PLENTY
Lk 10: 2 He said to them, "The harvest is p,

PLENTY → PLENTIFUL
Phil 4:12 and I know what it is to have p.

PLOT → PLOTTED
Ps 2: 1 and the peoples p in vain?
Nah 1: 9 Why do you p against the LORD?

PLOTTED → PLOT
Esth 9:24 p against the Jews to destroy them,

PLOWSHARES
Isa 2: 4 they shall beat their swords into p,
Joel 3:10 Beat your p into swords, and your

PLUNDER
Ex   3:22   and so you shall **p** the Egyptians."
Esth   9:10   but they did not touch the **p.**
Ezek   39:10   and **p** those who plundered them,

POISON
Ps   69:21   They gave me **p** for food,
Jas   3: 8   a restless evil, full of deadly **p.**

POLE → POLES
Num   21: 8   poisonous serpent, and set it on a **p;**
Deut   16:21   not plant any tree as a sacred **p**

POLES → POLE
2 Kings 17:10   for themselves pillars and sacred **p**

POLLUTED → POLLUTES
Acts   15:20   from things **p** by idols and from
Rev   21: 8   the cowardly, the faithless, the **p,**

POLLUTES* → POLLUTED
Num   35:33   blood **p** the land, and no expiation

POOR → POVERTY
Ex   23: 6   not pervert the justice due to your **p**
1 Sam   2: 8   He raises up the **p** from the dust;
Ps   113: 7   He raises the **p** from the dust,
Prov   19:22   and it is better to be **p** than a liar.
Mt   5: 3   "Blessed are the **p** in spirit,
Mk   10:21   own, and give the money to the **p,**
       12:42   **p** widow came and put in two small
Jn   12: 8   You always have the **p** with you,
2 Cor   6:10   as **p,** yet making many rich;
        8: 9   yet for your sakes he became **p,**
Jas   2: 5   Has not God chosen the **p** in the

PORTION → APPORTIONED
Deut   32: 9   the LORD's own **p** was his people,
Josh   18: 7   The Levites have no **p** among you,
Ps   142: 5   my **p** in the land of the living."
Sir   17:17   Israel is the Lord's own **p.**
Lam   3:24   "The LORD is my **p,**" says my soul,

POSSESS → POSSESSED, POSSESSION, POSSESSIONS
Deut   28:21   the land that you are entering to **p.**
Ezra   9:11   that you are entering to **p** is a land
Isa   60:21   they shall **p** the land forever.

POSSESSED → POSSESS
Mt   8:16   many who were **p** with demons;
Heb   10:34   you yourselves **p** something better

POSSESSION → POSSESS
Ex   19: 5   treasured **p** out of all the peoples.
Josh   1:11   to go in to take **p** of the land that
Ps   2: 8   and the ends of the earth your **p.**

POSSESSIONS → POSSESS
Lk   12:15   not consist in the abundance of **p.**"
1 Cor 13: 3   If I give away all my **p,**

POSSIBLE
Mt   19:26   but for God all things are **p.**"
       26:39   if it is **p,** let this cup pass from me;

POTIPHAR*
     Egyptian who bought Joseph (Gen 37:36; 39:1-6), sent him
     to prison (Gen 39:7-30).

POTTER → POTTER'S
Sir   33:13   Like clay in the hand of the **p,**
Isa   64: 8   we are the clay, and you are our **p;**
Rom   9:21   Has the **p** no right over the clay,

POTTER'S → POTTER
Jer   18: 2   go down to the **p** house,
Mt   27: 7   to buy the **p** field as a place to bury

POUR → POURED
Deut   12:16   **p** it out on the ground like water.
Isa   44: 3   I will **p** my spirit upon your
Ezek   39:29   I **p** out my spirit upon the house of
Joel   2:28   I will **p** out my spirit on all flesh;
Acts   2:17   I will **p** out my Spirit upon all flesh,
Rev   16: 1   **p** out on the earth the seven bowls

POURED → POUR
Mt   26:28   is **p** out for many for the forgiveness
Acts   2:33   he has **p** out this that you both see
Rom   5: 5   love has been **p** into our hearts

Titus   3: 6   This Spirit he **p** out on us richly

POVERTY → POOR
Prov   30: 8   give me neither **p** nor riches;
Sir   11:14   **p** and wealth, come from the Lord.
Mk   12:44   out of her **p** has put in everything
2 Cor   8: 9   by his **p** you might become rich.

POWER → POWERFUL, POWERS
Ex   9:16   show you my **p,** and to make
       15: 6   right hand, O LORD, glorious in **p—**
1 Chr 29:11   O LORD, are the greatness, the **p,**
Jdt   9:14   the God of all **p** and might,
Ps   68:34   Ascribe **p** to God, whose majesty is
Prov   18:21   and life are in the **p** of the tongue,
Sir   39:18   and none can limit his saving **p.**
Isa   40:29   He gives **p** to the faint,
Zech   4: 6   by might, nor by **p,** but by my spirit,
Mt   22:29   the scriptures nor the **p** of God.
Mk   13:26   coming in clouds' with great **p** and
Rom   1:20   creation of the world his eternal **p**
1 Cor   1:17   might not be emptied of its **p.**
       15:24   and every authority and **p.**
Eph   1:19   the immeasurable greatness of his **p**
Phil   3:10   Christ and the **p** of his resurrection
2 Tim   3: 5   form of godliness but denying its **p.**
2 Pet   1: 3   divine **p** has given us everything
Rev   1: 9   and glory and **p** to our God,
       20: 6   these the second death has no **p,**

POWERFUL → POWER
Mk   1: 7   one who is more **p** than I is coming
1 Cor   1:26   not many were **p,**
Heb   1: 3   he sustains all things by his **p** word.

POWERS → POWER
Rom   8:38   present, nor things to come, nor **p,**
Eph   6:12   against the cosmic **p** of this present

PRACTICE → PRACTICES
Sir   50:29   For if they put them into **p,**
Mt   23: 3   for they do not **p** what they teach.

PRACTICES → PRACTICE
Ex   23:24   or worship them, or follow their **p,**
Col   3: 9   stripped off the old self with its **p**

PRAISE → PRAISED, PRAISES
Ex   15: 2   this is my God, and I will **p** him,
Deut   10:21   He is your **p;** he is your God,
Tob   12: 6   Bless and sing **p** to his name.
Ps   56: 4   whose word I **p,** in God I trust;
      150: 6   that breathes **p** the LORD!
Prov   27: 2   Let another **p** you, and not your own
       31:31   let her works **p** her in the city gates.
Sir   24: 1   THE P OF WISDOM Wisdom praises
Mt   21:16   nursing babies you have prepared **p**
1 Cor 14:15   but I will sing **p** with the mind also.
Rev   19: 5   "**P** our God, all you his servants,

PRAISED → PRAISE
Ps   48: 1   is the LORD and greatly to be **p**
Lk   23:47   what had taken place, he **p** God and

PRAISES → PRAISE
Ps   47: 6   Sing **p** to God, sing **p;**

PRAY → PRAYED, PRAYER, PRAYERS, PRAYING, PRAYS
1 Sam 12:23   against the LORD by ceasing to **p**
2 Chr   7:14   humble themselves, **p,** seek my face
Ps   5: 2   King and my God, for to you I **p.**
      122: 6   **P** for the peace of Jerusalem:
Sir   37:15   But above all **p** to the Most High
Jer   7:16   As for you, do not **p** for this people,
Mt   5:44   and **p** for those who persecute you,
        6: 5   you **p,** do not be like the hypocrites;
Lk   11: 1   teach us to **p,** as John taught his
Rom   8:26   do not know how to **p** as we ought,
1 Cor 14:15   but I will **p** with the mind also;
1 Thess 5:17   **p** without ceasing,
Jas   5:16   and **p** for one another, so that you

PRAYED → PRAY
Mk   1:35   to a deserted place, and there he **p.**
       14:35   threw himself on the ground and **p**

PRAYER → PRAY
Ps   6: 9   the LORD accepts my **p.**

Prov 15:29 but he hears the **p** of the righteous.
Isa 56: 7 house shall be called a house of **p**
Mt 21:13 house shall be called a house of **p**';
Mk 11:24 I tell you, whatever you ask for in **p**,
Rom 12:12 patient in suffering, persevere in **p**.
Jas 5:16 The **p** of the righteous is powerful

PRAYERS → PRAY
Mk 12:40 the sake of appearance say long **p**.
Heb 5: 7 Jesus offered up **p** and supplications
Rev 5: 8 which are the **p** of the saints.

PRAYING → PRAY
2 Macc 12:42 they turned to supplication, **p** that the sin
15:12 was **p** with outstretched hands for the whole body

PRAYS → PRAY
2 Macc 15:14 and **p** much for the people and the holy city

PREACH → PREACHING
Titus 1: 9 able both to **p** with sound doctrine

PREACHING → PREACH
1 Tim 5:17 those who labor in **p** and teaching;

PRECEPT → PRECEPTS
Isa 28:10 For it is **p** upon **p**, **p** upon **p**,

PRECEPTS → PRECEPT
Ps 19: 8 the **p** of the LORD are right,
119:15 I will meditate on your **p**,
Mt 15: 9 teaching human **p** as doctrines.'"

PRECIOUS
Ps 72:14 and **p** is their blood in his sight.
Prov 3:15 She is more **p** than jewels,
Isa 28:16 a tested stone, a **p** cornerstone,
1 Pet 1:19 but with the **p** blood of Christ,
2: 6 a cornerstone chosen and **p**;
2 Pet 1: 1 received a faith as **p** as ours

PREDESTINED
Rom 8:30 those whom he **p** he also called;

PREDICTION* → PREDICTIONS
Isa 44:26 and fulfills the **p** of his messengers;

PREDICTIONS* → PREDICT
Jude 1:17 the **p** of the apostles of our Lord

PREPARE → PREPARED
Ps 23: 5 You **p** a table before me in the
Mal 3: 1 sending my messenger to **p** the way
Mt 3: 3 'P the way of the Lord, make his
Jn 14: 2 I have told you that I go to **p** a place

PREPARED → PREPARE
Lk 1:17 make ready a people **p** for the Lord.
1 Cor 2: 9 God has **p** for those who love him"

PRESENCE → PRESENT
Ex 25:30 the bread of the P on the table
33:14 He said, "My **p** will go with you,
Ps 51:11 Do not cast me away from your **p**,
139: 7 Or where can I flee from your **p**?
Jn 17: 5 with the glory that I had in your **p**
Heb 9:24 now to appear in the **p** of God

PRESENT → PRESENCE
Rom 6:13 but **p** yourselves to God as
1 Cor 3:22 or death or the **p** or the future—
Eph 5:27 **p** the church to himself in splendor,
2 Tim 2:15 **p** yourself to God as one approved

PRESS → PRESSED
Phil 3:14 I **p** on toward the goal for the prize

PRESSED → PRESS
Lk 6:38 A good measure, **p** down, shaken
Phil 1:23 I am hard **p** between the two:

PREVAIL → PREVAILED
1 Sam 2: 9 for not by might does one **p**.

PREVAILED → PREVAIL
Gen 32:28 God with humans, and have **p**."
Hos 12: 4 He strove with the angel and **p**,

PRICE
Mt 27: 9 the one on whom a **p** had been set,
1 Cor 6:20 For you were bought with a **p**;

PRIDE → PROUD
Ps 20: 7 our **p** is in the name of the LORD
Prov 16:18 P goes before destruction,
Sir 10:13 For the beginning of **p** is sin,
Mk 7:22 licentiousness, envy, slander, **p**,
1 Jn 2:16 the desire of the eyes, the **p** in riches

PRIEST → PRIESTHOOD, PRIESTS
Gen 14:18 he was **p** of God Most High.
Ex 2:16 **p** of Midian had seven daughters.
Neh 8: 9 and Ezra the **p** and scribe,
Ps 110: 4 "You are a **p** forever according to
Mk 14:63 Then the high **p** tore his clothes and
Heb 3: 1 apostle and high **p** of our confession
5:10 designated by God a high **p** according to
7: 3 the Son of God, he remains a **p**
10:21 since we have a great **p** over the

PRIESTHOOD → PRIEST
Ex 29: 9 the **p** shall be theirs by a perpetual
Heb 7:24 but he holds his **p** permanently,
1 Pet 2: 5 a holy **p**, to offer spiritual sacrifices

PRIESTS → PRIEST
Ex 28: 1 the Israelites, to serve me as **p**—
Deut 31: 9 this law, and gave it to the **p**,
Mic 3:11 its **p** teach for a price, its prophets
Mk 15: 3 the chief **p** accused him of many
Heb 7:27 Unlike the other high **p**, he has no
Rev 20: 6 they will be **p** of God and of Christ,

PRINCE → PRINCES
Isa 9: 6 Everlasting Father, P of Peace.
Ezek 37:25 David shall be their **p** forever.
Dan 10:21 princes except Michael, your **p**.

PRINCES → PRINCE
1 Sam 2: 8 to make them sit with **p** and inherit
Dan 8:25 even rise up against the Prince of **p**.

PRISCILLA*
Wife of Aquila, also called Prisca; co-worker with Paul (Acts 18; Rom 16:3; 1 Cor 16:19; 2 Tim 4:19); instructor of Apollos (Acts 18:24-28).

PRISON → PRISONER, PRISONERS
Gen 39:20 he remained there in **p**.
Mt 14:10 and had John beheaded in the **p**.
Acts 12: 5 While Peter was kept in **p**,
16:26 foundations of the **p** were shaken;

PRISONER → PRISON
Mk 15: 6 at the festival he used to release a **p**
Eph 3: 1 that I Paul am a **p** for Christ Jesus

PRISONERS → PRISON
Ps 146: 7 The LORD sets the **p** free;
Isa 61: 1 to the captives, and release to the **p**;

PRIZE
1 Cor 9:24 but only one receives the **p**?
Phil 3:14 the **p** of the heavenly call of God in

PROCLAIM → PROCLAIMED
Ex 33:19 **p** before you the name, 'The LORD';
Ps 97: 6 The heavens **p** his righteousness;
Mt 10:27 whispered, **p** from the housetops.
Mk 16:15 "Go into all the world and **p** the good news
Lk 4:19 to **p** the year of the Lord's favor."
Rom 10: 8 the word of faith that we **p**);

PROCLAIMED → PROCLAIM
Mk 13:10 the good news must first be **p** to all
Col 1:23 which has been **p** to every creature

PRODUCE → PRODUCES
Num 18:12 choice **p** that they give to the LORD,
Josh 5:11 they ate the **p** of the land,
Prov 3: 9 with the first fruits of all your **p**;

PRODUCES → PRODUCE
2 Cor 7:10 For godly grief **p** a repentance that
Jas 1: 3 testing of your faith **p** endurance;

PROFANE
Lev 22:32 You shall not **p** my holy name,
1 Macc 1:45 to **p** sabbaths and festivals,

PROFIT
Sir 29:11 and it will **p** you more than gold.

1574

Mt 16:26 For what will it **p** them if they gain

PROMISE → PROMISED, PROMISES
Ps 105:42 For he remembered his holy **p**,
Acts 2:39 the **p** is for you, for your children,
Eph 2:12 and strangers to the covenants of **p**,
1 Tim 4: 8 holding **p** for both the present life
2 Pet 3: 9 The Lord is not slow about his **p**,

PROMISED → PROMISE
Deut 1:11 and bless you, as he has **p** you!
2 Sam 7:28 **p** this good thing to your servant,
Lk 24:49 sending upon you what my Father **p**
Acts 13:23 to Israel a Savior, Jesus, as he **p**;
Eph 1:13 with the seal of the **p** Holy Spirit;
Heb 10:23 for he who has **p** is faithful.

PROMISES → PROMISE
Josh 21:45 the good **p** that the LORD had made
Ps 12: 6 **p** of the LORD are **p** that are pure,
2 Cor 1:20 every one of God's **p** is a "Yes."
Heb 8: 6 has been enacted through better **p**.

PROOFS* → PROVE
Isa 41:21 bring your **p**, says the King of Jacob
Acts 1: 3 to them by many convincing **p**,

PROPHECIES → PROPHESY
1 Cor 13: 8 as for **p**, they will come to an end;

PROPHECY → PROPHESY
Acts 21: 9 daughters who had the gift of **p**.
1 Cor 12:10 to another **p**, to another
2 Pet 1:20 that no **p** of scripture is a matter
Rev 22:18 who hears the words of the **p**

PROPHESY → PROPHECIES, PROPHECY, PROPHET, PROPHETS
Joel 2:28 sons and your daughters shall **p**,
Mt 7:22 Lord, did we not **p** in your name,
1 Cor 13: 9 only in part, and we **p** only in part;
Rev 11: 3 my two witnesses authority to **p**

PROPHET → PROPHESY
Ex 7: 1 your brother Aaron shall be your **p**.
Deut 18:18 a **p** like you from among their own
1 Macc 4:46 until a **p** should come to tell what
Mal 4: 5 the **p** Elijah before the great and
Lk 4:24 no **p** is accepted in the prophet's
20: 6 are convinced that John was a **p**."
Rev 16:13 and from the mouth of the false **p**,
20:10 where the beast and the false **p** were

PROPHETS → PROPHESY
Num 11:29 that all the LORD's people were **p**,
1 Kings 18:40 said to them, "Seize the **p** of Baal;
1 Macc 9:27 that **p** ceased to appear among them.
Ps 105:15 anointed ones; do my **p** no harm."
Mt 5:17 come to abolish the law or the **p**;
22:40 hang all the law and the **p**."
Lk 24:44 **p**, and the psalms must be fulfilled."
1 Cor 12:28 the church first apostles, second **p**,
Eph 2:20 the foundation of the apostles and **p**,
4:11 some **p**, some evangelists,
Rev 11:10 these two **p** had been a torment to
18:20 you saints and apostles and **p**!

PROSPER → PROSPERING, PROSPERITY, PROSPEROUS
Gen 39: 3 LORD caused all that he did to **p**
Ps 1: 3 In all that they do, they **p**.
Isa 53:10 the will of the LORD shall **p**.

PROSPERING → PROSPER
Deut 30: 9 will again take delight in **p** you,

PROSPERITY → PROSPER
Deut 30:15 have set before you today life and **p**,
Ps 73: 3 I saw the **p** of the wicked.
Isa 48:18 your **p** would have been like a river,

PROSPEROUS → PROSPER
Josh 1: 8 For then you shall make your way **p**

PROSTITUTE → PROSTITUTES
Ex 34:15 they **p** themselves to their gods
Josh 2: 1 a **p** whose name was Rahab,
1 Cor 6:15 and make them members of a **p**?
Heb 11:31 By faith Rahab the **p** did not perish

PROSTITUTES → PROSTITUTE
Sir 9: 6 Do not give yourself to **p**,
Mt 21:31 the **p** are going into the kingdom of
1 Cor 6: 9 idolaters, adulterers, male **p**,

PROTECT → PROTECTS
Ps 91:14 I will **p** those who know my name.
Jn 17:11 **p** them in your name that you have

PROTECTS → PROTECT
Jdt 9:14 no other who **p** the people of Israel
Ps 116: 6 The LORD **p** the simple;

PROUD → PRIDE
Ps 94: 2 give to the **p** what they deserve!
Prov 21: 4 Haughty eyes and a **p** heart—
Sir 10: 9 How can dust and ashes be **p**?
Jas 4: 6 God opposes the **p**, but gives grace

PROVE → PROOFS, PROVED
Heb 6:18 impossible that God would **p** false,

PROVED → PROVE
Rom 3: 4 let God be **p** true,

PROVERBS
1 Kings 4:32 He composed three thousand **p**,
Prov 1: 1 The **p** of Solomon son of David,
Eccl 12: 9 and studying and arranging many **p**.
Sir 39: 3 seeks out the hidden meanings of **p**

PROVIDE → PROVIDES
Gen 22: 8 "God himself will **p** the lamb for
1 Cor 10:13 testing he will also **p** the way out

PROVIDES → PROVIDE
Ps 111: 5 He **p** food for those who fear him;
1 Tim 6:17 who richly **p** us with everything

PROVOKE → PROVOKED
Deut 32:21 **p** them with a foolish nation.
Jer 25: 6 not **p** me to anger with the work of
Heb 10:24 how to **p** one another to love

PROVOKED → PROVOKE
Ps 78:41 and **p** the Holy One of Israel.

PROWLS*
1 Pet 5: 8 your adversary the devil **p** around,

PRUNES
Jn 15: 2 he **p** to make it bear more fruit.

PSALM → PSALMS
Jdt 16: 1 Raise to him a new **p**;
Ps 47: 7 sing praises with a **p**.

PSALMS → PSALM
Lk 24:44 and the **p** must be fulfilled."
Eph 5:19 you sing **p** and hymns and spiritual

PUBLIC
Mt 1:19 to expose her to **p** disgrace,
Col 2:15 and made a **p** example of them,
1 Tim 4:13 to the **p** reading of scripture,

PUFFED → PUFFS
Col 2:18 **p** up without cause by a human way
1 Tim 3: 6 or he may be **p** up with conceit

PUFFS* → PUFFED
1 Cor 8: 1 Knowledge **p** up, but love builds up.

PUNISH → PUNISHING, PUNISHMENT
Ex 32:34 I will **p** them for their sin."
2 Sam 7:14 I will **p** him with a rod such as
Jer 21:14 I will **p** you according to the fruit of
1 Pet 2:14 by him to **p** those who do wrong

PUNISHING → PUNISH
Deut 5: 9 **p** children for the iniquity of parents
Joel 2:13 in steadfast love, and relents from **p**.

PUNISHMENT → PUNISH
Gen 4:13 "My **p** is greater than I can bear!
Isa 53: 5 was the **p** that made us whole,
Mt 25:46 these will go away into eternal **p**,
1 Jn 4:18 for fear has to do with **p**,

PURE → PURIFICATION, PURIFIED, PURIFY, PURITY
2 Sam 22:27 with the **p** you show yourself **p**,
Ps 19: 9 the fear of the LORD is **p**, enduring

Ps	119: 9	can young people keep their way **p**?
Hab	1:13	Your eyes are too **p** to behold evil,
Mt	5: 8	"Blessed are the **p** in heart, for they
Phil	4: 8	whatever is **p**, whatever is pleasing,
Titus	1:15	To the **p** all things are **p**,
1 Jn	3: 3	purify themselves, just as he is **p**.

PURIFICATION → PURE

Jn	2: 6	water jars for the Jewish rites of **p**,
Heb	1: 3	When he had made **p** for sins,

PURIFIED → PURE

Dan	12:10	Many shall be **p**, cleansed, and
1 Pet	1:22	**p** your souls by your obedience to

PURIFY → PURE

Titus	2:14	**p** for himself a people of his own
Heb	9:14	**p** our conscience from dead works

PURIM

Esth	9:26	are called P, from the word Pur.

PURITY → PURE

2 Cor	6: 6	by **p**, knowledge, patience, kindness
1 Pet	3: 2	the **p** and reverence of your lives.

PURPLE

Ex	25: 4	**p**, and crimson yarns and fine linen,
Mk	15:17	And they clothed him in a **p** cloak;

PURPOSE

Ps	57: 2	to God who fulfills his **p** for me.
Isa	46:10	saying, "My **p** shall stand,
Rom	8:28	who are called according to his **p**.
Eph	3:11	was in accordance with the eternal **p**
2 Tim	1: 9	works but according to his own **p**

PURSUE → PURSUED, PURSUES

Ps	34:14	and do good; seek peace, and **p** it.
Sir	27: 8	If you **p** justice, you will attain it
Rom	14:19	Let us then **p** what makes for peace
1 Tim	6:11	**p** righteousness, godliness, faith,

PURSUED → PURSUE

Ex	14:23	Egyptians **p**, and went into the sea
Ps	18:37	I **p** my enemies and overtook them;

PURSUES → PURSUE

Prov	21:21	Whoever **p** righteousness
Sir	31: 5	**p** money will be led astray by it.

PUT

Isa	42: 1	I have **p** my spirit upon him;
Ezek	36:27	I will **p** my spirit within you,
Mt	12:18	I will **p** my Spirit upon him,
Eph	6:11	P on the whole armor of God,

Q

QUAILS

Ex	16:13	In the evening **q** came up
Num	11:31	and it brought **q** from the sea and

QUARRELED → QUARRELSOME

Ex	17: 7	the Israelites **q** and tested the LORD,
Num	20: 3	The people **q** with Moses and said,

QUARRELSOME → QUARRELED

1 Tim	3: 3	not **q**, and not a lover of money.
2 Tim	2:24	the Lord's servant must not be **q**

QUEEN

1 Kings	10: 1	the **q** of Sheba heard of the fame of
Esth	2:17	and made her **q** instead of Vashti.
Mt	12:42	The **q** of the South will rise up at
Rev	18: 7	in her heart she says, 'I rule as a **q**;

QUESTIONS

2 Chr	9: 1	to Jerusalem to test him with hard **q**,
Mt	22:46	anyone dare to ask him any more **q**.

QUICK → QUICKLY

Sir	5:11	Be **q** to hear, but deliberate
Jas	1:19	be **q** to listen, slow to speak,

QUICKLY → QUICK

Jn	13:27	"Do **q** what you are going to do."
Rom	9:28	execute his sentence on the earth **q**
Gal	1: 6	so **q** deserting the one who called

QUIET

1 Tim	2: 2	**q** and peaceable life in all godliness
1 Pet	3: 4	beauty of a gentle and **q** spirit,

QUIVER

Ps	127: 5	Happy is the man who has his **q** full of
Isa	49: 2	in his **q** he hid me away.

R

RABBI

Mt	23: 8	But you are not to be called **r**,
Jn	1:38	"R" (which translated means Teacher),

RACE

Eccl	9:11	the sun the **r** is not to the swift,
1 Cor	9:24	that in a **r** the runners all compete,
Heb	12: 1	let us run with perseverance the **r**
1 Pet	2: 9	But you are a chosen **r**, a royal

RACHEL

Daughter of Laban (Gen 29:16); wife of Jacob (Gen 29:28); bore two sons (Gen 30:22-24; 35:16-24; 46:19). Stole Laban's gods (Gen 31:19, 32-35). Death (Gen 35:19-20).

RAHAB

Prostitute who hid Israelite spies (Josh 2; 6:22-25; Heb 11:31; Jas 2:25). Mother of Boaz (Mt 1:5).

RAIN → RAINBOW, RAINED, RAINS

Gen	7: 4	For in seven days I will send **r** on
1 Kings	17: 1	neither dew nor **r** these years,
Isa	45: 8	let the skies **r** down righteousness;
Mt	5:45	sends **r** on the righteous and on the
Rev	11: 6	so that no **r** may fall during the days

RAINBOW → BOW

Rev	4: 3	the throne is a **r** that looks like an

RAINED → RAIN

Gen	19:24	**r** on Sodom and Gomorrah sulfur
Ex	9:23	LORD **r** hail on the land of Egypt;

RAINS → RAIN

Lev	26: 4	I will give you your **r** in their season
Jas	5: 7	receives the early and the late **r**.

RAISE → RISE

Deut	18:15	God will **r** up for you a prophet
2 Macc	7: 9	but the King of the universe will **r** us up
Jn	2:19	and in three days I will **r** it up."
2 Cor	4:14	who raised the Lord Jesus will **r** us

RAISED → RISE

Mt	17:23	and on the third day he will be **r**."
Acts	2:24	God **r** him up, having freed him
Rom	4:25	and was **r** for our justification.
1 Cor	15: 4	**r** on the third day in accordance

RAM → RAMS

Gen	22:13	and took the **r** and offered it up as
Ex	29:22	(for it is a **r** of ordination),
Dan	8: 3	saw a **r** standing beside the river.

RAMS → RAM

1 Sam	15:22	and to heed than the fat of **r**.

RANSOM → RANSOMED

Ps	49: 8	For the **r** of life is costly, and can
Mt	20:28	and to give his life a **r** for many."
1 Tim	2: 6	who gave himself a **r** for all

RANSOMED → RANSOM

Isa	35:10	And the **r** of the LORD shall return,
Rev	5: 9	by your blood you **r** for God saints

RAVENS

1 Kings	17: 6	**r** brought him bread and meat in
Lk	12:24	Consider the **r**: they neither sow

READ → READING

Ex	24: 7	and **r** it in the hearing of the people;
Josh	8:34	he **r** all the words of the law,
Neh	8: 8	they **r** from the book, from the law
Lk	4:16	as was his custom. He stood up to **r**,
2 Cor	3:15	this very day whenever Moses is **r**,

READING → READ

Acts	8:30	you understand what you are **r**?"

READY
| Lk | 1:17 | r a people prepared for the Lord." |
| Rev | 19: 7 | and his bride has made herself r; |

REAP
| Gal | 6: 7 | for you r whatever you sow. |
| Rev | 14:15 | for the hour to r has come, |

REBEKAH
Sister of Laban, secured as bride for Isaac (Gen 24). Mother of Esau and Jacob (Gen 25:19-26). Taken by Abimelech as sister of Isaac; returned (Gen 26:1-11). Encouraged Jacob to trick Isaac out of blessing (Gen 27:1-17).

REBEL → REBELLED, REBELLION
| Ex | 23:21 | do not r against him, for he will |
| 1 Sam | 12:14 | not r against the commandment |

REBELLED → REBEL
| Num | 20:24 | because you r against my command |
| Neh | 9:26 | they were disobedient and r |

REBELLION → REBEL
| 1 Sam | 15:23 | For r is no less a sin than divination, |
| 2 Thess | 2: 3 | the r comes first and the lawless one |

REBUILD → BUILD
Ezra	1: 3	and r the house of the LORD,
Neh	2:17	let us r the wall of Jerusalem,
Dan	9:25	went out to restore and r Jerusalem
Acts	15:16	and I will r the dwelling of David,

REBUKE
Ps	6: 1	O LORD, do not r me in your anger,
Prov	27: 5	Better is open r than hidden love.
Zech	3: 2	said to Satan, "The LORD r you,
Mk	8:32	Peter took him aside and began to r
2 Tim	4: 2	convince, r, and encourage,

RECEIVE → RECEIVED
Jn	3:27	"No one can r anything except
	16:24	Ask and you will r, so that your joy
	20:22	said to them, "R the Holy Spirit.
Acts	2:38	you will r the gift of the Holy Spirit.
	20:35	'It is more blessed to give than to r.'
1 Cor	4: 7	What do you have that you did not r?
Rev	4:11	to r glory and honor and power,

RECEIVED → RECEIVE
Mt	6: 2	I tell you, they have r their reward.
Jn	1:12	But to all who r him, who believed
1 Cor	11:23	I r from the Lord what I also handed

RECKONED → RECKONING
| Gen | 15: 6 | LORD r it to him as righteousness. |
| Rom | 4: 3 | it was r to him as righteousness." |

RECKONING → RECKONED
| Gen | 9: 5 | I will require a r for human life. |
| Sir | 2:14 | you do when the Lord's r comes? |

RECONCILE → RECONCILED, RECONCILIATION
| Acts | 7:26 | were quarreling and tried to r them, |
| Col | 1:20 | God was pleased to r to himself all |

RECONCILED → RECONCILE
| Mt | 5:24 | first be r to your brother or sister, |
| 1 Cor | 7:11 | let her remain unmarried or else be r |

RECONCILIATION → RECONCILE
| Rom | 5:11 | whom we have now received r. |
| 2 Cor | 5:18 | and has given us the ministry of r; |

RED
Ex	15: 4	officers were sunk in the R Sea.
Mt	16: 3	for the sky is r and threatening.'
Rev	12: 3	a great r dragon, with seven heads

REDEEM → REDEEMED, REDEEMER, REDEMPTION
Ex	6: 6	I will r you with an outstretched
2 Sam	7:23	whose God went to r it as a people,
Gal	4: 5	to r those who were under the law,

REDEEMED → REDEEM
| Deut | 15:15 | and the LORD your God r you; |
| Ps | 107: 2 | Let the r of the LORD say so, |

REDEEMER → REDEEM
Job	19:25	For I know that my R lives,
Ps	19:14	O LORD, my rock and my r.
Isa	48:17	Thus says the LORD, your R,

REDEMPTION → REDEEM
Lk	21:28	because your r is drawing near."
Rom	3:24	through the r that is in Christ Jesus,
Eph	1: 7	In him we have r through his blood,
Heb	9:12	own blood, thus obtaining eternal r.

REFINE → REFINED
| Jer | 9: 7 | I will now r and test them, |
| Zech | 13: 9 | r them as one refines silver, |

REFINED → REFINE
| Dan | 12:10 | shall be purified, cleansed, and r, |

REFLECTED → REFLECTION
| 2 Cor | 3:18 | though r in a mirror, |

REFLECTION → REFLECTED
| 1 Cor | 11: 7 | since he is the image and r of God; |
| Heb | 1: 3 | He is the r of God's glory |

REFUGE
Num	35:11	select cities to be cities of r for you,
Ps	2:12	Happy are all who take r in him.
Prov	30: 5	a shield to those who take r in him.
Jer	16:19	my r in the day of trouble,

REFUSE
Ex	8: 2	If you r to let them go,
Ezek	3:27	and let those who r to hear, r;
Heb	12:25	do not r the one who is speaking;

REGARD
Isa	8:13	of hosts, him you shall r as holy;
Phil	2: 6	did not r equality with God as
	3: 7	these I have come to r as loss
Heb	12: 5	not r lightly the discipline of the

REGULATIONS
| Col | 2:20 | Why do you submit to r, |
| Heb | 9:10 | r for the body imposed until the |

REHOBOAM
Son of Solomon (1 Kings 11:43; 1 Chr 3:10). Harsh treatment of subjects caused divided kingdom (1 Kings 12:1-24; 14:21-31; 2 Chr 10-12).

REIGN → REIGNS
Ex	15:18	The LORD will r forever and ever."
Ps	146:10	The LORD will r forever,
1 Cor	15:25	r until he has put all his enemies
2 Tim	2:12	we will also r with him;
Rev	11:15	and he will r forever and ever."
	22: 5	and they will r forever and ever.

REIGNS → REIGN
| Isa | 52: 7 | who says to Zion, "Your God r." |
| Rev | 19: 6 | the Lord our God the Almighty r. |

REJECT → REJECTED
| Ex | 20: 5 | generation of those who r me, |
| Isa | 30:12 | Because you r this word, |

REJECTED → REJECT
1 Sam	8: 7	but they have r me from being king
Ps	60: 1	O God, you have r us, broken our
	118:22	The stone that the builders r
Isa	53: 3	He was despised and r by others;
Mt	21:42	The stone that the builders r
1 Pet	2: 4	though r by mortals yet chosen and

REJOICE → REJOICING
Ps	5:11	But let all who take refuge in you r;
	118:24	let us r and be glad in it.
Isa	62: 5	so shall your God r over you.
Zeph	3:17	he will r over you with gladness,
Lk	6:23	R in that day and leap for joy,
Phil	4: 4	R in the Lord always; again I will say, R.

REJOICING → REJOICE
2 Sam	6:12	to the city of David with r.
Neh	8:17	And there was very great r.
2 Cor	6:10	as sorrowful, yet always r;

RELEASE
| Isa | 61: 1 | liberty to the captives, and r to |
| Mt | 27:15 | the governor was accustomed to r |

RELENT → RELENTED
| Ezek | 24:14 | I will not spare, I will not r. |
| Joel | 2:14 | whether he will not turn and r, |

Jon 3: 9 God may **r** and change his mind;

RELENTED → RELENT
1 Chr 21:15 LORD took note and **r** concerning
Jer 4:28 I have not **r** nor will I turn back.

RELIGION
Jas 1:27 **R** that is pure and undefiled before

RELY
2 Chr 14:11 O LORD our God, for we **r** on you,
Prov 3: 5 and do not **r** on your own insight.
Sir 5: 1 Do not **r** on your wealth,
Gal 3:10 all who **r** on the works of the law

REMAIN → REMAINS
1 Cor 7:20 Let each of you **r** in the condition
Heb 1:11 they will perish, but you **r;**

REMAINS → REMAIN
Josh 13: 2 This is the land that still **r:**
Heb 7: 3 Son of God, he **r** a priest forever.
10:26 there no longer **r** a sacrifice for sins,

REMEMBER → REMEMBERED, REMEMBRANCE
Gen 9:15 I will **r** my covenant that is between
Ex 20: 8 **R** the sabbath day, and keep it holy.
Deut 8:18 But **r** the LORD your God,
Job 10: 9 **R** that you fashioned me like clay;
Eccl 12: 1 **R** your creator in the days of your
Sir 23:18 The Most High will not **r** sins."
Jer 31:34 and **r** their sin no more.
2 Tim 2: 8 **R** Jesus Christ, raised from the dead
Heb 8:12 and I will **r** their sins no more."

REMEMBERED → REMEMBER
Ex 2:24 God **r** his covenant with Abraham,
Ps 78:35 They **r** that God was their rock,
106:45 For their sake he **r** his covenant,
Rev 16:19 God **r** great Babylon and gave her

REMEMBRANCE → REMEMBER
Lk 22:19 Do this in **r** of me."

REMNANT
Gen 45: 7 before you to preserve for you a **r**
Isa 10:21 A **r** will return, the **r** of Jacob,
Jer 50:20 will pardon the **r** that I have spared.
Rom 9:27 only a **r** of them will be saved;

REMOVE
Ezek 36:26 **r** from your body the heart of stone
Lk 22:42 if you are willing, **r** this cup from

RENEW → RENEWAL, RENEWED, RENEWING
Isa 40:31 for the LORD shall **r** their strength,
Lam 5:21 **r** our days as of old—

RENEWAL → RENEW
Mt 19:28 I tell you, at the **r** of all things,
Col 3:11 In that **r** there is no longer Greek

RENEWED → RENEW
2 Cor 4:16 inner nature is being **r** day by day.
Eph 4:23 to be **r** in the spirit of your minds,

RENEWING* → RENEW
Rom 12: 2 transformed by the **r** of your minds,

REPAY → PAY
Ps 28: 4 **R** them according to their work,
Isa 59:18 to their deeds, so will he **r;**
Rom 12:17 Do not **r** anyone evil for evil,
Rev 18: 6 and **r** her double for her deeds;

REPENT → REPENTANCE
1 Kings 8:47 **r,** and plead with you in the land
Job 42: 6 and **r** in dust and ashes."
Sir 18:21 and when you have sinned, **r.**
Mt 3: 2 **"R,** for the kingdom of heaven has
Acts 2:38 **"R,** and be baptized every one of
Rev 16: 9 they did not **r** and give him glory.

REPENTANCE → REPENT
Mk 1: 4 a baptism of **r** for the forgiveness
Lk 3: 8 Bear fruits worthy of **r.**
Rom 2: 4 kindness is meant to lead you to **r?**
2 Cor 7:10 **r** that leads to salvation and brings
2 Pet 3: 9 any to perish, but all to come to **r.**

REPROVE
Prov 19:25 **r** the intelligent, and they will gain
Titus 2:15 exhort and **r** with all authority.
Rev 3:19 **r** and discipline those whom I love.

REQUIRE
Deut 10:12 does the LORD your God **r** of you?
Mic 6: 8 the LORD **r** of you but to do justice,

RESCUE → RESCUED, RESCUES
Ps 22: 8 him **r** the one in whom he delights!"
Mt 6:13 but **r** us from the evil one.
2 Pet 2: 9 the Lord knows how to **r** the godly

RESCUED → RESCUE
Sir 51:12 and **r** me in time of trouble.
Col 1:13 has **r** us from the power of darkness

RESCUES → RESCUE
Ps 37:40 The LORD helps them and **r** them;
Dan 6:27 and **r,** he works signs and wonders
1 Thess 1:10 Jesus, who **r** us from the wrath that

RESIST
Mt 5:39 I say to you, Do not **r** an evildoer.
Rom 9:19 For who can **r** his will?"
Jas 4: 7 **R** the devil, and he will flee from

RESPECT
Mal 1: 6 if I am a master, where is the **r** due
Rom 13: 7 **r** to whom **r** is due,

REST → RESTED, RESTS
Ex 31:15 seventh day is a sabbath of solemn **r**
2 Sam 7:11 give you **r** from all your enemies.
Ps 95:11 swore, "They shall not enter my **r."**
Mt 11:28 and I will give you **r.**
Heb 4:10 those who enter God's **r** also cease

RESTED → REST
Gen 2: 2 he **r** on the seventh day from all the
Ex 20:11 all that is in them, but **r** the seventh

RESTORE → RESTORES
Deut 30: 3 LORD your God will **r** your fortunes
Ps 51:12 **R** to me the joy of your salvation,
Lam 5:21 **R** us to yourself, O LORD,
Dan 9:25 the word went out to **r** and rebuild
Mt 17:11 "Elijah is indeed coming and will **r**

RESTORES → RESTORE
Ps 23: 3 he **r** my soul. He leads me in right

RESTS → REST
Ps 16: 9 my body also **r** secure.
Prov 19:23 one **r** secure and suffers no harm.

RESURRECTION
Mt 22:30 For in the **r** they neither marry nor
Mk 12:18 Sadducees, who say there is no **r,**
Jn 11:25 said to her, "I am the **r** and the life.
1 Cor 15:12 you say there is no **r** of the dead?
Phil 3:10 know Christ and the power of his **r**
Rev 20: 5 This is the first **r.**

RETAIN
Jn 20:23 if you **r** the sins of any,

RETURN
Gen 3:19 you are dust, and to dust you shall **r.**
Deut 30: 2 and **r** to the LORD your God,
Ps 116:12 What shall I **r** to the LORD
Hos 14: 1 **R,** O Israel, to the LORD your God,
Mal 3: 7 **R** to me, and I will **r** to you,

REUBEN
Firstborn of Jacob by Leah (Gen 29:32; 46:8; 1 Chr 2:1). Attempted to rescue Joseph (Gen 37:21-30). Lost birthright for sleeping with Bilhah (Gen 35:22; 49:4). Tribe of blessed (Gen 49:3-4; Deut 33:6), numbered (Num 1:21; 26:7), allotted land east of Jordan (Num 32; 34:14; Josh 13:15), west (Ezek 48:6), failed to help Deborah (Judg 5:15-16), supported David (1 Chr 12:37), 12,000 from (Rev 7:5).

REVEAL → REVEALED, REVELATION, REVELATIONS
Mt 11:27 to whom the Son chooses to **r** him.

REVEALED → REVEAL
Isa 40: 5 the glory of the LORD shall be **r,**
Mt 16:17 flesh and blood has not **r** this to you

Lk 17:30 on the day that the Son of Man is **r**.
Rom 1:17 in it the righteousness of God is **r**
2 Thess 1: 7 the Lord Jesus is **r** from heaven
1 Jn 3: 2 we do know is this: when he is **r**,

REVELATION → REVEAL
1 Cor 14: 6 some **r** or knowledge or prophecy
Eph 3: 3 was made known to me by **r**,
Rev 1: 1 The **r** of Jesus Christ, which God

REVELATIONS → REVEAL
2 Cor 12: 1 but I will go on to visions and **r** of

REVERE → REVERENCE
Josh 24:14 "Now therefore **r** the LORD,
Tob 4: 5 "**R** the Lord all your days,
Mal 4: 2 But for you who **r** my name the sun

REVERENCE → REVERE
Eph 5:21 subject to one another out of **r** for
1 Pet 3: 2 see the purity and **r** of your lives.

REVILE → REVILED
Ex 22:28 You shall not **r** God, or curse
Mt 5:11 people **r** you and persecute you

REVILED → REVILE
1 Cor 4:12 When **r**, we bless;
1 Pet 4:14 If you are **r** for the name of Christ,

REWARD → REWARDED, REWARDS
Ps 19:11 in keeping them there is great **r**.
Isa 40:10 **r** is with him, and his recompense
Mt 6: 5 I tell you, they have received their **r**.
Lk 6:23 for surely your **r** is great in heaven;
Heb 11:26 for he was looking ahead to the **r**.
Rev 22:12 I am coming soon; my **r** is with me,

REWARDED → REWARD
2 Sam 22:21 The LORD **r** me according to my

REWARDS → REWARD
Heb 11: 6 and that he **r** those who seek him.

RIB
Gen 2:22 **r** that the LORD God had taken from

RICH → RICHES
Prov 23: 4 Do not wear yourself out to get **r**;
Mt 19:23 hard for a **r** person to enter the
Lk 12:21 but are not **r** toward God."
2 Cor 8: 9 by his poverty you might become **r**.
Eph 2: 4 But God, who is **r** in mercy,
1 Tim 6:18 to do good, to be **r** in good works,
Jas 1:10 and the **r** in being brought low,

RICHES → RICH
Ps 62:10 if **r** increase, do not set your heart
Prov 30: 8 give me neither poverty nor **r**;
Sir 13:24 **R** are good if they are free from sin;
Lk 8:14 they are choked by the cares and **r**
Rom 11:33 O the depth of the **r** and wisdom
1 Jn 2:16 the desire of the eyes, the pride in **r**

RID
Col 3: 8 But now you must get **r** of all such
1 Pet 2: 1 **R** yourselves, therefore, of all

RIDER → RIDES, RIDING
Rev 19:11 Its **r** is called Faithful and True,

RIDES → RIDER
Deut 33:26 **r** through the heavens to your help,
Ps 68: 4 a song to him who **r** upon the clouds

RIDING → RIDER
Zech 9: 9 humble and **r** on a donkey,

RIGHT → BIRTHRIGHT
Ex 15: 6 Your **r** hand, O LORD, glorious in
Deut 6:18 Do what is **r** and good in the sight
Job 42: 7 have not spoken of me what is **r**,
Ps 110: 1 says to my lord, "Sit at my **r** hand
Prov 14:12 a way that seems **r** to a person,
Mt 25:33 sheep at his **r** hand and the goats at
Acts 2:34 said to my Lord, "Sit at my **r** hand,
Heb 1:13 "Sit at my **r** hand until I make your
1 Pet 3:14 if you do suffer for doing what is **r**,

RIGHTEOUS → RIGHTEOUSNESS
Gen 18:23 "Will you indeed sweep away the **r**

Job 4:17 'Can mortals be **r** before God?
Ps 11: 7 For the LORD is **r**; he loves **r** deeds;
143: 2 for no one living is **r** before you.
Prov 10: 6 Blessings are on the head of the **r**,
11:23 desire of the **r** ends only in good;
15:29 but he hears the prayer of the **r**.
Wis 5:15 **r** live forever, and their reward
Sir 35:22 and does justice for the **r**,
Jer 23: 5 I will raise up for David a **r** Branch,
Ezek 3:20 if the **r** turn from their righteousness
Hab 2: 4 but the **r** live by their faith.
Mt 5:45 rain on the **r** and on the unrighteous.
Mk 2:17 come to call not the **r** but sinners."
Rom 1:17 one who is **r** will live by faith."
5:19 the many will be made **r**.
Heb 10:38 but my **r** one will live by faith.
1 Jn 2: 1 with the Father, Jesus Christ the **r**;
Rev 19: 8 the fine linen is the **r** deeds of the

RIGHTEOUSNESS → RIGHTEOUS
Gen 15: 6 the LORD reckoned it to him as **r**.
Ps 9: 8 He judges the world with **r**;
Prov 12:28 In the path of **r** there is life,
Eccl 7:15 people who perish in their **r**,
Isa 11: 5 **R** shall be the belt around his waist,
Jer 23: 6 be called: "The LORD is our **r**."
Dan 9:24 to bring in everlasting **r**,
12: 3 and those who lead many to **r**,
Hos 10:12 Sow for yourselves **r**; reap steadfast
Mt 5: 6 those who hunger and thirst for **r**,
Jn 16: 8 about sin and **r** and judgment:
Rom 3:22 the **r** of God through faith in Jesus
5:18 act of **r** leads to justification
10: 4 be **r** for everyone who believes.
Gal 3: 6 and it was reckoned to him as **r**,"
Eph 6:14 and put on the breastplate of **r**.
1 Pet 2:24 free from sins, we might live for **r**;
2 Pet 3:13 heavens and a new earth, where **r** is
Rev 19:11 and in **r** he judges and makes war.

RIPE
Joel 3:13 Put in the sickle, for the harvest is **r**.
Jn 4:35 how the fields are **r** for harvesting.
Rev 14:15 the harvest of the earth is fully **r**."

RISE → ARISE, RAISE, RAISED, ROSE
Num 24:17 and a scepter shall **r** out of Israel;
2 Macc 12:44 that those who had fallen would **r** again,
Ps 94: 2 **R** up, O judge of the earth;
Dan 12:13 shall **r** for your reward at the end of
Mal 4: 2 the sun of righteousness shall **r**,
Mt 27:63 'After three days I will **r** again.'
Eph 5:14 **R** from the dead, and Christ will
1 Thess 4:16 and the dead in Christ will **r** first.

RIVER → RIVERS
Ps 46: 4 a **r** whose streams make glad the
Isa 48:18 prosperity would have been like a **r**,
Ezek 47:12 On the banks, on both sides of the **r**,
Mt 3: 6 baptized by him in the **r** Jordan,
Rev 22: 1 showed me the **r** of the water of life,

RIVERS → RIVER
Ps 137: 1 By the **r** of Babylon—there we sat
Rev 8:10 it fell on a third of the **r** and on the

ROAD → CROSSROADS
Mt 7:13 and the **r** is easy that leads to

ROAR → ROARING, ROARS
Ps 46: 3 though its waters **r** and foam,
Jer 25:30 The LORD will **r** from on high,

ROARING → ROAR
1 Pet 5: 8 a **r** lion your adversary the devil

ROARS → ROAR
Hos 11:10 the LORD, who **r** like a lion;
Joel 3:16 The LORD **r** from Zion,

ROB → ROBBER, ROBBERS
Mal 3: 8 anyone **r** God? Yet you are robbing

ROBBER → ROB
1 Cor 5:11 an idolater, reviler, drunkard, or **r**.

ROBBERS → ROB
Jer 7:11 become a den of **r** in your sight?

Mt 21:13 but you are making it a den of **r**."

ROBE → ROBED, ROBES
Gen 37: 3 had made him a long **r** with sleeves.
Ex 28: 4 a breastpiece, an ephod, a **r**,
Lk 15:22 bring out a **r**—the best one—and put it on him;
Jn 19: 5 crown of thorns and the purple **r**.
Rev 6:11 They were each given a white **r** and
 19:13 He is clothed in a **r** dipped in blood,

ROBED → ROBE
Ps 93: 1 LORD is king, he is **r** in majesty;
Rev 15: 6 **r** in pure bright linen,

ROBES → ROBE
Mk 12:38 who like to walk around in long **r**,
Rev 22:14 Blessed are those who wash their **r**,

ROCK
Ex 17: 6 Strike the **r**, and water will come
Num 20: 8 you shall bring water out of the **r**
1 Sam 2: 2 there is no **R** like our God.
Ps 19:14 O LORD, my **r** and my redeemer.
Isa 44: 8 There is no other **r**; I know not one.
Mt 16:18 and on this **r** I will build my church,
Mk 15:46 that had been hewn out of the **r**.
1 Pet 2: 8 and a **r** that makes them fall."

ROD
2 Sam 7:14 I will punish him with a **r** such as
Ps 2: 9 shall break them with a **r** of iron,
 23: 4 your **r** and your staff—they comfort
Prov 13:24 who spare the **r** hate their children,
Heb 9: 4 and Aaron's **r** that budded,
Rev 2:27 to rule them with an iron **r**,

ROLL
Am 5:24 But let justice **r** down like waters,
Mk 16: 3 "Who will **r** away the stone for us

ROOF
Josh 2: 6 to the **r** and hidden them
2 Sam 11: 2 he saw from the **r** a woman bathing;
Mk 2: 4 they removed the **r** above him;

ROOM
Mk 14:15 He will show you a large **r** upstairs,
Rom 12:19 but leave **r** for the wrath of God;
Eph 4:27 and do not make **r** for the devil.

ROOT → ROOTED
Isa 11:10 On that day the **r** of Jesse
 53: 2 and like a **r** out of dry ground;
Rom 11:16 and if the **r** is holy, then the branches
 15:12 "The **r** of Jesse shall come,
1 Tim 6:10 For the love of money is a **r** of all
Rev 5: 5 the tribe of Judah, the **R** of David,

ROOTED → ROOT
Eph 3:17 are being **r** and grounded in love.

ROSE → RISE
Song 2: 1 I am a **r** of Sharon, a lily
1 Thess 4:14 believe that Jesus died and **r** again,

ROUGH
Isa 40: 4 and the **r** places a plain.
Lk 3: 5 and the **r** ways made smooth;

ROYAL
Jas 2: 8 if you really fulfill the **r** law
1 Pet 2: 9 are a chosen race, a **r** priesthood,

RUBBISH
1 Cor 4:13 have become like the **r** of the world,
Phil 3: 8 and I regard them as **r**,

RUIN → RUINS
Ezek 21:27 A **r**, a **r**, a **r**—I will make it!
Zeph 1:15 a day of **r** and devastation,

RUINS → RUIN
Ezra 9: 9 the house of our God, to repair its **r**,
Neh 2:17 Jerusalem lies in **r** with its gates
1 Macc 3:43 "Let us restore the **r** of our people,
Acts 15:16 from its **r** I will rebuild it,
1 Cor 15:33 "Bad company **r** good morals."

RULE → RULER, RULER'S, RULERS, RULES
Gen 3:16 husband, and he shall **r** over you."
Ps 110: 2 **R** in the midst of your foes.
Eph 1:21 far above all **r** and authority and
Col 3:15 the peace of Christ **r** in your hearts,
Rev 19:15 he will **r** them with a rod of iron;

RULER → RULE
Ex 2:14 made you a **r** and judge over us?
Mt 2: 6 a **r** who is to shepherd my people
1 Cor 15:24 after he has destroyed every **r**
Rev 1: 5 and the **r** of the kings of the earth.

RULER'S → RULE
Gen 49:10 the **r** staff from between his feet,

RULERS → RULE
Ps 2: 2 and the **r** take counsel together,
Isa 40:23 makes the **r** of the earth as nothing.
Eph 6:12 against the **r**, against the authorities,

RULES → RULE
Ps 66: 7 who **r** by his might forever,
Isa 40:10 and his arm **r** for him;
2 Tim 2: 5 competing according to the **r**.

RUMORS
Mt 24: 6 you will hear of wars and **r** of wars;

RUN → FORERUNNER, RUNNERS
Isa 40:31 they shall **r** and not be weary,
Gal 2: 2 or had not **r**, in vain.
Heb 12: 1 let us **r** with perseverance the race

RUNNERS* → RUN
1 Cor 9:24 that in a race the **r** all compete,

RUST
Bar 6:12 cannot save themselves from **r**
Mt 6:19 where moth and **r** consume

RUTH
 Moabitess; widow who went to Bethlehem with mother-in-law Naomi (Ruth 1). Gleaned in field of Boaz; shown favor (Ruth 2). Proposed marriage to Boaz (Ruth 3). Married (Ruth 4:1-12); bore Obed, ancestor of David (Ruth 4:13-22), Jesus (Mt 1:5).

S

SABBATH
Ex 20: 8 Remember the **s** day, and keep it holy.
2 Chr 36:21 the days that it lay desolate it kept **s**,
1 Macc 1:43 to idols and profaned the **s**.
Mt 12: 1 through the grainfields on the **s**;
Mk 2:28 Son of Man is lord even of the **s**."

SACKCLOTH → CLOTH
Dan 9: 3 supplication with fasting and **s** and
Mt 11:21 would have repented long ago in **s**

SACRED
Ex 28: 2 You shall make **s** vestments for
 34:13 and cut down their **s** poles

SACRIFICE → SACRIFICED, SACRIFICES
Ex 12:27 'It is the passover **s** to the LORD,
Lev 3: 1 If the offering is a **s** of well-being,
1 Sam 15:22 Surely, to obey is better than **s**,
Ps 40: 6 **S** and offering you do not desire,
Prov 15: 8 **s** of the wicked is an abomination
Dan 9:27 he shall make **s** and offering cease;
Hos 6: 6 For I desire steadfast love and not **s**,
Mt 9:13 this means, 'I desire mercy, not **s**.'
Rom 3:25 put forward as a **s** of atonement
Phil 4:18 a **s** acceptable and pleasing to God.
Heb 13:15 let us continually offer a **s** of praise
1 Jn 2: 2 and he is the atoning **s** for our sins,

SACRIFICED → SACRIFICE
1 Cor 5: 7 our paschal lamb, Christ, has been **s**.
 8: 1 Now concerning food **s** to idols:

SACRIFICES → SACRIFICE
Mk 12:33 all whole burnt offerings and **s**."
Heb 7:27 has no need to offer **s** day after day,

SADDUCEES
Mt 16: 6 the yeast of the Pharisees and **S**."

Mk   12:18 **S**, who say there is no resurrection,

SAFE → SAFETY
Ps   37:28 righteous shall be kept **s** forever,
Prov 18:10 the righteous run into it and are **s**.

SAFETY → SAFE
Deut 12:10 around so that you live in **s**,
Ezek 34:28 they shall live in **s**,

SAINTS
Ps   31:23 Love the LORD, all you his **s**.
Rom   8:27 the Spirit intercedes for the **s**
1 Cor 6: 2 that the **s** will judge the world?
Eph   4:12 equip the **s** for the work of ministry,
Rev   5: 9 by your blood you ransomed for God **s**

SALT
Gen   19:26 back, and she became a pillar of **s**.
Mt   5:13 "You are the **s** of the earth;

SALVATION → SAVE
Ex   15: 2 and he has become my **s**;
Ps   27: 1 The LORD is my light and my **s**;
      51:12 Restore to me the joy of your **s**,
Isa   12: 3 draw water from the wells of **s**.
      52: 7 brings good news, who announces **s**,
Lam   3:26 one should wait quietly for the **s**
Bar   4:29 everlasting joy with your **s**.
Hab   3:18 I will exult in the God of my **s**.
Lk   3: 6 all flesh shall see the **s** of God.'"
Acts   4:12 There is **s** in no one else,
2 Cor 6: 2 see, now is the day of **s**!
Phil   2:12 work out your own **s** with fear
Heb   2: 3 escape if we neglect so great a **s**?
2 Pet 3:15 regard the patience of our Lord as **s**.
Rev   19: 1 **S** and glory and power to our God,

SAMARIA → SAMARITAN
1 Kings 16:24 and called the city that he built, **S**,
2 Kings 17: 6 the king of Assyria captured **S**;
Jn   4: 4 But he had to go through **S**.
Acts   1: 8 in all Judea and **S**, and to the ends

SAMARITAN → SAMARIA
Lk   10:33 But a **S** while traveling came near
Jn   4: 7 A **S** woman came to draw water.

SAME
Rom   10:12 the **s** Lord is Lord of all
1 Cor 12: 4 varieties of gifts, but the **s** Spirit;
Heb   13: 8 Jesus Christ is the **s** yesterday and

SAMSON*
    Danite judge. Birth promised (Judg 13). Married a Philistine, but his wife given away (Judg 14). Vengeance on the Philistines (Judg 15). Betrayed by Delilah (Judg 16:1-22). Death (Judg 16:23-31). Feats of strength: killed lion (Judg 14:6), 30 Philistines (Judg 14:19), 1,000 Philistines with jawbone (Judg 15:13-17), carried off gates of Gaza (Judg 16:3), pushed down temple of Dagon (Judg 16:25-30; Heb 11:32).

SAMUEL
    Ephraimite judge and prophet (Heb 11:32). Birth prayed for (1 Sam 1:10-18). Dedicated to temple by Hannah (1 Sam 1:21-28). Raised by Eli (1 Sam 2:11, 18-26). Called as prophet (1 Sam 3). Led Israel to victory over Philistines (1 Sam 7). Asked by Israel for a king (1 Sam 8). Anointed Saul as king (1 Sam 9-10). Farewell speech (1 Sam 12). Rebuked Saul for sacrifice (1 Sam 13). Announced rejection of Saul (1 Sam 15). Anointed David as king (1 Sam 16). Protected David from Saul (1 Sam 19:18-24). Death (1 Sam 25:1). Returned from dead to condemn Saul (1 Sam 28).

SANCTIFICATION → SANCTIFY
Rom   6:19 as slaves to righteousness for **s**.
1 Thess 4: 3 For this is the will of God, your **s**:

SANCTIFIED → SANCTIFY
Ex   29:43 and it shall be **s** by my glory;
Jn   17:19 so that they also may be **s** in truth.
1 Cor 6:11 But you were washed, you were **s**,

SANCTIFY → SANCTIFICATION, SANCTIFIED
Lev   11:44 **s** yourselves therefore, and be holy,
Heb   13:12 to **s** the people by his own blood.

SANCTUARY
Ex   25: 8 And have them make me a **s**,

1 Chr 22:19 build the **s** of the LORD God
1 Macc 1:21 He arrogantly entered the **s**
       4:36 cleanse the **s** and dedicate it."
Ezek 37:26 and will set my **s** among them
Dan   9:26 shall destroy the city and the **s**.
Heb   9:24 Christ did not enter a **s** made by

SAND
Gen   22:17 as the stars of heaven and as the **s**
Hos   1:10 Israel shall be like the **s** of the sea,
Mt   7:26 foolish man who built his house on **s**.

SANDALS
Ex   3: 5 Remove the **s** from your feet,
Mt   3:11 I am not worthy to carry his **s**.

SARAH
    1. Wife of Abraham, originally named Sarai; barren (Gen 11:29-31; 1 Pet 3:6). Taken by Pharaoh as Abraham's sister; returned (Gen 12:10-20). Gave Hagar to Abraham; sent her away in pregnancy (Gen 16). Name changed; Isaac promised (Gen 17:15-21; 18:10-15; Heb 11:11). Taken by Abimelech as Abraham's sister; returned (Gen 20). Isaac born; Hagar and Ishmael sent away (Gen 21:1-21; Gal 4:21-31). Death (Gen 23).
    2. Daughter of Raguel, wife of Tobias (Tob 3; 6-8; 10-12).

SAT → SIT
Heb   10:12 "he **s** down at the right hand of God,
Rev   3:21 and **s** down with my Father

SATAN
1 Chr 21: 1 **S** stood up against Israel,
Job   1: 6 and **S** also came among them.
Zech   3: 2 "The LORD rebuke you, O **S**!
Mt   4:10 Jesus said to him, "Away with you, **S**!
      12:26 If **S** casts out **S**, he is divided
      16:23 said to Peter, "Get behind me, **S**!
2 Cor 11:14 **S** disguises himself as an angel of light.
Rev   12: 9 who is called the Devil and **S**,
      20: 7 **S** will be released from his prison

SATISFIED → SATISFY
Ps   17:15 I shall be **s**, beholding your likeness.
Joel   2:26 You shall eat in plenty and be **s**,

SATISFY → SATISFIED
Isa   55: 2 labor for that which does not **s**?
Jer   31:25 I will **s** the weary, and all who are

SAUL → =PAUL
    1. Benjamite; anointed by Samuel as first king of Israel (1 Sam 9-10). Defeated Ammonites (1 Sam 11). Rebuked for offering sacrifice (1 Sam 13:1-15). Defeated Philistines (1 Sam 14). Rejected as king for failing to annihilate Amalekites (1 Sam 15). Soothed from evil spirit by David (1 Sam 16:14-23). Sent David against Goliath (1 Sam 17). Jealousy and attempted murder of David (1 Sam 18:1-11). Gave David Michal as wife (1 Sam 18:12-30). Second attempt to kill David (1 Sam 19). Anger at Jonathan (1 Sam 20:26-34). Pursued David: killed priests at Nob (1 Sam 22), went to Keilah and Ziph (1 Sam 23), life spared by David at En Gedi (1 Sam 24) and in his tent (1 Sam 26). Rebuked by Samuel's spirit for consulting witch at Endor (1 Sam 28). Wounded by Philistines; took his own life (1 Sam 31; 1 Chr 10). Lamented by David (2 Sam 1:17-27). Children (1 Sam 14:49-51; 1 Chr 8).
    2. See Paul.

SAVE → SALVATION, SAVED, SAVIOR
Ps   54: 1 **S** me, O God, by your name,
Isa   59: 1 LORD's hand is not too short to **s**,
Jer   15:20 for I am with you to **s** you
Mt   1:21 he will **s** his people from their sins."
      16:25 who want to **s** their life will lose it,
Lk   19:10 came to seek out and to **s** the lost."
Heb   7:25 to **s** those who approach God

SAVED → SAVE
Isa   45:22 Turn to me and be **s**,
Joel   2:32 on the name of the LORD shall be **s**;
Mt   10:22 who endures to the end will be **s**.
Mk   15:31 He **s** others; he cannot save himself.
Lk   13:23 "Lord, will only a few be **s**?"
Acts   2:21 on the name of the Lord shall be **s**.'
      16:30 "Sirs, what must I do to be **s**?"
Rom   10:13 on the name of the Lord shall be **s**."
Eph   2: 8 For by grace you have been **s**

SAVIOR → SAVE

Ps	106: 21	They forgot God, their **S**,
Isa	49:16	know that I am the LORD your **S**,
Hos	13: 4	and besides me there is no **s**.
Lk	2: 11	this day in the city of David a **S**,
Acts	13:23	to Israel a **S**, Jesus, as he promised;
1 Tim	4: 10	who is the **S** of all people,
Titus	2: 13	of the glory of our great God and **S**,
2 Pet	3: 18	knowledge of our Lord and **S** Jesus

SCARLET

| Isa | 1: 18 | your sins are like **s**, they shall be |
| Mt | 27:28 | stripped him and put a **s** robe on him |

SCATTER → SCATTERED

| Deut | 4:27 | LORD will **s** you among the peoples; |
| Jer | 9:16 | I will **s** them among nations that |

SCATTERED → SCATTER

Deut	30: 3	the LORD your God has **s** you.
Jer	31:10	"He who **s** Israel will gather him,
Mk	14:27	the shepherd, and the sheep will be **s**.'

SCEPTER

Gen	49: 10	The **s** shall not depart from Judah,
Num	24:17	and a **s** shall rise out of Israel;
Heb	1: 8	righteous **s** is the **s** of your kingdom.

SCOFFED → SCOFFERS

| Lk | 23:35 | but the leaders **s** at him, saying, |

SCOFFERS → SCOFFED

Ps	1: 1	or sit in the seat of **s**;
Prov	19:29	Condemnation is ready for **s**,
2 Pet	3: 3	that in the last days **s** will come,

SCRIBES

| Mt | 7:29 | having authority, and not as their **s**. |
| | 23:13 | "But woe to you, **s** and Pharisees, |

SCRIPTURE → SCRIPTURES

Lk	4: 21	"Today this **s** has been fulfilled in
Jn	10:35	and the **s** cannot be annulled—
1 Tim	4:13	attention to the public reading of **s**,
2 Tim	3:16	All **s** is inspired by God and is useful

SCRIPTURES → SCRIPTURE

Mt	22:29	know neither the **s** nor the power
Lk	24:45	their minds to understand the **s**,
Jn	5:39	"You search the **s** because you think
1 Cor	15: 3	our sins in accordance with the **s**,

SCROLL

| Lk | 4:17 | the **s** of the prophet Isaiah was given |
| Rev | 5: 2 | to open the **s** and break its seals?" |

SEA

Gen	1:26	have dominion over the fish of the **s**,
Ex	15: 1	and rider he has thrown into the **s**.
Deut	30:13	Neither is it beyond the **s**, that you
Ps	95: 5	The **s** is his, for he made it,
Dan	7: 3	great beasts came up out of the **s**,
Mic	7:19	all our sins into the depths of the **s**.
Rev	4: 6	there is something like a **s** of glass,
	13: 1	a beast rising out of the **s** having
	21: 1	and the **s** was no more.

SEAL → SEALS

Dan	8:26	As for you, **s** up the vision,
2 Cor	1:22	by putting his **s** on us and giving us
Eph	1:13	the **s** of the promised Holy Spirit;
Rev	7: 3	our God with a **s** on their foreheads.
	22: 10	not **s** up the words of the prophecy

SEALS → SEAL

| Rev | 5: 2 | to open the scroll and break its **s**?" |

SEARCH → SEARCHES

Deut	4:29	if you **s** after him with all your heart
Ps	139:23	**S** me, O God, and know my heart;
Ezek	34: 11	I myself will **s** for my sheep,

SEARCHES → SEARCH

| Rom | 8:27 | And God, who **s** the heart, |
| 1 Cor | 2: 10 | the Spirit **s** everything, |

SEASON → SEASONS

| Ps | 1: 3 | which yield their fruit in its **s**, |
| Eccl | 3: 1 | For everything there is a **s**, |

SEASONS → SEASON

Gen	1:14	let them be for signs and for **s** and
Gal	4:10	and months, and **s**, and years.
1 Thess	5: 1	Now concerning the times and the **s**,

SEAT → SEATED

Ex	25:17	make a mercy **s** of pure gold;
Ps	1: 1	or sit in the **s** of scoffers;
Rom	14: 10	stand before the judgment **s** of God.
2 Cor	5: 10	must appear before the judgment **s**

SEATED → SEAT

Lk	22:69	the Son of Man will be **s** at the right
Eph	1:20	and **s** him at his right hand
Rev	4: 4	**s** on the thrones are twenty-four elders,
	19: 4	and worshiped God who is **s** on

SECOND → TWO

| Mt | 22:39 | And a **s** is like it: |
| Rev | 20:14 | This is the **s** death, the lake of fire; |

SECRET

| Deut | 29:29 | The **s** things belong to the LORD |
| Rom | 2:16 | will judge the **s** thoughts of all. |

SECURITY → SECURE

| Prov | 12: 3 | No one finds **s** by wickedness, |
| 1 Thess | 5: 3 | they say, "There is peace and **s**," |

SEE → FORESEEING, NEAR-SIGHTED, SEEN, SEES, SIGHT

Ex	12:13	when I **s** the blood, I will pass over
	33:20	for no one shall **s** me and live."
Ps	115: 5	eyes, but do not **s**.
Jn	9:25	that though I was blind, now I **s**."
1 Cor	13:12	we **s** in a mirror, dimly,
1 Jn	3: 2	for we will **s** him as he is.
Rev	1: 7	the clouds; every eye will **s** him,

SEED → SEEDS, SEEDTIME

Isa	6:13	The holy **s** is its stump.
Mt	17:20	have faith the size of a mustard **s**,
1 Pet	1:23	of perishable but of imperishable **s**,

SEEDS → SEED

| Mt | 13: 8 | Other **s** fell on good soil |
| Mk | 4:31 | the smallest of all the **s** on earth; |

SEEK

1 Chr	28: 9	If you **s** him, he will be found by
Ps	34:10	those who **s** the LORD lack no good
	119:10	With my whole heart I **s** you;
Isa	55: 6	**S** the LORD while he may be found,
	65: 1	found by those who did not **s** me.
Sir	2:16	who fear the Lord **s** to please him,
Lk	19:10	came to **s** out and to save
Heb	11: 6	that he rewards those who **s** him.

SEEMS

| Prov | 16:25 | there is a way that **s** to be right, |
| Heb | 12: 11 | discipline always **s** painful rather |

SEEN → SEE

Jn	1:18	No one has ever **s** God.
	14: 9	Whoever has **s** me has **s** the Father.
	20:29	Blessed are those who have not **s**
1 Pet	1: 8	you have not **s** him, you love him;

SELF-CONTROL → SELF-CONTROLLED

| 1 Cor | 7: 5 | tempt you because of your lack of **s**. |
| 2 Pet | 1: 6 | with **s**, and **s** with endurance, |

SELF-CONTROLLED → SELF-CONTROL

| Titus | 1: 8 | prudent, upright, devout, and **s**. |
| | 2: 5 | to be **s**, chaste, good managers |

SELFISH → SELFISHNESS

Ps	119:36	to your decrees, and not to **s** gain.
Phil	1:17	proclaim Christ out of **s** ambition,
Jas	3:14	if you have bitter envy and **s**

SELFISHNESS* → SELFISH

| 2 Cor | 12:20 | anger, **s**, slander, gossip, conceit, |

SELL

| Prov | 23:23 | Buy truth, and do not **s** it; |
| Mk | 10: 21 | **s** what you own, and give the money |

SEND → SENT

| Ex | 33: 2 | I will **s** an angel before you, |

Isa	6: 8	And I said, "Here am I; **s** me!"
Jn	3:17	God did not **s** the Son into the world to
	14:26	whom the Father will **s** in my name,

SENNACHERIB

Assyrian king; siege of Jerusalem was overthrown by the LORD following prayer of Hezekiah and Isaiah (2 Kings 18:13-19:37; 2 Chr 32:1-21; Isa 36-37).

SENT → SEND

Ex	3:14	'I AM has **s** me to you.'"
Lk	10:16	rejects me rejects the one who **s** me.
Jn	17:18	As you have **s** me into the world,
	20:21	the Father has **s** me, so I send you."
1 Jn	4:10	and **s** his Son to be the atoning

SEPARATE → SEPARATED

Mt	19: 6	joined together, let no one **s**."
Rom	8:35	will **s** us from the love of Christ?
1 Cor	7:10	wife should not **s** from her husband

SEPARATED → SEPARATE

| Lev | 20:24 | I have **s** you from the peoples. |
| Heb | 7:26 | **s** from sinners, and exalted above |

SERPENT → SERPENTS

Gen	3: 1	the **s** was more crafty than any other
Num	21: 9	Moses made a **s** of bronze,
2 Cor	11: 3	the **s** deceived Eve by its cunning,
Rev	20: 2	He seized the dragon, that ancient **s**,

SERPENTS → SERPENT

| Mt | 10:16 | wise as **s** and innocent as doves. |

SERVANT → SERVANTS

Ps	19:11	Moreover by them is your **s** warned;
Isa	42: 1	Here is my **s**, whom I uphold,
	43:10	and my **s** whom I have chosen,
	53:11	my **s**, shall make many righteous,
Zech	3: 8	going to bring my **s** the Branch.
Lk	1:38	"Here am I, the **s** of the Lord;
Acts	3:13	has glorified his **s** Jesus.
2 Tim	2:24	Lord's **s** must not be quarrelsome
Heb	3: 5	faithful in all God's house as a **s**,

SERVANTS → SERVANT

2 Kings	17:23	as he had foretold through all his **s**
Jn	15:15	I do not call you **s** any longer,
1 Pet	2:16	As **s** of God, live as free people,
Rev	7: 3	marked the **s** of our God with a seal

SERVE

Josh	24:15	my household, we will **s** the LORD."
1 Sam	12:20	but **s** the LORD with all your heart;
Mt	6:24	You cannot **s** God and wealth.
Mk	10:45	Son of Man came not to be served but to **s**,
1 Pet	4:10	**s** one another with whatever gift

SETH

| Gen | 4:25 | she bore a son and named him **S**, |

SETTLE

| Gen | 26: 2 | **s** in the land that I shall show you. |
| Num | 33:53 | possession of the land and **s** in it, |

SEVEN → SEVENTH

Gen	7: 2	with you **s** pairs of all clean animals,
Ex	25:37	You shall make the **s** lamps for it;
Josh	6: 4	march around the city **s** times,
Dan	9:25	prince, there shall be **s** weeks;
Mt	18:22	"Not **s** times, but, I tell you, seventy-seven
Rev	1:12	turning I saw **s** golden lampstands,
	5: 1	and on the back, sealed with **s** seals;
	8: 2	I saw the **s** angels who stand before
	12: 3	a great red dragon, with **s** heads and
	15: 1	**s** angels with **s** plagues,

SEVENTH → SEVEN

Gen	2: 2	on the **s** day God finished the work
Ex	20:10	the **s** day is a sabbath to the LORD
	23:11	but the **s** year you shall let it rest
Heb	4: 4	God rested on the **s** day from all his

SEVENTY → SEVENTY-SEVEN

Gen	46:27	who came into Egypt were **s**.
2 Chr	36:21	it kept sabbath, to fulfill **s** years.
Jer	25:12	Then after **s** years are completed,
Dan	9:24	**S** weeks are decreed for your people

SEVENTY-SEVEN → SEVENTY

| Mt | 18:22 | "Not seven times, but, I tell you, **s** |

SEXUAL

| 1 Cor | 10: 8 | not indulge in **s** immorality as some |

SHADOW

2 Kings	20:11	brought the **s** back the ten intervals,
Ps	17: 8	hide me in the **s** of your wings,
	91: 1	who abide in the **s** of the Almighty,
Mt	4:16	and **s** of death light has dawned."
Col	2:17	are only a **s** of what is to come,

SHADRACH → =HANANIAH

Hebrew exile to Babylon; name changed from Hananiah (Dan 1:6-7). Refused defilement by food (Dan 1:8-20). Refused to worship idol (Dan 3:1-18); saved from furnace (Dan 3:19-30).

SHALLUM

King of Israel (2 Kings 15:10-16).

SHALMANESER

King of Assyria; conquered and deported Israel (2 Kings 17:3-4; 18:9; Tob 1:2).

SHAME → ASHAMED, SHAMEFUL

Ps	69: 6	who hope in you be put to **s** because
Ezek	39:26	They shall forget their **s**, and all
Dan	12: 2	some to **s** and everlasting contempt.
1 Cor	1:27	foolish in the world to **s** the wise;
Heb	12: 2	endured the cross, disregarding its **s**,
1 Jn	2:28	be put to **s** before him at his coming.

SHAMEFUL → SHAME

| 2 Cor | 4: 2 | We have renounced the **s** things |
| Eph | 5:12 | For it is **s** even to mention |

SHAMGAR*

Judge; killed 600 Philistines (Judg 3:31; 5:6).

SHARE

Num	18:20	I am your **s** and your possession
Lk	3:11	"Whoever has two coats must **s**
Rom	15:27	for if the Gentiles have come to **s**
Col	1:12	to **s** in the inheritance of the saints
Heb	12:10	in order that we may **s** his holiness.
Jude	1: 3	to you about the salvation we **s**,

SHARP → SHARPENS, SHARPER

| Prov | 5: 4 | **s** as a two-edged sword. |
| Rev | 19:15 | a **s** sword with which to strike down |

SHARPENS → SHARP

| Prov | 27:17 | Iron **s** iron, and one person **s** |

SHARPER* → SHARP

| Heb | 4:12 | **s** than any two-edged sword, |

SHEBA

1. Benjamite; rebelled against David (2 Sam 20).
2. Queen of Sheba (1 Kings 10; 2 Chr 9; Mt 12:42; Lk 11:31).

SHECHEM

1. Raped Jacob's daughter Dinah; killed (Gen 34).
2. City where Joshua renewed the covenant (Josh 24). Abimelech as king (Judg 9).

SHED → BLOODSHED, SHEDDING

Gen	9: 6	shall that person's blood be **s**;
Prov	6:17	and hands that **s** innocent blood,
Mt	23:35	may come all the righteous blood **s**
Rev	16: 6	**s** the blood of saints and prophets,

SHEDDING → SHED

| Heb | 9:22 | without the **s** of blood there is no |
| | 12: 4 | resisted to the point of **s** your blood. |

SHEEP → SHEEPFOLD

1 Kings	22:17	like **s** that have no shepherd;
Ps	100: 3	people, and the **s** of his pasture.
Isa	53: 6	All we like **s** have gone astray;
Ezek	34:15	myself will be the shepherd of my **s**,
Zech	13: 7	shepherd, that the **s** may be scattered;
Mt	9:36	like **s** without a shepherd.
Lk	15: 4	a hundred **s** and losing one of them,
Jn	10: 7	I am the gate for the **s**.
	10:15	And I lay down my life for the **s**.
Heb	13:20	the great shepherd of the **s**,
1 Pet	2:25	For you were going astray like **s**,

SHEEPFOLD → SHEEP
Jn 10: 1 anyone who does not enter the **s** by the gate

SHELTER
Ps 91: 1 who live in the **s** of the Most High,
Rev 7:15 is seated on the throne will **s** them.

SHEM
Son of Noah (Gen 5:32; 6:10). Blessed (Gen 9:26). Descendants (Gen 10:21-31; 11:10-32; Lk 3:36).

SHEOL
Num 16:30 and they go down alive into **S,**
Job 26: 6 **S** is naked before God,
Ps 139: 8 if I make my bed in **S,** you are there.
Isa 28:15 and with **S** we have an agreement;
Hos 13:14 O **S,** where is your destruction?

SHEPHERD → SHEPHERDS
2 Sam 7: 7 whom I commanded to **s** my people
Ps 23: 1 The LORD is my **s,** I shall not want.
Eccl 12:11 sayings that are given by one **s.**
Isa 40:11 He will feed his flock like a **s;**
Mt 2: 6 ruler who is to **s** my people Israel.'"
26:31 strike the **s,** and the sheep of the flock
Jn 10:11 "I am the good **s.**
Heb 13:20 the great **s** of the sheep,
1 Pet 5: 4 And when the chief **s** appears,

SHEPHERDS → SHEPHERD
Ezek 34: 2 prophesy against the **s** of Israel:
Lk 2: 8 there were **s** living in the fields,

SHIELD
Gen 15: 1 I am your **s;** your reward shall be
Ps 7:10 God is my **s,** who saves the upright
Eph 6:16 With all of these, take the **s** of faith,

SHILOH
1 Sam 1:24 to the house of the LORD at **S;**

SHIMEI
Cursed David (2 Sam 16:5-14); spared (2 Sam 19:16-23). Killed by Solomon (1 Kings 2:8-9, 36-46).

SHINE → SHINES, SHINING
Num 6:25 LORD make his face to **s** upon you,
Ps 4: 6 light of your face **s** on us, O LORD!"
Isa 60: 1 **s;** for your light has come,
Dan 12: 3 Those who are wise shall **s** like the
Mt 5:16 let your light **s** before others,
Eph 5:14 the dead, and Christ will **s** on you."

SHINES → SHINE
Jn 1: 5 The light **s** in the darkness,

SHINING → SHINE
2 Pet 1:19 to this as to a lamp **s** in a dark place,
1 Jn 2: 8 and the true light is already **s.**

SHORT
Isa 59: 1 the LORD's hand is not too **s** to save,
Mt 24:22 if those days had not been cut **s,**
Rom 3:23 sinned and fall **s** of the glory of God;

SHOUT
Ps 47: 1 **s** to God with loud songs of joy.
Zech 9: 9 **S** aloud, O daughter Jerusalem!
Lk 19:40 were silent, the stones would **s** out."

SHOW → SHOWED
Gen 12: 1 to the land that I will **s** you.
Ex 33:18 Moses said, "**S** me your glory,
Ps 85: 7 **S** us your steadfast love, O LORD,
Jn 14: 8 said to him, "Lord, **s** us the Father,
1 Cor 12:31 will **s** you a still more excellent way
Rev 4: 1 I will **s** you what must take place

SHOWED → SHOW
Deut 34: 1 the LORD **s** him the whole land;
Jn 20:20 he **s** them his hands and his side.

SHOWERS
Deut 32: 2 rain on grass, like **s** on new growth.
Ezek 34:26 they shall be **s** of blessing.

SHUT
Isa 22:22 he shall open, and no one shall **s;**
Dan 6:22 God sent his angel and **s** the lions'
Rev 3: 7 who opens and no one will **s,**

SICK → SICKNESS
Mt 8:16 and cured all who were **s.**
9:12 of a physician, but those who are **s.**
Jas 5:14 Are any among you **s?**

SICKLE
Joel 3:13 Put in the **s,** for the harvest is ripe.
Rev 14:14 and a sharp **s** in his hand!

SICKNESS → SICK
Ex 23:25 I will take **s** away from among you.
Mt 4:23 and curing every disease and every **s**

SIDE → ASIDE
Ps 91: 7 A thousand may fall at your **s,**
124: 1 the LORD who was on our **s**
Jn 19:34 soldiers pierced his **s** with a spear,

SIFT
Isa 30:28 to **s** the nations with the sieve of
Lk 22:31 Satan has demanded to **s** all of you

SIGHT → SEE
Gen 6:11 the earth was corrupt in God's **s,**
Ps 72:14 and precious is their blood in his **s.**
Mt 11: 5 blind receive their **s,** the lame walk,
2 Cor 5: 7 for we walk by faith, not by **s.**
1 Pet 3: 4 which is very precious in God's **s.**

SIGN → SIGNS
Gen 9:12 the **s** of the covenant that I make
17:11 a **s** of the covenant between me
Isa 7:14 the Lord himself will give you a **s.**
Mt 24: 3 the **s** of your coming and of the end
Mk 8:12 does this generation ask for a **s?**

SIGNS → SIGN
Gen 1:14 be for **s** and for seasons and for days
Ex 7: 3 I will multiply my **s** and wonders in
Dan 6:27 he works **s** and wonders in heaven
Mt 16: 3 cannot interpret the **s** of the times.
Jn 20:30 Jesus did many other **s** in the
1 Cor 1:22 Jews demand **s** and Greeks desire
Rev 16:14 demonic spirits, performing **s,**

SILAS
Prophet (Acts 15:22-32); co-worker with Paul on second missionary journey (Acts 16-18; 2 Cor 1:19). Co-writer with Paul (1 Thess 1:1; 2 Thess 1:1); Peter (1 Pet 5:12).

SILENT
Isa 53: 7 a sheep that before its shearers is **s,**
Zeph 1: 7 Be **s** before the LORD GOD!
Mk 14:61 But he was **s** and did not answer.
1 Cor 14:34 women should be **s** in the churches.

SILVER
Ps 66:10 you have tried us as **s** is tried.
Prov 8:10 Take my instruction instead of **s,**
Isa 48:10 I have refined you, but not like **s;**
Zech 13: 9 refine them as one refines **s,**
Mt 26:15 They paid him thirty pieces of **s.**
Acts 3: 6 But Peter said, "I have no **s** or gold,
1 Cor 3:12 on the foundation with gold, **s,**

SIMEON → =SIMON
1. Son of Jacob by Leah (Gen 29:33; 35:23; 1 Chr 2:1). With Levi killed Shechem for rape of Dinah (Gen 34:25-29). Held hostage by Joseph in Egypt (Gen 42:24-43:23). Tribe of blessed (Gen 49:5-7), numbered (Num 1:23; 26:14), allotted land (Josh 19:1-9; Ezek 48:24), 12,000 from (Rev 7:7).
2. Godly Jew who blessed the infant Jesus (2:25-35).
3. See Peter (Acts 15:14; 2 Pet 1:1).

SIMON → =PETER, =SIMEON
1. See Peter.
2. Apostle, the Zealot (Mt 10:4; Mk 3:18; Lk 6:15; Acts 1:13).
3. Samaritan sorcerer (Acts 8:9-24).

SIMPLE
Ps 19: 7 are sure, making wise the **s;**
Prov 1:22 O **s** ones, will you love being **s?**
14:15 The **s** believe everything,

SIN → SINFUL, SINNED, SINNER, SINNERS, SINS
Gen 4: 7 not do well, **s** is lurking at the door;
Ex 32:32 if you will only forgive their **s**—
Num 32:23 and be sure your **s** will find you out.
1 Kings 8:46 "If they **s** against you—

2 Chr	7:14	forgive their **s** and heal their land.
Tob	12:10	but those who commit **s**
Ps	119:11	so that I may not **s** against you.
Wis	10:13	but delivered him from **s**.
Sir	3:30	so almsgiving atones for **s**.
Isa	53:12	yet he bore the **s** of many,
Dan	9:20	confessing my **s** and the **s** of my
Mt	5:29	If your right eye causes you to **s**,
Jn	1:29	who takes away the **s** of the world!
Rom	5:12	as **s** came into the world through one man,—
	6:23	For the wages of **s** is death,
2 Cor	5:21	made him to be **s** who knew no **s**,
Heb	4:15	tested as we are, yet without **s**.
1 Jn	1: 7	Jesus his Son cleanses us from all **s**.

SINAI → =HOREB

Ex	19:20	the Lord descended upon Mount S,
Ps	68:17	the Lord came from S into the holy
Gal	4:25	Now Hagar is Mount S in Arabia

SINFUL → SIN

1 Macc	1:10	From them came forth a **s** root,
Lk	5: 8	from me, Lord, for I am a **s** man!"
Rom	8: 3	Son in the likeness of **s** flesh,

SING → SINGERS, SONG, SONGS, SUNG

Ex	15: 1	"I will **s** to the Lord,
Jdt	16:13	I will **s** to my God a new song:
Ps	47: 6	**S** praises to God, **s** praises;
Isa	5: 1	**s** for my beloved my love-song
Dan	3:58	**s** praise to him and highly exalt him
1 Cor	14:15	I will **s** praise with the spirit,
Col	3:16	gratitude in your hearts **s** psalms,
Rev	5: 9	They **s** a new song:

SINGERS → SING

1 Chr	15:16	to appoint their kindred as the **s**
Ezra	2:70	and the **s**, the gatekeepers,

SINGLE

Mt	6:27	worrying add a **s** hour to your span
Rev	21:21	each of the gates is a **s** pearl,

SINNED → SIN

Num	14:40	Lord has promised, for we have **s**."
Ps	51: 4	Against you, you alone, have I **s**,
Sir	18:21	and when you have **s**, repent.
Lam	5: 7	Our ancestors **s**; they are no more,
Dan	9: 5	we have **s** and done wrong,
Rom	3:23	all have **s** and fall short of the glory of God;
1 Jn	1:10	If we say that we have not **s**,

SINNER → SIN

Lk	15: 7	over one **s** who repents than
Jas	5:20	that whoever brings back a **s**

SINNERS → SIN

Ps	1: 1	or take the path that **s** tread,
Prov	23:17	Do not let your heart envy **s**,
Lk	6:33	For even **s** do the same.
Rom	5: 8	we still were **s** Christ died for us.
1 Tim	1:15	Jesus came into the world to save **s**

SINS → SIN

1 Sam	2:25	but if someone **s** against the Lord,
Ps	103:10	not deal with us according to our **s**,
Sir	2:11	he forgives **s** and saves
Isa	1:18	your **s** are like scarlet, they shall be
Ezek	18: 4	only the person who **s** that shall die.
Mic	7:19	cast all our **s** into the depths of the
Mt	9: 6	has authority on earth to forgive **s**"—
Mk	1: 5	the river Jordan, confessing their **s**.
Lk	11: 4	forgive us our **s**, for we ourselves
Acts	3:19	to God so that your **s** may be wiped
1 Cor	15: 3	Christ died for our **s** in accordance
Heb	9:28	offered once to bear the **s** of many,
1 Jn	1: 9	If we confess our **s**, he who is faithful
Rev	1: 5	loves us and freed us from our **s**

SISTER

Gen	12:13	Say you are my **s**, so that it may go
	20: 2	of his wife Sarah, "She is my **s**."
Prov	7: 4	Say to wisdom, "You are my **s**,"
Mk	3:35	the will of God is my brother and **s**

SIT → SAT, SITS

Ps	1: 1	or **s** in the seat of scoffers;

Ps	110: 1	says to my lord, "**S** at my right hand
Jer	33:17	never lack a man to **s** on the throne
Mt	20:23	to **s** at my right hand and at my left,
Heb	1:13	"**S** at my right hand until I make

SITS → SIT

Ps	2: 4	He who **s** in the heavens laughs;
Isa	28: 6	to the one who **s** in judgment,

SIX

Ex	20: 9	**S** days you shall labor and do all
Prov	6:16	are **s** things that the Lord hates,
Isa	6: 2	above him; each had **s** wings:
Rev	4: 8	each of them with **s** wings,

SKILL

Ex	28: 3	whom I have endowed with **s**,
1 Kings	7:14	he was full of **s**, intelligence,

SKIN

Job	2: 4	Satan answered the Lord, "**S** for **s**!
	19:26	after my **s** has been thus destroyed,
Jer	13:23	Can Ethiopians change their **s**

SKULL

2 Kings	9:35	they found no more of her than the **s**
Mt	27:33	Golgotha (which means Place of a **S**)

SKY

Deut	28:23	**s** over your head shall be bronze,
Mt	16: 3	to interpret the appearance of the **s**,
Rev	6:14	The **s** vanished like a scroll rolling

SLANDER → SLANDERED

Ps	15: 3	who do not **s** with their tongue,
Prov	10:18	and whoever utters **s** is a fool.
Mt	15:19	fornication, theft, false witness, **s**.
1 Pet	2: 1	all guile, insincerity, envy, and all **s**.

SLANDERED → SLANDER

1 Cor	4:13	when **s**, we speak kindly.

SLAUGHTER → SLAUGHTERED

Prov	7:22	and goes like an ox to the **s**,
Isa	53: 7	like a lamb that is led to the **s**,
Zech	11: 4	a shepherd of the flock doomed to **s**.
Acts	8:32	"Like a sheep he was led to the **s**,

SLAUGHTERED → SLAUGHTER

Rev	5: 6	a Lamb standing as if it had been **s**,
	6: 9	who had been **s** for the word of God

SLAVE → ENSLAVE, ENSLAVED, SLAVERY, SLAVES

Gen	21:10	Cast out this **s** woman with her son;
Mk	10:44	first among you must be **s** of all.
Jn	8:34	who commits sin is a **s** to sin.
Gal	3:28	there is no longer **s** or free,
Phil	2: 7	taking the form of a **s**,
Philem	1:16	no longer as a **s** but more than a **s**, a beloved brother—

SLAVERY → SLAVE

Ex	20: 2	out of the house of **s**;
Rom	7:14	of the flesh, sold into **s** under sin.
	8:15	you did not receive a spirit of **s** to fall back
Gal	5: 1	do not submit again to a yoke of **s**.

SLAVES → SLAVE

Rom	6:16	are **s** of the one whom you obey,
	6:20	When you were **s** of sin,
2 Pet	2:19	people are **s** to whatever masters

SLEEP → ASLEEP, SLEEPER, SLEEPING

Gen	2:21	God caused a deep **s** to fall upon
	15:12	a deep **s** fell upon Abram,
Ps	121: 4	keeps Israel will neither slumber nor **s**.
Dan	12: 2	Many of those who **s** in the dust of

SLEEPER → SLEEP

Eph	5:14	"**S**, awake! Rise from the dead,

SLEEPING → SLEEP

Mt	9:24	for the girl is not dead but **s**."
	26:40	to the disciples and found them **s**;

SLING

1 Sam	17:50	over the Philistine with a **s** and a stone,

SLIP

Deut	32:35	for the time when their foot shall **s**;
Ps	37:31	their steps do not **s**.

SLOW → SLOWNESS

Ex	34: 6	merciful and gracious, **s** to anger,
Num	14:18	'The LORD is **s** to anger.
Tob	12: 6	Do not be **s** to acknowledge him.
Ps	145: 8	**s** to anger and abounding in
Sir	5: 4	for the Lord is **s** to anger.
Nah	1: 3	The LORD is **s** to anger but great in
Lk	24:25	and how **s** of heart to believe all that
2 Pet	3: 9	The Lord is not **s** about his promise,

SLOWNESS → SLOW

2 Pet	3: 9	think of **s**, but is patient with you,

SMALL → SMALLEST

Jas	3: 5	So also the tongue is a **s** member,

SMALLEST → SMALL

Mk	4:31	is the **s** of all the seeds on earth;

SMOKE → SMOKING

Ex	19:18	Now Mount Sinai was wrapped in **s**,
Isa	6: 4	and the house filled with **s**.
Joel	2:30	blood and fire and columns of **s**.
Rev	15: 8	with **s** from the glory of God and

SMOKING → SMOKE

Gen	15:17	**s** fire pot and a flaming torch passed
Ex	20:18	of the trumpet, and the mountain **s**,

SNAKE

Ex	4: 3	and it became a **s**; and Moses drew
Lk	11:11	will give a **s** instead of a fish?

SNARE

Ex	23:33	it will surely be a **s** to you.
Judg	2: 3	their gods shall be a **s** to you."

SNOW

Ps	51: 7	and I shall be whiter than **s**.
Isa	1:18	sins are like scarlet, they shall be like **s;**
Dan	7: 9	his clothing was white as **s,**
Rev	1:14	as white wool, white as **s;**

SOBER

1 Thess	5: 6	but let us keep awake and be **s;**
2 Tim	4: 5	always be **s**, endure suffering,

SODOM

Gen	19:24	rained on **S** and Gomorrah sulfur
Isa	1: 9	we would have been like **S,**
Lk	10:12	it will be more tolerable for **S** than
Rev	11: 8	city that is prophetically called **S**

SOLDIERS

Mt	28:12	give a large sum of money to the **s,**
Jn	19:23	When the **s** had crucified Jesus,

SOLID

1 Cor	3: 2	I fed you with milk, not **s** food,
Heb	5:14	But **s** food is for the mature,

SOLOMON

Son of David by Bathsheba; king of Judah (2 Sam 12:24; 1 Chr 3:5, 10). Appointed king by David (1 Kings 1); adversaries Adonijah, Joab, Shimei killed by Benaiah (1 Kings 2). Asked for wisdom (1 Kings 3; 2 Chr 1). Judged between two prostitutes (1 Kings 3:16-28). Built temple (1 Kings 5-7; 2 Chr 2-5); prayer of dedication (1 Kings 8; 2 Chr 6). Visited by Queen of Sheba (1 Kings 10; 2 Chr 9). Wives turned his heart from God (1 Kings 11:1-13). Jeroboam rebelled against (1 Kings 11:26-40). Death (1 Kings 11:41-43; 2 Chr 9:29-31). Proverbs of (1 Kings 4:32; Prov 1:1; 10:1; 25:1); psalms of (Ps 72; 127); song of (Song 1:1).

SON → SONS

Gen	21: 2	conceived and bore Abraham a **s**
Ex	4:23	now I will kill your firstborn **s.'"**
2 Sam	7:14	and he shall be a **s** to me.
Ps	2: 7	He said to me, "You are my **s;**
Sir	4:10	be like a **s** of the Most High,
Isa	7:14	is with child and shall bear a **s,**
Mt	1:23	virgin shall conceive and bear a **s,**
	2:15	"Out of Egypt I have called my **s.**"
	3:17	from heaven said, "This is my **S,**
	12: 8	the **S** of Man is lord of the sabbath."
	16:16	the Messiah, the **S** of the living God."
Mk	10:45	of Man came not to be served but to
Lk	1:35	he will be called **S** of God.
	20:44	so how can he be his **s?"**

SONG → SING

Ex	15: 1	sang this **s** to the LORD:
Deut	31:21	**s** will confront them as a witness,
Ps	40: 3	He put a new **s** in my mouth,
Rev	5: 9	They sing a new **s:** "You are worthy
	15: 3	and the **s** of the Lamb:

SONGS → SING

1 Kings	4:32	his **s** numbered a thousand and five.
Ps	137: 3	"Sing us one of the **s** of Zion!"
Col	3:16	hymns, and spiritual **s** to God.

SONS → SON

Gen	6: 2	the **s** of God saw that they were fair;
	35:22	Now the **s** of Jacob were twelve.
Deut	7: 3	giving your daughters to their **s**
Acts	2:17	**s** and your daughters shall prophesy,
2 Cor	6:18	you shall be my **s** and daughters,

SOON

Isa	56: 1	for **s** my salvation will come,
Rev	22:20	says, "Surely I am coming **s.**"

SORCERERS → SORCERY

Rev	22:15	Outside are the dogs and **s** and

SORCERY → SORCERERS

Gal	5:20	**s**, enmities, strife, jealousy, anger,
Rev	18:23	all nations were deceived by your **s**.

SORROW → SORROWFUL

Esth	9:22	turned for them from **s** into gladness
Eccl	1:18	who increase knowledge increase **s**.
Isa	35:10	and **s** and sighing shall flee away.

SORROWFUL → SORROW

2 Cor	6:10	as **s**, yet always rejoicing;

SOUL → SOULS

Deut	6: 5	all your **s**, and with all your might.
Josh	22: 5	all your heart and with all your **s.**"
Ps	16: 9	heart is glad, and my **s** rejoices;
	25: 1	To you, O LORD, I lift up my **s**.
	42: 1	so my **s** longs for you, O God.
Sir	7:29	With all your **s** fear the Lord,
Mic	6: 7	fruit of my body for the sin of my **s?**"
Mt	10:28	fear him who can destroy both **s** and
Heb	4:12	piercing until it divides **s** from spirit
Jas	5:20	will save the sinner's **s** from death
3 Jn	1: 2	just as it is well with your **s**.

SOULS → SOUL

Jer	6:16	walk in it, and find rest for your **s**.
Mt	11:29	and you will find rest for your **s**.
1 Pet	2:25	the shepherd and guardian of your **s**.

SOUND

Ezek	1:24	like the **s** of mighty waters,
1 Cor	15:52	For the trumpet will **s**, and the dead
2 Tim	4: 3	will not put up with **s** doctrine,
Titus	1: 9	able both to preach with **s** doctrine
Rev	1:15	voice was like the **s** of many waters.

SOUR

Jer	31:29	"The parents have eaten **s** grapes,
Mk	15:36	filled a sponge with **s** wine,

SOVEREIGN → SOVEREIGNTY

1 Kings	4:21	Solomon was **s** over all the
Rev	6:10	"**S** Lord, holy and true, how long

SOVEREIGNTY → SOVEREIGN

Dan	4:34	For his **s** is an everlasting **s,**

SOW → SOWED, SOWER, SOWS

Ex	23:10	For six years you shall **s** your land
Eccl	11: 6	In the morning **s** your seed,
Hos	10:12	**S** for yourselves righteousness;

Jn 1:34 testified that this is the **S** of God."
3:16 loved the world that he gave his only **S,**
Rom 8:29 be conformed to the image of his **S,**
1 Thess 1:10 to wait for his **S** from heaven,
Heb 1: 2 last days he has spoken to us by a **S,**
1: 5 my **S;** today I have begotten you"?
2 Pet 1:17 saying, "This is my **S,** my Beloved,
1 Jn 4: 9 God sent his only **S** into the world
Rev 12: 5 she gave birth to a **s,** a male child,
14:14 the cloud was one like the **S** of Man,

Mt	13: 3	A sower went out to **s**.
1 Cor	15:36	**s** does not come to life unless it dies.

SOWED → SOW

Mt	13:24	to someone who **s** good seed
Lk	13:19	took and **s** in the garden;

SOWER → SOW

Mk	4:14	The **s** sows the word.

SOWS → SOW

Jn	4:37	'One **s** and another reaps.'
2 Cor	9: 6	who **s** sparingly will also reap

SPAN

Isa	40:12	marked off the heavens with a **s**,
Mt	6:27	add a single hour to your **s** of life?

SPARE

Rom	11:21	perhaps he will not **s** you.
2 Pet	2: 4	if God did not **s** the angels when

SPARROWS

Lk	12: 7	you are of more value than many **s**.

SPEAK → SPEAKING, SPEECH, SPOKE

Gen	18:27	take it upon myself to **s** to the Lord,
Num	12: 8	With him I **s** face to face—
Deut	18:20	presumes to **s** in my name a word
Job	13: 3	But I would **s** to the Almighty,
Eccl	3: 7	time to keep silence, and a time to **s**;
Sir	4:25	Never **s** against the truth,
Mt	13:13	The reason I **s** to them in parables is
Acts	2: 4	began to **s** in other languages,
1 Cor	12:30	Do all **s** in tongues?
Jas	1:19	be quick to listen, slow to **s**,

SPEAKING → SPEAK

1 Cor	14:39	and do not forbid **s** in tongues;
Eph	4:15	But **s** the truth in love,

SPEAR → SPEARS

1 Sam	19:10	to pin David to the wall with the **s**;
Jn	19:34	the soldiers pierced his side with a **s**,

SPEARS → SPEAR

Joel	3:10	and your pruning hooks into **s**;
Mic	4: 3	and their **s** into pruning hooks;

SPECK

Mt	7: 4	'Let me take the **s** out of your eye, '

SPECTACLE

1 Cor	4: 9	we have become a **s** to the world,

SPEECH → SPEAK

Ex	4:10	I am slow of **s** and slow of tongue."
Ps	19: 3	There is no **s**, nor are there words;
Sir	4:29	Do not be reckless in your **s**,
1 Tim	4:12	set the believers an example in **s**
1 Jn	3:18	let us love, not in word or **s**,

SPICES

Ex	25: 6	**s** for the anointing oil and for
Jn	19:40	wrapped it with the **s** in linen cloths,

SPIES → SPY

Num	13:32	we have gone through as **s**
Josh	2: 1	two men secretly from Shittim as **s**,

SPIRIT → SPIRITS, SPIRITUAL

Gen	6: 3	My **s** shall not abide in mortals forever,
Num	11:25	**s** rested upon them, they prophesied.
2 Kings	2: 9	inherit a double share of your **s**."
Neh	9:20	You gave your good **s** to instruct
Job	33: 4	The **s** of God has made me,
Ps	31: 5	Into your hand I commit my **s**;
	51:17	acceptable to God is a broken **s**;
Prov	16:18	and a haughty **s** before a fall.
Isa	42: 1	I have put my **s** upon him;
Ezek	36:26	and a new **s** I will put within you;
Joel	2:28	I will pour out my **s** on all flesh;
Mt	1:18	to be with child from the Holy **S**.
	5: 3	"Blessed are the poor in **s**,
	12:31	against the **S** will not be forgiven.
	26:41	the **s** indeed is willing, but the flesh
Mk	1: 8	will baptize you with the Holy **S**."
Jn	3: 5	without being born of water and **S**.
	4:24	God is **s**, and those who worship him must worship in **s** and truth."

Jn	6:63	It is the **s** that gives life;
	14:26	But the Advocate, the Holy **S**,
Acts	2: 4	of them were filled with the Holy **S**
	2:38	will receive the gift of the Holy **S**.
Rom	8: 9	not in the flesh; you are in the **S**,
	8:26	the **S** helps us in our weakness;
1 Cor	6:19	your body is a temple of the Holy **S**
	12: 4	are varieties of gifts, but the same **S**;
2 Cor	3: 6	the letter kills, but the **S** gives life.
Gal	4: 6	sent the **S** of his Son into our hearts,
	5:22	the fruit of the **S** is love, joy, peace,
Eph	1:13	the seal of the promised Holy **S**;
	2:18	both of us have access in one **S**
	4:30	do not grieve the Holy **S** of God,
	5:18	but be filled with the **S**,
1 Thess	5:19	Do not quench the **S**.
Heb	4:12	piercing until it divides soul from **s**,
1 Pet	3: 4	lasting beauty of a gentle and quiet **s**
1 Jn	4: 1	Beloved, do not believe every **s**,
Rev	1:10	I was in the **s** on the Lord's day,

SPIRITS → SPIRIT

Num	16:22	the God of the **s** of all flesh,
Deut	18:11	or who consults ghosts or **s**,
Lk	4:36	power he commands the unclean **s**,
1 Cor	12:10	to another the discernment of **s**,
Gal	4: 3	we were enslaved to the elemental **s**
Rev	1: 4	seven **s** who are before his throne,

SPIRITUAL → SPIRIT

Rom	7:14	For we know that the law is **s**;
1 Cor	2:13	interpreting **s** things to those who are **s**.
	12: 1	Now concerning **s** gifts,
	14: 1	Pursue love and strive for the **s** gifts,
	15:46	the **s** that is first, but the physical,
Eph	1: 3	every **s** blessing in the heavenly
Col	1: 9	of God's will in all **s** wisdom
1 Pet	2: 2	infants, long for the pure, **s** milk,
	2: 5	yourselves be built into a **s** house,

SPIT

Mk	14:65	began to **s** on him, to blindfold him,
Rev	3:16	am about to **s** you out of my mouth.

SPLENDOR

1 Chr	16:29	Worship the Lord in holy **s**;
Eph	5:27	to present the church to himself in **s**,

SPOKE → SPEAK

Mk	4:33	many such parables he **s** the word
1 Cor	13:11	When I was a child, I **s** like a child,
Heb	1: 1	Long ago God **s** to our ancestors in
2 Pet	1:21	moved by the Holy Spirit **s** from

SPOT

Eph	5:27	without a **s** or wrinkle or anything
2 Pet	3:14	at peace, without **s** or blemish;

SPRING

Isa	45: 8	earth open, that salvation may **s** up,
Jn	4:14	a **s** of water gushing up to eternal life."
Rev	21: 6	from the **s** of the water of life.

SPRINKLE → SPRINKLED

Num	8: 7	**s** the water of purification on them,
Ezek	36:25	I will **s** clean water upon you,

SPRINKLED → SPRINKLE

Lev	8:11	He **s** some of it on the altar seven
Heb	10:22	with our hearts **s** clean from an evil
1 Pet	1: 2	and to be **s** with his blood:

SPY → SPIES

Num	13: 2	men to **s** out the land of Canaan,
Josh	6:25	whom Joshua sent to **s** out Jericho.

STAFF

Gen	49:10	the ruler's **s** from between his feet,
Ex	4: 4	and it became a **s** in his hand—
Num	17: 6	the **s** of Aaron was among theirs.
Ps	23: 4	your rod and your **s**—they comfort me.
Zech	11:10	I took my **s** Favor and broke it,

STAND → STANDING

Ex	14:13	"Do not be afraid, **s** firm,
Job	19:25	at the last he will **s** upon the earth;
Ps	1: 5	wicked will not **s** in the judgment,
Isa	7: 9	If you do not **s** firm in faith,

Mt	12:25	house divided against itself will **s.**
Rom	14: 4	for the Lord is able to make them **s.**
	14:10	all s before the judgment seat of God.
Eph	6:11	may be able to s against the wiles of

STANDARDS
Jn	8:15	You judge by human **s**; I judge no
1 Cor	1:26	of you were wise by human **s**,

STANDING → STAND
1 Cor	10:12	So if you think you are **s**,
Jas	5: 9	See, the Judge is **s** at the doors!
Rev	3:20	I am **s** at the door, knocking;

STAR → STARS
Num	24:17	a **s** shall come out of Jacob,
Isa	14:12	are fallen from heaven, O Day **S**,
Mt	2: 2	For we observed his **s** at its rising,
2 Pet	1:19	day dawns and the morning **s** rises
Rev	9: 1	saw a **s** that had fallen from heaven
	22:16	of David, the bright morning **s.**"

STARS → STAR
Gen	1:16	to rule the night—and the **s.**
Job	38: 7	when the morning **s** sang together
Ps	148: 3	praise him, all you shining **s**!
Dan	12: 3	like the **s** forever and ever.
Phil	2:15	you shine like **s** in the world.
Rev	1:16	In his right hand he held seven **s**,
	12: 4	a third of the **s** of heaven and threw

STATUE
Dan	2:31	there was a great **s.**

STATUTE → STATUTES
Lev	16:29	This shall be a **s** to you forever:
Num	19:21	It shall be a perpetual **s** for them.

STATUTES → STATUTE
Gen	26: 5	commandments, my **s**, and my laws.
Deut	4: 1	give heed to the **s** and ordinances
Neh	9:13	good **s** and commandments,
Ps	119: 8	I will observe your **s**;

STEADFAST
Ex	34: 6	abounding in **s** love and faithfulness
Num	14:18	and abounding in **s** love,
2 Sam	7:15	I will not take my **s** love from him,
Ps	57: 7	My heart is **s**, O God, my heart is **s.**
	136: 1	for his **s** love endures forever.
Heb	6:19	a sure and **s** anchor of the soul,
1 Pet	5: 9	Resist him, **s** in your faith,

STEAL
Ex	20:15	You shall not **s.**
Mt	6:19	and where thieves break in and **s**;
Jn	10:10	The thief comes only to **s** and kill

STEPHEN*
Early church leader (Acts 6:5). Arrested (Acts 6:8-15). Speech to Sanhedrin (Acts 7). Stoned (Acts 7:54-60; 8:2; 11:19; 22:20).

STEPS
Prov	16: 9	but the LORD directs the **s.**
1 Pet	2:21	so that you should follow in his **s.**

STIFF-NECKED → NECK
Ex	32: 9	"I have seen this people, how **s**
Acts	7:51	"You **s** people, uncircumcised in

STILL
Ex	14:14	and you have only to keep **s.**"
Josh	10:13	sun stood **s**, and the moon stopped,
Ps	46:10	"Be **s**, and know that I am God!
Mk	4:39	said to the sea, "Peace! Be **s**!"
Rom	5: 8	we **s** were sinners Christ died for us.
Heb	11: 4	but through his faith he **s** speaks.

STING
1 Cor	15:55	Where, O death, is your **s**?"

STONE → CORNERSTONE, MILLSTONE, STONED, STONES
Gen	28:18	the **s** that he had put under his head
Ex	28:10	six of their names on the one **s**,
	31:18	tablets of **s**, written with the finger of
1 Sam	17:50	the Philistine with a sling and a **s**,
Ps	118:22	The **s** that the builders rejected has

Isa	28:16	in Zion a foundation **s**, a tested **s**,
Ezek	36:26	from your body the heart of **s**
Mt	4: 6	will not dash your foot against a **s.**'"
Mk	12:10	'The **s** that the builders rejected has
	16: 3	"Who will roll away the **s** for us
Rom	9:32	have stumbled over the stumbling **s**,
2 Cor	3: 3	not on tablets of **s** but on tablets
1 Pet	2: 4	living **s**, though rejected by mortals
Rev	2:17	and I will give a white **s**,

STONED → STONE
2 Chr	24:21	by command of the king they **s** him
Acts	14:19	Then they **s** Paul and dragged him
Heb	11:37	**s** to death, they were sawn in two,

STONES → STONE
Ex	28:21	twelve **s** with names corresponding
Josh	4: 3	'Take twelve **s** from here out of the
1 Sam	17:40	chose five smooth **s** from the wadi,
Mt	3: 9	God is able from these **s** to raise
Lk	19:40	were silent, the **s** would shout out."
1 Cor	3:12	precious **s**, wood, hay, straw—
1 Pet	2: 5	like living **s**, let yourselves be built

STORE → SHOREHOUSE, STORING
Prov	7: 1	and **s** up my commandments
Mt	6:19	Do not **s** up for yourselves treasures

STOREHOUSE → HOUSE, STORING
Deut	28:12	LORD will open for you his rich **s**,
Mal	3:10	Bring the full tithe into the **s**,

STORING* → STORE
Rom	2: 5	you are **s** up wrath for yourself
1 Tim	6:19	**s** up for themselves the treasure of

STRAIGHT
Prov	3: 6	and he will make **s** your paths.
Sir	2: 6	make your ways **s**, and hope in him.
Isa	40: 3	**s** in the desert a highway for our God.
Mt	3: 3	way of the Lord, make his paths **s**.'"
Acts	9:11	Get up and go to the street called **S**,

STRANGE → STRANGER, STRANGERS
Deut	32:16	They made him jealous with **s** gods,
1 Cor	14:21	"By people of **s** tongues and by the

STRANGER → STRANGE
Deut	10:19	You shall also love the **s**,
Mt	25:35	I was a **s** and you welcomed me,

STRANGERS → STRANGE
Deut	10:19	for you were **s** in the land of Egypt.
Rom	12:13	extend hospitality to **s**.
Eph	2:12	and **s** to the covenants of promise,
Heb	11:13	They confessed that they were **s**

STRAW
Ex	5:10	says Pharaoh, 'I will not give you **s**.
1 Cor	3:12	precious stones, wood, hay, **s**—

STRAY → ASTRAY
Ps	119:10	not let me **s** from your commandments.
Prov	22: 6	and when old, they will not **s**.

STREAM → STREAMS
Isa	2: 2	all the nations shall **s** to it.
Am	5:24	righteousness like an ever-flowing **s**

STREAMS → STREAM
Ps	1: 3	like trees planted by **s** of water,
	42: 1	As a deer longs for flowing **s**,

STREET
Prov	1:20	Wisdom cries out in the **s**;
Mt	6: 5	the synagogues and at the **s** corners,
Rev	21:21	and the **s** of the city is pure gold,

STRENGTH → STRONG
Ex	15: 2	The LORD is my **s** and my might,
1 Chr	16:11	Seek the LORD and his **s**,
Neh	8:10	for the joy of the LORD is your **s**."
Jdt	9:11	your **s** does not depend on numbers,
1 Macc	3:19	but **s** comes from Heaven.
Ps	46: 1	God is our refuge and **s**,
	84: 7	They go from **s** to **s**;
Prov	31:25	**S** and dignity are her clothing,
Isa	40:31	for the LORD shall renew their **s**,
Mk	12:30	all your mind, and with all your **s**.'

1 Cor   1:25   God's weakness is stronger than human **s**.

STRENGTHEN → STRONG
Judg   16:28   and **s** me only this once, O God,
Ps   119:28   **s** me according to your word.
Lk   22:32   have turned back, **s** your brothers."
Heb   12:12   hands and **s** your weak knees,

STRENGTHENS → STRONG
Isa   40:29   to the faint, and **s** the powerless.
Phil   4:13   do all things through him who **s** me.

STRETCH → OUTSTRETCHED, STRETCHED
Ex   14:16   and **s** out your hand over the sea
Mk   3: 5   to the man, "**S** out your hand."

STRETCHED → STRETCH
2 Sam   24:16   angel **s** out his hand toward Jerusalem
Isa   5:25   and his hand is **s** out still.

STRIFE → STRIVE
Prov   23:29   Who has sorrow? Who has **s**?
Rom   1:29   Full of envy, murder, **s**, deceit,
Gal   5:20   enmities, **s**, jealousy, anger,

STRIKE
Gen   3:15   he will **s** your head, and you will **s**
Ex   17: 6   S the rock, and water will come out
Zech   13: 7   S the shepherd, that the sheep may
Mal   4: 6   come and **s** the land with a curse.
Mk   14:27   'I will **s** the shepherd, and the sheep
Rev   19:15   to **s** down the nations,

STRIVE → STRIFE
Mt   6:33   But **s** first for the kingdom of God
1 Cor   12:31   But **s** for the greater gifts.
2 Pet   3:14   **s** to be found by him at peace,

STRONG → STRENGTH, STRENGTHEN,
           STRENGTHENS, STRONGHOLD
Deut   31: 6   Be **s** and bold; have no fear
Josh   1: 6   Be **s** and courageous; for you shall
Ps   140: 7   O LORD, my Lord, my **s** deliverer,
Prov   18:10   The name of the LORD is a **s** tower;
Eccl   9:11   nor the battle to the **s**, nor bread to
Song   8: 6   for love is as death, passion fierce
Rom   15: 1   We who are **s** ought to put up with
1 Cor   1:27   in the world to shame the **s**;
2 Cor   12:10   whenever I am weak, then I am **s**.
Eph   6:10   be **s** in the Lord and in the strength

STRONGHOLD → STRONG
Ps   9: 9   The LORD is a **s** for the oppressed,
Nah   1: 7   a **s** in a day of trouble;

STRUGGLE
Eph   6:12   our **s** is not against enemies of
Heb   12: 4   In your **s** against sin you have not yet

STUBBORN
Deut   9: 6   for you are a **s** people.
Hos   4:16   Like a **s** heifer, Israel is **s**;

STUDY
Ezra   7:10   Ezra had set his heart to **s** the law
Eccl   12:12   much **s** is a weariness of the flesh.

STUMBLE → STUMBLING
Ps   37:24   we **s**, we shall not fall headlong,
Prov   4:12   and if you run, you will not **s**.
Mt   18: 9   And if your eye causes you to **s**,
Rom   9:33   a stone that will make people **s**,
1 Pet   2: 8   **s** because they disobey the word,

STUMBLING → STUMBLE
Ezek   14: 3   placed their iniquity as a **s** block
Mt   16:23   You are a **s** block to me;
Rom   11: 9   a **s** block and a retribution for them;
1 Cor   8: 9   not somehow become a **s** block to

STUMP
Isa   6:13   The holy seed is its **s**.
          11: 1   shall come out from the **s** of Jesse,

SUBDUE
Gen   1:28   and fill the earth and **s** it;
1 Chr   17:10   and I will **s** all your enemies.

SUBJECT → SUBJECTED
Rom   13: 1   be **s** to the governing authorities;

Gal   4:21   who desire to be **s** to the law,
Eph   5:21   **s** to one another out of reverence

SUBJECTED → SUBJECT
Rom   8:20   for the creation was **s** to futility,
1 Cor   15:28   When all things are **s** to him,

SUBMISSION* → SUBMIT
1 Tim   2:11   a woman learn in silence with full **s**.
Heb   5: 7   was heard because of his reverent **s**.

SUBMISSIVE → SUBMIT
1 Tim   3: 4   keeping his children **s** and respectful
Titus   2: 5   kind, being **s** to their husbands,

SUBMIT → SUBMISSION, SUBMISSIVE
Ps   81:11   Israel would not **s** to me.
Gal   5: 1   do not **s** again to a yoke of slavery.
Heb   13:17   Obey your leaders and **s** to them,

SUCCEED → SUCCESS, SUCCESSFUL
Prov   15:22   but with many advisers they **s**.
Eccl   10:10   but wisdom helps one to **s**.

SUCCESS → SUCCEED
Ps   118:25   O LORD, we beseech you, give us **s**!
Sir   10: 5   Human **s** is in the hand of the Lord,

SUCCESSFUL → SUCCEED
Josh   1: 7   that you may be **s** wherever you go.

SUDDENLY
Mal   3: 1   Lord whom you seek will **s** come to
Mk   13:36   find you asleep when he comes **s**.

SUFFER → SUFFERED, SUFFERING, SUFFERINGS,
           SUFFERS
Lk   22:15   this Passover with you before I **s**;
          24:46   the Messiah is to **s** and to rise from
Rom   8:17   we **s** with him so that we may also be glorified
Heb   9:26   then he would have had to **s** again
1 Pet   3:17   For it is better to **s** for doing good,

SUFFERED → SUFFER
Phil   3: 8   For his sake I have **s** the loss of all
1 Pet   2:21   because Christ also **s** for you,

SUFFERING → SUFFER
Job   2:13   they saw that his **s** was very great.
Isa   53: 3   a man of **s** and acquainted with
Mk   8:31   Son of Man must undergo great **s**,
Rom   12:12   Rejoice in hope, be patient in **s**,
Phil   1:29   but of **s** for him as well—

SUFFERINGS → SUFFER
Rom   8:18   the **s** of this present time are not
1 Pet   4:13   insofar as you are sharing Christ's **s**,

SUFFERS → SUFFER
1 Cor   12:26   If one member **s**, all suffer together

SUFFICIENT
2 Cor   12: 9   "My grace is **s** for you,

SULFUR
Gen   19:24   rained on Sodom and Gomorrah **s**
Ps   11: 6   he will rain coals of fire and **s**;
Rev   21: 8   in the lake that burns with fire and **s**,

SUMMED*
Rom   13: 9   commandment, are **s** up in this word
Gal   5:14   the whole law is **s** up in a single

SUN
Josh   10:13   And the **s** stood still,
Ps   84:11   For the LORD God is a **s** and shield;
Eccl   1: 9   there is nothing new under the **s**.
Joel   2:31   The **s** shall be turned to darkness
Mal   4: 2   the **s** of righteousness shall rise,
Mt   5:45   he makes his **s** rise on the evil and
Acts   2:20   The **s** shall be turned to darkness
Rev   1:16   his face was like the **s** shining with
          19:17   I saw an angel standing in the **s**,
          22: 5   they need no light of lamp or **s**,

SUPERIOR
Heb   1: 4   having become as much **s** to angels
          7: 7   that the inferior is blessed by the **s**.

SUPPER
Lk   22:20   he did the same with the cup after **s**,

Rev 19: 9 to the marriage **s** of the Lamb."

SUPPLICATION → SUPPLICATIONS
Ps 6: 9 The LORD has heard my **s**;
Zech 12:10 a spirit of compassion and **s**
Eph 6:18 at all times in every prayer and **s**.

SUPPLICATIONS → SUPPLICATION
1 Tim 2: 1 then, I urge that **s**, prayers,
Heb 5: 7 Jesus offered up prayers and **s**,

SUPPORT
Ps 18:18 but the LORD was my **s**.
Rom 11:18 that it is not you that **s** the root,

SURE
Num 32:23 and be **s** your sin will find you out.
Ps 19: 7 the decrees of the LORD are **s**,
Isa 28:16 a **s** foundation: "One who trusts
Heb 6:19 a **s** and steadfast anchor of the soul,

SURPASSES → SURPASSING
Sir 25:11 Fear of the Lord **s** everything;
Eph 3:19 the love of Christ that **s** knowledge,
Phil 4: 7 the peace of God, which **s** all

SURPASSING → SURPASSES
Ps 150: 2 according to his **s** greatness!
2 Cor 9:14 pray for you because of the **s** grace

SURPRISE → SURPRISED
1 Thess 5: 4 for that day to **s** you like a thief;

SURPRISED → SURPRISE
1 Pet 4:12 do not be **s** at the fiery ordeal that is

SURROUNDED → SURROUNDS
Lk 21:20 you see Jerusalem **s** by armies,
Heb 12: 1 **s** by so great a cloud of witnesses,
Rev 20: 9 of the earth and **s** the camp of

SURROUNDS → SURROUNDED
Ps 89: 8 Your faithfulness **s** you.
125: 2 so the LORD **s** his people,

SURVIVORS
Isa 1: 9 of hosts had not left us a few **s**,
Ezek 14:22 Yet, **s** shall be left in it,

SUSA
Neh 1: 1 while I was in S the capital,
Esth 1: 2 his royal throne in the citadel of S,

SUSANNA
Righteous woman wrongly accused of immorality (Dan 13:1-44); vindicated by Daniel (Dan 13:45-64).

SUSTAINS
Ps 3: 5 for the LORD **s** me.
Heb 1: 3 he **s** all things by his powerful word.

SWALLOW → SWALLOWED
Jon 1:17 provided a large fish to **s** up Jonah;
Mt 23:24 You strain out a gnat but **s** a camel!

SWALLOWED → SWALLOW
Gen 41: 7 The thin ears **s** up the seven plump
Num 16:32 earth opened its mouth and **s** them
1 Cor 15:54 "Death has been **s** up in victory."

SWEAR → SWORE, SWORN
Deut 10:20 and by his name you shall **s**.
Ps 24: 4 and do not **s** deceitfully.
Mt 5:34 Do not **s** at all, either by heaven,

SWEAT
Gen 3:19 By the **s** of your face you shall eat
Lk 22:44 ⟦ **s** became like great drops of blood⟧

SWEET → SWEETER
Ex 15:25 the water, and the water became **s**.
Ps 119:103 How **s** are your words to my taste,
Ezek 3: 3 in my mouth it was as **s** as honey.
Rev 10:10 it was **s** as honey in my mouth,

SWEETER → SWEET
Judg 14:18 "What is **s** than honey?
Ps 19:10 **s** also than honey, and drippings of

SWIFT
Eccl 9:11 the race is not to the **s**, nor the battle
2 Pet 2: 1 bringing **s** destruction on themselves

SWINE
1 Macc 1:47 sacrifice **s** and other unclean animals,
Mt 7: 6 do not throw your pearls before **s**,
Mk 5:12 "Send us into the **s**;

SWORD → SWORDS
Gen 3:24 and a **s** flaming and turning to guard
1 Sam 17:47 LORD does not save by **s** and spear;
1 Chr 21:30 he was afraid of the **s** of the angel
Sir 21: 3 All lawlessness is like a two-edged **s**
Isa 2: 4 shall not lift up **s** against nation,
49: 2 He made my mouth like a sharp **s**,
Hos 2:18 and I will abolish the bow, the **s**,
Mt 10:34 not come to bring peace, but a **s**."
Lk 2:35 a **s** will pierce your own soul too."
Eph 6:17 the **s** of the Spirit, which is the word
Heb 4:12 sharper than any two-edged **s**,
Rev 1:16 mouth came a sharp, two-edged **s**,
19:15 a sharp **s** with which to strike down

SWORDS → SWORD
Isa 2: 4 shall beat their **s** into plowshares,
Joel 3:10 Beat your plowshares into **s**,

SWORE → SWEAR
Ex 6: 8 the land that I **s** to give to Abraham,
32:13 how you **s** to them by your own self,
Ps 132:11 The LORD **s** to David a sure oath
Heb 6:13 by whom to swear, he **s** by himself,

SWORN → SWEAR
Gen 22:16 "By myself I have **s**, says the LORD;
Ps 110: 4 The LORD has **s** and will not change
Heb 7:21 "The Lord has **s** and will not change

SYMPATHIZE* → SYMPATHIZE
Heb 4:15 unable to **s** with our weaknesses,

SYMPATHY → SYMPATHIZE
Phil 2: 1 any compassion and **s**,
1 Pet 3: 8 all of you, have unity of spirit, **s**,

SYNAGOGUE → SYNAGOGUES
Lk 4:16 he went to the **s** on the sabbath day,
8:41 man named Jairus, a leader of the **s**.
Acts 18:26 He began to speak boldly in the **s**;

SYNAGOGUES → SYNAGOGUE
Mt 4:23 teaching in their **s** and proclaiming
Jn 18:20 always taught in **s** and in the temple,

T

TABERNACLE
Ex 25: 9 concerning the pattern of the **t**
40:34 the glory of the LORD filled the **t**.
1 Chr 6:48 for all the service of the **t** of the house

TABITHA* → See DORCAS

TABLE → TABLES
Ex 25:23 You shall make a **t** of acacia wood,
Ps 23: 5 a **t** before me in the presence of my

TABLES → TABLE
Mk 11:15 overturned the **t** of the money changers

TABLET → TABLETS
Prov 3: 3 write them on the **t** of your heart.

TABLETS → TABLET
Ex 31:18 gave him the two **t** of the covenant,
2 Cor 3: 3 not on **t** of stone but on **t** of human hearts.

TAKE → TAKEN, TAKES
Deut 12:32 do not add to it or **t** anything from
Mt 11:29 **T** my yoke upon you, and learn
Mk 8:34 deny themselves and **t** up their cross

TAKEN → TAKE
Eccl 3:14 added to it, nor anything **t** from it;
Sir 44:16 Enoch pleased the Lord and was **t**
Heb 11: 5 By faith Enoch was **t** so that he did

TAKES → TAKE
Jn 1:29 **t** away the sin of the world!
10:18 No one **t** it from me,
Rev 22:19 if anyone **t** away from the words of

TALENT
Mt 25:25 and hid your **t** in the ground.

TAMAR
1. Wife of Judah's sons Er and Onan (Gen 38:1-10). Children by Judah (Gen 38:11-30; Mt 1:3).
2. Daughter of David, raped by Amnon (2 Sam 13).

TASTE → TASTED
Ps 34: 8 O **t** and see that the LORD is good;
Mt 16:28 not **t** death before they see the Son
Col 2:21 not handle, Do not **t**, Do not touch"?

TASTED → TASTE
Heb 6: 4 and have **t** the heavenly gift,
1 Pet 2: 3 you have **t** that the Lord is good.

TAUGHT → TEACH
Isa 40:14 Who **t** him knowledge,
Jn 6:45 'And they shall all be **t** by God.'

TAX → TAXES
Mt 11:19 a friend of **t** collectors and sinners!'
Lk 18:10 Pharisee and the other a **t** collector.

TAXES → TAX
Mt 22:17 Is it lawful to pay **t** to the emperor,
Rom 13: 7 **t** to whom **t** are due,

TEACH → TAUGHT, TEACHER, TEACHERS,
TEACHING
Deut 6: 1 to **t** you to observe in the land that
Ps 90:12 So **t** us to count our days that we
Jer 31:34 No longer shall they **t** one another,
Jn 14:26 will **t** you everything,
Col 3:16 **t** and admonish one another in all
1 Tim 2:12 I permit no woman to **t** or
1 Jn 2:27 so you do not need anyone to **t** you.

TEACHER → TEACH
Eccl 1: 1 words of the **T**, the son of David,
Mt 10:24 "A disciple is not above the **t**,
Jn 1:38 "Rabbi" (which translated means **T**)
1 Tim 3: 2 respectable, hospitable, an apt **t**,

TEACHERS → TEACH
Ps 119:99 more understanding than all my **t**,
1 Cor 12:28 second prophets, third **t**;
Eph 4:11 evangelists, some pastors and **t**,
Jas 3: 1 Not many of you should become **t**,

TEACHING → TEACH
Mt 28:19 and **t** them to obey everything
Mk 1:27 A new **t**—with authority!
Titus 1:11 by **t** for sordid gain what it is not right
2 Jn 1: 9 who does not abide in the **t** of Christ,

TEAR → TORN
Mk 2:21 from the old, and a worse **t** is made.
Rev 7:17 God will wipe away every **t** from

TEETH → TOOTH
Mt 8:12 will be weeping and gnashing of **t**."

TEKEL
Dan 5:27 **T**, you have been weighed on the scales

TELL → FORETOLD
Ps 50:12 "If I were hungry, I would not **t** you,
     105: 2 **t** of all his wonderful works.
1 Cor 15:51 Listen, I will **t** you a mystery!

TEMPERATE
1 Tim 3: 2 married only once, **t**, sensible,
Titus 2: 2 Tell the older men to be **t**, serious,

TEMPLE
1 Sam 3: 3 Samuel was lying down in the **t** of the
2 Chr 2:12 who will build a **t** for the LORD,
1 Macc 4:48 sanctuary and the interior of the **t**,
Ps 11: 4 The LORD is in his holy **t**;
Mt 4: 5 placed him on the pinnacle of the **t**,
     12: 6 something greater than the **t** is here.
Jn 2:21 was speaking of the **t** of his body.
1 Cor 3:16 you are God's **t** and that God's Spirit
Eph 2:21 and grows into a holy **t** in the Lord;
Rev 21:22 its **t** is the Lord God the Almighty and

TEMPTATION* → TEMPTED, TEMPTER
1 Tim 6: 9 who want to be rich into **t** and

Jas 1:12 Blessed is anyone who endures **t**.

TEMPTED → TEMPTATION
Mk 1:13 wilderness forty days, **t** by Satan;
Gal 6: 1 care that you yourselves are not **t**.

TEMPTER* → TEMPTATION
Mt 4: 3 The **t** came and said to him,
1 Thess 3: 5 that somehow the **t** had tempted you

TEN → TENTH
Ex 34:28 the covenant, the **t** commandments.
Dan 7:24 out of this kingdom **t** kings shall arise,
Mt 25: 1 **T** bridesmaids took their lamps and
Rev 17:12 the **t** horns that you saw are **t** kings

TENDER → TENDERHEARTED
Hos 11: 8 my compassion grows warm and **t**.
Lk 1:78 By the **t** mercy of our God,

TENDERHEARTED* → HEART, TENDER
Eph 4:32 **t**, forgiving one another,

TENT
Ex 27:21 the **t** of meeting, outside the curtain
2 Sam 7: 2 but the ark of God stays in a **t**."
2 Cor 5: 1 the earthly **t** we live in is destroyed,

TENTH → TEN
Gen 14:20 Abram gave him one **t** of everything
Isa 6:13 Even if a **t** part remain in it,

TERROR
Ex 23:27 I will send my **t** in front of you,
Ps 91: 5 You will not fear the **t** of the night,
Rom 13: 3 rulers are not a **t** to good conduct,

TEST → TESTED, TESTING
Deut 6:16 not put the LORD your God to the **t**,
Sir 37:27 My child, **t** yourself while you live;
Lk 4:12 not put the Lord your God to the **t**.'
     10:25 then a lawyer stood up to **t** Jesus.
2 Cor 13: 5 indeed, you fail to meet the **t**!
1 Jn 4: 1 **t** the spirits to see whether they are

TESTED → TEST
Gen 22: 1 After these things God **t** Abraham.
Ps 78:41 They **t** God again and again,
Heb 4:15 been **t** as we are, yet without sin.

TESTIFIED → TESTIFY
Jn 1:15 (John **t** to him and cried out,
1 Pet 1:11 it **t** in advance to the sufferings

TESTIFIES → TESTIFY
1 Jn 5: 6 Spirit is the one that **t**,

TESTIFY → TESTIFIED, TESTIFIES, TESTIMONY
Jn 15:26 he will **t** on my behalf.
1 Jn 5: 7 There are three that **t**:

TESTIMONY → TESTIFY
Num 35:30 put to death on the **t** of a single
Mk 14:59 on this point their **t** did not agree.
Rev 1: 9 the word of God and the **t** of Jesus.

TESTING → TEST
1 Cor 10:13 No **t** has overtaken you that is not
Jas 1: 3 **t** of your faith produces endurance;

THADDAEUS* → =JUDAS
Apostle (Mt 10:3; Mk 3:18); probably also known as Judas son of James (Lk 6:16; Acts 1:13).

THANK → THANKS, THANKSGIVING
2 Chr 29:31 bring sacrifices and **t** offerings to
Ps 52: 9 I will **t** you forever,
Sir 35: 4 gives alms sacrifices a **t** offering.

THANKS → THANK
1 Chr 16: 8 give **t** to the LORD, call on his name,
Ps 107: 1 O give **t** to the LORD, for he is good;
Rom 1:21 not honor him as God or give **t** to
1 Cor 11:24 and when he had given **t**,
2 Cor 9:15 **T** be to God for his indescribable
Rev 4: 9 give glory and honor and **t** to

THANKSGIVING → THANK
Lev 7:12 If you offer it for **t**,
Ps 50:14 Offer to God a sacrifice of **t**,
Phil 4: 6 with **t** let your requests be made known

Rev   7:12 glory and wisdom and **t** and honor

THEFT → THIEF
Mt   15:19 fornication, **t**, false witness, slander.

THEFTS* → THIEF
Rev   9:21 or their fornication or their **t**.

THIEF → THEFT, THEFTS, THIEVES
Ex   22: 1 The **t** shall make restitution,
Jn   10:10 The **t** comes only to steal and kill
1 Thess 5: 2 day of the Lord will come like a **t** in
Rev   16:15 ("See, I am coming like a **t**!

THIEVES → THIEF
Mt   6:19 and where **t** break in and steal;
Eph   4:28 **T** must give up stealing;

THINK → THINKING, THOUGHT, THOUGHTS
Rom   12: 3 not to **t** of yourself more highly than
1 Cor   10:12 So if you **t** you are standing,

THINKING → THINK
Rom   1:21 but they became futile in their **t**,
1 Cor   14:20 infants in evil, but in **t** be adults.

THIRD → THREE
Hos   6: 2 on the **t** day he will raise us up,
Mt   26:44 and prayed for the **t** time,
Lk   18:33 and on the **t** day he will rise again."
2 Cor   12: 2 was caught up to the **t** heaven—

THIRST → THIRSTY
Mt   5: 6 who hunger and **t** for righteousness,
Rev   7:16 will hunger no more, and **t** no more;

THIRSTY → THIRST
Mt   25:35 I was **t** and you gave me something
Jn   6:35 believes in me will never be **t**.
Rev   22:17 And let everyone who is **t** come.

THOMAS*
    Apostle (Mt 10:3; Mk 3:18; Lk 6:15; Jn 11:16; 14:5; 21:2; Acts 1:13). Doubted resurrection (Jn 20:24-28).

THORN → THORNS
2 Cor   12: 7 a **t** was given me in the flesh,

THORNS → THORN
Gen   3:18 **t** and thistles it shall bring forth for
Mt   13: 7 Other seeds fell among **t**,
Jn   19: 2 the soldiers wove a crown of **t** and

THOUGHT → THINK
1 Cor   13:11 I spoke like a child, I **t** like a child,
2 Cor   10: 5 take every **t** captive to obey Christ.

THOUGHTS → THINK
Isa   55: 8 For my **t** are not your **t**,
1 Cor   3:20 "The Lord knows the **t** of the wise,
Heb   4:12 judge the **t** and intentions of the heart.

THOUSAND → THOUSANDS
Ps   50:10 the cattle on a **t** hills.
        90: 4 **t** years in your sight are like yesterday
2 Pet   3: 8 one day is like a **t** years, and a **t** years
Rev   20: 4 and reigned with Christ a **t** years.

THOUSANDS → THOUSAND
1 Sam   18: 7 has killed his **t**, and David his ten **t**."
Dan   7:10 A thousand **t** served him,
Rev   5:11 myriads of myriads and **t** of **t**,

THREE → THIRD
Gen   18: 2 and saw **t** men standing near him.
Ex   23:14 **T** times in the year you shall hold a
Mt   18:20 two or **t** are gathered in my name,
        26:34 you will deny me **t** times."
Mk   8:31 be killed, and after **t** days rise again.
2 Cor   12: 8 **T** times I appealed to the Lord
1 Jn   5: 7 There are **t** that testify:

THRONE → THRONES
2 Sam   7:13 the **t** of his kingdom forever.
Ps   45: 6 Your **t**, O God, endures forever
Isa   6: 1 I saw the Lord sitting on a **t**, high
Jer   33:21 not have a son to reign on his **t**,
Mt   19:28 the Son of Man is seated on the **t**
Heb   4:16 approach the **t** of grace with boldness,
        12: 2 his seat at the right hand of the **t**
Rev   4:10 they cast their crowns before the **t**,

Rev   20:11 I saw a great white **t** and the one

THRONES → THRONE
Dan   7: 9 **t** were set in place,
Rev   4: 4 Around the throne are twenty-four **t**,

THROW → THROWN
Ex   1:22 Hebrews you shall **t** into the Nile,
Mt   7: 6 do not **t** your pearls before swine,

THROWN → THROW
Ex   15: 1 horse and rider he has **t** into the sea.
Dan   3:21 **t** into the furnace of blazing fire.
         6:12 shall be **t** into a den of lions?"
Rev   20:10 **t** into the lake of fire and sulfur,

THUMMIM
Ex   28:30 you shall put the Urim and the **T**,

THUNDER → THUNDERS
Ex   9:23 and the LORD sent **t** and hail,
Rev   4: 5 and rumblings and peals of **t**,

THUNDERS → THUNDER
Rev   10: 3 he shouted, the seven **t** sounded.

TIBNI*
    King of Israel (1 Kings 16:21-22).

TIE
Prov   6:21 **t** them around your neck.
Mt   23: 4 **t** up heavy burdens, hard to bear,

TIME → TIMES
Esth   4:14 dignity for just such a **t** as this."
Eccl   3: 1 a **t** for every matter under heaven:
Dan   7:25 for a **t**, two times, and half a **t**.
Rom   5: 6 the right **t** Christ died for the ungodly.
2 Cor   6: 2 See, now is the acceptable **t**;
Gal   4: 4 when the fullness of **t** had come,
Col   4: 5 making the most of the **t**.
Rev   12:14 for a **t**, and times, and half a **t**.
        22:10 of this book, for the **t** is near.

TIMES → TIME
Josh   6: 4 march around the city seven **t**,
Sir   20:12 but pay for it seven **t** over.
Mt   16: 3 cannot interpret the signs of the **t**.
        18:22 seven **t**, but, I tell you, seventy-seven **t**.
Mk   14:30 you will deny me three **t**."

TIMOTHY
    Believer from Lystra (Acts 16:1). Joined Paul on second missionary journey (Acts 16-20). Sent to settle problems at Corinth (1 Cor 4:17; 16:10). Led church at Ephesus (1 Tim 1:3). Co-writer with Paul (1 Thess 1:1; 2 Thess 1:1; Philem 1).

TITHE
Deut   12:17 the **t** of your grain, your wine, and
Mal   3:10 Bring the full **t** into the storehouse,

TITUS
    Gentile co-worker of Paul (Gal 2:1-3; 2 Tim 4:10); sent to Corinth (2 Cor 2:13; 7-8; 12:18), Crete (Titus 1:4-5).

TOBIAH
    Enemy of Nehemiah (Neh 2:10-19; 4; 6; 13:4-9).

TOBIAS
Tob   7:12 he took her by the hand and gave her to **T**,
Tob   8: 5 **T** began by saying,

TOBIT
Tob   1: 1 This book tells the story of **T**

TODAY
Deut   30:15 set before you **t** life and prosperity,
Ps   2: 7 my son; **t** I have begotten you.
Lk   23:43 **t** you will be with me in Paradise."
Heb   1: 5 my Son; **t** I have begotten you"?
        13: 8 Christ is the same yesterday and **t** and

TOGETHER
Mt   19: 6 God has joined **t**, let no one separate."
Eph   2: 5 made us alive **t** with Christ—

TOLA
    A judge of Israel (Judg 10:1-2).

TOMB
Mk   15:46 laid it in a **t** that had been hewn out
Lk   24: 2 the stone rolled away from the **t**,

TOMORROW
Isa   22:13 "Let us eat and drink, for **t** we die."
Mt   6:34 "So do not worry about **t**,
Jas   4:14 do not even know what **t** will bring.

TONGUE → DOUBLE-TONGUED, TONGUES
Ex   4:10 I am slow of speech and slow of **t**."
Ps   139: 4 before a word is on my **t**, O LORD,
Prov   18:21 Death and life are in the power of the **t**,
Sir   20:18 is better than a slip of the **t**;
       23: 7 DISCIPLINE OF THE T
Isa   45:23 shall bow, every **t** shall swear."
1 Cor 14:19 than ten thousand words in a **t**.
Phil   2:11 every **t** should confess that Jesus Christ
Jas   3: 8 but no one can tame the **t**—

TONGUES → TONGUE
Acts   2: 3 Divided **t**, as of fire, appeared
1 Cor 12:10 of **t**, to another the interpretation of **t**.
       14: 5 in **t**, unless someone interprets,

TOOTH → TEETH
Ex   21:24 **t** for **t**, hand for hand, foot for foot,
Mt   5:38 'An eye for an eye and a **t** for a **t**.'

TORCHES
Dan   10: 6 lightning, his eyes like flaming **t**,
Rev   4: 5 of the throne burn seven flaming **t**,

TORMENTED
Rev   20:10 they will be **t** day and night forever

TORN → TEAR
1 Sam 28:17 has **t** the kingdom out of your hand,
Lk   23:45 curtain of the temple was **t** in two.

TORTURED
Mt   18:34 handed him over to be **t** until
Heb   11:35 were **t**, refusing to accept release,

TOUCH
Gen   3: 3 nor shall you **t** it, or you shall die.'"
Mt   9:21 only **t** his cloak, I will be made well.
Lk   24:39 **T** me and see;
Col   2:21 not handle, Do not taste, Do not **t**"?

TOWER
Gen   11: 4 and a **t** with its top in the heavens,
Prov   18:10 The name of the LORD is a strong **t**;

TRADITION
Mt   15: 2 disciples break the **t** of the elders?
Col   2: 8 empty deceit, according to human **t**,

TRAIN → TRAINING
Prov   22: 6 **T** children in the right way, and
1 Tim   4: 7 **T** yourself in godliness,

TRAINING → TRAIN
1 Tim   4: 8 while physical **t** is of some value,
2 Tim   3:16 and for **t** in righteousness,

TRAITOR
Lk   6:16 and Judas Iscariot, who became a **t**.

TRANSFIGURED
Mt   17: 2 And he was **t** before them,

TRANSFORM* → TRANSFORMED
Phil   3:21 will **t** the body of our humiliation

TRANSFORMED → TRANSFORM
Rom   12: 2 be **t** by the renewing of your minds,
2 Cor   3:18 are being **t** into the same image

TRANSGRESSION → TRANSGRESSIONS,
       TRANSGRESSORS
Ex   23:21 for he will not pardon your **t**;
Dan   9:24 to finish the **t**, to put an end to sin,
Gal   6: 1 if anyone is detected in a **t**,

TRANSGRESSIONS → TRANSGRESSION
Ps   103:12 so far he removes our **t** from us.
Isa   53: 5 But he was wounded for our **t**,

TRANSGRESSORS → TRANSGRESSION
Ps   51:13 Then I will teach **t** your ways,
Isa   53:12 and was numbered with the **t**;

TRAP
Lk   20:20 in order to **t** him by what he said,
Rom   11: 9 their table become a snare and a **t**,

TREAD → TREADING
Mic   7:19 he will **t** our iniquities under foot.
Rev   19:15 he will **t** the wine press of the fury

TREADING → TREAD
Deut   25: 4 not muzzle an ox while it is **t** out
1 Cor   9: 9 not muzzle an ox while it is **t** out

TREASURE → TREASURED, TREASURES
Ps   119:11 I **t** your word in my heart,
Mt   6:21 where your **t** is, there your heart
2 Cor   4: 7 But we have this **t** in clay jars,
2 Tim   1:14 Guard the good **t** entrusted to you,

TREASURED → TREASURE
Ex   19: 5 be my **t** possession out of all the
Lk   2:51 His mother **t** all these things in her heart.

TREASURES → TREASURE
Col   2: 3 are hidden all the **t** of wisdom

TREE → TREES
Gen   3:24 to guard the way to the **t** of life.
Deut   21:23 hung on a **t** is under God's curse.
Mt   12:33 for the **t** is known by its fruit.
Acts   5:30 had killed by hanging him on a **t**.
Rom   11:24 grafted back into their own olive **t**.
Rev   22: 2 the **t** of life with its twelve kinds

TREES → TREE
Ps   96:12 all the **t** of the forest sing for joy
Zech   4:11 "What are these two olive **t** on the
Rev   11: 4 two olive **t** and the two lampstands

TREMBLE → TREMBLED, TREMBLING
Ps   114: 7 **T**, O earth, at the presence of the LORD
Hab   3: 6 he looked and made the nations **t**.

TREMBLED → TREMBLE
Ex   20:18 they were afraid and **t** and stood at

TREMBLING → TREMBLE
Ps   2:11 Serve the LORD with fear, with **t**
Phil   2:12 your own salvation with fear and **t**;

TRESPASS → TRESPASSES
Rom   5:15 But the free gift is not like the **t**.

TRESPASSES → TRESPASS
Mt   6:14 For if you forgive others their **t**,
2 Cor   5:19 not counting their **t** against them,

TRIAL → TRIALS
Lk   4:13 do not bring us to the time of **t**."
2 Pet   2: 9 knows how to rescue the godly from **t**,
Rev   3:10 I will keep you from the hour of **t**

TRIALS → TRIAL
Jas   1: 2 whenever you face **t** of any kind,
1 Pet   1: 6 you have had to suffer various **t**,

TRIBE → TRIBES
Num   1: 4 A man from each **t** shall be with you
Ps   78:68 but he chose the **t** of Judah,
Rev   5: 5 See, the Lion of the **t** of Judah,

TRIBES → TRIBE
Gen   49:28 All these are the twelve **t** of Israel,
Ex   24: 4 to the twelve **t** of Israel.
Mt   19:28 judging the twelve **t** of Israel.
Rev   21:12 inscribed the names of the twelve **t**

TRIUMPH → TRIUMPHAL, TRIUMPHS
Ps   112: 8 they will look in **t** on their foes.
Prov   28:12 the righteous **t**, there is great glory,

TRIUMPHAL* → TRIUMPH
2 Cor   2:14 Christ always leads us in **t** procession,

TRIUMPHS → TRIUMPH
Jas   2:13 mercy **t** over judgment.

TROUBLE → TROUBLED
Job   14: 1 few of days and full of **t**,
Ps   9: 9 a stronghold in times of **t**.
Prov   11: 8 The righteous are delivered from **t**,
Sir   51:10 do not forsake me in the days of **t**,
Isa   33: 2 our salvation in the time of **t**.
Mt   6:34 Today's **t** is enough for today.

TROUBLED → TROUBLE
Jn   14: 1 "Do not let your hearts be **t**.

TRUE → TRUTH
Ps   119:151 and all your commandments are **t**.
Jn   1: 9 The **t** light, which enlightens
       21:24 and we know that his testimony is **t**.
Rom   3: 4 everyone is a liar, let God be proved **t**,
1 Jn   5:20 He is the **t** God and eternal life.
Rev   3:14 the Amen, the faithful and **t** witness,
       19:11 Its rider is called Faithful and **T**,
       22: 6 "These words are trustworthy and **t**,

TRUMPET → TRUMPETS
Ex   19:16 a blast of a **t** so loud that all the
Joel   2:15 Blow the **t** in Zion; sanctify a fast;
1 Cor   15:52 twinkling of an eye, at the last **t**.
1 Thess 4:16 and with the sound of God's **t**,

TRUMPETS → TRUMPET
Num   10: 2 Make two silver **t**; you shall make
Rev   8: 2 and seven **t** were given to them.

TRUST → ENTRUST, ENTRUSTED, TRUSTED,
     TRUSTEES, TRUSTS, TRUSTWORTHY
Ps   9:10 know your name put their **t** in you,
       37: 3 **T** in the LORD, and do good;
      119:42 for I **t** in your word.
Prov   3: 5 **T** in the LORD with all your heart,
Sir   2: 6 **T** in him, and he will help you;
Isa   12: 2 Surely God is my salvation; I will **t**,
Jer   17: 7 Blessed are those who **t** in the LORD,
Heb   2:13 And again, "I will put my **t** in him."

TRUSTED → TRUST
Ps   22: 4 they **t**, and you delivered them.
Dan   3:95 delivered his servants who **t** in him.
       6:23 because he had **t** in his God.
      13:35 for her heart **t** in the Lord.

TRUSTS → TRUST
Ps   86: 2 save your servant who **t** in you.
Mt   27:43 He **t** in God; let God deliver him

TRUSTWORTHY → TRUST
1 Macc 14: 41 until a **t** prophet should arise,
Ps   111: 7 and just; all his precepts are **t**.
1 Cor   7:25 as one who by the Lord's mercy is **t**.
Rev   22: 6 "These words are **t** and true,

TRUTH → TRUE
Tob   3: 2 all your ways are mercy and **t**;
Ps   25: 5 Lead me in your **t**, and teach me,
      119:142 and your law is the **t**.
Prov   23:23 Buy **t**, and do not sell it;
Jn   1:17 grace and **t** came through Jesus Christ.
        4:23 worship the Father in spirit and **t**,
        8:32 and the **t** will make you free."
       14: 6 "I am the way, and the **t**, and the life.
       14:17 This is the Spirit of **t**,
       16:13 he will guide you into all **t**;
Eph   4:15 But speaking the **t** in love,
1 Tim   3:15 the pillar and bulwark of the **t**.
2 Tim   2:15 rightly explaining the word of **t**.

TUNIC
Lk   9: 3 nor money—not even an extra **t**.
Jn   19:23 **t** was seamless, woven in one piece

TURN → TURNED
Ex   32:12 **T** from your fierce wrath;
Josh   1: 7 do not **t** from it to the right hand or
Isa   6:10 and **t** and be healed."
       45:22 **T** to me and be saved,
Mal   4: 6 He will **t** the hearts of parents to their
Lk   1:17 **t** the hearts of parents to their children

TURNED → TURN
Deut   23: 5 your God **t** the curse into a blessing
Isa   53: 6 we have all **t** to our own way,
Rom   3:12 All have **t** aside, together they have

TWELVE
Gen   49:28 All these are the **t** tribes of Israel,
Ex   24: 4 the mountain, and set up **t** pillars,
Josh   4: 3 Take **t** stones from here out of the
Mt   10: 1 Jesus summoned his **t** disciples
Lk   9:17 **t** baskets of broken pieces.
Rev   21:12 inscribed the names of the **t** tribes
       22: 2 tree of life with its **t** kinds of fruit,

TWINKLING*
1 Cor   15:52 in the **t** of an eye, at the last trumpet

TWO → TWICE, TWO-EDGED
Gen   1:16 God made the **t** great lights—
        6:19 bring **t** of every kind into the ark,
Ex   31:18 the **t** tablets of the covenant,
Deut   17: 6 of **t** or three witnesses the death
Mt   6:24 "No one can serve **t** masters;
       19: 5 and the **t** shall become one flesh'?

TWO-EDGED → TWO
Heb   4:12 sharper than any **t** sword,
Rev   1:16 his mouth came a sharp, **t** sword,

TYRE
1 Kings 5: 1 King Hiram of **T** sent his servants to
Ezek   28:12 a lamentation over the king of **T**,
Mt   11:22 be more tolerable for **T** and Sidon

U

UNBELIEF → UNBELIEVER, UNBELIEVERS
Mk   6: 6 And he was amazed at their **u**.
        9:24 cried out, "I believe; help my **u**!"
Rom   11:20 were broken off because of their **u**,
1 Tim   1:13 because I had acted ignorantly in **u**,

UNBELIEVER → UNBELIEF
1 Cor 10:27 If an **u** invites you to a meal and
2 Cor   6:15 does a believer share with an **u**?

UNBELIEVERS → UNBELIEF
2 Cor   6:14 Do not be mismatched with **u**.

UNCHASTITY*
Mt   5:32 except on the ground of **u**,
       19: 9 divorces his wife, except for **u**,

UNCIRCUMCISED → UNCIRCUMCISION
Ex   12:48 But no **u** person shall eat of it;
1 Macc 1:48 and to leave their sons **u**.
Acts   7:51 people, **u** in heart and ears,
Rom   4:11 he had by faith while he was still **u**.
Col   3:11 circumcised and **u**, barbarian,

UNCIRCUMCISION → UNCIRCUMCISED
1 Cor   7:19 Circumcision is nothing, and **u** is
Gal   5: 6 neither circumcision nor **u** counts

UNCLEAN → UNCLEANNESS
Lev   5: 2 when any of you touch any **u** thing
Isa   52:11 Touch no **u** thing;
       64: 6 We have all become like one who is **u**
Mk   3:11 Whenever the **u** spirits saw him,
Rev   21:27 But nothing **u** will enter it,

UNDER
Ps   8: 6 you have put all things **u** their feet,
Acts   4:12 for there is no other name **u** heaven
Rom   6:14 since you are not **u** law but **u** grace.
Eph   1:22 And he has put all things **u** his feet

UNDERSTAND → UNDERSTANDING
Job   42: 3 I have uttered what I did not **u**,
Prov   2: 5 then you will **u** the fear of the LORD
Hos   14: 9 Those who are wise **u** these things;
Mt   13:15 and **u** with their heart and turn—
Lk   24:45 opened their minds to **u** the scriptures,
Acts   8:30 "Do you **u** what you are reading?"
Eph   5:17 but **u** what the will of the Lord is.

UNDERSTANDING → UNDERSTAND
Ex   36: 1 has given skill and **u** to know how
Prov   2: 6 from his mouth come knowledge and **u**
Isa   40:14 and showed him the way of **u**?
Lk   2:47 heard him were amazed at his **u**
Phil   4: 7 peace of God, which surpasses all **u**,
2 Tim   2: 7 Lord will give you **u** in all things.

UNEXPECTED
Mt   24:44 Son of Man is coming at an **u** hour.

UNFAITHFUL → UNFAITHFULNESS
Rom   3: 3 What if some were **u**?

UNFAITHFULNESS → UNFAITHFUL
1 Chr   9: 1 exile in Babylon because of their **u**.

UNGODLY
Sir 12: 5 but do not give to the **u**;
Rom 5: 6 the right time Christ died for the **u**.
2 Pet 2: 6 example of what is coming to the **u**;

UNINTENTIONALLY
Lev 4: 2 When anyone sins **u** in any of
Num 15:22 if you **u** fail to observe all these

UNITY
Ps 133: 1 when kindred live together in **u**!
Eph 4: 3 to maintain the **u** of the Spirit in the

UNJUST
Rom 3: 5 That God is **u** to inflict wrath on us?
Heb 6:10 For God is not **u**; he will

UNLEAVENED
Ex 12:17 shall observe the festival of **u** bread,
Mt 26:17 first day of **U** Bread the disciples

UNPRODUCTIVE*
1 Cor 14:14 my spirit prays but my mind is **u**.
Titus 3:14 so that they may not be **u**.

UNRIGHTEOUS → UNRIGHTEOUSNESS
Mt 5:45 rain on the righteous and on the **u**.
2 Pet 2: 9 **u** under punishment until the day

UNRIGHTEOUSNESS → UNRIGHTEOUS
Ps 92:15 and there is no **u** in him.
1 Jn 1: 9 and cleanse us from all **u**.

UPHOLD
Isa 42: 1 my servant, whom I **u**, my chosen,
Rom 3:31 On the contrary, we **u** the law.

UPRIGHT
Job 1: 1 That man was blameless and **u**,
Ps 7:10 God is my shield, who saves the **u**
Titus 1: 8 a lover of goodness, prudent, **u**,
2:12 lives that are self-controlled, **u**, and godly,

UR
Gen 15: 7 LORD who brought you from **U** of

URIAH
Hittite husband of Bathsheba, killed (2 Sam 11).

URIM
Ex 28:30 of judgment you shall put the **U**

USE → USEFUL
Ex 20: 7 not make wrongful **u** of the name of
Gal 5:13 only do not **u** your freedom as an
2 Tim 2:20 for special **u**, some for ordinary.

USEFUL → USE
Eph 4:29 but only what is **u** for building up,
2 Tim 3:16 scripture is inspired by God and is **u**

UZZIAH → =AZARIAH
Son of Amaziah; king of Judah also known as Azariah (2 Kings 15:1-7; 1 Chr 6:24; 2 Chr 26). Struck with leprosy because of pride (2 Chr 26:16-23).

V

VAIN → VANITY
Lev 26:16 You shall sow your seed in **v**,
Ps 2: 1 and the peoples plot in **v**?
Mt 15: 9 in **v** do they worship me,
Phil 2:16 that I did not run in **v** or labor in **v**.

VALLEY
Ps 23: 4 through the darkest **v**, I fear no evil;
Isa 40: 4 Every **v** shall be lifted up,
Joel 3:14 multitudes, in the **v** of decision!
Lk 3: 5 Every **v** shall be filled, and every

VALUE
Mt 13:46 on finding one pearl of great **v**,
Rom 3: 1 Or what is the **v** of circumcision?
1 Tim 4: 8 while physical training is of some **v**,

VANITY → VAIN
Eccl 1: 2 **v** of vanities! All is **v**.
12: 8 **V** of vanities, says the Teacher; all is **v**.

VASHTI
Persian queen replaced by Esther (Esth 1-2).

VEIL
Ex 34:33 he put a **v** on his face;
2 Cor 3:15 a **v** lies over their minds;

VENGEANCE → AVENGE, AVENGER, AVENGING
Ps 94: 1 O LORD, you God of **v**,
Isa 34: 8 For the LORD has a day of **v**,
Nah 1: 2 the LORD takes **v** on his adversaries

VICTORY
Prov 21:31 but the **v** belongs to the LORD.
1 Cor 15:54 Death has been swallowed up in **v**."
1 Jn 5: 4 the **v** that conquers the world, our faith.

VINDICATE → VINDICATED
Ps 26: 1 **V** me, O LORD, for I have walked
135:14 For the LORD will **v** his people,

VINDICATED → VINDICATE
Job 13:18 I know that I shall be **v**.
Mt 11:19 Yet wisdom is **v** by her deeds."
1 Tim 3:16 He was revealed in flesh, **v** in spirit,

VINE → VINEYARD
Ps 80: 8 You brought a **v** out of Egypt;
Jer 2:21 Yet I planted you as a choice **v**,
Jn 15: 1 "I am the true **v**, and my Father is
Rev 14:18 gather the clusters of the **v** of the

VINEYARD → VINE
1 Kings 21: 1 Naboth the Jezreelite had a **v** in
Isa 5: 1 had a **v** on a very fertile hill.
Mt 21:33 a landowner who planted a **v**,

VIOLENCE → VIOLENT
Gen 6:11 and the earth was filled with **v**.
Isa 53: 9 although he had done no **v**,
Hab 2:17 because of human bloodshed and **v**

VIOLENT → VIOLENCE
1 Tim 3: 3 not **v** but gentle, not quarrelsome,
Titus 1: 7 or addicted to wine or **v** or greedy

VIPERS
Mt 23:33 You snakes, you brood of **v**!
Rom 3:13 venom of **v** is under their lips."

VIRGIN
Jer 31:21 Return, O **v** Israel, return to these
Mt 1:23 the **v** shall conceive and bear a son,
Lk 1:34 "How can this be, since I am a **v**?"
1 Cor 7:28 and if a **v** marries, she does not sin,
2 Cor 11: 2 present you as a chaste **v** to Christ.

VISION → VISIONS
Isa 22: 1 oracle concerning the valley of **v**.
Dan 8:26 As for you, seal up the **v**,
Acts 26:19 not disobedient to the heavenly **v**,

VISIONS → VISION
Num 12: 6 make myself known to them in **v**;
Ezek 1: 1 were opened, and I saw **v** of God.
Dan 1:17 Daniel also had insight into all **v**
Joel 2:28 and your young men shall see **v**.
Acts 2:17 and your young men shall see **v**,

VOICE
Isa 40: 3 A **v** cries out: "In the wilderness
Jn 1:23 **v** of one crying out in the wilderness
10: 3 and the sheep hear his **v**.
Heb 3: 7 says, "Today, if you hear his **v**,
Rev 3:20 if you hear my **v** and open the door,

VOID
Gen 1: 2 the earth was a formless **v**
Mt 15: 6 you make **v** the word of God.

VOW → VOWS
Eccl 5: 4 Fulfill what you **v**.
Sir 18:23 Before making a **v**, prepare yourself

VOWS → VOW
Ps 22:25 my **v** I will pay before those who fear

W

WAGES
Rom 6:23 For the **w** of sin is death,

WAIT → WAITS
Ps	27:14	**W** for the LORD; be strong,
Sir	2: 7	fear the Lord, **w** for his mercy;
Lam	3:26	should **w** quietly for the salvation of
Hab	2: 3	If it seems to tarry, **w** for it;
Rom	8:23	while we **w** for adoption,
1 Thess	1:10	to **w** for his Son from heaven,

WAITS → WAIT
Ps	130: 6	my soul **w** for the Lord more than
Rom	8:19	the creation **w** with eager longing

WALK → WALKED, WALKING
Gen	17: 1	**w** before me, and be blameless.
Deut	10:12	to **w** in all his ways, to love him,
Ps	23: 4	I **w** through the darkest valley, I fear no
Isa	2: 5	let us **w** in the light of the LORD!
	40:31	they shall **w** and not faint.
Jer	6:16	**w** in it, and find rest for your souls.
Jn	8:12	follows me will never **w** in darkness
2 Cor	5: 7	for we **w** by faith, not by sight.
Rev	21:24	The nations will **w** by its light,

WALKED → WALK
Gen	5:24	Enoch **w** with God; then he was no
	6: 9	Noah **w** with God.

WALKING → WALK
Mt	14:26	the disciples saw him **w** on the sea,

WALL
Josh	6:20	shout, and the **w** fell down flat;
Neh	2:17	let us rebuild the **w** of Jerusalem,
Zech	2: 5	I will be a **w** of fire all around it,
Eph	2:14	has broken down the dividing **w**,

WANT → WANTING
Ps	23: 1	LORD is my shepherd, I shall not **w**.
Phil	3:10	I **w** to know Christ and the power

WANTING → WANT
2 Pet	3: 9	not **w** any to perish, but all to come to

WAR → WARRIOR, WARS
Eccl	3: 8	a time for **w**, and a time for peace.
Dan	9:26	and to the end there shall be **w**.
Rom	7:23	in my members another law at **w**
Rev	19:11	righteousness he judges and makes **w**.

WARRIOR → WAR
Ex	15: 3	LORD is a **w**; the LORD is his name.

WARS → WAR
Mt	24: 6	you will hear of **w** and rumors of **w**;

WASH → WASHED
Ps	51: 7	**w** me, and I shall be whiter than snow.
Jn	13: 5	and began to **w** the disciples' feet
Rev	22:14	Blessed are those who **w** their robes,

WASHED → WASH
1 Cor	6:11	you were **w**, you were sanctified,
2 Pet	2:22	sow is **w** only to wallow in the mud.

WATCH → WATCHES
Lk	2: 8	keeping **w** over their flock by night.
Heb	13:17	they are keeping **w** over your souls

WATCHES → WATCH
Ps	1: 6	LORD **w** over the way of the righteous,
Wis	3: 9	and he **w** over his elect.

WATER → WATERS
Ex	17: 1	no **w** for the people to drink.
Num	20: 2	there was no **w** for the congregation;
Jer	2:13	the fountain of living **w**,
Ezek	36:25	I will sprinkle clean **w** upon you,
Mk	1: 8	I have baptized you with **w**;
Jn	2: 9	tasted the **w** that had become wine,
	3: 5	without being born of **w** and Spirit.
	4:10	he would have given you living **w**."
1 Jn	5: 6	the one who came by **w** and blood,
Rev	22: 1	showed me the river of the **w** of life,

WATERS → WATER
Gen	7: 7	the ark to escape the **w** of the flood.
Ex	14:21	dry land; and the **w** were divided.
Eccl	11: 1	Send out your bread upon the **w**,
Isa	55: 1	who thirsts, come to the **w**;

WAVERING
Heb	10:23	confession of our hope without **w**,
Jude	1:22	have mercy on some who are **w**;

WAY → WAYS
Ps	1: 6	watches over the **w** of the righteous,
	86:11	Teach me your **w**, O LORD,
Prov	12:15	Fools think their own **w** is right,
	22: 6	Train children in the right **w**,
Isa	40: 3	wilderness prepare the **w** of the LORD,
Mal	3: 1	sending my messenger to prepare the **w**
Mt	3: 3	'Prepare the **w** of the Lord,
Jn	14: 6	"I am the **w**, and the truth, and the life.
Acts	9: 2	found any who belonged to the **W**,
1 Cor	12:31	show you a still more excellent **w**.
Heb	10:20	the new and living **w** that he opened

WAYS → WAY
Deut	10:12	to walk in all his **w**, to love him,
Sir	2:15	who love him keep his **w**.
Hos	14: 9	For the **w** of the LORD are right,
Rev	15: 3	Just and true are your **w**, King of

WEAK → WEAKNESS, WEAKNESSES
Mt	26:41	indeed is willing, but the flesh is **w**."
Rom	14: 1	Welcome those who are **w** in faith,
1 Cor	1:27	God chose what is **w** in the world
2 Cor	12:10	whenever I am **w**, then I am strong.

WEAKNESS → WEAK
Rom	8:26	the Spirit helps us in our **w**;
1 Cor	15:43	It is sown in **w**, it is raised in power.

WEAKNESSES → WEAK
2 Cor	12:10	I am content with **w**, insults,
Heb	4:15	to sympathize with our **w**,

WEALTH
Ps	49: 6	those who trust in their **w** and boast
Prov	19: 4	**W** brings many friends,
Sir	5: 1	Do not rely on your **w**,
Mt	13:22	and the lure of **w** choke
Rev	5:12	receive power and **w** and wisdom

WEAPONS
Eccl	9:18	Wisdom is better than **w** of war,
2 Cor	6: 7	the **w** of righteousness for the right

WEAR
Isa	51: 6	the earth will **w** out like a garment,
Mt	6:31	or 'What will we **w**?'

WEARY
Isa	40:31	they shall run and not be **w**,
Heb	12: 3	you may not grow **w** or lose heart.

WEDDING
Jn	2: 1	there was a **w** in Cana of Galilee,

WEEKS
Ex	34:22	You shall observe the festival of **w**,
Lev	23:15	you shall count off seven **w**;
Dan	9:24	"Seventy **w** are decreed for your

WEEP → WEEPING
Eccl	3: 4	a time to **w**, and a time to laugh;
Rom	12:15	**w** with those who **w**.

WEEPING → WEEP
Ps	30: 5	**W** may linger for the night,
Mt	2:18	Rachel **w** for her children;
	8:12	will be **w** and gnashing of teeth."

WEIGHED
1 Sam	2: 3	and by him actions are **w**.
Dan	5:27	you have been **w** on the scales

WELL
Deut	6: 3	so that it may go **w** with you,
Mt	3:17	with whom I am **w** pleased."
	17: 5	I am **w** pleased; listen to him!"
2 Pet	1:17	with whom I am **w** pleased."

WEST
Ps	103:12	as far as the east is from the **w**,
Isa	43: 5	and from the **w** I will gather you;

WHEAT
Mt	13:25	and sowed weeds among the **w**,
Lk	22:31	demanded to sift all of you like **w**,

Jn 12:24 grain of w falls into the earth and dies,

WHIRLWIND → WIND
2 Kings 2:11 Elijah ascended in a w into heaven.
Nah 1:3 His way is in w and storm,

WHITE → WHITER
Dan 7:9 his clothing was w as snow,
Mt 5:36 cannot make one hair w or black.
Rev 1:14 his hair were w as w wool, w as snow;
20:11 a great w throne and the one who sat

WHITER → WHITE
Ps 51:7 wash me, and I shall be w than snow.

WICKED → WICKEDNESS
Gen 13:13 Now the people of Sodom were w,
18:23 the righteous with the w?
Ps 1:5 the w will not stand in the judgment,
73:3 I saw the prosperity of the w.
Isa 48:22 no peace," says the LORD, "for the w."
Ezek 18:23 any pleasure in the death of the w,
Dan 12:10 None of the w shall understand,

WICKEDNESS → WICKED
Gen 6:5 The LORD saw that the w of
Ps 45:7 you love righteousness and hate w.
Lk 11:39 inside you are full of greed and w.

WIDE
Mt 7:13 the gate is w and the road is easy

WIDOW → WIDOWS
Ex 22:22 shall not abuse any w or orphan.
Ps 146:9 he upholds the orphan and the w,
1 Tim 5:4 If a w has children or grandchildren,
Rev 18:7 I am no w, and I will never see grief

WIDOWS → WIDOW
1 Tim 5:3 Honor w who are really w.
Jas 1:27 to care for orphans and w in their

WIFE → WIVES
Gen 2:24 and his mother and clings to his w,
Ex 20:17 shall not covet your neighbor's w,
Tob 8:6 his w Eve as a helper and support.
Prov 18:22 who finds a w finds a good thing,
Sir 26:3 A good w is a great blessing;
Mt 5:32 that anyone who divorces his w,
19:3 to divorce his w for any cause?"
Eph 5:28 He who loves his w loves himself.
Rev 21:9 the bride, the w of the Lamb."

WILD
Ex 32:25 saw that the people were running w
Mk 1:13 and he was with the w beasts;
Rom 11:17 a w olive shoot,

WILDERNESS
Isa 40:3 the w prepare the way of the LORD,
Mt 3:3 voice of one crying out in the w:

WILL → FREEWILL, WILLING
Ps 40:8 I delight to do your w, O my God;
143:10 Teach me to do your w,
Isa 53:10 it was the w of the LORD to crush him
Mt 6:10 Your w be done, on earth as it is in
Lk 22:42 yet, not my w but yours be done."
Jn 4:34 "My food is to do the w of him who
Rom 9:19 For who can resist his w?"
Eph 6:6 doing the w of God from the heart.
1Jo 5:14 if we ask anything according to his w,

WILLING → WILL
Mt 26:41 spirit indeed is w, but the flesh is weak.
Lk 22:42 if you are w, remove this cup from

WIND → WHIRLWIND
1 Kings 19:11 but the LORD was not in the w;
Ps 1:4 like chaff that the w drives away.
Eccl 1:14 all is vanity and a chasing after w.
Jn 3:8 The w blows where it chooses,
Acts 2:2 a sound like the rush of a violent w,

WINE
Deut 7:13 your grain and your w and your oil,
Ps 104:15 and w to gladden the human heart,
Prov 20:1 W is a mocker, strong drink a
Song 1:2 For your love is better than w,

Sir 40:20 W and music gladden the heart,
Mt 9:17 is new w put into old wineskins;
Jn 2:9 tasted the water that had become w,
Eph 5:18 Do not get drunk with w, for that is
Rev 18:3 have drunk of the w of the wrath

WINGS
Ex 19:4 and how I bore you on eagles' w
Ps 17:8 hide me in the shadow of your w,
Mal 4:2 shall rise, with healing in its w.
Lk 13:34 hen gathers her brood under her w,

WIPE → WIPED
Isa 25:8 GOD will w away the tears from all faces,
Rev 21:4 he will w every tear from their eyes.

WIPED → WIPE
Acts 3:19 so that your sins may be w out,

WISDOM → WISE
Deut 4:6 will show your w and discernment
1 Kings 4:29 God gave Solomon very great w,
Job 11:6 the secrets of w! For w is many-sided.
Prov 1:20 W cries out in the street;
9:10 fear of the LORD is the beginning of w,
Eccl 1:13 to search out by w all that is done
Wis 6:12 W is radiant and unfading,
Sir 1:1 All w is from the Lord,
24:1 THE PRAISE OF W
Jer 9:23 Do not let the wise boast in their w,
Mt 13:54 this man get this w and these deeds
Lk 2:52 Jesus increased in w and in years,
Rom 11:33 the depth of the riches and w and
1 Cor 1:19 "I will destroy the w of the wise,
Col 2:3 whom are hidden all the treasures of w
Jas 3:17 But the w from above is first pure,
Rev 5:12 wealth and w and might and honor

WISE → WISDOM
Deut 4:6 great nation is a w and discerning
Ps 19:7 are sure, making w the simple;
Prov 3:7 Do not be w in your own eyes;
13:20 walks with the w becomes w,
Eccl 12:11 The sayings of the w are like goads,
Dan 12:3 are w shall shine like the brightness
Mt 25:2 were foolish, and five were w.
1 Cor 1:26 not many of you were w by human
Eph 5:15 not as unwise people but as w,

WITHER → WITHERED, WITHERS
Ps 1:3 and their leaves do not w.
Ezek 47:12 Their leaves will not w nor their

WITHERED → WITHER
Mt 13:6 since they had no root, they w away.
21:19 And the fig tree w at once.

WITHERS → WITHER
Jn 15:6 is thrown away like a branch and w;
1 Pet 1:24 The grass w, and the flower falls,

WITHHOLD
Ps 84:11 No good thing does the LORD w from
Rom 8:32 He who did not w his own Son,

WITHOUT
2 Chr 18:16 like sheep w a shepherd;
Prov 19:2 Desire w knowledge is not good,
Mt 9:36 helpless, like sheep w a shepherd.
Jn 3:34 for he gives the Spirit w measure.
Eph 2:12 no hope and w God in the world.
Heb 4:15 tested as we are, yet w sin.

WITNESS → EYEWITNESSES, WITNESSES
Deut 19:15 single w shall not suffice to convict
Job 16:19 in fact, my w is in heaven,
Rom 2:15 their own conscience also bears w;
Rev 1:5 faithful w, the firstborn of the dead,

WITNESSES → WITNESS
Mt 26:60 though many false w came forward.
Heb 12:1 surrounded by so great a cloud of w,
Rev 11:3 my two w authority to prophesy

WIVES → WIFE
1 Kings 11:3 and his w turned away his heart.
Eph 5:22 W, be subject to your husbands as
1 Pet 3:1 W, in the same way, accept the

WOE

Mt	23:13	"But **w** to you, scribes and Pharisees
Rev	8:13	"**W, w, w** to the inhabitants of the

WOLF → WOLVES

Isa	11: 6	The **w** shall live with the lamb,
Jn	10:12	sees the **w** coming and leaves the sheep

WOLVES → WOLF

Mt	7:15	but inwardly are ravenous **w**.

WOMAN → WOMEN

Gen	2:22	he made into a **w** and brought her to
	3:15	enmity between you and the **w**,
Jdt	16: 5	foiled them by the hand of a **w**.
Ps	113: 9	He gives the barren **w** a home,
Prov	11:16	A gracious **w** gets honor,
	31:30	**w** who fears the LORD is to be praised.
Isa	7:14	Look, the young **w** is with child
	54: 1	of the desolate **w** will be more than
Dan	13: 2	a very beautiful **w** and one who feared
Jn	19:26	his mother, "**W**, here is your son."
Gal	4: 4	born of a **w**, born under the law,
Rev	12: 1	a **w** clothed with the sun,

WOMB

Job	1:21	Naked I came from my mother's **w**,
Ps	139:13	knit me together in my mother's **w**.
Jer	1: 5	"Before I formed you in the **w** I knew you,
Lk	1:42	and blessed is the fruit of your **w**.
	1:44	the child in my **w** leaped for joy.

WOMEN → WOMAN

Ezra	10: 2	married foreign **w** from the peoples
Mt	24:41	Two **w** will be grinding meal
Lk	1:42	"Blessed are you among **w**,
	23:55	**w** who had come with him from
1 Pet	3: 5	that the holy **w** who hoped in God

WONDERFUL → WONDERS

Gen	18:14	Is anything too **w** for the LORD?
Judg	13:18	do you ask my name? It is too **w**."
Ps	107: 8	for his **w** works to humankind.
Isa	9: 6	named **W** Counselor, Mighty God,

WONDERS → WONDERFUL

Ex	3:20	and strike Egypt with all my **w** that
Ps	136: 4	who alone does great **w**,
Jn	4:48	signs and **w** you will not believe."
2 Thess	2: 9	who uses all power, signs, lying **w**,

WOOD

Deut	28:64	serve other gods, of **w** and stone,
1 Cor	3:12	silver, precious stones, **w**, hay,

WORD → BYWORD, WORDS

Deut	30:14	No, the **w** is very near to you;
1 Kings	8:56	not one **w** has failed of all his good
Ps	56: 4	In God, whose **w** I praise,
	119:105	Your **w** is a lamp to my feet and
Prov	30: 5	Every **w** of God proves true;
Isa	40: 8	the **w** of our God will stand forever.
	55:11	my **w** be that goes out from my mouth;
Mk	4:14	The sower sows the **w**.
Lk	1:38	let it be done to me according to your **w**."
Jn	1: 1	In the beginning was the **W**, and the **W** was
		with God, and the **W** was God.
	1:14	the **W** became flesh and lived among
	14:23	"Those who love me will keep my **w**,
	17:17	in the truth; your **w** is truth.
Rom	9: 6	as though the **w** of God had failed.
2 Tim	2:15	rightly explaining the **w** of truth.
Jas	1:22	But be doers of the **w**,
1 Jn	2: 5	but whoever obeys his **w**,
Rev	19:13	his name is called The **W** of God.

WORDS → WORD

Ex	20: 1	Then God spoke all these **w**:
Deut	11:18	put these **w** of mine in your heart
Ps	5: 1	Give ear to my **w**, O LORD;
Prov	30: 6	not add to his **w**, or else he will rebuke
Hos	6: 5	killed them by the **w** of my mouth,
Mt	24:35	but my **w** will not pass away.
Lk	6:47	hears my **w**, and acts on them.
1 Cor	2:13	in **w** not taught by human wisdom
Rev	22:19	takes away from the **w** of the book

WORK → WORKS

Gen	2: 2	the seventh day God finished the **w**
Ex	20:10	you shall not do any **w**—
Ps	8: 3	heavens, the **w** of your fingers,
Jn	6:27	Do not **w** for the food that perishes,
Phil	1: 6	who began a good **w** among you will
	2:12	**w** out your own salvation with fear
2 Tim	3:17	equipped for every good **w**.
Heb	6:10	not overlook your **w** and the love

WORKS → WORK

Ps	8: 6	given them dominion over the **w**
	92: 5	How great are your **w**, O LORD!
Gal	2:16	and not by doing the **w** of the law,
	5:19	the **w** of the flesh are obvious:
Eph	2: 9	not the result of **w**, so that no one may
1 Tim	6:18	to do good, to be rich in good **w**,
Jas	2:17	faith by itself, if it has no **w**, is dead

WORLD

Ps	9: 8	He judges the **w** with righteousness;
Mt	5:14	"You are the light of the **w**.
	16:26	gain the whole **w** but forfeit their life?
Jn	1:10	yet the **w** did not know him.
	3:16	loved the **w** that he gave his only Son,
	8:12	saying, "I am the light of the **w**.
	16:33	courage; I have conquered the **w**!"
1 Tim	6: 7	we brought nothing into the **w**,
Jas	4: 4	friend of the **w** becomes an enemy of
1 Jn	2: 2	but also for the sins of the whole **w**.
	2:15	not love the **w** or the things in the **w**.
Rev	11:15	kingdom of the **w** has become the

WORM

Ps	22: 6	But I am a **w**, and not human;
Mk	9:48	where their **w** never dies,

WORRY

Mt	6:25	do not **w** about your life,
	10:19	not **w** about how you are to speak

WORSHIP → WORSHIPED

Ex	20: 5	not bow down to them or **w** them;
Ps	100: 2	**W** the LORD with gladness;
Sir	35:10	Be generous when you **w** the Lord,
Mt	4: 9	if you will fall down and **w** me."
Jn	4:24	who **w** him must **w** in spirit and truth."
Rom	12: 1	which is your spiritual **w**.
Rev	22: 3	and his servants will **w** him;

WORSHIPED → WORSHIP

Mt	28: 9	took hold of his feet, and **w** him.
Rev	5:14	And the elders fell down and **w**.

WORTHY

2 Sam	22: 4	LORD, who is **w** to be praised,
Mt	10:38	and follow me is not **w** of me.
Eph	4: 1	to lead a life **w** of the calling
Heb	3: 3	Jesus is **w** of more glory than Moses
Rev	4:11	"You are **w**, our Lord and God,
	5:12	**W** is the Lamb that was slaughtered

WOUND → WOUNDS

Ex	21:25	burn for burn, **w** for **w**, stripe for
Rev	13: 3	but its mortal **w** had been healed.

WOUNDS → WOUND

Ps	147: 3	brokenhearted, and binds up their **w**.
1 Pet	2:24	by his **w** you have been healed.

WRAPPED

Mk	15:46	the body, **w** it in the linen cloth,
Lk	2: 7	**w** him in bands of cloth,

WRATH

Num	16:46	For **w** has gone out from the LORD;
Ps	2: 5	Then he will speak to them in his **w**,
	6: 1	or discipline me in your **w**.
Prov	15: 1	A soft answer turns away **w**,
Sir	16:11	For mercy and **w** are with the Lord;
Jer	25:15	my hand this cup of the wine of **w**,
Lam	4:11	The LORD gave full vent to his **w**;
Zeph	1:15	That day will be a day of **w**,
Mt	3: 7	you to flee from the **w** to come?
Rom	1:18	**w** of God is revealed from heaven
Eph	2: 3	we were by nature children of **w**,
1 Thess	1:10	rescues us from the **w** that is coming

Rev   6:17   the great day of their **w** has come,

WRESTLED

Gen   32:24   a man **w** with him until daybreak.

WRETCHED

Rom   7:24   **W** man that I am!

WRITE → WRITING, WRITTEN, WROTE

Ex   34:27   LORD said to Moses: **W** these words;
Num   17: 2   **W** each man's name on his staff,
Deut   6: 9   **w** them on the doorposts of your house
Prov   7: 3   **w** them on the tablet of your heart.
Jer   31:33   and I will **w** it on their hearts,
Heb   8:10   and **w** them on their hearts,
Rev   21: 5   "**W** this, for these words are trustworthy

WRITING → WRITE

Ex   32:16   and the **w** was the **w** of God,
Dan   5: 7   "Whoever can read this **w**

WRITTEN → WRITE

Josh   23: 6   to observe and do all that is **w** in
Dan   12: 1   who is found **w** in the book.
Lk   24:44   everything **w** about me in the law
Jn   21:25   if every one of them were **w** down,
Rev   21:27   are **w** in the Lamb's book of life.

WRONG → WRONGDOING, WRONGED

Num   5: 7   shall make full restitution for the **w**,
Lk   23:41   but this man has done nothing **w**."
Acts   23: 9   "We find nothing **w** with this man.
Rom   13:10   Love does no **w** to a neighbor;

WRONGDOING → DO, WRONG

Ex   23: 2   You shall not follow a majority in **w**
1 Jn   5:17   All **w** is sin, but there is sin that is not

WRONGED → WRONG

1 Cor   6: 7   Why not rather be **w**?

WROTE → WRITE

Ex   24: 4   And Moses **w** down all the words
       34:28   he **w** on the tablets the words of the
Jn   5:46   believe me, for he **w** about me.

Y

YEAR → YEARS

Ex   23:14   Three times in the **y** you shall hold a
Heb   10: 1   continually offered **y** after **y**,

YEARS → YEAR

Gen   1:14   and for seasons and for days and **y**,
Ex   12:40   in Egypt was four hundred thirty **y**.
Num   14:34   forty **y**, and you shall know my
2 Chr   36:21   it kept sabbath, to fulfill seventy **y**.
Ps   90: 4   For a thousand **y** in your sight are like
Jer   25:12   Then after seventy **y** are completed,
Dan   9: 2   of Jerusalem, namely, seventy **y**.
Gal   4:10   and months, and seasons, and **y**.
2 Pet   3: 8   the Lord one day is like a thousand **y**,
Rev   20: 2   and bound him for a thousand **y**,

YEAST

Mt   16: 6   beware of the **y** of the Pharisees and
Gal   5: 9   A little **y** leavens the whole batch of

YESTERDAY

Heb   13: 8   Jesus Christ is the same **y** and today

YOKE

Mt   11:30   my **y** is easy, and my burden is light."
Gal   5: 1   not submit again to a **y** of slavery.

YOUNG → YOUTH

Ps   119: 9   can **y** people keep their way pure?
Joel   2:28   and your **y** men shall see visions.
Acts   2:17   and your **y** men shall see visions,

YOUTH → YOUNG

Ps   71: 5   my trust, O LORD, from my **y**.
Eccl   12: 1   Remember your creator in the days of your **y**,

Z

ZACCHAEUS

Lk   19: 2   A man was there named **Z**;

ZEAL → ZEALOUS

1 Macc   2:26   Thus he burned with **z** for the law,
Ps   69: 9   **z** for your house that has consumed me
Isa   37:32   The **z** of the LORD of hosts will do this.
Jn   2:17   "**Z** for your house will consume me.
Rom   10: 2   testify that they have a **z** for God,
Phil   3: 6   as to **z**, a persecutor of the church;

ZEALOUS → ZEAL

Num   25:13   because he was **z** for his God,
1 Kings   19:10   "I have been very **z** for the LORD,

ZEBULUN

Son of Jacob by Leah (Gen 30:20; 35:23; 1 Chr 2:1). Tribe of blessed (Gen 49:13; Deut 33:18-19), numbered (Num 1:31; 26:27), allotted land (Josh 19:10-16; Ezek 48:26), failed to fully possess (Judg 1:30), supported Deborah (Judg 4:6-10; 5:14, 18), David (1 Chr 12:33), 12,000 from (Rev 7:8).

ZECHARIAH

   1. Son of Jeroboam II; king of Israel (2 Kings 15:8-12).
   2. Post-exilic prophet who encouraged rebuilding of temple (Ezra 5:1; 6:14; Zech 1:1).

ZEDEKIAH → =MATTANIAH

   1. False prophet (1 Kings 22:11-24; 2 Chr 18:10-23).
   2. Mattaniah, son of Josiah (1 Chr 3:15), made king of Judah by Nebuchadnezzar (2 Kings 24:17-25:7; 2 Chr 36:10-14; Jer 37-39; 52:1-11).

ZEPHANIAH

Prophet; descendant of Hezekiah (Zeph 1:1).

ZERUBBABEL

Descendant of David (1 Chr 3:19; Mt 1:3). Led return from exile (Ezra 2:2; Neh 7:7). Governor of Israel; helped rebuild temple (Ezra 3; Hag 1-2; Zech 4).

ZIMRI

King of Israel (1 Kings 16:9-20).

ZION

2 Sam   5: 7   David took the stronghold of **Z**,
Ps   2: 6   I have set my king on **Z**, my holy hill.
   48: 2   is the joy of all the earth, Mount **Z**,
   78:68   Mount **Z**, which he loves.
Isa   28:16   I am laying in **Z** a foundation stone,
Mic   4: 2   For out of **Z** shall go forth instruction,
Zech   9: 9   Rejoice greatly, O daughter **Z**!
Mt   21: 5   "Tell the daughter of **Z**,
Rom   11:26   "Out of **Z** will come the Deliverer;
1 Pet   2: 6   "See, I am laying in **Z** a stone,
Rev   14: 1   the Lamb, standing on Mount **Z**!

ZIPPORAH*

Daughter of Reuel; wife of Moses (Ex 2:21-22; 4:20-26; 18:1-6).

ZOPHAR*

One of Job's friends (Job 2:11; 11; 20; 42:9).

MAP 1

The Background of the Exodus

THE GREAT SEA

EGYPT

SINAI

MIDIAN

MOAB

EDOM

Memphis (Noph)

Heliopolis (On)

River Nile

Rameses (Qantir)

GOSHEN

Pithom

Pi-beseth

Baal-zephon

Zoan (Tanis)

Lake Menzaleh

Pelusium (Sin)

Zilu (Tjaru)

Lake Timsah

Succoth

Great Bitter Lake

Little Bitter Lake

Mons Casius

Lake Sirbonis

The Way to the Land of the Philistines

Wilderness of Shur

The Way to Shur

Brook of Egypt

Raphia

Gerar

Beer-sheba

Debir

Juttah

Hormah

Arad?

ARAD?

The Negeb

Salt Sea

Kir-hareseth

Bozrah

Punon

Selah

Teman

The King's Highway

Line of border fortresses

The Arabah

Ezion-geber

(Gulf of Aqaba)

Wilderness of Zin

Bene-jaakan (Beeroth)

Hazar-addar

Azmon

Kadesh-barnea (Meribah)

Oboth

Mt. Sinai? (Jebel Helal)

Wilderness of Paran

Wilderness of Sin?

Dophkah? (Serabit el Khadim)

Mt. Sinai (Horeb)? (Jebel Musa)

(Gulf of Suez)

© Oxford University Press

OUTER BORDER SHOWS 40 MILE SUBDIVISIONS

0   20   40 Miles

0   20   40 Kilometres

NOBM 23L

MAP 2

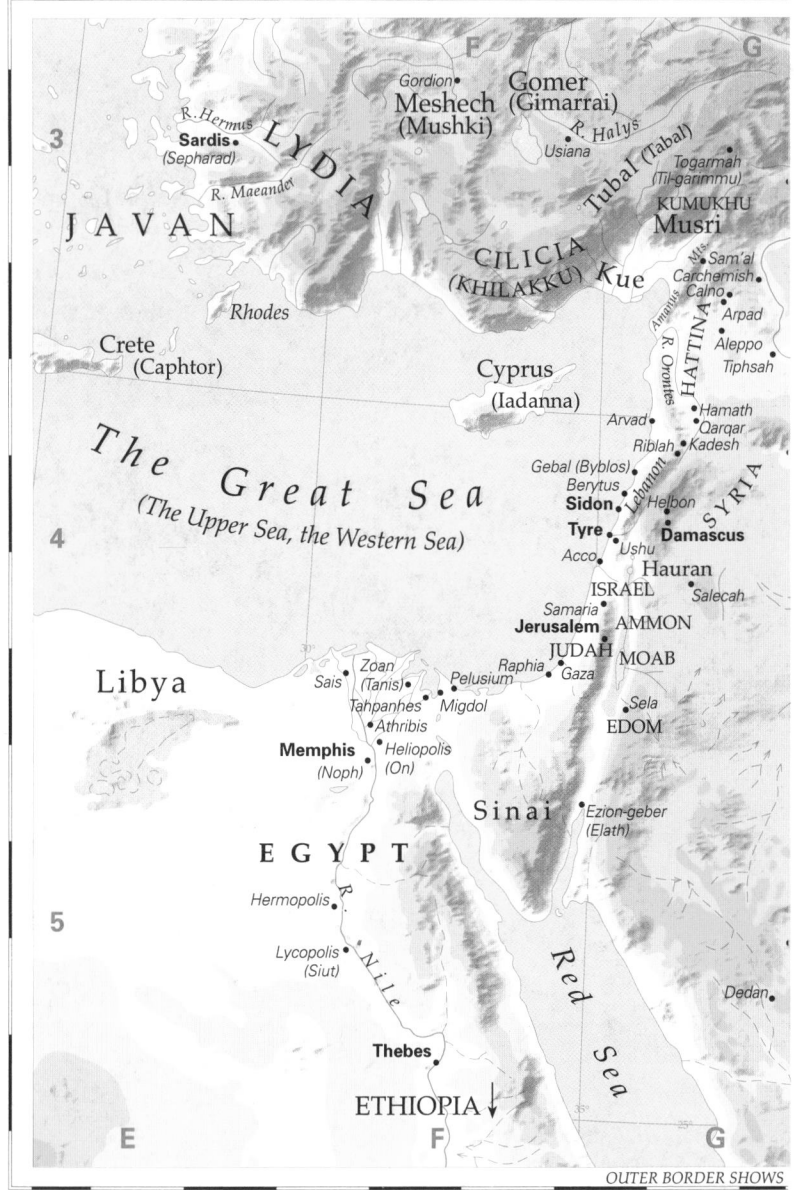

3

R. *Hermus*
Gordion•
Meshech
(Mushki)
Gomer
(Gimarrai)
Usiana•
R. *Halys*
Togarmah
(Til-garimmu)
Sardis•
(Sepharad)
LYDIA
KUMUKHU
Musri
R. *Maeander*

J A V A N
CILICIA
(KHILAKKU)
Kue
Tubal (Tabal)
Mts.
•Sam'al
Carchemish•
Calno•
Arpad
Rhodes
Aleppo•
Tiphsah•
HATTINA

Crete
(Caphtor)
Cyprus
(Iadanna)
Arvad•
•Hamath
•Qarqar
Riblah• Kadesh

4

The   Great   Sea
(The Upper Sea, the Western Sea)
Gebal (Byblos)•
Berytus•
Sidon•
Tyre•
Acco•
R. *Orontes*
Helbon•
Damascus
SYRIA
Lebanon
Ushu
Hauran
ISRAEL
Salecah•
Samaria•
Jerusalem
AMMON
JUDAH MOAB
Libya
Zoan
(Tanis)•
Raphia•
•Gaza
Pelusium•
•Sela
EDOM
Sais•
Tahpanhes•
•Athribis
Migdol

Memphis•
(Noph)
•Heliopolis
(On)
S i n a i
•Ezion-geber
(Elath)

E G Y P T

5

Hermopolis•
R. *Nile*
Lycopolis•
(Siut)
Red   Sea
Dedan•

Thebes•

ETHIOPIA ↓

E
F
G

MAP 2

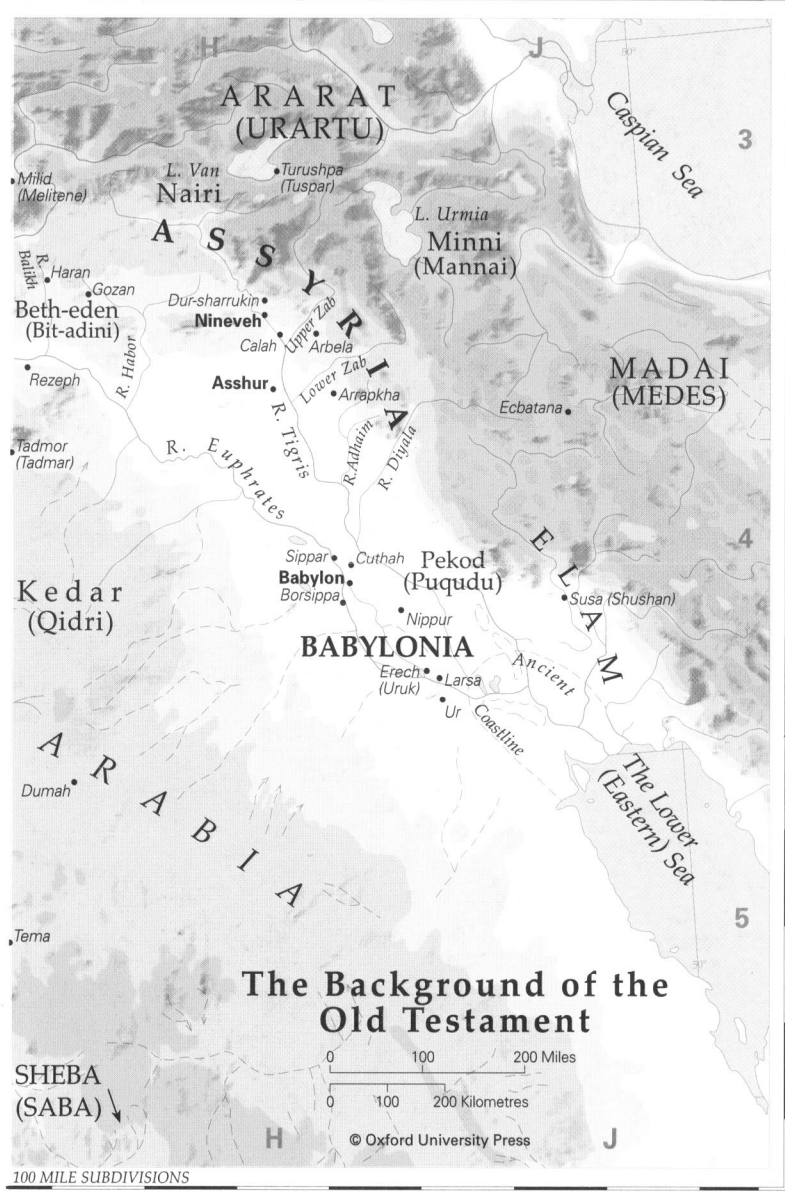

ARARAT
(URARTU)

Caspian Sea

Milid
(Melitene)

L. Van
Nairi

Turushpa
(Tuspar)

L. Urmia

Minni
(Mannai)

3

R. Balikh
Haran

Gozan

Beth-eden
(Bit-adini)

Dur-sharrukin
Nineveh

Calah

Upper Zab
Arbela

MADAI
(MEDES)

Rezeph

R. Habor

Asshur

Lower Zab
Arrapkha

Ecbatana

Tadmor
(Tadmar)

R. Euphrates

R. Tigris

R. Adhaim

R. Diyala

ELAM

Kedar
(Qidri)

Sippar
Babylon
Borsippa

Cuthah

Pekod
(Puqudu)

Nippur

Susa (Shushan)

BABYLONIA

Erech
(Uruk)

Larsa

Ur

Ancient

Coastline

The Lower
(Eastern) Sea

ARABIA

Dumah

Tema

5

The Background of the
Old Testament

0   100   200 Miles
0   100   200 Kilometres

© Oxford University Press

SHEBA
(SABA)

H

J

100 MILE SUBDIVISIONS

MAP 3

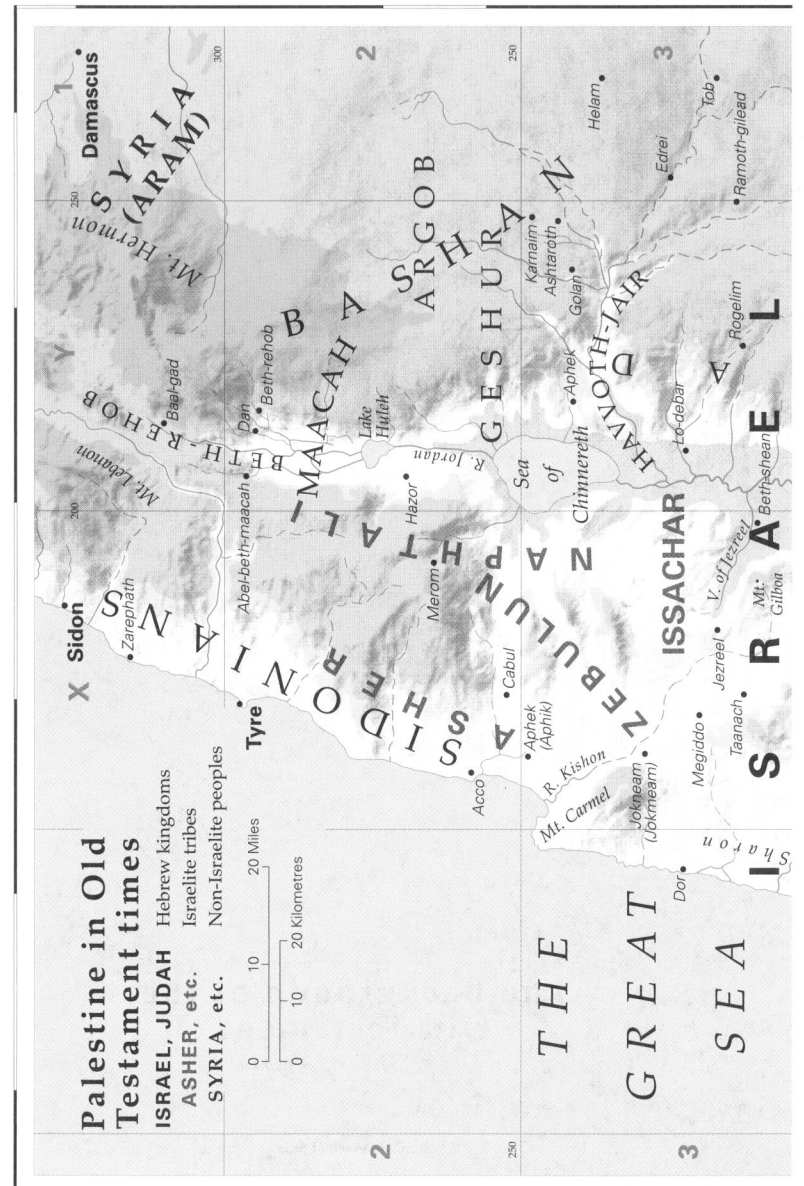

Palestine in Old Testament times

ISRAEL, JUDAH   Hebrew kingdoms
ASHER, etc.   Israelite tribes
SYRIA, etc.   Non-Israelite peoples

0   10   20 Miles
0   10   20 Kilometres

Damascus

S Y R I A
(A R A M)

Mt. Hermon

B A A R G O B

M A A C A H

G E S H U R A

Helam

Edrei

Tob

Ramoth-gilead

Baal-gad

Beth-rehob

Dan

BETH-REHOB

Mt. Lebanon

Lake
Huleh

R. Jordan

Karnaim
Ashtaroth
Golan
Aphek

HAVVOTH-JAIR

Rogelim

Lo-debar

Zarephath

Sidon

X

N A P H T A L I

Hazor

Merom

Sea
of
Chinnereth

D

G A L E A D

SIDONIANS

Z E B U L U N

ISSACHAR

Beth-shean

Tyre

Abel-beth-maacah

A S H E R

Cabul

Aphek
(Aphik)

V. of Jezreel

Mt.
Gilboa

I S R A E L

Acco

R. Kishon

Jokneam
(Jokmeam)

Mt. Carmel

Jezreel

Taanach

Megiddo

Dor

Sharon

T H E

G R E A T

S E A

MAP 3

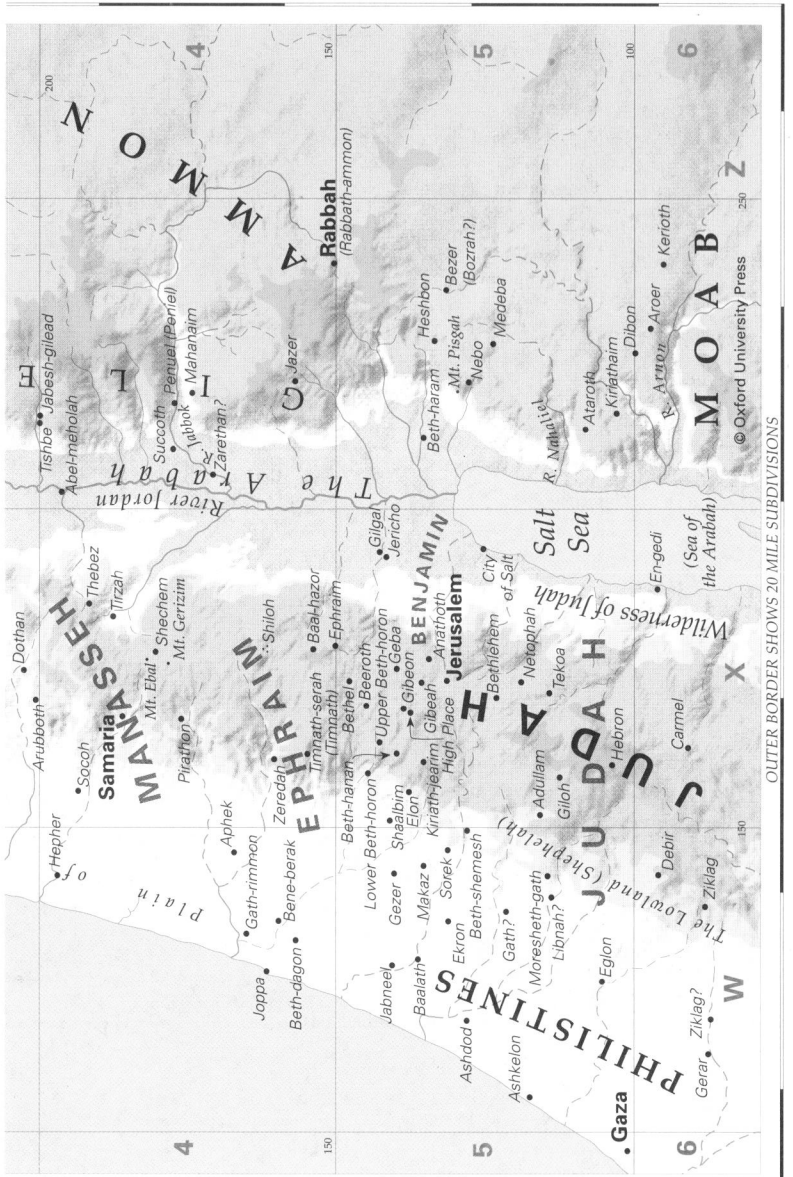

OUTER BORDER SHOWS 20 MILE SUBDIVISIONS

MAP 4

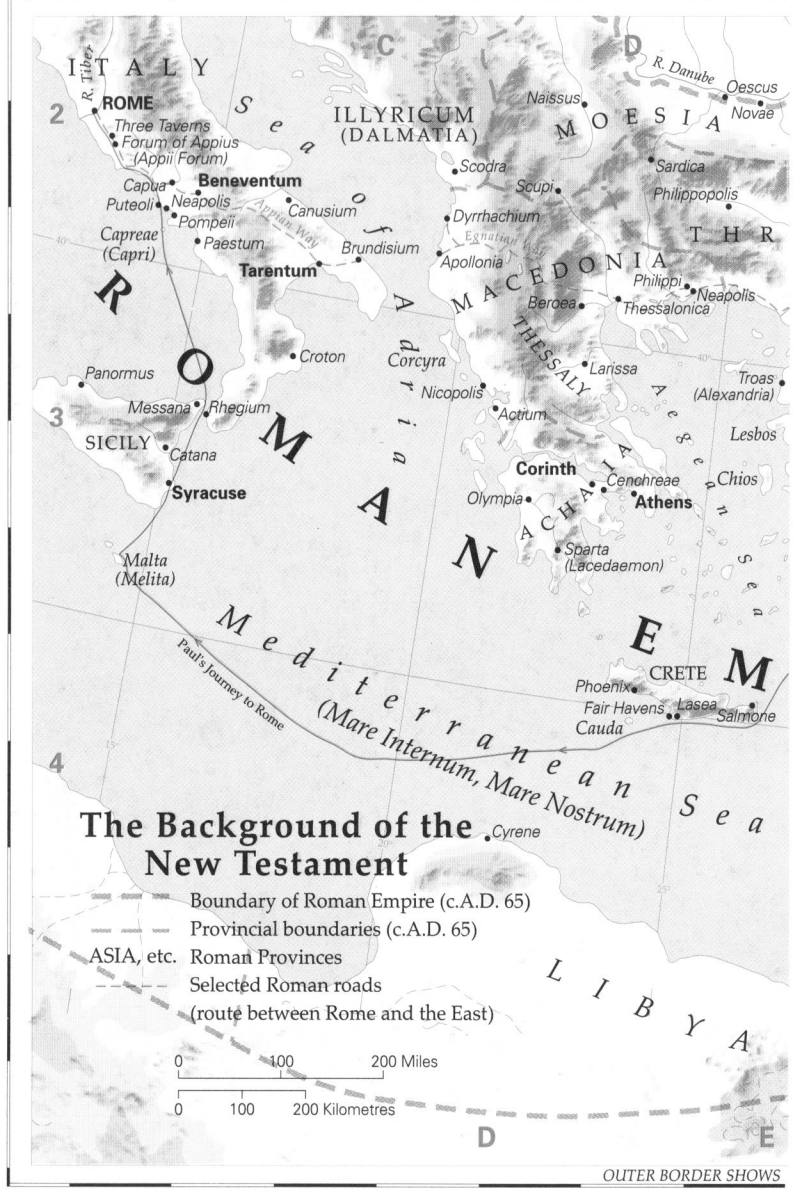

ITALY

ROME
Three Taverns
Forum of Appius
(Appii Forum)

R. Tiber

Capua
Puteoli **Beneventum**
Neapolis
Pompeii
Paestum
Capreae (Capri)
Canusium
Appian Way

Tarentum
Brundisium

Panormus
Messana *Rhegium*
Croton
SICILY *Catana*
Syracuse

Malta (Melita)

R O M A N   E M

Sea of Adriatic

C

ILLYRICUM (DALMATIA)
Scodra
Scupi
Dyrrhachium
Apollonia
Egnatian Way

MACEDONIA
THESSALY
Beroea
Larissa
Corcyra
Nicopolis
Actium

Naissus
Oescus
Novae

M O E S I A

D
R. Danube

Sardica
Philippopolis

T H R

Philippi *Neapolis*
Thessalonica

Troas (Alexandria)
Lesbos

Corinth
Olympia
Cenchreae
Athens
Chios
Sparta (Lacedaemon)

Aegean Sea

CRETE
Phoenix
Fair Havens *Lasea*
Cauda *Salmone*

Mediterranean Sea (Mare Internum, Mare Nostrum)

Paul's Journey to Rome

The Background of the New Testament

Cyrene

— — — Boundary of Roman Empire (c.A.D. 65)
— — — Provincial boundaries (c.A.D. 65)
ASIA, etc. Roman Provinces
— — — Selected Roman roads
(route between Rome and the East)

L I B Y A

0 — 100 — 200 Miles
0 — 100 — 200 Kilometres

D
E

MAP 4

E F G

Chersonesus

Odessus

E u x i n e   S e a

Mesembria

(*Pontus   Euxinus*)

A C E

2

Bosphorus

Amastris • *Sinope*

Egnatian Way **Heraclea** P O N T U S

Byzantium *Nicomedia* BITHYNIA and *Amisus*

Cyzicus *Nicaea* *Gangra* *Amasea* *Side* *Trapezus*

Prusa *Dorylaeum* G *Tavium* *Comana*

Assos *Adramyttium* **Ancyra** A Lesser

Pergamum *Gordium* L Armenia

Thyatira *Pessinus* A R. Halys

A S I A T *Caesarea (Mazaca)*

Smyrna **Sardis** I **CAPPADOCIA**

Philadelphia A *Archelais* *Melitene*

Ephesus *Laodicea* *Antioch* *Iconium*

Miletus *Colossae* PISIDIA *Lystra* Commagene *Samosata*

Cnidus PAMPHYLIA *Derbe* C I L I C I A OSROENE **Edessa**

LYCIA *Tarsus* *Zeugma*

Rhodes *Perga* Cilicia *Europus*

Rhodes *Patara* *Attalia* Trachea *Seleucia* (Carchemish)

P *Myra* I R E **Antioch**

Salamis R. Orontes *Apamea* and R. Euphrates

CYPRUS *Epiphania* S

Paphos *Tripolis* Arca *Emesa* *Palmyra*

Y

Berytus R *Abilene* I

Sidon A **Damascus**

Tyre *Caesarea*

Ptolemais *Philippi*

Tiberias

Caesarea

Joppa *Samaria*

Alexandria *Canopus* *Gaza* **Jerusalem**

Naucratis *Sais*

Pelusium Nabataean Kingdom

E G Y P T *Heliopolis* © Oxford University Press

Memphis *Babylon* **Petra**

F G

MAP 5

Palestine in New Testament times
A.D. 6–70

– – – – – – Political boundaries (A.D. 6–34)
JUDEA, etc. Political units
★ Fortresses
⊙ Cities of the Decapolis

0   10   20 Miles
0   10   20 Kilometres

Tyre
PHOENICIA
Ladder of Tyre
PROVINCE OF SYRIA
Caesarea Philippi (Paneas)
TETRARCHY OF PHILIP
L. Semechonitis (Lake Huleh)

Ptolemais
GALILEE
Chorazin
Capernaum
Gennesaret
Magdala (Dalmanutha)
Bethsaida
Sea of Galilee
Cana
Mt. Carmel
Sepphoris
Nazareth
Tabor
R. Kishon
The Great Plain (Esdraelon)
Nain
Tiberias
Hippos (Susithah)
Dion?
Gadara   Abila

Dora (Dor)

Caesarea
Mt. Gilboa
Scythopolis
Pella
Salim
Aenon
Brook Cherith

Sebaste (Samaria)
Gerasa
R. Jabbok
Neapolis
Mt. Ebal
Sychar
Mt. Gerizim
SAMARIA
administration

Antipatris (Pegai)
Alexandrium ★
Phasaelis
Joppa
Rathamin (Arimathea?)
Ephraim
Archelais
PEREA
Philadelphia (Rabbah)

Lydda
Jamnia
Emmaus (Nicopolis)
Jericho
Betharamphtha (Livias-Julias)
JUDEA (under Roman
Jerusalem
Bethany
Bethphage
(Kh. Qumran)
Medeba (Madaba)
Azotus
Bethlehem
Hyrcania ★
Ascalon
Bethsura (Beth-zur)
Herodium ★
R. Nahaliel
Gaza
Hebron
Lake Asphaltitis
★ Machaerus
NABATAEAN KINGDOM
River Jordan

IDUMEA
(Dead Sea)
Masada ★
R. Arnon
Areopolis (Rabbathmoab)

Beersheba

W   X   Y

© Oxford University Press

OUTER BORDER SHOWS 20 MILE SUBDIVISIONS